Women's History Sources

WOMEN'S
HISTORY SOURCES

A GUIDE TO ARCHIVES
AND MANUSCRIPT COLLECTIONS
IN THE UNITED STATES

Edited by
ANDREA HINDING

SUZANNA MOODY
Index Editor

In association with the University of Minnesota

VOLUME II / INDEX

R.R. BOWKER COMPANY
NEW YORK & LONDON · 1979

The Women's History Sources Survey
was made possible by a series of grants from
the National Endowment for the Humanities.

Published by R. R. Bowker Company
1180 Avenue of the Americas, New York, N.Y. 10036
Copyright © 1979 by Xerox Corporation
All rights reserved
Printed and bound in the United States of America

Library of Congress Cataloging in Publication Data
Main entry under title:

Women's history sources.

    Vol. 2 edited by Suzanna Moody.
    CONTENTS: v. 1. Collections.—v. 2. Index.
    1. Women—United States—History—Archival resources—
United States. I. Hinding, Andrea. II. Bower, Ames S.
Z7964.U49W64   [HQ1410]   016.30141'2'0973 78-15634

ISBN 0-8352-1103-7 (set)
ISBN 0-8352-1268-8 (Vol. II)

For the archivists, curators of manuscripts, librarians,
and other custodians of historical records
whose intelligent and generous cooperation
has made possible this work.

And for
Alice May Stahl • 1925–1978
cataloger, colleague, and friend,
whose strength and determination was characteristic
of so much of women's experience represented herein.

Women's History Sources Survey Staff

Cecelia Nelson Boone, writer and editor
Ames Sheldon Bower, writer and editor
Mary Jo Dobson, indexing assistant
Anna Bakuzis Glover, project manager
Andrea Hinding, project director and editor
David Klaassen, repository list compiler
Wendy Sue Larson, writer
Jeanne L'Heureux, indexing assistant
Doris Hanson Lunden, writer and fieldwork coordinator
Karen M. Mason, writer
Susan W. A. Mead, writer
Suzanna Moody, indexer
Randall Wallach, project assistant

Women's History Sources Survey Fieldworkers

Cathy F. Abernathy
Michele L. Aldrich
Nancy H. Burkett
Robert Conte
Howard A. Droker
Mathew J. Ferrero
Loretta Hefner
Heather Huyck
Patricia A. Michaelis
Dee Ann Montgomery
Mary Murphy
Ellen Newcombe
Mary Ostling
Cynthia H. Requardt
Kim Lacy Rogers
Darlene Roth-White
Marylynn Salmon
Phyllis Steele
Virginia Stewart
Sandra Van Burkleo

Women's History Sources Survey Advisory Board

Clarke A. Chambers, Professor of History, University of Minnesota
Maxine B. Clapp, University Archivist, University of Minnesota
Carl N. Degler, Professor of History, Stanford University
Lynn Bonfield Donovan, Archivist, California Historical Society
Frank B. Evans, Archivist, National Archives and Records Service
Elsie Freivogel, Archivist, National Archives and Records Service
Janet Wilson James, Professor of History, Boston College
Lucile M. Kane, Minnesota State Archivist, Minnesota Historical Society
Gerda Lerner, Professor of History, Sarah Lawrence College
Dorothy Porter, Librarian Emeritus, Howard University
Anne Firor Scott, Professor of History, Duke University
Joan Hoff Wilson, Professor of History, Arizona State University, Tempe

Preface

THIS VOLUME to *Women's History Sources* indexes the entries in Volume I, which were prepared by staff writers on the basis of questionnaires that were submitted by repositories or by fieldworkers, who surveyed the collections. The questionnaires describing the collections (or their counterparts, the record groups or subgroups), were prepared by working with the collections themselves and/or by examining published and unpublished guides and finding aids. Each proper name and corporate name was indexed as were collection titles where appropriate (when the title provided meaningful information). Subjects were entered when there was an indication that the collection contained more than passing reference to the subject. Geographic/subject access by state is also provided. In addition, types of records and manuscripts in which researchers have particular interest—such as oral histories, photograph collections, or diaries—were indexed.

Although the guiding principle behind the index is to provide as much accurate information, particularly name information, as possible, the characteristics of primary sources, the traditions in the archival profession, and the problems inherent in surveys of archival holdings limit the ability to do so. People represented in the vast majority of archives and manuscript collections are not prominent, and women represented are even less likely to be so. Because so few appeared in standard reference works such as *Who Was Who* or *Who's Who of American Women,* and because of a nineteenth-century practice of using the same given name for four or five generations of women and men, it was consequently difficult to distinguish, for example, between and among the 23 Mary Browns who were indexed from entries in the text. In addition, archivists have not developed a tradition of standard authority files for proper names, corporate names, and subject headings. This lack of uniformity in name and subject reporting complicated the task of indexing. A particular woman's name, for example, was spelled variously by a repository using it in several collections or by several repositories in a small area, and it was not always possible to reconcile the discrepancies.

In order to reduce the difficulties inherent in dealing with women's names and provide as much information as possible, a 25,000-name authority file was created from the indexes of *Notable American Women,* the *Dictionary of American Biography,* and *The National Union Catalog of Manuscript Collections.* Every woman's name reported by repositories was first checked against this in-house authority file for accuracy of spelling, birth and death dates, and maiden and marital name information. It was possible to verify many women's names through this procedure.

After the indexing of all entries was completed, all names that were alike and not clearly identified as differing from each other were again checked. Staff members compared text of entries to the questionnaires on which the entries were based and further consulted reference works. They searched for common denominators—similar correspondents or places where the women had lived or were educated. If the search proved unsatisfactory and doubt remained, the names were left separate. By the end of the survey, thousands of women's names had been recorded and entered in the index. The vast majority of these names were those of women who had not been documented in existing sources.

This index to *Women's History Sources* is itself a basis for research and analysis. The thousands of women's and men's names contained will assist genealogists and others with an interest in family history while also constituting a major addition to name authority control in the archives profession. To those ends, archivists, scholars, librarians, historians, students, and others who use these volumes, and then work directly with the source materials, are encouraged to write to the editor with additions or corrections to information in this index based on their latest research and investigation so that subsequent editions and related projects will be expanded and improved.

How to Use This Index

THIS INDEX provides name, subject, and geographic access to the archives and manuscript collections described in Volume I. Index numbers denote entry numbers and not page numbers. Boldface index numbers indicate that the collection is formed around the particular person, organization, or subject in the index entry.

PERSONAL NAME FORMAT

The name format indicates certain basic information that was available for any one person. Maiden names and birth and death dates are indicated by parentheses (birth and death dates, when given, appear at the end of a name entry preceding the collection numbers), and marital information is given in brackets (husbands' forenames and/or middle names are confined within the brackets, the surname remains outside).

> Lee, Mary Anna Randolph (Custis) [Mrs. Robert Edward] (1806–73), 2443, **2445**, 3552, 5350, 17,081
>
> Moses, Anna Mary (Robertson) "Grandma" [Mrs. Thomas Salmon] (1860–1961), **16,997**

The main listing for a woman appears in the index under the name by which she was best known, whether it be her professional, married, or maiden name. Cross-references from the woman's other names are provided where appropriate. For a married woman who did not use her husband's name in her work the married name appears at the end of the main listing separated by a period from the best-known name.

> Calderone, Mary (Steichen) (1904–), **6446**, 6987, 8672, 11,897
>
> *Cross-reference:*
> Steichen, Mary (1904–). *See* Calderone, Mary (Steichen) (1904–)
>
> Earhart, Amelia Mary. [Mrs. George Palmer] Putnam (1897–1937), 1594, 1605, 2198, 2863, 4395, **4681, 4756, 6550,** etc.
>
> *Cross-reference:*
> Putnam, Amelia Mary (Earhart) [Mrs. George Palmer] (1897–1937). *See* Earhart, Amelia Mary. [Mrs. George Palmer] Putnam (1897–1937)

Entries become more complicated for women who have married more than once. Cross-references are given from the maiden name and the names of previous husbands, where these are known.

> Luce, Clare (Boothe) [Mrs. George Tuttle] Brokaw [Mrs. Henry Robinson] (1903–), 1605, 2097, 2205, 2242, **2458,** 4640, 5123, etc.
>
> *Cross-references:*
> Boothe, Clare (1903–). *See* Luce, Clare (Boothe) [Mrs. George Tuttle] Brokaw [Mrs. Henry Robinson] (1903–)

> Brokaw, Clare (Boothe) [Mrs. George Tuttle] (1903–). *See* Luce, Clare (Boothe) [Mrs. George Tuttle] Brokaw [Mrs. Henry Robinson] (1903–)

> Madison, Dorothea "Dolley" (Payne) [Mrs. John, Jr.] Todd [Mrs. James] (1768–1849), **1460, 2468,** 3221, **5294,** 6653, **11,169, 12,255,** etc.
>
> *Cross-references:*
> Payne, Dolley (1768–1849). *See* Madison, Dorothea "Dolley" (Payne) [Mrs. John, Jr.] Todd [Mrs. James] (1768–1849)
> Todd, Dolley (Payne) [Mrs. John, Jr.] (1768–1849). *See* Madison, Dorothea "Dolley" (Payne) [Mrs. John, Jr.] Todd [Mrs. James] (1768–1849)

VARIANT NAMES AND SPELLINGS

In earlier times, it was not uncommon for a person to adopt first one name or variant spellings of a name, then another, apparently without legal process. In an index entry, variant names in most cases are separated by a period. Cross-references from all other names are provided where appropriate.

> Marlowe, Julia. Sarah Frances Frost. Fanny Brough. Fancy Brough. [Mrs. Robert] Taber [Mrs. Edward Hugh] Sothern (1866–1950), 2562, 2968, 3100, 10,025, 11,997, **12,173,** 12,535, etc.
>
> Oakley, Annie. Phoebe Ann Moses. [Mrs. Frank] Butler (1860–1926), 10,428, **14,101,** 15,935, **16,547, 17,932**

SAME OR SIMILAR NAMES

Multiple listings of the same name, e.g., Mary Brown, indicate that it was not always possible to confirm that those entered were the same Mary Brown. When filing personal names that are the same, the following rules apply: The simplest version (shortest form) of the name files first, followed by the simplest version and its *see* reference; next is the simplest version and its bracketed information, followed by the simplest version with its dates and then the simplest version with parenthetical information. When a woman's first name is unknown, or when a woman is known by her husband's first name, filing under the surname is by the term Miss or Mrs. (See below: Brown, Mrs. George William.)

> Brown, Mary,
> Brown, Mary. *See* Jones, Mary Eliza (Brown)
> Brown, Mary [Mrs.],
> Brown, Mary (1796–?). *See* Askew, Mary (Brown) (1796–?)
> Brown, Mary (Burr) [Mrs. Lloyd Warfield],
> Brown, Mary E.,
> Brown, Mary (Guion) [Mrs. Samuel] (1782–?),
> Brown, Mary R.,

Brown, Mary Taylor [Mrs. William John],
Brown, Mrs. George William,
Brown, Mrs. Nathan,
Brown, Myrtle,
Brown, N.,
Brown, Paula Watts (1909–74),

CORPORATE NAMES

Corporate names are listed under the most recent name ascertained, with appropriate cross-reference from earlier names, where these were known.

American Association of Group Workers. *See* National Association of Social Workers

National Association of Day Nurseries. *See* Child Welfare League of America

National Association of School Social Workers. *See* National Association of Social Workers

SUBJECT ENTRIES

The index uses Library of Congress subject headings modified as necessary to represent accurately historical sense and the content of the materials reported. The subject headings chosen·are as explicit as possible, however, general subject headings were used whenever the information given by the repositories did not allow for more specificity in indexing.

The subject heading "women" is used to indicate only those collections where women as a group are the subject of the source material or of the entire collection. Therefore, under the heading "women" will be found such subentries as attitudes toward, civil rights, education, employment, employment reentry, and history, all of which denote subject areas where women as a group are treated and discussed.

GEOGRAPHIC ACCESS

An important feature of this index is the subject listings under each state. While geographic/subject access duplicates the information to be found under general subject headings, it is an invaluable aid for anyone doing research on a particular state. When looking up information under a state name, a researcher finds a full range of subject headings. Below is a representative sample of subject headings that may be found under individual states.

Afro-Americans,	editors,
agriculture,	feminists,
archivists,	genealogy,
art,	German Americans,
authors,	governors,
businesswomen,	high school teachers,
charities,	hospital records,
church societies,	housewives,
clergy,	immigrants,
clergymen's wives,	interracial marriage,
clubs,	journalists,
diaries and journals,	juvenile delinquents,

laundresses,	public health officers,
legislators,	reformatories,
librarians,	single mothers,
Lutheran Church,	suffragists,
medical social workers,	teachers' wives,
Mexican Americans,	temperance societies,
minorities,	trust companies,
municipal charters,	women,
Native Americans,	education,
nurses,	employment,
Ojibwe Indians,	status of,
oral history,	women's colleges,
physicians,	women's studies,

ALPHABETIZATION

Alphabetization is word by word disregarding punctuation.

Ames, Ezra,
Ames Family (MS),
Ames, Fanny (Baker) [Mrs. Charles Gordon] (1840–1931),

Entries beginning with initials or arbitrary combinations of letters appear at the head of the appropriate letter.

"O, Fair New Mexico" (song),
O. Henry Award,
O. Henry Book Club (NC),
O.W.L.S. (DC),
Oahu College (HI),

Entries that are distinguished from each other by parenthetical geographic location are filed by the state abbreviation as if spelled.

American Legion Auxiliary (Hinsdale, IL),
American Legion Auxiliary (Garden City, KS),
American Legion Auxiliary (Horace Duffy Post, ME),
American Legion Auxiliary (MN),
American Legion Auxiliary (Mankato, MN),
American Legion Auxiliary (Morris, MN),
American Legion Auxiliary (Grand Island Post 53, NE),

Entries with parenthetical geographic locations precede those with parenthetical descriptions.

Bulletin (San Francisco, CA),
Bulletin (League of Women Voters),

Corporate names beginning with personal names are filed by the first letter of the first word. Cross-references are provided if necessary.

Phillis Wheatley. *See also* Phyllis Wheatley; Wheatley, Phillis
Phillis Wheatley Association,
Phillis Wheatley Association (OH),
Phillis Wheatley Foundation,
Phillis Wheatley Institute,

Surnames beginning with M' or Mc are filed as if spelled Mac.

Women's History Sources

Women's History Sources Index

AAUW Journal (periodical), 16,184
AAUW Journal Newspaper, 16,184
A. S. Lyons, Inc., 14,338
Aaron, Helen [Mrs. Ely M.] (ca. 1905-), **4,045**
Aars, Rosalie (Rueter) [Mrs. Calvert Pernell]
(1916-), **16,324**
Aa-Tik-Lik Club (MI). *See* Alpha Theta Sigma (MI)
Abandoned children, law and legislation, 9,351
Abbe, Charlotte (Colgate) [Mrs. George Waldo]
(1817-85), **11,506**
Abbe, Elfriede Martha (1919-), **11,505**
Abbe, George Waldo (1811-79), **11,506**
Abbe, Talitha Waldo (1789-?), 11,506
Abbett Family (OR), **14,498**
Abbett, John C., 14,498
Abbett, Mrs. J. T., 14,498
Abbett, Myra Leanne (?-1968). *See* Adams, Myra
Leanne (Abbett) (?-1968)
Abbey, Kathryn, 2,928
Abbey, Matilda Ormond (Taylor) Birchard, **14,056**
Abbey Theatre, 11,894
Abbeys, 6,907. *See also* Convents and nunneries
Abbot Academy (Andover, MA), **5,877**
Abbot, Elizabeth Bonsfield, **8,294**
Abbot, Ephraim (1779-1870), **7,597**
Abbot, John, 11,507
Abbot, Margaret Ella Lowe, 5,210
Abbot, Mary Holyoke Pearson [Mrs. Ephraim]
(1782-1829), 7,597
Abbott, Abiel Howard, 8,893
Abbott Academy (MA), 2,298
Abbott, Agnes, 7,583
Abbott, Albert J., 8,295
Abbott, Alice (Gilmour) Young [Mrs. Albert J.],
8,295
Abbott, Amy, 17,892
Abbott, Annette (1877-?). *See* Adams, Annette
(Abbott) (1877-1956)
Abbott, Berenice (1898-), **5,638, 11,252,** 12,789
Abbott, Caroline Younglove, 13,966
Abbott, Charlotte, 10,419
Abbott, Charlotte Helen (1844-1921), **5,876**
Abbott, Dorothy C., 11,599, 11,600
Abbott, Edith (1876-1957), 2,224, 2,411, 2,439, 3,828,
3,910, 4,003, 4,047, 4,052, 4,089, 4,103, 4,104,
4,110, 4,111, 4,117, 4,141, 4,146, 4,150, 4,166,
6,958, 8,651, 8,653, 8,662, **10,603,** 15,312
Abbott, Elizabeth. *See* Kerr, Elizabeth (Abbott)
Abbott, Emily, 9,145
Abbott, Emma. [Mrs. Eugene] Wetherell (1850-91),
672, 9,361, 10,651
Abbott, Eunice Strickland "Birdie" (1870-1956). *See*
Mercer, Eunice Strickland "Birdie" (Abbott)
[Mrs. David H.] (1870-1956)
Abbott, G. D., 14,206
Abbott, Grace [Miss] (1878-1939), 2,224, 2,336,
2,439, 2,519, 2,700, 3,910, 4,003, 4,047, 4,089,
4,103, 4,110, 4,117, 4,146, 4,166, 5,120, 5,122,
8,651, 8,662, 8,678, **10,419, 10,603,** 12,033,
12,534, 15,301, 15,311
Abbott, Hannah Tracy (Emery) [Mrs. Benjamin]
(1770?-93), 7,363
Abbott, Harriet [Miss], 17,018

Abbott, Harriet Elizabeth. [Mrs. Francis E.] Clark,
1,631
Abbott, Howard Strickland (1863-1944), Family
(MN), **8,893**
Abbott, Jane Ludlow Drake (1882-1962), **5,978**
Abbott, John S. C. (1805-77), 12,152
Abbott, Leonard D., 12,705
Abbott, Lucetta, 11,672
Abbott, Lyman, 14,062
Abbott, Mabel [Miss] (1874-1973), **12,863**
Abbott, Mary Adams, **6,340**
Abbott, Mary Ellen Strickland [Mrs. Abiel Howard],
8,893
Abbott, Mary (Stuart) [Mrs. E. C. "Teddy Blue"],
10,270
Abbott, Maude Elizabeth Seymour (1869-1940), **2,088**
Abbott, Nabia, 4,028
Abbott, Nora L., 955
Abbott, W., 11,672
Abbott's Institution (NY), **12,152**
Abby, Miss, 2,957
"ABC Book, An," 5,788
ABC Club (OR), **14,281**
ABC House, The, 17,821
Abduction, 1,564, 2,304, 2,467, 3,509, 7,539, 9,972,
11,227, 13,275, 16,876
Abeel, C. R., **11,067**
Abeel, Gustavus, 10,934
Abeel, Mary Stille, 10,934
Abel, Elizabeth, 12,867
Abel, Louise (1894-), 13,836
Abel-Henderson, Annie Heloise (1873-1947), **17,181**
Abell, Getelda F. Farward [Mrs. James Scott], 8,894
Abell, Hattie, 7,140
Abell, James Scott, Family, **8,894**
Abell, Maggie, 8,894
Abel's Daughter (book), 6,048
Abendanone, David, 7,524
Abendanone Family, **7,524**
Abendanone, Grace, 7,524
Abendpost, 3,878
Aberbach, Jean, 11,907
Abercrombie, Lelia [Miss] (1898-), **2,888,** 2,910
Abercrombie, Sarah (?-1871). *See* Shufeldt, Sarah
(Abercrombie) [Mrs. Robert Wilson] (?-1871)
Abercrombie Trail, 8,709
Aberdeen Church of Christ (MS), 9,537
Aberdeen Female College (MA), 9,538
Aberdeen Garden Club (MS), **9,529**
Aberdeen, Ishbel (1857-1939), 7,239
Aberdeen Woman's Club (MS), **9,530**
Aberfoyle Academy (NC), 13,363
Abernathy, Mildred. *See* Ridgely, Mildred
(Abernathy) [Mrs. Montgomery]
Abernathy, Ruth, **17,230**
Abernathy, Thomas, 15,548
Abernethy, Anne Pope [Mrs. George], **305**
Abernethy, George, 305
"Abigail Adams" (drama), 6,981
Abilene High School (KS), 5,153, 11,857
Able, Alta June [Mrs. John T.], 14,542
Able, Mary Ellen (1818-1902). *See* Kimball, Mary
Ellen (Able) [Mrs. Heber Chase] (1818-1902)

Abolition of slavery. *See* Abolitionists; Slavery,
anti-slavery movements
Abolitionists, **992, 1,902,** 1,948, **2,303, 2,368, 2,495,**
2,588, 2,614, **2,629,** 3,298, 3,300, **3,477, 4,421,**
4,603, 4,695, 4,708, 4,732, 4,838, 4,839, 4,940,
5,457, 5,467, **5,684, 5,907, 5,926,** 5,939, **5,963,**
6,374, 6,412, **6,458, 6,466, 6,575, 6,577, 6,595,**
6,598, 6,738, 6,741, **6,756,** 6,762, **6,783,** 6,830,
6,833, 6,842, 6,859, **6,891, 6,911, 6,940, 6,975,**
7,072, 7,082, 7,222, 7,233, **7,294,** 7,342, **7,430,**
7,561, 7,612, 7,629, 7,643, 7,677, **7,692, 7,751,**
8,002, 9,241, **9,282,** 9,320, **10,818,** 11,111,
11,412, **11,506,** 11,616, **11,998,** 12,003, **12,181,**
12,419, 12,576, 12,638, **12,693, 12,744,** 12,864,
13,587, 13,907, 13,914, 13,927, 14,000, **14,102,**
14,873, 14,893, 14,953, 14,989, 14,991, **15,069,**
15,229, 15,259, 15,291, **15,384,** 15,567, 16,077,
17,607
opposition to, 15,601
Abolitionists, Afro-American, **2,138, 2,154, 2,315,**
5,907, 7,846, **8,010,** 11,412
Abortion, 1,352, 3,968, 4,086, 4,124, 4,148, 4,241,
5,330, 5,842, 6,446, 6,475, 6,582, 7,242, 7,289,
7,324, 7,873, 8,078, 8,361, 8,624, 8,672, 8,699,
9,523, 10,345, 13,703, 14,507, 15,988, 15,993,
17,417, 17,663, 17,774, 17,787, 17,975
law and legislation, 8,630, 9,475, 10,736, 16,396,
17,358, 17,754
legal aspects, **1,984,** 4,046, 6,788, **7,856, 7,864,**
11,932, **14,825, 15,785,** 17,367, 17,754
opposition to. *See* Right to life movement
psychological aspects, 14,023, 17,754
public opinion, 7,274
religious aspects, 16,343
Abortion clinics and referral services, **6,897,** 11,932
Abortion Coalition, 3,827
Abortion counseling, 15,818
Abortion Interest Movement (SC), **15,785**
Abortion Rights Association of Illinois, **4,046,** 4,131
Above Earth's Sorrow (book), 4,622
Above Suspicion (book), 11,168
Abraham (slave, SC), 15,530
Abraham Lincoln Centre (Chicago, IL), **3,791,** 3,835
Abraham Lincoln Settlement House (Milwaukee, WI),
17,664, 17,841
Abraham, Lot (1838-1920), **4,789, 4,964**
Abraham, Sarah C. (Alden) [Mrs. Lot] (1841-88),
4,789, 4,964
Abrahams, Grace C. [Mrs.], **13,305**
Abram, Cynthia, 7,498
Abrams, Leonna, 11,774
Abrams, Maria Frank, **17,231**
Abrams, Mary Isabella, **14,282**
Abrams, Rita (1943-), 668, 1,068
Abrego, Doña Josefa, 1,278
Absence from school. *See* School attendance
Absenteeism (labor), 8,140
Absolutists War Objectors Association, 17,939
Abstract expressionism, 11,843
Abzug, Bella Savitsky (1920-), 4,168, **11,934**
Academic librarians. *See* College librarians
Academie Jullian (Paris, France), students, 3,634

Academy Awards (moving-pictures), 1,451, 17,792, 17,944
Academy of American Poets, 13,043
Academy of Fine Arts (IL), alumnae, 5,048
Academy of Fine Arts (Philadelphia, PA), 14,862
Academy of Medicine of New Jersey, **11,068**
Academy of Mercy (Merion, PA), 5,759
Academy of Mount St. Vincent (West Albany, NY), students, 14,392
Academy of Music (Northampton, MA), 7,195
Academy of Natural Sciences (PA), 14,877, 14,944
Academy of Pacific Coast History, 743
Academy of Sciences (France), 5,418
Academy of the New Church, 14,730, 14,735
Academy of the New Church College, 14,732
Academy of the New Church Girls' Seminary, 14,732
Academy of the Sisters of Notre Dame (San Jose, CA), 665
Academy of Visitation (DC), 2,327
Academy of Visitation (Kaskaskia, IL), **4,342**
Academy, The (Rome, Italy), students, 3,463
Academy, The (Salem Academy and College, NC), 13,634
Acadians, 5,410
Accidents, prevention, **3,976**, 3,977, **3,978**, 11,830
Accountants, **8,062**, 8,366, 9,046, 11,857, 12,231, **14,113**, **15,054**, 15,360
Accreditation of nursing schools. *See* Nursing schools, accreditation
Achenbach, Abbie (Bright) [Mrs. William M.] (1848-1926), **5,215**
Achenbach, William M., 5,215
Acheson, Alice S., 2,849
Acheson, Dean, 2,497
Achilles, Lillian A. [Miss] (1871-1941), **11,268**
Ackerman, Albert, 15,548
Ackerman, Barbara, 6,336
Ackerman, Carl William (1890-1970), **2,157**
Ackerman Drug Store (Yreka, CA), 1,663
Ackerman, Ethel C., 1,663
Ackerman, Judy, 1,779
Ackerman, Mabel L. (VanderHoof) [Mrs. Carl William] (?-1954), 2,157
Ackerman, Rhea Carolyn (1896-), **306**
Ackerman, Sarah, 15,548
Ackley, Louisa Maria, **12,368**
Acoma Indians, 11,227, 16,868
  medical care, 153
Acorn, The (periodical), 13,447, 15,300
Acquaintances, Old and New, Among Reformers (book), 17,852
Acree, Eugene G., **3,128**
"Across the Continent in a Brush Runabout, A Pioneer Trip in 1908," 1,786
Acrostics, 7,090
Acting, 3,980
Action Anthropology Project Among the Fox Indians, **2,832**
Action Committee for Decent Childcare (Chicago, IL), **3,792**
Actions and defenses, 1,134, 1,179, 1,180, 1,181
Activist Group, 14,423
Acton, A. E., 1,569
Acton, Augusta (Brasch) [Mrs. A. E.], 1,569
Actors, 60, 61, 226, 531, **950**, 970, 995, **1,073**, 1,077, 1,241, 1,426, **1,449**, 1,576, 1,779, **2,360**, **2,543**, **2,555**, **2,790**, 3,100, 3,210, 3,309, **3,477**, 3,564, 3,745, **4,493**, 4,743, 5,110, **5,478**, **6,005**, 6,008, **6,024**, 6,185, **7,250**, 7,272, 7,289, 8,001, 8,297, 9,199, 9,841, 9,878, 10,025, 10,868, 11,457, **11,461**, 11,817, **11,860**, 11,897, 11,907, **11,944**, 11,997, 12,006, 12,039, 12,367, **12,426**, **12,471**, 12,472, **12,527**, **12,530**, 12,535, **12,536**, 12,539, **12,559**, **12,610**, **12,612**, 12,803, **13,100**, **14,202**, 14,413, 16,150, 16,438, 16,485, 16,577, 16,893, 16,967, 17,197, 17,501, 17,792, 17,973, **18,001**
Actors Equity, 2,284, 2,625, 12,426
Actor's Fund, 12,634
Actors' Fund of America, 12,367
Actresses, 60, 61, 214, 226, **967**, 1,124, 1,189, 1,426, 1,634, **1,647**, **1,774**, **2,159**, 2,284, 2,288, 2,303,

2,330, **2,357**, **2,360**, **2,412**, **2,418**, 2,432, **2,434**, **2,555**, 2,562, **2,625**, 2,643, 3,309, **3,346**, **3,468**, **4,473**, 4,477, 4,732, **4,764**, 4,781, **4,826**, **5,622**, **5,625**, 5,919, 5,924, **5,954**, 5,980, **5,997**, **6,003**, **6,005**, 6,008, **6,018**, **6,033**, 6,185, **6,259**, 6,392, **6,400**, **6,773**, **6,787**, **6,882**, 7,065, **7,550**, 8,351, 9,057, 9,199, 9,361, 9,466, 9,841, 10,029, **10,176**, 10,393, 10,651, 11,445, **11,860**, 11,897, 11,907, 11,985, 12,006, **12,027**, 12,039, 12,173, 12,235, 12,394, **12,426**, **12,471**, **12,474**, 12,535, **12,539**, **12,568**, **12,579**, 12,610, **12,612**, 12,622, **12,629**, **12,630**, **12,631**, **12,689**, 12,798, **12,890**, 13,662, **14,686**, **15,618**, 16,149, **16,166**
Actresses, Afro-American, **5,478**, 12,684, 12,685, 12,690
Actresses, amateur, **16,410**
Actresses, British, 1,426, **1,449**, **3,477**, 6,495, 15,116
Actresses, children, 11,907, 18,016
Actresses, deaf, **2,104**, **2,105**, **2,113**
Actresses, Jewish, **13,809**
"Acts of Early Mill Valley and Surroundings, 1579-1947," 1,067
Ada County Republican Women's Club (ID), **3,658**
Adair, Augustus Dixon, **3,129**
Adair Family (OR), **14,515**
Adair Family (OR), **14,310**
Adair, Katie (1846-?). *See* Wilson, Katie (Adair) (1846-?)
Adair, Mary Ann (Dickinson), 14,310
Adair, Mrs. John, 14,515
Adair, Octavia Hammond, 3,129
Adamic, Louis, 2,879
Adams, A. G., **3,130**
Adams, Abigail "Nabby" (1780-1808). *See* Bixby, Abigail "Nabby" (Adams) [Mrs. Luke] (1780-1808)
Adams, Abigail (Smith) [Mrs. John] (1744-1818), 2,158, 2,571, 2,854, **5,904**, **6,341**, 6,712, 7,230, **7,337**, **7,598**, 7,662, 11,605, 11,821, 12,128, **12,153**, 12,369, 15,081
Adams, Ada Adelaide. *See* Vogdes, Ada Adelaide (Adams)
Adams, Adrienne (1906-), 8,531
Adams, Agatha (Boyd) (?-1950), **12,935**
Adams, Alice, 1,572
Adams, Andrew W., Family (MN, NH), **8,895**
Adams, Anna Hale (1923-), 8,896
Adams, Annette (Abbott) (1877-1956), 400, 863, 1,178
Adams, Annie. *See* Kingsbury, Annie (Adams) [Mrs. J. F.]
Adams, Annie (1834-1915). *See* Fields, Annie (Adams) [Mrs. Thomas] (1834-1915)
Adams, Ansel, 11,220
Adams, Austin, Family (IA), **4,684**
Adams, Barbara Ellen Metheson (1883-), **16,861**
Adams, Cecilia Emily McMillen [Mrs. William] (1829-67), **14,499**, 14,628
Adams, Celia A. (Mortimer) [Mrs. William], **9,580**
Adams, Charlotte. *See* Slocum, Charlotte (Adams) [Mrs. Christopher]
Adams, Colenda Chrilla (Rogers) [Mrs. Joseph] (1869-?), **16,578**
Adams, Dennis, 16,011
Adams, Dorothy, **16,493**
Adams, Dorothy Quincey (1894-). *See* Eschweiler, Dorothy Quincey (Adams) (1894-)
Adams, E. A., 4,054
Adams, Ebenezer, 10,857
Adams, Effie Mae, 7,830
Adams, Elisabeth [Mrs. Ephraim] (1821-1905), **4,889**
Adams, Eliza (1810-88). *See* Young, Eliza (Adams) [Mrs. Ira] (1810-88)
Adams, Eliza Leland (1806-98). *See* Crosby, Eliza Leland (Adams) [Mrs. John Leland] (1806-98)
Adams, Elizabeth, **5,285**
Adams, Elizabeth [Mrs. Peter Skipwith] Randolph [Mrs. Richard] (?-ca. 1810), 2,541
Adams, Ella, 11,547
Adams, Ellen Tompkins, 307
Adams, Elmer Ellsworth, Family (MN), **8,896**
Adams, Emily Campbell, 57
Adams, Ephraim (1818-1907), **4,889**

Adams, Eugenia (ca. 1850-?). *See* Jackson, Eugenia (Adams) [Mrs. Anson] (ca. 1850-?)
Adams, Eva B., 10,677
Adams Family (Acton, MA), **5,856**
Adams Family (UT), **16,862**
Adams, Fannie C., 17,029
Adams, Flora (1840-1910). *See* Darling, Flora (Adams) [Mrs. Edward Irving] (1840-1910)
Adams, Florence James [Mrs. Milward], 3,911
Adams, Frances (Cowles) [Mrs. Elmer Ellsworth] (1859-1937), 8,896
Adams Girls' School (Uttar Pradesh, India), 14,426
Adams, Grace E. (?-1939). *See* Hall, Grace E. (Adams) (?-1939)
Adams, Hannah [Miss] (1755-1831), 6,234, **6,342**, 6,741
Adams, Harriet B. Corbett [Mrs. Eben L.], **9,016**
Adams, Henry, 6,185, 15,601
Adams, Henry, 9,384
Adams, Inez (1904-67), **5,455**
Adams, J. D., 16,168
Adams, James Douglass, 4,889
Adams, John (1735-1826), 1,501, 2,158, 5,904, 6,341, 7,337, 7,598, 7,662, **12,369**, 15,041
Adams, John, Family, **2,158**, **2,854**
Adams, John Q., 9,259
Adams, John Quincy, 2,158, 2,608, 15,081, 15,256
Adams, Juliette Aurelia (Graves) [Mrs. Crosby] (1858-?), 13,331
Adams, Juliette Cecelia Bayles, 16,417
Adams, Katherine Rogers, 11,662
Adams, Lina D., **10,069**
Adams, Lizzie, 3,375, 16,049
Adams, Louisa (1773-1813). *See* Park, Louisa (Adams) [Mrs. John] (1773-1813)
Adams, Louisa Catherine (Johnson) [Mrs. John Quincy] (1775-1852), 2,158, 2,608, 3,907, 5,748, 11,654
Adams, Lucy Wilcox, 2,233
Adams, Luella (1889-1967). *See* Dalton, Luella (Adams) [Mrs. Harley Warren] (1889-1967)
Adams, Margaret (Webster) [Mrs. Hugh] (1831-62), **16,579**
Adams, Maria Abigail Henry (1836-1928), **1,227**
Adams, Marie (1890-), **4,518**, 4,532
Adams, Marion V. (Dunn), 14,778
Adams, Marjorie (1891-1951), 8,896
Adams, Martha (1751-1832). *See* Tufts, Martha (Adams) (1751-1832)
Adams, Mary, 13,052
Adams, Mary Ann. *See* Starr, Mary Ann (Adams) [Mrs. Cecil Franklin]
Adams, Mary Emma Guerard [Mrs. Richard W.], 3,515
Adams, Mary Evans [Mrs. Elmer], 8,896
Adams, Mary (Newbury) [Mrs. Austin] (1837-1901), 4,684, 4,732, 4,770, 4,786
Adams, Mary P., 11,495
Adams, Maude (1872-1953), **2,159**, 2,968, 3,100, 3,994, 4,781, 7,310, 11,453, 11,897, 11,997, 12,695
Adams, Melissa Jane Caldwell [Mrs. William Henry, Jr.] (1851-?), 16,862
Adams, Moses (1749-1819), 5,856
Adams, Myra Leanne (Abbett) (?-1968), 14,498, 14,628
Adams, Patience, 15,377
Adams, R. D., **16,398**
Adams, Richard, 2,541
Adams, Ruth, 7,574
Adams, Sarah Langston (1890-), 16,780
Adams, Sarah P., 7,135
Adams School Civic League (Minneapolis, MN), **8,897**
Adams, Sherman, 11,857
Adams Street Ladies' Woman's Investment Company, 1,429
Adams, Sue. *See* Vaughan, Sue (Adams) Landon [Mrs. Landon]
Adams, Susan (?-1839), **12,370**
Adams, Susan D., 12,589
Adams, Susan Maria Hazeltine [Mrs. Andrew W.] (1831-?), 8,895

Adams, Thomas Sewall, 17,757
Adams, Velma. *See* Dayton, Velma (Adams)
Adams, Wilhelmina (ca. 1900-), **12,680**
Adams, William (OH), 9,580
Adams, William (OR), 14,499
Adams, William Henry, Sr., 16,862
Adams, William Henry, Jr., 16,862
Adamson, Margaret (Lukens) Smith, 5,941
Adamson, Mary (Price) (1909-), 13,176
Adamson, Sarah Read (1829-1909). *See* Dolley,
   Sarah Read (Adamson) [Mrs. Lester Clinton]
   (1829-1909)
Adato, Perry Miller, **17,791**
Addams, 4,146
Addams, Anna (Hostetter) [Mrs. William] Haldeman
   [Mrs. John Huy] (1828-1919), 4,095, 4,154,
   4,477
Addams Family (IL), 4,095
Addams, Jane [Miss] (1860-1935), 540, 656, 677,
   756, 924, 1,224, 1,426, 1,559, 1,593, 1,680,
   2,186, 2,224, 2,359, 2,403, 2,432, 2,439, 2,451,
   2,502, 2,509, 2,602, 2,878, 3,280, 3,302, 3,787,
   3,803, 3,814, 3,828, 3,880, 3,889, 3,899, 3,910,
   3,992, 3,995, 4,003, 4,007, **4,047**, 4,048, 4,052,
   4,056, 4,066, 4,085, 4,089, 4,095, 4,100, 4,101,
   4,103, 4,110, 4,111, 4,117, 4,143, 4,153, 4,154,
   4,155, 4,161, 4,165, 4,166, 4,173, 4,211, 4,233,
   4,304, 4,330, 4,331, **4,343**, 4,477, 4,781, 4,823,
   4,958, 5,120, 5,121, 5,122, 5,209, 5,870, 6,427,
   6,499, 6,544, 6,602, 6,604, 6,712, 6,946, 6,978,
   7,172, 7,187, 7,210, 7,216, 7,217, 7,268, 7,300,
   7,731, 7,784, 7,792, 7,868, 7,923, 7,949, 8,144,
   8,651, 8,658, 8,659, 8,668, 8,678, 9,187, 9,302,
   9,443, 9,467, 9,494, 10,206, 11,299, 11,572,
   11,760, 12,026, 12,044, 12,518, 12,534, 13,801,
   15,269, 15,298, 15,301, 15,302, 15,305, 15,306,
   15,316, 15,946, **17,581**, 17,735
Addams, John Huy (1822-81), 4,095
Addams, Mary Catherine. *See* Linn, Mary Catherine
   (Addams)
Addams, Sarah Alice (1853-1915). *See* Haldeman,
   Sarah Alice (Addams) [Mrs. Henry Winfield]
   (1853-1915)
Addams, Sarah (Weber) [Mrs. John Huy] (1817-63),
   4,095
Addenbrooke, Alice Baltzell, **10,637**
Adderley's boarding school, 12,433
Addes, George (1910-), **8,136**
Addison Gallery of American Art, 17,407
Addy, Wesley, 12,367
Adelia Cheever House (MI), **7,697**
Adelphai Club (MN), **8,898**
Adelphai College (MO), 9,857
Adelphi University, faculty, 8,642
Adger, Elizabeth K. Shewsbury [Mrs. John B.],
   15,435
Adger Family (SC), **15,434**, 15,550, 15,726
Adger, James (1777-?), 15,434
Adger, Jane Ann, 15,418, 15,434
Adger, John B., **15,435**
Adger, John Bailey, 15,550
Adger, Margaret Milligan (1807-84). *See* Smythe,
   Margaret Milligan (Adger) [Mrs. Thomas]
   (1807-84)
Adger, Sarah Elizabeth Ellison [Mrs. James], 15,434
Adger, Susan D., 15,434
Ad Hoc Committee on the Status of Women (Morris,
   MN), **8,532**
Adivar, Halide Edib (1885-?), 7,191
Adix, Shauna, 16,971
Adjutants, **2,671**, 2,675
Adkins, Bertha S. (1906-), 99, **5,126**, 5,135, 5,137,
   11,857
Adkins, Edna M., 2,179
Adkins v. The Children's Hospital, 6,973
Adkinson, Florence Burlingame (1847-1925?),
   6,343
Adler, Alexandra, 2,491
Adler, Alfred (1870-1937), 6,224
Adler, Celia, 11,817
Adler, Gerhard, 2,631
Adler, Ruth (1915-68), 8,531
Adlerika (drug), 8,992
Adlord, H., 3,926

Adlow, Dorothy (1902-64), **6,344**
Administrative agencies, 1,897, 1,915, 1,917, 1,936,
   1,938, 2,679, 2,680, 2,681, 2,683, 2,684, 2,685,
   2,686, 2,687, 2,837, 3,665, 3,950, 17,015, 17,018,
   17,021, 17,022. *See also* Executive advisory
   bodies
Admirals, 4,822, 4,958, 6,557, 6,567, 9,308, 11,154,
   11,500, 12,191, 14,863, **15,080**
Adolescent Psychology (book), 13,870
Adoption, 1,236, 2,575, 4,103, 5,840, 6,259, 7,281,
   8,638, 8,640, 8,657, 9,140, 9,166, 9,422, 11,606,
   12,017, 13,795, 14,625, 17,991
   law and legislation, 8,633
   legal aspects, 3,852
Adorers of the Blood of Christ, Provincial House
   (Wichita, KS), **5,236**
Adorers of the Blood of Christ, Ruma Provincial
   House (Red Bud, IL), **4,314**
Adressebladet, 8,801
Adrian Daily Telegram (MI), 8,164
Adrian Dominican Sisters (Adrian, MI), **7,694**
Adrian Woman's Club (MI), **7,695**
Adriance, Fannie Amelia [Mrs. Jacob], 1,751
Adriance, Jacob, 1,751
Adult education, 2,516, 3,437, **3,651**, 3,971, **4,048**,
   4,115, 8,058, 8,074, 8,947, 9,020, 9,492, 11,844,
   12,473, 15,798, 17,029
Adult Education Council of Greater Chicago (IL),
   4,048
Adultery. *See* Extramarital relations
Advance (periodical), 15,979
Advent Christian Church, 3,741, 3,742
   missions, **7,064**
Advent Christian Church, Woman's Home and
   Foreign Mission Society, 3,742
Adventure (periodical), 393, 6,081
Adventure and adventurers, 1,476, 12,174, **14,660**.
   See also Explorers; Pioneers and settlers;
   Shipwrecks
*Adventure in Higher Education: The Story of the
   National College of Education, An* (book), 4,210
Adventurer's Club of Detroit (MI), **8,018**
"Adventures in World Understanding," 8,150
"Adventures of Grace Litchenfels, The," 5,788
Adventures of Pims (book), 17,553
Advertiser (AL), 63
Advertiser (Huntington, WV), 17,436
Advertising, 2,205, **6,345**, 6,523, 11,837, 12,547,
   17,623. *See also* Public relations; Radio
   advertising; Television advertising
   vocational guidance, **4,171**
Advertising agencies, 17,623
Advertising Careers for Women, 17,623
Advertising fliers, **10,659**
Advertising of Kate (book), 13,811
Advertising Women of New York, Inc., **6,345**, 6,523,
   17,582
"Advice for Young Folk" (column), 12,259
Advisor for Harvard Wives (MA), **6,264**
Advisory Committee of the State Park Contingency
   Fund (CA), 990
Advisory Council on Public Welfare, 8,632
Advocate (Bath, NY), 11,647
Advocate, The (periodical), **2,711**
Aeolian Ladies of Charity, 12,680
Aegerter, Adele Antoinette Agnes (1891-1970). *See*
   Bird, Adele Antoinette Agnes (Aegerter) [Mrs.
   Arthur D.] (1891-1970)
Aerial Nurse Corps of America, 13,762
Aero Club of America, 3,793, 17,217
Aero Club of Illinois, **3,793**
Aero Club of Philadelphia (PA), **14,946**
Aeronautical engineers, 11,831
Aeronautical societies, **31**, **1,060**, **3,793**, 5,132, 5,162,
   14,946, 17,217, 17,450
Aeronautics, **1,040**, **11,831**, 14,687, **14,946**, 17,566.
   See also Air pilots
   laws and regulations, 5,120
Aeronautics, commercial, 11,831
Aeronautics, military, study and teaching, 11,919,
   14,161
Aesthetic Club of Little Rock (AR), **276**
Aesthetics, 58, 17,235
Affiliated Schools for Workers, Inc., 6,893, 17,588

Affirmative action, 4,124, 5,873, 7,262, 14,023
Affirmative action programs, 4,043, 4,382, 6,571,
   8,550, 13,878, 15,236, **17,503**
Affleck, Afton Grant, 16,780
Affleck, Lady, 11,826
AFL-CIO. *See* American Federation of
   Labor-Congress of Industrial Organizations
AFL Magazine (periodical), 11,926
Africa, 2,339, 6,023, 6,109, 10,850, 13,276
   Americans in, 6,109
   antiquities, 45
   clinics, 5,475
   colonization, 9,991
   congresses and conventions, 2,130
   English language, study and teaching, 8,090
   factories, American owned, 15,765
   international education, 6,702
   labor and laboring classes, education, 8,071, 8,126
   missionaries to, 45, 87, 3,464, 7,129, 13,121
   missionaries to, Episcopal, 12,206
   missionaries to, lay, **15,669**
   missionaries to, Presbyterian, 93
   missions, 8,837
   orphans and orphan asylums, 5,475
   political and social conditions, 11,857
   politics and government, 13,280
   water resources development, 5,475
   women, status of, 87
   World War II, war work, 5,131
   Young Women's Christian Association, 12,724
Africa Before They Came (book), 6,110
Africa, South, race problems, 9,149
African Creeks I Have Been Up (book), 115
African Inland Mennonite Mission, **13,757**
African Journey (book), 3,291
African Methodist Episcopal Church, 3,038
African Methodist Episcopal Zion Church (KY),
   5,383
Afro-American Project (WA), **17,232**
"Afro-American Writers Published after 1835, With
   an Alphabetical List (tentative) of Imprints
   Written by American Authors, 1760-1835"
   (thesis), 2,146
Afro-Americans, 45, 90, 91, 122, 206, 659, 726, **727**,
   968, 993, **994**, 1,011, 1,017, 1,240, 1,332, **1,368**,
   1,567, **1,570**, 1,654, 1,655, **1,683**, 1,777, 1,837,
   2,124, **2,126**, **2,127**, **2,129**, **2,130**, **2,132**, **2,134**,
   2,143, 2,153, 2,368, 2,399, **2,490**, 2,587, **2,602**,
   2,643, 2,685, **2,880**, **2,945**, **2,946**, **2,947**, **2,948**,
   3,065, 3,115, **3,118**, 3,267, 3,279, 3,280, 3,282,
   3,290, **3,293**, **3,295**, 3,297, 3,303, **3,305**, 3,451,
   3,478, 3,593, **3,799**, **3,846**, 3,889, **3,934**, 4,032,
   4,049, 4,073, 4,087, 4,090, 4,093, 4,142, 5,064,
   5,121, 5,122, **5,314**, 5,378, **5,383**, **5,384**, **5,387**,
   5,458, **5,465**, 5,469, **5,533**, 5,718, **5,828**, 5,870,
   5,945, **6,628**, **7,211**, 7,243, 7,807, **8,056**, **8,065**,
   8,068, **8,097**, 8,098, 8,148, 8,164, 8,287, 8,639,
   9,041, 9,114, 9,241, 9,252, 9,259, 9,284, 9,467,
   9,527, 9,575, 9,583, 9,919, 9,962, 9,991, 10,021,
   10,030, 10,192, 11,013, 11,299, 11,390, 11,440,
   11,605, 11,616, 11,817, **12,004**, 12,100, 12,532,
   12,683, 12,686, **12,690**, 12,760, **12,865**, 12,939,
   13,073, 13,108, 13,120, **13,214**, 13,243, 13,635,
   13,682, 13,934, 13,937, 14,140, 14,241, 14,656,
   15,106, 15,176, 15,255, 15,281, 15,427, 15,439,
   15,451, 15,504, 15,507, 15,681, **15,782**, 15,917,
   16,261, 16,342, 16,351, 16,377, 16,780, 16,877,
   17,075, 17,163, **17,232**, 17,600, 17,663. *See also*
   Abolitionists, Afro-American; Freedmen;
   Mullatoes; Race problems; Slavery
   census, 15,069
   civil rights, 64, 889, **2,143**, 2,153, 2,303, 2,432,
      2,678, 6,814, 11,855, **12,682**, 15,197, **17,245**,
      17,299
   economic conditions, 3,283, 8,029, 9,252, 9,467
   education, 56, **88**, 89, 1,842, 1,856, 1,875, **1,898**,
      2,044, **2,130**, **2,313**, **2,486**, 3,281, 3,296, 3,580,
      5,457, 5,459, **5,469**, 5,472, 6,430, 6,997, 7,776,
      8,659, 9,542, 10,055, 11,057, 11,897, 12,236,
      13,215, 13,504, 13,859, 14,719, 14,850, 15,023,
      15,069, 15,541, 15,606, 15,744, **15,913**, 17,502
   employment, 3,414, 8,089, **8,115**, 13,950
   history, **3,298**, **3,748**, 3,915, 5,535, **16,205**
   housing, 15,205

medical care, **3,508**, 9,599, 15,011
pictorial works, 13,446
politics and suffrage, 2,502, 3,158, 4,732, 9,308
religion, 5,423, 7,656
segregation, 3,292, 9,605. *See also* Segregation in
 education; Segregation in higher education;
 Segregation in transportation
social conditions, 2,332, 5,540, 6,510, **6,745,** 9,342,
 12,317, 13,356, 13,618, 15,626
Afro-Americans and trade-unions, 8,121
Afro-Americans in literature, 81
Afro-Arts Bazaar, 5,465
After Barbed Wire (book), 10,252
"After Liberation, What?" (lecture), 15,197
"After the Manner of Bassanio" (article), 4,895
Aftermath Club (IN), **4,546**
Afternoon Women, The (book), 6,111
Afton, Lee. *See* Perry, Sally Randle [Mrs. John]
Agassiz, Alexander (1835-1910), 6,316, 6,681
Agassiz, Elizabeth Cabot (Cary) [Mrs. Louis]
 (1822-1907), 584, 2,643, 4,732, 6,339, **6,346,**
 6,358, 6,436, 6,593, 6,657, 6,659, 6,707, 11,742
Agassiz Family (MA), 6,593
Agassiz, Ida, 6,916
Agassiz, Louis (1807-73), 584, **6,316,** 6,346, 6,436,
 6,593, 6,657, 6,916, 9,753
Agassiz, Pauline (1841-1917). *See* Shaw, Pauline
 (Agassiz) [Mrs. Quincy Adams] (1841-1917)
Age Center of New England, **6,347,** 6,490
Age of consent, 8,633, 10,342
Age of Innocence, The, 4,491
Age of Reform, The (book), 11,912
Aged. *See* Senior citizens
Agerton, Zillah Lee (Bostick) Redd (1871-1967),
 3,358
Aggy (slave, VA), 2,132
Aging, 6,705, 7,817, 8,108, 8,674, 17,245, 17,341. *See
 also* Seniors
Agitator (periodical), 11,167
Agnes Blake Study Club (Hopkins, MN), 8,481
Agnes of Sorrento (book), 1,953
Agnes Scott College (GA), **3,452,** 13,398
 students, 3,430
Agnes Scott College (GA), Alumni Association, 3,343
Agnes Scott Institute (GA), 3,275
Agnew, Mary C., 4,697
Agnew, Paul, 6,778
Agnew, Spiro, 5,828
Agnosticism, 17,980
Agricultural administration, 6,343, 8,161, 8,171,
 14,202, 17,714
Agricultural Agent and Extension Service (MN),
 Anoka County, **9,469**
Agricultural colleges, 2,682, 6,624, **8,578, 8,607,**
 9,712, 11,703, 15,780, 16,402
Agricultural education, 4,920
Agricultural experiment stations, 4,386
Agricultural extension agents, **10,735**
Agricultural extension work, 453, **2,682, 5,871,** 6,585,
 9,052, **9,469, 10,015,** 10,023, 10,039. *See also*
 Home demonstration work
Agricultural industries, 6,315
Agricultural laborers. *See* Agricultural workers
Agricultural laws and legislation, 10,034, 11,695
Agricultural literature, 5,043, **10,504,** 13,698
Agricultural machinery, 8,741
 trade and manufacture, 8,302, 17,679
Agricultural prices, 9,975
Agricultural research, 2,682
Agricultural societies, 2,682, **4,687,** 4,839, 4,947,
 6,964, 8,112, 8,144, 8,161, 8,517, 8,518, 8,924,
 8,994, 9,788, 9,988, 10,047, **10,259,** 10,339,
 10,354, 10,479, **10,505, 11,437,** 11,550, 11,650,
 13,698, 13,720, 14,729, **16,963,** 17,638, 17,676,
 17,720, 17,926. *See also* Patrons of Husbandry
Agricultural Society of Northern Chautauqua (NY),
 11,650
Agricultural statistics, 2,676, **5,570,** 16,357
Agricultural workers, 1,614, 3,690, **6,963, 8,467,**
 9,467
 education, **17,448**
Agricultural workers, Afro-American, 15,712
Agricultural workers, Mexican-American, 16,003
Agriculture, 55, 108, 844, 1,428, 1,492, 1,626, 1,786,

3,739, 3,754, **3,756,** 4,424, 5,366, 5,644, 5,746,
 7,597, 7,680, 7,740, 8,288, 8,302, 8,352, 8,371,
 8,518, 8,687, 8,693, 8,765, 9,063, 9,107, 9,154,
 9,158, 9,312, 9,468, 9,975, 10,065, 10,638,
 10,680, 11,520, 12,402, 13,322, 13,540, 14,201,
 14,509, 14,522, 14,532, 14,622, 15,681, 16,078,
 16,092, 16,095, 16,148, 16,486, 16,867, 16,968,
 17,249, 17,271. *See also* Cattle; Crops and
 climate; Dairying; Farm life; Farm management;
 Farmers; Farmers' institutes; Farms; Forests and
 forestry; Gardening; Horticulture; Stock and
 stock-breeding; Viticulture; Women in agriculture
accounting, 6,206, 7,647, 9,787, 11,573, **12,392,**
 13,155
economic aspects, 1,173
experimentation, 9,625
Agriculture and state, 1,173, 2,682, 5,120, 10,505
Agriculture, cooperative, 8,518, 10,354, 14,509,
 17,676
Agriculturists, 349, **2,526, 6,896, 11,600, 11,683,**
 13,564, 14,904, 15,221, **17,055.** *See also*
 Farmers; Horticulturists; Plant pathologists
Agronomists. *See* Agriculturists
Agrostologists and agrostology. *See* Grass research
Aguilar, Grace, 13,079
Aguilar, Sarah, 13,079
Ah, Wilderness! (drama), 12,367
Ah, Wilderness (screen play), 17,799
Ahlstrom, June Claudia (Farrer), **16,399**
Ahn, Miss, 11,445
Ahrens, Gladys (Wheaton) [Mrs. B. F.] (1900-),
 9,434
Ahrens, Mary A. (1836-?), 3,862
Aichel, Alma, 15,551
Aichel Family (SC), **15,551**
Aichel, Johanna, 15,551
Aichel, Mrs. Oskar, 15,551
Aichel, Oskar, 15,551
Aid for the Shipwrecked, 12,931
Aid the Spanish Republic, 8,106
Aid to dependent children. *See* Child welfare
Aiken, Conrad, 15,900, 18,021
Aiken County Equal Suffrage League (SC), 15,706
Aiken, David, 15,552
Aiken, Ednah (Robinson) (1872-1960), **308**
Aiken, Eliza (Buckingham) [Mrs. William], 1,886
Aiken Family (GA), 3,088
Aiken Family (OR). *See* Aitken Family (OR)
Aiken Family (SC), **15,552**
Aiken, John Adams (1850-1927), **5,736**
Aiken, Kate Rennie. *See* Archer, Kate Rennie (Aiken)
Aiken, M. E. [Mrs. David], 5,736
Aiken, Mary Gayle, 15,552
Aiken, Mercy. *See* Welles, Mercy (Aiken) [Mrs.
 Roger]
Aiken, Nancy, 15,552
Aiken, Sarah, **4,344**
Ailshie, Margaret (Cobb) (1883-1959), 3,669
Aimwell Presbyterian Church (SC), **15,553**
Ainsworth, Amelia Ann. *See* Nichols, Amelia Ann
 (Ainsworth) [Mrs. Charles Sanders]
Ainsworth, Cynthia, 8,256
Ainsworth, Dorothy Sears (1894-1976), 7,158, **7,173**
Air bases, 1,769, 2,910, 9,587, 9,709
Air-brakes, 8,934
Air defenses, 14,203
Air defenses, civil, 5,737
Air force wives, 11,874, **11,919**
Air forces, volunteer, 11,861
Air Line Pilots Association, Steward and Stewardess
 Division, **8,055**
Air lines, flight attendants, 17,214
Air mail service, 11,831, 11,874
Air pilots, 36, **1,040,** 1,594, **2,179,** 2,450, 3,793,
 4,681, 4,756, 5,060, **5,132, 5,162,** 5,177, **5,311,**
 6,550, 6,573, **9,137,** 9,587, 11,235, 11,861,
 12,790, **14,161,** 14,203, **14,233,** 14,946, 17,450,
 17,731, **17,935**
Air pollution, 3,162
Air quality, 14,052
Air raid wardens, 5,755, **12,668**
Air travel, 7,170, **12,453,** 13,277
Aircraft drafting, 11,831
Aircraft industry workers, 17,214

Aircraft Warning Service, **5,737**
Airplane factories, **17,214**
Airplane racing, 11,831
Airplanes, 14,055
 accidents, 9,137
 ground handling, 11,861
Airports, 13,762, 14,946
Aitchison, Beatrice (1908-), **6,348**
Aitken, Alvord (1854-90), 14,500
Aitken, Carrie Fidelia (Johnson) [Mrs. Alvord]
 (1860-1947), 14,311, 14,500
Aitken Family (OR), **14,311, 14,500**
Aitken, Frances Alva (1889-1970), 14,311, 14,500
Aitken, Geraldine Lee, 14,311, 14,500
Aitken, Jane [Miss] (1764-1832), **14,881**
Aitken, John William Douglas (1824-1914), 14,500
Aitken, Maria Morrison (1834-83), 14,500
Aitken, Robert, 14,881
Aitkens Family (OR). *See* Aitken Family (OR)
Aitkens, Walter, 10,386
Aiton, Hannah, 8,899
Aiton, John Felix (1817-92), **8,899,** 9,446
Aiton, Mary Briggs [Mrs. John Felix], 8,899, 9,446
Aiton, Nancy (Hunter) [Mrs. John Felix] (ca.
 1820-53), 8,899
Ajzenberg-Selove, Fay (1926-), 1,097
Akehurst Family, **2,958**
Akehurst, Jennie, 2,958
Akerley, Elsie Ann (1842-83). *See* Faust, Elsie Ann
 (Akerley) [Mrs. Henry Jacob] (1842-83)
Akerly, Catherine. *See* Mitchill, Catherine (Akerly)
 Cock [Mrs. Samuel Latham]
Akerly, Margaret. *See* Miller, Margaret (Akerly)
 [Mrs. Silvanus]
Akers, A., 8,900
Akers, Charles N., 8,900
Akers, Elizabeth, 8,900
Akers, Elizabeth Anne (Chase) [Mrs. Benjamin Paul]
 (1832-1911). *See* Allen, Elizabeth Anne (Chase)
 [Mrs. Marshall S. M.] Taylor [Mrs. Benjamin
 Paul] Akers [Mrs. Elijah Marshall] (1832-1911)
Akers, Mary Dwight [Mrs. Charles N.], 8,900
Akers, Mrs. Peter, 8,900
Akers, Paul, 5,674
Akers, Peter, Family (MN), **8,900**
Akin Family (OR). *See* Aitken Family (OR)
Akin, Mabel M., 14,698
Akins, Ethel M. (1895-), **8,868**
Akins, Zoë. [Mrs. Hugo] Rumbold (1886-1958), 317,
 642, 1,025, **1,027, 1,390,** 10,154
Akre, Edna Honoria, 9,231
*ALA in Siberia, Letters Written by Harry Clemons,
 Representative of the ALA War Service with the
 A.E.F. in Siberia, The,* 4,727
Alabama, 20, **44, 45, 73,** 81, 9,699, 13,000
 Afro-Americans, 90
 education, **88**
 archive buildings, 76
 archives, 76
 archivists, **11, 57, 76**
 artists, 81
 associations, institutions, etc., **3, 12, 40, 53**
 authors, 38, **77,** 81, **113**
 boycott, **84,** 1,859, 8,117
 catalogs, college, 108, 114
 Catholic schools, 24
 Catholic universities and colleges, 24
 charitable societies, **118**
 charitable societies, Jewish, **13,806, 13,827**
 charities, medical, **21**
 Cherokee Indians, 62
 choirs (music), 122
 citizens' associations, 112, 3,283
 city councilwomen, 104
 civil rights workers, **64, 65**
 Civil War, 62, 69, 100, 13,518
 campaigns and battles, 13,090
 centennial celebrations, etc., **99,** 103
 personal narratives, 62, **66,** 68, 78, 79, 80, 10,584
 societies, **40**
 societies, Confederate, **9, 16,** 103, **119, 120**
 clergy, 53
 clergy, Presbyterian, 27, 9,801
 clergymen's children, Presbyterian, 65

clubs, **4, 7, 15, 50, 52, 74, 75,** 76, 116, 126
clubs, Afro-American, 91, 128
coal mines and mining, 63
coeducation, 81, 109, 117
college librarians, **82,** 105, 106, **107,** 120
college presidents, 81, **85**
college students, 109
college teachers, **97, 104**
college teachers, wives of, 4, 6
congressmen, 60, **61,** 76, 110
conservatories of music, 14
convict labor, 117
    opposition to, **53**
court-houses, 2,507
deans (in schools), **89, 96, 108,** 116
demonstrations, 11,855
diaries and journals, 19th C, 28, **71, 78,** 79,
    13,140
discrimination in transportation, 84
dormitories, 13
educational associations, 3
educators, 38, 56, **126, 128**
examinations, 117
farmers, 13,138
folklorists, 81
gardening, societies, **50**
genealogists, 11
governors, 53, 102, 105, 106
greek letter societies, 116
halls of fame, 32
high schools, 78
hospitals, administration, **21**
integration in higher education, 89, **102, 112**
journalists, Afro-American, 3,799
land trusts, 88
landlord and tenant, 90
lawyers, 20, 64, 65, 13,033
librarians, **11,** 123
libraries, university and college, 107
literary societies, 54, **57, 75,** 76
lobbyists, 76
lynching, prevention of, 3,279
missions, **17,219**
monasticism and religious orders for women,
    Catholic, **24**
music
    competitions, 51
    instruction and study, 51
music teachers, 83
musical societies, **17, 51**
Native Americans, 81
    education, 17,219
    government relations, 17,219
newsletters, 4
newspapers, 63, 81
nonviolence, moral and religious aspects, 1,859
novelists, 39, 47
nursing schools, **22**
officials and employees, **8,644**
patriotic societies, **40**
photographs, 9,699
pioneers and settlers, **62, 67,** 81, 106
plantation life, 2,221
politicians, 60, **61**
politics, practical, women's activism, **12, 53**
poll-tax, 7
prayer meetings, 16,097
prison reform, 81, 117
prisons for women, 117
prohibition, 13,388
public health nursing, 3,432
public welfare administration, 8,644
public works, 76
race problems, 1,859
reformatories, 91
riots, 112
scholarships, 51
schools, 44, 63, 71, 81
schools, Jewish, 13,827
senators, United States, 76, 110
slavery, **2,221**
social life and customs, 63, 81, 11,855, 12,653,
    13,463, 16,057
social reformers, 56, **117**

social work administration, **8,673**
societies, Jewish, **13,777**
soldiers' monuments, 121
state universities and colleges, **9,746**
student aid, 51
students, recreation, 18
students' societies, **18**
suffrage, 49
    law and legislation, 49
    opposition to, 76
suffrage societies, **5, 42,** 49, **55**
surveyors, 28
teachers, 111, 7,935
temperance societies, 56
tetanus, mortality, 106
trade and professional associations, 76
trade-unions, officials and employees, 3,448
universities and colleges, **1,** 81, 97, 9,671, 9,672
    archives, 33
    history, 126
women
    civil rights, 63
    education, 109
women's colleges, 14, 116, 9,698
"Alabama April," 73
Alabama Christian Movement, 1,859
Alabama Citizen, 112
Alabama Club Woman, The (periodical), 116
Alabama College, 116
    faculty, **104**
Alabama Department of Archives and History, 11
Alabama Equal Suffrage Association, 55
Alabama Federation of Colored Women's Clubs. *See*
    Alabama State Federation of Colored Women's
    Clubs
Alabama Federation of Garden Clubs, 50
Alabama Federation of Music Clubs, 51
Alabama Federation of Women's Clubs, 15, **52,** 76,
    116
Alabama Female Athenaeum, 63
Alabama Historical Quarterly, 69
Alabama League of Women Voters, Convict Lease
    System Abolition Activities, **53**
Alabama Pen Women, **54**
Alabama Polytechnic Institute. *See* Auburn
    University (AL)
Alabama School Journal (periodical), 116
Alabama State Federation of Colored Women's Clubs,
    91, 128
Alabama State University
    faculty, 82
    presidents, 83, **85**
Alabama Student Conference on Civil Rights, 89
Alabama Voter, 12
Alabama White Ribbon, 56
Alabama Woman's Anti-Ratification League, 55,
    15,964
Alabama Woman's Christian Temperance Union,
    Frances Willard Centenary Pictorial Review, 56
Alabama Women's Hall of Fame, 32
Alabama Writers Conclave, **57**
Aladdin Studio Tiffin Room (CA), 941
Alameda County Society for the Prevention of
    Cruelty to Children (CA), **309**
Alameda District Federation (CA), 1,341
Alamo (TX), 16,314
    siege (1836), 16,245
Alaska, 14,501, 14,562, 17,272
    aeronautics, 14,687
    artists, **134**
    charitable societies, 17,397
    church records and registers, Russian Orthodox,
        2,563
    civil defense, 17,217
    clergy, Presbyterian, 130
    clubs, 140, **147, 148**
    dentists, 17,217
    diaries and journals, travel, **129, 136**
    educators, **138**
    Eskimos, 14,415
    gold discoveries, 12,696
    gold mines and mining, 129, 130
    governors, **145, 17,217**
    housing managers, 140

    islands, 646
    medical records, 141
    mines and mineral resources, 7,935
    mining claims, 135
    missionaries, **1,504**
    missionaries, Friends, **137**
    missions, 4,848
        educational work, 1,168
    missions, Lutheran, 8,861
    Native Americans, 130, 2,563, 16,875
        history, 17,263
    nurses, **141**
    old age homes, 17,217
    oral history, 130
    patriotic societies, 145
    pioneers and settlers, **135,** 17,397
    political clubs, **133**
    politics, practical, women's activism, **139**
    prospecting, 2,528
    public libraries, 147
    reporters and reporting, **132**
    Russian Orthodox Greek Catholic Church of North
        America, **2,563**
    school superintendents and principals, 131
    societies, 144
    suffrage, 17,217
    teachers, 130, **143**
    temperance societies, 138
    wildlife, 5,487
Alaska Commercial Company, 619, 646
Alaska Dental Board, 17,217
Alaska Friends, 17,397
*Alaska: Its History, Resources, Geography and
    Government* (book), 143
Alaska Native Brotherhood and Sisterhood, 17,217
Alaska Packers Company, 412
Alaska Weekly (Fairbanks, AK), 132
Alaska Women's Patriotic League, 145
Alaskan Forget-me-nots (booklet), 1,439
Alaux, Alexander, **9,581**
Alaux, Louisa Antoinette, 9,581
Albany Argus (NY), 11,534
Albany Army Relief Bazaar (NY), **11,247**
Albany Female Academy (NY), 11,248
Albany Female Seminary (NY), **11,257,** 12,470
Albany Fresh Air Guild for Children (NY), 11,263
Albany Hospital Training School for Nurses, 6,238
Albany Inter-Racial Council (NY), 11,591
Albany Woman's Suffrage Society (NY), **11,258**
Albee, Edward, 16,161
Albers, Anni [Mrs. Josef] (1889-), **2,727, 13,307,**
    13,484
Albers, Hermina Charlotte (1899-), **14,502**
Albers, Josef, 13,307, 13,484
Albert, Dorothy, 11,774
Albert, Eleanor (?-1874). *See* Bliss, Eleanor (Albert)
    [Mrs. Alexander, II] (?-1874)
Albert, Emily, 2,188
Albertson, Ralph, 2,991
Albion College (MI), 8,168
    faculty, 9,448
Albion Monthly Meeting (IA), 4,842
Albrand, Martha (pseudonym). *See* Lamon, Heidi
    Huberta Freybe Loewengard (1911-)
Albrecht, Amy (Sadtler) (1857-1942), **14,796**
Albrecht, Evelyn [Mrs. Milton C.], 11,369
Albrecht, Milton C. (1904-), **11,369**
Albree, John, 17,122
Albrier, Frances (1898-), **8,056**
Albright, Erbie Claire (1895-1964), **17,445**
Albright, William, 13,308
Albrizio, Conrad, 5,488
Albums, 1,970, **3,794,** 4,432, **7,135, 8,334, 11,421,**
    12,202, 12,269, 12,332, 12,492, 12,603
Albuquerque Symphony Orchestra (NM), 11,217,
    11,218
Alcohol, 16,774, 16,863, 16,872, 16,875, 16,876
    physiological effects, 14,017
"Alcohol Education" (ms), 17,750
Alcoholic women, 8,984
Alcoholics, hospitals and asylums, 4,088, **4,164**
Alcoholism, 5,980
    study and teaching, 12,806
    treatment, 8,984

Alcorn, Amelia Walton (Glover) [Mrs. James L.] (ca. 1830-post 1903), 9,582, 9,709
Alcorn, James L. (1816-94), **9,582**
Alcott, Amos Bronson (1799-1888), 4,684, 5,949, 6,823, 7,042, 7,044, 7,046
Alcott, Anna Bronson (1831-1893). *See* Pratt, Anna, Bronson (Alcott) (1831-1893)
Alcott Hospital (Kuwait), 1,840
Alcott, Louisa May (1832-88), 951, 1,426, 3,927, **5,905**, 5,941, 6,762, **7,042**, 7,044, 7,055, 7,171, 7,185, 7,274, 7,294, 7,585, 11,344, 11,821, 12,292, 15,270, 17,053
Alcott, William A., 11,305
Alda, Frances, 2,968
Alden, Anne C., 14,816
Alden, Carroll Storrs, 2,521
Alden, Edesa [Mrs. Joseph], 4,961
Alden, Emily G., 4,374
Alden Ewell Library (NY), 11,270
Alden, Isabella (Macdonald) [Mrs. Gustavus Rosinbury] (1841-1930), 1,224
Alden, Joseph, 4,961
Alden Liberal Club (NY), **11,270**
Alden, Sarah C. (1841-88). *See* Abraham, Sarah C. (Alden) [Mrs. Lot] (1841-88)
Alder, Lydia (Dunford) [Mrs. George Alfred] (1846-1923), **16,580**
Alderman, Jacob Oliver, **13,309**
Alderson, Elizabeth Lena (1860-1933). *See* Houston, Elizabeth Lena (Alderson) (1860-1933)
Alderson Family (MT), **10,223**
Alderson, Floyd, 15,876
Alderson, Martha (1797-1885). *See* Feamster, Martha (Alderson) [Mrs. William] (1797-1885)
Alderson, Mary (Long) [Mrs. Matthew W.] (1860-1940), 8956, **10,271**
Alderson, Matthew W., 8956
Alderson, Mrs. M. W., 10,335, 10,381
Alderson, William W., 10,247
Aldinger, Ella H., **7847**
Aldington, Hilda (Doolittle) (1886-1961), 11,153
Aldis, Helen. *See* Lathrop, Helen (Aldis) [Mrs. Bryan]
Aldis, Mary (Reynolds) (1872-1949), 8,001
Aldis, Mrs. Arthur T., 3,813
Aldret, Anne S. [Miss], 15,436
Aldret, Mary [Mrs.], **15,436**
Aldrich, Abby (Chapman) [Mrs. Nelson Wilmarth], 2,160
Aldrich, Abby Greene (1874-1948). *See* Rockefeller, Abby Greene (Aldrich) [Mrs. John Davison, Jr.] (1874-1948)
Aldrich, Benton (1831-1918), **10,420**
Aldrich, Bess (Streeter) [Mrs. Charles S.] (1881-1954), 3,825, **4,965, 5,091, 10,421**, 10,491, 13,651
Aldrich, Charles, 4,747, 4,808
Aldrich, Gertrude, 8,349
Aldrich, Helen Reese, 5,861
Aldrich, Laura. *See* Neese, Laura (Aldrich) [Mrs. Albert H., Sr.]
Aldrich, Lucy, 2,160
Aldrich, Mark A. (1801-73), **178**
Aldrich, Matilda Olivia [Mrs. Charles] (1836-92), 4,732
Aldrich, Mildred (1853-1928), **6,349**
Aldrich, Mrs. Winthrop W., 12,708
Aldrich, Nelson Wilmarth (1841-1915), **2,160**
Aldrich, Roseltha (1837-?), **6,350**
Aldrich, Susan Helen (1818-1915). *See* DeKroyft, Susan Helen (Aldrich) [Mrs. William]
Aldrich, Vernice (1901-59), **13,698**
Aldridge, Amanda Ira, 12,690
Aldridge, Ira, 12,690
Aldridge, Mildred C., 11,662
Aleshire Family (OH), **17,432**
Aleshire, Mary, 17,432
Alethenai Literary Society (IL), 4,403
Aleuts
    language, 8,206
    medicine, 8,206
    rites and ceremonies, 8,206
Alexander, A. J., 311
Alexander, Abigail (Baldwin), 3,636

Alexander, Alexander, 12,328
Alexander, Alice Van Yeveren, 3,521
Alexander, Anna, 5,465
Alexander, Annie Montague [Miss] (1867-1950), **310**, 910
Alexander, Archer, 10,161
Alexander, Caroline, 3,967
Alexander, Caroline Bayard Stevens [Mrs.]. *See* Wittpen, Caroline Bayard Stevens [Mrs.] Alexander [Mrs. Otto]
Alexander, Deborah [Mrs. Dicks], 2,162
Alexander, Dicks, 2,162
Alexander, Eleanor (1905-). *See* Wiebeck, Eleanor (Alexander) (1905-)
Alexander, Elizabeth, 11,134
Alexander, Ella (1858-1952). *See* Boole, Ella (Alexander) [Mrs. William] (1858-1952)
Alexander, Evaline Throop (Martin) [Mrs. A. J.], **311**
Alexander Family, **2,162**
Alexander, Florence, 9,575
Alexander, Frances, **2,161**
Alexander, Francesca. Esther Frances Alexander [Miss] (1837-1917), **5,906**, 6,351
Alexander, Grace Maye (Forbes) (1874-1957), 169
Alexander, Harriet (1808-82). *See* Henry, Harriet (Alexander) [Mrs. Joseph] (1802-82)
Alexander, Iraminta Antoinette "Nettie," **3,359**
Alexander, Irme Elizabeth (1889-1947). *See* Bullis, Irme Elizabeth (Alexander) [Mrs. Harry Amos] (1889-1947)
Alexander, Janet, 11,453
Alexander, Julia G., **2,162**
Alexander, Lincoln (1873-?), **6,728**
Alexander, Louisa Frederika. *See* Gilmer, Louisa Frederika (Alexander) [Mrs. Jeremy F.]
Alexander, Lucia Gray Swett (1814-1916), 5,906
Alexander, Margaret Walker (1915-), 9,575, **9,583**, 9,585
Alexander, Maria, 12,328
Alexander, Mary, 11,134
Alexander, Mary (NY), 14,885
Alexander, Mary Ann (McKinney) [Mrs. William Patterson] (1810-88), 3,636
Alexander, Mary Jean [Mrs.], 4,868
Alexander, Mary L., **17,935**
Alexander, Melinda, 6,337
Alexander, Nancy N. (1816-?). *See* Tracy, Nancy N. (Alexander) [Mrs. Moses] (1816-?)
Alexander, Ruth, 5,123
Alexander, Sadie, 5,465
Alexander, Samuel T., 310
Alexander, Sarah Ann (Graham) (1807-39?), 2,162
Alexander, Sarah Jane (Kennedy) (1841-1912), 349
Alexander, Thea, 9,574
Alexander, Will Winton, 11,897
Alexander, William, 12,328
Alexander, William Patterson (1805-84), 3,636
Alexandria Hospital, 6,919
Alexandrovitch, Nikolai, Emperor, 12,497
Alexayeff, Lucy (Maude), 12,497
Alexian Brothers Hospital (San Jose, CA), 15,982
Alexian Brothers Hospital (Chicago, IL), **15,981**
Alexian Brothers Hospital (TN), Ladies Auxiliary, **15,983**
Alexian Brothers Hospital League (TN), **15,982**
Alexian Brothers Hospital, Woman's Board of the Alexian Brothers Hospital Foundation, 15,981
Alexian Brothers Rest Home (TN), Woman's Auxiliary, **15,984**
Alexine Learning Center (IL), 4,284
Aley, Maxwell, 14,378
Aley, Ruth, 6,337, 14,378
Alfalfa, 16,486
Alferez, Enrique, 5,488
Alfred A. Knopf (publisher), 14,475
Alfred A. Knopf, Inc., 16,157
Alfred University (NY), archives, **11,271**
Alfriend, Mary B. [Mrs.], 2,928
Algeo, Sarah M., 9,001
Alger, Abby Langdon (1850-?), 6,353
Alger Family (New England; PA), **6,352**
Alger, George William, 11,897

Alger, James, 17,007
Alger, Louisa Jackson (ca. 1900-), **6,353**
Alger, Sarah "Sally" (Rice) [Mrs. James] (ca. 1820-?), 17,007
Algology, 8,620
Algonquin Round Table, 11,867
Ali, Mohammed, 12,439
Alianza Hispano-Americana, 203
"Alice, a Minnesota Girl," 8,477
Alice Carr Trust Fund (AL), 2
Alice in Jungleland (book), 4,061
Alice Lloyd College, 17,063
Alice Shevlin Hall (MN), 8,616
Alien property, 10,740, 11,695
Aliens, 2,683, **9,481**. *See also* Naturalization
Aliesan, Jody, **17,233**
Alispaw, Fred, 1,751
Alispaw, Lucia Zora [Mrs. Fred], 1,751
All-American Girls' Baseball League, 15,320
All Saints Church (Atlanta, GA), 3,267
All Saints Church (Atlanta, GA), Women's Auxiliary, **3,438**
All Saints Episcopal Church (Minneapolis, MN), **8,901**
All Saints Sunday School Society (SC), 15,437
All Seasons Around the Sun, A Telescopic View of the First Centuries (book), 12,646
All Sorts and Conditions of Girls (NY), 7,217
All Souls Church (Chicago, IL), 3,791
All Star Music Concerts, 8,442
"All the Rights She Wants" (poem), 9,060
All This and Heaven Too (book), 5,694
All Those in Favor Say Something! (book), 3,111
Allabach, Lucy, 1,553
Allah and the Daughter of Abd Salam (book), 14,122
Allan, Maud (1879-1956), **1,028**
Allan, Ruth, 4,743
Allan, Virginia R., **7,699**
Allanson, Bertha [Mrs. George], 8,692
Allanson Family, 8,966
Allanson, George, 8,692
Allanson, Helen Margaret (1901-). *See* Burfiend, Helen Margaret (Allanson) (1901-)
Allard, Charles, 10,272
Allard, Lulu Spurgeon [Mrs. Charles], **10,272**
Allard, Sister Marie Amanda (1927-), 17,868
Allbritten, Alney (1903-). *See* Norell, Alney (Allbritten) [Mrs. Henry] (1903-)
Allbritten, Robert Alney, 5,397
Allder, Ann [Mrs. Conrad], 15,438
Allder, Conrad, **15,438**
Allegany County Woman's Temperance Union (NY). *See* Woman's Christian Temperance Union (Allegany County, NY)
Allegheny Bank (PA), 14,803
Allegheny County Industrial and Training School for Boys (PA), 15,246
Allegheny County Juvenile Court (PA), 15,246
Allegheny County League of Women Voters (PA), 15,251
Allegheny County Woman's Christian Temperance Union (PA), 15,254
Allegiance, 10,509
Allen, A. L., 16,325
Allen, Adaline Y., **11,069**
Allen, Agnes [Mrs. Amasa Orlando], 4,790
Allen, Alfred M. (1860-1927), Family (OH), **13,839**
Allen, Alice B. [Mrs.], 2,694
Allen, Alvira. *See* Vail, Alvira (Allen) [Mrs. William]
Allen, Amasa Orlando, **4,790**
Allen, Ambia W., 3,667
Allen, Ann (?-1830). *See* Penn, Ann (Allen) (?-1830)
Allen, Ann Hyde Andrews [Mrs. Hervey], 15,262
Allen, Anna [Miss], 15,153
Allen, Annie T. (1868-1921), 7,191
Allen, Annie Ware (Winsor) [Mrs. Joseph Allen] (1865-1955), **6,354**
Allen, Arthur Augustus, 11,507
Allen, Arthur J. (1891-1954), **11,935**
Allen, Bessie May (1882-1969), **17,869**
Allen, Caroline (Clarke), 12,814
Allen, Caroline Jerusha. *See* Jennings, Caroline Jerusha (Allen) [Mrs. Arthur Bates]

Allen, Catherine Ward (1883-), **14,185**
Allen, Cecyl (1890-1966). *See* Johnson, Cecyl (Allen) [Mrs. James W.] (1890-1966)
Allen, Clarissa. *See* Breck, Clarissa (Allen)
Allen, Corinne Marie (Tuckerman) (1856-1931), **6,355**, 7,174
Allen, Daisy. *See* White, Daisy (Allen)
Allen, David, Family, 582
Allen, Don B., **14,312**
Allen, Doris Twitchell (1901-), **13,735, 13,869**
Allen, Druscilla Chapman (1821-1913). *See* Stoddard, Druscilla Chapman (Allen) [Mrs. Ira Joy] (1821-1913)
Allen, Edith. *See* Milner, Edith (Allen) [Mrs. Charles H.]
Allen, Edna E., 14,378
Allen, Eleanor W., 6,962
Allen, Electa (Warner), 7,140
Allen, Elizabeth. *See* White, Elizabeth (Allen)
Allen, Elizabeth (1734-1824), **7,083**
Allen, Elizabeth Anne (Chase) [Mrs. Marshall S. M.] Taylor [Mrs. Benjamin Paul] Akers [Mrs. Elijah Marshall] (1832-1911), **5,669**, 5,674, 5,694, 12,525
Allen, Elizabeth Lee, 7,056
Allen, Ellen M., 2,945
Allen, Elsa Guerdrum [Mrs. Arthur Augustus] (1888-1969), **11,507**
Allen, Faith L., 11,938
Allen Family, 11,039
Allen Family (MA), **7,128**
Allen Family (NY), 12,229
Allen Family (NC), **13,310**
Allen, Florence Adams, 5,465
Allen, Florence Ellinwood (1884-1966), **2,163**, 2,166, **6,356, 6,357**, 6,687, **6,967**, 7,174, 8,678, 13,241, **13,904**, 13,979, 14,007, **16,918**
Allen, Frances Stebbins, 7,012
Allen, Frances Williams (1824-?), 7,650
Allen, Georgianna, 5,700, 5,701
Allen, Gideon Winan (1835-1912), **3,979**
Allen, Gladys [Miss] (1897-1953), **16,325**
Allen, Hannah Maria, **6,186**
Allen, Hannah (Smith) [Mrs. Alfred M.] (1861-1941), 13,839
Allen, Henrietta. *See* Mills, Henrietta (Allen)
Allen, Hervey (1889-1949), **15,262**
Allen, Ida (Elliot) (1880-1943), **14,313**
Allen, Ida Johnson (1893-), 1,068
Allen, Ivey [Mrs.], 13,322
Allen, Janet, **4,662**
Allen, Jeffie Obrea. *See* Conner, Jeffie Obrea (Allen) [Mrs. George Sherman]
Allen, Jennie (?-1881). *See* Casterline, Jennie (Allen) [Mrs. John Andrew] (?-1881)
Allen, John, 7,043
Allen, Joseph, 6,354
Allen, Judith, **312**
Allen, Katherine Fay (Worley) [Mrs. Charles] (1876-1971), **10,422**
Allen, Laura, 9,037
Allen, Lizzie C., **6,307**
Allen, Louisa (1856-?). *See* Gregory, Louisa (Allen) [Mrs. John M.] (1856-?)
Allen, Louise, **15,885**
Allen, Love (1786-1820). *See* Ripley, Love (Allen) [Mrs. Eleazar Wheelock] (1786-1820)
Allen, Lydia Augusta, **6,186**
Allen, M. Catherine, 7,043
Allen, M. M. S., **15,406**
Allen, Maria (Merrick) [Mrs. Samuel, Jr.] (1790-?), 7,649
Allen, Marie [Mrs.], 3,032
Allen, Marilyn, 14,686
Allen, Mary (NC), 13,470
Allen, Mary Barker [Mrs. Walter] (1784?-1861). *See* Farnum, Mary Barker [Mrs. Walter] Allen [Mrs. Moses] (1784?-1861)
Allen, Mary Cecil, 2,769
Allen, Mary Electa, 7,012
Allen, Mary J. [Mrs. Stafford], 5,061
Allen, Mary Louise, 8,647, 8,669
Allen, Mary Percival, 12,814
Allen, Mary S., 543

Allen, Maryland. *See* Tyson, Maryland Allen [Mrs. Edward T.]
Allen, Mr., 5,669
Allen, Nancy W., 8,924
Allen, Netta Powell [Mrs. Arthur J.] (1890-), 313, 11,846, 11,935
Allen, Pamela P. [Mrs. Robert L.] (1943-), **17,583**
Allen, Pearl (1875-1940). *See* Murdock, Pearl (Allen) [Mrs. Victor] (1875-1940)
Allen, Phoebe, 1,659
Allen, Rachel Stout, 13,310
Allen, Robert, 5,655
Allen, Robert A. (1886-1968), **10,638**
Allen, Robert L., 17,583
Allen, Robert P., 11,081
Allen, Roberta Etheridge, **9,783**
Allen, Ruth Alice (1889-), **15,986**
Allen, Ruth Robertson. *See* Dickinson, Ruth Robertson (Allen)
Allen, Sallie (Brown) "Sallie Fox" (?-1913), **1,229**
Allen, Sally (1880-1943) (pseudonym). *See* Allen, Ida (Elliot) (1880-1943)
Allen, Sarah Campbell, 15,429, 15,430
Allen, Sarah Elizabeth, **12,154**
Allen, T. D. (pseudonym). *See* Allen, Don B.; Allen, Thelma Diener [Mrs. Don B.]
Allen, Terry D. *See* Allen, Thelma Diener [Mrs. Don B.]
Allen, Thelma Diener [Mrs. Don B.], 14,312
Allen, Theodora (1903-), 4,495
Allen, Thomas, 7,128
Allen, Viola Emily (1867-1948). *See* Duryea, Viola Emily Allen [Mrs. Peter Edward Cornell] (1867-1948)
Allen, Walter, 7,623
Allen, Walter, 11,935
Allen, Willette A. [Miss], **3,131**, 3,140
Allen's Clipping Bureau, 1,068
Allensworth, Emma H., **12,936**
Allentown Association (NY), 11,358
Allerton Family, 14,059
Alley Dwelling Authority (DC), 6,656
Alley, Rewi, 1,564
Allgood, Andrew, 2,973
Allgood, de Forrest, 2,973
Allgood Family (GA), **2,973**
Allgood, Susan [Mrs. de Forrest] (?-1935), 2,973
Alliance for Guidance of Rural Youth, 13,189
Alliance Francaise (NC), 13,331
Alliance Woman's Club Company, 9,918
Allied Jewish Appeal, 14,908
Alling, Sarah MacKaye (1809-1904), 10,868
Allinson, Anne "Nancy" Crosby Emery, 17,723
Allinson, Mary (1768-1859), 14,836
Allison, Frances C. [Mrs. Ralph] (?-1943), 3,969
Allison, Isidore Johnson [Mrs. Duncan C.], **17,584**
Allison, Mary B., 8,201
Allison, Panthea, 13,311
Alliton, Silas (1842-?), **8,296**
Allow for the Skeleton (Dry Though It May Be)—and the Rest Revines (book), 12,646
Allred, Eliza Mariah (1848-1939). *See* Munson, Eliza Mariah (Allred) [Mrs. James Willard] (1848-1939)
Allred, Elizabeth [Mrs. James], 16,771
Allred, James, 16,771
Allred, Rhoda Luann B. (Smith) (1859-?), 16,968
Allston, Adele (1842-1915). *See* Vanderhorst, Adele (Allston) [Mrs. Arnoldus] (1842-1915)
Allston, Adele (Petigru) [Mrs. Robert Francis Withers], 15,554
Allston, Benjamin, 15,440, 15,554
Allston, Charles Petigru, 15,440, 15,554
Allston, Elizabeth Waties (1845-1921). *See* Pringle, Elizabeth Waties (Allston) [Mrs. John Julius] (1845-1921)
Allston Family (SC), **15,439, 15,554**
Allston, Jane Louise (1850-1937). *See* Hill, Jane Louise (Allston) [Mrs. Charles A.] (1850-1937)
Allston, Robert Francis Withers (1801-64), **15,440**, 15,525, 15,554, 15,698
Allyn, Abigail "Abba" B. *See* Francis, Abigail "Abba" B. (Allyn) [Mrs. Convers]
Allyn, Janet, 4,743

Alman, David (1919-), **5,979**
Alman, Emily (Arnow) [Mrs. David] (1922-), 5,979
Alman Family, **5,979**
Almanacs, 5,942
Almost Year, The (book), 6,072
Alms House (New York, NY), **12,423**
Alms House (NY), Commissioners, **12,371**
Alms House (Philadelphia, PA), 14,913, 14,916
Alms House (Charleston, SC), **15,402**, 15,404
Alms House Hospital (PA), 14,916
Almshouses, 1,939, 5,846, 6,662, 7,142, **11,117**, 12,127, 12,130, **12,371, 12,423**, 14,913, 14,916, **15,402**, 15,404
Almy (1770-1841), 14,963
Almy, Amy Celeste (Bruner) [Mrs. John Edwin] (1875-1943), 10,437
Almy, Anna Cabot (1886-), 6,358
Almy, Elizabeth (1892-), 6,358
Almy Family (MA), **6,358**
Almy, Helen Jackson (1884-1976), 6,358
Almy, Helen Jackson (Cabot) (1856-1938), 6,358
Almy, John J., 11,500
Almy, Lydia Hill, **7,338**
Almy, Mary (1883-1967), 6,358
Almy, Sarah [Mrs. John J.], 11,500
Aloha Club (Des Moines, IA), **4,725**
"Alone" (song), 2,639
Along Came the Witch (book), 41
Aloysius, Saint, 13,752
Aloysius, Sister Mary, **757**
Alpern, Anne X., 14,815
Alpern, Harriet (Cooper) [Mrs. Bryce] (1923-), **8,057**
Alpert, Pela Rosen (1920-), 17,744
Alpha Beta Chi, 8,740
Alpha Circle of the Chatauqua Literary and Scientific Circle (MA), **7,594**
Alpha Delphian Society of Mankato (MN), **8,484**
Alpha Delta Theta, 4,383
Alpha Kappa Alpha, **3,779**, 3,799, 3,800, 5,064, **10,191**, 13,945
Alpha Lambda Delta, 4,042, 4,390, 4,403, 11,388, **14,028**
Alpha Lambda Delta (MT), 10,222
Alpha Phi, 1,404, 4,403
Alpha Phi (Syracuse, NY), 1,404
"Alpha Suffrage Record, The," 4,147
Alpha Theta Sigma (MI), **8,041**
Alpha Xi Delta, 5,064
Alphin, Theresa (1877-1954). *See* Peterson, Theresa (Alphin) Taber Wilkinson (1877-1954)
Alpine Lakes Protection Society, 17,305
Alschuler, Rose Greenbaum (Haas) [Mrs. Alfred S.] (1887-), **4,049**
Alsop, Joseph, 4,476
Alsop, Mary, 12,461
Alsop, Mary (1885-). *See* O'Hara, Mary (1885-)
Alspaugh, Hannah Ditzler (1848-1938), **4,301**
Alston Family (MS), 9,656
Alston Family (NC), **13,312**
Alston Family (SC), **2,164**
Alston, Grace I., 5,465
Alston, Hessie. *See* Trapier, Hessie (Alston) [Mrs. Richard Shubrick]
Alston, Jacob Motte, 2,164
Alston, Joseph, 12,410
Alston, Mary Motte, 2,164
Alston, Theodosia (Burr) [Mrs. Joseph] (1783-1813), 850, 2,164, 2,322, 12,174, 12,410, 15,745
Alsup, Alice, 2,016
Alta Mira Ladies Club House (CA), 1,387
Altar guilds, 1,370, **3,936**, 5,826, 13,912
Altenheim Home for the Aged (Cleveland, OH), **13,905**
Altgeld, John P., 4,172
Altieri, Alice LaFond [Mrs.] (1894-1976), **15,373**
Altman, Brigette, 11,817
Alton Telegraph (IL), 4,347
Altose, Sophie, 17,282
Altrocchi, Julia (Cooley) [Mrs. Rudolph] (1893-1972), **315**, 353, 635, 1,085, 1,407, 1,448, 1,508
Altrocchi, Pauline Hemenway, 1,339
Altrusa Club of Columbus (OH), **13,985**
Altrusa Club of Neenah and Menasha (WI), **17,821**

Altrusa Club of Pittsburgh (PA), **15,220**
Altrusa International Club (NE), **10,423**
Altrusas, 11,237
Altschul, Helen [Mrs. Frank] (1887-), 11,875
Altschuler, Rebecca, 15,332
Alumnae Association of Mercyhurst College (Erie, PA), 14,788
Alumnae Magazine, The (NY), 11,302
Alumnae News (Wells College, NY), 11,281
Alumnae Record, The (Salem Academy and College, NC), 13,634
Alumnae War Work Committee (NC), 13,193
Alumni Journal (NC), 13,224
Alumni Register (Duke University, NC), 13,194
Alvara, Aloha Margaret (Hannah), 10,312
Alvarado, J. B., 331
Alverson, Rosana Margaret (Kroh) Blake (1836-1923), **316**
Alvo, Stella, 9,467
Alvord, Adeline, 14,324
Alvord, Anna Greene Grew [Mrs. James Church] (1812-92), 7,476
Alvord, Clarence Walworth (1868-1928), **4,406**
Alvord, Edith (Vosburg) (1876-1961), **8,019**
Alvord, Emily L. [Mrs. Benjamin], 684
Alvord, Idress Adaline (Head) (1874-?), **9,926**
Alvord, Katherine Sprague (1871-1959), **4,519**
Alward, Dennis R., 11,509
Alward, Emily Wight (Babcock) [Mrs. Dennis R.] (1836-1919), **11,509**
Always a River (book), 15,720
"Always a Silent Witness" (drawing), 6,883
Alyea, Dorothy C., 11,077
Amalgamated Clothing and Textile Workers Union, 1,577, 1,656, 3,447, 3,839, 5,515, **8,083,** 8,144, 9,493, 11,809, 12,861, 13,176, 15,998
Amalgamated Clothing and Textile Workers Union (Clearfield, PA), Local 628, 15,321
Amalgamated Clothing and Textile Workers Union (Curwensville, PA), Local 118, 15,321
Amalgamated Clothing and Textile Workers Union (Philipsburg, PA), Local 674, 15,321
Amalgamated Clothing and Textile Workers Union (TX), Farah Boycott Office, **15,987**
Amalgamated Clothing Workers of America. *See* Amalgamated Clothing and Textile Workers Union
Amalgamated Meat Cutters and Butcher Workmen of North America, 16,008
Amalie's Story (book), 5,008
Amana colonies (IA), **4,683**
Amanda (slave, NC), 13,188
Amarillo A&M Mothers' Club (TX), **16,183**
Amarillo Times, The (TX), 16,387
Amateur theatricals, 3,204
Amatruda, Catherine, 2,353
Ambassadors, 44, 1,605, 2,036, 2,292, 2,388, 2,456, 2,458, 2,542, **2,590,** 2,635, 2,965, **4,468,** 6,489, 7,539, 7,598, 7,886, **8,911,** 8,912, 9,037, 9,040, 9,160, 9,467, 10,800, **11,827,** 11,857, 12,022, 12,070, 12,273, 12,434, 13,931, 14,210, 14,237, 14,607, 15,059, 16,313, **17,116**
Ambassadors, French, **12,210**
Ambassadors, Indian, 4,030
Amber, Penelope [Mrs. Campbell] (?-1889), 5,063
Amberson, Katharine, 5,735
Ambler, Ann (1772-?). *See* Fisher, Ann (Ambler) (1772-?)
Ambler, Elizabeth Jacquelin (1765-1847). *See* Carrington, Elizabeth Jacquelin (Ambler) [Mrs. William] Brent [Mrs. Edward] (1765-1847)
Ambrose, Alice, 10,846
Amelia Earhart Memorial Airport (KS), 5,162
Amelia Gayle Gorgas Library (AL), 107
Amelia Pride Book Club of Rock Hill (SC), **15,786**
Amelia, Sister, **7,034**
Amena Church Ladies' Aid (ND), **13,666**
Amend, Dorothea, 1,641
America (periodical), 12,236
"America" (song), 1,487, 4,228
America (steamboat), 14,993
"America Bound" (radio program), 8,591
America, discovery by Norsemen, 4,327
America First Committee, 2,357

America First party, 14,686
"America the Beautiful" (poem), 7,563
"America When Feminized" (leaflet), 55
American Abstract Artists, 2,788
American Academy (Rome, Italy), School of Classical Studies, 14,744
American Academy and Institute of Arts and Letters, 11,161, **11,810,** 12,050, 12,888, 12,901
American Academy for the Advancement of Science, 10,459
American Academy of Arts and Letters. *See* American Academy and Institute of Arts and Letters
American Academy of Arts and Sciences, 7,094
American Academy of Dramatic Arts, 4,477
American Academy of Pediatrics, 1,348, 16,226
American Academy of Periodontology, 13,997
American Academy of Political and Social Science, 12,923
American-African Institute, 3,800
American Agriculturist, The (periodical), 11,350
American Ambulance Hospital (Neuilly-sur-Seine, France), 11,556
American Ambulance Hospital (Paris, France), 6,623, 9,277
American Ambulance Service, 13,889
American Annals of the Deaf, 2,102, 2,114
American Anthropological Association, 540
American Anti-Slavery Society, 3,297, 6,975, 7,233, 7,561, 12,419
American Arbitration Association, 11,767, 11,770
"American Army Song, The," 16,931
American Art Alliance, 12,011
American Art Annual (periodical), 2,781, 12,244
American Association for Adult Education of the USA, 2,233, 12,738
American Association for Health, Physical Education and Recreation, 7,173, **7,175,** 13,254, 17,230
American Association for Labor Legislation, 2,120, **11,760**
American Association for Social Workers, 8,658
American Association for Study and Prevention of Infant Mortality, 509
American Association for the Advancement of Science, 7,136, 8,822, 12,923
American Association for the United Nations, 1,530, 17,246
American Association of Anatomists, 1,738
American Association of Applied Psychology, 11,549
American Association of Deans of Women, 2,114
American Association of Group Workers. *See* National Association of Social Workers
American Association of Industrial Nurses, 5,417
American Association of Instructors of the Blind, 7,309
American Association of Marriage and Family Counselors, 6,987
American Association of Medical Social Workers. *See* National Association of Social Workers
American Association of Museums, 17,266
American Association of Psychiatric Social Workers. *See* National Association of Social Workers
American Association of Public Welfare Officials. *See* American Public Welfare Association
American Association of Schools of Social Work, 2,224, 6,900, 8,653, 8,663
American Association of Social Workers. *See* National Association of Social Workers
American Association of University Professors, 5,506, 8,559, 9,839, 11,281, 12,923, 16,358
American Association of University Women, 3, **58,** 104, 116, **150, 229,** 509, **909,** 1,078, 1,085, 1,526, 1,604, 1,618, 1,738, **2,064, 2,066, 2,073,** 2,076, 2,077, **2,079, 2,082,** 2,114, **2,728, 2,898,** 3,399, 3,653, 4,197, 4,630, 4,815, 4,888, **5,403, 5,438,** 5,506, 6,009, **6,359, 6,361, 6,362,** 6,368, 6,387, 6,388, 6,483, 6,687, 6,901, 6,941, **7,176, 7,184,** 7,198, 7,286, 7,572, 7,820, 8,209, **8,426, 8,485,** 8,492, 8,548, 8,552, 8,594, 8,689, 8,746, **8,819,** 9,385, 9,392, 9,526, **9,554,** 9,566, 9,647, 9,672, **9,927, 9,934,** 9,935, 9,998, **10,195, 10,273,** 10,488, 10,680, **10,746,** 10,755, 11,183, 11,228, 11,237, 11,349, 11,526, 11,706, 11,804, 11,806, 11,904, 11,999, **12,792,** 12,920, 12,923, 13,187,

13,189, 13,192, 13,255, **13,314,** 13,381, 13,390, 13,446, **13,667, 13,699, 13,747,** 13,754, **14,193, 14,708,** 14,900, 15,570, **15,787,** 15,789, 15,801, **16,294, 16,919,** 17,189, 17,369, **17,504, 17,763,** 17,822, 17,936
American Association of University Women (GA), **3,360**
American Association of University Women (Athens, GA), **2,959**
American Association of University Women (Savannah, GA), **3,480**
American Association of University Women (ID), **3,659**
American Association of University Women (Champaign-Urbana, IL), **4,407**
American Association of University Women (Chicago, IL), **3,795**
American Association of University Women (Hinsdale, IL), 4,278
American Association of University Women (Waukegan, IL), 4,452
American Association of University Women (IN), **4,547**
American Association of University Women (Evansville, IN), **4,498**
American Association of University Women (Hobart, IN), **4,588**
American Association of University Women (IA), **4,890**
American Association of University Women (Decorah, IA), **4,712**
American Association of University Women (Indianola, IA), **4,726**
American Association of University Women (Bonner Springs, KS), **5,176**
American Association of University Women (Manhattan, KS), **5,190**
American Association of University Women (KY), **5,395**
American Association of University Women (Lafayette, LA), **5,429**
American Association of University Women (Lowell, MA), **7,071**
American Association of University Women (Ann Arbor, MI), **7,700**
American Association of University Women (Ypsilanti, MI), **7,700**
American Association of University Women (MN), **8,902**
American Association of University Women (St. Cloud, MN), **8,840**
American Association of University Women (NE), **10,424, 10,425**
American Association of University Women (NV), **10,640**
American Association of University Women (Reno, NV), **10,639**
American Association of University Women (Sparks, NV), **10,641**
American Association of University Women (NH), **10,791**
American Association of University Women (Ithaca, NY), **11,510**
American Association of University Women (Chapel Hill, NC), **12,938**
American Association of University Women (OH), **13,987, 14,057**
American Association of University Women (Columbus, OH), **13,986**
American Association of University Women (Kent-Ravenna Branch, OH), **14,107**
American Association of University Women (Carlisle, PA), **14,750**
American Association of University Women (SC), **15,555**
American Association of University Women (TX), **16,177**
American Association of University Women (Bryan-College Station, TX), **16,184**
American Association of University Women (Lubbock, TX), **16,258,** 16,265
American Association of University Women (Waco, TX), **16,326**

American Association of University Women (UT), **16,494**

American Association of University Women (WV), **7368, 16,181**

American Association of University Women (Morgantown, WV), **17,446**

American Association of University Women (WI), **17,586**

American Association of University Women (Madison, WI), **17,585**

American Association of University Women, Arts Program, **2,065**

American Association of University Women, Board of Directors and General Director, **2,067**

American Association of University Women, Committee on the Economic and Legal Status of Women, 2,064, **2,068**, 6,362, 6,581

American Association of University Women, Community Arts Survey, **2,165**

American Association of University Women, Education Program, **2,069**

American Association of University Women, International, **6,360**

American Association of University Women, Legislative Program, **2,075**

American Association of University Women, Missouri Committee on Equal Pay, **9,831**

American Association of University Women, Women's Joint Congressional Committee, **2,074**

American Association of University Women, World Problems, 2,072

American Association of Women Ministers, 7,947

American Association of Women Preachers, 4,089

American Atlantic and Pacific Ship Canal Company, 12,046

American Author (periodical), 14,200

American Ballet Theatre, 12,360

American Baptist Convention, 161

American Baptist Foreign Mission Society, 14,443

American Baptist Foreign Mission Society and Woman's American Baptist Foreign Mission Society, **12,783**

American Baptist Missionary Union, 161

American Baptist Publication Society, 13,644

American Baptist Women, 5,203

American Bar Association, 1,723, 1,782, 7,174, 9,956, 10,440

American Benefit Association, 17,467

American Bible Society, 3,808, 5,760

American Bible Union, 11,506

American Biographical Dictionary, 1,998

American Birth Control League, Inc., 1,596, 5,739, 9,440

American Board of Commissioners for Foreign Missions, 86, 87, 880, 2,015, 2,019, 7,048, 7,517, **8,903**, 14,119, 14,470, 17,167, 17,212, 17,423, 17,424

American Board of Commissioners for Foreign Missions, Hawaiian Evangelical Association, **3,637**

American Branch of International Migration Service. *See* International Social Service, American Branch

American British Art Center, Inc. (NY), 2,820

American Cancer Society, 1,700, 4,698, 9,385, 11,445, 11,885

American Cancer Society, Women's Field Army, 4,698

American Catholic Historical Society, 10,990

American Child Health Association, 11,627

American Childhood (periodical), 13,366

American Children's Hospital (Poland), 8,045

American Church Temperance Society, 9,295

American Citizens Committee for Economic Aid Abroad, 12,061

American Civic Alliance, 12,574

American Civic Association, 14,819

American Civil Liberties Union, 931, 6,708, 6,790, **11,178**, 12,061, 12,701, 15,991, 15,993, 16,373, 17,238, 17,254, 17,260

American Civil Liberties Union, Northern California branch, 765

American College (Italy), 9,695

American College for Girls (Turkey). *See* Constantinople Woman's College (Turkey)

American College of Radiology, 4,698

American Collegiate Association, 3,899

American Colonial Charter, The (dissertation), 17,667

American Colonization Society, 15,470

American Committee for Devastated France, 2,354, 17,241

American Committee for Italian War Relief, **8,904**

American Committee for Protection of Foreign Born, 9,467

American Committee for Relief in the Near East, 12,559

American Committee in Aid of Chinese Industrial Cooperatives, 1,564

American Committee on Italian Migration, **12,860**

American Communist party, 993

American Community Theatre Wing, 5,232

American Conchology (book), 14,880

American Copyright League, 12,395

American Council for Nationalities Service, 7,302, **9,492**

officials and employees, 1,675

American Council of Guidance and Personnel Associations, 13,754

American Council of Railroad Women, 304, **7,177**

American Council on Education, 11,372

American Court Gossip or Life at the National Capitol, 4,732

American Cyanamid Company, 8,555

American Dependency Challenge, An, 8,632

American Design Awards, 6,879

American Dialect Society, 1,671

American Dilemma: The Negro Problem and Modern Democracy, An (book), 8,603

American Dramatic Fund Association, 8,297

American Education Theatre Association, 5,477

American Education Week, 4,946

American Emergency Food Committee for India, 12,061

American Equal Rights Association, 6,979

American Ethnological Society, **2,834**

American Eugenics Society, 6,223

American Evangelical Lutheran Church—Danish, publishing, 3,964

American Evangelical Lutheran Church—Danish, Women's Mission Society, **3,964**

American Evangelical Lutheran Mission Hospital (Guntur, India). *See* Kugler Memorial Hospital (Guntur, India)

American Expeditionary Force (World War I), 17,379, 17,755

American Express Company, 2,696, 11,278, 11,283

American Farm Bureau Women, 4,947

American Federation of Actors, 13,832

American Federation of Artists, 2,817

American Federation of Arts, 11,844

American Federation of Catholic Alumnae, 5,778

American Federation of International Institutes. *See* American Council for Nationalities Service

American Federation of Labor-Congress of Industrial Organizations, 1,577, 2,382, 3,449, 4,032, 8,085, 8,088, 8,135, 8,984, 9,054, 9,381, 11,924, 11,926, 13,212, 14,533, 15,327, 15,333
officials and employees, **11,484**, 11,765, 11,766
political activity, 11,916

American Federation of Labor-Congress of Industrial Organizations (IL), Local 1, 3,827

American Federation of Labor-Congress of Industrial Organizations (MI), **8,107**, 8,110

American Federation of Labor-Congress of Industrial Organizations, Bookkeepers, Stenographers and Accountants Union, 8,077

American Federation of Labor-Congress of Industrial Organizations, committee to abolish discrimination, 2,879

American Federation of Labor-Congress of Industrial Organizations, Food and Tobacco Workers Union, 3,442, 15,977

American Federation of Labor-Congress of Industrial Organizations, National Congress of Women's Auxiliaries, 8,124

American Federation of Labor-Congress of Industrial Organizations, Political Action Committee, 4,970

American Federation of Labor-Congress of Industrial Organizations, Region VIII, **3,442**

American Federation of Labor-Congress of Industrial Organizations, Steel Workers Union, 9,467

American Federation of Labor-Congress of Industrial Organizations, United Garment Workers, 17,635

American Federation of Sex Hygiene, 8,633

American Federation of Soroptimist Clubs, 6,387

American Federation of State, County and Municipal Employees, 9,381

American Federation of Teachers, 3,308, 4,124, **8,058**, 8,069, 8,093, 8,098, 8,101, 8,102, 8,104, 8,113, 8,120, 8,126, 8,128, 8,147

American Federation of Teachers (DC), Local 6, 8,109

American Federation of Teachers (MN), Local 28, **8,059**, 8,129

American Federation of Teachers (St. Louis, MO), Local 420, **8,060**

American Federation of Teachers (NY), Local 2, **11,761**

American Federation of Teachers (Philadelphia, PA), Local 192, 15,200

American Federation of Teachers (Pittsburgh, PA), Local 191, 15,332

American Federation of Teachers, Black Caucus, 8,097

American Federation of Teachers, Joint Progressive Caucus, 8,125

American Federation of Teachers, New Caucus, 8,121

American Federation of Teachers, Progressive Caucus, 8,128

American Federation of Television and Radio Artists, 2,284

American Female Guardian Society, 15,274

American Female Guardian Society and Home for the Friendless, 12,739

American Female Moral Reform Society, 17,707

American Field Service, 14,552, 17,821

American Forest History Foundation, **17,587**

American Forestry Association, 14,809

American Fork Training School, 16,554

American Foundation for the Blind, 6,691, **11,811**, 11,812

American Foundation for the Blind, Bureau of National and International Relations, 2,108

American Foundation for the Overseas Blind, 11,812

American Freedmen's Aid Commission, 6,943

American Friend of Southey, An (book), 12,002

American Friends, 12,263

American Friends of Greece, 12,180

American Friends Service Committee, 496, 965, 2,396, 7,809, 8,890, 9,095, 9,287, 13,221, 15,303, 15,315, 17,238

American Friends Service Committee, Chicago Regional Office (IL), **4,050**

American Frugal Housewife (book), 7,561

American Fund for French Wounded, 12,132

American Fund for French Wounded Children, 4,273

American Fund for Jewish War Sufferers, 7,531

American Fur Company, 9,371

American Geographical Society, 191

American Girl (periodical), 12,113, 14,421

American Girl, An (drama), 2,303

American Gold Star Mothers, **3,850**, 5,122, 15,693

American Gold Star Mothers of Wisconsin, **17,639**

American Gold Star Sons of the Chicago (IL) Historical Society, 3,850

American Gold Star Sons of the University of Chicago (IL), 3,850

American Guild of Music Teachers, Inc., **8,905**

American Guild of Organists (ME), **5,670**

American Hearing Society, 2,115, 6,919

American Heart Association, 11,885, 11,932

American Heritage (periodical), 6,201

American Heritage, Aladdin Books, 14,453

American Historical Association, 1,496, 1,604, 2,411, 4,684, 8,566

American Historical Review (periodical), 8,566

American History Class, The. *See* History Class, The

American History Forum (Tulsa, OK), **14,260**

American Home Economics Association, 2,673, 3,859, 4,380, 6,334, 8,567, 8,596, 9,978, 11,012, 11,806, 12,738, 12,923

American Home Economics Association, Home Economists in Business, **4,098**
American Home Missionary Society, **5,456**
American Hospital Number 3 (Spain), 6,511
American Humane Society, 12,923
American Hungarian Ladies Benevolent Society, **8,906**
American Ideals Conference, 16,331
American Immigration and Citizenship Conference, **8,631**
American Immigration Conference. *See* American Immigration and Citizenship Conference
American Indian Charter Convention, 17,266
American Institute of Archaeology, 11,706
American Institute of Architects, 1,191
American Institute of Banking, 11,440
American Institute of Family Relations, 8,634
American Institute of Home Grown Fats and Oils, 9,788
American Israelite, The (OH), 1,002
American Italian Historical Association, 9,497
American Jewish Archives, 2,929
American Jewish Committee, 4,045, 4,493
American Jewish Joint Distribution Committee, 7,531, 7,541
American Journal of Archaeology, 14,743
American Journal of Nursing, 6,122, 6,133, 6,157, 8,553, 12,137
American Journal of Nursing Company, Inc., **6,122**
American Labor Education Service, 6,895, **11,762,** 13,176, **17,588**
American Labor party, 8,077, 11,917
American League for Civic Improvement, 2,000
American League to Enforce Peace, 14,745
American Legation (Belgium), officials and employees, 9,277
American Legion, 6,826, 8,460, 10,426, 16,462
American Legion Auxiliary, 4,197, 9,385, 9,522, **13,315,** 13,446, 13,617, 13,618, 15,951
American Legion Auxiliary (Hinsdale, IL), 4,278
American Legion Auxiliary (Garden City, KS), 5,179
American Legion Auxiliary (Horace Duffy Post, ME), **5,597**
American Legion Auxiliary (MN), **8,907**
American Legion Auxiliary (Mankato, MN), 9,132
American Legion Auxiliary (Morris, MN), 8,696
American Legion Auxiliary (Grand Island Post 53, NE), **10,408**
American Legion Auxiliary (Saratoga Springs, NY), 12,851
American Legion Auxiliary (Hope, ND), 13,672
American Legion Auxiliary (Post 330, OH), **14,045**
American Legion, Koca-Reeder-Giddens Post No. 233, 9,914
American Legion Monahan Post Band (Sioux City, IA), 5,107
American Library (Paris, France), 11,930
American Library Association, 4,306, 4,350, 4,391, 4,402, **4,727,** 8,976, 9,020, 11,930, 12,395, 12,479, 12,526, 12,729, 17,394
American Library Association, Board of Education for Librarianship, **11,936**
American Library Association, Five State Regional Conference, 9,233
American Library Association, International Relations Committee, **11,937**
American Library Association, Library War Service (World War I), **4,727**
American Library Association, Training Class Section, **11,938**
American literature, 17,023
American loyalists, **2,191,** 4,418, 7,659, 7,665, 10,831, 11,196, 12,314, 15,007, **15,019,** 15,089
American Lutheran Church, Christian Deaconesses, 4,870
American Lutheran Church Women, **4,870, 8,861**
American McAll Association, 9,037
American Magazine (periodical), 4,484
American Magazine of Art (periodical), 12,821
American Mathematical Society, 5,506
American Matthay Association, 16,358
American Medical Women's Association, **6,363, 11,511,** 14,697, 14,698, **15,125,** 15,141
American Medical Writers Association, 5,230

American Memorial Hospital (Paris, France), 13,889
American Mental Health Association, 6,852
American Mercury, The (periodical), 73, 1,224, 12,466
American Missionary Association, 3,915, **5,457,** 5,461, 5,467, 5,468, 6,388, 15,716
American Missionary Association of New York, 4,359
American Missionary Society, 2,298
American Mother of the Year (1940), 8,823
American Mothers' Club (New Haven, CT), 1,997
American Mothers Committee, Inc., 8,421
American Mothers Platform to Prevent War, 10,048
American Museum of Immigration (NY), 9,509, 17,594
American Museum of Natural History (NY), 12,276, 14,235, 14,943
American Museum of Natural History, China expedition (1916-1917), 2,719
American Name Society, 15,789
American National Cowbelles, **17,937**
American National Red Cross. *See* American Red Cross
American National Theater and Academy, 2,625
American Negro Historical Society, 14,985
American Neutral Conference Committee, 7,923
American Newspaper Women's Club, 13,406, 17,070
American Nurses' Association, 2,205, 3,432, 3,444, 4,367, 5,000, **6,123,** 6,124, 6,127, 6,134, 6,139, 6,141, 6,147, 8,553, 8,610, 8,648, 11,667, 12,074, 13,680, 13,892, 17,291, 17,360
American Nurses' Association, Committee on Ethical Standards, 12,077
American Nurses' Association, Economic Security Section, 6,166
American Nurses' Association, Professional Counseling and Placement Service, 6,134, 6,147
American Nurses' Association, State Board of Nursing and Registration, 6,134
American Nurses' Foundation, 246, **6,124,** 8,553
American Orchid Society, 2,030
American Ouvroir Fund, 12,391
American Palestine Music Association, 14,908
American Parents Committee, 8,640
American Peace Crusade (1951), 5,979
American Peace Mobilization, 9,119
American Peace Society, 3,814, 13,439, **15,298,** 15,300
American Pen Women, 183, 6,867
American People's Encyclopedia, 3,999
American Philological Society, 14,744
American Philosophical Society, 14,944
American Planning and Civic Association, 14,819
American Play Company (NY), **12,372**
American Poetry Journal, 1,795
American Poetry League, 9,527
American Poetry Society, America Prize, 12,915
American Polish Women's Club (OH), **13,906**
American Political Tradition, The (book), 11,912
American Popular Revolutionary Alliance, 8,090
American Presbyterian Congo Mission, 95
American Presbyterian Mission, publishing, 14,425
American Press Association, 16,174
American Psychiatric Association, **2,086**
American Psychological Association, 11,549, 13,743
American Public Health Association, 12,998
American Public Welfare Association, 4,130, **8,632,** 8,644, 11,916, 11,958, 13,255
American Pure Food League, 2,633
American Purity Alliance, 8,633
American Red Cross, 167, 230, 236, 246, 247, 340, 710, 720, 945, 1,092, 1,114, **1,204, 1,400,** 1,534, 1,560, 1,563, 1,605, 1,837, 2,001, 2,052, **2,087,** 2,196, **2,214,** 2,280, 2,309, 2,336, 2,421, 2,424, 2,454, 2,515, 2,542, 2,650, 2,663, 2,868, 2,972, 3,135, 3,216, 3,274, 3,301, 3,311, 3,327, 3,335, 3,383, 3,432, 3,437, 3,530, 3,602, 3,653, 3,669, 3,729, 4,141, 4,350, 4,394, 4,791, 4,814, 4,843, 5,126, 5,228, 5,451, 5,506, 5,595, 5,854, 6,131, 6,142, 6,160, 6,223, 6,386, 6,520, 6,900, 6,939, 7,137, 7,188, 7,209, 7,332, 7,556, **7,600,** 7,701, 7,965, 8,047, 8,174, 8,228, 8,446, 8,535, 8,651, 8,991, 9,218, 9,277, 9,311, 9,374, 9,430, 9,467, 9,468, 9,709, 9,978, 10,197, 10,254, 10,509, 10,630, 10,658, 10,692, 10,720, 10,784, 10,886,

11,027, 11,063, 11,150, 11,247, 11,440, 11,444, 11,515, 11,719, 11,734, 11,944, 12,263, 12,751, 13,277, 13,366, 13,390, 13,543, 13,604, 13,617, 13,663, 13,696, 13,729, 13,860, 13,888, 13,889, 13,941, 13,953, 13,992, 14,026, 14,076, 14,136, 14,246, 14,741, **14,860,** 15,009, 15,246, 15,451, 16,092, 16,279, 16,999, **17,072,** 17,184, 17,267, 17,293, 17,304, 17,596, 17,686, 17,821, 17,856, 17,984, 17,998, 18,006
  WWI, **1,400,** 1,772, 6,647
American Red Cross (AZ), 167
American Red Cross (CA), **318,** 1,114, **1,204**
American Red Cross (San Francisco Chapter, CA), **318**
American Red Cross (GA), Nutrition Committee, **2,960**
American Red Cross (IL), 4,299
American Red Cross (IA), 4,702
American Red Cross (MN), **8,427,** 8,492, **8,824,** 8,908
American Red Cross (NE), 10,474
American Red Cross (NJ), 11,210
American Red Cross (NY), 12,506
American Red Cross (Greensboro, NC), **13,218**
American Red Cross (ND), **13,679**
American Red Cross (Carlisle Chapter, PA), 14,746
American Red Cross (Mount Sinai Hospital Auxiliary, PA), 15,161
American Red Cross (Galveston Chapter, TX), **16,216**
American Red Cross (WV), 6,129
American Red Cross (WI), **17,536**
American Red Cross, After Care, 8,908
American Red Cross, Civilian Relief Department, 8,908
American Red Cross, Edith Gray Canteen Reserve Corps, 2,885
American Red Cross, Family Service Board, 16,216
American Red Cross, Home Service, 8,908
American Red Cross Hospital (England, World War II), 6,153
American Red Cross, Naval Auxiliary, 2,292
American Red Cross, Nursing Service, 13,680
American Red Cross, Overseas Service League, 4,629
American Red Cross, Public Health Nursing Service, 16,216
American Red Cross Service Clubs, 7,258
American Repertory Theater, 2,625
American Revolution Bicentennial (1776-1976), 8,312, 10,878
American-Russian Review (periodical), 2,611
American Samoa, **1,177**
  census, 1,177
  court records, 1,177
  prisons, records and correspondence, 1,177
American-Scandinavian Review (periodical), 4,321
American Scholar, The (periodical), **2,166**
American School (Kikungshan, China), 8,878, 8,887
American School Citizenship League (MA), 6,368
American School Health Association, 11,627
"American School of the Air" (radio program), 17,666
American Scrapbooks (CT), **1,838**
American Service Committee, 13,183
American Shakespeare Festival Foundation, 11,944
American Short Horn Breeders' Association, 8,340
American Sisters of Charity, 4,645
American Slavery As It Is (tract), 2,629
American Social Credit Movement, 1,981
American Social Health Association, 6,223, 6,760, **8,633,** 12,736
American Social Hygiene Association. *See* American Social Health Association
American Society for Encouraging the Settlement of the Oregon Territory, 14,513
American Society for Ethnohistory, **2,835**
American Society for Nursing Service Administrators, **3,780**
American Society for Sanitary and Moral Prophylaxis, 8,633
American Society for the Prevention of Cruelty to Animals, 6,418
American Society for the Relief of French War Orphans, 2,352

American Society of Composers, Authors, and Publishers, 14,150
American Society of Contemporary Artists, 2,793
American Society of Landscape Architects, 303
American Society of Microbiologists, 13,259
American Society of Radiologic Technologists, 10,508
American Society of Superintendents of Training Schools, 12,074
American Sociological Association, 6,898
American Sojourn in China, An (book), 15,531
American Sunday-School Union, 13,932
American Telephone and Telegraph Company, 6,383
American Temperance Society, 453
American Theosophical Lodge (San Francisco, CA), 1,239
American Theosophical Society, 11,551
American Tobacco Company, 13,112
American Tract Society (NY, VA), 9,281, 12,370
American Tung Oil Association, 9,779
American Ukrainian Republican Association, 9,513
American Union Against Militarism, 8,658
American Unitarian Association, 9,413
American Unitarian Association (MA), 6,250
American University (Istanbul, Turkey), faculty, **1,556**
American Veterans of World War II, Iowa Auxiliary, **4,891**
American Veterinary Medical Association, Auxiliary to the Texas Student Chapter, **16,186**
American Vigilance Association. *See* American Social Health Association
American Vocational Association, 8,567
American Volunteer Group (WWII), 11,861
American War Mothers, 9,150, 10,032, 13,446, 13,618
American War Mothers (NC), **13,316**
American War Mothers (TX), **16,030**
American Way of Death, The (book), 16,162
American Weekly (periodical), 17,762
American Woman Suffrage Association. *See* National American Woman Suffrage Association
American Woman's Association, **6,456,** 6,483, 7,302, 8,142, 13,674
American Woman's Club, 13,674
American Woman's Educational Association, 1,951
American Woman's Society of Certified Public Accountants, **14,113**
American Women in Radio and Television, 2,844, 4,120
American Women in Radio and TV (project, MT), 10,330
"American Women Speak," 11,306
American Women's Club (France), 7,258
American Women's party, 14,686
American Women's Voluntary Service, 2,663, 7,209, **10,747,** 10,784, 16,222, 17,436
American Women's Volunteer Service Association, 8,635
American Youth Award, 13,535
American Youth Commission, 6,934, 10,035, 11,911
American Youth Congress, 8,104
American Zionist Medical Unit, 12,117
Americanization, 1,645, 1,891, 1,897, 1,997, 2,679, 2,683, 6,239, 8,668, 8,681, 9,254, 9,273, 9,487, 11,236, 13,993, 15,023, 17,902
"Americans All—Immigrants All" (radio program), 9,494
Americans for Democratic Action, 6,865, 12,061, 15,997, 17,238
America's First Spaceman (book), 1,534
Amertorp Corporation v. Lillian D. Reynolds et al., 2,678
Ames, Adelbert (1835-1933), 7,178
Ames, Alice Vivian (1865-1944). *See* Winter, Alice Vivian (Ames) [Mrs. Thomas Gerald] (1865-1944)
Ames, Blanche (Ames) [Mrs. Oakes] (1878-1969), **6,364,** 6,404, **6,968,** 7,178
Ames, Blanche (Butler) [Mrs. Adelbert] (1845-1939), 7,178, 9,709
Ames, Charles, 6,911
Ames, Elizabeth, 3,986
Ames, Elizabeth King, 12,844
Ames, Ethel. *See* Sagen, Ethel (Ames)
Ames, Ezra, 5,713

Ames Family (MS), **7,178**
Ames, Fanny (Baker) [Mrs. Charles Gordon] (1840-1931), 6,911, **6,969**
Ames, Harriet Ann (Moore) [Mrs. Solomon C.] Page [Mrs. Robert] Potter [Mrs. Charles] (1810-?), **2,167,** 13,537, 16,117
Ames, Helen Maude. *See* Peck, Helen Maude (Ames)
Ames, Jessie (Daniel) (1883-), 3,279, 3,283, 3,326, 3,347, **12,939**
Ames, Lillian Marion Norton (1844-1914). *See* Stevens, Lillian Marion Norton (Ames) [Mrs. Michael T.] (1844-1914)
Ames, Louise (Bates) (1908-), **2,168,** 2,353
Ames, Lucia True. Lucy James Ames (1856-1936). *See* Mead, Lucia True (Ames) [Mrs. Edwin Doak] (1856-1936)
Ames, Lucy Virginia (Semple) (1837-1925), **4,198**
Ames, Marcia Lucretia (1797-1896). *See* James, Marcia Lucretia (Ames) [Mrs. William] (1797-1896)
Ames, Mary E. (Clemmer) [Mrs. Daniel] (1831-84). *See* Hudson, Mary E. (Clemmer) [Mrs. Daniel] Ames [Mrs. Edmund] (1831-84)
Ames, Miss, 8,407
Ames, Oakes (1874-1950), 7,178
Ames, Serena Marie (1840-68). *See* Wright, Serena Marie (Ames) [Mrs. George Burdick] (1840-68)
Ames, Winthrop, 12,476
Ames Woman's Club (IA), 4,815
Amey, Mrs. William, 13,217
Amherst Book Club (NY), **11,334**
Amherst College (MA), 12,478
  faculty, 5,865, 11,957
  presidents, 5,713, 5,866, 5,868, **6,296**
Amherst H. Wilder Charity, 9,442
Amherst H. Wilder Foundation (MN), **8,909,** 9,359
Amick, Georgia (1903-), **14,186**
Amidon, Beulah, 8,679
Amidon, Paul, 9,232
Amis, Mary. *See* Hooper, Mary (Amis)
Amis, Sarah (Davis), 12,955
Amistad Defense Committee, 5,457
Amita Award, 9,496
Ammons, Edith Eudora (ca. 1884-1959). *See* Kohl, Edith Eudora (Ammons) [Mrs. Aaron Wesley] (ca. 1884-1959)
Amnesty, United States, 3,133, 12,703
Among the Girls, 4,473
Among Those Present: Fifty Years in the Old Home Town (book), 13,368
Amory Family (Ireland, SC, MA), **2,169**
Amory, Jonathon, 2,169
Amory, Martha, **11,783**
Amory, Martha [Mrs. Jonathon], 2,169
Amory, Rebekah (Holmes) [Mrs. Thomas], 2,169
Amory, Thomas (1682-1728), 2,169
Amos Abbott Company (MA), **7,113**
Amos Fortune, Free Man (book), 6,119
Amoskeag Foundation No. 12, 10,815
Amphibians, 2,717
Amphictyonic Council (Parma, ID), **3,660**
Amrud, Anna, 9,316
Amsler, Margaret (Harris) [Mrs. Sam] (1908-), **16,327**
Amusement parks, 1,751, 5,533
Anagnos, Michael (1837-1906), 7,684
Analytical Psychology Club of New York, 2,631
Anarchism and anarchists, 1,654, 4,145, 4,161, **4,229,** 4,433, **6,028,** 6,329, **7,223,** 7,997, 7,998, 9,900, 11,927, **12,487,** 12,698, **12,699, 12,701**
Anatomists, **14,900,** 14,943
Anatomy, 6,216, 14,965, 15,039
Anatomy (book), 4,710
Ancestry and Posterity of Joseph Smith and Emma Hale (book), 10,091
Anches, Libby, 17,282
Anchorage school (NY), 11,444
Ancient Order of United Workmen, 10,402
Ancon Hospital (Canal Zone), 1,665
Ancotty (Long Ago) (book), 14,546
And Promenade Home (book), 7,214
And the Bravest of These (book), 5,022
Anders, Mary, 5,063
Andersen, Andreas Martin (1869-1902), 2,170

Andersen, Annie Matilda Gerber (1881-), 16,780
Andersen, Ellen Wilson [Mrs. A. F.] (1847-1936), 9,042
Andersen, Hazel, **16,581**
Andersen, Hendrik Christian (1872-1940), Family, **2,170**
Andersen, Olivia Donaldson (Cushing) (1871-1917), 2,170
Anderson, Ada (Woodruff) [Mrs. Oliver Phelps], **17,387**
Anderson, Alexander (1775-1870), **12,155**
Anderson, Alfred (1899-1973), **8,061**
Anderson, Alice Brooks (?-1915), 16,478
Anderson, Alice K. (1905-), **8,869**
Anderson, Amanda Wilhelmina [Miss] (1859-?), **16,582**
Anderson, Ann. *See* Maverick, Ann (Anderson)
Anderson, Ann Jane (1811-18), 14,803
Anderson, Anna, **5,639**
Anderson, Anna (Magnuson), 17,862
Anderson, Balfour H., 1,566
Anderson, Belle (Kelley), 10,090
Anderson, Betty [Mrs. John], **16,259**
Anderson, Betty Baxter (1908-66), **4,966**
Anderson, Catherine. *See* McWillie, Catherine (Anderson)
Anderson, Charlena (van Vleck) [Mrs. Melville Best], 1,566
Anderson, Charles B., 10,386
Anderson, Charlotte Drees [Mrs.] (?-1969), **4,181**
Anderson, Colena M. (1891-), **8,870,** 14,459
Anderson College (IN), 4,465
Anderson College School of Theology (IN), **4,465**
Anderson, Connie, 3,442
Anderson, Constance Spalding [Mrs. Albert], **3,132**
Anderson, Cora (1897-). *See* Nygaard, Cora (Anderson) (1897-)
Anderson, Deborah [Mrs.], 7,372
Anderson, Delphine (1868-1961). *See* Squires, Delphine (Anderson) [Mrs. Charles Pemberton] (1868-1961)
Anderson, Dolly Brown, 1,339
Anderson, Dorothy (Moore) [Mrs. Edgar], 10,150
Anderson, Eba (1830-1919). *See* Lawton, Eba (Anderson) [Mrs. James Marsland] (1830-1919)
Anderson, Edgar, **10,150**
Anderson, Eleanor (Copenhaver), 13,176
Anderson, Elin L. [Miss], 17,018
Anderson, Eliza Bayard (Clinch) [Mrs. Robert], 2,174
Anderson, Elizabeth (Prall) [Mrs. Sherwood], 1,088
Anderson, Elizabeth (Preston) [Mrs. James] (1861-1954), **13,648,** 13,665, **13,668**
Anderson, Emma, 15,308
Anderson, Emma Augusta (1894-1969). *See* Ellsworth, Emma Augusta (Anderson) [Mrs. German Edgar] (1894-1969)
Anderson, Espy L., 14,803
Anderson, Ester, 17,901
Anderson, Eugenie Moore [Mrs. John P.] (1909-), 4,869, 6,710, **8,911, 8,912,** 9,040, 9,140, 9,287, 9,368, 9,449, 9,467
Anderson, Eunice G. (?-1964) **17,885,** 17,918, 17,985
Anderson Family (CA), **1,566**
Anderson Family (GA), **3,594**
Anderson Family (UT), 16,478
Anderson, Fannie Allen, 9,323
Anderson, Faye Louise, **7,701**
Anderson, Florence (1910-), 11,844
Anderson, Florence Bennett, 2,166
Anderson, Frances [Mrs.], 12,437
Anderson, Frances Hughes (Sanford) [Mrs. Robert] (1906-), 9,346
Anderson, George Wayne, 3,594
Anderson, Harriet, 2,694
Anderson, Helen (Best), 1,566
Anderson, Helen Marie (Nance) [Mrs. Walter L.] (1877-1966), **10,427**
Anderson, Helen Monsen (1842-?), 2,170
Anderson, Henry W., 17,059
Anderson, Inez, **1,205**
Anderson, Isabel Weld (Perkins) [Mrs. Larz] (1876-1948), **2,171,** 2,521
Anderson, James C. O'Gorman, 2,204, 6,366
Anderson, John (1770-1840), **14,803**

Anderson, John B. (1845-1925), **179**
Anderson, Judith, 11,459
Anderson, Katherine [Miss], **3,133**
Anderson, Katherine [Mrs. George Potter], **7,702**
Anderson, Laurine C., 15,913
Anderson, Lillian, 16,865
Anderson, Lily Strickland [Mrs. J. C.] (1887-1958),
   15,556
Anderson, Lizzie Crafton, **15,913**
Anderson, Louisa H. Watson (1817-84), 14,803
Anderson, Louisa Harrison (1850-1924), 14,803
Anderson, Lydia B., 12,351
Anderson, M. Margaret, 5,465
Anderson, Margaret, 2,331, 17,843
Anderson, Margaret Kay, 1,182
Anderson, Margaret M., 9,492
Anderson, Margarite [Mrs.], **2,172**
Anderson, Marguerite S. [Mrs.], **2,173**
Anderson, Maria Nelson [Mrs. Peter], 11,325
Anderson, Marian (1902-), **2,123**, 3,290, 3,294,
   3,303, 3,799, 5,469, 7,267, 12,004
Anderson, Marian Louise (1918-). See Larson,
   Marian Louise (Anderson) [Mrs. Robert M.]
   (1918-)
Anderson, Martha H. (1840-?). See Brown, Martha
   H. (Anderson) [Mrs. Francis A.] (1840-?)
Anderson, Mary, 3,976
Anderson, Mary [Miss] (1872-1964), 2,509, 2,878,
   6,365, 6,958, 8,122, 11,305
Anderson, Mary (1859-1940). See De Navarro, Mary
   (Anderson) [Madame Antonio] (1859-1940)
Anderson, Mary Audentia (Smith) [Mrs. Benjamin
   M.], **4,728**, 10,091, 16,813
Anderson, Mary Emma (Booth) [Mrs. John B.]
   (1854-1948), 179
Anderson, Mary (Espy) [Mrs. John] (1779-1815),
   14,803
Anderson, Mary Espy (1846-90), 14,803
Anderson, Mary Marvel (van Vleck) [Mrs. Balfour
   H.], 1,566
Anderson, Mary S. (van Vleck) [Mrs. Balfour H.],
   1,566
Anderson, Marybell (Harmon), **16,495**
Anderson, Mattie Belle, 16,132
Anderson, Maude (Case) [Mrs. Frank Maloy]
   (1871-?), **8,533**, 8,980
Anderson, Maxwell, 12,642, 16,156
Anderson, May [Miss] (1864-1946), 16,676
Anderson, Melville Best, 1,566
Anderson, Mother, 5,501
Anderson, Mrs. E. C., 3,594
Anderson, Mrs. Enbert, 9,070
Anderson, Mrs. Sherwood, 9,443
Anderson, Mrs. Warwick, 11,827
Anderson, Mrs. William E., Sr., **14,505**
Anderson, Nina, 3,523
Anderson, Pernilla (1850-?), 16,968
Anderson, Peter, 11,325
Anderson, Robert, 9,346
Anderson, Robert (1781-1859), **17,127**
Anderson, Robert (1805-71), **2,174**
Anderson, Rose [Mrs. Alfred] (1897-), **8,061**
Anderson School of Natural History (MA), 584,
   6,346
Anderson, Sherwood (1876-1941), 7,229, 11,867,
   12,821, 16,168
Anderson, Stella Benson [Mrs. James C. O'Gorman]
   (1892-1933), **2,204**, 2,628, 6,095, **6,366**, 12,499
Anderson, Walter L., 10,427
Anderson, Wendell R. (1933-), **9,475**
Anderson, William, **8,913**
Anderson, William (1888-), **8,910**
Anderson, William Patrick, 3,133
Anderson, William Watson, 14,803
Andersonville Prison, 7,188
Andersson, Hilda (1859-1968). See Erickson, Hilda
   (Andersson) [Mrs. John A.] (1859-1968)
"Andover" (song), 7,663
Andover-Newton Theological Seminary (MA),
   3,742
   students, 4,829
Andre, Alice I., 12,440
Andreasen, Anna Lena (Frandsen) [Mrs. Axel
   Ferdenand], 16,583

Andreen, Gustav Albert (1864-1940), **4,319**
Andreen, Mary (Strand) [Mrs. Gustav Albert]
   (1870-1948), 4,319
Andresen, August H., 9,041
Andrew Jackson Society, 16,061
Andrew, Louis Towers, 8,514
Andrew, Martha "Mattie" Freeman [Mrs. Louis
   Towers] (1877-1943), **8,514**
Andrew Methodist Church (WV), 17,471
Andrews, Alice, 9,435
Andrews, C. F., 12,715
Andrews, Charles (1814-52), 5,671
Andrews, Christopher C., 9,435
Andrews, Eliza Frances (1840-1931), **59**
Andrews, Elle (?-1900). See Wilson, Elle (Andrews)
   [Mrs. James Harrison] (?-1900)
Andrews, Ellen "Nellie" Miriam Gibson [Mrs. James
   Amasa] (?-1921), 8,914, 17,859
Andrews, Emily K., 16,060
Andrews, Emma B. [Mrs.] (?-1922), **14,882**
Andrews, Esther, 7,703
Andrews, Esther Myers (1861-1938), **6,367**
Andrews, Fannie Fern (Phillips) [Mrs. Edwin Gasper]
   (1867-1950), 1,559, **6,368**, 7,184, 15,316
Andrews, Fanny (1869-?), **16,101**
Andrews, Frances E. (ca. 1885-1961), 9,216, 9,302
Andrews Institute (OH), 11,003
Andrews, Irene Osgood, 11,760
Andrews, James Amasa, Family (WI), **8,914**, 17,859
Andrews, Jessie, 16,101
Andrews, Lila Juliet (1888-). See Wilson, Lila Juliet
   (Andrews) (1888-)
Andrews, Louise (1886-1969). See Kent, Louise
   (Andrews) (1886-1969)
Andrews, Lulah T., 5,122
Andrews, Mary Evans (ca. 1909-), 4,155
Andrews, Mary Garard [Mrs. Isaac R.] (1849-1936),
   9,406
Andrews, Myra Fithian (?-1935). See Arthur, Myra
   Fithian (Andrews) [Mrs. Chester Alan II]
   (?-1935)
Andrews, Persis (Sibley) [Mrs. Charles] (1813-91).
   See Black, Persis (Sibley) [Mrs. Charles]
   Andrews [Mrs. Alvah] (1813-91)
Andrews Pioneer Schools (TX), 16,031
Andrews, Ruth Caroline (1878-?), 8,914
Andrews, Sarah, **8,298**
Andrews, Sarah E., **8,915**
Andrews Sisters (singers), 18,001
Andrews, Whit, 16,031
Andrews, Willie [Mrs. Whit], **16,031**
Andrews, Winifred, **8,298**
Andrews, Yvette Borup, 2,719
Andrillon, Fernando, 12,160
Andrus, Lucy (Huber), 7,818
Andrus, Manomas Lavina (Gibson) (1842-1940),
   16,968
Andujar, Betty, **15,988**
"Andy Griffith Show, The" (television program),
   17,958
Anemia, 8,538
Anesi, Janet (1954?-), **17,886**
Anesthesia in obstetrics, 6,331
Anesthesiology, 11,727
Anesthetists, **8,823**, 13,055
Angel-Fish Aquarium Club, 11,967
Angel Grows Up, An (book), 17,731
Angel, Lydia, 17,282
Angel, Mary Ann (1803-82). See Young, Mary Ann
   (Angel) [Mrs. Brigham] (1803-82)
Angel on Snowshoes (book), 17,699
Angela Davis Defense Committee, **1,567**
Angelique, 9,604
Angell, Brenda (1890-1954). See Jepson, Brenda
   (Angell) [Mrs. Jesse Nightingale] (1890-1954)
Angell, Emma Frances (Hartley) [Mrs. Charles
   August] (1868-?), 16,713
Angell, James B., 7,704, 7,850
Angell, Lois Thompson. See McLaughlin, Lois
   Thompson (Angell) [Mrs. Andrew C.]
Angell, Sarah Swoope (Caswell) [Mrs. James B.]
   (1831-1903), **7,704**
Angels and Earthly Creatures (book), 2,658
Angermann, Dorothea, 2,403

Angier, Ida L. See Burnham, Ida L. (Angier)
Anglin, Margaret, 12,535
Anglo-Chinese College (Foochow, China), 14,089,
   14,441
Angola, American missionaries in, 86
"Angola, The Story of a Country Neighborhood"
   (ms), 9,552
Angus, Edith, 1,581
Angus, Mrs. Reginald, 8,378
Animal painters, **2,761**
Animals, treatment of, 4,105, 6,418, 7,305, 8,474,
   12,516, 14,867, 15,522, 16,301
   societies, etc., 6,418, 9,527
Ankeny Family (IA), **4,729**, 4,740
Ankeny, Harriet S. Giese, 4,740
Ankeny, Harriet Louise, **4,730**, 4,740
Ankeny, Jessie. See Lacy, Jessie (Ankeny) [Mrs.
   Henry Veere]
Ankeny, Joseph, 4,740
Ankeny, Louise, 14,404
Ankeny, Peter, 4,730
Ankeny, Rollin Valentine, 4,729
Anker, Anna (1949-). See Wasik, Anna (Anker)
   (1949-)
Ann Arbor Board of Education (MI), 7,926
Ann Arbor Business and Professional Women's Club
   (MI), **7,705**
Ann Arbor Transportation Authority (MI), 7,733
Ann Arbor Women for Peace (MI), 7,723
"Ann Sothern Show" (television program), 1,024
Ann Tillery Renshaw School of Speech, 13,366
Anna and the King of Siam (book), 2,435
Anna Jackson Book Club (NC), **13,317**
Anna Morgan Studio (IL), 3,880
Anna Teller (book), 6,082
Annals of Brattleboro, 1681-1895 (book), 17,024
Annals of Congress. See *Congressional Record*
"Annals of the Group" (ms), 3,404
Annals of Wyoming, 17,885
Anne L. Page Memorial School, 7,580
"Anne Royall—First 'Colyumist'" (article), 9,849
Anne Sullivan Macy Service for the Deaf-Blind, 2,111
Anneke, Fritz (1818-72), **17,589**
Anneke, Mathilde Franziska (Giesler) [Mrs. Fritz]
   (1817-84), **17,589**
Annette (slave, SC), 2,126
Annie Get Your Gun (drama), 12,366
Annie Laurie. See Bonfils, Winifred (Sweet) [Mrs.
   Orlow] Black [Mrs. Frederick G.] (1863-1936)
Annie Russell Theatre, 12,549, 12,612
Annie Wright Seminary, students, 17,185
Annis, Isaac, **12,176**
Annisquam Female Benevolent Society (Gloucester,
   MA). See Annisquam Sewing Circle (Gloucester,
   MA)
Annisquam Sewing Circle (Gloucester, MA), **7,032**
Anniston Star (AL), 112
Annulment (marriage). See Marriage, annulment
Annunciation Church, First Altar Guild (OH), 13,912
Another Mother for Peace, **7,179**, 7,278
"Another World" (soap opera), 17,705
Ansonia Library (CT), 6,910
Anspach, Lillian Sue (?-1942). See Keech, Lillian Sue
   (Anspach) [Mrs. Edward P.] (?-1942)
Ante Room (drama), 4,235
Antediluvian, or, the Infants' Clothing Association,
   The (PA), **14,947**
Antenuptial contracts. See Prenuptial contracts
Anthony, Bess Taylor [Mrs. Marc], 15,945
Anthony Family, **1,391**
Anthony, Helen, 7,413
Anthony, Janette, 8,462
Anthony, Jessie, 1,004
Anthony, John, 1,004
Anthony, Joseph, 1,391
Anthony, Katharine, 6,374, 12,537
Anthony League of the District of Columbia. See
   Susan B. Anthony Foundation
Anthony, Lucy Elmina, 1,391, **6,534**, 6,536, 6,637,
   12,835
Anthony, Lucy S., 15,851
Anthony, Margaret (1828-93), 7,413
Anthony, Mary S., 349, 1,004, 1,308, 1,391, 12,818,
   12,835

Anthony on Overtime (drama), 9,496
Anthony, Susan Brownell (1820-1906), 349, 589,
    1,004, **1,230**, 1,255, 1,304, 1,308, **1,391**, 1,404,
    1,414, 1,436, 1,437, 1,442, 1,475, 1,483, 1,492,
    1,494, 1,506, 1,552, 1,593, 1,751, 1,896, 1,950,
    2,175, 2,196, 2,218, 2,260, 2,303, 2,315, 2,346,
    2,374, 2,413, 2,542, 2,588, 2,605, 2,614, 2,648,
    3,862, 3,908, 4,172, 4,244, 4,623, 4,696, **4,731**,
    4,732, 4,781, 4,859, 5,334, 5,487, 6,244, **6,374**,
    6,412, 6,460, 6,526, 6,534, 6,588, 6,589, 6,629,
    6,637, 6,659, 6,712, 6,783, 6,804, 6,830, 6,836,
    6,859, 6,888, 6,891, 6,905, 6,932, 6,994, 7,171,
    7,180, 7,203, 7,222, 7,232, 7,243, 7,274, 7,430,
    7,808, 8,523, **8,916**, 9,060, 9,142, 9,241, 10,003,
    11,113, 11,349, 11,547, 11,590, 11,605, 11,741,
    11,742, 12,500, 12,529, 12,573, 12,625, 12,695,
    12,790, **12,791**, 12,799, 12,803, **12,811, 12,812**,
    12,818, 12,819, 12,828, 12,834, 12,835, 12,857,
    12,877, 12,917, 13,246, 13,668, 13,990, 14,144,
    14,206, 14,737, 15,283, 15,312, 17,010, 17,166,
    17,411, 17,589, 17,616, 17,852, 17,898
Anthrop, Mary, 4,635
Anthropo-geography, 5,323
Anthropological museums and collections, **919, 920**
Anthropological research, **2,832, 2,840**
Anthropological Society of Washington (DC), **2,836**
Anthropologists, 212, **919, 920**, 1,779, **1,887**, 2,464,
    2,716, **2,833, 2,836**, 2,838, 2,840, 2,841, 2,842,
    5,442, **5,455, 5,616, 5,874, 6,130, 6,324**, 6,325,
    6,326, 6,327, 6,328, 8,208, 8,848, **10,726, 11,387**,
    11,882, **12,067, 14,886, 14,894, 14,897, 17,252**
Anthropologists, Afro-American, **3,291**, 6,112
Anthropology, **3,951, 5,874, 6,130**, 6,327, 10,727
"Anthropology of the Americas" (television program),
    2,839
Anthropology publishing, 2,838
Anthroposophical Society in America, 13,855
Anthroposophy, 13,855
Anti-Catholicism, 3,437, 4,642, 8,070
Anti-Communist League of America, 15,755
Anti-communist movements, 9,359, 11,920, 15,374,
    15,755
Anti-discrimination laws. See Sex discrimination, law
    and legislation
Anti-Lottery League of Louisiana, 5,502
Anti-Mormonism, 16,565
Anti-Polygamous Ladies of Utah, 16,537
Anti-Saloon League, 2,886, 9,421, **10,642**
Anti-Semitism, 8,149, 8,662, 8,923, 8,963, **9,150**,
    9,467, 15,869
Anti Slavery Campaign, 1842-83, 7,233
Anti-Slavery Convention of American Women, 992
Anti-slavery Society of Philadelphia (PA), 14,953
Anti-Slavery Standard (periodical), 11,998
Anti-State Wide Prohibition Organization (TX),
    16,095
Anti-Suffrage Association (Albany, NY), 11,249
Anti-Tuberculosis Association (GA), **3,134**
Antibiotics, testing, 13,259
Antietam, battle of (1862), 4,490, 13,348
Antin, Mary (1881-1949). See Grabau, Mary Antin
    [Mrs. Amadeus William] (1881-1949)
Antioch Church (Pleasant View, KS), 5,187
Antioch College (OH), 6,435, 15,214
    presidents, 9,023, 11,694
Antique Collector's Club (MN), 8,460
Antique dealers, **8,358**
Antiques (periodical), **2,862**
Antiques, collectors and collecting, 12,452
Antiquities, 5,493
Antiquities, African, 45
Antiseptics, 3,146
Antitubercular agents, 11,862
Antonio Machado (book), 2,110
Antony and Cleopatra (drama), 871, 12,426
Ants, 14,877
Any Wednesday (drama), 2,546
Anybody's Woman (moving-picture), 1,025
AORN Journal, 1,691
Apache Indians, 16,497, **16,863**, 16,865, 16,868,
    16,877
    costume and adornment, 16,863
    education, 16,863
    government relations, 16,863

language, 16,863
    legends 16,863
Apcar, Diana Agabey, 1,559
Apostolic Christian church, 8,699, **8,711**
Apostolic Truth Tract Society, 8,335
Appalachia, 6,221, 14,013
Appalachian Economic and Political Action
    Conference, 17,608
Appalachian Oral History Project, **5,402**, 17,063
Appalachian State Teachers College (NC), 13,618
Appalachian State University (NC), **5,402**, 17,063
"Appeal Army" (column), 8,070
Appeal to Reason (newspaper), 8,070
"Appeal to the Christian Women of America, An,"
    7,295
"Appearance" (song), 7,663
Appel, Marie, **7,708**
Appel, R. P., 5,910
Appendicitis, 3,234
Apperson, Phoebe (1842-1919). See Hearst, Phoebe
    (Apperson) [Mrs. George] (1842-1919)
Apple, 14,683
Appleby, Cornelia Day (Wilder) [Mrs. T. E. W.
    Villiers] (1868-1903), 9,442
Appleby, Katherine Leslie (Lawson), 608
Applegarth, Laura Bride, 1,333
Applegarth, Mrs. George A., 1,333
Applegate, Bessie Bell, 14,506
Applegate, Cynthia [Mrs. Jesse], 14,506
Applegate Family (OR), 14,506, 14,549
Applegate, Frank, 11,220
Applegate, Jesse, 14,506, 14,552, 14,629, 14,680
Applegate, Lillian Gertrude, 14,506, 14,549
Applegate, Oliver Cromwell (1845-1938), **14,314**,
    14,506, 14,549
Applegate, Sallie. See Long, Sallie (Applegate)
Applegate trail, 14,611, 14,662
Applegate, Virginia (Watson), 14,506
Appleton, Agnes Morgan (Reeves) [Mrs. James H.]
    (1839-1901), **10,936**
Appleton Church Home (GA), 3,128
Appleton Company (North Andover, MA), **7,114**
Appleton Family (MA), **10,858**
Appleton Family (New England), **1,392, 7,522**
Appleton, Frances "Fanny" Elizabeth (1817-61). See
    Longfellow, Frances "Fanny" Elizabeth
    (Appleton) [Mrs. Henry Wadsworth] (1817-61)
Appleton, James H., 10,936
Appleton, Jane Means (1806-63). See Pierce, Jane
    Means (Appleton) [Mrs. Franklin] (1806-63)
Appleton, Mary. See Foster, Mary (Appleton) [Mrs.
    John Welch]
Appleton, Mary Ann [Mrs. William], 6,208
Appleton, Nathan (1779-1861), 6,331, 10,858
Appleton, Nathaniel Walker, 1,392
Appleton, Samuel (1766-1853), 10,858
Appleton, Sarah (Greenleaf) [Mrs. Nathaniel Walker]
    (?-1838). See Haven, Sarah (Greenleaf) [Mrs.
    Nathaniel Walker] Appleton [Mrs. Joseph]
    (?-1838)
Appleton, Thomas Gold (1812-84), 10,858
Appleton, Virginia (1824-1902). See Wilson, Virginia
    (Appleton) [Mrs. Franklin] (1824-1902)
Appleton, William (1786-1862), 10,858
Appletons of Beacon Hill, The (book), 10,858
Appointment on the Hill (book), 15,303
Apportionment (election law), 2,925, 7,861, 9,930,
    10,199
"Appraisals of Trends in Home Economics Research,"
    8,596
Apprentices, **12,227**, 12,563, 15,062
Apprentices Library (PA), **14,948**
Apprenticeships, 9,976
"Approach to Meaning" (ms), 6,082
Aquamaids (swim team, CA), 1,534
Aquinas, Sister, 17,731
Arab-Israeli conflicts, 6,023
Arabella and Her Aunts (book), 11,368
Arabia
    missionaries to, medical, **1,840**
    missionaries to, Reformed Church, **10,926, 10,927**
Arachnologists, **6,318**
Aram, Joseph (?-1898), **1,393**

Aram, Sarah Mahala (1836-1912). See Cool, Sarah
    Mahala (Aram) [Mrs. Peter Y.] (1836-1912)
Arapahoe County Hospital (CO), 1,753
Arapahoe Indians, 1,497, 1,779, 14,241, 17,921
    ethnology, 2,839
    missions, 5,196
Ararat (book), 6,115
Araucarian Indians, ethnology, 2,839
Arbella (ship), 7,127
Arber, Agnes (Robertson) (1879-1960), 10,152
Arbitration, industrial, 6,531, 6,640, 11,767, 11,770,
    11,772, 16,009. See also Mediation and
    conciliation, industrial; Strikes and lockouts
Arbitrators, industrial, **11,768**, 11,770, 11,776
Arbolado Parent Teacher Association of District 33,
    Ramsey County (MN), **8,917**
Arbolado School (MN), 8,917
Arbor Day, 3,881
Arboretums, 3,882
Arbus, Diane, 12,126
Arbuthnot, May H. [Mrs. C. C.], **13,879**
Arca de Salvacion (Philadelphia, PA), 14,868
Arcadia House (publishers), 14,329
Archaeological expeditions, 11,868, 14,882
"Archaeological Findings in Shantung Province"
    (speech), 6,992
Archaeological Institute of America, 6,324
Archaeological societies, 6,324, **6,325**, 11,387
Archaeologists, 2,207, **2,280**, 2,863, 7,288, 7,305,
    7,964, 9,448, 10,270, **10,459**, 10,726, **11,868**,
    14,743, 14,882, 15,116
Archaeology, 6,325, 6,327, 10,727, 12,489
Archambault, Anna Margaretta, **14,949**
Archbald, Mary Ann (Wodrow) (1762-1841), **7,181**
Archbell, Lillie (Vause) (1854?-1946), **12,940**
Arché Club (Chicago, IL), **3,796**
Arché Club (Wayne, MI), 8,387
Archer, Helen (Blackinton), 7,105, 7,109
Archer, Kate Rennie (Aiken), **1,394**, 1,407, 1,448,
    1,508
Archer, Mary Garland, 9,780
Archer, William, 17,208
Archers, 5,048
Archery, 11,445
Archibald, Abner P., 14,559
Archibald Family (MS), 9,816
Archibald, Mrs., 12,419
Architects, 257, **302, 678, 918**, 942, **1,198**, 1,837,
    2,354, 2,545, **2,608, 3,781, 3,782**, 4,224, 4,336,
    5,082, 5,823, **6,805**, 7,182, 9,250, **11,105, 12,216**,
    12,343, 12,349, 12,513, 12,859, 16,780
Architects and Engineers' Institute, Women's
    Auxiliary (GA), 3,374
Architect's Emergency Committee, 2,354
Architects' Small Home Service Bureau of the United
    States, **8,918**
Architectural design, 1,191
Architectural drawing, **1,191**, 12,216, **13,838**
Architectural League, 2,790
Architectural practice, 8,918
Architectural societies, 303, 1,191
Architecture, **544**, 2,414, 7,178, 14,740. See also
    Club-houses; Exhibition buildings; Historical
    buildings; Naval architecture; Palaces; School
    buildings
    designs and plans, 6,805, 9,250
    historiography, 2,790
Architecture, domestic, 5,082, 11,105, 12,988
    designs and plans, **8,918**, 9,049
Architecture League of New York, 12,892
Archive buildings, 76
Archive, The (Duke University, NC), 13,194
Archives, 76, **1,024, 1,025, 1,026, 1,114**, 1,420, **1,456**,
    1,480, **1,527, 2,064, 2,085**, 2,411, **2,926, 3,619**,
    5,409, 6,389, 6,433, 6,450, 6,495, 6,687, **6,801**,
    6,899, 6,966, **6,995**, 7,189, **9,230, 9,739, 9,861**,
    10,055, **10,096, 10,342**, 11,123, 11,143, **11,207**,
    11,246, **11,297**, 11,605, 11,835, 11,915, 13,189,
    14,900, **16,215, 16,408**
    inventories, calendars, etc., **5,424, 5,425**
Archives, Jewish, 17,282
Archivists, 11, 57, 76, 1,480, **2,446**, 2,553, 2,657,
    2,744, 2,981, 3,210, 4,522, 4,530, **5,050, 9,272**,
    9,599, 9,634, 9,673, 10,943, 10,990, **12,988**,

13,411, 13,522, 14,710, 15,302, 15,946, **16,083, 17,368**
Arctic Chandler Memorial (GA), **2,989**
Arctic regions, 2,535, 17,248
Arctic Wild (book), 17,248
Arden, Elizabeth, 698
Arden House Conference on Family Living (1962), 4,918
Ardent Years, The (book), 14,455
Ardis, Mamie (Haygood), 3,328
Areen, Emily Jane (1839-1918). *See* Hollister, Emily Jane (Areen) (1839-1918)
Arendell, Banks, **13,318**
Arendt, Hannah [Miss] (1906-75), **2,177,** 7,822, 11,810
Arensberg, Rose, 17,282
Arentz, Sam S., 10,679
Aretean Literary Society (New Concord, OH), 14,118
Arfsten, Marie. *See* Heinsen, Marie (Arfsten)
Argentina Good Neighbor Conference (1936), 6,433
Argentine Republic, 5,954, 8,164
  American actresses in, 5,954
  American teachers in, 10,937, 17,657
  diplomatic and consular service, 2,471
  education, 17,657
  missionaries to, 16,364
  missionaries to, Methodist, **4,203**
  teachers' colleges, 17,315
Argo Flastacowo, The (yearbook), 2,939
Argo of the Suwanee, The (yearbook), 2,939
Argonaut, 532
Argrett, Virginia M., 5,469
Arguello Boulevard Improvement Club (CA), 1,344
Argüello Family (CA), 314
Argüello, María de la Concepción (1791-1857). *See* Argüello, Sister Dominica, O.P. (1791-1857)
Argüello, Sister Dominica, O.P. (1791-1857), 314, **1,510**
Argus (IL), 3,746
Argus (Albany, NY), 12,556
Argyle Plantation (MS), 9,588
Argyle Plantation (SC), 15,635
Ariel (ship), 1,349
Aristes Fire Company Ladies' Auxiliary (Bloomsburg, PA), **14,720**
Aristocratic Journey, The: Being the Outspoken Letters of Mrs. Basil Hall Written During a Fourteen Months' Sojourn in America (book), 2,373
Arithmetical Tables for the Use of Schools (text-book), 1,898
Arizona, 196, 16,669, 16,709, 16,865, 16,901
  abortion, legal aspects, 1,984
  agriculture, 16,867
  astronomical observatories, 193
  authors, 156, 223
  bands (music), 203
  birth control, **154**
  business, 181
  businessmen, **198,** 222
  businesswomen, 156
  Catholic schools, 159
  cattle breeding, 202
  cattlemen, 190
  child welfare, 190, 200
  church societies, **164**
  churches, Methodist, 197
  citizens' associations, 203, 210
  citizens' associations, Japanese-American, 166
  clerks of court, 986
  clubs, **149, 152,** 167, 169, 198, 203, **208,** 210, **228**
  college teachers, **177, 224**
  community organization, 169
  congresswomen, 157, 184, **194,** 984, 9,155
  county government, records and correspondence, **162**
  court records, 162, **986, 987**
  cowboys, **189**
  crime and criminals, 165
  diaries and journals, **222**
  editors, 218
  educational associations, **150**
  elections, 175

farmers, **185**
gambling, 167
governors, 197, 207
  misconduct in office, 197
higher education, 193
historians, **172, 195,** 209
historical societies, 203
Hopi Indians, 173
hospitals, 153
housewives, 156
Hualapai Indians, medical care, 153
indictments, 178
interethnic marriage, 199
Japanese-Americans, evacuation and relocation (1942-1945), 1,415
journalism, societies, **9,747**
journalists, **214**
land settlement, 202, 16,715
lawyers, 184
legislators, **178, 196,** 16,351
literary societies, **158**
merchants, **199**
midwives, 162
miners, 190
mines and mineral resources, 202
mining engineers, **194**
minorities, 168, 203
missionaries, **185**
missions, 202
monasticism and religious orders for women, Catholic, **159**
Mormons and Mormonism, 160, 185, 191, 202, 207, 16,504, 16,707, 16,777, **16,903**
musical societies, 169
musicians, 156
National Guard, 196
Native Americans, 162, 187, 194, 202, 16,604
  education, 169
  missions, 10,187, 16,903, 17,820
  relations with whites, 16,715, 16,867
  reservations, 155
naturalization records, 162
news agencies, 169
newspapers, **151**
notaries, **179**
nuns, Catholic, 159
obituaries, 167
officials and employees, 168, **172,** 984
oral history, **156, 168, 169, 202,** 211
osteopaths, 219
Papago Indians, 3,671
patriotic societies, 203
pharmacists, 217
photograph collections, **206**
photographers, 169
pioneers and settlers, 160, **169,** 171, 187, 189, **199, 204, 207,** 1,229, 16,504, 16,512, 16,827, 16,915
poets, 5,988
politicians, **175**
politics and government, 202, 210
postal service, postmasters, **179**
prisoners, 210
prisons, **165**
  officials and employees, 190
  records and correspondence, **170**
prostitution, 167
public health nurses, **153**
Pueblo Indians, 2,843
race problems, 203
ranchers, 156, **184, 196, 223**
ranches, 216, 3,685
resorts, 169
retired teachers, 203
riding clubs, **227**
road construction, 181
school census, 162
school superintendents and principals, 190
secretaries of state, 168
senators, United States, **176,** 181
sheriffs, 190
social life and customs, 181, **199**
stores, retail, 178
students' societies, 14,029
suffrage, 200

taxation, 162
teachers, 169, 179, **187,** 197, **218,** 14,311
telephone, directories, **166**
temperance societies, 197, 203
theaters, 169, 203
United States marshals, 190
universities and colleges, faculty, **228**
vital statistics, 162
women, employment, 210
Young Women's Christian Association, 190
Arizona Champion-Coconino Sun Index, **151**
Arizona Children's Home, 190, 200
Arizona Daily Star, 214
Arizona Federation of Women's Clubs, **152,** 198, 203, 208, 210
Arizona Highways (periodical), 163
Arizona Historical Review, 209
Arizona Historical Society, 189, 198, 201, 203, 207, 209
Arizona National Guard, 196
Arizona Newsservice, 169
Arizona Photographic Associates, 169
Arizona Press Women, **163**
Arizona Retired Teacher's Association, 203
Arizona State Cowbelles, 203
Arizona State University, students, 174
Arizona Territory, 178, 187, 204
  governors, 168, 753, 1,430
Arizona Weekly Star, 197
Arizona Women's Commission, 210
Ark-adians (CA), 1,322
Arkansas 13,765
  architects, 257
  authors, **254, 262**
  autograph albums, 265
  bankers, 257
  beauty contests, 9,957
  camps, 16,257
  charitable societies, **269**
  charitable societies, Jewish, **13,768, 13,773**
  child welfare, 3,311
  citizens' associations, **295,** 3,283
  Civil War, 260
    personal narratives, **283**
  clinics, traveling, 231
  clubs, **250, 273, 274, 276, 277**
  college teachers, **265, 266**
  composers, 262, **264**
  conjunctivitis, granular, 231
  court records, 16,215
  deans (in schools), **235**
  diaries and journals, 19th C, **283, 291**
  educational associations, **229**
  elections, 7,194
  executive advisory bodies, 233
  farmers, 257, 9,645
  folk art, **234, 237, 240, 241, 244, 245, 248, 249**
  folk singers, **253**
  generals, 9,624
  governors, 257, 282
  health boards, 235, 238
  historians, **259**
  home nursing, 236
  hospitals, military, 233
  housewives, **296**
  intensive care units, 242
  Japanese-Americans, evacuation and relocation (1942-1945), 17,285
  judges, 297
  legislators, 5,537
  lynching, prevention of, 3,279
  maternal and infant welfare, 236
  medical care, 3,311
  migrant labor, 230
  missionaries, 292
  missionaries, Afro-American, **15,905**
  monasticism and religious orders for women, Catholic, **272, 275**
  newspapers, **294**
  novelists, **270**
  nurses, **230, 231, 232, 233, 235, 236, 238, 239, 242, 243, 247**
    in-service training, 235
    study and teaching, 230, 231, 232, 233, 236, 242

nursing, examinations, questions, etc., 230
nursing homes, administration, 242
nursing schools, 231, 235
    administration, 243
nursing service administration, 239, 247
patriotic societies, **279, 280, 281**
periodicals, **278**
physicians, 231, 287
plantation life, 260
poets, **289**
poliomyelitis, 8,621
poor, 16,215
psychiatric nursing, 231
public health nursing, 231, 236, 238, 239
race problems, 232
real estate agents, 247
registers of births, etc., 231
river steamers, 259
school integration, 295, 5,135
school nurses, 236
secretaries, **244**
senators, United States, **255,** 5,537, 9,942
social life and customs, 16,057, 17,455
social science research, 16,215
students' societies, 263, 268
suffrage societies, 16,252
trade and professional associations, 230, 231, 232,
    233, 236, 238, 239, 242, 243
venereal disease, clinics, 238
Young Women's Christian Association, **271**
Arkansas Business Woman, The, 277
Arkansas County Federation of Women's Clubs, **274**
Arkansas Democrat, 254
Arkansas Federation of Business and Professional
    Women's Clubs, **277**
Arkansas Federation of Garden Clubs, Inc., 278
Arkansas Federation of Women's Clubs, **250**
Arkansas Gardener, The (periodical), **278**
Arkansas Historical Society, 259
Arkansas History Commission, 259
Arkansas Industrial University, students, 265
Arkansas Joint Commission for the Improvement of
    Patient Care, 233
Arkansas Pioneers Association, **279**
Arkansas State Board of Health, 238
Arkansas State Board of Nurse Examiners, 230, 238
Arkansas State Nurses Association, 230, 231, 232,
    233, 236, 238, 239, 242, 243
    integration of, 238, 242, 243
Arkansas State Public Health Department, 235
Arkansas Territorial Restoration Commission, 297
Arkansas Territory, governors, 297
"Arkansas Traveler" (song), 3,764
Arkas, Maria (1900-). *See* Klepachivsky, Maria
    (Arkas) [Mrs. Konstantyn] (1900-)
Arkley, Mary (1923-). *See* Carter, Mary (Arkley)
    (1923-)
Arkwright, Dorothy (Colquitt) [Mrs. Preston S.],
    3,135, 3,253
Arkwright, Preston S., 3,135
Arlen, Alicia [Mrs. James] Hoge [Mrs. Michael],
    11,827
Arling, Emanie (Nahm) Sachs (1893-), **5,278**
Arlington County Board (VA), 17,050
Arlington County Ration Board (VA), 17,050
Arlington County Women's Democratic Club (VA),
    17,050
Arlington Hall Junior College (VA), **17,049**
Arlington Hills Mothers' Club (St. Paul, MN), **8,919**
Arlington Mansion (residence), 3,552
Arlington Street Church (MA), 6,503
Arlitt, Ada Hart (1890-), **13,870**
Arm and Hammer (periodical), 9,379
Armat, Ann [Mrs. Thomas] (?-1851), 15,043
Armat, Frances, 15,043
Armat, Jane (?-1856). *See* Skerrett, Jane (Armat)
    [Mrs. William] (?-1856)
Armat, Thomas, 15,043
Armbruster, Dorothy, 14,328
Armer, Laura Adams, 1,330
Armer, Ruth (1896-), **2,729**
Armes, Ethel [Miss] (1880-1945), 2,443, **4,246,**
    15,979
Armes, George Augustus, 15,979

Armes, Irene Headley, 8,634
Armies, officers, 5,690, **12,242**
Armistead, Meeta Rhodes. *See* Capehart, Meeta
    Rhodes (Armistead) [Mrs. B. A.]
Armitage, Merle, 16,163, 16,167
Armored vessels, 2,278
Armour Institute (IL), 11,893
Armour Institute (IL), library school, 4,396
Armour, Philip D., 11,547
Arms, Emaline Warner [Mrs. Myron Israel], 14,166
Arms Family (OH), **14,166**
Arms, Jennie Maria (1852-1938). *See* Sheldon,
    Jennie Maria (Arms) [Mrs. George Sheldon]
    (1852-1938)
Arms, Myron Israel, 14,166
Armstead Family (MS), 9,816
Armstrong, Alexander "Andy," 4,744
Armstrong, Barbara, 922
Armstrong, Barbara (1890-1976), 11,916
Armstrong, Barbara N., 8,670
Armstrong, Belle, **16,400**
Armstrong, Ben, 14,443
Armstrong, C. J., **9,832**
Armstrong, C. W., 12,431
Armstrong, Caroline, 2,178
Armstrong, Catherine, **17,065**
Armstrong, Charlotte (1905-69), 6,060
Armstrong, Chloe, **16,328**
Armstrong, Clarissa (Chapman) [Mrs. Richard], 2,178
Armstrong, Edith Hull (1872-?). *See* Talbot, Edith
    Hull (Armstrong) (1872-?)
Armstrong, Eleanor, **2,034**
Armstrong, Elsie Strawn (1789-1871), **4,345**
Armstrong, Emma Dean (Walker) [Mrs. Samuel
    Chapman] (1849-78), 7,590, **14,950**
Armstrong, Emzie Amelia (Covert) [Mrs. Alexander
    "Andy"] (1858-1947), **4,744**
Armstrong Family (MA), 7,590
Armstrong, Fred C., **4,092**
Armstrong, Hannah (1860-1958). *See* Porter, Hannah
    (Armstrong) [Mrs. Willard Hall] (1860-1958)
Armstrong, Hannah Henrietta Thacher [Mrs. William
    Frederick], 4,892
Armstrong, James Elder, 4,345
Armstrong, Jessie (1878-?), **320**
Armstrong, Lillian Hardin [Mrs. Louis] (ca.
    1898-1973), **5,529**
Armstrong, Lillie A. (1859-93). *See* Johnstone, Lillie
    A. (Armstrong) [Mrs. William] (1859-93)
Armstrong, Louis, 5,529, **5,534,** 17,944
Armstrong, Louise, 14,950
Armstrong, Louise (Van Voorhis) (1889-1948), **7,709**
Armstrong, Mary Alice Ford [Mrs. Samuel
    Chapman], 7,590
Armstrong, Mary Jane, 2,178
Armstrong, Mrs. Paul, 12,562
Armstrong, Paul, 12,562
Armstrong, Rhoda [Mrs. Ben], 14,443
Armstrong, Richard (1805-60), Family, **2,178**
Armstrong, Ruth Gallup (1891-1972), **4,685**
Armstrong, Samuel Chapman (1839-93), 7,590,
    14,950
Armstrong, T. I. F., 16,168
Armstrong, William Nevins, 2,178
Armstrong, William R., 10,678
Armstrong, Willimina Leonora [Miss] (1866-1947),
    1,029
Army and Navy Historical Association, Inc. (DC),
    2,414
Army Civilian Club (San Antonio, TX). *See* Military
    Civilian Club of San Antonio (TX)
Army of Tennessee (Civil War), 8,167
Army posts, 10,355, 14,277
"Army Wife's Forty Years in the Service, 1862-1902,
    An" (ms), 2,239
Army wives, **2,239,** 2,245, **5,779,** 9,041, 9,434, 9,899,
    10,236, 10,237, 10,289, **10,493, 10,557,** 12,718,
    12,729, 14,767, 14,768, 14,771, **14,773, 14,777,**
    17,069, 17,209
Arnett, Katharine, 8,149
Arney, Maude Baumann, **8,920**
Arnheim, Gus, 5,534
Arno, May. *See* Schwatt, May Arno [Mrs. Herman]
Arnold, Amelia Langworthy (1846-1929), **8,299**

Arnold, Annie S., **15,557**
Arnold, Benedict, 11,172
Arnold, Benedict, Family, **12,373**
Arnold, Bessie Haynes [Mrs. Fred], 18,025
Arnold, Edward, 12,373
Arnold, Eleanor A. (Poole) [Mrs. Henry Harley],
    2,179, 11,874
Arnold, Elizabeth, 6,987
Arnold, Harriet Kress [Mrs. W. J.], 9,048
Arnold, Henry Harley (1886-1950), **2,179, 11,874**
Arnold, Jean Carpenter, 4,211
Arnold, Jennie Waterman, **7,710**
Arnold, Lois E. *See* Snowden, Lois E. (Arnold) [Mrs.
    Ernest E.]
Arnold, Margaret "Peggy" (Shippen) [Mrs. Benedict]
    (1760-1804), 11,172, **12,373,** 14,970
Arnold, Maria, **17,938**
Arnold, Mary Augusta (1851-1920). *See* Ward, Mary
    Augusta (Arnold) [Mrs. Humphrey] (1851-1920)
Arnold, Mary Ellicott (1876-?), **6,375**
Arnold, Matthew, 2,384
Arnold, Richard Dennis (ca. 1808-76), **3,481,** 3,512,
    3,529
Arnold, Rose (1876-1961). *See* Powell, Rose
    (Arnold) (1876-1961)
Arnold, S. C., 4,852
Arnold, Sarah Louise (?-1943), 2,694, 6,237, 6,759,
    9,894
Arnold, Susan (1830-1907). *See* Wallace, Susan
    (Arnold) Elston [Mrs. Lewis] (1830-1907)
Arnold, Virginia A. (1907-), **6,125**
Arnold, William, 12,373
Arnot, Marianna. *See* Ogden, Marianna Arnot [Mrs.
    William B.]
Arnot Ogden Memorial Hospital (Elmira, NY),
    11,443
Arnott, Nellie Jane. *See* Darling, Nellie Jane (Arnott)
    [Mrs. P. L.]
Arnow, Harriette (1908-), 13,176
Arnstein, Flora (Jacobi) [Mrs. Lawrence] (1886?-),
    321, **931**
Arnstein, Helen. *See* Salz, Helen (Arnstein) [Mrs.
    Ansley K.]
Arnstein, Lawrence (1880-), 321
Arnstein, Margaret Gene (1904-72), **6,126**
Arny, Clara M. Brown, 11,662
"Around the Corner" (television program), 2,767
Arps, Louisa (Ward), 1,750
Arrangement (music), 5,531, **5,534**
Arrington, Katherine Pendleton [Mrs.], 13,334
Arrington, Mary Jones [Miss] (1874-1950), **12,941**
Arriwite, Haddi, 16,872
Arrow Rock Tavern Board (MO), **9,833**
Arrowsmith, Almeda, 4,893
Arrowsmith, Eunice, 4,893
Arrowsmith Family (IA), **4,893**
Arrowsmith, Lizzie, 4,893, **5,054**
Arrowsmith, Lucy, 4,893
Arrowsmith, Nettie, 4,893
Arsenal Technical High School (IL), 4,268
Arsenals, 2,700
Arsenic and Old Lace (drama), 2,357
Arson, 12,175
Art, 624, 1,428, 1,544, 2,804, 5,829, 7,178, 11,905,
    15,498
    catalogs, 2,851, **2,862, 3,783,** 12,914, 16,919,
        17,312
    collectors and collecting, **1,225,** 1,426, **1,638,** 1,837,
        2,475, **2,762, 2,778,** 2,781, **2,813, 2,817,** 3,077,
        5,721, **5,901, 6,185, 8,017,** 11,818, 17,286
    congresses, 2,828
    exhibitions, 241, 679, 2,131, 2,744, 2,777, 2,784,
        2,789, 2,792, 2,794, 2,816, 2,817, 2,820, 2,845,
        2,847, 2,849, 3,851, 4,766, 6,388, 6,876, 11,222,
        11,329, 11,956, 12,362, 12,889, 12,912, 13,820,
        17,236, 17,261, 17,296, 17,312, 17,320, 17,323,
        17,332, 17,362
    exhibitions, traveling, **2,728,** 3,980, **15,299**
    galleries and museums, 679, 760, 761, 918, **2,100,**
        2,734, 2,735, 2,746, 2,762, 2,767, 2,777, 2,778,
        2,787, 2,794, 2,803, **2,806, 2,808,** 3,980, **5,541,**
        5,829, **6,233,** 8,433, **8,622,** 10,530, 10,612,
        11,844, 12,709, 12,842, 15,424, 16,232, 17,235,
        17,243, 17,255, 17,261, 17,366, 17,846

history, 2,784, 15,302
prices, 17,366
study and teaching, 237, 240, 249, 2,741, 2,828,
   4,071, 7,667, 8,990, 11,835, 11,844, 11,897,
   12,446, 12,544, 17,320
study and teaching (secondary), 12,244
Art, abstract, 2,741, 2,788, 2,816
Art, African, 3,980, 17,294
Art, Afro-American, 2,131
"Art and Artists" (column), 11,213
Art and Life (book), 15,883
Art and state, 11,843, 11,883
Art and technology, 4,112
Art centers, 6,376
Art centers, Afro-American, 10,163
Art, Chinese, 1,564
Art Club (Fort Dodge, IA), **4,881**
Art clubs. *See* Art societies
Art, colonial (Spanish), 182
Art criticism, 1,949, 2,744, **2,764**, 2,777, 2,784, 2,799,
   2,801, 2,810, 2,820, 6,344, 10,363, 12,011, 17,320
Art critics, 2,520, 4,061, 6,331, 7,182, **10,363**
Art dealers, 2,662, 2,844, **17,243**, **17,255**, **17,261**,
   17,350
Art, decorative, **13,631**
Art Digest (periodical), 4,625
Art, feminist, 2,799
Art festivals, 4,275, 9,927
Art for World Friendship, **15,299**
Art historians, **10,955**
Art History Club (MN), **8,486**
Art, Humor, and Humanity of Mark Twain, The
   (book), 9,839
Art industries and trade, 12,917
Art Institute of Chicago (IL), 4,061, 4,071, 4,211,
   9,170, 12,912
   students, 14,707
Art Institute of St. Louis (MO), students,
   4,625
Art, Islamic, 17,478
Art, Jewish, 2,827
Art, modern, 1,265, 2,735, 2,808, 5,541
Art of Beatrix Potter, The (book), 12,570
Art of the Century, 2,794
"Art of Weaving, The," 3,747
Art, Oriental, 1,239, 1,471, 2,237
Art patronage, 2,065, **2,165**, 3,816, 3,980, 7,167,
   16,965, 17,366
Art patrons, 945, **1,282**, 2,720, 2,847, **6,185**, 10,163,
   11,897, 12,491, 12,709, 16,965, **17,366**
Art schools, 249, 1,883, 2,769, **2,797**, 3,587, **4,112**,
   4,847, **5,452**, 6,499, 7,667, 12,301, 12,577,
   13,446, 14,215, 17,846
Art societies, 1,261, **1,265**, 1,313, 1,673, 1,692, 1,754,
   1,766, 1,794, **1,884**, 1,949, 2,414, 2,738, 2,758,
   2,761, 2,763, 2,772, 2,782, 2,788, 2,789, 2,793,
   2,798, 2,817, 2,894, 3,374, 3,783, **3,816**, **3,980**,
   4,881, 5,488, **5,523**, **5,558**, 8,487, 8,545, 9,139,
   9,525, 9,646, 11,835, 11,844, 11,956, **12,131**,
   12,446, 12,888, 12,892, 12,901, 13,334, 13,853,
   13,854, 13,860, 14,707, 14,822, **15,288**, **15,299**,
   15,883, 16,195, 16,315, 17,179, 17,269, **17,288**,
   17,313
Art Spirit, The (book), 2,809
Art Students' League, 11,835
Art Students' League (DC), 2,414
Art Student's League (NY), 1,883, 2,769, 2,805,
   9,573, 12,438
Art, Swedish, 4,766
Art teachers, **1,678**, 1,767, **2,773**, 3,082, **4,688**, 4,847,
   6,245, **6,499**, 9,960, 10,435, 11,217, 11,222,
   11,440, 12,370, **12,446**, 12,884, **13,122**, **13,307**,
   13,855, **15,883**, **16,291**, 17,309
Art therapy, 13,122
Art, women's, 17,236, 17,296, 17,316, 17,323, 17,332,
   17,362
Art Workers Coalition, 2,782, 2,799
Art Workshop of the Rivington Neighborhood
   Association (NY), **6,376**
Arthur and Elizabeth Schlesinger Library on the
   History of Women in America (MA), 6,460,
   6,872, 6,966
Arthur, Charlotte (Wilson) [Mrs. Chester Alan, III],
   2,180

Arthur, Chester Alan (1830-86), 2,180, 8,962, 14,206
Arthur, Chester Alan,, II (1864-1937), 2,180
Arthur, Chester Alan, III (1901-72), 2,180
Arthur, Ellen Herndon (1875-1915). *See* Pinkerton,
   Ellen Herndon (Arthur)
Arthur, Ellen Lewis (Herndon) [Mrs. Chester Alan]
   (1837-80), 2,180
Arthur, Esther Murphy (Strachey) [Mrs. Chester
   Alan, III], 2,180
Arthur Family, **2,180**
Arthur, Grace, 2,840
Arthur H. Clarke Company, 180
Arthur Home for Blind Babies, 2,395
Arthur, Malvina Ann. *See* Haynesworth, Malvina
   Ann (Arthur)
Arthur, Myra Fithian (Andrews) [Mrs. Chester Alan,
   II] (?-1935), 2,180
Arthur, Regina. *See* Caw, Regina (Arthur)
Arthurdale Homestead Project (WV), **17,448**
Arthur's Home Magazine (periodical), **8,921**, 9,179
Artieda, Helen (Swett), 322
Artis, Letha, 13,217
Artists, 81, 215, 225, 508, 620, **657**, 710, 765, **824**,
   889, 931, **940**, 970, **1,124**, 1,167, **1,261**, **1,266**,
   1,318, **1,335**, 1,458, 1,534, 1,544, **1,601**, 1,734,
   1,751, 1,767, 1,779, 1,786, **1,794**, **1,800**, 1,804,
   1,878, 1,883, **1,948**, 2,100, **2,500**, 2,520, **2,716**,
   2,776, 2,784, 2,800, 2,813, 2,844, 2,847, 2,848,
   2,849, 2,850, **2,861**, 2,927, 3,082, 3,090, 3,311,
   3,462, **3,597**, **3,624**, **3,634**, 3,745, **3,783**, **4,472**,
   4,620, 4,625, **4,868**, 5,448, 5,541, 5,721, 5,829,
   5,899, **6,109**, 6,119, **6,185**, **6,245**, 6,308, **6,351**,
   6,364, 6,440, 6,597, 6,915, **6,968**, **7,182**, 7,301,
   7,305, **7,332**, **7,485**, **8,433**, 8,458, **8,522**, 8,604,
   9,139, 9,145, 9,318, **9,581**, 9,646, 9,694, 9,790,
   10,129, **10,133**, 10,152, 10,163, 10,347, 10,363,
   10,868, 11,234, 11,238, **11,261**, 11,419, 11,425,
   11,822, **11,834**, **11,835**, 12,427, 12,506, 12,619,
   12,670, 12,681, 12,842, **12,870**, **12,888**,
   12,912, 12,955, 13,176, **13,446**, 13,836, 14,838,
   15,354, 15,424, 15,575, **15,883**, 16,232, 16,277,
   16,291, 16,304, 16,315, 16,438, 16,448, 16,575,
   16,916, 16,970, 16,978, 16,981, 17,077, 17,102,
   17,284, 17,294, 17,310, 17,413, **17,496**
   18th C, **7,601**, 7,674, **15,485**
   19th C, **1,920**, 2,744, 2,749, 3,079, 5,606, **5,906**,
      5,933, 6,636, 7,227, 7,466, 7,601, 9,179, 11,152,
      12,265, 13,961, **14,779**, 14,878, 14,880, 14,883,
      14,901, **16,094**, 17,037
   19th-20th C, **191**, 543, 597, **1,306**, **2,722**, 2,753,
      2,807, 3,092, 3,782, 5,601, 8,990, 9,960, **11,136**,
      11,343, 12,293, 12,329, 12,438, 13,851, 13,853,
      13,963, **16,145**, 16,261
   20th C, **134**, 572, 2,746, 2,751, 2,760, 2,771, 2,802,
      2,815, **2,827**, 2,830, 4,238, 5,486, 6,924, 7,231,
      11,145, 11,434, 13,252, 14,184, 14,407, 16,997,
      17,235, **17,288**, 17,296, 17,309, 17,321, 17,323,
      17,362, 17,478
   indexes, 8,525
Artists, Afro-American, 2,945, 5,828, 9,252
Artists and Writers Guild, Incorporated, 14,453
Artists' Club (Denver, CO), 1,692, 1,754, 1,794
Artists' colonies, 10,852, 11,213
Artists, feminist, **6,883**
Artists Guild, 4,197
Artists materials, 2,789
Artists, Native American, **11,213**, 11,217, 11,235
Artists of the Dance (book), 12,364
Artists' Society of St. Paul (MN), 9,139
Artmobile, Inc., 12,416
Arts and Crafts Club of Hartford (CT), **1,884**
Arts and crafts movement, **7,012**
Arts Club of Chicago (IL), 3,848, **3,980**
Arts Resources Center, 2,064
Arundell Club (Baltimore, MD), **5,738**
Arundell Good Government Club (Baltimore, MD),
   5,738
Arvonen, Helen (1918-), **10,408**
Arzner, Dorothy, 1,025
As It Was in the Beginning (book), 8,806
"As Seen by Herself," 16,174
As the Earth Turns, 5,995
As the Pines, 17,792
"As weary pilgrim, now at rest" (poem), 7,127

As You Like It Club (South Bend, IN), **4,663**
Asberry, Nettie J. (1865-?), **17,234**
Asbill, J. J., **2,181**
Asbury, Francis, 4,202
Ascher, Charles, 11,897
Ascher, Mary (1900-), **2,730**, 2,793
Ascoli, Marion (Rosenwald), 5,469
Asgill, Lady Theresa, 11,195
Ash Hollow, Battle of, 10,433
Ash, Jessie Flora (1886-). *See* Maddan, Jessie Flora
   (Ash) [Mrs. Remington] Maddan [Mrs. Chester
   James] (1886-)
Ash, Philis, 5,718
Ash, Sister Ligouri, 1,513, 1,517
Ashbridge Family (PA), **15,338**
Ashbridge, Jeannette, 15,338
Ashbridge, Rachel S. (1833-1920), 15,338
Ashbridge, Rachel V., 15,338
Ashbridge, Rebecca, 15,338
Ashbrook, Harriette, 5,465
Ashburn, Bernice. *See* Mims, Bernice (Ashburn)
Ashburn, Betsy [Mrs. John] Ross [Mrs. Joseph]
   (1752-1836). *See* Claypoole, Betsy [Mrs. John]
   Ross [Mrs. Joseph] Ashburn [Mrs. John]
   (1752-1836)
Ashburn, Robert A., 17,127
Ashburner, Anne (1807-94), 7,505
Ashburner, Emilia (Field) [Mrs. William], 323
Ashburner Family (MA), **7,505**
Ashburner, Grace (1813-93), 7,505
Ashburner, Sarah, 7,505
Ashburner, William (1831-87), **323**
Ashby, Beth (1914-), **16,584**
Ashby, Dorothy (1895-). *See* Pownall, Dorothy
   (Ashby) (1895-)
Ashby, Ella Osmond, 9,274
Ashcraft, Annie Bickett, 13,533
Ashe, Samuel A'Court, **13,319**
Ashepoo Mission (SC), 15,412
Asheville Citizen (NC), 13,244
Asheville Female College (NC), 13,321
Ashfield, Elisabeth, **11,070**
Ashfield, Isabella, **11,070**
Ashforth, Frida, 10,866
Ashland (residence, KY), 2,270
Ashley, Angeline (Jackson), 1,505
Ashley, Constance Reed (1898-), 7,109
Ashley, Edward R., 6,204, 6,205
Ashley, Elizabeth, 12,367
Ashley Family (CO), 1,786
Ashley, Gertrude (Porter) [Mrs. Charles Hart], 7,012
Ashlock, Minerva Jane, 4,700
Ashmore, Grace Eulalie (Matthews) (1885-1972),
   12,374
Ashrams, 12,730
Ashtabula County Female Anti-slavery Society (OH),
   13,907
Ashton, Frances (Goodhue) [Mrs. William]
   (1779-1808), 12,695
Ashton, Henrietta (Rossi) [Mrs. Thomas B.], 1,083
Ashton, Margaret (1761-1850). *See* Roberts,
   Margaret (Ashton) [Mrs. Nathan] (1761-1850)
Ashton, Robert (1726-1816), **14,951**
Ashton-Warner, Sylvia, 6,045
Ashworth, Mary Elizabeth (Shepherd) [Mrs. William
   Booth] (1854-1932), **16,585**
Asia
   American travelers in, 1,841
   food relief, 1,557
   international education, 6,702
   labor and laboring classes, education, 8,071, 8,126
   Young Women's Christian Foundation, 12,724
Asia Foundation, 760
Askew, Mary (Brown) (1796-?), **14,952**
Asmonean, The (NY), 1,002
Asociación Insular de Mujeres Votantes (PR), 15,368
"Aspects of Religious Liberty in the Near East," 6,507
Aspel, Paulène, 5,063
Aspinwall Family (NE), **10,428**
Aspinwall, Louisa E., 11,498
Aspinwall, Mary Rebecca. *See* Roosevelt, Mary
   Rebecca (Aspinwall)
Aspinwall, Nan J. [Mrs. Frank Gable] (1880-),
   10,428

Aspinwall, Thomas, 12,274
Aspirant, The (periodical), 5,685
Asplund, Julia Brown [Mrs. Rupert] (1875-1958), 11,236
Asplund, Rupert, 11,236
Assassination, 9,384, 9,678, 11,486, 12,532, 15,948. *See also* Murder
Assault and battery, 2,161, 15,110
Assemblies of God, 161
Assembly of Captive European Nations, 17,978
Assembly of the Nebraska Independent Order of Odd Fellows, 10,411
Assembly of Women's Organizations for National Security, 6,901
Assessment, 1,120, **1,807**, **3,947**, **11,200**, **11,462**, **12,849**, 14,934
Assimilation (sociology), 1,350, 5,829, 8,631, 13,906, 17,216. *See also* Emigration and immigration
"Assiniboine Lullaby" (song), 13,674
Associate Reformed Presbyterian Church, 161
Associate Reformed Presbyterian Church (Hopewell, SC), **15,558**
Associated Alumnae of the Sacred Heart, 1,066
Associated Charities (Washington, DC), 2,397
Associated Charities (GA), 3,218
Associated Charities of St. Paul (MN). *See* Family Service of St. Paul (MN)
Associated Clubs of Woodlawn (IL), 3,931
Associated Colleges (Claremont, CA), 409
Associated Colleges of Upper New York, **11,285**
Associated Consultants in Education, Inc., 9,662
Associated Country Women of the World, 2,682, 4,947, 6,964, 8,144, **8,269**, 11,662, 13,685
Associated Country Women of the World, US Liaison Committee, 6,713
Associated Executive Committee of Friends on Indian Affairs, 4,653
Associated Garden Clubs of Skagit County (WA), **17,146**
Associated Negro Press, 3,799, 3,800, 3,851
Associated Press, 6,933, 11,489, 11,493, 17,762
Associated Women of the North Carolina Farm Bureau, 13,266
Association Against the Prohibition Amendment, 2,030
Association for Aid to Crippled Children, 2,115
Association for Befriending Children and Young Girls (White Plains, NY), 12,932
Association for Childhood Education International, 2,092, 2,093, 2,094, 2,095, 3,535, 4,211, 9,526
Association for Family Living (Chicago, IL), **4,051**, 4,079
Association for Jewish Children (Philadelphia, PA), **12,709**
Association for Relief of Aged and Destitute Women in Salem (MA), **7,339**
Association for the Advancement of Women, 2,606, 4,684, 6,664, **7,183**, 7,232, 7,298, 7,941, 8,822
Association for the Aid of Crippled Children, 6,919, **11,830**
Association for the Preservation of Virginia Antiquities, 17,121
Association for the Promotion of Female Education (MI). *See* Detroit Female Seminary (MI)
Association for the Relief of Jewish Widows and Orphans (LA), **13,764**
Association for the Relief of Respectable, Aged and Indigent Females (NY), **11,939**
Association for the Study of Community Organization. *See* National Association of Social Workers
Association for the Work of Mercy (MA), **6,175**
Association for Voluntary Sterilization, 8,634
Association Monthly (periodical), 12,712
Association of American Colleges, 1,125, 6,388
Association of American Foreign Service Women, 2,844
Association of American Library Schools, 4,391
Association of American Railroads, Bureau of Railway Economics Library, 304
Association of American State Geologists, 3,222
Association of American Universities, 10,892
Association of Bay Area Governments (CA), 661

Association of Collegiate Alumnae. *See* American Association of University Women
Association of Collegiate Schools of Nursing, 8,610
Association of Collegiate Schools of Nursing, Committee on Guidance, 12,077
Association of County Historians (NC), 13,609
Association of Day Nurseries of New York City. *See* Child Welfare League of America
Association of Deans of Women and Advisers to Girls in Negro Schools, 89
Association of Girl Scout Professional Workers, **12,092**
Association of Governing Boards of State Universities and Allied Institutions, 7,826
Association of Junior Leagues of America, **8,635**
Association of Land Grant Colleges and Universities, 8,567
Association of Minneapolis Jewish Women's Organizations (MN), **8,923**
Association of Minnesota State University Women, **8,392**
Association of Operating Room Nurses, **1,691**
Association of Pioneer Women of California, 1,256
Association of Research Libraries, 4,402
Association of Retired Persons, 15,570
Association of Southern Agricultural Workers, 9,788
Association of Southern Women for the Prevention of Lynching, **3,279**, 3,326, 12,731, 12,939
Association of Wisconsin Normal School Faculty, **17,505**
Association of Women Students (NY), **12,916**
Association of Women Students (WV), **17,449**
Association on American Indian Affairs, 17,266
Association Opposed to Woman Suffrage, 15,335
Association Record (newsletter), 929
Association to Promote Scientific Research by Women, 2,070
Associations, Institutions, etc., **40**, **705**, **1,132**, 2,149, 2,152, 2,193, 2,606, 3,166, **3,261**, **3,575**, 4,684, 4,799, 4,812, **5,421**, **5,500**, 6,103, 6,376, 6,388, 6,446, 6,456, **6,463**, 6,467, 6,483, 6,664, 6,687, **6,760**, 6,886, 6,978, 7,175, **7,183**, 7,201, 7,232, **7,270**, 7,293, 7,298, 7,299, 7,302, 7,669, **8,355**, **8,632**, **8,639**, 8,822, **9,238**, 11,240, 11,491, **12,736**, **13,203**, 13,381, 13,801, 14,004, **14,221**, 14,565, **14,920**, **15,365**, 15,570, 15,634, **15,819**, 17,245, 17,299, 17,341, **17,467**, 17,679. *See also* Bar associations; Clubs; Committees; Community life; Social group work; Societies
Associations, Jewish, **8,923**
Associations, Mexican-American, **2,666**
Associée des Beaux Arts, 13,854
Assumption College, trustees, 2,115
Assyriologists, 2,218
Astaire, Fred, 2,968
Astor, John Jacob, 14,549
Astor, Mary (1906-), **5,980**, **16,496**
Astor, Nancy Witcher (Langhorne) [Mrs. Waldor F.] (1879-1964), 2,163, 9,919
Astor, William B., 12,397
Astor, William Waldorf (1848-1919), **2,182**
Astrologers, **12,689**
Astrology, 9,131
Astronomers, **193**, 790, 1,403, **1,536**, **1,537**, **1,538**, **1,540**, **1,541**, **1,542**, 2,041, 2,464, **2,570**, 4,696, **6,267**, **6,269**, **6,280**, **6,285**, **6,305**, **6,312**, **6,902**, 6,986, 7,094, 7,820, 11,815, **11,816**, 12,009, **12,452**, 14,734, **14,895**
Astronomical observatories, 193, **6,285**
Astronomical photography, 12,452
Astronomical research, 5614
Astronomy, 7,671, 15,739
Astrophysicists, **6,337**
Astyanax (book), 3,158
Asylum Hill Congregational Church (CT), 1,958
Asylums, 12,156, 13,919, 15,048
At Fault (book), 10,158
"At Home in Lafayette County, Mississippi, 1860-1865" (ms), 9,596
At the End of the Rainbow (book), 17,033
Atcherson, Mary, 3,114
Atchison, David Rice (1807-86), **9,929**
Atchison, Katherine (Watkins) [Mrs. Jehu B.], 10,125

Atchison, Mary Elizabeth "Lizzie" (Watkins) [Mrs. William], 10,125
Atheists, civil rights, 16,373
Athena Club (Dorchester, MA), **7,020**
Athena Literary Society (IA), **4,968**
Athena Symposium (TX), 16,260
Athenea Club (NE), **10,429**
Atheneum Club (Muscatine, IA), 5,087
Athenian Literary Society and Young Tar Heel Farmers (NC), **13,320**
Athens College (AL), 9,672
Athens Female College (TN), 13,321
Athens Ladies Memorial Association (GA), **2,961**
Athens State College (AL), 1
Athens Woman's Music Club (OH), **13,748**
Atherton, George Henry Bowen, 1,395
Atherton, Gertrude Franklin (Horn) [Mrs. George Henry Bowen] (1857-1948), **325**, 378, 448, 569, 616, 691, 702, 712, 720, 922, 1,081, 1,082, 1,089, **1,231**, 1,291, 1,395, 1,416, 1,447, 1,510, **2,183**, 2,330, 2,403, 3,028, 5,713, 11,821, 12,496, 12,529, 12,648, 14,338, **16,151**
Atherton Police Department (CA), 324
Athletes, 995, 6,573
Athletic clubs, **1,554**, 4,041, 4,213, 4,220, **7,712**, 7,772, **7,985**, **8,037**, 10,218, 12,738
Athletic Federation of College Women, 7,712
Athletics, 997, 4,124
Athol Associated Charities (MA), **5,878**
Athol High School (MA), 5,879, 5,885
Athol Historical Society (MA), 5,892
Atiyeh, Victor (1923-), **14,507**
Atiyeh, Wadeeha (1903-73), **14,907**
Atkins, Elizabeth Mary, 8,600
Atkins Family (OH, NY), **326**
Atkins, Flora (1815-50). *See* Wheeler, Flora (Atkins) (1815-50)
Atkins, James W., 13,321
Atkins, Mary (1819-82). *See* Lynch, Mary (Atkins) [Mrs. John] (1819-82)
Atkins, Nannie Bell [Mrs. A. G.], 13,463
Atkins Park Garden Club (GA), 3,196
Atkins, Sarah Louisa (1806-52). *See* Wade, Sarah Louisa (Atkins) (1806-52)
Atkins, Sarah (Wright) (?-1853), 326
Atkins, Stella M. (1808-82). *See* Gaylord, Stella M. (Atkins) (1808-82)
Atkinson Academy (NH), 7,662
Atkinson, Brooks, 12,553
Atkinson, Buena [Mrs. Wallace] (1884-1966), **4,894**
Atkinson, Dorothy Dagmar (Bridgman) [Mrs. Frederick G.] (1890-1965). *See* Rood, Dorothy Dagmar (Bridgman) [Mrs. Frederick G.]
Atkinson [Mrs. John H.] (1890-1965)
Atkinson Family, 10,985
Atkinson Family (NJ), **10,937**
Atkinson, Florence (1863-89), 10,937
Atkinson, Frederich, 9,321
Atkinson, George Henry (1819-89), **14,508**
Atkinson, H. M., 3,179
Atkinson, Juliette P., 997
Atkinson, Mary Josephine (1854-1933), 10,937
Atkinson, Mary Jourdan [Mrs.], **16,032**
Atkinson, May. *See* Dick, May (Atkinson)
Atkinson, Mildred [Mrs.], 5,841
Atkinson, Nancy (Bates) [Mrs. George Henry], 14,508
Atkinson, Sallie Jane (Yeargin) (1857-1949), **327**
Atkinson, Sarah (1861-1956), 10,937
Atkinson, Ti-Grace, 3,827
Atkinson, Wallace (1878-?), **4,894**
Atkisson, Anne, 2,963
Atkisson, Eva, 2,963
Atkisson, Fannie [Miss], 2,963, 2,965
Atkisson, Frances Ann Harden, 2,963
Atkisson, George Baber, **2,963**
Atlanta (ship), 3,602
Atlanta (yacht), 12,214
Atlanta Amateurs (GA), 3,204
Atlanta Art Association (GA), 3,374
Atlanta Associated Charities (GA), 3,399
Atlanta Association for Childhood Education (GA), **3,136**

Atlanta Business and Professional Women's Club (GA), **3,361**
Atlanta Chamber of Commerce (GA), 3,229
Atlanta Civic Ballet (GA), 3,374
Atlanta Constitution (GA), 3,203, 3,227, 3,437
Atlanta Council of Church Women (GA), **3,137**
Atlanta Exposition (1895), 2,859
Atlanta Family Welfare Society (GA), 3,399
Atlanta Federation of Women's Clubs (GA), **3,138,** 3,236, 3,322, 3,350
Atlanta Female Academy (GA), 3,170
Atlanta Fire Department (GA), 3,215
Atlanta Free Kindergarten Association (GA), 3,140, 3,151
Atlanta Georgian (GA), 3,350
Atlanta High School for Girls (GA), 3,463
Atlanta Historical Society (GA), 3,131, 3,210, 3,222, 3,225
Atlanta Journal (GA), 3,197, 3,239, 3,262, 3,276, 3,423, 3,437, 13,001
Atlanta Journal Sunday Magazine (GA), 3,602
Atlanta Junior League (GA), 3,195, 3,245
Atlanta Kindergarten Alumnae Club (GA), **3,140**
Atlanta Kindergarten Normal School (GA), 3,130, 3,140
Atlanta Labor Council (GA), **3,443,** 3,449
Atlanta Law School (GA), alumnae, 3,374
Atlanta League of Women Voters (GA), **3,362**
Atlanta Music Club (GA), 3,195, 3,229, 3,374
Atlanta Musical Association (GA), 3,198
Atlanta Norwegian Evangelical Lutheran Church (MN), 9,271
Atlanta Pioneer Women's Society (GA), **3,141**
Atlanta Public School Teachers' Association (GA), 3,308
Atlanta Ranch (NV), 10,748
Atlanta Riot (GA, 1906), 3,301
Atlanta Social Planning Council (GA), 3,399
Atlanta Society (MA), **7,595**
Atlanta Symphony Guild (GA), 3,195, 3,374
Atlanta Symphony Orchestra (GA), 3,195
Atlanta Training School for Nurses, Presbyterian Hospital (GA), alumnae, 3,386
Atlanta Tulip Show Association (GA), 3,233
Atlanta Tulip Study Club (GA), 3,233
Atlanta Typographical Union Number 48 (GA), Women's Auxiliary, **2,964**
Atlanta University (GA), 3,304
  archives, **3,280**
  faculty, **3,305**
  presidents, **3,281**
  students, Afro-American, 7,595
Atlanta University Conferences (GA), 3,281
Atlanta Urban League (GA), 3,293, 3,469
Atlanta Woman's Club (GA), 3,128, 3,168, 3,218, 3,224
Atlanta Woman's Pioneer Society (GA), 3,204, 3,205
Atlanta Women's Thursday Study Club (TX), 16,126
Atlanta World Service Committee (GA), 3,316
Atlanta Writers' Club (GA), 2,977, **3,365**
Atlanta Yaarab Temple (GA), 3,165
Atlantic City Board Walk, 6,837
Atlantic Educational Journal, 5,834
Atlantic Institute, 11,857
Atlantic Monthly (periodical), 1,224, 1,426, 2,108, 5,085, 5,310, 9,771, 12,698, 14,080, 14,684
Atlantic Monthly Press, 5,036
Atlantic Union Conference, 7,885
Atomic bomb, 7,891, 9,146, 15,303
  testing, 4,438, 16,373
Atomic bomb shelters, 7,723
Atomic energy, 7,262, 7,288
Atomic energy research, 11,903
Atomic power, law and legislation, 11,920, 14,202
Atomic warfare, moral and religious aspects, 17,711
Atomic weapons and disarmament, 4,168, 7,322
Atsugewi Indians, 955
Attachment and garnishment, 3,554
Attendance officers, 4,341, 8,388
Atterbury, Catherine A., 12,318
Atterbury, Catherine (Boudinot), 11,075
Atterbury Family, 11,599
Attic Angel Association (Madison, WI), **17,590,** 17,733

Attic Angel Nursing Home (Madison, WI), 17,590
"Attica" (pseudonym), 3,234
"Attitudes of Entering College Freshmen Toward the Occupational Motivations of Married Women" (paper), 8,573
Attix, Frederick F., **10,274**
Attix, Ruth [Mrs. Frederick F.], 10,274
Attorneys. *See* Government attorneys; Lawyers
Attorneys general, 504, **592,** 645, **4,094, 4,982, 5,158,** 5,267, 5,824, 7,533, 8,353, 9,242, 9,416, **9,951,** 9,972, **10,342,** 10,740, 10,948, 14,982, 17,260, 17,680
Atwater, Adeline (Lobdell) [Mrs. Henry] (ca. 1887-). *See* Pynchon, Adeline (Lobdell) [Mrs. Henry] Atwater [Mrs. Henry C.] (ca. 1887-)
Atwater, Alice Merriam [Mrs. Charles], 1,974
Atwater, Caroline (1853-1939). *See* Mason, Caroline (Atwater) (1853-1939)
Atwater, Catherine, 1,974
Atwater, Charles (1885-1946), 1,974
Atwater, Dorence, 2,196
Atwater, Elizabeth Emerson (1812-78), 3,794
Atwater, Ella (1868-?). *See* Taylor, Ella (Atwater) (1868-?)
Atwater, Harriet [Mrs. L. R.], 1,974
Atwater, Helen Woodard (1876-1947), 1,974, 11,656
Atwater, Marcia (Woodard) [Mrs. Wilbur O.] (?-1933), 1,974
Atwater, Wilbur O. (1844-1907), **1,974**
Atwell, Grace Parthenia, **6,377**
Atwood, Augusta Allen [Mrs. Edwin H.], 8,924
Atwood, Edwin H. (1829-1900), Family (MN), **8,924**
Atwood, Elizabeth C., 17,855
Atwood, Elizabeth Garrett [Mrs. Edwin] (1800-33), **17,855**
Atwood, Eva [Miss] (1890-1975), **230**
Atwood, Harriet (1793-1812). *See* Newell, Harriet (Atwood) [Mrs. Samuel] (1793-1812)
Atwood, Hazel M., **14,316**
Atwood, Stella M. [Mrs. H. A.], 2,674
Aubbeenaubbee (school yearbook), 4,659
Aubrey, Estelle (1877-?). *See* Brown, Estelle (Aubrey) [Mrs. H. T.] (1877-?)
Aubrey, Katherin. *See* Johnston, Katherin (Aubrey) [Mrs. Mercer Green]
Auburn Art and Literature Club (ME), **5,557**
Auburn Art Club (ME), 5,557, **5,558**
Auburn Campus Club (AL), **4**
Auburn Campus Club Bulletin (AL), 4
Auburn Equal Suffrage Association (AL), **5**
Auburn University (AL), buildings, **13**
Auburn University (AL), Women's Music Club, **17**
Auburn University (AL), Women's Recreation Association, **18**
Auburn Woman's Club (MA), **5,893**
Auctioneers, 5,394
Auden, W. H., 14,423
Audio-visual materials, 8,057
Auditing, **9,480, 17,917**
Auditors, 8,062
Audrain, F. L., **17,182**
Audubon Artists, 12,892
Audubon Club, 12,869
Audubon, John James (1785-1851), **11,152, 14,883**
Audubon, Lucy Bakewell [Mrs. John James] (1788-1874), 11,152, 12,407, 14,883
Audubon societies, 7,874, **9,216,** 11,445, 12,869, 12,973, 15,252, 17,267
Audubon Society, 2,886, 11,445, 12,973, 14,646, 15,252
Audubon, Victor, 14,883
Auerbach; Matilda. *See* Elliott, Matilda (Auerbach) [Mrs. Richard]
Auerbach, Matilda Rice [Mrs. Maurice] (?-1945), 9,311
Auerbach, Robert Rice. *See* Rice, Robert Auerbach
Auerbach Service Bureau for Connecticut Organizations, **6,378,** 6,630
Aufbau (periodical), 2,177
Auger Family (CA), 1,232
Auger, Lina [Mrs.], **1,232**
Augsburg College (MN), faculty, 9,467
Augsburg Seminary (WI), 8,724

Augspurger, Cecilia. *See* Schultz, Cecilia (Augspurger)
Augspurger, Everett, 9,671
August, Rebecca, 1,016, 1,656
Augusta Bixler Farms (CA), **1,233**
Augusta Chronicle (GA), 3,437, 3,451
Augusta Herald (GA), 3,437
Augusta Mental Health Institute (ME), **5,562**
Augusta-Richmond County Public Library (GA), 3,451
Augustana College (IL), 4,319, 4,321, 4,326
  faculty, 4,320
Augustana College (SD), presidents, 8,797
Augustana College, faculty, 8,755
Augustana Endowment Society (IL), **4,320**
Augustana Lutheran Church (IL), 4,319, 4,325, 4,326
Augustana Lutheran Church (IL), Women's Missionary Society, 4,319
Augustana Lutheran Church Women (IL), 3,962
Augustana Swedish Institute (IL), **4,321**
Augustine Heard Company (MA), 6,196
Augustus, Nicholas, **9,531**
Aulls, Ina [Miss], 15,081
"Aunt" Clara Brown; the Story of a Black Pioneer (book), 1,750
Aunt Fannie's Cabin (GA), 3,425
"Aunt Magwire" (satire), 12,341
Aunt Patty's Scrap Bag (book), 111
Aunt Sally's Friends in Fur (book), 7,489
Auntie Kate (book), 14,096
Aurandt, Alfred, 15,322
Aurandt, Margaret, **15,322**
Aurora Club (St. Louis, MO), **10,192**
Aurora Club (Tacoma, WA), **17,399**
Aurora College (IL), archives, **3,741**
Aurora Colony (MO, OR), **14,268**
Auroras, 11,687
Ausherman, Clare E., 17,919
Austell, Mrs. Alfred, 3,141
Austin A&M Mothers' Clubs (TX), **16,185**
Austin, Abby Sheldon (Bagg) [Mrs. W. G.] (1824-?), 8,167
Austin, Alfred, 11,175
Austin, Andrew V., 8,169
Austin, Emmeline (1808-85). *See* Wadsworth, Emmeline (Austin) (1808-85)
Austin Family (TX), 16,083
Austin, Gladys [Mrs. Lloyd], 463
Austin, Harriet, 2,196
Austin, Hattie Foote [Mrs. A. V.], 8,154
Austin, Helen [Mrs. Horace], 8,925
Austin Home Culture Club (IL), 4,165
Austin Home Institute (TX), 16,031
Austin, Horace (1831-1905), Family (MN), **8,925**
Austin, Jane (Goodwin) (1831-94), **213,** 7,648
Austin, Jean, 9,160
Austin, Joyce P., **12,144**
Austin, Leonora. *See* Hamlin, Leonora (Austin) [Mrs. Conde]
Austin Literary Association (NV), **10,643**
Austin, Lloyd, 463
Austin, Mary C., 8,658
Austin, Mary (Hunter) [Mrs. Stafford Wallace] (1868-1934), **328,** 378, 732, 956, **1,030,** 1,081, 1,082, 1,089, **1,234,** 1,321, 1,395, **1,396,** 1,441, 1,447, 1,585, 2,376, 5,119, **11,220,** 11,235, 11,821, 11,944, 12,006
Austin, Mrs. Alfred, 11,175
Austin, Nancy, 8,778
Austin, Octavia A. (Lane) [Mrs. Julius Augustus Caesar] (1814-63), **16,586**
Austin, Rachel A., 2,946
Austin, Richard H. (1913-), **8,062**
Austin, Ruth (?-1939), 3,845, 4,047, 4,165
Austin, Sarah, 8,778
Austin Senior High School (TX), 16,038
Austin, Stafford Wallace, 1,030, 1,396
Austin, Stephen Fuller, 16,088
Austin Women's Suffrage Association (TX), **16,033**
Austine School for the Deaf (VT), 16,998
Australasian (ship), 12,326
Australia, 13,288
  American singers in, 5,911
  Americans in, 115

AUTHORS

women, status of, 6,981
Australian Paradox (book), 7,257
Austria
  American diplomats in, 5,134
  clinics, 11,908
Austrian, Mrs. Julius, 9,251
Autenrieth, Pauline (1833-?). *See* Tafel, Pauline (Autenrieth) [Mrs. Karl] (1833-?)
"Author Meets the Critics, The" (TV program), 6,065
Authors, 38, **43**, **54**, **73**, 81, **141**, **142**, **143**, 156, 159, 194, **317**, **433**, **442**, **499**, **538**, **567**, 602, 657, **799**, **873**, **934**, 956, **1,027**, **1,030**, **1,044**, 1,099, **1,250**, 1,340, **1,381**, **1, 386**, 1,395, **1,417**, **1, 420**, 1,434, **1,439**, 1,441, **1,443**, 1,447, **1,495**, 1,507, 1,509, 1,525, **1,580**, **1,582**, **1,583**, **1,601**, 1,605, **1,640**, 1,652, **1,750**, 1,751, **1,752**, 1,779, **1,795**, **1,801**, **1,860**, 1,866, 1,874, **1,876**, 1,959, 1,960, **2,130**, **2,273**, 2,283, 2,299, **2,318**, **2,349**, 2,369, **2,419**, **2,428**, **2,470**, **2,485**, **2,500**, **2,564**, **2,612**, **2,617**, **2,749**, **2,775**, 2,865, **2,918**, 2,927, **2,928**, 2,931, **2,932**, 2,942, **2,977**, **2,994**, **2,995**, **3,004**, **3,009**, **3,019**, **3,020**, 3,043, **3,078**, 3,111, **3,143**, 3,158, **3,159**, 3,167, 3,174, **3,177**, **3,194**, **3,195**, **3,197**, 3,210, **3,225**, **3,232**, 3,256, 3,257, **3,404**, **3,477**, 3,697, **3,707**, 4,143, 4,209, 4,227, **4,234**, **4,246**, **4,253**, **4,262**, **4,264**, 4,309, **4,312**, 4,468, 4,472, 4,473, 4,477, 4,484, **4,520**, **4,537**, **4,539**, 4,693, **4,766**, **4,785**, 4,821, 4,898, 4,957, **4,962**, **4,991**, **5,004**, **5,008**, **5,039**, **5,083**, **5,091**, **5,092**, 5,123, **5,205**, **5,261**, **5,264**, 5,269, 5,394, 5,442, 5,448, **5,524**, **5,528**, 5,536, 5,543, **5,619**, **5,621**, 5,736, 5,763, 5,805, **5,908**, **5,913**, **6,012**, **6,075**, 6,139, 6,144, 6,146, **6,153**, **6,185**, **6,242**, 6,329, 6,344, 6,349, 6,354, 6,366, 6,396, 6,399, **6,406**, **6,429**, **6,444**, **6,450**, **6,459**, **6,473**, **6,511**, 6,518, 6,565, **6,572**, **6,574**, **6,635**, 6,643, **6,649**, 6,653, **6,665**, 6,754, 6,762, 6,771, 6,796, **6,850**, **6,874**, 6,915, **6,955**, **7,189**, 7,195, 7,197, 7,301, 7,305, **7,602**, 7,605, **7,627**, 7,648, **7,685**, **7,775**, 7,846, **7,892**, **8,082**, 8,171, **8,275**, **8,314**, **8,318**, **8,329**, **8,342**, **8,428**, **8,495**, 9,057, 9,075, **9,313**, 9,414, **9,551**, **9,552**, 9,558, **9,567**, 9,572, **9,583**, 9,585, **9,640**, 9,656, 9,694, 9,699, **9,719**, **9,736**, **9,738**, **9,744**, **9,745**, 9,746, **9,763**, **9,768**, **9,769**, **9,770**, 9,790, 9,839, 9,841, **10,154**, **10,155**, **10,159**, **10,172**, **10,178**, **10,232**, **10,252**, **10,307**, **10,332**, 10,357, 10,366, **10,520**, **10,534**, 10,637, 10,759, **10,779**, **10,826**, 10,992, **11,084**, **11,156**, 11,165, 11,213, 11,238, 11,488, **11,491**, 11,637, 11,764, 11,846, **11,888**, 11,894, **11,927**, **11,940**, 11,954, **11,980**, 11,981, 11,983, **11,984**, **12,005**, 12,064, 12,314, **12,321**, 12,372, 12,469, 12,572, 12,646, 12,803, **12,817**, **12,879**, **12,888**, **12,893**, **12,894**, **12,899**, **12,900**, **12,903**, **12,904**, **12,905**, **12,906**, **12,908**, **12,912**, **12,914**, **12,915**, **13,007**, **13,017**, 13,176, **13,368**, **13,413**, **13,684**, **13,692**, **13,960**, **14,006**, **14,026**, 14,046, **14,056**, **14,081**, **14,084**, 14,085, **14,195**, **14,205**, **14,285**, **14,289**, **14,312**, 14,328, **14,369**, 14,395, 14,410, 14,427, 14,462, **14,465**, **14,501**, **14,503**, **14,510**, **14,575**, **14,608**, **14,610**, 14,656, **14,712**, **14,714**, 14,838, **14,842**, **14,872**, 14,949, 14,978, 14,995, **15,287**, 15,314, 15,319, **15,382**, **15,660**, **15,663**, **15,789**, **15,796**, 15,871, **15,878**, **15,892**, **15,896**, **15,899**, **15,900**, 15,916, **15,921**, **15,935**, **15,950**, **16,042**, **16,122**, **16,130**, 16,150, **16,290**, 16,438, **16,440**, 16,442, **16,464**, 16,485, **16,497**, **16,558**, **16,563**, 16,924, 16,971, 16,981, **16,983**, **17,025**, **17,027**, **17,053**, **17,059**, **17,098**, **17,131**, 17,169, 17,174, **17,175**, 17,197, **17,248**, **17,251**, **17,259**, 17,267, 17,310, **17,343**, 17,368, **17,369**, 17,400, 17,401, 17,406, 17,843, 17,868, 17,908, 17,921, 17,941, **17,946**, **17,959**, **17,991**, **17,999**, **18,006**, 18,010, **18,011**, 18,017
  18th C, 15,020
  18th-19th C, **2,372**, **2,560**, 2,608, 5,694, 5,824, **12,376**
  19th C, **77**, **213**, **254**, **568**, **1,167**, **1,275**, 1,426, 1,445, **1,485**, 1,488, **1,500**, **1,930**, **1,951**, **1,953**, **1,961**, **2,246**, **2,262**, **2,311**, **2,337**, 2,371, 2,454, **2,496**, 2,550, 2,566, **2,593**, 2,609, **4,327**, 4,444, **4,615**, **4,647**, **4,746**, 5,316, **5,714**, **5,899**, **5,905**, 5,907, **5,914**, **5,915**, **5,917**, **5,926**, **5,929**, **5,933**, **5,938**, **5,941**, **5,944**, **5,948**, **5,949**, **5,950**, **5,956**, **5,957**, **5,964**, **5,965**, **5,968**, **6,393**, **6,415**, **6,458**, **6,461**, **6,466**, 6,502, **6,541**, **6,559**, **6,587**, **6,617**, **6,636**, 6,663, **6,664**, **6,714**, **6,785**, **6,823**, **6,884**, **6,890**, **6,913**, **7,025**, **7,045**, **7,214**, **7,215**, **7,276**, 7,362, **7,364**, **7,377**, **7,398**, **7,561**, **7,612**, **7,651**, **7,657**, **7,681**, **7,682**, **8,526**, **10,130**, **10,158**, 10,431, **10,796**, 10,834, 10,858, **10,860**, **11,115**, 11,157, **11,315**, **11,676**, **11,953**, 11,960, **11,963**, **11,998**, **12,018**, **12,167**, **12,168**, **12,181**, **12,312**, **12,341**, 12,394, **12,419**, **12,430**, 12,431, 12,460, 12,461, **12,463**, 12,481, **12,519**, **12,624**, **12,636**, **12,662**, 12,818, **12,826**, **12,947**, 13,030, **13,134**, 13,172, **13,232**, **13,251**, **14,058**, 14,062, **14,073**, **14,779**, **15,002**, 15,256, **15,475**, **15,573**, **15,952**, **16,046**, 16,132, **17,010**, 17,037, **17,589**, **17,771**
  19th-20th C, **183**, **215**, 223, **325**, **328**, **346**, 355, **415**, **436**, **482**, **543**, **616**, **629**, **639**, **669**, 691, **692**, 710, **777**, **815**, **825**, **887**, **905**, **1,029**, **1,033**, **1,035**, 1,081, **1,082**, 1,087, **1,089**, **1,124**, **1,187**, 1,208, **1,224**, **1,231**, **1,234**, **1,240**, **1,241**, **1,322**, **1,377**, **1,529**, **1,540**, **1,565**, **1,581**, **1,592**, **1,699**, 1,952, **1,960**, **2,037**, **2,170**, **2,171**, **2,176**, **2,183**, 2,197, **2,198**, 2,202, **2,203**, 2,209, **2,218**, **2,244**, **2,250**, **2,256**, **2,258**, **2,264**, **2,282**, 2,298, **2,300**, 2,303, **2,309**, **2,316**, **2,317**, 2,319, **2,329**, **2,333**, **2,339**, **2,382**, 2,384, **2,395**, **2,399**, **2,401**, **2,415**, 2,420, **2,423**, **2,453**, 2,484, **2,498**, **2,510**, **2,520**, **2,533**, **2,549**, **2,551**, **2,562**, **2,586**, 2,587, **2,596**, **2,601**, 2,657, **2,658**, 2,720, 2,792, **2,804**, **3,028**, **3,090**, **3,339**, **3,633**, **3,778**, **3,797**, **3,804**, **3,825**, **3,985**, **3,993**, **3,996**, **4,007**, 4,059, **4,226**, 4,229, **4,250**, 4,326, **4,370**, 4,375, **4,419**, **4,491**, **4,508**, 4,654, 4,732, **4,758**, **4,808**, **4,965**, **4,973**, **4,988**, **4,995**, **5,015**, **5,025**, 5,093, **5,094**, **5,237**, 5,259, **5,273**, **5,274**, 5,275, **5,349**, **5,360**, **5,361**, **5,414**, **5,415**, **5,418**, **5,525**, **5,526**, **5,590**, **5,599**, **5,602**, **5,603**, 5,650, **5,694**, **5,734**, 5,768, **5,769**, **5,788**, 5,854, **5,863**, **5,870**, **5,906**, **5,921**, **5,925**, **5,935**, **5,940**, **5,951**, **5,959**, **5,970**, **5,973**, **5,976**, 6,009, **6,188**, **6,210**, **6,388**, **6,389**, **6,390**, 6,418, **6,500**, **6,507**, **6,513**, **6,601**, **6,602**, **6,671**, **6,696**, **6,773**, **6,809**, 6,855, **6,876**, **6,927**, **6,936**, **6,951**, 6,981, **7,069**, 7,158, **7,166**, **7,171**, **7,185**, **7,186**, **7,187**, 7,193, **7,206**, **7,212**, **7,217**, **7,220**, **7,221**, 7,227, **7,229**, 7,247, 7,249, **7,254**, **7,261**, **7,264**, 7,289, **7,292**, **7,293**, 7,308, **7,312**, **7,316**, **7,349**, **7,406**, **7,442**, **7,458**, 7,508, **7,509**, **7,888**, **8,751**, **8,779**, **8,784**, **8,852**, 8,962, 9,067, 9,960, **10,421**, **10,438**, **10,443**, **10,491**, **10,495**, **10,523**, **10,527**, **10,617**, **10,853**, 10,873, **11,091**, 11,126, **11,161**, **11,162**, **11,164**, **11,174**, **11,175**, **11,220**, **11,229**, **11,233**, **11,249**, **11,343**, **11,812**, 11,821, **11,854**, **11,967**, **11,979**, **11,993**, **11,996**, 12,015, **12,021**, **12,022**, **12,029**, **12,041**, 12,180, 12,185, **12,236**, **12,359**, 12,380, **12,406**, **12,409**, **12,412**, **12,414**, **12,427**, **12,436**, **12,437**, **12,455**, **12,473**, **12,476**, **12,480**, **12,488**, 12,491, **12,497**, **12,500**, **12,524**, **12,525**, **12,529**, **12,546**, **12,564**, **12,570**, **12,582**, **12,616**, **12,619**, **12,622**, **12,661**, **12,696**, **12,698**, **12,699**, 12,837, **12,877**, **12,930**, **12,992**, **13,027**, **13,043**, 13,051, 13,055, **13,073**, **13,104**, 13,130, 13,851, 13,963, 13,971, **14,080**, **14,258**, **14,366**, **14,392**, **14,549**, **14,663**, 14,697, **14,828**, **15,111**, 15,139, **15,261**, **15,263**, **15,318**, 15,377, 15,439, **15,445**, **15,672**, 15,688, 15,957, **16,102**, **16,145**, **16,166**, 16,274, **16,470**, **16,507**, **16,542**, 16,552, 16,555, **16,570**, **16,686**, **16,805**, **17,060**, **17,076**, **17,086**, **17,116**, **17,120**, 17,164, **17,208**, 17,221, **17,272**, **17,277**, **17,634**, 17,692, **17,718**, **17,723**, **17,734**, **17,739**, 17,899, **17,952**, **17,967**
  20th C, **113**, 115, **174**, **226**, **262**, **315**, **332**, **374**, **498**, **556**, **557**, **572**, **615**, **628**, **663**, **666**, **700**, **706**, **847**, **848**, 931, **937**, **947**, **962**, **1,020**, **1,039**, 1,189, **1,279**, **1,282**, **1,528**, 1,530, 1,564, **1,587**, **1,637**, **1,676**, **1,685**, **1,689**, **1,804**, 1,827, **1,981**, **2,051**, 2,093, **2,157**, 2,163, **2,177**, 2,180, **2,204**, **2,205**, **2,219**, **2,241**, **2,242**, **2,272**, **2,295**, **2,324**, **2,336**, **2,340**, 2,344, **2,365**, **2,385**, **2,396**, **2,410**, **2,435**, **2,450**, 2,456, **2,458**, **2,476**, **2,481**, **2,482**, **2,497**, **2,546**, 2,558, **2,591**, 2,625, **2,731**, **2,782**, **2,805**, **2,872**, **2,875**, **2,876**, **2,877**, **2,879**, **2,938**, **3,065**, **3,070**, 3,071, **3,073**, **3,075**, **3,278**, **3,287**, **3,288**, **3,332**, **3,350**, **3,351**, **3,368**, **3,471**, **3,514**, **3,555**, **3,657**, **3,771**, **3,775**, **3,879**, **3,981**, **3,986**, **3,988**, **4,053**, **4,061**, **4,131**, 4,161, **4,185**, **4,232**, **4,235**, **4,237**, **4,247**, **4,289**, **4,306**, **4,355**, **4,445**, **4,476**, **4,483**, **4,485**, **4,513**, **4,685**, **4,714**, **4,801**, **4,895**, **4,950**, **4,966**, **4,975**, **4,976**, **4,978**, **4,983**, **4,986**, **4,987**, **4,992**, **5,011**, **5,012**, **5,013**, **5,019**, **5,022**, **5,023**, **5,028**, **5,030**, **5,031**, **5,036**, **5,037**, **5,038**, **5,041**, **5,042**, 5,043, **5,047**, **5,127**, **5,206**, **5,208**, **5,263**, **5,270**, **5,304**, **5,315**, **5,342**, **5,439**, **5,441**, **5,450**, **5,501**, **5,580**, 5,633, **5,711**, **5,853**, **5,978**, **5,979**, **5,980**, **5,981**, **5,982**, **5,983**, **5,984**, **5,985**, **5,986**, **5,987**, **5,989**, **5,990**, **5,991**, **5,992**, **5,993**, **5,994**, **5,995**, **5,996**, **5,997**, **5,998**, **5,999**, **6,000**, **6,001**, **6,002**, **6,003**, **6,004**, **6,006**, **6,007**, **6,008**, **6,010**, **6,011**, **6,014**, **6,015**, **6,016**, **6,017**, **6,018**, **6,019**, **6,021**, **6,022**, **6,023**, **6,025**, **6,027**, **6,028**, **6,029**, **6,030**, **6,031**, **6,032**, **6,034**, **6,035**, **6,036**, **6,037**, **6,038**, **6,039**, **6,040**, **6,041**, **6,042**, **6,043**, **6,045**, **6,046**, **6,047**, **6,048**, **6,049**, **6,052**, **6,053**, **6,054**, **6,055**, **6,056**, **6,057**, **6,058**, **6,059**, **6,060**, **6,062**, **6,064**, 6,065, **6,067**, **6,068**, **6,069**, **6,070**, **6,071**, **6,072**, **6,073**, **6,074**, **6,076**, **6,077**, **6,078**, **6,080**, **6,081**, **6,082**, **6,083**, **6,084**, **6,086**, **6,087**, **6,089**, **6,090**, **6,091**, **6,092**, **6,093**, **6,094**, **6,095**, **6,096**, **6,098**, **6,099**, **6,100**, **6,101**, **6,102**, **6,103**, **6,104**, **6,105**, 6,106, 6,107, **6,108**, **6,109**, **6,110**, **6,111**, **6,113**, **6,114**, **6,115**, **6,116**, **6,117**, **6,118**, **6,119**, **6,120**, **6,121**, **6,475**, **6,512**, **6,569**, **6,573**, **6,582**, **6,637**, **6,682**, **6,708**, **6,722**, **6,726**, **6,739**, **6,767**, **6,841**, **6,872**, **6,904**, 6,908, **6,909**, **7,024**, 7,167, **7,170**, **7,202**, **7,230**, **7,235**, **7,257**, **7,265**, **7,296**, **7,304**, **7,688**, **7,689**, **7,691**, 7,709, **7,718**, **8,008**, 8,064, **8,435**, **8,489**, **8,726**, **8,850**, **8,935**, **9,360**, **9,949**, **10,027**, **10,126**, **10,127**, **10,262**, 10,292, **10,352**, **10,399**, **10,465**, **10,487**, **10,529**, 10,531, **10,608**, **10,760**, **10,848**, **10,854**, **10,867**, **10,869**, **10,871**, **10,875**, **10,894**, 10,921, **11,145**, **11,155**, **11,160**, **11,163**, **11,168**, 11,179, **11,182**, **11,214**, 11,221, 11,222, **11,223**, **11,224**, **11,226**, **11,286**, **11,287**, **11,310**, **11,368**, **11,385**, **11,485**, 11,555, **11,605**, **11,684**, **11,832**, **11,858**, **11,976**, **11,991**, **11,992**, 12,360, 12,362, 12,364, **12,396**, **12,441**, **12,466**, **12,496**, 12,520, **12,533**, **12,642**, **12,679**, **12,694**, **12,800**, **12,821**, 12,846, **12,880**, **12,890**, **13,131**, **13,190**, **13,252**, **13,267**, 13,289, **13,674**, **13,688**, 13,959, **14,096**, **14,203**, **14,215**, **14,218**, **14,231**, **14,313**, **14,315**, **14,319**, **14,320**, **14,321**, **14,324**, **14,326**, **14,327**, **14,333**, 14,334, **14,335**, **14,338**, **14,339**, **14,342**, **14,343**, **14,344**, **14,347**, **14,352**, **14,355**, **14,357**, **14,358**, **14,359**, **14,362**, **14,364**, **14,370**, **14,374**, **14,385**, **14,390**, **14,399**, **14,400**, **14,403**, **14,405**, **14,406**, **14,408**, **14,412**, **14,414**, **14,416**, **14,417**, **14,421**, 14,431, **14,438**, 14,447, **14,448**, **14,450**, **14,452**, **14,453**, 14,455, **14,458**, **14,460**, **14,463**, **14,464**, **14,467**, **14,468**, **14,475**, **14,476**, **14,574**, **14,684**, **14,736**, **15,188**, **15,199**, **15,262**, **15,286**, 15,303, **15,399**, **15,480**, **15,583**, **15,585**, **15,699**, **15,700**, **15,879**, **15,880**, 15,923, **15,927**, **15,929**, 15,933, **16,159**, **16,162**, **16,168**, 16,257, **16,301**, **16,302**, **16,370**, **16,371**, **16,881**, **16,882**, **16,884**, 16,905, **16,908**, 16,923, **16,972**, **17,023**, **17,192**, **17,193**, **17,198**, **17,336**, 17,373, **17,374**, **17,387**, **17,431**, **17,455**, **17,456**, **17,478**, **17,553**, **17,583**, **17,599**, **17,604**, **17,610**, **17,726**, **17,731**, **17,870**, **17,942**, **17,950**, **17,969**, **17,990**, **18,004**
Authors, Afro-American, 995, **1,854**, **1,856**, **2,137**, **2,143**, **2,144**, 2,145, 2,146, **2,153**, 5,535, **6,066**, **6,790**, 11,494
  19th-20th C, **2,602**
  20th C, 2,946, 2,948, 5,260, **15,782**
Authors and Composers Society of Arkansas, 250
Authors and publishers, 97, 1,221, 2,403, 4,237, 5,415, 5,984, 5,985, 5,994, 5,996, 6,006, 6,038, 6,069, 6,083, 6,102, 6,113, 6,121, 10,262, 11,166, 11,850, 11,870, 11,996, **12,499**, **12,537**, **12,661**, 14,319, 14,320, 14,324, 14,326, 14,327, 14,352, 14,359, 14,388, 14,390, 14,405, 14,407, 14,414, 14,458, 14,475, 14,476, 14,503, 15,482, 17,843.
  See also Literary agents
Authors, blind, **12,795**
Authors, British, **2,477**, **4,228**, **12,200**, 12,489, 13,079
Authors, child, **11,991**
Authors, deaf, 2,110, 2,112
Authors, deaf-blind, **2,108**
Authors, French, biography, 6,809
Authors Guild, 2,205

Authors, Jewish, **13,811**, **13,834**
Author's League of America, 325, 1,306, 12,395, 13,674
Authors, Native American, 11,217
Authors, Norwegian-American, **8,727**, 8,805
Authors, Scottish, **12,215**
Authors, Soviet, 5,875
Authors, Turkish, 7,191
Authors, Ukrainian-American, **9,499**
"Authors Who Have Lived in Brooklyn, Dates and Places" (ms), 11,320
Auto Labor Board, 8,099
Autobiographies, 67, 200, 586, 632, 899, 931, 1,254, **1,284**, **1,304**, 1,473, 1,772, 1,840, **1,960**, 2,159, 2,213, **2,320**, 2,384, 2,602, 2,733, 2,768, 2,872, 3,081, 3,143, 3,847, 4,143, 4,345, 4,736, **5,678**, 5,757, 6,031, 6,121, 6,144, 6,349, 6,412, **6,418**, 6,511, 6,590, 6,624, **6,641**, 6,816, 6,859, 6,958, 7,220, 7,292, 8,521, 8,732, 9,126, 9,192, **9,879**, 9,955, 10,355, 10,634, **10,902**, **11,158**, 11,305, 11,700, **11,813**, 11,944, 12,233, 12,528, 12,688, 12,700, 12,701, 12,976, 13,427, 13,668, 13,786, 13,833, 14,355, 14,643, 14,682, 15,583, **16,073**, **16,120**, 16,444, **16,467**, 16,472, 16,474, **16,634**, 16,645, 16,653, 16,664, 16,674, 16,683, 16,690, 16,715, 16,722, 16,756, 16,791, 16,804, 16,820, 16,832, 16,897, 16,903, 16,943, **16,967**, 17,258, **17,339**, 17,614, 17,948. *See also* Diaries and journals
Autobiography of John Ball (book), 14,513
Autobiography of Peggy Eaton, The (book), 2,320
Autograph albums, 265, **399**, 1,294, 3,418, 3,794, **5,111**, 5,749, 5,961, **6,915**, **6,998**, 8,791, 8,975, 9,274, 9,654, **9,789**, 10,799, 11,109, 12,003, 12,128, 12,483, 13,353, 13,477, 13,524, 14,967, 15,028, 15,065, **15,098**, 15,268, 15,280, 17,037
Autographs, **1,751**, **4,695**, **4,696**, **4,697**, **4,732**, **4,781**, 6,548, 7,037, 7,274, **11,144**, 12,250, 12,503, **14,838**, **17,197**
Automation, 9,379
Automobile agencies, 17,139
Automobile driving, 1,281
Automobile industry and trade, 6,315
Automobile industry workers, **8,100**, **8,110**, **8,143**
Automobile parking, 7,733
Automobile travel, 1,347, 3,621
Automobiles, 10,633
Automobiles, electric, 7,670
Automobiles, parts, 2,142
Automotive Industrial Workers Association, 8,099
Autonomous Industrial Colony Kuzbas (Russia), 8,072
Autopsy, 9,176
Autry, James L. (1859-1926), **16,243**
Autry, Martha W., 16,243
Auxiliary of Sons of Union Veterans (OR), 14,686
Auxiliary of the Dixie Highway on the Cumberland Divide, 15,964
Auxiliary of the United Spanish War Veterans, **15,848**
Avakian, Anne, **329**
Avakian, Sarah (Mahdesian), 330
Avard, Charles, **17,183**
Avard, Julia Hamacker Eastman [Mrs. Stephen] (1881-1956), **17,183**
Avard, Stephen, **17,183**
Avary, Myrta (Lockett), **3,143**, 3,256, 3,326
Averasboro, battle of (NC), 13,374, 13,602
Averill, Blaine, 5,651
Averill, Goldie [Mrs. Blaine], 5,651
Averill, Martha Jane (Weston) (1838-?), **7,340**
Averitt, Kay, 8,210
"Aversion to Anomalies, An," (pamphlet), 6,746
Avery-Bowman Company (NM), 11,237
Avery, Catherine Berry (Pilcher) [Mrs. Roy] (1894-), **15,939**
Avery Family (NY), **11,824**
Avery, Georgia. *See* Kendrick, Georgia (Avery)
Avery, Gladys (1897-). *See* Tillett, Gladys (Avery) (1897-)
Avery, Janet Pomeroy. *See* Dulles, Janet Pomeroy (Avery) [Mrs. John Foster]
Avery, Jennie M. [Miss] (1888-1976), **11,237**
Avery, Judith Ellen (Horton) [Mrs. Addison] (1840-1910). *See* Foster, Judith Ellen (Horton)

[Mrs. Addison] Avery [Mrs. Elijah Caleb O.] (1840-1910)
Avery, Leah, 13,142
Avery, Lizzie Little, 3,829
Avery, Margaret Dewees (1930-). *See* Ritchie, Margaret Dewees (Avery) (1930-)
Avery, Mary (Upson), 7,206
Avery, Mary Williamson, **17,368**
Avery, May (Bennett) [Mrs. Samuel] (1870-1960), **10,430**
Avery, Polly Mira (1779-1857). *See* Summey, Polly Mira (Avery) (1779-1857)
Avery, Rachel G. (Foster) [Mrs. Cyrus Miller] (1858-1919), 349, 1,436, 4,244, 7,239, 11,547, **12,811**
Avery, Roy, 15,939
Aviation mechanics (persons), 11,861
Ávila, María Inocenta (Pico) [Mrs. Miguel] (1811-?), **331**
Ávila, Miguel, 331
Awakening, The (book), 10,158
Awbry, Elizabeth Ann (1832-1920). *See* Miller, Elizabeth Ann (Awbry) [Mrs. John Napper Tandy] (1832-1920)
Axson, Ellen "Ellie" Louise (1860-1914). *See* Wilson, Ellen "Ellie" Louise (Axson) [Mrs. Woodrow] (1860-1914)
Ayars, Sara M., 9,323
Aycock, Charles Brantley, **13,323**
Aycock Family, 3,054
Aycock, Huda, 3,448
Aycock, Marguerite. *See* Blackstone, Marguerite (Aycock)
Aydelotte, Myrtle Elizabeth (Kitchell) (1917-), **4,969**
Ayer, Elizabeth, 5,700
Ayer, Elizabeth Taylor [Mrs. Frederick] (1803-98), **8,926**, 9,229, 9,230
Ayer, Elsie Johnson, 5,465
Ayer, Frederick, 8,926
Ayer, Harry Darius (1878-1966), Family (MN), **8,927**
Ayer, Janet Hopkins [Mrs. Benjamin F.], 3,816
Ayer, Janette Ora (Foster) [Mrs. Harry Darius] (1884-1966), 8,927
Ayer, Margaret. *See* Smith, Margaret Ayer [Mrs. Alfred Babington]
Ayer, Mary Catherine (Norton) (?-1921), **1,235**
Ayer, N. W., 17,623
Ayer, Sarah Connell [Mrs.] (1791-1835), **10,792**
Ayer, Timothy, 5,700
Ayers, Gertrude, 13,217
Ayers, Hester (Merwin) [Mrs. Edward L.], 3,745
Aynesworth, Kenneth Hazen (1873-1944), **16,225**
Ayres, Anne [Miss] (1816-96), 4,732
Ayres, D. C., 11,512
Ayres Family (NY), 11,717
Ayres, Sidney, **11,512**
Ayscough, Florence (Wheelock) [Mrs. Francis] (1878-1942). *See* MacNair, Florence (Wheelock) [Mrs. Francis] Ayscough [Mrs. Harley Farnsworth] (1878-1942)
Azalea Garden Club (FL), **2,899**
Azikiwe, Nnamdi, 5,460
B. H. Academy, 5,815
B. J. Brimmer Company (MA), 11,077
Baasch, Hans, 2,396
Baasch, Mrs. Hans, 2,396
Baasen, Francis (1820-1901), Family (MN), **8,928**
Baasen, Louise, 8,928
Baasen, Mary Belland (1842-1929), 8,928
Babashoff, Shirley, 997
Babb, Dot, 16,064
Babb, Mrs. E. S., **17,418**
Babb, Mrs. James E., 3,674
Babb, Sanora (1907-), **5,981**
Babbit Family (AZ), 196
Babbitt, Katharine, 2,160
Babcock, Caroline (Lexow) (1882-), **6,379**, 6,742, 15,314, 15,317, **17,939**
Babcock, Celia, 17,535
Babcock, Cora D. (1855-?), **15,849**
Babcock, Cornelia A. (1854-1941). *See* Upton, Cornelia A. (Babcock) (1854-1941)
Babcock, Elizabeth Celicia [Miss] (?-1899), 10,655

Babcock, Emily Wight (1836-1919). *See* Alward, Emily Wight (Babcock) [Mrs. Dennis R.] (1836-1919)
Babcock, Esther Van Deusen [Mrs. Cecil] (1907-77), 7,510
Babcock Family, 9,277
Babcock, Grace (Henshaw) [Mrs. Willoughby M., II], 8,929
Babcock, Helen, 3,920
Babcock, Helen E. Maynard [Mrs. Willoughby] (1838-?), 8,929
Babcock, James, 11,869
Babcock, Jessica (ca. 1860-?). *See* Moore, Jessica (Babcock) [Mrs. Gardner S.] (ca. 1860-?)
Babcock, Jessie (1865-?). *See* Pollock, Jessie (Babcock) [Mrs. John] (1865-?)
Babcock, Juline E. *See* Smith, Juline E. (Babcock) [Mrs. Peter]
Babcock, Katherine Guion (1866-1943), **15,559**
Babcock Kindergarten (Reno, NV), 10,655
Babcock, Louisa Atwater [Mrs. Samuel] (?-1850), 8,929
Babcock, Lucy, 4,063
Babcock, Margaret [Mrs.], 11,873
Babcock, Mary (1857-?). *See* Morrison, Mary (Babcock) [Mrs. John Henry] (1857-?)
Babcock, Mary Brown [Mrs. Dwight W.] (1829-1906), 9,277
Babcock, Mary Kent Davey [Mrs. Samuel G.] (1864-1947), **6,176**
Babcock, Mary (Potter), 11,509
Babcock, Samuel (?-1895), 8,929
Babcock, Samuel G., 6,176
Babcock, Willoughby (1832-64), Family (MN), **8,929**
Babcock, Willoughby M. (1864-1925), 8,929
Babcock, Willoughby M., II (1893-1967), 8,929
Baber, Ambrose (1793-1846), 2,965
Baber Family (GA), **2,965**
Baber, Mary Eliza (Sweet) [Mrs. Ambrose], **3,586**
Babies Aid Society of San Francisco (CA), **1,236**
Babies Home (St. Paul, MN), **8,930**
Babies Milk Fund, 13,860
Babion, Mable A., 8,167
Babson, Naomi Lane (1895-), **5,982**
Baby Black (book), 5,008
Bacall, Lauren (1924-), 11,827
Baccalaureate addresses, **9,563**, 9,998, 14,299
Bach, Ellen Botsford (1877-1960), **7,713**
Bach, Pearl (Day) [Mrs. William Everett] (1887-1968), **5,301**
Bach, William Everett, 5,301
Bache, Alexander, 14,895
Bache, Anna, **14,875**
Bache, Benjamin Franklin (1769-98), 14,884
Bache, Deborah. *See* Duane, Deborah (Bache) [Mrs. William John]
Bache Family, 8,781
Bache Family (PA), **14,884**
Bache, Richard (1737-1811), 14,884, 14,888
Bache, Sarah (Franklin) [Mrs. Richard] (1743-1808), 2,621, 14,884, 14,888, 14,890
Bacheller, Georgietta "Ettie," 11,392
Bachelor Ben (book), 17,718
Bachman, Anne. *See* Hyde, Anne (Bachman) [Mrs. Charles R.]
Bachman, Kate [Mrs. W. K.], **15,560**
Bachmann, Charles W., Family (MN), **8,931**
Bachmann, Ida Mackenroth (1837-?), 8,931
Bachmann, Mother Francis, 14,719
Bachmann, Sophie E., **2,184**
Back Bay Mission, 15,880
Backer, Miriam Lois, 6,765
"Background, Job Involvement, Perceived Discrimination and Job Dissatisfaction Among Academic Women at UMC, March, 1976" (report), 10,017
Background with Figures (book), 2,733
Backler, Eliza (Ridgely) White [Mrs. John Campbell], 5,822
Backus, Elizabeth Welch. *See* Mason, Elizabeth Welch (Backus)
Backus, Louise Burton (Laidlaw) (1906-), **6,380**
Backus, Marion A., 8,932

Backward Glance, A, 4,491
Bacmeister, Charles A., 4,346
Bacmeister, Emily, 4,346
Bacmeister, Laura (Ogle) [Mrs. Theodore], 4,346
Bacmeister, Laura Pauline, 4,346
Bacmeister, Louise, 4,346
Bacmeister, Otto, 4,346
Bacmeister, Theodore (1830-1911), **4,346**
Bacmeister, Theodore (son), 4,346
Bacmeister, William O., 4,346
Bacon, Albion (Fellows) [Mrs. Hilary Edwin]
  (1865-1933), 4,508
Bacon, Anne. See Fall, Anne (Bacon) [Mrs. Philip S.]
Bacon, Astrid Ihme (1903-), **8,722**
Bacon, Charles, 2,731
Bacon, Edward A. (1897-1968), **5,127**
Bacon, Elizabeth. See Williams, Elizabeth (Bacon)
  [Mrs. Howard Yolen]
Bacon, Elizabeth [Mrs. Charles], 2,731
Bacon, Elizabeth (1842-1933). See Custer, Elizabeth
  (Bacon) [Mrs. George Armstrong] (1842-1933)
Bacon, Ellen (Usher) (1817-), 5,689
Bacon, Evelyn (Smith) [Mrs. Walter R.], 801
Bacon Family, 9,443
Bacon Family (IN), **4,508**
Bacon, Gertrude M. (1866-1937), **11,363**
Bacon, Helen (Hazard) [Mrs. Nathaniel Terry],
  15,377
Bacon, Hilary Edwin, 4,508
Bacon, Isabel. See LaFollette, Isabel (Bacon) [Mrs.
  Philip Fox]
Bacon, Josephine Dodge (Daskam) (1876-1961),
  7,171, **7,186**
Bacon, Leonard, 12,035, 15,377
Bacon, Louise Agathe Josephine (1847-1929). See
  Sorbier, Louise Agathe Josephine (Bacon)
  (1847-1929)
Bacon, Lydia [Mrs. Josiah], 17,751
Bacon, Mae Hélène (1863-?). See Boggs, Mae Hélène
  (Bacon) [Mrs. Angus Gordon] (1863-1963)
Bacon, Martha, 1,525
Bacon, Mary Hannah (1833-1912). See Field, Mary
  Hannah (Bacon) (1833-1912)
Bacon, Mr., 7,042
Bacon, Moriah K. [Mrs.], **15,886**
Bacon, Nathaniel Terry (1857-1926), **15,377**
Bacon, Peggy. [Mrs. Alexander] Brook (1895-),
  2,731, 2,736, 2,824, **12,888**, 16,163
Bacot Family (SC), **15,441**
Bacot, Jane, 12,320
Bacot, Thomas W., I (1765-1834), 15,441
Bacteriologists, 2,329, **3,466**, 3,482, **7,558, 9,195,
  11,579, 11,629, 11,682, 14,943**
Bacteriology, marine, 7,558
Bade, Elizabeth (Marston) [Mrs. William Frederic]
  (1884-), **795**
Baden-Powell, Olave [Mrs. Robert] (1889-1977),
  12,093
Baden-Powell, Robert (1857-1941), **12,093**
Badger, Ella [Miss], **1,238**
Badger, Ella Louise (Smith) [Mrs. Robert A.]
  (1859-1949), **12,793**
Badger Family (NY), **11,513**
Badger, George E., 11,049
Badger, Ina, **14,194**
Badger, Mariette [Mrs. Daniel], 1,837
Badger, Mrs. George C., 13,619
Badgett, Thomas J., 13,324
Baer, Caroline (1913-75). See Rose, Caroline (Baer)
  [Mrs. Arnold M.] (1913-75)
Baer, Gertrude, 1,680, 15,305, 15,317
Baer, Jean Hitchcock (1918-74), **4,040**
Baer, Jennie Miller [Mrs.], **16,451**
Baer, Mildred, 1,655
Baer, Mrs. Jerome, 8,983
Baer, Myrtle [Miss] (1880-), **17,840**
Baer, Myrtle [Mrs.], **17,828**
Baer, William, 17,840
Bagby, Lelia Cocke [Mrs.] (1915-), **17,066**
Bagg, Abby Sheldon. See Austin, Abby Sheldon
  (Bagg)
Bagg, Gladys (1899-). See Taber, Gladys (Bagg)
  (1899-)
Baggerly, Cora Miranda (1876-1968). See Older,

Cora Miranda (Baggerly) [Mrs. Fremont]
  (1876-1968)
Baggerly, Margaret (1886-1971). See Bruner,
  Margaret (Baggerly) [Mrs. Vate] (1886-1971)
Baggett, Halcyon [Mrs. Hill], **16,260**
Baggett, Margaret (1914-74). See Dolan, Margaret
  (Baggett) (1914-74)
Baghdad School for Girls (Iraq), 10,926
Bagley, Adelaide "Addie" (1869-1943). See Daniels,
  Adelaide "Addie" (Bagley) [Mrs. Josephus]
  (1869-1943)
Bagley, Adelaide (Worth) (1844-?), 2,292
Bagley, Belle Worth (?-1939), 2,292
Bagley, Christina (1809-80). See Bickmore, Christina
  (Bagley) [Mrs. William] (1809-80)
Bagley, Ethel (?-1939), 2,292
Bagley, Grace Hodge (1860-1944), **6,970**
Bagley, Sarah G. [Miss], 7,069
Bagnold, Enid (1889-), 6,085
Bahaism, 12,507
Bahr, Susan, 9,462
Baier, Florence C., 9,323
Bailey, Antoinette (Crippen) [Mrs. James Monroe]
  (1834-1931), 17,862
Bailey, Barbara (1909-). See Hodges, Barbara
  (Bailey) [Mrs. J. Stanley] (1909-)
Bailey, Belle, **8,933**
Bailey, Benjamin, 3,144
Bailey, E. Morgan, 15,659
Bailey, Ella, **1,694**
Bailey, Eunice Miller [Mrs. E. Morgan] (1883-),
  15,659
Bailey, Everett Hoskins, Family (MN), **8,934**
Bailey, Florence Augusta (Merriam) [Mrs. Vernon]
  (1863-1948), 526, 2,484, 2,724
Bailey, Frank, 8,934
Bailey, George W., 8,168
Bailey, Hannah Clark (Johnston) [Mrs. Moses]
  (1839-1923), 15,298, **15,300**
Bailey, Harriet Frances (1918-38), **4874**
Bailey, Helen. See Twyford, Helen (Bailey) [Mrs.
  Loren C.]
Bailey, Jeannette (Jones) (1851-1923), 8,934
Bailey, Joel, 8,933
Bailey, John, 11,839
Bailey, Josiah W., 13,272
Bailey, Josiah W., 13,282
Bailey, Kate (1871-1970). See Hinman, Kate (Bailey)
  [Mrs. George W.] (1871-1970)
Bailey, Kay (1943-), 16,231
Bailey, Liberty Hyde, 11,662, 11,684, 11,691
Bailey, Louise (1869-?), 17,591
Bailey, Lottie Pendleton [Mrs. George W.], 8,168
Bailey, Lucy Antoinette (Crippen) [Mrs. James
  Monroe] (1834-1931), 17,592
Bailey, Maida Rossiter [Mrs. Meredith, Jr.] (?-1973),
  14,509
Bailey, Margaret, 9,884
Bailey, Margaret Hart. See Barbour, Margaret Hart
  (Bailey) [Mrs. Paul]
Bailey, Margaret Jewett (Smith) [Mrs. William J.],
  14,510, 14,645, 14,712
Bailey, Margery (1891-1963), **1,545**
Bailey, Martha E., 8,934
Bailey, Mary Abigail [Miss] (1838-ca. 1910), 5,706
Bailey, Mary E. (1845-1922), **12,942**
Bailey, Mary Stuart, 1,505
Bailey, Mrs. Joseph T., 2,035
Bailey, Orra B., **2,185**
Bailey, Rosalie Davis [Mrs. Benjamin], **3,144**
Bailhache, Adaline, 4,347
Bailhache Family (IL), **4,347**
Bailhache, John (1787-1857), 4,347
Bailhache, Sarah Adaline "Ada" (Brayman) [Mrs.
  William H.], 4,347
Bailhache, William H. (1826-1905), 4,347
Bailie, Helen (Tufts) [Mrs. William] (1874-1962),
  7,187, 12,698
Bailie, William (1867-1957), 12,698
Baillif, Matilda Victorine (1883-), **8,534, 8,935**
Bailly, Alexis, **8,936**
Bailly, Julia (Cory) [Mrs. Alexis], 9,018
Bailly, Lucy, **8,936**
Bailly, Sophie (Hortense), 8,936

Baily, Hannah J., 10,673
Bain, Emma. See Swiggett, Emma (Bain) [Mrs. Glen
  Levin]
Bain, Ione Branch [Mrs.], 13,617
Bain, Winifred E. (1889-1965), **2,093**
Bainbridge, Mary MacMath, 9,077
Bainter, Fay, 4,743
Bainton, Roland H., 11,594
Baintree, Mrs. W. S., 9,984
Baird, Elizabeth Thérèse (Fisher) [Mrs. Henry
  Samuel] (1810-90), 17,593
Baird, Emma Lilian (1859-1949), 3,897
Baird, Gertrude Luck (1885-), **16,587**
Baird, Henry Samuel (1800-75), **17,593**
Baird, Lenna E., **17,184**
Baird, Lucy Hunter (1848-1913), 2,712, 2,716, **2,855**
Baird, Mary Helen (Churchill) [Mrs. Spencer F.]
  (1821-1913), 2,712
Baird, Peggy, 11,873
Baird, R. Bruce (1891-1971), **14,511**
Baird, Sarah G. [Mrs. George W.] (1843-1923), **8,937**
Baird, Spencer F. (1823-87), **2,712**, 2,716, 2,855
Baird, Zebbie, 13,599
Baits, Vera (Burridge) (1892-1963), **7,714**
Baity, Minnie Martin (1864-1931), 9,972
Baker Act, The (FL). See Florida Mental Health Act,
  The
Baker, Ada (Nutting), 1,418
Baker, Ann G. [Miss], **14,954**
Baker, Ann Jane. See Graves, Ann Jane (Baker)
  [Mrs. John James]
Baker, Annie Laurie (1905-), **8,535**
Baker, Betsey (Metcalf) (1786-1867), 7,587
Baker, Blanche (1855-1943), **12,943**
Baker, Catherine (Ludlow), 17,992
Baker, Charlotte (1910-). See Montgomery,
  Charlotte (Baker) [Mrs. Roger] (1910-)
Baker, Charlotte Alice (1833-1909), **7,011**
Baker, Christine Otis (1689-1773), 10,846
Baker, Clara Belle (1885-1961), 4,210
Baker, Clara (Bradley) [Mrs. Presley C.] (1855-1954).
  See Burdette, Clara (Bradley) [Mrs. N. Milman]
  Wheeler [Mrs. Presley C.] Baker [Mrs. Robert J.]
  (1855-1954)
Baker, Dorothy (Dodds) (1907-68), **332, 11,832**
Baker, Edith M., 8,665
Baker, Edna Dean, 4,128, **4,210**, 4,212
Baker, Edward, 4,360
Baker, Elisabeth Annie (Nuttall) [Mrs. John Daniel]
  (1881-1968), **16,588**
Baker, Ella (1903-), 13,176
Baker Family, 6,650
Baker Family (GA), 3,025
Baker Family (GA), 2,999
Baker Family (MA), 7,587
Baker Family (NC), **13,325**
Baker, Florence, 5,644
Baker, Frances [Mrs. Frank], **14,195**
Baker, Gene Frances. See McComas, Gene Frances
  (Baker) [Mrs. Francis John]
Baker, Gertrude, **17,400**
Baker, Gertrude Margaret (1894-1977), **8,536**, 8,547
Baker, Grace (1874?-1961). See Diffendorf, Grace
  (Baker) (1874?-1961)
Baker, Helen Cody, 8,678
Baker, Helen Dorothy (1896-). See Reynolds, Helen
  Dorothy (Baker) [Mrs. Ralph A.] (1896-)
Baker, I. G., 10,242
Baker, Ida Strawn [Mrs. Walter D.] (1876-?), **4,620**
Baker, Irene Bailey [Mrs. Howard H.] (1901-),
  15,875
Baker, Ivy (1905-75). See Priest, Ivy (Baker)
  (1905-75)
Baker, James Heaton (1829-1913), 9,214
Baker, Jane Rio (Griffiths) [Mrs. Henry] (1810-83),
  16,589
Baker, Josephine (1906-), 12,004
Baker, Julia [Mrs. Edward], 4,360
Baker, Julia Kern (Wetherill) [Mrs. Marion A.]
  (1857-1931), 9,771
Baker, Karle (Wilson) [Mrs. Thomas E.] (1878-1960),
  16,295
Baker, Laura, 8,721
Baker, Laura Nelson (1911-), 8,531

Baker, Laura Virginia Lee (McNeil) [Mrs. George Varnadoe], 3,611
Baker, Lillian (1876-1955). *See* Griggs, Lillian (Baker) [Mrs. Alfred] (1876-1955)
Baker, Lydia Hamp [Mrs.] (1848-?), 16,486
Baker, Margaret Maranda (1853-1942). *See* Meredith, Margaret Maranda (Baker) [Mrs. Thomas Prentiss] Beebe [Mrs. John William] (1853-1942)
Baker, Marion A., 9,771
Baker, Mary (1821-1910). *See* Eddy, Mary (Baker) [Mrs. Asa] Gilbert [Mrs. George Washington] Glover [Mrs. Daniel Patterson] (1821-1910)
Baker, Maxine Eldridge (1898-), **6,381**
Baker, Mildred, **2,732**
Baker, Minnie Dell Sprague, 7,920
Baker, Mrs. Ashford, 646
Baker, Mrs. James H., 1,679
Baker, Mrs. James Heaton, 9,214
Baker, Mrs. Newton D., 13,942
Baker Orange (KS), 5,168
Baker, Ray Stannard (1870-1946), **2,186**
Baker, Rebecca Virginia (1868-?). *See* Moffett, Rebecca Virginia (Baker) (1868-?)
Baker, Sarah Ann (Miller) [Mrs. Edwin Franklin] (1853-1945), **17,419**
Baker, Sarah (Collins) [Mrs. William J.], 12,943
Baker, Simmons Jones, 13,325
Baker, Stella. *See* Hill, Stella Baker [Mrs. Benjamin]
Baker, Thomas Barwick Lloyd (1807-86), **12,375**
Baker, Thomas Frazier, III (1918-), **9,930**
Baker University (Baldwin City, KS)
  alumnae, 5,171, 13,284
  archives, **5,168**
  faculty, 5,170, 5,172
  students, 5,169
Baker, William J., 12,943
Baker, Zulu Bartlett [Mrs. James], 8,506
Bakers and bakeries, 8,717, 14,558
Bakewell Family, 11,599
Bakunin, Mikhail, 6,329
Bal Masque (Baton Rouge, LA), 5,419
Balabanoff, Angelica, 15,305
Balakirev, Mily Alexeyevich, 2,665
Balanchine, George, 12,364
Balanoff, Elizabeth [Mrs.], 13,428
Balboa Park (CA), 1,214
Balch, Emily Greene [Miss] (1867-1961), 1,680, 6,516, 6,563, 6,885, 7,278, 7,868, 7,923, 12,534, 15,269, **15,301,** 15,303, 15,305, 15,306, 15,311, 15,314, 15,316
Balch, Helene, 1,779
Balch, Nancy, 12,514
Bald Eagle Union Church (MN), Ladies Aid Society, **8,938**
Balderston, Katherine, 7,583
Baldwin, Abigail, 16,060, 17,029
Baldwin, Abigail. *See* Alexander, Abigail (Baldwin)
Baldwin, Alice (Blackwood) [Mrs. Frank Dwight], 1,398
Baldwin, Alice Mary (1879-1960), 40, 15,430
Baldwin, Amelia Muir (1876-1960), **6,382**
Baldwin Bird Club (NY), 12,869
Baldwin, Calvin Benham (1902-75), **4,970**
Baldwin, Charles A., 7,485
Baldwin, Charlotte (Fowler) [Mrs. Dwight] (1805-73), 3,636
Baldwin, Dwight (1798-1886), 3,636
Baldwin, Eleanore Florence, **14,512**
Baldwin, Elizabeth Bratt (?-1954), **13,700**
Baldwin, Eudocia (1829-?). *See* Marsh, Eudocia (Baldwin) (1829-?)
Baldwin, Faith (1893-), 4,227, **4,247, 5,983,** 10,992, 15,331
Baldwin Family, **1,397**
Baldwin, Fannie, 17,594
Baldwin, Frank Dwight (1842-1923), **1,398**
Baldwin, George J., 3,535
Baldwin, Harriet. *See* Dunnell, Harriet (Baldwin) [Mrs. John Henry]
Baldwin, Juanita. *See* Foote, Juanita (Baldwin) Williams
Baldwin, Juliet, 11,596

Baldwin, Lucy (Hull) [Mrs. George Johnson] (?-1923), **12,944**
Baldwin, Martha Harper [Mrs. John], **3,366**
Baldwin, Mary C., **7,341**
Baldwin, Mary (Gould), 11,600
Baldwin, Mary Newton, 17,006
Baldwin Methodist Episcopal Church (KS), Ladies Sewing Circle, 5,169
Baldwin, Michael (1719-87), 1,397
Baldwin, Mildred, 11,879
Baldwin, Nellie, 3,839
Baldwin, Roger Nash, 7,216, 7,223, 11,897, 12,518, 12,701, 15,303
Baldwin, Ruth (1756-1818). *See* Barlow, Ruth (Baldwin) [Mrs. Joel] (1756-1818)
Baldwin, Ruth Standish (Bowles), 7,868, 12,066, 17,594
Baldwin, Sarah L., 13,189
Baldwin School (St. Paul, MN). *See* Macalester College (St. Paul, MN)
Baldwin, Susan Bell [Mrs.], 13,463
Baldwin, Theron, 4,374
Baldwin University (St. Paul, MN). *See* Macalester College (St. Paul, MN)
Baldwin, William Henry (1891-), **17,594**
Baldy, Carrie (Munro), 3,559
Bale Family (CA), **333**
Bale, Mariano G., 333
Balenciaga, 16,210
Balfour, Emma, **9,586**
Balfour, M. L. G., 12,553
Balfour, Rhoda Brooks, 12,570
Balis, Lola A., 2,502
Ball, Catherine Grant, 14,688
Ball, Elias, 15,459
Ball, Elizabeth (Byle) [Mrs. William], 14,955
Ball, Eve, **16,497**
Ball Family, 2,206
Ball Family (SC), **15,562**
Ball, Flora. *See* Hopkins, Flora (Ball)
Ball, H. Belle, **7,715**
Ball, James F., 3,246
Ball, James M., 3,246
Ball, Jane [Mrs. John, Sr.] (1761-1804), 15,562
Ball, Jane (1823-?), 15,562
Ball, John, **15,442**
Ball, John (1794-1884), **8,300, 14,513**
Ball, John, Sr., 15,562
Ball, Joseph (1752-1821), **14,955**
Ball, Kate. *See* Powers, Kate (Ball)
Ball, Katherine M., **1,239**
Ball, Lucille, 950, 4,764, 12,111
Ball, Lucy, 14,513
Ball, Lydia [Mrs. Elias], 15,459
Ball, M. Margaret, 7,583
Ball, Margaret, 7,499
Ball, Maria L. Gibbs, 15,562
Ball, Mary [Mrs. John], 8,300
Ball, Mary (1708-89). *See* Washington, Mary Ball [Mrs. Augustine] (1708-89)
Ball, Mary Ann (1817-1901). *See* Bickerdyke, Mary Ann (Ball) "Mother" [Mrs. Robert] (1817-1901)
Ball, Mrs. S. C., 15,562
Ball, Mrs. W. W., **15,563**
Ball, Olivia Carolina, **15,443**
Ball, Sarah. *See* Matthews, Sarah (Ball) Williams [Mrs. John]
Ball, William, 14,955
"Ballad of Emma Sansom, A," 99
Ballad of the Sad Cafe (book), 16,161
Ballads, 590, 5,249, 5,624, 13,143
Ballads, English, 5,250
"Ballads of Murderer's Bar," 590
Ballads, Scottish, 5,250
Ballantine, Anna Eliza (Ena) Palmer Raymonde (1848-84). *See* McClary, Anna Eliza (Ena) Palmer Raymonde Ballantine (1848-84)
Ballantine, David Coulter (1877-1960), **10,431**
Ballantine, Stella, 12,487
Ballantyne Family, 16,961
Ballantyne, Jane (1813-?). *See* Taylor, Jane (Ballantyne) [Mrs. John] (1813-?)
Ballard, Lusina (Nash) [Mrs. Lyman] (1823-?), **7,716**
Ballard, Lyman, 7,716

Ballard, Martha Moore [Mrs.] (1735-1812), **5,574**
Ballard, Mary Ethel, **7,717**
Ballard, Matilda, 14,174
Ballard Normal School (GA), faculty, 5,468
Ballard, Russell Ward (1893-), **4,052**
Ballentine, L. Y., **13,326**
Ballet, 3,374, 3,980, 9,568, 12,360, 12,364, 14,240, 16,965
  study and teaching, 3,773
Ballet dancing, **14,047**
Ballet Russe de Monte Carlo, 12,360, 14,199, 14,239, 14,240
Ballet Theatre, 12,360
Ballet West, 16,965
Ballif, Algie, **16,498**
Balloonists, **2,523, 13,351**
Balloons, scientific applications, 2,523
Ballot, 15,755
Ballou, Eliza (1801?-?). *See* Garfield, Eliza (Ballou) [Mrs. Abram] (1801?-?)
Balls (parties), 493, 716, 1,305, 3,931, **5,546,** 12,272, 16,321
Balmanno, Mary [Mrs. Robert], 12,376
Balmanno, Robert (1780-1861), **12,376**
Baltimore and Ohio Railroad, 2,591, 5,746, 14,745
Baltimore and Ohio Railroad Transportation Museum, 5,783
Baltimore Association for the Relief of Friends in the South, 13,239
Baltimore Birth Control Clinic (MD), **5,739**
Baltimore Birth Control League (MD), 5,739
Baltimore City Water Department (MD), 5,829
Baltimore County Historical Society (MD), **5,850**
Baltimore Female College, Parthenian Society, 12,463
Baltimore Female Union Society for the Promotion of Sunday Schools (MD), 5,827
Baltimore Housing Authority (MD), 5,829
Baltimore, Lord, 11,960
Baltimore Museum of Art (MD), 5,829
Baltimore Sun (MD), 73
Baltimore Sunday School Union (MD), 5,841
Baltzelle, Adelaide. *See* Saylor, Adelaide (Baltzelle)
Baltzelle, Julia (Barnsley), 2,966
Baltzly, Mary Francis (1861-?), **17,887**
Balz, Arcada (Stark) [Mrs. Fred G.], **4,621**
Bambace, Angela (1898-1975), **9,493**
Bamman, Catherine A., 16,577
Banach, Sister Mary Lucille, 6,336
Banbury Family (IA), **4,919**
Banbury, Jane (Hoxie) [Mrs. James] Robinson [Mrs. Thomas] (1815-98), 4,919
Banbury, Thomas, 4,919
Bancker, Adrian, 12,377
Bancker, Anne Taylor, 14,885
Bancker, Charles Nicoll (1778?-1869), **14,885**
Bancker Family (NY), **12,377**
Bancker, Flores, 12,377
Bancker, Marie de Peyster [Mrs.], 14,885
Bancker, Martha [Mrs. Flores], 12,377
Bancker, Sarah N., 14,885
Bancroft, Aaron, 11,514
Bancroft, Albert Little, 14,514
Bancroft, Ann, 11,514
Bancroft, Anne. *See* Graham, Anne (Bancroft)
Bancroft, Anne (1931-), 11,449
Bancroft, Azariah Ashley, 14,514
Bancroft, Caroline (1900-), 1,751, **1,752**
Bancroft, Eliza (1791-1872). *See* Davis, Eliza (Bancroft) [Mrs. John] (1791-1872)
Bancroft, Elizabeth (1773-1867), **7,599**
Bancroft, Elizabeth (1886-1977). *See* Schlesinger, Elizabeth (Bancroft) [Mrs. Arthur Meier, Sr.] (1886-1977)
Bancroft, Elizabeth (Davis) [Mrs. Alexander] Bliss [Mrs. George] (1803-86), 2,188, **4,408,** 7,603, 11,514
Bancroft, Emily. *See* Pierce, Emily (Bancroft) Palmer
Bancroft, Emily (Ketchum), 334, 1,222
Bancroft, Ethel (Norton), 1,786
Bancroft Family, **2,188**
Bancroft Family (CA, OR), 334, **1,222,** 14,514
Bancroft Family (CO), 1,786
Bancroft, George (1800-91), 2,188, 4,408, 7,603, 7,615, **11,514,** 12,481

Bancroft, George, Jr., 11,514
Bancroft, Griffing, 335
Bancroft, Hubert Howe, 335, 699, 855, 856, 861, 1,222, 1,621, 14,514
"Bancroft Insurrection" (1915), 1,496
Bancroft, Jane Marie. [Mrs. George Orville] Robinson (1847-1932), 4,215
Bancroft, Jane Putnam. See Gherardi, Jane Putnam (Bancroft)
Bancroft, John Chandler, 11,514
Bancroft, Kate, 334, 1,222
Bancroft, Louisa, 11,514
Bancroft, Lucretia. See Farnum, Lucretia (Bancroft)
Bancroft, Lucretia [Mrs.], 12,434
Bancroft, Lucy Damaris (Howe), 335, 14,514
Bancroft, Mary, 11,514
Bancroft, Mary Melissa (1838-?). See Trevett, Mary Melissa (Bancroft) (1838-?)
Bancroft, Matilda Coley (Griffing) [Mrs. Hubert Howe], 335, 855, 856
Bancroft, Minnie L. (Smith) [Mrs. Edward], 336
Bancroft Reading Club (Kansas City, MO), 10,084
Bancroft, Sarah, 11,514
Bancroft, Sarah (Dwight) [Mrs. George] (?-1837), 11,514
Bancrofts (actors), 12,539
Bancroft's Works (books), 14,680
Bandel, Betty, 17,002
Bandel, Eugene (1835-89), 180
Bandel, Olga, 180
Bandemer, Susan (Franklin) (1751-1858), 4,029
Bandini Family, 370
"Bandit's Bride, The" (story), 9,949
Bands (music), 34, 203, 2,022, 5,107, 5,529, 5,534, 7,408, 11,907
Bane, Elizabeth Evans, 1,695
Bane Family (CO), 1,695
Bane, Lita (1887-1957), 4,378, 4,380
Banér, Johann Gustaf R., 17,553
Banér, Skulda Vanadis (ca. 1898-1964), 7,718, 17,553
Banfield Family (NY), 12,158
Banfield, John, 12,158
Banfield, Mary Ann, 12,158
Bangor Daily News (ME), 5,662
Bangs, John Kendrick, 12,006, 12,529
Bangs, Mrs. William, 10,275
Bangs, Tracy R., 13,652
Banister, Anne, 17,108
Banister, Anne Augusta. See Pryor, Anne Augusta (Banister) [Mrs. Archibald Campbell]
Banister, Elizabeth (Carter). See Izard, Elizabeth (Carter) Banister [Mrs. Thomas Lee] Shippen [Mrs. George]
Banister Family (VA), 17,108
Banister, Margaret Sandford, 5,984
Banister, Marion (Glass) (?-1951), 2,189
Banister, William, 7,494
Banister, William C., 17,093
Banister, Zilpah Polly (Grant) [Mrs. William] (1794-1874), 7,224, 7,493, 7,494, 7,496
Bank employees, 5,552
Bank of America, Woman's Banking Department (San Francisco, CA), 1,226
Bank of Augusta, 15,735
Bank of New York, 2,493
Bank of Pennsylvania (Pittsburgh, PA), 15,221
Bank of South Carolina, 15,441
Bank Street College of Education (NY), 674, 11,819, 12,048
Bank Street School (NY), 11,898
Bankatewa, Patrick, 16,877
Bankers, 257, 3,778, 3,923, 4,078, 4,095, 4,477, 4,479, 4,603, 4,707, 4,899, 4,951, 6,450, 6,638, 6,833, 7,469, 7,625, 7,680, 8,333, 8,719, 8,949, 9,028, 9,367, 9,401, 9,435, 9,501, 9,860, 10,748, 10,985, 11,037, 11,040, 11,129, 11,396, 11,440, 11,750, 12,069, 12,203, 12,383, 12,463, 12,467, 12,490, 12,619, 13,339, 13,930, 14,000, 14,026, 14,114, 14,284, 14,552, 14,709, 15,011, 15,221, 15,441, 16,040, 17,118, 17,185, 17,370
Bankers, Afro-American, 15,889
"Bankers Circular, The," 12,407
Bankhardt, Frederick, 14,325
Bankhead, John Hollis, II, 76

Bankhead, Marie (1869-1958). See Owen, Marie (Bankhead) [Mrs. Thomas M.] (1869-1958)
Bankhead, Tallulah Brockman (1902-68), 60, 61, 12,708, 13,008
Bankhead, William Brockman (1874-1940), 60, 61, 76
Bankruptcy, 1,809, 4,767, 8,934, 9,048, 9,857, 11,454, 12,246, 12,402, 12,554, 15,768
Banks and banking, 194, 1,226, 3,751, 4,479, 6,582, 6,673, 8,224, 8,333, 8,974, 9,501, 11,746, 11,896, 17,222. See also Bankers; Investment banking; Safe-deposit companies
Banks and banking, cooperative. See Credit unions
Banks and banking, women's, 6,945
Banks, Anna DeCosta, 15,430
Banks Family (MO), 9,906
Banks Family (SC), 15,828
Banks, Lucille Webb (1874-1966), 15,882
Banks, Lynn Stanton (1830-65), 9,906
Banks, Mary Rogers [Mrs. Lynn Stanton] (1833-1903), 9,906
Banks, Mr. (WA), 17,133
Banks, Mrs. M. L., 15,828
Banks, Sarah Gertrude (1839-1926), 7,719, 8,020
Banks, Virginia, 17,235
Banky, Vilma, 13,810
Bannarn, Henry, 9,252
Banner (IN), 4,538
Banner (TN), 15,966
Banner Boys, 14,144
Banner Publishing Company (NY), 11,407
Banner With a Strange Device, A (mss), 6,046
Banning, Margaret (Culkin) (1891-), 5,985, 8,428, 9,255
Bannister, Nettie (ca. 1868-?), 4,703
Bannistor, Nicholas, 15,478
Banyar Family, 12,342
Banyer, Maria (Jay) [Mrs. Goldsborough] (1702-1856), 11,795
Baptism, by force, 7,539
Baptist Association of Mississippi, 5,420
Baptist associations, 3,456, 3,458, 13,645
Baptist Church (Cherokee, IA), 4,701
Baptist Church (Chelsea, MI), 7,720
Baptist Church (Chelsea, MI), Women's Missionary Society, 7,720
Baptist Church (Hunterdon County, NJ), 12,378
Baptist churches, 1,802
  clergy, 1,487, 3,320, 5,205, 5,823, 8,304, 9,088, 9,697, 11,039, 12,966, 13,144, 13,957, 15,182, 15,184, 15,187, 16,362, 16,365
  clergy, Native American, 14,174
  education, 13,300
  government, 8,849
  membership, 13,636
  missionaries, 563, 2,017, 2,018, 5,710, 8,304, 8,870, 11,039, 11,056, 12,784, 12,788, 13,288, 13,635, 13,642, 13,643, 14,443, 14,459, 16,383, 17,196, 17,285, 17,301, 17,632
  missions, 563, 3,453, 8,034, 8,304, 8,870, 10,499, 11,039, 12,738, 13,641, 13,643, 14,443, 14,459, 15,394, 15,396, 16,383, 17,285, 17,301
  publishing, 3,454, 13,434
  societies, etc., 1,802, 3,453, 4,512, 5,203, 8,032, 8,033, 8,034, 8,035, 8,304, 10,499, 12,738
Baptist Convention (1880), 13,398
Baptist Female University (NC), 13,552
Baptist General Conference, 8,849
Baptist, Julia, 10,432
Baptist Ladies' Sewing Society, 1,726
Baptist Memorial Hospital (MO), employees, 239
Baptist Missionary Society (GA), 3,453
Baptist Missionary Society (MA), 8,304
Baptist Women's Missionary Society, 2,446
Baptist Women's Missionary Society (GA), 4,512
Baptist Women's Missionary Union, 13,434
Baptist Young People's Union (MS), 9,811
Baptists, 3,149, 3,168, 3,170, 3,267, 3,454, 3,457, 5,202, 5,420, 8,914, 9,070, 9,553, 10,936, 12,787, 13,398, 13,635, 14,173, 14,302, 15,718, 16,345, 16,382
Baptists, Afro-American, 13,644
Baptists, German, 16,365
  clergy, 16,362, 16,365

effect of World War I upon, 16,365
Baptists, Japanese, 17,301
Bar associations, 1,723, 1,782, 2,163, 4,076, 4,094, 4,533, 5,068, 5,175, 5,394, 6,467, 6,533, 6,789, 6,819, 7,174, 8,036, 8,828, 9,128, 9,525, 9,956, 10,440, 14,007, 15,358, 16,789, 17,260
Baraduc, Jeanne, 12,506
Baraka, Imamu Amiri (1934-), 11,221, 12,894
Barbe, Lizzie (Spiegel) [Mrs. Martin] (1856-?), 4,039
Barbeau, Rose [Mrs.] (1844-?), 8,939
Barbee, Mrs. Joshua, 9,984
Barber, Bette E. (?-1968). See Hammer, Bette E. Barber [Mrs. Harry] (?-1968)
Barber, C. W. [Miss], 3,006
Barber, George, 11,780
Barber, Jackson, 816
Barber, Janet, 5,465
Barber, Sister Josephine, 4,342
Barbot, Blanche Hermine [Madame], 15,444
Barbour, Harriot Buxton (1901-), 5,986
Barbour, Louise, 6,383
Barbour, Margaret Hart (Bailey) [Mrs. Paul], 2,016
Barbour, Thomas, 6,321, 6,322
Barbour, Willie Louise, 5,465
Barbourville College (WV), students, 5,313
Barcelon, Adelaide. See Martin, Adelaide (Barcelon)
Barcelon y Alvarado, Alta Gracia y (1840-1946), 1,062
Barclay, Julia Ann (Sowers) [Mrs. James Turner] (1813-1908), 15,904
Barclay, Katie, 14,618
Barclay Mission (GA), 3,140
Barclay Sewing Circle (GA), 3,253
Bard, Caroline, 11,941
Bard, Dorothy (Thompson) [Mrs. Josef] (1894-1961). See Thompson, Dorothy. [Mrs. Josef] Bard [Mrs. Sinclair] Lewis [Mrs. Maxim] Kopf (1894-1961)
Bard, Ehrgott, 1,507
Bard, Sally, 11,941
Bard, Samuel, 11,941
Bard, Sara (Field) [Mrs. Ehrgott] (1882-1974). See Wood, Sara (Field) [Mrs. Ehrgott] Bard [Mrs. Charles Erskine Scott] (1882-1974)
Bard, Susan. See Sands, Susan (Bard)
Barden, Emily [Mrs.], 8,239
Barden, Graham A., 13,272
Bardin, James, 9,631
Bardin, Mary Jane (Collins) [Mrs. James], 9,631
Bardwell, Mrs., 6,487
Barel, Constant Beauvais [Mrs. Pierre M. E.] (1866-1938), 5,418
Barel, Pierre M. E., 5,418
Barette, Leonore Gale (1880-?), 14,283
Barger, Fereba (Frost) [Mrs. William H.] (1818-1900). See Beatty, Fereba (Frost) [Mrs. William H.] Barger [Mrs. John Eli] (1818-1900)
Barger, William H., 16,590
Barili, Alfredo (1854-1935), 3,367
Barili, Emily Vezin [Mrs. Alfredo] (1856-1940), 3,367
Barili, Louise Vezin (1880-), 3,367
Barili School of Music (GA), 3,367
Baring Brothers and Company, 12,407
Barker, Agnes [Mrs. Charles P.], 17,506
Barker, Anna Miller (Newkirk) [Mrs. James W.] (1841-1918). See Place, Anna Miller (Newkirk) [Mrs. James W.] Barker [Mrs. James Keyes] (1841-1918)
Barker, Anna Morris, 14,515
Barker, Belle B., 14,515
Barker, Burt Brown, 6,384
Barker, Catherine (1806-?), 4,733
Barker, Charles P., 17,506
Barker, Clara [Mrs. Herbert C.], 17,506
Barker, E. Florence, 2,196
Barker, Elizabeth (1764-1858). See Rotch, Elizabeth (Barker) (1764-1858)
Barker Family (OR), 14,515
Barker, Florence (1891-?), 153
Barker, Frances Dana (1808-84). See Gage, Frances Dana (Barker) [Mrs. James L.] (1808-84)
Barker, George R., 14,515
Barker, Herbert C. (1872-1912), 17,506
Barker, James W., 11,020
Barker, Jennie Meta [Miss], 3,145

Barker, Laura Pindall Adair [Mrs. William M.], 14,515
Barker, Lillian Marion (1888-1968), 3,230, **3,368**
Barker, Mary Cornelia [Miss] (1879-1963), **3,308,** 3,347, 8,071
Barker, Mercy Truth (1835-1922). *See* Keetch, Mercy Truth (Barker) [Mrs. Charles Greenwood] (1835-1922)
Barker, Mrs. George R., 14,515
Barker, Nancy, **16,591**
Barker, Shirley (1911-65), **10,848**
Barker, Tommie Dora (1888-), 3,308
Barker, Veda Pauline (1898-). *See* Mason, Veda Pauline (Barker) [Mrs. Mirl Reese] (1898-)
Barker, William Morris, 14,515
Barkley, J. H., 5,331
Barkley, Marianne, **5,331**
Barkluff, Hattie V. [Miss], **4,734**
Barland, Betsy (1807-88). *See* Moffat, Betsy (Barland) [Mrs. George] (1807-88)
Barland School of Home Making, 6,188
Barlett, Bessie Herbert (?-1959). *See* Frankel, Bessie Herbert (Barlett) (?-1959)
Barlow, Anabella [Mrs.], 12,431
Barlow, Della [Miss], **13,256**
Barlow, Elizabeth (Haven) [Mrs. Israel] (1811-91), **16,592**
Barlow, Emma Louise, 17,125
Barlow, Ida. *See* Trotter, Ida (Barlow)
Barlow, J. L., 14,573
Barlow, Jennie. *See* Harding, Jennie (Barlow) [Mrs. George A.]
Barlow, Joel (1754-1812), 1,397
Barlow, Ruth (Baldwin) [Mrs. Joel] (1756-1818), 1,397
Barnard Club of the City of New York, **12,159**
Barnard College (NY), 4,167, 11,825, 11,890, 11,910, 12,159, 12,737, 12,740, 13,811
   alumnae, 2,542, 2,872, 11,053, 11,956, 12,042
   archives, **11,820**
   deans, 6,173
   faculty, 6,928, 12,047, 12,049
   students, 1,652, 2,481, 3,514, 11,698
   trustees, 12,632
Barnard, Daniel D. (1796-1861), 2,190
Barnard, E. Henry, 2,190
Barnard, Ebenezer, Jr. (1748-1827), 2,190
Barnard, Edith. *See* Delano, Edith (Barnard) [Mrs. James]
Barnard, Elizabeth, **8,211**
Barnard Family (CT, NY), **2,190**
Barnard, Harriet (1787-1847), 2,190
Barnard, Julia. *See* Hannaford, Julia (Barnard)
Barnard, Kate [Miss] (1875-1930), 14,248
Barnard Labor Education Program, 15,332
Barnard, Martha. *See* Reed, Martha (Barnard) [Mrs. Hezekiah H.]
Barnard, Sophia Griswold [Mrs. E. Henry], 2,190
Barnard, Sophye, 4,781
Barnard Summer School for Workers, 17,588
Barnard, Timothy (1756-1847), 2,190
Barndt, Elizabeth Williams, 10,714
Barnes, Anna, 14,995
Barnes, Carolina Gustafva (Roos) [Mrs. Frank] (1853-1910), 9,322
Barnes, Caroline (1807-83). *See* Crosby, Caroline (Barnes) [Mrs. Jonathan] (1807-83)
Barnes, Catherine Dean (1914-). *See* Bedell, Catherine Dean (Barnes) [Mrs.] May [Mrs.] (1914-)
Barnes, Christian [Mrs. Henry], **2,191**
Barnes, Clifford Webster (1864-1944), **3,798**
Barnes, Clive, 12,364
Barnes, Djuna, 11,810, 16,163
Barnes, Earl, 11,547
Barnes, Earl, 14,995
Barnes Family (NY), **12,379**
Barnes Family (VA), **17,107**
Barnes, Gary, 14,522
Barnes, James, 12,379
Barnes, Jehue, 14,517
Barnes, Katarina (McCormick), 11,225
Barnes, Kate, 6,310

Barnes, Louisa (1802-80). *See* Pratt, Louisa (Barnes) [Mrs. Addison] (1802-80)
Barnes, Margaret (Ayer) (1886-1967), 3,994, **14,736**
Barnes, Margaret W., 17,107
Barnes, Margaret W. Tomlin [Mrs. Newman Williamson B.] (?-1859), 17,107
Barnes, Marjorie Dean Mitchell (1909-?), **8,537**
Barnes, Mary, 14,522
Barnes, Mary Downing (Sheldon) [Mrs. Earl] (1850-98), 337, 1,595, **7,922,** 11,605, 12,762
Barnes, Mrs. Jehue, 14,517
Barnes, Newman Williamson B. (?-1858), 17,107
Barnes, Philinda. *See* Bucklin, Philinda (Barnes) [Mrs. John]
Barnes, Sarah Randleman (ca. 1827-?), **9,834**
Barnes, Sudie (McAlester), **14,196**
Barnes Textile Associates (MA), **7,115**
Barnes, Verda W., 2,701
Barnes, Virginia (Grant), **7,722**
Barneson, Pauline, 1,114
Barnett, Alice. *See* Stevenson, Alice (Barnett) [Mrs. George Roy]
Barnett, Alice T., 10,055
Barnett, Claude A. (1889-1967), **3,799,** 3,800
Barnett, Etta (Moten) [Mrs. Claude A.], 3,294, **3,800**
Barnett, Henrietta Octavia [Mrs.] (1851-1936), 4,003
Barnett, Ida Bell [Mrs. James] Wells [Mrs. Ferdinand Lee] (1862-1931). *See* Wells-Barnett, Ida Bell. [Mrs. James] Wells [Mrs. Ferdinand Lee] (1862-1931)
Barney, Anna Louise, **952**
Barney, Edna Locke, **1,371**
Barney, Elvira (Stevens) [Mrs. John S.] Woodbury [Mrs. Oliver B.] Huntington [Mrs. Royal] (1832-1909), **16,593**
Barney, Eunice. *See* Mitchell, Eunice (Barney) [Mrs. Benjamin]
Barney, Jane, 11,653
Barney, John, 1,837
Barney, L. Dreyfus, 15,310
Barney, Mary Allen, **8,256**
Barney, Nora (Stanton) [Mrs. Morgan], 1,837
Barney, Rhoda. *See* Jenkins, Rhoda (Barney)
Barnhart, Josephine, 9,091
Barnsley, Godfrey (1805-72), **2,966**
Barnsley, Julia. *See* Baltzelle, Julia (Barnsley)
Barnson, Zella. *See* Matheson, Zella (Barnson) [Mrs. Simon Alva]
Barnum and Bailey Circus. *See* Ringling Brothers and Barnum and Bailey Circus
Barnum, Caroline Cornelia (1833-1911). *See* Thompson, Caroline Cornelia (Barnum) [Mrs. David W.] (1833-1911)
Barnum, Lucy, 8,301
Barnum Museum (CT), 1,827
Barnum, Phineas T., 1,588, 1,823, 1,828, 17,491
Baron de Hirsch Fund, **7,525**
Barr, Agnes, **16,034**
Barr, Amelia Edith (Huddleston) (1831-1919), 16,097, 17,010
Barr, Katharine L. Kennedy [Mrs. John H.] (ca. 1863-?), **8,944**
Barr, Margaretta, 2,046
Barr, Mary (1853-1922). *See* Munroe, Mary (Barr) [Mrs. Kirk] (1853-1922)
Barr, Mildred, 9,809
Barr, William, 16,034
Barrabee, Marcia, **7,723**
Barratt, Marietta, 1,972
Barre Methodist-Episcopal Church (MA), 5,894
Barre Plains Chapel Association (MA), 5,894
Barre School Committee (MA), 5,895
Barreda, Rosa, 1,339
Barrell, Abigail, 11,942
Barrell, Charlotte. *See* Forbes, Charlotte (Barrell)
Barrell Family (Barbados, British Guiana, England, United States), **11,942**
Barrell, Sarah "Sally" Sayward (1759-1855). *See* Wood, Sarah "Sally" Sayward (Barrell) [Mrs. Richard] Keating [Mrs. Abiel] (1759-1855)
Barrell, Theodore, 11,942
Barrell, Walter, 11,942
Barrett, Alice E. [Mrs. Martin], **10,276**
Barrett, Clifton Waller, **17,053**

Barrett, Daisy, 2,198
Barrett, Dorothy (Pye), 16,797
Barrett, Elizabeth (1806-73). *See* Browning, Elizabeth (Barrett) [Mrs. Robert] (1806-73)
Barrett, Elizabeth B., **8,301**
Barrett, Ellen Marie, 12,085
Barrett, Evelyn (1891-1969). *See* Britten, Evelyn (Barrett) [Mrs. Walter] (1891-1969)
Barrett, General, 8,709
Barrett, Janie (Porter) [Mrs. Harris] (1865-1948), 3,302
Barrett, John (1866-1938), **2,192**
Barrett, John Walton, 2,192
Barrett, Kate Harwood (Waller) [Mrs. Robert South] (1857-1925), **2,193,** 8,669
Barrett, Marjorie [Mrs. William] (ca. 1886-), 7,510
Barrett, Martha Osborne (1827-?), **7,342**
Barrett, Martin, 10,276
Barrett, Mary X. (Ferguson) [Mrs. John Walton], 2,192
Barrett, Mrs. Halsey V., 12,070
Barrett, Reba. *See* Smith, Reba (Barrett)
Barrett, Robert South, 8,669
Barrett, Sara Randolph. *See* Bourne, Sara Randolph (Barrett)
Barrett, William H., Jr., 3,111
"Barrie and Daughter," 5,304
Barrie, James M., 2,330
Barrier, Fannie (1855-1944). *See* Williams, Fannie (Barrier) [Mrs. S. Laing] (1855-1944)
Barringer, Emily (Dunning) (1876-1961), 11,754
Barringer, Paul B., **13,327**
Barringer, Susanna Elisabeth [Mrs.], **12,945**
Barritt, Frances Auretta (Fuller) [Mrs. Jackson] (1826-1902). *See* Victor, Frances Auretta (Fuller) [Mrs. Jackson] Barritt [Mrs. Henry Clay] (1826-1902)
Barritt, Jackson, 862
Barron, Bertie R. (ca. 1880-), **16,329**
Barron, Jennie (Loitman) (1891-1969), **6,385**
Barron, Ruby, 16,329
Barrow, Clara, 2,967
Barrow, David Crenshaw, **2,967**
Barrow, David Crenshaw (1852-1929), 3,058, **3,126**
Barrow, Ella, 2,967
Barrow, Lucy, 2,967
Barrow, Mrs. James, Jr., 12,237
Barrow, Nancy (1812-85). *See* Pilcher, Nancy (Barrow) (1812-85)
Barrows, Alice Prentice (1878-1954), **5,615**
Barrows, Asenath B. (Vaill) [Mrs. Freeman], 9,835
Barrows, D. N., 9,686
Barrows, David Prescott, 525
Barrows, Ella (1898-). *See* Hagar, Ella (Barrows) [Mrs. Gerald Hanna] (1898-)
Barrows Family (MO), **9,835**
Barrows, Freeman, 9,835
Barrows, G. L. (1847-92), 10,897
Barrows, John, 9,835
Barrows, Mary Prentice (Lillie), 3,872
Barrows, Sarah, 9,835
Barrows, Sarah Tracy, 11,655
Barrus, Clara (1864-1931), 1,589, **12,380,** 12,449, 17,010
Barry, Clemmie (1901-), 1,356, 1,357
Barry Family (PA), 15,168
Barry, J. M., 13,871
Barry, J. Nielson, 14,594
Barry, Jane Powell (1925-), **5,987**
Barry, John, 15,168
Barry, Leonora Marie (Kearney) [Mrs. William E.] (1849-1930). *See* Lake, Leonora Marie (Kearney) [Mrs. William E.] Barry [Mrs. Obadiah Read] (1849-1930)
Barry, Mother Gerald, 7,694
Barry, Rachel. *See* Young, Rachel (Barry) Burnap
Barry, Sarah Austin [Mrs. John] (1754-1831), 15,168
Barry, Sister, 1,513
Barrymore, Ethel, 2,968, 3,100, 11,449, 11,453, 11,997, 12,129, 12,798, 16,149
Barrymore Family, 11,689
Barrymore, John, 12,610
Barsis, Olga, 2,491
Barsness, Nellie N., 9,323

Barstow, Alfred, **338**
Barstow, David Pierce, **339**
Barstow, Elizabeth Drew (1823-1902). *See* Stoddard, Elizabeth Drew (Barstow) [Mrs. Richard Henry] (1823-1902)
Barstow, Helen Augusta (1831-1924). *See* Whitney, Helen Augusta (Barstow) [Mrs. William Frank] (1831-1924)
Barstow, Marjorie. *See* Greenbie, Marjorie Barstow [Mrs. Sydney]
Barstow, William A., 17,595
Bartelme, Mary Margaret (1864-1954), 3,785, 4,165
Bartels, Marlene [Mrs. Don], 10,404
Barter, 16,452, 16,486
Barth Family (MO), **9,836**
Barth, Moses, 9,836
Bartholomew, Bryan, 4,971
Bartholomew Family (IA), **4,971**
Bartholomew, Harriet Ward [Mrs. Bryan], 4,971
Bartholomew, Ruth (1899-1969), **11,371**
Bartine, Mary Oakley [Miss] (1879-), **10,938**
Bartles, Nannie (Journeycake) (1843-1924), 14,173
Bartlesville High School (OK), 14,173
Bartlett, Abby Kane (DeWolf) [Mrs. Enoch] (1794-1842), 7,616
Bartlett, Ada. *See* Taft, Ada (Bartlett) [Mrs. Lorado]
Bartlett, Alice H., 2,376
Bartlett, Alice W. *See* Stimson, Alice W. (Bartlett) [Mrs. Henry Albert]
Bartlett, Carleton T., 641
Bartlett, Caroline Gardner [Mrs.] (1868-1934?), **10,793**
Bartlett, Edith, 17,498
Bartlett, Eliza Ann, **4,885**
Bartlett, Enoch, 7,616
Bartlett, Etta. *See* Vaughn, Etta Bartlett
Bartlett Family (CT), **1,958**
Bartlett Family (MA), 1,399
Bartlett, Frances Jane (McCulloh) [Mrs. Carleton T.], 641
Bartlett, George F. Hunter (1836-1931), **11,335**
Bartlett, Harriett M. (1897-), **8,636,** 8,665, 8,677, 8,683
Bartlett, Henry E., 11,666
Bartlett, Jennie, 11,543
Bartlett, Jessie (1859-1905). *See* Davis, Jessie (Bartlett) [Mrs. William James] (1859-1905)
Bartlett, Joseph H., 7,336
Bartlett, Josiah, **10,794**
Bartlett, Julia S., **1,399**
Bartlett, Latane (1916-). *See* Lambert, Latane (Bartlett) [Mrs. George] (1916-)
Bartlett, Margaret Abbott, 4,482
Bartlett, Mary, 17,498
Bartlett, Mary [Mrs. Josiah], 10,794
Bartlett, Mary (Buffum), 11,943
Bartlett, Mary Leeds Leffingwell (1850-1929). *See* Macdonald, Mary Leeds Leffingwell (Bartlett) [Mrs. Duncan Black] (1850-1929)
Bartlett, Mary (North) [Mrs. Roswell] Wright [Mrs. Henry E.], 11,666
Bartlett, Patty (1795-1892). *See* Sessions, Patty (Bartlett) [Mrs. David] (1795-1892)
Bartlett, Paul Wayland (1865-1925), **2,194**
Bartlett, Suzanne (Earle) [Mrs. Mahlon Ogden] Jones [Mrs. Samuel Franklin] Emmons [Mrs. Paul Wayland], 2,194
Bartlett, Vashti, 5,735
Bartlett, Willard (1846-1925), **11,943**
Bartlette, Sarah (French), 2,338
Bartling, Daniel, 4,352
Bartling, Harriet Ann (1811-40). *See* Buckmaster, Harriet Ann (Bartling) [Mrs. Nathaniel] (1811-40)
Bartling, Henry Tauzin, 4,352
Bartling, Mary (Tauzin) [Mrs. Daniel], 4,352
Barton, Ann Elizabeth (Jennison) [Mrs. William Sumner] (1827-69), 7,641
Barton, Bathsheba, **2,195**
Barton, Clara (1821-1912), **340**, 707, 900, **1,400**, 1,585, 2,009, **2,196**, 2,454, 2,972, 3,993, **4,791**, **6,386**, 7,044, **7,188**, 7,203, 7,556, **7,600**, 7,670,

8,831, 9,023, 9,373, 11,185, 14,062, **14,860,** 15,230, **17,596**
Barton, Clara Harlowe. *See* Barton, Clara
Barton, Clarissa Harlowe. *See* Barton, Clara
Barton, Eliza Anderson, 16,417
Barton, Esther Cox, 14,824
Barton, Florence Loring [Mrs.], 9,460
Barton, Ida Adelia (1847-1911). *See* Riccius, Ida Adelia (Barton) [Mrs. Adolf Gustav] (1847-1911)
Barton, Joab, 9,855
Barton, Lizzie, **7,724**
Barton, Malvina, **14,721**
Barton, Mary O. (1862-1964). *See* Luckie, Mary O. (Barton) [Mrs. S. Blair] (1862-1964)
Barton, Mrs. Theodosius, 3,564
Barton, Sally Ann, **11,071**
Barton, Sarah, 11,941
Barton, Sarah (ca. 1748-1817). *See* Murphy, Sarah (Barton) [Mrs. William] (ca. 1748-1817)
Barton, Stephen E., 2,196
Barton, Theodosia (?-ca. 1800). *See* Burr, Theodosia (Barton) Prevost [Mrs. Aaron] (?-ca. 1800)
Barton, Thorp, 15,588
Barton, William E., 2,196
Barton, William Sumner, 7,641
Bartow High School (FL), 2,868
Bartram, Isaac, 14,956
Bartram, John (1699-1777), 14,956
Bartram, Sarah, 14,956
Bartram, William (1739-1823), 14,956
Bartuska, Doris, 15,134
Baruch, Bernard, 12,553, 17,473
Bary, Helen Valeska [Miss] (1888-1973), **341**, 2,700
Barzee, Cleopatra (1892-). *See* McIntire, Cleopatra (Barzee) [Mrs. E. William] (1892-)
Bascom, Ethel (?-1974). *See* Sarjeant, Ethel (Bascom) (?-1974)
Bascom, Ezekiel Lysander (1779?-1841), 7,601
Bascom, Florence R. D. [Miss] (1862-1945), 608, 2,310
Bascom, Josephine Davis (?-1925), 15,106
Bascom, Ruth (Henshaw) [Mrs. Ezekiel Lysander] (1772-1848), **7,601**
Base Hospital Number 32 (Contrexeville, France), 4,258
Base Hospital Number 35, 14,778
Base Hospital Number 36, 14,778
Base Hospital Number 49, 14,778
Base Hospital Number 66, 14,778
Base Hospital Number 91 (France, 1918-19), 8,310
Baseball, 7,332
Baseball clubs, 11,405, **15,320**
Basford Family (MN), 8,927
Bashford, Herbert (1871-1928), **342**
Bashkirtseff, Marie (1860-84), **14,779**
Basic Nursing Defense Program, 8,045
Baskerville, Jessie B., **3,369**
Basket making, 7,012
Basketball, 8,544, 9,979
Basketball for women, 5,062
Baskin, Inez, 3,799
Baskin, Marjorie (Kinnan) [Mrs. Charles A.] Rawlings [Mrs. Norton] (1896-1953). *See* Rawlings, Marjorie (Kinnan) [Mrs. Charles A.] [Mrs. Norton] Baskin (1896-1953)
Baskin, Norton Sanford, 2,876, 12,800
Bass, Althea, **14,197**
Bass, Charlotta, 1,011, 4,970
Bass, Lorraine, 289
Bass, Sarah Ann (1827-1921). *See* Cooke, Sarah Ann (Bass) (1827-1921)
Basserman, Maude, 6,111
Bassett, Charlotte, 12,035
Bassett Family (MI), 8,020
Bassett, Joel B. (1817-1912), **8,940**
Bassett, Mary A., 9,323
Bassett, Mrs. Victor, 3,046
Bassett, Rachel, 2,044
Bassett, Sara Ware (1872-1968), **5,908**
Bassett, Victor Hugo (1871-1938), 3,046, **3,482**
Bastrop County Historical Society (TX), 16,176
Batavia, American travelers in, 6,907
Batavia Woman's Club (IL), 3,743
Batchelder, Amos, 343

Batchelder Family, **343**
Batchelder Family (IA, KS), **4,972**
Batchelder, Harriet Kipp Gearhart [Mrs. Joseph Mayo], 4,972
Batchelder, Isabella (1819-1901). *See* James, Isabella (Batchelder) (1819-1901)
Batchelder, Joseph Mayo, 4,972
Batchelder, Maria (?-1868). *See* Tuttle, Maria (Batchelder) [Mrs. Charles Albion] (?-1868)
Batchelder Mary Wellington, **5,909**
Batchelder, Nelly Alden. *See* Hassam, Nelly Alden (Batchelder)
Bateman, Ella Louise (Trowbridge) [Mrs. Warner M.] (ca. 1848-1906), **13,840**
Bateman, Mary E., **9,588, 12,946**
Bateman, Warner M., 13,840
Bates, Ann, 15,670
Bates, Anna May Lamb (1877-1953), **7,725**
Bates, Anson (1799-?), 1,885
Bates, Blanche Lyon. [Mrs. Milton F.] Davis [Mrs. George] Creel (1873-1941), 3,100
Bates, Carlos (1808-78), 1,885
Bates, Carol [Miss], 9,962, 10,174
Bates College (ME), 5,995
Bates, Daisy, 13,176
Bates, David, 5,347
Bates, Elizabeth (Fetzer) (1909-), 16,780
Bates, Estella, 8,944
Bates, Esther W., 12,739
Bates Family (CT), **1,885**
Bates Family (SC), 15,652
Bates, Flora (1806-?). *See* Metcalf, Flora (Bates) (1806-?)
Bates, George C., 16,812
Bates, Gladys E. [Mrs. Kenneth] (1895-), **12,889**
Bates, Helen Belfield. *See* Van Tyne, Helen Belfield (Bates) [Mrs. Josselyn]
Bates, James H. S., 14,318, 17,170
Bates, Kate (Stevens) [Mrs. Edward Wingard] Bingham [Mrs. James H. S.] (1852-1941), **14,318,** **17,164**
Bates, Katharine Lee [Miss] (1859-1929), 1,224, **7,563**
Bates, LaRue (Nielson), 16,780
Bates, Laura (1813-?). *See* Van Dorn, Laura (Bates) [Mrs. Harry] Trumbull [Mrs. Isaac] (1813-?)
Bates, Louise (1908-). *See* Ames, Louise (Bates) (1908-)
Bates, Lucy [Miss], **2,968**, 3,003, 3,020, 3,068
Bates, Mary, 17,002
Bates, Mary, 15,670
Bates, Mindwell Dorothy (1819-?), 1,885
Bates, Nancy. *See* Atkinson, Nancy (Bates) [Mrs. George Henry]
Bates, Sarah Marinda (1817-88). *See* Pratt, Sarah Marinda (Bates) [Mrs. Orson] (1817-88)
Bates, Stockton, 5,347
Bates, Therena. *See* Nicolay, Therena (Bates) [Mrs. John George]
Bathrick, Eunice (1794-1883), 7,047
Baths, public, 3,875, 4,114
Baton Rouge Business and Professional Women's Clubs, **5,411**
Batsto Furnace (NJ), **11,186**
Batten, Pluma B. [Mrs.] (1894-), **6,387**
Battey, Adrienne (ca. 1890-), **2,969,** 3,309
Battey, Martha Baldwin Allen (Smith) [Mrs. Robert] (1831-1922), 3,309
Battey, Mary. *See* Halsey, Mary (Battey)
Battey, Robert (1828-95), **3,146, 3,309**, 3,381
Battin, Lora, 14,445
Battle Creek, battle of, 16,486
Battle Creek Monument Committee, 16,648
Battle Hymn of China (book), 174
"Battle Hymn of the Republic" (song), 1,426, 1,442, 3,922
Battle, Kemp P., 13,581
Battle Lake Review (MN), 8,459
"Battle of Books" (radio program), 2,385
Battle of Flowers Association (San Antonio, TX), 16,313, **16,320**
Battle of the Overpass, 8,088
"Battle of Wilson's Creek, Memories of as a Little Girl," 4,795
Battles, Julia V. L., 9,663

Battleships, 9,032
Bauchle, Mary [Mrs.], 17,498
Baudelaire, Charles, 7,316, 12,047
Baudier, Roger, 5,493
Bauer, Catherine (1905-64). *See* Wurster, Catherine (Bauer) [Mrs. William Wilson] (1905-64)
Bauer, Frances (Myers) [Mrs. Edward E.] (ca. 1906-64), **4,379**
Bauer, Helen, 1,525
Bauer, Mother Benedicta (1803-65), 17,854
Bauer, Patti (Warashina). *See* Warashina, Patti
Baugh, Hansell, 2,969
Bauhaus, 2,727
Baum, Katrina (?-1843). *See* Mayer, Katrina (Baum) [Mrs. Christian] (?-1843)
Baum, Minette [Miss], 4,510
Baum, Willa (Klug), 657
Bauman, Mrs. Albert, **13,328**
Baumann, Eunice Nelson [Mrs.], **5,616**
Baumann, George, Family (MN), 8,920
Baumgartner, Florence Eikenberry (ca. 1900-76), **13,701**
Baumgartner, Leona (1902-). *See* Elias, Leona Baumgartner [Mrs. Nathaniel M.] (1902-)
Baur, Bertha [Mrs. Jacob], 4,066
Baxley, Catherine Virginia [Mrs.], **12,381**
Baxter, Anne, 1,025
Baxter, Bertha, 8,941
Baxter, Chauncey Luther (ca. 1858-1927), 8,941
Baxter, Edna May (1890-), **1,839**, 1,859
Baxter, Elizabeth Deuhs [Mrs. Chauncey Luther] (?-1947), 8,941
Baxter, Emily Poole (1874-1921), 5,606
Baxter, Emma Ward [Mrs. Luther Loren], 8,941
Baxter Family (GA, TX), 13,135
Baxter, James Phinney (1831-1921), **5,606**
Baxter, Jennie, 8,941
Baxter, Julia Blandina "Blandie" (1827-1902). *See* Springs, Julia Blandina "Blandie" (Baxter) [Mrs. Andrew Baxter] (1827-1902)
Baxter, Lucy, 15,601
Baxter, Luther Loren (1838-1915), Family (MN), **8,941**
Baxter, Madeleine Cummings (1879-1938). *See* Tomlinson, Madeleine Cummings (Baxter) (1879-1938)
Baxter, Mehetable Cummings (Proctor) [Mrs. James Phinney] (1837-1914), 5,606
Baxter, Nellie (ca. 1879-1950), 8,941
Baxter, Philene (?-1902), 8,941
Baxter, Sarah (Cone) (1787-1873), 5,606
Baxter, Sarah Kimball (Lewis) [Mrs. James Phinney] (1830-72), 5,606
Baxter, Sarah "Sally" Strong (1833-62). *See* Hampton, Sarah "Sally" Strong (Baxter) [Mrs. Frank] (1833-62)
Bay, J. Christian, 9,922
Bay, James Willard, Jr., 16,594
Bay, Mary Eva (LeBaron) [Mrs. James Willard, Jr.] (1867-1958), **16,594**
Bay View Club (Fenton, MI), **7,726**
Bayard Family (DE), **2,036**
Bayard, Florence (1866-1954). *See* Hilles, Florence (Bayard) [Mrs. William S.] (1866-1954)
Bayard, Jane (1772-1851). *See* Kirkpatrick, Jane (Bayard) [Mrs. Andrew] (1772-1851)
Bayard, Margaret (1778-1844). *See* Smith, Margaret (Bayard) [Mrs. Samuel Harrison] (1778-1844)
Bayard, Nicholas, 12,231
Bayard, Samuel, 2,141
Bayard, Sarah. *See* Hodge, Sarah (Bayard) [Mrs. William L.]
Bayard, Thomas Francis, 2,036
Bayes, Nora. [Mrs. Otto] Gressing [Mrs. Jack] Norworth [Mrs. Harry] Clarke [Mrs. Arthur A.] Gordon [Mrs. Benjamin L.] Friedland (1880?-1928), 3,100
Bayh, Birch Evans, 4,483
Bayles, Sarah (Staats) (1787-1870), **10,939**
Bayley, Betsy, 14,628
Bayley, Dorothy, 4,482
Bayley, Elizabeth (1774-1821). *See* Seton, St. Elizabeth (Bayley) (1774-1821)

Bayley, Mary (?-1929). *See* Pratt, Mary (Bayley) [Mrs. Joseph Hyde] (?-1929)
Bayley, William, 13,097
Bayliss, Celeste Chamberlain [Mrs. Willard] (1875-1935), **8,942**
Bayliss, Sarah Eleanor (1819-91). *See* Royce, Sarah Eleanor (Bayliss) [Mrs. Josiah] (1819-91)
Baylor, Mary, **16,035**
Baylor Nurse, The, 16,333
Baylor Round Table (TX), **16,330**
Baylor Star, The, 16,333
Baylor University (TX), 16,326, 16,329, 16,330, 16,340, 16,378
  alumnae, 16,349
  buildings, 16,339
  deans, **16,331**, 16,366, **16,382**
  department heads, 16,375
  endowments, **16,339**
  faculty, **16,328**, **16,347**, **16,358**, 16,388
  presidents, 16,337
  trustees, 16,325
Baylor University (TX), College of Medicine, 16,357
Baylor University (TX), Female College, 16,329, **16,369**, 16,385
Baylor University (TX), John K. Streckor Museum, 16,388
Baylor University (TX), Program for Oral History, 16,374
Baylor University (TX), School of Law, faculty, 16,327
Baylor University (TX), School of Nursing, **16,333**
Bayne, Margaret (1912-68). *See* Price, Margaret (Bayne) [Mrs. Hickman, Jr.] (1912-68)
Bayou Folk (book), 10,158
Bayou of Delisle (MS), 9,725
Bayou Suzette (book), 4,306
Bays, Bertie Cole [Mrs. Joshua Willingham], **5,205**
Baytown A&M Mothers' Club (TX), **16,187**
Bayview College (TX), **16,308**
Bazaars, charitable, 54, 6,837, **11,247**
BCG vaccination, 11,862
Beach, Amy Marcy (Cheney) [Mrs. Henry Harris Aubrey] (1867-1944), **5,910**, 7,267, **10,118**, 10,121, **10,835**
Beach, Anna S., 12,382
Beach, Cora M. (1878-), 17,908, **17,941**
Beach, David Nelson, 12,382
Beach, Eleanor Orbison [Mrs. Sylvester Woodbridge], 11,153
Beach, Elizabeth Jane, **9,589**
Beach, Elizabeth R. Porter [Mrs.], **12,160**
Beach Family, **12,382**
Beach, George, 1,879
Beach, Harlan Page, 12,382
Beach, Henry Harris Aubrey, 10,118
Beach, Joseph W., **11,072**
Beach, Joseph Wickliff (1822-91), 12,382
Beach, Lucy N., 12,382
Beach, Mary A. (Walkley) [Mrs. Joseph Wickliff] (1824-97), 12,382
Beach, Minnie Lee. *See* Parker, Minnie Lee (Beach) [Mrs. Joseph C.]
Beach, Myra. *See* Jordan, Myra (Beach)
Beach, Phebe Ann [Mrs. Joseph W.], **11,072**
Beach, Sylvester Woodbridge, 11,153
Beach, Sylvia [Miss] (1887-1962), **11,153**, 15,170
Beacham, Rosina [Mrs.] (1866-?), 16,486
Beacham, Sarah (1843-1909), 10,795
Beachy, Mary Swatzendruber [Mrs. Walter E.]. *See* Bender, Mary Swartzendruber [Mrs. Walter E.] Beachy [Mrs. Leroy]
Beachy, Walter E., 5,049
Beadle, George, 1,095
Beadle, W. H. H., 13,661
"Beadle's Frontier Series" (stories), 192
Beahan, Bessie DeWitt, 11,508
Beal, Alice (1886-1962). *See* Parsons, Alice (Beal) [Mrs. Hugh Graham] (1886-1962)
Beal, Charles E., 15,298
Beal, Phoebe Beers, 7,972
Beale, Elizabeth, 11,827
Beale Family, **2,197**
Beale, Sarah, 15,345
Beale Street Five (singers), 15,891

Beale, Truxtun (1856-1936), 2,197
Bealer, Emily Jane Winkler, **3,147**, **3,370**
Beall, Bettie, 16,097
Beall, Frances. *See* Knight, Frances (Beall)
Beall, Mary (Harper), **12,948**
Beall, Mrs. William J., **10,224**
Beals, Elvina S. [Mrs.], 808
Beals, Jessie Tarbox [Mrs. A. Tennyson B.] (1870-1942), 12,081
Beals, Katharine M., 9,339
Beals, Lydia (1789-1869). *See* Beecher, Lydia (Beals) Jackson (1789-1869)
Beam, Lura (1887-), 2,065, **6,388**, 7,198
Beaman, Louisa (1815-50). *See* Young, Louisa (Beaman) [Mrs. Joseph] Smith [Mrs. Brigham] (1815-50)
Beamon, Mary E. *See* Joralemon, Mary E. (Beamon)
Bean, Amanda O. (1843-1930). *See* Syford, Amanda O. (Bean) [Mrs. DeWitt N.] (1843-1930)
Bean, Catherine Ann (Bickham) [Mrs. James] (1909-), 4,055
Bean, Lillian (?-1974), 11,828
Bean, Margaret [Miss], 17,379, 17,384
Bean, Mary Florence. *See* James, Florence B. (1918-72)
Bean, Olive (Smoot) [Mrs. James William] (1860-1943), 16,559, **16,595**, 16,914
Bean, Paul W., **5,617**
Bean, Pearl, 1,663
Bean, Rose Jane. *See* Shaffer, Rose Jane (Bean)
Bean, Roy, 1,663
Beane, Ruth. *See* Irving, Ruth (Beane)
Bear River Lutheran Church (MN), 8,731
Beard, Charles, 11,123
Beard, Daniel Carter (1850-1941), **2,198**
Beard, Ezra J. H. (1842-1924), **4,735**
Beard, Frances (Birkhead) [Mrs. Cyrus] (1859-1964), **17,888**, 17,908, 17,918
Beard, Gertrude, 4,735
Beard, Grace M., **1,696**
Beard, Grace Pierson (James), **12,949**
Beard, James, 6,465
Beard, Julia (Dodge), 4,750
Beard, Lucy (Morgan), 13,089
Beard, Lura Alexander [Mrs. Ezra J. H.], 4,735
Beard, Mary (1876-1946), 2,087, **11,515**
Beard, Mary C., 2,215
Beard, Mary (Ritter) [Mrs. Charles] (1876-1958), 325, 656, 1,482, 2,085, 2,242, 2,403, 2,879, **4,520**, **6,389**, 6,399, 6,450, 6,542, 6,620, 6,692, 6,812, 6,872, 6,947, **7,189**, 7,210, 7,287, 11,123, 11,143, 11,605, 12,351, 12,739, 15,946
Beard, Richard Olding, 8,574
Beard, Theresa Virginia, 6,630
Beard, Vesta, 4,735
Bearden, Bessye [Mrs. Howard] (?-1943), **12,681**
Bearden, Howard, 12,681
Bearden, Romare, 12,681
Beardslee, Barbara, 17,006
Beardsley, Clarence B., **8,302**
Beardsley, Frances (1822-?). *See* Clark, Frances (Beardsley) [Mrs. Erasmus] (1822-?)
Beardsley, Lucy Luscombe [Mrs. Clarence B.], 8,302
Beardsley, Samuel (1790-1860), 10,948
Beardsley, W., 8,899
Beare, Thomas Marston, 12,302
Bearings for Re-Establishment, Incorporated, **17,597**
Beasley, Delilah Leontium (1871-1934), **1,240**
Beasley, Olive, **8,063**
Beath Family (ME), 7,669
Beatie, Beulah Augusta, 16,847
Beatrice, Sister (1868-1934?). *See* Bartlett, Caroline Gardner [Mrs.] (1868-1934?)
Beattie, Ellen, **8,252**
Beattie, Helen (Pruitt), 830
Beattie, Margaret Isabel (1893-1976), 344
Beatty, Bessie, 873
Beatty, Clara Smith [Mrs.] (1890-1967), 10,639, **10,644**, 10,692
Beatty, Eliza Watson Anderson (1848-1904), 14,803
Beatty, Fereba (Frost) [Mrs. William H.] Barger [Mrs. John Eli] (1818-1900), **16,590**
Beatty, Hetty Burlingame (1907-71), **14,319**
Beatty, John Eli, 16,590

Beatty, Louise Dilworth (1871-1947). *See* Homer, Louise Dilworth (Beatty) [Mrs. Sidney] (1871-1947)
Beatty, Sue (Smith), **16,499**, 16,545
Beaty, Delilah [Mrs. John], **4,792**
Beaty, John, **4,792**
Beau of Both, The (drama), 9,198
Beauchamp, Catherine, 9,931
Beauchamp, Clara, 9,931
Beauchamp, Dolly, 9,931
Beauchamp, Edwin, 9,931
Beauchamp Family (MO), **9,931**
Beauchamp, John, 9,931
Beauchamp, Lizzie (1890-), **231**
Beaumont, Abbey Louisa [Mrs.] (1803-ca. 1905), **4,736**
Beaumont, Hugh (1908-73), 6,085
Beaumont, Isa (Franklin), 486
Beaumont, Jane Lightfoot [Mrs. Charles], **11,516**
Beaumont, Matilda. *See* Greenleaf, Matilda (Beaumont) [Mrs. Daniel]
Beaupré, Olive Kennon (1883-1968). *See* Miller, Olive Kennon (Beaupré) (1883-1968)
Beauregard, Pierre Gustave Toutant (1818-93), **2,199,** 5,418
Beautiful Enemy (book), 6,118
Beautiful Lofty People (book), 13,190
Beauty contests, 1,534, 3,851, 15,186
Beauty culture, **9,483**
Beauty operators, 744, 1,906, 4,336, 9,480, **9,483,** 10,191, **10,469,** 13,217
  licenses, 1,136
Beauty, personal, 4,826, 6,523
Beauty queens, 8,476, 8,479
Beauty shops, 9,527
  law and legislation, **17,015**
Beauvais, Constant (1866-1938). *See* Barel, Constant Beauvais [Mrs. Pierre M. E.] (1866-1938)
Beauveau, Sophie. *See* Borie, Sophie (Beauveau) [Mrs. John Joseph]
Beauvoir (residence, MS), 2,296, 9,618, 9,657, 9,793, 9,795
Beaux, Cecilia (1855-1942), **2,733,** 6,185, 11,835
Beaver College (PA), faculty, 9,839
Beaver, Harriet, 3,379
Beaver, Jane, 3,379
Beaver, Mary Elizabeth (Brandon) (1840-?), **251**
Beaver Women's Suffrage Association (UT), **16,500**
Beaverton Band of Hope, Number 6 (OR), **14,516**
BeBerry Family (MS), 9,816
Bechko, Peggy Anne (1950-), **17,942**
Beck, Bertram, 8,655
Beck, Carla, 10,310
Beck, Cora Warren [Mrs.], **13,257**
Beck, Eleanor Nordhoff [Mrs. Broussais C.] (?-1966), **17,237**
Beck, Emma. *See* Coleman, Emma (Beck) [Mrs. Evans P.]
Beck, Mabel Lane (1892-1958), **7,015**
Beck, Mae Miller [Mrs.] (1891-), 94
Beck, Margaret W., 1,585
Beck, Robert F., 14,504
Beck, Sallie Didd. *See* Johnson, Sallie Didd Beck [Mrs. Joseph H.]
Beck, Sarah B., 15,619
Beck, Sarah G. [Mrs.], **12,950**
Beck, Simone, 6,465
Beckan, D'Nena Bridger, 3,131
Becker, Alice "Elsie" Theodora (Watson) [Mrs. George F.] (?-1880), 2,200
Becker, August, 16,362
Becker, Carl L., 11,526, 11,594
Becker Family (AZ), **181**
Becker, Florence S. D. [Mrs. George F.], 2,200
Becker, George F. (1847-1919), **2,200**
Becker, Gustav (1856-1959), 181
Becker, Jennie, 1,803
Becker, Lydia. *See* Hirsch, Lydia (Becker)
Becker, May Lamberton (1873-1958), **6,390**
Becker Mercantile Company (AZ), 181
Becker, Niles R., 6,519
Becker, Ruth, 1,803
Becker, Sarah Cary (Tuckerman) [Mrs. Andrew C.], 2,200

Becket, Thomas à, 15,876
Beckett, Samuel, 3,771
Beckham, Nellie, **14,517**
Beckius, Cecelia (Hammer) [Mrs. Michael], 9,154
Beckius, Michael, 9,154
Beckley, Josephine, 2,882
Beckley, Zoe, 7,868
Beckman, Ann, 17,598
Beckwith, Hazel Holland Wilson [Mrs. Robert T. Lincoln], 5,060
Beckwith, Jessie (Lincoln) [Mrs. Warren] (1875-1948). *See* Randolph, Jessie (Lincoln) [Mrs. Warren] Beckwith [Mrs. Frank Edward] Johnson [Mrs. Robert J.] (1875-1948)
Beckwith, Mary Lincoln (ca. 1898-?), 5,060
Beckwith, Robert T. Lincoln, 5,060
Beckwith, Warren, 5,060
Beckworth, James P., 17,950
Bedard, Irene R. [Mrs.] (1901-59) **8,429**
Bedell, Alice [Mrs.], **11,517**
Bedell, Caroline (1904-). *See* Thomas, Caroline (Bedell) [Mrs. Henry M.] (1904-)
Bedell, Catherine Dean (Barnes) [Mrs.] May [Mrs.] (1914-), 1,605, **17,200**
Bedell, Frederick (1868-1958), 7,311
Bedell, Harriet M., 2,931
Bedell, Henry, 17,029
Bedell, Virginia (1895-1975), 5,109
Bedford, Eliza. *See* Weakley, Eliza (Bedford) [Mrs. Samuel Davies]
Bedford Female Benevolent Sewing Society (OH), **13,908**
Bedford Mineral Springs (PA), 14,803
Bedford, Sybille (1911-), 6,023
Bedinger, Caroline Bowne (Lawrence) [Mrs. Henry] (1827-?), **6,391**
Bedinger, Henry, 6,391
Bedy-Schwimmer, Rosika [Mrs.] (1877-1948). *See* Schwimmer, Rosika (1877-1948)
Bee (Portland, OR), 14,456
Bee culture, 8,456, 16,486
Bee-Hive Girls, **12,094**
Bee, Rebecca (1815-98). *See* Turner, Rebecca (Bee) [Mrs. John C.] (1815-98)
Beebe, Clara M. Woodruff (1868-?), 16,911
Beebe, Elswyth Thane [Mrs. William] (1900-), **5,031,** 6,045, **6,103**
Beebe, Lucius, 10,677
Beebe, Margaret Maranda (Baker) [Mrs. Thomas Prentiss] (1853-1942). *See* Meredith, Margaret Maranda (Baker) [Mrs. Thomas Prentiss] Beebe [Mrs. John William] (1853-1942)
Beebe, Ruth W. [Mrs. Gilbert], 6,223
Beebe, Thomas Prentiss, 5,245
Beebe, William (1877-1962), 6,103
Beeby, Nell V. (1896-1957), 6,122
Beech Corporation, 5,239
Beech, Olive Ann, 5,239
Beecher, Catherine Esther (1800-78), 992, 1,865, 1,896, 1,950, **1,951,** 2,542, 3,797, 6,392, **6,393,** 7,183, 7,224, 7,493, 7,494, 8,526, 11,442, 11,709, 11,742, 17,689, 17,844
Beecher, Edward, 1,951
Beecher, Esther, 6,392
Beecher, Eunice White (Bullard) (1812-97), 6,392
Beecher Family, **6,392**
Beecher, Frances (Johnson) (1832-?). *See* Perkins, Frances (Johnson) Beecher [Mrs. James] (1832-?)
Beecher, Harriet Elizabeth (1811-96). *See* Stowe, Harriet Elizabeth (Beecher) [Mrs. Calvin Ellis] (1811-96)
Beecher, Harriet (Porter) (?-1835), 6,392
Beecher, Henry Ward (1813-87), 1,437, 1,896, 1,950, 3,778, 6,775, 7,430, 7,484, 10,825, 11,539, 12,003, 12,984, 14,062
Beecher, Isabella (1822-1907). *See* Hooker, Isabella (Beecher) [Mrs. John] (1822-1907)
Beecher, James C. (1828-86), **6,394**
Beecher, Julia (Jones) (1826-1905), 11,442
Beecher, Laura (1817-1900). *See* Comer, Laura (Beecher) (1817-1900)
Beecher, Lydia (Beals) Jackson (1789-1869), 6,392
Beecher, Lyman (1775-1863), 1,950, 1,951, 6,394, 6,553

Beecher, Margaret. *See* Ward, Margaret (Beecher)
Beecher, Mary (1805-1900). *See* Perkins, Mary (Beecher) [Mrs. Thomas Clap] (1805-1900)
Beecher, Mary E., 9,004
Beecher, Mary Frances (Beecher) (?-1952), 6,394
Beecher, Thomas Kinnicut, 1,950, 17,035
Beecher-Tilton case, 6,395
Beeching, Jane "Jennie" [Miss] (1855-1926), **16,596**
Beechwood Pleasant Circle (IN), **4,548**
Beed, Lottie. *See* Rohlf, Lottie (Beed) [Mrs. William A.]
Beeger, Gertrude, 1,114
Beehive, The (UT), **16,920**
Beekman, Azariah M., 11,034
Beekman, Lillian Grace [Miss] (1857-1946), **14,730**
Beeks, Gertrude Brackenridge (1867-1950). *See* Easley, Gertrude Brackenridge (Beeks) [Mrs. Ralph M.] (1867-1950)
Beeler, Emily (1838-1910). *See* Fletcher, Emily (Beeler) [Mrs. Calvin, Jr.] (1838-1910)
Beeman, Amanda, 8,989
Beeman, Eunice. *See* Chatfield, Eunice (Beeman) [Mrs. Andrew Gould]
Beer, William (1849-1929), **5,509**
Beerbohm, Max, 14,413
Beers, Sarah E., 3,755
Beery, John A., 4,792
Beery, Mary, 4,792
Beery, Noah, 4,792
Beery, Peter, 4,792
Beery, S. N., 4,792
Beeson, Martha [Mrs.], 4,773
Beetham, Asa, **2,201**
Beetham, Emily [Miss], 2,201
Beethoven Association of New York, 2,020
Beffel, John Nicholas (ca. 1895-), **8,064**
"Before Cock Crow" (story), 16,168
Begel, Father John Joseph, 15,336
Begelow, Mary Ann (Hayes) (1838-1925), 14,060
Beggar on Horseback (moving-picture), 18,003
Beggs, Helene Warder, 4,288
Beggs, Mrs. David, 14,020
Beggs, Thomas M., **2,848**
Beggs, Vera (Wadsworth) [Mrs. Frederic] (?-1968), **7,190,** 7,239, **10,940**
Behan, Mrs. W. J., 5,513
Behavior of the Newborn Infant, The (book), 14,010
Behind the Battle Line (book), 7,216
Behnke, Donna A., 3,742
Behrman, Samuel, 16,154
Behunin, Caroline (Hill) [Mrs. Mosiah Steven] (1854-1914), **16,597**
Behunin, Nancy Meribah (1839-1910). *See* Higgins, Nancy Meribah (Behunin) [Mrs. Nelson] (1839-1910)
Beidler, John X. (1831-90), 10,366
Beighley, Alice C., 1,641
Being Geniuses Together (book), 3,771
Beirne, Joseph A., 9,011
Beisel, Alice [Mrs. Robert], 8,212
Beisel, Robert, 8,212
Bel Geddes, Norman, 12,549
Belasco, David, 12,476
Belcher, Fannie S., 5,469
Belden, Anne E., Family, **14,059**
Belden, Charles F. D., 2,474
Belden, Ella Mary, 5,063
Belding Family, 14,059
Belfrage, Sally (1936-). *See* Pomerance, Sally Belfrage (1936-)
Belgian Relief Fund, 2,347
Belgium, 7,665
  cities and towns, 12,273
  German occupation, 16,780
  Mormons and Mormonism, 16,780
  school children, health and hygiene, 11,691
  World War I, 12,673
  war work, 8,436
Belgium Child Welfare Fund, 8,934
Belhaven College (MS), 9,699
Belin, Alice (1872-1944). *See* du Pont, Alice (Belin) [Mrs. Pierre Samuel] (1872-1944)
Belinson, Florence (Fenyvessy) [Mrs. Benjamin], **12,794**

Belk, Lucille M. (Bullard) [Mrs. Henry] (1895-), **13,193**
Bell, Adelaide "Addie" Merritt, 2,889
Bell, Alexander Graham (1847-1922), **2,202**
Bell, Amanda Lee [Mrs. Andrew Jackson], 9,259
Bell, Andrew (1757-1843), **12,161**
Bell, Andrew Jackson, 9,259
Bell, Anna, 2,889
Bell, Annie (Douglas), 11,091
Bell, Barbara, 9,145
Bell, Bianca Babb [Mrs. J. D.], 16,036
Bell, C. Jasper (1885-1978), **9,932**
Bell, Cara Georgina Whitmore [Mrs. William Abraham], 1,790
Bell, Catherine Jane (Mills), 345
Bell, Clara Lizette (Pierce) [Mrs. James H.] (1859-?), **5,612**
Bell, Clara Wiley [Mrs. James Hamilton], 8,945
Bell County A&M Mothers' Club (TX), **16,188**
Bell, Daisy. See Fairchild, Daisy (Bell) [Mrs. David]
Bell, Delphine [Mrs. James W.], 1,677
Bell, Eliza Grace (Symonds) [Mrs. Alexander Melville] (1809-97), 2,202
Bell, Elizabeth (Kennedy) [Mrs. Robert Mowry] (ca. 1871-?), 8,944
Bell, Elsie May (1878-1964). See Grosvenor, Elsie May (Bell) [Mrs. Gilbert] (1878-1964)
Bell, Emma [Mrs.] (1854-1913), 3,148
Bell, Eva. See Neal, Eva (Bell)
Bell Family, 9,259
Bell Family (FL), **2,889**
Bell Family (WI), **17,874**
Bell, George A. (?-1897), **6,395**
Bell, H. Anthony, 5,478
Bell, Helen Mary Hunt [Mrs. William Jefferson], 8,945
Bell, Henry Grady, 3,183
Bell House Boys (GA), **3,148**
Bell, Ione B., **8,495**
Bell, J. E., **13,329**
Bell, James Ford (1879-1961), **8,943**
Bell, James W., 1,677
Bell, Lilian (1867-1929). See Bogue, Lilian Bell [Mrs. Arthur Hoyt] (1867-1929)
Bell, Lizzie, **1,365**
Bell, Mabel Gardner (Hubbard) [Mrs. Alexander Graham] (1858-1923), 2,202, 2,420, 7,203, 17,197
Bell, Margaret, **7,727**
Bell, Margaret (Van Horn) Dwight (1790-?), **14,170**
Bell, Marian Hubbard (1880-1962). See Fairchild, Marian Hubbard (Bell) [Mrs. David G.] (1880-1962)
Bell, Martha McFarlane [Mrs. John] McGee [Mrs. William] (?-1820), **13,219**
Bell, Mary, 11,294
Bell, Mrs., 582
Bell, Myrtle (Johnson) [Mrs.] (1895-), **13,909**
Bell, Polly Mckean, 14,542
Bell, Portia (1901-). See Hume, Portia (Bell) [Mrs. Samuel James] (1901-)
Bell Quarterly (periodical), 6,383
Bell, Robert Mowry, Family, **8,944**
Bell, Rose, **1,697**
Bell, Rosetta Gordon Lipsia (1879-1974). See Wolcott, Rosetta Gordon Lipsia (Bell) [Mrs. Charles] (1879-1974)
Bell, Sarah M., 17,874
Bell, Susannah [Mrs. Andrew], 12,161
Bell, Theodore, 458
Bell, Thomas, **13,330**
Bell, William, 13,219
Bell, William Abraham, 1,790
Bell, William Jefferson (1888-), **8,945**
Bellamy Family (CO), **1,698**
Bellamy, Frederica (Le Fevre) [Mrs. Harry E.] (1884-1963), **1,698**
Bellamy, Harry E. (1874-1956), 1,698
Bellamy, Mary (Godat) (1861-1955), **17,889**
Belland, Henry, Family (MA), 8,981
Belle Isle Prisoner of War Camp, 5,689
Belle Meade (plantation, TN), 15,932
Belle Prairie School (MN), 8,926

Belle Springs Creamery (KS), 11,857
Belles Lettres Society, 12,863
Belles-lettres Society (NJ), 11,110
Bellevue Hospital (New York, NY), 2,384, 2,568, 3,743, 3,907, 5,326, 11,308, 11,869, **12,138**, 12,260
Bellevue Hospital (New York, NY), Nurses' Training School, 2,542
Bellevue in France, Anecdotal History of Base Hospital #1 (book), 11,727
Bellinger, Emily Simms. See Reynolds, Emily Simms Bellinger [Mrs. John Schreiner, Jr.]
Bellinger, Katie, **14,518**, 14,618
Bellingham Women's Music Club (WA), **17,132**
Bello, Jane. See Biddle, Jane (Bello) [Mrs. George]
Belloc, Marie Adelaide (1868-1947). See Lowndes, Marie Adelaide (Belloc) (1868-1947)
Bellos, Sybil [Mrs. George], 1,837
Bellow, Susan, 4,109
Bellows, Mrs. George, 2,775
Bellquist, Eric E., 843
Bells, 16,353
Bells, The (TX), 16,369
Belly dancers, 4,224
Belmont, Alva Erskine Smith Vanderbilt (1853-1933), 1,507
Belmont, August (1816-89), **12,383**
Belmont, Caroline Slidell (Perry) [Mrs. August], 12,383
Belmont College (Nashville, TN). See Ward-Belmont School (Nashville, TN)
Belmont, Eleanor (Robson) [Mrs. August B.] (1879-1979), 3,100, **11,944**, 12,050, 12,078, 12,079, 12,125, 12,496
Belmont, Ira J. (?-1964), 12,601
Belmont, Mrs. O. H. P., 12,575, 12,597
Belmont School Committee, 6,729
Belmont Woman's Club (IL), 4,165
Belnap, Adaline (Knight), 16,743
Belnap, Della Augusta [Miss] (1907-?), **16,598**
Belnap, Flora [Miss] (1884-1955), **16,599**
Belnap, Marion Adaline (1886-1972). See Kerr, Marion Adaline (Belnap) [Mrs. Walter Affleck] (1886-1972)
Belnap, Mary Louise. See Lowe, Mary Louise (Belnap) [Mrs. Joseph]
Belo, Jane, 11,940
Beloit College (WI), students, 14,401
Beloit Federation of Women's Clubs (WI), 17,494
"Beloved House" (recording), 6,669
Beloved Prophet (book), 16,167
Belshaw, Maria A., 14,628
Belt, Elizabeth Talbot [Mrs.], **2,970**
Belzner, Barbara (1902-), 232
Bemidji State University (MN), administration, 8,395
Bemidji State University (MN), Campus Human Rights Commission for Affirmative Action, **8,393**
Bemidji State University (MN), faculty wives, 8,394
Bemis, Caroline, 7,343
Bemis, Charles A., 3,661
Bemis, Martha (Wheatland) [Mrs. R. E.] (1807-?), **7,343**
Bemis, Polly [Mrs. Charles A.] (?-1933), 3,661
Bemo, John Douglas, 14,244
Bemo, Katie (Edwards) [Mrs. John Douglas] (1848-1933). See Mitchell, Katie (Edwards) [Mrs. John Douglas] Bemo [Mrs. L. S.] (1848-1933)
Ben (slave, NC), 2,124
Ben Follows Old Trails (book), 17,369
Ben Hur (book), 4,615
Benary-Isbert, Margot (1889-), 8,531, **14,320**
Benaszeski, Linda (1949-), **16,334**
Bench, Nancy Elvira (Cox) (1882-1964), **16,600**
Benchley, Robert, 11,867
Bendel, Henri, 12,086
Bendel, Winifred. See Stuart, Winifred (Bendel)
Bender, Albert M. (1866-1941), **1,081**, 1,082, 2,204, 2,628
Bender, Flora I., **10,645**
Bender, Ida C., 11,378
Bender, Lauretta (1897-), **11,308**
Bender, Leroy, 5,049

Bender, Mary Swartzendruber [Mrs. Walter E.] Beachy [Mrs. Leroy], **5,049**
Bender, Rose I. (Magil) (1895-1964), **14,908**
Bendick, Jeanne (1919-), **14,321**
Bendl, Gerta [Mrs.], **5,376**
Benedek, Therese, 3,914
Benedict, Agnes E., 2,205
Benedict, Ann (Kendrick), 12,524
Benedict, Anne (Scales) (1883-1958), **15,926**
Benedict, Cornelia, 6,998
Benedict, Enella, 4,056
Benedict, Francis G., 11,656
Benedict, Harriet, 8,303
Benedict, Mary Esther (1847-66). See Bitner, Mary Esther (Benedict) [Mrs. Breneman Barr] (1847-66)
Benedict, Mary March, 8,719
Benedict, Mrs. Elliott S., 11,449
Benedict, Ruth (Fulton) [Mrs. Stanley Rossiter] (1887-1948), 920, 2,166, 2,833, 2,834, 2,840, 14,886, 14,894, 14,897
Benedict, Stephen (1927-), **5,128**
Benedict, Vida Grenville Meister, 11,336
Benedictine Convent of Perpetual Adoration (St. Louis, MO), 10,138
Benedictine Convent of St. Martin (Rapid City, SD), 15,866
Benedictine Institute of Sacred Theology (Collegeville, MN), 10,138
Benedictine Sisters (MN), 9,323
Benedictine Sisters of Florida (St. Leo, FL), 2,920
Benedictine Sisters of Our Lady of Sorrows (Oak Forest, IL), 4,308
Benedictine Sisters of Pittsburgh (PA), 15,211
Benedictine Sisters of Pontifical Jurisdiction, Holy Family Convent (Benet Lake, WI), 17,499
Benedictine Sisters of Pontifical Jurisdiction, St. Bede Priory (Eau Claire, WI) 17,500
Benedictine Sisters of Sacred Heart Convent (Yankton, SD), 15,870
Benedictine Sisters of Virginia, 17,052
Benedictine Sisters, Queen of Angels Priory (Mount Angel, OR), 14,494
Benedictine Sisters, Sacred Heart Convent (Cullman, AL), 24
Benedictine Sisters, Sacred Heart Priory (Richardton, ND), 13,726
Benedictine Sisters, St. Gertrude Priory (Ridgely, MD), 5,851
Benedictine Sisters, St. Joseph Convent (Tulsa, OK), **14,259**
Benedictine Sisters, St. Scholastica Convent (Fort Smith, AR), **272**
Benedictine Sisters, St. Scholastica Priory (Covington, LA), **5,427**
Benedictine Superiors' Retreat and Novitiate Workshop (1953), 10,138
Benedum, Michael Late (1869-1959), **11,833**
Benedum, Pearl, 11,833
Benedum, Sophie, 11,833
Benefield, Hattie Stone [Mrs.], 1,525
Benét, Elinor Morton [Mrs. Philip] Hichborn [Mrs. Horace] Wylie [Mrs. William Rose] (1885-1929). See Wylie, Elinor Morton (Hoyt). [Mrs. Philip] Hichborn [Mrs. Horace] Wylie [Mrs. William Rose] Benét (1885-1929)
Benét, Laura, 7,209, 7,210, **11,309**
Benét, Marjorie Flack [Mrs. William Rose] (1897-), 12,537
Benét, Rosemary (Carr) [Mrs. Stephen Vincent] (1900-60), 2,216, 12,695
Benét, Stephen Vincent, 2,617, 4,482, 11,309, 11,944, 15,900, 18,021
Benét, William Rose, 2,658, 4,476, 4,482, 7,209, 7,221, 11,309, 12,642
Benevolent societies. See Charitable societies
Benfell, Edith Annie (1893-). See Gold, Edith Annie (Benfell) [Mrs. Cyrus Williams] (1893-)
Benham, Edith (1874-1962). See Helm, Edith (Benham) (1874-1962)
Benicia Young Ladies Seminary (CA), alumnae, 350
Benitt, Carsten, Family (MN), **8,946**
Benitt, Catherine (?-1780), 8,946
Benitt, Gierdt, 8,946

Benitt, Katherine, 8,946
Benitt, Linda (James) [Mrs. William A.], 8,947
Benitt, Peter, 8,946
Benitt, Rebecca, 8,946
Benitt, William A., Family (MN), **8,947**
Benjamin, Anna Northend, **7,344**
Benjamin, Blanche Grimshaw [Mrs. Arthur Edwin] (1870-1951), 8,948
Benjamin, Cornelia Juliaette. *See* Hagan, Cornelia Juliaette (Benjamin)
Benjamin, Elizabeth Garner [Mrs. John] (1830-1900), 8,948
Benjamin Franklin Butler Proclamation, **5,480**
Benjamin Franklin High School (NY), 3,437
Benjamin Franklin, Printer and Patriot (book), 5,041
Benjamin, Jeanette Smith, **7,728**
Benjamin, John (1823-?), Family (MN), **8,948**
Benjamin, Lucy Fassett (Robinson) (1822-1901). *See* Phelps, Lucy Fassett (Robinson) Benjamin [Mrs. Winthrop H.] (1822-1901)
Benjamin, Lulu [Mrs. E. E.] (1864-?), **10,277**
Benjamin, Mary Brower (Western), 11,945
Benjamin, Mary Gladding (Wheeler) [Mrs. Nathan], 11,945
Benjamin, Mary Judith (Gall) (1777-1848). *See* Lanman, Mary Judith (Gall) Benjamin [Mrs. James] (1777-1848)
Benjamin, Park, 11,945
Benjamin, Paul Lyman (1886-), **8,637**
Benjamin Sewall (ship), 6,831
Benjamin, Theodosia, 1,641
Benjamin West's Painting of Penn's Treaty with the Indians (book), 15,302
Benn, Mrs. Harold W., 17,967
Benners, John, **12,384**
Bennet, Belva Ann (1830-1917). *See* Lockwood, Belva Ann (Bennet) [Mrs. Uriah] McNall [Mrs. Ezekiel] (1830-1917)
Bennett, Alice (1851-1925). *See* Bennett, Mary Alice [Miss] (1851-1925)
Bennett, Anna, 300
Bennett, Audree Lauraine (1927-). *See* Norton, Audree Lauraine (Bennett) [Mrs. Ken] (1927-)
Bennett, Augustus P., **12,385**
Bennett, Bryant, 2,124
Bennett College (Greensboro, NC), **13,215**
alumnae, 15,914
Bennett, Dilys (1906-60). *See* Laing, Dilys (Bennett) [Mrs. Alexander Kinnan L.] (1906-60)
Bennett, Dorothy Agnes (1909-), 8,566
Bennett, Elizabeth, **2,124**
Bennett, Elizabeth H., **12,386**
Bennett, Ella Costillo (1865-1932), **346, 1,241, 1,699**
Bennett, Elmer F., 1,790
Bennett Family, 4,942
Bennett Family (NY), 11,709
Bennett, Fay, 8,112
Bennett, Genie F. (Carey) [Mrs. Augustus P.], 12,385
Bennett, Gertrude Ryder, 5,465
Bennett, Gwendolyn, 3,290, 5,465
Bennett, Helen, 4,066
Bennett, Henry Holcomb, 6,396
Bennett, Ismena (Densmore) (1798-1887), 9,041
Bennett, John (1865-1956), 6,396, **15,445**
Bennett, Kay, 11,231
Bennett, LaVerne, 4,132
Bennett, Louis, 17,450
Bennett, Louis, Jr., 17,450
Bennett, Malvina A. (Hart) [Mrs. William Kirby], 1,533
Bennett, Marion Tinsley (1914-), **9,933**
Bennett, Martha T. (1867-?), **6,396**
Bennett, Mary, **11,518**
Bennett, Mary A. [Miss], 10,623
Bennett, Mary Alice [Miss] (1851-1925), 17,678
Bennett, Mary E., 8,170
Bennett, Mary Katharine (Jones) [Mrs. Fred Smith] (1864-1950), 15,173
Bennett, Mary L., 346, 1,241
Bennett, Maxine, 15,134
Bennett, May (1870-1960). *See* Avery, May (Bennett) [Mrs. Samuel] (1870-1960)
Bennett, Mrs. John, **15,446**
Bennett, Philip Allen (1881-1942), 9,933

Bennett, Raphael, 346
Bennett, Ray, 1,241
Bennett, Sallie Maxwell [Mrs. Louis], **17,450**
Bennett, Sarah E., 5,805
Benning, Augustus H. (1840-1904), **3,149**
Benning Coal Company (GA), 3,149
Benning, Margaret Rowena (Russell) [Mrs. Augustus H.], **3,149**
Bennington College (VT), 12,737, 16,986, 16,988, 16,989, 16,990, 16,991, 16,992, 16,994, 16,995, 16,996, 17,045, 17,046
administration, **16,992**, 16,993
curricula, 16,988
faculty, 12,642
Bennington College (VT), Educational Counseling Committee, 16,989
Bennington College (VT), Office of Alumnae Service, **16,991**
Bennington School of Dance (VT), **16,987**
Bennion, Amelia Eliza (Slade) [Mrs. Alfred] (1854-1936), 16,601
Bennion, Desla Slade, **16,601**
Bennion, Mary. *See* Powell, Mary (Bennion)
Bens, Gwendolyn T. [Mrs.], **12,387**
Bense, Evangeline Isabelle [Miss], 12,388
Bense Family, **12,388**
Bense, J. Anne [Miss], 12,388
Benson, Anne (1898-). *See* Fisher, Anne (Benson) [Mrs. Walter Kenrick] (1898-)
Benson, Elizabeth English [Miss] (1904-72), **2,102**
Benson, Elmer Austin (1895-), **8,949**
Benson, Naomi Achenbach, **17,238**
Benson, Pamelia Frances (Loomis) [Mrs. Simon] (1865-1945), **14,519**
Benson, Simon, 14,519
Benson, Stella (1892-1933). *See* Anderson, Stella Benson [Mrs. James C. O'Gorman] (1892-1933)
Benson, Zoella (Palmer) [Mrs. Lamont], **16,401**
Bentham, Josephine, 11,165
Bentivoglio, Annetta (1834-1905). *See* Bentivoglio, Mother Mary Magdalen (1834-1905)
Bentivoglio, Mother Mary Magdalen (1834-1905), 8,414
Bentley, Anna (Briggs) [Mrs. Caleb?] (1796-?), 5,746
Bentley, Anna R., 12,238
Bentley, Anne Mary, 14,212
Bentley, Delich, 1,937
Bentley, Ellice Marie (1887-). *See* LeBaron, Ellice Marie (Bentley) [Mrs. William Farland] (1887-)
Bentley, Mary Ann (Mansfield) [Mrs. William Oscar], (1859-1949), **16,602**
Bentley, Nancy, 10,081
Bentley, William, 7,472
Benton House (Chicago, IL), **3,801**
Benton, Jessie Ann (1824-1902). *See* Frémont, Jessie Ann (Benton) [Mrs. John Charles] (1824-1902)
Benton, Maybell (Williams) [Mrs. John], 2,884
Benton, Patricia (1907-), **5,988**
Benton, Thomas Hart, 488, 680, 1,426, 1,430, 2,337, 9,929, 12,481, 15,900
Benton, William, 11,839
Bentzon, Theodore. *See* Blanc, Marie Therese (de Solms) (1840-1904)
Benz, Rose Matz, 1,319
Benzell, Mimi (1924-70), **17,943**
Benzonia Academy (MI), 7,706
Bequest From a Life (book), 7,198
Berch, Laura, 17,282
Berckman, Evelyn Domenica (1900-), 6,060
Berdahl, Evelyn, 8,784
Berdahl, Jennie Marie. *See* Rølvaag, Jennie Marie (Berdahl) [Mrs. Ole Edvart]
Berea College (KY), faculty, 5,251
Berenson, Bernard (1865-1959), 2,762, 4,491, 6,023, 6,185, 14,745
Berenson, Mary [Mrs. Bernard], 2,170, 2,762
Berg, Alban, 468
Berg, Gertrude (Edelstein) [Mrs. Lewis] (1899-1966), **12,890**
Berg, Johanne [Mrs. Ole-Iver], 8,739
Berg, Norman S., 3,075
Berg, Ole-Iver, 8,739
Berg, Patty, 4,700

Berg, Portia Willis, 7,312
Bergen, Christine [Mrs.] (1900-73), **17,444**
Bergen, Laura, 11,780
Berger, Meta [Mrs.], 17,749
Berger, Mother Mary Odilia (1823-80), 10,189
Berger, Sophie, 12,117
Bergh, Bolette Stub [Mrs. Johannes E.] (1852-1940), **8,723**
Bergland, Matilda (Christensen), 8,994
Bergman, Alan (1925-), 17,944
Bergman, Ingrid, 12,129
Bergman, Marilyn (Keith) [Mrs. Alan], **17,944**
Bergquist, Edith [Miss], 8,865
Bergsma, Nancy-Jane Nickerson [Mrs. William Lawrence], 1,587
Bergsma, William Lawrence, 1,587
Bering, Ada. *See* Wien, Ada (Bering)
Berk, Lane (1928-), 5,828
Berkeley Council of Camp Fire Girls (CA), 882
Berkeley Day Nursery (CA), 348
Berkeley fire (CA, 1929), 362
Berkeley High School (CA), 648
Berkeley Relief Committee (CA), **347**
Berkeley Sexual Freedom League, 8,207
Berkeley Street School (MA), **6,397**
Berkeley Street School Association (MA), **6,398**
Berkeley Suffrage Campaign Committee (CA), 530
Berkeleys and Their Neighbor, The (book), 17,098
Berkin, Solomon, 11,897
Berkman, Alexander (1870-1936), 6,028, 12,487, **12,699**
Berkow, Ira, **4,053**
Berkowitz, Ida (1892-), **17,744**
Berkshire County Suffrage Commission (MA), 1,948
Berkshire Hills (book), 7,509
Berkshires, The (book), 2,338
Berle, A. A., 12,553
Berle, Milton, 4,764
Berlin, Ben, 1,124
Berlin, Elaine, 11,774
Berlin, Ellen (Mackay) [Mrs. Irving], 12,843
Berlin, Irving, 12,843
Berman, Edward L., 12,362
Berman, Louise (Rosenberg) Bransten, 943
Berman, Theresa Beatrice [Mrs. Nathan] (1912-), 9,254
Bermuda, American singers in, 5,911
Bernadette of Lourdes, 15,876
Bernadette of Lourdes (book), 17,604
Bernadine, 14,335
Bernard, Bessie, 13,579
Bernard, Bessie (1862-1932). *See* Shields, Elizabeth (Smallwood) [Mrs. Bernard C.] (1862-1932)
Bernard, Helen, 15,324
Bernard, Jacqueline [Mrs.], **17,600**
Bernard, Jessie R. [Mrs. Luther Lee] (1903-), **15,323**, 15,324
Bernard, Joel, 17,600
Bernard, Luther Lee (1888-1951), **15,324**
Bernard, Mary Chenaille (1911-) 7,109
Bernardine Sisters, Generalate (Villanova, PA), **15,337**
Bernays, Anne F., 2,205
Bernays, Doris Elsa (Fleischman) [Mrs. Edward L.] (1891-), 2,205, **6,399**, 12,708, 14,377
Bernays, Edward L. (1891-), **2,205**, 11,897
Bernays, Thelka Mary (1856-1931), **10,154**
Bernhagen, Beatrice (1910-67), **8,638**
Bernhard, Dorothy Lehman, 12,069
Bernhard, Minnie, 17,282
Bernhardt, Sarah. [Mrs. M. Jacque] Damala (1845-1923), 605, 3,100, 3,889, 3,921, 6,185, **6,400**, 7,310, 10,025, 10,651, 11,459, 11,689, 11,897, 12,129, 12,539, 12,798, 17,197
Bernheim, Andre, 1,576
Bernhard, Mrs., 2,176
Bernstein, Barbara, 11,916
Bernstein, Jeannette Warsharsky (1896?-), **13,765, 17,890**
Bernstein, Leonard (1918-), 6,023, 12,013
Berri, Maud Lillian (1871-1958), **967**
Berrien, John McPherson, 12,168
Berrien, Laura M., **6,401**
Berries, 11,189
Berro, Rosa Scharhon, 17,282

Berry, Carrie, **3,150**
Berry, Charles Henry (1823-1900), 9,520
Berry, Eliza (Usher) [Mrs. William Augustus], **12,951**
Berry, Elizabeth Wright (Gould) [Mrs. William Bogardus], 11,633, 11,719, 11,734
Berry, Ella (1879-). *See* Leigh, Ella (Berry) [Mrs. William H.] (1879-)
Berry Family, 11,734
Berry Family, 6,650
Berry Family (MN), **9,520**
Berry Family (NY), **11,520**
Berry, Frances Eliza (Hubbel) [Mrs. Charles Henry], 9,520
Berry, Frances Miriam (1811-52). *See* Whitcher, Frances Miriam (Berry) [Mrs. Benjamin W.] (1811-52)
Berry, Hanna Shwayder, 1,786
Berry, Harriet Esselstyn. *See* Tyson, Harriet Esselstyn (Berry) [Mrs. James Wood]
Berry, Harriet Morehead [Miss] (1877-1940), **12,952**
Berry, Helen (Godfrey) [Mrs. Mark] (1839-1902), 9,099
Berry, Hilda Truslow (1916-). *See* Sanford, Hilda Truslow (Berry) (1916-)
Berry, Josephine T., 8,596
Berry, Kate. *See* Morey, Kate (Berry) [Mrs. Charles Anson]
Berry, Leanor, 2,443
Berry, Madeline, 8,676
Berry, Margaret, 8,651, 8,668
Berry, Martha McChesney [Miss] (1866-1942), 3,071, 3,117, **3,484**, 3,509
Berry, Modena (Lowrey) (1850-1942), 9,543
Berry, Olive (Nutting), 11,734
Berry, Romeyn, 11,644, 11,734
Berry, Ruth Seely (1913-). *See* McDonald, Ruth Seely (Berry) [Mrs. William Naylor, III] (1913-)
Berry Schools (GA), 3,476, 3,484
Berry, Walter, 4,491
Berry, William Augustus, 12,951
Berry, William Bogardus, 11,644
Berryman, Virginia (Smith), 1,534
Bersheba Presbyterian Church (SC), 15,571
Bertha Schaefer Gallery (NY), **2,734**
Berthelot, Helen W., **7,729**, 7,904
Bertin, Elizabeth, 2,520
Bertram, Julia (Godman) (1907-). *See* Ruuttila, Julia (Godman) Bertram Eaton (1907-)
Bertram, Lucy E., 2,196
Bertsche, William, Jr., 10,366
Bery, R. E., **16,603**
Besant, Annie (Wood) (1847-1933), 12,877, **14,751**
Bess, Maggie May Smith [Mrs.], 16,441
Bessesen, Beatrice (Gjertsen) [Mrs. William A.] (1886-1935), **8,950**
Bessesen, William A., 8,950
Bessie Mell Industrial Home (GA), 3,082, **3,083**
Besson, Babette, 13,331
Besson Family (NC), **13,331**
Best, Adelia Haughton [Mrs. Michael] (1838-1911), 14,132
Best Family (CA), 1,566
Best, Helen. *See* Anderson, Helen (Best)
Best, Isabella Playfair, 1,566
Best, Margaret, **14,132**
Beston, Elizabeth (Coatsworth) [Mrs. Henry] (1893-), 5,694, **11,337**
Beta Sigma Phi, 16,911
Betenson, Annette (Webster) [Mrs. Leland Stanley] (?-1971), **16,402**
Betenson, Lula Parker [Mrs.] (ca. 1880-), 16,485
Beth Israel Sinai Congregation Sisterhood (Racine, WI), **17,555**
Beth Meyer synagogue (NC), 13,472
Bethany College (KS), 4,319
Bethany College (Bethany, WV)
   archives, **17,430**
   students, 4,599
Bethany Congregational Church (Minneapolis, MN), Ladies Aid Society, **8,951**
Bethany Day Nursery Shelter, 2,421
Bethany Home (MN), 9,424

Bethany Lutheran Church (Remer, MN), Ladies' Aid Society, **8,952**
Bethel Colony, 2,464
Bethel Union Church (Honolulu, HI), 3,640
Bethell, Mary (Jeffreys) (1821-?), **12,954**
Bethers, Almira (Tiffany) [Mrs. Albert Francis] (1888-1966), **16,604**
Bethers, Jean Orme [Mrs. Pratt M.], **16,403**
Bethers, Pratt M., **16,403**
Bethesda Orphan Home, 3,488
Bethlehem Community Center (Chicago, IL). *See* Howell Neighborhood House (Chicago, IL)
Bethune-Cookman College (FL), 5,458
Bethune, Mary Jane (McLeod) (1875-1955), 127, 556, 2,502, 2,602, 2,685, 2,879, 2,931, 3,280, 3,283, 3,302, 3,303, 3,785, 3,830, 3,969, 5,122, **5,458**, 5,465, 5,828, 5,870, 8,116, 10,203, 11,812, 12,066, 12,681, 13,217
Betow, Emma J., 10,580
Betrothal, 13,424
Betsey Ross Club (PA), 14,946
Betsy-Tacy children's books, 8,489
Betsy-Tacy Day, 8,492
Bettelyoun, Susan Bordeaux (1857-?), **10,433**
Betten, Beatrice Argetsinger [Mrs. Cornelius], **11,521**
Betten, Cornelius, 11,521
Better America Federation, 7,187
Better Babies Movement, 16,127
Better Films Committee (GA), 3,224
Better Health Foundation (Durham, NC), 5,466
Better Homes in America, Inc., 5,122
Betteridge, Ellen Sarah Ballingham (1882-), 16,953
Betteridge, Mary Hadfield, 16,953
Bettle, Jane (Temple) [Mrs. Samuel] (ca. 1774-1840), **14,837**
Bettle, Samuel, 14,837
Betton, Elizabeth Ellis (Prescott) [Mrs. Charles], **7,345**
Betts, Doris June Waugh (1932-), **5,989**
Betts, Emma (1837-?). *See* Sterling, Emma (Betts) [Mrs. Frederick A.] (1837-?)
Betts, Howell P., 3,033
Betts, Lula [Mrs.], 3,033
Betts, Ruth (Teal), 14,675
"Betty Ragland at Adelphai College, Boonville, MO, 1854-1855" (essay), 9,857
Betty Parsons Gallery, 2,735
Betty Zane Frontier Days (OH), **14,112**
Between Two Novels (book), 3,177
Betz, Pauline, 997
Betzold, Estelle (1875-1958). *See* Doheny, Estelle (Betzold) [Mrs. Edward Lawrence] (1875-1958)
Beukema, John C., 8,167
Beulah Bunny Tells All (book), 10,399
Beulah Home for Babies (PA), 15,251
Bevan, Elizabeth N., 12,034
Bever Mission and Industrial School (Chicago, IL), 4,069
Beverly Country Club News (IL), 3,930
Beverly Female Charitable Society (MA), **5,898**
Bevier, Henrietta Cornelia, **12,389**
Bevier, Isabel [Miss] (1860-1942), 4,378, **4,380**
Bevington, Helen (Smith) [Mrs. Merle M.] (1906-), **13,190**, 13,511
Bewick, Clara Dorothy (1846-1916). *See* Colby, Clara Dorothy (Bewick) [Mrs. Leonard Wright] (1846-1916)
"Bewitched" (television program), 17,809, 17,958
Bewley, Lula Mary, **16,037**
Bewley's Bewitched (book), 15,720
Beyer, Audrey White [Mrs. Walter], 5,694
Beyer, Clara E. (Mortenson) (1892-), 2,700, **6,402**, 6,766, 6,848, 11,771
"Beyond Herself" (ms), 8,456
Beyond Our Selves (book), 2,476
Beyond the Blues (book), 2,145
Bezler, Anna Katherina (1832-1930). *See* Dicke, Anna Katherina (Bezler) [Mrs. Peter Heinrich] (1832-1930)
Bianchi, Martha Gilbert Dickinson, 5,861
Bianco, Margery (Williams) [Mrs. Francesco] (1881-1944), 12,570
Bibb Family (KY), 5,268

Bibb, John Booker (1789-1884), 5,268
Bibb, Mary (1782-1819). *See* Lewis, Mary (Bibb) [Mrs. Gabriel Jones] (1782-1819)
Bibbens Family (NY), **11,522**
Bibbens, Susan (1803-90). *See* Fox, Susan (Bibbens) [Mrs. Jonathan] (1803-90)
Biberman, Herbert (1900-), **17,792**
Bible
   publication and distribution, societies, etc., **2,046**
   societies, 2,009, **3,808**, 5,745, **5,760**, 8,914, 15,221
   study, 1,843, 2,116, 3,080, 3,872, 5,229, **8,487**, 10,571, 12,133
   translating, 1,877, 13,280, 14,243, 14,246
Bible colleges, 3,969, **3,970**
Bible Faith Mission, 7,064
Bibles, **15,829**
Biblical Recorder, 13,573
Bibliographers, **1,912**, 4,402, **7,654**, 7,681, 10,152, 12,593
Bibliographers, Afro-American, **17,693**
Bibliography, **3,707**, 4,048
   rare books, **6,813**, 7,660, **11,921**
"Bibliography of Dime Novels, 1860-1964," 192
Bibliography of Latvian Publications Outside Latvia, 1955, 8,604
"Bibliomania 1955," 8,586
Biblioteca Femina, 6,876, 7,293
Bibliotherapy, 123
Bicentennial celebrations, 8,728
Bickerdyke, Hiram, 2,206
Bickerdyke, James, 2,206
Bickerdyke, Mary Ann (Ball) "Mother" [Mrs. Robert] (1817-1901), **1,242**, **2,206**, 3,922, **4,248**
Bickett, Mrs. Thomas, 13,398
Bickham, Catherine Ann (1909-). *See* Bean, Catherine Ann (Bickham) [Mrs. James] (1909-)
Bickham, Edith Baker Reid [Mrs. Martin H.] (1877-ca. 1960), 4,055
Bickham, Emma Hayes (1915-). *See* Pitcher, Emma Hayes (Bickham) [Mrs. William] (1915-)
Bickham, Frances Louise (1922-). *See* Boyle, Frances Louise (Bickham) [Mrs. John] (1922-)
Bickham, Maria, 13,910
Bickham, Martin H. (1880-1976), **4,055**
Bickham, William D., Family (OH), **13,910**
Bickley, Beulah Vick, **9,590**
Bickmore, Christina (Bagley) [Mrs. William] (1809-80), **16,605**
Bidamon, Emma (Hale) [Mrs. Joseph, Jr.] Smith [Mrs. Lewis C.] (1804-79), 10,088, **10,092**, 16,641, **16,822**, 16,889
Bidamon, Lewis C. (1806-91), 10,088, 10,092
Biddie, Mary Minus, 2,946
Biddle, Ann (1757-1807). *See* Wilkinson, Ann (Biddle) [Mrs. James] (1757-1807)
Biddle, Anne "Nancy" (Coleman) [Mrs. George], 2,207
Biddle Family (NC), 12,962, **13,573**
Biddle Family (PA), 14,957, 15,104
Biddle Family (PA), **15,269**
Biddle, George (1885-), **2,207**
Biddle, Gertrude Gouverneur (Meredith), 14,829
Biddle, Grace Brosius, 15,269
Biddle, Hélène Sardeau [Mrs. George] (1899-), 2,207
Biddle, Henry D., 15,022
Biddle, Jane (Bello) [Mrs. George], 2,207
Biddle, Jane (Craig), 14,957
Biddle, John, 15,025
Biddle, Mary (Baird), 14,749
Biddle, Mrs. Edward W., 14,819
Biddle, Nicholas (1786-1844), 14,957
Biddle, Ora Patterson, **17,434**
Biddle, Rosa, 13,573
Biddle, Sally, 15,025
Biddle, William, 15,025
Biddlecom, Emma (1862-1951). *See* Sweet, Emma (Biddlecom) [Mrs. Fred G.] (1862-1951)
Bidgood, Maria (1832-?). *See* Ford, Maria (Bidgood) [Mrs. William] Jarman [Mrs. Robert Henry] (1832-?)
Bidwell, Annie Ellicott (Kennedy) [Mrs. John]

(1839-1918), 349, 491, 740, **953**, 955, 956, **1,153, 1,243**, 1,635
Bidwell, Daniel, 740
Bidwell Family (CA), **349**
Bidwell, John (1819-1900), 349, 491, 740, 953, 1,243
Biederman, Faye, 8,983
Bierce, Ambrose, 657
Bierce, Helen Ray (1875-?). *See* Cowden, Helen Ray (Bierce) (1875-?)
Bierce, Lora, 712
Bierstadt, Eliza, 9,841
Biester, Alice (1890-1969), **8,538**
Big Billy (slave, SC), 15,530
"Big Little Books," 192
Big Little Sister program (IL), 4,219
Big Oak Flat Road, The (book), 1,386
Big Sister Association, Inc.(MN), 8,583
Big Sister Association, Inc. (OH), **13,988**
Bigamy, 987, 9,972
Bigelow, Alice, 6,698
Bigelow, Hayes (1879-1956), Family, **14,060**
Bigelow, Louise, **7,602**
Bigelow, Mira Anne, 7,652
Bigelow, Mrs. A. J., 8,363
Bigelow, Mrs. J. W., 12,208
Bigelow, Pauline, 2,605
Bigelow, Russell A., 14,060
Bigelow, Susan Sturgis, 6,655
Bigelow, Suzanne, 16,971
Biggar, Elizabeth (1846-83). *See* Hart, Elizabeth (Biggar) [Mrs. Alexis Crane] (1846-83)
Biggart, Mabell, 16,314
Biggers, Caroline, 13,300
Biggs, Frankland (1877-1944), **11,073**
Biggs, Londa, **10,646**
Bigler, Bathsheba Wilson (1822-1910). *See* Smith, Bathsheba Wilson (Bigler) [Mrs. George A.] (1822-1910)
Bikur Cholim Sisterhood (WA), 17,282
Bilanksy, Anne Evards [Mrs. Stanislaus] (?-1860), 9,317
Bilansky, Mary Ann Evards Wright, 9,303
Bilbo, Linda (Gaddy), 9,709
Bilbo, Theodore G., 9,658, 9,688
Biles, Susan Isobel. *See* Drew, Susan Isobel (Biles)
Bill, Annie Cecilia (Bulmer) (1861-1936), **1,401**
Bill, Betsy Orcutt Davis [Mrs. Epaphras Chapman] (1826-57), 8,953
Bill, Clara McMaster [Mrs. Fred] (1852-1928), 8,953
Bill, Fred Adelbert, Family (MN), **8,953**
Bill, Jessie May (1878-?). *See* Clark, Jessie May (Bill) [Mrs. Harry] (1878-?)
Bill Keane, 17,947
Billau, Harriet (1868-1956), **14,061**
Billboards, 4,977
Billbrough, Marion. *See* Dreamer, Marion (Billbrough)
Billed-Magazin (periodical), 8,724
"Billie's Blues" (song), 5,530
Billings, Addie Melvina Stephenson (1858-1948), **6,403**
Billings, Florence (1879-1959), **7,191**
Billings, Frederica (Wade) [Mrs. John Shaw] (1901-63), 15,565
Billings, Frederica Wade, II, 15,565
Billings, Gretchen G. [Mrs.], 10,354
Billings, Harriet Elizabeth (1836-1927). *See* De Claire, Harriet Elizabeth (Billings) [Mrs. Hector Auguste] De Claire (1836-1927)
Billings, John Shaw (1898-1975), **15,564, 15,565**
Billings, Katharine (Hammond) [Mrs. John Sedgwick]. **15,566,** 15,600
Billings, Laura [Miss], 15,670
Billings, Lucy M., 1,751
Billings, Sara, **17,601**
Billings, Warren K., 12,702
Billington, Gertrude Weed, 3,595
Billone, Carol Jean [Miss] (1943-), **2,103**
Bills, Ella Mae Donohoo (1896-), **16,878**
Bills, Hattie M., **16,921**
Bills, legislative, 7, 1,010, **1,141,** 2,075, 2,356, 2,693, 2,697, 2,764, 3,622, 3,722, 4,149, 5,149, 5,313, 6,715, 6,944, 6,990, 8,205, 9,120, 9,225, **9,232,**
9,263, 9,452, 9,467, 9,560, 9,932, 10,168, 10,194, 10,658, 11,610, 12,910, 13,449, **14,251,** 14,994, 15,315, 15,686, 15,959, 15,971, 16,498, 17,376
Bills of lading, 7,664
Billups, Ida (Sykes) [Mrs. Thomas Carlton] (1858-91), 9,812
Billups, Joseph (1893-), **8,065**
Billups, Joseph Saunders, 9,812
Billups, Rose [Mrs. Joseph], 8,065
Billups, Thomas Carlton (1839-98), 9,812
Billups, Wildie (Sykes) [Mrs. Joseph Saunders], 9,812
Billy Graham Crusade, 14,231
Billy the Kid, 11,215, 11,227
Biloxi News (MS), 9,756
Bimetallic Association, 1,702
Bimetallism, 1,702, **10,558**
Binckley, Charlotte Stoker, 2,208
Binckley, John Milton, **2,208**
Binckley, Mary (Michel) [Mrs. John Milton], 2,208
Binder, Carroll, 9,426
Binder, Dorothy (Walton) [Mrs. Carroll] (1894-), 9,426, 9,427
Binford Family (NC), **13,221**
Binford, Helen [Mrs. Raymond] (1885-1952), 13,221
Binford, Jessie Florence (1876-1966), 3,828, 3,833, 4,047, 4,052, 4,066, 4,104, 4,114, 4,141
Bingham, Abel (1786-1865), **8,304**
Bingham, Angelina, 8,304
Bingham, Clarissa (Brewster) [Mrs. Hiram, II], 3,638
Bingham, Edward Wingard, 14,318
Bingham Family (HI), **3,638**
Bingham Family (MO), **9,837**
Bingham, Frances Payne (1885-). *See* Bolton, Frances Payne (Bingham) (1885-)
Bingham, George Caleb, 9,837
Bingham, Hannah [Mrs. Abel], 8,304
Bingham, Hannah Maria, 8,304
Bingham, Hiram (1789-1869), 3,638
Bingham, Hiram, II, 3,638
Bingham, Julia Scribner, 2,875
Bingham, June (Rossbach) [Mrs. Jonathan] (1919-), 2,513
Bingham, Kate (Stevens) [Mrs. Edward Wingard] (1852-1941). *See* Bates, Kate (Stevens) [Mrs. Edward Wingard] Bingham [Mrs. James H. S.] (1852-1941)
Bingham, Lydia. *See* Coan, Lydia (Bingham) [Mrs. Titus]
Bingham, Mary (Warden) [Mrs. Kinglsey Scott], 7,730
Bingham, Sophia, 8,304
Bingham, Sybil (Moseley) [Mrs. Hiram] (1792-1848), 3,638
Bingham, William, 15,077
Bingley, Sophronia, 3,395
Binion, L. B. (1904-), **10,733**
Binner, Mabel [Miss], 3,932
Binney, Amos, 14,878
Binney, Horace (1780-1875), **14,958**
Binney, Susan, 14,958
Bio-bibliography, 420, 6,119, 11,990
Biochemists, 6,336, 14,943
Biographers, 1,493, 1,495, 2,512, 2,610, **3,368,** 7,605, 7,691, 10,483, 11,827, 12,380, **13,871,** 14,680
Biographical Encyclopedia, The, 3,003
Biographical Sketch of Sue Landon Vaughan (book), 9,759
Biography, 54, 385, 443, 699, 1,289, 1,437, 1,507, 1,785, 2,129, 2,225, 2,232, 2,301, 2,341, 2,432, 2,877, 2,927, 2,931, **4,867, 4,899, 4,958,** 5,694, 5,949, 5,951, 6,077, 6,267, 6,284, 6,514, **6,528,** 6,575, **6,611,** 6,637, 6,681, 6,801, 6,920, 6,955, 7,198, 7,680, 8,122, 8,456, 8,491, 8,493, **8,737,** 8,786, 8,798, **8,845, 9,013,** 9,360, 9,842, **9,904, 10,151,** 10,417, 10,418, 10,526, 10,636, 10,758, **10,780, 11,213,** 11,307, **11,440,** 11,489, 11,491, **11,798,** 12,500, 12,765, 13,519, 13,572, 14,197, 14,203, 14,212, 14,438, 14,599, 14,602, **14,698,** 14,854, 14,982, 15,583, 16,041, **16,044,** 16,088, 16,149, **16,967, 17,413,** 17,493, 17,771, 17,865
indexes, **5,595**
Biography of an Old Cowboy, The (book), 18,007
Biological Abstracts, 8,555
Biological chemistry, 6,141
Biologists, **1,095,** 6,009, 6,336, 6,986
Biology, 6,916
Birch, Fannie. *See* Nichols, Fannie (Birch)
Birchard, Matilda Ormond (Taylor). *See* Abbey, Matilda Ormond (Taylor) Birchard
Birchard, Sardis, 14,071
Birchman, Anna (1872-?), **14,520**
Birckhead, Mary Lockhart (Lawson), 11,602
Bird, Annie Laurie (1893-1972), **3,662**
Bird Banding, 11,665
Bird, Caroline (1915-), 15,197
Bird, Adele Antoinette Agnes (Aegerter) [Mrs. Arthur D.] (1891-1970), **16,606**
Bird-Dumont, Ella, 16,117
Bird, Ellen George (1858-?), 16,486, 16,968
Bird Family (NY), 11,440
Bird, Isabella Lucy (1831-1904). *See* Bishop, Isabella Lucy (Bird) (1831-1904)
Bird, Mary, 12,315
Bird-song, 3,764
Bird, Sophia. *See* McClelland, Sophia (Bird) [Mrs. James L.]
Bird watching, 12,973
Birds, 2,724, 3,722, 10,534, 16,304
pictorial works, 11,152
protection of, **50**
Birds and Bird Babies (book), 4,785
"Birds for Beginners" (column), 17,267
Birds of Guyana (book), 7,487
Birds of Massachusetts, The (book), 7,487
Birds of the Bible (book), 4,226
Birge, Anna Grant, 17,775
Birk, Dolores (1907-73). *See* Hitchens, Dolores (Birk) Olsen (1907-73)
Birkhead, Frances (1859-1964). *See* Beard, Frances (Birkhead) [Mrs. Cyrus] (1859-1964)
Birkhoff, George David (1884-1944), **6,266**
Birkhoff, Margaret (Grafius) [Mrs. George David] (1885-1973), 6,266
Birkley, Dolan (pseudonym). *See* Hitchens, Dolores (Birk) Olsen (1907-73)
Birkley, Hannah (Vatteng) [Mrs. Iver], **10,434**
Birkley, Iver, 10,434
Birkman, Helen. *See* Blumenthal, Helen (Birkman)
Birmingham Age (AL), 15,979
Birmingham, Alma, **4,056**
Birmingham, Beatrice (1887-1972). *See* Stanley, Beatrice (Birmingham) [Mrs. Willoughby] Mason [Mrs. Lewis V.] (1887-1972)
Birmingham, J., 350
Birmingham News (AL), 112
Birmingham Post-Herald (AL), 112
Birney, Alice Josephine (McLellan) [Mrs. Alonzo J., Jr.] White [Mrs. Theodore Weld] (1858-1907), 4,133, 17,973
Birney, Alice M. [Mrs.], 3,143
Birth announcements, 872
Birth control, **154,** 174, **735,** 827, 1,047, 1,131, 1,529, 1,596, 1,652, 1,657, 2,120, 2,451, 2,883, 3,362, 3,895, 3,981, 4,074, 4,131, 4,145, 4,409, 5,842, 6,219, 6,221, 6,222, 6,223, **6,232,** 6,355, 6,364, 6,432, 6,446, 6,475, 6,602, 6,736, 6,846, 6,968, 6,978, **6,987,** 7,178, 7,189, **7,197,** 7,199, **7,283,** 7,284, 7,287, **7,289,** 7,294, 7,312, 7,317, 7,320, 7,920, 8,635, 8,647, 8,662, 8,699, **8,826,** 9,299, 9,440, 9,930, 11,017, 11,118, 12,652, **12,736,** 12,837, 13,430, 13,604, 13,725, 14,013, **14,221,** 14,637, 14,806, 14,897, 15,251, 17,659, 17,663, 17,787, 17,843. *See also* Abortion
law and legislation, 5,739, **6,404,** 6,564, 9,440
legal aspects, 7,192, 7,282, 7,289
religious aspects, 7,192, 7,283, 7,287
Catholic Church, 7,283, 8,634
research, 6,223, 6,227, **7,192,** 7,282, 7,283
Birth Control Clinical Research Bureau. *See* Margaret Sanger Bureau
Birth control clinics, 4,131, **5,739,** 6,223, 6,697, 6,987, 12,829
Birth Control Federation of America, 6,221
Birth Control League of Massachusetts, **6,404,** 6,432, 7,178
Birth Control League of Monroe County (NY). *See*

Planned Parenthood of Rochester and Monroe County (NY)
Birth Control Review (periodical), 6,223, 7,284
Birthright, 4,677
Birthright, Inc. *See* Association for Voluntary Sterilization
Bisbee, Dorothy Winsor, **6,405**
Bisbee, Eleanor, **1,556**
Biscaccianti, Elisa, **1,244**
Bischler, Mother M. Anastasia (1834-1917), 4,296
Biscoe, Helen Maria (1860-1946), **6,406**
Bish, Estella (1887-1960). *See* Nelson, Estella (Bish) (1887-1960)
Bishop, A. Hamilton (1810?-79), 11,314
Bishop, Agnes (Ware) [Mrs. J. L.], 57
Bishop, Anna, 8,954
Bishop, Anna (Rivière) (1810-84), **5,911**
Bishop, Della, **11,523**
Bishop, Dorothy Hubbard [Mrs. Merlin D.] (ca. 1910-), **8,066**
Bishop, Elena Brown [Mrs. John F.] (1810-1903), 8,954
Bishop, Elizabeth (1911-), 4,227, **14,322,** 15,170
Bishop, Ellen C., **16,607**
Bishop, Emily Mulkin, 2,432, 17,715
Bishop Family (NY), **11,314**
Bishop, Flora Ellice. *See* Stevens, Flora Ellice (Bishop)
Bishop, Harriet E. [Mrs. John] McConkey (1817-83), 9,038, 9,166
Bishop, Harriette (1846-1944), **8,042**
Bishop, Helen (1874-1947), **8,042**
Bishop, Isabel. [Mrs. Harold G.] Wolff (1902-), **2,736, 11,834,** 13,836
Bishop, Isabella Lucy (Bird) (1831-1904), 1,790
Bishop, Josephine (Hall) (1841-1917), 11,262
Bishop, Judson Wade (1831-1917), Family (MN), **8,954**
Bishop, Lena, 8,954
Bishop, Martha "Missouri" (1837-81). *See* Moore, Martha "Missouri" (Bishop) [Mrs. James Preston] (1837-81)
Bishop, Mary Axtell [Mrs. Judson Wade] (ca. 1859-1953), 8,954
Bishop, Miriam. *See* Cox, Miriam (Bishop)
Bishop, Mrs. I. G., 3,592
Bishop, Robert Haven, 8,954
Bishop, Susan Holmes [Mrs. A. Hamilton] (1817-47), 11,314
Bishop Tuttle School (Raleigh, NC), **16,022**
Bishop, W. D., **13,332**
Bishop Whitaker School for Girls (Reno, NV), 10,680, 10,681
Bishops, 9,645
Bishops, Catholic, 1,516, 3,971, 4,649, 7,049, 7,694, 8,934, 8,956, 9,695, 10,611, 12,933, 14,117, 14,269, **15,152,** 15,912, **16,018**
Bishops, Episcopal, **2,225,** 2,392, 5,827, 6,176, 6,784, 9,437, **9,438,** 10,821, 12,082, **12,087,** 12,089, 12,656, 13,121, 13,451, 15,048, 15,465
Bishops, Methodist, **3,328, 3,355,** 4,208, 4,774, **6,012,** 9,991
Bishops, Mormon, 16,705
Bishops, New Jerusalem Church, 14,734
Bishops, Russian Orthodox, 2,563
Bisland, John (1742-1821), 9,729
Bismarck Civic Improvement League (ND), **13,649**
Bismarck Federation of Women's Societies (ND), 13,649
Bison, American, 1,305, 10,272, 16,060
Bissart, Ellen, 1,221
Bissell, Bess G. (1876?-1974), **4,973**
Bissell, Eleanor, **1,402**
Bissell, Emily Perkins [Miss] (1868-1948), **2,037,** 2,063
Bissell Family (CT), 1,402
Bissinger, Elizabeth. *See* Ehrman, Elizabeth (Bissinger)
Bisttram, Emil, 1,779
Bitner, Breneman Barr (1837-1909), 351
Bitner Family, 351
Bitner, Mabel E. [Mrs.], 14,813

Bitner, Martina Marjorie (Halseth) [Mrs. Breneman Barr] (1847-1912), 351
Bitner, Mary Esther (Benedict) [Mrs. Breneman Barr] (1847-66), 3423
Bitner, Sarah Ann (Osguthorpe) [Mrs. Breneman Barr] (1847-1930), 351
Bittenbender, Ada Matilda (Cole) [Mrs. Henry Clay] (1848-1925), 17,411
Bitton, Davis, **16,890**
Bixby, Abigail "Nabby" (Adams) [Mrs. Luke] (1780-1808), 5,856
Bixby Family (MA), **5,856**
Bixby, Martha Abigail Adams (1806-97). *See* Faulkner, Martha Abigail Adams (Bixby) [Mrs. Winthrop Emerson] (1806-97)
Bixby, Mrs. A. F., 8,240
Bixler, David, 1,233
Bixler, Elizabeth Augusta (Hyde) (1838-1921), 1,233
Bizallion, Henry, 16,562
Bizallion, Lotta Van Buren [Mrs. Henry] (1877-1960), **1,818**
Bizell, Pattie [Mrs. H. C.], **9,591**
Bizot, Maguy, 9,425
Bjorklund, Ellen [Miss], 13,294
Bjorlie, Liv, **13,702**
Bjørnson, Bjørnstjerne, 8,793
Bjørnson, Einar, 8,793
Bjørnson, Freda [Mrs.], 8,690
Bjurstedt, Molla, 997
Blachly, Charles Dallas, **14,198**
Blachly Family, **12,673**
Blachly, Lucile (Spire), **14,198**
Black, Algernon David (1900-), **11,946**
Black, Annie [Mrs.], **1,245**
Black Bart (drama), 442
"Black Billy" (poem), 4,620
"Black, Cool and Collected: The Story of George A. Maston" (ms), 10,531
Black Creek Church (SC), 15,631
Black Diamond Gold Mine (CO), 1,799
Black, Doris (Gregory), 10,191
Black, Elizabeth (Gundaker) [Mrs. William M.] (1823-1902), **4,348**
Black, Ellen Engelman (1903-). *See* Winston, Ellen Engelman (Black) [Mrs. Sanford] (1903-)
Black Freemasons, 12,688
Black Gauntlet, The (book), 2,566
Black, George Robinson, 3,371
Black Hand, 16,965
Black Hawk, 6,609
Black Hawk (drama), 17,687
Black Hawk College Classified Committee (IL), **4,297**
Black Hawk War (1832), 3,897, 4,352
Black, Hortense Louise. *See* Pratt, Hortense Louise Black [Mrs. Schuyler]
Black, Hugo, 64, 11,855
Black, Irma S., 674
Black, James, **16,335**
Black, James, Family (TX), **1,619**
Black, John, 17,664
Black, John L. (1805-65), 9,592
Black Legion Citizens Committee, 8,106
Black, Lizzie (1858-1940). *See* Kander, Lizzie (Black) [Mrs. Simon] (1858-1940)
Black, Lucille, 2,502
"Black Mammy" (poem), 3,040
Black, Margaret J. [Miss] (1898-), **4,686**
Black, Martha C., 6,998
Black, Mary [Mrs. John], 17,664
Black, Mary Ellen "Nellie" [Mrs. George Robison] (1851-1919), **3,371**
Black, Misses, 14,945
Black Mountain College (NC), 13,307, **13,333,** 13,335, 13,446, 13,484, 13,616
    faculty, 2,727, 2,814
Black, Mrs. A. P., 1,268
Black, Mrs. E. E., 14,945
Black, Mrs. Robert L., 11,913
Black, Mrs. William D. (1838-1910), 2,024
Black Muslims, 8,148
Black, Nancy (1846-1918). *See* Wallace, Nancy (Black) (1846-1918)
Black, Narcissa L. [Mrs. John L.] (1810-post 1884), **9,592**

Black, Nellie (Peters) [Mrs. G. R.], 3,140, **3,151,** 3,189, 3,436
Black Panthers, 15,176
Black, Patience (Crain) [Mrs. James] (1842-69), 1,619, **16,335**
Black, Persis (Sibley) [Mrs. Charles] Andrews [Mrs. Alvah] (1813-91), **5,671**
Black Power, 11,855
"Black Priest of the Andes" (song), 5,534
Black Sparrow Press, **11,221**
Black Thoughts (book), 5,260
Black/White Sex (book), 6,031
Black, Winifred (Sweet) [Mrs. Orlow] (1863-1936). *See* Bonfils, Winifred (Sweet) [Mrs. Orlow] Black [Mrs. Frederick G.] (1863-1936)
Black Woman (book), 16,982
Black Woman: A Fictionalized Biography of Lucy Terry Prince (book), 12,692
"Black Woman in America, The," 11,663
"Black Women," 11,306
Blackall, Dorothy Brewer (ca. 1890-1949), **6,407**
Blackall, Gertrude, 2,315
Blackall, Sarah, 2,315
Blackburn, Freddie [Mrs. Paul], 1,221
Blackburn, Joan [Mrs. Paul], 1,221
Blackburn, Joyce Knight (1920-), 6,070
Blackburn, Katherine C. "Casey" [Miss] (1892-1972), **11,478**
Blackburn, Kathleen Bever (1892-1968), 10,151
Blackburn, Margaret. *See* Douglas, Margaret (Blackburn) [Mrs. Henry]
Blackburn, Mary J. [Mrs.], **3,152**
Blackburn, Mrs. Luke Pryor, 5,291
Blackburn, Paul, Family, 1,221
Blackburn, Sara, 1,221
Blackburn, W. Gordon, 1,221
Blackburn, Willie, 5,466
Blacke, Mary E., 9,058
Blackfoot Indians, 10,281
Blackford, Eliza Beulah, **6,308**
Blackford, Eugene (1840-1908), 5,770
Blackford, L. M., 5,770
Blackford, Rebecca (Gordon) [Mrs. Eugene] (1841-?), 5,770
Blackfriars Theatre (NY), 9,496
Blackinger, Dorothy (Eaton), 352
Blackinton, Charlotte Palmer [Mrs. John R.] (1814-99), **7,105**
Blackinton, Helen. *See* Archer, Helen (Blackinton)
Blackinton, John R., 7,105
Blackiston, Kate, 13,387
Blackjack, Adda, **10,859**
Blacklisting, **1,547**
Blacklisting in labor, 2,284, 6,365
Blacklisting of entertainers, 11,907, **17,792, 17,805**
Blackman, Ruth, 11,440
Blackmore, Beulah (1886-1964), 11,521, 11,661
Blacks. *See* Afro-Americans *as a main entry and as a subentry*
Blackshear Family (GA), **2,965**
Blacksmithing, 7,012
Blacksmiths, 4,437, **5,682,** 13,402
Blackstone, Marguerite (Aycock), 3,451
Blackwell, Agnes. *See* Jones, Agnes (Blackwell)
Blackwell, Alice Stone (1857-1950), 2,209, 2,256, 5,334, 6,009, 6,343, **6,408,** 6,412, 6,427, 6,469, 6,535, 6,536, 6,741, 6,864, 6,867, **6,971,** 6,974, 6,980, 7,222, 7,232, 7,274, 7,284, 7,294, 7,585, 13,204, 15,283, 15,851, 17,166, 17,411, 18,013
Blackwell, Anna, 2,209, **6,409**
Blackwell, Antoinette Louisa (Brown) [Mrs. Samuel] (1825-1921), 2,209, 4,708, 6,409, **6,410,** 6,741, 7,232, 11,590, 12,790, 13,204, 14,123
Blackwell, Betsey, 9,845
Blackwell, Eliza C. *See* Mayer, Eliza C. (Blackwell) [Mrs. Charles F.]
Blackwell, Elizabeth (1821-1910), 2,209, 5,724, **6,411,** 6,412, 6,741, 6,864, 7,274, 8,531, **11,467,** 11,605, **11,947,** 12,811, 13,204, 15,144, 17,010, 18,013
Blackwell, Emily (1826-1910), 2,209, 6,411, 6,412, 6,867, 11,947
Blackwell, Emma (Lawrence), 2,209
Blackwell, Ethel. *See* Robinson, Ethel (Blackwell)
Blackwell Family, **2,209, 6,412**

Blackwell, Henry Brown (1825-1909), 1,950, 2,209, 6,412, **6,413**, 6,867, 6,971, 9,291, 18,013
Blackwell, Howard Lane, 6,864
Blackwell, J. Whilden, 15,720
Blackwell, Kitty Barry (1848?-1936), 2,209
Blackwell, Louise, 2,928
Blackwell, Lucy (Stone) [Mrs. Henry]. *See* Stone, Lucy. [Mrs. Henry] Blackwell
Blackwell Medical Society (Rochester, NY), 12,841
Blackwell, Octavia. *See* Chilton, Octavia (Blackwell)
Blackwell, Ruby Chapin (1876-), **17,401**
Blackwell, Samuel, 6,412, 6,413
Blackwell's Island (NY), 12,130
Blackwood, Algernon, 15,967
Blackwood, Alice. *See* Baldwin, Alice (Blackwood) [Mrs. Frank Dwight]
Blackwood, Jane [Mrs. Thomas], 8,305
Blackwood, Lillian Caldwell, **14,323**
Blackwood, Richard, 14,323
Blackwood, Thomas (ca. 1800-56), **8,305**
Blagden, Sir Charles, 10,831
Blaikie, Jane Currie (1811-90). *See* Hoge, Jane Currie (Blaikie) [Mrs. Abraham Holmes] (1811-90)
Blain, Wilson, 14,614
Blaine, Anita (Emmons) McCormick (1866-1954), 3,787, 3,842, 3,910, 4,970, **17,602**
Blaine, Catherine V. (Paine) [Mrs. David E.] (1829-1908), **17,227**
Blaine, David E. (1824-1900), **17,227**
Blaine, Harriet (Stanwood) [Mrs. James Gillespie] (?-1903), 2,210
Blaine, James Gillespie (1830-93), **2,210**
Blaine, John, 17,621
Blaine, John G., 12,575
Blaine, Margaret. *See* Damrosch, Margaret (Blaine) [Mrs. Walter Johannes] (1865?-1949)
Blaine, Sarah E., 12,034
Blaine, Walker (?-1890), 2,210
Blair, Anne, 11,074
Blair, Aurelia, 11,074
Blair, Elizabeth. *See* Lee, Elizabeth (Blair) [Mrs. Samuel Phillips]
Blair, Emma, 11,074
Blair, Emma Helen (1851-1911), 2,553, **17,603**
Blair, Ernest W., 10,748
Blair Family, 12,531
Blair Family, **11,154**
Blair Family (VA), 17,108
Blair, Francis Preston, 11,154
Blair, Francis Preston, Family, **2,211**
Blair, Gist (1860-1940), 2,211
Blair, Hazel, 10,055
Blair, Helen McCormick, 4,100
Blair House (DC), 1,444
Blair, Ida, 3,753
Blair, James Thomas, Jr. (1902-62), **9,934**
Blair, Jane, 13,454
Blair, John (1732-1800), 17,108
Blair, John Insley (1802-99), **11,074**
Blair, John Jay, **13,334**
Blair, Laura (Lawson) [Mrs. Frank] Ellis [Mrs. Gist], 2,211
Blair, Lucy James. *See* Wheeler, Lucy James (Blair)
Blair, M. A. [Mrs. D. C.], 3,969
Blair, Mary. *See* Braxton, Mary (Blair)
Blair, Mary E., **10,796**
Blair, Mary Elizabeth (Woodbury) [Mrs. Montgomery], 2,211
Blair, Mary Serena Eliza (Jessup), 1,444
Blair, Minna. *See* Richey, Minna (Blair) [Mrs. Stephen Olin]
Blair, Minna P. (Nichols) [Mrs. Ernest W.] (1886-1973), 10,748
Blair, Montgomery, 2,211
Blair, Montgomery (1813-83), 2,211
Blair, Nan, 1,580
Blair, Nelly, 13,454
Blair, Roberta, **13,335**
Blair, Ruth, 3,131, 3,225
Blair, Sarah Maria Seymour [Mrs. William] (1832-1923), **3,802**
Blair, Susan (Shippen), 11,172

Blair, Violet. *See* Jain, Violet (Blair) [Mrs. Albert Covington]
Blair, William, 3,825
Blair, Woodbury, 2,211
Blaisdell, Anne (pseudonym). *See* Linington, Elizabeth (1921-)
Blaisdell, Dorothea C., 11,940
Blaisdell, Dorothea Chambers, 1,589
Blaisdell, Marie [Mrs. M. J.] (1846-1918), **8,454**
Blaise, Emma K., 4,869
Blake, Alde L. T., **6,414, 7,731**
Blake, Amanda (Farrington), **1,246**
Blake, Anita, 364
Blake, Anita Day (Symmes) [Mrs. Anson Stiles] (1872-1962), 353
Blake, Anna (?-1965). *See* Mezquida, Anna (Blake) [Mrs. Mateo M.] (?-1965)
Blake, Annie E. [Mrs. Charles H.], 1,790
Blake, Anson Stiles (1870-1959), 353
Blake, Bennett, 13,370
Blake, Bennett T., **13,336**
Blake, Betsey, 12,620
Blake, Betty. *See* Rogers, Betty (Blake) [Mrs. Will]
Blake, Carrie [Mrs.], 4,904
Blake, Charles H., 1,790
Blake, Effie A., **10,797**
Blake, Elizabeth W., 12,316
Blake, Euphemia Vale Smith [Mrs.] (1830?-1905), **11,315**
Blake Family, **7,193**
Blake Family (CA), **353**
Blake, Frances (Sledd) [Mrs. John], 2,884
Blake, Hannah, 7,047
Blake, Helen D., **5,740**
Blake, James L., **8,213**
Blake, Joseph, 12,843
Blake, Joseph, 15,519
Blake, Katherine (pseudonym). *See* Walter, Dorothy Blake (1908-)
Blake, Katherine Devereux [Miss] (1858-1950), **7,193**, 7,312, 9,443, 11,605
Blake, Katherine Duer [Mrs. Clarence H.] Mackay [Mrs. Joseph] (?-1930), 10,687, 12,843
Blake, Kay (pseudonym). *See* Walter, Dorothy Blake (1908-)
Blake, Lillie (Devereux) [Mrs. Frank Geoffrey Quay] Umsted [Mrs. Grinfill] (1833-1913), 1,255, 7,193, **10,155**, 11,605, 11,616, 12,811
Blake, Marion [Miss], 17,029
Blake, Mrs. William H., **11,835**
Blake, Rosana Margaret (Kroh) (1836-1923). *See* Alverson, Rosana Margaret (Kroh) Blake (1836-1923)
Blake, Sadie Evalena Hale, **17,891**
Blake, Sarah (Sindrey) [Mrs. Joseph], 15,519
Blakeley, Jane A. [Mrs. Johnston], 13,426
Blakelock, Denys, 4,235
Blakely, Kate, **17,945**
Blakely, Sara A., 3,834
Blakeslee, Maria S., 11,525
Blakey, Gladys McAlphine (Campbell) [Mrs. Roy Gillespie], 8,539
Blakey, Roy Gillespie (1880-1967), **8,539**
Blakiston, Anna (1869-1952). *See* Day, Anna (Blakiston) (1869-1952)
Blakiston Publishing Company (PA), 14,987
Blakney, Clara C., 1,786
Blanc, Archbishop, 16,018
Blanc, Marie Thérèse (de Solms) (1840-1904), **6,415**, 11,305
Blanc, Mrs. Lorenzo, 5,501
Blanchard, Adeline (1805-75). *See* Tyler, Adeline (Blanchard) [Mrs. John] (1805-75)
Blanchard, Elizabeth Amis Cameron (Hooper) [Mrs. John Osgood] (1873-1956), **12,955**
Blanchard, Emma W. Pendleton [Mrs. James, Jr.] (ca. 1847-70), 5,706
Blanchard Family (IA), **4,737**
Blanchard, Greta (1876-?). *See* Millikan, Greta (Blanchard) [Mrs. Robert Andrews] (1876-?)
Blanchard, Helen, 4,737
Blanchard, Henry E., 4,737
Blanchard, James, Jr., 5,706
Blanchard, John Osgood, 12,955

Blanchard, Louise [Mrs. Henry E.], 4,735
Blanchard, Maria, 4,737
Blanchard, Mary H. [Miss], **3,153**
Blanchard, Mrs., 3,287
Blanchard, Oliver, 4,737
Blanchard, Pearl R., **8,306**
Blanchard, Virginia, 17,125
Blanchfield, Florence A. (1884-1971), **6,127**
Blanck, Jacob, 6,396
Bland, Clara Ophelia, **2,971**, 3,071
Bland, Lillie Mae (1919-). *See* Carter, Lillie Mae (Bland) (1919-)
Bland, Martha Dangerfield, 2,621
Blanding, Lucy. *See* Carpenter, Lucy (Blanding)
Blanding, Rachel, 15,567
Blanding, Sarah Gibson (1898-), **6,416**, 6,475, 6,739, 11,661, 11,662
"Blanding Street" (article), 15,747
Blanding, Susan, 15,567
Blanding, William (1773-1857), **15,567**
Blank, Parthenia E., 14,499
Blank, Stephen, 14,499
Blankenburg, Ida May, 6,259
Blankenburg, Lucretia (Longshore) [Mrs. Rudolph] (1845-1937), 12,811
Blankenhorn, Ann Washington (Craton) [Mrs. Heber] (1891-1970), **8,067**
Blanton, Margaret Gray [Mrs. Smiley Jordan] (1887-1973), 15,876, **17,604**
Blanton, Smiley Jordan, 15,876, 17,604
Blase, Amelia (1874-?), **9,304**
Blashfield, Edwin Howland, 3,020
Blasienz, Ida Linda (1895-). *See* Hill, Ida Linda (Blasienz) (1895-)
Blaskfield, Linnie, 5,861
Blatch, Harriot Eaton (Stanton) [Mrs. William Henry] (1856-1940), 2,212, 4,210, **6,379**, 6,813, 6,858, 10,933, 12,834, 12,835
Blatchford, Carrie, 2,202
Blatchford, Mrs. R. M., 12,271
Blauvelt, Mary (Boggs), 12,166
Blavatsky, Helena Petrovna (Hahn) [Mrs. Nikifor Vasilievich] (1831-91), 2,213, 5,522, **6,246**, 11,542, 11,551
Blaylock, J. B., **13,337**
Bleckley, Annie E. (Hammond) [Mrs. Sylvester], 15,568
Bleckley, Sylvester (1832-96), **15,568**
Bledsoe, Geraldine [Mrs.], **8,068**
Bledsoe, Mary C., **12,162**
Bleeck, O. W., 9,967
Bleecker, Ann Eliza, 10,941
Bleecker, Catharine (1809-93). *See* Neilson, Catharine (Bleecker) [Mrs. James] (1809-93)
Bleecker, Leonard, 10,941
Bleeker, Mary Phillips, 11,662
Blegen, Theodore Christian (1891-), **8,910**
Bless This House (book), 14,231
Blessed Sacrament Monastery (Yonkers, NY), **12,934**
Blight, Mrs. T. J., 1,339
Blilie, Katharina, 8,867
Blind, 2,676, 4,074, 4,817, 5,123, 7,560, **7,602**, 10,919, **11,215**, 11,811, **12,795**, 17,553
   education, 2,919, 5,857, **7,309**, 7,560, **15,549**
   employment, 14,155
   institutional care, 5,570, 6,346
   law and legislation, 11,811, 17,463
   rehabilitation, 5,233
   research, 11,811
Blind, Afro-American, **15,549**
   education, 15,549
Blind Association, 11,445
Blind, books for the, 2,419, 5,270, 11,811
Blind-deaf, 1,426, **2,108**, **2,419**, 6,426, 6,484, **6,691**, **10,798**, **11,812**
   education, 4,732, 6,691, 7,560, **7,684**, 10,798
   institutional care, 12,171
   personal narratives, **15,587**
Blind Junky (drama), 12,367
"Blind Lamb, The" (poem), 2,603
Blind, libraries for the, **2,505**, 8,586
Blind, teachers of the, 1,133, **5,857**, 7,560, 15,549
Blind, workers for the, **5,318**, **6,691**

Blindness, 11,885
Blinn, Alice May, 11,662
Bliss, Alexander (1792-1827), 2,188, **7,603**
Bliss, Alexander, II (1827-96), 2,188, **4,408**
Bliss, Anais [Mrs. George] (?-1920), 12,163
Bliss, Anna C., 7,149
Bliss, Bell Rundlett [Mrs. M. N.], 17,605
Bliss, Cornelius N., 12,052
Bliss, Cynthia B., 10,193
Bliss, Eleanor (Albert) [Mrs. Alexander, II] (?-1874), 2,188
Bliss, Elizabeth B. [Miss], 2,188
Bliss, Elizabeth (Davis) [Mrs. Alexander] (1803-86).
    See Bancroft, Elizabeth (Davis) [Mrs. Alexander]
    Bliss [Mrs. George] (1803-86)
Bliss Family, **2,188**
Bliss Family (WI), **17,605**
Bliss, Florence (1890-), **10,193**
Bliss, George (1830-97), **12,163**
Bliss, George Theodore, **12,390**
Bliss, Ida, 17,605
Bliss, M. N., 17,605
Bliss, Marie (1887-1972), **10,193**
Bliss, Miriam E. (1862-1942). See Rains, Miriam E.
    (Bliss) [Mrs. J. Frank] (1862-1942)
Bliss, Mrs. George T., **12,391**
Bliss, Pearl (1894-). See Butt, Pearl (Bliss) (1894-)
Bliss, Sally (Hitchcock) [Mrs. David] (1791-1872),
    7,604
Bliss, Susan D., **12,391**
Bliss, Susan Dwight, **12,392**
Bliss, William D., 2,188
Blitch, Iris (Faircloth) [Mrs. Brooks Erwin] (1912-),
    3,372
Blitz, Anne Dudley, 8,594
Blitz, Constance, 2,763
Blizzard, Rae [Mrs. William], 2,241
Blizzards, 4,958, 4,655, 9,087, 11,181, 15,869
Bloch, Dorothy, 11,774
Bloch, Ernest (1880-1959), 749, 931, 2,020
Block, Minnie. See Brewer, Minnie (Block)
Blockade, 11,537
Blocker, Annie (Lane) [Mrs. J. R.], 16,312
Blocker, W. B., **16,312**
Blocklinger, Peggy Jeanne (O'More) (1897-1970),
    14,324
Blodgett, Avis Dodge, 3,891
Blodgett, Eusebia (1821-89). See Meeks, Eusebia
    (Blodgett) [Mrs. William] Harris [Mrs. Isaac]
    (1821-89)
Blodgett, Rebecca Smith [Mrs. Samuel] (1772-1837),
    12,174
Blome, Emma. See Peterson, Emma (Blome)
Blood and Banquets (book), 6,020
Blood, Charles H., 11,537
Blood, collection and preservation, 1,837
Blood on Her Shoes (book), 3,070
Blood on the Moon (drama), 2,576
Blood, Victoria (Claflin) [Mrs. Canning] Woodhull
    [Mrs. James Harvey]. See Martin, Victoria
    (Claflin) [Mrs. Canning] Woodhull [Mrs. James
    Harvey] Blood [Mrs. John Biddulph]
Bloodletting, 2,541
Bloom Family, 12,314
Bloom, Isabel, 4,868
Bloom, Levi, 5,339
Bloomer, Amelia (Jenks) [Mrs. Dexter Chamberlain]
    (1818-94), 1,436, 4,655, **4,708**, 4,738, 4,754,
    6,244, 6,460, 6,712, 9,241, **12,854**, 17,411
Bloomer costume, 2,629
Bloomer, Dexter Chamberlain (1816-1900), 4,708,
    4,738
Bloomer Girl (musical comedy), 12,360
Bloomer Girl on Pike's Peak, 1858, A (book), 1,790
Bloomer, Samuel, **8,955**
Bloomfield Art League (NJ), 10,889
Bloomfield, Fannie (1863-1927). See
    (Bloomfield)-Zeisler, Fannie [Mrs. Sigmund]
    (1863-1927)
Bloomfield Federation of Music (NJ), 10,889
Bloomfield Women's Club (NJ), 10,889
(Bloomfield)-Zeisler, Fannie [Mrs. Sigmund]
    (1863-1927), 3,788, **13,766**
Bloomington Auto Club (MN), 8,411

"Bloomington Community Service" (newsletter), 8,402
Bloomington Ferry School (MN), **8,400**
Bloomington High School (MN), 8,402
Bloomington Temperance Society (MN), 9,294
Bloomingtonian (periodical), **8,402**
Bloomquist, Nellie, 9,462
Bloomsburg Delta Club (PA), **14,722**
Bloomsburg Hospital Ladies' Auxiliary (PA), **14,723**
Bloor, Ella Reeve "Mother" (1862-1951), 8,144,
    9,119, 12,703, 14,393, 14,437
Blos, Joan W., 674
Blount, Ann C., 13,378
Blount, John Gray, **13,338**
Blount, Mildred, 13,217
Blount, Nancy. See Branch, Nancy (Blount) [Mrs.
    Lawrence O'Bryan]
Blow Family (MO), **10,156**
Blow, Henry Taylor, 10,156
Blow, Martha (1864-1934). See Wadsworth, Martha
    (Blow) (1864-1934)
Blow, Minerva Grimsley [Mrs. Henry Taylor], 10,156
Blow, Susan Elizabeth (1843-1916), **2,094**, 5,346,
    6,210, 10,149, 10,156
Bloyd Family, 256
Blue Anchor Society, 12,931
"Blue and the Grey, The" (poem), 100
"Blue Bird Twins, 4,764
"Blue Candle" (newsletter), 17,397
Blue Cross, 14,714
Blue Family (SC), **15,569**
Blue Hill Ladies Social Library (ME). See Blue Hill
    Public Library (ME)
Blue Hill Public Library (ME), 5,598
Blue, John Stuart, 15,569
Blue, Kate Lilly, 15,569
Blue Lake Advocate (CA), 1,628
Blue, Linden Stanley, 1,779
Blue Meadow (book), 15,196
Blue Mountain College (MS), 9,607
    history, **9,543**
"Blue Night" (song), 14,440
Blue Tea Literary Club of Salt Lake City (UT),
    16,879
Blue Valley Transportation, Inc. (NE), **10,404**
Blue, Virginia Neal, 1,779
Blueberries, 11,189
Blueford, Lucile H., 10,021, 10,030
Bluemel, Elinor, 1,786
Blues (songs, etc.), 5,532, 15,891
Bluestockings (VT), 17,004
Bluestone, Rose Whipple, 9,467
Bluethenthal, Janet (Weil) [Mrs. Herbert], 13,604
Bluffton College (OH), archives, **13,758**
Blum, Franz, 2,207
Blum, Nancy (Cory) [Mrs. Louis], 9,018
Blume, Julius, **10,647**
Blume, Netti, **10,647**
Blumenfeld, Lillian (Rifkin) [Mrs. Gustav] (1897-),
    15,353
Blumenschein, Ernest L. (1874-1960), 11,234
Blumenschein, Helen [Miss], 11,234
Blumenthal, Florence (Meyer), 945
Blumenthal, Gertrude, 14,475
Blumenthal, Helen (Birkman), 17,282
Blumenthal, Molly [Miss], 14,497
Blunden, Edmund Charles (1896-1974), **11,948**
Blunt, Sarah R., **12,165**
Bly, Alice (1878-1976), 7,151
Bly, Nellie. See Seaman, Elizabeth (Cochrane) [Mrs.
    Robert L.] (1865?-1922)
Blyche, Mrs. Harris, 9,605
B.M.Z. Women's Club (Chicago, IL), 3,866
B'nai Abraham Ladies Auxiliary (IN), **13,767**
B'nai B'rith, 9,083
B'nai B'rith, Bertha Rutz Fiterman Chapter
    (Minneapolis, MN), **9,218**
B'nai B'rith Women's Auxiliary (IL), 9,083
B'nai B'rith Women's Lodge, Annie Weinberg Lodge
    No. 567 (AR), **13,768**
B'nai Israel Congregation Sisterhood (Charleston,
    WV), **13,770**
B'nai Israel Congregation Sisterhood (Parkersburg,
    WV), **13,769**
Boak, Cada Castolas (1870-1954), **10,648**

Boan: A Memorial (book), 2,271
Board of Commissioners (ND), 13,661
Board of Control of the State Industrial School (MI),
    7,806
Board of National Popular Education, 8,526
Board of Public Charities (NC), 13,399
Board of Religious Organizations (MO), 6,467
Board of Selectmen (Amherst, MA), 6,753
Boarding schools, 5,426, 5,800, 7,514, **9,873**, 12,433,
    12,847, **13,234**, 13,238, 13,347, 13,407, 13,494,
    14,484, **15,452**, **15,940**, 16,031
Boardman, Alice L. [Mrs.], 7,424
Boardman, Anne Cawley, 8,600
Boardman, Douglass (1822-91), **11,524**, 11,525,
    11,645
Boardman, Emily [Miss] (?-1898), **11,525**
Boardman, Florence S., 2,542
Boardman, Frances [Miss] (1879-1953), **8,956**, 9,333
Boardman, Julia, 2,315
Boardman, Mabel Thorp [Miss] (1860-1946), 2,196,
    2,214, 2,411, 2,499, 2,542, 2,599, **2,972**
Boardman, Martha (1789-1863). See Shackford,
    Martha (Boardman) [Mrs. Seth Ring]
    (1789-1863)
Boardman, Martha (Lane) [Mrs. William], 10,882
Boardman, Nancy Ellen (1825-?). See Lord, Nancy
    Ellen Boardman [Mrs. Edward A.] (1825-?)
Boardman, Queen Walker, 2,243
Boardman, Sophia L., 11,547
Boardman, William, 10,882
Boards of trade, 623, 1,526, 3,229, **4,990**, **5,181**,
    9,334, 9,435, 9,622, 15,522, 16,535
    officials and employees, **17,086**
Boarman, Vivian. See Whitehouse, Vivian (Boarman)
Boas, Franz (1858-1942), **11,836**, **14,886**, 14,894,
    14,897, 17,252
Boas, Franziska, **11,836**
Boas, Helene. See Yampolsky, Helene (Boas)
Boas, Marie Krackowizer, 14,886
Boat of Longing, The (book), 8,788
Boatmen, 9,133
Boatner, Lillie Vidal [Mrs. S. A.], 9,813
Boatner, Maxine (Tull) [Mrs. Edmund Burke]
    (1903-), 2,341
"Bob Newhart Show, The" (television program),
    17,808
Bobb, Mae (1903-). See Urbanek, Mae (Bobb)
    (1903-)
Bobbs-Merrill Company, 13,267
Bodichon, Barbara Leigh (Smith) (1827-1891), **11,947**
Bodie Family (MS), **9,593**
Bodley Family (KY, MS), 9,807
Bodley, Rachel Littler [Miss] (1831-88), **15,126**
Boe, A. Sophie [Miss] (1879-1937), **8,724**
Boe, Borghild [Miss], 17,498
Boe, L. W., 8,815
Boe, N. E., 8,724
Boeckel, Florence (Brewer) (1885-), 15,308
Boehm, Margaret Donaldson (1894-1956), **5,726**
Boehme, Anthony William, 15,042
Boehner, Ruth P., **6,417**
Boeing Company, The, **17,214**
Boelté, Maria (1836-1918). See Kraus-(Boelté), Maria
    [Mrs. John] (1836-1918)
Boepple, Louise. See Graff, Louise (Boepple) [Mrs.
    Ulrich]
Boer Relief Fund, Women's Auxiliary League, 12,446
Boericke, Ruth (1888-1977). See Bowie, Ruth
    (Boericke) [Mrs. Ralston] White [Mrs. Robert]
    (1888-1977)
Boettcher, Charles, 1,720
Boettcher, Ruth (1890-1959). See Humphreys, Ruth
    (Boettcher) [Mrs. A. E., Jr.] (1890-1959)
Boettiger, Anna (Roosevelt), 12,044
Boetz, Johanna. See Clevans, Johanna (Boetz) [Mrs.
    Mark]
Boey, Vivan Hamilton, 3,224
Bogan, Louise (1897-1970), 3,986, 4,227, 5,580,
    5,860, 6,073, **11,155**, **12,393**, 15,170, 16,163
Bogardus Family (GA), **2,973**
Bogardus, Margaret, 2,973
Bogardus, Susan (?-1899). See Farmer, Susan
    (Bogardus) (?-1899)
Bogart, Humphrey, 11,822

Bogart, Maude Humphreys, 11,822
Bogert, Judith [Miss], **14,959**
Bogert, Margaret, 11,322
Bogert, Susan, 12,315
Boggs, Amelia Louise, 3,754
Boggs, Annie [Miss], 9,692
Boggs, Charles Stuart (1811-72), 12,166
Boggs, Corrine M. "Lindy" Claiborne, **5,504**
Boggs Family (NY), **12,166**
Boggs, L. Pearl, 1,340
Boggs, Mae Hélène (Bacon) [Mrs. Angus Gordon] (1863-1963), 354, 400, 1,265, **1,544**, 1,664
Boggs, Mary. *See* Blauvelt, Mary (Boggs)
Boggs, Mary L. (1777-?), 12,166
Boggs, Mrs. Hale, 9,239
Boggs, Robert (1766-1831), 12,166
Boggs, T. Hale, 5,504
Bogie, Mary (Hawn) (1879-), **8,691**
Bogin, R., 11,306
Bogue, Arthur Hoyt, 2,203
Bogue, Lilian Bell [Mrs. Arthur Hoyt] (1867-1929), **2,203**, 3,994
Bohannon, Mary Elizabeth (1905-63), **11,526**
Bohemian Flats, The (book), 9,463
Bohemian Settlement House (Chicago, IL). *See* Howell Neighborhood House (Chicago, IL)
Bohemian Women's Publishing Company (Chicago, IL). *See* Chicago Association of Czech-American Women (IL)
Bohn Aluminum, 8,105
Bohn, Belle C. [Mrs.] (1857-1948), **17,606**
Bohr Millinery and Dressmaker Shop (Westphalia, MI), **7,732**
Bohr, Niels, 11,814
Bohr, Theresa, 7,732
Bohrer, Florence (Fifer) [Mrs. Jacob A.] (1877-1960), 3,745, **3,749**, 3,764, 4,307, **4,349**
Bohrer, Gertrude, 4,349
Boice, Margaret McIntosh [Mrs. Fred] (1884-1967), **17,946**
Boies, Mrs. Herbert B., 4,954
Boiler-plates, 2,031
Boilermakers Union, **8,056**
Boinest Family (SC), 15,495
Boise Catholic Women's League (ID), **3,655**
Boise Civic Chorus (ID), 3,708
Boise Council of Church Women (ID), **3,656**
Boise State University (ID), 3,717
Boissevain, Inez (Milholland) (1886-1916), 6,615
Boissiere-Roumanille, Terese, 12,506
Bok, Edward, 2,414
Bolado, Dulce. *See* Davis, Dulce (Bolado)
Boley, Elijah, 13,650
Boley, Sarah (Lewallen or Llewelyn) [Mrs. Elijah], **13,650**
Boline, Sarah Metzler, 8,174
Bolitho, Hector, 1,579
Bolivia, **6,917**
Boll, Luellan H. [Miss] (1890-1973), **11,338**
Boll, N. Arnold, 5,232
Bolland, Adrienne, 11,831
Bolles, Charles Pattison, **13,339**
Bolles Family, 7,166
Bolles, George A., 6,821
Bolles, Maria DuBrutz Reston [Mrs. Charles Pattison], 13,339
Bolles, Mary L. *See* Branch, Mary L. (Bolles)
Bolling, Edith (1872-1961). *See* Wilson, Edith (Bolling) Galt [Mrs. Woodrow] (1872-1961)
Bollingen Foundation, **2,215**
Bollingen Prize in Poetry, 2,215
Bolsoadiris, Leide, **8,307**
Bolt, Beatrice Rebecca (French) [Mrs. Richard Arthur] (1880-1974), 1,620
Bolt, Elizabeth, 1,620
Bolt Family (CA), **1,620**
Bolt, Marrion Jane, 1,620
Bolt, Richard Arthur (1880-1959), 1,620
Bolt, Richard Henry, 1,620
Bolt, Robert, 1,620
Bolton, Ann (Laurance) [Mrs. George Wright] Hawkes [Mrs. Daniel], 12,220

Bolton, Charles Knowles (1867-1950), 6,176, **6,418**, 7,605
Bolton, Daniel, 12,220
Bolton, Ethel (Stanwood) [Mrs. Charles] (1874-1954), 7,605
Bolton Family (MA), **7,605**
Bolton, Frances Payne (Bingham) (1885-), 2,205, 2,242, 6,710, 6,766, **13,911**
Bolton, Gertrude. *See* Coleman, Gertrude (Bolton) [Mrs. Joseph Griswold, III]
Bolton, Gertrude (Janes) [Mrs. Herbert Eugene] (?-1954), 355
Bolton, Herbert Eugene (1870-1953), 355, 3,420
Bolton, Laura C., 3,980
Bolton, Mary H. (Lynch) [Mrs. William C.]. *See* Wilkes, Mary H. (Lynch) [Mrs. William C.] Bolton [Mrs. Charles]
Bolton, Sarah [Miss], **356**
Bolton, Sarah Knowles (1841-1916), 6,418, 7,605
Bolton, Susannah. *See* Moore, Susannah (Bolton) [Mrs. William]
Bolts of Melody (book), 5,862
Boltwood, Clarinda Boardman (Williams) [Mrs. Lucius Manlius], 8,021
Boltwood Family (MI), **8,021**
Bomar, Amaryllis. *See* Killian, Amaryllis (Bomar) [Mrs. Charles]
Bomar, Benjamin F., 3,154
Bomar Family (GA), **3,154**
Bomar, Sarah Elizabeth (Lumpkin) Hayes [Mrs. Benjamin F.], 3,154
Bombeck, Erma [Mrs. William] (1927-), **17,947**
Bombings, 15,709
Bombs, 14,200
Bonafield, Julia A. (1863-1956), **17,451**
Bonanza Trail (book), 1,804
Bonaparte, Charles Joseph (1851-1921), **5,741**
Bonaparte, Elisabeth (Patterson) [Mrs. Jerome] (1785-1879), 5,742, 5,820
Bonaparte, Jerome, 5,742
Bonaparte, Napoleon, 2,445, 5,742
Bonar, J. C., 17,199
Bonar, Mary Hetty (1860-?). *See* Martin, Mary Hetty (Bonar) (1860-?)
Bond, Alvan, **7,513**
Bond, Carrie Jacobs, 1,404
Bond, Catherine (Grayston), 11,527
Bond, Clara W. [Mrs.], 17,919
Bond, Elizabeth, 6,267
Bond, Elizabeth Powell (1841-1926), **15,270**
Bond Family (KS), **11,527**
Bond, George P. (1825-65), **6,267**
Bond, Joseph, 5,746
Bond, Priscilla "Mittie" Munnikhuysen, **9,594**
Bond, Sibby Ann (Waters) Davis [Mrs. Alvan], 7,513
Bond, Temperance (1771-?). *See* Mack, Temperance (Bond) [Mrs. Stephen] (1771-?)
Bond, William Cranch (1789-1859), **6,267**
Bonde party (Norway), 8,798
Bonds, 1,636, 1,882
Bonds, Confederate, 1,962
Bondurant, Alexander Joseph, 12,956
Bondurant, Emily (Morrison) [Mrs. Alexander Joseph] (1837-1926), **12,956**
Bone, Griselda Minerva (Burk) [Mrs. Robert Donnell], 3,310
Bone, Robert Donnell (1832-92), **3,310**
Bonebrake, Jeanette E. [Miss], **12,957**
Boner, John Henry, **13,340**
Bones, 6,323, 6,327
Bones, Helen Woodrow, 11,177
Boney, Mrs. Harvey, 13,523
Bonfield, Margaret, 2,878
Bonfils, Winifred (Sweet) [Mrs. Orlow] Black [Mrs. Frederick G.] (1863-1936), 689, 702
Bonham, Dora Dieterich [Mrs. Eugene] (1902-), **16,038**
Bonham, Eugene, 16,038
Bonham, Lillian, 1,124
Boniface, Isabella (Morrow) [Mrs. John J.], **14,773**
Boniface, John J., 14,773
Bonime, Florence Cummings (1907-), **5,990**
Bonitz, Fred W., **13,341**
Bonitz, Mary E. [Mrs.], 13,341

Bonne Femme Academy, 9,987
Bonneau, Catherine, 15,511
Bonneau Family (SC), **15,511**
Bonnell, Edith, 1,339
Bonner, Amy, 15,900
Bonner, Katherine Sherwood (1849-1883). *See* McDowell, Katherine Sherwood (Bonner) [Mrs. Edward] (1849-1883)
Bonner, Michael (pseudonym). *See* Glasscock, Anne Bonner (1924-)
Bonner, Miriam (1896-). *See* Camp, Miriam (Bonner) (1896-)
Bonner, Robert (1824-99), **12,394**
Bonnet, Edith Marguerite (1897-), **16,226**
Bonneville, Benjamin Louis Eulalie De (1796-1878), **252**
Bonneville, Susan Neis, 252
Bonney, Catherine Visscher (Van Rensselaer) [Mrs. Samuel W.], 11,260
Bonney, Eliza G., 7,090
Bonney, Emma, 11,260
Bonney Family (NY), 11,262
Bonney Family, The (book), 5,030
Bonney, Mabel Thérèse (1895-1978), **357**
Bonney, Samuel W., 11,260
Bonsal, Rebecca M. Wright (ca. 1839-?), 2,573
Bonsall, Anna, 11,949
Bonsall, Ellen C., 11,949
Bonsall Family (PA), **11,949**
Bonsall, Lydia, 11,949
Bonsall, Richard, 11,949
Bonsell, Margaret [Mrs.], 14,824
Bonsteel, Abbie Benton, 13,300
Bontecou, Eleanor (1891-1976), **10,070**
Bontemps, Arna Wendell (1902-), **3,284**, 3,285
Bonus system, 11,851. *See also* Piece-work
Book and a Love Affair, A (book), 13,190
Book clubs, **10,994**, 11,891, 12,040, **15,786**
Book collectors, **3,983**, 7,654
Book jackets, **8,531**
"Book Market, The" (column) 7,254
Book of Common Prayer, 6,180
"Book of Literacy Memoranda," 13,910
Book of Meditations, 7,300
Book of Mormon, 16,760
Book of Poems and Impressions, 4,304
Book of the Dance (book), 7,214
Book-of-the-Month Club, 2,216, **11,837**, 12,035
Book ornamentation, 1,464
Book-plates, 7,681, 8,531
Book selection, 11,837
Bookbinders, **7,300**, 12,879
Bookkeeping, 9,186
Bookmobiles, 5,341, 6,858, 11,228, 13,204
Bookniks (periodical), 11,331
Books and reading for children, 8,425
Books and You (book), 10,465
Books, reviews, 2,398, 4,227, 6,065, 6,110, 6,116, 6,120, 11,223, 12,393, 14,368, 17,076
Booksellers and bookselling, **11,153**, **12,001**, **12,178**, **12,249**, 12,622
colportage, subscription trade, etc., **2,216**, 11,485, **11,837**, 12,035
Booksellers League of New York, 12,570
Boole, Ella Alexander [Mrs. William H.] (1858-1952), 4,243, **11,838**
Boomer, Jorgine Slettede, 8,737
"Boomerang, The" (ms), 8,191
Boon, James, **13,342**, 13,428
Boon, Mahaly Buffaloe [Mrs. James], 13,428
Boone, Ada, 15,006
Boone, Agnes, 5,743
Boone, Alphonse D., 14,549
Boone, Daniel, 9,902, 17,624
Boone, Eliza Rowan (Harney) [Mrs. William Pendleton] (1815-?), 5,277
Boone Family (OR), 14,549
Boone, James, 17,624
Boone, Luther D., 14,549
Boone, Queen Victoria (1837-85). *See* Douglass, Queen Victoria (Boone) [Mrs. Benjamin Pennebaker] (1837-85)
Boone, Sarah P. (Kennedy) [Mrs. William Marshall] (1842-83), 5,743

Boone School (Hankow, China), 313
Boone, William Marshall (1836-79), 5,743
Boone, William Pendleton, 5,277
Boone, William Pendleton (1813-75), 5,277
Booth, Ada, 4,005
Booth, Almeda A., 2,346
Booth, Anne (Willson), **358**
Booth, Barbara M., 14,473
Booth, Edmund, Family (CA), **1,609**
Booth, Edwin, 6,329, 11,457, 12,235
Booth, Ellen M., 14,515
Booth, Evangeline Cory [Miss] (1865-1950), 138,
    2,198, 2,232, 7,868, 12,706, 17,868
Booth, Harriet (ca. 1814-1906). *See* Griswold,
    Harriet (Booth) (ca. 1814-1906)
Booth, Heather [Mrs. Paul] (ca. 1940-), 3,792
Booth, Hortense [Mrs. Arthur], 2,009
Booth, John Wilkes, 7,263
Booth, Junius Brutus, 11,457
Booth, Lillian (Clayson) [Mrs. Wayne Chipman]
    (1894-), **16,608**
Booth, Lucy A., 5,063
Booth, Marry Emma (1854-1948). *See* Anderson,
    Marry Emma (Booth) [Mrs. John B.] (1854-1948)
Booth, Mary, 17,589
Booth, Mary Ann [Mrs. Edmund], 1,609
Booth, Mary Humphrey (Corss) [Mrs. Sherman M.],
    17,607
Booth, Mary Josephine (1876-1965), **4,350**
Booth, Mary Louise [Miss] (1831-89), 2,542, **12,167**,
    14,058
Booth, Mattie (Hunter) [Mrs. John A.] (1889-),
    16,404
Booth, Maud Ballington (Charlesworth) (1865-1948),
    4,974, 7,203
Booth, Mrs. Lionel F., **2,217**
Booth, Orren B., 11,964
Booth, Samuel, 14,515
Booth, Sherman M. (1812-1904), **17,607**
Booth, William, 6,515, 12,706
Boothbay Harbor (ME), 7,669
Boothe, Clare (1903-). *See* Luce, Clare (Boothe)
    [Mrs. George Tuttle] Brokaw [Mrs. Henry
    Robinson] (1903-)
Boothe, Zina Olivia (1877-1901). *See* Woolley, Zina
    Olivia (Boothe) [Mrs. Dilworth] (1877-1901)
Boots and shoes, repairing, 5,422
Boots and shoes, trade and manufacture, 6,192, 6,315,
    9,467, **16,273**
Booze, Eugene P., 2,490
Booze, Mary, 5,121
Booze, Mary Cordelia (Montgomery) [Mrs. Eugene
    P.], 2,490
Borah, William Edgar, 3,669, 3,681, 3,684, 3,725,
    6,858
Borchardt, Selma Munter (1895-1968), **8,069**, 8,071,
    8,093
Borden, Ann. *See* Hopkinson, Ann (Borden) [Mrs.
    Francis]
Borden, Lizzie Andrew [Miss] (1860-1927), 2,009
Borden, Mary (1729-98). *See* Rodman, Mary
    (Borden) (1729-98)
Borden, Mary (1886-1968), **5,991**
Borel, Sophie. *See* Lewis, Sophie (Borel) [Mrs. John
    M.]
Borg, Carl Oscar, 215
Borgia, Mother, 14,791
Borgia, Emma Vignal [Mrs. Solon], **15,850**
Borglum, Gutzon (1871-1941). *See* Borglum, John
    Gutzon de la Mothe (1871-1941)
Borglum, John Gutzon de la Mothe (1871-1941),
    10,075, 17,986, 5006
Borglum, Mary (Montgomery) [Mrs. John Gutzon de
    la Mothe] (?-1955), 2,218
Borglum, Solon, 15,850
Bori, Lucrezia [Miss], 2,663, 12,125
Borie Family (PA), **14,960**
Borie, John Joseph (1776-1834), 14,960
Borie, Lysbeth Boyd, 11,877
Borie, Sophie (Beauveau) [Mrs. John Joseph], 14,960
Borland, Carroll. *See* Parten, Carroll (Borland)
Borland, Margaret [Mrs.] (?-1873), **16,039**
Born, Helena (1860-1901), 12,698
Borneman, Henry S., 7,043

Borneo, discovery and exploration, 5,177
Borner, Florence [Mrs.], 9,400
Borough Improvement Society (Metuchen, NJ),
    10,917
Borowik, Ann (1930-), **5,992**
Borsodi, Ralph (1888-), 4,151
Borthwick, Mary Frances, 11,414
Borthwick, William S., **11,414**
Bosanquet, Theodora, **6,419**
Bosch, Pat, 157
Boshart, Linda (1945-69), 5,063
Bosler Free Library (PA), 14,747
Bosley, Dolores J., 1,750
Bosley, Roberta, 3,305
Bosomworth, Mary. Cousaponakeesa. [Mrs. John]
    Musgrove [Mrs. Jacob] Mathews [Mrs. Thomas]
    (ca. 1700-63), **3,485**
Bosomworth, Thomas, 3,485
Bosone, Reva Beck (1895-), **16,880**
Bosquez, Maria J., 9,467
Boss, Francis Webster, 6,226
Bosshard Family, 17,636
Bost, Ethel W. [Miss], **13,258**
Bost, Marie, 14,893
Bostick, Alice, 8,149
Bostick, Alma, 3,358
Bostick, Sarah Lue (Howard) [Mrs. Mancil Mathis]
    (1868-1948), **15,905**
Bostick, Zillah Lee (1871-1967). *See* Agerton, Zillah
    Lee (Bostick) Redd (1871-1967)
Boston American (MA), 6,685
Boston and Barre Manufacturing Company (MA),
    5,896
Boston and Colorado Smelting Company, 1,719
Boston and Sandwich Glass Company (MA), 7,491
Boston Athenaeum, 6,176
Boston Authors Club (MA), 5,913, 5,934, 6,014,
    14,366
Boston Castilian Club (MA), 6,469
Boston City Hospital (MA), 6,128
Boston City Hospital Nurses' Alumnae Association
    (MA), 6,128
Boston City Hospital School of Nursing (MA), **6,128**,
    6,152, 6,163
Boston City Hospital Training School for Nurses
    (MA). *See* Boston City Hospital School of
    Nursing (MA)
Boston Club (IN), **4,549**
Boston Committee (MA), 6,648
Boston Daily Advertiser (MA), 7,227
Boston Equal Suffrage Association (MA), 6,969,
    6,980
Boston Equal Suffrage Association for Good
    Government, 6,477, 6,966, 6,978, 6,981, 6,984
Boston Evening Clinic (MA), 6,847
Boston Female Anti-Slavery Society (MA), 2,629
Boston Female Medical School (MA), 6,698
Boston Gleaning Cicle (MA), **5,912**
Boston Globe (MA), 7,691, 14,093
Boston Herald (MA), 6,104
Boston Insane Hospital (MA). *See* Boston State
    Hospital (MA)
Boston Insane Hospital (MA), Austin Farm, **6,211**
Boston Insane Hospital (MA), Pierce Farm, **6,212**
Boston Instructive District Nursing Association (MA),
    6,164
Boston Lunatic Asylum (MA). *See* Boston State
    Hospital (MA)
Boston Lying-In Hospital (MA), **6,213, 6,220**
Boston Lying-In Hospital Fertility and Endocrine
    Clinic (MA), 6,225
Boston Manufacturing Company (MA), **6,187**
Boston, Michaela (pseudonym). *See* Forbes, DeLoris
    Florine Stanton (1923-)
Boston Moral Reform Society (MA), 7,635
Boston, Nancy S. (Smith) [Mrs. John H.], **2,974**
Boston Parents' Council (MA), **6,420**
Boston Peace Congress (1904), 15,298
Boston Political Class (MA), 7,082
Boston Post, The (MA), 17,899
Boston Psychopathic Hospital (MA), 6,900
Boston Public Library (MA), 12,816, 14,392
Boston Public Library (MA), West End Branch,
    5,974, 13,787

Boston Public Library Quarterly (MA), 5,925
Boston School Committee (MA), 6,405, 6,497, 6,762
Boston School of Cooking (MA), 1,948
Boston Social Union (MA), 6,946
Boston State College (MA), faculty, **5,977**
Boston State Hospital (MA), **6,214**, 6,900
Boston State Hospital (MA), Training School for
    Nurses, **6,215**
Boston Symphony Orchestra (MA), 6,358, 10,835
Boston Times (MA), 9,085
Boston Transcript (MA), 5,694, 6,244
Boston University (MA), 6,051, 6,095, 6,751, 6,847
    alumnae, 5,061, **6,009**, 6,051
    faculty, 7,030, 14,447
    students, 9,198
Boston University Law School (MA), alumnae, 1,103
Boston University School of Medicine (MA),
    alumnae, 13,055
Boston University Settlement (MA), 5,079
Boston University Women's Education Society (MA).
    See Massachusetts Society for the University
    Education of Women
Boston Women's Trade Union League (MA), 11,773
Bostwick, Catherine, 12,316
Boswell, Connie, 18,001
Boswell, Martha, 13,604
Boswell Sisters (singers), 18,001
Bosworth, Eliza, **8,308**
Botanical gardens, 3,188, 7,580, 10,150, 10,153,
    11,297, 12,431
Botanical illustration, 2,107, **6,307, 6,308**
Botanical research, 786, 15,217
Botanical societies, 3,187, **3,188**
Botanists, **526**, 786, 1,409, 1,779, 2,927, **4,539**, 5,442,
    5,486, 5,601, 6,309, **6,310, 6,311**, 7,178, 8,595,
    8,620, 10,150, 10,151, 10,152, 11,170, 11,297,
    12,848, **13,632, 14,409, 14,944**, 15,213, 15,218,
    15,326, 16,060, 16,132, **16,316**
Botany, 1,099, **6,311**, 7,666, **11,297**, 11,628, 14,213,
    16,316
    classification, 6,310, 10,152
    morphology, 10,152
    pictorial works, **4,288**
Botello, Mary, 1,532
Botello, Vangie, 1,532
Bothwell, Jean (1892?-1977), **5,993**
Botsford, Alice Ansley [Mrs. Frank], 11,528
Botsford, Anna (1854-1930). *See* Comstock, Anna
    (Botsford) [Mrs. John Henry] (1854-1930)
Botsford, Elizabeth, 11,528
Botsford, Frank, Family (NY), **11,528**
Botsford, Franklin, 11,528
Botsford, Kathleen, 11,528
Botsford, Mary, 11,528
Botsford, Myrtie, 11,528
Botsford, Phoebe, 11,543
Botsford, Samuel, 11,528
Botta, Anne Charlotte (Lynch) [Mrs. Vincenzo]
    (1815-91), 11,742, 12,168, 12,481, 17,010
Bottin, Fanny Burgess, 12,407
Bottolfsen, C. A., 3,667
Bottome, Phyllis, 3,110
"Bottoms and Hills: Virginia Tales, The" (book),
    15,660
Bottrall, Ronald, 16,165
Botts, Benson [Miss], **9,838**
Botts, Effie [Miss], 986
Botts, John Minor, 5,750
Botts, Lee [Mrs.], 4,119
Botume, Elizabeth Hyde, 5,917
Boucher, Mae, **14,325**
Bouchier, Arthur, 12,539
Boudin, Anna P., 11,950
Boudin, Leah, 11,950
Boudin, Louis B., **11,950**
Boudinot, Catherine. *See* Atterbury, Catherine
    (Boudinot)
Boudinot, Elisha, 11,075
Boudinot Family (NJ), **11,075**
Boughey, Grace Greenstead, 8,309
Boughey, Herbert F., **8,309**
Bouknight, Lula, 3,486
Bouknight, Mary Elinor. *See* Poppenheim, Mary
    Elinor Bouknight [Mrs. Christopher Pritchard]

Boulanger, Nadia, 3,980
Boulter, Grace (Foutz), **16,576**
Boulton, Sadie J., 1,786
Boulware, Amanda (?-1872). *See* Lumpkin, Amanda (Boulware) [Mrs. Richardson] (?-1872)
Boulware, Bertha, **3,663**
Boulware, Caroline (?-1848). *See* Broaddus, Caroline (Boulware) [Mrs. Andrew] (?-1848)
Boulware, Caroline Miller [Mrs. Lee], 3,373
Boulware, Catherine (?-1867). *See* Kidd, Catherine (Boulware) [Mrs. John] (?-1867)
Boulware Family (GA), **3,373**
Boulware Family (SC), **15,788**
Boulware, Josephine. *See* Ryland, Josephine (Boulware) [Mrs. Robert]
Boulware, Lee, 3,373
Boulware, Susan. *See* Taliaferro, Susan (Boulware) [Mrs. Alexander]
Bound Brook Presbyterian Church (NJ), 10,939
Boundaries, state, 10,673
Bouney, Emma, 12,527
Bounties, military, 2,698, 12,264
Bourgeois, Julia, 8,310
Bourgeois, Mary (1884-), **8,310**
Bourke-White, Margaret. [Mrs. Erskine] Caldwell (1904-71), **12,891**
Bourland, Caroline Brown (1871-1956), 7,158
Bourn Family (CA), **359**
Bourn, Hannah. *See* Ingalls, Hannah (Bourn)
Bourne, Bertha, 12,532
Bourne Family, 12,532
Bourne, Linnie H. [Mrs.], 12,532
Bourne, Randolph Silliman (1886-1918), **11,951**
Bourne, Sara Randolph (Barrett), 11,951
Bournonville and Ballet Technique (book), 12,364
Bournonville, Auguste, 12,364
Bouske, Nancy, 8,936
Boutemps, Anna, 2,882
Bouton, Hulda. *See* Holmes, Hulda Bouton [Mrs. Samuel Leek]
Bouton, Louie (1850-1928). *See* Felt, Louie (Bouton) [Mrs. Joseph H.] (1850-1928)
Boutwell, Hester Crooks [Mrs. William] (1817-53), **8,903**
Bouvier, Hannah Mary. *See* Peterson, Hannah Mary (Bouvier)
Bouvier, Jacqueline. *See* Onassis, Jacqueline (Bouvier) [Mrs. John Fitzgerald] Kennedy [Mrs. Aristotle]
Bouvier, John (1787-1851), **1,403**
Bovasso, Julie [Miss], 12,367
Bove, Linda Ann Marie. [Mrs. Edmund, Jr.] Waterstreet (1945-), **2,104**
Bovett, Florence Biggar [Mrs. Clifford Alfred] (1890-), 10,658, 10,677, 10,692
Bovey, Margaret (Jackson) [Mrs. John] (1887-), **8,957**
Bowden, Artemesia (1879-1954), 16,318
Bowditch, Charles Pickering (1842-1921), **6,324**
Bowditch, Elizabeth Ingersoll. *See* van Loon, Elizabeth Ingersoll (Bowditch) [Mrs. Hendrik Willem]
Bowditch, Fanny (1874-1967). *See* Katz, Fanny (Bowditch) [Mrs. Johann Rudolf] (1874-1967)
Bowditch, Henry Pickering (1840-1911), 6,933
Bowditch, Nancy Douglas (Brush) [Mrs. William Robert] Pearmain (1890-), **2,737**
Bowditch, Sarah R., **6,422**
Bowditch, Sylvia Church Scudder, **6,421**
Bowditch, William L., **6,422**
Bowdoin medical school (ME), 12,055
Bowe, Ave [Mrs. Earl], 1,532
Bowe Family, 4,058
Bowe, Mary Gwinn [Mrs. William John] (1901-), **4,058**
Bowe, Sister Camilla, 9,467
Bowen, Albert E., 16,577
Bowen, Amanda Blake [Mrs. Nathaniel], 15,447
Bowen, Catherine (Drinker) [Mrs. Ezra] (1897-1973), **2,219**, 2,336, 6,584, 11,165, 15,892
Bowen, Clarissa Adger [Mrs.] (1837-1915), **15,778**
Bowen Country Club (IL), 4,452

Bowen, Elizabeth (1734-?), **7,346**
Bowen, Elizabeth Dorothea (1899-), 4,485, 16,172
Bowen, Emma Lucy (Gates) [Mrs. Albert E.] (1880-1951), **16,577, 16,922**
Bowen Family (SC), **15,447**
Bowen, George, 4,172
Bowen, Georgene Esther (1898-), **6,247**
Bowen, Katharine Giltinan [Mrs. Trevor R.], 9,467
Bowen, Louise Hadduck (deKoven) [Mrs. Joseph T.] (1859-1953), **3,803**, 3,814, 3,820, 3,825, 3,828, 3,899, 3,910, 3,932, 3,995, 4,047, 4,052, 4,056, 4,100, 4,101, 4,103, 4,146, 4,165, 4,166, 4,452, 7,210
Bowen, Lydia (ca. 1752-?). *See* Clark, Lydia (Bowen) [Mrs. John Innes] (ca. 1752-?)
Bowen, Mary, 2,344
Bowen, Mary E., **360**
Bowen, Mildred, 466
Bowen, Mrs. J. T., 2,878
Bowen, Mrs. Penuel, 15,447
Bowen, Nathaniel (?-1838), 15,447
Bowen, Penuel (?-1788), 15,447
Bowen, William, 1,248
Bower, Helena May, **2,220**
Bowers, Caroline. *See* Woodman, Caroline (Bowers) [Mrs. Edward]
Bowers, Claude Gernade (1878-1958), **4,468**
Bowers, Eaton J., 9,706
Bowers, Eilley (Orrum) [Mrs. Stephen] Hunter [Mrs. Alexander] Cowan [Mrs. Lemuel Sanford "Sandy"] (1826-1903), 10,731
Bowers, Fidelia March, 1,505
Bowers, Gracie (1906-63). *See* Pfost, Gracie (Bowers) (1906-63)
Bowers, Lemuel Sanford "Sandy" (1830-68), 10,731
Bowers, Mabel, 8,321
Bowers, Patricia (1915-75), 4,468
Bowers, Sybil (McCaslin), 4,468
Bowers, Tallulah Gaines [Mrs. Eaton J.], 9,706
Bowers' Mansion (NV), 10,637, 10,662
Bowie Family (MD), 5,744
Bowie, Lucy Leigh (1872-1966), **5,744**
Bowie, Margaret Armstrong, 16,060
Bowie, Mrs. James, 16,106
Bowie, Ruth (Boericke) [Mrs. Ralston] White [Mrs. Robert] (1888-1977), **361**, 1,068
Bowker, Martha (1822-90). *See* Young, Martha (Bowker) [Mrs. Brigham] (1822-90)
Bowker, Richard Rogers (1848-1933), **12,395**
Bowler, Alida Cynthia, 863
Bowler, Isabel (1886-1961). *See* Paterson, Isabel (Bowler) (1886-1961)
Bowles, Chester B., 11,839, 17,594
Bowles, Dorothy Stebbins [Mrs. Chester], **11,839**
Bowles, Eva del Vakia [Miss] (1875-1943), 10,201
Bowles, Paul, 2,997
Bowles, Ruth Standish. *See* Baldwin, Ruth Standish (Bowles)
Bowling Green State University (OH), Faculty Dames, **13,760**
Bowman, Frances Willard [Mrs.], **13,259**
Bowman, Gladys (1899-). *See* Knight, Gladys (Bowman) [Mrs. Leonard R.] (1899-)
Bowman, Grace [Miss] (1875-1951), 11,237
Bowman, Lillie Lewin (1899-1968?), **13,736**
Bowman, Mary E., 11,616
Bowman, Mrs. E. A., 16,097
Bowman, Sallie (1863-1948). *See* Caldwell, Sallie (Bowman) (1863-1948)
Bowman, Thomas, 4,521
Bowmer Family, 5,780
Bowne, Elizabeth Southgate, 6,391
Bowne, Lydia C., 11,077
Box Sisters, 1,790
Boxer, Charles R., 4,476
Boxers, 9,308, 13,288, 13,809, 14,119, 14,129
Boxing, 17,376
Boy From Nowhere (book), 17,969
Boy Scouts of America, 2,198, 3,946, **8,463**, 9,104, 12,093, **12,096**
Boyce, Ellen Ruth, 15,225
Boyce, Mr., 10,230

Boycott, 64, **84**, 1,014, 1,859, 8,117, 11,855, **15,987**, 16,010
Boyd, Agatha (?-1950). *See* Adams, Agatha (Boyd) (?-1950)
Boyd, Alice Webster, **7,347**
Boyd, Belle (1844-1900). [Mrs. Samuel Wylde, Jr.] Hardinge [Mrs. John Swainston] Hammond [Mrs. Nathaniel Rue, Jr.] High, 15,610
Boyd, Caroline (1848-82), 11,602
Boyd, E. [Miss], 182
Boyd, Edith, 8,574
Boyd, Edith L., **17,369**
Boyd, Elizabeth, 11,238
Boyd, George (1832-79), Family (MN), **8,958**
Boyd, Isabelle "Belle" (1844-1900). *See* High, Isabelle "Belle" (Boyd) [Mrs. Samuel Wylde, Jr.] Harding [Mrs. John Swainston] Hammond [Mrs. Nathaniel Rue, Jr.] (1844-1900)
Boyd, John W., 11,602
Boyd, Katherine, 559
Boyd, Laura Johnson (Broyles) [Mrs. Montague Lafitte], **3,487**
Boyd, Louie Croft, **1,753**
Boyd, Louise A., 1,085
Boyd, Madeleine Elise (Reynier), 10,866, 10,871
Boyd, Margaret (1846-?), **13,749**
Boyd, Mary Brown (Sumner), 6,223, 10,658, **14,521**
Boyd, Montague Lafitte, 3,487
Boyd, Nancy (pseudonym). *See* Millay, Edna St. Vincent
Boyd, Nancy Williams [Mrs. George] (?-1857), 8,958
Boyd, Neva Leona (1876-1963), 4,047, **4,059**, 4,141, 4,146, 4,958
Boyd, Nicholas E., 11,547
Boyd, Rosamonde Ramsay (1900-), **6,423**, 13,176, **15,570**
Boyd, Rosanna (1789-1872). *See* Hamilton, Rosanna (Boyd) [Mrs. Hugh] (1789-1872)
Boyd, Sarah A. Williams [Mrs. George] (?-1899), 8,958
Boyd, Sarah Hollenback, 3,897
Boyd, Sarah Taylor (Johnson) [Mrs. Alfred Davis, Jr.], **2,221**
Boyd, Sheila (Rule), 10,191
Boyd, Susan. *See* Grant, Susan (Boyd)
Boyd, Welthea Hannah (Hatheway) [Mrs. John W.] (1817-55), 11,602
Boyden, Emily Maria Blakeslee (1828-?), **3,804**, 3,902
Boyden, Helen W., 3,902
Boyden, Sarah Brown [Mrs. William Cowper], 4,060
Boyden, William Cowper (1894-1965), **4,060**
Boye, Karin, 12,880
Boyer, Alice (Davidson), **16,336**
Boyer, Augustine C. (?-1884), 12,267
Boyer, Charlotte (Morrell) [Mrs. Augustine C.] (1816-1901), 12,267
Boyer, Edith Mayse (1900-), **14,187**
Boyer, Florence M. (Squires) Doherty (1890-), **10,749**
Boyer, Harriet Amelia, 11,596
Boyer, Ida Porter, 2,501
Boyer, Maria Comegys, 12,267
Boyer, Richard Montgomery, 9,120
Boyes, Martha Benbow, 5,063
Boyesen, Bayard, 12,487
Boyich, Dorothy (Davis), 522
Boykin, Anne Catherine "Kate." *See* Jones, Anne Catherine "Kate" (Boykin) [Mrs. J. R.]
Boyko, Anna Kobryn [Mrs.] (1889-1973), **14,909**
Boylan Industrial Home (Jacksonville, FL), 5,073
Boyle, Emmet Derby (1879-1927), **10,649**, 10,750
Boyle Family, 1,484
Boyle Family (SC), 15,473
Boyle, Frances Louise (Bickham) [Mrs. John] (1922-), 4,055
Boyle, Kate Satterlee, 12,303
Boyle, Kay. [Mrs. Laurence] Vail [Mrs. Joseph] Franckenstein (1903-), 2,331, **3,771**, 7,171, **16,152**, 16,164
Boyle, Maria (1801-64). *See* Ewing, Maria (Boyle) [Mrs. Thomas, Sr.] (1801-64)
Boyle, Sister Electa, 14,800
Boyle, Vida Margaret (McClure) [Mrs. Emmet Derby] (1880-?), 10,649, **10,750**

Boyles, Katherine, 17,535
Boynton, Anna T., 2,346
Boynton, Charles C., 662
Boynton, Elizabeth Morrison (1843-1925). *See* Harbert, Elizabeth Morrison (Boynton) (1843-1925)
Boynton Family (CA), **362**
Boynton, Grace Morrison (1890-), **6,424**
Boynton, Julia (1861-1957). *See* Green, Julia (Boynton) [Mrs. L. Worthington] (1861-1957)
Boynton, May Olive, 17,006
Boynton, Olive (1805-46). *See* Hale, Olive (Boynton) [Mrs. Jonathan Harriman] (1805-46)
Boynton, Rhea. *See* Hildebrand, Rhea (Boynton)
Boynton, Ruth Evelyn (1896-), **8,540**
Boys, 14,537
    societies and clubs, 2,682, 6,665
Boys Aid Society of California (San Francisco, CA), **363**
Boys and Girls Aid Society (San Francisco, CA). *See* Boys Aid Society of California (San Francisco, CA)
Boys Club (MA), 6,665
Boysville, 16,321
Bozarth, Mrs. L. A., 14,628
Bozeman Academy (MT), 17,315
Bozeman Deaconess Hospital (MT), 10,220
Brace, Charles Loring, 1,998
Brace, Helen. *See* Emerson, Helen (Brace)
Brace, John Pierce, 1,998
Brace, Mabel (Maxwell) [Mrs. Charles], 1,730
Bracelin, Nina Floy [Mrs.], **364**
Brack, Ruth M., 2,016
Brackenridge, Caroline Marie [Mrs. Henry], 15,256
Brackenridge, Cornelia, 15,256
Brackenridge, Henry Marie (1786-1871), **15,256**
Brackenridge, Mary Eleanor (1837-1924), **16,040**, 16,313
Brackett Academy (NH), 7,597
Brackett, Anna Callender [Miss] (1836-1911), 2,542
Brackett, Elizabeth W., 12,739
Bracknell, Barbara Smith [Mrs. Robert] (1922-), 7,510
Bradbury, Annie J. [Miss], 17,750
Bradbury Family, 8,927
Bradbury, Janette Lane, 3,374
Bradbury, Janette Lane [Mrs. Thomas] (1908-68), **3,374**
Bradbury, Lavinia, 8,927
Bradbury, Lynda Lane, 3,374
Bradbury, Thomas Lane, 3,374
Braddock, General, 3,509
Braden, Amy (Steinhart) [Mrs. Robert] (1879-?), **365**
Braden, Anne Gambrell (McCarty) [Mrs. Carl] (1924-), 127, **5,377, 11,840, 15,877, 17,608**
Braden, Carl (1914-75), 5,377, 11,840, **15,877, 17,608**
Braden, Hector W., 2,930
Bradford College (MA), **7,048**, 7,658
    alumnae, 7,357
    students, 4,829
Bradford, Ellen Knight, **2,222**
Bradford Female Academy (MA). *See* Bradford College (MA)
Bradford Female Benevolent Society (MA), **7,348**
Bradford Female Charitable Society (MA), **7,348**
Bradford, Gamaliel, 17,114
Bradford, Moses, 2,038
Bradford, Phoebe (George) [Mrs. Moses] (1794-1840), **2,038, 5,745**
Bradford, Sarah Alden (1793-1867). *See* Ripley, Sarah Alden (Bradford) [Mrs. Samuel] (1793-1867)
Bradford, Sister Vincent Ferrer (1889-1972), 17,868
Bradford Society (WI), 17,724
Bradford, Susan. *See* Eppes, Susan (Bradford) [Mrs. Nicholas Ware]
Bradlee, Alice Crowninshield [Mrs. Josiah], 7,361
Bradlee, F. B. C., 7,361
Bradlee, Sarah Crowninshield, 7,361
Bradley, Celia (Walsh), 12,658
Bradley, Clara (1855-1954). *See* Burdette, Clara (Bradley) [Mrs. N. Milman] Wheeler [Mrs. Presley C.] Baker [Mrs. Robert J.] (1855-1954)
Bradley, Duane (1914-), **4,975**

Bradley, Frances (Sage) [Mrs. Horace James] (ca. 1862-1949), **3,311**
Bradley, Grace E. [Miss], 8,170
Bradley, Horace James, 3,311
Bradley-Hyde Family (CT, MA), **6,425**
Bradley, Ione (Dewey) [Mrs. Luther P.], 14,767
Bradley, Joseph P. (1813-92), **11,076**
Bradley, Laura, 11,975
Bradley, Laura [Mrs.], **8,264**
Bradley, Luther P., **14,767**
Bradley, Madge, 1,186, 1,188
Bradley, Martha C., 8,164
Bradley, Mary. *See* Cowles, Mary (Bradley) [Mrs. George]
Bradley, S. Grace, 3,799
Bradley University (Peoria, IL), Chimes, 14,029
Bradley, Walter Wadsworth (1878-1950), **366**
Bradner, Clara (Harwood) (1855-1956), **367**
Bradner, Judith, 3,754
Bradshaw, Doris Crump [Mrs. William L.], 9,935
Bradshaw, Elizabeth, 16,451
Bradshaw, Harriet Olive (Ririe) [Mrs. Richard] (1892-), **16,609**
Bradshaw, Helen (1878-1954). *See* Stevens, Helen (Bradshaw) [Mrs. Thomas Wood] (1878-1954)
Bradshaw, Nellie Kemp, 1,319
Bradshaw, William L., 9,935
Bradshaw, William L., Jr., 9,935
Bradstreet, Anne (Dudley) [Mrs. Simon] (1612-72), **7,127**
Bradstreet, Simon, 7,127
Bradwell, Annie (Campbell), **12,958**
Bradwell, James Bolesworth, 4,351
Bradwell, Myra (Colby) [Mrs. James Bolesworth] (1831-94), 3,797, **4,351**
Brady, Benton, 3,375
Brady, John David, **10,435**
Brady, Julia [Mrs.], 11,780
Brady, Marna V., 2,884
Brady, Mary A., **12,169**
Brady, Mildred, 11,805
Brady, Sara M. [Mrs.], **3,375**
Brady, Thomas A. (1902-64), **9,936**
Braffett, Amanda Lucretia (1830-1910). *See* Hofheins, Amanda Lucretia (Braffett) [Mrs. Jacob Michael] (1830-1910)
Bragdon, Helen, 12,836
Bragg, Fannie May (1920-). *See* Duncan, Fannie May (Bragg) [Mrs. Edward R.] (1920-)
Bragg, Fred, 17,907
Bragg, Laura Ingham [Mrs. Fred], 17,907
Bragg, Lillian (Chaplin) (1895-1967), **3,488**
Bragg, Mary (Rankin), 6,846
Bragg, Mrs. Braxton, 16,097
Braginton, Mary V., 5,110
Brahms and His Women's Choruses (book), 7,218
Brahms, Johannes, 6,185, 7,218
Brailsford, Samuel, 15,716
Brain
    diseases, 6,216
    weight, 9,235
Brainard, B. M., 368
Brainard Cherokee Mission School (MN), 11,709
Brainard, Clementine H. [Mrs. B. M.], 368
Brainard, Laura Russell [Mrs.], **10,225**
Brainard Mission (MN), 15,463
Brainerd, Heloise [Miss] (1881-1954?), 1,604, 15,316
Brainerd, Mary Kinney, 3,993
Brainerd Senior High School (MN), 8,593
Braithwaite, William Stanley Beaumont, 3,288, **11,077**, 11,897
Brakeman, Esther (1826-1917). *See* Butler, Esther (Brakeman) [Mrs. Joseph] Lyman [Mrs. Thomas] (1826-1917)
Braley, Grace (Madden) [Mrs. Gerald], 4,599
Braly, Susannah Hyde [Mrs. John Eusebius] (1805-97), **1,247**
Bramblett, Agnes Cochran (1886-), 3,071, **3,312**
Brame, Herbert, **1,621**
Bramer, Electa (Snow) (1796-?), **369**
Branch Agricultural College (UT), 16,402

Branch, Anna Hempstead [Miss] (1875-1937), 2,376, 4,005, 5,273, 7,131, **7,166**, 7,868
Branch, Charlotte Sawyer [Mrs.] (1814-94), 3,086
Branch Family, 7,166
Branch, Hamilton McDevitt (1843-99), 3,086
Branch Herald (Topeka, KS), 10,579
Branch, John Lufburrow (1838-61), 3,086
Branch, Lawrence O'Bryan, 13,343
Branch, Mary Elizabeth (1882-1944), **2,125**
Branch, Mary L. (Bolles), 7,166
Branch, Nancy (Blount) [Mrs. Lawrence O'Bryan], **13,344**
Branch, Nannie, 13,344
Branch Normal School (UT). *See* Southern Utah State College
Branch, Sanford W., 3,086
Brand Family (WV), **17,452**
Brand, Frank M., 17,452
Brand, John M., 17,452
Brand, Katharine E., 2,186
Brand, Millen, 14,455
Brand, Willa, 17,452
Brand, William N., 17,452
Brandegee, Mary Katharine (Layne) [Mrs. Towshend Stith] Curran (1844-1920), 526, 6,310
Brandegee, Sarah Canfield (De Camp), 12,191
Brandeis, Alice (Goldmark) [Mrs. Louis Dembitz], 441, 2,432, 6,565
Brandeis, Elizabeth. [Mrs. Paul] Raushenbush (1896-), 11,760, **17,765**, 17,775
Brandeis, Irma, 2,215
Brandeis, Jean (1894-1978). *See* Tachau, Jean (Brandeis) [Mrs. Charles G.] (1894-1978)
Brandeis, Louis Dembitz, 945, 2,359, 5,365, 6,565, 11,855, 12,534
Branden, Amy Steinhardt, 942
Brandenburg, Linn [Mrs.], 4,079
Brandenstein, Edith. *See* Jacobi, Edith Brandenstein [Mrs. Jacob]
Brandon, Emma, **13,771**
Brandon Family, 9,738
Brandon, Francis Lawson, 62
Brandon, Mary Elizabeth (1840-?). *See* Beaver, Mary Elizabeth (Brandon) (1840-?)
Brandon News, The (MS), 9,703
Brandon, William, 53
Brandon, Zillah (Haynie) [Mrs. Francis Lawson] (1801-post 1871), **62**
Brandsmark, Gertrude Marie. *See* Longbrake, Gertrude Marie Brandsmark [Mrs. George R.]
Brandt and Brandt (literary agency), 5,273, 5,985, 5,996, 6,110, 11,490
Brandt, Carol (Denny) (1904-), 2,295, 4,476
Brandt, Diderikke Ottesen (1827-85), 8,737
Brandt, Isaac, 4,838
Brann, Esther. *See* Schorr, Esther Brann [Mrs. Richard]
Brannan, Eleanor, 15,308
Brannan, Samual, 16,586
Brannigan, Daliah. *See* Hall, Daliah (Brannigan) [Mrs. R.]
Brannigan, Felix (1843-1907), **2,223**
Brannock, Edwin, 9,937
Brannock, Lizzia E., **9,937**
Branscombe, Martha, 4,084
Branson, Emily, 13,345, 13,369
Branson, Grace, 13,345
Brant, Mary "Molly" (ca. 1736-96), 11,440, 12,615
Brantley, Ella Thomas (Foreacre) [Mrs. Archibald Philip], **3,185**
Brasch, Augusta. *See* Acton, Augusta (Brasch) [Mrs. A. E.]
Brasch, Betty. *See* Picard, Betty (Brasch) [Mrs. Joseph]
Brasch, Caroline [Mrs. Otto], 1,569
Brasch Family (CA), **1,569**
Brasch, Frederick E., 1,569
Brasch, Louise. *See* Schmidt, Louise (Brasch) [Mrs. Albert]
Brasch, Otto, 1,569
Brashear, Margaret M. (1874-1963), **9,839**
Brasher, Helen (Kortwright) [Mrs. Abraham] (1739-1819), **12,170**
Brass, Maggie, 9,355

Bratager, Laura [Mrs.], 9,190
Brathwaite, Yvonne. *See* Burke, Yvonne (Watson) Brathwaite
Brattleboro High School (VT), 16,998
Bratton, Helen (1899-), **14,327**
Braun, Emma Lucy (1889-1971), **2,713**
Braun, Evelyn M., **1,700**
Braun, Oelóel (Quitzow), 362
Braxton, Carter M., 2,404
Braxton Family (VA), 17,107, 17,108
Braxton, Fannie Page (Hume) [Mrs. Carter M.] (1838-65), **2,404**, **13,036**
Braxton, Mary (Blair), 17,108
Bray, Avis **10,405**
Bray, Evelina (1810-95). *See* Downey, Evelina (Bray) (1810-95)
Bray, Gertrude C. [Miss] (1888-1975), **15,378**
Brayman Family (IL), **4,347**
Brayman, Mary (Williams) [Mrs. Mason] (1816-86), 4,347
Brayman, Mason, 4,347
Brayman, Nellie, 4,347
Brayman, Sarah, 4,347
Brayman, Sarah Adaline "Ada." *See* Bailhache, Sarah Adaline "Ada" (Brayman) [Mrs. William H.]
Brayton, Cynthia, 11,529
Brayton, Ellen M. (1836-?), 11,529
Brayton Family (NY), **11,529**
Brayton, Katy C., 11,529
Brayton, Mary Clark, 13,966
Brayton, Mr., 11,440
Brayton, Mrs., 11,440
Brayton, Patience, **13,346**
Brazer, Marjorie C., **7,733**
Brazil
   American ambassadors to, 11,857
   art, abstract, 2,741
   emigrés, American, **69**, 70, 114, 13,025, 13,049
   missionaries to, 1,786
   missionaries to, Methodist, 13,294
   Peace Corps Volunteers in, **8,261**
   social life and customs, 70
   Young Women's Christian Association, 1,655
Breach of contract, 17,230
Breach of promise, 10,153
Bread upon the Waters (book), 12,589
"Breadfruit in the Baggage" (speech), 6,992
Breadgivers, The (book), 947
Break in the Weather, A (book), 6,091
Breakaway College (San Francisco, CA), 17,663
Breakaway Conferences (1970-1971), 17,583
Breakfast at Tiffany's (moving-picture), 17,802
Breakwater (plantation, SC), 15,440
Brearley School, 11,890
Breast cancer, 4,698, 5,757
Breastfeeding, 3,968, 8,639
Brebner, Eva M. [Mrs.] (1875-?), 4,899
Brecht, Berthold, 12,367
Breck, Clarissa (Allen), 7,128
Breck, Hannah. *See* Lloyd, Hannah (Breck)
Breck, Jean Ross [Mrs. Samuel], 14,961
Breck, Lucy, 14,961
Breck, Martha Cunnable, 7,661
Breck Mission and Farm School (Wilder, MN), 9,442
Breck, Nathaniel, 7,661
Breck, Samuel (1771-1862), **14,961**
Breck, Sarah (1710-53). *See* Pierpont, Sarah (Breck) [Mrs. James] (1710-53)
Breck School (MN), 9,438
Breckenridge, Clarence Edward (1877-1963), **9,840**
Breckenridge, William Clark (1862-1927), **9,841**
Breckens, Mrs. Joe, 17,894
Breckinridge, Aida de Acosta, 5,123
Breckinridge, Elizabeth E. (1859-1942), Family (MN), **8,959**
Breckinridge Family (KY), **5,332**
Breckinridge, John Cabell (1821-75), 5,303, 5,332
Breckinridge, Leola [Mrs.], 9,986
Breckinridge, Madeline (McDowell) [Mrs. Desha] (1872-1920), **5,302**
Breckinridge, Mary, 5,252
Breckinridge, Mary Cyrene (Burch) [Mrs. John Cabell] (1822-1906), **5,303**, 5,332
Breckinridge, Robert J., 5,750

Breckinridge, Robert Jefferson (1800-71), 5,343
Breckinridge, Sophonisba Preston [Miss] (1866-1948), **2,224**, 2,439, 2,446, 2,509, 2,519, 3,828, 4,003, 4,047, 4,052, 4,101, 4,103, 4,104, 4,110, 4,117, 4,150, 4,161, 7,923, 8,653
Breckinridge, Virginia (Hart) [Mrs. Alfred] Shelby [Mrs. Robert Jefferson] (1809-59), 5,343
Breda, O. J., 8,725
Brede Place (residence, England), 11,979
Bree, Germaine, 7,822
Breed, Augustus Baxter, 4,844
Breed, Betsy (Niles), 4,904
Breeden, Jane Rooker (Smith) (1853-1955), **15,851**, 15,857
Breeden, Mrs. William H., 11,440
Breeding, W. P., 690
Breedlove, Mildred [Mrs. Crongy P.] (1904-), **10,650**
Breen Family, 644
Breen, Genevieve Rose, 9,313
Breen, Mae, 7,109
Breen, Ruth S., 2,927
Breese Family (NY), 11,440
Breese, Zona Gale [Mrs. William Llywelyn] (1874-1938). *See* Gale, Zona. [Mrs. William Llywelyn] Breese (1874-1938)
Breeskin, Adelyn (Dohme) (1896-), 2,844, 2,845, 5,829
Bregman, Buddy, 6,013
Bregman, Elsie Oschrin (1896-1969), 13,737
Breinholt, Maxine (Lund) [Mrs. Harvey Cowley] (1926-), **16,611**
Breit, Harvey, **4,227**
Breitenbaugh, Dolly [Miss], 9,991
Brelsford, Sarah E., 1,533
Bremer, Anne M., 1,081
Bremer, Edith Terry, 9,492
Bremer, Edna Thayer, 1,659
Bremer, Fredrika (1801-65), **4,322**, 7,585, **8,960**, 11,125, **14,905**, 15,601
Bremer, Mrs. Alexander, 11,597
Bremer, Mrs. Thayer, 1,658
Brenau College, alumnae, 3,437
Brennan, Angela Juanita (Stott) [Mrs. Gerton] Colling [Mrs. James] Murray [Mrs. James Arthur] Connery [Mrs. Don] (1919-), **13,669**
Brennan, Arcadia Bandini (Scott) (1885-), **370**
Brennan, Don, 13,669
Brenner, Ann Reed, 8,658, 8,678
Brenner, Rose (?-1926), 8,963
Brenner, Ruth Kutoff Lukov, 17,282
Brenny, Bertha (1906-), **8,841**
Brent, Charles Henry (1862-1929), **2,225**
Brent, Elizabeth Jacquelin (Ambler) [Mrs. William] (1765-?). *See* Carrington, Elizabeth Jacquelin (Ambler) [Mrs. William] Brent [Mrs. Edward]
Brent, Helen C. [Miss], 2,225
Brent, Madame, 5,501
Brent, Sylvia. *See* Elliot, Sylvia (Brent)
Brent, William (?-1785), 2,248, 17,126
Brentano, Frances Isabella (Hyams) [Mrs. Lowell], 14,328
Brentano, Lowell (1895-1950), **14,328**
Brenton, Alice, 4,916
Brenton, Fanny [Miss], 12,166
Brenton, Maria [Miss], 12,166
Brenum Family, 8,765
Brenvold, Emma (1883-), 8,709
Brescia College (Owensboro, KY), curricula, **5,399**
Bressler, Allen, 10,436
Bressler Family (NE), **10,436**
Bressler, Julia (Nelson) [Mrs. Calvin] (1881-), 10,436
Bretag, Rose Anna (1862-1929), 9,025
Bretherton, Alice Gertrude, 14,542
Breton, Adela C. (1850-1923), 6,323, 6,324, 6,328
Brett, Dorothy, 1,779
Brett, Dorothy (1883-), 572, **13,871**
Brett, Dorothy (1891-), **4,228**
Brett, Phillip M., **10,929**
Bretz, Martha Grubb, 1,788
Brevard, Alexander, **13,347**
Brevard, Harriet, 13,347
Brevoort, Henrietta. *See* Lindsey, Henrietta (Brevoort) [Mrs. Benjamin Barr]
Brewen, Mrs., 6,609

Brewer, Alice. *See* Gardner, Alice (Brewer)
Brewer, Ellen, 13,479
Brewer, Florence (1885-). *See* Boeckel, Florence (Brewer) (1885-)
Brewer, George, **8,070**
Brewer, Grace [Mrs. George] (1881-), **8,070**
Brewer, Henry Bridgeman, **17,402**
Brewer, Laura Giddings [Mrs. Henry Bridgeman], 17,402
Brewer, Leslie R., 17,892
Brewer, Luther A., 1,224
Brewer, Minnie (Block), 9,709
Brewer, Mrs. George, 4,675
Brewer, Nina (Brinkerhoff) [Mrs. Leslie Odell] (1908-), **16,610**
Brewer, Vivion Mercer (Lenon) [Mrs. Joe Robinson] (1900-), **7,194**, 11,857, 13,176
Brewer, William H., 323
Brewer, William Henry (1828-1910), **371**
Brewing industries, 2,706
Brewster, Anna Gertrude, 7,195
Brewster, Anne Maria Hampton (1819-92), **14,962**
Brewster, Caroline, 7,195
Brewster, Clarissa. *See* Bingham, Clarissa (Brewster) [Mrs. Hiram, II]
Brewster Family (MA), **7,195**
Brewster Family (NY), 11,709
Brewster, Helen, 7,195
Brewster, Helen (1881-). *See* Owens, Helen (Brewster) [Mrs. Fred] (1881-)
Brewster, Juanita Gilmore (1895-1970), **122**
Brewster Ladies Library Association (MA), **6,241**
Brewster, Mary, 8,655
Brewster, Mary K., 7,195
Brewster, S. Harriette. *See* Conwell, S. Harriette (Brewster) [Mrs. Leon M.]
Brewster, William (1851-1919), **6,317**
Brezhnev, Leonid, 12,111
Brian, Sarah, **2,039**
Briarcreek Institute (GA), 3,417
Briarcreek Presbyterian Church (Bloomsburg, PA), Women's Foreign Missionary Society, 14,724
Brice, C. Olivia, 12,440
Brice, Carol. [Mrs. Thomas] Carey, **5,459**
Brice, Eugene, 5,459
Brice, Fanny Borach (1891-1951), 12,129, 12,798
Brice, Jonathan, 5,459
Bricelin, Susan (ca. 1838-?). *See* Fletcher, Susan (Bricelin) [Mrs. Henry Lewis] (ca. 1838-?)
Brickell, Herschel, 12,035
Brickell, James B., **13,348**
Bricker, Mrs. Marvin, 4,923
Brickett, Huldah (Gragg), 14,375
Brickmaking, 3,270
Bricks, 15,518
Bricks and People (book), 13,244
Brico, Antonia, **372**, 1,788
Brico Symphony, The (CO), 1,788
Bride and the Burglar, The (drama), 6,904
Bride of Innisfallen and Other Stories (book), 9,770, 16,172
Bridel, Genevieve, 9,449
Bride's Club (Ithaca, NY), **11,530**
Bridewell Prison (NY), Commissioners, **12,423**
Bridge, Ann, 3,110
Bridge, Elizabeth, 6,310
Bridge, Mr., 6,246
Bridge to Brotherhood, 3,288
Bridgeport Board of Education (CT), 1,829
Bridgeport War Bureau (CT), 1,820
Bridgers, Ann Preston, **12,959**, 13,391
Bridgers, Robert R., **13,349**
Bridges, 5,538, 5,542
Bridges, Bernice, 8,670
Bridges, Grace, 826
Bridges, J. R., 13,179
Bridges, Margaret, 13,300
Bridgeton Female Seminary (NJ), 6,601
Bridgman, Amy (1866-1948). *See* Cowles, Amy (Bridgman) (1866-1948)
Bridgman, Annie Cleaveland (1857-1936), 7,131
Bridgman, Dorothy Dagmar (1890-1965). *See* Rood, Dorothy Dagmar (Bridgman) [Mrs. Frederick Grant] Atkinson [Mrs. John H.] (1890-1965)

Bridgman, Eliza Jane (Gillett) [Mrs. Elijah] (1805-71), 2,016
Bridgman Family (MA), **7,129**
Bridgman, Laura Brainerd Nichols (1834-1923), 6,663, 7,129
Bridgman, Laura Dewey (1829-89), 3,927, 4,732, **6,426**, 7,560, **10,798**
Bridgman, Ralph P., 13,870
Bridgwater, Lucy, 16,097
Bridson, Diane Mary (1942-), 10,151
Brief Historical Rhetoric, A (book), 12,031
Brief History of the Delta Kappa Society, 6,514
Briffault, Herma (Hoyt) (1898-), 6,947, **12,396**
Briggs, Anna (1796-?). *See* Bentley, Anna (Briggs) [Mrs. Caleb] (1796-?)
Briggs, Annie Frances, 1,261
Briggs, Deborah, 5,746
Briggs, Dorothy (1912-), 7,109
Briggs, Elizabeth, 5,746
Briggs, Emma, 3,834
Briggs, Hannah (Brooke) [Mrs. Isaac] (?-ca. 1851), 5,746
Briggs, Harriet, 12,379
Briggs, Isaac (1763-1825), 5,746
Briggs, J. A., 13,397
Briggs, L. B. R. (1855-1934), 6,484
Briggs, Maria Antoinette (?-1903). *See* Haskell, Maria Antoinette (Briggs) [Mrs. Edward Wilder] (?-1903)
Briggs, Mary, 5,746
Briggs, Mary Edith. *See* Moses, Mary Edith (Briggs) [Mrs. Bernard]
Briggs, Melissa (Chapin) [Mrs. Welcolm] (?-1861), **8,961**
Briggs, Minerva (1825-96), **4,739**
Briggs, Mrs. Willis, 13,350
Briggs, Ruth M., **5,129**
Briggs, Sarah, 5,746
Briggs, Sarah, 13,350
Briggs, Sarah (Grandy) [Mrs. Thomas Henry, Jr.], 13,350
Briggs, Thomas Henry, Jr., 13,350
Briggs, Welcolm (1823-?), **8,961**
Briggs, Willis G., **13,350**
Brigham, Cephas (1822?-?), **7,606**
Brigham, Florence May (?-1956). *See* Stetson, Florence May (Brigham) [Mrs. Harlan True] (?-1956)
Brigham, Johnson, 4,731
Brigham, Lucy Elmira Graves (1827-87), 7,606
Brigham Young (moving-picture), 16,496
Brigham Young Academy (UT). *See* Brigham Young University (Provo, UT)
Brigham Young University (Provo, UT), 16,505, 16,635, 16,640, 16,874
  deans, 16,518, 16,608
  faculty, 3,738, 16,530, 16,536, 16,802, 16,843
  students, 16,546, 16,550, 16,720, 16,810
Brigham Young University (Provo, UT), Training School, 16,549
Brigham Young University (Provo, UT), University Emeritus Club, 16,536
Bright, Abbie (1848-1926). *See* Achenbach, Abbie (Bright) [Mrs. William M.] (1848-1926)
Bright, Carrie Lena McMullen (1915-), **8,871**
Bright College Year (book), 5,028
Bright, R. Golding, 14,366
Bright, Sallie, 8,670
"Brighter Day, The" (soap opera), 17,705
Brill, Alice Cora (1889-1968), 8,962
Brill, Cora Amelia (Gray) [Mrs. Hascal Russell] (1850-1927), 8,962
Brill, Edith (1876-1961), 8,962
Brill, Ethel Claire (1877-1962), 8,962
Brill, Hascal Russell (1846-1922), Family (MN), **8,962**
Brin, Fanny (Fligelman) (1884-1961), **8,963**
Brinckerhoff, Catherine, **11,078**
Brinckerhoff, Charlotte Troup (1818-61). *See* Bronson, Charlotte Troup (Brinckerhoff) (1818-61)
Brinckerhoff, Elizabeth Susan, 11,083
Brinckerhoff Family, 12,607
Brinckerhoff, Louisa Troup, 12,398

Bringhurst, Anna [Mrs. James] (?-1777), 14,963
Bringhurst, Deborah, 2,045
Bringhurst, Hannah [Mrs. James] (ca. 1751-82), **14,963**
Bringhurst, James (?-1810), 14,963
Bringloe, Frances, **17,239**
Brink, Carol Ryrie (1895-), 8,531, 8,600
Brink, Sarah Ann, 12,337
Brinkerhoff, Lucy, 11,547
Brinkerhoff, Nina (1908-). *See* Brewer, Nina (Brinkerhoff) [Mrs. Leslie Odell] (1908-)
Brinkley, Roberta Florence (1893-1967), **13,191**
Brinley, Katherine Johnstone (?-1926). *See* Wharton, Katherine Johnstone (Brinley) (?-1926)
Brinton, Anna Cox, 705
Brinton, Cassandra, **15,339**
Brinton, Ellen Starr (1886-1954), **15,302**
Brinton, Howard, 705
Brisbane, Albert (1809-90), **4,409**
Brisbane, Lodoiska M. [Mrs. Albert], 4,409
Brisbane, Redelia Bates [Mrs. Albert], 4,409
Brisco, Mary Susan (High) Casey (1875-1958), **253**
Briscoe, Adele Lubbock (1848-1935). *See* Looscan, Adele Lubbock (Briscoe) (1848-1935)
Briscoe, Mary Jane Harris (1819-1903), **16,041**
Brish, Eleanor (Cary) [Mrs. Henry Colgate], 2,328
Bristol, Edith. *See* Tigert, Edith (Bristol) [Mrs. John J.]
Bristol, Fanny L., **12,397**
Bristol, Helen (Moore) [Mrs. William Bailey] Thomas [Mrs. Mark Lambert] (1867?-1945), 2,226
Bristol, Mark Lambert (1868-1939), **2,226**
Bristol, Myrl Lewark, **4,895**
Bristol Sewing Society (WI), **17,556**
Bristol Socialist Society (England), 12,698
Bristow, Darwin (1862-1951), 14,284
Bristow, Elijah (1788-1872), 14,284
Bristow, Elizabeth Coffey, 14,284
Bristow, Evelyn, 14,284
Bristow Family (OR), **14,284**
Bristow, Helen, 14,284
Bristow, Lisette "Lizzie" (1867-1962). *See* Stephens, Lisette "Lizzie" (Bristow) [Mrs. John H.] (1867-1962)
British Columbia
  monasticism and religious orders, Catholic, **17,415**
  Native Americans, 17,263
  nuns, Catholic, **17,415**
British Columbia Rides a Star (book), 13,674
British Expeditionary Forces, France, World War I, 6,152
British Guiana, 8,555
British occupation of Philadelphia, 14,847, 15,118
British Social Hygiene Council, 12,736
British War Relief Society, Inc., 10,452, 10,488, 15,446
British Women's Temperance Association, 17,916
Brittain, Vera Mary (1893-1970), 3,980
Britten, Evelyn (Barrett) [Mrs. Walter] (1891-1969), **12,846**
Brittle Heaven (book), 12,441
Britton, Elizabeth Gertrude (Knight) [Mrs. Nathaniel Lord] (1858-1934), 6,309, 6,310, 11,297, 15,213
Broad, Verna S., 10,478
Broaddus, Caroline (Boulware) [Mrs. Andrew] (?-1848), 3,373
Broader Learnings Through Poetry, 5,083
Broadhurst, Mrs. Thomas, 11,596
"Broadwalk Tattler, The" (column), 4,379
Broadway Hospital Unit (Decorah, IA), **4,713**
"Broadway or Theater" (lecture), 17,811
Broadway Tabernacle (NY), 7,168
Broadwick, Charles, 13,351
Broadwick, Tiny. Georgia Ann Thompson, 13,322, **13,351**, 13,446
Broberg, Amanda (?-1919), 9,119
Broch, Hermann, 12,035
Brock, Emma Lillian (1886-?), 8,531
Brock, G. W., 81
Brock, Genevra, 17,919
Brock, Leah. *See* McCartney, Leah (Brock)
Brock, Lulu Wash Chapoose, 16,876
Brockenbrough, Judith. *See* McGuire, Judith (Brockenbrough) [Mrs. John P.]

Brockhost, Mrs., 11,318
Brockport Collegiate Institute (NY). *See* State University of New York College at Brockport
Brockport State Teachers College (NY). *See* State University of New York College at Brockport
Brockway, Betsy Ann, 9,041
Brockway, Margaret Rice, **14,522**, 14,618
Brode, Bernice (1901-), **373**
Brodeau, Anna Maria (1774?-?). *See* Thornton, Anna Maria (Brodeau) [Mrs. William] (1774?-?)
Brodie, Fawn (McKay) [Mrs. Richard] (1915-), **16,612**, 16,881, 16,923
Brodie, Jennie Imogene (Harding) (1878-1956), 14,573
Brodie, Jessie L., 14,698
Brodine, Virginia (1915-), **4,492**
Brodman, Estelle, 10,152
Brodnik, Cecilia (1880-1974), **13,912**
Brodt, Elizabeth Elaine. *See* Loring, Elizabeth Elaine (Brodt)
Brodwell, Elizabeth Lytle, 8,900
Broedel, Max, 8,574
Broer, Marion Ruth (1910-), **17,240**
Broidrick, Annie Laurie (Harris), **12,960**
Broiler Festival (ME), 5,644
Brokaw, Ada, 10,901
Brokaw, Clare (Boothe) [Mrs. George Tuttle] (1903-). *See* Luce, Clare (Boothe) [Mrs. George Tuttle] Brokaw [Mrs. Henry Robinson] (1903-)
Brokaw, Cornelia, **11,079**
Brokaw, George Tuttle, 2,458
Brokaw, Josephine, **7,734**
Broke, Frederica Sophia (Mure) [Mrs. Horatio George], **12,813**
Broke, Horace, 12,813
Broke, Horatio George (1790-1860), 12,813
Brokers, 1,081, 10,784
Bromfield Family (NY), 12,298
Bromley, Louise Love, 9,289
Bromley, Marion (1880-ca. 1960). *See* Newton, Marion (Bromley) (1880-ca. 1960)
Bromley, Shirlee M., 3,742
Bromwell, Henrietta Elizabeth [Miss] (1859-1946), **1,692**, 1,754
Bromwell, Judge, 1,759
Bromwell, Mrs. Charles S., 11,704
Bronck Family (NY), **11,415**
Bronck, Jan Leonard, 11,416
Bronck, Jonas, 11,415
Bronck, Susannah [Mrs. Jan Leonard] (?-1814), **11,416**
Bronk, Elizabeth [Miss], 1,837
Bronson, Ann, 12,398
Bronson, Ann Eliza Bailey [Mrs.], 12,398
Bronson, Anna Olcott [Mrs.], 12,398
Bronson, Arthur (1801-44), 12,398
Bronson, Charlotte Troup (Brinckerhoff) (1818-61), 12,398
Bronson, Christine Frederica, **7,735**
Bronson, Deborah [Mrs.], 11,823
Bronson, Ethel (1765-1825), 12,398
Bronson Family (NY, CT), **12,398**
Bronson, Fredric (1802-68), 12,398
Bronson, Harriet, 12,398
Bronson, Isaac (1760-1838), 12,398
Bronson, Loosie (ca. 1867-?), **5,747**
Bronson, Mary, 12,398
Bronson, Miles, **10,942**
Bronson, Oliver (1799-1875), 12,398
Bronson, Ruth M. Lucas [Mrs. Miles], 10,942
Bronstad, Anna, 8,747
Bronstad, Johan, 8,747
Brontë, Charlotte (1816-55), 15,753, 16,501
Brontë, Emily (1818-48), 16,501
Brontë Society (UT), **16,501**
Brontës, 1,488
Brook, Alexander, 2,824
Brook Farm (MA), 1,426, 4,434, **7,043**, 7,044
Brook, Libbie (1850-1933). *See* Gaddis, Libbie (Brook) (1850-1933)
Brook, Madge Ann. *See* De Jonge, Madge Ann (Brook)
Brooke, Florence Ralston (1858-1944), 16,132

Brooke, Hannah (?-ca. 1851). *See* Briggs, Hannah (Brooke) [Mrs. Isaac] (?-ca. 1851)

Brooke, L. Leslie, 12,570

Brooke, Nan (ca. 1888-1958). *See* Harold, Nan (Brooke) (ca. 1888-1958)

Brooke, St. George Tucker, 17,461

Brookes, Sybil D., 12,570

Brookes, Stella B., 3,290

Brookfield, Kate (Morgan) [Mrs. William], 12,052

Brookgreen Gardens (SC), 12,901

Brookhaven National Laboratory, officials and employees, 6,336

Brookings Institution Survey of Indian Affairs, 14,006

Brookins, Jean, 9,049

Brooklyn (ship), 16,586

Brooklyn Association (NY), 6,979

Brooklyn College (NY), faculty, 5,455, 5,460

Brooklyn Congregational Church (OH), Woman's Missionary Society, **13,913**

Brooklyn Daily Eagle (NY), 2,801, 7,182, **11,311,** 12,556

Brooklyn Daily Union (NY), 14,058

Brooklyn Dodgers (NY), 9,951

Brooklyn Female Academy (NY). *See* Packer Collegiate Institute (NY)

Brooklyn Fire Insurance Company (NY), 11,324

Brooklyn Heights Seminary (NY), 11,719

Brooklyn Navy Yard (NY), 2,679

Brooklyn Society of New England Women (NY), **11,317**

Brooklyn Women's Bar Association (NY), 6,819

Brooks, Abbie M. [Miss], **3,155**

Brooks, Anne (Tedlock) (1905-), **5,206, 14,329**

Brooks, Charles (1795-1872), 2,477, **12,171**

Brooks, Charles Timothy, 12,457

Brooks, Charlotte [Mrs. Charles], 12,171

Brooks, Cleanth (1906-), 9,769

Brooks, E. C., **13,332**

Brooks, Eleanor (Stimson) [Mrs. Van Wyck], 794

Brooks, Elizabeth, 12,171

Brooks, Ethel Grant (1887-1976), **6,129**

Brooks Family, 15,942

Brooks, Fern E., **8,964**

Brooks, Gladys [Mrs. Van Wyck], 794, 11,952

Brooks, Gladys Sinclair [Mrs. Wright W.] (1914-), 9,159

Brooks, Gwendolyn, 3,290

Brooks, Hallie B., 3,290

Brooks, Helen, 13,617

Brooks, Jabez, 8,602

Brooks, John Graham (1846-1938), **6,427**

Brooks, Juanita (Leavitt) [Mrs. L. Ernest] Pulsipher [Mrs. William] (ca. 1900-), 16,488, **16,882,** 16,900, **16,924,** 16,971

Brooks, Leona. *See* Morgan, Leona (Brooks) [Mrs. Arthur]

Brooks, Margaret Hessler, 4,070

Brooks, Margarette W., **7,467**

Brooks, Maria (Gowen). [Mrs. John] Abigail Gowen. Mary Abigail Brooks (ca. 1794-1845), 12,002, **12,399**

Brooks, Mary E. [Miss], 1,926

Brooks, Mary (Thomas) [Mrs. A. J., Jr.] Peavey [Mrs.], 3,682

Brooks Memorial Art Gallery (TN), 15,883

Brooks, Mrs. Morgan, **6,428**

Brooks, Phyllis 4,764

Brooks, Rachel (1884-), **12,400,** 13,799

Brooks, Romaine, 2,845

Brooks, Samuel Palmer (1863-1931), **16,337**

Brooks, Thelma, 400

Brooks, Van Wyck, 2,463, 11,286, **11,952**

Brooks, Will, 16,924

Brookwood Labor College (Katonah, NY), 4,032, **8,071,** 8,085, 12,422, 15,332
faculty, **8,126**

Broom and brush industry, 7,606

Broom, Mary Louise, 5,469

Broomall, Anna Elizabeth [Miss] (1847-1931), **15,127**

Broomall Club, 15,145

Broome, Christine [Miss] (1894-1976), **3,459**

Broomhall, Estella Baird, 14,155

Brophy, John, 8,085, 11,766, 15,327

Brossman, Adeline H., **17,948**

Brother Angel (book), 17,731

Brotherhood of Locomotive Engineers Journal, 17,635

Brotherhood of Locomotive Firemen, 4,675

Brotherhood of Locomotive Firemen and Engineers, Women's Auxiliary, **16,255**

Brotherhood of Railroad Trainmen, Ladies Auxiliary, **8,842**

Brotherhood of Railway Carmen of America, 3,220

Brotherhood of Sleeping Car Porters, Chicago Division (IL), **3,805**

Brotherhood of Sleeping Car Porters, International Ladies Auxiliary, 3,805

Brothers Family, 15,942

Brotherton, Belle [Mrs.], **8,266**

Brott, George F., 9,398

Brouaugh, Anne, 4,743

Brough, Charles Hillman, 271

Brough, Fanny "Fancy" (1866-1950). *See* Marlowe, Julia. Sarah Frances Frost. Fanny Brough. Fancy Brough. [Mrs. Robert] Taber [Mrs. Edward Hugh] Sothern (1866-1950)

Brough, Jane (1820-1908). *See* Davis, Jane (Brough) [Mrs. William] (1820-1908)

Broughton, Ann [Miss], 15,516

Broughton, Celeste, 11,953

Broughton, Elizabeth Damaris, 15,448

Broughton Family (SC), **15,448, 15,516**

Broughton, Governor, 13,323

Broughton, Philip Porcher, 15,448

Broughton, Sarah (Sumner) [Mrs. Shebuel] (1802-53), **11,953**

Broughton, Shebuel, 11,953

Broughton, Thomas, 15,448

Broun, Anne Hinman (1848-1932). *See* Singleton, Anne Hinman (Broun) (1848-1932)

Broun, Catherine Hopkins (ca. 1843-1903), **16,244**

Broun, Heywood, 11,867

Browder, Mary P., 10,651

Brower, Helen (Pierson), 10,913

Brown, **1,755**

Brown, Abbie Farwell (1871-1927), 1,224, **6,429**

Brown, Abigail, 14,965

Brown, Abigail (1792-?), 5,672

Brown, Addie, 1,875

Brown, Adelaide (1868-1940), **1,607**

Brown, Agnes, 14,965

Brown, Alice, 14,943

Brown, Alice, 7,307

Brown, Alice [Miss] (1856-1948), 2,370, 5,714, **5,913,** 7,349, 8,001, 10,853, 12,529

Brown, Alice (1852-1935). *See* Davis, Alice (Brown) [Mrs. George Rollin] (1852-1935)

Brown, Allen, 17,069

Brown, Alpha, 1,229

Brown, Alta [Mrs.], 8,399

Brown, Amy Cassandra (1872-1959). *See* Lyman, Amy Cassandra (Brown) [Mrs. Richard R.] (1872-1959)

Brown, Angie Mitchell (ca. 1870s-1909), **171**

Brown, Ann. *See* Chauncey, Ann (Brown) [Mrs. Wolcott]

Brown, Ann Regan, **9,595**

Brown, Anna [Mrs. John J.], 17,370

Brown, Anna C. (Hutchinson), 1,450

Brown, Anna Christine. *See* Glaser, Anna Christine (Brown)

Brown, Annie May, 2,941

Brown, Antoinette Louisa (1825-1921). *See* Blackwell, Antoinette Louisa (Brown) [Mrs. Samuel] (1825-1921)

Brown, Arvin, 12,367

Brown, Aunt Clara, 1,776

Brown, Belle (1846-1924). *See* Brown, Mary Belle (1846-1924)

Brown, Benjamin, 10,915

Brown, Bernice Veazey (1893-). *See* Cronkhite, Bernice Veazey (Brown) [Mrs. Leonard Wolsey] (1893-)

Brown, Bill, 374

Brown, Caroline Thela (Cameron) [Mrs. Thomas A.] (1834-1922), 654

Brown, Charles Brockden (1771-1810), **14,964**

Brown, Charlotte (Hawkins) [Mrs. Edward S.] (1882-1961), 3,280, 3,283, 3,302, 3,303, 5,459, **6,430,** 13,217

Brown, Charlotte Hays (1862-1951), 7,279

Brown, Charlotte L. [Mrs.], 1,248

Brown, Clara, 17,744

Brown, Clara E. (1850-1919). *See* Fisher, Clara E. (Brown) [Mrs. George] (1850-1919)

Brown, Claud, 2,975

Brown, Cora Inez. *See* Brownson, Cora Inez (Brown)

Brown County A&M Mothers' Club (TX), **16,189**

Brown, Dorothy (1919-), 15,134, **15,914**

Brown, Dorothy Kirchwey (1888-), **6,431, 6,432**

Brown, Edmund G., 515

Brown, Edward Josiah (1851-1938), **8,965**

Brown, Elam, Family, 582

Brown, Elijah, 14,964

Brown, Eliza Jane [Mrs.], 2,979

Brown, Elizabeth Athenais, 5,435

Brown, Elizabeth Gillenwaters (1847-?). *See* Daniel, Elizabeth Gillenwaters (Brown) [Mrs. Henry Clay] (1847-?)

Brown Elizabeth (Grisham) [Mrs. Joseph Emerson] (1826-96), **2,976, 3,156,** 3,160

Brown, Ella H., **14,330**

Brown, Ellen "Brownie." *See* Schrumpf, Ellen "Brownie" (Brown) [Mrs. William]

Brown, Ellen Burgess (Senkler) [Mrs. J. Fuller], 9,364

Brown, Ellen Coit (1860-1957). *See* Elliott, Ellen Coit Brown [Mrs. Orrin Leslie] (1860-1957)

Brown, Ellen M., 4,060

Brown, Emma (1839-1920), 5,672

Brown, Emma V., 11,616

Brown, Ephraim (1765-1840), 5,672

Brown, Estelle (Aubrey) [Mrs. H. T.] (1877-?), **183**

Brown, Esther, 10,216

Brown, Esther Lucile, **6,130**

Brown, Euphemie Labranche [Mrs. William], 5,435

Brown, Eva Nellie (1908-), 7,109

Brown, F. Delos, 17,651

Brown Family (CT, MA, RI), 7,520

Brown Family (IA, MA, RI), **4,701, 4,704**

Brown Family (KY), **5,333**

Brown Family (ME), **5,672**

Brown Family (MA), 7,014

Brown Family (PA), **14,965**

Brown Family (VA), 17,109

Brown Family (WA), **17,165**

Brown, Frances, 9,841

Brown, Frances Bland Coalter (1835-94), 17,109

Brown, Frances Campbell (1906-), **13,192**

Brown, Francis A., 855

Brown, George William, 6,868

Brown, Georgia T., 11,831

Brown, Gertrude Foster [Mrs. Raymond] (1867-1956), **6,433,** 6,960

Brown, Gloria, **7,736**

Brown, Greta Weitz [Mrs. Robert A.], **4,740**

Brown, Hallie Quinn (1850-1949), 4,768

Brown, Hannah (1800-26), 5,672

Brown, Hannah (1830-1923), 5,672

Brown, Hannah Helen (Mendelsohn) [Mrs. Samuel] (ca. 1901-), 15,425

Brown, Hannah Tuttle King, 11,717

Brown, Harriet S., **16,613**

Brown, Harriett Johnson [Mrs. Elijah A.], **3,157**

Brown, Hazel E., **4,976**

Brown, Helen Davenport (1882-1960). *See* Gibbons, Helen Davenport (Brown) [Mrs. Herbert Adams] (1882-1960)

Brown, Helen E. (Foote) [Mrs. Charles Kent], **9,628**

Brown, Helen Gilman (Noyes) [Mrs. William Adams], 12,401

Brown, Helen (Gurley) (1922-), **7,196**

Brown, Helen Tyler, **17,023**

Brown, Henry Armitt, 14,952

Brown, Henry C., **13,353**

Brown, Izetta Jewell [Mrs. William Gay, Jr.] (1882-). *See* Miller , Izetta Jewell [Mrs. William Gay, Jr.] Brown [Mrs. Hugh] (1882-)

Brown, J. Fuller, 9,364

Brown, J. Mabel [Miss] (ca. 1880-), 10,915

Brown, J. Wistar, 14,965

Brown, Jacob, 11,654
Brown, James A., 16,718
Brown, James A. (1820-1902), 4,701, 4,704
Brown, James Oliver, **11,954**
Brown, James Wright (1873-1959), **12,172**
Brown, Jane, 8,672
Brown, Jeanie Valliant, 16,243
Brown, John, 15,959
Brown, John, 11,001
Brown, John, 5,333
Brown, John (1800-59), 956, 4,838, 7,295, 7,561,
   11,616, 12,419
Brown, John Evans, 13,355
Brown, John, Family (Bahamas), **12,230**
Brown, John, Family (MN), 8,981
Brown, John Henry, 16,060
Brown, John Mason, 11,164
Brown, John Thompson (1802-36), 17,109
Brown, Joseph, 8,692
Brown, Joseph Emerson, **2,976**, 3,008, 3,160, 3,168
Brown, Joseph M., 2,976
Brown, Joseph Mackey, **3,158**
Brown, Joseph P., 1,756
Brown, Joseph Renshaw (1805-70), **8,966**
Brown, Josephine Chapin, 8,670, 12,033
Brown, Juanita, **9,815**
Brown, Julius L., 2,976
Brown, Kark (1895-), 11,955
Brown, Katherine. See Kerr, Katherine Brown [Mrs.
   Alexander], 14,401
Brown, Katherine Holland, **4,312**
Brown, Katherine Kennedy **6,434**, 11,913
Brown, Laura, 5,644
Brown, Laura (1869-1944). See Zook, Laura (Brown)
   (1869-1944)
Brown, Lillian, 11,717
Brown, Lillie (West) [Mrs. Harry] (1855-1939). See
   Buck, Lillie (West) [Mrs. Harry] Brown [Mrs.
   Franklyn Howard] (1855-1939)
Brown, Lizzie. See Knappen, Lizzie Brown [Mrs.
   Eugene]
Brown, Louis Nicholia [Mrs. Nathan Atkinson], 2,978
Brown, Lucy Hughes (?-1911), 15,430
Brown, Lucy Shands (Rives) 9,762
Brown, Lydia Ann (1818-1905). See Carli, Lydia
   Ann (Brown) [Mrs. Christopher] (1818-1905)
Brown, Lydia Lax, 14,497
Brown, Madaline (1898-), 6,698
Brown, Madie D. [Mrs. Edmund N.]. See Empafan,
   Madie D. [Mrs. Edmund N.] Brown [Mrs.
   Richard Raoul]
Brown, Marel [Mrs.], **2,977, 3,159**
Brown, Margaret (Tobin) [Mrs. James J.]
   (1867-1932), 1,752, **1,756**
Brown, Margaret Wise (1910-52), 8,531, **15,399**
Brown, Margaretta (Mason) [Mrs. John] (1772-1838),
   5,333
Brown, Maria Smith [Mrs. Morris], 8,311
Brown, Marian Katherine, **2,227**
Brown, Marie A. (pseudonym). See Shipley, Marie
   Adelaide (Brown) (1842-1900)
Brown, Marie Adelaide (1842-1900). See Shipley,
   Marie Adelaide (Brown) (1842-1900)
Brown, Marjorie P. M., **14,966**
Brown, Martha A., **7,737**
Brown, Martha H. (Anderson) [Mrs. Francis A.]
   (1840-?), 855
Brown, Mary, 12,377
Brown, Mary [Mrs.], 8,214
Brown, Mary [Mrs. John], 956
Brown, Mary (1796-?). See Askew, Mary (Brown)
   (1796-?)
Brown, Mary Armitt, 14,964
Brown, Mary Burnham, 5,672
Brown, Mary (Burr) [Mrs. Lloyd Warfield], 4,410
Brown, Mary Butler (1860-1957), **1,701**
Brown, Mary Celestine Mitchell [Mrs. Edward T.],
   3,018
Brown, Mary Davis (1822-1903), **15,571**
Brown, Mary E., **7,052**
Brown, Mary E. (1869-1952). See Lee, Mary E.
   (Brown) (1869-1952)
Brown, Mary Eliza (Brown) [Mrs. James A.]

(1836-1916). See Jones, Mary Eliza (Brown)
   [Mrs. James A.] Brown [Mrs. Nathaniel Vary]
   (1836-1916)
Brown, Mary (Guion) [Mrs. Samuel] (1782-?), **12,217**
Brown, Mary Hartley, 12,256
Brown, Mary Jeannette (Robison) [Mrs. Edward H.]
   Gore [Mrs. Augustus Homer] (1858-1942). See
   Robson, May. Mary Jeannette Robson. [Mrs.
   Charles Livingston] Gore [Mrs. Augustus Homer]
   (1858-1942)
Brown, Mary Magoun (1869-1962), **6,131**
Brown, Mary Milbank, 6,542, 6,947
Brown, Mary (Olney) [Mrs. Benjamin] (1821-86),
   17,165
Brown, Mary Quincy, **7,350**
Brown, Mary R., **11,531**
Brown, Mary Taylor [Mrs. William John], 13,355
Brown, Mason, 5,333
Brown, Matilda [Miss], 10,085, 10,087
Brown, Maud (Morrow) [Mrs. Calvin S.], **9,596**
Brown, Maurine (1907-). See Neuberger, Maurine
   (Brown) [Mrs. Richard L.] (1907-)
Brown, May (Robson) [Mrs. Charles Livingston] Gore
   [Mrs. Augustus Homer] (1858-1942). See
   Robson, May. Mary Jeannette Robson. [Mrs.
   Charles Livingston] Gore [Mrs. Augustus Homer]
   Brown (1858-1942)
Brown, Mollie. See Carran, Mollie (Brown)
Brown, Mollie E. Merritt [Mrs. Henry C.], 13,353
Brown, Morris (?-1878), **8,311**
Brown, Mrs. Alpha, 1,229
Brown, Mrs. Claud, 2,975
Brown, Mrs. David, 13,835
Brown, Mrs. George William, 6,868
Brown, Mrs. Nathan, 10,942
Brown, Mrs. Terrel, 9,815
Brown, Myrtle, 14,946
Brown, N., 7,350
Brown, Nathan, 10,942
Brown, Nathan Atkinson, **2,978**
Brown, Nellie Somers [Mrs.], **3,664**
Brown, Olivia A. See Hazeltine, Olivia A. (Brown)
Brown, Ollie L. (1891-1972), 82
Brown, Olympia [Mrs. Willis] (1835-1926), 1,950,
   6,435, 11,391, 17,665, 17,749, **17,852**
Brown, Orlando, 5,333
Brown, Paula Watts (1909-74), **4,977**
Brown, Pearl (1879-1957). See Smith, Pearl (Brown)
   (1879-1957)
Brown, Peter, 4,410
Brown, Phoebe Robinson [Mrs. Samuel Jerome (?-ca.
   1910), 8,966
Brown, Rebecca McClure (1860-1911). See Pearce,
   Rebecca McClure (Brown) (1860-1911)
Brown, Roberta (Young), 9,709
Brown, Rosalie (Moore) [Mrs. Bill] (1910-), 374,
   14,423
Brown, Roxanna. See Watts, Roxanna (Brown)
   Walbridge
Brown, S. Janie [Miss], **13,354**
Brown, Sallie Eugenia (1862-1942), **3,160**
Brown, Sallie "Sallie Fox" (?-1913). See Allen, Sallie
   "Sallie Fox" (Brown) (?-1913)
Brown, Sally. See Dover, Sally (Brown)
Brown, Samuel, 8,718
Brown, Samuel Jerome (1845-1925), **8,966**
Brown, Sanger, 17,678
Brown, Sarah, 956
Brown, Sarah D. [Mrs. R. B.], 3,891
Brown, Sterling, 3,288
Brown, Susan Freniere [Mrs. Joseph Renshaw], 8,966
Brown, Susannah, 12,230
Brown, Susie (ca. 1895-1960?), **17,893**
Brown, Tabitha (Moffat) (1780-1858), **14,477,** 14,478
Brown, Terrel, 9,815
Brown, Theodora (Kracaw). See Kroeber, Theodora
   (Kracaw) Brown [Mrs. Alfred Louis]
Brown University (RI), 7,620, 11,915
   alumnae, 1,553, 4,682, 13,674
Brown v. Board of Education of Topeka (KS), 1,856,
   8,098
Brown, Van Dyck (pseudonym). See Heyneman,
   Julie Helen [Miss] (1868-?)
Brown, Velva V., **2,010**

Brown, W. C., 3,713
Brown, W. Vance, **13,355**
Brown, Weltha, 6,653
Brown, William, 4,410
Brown, William (1752-1834), 14,965
Brown, William Adams (1865-1943), **12,401**
Brown, William Gay, Jr., 17,472
Brown, Willis Gertrude (?-1949), 9,289
Browne, Alice. See Quan, Alice (Browne)
Browne and Nichols School (MA), 6,805
Browne, Charles O., 11,547
Browne, Charlotte [Mrs.], **2,228**
Browne Family, **8,001**
Browne Family (CA), 1,648
Browne, John J., **17,370**
Browne, Lucy (1846-1937). See Johnston, Lucy
   (Browne) [Mrs. William Agnew] (1846-1937)
Browne, M. S. (physician), **3,161**
Browne, Maimee Lee Robinson [Mrs. Virgil], **14,230**
Browne, Margaret (Stevens), 63
Browne, Maurice (1881-1955), 8,001
Browne, Mr. and Mrs., 2,392
Browne, Nina. See DeCottes, Nina (Browne)
Browne, Ruth, 7,109
Browne, Sarah Ellen, **6,436**
Browne, William M., **2,979**
Browne William Phineas (1804-69), **63**
Brownell, Abner (1756-1851), **7,607**
Brownell, C. L., 17,230
Brownell, Elizabeth "Beezie" (Hyde) [Mrs. Kenneth
   C.], 1,837
Brownell, Sarah, **5,111**
Brownell, William Crary (1851-1928), 3,019, **5,861**
Brownie Reader (periodical). See *Daisy* (periodical)
Brownie Scouts, **12,097**
Browning, Charles Henry (1846-1926), 2,229
Browning, Elizabeth (Barrett) [Mrs. Robert]
   (1806-61), 951, 3,077, **6,437,** 6,659, 10,085,
   10,086, 16,170
Browning Family (FL), 2,923
Browning Family (NH, OH), **2,229**
Browning, Flo (Crouch) [Mrs. Jack], 3,451
Browning, Leanor (Hanlon) [Mrs. Robert Lewright]
   (1809-57), 2,229
Browning, Robert (1812-89), 3,077, 5,815, 5,910,
   6,659, 10,085, 10,086, 16,170
Browning, Robert Lewright (1803-50), 2,229
Browning, Robert Lewright, Jr. (1835-60), 2,229
Browning Society (Canton, NY), **11,392**
Brownlee, Charlotte (1876-1970), 5,394
Brownlee, Clara (1850-1931). See Hutchinson, Clara
   (Brownlee) (1850-1931)
Brownlee, Emma (1848-1925). See Kilgore, Emma
   (Brownlee) (1848-1925)
Brownmiller, Susan, 4,981
Brownson, Cora Inez (Brown), **8,542**
Browntown-Madison Township Parents' and Teachers'
   Association (NJ), **11,146**
Brownyard, Maggie, 12,790
Brownyard, Mary Jane "Jennie," 12,790
Broyles, Laura Johnson. See Boyd, Laura Johnson
   (Broyles) [Mrs. Montague Lafitte]
Broyles, Margaret Caroline. See Van Wyck, Margaret
   Caroline (Broyles)
Broyles, Nellie, 9,538
Broyles, Oze Robert, 15,649
Bruce, Annie J., **2,980**
Bruce, Blanche Kelso (1841-98), **2,230**
Bruce, Charles K., **12,402**
Bruce, Charlotte Ann (1819-?), 7,653
Bruce, Elizabeth Gordon, 2,016
Bruce, Elvira A. (Cabell) [Mrs. Patrick, Jr.] Henry
   [Mrs. James] (?-1858), 2,231
Bruce, Evangeline [Mrs. David], 6,489
Bruce Family, **2,231**
Bruce, Georgiana [Miss], 1,565
Bruce, Ida Lovell [Mrs.], **10,278**
Bruce, Josephine B. (Wilson) [Mrs. Blanche Kelso],
   2,230
Bruce, Mary Stone, 1,224
Bruce, Robert E., **2,980**
Bruce, Upton, 12,402
Brucellosis, 11,579
Bruch, Clara, 3,110

Bruch, Hilde [Miss], 2,086
Bruch, Margaret, 3,110
Bruchholz, Elizabeth Roy (Ware) [Mrs. Henry], **8,543**
Bruchholz, Henry, 8,543
Brucker, Clara (Hantel) [Mrs. Wilber M.], **7,738**
Bruemerhoff, Lilly [Miss], 4,173
Bruen, Ada (1848-1924). *See* Grier, Ada (Bruen) (1848-1924)
Bruen Family (NY), 12,020
Bruff, Nancy (1915-). *See* Gardner, Nancy (Bruff) (1915-)
Bruhn, Erik, 12,364
Bruington Memorial Baptist Church (NC), **13,636**
Brumby, Ann Eliza, **12,961**
Brumby, Richard Trapier (1804-75), 12,961
Brunck, Catharine L. [Mrs. Francis C.], **11,348**
Brundin, Agnes (Smedley) [Mrs. Ernest] (1894?-1950). *See* Smedley, Agnes (1894?-1950)
Brundin, Ernest, 174
Brune, Ellen Judith (1868-1936). *See* Debell, Ellen Judith (Bruner) (1868-1936)
Brunelle, Adelaide, 9,323
Bruner, Amelia Phoneta (1854-?). *See* Monroe, Amelia Phoneta (Bruner) [Mrs. James W.] (1854-?)
Bruner, Amy Celeste (1875-1943). *See* Almy, Amy Celeste (Bruner) [Mrs. John Edwin] (1875-1943)
Bruner Family (NE), 10,437
Bruner, Ida M. *See* King, Ida M. (Bruner) [Mrs. J. J.]
Bruner, Lillie C. (1864-1957), 10,437
Bruner, Margaret (Baggerly) [Mrs. Vate] (1886-1971), **4,622**
Brunner-Orne, Martha, 6,698
Bruno, Harry A., 11,831
Bruns, Eugenia "Jennie" Mary (1877-1970), **10,751**
Brunsdale, Anna Margaret (1860-1927), 8,737
Brunt, Stella (1894-). *See* Osborn, Stella (Brunt) [Mrs. Chase S.] (1894-)
Brunyate, Josephine (1879-1965). *See* Meredith, Josephine (Brunyate) [Mrs. Arthur J.] (1879-1965)
Bruot, Blanche (1862-1953). *See* Hower, Blanche (Bruot) (1862-1953)
Brush, Dorothy (1896?-1968), 7,189, **7,197**, 7,289
Brush, George De Forest, 2,737
Brush, Katharine (Ingham) (1902-52), 691, 15,060
Brush, Marjorie E., 1,348
Brush, Nancy Douglas (1890-). *See* Bowditch, Nancy Douglas (Brush) [Mrs. William Robert] Pearmain (1890-)
Brussels World Fair (Belgium, 1957-58), 6,662, 17,716
Bruyn, Kathleen [Mrs.] (1903-), 1,750
Bry, Edith (1898-), **2,738**
Bryan, Alice Cheever [Mrs. A. H.] (1854-1917), **4,381**
Bryan, Anna E. [Miss] (1858-1901), 5,346
Bryan, Bettie, 13,466
Bryan, Cornelia Ann. *See* Robinson, Cornelia Ann (Bryan) [Mrs. David M.] Hickman [Mrs. John M.]
Bryan, Delia [Mrs.], 3,505
Bryan, Dorothy M., 14,475
Bryan, Elizabeth Tucker (Coalter) (1805-56), 17,109
Bryan, Eveleen K., 1,186
Bryan Family (GA), **3,505**
Bryan Family (LA, MO), **9,987**
Bryan Family (NC), 12,962
Bryan Family (SC), **15,600**
Bryan Family (SC, GA), **3,376**
Bryan, Fannie Morton [Miss] (1870-1964), **5,258**
Bryan, Grace Dexter. *See* Hargreaves, Grace Dexter (Bryan)
Bryan, H. Georgia. *See* Screven, H. Georgia (Bryan) [Mrs. James Proctor]
Bryan, Hally Ballinger (1868-1955). *See* Perry, Hally Ballinger (Bryan) [Mrs. Emmett L.] (1868-1955)
Bryan, Hannah P. [Miss], **14,967**
Bryan, Henry Ravenscroft (1836-1919) 12,962
Bryan, Isabel [Mrs. A. P.], 13,356
Bryan, James West, 13,356
Bryan, John Herritage, **13,356**, 13,466
Bryan, Julia. *See* Cumming, Julia (Bryan) [Mrs. Henry Harford]

Bryan, Margaret Anna. *See* Vold, Margaret Anna (Bryan)
Bryan, Maria, 15,600
Bryan, Mary B. [Mrs. William J.], 9,048
Bryan, Mary Biddle (Norcott) [Mrs. Henry Ravenscroft] (1841-1925), **12,962**, 13,573
Bryan, Mary Givens (1910-64), **2,981**
Bryan, Mary Shepard [Mrs. John Herritage], 13,356
Bryan, Milton, 9,987
Bryan, Morgan, 9,987
Bryan, Mrs. Joseph, 3,505
Bryan, Richard Dobbs Spaight, **13,357**
Bryan, Ruth (1885-1954). *See* Rohde, Ruth (Bryan) Owen (1885-1954)
Bryan, S. C., 3,376
Bryan, Sarah [Mrs. Morgan], 9,987
Bryan, Sarah Jane Willingham, 3,376
Bryan, Shirley, 4,111
Bryan, Virginia S., 3,505
Bryan, William Jennings (1860-1925), **2,232**, 2,596, 8,450
Bryan, William Lowe, 4,494
Bryan, William W., 9,987
Bryant, Ada. *See* Leigh, Ada (Bryant) [Mrs. Francis Webster]
Bryant, Anita (1941-). *See* Green, Anita (Bryant) [Mrs. Bob] (1941-)
Bryant Birthday Book of Verses, 7,654
Bryant, Cyrus, 12,404
Bryant, Dorothy, 14,352
Bryant, Elizabeth Bangs, **6,318**
Bryant Family (IL), **12,403, 12,404**
Bryant, H. E. C., **13,358**
Bryant, Hazel, 12,367
Bryant, John Howard (1807-1902), 12,404
Bryant, Julia S., 12,404
Bryant, Laura (1878-1961), **11,532**
Bryant, Louise Frances (Stevens) (1885-1956), 6,223, **7,198**, 7,320
Bryant, Margaret (Clifford), 3,304
Bryant, Margaret Mae (1900-), **15,789**
Bryant, Mrs. E. Roy, 8,016
Bryant, Sarah (Snell), 12,404
Bryant, Susanna (1905-66). *See* Dakin, Susanna (Bryant) (1905-66)
Bryant, William Cullen (1794-1878), 12,403, 12,404
Bryce, Cornelia Elizabeth (1881-1960). *See* Pinchot, Cornelia Elizabeth (Bryce) [Mrs. Gifford] (1881-1960)
Bryce, James, 12,032
Brye, Martha M. (1864-1946), **8,725**
Bryn Mawr College (PA), 2,700, 4,167, 4,477, 5,731, 6,239, 8,142, 11,890, 11,931, 12,737, 14,738, 14,844, 14,857
alumnae, 2,523, 5,318, 6,238, 11,501, **14,737**, 15,011, 17,723
deans, 11,501
faculty, **2,423**, 8,653, 11,857, 14,742, 14,743, 14,744
presidents, 2,473, 14,745, 14,889
students, 1,948, 2,030, 2,333, 2,345, 2,359, 2,875, 5,321, 5,755, 8,073, 9,464
Bryn Mawr College (PA), Resident Summer School for Women Workers. *See* Bryn Mawr Summer School for Women Workers in Industry (PA)
Bryn Mawr School (Baltimore, MD), 11,164, 11,890, 14,738, 14,745
Bryn Mawr Summer School for Women Workers in Industry (PA), 4,032, 6,893, 11,762, 11,806, 13,176, 14,737, 14,745, 15,011
Bryne, Eulella (1905-), 16,488
Bryson, Cassie L., 3,377
Bryson Family (GA), **3,377**
Bryson, Lyman Lloyd (1888-1959), **2,233**
Buchanan, Ann "Nannie" Lloyd, 5,789
Buchanan, Carolina Virginia Marylandia (Johnson) [Mrs. Andrew]. *See* Frye, Carolina Virginia Marylandia (Johnson) [Mrs. Andrew] Buchanan [Mrs. Nathaniel, Jr.]
Buchanan County Agricultural Fair (MO), 9,902
Buchanan, Dorothy Jacobs, 16,965
Buchanan, Elizabeth, 14,968
Buchanan Family (MD), 5,751
Buchanan, Hannah, 6,653

Buchanan, Harriet. *See* Henry, Harriet (Buchanan) [Mrs. Robert]
Buchanan, James (1791-1868), 2,234, 5,303, 10,170, 13,262, 14,863, **14,968**
Buchanan, James, Family, **2,234**
Buchanan, Maria, 16,468
Buchanan, Marie. *See* Sullivan, Marie (Buchanan) [Mrs. Mark]
Buchanan, Mildred (1886-). *See* Flagg, Mildred (Buchanan) (1886-)
Buchanan, Robert Christie (1811-78), **5,748**
Buchanan, Ruth Bacon (1882-1953), **7,739**
Buchannan, Charles M., 17,387
Buchele, Estelle, 2,284
Buchignani, Antonio, 2,320
Buchignani, Margaret L. (O'Neale) [Mrs. John B.] Timberlake [Mrs. John Henry] Eaton [Mrs. Antonio] (1799?-1879). *See* Eaton, Margaret L. (O'Neale) [Mrs. John Henry]. [Mrs. John B.] Timberlake [Mrs. Antonio] Buchignani (1799?-1879)
Buchman, Carrie. *See* Roberts, Carrie (Buchman)
Buck, Harriet D. (1823-99?), **17,609**
Buck, Hazle. *See* Ewing, Hazle (Buck) [Mrs. Davis]
Buck, Lillie (West) [Mrs. Harry] Brown [Mrs. Franklyn Howard] (1855-1939), 3,994, 10,860
Buck, Luella, **10,105**
Buck, Mina (Van Cleave) [Mrs. Frank] (1879-), 2,016
Buck, Muriel. *See* Humphrey, Muriel (Buck) [Mrs. Hubert Horatio]
Buck, Oral, 3,754
Buck, Pearl Comfort (Sydenstricker) (1892-1973), 1,565, 2,403, 2,424, 2,482, 3,290, 4,005, 4,067, 5,469, 7,272, 7,287, 8,657, 9,081, 11,144, 11,165, 11,812, 11,821, 12,044, 12,553, 13,391, 14,377, 14,815, 15,060, 15,305, 15,331, 15,377, **16,153**, 17,197, **17,431, 17,610**
Buck, T. L., 3,754
Buck, William J., 15,006
Buckalew, Charles Rollin (1821-99), **2,235**
Buckalew, Permelia Stevens (Wadsworth) [Mrs. Charles Rollin], 2,235
Buckbee, Edna Bryan, **1,250**, 1,516
Buckel, Chloe Annette [Miss] (1833-1912), **1,251**
Bucketful Full of Diamonds (book), 18,012
Buckeye Boys Ranch (OH), 14,010
Buckhead Business and Professional Women's Club (GA), **3,378**
Buckhout, William A., 15,326
Buckingham, Edgar, 11,814
Buckingham, Eliza. *See* Aiken, Eliza (Buckingham) [Mrs. William]
Buckingham, Eliza (Ripley) [Mrs. William Alfred] (?-1868), 1,886
Buckingham, Elizabeth Lee, **1,546**
Buckingham Family, 14,531
Buckingham, Harriet T. (1832-90). *See* Clarke, Harriet T. (Buckingham) (1832-90)
Buckingham, Margaret C., 14,816
Buckingham Monthly Meeting of Friends (PA), 14,821
Buckingham, William Alfred (1804-75), **1,886**
Buckler, Eliza "Didy" (Ridgely) [Mrs. John Campbell] White [Mrs. Thomas H.], 5,805
Buckler, Georgina, 12,572
Buckley, Deloris, 17,862
Buckley, Iona C., 3,606
Buckley, J. D. M., 4,208
Buckley, Joan Naglestad [Mrs.], **8,805**
Buckley, Margaret [Mrs. James], 11,440
Buckley, William F., Sr., 14,345
Buckley, William F., Jr., 1,017
Bucklin, Abby [Mrs. George], **8,967**
Bucklin, John, 12,379
Bucklin, Philinda (Barnes) [Mrs. John], 12,379
Buckmaster, Catherine M. (1837-1918). *See* Curran, Catherine M. (Buckmaster) [Mrs. Isaac Bush] (1837-1918)
Buckmaster Family (IL), **4,352**
Buckmaster, Harriet Ann (Bartling) [Mrs. Nathaniel] (1811-40), 4,352

Buckmaster, Nathaniel, 4,352
Buckminister, Eliza (ca. 1788-1864). *See* Lee, Eliza (Buckminister) (ca. 1788-1864)
Bucknall, Joanna Rooker (1816?-95), **6,438**
Bucknall, Martha Elizabeth (?-1880), **6,438**
Bucknall, Mary (Davis) [Mrs. George] (1845-?), **376**
Buckner, Cornelia Matilda (Scudder), 3,576
Buckner, Delia Claiborn [Mrs. S. B.], 5,291
Buckner, Emory R., 4,208
Buckner Family (MS), 9,816
Buckner, Mrs. N., 13,617
Buckner, Mrs. Simon Bolivar, 5,337
Bucy, Merissa [Mrs. Paul], 4,012
Bucyrus Evening Telegraph (OH), 13,999
Budenz, Louis F. (1891-1972), **15,374**
Budgets, family. *See* Home economics, accounting
Budlong, Caroline Gale, 14,542
Buechner, Mrs. J., 8,215
Buehermann, Elizabeth, **12,405**
Buehler, Betty Hicks [Mrs.], 5,322
Buel, Mary, 1,970
Buell, Ellen L. [Mrs.], **13,880**
Buell, Jennie (1891-), **7,740**
Buell, Sarah Josepha (1788-1879). *See* Hale, Sarah Josepha (Buell) [Mrs. David] (1788-1879)
Buena Vista College (Storm Lake, IA), Honor Iowans Convocation, **5,110**
Buenos Aires Peace Treaties (1937), 15,311
Buerbaum, Minnie. *See* Morgan, Minnie (Buerbaum)
Buerger, Mrs. David B., 6,964
Bufano, Benjamino, 761, 945
Bufano, Virginia, 1,507
Buff and Blue, The (Gallaudet College, DC), 2,110
"Buffalo Bill Stories, The," 192
Buffalo Bill's Wild West Show, 10,428, 14,101, 16,547, 17,932
Buffalo Bird Woman (ca. 1839-?), 9,447
Buffalo-Courier (NY), 11,355
Buffalo District Nurses' Association (NY), 12,759
Buffalo Evening News (NY), 11,344
Buffalo Foundation (NY), 11,346
Buffalo General Hospital (NY), 12,759
Buffalo King, The (book), 5,037
Buffalo Library, 11,893
Buffalo Orphan Asylum (NY), 12,759
Buffalo Seminary Graduates' Association (NY), 11,356
Buffalo State Hospital (NY), 11,357
Buffaloe, Mahaly. *See* Boon, Mahaly Buffaloe [Mrs. James]
Buffalow, Mahalia [Miss], 13,428
"Buffer, The" (story), 5,360
Buffett, Mary E. *See* Durant, Mary E. (Buffett) [Mrs. Henry]
Buffington, Mrs. W. R., **12,963**
Buffum Family, 11,943
Buffum, Mary. *See* Bartlett, Mary (Buffum)
Buffum, Rebekah Maria (Northey) [Mrs. John Henry] (1825-?), 7,413
Buford College (Nashville, TN), **15,940**
Buford, Elizabeth Burgess, 15,940
Bug, Emma, 8,927
Bugbee, Lester G., 16,097
Bugbee, Mrs. A. (?-1898), 16,097
Buhler, Charlotte (Malachowski), 2,086, 2,353
Buhlmann, Marie Catherine (1897-). *See* Jahn, Marie Catherine (Buhlmann) (1897-)
Buie, Emma McRae [Mrs. Prentiss], 9,597
Buie, Estelle, 9,597
Buie Family (MS), **9,597**
Buie, Hallie, 9,597
Buie, Mary, 9,597
Buie, Prential. *See* Rew, Prential (Buie) [Mrs. R. G.]
Buie, Prentiss, 9,597
Building and loan associations, **17,276**
Building materials industry, **9,433**
"Building of the Michigan Road, The" (dissertation), **4,657**
Buisson, Nancy G., 8,936
Bukowska, Eugenia (Fronczak), 11,367
Bulette, Julia [Miss], 10,721
Bulette, Sara, 6,713
Bulgaria
  American diplomats in, 2,304

  missionaries to, Methodist, 13,294
  United States public officials in, 10,074
Bulkeley, Virginia [Mrs. Houghton], 1,882
Bulkley Family (MO), **10,157**
Bulkley, Mary E., 10,157
Bulkley, Sarah Adams, 13,357
Bull, Alexander, 17,692
Bull, Dorothy, **1,966**
Bull, Emma Anna, 15,521
Bull, Ethel, 11,717
Bull Family, 5,780
Bull Family (SC), 15,521
Bull-fights, 335
Bull, Gracia, 15,521
Bull, Marianne. *See* Cozens, Marianne (Bull)
Bull Moose campaign, 11,922
Bull, Ole, 17,692
Bullard, Eunice White (1812-97). *See* Beecher, Eunice White (Bullard) (1812-97)
Bullard, Helen E., 11,508
Bullard, Lola, **17,829**
Bullard, Lucille M. (1895-). *See* Belk, Lucille M. (Bullard) [Mrs. Henry] (1895-)
Bullard, Marjorie A., **8,968**
Bullard, Mrs. B. F., 3,572
Bullard, Polly Caroline (1881-1949), **8,969**
Bulletin (San Francisco, CA), 342
Bulletin (League of Women Voters), 15,359
Bulletin Index, The (periodical), 15,228
Bulletin of the Menninger Clinic, 5,230
Bulletins (Duke University, NC), 13,194
Bulletins (periodical), 2,863
Bullette, Julia [Miss], 10,721
Bullis, Buckskin Jim, 10,487
Bullis, Glenna, 2,353
Bullis, Harry Amos (1890-1963), **8,970**
Bullis, Irme Elizabeth (Alexander) [Mrs. Harry Amos] (1889-1947), 8,970
Bullis, Maria Robert Smorczewska [Mrs. Harry Amos], 8,970, 9,159
Bulloch, Catherine, 3,596
Bulloch, Emma Hamilton, **2,982**
Bulloch, William B., 3,515
Bullock, Dillman S., 8,164
Bullock, Edith Willets [Miss], **14,969**
Bullock, Electa Wood (1834-1911), **16,883**
Bullock, Flora (1871-1962), 3,983, **10,438**
Bullock, Georgia Philipps (Morgan) (1878-), **1,031,** 2,243
Bullock, Helen D., 17,125
Bullock, Helen L., 11,440
Bullock Home for Girls (NY), 11,443
Bullock, Katie (Kelly) [Mrs. Dillman S.], 8,164
Bullock, Robert William, 16,425
Bulmer, Annie Cecilia. *See* Bill, Annie Cecilia (Bulmer)
Bum Hill Gazette (CA), 377
Bumstead Family (MA), 7,014
Bumstead, Horace, **3,281**
Bumstead, Mary, 7,014
Bunce, Grace. *See* Paulding, Grace (Bunce) [Mrs. William]
Bunche, Ralph J., 6,579
Bundle of Life, The (book), 2,236
Bundock, Mary, 15,031
Bundy, John C. (1841-?), **4,062**
Bundy, Mary [Mrs. John C.], 4,062
Bundy, May Sutton, 15,371
Bunker, Belle H. [Mrs. Fred R.], 87
Bunker, Chang, 13,432, **13,572**
Bunker, Eng, **13,572**
Bunker, Fred R., **87**
Bunker, Hannah Adelia (1853-1932). *See* Crosby, Hannah Adelia (Bunker) [Mrs. Samuel Obed]
Bunker Hill Monument Ladies Appeal, **6,439**
Bunker, Louisa. *See* Haynes, Louisa (Bunker)
Bunker, Nancy "Nannie," 13,572
Bunnell, Esther Romania (1839-1932). *See* Penrose, Esther Romania (Bunnell) [Mrs. Parley P.] Pratt [Mrs. Charles W.] (1839-1932)
Bunnell, Kate M., 1,252
Bunnell, Louise, **1,252**
Bunnell, Louise Mapes (1877-1907). *See* Keeler, Louise Mapes (Bunnell) [Mrs. Charles Augustus]

Bunting, Estelle Vining (1864-1965), 8,388
Bunting, Mary I., 6,633
Bunting, Pauline [Miss], **17,949**
Bunzel, Ruth, 2,833
Bunzl, Mrs. Walter, **11,841**
Burack, A. S., 14,414
Burbank, E. A., 215
Burbank, Elizabeth [Mrs. Luther], 4,675
Burbank, Luther, 17,950
Burbank, Minerva, **14,523,** 14,618
Burbank, Timothy, **7,351**
Burch, Mary Cyrene (1822-1906). *See* Breckinridge, Mary Cyrene (Burch) [Mrs. John Cabell] (1822-1906)
Burch, Suzanne (1929-). *See* Powell, Jane (1929-)
Burckmyer, C. R. [Mrs. Cornelius], **15,407**
Burckmyer, Cornelius L., **15,407**
Burckmyer Letters, March, 1863-June, 1865, The (book), 15,407
Burd, Eliza, 7,972
Burd Family (PA), **14,970,** 15,087
Burd, Margaret (1761-?). *See* Hubley, Margaret (Burd) (1761-?)
Burd, Sarah (Shippen) (1731-84), **14,970,** 15,087
Burdette, Clara (Bradley) [Mrs. N. Milman] Wheeler [Mrs. Presley C.] Baker [Mrs. Robert J.] (1855-1954), **1,404,** 5,121, 5,123
Burdge, Emma Spencer, **7,741**
Burdick, Anna Lalor [Mrs.], 11,003, 11,047
Burdick, Medora [Miss], 8,221
Burdick, Polly [Mrs.], 8,221
Bureau of Human Resources (OR), 14,605
Bureau of Information and Employment, 13,966
Bureau of Jewish Education (Los Angeles, CA), 1,000
Bureau of Refugees, Freedmen, and Abandoned Lands, 7,055, 13,859
Bureau of Social Hygiene, 12,736
Bureau of Vocational Information (NY), **6,440,** 12,738
Bureau of Women in Industry, 6,686
Burfiend, Helen Margaret (Allanson) [Mrs.] (1901-), **8,692**
Burge, Adelaide Lasheck [Mrs.] (1876-1947), 5,035
Burge, Dolly Sumner (Lunt) [Mrs. Thomas] (1817-91). *See* Parks, Dolly Sumner (Lunt) [Mrs. Samuel Harding] Lewis [Mrs. Thomas] Burge [Mrs. William Justice] (1817-91)
Burge Family (GA), **3,313**
Burge, J. H., 12,406
Burge, Louisiana, 3,313
Burge, Marie Louise [Miss], **12,406**
Burge, Sadai. *See* Gray, Sadai (Burge)
Burgess, Anna [Mrs. Edward], 12,407
Burgess, Annette Louise (Curnen) [Mrs. Elisha Payne Jewett], 11,956
Burgess, Charles Henry, 12,407
Burgess, Edward, 12,407
Burgess, Elisha Payne Jewett, 11,956
Burgess, Elizabeth, 5,735
Burgess, Estelle (Loomis) [Mrs. Gelett], 378
Burgess Family (England, NY), **12,407**
Burgess Family (NY), **11,956**
Burgess, Frances [Mrs. Henry], 12,407
Burgess, Gelett (1866-1951), **378**
Burgess, George, 12,407
Burgess, Henry, 12,407
Burgess, John William (1844-1931), 11,956, **11,957**
Burgess, Joseph, 12,407
Burgess, Lillie May [Mrs.], 3,839
Burgess, Martha Palmer (1905-), **6,441**
Burgess, Ruth Payne (Jewett) [Mrs. John William] (?-1934), 11,956, 11,957
Burgess, Ruth Payne Jewett, II. *See* Jaeggi, Ruth Payne Jewett (Burgess, II) [Mrs. Walter E. A.]
Burgess, Thomas Foljambe, 12,407
Burgess, Thornton W. (1874-1965), 7,489, 7,491
Burgess, Valeria [Mrs. George], 12,407
Burgess, W. Randolf (1889-), **5,130**
Burghardt, Clara Esther. *See* Meharry, Clara Esther (Burghardt) [Mrs. Charles Leo]
Burgin, William O., 13,282
Burgoyne, Mrs. David H., 16,461
Burgum, Emma Gannell [Mrs. John] (1826-1923), 10,799
Burgum Family (NH), **10,799**

Burgum, John, 10,799
Burgwin, Eliza Carolina (1784-1863). *See* Clitherall, Eliza Carolina (Burgwin) [Mrs. George Campbell] (1784-1863)
Burgwyn, Margaret C. D., 13,383
Burgwyn, [Miss], 13,359
Burgwyn, Mrs. William Hyslop Sumner, 13,359
Burgwyn, William Hyslop Sumner, **13,359**, 13,420
Burhans, Eliza Wood (1815-64). *See* Fitzpatrick, Eliza Wood (Burhans) [Mrs. Thomas Jefferson] Farnham [Mrs. William] (1815-64)
"Burial of a Fallen Poet, The" (ms), 6,349
Burial societies, 4,162
Burk, Antoinette (Naglee) (1869-1952), 684
Burk, Griselda Minerva. *See* Bone, Griselda Minerva (Burk) [Mrs. Robert Donnell]
Burk, Martha "Calamity Jane" (Cannary) [Mrs. Clinton] (ca. 1852-1903), 9,846, 13,682
Burk, Mary (Naglee) [Mrs. James Alexander] (?-1911), 684
Burke, Agnes (?-1974), **11,842**, 11,864
Burke, Annie Elizabeth [Mrs. Russell W.], **12,173**
Burke, Billie, 11,453
Burke, Billie, 3,084
Burke, Caroline Ethel (McGilvra) [Mrs. Thomas] (1858-1932), **17,241**
Burke, Emma, **379**
Burke, Fielding (pseudonym). *See* Dargan, Olive (Tilford) [Mrs. Peagram] (1868-1968)
Burke, Jane Revere [Mrs. Nicholas P. Trist], **2,236**
Burke, Katherine, 945
Burke, Margaret 17,918
Burke, Margaret Jane (1859-1952). *See* Carns, Margaret Jane (Burke) [Mrs. Edmund C.] (1859-1952)
Burke, Noel (pseudonym). *See* Hitchens, Dolores (Birk) Olsen (1907-73)
Burke, Pauline (Wilcox) [Mrs. Moncure], 2,312
Burke, Selma H., 3,290
Burke, Thomas, 17,241
Burke, Yvonne (Watson) Brathwaite, **1,010**, 1,017, 2,438
Burkhalter, Savina Karl (1888-1959), 4,249
Burleigh, Celia, 9,452
Burleigh County Pioneers (ND), 13,661
Burleigh, Mary Lou. *See* Williams, Mary Lou [Mrs. John] (1910-)
Burleson, Adele Steiner, **16,042**
Burling, Judith [Mrs. Arthur Hart] (1900-), **2,237**
Burlingame, Anson (1820-70), 2,238
Burlingame, Edward Livermore (1848-1922), 2,238
Burlingame Family, **2,238**
Burlingame, Jane Cornelia (Livermore) [Mrs. Anson], 2,238
Burlingame, Walter, 2,238
Burlingham, Elizabeth, **12,408**
Burlingham, Gertrude S., 6,307
Burlington Garden Club (WA), **17,147**
Burlington Starry Journal (NJ), 11,080
Burlington Study Club (IA), 4,960
Burma
  American teachers in, **6,826**
  missionaries to, Methodist, 13,294
  World War II, 11,861
Burma Road, 11,861
Burn Then, Little Lamp (book), 5,984
Burnaby, Minna (1882-), 17,116
Burnam Family (TX), 16,261
Burnap, Rachel (Barry). *See* Young, Rachel (Barry) Burnap
Burnes, Catherine (1853-1926), 8,465, 8,477
Burnet, Bernice. *See* Taylor, Bernice (Burnet)
Burnet, Duncan, 3,063, 3,106
Burnet, John, 14,896
Burnet, John, Jr., 14,896
Burnet, Mrs. M. G., 15,904
Burnett, Carol, 950, 1,024
Burnett, Frances Eliza (Hodgson) [Mrs. Swan Moses]. [Mrs. Stephen] Townesend (1849-1924), 1,950, 11,944, **12,409**, 12,467, 12,498, 12,529, 17,053
Burnett, Jane Cromwell (Cleveland) (1834-1923), **1,253**
Burnett, Jennie (Cleveland) [Mrs. Wellington C.], 1,405
Burnett, Mary Weeks, 2,196
Burnett, Virginia Stiles (1903-47), **10,943**

Burnett, Wellington C. (1828-1907), 1,248, **1,405**
Burnham, Clara Louise Root (1854-1927), **4,250**
Burnham, Daniel Hudson (1846-1912), **3,781**
Burnham, Elizabeth [Miss] (1894-), **380**
Burnham, Elizabeth [Mrs.], 4,868
Burnham Family (MA), **7,352**
Burnham Family (TX), 16,261
Burnham, Ida L. (Angier), 7,352
Burnham, Mary Ann (1845-1912). *See* Freeze, Mary Ann (Burnham) (1845-1912)
Burnham, Nancy, 16,261
Burnham, Rebecca Dodge (1797-1869). *See* Manning, Rebecca Dodge (Burnham) (1797-1869)
Burnham, Sally [Mrs. Samuel], 7,352
Burnhans, Amy F. [Mrs.], 1,080
"Burning, The" (story), 9,770, 16,172
Burning Tide (drama), 15,700
Burnley, Edwina, 9,744
Burnquist, Joseph Alfred Arner (1879-1961), **8,971**
Burns, Annie Johnson, 3,072
Burns, Eunice L., **7,742**
Burns, Eveline Mabel (Richardson) (1900-), 11,916, **11,958**, 12,078
Burns Family, 11,730
Burns, Florence M. (1874-?). *See* Culp, Florence M. (Burns) [Mrs. Cordie Jacob] (1874-?)
Burns, Frances, 17,125
Burns, Joan Simpson [Mrs.], 11,829
Burns, Julie C., **7,743**
Burns, Lucy, 2,508
Burns, Lugenia. *See* Hope, Lugenia (Burns) [Mrs. John]
Burns, Robert, 3,211
Burns, Susan, **3,314**
Burns, William, 8,657
Burnside, Sophia Dwight (Foster) [Mrs. Samuel M'Gregore] (1787-1872?), 7,630
Burnsville Academy (NC), 13,599
Burpee, Louise Coburn [Miss] (?-1941). *See* Sawtelle, Louise Coburn (Burpee) [Mrs. William Otis] (?-1941)
Burr, A. Regina [Mrs.], **129**
Burr, Aaron (1756-1836), 2,164, **12,174**, **12,410**, 15,585, 15,745
Burr, Adeline. *See* Davis, Adeline (Burr) [Mrs. David]
Burr, Amos Shelton (1848-1911), **4,410**
Burr, Anna Robeson, 14,889
Burr Conspiracy (1805-07), 9,721
Burr, Ellen. *See* Simpson, Ellen (Burr) [Mrs. Randolph S.]
Burr, Emma Lucretia (Quigly) [Mrs. Isaac Post], 5,084
Burr Family (MI), **7,744**
Burr, Frances E., 1,896
Burr, George Lincoln, 11,575, 11,707, 11,731
Burr-Hamilton Duel, 12,554
Burr, Isaac Post, 5,084
Burr, Jane (pseudonym). *See* Winslow, Rosalind Mae (Guggenheim) (1882-1958)
Burr, Kate Ancrum (1881-1968). *See* Johnson, Kate Ancrum (Burr) [Mrs. Clarence A.] (1881-1968)
Burr, Lincoln, 11,621
Burr, Loie (1905-72). *See* Cleveland, Loie (Burr) [Mrs. Walter H.] (1905-72)
Burr, Mary. *See* Brown, Mary (Burr) [Mrs. Lloyd Warfield]
Burr, Mary Florence (1852-1950). *See* Norton, Mary Florence (Burr) [Mrs. William Harmon] (1852-1950)
Burr, Mary L., 7,744
Burr, Sarah. *See* Reeves, Sarah (Burr) [Mrs. Tapping]
Burr, Sydney Amelic (Compton) [Mrs. Amos Shelton], 4,410
Burr, Theodosia (1783-1813). *See* Alston, Theodosia (Burr) [Mrs. Joseph] (1783-1813)
Burr, Theodosia (Barton) Prevost [Mrs. Aaron] (?-ca. 1800), 12,174, 12,410
Burr, William, 7,744
Burrage, Frances Morse (1839-1934). *See* Lang, Frances Morse (Burrage) [Mrs. Benjamin Johnson] (1839-1934)
Burrall, Frances, 12,315

Burrell, Helen (1842-1915). *See* D'Apery, Helen (Burrell) (1842-1915)
Burrell, Rosa Frazar, 14,618
Burridge, Vera (1892-1963). *See* Baits, Vera (Burridge) (1892-1963)
Burrill, Florence (?-1978). *See* Jacobs, Florence (Burrill) (?-1978)
Burrill, Thomas J., 4,394
Burris, Edith S., 9,842
Burritt, Elihu, 11,520, 15,302
Burritt, Jane, 63
Burroughs, Benjamin, 3,489
Burroughs, John (1837-1921), 2,413, 3,097, 12,032, 12,380, 12,449
Burroughs, Marie (1866-1926), 16,150
Burroughs, Nannie Helen (1883-1961), 3,280, 13,217
Burroughs, Rosa M. E. (Williams) [Mrs. Benjamin] (ca. 1799-1853), **3,489**
Burroughs, Valeria G. Berrien [Mrs. Joseph H.], 3,567
Burroughs, William, 12,064, 12,894
Burroways, Janet, 2,928
Burrows, Emily L., 14,618
Burrows, Frances (Peck) [Mrs. Julius] (?-1916), **7,745**
Burrows, Julius, 7,745
Burrows, Vinnie, 9,575
Burrus, Florence [Miss], 9,741
Burrus, John, 9,756
Burson, Josie [Mrs. Leo R.], **15,887**
Burstyn, Ellen, 15,334
Burt, Agnes. *See* Van Santan, Agnes (Burt)
Burt, Andrew Sheridan, 2,239
Burt, Bradley Benedict (1814-98), **12,755**
Burt, Clara M. (1857-?), **381**
Burt, Cora Gardner, 1,067
Burt, Edith Sanders (1867-?). *See* Trout, Edith Sanders (Burt) [Mrs. Harry] (1867-?)
Burt, Elinor, 1,068
Burt, Elizabeth Johnston (Reynolds), Family, **2,239**
Burt, Emma, 12,755
Burt Family (CA), 381
Burt Family (MA), 16,531
Burt, James, 12,755
Burt, Jane (Rutherford) [Mrs. John H.], **16,614**
Burt, John, 12,755
Burt, John H., 16,614
Burt, Katharine Newlin [Mrs. Struthers], 11,878
Burt, Libbie, 12,755
Burt, Lilian (Stewart) [Mrs. Reynolds J.], 14,768
Burt, Marguerite (1818-), **233**
Burt, Mary Elizabeth (1850-1918), 12,755
Burt, Olive W. (1894-), **16,884**, **17,950**
Burton Academy (OH), 13,949
Burton, Agatha, 13,360
Burton, Alice Irene (1890-?), **382**
Burton, Ester [Mrs.], 5,644
Burton, Florence, 1,767
Burton, Hannah (Wolfe) [Mrs. Josiah], **2,040**
Burton, Harriet Wright (1873-1949). *See* Laidlaw, Harriet Wright (Burton) [Mrs. James Lee] (1873-1949)
Burton Homemakers (Rochester, IN), 4,661
Burton, Josiah, 2,040
Burton, Margaret Ernestine, 12,715
Burton, Naomi, 14,405, 14,414
Burton, Rebecca Diamond, 3,001
Burton, Richard, 8,602
Burton, Robert, **13,360**
Burton, Sarah Fenn, **4,251**
Burton, Sarah Josephine Evans, 10,693
Burton, Theodora, 772
Burtschi, Joseph Charles, 4,444, 4,445
Burtschi, Josephine "Jo" Frances (1909-), **4,444**, 4,445, 4,446
Burtschi, Mary (1911-), 4,444, **4,445**, 4,446
Burtschi, Olivia [Mrs. Joseph Charles] (1876-1959), 4,444, 4,445, **4,446**
Buruson, Anna. *See* Vardaman, Anna (Buruson)
Burwell, Bryant, 11,347
Burwell, Esther Ann. *See* Glenny, Esther Ann (Burwell) [Mrs. William H.]
Burwell, Lewis (?-1710), 12,578
Burwell, Louise, **8,464**
Burwell, Lucy (1683-1716), 12,578

Burwell, Margaret Anna (Robertson) [Mrs. Robert] (1810-71), **13,177**
Burwell, Mary, **8,464**
Burwell, Mary, 11,347
Burwell, Mary [Mrs.], 17,108
Busbee, Jacques, 13,447
Busbee, Juliana [Mrs. Jacques], **13,361**, 13,391, 13,447
Busbee, Thelma Ecord [Mrs.] (1910-), **15,790**
Busbey, Mary, 4,313
Busch, Anna (1891-). *See* Metzger, Zerline Muhlman [Mrs. Fritz] (1891-)
Busch Music Conservatory (IL), 9,467
Busenbark, Louisa. *See* Rice, Louisa Busenbark [Mrs. Asaph]
Busenbark, Mary. *See* Rice, Mary Busenbark [Mrs. Asaph]
Busey, Marietta (1879-1949). *See* Tawney, Marietta (Busey) [Mrs. Guy] (1879-1949)
Bush-Brown Family, **7,200**
Bush-Brown, Margaret Lesley (1857-1944), 7,200
Bush, Eugenia Zieber, 14,709
Bush Family (OR), **14,709**
Bush, Gladys, 13,890
Bush, Harry, 1,550
Bush, Lewis, **13,362**
Bush, Nellie (Trent) [Mrs. Joseph E.] (1888-1963), **184**
Bush, Sally, 14,709
Bush Temple Theater (Chicago, IL), 3,878
Bush, Thetis, 5,420
Bushell, Bertha [Mrs.], **8,216**
Bushfield, Mrs. Harlan, 15,869
Bushman, John (1843-1946), **185**
Bushman, Lois Angeline (Smith) [Mrs. John] (1844-1921), 16,827
Bushman, Maria Elizabeth (1869-?). *See* Smith, Maria Elizabeth (Bushman) [Mrs. Silas Derryfield] (1869-?)
Bushnell, Hannah, 11,414
Bushnell, Rosetta (Hammond) (1842-1915), **11,470**
Bushongo language, 92
Busick, Mary Ann, **10,226**
Business, **1,406**, 9,407. *See also* Businessmen; Businesswomen; Department stores; Executives; Merchants; Occupations; Secretaries
vocational guidance, 6,440
Business and Professional Club (NY), 6,829
Business and Professional Women (IN), **4,550**
Business and Professional Women's Clubs, 76, 116, 9,647, 9,779, 10,197, 11,349, 13,111, 13,446
Business and Professional Women's Club (Ontario, CA), 1,092
Business and Professional Women's Club (HI), 3,653
Business and Professional Women's Club (Bloomington, IL), **3,750**
Business and Professional Women's Club (Monmouth, IL), **4,094**
Business and Professional Women's Club (Muscatine, IA), 5,087
Business and Professional Women's Club (Webster City, IA), **5,117**
Business and Professional Women's Club (Garden City, KS), 5,179
Business and Professional Women's Club (Monroe, MI), 7,934
Business and Professional Women's Club (Ypsilanti, MI), **7,746**
Business and Professional Women's Club (MN), 8,460, 8,821, 8,833
Business and Professional Women's Club (Carlton, MN), **8,422**
Business and Professional Women's Club (Columbia, MO), **9,843**
Business and Professional Women's Club (Grand Island, NE), **10,409**
Business and Professional Women's Club (NV), 10,658, 10,671
Business and Professional Women's Club (Madison, WI), **17,611**
Business and Professional Women's Club of Auburn (AL), 7
Business and Professional Women's Club of Atlanta (GA), **3,162**

Business and Professional Women's Club of Wausau (WI), **17,883**
Business and Professional Women's Clubs (DC), 6,994
Business and Professional Women's Clubs (NY), 12,924
Business and Professional Women's Clubs of Jackson (MS), 6,901
Business and Professional Women's Foundation (DC), **2,097**
Business cycles, 5,120
Business education, 7, **6,236**, **6,643**, 10,197, **10,198**, **11,379**, 12,271. *See also* Accounting; Education; Secretaries; Shorthand
Business Girls' Inn (LA), **5,544**
Business records, 14,945
Business Woman's Equal Suffrage Club (Helena, MT), 3,681
Business Women's Club (Minneapolis, MN), 8,972
Business Women's Holding Company (MN), **8,972**
Business Women's Legislative Council of California, **1,406**
Businessmen, 198, 222, 1,698, **2,249**, **2,267**, **2,317**, 2,558, **2,572**, 2,725, 2,929, **3,270**, 3,757, **3,882**, **3,893**, 3,923, 4,469, 4,614, **4,799**, 4,906, **4,941**, **4,951**, 5,127, 5,431, 5,743, 5,754, 5,826, 6,873, 7,608, **8,000**, 8,007, 8,306, **8,374**, **8,558**, 8,709, 8,909, **8,943**, **9,050**, **9,202**, **9,431**, **9,435**, **9,442**, **9,841**, 9,987, 10,041, 10,331, 10,381, 10,482, 10,752, **10,920**, 11,005, **11,031**, **11,335**, 11,347, **11,550**, **11,710**, **11,875**, 12,180, **12,547**, 12,814, 13,117, 14,498, 14,803, 14,835, 14,977, 14,993, 15,004, **15,115**, **15,222**, 15,257, **15,258**, **15,271**, 15,291, **15,333**, 15,616, **15,626**, **15,637**, 16,257, **16,449**, 17,118, 17,169, 17,293, **17,335**, 17,390, **17,535**, 17,607
Businessmen, Afro-American, **2,490**
Businesswomen, 156, 688, 1,346, 1,402, 1,747, 2,031, **2,428**, 2,558, 2,635, **2,922**, 3,149, 3,222, 3,451, 3,682, **4,198**, 4,863, 4,899, **4,922**, 5,272, 6,672, **7,196**, 7,249, 7,624, **7,699**, **7,875**, 8,007, 8,388, **9,518**, 10,075, **10,197**, **10,471**, 10,680, **11,209**, **11,237**, 11,661, 12,803, 12,993, **13,272**, 13,299, 13,610, **13,689**, 14,885, **15,629**, **15,840**, 15,869, **16,002**, 16,038, 16,510, 16,780, **17,171**, 17,186, **17,241**, **17,496**, 17,679
Businesswomen, Afro-American, 9,575
Businger, Ruth A., 2,663
Busk, Sir Douglas, 12,023
Buss Family, 4,942
Bussard, Nettie, **14,524**
Busse, Frank, 2,022
Bussey, Ella, 14,525
Bussey, Gertrude, 1,680
Bussey, Minnie, **14,525**
Butcher, Fanny. [Mrs. Richard Drumond] Bokum (1888-), 3,825, 4,005
Butchers, 8,339, 13,217
Butforth Place, Inc., 8,984
Butler, A. L., 2,636
Butler, Anna Cady (1878-1973), 8,388
Butler, Anne, 4,598
Butler, Anne. *See* Thomas, Anne (Butler) [Mrs. David Owen]
Butler, Annie Oakley [Mrs. Frank] (1860-1926). *See* Oakley, Annie. Phoebe Ann Moses. [Mrs. Frank] Butler (1860-1926)
Butler, Benjamin Franklin (?-1864), **1,254**
Butler, Benjamin Franklin (1818-93), 2,522, 2,557, 2,659, 5,480
Butler, Beulah, 3,753
Butler, Blanche (1845-1939). *See* Ames, Blanche (Butler) [Mrs. Adelbert] (1845-1939)
Butler, C. Ann [Mrs. William], **3,490**
Butler, Clementina (Ware) (1820-1913), **10,907**
Butler, Edward George Washington (1800-88), 5,481, 9,753
Butler, Eloise [Miss], **8,973**
Butler, Esther (Brakeman) [Mrs. Joseph] Lyman [Mrs. Thomas] (1826-1917), 606, 1,505, **14,294**
Butler, Eva L. [Mrs.], **1,887**
Butler Family (IN), **4,598**
Butler Family (LA), **5,481**
Butler, Florence (Faison) [Mrs. Marion], **12,965**

Butler, Frances "Fanny" Anne (Kemble) [Mrs. Pierce] (1809-93). *See* Kemble, Frances "Fanny" Anne. [Mrs. Pierce] Butler (1809-93)
Butler, Frances (1838-1910). *See* Leigh, Frances (Butler) [Mrs. James Wentworth] (1838-1910)
Butler, Frances Parke Lewis [Mrs. Edward George Washington], 5,481
Butler, Francis E., **10,944**
Butler, General, 12,503
Butler, Hannah M., **7,130**
Butler, Helen (Tooke), 11,730
Butler, Henry V., 10,944
Butler, Hilda H., **5,378**
Butler, Ida F., 2,087
Butler, James L., 10,648
Butler, Jane Elizabeth Lee (1875-1963), **16,885**
Butler, Jessie (Haver) (1886-), 827, 1,652
Butler, Josephine, 18,013
Butler, Julia Colt (1872-?), 10,944
Butler, Lucy (Wood) (1841-), **12,964**
Butler, Mabel (Churchill), **6,442**
Butler, Marion, 12,965
Butler, Mary Lupton [Mrs.], 15,712
Butler, Mary Macel. *See* Goulet, Mary Macel (Butler) [Mrs. Alfred W.]
Butler, Mr., 15,355
Butler, Mrs. E. B. (1834-?), 13,683
Butler, Mrs. James L., 10,648
Butler, Nicholas Murray, 11,849, 11,930, 12,038, 12,553
Butler, Nellie, **100**
Butler, Orma Fitch (1874-1938), **7,747**
Butler, Ovid (1801-81), 4,598, 4,614
Butler, Pierce, 1,426, 2,643, 3,477, 15,041
Butler, Reba [Mrs. A. L.], 2,636
Butler, Rebecca A. [Mrs.], 2,985
Butler, Rose, **12,175**
Butler, Sarah (1835-1908). *See* Wister, Sarah (Butler) [Mrs. Owen Jones] (1835-1908)
Butler University (IN), 4,598, 4,600, 4,614
alumnae, 4,623, 10,926
presidents, 4,598
Butler University (IN), Chimes, 14,029
Butler, Warren, 6,635, 6,669
Butler, William, 3,490
Butman Family, **14,071**
Butner, Anne Maud (1870-1932), **8,544**
Butt, Pearl (Bliss) (1894-), **16,502**
Buttenheim, Mrs. Harold S., **10,945**
Butter, 17,418
marketing, 7,672
Butterfield, Eleanor, **7,748**
Butterfield, Frances Westgate [Miss], **9,598**
Butterfield, Jacob K., **16,925**
Butterfield, Persis, 16,925
Butterfly Association (Chicago, IL), 4,143
Butterfly Club (Nevada City, CA), 1,079
Butterfly, The (periodical), 4,143
Butterick Company, **11,822**
"Butternut Wisdom" (column), 6,101
Butters, Dorothy Gilman (pseudonym). *See* Gilman, Dorothy (1923-)
Butters, Ella S. King [Mrs. William] (?-1916), 8,974
Butters, William (1849-1902), Family (MA, MN), **8,974**
Butterworth Family (NY), 12,020
Buttler, Jane. [Mrs. Gustave] Salevski, 522
Buttrick, Caroline I., **14,966**
Buttrick, Wallace Henry (1853-1926), 12,966
Butts, Frances Amelia (Buss) [Mrs. George Edgar] (1834-84), 16,452, **16,926**
Butts, George Edgar, 16,452
Butts, June, 5,466
Butts, Mary, 15,170
Butts, Orilla Wright (1904-), 11,661, 11,662
Buxton, Huldah G. [Mrs. Joshua, Jr.], **7,353**
Buxton, Mary Jane (1821-1915), **7,354**
Buyse, Zedie Jane (Morrison), **8,516**
Buzell, Mrs. R. L., **10,227**
By the King's Command (book), 6,084
By the Political Sea (book), 2,456
By the Thorn Road (book), 4,956

"By Wagon from Bannack City to the Bitter Root Valley," 10,337
Bybee, Minnie Ida (1871-1952). *See* Luy, Minnie Ida (Bybee) [Mrs. Fred, Jr.] (1871-1952)
Bye, George T., 11,954
Bye, Ruth, 9,140
Byers, Elizabeth [Mrs. William Newton], 1,757
Byers, Emma F. [Mrs.], 10,518
Byers Junior High School (Denver, CO), 1,713
Byers, Mary Eve. *See* Robinson, Mary Eve (Byers)
Byers, William Newton (1831-1903), **1,757,** 1,764
Byington, Margaret, 8,670
Byle, Elizabeth. *See* Ball, Elizabeth (Byle) [Mrs. William]
Bynner, Witter, 4,482, 4,483, 11,220, 12,029, 12,035, 16,168, 16,169
Bynum, Caroline W., 6,482
Byrd Family, 3,099
Byrd Family (MS), 9,816
Byrne, Clarissa (Young) (1895-), **383,** 1,068
Byrne, Elizabeth (1828-1906). *See* Williams, Elizabeth Byrne [Mrs. William W.] (1828-1906)
Byrne, Eva. *See* Smith, Eva (Byrne) Rizzi
Byrnes, Roane Fleming [Mrs. Ferriday], 9,813
Byrns, Elinor, 6,379
Byron, Elsa (Spear) Edwards (1897-), 17,894, **17,951**
Byron, Joseph (1844-1923), **12,127**
Byron, Percy (1878-1959), **12,127**
CBS, **2,274,** 2,622, 5,123, 11,493, 17,666
CBS radio, 13,261
"Cabaret Love," 3,368
Cabell, Elvira A. (?-1858). *See* Bruce, Elvira A. (Cabell) [Mrs. Patrick, Jr.] Henry [Mrs. James] (?-1858)
Cabell, Emily Corbett (Failing), 14,552
Cabell Family, 9,762
Cabell, Henry F., 14,552
Cabell, James Branch, 2,875, 2,876
Cabell, Mary (Malarckey) Cartwright [Mrs. Henry Failing], 14,552
Cabet, Etienne, 4,767
Cabin Creek coal field (WV), 17,482
Cabinet Committee on Economic Security, 1,675
Cabinet officers, **1,424,** 1,530, 2,036, **2,210, 2,232, 2,259,** 2,270, **2,292,** 2,320, 2,322, 2,388, 2,393, 2,429, **2,472,** 2,592, **2,651,** 2,700, 3,881, 4,643, 4,727, 4,732, 5,060, **5,120,** 5,121, **5,149,** 9,160, 9,242, 9,962, 10,832, 10,862, 11,158, **11,159,** 11,676, 12,069, **12,538,** 12,553, 12,833, 17,065, 17,633
Cable, George W., **6,443**
Cable, George Washington (1844-1925), 1,954, **11,959,** 12,006
Cable, Maria, 14,542, 14,628
Cables, submarine, Atlantic, 12,541
Cabot, Eliza Lee (1787-1860). *See* Follen, Eliza Lee (Cabot) [Mrs. Charles] (1787-1860)
Cabot, Elizabeth (Dwight) (1840-1902), 6,445
Cabot, Ella (Lyman) [Mrs. Richard Clarke] (1866-1934), **6,188,** 6,268, **6,444,** 6,484, 6,613
Cabot Family (MA), 6,358
Cabot, Hannah, 7,372
Cabot, Hannah (Clarke) [Mrs. John], 7,372
Cabot, Hannah Lowell (Jackson) [Mrs. Samuel] (1820-79), 6,358
Cabot, Helen Jackson (1856-1938). *See* Almy, Helen Jackson (Cabot) (1856-1938)
Cabot, Hugh, **6,445**
Cabot, Hugh, Jr., 6,445
Cabot, Lizzie Perkins (1791-1885), 6,445
Cabot, Mary Anderson Boit, 6,445
Cabot, Mary R. (1856-?), **17,024**
Cabot, Mrs. J. S., 7,366
Cabot Overseers of the Poor (VT), 17,029
Cabot, Richard Clarke (1868-1939), **6,268,** 6,613
Cabot, Samuel (1815-85), 6,358
Cabrini, Mother Frances Xavier (1850-1917), 4,165
Cache County Board of Education (UT), **16,453**
Cadbury, Lydia Shinn [Mrs. Richard Tapper, Sr.], 15,271
Cadbury, Richard Tapper, Sr. (1853-1929), **15,271**
Cadbury, Sarah, 14,850
Caddie Woodlawn (book), 8,531
Cadet Corps, 15,426

Cadman, Charles Wakefield (1881-1946), 2,020, 10,483
Cadott, Charlotte. *See* Ermatinger, Charlotte (Cadott) [Mrs. James]
Cadwalader, Priscilla (Coffin) [Mrs. Jabez] Hunt [Mrs. Joseph] (1786-1860), 15,295
Cadwallader Family (PA), 15,044
Cadwallader, Mary (1820-1907). *See* Lightfoot, Mary (Cadwallader) [Mrs. Thomas] (1820-1907)
Cadwallader, Mary I. (Paul) [Mrs. Sylvanus], 2,240
Cadwallader, Mrs. Rawlins, 1,169
Cadwallader, Sylvanus (1825 or 1826-1905?), **2,240**
Cady, Alonzo D. (ca. 1823-1917), 8,975
Cady, Daniel, 2,588
Cady, Elizabeth (1815-1902). *See* Stanton, Elizabeth (Cady) [Mrs. Henry Brewster] (1815-1902)
Cady, Emma (ca. 1860-1940). *See* Randolph, Emma (Cady) [Mrs. John M.] (ca. 1860-1940)
Cady Family 12,276
Cady Family, **8,975**
Cady, Lee D. (1896-), **9,844**
Cady, Mary, 17,010
Cady, Sabrina E. Ellis [Mrs. Alonzo D.], 8,975
Cady, Sarah L., 1,998
Cadzow-Hokanson, Dorothy (1916-), 4,242
Caen, Herb, 10,677
"Caesar's Hour" (television program), 2,105
Caesars of the Wilderness (book), 8,441, 9,272
Caeser, Doris (Porter) [Mrs. Harry I.] (1892-1971), **12,892**
Cage, Minerva. *See* Sharkey, Minerva (Cage)
Cagwin, Eunice Adelaide, **10,652**
Cahill, Dorothy Canning Miller [Mrs. Holger], 11,843
Cahill, Holger (1893-1960), **11,843**
Cahill, Sister Agnes, 1,513
Cahlan, Charlotte Farley, 10,653
Cahlan-Edmunds Family (NV), 10,653
Cahlan, Florence Lee Jones, **10,653**
Cahn, Marjorie Winfield, 2,284
Cahoon, Frances Evelyn [Mrs. George C.], 8,987
Cahoon, Hannah (1799-?), **7,036**
Cain, Ethel [Miss], 9,650
Cain, Genevieve, 2,241
Cain, James Mallahan (1892-1977), 2,241
Cain, Lillian, **15,830**
Cain, Rosalie. *See* McComas, Rosalie (Cain)
Cain, Rose C. [Mrs. James W.], 2,241
Caines, Frances, 2,248, 17,126
Cairns, A. W., 17,857
Cairns, Abbie S. Leavitt [Mrs. George W.], 17,857
Cairns, George W. (1826-1900), 17,857
Cairns, Gertrude M. (1872-1959), **17,857**
Cairns, Huntington (1904-), **2,242**
Cairns, Rollo, 17,857
Cairns, William, 17,857
Cajun, The, 5,439
Calabria, the First Italy (book), 17,723
Calamity Jane (ca. 1852-1903). *See* Burk, Martha "Calamity Jane" (Cannary) [Mrs. Clinton] (ca. 1852-1903)
Calbreath Family (OR), **14,331,** 14,526
Calbreath, Helen, 14,331
Calbreath, Irene (Smith) [Mrs. John], 14,331, 14,526
Calbreath, John Franklin (1854-1939), 14,331, **14,526**
Calbreath, Mary Evelene (?-1972), 14,331, **14,527**
Calculi, biliary, 1,371
Caldecott Award, 11,368
Caldecott medal books, 8,531
Calder, Alexander, 12,642
Calderone, Mary (Steichen) (1904-), **6,446,** 6,987, 8,672, 11,897
Caldwell, Adelaide Williams [Mrs. Joseph], 13,358
Caldwell, Barzilla Guyman, 16,862
Caldwell, Edward, 4,265
Caldwell, Elizabeth (1808-76). *See* Duncan, Elizabeth (Caldwell) [Mrs. Joseph] (1808-76)
Caldwell, Erskine, 2,879, 12,891
Caldwell, Eunice, 7,056
Caldwell Family (IN), 9,738
Caldwell Family (NC), 13,164
Caldwell Family (SC), 15,647
Caldwell, Louise (1858-1915). *See* Murdock, Louise (Caldwell) [Mrs. Roland Pierpont] (1858-1915)

Caldwell, Lucy Smith (Morse) [Mrs. Edward] (1864-1941), **4,265**
Caldwell, Margaret (Bourke-White) [Mrs. Erskine] (1904-71). *See* Bourke-White, Margaret. [Mrs. Erskine] Caldwell] (1904-71)
Caldwell, Mary, 2,229
Caldwell, Matthew, 16,862
Caldwell, Maude Elaine (1873-1963). *See* Perry, Maude Elaine (Caldwell) [Mrs. Stuart H.] (1873-1963)
Caldwell, Sallie (Bowman) (1863-1948), **4,521**
Caldwell, Sarah, 7,267
Caldwell Sisters (NC), 13,217
Caldwell, Taylor, 15,331
Caldwell, Willie W., 5,121
Calendar art, 14,204
Calendars, Mexican, 6,326
Caley, Annie, 15,293
Calhoun, Anna Maria (1817-75). *See* Clemson, Anna Maria (Calhoun) [Mrs. Thomas Green] (1817-75)
Calhoun, Arthur, 15,332
Calhoun, Daisy B., 9,995
Calhoun, Floride (Colhoun) [Mrs. John C.] (1782-1866), **15,779**
Calhoun, J. H. H., 7,717
Calhoun, John C., 5,750, 10,170, 11,049, 15,041, 15,779
Calhoun Land Trust (AL), 88
Calhoun, Lucy (Monroe) [Mrs. William James], **3,982,** 3,992
Calhoun, Mary (1926-), **4,978**
Calhoun School (AL), 88
Calhoun Times (GA), 3,078
Calhoun, William James (1848-1916), **3,982**
Calico Captive (book), 6,093
California, 354, **397,** 494, **544,** 653, 709, 748, 777, 794, 807, 879, 886, 907, 982, **995, 1,067, 1,074, 1,115, 1,117,** 1,187, 1,249, **1,285,** 1,345, **1,459, 1,486,** 1,628, 1,638, 1,663, **1,664,** 8,722, 10,678, 12,195, 13,414
  abortion, legal aspects, 1,984
  actors, 1,077
  actresses, 1,077, **1,238, 1,270,** 14,202
  Afro-Americans, 726, **727,** 968, 1,011, 1,240, **1,368**
  agricultural extension work, 453
  agriculture, 844, 1,626
  agriculturists, 349
  altar gilds, 1,370
  antenuptial contracts, 333
  anthropological museums and collections, **919, 920**
  architects, 302, 678, **1,198**
  architecture, **544**
  archives, 1,114, **1,456, 1,527**
  art, 624
    collectors and collecting, **1,225**
    exhibitions, 2,820
    galleries and museums, 679, 760, 761, 918
  art, Oriental, collectors and collecting, 1,239
  art patrons, **1,282**
  art societies, 1,261, **1,265,** 1,313, 14,707
  artists, 597, 657, 889, **1,261,** 1,318, **1,335**
  assessment, 1,120
  associations, institutions, etc., **705, 1,132**
  astronomers, **1,541, 1,542**
  athletic clubs, **1,554**
  attorneys general, 592, 645
  authors, 433, 442, 657, 1,030, 1,099, 1,124, **1,250,** 1,340, **1,386, 1,396,** 1,417, 1,439, 1,640
    19th-20th C, 415, 436, 1,020, 1,082, 1,087, 1,089, 1,208, **1,231, 1,234,** 1,240, 1,241, **1,377**
  autobiography, **1,284**
  autograph albums, 1,294
  balls (parties), 493, 716
  banks and banking, **1,226**
  beauty contests, 1,534
  beauty operators, licenses, 1,136
  bills, legislative, **1,141**
  biography, 385
  birth announcements, **872**
  birth control, 1,047
  bishops, 1,516
  blacklisting, **1,547**
  blind, teachers of the, 1,133
  boards of trade, 623, 1,526

bonds, 1,636
botanists, **526, 1,409**
botany, 1,099
boundaries, 10,673
boycott, 16,010
brokers, 1,081
businesswomen, 688, 1,346
Camp Fire Girls, 882, **1,622**
campaign management, 1,043
camps, 2,685
cantors, Jewish, 749
carriages and carts, 1,544
Catholic Church, societies, 1,078
Catholic hospitals, 1,518
Catholic schools, 665, 1,066, 1,387, 1,515, **1,518**
Catholic universities and colleges, **1,005, 1,006**
census, **1,135**
centennial celebrations, 1,387
charitable societies, **309, 347, 363, 389, 394, 408,**
    675, 1,121, **1,200,** 1,632
charitable societies, Jewish, **574**
charities, 341, 760, 1,078, **1,237,** 1,328
charities, Jewish, 1,000, 1,003
child care centers, 348, 1,140, 1,309, 1,534, 1,636
child custody, 1,143
child psychiatrists, **935**
child welfare, 365
Chinese, 5,457
Chinese-Americans, 497, 772, 1,171, **1,644**
choral societies, **1,212**
church colleges, **1,512,** 1,516
church records and registers, 319, 673, 695, 723,
    733, 766, 767, 768, 769, 770, 773, 774, 775, 776,
    778, 985
church records and registers, Episcopal, **1,370**
church records and registers, Lutheran, **1,364**
church records and registers, Unitarian, **1,362**
church societies, **446, 763**
church societies, Mormon, 16,758
church societies, Presbyterian, **1,171, 1,260,** 1,387
church societies, Unitarian, **1,363**
church work with immigrants, **1,156**
churches, 1,595
churches, Congregational, 1,632
cities and towns, 391, 943, 1,092
    planning, 470
citizens' associations, 387, 1,313
city councilwomen, 661, 895, 1,642
civil rights workers, **1,012**
Civil War
    public opinion, 1,639
    societies, Confederate, **513, 1,264**
clergy, Congregational, 703
clergy, Presbyterian, **953, 1,243,** 1,247
clergymen's wives, 327
clerks, **944**
clinics, 1,121, 1,236, 9,514
club-houses, 1,193
clubs, 324, 507, 901, **932,** 935, **966, 977, 1,036,**
    1,063, 1,067, 1,079, 1,092, **1,094, 1,106, 1,109,**
    1,115, 1,117, 1,132, 1,140, **1,155, 1,214, 1,215,**
    1,220, 1,295, 1,310, 1,318, **1,341,** 1,344, 1,355,
    1,382, 1,385, 1,387, 1,483, 1,525, 1,591, **1,616,**
    5,893, 10,358
clubs, Afro-American, **1,105**
collectors and collecting, **1,481**
college administrators, 449, **487,** 1,053
college and school drama, **911, 913**
college and school journalism, **912, 914**
college librarians, **757, 1,549**
college presidents, 355, 674, **924,** 1,547, **1,559**
college students, 1,130, **1,553,** 6,862
college teachers, 337, **344,** 650, **821, 930, 952,**
    1,125, **1,128,** 1,130, **1,161,** 1,162, 1,409, 1,509,
    1,545, **1,546, 1,548, 1,550,** 1,551, **1,645,** 1,655
college trustees, 1,081
commonplace books, 839
communist party, 993, 14,453
communists, 903, 1,356, 1,357
community and school, **708**
community colleges, 17,663
community leadership, **1,429,** 1,492
community mental health services, 458
community music, 1,038

community organization, **386,** 412, 470
composers, **1,021**
congressmen, 349, **936,** 953, **1,605**
congresswomen, 387, **936, 1,010,** 1,043, **14,202**
conservationists, 637, 660, 1,526, 1,634
conservatories of music, 755, 1,313
convents and nunneries, Catholic, **1,651**
cooperative societies, 623, **1,319**
cost and standard of living, 398, 2,317
county attorneys, **1,405**
county government, records and correspondence,
    1,004, **1,149**
county officials and employees, 306, **1,428,** 6,934
court records, **186, 988, 989, 1,134, 1,143, 1,178,**
    1,180, 1,181
courts, 623, 1,031
crime and criminals, 338, **1,138**
crime prevention, citizen participation,
    1,207
dancers, **440,** 718
deaf, education, 16,654
deans (in schools), **435,** 449, 674, 843, 1,020, 6,149,
    11,898
demonstrations, 564
dental schools, **1,061**
department heads (universities), **1,088**
diaries and journals, 368, **438, 581, 594, 701,** 1,062,
    1,102, 1,258, 1,524, 1,610
19th C, 415, **502,** 636, **1,228,** 1,329, **1,367**
Diegueno Indians, 11,293
disaster relief, 347
divorce, 1,143
dormitories, 925
drama, **459**
drama critics, **712**
drugstores, 1,663
early development of, 1,409, **1,459, 1,475,** 17,740
earthquakes, 347, 391, 551, 612, 619, 664, 685,
    729, 755, **771,** 772, 1,231, 1,281, 1,308, 1,311,
    1,339, 1,569, 1,627, 10,633, 15,568
editors, **611**
education, 331, 529, 844, **1,137**
    experimental methods, 321
educational associations, 485, **909,** 1,078
educational associations, Jewish, 1,000
educators, 931, 1,054, 1,115, **1,429**
elections, 349, 1,091, **1,139,** 1,361, 8,077
elementary school teachers, 641
elementary schools, 888, **1,055**
embroidery, 1,331
endowments, **997**
engravers, **1,298,** 1,335, 1,358
environmental policy, 470
equal rights amendment (proposed), 1,140
executive advisory bodies, 645, 1,525
exhibitions, 941, 1,377, 16,965
farm life, 14,491
farms, **1,233**
festivals, 1,263, 1,387
financial federations (social service), 945
firefighters, 1,086
fires, 362, 391, 405, 471, 544, 551, 612, 685, 729,
    755, **771,** 772, 1,231, 1,254, 1,281, 1,308, 1,311,
    1,339, 1,569
folklore, 1,128
food industry and trade, 943
Friends, 496
gardeners, 324
gardening, societies, etc., **1,211,** 1,526
gardens, 303
genealogists, 1,620, **1,648**
genealogy, **1,533,** 16,684
German-Americans, 1,534
girls, societies and clubs, **501, 565**
gold discoveries, **388,** 1,418, 1,621, 2,661, 8,305
gold dredging, **959**
gold miners, 338, 10,993, **12,176**
gold mines and mining, 338, 497, **1,393,** 8,374,
    10,061, 10,763
governors, 331, 504, **575,** 645, 870, 1,140, **1,152,**
    1,552
greek letter societies, 914, **922,** 1,085, **1,613,** 1,625
handicapped children, education, 1,348
hatters, 6,641

health boards, **1,121**
high school teachers, **1,610**
high schools, 789, **1,300,** 1,534
historians, **1,333,** 1,638
historic sites, conservation and restoration, 990,
    991, 1,198, 1,649
historical societies, **1,076, 1,216,** 1,258, **1,324,**
    1,333, 1,526, 1,649, **1,659**
home economics, accounting, **1,232**
horticulturists, **1,194, 1,218**
hospital records, 1,149
hospitals, 472, 1,374, 2,542
hotels, taverns, etc., 400, 438, 1,336, 1,624
    employees, 982
hours of labor, 441
housewives, **502, 1,287, 1,299**
housing, 470, **517**
Hupa Indians, 965
illustrators, **1,617**
immigrants, 1,472
immigrants, Chinese, 1,181
immigrants, German, **688**
immigrants, Norwegian, **8,722**
immigrants, Russian, **650**
Indian agents, **1,481**
insurance, health, 1,140
interior decorators, 1,068
Japanese-Americans, 15,059
    evacuation and relocation (1942-1945), 566, **785,**
    1,292
Jews, 601, 619
    oral history, **1,001**
journalists, 974, 1,193, **1,205, 1,441,** 1,638
judges, **400,** 592, 698, 895, 1,186, **1,190**
junior colleges, archives, **1,543**
jury, **1,185**
juvenile courts, 2,451
juvenile detention homes, 306, 1,525
Karok Indians, 965, **1,662**
kindergarten, 1,385
labor and laboring classes, 1,047
    housing, 396
labor disputes, 348
labor law and legislation, 441
land grants, 626, **1,145**
landlord and tenant, cases, 186
landscape gardening, 1,214
law, cases, 393, 689, 1,134
lawyers, **441, 644, 689,** 844, **1,144, 1,183, 1,184,**
    1,186, 1,188, **1,189, 1,427, 1,611, 5,058,** 6,403,
    6,620, 6,720
lecturers, 1,461
legal instruments, 333
legal secretaries, **645**
legislative councils, **1,406**
legislative hearings, 1,141
legislators, 453, 540, 592, 1,010, 1,013, 1,043,
    1,253, **1,393, 1,405,** 1,413, 10,678
liberty of speech, **915**
librarians, **420,** 1,090, **1,374,** 1,386, **1,429,** 1,532,
    8,564
libraries, 324, 1,385, 12,902
libraries, special, 303
library administration, 1,425
library resources, 1,425
licenses, 1,119
literary societies, **1,107, 1,108, 1,110,** 1,258, **1,307,**
    1,322, **1,625, 1,641**
lithographers, **1,254**
Luiseno Indians, 11,293
lumbering, 497
lynching, 338, 339
mayors, 895
Mechoopda Indians, marriage rites and customs,
    1,243
medical colleges, 1,020
medical education, 1,020
medical societies, 1,045
medical students, 1,380
memorials, 945
mental health services, **458**
merchants, 368, **963, 7,675**
Mexican-Americans, **968**
migrant agricultural laborers, 380

housing, **1,176**
migrant labor, 677
militia, 390
milk hygiene, 1,237, 1,251
mine management, 1,072
miners, medical care, 1,080
mines and mineral resources, 412, 1,516, 1,627
mining claims, 1,334
mining law, 1,072
minorities, 365, **968**
missionaries, 1,243, 11,639
missions, 331, **392**, 446, 1,222, 1,384, 1,595
missions, Presbyterian, **1,171**
Modoc Indians, 1,662
  wars, 804
monasteries, 831, 998, **1,065**, 1,534
monasticism and religious orders for women,
  Catholic, **299, 996, 998, 999, 1,007, 1,008, 1,009,
  1,066, 1,093, 1,118**, 1,339, **1,369, 1,513, 1,519,**
  1,525, 1,534, **1,651**
Mormons and Mormonism, 391, 16,758, 16,792
  education, 713
mothers general, **1,515, 1,516, 1,517**
motion picture industry, 4,473
municipal government, records and correspondence,
  1,119, 1,120
municipal officials and employees, 480, **981**, 1,119,
  1,190, **1,650**, 13,762
municipal universities and colleges, 17,663
murder, 677
museum directors, 310, 910, 1,004, 1,080, 1,634
museums, 849, 1,465
music critics, **1,210**
music-halls (variety theaters, cabarets, etc.), 396,
  941
music teachers, 468
musical societies, 1,038, 1,123
names, personal, **1,660**
Native Americans, 370, 491, 496, 497, 748, 991,
  1,396, **1,475**, 1,664
  legends, 1,471
  missions, 631, 1,243, 1,504
  names, 723
  reservations, 740, 11,293
  social life and customs, 798
  wars, 1,323, 10,632
naturalists, 668, 1,068
newsletters, **1,126, 1,129**
newspapers, **377, 912, 914, 1,011, 1,116**
  illustrations, **1,617**
  indexes, **1,166, 1,535, 1,618**
notaries, **1,142, 1,334**
novelists, 1,416
nuns, Catholic, **1,513, 1,519, 1,520**
nurseries (horticulture), 1,331, 1,482
nurses, 631, 1,068, **1,313**
  licenses, 1,136
nurses aides, Native American, 1,662
nursing, 406, 1,121
nursing schools, 955, 1,534, 6,149
observatories (astronomy), 790
officials and employees, **365, 375, 396, 942, 973,
  1,132**
  appointments, qualifications, etc., 1,140
old age homes, 813, 877
old age pensions, 1,334
open air schools, 321, 765
opera, 1,123
oral history, 668, 772, 925, **942, 955, 968, 982,
  1,049, 1,054, 1,068, 1,080**, 1,114, 1,189, **1,345,
  1,357, 1,532, 1,663**
ornithologists, **1,447**
orphans and orphan asylums, 546, **1,213, 1,236**
orphans and orphan asylums, Jewish, **1,327**
osteopaths, **1,045**, 1,111
pageants, 921
painters, **1,522, 2,729, 2,740, 2,774, 14,707**
Paiute Indians, 965, 1,243
parades, 1,387
parents' and teachers' associations, 539, **979**, 1,304,
  1,615
parks, 990, 1,385
  management, 375
parole, 1,503

patriotic societies, **431, 432**, 513, 1,078, 1,092,
  1,253, 1,264, **1,276, 1,277**, 1,297
peace societies, 15,316
pharmacists, licenses, 1,136
philanthropists, **1,153, 1,193, 1,217**
photograph collections, **978, 1,064, 1,079, 1,157,
  1,330, 1,531**
photographers, **2,745**
photographs, **923**
physical education and training, **1,555**
physical education teachers, **402**
physicians, **935**, 1,020, 1,058, 1,062, 1,136, **1,251,
  1,348**, 1,374, **1,417, 1,521**, 1,551, 1,607, 1,608,
  1,620, **1,629**
  licenses, 1,136
pioneers and settlers, 315, **338**, 457, 591, 618, **724,
  798**, 813, 899, 956, **960**, 971, **975**, 1,114, 1,115,
  1,256, 1,257, 1,278, **1,355, 1,393**, 1,396, 1,418,
  1,525, **1,609**, 1,621, 1,632, **1,634**, 1,640, 1,658,
  1,661, 2,561, 16,751, 17,626
playgrounds, 1,385
poetry, study and teaching, 1,394
poets, **436**, 635, **874**, 889, **1,268, 1,394, 1,407,
  1,432, 1,441, 1,447, 1,448, 1,453, 1,461, 1,489,
  1,508**, 17,327
poets laureate, **1,090**, 1,307, 1,395, 1,416, 1,417,
  1,429, 1,447, 1,489
police, 612
  complaints against, 1,122
  records and correspondence, 1,122
poliomyelitis, 8,621
political activists, women, 972
political clubs, 1,503
politicians, **1,642**, 4,493
politics and government, 611, 1,503
politics, practical, **1,014**
politics, practical, women's activism, 453, 485, **610,**
  720, **1,316, 1,317**
Pomo Indians, 965
poor, Jewish, 1,003
Portuguese Americans, 1,532, 1,534
postal service, postmistresses, 982
potters, **2,828**
prenatal care, 1,607
priests, 715, 733
printers, 1,358
prisoners, 1,140
prisons
  officials and employees, 1,147
  records and correspondence, 1,147, 1,149
  reform of, 6,811
prisons for women, 1,140
  records and correspondence, 1,146
private schools, 888, 931, 1,104
prospecting, 8,305
prostitution, 186, 400, 1,181
public health, 321, **1,148**
public health nurses, **1,148**
public health nursing, 1,655
public institutions, for teen agers, **1,151**
public libraries, 966, 1,068, **1,114**
public records, **1,422**
public schools, 1,010
public welfare, 321, 380, 973, **1,150**
ranch life, **1,101**, 1,312
ranchers, 426, 1,208, 1,634
ranches, 333, 349, 370, 428, 477, 627, 636, 731,
  733, 870, 906, 1,412, 1,441, 1,492, 5,132
recreation centers, 945, 1,615
reformatories (female), 1,151
refugees, 462
regional planning, 1,503
registers of births, etc., **1,384**
religion in the public schools, 485
school boards, 485, 500, 936
school buildings, 713
school librarians, 1,633
school superintendents and principals, 326, 788,
  789, 1,137, 10,751
schools, 350, **506**, 596, 955, **1,137**, 1,353
schools of public health, 344
science museums, 310
scientific societies, 546
scrapbooks, **926, 980**

sculptors, **2,748, 2,774**
secret societies, **1,075, 1,207**
secretaries, **1,037**
seed industry and trade, 1,052
senators, United States, 540, 575, 1,552, 12,828
sex discrimination in education, 1,125
sex discrimination in employment, 1,162
sheep ranches, 1,621
Shoshone Indians, 965
singers, 316, **994**, 14,202
sisterhoods, Jewish, **932**, 939, **946**
social action, 393
social life and customs, 532, 619, 647, 722, 777,
  1,117, 1,638
social reformers, **1,047**, 1,356
social service, 754
social settlements, 365
social work education, 393, 8,641
social workers, 648, 8,077
  licenses, 1,136
Socialist party, **808**, 12,702
societies, **1,071**
societies, Afro-American, 726
societies, Jewish, 1,000
soldiers, 748
Spanish-Americans, **968**
Spanish in, 1,510, 2,197
Spanish missions of, 985, 1,459
state departments of education, 1,137
state libraries, **1,133**
state universities and colleges, faculty, **440**, 468
stock and stock breeding, 647
stores, retail, 1,419
strikes and lockouts, 11,905
  agricultural laborers, 842, 1,577
student housing, 449
students, 1,263
students' societies, 578, **908, 925, 927, 1,164**, 1,543,
  1,625, 14,029
suffrage, 530, 1,058, **1,255, 1,359, 1,360**, 1,473,
  1,618
  law and legislation, 1,255
  opposition to, 2,508
suffrage societies, 530, 648, **1,158, 1,202**, 1,255,
  1,344, 1,359, 1,629
suffragists, **1,304, 1,351**, 1,506
Sunday schools, 1,114
symphony orchestra societies, **1,389**
symphony orchestras, 1,038, 1,429
teachers, **381**, 631, 649, 668, **788**, 955, 956, **969,**
  1,068, 1,137, 1,193, **1,197**, 1,208, **1,261, 1,301,**
  1,461, **1,522**, 1,532, 1,628, 1,634, **1,643, 1,651,**
  1,655, 2,745, **10,751**
  out-of-school activities, 1,197
teachers' colleges, 954, **1,042**
teachers' unions, 1,636, 8,128
teen agers
  employment, 14,202
  welfare, 402
telegraph operators, 956
temperance societies, 400, 509, **1,056, 1,169**, 1,632
theater, 1,115
  study and teaching, 440
theaters, **1,077**
theatrical producers and directors, 871
trade and professional associations, **384, 393, 948,
  1,159, 1,160**, 1,344
trade-unions, 1,356
  agricultural laborers, 797, 16,003
  clerks, retail, 944
  clothing workers, 659, 1,656
  longshoremen, 1,280
  officials and employees, 640, 1,357
  printing industry, **1,358**
transportation, 1,664
travel, 398
trials, 341, 8,127
trolley buses, 1,313
tuberculosis, hospitals and sanitoriums, 7,526
tugboats, 412
undercover operations, 1,122
United Methodist Church, 1,393, **1,459**
universities and colleges, 760, 786, 917, **923**, 1,163,
  1,377, 1,534, 1,552, 3,165, 6,862

archives, **1,085**
buildings, 918
faculty, **916, 928**
graduate work, 11,846
records and correspondence, **1,095**
religion, 521
university presses, 11,925
urban renewal, 470
vacation schools, 1,385
veterans, 1,140
veterans, disabled, vocational rehabilitation, 543
vigilance committees, 1,254
vital statistics, 392, 432
voice culture, 316, **1,192**
volunteer workers in hospitals, 955, **1,388**
volunteer workers in social service, 365, **380, 647**
wages, 398
    minimum wage, 2,336
walnuts, 1,229
water-supply, 1,492
weavers, 1,068
welders, Afro-American, **8,056**
welfare rights movement, 393
women
    employment, 1,140
    institutional care, **1,146**
women's centers, 1,543
women's colleges, 864
women's liberation movement (1960-), 17,663
women's studies, 1,125, **1,131, 1,165**
work relief, 14,202
World War I
    civilians' work, 849, **1,206**
    food question, 1,404
Young Women's Christian Association, 929, 12,719
Yurok Indians, 965
zoological museums, **910**
California (ship), 1,505
California Academy of Sciences, 546
California Advisory Council of Vocational Education, 2,103
California Alumni Association, 509
California Anti-Saloon League, 400
California Assembly, committees, 1,013
California Association for Adult Education, 2,233
California Association of Negro Women's Clubs, 726
California Association of Women Deans and Vice-Principals, **384**
California Centennial series, 830
California Civic League, 509
California Civic League, San Francisco Center, Public Dance Hall Committee, **386**
California College of Arts and Crafts, 2,745
California Committee for Parole Reform, 1,503
California Committee on Indian Relief Work, 389
California Conference of the National Negro Congress, 993
California Constitutional Convention, 1,393
California Coralettes (swim team), 1,534
California Council of Defense, San Diego Division, Women's Committee, **1,206**
California Council of Negro Women, 726
California Council of Republican Women, Southern Division, 453
California Cousins (drama), 12,651
California Democratic Council, 1,018, 1,037
California, Department of Consumer Affairs, **1,136**
California, Department of Justice, **1,138**
California, Department of Professional and Vocational Standards. *See* California, Department of Consumer Affairs
California, Department of Public Health, **1,148**
California Eagle, **1,011**
California Equal Suffrage Association, 530, 1,359, 1,629
California Farmer, 869
California Farmer-Labor Association, 11,769
California Federation, 1,341
California Federation for Civic Unity, **387**
California Federation of Music Clubs, 1,038
California Federation of Women's Clubs, 507, 900, 1,385, 1,404

California Foundation for Economic Opportunity, 393
California Garden Club, 1,526
California Historical Society, 1,258
California House for Belgian soldiers, 543
California Institute of Technology, administration, 1,098
California Institute of Technology, Biology Division, **1,095**
California Institution for Women (Tehachapi, CA), 1,140
California Justice Court, **186**
California League for American Indians, **389**
California Library Week, 1,386
California Literary Society, 1,090, 1,258, 1,322
California Medical Association, 1,045
California Militia, **390**
California Militia, First Regiment of Infantry, 390
California Mission Indians, 1,475
California Osteopathic Association. *See* California Medical Association
California School of Design (San Francisco, CA), students, 14,381
California School Women's Club (Oakland, CA), **1,636**
California, Secretary of State, 1,144
California Social Workers Organization, Inc., **393**
California, Spanish Archives, **1,145**
California, State Board of Social Welfare, 647
California State College, Sonoma. *See* Sonoma State University (CA)
California State Company, 1,544
California, State Department of Corrections, **1,146**
California, State Department of Mental Hygiene, officials and employees, 458
California, State Department of Social Welfare, 973, **1,149**
California State Emergency Relief Administration, **394**
California State Employees Associaton, **1,132**
California State Library, **1,133**
California State Park Commission, 375
California State Planning Commission, 1,503
California, State Relief Administration, **1,150**
California State University, Sacramento, faculty, 1,161
California State University, Sacramento, Women's Advocate, **1,163**
California State University, Sacramento, Women's Caucus, **1,164**
California State University, Sacramento, Women's Studies, **1,165**
California State University, San Diego, women, 1,125
California State Welfare Department, 1,334
California State Woman Suffrage Educational Association, 1,344
California State Women's Club, 1,132
California, State Youth Authority, **1,151**
California Superior Court, 1,031
California Teachers' Association, 1,636
California—The Name (book), 734
California Women of the Golden West, **2,243**
California Writers Club, 1,258
California Youth Authority, 402
Calisher, Hortense, 4,476
Calkins, Angelina (1818-1900). *See* Farley, Angelina (Calkins) [Mrs. Winthrop] (1818-1900)
Calkins, Earnest Elmo, 4,257
Calkins, Frank, 16,485
Calkins, Marion Clinch (1895-1968), 8,658, 8,678
Calkins, Mary Whiton [Miss] (1863-1930), 1,340, 7,567
Calkins, Rodello Hunter [Mrs. Frank], **16,464**, 16,485
Calkins, William S., 8,164
Call, 17,259
Call (San Francisco, CA), 712
Call, Alice (Hawthorne) [Mrs. George R.], 5,104
Call, Annie Payson (1854-1940), **2,244**
"Call Board" (radio program), 16,277
Call, Ellen (1826-1904?). *See* Long, Ellen (Call) (1826-1904?)
Call, George R. (1898-1974), **5,104**
Call, Mary L. [Mrs. Richard Keith], 2,942
Call, Richard Keith (1792-1862), **2,942**
Call, Una (1885-1950). *See* Jeffers, Una (Call) [Mrs. Robinson] (1885-1950)

Callahan, Margaret, 4,764
Callahan, Mary, 15,332
Callahan, Ola Eugene [Miss], **13,260**
Callahan, P. H., 2,878
Callan, Louise, 4,445
Callan, Martha C., 1,059
Callanan, Martha, 4,731
Callanan, Martha (Cooney) [Mrs. James] (1826-1901), **4,793**
Callanan University (Des Moines, IA), students, 4,896
Callaway, James, 3,491
Callaway, Leila (Hinton) [Mrs. Morgan], **2,983**
Callaway, Mary Ann (Irwin) [Mrs. Merrell Price] (ca. 1817-82), **3,491**
Callaway, Morgan, **2,983**
Callegari, Maria Giovanni, 5,418
Callen, Jane [Mrs. Martin], **4,794**
Callen, Martin, **4,794**
Callender, Eunice (1785-?), **6,447**, 6,906
Callender, Martha Brown [Mrs. James Rorke] (?-1864). *See* Forman, Martha Brown [Mrs. James Rorke] Callender [Mrs. Thomas Marsh] (?-1864)
Callis, Susan M., 3,829
Callister, Helen Marr (Clark) [Mrs. Thomas] (1829-1917), **16,615**
Callister, Henry (1716?-1768?), **12,411**
Callister, Sarah Trippe [Mrs. Henry], 12,411
Calloway, Cab, 5,534
Calloway, DeVerne Lee (ca. 1918-), 10,191, **10,194**
Calloway, Ernest, 10,194
Calohan, Mrs. W. L. (1847-?), **16,043**
Calumet Historical Society (IL), 3,919
Calvary Episcopal Church (Williamsville, NY), Women's Auxiliary, 11,359
Calvé, Emma (1858-1942), 16,150, 17,197
Calver, Amelia J. (1844-1929), **7,037**
Calverly, Edwin Elliott (1882-1971), **1,840**
Calverly, Eleanor Jane (Taylor) [Mrs. Edwin Elliott] (1886-1968), **1,840**
Calvert, Amelia Catherine (Smith) [Mrs. Philip P.] (1876-?), **14,876**
Calvert Family (KY), **5,259**
Calvert Family (NY), **11,960**
Calvert, George Henry (1803-89), 11,960
Calvert, Herbert S. (ca. 1888-), **8,072**
Calvert, Josephine (1864-1956), 5,259
Calvert, Lida (1856-1935). *See* Obenchain, Lida (Calvert) [Mrs. William Alexander] (1856-1935)
Calvert, Margaret (1860-1947), 5,259
Calvert, Margaret (Younglove) [Mrs. Thomas] (1829-1920), 5,259
Calvert, Maude Richman [Mrs. George E.] (1893-), **14,232**
Calvert, Mellie M. [Mrs. Herbert S.] (ca. 1895-), **8,072**
Calvert, Philip P., 14,876
Calvert, Rosalie Eugenia (Stier), 11,960
Calvert, Samuel Wilson (1796-1837), 5,259
Calvert, Thomas (1826-98), 5,259
Calvo, Selma, 17,282
Cam, Helen Maud (1885-1968), **6,448**
Camak Family (GA), **2,984**
Camak, James A., 2,984
Camak, Louis, 2,984
Camak, Mary W. [Mrs.], 2,984
Camber, Sarah, 3,509
Cambridge Hebrew Women's Aid Society (MA), **7,526**
Cambridge Laboratory Experimentation Review Board, 6,336
Cambridge Political Equality Association (MA). *See* League of Women Voters of Cambridge (MA)
Cambridge School Committee (MA), 6,872
Cambridge School of Architecture and Landscape Architecture (MA), 7,159
Cambridge Sewing Club (MA), **6,449**
Cambridge University (England), 6,448
Camden Female Institute (SC), **15,572**
Camelback Inn (AZ), 169
Camerer, Josephine Fredericke Clotilde (1830-64).

See Grunsky, Josephine Fredericke Clotilde (Camerer) [Mrs. Charles] (1830-64)
Cameron, Agnes, 1,083
Cameron, Alice Frances (Marsh) [Mrs. William Walker] (1852-1927), 654
Cameron, Amy Gertrude (1872-?), 654
Cameron, Anna, **10,439**
Cameron, Beatrice. *See* Mansfield, Beatrice (Cameron) [Mrs. Richard]
Cameron, Caroline Thela (1834-1922). *See* Brown, Caroline Thela (Cameron) [Mrs. Thomas A.] (1834-1922)
Cameron, Donaldina M. [Miss], 1,171
Cameron, Emma [Mrs. James], 1,083
Cameron Family (CA), **1,256**
Cameron, Goldie Griffith [Mrs.], 1,779
Cameron, Hannah H., 1,256
Cameron, James, (1816-?), **1,083**
Cameron, Jessie Anderson (1822-1906), **1,257**
Cameron, Margaret (1838-1929). *See* Pierce, Margaret (Cameron) [Mrs. James Manning] (1838-1929)
Cameron, May, 14,329
Cameron, Meribeth E., 2,166
Cameron, Minnie B., **16,044**
Cameron, Mr., 3,683
Cameron, Viola J., 654
Cameron, William Walker, 654
Cameroon, American missionaries to, 16,367
Camerson, Mrs., 8,399
"Camillia's Snuff Box" (poem), 11,161
Cammack, Eleanore [Miss] (1906-), **4,522**, 4,530
Camp, Anna Rachel (1876-1956). *See* Edwards, Anna Rachel (Camp) [Mrs. Richard Henry] (1876-1956)
Camp Butler (IL), 4,362
Camp, Charles Lewis (1893-1975), **395**
Camp Cooke (MT), 13,651
Camp Dennison (OH), 4,347
Camp Dix, 12,479
Camp Drum (OR), 14,655
Camp, Elizabeth Francis Osborn [Mrs. Jacob Andrus] (1835-1920), 11,533
Camp Family (NY), **11,533**
Camp Fire Girls, 389, 882, 1,534, **1,622**, 1,817, 2,198, 3,163, **8,490**, 8,497, 8,665, 8,670, **12,098**, 12,738
Camp Fire Girls (OH), **13,989**
Camp Fire Girls, Chicago (IL) Area Council, 4,079
Camp Fire Girls, Salt Creek Council (IL), **4,063**
Camp, Georgia Douglas (1886-). *See* Johnson, Georgia Douglas (Camp) (1886-)
Camp, Katherine. *See* Mayhew, Katherine (Camp)
Camp, Katherine (Lindsley) [Mrs. William P.] (1918-), 15,316
Camp Lewis, 14,277
Camp Lincoln Library (MN), 9,238
Camp, Mary G. (1799-1841), 1,901
Camp-meetings, 5,614, 7,604, 9,036, 11,602, 15,463, 15,968
Camp, Miriam (Bonner) (1896-), 13,176
Camp Onward (LA), 5,515
Camp sites, facilities, etc., 5,614
Camp Stebbins, 4,362
Camp Upton (NJ), 3,302
Camp Wanakiwin (MN), 8,451
Camp Waziyatah (ME), 6,614
Camp Winder Hospital (Richmond, VA), 5,812
Campaign literature, 808, 8,984, 11,503, 13,533, 13,551
Campaign management, 860, 878, 1,043, 3,293, 4,970, 5,128, 6,939, 7,729, 11,486, 11,502, 13,266, 13,566, 13,999
Campaign songs, 5,854
Campbell, A. Hartwell, 13,404
Campbell, Ada (1866-1963). *See* Larew, Ada (Campbell) [Mrs. Charles L.] (1866-1963)
Campbell, Alexander, 1,673
Campbell, Ann, 11,134
Campbell, Ann C., 14,592
Campbell, Annie. *See* Bradwell, Annie (Campbell)
Campbell, Beatrice Stella (Tanner) [Mrs. Patrick] (1865-1940), 3,980, 12,005, 16,166
Campbell, Caroline Bezora (Portman) [Mrs. James H.] (1859-1926), 2,187, **7,749**

Campbell, Clara (Cooley) (1883-), 7,151
Campbell, Diana Burnes [Mrs. Samuel C.] (1856-1938), 8,465
Campbell, Doak Sheridan, 2,928
Campbell, Dorcas (?-1959), **6,450**
Campbell, Duward, **16,886**
Campbell, Elizabeth, 9,492
Campbell, Elizabeth Barker Stevens, 14,454
Campbell, Elizabeth "Bessie" (1878-1974). *See* Feiker, Elizabeth "Bessie" (Campbell) [Mrs. Frederick] (1878-1974)
Campbell, Ella, **16,616**
Campbell, Emma A. (?-1883), **16,338**
Campbell Family (IL, MT), **10,228**
Campbell, Esther [Mrs. Duward], 1,786, **16,886**
Campbell, Fay Strawn, 4,620
Campbell, Flora, 15,427
Campbell, Francis, **5,857**
Campbell, George W., 9,748
Campbell, Gladys McAlphine. *See* Blakey, Gladys McAlphine (Campbell) [Mrs. Roy Gillespie]
Campbell, Gordon, 10,228
Campbell, Harriet (Parker) [Mrs. John], 4,940
Campbell, Helen [Mrs.], 11,748
Campbell, Helen L., 15,449
Campbell, James, 15,449
Campbell, James B., 10,228
Campbell, James H., 7,749
Campbell, Jane, **12,139**
Campbell, Jane. *See* Foss, Jane (Campbell)
Campbell, Jane (1800-71). *See* McKeever, Jane (Campbell) [Mrs. Matthew] (1800-71)
Campbell, John Archibald, **2,985**
Campbell, Lily Bess, 12,360
Campbell, Loraine Leeson (1905-), 6,987, 7,283
Campbell, Louisa (1848-?). *See* Sheppard, Louisa (Campbell) (1848-?)
Campbell, Margaret (1846-1936), 10,185
Campbell, Margaret Bennett [Mrs. James], 15,449
Campbell, Margaret (Patterson), 1,673
Campbell, Margaret V., 2,927
Campbell, Margaret W. [Mrs. John], 4,732
Campbell, Margaret Wade (1857-1945). *See* Deland, Margaretta "Margaret" Wade (Campbell) [Mrs. Lorin Fuller] (1857-1945)
Campbell, Margaretta Wade (1857-1945). *See* Deland, Margaretta "Margaret" Wade (Campbell) [Mrs. Lorin Fuller] (1857-1945)
Campbell, Marguerite [Mrs. Rollie] (1895-1966), 3,667
Campbell, Marie [Mrs.], **5,430**
Campbell, Mary, 15,449
Campbell, Mary Bennett [Miss], **15,450**
Campbell, Mary Sophia [Mrs. J. W.], 14,665
Campbell, Matilda Jane (1846-1943). *See* Wilkin, Matilda Jane (Campbell) (1846-1943)
Campbell, Mildred Hall, 5,123
Campbell, Miriam S., 1,779
Campbell, Mrs. E. V., 15,769
Campbell, Mrs. Patrick (1865-1940). *See* Campbell, Beatrice Stella (Tanner) [Mrs. Patrick] (1865-1940)
Campbell, Mrs. S. H., 15,904
Campbell, Mrs. W. N., 9,659
Campbell, Oliver Arnold (Dame) [Mrs. John Charles] (1882-1954), **5,249**
Campbell, Patience, 2,946
Campbell, Persia Crawford [Mrs. Edward Rice, Jr.] (1898-1974), **11,804**, 11,805, 11,806
Campbell, Rollie, 3,667
Campbell, Samuel C., 8,465
Campbell, Serita. *See* Tamplet, Serita (Campbell)
Campbell, Sophia Elizabeth (Faulkner) [Mrs. Francis] (1849-1933), **5,857**
Campbell, William J., **3,946**
Campbell, William S., 2,633
"Campfire Library, The" (stories), 192
Camping, 3,678, 10,829, 12,112
"Camping Expedition to Colorado," 1,790
Campobello (residence), 11,853
Camps, 396, 938, 1,798, 2,685, 3,068, 3,903, 4,134, 4,452, 4,920, 5,515, 5,654, 6,516, 6,808, 8,134, 8,451, 8,655, 8,684, 8,754, 9,456, 9,506, 10,518,

12,078, 12,079, 12,100, 13,221, 13,994, 15,209, 16,257
administration, 2,685, 6,614
Campus, The (NY), 11,302
Can Women Be Gentlemen? (book), 325
"Can Women Stop Crime?" (article), 1,207
Canada, 12,268, 16,690
American ambassadors to, 2,590
American singers in, 5,911
armed forces, women, 6,850
bar associations, 1,723
community leadership, 8,635
country music, **5,642**
Mormons and Mormonism, 16,609, 16,740
pioneers and settlers, 9,325
slavery, fugitive slaves, 5,457
theaters, 8,956
trade and professional associations, 6,164
Canadian-American Women's Association, **7,201**
Canadian-American Women's Committee, **7,190**
Canadian Bar Association, 1,723
Canadian Medical Corps, 5,081
Canal-boats, 12,887
Canal Zone, nurses, **1,665**
Canals, 1,901, 2,696, **7,070**, 12,402, 12,886, 14,142
Canals, interoceanic, 1,666
Canan, Jessie, 14,861
Canandaigua Academy (NY), 11,708
Canavan, Myrtelle Mary Moore (1879-1953), **6,216**
Canby, Fanny, 2,045
Canby, Louise Hawkins [Mrs. E. R. S.] (1819-?), 1,786
Canby, Margaret, 2,045
Canby, Marion G. [Mrs. Henry Seidel], 2,263
Canby, Mary, 2,045
Cancer, 15,507
nursing, **3,239**
radiotherapy, **4,698**
surgery, 4,436
Cancer patients, 7,383, 10,535
personal narratives, 97
Cancer research, 7,327, **10,210**, 11,885, 14,900
Cancer Research Center (CT), 2,005
Cancer Society, 8,697
Candida (drama), 11,457
Candle molds, 16,402
Candlemaking, 13,141
Candles, Amelia, 9,437
Caney Creek Community Center (PR), 7,225
Canfield, Andrew N., **10,279**
Canfield, Cass, 11,870, 11,897
Canfield, Dorothea "Dorothy" Frances (1879-1958). *See* Fisher, Dorothea "Dorothy" Frances (Canfield) [Mrs. John Redwood] (1879-1958)
Canfield, Flavia C. [Mrs. James H.], **16,978**
Canfield, Harriet Augusta Graves [Mrs. Malcolm], 11,259
Canfield, Harriet Vail (1849-?), 10,920
Canfield, James H., 16,978
Canfield, Lucy Marie (1846-1915). *See* Margetts, Lucy Marie (Canfield) [Mrs. John W.] Young [Mrs. Ara W.] Sabin [Mrs. Phillip H.] (1846-1915)
Canfield, Malcolm (1822-92), **11,259**
Canfield, Martha [Miss], **16,979**
Canfield, Mary Grace [Mrs.], **17,025**
Canfield, Prudence, 16,605
Canfield, Sarah Elizabeth (Haas) [Mrs. Andrew Nahum], **10,279**, 13,651
Caniff, Milton, 4,476
Cannary, Martha "Calamity Jane" (ca. 1852-1903). *See* Burk, Martha "Calamity Jane" (Cannary) [Mrs. Clinton] (ca. 1852-1903)
Canneries, 12,130
Cannery workers, 5,829
Canning and preserving, 54, 5,359, 10,015, 11,851, 13,617, 15,961, 16,968
Cannon, Alice (1882-1967). *See* Cheney, Alice (Cannon) [Mrs. Joseph LeRoy] (1882-1967)
Cannon, Angus Munn, 16,617, 16,946
Cannon, Annie Jump [Miss] (1863-1941), **1,536, 2,041, 6,269,** 6,285
Cannon, Clara Cordelia (Moses) [Mrs. Angus Munn] (1839-1926), **16,618**

Cannon, Clarence A. (1879-1964), **9,938**
Cannon, Elizabeth. *See* McCrimmon, Elizabeth (Cannon) Porter
Cannon, Elizabeth Ann (1821-1910), 9,241
Cannon Family, 9,241
Cannon, Frank Jenne (1859-1933), **1,702**
Cannon, George Q., 16,676, 16,765
Cannon, Ida M., 8,665
Cannon, Jane Grey (1815-84). *See* Swisshelm, Jane Grey (Cannon) [Mrs. James] (1815-84)
Cannon, Jenny, 6,815
Cannon, Jenny (Curtis) [Mrs. Henry M.], 9,028
Cannon, Joe, 13,228
Cannon, Leonora (1840-1924). *See* Gardner, Leonora (Cannon) [Mrs. Robert] (1840-1924)
Cannon, Lucy A., **5,749**
Cannon, M. Antoinette, 8,665
Cannon, Martha Hughes [Mrs. Angus Munn] (1857-1932), 16,617, 16,946
Cannon, Mary Alice (1828-?). *See* Lambert, Mary Alice (Cannon) [Mrs. Charles] (1828-?)
Cannon, Ruth Louise (Coltrane) [Mrs. Charles Albert] (1891-1966), **12,967**, 13,514
Cannon, Sarah Maria (Mousley) [Mrs. Angus Munn], **16,887, 16,927**
Cannor, Emma F. [Mrs.], 13,363
Canoes and canoeing, 13,947
Canon, Helen, 11,662
Canonza Ladies Chorus (UT), **16,405**
Canonza Society (UT), **16,406**
Canoyer, Helen G., 11,662, 11,805, 11,806
Can't Get a Redbird (book), 16,384
Canteen, The (Albany, NY), 11,247
Canteens (war-time, emergency, etc.), 11,566, 12,132, **13,156**, 14,741, **17,072**, 17,184, 17,815
Canterbury, Hazel, **17,894**
Cantey, Floride. *See* Johnson, Floride Cantey [Mrs. John]
Cantine, Christina M., **11,534**
Cantine des Deux Drapeaux (Chalon-sur-Marne, France), 14,741
Cantine Family (Ithaca, NY), 11,534
Cantine, Moses I. (1774-1823), 11,534
Canton Asylum for Insane Indians (SD), **10,097**
Canton Ladies Anti-slavery Society (OH), **13,914**
Cantonment Indians, 14,241
Cantors, Jewish, 749
Cantrell, Ellen Maria (Harrell) (1833-1909), **254**
Cantwell, Catherine Simmons [Mrs. James C.], 17,170
Cantwell, Charles A., 10,679
Cantwell, Ellen. *See* Sargent, Ellen (Cantwell)
Cantwell, James C., 17,170
Cantwell, Jessie (1887-1971). *See* Hilburger, Jessie (Cantwell) (1887-1971)
Canwell Committee (WA), 17,281
Cape Cod, 6,621, 7,023
Capehart, B. A., 12,968
Capehart, Meeta Rhodes (Armistead) [Mrs. B. A.], **12,968**
Capen, Bessie Tilsen (1837-1920), 6,851
Capen, Betsey Estey Talbot (1807-87), 6,851
Capen, Charles, 3,764
Capen, Edward Warren (1870-1947), **1,841**
Capen, Elizabeth Lydia (Sanderson) (1872-1955), **1,841**
Capen, Grace Duncan (Wright) [Mrs. Samuel Paul] (1874-1951), 11,372
Capen, Samuel Paul (1878-1956), **11,372**
Capener, Clara (Oyler) [Mrs. Samuel William] (1891-) **16,619**
Capers, Charlotte [Miss] (1913-), 9,585, **9,599**, 9,694, 9,769
Capers, Roberta, 11,844
Caperton, Helena Trench (Lefroy) [Mrs. Clifford Randolph] (1878-1962), **17,076**
Capetown School of Art (South Africa), students, 3,634
Capital City Club (GA), 3,130, 3,254
Capital City School of Nursing (DC), **2,306, 6,132**
Capital punishment, 7,031, 11,827, 17,463. *See also* Executions and executioners
    abolishment of, 12,419
    public opinion, 6,379, 10,354
Capital Times (Madison, WI), 17,598, 17,675

Capitalism, 8,082
Capitalists and financiers, **2,182, 2,472, 9,055, 10,776, 11,074, 11,720, 11,896, 12,600**, 13,943, **14,885**, 14,957, **15,054**
Capitol Girls Club (Salt Lake City, UT), **16,928**
Capitol School (NE), 10,488
Caples, Louise Skinner Leigh [Mrs. D. Delmas] (1915-), **5,849**
Caplinger, Leonard J., **1,408**
Caplinger, Mary P. [Mrs. Leonard J.], 1,408
Capron, Sarah Brown (Hooker) (1828-?), 3,969, 3,970
Captain Archer's Daughter (book), 2,300
Captive Wild (book), 17,248
Capture at Sea (book), 5,694
Car, Benjamin, **1,703**
Caravan Family, 4,058
Caraway, Hattie Ophelia (Wyatt) [Mrs. Thaddeus Horatius] (1878-1950), 255, 282, 5,537
Caraway, Thaddeus Horatius (1871-1931), 255
Carbery, Muriel, 12,351
Card Family (TX), 16,261
Card, Lottie (Holman) [Mrs. James R.] (1882-1964), **16,261**
Card, Zina Priscenda (Young) [Mrs. Thomas] Williams [Mrs. Charles Ora] (1850-1931), 3,738, **16,620**, 16,676
Carden, Georgiana Caroline [Miss], **396**
Carden, I. Myrtle, 9,114
Carden, Mary Elizabeth (1903-), 5,394
Cardiac Clinic, 11,932
Cardillo, Mrs., 7,109
Cardinal (Wells College, NY), 11,281
Cardiologists, 11,932
Cardiology, research, 11,885
Cardiovascular research, 2,088
Cardiovascular system
    abnormalities and deformities, 2,088
    surgery, 9,979
Cardoza Night School (DC), 2,131
Cardozo, Benjamin N., 13,811
Cardwell, Minnie Lee. *See* Miller, Minnie Lee (Cardwell)
Cardwell, Mrs. B. P., 14,542
CARE. *See* Cooperation for American Relief Everywhere
Career Equity for Workers program, 2,122
Carel, Alexis, 12,405
Carey, Alice, 8,375
Carey, Amelia L. (?-1891), **4,252**
Carey and Hart (PA), **12,178**
Carey, Anne G. (Hall) [Mrs. Francis K.] (1864-1943), 5,741
Carey, Cora E. (White) [Mrs. Will] Watson [Mrs. S. E.] (1843-1911), **9,600**
Carey, Ernestine Moller (Gilbreth) (1908-), **7,202**
Carey Family, 7,202
Carey, Genie F. *See* Bennett, Genie F. (Carey) [Mrs. Augustus P.]
Carey, James B., 8,085
Carey, Jean Wallace (1907-75), 12,078
Carey, Mary (1857-1950), **10,229**
Carey, Miriam Eliza (1858-1937), 8,976
Carey, Phoebe, 8,375
Carey, S. E., 9,600
Carey, Thomas, 5,459
Cargill, Benjamin, Sr. (1737-1813), 7,608
Cargill, Benjamin, Jr. (1769-1822), 7,608
Cargill Family (CT, RI), **7,608**
Cargill Family (ME), **5,673**
Cargill, John Milton (1806?-90), 7,608
Cargill, Mary H., 7,608
Carhart, J. W., 14,552
Carhart, Mrs. Louis, 12,504
Caricatures and cartoons, 1,576, 3,111, 7,178, 10,178, **11,997**
Carigen, Mrs. Thomas, 17,894
Carithers, Elizabeth (1874-?), 3,024
Carithers Family (GA), **3,024**
Carithers, John, 2,962
Carkeek, Emily [Mrs. Morgan], **17,220**
Carkeek, Morgan, 17,220
Carle, Nancy Charlotte Emmaline Matchett, **4,795**
Carleton, Annie, 3,026

Carleton College (Northfield, MN), 6,670, 8,797, 9,076
    deans, 8,721
    faculty, 8,995
    students, 9,376
Carleton, Margaret K. *See* Farrand, Margaret K. (Carleton) [Mrs. Livingston]
Carley, Maurine, 17,921
Carlgren, Maud (Mullan), 9,078, 17,587
Carli Family, 8,966
Carli, Lydia Ann (Brown) [Mrs. Christopher] (1818-1905), 9,096
Carlin, Katie, 9,025
Carlin, Margot R., **8,312**
Carlin, Thomas, 10,092
Carlisle Arrow, 14,748
Carlisle Civic Club (PA), **14,746**
Carlisle Fortnightly Club (PA), **14,747**
Carlisle Indian Industrial School, 2,674
Carlisle Indian School (PA), **14,748**, 14,761
Carlisle, Kitty, 11,817, **17,801**
Carlisle, Mary (1882-1964). *See* Howe, Mary (Carlisle) (1882-1964)
Carlisle, Sally (1805-?). *See* Randall, Sally (Carlisle) [Mrs. James] (1805-?)
Carlow College (Pittsburgh, PA), archives, **15,212**
Carlsey, Ina Donna [Mrs. Robert B.] (1841-1928). *See* Coolbrith, Ina Donna. [Mrs. Robert B. Carlsey] (1841-1928)
Carlson, Catharine [Mrs. Pehr], 8,977
Carlson, Grace Holmes, 9,380
Carlson, June, **8,466**
Carlson, Katherine, **8,466**
Carlson, Minne, 8,462
Carlson, Natalie Savage (1906-), 8,531
Carlson, Pehr (?-1904), Family (MN), **8,977**
Carlson, Peter (?-1904). *See* Carlson, Pehr (?-1904), Family (MN)
Carlson, Ruth Elizabeth (Kearney), **397**
Carlsson, Emmy. *See* Evald, Emmy (Carlsson) [Mrs. Carl A.]
Carlton, Caleb Henry (1836-1923), **2,245**
Carlton, Elizabeth (1726-1804). *See* Shackleton, Elizabeth (Carlton) (1726-1804)
Carlton, Elizabeth Ann Espey, 2,986
Carlton Family (GA), **2,986**
Carlton, Mabel (?-1961). *See* Horner, Mabel (Carlton) [Mrs. John K.] (?-1961)
Carlton, Marian, 2,986
Carlton, Rosemary, 4,743
Carlton, Sadie (Pollock) [Mrs. Caleb Henry], 2,245
Carlyle, Sarah Fairfax, 2,621
Carmalt, Ethel (1865-1959), **1,992**
Carmalt, William Henry, 1,992
Carmel Mission (CA), 657
Carmel Museum of Art (CA), 597
Carmel Presbyterian Esther Circle (MN), **8,487**
Carmelite Monastery (Santa Clara, CA), 1,534
Carmelite Monastery (Eldridge, IA), **4,876**
Carmelite Monastery (MD), **5,722**
Carmelite Monastery (Saranac Lake, NY), **12,845**
Carmelite Sisters of St. Therese, Villa Teresa Convent (Oklahoma City, OK), **14,226**
Carmen (opera), 7,213, 7,303
Carmer, Carl, 12,035
Carmichael, Stokely, **1,570**
Carmouche, Annie (Jeter) [Mrs. Emile A.] (1843-?), **12,969**
Carmouche, Emile A. (?-1885), 12,969
Carnahan, Ann, **9,654**
Carnahan, R. B., 15,226
Carne Humana Rancho (CA), 333
Carnegie, Andrew, 2,384, 4,396, 11,844, 14,733
Carnegie Corporation, **11,844**, 11,845
Carnegie Hero Medal, 4,949
Carnegie Institute of Technology (Pittsburgh, PA). *See* Carnegie-Mellon University (Pittsburgh, PA)
Carnegie Institution of Washington, **6,325**
Carnegie Library (GA), 3,200
Carnegie, Louise (Whitfield) [Mrs. Andrew] (1857-1946), 4,696, 12,087
Carnegie, Mary Elizabeth Lancaster (1916-), **6,133**
Carnegie-Mellon University (Pittsburgh, PA), 2,107, 2,798

faculty, 10,238, 11,618
students, 14,235
Carnegie, Nancy. *See* Rockefeller, Nancy (Carnegie) [Mrs. J. Stillman]
Carnell, Laura Horner (1867-1929), **15,182**
Carner, Lucy Perkins (1886-), 9,443, **12,710**, 15,316
Carnes, Rebecca (1813-97). *See* Rowan, Rebecca (Carnes) [Mrs. John, Jr.] (1813-97)
Carney, Elizabeth J., 9,145
Carney, Ellen, 9,145
Carney, Julia Fletcher, 4,696
Carney, Kate S. (1842-?), **12,970**
Carney, Mabel, **1,842**
Carnival, 5,497
"Carnival of Books" (radio program), 2,385
Carnival of Rhythm, 3,773
Carns, Margaret Jane (Burke) [Mrs. Edmund C.] (1859-1952), **10,440**
"Carolina" (song), 15,804
Carolina College (NC), **13,364**
Carolina Echoes (book), 13,364
Carolina Female College, 15,588
Carolina Playmakers, 13,100
Caroline Islands
missionaries to, 3,642, **14,650**
missionaries to, Congregational, 14,470
Carolinians, The (book), 5,987
Caron, Patricia. *See* Crowley, Patricia (Caron) [Mrs. Patrick]
Carousel (musical comedy), 12,360
Carow, Edith Kermit (1861-1948). *See* Roosevelt, Edith Kermit (Carow) [Mrs. Theodore] (1861-1948)
Carp Lake Lumber Company (MI), 8,309
Carpenter, Alice, 7,312
Carpenter, Carrol C., 9,323
Carpenter, Clarina Irene (Howard) [Mrs. Justin] (1810-85). *See* Nichols, Clarina Irene (Howard) [Mrs. Justin] Carpenter [Mrs. George W.] (1810-85)
Carpenter, Edwin H., Jr., 10,677
Carpenter, Elizabeth, 15,567
Carpenter, Elva H., 5,123, 10,679
Carpenter, Emily M. (1830-1907), 10,449
Carpenter, Esther Bernon [Miss] (1848-?), **2,246**
Carpenter Family (WA), **17,185**
Carpenter, Frances (1909-). *See* Huntington, Frances (Carpenter) [Mrs. William Chapin] (1909-)
Carpenter, Frank, 17,185
Carpenter, Frank G. (1855-1924), **2,247, 7,203**
Carpenter, George F., 10,287
Carpenter, Hannah, 12,563
Carpenter, Helen McCowen, 1,505
Carpenter, Julia M. [Mrs.] (1838-1906), **398**
Carpenter, Laura Clarke [Mrs.] (1825-60), 16,132
Carpenter, Louise, **8,150**
Carpenter, Lucy (Blanding), 15,567
Carpenter, Mamie (ca. 1864-?). *See* Hurd, Mamie (Carpenter) [Mrs. Charles] (ca. 1864-?)
Carpenter, Margaret (1910-73). *See* Richardson, Margaret (Carpenter) [Mrs. John P.] (1910-73)
Carpenter, Marguerite MacDonald, 11,123
Carpenter, Martha. *See* Meredith, Martha Carpenter [Mrs. Reese]
Carpenter, Mary, 2,315
Carpenter, Mary E. (Lovell) [Mrs. George] (1840-1925), Family (MN), **8,978**
Carpenter, Mrs. Elbert, 8,963
Carpenter, Mrs. John, 11,827
Carpenter, Mrs. William O., 3,812
Carpenter, Nancy Crouse, 10,860
Carpenter, Norah Carr [Mrs. Frank] (ca. 1875-1962), 17,185
Carpenter, Ruth Haynes, 8,913
Carpenter, Sylvia Macomber (ca. 1845-?), Family (MN), **8,979**
Carpenter, Thorne M., 11,656
Carpenter, Wroz, 9,903
Carpenters, **3,337, 11,620,** 12,432, 14,910, 15,018
Carper, Madelone, 1,623
Carp's Washington (book), 2,247
Carr, Austin Heaton (?-1942), 12,971
Carr, Austin Heaton, Jr., 12,971

Carr, Catherine Burgess [Miss], 17,186
Carr, Charles Noell, 12,971
Carr, Charlotte (1890-1957), 4,047, 4,052, 4,100, 4,101, 4,165
Carr, Cornelia, 6,659
Carr, Ezra Slocum, **1,409**
Carr Family (CA), **1,099**
Carr Family (IL), 17,185
Carr, Hamptonetta Burgess [Miss], **17,186**
Carr, Harriet [Mrs. Benjamin], 1,703
Carr, Jeanne C. (Smith) [Mrs. Ezra Slocum] (ca. 1823-1903), 1,099, **1,409,** 1,635
Carr, Laura Noell [Mrs. Austin Heaton]. *See* Chapman, Laura Noell [Mrs. Austin Heaton] Carr [Mrs. Robert Hett]
Carr, Mary A., **2,126**
Carr, Rosemary (1900-60). *See* Benét, Rosemary (Carr) [Mrs. Stephen Vincent] (1900-60)
Carr, Ruth M. (White) [Mrs. Clarence] (1889-), **2,011**
Carr, Sarah Ann (Rogers) (1849-1929), 14,173
Carr, Sarah E., 2,126
Carrall, Maria L., **399**
Carran, Mollie (Brown), 4,958
Carrau, Catherine Walkins (1887-), **14,936**
Carraway, Gertrude Sprague [Miss], **13,365,** 13,421, 13,511
Carrel, Ruth E., 8,174
Carreño, Teresa. [Mrs. Emile] Sauret [Mrs. Giovanni] Tagliapietra [Mrs. Eugen] d'Albert [Mrs. Arturo] Tagliapietra (1853-1917), 2,023
Carrera, Anna Held [Mrs. Maximo] (1865?-1918). *See* Ziegfeld, Anna Held [Mrs. Maximo] Carrera [Mrs. Florenz] (1865?-1918)
Carretero, J. M., 215
Carriages and carts, 1,544, 7,601, 12,286
Carrie Chapman Catt Memorial Foundation, 11,886
Carrie Chapman Catt Memorial Fund, 6,702, 7,190, 7,302
Carriel, H. F., 4,411
Carriel, Mary (Turner) [Mrs. H. F.] (1845-1928), **4,411**
Carrier, N. K. *See* Schopp, N. K. (Carrier) [Mrs. William]
Carrigan, Minnie Bruce [Mrs.] (1856-?), **8,515**
Carrigan, William Andrew, 15,613
Carrighar, Sally, **5,994,** 7,578
Carrillo, Francisca Benicia (1815-91). *See* Vallejo, Francisca Benicia (Carrillo) [Mrs. Mariano Guadalupe] (1815-91)
Carrillo, Josefa (1810-?). *See* Fitch, Josefa (Carrillo) [Mrs. Henry Delano] de (1810-?)
Carrington, Edward, 2,248
Carrington, Elizabeth Jacquelin (Ambler) [Mrs. William] Brent [Mrs. Edward] (1765-1847), **2,248, 17,126**
Carrithers, Etta Havens, 3,754
Carroll, Anna Ella [Miss] (1815-94), **5,750,** 5,753, 11,345, 12,757
Carroll, Anne C. [Miss], 2,249
Carroll, Catharine (1775-1861). *See* Harper, Catharine (Carroll) [Mrs. Robert Goodloe] (1775-1861)
Carroll, Charles N., 16,621
Carroll College (WI)
alumnae, 17,876
faculty, 17,872
presidents, 17,872, 17,880
Carroll County League of Republican Women (MD), 5,854
Carroll, Daniel (1764-1849), **2,249**
Carroll, Delia Dixon, 13,508
Carroll, Eileen, 9,397
Carroll, Elva Haskell (1877-?), **396**
Carroll, Emma Isabella (1868-1954). *See* Higbee, Emma Isabella (Carroll) [Mrs. Daniel] Seegmiller [Mrs. Myron D.] (1868-1954)
Carroll Family (MD), 2,425
Carroll, Gladys (Hasty) [Mrs. Herbert Allen] (1904-), 5,580, 5,694, **5,995,** 9,276
Carroll, Jennie Dodson [Mrs. Beryl F.], **4,741**
Carroll, Katharine R., **1,258**

Carroll, Kezia (Giles) [Mrs. Charles N.] (1840-1927), **16,621**
Carroll, Lewis, 1,224
Carroll, Louisa Thomas, **4,253**
Carroll, Mary, 4,433
Carroll, Mary (Tarver) [Mrs. M. C.], 57
Carroll, May. *See* Waters, May Carroll [Mrs. Henry Harcourt]
Carroll, Mrs. Howard, 12,348
Carroll, Nira (Cook) [Mrs. Henry], 9,095
Carroll, Sister Elizabeth, 15,212
Carroway, Daphne [Miss], **13,366**
Carroway, Sue [Miss], 13,420
Carruth, Fred Hayden (1862-1932), **12,412**
Carruth, Katharine (1911-). *See* Grover, Katharine (Carruth) (1911-)
Carruth, Mary (Veeder) [Mrs. Oliver Powers], 12,412
Carruth, Oliver Powers, 12,412
Carruthers, Olive, 2,540
"Carry On" (song), 16,837
Carson, Anna Josephine, 9,467
Carson, Caroline McKinley, **4,896**
Carson, Caroline Petigru (1820-92), **15,573**
Carson, Carrie Gordon (Cubbedge) [Mrs. John Avery Gere], 3,492
Carson, Catherine. *See* Pullen, Catherine (Carson) [Mrs. William H., Jr.]
Carson City Leisure Hour Club (NV), 10,689
Carson County Children's Council (TX), 16,279
Carson, Elvira (Egbert) (1821-1908), **16,503**
Carson, Estelle, 9,711
Carson, Florence. *See* Graves, Florence (Carson) [Mrs. Nat]
Carson, Henry Garrison, 14,254
Carson, James, 9,545
Carson, John Avery Gere (1856-1930), 3,492
Carson, Josephine [Mrs.] (1886-), **8,693**
Carson, Kit, 311
Carson, Luella Clay (1856-1938), 1,085, **14,332**
Carson McCullers: Her Life and Work (book), 16,161
Carson, Mary Anderson. *See* Warfield, Mary Anderson (Carson) [Mrs. Elisha]
Carson, Mrs. Joseph, 11,877
Carson Naval Stores Company (Savannah, GA), 3,492
Carson, Rachel Louise (1907-64), 2,097, 6,034, 11,810, 14,452
Carson, Thomas James, 9,711
Carstang, Effie [Miss], 10,153
Carstarphen, Frank Ellice (1871-1952), **12,413**
Carstens, Vern, 5,177
Cart, John, 15,533
Carter, Ada. *See* Corson, Ada (Carter) [Mrs. Joseph K.]
Carter, Anna Rogers, 2,250
Carter, Antoinette (1864-1945). *See* Hughes, Antoinette (Carter) [Mrs. Charles Evans] (1864-1945)
Carter, Catherine (ca. 1900-). *See* Conkling, Catherine (Carter) [Mrs. Cook] (ca. 1900-)
Carter, Catherine McRee, **3,603**
Carter, Charles, 10,672
Carter, Clarence Edwin (1881-), **2,250**
Carter, Daisie Chaney [Mrs. Hobart] (1897-), 5,394
Carter, Elizabeth, 13,538
Carter, Elizabeth. *See* Izard, Elizabeth (Carter) Banister [Mrs. Thomas Lee] Shippen [Mrs. George]
Carter, Elizabeth Margaret (1799-1866). *See* Reynolds, Elizabeth Margaret Carter [Mrs. William B.] (1799-1866)
Carter, Ella B., 11,114
Carter, Ellen (Galen) [Mrs. Thomas Henry], 2,251
Carter, Evelyn [Mrs.] (ca. 1920-), 10,915
Carter Family (MS), 9,816
Carter Family (TX), 16,085
Carter, Farish (1780-1861), 13,144
Carter, Gwendolyn (1906-), 4,067
Carter, Hilda, 17,548
Carter, Jeannette, **2,127**
Carter, Jesse Washington (1888-1959), **400**
Carter, Jimmy, 3,088, 8,096
Carter, Kate B. (1892-1976), 3,739, 16,525

Carter, Lillie Mae (Bland) (1919-), **5,260**
Carter, Louise Dudley [Mrs. Leslie], 9,878
Carter, Lucy Lee [Mrs. Bernard], 2,443
Carter, Margaret [Mrs. Jack], **15,989**
Carter, Marguerite (Dorsey), 3,799, **5,460**
Carter, Mary, 7,387
Carter, Mary (1766-?). *See* Cutts, Mary Carter [Mrs. Edward] (1766-?)
Carter, Mary (Arkley) (1923-), **5,996**
Carter, Mary D., **16,045**
Carter, Mary Elizabeth (1829-1900). *See* Rives, Mary Elizabeth (Carter) (1829-1900)
Carter, Mary Elizabeth (Hamilton) [Mrs. William Alexander], 419
Carter, Mary Sarah (1890-1975). *See* Winter, Mary Sarah (Carter) [Mrs. Rogers] (1890-1975)
Carter, Maude, **1,259**
Carter, Morris (1877-1965), 6,185, **6,452**
Carter, Mother Celine, 14,226
Carter, Mrs. Joshua, 7,355
Carter, Mrs. Leslie, 3,100
Carter, Mrs. W. A., 201
Carter, Myrtle [Mrs.], **4,656**
Carter, Naamah Kendel Jenkins (1821-1909). *See* Young, Naamah Kendel Jenkins (Carter) [Mrs. John Saunders] Twiss [Mrs. Brigham] (1821-1909)
Carter, Orpha Lankton, **14,528**
Carter, Patricia A., 15,429
Carter, Pearl (1896-1970). *See* Pace, Pearl (Carter) (1896-1970)
Carter, Phebe Whittimore (1807-85). *See* Woodruff, Phebe Whittimore (Carter) [Mrs. Wilford] (1807-85)
Carter, Susan, 6,451
Carter, Susan Ophelia (1860-1946), **10,441**
Carter, Thomas Henry (1854-1911), **2,251**
Carter, Tiny (Gish) [Mrs. Jesse Washington], 400
Carter, W. A., 201
Carter-White Family (MA), **6,451**
Carter, William, 15,524
Carter, William A., 1,786
Carter, William Alexander, 419
Carter, William Justin, 2,127
Carter, William R., **9,939**
Cartographers, **10,298**
Cartoonists, 11,997, 14,046
Cartter, David Kellogg (1812-87), 2,252
Cartter, David Kellogg, Jr. (?-1862?), 2,252
Cartter Family, **4,849**
Cartter, Nancy (Hanford) [Mrs. David Kellogg], 2,252
Cartter, William H., 2,252
Cartwright, Frank T., 14,325
Cartwright, Jessie Whitney (ca. 1891-1977), **4,064**
Cartwright, Mabel (Stone) [Mrs. Paul] (1886-), **8,694**
Cartwright, Mary (Malarckey). *See* Cabell, Mary (Malarckey) Cartwright [Mrs. Henry Failing]
Cartwright, Peter, **4,432**
Caruso, Enrico, 3,369
Carver, Ada Jack (ca. 1895-?), **5,439**, 5,448
Carver, George Washington, **2,987**, 4,800, 4,847, 7,229, 13,264
Carver Hospital (DC), 17,737
Carver, Margaret (1896-). *See* Leighton, Margaret (Carver) (1896-)
Carver School of Missions and Social Work, 13,641
Cary, Alice (1820-71), 1,426, 4,732, **5,914**, **6,453**
Cary, Ann M. [Miss], 2,200
Cary, Charlotte Amelia (1859-1936), 3,969
Cary, Constance (1843-1920). *See* Harrison, Constance (Cary) [Mrs. Burton Norvell] (1843-1920)
Cary, Eleanor. *See* Brish, Eleanor (Cary) [Mrs. Henry Colgate]
Cary, Eliza. *See* Green, Eliza (Cary)
Cary, Elizabeth Love (1841 or 1842-1924), 11,339
Cary Family (FL), **2,890**
Cary Family (New England), 6,346, 6,593
Cary Family (NY), **11,339**
Cary Family (OH, VA), **2,328**
Cary, Harriet [Miss], 2,200
Cary, Harriette (1838-post 1926). *See* Christian, Harriette Cary [Mrs. William] (1838-post 1926)

Cary, Hetty. *See* Harrison, Hetty (Cary) [Mrs. Fairfax]
Cary, Julia Love (1826 or 1827-1915), 11,339
Cary, Mary Ann (Shadd) (1823-93), **2,128**
Cary, Mrs., 12,447
Cary, Ophelia (Mathews) [Mrs. William], 2,328
Cary, Phoebe (1824-71), **5,915**, **6,454**
Cary, William (1798-1857), 2,328
Casa de Estudillo (CA), 1,198
Casa Hispanica de Bellas Artes, 17,619
Casad Club (Smith River, OR), **14,700**
Casals, Pablo, 573
Case Against Colonel Sutton, The (moving-picture), 17,972
Case, Anna M. *See* Wilcox, Anna M. Case [Mrs. Howard]
Case, Belle (1859-1931). *See* La Follette, Belle (Case) [Mrs. Robert Marion, Sr.] (1859-1931)
Case, Carlotta (1880-?). *See* Hall, Carlotta (Case) [Mrs. Harvey Monroe] (1880-?)
Case, Catherine Norton, **401**
Case, Ellen, 13,881
Case, Eula [Miss], **8,217**
Case Family (PA), 14,648
Case, George E., Family (MN), **8,980**
Case, Hannah. *See* Harley, Hannah (Case)
Case, Isaac (ca. 1761-1852), **5,710**
Case, Jannette, 8,981
Case, Joanna [Mrs. Isaac], 5,710
Case, John Higley, **8,981**
Case, Kate Hunt [Mrs. George E.] (1849-1927), 8,980
Case, Laura Abigail (1815-94), **11,535**
Case, Lawrence, 17,815
Case, Lucy Elizabeth (Merriam), 3,305
Case, Luella J. B., 6,653
Case, Lura. *See* Smith, Lura (Case) [Mrs. Jesse]
Case, Mabel Almeria (1877-1933), 8,980
Case, Marie (Stevens) [Mrs. Lyman] (1836?-1921). *See* Howland, Marie (Stevens) [Mrs. Lyman] Case [Mrs. Edward] (1836?-1921)
Case, Mary, 13,881
Case, Mary Ann Humble [Mrs.], **11,536**
Case, Maude (1871-?). *See* Anderson, Maude (Case) [Mrs. Frank Maloy] (1871-?)
Case, Minna, 13,881
Case, Victoria (1897-1973), **14,333**
Case Western Reserve University (OH), 9,770, 13,886, 13,887, 13,890
  alumnae, 13,904
  faculty, **13,879**, 13,880, **13,882**, 13,883, **13,891**, 13,896
  students, 11,572
Case Western Reserve University (OH), Institute of Technology, Fortnightly Club, 13,881
Casement, Frances Jennings, **13,990**
Casement, Frances M. (1840-1928), **7,204**
Casey, Anna Z., **9,601**
Casey, Mary Susan (High) (1875-1958). *See* Brisco, Mary Susan (High) Casey (1875-1958)
Cashier, Albert D. J., 3,752
Casket and Budget, The (IL), 4,215
"Casket, The" (ms), 13,969
Cason, Zelma, 2,873, 2,876
Caspary, Vera (1904-68), 6,045, **17,793**
Cass, Lewis (1782-1866), 11,602
Cassandra (periodical), 3,827
Cassandra at the Wedding (book), 11,832
Cassatt, Mary (1844-1926), 2,207, **2,739**, 2,847, 2,850, 5,829, 12,506
Casseday, Fannie. *See* Duncan, Fannie (Casseday)
Casserly, Teresa, **1,366**
Cassettari, Rosa (ca. 1867-1943), 9,495
Cassety, Louise M. (1873-1931), **11,364**
Cassidy, Butch, 16,485, 16,965
Cassidy, Florence, 9,508, 9,512
Cassidy, Gerald, 328, 11,213, 11,233
Cassidy, Ina (Sizer) [Mrs. Gerald] (1869-1965), 328, 11,213, **11,233**, 11,234, 11,235
Cassidy, Reverend Mother Francis de Sales, 3,601
Cassidy, Rosalind Frances (1895-?), **402**, 1,655
Cassill, Christine (1894-?), 17,924
Casson, Esley D. (Hake), **2,253**
Cassville Female College (GA), 3,379
Castaways (book), 2,875

Caste of Heroes, A (book), 6,041
Casteen, Lucinda (1797-1839), **4,353**
Castell, Mrs. Maurice, 8,016
Castellaw, Janie (Pender) (?-1969), **16,339**
Casterline, Jennie (Allen) [Mrs. John Andrew] (?-1881), **11,081**
Casterline, John Andrew, 11,081
Castilian Club (Boston, MA), **5,916**
Castilian Club of Rock Hill (SC), **15,791**
Castle, Amos, 9,975
Castle Club, 11,537
Castle, Emily (1820-88). *See* Cornell, Emily (Castle) (1820-88)
Castle Family (CA), **403**
Castle Family (IL), 3,754
Castle, Frances A. (Ferry) (1827-60), 403
Castle, Henry A., 9,044
Castle, Irene [Mrs. Vernon], Management, 11,537
Castle, Irene (Foote) [Mrs. Vernon]. [Mrs. Robert Elias] Treman [Mrs. Frederic] McLaughlin [Mrs. George] Enzinger (1893-1969), **11,537**, 11,607
Castle, Mabel Wing, 4,089
Castle, Marian, 1,750
Castle, Molly. [Mrs. William] Tucker, 1,600
Castle, Vernon (?-1918), 11,537
Caston, Jennie, 17,282
Castor, Laura Rice, **14,529**
Castro, Anita, 1,656
Castro, Jill, 15,198
Castro, José, 331
Castro, Manuel de Jesús (1821-?), **404**
Castro, Martina (1807?-1890). *See* Lodge, Martina (Castro) [Mrs. Michael] (1807?-1890)
Caswell Family, 7,704
Caswell, Hollis, 11,897
Caswell, Mina Holway, **5,575**
Caswell, Sarah Swope (1831-1903). *See* Angell, Sarah Swope (Caswell) [Mrs. James B.] (1831-1903)
Cat on a Hot Tin Roof (drama), 12,367
Catalog (Wells College, NY), 11,281
Catalogs, college, 108, 114, 1,815, **2,935**, **3,423**, **3,428**, 7,110, **9,555**, **9,576**, 13,194, **13,225**
Catalogs, school, 8,954, 12,088, 15,940
Catania, Susan (1941-), 4,106, 4,109
Catawba Indians, 2,883
Catch 22 (moving picture), 17,804
Cate, Catherine. *See* Coblentz, Catherine (Cate) [Mrs. William Weber]
Cate, Helen, 2,941
Cate, Margaret Davis [Mrs.], **2,988**, 3,046
Catechists, 2,919
Cater, Douglas J., **2,254**
Cater, Fannie S. [Mrs.], 2,254
Cater, Rufus W., **2,254**
Caterers and catering, 1,655, **4,939**
Cates, John Wesley (1847-1918), **13,637**
Cates, Sarah Elizabeth [Mrs. John Wesley], 13,637
Cates, Tulah. *See* Perry, Tulah (Cates)
Cates, Verna. *See* Stackhouse, Verna (Cates)
Cathcart, Alexander Henry (1820-99), Family (MN), **8,982**
Cathcart, Catherine, 8,982
Cathcart, E. P., 11,656
Cathcart, Ellen Weir [Mrs.], **15,213**
Cathcart, Rebecca Lowry (Marshall) [Mrs. Alexander Henry] (1830-1925), 8,982
Cathedral of St. John the Divine (New York, NY), 12,089
Cathedrals, 9,022
Cather Family (NE), **10,442**
Cather, Willa Sibert (1873-1947), 267, 378, 556, 924, 1,390, 2,283, 2,617, **3,983**, **3,984**, 3,986, 5,863, 7,171, 7,185, 7,648, **10,443**, **10,617**, 10,853, 11,156, 11,897, 12,044, **12,414**, 12,695, 17,010, 17,053, **17,952**
"Catherine Beecher and the Dubuque Female College" (article), 4,752
Catherine Innes Ireland Travelling Scholarship, 6,563
Catherine, Mother, 5,501
Catherwood, Mary (Hartwell) [Mrs. James Steele] (1847-1902), **3,985**
Catholic action, 15,146
Catholic Archives at San Antonio (TX), 16,311

Catholic Association of International Peace, 17,868
Catholic Big Sisters, 11,397
Catholic Caucus, 6,794
Catholic Church, 3,946, 6,446, 8,164, 16,866, 17,416
  charities, 4,308, **15,705**
  clergy, **12,236**, 12,933
  dioceses, **16,311**
  education, 1,518, 1,784, **5,689**, 5,832, 8,292,
    10,916, 11,808, 11,932, 14,719, 14,783, 15,180,
    15,639, 17,052, 17,820, 17,868
  history, 15,870
  missionaries, 12,069
  missions, **1,514**, 5,184, 6,945, 9,022, 11,568, 11,803,
    14,116, 14,225
  societies, 355, 1,078, **3,655**, 3,946, **4,447**, **4,641**,
    8,383, 11,397, 14,259, 14,909, **16,017**, **17,551**,
    17,741
Catholic Church and abortion, 16,343
Catholic Church and birth control. *See* Birth control,
  religious aspects
Catholic Church in the United States, 10,144
Catholic Gold Star Mothers, 9,963
Catholic high schools, **4,148**
Catholic hospitals, **5,493**, 8,848, **10,732**, 11,298,
  14,794, 15,181, 15,433
  records and correspondence, **15,232**, 17,487
Catholic Ladies Relief Society and Donation Day
  Association (CA), 1,078
Catholic Library Association, 4,640
Catholic Man (book), 5,815
Catholic Poetry Society of America, 4,640
Catholic schools, 24, 159, 665, 1,066, 1,387, 1,515,
  1,786, 1,985, **2,121**, 2,919, 4,284, 4,328, 4,335,
  4,342, 4,872, 4,874, 5,556, 5,722, 5,759, 5,778,
  5,800, 5,831, 5,832, 7,694, 8,176, 8,292, 8,425,
  8,848, 9,022, 9,490, 10,144, 10,188, 10,890,
  12,733, **13,752**, **13,867**, 13,903, 14,145, 14,493,
  14,794, 14,795, 15,181, 15,211, 15,235, 15,264,
  15,433, 15,497, 15,912, 16,251, 17,229, 17,572,
  17,820, 17,839, 17,854
Catholic universities and colleges, 24, **1,005**, **1,006**,
  3,971, 4,316, 4,509, 4,649, **4,709**, **5,373**, 5,389,
  9,467, 10,188, 10,888, **11,807**, **14,789**, 14,794,
  15,179, 16,230, 17,854
  archives, **2,864**, **4,632**, **10,892**, **11,251**, **14,788**,
    14,790, 14,911
  history, **4,648**
  pictorial works, **3,973**, 14,791
Catholic Youth Organization, 3,946
Catholicity, 110, 16,438
Catholics, 5,821
Catholics, Ukrainian, in the United States, **14,909**
Catledge, Turner, 9,706
Catlin, Claiborne. *See* Elliman, Claiborne (Catlin)
  [Mrs. Kenneth]
Catlin, George, 12,035
Caton, John Dean (1812-95), **2,255**
Caton, Laura A. (Sherrill) [Mrs. John Dean] (?-1892),
  2,255
Catonsville High School (MD), 5,829
Catskill Travel Club (NY), **11,417**
Catskill Valley Grange, No. 1557 (East Durham,
  NY), **11,437**
Catt, Carrie Clinton (Lane) [Mrs. Leo] Chapman
  [Mrs. George William] (1859-1947), 138, 509,
  1,059, 1,255, 1,437, 1,451, 1,652, 2,084, 2,186,
  2,256, 2,439, 2,451, 2,602, 2,679, 2,878, 4,244,
  4,304, 4,623, 4,631, **4,742**, 4,859, **4,897**, 4,930,
  5,002, 5,587, 6,433, **6,455**, **6,525**, **6,532**, 6,534,
  6,536, 6,596, 6,629, 6,741, 6,858, **6,972**, 7,187,
  7,205, 7,217, 7,221, 7,232, 7,268, 7,290, 8,963,
  8,971, 9,142, 9,291, 10,155, 10,658, 10,687,
  11,579, 11,605, 11,812, 12,044, 12,387, **12,415**,
  12,464, 12,505, 12,534, 12,811, 12,819, 12,834,
  12,835, 14,144, 14,737, 14,739, 14,900, 15,095,
  15,252, 15,306, 15,307, 15,311, 15,312, 15,316,
  15,706, 15,857, 15,868, **15,941**, 16,789, 17,166,
  17,328, **17,612**, 17,616, 17,654, 17,749, **17,916**,
  17,940, **17,953**, 17,974, 18,013
Catt, Charles William, 7,205
Catt, George William, 17,953
Catt, Mrs. Reeves, 16,060
Cattanach, Anna (Metschan), 14,615
Cattell, J. W., 4,793

Cattle, 8,316, 16,039, **16,312**
Cattle brands, 10,722
Cattle breeders, 190, 875, 7,826, **8,340**, 10,336,
  10,382, 16,529
Cattle breeders' societies, 8,340
Cattle breeding, 202, 2,922, 8,161, 10,250
Cattle ranches. *See* Ranches
Cattle stealing, 1,786, 16,877, 16,904
Cattle trails, **14,676**, 16,039
Caucus, 176, **4,109**, 4,982, **5,003**, 5,330, 6,582, 8,101,
  8,125, **8,210**, 8,287, **9,947**
Caudell, Myrtle Viola (1878-1963), **11,365**
Caudill, Rebecca (1899-), **5,304**
Caulfield, Genevieve (1888-1972), 11,812
Caulfield, Henry S. (1873-1966), **9,940**
"Cavalcade of America" (radio program), 13,626
"Cavalcade of America Broadcast Number 175—The
  People vs. Anne Newport Royall, The"
  (program), 9,849
Cavallo, Diana, 11,165
Cavanaugh, Lucy, 3,683
Cavanaugh, Mother Agnes Teresa, 14,226
Cave temples, 4,518
Cavelier, Robert, 8,441
Cavell, Edith, 5,119
Cavell, Edith Louisa (1865-1915), 12,535
Caverno, Julia H., 7,158
Caves, 13,250
Cavett, Allie. *See* Swann, Allie (Cavett)
Cavett, E. D., 9,806
Cavett Family (MS), **9,806**
Cavileer, Charles, 13,652, 13,661
Cavileer, Lulah [Miss], **13,652**
Caw, Regina (Arthur), 8,962
Cawein, Madison, 5,352
Caxton Printers (Caldwell, ID), 3,687
Cayce Family (SC), **15,574**
Caylor, George N. (1885-1974), **12,700**
Cayton, Inc., 11,269
Cayuga County Historical Society (NY), 11,823
Cayuga Heights School (Ithaca, NY), 11,611
Cayuga Pictures (NY), 11,537
Cayuse Indians, 880
  missions, 17,213
Cazalet, William L., 9,888
Cazneau, Jane McManus Storme [Mrs.] (1807-78),
  16,046
Cech, Nancy, 4,063
"Cecile Taylor Circle of King's Daughters, 1948-69,
  The," **9,944**
Cecilian Chorale Society (MN), **8,430**, 8,444
Cecilian Club (Richmond, KY), **5,405**
Cecilie, Crown Princess (Germany), 2,663
Cedar City Opera House (UT), 16,399
Cedar City Primary Organization (UT), 16,430
Cedar Crest College (Allentown, PA), archives,
  14,716
Cedar Grove Plantation (SC), 15,582
Cedar Rapids Ladies Literary Club (IA), 4,770
Celebrity Breakfasts, 6,573
"Celia and Winnie Mae Murphree," 99
Celibacy, 9,996
Celtic literature, 1,509
Cemanahuac educational community (Mexico), 6,511
Cemeteries, 633, 3,387, **3,613**, 4,197, 4,302, 4,448,
  5,041, 5,709, 5,805, **8,398**, 9,117, 9,869, 10,943,
  11,274, 11,441, 17,700
Cemetery Beautifying and Anti-Removal Association
  (CA), 1,344
*Cemetery Directory of Amish and Mennonites in
  Iowa, Johnson, and Washington Counties of Iowa*
  (book), 5,050
Censorship, 11,178
Census, **1,135**, **1,895**, 1,935, **3,945**, 5,409, 5,497,
  5,566, 7,142, 9,532, **11,797**, 14,290, 14,655,
  16,215. *See also as a subhead under specific
  subjects*
Centenarians, 10,568
Centenary College (LA)
  faculty, **5,550**
  finance, 5,545
Centenary College (NJ), alumnae, 10,903
Centenary College (TN), deans, 3,462
Centenary Opera Workshop (LA), 5,550

Centenary Women's Club (LA), **5,545**
"Centennial" (ms), 3,075
Centennial Celebration of the Invention of
  Lithography (1896), 7,667
Centennial celebrations, **9,479**, 10,677, 12,346,
  14,923, **14,924**, **15,853**. *See also as a subhead
  under specific states*
Centennial Christian Church, 3,762
Centennial Club (Warrensburg, MO), 10,211
Centennial Club (Nashville, TN), 15,967
Centennial International Exposition (PA, 1876),
  1,730, 4,835
Centennial International Exposition (PA, 1876),
  Register of Visitors, Women's Department,
  14,971
Centennial International Exposition (PA, 1876),
  Women's Centennial Executive Committee,
  12,417
Center Congregational Church of Manchester Ladies
  Benevolent Society (CT), 1,889
Center for a Woman's Own Name, 17,680
Center for Advanced Film Studies (CA), 950
Center for Continuing Education of Women (MI),
  7,955
Center for the Study of the Consumer Movement,
  11,805
Center of the Web (book), 5,022
Centinel of Freedom (NJ), 11,122
Central America
  culture, 2,777
  fauna, 2,714
Central American Mission, 16,610
Central Baptist Children's Home (Lake Villa, IL),
  4,065
Central Baptist Children's Home (Lake Villa, IL),
  Woman's Auxiliary Board, 4,065
Central Baptist Church (CO), 1,802
Central Baptist Orphanage (Chicago, IL). *See
  Central Baptist Children's Home (Lake Villa, IL)*
Central Bureau of Nursing (MI), 8,045
Central Business and Professional Women's Club (IL),
  4,076
Central Carolina Colony, 13,580
Central Christian Church (Austin, TX), 16,032
Central Christian (Disciples) Church (NY), 12,400
Central City Play Festival (CO), 1,751
Central Committee on Friendship Dinners, **6,456**
Central Community House, Inc. (St. Paul, MN),
  8,983
Central Congregational Church (PA), **14,972**
Central Congregational Society of Philadelphia (PA),
  14,972
Central Cooperative Wholesale, 9,502, 9,506
Central Cooperative Wholesale (WI), 17,676
Central Council for Nursing Education (Chicago, IL).
  See Chicago Council on Community Nursing
  (IL)
Central Council of Childhood Education (Chicago,
  IL), 3,974
Central Council of Social Welfare Agencies of St.
  Paul (MN), 9,442
Central Employment Association, **15,272**
Central Friendly Inn (Cleveland, OH), 13,976
Central High School (KY), 5,384
Central High School (St. Paul, MN), 9,382
Central Homeopathic Society, 3,826
Central Labor Union, 9,467
Central Labor Union of Minneapolis and Hennepin
  County (MN), **8,984**
Central Library (Paris, France), 4,350
Central Michigan Normal School (MI). *See* Central
  Michigan University (Mt. Pleasant, MI)
Central Michigan University (Mt. Pleasant, MI),
  8,310, 8,348, 8,378
Central National Society for Women's Suffrage,
  17,895, 17,916
Central Normal College (IN), alumnae, 4,625
Central of Georgia Railroad, 3,246
"Central Organization for a Durable Peace, The"
  (dissertation), 7,216
Central Presbyterian Church (San Francisco, CA),
  Young Peoples Aid Society, **1,260**
Central Presbyterian Church (Atlanta, GA), 3,266
Central Presbyterian Church (St. Paul, MN), Foreign

Missionary Society. *See* Central Presbyterian Church (St. Paul, MN), Woman's Missionary Society

Central Presbyterian Church (St. Paul, MN), Woman's Home Society. *See* Central Presbyterian Church (St. Paul, MN), Woman's Missionary Society

Central Presbyterian Church (St. Paul, MN), Woman's Missionary Society, 9,310

Central Railroad and Ocean Steamship Company (GA), 3,086

Central Seattle Community Council (WA), 17,357

Central State College (OH), faculty, **6,997**

Central State Normal School (MI). *See* Central Michigan University

Central University (IA), 11,039

Central Woman's Christian Temperance Union (MN), **8,985**

"Centralia, First 50 Years" (ms), 17,140

Centralia Ladies Civic Club (WA), 17,134

Centralia Ladies Civic Club (WA), Music Department. *See* Centralia Music Club (WA)

Centralia Music Club (WA), **17,134**

Centreville Book Club (MS), 9,667

Centro Mexicano de Escritores, 6,089

Century (periodical), **1,410**, 1,500, 7,221, 9,771, 11,996, 12,022, 17,387

"Century Book of Facts, The," 9,954

Century Club, 12,050

Century Club (San Francisco, CA), 540

Century Club (Holland, MI), 8,190

Century Club (SC), **15,408**

Century Club (TX), 16,336

Century Company, The, 5,273

Century Magazine (periodical). See *Century* (periodical)

"Century of Progress in the Higher Education of Women" (ms), 9,610

Century of Progress International Exposition, A (Chicago, IL, 1933-1934), **4,066**, 4,091, 4,123, 9,610

Century of Progress International Exposition (Chicago, IL, 1933-1934), Hall of Religion, 14,026

Century of Service, A (book), 5,493

Ceramics, 2,821, **13,852**

Ceramists, **5,542**

Cereal, prepared, 7,655, 10,913

Cerebral palsy, 1,348, 4,506

Ceresi, Rose, 8,904

Cerf, Bennett, 4,482, 5,983, 11,897

Cerf, Phyllis Fraser [Mrs. Bennett], 11,897

Cerf, Sylvia Sidney [Mrs. Bennett], 11,897

Certain Measure, A (book), 17,059

Cervanties, Alfonso J., 10,203

Cerveri, Doris, **10,654**

Cesarean section, 779, 11,068

Cha' kwena Order, 16,868

Chabot, Catherine. *See* Dunn, Catherine (Chabot) [Mrs. J. P. H.]

Chabot College (Hayward, CA), Readers Theatre Group, 459

Chabot, Frederick C., 16,315

Chace, Elizabeth (Buffum) (1806-99), 5,907

Chace, Mary (Tyler) [Mrs. Charles, Jr.] (1797-?), **7,609**

Chadbourne, Ava Harriet (1875-1964), **5,618**

Chadbourne, Paul, 17,615

Chadick, Mary Cook, 99

Chadron State Teachers College (NE), faculty, **10,556**

Chadwick, Bessie Stark, 8,280

Chadwick, Florence, 4,700

Chadwick, George Whitefield (1854-1931), 2,020

Chadwick, James Read (1844-1905), **6,217**

Chadwick, John White, 7,131

Chadwick, May (1884-). *See* Jones, May (Chadwick) [Mrs. Charles] (1884-)

Chaff, Sandra L., 15,138

Chaffee, Harriet. *See* Ross, Harriet (Chaffee) [Mrs. Frederick R.]

Chaffey Family (CA), 1,092

Chaffin, Sarah, 16,417

Chain, Helen, 1,767

Chain stores, catalogs, **4,033**

Chalfonte Hotel (NJ), 14,851

Chalk Line, The (drama), 12,413

Chalmers, W. Ellison (1903-), **8,073**

Chamber music, 1,788

Chamber of Commerce (TX), 16,260

Chamber of Commerce (UT), 16,419

Chamberlain, General, 5,668

Chamberlain, Genevieve (1905-), **16,621**

Chamberlain, Hazel, **14,334**

Chamberlain, Hope (Summerell) (1870-1960), **12,972**, **13,368**, 13,447, 13,468

Chamberlain, Joseph, 8,660

Chamberlain, Leila (Curtis) [Mrs.], 1,335, 1,358

Chamberlain, Lucy (Parker) (1829-?), **6,457**

Chamberlain, Mary E. [Miss], **5,461**

Chamberlain, Mary Foster. *See* Crosby, Mary Foster (Chamberlain) [Mrs. Hale Estabrook]

Chamberlain, Mary (Spalding) [Mrs. C. P.], 7,935

Chamberlain, Mellen (1821-1900), 5,929, 5,935, 5,976

Chamberlain, Neville, 13,015

Chamberlain, Ruth [Mrs. Arthur], 1,837

Chamberlain, Samuel, 2,338

Chamberlain, Willard, 8,942

Chambers, Alexander, Family, **8,986**

Chambers, Andrew Jackson, **17,242**

Chambers, Ann, 9,140

Chambers, Augusta Stokes [Mrs. Paschal H.], **9,916**

Chambers, Clarke, 8,986

Chambers, Edith Kerns (1876-1962), **14,285**

Chambers, Elizabeth. *See* Morgan, Elizabeth (Chambers) [Mrs. Thomas J.]

Chambers Family, **17,992**

Chambers Family (PA), **14,973**

Chambers, Fanny Winslow, 8,986

Chambers, Frank Ross (1850-1940), **12,179**

Chambers, Helen, 15,122

Chambers, Ida (Hendricks), 14,301

Chambers, Kate Waller [Mrs. Frank Ross] (?-1947), 12,179

Chambers, Letitia A., 14,618

Chambers, Lucy Johnson [Mrs. Clarke] (ca. 1850-?), 8,986

Chambers, Margaret Barker [Mrs. Josiah Pugh] Wilbarger [Mrs. Thomas Washington] (ca. 1802-?), 16,176

Chambers, Margaret M., 10,611

Chambers, Margaret White, 14,628

Chambers, Mary Ballard, 14,973

Chambers, Mrs. J. W., 3,161

Chambers, Odessa [Miss], 13,617

Chambers, Paschal H., 9,916

Chambers, Samuel, 16,780

Chambers, Sarabella. *See* McAllister, Sarabella (Chambers) Dunlop

Chambers, Sarah (1801-?), 8,986

Chambers, Whittaker, 14,451

Chambersburg and Bedford Turnpike Road Company, 14,803

Chamblee, Oma Edna Spiva (1894-?), 16,126

Chaminade Music Club (IN), **4,551**

Chamness, Ivy Leone, 4,494

Champ, Elizabeth Ann (Nation) [Mrs. George W.] (1833-?), 4,469

Champ, Flora A., 4,469

Champ, George W. (1830-1905), 4,469

Champaign Business and Professional Women's Club (IL), **4,412**

Champaign County Gazette (IL), 3,676

Champion, Deborah, **2,257**

Champions of the Red Cross of the State of California, **1,071**

Champlain College (NY), 11,285

Champney, Elizabeth (Williams) [Mrs. James Wells], 6,245, 7,012

Champney, Etta, 6,245

Champney, James Wells (1843-1903), **6,245**

Champney, Marie M. *See* Humphreys, Marie M. (Champney)

Champney, Sarah E. (Wells), 6,245

Chance, Janet, 12,877

Chance Meeting, A (book), 12,414

Chancellorsville, Battle of (1863), 5,362

Chancery Court (NJ), **11,187**

Chandler, Alban B., **13,369**

Chandler, Alice Greene [Miss] (1851-1935), **7,060**

Chandler, Alice Victoria (1867-?), **16,047**

Chandler, Amélie (Rives) (1863-1945). *See* Troubetzkoy, Amélie (Rives) Chandler (1863-1945)

Chandler, Anna Craig [Mrs. Charles Frederick], 11,961

Chandler, Augusta Berard [Mrs. Charles Frederick], 11,961

Chandler, Beatrice (1875-1965). *See* Gesell, Beatrice (Chandler) [Mrs. Arnold Lucius] (1875-1965)

Chandler, Charles Frederick (1836-1925), **11,961**

Chandler, Elizabeth Margaret (1807-34), 5,907, **7,751**, 8,164

Chandler, Ellen Louise (1835-1908). *See* Moulton, Ellen Louise (Chandler) [Mrs. William Upham] (1835-1908)

Chandler Family (MA), 7,659

Chandler Family (NH), **10,862**

Chandler, Fanny (1852-1939). *See* Lincoln, Fanny (Chandler) (1852-1939)

Chandler, George C., 14,418

Chandler, George Clinton (1807-81), 14,581

Chandler, Julia (1844-1932). *See* Hill, Julia (Chandler) [Mrs. William Lair] (1844-1932)

Chandler, Louise, 2,294

Chandler, Louise (1835-1908). *See* Moulton, Ellen Louise (Chandler) [Mrs. William Upham] (1835-1908)

Chandler, Lucinda B., 4,172

Chandler, Lucy Lambert (Hale) [Mrs. William Eaton] (1842-1915), 10,800, 10,862

Chandler, Mary, 13,369

Chandler, Mary Ann, **14,974**

Chandler, Mary Ann (1847-1929). *See* Dowdle, Mary Ann (Chandler) [Mrs. John Clark] (1847-1929)

Chandler, Mary Ann Tucker, 10,800

Chandler, Mrs. Lloyd, 1,525

Chandler Normal School (KY), faculty, 5,468

Chandler, Persis Warren Heald [Mrs. George Clinton] (1814-1906), 14,581

Chandler, Sarah (1726-1811). *See* Paine, Sarah (Chandler) [Mrs. Timothy] (1726-1811)

Chandler, Sarah Ann Quarles [Mrs.], **17,080**, 17,613

Chandler, Sarah Elizabeth [Miss], **1,261**

Chandler, Thomas, 7,751

Chandler, William Eaton (1835-1917), **10,800**, 10,825, 10,862

Chaney, Abigail [Mrs. John], 8,987

Chaney, Alma (Effert) [Mrs. Ralph], 3,451

Chaney, Delia E., 8,987

Chaney, Josiah B. (?-1908), **8,987**

Chaney, Melissa [Mrs. Josiah B.], 8,987

Change and a Parting, A: My Story of Amana (book), 5,047

"Change, the Women's Newsletter" (CA), **1,126**

Changelings, The (book), 6,082

Changing Hands (drama), 6,602

Changing New York (book), 11,252

Chanler, Beatrice Winthrop Ashley [Mrs. William] (1886-1946), 12,180

Chanler, Mrs. John Winthrop, 12,237

Chanler, William (1867-1934), 12,180

Chanler, William Astor, **12,180**

Channing, Dr., 2,495

Channing, Eliza (Wainwright), 12,656

Channing, Ellen, 17,010

Channing, Eva, 6,009

Channing, Eva, 2,502

Channing-Stetson, Gracy Elly [Mrs.], 2,170

Channing, William Ellery, 6,009

Channing, William Henry (1810-84), 2,588, 5,949

Chanticleer (Duke University, NC), 13,194

Chapel Hill Bird Club (NC), **12,973**

Chapel Hill Business and Professional Women's Club (NC), **12,974**

Chapel Hill Weekly (NC), 13,016

Chapelbrook Foundation, 7,167

Chapelle, Georgette L. "Dickey" Meyer [Mrs. Tony] (1918-65), **17,614**

Chapelle, Tony, 17,614

"Chaperon and Housemother, Builders of Youth, The," 4,390

Chapin, Ada Mary. *See* Chivvis, Ada Mary (Chapin)
Chapin, Augusta Jane [Miss] (1836-1905), 7,941
Chapin, Barbara, **12,416**
Chapin, Blanche I. (ca. 1865-?), 8,988
Chapin, Calvin (1763-1851), **15,358**
Chapin, Cornelia Van A., 11,505
Chapin, Edward (1799-1868), 15,358
Chapin, Eliza. *See* Robbins, Eliza (Chapin)
Chapin, Eliza Baylies (1809-1905). *See* Wheaton,
    Eliza Baylies (Chapin) [Mrs. Laban Morey]
    (1809-1905)
Chapin, G. L. (pseudonym). *See* Linington, Elizabeth
    (1921-)
Chapin, George A., Family (MN), **8,988**
Chapin Hall for Children (Chicago, IL), **3,806**, 4,079
Chapin, Helen (1882-1950), **14,740**
Chapin, Jerusha, 15,358
Chapin, Katherine Garrison (1890-?), 7,171
Chapin, Mary Cheever (Pennie) (ca. 1847-?), **1,262**
Chapin, Melissa (?-1861). *See* Briggs, Melissa
    (Chapin) [Mrs. Welcolm] (?-1861)
Chapin, Mrs. Nelson, 8,961
Chapin, Myrtle, 1,319
Chapin, Nettie Sanford, 4,732
Chapin, Sarah D. (1847-1947), 8,988
Chapin, Sarah Davis [Mrs. George A.] (ca. 1825-?),
    8,988
Chapin, Walter Leeds (1863-1947), 8,988
Chaplains, 1,922, 9,422, 15,042
Chaplains, hospital, 3,173
Chaplains, military, 9,281
Chaplet of Memories, A (book), 10,591
Chaplin, Addie F., **7,752**
Chaplin, Albert Vernon, 3,488
Chaplin, Lillian (1895-1967). *See* Bragg, Lillian
    (Chaplin) (1895-1967)
Chaplin, Mary F. *See* Hodson, Mary F. (Chaplin)
Chaplin, Nellie Wallis [Mrs. Albert Vernon], 3,488
Chaplin, Serena M., 5,617
Chapman, Abby. *See* Aldrich, Abby (Chapman)
    [Mrs. Nelson Wilmarth]
Chapman, Ann, 6,337
Chapman, Ann Elizabeth Seed [Mrs. Samuel Henry],
    1,242
Chapman, Anne T. (1884-1954), **17,110**
Chapman, Blanche, 10,717
Chapman, Caroline, 10,717
Chapman, Caroline (1793 or 1794-1868). *See* Gilbert,
    Caroline (Chapman) [Mrs. Joseph T.] (1793 or
    1794-1868)
Chapman, Carrie Clinton (Lane) [Mrs. Leo]
    (1859-1947). *See* Catt, Carrie Clinton (Lane)
    [Mrs. Leo] Chapman [Mrs. George William]
    (1859-1947)
Chapman, Clara B., 10,055
Chapman, Clarissa. *See* Armstrong, Clarissa
    (Chapman) [Mrs. Richard]
Chapman, Croydon, 11,962
Chapman, Ella, 10,717
Chapman, Emil (?-ca. 1852). *See* Gordon, Emily
    (Chapman) [Mrs. John Montgomery] (?-ca. 1852)
Chapman, Ethelyn Bryant, 16,570
Chapman Family (NY), 12,020
Chapman Family (SC), **15,511**
Chapman, Fanny, 1,574
Chapman, Laura Noell [Mrs. Austin Heaton] Carr
    [Mrs. Robert Hett], **12,971**
Chapman, Leo, 17,953
Chapman, Leo, 7,205
Chapman, Leonard Bond (1834-1915), **5,674**
Chapman, Louisa (1815-?), **7,356**
Chapman, Lucinda Bewley [Mrs. William], 881
Chapman, Maria (Weston) [Mrs. Henry Grafton]
    (1806-85), 992, 5,907, 5,926, 5,972, **6,458**, 6,741,
    7,274, 7,295, 7,585, 7,629, 12,971
Chapman, Mary (1881-1975). *See* Ghostley, Mary
    (Chapman) [Mrs. Fred] (1881-1975)
Chapman, Mary Adelaide, 11,962
Chapman, Mary "Mollie" F., 4,374
Chapman, Mary (Sumner), **11,962**
Chapman, Oscar, 11,962
Chapman, Oscar L., 2,123
Chapman, Rebecca [Mrs. William Parsons], 15,511
Chapman, Robert Hett, 12,971

Chapman, William Parsons, 15,511
Chapoose, Conner, 16,876
Chapoose, Ina Lou, 16,876
Chappell Hill Female College (TX), **16,048,
    16,108**
Chappell, Naomi [Mrs.], 17,096
Chappuis, Flore Guillemine Catherine Lahon
    (1909-), 16,780
Chapters in the History of Organized Labor in Texas
    (book), 15,986
Chard, Marie, 17,618
Chariots of the Sun (book), 14,185
Charitable bequests, 3,216, **12,738**
Charitable societies, 118, 269, 309, 347, 363, 389,
    394, 408, 675, 1,121, **1,200**, 1,632, 1,693, **1,864,
    1,888**, 1,900, 2,005, **2,026, 2,045,** 2,099, 2,518,
    2,706, **3,253,** 3,404, **3,507, 3,955, 4,092, 4,118,
    4,140, 4,157,** 4,278, **4,372, 4,678,** 4,973, **5,069,
    5,510, 5,516,** 5,605, 5,608, 5,686, 5,687, 5,709,
    5,766, 5,878, 5,898, 6,449, 6,462, 6,926, 7,032,
    7,073, 7,074, 7,086, 7,093, 7,095, 7,120, 7,319,
    7,331, 7,339,** 7,348, **7,365, 7,404, 7,431,** 7,517,
    7,595, 7,637, 7,753, 7,913, **7,939,** 8,006, 8,040,
    8,896, 9,166, 9,451, 9,515, 10,896, 10,956,
    10,965, 10,969, 10,973, **11,022,** 11,059, **11,067,
    11,094,** 11,103, **11,119,** 11,133, **11,410,** 11,445,
    11,636, 11,939, **12,156,** 12,169, **12,263, 12,315,
    12,322, 12,348, 12,576,** 12,680, **12,802, 12,830,**
    12,931, 13,239, 13,446, 13,785, **13,933, 13,937,**
    13,988, 13,996, 14,083, 14,749, 14,841, 14,866,
    14,867, 14,947, 14,953, 14,972, **14,985, 15,022,**
    15,023, 15,026, 15,048, 15,062, 15,094, **15,187,**
    15,272, 15,277, 15,292, 15,388, 15,397, 15,490,
    15,491, 15,520, 15,727, 15,775, 16,657, 17,111,
    17,397, 17,459, 17,562, 17,590, 17,672, 17,684,
    17,821, 17,825, **17,833**. *See also* Charities;
    Societies
Charitable societies, Finnish-American,
    9,504
Charitable societies, Jewish, 574, 946, **4,038,** 8,906,
    9,123, 9,165, **12,822,** 13,768, **13,769, 13,770,
    13,772, 13,773, 13,774, 13,781, 13,782,
    13,789, 13,791, 13,792, 13,793, 13,797, 13,798,
    13,802, 13,804, 13,806, 13,807, 13,808, 13,812,
    13,821, 13,822, 13,825, 13,826, 13,827, 13,831,
    13,835,** 14,497, **15,153,** 15,161, **15,165**
Charitable societies, Scandinavian, 9,182
Charitable Society of Vernon (CT), **1,888**
Charitable uses, trusts, and foundations, 4,084, 6,125,
    6,130, **7,525, 12,739,** 14,047. *See also*
    Endowments
Charities, 52, 341, 760, 945, 1,046, 1,078, **1,237,**
    1,328, 1,673, 1,709, 2,397, 2,568, 2,663, 2,671,
    3,027, 3,082, **3,083, 3,135, 3,193,** 3,218, 3,368,
    3,399, 3,451, **3,543,** 3,851, 4,047, **4,072, 4,079,
    4,103, 4,114, 4,150, 4,617,** 4,670, **5,125,** 5,484,
    5,575, 6,175, 6,515, 6,729, 6,748, 6,752, 7,209,
    7,477, 7,542, **8,031, 8,481, 8,645, 8,647, 8,669,
    8,922,** 8,962, **9,140, 9,222, 9,341, 9,351, 9,352,**
    9,442, 9,460, 9,492, 9,978, 10,048, 10,484,
    10,518, 10,747, 10,784, 11,013, **11,030,** 12,297,
    12,375, **12,417, 12,634, 12,706,** 13,618, 13,860,
    13,964, 13,995, 14,070, 14,138, 14,192, **14,418,**
    14,625, 14,642, 14,644, 14,704, 14,893, 14,924,
    15,072, 15,101, 15,206, 15,251, **15,462,** 15,471,
    15,570, 15,811, 16,132, 16,260, 16,275, **16,321,**
    16,744, 16,968, 17,220, 17,260, 17,314, **17,579,**
    17,580. *See also* Almshouses; Bazaars; Blind,
    institutional care; Charitable bequests; Charitable
    societies; Charitable uses, trusts, and foundations;
    Child care centers; Child welfare; Community
    organizations; Endowments; Food relief;
    Hospitals; International relief; Old age homes;
    Orphans and orphan asylums; Poor; Public
    welfare
Charities, Afro-American, **3,302**
Charities Department (Charleston, SC), 15,404
Charities, Finnish, **8,184**
Charities, Italian-American, **12,862**
Charities, Jewish, 1,000, 1,003, 3,807, **3,865, 4,162,**
    6,114, 7,525, **7,526,** 7,531, **7,535, 7,538,** 7,541,
    7,546, **7,551,** 7,554, **9,083,** 9,109, **9,151,** 12,729,
    13,764, 13,778, 13,795, 15,154, 15,155, 15,157,
    15,161, **17,247,** 17,282, **17,833**

Charities, medical, 11,885. *See also* Blind,
    institutional care; Children, hospitals; Hospitals;
    Medical social work; Poor; Psychiatric hospitals;
    Tuberculosis, hospitals and sanitoriums
Charities, Ukrainian-American, 9,508, **9,512**
Chariton Suffrage Club (IA), 4,859
Charity, 5,906
Charity Ball Association (San Antonio, TX). *See*
    Chrysanthemum Ball Association of San Antonio
    (TX)
Charity organization, 3,903, 8,664, 12,252, **17,892**
Charity schools, 12,830, 13,619. *See also* Charities;
    Child welfare; Education; Orphans and orphan
    asylums; Schools
Charles City Equality Club (IA), 4,960
Charles, Ellen (McRaven) [Mrs. Thomas C.], 9,602
Charles Family (IL), 9,602
Charles Female Seminary (SC), **15,452**
Charles H. and Rachel M. Schwab Rehabilitation
    Hospital (Chicago, IL), 3,807
Charles, Lucile Marie Hoerr (1903-65), **13,261**
"Charles Mayse, Pioneer Aviator" (ms), 201
Charles Scribner's Sons (publishers), 1,221, **11,156,**
    14,458
Charles Street Jail (MA), 6,367
Charles, Thomas C., 9,602
Charleston Chamber of Commerce (SC), 15,522
Charleston Civic Club (SC), 15,522
Charleston Civic Union (SC), **15,451**
Charleston Courier, The (SC), 15,419
Charleston Daily Courier, The (SC), 15,419
Charleston Female Seminary (SC), 15,551
Charleston Independent or Congregational Church
    (SC), **15,453**
Charleston Independent or Congregational Church
    (SC), Charleston Benevolent Society, 15,453
Charleston Independent or Congregational Church
    (SC), Clergy Society, 15,453
Charleston Independent or Congregational Church
    (SC), Society for the Relief of Elderly and
    Disabled Ministers, 15,453
Charleston Mercury, The (SC), 15,419
Charleston Musical Association (SC), 15,444
Charleston Orphan House (SC), 15,404
Charleston Preservation Society (SC), 15,522
Charleston Protestant Episcopal Female Domestic
    Missionary Society (SC), **15,454**
Charleston, the Place and the People (book), 15,688
Charlestown Gazette (SC), 15,419
Charlesworth, Maud Ballington (1865-1948). *See*
    Booth, Maud Ballington (Charlesworth)
    (1865-1948)
Charley Smith's Girl (book), 13,190
Charlotte Board of School Commissioners (NC),
    13,181
Charlotte, 1863-1963 (book), 6,514
Charlotte Observer (NC), 13,001, 13,277
Charlotte, Sister, **5,640**
Charlotte Sophia, Queen of England (1744-1818),
    17,197
Charlotte Unitarian Church (NC), **13,182**
Charlotte Unitarian Church (NC), Woman's Alliance,
    13,182, **13,183**
Charlottesville Business and Professional Women's
    Club (VA), **17,054**
Charlottesville Woolen Mills (MA), **7,116**
Charlton, Lillian, 11,889
Charlton, Mary, 17,127
Charlton, Mary Waldon Johnson, 3,532
"Charmer, The" (story), 14,736
Charmley, Buelah Jackson, 17,498
Charpenning, Charlotte, 3,924
Charwomen and cleaners, 6,708
Chase, Agnes (1869-1963). *See* Chase, Mary "Agnes"
    (Merrill) [Mrs. William Ingraham] (1869-1963)
Chase, Alice, 8,127
Chase, Alice, **16,929**
Chase, Ann, 11,316
Chase, Anne A., 2,258
Chase, Anthony (1791-1879), 7,610
Chase, Augusta (Field) [Mrs. Ethan Allen], 2,258
Chase, Catherine "Kate" Jane (1840-99). *See* Sprague,
    Catherine "Kate" Jane (Chase) [Mrs. William]
    (1840-99)

Chase, Charles, **10,801**
Chase, Charles Augustus (1833-1911), 7,610
Chase, Cornelia [Mrs. John Smith] (1815-1905), **7,753**
Chase, Edna Woolman, 12,086
Chase, Elizabeth Anne (1832-1911). *See* Allen, Elizabeth Anne (Chase) [Mrs. Marshall S. M.] Taylor [Mrs. Benjamin Paul] Akers [Mrs. Elijah Marshall] (1832-1911)
Chase, Emma Service (Lester) [Mrs. Lewis Nathaniel], 2,258
Chase, Emma (Wendt) (189?-?), **14,480**
Chase, Ethel Winifred Bennett (1877-1949), **8,043**
Chase Family, 11,717
Chase Family (MA), **7,610**
Chase, Florence. *See* Newell, Florence (Chase)
Chase, Gail, **17,243**
Chase, Hannah [Mrs. Charles], 10,801
Chase, Hannah Abby (1833-?). *See* Goodnow, Hannah Abby (Chase) [Mrs. George Franklin] (1833-?)
Chase, Harold, 1,526
Chase, Helen, 2,815
Chase, Ilka (1905-), **5,997**
Chase, Janette. *See* Hoyt, Janette (Chase) [Mrs. William S.]
Chase, Lewis Nathaniel (1873-1937), **2,258**
Chase, Lucia, 12,360
Chase, Lucy (1822-1909), 7,610
Chase, Margaret, **5,131**
Chase, Maria, 7,277
Chase, Martha, 4,433
Chase, Mary, 2,258
Chase, Mary. *See* Cornelius, Mary (Chase)
Chase, Mary "Agnes" (Merrill) [Mrs. William Ingraham] (1869-1963), 10,151, 10,152, **15,215**
Chase, Mary (Coyle) (1907-), **14,335**
Chase, Mary Ellen (1887-1973), 5,580, **5,599, 5,619, 5,711, 5,998, 6,459,** 7,158, 7,171, 8,600, 12,035
Chase, Mary S. Heywood [Mrs. George L.] (1864-1946), 9,077
Chase, Mrs. George O., 16,929
Chase, Nelson, 12,234
Chase, Pauline, 11,453
Chase, Pearl [Miss], 990, 1,526
Chase, Pearl Adell (Rowell) Mikesell [Mrs. Lewis Nathaniel], 2,258
Chase, Rebecca. *See* Kinsman, Rebecca (Chase) [Mrs. Nathaniel]
Chase, Salmon Portland (1808-73), **2,259,** 5,690, 17,992
Chase, Sarah Bella (Ludlow) [Mrs. Salmon] (?-1852), 2,259
Chase, Sarah Earle (1836-1915), 7,610
Chase Sarah Tyng (Winslow) [Mrs. Samuel] Waldo [Mrs. Salmon] (1765-1826), 5,690
Chase, Susan Frances (1859-1927), **11,366**
Chase, Tirzah Wells (1796-1867), 16,911
Chase, Virginia. *See* Perkins, Virginia (Chase) [Mrs. Wallace]
Chase, William Merritt, 1,948
Chase, Winifred B., 14,409
Chaska Fairway grocery (MN), 8,941
Chatfield Academy, 8,954
Chatfield, Andrew Gould (1810-75), Family, **8,989**
Chatfield, Eunice (Beeman) [Mrs. Andrew Gould], 8,989
Chatfield, Levi B., 8,989
Chatfield, Reaia. *See* Yeatman, Reaia (Chatfield) [Mrs. W. E.]
Chatham Academy (GA), 3,577
Chatham College (Pittsburgh, PA), archives, **15,219**
Chatham County (GA), department of family and children's services, 3,572
Chatham County (GA), 3,492
Chatham County Commission (GA), 3,492
Chatham County PTA (GA), **3,493**
Chatham, Thurmond, **13,370**
Chattanooga Railroad Expedition (1862), 3,210
Chattanooga Southern Association Club, 11,405
Chatterly, Sarah Whittaker, 16,401
Chatterton, Ruth, 7,310
Chatwork (Portland, TX), **16,309**
Chaudron, Adelaïde de Vendel, **38**
Chaun, Dee C., 1,564

Chauncey, Ann (Brown) [Mrs. Wolcott], 12,418
Chauncey, Catharine Sickle [Mrs. Isaac], 12,418
Chauncey, Charles (1747-1823), 12,418
Chauncey, Charles (1777-1849), 12,418
Chauncey Family (CT), **12,418**
Chauncey, Isaac (1772-1840), 12,418
Chauncey, Wolcott, 12,418
Chauncy, Mary Griswold, 2,009
Chautauqua Circle (GA), **3,282**
Chautauqua Circle (NC), 13,604
Chautauqua Club (Winona, MN), 9,385
Chautauqua Institute, 9,568
Chautauqua Institution, 16,115
Chautauqua Woman's Club, 7,290
Chautauqua Woman's Club (IA), 4,918
Chautauquas, 3,282, 4,944, **5,021,** 5,070, 5,426, 5,549, 8,832, 9,103, 9,268, 10,571, 11,126, 11,406, 13,366, 14,333, 14,595, 15,182, 16,115
Cheaper by the Dozen (book), 3,077, 11,144
Cheaper by the Dozen (moving-picture), 7,202
Cheatham, Mary (1796-1865). *See* Washington, Mary (Cheatham) (1796-1865)
Cheb Shalom Congregation (NJ), Miriam Auxiliary, 7,542
Cheek, Jeannette Bailey, **6,460**
Cheery Chatter (periodical), 11,443
Cheever, Alice (1854-1917). *See* Bryan, Alice Cheever [Mrs. A. H.] (1854-1917)
Cheever, Charlotte Barrell (1778-1854), 7,611
Cheever, Charlotte Barrell (1858-1944). *See* Tucker, Charlotte Barrell (Cheever) [Mrs. William Jewett] (1858-1944)
Cheever, Elizabeth Bancroft (1812-98). *See* Washburn, Elizabeth Bancroft (Cheever) [Mrs. Ichabod] (1812-98)
Cheever, Elizabeth Hoppin Wetmore [Mrs. George Barrell] (?-1886), 7,611
Cheever Family (MA), **7,611**
Cheever, George Barrell (1807-90), 7,611
Cheever, Helen, 6,516
Cheever House (MN), 8,533
Cheever, Nathaniel (1778-1819), 7,611
Cheevertown (MN), 8,533
Chelette, Atala, **9,604**
Chelette Family (LA), **9,604**
Chelette, Manuel, 9,604
Chemistry, 5,512, 6,673
Chemists, **930, 1,974,** 2,523, 4,495, **6,334, 6,496,** 6,986, **7,286,** 7,328, 8,555, **11,961**
Chemonie Plantation (FL), 2,930, 2,943
Chenault, Sarah F., 3,290
Cheney, Alice (Cannon) [Mrs. Joseph LeRoy] (1882-1967), **16,622**
Cheney, Amy Marcy (1867-1944). *See* Beach, Amy Marcy (Cheney) [Mrs. Henry Harris Aubrey] (1867-1944)
Cheney, Brainard (1900-), **15,927**
Cheney, Camilla S., 16,097
Cheney, Charles W., 9,304
Cheney, Cora, 2,928
Cheney, Ednah Dow (Littlehale) (1824-1904), 4,684, **5,917,** 6,427, 6,460, **6,461,** 6,664, 6,762, 7,044, 7,274
Cheney Family (GA), **2,990**
Cheney, Fannie, **1,263**
Cheney, Frances, 2,990
Cheney, John Vance (1848-1922), **2,260**
Cheney, Lucia T., 3,290
Cheney, Mary Moulton (1871-1957), 8,990, 9,304
Cheney, Mary Moulton (1871-1957), Family (MN), **8,990**
Cheney, Maude, 2,990
Cheney, May Lucretia (Shepard) [Mrs. Warren], 530, 792
Cheney, Monona L., **14,336**
Cheney, Seth W., 6,461
Cheney, Sheldon, 436
Cheney Women's Club (KS), **5,216**
Chenier, Celine, 13,108
Chennault, Anna [Mrs. Claire Lee], 11,861
Chennault, Claire Lee (1890-?), 11,861
Chenoa Methodist Church (IL), 3,762
Chenoweth, Alice (1853-1925). *See* Gardener, Helen

Hamilton. [Mrs. Charles Selden] Smart [Mrs. Selden Allen] Day (1853-1925)
Chercassen, Eva, 8,206
Chern, Fanny I., **3,807**
Cherokee Columbian Club (IA), 4,705
Cherokee County Republican central committee (IA), 5,009
Cherokee Hills Church (Overland Park, KS), 5,187
Cherokee Indians, 243, 247, 1,475, 2,883, 3,421, 7,660, 10,987, 11,639, 13,055, 13,448, 14,174, 14,175, 14,241, 14,243, 14,246, 15,463, **15,528,** 16,215, 16,877
   history, **14,197, 14,206**
   missions, 14,246
   relations with whites, 62
Cherokee Nation, The (book), 6,095
Cherokee-Oklahoma-Kansas Gateway Association, 14,192
Cherokee Outlet Case, 14,206
Cherrington, Edith, 1,224
Cherry, E. E., Sr., 6,862
Cherry, E. Richardson (1892-1953), **16,232**
Cherry Festival Parade (San Leandro, CA), 1,387
Cherry, Marguerite, 6,862
Cherry, Marjorie (1910-). *See* Rohfleisch, Marjorie (Cherry) [Mrs. Kramer] (1910-)
Cherry, Mildred [Mrs. R. Gregg], 13,371
Cherry, R. Gregg, **13,371**
Cherry Valley Female Seminary (NY), 17,651
Cheryl James Defense Committee, 14,592
Chesky, Jane, 2,840
Chesley, Albert Justus (1877-1955), **8,991**
Chesley, Placida (Gardner) [Mrs. Albert Justus], 8,991
Chesley, Sophia Mary (1831-1905). *See* Dunlap, Sophia Mary (Chesley) [Mrs. Robert] (1831-1905)
Chesnut Family (SC), **15,455**
Chesnut, Harriet, 15,455
Chesnut, Helen (Van Valkenburgh), 405
Chesnut, Mary Boykin (Miller) [Mrs. James, Jr.] (1823-86), 11,305
Chester, Cordelia Adelaid (Perrine) [Mrs. Lewis Harvey [Mrs.], **4,354**
Chester County Federation of Women's Clubs (PA), **15,340**
Chester, Edward, 2,394
Chester, Eliza, 12,316
Chester, Elizabeth (1846-1927). *See* Fisk, Elizabeth (Chester) [Mrs. Robert E.] (1846-1927)
Chester Family (TN), **15,888**
Chester Female Institute (VA), 15,799
Chester, Giraud, 2,303
Chester-Kent, Inc. (St. Paul, MN), **8,992**
Chester, Ruth M., 2,016
Chester, Sophy (Hoffman) [Mrs. Edward], **2,261,** 2,394
Chester, William, 14,656
Chesterfield Female Benevolent Society (NH), **6,462**
Chesterfield Friends (NJ), 11,184
Chestner, Rosella, 3,445
Chestnut Grove (residence, KY), 5,327
Chestnut, Helen (1880-), 1,068
Chestnut Hill College (PA), archives, **14,911**
Cheston, Cornelia, 12,513
Cheston, Mary Godley Starr (1902-), **8,687**
Chevalier, Elizabeth Pickett, 2,309
Chevallié, Catharine Power [Mrs.], 1,411
Chevallié Family, **1,411**
Chevallié, Sarah Magee [Mrs.], 1,411
Cheves Family (SC), **15,456,** 15,457, 15,726
Cheves, Langdon, 15,457
Cheves, Louisa Susannah (1810-79). *See* McCord, Louisa Susannah (Cheves) [Mrs. David James] (1810-79)
Cheves, Mary Elizabeth [Mrs. Langdon], 15,457
Cheves, Sophia Lovell (Haskell) (1846-1922), 15,456, 15,477
Chevy Chase College, 16,390
Chevy Chase French and English School for Girls, 13,430
Chew, Benjamin (?-1844), 17,081
Chewing-gum, 3,745
Cheyenne-Black Hill Trail, 17,961

Cheyenne Indians, 10,496, 14,241
  missions, 5,199
  wars, 1,790
Cheyenne language, 1,497
Chi Gamma, **11,712**
Chiang Kai-shek, 1,564
Chiang Kai-shek, Madame, 3,856, 4,476, 5,123, 7,578, 7,738, 17,978
Chicago and Northern District Association of Colored Women (IL), 3,846
Chicago and Vicinity Bible Society (IL). *See* Chicago Bible Society (IL)
Chicago Art Institute (IL), 5,118
Chicago Association of Collegiate Alumnae (IL). *See* American Association of University Women (Chicago, IL)
Chicago Association of Czech-American Women (IL), 3,928, **4,057**
Chicago Bar Association (IL), 4,290
Chicago Bible Society (IL), **3,808**
Chicago Bible Society (IL), Woman's Council, 3,808
Chicago Board of Education (IL), **3,784**, 3,911, 4,081, 4,150
Chicago Boys' Club, girls division (IL), 4,176
Chicago Boy's Court (IL), 4,141
Chicago Bureau of Charities (IL). *See* United Charities of Chicago (IL)
Chicago Child Care Society (IL), 4,079
Chicago Child Saving League (IL), 3,899
Chicago Chronicle (IL), 15,979
Chicago Citizens Schools Committee (IL), 4,125
Chicago Civic Federation (IL), 12,574
Chicago City Garden Association (IL), 4,097
Chicago Commission on Human Relations (IL), 4,045
Chicago Committee to Defend the Bill of Rights, 3,852
Chicago Commons (IL), **3,809**, **3,836**, 3,901, 3,974, 4,003, 4,047, 4,105, 4,158, 9,495
Chicago Commons Woman's Club (IL), 3,809
Chicago Community Trust (IL), 4,084
Chicago Conservatory (IL). *See* Chicago Conservatory College (IL)
Chicago Conservatory College (IL), **3,788**
  faculty, 3,880
Chicago Council of Negro Organizations (IL), 3,846
Chicago Council on Community Nursing (IL), **3,810**
Chicago Council on Foreign Relations (IL), **4,067**
Chicago Daily News (IL), 3,989, 5,208, 10,444, 12,863
Chicago Daily Tribune, South, 112
Chicago Equal Suffrage Association (IL), 3,803
Chicago Evangelical Institution (IL), 16,364
Chicago Evangelization Society (IL), 3,969
Chicago Evangelization Society (IL), Bible Institute for Home and Foreign Missions, 3,969
Chicago Exchange for Woman's Work (IL), **3,811**, **4,068**
Chicago Exposition (1933), 17,468
Chicago Federation of Labor (IL), 2,878, 3,839, 4,032
Chicago Federation of Settlements and Neighborhood Centers (IL), 3,901, 4,130, 4,158
Chicago Forum Council (IL). *See* Adult Education Council of Greater Chicago (IL)
Chicago Grace Methodist Episcopal Church, Epworth League (IL), 9,052
Chicago Hearing Society (IL), 4,130
Chicago Hebrew Institute (IL). *See* Jewish Community Centers of Chicago (IL)
Chicago Herald (IL), 12,863
Chicago Herald and Examiner (IL), 3,873
Chicago Historical Society (IL), 3,998
Chicago Home for the Friendless (IL), **4,069**
Chicago Home Mission (IL), 4,515
Chicago Hospital for Women and Children (IL), 4,027
Chicago Housing Authority (IL), 3,874, 4,096, 4,147
Chicago Industrial Union Council (IL), 4,032
Chicago Institute for Psychoanalysis (IL), 3,914
Chicago-Kent College of Law, students, 4,269
Chicago Kindergarten Club (IL), 4,212
Chicago Kindergarten Institute (IL), 4,059
Chicago Lawn Historical Society (IL), **3,916**
Chicago Lawn Woman's Club (IL), 3,916
Chicago Legal News (IL), 4,351

Chicago Little Theatre (IL), 8,001
Chicago Lung Association (IL), **3,813**
Chicago Lying-In Hospital (IL), 5,081
Chicago Maternity Center (IL), 4,021, 4,053
Chicago Medical Women's Club (IL), 15,145
Chicago Memorial Hospital (IL), **4,015**, 4,016
Chicago Memorial Hospital School of Nursing Alumnae Association (IL), **4,011**
Chicago Memorial School of Nursing (IL), **4,013**
Chicago Negro Old Timers or Early Settlers Club (IL), 3,934
Chicago Negro School of Ballet Theatre, The (IL), 3,773
Chicago News (IL), 5,048
Chicago Nursery and Half Orphan Asylum (IL). *See* Chapin Hall for Children (Chicago, IL)
Chicago Nutrition Association (IL), **4,070**
Chicago Nutritional Committee (IL), 4,070
Chicago Old Settlers Social Club (IL), 3,934
Chicago Opera (IL), 3,848
Chicago Opera Ballet (IL), 17,965
"Chicago Overseas Dead and Chicago Gold Star Mothers," 3,850
Chicago Park District Children's Opera Guild (IL), 3,878
Chicago Peace Action Coalition (IL), 3,827
Chicago Peace Society (IL), **3,814**, 17,735
Chicago Political Equality League (IL), 4,121
Chicago Poor Clares Monastery (IL), **4,274**
Chicago Public Library (IL), **3,925**, 4,165
Chicago Public Library (IL), Hall branch, 3,915
Chicago Public Library (IL), Staff Association, 3,925
Chicago Public School Art Society (IL), **4,071**
Chicago Railroad Fair (1948, 1949), 4,091
Chicago Recreation Commission (IL), 3,901
Chicago Relief and Aid Society (IL). *See* United Charities of Chicago (Chicago, IL)
Chicago Resettlers' Committee (IL). *See* Japanese-American Service Committee (Chicago, IL)
Chicago School of Civics and Philanthropy. *See* University of Chicago, graduate school of social service administration
Chicago Seven, 16,162
Chicago Society for the Prevention of Veneral Disease (IL), 4,145
Chicago Society of Decorative Art (IL), **3,816**
Chicago Soldiers' Home (IL), 3,897
Chicago Sun-Times (IL), 6,056
Chicago Syphilis Control Program (IL), 4,145
Chicago Teachers College (IL), 3,918
Chicago Teachers' Federation, 3,787, **3,817**, 3,818, 3,839
Chicago Teachers' Union (IL), 3,787, **3,818**, 3,824, 4,124
Chicago Temperance Union (IL), **3,819**
Chicago Training School for City, Home and Foreign Missions (Chicago, IL). *See* Wesley-Passavant School of Nursing (Chicago, IL)
Chicago Tribune (IL), 3,825, 4,289, 11,998
Chicago Tribune-New York News syndicate, 14,354
Chicago Tuberculosis Institute (IL). *See* Chicago Lung Association (IL)
Chicago University (IL), 13,189
Chicago Urban League (IL), 3,915, **4,073**
Chicago Urban League (IL), Junior Women's Auxiliary, 4,073
Chicago Urban League (IL), Urbaniades, 4,073
Chicago Urban League (IL), West Side Women's Division, 4,073
Chicago Urban League (IL), Women's Joint Committee on Adequate Housing, 4,073
Chicago Wesley Memorial Hospital (IL), School of Neurological Nursing, **4,014**
Chicago Woman's Aid (IL), **4,074**, 4,152, 4,162, 13,785
Chicago Woman's Club (IL), **3,820**, 3,899, 3,974, 4,144, 4,211
Chicago Women in Broadcasting, 4,075
Chicago Women's Liberation Union (IL), **3,821**, 3,827, 4,241
Chicago Women's Medical College (IL), alumnae, 14,442
Chicago Women's Political Caucus (IL), 4,109

Chicago Women's Trade Union League, 3,887
Chicago World's Fair (1893). *See* World's Columbian Exposition (Chicago, IL, 1893)
"Chicago's Advertising Woman" (newsletter), 4,171
Chicanos. *See* Mexican Americans
Chickasaw Female College (MS), **9,785**
Chickasaw Indians, 1,475, 14,235, 14,241
Chicken Family (SC), **15,459**
Chicken, George, **15,458**
Chicken, Lydia (Child) [Mrs. George], 15,458
Chico State College (CA), 955
  faculty, 1,128
Chico State Teachers College (CA), faculty, 952
Chicora Wood (plantation, SC), 15,440
Chief Timothy (Nez Percé Tribe), 14,660
Chief Washakie (book), 18,017
Chien Ching Middle School (China), 14,379
Child abuse, 5,840, 8,638, 12,687, 14,867, 17,511, 17,567
  legal aspects, 3,932
Child care, 1,997, 2,097, 2,691, 2,704, **3,792**, 3,821, 3,905, 4,065, 4,102, 4,124, 4,241, 5,873, 7,062, 7,248, 7,262, 7,324, 8,057, 8,075, 8,095, 8,135, 8,139, 8,140, 8,624, 8,637, 8,655, 8,681, 8,999, 9,140, 9,159, 9,951, 11,764, 12,357, 14,023, 14,027, 15,205, 15,209, 17,975
Child Care and Development (book), 2,168
Child Care Center Parents Association of New York (NY), **6,463**
Child care centers, 52, **348**, 1,140, 1,309, 1,317, 1,534, 1,636, 2,686, 2,687, 3,135, **3,253**, 3,653, 3,690, 3,792, 3,865, 3,903, 3,905, 4,054, 4,148, 4,286, 5,401, 5,474, 5,758, 5,841, **6,463**, 6,482, 6,808, 7,266, 8,434, 8,485, **8,640**, 8,836, 9,210, 9,467, 9,542, 9,950, 10,013, 10,203, 10,965, 11,965, 12,574, 13,618, **14,020**, 14,671, 14,695, 15,160, **15,206**, 17,220, 17,663, **17,988**
Child care centers, Jewish, 15,161
Child custody, 1,143, 2,574, 8,657, 9,317, 12,174, 14,914, 16,932
Child, David Lee (1794-1874), 1,426, 2,262, **6,464**, 12,419
Child, Dorothy, 14,900
Child Family (SC), 15,523
Child, Francis, 5,250
Child, George, 407
Child Guidance (book), 17,604
Child guidance clinics, 11,908
Child Health Act, 4,117
Child Health Organization of America, 11,627
Child health services, 6,770, 17,590
Child, Henrietta [Miss] (1867-1968), **5,250**
Child, Isaac, 15,458
Child, James, 15,523
Child, Julia (McWilliams) (1912-), **6,465**
Child labor. *See* Children, employment
Child Labor Amendment, 6,431, 6,486
Child Labor Committee (Minneapolis, MN), **8,993**
Child Life, 14,408
Child, Lydia. *See* Chicken, Lydia (Child) [Mrs. George]
Child, Lydia Maria (Francis) [Mrs. David Lee] (1802-80), 992, 1,426, **2,262**, 2,588, 2,614, 3,298, 5,907, 6,466, 6,578, 6,659, 6,738, 6,741, 7,044, 7,171, 7,274, 7,390, 7,561, 7,585, 7,612, **8,002**, 11,125, 11,305, 11,605, 11,821, **11,963**, **12,181**, 12,403, **12,419**, 12,621, 14,893, 15,355
Child, Maria M. (Eastman) [Mrs. Isaac], 617
Child marriage, 9,934
Child mental health services, 11,308
Child of Icaria (book), 4,767
Child psychiatrists, **935**
Child psychiatry, 6,260, 8,639, 11,308
Child psychologists, **2,168**, **14,010**
Child psychology, **2,168**, 6,490, 8,639, 9,053, **17,270**
Child Psychology Study Circle, 9,053
Child rearing. *See* Children, Development and guidance
Child Research Council, 1,786, 12,739
Child, Sarah "Sade" B. (Treat) [Mrs. George], 407
Child study, 11,756
Child Study Association, 12,738
Child Study Association of America. *See* Family Development Association

Child Study Club (Ann Arbor, MI), **7,754**
Child Study Club (Ypsilanti, MI), **7,755**
Child support (law), **6,293**, 8,657, 14,914, 14,916
Child welfare, 52, 190, 200, 365, 1,473, 1,806, 1,906,
  1,917, **1,925**, 2,451, 2,677, 2,686, 2,693, 3,311,
  3,362, 3,852, 3,863, 3,877, 3,905, 3,910, 4,047,
  4,084, 4,101, 4,114, 4,117, 4,166, 4,211, 4,915,
  4,921, 5,120, 5,123, 5,305, 5,474, 5,840, 5,846,
  6,402, 6,420, 6,431, 6,467, 6,558, 6,689, 6,715,
  6,748, 6,766, 6,860, 6,981, 6,987, 7,216, **7,536**,
  8,062, 8,108, 8,119, 8,456, 8,632, 8,638, **8,640**,
  8,647, 8,668, 8,676, 8,678, 8,681, 8,922, 9,015,
  9,151, **9,222**, 9,656, 9,779, 10,168, 10,945,
  11,000, 12,037, 12,118, 12,180, **12,238**, 13,795,
  13,891, 13,996, 14,002, 14,644, 15,811, 15,884,
  17,220, 17,845. *See also* Charities; Child health
  services; Children; Children, hospitals; Children, law;
  Juvenile delinquency; Maternal and infant
  welfare; Orphans and orphan asylums;
  Playgrounds; Public welfare
  law and legislation, 9,299
  legal aspects, 10,161
Child Welfare League of America, 3,399, **8,640**,
  8,647, 8,669, 13,255
Child Welfare Magazine, 13,870
Child Welfare Week (OR), 14,551
Child Went Forth, A (book), 1,372
"Childbearing, Child Rearing, Abortion, and
  Contraception," 11,663
Childbirth, 6,331, 8,518, 8,989, 9,376, 9,467, 10,898,
  11,536, 12,353, 13,446, 15,427, 16,463, 16,865,
  16,867, 16,876. *See also* Obstetrics
Childe, Rheta (1866-1948). *See* Dorr, Rheta (Childe)
  [Mrs. John Pixley] (1866-1948)
Childers, [Mrs.] Boyce [Mrs. John], **10,230**
Childhood Education (periodical), 2,093
*Childhood Memories of the Civil War Years,
  1861-1865* (book), 2,058
Children, 1,838, **2,083**, 7,270, 17,975, 17,991
  care and hygiene, 1,303, 1,607, 2,673, 4,084, 5,123,
    7,198, 7,259, 8,671, 11,932, 12,355, 17,515
  civil rights, 12,106
  dental care, 4,273
  development and guidance, 62, 792, 1,657, 2,001,
    2,353, **4,996**, 5,233, 5,412, 5,805, 5,824, **6,354**,
    6,420, 6,490, **6,556**, 6,730, **6,779**, 7,186,
    7,517, 8,048, **8,355**, 8,485, 8,618, **8,639**, 8,642,
    8,676, 8,798, 8,919, 8,962, 8,987, 8,989, 9,095,
    9,254, 9,467, 10,052, 10,168, **10,202**, 10,217,
    11,739, 11,819, 11,908, 12,100, 12,420, 12,737,
    12,738, 12,739, 12,807, 12,923, 13,219, 13,221,
    13,445, 13,875, 15,030, 15,811, 16,128, 17,270
  diseases, 2,677
  education, 15,631
  employment, 52, 63, 1,731, 2,120, 2,432, 2,451,
    2,503, 2,504, **3,037**, 3,362, 3,887, 3,899, **4,104**,
    4,114, 4,117, 4,172, 4,175, 5,302, 5,846, **6,135**,
    6,431, 6,485, 6,486, 6,686, 6,810, 7,172, 7,318,
    8,069, 8,144, 8,658, 8,686, 8,993, 9,263, 10,603,
    10,946, 10,953, 11,596, 11,771, 11,916, 11,964,
    11,965, 12,037, 12,574, 13,996, 14,551, 14,939,
    16,153, 17,486
  economic aspects, **8,067**
  hospitals, **3,932**, **6,150**, 6,407, 6,698, **6,797**, 7,255,
    8,621, **12,272**, **12,356**, **12,357**, 17,118, 17,241,
    17,831
  institutional care, 2,047, 3,572, 4,103, **10,691**,
    11,030. *See also* Child welfare; Foster home
    care; Orphans and orphan asylums
  language, 11,819
  law, 2,677, 3,932, 17,845. *See also* Child welfare;
    Children, employment; Illegitimacy; Juvenile
    courts; Juvenile delinquency
  mortality, 1,350, 2,677, 13,555
  religious life, **10,572**, **10,573**
  research, 2,069, 13,738
Children, adopted, 13,696
Children and Other People (book), 5,030
*Children in Old Paris, From the Notes of a Journal
  by Their Mother, The* (book), 17,723
Children, Native American
  development and guidance, 2,832
  research, **2,840**
Children of Democracy Conference, 8,171

Children of immigrants, **8,797**, **9,118**, 9,124
Children of migrant laborers, 797, 5,841
  education, 396
Children of missionaries, **3,639**, **8,871**, 8,887
Children of single parents, 3,905, **8,647**
Children of the Albatross (book), 4,232
Children of the American Revolution, **13,372**, 17,293
Children of the Confederacy, 3,080
Children of the Confederacy (San Francisco, CA),
  Nannie Crittenden Van Wyck Chapter, **1,264**
Children of the Confederacy, Alfred Holt Colquitt
  Chapter (GA), 3,164
Children of the Confederacy, Carrie Johnston
  Gillespie Chapter (MS), 9,757
Children's Aid Society (NY), 12,263, 12,297
Children's art, 11,213
Children's Civic Theatre (Atlanta, GA), 13,026
Children's clothing, 12,267
Children's clubs, **4,136**, **8,897**
Children's Crusade for Amnesty, 10,177
Children's Crusade for Children, **2,263**
Children's Crusade to Free Political Prisoners, 10,177
Children's Farm Home (OR), 14,641
Children's Fold, 11,030
Children's Fund of Michigan, 7,817
Children's Home (AL), 74
Children's Home Society (MN), 8,896, 9,351
Children's Hospital (CA), 1,380
Children's Hospital (San Francisco, CA), 939
Children's Hospital (San Francisco, CA), pediatrics
  department, 1,348
Children's Hospital (San Francisco, CA), Women's
  Board, 760
Children's Hospital Association (Berkeley, CA), 793
Children's Hour, The (drama), 3,468
Children's librarians, **12,435**, **12,570**, **15,392**
Children's libraries. *See* Libraries, children's
Children's literature, 615, 4,185, 4,508, 5,694, 8,639,
  9,572, 11,182, 12,570, 14,217, 14,381, 14,458,
  14,467, 15,399, 17,956, 17,990
  publishing, 11,893
  technique, 14,475
Children's Lobby, 7,248
Children's Medical Center of the Philippines, 6,770
Children's Memorial Hospital (Chicago, IL), **3,932**
Children's museums, 2,069
Children's Orthopedic Hospital (WA), 17,241
Children's periodicals, 1,421, 5,941, 6,040, 7,605,
  9,633, 11,157, 11,963, 12,007, 12,054, 12,419,
  14,407
Children's Protective Society of San Francisco (CA),
  408
Children's Scholarship Association (IL), 4,150
Children's stories, 1,421, 1,426, 2,272, 2,428, **2,775**,
  2,938, 4,306, 4,801, 4,991, 5,070, 5,206, 5,304,
  5,633, 6,077, 6,093, 6,119, 6,429, 6,575, 7,261,
  8,329, **8,531**, 8,852, 10,172, **11,368**, 11,485,
  11,988, **12,570**, 12,904, 14,215, 14,326, 14,347,
  14,357, 14,359, 14,463, **16,301**, 17,272, 17,478
Children's Television Workshop, 11,845
Children's Theatre, **12,557**
Children's Theatre of Evanston (IL), 4,222, 15,901
Children's University School (NY), 7,541
Childress, Sarah (1803-91). *See* Polk, Sarah
  (Childress) [Mrs. James Knox] (1803-91)
Childs, Catherine (?-1899). *See* Smith, Catherine
  (Childs) [Mrs. Augustus W.] (?-1899)
"Child's Christmas in Wales, A" (television program),
  2,104
Childs-Coate, Louisa [Mrs.], 4,773
Childs, Emma [Miss], **9,786**
Childs Family (SC), **15,459**
Childs, Isaac, 15,459
Childs, James, 15,459
Childs, John, 11,572
Childs, Margaret Tunsteed [Mrs. Isaac], 15,459
Childs, Mrs., 6,554
Childs, William, 15,459
Childsbury Family (SC), **15,459**
Chile, 5,954, 8,164
  American actresses in, 5,954
  American consuls in, 10,816
Chiles, Joseph B., 582
Chiles, Rosa Pendleton, 12,335

Chilson, Charlotte Grace (Light), 14,778
Chilton, Octavia (Blackwell), **9,845**
Chimborazo Hospital (Richmond, VA), 13,087
Chimes, 14,029
China, 6,099, 6,709, 7,262, 7,407, 7,441, 7,704,
  11,540, 12,701
  American ambassadors to, 44
  American college presidents in, 44
  American deans (in schools) in, **893**
  American diplomats in, 2,238, 3,982
  American educators in, **8,881**
  American nurses in, 447, **8,877**, **8,890**
  American physicians in, 1,219, 8,884, **14,397**
  American school superintendents and principals in,
    758, 2,015, 6,651, 14,393
  American teachers in, **817**, **6,826**, 14,396, **14,435**,
    14,441, **14,445**
  Americans in, 6,099, 7,053, 7,054, 7,850, **8,873**,
    14,768, **15,097**
  cave temples, 4,518
  commerce, with United States, 15,097
  disaster relief, 1,558
  economic conditions, 1,634, 7,231
  English language, study and teaching, 8,090
  foreign relations, 12,012
  history
    (1900-), 2,266, 10,833
    (1912-1937), 8,074, 14,397
    Republic (1912-1949), 174, 3,966, 14,116
    (1937-1945), 555, 9,467
    Civil War (1945-1949), 13,279, 13,290
    (1949-), 12,726
  home economics, 14,272
  hospitals, 7,285
  industry, social aspects, 12,715
  medical colleges, 11,754
  mission schools, 14,396
  missionaries in, 313, **409**, **421**, **555**, 563, 580, 796,
    812, **866**, **1,571**, 1,822, **2,011**, **2,012**, **2,013**,
    2,014, **2,015**, **2,016**, **2,017**, 2,018, 2,019, 3,328,
    4,185, 5,187, **6,012**, **7,407**, **9,081**, 9,543, **10,143**,
    10,460, **10,545**, 11,249, 11,260, 11,639, **11,846**,
    11,935, 12,448, 12,776, **12,788**, 13,279, 13,294,
    13,439, 13,799, **14,089**, **14,116**, **14,119**, 14,126,
    14,129, 14,397, 14,435, **14,441**, 14,457, 14,877,
    15,531, **16,383**, **17,307**, **17,429**, **17,451**
  missionaries to, Baptist, 563, **2,017**, 2,018, 8,870,
    13,288, **13,642**, 17,196
  missionaries to, Catholic, **638**
  missionaries to, Christian Church (Disciples of
    Christ), 14,457
  missionaries to, Congregational, **742**, **884**
  missionaries to, Dutch Reformed Church, 12,448
  missionaries to, Episcopal, **11,935**, 13,263
  missionaries to, Lutheran, 8,858, **8,868**, 8,869,
    8,874, **8,878**, **8,880**, **8,882**, **8,883**, **8,884**, **8,887**,
    8,888, **8,889**, 10,143
  missionaries to, medical, **2,010**, **7,231**, 7,293, **8,886**,
    9,159, **14,442**
  missionaries to, medical, Congregational, 14,316
  missionaries to, medical, Lutheran, 8,875
  missionaries to, medical, Presbyterian, 14,425
  missionaries to, Mennonite, **5,197**, 5,198
  missionaries to, Methodist, 2,258, 3,328, 5,171,
    5,246, **6,012**, 8,876, **8,879**, **8,891**, **8,892**, 13,258,
    13,290, **14,325**, 14,336, 14,379, 14,389, **14,404**,
    14,419, **14,444**, **14,445**, **14,466**
  missionaries to, Presbyterian, **44**, 8,871, **8,879**,
    11,639, 13,439
  missionaries to, Reformed Church, **8,198**
  missionaries' wives in, 9,991
  missionary movement, effect upon (1900-1950),
    7,285, **11,846**
  missions, 742, 8,858
  missions, medical, 9,081, 10,580
  missions, Methodist, 14,396
  orphans and orphan asylums, 2,013
  palaces, 4,393
  politics and government, 14,380
  schools, 2,013, 14,393
  scientific expeditions (1916-1917), 2,719
  Sino-Japanese Conflict (1937-1945), 4,476
  social life and customs, 6,366, 9,164, 14,380
  teachers' colleges, 6,651

theologians, **8,872**
universities and colleges, 6,424, 7,574
women, status, 7,285
Young Men's Christian Association, 12,400
Young Women's Christian Association, 576, 1,219, 1,558, 8,885, 10,609, 12,724, 12,725, 12,726, **12,732,** 12,999
China Aid committee, 8,106
China Christian Education Association, 14,419
China Eighth Route (Communist) Army, 9,081
China Maritime Customs Service, 14,380
China National Aviation Corps (World War II), 11,861
China Polly. *See* Bemis, Polly [Mrs. Charles A.] (?-1933)
China Records Project (Yale University, CT), 2,019
China, The (steamboat), 3,538
China's Book of Martyrs (book), 17,307
Chinese Americans, 497, 659, 772, 1,171, 1,332, **1,644,** 3,856, 9,390, 9,550, 10,633, 10,763, 11,639, 16,968
education, 5,457
Chinese Christian Church of Peking (China), 7,407
Chinese Christian Institute (CA), 446
Chinese Christian Union Church (Chicago, IL), 3,856
Chinese literature, 1,113
Chinese Women's Anti-Aggression League, 2,746
Chinn, Alice B., 7,090
"Chinook Hour" (radio program), 10,330
Chipman, Caroline E., 1,412
Chipman Family (CA), **1,412**
Chipman, John, 12,377
Chipman, William W., 1,412
Chippewa Indian Dancers (WI), 9,041
Chippewa Indians. *See* Ojibwe Indians
Chipps, Nettie R., **3,666**
Chiropractic, 4,711
Chisholm, John A. (?-1910), 8,293
Chisholm, Mrs. W. S., **12,975**
Chisholm, Nellie B. (O'Connell) [Mrs. John A.] (1870-1958), **8,293**
Chisholm, Shirley (St. Hill) (1924-), 2,438
Chisum, John, 16,529
Chittenden, Alice B. (1859-1944), **2,740**
Chivers, Margaret Alyce Ruth. *See* Ramsland, Margaret Alyce Ruth (Chivers)
Chivvis, Ada Mary (Chapin) (1864-1937), **6,467**
Chlapowski, Karol Bozenta, 1,426
Chlorine, spectra, 11,814
Chmiel, Elizabeth McKinney, **10,444**
Choate, Abby Parker (Cogswell) (1832-?), **7,357**
Choate, Anna N. (1870-?), **7,358**
Choate, Anne Hyde, 12,111
Choate, Caroline Dutcher (Sterling) [Mrs. Joseph Hodges], 2,264
Choate, Hannah, 14,688
Choate, John N., 14,748
Choate, Joseph Hodges (1832-1917), **2,264**
Choate, Mabel, 2,264, 12,738
Choate, Margaret Manning (Hodges) [Mrs. George], 2,264
Chocolate processing, **6,207**
Choctaw Indians, 81, 1,475, 2,883, 6,652, 9,695, 9,710, 9,782, 14,214, 14,241
Chodorov, Jerome, 9,769
Choice Seed in the Wilderness (book), 17,706
Choirs (music), 122, 8,792, 8,814, **9,338**
Cholera, 4,347
Cholera epidemics, 3,897, 5,398, 13,173, 13,250, 15,041
Chomeau, Henri, **9,941**
Chomperey, Elizabeth (William), 12,506
Chopin, Kate (O'Flaherty) [Mrs. Oscar] (1851-1904), 9,841, **10,158**
Chopin, Oscar, 10,158
Choral music, 8,792
Choral singing, **16,405, 16,406**
Choral societies, **1,212, 2,007, 16,223**
Choreographers, 7,214, 11,312, 12,360, 12,362, **12,363,** 12,366, 17,965
Choreography, 4,277, **6,024**
Chosen Sparrow, A, 17,793
Chotard, Eliza William (1798-?). *See* Gould, Eliza

William (Chotard) [Mrs. William Proctor] (1798-?)
Chou En-Lai, 17,343
Chou, Ivy (1914-), **8,872**
Chouteau, Auguste P., **14,199**
Chouteau, Yvonne (1929-). *See* Terekhov, Yvonne (Chouteau) [Mrs. Miguel] (1929-)
Chowan Baptist Female Institute (NC). *See* Chowan College (NC)
Chowan College (NC), 13,262, **13,373,** 13,420, 13,563, 13,605
Chowning, Anna, 6,325
Chowning, Jennie Ennis (1863-1951), **10,231**
Chrisman, L. R., **9,846**
Chrisman, Mildred Douglas [Mrs. Pat] (1895-), 14,182
Chrisman, Pat, 14,182
Christ Child School (MN), 9,467
Christ Child Society, 2,099
Christ Church (Greenwich, CT), 1,837
Christ Church (Savannah, GA), **3,494**
Christ Church (Savannah, GA), Altar Society, 3,494
Christ Church (Savannah, GA), Sacristan Society, 3,494
Christ Church (Savannah, GA), Widows and Orphans Fund, 3,494
Christ Church (Boston, MA). *See* Old North Church (Boston, MA)
Christ Church (Pompey, NY), 17,725
Christ Episcopal Church (NE), Altar Guild, 10,447
Christ Hospital (KS), **5,213**
Christ Hospital School of Nursing (KS), **5,213**
Christ, Lydia B., 8,666
Christadora settlement house, 7,166
Christensen, Edith J. [Miss], 13,294
Christensen, Ethel, 8,994
Christensen, Ethlyn, 12,717
Christensen, Gertrude [Mrs.] (1875-1976), 16,485
Christensen, Matilda. *See* Bergland, Matilda (Christensen)
Christensen, Nellie May, 15,869
Christensen, Oscar A., 8,994
Christensen, Otto Augustus (1851-1918), Family (MN), **8,994**
Christenson, Edith L. (1893-), **8,074**
Christian Americanization Program, 17,902
Christian Association of Mothers for Peace, Inc., 4,050
Christian Catholic Church, 4,461
Christian Children's Fund, 15,811
Christian Church (Morganfield, KY), 4,599
Christian Church (Unadilla, NE), **10,546**
Christian Church (Unadilla, NE), Christian Women's Board of Missions, 10,546
Christian Church (Disciples of Christ), 161, **5,299,** 5,393, 15,904, **17,309**
membership, 5,299
missions, 5,300
Christian Church (Disciples of Christ), Christian Women's Fellowship of Tennessee, **4,186**
Christian Church in America, 1,673
Christian College (MO), 9,829, **9,942,** 10,026
alumnae, 10,056
faculty, 9,826
Christian College Chronicle, 9,824
Christian College Microphone, 9,824
Christian Commonwealth (GA), **2,991**
Christian Endeavor (Chicago, IL), 4,054
Christian Endeavor Society. *See* International Society of Christian Endeavor
Christian Endeavor World, 1,224
Christian Family (VA), **17,111**
Christian Family Movement, **4,641**
Christian Female College (Columbia, MO). *See* Columbia College (MO)
Christian Friends of Racial Equality, 17,245
Christian, Harriette Cary [Mrs. William] (1838-post 1926), **17,079**
Christian Index (newspaper), **3,454**
Christian life. *See* Religious life (Christianity)
Christian, Marcus Bruce (1900-76), **5,535**
Christian, Mrs. George Chase (1875-1964), **8,545**
Christian Sanitary Commission, 3,752

Christian Science, **1,399, 1,401,** 1,490, **1,491,** 5,712, **6,184,** 16,438
Christian Science Church (GA), 3,227
Christian Science Monitor, 5,999, 6,167, 6,168, 6,344, 11,226, 11,493, 13,692
Christian Scientists, 1,948, **4,199,** 10,800, **10,808,** 11,217
Christian Service Guild (NE), 10,599
Christian Spectator (periodical), 5,234
Christian, William, 17,104
Christian Woman's Exchange (New Orleans, LA), **5,510**
Christian Women's Fellowship, **5,300,** 10,001
Christian Writers and Editors Conference (1962), 14,475
Christianity, 3,038
Christianity and other religions, Judaism, 4,048
Christianity Culture Civism (periodical), 11,443
Christiansen, F. Melius, 8,792
Christiansen, Gerald Niels, 16,568
Christiansen, Therese. *See* Hill, Therese (Christiansen) [Mrs. Reuben]
Christianson, Donna Andrae [Mrs. Marvin E.] (1931-), **8,688**
Christianson, Elaine. *See* Southwick, Elaine (Christianson) [Mrs. Edward H.]
Christie, Agnes (1887-1920), 8,996
Christie, Alexander, 8,995
Christie, Anna (1876-1910), 8,996
Christie, Augusta (Kalloch) [Mrs. Walter A.] (1887-), **5,641**
Christie, Carmelite Brewer [Mrs. Thomas] (1852-1931), **8,996**
Christie, David, 8,995
Christie, James C., Family (MN), **8,995**
Christie, Jeanne, **4,898**
Christie, Julie, 17,973
Christie, Sarah Jane (1844-1919). *See* Stevens, Sarah Jane (Christie) (1844-1919)
Christie, Thomas, 8,995, **8,996**
Christie, William, 8,995
Christman, Elizabeth, 8,122
Christman, Elizabeth, 2,509
Christmas, 9,378, 9,422, 16,809
Christmas cards, 1,335, 6,678, 6,909, 8,349
"Christmas Adventure," 8,150
"Christmas at Uncle Richard's in 1845," 4,771
Christmas Carol, A (drama), 15,699
Christmas Dramatic News, 1,745
Christmas, Franklin B., 14,447
Christmas Gift (drama), 15,699
"Christmas Hymn" (song), 7,663
"Christmas Pilgrimage in the Southwest, A," 1,786
Christmas Seal campaigns (DE), 2,037
Christmas Seal Fund (FL), 2,885
Christmas Seal program (IL), 3,813
Christopher, Adrienne Tinker, **9,847**
Christopher Columbus, Discoverer (book), 4,988
Christopher House (Chicago, IL), **3,822**
Christopherson, Mary, 8,948
Christy, E. A., **9,848**
Christy, Susan (Preston). *See* Hepburn, Susan (Preston) Christy
Chronically ill, 3,252, 7,673, 15,314
Chronicle (Penn Yan, NY), 11,512
Chronicle (Wells College, NY), 11,281
Chronicle (Duke University, NC), 13,194
Chronicle News (CO), 1,790
Chronicle, The (OH), 13,997
Chronicles of Chicora Wood (book), 15,439
Chrysanthemum Ball Association of San Antonio (TX), **16,321**
Chrysolite Club (MI), **8,218**
Chrystie, Mary, **12,182**
Chu Lai Air Base (Vietnam), 17,614
Chubb, Irene Sylvester, 11,760
Chubbuck, Emily (1817-54). *See* Judson, Emily (Chubbuck) [Mrs. Adoniram] (1817-54)
Chuck Wagon Windies (book), 16,387
Chunn, Elizabeth Word [Mrs. Samuel Love], 3,379
Chunn Family (GA), **3,379**
Chunn, Florence "Bettie," 9,747
Chunn, Lila (Land) [Mrs. William Augustus], 3,315, 3,379

Chunn, Samuel Love (1806-63), 3,379
Chunn, William Augustus (1840-1921), **3,315**, 3,379
Church, Amanda, 12,752
Church and education, 14, 12,713
Church and race problems, Catholic Church, **3,844**
Church and social problems, 5,380
  Catholic Church, **1,008, 14,671**
Church and state, 9,150, 13,413
  Catholic Church, **5,389**, 7,306
  Mormonism, 410, 16,620, 16,756, 16,812, 16,839, 16,933, 16,965, 16,967
Church architecture, 11,105
Church Auxiliary of the Eastern Connecticut Branch of the Woman's Board of Missions (CT), 1,890
Church colleges, **1,512**, 1,516, **4,281**, 4,914, 6,784, **8,817, 13,278**, 13,370, 13,552, 14,732, **15,536, 15,837, 15,960**, 16,125. *See also* Bible colleges; Catholic universities and colleges
  archives, 3,746, **5,188, 5,212**
  faculty wives, **1,980**
Church-Community Action Program (OR), 14,671
Church councils, local. *See* Local church councils
Church, Eliza, 12,752
Church, Ellen, 11,831
Church Family (NY), **12,752**
Church, Fidelia (1810-72). *See* Coan, Fidelia (Church) [Mrs. Titus] (1810-72)
Church, Frank, 3,722
Church group work, 4,319
Church historians, 3,358, **6,176**, 6,355, 8,867, 9,596, **13,411**, 16,430, **17,471**
Church history, **10,574**, 10,580, 10,591
Church Home and Infirmary (Baltimore, MD), 5,827
Church, Isabel (1862-1941), **11,393**
Church, J. E., Jr., 10,655
Church, John Barker, 12,420
Church, Julia, 12,752
Church, Marguerite Stitt (1892-), 99, 1,605
Church, Maria Trumbull (Silliman) [Mrs. John Barker] (1810-80), **12,420**
Church, Marie, 4,536
Church, Mary. *See* Robinson, Mary (Church)
Church, Mary (1863-1954). *See* Terrell, Mary (Church) (1863-1954)
Church, Mary Jane [Miss] (1847-?), **11,539**
Church, Mary Louise (Crane) (1861-1949), **14,530**
Church, Maureen Elizabeth (1930-), 10,151
Church meetings, 6,553
Church Militant (newspaper), 6,176
Church of Christ (Englishville, MI), 7,716
Church of Christ, Scientist, 1,491, 2,321, **6,184**
Church of England, 10,230
Church of God, **4,463**
Church of God (Barre, MA). *See* First Parish Unitarian Church (Barre, MA)
Church of God, National Woman's Missionary Society, **4,464**
Church of Jesus Christ of Latter-day Saints, 5,567, 6,092, 16,430, 16,533, 16,539, 16,565, 16,571, 16,582, 16,767, 16,900, 16,911. *See also* Mormons and Mormonism
  clergy, 16,888
  missionaries, 1,755, 10,090, **12,465**, 16,554, 16,574, **16,626**
  missions, 16,448, 16,554, **16,716**, 16,898
  women, status of, 16,431
Church of Jesus Christ of Latter-day Saints, Argentina Mission Conference, 16,760
Church of Jesus Christ of Latter-day Saints, California Mission, 16,684
Church of Jesus Christ of Latter-day Saints, Eastern States Mission, 16,648, 16,755
Church of Jesus Christ of Latter-day Saints, Female Relief Society, 806, 16,557
Church of Jesus Christ of Latter-day Saints, Genealogical Society, 16,587
Church of Jesus Christ of Latter-day Saints, New England Mission, 16,780
Church of Jesus Christ of Latter-day Saints, Northwestern States Mission, 16,601
Church of Jesus Christ of Latter-day Saints, Palestine-Syria Mission, 16,780
Church of Jesus Christ of Latter-day Saints, Primary Association, 16,618, 16,769, 16,809, 16,830

Church of Jesus Christ of Latter-day Saints, Primary General Board, 16,780
Church of Jesus Christ of Latter-day Saints, Relief Society, 16,460, 16,479, 16,500, **16,511**, 16,536, 16,555, 16,560, 16,566, 16,595, 16,664, 16,681, 16,731, 16,743, 16,748, 16,758, 16,760, 16,761, 16,780, 16,786, 16,787, 16,789, 16,802, 16,819, 16,820, 16,830, 16,839, 16,860, 16,883, 16,911, 16,958
Church of Jesus Christ of Latter-day Saints, Relief Society (Laketown, UT), **16,930**
Church of Jesus Christ of Latter-day Saints, Relief Society, Davis Stake, 16,685
Church of Jesus Christ of Latter-day Saints, Relief Society, Lewiston First Ward (UT), **16,801**
Church of Jesus Christ of Latter-day Saints, Relief Society, Liberty Stake, 16,811
Church of Jesus Christ of Latter-day Saints, Relief Society, St. Joseph Stake, 16,731
Church of Jesus Christ of Latter-day Saints, San Bernardino Stake (CA), 16,758
Church of Jesus Christ of Latter-day Saints, Society Island Mission, 16,793
Church of Jesus Christ of Latter-day Saints, Spanish American Mission, 16,716
Church of Jesus Christ of Latter-day Saints, Texas-Louisiana Mission, 16,778
Church of Jesus Christ of Latter-day Saints, Young Ladies Mutual Improvement Association, 16,681, 16,689
  Manuta Ward, **16,851**
  Second Ward (Brigham City, UT), **16,850**
  Willard Ward (UT), 16,764
Church of Jesus Christ of Latter-day Saints, Young Women's Mutual Improvement Association, 16,513, 16,780, 16,837
Church of St. John's on the Hill (Lake Benton, MN), St. Agnes Guild, **8,997**
Church of the Brethren, **5,187**, 5,188
Church of the Good Shepherd (St. Paul, MN), 9,295
Church of the Messiah (St. Paul, MN), **8,998**
Church of the Transfiguration, Little Church around the Corner (New York, NY), 9,706
Church of the United Brethren in Christ. *See* United Methodist Church
Church records and registers, **319, 673, 695**, 723, **733, 766, 767, 768, 769**, 770, **773, 774, 775, 776, 778**, 985, 1,004, **1,889, 1,890, 2,563, 3,114, 3,479, 3,494**, 4,054, 4,099, **4,441, 4,774, 5,169**, 5,187, 5,234, 5,425, **7,092, 7,857, 8,938, 9,326**, 9,728, 10,055, **10,212, 10,532, 10,546**, 10,662, 11,074, **12,781**, 13,635, 15,006, 15,328, **15,432**, 16,311, 17,725, 17,904
Church records and registers, Assemblies of God, 161
Church records and registers, Baptist, 161, 3,132, **3,455, 7,720, 7,759**, 8,389, **9,070**, 9,553, **11,587, 12,378, 13,636**, 17,962
Church records and registers, Catholic, 8,389
Church records and registers, Christian Church (Disciples of Christ), 161
Church records and registers, Congregational, 161, **7,001, 7,004**, 8,389, **9,071, 9,344**, 10,460, 10,461, **10,464**, 10,550, 14,972, 15,453
Church records and registers, Episcopal, **1,370**, 5,827, **7,905, 7,907, 7,908, 7,909**, 8,389, **8,901, 8,997, 8,998, 9,093, 9,300, 9,301, 9,329, 9,331, 9,343**, 12,082, 12,083, 17,518
Church records and registers, Lutheran, 161, **1,364, 5,433**, 8,389, 8,746, **9,271, 15,855**
Church records and registers, Methodist, **5,171**, 5,894, **8,528, 9,332, 9,704**, 9,750, **9,895**, 10,476, 10,910, 11,095, 11,624, 11,802, 15,586, 15,614, 15,615, 15,632, 15,655, **17,157**, 17,962
Church records and registers, Presbyterian, 161, 3,114, 3,416, **7,863, 7,898, 7,899, 7,900, 7,901, 7,902**, 10,943, **10,956, 12,256, 12,781**, 15,592, **15,599**, 17,962
Church records and registers, Reformed Church, **11,023**
Church records and registers, Russian Orthodox, **2,563**
Church records and registers, Seventh-Day Adventist, 161

Church records and registers, Unitarian, **1,362**, 5,894, **7,952, 9,413, 13,182**
Church records and registers, United Brethren in Christ, 161, **4,849**
Church records and registers, United Church of Christ, **10,501**
Church records and registers, Universalist, **5,859, 9,406**
Church, Rita B. (1838-1928), 11,440
Church, Robert R., Sr. (1839-1912), 15,889
Church, Robert R., Jr. (1885-1952), 15,889
Church, Robert T., Family (TN), **15,889**
Church, Roberta (ca. 1915-), 15,889
Church, Roberta (ca. 1923-), **6,468**
Church schools, **1,740**, 1,786, 1,790, **1,803**, 5,713, **6,257**, 6,520, 6,641, 6,817, **8,762**, 8,858, **8,864**, 9,413, 9,438, 9,597, 9,620, **10,146**, 10,169, 15,463, **16,022, 16,027**, 16,249, 16,318. *See also* Church colleges
Church schools, Episcopal, 3,717
Church societies, 96, **164**, 446, 763, 1,363, 1,631, 1,632, 1,726, 1,868, 1,889, **1,947**, 2,009, **2,026**, 2,609, **2,913, 2,937**, 3,250, **3,438**, 3,742, **3,940**, 4,147, **4,193, 4,292**, 4,469, **4,540, 4,541, 4,542, 4,543, 4,544, 4,545**, 4,650, 4,815, **4,959, 4,979**, 5,300, 5,426, 5,544, 5,551, **5,604, 5,701, 5,859, 6,173, 6,174, 6,177, 6,183, 6,294**, 6,794, **7,099, 7,102, 7,103**, 7,720, **7,823, 7,839, 7,899**, 7,901, 7,902, 8,366, **8,379**, 8,795, 8,849, **8,857, 8,865**, 8,867, 8,987, **8,997**, 9,037, 9,052, 9,102, 9,218, **9,283**, 9,326, **9,406**, 9,448, **9,507, 9,723**, 9,750, **9,944, 10,094, 10,140**, 10,331, 10,447, 10,546, **10,570**, 10,599, **11,008, 11,067**, 11,095, **11,107**, 11,443, **11,697, 12,324, 12,520, 12,783**, 12,986, 13,235, 13,559, **13,666**, 13,872, **13,980**, 14,026, **14,439**, 14,667, **14,735, 15,122, 15,227**, 15,230, **15,373, 15,437**, 15,447, 16,265, 16,278, 16,430, **16,465**, 16,479, 16,500, **16,574**, 16,587, 16,731, 16,748, 16,787, **16,850**, 16,911, **17,113**, 17,262, **17,683**
Church societies, Advent Christian, 7,064
Church societies, Baptist, 1,103, 1,889, 3,256, **3,453**, 3,455, **3,456, 3,457, 3,458, 4,512**, 4,661, 4,959, **5,203**, 5,894, **7,098, 7,100, 7,101, 7,104, 7,396, 8,032, 8,033, 8,034, 8,035**, 8,304, 9,068, 9,069, **9,070, 9,659**, 9,811, 10,499, 10,900, 11,587, **12,783**, 13,297, 13,635, 13,639, 13,641, **13,643, 13,645, 13,923**, 14,595, **15,394, 15,396**, 16,382, 17,246
Church societies, Church of God, 4,464
Church societies, Congregational, 1,965, 4,779, **5,234, 5,456, 5,463, 5,464**, 5,894, **6,169, 6,172, 7,001, 7,004**, 7,371, 7,857, **8,255**, 8,951, 9,012, 9,071, **9,290**, 9,365, **10,145, 10,147**, 10,460, 10,461, 10,550, **13,913**, 14,340, 14,972, **15,453, 15,454, 17,563**
Church societies, Episcopal, 2,913, 3,939, 3,941, **3,942**, 4,959, **5,214**, 5,827, **6,181, 6,182**, 7,905, 7,907, 7,908, 7,909, 8,901, **8,998**, 9,093, 9,301, 9,331, **11,359, 12,084**, 12,088, **12,237**, 12,520, **15,380, 15,754, 16,024, 16,025, 16,028**
Church societies, Evangelical Covenant, 3,943
Church societies, Friends, 4,959, 9,220
Church societies, Lutheran, 3,957, **3,959, 3,960, 3,961, 3,962, 3,963, 3,964, 3,965, 3,966**, 4,319, **4,724, 4,870**, 4,959, **5,224**, 8,418, 8,731, **8,804, 8,860, 8,861, 8,865, 8,867, 8,952, 9,271, 9,405**, 10,139, **10,140, 10,141**, 14,496, 15,704, 15,855
Church societies, Mennonite, 4,514, 4,517, 5,051, **5,052**, 5,196, **5,200, 5,201**, 14,869
Church societies, Methodist, 1,813, 1,900, **3,307**, 3,353, **3,479, 3,765, 3,766, 3,767, 3,768, 3,769, 3,770**, 4,127, **4,540, 4,541, 4,543, 4,544, 4,545, 4,597**, 4,774, 4,849, 4,906, 4,959, **5,073, 5,075, 5,076, 5,169**, 5,171, **5,173, 5,179, 5,244, 5,247, 5,248, 5,400, 5,554**, 5,740, **7,862**, 7,947, 7,972, 9,072, 9,101, 9,332, 9,448, **9,704**, 9,750, **9,896, 9,923, 10,066, 10,457**, 10,476, **10,566, 10,567, 10,569**, 10,571, **10,572, 10,573, 10,575, 10,576, 10,577, 10,578, 10,579, 10,580, 10,581, 10,582, 10,583, 10,584, 10,585, 10,586, 10,587, 10,588, 10,589, 10,590, 10,591, 10,592, 10,593, 10,594, 10,595, 10,596, 10,597, 10,598, 10,599, 10,601**, 10,907, **10,910**, 11,350, 11,624, 13,176, 13,211,

13,296, 13,944, 14,485, 15,642, 15,654, 15,838, 16,059, **16,084**, **16,209**, 16,265
Church societies, Mormon, 806, **16,511**, 16,513, 16,536, 16,555, 16,557, 16,560, 16,566, **16,583**, 16,595, 16,618, 16,619, **16,657**, **16,662**, 16,663, 16,664, 16,679, 16,681, 16,685, **16,689**, 16,722, 16,743, 16,758, 16,760, 16,761, 16,764, 16,769, 16,780, 16,786, 16,789, **16,796**, **16,800**, **16,801**, 16,802, 16,811, 16,812, 16,819, 16,820, 16,830, 16,837, 16,839, **16,851**, **16,859**, 16,860, 16,883, 16,911, 16,916, **16,930**, 16,957, 16,958, 16,967
Church societies, Presbyterian, 98, **1,171**, **1,260**, 1,387, 3,358, 3,802, 4,099, 4,959, **5,370**, **5,456**, **7,863**, 7,898, 7,900, 7,903, 7,906, **7,989**, **7,990**, **8,487**, 9,191, 9,310, 9,432, 9,453, 9,454, 9,660, **10,304**, 10,956, 11,740, 12,256, **13,951**, **13,952**, **14,724**, **14,727**, **15,173**, 15,174, 15,176, **15,558**, **15,592**, 15,593, 15,599
Church societies, Reformed Church, **10,925**, 11,023
Church societies, Unitarian, 4,959, **6,252**, **6,254**, **6,255**, **6,258**, 7,941, 7,952, 9,392, **9,413**, 13,182, **13,183**
Church societies, Universalist, 9,406
Church Women United, 9,192
Church Women United, Arizona, **164**
Church Women United, Iowa, **4,979**
Church Women's Federation of Lubbock (TX), 16,278
Church work, 4,477, 6,775, 7,564, 13,280, 16,447. *See also* Church group work; Deaconesses; Sunday-schools
Church work with criminals, 13,639
Church work with immigrants, **1,156**, 15,173
Church work with military personnel, 3,808
Church work with seniors, 11,469
Church work with teen agers, Presbyterian Church, 15,173
Church work with the sick, Catholic Church, 10,189
Church work with women, Catholic Church, 9,491, 11,477
Church World Service, 164
Churches, 1,595, 3,219, 6,503, 7,804, 8,699, 9,989, **15,839**, 16,876, 17,227. *See also names of denominations*
Churches, Baptist, 3,168, 3,170, 3,256, 3,267, 4,701, 5,644, 7,720, 9,697, 9,906, 12,324, 13,991, 14,031, 15,093, 16,365, 17,285
Churches, Catholic, 5,239, 14,909, 15,839
Churches, Congregational, 9,090, 15,839
Churches, Episcopal, 3,141, 9,120, 9,606, 9,649, 9,706, 10,331, 10,680, 12,489, 17,502, **17,518**
Churches, Lutheran, 642, 4,319, 4,325, 4,326, 8,752, 8,774
Churches, Methodist, 197, 3,762, **10,574**, **11,095**, 15,839
Churches of Christ, 161
Churches, Presbyterian, 3,266, 9,596, 9,709, 11,626, 11,750, **12,256**, 15,553, 15,839
Churches, Unitarian, 6,249, 15,252
Churchill, A. B. (Pierson), 10,913
Churchill, Ann Maria (1818?-?), **2,265**
Churchill, Anna (1884-), 6,698
Churchill, Claire (Warner), 14,462
Churchill, Emeline, 8,164
Churchill, Eunice Malvina, 9,023
Churchill Family, 9,023
Churchill, Isabell (1901-). *See* Mooney, Isabell (Churchill) [Mrs. Matthew] (1901-)
Churchill, Jennie (Jerome) [Lady Randolph] (1854-1921), 12,053, 12,326
Churchill, Mable (Hall), 6,442
Churchill, Mary Adelaide (1828-79). *See* Craig, Mary Adelaide (Churchill) [Mrs. Austin] (1828-79)
Churchill, Mary Helen (1821-1913). *See* Baird, Mary Helen (Churchill) [Mrs. Spencer F.] (1821-1913)
Churchill, Owen, 8,170
Churchill, Sarah J. (Starkweather) (1835-1915), **2,266**, 10,919, **11,082**
Churchill, Winston, 2,108, 15,564
Churchwomen of St. Lukes (MI), 7,908
Chute, Charles Lionel (1882-1953), **11,964**
Chute, Joy, 8,600
Chute, Marchette Gaylord (1909-), 8,600, 11,810, 11,969

Chynoweth, Edna E. Phillips [Mrs.] (1852-1950), **17,615**
Ciardi, John, 12,001
Cieminski, Lorraine [Mrs.], 9,527
Cigar makers, 1,653
Cihak, Anna M., 9,467
Cilley, Lavina Bayley Kelly, 10,817
Cimarron (moving-picture), 17,795
Cincinnati Art Academy (OH), faculty, **13,855**
Cincinnati Art Museum (OH), 13,845, 13,851, 13,857
Cincinnati Conservatory of Music (OH), 16,381
Cincinnati Crafters Company (OH), **13,841**, 13,851, 13,853
Cincinnati Enquirer (OH), 2,467
Cincinnati Human Relations Committee (OH), 13,872
Cincinnati League of Women Voters (OH), **13,842**
Cincinnati League of Women Voters (OH), Woman's Suffrage Committee, 13,842
Cincinnati Pottery Club (OH), 13,853
Cincinnati School of Expression (OH), 13,810
Cincinnati Symphony Orchestra (OH), 13,857
"Cincinnati, The," 9,280
Cincinnati Training School for Deaconesses (OH), 5,394
Cincinnati Wesleyan College for Young Women (OH), 13,749
Cincinnati Women's Club (OH), 13,853
Cincinnati Women's Pottery Club (OH), 13,856
Cinderella Theatre Company v. Sign Workers' Local No. 591, 6,314
Ciphers, 11,083
"Circe" (story), 16,172
Circle C Ranch (ID), **3,667**
Circle Repertory Theatre Company (NY), 11,860
Circuit Court of Alchua County (FL), 2,873
Circuit Rider's Wife, A (book), 3,197
Circus, 1,827, 9,390, **12,858**, **17,490**
    pictorial works, 17,488, 17,489
"Circus Lore," 3,747
Cirese, Helen Mathilde (1899-), **4,076**
Cities and towns, 391, 943, 1,092, 3,753, **3,917**, **3,919**, **3,920**, **3,931**, 5,644, 6,650, **7,635**, **8,470**, 9,477, 9,907, 10,686, **12,128**, 14,196, **15,036**, 15,869, 16,714
    civic improvement, **50**, **4,676**, **4,888**, 5,302, 5,611, 7,508, 8,223, 8,481, 8,487, 8,493, **8,836**, 9,330, 9,347, **10,917**, **10,946**, 11,270, **12,347**, **13,649**, 13,991, 14,222, 16,302, **16,435**, 17,138, 17,863
    planning, 470, 3,879, 4,129, 5,829, **5,837**, 7,841, 8,659, 12,148, 14,605, 16,259
Citizen Kane (moving-picture), 17,809
Citizen's Advisory Commission (TX), 16,259
Citizens Advisory Committee on Health, Physical Education, and Physical Fitness in the Detroit Public Schools (MI), 8,103
Citizen's Advisory Committee on Recreation and Natural Beauty, 7,794
Citizens Advisory Committee on School Needs (MI), 8,103
Citizen's Advisory Committee on Voluntary Foreign Aid, 10,197
Citizens' advisory committees in education, 8,103, 10,472
Citizen's Advisory Council on the Status of Women, 10,197
Citizens' associations, 112, 203, 210, **295**, **387**, 566, 1,313, 1,948, **2,083**, 2,633, **3,283**, 3,293, 3,430, 3,469, **3,792**, 3,798, **3,823**, **3,824**, 3,905, **4,073**, **4,090**, 4,125, **4,170**, 4,627, **4,671**, **4,899**, 4,921, **5,462**, 5,829, **5,837**, **7,508**, **7,856**, **7,864**, 7,967, 8,106, 8,112, 8,130, 8,131, 8,148, 8,630, 8,984, **9,209**, 9,289, **9,342**, 9,435, 11,914, **11,965**, 12,042, 12,061, 12,066, 12,266, **15,376**, **15,451**, 16,259, 16,342, 17,110, **17,124**, 17,262, 17,304, 17,314, 17,357
Citizens' associations, Japanese American, 166
Citizen's Charter Committee of Minneapolis (MN), 9,440
Citizens' Committee for Voluntary School Transfer (WA), 17,342
Citizens Committee on Displaced Persons, 8,984
Citizens Committee on the Family Court (IL). *See* Citizens Committee on the Juvenile Court (IL)
Citizens Committee on the Juvenile Court (IL), **3,823**

Citizens Committee on the State Legislature (MT), **10,280**
Citizens Committee to Save the Cable Cars (CA), 1,313
Citizens Committees for Reorganizing Executive Government and for the Courts, 6,914
Citizens' Council for Legislation (IA), 4,921
Citizens' Council Forum Films (MS), **9,605**
Citizen's Crusade against Poverty, 8,112
Citizen's Fact-Finding Committee (GA), 3,347
Citizens for Eisenhower, 5,128, 5,143
Citizens for Farm Labor, 1,283, 1,577
Citizens for Michigan, 8,130
Citizens for School, 8,130
Citizens for the Extension of Birth Control Services, 4,046
Citizens Historical Association (IA), **4,899**
Citizens' Housing Council, 11,914
Citizens League (Kansas City, MO), 10,112
Citizens of Greater Chicago (IL), 4,125
Citizens Planning and Housing Association (MD), 5,829, **5,837**
Citizens' Save Our Schools Committee (Chicago, IL). *See* Citizens Schools Committee (Chicago, IL)
Citizens Savings Athletic Foundation (Los Angeles, CA), **997**
Citizens Savings Athletic Foundation, World Trophy Award, 997
Citizens Schools Committee (Chicago, IL), 3,787, **3,824**, 3,901
Citizen's School Tax Campaign Committee (MO), 9,984
Citizens Service Corps, **8,999**, 13,618
Citizens Temperance Union (PA), 14,953
Citizen's Union of the City of New York, 1,948, 11,841, 12,403
Citizen's Volunteer Committee (MN), 8,913
Citizenship, 1,179, 2,569, 6,702, 7,237, 7,524, 13,912
Citizenship Class (Sharon, WI), 17,721
Citron, Minna Wright (1896-), **2,741**, 2,763
Citrus fruit, 14,060
City and State, 2,643
City attorneys, 8,988, 14,600
City Board of School Commissioners (Charleston, SC), **15,403**
City Cemetery (MS), 9,686
City Club of Denver (CO), 1,750
City College (New York, NY), 6,354
    faculty, 11,631
City councilmen, 3,492, 9,315, **10,062**, 10,743, 12,297, 14,142, 14,619, 15,000
City councilwomen, 104, 661, 895, 1,642, 1,779, **3,853**, **4,149**, **5,007**, 5,172, **5,386**, 6,336, **7,742**, **11,987**, 12,145, **13,872**, 13,972, 14,236, **14,983**, **16,289**, 17,257, **17,289**, 17,314, 17,324, 17,342
City Federation of Women's Clubs (San Antoinio, TX), **16,322**
City Hospital (San Francisco, CA), 406
City Improvement Society of New Brunswick (NJ), **10,946**
City missions, **5,762**
City of Hope, 4,149
City of Richmond (ship), 7,588
City planners, 1,779, **3,781**, **17,279**
City Union of Mothers Clubs (IA), 4,915
City University of New York, Brooklyn College, School of General Studies, 6,683
City University of New York, faculty, 17,738
Civic Center (Columbus, OH), 14,022
Civic Club (Harrisburg, PA), 14,822
Civic Club of Philadelphia (PA), 2,643
Civic Council (New York, NY), 11,261
Civic Federation (Arlington, VA), 17,050
Civic Garden Club (CO), 1,734
Civic improvement. *See* Cities and towns, Civic improvement
Civic League (MD), 5,854
Civic League Day Nursery (Rochester, MN), 8,836
Civic Legislative League (NY), **11,965**
Civic Music Association (Tulsa, OK), **14,261**
Civic planning. *See* Cities and towns, Civic improvement
Civic Unity Committee (WA), 17,341
Civil Air Patrol, New Mexico, 14,202

Civil defense, 1,206, **2,686**, 2,694, 3,214, **3,383**, 4,727, 4,937, 5,228, 5,755, 6,123, 6,586, 6,606, 6,662, 7,160, 7,546, 7,705, 7,723, **7,954**, 7,965, 8,223, 8,446, 8,635, 8,666, 9,333, 9,481, **9,486, 9,487, 9,894, 10,013, 10,509,** 10,671, **10,692,** 11,857, 12,573, 12,751, 13,557, 13,617, 13,618, 15,451, 15,755, 17,217, 17,278

Civil engineers, 1,837, 4,749, 5,746, **9,804,** 10,678, **12,277,** 15,440, **17,440**

Civil law, cases, 10,103, 16,215, 17,218

Civil Liberties Committee, 10,193

Civil rights, **65**, 164, 459, 592, 621, 726, 943, 1,049, 1,507, 1,559, 1,561, 1,605, 2,143, 2,153, **2,438**, 2,504, 2,509, 2,562, 2,589, **2,865**, 3,805, 4,073, 5,455, 6,314, 6,547, 6,622, 6,682, 6,838, 6,848, 7,323, 8,058, 8,068, 8,078, 8,104, 8,131, 8,132, 8,149, 8,591, 8,668, 8,678, 9,150, 9,289, 9,379, 9,402, 10,199, 11,389, 11,772, 11,920, 11,928, 12,061, **12,682**, 12,703, 12,870, 13,993, 14,023, 14,637, 14,691, 15,204, 15,316, 15,951, **15,991, 15,993,** 17,238, 17,245, 17,254, 17,290, 17,299, 17,365, 17,787. *See also* Liberty; Race discrimination, law and legislation; Right of property; *and as a subhead under subjects, e.g.,* Afro-Americans, civil rights
  law and legislation, 8,077, 8,093, 11,695

Civil Rights Act, 2,438

Civil Rights Commission (MI), 8,063

Civil Rights Congress, 8,104, **12,682**

Civil Rights Congress of Los Angeles (CA), **1,012**

Civil Rights Defense Committee, 17,365

Civil Rights Federation, 8,104

Civil rights, Socialist involvement in, 11,917

Civil rights workers, 64, 65, 89, 717, **1,012, 1,570**, 1,654, **3,353, 3,469**, 3,852, 4,055, **5,377, 5,476, 5,477, 6,980, 7,194, 7,807, 8,106,** 8,116, **8,117,** 9,694, **11,840, 11,855,** 11,914, 12,066, 13,176, 13,333, 14,453, 14,656, 14,671, 15,376, **15,877, 15,880,** 15,977, **17,234, 17,259, 17,262, 17,304, 17,357, 17,599, 17,600, 17,608,** 17,630, **17,649, 17,691, 17,714,** 17,726

Civil rights workers, Afro-American, 2,315, 4,147, **5,828,** 8,531, 12,690, **17,232**

Civil service, 255, 6,358, 6,561, 7,861, 11,920. *See also* Municipal officials and employees; Public officers

Civil service reform, 5,305, 5,741, **7,081,** 7,827

Civil supremacy over the military, 16,323

Civil War Centennial Commission, 15,806

"Civil War Letters of Cordelia Scales, The" (article), 9,726

Civil War Sanitary Commission, 10,160

Civilian Civic Center (China), 14,466

Civilian defense, 2,397, 4,850, 13,246

Civilian Defense Council (NC), 13,618

Civilian Defense Homemakers Corps, 8,446

Civilian Defense Volunteer office, 5,228

Civinette Club (NC), 13,185

Claassen, Evelyn [Mrs. Peter Walter], **11,540**

Claassen, Peter Walter, 11,540

Clackamas Female Seminary (OR), 14,508

Claflin, Adelaide Avery (1846-?), **6,469**

Claflin, Mary Bucklin (Davenport) [Mrs. William] (1825-96), 14,062

Claflin, Tennessee, 3,778

Claflin, Victoria (1838-1927). *See* Woodhull, Victoria (Claflin) [Mrs. Canning]. [Mrs. James Harvey] Blood [Mrs. John Biddulph] Martin (1838-1927)

Claflin, William (1818-1905), **14,062**

"Claiborne County, Mississippi, The Promised Land" (ms), 9,641

Claiborne, Magdalene (Hutchins) [Mrs. Ferdinand Leigh], 12,963, **12,977**

Claiborne, William Charles Coles, 12,963

"Claim of Being a Western Pioneer, 1902-1932, The" (ms), 200

"Claimed by the Prairies" (ms), 13,682

Clair, Blanche, 17,623

Clair, Mary F. (1890-), 11,851

Claire, Ina, 12,444

Clanjamfry (Baton Rouge, LA), 5,419

Clanton, Ella Gertrude (1834-?). *See* Thomas, Ella Gertrude (Clanton) (1834-?)

Clapesattle, Helen B. (1908-), 8,566, 9,360

Clapp, Alice B., 9,230

Clapp, Caledonia Wright (1830-70), 16,148

Clapp, Cornelia Maria [Miss] (1849-1934), 7,499

Clapp, Elizabeth. *See* Woodbury, Elizabeth (Clapp) [Mrs. Levi]

Clapp, Ella, 9,000

Clapp, Elsie Ripley [Miss] (1879-1965), **3,772**

Clapp, Eva Katherine (1875-1916). *See* Gibson, Eva Katherine (Clapp) [Mrs. C. B.] (1875-1916)

Clapp Family (MA), **7,614**

Clapp, Florence Julia Tilton [Mrs. Harrie Winter] (1858-1946), 9,000

Clapp, George Christopher (1823-91), Family (MN), **9,000**

Clapp, George Frederic (1867-1955), 9,000

Clapp, Hannah J., 1,230

Clapp, Hannah Keziah [Miss] (1824-1908), **10,655,** 10,779

Clapp, Harrie Winter (1858-1949), 9,000

Clapp, Harriet Cecelia (Snow) [Mrs. Elisha Drown] (1861-1937), **16,623**

Clapp, Hattie Allen [Mrs. Moses E.] (1850-1924), 9,001

Clapp, Isabelle, 9,000

Clapp, John Drury (1822-98), 7,614

Clapp, Katherina (ca. 1880-1903), 9,001

Clapp, Levi (1794-1854), 7,614

Clapp, Margaret Antoinette, 6,877, 7,574, 7,583

Clapp, Mariette Warner [Mrs. George Christopher] (1824-1903), 9,000

Clapp, Maud, 5,863

Clapp, Moses E. (1851-1929), **9,001**

Clapp, Sarah Huntington (1824-69). *See* Holmes, Sarah Huntington (Clapp) (1824-69)

Clapper, Olive Ewing [Mrs. Raymond] (1896-1968), **17,954**

Clapper, R., 17,992

Clapper, Raymond, 17,954

Clappison, Gladys Bonner, 6,161

Clara Barton (book), 6,955

Clara Barton, Red Cross Pioneer (book), 4,988

Clara de Hirsch Home for Working and Immigrant Girls (NY), 7,525

Clara de Hirsch School for Immigrant Girls, 7,537

Clardy, Josephine (1881-1970). *See* Fox, Josephine (Clardy) (1881-1970)

Clare, Ada A. Jane (McElhenney) [Mrs. J. Franklin] Noyes (1836-74), **15,629**

Claremont School (CA), Oral History Program, 11,846

Clarenbach, Kathryn F., 17,769, 17,774

Clarence Darrow Community Center (Chicago, IL), **4,077,** 4,130

Clarence Walworth Alvord Memorial Commission, **9,002**

Clarinda High School (IA), 4,819

Clarion (MS), 9,686

Clarissa D. Spaulding Girls' School (NJ), **10,947**

Clark. *See also* Clarke

Clark, A. H., 9,596

Clark, A. M. [Miss], 12,369

Clark, Ada. *See* Smith, Ada (Clark) [Mrs. Joseph, III]

Clark, Ada Bacot, **15,561**

Clark, Addison N., 10,728

Clark, Adele [Miss] (1884?-), **2,742, 17,077**

Clark, Alden, 1,224

Clark, Alice, 3,668

Clark, Amelia, 7,140

Clark, Ann (1871-?). *See* Hart, Ann Clark [Mrs. Jerome Alfred] (1871-?)

Clark, Ann Eliza (Darden), 9,709

Clark, Anna (1842-?), 9,004

Clark, Anna P., 1,084

Clark, Annetta I. (1883-1961), 7,158

Clark, Annie E. *See* Jacobs, Annie E. (Clark)

Clark, Arianna [Mrs. John Calvin], 10,445

Clark, Ava Milam, **14,272**

Clark, Barzilla W., 3,687

Clark, Benjamin, 8,372

Clark, Betsey Brickett [Mrs. Nathaniel], **10,802**

Clark, Bettie, 13,420

Clark, Caroline Hopkins [Mrs.], **16,454**

Clark, Carrie, 9,004

Clark, Carroll [Mrs. George], 2,851

Clark, Cary Ann (Freeman) [Mrs. Edward D.] (1849-1922), 9,573

Clark, Charles, 9,653

Clark, Charles Asa, Family, **9,003**

Clark, Charles H., 8,151

Clark, Charles Henry, Family (MN), **9,004**

Clark, Charlotte Ouisconsin (1819-1907). *See* Van Cleve, Charlotte Ouisconsin (Clark) [Mrs. Horatio Phillips] (1819-1907)

Clark, Chloe, **7,756**

Clark College (Atlanta, GA), faculty, 3,304, 3,777

Clark College, presidents, 11,372

Clark, D. Worth, 3,712

Clark, David Francis, 9,005

Clark, Donald Lumen (1888-1966), **11,966**

Clark, Dorcas A., 7,140

Clark, Edith K. O. (1881-1936), **17,896,** 17,901, 18,010

Clark, Edward Hardy, 17,973

Clark, Edward Tracy (1878-1935), **2,267**

Clark, Eliza (1829-?). *See* Darrah, Eliza (Clark) (1829-?)

Clark, Eliza A. *See* Johnson, Eliza A. (Clark) [Mrs. Samuel]

Clark, Elizabeth, 15,285

Clark, Elizabeth Hannah, 6,316

Clark, Elizabeth Jenks, 2,331

Clark, Elizabeth W., 8,657

Clark, Elizabeth Zane [Mrs. John (or Henry)] McGloughlin (or McGlaughlin or McLaughlin) [Mrs. Jacob (or John)] (1766?-1831?), 17,624

Clark, Ella Elizabeth (1896-), **17,187**

Clark, Ella Sterling (1853-1934). *See* Mighels, Ella Sterling (Clark) (1853-1934)

Clark, Eloise W., 5,469

Clark, Emma Cornelia (ca. 1806-?). *See* Strobel, Emma Cornelia (Clark) [Mrs. William D.] (ca. 1806-?)

Clark, Emma H., 17,474

Clark, Erasmus, 10,948

Clark, Esther Bridgman, 15,134

Clark, Eugenie, 2,863

Clark Family, 9,373

Clark Family (CA), **595**

Clark Family (CO), 1,742

Clark Family (ID), **3,668**

Clark Family (MA), 7,014

Clark Family (MI), **8,151**

Clark Family (NJ), **11,180**

Clark Family (NY), 11,440

Clark Family (VA, TN), **15,928**

Clark, Frances (Beardsley) [Mrs. Erasmus] (1822-?), **10,948**

Clark, Georgia Neese, 13,391

Clark, Gertrude B., 12,513

Clark, Gertrude (Voorheis) [Mrs. Baylies Coleman], 595

Clark, Grace, 9,004

Clark, Grace (Johnson) [Mrs. Deane L.] (1887-), 5,665

Clark, Hannah A. *See* Jennings, Hannah A. (Clark)

Clark, Harriet. *See* Myles, Harriet (Clark)

Clark, Harriet Elizabeth "Mother" [Mrs. Francis E.]. *See* Abbott, Harriet Elizabeth. [Mrs. Francis E.] Clark

Clark Helen E., 1,790

Clark, Helen Marr (1829-1917). *See* Callister, Helen Marr (Clark) [Mrs. Thomas] (1829-1917)

Clark, Helen P. [Miss], **10,281**

Clark Henry Toole, **13,375**

Clark, Herma Naomi (1871-1959), **3,825,** 3,969

Clark, Isabella Duncan (?-1903), 532

Clark, James Freeman, 12,419

Clark, Jane. *See* Kirkwood, Jane (Clark) [Mrs. Samuel J.]

Clark, Janet H., 11,662, 12,836

Clark, Jessie May (Bill) [Mrs. Harry] (1878-?), 8,953

Clark, John Calvin (1829-?), **10,445**

Clark, John Innes, 15,379

Clark, Jonas Gilman (1815-1900), **7,687**

Clark, Jonathan, 9,596

Clark, Joseph Sill, **14,975**

Clark, Joshua Reuben, **16,624**

Clark, Julia A. B., 15,928

Clark, Julia A. (Smith) [Mrs. Lincoln], **1,413**
Clark, Kate Freeman [Miss] (1875-1956), **9,573**
Clark, Kate (Upson) (1851-1935), **7,206**
Clark, Kenneth, 4,491
Clark, Kenneth, 8,097
Clark, L. S., Family (MN) **9,005**
Clark, Lena (Simmons), **9,787**
Clark, Lincoln (1800-86), **1,413**
Clark, Lucy A. Rice, **16,931**
Clark, Lydia (Bowen) [Mrs. John Innes] (ca. 1752-?), 15,379
Clark, Margaret Miller, 10,962
Clark, Margaret Miller (Davidson), **10,949**
Clark, Margery B. Rogers [Mrs. T. G.], 9,596
Clark, Marguerite, 2,205
Clark, Marguerite H. Gosse, **10,758**
Clark, Marianne, 9,241
Clark, Martha Cowper Pierce (1837-?), 9,004
Clark, Mary [Mrs.], 1,017
Clark, Mary [Mrs. Alden], 1,224
Clark, Mary [Mrs. E. G.], 4,175
Clark, Mary Barnard (1871-1963). *See* Putnam, Mary Barnard (Clark) (1871-1963)
Clark, Mary Ellen, 4,740
Clark, Mary H., 7,882
Clark, Mary Jean [Miss], 3,932
Clark, Mary Louisa (Woolley) [Mrs. Joshua Reuben], **16,624**
Clark, Mary "Mollie" [Miss], **12,421**
Clark, Mary Montressor Sears [Mrs. David Francis] (ca. 1868-?), 9,005
Clark, Matilda. *See* Sillers, Matilda (Clark)
Clark, Maud, 11,889
Clark, May S., 2,722
Clark, Michael, 6,694
Clark, Miss, 1,543
Clark, Mrs. B. B., 4,923
Clark, Mrs. Charles H., 8,151
Clark, Mrs. E., **17,382**
Clark, Mrs. Harry Hayden, 17,775
Clark, Mrs. S. G., 9,593
Clark, Myra (1805-1885). *See* Gaines, Myra (Clark) [Mrs. William Wallace] Whitney [Mrs. Edmund Pendleton] (1805-1885)
Clark, Nathan, 9,416
Clark, Nellie M. (1876-?), **8,044**
Clark, Orah Dee [Miss] (1875-1965), **131**
Clark, Pauline [Mrs.], 10,254
Clark, Pearl (1872-1963), 9,003
Clark, Phebe, 15,285
Clark, Rebecca Angeline (1832-?). *See* Trevett, Rebecca Angeline (Clark) [Mrs. Sewell S.] (1832-?)
Clark, Robert (?-1837), **8,313**
Clark, Rosamond, 6,470
Clark, Rozana P., 2,190
Clark, Ruth E., **6,471**
Clark, Ruth Swan (1887-?), 7,158
Clark, Sarah, 2,190
Clark, Septima (Poinsetta) (1898-), 13,176
Clark, Sister M. Ferdinand, 15,232
Clark, Susan. *See* Knight, Susan (Clark) [Mrs. John H.]
Clark, Susan (Wright) [Mrs. Jonas Gilman] (1816-1904), **7,687**
Clark, Susanna Boylston, 12,369
Clark, T. G., 9,596
Clark, Thomas A., 4,394
Clark University (MA), 7,687
archives, **7,686**
faculty, 5,323
Clark, Walter, **13,376**
Clarke, Adelle (1882-), 13,176
Clarke, Alice R., **6,134**
Clarke, Anna Laura (1788-1861), **7,146**
Clarke, Annie, 3,100
Clarke, Caroline. *See* Allen, Caroline (Clarke)
Clarke, Charity. *See* Moore, Charity (Clarke) [Mrs. Benjamin]
Clarke, Dorothy, 772
Clarke, E. Malcolm, 10,281
Clarke, Edward Smith, 12,814
Clarke, Eliza Ann Redmond [Mrs. Thomas Clarke], 9,464

Clarke, Elizabeth Lawrence, 6,472
Clarke, Elizabeth Mickel [Mrs. Ethan Case] (1826-?), 9,006
Clarke, Emily Edith, 17,006
Clarke, Emma Cornelia (ca. 1806-?). *See* Strobel, Emma Cornelia (Clark) [Mrs. William D.] (ca. 1806-?)
Clarke, Emma R., **2,129**
Clarke, Erminda R., 10,508
Clark, Ethan Case, Family (MN), **9,006**
Clarke, F. C., 11,547
Clarke, Freeman (1809-87), Family (NY), **12,814**
Clarke, Grace Giddings (Julian) [Mrs. Charles B.] (1865-1938), **4,623**
Clarke, Hannah. *See* Cabot, Hannah (Clarke) [Mrs. John]
Clarke, Harriet T. (Buckingham) (1832-90), **410, 14,531**
Clarke, Henrietta Jaquelina (Ward) [Mrs. Freeman] (1814-90), 12,814
Clarke, Herbert Edwin (1852-?), 7,651
Clarke, Institute (San Francisco, CA), 1,291
Clarke, J. Eric G., **1,571**
Clarke, James Frederic, 4,880
Clarke, James Freeman, 6,500
Clarke, Mary Bayard (Devereux) [Mrs. William John] (1827-86), 13,172, 13,421, 13,581
Clarke, Mary Cowden, 11,551
Clarke, Mary Stetson (1911-), **5,999**
Clarke, Mrs. R. P., 6,500
Clarke, Olivia, 13,217
Clarke, Philip Ream (1889-1966), **4,078**
Clarke, Ruth Johnson [Mrs. J. Eric G.], **1,571**
Clarke, Sara Jane (1823-1904). *See* Lippincott, Sara Jane (Clarke) [Mrs. Leander K.] (1823-1904)
Clarke, Sarah (1824-80). *See* Sim, Sarah (Clarke) [Mrs. Francis] (1824-80)
Clarke, Sarah Freeman, 5,950
Clarke, Sherman, 12,814
Clarke, Shirley (1927-), **17,794**
Clarke, Sidney, 11,516
Clarke-Smith, Linda [Miss], **2,280**
Clarke, Thomas William, Family, 9,464
Clarks, Helen, **17,955**
Clarksburg Women's Club (WV), 6,868
Clarkson, Catharine. *See* Stevens, Catharine (Clarkson) [Mrs. Henry]
Clarkson, Catharine Rutherfurd (1794-1861). *See* Goodhue, Catharine Rutherfurd (Clarkson) [Mrs. Jonathan] (1794-1861)
Clarkson, Charlotte (Dunlop), 17,992
Clarkson, Elizabeth (1793-1820), 12,695
Clarkson Family (NY), 12,020
Clarkson Family (SC), **15,710**
Clarkson, H. F. [Miss], 12,317
Clarkson, Levinus, **2,268**
Clarkson, Matthew (1758-1825), 12,695
Clarkson, Polly, 15,691
Clarkson, Ruth (1857-1947). *See* Crockett, Ruth (Clarkson) [Mrs. Ozro O.] (1857-1947)
Clary, H. L., 13,636
Clasen, Jeannie M., **10,656**
Class meetings, Methodist, **10,911**
Claude, Sister Mary, 4,848
Claudel, Paul, 12,047
Clausen, Claus L., 8,774
Clauson, Bertha E., 6,343
Clavier Club (ME). *See* Philharmonic Club (ME)
Clawson, Ellen Spencer, 16,888
Clawson, Hiram B. (1826-1912), Family, **16,888**
Clawson, Margaret Gay (Judd) [Mrs. Hiram Bradley] (1831-1912), **16,625**
Clawson, Nabbie Howe Young (1891-). *See* McMaster, Nabbie Howe Young (Clawson) [Mrs. Frank Athol] (1891-)
Clay, Cassius Marcellus (1810-1903), 5,305, **5,334**
Clay, Clement Clairborne, 13,610
Clay, Henry (1777-1852), 1,435, 2,269, 2,270, 5,265, 11,602, 11,654, 15,256, 17,992
Clay Hills Garden Club (GA), 3,187
Clay, James Brown (1817-64), 2,270
Clay, Josephine. *See* Habersham, Josephine (Clay) [Mrs. William Neyle]
Clay, Laura (1849-1941), **5,305**

Clay, Lucretia H., 2,270
Clay, Lucretia (Hart) [Mrs. Henry] (?-1864), 2,270
Clay, Mary [Mrs. Thomas H.], 2,269
Clay, Mary (1766-1803), **12,978**
Clay, Mary Barr (1839-?), 5,334, **5,336**
Clay, Mrs. Clement Clairborne, 13,610
Clay Seminary (MO), **9,943**
Clay, Susan M. (Jacob) [Mrs. James Brown] (1823-1905), 2,270
Clay, Thomas H., **2,269**
Clay, Thomas J., **2,270**
Clay, William H., 10,191
Clayburn, Juliet, 15,763
Claypoole, Betsy [Mrs. John] Ross [Mrs. Joseph] Ashburn [Mrs. John] (1752-1836), 2,580
Clayson, Esther (1869-1967). *See* Lovejoy, Esther (Clayson) Pohl (1869-1967)
Clayson, Lillian (1894-). *See* Booth, Lillian (Clayson) [Mrs. Wayne Chipman] (1894-)
Clayton, Anna (Colton) [Mrs. John] (1820-?), 14,976
Clayton, Annie Dexter (1893-), 16,780
Clayton, C. T., 2,700
Clayton, Edward (1840-1925), Family (UT), 16,477
Clayton, Edward P., 3,089
Clayton, Ellen Morrison [Mrs. Edward] (?-1911), 16,477
Clayton Family (TX), 16,341
Clayton, Florida, 2,945
Clayton, John (1819-81), **14,976**
Clayton, Marion. *See* Link, Marion (Clayton) [Mrs. Edwin A.]
Clayton, Mary [Miss], **16,341**
Clayton, Philip, 3,089
Clayton, Roberta (Flake) (1877-), **16,504**
Clayton, Sarah Lillian (1874-1930), 6,122, 6,131
Clayton, Sarah (Medford) (1786-1849), 14,976
Clayton, William, Family, 16,780
Claywell, Allen. *See* Irvine, Allen (Claywell)
Claywell Family, 13,016
Claywell, Mary (Moses), 13,016
Cle Elum State Bank (WA), 17,185
Cleaning women. *See* Charwomen and cleaners
Clear Springs Creek School (MN), 8,476
Clearman, Hattie, 3,683
Clearwater Fire Protective Association (ID), 3,664
Clearwater Timber Company (ID), 3,664
Cleary College (MI), 7,800
Cleasby, E. A., 17,516
Cleaveland, Elizabeth Hannah (Jocelyn) [Mrs. James Bradford], 1,870
Cleaver, Emma O., 5,735
Clef Club (ME). *See* Philharmonic Club (ME)
Clef Club (Northampton, MA), 7,147
Clegg, Dorah, 16,060
Clegg Family, **5,362**
Clegg, Helen (Gifford) [Mrs. William], 5,362
Clegg, William, 5,362
Cleghorn, Sarah Norcliffe (1876-1959), **6,473**, 6,867, **15,273**, 15,290, 15,305, 17,013
Clein, Ruby. *See* Webber, Ruby (Clein)
Cleiorhetia Society (Westerville, OH), **14,158**
Cleland, Anne Isabella. *See* Kinloch, Anne Isabella (Cleland)
Cleland, Elizabeth (1901-), 4,495
Clem, Jane, 18,025
Clemens, Clara Langdon (1874-1962). *See* Gabrilovich, Clara Langdon (Clemens) (1874-1962)
Clemens, Cyril, 628
Clemens, Drusilla [Mrs.] (?-1954), 14,140
Clemens, Samuel L. (1835-1910), 792, 1,493, 1,495, 1,643, 1,954, 2,108, 5,414, 6,329, 9,425, 9,832, 9,839, **10,130**, 10,677, 11,637, **11,967**, 12,529
Clement (bark), 7,480
Clement, Carrie, 13,363
Clement, Grace Groves, **3,826**
Clement, Josephine, 5,466
Clement, Loretta [Miss], **16,627**
Clement, Mary Greenleaf (1830-1912). *See* Leavitt, Mary Greenleaf (Clement) [Mrs. Thomas Hooker] (1830-1912)
Clement, Nancy Abigail (1872-1954). *See* Williams, Nancy Abigail (Clement) [Mrs. Frederick Granger] (1872-1954)

Clements, Edith Gertrude (Schwartz) [Mrs. Frederick E.] (?-1971), **10,446**
Clemmer, Mary E. (1831-84). *See* Hudson, Mary E. (Clemmer) [Mrs. Daniel] Ames [Mrs. Edmund] (1831-84)
Clemmons, Ella May, 1,279
Clemson, Anna Maria (Calhoun) [Mrs. Thomas Green] (1817-75), **15,780**
Clemson College, 7,717
Clemson, Thomas Green, 15,780
Clendenning, Arminda Holliday, 17,435
Clendenning Family (OH, WV), **17,435**
Clendenning, Florence, 12,520
Clergy, 14, 53, 521, 736, **1,172**, 1,304, **1,847, 1,860, 1,914, 1,942,** 1,956, 1,957, 2,040, **2,138,** 2,371, 2,477, 3,007, 3,008, 3,036, 3,313, 3,405, 3,464, 3,489, 3,496, **3,640,** 3,778, 4,003, 4,054, **4,405,** 4,489, 4,972, 5,285, 5,286, 5,287, 5,289, 5,362, **5,492,** 5,699, 5,903, 6,119, 6,354, 6,395, **6,410,** 6,412, **6,435,** 6,500, **6,515, 6,534, 6,543,** 6,556, 6,561, 6,573, 6,578, 6,706, **6,744,** 6,833, 6,845, 6,857, 6,911, **6,925,** 6,983, 7,163, 7,223, 7,227, 7,385, **7,390, 7,472, 7,513, 7,597, 7,622,** 7,645, 7,656, 7,661, 7,673, 7,674, **7,676,** 7,681, 7,767, 8,068, **8,223, 8,332,** 8,667, 8,780, 8,916, **9,023,** **9,351,** 9,634, 9,706, **9,832,** 9,989, 10,347, 10,826, 10,909, 10,936, 10,942, 10,975, **11,029,** 11,030, 11,099, **11,102,** 11,314, **11,572,** 11,846, 11,855, 12,197, **12,198,** 12,206, 12,341, 12,464, **12,478,** 12,619, 12,770, 12,779, 13,076, **13,246,** 14,351, **14,470, 14,564,** 14,566, 14,588, 14,603, 15,077, 15,079, **15,358,** 15,435, 15,447, 15,533, 15,631, 15,634, 15,661, **16,359, 16,386,** 17,036, 17,150, 17,665, 17,749, 17,862
Clergy, Afro-American, **2,138,** 3,519, 5,828, **6,410,** 6,414
Clergymen's families, 8,751, 8,780
Clergymen's wives, 130, 327, **736, 1,247,** 1,751, 1,786, **1,956,** 2,040, 2,106, **3,939,** 4,205, 4,319, 4,334, **4,721,** 4,779, **4,809, 5,205, 5,220, 5,801,** 5,823, **5,918,** 6,561, **6,845, 6,857,** 7,042, **7,335, 7,601, 8,285,** 8,367, **8,432, 8,723, 8,738, 8,748, 8,749, 8,752,** 8,757, **8,774, 8,856,** 8,860, **8,866, 10,002, 10,530, 10,879,** 10,908, 10,958, 10,988, 11,246, **11,424, 12,771,** 14,837, 15,079, **15,475, 16,014,** 16,060, 17,029, 17,090
Clerk, Herma (?-1959), 3,994
Clerke, Agnes M., 4,696
Clerks, **944, 1,822,** 11,851, 14,994
Clerks (retail), 8,476, 8,690
Clerks of court, 986, 9,369, **14,914,** 14,921, 17,125
Clevans, Johanna (Boetz) [Mrs. Mark], 7,998
Clevans, Mark, 7,998
Cleve, Constance (pseudonym). *See* Berckman, Evelyn Domenica (1900-)
Cleveland Academy (OH), faculty, 13,930
Cleveland Advisory Board of Playgrounds and Recreation (OH), 13,909
Cleveland Association for the Hard of Hearing (OH), 2,347
Cleveland Board of Education (OH), 13,961
Cleveland, Catherine, 12,275
Cleveland County Nursing Home (AR), 242
Cleveland, Elizabeth H., **7,359**
Cleveland Federation of Women's Clubs (OH), 13,917
Cleveland Female Seminary, 8,986
Cleveland Female Seminary (OH), faculty, 13,966
Cleveland, Frances (Folsom) [Mrs. Grover]. [Mrs. Thomas Jex] Preston (1864-1947), 2,384, 2,414, 2,472, 3,907, 4,244, 4,375, 4,695, 4,696, 9,438, 11,249, 11,339, 11,358, 11,621, 12,184, 15,355
Cleveland, Grover (1837-1908), 2,009, 2,108, 3,227, 9,437, 10,165, 11,242, 11,249, 11,339, **11,340, 12,184,** 12,203, 12,322, 15,355
Cleveland Humane Society (OH), 13,970
Cleveland, Jane Cromwell (1834-1923). *See* Burnett, Jane Cromwell (Cleveland) (1834-1923)
Cleveland, Jennie. *See* Burnett, Jennie (Cleveland) [Mrs. Wellington C.]
Cleveland Job Corps (OH), 1,600
Cleveland Job Corps for Women (OH), 13,945
Cleveland, Loie (Burr) [Mrs. Walter H.] (1905-72), **12,775**

Cleveland Maternal Health Association (OH), 6,223
Cleveland Mental Health Association (OH), 13,945
Cleveland, Mrs. Stafford Canning, 11,710
Cleveland Music School Settlement (OH), 13,932
Cleveland News (OH), 13,898
Cleveland Orchestra (OH), 13,932
Cleveland Play House, 14,413
Cleveland Police Department, women's bureau (OH), 13,964
Cleveland Public Library (OH), 6,551, 12,479, 13,954
Cleveland, Rose Elizabeth (1846-1918), 9,048, 9,437, 9,438, 11,339
Cleveland School of Art (OH), faculty, 2,859
Cleveland Sorosis (OH), 13,916
Cleveland Travelers Aid Society (OH), **13,964**
Cleveland Welfare Federation (OH), 13,950
Cleveland, William Henry, 14,552
Cleveland Writers' Club (OH), **13,917**
Cleveland, Zuleika Haralson [Miss], **12,979**
Clewer Sisterhood, 5,827
Clews, Elsie (1875-1941). *See* Parsons, Elsie (Clews) [Mrs. Herbert] (1875-1941)
Clifford, Emily (Orr) [Mrs. George S.] (1866-1952), **4,504**
Clifford, Eth (Rosenberg), **17,956**
Clifford, Josephine (Wompner) [Mrs. James A.] (1838-1920). *See* McCrackin, Josephine (Wompner) [Mrs. James A.] Clifford [Mrs. Jackson] (1838-1920)
Clifford, Margaret. *See* Bryant, Margaret (Clifford)
Clifford, Wesley N., 3,304
Clift, Elizabeth [Mrs. William], 15,942
Clift Family (TN), **15,942**
Clift, William (1794?-1886), 15,942
Clifton Road Garden Club (GA), 3,187
Clifton, Susie, 4,493
Climb the Hills of Gordon (book), 3,078
"Climb Up Mount Hood, A," 14,553
Clinard, Frank A., **13,377**
Clinch, Eliza Bayard. *See* Anderson, Eliza Bayard (Clinch) [Mrs. Robert]
Clinch, Loisa, 12,228
Clinch, Sophie H. Gibbes Couper [Mrs. Duncan L.], 3,589
Cline, Carolynne Helen [Miss], **11,541**
Cline, Dorothy I., **11,239**
Cline, Gloria Grace (Griffen) (1929-73). *See* Harrison, Gloria Grace (Griffen) Cline (1929-73)
Cline, Maranda J., 4,904
Cline, Vassie, 10,714
Clinical psychologists, **12,060**
Clinical psychology, 8,049
Clinics, 1,121, 1,236, 5,373, 5,410, 5,475, 6,225, 6,232, 6,516, 6,688, 6,847, 7,088, 8,045, 8,645, 8,823, 9,442, 9,514, 10,189, 10,878, 11,869, 11,908, 11,932, 12,079, 12,841, 13,660, 13,823, **15,130,** 17,831. *See also* Birth control clinics
Clinics, traveling, 231
Clinton, Anna L. (1871-1960), **7,757**
Clinton, Cornelia Tappen. [Mrs. Edmund Charles Genet], 12,210
Clinton Domestic Seminary (NY), 11,471
Clinton Farms (NJ), 11,003
Clinton, Florence (1865-1906). *See* Sutro, Florence (Clinton) (1865-1906)
Clinton, George, 2,281, 12,210, 12,320
Clinton, Hannah, 12,207
Clinton, Helen (Davis) (1880-1978), 668, 1,068
Clinton Liberal Institute (Fort Plain, NY), 9,023
Clinton, Sharen, 12,210
Clio Circle (South Bend, IN), **4,664**
Clio Club, **4,796**
Clio Club (Carroll, IA), 4,960
Clio Club (Mankato, MN), **8,488**
Clio Club (Minneapolis, MN), 9,227
Clionian Club (IA), 4,732
Clipping bureaus, 1,268
"Cliquot" (story), 5,413
Clitherall, Eliza Carolina (Burgwin) [Mrs. George Campbell] (1784-1863), **12,980**
Clitherall, George Campbell, 12,980
Clithers, Electra Thomas, 3,673
Cliveden (residence, England), 2,182

Clock and the Fountain, A Masque in Three Parts, The (drama), 9,564
Clock, The, 5,439
Clock without Hands (book), 16,161
Clocks and watches, **2,853**
Cloistered Dominican Nuns of Perpetual Adoration, Monastery of the Angels (CA), **998**
Cloon, Mary (King) [Mrs. William G.], **7,758**
Cloon, William G., 7,758
Clooney, Rosemary, 16,208, 17,944
Clopath, Henrietta [Miss] (?-1936), **8,546**
Cloran, Mrs. Timothy, **14,337**
Close Her Pale Blue Eyes (book), 12,016
Clothier, Florence [Mrs. George Wislocki] (1903-), 6,987
Clothier, Hannah (1872-1958). *See* Hull, Hannah (Clothier) (1872-1958)
Clothier, Robert Clarkson, **10,929**
Clothing and dress, 3,133, 8,352, **11,342,** 11,851, 16,402
  reform of, 5,976, 6,602
Clothing factories, 13,823
Clothing trade, economic aspects, 8,067
Clothing workers, 659, **1,656,** 1,779, 2,700, 6,795, 8,064, 10,789, **15,992**
Clotworthy, Mrs. John B., **12,981**
Cloud Clap Inn (OR), 14,664
Cloud Shoes (book), 8,531
Cloudcraft Recreation Camp (TX), 938
Clough, Alexander, 16,799
Clouse, Ruth Cowan (1892-?), 4,070
Cloutier Family (LA), **5,440**
Cloutier, Helen H. (1909-), **8,314**
Cloverleaf School, Towns of Grant and Grow, School District No. 3, Rusk County (WI), **17,508**
Clow, Alice, **16,049**
Clow, Robert J., 16,049
Clowes, Florence, 15,332
"Clowns at the Inn at Deya" (story), 11,145
Club Alabama (NY), 5,478
Club Beaux Arts (San Francisco, CA), **1,265**
Club-houses, 1,193, 6,805
Club Montparnasse (St. Paul, MN), 9,007
Clubbs, A. V., 2,900
Clubbs, Occie [Miss] (1888-1971), **2,900**
Clubs, 4, 7, 15, 50, 52, 74, 75, 116, 126, 140, **147, 148, 149, 152, 158,** 167, 169, 203, **208,** 210, **228, 250, 273, 274, 276, 277,** 324, 507, 720, 901, **932,** 935, 938, **966, 977, 1,036,** 1,063, 1,067, 1,079, **1,092, 1,094, 1,106, 1,108, 1,109,** 1,115, 1,117, **1,127,** 1,132, 1,140, **1,155, 1,214, 1,215, 1,220,** 1,295, 1,310, 1,318, **1,341,** 1,344, 1,355, **1,382,** 1,385, 1,387, 1,483, 1,496, 1,525, 1,582, 1,591, **1,616, 1,667,** 1,673, **1,679,** 1,700, 1,716, 1,721, 1,732, **1,734, 1,735,** 1,741, 1,744, **1,750, 1,758, 1,767,** 1,771, 1,775, **1,776, 1,781,** 1,785, 1,791, **1,792, 1,793, 1,797, 1,817, 1,818, 1,825, 1,834, 1,891, 1,893, 1,903, 1,910, 1,913, 1,921, 1,925, 1,945,** 1,948, **1,954, 1,980,** 1,992, **1,994, 1,997, 1,999,** 2,000, **2,001, 2,004,** 2,009, 2,058, **2,117, 2,147,** 2,170, 2,597, 2,633, 2,643, 2,704, **2,705,** 2,875, 2,886, 2,955, **2,964,** 3,077, 3,113, **3,127,** 3,130, **3,138, 3,141,** 3,142, **3,148,** 3,151, 3,159, 3,168, 3,169, **3,189,** 3,198, 3,204, 3,205, **3,209,** 3,224, 3,229, **3,231, 3,236, 3,237, 3,243,** 3,245, 3,254, 3,265, **3,274, 3,277,** 3,305, **3,322,** 3,358, **3,365,** 3,371, 3,374, 3,384, 3,403, 3,419, 3,430, 3,439, **3,558, 3,574,** 3,585, **3,660, 3,670, 3,693,** 3,743, **3,750, 3,796,** 3,809, 3,820, 3,828, 3,848, 3,851, 3,855, **3,857, 3,868, 3,876, 3,877, 3,891,** 3,899, **3,900, 3,910,** 3,916, 3,917, 3,918, 3,920, 3,930, 3,931, **3,992, 3,997,** 4,044, 4,074, 4,094, 4,154, 4,155, 4,163, 4,165, **4,166, 4,171, 4,176, 4,179, 4,187, 4,188, 4,189, 4,190, 4,192, 4,195,** 4,197, **4,273, 4,278, 4,291, 4,298, 4,299, 4,309, 4,310, 4,311, 4,318, 4,334,** 4,366, **4,400, 4,401, 4,412,** 4,448, **4,451, 4,458, 4,459, 4,462,** 4,477, 4,532, 4,548, 4,549, **4,554, 4,560, 4,561, 4,562, 4,565, 4,566, 4,567, 4,570, 4,571, 4,572, 4,574, 4,575, 4,576,** 4,578, 4,579, **4,580, 4,582, 4,584, 4,585, 4,586,** 4,587, 4,591, 4,621, 4,623, 4,625, 4,630, **4,661, 4,664, 4,665, 4,667, 4,668, 4,669, 4,677,** 4,710, **4,711,** 4,719, **4,720, 4,723, 4,725,**

4,729, 4,732, **4,748**, **4,751**, **4,753**, **4,769**, **4,770**,
4,775, **4,780**, **4,796**, 4,800, 4,815, **4,838**, **4,846**,
4,851, **4,864**, 4,866, **4,878**, **4,883**, 4,888, 4,918,
4,922, **4,923**, 4,957, **4,960**, **4,997**, **4,998**, 5,059,
5,066, **5,087**, **5,099**, 5,109, 5,112, 5,113, 5,117,
5,123, **5,176**, 5,179, 5,191, 5,193, **5,194**, 5,195,
5,216, 5,270, 5,301, 5,305, 5,321, **5,352**, 5,357,
5,396, 5,405, **5,407**, 5,411, 5,419, 5,426, 5,443,
5,445, **5,447**, **5,508**, 5,545, 5,546, 5,549, **5,557**,
5,579, **5,607**, 5,611, 5,613, 5,614, 5,631, **5,696**,
5,738, 5,739, **5,809**, 5,815, **5,825**, **5,886**, **5,916**,
5,945, **5,971**, **6,265**, 6,354, 6,355, 6,358, 6,399,
6,449, 6,467, 6,469, 6,494, 6,516, 6,546, **6,563**,
6,630, 6,638, 6,670, 6,700, 6,704, 6,740, 6,748,
6,762, **6,779**, **6,780**, 6,781, **6,782**, **6,798**, 6,806,
6,822, 6,868, **6,870**, 6,871, 6,886, 6,950, **6,989**,
6,990, **6,992**, **7,000**, 7,020, 7,021, 7,050, 7,051,
7,059, 7,075, 7,077, **7,078**, 7,079, **7,082**, **7,089**,
7,132, 7,190, 7,217, 7,258, 7,270, **7,373**, **7,397**,
7,434, **7,436**, 7,449, **7,507**, **7,512**, 7,517, **7,519**,
7,592, 7,593, 7,594, 7,596, 7,635, 7,695, 7,696,
7,705, 7,726, 7,738, **7,746**, **7,754**, 7,755, **7,771**,
7,780, **7,781**, 7,787, 7,788, **7,799**, **7,813**, **7,836**,
7,865, **7,912**, 7,925, 7,934, 7,936, **7,938**, 7,957,
7,960, 7,962, 7,963, **7,971**, **7,984**, 7,986, 7,987,
8,012, **8,014**, **8,015**, **8,016**, 8,018, 8,019, 8,038,
8,046, 8,047, **8,174**, 8,177, **8,187**, 8,188, **8,193**,
8,212, 8,213, **8,215**, 8,218, 8,220, 8,227, **8,234**,
8,235, 8,240, 8,243, **8,254**, 8,262, **8,263**, **8,267**,
8,273, **8,281**, **8,325**, 8,330, 8,339, 8,369, **8,381**,
8,382, **8,384**, **8,386**, 8,387, **8,394**, **8,415**, **8,416**,
8,417, **8,422**, 8,429, **8,431**, 8,434, 8,438, **8,445**,
8,449, 8,450, 8,456, 8,460, 8,476, **8,481**, 8,482,
8,484, **8,486**, **8,491**, **8,493**, **8,504**, **8,508**,
8,511, **8,562**, **8,563**, 8,615, 8,622, 8,681, 8,696,
8,697, **8,766**, 8,768, **8,821**, **8,825**, **8,827**, **8,829**,
8,832, 8,833, **8,837**, 8,896, 8,902, 8,919, 8,942,
8,964, 8,972, **9,007**, **9,010**, 9,080, 9,103, **9,143**,
9,144, **9,145**, 9,164, **9,227**, **9,228**, **9,243**,
9,260, **9,267**, **9,324**, **9,330**, **9,340**, **9,346**, 9,347,
9,349, 9,385, **9,404**, **9,420**, **9,455**, **9,459**, 9,466,
9,505, 9,511, **9,516**, **9,518**, **9,530**, **9,536**, **9,541**,
9,551, 9,644, 9,647, 9,667, **9,673**, **9,681**, **9,682**,
9,689, **9,691**, 9,708, 9,749, 9,750, **9,776**, **9,777**,
9,779, **9,801**, **9,805**, 9,811, 9,819, **9,822**, **9,843**,
9,856, **9,885**, 9,892, **9,910**, **9,915**, 9,918, 9,938,
9,959, **9,968**, **9,968**, 9,978, 9,986, 9,993, 10,012,
10,058, **10,084**, **10,085**, **10,086**, **10,087**, 10,101,
10,102, **10,108**, **10,112**, 10,195, 10,254, 10,257,
10,331, **10,339**, **10,341**, 10,376, **10,396**, **10,406**,
10,409, **10,413**, **10,415**, **10,416**, 10,420, 10,422,
10,423, **10,429**, **10,470**, 10,484, **10,506**, **10,507**,
10,528, 10,534, **10,536**, 10,643, 10,658, 10,679,
10,680, **10,685**, **10,689**, **10,705**, 10,720, **10,754**,
10,757, **10,770**, **10,771**, 10,782, **10,783**, 10,820,
10,841, **10,843**, **10,845**, 10,849, **10,856**, **10,878**,
10,884, 10,886, 10,887, **10,889**, **10,891**, **10,899**,
10,906, 10,918, 10,919, 10,930, 10,932, 10,940,
10,994, **11,007**, **11,009**, **11,010**, **11,045**, 11,091,
11,121, **11,126**, **11,141**, 11,210, 11,222, **11,236**,
11,270, **11,324**, **11,334**, 11,344, **11,349**, 11,351,
11,381, **11,384**, **11,392**, 11,406, 11,411, 11,412,
11,413, 11,417, **11,420**, 11,445, 11,447, **11,530**,
11,576, **11,581**, **11,623**, 11,625, **11,692**, 11,696,
11,713, **11,716**, **11,794**, 11,959, 11,967, **12,159**,
12,208, 12,297, **12,323**, 12,346, 12,347, **12,484**,
12,521, 12,524, 12,598, 12,734, 12,737, 12,804,
12,807, **12,839**, 12,851, **12,851**, **12,882**, 12,893,
12,941, **12,973**, **12,974**, 13,083, 13,124, 13,195,
13,198, 13,205, **13,220**, 13,253, 13,265, 13,274,
13,304, **13,317**, 13,331, 13,334, 13,352, **13,380**,
13,383, **13,410**, 13,439, 13,446, 13,447, **13,461**,
13,468, **13,471**, **13,508**, **13,509**, **13,511**, **13,515**,
13,517, **13,521**, 13,557, 13,566, **13,574**, 13,576,
13,596, 13,617, 13,618, 13,649, 13,658, 13,659,
13,660, 13,670, **13,671**, **13,683**, **13,685**, **13,687**,
13,695, **13,696**, **13,705**, 13,706, **13,708**, 13,713,
13,714, **13,725**, **13,751**, **13,753**, **13,755**, **13,756**,
13,760, **13,850**, 13,853, 13,856, **13,858**, **13,881**,
13,898, **13,906**, **13,908**, **13,916**, 13,917, **13,922**,
13,932, 13,938, 13,969, **13,979**, **13,985**, **13,991**,
13,992, 13,997, **14,001**, **14,022**, **14,023**, **14,031**,
14,032, 14,035, **14,036**, **14,043**, 14,067, **14,108**,
14,109, 14,110, 14,118, **14,121**, **14,147**, **14,149**,

14,158, 14,160, **14,171**, **14,177**, **14,219**, **14,222**,
14,223, **14,260**, **14,262**, **14,265**, **14,266**, **14,267**,
14,281, **14,287**, **14,295**, 14,356, **14,472**, 14,478,
14,500, **14,564**, 14,635, **14,640**, **14,641**, **14,700**,
14,705, **14,711**, **14,722**, **14,725**, **14,746**, 14,822,
14,929, **14,931**, 14,949, 14,953, **14,987**, **15,071**,
15,076, **15,108**, 15,145, **15,190**, **15,194**, 15,207,
15,220, **15,231**, **15,243**, **15,244**, **15,249**, **15,340**,
15,383, **15,390**, **15,408**, **15,421**, **15,422**, **15,431**,
15,461, 15,515, **15,522**, 15,578, **15,664**, **15,728**,
15,790, 15,795, 15,797, **15,812**, 15,814, **15,846**,
15,847, 15,851, 15,858, **15,861**, 15,897, 15,967,
15,971, 16,115, **16,119**, 16,126, 16,127, 16,128,
16,138, 16,145, 16,146, **16,183**, **16,185**, **16,186**,
16,187, **16,188**, **16,189**, **16,190**, **16,192**, **16,193**,
16,194, **16,195**, **16,196**, **16,198**, **16,199**, **16,200**,
16,201, **16,202**, **16,203**, **16,211**, 16,224, **16,228**,
16,255, **16,263**, **16,267**, **16,277**, **16,278**, 16,279,
16,293, **16,296**, **16,297**, **16,300**, 16,303, **16,309**,
16,313, **16,320**, **16,322**, **16,330**, 16,336, 16,341,
16,350, 16,354, **16,389**, **16,397**, **16,413**, **16,419**,
16,444, 16,461, 16,542, 16,555, 16,566, 16,625,
16,753, **16,879**, **16,899**, 16,916, **16,928**, **16,966**,
16,984, 16,998, **17,041**, **17,054**, 17,067, 17,091,
17,134, 17,135, **17,136**, **17,138**, 17,158, 17,177,
17,211, **17,228**, 17,246, **17,267**, 17,299, 17,375,
17,376, **17,388**, **17,394**, **17,399**, **17,412**, **17,424**,
17,426, **17,458**, 17,494, **17,546**, **17,556**, **17,577**,
17,611, 17,671, 17,675, **17,682**, **17,690**, **17,730**,
17,742, **17,747**, **17,786**, **17,821**, **17,823**, **17,825**,
17,856, **17,861**, **17,863**, **17,864**, **17,883**, 17,894,
17,908, **17,928**, 17,931, 17,940, **17,987**

Clubs, Afro-American, 91, 128, **1,105**, 1,760, **1,762**,
    3,282, 3,846, **4,768**, 8,029, 8,284, 8,898, 10,205
Clubs, Jewish, 1,993, 2,005
Clubs, Norwegian-American, **8,769**
Clubs, Welsh, 9,952
Clubwoman (periodical), 17,468
Clubwoman's Monthly News Magazine, The, 15,244
Clues to Burn (book), 700
Cluff, Sarah (Eggertsen) [Mrs. Harvey Harris]
    (1858-1944), **16,628**
Clunas, Elizabeth (Randall) [Mrs. J. A.?] (ca. 1830-?),
    5,802
Clunas Family (MD), **5,802**
Clunie Opera House (Sacramento, CA), 939
Clure, W. O., 4,847
Clyens, Mary Elizabeth (1850-1933). *See* Lease,
    Mary Elizabeth (Clyens) [Mrs. Charles L.]
    (1850-1933)
Coaches (athletics), 1,534, **10,739**
Coaching, 10,724
Coad, Henrietta "Retta," 14,554
Coad, Pauline Corson [Mrs.], **11,542**
Coahuila y Texas, 16,310
Coal Camp Girl (book), 4,306
Coal miners, **8,091**, 17,232
Coal mines and mining, 63, 5,367, **17,482**
    economic aspects, 8,067
Coalachy (Native American, NC), 13,448
Coale, Anne (Hopkinson) [Mrs. Samuel Stringer]
    (1745-1817), 5,803, 15,079
Coale, Eliza (1786-1838). *See* Proud, Eliza (Coale)
    [Mrs. John Greene] (1786-1838)
Coale, Elizabeth [Mrs.], 3,762
Coale Family (MD), **5,751**
Coale, Mary Abigail Willing (?-1831). *See* Proud,
    Mary Abigail Willing (Coale) [Mrs. William T.]
    (?-1831)
Coale, Mary B. (1861-1940). *See* Redwood, Mary B.
    (Coale) [Mrs. Francis T.] (1861-1940)
Coale, Samuel Stringer, 5,803
Coalition for a Democratic Union, 8,128
Coalition for Economic Survival, **1,013**
Coalition for Protective Legislation, 8,076
Coalition of Labor Union Women, 4,124, **8,075**,
    8,076, 8,103, 8,128
Coalter, Elizabeth Tucker (1805-56). *See* Bryan,
    Elizabeth Tucker (Coalter) (1805-56)
Coalter Family (SC), 15,652
Coalter Family (VA), 17,107, 17,109
Coalter, Frances Bland (Tucker) [Mrs. John]
    (1785-1813), 17,109
Coalter, John (1769-1838), 17,109

Coalter, Judith H. Tomlin (1808-59), 17,109
Coan, Carol, 2,678
Coan, Fidelia Church [Mrs. Titus] (1810-72), 2,271,
    12,185
Coan, Harriet Fidelia (1839-1906), 2,271
Coan, Lydia (Bingham) [Mrs. Titus], 2,271, 3,638
Coan, Sara, 12,208
Coan, Sarah Eliza (1843-1916), 12,185
Coan, Titus (1801-82), **2,271**, **12,185**
Coan, Titus Munson (1836-1921), 12,185
Coast, Marjorie Eames (?-ca. 1920). *See* McClain,
    Marjorie Eames (Coast) [Mrs. Donald] (?-ca.
    1920)
Coast Seamen's Union, 535
Coates, Aurora (Walker) (1826-1900), **12,753**
Coates, Beulah, 14,887
Coates Family (PA), **14,977**
Coates, Grace Stone, **10,232**, 10,327
Coates, Margaret, **14,887**
Coates, Mary, **14,887**, 14,945
Coates, Samuel (1748-1830), 14,977
Coatsworth, Elizabeth (1893-). *See* Beston, Elizabeth
    (Coatsworth) [Mrs. Henry] (1893-)
Coatsworth, Elizabeth Jane (1893-), **5,620**, 8,531,
    11,940, 15,900
Coatsworth Family (NY), 11,337, **11,341**
Cobb, Calvin, **3,669**
Cobb, Collier (1863-1934), 12,982
Cobb, Collier, Jr. (1893-), 12,982
Cobb, Ella Waite, 4,697
Cobb, Eunice Hale Waite, **5,918**
Cobb Family, 11,130
Cobb Family (GA), **2,992**
Cobb Family (NC), **12,982**
Cobb, Howell (1815-68), 2,992, 3,266
Cobb, Howell, Jr., 2,979
Cobb, Jerrie (1931-), 11,831, **14,233**
Cobb, John A., 2,979
Cobb, Lois P. (Dowdle), **9,788**
Cobb, Lucy, 12,982
Cobb, Lucy (Barrow) [Mrs. John A.], 2,979
Cobb, Lucy Battle [Mrs. Collier] (1861-1905), 12,982
Cobb, Margaret (1883-1959). *See* Ailshie, Margaret
    (Cobb) (1883-1959)
Cobb, Mary Ann (Lamar) [Mrs. Howell] (1818-99),
    2,992
Cobb, Mary Ann Lamar (1850-1930). *See* Erwin,
    Mary Ann Lamar (Cobb) [Mrs. Alexander S.]
    (1850-1930)
Cobb, Mary Battle [Mrs. Collier] (1864-1900), 12,982
Cobb, Mary Gatlin [Mrs. Collier] (1871-1973), 12,982
Cobb, Mary Louisa (1899-1976), 12,982
Cobb, Mary McK. [Mrs. Howell, Jr.], 2,979
Cobb, Mrs. Howell, 12,190
Cobb, Penelope, 12,982
Cobb, Sarah Martha. *See* Whitner, Sarah Martha
    (Cobb) [Mrs. John C.]
Cobb, Sylvanus (1798-1866), 5,918
Cobb, Thomas R. R., 3,266
Cobb, William Battle (1891-1933), 12,982
Cobbe, Frances Power (1822-1904), 15,116
Cobden-Sanderson, Thomas J., 7,300
Coblentz, Catherine (Cate) [Mrs. William Weber],
    2,272, 2,479
Coblentz, Dorothy Wormer, 544, 942
Coblentz, Edmond David (1882-1962), 411
Coblentz, Staton, 14,383
Coblentz, William Weber, 2,272
Coburn, Charles, 7,209
Coburn, Emma, 12,759
Coburn Family (UT), 16,455
Coburn, Mary. *See* Dewees, Mary (Coburn)
Coburn, Mary Hulet (1882-1958), **16,455**
Coca, Imogene, 16,208
Cochran, Betty Holmes, 9,944
Cochran, Doris Mabel (1898-1968), **2,714**, 2,717,
    2,723
Cochran Family (SC), 15,441
Cochran, Jacqueline. [Mrs. Floyd] Odlum, 36, **5,132**,
    5,135, 5,137, 5,311
Cochran, Jean [Miss], 3,451
Cochran, Miriah Shelnut [Mrs. George Washington],
    3,421
Cochran, Mrs. W. Edward (1908-), **15,792**

Cochrane, Adelaide (Griffith), **412**
Cochrane, Elizabeth (1865?-1922). *See* Seaman, Elizabeth (Cochrane) [Mrs. Robert L.] (1865?-1922)
Cochrane Family, 8,374
Cochrane, Janet Craig, 8,374
Cock, Elizabeth F., 12,316, 12,354
Cockburn, Carlotta (Crabtree), 6,259
Cockburn, John Cassilis (1842-1911), **9,008**
Cocke Family (VA), **17,055**
Cocke, John Hartwell (1780-1866), 17,055
Cocke, Louisa Maxwell Holmes [Mrs. John Hartwell], 17,055
Cocke, Lucy, 17,055
Cocke, Sarah F., 5,752
Cockerell, Sydney, 11,993
Cockerill, Eleanor, 8,665
Cockett, Margaret, 15,144
Cockett, Marguerite Standish (1878-?), **12,132**
Cockrell, Marian Brown (1909-), **6,000**
Code, Marion Osborne Graves (189?-1955), **6,476**
Codman, Catherine, 7,128
Codman, Katharine Putnam Bowditch, 6,622
Codwise, Cornelia Josepha (1810-90). *See* Van Rensselaer, Cornelia Josepha (Codwise) (1810-90)
Cody, Annie E. (1890-1957), **15,943**
Cody Enterprise, The (WY), 17,899
Cody, William Frederick, 1,751, 1,786
Coe College, 4,918
Coe, Evelyn Peverley (1881-1967?), **6,477**
Coe Family (OR), **14,532**
Coe, Frances, 5,474, **15,890**
Coe, Helen Louise. *See* Howard, Helen Louise (Coe) [Mrs. John Lawrence]
Coe, Louise (1896-), 11,213, 11,217
Coe, Mary White [Mrs. Nathaniel] (1801-92), 14,532
Coe, Nathaniel (1788-1868), 14,532
Coeducation, 81, 109, 117, 1,848, **1,975**, 3,328, 4,470, **5,725, 5,729, 6,270, 6,271,** 6,303, **7,646,** 7,662, 8,578, 9,699, 9,809, **10,014,** 10,038, 11,300, 11,694, 12,807, 12,836, 13,467, 14,123, 14,165, **14,752,** 14,941, 15,034, 15,824, 16,031, 17,091
Coes, Mary (1861-1913), **6,189,** 6,339, **6,478**
Coeur d'Alene Mission (OR), 690
Cofax, Nellie [Mrs. Schuyler], 10,392
Cofer, Mrs. C. J., **3,380**
Coffee, A. D., 27
Coffee, Andrew J., 15,898
Coffee, Ann Eliza (Sloss) [Mrs. A. D.], **27**
Coffee-houses, 6,477
Coffee, Mary (Donelson), 15,898
Coffee plantation workers, **11,733**
Coffey, Julia Morgan, 14,943
Coffin, Charles Fisher (1823-1916), 4,624, **4,652,** 15,274
Coffin, Charlotte. *See* Gardner, Charlotte (Coffin)
Coffin, Ebenezer (?-1816), 15,460
Coffin Family, **15,274**
Coffin, Lucretia (1793-1880). *See* Mott, Lucretia (Coffin) [Mrs. James] (1793-1880)
Coffin, Marie Louise [Mrs. Trenmor], 10,752
Coffin, Martha (1806-75). *See* Wright, Martha (Coffin) [Mrs. Peter] Pelham [Mrs. David] (1806-75)
Coffin, Phebe Ann (1829-1921). *See* Hanaford, Phebe Ann (Coffin) [Mrs. Joseph Hibbard] (1829-1921)
Coffin, Priscilla (1786-1860). *See* Cadwalader, Priscilla (Coffin) [Mrs. Jabez] Hunt [Mrs. Joseph] (1786-1860)
Coffin, Rhoda M. (Johnson) [Mrs. Charles Fisher] (1826-1909), **4,624, 4,652,** 15,274
Coffin, Trenmor (1848-1904), **10,752**
Coffing, Marcia. *See* Holley, Marcia (Coffing)
Coffin's Point (plantation, SC), **15,460**
Cog Road (CO), 1,790
Cogen, Charles, 8,093
Coggeshall, Mary Jane Whitely (1836-1911), **6,479**
Coggins, Elsie (Shirpser), 574
Cogswell, Abby Parker (1832-?). *See* Choate, Abby Parker (Cogswell) (1832-?)
Cogswell Celia, **4,743**
Cohan, George M., 4,764
Cohen, Cecilia, 3,496

Cohen, Esther Shapiro (1895-), 17,744
Cohen, George N. (1885-1974). *See* Caylor, George N. (1885-1974)
Cohen, Joseph E., 12,700, 12,704
Cohen, Lillian (1878-1949), 8,609
Cohen, Maria, 1,248, 3,481
Cohen, Miriam Gratz Moses [Mrs. Solomon], **13,079**
Cohen, Moses C., 3,496
Cohen, Natalie [Miss], **3,165**
Cohen, Nina (Morais) (1855-1918), 8,963, 9,254, 9,347
Cohen, Wilbur, 8,085
Cohn, Amy [Mrs. Abraham], **10,657,** 10,703
Cohn, Daisy (?-1938). *See* Liederman, Daisy (Cohn) [Mrs. Benjamin] (?-1938)
Cohn, Fannia Mary (1885-1962), 8,071, 8,126, **12,422**
Cohn, Felice (1884-1961), **10,658,** 10,687
Cohrsen, Hanny, 9,492
Coit, Eleanor G. (?-1976), 8,085, 9,443, 12,717, 13,176
Coit, Eliza "Lillie" W. (Hitchcock) (1843-1929), 532, 545, **1,086, 1,367**
Coit, Laura, 13,245
Coit, Mary Ann. *See* Parker, Mary Ann (Coit) [Mrs. Willard]
Coker, Mrs. J. L., 15,609
Coker, Sarah E., 15,776
Cokesbury School, 15,588
Colaw, Mrs. James S., 1,751
Colbert, Claudette, 1,025, 1,576
Colbert, Elizabeth Stroud [Mrs. William], 4,202
Colbert, Mrs. William B., 9,606
Colbert, William (1765-1833), **4,202**
Colburn. Ellen [Miss], 13,526
Colburn, Fern, 8,668
Colburn, Mary E. G., **7,588**
Colburn, Nancy (?-1864). *See* Hartford, Nancy (Colburn) (?-1864)
Colby, Celestia R., 4,304
Colby, Clara Dorothy (Bewick) [Mrs. Leonard Wright] (1846-1916), **1,414,** 1,436, 15,864, **17,616,** 17,909
Colby College (ME), 4,404, 5,711, 6,724
  students, 2,446
Colby Family (NY), **12,585**
Colby, Francelia, 3,897
Colby, Hannah M., 12,585
Colby, Jean Poindexter, 14,390
Colby, Josephine, 8,071, 8,126
Colby, June Rose [Miss], **4,304**
Colby, Mrs., 14,473
Colby, Myra (1831-94). *See* Bradwell, Myra (Colby) [Mrs. James Bolesworth] (1831-94)
Colby, Pauline (1853-1944), **9,009,** 9,042
Colby, Ruth Gage [Mrs. Woodward L.], 9,150, 9,341, 9,352, 9,456
Colby, Veronica, 16,890
Colchester, First Congregational Church (CT), 1,890
Colcord, Joanna Carver. [Mrs. Frank] Bruno (1882-1960), 8,670, 8,685, 12,080
Colcorton (book), 2,875
Colden, Alexander, 11,745
Colden, Henrietta Maria, 11,745
Colden, Richard Nicholas, 11,745
Coldiron, D. F., 14,200
Coldiron, Daisy (Lemon) (1876-1946), **14,200**
Coldwell, Ethel Hunley, 1,085
Cole, Ada A., 6,009
Cole, Ada Matilda (1848-1925). *See* Bittenbender, Ada Matilda (Cole) [Mrs. Henry Clay] (1848-1925)
Cole, Adeline P. (Dodge), 7,465
Cole, Catherine (pseudonym). *See* Field, Martha (Smallwood)
Cole, Dorothy Ethlyn (1907-), **11,968**
Cole, Edda A., **3,166**
Cole, Ella, 16,060
Cole Family (CA), **1,032**
Cole Family (Jamaica), 15,077
Cole, Fred P., 7,481
Cole, Helen Moore [Mrs. Whitford], 2,491
Cole, Ida S., 1,319
Cole, Laura M., 16,097

Cole, Lucretia. *See* Waring, Lucretia (Cole) [Mrs. Howard S.]
Cole, Mary Jane. *See* Megquier, Mary Jane (Cole)
Cole, Mr., 5,779
Cole, Nellie Wurtsmith (1864-1955), **10,447**
Cole, Olive [Mrs. Cornelius], 1,032
Cole, Paul Boneau, **3,167**
Cole, Susan A. [Mrs. Fred P.], 7,481
Coleman, Ann, 10,846
Coleman, Ann Raney Thomas (1810-92), **16,050**
Coleman, Anne Caroline (1818-96), **5,752,** 14,816
Coleman, Anne "Nancy." *See* Biddle, Anne "Nancy" (Coleman) [Mrs. George]
Coleman, Cataline Storms, **1,100**
Coleman, Charles Washington, 17,121
Coleman, Cynthia Beverley (Tucker) [Mrs. Charles Washington] (1832-1908), 17,121
Coleman, Elinor (1912-). *See* Guggenheimer, Elinor (Coleman) [Mrs. Randolph] (1912-)
Coleman, Emma A., **14,201**
Coleman, Emma (Beck) [Mrs. Evans P.], 189
Coleman, Emma Lewis, 7,012
Coleman, Evans P. (1874-1954), **189**
Coleman Family (AZ), 189
Coleman Family (GA), **2,993**
Coleman Family (PA), 14,816
Coleman Family (VA), **17,121**
Coleman, Frances (1835-1920?). *See* Forsythe, Frances (Coleman) (1835-1920?)
Coleman, George, 9,521
Coleman, Gertrude (Bolton) [Mrs. Joseph Griswold, III], 355
Coleman, Juliet Cox [Mrs.], **2,273**
Coleman, Kenneth, **2,994**
Coleman, Leodel, **3,602**
Coleman, Marion, 15,179
Coleman, Mary H. B. [Mrs. George], 17,125
Coleman, Mary (Haldane) [Mrs. George] (1874 or 1875-1967), **9,521**
Coleman, Mildred Brown [Mrs.] (1924-), 94
Coleman, Mrs. Albert J., 1,757
Coleman-Norton, Marion (Stephenson) [Mrs. Paul] (1888-). *See* Olden, Marion (Stephenson) [Mrs. James, Jr.] Henry [Mrs. William K.] DeVictor [Mrs. Paul] Coleman-Norton [Mrs. Roger] (1888-)
Coleman, Patricia [Miss] (1916-?), **5,453**
Coleman, Sarah H., 14,816
Coleman, Susan (1839-?). *See* Henrie, Susan (Coleman) (1839-?)
Coleman, William Lewis, Jr. (1853-1940), 2,993
Coleman's Lake View Improvement Association (MN), 8,917
Coles, Annie Cadwallader (1883-1969), **15,575**
Coles, Bertha Horstmann (Lippincott) [Mrs. Stricker] (1880-1963), 14,978
Coles Family (PA), **14,978**
Coles, Grace M. (?-1967). *See* Currie, Grace M. (Coles) (?-1967)
Coles, Ida B., **16,629**
Coles, Marshall [Miss], 2,684
Coles, Mary [Mrs. S. L.], 9,438
Coles, Rebecca T. (?-1849). *See* Singleton, Rebecca T. (Coles) [Mrs. Richard] (?-1849)
Colesbury, Jean, 15,202
Colfax, Schuyler, 10,392
Colgate, Charlotte (1817-85). *See* Abbe, Charlotte (Colgate) [Mrs. George Waldo] (1817-85)
Colgate, Florence (1873-1951). *See* Speranza, Florence (Colgate) (1873-1951)
Colgate-Palmolive case, 6,849
Colgate University, 11,039
Colhecon (periodical), 3,124
Colhoun, Floride (1782-1866). *See* Calhoun, Floride (Colhoun) [Mrs. John C.] (1782-1866)
Colin, Rosica, 14,465
Collatz, Leonora J., 7,905
Collected Stories, 16,164
Collective bargaining, 8,058
  nursing, 3,444
  teachers, 8,060
Collective settlements
  Israel, 7,301
  Russia, 8,072

Collectors and collecting, **1,471**, **1,481**, **2,909**, 10,861, **11,899**, **12,376**, 12,467
College, a Smith Mosaic (book), 7,162
College administrators, 107, 449, **487**, 1,053, 1,975, **3,066**, 3,126, 4,495, 5,035, **5,834**, **6,279**, 6,339, **6,493**, 6,739, 7,158, **7,590**, **8,395**, 8,544, **8,553**, 8,566, **8,567**, **10,035**, **11,365**, 11,372, 11,375, **11,386**, 11,691, **13,187**, 13,189, **14,889**, **15,182**, 15,197, **17,270**
College and school drama, **911**, **913**, 4,690
College and school journalism, **912**, **914**, 1,814, 2,110, 3,124, 3,746, **4,316**, **4,317**, 4,595, 4,632, 5,075, 5,085, 5,188, 6,010, 7,330, 8,600, 9,282, **9,557**, **9,570**, 9,824, **10,623**, **11,281**, 11,302, 11,650, 13,194, 13,634, 14,748, **15,351**, 15,536, 17,716, **17,849**
College and school periodicals, **2,933**, **2,936**, 5,685, **8,402**, **11,108**, 12,746, **13,227**, **13,228**, 13,447, 15,897, 16,341, 16,369
College attendance, 1,845
College Baptist Church (Hillsdale, MI), **7,759**
College Baptist Church (Hillsdale, MI), Women's Missionary Society, 7,759
College Club (Boston, MA), **6,480**
College Club (St. Louis, MO), **10,195**
College Club of Hartford (CT), **1,891**
College Dance Group Tours, 16,987
College discipline, 2,935, 8,740, 10,604, 17,354, 17,449
College Equal Suffrage League, 6,981
College Equal Suffrage League of California, 648
College for Women (SC), **15,648**
"College Freshmen's Attitudes Toward Working Wives" (paper), 8,573
College in Crinoline (book), 5,012
College integration. *See* Segregation in higher education
College librarians, **82**, 105, 106, 107, 120, **757**, 905, **1,549**, 1,995, 2,927, 3,106, **4,396**, **4,398**, **4,402**, **4,522**, **4,523**, 5,241, **5,509**, **6,277**, **6,302**, 7,499, **7,924**, **8,564**, **8,582**, **8,588**, 8,595, **8,604**, 9,467, 9,712, 9,803, **10,932**, **11,371**, 11,660, 11,824, 11,930, 11,971, 11,972, **11,988**, **12,007**, **12,054**, 12,479, **12,935**, **13,178**, **13,204**, 13,333, 13,390, **13,954**, **14,128**, 14,277, 15,980, 16,131, 17,002, 17,012, 17,209
College of Charleston (SC), 15,515
   faculty, **15,683**
College of New Rochelle (NY), Alumnae Association, 11,807
College of New Rochelle (NY), archives, **11,807**
College of New Rochelle (NY), Ursuline Guild, 11,807
College of Notre Dame of Maryland (Baltimore, MD), faculty, 4,814, 5,829
College of Physicians and Surgeons of the Western District, 880
College of Racine (WI), **17,557**
College of St. Catherine (St. Paul, MN), 9,192, 9,467
   faculty, **8,853**
   presidents, **8,851**, 9,490
   trustees, 9,193
College of Saint Elizabeth (Convent Station, NJ), archives, **10,892**
College of St. Rose (NY), archives, **11,251**
College of St. Teresa (MN), 9,467
   archives, **9,519**
College of the Ozarks, alumnae, 15,977
College of the Sisters of Bethany (KS). *See* Washburn University (KS)
College of William and Mary (VA), 13,451
   faculty, 17,115
   students, 3,430
College Park Woman's Club (GA), 3,384
College Poetry Society of America, 18,021
College presidents, 44, 81, **85**, 355, 674, **924**, 1,085, 1,547, **1,559**, **1,562**, 1,859, 1,956, **1,976**, 1,977, 1,982, 1,983, **2,093**, **2,125**, 2,130, 2,580, 2,884, 2,927, **3,281**, **3,328**, 3,405, 3,974, 4,210, 4,211, 4,212, **4,305**, **4,319**, 4,326, 4,374, 4,395, 4,494, 4,521, 4,598, **4,640**, 4,709, 5,060, 5,063, 5,068, 5,362, 5,373, 5,458, **5,731**, 5,834, **5,836**, **5,866**, 5,868, 6,095, **6,278**, **6,290**, **6,291**, **6,299**, 6,346,

6,416, 6,436, **6,483**, **6,484**, 6,573, 6,617, **6,658**, 6,708, 6,877, **7,161**, 7,212, 7,264, 7,569, 7,572, **7,574**, 7,639, 8,565, 8,566, 8,689, 8,797, **8,851**, **9,023**, 9,077, 9,558, 9,610, 9,671, 9,824, 9,825, **10,022**, 10,038, **10,928**, **10,929**, 10,989, **11,172**, 11,251, 11,575, 11,661, 11,694, **11,742**, 11,807, 11,849, 11,879, 11,890, 11,910, 11,930, 12,036, 12,283, 12,619, 12,941, 13,147, **13,179**, **13,185**, **13,186**, **13,242**, **13,245**, 13,350, 13,436, 14,332, 14,706, 14,737, **14,745**, **14,787**, 15,212, 15,377, **16,992**, **16,993**, 17,586, 17,689, 17,832, 17,868, 17,872, 17,880
College registrars, **6,235**, **8,808**, 14,699, **17,443**
College Settlement (NY), 7,292
College Settlement (Philadelphia, PA), 15,208
College Settlement Association, 6,376
College sports, 7,164, 10,739, 15,186
College students, 109, 1,005, 1,006, 1,130, **1,553**, 3,015, 4,430, **4,612**, 5,306, 5,331, 6,008, **6,332**, 6,338, 6,817, 6,862, **7,156**, **7,495**, **7,575**, **7,578**, **7,725**, 7,735, 7,748, 7,777, 7,814, 7,819, 7,833, 7,893, 8,172, 8,367, 8,599, 8,601, 8,613, **8,614**, 8,748, **8,800**, 8,807, 9,161, **9,569**, **9,802**, 9,827, 9,838, 10,005, 10,022, 10,775, **11,151**, **11,302**, 11,520, 11,531, **11,552**, 11,641, 11,652, 11,707, **12,012**, **12,918**, **12,919**, **12,922**, 13,155, 13,257, **13,335**, 13,470, **13,886**, 14,033, 14,654, **14,757**, 15,189, 15,241, 15,242, 15,953, 16,006, 16,329, **16,332**, **16,338**, **16,361**, 16,390, 16,810, 16,873, **16,990**, **16,995**, 17,043, 17,195, 17,461, 17,615, **17,628**, **17,778**, **17,780**, **17,781**, **17,782**
   health and hygiene, 2,069, 7,577, 8,540, 9,942
   political activities, 10,020, 11,847
   wives, **13,197**
College students, Afro-American, 2,880, 4,382
College students, Jewish, 7,545
College teachers, 97, 104, 177, 224, 265, **266**, 337, **344**, **395**, **479**, 561, 650, **821**, **930**, **952**, **1,088**, 1,125, **1,128**, 1,130, **1,161**, 1,162, 1,409, **1,425**, 1,509, 1,545, **1,546**, **1,548**, **1,550**, 1,551, **1,556**, **1,604**, 1,645, 1,655, **1,671**, **1,674**, **1,677**, 1,804, **1,839**, 1,842, 1,843, 1,844, 1,845, 1,846, 1,849, 1,851, 1,858, 1,859, 1,921, **1,983**, 1,998, 2,125, **2,130**, 2,540, **2,660**, 2,784, 2,884, 2,927, 2,931, 3,126, **3,305**, 3,316, 3,318, 3,347, 3,405, 4,028, 4,040, **4,272**, **4,304**, **4,319**, 4,361, 4,374, **4,378**, **4,385**, **4,387**, **4,389**, **4,393**, **4,397**, 4,406, 4,489, **4,539**, **4,682**, **4,686**, **4,690**, **4,691**, **4,710**, **4,916**, **4,935**, **4,940**, 4,958, 5,035, **5,063**, **5,068**, **5,070**, **5,079**, 5,082, 5,083, 5,084, 5,085, 5,101, 5,102, 5,103, 5,170, 5,172, **5,211**, 5,251, 5,259, **5,300**, **5,323**, 5,372, **5,394**, **5,432**, **5,455**, **5,460**, 5,466, **5,468**, **5,477**, **5,512**, **5,550**, **5,632**, 5,829, **5,865**, 5,868, **5,977**, 5,998, 6,087, 6,095, **6,126**, **6,143**, 6,223, **6,239**, **6,266**, **6,268**, **6,283**, **6,284**, 6,293, **6,295**, **6,296**, **6,297**, **6,305**, **6,334**, **6,354**, **6,379**, **6,448**, 6,459, **6,590**, **6,607**, 6,622, **6,651**, **6,684**, **6,726**, **6,733**, **6,754**, **6,835**, **6,848**, **6,852**, 6,870, **6,904**, 6,928, 6,933, **6,935**, **6,946**, 6,955, 6,987, **6,997**, 7,158, **7,499**, 7,567, 7,620, 7,680, **7,747**, 7,818, 7,851, 7,873, **7,876**, **7,891**, **8,042**, **8,043**, 8,049, 8,050, 8,058, 8,073, **8,126**, **8,150**, **8,155**, 8,189, **8,191**, **8,192**, **8,232**, **8,244**, **8,247**, **8,348**, 8,492, 8,530, 8,535, 8,538, 8,539, 8,555, **8,557**, **8,559**, **8,575**, **8,580**, 8,593, 8,596, **8,597**, **8,603**, 8,607, 8,609, **8,611**, 8,617, **8,619**, **8,623**, **8,642**, **8,653**, **8,755**, **8,759**, 8,788, 8,793, **8,805**, **8,806**, 8,807, **8,809**, **8,814**, **8,815**, **8,913**, 8,995, 9,047, 9,052, 9,081, **9,120**, 9,176, **9,347**, 9,359, **9,425**, 9,467, **9,569**, 9,572, **9,610**, **9,650**, 9,828, **9,839**, 9,857, **9,936**, 9,948, **9,960**, 9,997, 9,998, 10,027, 10,049, 10,060, **10,062**, **10,073**, **10,207**, **10,208**, **10,209**, 10,210, **10,477**, 10,492, **10,522**, **10,554**, **10,556**, 10,568, 10,603, 10,766, 10,775, 10,971, 10,974, 11,029, **11,170**, **11,239**, 11,244, **11,246**, 11,278, 11,282, 11,285, **11,297**, **11,306**, **11,363**, **11,364**, **11,366**, **11,374**, **11,383**, 11,526, **11,543**, **11,545**, 11,551, 11,575, **11,593**, **11,619**, **11,631**, **11,656**, 11,659, **11,677**, **11,682**, 11,685, 11,688, 11,707, **11,735**, **11,739**, 11,747, 11,748, 11,749, 11,764, 11,770, 11,776, 11,807, 11,857, 11,858, 11,888, **11,912**, **11,957**, 11,968, 11,982, **11,986**, **12,009**, **12,016**, **12,017**, **12,024**, 12,031, **12,043**, 12,047, **12,049**, **12,055**, **12,063**, 12,622, **12,642**,

12,765, 12,774, 12,803, **12,884**, **12,920**, **12,923**, 12,982, 12,998, **13,138**, 13,170, **13,177**, **13,189**, **13,190**, **13,191**, **13,192**, **13,207**, 13,225, 13,231, **13,240**, 13,243, **13,261**, **13,271**, 13,273, **13,289**, **13,632**, **13,671**, **13,698**, **13,746**, **13,749**, **13,755**, **13,870**, **13,879**, **13,882**, **13,883**, **13,891**, **13,895**, **13,896**, **13,954**, 14,005, 14,006, 14,122, 14,186, **14,216**, **14,217**, **14,272**, **14,273**, 14,332, 14,392, **14,402**, **14,577**, **14,706**, **14,742**, **14,744**, **14,759**, **14,798**, **15,092**, 15,196, 15,197, 15,217, **15,366**, **15,683**, **15,806**, **15,811**, 15,924, **15,925**, **15,929**, **15,934**, **15,964**, **15,986**, **16,212**, **16,249**, **16,295**, **16,304**, **16,328**, **16,347**, 16,351, **16,358**, **16,360**, **16,384**, **16,385**, 16,388, 16,485, 16,553, **16,555**, **16,881**, 16,890, 16,923, 16,971, **17,002**, 17,115, **17,187**, **17,240**, **17,263**, **17,266**, **17,303**, **17,322**, **17,463**, 17,520, 17,589, **17,626**, **17,662**, **17,712**, **17,735**, 17,764, 17,765, **17,770**, **17,773**, **17,775**, **17,777**, **17,788**, 17,817, 17,859, **17,860**, **17,868**, **17,869**, **17,870**, **17,872**, **18,008**, **18,019**, **18,021**
   salaries, pensions, etc., 14,274
   women, status of, **6,276**
College teachers, Afro-American, 6,790, 10,191, **15,918**
College teachers, Jewish, **13,810**
College teachers, part-time, 6,482
College Temple (GA), 3,422
College theater, 1,678, **11,480**, **15,193**, 17,792
College trustees, 1,081, 1,404, 2,047, 3,293, 3,321, 3,381, 3,667, 4,214, 4,388, 4,411, **4,470**, 4,494, 4,504, 5,063, **5,065**, 5,470, **5,995**, 6,201, 6,881, **7,165**, 7,264, 7,584, 7,714, 7,875, 8,096, 8,171, 9,193, **9,785**, 9,956, 10,989, **11,280**, 11,556, **11,569**, 11,600, 11,700, 11,701, 12,632, 12,712, 13,244, 13,249, **13,436**, **14,271**, 15,631, 16,225, 16,325, **16,996**
College Verse, 18,021
College Women's Club (NJ), 11,121
Colleges. *See* Universities and colleges; Women's Colleges
Collegian (IA), 5,079
Collegian (NC), **13,226**
Collegiate Methodist Church (Ames, IA), Ladies Aid Society, 4,815
Colles Family, **12,673**
Colles, Gertrude, **11,261**
Colles, Julia Keese, **11,084**
Colles, Mary A., 12,673
Collet, Emma, 8,315
Collet Family (IN, IA, MI), **8,315**
Colleton, Eleanor M., 9,964
Collett, Glenna, 997
Collier, Alfred, 7,047
Collier, Alice Light, **1,704**
Collier, Catherine [Mrs.], 10,134
Collier, Constance, 12,637
Collier, Daisy Adams [Mrs.], 2,901
Collier, Elizabeth (ca. 1844-?), **12,983**
Collier Family (CO), 1,704
Collier Family (FL), **2,901**
Collier, John (1874-1947), **8,077**
Collier, Julia Florida (1875-1967). *See* Harris, Julia Florida (Collier) [Mrs. Julian LaRose] (1875-1967)
Collier, Nina Perera, **2,743**
Collier, Phyllis (Feningston) [Mrs. John] (1896-), **8,077**
Collier, Robert, 1,704
Collier, Sybel A., 14,618
Collier, William Armistead, 1,279
Collier, William Armistead, Jr. (1874-1947). *See* Collier, John (1874-1947)
Collier's (periodical), 4,061, 10,894, 11,974
Collier's Encyclopedia, 6,947
Collin Family (NY), 11,440
Colling, Angela Juanita (Stott) [Mrs. Gerton] (1919-). *See* Brennan, Angela Juanita (Stott) [Mrs. Gerton] Colling [Mrs. James] Murray [Mrs. James Arthur] Connery [Mrs. Don] (1919-)
Colling, Berton, 13,669
Collings, Ada, 8,219
Collins, Annie Maria, 5,306
Collins, Betty, 4,063

Collins, Carrie B. H., **15,915**
Collins, Catherine, 6,068
Collins, Catherine [Mrs. William Oliver], 1,751
Collins, Catherine (Wever), 17,992
Collins, Charles, **9,849**
Collins, Deborah Morris Smith (1760-1822), **14,854**
Collins, Dorothy, 4,494
Collins, Dorothy (Spencer), **5,511**
Collins Family (MS), 9,631
Collins Family (NY), **11,412**
Collins Family (SC), 15,622
Collins, Fannie Belle (1867-?), **10,282**
Collins, Hannah (Daggett) [Mrs. Joseph M.] Buckland
  [Mrs.] (1802-?), **16,630**
Collins, Hannah (Pickering) [Mrs. Adoniram]
  (1708-?), **7,351**
Collins, Isabel Margaret (Porter) (1875-1954), **1,266,**
  1,330
Collins, Jean (1923-). *See* Kerr, Jean (Collins) [Mrs.
  Walter] (1923-)
Collins, John, 12,288
Collins, Josiah, **13,378**
Collins, LeRoy (1909-), **2,953**
Collins, Lizzie (1839-?), **17,420**
Collins, Lucile (ca. 1887-1968). *See* Dooley, Lucile
  (Collins) [Mrs. Patrick V.] (ca. 1887-1968)
Collins, Marie. *See* McGuire, Marie (Collins)
Collins, Mary [Mrs.], 13,378
Collins, Mary Ellen, 5,306
Collins, Mary (Garden), **14,338**
Collins, Mary Jane. *See* Bardin, Mary Jane (Collins)
  [Mrs. James]
Collins, Mary (Mudge) (1841-89), 11,412
Collins, Moses, 9,631
Collins, Mrs. E. Burke, 1,224
Collins, Richard (1824-89), Family (KY), **5,306**
Collins, Sarah. *See* Baker, Sarah (Collins) [Mrs.
  William J.]
Collins, Sarah. *See* Tyler, Sarah (Collins)
Collins, Sarah (1827-94). *See* McElroy, Sarah Collins
  [Mrs. Thornton Fleming] (1827-94)
Collins, Thelma [Mrs.], 7,064
Collins, William Oliver, 1,751
Collisions at sea, 14,993
Collitz, Klara Hechtenberg [Mrs. Hermann]
  (1863-1944), **5,727**
Collums, Thelma T., **9,607**
Collver, Harriet Russell, 5,582
Colman, Hila, **14,339**
Colombia, South America, medical projects in,
  13,206
Colonel Arthur Woods Committee. *See* United States
  (government), President's Organization on
  Unemployment Relief
Colonel Carroll Junior Club (ND), 13,696
Colonel Timothy Bigelow: A Historical Novel, 7,602
Colonia Juarez (book), 16,520
Colonial Club (Northampton, MA), 7,132
Colonial Dames of America. *See* National Society,
  Colonial Dames of America
Colonial Dames of the Seventeenth Century, 5,850,
  13,380
Colonial Dames of the Seventeenth Century,
  Arkansas Society, **280**
Colonial Dames of the Seventeenth Century, Sir John
  Ogle Chapter (IN), **4,552**
Colonial Records of North Carolina, 13,561
Colonial Records of Spanish Florida (book), 2,275
Colonial Williamsburg Foundation (VA), 17,110,
  17,125
Colonie Icarienne (newspaper), 4,302
Colonies
  administration, 1,510, **5,495, 5,496**
  law, 5,495, 5,496
  research, 16,296
Colonization, 16,083
Color-blindness, 11,659
Color-sense, 1,948, 11,659, 11,995
Colorado, 1,678, 1,709, 1,713, 1,732, 1,741, 1,750,
  1,758, 1,775, 1,790, 12,425, 14,680
  abortion, legal aspects, 1,984
  Afro-Americans, **1,683, 1,777,** 1,779
  agriculture, 1,786
  air bases, 1,769

amusement parks, 1,751
art societies, 1,673, 1,692, 1,754, **1,766,** 1,794
art teachers, **1,678,** 1,767
artists, 1,734, 1,751, 1,767, 1,779, 1,786, **1,800,**
  1,804
assessment, 1,807
authors, **1,685, 1,689, 1,750,** 1,751, **1,752,** 1,779,
  1,795, 1,801, 1,804, 14,335
autographs, **1,751**
biographies, 1,785
botanists, 1,779
businessmen, 1,698
businesswomen, 1,747
Camp Fire Girls, 1,817
camps, 1,798
cattle stealing, 1,786
chamber music, 1,788
charitable societies, **1,693**
charities, 1,673
children, employment, 1,731
Chinese in, 1,782
church schools, **1,740,** 1,786, **1,803**
church societies, Methodist, **1,813**
city councilwomen, 1,779
city planners, 1,779
clothing workers, 1,779
clubs, **1,667,** 1,673, **1,679,** 1,700, 1,716, 1,721,
  1,732, **1,734, 1,735,** 1,741, 1,744, 1,750, **1,758,**
  1,767, 1,771, 1,775, **1,776, 1,781,** 1,785, 1,791,
  1,792, 1,793, 1,797, 1,817, 1,818
college and school journalism, 1,814
college teachers, **1,671, 1,674, 1,677,** 1,804, 12,921
college theater, 1,678
community leadership, **1,684,** 1,779
composers, 1,788
congressmen, 1,670
constitutional conventions, 1,759
convents and nunneries, 1,786
corporations, **1,719**
councils and synods, 1,750
country life, 1,750
court records, 1,808, 1,809
crime and criminals, 1,771, 1,786
dancers, 1,750
deaconesses, **1,812**
department heads (universities), 1,751
diaries and journals, 19th C, **1,694, 1,727,** 1,737,
  1,816
drama, 1,798
  study and teaching, 1,749
dramatists, **1,795, 14,335**
editors, 1,686
education, 1,707
educational associations, 1,681
educators, 1,747
festivals, 1,751
flags, 1,786
folklore, 1,671
freedwomen, 1,776
gangs, 1,786
gardening, societies, etc., 1,734
gold mines and mining, 1,750, 1,799
governors, 4,700
hardware, 1,732
high school students, 1,779
historians, **1,676, 1,752**
historic buildings, conservation and restoration,
  1,756
home economics, rural, 2,673
hospitals, 1,753
hotels, taverns, etc., 1,750
insurance companies, management, 1,688
interviews, **1,779**
journalism, societies, **1,710, 1,761, 1,768**
journalists, **1,670,** 1,750, **18,009**
judges, 1,783
junior high schools, 1,713
jury, 1,817
juvenile courts, 1,675, 2,451
juvenile detention homes, 1,682
kindergarten, 1,721
kindergarten teachers, 1,721
land settlement, 10,059
laundries, 1,776

lawyers, **1,733, 1,782,** 1,783
legislators, **1,763**
librarians, 1,786
libraries and community, 1,777
lieutenant governors, **1,746**
linguistic research, 1,671
literary societies, 1,674, 1,749, 1,750, **1,787, 1,789,**
  1,791
luggage industry, 1,786
merchants, 1,790
military posts, 1,751, 1,786
mineral industries, 1,750
miners, 1,752
mines and mineral resources, 745, 833, 1,732,
  1,804, 17,209
mining camps, 10,756
mining corporations, 1,675
monasticism and religious orders for women,
  Catholic, **1,690,** 1,750, 1,786, **1,819**
mothers, 1,705
municipal officials and employees, 1,721, **1,722**
museum directors, 1,676
museums, 1,730, 1,785
music festivals, 1,788
music halls (variety-theaters, cabarets, etc.), 1,683
music, study and teaching, 1,749
music teachers, **1,686,** 1,788
musical societies, 1,788
musicians, 1,716, 1,788
Native Americans, 1,780
  reservations, 6,650
naturalists, **1,730**
newspapers, 1,757, 1,764, 1,790
  sections, columns, etc., 1,750, 1,800
novelists, **1,745**
nurses, Afro-American, 1,779
nursing, law and legislation, 1,753
nursing schools, **1,739,** 1,753
parks, 1,682, 1,817
patriotic societies, **1,708, 1,765**
peace societies, 15,316
pediatrics, study and teaching, 6,679
philanthropists, 1,747
physicians, **1,672, 1,733,** 1,779, 1,786, 1,790
pioneers and settlers, 1,630, 1,736, 1,750, 1,753,
  1,757, 1,780, 1,785, **1,790,** 7,677
poets, **1,795**
poets laureate, **1,718**
politics, practical, women's activism, **1,682**
postal service, postmasters, 1,746
prisons, officials and employees, 1,771
private schools, 1,786
prostitution, 1,751, 1,779, 1,786
psychiatry, study and teaching, 6,679
public health nursing, 1,706, 1,779
public officers, 1,747, 1,779
public schools, 1,713
public works, **1,798**
publishers and publishing, 1,786
quarries and quarrying, 1,750
radio programs, 1,786
railroads, 1,790
ranchers, 1,786
real estate agents, 1,779
real property, cases, 1,811
recreation leadership, 1,769
rescue work, 1,750
sanatoriums, 1,700
school boards, 1,779
school superintendents and principals, **1,707,** 1,814
scrapbooks, 1,698, 1,736, 1,786
secret societies, **1,796**
senators, United States, 1,669, 1,673, 1,746, 9,965
singers, **1,799**
social workers, 1,731
societies, Jewish, **13,790**
sociologists, 1,779
state universities and colleges, administration, 1,779
student counselors, 1,779
suffrage, 1,673, **1,759**
suffragists, **1,731, 1,745**
summer theater, 1,674, 1,751
Sunday-schools, 1,776
surplus government property, 1,811

symphony orchestras, 1,734, 1,788
taxidermists, **1,730**
teachers, **1,713,** 1,779, 1,803
teachers' unions, 1,713
temperance societies, **1,668, 1,805**
theater, little theater movement, 1,734
theaters, 1,774
toll roads, 1,750
trade and professional associations, **1,706**
tuberculosis, hospitals and sanatoriums, 1,672, 7,526
unemployed, 1,798
universities and colleges, 1,751, **1,784, 1,815,** 6,679
  administration, 12,921
  archives, **1,681, 1,814**
  urban transportation, 1,682
  Ute Indians, 965
  views, 14,204
  women's colleges, archives, **1,748**
  World War I, 1,689
  zoning law, 1,779
Colorado (brig), 406
Colorado and Red River (TX) Land Company, 2,624
Colorado Authors' League, 1,749
Colorado Club (TX), 16,263
Colorado College (Colorado Springs, CO)
  archives, **1,681**
  presidents, 14,706
Colorado Constitutional Convention, **1,759**
Colorado Council of Churches, 1,750
Colorado Federation of Colored Women's Clubs,
  1,760
Colorado Federation of Music Clubs, 1,788
Colorado Folklore Society, 1,671
Colorado Genealogical Society, 1,775
Colorado Mothers' Committee, **1,705**
Colorado Nurses' Association, **1,706**
Colorado Pen Women, 1,749
Colorado Press Women, Inc., **1,761**
Colorado Progressive Party, 1,669
Colorado River expedition (1871-72), 191
Colorado River Relocation Center, **1,415**
Colorado River, The (book), 308
Colorado Shakespeare Festival, 1,674
Colorado State Association of Colored Women's
  Clubs, **1,762**
Colorado State Federation of Women's Clubs, **1,667,**
  1,679, 1,734, 1,791
Colorado State Historical Society Museum, 1,676
Colorado State University, archives, **1,814**
Colorado Territory, 7,677
  pioneers and settlers, **1,703**
Colorado Training School for Nurses, 1,753
Colorado Woman, The (periodical), 1,814
Colorado Woman's Christian Temperance Union,
  1,668
Colorado Woman's Service Club, 1,734
Colorado Women's College, archives, **1,748**
"Colored Mammy and Her White Foster-Child, A
  True Story, The" (ms), 12,181
Colored National Democratic League, 3,301
Colored Woman in a White World, A (book), 2,602
Colored Women's Federation of Washington and
  Jurisdiction, 17,234
Colquitt, Alfred H., 3,135
Colquitt, Alice F. Murrell [Mrs.], **16,051**
Colquitt, Dorothy. *See* Arkwright, Dorothy
  (Colquitt) [Mrs. Preston S.]
Colquitt, Harriet Ross, 3,585
Colsan, Jennie Miller, 9,323
Colson, Mary J., 1,505
Colston, Mary B. [Mrs.], 14,809
Colston, W. H., 5,369
Colt, Miriam Davis [Mrs. William H.] (1817-post
  1899), **9,850**
Colt Press, 505, **1,573**
Colt, William H., 9,850
Coltman, E., 7,476
Coltman, Elizabeth (1769-1831). *See* Heydrick,
  Elizabeth (Coltman) (1769-1831)
Colton, Anna. *See* Clayton, Anna (Colton) [Mrs.
  John] (1820-?)
Colton, Elizabeth Avery, **13,381**
Colton, Olive A. [Miss] (1874-1972), **14,133,** 14,144
Coltrane, David S., **13,382**

Coltrane, Mrs. David S., 13,382
Coltrane, Ruth Louise (1891-1966). *See* Cannon,
  Ruth Louise (Coltrane) [Mrs. Charles Albert]
  (1891-1966)
Colum Family (NY), **11,286**
Colum, Mary (Maguire) [Mrs. Padraic] (1887-1956),
  11,286
Colum, Padraic (1881-1972), 11,286, 12,642
Columbia Art Association (SC), 15,719
Columbia Broadcasting System. *See* CBS
Columbia Circle (Clarence, IA), 4,960
Columbia College (MO), 9,951, 9,981, 10,001, 10,048
  archives, **9,824**
  faculty, 10,000
Columbia College (SC), **15,536**
Columbia College of Expression (IL), 4,762
Columbia Council of Jewish Women, 15,251
Columbia Equal Suffrage Association (MO), 9,851
Columbia Female Academy (MO), 9,942, **9,945,**
  9,972
Columbia Female College (SC). *See* Columbia
  College (SC)
Columbia Female Institute (Columbia, TN), 15,976
Columbia Female School (SC), 15,834
Columbia Garden Club (MO), 9,918, 9,935
Columbia, Hazel, 11,717
Columbia Heights Garden Club (MN), **8,390**
Columbia High School for Young Ladies and Little
  Girls (SC), 15,644
Columbia Interstate Compact Commission, 14,507
Columbia Law School (NY), alumnae, 8,957
Columbia League of Women Voters (MO), **9,946**
Columbia Literary Club (Dundee, IL), **4,186**
Columbia Memorial Association (SC), 15,775
Columbia-Presbyterian Medical Center (NY), 6,721
Columbia Public Library (MO), 9,935
Columbia Region Association of Governments (WA),
  17,311
Columbia Religious and Industrial School for Jewish
  Girls (NY), 7,527
Columbia River Gorge Commission, 14,398
Columbia River, mythology, 14,669
Columbia School of Oratory, 5,070
Columbia Street Baptist Church (ME), 5,644
Columbia University (NY), 2,146, 2,882, 4,528, 9,803,
  11,828, **11,847, 11,849,** 11,879, 11,940, 12,526,
  13,742, 17,445
  alumnae, 952, 5,477, 8,583, 8,597, 8,604, 8,746,
    10,974, 11,670, 12,009, 13,249, 13,289, 14,236
  deans, 2,157
  faculty, 5,869, 6,238, 10,475, 11,490, 11,660,
    11,835, 11,848, **11,912,** 11,941, 11,956, 11,957,
    11,966, 11,986, 11,990, **12,007,** 12,009, **12,016,**
    12,023, 12,028, 12,031, 12,050, 12,054, 12,055,
    12,063, **13,954**
  presidents, 11,826, 11,849, 12,036, 12,553
  strike (1968), 11,847
  students, 656, 1,675, 1,948, 3,514, 3,974, 6,239,
    8,962, 10,523, 11,054, **12,012,** 13,001, 14,135,
    14,453, 15,353
Columbia University (NY), Avery Architectural
  Library, 11,824
Columbia University (NY), College of Physicians and
  Surgeons, 11,068
Columbia University (NY), English Department,
  11,969
Columbia University (NY), Faculty of Medicine,
  6,721
Columbia University (NY), Institute of Arts and
  Science, **11,970**
Columbia University (NY), Libraries, 11,930
  Library Office, **11,971**
  Reference Department, **11,972**
  Staff Association, **11,973**
Columbia University (NY), New College, 13,261
Columbia University (NY), Oral History Project,
  9,415
Columbia University (NY), Rare Book Collection,
  11,921
Columbia University (NY), School of Social Work,
  faculty, 11,958
Columbia University (NY), Teachers College, 246,
  1,842, 6,157, 6,490, 9,909, 11,842, 11,864,
  11,897, 11,918

administrators, 12,712
alumnae, 9,526
faculty, 2,093, 5,346, 15,312
graduate students, 11,374
Columbia University (NY), Teachers College Alumni
  Association, 9,526
Columbia University (NY), Teachers College,
  Department of Nursing Education, **12,074**
Columbia University (NY), Teachers College, Lincoln
  School, 11,988
Columbia University (NY), Women's Counseling
  Project, 11,825
Columbia University (NY), Women's Graduate Club,
  11,825
Columbia University Teacher's College (MO), faculty,
  9,909
Columbian Women, 2,633
Columbia Women's Political Caucus (MO), **9,947**
Columbian Club (Boise, ID), **3,670**
Columbian Club (Minneapolis, MN), **9,010**
Columbian Club of Flint (MI), **8,177**
Columbian College, 5,823
Columbian Ode, The (poem), 3,923
Columbian Sentinel and Massachusetts Observer,
  9,636
Columbian Star (newspaper). *See Christian Index*
Columbian, The, 15,536
Columbus Baby Camp (OH), 13,994
Columbus Business and Professional Women's Club
  (OH), 13,997
Columbus, Christopher, 2,361
Columbus City Light Rifles (GA), 9,730
Columbus Day Purple Line (NY), 12,146
Columbus Enquirer Sun (GA), 15,585
Columbus Federation of Business and Professional
  Women's Clubs (OH), **13,991**
Columbus Federation of Women's Clubs (OH),
  13,992
Columbus Female Benevolent Society (OH), 13,996
Columbus Health Department (OH), 13,994
Columbus Motion Picture Council (OH), 14,022
Columbus School for the Blind (OH), 5,857
Columbus Section of The National Council of Jewish
  Women (OH), **13,993**
Columbus Symphony Orchestra (OH), 13,991
Colville Indian Reservation, 17,183
Colville Indians, **17,383**
Colville Mission (WA), 17,383
Colvin, Winifred Marie (?-1965), **13,843**
Coman, Katharine (1857-1915), 7,567
Comanche Indians, 13,682, 14,207, 16,097
  captivities, **16,036**
  wars, 16,117
Comanche Study Club (TX), **16,203**
Comandine, Adele, 17,699
Combined Chiefs of Staff, World War II, 11,874
Combs Family, 256
Comden, Betty (1919-), 11,907
Come Back Little Sheba (screen play), 17,797
Comedians, 967, **15,894**
Comedy, slapstick, 11,907
Comer, James (1797-1864), 12,984
Comer, John P., 2,345
Comer, Laura (Beecher) [Mrs. James] (1817-1900),
  12,984, 15,585
Comer, Lucretia (Garfield) [Mrs. John P.]
  (1894-1968), 2,345
Comer, Mrs. L. H., 15,549
Comer, Professor, 15,549
Comfort, Anna (Manning) [Mrs. George Fisk]
  (1845-1931), **12,917**
Comfort, Buelah Walton [Mrs. David], 15,271
Comfort, David, 15,271
Comfort Family, **12,917**
Comfort, George Fisk, 12,917
Comfort, Joanna [Mrs. Thornton], 15,271
Comfort, Lydia, 15,271
Comfort, Martha (Patty), 15,271
Comfort, Sarah, 9,274
Comfort, Thornton, 15,271
Comings, Sherman, 8,220
Comins, Verna. *See* Higgins, Verna (Comins) [Mrs.
  Rosco]

Comité Franco-Américain pour la Protection des Enfants de la Frontière, 6,619
Comly-Howell, Elizabeth, 15,142
Command Performance (drama), 17,797
Commemorative porcelain, 3,260
Commemorative postage stamps, 4,731, 4,756
Commentators. *See* Journalists
Commerce, 611, 6,193, 6,196, 12,213, 14,622, 15,765
Commercial Advertiser, 12,403
Commercial artists, 15,575, **17,437**
Commercial education. *See* Business education
Commercial Telegraphers Union, 14,533
Commercial travelers, 1,653, **4,810**, 8,344
Commins, Dorothy Berliner [Mrs. Saxe], **11,850**
Commins, Saxe, 11,850
Commission for the Feeble-Minded (GA), 3,399
Commission merchants, 3,496, 8,781, 9,055, 9,747, 13,121, 15,441, 15,532, 15,533, 15,613
Commission on County Government (NC), 13,352
Commission on Free Schools of the Parish of St. Philip's and St. Michael's (Charleston, SC). *See* City Board of School Commissioners (Charleston, SC)
Commission on Health Careers, 6,123
Commission on Indian Affairs, 17,266
Commission on Indian Affairs of the State of Michigan, officials and employees, **7,945**
Commission on Interracial Cooperation (Atlanta, GA). *See* Southern Regional Council
Commission on the Education and Employment of Women (NC), 13,565
Commission on the Education of Women, American Council on Education, **6,481**, 11,999
Commission on the Education of Women, American Council on Education, War Services Opportunities, **9,928**
Commission on the Status of Women, 10,197, 12,707
Commission on the Status of Women of the Commonwealth of Pennsylvania, 15,158
Commission on Women (KY), **5,282**
Commission on Women's Work and Industrial Studies, 8,142
Commissioner of Immigration, 6,925
Commissioner of the Poor (Eau Claire, WI), **17,509**
Commitment of the insane. *See* Mentally ill, commitment and detention
Committee for a More Beautiful Capitol, 2,456
Committee for a Women's National Abortion Coalition, 17,975
Committee for Completion of the Riverfront Memorial (MO), 10,203
Committee for Cultural Freedom, 2,284, 12,906
Committee for Defending America, 12,180
Committee for Economic Development, 6,914
Committee for Georgia of the Southern Conference for Human Welfare, 3,347
Committee for Modern Courts in Illinois, 4,125
Committee for Nuclear Responsibility, 12,042
Committee for Paradise Dam Project (MT), 10,328
Committee for the Extension of Labor Education, 6,895
Committee for the Improvement of Child Health, 1,348
Committee for the Lake Brazos Drive Median Strip Beautification Project (TX), 16,394
Committee for the White House Conference on Education, 7,826
Committee of Colonial Dames (NC), 13,617
Committee of Correspondence, 6,380, **7,207**
Committee of Fifteen, 138
Committee of Fifteen (Chicago, IL), 3,798
Committee of Fifteen (New York City, NY), **12,424**
Committee of Mercy, 12,180
Committee of Six Hundred (San Diego, CA), **1,207**
Committee on American Principles and Fair Play (Palo Alto, CA), 566
Committee on Care of Transients and Homeless, 8,679
Committee on Civil Rights in Metropolitan New York, **5,462**
Committee on Conservation of Cultural Resources (NC), 13,618
Committee on Economic Security, 6,982, 11,916

Committee on Environmental Information, 4,492
Committee on Exhibitions (PA). *See* Franklin Institute (PA)
Committee on Grading of Nursing Schools, 5,735
Committee on Human Relations (Highland Park, IL), 4,158
Committee on Instruction (PA). *See* Franklin Institute (PA)
Committee on Maternal Health, 12,736
Committee on Municipal Affairs (NY), 12,266
Committee on Northwest Indian Affairs, 17,266
Committee on Political Education, AFL-CIO, Area 8 (TX), **15,990**
Committee on Political Education, AFL-CIO, Women's Activities Department, 15,990
Committee on Political Education, congressional district 20 (PA), 15,321
Committee on Public Progress, 7,287
Committee on Racial Equality, 5,828
Committee on Relations with Radcliffe College (MA), **6,274**
Committee on Research in Home Economics, 8,567
Committee on Services and Shelter Care for Unwed Mothers (Santa Clara, CA), 1,534
Committee on Social Trends, 6,622
Committee on State Institutions and Properties (MO), 10,194
Committee on Streets (NY), 12,266
Committee on the Cause and Cure of War, 2,072, 14,987
Committee on the Harvard-Radcliffe Relationship. *See* Harvard University
Committee on the Status of Women at Harvard (MA). *See* Harvard University
Committee to Eliminate Discrimination Against Women, 11,143
Committee to Re-elect the President, 11,817
Committee to Secure Justice for Morton Sobell, **17,617**
Common Council for American Unity. *See* American Council for Nationalities Service
Common law marriage, 13,342
Commonplace books, 839, 2,522, 3,483, 3,496, 3,501, 3,526, **3,553**, 3,584, 3,586, 4,738, 5,929, 5,961, 7,039, 10,988, **11,078**, **11,120**, **11,137**, 11,173, 11,792, **12,228**, 12,469, 12,555, 12,580, **12,596**, 12,618, 14,951, **14,954**, 14,958, 15,065, **15,100**, 15,268, 15,492
Commons, John R., 17,757
Commonweal (periodical), 5,310
Communal family. *See* Utopias
Communally organized groups. *See* Utopias
Communicable diseases, 73, 344, 1,121, 7,208, 14,290, 14,854, 17,515. *See also* Epidemics; *and* names of diseases, e.g., Yellow fever
Communication, 7,729, 8,731
societies, etc., **16,175**
Communications Workers of America, 6,893, 7,729, **9,011**
Communications Workers of America, Local 3204 (GA), 3,449
Communications Workers of America, Local 7200 (MN), 9,011, 17,314
Communism, 1,564, 8,071, 8,126, 8,963, 9,605, 11,596, 11,761, 12,574, 12,702, 13,468, 14,451, 15,374
Communist countries, 11,857
Communist International, 12,705
Communist parties, 689, 993, 1,654, 11,917, 12,705, 14,453, 17,254, 17,278
Communists, 788, 903, 1,356, 1,357, 3,303, 6,365, 8,058, 8,069, **8,087**, 8,093, 9,159, 9,467, **10,872**, **12,705**, 12,884, 14,002, 15,332, 17,254, **17,635**
Community, 8,642
Community Achievement Contest (IA), 4,748
Community and school, 708, 3,787, **3,824**, **6,511**
Community art centers, 2,732, 4,977
Community art projects, 17,255, **17,334**, 17,366
Community Arts Association (Santa Barbara, CA), 1,526
"Community—Brook Farm, The" (poem), 6,655
Community centers, 1,817, 1,837, 3,905, **4,054**, **4,077**, 4,114, **4,139**, 4,308, 5,709, 6,701, 7,225, 7,242,

8,182, 9,104, 10,484, 11,623, **15,160**, 17,599, **17,827**
Community centers, Jewish, **8,983**, 17,664, 17,841
Community Chest, 2,885
Community Chest (San Francisco, CA), 647, 945
Community Chest (Colorado Springs, CO), 1,684
Community Chest (Greenwich, CT), 1,837
Community Chest (GA), 3,135
Community Chest (TX), 16,260
Community Chest-United Fund (PA), 15,201
Community chests. *See* Federations, financial (social service)
Community Church of New York City, 8,116
Community churches, **9,275**, **17,161**
Community Club of Charleston (SC), 15,522
Community Club of Enlisted Men (Charleston, SC), **15,461**
Community Club of Wellesley Lower Falls (MA), 6,806
Community College of Allegheny County (PA), faculty, 15,228
Community colleges, 16,242, 17,663
Community Fund (Columbus, OH), 14,022
Community Fund of Chicago, Inc. (IL). *See* United Way of Metropolitan Chicago (IL)
Community Fund-Red Cross Joint Appeal (Chicago, IL), 4,078
Community Health and Nursing Service (OH), **13,994**
Community Health Association (NY), 11,515
Community health facilities, 8,651
Community health nursing, **13,994**, **17,826**
Community health services, 8,713, 9,467, **11,225**, 15,264. *See also* Clinics
Community health services for children, 8,635
Community House, 14,437
Community leadership, **1,429**, 1,492, **1,684**, 3,316, 4,477, **4,502**, **5,538**, **5,542**, **6,355**, 6,467, 6,615, **6,682**, **6,727**, 6,803, 6,881, **7,542**, 7,648, 7,659, 7,671, **8,635**, **8,842**, **9,275**, 10,469, **10,472**, **10,484**, 10,521, 11,170, 11,914, **11,920**, 12,066, 12,505, 12,507, 12,803, 13,382, **13,442**, **13,604**, **13,615**, **14,535**, 14,552, **15,005**, **15,790**, **17,237**, **17,245**, 17,260, 17,341
Community leadership, Afro-American, 122, **6,716**
Community life, **5,688**, 7,716, **8,361**, 8,518, 9,058, 14,061, 14,695, 16,457, 16,488
Community Magazine (Boone, IA). *See Community Visitor* (Boone, IA)
Community mental health services, 458
Community music, 1,038, **16,432**, 16,446
Community Music School (San Francisco, CA), 755, 1,313
Community organization, 169, **386**, 412, 470, 3,302, 3,853, 3,905, **4,093**, **4,102**, **4,134**, **5,422**, **5,540**, 5,542, 7,926, 8,026, **8,487**, 8,654, 8,668, 8,671, 8,676, **8,681**, **8,836**, 9,150, 10,117, **11,006**, **11,007**, **12,078**, **12,079**, 12,751, 13,352, 13,783, 13,909, **14,021**, 14,605, **15,386**, **15,813**, **15,961**, **16,297**, **17,138**, 17,357, **17,475**
Community organization, Jewish, **13,899**, **13,900**, **13,901**
Community Relations Board (Cleveland, OH), 13,909
Community Relations Commission (Atlanta, GA), 3,343
Community Resources Council (KS), 5,228
Community Resources Pool, 6,582
Community Service Society (NY), 6,928, 8,664, 8,674, 8,678, 12,078, **12,079**, **12,080**, 12,081
Community, The (periodical), 17,635
Community Visitor (Boone, IA), 4,693
Community welfare councils, 8,360, 8,428, **11,013**, 13,686
Company A, Fifteenth New Jersey Volunteers, 11,092
Company E, Third Virginia Volunteer Infantry, 17,477
Company Flagmakers (NY), 3,687
Company H, Nineteenth Iowa Volunteer Infantry, 3,700
Company K, Fifth Ohio Volunteer Infantry, 3,922
Company Q (MN), 8,551
Company towns, 1,505, 16,965
"Comparative Study of Private Industrial Law, A" (thesis), 6,848

Compendious Lexicon of the Hebrew Language, A (book), 11,826
"Complete Book of Fiddling, The," 10,418
Complete Writings of Thomas Say on the Conchology of the United States, The (book), 14,901
Composers, 51, 262, 264, 372, 931, **1,021, 1,022, 1,023, 1,038,** 1,068, **1,195, 1,209,** 1,451, 1,788, 2,020, **2,021,** 2,023, **2,580,** 2,601, **2,641, 3,109, 3,628, 3,632,** 4,319, 4,689, **5,413, 5,483, 5,529, 5,531,** 5,534, **5,582, 5,910, 5,920, 5,936, 5,937, 6,503,** 6,908, **7,267,** 7,270, 7,316, **8,444,** 9,467, 9,745, **10,118, 10,119,** 10,120, **10,121, 10,131,** 10,438, **10,478,** 10,481, **10,540,** 10,626, 10,651, **10,835,** 10,852, **11,215, 11,219, 11,230,** 11,907, **12,038, 12,050,** 12,160, 12,362, 12,685, **14,150, 14,440, 14,469,** 15,364, 15,367, **15,556, 15,915, 16,135, 16,317,** 16,438, 16,780, 17,400, 17,983, **17,999**
Composers, Afro-American, **2,852,** 3,294, **6,013,** 12,690
Composers and Authors Association of America, The, 4,758
Composition (music), **3,790**
Compton, Arthur Holly, 11,814, 11,815
Compton, Betty Charity (McCloskey) [Mrs. Arthur Holly], 11,815
Compton, Beulah, 8,676
Compton, Cyrus, **8,316**
Compton, Isa, 13,870
Compton, Martha (Lumpkin) (1827-1917), 3,058, **3,221, 3,381**
Compton, Mary [Mrs. Cyrus], 8,316
Compton, Pattie [Mrs.], 247
Compton, Sydney Amelie. *See* Burr, Sydney Amelie (Compton) [Mrs. Amos Shelton]
Compulsory military service, 9,159
Comstock, Ada Louise. [Mrs.] Notestein (1876-1973), 2,336, 5,122, 6,427, 6,452, **6,483, 6,484,** 6,503, 6,961, 7,158, 7,221, 8,558, 8,566, 8,896
Comstock, Alice (Van Hoosen) Jones [Mrs. Joseph C.] (1855-1950), **7,825,** 7,826
Comstock, Anna (Botsford) [Mrs. John Henry] (1854-1930), 832, 9,302, 11,508, 11,510, 11,528, **11,543,** 11,714, 11,742
Comstock, Elizabeth (1875-1972), 17,574, **17,618**
Comstock Family (WI), **17,574**
Comstock, George, 8,689
Comstock, Grace [Miss], 1,543
Comstock, Jane, 8,164
Comstock, Jesse, 8,689
Comstock, John, 17,859
Comstock, John Henry (1849-1931), **11,543,** 11,714
Comstock, Joseph C., 7,825
Comstock, Julia (1857-1937). *See* Field, Julia (Comstock) [Mrs. Eugene] (1857-1937)
Comstock Lode, 10,664, 10,677, 10,678, 10,717
Comstock, Noah D. (1832-90), 17,618
Comstock, Soloman Gilman, **8,689**
Comtes Rendus de l'Athénée Louisianais, 5,418
Conant, Isabel (Fiske), 7,868, 15,377
Conant, James Bryant, 6,299, 7,489
Conant, Lucy, 7,222
Concentration camps, 4,061, 14,445
Concentration camps, pictorial works, 12,891
Concerts, 2,743, 4,056, 8,611, 11,647, 16,013
Conchologists, **14,901**
Concilio Mujeres, **17,619**
Concord Female College (NC), students, 13,052
Concord Monitor (NH), 10,808
Concord School of Philosophy (MA), 4,684, 7,082
Concord, The (periodical), 16,565
Concordia College (Moorhead, MN)
  alumnae, 8,397
  faculty, **8,805**
Condict, Alice, 7,761
Condict, Anna, 7,761
Condict Family (MI), **7,761**
Condict, Ira, 11,086
Condict, Jemima [Miss] (1757-79), **11,085**
Condict, John H. N., 10,950, 10,973
Condict, Marion Angevine (Freeman) [Mrs. John H. N.] (1876-?), **10,950,** 10,973
Condict, Ruth W. (1798-1815), **11,086**

Condit, Caroline W. (1830-?), 11,122
Condit, Phebe Williams, 11,138
Condit-Smith, Louise A. (1869-1943). *See* Wood, Louise A. (Condit-Smith) [Mrs. Leonard] (1869-1943)
Conditions in the Millinery Industry in the United States (bulletin), 2,703
Conditions of labor, 9,473
Condon, Kate. [Mrs. Edward Burke] Scott, 3,745
Condor (ship), 13,419
Condottiere (book), 6,113
Conduct of life, 7,650, 13,490. *See also* Family life education
Conductors (music), 2,020, 2,023, 2,123, 11,218, 14,639, 17,425
Conductors (music), Afro-American, 12,690
Cone, Bonnie Ethel [Miss] (1907-), 13,185, 13,186, 13,187
Cone, Claribel [Miss] (1864-1929), 5,721
Cone, Etta [Miss] (1870-1949), 5,721
Cone, Mary Elizabeth (Thropp), 11,602
Cone, Sara A., 14,542
Cone, Sarah (1787-1873). *See* Baxter, Sarah (Cone) (1787-1873)
Conellian, 5,079
Conelly, Catherine, 11,445
Coney, Delphine (1853-95), **11,544**
Coney Female Academy (ME), 5,679
Coney, Thelma, **17,244**
Confectionary, 8,269
Confederate Congress, 5,549
Confederate Home and College (Charleston, SC), **15,462,** 15,535, 15,692, 15,727
Confederate Home Commission (SC), **15,538**
Confederate Home School (SC). *See* Confederate Home and College (Charleston, SC)
Confederate States of America, 101, 3,254, 3,551, 5,415, 5,818, 9,715, 13,571, 15,477, 17,079, 17,092, 17,099, 17,103. *See also* United States, Civil War (1861-1865)
  communications, 3,319
  defenses, 1,619, 15,658, 16,144, 17,093
  economic conditions, 7,613, 15,621
  flag, 13,374
  history, 2,381, 3,262, 9,799, 15,475
  hospitals, charities, etc., 68, 3,146, 3,151
  monuments, 13,340
  officials and employees, 2,892, 2,907, 7,613
  politics and government, 13,136, 15,766
  printers' marks, 38
  registers, 3,262
  social conditions, 80, 5,436, 13,374, 13,598, **15,954,** 17,100
  social life and customs, 68, 79
Confederate States of America, Army, 19, 3,176, 3,315
  cavalry, 13,059
    surgeons, 9,630
  chaplains, 2,455, **2,983,** 9,801, 15,550
  Fifth Missouri Volunteers, 10,196
  infantry, 3,315, 3,317, 3,320, 3,323, 3,331, 3,344
    Company K, Fourteenth Mississippi Regiment, 9,651
    officers, 9,651
  officers, 68, 107, **1,457,** 1,619, **2,199,** 2,635, **2,978,** 3,247, 3,394, **3,593,** 5,321, 5,343, 5,350, 5,362, 5,770, 5,771, 9,696, **9,790,** 12,552, 12,943, 12,968, 13,028, 13,085, 13,171, 13,344, 15,401, 15,932, 16,029, 16,097, 17,103, 17,106, 17,477
  recruiting, enlistment, etc., 9,836
  registers, 19
  sanitary affairs, 15,769
  surgeons, 3,559, 15,533
Confederate States of America, Department of the Treasury, 7,613
Confederate States of America, Navy, officers, 3,334, 15,895
Confederate States of America, Quartermaster Department, 13,374
Confederate Veterans' Organization, 3,104
Confederated Southern Memorial Association, 3,419, 5,513
Conference for the Protection of Civil Rights (1937-38), 8,106

Conference for the Reduction and Limitation of Armaments (Geneva, Switzerland, 1932), 15,310
Conference Group of United States Organizations for the United Nations, 4,480
Conference News, W. S. C. S. (NE), 10,598
Conference of Allied Ministers of Education, London (1944), 3,257
Conference of Consultative Non-Governmental Organizations (1949-54), 2,407
Conference on Law Enforcement (DC), 9,372
Conference on Roles of Women, Iowa State University, **4,861**
Conference on the Cause and Cure of War, 4,897, 9,197, 17,654
"Confessions of a Breadwinner" (ms), 6,349
Confessions to a Heathen Idol (book), 11,543
Confidential Council, No. 13 (CO), 1,771
Conflict of generations, 11,890
Confraternity of Christian Doctrine, 8,383
Congden Family (VT), **17,039**
Congenial Circle of King's Daughters, Mary Fitch Circle (OH), **14,063**
Conger, Laura Darby [Miss], 2,285
Conger, Lesley (pseudonym). *See* Suttles, Shirley Smith (1922-)
Congo Polytechnique Institute (Africa), 13,276
Congregation Anshe Emeth Sisterhood (OH), **13,772**
Congregation B'nai Israel Ladies Temple Aid Society (AR), **13,773**
Congregation Emanu-El Sisterhood (WV), **13,774**
Congregation Emanuel Sisterhood (MI), **13,775**
Congregation of Our Lady of the Retreat in the Cenacle (Chicago, IL), **3,933**
Congregation of St. Scholastica (Atchison, KS), **5,164**
Congregation of the Holy Cross, 4,643
Congregation of the Sisters of the Holy Cross, 4,640
Congregation Rodeph Shalom Sisterhood (PA), **13,776**
Congregation Shearith Israel (NY), 7,549
Congregation Sherith Israel (San Francisco, CA), 939
Congregational Church (Albany, OR), Women's Missionary Society, **14,340**
Congregational Church Extension Boards, 5,463
Congregational Church of Anoka (MN), 8,389
Congregational Church of Bloomfield (CT), Ladies' Reading Circle, 1,889
Congregational Church of Christ (Ladysmith, WI), 9,005
Congregational Church of East Haven (CT), Ladies Benevolent Society, 1,889
Congregational churches, 161, 447, 6,775, **7,004,** 7,857, 8,255, 9,012, 9,290, 9,344, **10,460, 10,461, 10,464,** 10,534, **10,550**
  charities, 1,889, 7,001, 7,004
  clergy, 703, **3,991,** 4,436, **4,829, 4,889,** 5,856, 7,335, 7,611, 7,616, 7,652, **7,662, 9,443,** 10,806, **12,318, 12,540,** 12,790, 14,508, 17,029, 17,971
  education, 6,817
  missionaries, **742,** 812, **884,** 7,678, 10,460, **14,119, 14,470,** 17,373
  missionaries, medical, **14,316**
  missions, 447, 5,701, **6,173,** 7,678, 14,119, 14,470
Congregational Churches, Woman's Home Missionary Federation, 5,701
Congregational Conference of Minnesota (Minneapolis, MN), **9,012**
Congregational Conference of Minnesota (Minneapolis, MN), Minnesota Congregational Woman's Missionary Society, 9,012
Congregational Conference of Minnesota (Minneapolis, MN), Minnesota Woman's Home Missionary Union, 9,012
Congregational Conference of Minnesota (Minneapolis, MN), Widows and Orphans Aid Society, 9,012
Congregational Home Extension Boards, **5,464**
Congregational House (Boston, MA), 8,903
Congregational Way, The (book), 6,095
Congregationalism, 5,457, 5,467
Congregationalist, The (periodical), 2,311
Congress for Democracy in South Carolina, 2,879
Congress Lantern, The (PA), 15,244
Congress of American Women, 7,322

Congress of Mothers. *See* Parents' and Teachers' Association

Congress of Racial Equality, 14,453, 17,630

Congress of Racial Equality (Detroit, MI), 7,736

Congress of Southern Mountain Workers, 2,879

Congress of Women's Clubs of Western Pennsylvania, **15,244**

Congress Outlet (PA), 15,244

Congress to Unite Women, 17,975

Congresses and conventions, 113, 1,017, **1,069, 1,170,** 1,341, **2,084,** 2,095, **2,519,** 2,831, 2,878, 3,257, 3,704, 4,082, 4,100, 4,106, 4,624, 4,859, 4,861, 4,897, 4,918, 4,946, 6,368, 6,373, 6,423, 6,433, 6,582, 6,585, **6,675,** 6,729, 6,741, 6,812, 6,958, 6,990, 7,160, 7,183, 7,217, **7,238,** 7,239, 7,274, 7,318, 7,322, 7,729, **7,822,** 8,009, 8,093, 8,121, 8,144, 8,362, 8,540, 8,819, 8,834, 9,197, 9,201, 9,240, 9,368, 9,372, 9,956, 9,983, **10,754, 11,663,** **11,744,** 11,853, 11,958, 11,999, 12,415, 12,639, **12,707, 12,855, 12,857,** 12,921, 13,255, 13,398, 15,061, 15,269, 15,316, 15,877, 16,331, 16,789, 17,663, 17,776, **17,785**

Congressional Club, 1,670

Congressional Globe. See *Congressional Record*

Congressional hearings. *See* Legislative hearings

Congressional investigations. *See* Governmental investigations

Congressional Medal of Honor, 2,332, 12,754, 12,765, 12,770

Congressional Record, 2,697, 3,735, 6,435, 14,622, 15,889

Congressional Serial Set. See *Congressional Record*

Congressional Union for Woman Suffrage, 7,803

Congressmen, 110, 349, 699, **936,** 953, 1,506, **1,605,** 1,670, 2,190, **2,210,** 2,238, **2,251, 2,270, 2,298,** 2,322, 2,325, 2,379, 2,454, 2,489, 2,499, 2,508, 2,550, **2,638,** 2,972, 3,008, 3,712, 4,358, 4,375, 4,695, 4,747, 4,749, 4,759, 4,784, 4,906, 4,914, 5,010, 5,265, 5,267, 5,276, 5,321, 5,671, **5,676,** 5,775, 5,868, 6,330, 7,205, **7,544,** 7,615, 7,802, 8,117, 9,048, 9,084, 9,155, 9,159, **9,181,** 9,200, 9,225, 9,268, 9,400, **9,421,** 9,605, 9,624, 9,688, 9,706, 9,733, **9,932, 9,933, 9,938, 9,950, 9,957,** 9,986, **9,994, 9,996,** 10,062, **10,513,** 10,740, 10,800, 10,858, 10,862, 10,872, 10,948, 11,049, 11,602, 12,052, 12,180, 12,284, **12,342,** 12,485, 12,611, 12,814, 12,847, 13,091, 13,228, 13,926, 14,046, 14,062, 14,077, 14,284, 14,619, 14,822, 15,020, **15,030, 15,115,** 15,221, **15,695,** 16,058, 16,379, 16,965, **17,455, 17,466,** 17,472, **17,627**

Congresswomen, 99, 157, 184, **194,** 387, 863, 933, **936,** 984, **1,010,** 1,043, 1,605, **2,379,** 2,458, **3,372, 3,735,** 4,627, **5,504,** 6,710, **6,861,** 6,939, 7,203, **7,262, 8,397,** 9,001, 9,040, 9,155, 9,287, 9,467, 9,605, 9,934, **10,360, 11,016,** 11,123, 11,225, 11,243, **11,695,** 11,817, **11,934,** 12,069, 12,790, **13,282, 13,911,** 14,046, **14,202, 14,391,** 14,504, 14,587, **15,875, 16,880, 17,200, 17,268,** **17,466**

Conine, Eytje, **11,418**

Conine, Martha A. Bushnell, 1,751, **1,763**

Conjunctivitis, granular, 231, 5,318

Conklin, Annie F., 1,324

Conklin, Hannah. *See* Woodhull, Hannah (Conklin) [Mrs. Noah Hallock]

Conklin, Harriett V., 4,880

Conklin, Robert S., 15,326

Conkling, Catherine (Carter) [Mrs. Cook] (ca. 1900-), 11,181

Conkling, Grace Walcott (Hazard) (1878-1958), 7,158, 7,171, **12,641**

Conlan, Mildred, 8,676

Conley Family (KS), **5,174**

Conley, Frances, 15,134

Conley, Hattie, 17,379

Conley, Helena "Lena" (?-1958), 5,174

Conley, Ida, 5,174

Conley, Lyda Burton (?-1946), 5,174

Conlin, Roxanne Barton (1944-), 4,869, **4,982**

Connally, Elijah L., 3,256

Connally, Elijah L., Family (GA), 3,168, 3,256

Connally, Mary. *See* Spalding, Mary (Connally)

Connally, Mary V. [Mrs. E. L.], **3,168**

Connally, Mrs. Elijah L., 3,256

Connaway, Eleanor (Ficklin) [Mrs. John Waldo], 9,948

Connaway, John Waldo (1859-1947), **9,948**

Connaway, Penelope, 9,948

Connecticut, 1,887, 1,911, 1,918, 1,929, 1,958, **1,959,** **1,979**

abolitionists, **1,902**

abortion, legal aspects, 1,984

administrative agencies, **1,897, 1,915, 1,917, 1,936,** **1,938**

Afro-Americans, 1,837

education, **1,898**

agriculture, accounting, 12,392

almshouses, 1,939

Americanization, 1,891, 1,997

art societies, **1,884, 1,949**

artists, 1,920

associations, institutions, etc., 1,932

authors, **1,930**

beauty operators, 1,906

bible, societies, etc., 2,009

bibliographers, **1,912**

bonds, 1,882

businessmen, 7,608

census, **1,895**

chaplains, 1,922

charitable societies, **1,864, 1,888,** 1,900, 2,005, **2,026,** 7,517, **8,006**

chemists, **1,974**

child study, 1,910

child welfare, 1,906, 1,917, **1,925**

children

development and guidance, **2,353**

employment, 6,485

choral societies, **2,007**

church charities, 1,889, 1,890

church charities, Episcopal, **1,879**

church colleges, faculty wives, **1,980**

church records and registers, **1,889, 1,890**

church societies, 1,889, 1,890, **1,947,** 2,009, **2,026**

church societies, Baptist, 1,889

church societies, Congregational, **1,965**

civil defense, **1,936**

Civil War, **1,962**

clergy, 1,914, **1,942,** 4,484, 7,656

clergy, Methodist, **1,976, 1,977, 1,982**

clerks, **1,822**

clubs, **1,825, 1,834, 1,891, 1,893, 1,903, 1,910,** **1,913, 1,921, 1,925, 1,945, 1,954, 1,980,** 1,992, **1,994, 1,997, 1,999,** 2,000, **2,001, 2,004,** 2,009

clubs, Jewish, **1,993, 2,005**

coeducation, **1,975**

college librarians, 1,995

college presidents, 1,859, 1,956, **1,976,** 1,977, 1,982, 1,983

college teachers, **1,839, 1,842, 1,843, 1,844, 1,845,** 1,846, 1,849, 1,851, 1,858, 1,859, 1,921, **6,126,** 7,680

colonial period, 1,906, 1,915

community centers, 1,837

congresswomen, 1,605, 2,458

conservation of natural resources, 1,897

conservation of wild life, 1,835

constitution, amendments, 1,927

consumers' leagues, **6,485**

county courts, 1,915

courts, colonial, **1,915**

deans (in schools), **6,126,** 6,143

diaries and journals, **1,901, 1,970,** 2,009

travel, 1,425, 1,841, 1,852

divorce, 1,914, 1,915, **1,919**

editors, **7,675**

elections, local, 1,829

Equal Rights Amendment (proposed), 6,695

farm management, 1,885

floods, 1,901

friendly societies, **2,008**

gardening, societies, etc., **1,833, 1,835**

genealogists, 1,901, **1,940**

genealogy, 1,852, **1,905,** 1,918, 6,234

governors, **1,906**

high schools, 17,035

historians, **1,926, 1,939**

historic buildings, conservation and restoration, 1,892

home labor, 6,485

hospitals, 1,837

housing authorities, 1,837

housing subsidies, 1,879

inmates of institutions, 1,906

Irish Americans, 1,998

Italian Americans, 1,837

jewelry trade, 1,941

Jews, 1,837

judgments, 1,898

judicial statistics, 1,915

labor bureaus, **1,917**

labor law and legislation, 6,485

lawyers, **1,916,** 1,982, **7,672**

legislators, 1,937

libraries, **1,931,** 6,910

library associations, **2,025**

literary societies, **1,873**

local church councils, **1,965**

manufacturing, 1,955

medical colleges, 6,679

medical societies, 15,145

missions, finance, **1,904**

monasticism and religious orders for women, Catholic, **1,985, 2,027**

municipal government, records and correspondence, **1,933**

museum directors, 1,827

musical societies, **1,830**

Native Americans, 1,887

newspapers, 11,867

nurses, 1,895, 1,906

nursing schools, 6,126, 6,143

nursing, study and teaching, 6,126

oral history, **1,837**

orphans and orphan asylums, 1,938

patriotic societies, **1,899,** 1,905, **1,934**

peace societies, 6,695

pediatrics, study and teaching, 6,679

pensions, military, **1,924**

periodicals, 1,910

Polish Americans, 1,837

political parties, 2,218

politicians, **1,868,** 1,878, **1,886, 1,928**

politics and government, 6,673

politics, practical, women's activism, 1,837, **1,894,** 6,723

prisons, 1,939

private schools, **1,836,** 1,837, **1,967, 2,003, 2,024**

psychiatry, study and teaching, 6,679

public health nursing, 1,837

public schools, records and correspondence, **2,003**

publishers and publishing, 7,675

reformatories (female), 1,979

school boards, 1,829, 7,941

schools, **1,865,** 1,874, 1,876, 1,901, 1,979, **2,006,** 4,489, 6,548

seed industry and trade, 1,939

Seton Indians, 1,837

sex discrimination, law and legislation, **1,927**

social service, **6,378**

social settlements, 1,891, 1,997, 7,243

societies, **1,923**

stores, retail, 1,837

students, Afro-American, 1,874

students' societies, 14,030

suffrage, 6,695

suffrage societies, **1,872, 1,896, 1,908,** 1,950, 6,876, 7,941

suffragists, 1,820, **6,256**

Sunday-schools, 1,890, 1,958

teachers, 1,863, 1,900, 1,933, 1,971, 7,935

temperance societies, **1,943, 1,944, 1,946**

theater, little theater movement, **1,996**

theological seminaries, 1,839, 1,841, 1,842, 1,843, 1,844, 1,845, 1,846, **1,848,** 1,849, 1,851, 1,853, 1,855, 1,856, 1,858, 1,859, 6,379, 6,397

universities and colleges, 1,870, 7,680

administration, **1,841**

utopias, 1,590

veterans, societies, etc., **1,907**
vital statistics, 1,889, 1,933, **1,935**
voters, registration of, 1,933
wages, minimum wage, 6,485
War of 1812, personal narrative, 2,009
widows, housing, 1,879
wild life refuges, 3,062
women, education, 1,933
women's colleges, 1,906
World War I, war work, 1,891
Young Men's Christian Association, auxiliaries, 1,821, **1,831**
Connecticut Association of Women's Groups of the Young Men's Christian Association, 1,831
Connecticut Child Welfare Survey, 2,353
Connecticut College (New London, CT), 1,906, 6,914, 12,737
Connecticut College for Women. *See* Connecticut College (New London, CT)
Connecticut Committee for the Equal Rights Amendment, 6,695
Connecticut Federation of Women's Clubs, **1,893**
Connecticut Indian Association, 1,932
Connecticut Industrial School for Girls, 1,979
Connecticut League of Nations Association, 6,695
Connecticut League of Women Voters, **1,894**
Connecticut Military Census, **1,895**
Connecticut Nutmeg, 11,867
Connecticut State Federation of Music Clubs, 2,007
Connecticut State Federation of Women's Clubs, 2,000
Connecticut State Labor Department, Women's Division, 1,917
Connecticut Welfare Department, **1,938**
Connecticut Woman Suffrage Association, 1,872, **1,896**, 1,950, 6,876, 7,941
Connecticut Women's Indian Association, 10,483
Connelly, Bridget [Mrs. Michael] (1853-1952), **10,283**
Connelly, Cornelia Augusta (Peacock) (1809-79), 15,265
Connelly, Heidi G., 9,986
Connelly, Karin Lundquist (1896-), 1,068
Connelly, Michael (1848-1944), **10,283**
Connelly, Polly (1940-), **3,827**
Conner, Alma Graham, 9,709
Conner, Ann S. (1826-1918). *See* Hartsuck, Ann S. (Conner) [Mrs. Mark] (1826-1918)
Conner, B. Pearl [Mrs.], **10,284**
Conner, David (1792-1856), 11,500, 15,167
Conner Family (PA), **15,167**
Conner, George Sherman (1895-1972), **16,342**
Conner, Henry Workman, 12,985
Conner, J. S. (1838-84), 413
Conner, James, 12,985
Conner, Jeffie Obrea (Allen) [Mrs. George Sherman], **16,342**
Conner, Julia Ann M. [Mrs.], **15,463**
Conner, Juliana Margaret (Courtney) [Mrs. Henry Workman], 12,985, 13,347, **15,577**
Conner, Louisa A. [Mrs. J. S.], **413**
Conner, Mary, 8,936
Conner, Stuart W., 10,284
Conner, Susan Dillwyn (Physick) [Mrs. David] (1803-56), 11,500, **15,167**
Conner, Virginia, **10,951**
Connery, Angela Juanita (Stott) [Mrs. Gerton] Colling [Mrs. James] Murray [Mrs. James Arthur] (1919-). *See* Brennan, Angela Juanita (Stott) [Mrs. Gerton] Colling [Mrs. James] Murray [Mrs. James Arthur] Connery [Mrs. Don] (1919-)
Connery, Debra. *See* Lockwood, Debra (Connery)
Connery Family (ND), 13,669
Connery, James Arthur (?-1959), 13,669
Connery, Kevin Michael, 13,669
Connery, Kimberly Francine, 13,669
Connett, Cornelia Ett (Thompson) [Mrs. Earl Fairchild] (1836-1919), **10,952**
Connett, Earl Fairchild (1826-1914), 10,952
Connolly, James, 11,597
Connolly, Vera Leona (1888-1964), **11,974**
Connor, Jeannette Thurber [Mrs. Washington Everett] (?-1927), **2,275**

Connor, Mabel [Miss], 5,587
Connor, Mamie E., **7,762**
Connor, Otelia Carrington (Cuningham) [Mrs. David M.] (1894-1969), **12,986**
Conover, Allan Darst (1854-1929), 17,620
Conover, Charlotte Reeve, 14,046
Conover, Edith Williams (1852-1931), 17,620
Conover, Frederic King (1857-1919), 17,620
Conover, Julia Ann (1781-1834). *See* Schureman, Julia Ann (Conover) [Mrs. John] (1781-1834)
Conover, Julia Darst [Mrs. Obadiah Milton] (?-1863), 17,620
Conover, Mary, 10,901
Conover, Obadiah Milton (1825-84), **17,620**
Conover, Sarah Fairchild [Mrs. Eliab B.] Dean [Mrs. Obadiah Milton], 17,620, 17,629
Conover, Sinechy, 10,901
Conover, Wilbur, 17,620
Conqueror or Conquered? (book), 9,658
"Conqueror, The" (ms), 1,395
"Conquest Through Self Conquest" (ms), 7,233
Conrad brothers, 10,242
Conrad, Earl, **12,683**
Conrad, Joseph, 11,979, 16,164
Conrad, Peter, 17,632
Conradi, Edward, 2,927
Conroy, Hillary, 3,763
Conscientious Objector, The (periodical), 15,313
Conscientious objectors, 8,149, **9,900**, 10,692, 11,931, 12,703, 13,230, 15,314, 17,262
Conservation of natural resources, 518, 577, 1,837, 8,103, 8,715, 8,716, 9,381, 9,733, 10,689, 11,236, 11,495, 14,429
law and legislation, 1,897, 5,443, 11,695, 14,622
study and teaching, 4,686, 7,976, 16,256, 17,842
"Conservation of Womanhood and Childhood, The" (ms), 12,299
Conservationists, 637, 660, 781, **795**, 1,526, 1,594, 1,634, 2,310, 2,526, 3,735, **4,119**, **4,492**, 4,686, 6,336, 7,305, **7,794**, **9,302**, 9,467, **12,875**, 14,052, **14,398**, **14,819**, 16,197, **16,256**, **17,305**, **17,364**, **17,671**, **17,842**, **17,945**
Conservatism, 14,345, 16,253
Conservator, The (periodical), 2,610
Conservatories of music, 14, 755, 1,313, 2,151, **2,155**, 2,664, 3,180, 3,204, 3,367, 3,582, **3,788**, **3,789**, 4,056, 4,153, 5,543, 8,950, 9,467, **12,124**, 12,796, 13,932, 14,008, 14,346, **15,208**
Conservatorium (Stuttgart, Germany), 13,840
Considine, Mrs. M. H., **10,233**
Consignment sales shops, **13,841**
Consolidated Mining Syndicate (ID), 3,698
Consolidated University of North Carolina, trustees, 13,244
Conspiracies, 9,528, 9,721
Constance Lindsay Skinner medal, 12,570
Constant Circle, The: H. L. Mencken and His Friends (book), 113
Constant Heart, The (book), 4,622
Constantinople College (Turkey), trustees, 12,712
Constantinople Woman's College (Turkey), 1,562, 7,279
Constellation, The (periodical), 5,685
Constitution (ship), 481, 5,946
Constitutional conventions, 1,759, 3,389, 7,861, 8,160, 9,855, 10,046, 10,171, 10,199, 10,285, 10,334, **10,344**, 13,690, **14,247**, **15,068**
"Constitutions, Electoral Laws and Treaties of States in the Near and Middle East," 6,507
Constitutions, state, 2,925, 2,926, 10,286, 11,064, 13,532
amendments, **1,927**, 8,118, **9,450**
citizen participation, 16,259, 16,264
Construction workers, 1,666
Consuls, 261, **1,044**, 2,048, **2,604**, 9,204, 10,816, 11,316, **12,068**, 12,274, 14,634
Consuls, British, 2,966
Consuls, Italian, 9,277
Consultants Directory, 15,124
Consumer Advisory Council, 11,804
Consumer cooperatives, 11,804, **11,805**, 11,806, 17,340. *See also* Consumers' leagues

Consumer education, 3,805, 3,859, 3,978, **7,251**, 8,651, 8,655, 9,349, 11,805
Consumer Federation of America, 11,806
Consumer Interests of Minneapolis (MN), 9,349
Consumer protection, **1,013**, 11,805
Consumer rationing. *See* Rationing, consumer
Consumers, 2,688, 6,034, 6,345, 6,523
Consumers' League, 6,604, 6,765, 6,953, 13,972
Consumers' League of Connecticut, **6,485**
Consumers' League of Kentucky, **7,208**
Consumers' League of Maryland, 5,741
Consumers' League of Massachusetts, **6,486**, 6,707, 6,708
Consumers' League of New Jersey, 10,953, 11,011
Consumers' League of New York, 1,948, **11,763**, 11,905, 11,916
Consumers League of Ohio, 13,942
Consumers' leagues, 827, 1,652, 1,669, 1,948, 2,336, 2,359, **2,504**, 2,633, 2,647, 3,899, 5,741, 6,427, **6,485**, **6,486**, 6,520, 6,604, 6,707, 6,708, 6,765, 6,791, **6,793**, 6,953, 6,982, **7,208**, 8,144, **10,953**, 11,011, 11,143, 11,369, **11,763**, **11,771**, 11,897, 11,905, 11,916, 13,212, 13,942, 13,972, 14,144, 14,437. *See also* Boycott; Comsumer cooperatives; Consumer education
Consumers Union of the United States, Inc., 11,804, 11,805, 11,806
Consumption (economics), 453
Contemplative orders, **2,871**, **3,601**, **4,329**, **4,503**, **4,871**, 4,881, **10,613**, **11,448**, **12,845**, **14,782**, **14,785**, **15,147**
Contemporaries, The (NY), 2,767
Contemporary Arts Festivals, 4,384
Contemporary Club (Indianapolis, IN), 4,631
Contemporary German Poetry (book), 12,441
Contempt of court, 3,224
Conti, Bianca (1874?-1954), **414**
Continental Congress, 3,093, 17,083
Continental Group (Con Can), **11,851**
Continuing education centers, 3,308, 7,955, 11,910
Contraceptives, 1,529, 8,633
Contracts for work and labor, 3,223
Contracts, of married women, 13,396
Convent of the Annunciation (CO), 1,786
Convent of the Holy Child Jesus (Lincoln, NE), 10,611
Convent of the Holy Child Jesus (Cheyenne, WY), 10,611
Convents and nunneries, Catholic, 1,513, **1,651**, 1,786, 1,985, **2,121**, **3,744**, 4,466, **4,649**, **4,875**, **5,090**, **5,184**, 5,596, 5,689, **5,831**, 8,383, 8,848, 10,129, 10,188, 10,611, 10,916, **12,859**, **13,727**, **13,866**, 14,145, 14,225, **14,874**, 15,265, **15,492**, 15,639, 15,696, **15,845**, **15,866**, 16,019, **17,499**, **17,552**, **17,572**, 17,839
"Conversation with an Artist" (radio program), 17,325, 17,350
Conversational Club (Des Moines, IA), 4,729
Conversational Club (Dubuque, IA), 4,786
Conversational Club (OH), **13,918**
Converse, Amelia, **13,919**
Converse, August L., 2,578
Converse College (SC), 6,423
alumnae, 15,575
faculty, **15,570**
Converse, Florence, 7,585
Converse, John Phelps, 13,919
Converse, Marion (Singleton) [Mrs. Robert Marion] Deveaux [Mrs. August L.] (1815-?), 2,578
Converse, Martha, 13,919
Conversion, 7,607, 9,246, 9,886, 14,964, 16,428
Converts, Baptist, 4,601
Converts, Catholic, 3,872, 5,980, 9,991, 17,868
Converts, Methodist, 5,245
Converts, Mormon, 416, 554, **562**, 805, 855, 10,731, **16,409**, **16,433**, **16,463**, **16,467**, **16,468**, **16,474**, 16,486, 16,487, 16,489, 16,490, 16,525, 16,537, 16,557, 16,614, 16,674, 16,684, 16,691, 16,692, 16,693, 16,713, 16,723, 16,730, 16,735, 16,756, 16,761, 16,776, 16,838, 16,853, 16,892, 16,895, 16,897, **16,910**, 16,925, 16,943, 16,947, 16,952, 16,968, 16,974

Conveyancing, 15,499
Convict labor, 117, 6,106, 13,371
  abolition of, 53
Conway, Carle C., 11,851
Conway, Charity Anne [Mrs. William B.], 4,900
Conway Company, 11,851
Conway, William B. (1802-), 4,900
Conwell, Jennie (Hayden) [Mrs. Russell H.]
  (1844-72), 15,184
Conwell, Nima (1868-1950). See Tuttle, Nima
  (Conwell) (1868-1950)
Conwell, Russell H. (1843-1925), 15,182, 15,184,
  15,187
Conwell, S. Harriette (Brewster) [Mrs. Leon M.],
  15,184
Conwell, Sarah (Sanborn) [Mrs. Russell H.]
  (1842-1910), 15,184
Conyers, John, 8,117
Coody, W. J., 3,618
Cook, Addison Melville, 11,784
Cook, Alfred P., 11,546
Cook, Alice Hanson [Mrs.] (1903-), 11,545, 11,764,
  13,176
Cook, Anna Rose [Mrs. Addison Melville] (ca.
  1847-1920s), 11,784
Cook, Anne M., 5,469
Cook, Bessie Catherine Smith (1902-). See Kelsey,
  Bessie Catherine Smith (Cook) [Mrs. Leander]
  (1902-)
Cook, Betsey [Miss], 11,784
Cook, Cara, 8,071
Cook, Carol Halsey. See Stoots, Carol Halsey (Cook)
  [Mrs. William D.]
Cook, Caroline Halsey [Mrs. Allanson Melville],
  11,784
Cook, Cathleen, 11,847
Cook, Charlotte, 8,270
Cook, Charlotte Augusta Langdon (?-1902?). See
  Sibley, Charlotte Augusta Langdon (Cook) [Mrs.
  John Langdon] (?-1902?)
Cook, Constance Knowles Eberhardt [Mrs. Alfred P.]
  (1919-), 11,546
Cook County Department of Welfare (IL), 4,117
Cook County Hospital (Chicago, IL), 3,861, 4,108
Cook County Jail School (Chicago, IL), 3,826
Cook County Normal School (IL). See Chicago
  Teachers College (IL)
Cook County School of Nursing (Chicago, IL), 3,954,
  4,108, 4,117
Cook County Socialist Party (IL), 4,080
Cook County Taxpayers' Warrant Trust (IL), 4,078
Cook, Dana G., 7,920
Cook, Edith Clemons, Family (MN), 9,014
Cook, Elizabeth Sue (1936-77), 14,118
Cook, Emma. See Crane, Emma (Cook)
Cook, Estelle, 8,608
Cook Family (MI, NY), 8,270
Cook Family (NY), 11,784
Cook Family (NC), 13,269
Cook, Fannie (Frank) [Mrs. Jerome E.] (1893-1949),
  10,159
Cook, Florence, 9,232
Cook, Francis "Frank" M. See Patton, Francis
  "Frank" M. (Cook) [Mrs. Thomas McFadden]
Cook, George Cram, 12,029
Cook, George Hammell, 10,954
Cook, Georgia. See Thompson, Georgia (Cook)
  [Mrs. Ben]
Cook, Gertrude (Fallin), 256
Cook, Guy, 1,623
Cook, Helen Rawson, 10,961
Cook, James H., 2,206
Cook, James P., 13,383
Cook, June Osborn (1888-), 168
Cook, Katherine Augusta Westcott [Mrs. Richard
  Henry] (1847-1929). See Tingley, Katherine
  Augusta Westcott [Mrs. Richard Henry] Cook
  [Mrs. George W.] Parent [Mrs. Philo Buchanan]
  (1847-1929)
Cook, Lilla, 18,026
Cook, Louisa (1833-?), 14,134
Cook, Lucy (1851-1902). See McCandless, Lucy
  (Cook) (1851-1902)
Cook, M. F., 14,547

Cook, Madeline Grace "Madge" (1889-1972). See
  Tennent, Madeline Grace "Madge" (Cook) [Mrs.
  Hugh Cowper] (1889-1972)
Cook, Margaret, 15,290
Cook, May Estelle (1865-1961), 4,309
Cook, Minerva Hynes [Mrs. Jared Reese], 9,609
Cook, Mollie Price [Mrs. George Cram], 3,988
Cook, Mrs. Finlay, 1,307
Cook, Nancy Smith, 16,631
Cook, Nilla, 14,378
Cook, Nira. See Carroll, Nira (Cook) [Mrs. Henry]
Cook, Ola Delight (Lloyd) (1880-1958), 14,533
Cook, Richard Henry, 1,196
Cook, Ruth (Meyer), 945
Cook, Sarah, 8,270
Cook, Sarah (1849-78). See Williamson, Sarah
  (Cook) [Mrs. Nicholas] (1849-78)
Cook, Susan Keating (Glaspell) (1876?-1948). See
  (Glaspell), Susan Keating. [Mrs. George Cram]
  Cook [Mrs. Norman Haghejm] Matson
  (1876?-1948)
Cook, Wallace, 8,221
Cooke, Alice Rebecca [Miss] (1861-1956), 7,489
Cooke, Belle W. [Mrs. Joseph], 14,603
Cooke, Catheryne (1880-1954). See Gilman,
  Catheryne (Cooke) [Mrs. Robbins] (1880-1954)
Cooke, Charles Clyde Benton, 14,603
Cooke, Clinton Tyng, 14,603
Cooke Family (CA), 415
Cooke Family (MI, NY). See Cook Family (MI,
  NY)
Cooke Family (SC), 15,447
Cooke, Flora Juliette (1864-1953), 3,842
Cooke, Gaylord W., 14,603
Cooke, George (1793-1849), 3,079
Cooke, George (1848-1923), 7,044
Cooke, George Willis (1848-1923), 7,044
Cooke, Grace (MacGowan) (1863-1944), 415
Cooke, Harriette Jay [Miss] (1830-1914), 5,079
Cooke, Helen Temple (1865-1955), 6,487
Cooke, J. F., 3,527
Cooke, Joseph, 14,603
Cooke, Louise Stephens, 1,574
Cooke, Lucy (1827-1921). See Lester, Lucy (Cooke)
  [Mrs. Charles] (1827-1921)
Cooke, Lucy Rutledge [Mrs.], 1,267
Cooke, Mary. See Hopkins, Mary (Cooke) [Mrs.
  John L., II]
Cooke, Nattie Anna. See Lee, Nattie Anna (Cooke)
  [Mrs. George Hewit]
Cooke, Philos, 1,574
Cooke, Rollin H., 1,426
Cooke, Rose (Terry) [Mrs. Rollin] (1827-92), 672,
  1,426, 1,878, 17,010
Cooke, Sarah A. [Mrs. William], 416
Cooke, Sarah Ann (Bass) (1827-1921), 3,969
Cooke, Sarah M., 11,087
Cooke, William, 416
Cooke, William W., 13,384
Cookery, 1,167, 2,035, 2,048, 2,062, 2,510, 3,221,
  3,568, 3,598, 5,659, 5,858, 6,371, 6,387, 6,488,
  6,566, 6,572, 6,707, 6,907, 8,813, 9,098, 9,670,
  10,053, 11,070, 11,079, 11,089, 11,173, 11,573,
  12,248, 12,262, 12,306, 12,606, 13,463, 13,495,
  13,548, 14,155, 14,204, 14,854, 14,999, 15,345,
  15,450, 15,474, 15,532, 16,425, 17,027, 17,095,
  17,840, 17,841
Cookery, Arab, 14,907
Cookery, French, 6,465
Cookery, Scottish, 12,306
Cooks, 5,651, 9,874, 10,630
Cool, Peter Y., 1,393
Cool, Sarah Mahala (Aram) [Mrs. Peter Y.]
  (1836-1912), 1,393, 5,599
Coolbrith, Ina Donna. [Mrs. Robert B.] Carsley
  (1841-1928), 342, 448, 616, 707, 712, 720, 737,
  757, 1,081, 1,082, 1,090, 1,231, 1,268, 1,307,
  1,340, 1,395, 1,416, 1,417, 1,429, 1,447, 1,565,
  1,585, 1,602, 1,635, 10,029, 16,632
Cooleemee (book), 13,251
Cooley, C. W., 10,280
Cooley, Clara (1883-). See Campbell, Clara
  (Cooley) (1883-)
Cooley, Julia (1893-1972). See Altrocchi, Julia
  (Cooley) [Mrs. Rudolph] (1893-1972)

Cooley, Lucy, 1,072
Cooley, Rossa B., 8,678
Coolidge, Calvin (1872-1933), 2,267, 2,538, 2,542,
  2,640, 6,925, 7,133, 11,944, 13,999, 17,029,
  17,978
Coolidge, Dane (1873-1940), 418
Coolidge, Ellen W. [Mrs. Joseph], 6,196, 8,668
Coolidge, Ellen Wayles (Randolph) [Mrs. Joseph IV]
  (1796-1879), 17,056
Coolidge Family (VA), 17,056
Coolidge, Grace Anna (Goodhue) [Mrs. Calvin]
  (1879-1957), 255, 1,593, 2,267, 2,640, 3,907,
  6,925, 7,133, 7,138, 7,151, 17,029, 17,978
Coolidge, Joseph, IV, 17,056
Coolidge, Mary Elizabeth Burroughs (Roberts) Smith
  [Mrs. Dane] (1860-1945), 418, 621
Coolidge, Mrs. C. W., 3,382
Coolidge, Mrs. Marshall H., 9,015
Coolidge, Susan (pseudonym). See Woolsey, Sarah
  Chauncey (1835-1905)
Coolville Seminary (OH), 13,749
Commaraswamy, Ananda K., 14,740
Coombe Cottage (Ann Arbor, MI), 8,279
Coombe Family (PA), 14,979
Coombe, Sarah. See Shields, Sarah Coombe
Coombs, Mrs. R. H., 16,052
Coombs, Sarah Ellis (Day) [Mrs. Leslie McLean]
  (1883-), 16,634
"Coon Dog, The" (ms), 1,445
Cooney, Barbara (1917-), 5,999
Cooney, Cynthia Agatha, 3,891
Cooney, Joan Ganz, 11,845
Cooney, Laurette (1884-1946). See Taylor, Laurette
  (Cooney) [Mrs. Charles Alonzo]. [Mrs. Hartley]
  Manners (1884-1946)
Cooney, Martha (1826-1901). See Callanan, Martha
  (Cooney) [Mrs. James] (1826-1901)
Coons Family (MO), 9,878
Cooper, Anna Julia (1858-1964), 2,130
Cooper, Arvazena Angeline Spillman [Mrs. Daniel
  Jackson] (1845-1929), 9,852, 14,341, 14,534
Cooper, Augusta (Skeen) [Mrs. Samuel Inman], 3,316
Cooper, Barbara, 17,957
Cooper, Bella Taylor McKnight [Mrs. Felix], 17,245
Cooper, Caroline (Kendrick), 12,524
Cooper, Dorothy Pendleton (1900-73), 14,731
Cooper, Elias C., 1,608
Cooper, Elizabeth (1877-?), 4,005
Cooper, Elizabeth (1909-). See Terwilliger, Elizabeth
  (Cooper) (1909-)
Cooper, Elvira (Langdon) (?-1898), 8,195
Cooper, Evelyn N., 2,678
Cooper, Frank, 17,957
Cooper, Gary, 8,531
Cooper, Harriet (1856-96), 11,547
Cooper, Harriet (1923-). See Alpern, Harriet
  (Cooper) [Mrs. Bryce] (1923-)
Cooper, I. W., 9,610
Cooper, Ida A. See Douglas, Ida A. (Cooper) [Mrs.
  Thurlow]
Cooper Institute, students, 1,581
Cooper, Jacob Calvin (1845-1937), 14,535
Cooper, James Fenimore, 5,951, 15,717
Cooper, Jamie Lee, 6,001
Cooper, Jane, 16,163
Cooper, Jane (Drake) [Mrs. I. W.] (1875-1963),
  9,610
Cooper, John Sherman, 6,489
Cooper, Kate (Wheeler) (1833-1912), 13,262
Cooper, Katherine (Wakeman), 890
Cooper Laboratories (CT), 6,743
Cooper, Lorraine (Rowan) [Mrs. John Sherman]
  (1906-), 6,489
Cooper, Lucy C. (Vrooman) [Mrs. William Jonathan]
  (1878-1947), 3,621
Cooper, Margaret Cochrane, 7,920
Cooper, Martha (1747-1823). See Allinson, Martha
  (Cooper) (1747-1823)
Cooper, Mary Ophelia (1857-?). See Myers, Mary
  Ophelia (Cooper) [Mrs. John Ephraim] (1857-?)
Cooper, Maude (Doyle) Prickett (1914-76), 17,958
Cooper, May I. [Miss], 4,779
Cooper, Mrs. James Fenimore, 15,717
Cooper, Nan P., 9,852

Cooper, Petra, 1,114
Cooper Ranch Inn (Oahu, HI), 3,621
Cooper, Robert, 16,505
Cooper, Sarah Brown (Ingersoll) [Mrs. Halsey
  Fenimore] (1835-96), 1,083, **11,547**
Cooper, Sarah Paxen, 6,310
Cooper, Signe S., **17,766**
Cooper, Sue Hamilton (1887-1968), **17,246**
Cooper, Susan Augusta Fenimore (1813-94), 3,908
Cooper Union (NY), 6,451
Cooper, Vera Southwick (1890-), **4,523**, 11,938
Cooperation for American Relief Everywhere, 17,823
Co-operative Club (CO), 1,734
Cooperative for American Relief to Everywhere
  (CARE), 10,048
Cooperative societies, 623, **1,319**, 1,564, **9,136, 9,506,**
  10,674, 16,486, 16,489, 16,867. *See also* Utopias
Cooperative Union Activities, 8,994
Cooperatives, 5,829, 8,651, 8,655
Co-Operettes (CO), 1,734
Coopers and cooperage, 15,535
Co-ordinate College League, 17,091
Coordinating Council of Women's Organizations for
  War Service, 9,707
Coors, Dorothea Clara (Morse), 11,658
Copani, Peter, 12,367
Cope, Anna Garrett [Mrs. Gilbert] (1848-1918),
  15,341
Cope, Annette, 14,805
Cope, Caroline, 14,805
Cope, Clementine, 14,805
Cope, Ellen [Miss] (ca. 1885-), **15,341**
Cope, Emily (Kilbourn) (1808-1901), 11,471
Cope Family (NY), **11,471**
Cope Family (PA), **14,805**
Cope, Gilbert (1840-1928), 15,341
Cope, Mary (Drinker) [Mrs. Thomas P.], 14,805
Cope, Susan L. (Newbold) [Mrs. William Drinker],
  14,805
Cope, Thomas P. (1768-1854), 14,805
Cope, William Drinker (1798-1870s), 14,805
Copeland Family, 11,582
Copeland, John, 7,490
Copelin, Nida, 8,894
Copenhaver, Eleanor. *See* Anderson, Eleanor
  (Copenhaver)
Copiah-Lincoln Junior College (MS), 9,664
"Copied From My Mother's Writings—Elizabeth
  Millar Wilson" (ms), 14,689
Coplin, W. M. L., 6,215
Coply, Betsy (1796-1870), 7,035
Copper mines and mining, 8,373
Copperfield, Anna May [Mrs.], 1,662
Coppinger, William, 15,470
Coppock, Grace, 10,609
Copyright, cases, 14,736
Coquette (drama), 13,391
Coquette, or, the History of Eliza Wharton, The
  (book), 1,397
Cora (slave, NC), 2,124
Coral Island Club Hotel (Bermuda), 10,935
Coray, Harriet Knowlton Virginia (1846-72). *See*
  Dusenberry, Harriet Knowlton Virginia (Coray)
  [Mrs. Wilson Howard] (1846-72)
Coray, Martha Jane (Knowlton) [Mrs. Howard]
  (1821-81), **16,505, 16,635**
Corazon (book), 10,867
Corazza, Lorraine, 4,700
Corbett, Elizabeth Frances (1887-), **6,002, 14,342**
Corbett, Harriet B. *See* Adams, Harriet B. Corbett
  [Mrs. Eben L.]
Corbett, Marion, **12,186**
Corbin, Caroline Elizabeth, 3,908
Corbin, Hazel (1895-), **11,852**
Corbitt, David Leroy, **13,385**
Corcoran, Catherine, 11,457
Corcoran Gallery of Art (DC), **2,100**, 2,792, 12,912
Cord, William, 8,113
Corder, Charlotte, 9,979
Cordes, Esther, 15,499
Cordes, John, 15,499
Cordiner, Jessie C. (Turner), **4,413**
Cordner, Elizabeth P., 6,162
Cordon, The (Chicago, IL), **3,828**

Corell, Margaret [Mrs. Fred], 8,482
Corelli, Marie, 12,005
Corey, Alice, 11,443
Corey, Ashbel, **11,088**
Corey, Elizabeth "Bess" (1887-?), **15,852**
Corey, Mrs. Ashbel, **11,088**
Corey, Paul F., 15,852
Cori, Gerty Theresa (Radnitz) [Mrs. Carl F.], 2,668
Corica, Clara (1906-). *See* Grillo, Clara (Corica)
  [Mrs. Dominic] (1906-)
Cork, Anne McNeil Ward, 3,611
Corkhill, Emma Kate, 5,061
Corlett, John, 3,667
Corlies, Emma, **1,269**
Corliss, Florence Haskell (1873-1952). *See* Lamont,
  Florence Haskell (Corliss) (1873-1952)
Cormack, Maribelle (1902-), **14,343**, 14,470
Corman, Cid, 16,163
Corn Farm Boy (book), 4,306
Corneau, Barton, 4,355
Corneau, Octavia Roberts [Mrs. Barton] (?-1972),
  4,355
Corneil, Mrs. R. F., **9,611**
Cornelia Jackson Moore Day Care Center (GA),
  3,253
Cornelia Moore Day Nursery (GA), 3,135
Cornelius, Elias (1794-1832), **1,861**
Cornelius, Mary (Chase), 57
Cornelius, Sarah. *See* Perry, Sarah (Cornelius)
Cornell, Alonzo B., 11,550
Cornell Alumni Corporation, 11,556
Cornell Association for the Higher Education of
  Women (IA), 5,079
Cornell Association of Class Secretaries, 11,667
Cornell Child Study Clubs (NY), 11,756
Cornell College (Mount Vernon, IA), 5,110
  alumnae, 5,080, 5,082
  employees, 5,081
  faculty, 5,079, 5,083, 5,084, 5,085
Cornell College Alumnus, 5,082
Cornell College Bulletin (IA), 5,084
Cornell College Bulletin, Alumni Number, 5,085
Cornell, Dorothy, **11,548**
Cornell, Edward W., 14,536
Cornell, Emily (Castle) (1820-88), 14,536
Cornell, Esther, 11,951
Cornell, Ethel Letitia (1892-1963), **11,549**
Cornell, Ezra (1807-74), **11,550**
Cornell Family (OR), **14,536**
Cornell-in-Thailand Project, 11,603
Cornell, Katharine. [Mrs. Guthrie] McClintic
  (1898-1974), 2,424, 7,310, 11,344, 11,812,
  11,907, 11,997, 12,610
Cornell, Mary Ann [Mrs. Ezra], 11,550
Cornell Pay Clinic (NY), 11,869
Cornell Public Library (NY), 11,577
Cornell, Sara (Hughes) (1862-1938), **1,417**
Cornell Twin Study Club (Jamestown, NY), 11,756
Cornell University (NY), 1,652, 4,949, 6,223, 6,416,
  6,592, 7,209, 11,542, 11,555, 11,584, 11,586,
  11,599, 11,660, 11,743, 11,748, 11,903, 13,189,
  13,604, 14,745, 17,716
  administration, **11,538**
  alumnae, 2,070, 8,596, 11,505, 11,541, 11,546,
  11,591, 11,687, 11,688, 11,699, 11,702, 11,706,
  12,352
  buildings, 11,687
  curriculum, 11,661
  deans, **11,561**
  employees, 11,642
  faculty, 1,088, 1,748, 11,507, 11,521, 11,532,
  11,545, 11,566, 11,578, 11,580, **11,581,** 11,603,
  11,612, 11,619, 11,645, 11,656, 11,659, 11,676,
  11,677, 11,756, 13,176, 14,392, 14,706, 15,319
  history, 11,550
  presidents, 11,524, 11,543, 11,575, 11,635
  students, 11,526, 11,552, 11,557, 11,575, 11,610,
  11,641, 11,652, 11,661, 11,692, 11,707, 11,736,
  11,759, 15,341, 15,773, 15,936
  trustees, 11,556, 11,569, 11,600, 11,700, 11,701
Cornell University (NY), Agricultural Circle, 11,581
Cornell University (NY), Alumni Association, **11,508**
Cornell University (NY), Biological Society, 11,721
Cornell University (NY), Brides' Club, 11,581

Cornell University (NY), Campus Book Club, 11,581
Cornell University (NY), Campus Club, 11,581
Cornell University (NY), Campus Club Choral
  Group, 11,581
Cornell University (NY), Classical Association,
  11,721
Cornell University (NY), Cornell Dramatic Club,
  11,567
Cornell University (NY), Cornell Women's Dramatic
  Club. *See* Cornell University (NY), Cornell
  Dramatic Club
Cornell University (NY), Department of Household
  Economics and Management, **11,564, 11,565**
Cornell University (NY), Department of Institution
  Management, **11,566**
Cornell University (NY), Department of Speech and
  Drama, **11,567**
Cornell University (NY), Engineering Women's Club,
  11,581
Cornell University (NY), Ladies' Auxiliary to the
  Sage Infirmary, **11,635**
Cornell University (NY), Medical College, 11,869,
  14,943
  faculty, 7,226, 12,352
Cornell University (NY), Medical College, Dr.
  Connie Guion Building, 12,352
Cornell University (NY), Prudence Risley Hall,
  11,679, **11,680**
Cornell University (NY), Sage College, **11,694**
  students, 11,543
Cornell University (NY), Sibley Faculty Wives
  Society, 11,581
Cornell University (NY), Teachers' Association,
  11,721
Cornell University (NY), Wayside-Aftermath Literary
  Club, 11,721
Cornell University (NY), Willard Straight Hall,
  11,521
Cornell University (NY), Women Graduates'
  Association, 11,508
Cornell University (NY), Women's Club, 11,692
Cornell University (NY), Women's Festival (1971),
  11,751
Cornell University (NY), Women's Judiciary Board,
  11,752
Cornell University (NY), Women's Self-Government
  Association, 11,561, **11,755**
Cornell University (NY), Women's Southern Club,
  11,721
Cornell University Council (NY), 11,508
Cornell University-New York Hospital School of
  Nursing (NY), **12,351**
Cornell University Presbyterian Union (NY),
  11,721
Cornell, William (1812-91), 14,536
Cornell Women's Club (Chicago, IL), 11,713
Cornell Women's Club (NY), 11,622
Cornett, J. A., 14,980
Cornett, Jane, **14,980**
Corning, Charles R., **10,803**
Corning Clionian Circle (NY), **11,406**
Corning, Erastus (1794-1872), 12,191
Corning Glass Works (NY), 11,407, **11,408**
Corning, Harriet (Weld) [Mrs. Erastus], 12,191
Corning, Lizzie M., 10,803
Corning, Mary A. G. (De Camp) [Mrs. Edwin Weld]
  (1843-?), 12,191
Cornish, Alison. *See* Thorne, Alison (Cornish)
Cornish, Lena, 8,222
Cornish Theater, 17,281
Cornman, Ada, 8,955
Cornwall, Susan (1825-1905). *See* Shemwake, Susan
  (Cornwall) [Mrs. Oscar Lassiter] (1825-1905)
Cornwell, Irene, **9,017**
Coronary heart disease, research, 7,311
"Coronation, The" (story), 12,480
Coronations, 12,273
  Great Britain, 4,383
Coroners, 11,452, **15,427**
Coroners' inquests. *See* Inquisitions post mortem
Corozon Club (Los Angeles, CA), 10,358
Corporation for the Relief of Widows and Children of
  Deceased Clergymen, 5,827

Corporation for the Relief of Widows and Orphans (New York, NY), 12,088
Corporation law, 16,327
  cases, **10,104**
Corporation of the Sisters of Mercy of Erie County (PA), 14,794
Corporations, 1,014, **1,719**, 2,205, 2,624, 2,635, 3,623, 3,669, 3,682, 5,144, **6,960**, 8,057, 8,133, **11,851**, 12,203
Corporations, government, **2,695**, 9,733, 11,896
Corpus Christi Monastery of Poor Clares (Rockford, IL), **4,329**
Corr, Maureen, 11,485
Correctional personnel, 7,770, **7,806**
Correctional School for Women (PA), 11,003
Corrections, 3,430, 7,244, 11,965
Correll, Erasmus Michael (1846-95), **10,448**
Correspondence (newspaper), 8,082
Correspondence schools and courses, **5,958**
Correvan, Henry, 353
"Corridors of Power in Contemporary American Life" (photographs), 2,730
Corrigan, Mary Foutz, 16,576
Corrigan, Sister Monica, 1,007
Corruption (in politics), 10,050
Corse, Israel (1819-85), **12,187**
Corset, 9,918
Corson, Ada (Carter) [Mrs. Joseph K.], 419
Corson, Caroline [Mrs. Hiram], 11,551, 11,558
Corson, Eugene, 11,551
Corson Family, **419**
Corson, Hiram (1828-1911), 11,542, **11,551**, 11,655
Corson, Joseph K., 419
Corss, Mary Humphrey. *See* Booth, Mary Humphrey (Corss) [Mrs. Sherman M.]
Corthell, Evelyn. *See* Hill, Evelyn (Corthell) [Mrs. John]
Cortissoz, Royal, 12,648
Cortland Library Association (NY), 11,412
Cortot, Alfred (1881-1962), 2,020
Corum Family, 256
Corwin, Lena Rickords, 4,061
Cory, Amanda. *See* Forbes, Amanda (Cory) [Mrs. William H.]
Cory Family, **9,018**
Cory, Harriet S., 9,844
Cory, Johanna [Mrs. Arthur S.], **17,135**
Cory, Julia. *See* Bailly, Julia (Cory) [Mrs. Alexis]
Cory, Kate (1861-1958), **173**
Cory, Mabel (1873?-1951). *See* Costigan, Mabel (Cory) [Mrs. Edward P.] (1873?-1951)
Cory, Nancy. *See* Blum, Nancy (Cory) [Mrs. Louis]
Cory, Phoebe Frances, 9,018
Cosandy, Evelyn Graber [Mrs. Everett Wallace], 9,101
Cosho, Maude L. (1896-), **3,671**
Cosmé, Eusebia (1911-), **12,684**
Cosmetics, 4,716, 5,132, 9,841, 14,351
Cosmopolitan Club (NY), 1,948, 12,074
Cosmopolitan Club (Fremont, OH), **14,064**
Cosmopolitan Magazine (periodical), 4,061, 7,196
Coss, Warren, 13,707
Coss, William, 13,707
Cosseboom, Kathy (Groehn) (1946-). *See* El-Messidi, Kathy (Groehn) Cosseboom (1946-)
Cost and standard of living, 398, 2,317
Costigan, Edward P., **1,669**
Costigan, Mabel (Cory) [Mrs. Edward P.] (1873?-1951), 1,669
Costillo, Mary L. *See* Nichols, Mary L. (Costillo)
Costin, Ada Amelia, 13,268
Costley, Clara, **5,715**
"Costliness of Human Progress, The," 4,844
Coston, Nellie, 16,876
Costume, 1,080, 1,657, 6,032, 7,146, 8,765, 9,468, **17,802**
  conservation and restoration, 17,239
  history, 17,322
Costume design, 3,192
Costume designers, 12,086, **16,210**, **17,802**, **17,804**
Costume, Shaker, **7,040**, 7,047
Costume/Textile Study Center, 17,322
Cosulich, Bernice (1896-1956), **214**

Cosway, Maria Cecilia Louisa (Hadfield) [Mrs. Richard] (1759-1838), **2,276**
Coterie (IN), **4,553**
Coterie Club (Fremont, OH), **14,065**
Cotillion Club (GA), 3,254
Cotillion Club (Charleston, SC), 15,515
Cotrell and Leonard, Furriers (Albany, NY), 11,263
Cotsworth, Staats, 12,367
Cotten, Elizabeth Brownrigg (Henderson) [Mrs. Lyman A.] (1875-1975), **12,988**
Cotterill, George, 17,264
Cottin, Charlotte. *See* Gardner, Charlotte (Cottin) [Mrs. William Bunker]
Cottle, Barzelia, 10,777
Cottle Family (NV), 10,777
Cottle, Rebecca Rich, 10,777
Cotton, 3,115, 3,270
  marketing, 15,525, 15,723
Cotton, Ann (Steece) [Mrs. Josiah Dexter], 2,277
Cotton Blossoms (periodical), 3,209
Cotton carding, 13,322
Cotton Club (Colorado Springs, CO), 1,683
Cotton, Eugénie, 7,322
Cotton, Flora. *See* Etter, Flora (Cotton) [Mrs. W. L.]
Cotton, Helen, **9,019**
Cotton History Review, 3,052
Cotton, Josiah Dexter (1822-?), **2,277**
Cotton manufacture, **5,896**, 15,285
Cotton, Nancy (Zumwalt). *See* Hunt, Nancy (Zumwalt) Cotton
Cotton picking, 15,595
Cotton-picking machinery, 2,579
Cotton spinning, 13,322
Cotton States International Expositon (Atlanta, GA, 1895), 1,932, 3,151, 3,275
Cotton, Sylvia (1913-), **4,081**
Cotton textiles, **6,202**
Cottonwood Baptist Church (TX), 16,365
Cottrell, Ann, 11,493
Coues, Lucy Louisa (1837-1921). *See* Flower, Lucy Louisa (Coues) (1837-1921)
Cougar Lakes Wilderness Area (WA), 17,251
Coughlin, Sister Mary Samuel (1868-1959), 17,868
Coulson, Mrs. Kenneth, 1,791
Coulson, Mrs. M. B., 9,466
Coultas Family (WA), **17,406**
Coultas, Mary Fife Smith, 17,406
Coulter, Edith Margaret [Miss] (1880-1963), **420**
Coulter, Margaret Elizabeth (1881-1939), **11,552**
Council Bulletin (newsletter), 17,695
Council for Lay Life and Work, 2,019
Council for University Women's Progress (MN), 8,587
Council of Church Boards of Education, 6,388
Council of Church Women (Ypsilanti, MI), **7,763**
Council of Clubs (IN), **4,554**
Council of Clubs (KS), 5,176
Council of Federated Organizations, 14,453, 17,599, 17,600, 17,714
Council of Foreign Ministers to Russia, 4,932
Council of Jewish Federations and Welfare Funds, 8,662
Council of Jewish Women (Marion, OH). *See* Temple Israel Sisterhood (Marion, OH)
Council of National Defense (WWI), **1,897**, 2,397, 4,850, 4,954, **9,487**, 13,241, 13,246, 17,685
Council of National Defense and Home Economics, women's committee (MA), **6644**
Council of National Defense, Committee on Nursing, 6,606
Council of National Defense, Georgia Division, Woman's Committee, **3,383**
Council of National Defense, Iowa Division, 4,727
Council of National Defense, Minnesota division, woman's committee, 9,481
Council of National Defense, Tama County Unit, Women's Committee (IA), **5,114**
Council of National Defense, Woman's Committee, 6,606
Council of National Defense, Woman's Division (CT), 1,897
Council of National Library Associations, 4,402
Council of Social Agencies, 8,637
Council of Social Agencies (Philadelphia, PA), 15,161

Council of Social Agencies, Negro civic welfare committee (GA), 3,302
Council of the Southern Mountains, 5,251
Council of the Twelve (Mormons), 16,842
Council of the United Church Women of Iowa City (IA), 4,959
Council of Ukrainian Women in America, 14,909
Council of Women (San Leandro, CA), 1,385
Council of Women for Home Missions, 1,170
Council on Population and Environment, **4,082**
Councils and synods, 1,750, 3,690, **7,042**, **10,139**, 12,907, 13,230, **13,505**, 14,682. *See also* Local church councils
Counselbaum, Stella Levinkind (ca. 1910-), **3,830**
Counseling, 3,903, 4,051, 8,573
Counselman, Jennie Elizabeth Otis (1853-1936), 3,812
"Count Joannes." *See* Jones, George (?-1878)
Count Rumford (book), 4,975
Counterattack (drama), 14,455
Countess Mara, Inc., 2,205
"Country Constituents Visit to the Legislature, The" (poem), 4,766
Country-dance, **5,643**
Country Gentleman (periodical), 6,713
"Country Gentlewomen," 6,713
Country life, 1,750, 3,310, 8,373, 9,594, 9,975, 10,751
Country Life Readers, 5,325
Country music, **5,642**
Country of the Pointed Firs, The (book), 5,650, 5,694
"Country Poor House" (poem), 2,565
Country Reading Club (IN), **4,555**
Country Women's League, 6,713
Countryman, Alta Chamberlain [Mrs. Levi Newton], 9,020
Countryman, Gratia Alta (1866-1953), Family (MN), **8,551**, 8,913, 8,963, **9,020**, **9,021**, 9,270
Countryman Family (MN), 8,981
Countryman, Levi Newton (1832-1924), 9,020, 9,021
County agricultural agents, **5,180**
County attorneys, **1,405**, 8,034
County Bard (periodical), 9,043
County Commissioners of Sweetwater County (WY), **17,933**
County courts, 2,926, **17,884**
County government, 6,692, 7,841
  records and correspondence, 162, 1,004, **1,149**, **1,422**, **3,002**, 5,409, **9,532**, 10,055, **11,207**, **13,386**, 13,661, **14,290**, 15,542, 15,544, **17,143**
County officials and employees, 306, **1,428**, 4,899, 6,934, 7,610, **7,709**, 8,062, 8,293, 9,304, 9,527, 10,741, **10,749**, **10,967**, 11,064, 13,965, 14,554, 17,050, 17,051, **17,511**, 17,512, **17,542**, **17,543**, 17,857, **17,933**
  salaries, allowances, etc., 17,661
County school systems, 13,184
Couper, Caroline G., 3,506
Couper Family (GA), **3,506**
Couper, Isabella H., 3,506
"Courage," 5,694
Courage Is Not Given (book), 15,720
Courage to Change: An Introduction to the Life and Thought of Reinhold Niebuhr (book), 2,513
Courier (Evansville, IN), 5,310
Courier (Wells College, NY), 11,281
Courier-Journal (Louisville, KY), 5,339, 17,076
Court, Cora May (Trawick) (1875-?), **6,490**
Court-houses, **2,507**, 9,258
Court of St. James (England), ambassadors to, 7,598
Court records, 162, **186**, 983, **986**, **987**, 988, 989, **1,134**, **1,143**, 1,177, **1,178**, **1,179**, 1,180, 1,181, **1,808**, **1,809**, 2,873, 2,926, 5,497, **5,568**, **7,106**, 7,659, 9,739, **10,103**, 10,104, **11,187**, 11,205, **11,450**, **11,454**, **11,460**, **13,874**, 14,105, **14,696**, **14,832**, 14,914, 14,921, 14,937, 14,938, 15,039, **15,547**, 15,548, 16,215, 17,016, 17,218, **17,514**
Court records, colonial, 13,448
Court reporters, **7,797**
Court, The (brothel), 11,978
Courtland, Roberta (pseudonym). *See* Dern, Peggy Gaddis (1895-1966)
Courtney, Juliana Margaret. *See* Conner, Juliana Margaret (Courtney) [Mrs. Henry Workman]
Courtney, Kathleen D., 15,310

Courtney, Mrs. M. S., 14,323

Courts, 623, 1,031, 2,163, 3,760, 4,166, 6,357, 6,666, 6,886, 6,980, **10,385**, 10,392. *See also* Judges; Judgments; Juvenile courts; Vigilance committees officials and employees, 8,089

Courts, colonial, 5,495, **5,496**

Courts-martial and courts of inquiry, 2,594, 3,620, 5,394

    Confederate States of America, 13,412

Courtship, 7,619, 7,624, 7,673, 7,677, 10,809, 13,427, 13,498, 14,348, 15,045, 16,443, 16,968

Cousaponakeesa (ca. 1700-63). *See* Bosomworth, Mary. Cousaponakeesa. [Mrs. John] Musgrove [Mrs. Jacob] Mathews [Mrs. Thomas] (ca. 1700-63)

Cousey, Eliza, 4,239

Cousin, Anatole, 5,418

"Cousin Dorothy" (column), 17,623

Cousins, Leathia (1876-1963). *See* Fleming, Leathia (Cousins) [Mrs. Thomas W.] (1876-1963)

Cousins, Margaret (1905-), 4,482, 6,006, **16,154**

Cousins, Norman, 16,153, 16,173

Cousins, Sue Margaret (1905-). *See* Cousins, Margaret

Couture, Theresa, **5,648**

Couzens, James, 8,360

Couzens, Mathew K., 11,330

Couzens, Virginia [Mrs. Harry D.], 4,958

Couzins, John E. D. (1813-86), **10,160**

Couzins, Phoebe Wilson [Miss] (1839?-1913), 832, 5,334, 10,160

Covel, Iantha T. (Starbird) (1860-?), **969**

Covell Family (NY), 12,278

Covell, William King, 6,176

Covenant Garden Club (GA), 3,374

Covenhoven, Deborah [Mrs.], 11,325

Covered bridges, 7,739

Covered Wagon Babies Club (CA), 1,591

Covert, Emzic Amelia (1858-1947). *See* Armstrong, Emzie Amelia (Covert) [Mrs. Alexander "Andy"] (1858-1947)

Covert, George Washington, 4,744

Covert, Jeannette (1897-1974). *See* Nolan, Jeannette (Covert) [Mrs. Val Francis] (1897-1974)

Covert, Mary Jane Judd [Mrs. George Washington], 4,744

Coves, Lucy Louisa (1837-1921). *See* Flower, Lucy Louisa (Coves) [Mrs. James Monroe] (1837-1921)

Covey, Almira (Mack) [Mrs. Benjamin] (1805-86), **16,636**

Covey, Arthur S., 4,306, 13,252, 14,215, 17,990

Covey, Lois Lenski [Mrs. Arthur] (1892-1974). *See* Lenski, Lois. [Mrs. Arthur] Covey (1892-1974)

Covington Female Seminary (KY), 5,289

Covington, Joe, 5,263

Covington, Mary Ann. *See* Wilson, Mary Ann (Covington) [Mrs. Thomas M.]

Cowan, A. Hortense, 13,052

Cowan, Charles E., 15,393

Cowan, Cora, 1,719

Cowan, Eilley (Orrum) [Mrs. Stephen] Hunter [Mrs. Alexander] (1826-1903). *See* Bowers, Eilley (Orrum) [Mrs. Stephen] Hunter [Mrs. Alexander] Cowan [Mrs. Lemuel Sanford "Sandy"] (1826-1903)

Cowan, Emma Carpenter [Mrs. George F.], **10,287**

Cowan, Louise S., 15,929

Cowan, Mrs. Arthur, **10,234**

Cowan, Naomi (Read) (1857-?), 16,968

Cowan's Tavern (ME), 5,644

Coward-McCann, 11,989

Coward, Noel, 60, 4,764

"Cowboy on the Plain, The" (song), 10,436

Cowboys, 189, 1,676, 10,324, **16,450**

    songs and music, 189

"Cowboy's Return, The" (song), 10,478

Cowden Family (ME), 7,669

Cowden, Helen Ray (Bierce) (1875-?), 712

Cowden, Margaret, 4,106

Cowdery, Patience (Simonds) [Mrs. Warren F.] (1794-1862), **16,637**

Cowdrey, Mary Bartlett [Miss] (1910-74), **2,744, 10,955**

Cowdry, Belle (1838-1922), **11,777**

Cowgirls, 1,779

Cowing, Julia Radcliffe, **12,425**

Cowl, Jane. Grace Bailey. Jane Cowles. [Mrs. Adolph] Klauber (1833-1950), **12,426**

Cowles, Amy (Bridgman) (1866-1948), 7,129

Cowles, Anna (Roosevelt) (1855-1931), 2,643

Cowles, Betsey Mix [Miss] (1810-76), 5,907, **14,102**, 14,123

Cowles, Calvin J., **13,387**

Cowles, Edith, 12,427

Cowles Family (VT), **11,975**

Cowles, Fleur Fenton [Mrs. Gardner], 9,159

Cowles, Frances, 11,975

Cowles, Frances (1859-1937). *See* Adams, Frances (Cowles) [Mrs. Elmer Ellsworth] (1859-1937)

Cowles, Genevieve Almeda, 12,427

Cowles, George, 11,975

Cowles, Helen. *See* Reynolds, Helen (Cowles) [Mrs. Reginald M.]

Cowles, Henry C., 4,289

Cowles, James Lewis (1843-1922), **12,427**

Cowles, Jennie, 11,975

Cowles, Laura, 17,029

Cowles, Mary (Bradley) [Mrs. George], 11,975

Cowles, Mary (Evans) [Mrs. Josiah, Jr.], 13,387

Cowles, Mrs. John, 8,672

Cowles, Myra G. (1878-1966), **14,103**

Cowles, S. H., 11,975

Cowley, Abigail "Abbie" (Hyde) [Mrs. Matthias Foss] (1863-1931), **16,638**

Cowley, Lucy Abigail (Peet) (1837-1900), 17,373

Cowley, Malcolm (1898-), **3,986**, 8,077

Cowley, Matthias Foss, 16,638, 16,780

Cowley, Moses F., 16,638

Cowperthwaite, Margaret [Mrs. L. LeRoy], **17,858**

Cox, Alethea (Crawford) Parcells (?-1909), 2,280

Cox, Ann, 14,845

Cox, Ann [Mrs. John], 14,981

Cox, Anna P., **6,491**

Cox, Annie Poad, 3,979

Cox, Clara I. (1879-1939), **13,222**

Cox, Codelia (Morley) (1823-1915), **16,456**

Cox College (GA), **3,095**, 3,384, 3,427

Cox, Elizabeth Threlkeld (1818-84). *See* Underwood, Elizabeth Threlkeld (Cox) [Mrs. Joseph Rogers] (1818-84)

Cox, Ellen (1833-1919). *See* Ewing, Ellen (Cox) [Mrs. Thomas II] (1833-1919)

Cox, Elvira Euphrasia (1864-1944). *See* Day, Elvira Euphrasia (Cox) [Mrs. Eli Azariah] (1864-1944)

Cox, F. Antoinette [Mrs.], 12,532

Cox Family (NY), **12,331**

Cox Family (NY), **11,472**

Cox Family (PA), **14,981**

Cox, Gertrude Castle, 3,753

Cox, Hannah (Gilbert) [Mrs. James] (1830-85), 11,472, 11,474

Cox, Henry Givin (1879-ca. 1965), **4,901**

Cox, I. F., 3,095

Cox, Ida, 5,532

Cox, Isabella Vache (1857-1947), 12,331

Cox, James, 11,472

Cox, James M. (1870-1957), 5,328, 13,318, 13,453, **14,046**

Cox, Jemima Lossee, 16,449

Cox, John (1754-1847), 14,981

Cox, Joseph Aloysius, 11,897

Cox, Lizzie, 5,306

Cox-McCormack, Nancy (1885-1967). *See* Cushman, Nancy Cox-McCormack [Mrs. Charles Thomas] (1885-1967)

Cox, Margaretta [Mrs. James M.] (?-1960), 14,046

Cox, Martha (Cragun) [Mrs. Isaiah] (1852-?), **16,506, 16,639**

Cox, Mary Peachy, **10,288**

Cox, Miriam (Bishop), **12,989**

Cox, Mrs. D. Mitchell, **3,169**

Cox, Mrs. E. E., 3,755, 3,762

Cox, Mrs. William H., 651

Cox, Nancy Elvira (1882-1964). *See* Bench, Nancy Elvira (Cox) (1882-1964)

Cox, Nellie Stedman (1855-1908), **16,053**

Cox, Phebe. *See* Thurber, Phebe (Cox)

Cox, Queen Hortense Snow [Mrs. Henry Givin] (1881-), 4,901

Cox, Rachel, 11,134

Cox, S. Myra (1822-87). *See* Smith, S. Myra (Cox) (1822-87)

Cox, Sister Ignatius Loyola, **9,022**

Cox, Susannah (1788-1851). *See* Parrish, Susannah (Cox) [Mrs. Joseph] (1788-1851)

Cox, Venetia [Miss], **13,263**

Coxe, Mrs. Daniel W., 14,945

Coye, Laura Parker, **12,756**

Coyle, Grace, 8,683, **13,882**

Coyle, Mary (1907-). *See* Chase, Mary (Coyle) (1907-)

Coyle, Mary Fallon, 1,659

Cozart, Toccoa Page, **13,388**

Cozens, Marianne (Bull), **12,990**

Cozens, Mary York (1830-1909), 1,790

Cozens, Sarah Varick (1814-?). *See* Morrison, Sarah Varick (Cozens) [Mrs. William N.] (1814-?)

Cozzini, Georgia P., 9,379

Crabbe, Hannah Frances, 1,634

Crabtree, Carlotta. *See* Cockburn, Carlotta (Crabtree)

Crabtree, Charlotte "Lotta" Mignon (1847-1924), 537, 820, 1,073, 1,077, **1,270**, 1,324, 4,695, **6,259**, 9,033, 10,717, 11,185, 16,149

Crabtree, Jack, 6,259

Crabtree, Mattaline G. [Miss], 1,029

Cracfrot, Sophia, 3,654

Crack in the Sidewalk, A (book), 6,117

Craddoc, Helen Hardin, 11,213, 11,217

Craddock, Charles Egbert (pseudonym). *See* Murfree, Mary Noailles [Miss] (1850-1922)

Craddock Family (Weedsport, NY), **11,748**

Craddock, Samuel, 11,748

Cradlebaugh, Miss, 3,752

Cradock Family (MD), **5,753**

Craft, Ellen (ca. 1826-97), 5,907

Craft, Lucy (1854-1933). *See* Laney, Lucy (Craft) (1854-1933)

Craft, Marcella [Miss] (1874 or 1880-1959), **1,123**

Craft, Nina, 16,176

Crafte, Sally G., 8,936

Cragun, Martha (1852-?). *See* Cox, Martha (Cragun) [Mrs. Isaiah] (1852-?)

Craig, Austin (1824-81), Family (MN), **9,023**

Craig, Ceyce (Dodd). *See* Eastman, Ceyce (Dodd) Craig

Craig, Edward Gordon (1872-1966), **12,359**

Craig Family (MI), 8,374

Craig Family (MS), 9,816

Craig Family (PA), 14,957

Craig, Genieve Woodruff [Mrs. Nalin], **10,289**

Craig, Georgia (pseudonym). *See* Dern, Peggy Gaddis (1895-1966)

Craig, Gordon, 12,361

Craig, Helen, 2,112

Craig, Ina Cook [Mrs.], 1,307

Craig, Jane. *See* Biddle, Jane (Craig)

Craig, Josephine, 9,023

Craig, Katherine (1876-1934), **1,707**

Craig, Lewis, 2,414

Craig, Lizzie. *See* Pitts, Lizzie (Craig) [Mrs. Thomas Henry]

Craig, Marjorie [Miss] (?-1955), **12,991**

Craig, Mary Adelaide (Churchill) [Mrs. Austin] (1828-79), 9,023

Craig, Mary Francis (1923-), **14,344**

Craig, Minnie D. (Davenport) [Mrs. Edward O.] (1883-1966), **13,670**

Craig, Mrs. John, 14,957

Craig, Roger (1933-), **8,078**

Craigie, Dorothy (1901-), **11,976**

Craigie, Pearl Mary Teresa (Richards) (1867-1906), **11,977**

Crain, Lucille Cardin (1901-), **14,345**

Crain, Patience. *See* Black, Patience (Crain) [Mrs. James]

Cram, Anna Brown [Mrs.] (1756-1849), 10,804

Cram Family (NH), **10,804**

Cram, Ralph Adams, 7,690

Cramer, Alice Bulfinch, 2,293

Cramer, Mary Grant, 17,992
Cranberries, 9,107, 11,189
Cranch, Lucy (1767-1846). *See* Greenleaf, Lucy (Cranch) (1767-1846)
Cranch, Mary, **7,360**
Cranch, Mary (Smith) (1741-1811), 7,598
Crandall, Amanda, **14,537**
Crandall, Ella Phillips (1871-1939), 6,162
Crandall, Eva (Maeser) [Mrs. Myron E.] (1876-1967), **16,640**
Crandall, Lulu Donnell Brown (1854-1931), **17,188**
Crandall, Madge (1886-?), 5,652
Crandall, Myra R., 14,706
Crandall, Prudence (1803-89). *See* Philleo, Prudence Crandall [Mrs. Calvin] (1803-89)
Cranc, Agnes, 4,696
Crane, Alice E., 11,077
Crane, Augustus C., 8,223
Crane, Caroline Bartlett [Mrs. Augustus C.] (1858-1935), 7,941, **8,223**
Crane, Carolyn G., **3,234**
Crane, Carrie, 11,324
Crane, Charlotte E. [Miss], 12,598
Crane, Cora Ethel Eaton (Howarth) [Mrs. Stephen] (1865-1910). *See* McNeil, Cora Ethel Eaton (Howarth) [Mrs. Stephen] Crane [Mrs. Hammon P.] (1865-1910)
Crane, Elizabeth "Betsey" (Mulford) [Mrs. John] (1775-1828), **10,957**
Crane, Elize Prentice, 3,872
Crane, Emma (Cook), 14,134
Crane, Esther, 11,902
Crane Family (NJ), 10,905
Crane, Frances Jane (Timmons) [Mrs. Andrew Jackson] Grayson [Mrs. George Belden] (1823-1908), 512
Crane Fund for Widows and Children, 3,872
Crane, Hart, **11,873**
Crane, Laura B., 11,696
Crane, Mary C. [Mrs. Horace A.], 3,592
Crane, Mary Louise (1861-1949). *See* Church, Mary Louise (Crane) (1861-1949)
Crane, Mary Prentice [Mrs. Richard T.], 3,872
Crane, Nathaniel, 10,905
Crane, Richard T., 3,872, 4,128
Crane, Sara Clayton [Mrs.], **3,170**
Crane, Stephen (1871-1900), **10,860**, 11,978, **11,979**
Crangle, Emily Elkus [Mrs. Roland] (1878-?), **11,553**
Crangle, Roland (1862-1945), **11,553**
Craniotomy, 3,234
Crank, Mary Agnes, **1,101**
Cranmer, Helen [Mrs. John] Erskine [Mrs. W. H. H.] (1896-), **11,858**
Cranston, Martha S., 2,042, 2,063
Cranstone, Mildred (Welch) (1898-?), **421**, 11,846
Cranstone, Sarah (Marsh) (1829-57), **422**
Cranstone, Susan Marsh, **1,271**
Crapleve, Anne, 9,512
Crapsey, Adelaide [Miss] (1878-1914), **12,815**
Crary, Catherine S., **11,980**
Crary, Margaret (1906-), **4,983**
Craton, Ann Washington (1891-1970). *See* Blankenhorn, Ann Washington (Craton) [Mrs. Heber] (1891-1970)
Cratty, Mabel [Miss] (1868-1928), **12,711**
"Crave, The" (song), 5,531
Craven, Beulah. *See* Hart, Beulah (Craven)
Craven, Catherine S. (Tichenor) [Mrs. John Joseph], 2,278
Craven, Elijah R., 11,099
Craven, Jennie (1862-1954). *See* Ralston, Jennie (Craven) [Mrs. Samuel Moffett] (1862-1954)
Craven, John Joseph (1822-93), **2,278**
Craven, Liola. *See* Woffort, Liola (Craven)
Craven, Mrs. Walter, 13,618
Craw, Elizabeth (1819-ca. 1909), **16,245**
Craw, Frances (Whipple) [Mrs. Frank G.]. *See* Jackson, Frances (Whipple) [Mrs. Frank G.] Craw [Mrs. Freedom W.]
Crawford, Ada L. [Miss], **11,554**
Crawford, Alethea (?-1909). *See* Cox, Alethea (Crawford) Parcells (?-1909)
Crawford, Amanda Melvin (Morgin), **14,538**
Crawford, Anna Harriette (1834-1914). *See*

Leonowens, Anna Harriette (Crawford) [Mrs. T. L.] (1834-1914)
Crawford, Anne. *See* Flexner, Anne (Crawford) [Mrs. Abraham]
Crawford, Annie I. (1857-1942), **11,343**
Crawford, Carrie Lena (?-1898). *See* Moffett, Carrie Lena Crawford [Mrs. A. L.] (?-1898)
Crawford, Charlotte Holmes (1885-1971), **11,555**, 11,690, 12,599
Crawford, Cheryl (1902-), 2,625
Crawford, Elizabeth (?-1925), 3,706
Crawford, F. Marion, 6,185
Crawford, Harry Love (1879-1959), **10,449**
Crawford, Isabel Alice Hartley (1865-1961), **12,784**
Crawford, Jean V., 7,583
Crawford, Joan, 12,129
Crawford, Joanna (1941-), **6,003**
Crawford, Kate, 8,077
Crawford, Laura Jones [Mrs.] (1838?-?), **2,279**
Crawford, Martha (Everitt) (ca. 1820-?), 46
Crawford, Mary (1861-1945), 3,706
Crawford, Mary Merritt [Mrs. Edward] Schuster, 11,508, **11,556**
Crawford, Mrs. E., 12,335
Crawford, Mrs. R. L., 12,335
Crawford, R. R., 2,279
Crawford, Rebekah [Miss] (1845-1934), **2,280**, 2,653
Crawford, Robert Leighton (1799-1853), 46, 12,335
Crawford, Thomas, 12,607
Crawford, Vesta Maude (Pierce) [Mrs. Arthur Lorenzo] (1899-), **16,641**, **16,889**
Crawford, Vivian Henrie, 16,523
Crawley, Elizabeth, 4,369
Crazy Horse (Native American), 10,433, 10,473, 15,856
Crazy Jane Society (NJ), 11,119
Crazy Snake uprising, 14,206
Creameries, 11,857
"Created in God's Image: Religious Issues in the Woman's Rights Movement of the Nineteenth Century" (dissertation), 3,742
Creath, Jacob, Jr. (1799-1886), 5,262
Creath, Prudence (Dunn) Rogers [Mrs. Jacob, Jr.] (1798-188?), 5,262
Creation and Other Biblical Plays (drama), 2,170
Creative Arts in Democratic Living, The (book), 9,960
Credit Foncier, 2,401
Credit unions, 6,808, 8,085, 8,651, 8,655, 9,180
Creech, Margaret, 8,670
Creedy, Brooks Spivey (1917-), 13,176
Creek Indians, 1,475, 2,883, 9,719, 11,639, 14,241, 14,244
  history, **14,197**
  missions, 14,243, 14,246
Creek language, 14,243
Creel, George, 9,853
Creel, Virginia Fackler (1845-1937), **9,853**
Creighton, Robert (1910-), 169
Creole dialects, 1,493
Creole Families of New Orleans (book), 5,536
Creoles, 5,418, 9,841
Crepeau, Sister Rosemary (1884-1974), 17,868
Cresap, Helen Holmes [Mrs. Robert D.], 4,958
Crescent Club (IN), **4,556**
Crescent Council of Civic Associations (LA), 5,542
Creshkoff, Nancy, 6,907
Cresson, Margaret (French) [Mrs. William Penn] (1889-1973), 2,338, **7,503**, 7,504, 7,509, 7,510
Cresson, Sarah, 14,847
Cresson, William Penn, 2,338
Cresswell, Sadie (Peterson), 17,862
Creswell, Cordelia (1868?-1950), **7,764**
Creswell, Margaret, 7,764
Creswell, Mary Ethel [Miss], **3,123**
Crew, James R., 3,171
Crew, Jane Louisa Killian [Mrs. James R.], **3,171**
Crews, Angelina (Smith) (?-1886), 14,662
Crichton, Frances E., **13,389**
Crigler, S. G., **15,409**
Crime and criminals, 52, 165, 338, **987**, **1,138**, 1,676, 1,771, 1,786, 6,259, 6,260, 7,142, 8,144, 9,299, 9,303, 11,227, 11,440, **12,175**, 12,375, 12,702,

13,537, 14,173, **15,537**, 16,485, 16,486, 16,886, 16,904, 16,965, 17,961
  public opinion, 17,256
  research, 6,282
Crime and criminals, Afro-American, 15,110
Crime prevention, 9,477, 9,523
  citizen participation, **1,207**, **3,279**
Criminal law, 6,260
  cases, 1,134, 1,179, 1,180, 1,181, 2,161, 5,175, 10,103, 13,448, 16,215, 17,218
Criminal statistics, 5,570
Criminal syndicalism, 689, 1,357, 8,127, 8,144, 17,635
Criminologists, 863, **6,260**, 13,108
"Crimson Canary," 18,000
Crimson White (AL), 112
Cripliver, Elizabeth (1893-1956). *See* Wherry, Elizabeth (Cripliver) (1893-1956)
Crippen, Lucy Antoinette (1834-1931). *See* Bailey, Lucy Antoinette (Crippen) [Mrs. James Monroe] (1834-1931)
Crippled children, institutional care, 8,621
Crisis, The (periodical), 5,870
Crisler, Clara M. [Miss] (1882-1957), **10,660**
Crisler, Lois Brown [Mrs. Herb] (1897-1971), **17,248**
Crisp, Lucy Cherry [Miss] (1899-1977), **13,264**
Crisson, Margaret, **3,172**
Cristman, Elizabeth, 2,878
Cristo Rey Church (Lansing, MI), 7,743
Critchlow, Hattie (1864-1948). *See* Jensen, Hattie (Critchlow) [Mrs. Ephraim] (1864-1948)
Criterion, The (periodical), 15,536
Critic (periodical), 6,601, 9,771
Criticism, 3,983, 3,990
Critics, **2,610**, **5,863**, **10,871**, **11,286**, 12,539, 12,602, **16,165**, **16,169**, **17,979**
Crittenden, Ann Lane. *See* Griffiths, Ann Lane (Crittenden)
Crittenden, Ann M., 16,057
Crittenden, Annie. *See* Severance, Annie (Crittenden)
Crittenden, Christopher, **13,390**, 13,575
Crittenden, Cornelia Williams (1895-1959), **10,450**
Crittenden, Ethel Taylor, 13,390
Crittenden Family (TX), **16,057**
Crittenden Home (MN), 9,099
Crittenden, Janet Quinlan [Mrs. Christopher], 13,390
Crittenden, John Jorden (1787-1863), 11,131
Crittenden, Mariette C. (1825-?), **8,153**
Crittenden, Marion Brown, 10,450
Crittenden, May, 407
Crittenton, Charles Nelson (1833-1909), 4,088, 8,669
Crocetti, Mary, 9,492
Crocheron, Helen, **16,054**
Crocheron, Mabel, **8**
Crocker, Ada R., 3,954
Crocker, Anna, 14,594
Crocker, Betty, 6,495
Crocker, Celia May (1874-?). *See* Thompson, Celia May (Crocker) (1874-?)
Crocker, Ellen May (Hall) [Mrs. Henry Robinson] (1848-1935), 837
Crocker, Helen (?-1966). *See* Russell, Helen (Crocker) (?-1966)
Crocker, Henry Robinson, 837
Crocker, Marion A., 2,310
Crocker, Mary Deming [Mrs. Charles], **1,272**
Crocker, Mrs., 11,543
Crocker, Mrs. Henry, 1,314
Crocker, Samuel, 15,533
Crocker's Station (Bronson, CA), 837
Crockett, Fannie E., **16,055**
Crockett, Ruth (Clarkson) [Mrs. Ozro O.] (1857-1947), **16,457**, **16,642**
Croffut, Bessie Nicholls [Mrs. William Augustus], 2,282, **2,715**
Croffut, William Augustus (1835-1915), **2,282**, 2,715
Crofts, Margaret (Lee) [Mrs. F. S.], **2,283**
Croghan Family, **15,257**
Croghan, Mary (1826-1903). *See* Schenley, Mary (Croghan) [Mrs. Edward] (1826-1903)
Croghan, William (?-1850), 15,257
Croix de Guerre, 3,203
Croly, Jane "Jennie June" (Cunningham) [Mrs. David

Goodman] (1829-1901), 2,542, **6,492**, 6,872, 7,298, 17,692
Cromartie, Ellen, 13,437
Cromartie Family (NC), **13,478**
Cromer, Marie Samuella, **15,578**
Cromwell, Marion [Mrs.], 17,395
Cronin, Kathleen (pseudonym). *See* Ruuttila, Julia (Godman) Bertram Eaton (1907-)
Cronin, Mary [Mrs. Patrick], **1,273**
Cronkhite, Adelbert, 17,086
Cronkhite, Bernice Veazey (Brown) [Mrs. Leonard Wolsey] (1893-), 6,339, **6,493**
Cronyn, Hume (1911-), **2,284**
Crook Family (SC), **15,832**
Crook, Margaret Brackenbury (?-1972), 7,158
Crooks, Heléne [Miss], **11,479**
Crooks, Mrs. F., 6,735
Crooks, Virginia, 14,618
Crookston, Alice Rice (1860-1925), **16,458**
Cropper, Jacintha Simonton, 9,976
Cropper, Levin, 9,976
Cropper, Mary [Mrs. Levin], 9,976
Cropper, Mary Stephens, 9,976
Cropper, Sara, 9,976
Cropper, Vincent, 9,976
Crops and climate, 3,558, 7,678, 8,741, 10,036
Crosby, Bing, 17,944
Crosby, Caroline (Barnes) [Mrs. Jonathan] (1807-83), **16,643**
Crosby, Caroline M. (?-1921), 9,058
Crosby, Catharine Clarkson (1812-82). *See* Stevens, Catharine Clarkson (Crosby) [Mrs. Henry H.] (1812-82)
Crosby, Cornelia "Flyrod" Thurza (1854-1946), **5,586**
Crosby, Eliza Leland (Adams) [Mrs. John Leland] (1806-98), **5,589**
Crosby Family, 14,059
Crosby, Florence. *See* Stone, Florence (Crosby) [Mrs. Henry]
Crosby, Frances "Fanny" Jane. [Mrs. Alexander] Van Alstyne (1820-1915), 3,969
Crosby, Frances Marion, Family (MN), **9,024**
Crosby, George, **9,025**
Crosby, Hale Estabrook, 8,154
Crosby, Hannah Adelia (Bunker) [Mrs. Samuel Obed] (1853-1932), **16,644**
Crosby, Harriet Aston [Mrs. William Bedlow], 12,317
Crosby, Helen Sophia Bates [Mrs. Francis Marion] (?-1909), 9,024
Crosby, Henrietta. *See* Ingersoll, Henrietta (Crosby) [Mrs. George W.]
Crosby, Lillian, 9,025
Crosby, Marion Emma, 9,024
Crosby, Mary (1822-?), **12,188**
Crosby, Mary Foster (Chamberlain) [Mrs. Hale Estabrook], 8,154
Crosby, May, 10,382
Crosby, Nellie P. *See* DeWolfe, Nellie P. (Crosby)
Crosby, Sarah Adella. *See* Rayner, Sarah Adella (Crosby) [Mrs. John]
Crosby, William Bedlow, 11,037, 12,188
Crosby's Opera House (IL), 12,639
Crosfield, Jane, 15,290
Crosley, Willierean Jackson [Mrs.] (1938-), 94
Cross, Ada (ca. 1858-?), 9,026
Cross, Anna R., 4,218
Cross Creek (book), 2,873, 2,876
Cross, Dorothy Child (1890-). *See* Zeiger, Dorothy Child (Cross) Remington (1890-)
Cross, Eleanor (1874-1950). *See* Marquand, Eleanor (Cross) [Mrs. Allen] (1874-1950)
Cross, Elsie H., 1,339
Cross, Eva (McDonald) [Mrs. Frank] Valesh [Mrs. Benjamin F.] (1866-1956). *See* Valesh, Eva (McDonald) [Mrs. Frank]. [Mrs. Benjamin F.] Cross (1866-1956)
Cross, Florence Ledyard (1874-1961). *See* Kitchelt, Florence Ledyard (Cross) [Mrs. Richard] (1874-1961)
Cross, Helen M., 12,265
Cross, Milton, 7,303
Cross, Ruth (ca. 1895-), **5,441**
Cross, William, Family (MN), **9,026**
Crossett, Ella (Hawley) [Mrs. John B.], 12,834

Crossman, Abigail (1801-89), 7,035
Crossnore School (NC), 13,128
Crosson, Elizabeth "Lizzie" [Mrs. George] (1844-1924), 15,985
Crosson, George (1812-85), 15,985
Crosson, Jane Elizabeth (1847-1927), 10,632
Crosson Ranch (TX), **15,985**
Crosswaith, Frank R., 8,141
Croswell, Esther (Ellis), 8,487
Croswell, Ruth, 11,534
Crothers, Rachel (1878-1958), 3,745, 3,764, 3,994, 7,310, 7,559
Crothers, Sally Jane, 11,457
Crotte, Mrs. Andre, 13,988
Crouch, Flo. *See* Browning, Flo (Crouch) [Mrs. Jack]
Crouch, Jordon J., 10,677
Crouch, Mabel C., 12,487
Crouch, Malinda (Sutherlin) (1835-1930), **14,539**
Crouse, Mrs. John N., 4,211
Crow Butte legend, 10,433
Crow, Catherine Diamond, 3,001
Crow Creek Agency, 9,294
Crow Creek Reservation (SD), 15,850
Crow, Evelyn. *See* Simmons, Evelyn (Crow)
Crow, Evelyn [Mrs.], 978
Crow Family (CA), **1,274**
Crow Indians, 17,950
Crow, John Bradford, 1,274
Crow, Martha (Foote) [Mrs. John M.] (1854-1924), 12,484, **12,893**
Crow, Myra. *See* Marshall, Myra (Crow) [Mrs. Robert Bradford]
Crow, Perthania Eastin [Mrs. John Bradford], 1,274
Crow, Wayman, 6,659
Crowe, Cecily, 6,060
Crowell, F. Elizabeth, 12,739
Crowell, Florance H., 1,589
Crowell, Grace Noll, 16,137
Crowell, Rhoda, **6,494**
Crowell, Vivian G. [Mrs.], **5,379, 5,382**
Crowley, Ellen, 17,918
Crowley, Mary Ellen, 17,919
Crowley, Patricia (Caron) [Mrs. Patrick], 4,641
Crowley, Patrick, 4,641
Crown of Thorns (drama), 2,303
Crown Publishers, 14,324, 14,455
Crownhart, Charles H., Sr., and Family (WI), **17,621**
Crownhart, Charles, Jr., 17,621
Crownhart, Jesse George, 17,621
Crownhart, Jessie (Evans) [Mrs. Charles H., Sr.], 17,621
Crowninshield, Benjamin Williams (1773-1851), 7,468
Crowninshield, Clarissa (1810-1907). *See* Thies, Clarissa (Crowninshield) [Mrs. Louis] (1810-1907)
Crowninshield Family (MA), **7,361**
Crowninshield, Francis Boardman (1809-77), **7,470**
Crowninshield, Francis Boardman (1869-1950), **2,028**
Crowninshield, Hannah B. Armstrong, **7,471**
Crowninshield, Jacob (1770-1808), **7,472**
Crowninshield, Katherine M., 7,361
Crowninshield, Louise Evelina (du Pont) [Mrs. Francis Boardman] (1877-1958), **2,028**, 7,361
Crowninshield, Maria Louisa, **7,473**
Crowninshield, Mary Boardman [Mrs. Benjamin Williams], 7,468, 7,470
Crowninshield, Sally Gardner [Mrs. Jacob] (?-1807), 7,472
Crowninshield, Sarah Putnam [Mrs. Francis Boardman], 7,470
Crowninshield, Walter, 14,680
Crow's Nest (residence, NY), 12,179
Croy, Homer (1883-1965), **9,949**
Crozier, Chell (1884-). *See* Meachem, Chell (Crozier) [Mrs. Colo W.] (1884-)
Crozier, Gordon T., 3,608
Cruickshank, Helen [Mrs.], 2,928
Cruikshank Family (NY), **11,318**
Crum, Ethel Katherine (1886-1943), 10,151
Crumbaker, Martha, **17,249**
Crumbo, Mentora Daniels, 16,876
Crumley Family (GA), **3,173**
Crumley, Flora [Miss] (1870-1961), 10,435
Crumley, W. M., 3,173

Crumley, William, 3,173
Crumley, Zulette, 3,173
Crump, Louise Eskrigge, 9,567, **9,612**
Crump, Maria, 17,127
Crump, Mary Alletta (1887-1970), **7,209**
Crump, Sarah E. *See* Helm, Sarah E. (Crump) "Crumpsie"
Crusade for Children, 8,984
Crusader, The (newspaper), 15,952
Crustacea, physiology, **13,207**
Crutcher, Emma C., 9,602
Crutcher, Emma (Shannon) [Mrs. William O.], 9,613
Crutcher Family (MS), **9,602**
Cruzen, Mary Edna [Mrs.], 10,032
Cry for Love, The (book), 6,019
Cry of Laughter, The (drama), 5,783
Cry of Winter (drama), 11,310
Cry to the Hills (book), 6,040
Cryer, Gretchen, 12,367
Cryer, Jennie Helen. *See* Haskell, Jennie Helen (Cryer) [Mrs. Edward Prince]
Cryptograms, scientific. *See* Scientific cryptograms
Cryptography, 5,599
Crystal City (TX), Independent School District, 16,334, 16,368, 16,376
Crystallographers, **7,328**
Cuba, 5,954, 6,709, 12,247
    Americans in, 5,954, 7,610
    art, abstract, 2,741
    missions, 13,230
    prisoners of war, 12,532
    revolution (1895-1898), 15,743
    slavery, 15,601
    social life and customs, 7,610, 12,270
Cuba (steamboat), 15,090
Cuban Educational Association of the United States of America, **2,285**
Cuban Missile Crisis (1962), 11,827
Cubbedge, Carrie Gordon. *See* Carson, Carrie Gordon (Cubbedge) [Mrs. John Avery Gere]
Cudahy Jean (Morton) [Mrs. Joseph] (?-1953), 3,882
Cuddeback, Elizabeth, 1,655
Cuddihy, Joan F., **7,765**
Culbertson, Helen. *See* Kip, Helen (Culbertson)
Culbertson, Mary Virginia (Pond) [Mrs. Jack Arthur], 589
Culbertson, Matthew Simpson, 423
Culkin, Margaret (1891-). *See* Banning, Margaret (Culkin) (1891-)
Cullen, Ann (1913-). *See* Presley, Ann (Cullen) [Mrs. Walter] (1913-)
Cullen, Countee (1903-46), **3,285, 5,465**, 6,112
Cullen, Elizabeth O., 304
Cullen, Ida Mae (Roberson) [Mrs. Countee], 3,285, 5,465
Cullen, Mary Bartlett Dixon, 7,306
Cullman, Marguerite Wagner [Mrs.] (1908-), **6,004**
Cullum, Catharine. *See* Huidekoper, Catharine (Cullum) [Mrs. Alfred]
Cullum, George Washington (1809-92), **2,286**
Culp, Cordie Jacob (1872-1952), **10,958**
Culp, Florence M. (Burns) [Mrs. Cordie Jacob] (1874-?), 10,958
Culp, Oveta (1905-). *See* Hobby, Oveta (Culp) (1905-)
Culpepper Family (SC), **15,622**
Culpepper Institute (VA), 4,817
Cults, 9,841
Cultural anthropology. *See* Ethnology
Cultural Gardens Association, 13,953
Cultural relations, 2,133, **4,321**, 6,355, 6,368, 6,408, **6,419**, 6,456, 8,493, 9,467, 11,846, 14,219, 14,223
Culture, **11,829**
Culver, Barbara G. [Mrs. John R.], **16,264**
Culver Family (IL), **4,100**
Culver, Helen, 5,063
Culver, Helen (1832-1925), 4,100
Culver, Lillian E. H. [Mrs. William N.], **10,290**
Cum Concilio Club (Nacogdoches, TX), **16,297**
Cumberland Bay Works (NY), 12,770
Cumberland College (Williamsburg, KY), alumnae, 15,964
Cumberland County Tuberculosis Association (PA), 14,746

Cumberland Female Seamans Friends Society (ME), **5,605**

Cumberland Presbyterian Church (TN), 161

Cumberland Womans Missionary Society (ME), **5,604**

Cumings, Grace P. (1866-?), **7,766**

Cumings, Mrs., 7,880

Cumming, Adelaide (Fish) Hawley (1905-), **6,495**

Cumming, Alfred (1792-1889), **424, 16,932,** 16,933

Cumming, Alice McKee [Mrs.], 4,868

Cumming, Elizabeth Wells (Randall) [Mrs. Alfred], 424, **16,933**

Cumming, Emily. See Hammond, Emily (Cumming) [Mrs. Harry]

Cumming Family (SC), **15,600**

Cumming, Henry Harford, 15,600

Cumming, Julia (Bryan) [Mrs. Henry Harford], 15,600

Cumming, Kate [Miss] (1828?-1909), 99

Cumming, Sarah W. [Miss], 3,051

Cumming, Thomas W., 3,051

Cummings, Clara E. (1855-1906), 10,151

Cummings, E. E. (1894-1962), 6,353, 16,163

Cummings, Marion [Mrs. Stanley] (1876-1941). See Slonimsky, Marion [Mrs. Stanley] Cummings [Mrs. Henry] (1876-1941)

Cummings, Mary (Lanphear) [Mrs. Frank], 9,366

Cummings, Mildred (Francis), **14,540**

Cummings, Stanley, 3,987

Cummings, Wanda Catherine [Mrs. Edward H.] (1914-), 5,394

Cummins, Annie Blair (Titman) [Mrs. George Wyckoff] (1867-1952), **10,903**

Cummins Family (MA), **7,362**

Cummins, George Wyckoff (1865-1942), **10,903**

Cummins, Lucile (?-1975), **14,346**

Cummins, Maria Susannah [Miss] (1827-66), 7,362

Cummins, Sarah J., 14,628

Cunard, Nancy, 2,331, 3,290, 3,799, 16,152

Cuney, Maud (1874-1936). See Hare, Maud (Cuney) (1874-1936)

Cuningham, Mrs. John S., 12,986

Cuningham, Otelia Carrington (1894-1969). See Connor, Otelia Carrington (Cuningham) [Mrs. David M.] (1894-1969)

Cunningham, Agnes (O'Leary) (1907-), **8,695**

Cunningham and Moore Funeral Home (St. Louis, MO), 10,191

Cunningham, Ann Pamelia [Miss] (1816-75), 15,510

Cunningham, Charles C., 10,177, 15,309

Cunningham, Imogen. [Mrs. Roi] Partridge (1883-1976), 317, **425, 2,745,** 12,126, 12,789, **17,250**

Cunningham, Jane "Jennie June" (1829-1901). See Croly, Jane "Jennie June" (Cunningham) [Mrs. David Goodman] (1829-1901)

Cunningham, Julia Woolfolk (1916-), 1,525, **14,347**

Cunningham, Kate (Richards) [Mrs. Francis "Frank" Patrick] O'Hare [Mrs. Charles C.] (1877-1948), 1,321, **6,811, 9,900,** 10,103, 10,104, 10,177, 12,699, **14,432, 15,309**

Cunningham, Lucy H. King (1872-1940). See Smith, Lucy H. King (Cunningham) [Mrs. Alfred Franklin] (1872-1940)

Cunningham, Mary Simmerson (1838-1923). See Logan, Mary Simmerson (Cunningham) [Mrs. John Alexander] (1838-1923)

Cunningham, Merce, 4,384

Cunningham, Minnie (Fisher) [Mrs. B. J.], 6,432, 16,015, **16,235, 16,252,** 17,654

Cunningham, Nettie, 10,191

Cup and the Sword, The (book), 14,388

Cupid and Psyche (drama), 12,476

Curators. See Museum directors

Curet, Sister Mary Adrienne, 9,542

Curfew, 8,633, 10,703, 10,886

Curie, Eve, 8,450, 12,045

Curie, Iréne. See Joliot-(Curie), Iréne [Mrs. Frederic]

Curie, Marie (Sklodowska) (1867-1934), 1,026, 5,122, **6,496,** 8,450, 12,045, 15,179

Curl, Samuel, Inc., 14,329

Curle, Richard, 2,997

Curley Family (ND), 13,669

Curley, James, 6,185

Curnen, Annette Louise. See Burgess, Annette Louise (Curnen) [Mrs. Elisha Payne Jewett]

Curnen, James Francis, 11,956

Curnen, Mrs. James Francis, 11,956

Curran, Catherine M. (Buckmaster) [Mrs. Isaac Bush] (1837-1918), 4,352

Curran Family (IL), **4,352**

Curran, Isaac Bush, 4,352

Curran, Mary Harris (Ellison) [Mrs. Nicholas F.] (1839-1917), **5,590**

Curran, Mary Katherine (Layne) (1844-1920). See Brandegee, Mary Katherine (Layne) Curran (1844-1920)

Curran, Pearl [Mrs. John W.], 9,841, 10,184

Currell, Leila, 982

Currency convertibility, 11,857

Current events, 4,495

Current Events Club (Crookston, MN), **9,027,** 9,260

Current Events Club of Troy (OH), 14,147

Current, Gloster, 8,116

Current, Ruth, **13,391**

Currie, Grace M. (Coles) (?-1967), 5,063

Currie Line (MN), 8,518

Currier and Ives, 2,825

Curry, Chancy (D'Elia) [Mrs. J. Lane], 1,837

Curry Family (OR), 14,549

Curry, George L., 14,549

Curry, Helen Brown, **8,400**

Curry, Peggy Simon (1911-), **17,959**

Curti, Margaret (1891-1961), **13,738**

Curtin, Mary Amelia (1836-87). See Taylor, Mary Amelia Curtin [Mrs. Samuel] (1836-87)

Curtis, Ann, 997

Curtis, Anna Mary (ca. 1830-?). See Morris, Anna Mary (Curtis) (ca. 1830-?)

Curtis, Bardella (Shipp) [Mrs. Theodore E.] (1874-1957), **16,645**

Curtis Brown (publishers), 14,405

Curtis, Charles William, **11,557**

Curtis, Charlotte, 6,584

Curtis, Ellen Louise (1824-98). See Demorest, Ellen Louise (Curtis) (1824-98)

Curtis Family (CT), 1,955

Curtis, Fanniebelle [Miss], 2,094

Curtis, Frances Greeley (1867-1957), **6,497**

Curtis, George William (1824-92), **12,864**

Curtis, Gold, 9,028

Curtis, Harriot, 7,069

Curtis, Henrietta. See Porter, Henrietta (Curtis) [Mrs. James R.]

Curtis, Jenny. See Cannon, Jenny (Curtis) [Mrs. Henry M.]

Curtis, Leila. See Chamberlain, Leila (Curtis)

Curtis, Lydia Krueger [Mrs. James H.], 4,927

Curtis, Margaret, 8,657

Curtis, Marie, **8,317**

Curtis, Martha (Leach) [Mrs. William S.], **7,767**

Curtis, Mary (1821-88). See Reed, Mary (Curtis) [Mrs. Calvin] (1821-88)

Curtis, Mary (1847?-?). See Richardson, Mary (Curtis) (1847?-?)

Curtis, Mary A. [Mrs. Gold Tompkins], 9,028

Curtis, Mary Ann (Scovill) [Mrs. William Edmond] (1830-1908), 1,955

Curtis, Nellie M. (1865-1943), **10,564**

Curtis, Permelia (?-1949). See Porter, Permelia (Curtis) [Mrs. William Earl] (?-1949)

Curtis, Richard, 9,697

Curtis, Sarah, **6,190**

Curtis, Sarah Wells (Hartley) [Mrs. Richard] Soper [Mrs. Lyman] (1836-1921), **16,646**

Curtis, Stephanie (Marx) [Mrs. Charles William], **11,557**

Curtis, Thomas B. (1911-), **9,950**

Curtis, Vera (1879-1962), **6,498**

Curtis, William Edmond (1823-80), 1,955

Curtis, William S., 7,767

Curtiss, Charles, **11,558**

Curtiss, Cornelia, 11,558

Curtiss, Floretta A. (1822-?), 6,309

Curtiss, Mina (Kirstein) [Mrs. Henry T.] (1896-), 7,158

Curtiss, Ursula Reilly (1923-), 6,060

Cusabo Indians, 15,713

land transfers, **15,713**

Cushing, Anne M. (Kennedy), 14,705

Cushing, Caroline Moreland (1871-1926). See Duniway, Caroline Moreland (Cushing) [Mrs. Clyde Augustus] (1871-1926)

Cushing Family (MA), 6,593

Cushing, Frank H., 11,295

Cushing, Lily Emmet (1909-69), **2,746**

Cushing, Olivia Donaldson (1871-1917). See Andersen, Olivia Donaldson (Cushing) (1871-1917)

Cushing, Sarah P. See Morris, Sarah P. (Cushing) [Mrs. Thomas John]

Cushing, Stella Marek, **12,428**

Cushman, Charlotte Saunders (1816-76), **2,288,** 2,542, 3,889, 3,921, 4,695, **5,919,** 6,392, 11,985, 12,342, 12,431, 12,833, 16,040

Cushman, Harriette E. [Miss] (1890-), **10,215**

Cushman, Maria S., **7,168**

Cushman, Nancy Cox-McCormack [Mrs. Charles Thomas] (1885-1967), **6,499,** 6,597, **7,210, 15,946**

Cushman, Pauline (1835-93), 3,922

Cusimano, Sister Josephine. Sister Austin (1918-), **16,343**

Custer, Elizabeth (Bacon) [Mrs. George Armstrong] (1842-1933), 342, 2,198, 7,171, **8,318,** 10,213, **16,507**

Custer, George Armstrong (1839-76), 12,564, 13,682, 16,507

Custer Park (ND), 13,649

Custis, Eleanor Parke (1779-1852). See Lewis, Eleanor Parke (Custis) [Mrs. Lawrence] (1779-1852)

Custis, Eliza Parke [Mrs.] (1777-1832), 5,820

Custis Family (VA), **17,081**

Custis, George Washington Parke, 17,081

Custis, Martha (Dandridge) [Mrs. Daniel Parke] (1731-1802). See Washington, Martha (Dandridge) [Mrs. Daniel Parke] Custis [Mrs. George] (1731-1802)

Custis, Mary Anne Randolph (1806-73). See Lee, Mary Anne Randolph (Custis) [Mrs. Robert Edward] (1806-73)

Custis, Mary Lee Fitzhugh [Mrs. George Washington Parke], 17,081

Custis, Nelly Parke. See Lewis, Nelly Parke (Custis)

Customer Is Always Right, The (book), 5,261

Customhouse brokers, **15,162**

Customs administration, **1,174,** 6,366, 8,433, 9,205, 14,587, 14,979

Cuthbert, Anne Emily (Rush) [Mrs. Ross] (1779-1850), 15,084

Cuthbert, Norma, 2,540

Cuthrell, Faith (Baldwin) (1893-). See Baldwin, Faith (1893-)

Cutler, Kathleen L. [Miss], 11,566

Cutler, Anna Alice (1864-1957), 7,158

Cutler, Ephraim (1767-1853), 14,111

Cutler Family, 6,663

Cutler Family (OH), **14,111**

Cutler, Jane Elizabeth (1837-1915), 10,920

Cutler, Julia Perkins (1814-1904), 14,111

Cutler, Manasseh (1742-1823), 14,111

Cutler, Mary Reed (1806-73). See Goodenow, Mary Reed (Cutler) [Mrs. Robert] (1806-73)

Cutler, Mrs. R., 18,025

Cutler, Sarah Cecelia (1842-83), 10,920

Cutler, Sarah Jane Cutler (1856-1933), 14,111

Cutler, William P., 9,899

Cutler, William Parker (1812-89), 14,111

Cutter (slave), 2,156

Cutter, Carrie Eliza (1842-62), **2,289**

Cutter, Eliza Ann. See Whittemore, Eliza Ann (Cutter) [Mrs. Henry]

Cutter, Elizabeth Reeve (1873-1955). See Morrow, Elizabeth Reeve (Cutter) [Mrs. Dwight] (1873-1955)

Cutter, Maria Ygnacia (Vallejo) [Mrs. James Harry] (1857-1932), 858

Cuttington College (Liberia), 5,083

Cuttino Family (GA), 3,323

Cutts, Adele (1835-99). See Williams, Adele (Cutts) [Mrs. Stephen A.] Douglas [Mrs. Robert] (1835-99)

Cutts, Anna (Holyoke) [Mrs. Samuel] (1735-1812), 2,290, 7,385
Cutts, Betsey, 5,695
Cutts, Charles (1769-1846), 2,290
Cutts, Edward, 7,363
Cutts, Eunice [Miss], 5,695
Cutts Family, **2,290**
Cutts Family (ME), **5,695**
Cutts Family (MA), **7,363**
Cutts, Foxwell, 5,695
Cutts, Lucy Henry [Mrs. Charles] (1786-1868), 2,290
Cutts, Mary, 7,387
Cutts, Mary Carter [Mrs. Edward] (1766-?), 7,363
Cutts, Sarah Chauncey, 5,695
Cuyler, Benjamin Ledyard (1802-?), 12,267
Cuyler, Louisa (Morrell) [Mrs. Benjamin Ledyard] (1802-?), 12,267
Cycling, **15,071**
Cypress Creek Cotton Mills, 28
Cypress Lawn Memorial Park, 575
Cytologists, 1,095
Cytomegalic inclusion disease, 10,209
Czech-American periodicals, **3,928**
Czech-Americans, 13,965
Czechoslovakia, 16,831
  American ambassadors to, 2,590
  American National Red Cross (1920-21), 3,327
  nursing schools, 6,152
Czechoslovakian Academy of Commerce (Czechoslovakia), 13,953
Czechoslovakian-American National Alliance, 13,965
Czechoslovakian Cultural Gardens, 13,953
Czechoslovakian Singing Society, 13,953
Czechoslovakian Society of America, 13,953
D. A. Ranch (AZ), 216, 3,685
D. H. Lawrence, An Unprofessional Study (book), 4,232
DHS ranch (MT), 10,270
D. Lothrop and Company, 5,940. *See also* Lothrop, Lee and Shepard (publishers)
D. Mackintosh and Sons Company (MA), **6,191**
Dabbs, Edith (Mitchell) (1906-), 13,176
Dabney, Lucy Jane (1880-), **16,056**
Dabney, Susan (1840-1913). *See* Smedes, Susan (Dabney) (1840-1913)
Dabney, Walter Scates, 16,056
Dace, Catherine (Hubbard) Egbert (1886-1961), **426**
Daddy, Come Home (drama), 9,496
Daddy Was a Number Runner (book), 15,921
Dade, Laura H., 15,093
Daems, Marie L. (?-1904), **10,291**
da Gama, Vasco, 2,485
Daggett, Hannah (1802-?). *See* Collins, Hannah (Daggett) [Mrs. Joseph M.] Buckland [Mrs.] (1802-?)
Daggett, Laura Gilbert, 2,009
Daguerreotype, 2,740
Dahl, Borghild Margarethe (1890-), **4,714**, 8,531, **8,726**
Dahl, Dorthea (1883-1958), **8,727**
Dahl, Lena (Gjertsen) [Mrs. T. H.], 8,867
Dahl, Rebekka Oline Gjertsen (1849-1922), 8,737
Dahlberg, Edward, 16,152
Dahle, John, **8,750**
Dahlem, Margaret M. (ca. 1898-), **3,831**
Dahlgren, John Adolphus Bernard (1809-70), **12,429**
Dahlgren, Sarah Madeleine (Vinton) [Mrs. John Adolphus Bernard] (1825-98), 2,609, 12,429, 14,058
Dahlia Club (MS), **9,533**
Dahlias, **9,533**
Dahlin, Helen (DePass) (1923-), **8,873**
Dahlquist, John, **17,960**
Dahlquist, Laura, **17,960**
Dahme, Florence [Miss], 11,567
Dahn, Adelaide H. [Miss] (1882-1974), **14,135**
Dailey, Grace [Miss] (1874-1961), 1,764
Dailey, John Lewis (1833-1908), **1,764**
Dailey, Margaret (Pryor), **16,409**
Dailey, Mary G., 7,109
Daily Californian (CA), **912**
Daily Doings (newsletter, TX), 16,275
Daily Gator, The, 17,663
Daily Independent (Ashland, KY), 5,313

Daily Journal (MN), 8,457
Daily News (DC), 11,493
Daily News (IN), 12,500
Daily News (NY), 11,493
Daily News (Dayton, OH), 14,046
Daily, Ray K. (1891-1975), **16,236**
Daily Sentinel (Grand Junction, CO), 18,009
Daily Socialist (IL), 10,475
Daily Socialists, The, 4,161
Daily Star (AZ), 197
Daily Times (OH), 13,999
Daily Tribune (MN), 8,429
Daily Worker, The 15,374
Dair, Bessie (1886-1968), 8,167
Dairy bacteriology, 11,579
Dairy cattle, 11,629, 13,272
Dairy cattle breeding, **17,655**
Dairy laws, 5,809, 8,485
Dairy plants, 3,482
Dairying, 16,436, 16,475
Daisy (periodical), 12,106
Dakin, Alice Laura, (1864-?), 1,275
Dakin, Henry Robert (1863-?), 1,275
Dakin, Irene (1888-1974). *See* Paden, Irene (Dakin) (1888-1974)
Dakin, Isaac, 1,275
Dakin, Laura Maria (Jameson) [Mrs. Isaac] (1836-93), **1,275**
Dakin, Susanna (Bryant) (1905-66), **427, 428**
Dakin, Wilbur Jameson (1860-1947), 1,275
Dakota Business College (Fargo, ND), students, 13,669
Dakota Indians, 8,899, 8,936, 8,966, 9,371, 9,446, 9,467, 9,468
  captivities, 9,423
  language, 14,886
  legends, 9,447
  missions, 8,903, 9,185, 9,294, 9,438
  music, 9,042
  wars (1862-1865), 9,045, 9,085, 9,341, 9,371, 9,423, 9,436, 9,462
  reparations, 9,423
  wars (1890-1891), 17,891
Dakota League (MA), **6,177**
Dakota Territorial Centennial Commission, **15,853**
Dakota Territory, 8,316, 8,978, 9,431, 11,630
  cattle, 8,316
  land settlement, 9,158
  military posts, 8,412
  pioneers and settlers, **8,763**
Dalby, Bettie Scoggin (1850-1929), 16,132
Daley, Clara May [Miss] (1871-1955), 5,035
Daley, Gertrude (Donahue) [Mrs. James], 3,451
Daley, Maria L., 14,618
Daley, Richard J., 11,827
Dall, Caroline Wells (Healey) [Mrs. Charles Henry Appleton] (1822-1912), 2,716, 6,500, 6,578, 7,044
Dall, Charles Henry Appleton, 6,500
Dall, William Healey (1845-1927), **1,575, 2,716**
Dallam, Annie Pleasants Fisher [Mrs. Wilbur] (1823-?). *See* Harris, Annie Pleasants Fisher [Mrs. Wilbur] Dallam [Mrs. John W.] (1823-?)
Dallas A&M Mothers' Club (TX), **16,192**
Dallas Academy (Selma, AL), 16,065
Dallas, Alexander James (1759-1817), 14,982
Dallas, Arabella Maria, 14,982
Dallas Civil Liberties Union (TX), **15,991**
Dallas, Constance H. [Mrs.] (1902-), **14,983**
Dallas County Democratic Association (TX), 15,998
Dallas Family (PA), **14,982**
Dallas, George Mifflin (1792-1864), 14,982
Dallas Indian Urbanization Project (TX), **16,344**
Dallas Museum of Fashion (TX), **16,210**
Dallas, Sophia Chew (Nicklin) [Mrs. George Mifflin] (1798-?), 14,982
Dallas, Susan, 14,982
Dalles, The (MN), 9,075
Dalley Family (NY), **11,559**
Dalley, Gretta M., 11,559
Dallin, Cyrus Edwin (1861-1944), 16,934
Dallin, Victoria Colonna (Murray) [Mrs. Cyrus Edwin] (1861-?), **16,934**

Dally, Bea. *See* Lingenfelter, Bea (Dally) [Mrs. C. H.]
Dalton, Alice Ann Langston [Mrs.] (1865-?), 16,486
Dalton, Emily Stevens, 16,915
Dalton, Frances, **13,292**
Dalton, Hannah Daphne (Smith), **16,508**
Dalton, Jack, 11,937
Dalton, John M. (1900-72), **9,951**
Dalton, Julia (Johnson) Whiteturkey [Mrs. Bob] Gilstrap [Mrs. Earnest] Lewis [Mrs. Emmett], 14,173
Dalton laboratory plan, **17,870**
Dalton, Lucinda (Lee) [Mrs. Charles W.] (1847-1925), **429**
Dalton, Luella (Adams) [Mrs. Harley Warren] (1889-1967), **16,410, 16,647**
Dalton, Mary Louise [Miss], 10,046
Dalton, Pleasant Hunter (1821-96), 13,292
Dalton School of Art (New York, NY), 13,122
Daly, Augustin, 4,695, 12,235
Daly, Kathleen E., 2,325
Daly, Charles Patrick (1816-99), **12,430**, 12,431
Daly, Maria (Lydig) [Mrs. Charles Patrick] (1824-94), 12,430, **12,431**
Daly, Mary, 12,629
Dam for Nothing, A (book), 6,096
Damala, Jacques, 6,400
Damala, Sarah (Bernhardt) [Mrs. Jacques] (1845-1923). *See* Bernhardt, Sarah. [Mrs. Jacques] Damala (1845-1923)
D'Amant, Mae [Mrs.], **3,672**
d'Amblimont, Madame, 15,745
Dame, Harriet Patience (1815-1900), **6,501**
Dame, Louinna [Mrs. William H.], 16,411
Dame, Olive Arnold (1882-1954). *See* Campbell, Olive Arnold (Dame) [Mrs. John Charles] (1882-1954)
Dame, Susan, 16,411
Dame, William H. (?-1884), **16,411**
Dameron, Josie, 13,610
Dameron, Julia Mangum, 13,610
Damned Engineers, The (book), 5,264
Damned If You Do—Damned If You Don't (book), 6,062
Damon, Abby Perrin [Mrs. Edward], 10,891
Damon, Bertha Clark Pope [Mrs.], 635, 1,081, 1,082
Damon, Julia Sherman (Mills) [Mrs. Samuel Chenery] (1817-90), 3,640
Damon, Samuel Chenery (1815-85), **3,640**
Damon, Susan (1833-1908). *See* Gale, Susan Damon [Mrs. Samuel Chester] (1833-1908)
Damrosch, Alice Blaine, 12,496
Damrosch, Anita. *See* Littell, Anita (Damrosch) [Mrs. Robert]
Damrosch Family, 556
Damrosch, Frank (1859-1937), 2,020
Damrosch, Leopoldine "Polly" Blaine. *See* Coe, Leopoldine "Polly" Blaine (Damrosch) [Mrs. Sidney Coe]
Damrosch, Margaret (Blaine) [Mrs. Walter Johannes] (1865?-1949), 2,210
Dams, 3,735, 9,133, 9,464, 10,328, 10,781
Dana, Caroline (?-1822). *See* Jarvis, Caroline (Dana) [Mrs. Russell] (?-1822)
Dana, Charles D., 9,624
Dana, Edith (Longfellow) (1853-1915), 6,330
Dana Family, **6,502**
Dana Hall (MA), 6,487
  students, 8,896
Dana, Henrietta (Silliman) [Mrs. James Dwight], 12,420
Dana, Lucile Olive (Davis) (1891-1974), **17,189**
Dana, Lucy, 2,291
Dana, Marietta Hungerford, 10,763
Dana, Mary Amelia (1836-1927). *See* Prang, Mary Amelia (Dana) [Mrs. Charles Spencer] Hicks [Mrs. Louis] (1836-1927)
Dana Natural History Society (Albany, NY), **11,248**
Dana, Olive E. (1859-?), **5,621**
Dana, Richard, 9,624
Dana, Richard H., III, 6,502
Dana, Richard Henry, Jr. (1815-82), 6,502
Dana, Ruth Charlotte (1814-1901), 6,502
Dana, Sarah Watson (1814-1907), 6,502

Danby Baptist Church (NY), 11,587
Dance, 711, 2,804, 9,568, 11,985, 12,260
Dance Club (Elmhurst, IL), 4,197
Dance Encyclopedia, 12,364
Dance Magazine (periodical), 10,894
Dance News (periodical), 12,364
Dance to the Piper (book), 7,214
Dancers, 362, **440**, 687, 718, **764, 1,028, 1,051,** 1,750,
   2,631, 2,968, 3,100, **3,202, 3,773,** 3,856, 4,277,
   4,384, **5,478,** 6,024, **6,067,** 7,167, **7,214,** 9,346,
   10,111, 10,894, 11,312, 11,537, 11,907, **12,359,**
   12,360, 12,361, 12,362, 12,363, 12,364, 12,365,
   12,366, 13,333, **14,199, 14,239, 14,240,** 16,208,
   17,794, **17,965**
Dancers, Afro-American, **12,685,** 14,907
Dancers, Native American, **14,235**
Dancing, 7,214, 7,599, 8,633, **15,110**
   study and teaching, 16,987
Dancing Gods (book), 11,223
d'Andigne, Marquise, 15,385
Dandridge, Danske (1858-1914), **17,454**
Dandridge, Martha (1731-1802). *See* Washington,
   Martha (Dandridge) [Mrs. Daniel Parke] Custis
   [Mrs. George] (1731-1802)
Dane County Young Republicans (WI), 17,628
Dane, Ezra (1828-1921), 1,418
Dane Family (CA), **1,418**
Dane, Henry C., 11,547
Dane, Lois Anna (Nutting) [Mrs. Ezra], 1,418
Dangberg, Grace M. [Miss], **10,661,** 10,750
Dangberg Land and Livestock Company (NV),
   10,661
Dangberg, Mrs. John, 10,750
Dangerfield, Ethel, 2,631
Dangerfield, George, 12,035
"Dangerous Dick" (criminal), 17,961
Daniel Barnes (ship), 1,989
Daniel, Berthe, **8,079**
Daniel, Edna Cain, 3,602
Daniel, Elizabeth Gillenwaters (Brown) [Mrs. Henry
   Clay] (1847-?), 10,026
Daniel, Frank, **2,969,** 2,995, **3,174,** 3,197
Daniel, Jessie (1883-). *See* Ames, Jessie (Daniel)
   (1883-)
Daniel, Joseph, 9,391
Daniel, Kate, 7,222
Daniel, Margaret (Truman) [Mrs. Clifton], 9,962,
   10,048, 10,073, 10,076, 10,082, 10,083, 13,566,
   16,154
Daniel, Mary Brown (1875-?). *See* Moore, Mary
   Brown (Daniel) [Mrs. John Trotwood] (1875-?)
Daniel, Portia Bird, **2,131**
Daniel, Price, 16,000
Daniell, Dorothy (1908-). *See* Schramm, Dorothy
   (Daniell) (1908-)
Daniell, Miriam (1833-189?), 12,698
Daniels, Adelaide "Addie" (Bagley) [Mrs. Josephus]
   (1869-1943), 2,292
Daniels, Agness Powell [Mrs. Richard] Williams [Mrs.
   Francis] Jones [Mrs. David] (1827-94), **9,952**
Daniels, Annie (Stakebake) [Mrs. H. J.] Seayrs [Mrs.
   Benjamin F.] (1869-1946), 190
Daniels, Benjamin F. (1852-1923), **190**
Daniels, Davis, 9,952
Daniels, Edward (1854-1918), **4,470**
Daniels, Florence Hibbs, 9,467
Daniels, George F., 6,503
Daniels, Josephus (1862-1948), **2,292,** 13,228
Daniels, Mabel Wheeler (1878-), **5,920, 6,503**
Daniels, Maria H., 12,551
Daniels, Mary Louise (Underwood) (?-1933), **1,843**
Daniels, Rose, 16,876
Daniels, Sallie, 9,908
Daniels, Vesta Marie (Eaton) Smith (?-1926), 462
Danielson, Sarah, **6,504**
Danilova, Alexandra (ca. 1900-), 3,980
Dann, Anne E. *See* Mason, Anne E. (Dann)
Dann, Hollis, 11,532
Dannat, Mary Caroline. *See* Starr, Mother M.
   Veronica
Dannett, Sylvia G. L., **11,299**
Danniel, Pearl Sparks (1885-), **10,292**
Danske Kvinders Missionsfond (periodical), 3,964
Danskin Family (WA), **17,141**

Danskin, Floyd B., 17,141
Danskin, Hannah (Mitchell) [Mrs. Floyd B.], 17,141
Dantas, Elise (Meyer) Stern de Souze, 945
Dantzler, Cornelia, 15,834
Dantzler, Sophia C., 15,834
Danver, Edna, 16,877
Danvers Women's Association (MA), **7,000**
Danzig, Sarah Palfrey, 15,371
Da-O-Ma (opera), 10,483
d'Aoust, Blancharel, 12,405
D'Apery, Helen (Burrell) (1842-1915), **430**
D'Aquino, Iva Toguri [Mrs.], 1,178
D'Arcy, Barbara O'Neill [Mrs. Peter, Sr.]
   (1823-1901), 17,371
D'Arcy, Belle [Miss], **5,622**
Darcy, Eliza [Miss] (1835?-?), 10,959
D'Arcy Family (OR), **17,371**
D'Arcy, Maria, 17,371
D'Arcy, Marianne (Hunsaker) (1842-?), **14,348**
D'Arcy, Peter, Sr., 17,371
D'Arcy, Theresa, 17,371
Darcy, Timothy Johnes (1790-1878), **10,959**
Darden, Annie "Nannie," **13,392**
Darden, Elizabeth, 9,614
Darden Family (MS), **9,614**
Darden, Ida [Mrs.], **16,253**
Darden, James T., 9,614
Darden, Jesse H., 9,614
Darden, Sarah Annette, 9,614
Darden, Susan (Sillers) [Mrs. Jesse H.], 9,614
Darden, Thomas E., 5,362
Dare, Hazel T., **17,372**
Dare, Virginia (1587-?), 10,764, 12,988
"Dare We Not Discriminate" (forum), 6,633
Dargan, Olive (Tilford) [Mrs. Peagram] (1868-1968),
   5,861, 12,705, **12,992,** 13,055, 13,511
Dargan, Peagram, 13,055
"Dark Eyes" (drama), 2,487
Dark of the Moon (drama), 13,100
Darland, Grace. *See* Needham, Grace (Darland)
   [Mrs. Sherman W.]
Darland, Mary Vermillion [Mrs.], 4,816
Darling, Flora (Adams) [Mrs. Edward Irving]
   (1840-1910), **17,112**
Darling, Isabel, 342
Darling, Lucia (1839-1905). *See* Parks, Lucia
   (Darling) (1839-1905)
Darling, Lucia A., **10,293**
Darling, Nellie J. (Arnott) [Mrs. P. L.], 3,969
Darlington (book), 15,952
Darlington, Georgine "Nina" Kelton (Murphy)
   (1866-?), **14,984**
Darnell, James Samuel, 5,307
Darnell, Maude, 16,876
Darnell, Mrs. James Samuel (1880-1957), **5,307**
Darnley Family (NY), **12,432**
Darnley, William, 12,432
Darrah, Eliza (Clark) (1829-?), 9,004
Darrow, Bob, 17,961
Darrow, Clara [Mrs.], 13,721
Darrow, Clarence, 4,675, 5,209, 7,796
Darrow, Ruby H. [Mrs. Clarence Seward], 2,502,
   2,562
Dart and Dart (LA), **5,536**
Dart Family, 960
Dart, Henry P., 5,414
Dart, Mary Minerva (1838-?). *See* Judd, Mary
   Minerva (Dart) [Mrs. Zadok Knapp] (1838-?)
Dartmouth College (NH), 5,475, 7,584
   alumni, 10,863
   faculty, 10,857, 10,865, 10,869, 10,874, 12,063
   presidents, 5,858
   students, 5,736, 12,055
Dartt, Amy (Sanford) [Mrs. Josiah], 1,730
Dartt, Elizabeth. *See* Sayre, Elizabeth (Dartt) [Mrs.
   Hal]
Dartt, Josiah, 1,730
Dartt, Mary. *See* Thompson, Mary (Dartt) [Mrs.
   Nathan]
Dartt-Maxwell Family, 1,730
D'Arusmont, Frances [Mrs. Guillaume Sylvan Casimir
   Phiquepal] (1795-1852). *See* Wright, Frances.
   [Mrs. Guillaume Sylvan Casimir Phiquepal]
   D'Arusmont (1795-1852)

D'Arusmont, Guillaume Sylvan Casimir Phiquepal,
   2,656, 13,846
D'Arusmont, Sylva. *See* Guthrie, Sylva
   (D'Arusmont)
Das Illustrirte Mississippithal, 9,125
Dashiell, Margaret (May) [Mrs. John Parker]
   (1869-1958), 2,877, **12,993**
Dashiell, Sarah. *See* Stone, Sarah (Dashiell) [Mrs.
   David]
Daskam, Josephine Dodge (1876-1961). *See* Bacon,
   Josephine Dodge (Daskam) (1876-1961)
Dat-So-La-Lee (?-1925), 10,657, 10,680
Daugherty, James H., 12,570
Daughter of Earth (book), 174
Daughters from Afar (book), 7,301
Daughters of Africa Society (PA), 14,985
Daughters of America, Baxter Council Thirty-four
   (KY), **5,338**
Daughters of Charity of St. Vincent de Paul, 5,493,
   5,494, 16,343
Daughters of Charity of St. Vincent de Paul, East
   Central Province (Evansville, IN), **4,497**
Daughters of Charity of St. Vincent de Paul, Marillac
   Provincial House (St. Louis, MO), **10,144**
Daughters of Charity of St. Vincent de Paul, St.
   Joseph's Provincial House (Emmitsburg, MD),
   5,847
Daughters of Charity of St. Vincent de Paul, Seton
   Provincialate (Los Altos Hills, CA), 996
Daughters of Christ Church (Adrian, MI), Women's
   Auxiliary, **7,906**
Daughters of Colonial Wars, 7,669, **13,393**
Daughters of Confederate Veterans, **9,615**
Daughters of 1812. *See* United States Daughters of
   1812
Daughters of 1812 (IN), **4,558**
Daughters of 1812 (Peter Navarre Chapter), 14,137
Daughters of '53 (New Haven, CT), **1,993**
Daughters of Founders and Patriots of America (MS),
   9,551
Daughters of Founders and Patriots of America (PA),
   14,986
Daughters of Founders and Patriots of America,
   California Chapter, **1,276**
Daughters of Hawaii, 3,653
Daughters of Hope (Providence, RI), **15,380**
Daughters of Isabella, 4,165
Daughters of Israel Relief Society, 946
Daughters of Pioneers of Washington, 14,676, **17,136**
Daughters of Temperance, 3,069
Daughters of the American Colonists, 3,415, **8,319,**
   9,962, **17,962**
Daughters of the American Colonists, Dr. Henry
   Woodward Chapter (SC), **15,579**
Daughters of the American Colonists, Georgia
   Society, 3,439
Daughters of the American Colonists, Iowa, 4,960
Daughters of the American Colonists, James Edward
   Oglethorpe Chapter (GA), **3,175**
Daughters of the American Colonists, South Carolina
   Society, **15,580**
Daughters of the American Republic, 4,815, 11,324,
   15,881
Daughters of the American Republic, Captain
   Hubbard Burrows Chapter (Hinsdale, IL), 4,278
Daughters of the American Republic, Commodore
   Samuel Tucker Chapter (MA), 7,090
Daughters of the American Republic, Mercy Otis
   Chapter (IA), 4,860
Daughters of the American Revolution, 9, 203, **281,**
   589, 1,078, 1,092, 1,534, **1,547,** 1,688, **1,899,**
   1,948, 1,969, 2,114, **2,123,** 2,193, **2,293,** 2,844,
   2,901, 2,955, 3,169, 3,383, 3,423, **3,497, 3,605,**
   3,653, 3,930, 4,539, 4,661, 4,689, 4,732, 4,799,
   4,918, 5,109, 5,123, 5,136, 5,307, 5,308, 5,326,
   5,549, 5,641, 5,850, 6,355, 6,365, 6,901, 6,953,
   7,187, 7,546, 7,669, 7,704, 8,167, 8,301, **8,320,**
   8,436, 8,606, **8,820,** 8,948, 8,962, 9,015, 9,113,
   9,280, 9,550, 9,551, 9,596, **9,616,** 9,647, 9,692,
   9,697, 9,706, 9,719, 9,731, 9,779, 9,870, 9,935,
   9,940, 9,986, 9,993, 10,032, 10,048, 10,112,
   10,211, 10,407, 10,666, 10,679, 10,773, **10,924,**
   11,154, 11,222, 11,274, 11,445, 11,704, 12,532,
   12,847, 13,070, 13,159, 13,344, 13,375, 13,388,

13,394, 13,395, 13,439, 13,446, 13,557, 13,576, 13,595, 13,617, 13,618, 13,629, 13,853, 14,005, 14,153, **14,167,** 14,230, 15,221, 15,302, 15,597, 15,620, 15,942, 15,951, 16,116, 16,127, 16,265, **16,298,** 16,997, 17,029, **17,112,** 17,170, 17,189, 17,293, 17,390, 17,394, 17,434, 17,441

Daughters of the American Revolution (CA), **432, 1,277,** 1,297

Daughters of the American Revolution (Berkeley Hills, CA), **431**

Daughters of the American Revolution (Sequoia Chapter, CA), 1,253

Daughters of the American Revolution (CO), **1,708, 1,765**

Daughters of the American Revolution (Ruth Wyllys Chapter, Hartford, CT), **1,899**

Daughters of the American Revolution (Cherokee Chapter, GA), 3,374, **3,385**

Daughters of the American Revolution (Edmund Burke Chapter, GA), 3,358

Daughters of the American Revolution (General James Jackson Chapter 1010, GA), 3,615

Daughters of the American Revolution (Hannah Clarke Chapter, GA), 3,385

Daughters of the American Revolution (Lachlan McIntosh Chapter, GA), 3,498

Daughters of the American Revolution (Peachtree Chapter, GA), 3,385

Daughters of the American Revolution (Sarah Dickinson Chapter, GA), 3,418

Daughters of the American Revolution (ID), **3,673, 3,674**

Daughters of the American Revolution (Alliance Chapter No. 462, IL), **4,414**

Daughters of the American Revolution (Illinois Chapter), **4,415**

Daughters of the American Revolution (IN), **4,557**

Daughters of the American Revolution (IA), **4,902**

Daughters of the American Revolution (Pilgrim Chapter, IA), 4,916

Daughters of the American Revolution (James Ross Chapter, KS), 5,176

Daughters of the American Revolution (William Wilson Chapter, Garden City, KS), 5,179

Daughters of the American Revolution (Boonesborough Chapter, KY), **5,404**

Daughters of the American Revolution (Bryan Station Chapter, KY), 5,326

Daughters of the American Revolution (Attakapas Chapter, LA), 633

Daughters of the American Revolution (Hannah Weston Chapter, Machias, ME), **5,610**

Daughters of the American Revolution (Silence Howard Hayden Chapter, Waterville, ME), **5,717**

Daughters of the American Revolution (MI), **7,768**

Daughters of the American Revolution (Dearborn, MI), **8,011**

Daughters of the American Revolution (Genesee Chapter, MI), **8,178**

Daughters of the American Revolution (John Biddle Chapter, Trenton, MI), 7,858

Daughters of the American Revolution (Keziah Cooley Goss Chapter, Ann Arbor, MI), 7,858

Daughters of the American Revolution (Lewis Cass Chapter, Escanaba, MI), 7,858

Daughters of the American Revolution (Menominee, MI), 7,858

Daughters of the American Revolution (Sarah Caswell Angell Chapter, Ann Arbor, MI), 7,858

Daughters of the American Revolution (MN), **9,029, 9,030, 9,031**

Daughters of the American Revolution (Anthony Wayne Chapter, MN), **8,496**

Daughters of the American Revolution (Sibley House Association, MN), **9,032**

Daughters of the American Revolution (MS), 9,626

Daughters of the American Revolution (Barnard Romans Chapter, MS), 9,638

Daughters of the American Revolution (Copiah Chapter, MS), **9,616**

Daughters of the American Revolution (David Reese Chapter, MS), **9,816**

Daughters of the American Revolution (Hic-a-sha-ba-ha Chapter, MS), **16,086**

Daughters of the American Revolution (Magnolia State Chapter, MS), **9,616**

Daughters of the American Revolution (Mississippi Delta Chapter, MS), 9,731

Daughters of the American Revolution (Ralph Humphreys Chapter, MS), **9,616**

Daughters of the American Revolution (Columbia Chapter, MO), **9,953**

Daughters of the American Revolution (Elizabeth Benton Chapter, MO), **10,109**

Daughters of the American Revolution (Kansas City Chapter, MO), **10,109**

Daughters of the American Revolution (Black Eagle Chapter, Great Falls, MT), **10,294**

Daughters of the American Revolution (Oro Fino Chapter, Helena, MT), **10,295**

Daughters of the American Revolution (Betsey Hager Chapter, Grand Island, NE), **10,410**

Daughters of the American Revolution (Deborah Avery Chapter, NE), **10,451**

Daughters of the American Revolution (NV), **10,662**

Daughters of the American Revolution (John C. Fremont Chapter, NV), 10,662

Daughters of the American Revolution (Margery Sullivan Chapter (NH), **10,840**

Daughters of the American Revolution (Mary Torr Chapter, Rochester, NH), 10,887

Daughters of the American Revolution (Camp Middlebrook Chapter, NJ), **10,960**

Daughters of the American Revolution (General Frelinghuysen Chapter, NJ), **10,961**

Daughters of the American Revolution (Jersey Blue Chapter, New Brunswick, NJ), **10,963**

Daughters of the American Revolution (Whitehouse Chapter, NJ), 10,961

Daughters of the American Revolution (William Maxwell Chapter, NJ), **10,903**

Daughters of the American Revolution (Brooklyn Battle Pass Chapter, NY), **11,319**

Daughters of the American Revolution (Meeting House Hill Chapter, East Durham, NY), **11,438**

Daughters of the American Revolution (Tioughnioga Chapter, Cortland, NY), **11,409**

Daughters of the American Revolution (Yennicott Chapter, NY), **12,776**

Daughters of the American Revolution (Caswell-Nash Chapter, Raleigh, NC), 13,394

Daughters of the American Revolution (Col. Polk Chapter, Raleigh, NC), 13,394

Daughters of the American Revolution (Davie Chapter, Durham, NC), 13,394

Daughters of the American Revolution (Davie Poplar Chapter, NC), **12,994**

Daughters of the American Revolution (Fort Industry Chapter, OH), 14,137

Daughters of the American Revolution (George Crogham Chapter, OH), **14,066**

Daughters of the American Revolution (Ursula Wolcott Chapter, OH), 14,137

Daughters of the American Revolution (War Emergency Relief Board, OH), **13,968**

Daughters of the American Revolution (Western Reserve Chapter, OH), **13,920**

Daughters of the American Revolution (OR), **14,349**

Daughters of the American Revolution (West Chester, PA), **15,342**

Daughters of the American Revolution (Rebecca Motte Chapter, SC), 15,405

Daughters of the American Revolution (University of South Carolina Chapter), **15,581**

Daughters of the American Revolution (Daniel Newcomb Chapter, SD), 2,293

Daughters of the American Revolution (TN), **15,947**

Daughters of the American Revolution (Colonel George Moffett Chapter, TX), 16,178

Daughters of the American Revolution (San Antonio de Bexar Chapter, TX), 16,040, 16,313

Daughters of the American Revolution (General Lewis Morris Chapter, Springfield, VT), 17,048

Daughters of the American Revolution (Albemarle County, VA), 17,057

Daughters of the American Revolution (Jack Jouette Chapter, VA), 17,057

Daughters of the American Revolution (Point of Fork Chapter, VA), 17,057

Daughters of the American Revolution (Mary Ball Chapter No. 29, WA), **17,403**

Daughters of the American Revolution, Chapter 292 (Lansing, MI), **8,271**

Daughters of the American Revolution, Elizabeth Benton Chapter, 10,109

Daughters of the American Revolution, Gulf Coast Chapter, 9,706

Daughters of the American Revolution, Marian Anderson controversy (DC), **2,123**

Daughters of the American Revolution, National Board of Management, 4,902

Daughters of the American Revolution, William Maxwell Chapter, 10,903

Daughters of the Grand Army of the Republic (MI), **8,272**

Daughters of the Grand Army of the Republic, General Alpheus S. Williams Fortress (MI), 8,272

Daughters of the King, Chicago Chapter (IL), **3,940**

Daughters of the Military Order of the Loyal Region, **12,189**

Daughters of the Pioneers, 17,170

Daughters of the Pioneers (Skagit Chapter No. II, WA), **17,149**

Daughters of the Republic of Texas, 16,014, 16,058, 16,116, 16,127, 16,178, **16,299,** 16,314, 16,382

Daughters of the Revolution, 17,112

Daughters of the Snake River Pioneers (ID), **3,736**

Daughters of the Utah Pioneers, **3,737,** 3,739, 16,401, **16,412,** 16,430, 16,441, 16,445, 16,447, 16,525, **16,648,** 16,755

Daughters of the Utah Pioneers (Camp G, UT), 16,648

Daughters of the Utah Pioneers (Camp 10), 16,648, 16,790

Daughters of the Utah Pioneers (Wandamere Camp), 16,611

Daughters of the War of 1812. *See* United States Daughters of 1812

Daughters of the World, **4,187**

Daughters of Union Veterans of the Civil War, **2,294, 4,745, 4,903,** 5,176, 10,622

Daughters of Union Veterans of the Civil War (Clara Barton Tent No. 5, York, NE), 10,619

Daughters of Zion, 3,865

D'Auliffe, **12,433**

Daum, Kate (1892-1955), 5,035

Dautin, Amelia [Mrs.], 3,599

D'Autremont, **6,505**

Davenport Academy of Science (IA), 4,732

Davenport, Charles B., 2,464

Davenport, Edward Loomis (1815-77), 961

Davenport, Eleanor [Mrs.], 1,268

Davenport, Ellen Miller, 16,417

Davenport, Eugene, 4,380, 4,386

Davenport Family, **961**

Davenport Family (NY), **11,560**

Davenport Family (TX), **16,057**

Davenport, Fanny (1850-98). *See* Davenport, Fanny Lily Gypsy (1850-98)

Davenport, Fanny Lily Gypsy. [Mrs. Edwin H.] Price [Mrs. William Melbourne] MacDowell (1850-98), 961, 2,303, 4,695, 8,297, 12,832

Davenport, Fanny Vining [Mrs. Edward Loomis], 961

Davenport Home for Female Orphan Children, 11,560

Davenport, Jean Margaret (1829-1903). *See* Lander, Jean Margaret (Davenport) [Mrs. Frederick West] (1829-1903)

Davenport, Marcia (Gluck) [Mrs. Russell W.] (1903-), **2,295,** 2,876, 12,035

Davenport, Mary Bucklin (1825-96). *See* Claflin, Mary Bucklin (Davenport) [Mrs. William] (1825-96)

Davenport, Minnie D. (1883-1966). *See* Craig, Minnie D. (Davenport) [Mrs. Edward O.] (1883-1966)

Davenport, Mrs. Dixwell, 1,315

Davenport, Nancy, 16,057

Davenport, Russell Wheeler (1899-1954), 2,295, 14,447

Davenport, Samuel, 16,034

Davenport, Sarah Rosamund, 3,549
Davenport, Thomas Donald, 2,434
Daves, Delmer, **1,576**
Daves, Mary Haynes, 13,411
Daves, Mary Lou, 1,576
Davey (slave, SC), 15,530
Davey, Marie Augusta "Minnie Maddern" (1865-1932). *See* Fiske, Marie Augusta "Minnie Maddern" (Davey) [Mrs. LeGrand] White [Mrs. Harrison Grey] (1865-1932)
"David and Anna Mattson" (poem), 14,703
David Bispham Memorial Medal, 1,022
David, Elizabeth Ruggles, 11,176
David McKay Company, 14,327
David, Theodore M. (1837-1915), 14,882
Davidian, Nectar, 433
Davids, May (Dow) [Mrs. George W.]. *See* Young, May (Dow) [Mrs. George W.] Davids [Mrs. John Russell]
Davidson, Alice. *See* Boyer, Alice (Davidson)
Davidson, Allen T., 13,396
Davidson, Donald (1893-1968), **15,929**
Davidson, Doris, 6,221
Davidson, Ellinor C., 434
Davidson, Ellinor (Fauntleroy) [Mrs. George], 434
Davidson Family, **10,962**
Davidson Family (MO), **9,870**
Davidson, Frances Stillman [Mrs. Gaylord] (1873-1959), 9,216
Davidson, George (1825-1911), **434**
Davidson, Jane W. *See* Kops, Jane W. Davidson de Bruyn [Mrs.]
Davidson, John, 1,187
Davidson, John L., 3,176
Davidson, John Mitchell (1829-1917), **3,176, 3,317**
Davidson, Julia B. [Mrs.], 9,033
Davidson, Julia (Dunn) [Mrs. John Mitchell] (1836-90), **3,176,** 3,317
Davidson, Lucretia Maria (1808-25), 1,084, 10,962
Davidson, Margaret. *See* Clark, Margaret Miller (Davidson)
Davidson, Margaret Miller [Miss], 10,962
Davidson, Mary Aileen, 9,870
Davidson, Mary Blossom (?-1968), **435**
Davidson, Mrs. James Frank, 9,870
Davidson, Ophelia, 15,767
Davidson, Sallie Davenport (1857-1935), 10,296
Davidson, Sarah A. *See* Wangensteen, Sarah A. Davidson [Mrs. Owen]
Davidson, Sarah Anne (Johnston) [Mrs. William F.], 9,033
Davidson, Sarah Matilda (1874-1945). *See* Davidson, Sarah Matilda (Davidson) [Mrs. W. P.] (1874-1945)
Davidson, Sarah Matilda (Davidson) [Mrs. W. P.] (1874-1945), 9,033
Davidson, Sylvia, **7,769**
Davidson, Theodore F., **13,396**
Davidson, William Fuson, Family (MN), **9,033**
Davidson, Winifred [Mrs. John] (1874-1964), **1,187**
Davie, Eugenie Mary [Mrs. Preston] (1895-1975), 11,913
Davie, Marie Augusta (1865-1932). *See* Fiske, Marie Augusta "Minnie Maddern" (Davey) [Mrs. LeGrand] White [Mrs. Harrison Grey] (1865-1932)
Davies, Daisy Bell (Hitch) (1877-1938), **6,506**
Davies Family (PA), 15,053
Davies, Jane (1830-1922). *See* Kellogg, Jane (Davies) (1830-1922)
Davies, Maria (1865-1951). *See* McGrath, Maria (Davies) (1865-1951)
Davies, Mary Ann. *See* Whittle, Mary Ann Davies [Mrs. Fortescue]
Davies, Mary Carolyn (1888-?), **436,** 14,350, 15,060
Davies, Mary Murray, 3,436
Davis, A. J., 8,407
Davis, Ada M., 14,504
Davis, Adeline (Burr) [Mrs. David], 4,356
Davis, Adelle (1904-74), 6,034
Davis, Alice [Mrs. William J.], 7,507
Davis, Alice (1870-1936). *See* Menken, Alice (Davis) (1870-1936)
Davis, Alice (Brown) [Mrs. George Rollin] (1852-1935), **14,234**

Davis, Alice Taylor [Mrs. Michael], 8,677
Davis, Allen Bowie (1809-89), **5,754**
Davis, Alpha. *See* Edge, Alpha (Davis) [Mrs. Andrew J.]
Davis, Amanda, **9,954**
Davis, Amelia, 14,618
Davis, Angela (1944-), **1,567, 7,211,** 14,691, 15,176, 17,759
Davis, Ann B., 16,208
Davis, Anna M., **9,854**
Davis, Anne, 4,150
Davis, Anne (Pence), **5,261**
Davis, Apollonia (Weyerhaeuser) [Mrs. S. S.] (1864-1953), 9,433
Davis, Belle Fremont (1879-1901), 3,832
Davis, Bette (1908-), **6,005**
Davis, Catherine (1757-?), **17,082**
Davis, Charles Augustus, 5,347
Davis, Charles E., 8,307
Davis, Clara Addie (1850-?). *See* Lester, Clara Addie (Davis) [Mrs. Anson Wood]
Davis, Cornelia (Whipple) [Mrs. William Wilkins] (1845-84). *See* Rose, Cornelia (Whipple) [Mrs. William Wilkins] Davis [Mrs. Francis Marion] (1845-84)
Davis, Daniel, 16,812
Davis, David (1815-86), 3,760, **4,356**
Davis, Doreen, 11,861
Davis, Dorothy. *See* Boyich, Dorothy (Davis)
Davis, Dorothy Salisbury [Mrs.] (1916-), **11,310**
Davis, Dulce (Bolado), **1,278**
Davis, Eliza (Bancroft) [Mrs. John] (1791-1872), 7,615, 11,514
Davis, Eliza (Patten). *See* Hodge, Eliza (Patten) Davis [Mrs. Benjamin]
Davis, Eliza Van Benthuysen [Mrs. Joseph E.], 5,518
Davis, Elizabeth (1803-86). *See* Bancroft, Elizabeth (Davis) [Mrs. Alexander] Bliss [Mrs. George] (1803-86)
Davis, Elizabeth Jeffords (Drake) [Mrs. Daniel] (1830-1916). *See* Roundy, Elizabeth Jeffords (Drake) [Mrs. Daniel] Davis [Mrs. Jared Curtis] (1830-1916)
Davis, Elizabeth Lindsay [Mrs.], 4,142
Davis, Elizabeth S., **10,963,** 11,045
Davis, Elkanah, 8,967
Davis, Ella Hanna [Mrs. George Perrin], 4,356
Davis, Ellabelle, 3,290
Davis, Ellen, 9,467
Davis, Emily, **4,471**
Davis, Ester, 5,754
Davis, Esther, 9,397
Davis, Ethelreda C., 437
Davis, Eunice Cady [Mrs. Alden] (1817-?), 1,900
Davis, F. J., 9,114
Davis Family, 14,651
Davis Family (CT), 1,900
Davis Family (MD), 5,744
Davis Family (NE), 10,452
Davis Family (SC), 15,652
Davis, Fannie (1867-1955). *See* Ennis, Fannie (Davis) (1867-1955)
Davis, Francis W., 14,119
Davis, Fred C., **1,900**
Davis, George Rollin, 14,234
Davis, Gherardi (1858-1941), **12,434**
Davis, Gladys Riley, **3,675**
Davis, Gladys Rockmore (1901-67), **2,747**
Davis, Grace (ca. 1885-1953), 17,189
Davis, Hallie (Ferguson) Flanagan (1890-1969), **2,759, 11,480,** 12,884
Davis, Harriet Tubman [Mrs. John] Ross [Mrs. Nelson] (ca. 1815-1913). *See* Tubman, Harriet. [Mrs. John] Ross [Mrs. Nelson] Davis (ca. 1815-1913)
Davis, Helen (1880-). *See* Clinton, Helen (Davis) (1880-)
Davis, Helen Clarkson (Miller) [Mrs. Harvey N.] (1879-1968), **6,507**
Davis, Helen Elvira (1909-). *See* McMillan, Helen Elvira (Davis) [Mrs. Kenneth] (1909-)
Davis, Helen Louise. *See* Stevenson, Helen Louise (Davis) [Mrs. Lewis Green]

Davis, Helen Stuart (1869-1966), **2,748**
Davis, Helene (Hinz) [Mrs. Edwin W.], 522
Davis, Henrietta Vinton, 9,048
Davis, Hester A. (Wilkins) [Mrs. Allen Bowie] (1809-88), 5,754
Davis, Hilda Andrea (1905-), 89
Davis, Horatio, 2,887
Davis, Inez (Smith) (1889-1964), **10,089**
Davis, Jacquatta, 13,108
Davis, Jane (Brough) [Mrs. William] (1820-1908), **16,649**
Davis, Jeannette P., 11,662
Davis, Jefferson (1808-89), **101, 2,296,** 2,384, 2,490, 2,996, 3,227, 3,570, 5,350, 5,413, 5,415, 5,482, 5,518, 6,509, 9,600, **9,617, 9,618,** 9,619, 9,657, 9,658, 9,678, 9,737, 9,748, 9,783, 9,795, 9,884, **12,190,** 12,503, 13,054, 13,136, 13,268, 13,344, **13,397,** 15,585, 16,114, 17,992
Davis, Jerome, 8,113
Davis, Jessie (Bartlett) [Mrs. William James] (1859-1905), 3,832
Davis, John, 14,119
Davis, John (1787-1854), **7,615**
Davis, John Burton, 16,151
Davis, John J., **17,455**
Davis, John Jefferson, 17,853
Davis, John W., 17,455, 17,456, 17,472
Davis, Joseph E., 2,490, 5,518, 9,714
Davis, Joy P., 2,678
Davis, Julia, 10,191
Davis, Julia McDonald (1900-), 17,455
Davis, Justina. *See* Nash, Justina Davis [Mrs.] Dobbs [Mrs. Abner]
Davis, Kate (Winslow), 10,452
Davis, Katharine Bement (1860-1935), 12,736
Davis, Katherine (1894 or 1895-), **5,645**
Davis, Katherine K., 7,578
Davis, Lambert, 9,769
Davis, Laura, **12,918**
Davis, Lemuel Clarke, 1,426
Davis, Lena B., 13,446
Davis, Lewis, 14,119
Davis, Lizzie, 376
Davis, Lucile Olive (1891-1974). *See* Dana, Lucile Olive (Davis) (1891-1974)
Davis, Lucy I., 14,699
Davis, Lydia (Lord) [Mrs. Francis W.] (?-1952), **14,119**
Davis, Madeline, 1,662
Davis, Margaret, 9,701
Davis, Margaret [Miss] (1875-1958), **10,452**
Davis, Margaret E. (1892-), 11,833
Davis, Margaret Howell Jefferson. *See* Hayes, Margaret Howell Jefferson (Davis)
Davis, Margaret M. (1891-), 94
Davis, Margaret (Stout) [Mrs. Will] (1870-?), **9,955**
Davis, Marguerite (1887-1967), **17,853**
Davis, Maria Gibbs, 9,346
Davis, Maria H., 7,383
Davis, Martha Jenks [Mrs. William H.] (1869-1955), 17,189
Davis, Mary, 7,150
Davis, Mary. *See* Mitchell, Mary (Davis) [Mrs. Charles Jewett]
Davis, Mary (1845-?). *See* Bucknall, Mary (Davis) [Mrs. George] (1845-?)
Davis, Mary Alice (1872-?), 17,924
Davis, Mary Dorsey (?-1939), 5,754
Davis, Mary Eliza, 1,440
Davis, Mary (Gardiner) [Mrs. William Nye], 6,593
Davis, Mary Gould [Miss] (1882-1956), **12,435**
Davis, Mary J., **2,297**
Davis, Mary O. (1881-1964), **1,709**
Davis, Mary P., **7,770**
Davis, Mary Roselle, 16,060
Davis, Melissa Jane Lambson. *See* Rice, Melissa Jane Lambson Davis [Mrs. Asaph]
Davis, Mildred, 6,060
Davis, Mollie Evelyn (Moore) [Mrs. Thomas E.] (1844-1909), 5,418, **5,498,** 5,524
Davis, Mrs. Cushman K., 8,925
Davis, Mrs. Henry C., 15,593
Davis, Mrs. John, 10,449

Davis, Mrs. Robert, 12,630
Davis, Mrs. Stuart, 2,847
Davis, Myrtie Harwood [Mrs. George William], 1,900
Davis, Olive Bell, **3,177**
Davis, Paulina (Kellogg) Wright (1813-76), 5,907, **6,508**, 15,389
Davis, Peter, 12,628
Davis, Purley B., 12,435
Davis, Rebecca Blaine (Harding) [Mrs. Lemuel Clarke] (1831-1910), 1,426, 11,821
Davis, Rebecca Dorsey (ca. 1844-1921), 5,754
Davis, Reuben, 9,717
Davis, Robert Hobart (1869-1942), **12,436,** 12,630
Davis, Roleta (1913-). See Teal, Roleta (Davis) [Mrs. Talmadge Theodore] (1913-)
Davis, Ruby Sheppard, **12,685**
Davis, Ruth (1914-67). See Hill, Ruth (Davis) [Mrs. Roscoe] (1914-67)
Davis, Sarah, **4,797**
Davis, Sarah. See Lilliard, Sarah (Davis) Swayne [Mrs. John T.]
Davis, Sarah [Mrs. A. J.], 15,506
Davis, Sarah (McCauley) [Mrs. Elkanah], 8,967
Davis, Sarah Olive Packard, 15,506
Davis, Sarah (Walker) [Mrs. David] (1814-79), 4,356, 7,590
Davis, Sibby Ann (Waters). See Bond, Sibby Ann (Waters) Davis [Mrs. Alvan]
Davis, Sophia (Lowe) [Mrs. Nicholas], **72**
Davis, Stuart, 2,748
Davis, Thomas, 8,167
Davis, Thomas, 9,747
Davis, Varina Anne (Howell) [Mrs. Jefferson] (1826-1906), 101, 1,963, 2,211, 2,296, 2,384, 2,522, 2,892, **2,996,** 3,103, 3,570, 3,889, 4,244, 4,695, **4,746,** 5,350, **5,482, 6,509,** 7,613, **9,617, 9,618, 9,619,** 9,658, 9,696, 9,714, 9,783, 9,793, 9,795, 10,417, 12,190, 12,327, 13,344, 13,359, 13,385, 13,397
Davis, Varina Anne "Winnie" Jefferson (1864-98), 2,996, 3,166, 9,619, 9,737
Davis, W. Wilkins, 5,754
Davis, Will, 9,955
Davis, William, 14,119
Davis, William H., 17,189
Davis, William Heath (1822-1909), **1,419**
Davis, William James (1844-1919), **3,832**
Davison, Ada Clark, **10,895**
Davison, Ann Maria (1783-?), **6,510**
Davison, Benoni Richmond, 3,628
Davison, Birta M., 5,675
Davison, Eliza Ann (Gannett) [Mrs. John] (1811-?), **5,675**
Davison, Emma Ahuena (1866-1937). See Taylor, Emma Ahuena (Davison) [Mrs. Albert Pierce] (1866-1937)
Davison, John, 5,675
Davison, John A., 5,675
Davison, Mary Jane Kekulani (Fayerweather) [Mrs. Benoni Richmond] (1842-1930). See Montano, Mary Jane Kekulani (Fayerweather) [Mrs. Benoni Richmond] Davison [Mrs. Andres Avelino] (1842-1930)
Davison, Natalie, 2,691
Davison, Peter, 4,485
Davisson, Ida, 195
Dawes, Anna L. (1851-1938), 2,298
Dawes Commission, 14,234
Dawes, Elta (Sanderson) [Mrs. Henry Laurens] (1822-1901), 2,298
Dawes General Allotment Act (1887), 10,459
Dawes, Henry Laurens (1816-1903), **2,298**
Dawes, Mrs. Rufus, 4,066
Dawn, Day and Eventide (book), 1,772
Dawn in Carolina (drama), 15,612
Dawn's Early Light (book), 5,031
Dawsey, Marie, 3,499
Dawson, Anna Cheney, 3,763
Dawson, Carley (Robinson), 14,322, **14,351**
Dawson, Elizabeth, 8,948
Dawson, Emma Frances (1851-1926), 616, 1,082
Dawson Family, 12,020
Dawson, Henry B., 12,167

Dawson, Irene J., 9,397
Dawson, John Wells, 3,763
Dawson, Mary Cardwell, **12,686**
Dawson, Mary E. S., **2,012**
Dawson, Nancy [Mrs. Ralph Burk] (1920-), **11,981**
Dawson, Nelle (1895-?), **3,676**
Dawson, Mrs. P., 13,454
Dawson-Paist, Maria, 3,754
Dawson, Roper, 11,318
Day, Alice. See Jackson, Alice (Day)
Day, Alice Chenoweth [Mrs. Charles Selden] Smart [Mrs. Selden Allen] (1853-1925), **6,592, 6,976**
Day, Alice (Hooker) [Mrs. John C.] (1847-1928), 1,948, 1,952
Day, Anna [Mrs.], **155**
Day, Anna (Blakiston) (1869-1952), 14,987
Day Care and Child Development Council of America, 7,248
Day Care and Child Development Council of Oregon, 14,605
Day care centers. See Child care centers
Day Care Crisis Council of Chicago (IL), 4,081
Day, Caroline E., 6,631
Day, Dorothy (1899-), 12,884
Day, Eli Azariah (1856-?), **16,935**
Day, Elvira Euphrasia (Cox) [Mrs. Eli Azariah] (1864-1944), **16,650**
Day, Emeline (Hubbard), **438**
Day, Emma Ellen (1862-1952). See Newsom, Emma Ellen (Day) [Mrs. John Edward] (1862-1952)
Day, Emma Rebecca (Hunt) [Mrs. John T.] Ewing [Mrs. James Collins], **9,034**
Day, Ethelmary. See Russell, Ethelmary (Day)
Day Family (IL, IN, ME, OH), **17,622**
Day, Frank Arah (1855-1928), **9,035**
Day, Frederick Holland, 2,370
Day, George E., 17,622
Day, James Collins (1822-1911), 9,034
Day, Katharine Seymour [Miss] (1870-1964), **1,948,** 1,952, 1,953
Day, Lionel Warrington, 17,622
Day, Marian MacDowell, 2,463
Day, Mary Anna (1852-1924), **6,277,** 10,152
Day, Maureen, 3,762
Day, Mrs. James C., **10,297**
"Day of My Advent in the Legal Profession, The," 14,553
Day, Orville, 16,876
Day, Pearl (1887-1968). See Bach, Pearl (Day) [Mrs. William Everett] (1887-1968)
Day, Ruth, 11,662
Day, Sarah Ellis (1883-). See Coombs, Sarah Ellis (Day) [Mrs. Leslie McLean] (1883-)
Day, Selden Allen, 6,592
"Day We Celebrate, The," 16,174
Days of Jeanne d'Arc, The (book), 3,985
Days of My Life (book), 5,229
Days of Our Lives (book), 12,589
"Days of Our Lives" (television program), 18,000
Dayton Art Institute (OH), 2,817
Dayton Ballet Company (OH), **14,047**
Dayton Civic Ballet (OH), **14,047**
Dayton Division of Health (OH), 6,154
Dayton Family, 9,388
Dayton, Ida May (1872-?). See Young, Ida May (Dayton) (1872-?)
Dayton, Mary, 12,154
Dayton, Rachel. See Gillett, Rachel (Dayton)
Dayton, Velma (Adams), 982
Deaconess Home (Oslo, Norway), 8,732
Deaconess Home (OR), 10,564
Deaconess Order of the Synod, 10,212
Deaconess School of Nursing (IL), 8,862
Deaconess Training School of the Pacific, 16,027
Deaconesses, **1,812,** 2,931, **3,937, 3,938,** 4,026, 4,201, 5,394, **5,817,** 5,827, **7,038, 8,732,** 8,760, **8,761,** 8,770, 8,859, 8,862, 10,447, **10,565,** 10,598, 11,140, 15,202
Dead Lovers Are Faithful Lovers (book), 2,969, 3,232
Deadwyler, Alice Ann Mildred, 3,002
Deady Family (OR), **14,541**
Deady, Lucy Ann (Henderson) [Mrs. Matthew] (1835-1923), 14,541

Deady, Matthew Paul (1824-93), 14,541
Deaf, 1,609, **2,103,** 2,106, **2,107, 2,109, 2,110, 2,112, 2,113,** 2,676, **6,426,** 6,919, 7,560, 8,618, **10,982**
education, 2,104, 2,105, 2,110, 2,308, **2,341,** 2,919, 10,188, 13,432, 13,673, **15,549,** 16,654, 16,998, 17,821
institutional care, 5,570
personal narratives, 15,796
rehabilitation, 2,115
Deaf, Afro-American, education, 15,549
Deaf, Jewish, 15,154
Deaf-mute, education, 13,067
Deaf Woman, The (book), 2,112
Deal, Babs Hodges (1929-), **6,006**
Dean Bond of Swarthmore: A Quaker Humanist (book), 15,286
Dean, Catharine (1802-69). See Flint, Catharine (Dean) [Mrs. Waldo] (1802-69)
Dean Creek Thrashing Company (MI), 8,302
Dean, Elizabeth, 5,063
Dean, Emily (Washburn) (1870-1958), **3,833**
Dean, Harriet, 657
Dean, Helen Ryan [Mrs.] (1892-1971), **8,022**
Dean, Jennette Cordelia, 9,294
Dean, Laura (Winter) [Mrs. William John] (1870-1968), 9,037
Dean, Lydia (Rotch) (1770-1822), 15,294
Dean, Marie, 7,109
Dean, Mary Ann [Miss], **12,868**
Dean, Prudence (1799-). See Fish, Prudence (Dean) [Mrs. Asa] (1799-?)
Dean, Rebecca Cordelia (Pond) [Mrs. William J.] (1844-1910), 9,294
Dean, Rebekah Scott (1812-43). See Salisbury, Rebekah Scott (Dean) (1812-43)
Dean, Sarah Fairchild [Mrs. Eliab B.]. See Conover, Sarah Fairchild [Mrs. Eliab B.] Dean [Mrs. Obadiah Milton]
Dean, Susan Ann [Mrs. Lawrence], 4,696
Dean, Vera Micheles [Mrs.] (1903-72), **6,512,** 12,739
Dean, William Blake, Family (MN), **9,036, 9,037**
Deane, Martha Blanchard (1896-?), **440**
De Angeli, Marguerite, 8,531
DeAngelis, Elizabeth Webb [Mrs. Pascal Charles Joseph], 12,759
DeAngelis Family (NY), **12,759**
DeAngelis, Hannah (1802-90). See Wells, Hannah (DeAngelis) Lemoyne [Mrs. Chester] (1802-90)
DeAngelis, Millicent Ann (1813-87). See Marshall, Millicent Ann (DeAngelis) [Mrs. Orsamus Holmes] (1813-87)
DeAngelis, Pascal Charles Joseph, 12,759, 12,763
Deans (in schools), **89, 96, 108,** 116, **235, 435,** 449, 674, 843, **893,** 952, 1,020, **1,853, 1,855,** 2,927, 2,931, **3,125,** 3,257, 3,356, 3,462, 3,463, **4,042,** 4,181, 4,215, 4,223, 4,374, **4,382,** 4,385, **4,390,** 4,494, **4,519,** 4,906, 4,969, 5,035, 5,063, **5,101,** 5,394, **5,419,** 5,506, **5,833,** 6,126, 6,133, 6,143, 6,149, 6,158, 6,165, **6,189,** 6,237, **6,284,** 6,339, **6,423,** 6,478, **6,493,** 6,670, 6,677, **6,683,** 6,769, **6,899, 6,941,** 7,572, **7,582, 7,845, 7,872, 7,959, 8,053, 8,552,** 8,557, **8,594,** 8,689, 8,721, **8,746,** 8,809, 9,333, **9,610, 9,671,** 9,809, **9,829, 10,216,** 10,928, 10,929, 10,930, 11,377, 11,501, **11,502, 11,508, 11,561,** 11,807, 11,898, 11,906, **11,925, 11,999,** 12,836, 12,917, 12,921, 12,923, **12,924, 13,189, 13,191, 13,209,** 13,241, 13,299, 13,350, 13,604, **13,754, 13,892,** 14,122, 14,123, **14,275,** 14,280, 14,620, 14,732, 14,826, **15,126, 15,131, 15,140,** 15,186, 15,189, 15,228, **15,237,** 15,239, **15,922,** 15,926, **15,930,** 16,037, **16,134, 16,288, 16,331, 16,332, 16,366, 16,382,** 16,608, 16,971, 16,988, 17,001, 17,002, **17,203,** 17,291, **17,297, 17,352,** 17,653, 17,723, **17,767,** 17,776, **17,783**
Deans (in schools), Afro-American, **2,149**
Deans, Anna Maria. See Garretson, Anna Maria (Deans)
Deans of Women Conference (1948), 6,423
Dear Lady (book), 1,496
Dear Ones at Home (book), 7,610
Dearborn, Ella K., 14,473
Dearborn Seminary (Chicago, IL), 3,911, 4,477
Dearborn Woman's Club (MI), **8,012**
Deardorff, Minnie, 5,419

Deardorff, Neva Ruth (1887-1958), 8,665
Dearing, Katherine G., **2,998**
Dearmont, Russell L. (1891-1967), **9,956**
DeArnold, Martha (1887-1976). *See* McKelvie,
  Martha (DeArnold) [Mrs. Sam R.] (1887-1976)
Deas, Alston, 15,464, 15,582
Deas, Anne [Miss], **15,464**
Deas, Anne Izard, 15,498
Deas, Anne Simons, **15,582**
Death, 1,274, 1,485, 9,446, 13,537
  causes, 7,683, 9,008, **11,452**, 15,427, 17,879
  proof and certification, 17,528
"Death of a Traveling Salesman" (story), 9,769
Death Stalks the Philippine Wilds (book), 8,600
De Baillou, Katherine Cowan, **2,997**
de Baker, Arcadia Bandini Stearns, 370
de Bale, María Ignacia (Soberanes) [Mrs. Edward
  Turner]. *See* Peabody, María Ignacia
  (Soberanes) [Mrs. Edward Turner] de Bale [Mrs.
  Edward T.]
de Banke, Cecile, 7,567
Debates and debating, 3,897, 4,788, 8,485
de Beaumarchais, Baron, 1,411
Debell, Ellen Judith (Bruner) (1868-1936), 10,437
"Deborah Sampson, Maiden Soldier of the
  Revolution" (article), 8,271
de Bosis, Lillian (Vernon) [Mrs. Adolfo], 12,632
de Brabant, Jean Baptiste (1801-80), 7,033
de Bretteville, Alma (1881-1968). *See* Spreckels,
  Alma (de Bretteville) (1881-1968)
de Bryas, Comtesse Madeline, 9,894
Debs, Eugene V. (1855-1926), 4,675, 8,070, 11,917,
  12,701, 12,702
Debs, Katherine Metzel [Mrs. Eugene V.]
  (1857-1936), **4,675**, 8,070
Debs, Theodore, 12,702
Debtor and creditor, **11,192**
Debts, public, 9,755
Debunker, The, 4,095
Decals, 2,823
De Camp, Anna Maria Jackson. *See* Morris, Anna
  Maria Jackson (De Camp) [Mrs. Gouverneur]
DeCamp, Edith [Mrs. Ralph], 10,905
De Camp Family (NY), **12,191**
De Camp, John (1812-75), 12,191
De Camp, Mary A. G. (1843-?). *See* Corning, Mary
  A. G. (De Camp) [Mrs. Edwin Weld] (1843-?)
De Camp, Samuel G. J., 12,191
De Camp, Sarah Canfield. *See* Brandegee, Sarah
  Canfield (De Camp)
De Camp, Susan (Grandin), 12,191
Decatur House (residence), 2,197
Decatur, Stephen (1779-1820), 5,718, **12,194**
Decatur, Susan [Mrs. Stephen], 9,120, **12,194**
de Chateaubriand, Rene, **9,603**
Decherd, Mary, **16,059**
"Decision" (television program), 5,240
Decision at Delphi (book), 11,168
Decker, Anna M. (1884-), 4,899
Decker, Aurelia [Mrs. Henry], **11,563**
Decker, Clara (1828-89). *See* Young, Clara (Decker)
  [Mrs. Brigham] (1828-89)
Decker, Henry, 11,563
Decker, Hermine Duthie (1908-), **17,190**
Decker, Katharine M., **11,419**
Decker, Perl D. (1875-1934), **9,957**
De Claire, Adelaide (1864-1945). *See* Thayer,
  Adelaide (De Claire) (1864-1945)
De Claire, Harriet Elizabeth (Billings). [Mrs. Hector
  Auguste] De Claire (1836-1927), 7,997
De Claire, Hector Auguste, 7,997
Declaration of Independence, 11,173, 15,041
De Cleyre, Harry (1890-1974), 7,997
DeCleyre, Voltairine (1866-1912), **7,997**, 8,064
Decorah College for Women (IA). *See* Luther
  College (Decorah, IA)
Decorah-Posten, 8,751
Decoration Day Services, 3,922
DeCottes, Nina (Browne), 63
de Crevecoeur, Michel-Guillaume St. Jean, **2,281**
Dee, Sylvia. *See* Moore, Josephine Proffitt
Deeds, 3,679, 3,871, 4,920, 5,690, 7,635, 9,085,
  9,815, 10,712, **11,188**, 11,737, 12,218, 13,448,
  15,417, 15,469, 15,645. *See also* Land titles

Deems, Hilda Cox [Mrs.], 3,756
Deen-Crist, **2,912**
Deen, Mrs. E. W., **2,299**
Deen, Tilla R. Dahl (1868-?), **8,729**
Deerfield Society of Arts and Crafts (MA), **7,012**
Deering, Mrs. N. C., **4,747**
Deering, Nathaniel Cobb (1827-87), 4,747
Defense Advisory Committee on Women in the
  Services, 7,904, 9,349
Defense Committee on Womanpower, 8,553
deForbes (pseudonym). *See* Forbes, DeLoris Florine
  Stanton (1923-)
de Force, Laura (1838-1907). *See* Gordon, Laura (de
  Force) [Mrs. Charles H.] (1838-1907)
de Ford, Lydia Howard. *See* De Roth, Lydia Howard
  (de Ford) [Mrs. Herbert Charles]
De Ford, Miriam Allen (1888-1975). *See* Shipley,
  Miriam De Ford [Mrs. Maynard] (1888-1975)
De Forest, Charlotte Burgis (1879-1973), **7,212,**
  10,037
DeForest Family, 14,059
De Forest, Julie Morrow (1882-), 13,836
de Forest, Lockwood, 14,745
DeForest, Marian [Miss] (1864-1935), **11,344**
Deformities, 15,427
DeFrance, Laura M. S., 9,602
De Frehn, Edna, **15,185**
Degginger, Bernice. *See* Greengard, Bernice
  (Degginger)
de Gogorza, Emilio, 6,549
de Gogorza, Emma Hayden (Eames) [Mrs. Emilio]
  (1865-1952). *See* Eames, Emma Hayden. [Mrs.
  Julian] Story [Mrs. Emilio] de Gogorza
  (1865-1952)
DeGraffenried Family (NC), **13,312**
DeGraffenried, Mrs. John, 13,312
de Greayer, Josephine Morris [Mrs.]. *See* Rowan,
  Josephine Morris [Mrs.] de Greayer [Mrs.
  Andrew S.]
Degrees, academic, 4,520, **16,340**
De Groot, Adelaide Milton, 12,192
De Groot, Elizabeth King Hawley [Mrs. William],
  12,192
De Groot Family (NY), **12,192**
De Grummond, Lena Y., **9,572**
DeHaven, Mary (Redfield) Lindsey (1892-1972),
  10,235
de Havilland, Olivia, 1,025, 3,210
DeHay, Elizabeth (Norton) [Mrs. P. S.], **9,620**
de Hirsch, Baroness, 7,525, 7,540
Dehner, Dorothy [Mrs. Davis Smith] (1908-), **2,750**
Dehon, Anne Middleton [Mrs. William], 15,465
Dehon Family (SC), **15,465**
Dehon, Theodore, 15,465
Dehon, William, 15,465
De Huff, Elizabeth (1892-), **11,222**
Deichmann, Christine, 2,848
Deichmann, Elizabeth (1896-1975), **6,319**
Deinard, Hortense Honig [Mrs. Amos S.], 9,130
Deism, 6,602
DeJong, Nettie R. (?-1972), 2,016
De Jonge, Madge Ann (Brook), **7,771**
De Kalb, Courtenay, 215
De Kalb, Frances Douglas [Mrs. Charles Fletcher]
  Lummis [Mrs. Courtenay] (1870-1969), **215**
deKay, Helena. *See* Gilder, Helena (deKay)
de Kleven, Concha Ortiz y Pino [Mrs. Victor]
  (1914-), 11,217
DeKroyft, Susan Helen (Aldrich) [Mrs. William]
  (1818-1915), **12,795**
de Kruif, Paul, 11,579
DeLacey, Zdenka Cerny (1895-), 3,897
de la Chapelle, Clarence E., 11,897
de la Cruz, Sor Juana Ines, 9,425
De Lacy, Fannie, 10,298
De Lacy, Walter Washington (1819-92), **10,298**
De Lacy, William, 10,298
Delafield, Emily, 12,195
Delafield, Emily (Prime) [Mrs. Lewis Levingston]
  (1840-1909), **12,195**
Delafield, Julia, 12,195
de La Fite de Pelleport, Gabrielle Josephine
  (1770-1837). *See* du Pont, Gabrielle Josephine

(de La Fite de Pelleport) [Mrs. Victor]
  (1770-1837)
Delage Family (SC), **15,745**
de la Guerra, María de las Augustias (1815-?). *See*
  Ord, María de las Augustias (de la Guerra) [Mrs.
  Manuel] Jimeno Cesarín [Mrs. James L.]
  (1815-?)
de la Guerra y Noriega, José, 599
de la Guerra y Noriega, María Antonia (1827-).
  See de Oreña, Maria Antonia (de la Guerra y
  Noriega) [Mrs. Cesáreo] Lataillade [Mrs. Gaspar]
  (1827-)
de Laguna, Frederica, 2,833
Delahunt, Mary Abbott [Mrs.], 5,074
de la Mare, Walter, 3,201, 7,247, 12,570
De La Motta, Jacob, 7,524
De Lancey, Alice. *See* Izard, Alice (De Lancey)
  [Mrs. Ralph, Sr.]
DeLancey, Ann, 12,643
DeLancey, Helen Watts (?-1872). *See* Floyd-Jones,
  Helen Watts (DeLancey) [Mrs. Henry] (?-1872)
DeLancey, Mrs. Peter, 12,643
Deland, Lorin Fuller, 1,420, 1,426, 12,437
Deland, Margaretta "Margaret" Wade (Campbell)
  [Mrs. Lorin Fuller] (1857-1945), 467, **1,420,**
  1,426, 2,300, 2,605, 3,927, 5,694, **5,921,** 5,973,
  6,513, 6,907, 7,274, 11,821, **12,437,** 12,529,
  14,062, 14,828, 15,060
Delaney, Matilda Jane (Sager), 17,422
Delaney, Sadie Peterson (1889-1958), 123
Delano, Alonzo, 11,278
Delano, Annie. *See* Hitch, Annie (Delano)
Delano, Annita (1894-), **2,751**
Delano, Catherine Robbins Lyman [Mrs. Warren, II],
  11,481, 11,482
Delano, Dora. *See* Forbes, Dora (Delano)
Delano, Edith (Barnard) [Mrs. James], 7,012
Delano, Elizabeth (Hartwell) [Mrs. Washington
  Warren] (1847-1922), **5,623**
Delano Family, 11,481
Delano, Frederic Adrian (1863-1953), 11,482
Delano, Harriet (1843-?), 11,278
Delano, Jane Arminda [Miss] (1862-1919), 2,087,
  6,122
Delano, Laura A. [Mrs.], 11,481, 12,431
Delano, Lucile Kathryn (1902-), **15,793**
Delano, Mary Burt [Mrs. Alonzo] (1808-71), 11,278
Delano, Sara (1857-1941). *See* Roosevelt, Sara
  (Delano) [Mrs. James] (1857-1941)
Delano, Sarah Alvey, 11,481
de la Noye, Phillippe, 11,481
De la Pole, Dorothy, 8,670
de la Ramee, Marie Louise (1839-1908), 2,598
De la Rocheaulion, Aimé Marie, 3,521
De la Rocheaulion, Sarah Catherine Wigg Floyd
  [Mrs. Aimé Marie], 3,521
de La Salle, Sieur, 8,441
de la Torre, Victor Raúl Haya, 8,090
Delaunay, Robert, 2,751
Delaunay, Sonia, 2,751
Delaware, 12,270
  Afro-Americans, education, **2,044**
  bible, societies, etc., 5,745
  charitable societies, **2,045**
  church records and registers, 15,006
  cities and towns, **15,036**
  clergymen's wives, **2,040**
  club-houses, 6,805
  clubs, 2,058
  diaries and journals, 2,040, 2,047, **2,050, 2,056,**
    5,745
  educational associations, **2,044**
  federal aid to the arts, **2,754**
  freedmen, 7,677
  Friends, 15,006
  Friends, Society of, **2,060**
  hotels, taverns, etc., 15,036
  housewives, **2,040, 2,062**
  junior high schools, 2,058
  physicians, 7,677
  real property, 2,028
  schools, 13,350
  secretaries of state, 10,740
  silversmiths, **2,054**

social science research, 14,936
  suffrage societies, **2,042**
  temperance societies, 2,059
  women, employment, 2,045
Delaware Equal Rights Association, **2,042**
Delaware Expressway (PA), 15,202
Delaware Gazette, 2,038
Delaware Indians, 9,841, 14,173, 14,174, **14,175**
  treaties, 14,175
Delaware Journal, 2,038
del Caribe, La Hija (pseudonym). *See* Padilla de
  Sanz, Doña Trina (1864-1957)
de Leon, Ponce, 2,485
Delgado, Rafel, 215
D'Elia, Chancy. *See* Curry, Chancy (D'Elia) [Mrs. J.
  Lane]
Delille Olive [Mrs. Henry A.] (1839-1909). *See*
  Logan, Olive [Mrs. Henry A.] Delille [Mrs.
  William Wirt] Sikes [Mrs. James O'Neill]
  (1839-1909)
De Lima, Agnes, 11,951
Delineator (charity), 9,277
Delineator (periodical), 1,718, 11,304, 11,974, 12,044,
  17,716
Delinquent women, 14,367
Delinquents, Jewish, 15,153
Deliz, Monserrate (1896-1968), **15,364**
Dell, Berta Marie (Gage) [Mrs. Floyd], 3,988
Dell, Floyd (1897-1969), **3,988**
Dell, Margery Currey [Mrs. Floyd], 3,988
Dellenbaugh, Frederick Samuel (1853-1935), **191**
Delmar, Vina, 10,992
del Mundo, Fe, 6,770
del Occidente, Maria (pseudonym). *See* Brooks,
  Maria (Gowen) [Mrs. John]. Abigail Gowen.
  Mary Abigail Brooks (ca. 1794-1845)
de Long, Ethel, 5,256
DeLonne, Mrs. H. P., 9,621
Delony Family, 2,999
Delony, Rosa Huguenin [Mrs. William Gaston], 2,999
Delony, William Gaston, **2,999**
Delord, Elizabeth (Ketchum) [Mrs. Henry]. *See*
  Swetland, Elizabeth (Ketchum) [Mrs. Henry]
  Delord [Mrs. William]
Delord Family (NY), **12,769**
Delord, Frances Henrietta, 12,769
Delord, Henry (1764-1825), 12,769, 12,773
Deloria, Ella, 14,886
De Losada, Betty Baget [Mrs. Horace "Ace"]
  (1921-), **1,280**, 1,356, 1,357
De Losada, Horace "Ace," 1,280
Delp, Flo, 4,658
Delphian Chapter (Rockwell City, IA), **5,099**
Delphian Society, Alpha Chapter (Blue Earth, MN),
  8,415
Delphic Studio (NY), 12,912
Del Rio, Delores, 11,461
Delroy, Irene (pseudonym). *See* Sanders, Josephine
Delsarte, Francois, 10,863
Delsarte system, 17,715
Delta Delta Delta, 14,365
Delta Gamma, 1,625
Delta Kappa Gamma, 116, 3,077, 4,532, **4,559, 6,514,
8,321**, 8,567, **9,038**, 9,839, **10,453, 10,663,**
13,391, 17,924
Delta Kappa Gamma Bulletin, The, 6,514
Delta Oral History Project (PA), **15,357**
Delta Review (periodical), 9,599
Delta Sigma Theta, 3,799
Delta State Teachers College (MS), 9,650
Delta Wedding (book), 9,770
Delta Zeta, **4,524**
De Lussan, Zelie. [Mrs. Angelo] Fronani
  (1863-1949), **7,213**
De Mare, Marie, **2,749**
Demarest, Catharine Louisa (Nevius) [Mrs. David
  D.], 10,964
Demarest, David D., **10,964**
Demarest, Victoria Booth (ca. 1890s-), **6,515**
Demarest, William H. S., **10,928**, 10,931
de Maupassant, Guy, 10,158
De Mille, Agnes (1908-), 4,384, **7,214, 12,360**
DeMille, Anna Angela (George) [Mrs. William
  Churchill] (1877-1947), 2,198, **2,301**, 7,214

DeMille, Cecil B., 14,366
DeMilly, Marie Louise (Morris), **12,995**
De Milt, Clara (1880-1958), **5,512**
Deming, Abigail Barnum [Mrs. Minor Rudd], **4,254,
4,416**
Deming, Edwin Willard (1860-1942), **12,438**
Deming, Eleanor, 355
Deming, Minor Rudd (1810-45), **4,416**
Democracy for All (book), 8,591
Democracy Unlimited, 7,779
Democrat (Wichita, KS), 5,243
Democratic Central Committee, 10,078, 17,268
Democratic Central Committee (MO), 10,078
Democratic Digest, The, 48, 11,503
Democratic-Farmer-Labor Party, 2,070, 8,844, 8,912,
  8,949, 9,062, 9,084, 9,119, 9,127, 9,140, 9,174,
  9,177, 9,287, 9,381, 9,396, 9,400, 9,443, 9,467
Democratic-Farmer-Labor Party, State Central
  Committee (MN), **9,039, 9,040**
Democratic National Committee, 2,189, 2,456, 3,372,
  4,909, 4,930, 5,829, 6,520, 6,765, 6,949, 6,973,
  7,290, 7,904, 9,239, 9,643, 9,779, 10,069, 11,483,
  11,926, 12,680, 13,274, 13,406, 16,115, 16,252,
  17,117, 17,304
Democratic National Committee, publicity division,
  10,077
Democratic National Committee, Women's Division,
  11,503
Democratic National Convention, 5,459, 11,545,
  11,817, 13,271, 13,274, 15,304
Democratic National Convention (1920), 16,252
Democratic National Convention (1924), 11,249,
  12,952
Democratic National Convention (1928), 11,243
Democratic National Convention (1960), 2,349
Democratic National Convention (1968), riots, 6,079
Democratic Party, 48, 793, 2,941, 3,735, 4,623, 5,156,
  5,305, 6,432, 6,582, 6,765, 6,973, 7,904, 8,116,
  9,550, 9,956, 10,069, **10,077**, 10,078, 10,079,
  10,127, 11,134, 11,483, 11,503, 11,827, 11,853,
  11,872, 11,905, 12,986, 13,249, 13,702, 15,941,
  15,997, 16,128, 17,117, 17,238, 17,304, 17,340,
  17,377
  committees, 2,189, 2,456, 3,117, 3,293, 3,372,
    4,486, 6,949, 7,904, 8,116, 9,239, 9,643, 9,984,
    11,483, **11,503**, 13,266, 13,271, 13,274, 13,371,
    13,406, 16,115, 17,268
Democratic Party, Alabama, 48
Democratic Party, California, 793
Democratic Party, Georgia, **3,178**
Democratic Party, Idaho, 3,698
Democratic Party, Indiana, 4,486
Democratic Party, Kentucky, 5,328, 5,329
Democratic Party, Michigan, 7,729, **7,810**, 7,883,
  8,157
Democratic Party, Minnesota, 9,197
Democratic Party, Mississippi, 9,643
Democratic Party, Missouri, 10,080
Democratic Party, Montana, 10,328, 10,334
Democratic Party, New York, 6,819, 11,576, 12,203,
  12,342
Democratic Party, North Carolina, 13,266, 13,271,
  13,274, 13,286, 13,371
Democratic Party, North Dakota, 13,702
Democratic Party, Oregon, 17,304
Democratic Party, South Carolina, **15,825**
Democratic Party, Tennessee, 15,890, **15,945**
Democratic Party, Texas, 15,890, 15,989, 15,997,
  15,998, 16,007, 16,240
Democratic Party, Utah, 16,965, 16,975
Democratic Party, Virginia, 17,117
Democratic Party, Washington, 17,260, **17,326,**
  17,347, 17,356, 17,377
Democratic Party, Wisconsin, 17,654
Democratic State Committee (NY), 11,576
Democratic Union, 11,576
Democratic Woman's Club of Kentucky, 5,313
Democratic Woman's Day (1946), 13,266
Democratic Women of Pitt County (NC), 13,271
Democratic Women's Convention (1964), 13,565
Democrats for Eisenhower, 5,143
Demography, 14,290, 15,155, 16,215
Demoiselle Ball (LA), **5,546**
Demoiselle Club (LA), **5,546**

Demonstrations, 564, 2,063, 4,161, 4,170, 5,455,
  6,694, 8,065, 11,855, 12,523, 14,453, 17,583,
  17,630, **17,858**
Demorest, Ellen Louise (Curtis) (1824-1898), 6,772
Demorest's Magazine (periodical), 13,400, 17,692
Dempster, Arthur J., 11,814
Dempster, John (1794-1863), **4,203**
Dempster, Sara. *See* McKee, Sara (Dempster)
Dempster, William, 4,203
De Muth, Sister M. Ethelbert, 9,695
Den burtkomne faderen (book), 8,735
Den gamle Richards Kunst at blive rig og lykkelig
  (book), 8,734
Den, Ysabel Argüello [Mrs.], 314
Denargo Land Company, 1,719
De Navarro, Mary (Anderson) [Mrs. Antonio
  Fernando] (1859-1940), 3,100, **5,339**, 10,651
Denbo, Amzi, 5,431
Denbo, Anna Marshall [Mrs. Amzi] (ca.
  1860s-1940s], **5,431**
Dendy, Clary, 15,524
Dendy, William, 15,524
de Nemours, Nicole Charlotte Marie Louise Le Dee
  de Roccourt [Mrs. Pierre Samuel du Pont]
  (1743-84), 2,033
de Nemours, Pierre Samuel du Pont, 2,033
Denise, Carrie L., 5,063
Denishawn School, 12,363, 12,365
Denison, Fanny, 6,325
Denison House (Boston, MA), **6,516**
Denison, Minerva (1784-1877). *See* Rodgers,
  Minerva (Denison) [Mrs. John] (1784-1877)
Denison, Sara M., 2,009
Denison University (OH), curricula, 4,399
Denlinger, Nelle May (Hill) (1868-1900), 14,387
Denman, Leslie (Van Ness) [Mrs. William]
  (1867-1959), 441
Denman, Marion (?-1975). *See* Frankfurter, Marion
  (Denman) [Mrs. Felix] (?-1975)
Denman, William (1872-1959), **441**
Denmark
  American ambassadors to, **8,911**, 8,912, 9,040
  American diplomats in, 6,391
  sex customs, 8,207
  social life and customs, 6,391
Denmark Industrial School (SC). *See* Voorhees
  College (SC)
Denmark, Juanita "Nita" (Polk) [Mrs. James W.],
  13,398
Denmark, Leonidas Polk, **13,398**
Denmark, Leonita [Miss], 13,398
Dennett, Mary Coffin (Ware) [Mrs. William Hartley]
  (1872-1947), 1,596, 6,223, 6,579, 6,812, 7,284,
  12,652
Dennis, Eleanor Geiser [Mrs.], 247
Dennis, Elizabeth. *See* Matthews, Elizabeth (Dennis)
  [Mrs. Horace]
Dennis, Eugene (1901-48). *See* Von Herberg, Eugene
  (Dennis) [Mrs. J. C.] (1901-48)
Dennis, Gene (1901-48). *See* Von Herberg, Eugene
  (Dennis) [Mrs. J. C.] (1901-48)
Dennis, Gertrude. *See* Leland, Gertrude (Dennis)
  [Mrs. Waldo Gifford]
Dennis, May A. [Mrs.], 9,167
Dennis, Ruth (1878-1968). *See* St. Denis, Ruth.
  [Mrs. Edwin M.] Shawn (1878-1968)
Dennis, Shirley, 15,201
Dennis, Wesley (?-1966?), 6,092
Denny, Carol (1904-). *See* Brandt, Carol (Denny)
  (1904-)
Denny, David, 17,221
Denny, Dorothy (Detzer) [Mrs. Ludwell] (1893-),
  10,730, 15,301, **15,303**, 15,307, 15,316
Denny, Ebenezer (1761-1822), 15,221
Denny, Emily Inez (ca. 1860-1940), **17,221**
Denny Family (PA), **15,221**
Denny, Harmar (1794-1852), 15,221
Denny, Melcena Burns, **442**
Denny, Osward T., 13,693
de Nogarola, Comtesse, 10,831
de Normandie, Henriett Elizabeth, 11,941
Densen-Gerber, Judianne (1934-), **6,517**
Densford, Katherine Jane (1890-). *See* Dreeves,
  Katherine Jane (Densford) [Mrs. Carl] (1890-)

Denslow, Dwight B., **12,439**
Denslow, Louise A., **12,439**
Densmore, Benjamin, Family (MN, NY, WI), **9,041**
Densmore, Elizabeth (Fowle) [Mrs. Orrin] (1805-91), 9,041
Densmore, Frances Theresa (1867-1957), 2,837, 9,041, **9,042**, 9,073, 9,302, 9,462
Densmore, Ismena (1798-1887). See Bennett, Ismena (Densmore) (1798-1887)
Densmore, Margaret Louise (1874-?), 9,041
Densmore, Margaret Seaton (Hartshorn) (1776-1823), 9,041
Densmore, Martha Elizabeth (1838-1908). See Hodgman, Martha Elizabeth Densmore [Mrs.] (1838-1908)
Densmore, Orrin, 9,041
Densmore, Sarah Adelaide, 9,041
Denson, Daisy [Miss], 13,399, 13,504, 13,512
Denson, Olive McGehee, **16,345**
Dent, Jessie Covington, 5,469
Dent, Julia (1826-1902). See Grant, Julia (Dent) [Mrs. Ulysses S.] (1826-1902)
Dental clinics, 5,607, 12,079, 15,202, 17,826
Dental hygiene, 1,061, **1,832**
Dental hygienists, 4,336, 9,467
Dental schools, **1,061**
Dental technicians, 8,984, **10,787**
Dentists, 1,061, 1,832, 1,995, 4,336, 4,341, 4,373, **4,948**, 5,478, 5,763, **13,997**, **15,095**, **15,120**, 17,217
Dentists, Afro-American, **3,038**
Denton, Bertha M. (1870-1957). See Snell, Bertha M. (Denton) [Mrs. Marshall K.] (1870-1957)
Denton, Marilda Cassa (1833-1908). See Mexey, Marilda Cassa (Denton) [Mrs. Samuel Bell] (1833-1908)
Denver and Gulf Railway Company, 4,749
Denver Area Music Teachers' Association (CO), 1,788
Denver Art League, Inc. (CO), **1,766**
Denver Artists' Club (CO), 1,673
Denver Board of Education (CO), 1,779
Denver Bureau of Public Welfare (CO), 1,722
Denver Businessmen's Orchestra (CO). See Brico Symphony, The (CO)
Denver City Planning Office (CO), 1,779
Denver Civic Symphony, 1,734
Denver Community Players (CO), 1,734
Denver Fortnightly Club (CO), 1,744, **1,767**
Denver General Hospital (CO), 1,753
Denver Juvenile Court (CO), 1,675
Denver Keramic Club (CO), 1,734
Denver Metropolitan Piano Festival (CO), 1,788
Denver Pioneer Museum (CO), 1,785
Denver Post (CO), 1,670, 17,899
Denver Public Library (CO), 1,777, 1,786
Denver Symphony Orchestra (CO), 1,788
Denver Symphony Society (CO), 1,788
Denver Tuberculosis Society (CO), 1,706
Denver Visiting Nurses' Association (CO), 1,706
Denver Woman's Club (CO), 1,673, 17,908
Denver Woman's Press Club (CO), **1,710**, **1,768**
"Denver's Historic Mansions" (column), 1,750
de Oreña, Gaspar, 599
de Oreña, María Antonia (de la Guerra y Noriega) [Mrs. Cesáreo] Laitaillade [Mrs. Gaspar] (1827-?), 599
deOsborne, Claudia, 16,210
Departamento de Estado, Corporaciones Sin Fines de Lucro (PR), **15,365**
Departamento de Instrucción, Expedientes de Maestros (PR), **15,366**
Department heads (universities), 104, 656, **1,088**, 1,674, 1,678, 1,751, 2,070, **3,123**, 6,900, **6,924**, **7,727**, 7,829, **8,546**, 8,547, **8,611**, **10,605**, **10,607**, 10,727, 11,637, 11,844, 12,050, 13,255, **13,880**, **13,894**, 14,800, **16,375**, 17,230, **17,766**, **17,772**, **17,777**, **17,788**, 17,994
Department of Community Development (Seattle, WA), 17,279
Department of Iowa Woman's Relief Corps, **4,862**
Department of Justice, Bureau of Corrections, Kentucky Correctional Institution for Women, **5,283**

Department of Labor and Industry, Industrial Safety Division (ME), **5,564**
Department Store Employees Union, Local 110 (San Francisco, CA), 944
Department stores, 5,394, **6,203**, 6,879, 7,628, 16,210, 16,569, 16,888
  employees, 9,517
  management, **11,859**, **13,817**
DePass, Helen (1923-). See Dahlin, Helen (DePass) (1923-)
DePass, M. B., 8,873
De Paul University (IL), alumnae, 4,076
DePauw Female College (New Albany, IN), presidents, 5,362
DePauw University (IN), 4,481, 4,519, 4,520, 4,521, 4,522, 4,523, 4,527, 4,530, 4,532
  faculty, 5,068
DePauw Women's Club (IN), 4,532
Depelchin, Kenzia Payne (1828-93), **16,246**
Depew, Chauncey Mitchell (1834-1928), **12,440**
de Peyster, Anna, 14,885
De Peyster, Cornelia, 12,193
DePeyster, Elizabeth Van Rensselaer, **12,196**
De Peyster, Eve, 12,193
De Peyster Family (NY), **12,193**
De Peyster, Frederick (1758-1834), 12,193
DePierri, Kate Pinsdorf, 2,344
Deportation, 3,464, 3,852, 8,657, 8,949, 12,487, 12,703, 14,933, 17,633
Depressions, 15,869
  (1857), United States, 4,767, 12,303
  (1929), United States, 230, 232, 242, 1,532, 2,684, 2,692, 2,891, 4,688, 5,829, 6,506, 8,065, 8,085, 8,148, 8,690, 8,703, 8,704, 9,468, 9,699, 11,851, 11,870, 11,874, 13,273, 13,604, 15,054, 16,488, 16,554, 16,791, 16,965, 16,967
DePriest, Mrs. Oscar, 5,122
DePuy, Blanche, 7,583
Derby, Cora, 11,442
Derby, Ethel Carow Roosevelt [Mrs. Richard], 2,596, 12,044, 12,299
Derby, Frances (Janney) [Mrs. Samuel C.], 14,000
Derby, James Cephas, 5,347
Derbyshire, Mamie C., **1,711**
De Renne, George Wimberly, 3,537
De Renne, Letitia, 3,521
DeReyter, Nellie Molenar (ca. 1892-), **8,554**
Der Ithaca Frauen Mission Verein, Ithaca Bezirk (NE). See Ithaca Church (NE), Woman's Missionary Society
Derleth, August, 15,331
Dern, George H., 3,133
Dern, Peggy Gaddis [Mrs.] (1895-1966), **3,000**
De Roth, Lydia Howard (de Ford) [Mrs. Herbert Charles], **5,755**
de Rothschild, Pauline, 11,165
Derricotte, Frances Ada (Martin) (1865-?), **443**
Derricotte, Juliette, 3,302
Derry, Laura Ellen (Miller) [Mrs. Stephen A.] (1905-), 5,394
de Ruiz, Pauline B., 12,572
Derwood, Gene. [Mrs. Oscar] Williams (1909-54), **4,472**
DeRyke, DeLores, 10,418
de St. Leger, Henriette, 15,258
de St. Roman, Marie Rosine, 5,415
de San Vicente, Agustín Fernández, 331
DeSaussure Family (SC), 15,441, **15,466**
de Saussure, Frances. See Gibbes, Frances (de Saussure) [Mrs. William Stuart]
DeSavary, Edith L., 2,180
Descendants of Hugh Amory (book), 2,169
Deschin, Celia, 8,633
Deschine, Celia S. (ca. 1902-), **8,642**
Deschutes Farmer's Co-op (OR), 14,509
de Schweinitz, Elizabeth McCord [Mrs. Karl] (1895-1978), **8,641**
de Schweinitz, Karl (1887-1975), **8,641**, 8,653
de Schweinitz, Louise, 15,134
Desdemona (opera), 7,213
Desegregation. See Segregation
Deseret News (UT), 16,403, 16,486
"Desert Night," 208

Desertion and nonsupport, 2,167, 2,677, 5,057, 10,100, 13,537, 14,914
Desertion, military, 12,703, 13,567
"De-sexing the Ballot Box: The History of Woman Suffrage in Arizona, 1883-1912" (paper), 210
Desha, Mary [Miss], **5,308**
Deshon, Florence (1896-1922), **4,473**
de Sibour, Jean Antoine Gabriel, 1,960
de Sibour, Mary Louisa [Mrs. Jean Antoine Gabriel] (ca. 1837-?), 1,960
Design Laboratory, 2,795
Designer, The (periodical), 5,048
DeSilver, Margaret, 8,064
Des Moines Art Center (IA), 4,977
Des Moines College (IA), 10,390
  alumnae, 4,960
Des Moines Equal Suffrage Council (IA), 4,859
Des Moines Federation of Women's Clubs (IA), **4,748**
Des Moines Home for the Aged (IA), 4,817
Des Moines Junior Federation of Women's Clubs (IA), 4,800
Des Moines Junior League (IA), 4,866
Des Moines Pioneer Club (IA), 4,851
Des Moines Political Equality League (IA), 4,859
Des Moines University (IA), 5,070
  alumnae, 4,960
Des Moines Woman's Press Club (IA), 4,960
Des Moines Woman's Club (IA), 4,729, 4,732, 4,800
Desmond, Alice Curtis (1897-), **14,352**
Desmond, Dagmar. Dagmar Frisselle Haarbauer (1895-), **970**
de Solms, Marie Therese (1840-1907). See Blanc, Marie Therese (de Solms) (1840-1907)
DeSoto Discovers the Mississippi (painting), 9,581
De Soto Fort (AL), 13,000
Des Plaines Woman's Club (IL), **4,179**
Desprez, Mary (McClellan) [Mrs. Paul] (1861-1945), 2,462
Desteiger, Julia W. [Mrs.] (1848-?), **10**
Desti, Mary (1871-1931), **1,033**
Destinn, Emmy, 2,968
Detective and mystery stories, **6,060**, 9,640, 11,310, 14,338, 14,364
  juvenile, 5,628
Detectives, 11,440
De Tilly, James Alexander, Comte, 14,988
De Tilly, Maria Matilda Bingham [Mrs. James Alexander], **14,988**
de Tolna, Countess Festeties (1874-1939). See McKee, Eila Butterworth Haggin [Countess Festeties] de Tolna [Mrs. Robert T.] (1874-1939)
Detroit Board of Education (MI), 8,030
Detroit City College (MI), 9,467
Detroit Commission on Community Relations (MI), 8,148
Detroit Common Council (MI), 8,095
Detroit Conference of Home Missions (MI), 8,379
Detroit Council on Community Nursing (MI), 8,045
Detroit Equal Suffrage Club (MI), 7,803, 8,028
Detroit Federation of Women's Clubs (MI), **8,273**
Detroit Female Seminary (MI), **7,711**, **8,023**
Detroit High School (MI), 8,044
Detroit House of Corrections (MI), 7,770, 7,806
Detroit Household Workers Organization (MI), **8,080**
Detroit Housing Commission (MI), 7,796
  officials and employees, 8,089
Detroit Institute of Cancer Research (MI), 7,817
Detroit Job Training Center for Women, Inc. (MI), 8,062
Detroit Junior College (MI). See Wayne State University (MI)
Detroit Model Neighborhood Region Three (MI), 8,026
Detroit News (MI), 12,863
Detroit Normal School (MI), alumnae, 8,044
Detroit School of Government (MI), 7,738
Detroit Urban League (MI), 8,131
Detroit Welfare Department (MI), 8,148
Detroit Women Writers' Club (MI), **8,024**
Detroit Women's Press Club (MI). See Detroit Women Writers' Club (MI)
Detzer, Dorothy (1893-). See Denny, Dorothy (Detzer) [Mrs. Ludwell] (1893-)
Deueff, William, 14,518

Deutsch, Babette (1895-), 2,166, 2,207, 2,403, 2,491, 2,805, 9,443, 12,035, **12,441**, 15,900, 16,163
Deutsch, Felix, 340
Deutsch, Helen, **6,008**
Deutsch, Hermann B. (1889-1970), **5,537**
Deutsch, Naomi (1890-), **6,135**, 12,657
Deutsche Damen Club (CO), 1,673
Devall, Josephine R., 9,753
de Valois, Ninette, 3,980
Devan, Irene (Sanford) (1882-1964), **11,785**
deVarona, Donna, 1,534
Deveau Family (SC), 15,722
Deveaux, Marion (Singleton) [Mrs. Robert Marion] (1815-?). *See* Converse, Marion (Singleton) [Mrs. Robert Marion] Deveaux [Mrs. August L.] (1815-?)
Deveaux, Robert Marion, 2,578
De Vere, Mary A., 17,010
Devereux, Abigail, 7,461
Devereux, John, 12,996
Devereux, Lillie (1833-1913). *See* Blake, Lillie (Devereux) [Mrs. Frank Geoffrey Quay] Umsted [Mrs. Grinfill] (1833-1913)
Devereux, Margaret (Mordecai) [Mrs. John], **12,996**
Devereux, Marianne Cabot (1812-99). *See* Silsbee, Marianne Cabot (Devereux) [Mrs. Nathaniel] (1812-99)
Devereux, Mary Bayard (1827-86). *See* Clarke, Mary Bayard (Devereux) [Mrs. William John] (1827-86)
Devereux, Mary D., **11,568**
Devereux, Nicholas, 11,568
De Vergennes, Count, 11,195
DeVictor, Marian S., 6,623
DeVictor, Marion (Stephenson) [Mrs. James, Jr.] Henry [Mrs. William K.] (1888-). *See* Olden, Marion (Stephenson) [Mrs. James, Jr.] Henry [Mrs. William K.] DeVictor [Mrs. Paul] Coleman-Norton [Mrs. Roger] (1888-)
Devil in Massachusetts, The (book), 6,095
"Devil, The" (song), 5,534
DeVilbiss, Lydia Allen, 7,282, 7,289, 7,320
Devil's Elbow (book), 15,927
Devil's Hand, The (book), 3,775
Devin, Alice, **7,773**
Devine, Amelia, 14,861
Devlin, Annie, 11,602
Devoe, Allan, 12,360
DeVoe, Emma (Smith) (1858-1927), **17,166**, 17,171, 17,377
de Volude, Natalie de Delage (1782-1841). *See* Sumter, Natalie de Delage de Volude [Mrs. Thomas, Jr.] (1782-1841)
DeVoto, Avis [Mrs. Bernard] (1904-), **6,518**
DeVoto, Bernard Augustine (1897-1955), 1,550, 4,483, 6,518
DeVoto, Ella B. (1889-1929), 16,936
deVou, Mary, 2,042
De Vree, Anna, 8,195
De Vries, Lini Moerkerk, **6,511**
Dewald, Kathryn [Miss], 15,869
de Weerth, Ernst, 12,374
Dewees, Carroll F., 10,005
Dewees, Mary (Coburn), 15,939
DeWeese, Alice Christine (Towne) [Mrs. Fred M.] (1884-), **10,454**
Dewell, Margaret O., 449
Dewey, Ethel, 4,047
Dewey, Evelyn, 11,572
Dewey, Frances E. (Hutt) [Mrs. Thomas E.] (1903-70), **6,519**
Dewey, George (1837-1917), **2,302**
Dewey, Ione. *See* Bradley, Ione (Dewey) [Mrs. Luther P.]
Dewey, John (1859-1952), 3,772, 5,977, 6,614, 8,144, 8,145, 11,572, 11,864, **11,982**, 15,353
Dewey, Malcolm H., 3,318
Dewey, Marcia. *See* Lyman, Marcia (Dewey) [Mrs. Orange]
Dewey, Maria Lucy. *See* Woolley, Maria Lucy (Dewey)
Dewey, Maybelle Jones [Mrs. Malcolm H.] (1888-1963), **3,318**
Dewey, Melvil, 4,396

Dewey, Mildred (McLean) Hazen [Mrs. George], 2,302
Dewey, Mrs. Elliott Todhunter, **1,769**
Dewey, Sylvina Maria (1832-?). *See* Green, Sylvina Maria (Dewey) (1832-?)
Dewey, Thomas Edmund, 6,519, 10,487, 11,546, 11,592
de White, María del Rosario (Pérez), 715
Dewing, E. B., 16,158
De Witt, Alfred, 439
De Witt Family (CA), **439**
DeWitt, Katharine (1867-1963), 6,122
De Witt, Margaret [Mrs. Alfred], 439
De Witt, Ruth, **8,728**
DeWolf, Abby Kane (1794-1842). *See* Bartlett, Abby Kane (DeWolf) [Mrs. Enoch] (1794-1842)
De Wolf, Anna Elizabeth (1815-?). *See* Middleton, Anna Elizabeth (De Wolf) (1815-?)
DeWolf, James (1762-1834), **7,616**
De Wolf, Nancy (Lawrence) [Mrs. James] (1764-1807), **7,616**
DeWolfe, Nellie P. (Crosby), 9,025
Dewson, Elizabeth Weld (Williams) (1836-1912), 6,520
Dewson, Mary "Molly" M. Williams [Miss] (1874-1962), 2,336, 2,403, 2,504, 2,693, **6,520**, 6,765, 6,958, **6,973**, **11,483**, 11,503, 11,771, 11,916, 12,069, 13,241
Dexter, Katharine (1875-1967). *See* McCormick, Katharine (Dexter) [Mrs. Stanley] (1875-1967)
Dexter, Mary, 18,026
DeYampert, Lillian Thomas (?-1929), 86
de Zavala, Adina Emilia (1861-1955), **16,058**
de Zavala, Manuel Lorenzo Justiniano (1789-1836), 16,058
d'Happart, Elizabeth (Thompson) [Mrs. Joseph St. Leger], 15,258
d'Happart, Joseph St. Leger, **15,258**
Diabetes, research, 10,208
"Dial-a-Ride" system, 7,733
Dial, Nathaniel Barksdale, 15,583
Dial, Rebecca (1894-), **15,583**
Dial, The (periodical), 5,949, 7,044
Dialect Mixture in Three New England Pronunciation Patterns (book), 12,031
Diamond, Amanda J., 3,001
Diamond, Emma, 3,001
Diamond, James, Family (GA), **3,001**
Diamond, Julius, 2,929
Diamond, Lizzie Towles, 3,001
Diamond, Nancy Cornwell [Mrs. James], 3,001
Diamond, Nancy Jane, 3,001
Diamond, Ruby, **2,929**, 2,941, **13,780**
Diamond, Sallie, 3,001
Diaries and journals, 222, 360, 368, 438, **581, 594, 701**, 1,062, **1,102**, 1,258, 1,281, 1,290, 1,431, 1,524, 1,610, **1,714**, 1,755, **1,841**, 1,847, **1,852**, 1,860, 2,009, 2,011, **2,056**, 2,170, 2,173, 2,498, 2,563, 2,757, **2,765**, **2,776**, 3,147, 3,419, **3,426**, 3,487, **3,563**, **3,621**, **3,643**, 3,678, **3,834**, 4,019, 4,178, 4,294, **4,428**, 4,481, 4,620, 4,656, **4,762**, 4,893, 4,894, 4,896, 4,911, **4,925**, 5,049, **5,215**, 5,217, **5,218**, **5,295**, **5,585**, 5,617, 5,634, 5,635, **5,677**, 5,716, **5,740**, 5,779, **5,943**, **5,947**, 6,008, 6,020, **6,096**, 6,099, 6,354, 6,418, **6,690**, **7,047**, **7,052**, **7,140**, 7,314, **7,376**, 7,471, 7,496, 7,605, **7,706**, **7,762**, **7,782**, **7,783**, **7,812**, 7,815, **7,897**, **7,929**, **8,154**, **8,217**, **8,229**, **8,246**, **8,248**, **8,249**, 8,252, 8,294, **8,322**, **8,330**, 8,339, **8,359**, 8.363, 8,365, 8,370, **8,514**, 8,782, 8,896, 8,914, 8,937, 8,944, 8,980, 9,004, 9,026, 9,063, 9,067, 9,079, 9,086, 9,099, 9,247, 9,303, 9,356, 9,378, 9,445, **9,461**, **9,548**, 9,588, 9,591, 9,609, **9,753**, 9,796, **9,800**, 9,819, 9,870, 10,034, 10,051, **10,105**, **10,106**, **10,107**, 10,202, 10,232, 10,265, 10,274, 10,293, 10,362, 10,380, 10,638, 10,799, 10,807, 10,821, 10,829, **10,859**, **10,895**, 10,903, 10,950, **10,973**, 10,975, **10,983**, 10,985, 11,041, **11,053**, 11,069, **11,087**, 11,096, **11,127**, 11,249, 11,305, **11,429**, **11,475**, 11,723, 11,792, **12,221**, **12,295**, **12,326**, **12,368**, **12,374**, **12,442**, **12,454**, 12,465, **12,586**, **12,640**, **12,671**, 12,673, **12,718**, 13,071, 13,155, 13,230, 13,341, 13,392, 13,445, 13,603, 13,643, 13,650, 13,652, 13,711, 13,873, **14,244**,

14,283, 14,305, 14,311, 14,318, 14,337, 14,461, **14,484**, **14,490**, 14,498, 14,514, **14,529**, **14,560**, **14,568**, 14,620, 14,646, **14,649**, **14,673**, 14,678, **14,729**, 15,046, **15,090**, **15,091**, **15,284**, **15,343**, **15,625**, **15,640**, **15,643**, 15,724, 15,809, 15,856, **16,060**, 16,247, 16,300, 16,305, 16,457, 16,495, 16,518, **16,566**, **16,578**, 16,596, 16,601, 16,623, **16,631**, **16,642**, 16,650, **16,678**, **16,709**, **16,738**, 16,778, 16,803, **16,896**, **16,921**, **16,934**, 17,026, 17,029, **17,101**, **17,440**, **17,470**, 17,591, **17,645**, 17,782, 17,857, **17,859**, 17,876, **17,938**, 17,982, 18,015
18th C, 1,956, **5,576**, **5,928**, 6,447, 7,181, **7,338**, 7,346, 7,351, 7,660, 7,661, 7,671, 7,673, **7,676**, **11,061**, 11,085, 11,284, **12,217**, **12,545**, 14,847, **15,290**, 15,939, **17,082**
18th-19th C, 62, 1,007, **1,597**, 1,753, 1,773, **1,901**, **1,970**, 2,049, 2,582, 2,608, 2,644, **2,655**, 2,659, 2,889, **3,538**, 5,574, **5,691**, 5,772, 7,333, 7,453, **7,460**, 7,601, 7,619, 7,659, 7,660, 10,417, 10,908, **10,957**, 10,989, 11,042, 12,170, **12,217**, 12,324, **12,980**, 14,286, **14,371**, **14,372**, **14,456**, 14,462, 14,836, **14,837**, **14,961**, **14,963**, 15,041, 15,463, **15,746**, 16,589, **16,666**, 16,670, **16,712**, 16,806, **16,814**, 16,816, 16,924, **16,927**, 16,957, 17,037
19th C, 25, 26, 28, **59**, 62, **68**, 69, **71**, **78**, 79, **283**, **291**, 336, 445, 502, 736, 802, 814, 834, 846, **865**, **1,112**, **1,227**, **1,228**, **1,247**, 1,329, **1,336**, **1,350**, **1,367**, 1,402, 1,425, **1,694**, **1,697**, **1,711**, **1,725**, **1,727**, 1,737, 1,816, **1,828**, 1,877, **2,040**, 2,044, **2,050**, **2,061**, 2,138, **2,404**, 2,455, 2,457, 2,478, **2,531**, 2,545, **2,548**, 2,957, 2,958, **3,150**, 3,155, 3,173, 3,247, **3,349**, 3,390, **3,540**, **3,546**, 3,565, **3,624**, **3,776**, 4,348, 4,365, 4,437, 4,456, 4,475, **4,602**, 4,604, **4,607**, **4,610**, 4,613, **4,637**, 4,651, **4,717**, **4,882**, 4,920, 4,964, 5,027, 5,219, 5,259, 5,279, **5,298**, 5,312, 5,518, 5,553, **5,671**, 5,689, 5,699, 5,706, **5,743**, **5,745**, **5,747**, **5,749**, 5,754, 5,765, **5,775**, **5,790**, **5,799**, 5,812, **5,819**, **5,821**, **5,887**, 5,900, 5,909, 5,919, 5,942, **5,952**, 5,955, 6,445, **6,510**, **6,521**, 6,845, 6,851, **6,878**, 6,906, **7,008**, **7,018**, 7,027, **7,029**, **7,057**, **7,061**, 7,094, 7,148, 7,150, 7,152, 7,181, 7,206, **7,335**, 7,340, 7,341, **7,353**, **7,354**, **7,356**, **7,357**, **7,358**, 7,359, 7,368, **7,369**, **7,378**, **7,380**, 7,384, **7,386**, **7,388**, **7,391**, **7,395**, **7,399**, **7,400**, **7,401**, **7,402**, **7,412**, **7,414**, **7,415**, 7,417, **7,419**, **7,420**, 7,423, **7,425**, **7,426**, 7,438, **7,444**, 7,454, **7,457**, 7,463, 7,492, 7,513, **7,603**, 7,606, **7,613**, 7,641, 7,644, **7,645**, 7,683, 7,704, **7,716**, **7,730**, 7,745, **7,752**, **7,753**, 7,778, **7,805**, 7,928, **7,931**, **7,969**, **7,972**, 8,166, **8,214**, **8,219**, **8,221**, **8,225**, **8,230**, **8,231**, **8,237**, **8,239**, **8,241**, **8,250**, **8,251**, **8,256**, **8,279**, **8,291**, **8,347**, **8,433**, **8,516**, **8,895**, 8,945, 8,968, 8,974, **9,019**, 9,045, 9,074, **9,090**, **9,091**, **9,105**, **9,207**, **9,294**, 9,363, 9,574, **9,584**, **9,586**, 9,594, **9,595**, **9,645**, 9,651, 9,675, **9,743**, 9,774, 9,781, **9,860**, **9,920**, 9,970, **9,992**, 10,234, 10,279, 10,365, **10,788**, **10,790**, **10,792**, 10,795, 10,800, 10,801, 10,802, 10,803, **10,805**, **10,806**, 10,810, **10,811**, **10,813**, **10,815**, 10,817, **10,819**, **10,827**, **10,882**, **10,914**, 10,938, 10,939, 10,944, **10,948**, **10,951**, **10,952**, 10,954, 10,959, **10,968**, **10,980**, **10,988**, **10,991**, 10,999, **11,015**, 11,031, 11,035, 11,041, 11,044, 11,046, **11,048**, 11,049, 11,050, **11,051**, 11,056, 11,057, **11,081**, 11,086, 11,104, **11,211**, 11,316, **11,348**, **11,352**, 11,354, 11,419, 11,443, **11,470**, 11,522, **11,544**, 11,570, **11,609**, **11,778**, **11,779**, 11,789, 12,028, **12,188**, **12,243**, 12,254, 12,278, **12,333**, 12,335, 12,381, **12,389**, 12,412, 12,430, 12,432, 12,458, 12,464, **12,490**, 12,528, **12,541**, **12,633**, **12,660**, **12,663**, **12,664**, 12,670, 12,742, 12,753, 12,824, 12,936, **12,942**, **12,946**, **12,954**, **12,970**, **12,983**, **12,984**, 13,002, 13,003, 13,005, **13,009**, **13,019**, **13,021**, **13,036**, **13,040**, **13,045**, 13,056, **13,057**, **13,072**, **13,091**, **13,096**, **13,102**, **13,103**, **13,106**, **13,113**, **13,114**, **13,151**, **13,152**, 13,157, **13,167**, **13,171**, 13,189, **13,268**, **13,270**, **13,321**, 13,403, 13,419, 13,465, 13,624, 13,919, 13,925, **13,946**, **13,957**, 14,117, 14,132, 14,162, 14,302, 14,420, 14,424, **14,491**, 14,519, 14,531, **14,636**, 14,667, **14,702**, **14,775**, **14,792**, 14,808, **14,899**, 14,950, **14,952**, 15,002, 15,028, **15,047**, **15,096**, **15,105**, **15,113**, 15,167, 15,280,

15,290, 15,370, **15,414**, 15,477, **15,494**, 15,582,
15,595, 15,608, 15,657, 15,662, **15,685, 15,751,**
15,759, 15,763, 15,939, **15,952, 15,955**, 16,060,
16,372, 16,378, **16,452**, 16,461, **16,472, 16,479,**
16,482, 16,483, 16,489, 16,505, **16,513**, 16,537,
16,541, **16,543**, 16,544, 16,546, 16,559, **16,561,**
16,635, **16,637**, 16,643, **16,655, 16,656, 16,665,**
16,669, **16,671, 16,672**, 16,685, **16,691, 16,717,**
16,725, 16,727, **16,728**, 16,731, **16,741**, 16,763,
16,775, **16,784**, 16,793, **16,825**, 16,830, **16,848,**
16,856, 16,895, 16,902, 16,909, 16,911, 16,913,
16,914, 16,915, 16,917, 16,962, 17,079, **17,090,**
17,100, 17,103, **17,105**, 17,106, 17,123, 17,199,
17,225, **17,287, 17,464, 17,477, 17,479**, 17,595,
17,605, **17,644, 17,660**, 17,668, **17,669, 17,688,**
17,703, **17,708**, 17,709, **17,873, 17,875, 17,878**
19th-20th C, 415, 636, 3,627, **3,849**, 4,468, 5,172,
5,623, **6,773, 7,005**, 7,628, 7,675, 10,937, **10,974,**
12,023, **12,793, 15,112, 17,120**
travel, 41, 72, **129, 136, 307, 524**, 585, 1,637,
1,717, 1,783, 1,841, **1,852**, 1,854, **2,228, 2,237,**
2,266, 2,367, 2,400, 2,747, 2,790, 3,314, **3,683,**
3,700, 3,727, **3,763**, 3,902, 4,411, 4,600, **4,611,**
4,904, 5,055, 5,458, **5,591, 5,804, 5,953**, 6,208,
6,340, 6,419, 6,429, 6,445, **6,476**, 6,503, 6,678,
6,803, 6,907, 7,344, **7,366, 7,462, 7,623, 8,222,**
8,323, 8,326, 8,520, 9,051, 9,108, 9,212, 9,242,
9,248, **9,264**, 9,321, 9,358, **9,601, 9,905**, 9,983,
10,040, 10,042, 10,166, 10,180, 10,242, **10,314,**
10,427, 10,645, **10,695**, 10,949, **10,958, 10,982,**
10,986, **11,004**, 11,014, **11,020, 11,054, 11,058,**
11,106, 11,424, 11,431, 11,646, 11,686, **11,731,**
12,157, **12,183**, 12,186, **12,196, 12,247, 12,285,**
12,289, 12,330, 12,428, **12,439, 12,546, 12,566,**
12,609, 12,650, 12,665, 13,931, **13,947, 14,179,**
14,520, 14,847, 15,057, **15,063, 15,066, 15,114,**
15,417, 15,591, 15,793, 15,886, 16,060, 17,038,
17,080, 17,135, **17,315**, 17,452, **17,612**
17th-18th C, **2,032, 2,440, 4,797, 10,966, 13,146,**
15,058
18th-19th C, 193, **251, 292, 311**, 326, **358, 422,**
444, 455, 465, 478, 489, 527, 528, 547, 571,
579, 606, 652, 683, 694, 738, 747, 759, 782,
841, **852**, 864, 867, **1,269, 1,286**, 1,288, **1,303,**
1,320, 1,332, 1,342, 1,343, 1,349, **1,365, 1,505,**
1,726, **1,987**, 1,989, 2,457, 2,557, 2,583, **2,642,**
2,661, **3,366**, 3,872, **4,251, 4,420, 4,439, 4,782,**
4,825, 5,271, **5,280, 5,707, 5,813**, 5,822, 6,194,
6,196, 6,261, 6,487, **6,576**, 6,910, **7,392, 7,421,**
7,427, 7,588, 7,631, **7,756**, 7,766, **7,991**, 8,305,
9,319, 9,354, 9,631, 9,696, 9,833, 10,031,
10,175, 10,260, **10,268, 10,329**, 10,389, **10,675,**
10,811, **10,987, 10,993, 11,002**, 11,005, **11,024,**
11,037, 11,648, 11,681, **11,732**, 11,795, **12,226,**
12,268, **12,270, 12,388, 12,456**, 12,463, **12,482,**
12,494, 12,542, **12,607, 12,645, 12,813, 12,985,**
12,990, 13,042, 13,149, 13,154, 13,346, **13,651,**
13,818, 13,921, 13,928, 13,930, **14,170, 14,288,**
14,293, 14,297, 14,298, 14,307, 14,483, 14,489,
14,532, 14,545, 14,550, 14,566, **14,569, 14,572,**
14,612, 14,709, **14,754**, 14,902, 14,958, 14,961,
15,406, 15,577, **16,245, 16,454**, 16,573, **16,887,**
17,172, 17,176, 17,206, 17,408, 17,410, **17,613,**
17,681, 17,758, 17,815, 17,857, 17,881
Diary from Dixie (book), 3,143
Diary of Anne Frank, The (drama), 17,799
"Diary of Domesticity" (column), 6,101
Diary of Sarah Connell Ayer (book), 10,792
"Diary of the Invasion of Canada," 10,877
Diaz, Abby (Morton) [Mrs. Manuel A.] (1821-1904),
1,426, **7,215**, 7,274, 11,742
Díaz Peña, Harriet Amelia (Kearsing), 587
Díaz Peña, Mary H., 587
Díaz, Profirio, 335
Diaz Union (Saco, ME), **5,696**
"Dibbie Dear" (ms), 5,127
Dibble Family (MI), **8,224**
Dibble, Philo, 8,224
Dick, Jackson P., Sr., **3,179**
Dick, Jackson P., Jr., 3,179
Dick, Jane [Mrs. Edison] (1906-), 11,827
Dick, Jane (LeRoux) [Mrs. Jackson P. Dick, Jr.],
3,179
Dick, May (Atkinson), **3,179**

Dicke, Anna Katherina (Bezler) [Mrs. Peter Heinrich]
(1832-1930), 17,862
Dicke, Peter Heinrich, 17,862
Dicken, Anna (1839-1909). *See* Troutman, Anna
(Dicken) [Mrs. Francis] (1839-1909)
Dicken Family (KY), **5,309**
Dicken, George D. (1809-74), 5,309
Dickens, Charles, 3,077, 6,185, 6,329, 7,596, 10,170
Dickens Club of Winchendon (MA), **7,596**
Dickenson, Kathleen (1895-1969). *See* Mellen,
Kathleen (Dickenson) [Mrs. George] (1895-1969)
Dickerman, Carolyn Gorham, 1,998
Dickerman, Marion (1890-), **11,853**
Dickerson, Anna, 11,662
Dickerson, Denver S. (1872-?), 10,753
Dickerson Family (NV), **10,753**
Dickerson, Nancy H., 1,605
Dickerson, Una Reiley [Mrs. Denver S.], 10,753
Dickey Family, 12,531
Dickinson, Anna Elizabeth [Miss] (1842-1932), 1,963,
2,303, 2,315, 4,244, 4,732, **6,522**, 6,712, 12,003
Dickinson, Catherine (Willard) [Mrs. Samuel
Philemon], 5,756
Dickinson, Charles Monroe (1842-1924), **2,304**
Dickinson College (PA), 14,752, 14,761, 14,765
alumnae, 14,763
faculty, 14,759
Dickinson College (PA), Independent Women, **14,757**
Dickinson College (PA), Panhellenic Council, 14,764
Dickinson College (PA), Women's Student
Government Association, 14,764
Dickinson College (PA), Women's Student Senate,
14,764
Dickinson, Emily (1830-86), 896, 5,211, **5,862, 5,922**,
7,131, 7,171, 7,185, 8,021, **11,307**, 11,821,
12,443, 12,642, **15,169**, 17,010
Dickinson Family (MD), **5,756**
Dickinson Family (NY), **14,071**
Dickinson Family (PA), 15,039
Dickinson, Irene Hallock [Miss] (1888-), **12,777**
Dickinson, John (1732-1808), 15,039
Dickinson, John (1894-1952), 13,245
Dickinson, Laura D. (1856-1934), 5,756
Dickinson, Lora (Townsend) [Mrs. Frederick]
(1878-), **4,255**
Dickinson, Lula Martin (McIver) [Mrs. John], 13,245
Dickinson, Martha (1882-). *See* Galbraith, Martha
(Dickinson) [Mrs. Archibald] (1882-)
Dickinson, Mary, **11,089**
Dickinson, Mary, 3,140
Dickinson, Mary, 15,013
Dickinson, Mary Ann. *See* Adair, Mary Ann
(Dickinson)
Dickinson, Mary Norris [Mrs. John], 15,039
Dickinson, Minna F., 1,786
Dickinson, Mrs. Israel, 7,140
Dickinson, Philemon (1739-1809), 11,090
Dickinson, Rebecca [Mrs. Philemon], **11,090**
Dickinson, Robert Latou (1861-1950), **6,219**, 7,320,
8,634
Dickinson, Ruth Robertson (Allen), **8,643**
Dickinson, Sally A., 15,042
Dickinson, Sally Norris (1774-1855), 14,836
Dickinson, Samuel, 5,756, 11,090
Dickinson State College (ND), 9,527
Dickinson, Statira. *See* Grant, Statira (Dickinson)
Dickinson, Thomas H., 17,815
Dickmann, Bernard "Barney" F. (1888-1971), **9,958**
Dickson, Abigail Louise (1871-1961). *See* Senkler,
Abigail Louise (Dickson) [Mrs. George Easton]
(1871-1961)
Dickson, Alice M., 2,692, 5,123
Dickson, Emma, 15,325
Dickson, Eudora M. [Miss], 9,967
Dickson Family, 3,650
Dickson, Jack F., 1,281
Dickson, Lillian M. [Mrs. Jack F.] (1872-?), **1,281**
Dickson, Margarette Ball [Mrs.] (?-1963), **9,043**
Dickson, N. T., 8,801
Dickson, Susan Layman, 8,251
Dickson, William B., **15,325**
Dictionaries and encyclopedias, 14,609, 17,693
Dictionaries, polyglot, 173, 3,706
Dictionary of American Biography, 2,411

"Did You Carry the Flag Today, Charley?" 5,304
Diddock, Marguerite (La Flesche) [Mrs. Walter T.],
10,483
Dido, Queen of Hearts (book), 325
Didrickson, Babe, 15,935
Die Heilige Elisabeth, 8,597
Die Neue Zeit (periodical), 7,999
Diebitsch, Josephine (1863-1955). *See* Peary,
Josephine (Diebitsch) [Mrs. Robert E.]
(1863-1955)
Dieckmann, Annetta Maria (1892-1974), **4,083**
Diegueno Tribe, 11,293
Diekema, Martha (1867-1960). *See* Kollen, Martha
(Diekema) [Mrs. George E.] (1867-1960)
Dielectrics, 11,814
Diem, Ngo-dinh- (1901-1963), 9,286
Diepenbrock, Catherine George [Mrs. George W.]
(1845-?), 9,042
Dier, Carolyn Lawrence, 1,786
Dierssen, Anna (1884-1969), **9,959**
Dieson, Georgina (1882-). *See* Hegland, Georgina
Dieson [Mrs. Martin] (1882-)
Diet, 9,841, 10,364, 10,379, 14,827, 16,965
Dieter, Alice (1928-), **3,677**
Dieterich, Dora (1902-). *See* Bonham, Dora
Dieterich [Mrs. Eugene] (1902-)
Dieterich Family (TX), 16,038
Dieticians, 4,258, 8,530
Dietrich, Margretta (Shaw) [Mrs. Charles H.]
(1881-), **11,240**
Dietrich, Marlene, 1,025, 12,129
Dietrickson, Mathine M., 5,063
Dietz, Betty, 14,046
Diffendorf, Grace (Baker) [Mrs. Walter]
(1874?-1961), **1,208**
Difficult Courtship (book), 10,399
Diggs, Irene, 3,799
Dighton Rock Grange No. 314 (MA), 7,017
Dignam, Dorothy (1896?-), **6,523, 17,623**
Dignam, J. B., 17,623
Dignam's Magazine (periodical), 17,623
Dike, Abbie T. Griffin [Mrs. S. Clint] (1851-?), **9,105**
Dike, Priscilla Miriam (Manning) (1790-1873), 7,383
Dike, S. Clint, 9,105
Dildine, Jeannette (Drew) [Mrs. Marcene H.]
(1843-1918), 9,052
Dill, Max M., 967
Dill, Minnie, 16,132
Dill Pickle, The (CA), **914**
Dill, Theresa Mae (Varney) [Mrs. Robie L.], **1,154**
Dillard University (LA)
alumnae, 5,470
faculty, 5,468
trustees, 5,470
Dillavou, Leta. *See* Jaquis, Leta (Dillavou)
Dille, Thomas Ray, **17,457**
Dilletanti (periodical), **9,557**
Dilling, Elizabeth [Mrs.], 9,150
Dillingham, Charles Bancroft (1868-1934), **12,444**
Dillingham, Howard A., 11,592
Dillingham, Mabel W., 88
Dillingham, Mary Pauline [Miss] (1875-1964), **16,247**
Dillman, Mildred Myrtle (Miles) [Mrs. Ray Eugene]
(1893-), **16,651**
Dillman, Ray Eugene, 16,651
Dillon, Anna (Price) [Mrs. John Forest] (1835-93),
4,695
Dillon Family (IL), 3,751
Dillon, Fannie Fairchild (Fairley) [Mrs. John L.],
11,582
Dillon, Frances "Fannie" Charles (1881-1947), **1,021**
Dillon, Helen A. (1914-), 853
Dillon, John Forest, 4,695
Dillon, John L., 11,582
Dillon, Julia (Lester) [Mrs. William Bennett], 2,258
Dillon, Margie (1926-), **234**
Dillwyn, Susanna (1769-1819). *See* Emlen, Susanna
(Dillwyn) [Mrs. Samuel] (1769-1819)
Dillwyn, William (1743-1824), **14,989**
Dilts, Adda, **7,774**
Dilts, Marion M., 12,739
Dilworth, Richardson, 15,332
Dime novels, **192**, 10,027
Dimmitt, Lillian E. (1867-1965), **5,101**

Dimmitt, Marjorie Alma (1895-1965), **4,525,** 4,532
Dimock Community Health Center (MA), **6,150,**
  6,228, 6,364, 6,407, 6,698, **6,797,** 6,968, 7,178,
  7,274
Dimock Community Health Center, New England
  Hospital for Women and Children, School of
  Nursing (MA), 6,150
Dimock Farm (VT), 6,472, 6,896
Dimock, Susan (1847-75), 6,226, 7,274
Dimond, Susan B., **5,217**
Dines, Alta (?-1965), 12,079
Dinesen, Isak, 2,331
Dingham, Mary Agnes, 15,310
Dingley Normal Training School (ME), 5,577
Dingley, Susan. *See* Manning, Susan (Dingley)
Dingman, Helen (1885-1978), **5,251**
Dingman, Mary Agnes (1875-1961), **6,538,** 6,958
Dingus, Georgia (Wilson) [Mrs. William G.] (1886-),
  16,265
Dinner Gang (St. Paul, MN), **9,044**
Dinners and dining, **9,044**
Dinosaur National Monument (UT), 451
Dinsmore, Florence [Mrs.], **5,646**
Diocesan Council of Catholic Women (Green Bay,
  WI), **17,551**
Dionne family, 3,368
Diplomats, **2,140,** 2,188, 2,190, **2,192,** 2,197, **2,226,**
  2,235, 2,238, 2,252, 2,264, 2,270, **2,304,** 2,312,
  2,322, 2,382, 2,441, **2,493,** 2,527, 2,550, **2,661,**
  3,982, 4,370, 4,375, **4,615, 5,134,** 5,321, **5,791,**
  5,820, 6,391, **6,737, 6,766,** 6,912, 7,264, **7,281,**
  7,704, 7,850, 8,450, 10,862, 11,140, 11,509,
  11,514, 11,720, 11,742, 11,839, **11,872,** 11,956,
  12,044, **12,070,** 12,383, 12,619, 12,640, **12,694,**
  13,146, 13,262, 14,890, **14,904,** 17,629. *See also*
  Ambassadors; Consuls
Diplomats, Afro-American, **2,140,** 2,315
Di Prima, Diane (1934-), **5,374,** 12,064, 12,877,
  12,894
Diptheria epidemics, 8,701, 8,709, 16,968
Directory of Medical Women, 11,511
"Dirge Blues" (song), 5,534
Dirlston Plantation (SC), **15,467**
"Dis N Dat" (column), 9,550
Disarmament, 2,407, 2,432, 4,243, 4,480, 5,839,
  6,771, 6,978, 7,187, 7,290, 7,312, 7,723, 8,149,
  9,379, 9,656, 11,389, 14,691, 15,310, 15,316,
  17,468, 17,654
Disaster relief, 347, 2,087, 3,812, 4,072, 4,157, 4,500,
  5,120, 5,608, 8,908, 9,477, 10,620, 12,738,
  13,729, 14,742, 14,860, **15,471**
Disbro, Johanna, 9,323
Disbrow, Mrs. F. W., 3,764
Discalced Carmelite nuns, 12,845
Discalced Carmelite Nuns Monastery (Elysburg, PA),
  14,785
Discalced Carmelite Nuns Monastery (Seattle, WA),
  17,215
Disciples of Christ, 2,009, 2,346, 9,824, 9,981
  clergy, 5,262, **9,971, 10,001,** 10,002
  missions, 14,457
Disciples of Christ, United Christian Missionary
  Society, 8,886
Disciples of Christ, Woman's Missionary Society,
  California North, **446**
"Discrepancies in the Value Climate of Nursing
  Students: A Comparison of Head Nurses and
  Nursing Educators" (dissertation), 1,379
Discrimination, 83, 835, 6,353, 6,751, 11,591, 11,932,
  15,210, 15,993, 16,488. *See also* Civil rights;
  Discrimination in education; Discrimination in
  employment; Minorities; Race discrimination;
  Segregation; Sex discrimination
  legal aspects, 658
Discrimination in education, 4,382, 8,121, 10,030,
  10,159. *See also* Segregation in education
Discrimination in employment, 1,280, **2,678,** 3,915,
  5,378, 6,751, 8,063, 8,115, 8,139, 8,984, 9,196,
  9,932, 9,951, 10,012, 11,771, 12,691, 14,023,
  15,332, 17,663. *See also* Affirmative action
  programs; Blacklisting; Equal pay for equal work;
  Labor
Discrimination in housing, 3,835, 5,462, 7,794
Discrimination in public accommodations, 5,828

Discrimination in transportation. *See* Segregation in
  transportation
Discrimination, racial. *See* Race discrimination
Disease, 2,317, 3,482, 9,312, 9,800, 15,474, 15,479,
  16,117, 17,423
Dishonest Lady (drama), 14,736
Disney, Doris Miles (1907-76), 6,060
Disney, Walt, 17,248
Dispatch (Columbus, OH), 14,041
Displaced persons, 8,984
Dissenters, religious, 15,526
Dissertations, academic, 270, 312, 1,379, 2,752, 2,900,
  3,503, 3,742, 3,790, 4,525, 4,537, **4,657,** 4,759,
  6,104, 6,339, 6,683, 6,692, 6,815, 6,848, 7,216,
  7,579, 7,785, 8,750, 8,812, 9,231, **9,544, 9,547,**
  9,764, 9,770, 9,893, 10,717, **11,303,** 12,012,
  12,991, 14,163, **15,143, 15,191, 15,409,** 16,164,
  16,994
d'Issertelle, Edna, 8,665
Distaff (periodical), 2,936
Distilling, illicit, 9,995
Distilling industries, 2,706
Distinguished Citizens Award, 4,125
Distinguished Daughters of Pennsylvania, 14,823
District Nurses Board of Examiners (DC), 2,332
District Nursing Association, 11,515
District of Columbia, 2,135, 2,378, 2,608, 12,186,
  12,270, 12,475, 16,371
  abolitionists, Afro-American, 2,138
  Afro-Americans, **2,143,** 3,889
    civil rights, 2,123
    education, **2,313, 2,486**
    social conditions, 2,332
  archives, 6,687
  art
    exhibitions, 2,131
    galleries and museums, **2,100,** 12,912
  art, Afro-American, 2,131
  art patrons, 2,720
  Catholic schools, **2,121**
  Catholic universities and colleges, archives, **2,864**
  charities, 2,397, 3,027
  church and race problems, Catholic Church, 3,844
  church societies, 2,609
  civil rights, 2,143
  clergy, **2,138**
  clubs, 2,597, 2,633, 6,704, 11,249
  college teachers, 5,829
  conservatories of music, **2,155**
  consumers' leagues, 827
  convents and nunneries, **2,121**
  demonstrations, 2,063
  educational associations, 6,934, 10,035, 11,911
  evening and continuation schools, 2,131
  government social functions, 10,083
  governors, **2,572**
  historical societies, 2,414
  hospitals, military, 8,987
  housing authorities, 6,656
  journalists, **6,474, 6,767**
  lawyers, **6,668**
  librarians, Afro-American, **2,146**
  Lumbee Indians, 2,883
  manual training, 2,313
  mayors, 2,279
  mentally ill children, care and treatment, 2,391
  Mormons and Mormonism, 5,829
  museums, 2,131
  music, instruction and study, 2,134
  musicians, Afro-American, **2,155**
  newspapers, 11,896
  nursing schools, **2,306, 6,132**
  nursing service administration, 2,332
  officials and employees, 8,656
  orphans and orphan asylums, 2,391, 6,704
  patriotic societies, **2,307**
  political clubs, 11,249
  public housing, 2,695
  race problems, 2,143, 2,602
  real property, 2,028
  school administrators, Afro-American, **2,155**
  school boards, 6,771
  schools, 65, 2,130, 2,134, **2,305**
  slums, 6,656

  social life and customs, 2,287, 2,456, 2,467, 2,715,
    7,968, 9,303, 11,049, 11,249, 12,611, 14,962
  social work education, 8,641
  social workers, 8,654
  suffrage societies, 2,597
  teachers, Afro-American, 2,138
  teachers unions, 8,109
  teen agers, research, 6,934, 10,035, 11,911
  trade and professional associations, **2,836**
  universities and colleges, 2,143, 2,146, 2,149, 2,680
    archives, **2,118**
  wages, minimum wage, 6,402, 6,848
District of Columbia Belgian Relief Fund, 2,454
District of Columbia Board of Education, 2,123
District of Columbia board of public health, 8,641
District of Columbia department of public health,
  8,656
District of Columbia Federation of Women's Clubs,
  2,597, 2,633
District of Columbia Minimum Wage Board, 6,402,
  6,848
District of Columbia Woman Suffrage Association,
  2,597
Disturbing Death of Jenkin Delaney, The (book), 962
Ditmars, Jane, 11,322
Ditmer Family (PA), **14,808**
Ditmer, Joanne, 1,750
Ditmer, Lydia M., 14,808
Ditmer, Sarah A. *See* Lehmer, Sarah A. (Ditmer)
  [Mrs. Jacob F.]
Ditmer, Susan, 14,808
Ditzer, Dorothy, 17,254
Diven Family (NY), 11,440
Divers, 997
Divine Science, 14,351
Divining-rod, **5,648, 5,656**
Division of Negro Service, 7,287
Divoire, Fernand, 12,361
Divorce, 1,143, 1,167, 1,177, 1,344, 1,655, 1,686,
  1,753, 1,786, 1,806, 1,914, 1,915, **1,919,** 2,211,
  2,258, 2,259, 2,356, 2,451, 2,458, 2,467, 2,488,
  2,569, 2,656, 2,761, 3,525, 3,771, 3,981, 4,409,
  4,912, 5,060, 5,278, 5,334, 5,568, 6,196, 6,343,
  6,789, 7,065, 7,199, **8,200,** 8,311, 8,941,
  9,206, 9,532, 9,841, 9,933, 9,934, 9,940, 9,951,
  9,976, 9,991, 10,025, 10,043, 10,100, 10,101,
  10,102, 10,177, 10,680, 10,684, 10,711, 12,087,
  12,174, 12,612, 12,617, 12,705, 12,847, 12,913,
  13,386, 13,669, 13,725, 13,846, 13,874, 14,510,
  14,832, 15,258, 16,180, 16,411, 16,486, 16,893,
  16,932, 16,968, 17,216, 17,236, 17,378, 17,514,
  17,975, 17,991
  law and legislation, 3,381, 9,963, 9,972, 14,023,
  14,829
Divorce suits, 1,957, 14,921, **15,958**
Dix, Agnes A., 955
Dix, Beulah Marie (1876-1970). *See* Flebbe, Beulah
  Marie (Dix) [Mrs. Georg Heinrich] (1876-1970)
Dix, Dorothea Lynde (1802-87), 1,452, 1,480, **2,308,**
  2,721, 2,972, 5,226, **5,923, 6,539,** 6,540, 6,556,
  7,477, 11,103, 11,185, 11,303, 11,345, **12,445,**
  12,757, 13,446, 13,512, 13,593, 14,718, 14,824,
  14,831, 14,895, 15,077, 17,128
Dix, Dorothy (pseudonym). *See* Gilmer, Elizabeth
  (Meriwether) (1861-1951)
Dix, Mary Augusta (1810-81). *See* Gray, Mary
  Augusta (Dix) (1810-81)
"Dixie Story Lady," 13,366
Dixon, Ann Lilley [Mrs. George], **7,617**
Dixon, Annie Hughes [Mrs.], **9,622**
Dixon, Eileen, 3,762
Dixon, Elizabeth. *See* Geer, Elizabeth (Dixon) Smith
Dixon, Gertrude (?-1969). *See* Enfield, Gertrude
  (Dixon) (?-1969)
Dixon, Hannah, 13,308
Dixon, Harriet [Mrs. Joseph], 9,813
Dixon, Hazel. *See* Payne, Hazel (Dixon)
Dixon, J. Curtis, 11,897
Dixon, Jeanne, 16,371
Dixon, Marian (Homes), **12,997**
Dixon, Mary C., 16,114
Dixon, Maynard, 607
Dixon, Sarah, 13,308

Dixwell, Fanny Bowditch. *See* Holmes, Fanny Bowditch (Dixwell) [Mrs. Oliver Wendell, Jr.]
Dizney, Helen (1894-?), **447**, 11,846
"Do Men Like Flirts?" 16,174
"Do We Exercise Our Right of Franchise?" (article), 9,988
Doane College (Crete, NE), 10,407
Doane Family, 4,942
Doane, Gustavus C. (?-1892), **10,236**, 10,237
Doane, Mary (Hunter) [Mrs. Gustavus C.] (1859-1952), 10,236, **10,237**
Doane, Sarah W., 14,650
Dobbins, Emma Jane (1853-1932), 17,897
Dobbins, Gertrude Wyoming, **17,898**
Dobbins, Mary Emma, 3,319
Dobbins, John S. (1800-66), Family, **3,319**
Dobbins, Natalia (?-1975), **1,282**
Dobbins, Sarah (Williams) [Mrs. John S.] (1816-?), 3,319
Dobbs, Catherine R. (1909-74), **13,728**
Dobbs, Ella Victoria (1866-1952), 9,894, **9,960**
Dobbs, Governor, 13,488
Dobbs, John Wesley (1881-1961), Family, **5,466**
Dobbs, Justina Davis [Mrs.]. *See* Nash, Justina Davis [Mrs.] Dobbs [Mrs. Abner]
Dobbs, Mary Butts Griffith, **3,180**
Dobie, Bertha (McKee) [Mrs. J. Frank] (1890-1974), **16,346**
Dobie, Charles Caldwell (1881-1943), **448**
Dobie, J. Frank, 16,154, 16,159, 16,164
Doble, John, 9,961
Doble, Margaret McFarland, **9,961**
Dochterman, Lillian, **2,752**
Dock Family (PA), **14,809**
Dock, George (1823-7?), 14,809
Dock, George (1860-1951), 2,309, 14,809
Dock, Gilliard (1827-95), 14,809
Dock, Lavinia Lloyd (1858-1956), **2,309**, 6,122, 12,074
Dock, Mira C. (?-1945), **15,326**
Dock, Mira Lloyd (1853-1945), **2,310**, 14,809, 14,819, 15,240
Dock, William (1793-1868), 14,809
Dockery, Alexander M., 9,624
Dockery, Octavia [Miss] (?-1949), **9,623, 9,624**
Dockery, Thomas P., 9,624
Docks, 14,555
Dr. Brown's Institution for Feeble Minded Youth (Barre, MA), 5,895
Dr. Clearwater Medicine Company, **5,647**
Doctor Faustus Lights the Lights (opera), 819
*Dr. Jane Hodgson Legal Defense Fund, 8,630
Dr. Jekyll and Mr. Hyde (drama), 15,699
"Dr. Kate Woodhull—Pioneer Doctor for Women in Foochow" (pamphlet), 12,776
Dr. Mary Walker: The Little Lady in Pants (book), 12,765
Dr. Zay (book), 6,714
Doctors and nurses, 231, 233
Doctors Jacobi, The (book), 15,144
Doctors Mayo, The (book), 8,566
Doctors, The (drama), 2,576
Documents Relating to Northwest Missions (book), 9,002
Dod, Martha, 11,134
Dodd, Bella (Visono) (1904-), 12,884
Dodd, Ceyce. *See* Eastman, Ceyce (Dodd) Craig
Dodd College (LA), **5,547**
Dodd, Dorothy, 2,931
Dodd Family, 11,130
Dodd, Lillian, **13,400**
Dodd, Mead and Company (publishers), 5,712, 6,083, 14,352, 14,382, 14,475
Dodd, S. C. [Mrs. James], 13,400
Dodd, William B., Family (MN), **9,045**
Dodds, Dorothy (1907-). *See* Baker, Dorothy (Dodds) (1907-)
Dodge, Adeline P. *See* Cole, Adeline P. (Dodge)
Dodge, Alice [Mrs.], 8,829
Dodge, Anne, 4,749
Dodge, Anne [Mrs. Grenville M.], 1,770, 4,749
Dodge, Augustus Caesar (1812-83), **4,905**
Dodge, Caroline E. (Marshall) [Mrs. George A.], **10,455**

Dodge, Clara A. [Mrs. Augustus Caesar], 4,696, 4,905
Dodge, Elizabeth Clementine (1810-89). *See* Kinney, Elizabeth Clementine (Dodge) Stedman (1810-89)
Dodge, Ella, 4,749
Dodge Family (IA), 4,750
Dodge, Grace Hoadley [Miss] (1856-1914), 11,864, **12,075, 12,712**
Dodge, Grenville M. (1831-1916), **1,770, 4,749**, 4,750
Dodge, Harriet Hazen, 9,964
Dodge, Jane Gay, **6,540**
Dodge, Julia. *See* Beard, Julia (Dodge)
Dodge, Julia Theresa (Phillips) [Mrs. Sylvanus] (1802-88), 1,770, 4,749, 4,750
Dodge, Lettie. *See* Montgomery, Lettie (Dodge)
Dodge, Mary Abigail [Miss] (1833-96), 1,585, 2,210, **2,311**, 2,542, 2,641, **6,541, 7,025, 7,364**, 7,605, 8,375
Dodge, Mary Bourne Thompson [Mrs.], 14,639
Dodge, Mary Elizabeth (Mapes) [Mrs. William] (1831-1905), 1,304, **1,421**, 1,447, 1,963, 3,797, 3,927, 11,144, **11,157**, 11,167, 12,022
Dodge, Mrs. Horace O., 1,679
Dodge, Mrs. William, 8,925
Dodge, Nathan P., 1,770, **4,750**
Dodge, Sylvanus, 1,770
Dodge, William, 8,925
Dodgson, Anna, 7,047
Dodson, Emeline, 3,763
Doe, Elizabeth Bondvel "Baby Doe" (McCourt) [Mrs. Harvey] (1854-1935). *See* Tabor, Elizabeth Bondvel "Baby Doe" (McCourt) [Mrs. Harvey] Doe [Mrs. Horace Austin Warner] (1854-1935)
Doe, Harvey, 1,786
d'Oegreda, Ven. Mère Marie de Jesus, 1,513
Doerschuk, Beatrice, 6,440, 11,910
Doggett, Kate Newell [Mrs. William] (ca. 1828-84), 3,992, 14,062
Dogwood Garden Club (SC), **15,584**
Doheny, Edward Lawrence, 951
Doheny, Estelle (Betzold) [Mrs. Edward Lawrence] (1875-1958), 951
Doherty, Catherine de Hueck (1900-), 3,844
Doherty, Florence (Squires) (1890-). *See* Boyer, Florence (Squires) Doherty (1890-)
Doherty, Mrs. C., 9,580
Dohme, Adelyn. *See* Breeskin, Adelyn (Dohme)
Doing It Our Way (book), 5,260
Dolan, Margaret (Baggett) (1914-74), **12,998**
Dolan, Mary, 3,844
Dolan, Sister Angelico (1867-1947), 17,868
Dolan, Thomas F., **4,642**
Dolbear, Angeline Louise Bailey, 9,728
Dolbee, Cora (?-1956), **6,248**
Dolbey, Dorothy (1908-), **13,872**
Dole, Charlotte C., 14,650
Dole, Clara (Rowell), 2,002
Dole Family (HI), **3,641**
Dole, Sanford Ballard (1844-1926), 3,641
Dolgoff, Esther [Mrs. Sam], 4,032
Dolgoff, Sam, 4,032
Dolim, Mary Nuzum (1925-), **6,010**
Doll, Edgar A., 13,746
Dollenmayer, Albert, Family (MN), **9,046**
Dollenmayer, Emma (1859-?). *See* Taylor, Emma (Dollenmayer) (1859-?)
Dolley, Charles Sumner, 12,840
Dolley Family, 12,840
Dolley, Sarah Read (Adamson) [Mrs. Lester Clinton] (1829-1909), **12,840**
Dolley Todd Madison House, 14,935
Dollinger, Genora Johnson (1913-), 1,654, 1,656, **8,081**
Dollinger, Renate, 1,534
Dolliver, Augusta (Larrabee) [Mrs. Victor], 4,928
Dolliver, Jonathan Prentiss (1858-1910), **4,906**
Dolliver, Louise (Pearsons) [Mrs. Jonathan Prentiss] (1866-1937), 4,906
Dolliver, Mary (1860-1919). *See* Graham, Mary (Dolliver) (1860-1919)
Dollmakers, 13,217, **17,239**
Dollmaking, 17,239
Dolloff Family (NH), **10,807**
Dolloff, Myra E. (1864-ca. 1933), 10,807

Dolls, **10,133**, 11,442
collectors and collecting, 5,093, 17,239
"Doll's Dressmaker: A Magazine for Girls, The," 1,224
"Dolly Dump" (ms), 1,745
Dolly Kneeland et al. v. Waitsill Goodrich et al., 4,809
Dolly Varden Mining Company, 1,719
Dolson, Hildegarde, 9,770, 14,828
Dombois Family, 15,956
Dombois, Thekla. *See* Hasslock, Thekla (Dombois) [Mrs. Herman Wilhelm]
Dombrowski, James, 6,547, 17,608
Dome Club (MN), 9,080
Döme, Lillian (Norton) [Mrs. Frederick Allen] Gower [Mrs. Zoltan] (1857-1914). *See* Nordica, Lillian. Lillian (Norton) [Mrs. Frederick Allen] Gower [Mrs. Zoltan] Döme [Mrs. George Washington] Young (1857-1914)
Domesday Book, 11,894
Domestic Reform League, 7,184
Domestic relations, 6,223, 8,488. *See also* Children, law; Family; Marriage law
cases, 14,914
Domestic relations courts, 11,897
Domestic Science Club (IN), **4,560**
Domestic Science Club (Manhattan, KS), **5,191**
Domestic workers. *See* Household workers
Dominga, Sister M., 10,732
Dominican College of San Rafael (CA), 1,516
archives, **1,512**
Dominican Convent of Our Lady of Prouille (Elkins Park, PA), 14,783
Dominican Convent of Our Lady of the Rosary (Sparkill, NY), **12,859**
Dominican Nuns of Perpetual Adoration, 10,732
Dominican Nuns of Perpetual Adoration, Corpus Christi Monastery (Menlo Park, CA), **1,065**
Dominican Nuns of Perpetual Adoration, Corpus Christi Monastery (Bronx, NY), **11,292**
Dominican Order of Monterey (CA), 1,510
Dominican Republic, 2,134, 5,134
Dominican Sisters, Congregation of Holy Cross (Edmonds, WA), **17,145**
Dominican Sisters, Congregation of the Most Holy Rosary (Newburgh, NY), **12,733**
Dominican Sisters of St. Catherine (KY), 10,611
Dominican Sisters of St. Catharine of Siena, Motherhouse (KY), **5,408**
Dominican Sisters of St. Cecilia Congregation (Nashville, TN), **15,912**
Dominican Sisters of Springfield, Sacred Heart Convent (IL), **4,335**
Dominican Sisters of the Sick Poor, Center House (Ossining, NY), **12,749**
Dominican Sisters, St. Mary of the Springs Motherhouse (Columbus, OH), **13,984**
Dominick, David (1937-), **17,899**
Dominick, Mary [Mrs.] (ca. 1890-), 10,915
Dominis, John, 3,632
Dominis, John Owen, 3,632
Dominis, Mary [Mrs. John], 3,632
Doña Maria Concepción Argüello (1791-1857). *See* Argüello, Sister Dominica, O.P. (1791-1857)
Donaghey, George Washington (1856-1937), **257**, 282
Donaghey, Martha Louvenia (Wallace) [Mrs. George Washington] (1862-1947), 257, **282**
Donaghey, Raymond Ruskin (1897-), 282
Donahue, Gertrude. *See* Daley, Gertrude (Donahue) [Mrs. James]
Donald, Kate Lea (Gazzam) [Mrs. H.G.], 54
Donald, Warren, 15,537
Donaldson, Jessie (1867-1931). *See* Hodder, Jessie (Donaldson) (1867-1931)
Donaldson, Mrs. Robert, 12,397
Donalson, Agnes Graves, **3,386**
Donation Land Claim, 14,702
Dondore, Dorothy Anne (1894-1946), **9,047**
Done, John Haynie, 5,757
Done, Josiah Bayly (1845-?), 5,757
Done, Rachel Anne (Kerr) [Mrs. John Haynie] (1814-92), 5,757
Donelley, Ignatius, 9,467
Donelson, Andrew Jackson (1799-1871), **2,312**

Donelson, Bettie Mizell [Mrs. William Alexander] (1862-1939), **15,948**, 16,061
Donelson, Emily Tennessee (1807-36). *See* Donelson, Emily Tennessee (Donelson) [Mrs. Andrew Jackson] (1807-36)
Donelson, Emily Tennessee (Donelson) [Mrs. Andrew Jackson] (1807-36), 2,312
Donelson, John, 2,312
Donelson, Mary. *See* Coffee, Mary (Donelson)
Donelson, Mary Emily (1829-?). *See* Wilcox, Mary Emily (Donelson) (1829-?)
Donelson, Mary P. [Mrs. John], 2,312
Donelson Methodist Church (CT), Ladies Foreign Missionary Society, 1,890
Donelson, William A., **16,061**
Donelson, William Alexander, 15,948
Doner, Mary Frances, **7,775**
Donham, S. Agnes, 6,989
Donlevy, Alice Heighes [Miss] (1846-1929), **12,446**, 15,288
Donlon, Mary Honor (1893-), 11,508, **11,569**, 11,662
"Donna Reed Show, The" (television program), 18,000
Donnan, Elizabeth (1883-1955), 2,411
Donnell, Forrest C., **9,962**
Donnelly, Betty Hawley, **11,765**
Donnelly, Catharine Gavin [Mrs. Philip C.], 9,048
Donnelly, Eleanor Cecelia (1838-1917), 9,048
Donnelly, Ignatius (1831-1901), **9,048**
Donnelly, Katharine "Kate" McCaffrey [Mrs. Ignatius] (1833-94), 9,048
Donnelly, Lucy Martin [Miss] (1870-1948), 14,745
Donnelly, Marion O. Hanson [Mrs. Ignatius] (1877-1964). *See* Woltman, Marion O. Hanson [Mrs. Ignatius] Donnelly [Mrs. Henry L.] (1877-1964)
Donnelly, Phil M. (1891-1961), **9,963**
Donnelly, Ruth (Norton) (1903-), **449**
Donner, Eliza Poor (1843-1922). *See* Houghton, Eliza Poor (Donner) [Mrs. Sherman Otis] (1843-1922)
Donner Family, 644
Donner Party, 516, 644, 743, 956, 1,621
Donohugh, Agnes Crawford Leaycraft (1876-1966), **1,844**
Donovan, John, **12,447**
Donovan, Joseph L., 8,928
Donovan, Mrs. John, 12,447
"Don't Buy Anything Day" (1973), 1,014
Don't Push Your Pre-Schooler (book), 2,168
Don't Put Your Daughter on the Stage (book), 2,625
Doodletown Pipers (singers), 17,944
Dooley, Lucile (Collins) [Mrs. Patrick V.] (ca. 1887-1968), **8,556**
Dooley, Mother Lucy, 5,164
Doolittle, Ethelwyn, 2,396
Doolittle, Hilda (1886-1961) 15,170. *See also* Aldington, Hilda (Doolittle) (1886-1961)
Doolittle, Lucy (Salisbury) [Mrs. Myrick H.] (1832-1908), **2,313**
Doorenbos, Grace E., 10,373
Doorways into History (book), 14,289
Dorcas and Day Nursery Society of New Brunswick (NJ), **10,965**
Dorcas Society (Salem, MA), **7,365**
Dorcas Society for the Relief of Poor Female Professors of Religion (CT), 2,009
Dorchester Abbey (England), 6,907
Dorchester Academy (GA), 8,572
Dorchester Community Medical Fund (NE), 10,405
Dorchester Woman's Club (NE), **10,406**
Dorchester Women's Club (MA), **7,021**
Dorchester Workhouse (MA), 6,206
Doremus, Mrs. Thomas C., 12,271
Doren, Alice M., 14,046
Dorfman, Elsa [Miss], **11,983**
Doris Duke American Indian Oral History (project), 211
Doris Ulman Foundation, 5,257
Dorius, Anne Maria (Stalleson) [Mrs. John F. F.] (1857-1939), **16,652**
d'Orleans, Henry, 14,684
Dorman, Deborah, **2,314**
Dorman, Edward O., 13,388

Dorman, Florence Bailey, 8,934
Dormitories, 13, 925, **3,053**, **4,295**, 4,366, **7,697**, 7,831, **7,852**, **7,854**, 8,558, 8,566, **11,680**, 11,687, 13,231, **14,033**, 15,926
Dormon, Caroline (1889-1971), **5,442**, 5,448, 5,449
Dorn, Augustus, 11,778
Dorn, Eugene, 11,778
Dorn, Juliett Georgia [Mrs. Seth] (1843-?), **11,778**
Dorn, Seth, 11,778
Dorothy Arkwright Day Care Center (GA), 3,253
Dorothy Canfield Fisher Children's Book Award, 11,182
Dorr, Gertrude Horton (1844-1917). *See* Swift, Gertrude Horton (Dorr) [Mrs. Joseph] (1844-1917)
Dorr, Julia Caroline (Ripley) (1825-1913), 1,224, 5,714, 7,131, 12,403, **17,009**, 17,043
Dorr, Rheta (Childe) [Mrs. John Pixley] (1866-1948), 4,005
Dorrance, Frances [Miss], 14,813
Dorsett, Charles, 3,499
Dorsett Family (GA), **3,499**
Dorsett, Fannie A., 3,499
Dorsett, Josie, 3,499
Dorsey, Jessie, 15,777
Dorsey, Marguerite. *See* Cartwright, Marguerite (Dorsey)
Dorsey, Owen, 9,618
Dorsey, Sarah A., 9,793
Dorsey, Tommy, 5,534
Dos Passos, John, 2,497, 8,144
Dos Passos, Katy, 8,144
Doshisha Women's College (Kyoto, Japan), 17,653
d'Ossoli, Sarah Margaret Fuller [Mrs. Giovanni Angelo] (1810-50). *See* Fuller, Sarah Margaret. [Mrs. Giovanni Angelo] d'Ossoli (1810-50)
Doster, Daphine De Luxe [Miss] (1906-), **235**
Dot S Dot Ranch (MT), 10,238
Doten, Elizabeth, 10,664
Doten Family (NV), **10,664**
Dothan Eagle (AL), 112
Dotty Dunn Hat Shop (MN), 8,460
Doty-Dubois, Amelia C. [Miss], 12,448
Doty-Dubois Family (NY), **12,448**
Doty, Elihu (1809-64), 12,448
Doty, Madeleine Zabriskie. [Mrs. Roger] Baldwin (1879-1963), **7,216**
Doty, Mary T., 11,570
Doty, Stella. *See* Hare, Stella (Doty) Smith
Doub, Laura, 13,336
Double K Mountain Ranch (WA), **17,251**
Doubleday and Company, 1,221, 9,769, 11,893, 14,405, 14,407, 14,475
Doubleday, Frank, 11,893
Doubleday, Russell, 17,473
Doud, Elivera M. (1878-1960), **5,133**
Doudna, Viola (1863-1946). *See* Romans, Viola (Doudna) [Mrs. C. D.] (1863-1946)
Dougan, Ronald Arthur, 17,494
Dougan, Vera Wardner [Mrs. Ronald Arthur] (1898-?), **17,494**
Dougherty, Amanda (1805-?). *See* Worthington, Amanda (Dougherty) [Mrs. Samuel] (1805-?)
Dougherty, Celius, 2,664
Dougherty, John Alley, **9,049**
Dougherty, Thomas, 9,781, 13,173
Doughton, Robert Lee, 13,282
Doughty, Emma Hillman [Mrs. Daniel] (1790-1851), 11,180
Doughty Family, 15,942
Doughty Family (NJ), **11,180**
Doughty, Nanelia S. [Mrs.], **10,665**
Douglas, Adele (Cutts) [Mrs. Stephen A.] (1835-99). *See* Williams, Adele (Cutts) [Mrs. Stephen A.] Douglas [Mrs. Robert] (1835-99)
Douglas, Amanda Minnie [Miss] (1831-1916), **11,091**, 11,126
Douglas, Annie. *See* Bell, Annie (Douglas)
Douglas, Emily (Taft) [Mrs. Paul H.], 4,067, 9,170, 13,942
Douglas, Frances [Miss] (1870-1969). *See* De Kalb, Frances Douglas [Mrs. Charles Fletcher] Lummis [Mrs. Courtenay] (1870-1969)

Douglas, Georgia "Georgia Boy." *See* Johnson, Georgia "Georgia Boy" (Douglas)
Douglas, Helen (Gahagan) (1900-), 387, 453, 592, 698, 1,043, 2,513, 4,493, **14,202**
Douglas, Henry, 10,720
Douglas, Ida A. (Cooper) [Mrs. Thurlow], **10,666**
Douglas, Jennifer, 1,221
Douglas, Lloyd C., 13,264
Douglas, Mabel (Smith), 10,930
Douglas, Margaret (Blackburn) [Mrs. Henry], 10,720
Douglas, Marjorie Stoneman, 2,876, 2,932, 2,944, 15,892
Douglas, Melvyn, **4,493**, 14,202
Douglas, Paul, 8,093
Douglas, Paul H., 9,170
Douglas, Stephen A., 4,357
Douglas, William O., 64, 17,251
Douglas, Wiwona, 1,067
Douglass, Amelia, 2,315
Douglass, Andrew Ellicott (1867-1962), **193**
Douglass, Anna (Murray) [Mrs. Frederick] (?-1882), 2,315
Douglass, Benjamin Pennebaker (1820-1904), 4,467
Douglass, Carrie Church, 12,752
Douglass College (NJ), 10,928, 10,929, **10,930**, 10,981
    deans, 10,928, 10,929
    history, 10,932
    students, 10,928
Douglass, Edith (?-1948). *See* Roth, Edith (Douglass) (?-1948)
Douglass, Esther, **7,776**
Douglass Family (NY), **12,752**
Douglass, Frederick, Sr. (1817?-95), 1,437, **2,315**, 2,588, **3,296**, 5,684, 11,777, 12,857
Douglass, Frederick, Jr., **3,295**
Douglass, Harlan Paul, **5,467**
Douglass, Helen (Pitts) [Mrs. Frederick], 2,315
Douglass, Mabel (Smith) [Mrs. William Shipman] (1877-1933), 10,928, 10,929, **10,931**, 10,932, 10,981
Douglass, Margaret. *See* Gould, Margaret (Douglass) [Mrs. Warren H.]
Douglass, Maria Greene [Mrs. Truman O.], 5,467
Douglass, Mary Carolyn, 193
Douglass, Queen Victoria (Boone) [Mrs. Benjamin Pennebaker] (1837-85), 4,467
Douglass, Rosetta. *See* Sprague, Rosetta (Douglass)
Douglass, Sarah Mapps (1806-82). *See* Douglass, Sarah Mapps (Douglass) (1806-82)
Douglass, Sarah Mapps (Douglass) (1806-82), 2,368, 3,298, 5,907
Douglass, Truman O., 5,467
Douglass, William, 2,368
Dousman, Hercules Louis (1800-68), **9,050**
Dousman, Hercules Louis (1848-86), 9,050
Dousman, Nina Sturgis [Mrs. Hercules Louis], 9,050
Douthit, Mary Osburn, 14,551
Dover Anti-Slavery Sewing Circle (NH), 10,818
Dover, Sally (Brown), 9,284
Dover Women's Club (NH), **14,705**
Dow, James Gilman, 2,661
Dow, Margaret Elder (?-1962), **10,861**
Dow, Mary Ann [Mrs. James Gilman], 2,661
Dow, May. *See* Young, May (Dow) [Mrs. George W.] Davids [Mrs. John Russell]
Dow, Mrs. Daniel, 8,472
Dowd, Margaret (Wosser) (1906-), **450**, 1,068
Dowd, Tessie, 1,339
Dowda, Earline, **3,387**
Dowden, Edward (1843-1913), 12,449
Dowden, Elizabeth Dickinson (West) [Mrs. Edward], **12,449**
Dowdle, Hannah C., 16,653
Dowdle, John Clark (1836-?), **16,653**
Dowdle, Lois P. *See* Cobb, Lois P. (Dowdle)
Dowdle, Mary Ann (Chandler) [Mrs. John Clark] (1847-1929), 16,653
Dowell, Benjamin Franklin (1826-97), **14,353**
Dowell, Julia Gray, 1,203
Dower, 3,550, 13,486, **15,542**, 15,548
Dowie, Jane [Mrs. John Alexander], 4,461
Dowie, John Alexander (?-1907), 4,461
Dowling, Eddie, 11,897

Dowling, Nannie, **9,789**
Down-Town Hebrew Day Nursery (Philadelphia, PA), 15,161
Downer College (WI), students, 4,914
Downer, Jason, 17,689
Downers Grove North High School (IL), 4,181
Downes Family (SC), **15,493**
Downes, Mary LeJau (Huger) [Mrs. Richard], 15,493
Downey Baptist Church (IA), Woman's Mission Society, 4,959
Downey City Library (CA), 966
Downey, Evelina (Bray) (1810-95), 8,526
Downey, Jane, 4,112
Downey, June Etta [Miss] (1875-1932), 17,908
"Downhearted Blues" (song), 5,533
Downing, Andrew J., 8,960
Downing, Anna, 5,187
Downing, Jennie, **14,543**
Downing, Lydia, **5,286**
Downs, Lucinda Goodrich, **7,777**
Downs, Marjorie Mead, **10,646**
Dowry, 5,435, 7,535, 9,861, 12,542
Dowsett, Deborah Melville (1827-53). *See* Howland, Deborah Melville (Dowsett) [Mrs. Henry] (1827-53)
Dowsett, James, 3,624
Dowsett, Mary [Mrs. James], 3,624
Dowsing. *See* Divining-rod
Doyier, Carrie L., 9,467
Doyle, Alice Phelan (1923-?). *See* Mahoney, Alice Phelan (Doyle) [Mrs. William Patrick] (1923-?)
Doyle, Arthur Conan, 12,005
Doyle, Gladys (Sullivan) (1889-1933), 682, 828, 831
Doyle, Helen MacKnight (1872-1957), **1,372**
Doyle, Marian Wade, 2,123
Doyle, Maude (1914-76). *See* Cooper, Maude (Doyle) Prickett (1914-76)
Doyle, Thomas H., 14,212
Doyle-Carte Company, 2,009
Doyley, Rebecca, 15,676
Draft horses, 3,751
"Drag 'Em" (song), 5,534
Draginda, Joanne, 9,512
Dragonette, Jessica [Miss], **11,984**
Dragonette, Ree (1918-), **15,198**
Drahosh, Anna [Mrs. Joseph] Stodola [Mrs. Joseph] (1856-1952), **8,467**
Drahosh, Joseph (?-1922), 8,467
Drain High School (OR), 14,540
Drainage, 4,410
Drake, Benjamin, **12,450**
Drake, Benjamin Michael (1800-60), 9,610, 12,941
Drake, Claribel [Miss], 9,610
Drake, Elizabeth Jeffords (1830-1916). *See* Roundy, Elizabeth Jeffords (Drake) [Mrs. Daniel] Davis [Mrs. Jared Curtis] (1830-1916)
Drake, James Perry (1797-1876), 12,941
Drake, Janie (1875-1963). *See* Cooper, Janie (Drake) [Mrs. I. W.] (1875-1963)
Drake, Julia A., 654
Drake, June (1881-1969), **14,544**
Drake, Kate Archer, 9,704
Drake, Leah Bodine [Miss] (1904-64), **5,310**
Drake, Sir Francis, 762
Drake University (IA), 4,796
  alumnae, 8,607
  faculty, **4,686**
Drama, 459, 536, 1,027, 1,798, 5,477, 6,016, 6,022, 6,085, **6,372**, 7,221, 8,444, 11,985, 12,006, 12,562, 12,959, 17,634
  history and criticism, 6,834
  study and teaching, 1,749, 1,774, 3,880, 13,261, 13,810
"Drama Among Primitives and in Our Schools" (article), 13,261
Drama critics, **712**, **12,496**, 14,411
Drama, Finnish, 9,175
Drama, Yiddish, 7,530, 7,550
Dramatic criticism, 6,008
Dramatists, 111, 225, **226**, 556, 642, **1,030**, 1,167, **1,390**, **1,396**, 1,605, 1,647, 1,750, **1,795**, 1,978, 2,170, **2,171**, 2,319, 2,333, **2,360**, **2,426**, 2,458, **2,487**, **2,546**, **2,576**, 2,619, **3,084**, 3,745, **3,847**, 3,848, **3,994**, 4,989, **5,374**, 5,418, 5,441, **5,453**,

5,694, **5,783**, **5,965**, **6,063**, **6,597**, **6,749**, **6,787**, **6,824**, **6,904**, 7,249, **7,260**, 7,307, 7,310, 7,550, 8,001, 9,175, **9,198**, 9,502, 9,981, 10,863, 10,868, 11,038, 11,174, 11,220, 11,221, 11,344, 11,907, **11,977**, **11,994**, 12,068, **12,173**, 12,180, 12,367, **12,413**, **12,426**, 12,436, **12,451**, **12,476**, 12,529, 12,535, **12,651**, **12,959**, 13,469, 13,724, **14,313**, **14,335**, 14,366, 14,413, **14,423**, 14,455, **14,663**, **14,736**, **15,612**, 15,927, **16,156**, 16,517, **17,190**, **17,391**, 17,393, **17,793**, 17,797, 17,798, 17,799, **17,801**, **17,806**
Dramatists, Afro-American, **3,285**, **3,287**, **5,465**, **11,442**
Dramatists Alliance, 1,545
Dramatists, Italian-American, 9,496
Dramus Guild (CO), 1,749
Dransfield, Jane (1875-1957), **12,451**
Draper, Anna (Palmer) [Mrs. Henry] (ca. 1845-1914), **12,452**
Draper, Anne (1916-73), **1,577**
Draper, Anne Pauline (Kracik) [Mrs. Hal] (1917-73), **1,283**
Draper, Barbara M., **451**
Draper, Constance (Knowles) [Mrs. Jesse], 3,181
Draper, Edythe Squier (1882-1964), **5,208**
Draper, Emeline (1806-54). *See* Rice, Emeline (Draper) [Mrs. William E.] (1806-54)
Draper Family (MA), **7,618**
Draper, Frances L., 10,580
Draper, Hal, 1,283
Draper, Henry (1837-82), **12,452**
Draper, James (1778-1868), 7,618
Draper, Jessie, **3,181**
Draper, Julia Ann (1808-41). *See* Pratt, Julia Ann (Draper) Lazell (1808-41)
Draper, Lucy (1813-?). *See* Rider, Lucy (Draper) (1813-?)
Draper, Lucy Watson [Mrs. James] (1788-1848), 7,618
Draper, Lyman C. (1815-91), **17,624**
Draper, Muriel (1886-), 831, **12,453**, 13,871
Draper, Paul, 1,689
Draper, Ruth (1884-1956), 543
Draper, Ruth Dana [Mrs.], 12,431
Draper, Sophia A. (1811-67). *See* White, Sophia A. (Draper) (1811-67)
Draper, Wanetta (White) [Mrs. Paul] (1918-). *See* Tesker, Wanetta (White) [Mrs. Paul] Draper [Mrs. Elmer H.] (1918-)
Drawing, 7,658
Drawing-books, 343, 7,667
Draxton, Carol, 8,462
Dreamer, Marion (Billbrough), **17,191**
Dreaming America (book), 10,854
Dreams, 7,660
Dreams and Idols (book), 9,103
Dreams in Me, 3,288
Dred Scott case, 10,096
Dreer, Mary L., 2,363
Dreeves, Carl, 8,553
Dreeves, Katherine Jane (Densford) [Mrs. Carl] (1890-), **8,553**, 8,610
Dreier, Dorothea (1870-1923), **2,753**
Dreier, Ethel Eyre (Valentine) [Mrs. H. Edward] (1872-1958), **7,217**
Dreier, Katherine (1877-1952), 2,878, 6,812
Dreier, Katherine S., 7,182
Dreier, Margaret (1868-1945). *See* Robins, Margaret (Dreier) [Mrs. Raymond] (1868-1945)
Dreier, Mary E. (1875-1963), 2,424, 2,878, 6,812, 11,760, 12,069
Dreifus, Betty, 17,282
Dreiser Family (IN), 4,474
Dreiser, Theodore, 1,600, 2,617, 4,474, 7,209, 8,077, 11,894, 12,029, 12,821
Dresbach, Beverly (Githens) [Mrs. Glenn Ward] (1903-71), **258**
Dresbach, Glenn Ward, 258
Drescher, Rudolf, 5,951
Dresel, Anna (Loring) (1830-96), 6,466, 6,738
Dresel, Ellis Loring (1865-1925), 6,738
Dresel Family (MA), 6,738
Dresel, Louisa Loring (1864-195?), 6,738
Dresel, Otto (1826-90), 6,738

Dress Doctor, The (book), 17,802
Dresselhaus, Mildred S., 6,335
Dresser, Julius, 2,321
Dressler, Marie. [Mrs. George Francis] Hoppert [Mrs. James H.] Dalton (1868?-1934), 3,100, 11,579
Dressmakers, 3,751, **7,061**, **7,732**, **12,340**, 12,689, **15,360**, 16,486, 16,968, 17,170. *See also* Seamstresses
Dressmaking
  accounting, 12,340
  pattern books, **11,822**
  pattern design, **11,822**
Dreves, Louise M., **9,051**
Drew, Abigail (Gardner) [Mrs. Gershom, Jr.] (1777-1868), 7,619
Drew, Benjamin Franklin (1831-82), 9,052
Drew, Edward Bolivar (1827-1902), 9,052
Drew, Elizabeth A. (1887-1965), 7,158
Drew, Elsie Salisbury [Mrs. James Meddick] (1865-1945), 9,052
Drew, Helen L. (ca. 1892-). *See* Richardson, Helen L. (Drew) [Mrs. Robert Kimball] (ca. 1892-)
Drew, James Meddick (1863-1948), and Family (MN), 8,530, **9,052**
Drew, Jeanette (?-1895), 9,052
Drew, Jeannette (1843-1918). *See* Dildine, Jeannette (Drew) [Mrs. Marcene H.] (1843-1918)
Drew, John D., 4,695
Drew, Laurel, 11,216
Drew, Louisa (Lane) [Mrs. Henry Blaine] Hunt [Mrs. George] Mossop [Mrs. John D.] (1820-97), 3,921, 4,695
Drew, Lydia Rider. *See* Nye, Lydia Rider (Drew) [Mrs. Gorham]
Drew, Margaret Salisbury (1894-1966), 8,530
Drew, Mary, 9,052
Drew, Matilda Sherwood [Mrs. John S.] (1802-67), 9,052
Drew, Pamela. *See* Kerr, Pamela (Drew)
Drew, Susan Isobel (Biles), 14,628
Drew Theological Seminary (NJ), 5,246
  faculty, 10,988
Drew Timber Company, 14,565
Drew, Virginia, 1,838
Drewsen, Gudrun Løchen, 8,737
Drexel, Louise (1863-1945). *See* Morrell, Louise (Drexel) (1863-1945)
Drexel, Mother Mary Katharine (1858-1955), 14,781, 15,152
Drexel University (PA), Drexel Women's Club, **14,929**
Drexel University (PA), Graduate School of Library and Information Science, **14,930**
Dreyfus, Helen Thompson (1908-), 1,068
Driggs, Alice Nevada (Watson) [Mrs. Burton] (1891-1976), **16,654**
Driggs, George T., 12,003
Driggs, Olive Russell (Harrington) [Mrs. Benjamin Woodbury] (1861-93), **16,655**
Drinker, Catherine (1897-1973). *See* Bowen, Catherine (Drinker) [Mrs. Ezra] (1897-1973)
Drinker, Catherine Anne (1841-1922). *See* Janvier, Catherine Anne (Drinker) (1841-1922)
Drinker, Elizabeth (Sandwith) [Mrs. Henry] (1734-1807), 14,839, **14,990**
Drinker Family, 2,733
Drinker, Henry, 14,839
Drinker, Mary. *See* Cope, Mary (Drinker) [Mrs. Thomas P.]
Drinker, Sophie Lewis (Hutchinson) [Mrs. Henry Sandwith] (1888-1967), **6,542**, 7,218, 14,377, 14,378
Drinkwater Family, 452
Drinkwater, Leoline Howell, 452
Drinkwater, Sarah Bradley (Merrill) [Mrs. Leoline Howell], **452**
Driscoll, Katharine (1894-), 6,432
Drobish, Harry Everett (1893-1954), **453**
Droesel, Louise, 12,021
Dromgoole, Will Allen [Miss] (?-1934), **15,878**
Dropouts, 4,150
  education, 3,787
Droughts, 15,869

Drown, Lucy Lincoln (1848-1934), 6,128
Droze, Mary Elizabeth, 15,548
Druck, Rae [Mrs. Bernard], **9,053**
Drug abuse, 2,433, 10,203, 16,242
  study and teaching, 12,805
  treatment, 6,516, 8,633, 8,655
Drug factories, **8,992**
Drug rehabilitation. *See* Drug abuse, treatment
Drug trade, 4,716
Druggists, 14,089
Drugs, 459, 2,504
  purification, **13,259**
Drugstores, 1,663, 14,573, 16,425
Druid Hills Garden Club (GA), 14,570
Drum, Lucia S. *See* Fear, Lucia S. (Drum) [Mrs. William H.]
Drumm, Erma O. (1905-). *See* Godbey, Erma O. (Drumm) [Mrs. Thomas] (1905-)
Drums of Khartoum (book), 6,022
Drury, Clifford M. (1897-), **17,373**, 17,423
Drury, John (1898-1972), **3,989**
Drury, Marion Neveille [Mrs. John] (?-1968), 3,989
Drury, Mr., 1,172
Dry-goods, 4,184, 8,961, 8,982, 11,099, 15,085
  accounting, 6,190
Dryer, Emma (?-1925), 3,969, 3,970
Dryer Family (NY), **12,197**
Dryer, Harriet L., 12,197
Dryer, Horatio N. (1805-87), 12,197
Dryer, Mary, 12,197
Drysdale, Euphemia, **6,543**
Duane, Deborah (Bache) [Mrs. William John], 14,888
Duane Family (PA), **14,888**
Duane, Mrs. Russell, 14,888
Duane, William John (1780-1865), 14,888
Dubinsky, David, 8,144
Dublin, Mary, 11,771
Dublin Yearly Meeting, 14,858
DuBois, Adele Gourgas [Mrs. John], 9,866
Du Bois, Constance Goddard, **11,293**
DuBois, Cora A., 920, 2,833
Du Bois Family (NY), 12,020
DuBois, Henry Osgood, **12,198**
Du Bois Hospital (Du Bois, PA), 14,794
Dubois, John, 12,448
Dubois, John, 9,866
Du Bois, Marguerite Delavarre (?-1947?), **12,454**
Dubois, Mary A. [Mrs.], 12,272
DuBois, Rachel Davis (1892-), **9,494**
Du Bois, Shirley Lola (Graham) [Mrs. William Edward Burghardt] (1906-), 3,290, 5,870, 9,259, 12,884
Du Bois, W. E. B. (1868-1963), 2,879, 3,281, 3,285, **5,870**, 15,303
Dubos, René, 12,072
DuBose, Louise (Jones) (1901-), **15,585**
DuBrutz, Marie Louise. *See* Reston, Marie Louise (DuBrutz)
Dubs, Emma M., 10,591
Dubuque Benevolent Society (IA), 4,973
Dubuque Conversational Club (IA), **4,751**
Dubuque Female College (IA), **4,752**
Dubuque Ladies Literary Association (IA), **4,770**
DuCasse, Micaela [Mrs. Ralph], 657
DuCasse, Ralph, 657
Duché, Elizabeth (Hopkinson) [Mrs. Jacob] (1738-?), 15,079
Duché, Jacob, 15,077
Duchesne, Mother Rose Philippine (1769-1852), 10,134
Duck, Ramona. *See* Sutfin, Ramona (Duck)
Duckett, Eleanor Shipley (1880-1976), 7,158
Duclaux, Agnes Mary Frances (Robinson) (1857-1944), **2,316**
Duclos, Marie (1783-1833). *See* Fretageot, Marie (Duclos) (1783-1833)
Dude ranches, 10,238, 10,253, 10,256
Dudley, Anne (1612-72). *See* Bradstreet, Anne (Dudley) [Mrs. Simon] (1612-72)
Dudley, Dorothy [Mrs. Thomas], 7,127
Dudley, Dorothy (1884-1962). *See* Harvey, Dorothy (Dudley) [Mrs. Henry Blodgett] (1884-1962)
Dudley, Helena Stuart [Miss] (1858-1932), 6,516
Dudley, John Stuart (1893-1966), 12,999

Dudley, Marion (1895-), **12,999**
Dudley, Mildred (Smilks), 2,248
Dudley, Mildred Smith, 17,126
Dudley, Sarah Frances [Mrs.], 14,628
Dudley, Susan J., **16,509**
Dudley, Thomas, 7,127
Dudzik, Josephine (1860-1918). *See* Dudzik, Mother Mary Theresa (1860-1918)
Dudzik, Mother Mary Theresa (1860-1918), 4,286
Dueling, 3,516, 12,554
Duer, Alice (1874-1942). *See* Miller, Alice (Duer) (1874-1942)
Duer, Caroline King (1865-1956), **11,854**
Duff, James H. (1883-1969), **10,595**
Duffee, Mary Gordon, **13,000**
Duffy, Ethel (1885-1969). *See* Turner, Ethel (Duffy) [Mrs. John Kenneth] (1885-1969)
DuFlon, Constance, 12,832
Dufour, Viola A. (Stow) [Mrs. Francis R.], 4,613
Dugan, Caro (?-1941), **6,242**
Dugdale, Joseph A. (1810-?), 4,731, **4,754**, 15,291
Dugdale, Ruth [Mrs. Joseph A.], 4,754
Duggan, A. P., Sr., 16,268
Duggan, Alice. *See* Gracy, Alice (Duggan) [Mrs. David C.]
Duggan Family (TX), 16,268, 16,269
Duggan, Julia (1873-1970). *See* Hart, Julia (Duggan) [Mrs. Edward M.] (1873-1970)
Dugger, Minnie L., **1,624**
Duke, Carrie, 2,877
Duke, Eleanor (Lyon), **16,212**
Duke, Eliza Hoppe, 8,936
Duke Endowment, 11,879
Duke, James B. (1857-1925), **11,879**
Duke, John F., 16,097
Duke, Mattie A., 16,097
Duke, Myrtle, 15,360
Duke Power Company (NC), 11,879
Duke University (NC), 11,879, 13,189, 13,190, 13,191, 13,192, 13,193, 13,195, 13,196, 13,197, 13,198, 13,199, 13,200, 13,201, 13,202, 13,203, 13,204, 13,205, 13,206, 13,207, 13,208, 13,209
  alumni, 13,194, 15,570
Duke University (NC), Associated Students, 13,202
Duke University (NC), Campus Club, **13,195**
Duke University (NC), Career Development and Continuing Education Program, 13,196
Duke University (NC), Divinity Dames, **13,197**
Duke University (NC), Divinity school, 13,197
Duke University (NC), Law Dames, **13,198**
Duke University (NC), Order of the White Duchy, **13,199**
Duke University (NC), Trinity College, 13,201, 13,202
Duke University (NC), Trinity College Coordinate College for Women, **13,208**
Duke University (NC), Woman's College, 13,191, 13,199, 13,200, **13,201**, 13,202, 13,204, 13,205, 13,208
Duke University (NC), Women's Student Government Association. *See* Duke University (NC), Associated Students
Duke University (NC), Young Women's Christian Association, **13,203**
Duke University Centennial Celebration (NC), **13,401**
Dukes, Hope (Shellenberger), 10,780
Dukes, Laura (1907-), **15,891**
Dulan, Elva Jones, 1,779
Dullea, Keir, 12,367
Dulles, Allen, 5,134, 11,857
Dulles, Edith Foster (1863-1941), **11,158**
Dulles, Eleanor Lansing (1895-), **5,134**, 5,135, 11,857
Dulles, Janet Pomeroy (Avery) [Mrs. John Foster], 11,159
Dulles, John Foster (1888-1959), 5,134, 11,158, **11,159**, 11,857, 11,956, 12,553
Duluth Business and Professional Women's Club (MN), 8,429
Duluth Charter Commission (MN), 8,913
Duluth Federated Trades and Labor Assembly (MN), **9,054**
Duluth Iron Range Railroad, 9,467
Duluth State Teachers College (MN), 9,467

Duluth Women's Club (MN), 8,431, **8,449**
Dumbarton Oaks Conference, 11,999
Dummeier, Binna Mason, 17,379
Dummer, Ethel (Sturges) (1866-1954), 6,432, **6,544**
Dummer family (IL), 6,544
Dummer, Katharine (1892-1961). *See* Fisher, Katharine (Dummer) (1892-1961)
DuMond, Neva [Miss], **8,274**
Dumont, Henry (1878-1942), 816, **2,317**
Dumont, Nina (Webster) [Mrs. Leslie D.] Smith [Mrs. Henry] (1887-), **2,317**
Dun, Marie de Nervaud (1884-1973), 14,354
Dunagan, Lyda E. [Mrs. Jesse Jackson] (?-1932), **1,771**
Dunaway, Alice, 1,662
Dunaway, Don Carlos, 6,545
Dunaway, Dorothy, 6,545
Dunaway, James S., 16,446
Dunaway, Margaret Fowler. [Mrs. Maurice Don Carlos], **6,545**
Dunaway, Mrs. B. L., **9,855**
Dunayevskaya, Raya, **8,082**
Dunbar, Alice N. [Mrs. Paul Lawrence], 3,286
Dunbar, Belle Hanchett [Mrs.], 4,383
Dunbar, Dinah Clark [Mrs. William] (1769-1821), **9,625**
Dunbar, Elizabeth G. Lewis (1886-1960), **14,355**
Dunbar, Elsie S., 1,623
Dunbar, Etta C., **3,678**
Dunbar Family (MS), 9,767
Dunbar High School (DC), 2,130
Dunbar High School (Lexington, KY), 5,314
Dunbar, Joseph, 9,675
Dunbar, Louise B. (1894-1975), 4,383
Dunbar, Olivia (1873-1953). *See* Torrence, Olivia (Dunbar) [Mrs. Frederick Ridgely] (1873-1953)
Dunbar, Paul Lawrence (1872-1906), **3,286**
Dunbar, Sadie Orr (1889-1960), 8,670, **14,356**
Dunbar, Virginia M. (1897-), **6,136**, 16,742
Dunbar, William, **9,625**
Duncan, Anna, 2,205
Duncan, Augustin, 12,359
Duncan, Barbara [Miss] (1882-1965), **12,816**
Duncan Dancer, 12,361
Duncan, Dorothy (Packer), 10,258
Duncan, Elizabeth (1871-1948), 12,359
Duncan, Elizabeth (Caldwell) [Mrs. Joseph] (1808-76), 4,358, 4,417
Duncan Family (IL), 4,417
Duncan, Fannie (Casseday), 5,348
Duncan, Fannie May (Bragg) [Mrs. Edward R.] (1920-), **1,683**
Duncan, Fanny. *See* McBlair, Fanny (Duncan) [Mrs. Charles H.]
Duncan, Father William, 17,219
Duncan, Helen. [Mrs. Dana] Howe (?-1928), 4,099
Duncan, Irma. *See* Rogers, Irma Duncan
Duncan, Isadora. [Mrs. Sergei] Esenin [Mrs. Gordon] Craig (1878-1927), 362, 764, 1,033, 2,968, 3,100, 12,129, 12,359, 12,361
Duncan, James, 2,440
Duncan, Janice K., 14,510
Duncan, Joseph (1794-1844), 4,358, 4,417
Duncan, Julia, 4,358
Duncan, Lucinda, 10,654, 10,702
Duncan, Margaret S., 12,552
Duncan Memorial Methodist Episcopal Church (SC), **15,586**
Duncan, Mrs. Walter E., 15,609
Duncan, Raymond, 12,359
Duncan, Robert Edward, **454**
Duncan Sisters, 941
Duncan, Susan Lear [Mrs. James] (ca. 1770-?), **2,440**, 10,966
Duncan, William, **3,500**
Duncombe, Frances E. [Miss] (1870-1958), **10,456**
Dundas, Harriet Thompson Palmer [Mrs.] (1875-), **1,284**
Dundee Home Welfare Club (IL), **4,188**
Dundee Woman's Club (IL), **4,189**
Dunford, Alma Bailey, 16,681
Dunford, Leah Eudora (1874-1965). *See* Widtsoe, Leah Eudora (Dunford) [Mrs. John Andrew] (1874-1965)

Dunford, Lydia (1846-1923). *See* Alder, Lydia (Dunford) [Mrs. George Alfred] (1846-1923)

Dunford, Susa Amelia (Young) [Mrs. Alma Bailey] (1856-1933). *See* Gates, Susa Amelia (Young) [Mrs. Alma Bailey] Dunsford [Mrs. Jacob Forsberry] (1856-1933)

Dunham, Catherine Devenney [Mrs. William], **6,546**

Dunham Company, 3,773

Dunham, Ellen Ann (1911-), 11,661

Dunham, Katherine Mary (1910-), 3,290, **3,773,** 3,799

Dunham, Mrs. Montrew, 4,185

Duniway, Abigail Jane "Jennie" (Scott) [Mrs. Benjamin Charles] (1834-1915), 14,473, 14,545, **14,703,** 14,704, 14,705, 14,706, 14,710, 14,713, 17,166, 17,226

Duniway, Alice (MacCormick) [Mrs. Willis Scott] (1864-1953), **14,704**

Duniway, Caroline Moreland (Cushing) [Mrs. Clyde Augustus] (1871-1926), **14,705,** 14,706

Duniway, Clyde Augustus (1866-1944), 14,705, **14,706**

Duniway, David C., 14,703, 14,704, 14,705, 14,706

Duniway Publishing Company (OR), 14,545

Dunkerly, Sister Dorothea, 11,807

Dunkley, Ferdinand L. (1869-?), **12,455**

Dunklin, Jennie [Mrs. William A.], 4,755

Dunklin, William A., **4,755**

Dunlap, Adella H., 3,969

Dunlap, Caroline Cock, **14,546**

Dunlap, Eule Wellmon [Mrs.], 5,472

Dunlap, Flora, 4,823

Dunlap, Harriet "Hattie" Ball, 17,154

Dunlap, Henrietta, 9,931

Dunlap, Katharine [Mrs. Robert H.], **2,318**

Dunlap, Katherine [Mrs.], 455

Dunlap, Robert (1816-79) 17,875

Dunlap, Sophia Mary (Chesley) [Mrs. Robert] (1831-1905), **17,875**

Dunlevy, Harriet Farley, 7,069

Dunlevy, Louisiana. *See* Garrett, Louisiana (Dunlevy) [Mrs. Fontaine D.]

Dunlop, Charlotte. *See* Clarkson, Charlotte (Dunlop)

Dunlop Family, **17,992**

Dunlop, Jane Catherine. *See* Wever, Jane Catherine (Dunlop) [Mrs. Caspar W.]

Dunlop, Josephine. *See* Ludlow, Josephine (Dunlop)

Dunlop, Sarabella (Chambers). *See* McAllister, Sarabella (Chambers) Dunlop

Dunmore, Hope I., **3,934**

"Dunmore's Family Magazine," 3,934

Dunn, Anna, 13,402

Dunn, Berry Walker (1823-98), **14,547**

Dunn, Catherine (Chabot) [Mrs. J. P. H.], 472

Dunn, Elizabeth Robinson Potter, 7,620

Dunn Family (FL), 2,923

Dunn Family (KY), **5,262**

Dunn Family (MI), 7,927

Dunn, Fannie (1876-1950). *See* Quain, Fannie (Dunn) [Mrs. Eric P.] (1876-1950)

Dunn, Gertrude, **12,456**

Dunn, Helen. *See* Gates, Helen (Dunn)

Dunn, Henrietta M., 16,063

Dunn, Inez, 3,751

Dunn, James R. (1802?-81), 5,262

Dunn, John Piatt, 13,660

Dunn, Julia (1836-90). *See* Davidson, Julia (Dunn) [Mrs. John Mitchell] (1836-90)

Dunn, Julia Elizabeth, **12,457**

Dunn, Loula Friend [Miss] (ca. 1900-), 8,632, **8,644,** 11,916

Dunn, Marion V. *See* Adams, Marion V. (Dunn)

Dunn, Mary [Miss] (1888-), **16,062,** 16,266

Dunn, Mary Margaret (Masterson) (1859-?), **14,548**

Dunn, Mary Marshall (1859?-ca. 1930), **16,063**

Dunn, Mary (Rogers) (?-1857), 5,262

Dunn, Mary Stiles Foster [Mrs. Robinson Potter] (?-1900), 7,620

Dunn, Maud, 16,168

Dunn, Mrs. John Piatt, 13,660

Dunn, Prudence (1798-188?). *See* Creath, Prudence (Dunn) Rogers [Mrs. Jacob, Jr.]

Dunn, Rebecca. *See* Robinson, Rebecca (Dunn)

Dunn, Robinson Potter (1825-67), **7,620**

Dunn, Sara Anna, 12,457

Dunn, Sarah Abbie (1853-1926). *See* Slayton, Sarah Abbie (Dunn) (1853-1926)

Dunn, Sarah Thompson [Mrs. Richard] (1764-1821), **15,100**

Dunn, Theophilus Colhoun (?-1871), 7,620

Dunn, Zachariah James (1842-1918), 5,262

Dunne, Alice, 4,000

Dunne, Irene, 1,025, 4,640

Dunnell, Harriet (Baldwin) [Mrs. John Henry], 456

Dunnell, John Henry (1813-1904), **456**

Dunnigan, Alice, 3,799

Dunning, Charlotte, 11,986

Dunning, Ellen (Sweets), 10,191

Dunning, Emily (1876-1961). *See* Barringer, Emily (Dunning) (1876-1961)

Dunning, Helen [Mrs.], 1,172

Dunning, Matilda M., 11,986

Dunning, William A. (1857-1922), **11,986**

Dunnovant, Emma Anderson, 15,733

Dun's Review, 17,975

Dunsany, Beatrice, 11,287

Dunsany, Edward, 11,287

Dunshee, Mariah L. B., **7,778**

Dunstan, Caroline A., **12,458**

Dunster, Edward, 7,715

Dunwell, Amelia L. *See* Streeter, Amelia L. Dunwell [Mrs. Benjamin H.]

Dunwoody, Catherine Lane (Patten) [Mrs. William Hood] (1845-1914), 9,055

Dunwoody, Frank, 9,055

Dunwoody Institute (MN), 9,055

Dunwoody, James Penrose (1849-88), 9,055

Dunwoody John, 9,055

Dunwoody, Kate [Mrs. Frank], 9,055

Dunwoody, William Hood (1841-1914), **8,558, 9,055**

du Pont, Alice (Belin) [Mrs. Pierre Samuel] (1872-1944), 2,030

du Pont, E. I., 2,033

du Pont, Gabrielle Josephine (de La Fite de Pelleport) [Mrs. Victor] (1770-1837), 2,033

du Pont, Henry A., 2,033

du Pont, Henry Francis, **2,033**

duPont, Louise Evelina (1877-1958). *See* Crowninshield, Louise Evelina (duPont) [Mrs. Francis Boardman] (1877-1958)

duPont, Margaret O., 15,371

du Pont, Mary Pauline (Foster) [Mrs. Henry A.] (1849-1902), 2,033

du Pont, Mrs. Pierre S., 11,887

du Pont, Pierre Samuel (1870-1954), **2,030,** 11,887, 15,319, 15,585

Du Pont, Samuel Francis, 2,033

du Pont, Sophie Madeleine Dalmas [Mrs. Eleuthère Irénée], 2,033

Du Pont, Sophie Madeleine (du Pont) [Mrs. Samuel Francis] (1810-88), 2,033, 2,271

Dupré, Edith Garland [Miss] (1881-1970), **5,432**

DuPre School (SC), 15,729

Duprey, Annie (?-1916), **3,679**

DuPuy, Elisabeth (1868-1932), **2,319**

DuPuy, Elizabethe (1868-1932). *See* DuPuy, Elisabeth (1868-1932)

Duquesne University (Pittsburgh, PA), deans, 15,228

Durand, Asher Brown (1796-1886), **12,459**

Durand, Mary [Mrs. Asher Brown], 12,459

Durant Family (CA), 457

Durant, Genevieve Taggard [Mrs. Robert] Wolf [Mrs. Kenneth] (1894-1948). *See* Taggard, Genevieve. [Mrs. Robert] Wolf [Mrs. Kenneth] Durant (1894-1948)

Durant, Henry Fowle (1822-81), 7,568

Durant, Mary E. (Buffett) [Mrs. Henry], 457

Durant, Pauline Cazenove [Mrs. Henry Fowle] (1832-1917), 7,568

Durant, Thomas Jefferson, 12,162

Durbin, Margaret Cook (1830-86). *See* Harper, Margaret Cook (Durbin) [Mrs. Fletcher, Jr.] (1830-86)

Durell, Edward Henry, 12,200

Durell, Elizabeth S., 12,200

Durell Family (NY), **12,200**

Durell, Fanny Poor, 12,200

Durell, Mary Seitz Gebhart [Mrs. Edward Henry], 12,200

Duren Family (MA), **6,192**

Duren, Samuel, 6,192

Durham, Chris, 16,971

Durham, Frances [Mrs.], 54

Durham, Marilyn Wall, 4,483

Durham, Ruth, **10,967**

Durham Tuesday Afternoon Club (NH), **10,849**

Duricy, Anna (1898-). *See* Raicoff, Anna (Duricy) [Mrs. James] (1898-)

Durieux, Caroline, 5,488

Durkee, Anna (1753-1839). *See* Young, Anna [Mrs. Dominic] Tauzin [Mrs.] (1753-1839)

Durkee, Cora Dana [Miss], **3,990**

Durkee, John, 4,352

Durket Sperret, The (book), 15,980

Durkin Family (OH), **14,786**

Durkin, Mary Blaise (Walsh) [Mrs. Edmund J., Sr.] (1883-1968), 14,786

Durley, Ella Adaline Hamilton [Mrs. Preston B.] (1852-1922), 4,732

Durr, Clifford Judkins (1899-1975), **64,** 65, 6,547, 11,855

Durr, Virginia Foster [Mrs. Clifford Judkins] (1903-), **65,** 125, 127, 4,970, **6,547, 11,855,** 13,176

d'Ursel, Louise, 8,934

Duryea American Relief Clearing House, 2,352

Duryea, Anna Sturges [Mrs.], 2,170

Duryea Committee of War Relief, 2,280

Duryea, Nina Larrey (1868-1951), 2,280, 7,509

Duryea, Viola Emily Allen [Mrs. Peter Edward Cornell] (1867-1948), 4,781

Duryee, Catherine, 11,318, 11,322

DuSable High School (Chicago, IL), 4,147

Dusanek, Rosa [Mrs.], 10,405

Dusanne, Zoe, 17,284

Dusch, Willa Adams (ca. 1880-1957), **14,255**

Duse, Eleanora (1859-1924), 11,453, 12,361

Dusenberry, Harriety Knowlton Virginia (Coray) [Mrs. Wilson Howard] (1846-72), **16,656**

Dusenbury, Grace [Mrs.], 10,905

Dushkin, Julia, 12,117

Dust Tracks on the Road (book), 2,872

Dutch Reformed Church
clergy, 11,086
missionaries, **12,448**

Dutcher, Caroline M., **6,548**

Dutcher, Phoebe [Mrs. William] (1905-), **4,182**

"Duties and Demands of the New Women, The," 17,675

Dutton, Bertha Pauline (1903-), 11,217

Dutton, Celinda Parker [Mrs. Jerome], 4,798, 4,799

Dutton, Claude Webb, **4,798**

Dutton Hotel (Jolon, CA), 982

Dutton, Jerome (1826-93), **4,799**

Duty, Jennie F., 12,740

Duval, Elga (Liverman), 12,877

Duval, Ione, 4,110

Duveneck, Josephine (Whitney) (1891-), 496

Duyckinck, Evert, 12,460

Duyckinck, Evert Augustus (1816-78), 12,460

Duyckinck Family (NY), **12,460**

Duyckinck, Margaret Wolfe (Panton) [Mrs. Evert Augustus], 11,318, 12,460

Dvorak, Antonin, 4,689, 9,467

Dwellings, 9,907, 14,285

Dwight, Abigail [Mrs. Theodore, Sr.], 12,461

Dwight, Amos T., 12,390

Dwight, Annie A. (?-1936). *See* Tyler, Annie A. (Dwight) [Mrs. Richard] (?-1936)

Dwight Family (NY), **12,461**

Dwight, Harrison Griswold (1875-1959), **5,863**

Dwight, John Sullivan (1813-93), 5,950

Dwight, Margaret Van Horn (1790-1834), **13,921**

Dwight, Marianne (1816-1901). *See* Orvis, Marianne (Dwight). Mary Ann. [Mrs. John] (1816-1901)

Dwight, Mary A. *See* Patrick, Mary A. (Dwight) [Mrs. Matthew]

Dwight, Mary Ann (1816-1901). *See* Orvis, Marianne (Dwight). Mary Ann. [Mrs. John] (1816-1901)

Dwight Mission (AR), 292

Dwight, Rae Mortimer, 2,009

Dwight, Sally, 12,461
Dwight, Sarah (?-1837). *See* Bancroft, Sarah (Dwight) [Mrs. George] (?-1837)
Dwight, Theodore (1764-1846), **1,862**, 12,461
Dwight, Theodore, Jr. (1796-1850), 12,461
Dwight, William E., 12,461
Dwinelle Family (CA), **1,412**
Dwinelle, John W., 1,412
Dworshak, Henry Clarence (1894-1962), 3,667, 3,712
Dwyer, Anita. *See* Withers, Anita (Dwyer) [Mrs. John]
Dwyer, John, 13,171
Dwyer, Mary Ann. *See* McIntosh, Mary Ann Dwyer
Dyas, Ralph, 10,387
Dyckman, Fannie Fredericks. *See* Welch, Fannie Fredericks Dyckman [Mrs. Alexander McMillan]
Dyckman, Mary L., 10,953
Dye, Charles Henry, 14,549
Dye, Eva (Emery) [Mrs. Charles Henry] (1855-1947), 4,695, 14,473, 14,513, 14,549
Dye, Marie (1891-1974), **8,155**
Dyer, Caroline. *See* Whitfield, Caroline (Dyer)
Dyer, Frank H., **16,936**
Dyer, Mrs. Edward, 16,060
Dyes, 15,968
Dyes and dyeing, **7,035**, 7,667, 13,141
Dyhr, Helmi Saari, 9,467
Dying patient. *See* Terminal care
Dykes, Mattie (1890-), **10,126**
Dykstra, Adelphos A., **8,197**
Dykstra, Bernice Mollema, **8,197**
Dykstra, Lillian, 17,775
Dyson, Absalom Roby (1832-64), **10,196**
Dyson, Cornelia (1860-?), 10,196
Dyson, Louisa (Johnson) [Mrs. Absalom Roby] (1833-98), 10,196
E. Dole and Company (MA), **7,117**
E. I. du Pont de Nemours and Company, **2,030**
E. J. Meyer Memorial Hospital (NY), 11,357
Eadle Keatah Toh, 14,748
Eagan, Henry E., 13,001
Eagan, Julia Goode [Mrs. Henry E.] (1888-1963), **13,001**
Eager, Sarah Elizabeth (Riddle) [Mrs. Robert] (1842-1947), **16,314**
Eagle (Wichita, KS), 5,239
Eagle Feathers Club (WA), 17,383
Eagle Grove Equality Club (IA), 4,960
Eagle, Lucinda (Harris) (1792-post 1885). *See* Kennedy, Lucinda (Harris) Eagle (1792-post 1885)
Eagles, Aloha [Mrs.] (1916-), **13,703**
Eagleswood School (Perth Amboy, NJ), 4,421
Eagleton, Davis Foute (1861-1916), 13,052
Eakin, Jane Paul (ca. 1850-?), **14,286**
Eakin, Stewart Bates, Sr., 14,286
Eakle, Arlene, **16,937**
Eakle, Mary Alice, **16,937**
Eames, Camilla (Hendricks) [Mrs. Earl] (ca. 1898-), **8,696**
Eames Celebration, An (moving-picture), 17,791
Eames, Charles, 17,791
Eames, Emma Hayden. [Mrs. Julian] Story. [Mrs. Emilio] de Gogorza (1865-1952), 2,663, 2,968, **6,549**, 10,651
Eames, Wilberforce (1855-1937), 12,593
Earhart, Amelia Mary. [Mrs. George Palmer] Putnam (1897-1937), 1,594, 1,605, 2,198, 2,863, 4,395, **4,681**, **4,756**, **5,162**, **6,550**, 11,831, 13,301, 14,946, 17,935
Earhart Amy (Otis) [Mrs. Edwin S.], 5,162, 6,550
Earhart, Edwin S., 5,162, 6,550
Earhart, Muriel. *See* Morrissey, Muriel (Earhart)
Earhart, Rockey P., 14,634
Earie, J. P., **16,064**
Earl, Phillip Irving, **10,667**
Earle, Adaline (Graves) [Mrs. Isham Harrison] (1835-1906), 16,357
Earle, Alice (Morse) [Mrs. Henry] (1851-1911), 4,226
Earle, Dorothy, 8,297
Earle Family (TX), **16,357**
Earle, Genevieve Beavers [Mrs. William P.] (1883-1956), **11,856**, **11,987**, **12,145**
Earle, Hallie (1880-1963), 16,357

Earle, Isham Harrison, 16,357
Earle, Joseph F., 284
Earle, Suzanne. *See* Bartlett, Suzanne (Earle) [Mrs. Mahlon Ogden] Jones [Mrs. Samuel Franklin] Emmons [Mrs. Paul Wayland]
Earle, William P., 11,856
Earley, Elisabeth (1917-), 11,912
"Earliest Protestantism in Mississippi," 9,773
Earll, Irene, 6,706
Early, Anna, 16,863
Early Architecture of North Carolina (book), 2,414
Early Childhood Academy (Fort Myers, FL), 15,353
Early Courthouses of Alabama Prior to 1860 (book), 2,507
"Early Day Mansion on Rose Hill" (ms), 5,104
"Early Days in Virginia City" (ms), 10,239
Early Development of Henry James, The (book), 4,404
"Early History of Mankato," 8,510
"Early Iowa Trails," 4,773
"Early Women Jurors in San Diego" (article), 1,185
"Earnings of Women, The" (ms), 4,156
Earth and Its Atmosphere, The (book), 6,061
Earth paintings, 11,213
Earthquakes, 347, 391, 551, 612, 619, 664, 685, 729, 755, **771**, 772, 846, 1,231, 1,281, 1,308, 1,311, **1,339**, 1,569, 1,627, 10,633, 11,733, 12,384, 14,848, 15,471, 15,568, 15,571, 15,631, 15,656, 15,707
Earth's the Right Place for Love: A Portrait of the '60s, 459
Easley, Gertrude Brackenridge (Beeks) [Mrs. Ralph M.] (1867-1950), 2,397, 12,574
Easley, Ralph M. (1856-1929), 12,574
Eason, Winefred, 10,714
East (Far East), World War II, 6,011
East Bay Girls Service Association (CA), 882
East Carolina College (Greenville, NC). *See* East Carolina University (Greenville, NC)
East Carolina Teachers Training School (Greenville, NC). *See* East Carolina University (Greenville, NC)
East Carolina University (Greenville, NC), 13,286, 13,446, 13,617
    faculty, 13,261, 13,271, 13,273, 13,289
East Carolina University (Greenville, NC), Alumni Award, 13,259
East Carolina University (Greenville, NC), Baptist Student Union, **13,638**
East Commerce High School (MI), 8,317
East Glastonbury Methodist Episcopal Church Ladies Aid Society (CT), 1,889
East Hartford Woman's Club, Inc. (CT), **1,834**
East High School (CO), 1,779
East India Company (England), 14,994
East India, economics, 6,709
East Indians, 6,012, 6,071
East Los Angeles Girls' Vocational High School (CA). *See* Ramona High School (Los Angeles, CA)
East Lynn Railroad, 11,595
East, Selina Jewel. *See* Green, Selina Jewel (East) [Mrs. Theophilus Walton] (1887-1971)
East Side Commercial Club (St. Paul, MN), 9,243
East Side High School (Milwaukee, WI), 17,664
East Side House Settlement (NY), 9,095
East Side Thimble Club (Ontario, CA), 1,092
East Side, West Side (moving-picture), 17,989
East Texas Register, 16,132
East Texas State University, students, **16,204**
East Wind: West Wind (book), 16,153
Eastburn, Margaret Roberts (1880-1964), **15,275**
Easterby, Hattie, **15,587**
Easterby, Jessie, **15,587**
Easterling, Edward C., 15,588
Easterling, Narena [Mrs. Lamar F.], **9,626**
Easterling, Rebecca, **15,588**
Eastern Association for the Physical Education of College Women, **7,219**
Eastern Michigan College (Ypsilanti, MI). *See* Eastern Michigan University (Ypsilanti, MI)
Eastern Michigan University (Ypsilanti, MI)
    faculty, 7,891
    students, 8,293

Eastern Star, Order of the. *See* Order of the Eastern Star
Eastern States Archaeological Federation, 11,387
Eastern States Association of College and University Business Officers: Fifty Years in Review (book), 11,386
Eastern Washington University, archives, **17,142**
Eastern Women Today and Tomorrow (book), 7,326
Eastin, Nancy J. [Mrs.], 1,185
Eastlake, Martha Lee (Simpson), 14,903
Eastlick, Mrs. L. John (1833-?), **9,056**
Eastman, Barbara [Mrs. George W.], **1,285**
Eastman, Crystal [Mrs. Wallace] Benedict [Mrs. Walter] Fuller (1881-1928), 8,678
Eastman, Edward R., 11,592
Eastman, Elaine (Goodale) [Mrs. Charles A.] (1863-1953), **7,220**
Eastman Family, **460**
Eastman, George (1854-1932), 12,789
Eastman, Harrison, 406
Eastman, Ida Rauh (1877-1970), **17,964**
Eastman Kodak Company, 11,121, 12,789
Eastman, Linda Anne (1867-1963), **6,551**
Eastman, Lucy Ann. *See* Smith, Lucy Ann (Eastman)
Eastman, Maria M. *See* Child, Maria M. (Eastman) [Mrs. Isaac]
Eastman, Mary F., **6,552**
Eastman, Mary (Henderson) [Mrs. Seth] (1818-87), 8,921, 9,179
Eastman, Mary (Reed) [Mrs. Ornan] (1806-78), **6,553**
Eastman, Max (1883-1969), 4,473, 8,077, 12,642
Eastman, Mrs. Lucius R., 12,708
Eastman, Ornan, 6,553
Eastman School of Music (NY), 12,796
Eastman, Sophia A. *See* Eastman, Sophia A. (Eastman) [Mrs. Harrison]
Eastman, Sophia A. (Eastman) [Mrs. Harrison], 406, **461**, 17,010
Easton-Avery Far Woman's Club (WV), **17,458**
Easton, Elizabeth, 2,216
Easton, Mary (1800-78). *See* Sibley, Mary (Easton) [Mrs. George Champlin] (1800-78)
Easton, Mrs. Charles, 12,237
Eastwood, Alice (1859-1953), 473, 526, 1,779, 10,151, 10,152
"Easy Living" (song), 5,530
Eaton, Anne Thaxter [Miss] (1881-1971), **11,988**
Eaton, Burt W., 8,821
Eaton, Charles, 6,353
Eaton, Dorothy. *See* Blackinger, Dorothy (Eaton)
Eaton, Dorothy Ervin [Mrs.] (1920-70), **13,302**
Eaton, Emily (1886-1955). *See* Hepburn, Emily (Eaton) [Mrs. A. Barton] (1886-1955)
Eaton, Evelyn Sybil Mary (1902-), **6,011**
Eaton Family (CA), **462**
Eaton, Florence, 2,968
Eaton, George, 6,353
Eaton, Harriet H. A. [Mrs.], **13,002**
Eaton, John, 11,547
Eaton, John Henry (1790-1856), 2,320
Eaton, Julia (Godman) Bertram (1907-). *See* Ruuttila, Julia (Godman) Bertram Eaton (1907-)
Eaton, Lydia Ellen (1839-1903). *See* Peirce, Lydia Ellen (Eaton) [Mrs. George H.] (1839-1903)
Eaton, Margaret L. (O'Neale) [Mrs. John Henry]. [Mrs. John B.] Timberlake [Mrs. Antonio] Buchignani (1799?-1879), **2,320**, 2,542
Eaton, Seigniora [Mrs. William], 13,482
Eaton, Susan M. (Sparrow) [Mrs. Solomon], 9,383
Eaton, Vesta Marie (?-1926). *See* Daniels, Vesta Marie (Eaton) Smith (?-1926)
Eaton, Willard Gould, 462
Eaton, William, 6,504
Eatontown Institute (NJ), students, 10,997
Eau Claire Circuit Court (WI), **17,514**
Eau Claire County Relief Group (WI), **17,513**
Eau Claire Health Council (WI), **17,517**
Ebb, Fred, 12,367
Ebb Tide (book), 13,021
Ebell Club (Pomona, CA), **1,108**
Ebenezer Baptist Association (GA), **3,456**

Ebenezer Baptist Association (GA), Women's
Missionary Union, 3,456
Eberhard, Freelove, 1,532
Eberhard Tannery (Santa Clara, CA), 1,532
Eberhart, Lovicy Ann (May) [Mrs. Uriah] (1832-?),
4,359
Eberhart, Mignon (Good) (1899-), 6,060
Eberhart, Nelle Richmond, 10,483
Eberle, Abastenia St. Leger (1878-1942), **5,118**
Eberle, Agnes St. Leger (1878-1942). *See* Eberle,
Abastenia St. Leger (1878-1942)
Eberle, Irmengarde (1898-). *See* Koehler, Irmengarde
(Eberle) (1898-)
Eberly, Margaret, 16,876
Ebert, Reva, 4,063
Ebey Family (WA), 17,329
Ebony (periodical), 3,301
Eby, Clara (1873-1929). *See* Steiner, Clara (Eby)
[Mrs. Menno] (1873-1929)
Eby, Frederick (1874-1967), **16,347**
Eccles, Patrick, 1,549
Echo of the Flute (book), 6,037
Echoes from the Houseboat on the Styx (drama),
13,469
"Echoing Ages, The" (ms), 3,437
Echols County Centennial History Committee (GA),
3,606
Echols County High School (GA), 3,604
Echonodermologists, 6,321
Echovarria, Helen, 1,779
Eckberg, Minnie, **4,800**
Eckels, George M., 12,184
Eckert, Ruth Elizabeth (1905-). *See* McComb, Ruth
Elizabeth Eckert [Mrs. John H.] (1905-)
Eckles, Isabel Lancaster, 11,227
Eckman, Jeanette, **2,754**
Eckstein, Anna B. (1868-1947), 15,298
Eckstein, Joanna, 17,282
Eckstorm, Fannie Pearson (Hardy) [Mrs. Jacob
Andreason] (1865-1946), 5,580, **5,592, 5,624,**
7,474
Eclipse (steamboat), 10,306
Eclipses, lunar, 17,029
Ecole des Beaux Arts (Paris, France), 302
Ecologists, **10,446**
Ecology, 7,286, 10,199, 11,495
Economic assistance, 5,120, 12,042, 15,204
Economic assistance, domestic, 9,155, 13,972. *See
also* Public works; Unemployed; Work relief
"Economic Background of Southern Populism, The"
(article), 104
Economic Opportunity Act (1964), 14,936
Economic policy, 8,678
Economic policy, domestic, 8,665
Economic security, 2,680, 6,565, 6,973, 6,982. *See
also* Public welfare; Social security; Wages,
minimum wage
Economic stabilization, **1,810**
"Economic Status of University Women in the USA,"
2,068
Economic Survey of Mississippi, 9,647
Economics, 8,077, 14,641, 15,986, 17,303
Economics Club (Neenah-Menasha, WI). *See*
Neenah-Menasha Federated Woman's Club (WI)
Economist Press, 12,395
Economists, 561, 2,301, 5,134, **6,166,** 6,402, **6,600,**
6,672, 6,709, 6,833, **6,848, 6,874, 6,973, 6,977,**
8,085, 9,077, 11,661, **11,804, 11,806,** 11,857,
11,916, **11,929, 11,958,** 12,069, **12,072,** 12,078,
12,407, **12,485,** 12,694, **13,015,** 14,203, **14,758,**
14,904, 17,757. *See also* Labor economists
Economous, Rose, 4,109
Ecuador
American diplomats in, 2,235
volunteer workers in social service, American,
7,970
Ecumenical movement, 9,192, 12,787
Ecumenical Task Force on Women and Religion,
6,794
Ed Curran Quartet, 15,198
Eddie, Bernice U. (1903-69), **1,373**
Eddington, Henry Charles, **16,938**
Eddington, Sarah [Mrs. Henry Charles], 16,938
Eddy, Bessy, 15,549

Eddy Breeding Station, The: Institute of Forest
Genetics (CA), **463**
Eddy, Cordelia [Mrs. Robert C.], 11,020
Eddy, E. J. Foster, 10,808
Eddy, Josephine (1889-), **8,697**
Eddy, Lucy H. [Miss] (1796-?), **10,968**
Eddy, Martha, **12,462**
Eddy, Martha H. (1836-1957), **11,571**
Eddy, Mary (Baker) [Mrs. George Washington]
Glover [Mrs. Daniel] Patterson [Mrs. Asa
Gilbert] (1821-1910), 1,491, **2,321,** 3,889, 3,897,
6,184, 10,800, **10,808**
Eddy, Robert C., 11,020
Eddy, Sarah Jackson, 7,182
Eddy, Sherwood, 11,572
Eddy, Thomas, 10,968
Edeau, Sadie, 677
Edel, Leon, 4,404, 12,001
Edel, May Mandelbaum (1909-65), **17,252**
Edelman, John W. (1893-1971), 8,083, 11,897
Edelstein, Eleanor, 16,163
Edelstein, Gertrude (1899-1966). *See* Berg, Gertrude
(Edelstein) [Mrs. Lewis] (1899-1966)
Edelweiss Study Club (Tacoma, WA), **17,388**
Eden, Elizabeth Maltbie. *See* Guillet, Elizabeth
Maltbie (Eden) [Mrs. Isadore]
Eden Historical Society (NY), **11,439**
Eden, Rachel Maltbie [Mrs. Medcef], 12,174
Eden, Rebecca Maltbie. *See* Wilson, Rebecca Maltbie
(Eden) [Mrs. John Lyde]
Edenfield, Vernon, 3,074
Edens, Bessie (1893-), 13,176
Eder, Bessie N. [Mrs. Ernest] (1895?-), **17,900**
Ederle, Gertrude, 15,935
Edes, Henry Augustus (1824-51), 7,621
Edes, Sarah Louisa Lincoln [Mrs. Henry Augustus]
(1823-?), **7,621**
Edgar, Anne Randolph Page (Robinson) [Mrs.
William Crowell] (ca. 1860-1949), 9,057
Edgar, Marjorie (1889-1960), 9,057, 9,073, 9,230
Edgar, Mary. *See* Sill, Mary (Edgar) [Mrs. William
Raymond]
Edgar, Mary L. [Miss] (1865-1955), **17,625**
Edgar, William Crowell (1856-1932), Family (MN),
9,057
Edgarton, Muriel, 1,576
Edgarton, Sarah, 6,653
Edge, Alpha (Davis) [Mrs. Andrew J.], 3,320
Edge, Andrew J. (1836-1926), 3,320
Edgefield Female Institute (SC), **15,589**
Edgehill (residence, VA), 17,058
Edgehill Plantation (SC), 15,604
Edgerton, Ethel (1845-1929). *See* Hurd, Ethel
(Edgerton) [Mrs. Tyrus I.] (1845-1929)
Edgerton Family (MT), **10,300**
Edgerton, Martha "Mattie" A., 10,300
Edgerton, Mary [Mrs. Sidney], 10,300
Edgerton, Mary Pauline, 10,300
Edgerton, Sidney, 10,293, 10,300
Edgerton, Winifred H. *See* Merrill, Winifred H.
Edgerton [Mrs. J. H.]
Edgett, Edwin F., 5,602
Edgette, C. De Ette [Miss] (1895-1966), **14,871**
Edgewood College (Madison, WI), 17,868
Edgewood Public School (GA), 3,226
Edick, Helen, 1,859
Edict of Nantes, 15,410
Edifying Discourses, A Selection (book), 8,617
Edinburg Study Club (TX), **16,211**
Edinburgh Women's Suffrage Society (Scotland),
17,916
Edinger, Dora, 6,947
Edinger, Tilly (1897-1967), **6,320**
Edison Electric Illuminating Company, 12,395
Edison General Electric Company, 1,778
Edison National Historic Site, 11,923
Edison, Thomas Alva (1847-1931), 6,329, **11,923,**
15,554
Edith Wharton: A Biography (book), 4,491
Editors, 63, 73, 218, 342, **536, 611,** 792, 869, **1,325,**
1,340, 1,403, 1,410, **1,414,** 1,421, **1,426, 1,435,**
1,448, 1,452, 1,500, 1,581, 1,686, **1,981,** 2,038,
2,128, 2,189, 2,209, **2,250, 2,258,** 2,304, 2,372,
2,436, 2,499, 2,553, 2,604, **2,611, 2,617,** 2,632,

2,716, **2,781, 3,462, 3,514,** 3,778, **3,797, 3,986,**
3,999, 4,062, 4,130, 4,270, 4,347, 4,481, **4,484,**
4,695, **4,816, 4,956,** 5,121, **5,243,** 5,268, 5,602,
5,694, **5,861, 5,899,** 5,938, **6,040,** 6,049, 6,053,
6,106, **6,133, 6,134,** 6,143, 6,157, **6,201, 6,250,**
6,390, 6,408, 6,500, **6,512, 6,518, 6,617,** 6,684,
6,694, 6,714, 6,730, **6,739, 6,804, 6,834,** 6,867,
6,955, 7,136, 7,221, **7,256,** 7,605, **7,675, 7,690,**
8,064, **8,114, 8,293,** 8,566, **8,649, 8,658,** 8,843,
9,048, **9,434,** 9,466, 9,503, 9,575, 9,600, 9,706,
9,709, 9,768, 9,769, 9,983, 10,027, **10,071,**
10,197, 10,448, 10,808, **11,077, 11,157,** 11,174,
11,850, **11,866, 11,893, 11,998,** 12,011, **12,016,**
12,022, 12,044, 12,045, **12,167, 12,172,** 12,185,
12,236, **12,240, 12,244, 12,292, 12,350, 12,395,**
12,403, **12,524, 12,525,** 12,529, **12,556, 12,572,**
12,622, **12,648,** 12,778, 12,864, 13,388, 13,413,
13,561, **13,834,** 13,999, **14,052,** 14,080, 14,085,
14,223, 14,345, 14,368, **14,411,** 14,437, 14,446,
14,453, 14,581, **14,582,** 14,648, **14,703, 14,733,**
14,863, **15,374, 15,564,** 15,634, **15,637, 15,966,**
15,976, 15,979, 16,154, 16,282, **16,805,** 17,030,
17,043, 17,114, **17,328,** 17,589, **17,716,** 17,921,
17,975
Editors, Afro-American, 6,112, 9,259
Edman, Irwin, 12,042
Edmister, Grace Thompson [Mrs. William R.]
(1893-), 11,217, **11,218**
Edmiston, Althea Brown (1874-1937), **92**
Edmond, Kate [Miss] (?-1940), **16,065**
Edmond, Katherine "Kate" McKinnon [Miss]
(1880-1963), **16,348**
Edmonds, Gertrude Barron, 10,653
Edmonds, Katherine (1904-56). *See* Leighly,
Katherine (Edmonds) [Mrs. John Barger]
(1904-56)
Edmonsen Family (AR), **283**
Edmondson, Belle [Miss], **13,003**
Edmondson, Mildred (1914-), 1,356, 1,357
Edmonson, Mary Frances (Sale) [Mrs. Albert G.],
283
Edmonston, Catherine Ann [Mrs.], **13,403**
*Edmund Booth, 1810-1905, Forty-Niner: The Life
Story of a Deaf Pioneer* (book), 1,609
Edmund, Susan M., 12,203
Edmunds, H. L., 4,904
Edmunds, Mrs. H. L., 4,904
Edmunds, Susan M., **6,554**
Edmundson, Matilda Greer (Wilson) [Mrs. John
King], 15,976
Edmundson, Mildred, 13,418
Edmundson, Sarah Emma (Seelye) (1841-98),
8,324
Ednie, Mrs. William, 8,225
Edrington, Sarah, 982
Edson, Elizabeth Mason [Miss], 6,178
Edson Family (ID), 3,727
Edson, Katherine (Philips) (1870-1933), **1,034**
Educate a Woman (book), 13,244
Education, 299, 331, 529, 817, 844, 1,049, 1,137,
1,428, 1,473, 1,474, 1,680, 1,707, 1,842, 1,856,
2,399, 2,432, **3,472,** 3,580, 3,619, 3,905, 4,003,
4,125, 4,166, 4,344, 4,431, 4,596, 4,873, 4,977,
5,426, 5,570, 6,168, 6,346, 6,354, 6,359, 6,430,
6,504, 6,728, 6,838, 6,984, 7,178, 7,239, 7,326,
7,729, 8,057, 8,176, 8,661, 8,798, 9,381, 9,477,
9,662, 10,199, 10,317, 10,707, 11,213, 11,879,
11,951, 12,061, 12,724, 12,738, 12,740, 13,221,
13,261, 13,287, 13,414, 13,718, 13,979, 14,473,
14,637, 14,640, 14,821, 14,849, 14,905, 15,260,
15,422, 15,634, 15,663, 15,802, 16,347, 17,303,
17,341. *See also specific types of education and
specific types of schools; and* education *as a
subhead under specific subjects and groups, e.g.,*
Luthern Church, education
costs, 15,628
curricula, **3,786,** 4,341, 6,354, 6,438, 7,655, 9,472,
13,632
directories, **17,537**
exhibits and museums, 11,118
experimental methods, 321, 788, 3,772, **4,151,**
4,958, 5,977, 6,544, 6,614, 8,548, 11,719, 11,864,
11,890, 11,898, 11,910, 12,048
finance, 4,341, 7,662, 10,789, 10,886, 17,463

research, 13,736
study and teaching, **9,194,** 12,762
Education at The Principia (book), 4,199
Education, bilingual, 9,210, 11,217, 15,235, 16,376
Education, compulsory, 2,886, 4,366, 7,208
"Education for Girls and Women in Upper South
   Carolina Prior to 1890" (dissertation), **15,409**
Education, higher, 193, 550, 6,051, 11,895. *See also*
   Junior colleges; Universities and colleges
   curricula, 11,890
   research, social aspects, 17,698
Education, Jewish, **7,527**
Education of children, 1,341, **2,092**
Education on the Dalton Plan (book), 17,870
Education, preschool, **4,116,** 4,128, 6,556, 11,845
Education, primary, 8,282, 13,879
Education, rural, 2,080, 3,327, 5,469, 6,585, 9,442,
   9,975, 14,301, 16,132
   Latin America, 1,842
Education, secondary, **7,668,** 8,282, 11,549
Educational administration. *See* School management
   and organization
Educational associations, 58, 485, 1,681, 1,951, 2,000,
   2,044, 2,069, 2,071, 2,080, **2,092,** 2,093, 2,095,
   2,103, 2,233, **2,285,** 2,647, 3,136, 3,140, 3,151,
   3,535, **3,573, 3,574, 3,659,** 3,842, 3,974, 4,008,
   4,048, 4,051, 4,067, 4,119, 4,150, 4,211, 4,278,
   4,321, 4,577, 4,815, 4,830, 4,888, 4,946, 5,048,
   5,079, **5,097,** 5,176, 5,251, 5,506, 5,883, **5,974,**
   6,009, **6,359, 6,360, 6,361, 6,362,** 6,368, 6,387,
   6,388, 6,428, **6,463,** 6,481, 6,483, 6,514, 6,581,
   6,687, 6,901, 6,934, **6,962, 7,071,** 7,173, 7,184,
   7,193, 7,219, 7,286, 7,293, 7,309, **7,312, 7,711,**
   8,039, 8,171, **8,173, 8,426, 8,485,** 8,492, 8,567,
   8,573, **8,576, 8,819, 8,847,** 9,440, 9,526, 9,928,
   10,035, **10,128, 10,627,** 10,707, 11,351, 11,372,
   11,762, 11,906, 11,911, 11,958, 11,999, **12,076,**
   12,238, 12,738, 12,920, 12,921, **12,937,** 13,189,
   13,254, 13,667, 13,677, 13,718, 13,720, **13,761,**
   14,107, 14,193, 14,221, **16,294,** 16,344, **17,040,**
   17,091, 17,356, **17,442,** 17,445, **17,698, 17,748,**
   17,936
Educational associations, Afro-American, 3,290
Educational associations, Jewish, 1,000, 12,009
Educational associations, Methodist, **10,600**
Educational broadcasting, 17,665
Educational Dramatic League, 11,944
Educational endowments. *See* Endowments; *and
   names of specific endowments, e.g.,* Carnegie
   Corporation
Educational exchanges, 7,153
Educational publishing, 11,889
Educational Reviewer (periodical), 14,345
Educational Society (SC), 15,544
Educational surveys, **2,165**
Educational Testing Service, **11,150**
Educational tests and measurements, **11,150,**
   13,737
Educational toys, 11,864, 15,353
Educators, 38, 56, 109, **122, 124, 126, 128, 131, 138,**
   159, **667, 674,** 792, 931, 936, 1,035, 1,054, 1,115,
   1,429, 1,452, 1,487, **1,603,** 1,747, **1,847, 1,850,**
   1,951, 1,966, 1,967, 1,979, **2,093, 2,094, 2,095,**
   2,125, 2,130, **2,233,** 2,258, 2,310, **2,333, 2,344,**
   2,345, 2,369, **2,383,** 2,415, 2,459, 2,460, 2,471,
   2,473, 2,523, **2,821,** 2,841, **2,911,** 3,088, 3,131,
   3,257, 3,327, 3,328, 3,342, 3,733, **3,798, 3,841,**
   4,052, 4,059, 4,081, **4,089,** 4,115, **4,205,** 4,209,
   4,210, 4,211, 4,305, 4,319, 4,487, **4,533, 4,534,**
   4,535, 4,640, 4,853, **4,946,** 5,275, **5,325,** 5,394,
   5,426, 5,458, 5,500, 5,543, **5,615, 5,616, 5,618,**
   5,731, 5,764, 5,827, 5,860, 5,907, 6,009, **6,188,**
   6,268, 6,354, **6,387, 6,393, 6,416, 6,430, 6,444,**
   6,487, 6,528, **6,544,** 6,616, **6,630, 6,700, 6,823,**
   6,831, 6,851, **7,296, 7,416, 7,541, 7,563, 7,569,**
   7,591, 7,597, 7,651, **7,829, 7,941, 7,973,** 8,003,
   8,079, 8,089, **8,102,** 8,113, **8,121, 8,129,** 8,145,
   8,321, 8,526, **8,540, 8,553, 8,583, 8,591, 8,603,**
   8,618, 8,620, 8,641, 8,663, 8,667, 8,784, 8,851,
   8,854, 8,881, 8,896, 9,024, **9,526,** 9,575, **9,583,**
   9,673, **9,839,** 10,035, 10,156, 10,466, **10,473,**
   10,475, 10,488, 10,537, 10,562, 10,608, 10,630,
   10,677, 10,680, 10,741, 10,745, 10,975, 11,039,
   11,125, 11,164, 11,213, 11,229, **11,279,** 11,297,
   11,351, 11,547, 11,616, 11,640, **11,683, 11,742,**
   11,816, 11,842, 11,844, 11,846, **11,853, 11,864,**
   11,867, 11,888, 11,890, 11,897, **11,898, 11,906,**
   12,044, **12,075, 12,171, 12,422,** 12,461, 12,478,
   12,493, **12,515, 12,544, 12,632,** 12,740, 12,818,
   12,921, 13,176, **13,211,** 13,217, 13,289, 13,302,
   13,369, 13,642, 13,763, 13,999, **14,102, 14,267,**
   14,378, 14,508, **14,629,** 14,838, 14,873, 15,051,
   15,182, 15,270, 15,281, 15,283, **15,312, 15,353,**
   15,617, 15,634, **15,789, 15,793, 15,802, 15,816,**
   15,917, 15,920, 15,923, **15,929, 15,933, 15,964,**
   16,059, 16,337, **16,552,** 16,640, 16,965, 16,967,
   17,037, 17,191, **17,194, 17,291, 17,296, 17,307,**
   17,341, 17,474, 17,494, 17,589, 17,675, 17,870,
   17,896, 17,914, 17,924, 17,974. *See also* Deans
   (in schools); Teachers
Educators, Afro-American, 1,875, 2,139, 2,151, 2,931,
   6,430, **6,680,** 9,575, 10,191, 12,690, **15,777**
Educators, British, 6,889
Educators, Jewish, **13,799**
Educators, Native American, 10,483
Edward VIII (king), 5,209
Edward F. Waite Neighborhood House (Minneapolis,
   MN), **9,058**
Edward MacDowell Association (NY), 8,428
Edward MacDowell Association, Inc., 2,463, 6,867,
   12,050
Edward MacDowell Colony (NH), 2,463, 4,689,
   5,993, 6,011, 7,316
Edward Markham School (Hayward, CA), 979
Edwardian Days (book), 799
Edwards, Ann (?-1962), **7,779**
Edwards, Anna Cheney (1835-?), **7,134,** 7,497
Edwards, Anna McBride (James) [Mrs. Isaac]
   (1826-1907), 5,713
Edwards, Anna Rachel (Camp) [Mrs. Richard Henry]
   (1876-1956), 11,533, 11,572
Edwards, Anna Rebecca (1863-?), **8,156**
Edwards, Bruce, 12,444
Edwards, Camilla (Leonard) [Mrs. Walter], 12,242
Edwards, Catherine, **15,468**
Edwards, Charlotte [Mrs.], 11,634
Edwards, Christine (1897-). *See* Needham,
   Christine [Mrs. James Leland] (1897-)
Edwards, Dwight, 1,564
Edwards, Elbert (1907-), **10,734**
Edwards, Eliza, 4,164
Edwards, Elizabeth Parker (Todd) [Mrs. Ninian Wirt]
   (1813-88), **4,360**
Edwards Family (NJ), 10,905
Edwards Family (SC), **15,710**
Edwards Family (SC), 15,622
Edwards, Florence Mildred (1868-?), 3,755
Edwards, Gladys Talbott [Mrs.], 13,720
Edwards, Guy M., 5,412
Edwards, Helen M., 2,928
Edwards Hotel (MS), 9,694
Edwards, India, 11,483
Edwards, Isaac, 5,713
Edwards, Jennie, 13,298
Edwards, Jonathan, 14,170
Edwards, Jonathan, Jr. (1745-1801), **15,358**
Edwards, Julia. *See* Baker, Julia (Edwards) [Mrs.
   Edward]
Edwards, Katherine James, 5,713
Edwards, Katie (1848-1933). *See* Mitchell, Katie
   (Edwards) [Mrs. John Douglas] Bemo [Mrs. L.
   S.] (1848-1933)
Edwards, Lana (1900-), 6,697
Edwards, Laura [Mrs.], 9,984
Edwards, Louisa M. [Miss] (1859-1941), 14,168
Edwards, Margaret (Royalty) [Mrs. Herbert R.]
   (1895-1969), **16,349**
Edwards, Marianne [Mrs. Guy M.], **5,412**
Edwards, Martha Letitia (?-1926), **17,626**
Edwards, Mrs. Ninian, 5,291
Edwards, Ninian, 4,360
Edwards, Rebecca, **15,468**
Edwards, Richard, 3,755
Edwards, Richard Henry (1877-1954), Family, **11,572**
Edwards, S. S., 15,710
Edwards, Sara E., 9,409
Edwards, Sara K. (Upton), **464**
Edwards, Sarah, 831

Edwards, Sarah J. Cleveland, 17,626
Edwards, Sarah (Pierpont) [Mrs. Jonathan] (1710-58),
   11,728
Edwards, Sarah "Sallie" Screven, 15,710
Edwards, Thyra, 3,791, 3,799, **3,835**
Edwards-Tryon-Nash house (NC), 12,988
Edwardsville Social and Literary Club (KS), 5,176
Eells, Abbie Foster [Mrs. Edwin] (1844-1922), 17,404
Eells, Cushing, **14,550,** 17,167, 17,404, 17,419
Eells, Edwin (1841-1917), 14,550, **17,404**
Eells, Eva Alice (1876-98), 17,404
Eells Family (NY), **11,573**
Eells Family (OR), 17,422
Eells, Ida Myra, **17,167,** 17,404
Eells, Mrs. H. B., 11,573
Eells, Myra (Fairbanks) [Mrs. Cushing] (1805-78),
   14,478, 14,550, 17,167, 17,373, 17,402, 17,404
Eells, Myron (1843-1907), 14,550, **17,421**
"Effect of Changes of Sovereignty on Nationality,
   The" (thesis), 6,692
Effert, Alma. *See* Chaney, Alma (Effert) [Mrs. Ralph]
Effingham High School (IL), 4,445
Efland School (NC), 13,504
Egan, Barbara (pseudonym). *See* Linington, Elizabeth
   (1921-)
Egan, Dale (pseudonym). *See* Linington, Elizabeth
   (1921-)
Egan, Emma A. [Miss], 12,348
Egan Family (LA), **5,444**
Egan, Lesley (pseudonym). *See* Linington, Elizabeth
   (1921-)
Egan, Sister Eileen, S.C.N., 5,373
Egbert, Catherine (Hubbard) (1886-1961). *See* Dace,
   Catherine (Hubbard) Egbert (1886-1961)
Egbert, Eliza Ann (McAuley) (1835-?), 465, **1,286**
Egbert, Elvira (1821-1908). *See* Carson, Elvira
   (Egbert) (1821-1908)
Egenes, Sonja Carlsen (1930-), 4,869
Eggertsen, Sarah (1858-1944). *See* Cluff, Sarah
   (Eggertsen) [Mrs. Harvey Harris] (1858-1944)
Eggertsen, Virginia (1912-). *See* Sorensen, Virginia
   (Eggertsen) (1912-)
Eggleston, Arthur Dupuy (1899-1959), **466**
Eggleston, Blanche (Stokes) [Mrs. William Green],
   467
Eggleston, Jennie M., 9,294
Eggleston, William Green (1859-1937), 467
Eggs, 11,629
   collectors and collecting, 7,487
Egleston, Sophie (Lyon) (1856-?), **13,004**
Egypt
   American consuls in, 2,604
   American travelers in, 1,854
   antiquities, 14,882
   economic assistance to, 6,125
   international relief, 11,593
   missionaries to, Presbyterian, **15,175**
Egypt, Ophelia Settle, **15,916**
Egyptologists, 12,492
Ehlers, Alice (1887-?), **468**
Ehrenreich Family, **7,528**
Ehrhorn, Alma (1906-). *See* Kincannon, Alma
   (Ehrhorn) [Mrs. Claud] (1906-)
Ehrhorn, Julius Ernest, 16,365
Ehrlich, Bettina (1903-), **14,358**
Ehrman, Elizabeth (Bissinger), **469**
Ehrman, Marli, 4,112
Ehrmann, Sara Emelie (Rosenfeld) [Mrs. Herbert]
   (1895-), **6,555**
Eichelberger, Bessie Reese, 826, **10,668**
Eichelberger, Brenda, **4,132**
Eichorn, Gertrude, 9,986
Eichstaedt, Donna M. [Mrs.], 3,751
Eickbush, Edna (Mason) [Mrs. William Henry]
   (1870-1918), 10,682
"Eight Hour Day," 6,812
Eight hour movement, 4,173, 6,812, 17,376
Eighteenth Amendment, 12,806, 13,533
Eighteenth Avenue Youth Center (Nashville, TN),
   5,477
Eighth Michigan Infantry, 8,164
Eightieth Division Veterans Association, 17,086
81 Club, The (MO), 10,112

"Eighty Years at the Gopher Hole: 1867-1947," 9,399
Einstein, Albert, 2,382, 5,991, 8,443, 13,801
Einstein, Sarah. *See* Weil, Sarah (Einstein) [Mrs. Sol]
Einstien, Vera Lustig, 1,186
Eirene, or a Woman's Right (book), 14,058
Eisely, Mrs. Loren, 12,879
Eisenbrey, Augusta (Frost) (1883-?), 15,004
Eisenhower, A. B., 5,151
Eisenhower, Dwight David (1890-1969), 31, 1,712, 2,542, 2,640, 5,131, 5,133, 5,135, **5,136, 5,137,** 5,138, 5,148, 5,151, 5,153, 5,155, 5,158, 5,159, 5,307, 6,662, 6,720, 11,744, **11,857,** 11,944, 14,686, 14,822, 15,889, 17,984
Eisenhower Family, 5,157
Eisenhower, Ida Stover, 5,151
Eisenhower, Mamie (Doud) [Mrs. Dwight David] (1896-), **1,712,** 2,640, 3,907, 5,110, 5,133, **5,138,** 5,151, 5,161, 11,825, 11,857, 17,984
Eisenhower, Milton, 14,822
Eisler, Edwin, 3,914
Eisslinger, Elsie [Mrs. H. O.], 4,961
Ekelof, Gunnar, 12,880
Ekstrom, Laura Allyn, **17,902**
El Caribe (pseudonym). *See* Padilla, Don José Gualberto (1829-96)
El-Dabh, Halim, 4,384
El Destino (plantation, FL), 2,930, **2,943**
El-Messidi, Kathy (Groehn) Cosseboom (1946-), **8,084**
El Paso Historical Society (TX), 938
El Retiro (CA), 6,934
El Tecolote (newspaper), 17,619
Elam House (Chicago, IL), 3,935
Ela, Ida L. (1855-1934), **17,558**
Elam, Mellissia Ann [Mrs.], **3,935**
Elanto Company (MN), 9,136
Elbert Hubbard library museum (NY), **11,435**
Elbow Lake High School (MN), 8,709, 8,710
Elder, Charles, 14,386
Elder Daughters (IA), 4,960
Elder, Dixie [Mrs. A. L.], 4,063
Elder, Edith Ashmore [Mrs. Charles] (1882-1975). *See* Hensolt, Edith Ashmore [Mrs. Charles] Elder [Mrs. Fred] (1882-1975)
Elders, Pauline, 13,332
Eldert, Margaret, 11,325
Eldora Federation of Club Women (IA), 4,815
Eldredge, Clarence, 16,657
Eldredge, Helen (Woodsmall) (1879-1959), **1,035**
Eldredge, Leila (Moss) [Mrs. Horace J.] Grant [Mrs. John E.] Lee [Mrs. Clarence] (1895-1962), **16,657**
Eldredge, Sara Payson (Willis) [Mrs. Charles H.] (1811-72). *See* Parton, Sara Payson (Willis) [Mrs. Charles H.] Eldredge [Mrs. Samuel P.] Farrington [Mrs. James] (1811-72)
Eldress, Ruth (Shaker), 7,047
Eldridge, Emelyn (1821-94). *See* Story, Emelyn (Eldridge) [Mrs. William Wetmore] (1821-94)
Eldridge, James William (1841-1909), **1,423**
Eldridge, Mary Moffitt (1875-), **15,381**
Eldridge, Phebe, 15,285
Eleanor, Empress of the Holy Roman Empire (?-1720), 17,197
Eleanor McMain Girls' High School, 5,515
Electing a President (book), 4,975
Elections, 175, 1,034, **1,139,** 2,525, 3,158, 4,125, 4,623, 4,628, 5,132, 5,328, 6,432, 6,973, 7,678, 8,077, 8,114, 8,236, **8,844,** 9,040, 9,048, 10,082, 11,897, 11,905, 14,163, 14,202, 14,252, 15,634, 15,890, 15,941, 15,945, 16,386, **17,417,** 17,428. *See also* Afro-Americans, politics and suffrage; Campaign management; Suffrage; Voters, registration of; Voting
Electoral college. *See* Presidents, US, elections
Electric lighting, 4,436, 8,957
Electric power, 11,495
Electric power development. *See* Electrification
Electric Sewing Machine Society (Baltimore, MD), **5,758**
Electric Steel Foundry Company (OR), 14,674
Electric utilities, 14,653
Electrical engineering, 17,222

Electrical engineers, **1,778**
Electrification, 8,517, 10,354
Electrocution, 11,445
Elementary education of adults, 13,309
Elementary School Teacher, The, 4,305
Elementary school teachers, 641, **7,491, 8,841, 10,904, 13,071, 14,135,** 15,178
Elementary schools, 888, **1,055**
"Elements of Happiness" (article), 15,270
Elements of Love and Marriage, The (book), 6,789
Eleventh National Women's Rights Convention (1886), 5,961
Eleventh Ward Retrenchment Society (UT), 16,513
Elgin Academy and Junior College (IL), faculty, 8,710
Eli and Sybil Jones Mission (Israel), 14,846
Elias, Leona Baumgartner [Mrs. Nathaniel M.] (1902-), **6,209**
Elias, Nathaniel M., 6,209
Eliason Sisters (UT), **16,459**
Eliel, Harriet Judd, 1,356
Elim Baptist Church (Anoka, MN), 8,389
Eliot, A. C. (pseudonym). *See* Jewett, Sarah Orne (1849-1909)
Eliot, Abigail Adams (1892-), **6,556**
Eliot, Alice (pseudonym). *See* Jewett, Sarah Orne (1849-1909)
Eliot, Charles William (1834-1926), **6,278,** 6,358
Eliot, Charlotte Champe (Stearns) [Mrs. Henry Ware] (1843-1929), 10,161
Eliot, Emily Marshall (1857-?). *See* Morison, Emily Marshall (Eliot) (1857-?)
Eliot, Emily Marshall (Otis) [Mrs. Samuel] (1832-1906), 5,903, 6,557
Eliot, Emmy. *See* Morison, Emmy (Eliot) [Mrs. John Homes]
Eliot, George, 1,488, 3,077, 3,927
Elliot, Ida (1880-1943). *See* Allen, Ida (Elliot) (1880-1943)
Eliot, Henry Ware, **10,161**
Eliot, Mabel, **11,574**
Eliot, Martha May (1891-1978), 2,686, 6,556, **6,558,** 6,987, 11,916
Eliot, Mary. *See* Guild, Mary (Eliot) [Mrs. Charles E.]
Eliot, Mary [Mrs. Samuel Atkins], 6,279
Eliot, Samuel (1821-98), 5,903
Eliot, Samuel Atkins (1798-1862), **6,279**
Eliot, T. L., 6,556
Eliot, Thomas Lamb, 14,311
Eliot, T. S., 8,260, 11,969, 15,900, 16,163
Eliot, William G., 6,556
Elitch's Theater (CO), 1,774
Elizabeth (ship), 5,707
Elizabeth McCormick Memorial Fund, **4,084**
Elizabeth Peabody House (Boston, MA), 6,239, 6,946
Elizabeth II, Queen of England, 3,260, 5,140, 9,057, 12,111
Elizabeth Skelton Danford Memorial Scholarship, 4,217
Elizabeth Town Female Humane Society (NJ), 10,969
Elkhorn Dude Ranch (MT), 10,256
Elkins, Kate Felton [Mrs.], **1,578**
Elkinton, Anna Bassett Griscom [Mrs. J. Passmore] (1889-1974), **15,279**
Elks Club, 939
Elkus, Elizabeth [Mrs. Albert I.], 942
Ellae, Ennaes (pseudonym). *See* Steelink, Nicolaas (1890-)
Elledge, Elizabeth, 14,618
Ellen H. Easton Girls High School (AL), 78
Ellender, Allen, 9,605
Ellers, Mrs. Charles, 11,270
Ellet, Elizabeth Fries (Lummis) (1812?-77), 850, 5,948, **6,559**
Ellickson, Katherine (Pollak) [Mrs. John Chester] (1905-), 8,071, **8,085,** 8,126, **11,484, 11,766,** 11,916, **15,327**
Ellicott Family, 349
Elliff, Joseph D. (1863-1959), **9,964**
Elliman, Claiborne (Catlin) [Mrs. Kenneth], **6,560**
Ellinger, Flora Hofmeister (1862-1966), **17,559**
Ellingham, Emily (1821-92). *See* Hart, Emily (Ellingham) [Mrs. James Henry] (1821-92)

Ellingson, Ethel (1896-). *See* Hanson, Ethel (Ellingston) [Mrs. Oliver] (1896-)
Ellington Airfield (TX), 12,729
Ellington, Buford, 15,887
Ellington, Duke, 2,382, 5,534
Ellington, S. R., 3,013
Elliot, Harriet, 13,604
Elliot, Sylvia (Brent), 10,191
Elliott, Amanda (1789-1839), 1,901
Elliott, Barnard (?-1806), 15,411
Elliott, Charles, 5,063
Elliott, Clarice May, 10,807
Elliott, Collins D. (1810-99), **15,949**
Elliott, Elizabeth B., **15,469**
Elliott, Elizabeth "Lizzie" Porterfield (1860-1932), 15,949
Elliott, Ellen Coit (Brown) [Mrs. Orrin Leslie] (1860-1957), **11,575,** 11,742
Elliott Family (SC), **15,411**
Elliott, Habersham, 15,980
Elliott, Harriet Wiesman (1884-1947), 2,688, **13,241**
Elliott, Jane Whiteside, **9,544**
Elliott, John F., 46
Elliott, Juliet Georgiana (Gibbes) [Mrs. Barnard], 15,411, **15,412**
Elliott, Lillian A. [Miss] (1880-), **10,458**
Elliott, Lola [Mrs. E. A.], 4,745
Elliott, Maria J. *See* Norton, Maria J. (Elliott)
Elliott, Mary (1867-1933). *See* Flanery, Mary (Elliott) [Mrs. William Harvey] (1867-1933)
Elliott, Mary Habersham, 3,518
Elliott, Matilda (Auerbach) [Mrs. Richard], 9,311
Elliott, Maxine (1868-1940), **5,625**
Elliott, Mrs. Charles, 5,846
Elliott, Orrin Leslie, 11,575
Elliott, Phebe Leech (1839-1923), 5,063
Elliott, Sarah Barnwell [Miss] (1848-1928), **15,980**
Elliott, Stephen, **3,502**
Ellis, Augusta. *See* Johnson, Augusta (Ellis)
Ellis, Edith Anna, 11,510
Ellis, Edith M. [Mrs. Willard W.], **11,576**
Ellis, Eliza, 8,975
Ellis, Ella Neuman (1903-), **14,188**
Ellis, Elmer, **9,965**
Ellis, Emily Caroline [Mrs.] (1838-78), **15,590**
Ellis, Evelyn, 3,290
Ellis, Havelock, 6,544, 7,199, 12,701
Ellis, Helen H., 7,897
Ellis, Henry, 3,485
Ellis, Ida H., 955
Ellis, Irene. *See* Murphy, Irene (Ellis) [Mrs. Harold]
Ellis Island, 17,633
Ellis, Iva, 11,596
Ellis, Laura (Lawson) [Mrs. Frank]. *See* Blair, Laura (Lawson) [Mrs. Frank] Ellis [Mrs. Gist]
Ellis, "Ma" [Mrs. E.], **1,287**
Ellis, Margaret, 14,847, 15,290
Ellis, Margaret Dye, 10,673
Ellis, Martha (1870-1959). *See* Hopkins, Martha (Ellis) [Mrs. Arthur Herbert] (1870-1959)
Ellis, Mary [Miss] (1875-1972), **17,048**
Ellis, Mina Benson [Mrs. Leonidas, Jr.] Hubbard [Mrs.], 10,864
Ellis, Mollie, 13,420
Ellis, Mrs. James, 10,680
Ellis, Richard T., 2,689
Ellis, Sallie F., **9,966**
Ellison, Elizabeth Julia (1831-?). *See* Farrington, Elizabeth Julia (Ellison) [Mrs. Nelson] Goltra [Mrs. Keeler] (1831-?)
Ellison, Mary Harris (1839-1917). *See* Curran, Mary Harris (Ellison) [Mrs. Nicholas F.] (1839-1917)
Ellison, Smith, 9,078
Elliston, George [Miss] (1883-1946), **13,844**
Ellmann, Erwin B., **8,086**
Elloie, Pearlie Hardin, 5,470, 5,473
Ellsworth, Abigail. *See* Williams, Abigail (Ellsworth)
Ellsworth, Edgar, 16,658
Ellsworth, Emily. *See* Ford, Emily (Ellsworth) [Mrs. Gordon Lester]
Ellsworth, Emma Augusta (Anderson) [Mrs. German Edgar] (1894-1969), **16,658**
Ellsworth, James (1849-1925), **3,923**
Ellsworth, Laura. *See* Seiler, Laura (Ellsworth)

Ellsworth, Louisa, 11,318
Ellsworth Pioneer School Girls' Club (WI), 17,857
Ellsworth Press (IA), 4,734
Ellsworth, William, 11,318
Ellzey, Maude, **9,627**
Elmendorf Family (NY), 11,260
Elmendorf, Harriet. *See* Gould, Harriet (Elmendorf)
Elmendorf, Harriet Maria, 11,260
Elmer, William, **10,970**
Elmhirst, Leonard, 11,521
Elmhurst Choral Women's Club (IL), 4,195
Elmhurst Evening Woman's Club (IL), **4,190**
Elmhurst Garden Club (IL), **4,191**
Elmhurst Junior Woman's Club (IL), **4,192**
Elmhurst Lioness Club (IL), 4,197
Elmhurst Methodist Church, Women's Society of
    Christian Service (IL), **4,193**
Elmhurst Panhellenic (IL), **4,194**
Elmhurst Woman's Club (IL), **4,195**
Elmira Academy (NY), 11,440
Elmira Business and Professional Women's Club
    (NY), 11,445
Elmira College (NY), 11,443
    archives, **11,446**
    faculty, 9,047, 11,637, 11,707
    students, 2,424
Elmira Free Academy (NY), 11,443
Elmira Water Cure, 11,443
Elmira Women's News Magazine (NY), 11,444
Elmore, Grace B. [Miss] (1839-?), **13,005**
Elmwood Seminary (MO), **9,967**
Elocutionists, **9,876**, 11,440
Elsbree, Anna, **11,577**
Elsbree, Llewellyn, 11,577
Elsensohn, Sister M. Alfreda, **3,680**
Elsey, George M., 10,197
Elsey, Sara Walsh, 12,658
Elshin, Jacob, 17,284
"Elspeth Bynor" (ms), 12,519
Elston, Mary O., 7,047
Elston, Susan (Arnold) (1830-1907). *See* Wallace,
    Susan (Arnold) Elston [Mrs. Lewis] (1830-1907)
Elwell, Sara. *See* Jameson, Sara (Elwell) [Mrs. John
    Franklin]
Ely, Catherine Bissell [Mrs. E. F.] (1817-80), **8,432**
Ely, Charles Arthur, **1,288**
Ely, Charlotte, 7,498
Ely, Smith, 12,187
Ely, Gertrude, 8,657
Ely, Helen M., 9,378
Ely, Helena Rutherford, 17,009
Ely, Louise (Foot) [Mrs. Charles Arthur] (1831-?),
    1,288
Ely, Mary, 7,498
Ely, Mary L., 2,233
Ely, Mrs. D. J., 12,238
Ely Tribe, 10,718
Ely Women's Club (NY), 10,689
Emanu-El (CA), 1,002
Emanu-El Sisterhood for Personal Service (San
    Francisco, CA), **932**
Emanu-El, The (periodical), 939
Embargo, tea, 14,994
"Embattled Ladies of Little Rock, The," 7,194
Embattled Maiden (book), 2,303
Emblems, state, 3,687, 7,749
Embree, Henrietta [Mrs. J. W.] (1834-61), 16,060
Embree, Tennessee Keys [Mrs.], 16,060
"Embroglio" (ms), 17,731
Embroidery, 1,331, 15,896. *See also* Needlework
    patterns, 7,012, 12,462
Embryo (periodical), 2,936
Embryology, human, research, 11,830
Embury, Daniel, 12,463
Embury, Emma Catherine (Manley) [Mrs. Daniel]
    (ca. 1806-63), **12,463**
Embury, Philip Augustus, 12,463
Emer, Margaret (1875-1964), **17,830**
Emera Club (IN), **4,561**
Emerald Street Mission (MA). *See* Warren Street
    Mission (MA)
Emergency Civil Liberties Committee, 17,608
Emergency housing, 6,892
Emergency Peace Federation, 7,923

Emergency relief. *See* Disaster relief
Emergency Relief Administration, 231
Emergency Relief Association (NJ), 11,013
Emerich, Regina, **1,289**
Emerson, Alfred Edwin, Jr., 11,578, 12,464
Emerson, Alice Edwards [Mrs. Alfred] (1862-1933),
    11,578
Emerson, Amelia [Mrs. Raymond], 8,657
Emerson, Benjamin Kendall (1843-1932), **5,864**
Emerson Club (TX), **16,350**
Emerson, Edwin, 1,417
Emerson, Edwin, 12,464
Emerson, Ellen Russell (1837-1907), 2,836, 15,270
Emerson, Ellen Tucker (1839-1909), 6,358, **6,562,**
    7,044, 12,021
Emerson, Emma E. [Mrs. Nicholas Newman]. *See*
    Newman, Emma E. [Mrs. Nicholas Newman
    Emerson]
Emerson, Eugenie Homer [Mrs. Oliver P.]
    (1854-1940), **6,561**
Emerson Family, **12,464**
Emerson Family (MA), 6,281
Emerson, George Barrell (1797-1881), 5,923
Emerson, George Harrington, 12,464
Emerson, Harriet Josephine, 1,224
Emerson, Helen (Brace), 17,498
Emerson House (Chicago, IL). *See* Chicago
    Commons (IL)
Emerson, Lucy, 17,029
Emerson, Lydia "Lidian" [Mrs. Ralph Waldo], 7,055,
    7,416
Emerson, Margaret (1863-1948), 12,464
Emerson, Mary, 11,897
Emerson, Mary Edith Griswold [Mrs. Edwin], 1,417
Emerson, Mary Ingham [Mrs. Edwin], 12,464
Emerson, Mary Moody (1774-1863), 2,818, 6,857,
    17,010
Emerson, Mercy, 5,700
Emerson, Mrs. Harry, 11,596
Emerson, Oliver P. (1845-1938), 6,561
Emerson Public School (Minneapolis, MN), 9,390
Emerson, Ralph Waldo (1803-82), 1,426, 2,406,
    4,684, 5,949, 6,329, 6,358, 6,562, 6,738, 6,857,
    6,870, 7,025, 7,044, 7,416, 7,430, 12,032, 17,692
Emerson, Samuel, 12,464
Emerson, Sarah Marsh (1835-1915), **7,366**
Emerson, Sarah White Davis, 6,569
Emerson, Susanna Hovey Perkins (1737-?), **5,576**
Emery, Alla M. [Mrs. John R.], **11,092**
Emery, Anne McGuigan (1907-), **14,359**
Emery, Ella Maria [Mrs. Moses], 7,367
Emery, Ellen Vesta (1832-1920). *See* Hamlin, Ellen
    Vesta (Emery) [Mrs. Hannibal] (1832-1920)
Emery, Eva (1855-1947). *See* Dye, Eva (Emery)
    [Mrs. Charles Henry] (1855-1947)
Emery Family (MA), **7,367**
Emery, Hannah Tracy (1770?-93). *See* Abbott,
    Hannah Tracy (Emery) [Mrs. Benjamin]
    (1770?-93)
Emery, John R., **11,092**
Emery, Margaret "Meta" [Miss], 7,367
Emery, Mary Elizabeth "Lizzie," **7,368**
Emery, Moses, 7,367
Emery, Rebecca (Hitchcock) (1697-1786), 5,595
Emigrants and immigrants, personal narratives, 17,938
Emigration and immigration, 110, 387, 1,177, 1,559,
    3,362, **3,815,** 4,047, 6,365, 6,978, 7,315, 8,007,
    8,631, 8,657, 8,678, 9,042, 9,418, 9,419, 9,492,
    9,974, 10,603, 12,724, 12,860, 13,414, 13,795,
    13,982, 14,522, 14,686, 17,282. *See also*
    Assimilation (sociology)
    economic aspects, 7,557
    psychological aspects, 3,815
Emigration and immigration law, 1,174, 2,683, 4,110,
    8,631, 9,254, 9,492, 10,419, 14,933
Emigres, American, 114
Emily Bishop League, 2,432
Emlen, Anne, 14,991
Emlen, Anne. *See* Mifflin, Anne (Emlen) [Mrs.
    Warner]
Emlen, Deborah, 14,992
Emlen, Elizabeth, 14,992
Emlen Family, **14,991,** 15,104, **15,276**
Emlen, James, 15,276

Emlen, Margaret, 14,966
Emlen, Samuel, 14,991
Emlen, Samuel (1730-99), **14,992**
Emlen, Samuel, Jr., 14,992
Emlen, Sarah (Foulke) Farquhar [Mrs.
    James] (1787-1849), 15,276, 15,290
Emlen, Sarah Mott [Mrs. Samuel], 14,992
Emlen, Susanna (Dillwyn) [Mrs. Samuel] (1769-1819),
    14,845, 14,989
Emma (sculpture), 9,170
Emma A. Fox Foundation, 8,018
"Emma Goldman Speaks" (ms), 12,701
Emma Lazarus Jewish Woman's Clubs, 1,018
Emma, Queen. [Mrs. Alexander Liholiho, King
    Kamehameha IV]. Emma Rooke (1836-85),
    3,631, 3,654, 16,249
Emma Willard School (NY, VT), 63, **12,927, 12,928,**
    17,031
Emmel, Zillah, 3,436
Emmeline B. Wells Centennial Memorial Committee,
    16,659
Emmet, Jean Reeder, 6,927
Emmet, Jessie [Mrs. Richard], 11,830
Emmett, Gracie, 9,361
Emmons, Anita (1866-1954). *See* Blaine, Anita
    (Emmons) McCormick (1866-1954)
Emmons, Charlotte, 14,046
Emmons, Ed M., 10,684
Emmons, Elizabeth, 12,513
Emmons, Hannah Elizabeth "Libbie" [Mrs. Ed M.]
    (1843?-1935). *See* Molan, Hannah Elizabeth
    "Libbie" [Mrs. Ed M.] Emmons [Mrs. Thomas]
    (1843?-1935)
Emmons, Martha Lena (1894-), **16,351**
Emmons, Samuel Franklin, 2,194
Emmons, Suzanne (Earle) [Mrs. Mahlon Ogden]
    Jones [Mrs. Samuel Franklin]. *See* Bartlett,
    Suzanne (Earle) [Mrs. Mahlon Ogden] Jones
    [Mrs. Samuel Franklin] Emmons [Mrs. Paul
    Wayland]
Emmy Awards, 2,105, 17,983
Emory and Henry College (VA), 5,402, 17,063
Emory College (GA), 3,313, 3,328, 3,467
Emory Glee Club (GA), 3,318
Emory University (GA), 3,316, 3,318, 3,321, 3,356
    alumnae, 3,464
"Emotional Factors in Learning," 11,306
Emotional Life of Children (book), 17,604
Emotionally disturbed children. *See* Mentally ill
    children
Empanger, Joseph, **8,468**
Empáran Family (CA), 858
Empáran, Luisa Eugenia "Lulu" (Vallejo) [Mrs.
    Ricardo] de (1856-1943), 858
Empáran, Madie D. [Mrs. Edmund N.] Brown [Mrs.
    Richard Raoul], 375, **1,249,** 1,634
Emperor and Pope (drama), 2,170
"Empire" (television program), 5,240
Empire and the Berthoud Pass (book), 1,750
Empire Mines (CA), 412
Empire on the Columbia (book), 14,594
Empire State Campaign Committee (NY), 12,415
Empire State Suffrage Association (NY), 6,815
Empire Theatre Dramatic School (NY), alumnae,
    17,815
Employee-management relations in government,
    11,770
Employees magazines, handbooks, etc., 11,851
Employment, 4,124, **6,675,** 7,729, 8,128, 8,754,
    12,724, 14,671, 15,887
Employment agencies, 1,917, **3,811, 4,068,** 4,162,
    6,705, **7,432, 11,622, 11,787,** 12,808, **15,272,**
    17,196, 17,597
Employment exchanges. *See* Employment agencies
"Empress of Treasure Island," 687
Empty Sleeve, The (book), 10,487
Ena, Anna Eliza (1848-84). *See* McClary, Anna
    Eliza (Ena) Palmer Raymonde Ballantine
    (1848-84)
Enamelists, **17,331**
Enches, Evelyn Leslie, **8,560**
Encinal San Antonio (CA), 1,412
Encyclopaedia Britannica, 6,947, 8,441
Encyclopaedia Britannica Foundation, 8,689

Encyclopedia Americana, 1,452
Encyclopedias and dictionaries, 1,452
   treatment of women, 6,947
End of the Century Book Club (Greenville, NC), **13,265**
Endicott, Clarissa (1807-91). *See* Peabody, Clarissa (Endicott) [Mrs. George] (1807-91)
Endicott, Mary (1800-77), **7,369**
Endicott, William Crowninshield, 5,718
Endocrinology, 2,667, 2,669
Endowments, **997, 2,215, 3,626,** 3,872, 4,320, **5,469, 5,474,** 6,914, 7,157, **7,167, 8,909, 11,830,** 11,879, 12,233, **12,737,** 12,966, 14,745, 16,339. *See also* Charitable uses, trusts, and foundations; Charities
   officials and employees, **11,862,** 11,892, **11,911**
Enfield, Gertrude (Dixon) (?-1969), **13,006**
Enfield, Marjorie (Marsh), 7,258
Engagement. *See* Betrothal
Engel, Joe, 11,405
Engel, Lehman, 9,745, 12,367
Engel, Samuel G., 2,476
Engineering, 11,288
Engineering societies, 4,221
Engineers, **1,867,** 2,199, **2,511, 4,221,** 5,434, 6,335, 9,074, 10,312, 10,324, **10,638,** 11,555, **11,903, 12,599, 14,898,** 14,902, **15,618,** 17,164, 17,889
Engines and Brass Bands (book), 7,261
England, 12,196
   American ambassadors to, 9,160
   American consuls in, 12,274
   American diplomats in, 2,188, 11,509
   American travelers in, 6,907
   architecture, conservation and restoration, 6,907
   art, galleries and museums, **2,794**
   congresses and conventions, 1,374, 6,741, 6,842, 8,362
   government, local, 6,448
   medicine, 6,681
   missionaries to, 16,448
   Mormons and Mormonism, 16,806
   suffrage, 17,616
   universities and colleges, 11,857
   World War I, 6,618, 15,112
   World War II, 16,890
      civilian relief, **3,182**
      civilians' work, 3,343, 5,131
      civilians' work, industrial, 9,449
      nurses and nursing, **17,306**
England, Mrs. C. H., 10,101
England, Olive Stanton, 14,618
"England to America" (story), 17,473
Engle, Eleanor, 11,405
Engle, Lavinia, 5,846, 11,916
Engle, Mary Edith B. [Mrs.] (1916-), **5,311**
Engle, Paul Hamilton, 4,485
Engleman, Ellen (Black). *See* Winston, Ellen (Black) Engelman [Mrs. Sanford]
Engles, Friedrich, 12,534
Englewood Historical Society (IL), **3,918**
Englewood News (IL), 3,918
Englewood Women's Club (IL), 3,918
English Academy (Savannah, GA), 3,503
English, Ada [Mrs.], **10,932**
English, Albert D., 8,157
English, Annette, 8,157
English, Elisabeth Doby (1887-1978), **15,591**
English Family (MI), **8,157**
"English from the Inside," 9,770
English immigrants, **16,433, 17,099**
English, Jean. *See* Wisner, Jean (English)
English, Jennie (Wright), 2,655
English language, study and teaching, foreign students, 1,645, 1,845, **8,090**
English, Marion Brown (Monteith) [Mrs. Albert D.], 8,157
English, Ruby, 955
English Speaking Union, **3,182,** 3,734
Engravers, **1,298,** 1,335, 1,358, 2,783, 7,789, **12,260,** 12,376, **12,459,** 14,878
En-lai, Chou, 9,081
Enloe, Rachael (1853-?), **1,290**
Enlow Family (IA), **4,907**
Enlow, Hulda, 4,907

Ennis, Fannie (Davis) (1867-1955), **10,239**
Eno, Amanda. *See* Vail, Amanda (Eno) [Mrs. Alfred]
Eno, Clara Bertha (1854-1951), **259**
Enoch Arden (book), 12,381
Enochs, Elisabeth Shirley, 2,863
Enochson, Marie Johnson (1864-1953), **8,730**
Enote, Mrs. Nunuche, 16,877
Enquirer-Sun (GA), 7,229
Ensemble Club (TX), **16,352**
Ensey, Grace E. [Miss] (?-1935), **1,772**
Ensfield, Mary [Miss], **8,226**
Ensign, Mary W. [Mrs. Horace S.], **12,465**
Enslow, Catherine Bliss [Miss], **17,436**
Enslow, Mary Constance [Miss], **17,437**
Enterline, Helen J. [Mrs.] (ca. 1920-), 10,915
Enters, Angna (1907-), **3,003, 12,362**
Entertainers, 1,024, 2,931, 7,310, 9,575, 10,182, **10,717, 14,182,** 16,208, **17,970**
Entertainers, children, 1,073
Entertainment, 9,407
Entomologists, **2,089,** 6,321, **7,467, 8,555,** 11,540, 11,543, **11,589,** 14,892, **14,901,** 14,943
Entrepreneurs, 13,637
Entz, Frieda (Voth) Regier (1855-1949), **5,196,** 5,201
Environment (periodical), 4,492
Environmental education. *See* Conservation of natural resources, study and teaching
Environmental policy, 470, 17,945
   citizen participation, 5,538, 5,542, **12,875**
Environmentalists. *See* Conservationists
Enzinger, George (?-1959), 11,537
Eola Village, Gleaners Chapel (OR), 14,459
Eoline, or Magnolia Vale (book), 111
Epes, Mary (?-1790). *See* Holyoke, Mary (Epes) [Mrs. Edward] (?-1790)
Ephron, Phoebe, 1,025
Epidemics, 3,170, 5,492, 7,288, 8,765, 10,134, 12,384, 14,854, 15,427, 15,869, 16,868. *See also* Communicable diseases; *and specific types of epidemics, e.g.,* Cholera epidemics
Episcopal Christ Church (Red Wing, MN), 9,120
Episcopal church, 2,523, 3,141, 5,305, 5,511, 9,606, 9,649, 9,706, 15,621, 16,965
   charities, **1,879, 12,237, 16,023**
   clergy, 1,823, **2,225, 2,415,** 2,523, 5,319, **5,492,** 5,827, 6,784, 7,088, **7,198, 9,295, 9,438,** 11,034, 11,190, 12,083, **12,089, 12,660,** 13,176, 13,451, 15,465
   clergy, Afro-American, **6,790**
   deaconesses, training of, **3,938**
   dioceses, 5,827, **12,083**
   education, **12,090**
   missionaries, 2,931, 9,042, **9,081,** 9,438, **11,935,** 12,206, **13,263, 13,269,** 13,284, 16,024
   missions, 313, 5,511, 12,206, **14,996,** 16,024
Episcopal Church, Connecticut Branch of the Woman's Auxiliary to the National Convention, **1,947**
Episcopal Church, Domestic and Foreign Missionary Society, **16,024**
Episcopal Churchwomen, 7,908, **12,084, 16,028**
Episcopal Churchwomen (KS), **5,214**
Episcopal Churchwomen, Diocese of Chicago (IL), **3,941**
Episcopal Churchwomen, Diocese of New York, **12,084**
Episcopal Churchwomen of the Diocese of Missouri, **10,147**
Episcopal Diocese of Chicago (IL), 3,801
Episcopal Diocese of Chicago (IL), Altar Guild, **3,936**
Episcopal Diocese of Chicago (IL), Central House for Deaconesses, **3,937**
Episcopal Diocese of Chicago (IL), "Clerica," **3,939**
Episcopal Diocese of Eau Claire (WI), **17,518**
Episcopal Diocese of New York, **12,082**
Episcopal Diocese of New York, Diocesan Convention, **12,083**
Episcopal Diocese of New York Standing Committee Proceedings, **12,085**
Episcopal High School of Virginia, 5,770, 13,062
Episcopalians, **7,679,** 9,314, 13,102
Epistolary Autobiography, An (book), 10,933
Epitaphs, 7,635
"Epochs in the Life of Jefferson Davis" (ms), 9,627

Eppes, John Wayles (1772-1823), 17,083
Eppes, Martha Burke (Jones) [Mrs. John Wayles] (1790-1863), **17,083**
Eppes, Mary "Maria" "Polly" (Jefferson) [Mrs. John Wayles], 17,083
Eppes, Susan (Bradford) [Mrs. Nicholas Ware], **13,007**
Epps Family (TN), 9,872
Epsilon Lambda Sigma (CA), **1,625**
Epstein, Alice [Mrs. Paul S.], 1,096
Epstein, Berthan, 4,053
Epstein, Cynthia Fuchs, 15,197
Epstein, Lida Hedwig, 1,096
Epstein, Lillian (1898?-1960). *See* Levine, Lillian (Epstein) [Mrs. Murray] (1898?-1960)
Epstein, Paul S. (1883-1966), **1,096**
Epstein, Sara Lurie, 1,096
Epworth League, 14,595
Epworth Methodist Church (NE), Wesleyan Service Guild, **10,575**
Epworth Village (York, NE), **10,621**
"E. Q. B." (poem), 15,980
Equal Employment Opportunity Enforcement Act (1971), 8,103
Equal Franchise Federation of Pittsburgh (PA), 17,217
Equal Franchise Society (NY), 12,843
Equal Franchise Society of Nevada, 10,679
Equal Franchise Society of New Jersey, 10,984
Equal Opportunity Committee of Clark County (WA), 17,314
Equal pay for equal work, 2,075, 2,545, 6,365, 6,892, 7,237, 7,257, 8,069, 8,083, 8,107, 8,135, 8,140, **9,831,** 9,951, 10,194, 11,729, 13,610, 14,939, 15,819, 17,217
Equal rights. *See* Civil rights
"Equal Rights" (lecture), 11,167
Equal Rights (periodical), **2,043,** 6,742, 6,944, 6,953
Equal Rights Amendment (proposed), 177, 658, 714, 1,140, 2,120, 2,504, 2,705, 4,075, 4,124, 5,388, 5,429, 6,695, 6,742, 6,892, 6,944, 7,193, 7,242, 7,272, 7,325, 7,699, 7,889, 8,057, 8,075, 9,140, 9,947, 9,950, 9,986, 10,204, 10,345, 11,123, 11,695, 11,876, 11,920, 12,106, **13,404, 13,704,** 13,706, 13,712, **14,009, 14,011,** 14,023, 14,814, **15,794,** 15,805, 15,819, 15,971, **16,660,** 16,971, 17,217, **17,253,** 17,317, 17,348, 17,746
   opposition to, 4,173, 7,273, 11,904
Equal Rights Association, 13,990
"Equal Rights Banner" (newspaper), 16,500
Equal Rights Commission, 3,653
Equal Rights party, 1,091, 3,778, 4,695
Equal Suffrage Amendment. *See* United States (government), Constitution, amendments
Equal Suffrage Association, 49
Equal Suffrage Association (IA), 4,960
Equal Suffrage Association (NC), 13,405
Equal Suffrage Association of Idaho, 3,681
Equal Suffrage Club of Pierre (SD), 15,864
Equal Suffrage League, 13,557, 15,733
Equal Suffrage League of Baltimore (MD), **6,757**
Equal Suffrage League of Virginia, 17,104
Equal Suffrage Party of Georgia, 3,183
Equal Suffrage Society (Indianapolis, IN), 4,623
Equal Suffrage: The Results of an Investigation in Colorado Made for the Collegiate Equal Suffrage League of New York State (book), 17,757
Equinox, The (book), 6,078
Equity Club, 6,533
Equity pleading and procedure, 986, 11,450, 11,454, **15,547**
Era Civic Association (LA), 5,549
ERA Club (New Orleans, LA), **5,499**
ERA South Carolina, **15,794**
ERA United (NC), 13,176
Erasmus Hall High School, 11,555
Erasmus Hall School (NY), 11,322
Erasmus, Joanna G. (1933-), 10,151
Erb, Caroyl [Mrs. Edward G.], 1,837
Erb, Mary, 8,122
Eric Dolphy Quintet, 15,198
Ericksen, Theresa (1867-?), 8,648, **9,059**
Erickson, Elaine, 16,875

Erickson, Grace Vance [Mrs. John E.], **10,301**, 10,302, 10,397
Erickson, Hilda (Andersson) [Mrs. John A.] (1859-1968), **16,510**, **16,661**
Erickson, John A., 16,510
Erickson, John E., 10,301
Erickson, Phoebe (1907-), 8,531
Erickson, Ruth (?-1970), **14,360**
Erie Canal, 11,464, 12,886
Erie Chapel Sunday School (Chicago, IL), 3,837
Erie Neighborhood House (Chicago, IL), **3,837**
Erin-Go-Bragh Club (MA), **6,563**
Erlanger, Elizabeth N. (1901-75), **2,755**
Erlanger, Margaret [Miss] (1908-75), **4,384**
Ermatinger, Annie, 17,519
Ermatinger, Caroline [Mrs. George], 17,519
Ermatinger, Charlotte (Cadott) [Mrs. James], 17,519
Ermatinger, George, 17,519
Ermatinger, James (?-1866), **17,519**
Ermatinger, Ralph, 17,519
Ernest Endeavor Study Club (TX), 16,336
Ernst, Agnes Elizabeth (1887-1970). *See* Meyer, Agnes Elizabeth (Ernst) [Mrs. Eugene, Jr.] (1887-1970)
Ernst, Juliette, 14,744
Ernst, Margaret [Mrs. Morris L.], 12,537
Ernst, Morris Leopold, (1888-1976), **6,564**
Ernstsen, Oline [Mrs. Daniel] (1882-?), **8,731**
Erodelphian Literary Society (IA), **4,985**
Erodelphian Literary Society (New Concord, OH), 14,118
Erotica, 8,207
Erskine, Arthur W. (1885-1952), **4,698**
Erskine, Dorothy (Ward) [Mrs. Morse], 470, 831
Erskine, Helen W. [Mrs. John] (1896-). *See* Cranmer, Helen W. [Mrs. John] Erskine [Mrs. W. H. H.] (1896-)
Erskine, John, 11,858
Erskine, Katherine Anne (Porter) [Mrs. Albert Russel] (1890-). *See* Porter, Katherine Anne. Mrs. Albert Russel Erskine, Jr.
Erskine, Marjorie, 4,445
Ertmann, Anna E., **16,662**
Ertz, Susan, 11,966
Erwin, Alexander S., 2,992
Erwin Family (GA), **2,992**
Erwin, Marie H., **17,903**, 17,918
Erwin, Mary Ann Lamar (Cobb) [Mrs. Alexander S.] (1850-1930), 2,992
Erwin, Meryl (1883-), **10,303**
Esa Senora (drama), 4,235
Esau, Katharine (1898-), 10,151
Esberg, Mrs. Milton, 1,293
"Escape into Living" (story), 16,168
"Escape-thought, An" (ms), 12,473
Esch, John J. (1861-1941), **17,627**
Eschweiler, Dorothy Quincey (Adams) (1894-), 8,896
Escuela Normal de San Juan (Argentina), 10,937
Esdaile, Arundell, 1,549
Esenin, Sergei, 12,361
Eshman, Caroline Louise (1901-). *See* Liebig, Caroline Louise (Eshman) (1901-)
Eskew, Ruby Wilson, 12,532
Eskimos, 132, 134, 211, 2,674, 14,415
    language, gender, 8,206
    rites and ceremonies, 8,206
    sex customs, 8,207
Eskridge, Mary (1901-73). *See* King, Mary (Eskridge) (1901-73)
Esperanto, 15,218
Espina, Concha, 215
Espionage, 6,020, 6,106, 11,931. *See also* Intelligence service; Spies
Espionage Act, 10,177, 11,931, 14,432, 15,309
Esplin, Ann Amelia Chamberlain (1896-), 16,780
Espy, David, 14,803
Espy, Harriet N. (?-1878). *See* Baird, Harriet N. (Espy) [Mrs. Zebulon] (?-1878)
Espy, Mary (1779-1815). *See* Anderson, Mary (Espy) [Mrs. John] (1779-1815)
Espy, Sarah Rodgers (Rousseau) [Mrs. Thomas] (1815-98), 66
Essary, Helen, 48

Essayists, 54, **1,433**, **2,406**
Essays, 4,908, 5,931
"Essays of Sarah Worcester" (ms), 14,197
Essex County Teachers Association (MA), **7,370**
Essex House Hotel, Inc. (NY), 12,601
Essex North Branch, Women's Board of Missions (MA), **7,371**
Essex North Home Missionary Alliance (MA), 7,371
Essex North Missionary Association (MA), 7,371
Essex North Women's Congregational Fellowship (MA), **7,371**
Estabrook, Ann, 9,274
Estabrook, Helen [Miss], **14,120**
Estabrook Woman's Relief Corps (Ann Arbor, MI), 7,860
Estate of Memory, An (book), 6,039
Estates (law), 5,599, 7,504, 11,139, **11,189**, 11,525, 11,583, 15,018, 15,519, 15,641, 15,661, 15,834, 17,081
    cases, 6,259, 16,034
Estaugh, Elizabeth (Haddon) [Mrs. John], 14,843
Estaugh family (NJ), **14,843**
Estaugh, John, 14,843
Estes Kefauver for President Committee, 793
Estes, Lydia (1819-83). *See* Pinkham, Lydia (Estes) (1819-83)
Estlin, Mary Ann, 5,926
Estranged—But They Still Love, 11,038
Etchers, **2,520**, **2,736**, **2,809**, **2,825**, **12,282**, **12,293**, **12,637**
Etcheverry, Marion. *See* McVitty, Marion (Etcheverry) [Mrs. Edward W.]
Etching, 13,447
Eternal Quest (book), 4,622
Ether (anesthetic), 3,054
Etheridge, Mary Lee, 7,090
Etheridge, Miss, 9,838
Ethical Culture School (NY), faculty, 15,278
Ethical Humanist Society of Chicago (IL), **4,085**, 4,096
Ethics, 4,409, 12,807
Ethics Club (Muscatine, IA), 5,087
Ethiopia
    American ambassadors to, 9,467
    American nurses in, 233
    insurgency (1960), 11,857
Ethnic groups. *See* Minorities; Race problems; *and names of individual groups*
Ethnobotany, 14,213
Ethnohistory (periodical), 2,835
Ethnologists, 2,298, **2,839**, **2,843**, **12,593**, 15,004
Ethnologists, Native American, 10,483
Ethnology, 1,844, **2,837**
    Aleutian Islands, **8,206**
Ethnology, Native American, **2,839**
Ethnomusicologists, **15,923**
Ethridge, Willie Snow, **3,004**, 3,065, 3,117
Etiquette, 2,533, 2,616, 8,798, 12,433
Etiquette for children and youth, 6,682
Ets, Marie Hall [Mrs.] (1895-), 8,531, **9,495**
Etter, Flora (Cotton) [Mrs. W. L.], **4,909**
Etting Family, 7,555
Ettor, Iva, 12,702
Eubanks, Delphine, 2,502
Eubanks Family, **16,066**
Eubanks, Mary, **16,066**
Eugene City Temperance Alliance (OR), **14,361**
Eugene Field foundation, 9,978
Eugene Field house (CO), 1,756
Eugene Fortnightly Club (OR), **14,287**
Eugene O'Neill Foundation, 2,105
Eugenia Price Productions, 6,070
Eugenics, 4,409, 7,198, 7,283, 7,289, 11,403, **17,018**
Eugenics Record Office (NY), 17,018
Eugenics Survey and Country Life Commission (VT), **17,018**
Eulogies, 17,150
"Eunice Richmond's Confirmation" (story), 11,091
Eunomian Literary Society (MO), 9,943
Eureka College, faculty, 4,428
Eureka National Bank (SD), 15,869
Eureka Springs Sanatarium (MI), 8,307
Euren, Gustaf, 8,690
Europe, 12,195, 17,282

American travelers in, 7,610
    food relief, 1,557
    international education, 6,702
    labor and laboring classes, education, 8,071, 8,126
    medicine, practice, 2,282
    missionaries to, **14,992**
    Young Women's Christian Association, 12,724
Europe in Retreat (book), 6,512
European Woodcock Research Group, 8,626
"Europe's Teenagers" (article), 17,762
Eurydice Club (Toledo, OH), 14,141
Eustis, Caroline (Langdon) [Mrs. William] (?-1865?), 2,322
Eustis, William (1753-1825), **2,322**
Euthanasia, 6,475, 14,473
Evacuation 114 (book), 7,332
Evald, Carl A., 4,319
Evald, Emmy (Carlsson) [Mrs. Carl A.] (1857-1946), **3,957**, 4,319
Evance, Rebecca, 15,716
Evangelical Church (NE), Woman's Missionary Society, **10,591**
Evangelical Covenant Church of America, Covenant Women, **3,943**
Evangelical Lutheran Augustana Synod, Women's Missionary Society, 3,957
Evangelical Lutheran Church, Board of Charities, **8,857**
Evangelical Lutheran Church, Board of Foreign Missions, **8,858**
Evangelical Lutheran Church, Christian Service Institute, 8,859
Evangelical Lutheran Church, Commission on Diaconic Service, 8,859
Evangelical Lutheran Church, Diaconate, **8,859**
Evangelical Lutheran Church, missions, 8,875
Evangelical Lutheran Church, Women's Missionary Federation, **4,724**
Evangelical United Brethren Church of Prairie Gem (NE), Women's Society of World Service, **10,595**
Evangelical United Brethren, Woman's Society of World Service (IN), **4,544**
Evangelism, 3,969
Evangelists, 326, **1,470**, 2,232, **2,518**, **2,613**, 3,777, **6,515**, **9,971**, 10,911, 14,254
Evans, Alice Catherine [Miss] (1881-), **11,579**
Evans, Anne [Miss] (ca. 1871-1941), 9,479
Evans, Augusta Jane (1835-1909). *See* Wilson, Augusta Jane (Evans) [Mrs. Lorenzo Madison] (1835-1909)
Evans, Carol, 11,827
Evans, Caroline, 1,702
Evans, Catherine (Peter), **5,312**
Evans, Charles, 14,840
Evans, Claiborne, **2,132**
Evans, Dorothy, 9,256
Evans, Elizabeth, 9,341
Evans, Elizabeth (Shober) [Mrs. William] (1834-?), 9,369
Evans, Elizabeth Gardiner [Mrs. Glendower] (1856-1937), 2,432, **6,565**, 6,642, 6,843, **6,974**
Evans, Emily Helen, 9,770
Evans, Ernestine (1889-1967), **11,989**
Evans Family (CO), 1,695
Evans, George, 15,413
Evans, Gladys C., 9,819
Evans, Harriet Myrick, 9,032
Evans, Ida, 3,764
Evans, Ida Suella Elliott, **10,669**
Evans, Jessie. *See* Crownhart, Jessie (Evans) [Mrs. Charles H., Sr.]
Evans, Jessie Ella (1902-71). *See* Smith, Jessie Ella (Evans) [Mrs. Joseph Fielding] (1902-71)
Evans, Johanna Lovisa Lofdahl [Mrs. Morgan] (1834-1912), 16,481
Evans, Laura, 1,751
Evans, Lena Cadwallader [Miss], 12,187
Evans, Letitia (Pate) (?-1953), **3,321**
Evans, Lizzie, 9,361
Evans, Louisa A. (Thompson) [Mrs. Samuel D.] (?-1912), 14,677
Evans, Louise, **3,005**
Evans, Margaret (1889-1973). *See* Price, Margaret (Evans) [Mrs. Irving] (1889-1973)

Evans, Margaret Jane (1842-1926). *See* Huntington, Margaret Jane (Evans) [Mrs. George] (1842-1926)
Evans, Maria Holliday Elkin [Mrs. Julian, Sr.], **9,534**
Evans, Mary, 3,114
Evans, Mary. *See* Adams, Mary Evans [Mrs. Elmer]
Evans, Mary. *See* Cowles, Mary (Evans) [Mrs. Josiah, Jr.]
Evans, Mary (1884-). *See* Oxborough, Mary (Evans) [Mrs. Robert] (1884-)
Evans, Mary Ann, 4,949
Evans, Mary Ellen (1912-), **4,986**
Evans, Mary Lee (?-1888). *See* Gibbes, Mary Lee (Evans) [Mrs. James Schoolbred] (?-1888)
Evans, Mary Lucretia Parke [Mrs.], 3,752, 3,764
Evans, Mary Rees Phillips [Mrs.] (1828-92), 16,460
Evans, Matilda A., 15,430
Evans, Matilda "Tilly" Coxe (1849-1915). *See* Stevenson, Matilda "Tilly" Coxe (Evans) [Mrs. James] (1849-1915)
Evans, Maurice, 9,769
Evans, May (Thompson) (1901-), 2,701, **13,406**
Evans, Morgan, 16,481
Evans, Morgan S., **16,460**
Evans, Mrs. J. Wistar, 14,986
Evans, Mrs. Wealthy Cleveland, **2,323**
Evans, Portia Lee. *See* Jennifer, Portia Lee (Evans) [Mrs. Harper Councill] Trenholm
Evans, Priscilla (Livingston) [Mrs. Frank] (1881-1957), **16,663**
Evans, Nora (1887-), **471, 795,** 1,068
Evans, Oliver, 16,161, 16,163
Evans, Pearlie I., 10,191
Evans, Priscilla (Merriman) [Mrs. Thomas David] (1835-1914), **16,664**
Evans, Samuel, 16,245
Evans, Samuel D., 14,677
Evans, Sarah, 15,413
Evanston College for Ladies (IL). *See* Northwestern University (IL)
Evanston King's Daughters (IL), 6,748
Evening and continuation schools, 2,131, 5,325, 5,426, 6,490
Evening Garden Club (Wilmette, IL), 4,454
Evening of the Good Samaritan, The (book), 11,310
"Evening Prayer, The" (song), 12,160
Evening Star (DC), 5,080
Evens, Harriet (ca. 1828-1914). *See* Peet, Harriet Evens [Mrs. James] (ca. 1828-1914)
Evens, Mrs. George H., 3,922
Ever-Present Past, The (book), 11,164
Ever Tomorrow (book), 5,023
Everest, Myrtle [Mrs.], 1,658
Everett, Anna, 11,093
Everett Consumer's Co-op Association (WA), 17,238
Everett, Cynthia (1839-76), 3,991
Everett, Elizabeth [Mrs. Robert] (179?-1878), 3,991
Everett, Ella, 9,323
Everett Family, **7,227**
Everett Family (NJ), **11,093**
Everett, Laura Bell, 1,602
Everett, Lillie (Moore) (1870-?), 13,473
Everett, Lizzie L., 11,093
Everett, Louella D. (?-1967), 11,516
Everett, Mary (Leonard) [Mrs. Horace], 9,884
Everett, Mary Holywell (1830-1916), 9,991
Everett, Nettie Ward Frierson [Mrs.] (1886-1971), **3,460**
Everett, Robert (1791-1875), Family (NY), **3,991**
Everett, Sallie Baker [Mrs.] (1888-1975), **13,266**
Everett, Sarah Preston (1796-1866). *See* Hale, Sarah Preston (Everett) [Mrs. Nathan] (1796-1866)
Evergood, Philip, 2,782
Evergreen State College (Olympia, WA), faculty, 6,336
Everhard, Carolyn (McCullough) (1834-1902), 13,967, **14,114**
Everhart, Adelaide, 3,184
Everhart Family (GA), **3,184**
Everhart, Lay H., 3,184
Everitt Family (GA), **3,388**
Everitt, Julia (1852-?), 3,388
Everitt, Richard Mills (1823-?), 3,388

Evers, A Frank Autobiography of Charles Evers (book), 6,031
Everston Family, 12,314
Everts, Lillian (pseudonym). *See* Levine, Lillian (Epstein) [Mrs. Murray] (1898?-1960)
Every Bite: A Patriotic Burlesque (drama), 4,727
"Every Day Poem" (column), 13,844
Every Friday Club (MI), **8,227**
Every One His Own Way (book), 4,007
Every Saturday Club (GA), **3,322**
Everyman and Roach (drama), 12,367
Evjue, William, 17,675
Ewer, Annie (1867-1972). *See* Rose, Annie (Ewer) [Mrs. William J.] (1867-1972)
Ewer, Mary Anita [Miss] (1892-1961), **11,580**
Ewing, Charles (1835-83), 2,325
Ewing, Charles, Family, **2,325**
Ewing, Charles, II, 2,325
Ewing, Ellen Boyle (1824-88). *See* Sherman, Ellen Boyle (Ewing) [Mrs. William Tecumseh] (1824-88)
Ewing, Eleanor Boyle (1824-88). *See* Sherman, Ellen Boyle (Ewing) [Mrs. William Tecumseh] (1824-88)
Ewing, Ellen (Cox) [Mrs. Thomas II] (1833-1919), 2,327
Ewing, Emma Rebecca (Hunt) [Mrs. John T.]. *See* Day, Emma Rebecca (Hunt) [Mrs. John T.] Ewing [Mrs. James Collins]
Ewing Family (OH), 1,484, **4,643**
Ewing, Hazle (Buck) [Mrs. Davis], 3,745
Ewing, Henrietta, 1,659
Ewing, Jane, **2,326,** 11,184
Ewing, John K. M., 2,325
Ewing, John T., 9,034
Ewing, Judge, 13,250
Ewing, Lizzie Alberta (Merchant), **1,773**
Ewing, Maria, 2,325
Ewing, Maria (Boyle) [Mrs. Thomas, Sr.] (1801-64), 1,484, 2,327, 4,643
Ewing, Maria Rebecca (Gillespie) (1828-?), 4,643
Ewing, Maria Theresa. *See* Steele, Maria Theresa (Ewing) [Mrs. Clement F.]
Ewing, Thomas, Family, **2,327**
Ewing, Thomas, Sr. (1789-1871), 2,327, 4,643
Ewing, Thomas II (1829-96), 2,327
Ewing, Virginia Larwill (Miller) [Mrs. Charles] (1846-1937), 2,325
Ex-clergy, 17,597
Ex-nuns, 999
  personal narratives, **5,640**
Ex-priests, Catholic, 17,597
Ex-rabbis, 17,597
Examination, 117, 8,308
Examinations, 4,336
Examiner, 9,717
Excavations (archaeology), 3,753, 14,882
Excelsior Study Club (Milbank, SD), **15,846**
Exceptional children, 11,549. *See also* Gifted children
  education, 7,684, 7,764, 8,030, 9,467
Exchange (plantation, SC), 15,440
Exchange of persons programs, **5,475,** 12,100. *See also* Students, interchange of
Executions and executioners, 3,396, 5,979, 9,317, 11,718, 12,175
Executive advisory bodies, 233, 645, 1,525, 1,675, 2,397, **2,667, 2,668,** 3,399, 3,430, 3,469, 4,397, 4,850, 4,861, 4,921, 5,122, 5,136, 5,147, 5,155, **5,282,** 5,325, 5,828, 6,263, 6,367, 6,723, 6,751, 6,914, 6,939, 6,949, 7,031, 7,325, **7,326,** 7,699, 7,794, 8,027, 8,063, 8,085, 8,553, 8,651, 8,984, **9,237,** 9,276, 9,392, 9,474, 9,930, 10,197, **10,280, 11,011,** 11,484, 11,744, 11,756, 11,765, 11,770, 11,804, 11,916, 11,958, 12,694, 13,241, 13,246, 13,565, 13,909, **14,249,** 14,822, 14,942, 15,570, 15,889, 16,264, 16,342, 17,238, 17,300, 17,340, **17,769**
Executive advisory committees, 8,636
Executive advisory councils, 8,632
Executive Relief Committee (Charleston, SC) 15,471
Executives, **2,030, 2,095,** 3,135, 3,179, 3,229, 3,246, 3,268, **3,399, 3,698, 3,927, 4,123,** 5,143, **5,144,** 5,239, **5,378,** 5,394, **6,879,** 8,112, **8,970, 9,131,**

9,401, **11,073,** 11,822, 11,831, 11,909, **12,086, 12,710, 12,713, 12,726, 12,727, 14,674, 15,000, 16,273**
Executives, Jewish, **13,817**
Executors and administrators, 2,169, 2,268, 5,515, 11,524, 14,204, 15,056, 15,481
Exhibition buildings, 441, 1,932, 2,859, 2,922, 3,781, 3,912, 4,786, 6,805
Exhibitions, 761, 941, **1,170,** 1,377, 1,730, 1,790, 2,454, 2,472, 2,506, 2,743, 3,234, 3,275, 4,018, **4,066,** 4,123, **4,337,** 4,368, 4,369, 4,609, 4,835, 4,904, 5,418, 5,805, 6,346, 6,664, 7,632, 7,677, 7,678, 7,887, 8,177, 8,362, 9,334, 9,610, 9,705, 9,858, **10,043,** 10,319, 10,343, 10,370, **11,266,** 11,326, **12,416,** 12,417, 12,936, 13,307, 13,535, **13,863,** 13,993, 13,999, 14,026, 14,535, 14,549, 14,940, **14,971,** 15,182, 15,194, 16,060, 16,965, 17,468, 17,616. 17,716. *See also* Fairs; and specific *exhibitions;* and as a subhead under subjects, e.g., Art, exhibitions
Exile of a Race (book), 17,259
Exile, The (book), 16,153
Exiles from Paradise: Zelda and Scott Fitzgerald (book), 113
Exclusion Act (1882), 1,174
Exodus: 20 (ms), 3,177
"Experience of a Mormon Wife" (article), 16,559
"Experiences with Miss Clara Barton" (report), 12,497
Experiment in Silk-Culture, An (pamphlet), 7,467
Experimental farms, 7,224
Experimental films, 17,794
Experimental theater, **964, 17,815**
Expiation (book), 17,009
Explorations Holding Company (CA), 11,517
Explorers, 801, 1,426, 1,430, **1,468, 1,478,** 2,202, 2,339, **2,364, 2,420,** 2,485, 2,558, 2,566, 2,575, **2,600, 2,634,** 2,719, 3,654, 4,696, **5,177,** 6,573, 7,293, **8,208,** 8,441, 10,236, 10,237, 10,531, 10,864, 12,180, **12,481,** 12,619, 12,622, **14,501, 14,660, 14,891,** 15,472
Exploring the Child's World (book), 17,870
Exploring the Great Basin (book), 10,760
Explosives industry, 15,963
Export marketing, 11,851
Expositions. *See* Exhibitions.
Expositor (newspaper), 4,302
Express (Wells College, NY), 11,281
Express highways, public opinion, 9,467
Expression, 3,252, 13,366
  schools of, 13,810
"Expressions of dying sayings," 14,981
Exquisite Thing, The (ms), 6,047
Extended care facilities, 14,494, 15,984
Extension Service Wives Club (TX), **16,193**
Extradition, 987
Extramarital relations, 987, 1,919, 3,778, 13,356
Extremities (anatomy), morphology, 11,830
Exxon Corporation, 1,014
Eye, diseases and defects, 2,335
Eye, The (IL), 3,918
Eyre, Alice McFadden Brinton [Mrs. Lawrence], 12,468
Eyre, Lawrence, 12,468, 12,474
Eyerly, Jeannette Hyde (1908-), **4,987**
Eyrich, Gladys [Miss], 1,061
Eyster, Nellie B., 11,547
Eytinge, Pearl (?-1914), 3,969
Eytinge, Rose (1835-1911), 16,150
F Club (FL), 2,939
"F. B. I. in Peace and War, The" (radio program), 1,026
F.D.R. labor camps, 8,134
"FDR Was My Boss" (article), 3,301
F. Jasmine Addams (drama), 12,367
Faber, Georgia Lydia (Knox) [Mrs. W. L.], 287
Faber, Judith Ann (1945-), **17,628**
Fabian, Josephine [Mrs.] (1885-), 16,485
Fabilli, Mary, 454
Fabiola Hospital (Oakland, CA). *See* Samuel Merritt Hospital (Oakland, CA)
Fabiola Hospital Association (Oakland, CA), **472**
Fables of La Fontaine, The (book), 11,171
Fables, The (book), 7,193
Fabray, Nanette. [Mrs. Ranald] MacDougall, **2,105**

Fabric of Memory (book), 11,944
Face of Fear, The (book), 9,612
Fackrell, Mary Susannah Sumner (1862-1920). *See* Fowler, Mary Susannah Sumner (Fackrell) [Mrs. Henry Ammon] (1862-1920)
Fact Feature Syndicate, 14,324
Factories, 4,259
  fires and fire prevention, 11,597
  safety measures, 4,173
Factors. *See* Commission merchants.
Factory inspection, 4,101, 4,173, 7,834
Factory inspectors, **4,824, 11,597**
Factory sanitation, 11,597
Factory workers, 11,255, 12,760, 15,332, 16,967
Facts (periodical), 3,217
Facts and Fancies (yearbook), 3,435
Faculty Ladies Club (UT), **16,413**
Faculty Wives Club (MI), **8,046**
Faculty Women's Club, North Dakota State University, **13,671**
Faddis, Margene O., **13,883**
Fadem, Joyce Abrams [Mrs.] (1932-), **1,037**
Fader, Anna (1858-1942). *See* Haskell, Anna (Fader) [Mrs. Burnette Gregor] (1858-1942)
Fader, Anne Keith (Hayden) [Mrs. Christian] (1835-96). *See* Field, Anne Keith (Hayden) [Mrs. Christian] Fader [Mrs. J. C.] (1835-96)
Fader Family, 535
Fagan, Eleanora (1915-59). *See* Holiday, Billie. Eleanora Fagan. [Mrs. Joe] Guy [Mrs. Louis] McKay (1915-59)
Fagg Family (CA), 1,648
Fagot Club (OR), 14,500
Fahley, Agnes, 8,399
Fahnestock, Anna Maria (Wolff) (1803-?), **14,993**
Fahnestock, Elizabeth Shenk Dickey (1840-1924), **6,566**
Fahnestock, George Wolff (1823-68), **14,993**
Fahnestock, Grace, 14,993
Fahs, Sophia Blanche (Lyon) (1876-), **6,250**
Failing, Emily Corbett. *See* Cabell, Emily Corbett (Failing)
Failing, Henrietta Ellison, 14,552
Failing, Henry (1834-98), **14,552**
Failing, Josiah, 14,552
Failing, Mary. *See* Merrill, Mary (Failing)
Failing, Mary [Miss], 14,024
Failing, Melinda Forbush, 14,552
Fain, Esther [Mrs. Benjamin] (1907-77), 4,048
Fair employment practice. *See* Discrimination in employment
Fair Employment Practices Commission, 9,196
Fair Labor Standards Act (1938), 2,504, 14,939
Fairbairn, Ann (pseudonym). *See* Tait, Dorothy Fairbairn (?-1972)
Fairbank, Deborah (Clark) [Mrs. Josiah, Sr.]. *See* Stone, Deborah (Clark) [Mrs. Josiah, Sr.] Fairbank [Mrs. Benjamin]
Fairbank Family (MA), **7,014**
Fairbank, Josiah, Sr. (1761-95), 7,014
Fairbank, Josiah (1794-1878), 7,014
Fairbank, Mary (Clark) [Mrs. Josiah, Sr.], 7,014
Fairbank, Mrs. Kellogg, 4,066
Fairbank, Sarah Elizabeth Gulliver [Mrs. Josiah] (1801-70), 7,014
Fairbanks, Ellen M., 9,323
Fairbanks Family, 9,384
Fairbanks, Lulu M. (1888-1968), **132**
Fairbanks, Mrs. Douglas. *See* Pickford, Mary. Gladys Smith. [Mrs. Douglas] Fairbanks, Sr. [Mrs. Charles "Buddy"] Rogers (1893-1979)
Fairbanks, Myra (1805-78). *See* Eells, Myra (Fairbanks) "Mother" [Mrs. Cushing] (1805-78)
Fairbanks Republican Women's Club (AK), **133**
Fairbanks Women's Club (AK), **140**
Fairchild, Charles Stebbins (1842-1924), **12,203**
Fairchild, Daisy (Bell) [Mrs. David], 2,420
Fairchild, Helen G., 11,547
Fairchild, Helen (Lincklaen) [Mrs. Charles Stebbins] (1845-ca. 1931), 12,203, 12,247, 12,252
Fairchild, Huldah, 422
Fairchild, J. H., 14,124
Fairchild, James, 11,694
Fairchild, James T., 14,123

Fairchild, Lilly Nelson [Mrs. Charles] (1845-1924), 5,906, 5,935
Fairchild, Lucia (1870-1924). *See* Fuller, Lucia (Fairchild) [Mrs. Henry Brown] (1870-1924)
Fairchild, Lucius (1831-96), **17,629**
Fairchild, Marguerite [Mrs. I. D.] (1885-1974), 16,225
Fairchild, Marian Hubbard (Bell) [Mrs. David G.] (1880-1962), 2,202
Fairchild, Mary [Mrs. J. H.], 14,124
Fairchild, Reuben, 422
Fairchild, Sarah, 17,640
Fairchild, Thomas B., **7,622**
Faircloth, Iris (1912-). *See* Blitch, Iris (Faircloth) [Mrs. Brooks Erwin] (1912-)
Faircloth, Jean Marie. *See* MacArthur, Jean Marie (Faircloth) [Mrs. Douglas]
Fairfax-Cholmeley, 1,564
Fairfax Development Corporation, 2,635
Fairfax Family (MA), **7,372**
Fairfax, Hannah (ca. 1738-1810). *See* Washington, Hannah (Fairfax) (ca. 1738-1810)
Fairfield, Anne Payne, 5,697
Fairfield divorce, 9,933
Fairfield Family (ME), **5,697**
Fairfield, Mary, 11,846
Fairfield Musical Club (IA), **4,877**
Fairfield Seminary, 11,728
Fairfield Woman's Club (IA), **4,878**
Fairley, Catherine [Mrs. William D.]. *See* Stevens, Catherine [Mrs. William D.] Fairley [Mrs. Melvin James]
Fairley, Charles, 11,582
Fairley Family, **11,582**
Fairley, Fannie Fairchild. *See* Dillon, Fannie Fairchild (Fairley) [Mrs. John L.]
Fairley, William D. (?-1871) 11,582
Fairmont Daily Sentinel (MN), 9,183
Fairs, 5,946, 5,964, 6,662, **8,345**, 8,456, 8,709, 9,154, 9,207, 9,468, 9,902, 11,650, **15,085**, 15,611. *See also* Exhibitions
Fairview School (IA), 4,958
"Fairy Tale of the Natchez Trace, The" (story), 9,770
Fairyland Around Us, The (book), 14,468
Faison, Florence. *See* Butler, Florence (Faison) [Mrs. Marion]
Faith and Fire Within Us, The (book), 8,580
Faith and Works (periodical), 15,209
Faith Is A Song (book), 11,984
Faith on the Frontier (book), 1,750
Fake, Effie J. [Mrs. Frederic L.], 3,919, 4,175
Falconer, Marjorie (Ward) [Mrs.] (1898-), **236**
Fales, De Coursey (1888-1966), **12,467**
Falkener, Mrs. William, 13,407
Falkener, William, **13,407**
Falkett, Camille, 6,917
Falkner, Virginia Louise, 4,482
Fall, Albert Bacon (1861-1944), **1,424**
Fall, Anne (Bacon) [Mrs. Philip S.], 5,285, **5,287,** 5,288, 5,297
Fall City Methodist Church (North Bend, WA), **17,157**
Fall City Study Club (WA), **17,158**
Fall, Mary. *See* Temple, Mary (Fall)
Fall, Mrs. Anne A., 5,285
Fall, Nancy, 5,285
Fall, Philip S., 5,285, 5,286, 5,287, 5,288
Fallandy, Yvette, 1,125
Fallin Family, 256
Fallin, Gertrude. *See* Cook, Gertrude (Fallin)
Fallon, Genevieve (1899-). *See* Steefel, Genevieve (Fallon) [Mrs. Lawrence D.] (1899-)
Falter, Sarah Nunes, 13,785
Falvey, Katherine (Mull) [Mrs. Lawrence (1904-). *See* Zastrow, Katherine (Mull) [Mrs. Lawrence] Falvey [Mrs. Ralph] (1904-)
Falvey, Lawrence, **4,910**
Familiar Astronomy; or, An Introduction to the Study of the Heavens (book), 1,403
Familiar Quotations (book), 11,516
Familiens Magasin (periodical), 8,738
Family, 1,860, 3,988, 7,453, 8,637, 10,073, 15,811, 17,991. *See also* Children; Divorce; Domestic relations; Family life education; Marriage; Mothers; Polygamy

Family, Afro-American, 5,471
Family and Children's Society (NJ), 11,000
Family Circle (periodical), 849, 6,101, 11,866
Family Comprehensive Care Program, 11,869
Family Counseling Service (OR), 14,671
Family Development Association, **8,639**
Family farms, 2,644, 8,947
  management, 2,208, 2,673, 7,640, 8,260, 10,445, 10,471
"Family Grows Up, The" (radio program), 11,756
Family law. *See* Domestic relations
Family life, 164, 8,518, 9,058, 13,221
Family life education, 6,490, 6,760, **8,048**, 8,633, 11,756, 12,724, 12,738, **13,506, 14,849**. *See also* Home economics; Marriage counseling; Sex instruction
Family of Isaac and Rebecca Harris, The (book), 940
Family planning, 1,596, 1,837, 3,690, **3,895, 5,842**, 6,788, **7,840**, 8,196, **8,672**, 11,857, 11,885, 11,932, **12,829, 14,013**, 15,176, 15,323, 15,802. *See also* Adoption; Birth control
Family Portrait (book), 2,219
Family Service Association of America, 6,928, 8,647
Family Service of St. Paul (MN), **8,645, 8,922**, 8,962, 9,442
Family social work, 4,051, 6,729, 6,788, **8,667**. *See also* Family life education; Marriage counseling
"Family Talk," 15,953
Family Visitor (periodical), 3,006
Family Welfare Association, 15,251
Family Welfare Association (Minneapolis, MN), 9,140
Family Welfare Association of America, Southern Institute, 6,729
Family Welfare Foundation, 6,364
Family Welfare Society (GA), 3,356
Family Welfare Society of Boston (MA), 6,729
Famous American Humorists (book), 11,309
Famous Old Euclid Avenue (book), 13,971
Fancher, Catherine (ca. 1880-1970s). *See* Vleit, Catherine (Fancher) [Mrs. Frank] (ca. 1880-1970s)
Fancher, Jannette. *See* Wilcox, Jannette Fancher [Mrs. Howard]
Fancher, Penelope, 12,504
Fancy's Knell (book), 6,006
Fannin massacre, 16,117
Fanning, Caroline E., 7,792
Fanning, Charlotte Fall, **5,288**
Fanny Kemble and the Lovely Land (book), 6,118
Fant, John Clayton (1870-1929), **9,558**
Fant, Mabel Beckett [Mrs. John Clayton] (?-1927), 9,558
"Fantasie Indienne" (music), 5,418
Far Eastern Commission, 11,902
Far West and the Rockies, The (book), 16,516
Far West Sketches (book), 12,481
Farah Manufacturing Company (TX), 15,987
Farbman, Ruth, **12,146**
"Farce, The" (ms), 6,722
Farewell to Fear (book), 6,019
Farey, Edith, 1,641
Fargo Community Welfare Association (ND), 13,686
Fargo Family, **1,291**
Fargo, Jerome Bonaparte, 1,291
Fargo, Louise (Mears), 17,687
Fargo, Martha (True) [Mrs. Jerome Bonaparte] (1834-73), 1,291
Fargo Masonic Grand Lodge Library (ND), 13,686
Faribault County Federation of Women's Clubs (MN), **8,416**
Faribault, Emily R., 8,936
Faribault Family (MN), **8,981**
Faribault Public Library (MN), 8,586
Faribault School for the Blind (MN), 8,586
Fariss, Mary Ward, **284**
Farjeon, Eleanor (1881-1965), 12,570
Farley, Angelina (Calkins) [Mrs. Winthrop] (1818-1900), **16,665**
Farley, James Aloysius, 255, 8,116, 11,576
Farley, Rosalie (La Flesche), 10,483
Farlow, William Gilson (1844-1919), **6,309**
Farm and Garden Magazine (periodical), 6,964
Farm Bureau, 8,517

Farm Camp (PA),
Farm Defense Program, 13,350
Farm Holiday Association, 8,517, 8,518
Farm income, 17,606
Farm Labor party, 1,654
Farm life, 66, 4,002, 4,294, 4,607, 4,610, 4,882, 4,904, 5,644, **5,665**, 7,624, 7,812, 8,154, **8,217**, 8,243, 8,343, 8,344, 8,352, 8,361, 8,514, 8,516, 8,704, 8,748, 8,787, 8,978, 9,026, 9,279, 9,938, 10,420, **10,790**, 10,807, 10,999, 11,259, **11,664**, 14,491, 16,530, 17,138, 17,199, 17,379, 17,641, 17,703, 17,720. *See also* Rural teenagers
  research, **11,562**
Farm management, 1,173, 1,885, 5,359
  records and correspondence, 9,538
Farm ownership, 14,202
Farm rents, 13,355
Farm tenancy, 1,653, 3,576
Farmer Consumer Reporter (bulletin), 11,769
Farmer, Eliza, **14,994**
Farmer, Eugenia B. [Mrs.] (1845-1926), **9,060, 9,061**, 9,327
Farmer, Foy Johnson, 13,643
Farmer, Hallie (1891-ca. 1960), **104**
Farmer-Labor Association of Minnesota, **9,062**
Farmer-Labor Party. *See* Democratic-Farmer-Labor Party
Farmer Labor Political Federation, 9,443
Farmer-Labor Women's Federation, 9,119
Farmer-Labor Women's Federation of Minnesota, 9,396
Farmer, Mrs. W. R., Jr., 13,638
Farmer, Sarah J., 7,044
Farmer, Susan (Bogardus) (?-1899), 2,973
Farmers, 185, 257, 2,614, **3,315, 3,320, 3,331,** 3,344, 3,757, **4,410, 4,425, 4,430, 4,651, 4,911,** 4,924, 4,952, 4,953, **4,955, 4,963,** 5,268, **5,672, 6,206,** 6,375, **7,826,** 8,157, **8,161, 8,302, 8,340, 8,344,** 8,370, 8,372, **8,403, 8,506,** 8,929, 9,155, 9,241, **9,370, 9,394,** 9,582, 9,592, 9,614, **9,760,** 9,803, 9,884, **9,917,** 10,466, 10,748, 11,414, 11,415, **11,723,** 11,780, 13,138, 13,471, **13,650,** 14,668, 14,808, 15,439, 15,440, **15,496, 15,529, 15,616,** 15,682, 15,932, 16,306, 16,357, **16,411, 16,416, 16,436, 17,007,** 17,183, **17,402, 17,472,** 17,540, **17,720, 17,724**
  18th-19th C, 5,803, 10,957, 14,981, 15,040, **15,626, 15,677, 15,678**
  19th C, **3,319,** 4,799, 5,262, 5,281, **5,420,** 5,549, **5,754,** 5,789, 7,618, 7,632, 7,647, **8,961,** 10,196, **10,959,** 12,199, 14,805, 14,835, **15,628, 15,694, 15,695**
  political activity, 8,518, 9,278, 9,443, 11,769
Farmers' Alliance (MN), 9,046, 9,415
Farmers cooperatives. *See* Agriculture, cooperative
Farmers Holiday Association, 8,144
Farmers Holiday Movement, 8,994
Farmers Institute (NY), 11,650
Farmers' institutes, 4,380, 4,920, 17,655
Farmers' organizations. *See* Agricultural societies
Farmers State Alliance (NC), **13,408**
Farmers Union, 8,518, 8,994
Farmers Union Cooperative Education Service, 13,720
Farmer's Wife, The (periodical), 9,103
Farmhouses, 4,380
Farmington Female Seminary (CT), 1,836
Farms, **1,233,** 8,456, 9,241, 10,905, **11,643**. *See also* Family farms; Farm ownership; Plantations; Ranches
Farnam, Mrs. Henry, 12,238
Farnam, Thornton J., 4,752
Farner, Eugene, 3,708
Farnham, Eliza Wood (Burhans) [Mrs. Thomas Jefferson] (1815-64). *See* Fitzpatrick Eliza Wood (Burhans) [Mrs. Thomas Jefferson] Farnham [Mrs. William] (1815-64)
Farnham, Jerusha Brewster (Loomis) [Mrs. Eli] (1806-72), **4,256**
Farnsley, Alexander, 16,443
Farnsworth, Charlotte (1825-47), **4,405**
Farnsworth, Martha O. (Van Orsdol) [Mrs. John] Shaw [Mrs. Fred C.], **5,218**
Farnsworth, Mary (Wing) [Mrs. Thomas S.]

(1822?-92). *See* Merriman, Mary (Wing) [Mrs. Thomas S.] Farnsworth [Mrs. Dwight] (1822?-92)
Farnum, Elizabeth (Whipple) [Mrs. Charles Augustus] (1843-ca. 1918), 9,437
Farnum, Lucretia (Bancroft) (1819-72), 11,514
Farnum, Mary Barker [Mrs. Walter] Allen [Mrs. Moses] (1784?-1861), **7,623**
Farnum, Moses, 7,623
Farquhar, Francis Peloubet (1887-1974), **473**
Farquhar, Sarah (Foulke) [Mrs. William]. *See* Emlen, Sarah (Foulke) [Mrs. William] Farquhar [Mrs. James]
Farquharson, B. F., 17,254
Farquharson, Mary [Mrs. B. F.] (1902-), **17,254**
Farr, Ann, 11,196
Farr, Clara, 16,648
Farr Family (SC), 15,473
Farr, Fred, **1,292**
Farr, Nancy B. Chase (1823-92), 16,911
Farragut, David, 6,567
Farragut, Virginia (Loyall) [Mrs. David], **6,567**, 12,431
Farrand, Beatrix (1872-1959), 303
Farrand, Margaret K. (Carleton) [Mrs. Livingston], 11,510, 11,541
Farrand, Max (1869-1945), **1,425**, 13,921
Farrar, Agnes Freeman (ca. 1870-?), 9,304
Farrar and Rinehart, 14,421
Farrar, Clarissa Palmer (1899-1963), **11,990**
Farrar, Geraldine [Miss] (1882-1967), **2,663**, 2,968, 3,326, 7,229, 7,267, 12,436, **12,468**, 16,149
Farrars, Professor, 6,902
Farrell Family, **12,516**
Farrell, Glenda (1904-), 11,907
Farrell, Hazel M., 324
Farrell, Mrs. Clinton P., 12,516
Farrell, Warren, 15,197
Farren, Catherine Mary "Kate" (Reignolds) [Mrs. Henry] (1836-1911). *See* Winslow, Catherine Mary "Kate" (Reignolds) [Mrs. Henry] Farren [Mrs. Alfred Erving] (1836-1911)
Farrer, Edith. *See* Steuenberg, Edith (Farrer)
Farrer, June Claudia. *See* Ahlstrom, June Claudia (Farrer)
Farrester Family (ND), 13,669
Farrington, Amanda. *See* Blake, Amanda (Farrington)
Farrington, Charlotte [Mrs. Daniel], 1,246
Farrington, Daniel, 1,246, 14,650
Farrington, Elizabeth Julia (Ellison) [Mrs. Nelson] Goltra [Mrs. Keeler] (1831-?), 606, **14,288**, 14,372, 14,628
Farrington, Elizabeth (Pruett) [Mrs. Joseph R.] (1898-), **3,622**
Farrington, Elizabeth R. (1898-?), 1,605
Farrington, Grace (1871-1935). *See* Gray, Grace (Farrington) [Mrs. James] (1871-1935)
Farrington, Mrs. Joseph, 5,150
Farrington, Myra (1835-1912). *See* Roberts, Myra (Farrington) [Mrs. Ephraim Peters] (1835-1912)
Farrington, Sara Payson (Willis) [Mrs. Charles H.] Eldredge [Mrs. Samuel P.] (1811-72). *See* Parton, Sara Payson (Willis) [Mrs. Charles H.] Eldredge [Mrs. Samuel P.] Farrington [Mrs. James] (1811-72)
Farris, Anna Leonard (Webb) [Mrs. Thomas C.] (1821-68), 7,677
Farris, Linda, **17,255**
Farris, Thomas C., 7,677
Farrow, Henry Patillo, **3,007**
Farrow, Tiera [Miss] (ca. 1880-), **5,175**
Farwell, Margaret M. [Mrs. John V., III], 11,827
Farwell, Mary M., 13,919
Fasano, Clara (1900-), **2,757**
Fashion, 3,228, 8,518, **12,086**, 13,322, 13,446, 13,480, 15,774, **16,210**
  pictorial works, 13,528
"Fashion" (drama), 6,787
Fashion Group, Inc., The, **12,086**
Fashion shows, 1,353
Fashionable Women Shipwreck (book), 10,933
Fast, Aganetha (1888-), **5,197**
Fast, Aganetha Becker [Mrs. Hermann J.] (1865-1930), 9,063

Fast, Hermann J., Family (MN), **9,063**
Fast, Louisa K. (1878-), 7,269
Fast, Marie K., 5,197
Fasts and feasts
  Islam, 10,927
  Judaism, 7,552
Fata Morgana (book), 9,738
Fate of the Fenwicks, The (book), 12,206
"Father Knows Best" (television program), 17,966
"Father Never Gets a Valentine" (story), 7,138
Father of the Bride (screen play), 17,799
Father Shipherd's Magna Carta (book), 14,123
Father Struck It Rich (book), 2,467
Fatherland Farm (MA), 7,628
Fatherless Children of Europe, 9,642
Fatherless Children of France, Inc., 945, 2,347, 9,037, 9,346
Fatigue, 2,667, 4,682
Fatigue and Efficiency (book), 2,359
Fatima and Her Sisters (book), 10,927
Faubion, Nina (Lane) (1884-1945), **14,362**
Faulkner, Charlotte "Lottie" Cornelia (1838-1909). *See* Flagg, Charlotte "Lottie" Cornelia (Faulkner) [Mrs. George F.] (1838-1909)
Faulkner, Elizabeth "Betsey" (1765-1813), 5,858
Faulkner Family (MA), **5,858**
Faulkner, Martha A. A. (Bixby), 5,858
Faulkner, Martha Abigail Adams (Bixby) [Mrs. Winthrop Emerson] (1806-97), 5,856
Faulkner, Mary (Wright) [Mrs. Winthrop] (1777-1855), 5,858
Faulkner, Rebecca (Keyes) [Mrs. Francis] (1736-1812), 5,858
Faulkner, Sophia Elizabeth (1849-1933). *See* Campbell, Sophia Elizabeth (Faulkner) [Mrs. Francis] (1849-1933)
Faulkner, William, 11,850
Faulks, Theodosia, 12,648
Faunt, Joan (Reynolds), 15,693
Fauntleroy, Ellinor. *See* Davidson, Ellinor (Fauntleroy) [Mrs. George]
Fauntleroy, Jane Dale (Owen), 434
Fauntleroy, Jane Owen, 4,637
Fauset, Crystal (Bird) (?-1965), **2,133**
Fauset, Jessie, 5,465
Faust, Elsie Ann (Akerley) [Mrs. Henry Jacob] (1832-83), **16,666**
Favill, Louise Baird, 17,593
Favill, Therese S., 17,593
Faville, Katharine, 8,045
Fawcett, Charles Edward (1869-1939), **9,064**
Fawdry, Dallas (1933-72), 10,151
Faxon, Henrietta (?-1951). *See* Pease, Henrietta (Faxon) [Mrs. Arthur Stanley] (?-1951)
Fay, Agnes (1884-). *See* Morgan, Agnes (Fay) [Mrs. Arthur Ivason] (1884-)
Fay, Annah C. (Harthan) [Mrs. Arthur] (1853-1938), **7,624**
Fay, Bernard, 5,525
Fay, Edwin Hedge, 16,155
Fay, Esther Merrill, 544
Fay, Harriet (Howard), 7,634
Fay House, 6,817
Fay, Lois (1883-1960). *See* Powell, Lois (Fay) (1883-1960)
Fay, Polly, 5,718
Fay, Sarah Elizabeth (Shields) [Mrs. Edwin Hedge] (?-1919), **16,155**
Fayerweather Family, 3,633
Fayerweather, Hannah (?-1790). *See* Winthrop, Hannah (Fayerweather) Tolman [Mrs. John] (?-1790)
Fayerweather, Mary Jane Kekulani (1842-1930). *See* Montano, Mary Jane Kekulani (Fayerweather) [Mrs. Benoni Richmond] Davison [Mrs. Andres Avelino] (1842-1930)
Fayerweather, Sarah (Harris), 1,874
Fayette County Associated Charities (KY), 5,302
Fayette County Tuberculosis Sanitarium (KY), 5,302
Fayhey, Nellie, **5,759**
Fealy, Maude Hawk (1881-1971), **1,774**, 1,779
Feamster Family, **2,328**
Feamster, Martha (Alderson) [Mrs. William] (1797-1885), 2,328

Feamster, Maude Inez (Simmons) [Mrs. Claude N.], 2,328
Feamster, Thomas L. (1829-1906), 2,328
Fear and Tenderness (book), 15,893
Fear Is the Enemy (book), 538
Fear, Lois, 14,363
Fear, Lucia S. (Drum) [Mrs. William H.], 14,476, **14,553**
Fear, Lyle, 14,363
Fear, William H., **14,363**
Fearing, Maria [Miss] (1838-1937), 86, **93**
"Feast of Good Things" (cookery), 4,661
Featherlegs, "Mother" (?-1879), 17,961
Featherston Family (GA), **3,323**
Featherston, Lucius H. (1814-86), **3,323**
Featherston, Mary. *See* Wright, Mary (Featherston)
Featherstone, Louise D. (1899-), 9,467
Fedde, Margaret (1883-), **10,605**
Fedde, Sister Elizabeth (1850-1921), **8,732**, 8,761, 8,768, 8,770
Federal Advisory Council, 11,958
Federal aid to education, 2,075, 2,680, 4,341, 8,058, 8,069, 8,093
Federal aid to health facilities, 2,677
Federal aid to higher education, 8,547
Federal aid to medical education, 11,885
Federal aid to the arts, **2,732, 2,742**, 2,743, 2,748, 2,754, 2,795, 8,905, 9,145, 9,462, 10,163, **11,143**, 11,480
Federal aid to theater, 17,281
Federal aid to vocational education, 4,382
Federal Board of Vocational Education, 6,236
Federal Civil Defense Administration, 6,939 officials and employees, 6,586
Federal Civil Defense Administration, National Women's Advisory Commission, 5,136
Federal Communications Commission, 64, 10,072, 11,909
Federal Council of Churches of Christ in America, 9,219
Federal Court of Appeals, 2,163
Federal Educational Camp for Unemployed Women (CO), 1,798
Federal Emergency Relief Administration, 6,420 officials and employees, **2,743**
Federal Emergency Relief Administration, Women's Division, officials and employees, 9,779
Federal Emergency Relief Administration, Workers Service Program, 6,893
Federal Food Administration, executive committee, 16,128
Federal government, 8,443, 13,454, 17,268 information services, **2,672**
Federal Housing Administration, 194
Federal Industrial Relations Commission, 2,382
Federal Land Bank (Grantsville, UT), 16,510
Federal magistrates, 945, **2,336, 11,076, 13,210**, 16,171, 17,251. *See also* Judges
Federal Negro Theatre Project, 2,872
Federal Office of Vocational Rehabilitation, officials and employees, **6,919**
"Federal Old-Age and Survivor's Insurance for Employees of the College of New York" (thesis), 6,683
Federal Power Commission, officials and employees, 11,495
Federal Public Housing Administration, officials and employees, 11,501
Federal Records Council, officials and employees, 5,157
Federal Reserve banks, 11,896, 13,617
Federal Screw strike, 8,088, 8,120
Federal Suffrage Association of the United States, 6,435, 17,616
Federal Union, Inc., 7,885
Federal Woman's Award, 13,259
Federal Works Agency, officials and employees, **11,883**
Federally Employed Women, 13,864
Federated Club (New Concord, OH), 14,118
Federated Council of Art Education, 12,544
Federated Department Stores, **11,859**
Federated Economics Club (Neenah-Menasha, WI).

See Neenah-Menasha Federated Woman's Club (WI)
Federated Garden Clubs of Missouri, 10,057
Federated Garden Clubs of New York, 12,869
Federated Garden Clubs of West Virginia, 17,468
Federated Republican Women's Club (MO), **9,856**
Federated Women's Clubs. *See* General Federation of Women's Clubs
Federated Women's Clubs (Waukegan, IL), 4,451
Federated Women's Club (Muscatine, IA), 5,087
Federated Women's Club (LA), 5,445
Federation for Child Study. *See* Family Development Association
Federation for Sex Hygiene. *See* American Social Health Association
Fédération Internationale de Documentation, 11,937
Federation News (IA), 4,748
Federation of Business and Professional Women, 4,094
Federation of Clubs (IN), **4,562**
Federation of Cornell Women's Clubs, 11,508
Federation of Democratic Women's Clubs, 10,032
Federation of Handicapped Citizens, 5,193
Federation of Jewish Philanthropies of New York, 7,531
Federation of Jewish Women's Organizations. *See* Pittsburgh Conference of Jewish Women's Organizations (PA)
Federation of Jewish Women's Organizations (Cleveland, OH). *See* Jewish Community Federation, Women's Organization (Cleveland, OH)
Federation of Modern Painters and Sculptors, 2,738, 2,758, 12,892
Federation of Motion Picture Councils, 17,326
Federation of North Dakota Business and Professional Women's Clubs, 13,706
Federation of Norwegian Women's Societies, 8,777
Federation of Settlements and Neighborhood Centers, 9,270
Federation of Texas A&M Mothers' Clubs, **16,194**
Federation of the Sisters of Mercy of America, 15,233
Federation of Western Outdoor Clubs, 781, 17,267
Federation of Woman Dentists, 13,997, 15,095, **15,120**
Federation of Woman's Boards of Foreign Missions, 1,170
Federation of Women High School Teachers, 3,818
Federation of Women's Clubs (GA), 3,198
Federation of Women's Clubs (MI), 8,019
Federation of Women's Clubs (Washtenaw County, MI), **7,780**
Federation of Women's Clubs (Ypsilanti, MI), **7,781**
Federation of Women's Clubs (MN), 9,287
Federation of Women's Clubs of Greater Cleveland (OH), **13,922**
Federation of Woolen and Worsted Workers Union, 3,450
Federations, financial (social service), 945, 1,237, **3,905**, 4,078, **4,079**, 4,440, **9,104**
Federations, financial (social service), Jewish, **4,037**
Fedorova-Fokine, Alexandra, 12,364
Fedou, Mother M. Anglea, 9,695
Feeds, analysis, 13,531
Feibleman, Gertrude, 8,963
Feigin, Dorothy Lubell [Mrs.] (1903-69), **2,758**
Feiker, Elizabeth "Bessie" (Campbell) [Mrs. Frederick] (1878-1974), 7,151
Feil, Helen R., 11,837
Fein, Leah Gold (1910-), **13,739**
Feinberg, Ann (Kaplan) Williams, 12,705
Feineman, Ethel, 932
Feingold, Miriam (1941-), **17,630**
Feinter, Fannie Bloomfield, 3,828
Fejes, Claire (1920-), **134**
Felch, Alpheus, 7,722
Felch, Ella M. (1860-), 9,394
Feldman, Dorothy [Mrs. Joe E.] (ca. 1950-), **17,904**
Felician Sisters, Assumption of Our Lady Provincial House (NM), **11,232**
Feliciana archives, 5,425
Felion, Phebe, **7,782**
Felland, O. G. (1853-1938), **8,807**

Fellows, Albion (1865-1933). *See* Bacon, Albion (Fellows) [Mrs. Hilary Edwin] (1865-1933)
Fellows, Alma. *See* Latimer, Alma (Fellows)
Fellows, Annie (1863-1931). *See* Johnston, Annie (Fellows) [Mrs. William "Will" L.] (1863-1931)
Fellows, Anstice, 7,032
Fellows, Dora. *See* Haynes, Dora (Fellows) [Mrs. John Randolph]
Fellows, Eunice C. [Miss] (1802-83), 7,032
Fellows, Joseph, 1,661
Fellows, Josephine (1892-1975). *See* Gomon, Josephine (Fellows) (1892-1975)
Fellows, Sophia Bullock "Auntie" [Mrs. Joseph], 1,661
Fellowship of Reconciliation, 4,089, 7,868, 7,923, 10,193, 14,393, 17,262
Fellowship of Southern Churchmen, 2,879
Fellowship of the Concerned, 3,353
Fellowships, 9,360
Felmley, David (1857-1930), **4,305**
Fels, Joseph, 14,995
Fels, Mary [Mrs. Joseph] (1907-40), 14,995
Felshaw, Mary (Nelson) Johnson (1858-?), 16,968
Felt, Abigail Adams (Shaw) [Mrs. Joseph Barlow] (1790-1859), 2,571
Felt, Louie (Bouton) [Mrs. Joseph H.] (1850-1928), **16,667**, 16,673
Felt, Margaret, **1,713**
Felton, Katharine Conway (1873-1940), 396
Felton, Rebecca Ann (Latimer) [Mrs. William Harrell] (1835-1930), 3,007, **3,008**, 3,362, 3,585
Felton, William Harrell, 3,007, 3,008
Female Academy (Albany, NY), 9,277
Female Academy (Yorkville, SC), 15,543
Female African School Society (DE), **2,044**
Female Anti-Slavery Society (MA), **7,072**, 15,069
Female Anti-Slavery Society of Brooklyn (CT), **1,902**
Female Association of Philadelphia (PA), **15,277**, 15,285
Female Auxiliary Bible Society of New Haven (CT), 2,009
Female Benevolent Society (DE), **2,045**, 2,047
Female Benevolent Society (Brimfield, MA), 7,517
Female Benevolent Society (Danvers, MA), 7,006
Female Benevolent Society (Lynn, MA). *See* Ladies Benevolent Society (Lynn, MA)
Female Benevolent Society (Newton, MA), 7,095
Female Benevolent Society of Carlisle (PA), **14,749**
Female Benevolent Society of Cumberland (ME), **5,605**
Female Bible Class (Goshen, CT), 1,926
Female Bible Society (DE), **2,046**, 5,745
Female Bible Society (NY), 12,324
Female Bible Society (PA), 15,221
Female Bible Society of Annapolis (MD), **5,760**
Female Cent Society of Lebanon (CT), **1,903**
Female Charitable Society (NY), **12,204**
Female Charitable Society of Cranbury (NJ), 10,956
Female Christian Home (MD), **5,761**
Female City Mission of Baltimore (MD), **5,762**
Female College (SC), 15,571
Female College (Athens, TN), presidents, 5,362
Female Collegiate Institute (MO). *See* Adelphai College (MO)
Female Collegiate Institute (Buckingham, VA), 2,635
Female Colonial Society (Wilmington, DE), 5,745
Female Colonization Society, 2,038
Female Domestic Missionary Society (Danvers, MA), 7,001
Female Eclectic Institute (Frankfort, KY), faculty, 5,287
"Female Education" (ms), 6,845
Female Foreign Missionary Society of South Preston (CT), **1,904**
Female Fragment Society (Coventry, CT), 7,517
Female Free Masons, 4,697
Female Friendly Society of Coventry (CT), 7,517
Female Hebrew Benevolent Society (VA), 13,781
Female High School (Louisville, KY), **5,340**
Female Hospitable Society (Wilmington, DE), 5,745
Female Liberation, 17,975
Female Poets of America (book), 5,930
"Female Preachers in the Advent Christian Denomination" (dissertation), 3,742

Female Religious and Biographical Reading Society (Salem, MA), **7,373**

Female Seminary, The (New Haven, CT), 2,003

Female Society (Danvers, MA), 7,001

Female Society of Philadelphia for Relief and Employment of the Poor, **14,841**

Female Society of Vernon (CT). *See* Charitable Society of Vernon (CT)

Female Temperance Society (West Bradford, MA), **7,374**

Female Temperance Society of Saco and Biddleford (ME), **5,698**

Female Tract Society (MI), **8,325**

Female Tract Society (PA), **14,996**

Female Union School Association (NJ), **11,094**

Feminine Mystique, The (book), 6,582

Feminism, 300, 827, 1,561, 2,523, 3,988, 4,238, 4,241, 6,789, 7,257, 7,283, 8,659, 13,398, 14,637, 15,252, 17,680

"Feminism and Literature" (lecture), 15,197

"Feminism-Cause or Effect?" (article), 1,279

Feminism, radical, 17,583

Feminism: The Essential Historical Writings (book), 6,079

Feminist Coordinating Council (WA), 4,241, **17,256**

Feminist credit unions, 15,821

Feminist Press, 7,324

Feminist Voice, The (newspaper), **4,086**

Feminists, 63, **1,279**, 1,483, **1,652**, **1,952**, **2,569**, **2,633**, **2,636**, 2,716, **3,778**, **3,821**, **3,827**, 4,241, **4,322**, 4,867, **5,458**, **5,949**, **5,963**, 6,009, **6,333**, **6,374**, 6,408, **6,508**, 6,582, 6,587, 6,633, **6,846**, **6,911**, **6,954**, 7,045, 7,189, **7,216**, **7,223**, **7,249**, **7,289**, 7,293, 7,998, 8,000, 8,114, **8,362**, **8,495**, **8,603**, **8,624**, 8,721, **8,855**, **9,127**, **9,546**, **9,647**, **10,180**, 11,134, 11,776, **11,804**, 11,821, **11,904**, 12,123, **12,597**, 12,619, **12,704**, 12,765, 13,468, 15,116, **17,233**, 17,256, **17,365**, 17,367, **17,583**, **17,652**, 17,975

Feminists, Afro-American, **4,132**

Feminists, The, 17,975

Feminists, Turkish, 7,191

Fence Corners (book), 3,159

Fenceless Range, The (book), 10,487

Fenichel, Carol, 15,138

Feningston, Phyllis (1896-). *See* Collier, Phyllis (Feningston) [Mrs. John] (1896-)

Fenn, Jane, 15,290

Fennell Family, 12,485

Fenno, Ann M. (1839-81?), 12,469

Fenno, August, 12,469

Fenno Family, **12,469**

Fenno, Henry, 12,469

Fenno, Maria E. *See* Hoffman, Maria E. Fenno [Mrs. Ogden]

Fenno, Mary Eliza. *See* Verplanck, Mary Eliza Fenno [Mrs. Gulian C.]

Fenollosa, Mary McNeill, 39

Fenton, Beatrice (1887-), **12,895**

Fenton, Fleur (1910-), **10,071**

Fenton, Henry Lee (1863-1930), **14,554**

Fenton, Susan J., 309

Fenton, Thelma (1893-), 668, 1,068

Fenwick, David P., 1,800

Fenwick, Elizabeth (pseudonym). *See* Way, Elizabeth Fenwick

Fenwick, Elizabeth [Mrs. John] (1767-1840), 12,206

Fenwick Family (NY), **12,206**

Fenwick, Harriet, 5,752

Fenwicke, Sarah, 15,526

Fenyvessy, Florence. *See* Belinson, Florence (Fenyvessy) [Mrs. Benjamin]

Feodorovna, Alexandra, Empress, 12,497

Ferber, Edna (1887-1968), 556, 691, 2,360, 2,499, 3,825, 3,927, 3,994, 4,155, **5,092**, 10,992, 11,812, 11,970, 12,367, 12,499, **17,795**, 18,021

Ferdinand, King of Spain, 2,944

Ferebee, Sarah Elizabeth. *See* Grandy, Sarah Elizabeth (Ferebee) [Mrs. J.] Lamb [Mrs.]

Fergus Falls State Hospital (MN), 8,458

Fergus, Maria (?-1881). *See* Pizzini, Maria Fergus [Mrs. John] (?-1881)

Ferguson, A. E., **8,326**

Ferguson, Agnes Beveridge (1868-1924), **5,102**

Ferguson, Blanche (Smith) [Mrs. James Henry, Jr.], 3,290, **5,763**

Ferguson, Charlotte [Mrs. Duncan], 9,302

Ferguson, Elizabeth Graeme [Mrs. Henry Hugh] (1737-1801), 2,621, **14,753**, 14,884, **14,997**, **14,998**, 15,084

Ferguson, Elsie, 12,637

Ferguson, Elva Shartel [Mrs.Tom], 6,568

Ferguson Family, 9,372

Ferguson Family, 3,099

Ferguson, Frances (Hand) [Mrs. Robert M.] (1907-), 6,987

Ferguson, Hallie (1890-1969). *See* Davis, Hallie (Ferguson) Flanagan (1890-1969)

Ferguson, James, 15,229

Ferguson, James E., 16,014

Ferguson, James H., Jr., 5,763

Ferguson, Kate Lee [Mrs. Samuel Wragg] (1841-post 1911), **5,413**

Ferguson, Lucia, **6,568**

Ferguson, Lydia Dale Estey [Mrs. William Henry] (1825-95), 9,065

Ferguson, Margaret, 7,567

Ferguson, Mary L., 14,515

Ferguson, Mary X., 10,211

Ferguson, Mary X. *See* Barrett, Mary X. (Ferguson) [Mrs. John Walton]

Ferguson, Matilda. *See* Todd, Matilda (Ferguson) [Mrs. Roger North]

Ferguson, Miriam Amanda "Ma" (Wallace) [Mrs. Jim] (1875-1961), 16,313

Ferguson, Samuel Wragg, 5,413

Ferguson, Sarah J., **8,327**

Ferguson, Sue Ramsey (Johnston) [Mrs. Raymond S.] (1897-), **13,249**

Ferguson, Tom, 6,568

Ferguson vs. Austin American and Webb, 16,391

Ferguson, William Henry (1816-57), Family (MN), **9,065**

Fergusson, Erna (1888-1964), **11,214**, **11,223**

Ferlinghetti, Lawrence, 12,894

Fern, Fanny (pseudonym). *See* Parton, Sara Payson (Willis) [Mrs. Charles H.] Eldredge [Mrs. Samuel P.] Farrington [Mrs. James] (1811-72)

Fernandez, Josefa Peralta de (1847-88), 1,531

Fernbach, Frank, 15,332

Fernbank Science Center (GA), 3,316

Ferrar, Geraldine, 12,321

Ferré, Ella, 474

Ferree School of Art (NC), 13,446

Ferrell, Conchata, **11,860**

Ferrell, Mrs. Theodore F., 4,697

Ferrer Colony (NJ), 1,654

Ferrer, Helene. *See* Harding, Helene (Ferrer)

Ferries, 17,205

Ferril, Alice MacHarg, 1,751

Ferris, Ada E., 9,679

Ferris, Ann, 2,045

Ferris, Anna M. [Miss] (1815-90), **2,047**

Ferris, Benjamin G., **16,939**

Ferris, Donna [Mrs.], **8,275**

Ferris, Eddy R., 10,240

Ferris, Edith, 2,045

Ferris Family (NY), 11,583

Ferris, Fanny, 2,060

Ferris, George Washington Gale, Sr., 10,698

Ferris Girls' School (Yokohama, Japan), 5,088

Ferris, Gratia F., **9,066**

Ferris, Helen [Miss] (1891-1969), **11,485**

Ferris Institute, 7,710

Ferris, Isaac (1798-1873), **12,470**

Ferris, Margaret [Mrs. Eddy R.] (?-1889), **10,240**

Ferris, Mary L. D., 2,596

Ferris, Mrs. Morris P., 12,088, **12,201**

Ferris, Rachel, 11,318

Ferris, Ruth, 9,857

Ferris wheel, 10,698

Ferris, Woodbridge N., 7,710

Ferry, Amanda (White) [Mrs. William Montague], 8,164

Ferry, Elisha P., 17,226, 17,293

Ferry, Eliza (ca. 1851-1936). *See* Leary, Eliza (Ferry) [Mrs. John] (ca. 1851-1936)

Ferry Family (KY), **5,320**

Ferry, Frances A. (1827-60). *See* Castle, Frances A. (Ferry) (1827-60)

Ferry, Priscilla [Miss], **11,584**

Ferry, William Montague, 8,164

Fertility, human, 6,227, 12,358

Fertilizers and manures, 4,410

Fessenden, William Pitt, 17,992

Fessler, Ruth. *See* Lippman, Ruth (Fessler)

Festival of Missouri Women in the Arts (1974), 9,927

Festivals, 234, 1,263, 1,387, 1,545, 1,751, 4,384, 4,981, 5,644, **8,479**, 8,725, 9,828, **11,751**, **14,112**. *See also* Music festivals; Pageants

Fetter, Elizabeth Head (1904-72), **14,364**

Fetus, research, 11,932

Fetzer, Elizabeth (1909-). *See* Bates, Elizabeth (Fetzer) (1909-)

Fetzer, John, 16,780

Feuchette, Cherry Noble, 5,657

"Feud, The" (ms), 14,663

Feudel, Alma Wright [Mrs. Arthur], 1,751

Feuilletons, 12,219

Feves, Gertrude, 14,497

Few Are Chosen (book), 6,710

Few, Catharine, 12,315

Few, Mary, 3,389

Few, Mary Reamey Thomas [Mrs. William Preston], 11,879

Few Memories, A (book), 5,339

Few, William (1748-1829), **3,389**

Few, William Preston, 11,879

Fiber plants, 4,807

Fibers, 2,673

Ficher, Mrs. Edgar S., 17,425

Fick, Nellie Mitchell, **17,257**

Ficke, Gladys [Mrs. Arthur], 3,988

Ficklin, Eleanor. *See* Connaway, Eleanor (Ficklin) [Mrs. John Waldo]

Fiction, 1,750, 8,485. *See also* Children's stories; Dime novels; Historical fiction; Novelists; Western stories

Fiddler's Association, 10,418

"Fidelia" (pseudonym). *See* Griffitts, Hannah [Miss] (1727-1817)

Fidelity Title and Trust Company (PA), 15,222

Fidelity Trust Company, 16,243

Field, Amanda, 1,641

Field, Anne Keith (Hayden) [Mrs. Christian] Fader [Mrs. J. C.] (1835-96), 535

Field, Augusta. *See* Chase, Augusta (Field) [Mrs. Ethan Allen]

Field, Betty (1918-), 11,907

Field, Charles Kellogg, 11,956

Field, Edward, 11,983

Field, Edward Salisbury, 1,167

Field, Eleanor Kingsland (1819-1909). *See* Jay, Eleanor Kingsland (Field) [Mrs. John] (1819-1909)

Field, Elizabeth (1891-), 7,506, 7,508, 7,509

Field, Emilia. *See* Ashburner, Emilia (Field) [Mrs. William]

Field, Eugene (1850-95), 9,889, 9,941, **10,148**, **10,162**, 16,174

Field Family, 11,956

Field Family (MA), **7,506**

Field Family (NY), 12,020

Field, Henriette Desportes (1813-75), 7,506

Field, Herta, 6,106

Field hospitals. *See* Hospitals, military; Medicine, military; Red Cross; War, Relief of sick and wounded

Field, Isobel (Osbourne) [Mrs. Joseph Dwight] Strong [Mrs. Edward Salisbury] (1858-1953), **475**, 820, 1,167, 1,525, **1,579**

Fiedel, Jennie (Hayes), 14,060

Field, Jessie, 4,920

Field, Julia (Comstock) [Mrs. Eugene] (1857-1937), 10,148

Field, Kate. Mary Katherine Keemle Field (1838-96), 5,919, **5,924**, 5,934, 5,954, 5,966, 10,162, 12,172, 12,394, 14,062, **16,668**, **16,940**

Field, Martha (Smallwood), 6,882

Field, Mary (1836-1943). *See* Garner, Mary (Field) [Mrs. William, Jr.] (1836-1943)

Field, Mary Hannah (Bacon) (1833-1912), 317

Field, Mary Hyde [Mrs. William R.], 11,585
Field, Mary Katherine Keemle [Miss] (1838-96). *See* Field, Kate. Mary Katherine Keemle Field (1838-96)
Field, Mrs. John, 12,203
Field Museum of Natural History, Board of Trustees (Chicago, IL), **3,953**
Field Museum of Natural History, Department of Anthropology (Chicago, IL), **3,951**
Field Museum of Natural History, Division of Planning and Development, Women's Board (Chicago, IL), **3,952**, 3,953
Field, Noel, 6,106
Field, Rachel Lyman. [Mrs. Arthur Siegfried] Pederson (1894-1942), 569, 5,448, **5,450**, 5,694, **6,569**, 7,506, 7,508, 7,509, 14,399, 16,150
Field, Roswell M., 9,941
Field, Ruth [Mrs. Marshall], 11,827
Field, Sara. [Mrs. Ehrgott] Bard [Mrs. Charles Erskine Scott] Wood (1882-1974), **476**, 635, 642, 831, 859, 873, 896, 945, 1,081, 1,082, 1,321, 1,507, 8,001
Field, Stanley, 3,953
Field, Susan Kilteridge (Osgood) [Mrs. Moses], **12,207**
Field, William R., **11,585**
"Field Work in College Education," 11,306
Fielde, Adele Marion [Miss] (1839-1916), **14,877**
Fielden Family (SC), **15,472**
Fielden, Henry Wemyss (?-1921), 15,472
Fielden, Julia (McCord) [Mrs. Henry Wemyss], 15,472
Fielding, Anna Marie (1800-81). *See* Hall, Anna Marie (Fielding) (1800-81)
Fielding, Elizabeth, **3,504**
Fielding, Mercy Rachel (1807-93). *See* Thompson, Mercy Rachel (Fielding) [Mrs. Hyrum] Smith [Mrs. Robert Blashel] (1807-93)
Fielding, Merdean, 10,191
Fields, Annie (Adams) [Mrs. James Thomas] (1834-1915), 1,426, 1,963, 2,370, **5,925**, 5,933, 5,966, 5,975, **6,570**, 6,659, 6,714, 6,870, 7,044, 8,375, 10,853, 11,742, 12,022, 12,403
Fields, Bertram, 11,782
Fields, Bruce Eric (1959-), 11,782
Fields, Daisy B., **6,571**
Fields, Dorothy (1905-74), 11,907
Fields, E. C., 15,288
Fields, Gracie (1898-), 11,907
Fields, Gulielma, 15,288
Fields, James Thomas (1817-81), **1,426**, 5,925, 5,933, 5,950, 5,966, 6,870
Fields, Joseph A., 9,769
Fields, Mrs., **14,999**
Fields, Mrs. B. O., 6,955
Fields, Paul Adam (1957-), 11,782
Fields, Verna, 950
Fields, William, 13,264
Fiero Family (NY), **11,427**
Fiesta in Mexico (book), 11,223
Fiester, Fanny Gray Kimball, 9,323
Fife Family (WA), **17,406**
Fife, Hilda M., 5,650
Fife Hotel (Tacoma, WA), 17,406
Fife, William H., 17,406
Fifer, Florence (1877-1960). *See* Bohrer, Florence (Fifer) [Mrs. Jacob A.] (1877-1960)
Fifer, Joseph, 3,749, 4,349
Fifteen Regiment New Jersey Volunteer Veterans Association, 11,092
Fifteen Years of a Dancer's Life (book), 4,277
Fifteenth Pelican, The (book), 17,731
Fifth Congressional District Committee on Political Education (GA), 3,443
Fifth Federal Reserve District, savings division, education, 13,617
Fifth New Hampshire Volunteers, 10,819
Fifty-first Iowa Mother's Prayer Circle, **4,757**
Fifty-first Iowa Regiment, 4,757
Fifty-second Georgia Infantry, Company C, 3,320
Fifty-sixth Georgia Infantry, 3,323
Fifty Years Club (UT), **16,414**
"Fig Tree, The" (story), 16,164
Fight for Freedom Committee, 11,555

Fight Inflation Together, **1,014**
Figure painting, 2,733, 2,768
Fiji Islands, American travelers in, 7,488
Fike, Ellie, 10,107
Fike, Ellie [Miss], **10,106**
Fike, Ellie (1861-?), **9,858**
Fike, Lucy Cimbaline, 10,106
Fike, Lucy Cimbaline [Mrs.], **10,107**
Filaria and filariasis, 14,459
Filbey, Edward J. (1879-1959), 4,385
Filbey Family (IL), **4,385**
Filbey, Mary L. [Mrs.], 4,385
Filene, Edward A., 6,873
Filiatrault, Shirley, 9,140
Filion, June Parsons, 7,151
Filipino Community Association (CA), 1,525
Fillmore, Abigail (Powers) [Mrs. Millard] (1798-1853), 11,345, 12,757, **12,867**
Fillmore, Caroline C. [Mrs. Millard], 11,345, 12,757
Fillmore, Mary Abigail (1832-54), 11,345, 11,436
Fillmore, Millard (1800-74), 1,435, 5,750, **11,345**, 11,434, 11,436, **12,757**, 12,867
Films. *See* Moving-pictures
Filmstrips, **8,524**
Filsinger, Sara Teasdale [Mrs. Ernst B.]. *See* Teasdale, Sara. [Mrs. Ernst B.] Filsinger (1884-1933)
Filson, Bertha Steinbach [Mrs.], **17,438**
Filson Club, The (KY), 5,342
Filter Centers, 5,737
Final Analysis, The (drama), 12,367
Final Report on the Woman Pilot Program, 5,311
"Final Triumph of Jeremiah Prophet Elizah, The," 5,526
Finance, public, 7,138
Financiers. *See* Capitalists and financiers
Finberg, Barbara, 11,845
Finch, Adelaide Victoria [Miss] (1864-?), **5,577**, 5,609
Finch, Alida Elizabeth (1871-1954), **4,257**
Finch, Florence (1858-1939). *See* Kelly, Florence (Finch) [Mrs. Allen P.] (1858-1939)
Finch, Harold C., 3,678
Finch, Harriet, **11,586**
Finch, Julia (1862-1952). *See* Gilbert, Julia (Finch) [Mrs. Cass] (1862-1952)
Finch, Robert Voris (1909-59), 13,131
Finding Hardware Company (CO), 1,732
Findlay, Mary, 15,308
"Fine and Mellow" (song), 5,530
Fine Art of Nourathar (Light-Color Playing), The (book), 2,366
Fine Art Opera (Chicago, IL), **3,838**, 3,878
Fine Art Opera Club (Chicago, IL). *See* Fine Art Opera (Chicago, IL)
Fine Art Opera Company (Chicago, IL), 3,838
Fine Arts Group of A&M Women's Social Club, **16,195**
Fineman, Irving, 6,920
Finger painting, **13,122**
Finholt, Elea, **4,716**
Finholt, Mark, **4,716**
Finitimi Society (Oberlin, OH), **14,121**
Finkelstein, Minna, 11,774
Finland, women, status of, 6,981
Finlay, Helen [Miss], 9,741
Finley, Emma, 9,574
Finley, Georgia E. (1872-1943), **4,258**
Finley, Howard J., 11,522
Finley, John E., 17,624
Finley, Louise [Miss], 15,980
Finley, Louise [Mrs. Kellogg B.], 464
Finley, Vesta (1909-), 13,176
Finnegan, Elizabeth, 1,534
Finneran, Betty, 8,060
Finney, Charles Grandison (1792-1875), 326, 11,616
Finney, J. M. T., 5,806
Finney, Mrs. Charles (1832-1910), 13,683
Finnish-American Historical Society, 9,127
Finnish-American newspapers, 9,503
Finnish-Americans, 5,829, **8,183**, 8,185, 8,455, 9,498, **9,500**, 9,502, 9,503, 9,506
social life and customs, 9,467
Finnish Apostolic Lutheran Church (Aberdeen, SD), 15,839

Finnish Lutheran Church, 8,185
Finnish Socialist party, 9,175
Finnochietti, Rosa Marie (1878-1959). *See* Levis, Rosa Marie (Finnochietti) (1878-1959)
Finns in Minnesota, 9,462
FINS Club (Denver, CO), 1,700
Fire (drama), 328
"Fire and Ice" (poem), 1,508
Fire Bell in the Night (book), 12,908
Fire-departments, 3,215
finance, 14,720
Fire drills (in schools), 8,486
Fire fighters, 1,086, 10,013, 10,111, 11,863
"Fire Guard" (story), 12,644
Fireman, Bert, 210
Fires, 362, 391, 405, 471, 544, 551, 612, 685, 729, 755, **771**, 772, 1,254, 1,281, 1,308, 1,311, **1,339**, 1,569, 3,802, **3,812**, 3,834, 3,897, 5,644, 7,160, 7,376, 7,877, 12,554, 13,682, 15,475
Fires, Francis (1812-63), 13,149
Firkins, Ina Ten Eyck [Miss] (1866-1937), **8,564**, 8,600, 9,067
Firkins, Oscar W. (1864-1932), Family, 8,602, **9,067**
Firman House (Chicago, IL), **4,087**
First aid in illness and injury, study and teaching, 13,993
First Baptist Church (New Haven, CT), 1,999
First Baptist Church (Atlanta, GA), 3,267
First Baptist Church (Rochester, IN), Woman's Missionary Society, 4,661
First Baptist Church (Boston, MA), Benevolent Circle and Society, **7,099**
First Baptist Church (Framingham, MA), Female Mite Society, **7,101**
First Baptist Church (Salem, MA), Ladies Foreign Missionary Society, **7,396**
First Baptist Church (Watertown, MA), Female Foreign Mission Society, **7,100**
First Baptist Church (Watertown, MA), Female Missionary Society, **7,098**
First Baptist Church (Watertown, MA), Ladies Home Mission Sewing Circle, **7,103**
First Baptist Church (Detroit, MI), 8,018
First Baptist Church (Anoka, MN), 8,389
First Baptist Church (Northfield, MN), Baptist Women's Missionary Society, **9,068**
First Baptist Church (St. Paul, MN), **9,070**
First Baptist Church (St. Paul, MN), Home Mission Circle, 9,070
First Baptist Church (St. Paul, MN), Ladies Benevolent Society, 9,070
First Baptist Church (St. Paul, MN), Ladies Society, 9,070
First Baptist Church (St. Paul, MN), Woman's Missionary Society, 9,070
First Baptist Church (St. Paul, MN), Young Woman's Tuesday Club, 9,070
First Baptist Church (Waseca, MN), Women's Foreign Missionary Society, **9,069**
First Baptist Church (McComb, MS), 9,697
First Baptist Church (Omaha, NE), 10,499
First Baptist Church (Elyria, OH), Women's Baptist Home Mission Society, **13,923**
First Baptist Church (Dewey, OK), 14,173
First Baptist Church (Laramie, WY), 17,962
First Baptist Church of Christ (Ithaca, NY), 11,587
First Baptist Church of Hartford Women's Missionary Society (CT), 1,889
First Baptist Church of Ithaca (NY), Northrup Circle, 11,587
First Baptist Church of Ithaca (NY), Woman's Mission Circle and Missionary Society, 11,587
First Baptist Church of Ithaca (NY), Woman's Union, 11,587
First Baptist Church of Ithaca (NY), Young People's Society of Christian Endeavor, 11,587
First Baptist Church of Jackson (MS), Ladies Aid Society, **9,659**
First Baptist Church of Macon (GA), Women's Missionary Society, 3,455
First Baptist Church of Middletown (CT), Young Women's Class Sunday School Meetings, 1,890
First Baptist Church of Shrewsbury-Red Bank (NJ), Ladies' Aid Society, 10,900

First Baptist Society of Barre (MA), 5,894
First Benevolent Association of Hebrew Ladies (IL), **13,782**
"First Bill of Rights for Women, The," 12,575, 12,597
First Capitol Restoration Committee (MO), 10,194
First Christian Church (Hannibal, MO), 9,832
First Church (Brookline, MA), 6,833
First Church (Waltham, MA), 6,857
First Church (Omaha, NE), Woman's Missionary Society, **10,589**
First Church, Congregational (Danvers, MA), **7,001**
First Church of Christ, Scientist, 10,800, 10,808
First Congregational Church (Lockeford, CA), 1,632
First Congregational Church (Oakland, CA), 703
First Congregational Church (Burlington, IA), 4,829
First Congregational Church (MA) 6,817
First Congregational Church (Amherst, MA), Ladies Benevolent Society, 4,779
First Congregational Church (MI), 8,162
First Congregational Church (MI), Ladies' Aid Society, **8,255**
First Congregational Church (Marine, MN), 9,071
First Congregational Church (Marine, MN), Ladies Church Aid Society, 9,071
First Congregational Church (Marine, MN), Ladies Union League, 9,071
First Congregational Church (Marine, MN), Marine Mite Society, 9,071
First Congregational Church (Marine, MN), Marine Sewing Society, 9,071
First Congregational Church (Moorhead, MN), Ladies' Union, 9,365
First Congregational Church, UCC (Fremont, NE), **10,460**
First Congregational Church, UCC (Fremont, NE), Women's Missionary Society, 10,460
First Congregational Church (Friend, NE), **10,461**
First Congregational Church (Friend, NE), Dorcas Federated Missionary Society. *See* First Congregational Church (Friend, NE), Women's Fellowship
First Congregational Church (Friend, NE), Women's Missionary Society. *See* First Congregational Church (Friend, NE), Women's Fellowship
First Congregational Church (Friend, NE), Women's Fellowship, 10,461
First Congregational Church (Grant, NE), Ladies Aid Society, **10,464**
First Congregational Church (Weeping Water, NE), **10,550**
First Congregational Church (Weeping Water, NE), Woman's Missionary Society, 10,550
First Congregational Church (Portland, OR), 14,508
First Congregational Church (Jericho Centre, VT), Ladies Cent Society, 6,169
First Congregational Church (Jericho Centre, VT), Woman's Foreign Missionary Society, 6,169
First Congregational Church (Jericho Centre, VT), Woman's Home Missionary Society, 6,169
First Congregational Church (Jericho Centre, VT), Women's Missionary Society, 6,169
First Congregational Church of Atkinson (NH), 7,662
First Congregational Church of Norwich (CT), Ladies Home Missionary Society, 1,890
First Congregational Church of Oakland (CA), Women's Missionary Society, 309
First Congregational Church of Preston (CT), Ladies Benevolent Society, 1,889
First Congregational Church of Suffield (CT), Woman's Missionary Society, 1,889
First Day Women Suffrage Stamp Ceremonies (MA), 7,180
First English Lutheran Church (Cedar Rapids, IA), Ladies Aid Society, 4,959
First English Lutheran Church (Cedar Rapids, IA), Society of Woman's Home and Foreign Missions, 4,959
First Evangelical Church (Aberdeen, SD), 15,839
First Families of Virginia, 9,870
First Female Beneficial Society of Philadelphia (PA), 14,953
"First Fourth of July, The" (story), 7,090
First Gentleman of Europe, The (drama), 12,409
First Georgia Volunteers, 3,247

First Illinois Artillery, 4,362
First in Peace (drama), 2,170
First Independent Church (Philadelphia, PA), 15,122
First International Congress on Mental Hygiene, 6,748
First International Women's Year Conference (1977, SC), 15,430
First Jobs of College Women—Report of Women Graduates, Class of 1957 (bulletin), 2,703
First Kentucky Regiment, Women's Auxiliary, Battery A, 138th Field Artillery, **5,369**
"First Ladies of Mississippi, The", 9,709
First Lady of the Renaissance (ms), 6,053
First Lutheran Church (Cedar Rapids, IA), Women's Missionary Society, 4,959
First Lutheran Church (Cedar Rapids, IA), Young Women's Missionary Society, 4,959
First Lutheran Church (Crowley, LA), **5,433**
First Lutheran Church (Duluth, MN), 9,116
First Lutheran Church board (Morris, MN), 8,696
First Methodist Church (Evanston, IL), 4,127
First Methodist Church (Newton, IA), Women's Home Missionary Society, 4,744
First Methodist Church (Garden City, KS), Wesleyan Service Guild, 5,179
First Methodist Church (Frankfort, KY), 5,307
First Methodist Church (Mansfield, LA), 5,554
First Methodist Church (Ann Arbor, MI), Ladies Aid Society, 7,972
First Methodist Church (Grand Rapids, MI), 7,973
First Methodist Church (Minneapolis, MN), Mnemosyne Club, 9,101
First Methodist Church (Minneapolis, MN), Woman's Foreign Missionary Association, 9,448
First Methodist Church (Greenville, MS), 6,901
First Methodist Church (Aberdeen, SD), 15,839
First Methodist Church of Bloomington (IL), 3,762
First Methodist Church of Hartford (CT), Ladies Benevolent Society, 1,889
First Methodist Episcopal Church (NE), Woman's Foreign Missionary Society, **10,577**
First Methodist Episcopal Church (NE), Woman's Home Missionary Society, **10,583**
First Michigan Cavalry, Company H, 8,372
First Minnesota Conservation and Development Congress (MN, 1910), 9,372
First Missouri Cavalry, Company B, 4,961
First National Bank (Normal, IL), 3,751
First National Bank (MI), 8,333
First National Bank (Austin, MN), 9,435
First National Congress on Optimum Population and Environment (1970), 4,082
First National Radical Women's Conference, 17,583
First North Carolina Colored Volunteers, 6,394
First Parish Unitarian Church (Barre, MA), 5,894
First Parting (book), 7,718
First Pennsylvania Artillery, Battery E, 4,817
First Person Plural (book), 12,362
First Presbyterian Church (San Leadro, CA), Ladies Aid Society, 1,387
First Presbyterian Church (DC), Ladies Association, 2,609
First Presbyterian Church (Ann Arbor, MI), Women's Foreign Missionary Society, **7,898**
First Presbyterian Church (Blissfield, MI), 7,900
First Presbyterian Church (Blissfield, MI), Afternoon Circle, 7,900
First Presbyterian Church (Blissfield, MI), Ladies Church Society, 7,900
First Presbyterian Church (Blissfield, MI), Priscilla Circle, 7,900
First Presbyterian Church (Blissfield, MI), Sewing Society, 7,900
First Presbyterian Church (Blissfield, MI), Women's Association, 7,900
First Presbyterian Church (Blissfield, MI), Women's Home Missionary Society, 7,900
First Presbyterian Church (Blissfield, MI), Young Ladies Guild, 7,900
First Presbyterian Church (Evart, MI), Women's Missionary Society, 7,863
First Presbyterian Church (Lapeer, MI), Women's Missionary Society, 7,863
First Presbyterian Church (Saline, MI), **7,901**

First Presbyterian Church (Ypsilanti, MI), **7,903**
First Presbyterian Church (Jackson, MN), 9,709
First Presbyterian Church (Oxford, MS), 9,596
First Presbyterian Church (Helena, MT), Ladies Aid Society, **10,304**
First Presbyterian Church (Cranbury, NJ), **10,956**
First Presbyterian Church (Princeton, NJ), 11,153
First Presbyterian Church (Buffalo, NY), 12,759
First Presbyterian Church (Elmira, NY), Elizabeth Guild, 11,443
First Presbyterian Church (SC), Ella C. Davidson Auxiliary, **15,592**
First Presbyterian Church (Aberdeen, SD), 15,839
First Presbyterian Church (Bloomsburg, VA), Mary Vance Auxiliary Society, **14,727**
First Presbyterian Church (Cheyenne, WY), 17,962
First Presbyterian Church of Allegheny (PA), 14,833
First Presbyterian Church of Cranbury (NJ), Ladies Benevolent Society, 10,956
First Presbyterian Church of Evanston (IL), 3,822
First Presbyterian Church of Oregon, 14,606
First Presbyterian Church Woman's Auxiliary (SC), **15,593**
First Presbyterian Congregation of Cranbury (NJ), Female Benevolent Society, 10,956
First Society of Free Inquirers (Boston, MA), 4,809
"First Steamboat on Western Waters, The" (article), 9,763
First Swedish Methodist Episcopal Church (St. Paul, MN), **9,072**
First Swedish Methodist Episcopal Church (St. Paul, MN), Ladies Aid Society, 9,072
First Swedish Methodist Episcopal Church (St. Paul, MN), Sunday School Board, 9,072
First Unitarian Church (San Francisco, CA), **1,362**
First Unitarian Church (San Francisco, CA), Society for Christian Work, **1,363**
First Unitarian Church (Iowa City, IA), Woman's Alliance, 4,959
First Unitarian Church (Ann Arbor, MI), **7,952**
First Unitarian Church (Ann Arbor, MI), King's Daughters, 7,952
First Unitarian Church (Ann Arbor, MI), Ladies Union, 7,952
First Unitarian Church (Pittsburgh, PA), 15,252
First Unitarian Society (Minneapolis, MN), 9,392
First United Evangelical Church (Omaha, NE), Woman's Foreign Missionary Society, **10,578**
First United Methodist Church (Newark, NJ), **11,095**
First United Methodist Church (Newark, NJ), Ladies Aid Society, 11,095
First United Presbyterian Church (Pittsburgh, PA), 15,226
First Universalist Church (Acton, MA), Social Circle, **5,859**
First Ward Industrial School (NJ), 11,067
First White Women Over the Rockies (book), 1,790, 17,373, 17,423
First Woman's Congress (1873), 7,183
Firth, Lila Hannah, **17,258**
Fischel, Edna (1898-1970). *See* Gellhorn, Edna (Fischel) [Mrs. George] (1878-1970)
Fischer, Alice. [Mrs. William Harcourt] King (1869-1947), **12,471**
Fischer, Bella. *See* Resek, Bella (Fischer)
Fischer, Katherine Browning (1858-1960). *See* Miller, Katherine Browning (Fischer) (1858-1960)
Fischer, Lillian. [Mrs. Frank] Farley, 12,582
Fischer, Mrs. Aaron, 10,200
Fish, Adelaide (1905-). *See* Cumming, Adelaide (Fish) Hawley (1905-)
Fish and game licenses, 17,842
Fish and Game Protective Association (OH), 14,004
Fish, Asa (1790-1861), 1,986
Fish, Asa (1828-?), 1,986
Fish, Benjamin (1834-?), 1,986
Fish, Caroline, 477
Fish, Catherine. *See* Stebbins, Catherine (Fish)
Fish, Catherine Delphina "Della" (1864-1934). *See* Smith, Catherine Delphina "Della" (Fish) [Mrs. Joseph West] (1864-1934)
Fish, Charles, 477
Fish, Clara. *See* Roberts, Clara (Fish)
Fish, Cornelia, 477

Fish, Dorothy (1889-1971). *See* Kerr, Dorothy (Fish) [Mrs. William John] (1889-1971)
Fish, Eliza Lewis [Mrs. Joseph], 16,915
Fish Family (CA), **477**
Fish Family (CT), **1,986**
Fish, Fanny D. (1839-?), 1,986
Fish, Hannah (1823-?), 1,986
Fish, Horace P., 8,574
Fish inspection, 9,467
Fish, James D. (1819-?), 1,986
Fish, Jean E. (Hirsch) [Mrs. Horace P.] (1893-1974), **8,574**
Fish, Joseph, 16,915
Fish, Joseph (1705 or 1706-81), 7,656
Fish, Julia (Kean) [Mrs. Hamilton], 12,237, 15,717
Fish, Juliette G., 1,505
Fish, Lafayette, 477
Fish, Leah, 17,288
Fish, Mary C., **478**
Fish, Prudence (1830-?), 1,986
Fish, Prudence (Dean) [Mrs. Asa] (1799-?), 1,986
Fish, Sands H. (1821-?), 1,986
Fish, Silas (1825-?), 1,986
Fishbourn, William, 12,563
Fishburn, Mrs. M. P., 17,631
Fisher, Albert Kenrick (1856-1948), **2,329**
Fisher, Ann Eliza (1839-?). *See* Latourette, Ann Eliza Fisher [Mrs. Lyman Daniel Cornwall] (1839-?)
Fisher, Ann Eliza George, 15,002
Fisher, Ann "Nancy" (Ambler) (1772-?), 2,248, 17,126
Fisher, Anne, **17,259**
Fisher, Anne, 1,245
Fisher, Anne (Benson) [Mrs. Walter Kenrick] (1898-), 2,329
Fisher, Annie **1,845**
Fisher, Annie E. (1871-). *See* Johnson, Annie E. (Fisher) Swanson [Mrs. Aron] (1871-)
Fisher, Annie Pleasants (1823-?). *See* Harris, Annie Pleasants Fisher [Mrs. Wilbur] Dallam [Mrs. John W.] (1823-?)
Fisher, Charlotte Vinette Gardner, 7,632
Fisher, Clara E. (Brown) [Mrs. George] (1850-1919), 4,701, 4,704
Fisher, Clyde, 14,235
Fisher, Dorothea Frances (Canfield) [Mrs. John] (1879-1958), 2,263, 2,336, 3,983, 3,994, 5,870, 6,770, 7,227, 7,229, 7,718, 11,837, 12,111, **12,473**, 12,570, 15,311, **16,980**, 17,010, 17,043
Fisher, Dorothy (Canfield) (1879-1958). *See* Fisher, Dorothea Frances (Canfield) [Mrs. John] (1879-1958)
Fisher, Elizabeth (Ingersoll) [Mrs. Sidney George] (1815-72), **15,002**
Fisher, Elizabeth (Rhoads) [Mrs. Samuel W.] (1770-96), 15,000
Fisher, Elizabeth Thérèse (1810-90). *See* Baird, Elizabeth Thérèse (Fisher) [Mrs. Henry Samuel] (1810-90)
Fisher Family (IA), **4,911**
Fisher Family (IA), **4,701, 4,704**
Fisher, Florence (1873-?), 4,704
Fisher, Frances Christine (1846-1920). *See* Tiernan, Frances Christine (Fisher) [Mrs. James Marquis] (1846-1920)
Fisher, Frederick (1882-1938), **6,012**
Fisher, Galen M., 11,572
Fisher, George, 4,701, 4,704
Fisher, Gustavus (1815-93), **10,971**
Fisher, Guy (1892-1965?), **14,555**
Fisher, Hannah (Rodman) (1764-1819), 15,294
Fisher, Hiram, 2,329
Fisher, Ida A. Graham Wart [Mrs. Guy], 14,555
Fisher, Jane A. (1829-97). *See* Lees, Jane A. (Fisher) [Mrs. Isaiah W.] (1829-97)
Fisher, Julia (Johnson) [Mrs. William] (1814-85), **13,009**
Fisher, Katharine, A., 2,596
Fisher, Katharine (Dummer) (1892-1961), **6,544**
Fisher, Lillian E., **479**
Fisher, Louise A., **1,714**
Fisher, Louise B., 17,125

Fisher, M. F. K. (1908-), 6,465, **6,572**
Fisher, Margaret L., 3,290
Fisher, Mary [Mrs. Irving M.], 4,911
Fisher, Mary Frances (Kennedy) (1908-), 569
Fisher, Mary (Rodman) (1781-1813), 15,294
Fisher, Mary (Thompson) [Mrs. Clyde] (1895-), **14,235**
Fisher, Minnie. *See* Cunningham, Minnie (Fisher) [Mrs. B. J.]
Fisher, Mrs. Irving, 138
Fisher, Pearl, 3,290
Fisher-Price Toys, 11,434
Fisher, Rachel (Joy) (?-1868). *See* Mills, Rachel (Joy) Fisher (?-1868)
Fisher, Rebecca Jane (Gilleland) [Mrs. Orceneth] (1831-1926), 16,014
Fisher, Ruth (Freeman) (1906-), **6,138**
Fisher, Ruth Page (1900?-), **17,965**
Fisher, Sally, 4,911
Fisher, Samuel W. (ca. 1765-1817), **15,000**
Fisher, Sarah (Logan) [Mrs. Thomas] (1751-96), 14,847, 14,966, **15,001**
Fisher, Sarah Logan [Mrs. William Wister] (1806-91), **14,754**
Fisher Sidney George (1809-71), **15,002**
Fisher, Susan [Miss] **13,010**
Fisher, Susan Elizabeth (Townsend) [Mrs. Hiram] (1817-1906), 2,329
Fisher, Sydney George, 15,002
Fisher, Te Ata (Thompson) [Mrs. Clyde] (1895-). *See* Fisher, Mary (Thompson) [Mrs. Clyde] (1895-)
Fisher, Theodore Willis (1827-1914), 6,214
Fisher, Walter Kenrick (1878-1953), 2,329
Fisher, Welthy Blakesley (Honsinger) [Mrs. Frederick] (1879-), **6,012**
Fisher, William, 13,009
Fisheries, 9,467, 11,209
Fishermen, 6,375
Fishing, 5,410, 8,167, 8,927, 9,467, 12,184
Fishing Creek Church (SC), 15,623
Fishing nets, 7,640
Fisk, Andrew J., 10,305
Fisk, Charity Babcock, 5,735
Fisk, Elizabeth (Chester) [Mrs. Robert E.] (1846-1927), 10,305
Fisk Family (MT), **10,305**
Fisk, James L., 10,305
Fisk Jubilee Singers, 122, 2,150
Fisk Normal School (TN). *See* Fisk University (TN)
Fisk, Robert E., 10,305
Fisk, Ruth (Peck) [Mrs. Wilbur] (1795-1884), 1,976
Fisk Stagecrafters (TN), 15,925
Fisk Union Church, 5,477
Fisk University (TN)
    deans, 15,922
    faculty, 5,455, 5,461, 5,477, 15,924, 15,925
    students, 5,529
Fisk University dining hall, 15,919
Fisk University, Second Annual Institute on Race Relations (1945), 5,460
Fisk, Van Hayden, 10,305
Fisk, Wilbur (1792-1839), **1,982**
Fiske, A. S., 11,750
Fiske, Annette (1873-1953), 6,164
Fiske, Eliza Wilkins [Mrs.], 9,737
Fiske, Fidelia [Miss] (1816-64), 7,500
Fiske, Frances (1819-73). *See* Lincoln, Frances (Fiske) [Mrs. Daniel Waldo] (1819-73)
Fiske, Harrison Grey, 12,474
Fiske, Helen Maria (1830-85). *See* Jackson, Helen Maria (Fiske) [Mrs. Edward Bissell] Hunt [Mrs. William Sharpless] (1830-85)
Fiske, Isabel. *See* Conant, Isabel (Fiske)
Fiske, Jennie (McGraw) [Mrs. Willard] (1840-81), **8,328**, 11,524, **11,588**, 11,645
Fiske, Marie Augusta "Minnie Maddern" (Davey) [Mrs. LeGrand] White [Mrs. Harrison Grey] (1865-1932), 536, **2,330**, 2,384, 2,610, 9,057, 10,029, **12,474**, 12,496, 12,535, 12,556, 12,659, 16,149
Fiske, Minnie Maddern (1865-1932). *See* Fiske, Marie Augusta "Minnie Maddern" (Davey) [Mrs.

LeGrand] White [Mrs. Harrison Grey] (1865-1932)
Fiske, Mrs. C. W., 11,558
Fiske, Samuel Augustus, 6,226
Fiske, Turbese Lummis, **1,580**
Fiske, Willard, 11,558, 11,645
Fiske, Zoe, 11,750
Fiste, Louise. *See* Bombeck, Erma [Mrs. William] (1927-)
Fitch, Asa (1809-79), **11,589**
Fitch, Caroline M., 7,514
Fitch, Clyde, 12,559
Fitch Creche nursery (NY), 11,339
Fitch, Emma Monroe, 14,123
Fitch Family (CA), **480**
Fitch Family (NY), 11,440
Fitch, Florence M. (1875-1959), **14,122**
Fitch, Frank, 14,122
Fitch, Geraldine, 1,564
Fitch, Henry Delano (1799-1849), **480**, 724
Fitch, Josefa (Carrillo) [Mrs. Henry Delano] (1810-?), 480, 724
Fitch, Lucy (1865-1937). *See* Perkins, Lucy (Fitch) (1865-1937)
Fitch, Mary R. *See* Jenks, Mary R. (Fitch) [Mrs. I. Henry]
Fitch, Rachel Louise (1878-), 11,541, **14,365**
Fitch, Sarah Elizabeth. *See* Poates, Sarah Elizabeth (Fitch)
Fitts, Robert, 7,150
FitzGerald, Alice [Mrs. William], 11,830
Fitzgerald, Alice Louise Florence (1874-1962), 5,735, **5,764**
Fitzgerald, Claudia, 4,727
Fitzgerald, Clifford K. (1896-1971), 1,183
Fitzgerald, Eleanor, 8,311
Fitzgerald, Ella (1918-), **6,013, 17,796**, 18,001
Fitzgerald, F. Scott, 1,451, 9,467, 11,160
Fitzgerald, Florence (McCartney) [Mrs. Clifford K.], **1,183**
Fitzgerald, Frances Scott, 11,160
Fitzgerald, Geraldine, **12,367**
Fitzgerald, Ida F. (Jefferis), 1,505
Fitzgerald, James, 17,350
Fitzgerald, John (?-1799), 2,425
Fitzgerald, John J., 2,972
Fitzgerald, M. Eleanor, 12,701, 12,703
Fitzgerald, Zelda (Sayre) [Mrs. F. Scott], 113, 1,451, 9,467, 11,156, **11,160**
Fitzhugh, Elizabeth Lee [Miss], **16,353**
Fitzhugh, Mary Darby, **12,475**
Fitzmaurice, Mrs. John, 4,923
Fitzpatrick, Eliza Wood (Burhans) [Mrs. Thomas Jefferson] Farnham [Mrs. William] (1815-64), 869, 1,312, 12,403
Fitzpatrick Family, 79
Fitzpatrick, John (1872-1946), **3,839**
Fitzwater, Fanny Fern, 2,542
Fitzwilliam, Sarah E. (Raymond) [Mrs. Francis J.], 3,745, 3,764
Five Civilized Tribes, 1,475, 14,241
Five Families and Eight Young Men (book), 15,950
Five Little Kachinas (book), 11,222
Five Towns Community House (Lawrence, NY), **8,646**
"Five Towns, The: A Community Self-Portrait," 8,642
Fiveash, Virgie (Hill) [Mrs. Wilburn] (1915-), 237
"Fixed Stars, The; or, The Goddess of Truth and Justice," 2,299
Fjoslien, Mrs. Tena (1872-), 8,709
Flachmeier, Jeanette H. [Mrs. W. A.], **16,067**
Flack, Astrid. *See* Forde, Astrid (Flack) [Mrs. G. O.]
Flacks, Mildred, 11,774
Flagellants, The (book), 6,067
Flagg, Charlotte "Lottie" Cornelia (Faulkner) [Mrs. George F.] (1838-1909), 5,858
Flagg, Mary Magdalen, **12,338**
Flagg, Mildred (Buchanan) (1886-), **6,014, 6,573**
Flagg, Miss, 2,502
Flags, 1,786, 2,615, 9,748, 13,374, 13,576, 17,985
    Confederate States of America, 15,954
Flagstad, Kirsten (1895-1968?), **1,293**

Flagstaff City-Coconino County Public Library Oral History (AZ), **156**
Flagstaff Cooperative Newspaper Indexing Project, 151
Flagstaff Women's Club (AZ), 152
Flaherty, Frances (Hubbard) [Mrs. Robert J.], 12,015
Flaherty, Marie (1874-), **10,241**
Flaherty, Marjorie. *See* Paisley, Marjorie (Flaherty)
Flaherty, Robert J., 11,989, 12,015
Flake, Lucy Hannah (White) [Mrs. William Jordan] (1842-1900), **16,512, 16,669**, 16,903
Flake, Roberta (1877-). *See* Clayton, Roberta (Flake) (1877-)
"Flambeau" (ms), 15,876
Flame on the Frontier (book), 10,399
Flaming Arrow, The (opera), 1,022
Flanagan, Emma Cecelia (Rector) [Mrs. Edward E.] (1870-1964), **4,474**
Flanagan, May G. (1874-1958), **10,242, 10,306**
Flanagan, Michael A., 10,306
Flancher incident (Mountain Meadow, UT), 16,430
Flanders, Caroline W. (1873-1970), 14,556
Flanders Family (OR), **14,556**
Flanders, George Hall (1821-92), 14,556
Flanders, Helen (Hartness), 17,010
Flanders, Jesse Evan, 14,615
Flanders, Lillian (Metschan) [Mrs. Jesse Evan], 14,615
Flanders, Marie Louise (?-1958), 14,556
Flandrau, Charles E., 9,045
Flandrau, Charles M., 194
Flanery, Dawn. *See* Parker, Dawn (Flanery) [Mrs. H. Leslie]
Flanery, Dew. *See* Haffler, Dew (Flanery) [Mrs. Whayne W.]
Flanery, John Elliott, 5,313
Flanery, Mary (Elliott) [Mrs. William Harvey] (1867-1933), **5,313**
Flanery, Merle. *See* Howerton, Merle (Flanery) [Mrs. Davis Monroe]
Flanery, William Harvey, 5,313
Flanner, Hildegarde, 317, 635, 1,081, 1,082
Flanner, Janet [Miss] (1892-), **2,331**, 14,377
Flannery, Agnes Veronica (1879-), **4,758**
Flanningan, Minnie, 826
Flash (periodical), 5,737
Flat Top Sheep Company (ID), **3,682**
Flathead Tribe, land tenure, 10,272
Flatt, Anna Hall, 7,920
Flatt, Caroline, 3,764
Flaubert, Gustave, 2,339
Flavelle, Mary E. (1847-1914), **3,840**
Flax, 8,596, 14,278, 14,653, 16,628
Flebbe, Beulah Marie (Dix) [Mrs. Georg Heinrich] (1876-1970), 6,406, 12,360, **14,366**
Flebbe, Georg Heinrich, 14,366
Flechine, Mollie Steimer, 12,589
Fleck, Ella Conover (Gray) [Mrs. H. Willard] (1875/76-1972), **1,820**
Fledderus, Mary L., 7,315, 8,142
Fleetwood, Ann Maria, 2,332
Fleetwood, Christian Abraham (1840-1914), **2,332**
Fleetwood, Edith, 2,332
Fleetwood, Kate, 13,309
Fleetwood, Sara (Iredell) [Mrs. Christian Abraham] (1811-1908), 2,332
Fleischman, Doris Elsa (1891-). *See* Bernays, Doris Elsa (Fleischman) [Mrs. Edward L.] (1891-)
Fleischman, Raoul, 14,377
Fleishhacker, Delia, 601
Fleming, Benjamin (1806-91), 17,459
Fleming, E. McClung, 12,395
Fleming Family (WV), **17,459**
Fleming, Florence, 17,459
Fleming, Greta Wolfe [Mrs.], **8,228**
Fleming, Honora [Mrs. John], 11,620
Fleming, John, 11,620
Fleming, John Giles, **13,409**
Fleming, Leathia (Cousins) [Mrs. Thomas W.] (1876-1963), 3,799, **13,924**
Fleming, Margaret [Mrs. John Giles], 13,409
Fleming, Mary Louise Robson [Mrs.] (ca. 1917-), **2,891**

Fleming, Myrtha [Miss], 13,566
Fleming, Thomas W., 13,924
Fleming, Thurston Worth (1846-?), 17,459
Fleming, Vivian Minor [Mrs.], 17,064
Fleming, Williamina "Mina" Paton (Stevens) [Mrs. James Orr] (1857-1911), **6,280**, 6,285
Flemming, T. P., 8,588
Fles, Berthold, 14,455
Fletcher, Alice Cunningham [Miss] (1838-1923), 876, 1,340, 2,298, 2,512, 2,716, 2,722, 2,837, **2,838**, 6,323, 6,324, 6,541, **10,459**, 10,483
Fletcher, Benjamin F., 14,557
Fletcher, Calvin (?-1866), 4,603
Fletcher, Calvin, Jr., 4,602
Fletcher, Charlie May Simon [Mrs. John Donald], **15,900**
Fletcher, Dix, 3,390
Fletcher, Edna, 8,462
Fletcher, Elizabeth (1816-?), 7,637
Fletcher, Ella May (1874-1959), **8,497**
Fletcher, Ellen Louise [Mrs.] (1841-?), **10,243**
Fletcher, Ellsworth Benjamin, 14,557
Fletcher, Emilie C. [Mrs.] (1847-?), **17,632**
Fletcher, Emily (185?-1927), 4,602
Fletcher, Emily (Beeler) [Mrs. Calvin, Jr.] (1838-1910), **4,602**
Fletcher Family (OR), **14,557**
Fletcher, Fannie [Miss], 288
Fletcher farm (VT), 12,716
Fletcher, Grace (Nies) (1895-), **6,015**
Fletcher, Grace (1781-1828). *See* Webster, Grace (Fletcher) [Mrs. Daniel] (1781-1828)
Fletcher, Ifan Kyrle, 12,364
Fletcher, Inglis (1888-1969), **13,267**, 13,511
Fletcher, J. I., 7,816
Fletcher, John Elliot, **14,558**
Fletcher, John Gould, 12,035
Fletcher, L. G. M., 8,497, 8,498
Fletcher, Laurel Louise. *See* Tarkington, Laurel Louise (Fletcher) [Mrs. Booth]
Fletcher, Lois Lorraine, 14,557
Fletcher, Louisa Warren Patch (1808-84) [Mrs. Dix], **3,390**
Fletcher, Lucille, 1,026
Fletcher, Lydia Bates, **3,391**
Fletcher, Mary Augusta, 3,683
Fletcher, Mary T. (MacMurray) [Mrs. Donald A.], **12,869**
Fletcher, Ruth, 14,558
Fletcher, Ruth, 3,391
Fletcher, Sarah. *See* Jones, Sarah (Fletcher) [Mrs. Albert]
Fletcher, Sarah (Hill) [Mrs. Calvin] (1801-54), **4,603**
Fletcher, Sarah Hill (1854-?), 4,602
Fletcher, Susan (Bricelen) [Mrs. Henry Lewis] (ca. 1838-?), **260**
Fletcher, Susan Marshman Dyer [Mrs. L. G. M.] (1845-1941), 8,497, **8,498**
Flewellen, Elvira. *See* Shingleur, Elvira (Flewellen) [Mrs. J. A.]
Flexner, Abraham (1866-1959), **2,333**
Flexner, Anne (Crawford) [Mrs. Abraham], 2,333
Flexner, Carolin A., 11,875
Flexner, Eleanor, 2,333
Flexner, Helen (Thomas) [Mrs. Simon], 14,889
Flexner, Hortense (1885-), 6,023
Flexner, Jean. *See* Lewinson, Jean (Flexner) [Mrs. Paul]
Flexner, Simon (1863-1946), 14,745, **14,889**
Flexner, Vivian, 14,579
Flick, Beatrice Ludlow, 1,356
"Flicker and the Flame, The" (poem), 18,021
Flickinger Family (PA),
Fligelman, Fanny (1884-1961). *See* Brin, Fanny (Fligelman) (1884-1961)
Flight into America's Past: Inca Peaks and Maya Jungles (book), 2,197
Flight radio operators, 11,861
Flinn, Helen (1895-?), **13,740**
Flinn, Maria, 10,901
Flint, Annie, 5,861
Flint, Catharine (Dean) [Mrs. Waldo] (1802-69), 7,625
Flint-Goodridge Hospital, 5,470

Flint, Hallie Rienzi, **16,248**
Flint High School (MI), 7,829
Flint, Margaret (1891-1960). *See* Jacobs, Margaret Flint [Mrs. Lester W.] (1891-1960)
Flint, Maria Florilla. *See* Hamblen, Maria Florilla (Flint)
Flint Parliamentary Law Club (MI), **8,179**
Flint, Seneca R., 693
Flint, Waldo (1794-1879), **7,625**
Flippin, Kay, 1,348
Floating Bear (newsletter), 12,894
Floating Hospital Nashville (MS), 1,251
Floating University, 14,378
Floersheim, Bertha (1865-1952). *See* Rauth, Bertha (Floersheim) [Mrs. Enoch] (1865-1952)
Flood control, 4,627, 9,733, 9,800
  law and legislation, 11,695
Floods, 1,901, 3,302, 4,500, 5,644, 9,551, 9,694, 10,686, 13,729, 14,656, 14,694, 14,860, **14,861,** 15,869
Floore, Florence C. [Mrs.], 16,072
Flora (slave), 3,300
Flora (slave, SC), 4,239
Flora Macdonald College (NC), 13,436, 13,446, 13,584, 13,588
Flora Stone Mather College (OH)
  alumnae, **13,890**
  faculty, **13,894**
  students, **13,886**
Flora Stone Mather College (OH), Alumnae Association, **13,885**
Floral College (NC), 13,437, 13,439, 13,470
Florance, Julia (1898-). *See* Newell, Julia (Florance) [Mrs. Duncan H.] (1898-)
Florance, William E., 11,014
Flora's Dictionary (book), 5,824
Florence, Annie, 4,695
Florence Crittenton Anchorage (Chicago, IL), 4,088
Florence Crittenton Association (Chicago, IL), 4,130
Florence Crittenton Association of America. *See* Child Welfare League of America
Florence Crittenton Home (San Francisco, CA), 832
Florence Crittenton Home (CO), 1,672
Florence Crittenton Homes Association. *See* Child Welfare League of America
Florence Crittenton League, 7,546
Florence Crittenton Refuge Home (Portland, OR), **14,367**
Florence Crittenton Services of Columbus (OH), **13,995**
Florence Insurance and Banking Company (AL), 28
Florence Mission (NJ), **10,972**
Florence Nightingale International Foundation, 6,136
Florence Nightingale Medal, 17,686
Florence Synodical Female College (AL), 28
Florence Wesleyan University (AL), 28
Florer, Alice [Miss], 10,626
Flores, Florence (1903?-), **6,137**
Floriculture, 17,137
Florida 2,657, **2,869, 2,881,** 2,897, 2,903, 2,907, 2,916, **2,944,** 9,699, 12,247, 13,780
  abortion, legal aspects, 1,984
  Afro-Americans, **2,880, 2,945, 2,946, 2,947, 2,948**
  air bases, 2,910, 9,709
  art societies, 2,894
  Audubon societies, 2,886
  authors, **2,918, 2,928, 2,932,** 13,007
  bills, legislative, 6,944
  businessmen, 2,929
  businesswomen, **2,922**
  catalogs, college, **2,935**
  cattle breeding, 2,922
  Choctaw Indians, 2,883
  church societies **2,937**
  church societies, Episcopal, **2,913**
  citizens associations, 3,283
  Civil War, 13,518
    societies, Confederate, 2,955
  clubs, 2,875, **2,885,** 2,886, 2,955
  collectors and collecting, **2,909**
  college and school periodicals, **2,933, 2,936**
  college librarians, 2,927
  college presidents, 2,884, 2,927
  college students, Afro-American, 2,880

college teachers, 2,884, 2,927, 2,931
colonial period, 2,275, 2,553
constitution, 2,925, 2,926
contemplative orders, **2,871**
court records, 2,873, 2,926
deans (in schools), 2,927, 2,931
diaries and journals, 12,942
education, experimental methods, 4,151
educational associations, **2,898**, 12,937
educators, **2,911**
elections, 2,953
folklorists, 2,882
food, 2,947
freedmen, 2,919, 2,945, 7,610
gambling, 2,948
gardening, societies, etc., **2,899**, 2,901
Girl Scouts, 2,905
government librarians, 2,931
governors, 2,320, 2,868, 2,870, 2,882, 2,886, **2,942,** 2,950, **2,953**
greek letter societies, 2,939
high school teachers, 2,868
historians, **2,900**
historical museums, 2,888
historical societies, 2,900
hospitals, 2,945
insurance agents, 2,941
journalists, **6,944**
lawyers, **2,873, 2,887, 6,944**
legislators, 2,886, **2,925,** 2,931, **6,381**
legislators, Afro-American, 2,940
library associations, **2,924**
literary societies, **2,914**
lumber trade, 2,915
lynching, prevention of, 3,279
massacres, 2,952
mental health law, 6,381
mentally handicapped, institutional care, 2,886
monasteries, 2,871
monasticism and religious orders for women, Catholic, **2,919, 2,920**
nursing schools, 6,133
oral history, **2,880, 2,881, 2,882, 2,884, 2,910, 2,941**
parks, 2,886
philanthropists, **2,929,** 2,941
photograph collections, **2,870, 2,923, 2,940**
pianists, **2,908**
pioneers and settlers, 2,923, 2,931, 2,940, 9,118, 15,774
pioneers and settlers, Jewish, 13,780
plantations, **2,930, 2,943,** 2,947
playgrounds, 2,955
poets laureate, **2,437**
politics and government, 2,909
politics, practical, women's activism, **2,906**
public health nursing, 3,432
public officers, Afro-American, 2,880
public records, **2,926**
race problems, 2,885
railroads, employees, 5,319
real estate agents, **2,909**
recreation, Afro-American, **2,911**
school librarians, **2,924**
school superintendents and principals, **2,900,** 2,955
school yearbooks, **2,939**
sculptors **2,748**
secret societies, 7,849
Seminole Indians, 2,883, 2,947, 15,494
    costume and dress, 2,951
    food, 2,951
    religion, 2,951
    wars, 2,952
senators, United States, 2,868, 2,875
slave records, 2,930
slave trade, 2,943
slavery, **2,946, 2,947**
    fugitive slaves, 2,947
social life and customs, 15,735, 16,057
Spanish occupation of, 3,420
students' societies, 2,939
superstitions, 2,948
teachers, **2,874, 2,891, 2,900, 2,902, 2,910, 2,912**
teachers, Afro-American, 2,948

theaters, 12,612
tourist trade, 2,922
trade and professional associations, **2,924**
universities and colleges, **2,884**
    alumnae, **2,934**
    employees, **2,918**
    faculty, **2,927**
urban beautification, **2,921**
voodoo, 2,948
war of 1898, 2,904
yearbooks, **2,885**
Florida Agricultural and Mechanical College, School of Nursing, 6,133
Florida Agricultural and Mechanical College, School of Nursing, deans, 6,133
Florida Association for Health, Physical Education and Recreation, 12,937
Florida Breezes (book), 2,942
Florida Federation of Women's Clubs, 2,886, 2,955
Florida Flambeau (FL), **2,933**
Florida Historical Society, 2,900
Florida Mental Health Act, The, 6,381
Florida State College, 2,928
Florida State Historical Society, 2,657
Florida State University (Tallahassee, FL), 2,932, 2,933, **2,935,** 2,939, 2,941
    alumnae, **2,934**
    faculty, **2,927,** 2,931
Florida Supreme Court, 2,873, 2,887
Florists, 10,043, 13,217, **13,971, 17,440**
Florists, Afro-American, 10,191, **12,680**
Flour-mills, 14,632
Flournoy, Anna E. (Winship) [Mrs. Josiah A.], 3,271
Flournoy Family (GA), **3,271**
Flournoy, Josiah A., 3,271
Flournoy, Robert, 3,271
Flower Chronicles (book), 6,646
Flower, Elsie (1886-1968), **1,626**
Flower, Lucy Louisa (Coues) [Mrs. James Monroe] (1837-1921), 3,785, 3,819, **3,841,** 3,861
Flower, Mark D., 9,044
Flower, Mrs. J., **5,843**
Flower of May, The (book), 4,235
Flower of May, The (drama), 4,235
Flower shows, 3,050, 3,082, 3,196, 5,559, 7,519, 17,146. *See also* Exhibitions
Flowers, Paul, **15,892**
Flowers, Ruth (Payne), 10,191
Floyd, Dolores Boisfeuillet, **3,009**
Floyd, John (1783-1837), 13,011
Floyd-Jones Family (CA), **481**
Floyd-Jones, Helen Watts (DeLancey) [Mrs. Henry] (?-1872), 481
Floyd-Jones, Isabelle (Mizner) [Mrs. Charles], 481
Floyd-Jones, Mary (Lord) [Mrs. Edward] (?-1874), 481
Floyd-Jones, Sarah, 481
Floyd, Letitia (Preston) [Mrs. John], **13,011**
Floyd, Olive B., **6,574,** 6,855
Floyd School Parents' and Teachers' Association (IA), **5,105**
Flucker, Lucy (?-1824). *See* Knox, Lucy (Flucker) [Mrs. Henry] (?-1824)
Flucker, Thomas, 12,538
Fluetsch, Lois (1914-). *See* Vogel, Lois (Fluetsch) [Mrs. Mort R.] (1914-)
Fluhrer, Emma Caroline (Pullman) [Mrs. William F.], 3,896
Flute-players, 14,498
Fly Family (TX), 16,087
Fly, William Seat, **16,087**
Flying Club (MA), 7,164
Flying Nun, The (book), 17,731
Flying saucers, 212, 3,712
Flying Tigers, **11,861**
Flynn, Elizabeth Gurley (1890-1964), 621, 2,403, 8,064, 8,067, 8,071, 8,077, **8,087,** 8,094, 9,119, 10,872, 11,305, 11,812, 12,700, 12,705, 12,884, 17,633
Flynn Family (SC), **15,550**
Flynn, John, 3,206
Foard, Rebecca, 9,859
Fobes, P. [Miss], 7,398
Foch, the Man (book), 7,249

Foerester, Robert Franz, 6,293
Fogarty, Kate Hammond, **10,307**
Fogg, Emily, 15,335
Fogg, Georgia, **1,294**
Fokes, Abigail McLennan, 16,100
Foley, Alma, 9,467
Foley, Cora H., 1,751
Foley, Doris E., 1,077
Foley, Eileen, 3,753
Foley, James W., 13,660
Foley, May E., 5,871
Foley, Teresa, 10,853
Folger Shakespeare Library, 11,526
Folies Bergere (Paris, France), 10,894
Folk art, **234, 237, 240, 241, 244, 245, 248, 249, 9,073**
Folk Arts Foundation of America, Inc., **9,073**
Folk dancing, 9,073
Folk literature, **5,652, 5,666,** 17,263
Folk-lore, 1,128, 1,671, 5,539, **5,655,** 11,591, 15,445, 15,933, 16,261, 16,552
Folk-lore, Afro-American, 5,423
Folk-lore, Appalachian, **5,375**
Folk-lore, Native American, 11,315
Folk-lore, Native American, **1,396,** 14,220
Folklore Society, 10,459
Folklorists, 81, **209,** 2,872, 2,882, **3,532, 3,628, 3,633, 5,375, 5,539,** 9,057, 10,131, **10,522, 12,772, 13,143, 14,897,** 16,346, **16,351**
Folklorists, Afro-American, 2,946
Folk medicine, 3,395, 9,542, **9,901,** 15,933
Folk music, 51, 9,073, 9,387, 9,585, 9,810, 13,298, **15,977**
"Folk Sayings from Colorado," 1,671
Folk singers, **253**
Folk-songs, **9,814,** 12,428, 15,933, **15,977**
    Finland, 9,057
    Trinidad, 5,155
Folk-songs, Creole, Louisiana, 5,410
Folk-songs, French, 5,410
    Louisiana, 5,539
Folk-songs, Latvian, 8,604
Folk-tales. *See* Folk literature
Folkedahl, Beulah [Miss] (1896-1971), **8,733**
Folks, Gertrude (1894?-1966). *See* Zimand, Gertrude (Folks) [Mrs. Savel] (1894?-1966)
Folks, Homer (1867-1963), 8,686, 11,897
Follansbee, Aphia-Ann Russell (Tyler), 1,505
Follen, Charles, 6,575
Follen, Eliza Lee (Cabot) [Mrs. Charles] (1787-1860), **5,926, 6,575**
Follen, Mrs. B. L., 992
Follett, Barbara Newhall (1914-?), **11,991,** 11,992
Follett, Helen (Thomas) [Mrs. Wilson] (?-1970), 11,991, **11,992**
Follett, Wilson, 11,991
Follette, Mary Parker (1868-1933), 6,946
"Follies of Fashion—The Fashionable Girl's Soliloquy on a Practical and Pressing Subject, The" (poem), 9,854
Folline, Miriam Florence (1836-1914). *See* Leslie, Miriam Florence (Folline) [Mrs. David Charles] Peacock [Mrs. Ephraim George] Squier [Mrs. Frank] (1836-1914)
Following the Monkey (book), 4,145
Folrvard, Marie (1877-1968), 8,737
Folsom, Charles (1794-1872), 5,950
Folsom, Frances (1864-1927). *See* Preston, Frances (Folsom) [Mrs. Grover] Cleveland [Mrs. Thomas Jex] (1864-1947)
Folsom, Margie E. [Mrs. Fred W.], 1,339
Folsom, Mary C. Wieck [Mrs. Wyman X.] (1860-96), 9,076
Folsom, Mary Jane Wyman [Mrs. William Henry Carman] (1818-96), 9,076
Folsom, Simeon Pearl, **9,074**
Folsom, William Henry Carman (1817-1900), **9,076**
Folsom, William Henry Carman Family (MN), **9,075, 9,076**
Foltz, Clara (Shortridge) [Mrs. Jeremiah Richard] (1849-1934), 1,144, **1,184, 1,427,** 5,058
Foltz, Jeremiah Richard, 1,427
Folwell Family (MN), **8,565**
Folwell Family (PA), **14,973**

Folwell, Joanna Bainbridge, 9,077
Folwell, Mary Chambers (1881-1966), 14,973
Folwell, Mary Heywood (1865?-1946), 8,565, 9,077
Folwell, Sarah (Heywood) [Mrs. William Watts] (1838-1931), 8,565, 9,077
Folwell, William Bainbridge, 8,565
Folwell, William Watts (1833-1929), Family (MN), 8,565, **9,077**
Fones, Alfred Civilion, 1,832
Fontaine, Edward, **9,790**
Fontaine, Joan, 1,025
Fontaine, Lamar, 9,790
Fontaine, Lemuella S. Brickell [Mrs. Lamar], 9,790
Fontaine, Lucretia, 9,747
Fontaine, Susan C. [Mrs. Edward], 9,790
Fontaine, Susan "Susette." See Sawyer, Susan "Susette" (Fontaine)
Fonvieille, Adeline, 9,449
Foochow College (China), faculty, 2,013
Foochow Woman's Conference (China), 5,073
Food, 2,504, 2,947, 6,863, 7,286, 8,741, 9,407, 13,261, 14,348. See also Cookery; Food, natural; Nutrition
  preservation, **5,659**, 9,467
  public opinion,
  research, 364, 2,673
Food additives, 10,953
Food adulteration and inspection, 7,208, 8,486, 9,893. See also Meat inspection
Food, dried, 364
Food, enriched, 4,070
Food for the Small Democracies, 5,123
Food, frozen, 364
Food industry and trade, 943
Food, natural, 6,034, 11,718
Food poisoning, 1,373
Food prices, 3,558, 9,138, 10,953, 11,443, 11,718
Food processing plants, 7,655. See also Creameries
Food relief, 1,557, 4,038, 7,287, 10,071, 12,061, 13,589. See also Food stamp program
Food service, legal aspects, 15,822
Food service management, 15,822
Food service, quality control, **15,822**
Food stamp program, **15,826**
Food supply, 7,198
"Foolin' Myself" (song), 5,530
Fooshe and Sample (SC), 15,594
Fooshe, James W., 15,594
Fooshe, Melissa A., 15,594
Foot, Louise (1831-?). See Ely, Louise (Foot) [Mrs. Charles Arthur] (1831-?)
Football, women's, 10,739
Footbinding, 2,013
Foote, Arthur (1853-1937) 2,020
Foote, Arthur De Wint, 1,426
Foote, Dorothy Cooper (1911?-), **17,966**
Foote, Elizabeth Winter, 9,709
Foote Family (MI), 8,169
Foote, Harriet Ward (1831-86). See Hawley, Harriet Ward (Foote) [Mrs. Joseph Roswell] (1831-86)
Foote, Hattie, 8,169
Foote, Helen E. See Brown, Helen E. (Foote) [Mrs. Charles Kent]
Foote, Henry Wilder (1875-1964), **6,251**
Foote, Irene (1893-1969). See Castle, Irene (Foote) [Mrs. Vernon]. [Mrs. Robert Elias] Treman [Mrs. Frederic] McLaughlin [Mrs. George] Enzinger (1893-1969)
Foote, Juanita (Baldwin) Williams, 1,398
Foote, Martha (1854-1924). See Crowe, Martha (Foote) [Mrs. John M.] (1854-1924)
Foote, Mary (1841-1931). See Henderson, Mary (Foote) [Mrs. John Brooks] (1841-1931)
Foote, Mary Anna (Hallock) [Mrs. Arthur De Wint] (1847-1938), **482**, 1,224, 1,434, **1,581**, 1,601, 9,057, **17,967**
Foote, Mary Kennedy, 1,589
Foote, Sarah H. [Mrs. George], 8,263
"For a Grand Child" (poem), 11,145
"For George Washington Carver" (poem), 2,469
For Goodness' Sake! (ms), 6,053
For My People (book), 9,583
For Stutterers (book), 17,604
For the Leg of a Chicken (book), 14,358

For the Love of Mike (book), 17,638
For True (book), 5,083
"For Women Only," 2,811
Forbes, Addie L., 12,220
Forbes, Alexander B., 7,628
Forbes, Amanda (Cory) [Mrs. William H.], 9,018
Forbes and Wallace Department Stores (NH), 7,628
Forbes, Anna H., 6,193
Forbes, Charlotte (Barrell), 11,942
Forbes, DeCourcey, 6,193
Forbes, DeLoris Florine Stanton (1923-), 6,060
Forbes, Dolly (Murray), 6,193
Forbes, Dora (Delano) (1847-1940), 11,481, 11,482
Forbes, Dorothy (Murray), 2,191
Forbes, Dorothy Virginia. See Sabin, Dorothy Virginia (Forbes) [Mrs. Joseph Percy]
Forbes, Edward Waldo (1873-1969), **6,281**
Forbes, Eliza D., 12,220
Forbes, Elizabeth, 14,896
Forbes, Emma P., 6,193
Forbes, Esther [Miss] (1891-1967), 6,353, 7,138, **7,626, 7,688**
Forbes Family, 6,281
Forbes Family, **9,018**
Forbes Family (MA), **6,193**
Forbes, Grace Maye (1874-1957). See Alexander, Grace Maye (Forbes) (1874-1957)
Forbes, Harriette (Merrifield) (1856-1951), **7,627**
Forbes, Helen. See Ross, Helen (Forbes) [Mrs. E. A.]
Forbes, Josephine, 6,193
Forbes, Julia [Mrs.], 990
Forbes, Kathryn (1909-66), **6,016**
Forbes Library (MA),
Forbes, Mrs. Ralph Bennet, 6,193
Forbes, Nellie, 6,193
Forbes, Robert Bennet, 6,193
Forbes-Robertson Company, 14,686
Forbes, Rose Dabney Malcolm [Mrs. J. Malcolm], **15,304**
Forbes, Sally, 2,380
Forbes, Stanton (pseudonym). See Forbes, DeLoris Florine Stanton (1923-)
Forbes, Susan E. P. Brown [Mrs. Alexander B.] (1824-1910), **7,628**
Forbes, Valeria Wright [Mrs. Paul Siemen], 6,193
Forbes, Walter Tillou, I, **3,010**
Forbus, Lady Willie (1892-), **17,260**
Forbush, Gabrielle [Mrs.], **11,486**
Force of Women in Japanese History, The (book), 7,189
Force, W. B., 12,399
Forchet, Juaneta, 9,861
"Ford Anniversary Show, The" (television program), 12,367
Ford, Antonia (1838-71). See Willard, Antonia (Ford) [Mrs. Joseph Clapp] (1838-71)
Ford, Arthur Peronneau, 15,682
Ford, Beatrice (1881-1975), **10,127**
Ford, Charles Henri, 16,160
Ford, Clara J. (Bryant) [Mrs. Henry], 8,016
Ford, Cora, 17,502
Ford, Emily (Ellsworth) [Mrs. Gordon Lester], 12,592
Ford Family (ND), 13,669
Ford Family (SC), **15,682**
Ford, Ford Maddox, 9,769
Ford Foundation, 11,845
Ford Foundation Fund for the Advancement of Education, 7,584
Ford, Frances Emily, 15,689
Ford, George, 1,428
Ford, Gerald R., 7,889
Ford, Geraldine Bledsoe, 8,062
Ford, Grace [Mrs. Guy Stanton], 8,617
Ford, Guy Stanton, **8,566**
Ford, Harriet [Miss] (1868-1949). See Morgan, Harriet French Ford (1868-1949)
Ford, Harriet Bliss Chalmers (1876-1964), 2,451, 7,165, **7,221**
Ford, Henry, 6,329, 8,000, 8,342
Ford Hunger March, 8,065, 8,089
Ford, Jeanette T., 1,428
Ford, John Anson (1883-), **1,428**
Ford, Justina, 1,777
Ford, Katherine, 11,844

Ford, Marcia (pseudonym). See Radford, Ruby Lorraine
Ford, Maria (Bidgood) [Mrs. William] Jarman [Mrs. Robert Henry] (1832-?), **16,670**
Ford, Mary (1907-), 11,661
Ford, Mary A., 9,841
Ford, Mary Frances (ca. 1854-1956), 10,444
Ford Motor Company (MI), 7,796
Ford Motor Company, Highland Park plant, 8,115
Ford Motor Company, River Rouge plant, 8,088
Ford Motor Company, Willow Run Plant, 8,089
Ford, Mr. 12,602
Ford, Nancy, 12,367
Ford Organizing Drive, 8,065
Ford Peace Expedition (1915), 1,561, 8,000, 17,735
Ford, Roxana Ruth (1910-), **8,567**
Ford, Sina Hutchison [Mrs.], **8,229**
Ford Theatre, 5,828
Ford, Worthington C., 14,758
Forde, Astrid (Flack) [Mrs. G. O.], **8,698**
Forde, Dorothy, 772
Fordham University (NY), 6,087
Fordham University (NY), Bensalem, The Experimental College, 6,087
Ford's Theater, 2,418
Fordyce, Alice (1905-), **11,862**
Foreacre, Ella Thomas. See Brantley, Ella Thomas (Foreacre) [Mrs. Archibald Philip]
Foreacre, Mrs. G. J., 3,141
Foreign Affairs Committee, 9,159
Foreign Assistance Act, 6,402
Foreign correspondents, 174, 6,023, **6,044, 6,054, 6,075**, 6,110, **6,111, 11,179**, 11,817, **14,962, 17,589, 17,677**, 17,762
Foreign Language Information Service. See American Council for Nationalities Service
Foreign Mission Board, 13,279
Foreign Missionary Association, 9,448
Foreign Missionary Society of America, 8,837
Foreign Operations Administration, officials and employees, **6,660**
Foreign Policy Association, 6,512, 6,978, 8,658, 8,660, 9,092, 13,801
Foreign Policy Without Fear (book), 6,512
Foreman, Clark, 6,547
Foreman, Mairi, 6,547
Forerunner (periodical), 11,305
Forest conservation, 2,371
Forest ecology, **2,713**
Forest fires, 9,097
Forest Hill Cemetery (Madison, WI), 17,700
Forest History Society, **9,078, 11,863**
Forest, N. B., 9,756
Forest nurseries, 9,467
Forest reserves, **9,397**
Forest, The (plantation, MS), 9,625
Foresters, **9,466**, 13,129
Forestier, Auber (pseudonym). See Moore, Aubertine Woodward [Miss] (1841-1929)
Forestry societies, **9,078, 11,863**
Forests and forestry, 3,357, 3,944, 6,359, 11,863, 14,809, 17,842
  safety measures, 11,863
Forgery, 11,440
Forgotten Chapter in American Education, A: Jane Andrews of Newburyport (book), 10,465
Forgotten Frontiers: Dreiser and the Land of the Free (book), 12,821
Forman, Augusta, 3,505
Forman Family, 12,203
Forman Family (MD), **3,505**
Forman Family (PA), 15,053
Forman, Lewis Leaming, 11,555, 11,690
Forman, Martha Brown [Mrs. James Rorke] Callender [Mrs. Thomas Marsh] (?-1864), **5,765**
Forman, Mrs. Lewis Leaming, 11,555, 11,690
Forman, Thomas Marsh (1758-1845), **5,765**
Forney, Pauline, 5,861
Forrest, Edwin, 12,235
Forrest, William, 13,423
Forshee, Jesse, 1,740
Forster, E. M., 2,617, 4,491
Förster-Nietzsche, Elizabeth, 783
Forsyth, Gloria, 1,525

Forsyth, Natalie L. B., 10,029
Forsyth Post Ladies Society, 14,138
Forsyth Relief Corps, 14,138
Forsythe, Effie M., 11,443
Forsythe, Frances (Coleman) (1835-1920?), 4,178
Forsythe, Lucy Jane, **5,289**
Forsythe, Nellie (1869-post 1922). *See* Woodbury, Nellie (Forsythe) (1869-post 1922)
Fort Benjamin Harrison, 4,632
Fort Berthold, 13,651
Fort Boise, 14,294
Fort Churchill, 10,637
Fort Dalles (OR), 14,655
Fort Davis, 16,060
Fort Dearborn, 3,829, 3,897
Fort Delaware (MD), 3,721
Fort Des Moines Training Camp (IA), 14,774
Fort Fetterman (Wyoming Territory), 1,497
Fort Garland, 1,786
Fort Gibson Female College (MS), 9,628
Fort Hall Reservation (ID), 14,763
Fort Hall Reservation Church (ID), 3,719
Fort Hays Kansas State College (Hays, KS), **5,185**
Fort Hays Kansas State College (Hays, KS), Faculty Wives Club, 5,185
Fort Hays Kansas State College (Hays, KS), Faculty Women's Club, 5,185
Fort Hays Kansas State College (Hays, KS), Mortar Board, 5,185
Fort Hays Kansas State College (Hays, KS), Quill Club, 5,185
Fort Hays Kansas State College, Graduate Club 5,185
Fort Henry, Battle of (WV, 1782), 14,112
Fort La Fayette, 2,465
Fort Laramie (WY), 1,497
Fort Lewis College (Durango, CO), 16,875
Fort, Louis, 9,604
Fort MacPherson, 3,229
Fort Moultrie (SC), 15,683
Fort Pickens, 2,893
Fort Ripley Reservation, 9,085
Fort Sill (OK), 4,953, 14,777
Fort Simcoe, 538
Fort Snelling (MN), 9,041, 9,113
Fort Stevens (OR), shelling of (1943), 14,505
Fort Sumter (SC), 2,600, 15,627
bombardment of, Civil War, 15,606, 15,749
Fort Thompson (Dakota Territory), 8,412
Fort Union (CO), 1,786
Fort Vancouver, 534
Fort Vancouver Civic Club (WA), 17,314
Fort Winnebago (WI), 9,416
Fort Worth A&M Mothers' Club (TX), **16,196**
Fort Worth Independent School District (TX), 15,993
Fort Worth Police Department (TX), 15,993
Forten, Charlotte L. (1837-1914). *See* Grimké, Charlotte L. (Forten) [Mrs. Francis James] (1837-1914)
Forten, Sarah L., 8,375
Fortner, Ethel Nestell (1907-), **14,368**
Fortnightly (Chicago, IL), **3,992**
Fortnightly Club (Boulder, CO), 1,674, **1,679**
Fortnightly Club (New Haven, CT), **1,994**
Fortnightly Club (Peoria, IL), **4,311**
Fortnightly Club (IN), **4,563**
Fortnightly Club (Mount Pleasant, IA), **5,059**
Fortnightly Club (Winona, MN), 9,520
Fortnightly Club (MS), 9,673
Fortnightly Club (MO), **9,968**
Fortnightly Club (MO), Newcomers Group, **9,969**
Fortnightly Club (Columbia, MO), 9,935
Fortnightly Club (ND), 13,660
Fortnightly Club (OH), **14,148**
Fortnightly Club of San Francisco (CA), **1,295**
Fortnightly Musical Club (OH), 13,932
Fortnightly Review Club (NC), **13,410**
"Fortress of Freedom" (ms), 2,564
Fortt, Inez, 14,468
Fortun, Myrtle E. (ca. 1912-), **9,079**
Fortune and Men's Eyes: New Poem with a Play, 1,087
Fortune, Reo P., 14,886, 14,894
Fortune, Smile Once More (book), 887
Fortune-tellers, 10,731

Forty-Fourth Georgia Infantry, 4,755
Forty-second (Rainbow) Division, One-hundred sixty-seventh regiment (World War I), 15,378
Forty-third General Hospital Unit "Emory Unit" (France, World War I), 3,172
Forums, (discussion and debate), **6,633**, 11,897, 12,690, 16,236, 16,773, **16,942**
"Forward Minneapolis" (pamphlet), 9,103
Forwood, Rachel [Mrs. S.] (1806-30), 5,811
Forwood, William Stump (1830-92), 5,811
Fosdick, Lucy H., **6,576**
Fosnot, Pearl (1891-?). *See* Winans, Pearl (Fosnot) (1891-?)
Foss, Amelia (Robertson) [Mrs. Cyrus David], 1,977
Foss, Archibald, 1,977
Foss, Cyrus David (1834-1910), **1,977**
Foss, Jane (Campbell), 1,977
Foss, William, 1,977
Fosseen, Carrie Secelia Jorgens [Mrs. Manley Lewis] (1875-1963), 8,737, **9,080**, 9,297
Fossils, 15,956
Foster, Abigail "Abby" (Kelley) [Mrs. Stephen Symonds] (1810-87), 2,501, 5,907, **6,577**, 6,741, **6,975**, 7,072, 7,233, **7,629**, 7,692
Foster, Agnes Perry, 11,096
Foster, Anna E., 12,297
Foster, Anna M. [Mrs.], 900
Foster, Charles, 12,052
Foster, Clara (Hess) [Mrs. John Marshall] (1859-1945), 2,017
Foster, Dorothea Cornelia (Jocelyn) [Mrs. William Hammond], 1,870
Foster, Dwight, 7,630
Foster, Edythe, 1,335
Foster, Elmina (1827-1917), **13,012**
Foster Family **1,392**
Foster Family, **2,017**
Foster Family (MA), **7,630**
Foster Family (MA), **7,692**
Foster Family (MN), 8,927
Foster, Fannie (pseudonym). *See* Judson, Emily Chubbuck [Mrs. Adoniram] (1817-54)
Foster, Flora Hale, 12,556
Foster, Flora Shaw [Mrs. Charles E.], **11,096**
Foster, Hannah Webster, 1,397
Foster, Harriet N., 7,586
Foster, Hazel E. (1885-), **4,089**
Foster home care, 1,236, 3,725, 4,065, 4,103, 7,281, 8,640, 8,686, 9,351, 10,669, **11,030**, 12,017. *See also* Children, institutional care research, 8,909
Foster homes, 8,637
Foster, Isaac (1740-81), Family, **2,334**
Foster, J. E., 12,740
Foster, Jane, 9,081
Foster, Janette Ora (1884-1966). *See* Ayer, Janette Ora (Foster) [Mrs. Harry Darius] (1884-1966)
Foster, Jeanne Robert [Mrs.] (1884-1970), **12,477**
Foster, John Burt (1911-), **9,081**
Foster, John Harold, **10,809**
Foster, John Marshall, 2,017
Foster, Judith Ellen (Horton) [Mrs. Addison] Avery [Mrs. Elijah Caleb C.] (1840-1910), 4,732
Foster, Julia (1846-1936). *See* Porter, Julia (Foster) [Mrs. Edward C.] (1846-1936)
Foster, Julie Putman, 16,915
Foster, June, **1,296**
Foster, Lydia (Stiles) [Mrs. Alfred Dwight] (1806-87), 7,630
Foster, Lysander Patterson (1836-1924), **9,082**
Foster, Maria (1821-97), 7,047
Foster, Martha, **5,290**
Foster, Mary (Appleton) [Mrs. John Welch], 1,392
Foster, Mary Elizabeth (Robinson) [Mrs. Thomas R.] (1844-1930), **3,623**
Foster, Mary Elliott (?-ca. 1920), 10,809
Foster, Mary Louise (1865-1960), 7,158
Foster, Mary Pauline (1849-1902). *See* du Pont, Mary Pauline (Foster) [Mrs. Henry A.] (1849-1902)
Foster, Mary (Russell) [Mrs. Isaac], 2,334
Foster, Mary Stiles (1830-1900), 7,630
Foster, May Phoebe (?-1942), **14,136**
Foster, Pamela (1784-1807), 7,630

Foster Parent's Plan for War Children, 2,396
Foster, Pauline. *See* Stephens, Pauline (Foster)
Foster, Rachel G., 2,196
Foster, Rebecca, 16,932
Foster, Rebecca Faulkner [Mrs. Dwight] (1761-1834), 7,630
Foster, Sallie Independence, **25**
Foster, Sarah Shaw, 11,096
Foster, Sophia Dwight (1787-1872?). *See* Burnside, Sophia Dwight (Foster) [Mrs. Samuel M'Gregore] (1787-1872?)
Foster, Stephen Symonds (1809-81), 7,629, 7,692
Foster, Virginia Heard (1903-). *See* Durr, Virginia Heard (Foster) [Mrs. Clifford Judkins] (1903-)
Fotheringill, Samuel, 12,628
Fouch, Altha [Mrs.] (1868-1937), **3,684**
Fouché and Duckett (SC), 15,594
Fouché Family (SC), **15,594**
Fouché, Sallie, 15,594
Fouke, Mary M. T., 10,591
Foulk, Nina, **1,627**
Foulke, Sarah. *See* Emlen, Sarah (Foulke) [Mrs. William] Farquhar [Mrs. James]
Foundation of the National Federation of Business and Professional Women, 12,921
Foundations (charitable). *See* Charitable uses, trusts, and foundations
Founders Memorial Garden (GA), 3,050
Foundling Hospital (NY), 11,298
"Foundling's Heritage" (ms), 6,611
Fountain, Ethel (1865-1915). *See* Hussey, Ethel (Fountain) [Mrs. William J.] (1865-1915)
Fountain, Leatrice (1924-), **6,017**
Fountain, Susie Baker, **1,628**
Four Gospels, The (book), 10,844
4-H clubs, 116, 4,947, 4,960, 4,961, 5,180, 5,662, 9,469, 9,708, 9,892, 10,217, 12,737, 13,566, 13,618, 14,700, **17,481**, 17,619
Four Lights (periodical), 7,988
Four Score Years (book), 1,085
Four Seasons Garden Club (GA), 3,374
Four-Square Bridge Club (Baton Rouge, LA), 5,419
Four Young Lady Poets (book), 11,221
Foure, Helene, 15,319
"Fourteen to One" (story), 5,970
Fourteenth Army Volunteer Air Force, 11,861
Fourth District Minnesota Nurses' Association, **8,648**
Fourth District Minnesota Nursing Students' Association, 8,648
Fourth District Minnesota State Registered Nurses' Association. *See* Fourth District Minnesota Nurses' Association
Fourth Iowa Cavalry, 4,964
Fourth National Conference on Health in Colleges, 8,540
Fourth of July, 8,754, 9,207, 10,920
Fourth Presbyterian Church (NY), 12,561
Fousche Family, 4,942
Fouse Family (KY), **5,314**
Fouse, L. B., 5,314
Fouse, Mrs. L. B., 5,314
Foust, Julius Isaac (1865-1946), **13,242**
Fouts, Mary E., 8,167
Fouts, Virginia Ruth. *See* Pochmann, Virginia (Fouts) [Mrs. Henry A.]
Foutz, Grace. *See* Boulter, Grace (Foutz)
Fowle, Elizabeth (1805-91). *See* Densmore, Elizabeth (Fowle) [Mrs. Orrin] (1805-91)
Fowle, James, 9,041
Fowle, Susan (1802-72). *See* Hanford, Susan (Fowle) [Mrs. Charles] (1802-72)
Fowler, Adaline "Addie" Chamberlin [Mrs. J. C.] McTarnahan [Mrs.] (1845-?), 1,245
Fowler and Wells Phrenological Cabinet (NY), 5,029
Fowler, Charlotte (1805-73). *See* Baldwin, Charlotte (Fowler) [Mrs. Dwight] (1805-73)
Fowler, Charlotte (1814-1901). *See* Wells, Charlotte (Fowler) [Mrs. Samuel Robert] (1814-1901)
Fowler, Eldridge, 17,679
Fowler Family, **12,478**
Fowler Family, 15,942
Fowler Family (NY), **11,590**
Fowler, Grace Georgia [Miss] (1890-), **1,610**

Fowler, Harriet (Webster) [Mrs. William Chauncey], 12,478
Fowler, Harriet P. (1806-91), 6,998, **7,002**
Fowler, Kate, 11,596
Fowler, L. N., 11,741
Fowler, Marcia Gaylord, 326
Fowler, Maria, 17,679
Fowler, Mary Susannah Sumner (Fackrell) [Mrs. Henry Ammon] (1862-1920), **16,671, 16,891**
Fowler, Minnie (Osborne) (1862-?), **7,783**
Fowler, Mrs. Warren R. (ca. 1820-?), **483**
Fowler, Nancy Maria "Nettie." See McCormick, Nancy Maria "Nettie" (Fowler) [Mrs. Cyrus Hall]
Fowler, Orson Squire, 11,602, 14,152
Fowler, Sister Mary Charlotte, S.C.N., 5,373
Fowler, William Chauncey (1793-1881), 12,478
Fowlie, Wallace, 12,001
Fox, Aim [Mrs. James], 3,550
Fox, Anna Barlett [Mrs.] (1870/71-1959), **11,346**
Fox, Annie. See George, Annie (Fox) [Mrs. Henry]
Fox, Captain, 11,554
Fox, Chastity, 16,208
Fox, Della (1870-1913), 16,150
Fox, Dixon R., 6,921
Fox, Eleanor. See Ponder, Eleanor (Fox)
Fox, Elizabeth, 16,492
Fox, Emily Read, 15,517
Fox, Emma Augusta (Stowell) (1847-1945), **7,784, 8,025**
Fox, Fannie, 9,932
Fox, Fannie Ferber, 10,992
Fox, Fontaine T., 5,315
Fox, Frances Barton [Miss] (1887-1967), **5,315**
Fox, Frances Margaret (1870-1959), **8,329**
Fox, Frederic E. (1917-), **5,139**
Fox, George, 12,627
Fox, Gustavus Vasa, 2,651
Fox, Helen Morganthau (1884-1974), 11,297
Fox, Jonathan, 11,522
Fox, Josephine (Clardy) (1881-1970), **16,213**
Fox, Margaret (1833-93), 14,891
Fox, Margaret M. [Mrs.], 9,635
Fox, Nita, **13,706**
Fox, Ruth May, 16,837, 16,966
Fox-Shawnee Indians, 14,241
Fox, Susan (Bibbens) [Mrs. Jonathan] (1803-90), 11,522
Fox Tribe, 2,832, 7,224, 15,289
Fox, Virginia L. (Woodbury) [Mrs. Gustavus Vasa], 2,651
Foy, Mary Emily (1862-1958), **1,429**
Foye, Lizzie, 12,527
Fraenkel, Ernst, 9,986
Fraenkel, Hanna, 9,986
Fragment of an Autobiography (book), 6,850
"Frail Emma" (ms), 14,663
Frampton, Eleanor, 12,363
France, 5,954, 12,196, 12,285, 12,289
  American actresses in, 5,954
  American diplomats in, 2,550
  American nurses in, 13,657
  Americans in, 15,063, 17,035
  army wives, 12,718
  colonies, **5,436**
  exhibitions, 13,999
  hospitals, military, 9,277
  medicine, 6,681
  missions, medical, 9,425
  orphans and orphan asylums, 6,359
  refugees, Vietnamese, 6,709
  Revolution (1789-99), 2,445, 7,660
  riots, student, 11,857
  schools, 9,017
  social life and customs 14,961
  women, employment, 14,365
  World War I, 6,618
    civilian relief, 2,280, 6,613, 7,191, 7,307
    communications, 6,383
    hospitals, charities, etc., 5,991, 6,623, 9,277
    nurses, **8,932**, 13,336
    war work, 2,052, 3,669, 6,152, 6,647, 7,003, 9,427, 10,538, 13,193, 15,325
    war work, Red Cross, 1,560, **2,515**, 4,394, 5,451, 6,520, 6,605, 8,228, 8,436, 9,277, **9,362**, 9,374,

9,425, 9,467, 13,193, 13,243, 13,604, 13,941, 14,136, 14,741, 15,009
    war work, Young Women's Christian Association, 8, 12,718, 13,617
  World War II, 6,023, 6,903
    hospitals, charities, etc., 5,991
    war work, Red Cross, 5,131
  Young Men's Christian Association, 7,003, 12,132
France, Anatole, 11,944
France, Beulah, 2,166
France, Charles B. (1835-95), **9,860**
France Family (MO), **9,970**
France, Mrs., 9,970
France, Sara, 9,970
Frances Payne Bolton School of Nursing (OH), **13,887**, 13,888, 13,892
  alumnae, 13,889
  faculty, 13,883
Frances Stern Food Clinic, 13,823
Franchere, Ruth Myers, **14,369**
Francis, Abigail "Abba" B. (Allyn) [Mrs. Convers], **6,578**, 6,857
Francis, Anne Maria (1831-?), 1,863
Francis Bacon Society 4,895
Francis, Convers, 6,578
Francis Family (CT), **1,863**
"Francis Ferrer is No More!," 6,812
Francis, Jane Clarissa (1834-ca. 1912), 1,863
Francis, Lydia Maria (1802-80). See Child, Lydia Maria (Francis) [Mrs. David Lee] (1802-80)
Francis, Maria M. [Mrs. John] (1801-68), 1,863
Francis, Mary Lou. See Paul, Mary Lou (Francis)
Francis, Mildred. See Cummings, Mildred (Francis)
Francis, Mother Kate, 5,501
Francis, Myrtle (Shepherd), **484**, 1,052
Francis Scott Key Memorial Association, 4,799
Francis, Sir Frank, 1,549
Francis W. Parker School (Chicago, IL), 3,777, **3,842**, 4,091
Franciscan Missionary Sisters of the Divine Child (Williamsville, NY), **12,933**
Franciscan Missionary Sisters of the Sacred Heart (Peekskill, NY), **12,767**
Franciscan Sisters of Allegany, St. Elizabeth Motherhouse (NY), **11,272**
Franciscan Sisters of Blessed Kunegunda. See Franciscan Sisters of Chicago (IL)
Franciscan Sisters of Chicago (IL), **4,286**
Franciscan Sisters of Christian Charity, Holy Family Convent (Manitowoc, WI), **17,820**
Franciscan Sisters of Little Falls, Motherhouse (MN), **8,483**
Franciscan Sisters of Perpetual Adoration, St. Rose Convent (WI), **17,572**
Franciscan Sisters of St. Joseph, Immaculate Conception Convent (Hamburg, NY), **11,476**
Franciscan Sisters of the Atonement, St. Francis Convent (Garrison, NY), **11,465**
Franciscan Sisters of the Poor, Community Service Center (Brooklyn, NY), **11,313**
Franciscan Sisters of the Sacred Heart (Santa Barbara, CA), **1,525**
Franciscan Sisters of the Sacred Heart (Mokena, IL), **4,296**
Franciscan Sisters, Our Lady of the Angels Convent (Wheaton, IL), **4,453**
Francisco Family, 4,942
Franck, John Martin (?-1868), 13,013
Franck, Maria (Miller) [Mrs. Samuel] Hill [Mrs. John Martin], **13,013**
Francke, Katharine (Gilbert) [Mrs. Kuno] (1860-1956), **11,473**
Francke, Kuno, 11,473
Franco-German War (1870-71), 5,485, 6,457
François, Jocelyn, 3,799
Frandsen, Anna Lena. See Andreasen, Anna Lena (Frandsen) [Mrs. Axel Ferdenand]
Frank, Adelaide (Schulkind), 6,579
Frank, Clara C. S. [Miss], **2,335**
Frank, Fannie (1893-1949). See Cook, Fannie (Frank) [Mrs. Jerome E.] (1893-1949)
Frank, Fedora (Small), **15,950**
Frank, Josette (1893-), 8,639
Frank Knox Memorial Fellowship, 2,429

Frank, Leo Max (1884-1915), **3,186**
Frank Leslie's Lady's Magazine (periodical), 13,312
Frank, Lucile [Mrs. Leo Max], 3,186
Frank, Maude Morrison [Miss] (1870-1956), **11,993**
Frank, Nan Bamburg [Mrs. Ludwig], **485**, 1,356
Frank, Patricia M., **7,785**
Frank, Ray (1864 or 1865-1948). See Litman, Ray (Frank) (1864 or 1865-1948)
Frankau, Pamela (1908-), 6,045
Frankel, Bessie Herbert (Barlett) (?-1959), **1,038**
Frankel, Hiram S. (1882-1931), **9,083**
Franken, Rose (1895-), **11,994**
Frankfurter, Felix (1882-1965), 64, 945, **2,336**, 6,544, 12,534
Frankfurter, Marion (Denman) [Mrs. Felix] (?-1975), 2,336
Frankfurter Zeitung (Germany), 174
Franklin, Anna [Miss], 2,989
Franklin, Benjamin (1706-90), 14,884, **14,890**, 15,041
Franklin, Christine (Ladd) [Mrs. Fabian] (1847-1930), **5,728, 11,995**
Franklin College, 3,381
Franklin County Equal Suffrage Association (ME), 5,626
Franklin Debating Society (PA), 14,818
Franklin, Deborah (Read) [Mrs. Benjamin] (ca. 1707-74), 14,890
Franklin, Edith A., **17,084**
Franklin, Eulalia (Rogers), 9,629
Franklin, Fabian (1853-1939), **11,995**
Franklin Family (GA), 3,419
Franklin Female College (MS), 9,614
Franklin Forensic Association (ME), 7,669
Franklin, Helen Graham Rogers (1870-1938), 3,419
Franklin Institute, The (PA)
  attendance reports, 14,941
  students, 14,941
Franklin Institute, The (PA), Committee on Exhibitions, **14,940**
Franklin Institute, The (PA), Committee on Instruction, **14,941**
Franklin Institute, The (PA), Committee on Science and the Arts, **14,942**
Franklin Institute, The (PA), Drawing School. See Franklin Institute, The (PA), School of Mechanic Arts
Franklin Institute, The (PA), School of Design for Women. See Moore College of Art (PA)
Franklin Institute, The (PA), School of Mechanic Arts, 14,941
Franklin, Isa. See Beaumont, Isa (Franklin)
Franklin, Jane (1712-ca. 1794). See Mecom, Jane (Franklin) [Mrs. Edward] (1712-ca. 1794)
Franklin, Jane (Griffin) [Mrs. John]. Lady Jane Franklin (1792-1875), **3,654**
Franklin, Jennie (1873-1958). See Purvin, Jennie (Franklin) (1873-1958)
Franklin, John, 3,654
Franklin, Lucy A. (Harrison) (?-1882), **486**
Franklin, Lulu, 1,777
Franklin, Mary [Miss], **3,011**
Franklin, Mrs. Jesse, 13,411
Franklin party, 14,987
Franklin, Samuel, 94
Franklin, Sarah (1743-1808). See Bache, Sarah (Franklin) [Mrs. Richard] (1743-1808)
Franklin School (Buffalo, NY), faculty, 11,351
Franklin School controversy (MO), 10,159
Franklin Settlement (MI), 8,022
Franklin, Susan (1751-1858). See Bandemer, Susan (Franklin) (1751-1858)
Franklin, Willie, 12,421
Franks, Barbara, 6,336
Franks, Bilhah Abigail (Levy) [Mrs. Jacob] (1696-1756), **7,529**
Franks, Rebecca (ca. 1760-1823), **15,003**
Frankstein, Emily, 3,834
Frantz, Marie J. (Regier), **5,198**
Franz, Amelia Radell [Mrs. Joseph] (1890-), 7,510
Franz, Robert, 12,457
Fraser, Ann L., 3,506
Fraser, Anne Rebecca, 3,506
Fraser, Arvonne [Mrs. Donald], 6,584, **9,084**, 9,140
Fraser, Cynthia, 2,396

Fraser, Donald, 9,084
Fraser, Elizabeth (Ramsay) [Mrs. George] (1857-1924), **16,672**
Fraser Family (AR), **285**
Fraser Family (GA), **3,506**
Fraser, Georgia. *See* Goins, Georgia (Fraser)
Fraser, Gus, 2,396
Fraser, Helen Anderson [Miss] (1902-), **11,591**
Fraser, James Earle, **12,896**
Fraser, James H., 285
Fraser, Laura (Gardin) (1889-1966), **12,896**
Fraser, Margaret Ethel V. (1871-1962), 1,786
Fraser, Martha Ann Wyche, 285
Fraser, Mary R., 11,591
Fraser, Mrs. John, 3,506
Fraser, Rebecca L. M., 3,506
Fraser, Rees, 15,523
Fraser, Sarah Marinda Loguen, 2,134
Frass, Emelia (?-ca. 1969). *See* Mason, Emelia (Frass) (?-ca. 1969)
Frass, Henry, **10,123**
Frass, Teresa. *See* Weber, Teresa (Frass)
Fraternité Franco-Américaine, 9,037
Fraternity, The (NY), **12,208**
Fratricide, 12,847
Fratto, Catherine (1925-), 16,890
Frauen Mission Verein (Hastings, NE), **10,567**
Frauen Mission Verein (NE). *See* Woman's Missionary Society, First Church, Omaha (NE).
Frayser, Mary Elizabeth (1868-1968), **15,795**
Frayseth, Inez [Miss] (1912-), **8,808**
Frazer, Laura Hawkins, 9,832, 10,130
Frazier, Lynn J., 15,317
Frazier, Neta Lohnes (1890-1959), **17,374**
Frazier, Roberta, 4,768
Frazier, Susan R., 10,453
Frechette, Annie (Howells), 14,080
Fred Olds School (NC), 13,369
Frederick Ayer Mission School (MN), 9,265
Frederick, Christine (McGaffey) (1883-1970), 6,523, **6,580**
Frederick Douglass Junior High School (NY), 5,465
Frederick Female Seminary (MD), faculty, 10,974
Frederick, Pauline, 4,981
Fredericksburg Normal School (NC), 13,489
Frederickson, Florence [Mrs.], 9,040
Frederickson, Hansena, **487**
Fredgant, Sarah, 15,332
"Fredi Says" (column), 5,478
Fredonia Mine (CO), 1,732
Fredonia State Normal School (NY), 11,650
Fredricksen, Mabel [Mrs.], **8,734**
Free Acres (NJ), 11,028
Free Acres Community (NJ), 11,028
Free China Movement, 12,061
Free Claim Agency, 13,966
Free Germany Movement, 12,061
Free, Hannah Corrilla (1829-1913). *See* Wells, Hannah Corrilla (Free) [Mrs. Daniel H.] (1829-1913)
Free Hospital for Women (Boston, MA). *See* Boston Lying-In Hospital (MA)
Free love, 3,778
Free Masons, 4,736
Free Night School for Working Men and Boys (New Orleans, LA), 5,426
Free Presbyterian Church, 5,457
Free Press, 14,686
Free Soil Party (IA), 4,829
Free Space: A Perspective on the Small Group in Women's Liberation (pamphlet), 17,583
Free Speech Movement, 843
Free State party, 5,222
Free Summer Excursion Society (Baltimore, MD), **5,766**
Free thought, 4,809, 6,602, 17,980
Free Town Library (NY), 11,268
Free trade and protection, 7,222
Freeborn, Edith (George), 11,596
Freedgood, Anne, 1,221
Freedman, Benedict (1919-), **6,018**
Freedman, Nancy (Mars) [Mrs. Benedict] (1920-), **6,018**
Freedman's Camp (AR), 2,471

Freedmen, 1,776, 1,875, **2,136**, 2,148, 2,154, 2,618, **2,675**, 2,919, 2,945, 3,300, 3,481, 3,991, 6,394, 6,650, 7,424, 7,677, 8,906, **9,604**, 9,717, 9,841, 9,861, 11,616, **12,692**, 13,020, **13,342**, 13,428, 13,573, 13,859, 15,405, 15,630, 15,744, 16,356
  education, 4,359, 5,457, 5,907, 6,943, 7,610
  employment, 3,296, 16,148
  relations with whites, 15,711
Freedmen's Bureau. *See* United States (government), Bureau of Refugees, Freedmen, and Abandoned Lands
Freedmen's Bureau Act, **2,148**
Freedmen's Hospital (DC), 2,332
Freedmen's Village (LA), 2,154
Freedmens Village (VA) 3,490
Freedom Democratic party, 17,714
Freedom of speech. *See* Liberty of speech
Freedom Ship of Robert Smalls, The (book), 15,921
Freedom Summer (book), 1,570, 17,599
Freehold Military Academy (NJ), **10,897**
  faculty, 10,974
Freehold Sewing Association (Freehold, NJ), **10,896**
Freehold Young Ladies' Seminary (NJ). *See* Freehold Military Academy (NJ)
"Freehold Young Ladies Seminary: A Justifiable End to an Era, The," 10,897
Freeland, Eunice M. Hilton [Mrs. John] (1899-1975). *See* Vreeland, Eunice M. Hilton [Mrs. John] Freeland [Mrs.] (1899-1975)
Freeland, John, 12,921
Freeland, Lucy, 920
Freeman (WI), 17,881
Freeman, Alexander H. (?-1883), 10,973
Freeman, Alice Elvira (1855-1902). *See* Palmer, Alice Elvira (Freeman) (1855-1902)
Freeman, Amelia [Mrs.], 2,224
Freeman, Cary Ann (1849-1922). *See* Clark, Cary Ann (Freeman) [Mrs. Edward D.] (1849-1922)
Freeman, Corinne (Keen) [Mrs. Walter Jackson] (1868-?), **15,005**
Freeman, Douglas Southall, 2,876
Freeman, Edythe, 1,576
Freeman, Eeta Bayla [Mrs. Irwin Gershaw], **7,786**
Freeman, Emily D. *See* Scott, Emily D. (Freeman) [Mrs. George]
Freeman, Erika, 212
Freeman, Ethel Hale, 7,158
Freeman, Eva, 5,061
Freeman Family (PA), **15,004**
Freeman, Frances Tuckerman [Mrs.], **6,581**
Freeman, G. W., 9,713
Freeman Ginevra (1839-?), **10,973**
Freeman, Grace Beacham (1916-), **15,796**
Freeman, Harriet Elizabeth [Miss], 2,371
Freeman, Inez, 2,877
Freeman, Isabel (1849-1929). *See* Frost, Isabel (Freeman) (1849-1929)
Freeman, Isabel C., 14,816
Freeman, Jane (Shields) [Mrs. Orville], 9,467
Freeman, Jessie Wheeler, 5,694
Freeman, John Shaw, 15,951
Freeman, Julia Deane, 5,347
Freeman, Kate Whitehall, 9,819
Freeman, Katharine M. Kirtland [Mrs. Wilberforce] (?-1912), 10,973
Freeman, Laura A., 17,026
Freeman, Lucia, 6,223
Freeman, Lucinda Crane [Mrs. Alexander H.] (?-1889), 10,973
Freeman, Lucy Greenbaum (1916-), **6,019**
Freeman, Lucy (West) [Mrs. Frederick], **17,026**
Freeman, Margaret C., 14,816
Freeman, Margaret C. "Kate" (Walthall) [Mrs. George R.] (1828-1919), 9,573
Freeman, Marilla Waite (1870-1961), **12,479**
Freeman, Marion Angevine (1876-?). *See* Condict, Marion Angevine (Freeman) [Mrs. John H. N.] (1876-?)
Freeman, Mary Barry (Martin) [Mrs. John Shaw] (1882-1963), **15,951**
Freeman, Mary Eleanor (Wilkins) [Mrs. Charles M.] (1852-1930), 5,714, **11,161**, **11,996**, **12,480**, 12,529, 17,010, 17,053
Freeman, Mary L. [Mrs.], **8,330**

Freeman, Orville L., 9,040, 9,187
Freeman, Rosa. *See* Keller, Rosa (Freeman)
Freeman, Ruth Benson (1906-). *See* Fisher, Ruth Benson (Freeman) (1906-)
Freeman, Tristram William L. (?-ca. 1848), 15,004
Freeman, Warren Samuel (1911-), 5,986
Freeman, Wilberforce (?-1907), 10,973
Freer, Florence, 11,662
Freeze, Leila "Lillie" (Tuckett) [Mrs. James Perry] (1855-1937), **16,673**
Freeze, Mary Ann (Burnham) (1845-1912), **16,513**
Freibert, Sister Lucy, **5,380**
Freie Arbeiter Stimme, 7,998
Freight and freightage, 11,259
Frelick, Robert "Alcy," 6,353
Freligh, Lizzie, 69
Frelinghuysen University, 2,130
Frémont, Elizabeth Benton (1842-1919), 488, 680
Frémont Family (CA), **488**
Fremont Federation of Women's Clubs (OH), 14,067
Frémont, Francis, 488
Fremont Garden Club (OH), **14,068**
Frémont, Jessie Ann (Benton) [Mrs. John Charles] (1824-1902), 464, 488, 680, 753, 1,426, **1,430**, 1,432, 1,481, 1,483, 1,595, 1,640, **2,337**, 2,448, 2,600, 8,375, 9,841, 12,431, 12,481
Frémont, John Charles (1813-90), 488, 753, 1,426, 1,430, 2,337, 2,600, 9,241, **12,481**
Fremont Matinee Musical Club (OH), **14,069**
Fremstad, Olive, 2,663
French, Adelaide A. [Miss] (1878-1974), **1,775**
French, Alice (1850-1934), **3,993**, 4,781, 9,057
French-American literature, 5,418
French, Amos Willard, 4,373
French, Augusta (1849-89). *See* Wicker, Augusta (French) [Mrs. Cassius] (1849-89)
French, Augustus C. (1808-61), Family (IL), **1,361**
French Azilum (PA), 15,319
French Baby Fund, 6,847
French, Barsina (Rogers), 1,505
French, Beatrice Rebecca (1880-1974). *See* Bolt, Beatrice Rebecca (French) [Mrs. Richard Arthur] (1880-1974)
French, Belle. *See* (French)-Patterson, Belle
French Broad Baptist Association (NC), Women's Missionary Union, 13,297
"French Chef" (television program), 6,465
French, Cornelia (1840-1914), 7,039
French, Daniel Chester (1850-1931), **2,338**, 2,521, 7,503, 7,504
French, Eleanor (1904-71), **12,713**
French, Elizabeth B. [Miss], 10,919
French, Elizabeth Denison (Lance), 15,354
French, Emily, 17,165
French, Fanny. *See* Matheny, Fanny (French) [Mrs. James H., Jr.]
French, Harriette V. *See* Hollis, Harriette V. (French) [Mrs. Abijah]
French Heels (moving-picture), 11,537
French, Henry M. (1851-1916), 1,620
French Hospital (San Francisco, CA), 3,621
French, in Louisiana, **5,495**
French, Kate. *See* Wheelock, Kate (French) [Mrs. Joseph Albert]
French, Lucy [Mrs. Augustus C.] (1818-?), 4,361
French, Lucy Virginia (Smith) [Mrs. John Hopkins] (1825-81), **15,952**
French, Margaret (1889-1973). *See* Cresson, Margaret (French) [Mrs. William Penn] (1889-1973)
French, Mary (1847-1936). *See* (French)-Sheldon, Mary [Mrs. Eli Lemon] (1847-1936)
French, Mary Adams (1859-1939). *See* French, Mary Adams (French) [Mrs. Daniel Chester] (1859-1939)
French, Mary Adams (French) [Mrs. Daniel Chester] (1859-1939), 2,338, **7,504**
French, Mary E., **7,375**
French, Nora May (1881-1907), 312, 712
French, Pamela M. (Prentiss) [Mrs. Henry Flagg], 2,338
(French)-Patterson, Belle, 2,339
French, Sarah. *See* Bartlette, Sarah (French)

(French)-Sheldon, Mary [Mrs. Eli Lemon] (1847-1936), **2,339**
French Superior Council of Louisiana, **5,495**
French, Susannah "Sukey." *See* Livingston, Susannah "Sukey" (French) [Mrs. William]
Freneau Family, 12,203
Freniere Family, 8,966
Fresh Air Association (Hinsdale, IL), **4,276**, 4,279
Fresh-air charity, **4,276**, 11,263, 17,840
Fresh Air Home (GA), 3,507
Freshel, 6,867
Freshwater Univalve Molluska of the United States (book), 14,878
Fresno Armenians (book), 433
Fresno Morning Republican (CA), 974
Fretageot, Marie (Duclos) (1783-1883), **4,429**, 4,433, 4,435, **4,638**
Freud, Sigmund, 2,205, 6,544, 6,602, 11,908
Freudenthal, Elsbeth Estelle (1902-53), **14,203**
Freuh, Alfred (1880-1968), **11,997**
Frewen, Clare (Jerome) [Mrs. Moreton], 12,053
Frey, Caroline (1841-1922). *See* Winne, Caroline (Frey) [Mrs. Charles K.] (1841-1922)
Friars, Spanish, 7,539
Frick, Henry Clay, 14,706
Frick, Mildred (1905-). *See* Taylor, Mildred (Frick) [Mrs. E. Paul] (1905-)
Fricke, Achsah (1893-), 8,518
Friday Afternoon Club (Ontario, CA), 1,092
Friday Afternoon Club (Downey, CA). *See* Woman's Club of Downey (CA)
Friday Club (Jackson, MI), **7,787**
Friday Club (Leeds, NY), **11,420**
Friday Club (Hillsboro, OH), 2,607
Friday Club (Wellsboro, PA), 11,407
Friday Evening Club, Moot Court (Baltimore, MD), 5,800
Friday, Lucy F., 5,809
Friday Musical Club (Boulder, CO), 1,679
Fried, Lucy, 1,013
Fried, Rose [Miss], 2,806
Friedan, Betty Naomi (Goldstein). [Mrs. Carl] Friedan (1921-), 1,017, **6,582**, 6,633, 11,663
Friedberg, Lillian A., **13,783**, 15,250
Friedburger, Tibbie Damon, 16,176
Frieden German Evangelical Church (Seward, NE), **10,532**
Friedl, Ernestine, 2,834
Friedlander, Polly, **17,261**
Friedline, Cora L. (1893-1975), **13,741**
Friedman, Ernestine, 6,365
Friedman, Esther, 17,282
Friedman, Sophie G. (1880-1957), **13,784**
Friedmann, Ernestine, 15,332
Friend, John S., 838
Friend, Kate Harrison [Miss] (1856-1949), **16,354**
Friend, Matilda Jane (Jones) [Mrs. John S.] (1848-1909), 838
Friend, The (HI), 3,640
Friendly Club of Cambridge (MA), 6,871
"Friendly Nurse," 6,648
Friendly societies, **2,008**, **11,598**, 13,446, 14,010, **16,025**
Friendly World (periodical), 11,331
Friends, 496, 1,652, 3,688, 3,762, 4,050, 4,651, **4,652**, 4,654, 4,936, 4,953, **5,317**, **5,772**, 6,747, **7,029**, 7,490, 8,166, 9,207, 10,846, 10,997, 11,048, **11,061**, 11,599, 12,989, **13,221**, 13,223, **13,233**, 13,234, **13,236**, **13,237**, 13,239, **13,956**, 14,000, 14,745, 14,755, 14,821, 14,839, 14,856, **14,963**, 14,981, 14,989, 15,001, **15,006**, 15,022, 15,042, **15,058**, 15,067, **15,089**, 15,104, **15,118**, **15,273**, **15,274**, **15,279**, 15,281, **15,284**, **15,285**, **15,286**, 15,288, **15,289**, **15,290**, 15,293, **15,294**, **15,300**, **15,306**, **15,341**, 15,349, **15,391**
  persecution of, in England, 15,035
Friends Ambulance Unit (China), 8,877, 8,890
Friend's Boarding School (DC), 12,197
Friends Central School (PA), 15,088
Friends Freedmans Association, school operated by, 14,850
Friends in Action, 14,010
Friends in Council (Kansas City, MO), 10,112
Friends Instruction Association (PA), **15,293**

Friends Interracial Committee, 13,222
Friends Library Association, 9,207
Friends of Alliance, 6,766
Friends of American Writers, **3,843**
Friends of Greece, 12,180
Friends of Ida Kaminska Theatre Foundation, Inc., **7,530**
Friends of Jesus (periodical), 3,777
Friends of Kentucky Libraries, **5,341**
Friends of Literature, 4,094
Friends of Russian Freedom, 6,408
Friends of Temperance (OH), 14,114
Friends of the Ann Arbor Public Library (MI), 7,926
Friends of the Deaf (Philadelphia, PA), **15,154**
Friends of the Earth, 6,336
Friends of the Framingham Reformatory (MA), 6,382, **6,583**
Friends of the Library (Santa Clara, CA), 1,534
Friends of the Schlesinger Library, **6,584**
Friends School, students, 8,664
Friend's Society (NY), 11,440
Friends, Society of, 1,004, **2,060**, 4,653, 4,842, **5,927**, 7,607, 7,774, **9,220**, **9,221**, 10,968, 11,120, 11,184, 11,649, 11,904, **12,224**, **12,627**, 13,013, 13,222, 13,230, 13,232, **13,235**, 13,240, 14,742, 14,821, 14,843, 14,845, **14,849**, **14,850**, **14,854**, **14,858**, 15,041, 15,053, 15,352, **15,391**, 17,029
  clergy, **2,032**, **2,495**, 4,731, **4,754**, 5,907, **6,783**, **7,623**, 14,836, 14,837, **14,840**, 14,843, 14,846, 14,847, 14,853, 14,965, **15,031**, 15,276, 15,291, 15,295, **15,297**
  doctrinal and controversial works, 12,627
  education, 13,322, 14,848
  history, 14,842
  membership, 13,235
  missionaries, 137, 13,226, 14,846
  missions, 137, 796, 14,846
Friends, Society of (Hicksite), 15,006
Friends, Society of, New York Yearly Meetings, **11,032**
Friends, Society of, Philadelphia Yearly Meeting of Women Friends, **5,927**
Friends, Society of, Rancocas Preparative Meeting (NJ), **11,033**
Friends, Society of (Rhode Island), **12,628**
Friends, Society of, Women's Foreign Missionary Society, 15,391
Friends United Meeting, 9,221
Friends World Committee, 13,240
Friends World Conference (1937), 13,230
Friends World Conference Committee, 15,279
Friendship, **7,135**
Friendship Forest (KS), 5,162
Friendship House (Chicago, IL), **3,844**
Friermood, Elisabeth (Hamilton) (1903-), **14,370**
Fries, Adelaide Lizetta, 13,319, 13,376, 13,385, **13,411**, 13,511, 13,514, 13,528, 13,609
Fries, Carrie, 13,568
Fries, Francis, 13,086
Fries, Lisetta Maria Vogler [Mrs. Francis] (1820-1903), **13,149**
Fries, Mary (1844-1927). *See* Patterson, Mary (Fries) [Mrs. Rufus Lenoir] (1844-1927)
Friess, Mother Caroline, 5,832
Frietchie, Barbara (Haver) [Mrs. John Casper] (1766-1862), 11,599
Friganza, Trixie, 4,781
Frilk, Mrs. Ernest, 4,923
Friman, Maude M., 4,767
Frings, Katherine "Ketti" (1921-62), **17,797**
Frink, Miriam, 17,846
Fripp, Alice Louisa, 15,595
Fripp Family (SC), **15,595**
Frisbee, Harriet, 6,698
Frisbie, Adelayde "Adela" (Vallejo) [Mrs. Levi C.] (1837-95), 858
Frisbie, Epifania de Guadalupe "Fannie" (Vallejo) [Mrs. John E.] (1835-1905), 858
Frisbie, Ruth E. (1906-), **2,760**
Frisch, Teresa G., 7,583
Frishmuth, Harriet D. (1880-), **12,897**
Fritch, Mary Fry [Mrs.] (1910-), 17,067
Fritter, Caroline, 11,077
Fritts, Stella [Mrs.], **9,862**

Fritz, Anna M. (1840-?). *See* Marti, Anna M. (Fritz) (1840-?)
Fritz, Edna Lillian (1918-), 8,610
Fritz, Florence, 2,928
Fritz, Frances (Sthamm) [Mrs. Philip], 10,010
Frizzell, Lodisa, **12,482**
Froebel Circle (GA), **3,507**
Froebel, Friedrich, 2,430, 4,211, 5,346, 7,788, 9,871, 10,156
Froebel League School (NY), 12,241
Froebel Study Club (Grand Rapids, MI), **7,788**, 7,973
Froelicher, Frances Morton [Mrs. Hans, Jr.] (1912-), 5,829, 5,837
Frog Pond, The (drama), 6,047
"Froggy Bottom" (song), 5,534
Frohlicher, Vera Hanawalt, 8,819
Frohman, Charles, 14,736
Frohman, Daniel (1851-1940), 12,065
From Brilliant Feather Cape to Eagle (book), 3,633
From Canoe to Steel Barge on the Upper Mississippi (book), 6,203
From Little Acorns (book), 9,598
From Sunrise to Sunset (book), 11,700
From the Mixed-Up Files of Mrs. Basil E. Frankweiler (moving-picture), 17,972
Fromberger, Susan Maria (?-ca. 1863). *See* Rodney, Susan Maria (Fromberger) [Mrs. Thomas McKean] (?-ca. 1863)
Fromm, Bella (1890-1972), **6,020**
Fromm, Erich, 10,197
Fronani, Angelo, 7,213
Fronczak, Eugenia. *See* Bukowska, Eugenia (Fronczak)
Fronczak, Francis Eustachius (1874-1955), **11,367**
Fronczak, Lucy Rosalie (Tucholka) [Mrs. Francis Eustachius] (1880-1933), 11,367
Front Door Lobby (book), 6,981
Front, Maxine (Redd), **16,514**
Front, Thressa (Lewis), **16,515**
Frontier Lady, A (book), 759
"Frontier Life in the Army 1854-1861" (ms), 180
Frontier Mother (book), 8,768
Frontier Nursing Service (KY), **5,252**, 6,201
Frontier Parsonage (book), 8,768
Frost, Adelaide Gail [Miss] (1868-?), 13,949
Frost, Amelia J., 3,719
Frost, Augusta (1883-?). *See* Eisenbrey, Augusta (Frost) (1883-?)
Frost, Belle (Moodie) [Mrs. William Prescott], 2,517, 6,818
Frost Block Company (PA), 15,004
Frost, Corinne Chesholm [Mrs.], 11,982
Frost, Elizabeth (Hollister) [Mrs. Elliott Park] (?-1958), **12,817**
Frost, Elliott Park (1884-1926), 12,817
Frost Family (PA), **15,004**
Frost Family (SC), **15,493**
Frost, Fereba (1818-1900) *See* Beatty, Fereba (Frost) [Mrs. William H.] Barger [Mrs. John Eli] (1818-1900)
Frost, Frances. [Mrs. W. Gordon] Blackburn (1905-59), 1,221, 2,166
Frost, Grace Inglis (?-ca. 1940), 16,889
Frost, Isabel (Freeman) (1849-1929), 15,004
Frost, J. H., 14,602
Frost, Robert (1874-1963), 2,517, 6,818, 11,832, 11,969, 11,970, 15,967, 18,021
Frost, Sarah Frances (1866-1950). *See* Marlowe, Julia. Sarah Frances Frost. Fanny Brough. Fancy Brough. [Mrs. Robert] Taber [Mrs. Edward Hugh] Sothern (1866-1950)
Frost, Sigrid, 8,518
Frost, W. G., 14,123
Frostic, Gwen, **7,789**
Frothingham, Cornelia [Miss], 15,055
Frothingham, Ellen, 12,457
Fruit and Flower Mission (OH). *See* Public Health Nursing Service of Dayton and Montgomery County (OH)
Fruit, prices, 10,059
Fruitlands (MA), **7,046**
Fry, Elizabeth (Gurney) [Mrs. Joseph] (1780-1845), **14,755**

Fry, Ellen Jean, 8,174
Fry, Laura B., 14,274
Fry, Mary Fourqurean, **17,067**
Frye, Carolina Virginia Marylandia (Johnson) [Mrs. Andrew] Buchanan [Mrs. Nathaniel, Jr.], 5,748
Frye, Clara, 2,945
Frye, Elizabeth, House (Philadelphia, PA), 15,210
Fryer, H. H., 16,095
Frye, Helene, 11,889
Fryer, Mary Margaretta (1845-1928). *See* Manning, Mary Margaretta (Fryer) [Mrs. Daniel] (1845-1928)
Frysinger, Grace Elizabeth [Miss] (1885-ca. 1973), **6,585**
Fu, Lo (pseudonym). *See* Snow, Helen Foster (1907-)
Fuertes, Katharine "Kip," 11,644
Fuertes, Louis Agassiz, 11,644
Fugin Home (Seattle, WA), 17,285, 17,301
Fugitive Group, The, 15,929
"Fugitive Poems," 16,482
Fugitive slave law, 2,495
Fugitive, The (periodical), 15,936
Fugitive writer's circle, 15,900
Fugitive writers group, 54, 15,936, 15,938
Fukien Christian University (China), faculty, 409
Fulbright Conference (1963), 17,776
Fulbright scholars, 8,586, 13,261
Fulbright, William J., 9,942
Fulda, Carl, 2,761
Fulda, Elisabeth (Rungius) [Mrs. Carl] (1879-1968), 2,761
Fulkerth, Abby E. [Mrs. William], **489**
Fulkerth, William, 489
Fulkes, Elizabeth Houston, 16,038
Fulkes Family (TX), 16,038
Full Employment Act, 1,013
Fuller, Abby Abbe, Family (MN), **9,005**
Fuller Anne E., 8,896
Fuller, Barbara (1925-), **7,790**
Fuller, Caroline, 11,077
Fuller, Clara C. [Miss], 12,750
Fuller, Clement A. (1873-?), 1,995
Fuller, Cordelia Ellen (1833-1916), **14,371**
Fuller, Emeline L., 14,628
Fuller, Ethel Romig (1883-1965), 14,383
Fuller, Evelyn [Miss] (1878-ca. 1946), **5,880**
Fuller Family (IL), **4,277**
Fuller Family (OH), **14,104**
Fuller, Frances Auretta (1826-1902). *See* Victor, Frances Auretta (Fuller) [Mrs. Jackson] Barritt [Mrs. Henry Clay] (1826-1902)
Fuller, Frank, 10,913
Fuller, Gertrude B., 14,813
Fuller, Grace Pierpont (1883-1965), 1,995
Fuller, Hattie, **12,483**
Fuller, Hattie (Pierpont) [Mrs. Austin B.] (1847-1923), **1,995**
Fuller, Hiram, 14,371
Fuller, Jacob, 4,277
Fuller, Jean Wood [Mrs.] (1913-), **6,586**
Fuller, Jeannette (1868-1952), 14,104
Fuller-Kurtz Family (GA), 3,210
Fuller, Loie (1862-1928), 4,277, 4,279, 9,346, 16,150
Fuller, Lucia (Fairchild) [Mrs. Henry Brown] (1870-1924), 5,861
Fuller, Margaret (1810-50). *See* Fuller, Sarah Margaret. [Mrs. Giovanni Angelo] Marchesa d'Ossoli (1810-50)
Fuller, Maria Augusta, 12,649
Fuller, Mary, 2,346
Fuller, Mary. *See* Van Velser, Mary (Fuller)
Fuller, Maud Jeannie (1826-82). *See* Young, Maud Jeannie (Fuller) [Mrs.] (1826-82)
Fuller, Meta Vaux Warwick [Mrs. Solomon] (1877-1968), **7,030**
Fuller, Mrs. Jacob, 4,277, 4,279
Fuller, Muriel, 15,196
Fuller, Nella, 4,277
Fuller, Pierpont, 1,995
Fuller, Sarah Margaret. [Mrs. Giovanni Angelo] Marchesa d'Ossoli (1810-50), 317, 1,565, **5,949,** 6,500, **6,587, 7,045,** 7,185, 7,230, 7,631, 11,125, 11,605, 17,010, 17,616

Fuller, Solomon, 7,030
Fuller, William A., 3,210
Fullerton, Caroline, 9,282
Fullerton Family (ME), 7,669
Fullerton, Katharine Elizabeth (1879-1944). *See* Gerould, Katharine Elizabeth (Fullerton) [Mrs. Gordon Hall] (1879-1944)
Fullinwider, Pat, 175
Fullmer, Desdemona Wadsworth [Miss] (1809-86), **16,674**
Fullmer, Jane Griffiths, 16,616
Fullmer, Rhoda Ann (Marvin) [Mrs. David] (1813-92), **16,675**
Fulmer, Harriet [Miss], 3,813
Fulstone, Maggie [Mrs. Joseph H.], **10,670**
Fulton, Christine (Zdulezna) (1898?-), **12,714**
Fulton County Bimetallic League (GA), 3,266
Fulton County Juvenile Board (GA), 3,430
Fulton, Ellen, 14,378
Fulton Female Seminary (NY), 7,653
Fulton, Jean Boyd (1860-?), **5,767**
Fulton, Ruth (1887-1948). *See* Benedict, Ruth (Fulton) [Mrs. Stanley Rossiter] (1887-1948)
Fulton, Susan Elizabeth (1905-). *See* Welty, Susan Elizabeth (Fulton) (1905-)
Fund for the Republic, 17,805
Fund-raising, 2,037, 2,197, **3,952,** 4,015, 4,105, 4,128, 4,273, 5,228, 7,274, 8,193, **12,261,** 12,708, 12,802, 15,730, 16,183, 16,185, 16,186, 16,188, 16,189, 16,192, 16,196, 16,198, 16,202, 17,475, 17,716
Fund-raising, Jewish, **13,900**
Funeral rites and ceremonies, 8,701, 12,507
Funeral service, **16,676**
Fungi, pictorial works, 6,307, 6,308
Funicello, Annette, 11,461
Funk and Wagnall (publishers), 3,462
Funk, Antoinette, 904
Funk, Antoinette [Mrs.], 17,749
Funk, Dorothea M. (Johnson) [Mrs. Frank] (1916-), **238**
Funk, Goldie R. [Mrs. George H.], **17,168**
Funk, Helen (Muir), **490,** 1,635
Funk, Rose, **14,204**
Funny Girl (moving-picture), 17,989
Fur, 2,718
Fur trade, 1,476, 8,357, 8,441, 8,709, 9,074, 9,272, 9,371, 10,306, 10,400, 10,433, 11,263, 17,459, 17,674
Fur traders, 801, 8,936, **9,050, 17,519**
Furber, Lucy Metcalfe [Mrs.], 9,086
Furber, Pierce P., Family, **9,086**
Furbish, Kate [Miss] (1834-1931), **5,601,** 6,310
Furcht, Clara Euren [Mrs.], 8,690
Furey, Marie L., 2,832
Furlong, Mary [Mrs.], **1,297**
Furman, Abigail Spicer. *See* Irving, Abigail Spicer (Furman) [Mrs. John Treat, Sr.]
Furman, Bess (1894-1969), **2,340**
Furman, Elizabeth. *See* Talley, Elizabeth (Furman)
Furman, Emma (LeConte) [Mrs. Farish Carter], 609, 3,541, **13,057**
Furman Family (GA, SC), **3,541,** 13,144
Furman Family (LA), **5,549,** 5,555
Furman Family (NY), 12,019
Furman, Farish Carter, 3,541
Furman, Margaret Manix (1864-1932), 10,333
Furman, Mary Taylor (?-1913), 5,549
Furman, Richard (1755-1825), 13,144
Furman, Sarah Chandler (?-1910), 5,549
Furman University (SC), 15,585, 15,610
Furness, Anna Earl Ramsey (1876-1964), 9,303, 9,467
Furness, Caroline E. (1869-1936), **1,537**
Furness, Laura (1882-1959), 9,303
Furness, Marion (Ramsey) [Mrs. Charles Eliot] (1853-1935), 9,303
Furness, Rebecca, 9,303
Furniture design, 2,734
Furniture industry and trade, 3,199, 8,347, 10,449, 15,682
Furtwangler, Selma Tharin, 15,700
"Fury" (television program), 17,958
Fussell Family (PA), **14,873**
Fussell, Lydia Ada (1837-1900), 14,873

Fussell, Rebecca (Lewis) [Mrs. Edwin] (1820-93), 14,873
Fussell, Susan (1832-89), 14,873
Futch, John, **13,412**
Futch, Martha [Mrs. John], **13,412**
Future Citizens All, 8,632
Future Homemakers, 13,446
Future Homemakers of America (NV), **10,627**
"Future of Women in America," 11,663
Future Teachers of America, 4,008
Futures (periodical), 15,199
Fyervary Celestine, 3,993
Fyffe, David Maxwell (1856-1934), **9,087**
Fyffe, Jessie Smith Allan [Mrs. David Maxwell] (?-1946), **9,087**
G. I. Bill of Rights, 6,861
G. I. Journal of Sergeant Giles (book), 5,264
G. P. Putnam's Sons, 17,454
Gable, Frank, 10,429
Gabriel et. al. v. Gallatin, 4,798
Gabrilovich Clara Langdon (Clemens) (1874-1962), 9,832
Gaddis, Libbie (Brook) (1850-1933), 10,185
Gaddis, Peggy (pseudonym). *See* Dern, Peggy Gaddis (1895-1966)
Gaddy, Linda. *See* Bilbo, Linda (Gaddy)
Gaden, George T., 11,547
Gaden, Minna V., 11,547
Gads Hill Center (Chicago, IL), **3,845,** 4,047
Gadsden, Jeanne [Miss], **15,473**
Gadsden, John (1853-1902), 15,473
Gadsden, John B. (1877-1924), 15,473
Gadsden, Philip (1864-95), 15,473
Gaekle, Louise [Miss], 5,086
Gaelic (ship), 1,174
Gág, Stella, 9,360
Gág, Wanda Hazel. [Mrs. Earle] Humphreys (1893-1946), 8,531, 9,145, 9,360
Gage, Berta Marie. *See* Dell, Berta Marie (Gage) [Mrs. Floyd]
Gage, Fern (1893-1963), **17,262**
Gage, Frances Dana (Barker) [Mrs. James L.] (1808-84), 2,818, 4,733, 5,907, **6,588**
Gage, Helen Sommer (1888-?), **491**
Gage, Matilda (Joslyn) (1826-98), 1,950, 3,886, **6,589,** 6,859, 7,193, 7,222
Gage, Mrs. E. L., 10,010
Gage Park High School (Chicago, IL), 4,158
Gaillard, T., 11,068
Gainer vs. Dohrman, 6,973
Gaines, Anna, 14,559
Gaines, Cammie Pendleton (1863-1920), 11,394
Gaines, Chloe S. (1880-1944), 11,394
Gaines Family (MS), 9,816
Gaines Family (NY), **11,394**
Gaines Family (OR), 14,559
Gaines, Irene (McCoy) (ca. 1896-1964), **3,846**
Gaines, Mary [Mrs.], 3,002
Gaines, Mrs. Reuben R., 16,068
Gaines, Myra (Clark) [Mrs. William Wallace] Whitney [Mrs. Edmund Pendleton] (1805-1885), 5,410
Gaines v. Dohrman, 6,973
Gaines, W. W., 3,215
Gaines, Wiley S., 3,002
Gaiser, Mary Cooper Jewett, 7,583
Galbraith Family (NE), 10,454
Galbraith, Lillian, 11,691
Galbraith, Martha (Dickinson) [Mrs. Archibald] (1882-), 7,151
Gale, Amory (1815-74), Family (MN), **9,088**
Gale, Caroline (1874-?). *See* Johnston, Caroline (Gale) [Mrs. George H.] (1874-?)
Gale, Caroline E. Goddard [Mrs. Amory], 9,088
Gale, Eliza Beers, 17,634
Gale Family (MA), **7,631**
Gale, Frederick William (1816-54), 7,631
Gale, George W., 11,705
Gale, Hannah "Anna" Davis (1818-51), 7,631
Gale, Harriet (Selden) (?-1840), 11,705
Gale, Harriet Yvonnet (1823-?), 11,705
Gale, Isabel (ca. 1860-?), **8,568**
Gale, Justin Edwards, 6,398

Gale, Margaret (1831-1914). *See* Hitchcock, Margaret (Gale) [Mrs. Henry Ethan] (1831-1914)

Gale, Martha J. (1826-1903). *See* Hockersmith, Martha J. (Gale) (1826-1903)

Gale, Mary Louisa Bigelow [Mrs. Wakefield] (1807-61), **7,335**

Gale, Richard Pillsbury, **9,089**

Gale, Samuel, 15,765

Gale, Samuel Chester (1827-1916), **9,090**

Gale, Susan Damon [Mrs. Samuel Chester] (1833-1908), **9,090**

Gale, Wakefield (1797-1881), 7,335

Gale, Zona. [Mrs. William Llywelyn] Breese (1874-1938), 3,797, 3,927, 3,994, 4,007, 4,155, 6,712, 8,976, 9,103, 9,302, 9,443, 11,821, 12,537, 12,575, 12,597, **17,634**, 17,749, 17,815

Galen, Ellen. *See* Carter, Ellen (Galen) [Mrs. Thomas Henry]

Galerie Beaux Arts (San Francisco, CA), 761

Gales, Anne. *See* Root, Anne (Gales) [Mrs. Charles B.]

Gales, Weston Raleigh (1803-48), 13,117

Gales, Winifred (Marshall) (1761-1839), **13,413**

Galesburg High School (IL), 4,255

Gall, Mary Judith (1777-1848). *See* Lanman, Mary Judith (Gall) Benjamin [Mrs. James] (1777-1848)

Gallagher, Dorothy [Mrs.], **10,117**

Gallagher, Gladys (1904-), 11,851

Gallagher, Marguerite, 504

Gallagher, Mary Eleanora. [Mrs. Douglas] Robson (1883-1966), **492**

Gallagher, Sister Mary Annette, **4,759**

Gallaher, Ruth A., 4,767

"Gallant American Women" (radio program), 6,625, 7,228

Gallant, Ceil, **12,147**

Gallatin County Historical Society (IL), **4,315**

Gallatin Female College (TN), students, 15,964

Gallatin, Grace (1872-1959). *See* Seton, Grace (Gallatin) [Mrs. Ernest Thompson] (1872-1959)

Gallatin, Hannah (Nicholson), 12,255

Gallaudet College (DC), 2,106, 2,112, 2,680 faculty, 2,102, 2,114

Gallaudet, Edward Miner (1837-1917), **2,341**

Gallaudet, Thomas Hopkins (1787-1851), **2,341**

"Gallery of Women" (radio program), 6,625

Galli-Curci, Amelita (1889-1963), 2,376, 2,663, 2,968

Gallico, Paul, 4,482

Gallinger General Hospital School of Nursing (DC). *See* Capital City School of Nursing (DC)

Gallison, Henry, 6,590

Gallison, Marie (Reuter) [Mrs. Henry] (1861-?), **6,590**

Gallison, Martha, 12,051

Gallon, Rosemary K., 210

Galloway, Anna G., 1,635

Galloway, Beverly Tucker (1863-1938), 11,662

Galloway, Cecilia, 1,635

Galloway, Elizabeth, 2,342

Galloway Family, **2,343**

Galloway, Grace (Growden) [Mrs. Joseph] (?-1782), 2,342, **4,418**, **15,007**

Galloway, Joseph (1731-1803), 2,342, 4,418, 14,991

Galloway, Joseph, Family (PA), **2,342**

Galloway, Mary (1787-1849). *See* Maxcy, Mary (Galloway) [Mrs. Virgil] (1787-1849)

Galloway Memorial Methodist Episcopal Church, South (MS), 9,750

Galloway Memorial Women's Bible Class (MS), 9,644

Galloway, Mollie, 2,502

Galloway, Sarah, 1,635

Galloways, John, 11,322

Gallup Family, 12,314

Gallup-Wilson, Gladys, 5,048

Gallupe, Vivian [Mrs.], 5,644

Galpin, Bernice. *See* Wade, Bernice (Galpin) [Mrs. Decius S.]

Galsworthy, John, 7,216, 11,944, 11,993, 16,166, 17,208

Galsworthy, John, 15,967

Galt, Alexander D. (1771-1841), 17,128

Galt, Alexander D., Jr., 17,128

Galt, Edith (Bolling) (1872-1961). *See* Wilson, Edith (Bolling) Galt [Mrs. Woodrow] (1872-1961)

Galt, Elizabeth (1816-54), 17,128

Galt Family (VA), **17,128**

Galt, John M. (1744-1808), 17,128

Galt, John M., II (1819-62), 17,128

Galt, John M., III, 17,128

Galt, Judith C. [Mrs. John M.] (ca. 1749-?), 17,128

Galt, Sarah Maria (1822-80), 17,128

Galveston Chamber of Commerce (TX), 16,222

Galveston County Medical Assistants Society (TX), **16,227**

Galveston Equal Suffrage Association (TX), **16,218**

Galveston Garden Club (TX), **16,219**

Galvin, Sister Eucharista, 9,467

Gambino, Monsignor Joseph, 12,933

Gamble, Anna Dill (1878-1956), 15,361

Gamble, Clarence James (1894-1966), **6,221**, 8,634

Gamble, Elizabeth (1784-1857). *See* Wirt, Elizabeth (Gamble) [Mrs. William] (1784-1857)

Gamble, Harriet Douglas (Whetten) (pre-1822-?), **17,737**

Gamble, John R., Jr., 13,404

Gamble, Vanessa, 15,134

Gambling, 167, 2,948, 4,114, 10,050, 10,711, **10,733**, 10,738, 12,424, 15,451

Game and game-birds, 9,154

Game-laws, 8,456

Game protection, 14,004

Games Around the World: Four Hundred Folk Games for an Integrated Program in the Elementary School (book), 9,650

Games, Mrs. A. B., 617

Gamewell, Mary (Porter) [Mrs. Francis] (1848-1906), 2,016

Gamewell School (Peking, China), 14,336, 14,396, 14,466

Gaming Industry Association of Nevada, 10,738

Gamma Phi Beta, 17,003, 17,110

Gamma Sigma Delta, 8,567

Gammell, Harriet Ives. *See* Safe, Harriet Ives (Gammell) [Mrs. Thomas]

Gamow, Barbara (Perkins) [Mrs. J. R. de la Torre] Bueno [Mrs. George Antony] (1905-76), **2,344**

Gamow, George Antony (1904-68), **2,344**

Gandhi, Indira, 17,978

Gandhi, Mohandas Karamchand, 6,012, 6,499, 6,978, 7,210, 12,715, 12,730

Gandy, Evelyn, 9,585

Gangs, 1,786

Ganier, Amanda M., 5,518

Gann, Dolly [Mrs. Edward E.], 5,122

Gannett, Betty (1906-70), **17,635**

Gannett, Caroline Werner [Mrs. Frank E.] (1894-), **11,592**, 12,790

Gannett, Deborah (Sampson) [Mrs. Benjamin] (1760-1827), 8,271, **10,876**

Gannett, Eliza Ann (1811-?). *See* Davison, Eliza Ann (Gannett) [Mrs. John] (1811-?)

Gannett, Frank, Newspaperboy Scholarship, Inc., 11,592

Gannett, George, 5,675

Gannett, Kate (1838-1911). *See* Wells, Kate (Gannett) [Mrs. Samuel] (1838-1911)

Gannett, Mary Thorn (Lewis) [Mrs. William Channing] (1854-1952), 12,818

Gannett Newspaper Foundation, 11,592

Gannett, Olive, 5,675

Gannett, William Channing (1840-1923), **12,818**, 12,835

Gannon, Nell Upshaw, **3,012**

Gano, John Allen, Family, **9,971**

Gano, Mary, 2,239

Gano, Mary Catherine [Mrs. John Allen], 9,971

Gano, Mary E., 9,971

Ganson, Mabel (1879-1962). *See* Dodge, Mabel (Ganson) (1879-1962)

Gantt, Eliza, 2,592

Gaposchkin, Cecilia (Payne). *See* (Payne)-Gaposchkin, Cecilia

Garant, Rita B., 1,125

Garbe, Raymond W., 3,879

Garbe, Ruth (Moore) [Mrs. Raymond W.] (1920-), **3,879**

Garber, Lily (1925-). *See* Schwartz, Lily (Garber) [Mrs. Ernest] (1925-)

Garbo, Greta, 11,461, 12,129

Garborg, Arne, **8,735**, 8,736

Garborg, Hulda [Mrs. Arne], **8,736**

García, Manuel Rafael, 2,471

García, Marcelino, **493**

Gardella, Louie A. (1908-), **10,735**

Garden, Alexander, 15,474

Garden architecture. *See* Landscape gardening

Garden City Chamber of Commerce (KS), **5,181**

Garden City Garden Club (KS), 5,179

Garden City Music Study Club (KS), 5,179

Garden Club (Williamsburg, VA), 17,110

Garden Club Fellowship (CA), 760

Garden Club of America, 2,028

Garden Club of Cincinnati (OH), 13,845

Garden Club of Cornwall (CT), **1,833**

Garden Club of Dearborn (MI), 8,013

Garden Club of Georgia, 3,050, 3,187, 3,196, 3,439

Garden Department of Women's Civic Club (WA), **17,137**

Garden Gateways (periodical), 3,050

Garden, Mary. *See* Collins, Mary (Garden)

Garden, Mary (1877-1967), 3,980, 12,798

Garden of Allah (CA), 361

"Garden of Memories" (song), 3,014

Gardener, Helen Hamilton (pseudonym). *See* Day, Alice Chenoweth [Mrs. Charles Selden] Smart [Mrs. Selden Allen] (1853-1925)

Gardeners, 324, 955, 13,709

Gardeners' Union of Lewiston and Auburn (ME), **5,559**

Gardening, 2,310, 5,486, 8,269, 10,233. *See also* Gardens; Horticulture; Horticulturists; Landscape gardening; Organic gardening societies, etc., **50**, **1,211**, 1,526, 1,734, **1,833**, **1,835**, 2,028, 2,134, **2,899**, 2,901, **3,050**, 3,082, **3,187**, 3,196, 3,233, 3,358, 3,374, 3,439, 4,097, **4,191**, 4,273, **4,454**, **4,501**, **4,590**, 5,179, 5,443, **7,087**, **8,013**, 8,211, 8,360, **8,390**, 8,481, **8,830**, 9,529, **9,533**, **9,813**, 9,918, 10,057, **10,704**, 10,709, **10,838**, 10,842, **10,883**, 12,851, 12,869, 12,916, **13,293**, 13,303, **13,845**, 14,068, 15,074, 15,584, **16,219**, 16,302, 17,110, **17,137**, 17,146, **17,147**, **17,155**, 17,267, 17,314, 17,468

Gardening in North Dakota (book), 13,709

Gardens, 303, 2,414, 3,050, 3,077, 3,082, 8,089, **11,887**, 12,901, 12,988

Gardescu, Pauline, 6,778, 9,492

Gardin, Laura (1889-1966). *See* Fraser, Laura (Gardin) (1889-1966)

Gardiner, Caroline Perkins [Mrs. William H.], 6,593

Gardiner, Eliza C. [Mrs.], 5,744

Gardiner, Eliza Doane, 11,593

Gardiner, Elizabeth (1856-1937). *See* Evans, Elizabeth (Gardiner) [Mrs. Glendower] (1856-1937)

Gardiner, Elizabeth Greene (1890-), **11,593**

Gardiner Family (MD), 5,744

Gardiner Family (MA), **6,593**

Gardiner Family (MN), 9,172

Gardiner, Henrietta, 1,959

Gardiner, Lottie Leigh, 5,744

Gardiner, Lucy Leigh, 15,894

Gardiner, Mary. *See* Davis, Mary (Gardiner) [Mrs. William Nye]

Gardiner, William H., 6,593

Gardner, Abigail (1777-1868). *See* Drew, Abigail (Gardner) [Mrs. Gershom, Jr.] (1777-1868)

Gardner, Alice (Brewer), 10,628

Gardner, Ann (Jones) [Mrs. Robert Snow], 16,415

Gardner, Bernella Elizabeth (Snow) [Mrs. Robert Berry] (1866-1952), **16,677**

Gardner, Catherine Endicott (Peabody) (1808-83), 6,194

Gardner, Charlotte (Coffin) [Mrs. William Bunker], 1,431, **14,560**

Gardner, Edith, 9,049

Gardner, Elizabeth, 8,666

Gardner, Elizabeth F., **16,069**

Gardner, Eunice, 7,632

Gardner Family (MA), **6,194**, **7,632**

Gardner Family (MN), 9,049

Gardner Family (UT), 16,686

Gardner Family (WA), **17,159**

Gardner, Flora [Mrs. Edward M.] (1839-1910), **10,308**
Gardner, Florence (Guild) Bruce, **14,205**
Gardner, Frances Tomlinson (?-1954), **1,374**, 1,383
Gardner, George, 7,619
Gardner, Grace Brown, 1,431
Gardner, Harriet [Mrs. Jared M.], 7,632
Gardner, Isabella (Stewart) [Mrs. John Lowell] (1840-1924), 1,426, **2,762, 6,185**
Gardner, Jane (1829-1914). *See* Waterman, Jane (Gardner) [Mrs. Robert Whitney] (1829-1914)
Gardner, Jared M. (1818-76?), 7,632
Gardner, John, 11,844
Gardner, John Lowell 1,426
Gardner, Katherine [Mrs. Augustine Vincent] (?-1966), 9,049
Gardner, Leonora (Cannon) [Mrs. Robert] (1840-1924), **16,678**
Gardner, Mabel Mary (1875-1967), 9,049
Gardner, Marjorie, 14,501
Gardner, Mary Sewall (1871-1961), **6,594**
Gardner Museum (MA), 2,762, 6,185
Gardner, Nancy (Bruff) (1915-), **6,021**
Gardner, Nannette Brown Ellingwood (1828-1900), **7,791**
Gardner, Placida. *See* Chesley, Placida (Gardner) [Mrs. Albert Justus]
Gardner, Rebecca Coffin [Mrs. George], 7,619
Gardner, Sarah M., 7,791
Gardner, Thomas J., 3,013
Gardner, William Bunker, **1,431**
Garebold, Elizabeth, **3,014**
Garebold, John A., 3,014
Garey, Hannah, 15,537
Garfield, Abram, 2,348
Garfield, Belle (Mason) [Mrs. Harry Augustus] (1865?-1944), 2,345
Garfield, Eliza (Ballou) [Mrs. Abram] (1801-88), 2,346, **13,925**, 14,206, 17,204
Garfield, Harry Augustus (1863-1942), **2,345**
Garfield, Helen (Newell) [Mrs. James Rudolph] (1866-1930), 2,347
Garfield, Irvin McDowell, 2,348
Garfield, James Abram (1831-81), 2,210, 2,345, **2,346,** 2,348, 8,725, 13,925, **13,926,** 13,954
Garfield, James Rudolph (1865-1950), **2,347**
Garfield, Josephine. *See* Russell, Josephine (Garfield) [Mrs. Milo]
Garfield, Lucretia (1894-1968). *See* Comer, Lucretia (Garfield) [Mrs. John P.] (1894-1968)
Garfield, Lucretia (Rudolph) [Mrs. James A.] (1832-1918), 14,916, 7784, **7122,** 6863, 6866, 6862, 6831, 16,270, 16,604
Garfield, Mary (1867-1947). *See* Stanley-Brown, Mary (Garfield) [Mrs. Joseph] (1867-1947)
Garfield, Mary Elizabeth (Parker) [Mrs. John P.] (1839-70), Family (MN), **9,091**
Garfield, Viola (1898-), 2,834, **17,263**
Garfinkle, Clara (1901-). *See* Shirpser, Clara (Garfinkle) [Mrs. Adolph J.] (1901-)
Garlach, Anna, **14,769**
Garland Farm, 8,077
Garland Fund, 8,077
Garland, Hamlin, 11,979, 14,206
Garland, Judy, 12,129
Garland, The (periodical), 2,566, 13,969
Garland Ward Relief Society (UT), 16,619
Garland, William H., 2,136
Garlick, Hope. *See* Mineau, Hope (Garlick) [Mrs. Wirt]
Garlick, Elizabeth Rebecca (Rawson) [Mrs. Joseph Elsbury] (1873-1961), **16,679**
Garlick Family, 9,078
Garlin, Anna Carpenter (1851-1931). *See* Spencer, Anna Carpenter (Garlin) [Mrs. William Henry] (1851-1931)
Garman, Charles Edward (1850-1907), **5,865**
Garman, Eliza, 5,865
Garment Workers (periodical), 15,329
Garner, Isabel Irwin [Mrs. Perkins], 8,167
Garner, Lizzie, 13,424
Garner, Marian, 8,948
Garner, Mary (Field) [Mrs. William, Jr.] (1836-1943), 16,676, **16,680**

Garner, Perkins, 8,167
Garner, Richard, 8,948
Garner, Stella Wheelock [Mrs.] (1887-), 13,639
Garnet Family, 12,635
Garnet Key (FL), 2,939
Garnett, Maria Champe. *See* Garnett, Maria Champe (Garnett)
Garnett, Maria Champe (Garnett), 545
Garnett, Porter, 743
Garrecht, Gertrude (Lang) (1844-?), 10,632
Garretson, Anna Maria (Deans), **13,014**
Garrett Biblical Institute (IL). *See* Garrett-Evangelical Theological Seminary (IL)
Garrett, Cammie. *See* Henry, Cammie (Garrett) [Mrs. J. H.]
Garrett, Cecilia (Vincent) [Mrs. Milton W.], **8,331**
Garrett, Edward J., Family, 2,461
Garrett, Elizabeth (?-1947), **11,215**
Garrett-Evangelical Theological Seminary (IL), 4,201, 4,203, 4,206, 4,207, 4,208
Garrett Family (TX), **16,355**
Garrett, Fontaine D., 9,630
Garrett, Franklin, 3,176
Garrett, John W., 5,734
Garrett, Louisiana (Dunlevy) [Mrs. Fontaine D.], **9,630**
Garrett, Margaret (1901-). *See* Smythe, Margaret (Garrett) (1901-)
Garrett, Mary E., **5,729**
Garrett, Mary Elizabeth (1854-1915), 14,738, 14,745
Garrett, Mrs. C. C., **16,070**
Garrett, Mrs. John W., 5,734
Garrett, Mrs. S. D., 9,630
Garrett, Pat, 11,215
Garrette, Eve, 5,123
Garrettson, Catherine (Livingston) [Mrs. Freeborn] (1752?-1849), 10,908
Garrettson, Freeborn, 10,908
Garrigue, Charlotte (1850-1923). *See* Masaryk, Charlotte (Garrigue) [Mrs. Thomas] (1850-1923)
Garrison, Charlotte (1881-1972), **11,864**
Garrison, Ellen Wright [Mrs. William Lloyd, II] (1840-1931), 11,125
Garrison Family, **7,222**
Garrison, Fanny (1844-1928). *See* Villard, Fanny (Garrison) [Mrs. Henry] (1844-1928)
Garrison, Helen Eliza Benson (1811-76), 5,907
Garrison, Helen Frances "Fanny" (1844-1928). *See* Villard, Helen Frances "Fanny" (Garrison) [Mrs. Henry] (1844-1928)
Garrison, Martha Ellen Rogers, **14,561**
Garrison, Mr., 6,458
Garrison, Wendell Phillips (1840-1907), 12,572
Garrison, William Lloyd (1805-79), 1,437, 1,896, 1,950, 2,327, 2,501, **3,297,** 5,684, 5,907, 5,939, 5,961, 5,963, 5,964, 6,491, **6,595,** 6,738, 6,961, 7,222, 12,419, 12,485, 15,270, 15,291
Garrison, William Lloyd, II (1838-1909), 7,222
"Garrulity of Age, The" (ms), 7,112
Garson, Barbara, 2,349
Garth, Helen K., 10,130
Gartner, Chloe Maria (1916-), **6,022**
Garvey, Amy, 5,870
Garvin, Henry B., 3,451
Garvin, J. L., 16,166
Garvin, Laura [Miss], 3,451
Gary, Mrs. Sterling, 13,322
Gary Urban League (IN), **4,090**
Gas companies, 3,898, 5,316
Gas industry, 11,833
Gas manufacture and works, 3,898
Gash Family (NC), **13,414**
Gash, Mary, **13,414**
Gaskell, Elizabeth Cleghorn (Stevenson) (1810-65), 16,170
Gaskill, Annie Florence (Porter) [Mrs. Varne
Gaskill, Gussie Esther (1898-), **11,594**
Gasquet, Martha (1883-1960). *See* Westfeldt, Martha (Gasquet) (1883-1960)
Gassaway Family (MS), **9,631**
Gassaway, Mary [Miss], **9,631**
Gastanaga Family (NV), **10,671**
Gastanaga, Lola Jimella Harvey, 10,671
Gaston Family, 3,612

Gaston, Marjorie (1906-74), **4,526**
Gastroenterology, 6,688
Gatenby, Rosemary (1918-), 6,060
Gates, Adelia [Miss] (ca. 1817-80), **15,214**
Gates Ajar (book), **1,500**
Gates, Ellen M. (Huntington) [Mrs. J. E.] (1845-1920), **2,350**
Gates, Emma Lucy (1880-1951). *See* Bowen, Emma Lucy (Gates) (1880-1951)
Gates, Eva (1888-1968), 10,244
Gates Family (Savona, NY), **11,595**
Gates, General, 7,638
Gates, Gertrude Edna (Lewis), **216**
Gates, Gertrude Lewis [Mrs.], **3,685**
Gates, Helen (Dunn), 7,927
Gates, Horatio, **12,569**
Gates, Irwin W., 9,006
Gates, Isabel Likins, **2,351**
Gates, Jacob Forsberry, 16,681
Gates, Katherine (Van Akin) (?-1949), **1,846,** 17,498
Gates, Lillian, 11,595
Gates, Madge. *See* Wallace, Madge (Gates) [Mrs. George]
Gates, Mary Johnston [Mrs.] (1920-), **15,797**
Gates, Mimosa (1872-1952). *See* Pittman, Mimosa (Gates) [Mrs. Key] (1872-1952)
Gates, Rosalie, 2,941
Gates, Susa Amelia (Young) [Mrs. Alma Bailey] Dunford [Mrs. Jacob Forsberry] (1856-1933), 3,738, 16,620, 16,676, **16,681,** 16,789, 16,842, 16,843, 16,922, **16,941,** 16,973
Gatewood, James Duncan (1857-1924), **5,844**
Gathings, Lucy (1851 or 1853-1942). *See* Parsons, Lucy (Gathings) [Mrs. Albert] (1851 or 1853-1942)
Gattiker, Emma [Miss] (1860-?), **17,636**
Gattini, Pearl (Heckman) (1886-?), **494,** 1,068
Gatzert, Babette (Schwabacher) [Mrs. Bailey], 495
Gatzert, Bailey, 495
Gatzert Family (WA), **495**
Gauger, May S. (1892-1949), **14,868**
Gauld, Charles Anderson, 496
Gault, Alma Elizabeth [Miss] (1891-), **15,931**
Gaultlett, Dorothy [Mrs. Jack], 8,227
Gauntlett, Anna (Winsor), **14,562,** 14,618
Gauntlett, Mary Celesita "Lettie" McGraw [Mrs. John C.], 11,645
Gauntlett, Minna, 11,645
Gause, M. Jeanette, 1,594
Gauthier, Eva, 10,894
Gautreaux, Michele, 4,132
Gavit, Bernard C., 2,701
Gawboy, Helmi Jarvinen, 9,467
Gawthorne, J. E., 12,543
Gay, E. Jane [Miss], 6,540
Gay, Ebenezer, 11,998
Gay, Edwin F., 2,596
Gay, Elizabeth (Neall) [Mrs. Sydney Howard], 11,998
Gay, Fidelia Thompson [Mrs. Horace], 12,209
Gay, Horace, **12,209**
Gay, Katharine, 2,596
Gay liberation movement, 8,624
Gay, Sydney Howard (1814-88), **11,998**
Gay, Theresa, **497, 1,582**
Gay, Tirzah Farr (1852-1946), 16,911
Gay, Warren, 7,514
Gay, Margaret (1864-1938), 4,906
Gay, Martha Ann, 14,628
Gay, Mary Allyne (Otis) [Mrs. Ebenezer], 11,998
Gay, Olive, 7,514
Gay, Sarah, 11,998
Gayarre, Mrs. Charles, 13,051
Gayle, Amelia (1826-1913). *See* Gorgas, Amelia (Gayle) [Mrs. Josiah] (1826-1913)
Gayle, Clarissa Steadman Peck [Mrs. John], 105
Gayle, John, 105, 106
Gayle, Martha, 5,320
Gayle, Sarah Haynesworth [Mrs. John] (ca. 1795-1835), 105, **106**
Gaylord, Edith, 11,493
Gaylord, Gladys, 6,223
Gaylord, Mrs. E. L., 3,813
Gaylord, Stella M. (Atkins) (1808-82), 326
Gayman, Esther Palm (1891-1974), **4,259**

Gaynor, Janet (1906-), 11,907
Gaynor, Lizzie Mahon, **1,715**
Gayton, Anna Hadwick, 920
Gayton Virginia, 17,232
Gazette (periodical), 12,341
Gazette of the State of South Carolina, 15,419
Gazette-Telegraph (Colorado Springs, CO), 1,686
Gazzam, Kate Lea. *See* Donald, Kate Lea (Gazzam) [Mrs. H. G.]
Gbedemah, Komla, 5,460
Gearhart, Lucy [Mrs. John W.], **17,264**
Gearing, Marjorie, 2,832
Gebhart, Mary Seitz. *See* Durell, Mary Seitz Gebhart [Mrs. Edward Henry]
Gee, Christine South [Mrs.] (1884-), **15,798**
Geer, Clara (1893-1976). *See* Reynolds, Clara (Geer) [Mrs. Clyde] (1893-1976)
Geer, Elizabeth (Dixon) Smith, **14,563**
Geer, Mrs. A. D. (1846-1936), 10,632
Gehr, Agnes R., 13,890
Gehrig, Lou, 11,405
Geiger, E. Elizabeth, 3,954
Geiger, Lizzie K., **15,596**
Geiringer, Hilda (1893-1973). *See* Mises, Hilda (Geiringer) [Mrs. Richard von] (1893-1973)
Geister, Janet Marie Louise Sophie (1885-1964), 6,134, 6,138, **6,139**
Geittmann, Ida, **8,395**
Gelb, Jan (1906-), 2,741, **2,763**
Gelders Emma (1894-). *See* Sterne, Emma (Gelders) (1894-)
Gelin, Leona. *See* Kent, Leona (Gelin) [Mrs. William C.]
Gelispe, Maria, 16,862
Gelles, Catherine "Babe" [Mrs. Albert], **8,088**
Gellhorn, Edna (Fischel) [Mrs. George] (1878-1970), **6,596**, 8,685, 9,984, 10,195, 10,200, **11,865**, 15,706
Gellhorn, Martha Ellis [Mrs. Ernest Hemingway] (1908-), **6,023**, 14,433
Gelston, Anna, 7,792
Gelston, Caroline, 7,792
Gelston Family (MI, NY), **7,792**
Gem City Business College, alumnae, 4,094
Gem State Signal, 3,666
Gemini (book), 6,026
Genauer, Emily [Miss] (1910-), **2,764**
Genealogical Institute (Salt Lake City, UT), 16,937
Genealogical societies, 10,851
Genealogical Society, 16,681
Genealogists, 11, 1,620, **1,648**, **1,824**, 1,854, 1,901, **1,940**, 1,948, **1,958**, 2,229, **2,532**, 2,545, 3,358, **3,415**, 4,689, **4,942**, 5,123, **5,157**, **5,291**, **5,301**, **5,674**, **5,780**, **7,134**, **7,555**, 8,935, 9,075, **9,414**, **9,697**, 10,076, 10,135, **10,454**, **10,562**, 11,101, **12,863**, 13,098, 15,328, 15,370, **15,951**, 16,429, **16,434**, **16,599**, 16,782, **17,437**, **17,444**, **17,457**
Genealogy, 73, 281, 781, **1,533**, 1,726, 1,730, 1,852, **1,905**, 1,958, 1,960, 3,054, 3,088, 3,222, **3,460**, **3,606**, 3,612, 3,618, 3,754, 5,567, **5,876**, 6,012, **6,234**, 6,467, 6,650, 6,701, 7,609, 7,669, 7,670, 8,452, 8,756, 8,779, 8,783, 8,962, 9,036, **9,527**, 9,656, 9,762, 9,816, 9,926, 10,068, 10,076, **11,208**, 11,245, 11,440, 11,577, 12,373, **12,531**, 12,755, 12,981, 13,684, 14,056, 14,506, 14,599, 14,606, 14,854, 15,221, 15,521, **15,622**, 15,788, 15,942, 15,975, 16,587, 16,684, 16,819, 16,832, 16,836, 17,266
Genealogy, Native American, 9,296
Genee, Adeline, 2,968
General Alliance of Unitarian-Universalist Women, 13,183
General Archives of the Indies (Spain), 2,657
General Church of the New Jerusalem, 14,734
General Conference Mennonite Church, Board of Christian Service, Women in Christian Church Vocation, **5,200**
General Conference Mennonite Church, Central District, **13,759**
General Conference Mennonite Church, missions, 5,197, 5,198, **5,199**, 5,201
General Conference Mennonite Church, Women's Missionary Association, 5,196, **5,201**

General Director's Letter (AAUW, newsletter), 16,184
General Education Board (NY), **5,146**, 11,911
General Electric Company, 11,903
"General Electric Theatre" (television program), 5,240
General Federation Magazine (periodical), 250, 2,170
General Federation of Women's Clubs, 148, 250, 389, 540, 1,341, 1,385, 1,679, 1,734, **2,117**, 2,170, 2,595, 2,597, 2,674, 2,886, 3,670, 3,877, 3,899, 4,623, 4,630, 4,769, 4,775, 4,846, 4,918, 4,957, 5,112, 5,136, 5,426, 6,355, 6,638, 6,740, 6,798, 7,059, 7,190, 7,270, 7,738, 7,868, 8,187, 8,438, 8,482, 8,493, 8,633, 10,084, 10,101, 10,102, 10,534, **10,754**, 10,878, 10,886, 10,906, 10,940, 11,141, 11,236, 12,598, 12,893, 13,352, 13,439, 13,604, 13,753, 13,916, 14,219, 14,223, 14,553, 14,703, 14,705, 14,809, 16,115, 16,555, 17,158, 17,468, 17,654, 17,747
General Federation of Women's Clubs, consumer division, 9,349
General Federation of Women's Clubs, Department of literature, **12,484**
General Federation of Women's Clubs, Fifth District, **9,092**
"General Flight, The," 9,077
General Foods Corporation, Maxwell House division, 3,977
General Hospital No. 8 (New Albany, IN), 4,844
General Mills, 2,523, 6,495, 8,943, 8,970
General Mills, Home Service Department, 6,672
General Motors Corporation, 2,030
General Motors Corporation, Delco-Remy division, 8,133
General Motors, strike (1937), 11,905
General Pershing (book), 10,531
General Society of Mayflower Descendants, 14,230
General stores, 2,993, 3,413, 4,854, 4,892, 5,636, 7,409, 7,633, 7,647, 8,151, 9,467, 9,955, 10,515, 12,408, 16,510
General Theological Seminary (New York, NY), archives, **12,090**
Generals, 34, **68**, **1,398**, 1,444, 1,457, 1,484, 1,770, 1,786, 1,924, 2,061, **2,979**, 3,144, 3,219, **3,299**, 4,749, 5,040, 5,991, 6,504, 7,178, 7,225, 7,638, 7,677, 8,318, 8,351, 9,624, 9,678, 9,717, 9,912, 11,184, **11,874**, **11,876**, 12,326, 13,054, 13,344, 14,950, 15,025, 15,044, 16,097, **17,074**, 17,079, 17,083, 17,103, 17,420
Generation gap. *See* Conflict of generations
Genet, Cornelia Tappen (Clinton) [Mrs. Edmund Charles]. *See* Clinton, Cornelia Tappen. [Mrs. Edmund Charles] Genet
Genet, Edmund Charles (1763-1834), **12,210**
Genet, Martha B. [Mrs. Edmund Charles]. *See* Osgood, Martha B. [Mrs. Edmund Charles Genet]
Genetic code, 2,344
Genetic engineering, **6,336**
Genetic research, 11,830
Geneticists, 1,095
Geneva Community Club (IL), 4,273
Geneva Disarmament Conferences (1932-1935, 1935-1937), 6,771, 15,306
Geneva Female Seminary (NY), 12,368
Geneva Garden Club (IL), 4,273
Geneva Improvement Association (IL), 4,273
Geneva Medical College, 11,467, 11,748
Geneva Woman's Club (IL), 4,273
Gengalo, Oksana, 9,512
Genin, Jean Baptiste Marie, 13,661
Gens, Fannie, 17,282
Genthe, Arnold, 607
Gentle Living Publications, 1,786
Gentry, Ann Hawkins (1791-1870), 9,972, **9,974**
Gentry, Bobbie, 9,819
Gentry, Elizabeth, 9,833
Gentry, Eugenia "Eugie" [Mrs. Thomas Benton], 9,864
Gentry, Mary, 9,972
Gentry, Mary E., **9,863**
Gentry, Mary "Molly" [Mrs. Thomas Benton], 9,864
Gentry, Mary Wyatt [Mrs. Richard Harrison], 9,973
Gentry, Meredith Poindexter, 9,972
Gentry, North Todd (1866-1944), **9,972**

Gentry, Richard Harrison, **9,973**
Gentry, Sue, 9,972, 10,000
Gentry, Thomas Benton (1830-1906), **9,864**
Gentry, William R., Jr., 9,864, **9,974**
Genung, Ursula (1913-). *See* Walker, Ursula (Genung) [Mrs. Kenneth James] (1913-)
Geographers, **2,863**, **3,420**, 7,235
Geographical societies, **1,594**, 2,339, **2,863**, 14,235
Geography, 7,671, 16,054
Geological societies, 3,222
Geologists, 265, **608**, **1,478**, **2,200**, 2,566, **2,726**, **3,222**, **4,429**, **5,864**, 5,866, **6,316**, 6,986, 9,448, 10,726, 10,954, **11,262**, 12,015, 12,848, 12,961, 12,982, 13,048, 13,144, **14,005**, **14,893**, **15,956**, 16,274
Geology, 451, 6,916, 11,833, 13,593, 14,608
George, Alice, 6,800
George and Susan, The (ship), 1,505
George, Anna Angela (1877-1947). *See* DeMille, Anna Angela (George) [Mrs. William Churchill] (1877-1947)
George, Annie (Fox) [Mrs. Henry], 12,485
George B. Sohier Prize, 14,366
George Chamberlain (ship), 634
George, Edith. *See* Freeborn, Edith (George)
George Eliot Club (NE), **10,415**
George, Ellen (1858-?). *See* Bird, Ellen (George) (1858-?)
George, Emma L., **2,352**
George, Esther Ide Brewster [Mrs. William Reuben] (1872-1962), 11,596
George, Henry (1839-97), 2,301, **12,485**
George, Henry (1862-1916), 12,485
George, Julia [Miss] (?-1944), 318, 408
George Junior Republic, **11,596**, 11,633
George, Katherine, 1,663
George, Mary (Ormond) [Mrs. William] (1821-92). *See* Morris, Mary (Ormond) [Mrs. William] George [Mrs. John] (1821-92)
George Nugent Home for Baptists (PA), 11,056
George, Owen, and Brehmer (law firm, MN), 9,525
George Peabody College for Teachers (TN), faculty, 233, 266
George, Phoebe (1794-1840). *See* Bradford, Phoebe (George) [Mrs. Moses] (1794-1840)
George Polk Memorial Award (1962), 17,614
George, Prince of Denmark, 15,042
George Rogers Clark Memorial (KY), 5,307
George, Theodora, 2,233
George, Walter F., 3,133
George Washington Bicentennial Committee, 17,468
George Washington University, 2,171
  alumnae, 5,048
  faculty, 17,472
  graduate students, 11,629
George Washington University, Columbian Women, 2,114
George, William Reuben (1866-1936), 11,596
George, Zelma Watson, 3,799
Georgetown Shakespeare Club (CO), 1,716
Georgetown University (DC)
  archives, **2,118**
  faculty, 5,134
Georgetown Visitation Convent and Preparatory School (DC), **2,121**
Georgia, 2,994, 3,034, 3,081, 3,139, 3,141, 3,145, 3,206, 3,218, 3,222, 3,488, 3,603, 3,604, **3,607**, 3,617, 9,699, 12,958, 13,133
  abortion, legal aspects, 1,984
  actors and actresses, **3,477**
  Afro-Americans, 2,643, 3,115, **3,293**, 3,451, 3,593, 6,628
  agriculture, accounting, 13,155
  air, pollution, 3,162
  amateur theatricals, 3,204
  archivists, **2,981**, **3,210**
  art, decorative, 13,631
  art schools, 3,587
  art societies, 3,374
  artists, **3,082**, 3,090, **3,597**
  associations, institutions, etc., 3,166, **3,261**, **3,575**
  authors, 2,995, 3,009, 3,019, 3,020, 3,043, 3,071, **3,078**, **3,143**, 3,158, **3,159**, 3,174, **3,177**, **3,194**, **3,195**, **3,197**, 3,210, 3,225, 3,232, 3,256

19th-20th C, **3,028, 3,090, 13,027**
20th C, **3,073, 3,332, 3,350, 3,351**
ballet, 3,374
Baptists, **3,457**
boards of trade, 3,229
botanical gardens, 3,188
botanical societies, **3,188**
brickmaking, 3,270
businessmen, 3,148, **3,270**
businesswomen, **3,149,** 3,222, 3,451
Camp Fire Girls, **3,163**
cancer, nursing, **3,239**
canteens (war-time, emergency, etc.), 13,156
catalogs, college, **3,423, 3,428**
cemeteries, 3,387, 3,613
census, 3,606, **3,609**
centennial celebrations, 3,265
chaplains, hospital, Civil War, 3,173
charitable societies, **3,253,** 3,404, **3,507**
charitable societies, Jewish, **13,792, 13,797**
charities, 3,082, **3,083,** 3,135, **3,193,** 3,218, 3,399,
   3,451, **3,543**
charities, Afro-American, **3,302**
Cherokee Indians, 7,660
child care centers, 3,135, **3,253**
children, employment, **3,037**
Christian Science, 3,227
Christmas, 3,141
church records and registers, **3,494**
church records and registers, Baptist, 3,132, **3,455**
church records and registers, Methodist, **3,479**
church records and registers, Presbyterian, **3,114,
   3,416**
church societies, **3,363**
church societies, Baptist, 3,256, **3,453, 3,456, 3,457,
   3,458**
church societies, Methodist, **3,307, 3,479**
church societies, Presbyterian, **3,049,** 3,358
churches, 3,132, 3,218
churches, Baptist, 3,149, 3,168, 3,170, 3,256, 3,267
churches, Episcopal, 3,141
churches, Presbyterian, 3,266
citizens' associations, **3,283,** 3,293, 3,430, 3,469
city councilmen, 3,492
civil defense, 3,383
civil rights workers, **3,353, 3,469, 17,649**
Civil War, 3,145, 3,349, 9,661, 12,944
   campaigns and battles, 3,150, 3,210, 3,256, 3,271,
      3,419
   communications, 3,319
   nurses, 13,087
   personal narratives, **59,** 3,129, 3,173, 3,330,
      3,390, **13,257**
   prisoners and prisons, 3,208
   societies, Confederate, 3,076, 3,080, **3,164,** 3,169,
      3,219, **3,262,** 3,345, 3,419, **3,431,** 3,440, **3,537,
      3,616**
   war work, 3,249
clergy, 3,007, 3,008, 3,489
clergy, Baptist, **3,320**
clergy, German Baptist, 16,365
clergy, Methodist, 3,091, **3,333,** 3,524, **3,546**
clergy, Presbyterian, 3,208
clubs, 19, **2,964,** 3,077, 3,113, **3,127,** 3,130, **3,138,
   3,141, 3,142, 3,148,** 3,151, 3,159, 3,168, 3,169,
   3,189, 3,198, 3,204, 3,205, **3,209,** 3,218, 3,224,
   3,229, **3,231,** 3,236, **3,237, 3,243,** 3,245, 3,254,
   3,265, **3,274, 3,277,** 3,305, **3,322,** 3,358, **3,365,**
   3,371, 3,374, 3,384, **3,403,** 3,419, 3,430, 3,439,
   3,571, 3,574, 3,585, **3,592**
clubs, Afro-American, **3,282**
coeducation, 3,328
college administrators, **3,066,** 3,126
college librarians, 3,106
college presidents, **3,281, 3,328,** 3,405
college students, 3,015, 13,257
college teachers, 3,126, **3,305, 3,316,** 3,318, **3,347,**
   3,405, **3,459**
college trustees, 3,321
colonial period, 3,550
commemorative porcelain, 3,260
commission merchants, 3,496
commonplace books, 3,496, 3,501, 3,526, **3,553**
community leadership, 3,316

community organization, 3,302
congresses and conventions, 6,729
congressmen, 3,008
congresswomen, **3,372**
conservatories of music, 3,180, 3,367, 3,582
consuls, British, in, 2,966
contemplative orders, **3,601**
corrections, 3,430
cotton, 3,115, 3,270
county government, records and correspondence,
   3,002
deans (in schools), **3,125, 3,234,** 3,356, 3,463
dentists, Afro-American, **3,038**
department heads (universities), **3,123**
diaries and journals, 59, **3,147, 3,150,** 3,173, 3,390,
   3,419, **3,426,** 3,487, **3,546, 13,021**
divorce, 3,525
dormitories, **3,053**
economic conditions, 3,323
education, 3,323, **3,472**
educational associations, **2,959,** 3,136, 3,140, 3,151,
   3,360, 3,480, 3,535, **3,573, 3,574**
educators, **3,088, 3,131, 3,327,** 3,342
elections, 3,430
epidemics, 3,170, 3,205
executions, 3,396
executive advisory bodies, 3,430
executives, 3,135, 3,179, 3,229, 3,246
exhibition buildings, 3,151
exhibitions (1895), 3,275
farm tenancy, 3,576
farmers, **3,315, 3,319, 3,320, 3,331, 3,344**
fire departments, 3,215
flower shows, 3,050
forests and forestry, 3,357
freedmen, 2,919
freedwomen, 3,481
furniture industry and trade, 3,199
gardening, societies, **3,050,** 3,082, **3,187,** 3,196,
   3,233, 3,358, 3,374, 3,439
gardens, 3,077, 3,082
genealogists, 3,358
genealogy, 3,054, 3,088, 3,222, **3,606,** 3,612, 3,618
general stores, 2,993, 3,413
geologists, **3,222**
governors, 3,135, **3,158,** 3,266, 3,381, 3,389, 3,394,
   3,429, **3,516,** 3,587, 13,144
gravestones, **3,615**
greek letter societies, 3,077
grocers, 3,496, 3,562
gynecologists, **3,146, 3,309**
halls of fame, 3,225
health boards, **3,608**
health-officers, 3,482
high school principals, 3,191
high schools, 3,132, 3,153, 3,165, **3,191,** 3,215,
   3,224, 3,241, 3,255, 3,256
historians, 3,418
historic buildings, 3,549, 3,561
   conservation and restoration, 3,600
historic sites, conservation and restoration, 3,440,
   3,441
historical societies, 3,131, **3,139,** 3,210, 3,222,
   3,225, 3,587, **3,610**
hospitals, 3,216, 3,268, 3,275, **3,588**
hospitals, Afro-American, 3,293, **3,508**
hotels, taverns, etc. 3,007, 3,148, 3,388, 3,390,
   3,425, 3,545
housewives, 3,317
islands, 3,132
Jews, 3,147
journalism, societies, 3,117, 3,357
journalists, **3,143,** 3,225, 3,251, **3,325, 3,327, 3,335,
   3,336, 3,338,** 3,340, 3,350, 3,357, **3,437,** 3,488,
   3,491, 3,602
judges, 3,323, 15,565
justices of the peace, 3,414
kindergarten, 3,131, 3,136, 3,140, 3,522, **3,535,**
   3,573, **3,574**
land grants, 3,246, 3,258, 3,509
land titles, 3,271
law, cases, 3,224
lawyers, 3,158, **3,218, 3,323,** 3,436
legal documents, 3,414

legal secretaries,
legislators, 3,133
legislators, Afro-American, **3,293**
librarians, 3,090, 3,451
libraries, 3,200
library administration, 3,200
library finance, 3,520
literary societies, 2,977, 3,159, **3,201, 3,211**
local church councils, 3,137
lynching, 3,186
   prevention of, 3,279
mayors, 3,154, 3,203, 3,481
medical colleges, 3,234
medical societies, auxiliaries, **3,273**
mental hygiene, 3,273
merchants, 3,033, **3,319, 3,344,** 3,352, **3,556**
midwives, 3,482
monasteries, **3,601**
municipal government, records and correspondence,
   3,384
murder, 3,186, 12,682
music teachers, **3,582**
musical societies, 3,195, 3,198, 3,229, 3,318, 3,374
national cemeteries, 3,274
Native Americans, 3,485
   mortuary customs, 3,121
   religion, 3,121
   social life and customs, 3,121
   wars, 3,402
newspapers, 3,197, 3,203, 3,224, 3,227, 3,239,
   3,240, 3,271, 3,326, 3,340, 3,419
   sections, columns, etc., 3,251, 3,262, 3,276, 3,350
novelists, **3,325, 3,336, 3,338**
nurses, history, 6,160
nursing homes, **3,239**
obstetricians, **3,309**
obstetrics, study and teaching, 3,482
officials and employees, 2,981, **3,222,** 3,399
open-air schools, 3,226
opera, 3,275
oral history, **3,451, 3,474**
ordinaries, 3,379
orphans and orphan asylums, 3,371
parents' and teachers' associations, **3,493**
parks, 3,130, 3,276
patriotic societies, 3,076, 3,169, **3,175, 3,212, 3,213,**
   3,214, **3,219,** 3,345, 3,358, **3,385,** 3,423, 3,439,
   3,497, 3,498, 3,509, 3,605, 3,615
periodicals, **3,006,** 3,209
philanthropists, **3,321,** 3,587
photographers, **3,115**
physicians, **2,963,** 2,965, 3,007, 3,008, **3,091, 3,161,**
   3,333, 3,381, **3,481, 3,482,** 3,487
pioneers and settlers, **62,** 3,141
place names, 3,381
plantation life, 3,419, 13,257
plantations, 3,410, 3,477
poets, **2,982, 3,177**
poets laureate, **3,312,** 3,358
politics and government, 3,008, 3,357, 13,010
politics, practical, women's activism, **3,217,** 3,308,
   3,324, 3,356, **3,362,** 13,176
power-plants, 3,179
private schools, **3,055, 3,094,** 3,130, 3,170, 3,245,
   3,264, 3,266, 3,435
public health, 3,145, 3,273
public health nursing, 3,432
public housing, 3,293
public institutions, **3,572**
public prosecutors, 3,524
public records, **3,119**
public schools, 3,088, 3,140, 3,215, **3,364**
public welfare, 3,356
public works, **3,119, 3,120**
race problems, 3,145, 3,157, 3,302, 3,343, 3,347,
   3,357, 12,939
railroad companies, 3,086
railroad societies, 3,220
railroads, 3,145, 3,246
reading interests, **3,107**
real estate business, 3,149, 3,152, 3,270
Reconstruction, 3,007, 3,145, 3,227, 3,319
Red Cross, **2,960**
reformatories, 3,356

reformatories for women, 3,469
religious education, 16,257
riots, 3,301
rural schools, **3,244**
sanatoriums, 3,158
scholarships, 3,066
school administrators, 3,474
school boards, **3,105**, 3,206
school census, **3,102**
school superintendents and principals, 3,080, **3,226**, 3,265, 3,342, **3,409**
school yearbooks, 3,435
schools, 3,039, **3,042**, **3,068**, **3,122**, **3,397**, **3,434**, **3,475**, 3,484, **3,523**
scrapbooks, 3,489, 3,534
senators, United States, **3,008**, 3,389, 3,394
sewing, **2,998**
sex discrimination in employment, 3,451
Sherman's march to the sea, 2,277
singers, **3,267**
slave records, 2,985, 3,270, 3,271, 3,373, 3,506
slave trade, 3,043, **3,089**, 3,215
slavery, 3,396, 6,628
slaves, 3,373, 3,478, **6,628**
  pictorial works, **3,478**
social life and customs, 63, **2,962**, 3,012, 3,024, 3,141, 3,323, 3,389, 3,581, 3,585, 16,057
social workers, **3,399**
socialists, **3,329**
sociologists, **3,356**
soft drink industry, 3,210
soldiers
  Civil War, Confederate, 3,262, **3,315**, 3,320, **3,331, 3,344**
  World War I, 3,250
soldiers' monuments, **2,961**, 3,345, 13,053
Spanish occupation, 3,420
speech clinics,
speech therapy,
storekeepers, 3,317
stores, retail, 13,010
student aid, Afro-Americans, 3,280
students, 3,474
students' societies, **3,124**, 3,191, 3,281
suffrage, 3,169, **3,240**, 3,362
suffrage societies, **3,183**, 3,240
suffragists, 3,324
surgeons, **3,054**
symphony orchestras, 3,195
teachers, **3,013**, **3,215**, 3,265, **3,308**, 3,329, **3,409**, 3,413, 3,419, 3,451, 3,474, 3,610, 6,650
teachers' colleges, 2,986, 3,131, 3,140, **3,363**
teachers' unions, 3,308
telephone operators, 3,451
temperance, 3,069
temperance societies, **3,306**
tenant farmers, Afro-American, 12,682
textbooks, 3,434
theater, 3,145, 13,026
theaters, 3,267
titles of honor, **3,272**
trade and professional associations, **3,162**, **3,190**, **3,361**, **3,378**, 3,432, 3,439, 3,444
trade-unions, 3,145
  officials and employees, **3,449**
  political activity, **3,443**
tropical crops, 3,477
tuberculosis, cases, clinical reports, statistics, **3,134**
typhoid epidemics, 2,991
United Nations associations, 3,399
universities and colleges, **3,095**, **3,098**, 3,157, 3,218, 3,258, 3,305, 3,313, 3,328, 3,356, **3,384**, **3,473**, 13,398
  admission, 3,381
  archives, **3,280**, **3,470**
  history, **3,085**
utopias, **2,991**, 3,603
vital statistics, 3,482
voters, registration of, 3,443
war memorials, 3,437
widows, **3,370**
wills, 3,481
women, education, 3,245, 3,264, 3,266

women's colleges, 3,157, 3,271, 3,379, **3,392**, 3,422, **3,452**
women's liberation movement, 3,451
World War I, civilians' work, **3,383**
World War II, civilians' work, 3,451
yellow fever epidemics, 3,564
Young Women's Christian Association, 3,302, 3,305
Georgia Association of Legal Secretaries, Atlanta Chapter,
Georgia Association of Women Lawyers, 3,439
Georgia Board of Examiners, 3,432
Georgia Botanical Society, 3,187, **3,188**
Georgia Citizens Committee for Children and Youth, 3,430
Georgia College, **3,392, 3,473**
Georgia College (GA), archives, **3,470**
Georgia Colony, 3,509
Georgia, Commission on Constitutional Government, 3,437
Georgia Committee on Interracial Cooperation, 3,157
Georgia Confederate Memorial, 2,218
Georgia Conference on Social Work, 3,356
Georgia Council on Human Relations, 13,176
Georgia Court of Appeals, 15,565
Georgia Department of Natural Resources, Historic Preservation Section, 3,441
Georgia Department of Welfare, 3,356, 3,399
Georgia Dietetic Association, 3,439
Georgia Education Association, 3,140
Georgia Episcopal Institute (GA), 3,419
Georgia Federation of Business and Professional Women's Clubs, 3,439
Georgia Federation of Women's Clubs, 3,113, 3,138, 3,151, 3,159, 3,169, **3,189**, 3,371, 3,383, 3,430, 3,439, 3,574
Georgia Female College (Madison, GA), 3,015, 3,072
Georgia, Florida, and Alabama Railroad, 3,268
Georgia Forestry Association, 3,357
Georgia Gladiolus Society, 3,187
Georgia Hall of Fame, 3,225
Georgia Historical Commission, 3,441
Georgia Historical Quarterly, 3,048
Georgia Historical Society, 3,514, 3,587
Georgia Home Economics Association, 3,439
Georgia Home Journal (periodical), 3,017
Georgia Hussars, Jefferson Davis Legion, 3,593
Georgia Infantry, Company I, Fortieth Regiment, 3,315
Georgia Infirmary, **3,508**
Georgia Interracial Committee, 3,469
Georgia Journeys (book), 2,994
Georgia Kindergarten Association, 3,140
Georgia Legislative Forum for Women, 3,430
Georgia Library Association, 3,107
Georgia Military Institute, 13,079
Georgia Militia, 3,412
Georgia Mothers' Committee, 3,439
Georgia Negro Training School for Delinquent Girls, 3,469
Georgia Normal and Agricultural College, presidents, 15,377
Georgia Normal and Industrial College. *See* Georgia College
Georgia Nurses Association, **3,444**
"Georgia Nursing" (periodical), 3,190
Georgia Nutrition Council, 3,439
Georgia Patriot, The (newspaper), 3,240
Georgia Power Co., 3,135, 3,179
Georgia Press Association, 3,117, 3,357
Georgia Press Institute, 3,357
Georgia Public Forums, 3,357
Georgia Railroad, 2,984
Georgia Scenes (book), 3,404
Georgia School of Technology, students, 13,064
Georgia Society of Colonial Dames of the 17th Century, 3,439
Georgia State
  Baptist associations, **3,456**, 3,458
  Baptists, 3,454
    societies, etc., **3,453**
  church records and registers, **3,455**
  church societies, Baptist, 3,455, **3,458**
Georgia, State Board of Family and Children's Services, 3,430

Georgia State College for Women. *See* Georgia College
Georgia State Council of Social Agencies, 3,399
Georgia State Lunatic Asylum, 3,512
Georgia State Normal School (Athens, GA), **3,098**, 3,108, 3,125
Georgia State Normal School (Athens, GA), history, **3,085**
Georgia State Nursing Association, **3,190**, 3,432
Georgia State Teachers' Colleges, 2,986
Georgia State Troops, Company I, First Regiment, First Brigade, 3,315
Georgia States Rights Democratic party, 3,437
Georgia Training School for Girls, 3,356
Georgia Volunteers, Fifty-first Regiment, 3,559
Georgia Voters League, 5,466
Georgia Woman's Suffrage Association, 3,240
Georgia Workers Education Service, 4,126
Georgia Writers' Association, 2,977
Georgian-American (newspaper), 3,251
Geraghty, Helen Tieken [Mrs. Maurice P.] (1902-), 4,066, **4,091**
Gerald, Florence, 1,224
Geraldine (book), 13,594
Geraldine, Sister M., 17,371
Gerard, Sister M., 10,732
Gerber, Merrill Joan, **1,583**
Gerbich, Helen. *See* Wittenberg, Helen (Gerbich) [Mrs. Ralph K.]
Gerhardi, William. *See* Gerhardie, William
Gerhardie, William, 4,491, 16,173
Geriatric nursing, 6,123
Geriatrics, 17,295
Gerlach, George, 16,071
Gerlach, John, 16,071
Gerlach, Margaret Moody, **16,071**
Germain, Lucy D., **6,140**
German Aid Society of Chicago (IL), **4,092**
German-American periodicals, 7,999
German-Americans, 1,534, 8,704, 10,509
  evacuation and relocation (1942-1945), 2,702
German Council of Women, 16,580
German Democratic Republic, 6,489
German Land Association of Minnesota, 14,910
German Methodist Church (Humboldt, NE), 10,476
German Teachers' Seminary (Milwaukee, WI), 13,905
Germann, Gertrude (1881-?), 3,969
Germany, 12,285, 12,289
  ambassadors to, 12,434
  American diplomats in, 2,188
  Americans in, 7,469
  congresses and conventions, 8,362
  feminism, 6,789
  international relief, 11,593
  reconstruction (1914-1939), 12,487
  school administrators, 14,943
  social life and customs, 6,862
  World War I, **6,470**
    nurses, 13,336
Germany, East, political prisoners, personal narratives, 6,106
Germany, Mrs. C. C., Jr., 9,667
"Germs of Thought," 15,117
Geronimo, 14,777
Gerontologists, **7,241**, **8,674**
Gerould, Katharine Elizabeth (Fullerton) [Mrs. Gordon Hall] (1879-1944), **11,162**
Gerrard, Elizabeth Caroline (Weaver) [Mrs. Leonard] (1852-1924), **10,462**
Gerrish, W. B., 14,123
Gerry, Elbridge, 1,501
Gerry, Eliza [Mrs. Elbridge], 1,501
Gerry, Eloise [Miss], **17,768**
Gershoy, Eugenie (1905-), **12,898**
Gershwin, George, 1,451
Gershwin, Ira, 1,451, 17,796
Gerstenberg, Alice (1885-1972), 3,825, 3,828, **3,847**, 3,848, **3,994**, 3,997, 3,999, 4,007, **6,597**
Gerstenberg, Julia (Wieschendorff) [Mrs. E.] (1861-1938), **3,848**
Gerstle, Alice (1873-?). *See* Levison, Alice (Gerstle) [Mrs. Jacob Bertha] (1873-?)
Gerstley, Jennie R. [Mrs. Henry M.], **13,785**
Gesell, Arnold Lucius (1880-1961), **2,353**

Gesell, Beatrice (Chandler) [Mrs. Arnold Lucius] (1875-1965), 2,353

Gesell Institute of Child Development (CT), 2,168, 2,353

Gesell, Katherine. See Walden, Katherine (Gesell) [Mrs. Joseph Whitelsen]

Get Out of the Garden, Nellie, the Flowers are Gone! (book), 6,017

"Get Smart" (television program), 17,958

Gethsemane Episcopal Church (Minneapolis, MN), Woman's Guild, 9,093

Gettemy, James N., 1,859

"Getting Ready to Be an Old Maid" (story), 12,473

Getty, Annie (?-1926). See McClure, Annie (Getty) [Mrs. Charles] (?-1926)

Getty Family (NM), 11,241

Getty, George W., 11,241

Gettys, Luella. See Key, Luella (Gettys) [Mrs. V. A., Jr.]

Getz, Ann. See Lake, Ann (Getz) [Mrs. Edward] Hutchinson [Mrs. Andrew Leech] (ca. 1800-?)

Geva, Tamara, 6,024

Geyer, Georgie Anne (1935-), 6,025

Geyer, Henry S., 9,865

Geyers, Thomas, 5,695

Gherardi, Jane Putnam (Bancroft), 11,514, 12,434

Gholson, William Yates (1807-70), 13,846

Ghost Cities of Colorado (book), 1,804

"Ghost Dance War and Wounded Knee Massacre of 1890-91, The," 7,220

Ghostley, Mary (Chapman) [Mrs. Fred] (1881-1975), 8,396, 8,995

Ghosts with Southern Accents and Evidence of Extrasensory Perception (book), 9,727

Giambarresi, Anna Porter, 5,171

Giant Joshua, The (book), 16,972

Gibb, Walcott, 5,512

Gibbes, Ann [Mrs. Robert], 15,474

Gibbes Art Gallery (SC), 15,424

Gibbes, Eliza Ford (1808-75). See Holmes, Eliza Ford (Gibbes) (1808-75)

Gibbes Family (SC), 15,474

Gibbes, Frances (de Saussure) [Mrs. William Stuart], 15,411

Gibbes, James Schoolbred, 15,413

Gibbes, John, 15,474

Gibbes, Juliet Georgiana. See Elliott, Juliet Georgiana (Gibbes) [Mrs. Barnard]

Gibbes, Maria H. Drayton (1784-1826), 15,474

Gibbes, Mary Ann, 15,474

Gibbes, Mary Lee (Evans) [Mrs. James Schoolbred] (?-1888), 15,413

Gibbes, Mrs. Arthur S., 15,742

Gibbes, Robert (1732-94), 15,474

Gibbons, A. S., 1,584

Gibbons, Abigail (Hopper) (1801-93), 5,907, 6,598

Gibbons, Abraham, Jr., 2,031

Gibbons, Alice Howe. See James, Alice Howe (Gibbons) [Mrs. William]

Gibbons, Eleanor P. See Sharp, Eleanor P. (Gibbons) [Mrs. Louis H.]

Gibbons Family (GA), 3,587

Gibbons Family (PA), 15,021

Gibbons, Fanny (1818-61). See Montez, Lola. Marie Dolores Eliza Rosanna Gilbert. [Mrs. Thomas] James [Mrs. George] Trafford [Mrs. Patrick Purdy] Hall. Fanny Gibbons (1818-61)

Gibbons, Frances North (Moale) [Mrs. John], 15,008

Gibbons, Hannah, 2,060

Gibbons, Helen Davenport (Brown) [Mrs. Herbert Adams] (1882-1960), 11,179

Gibbons, Herbert Adams (1880-1934), 11,179

Gibbons, John, 3,554

Gibbons, John (1827-86), 15,008

Gibbons, Joseph, 3,554

Gibbons, Katherine Clark, 11,827

Gibbons, Maggie (McLennan) (1885-), 16,356

Gibbons, Sarah, 15,021

Gibbons, Sarah Cloud [Mrs. A. S.], 1,584

Gibbs, Elizabeth Sheafe (?-1718), 7,633

Gibbs, Jane [Miss], 17,085

Gibbs, Jane DeBow, 8,404

Gibbs, Lillian, 12,486

Gibbs, Lucy (Weston), 17,029

Gibbs, Mrs. Addison C., 14,418

Gibbs, Robert (1634-74), 7,633

Giberson, Bonnie (1918-). See Stahler, Bonnie (Giberson) (1918-)

Gibran, Kahlil, 2,283, 12,705

Gibson, Althea, 12,004

Gibson, Anson Wright, 11,676

Gibson, C. B., 4,419

Gibson, Charles Dana, 6,599, 7,254

Gibson, Dorothy M. [Mrs. Anson Wright], 11,676

Gibson, Eleanor B., 11,407

Gibson, Elizabeth Bordley [Mrs. James] (1777-1863), 15,037

Gibson, Elvena Miller [Mrs. J. H.] (1905-63), 5,394

Gibson, Eva Katherine (Clapp) [Mrs. C. B.] (1875-1916), 4,419

Gibson Family, 864

Gibson Family (LA), 5,343

Gibson, Irene (Langhorne) [Mrs. Charles Dana], 2,198, 6,599

Gibson, Manomas Lavina (1842-1940). See Andrus, Manomas Lavina (Gibson) (1842-1940)

Gibson, Margaret, 12,520

Gibson, Margaret Purdy [Mrs.] (1849-?), 11,597

Gibson, Mary, 5,119

Gibson, Mary, 17,365

Gibson, Mary Bass (1905-), 11,866

Gibson, Mrs. Peter, 5,150

Gibson, Sarah Ellen (?-1908), 135

Gibson, Sarah (Hollingsworth) [Mrs. William], 13,063

Gibson, Sarah Huger, 15,441

Giddings, Allan M., 8,230

Giddings, Catherine (Randall) [Mrs. Luther?] (ca. 1829-?), 5,802

Giddings Family (MD), 5,802

Giddings, Mary Coult, 10,810

Giddings, Paula, 9,575

Giddy Moment (book), 7,202

Gide, André, 11,153

Gidlow, Elsa, 1,082

Giese-Cronin defense, 14,691

Giesler, Mathilde Franziska (1817-84). See Anneke, Mathilde Franziska (Giesler) [Mrs. Fritz] (1817-84)

Giffen, Helen (Smith) (1893-?), 498, 830

Giffen, R. L., 16,151

Giffin, Etta Josselyn [Miss] (?-1932), 2,505

Gifford, Ellen M. See Leland, Ellen M. (Gifford) [Mrs. Luther E.]

Gifford Family, 5,362

Gifford, Frances, 15,370

Gifford, Harley Nelson, 5,362

Gifford, Helen. See Clegg, Helen (Gifford) [Mrs. William]

Gift-books (annuals, etc.), 12,337

Gifted children, 10,475
   education, 6,808, 13,742
   research, 13,736

Gifts, spiritual, 16,359

Gigous Family (MO), 9,975

Gigous, George, 9,975

Gigous, Mary [Mrs. George], 9,975

Gilbert, Adelia F. [Mrs. Joseph Lucien], 14,564

Gilbert, Amy M., 11,285

Gilbert, Anne Jane (Hartley) [Mrs. George Henry] (1821-1904), 11,985

Gilbert, Barclay, 13,927

Gilbert, Caroline (Chapman) [Mrs. Joseph T.] (1793 or 1794-1868), 11,474

Gilbert, Cass (1859-1934), 2,354

Gilbert, Clara, 11,440

Gilbert, E. P., 11,743

Gilbert, Elizabeth (Lathrop) [Mrs. John Henry] (1825-1910), 11,475

Gilbert, Fabiola Cabeza de Baca (1898-), 11,217

Gilbert Family (IL), 4,420

Gilbert, Hannah (1830-85). See Cox, Hannah (Gilbert) [Mrs. James] (1830-85)

Gilbert Islands, missionaries to, 3,642

Gilbert, James H., 4,420

Gilbert, John Henry, 11,475

Gilbert, Joseph Lucien, 14,564

Gilbert, Joseph T., 11,474

Gilbert, Julia, 1,585

Gilbert, Julia (Finch) [Mrs. Cass] (1862-1952), 2,354

Gilbert, Katharine (1860-1956). See Francke, Katharine (Gilbert) [Mrs. Kuno] (1860-1956)

Gilbert, Lida, 10,714

Gilbert, Mabelle Agnes, 7,793

Gilbert, Maria Rita Madam [Mrs.], 3,510

Gilbert, Mary, 11,294

Gilbert, Mary (Baker) [Mrs. Asa] (1821-1910). See Eddy, Mary (Baker) [Mrs. Asa] Gilbert [Mrs. George Washington] Glover [Mrs. Daniel Patterson] (1821-1910)

Gilbert, Mary Lukens, 13,927

Gilbert, Mary Morse [Mrs.], 4,420

Gilbert, Mrs., 880

Gilbert, Mrs. J. L., 13,322

Gilbert, Page Morris [Mrs. Wells Smith], 14,565

Gilbert, Perry, 11,541

Gilbert vs. Parsons, Bros., Linn Company, 14,564

Gilbert, Wells Smith (1870-1965), 14,565

Gilbert, Yvette, 11,997

Gilbertson, Vera, 17,497

Gilboy, Elizabeth Waterman [Mrs.] (1903-73), 6,600

Gilbreath, Olive. See McLorn, Olive (Gilbreath)

Gilbreth, Ernestine Moller (1908-). See Carey, Ernestine Moller (Gilbreth) (1908-)

Gilbreth Family, 7,202

Gilbreth, Frank (1868-1924), 4,682

Gilbreth, Lillian Evelyn (Moller) [Mrs. Frank B.] (1878-1972), 2,692, 4,682, 5,122, 5,123, 6,958, 7,241, 11,144, 11,900, 12,095

Gilchrist, Adeline, 886

Gilchrist, Emma S., 15,474

Gilchrist Family (SC), 15,474

Gilchrist, Margaret, 5,063

Gilchrist, Mary Wilson, 17,439

Gilchrist, Robert, Family (OH), 17,439

Gilder Family, 2,733

Gilder, Helena (de Kay) [Mrs. Richard Watson], 1,434, 1,581, 2,370, 6,451

Gilder, Jeannette Leonard [Miss] (1849-1916), 6,601, 11,036

Gilder, Richard Watson (1844-1909), 1,410, 1,500, 1,581, 5,414, 6,601, 11,996, 12,029, 12,380

Gilder, Rosamond (1896-), 7,310

Gildersleeve, Anna Maria, 11,097

Gildersleeve Family (NJ), 11,097

Gildersleeve, Virginia Crocheron (1877-1965), 2,067, 11,825, 11,849, 11,999

Gildez, Jeanette L., 11,084

Gilds, 5,670, 6,008

Gile, Elizabeth, 11,889

Giles, Aguila, 11,318

Giles, Eliza, 11,318

Giles, Ella (1851-1915). See Ruddy, Ella (Giles) (1851-1915)

Giles, Gwen, 10,191

Giles, Harriet E., 3,280, 12,740

Giles, Janice (Holt) Moore [Mrs. Henry] (1909-), 5,263, 5,264, 5,342

Giles, Kezia (1840-1927). See Carroll, Kezia (Giles) [Mrs. Charles N.] (1840-1927)

Giles, Kris (pseudonym). See Nielsen, Helen Bernice (1918-)

Giles, Rosena A., 830

Gilkey, Charles W., 6,696

Gilkey, Helen, 14,273

Gilkinson, Bernice, 2,876

Gill, Bessie Faunce, 6,851

Gill, Brendan, 12,367

Gill, Daisy Sanial [Mrs.], 2,355

Gill, Irving J., 1,198

Gill, Isabella. See Knight, Isabella (Gill) [Mrs. Harvey J.]

Gill, Lucy (1855-1935). See Gill, Mother Irene (1855-1935)

Gill, Martha. See Mack, Martha (Gill) Mack [Mrs. John T.]

Gill, Mary Jane, 16,176

Gill, Mother Irene (1855-1935), 11,807

Gill, Sarah Prince (1728-71), 5,928

Gilleland, Rebecca Jane (1831-1926). See Fisher, Rebecca Jane (Gilleland) [Mrs Orceneth] (1831-1926)

Gillespie, Eliza Maria (1824-87). *See* Gillespie, Mother Angela (1824-87)
Gillespie, Emily Elizabeth (Hawley), 4,920
Gillespie Family (FL), 2,923
Gillespie, Maria Rebecca (1828-?). *See* Ewing, Maria Rebecca (Gillespie) (1828-?)
Gillespie, Mother Angela (1824-87), 4,643
Gillespie, Robert, 13,583
Gillespie, Sarah (1865-1952?). *See* Huftalen, Sarah (Gillespie) (1865-1952?)
Gillespy, Frances (1875-1967). *See* Wickes, Frances (Gillespy) (1875-1967)
Gillet, Lily, 9,425
Gillett, Arthur Lincoln (1859-1938), **1,847**
Gillett, Eliza Jane (1805-71). *See* Bridgman, Eliza Jane (Gillett) [Mrs. Elijah] (1805-71)
Gillett, Lucy H. (1880-1975), 12,079
Gillett, Rachel (Dayton), 982
Gillett, Sarah Colton Phillips (?-1951), **1,847**
Gillette, Elisabeth "Lilly" (1835-1915). *See* Warner, Elisabeth "Lilly" (Gillette) [Mrs. George] (1835-1915)
Gillette, Emma Genevieve (1898-), **7,794**
Gillette, Genevieve, 7,785
Gillette, Mabel "Daisy" Hyde, 1,233
Gillette State Hospital for Crippled Children (MN), 8,621
Gillette, Viola (Pratt) (1871-1956). *See* McFarlane, Viola (Pratt) Gillette (1871-1956)
Gillhouse, Eva Olenna, **499**
Gilliam, Beverly, **12,654**
Gillies, May, 17,919
Gilliland, Atma Dorthea, 1,124
Gillingham, Anna (1878-1964), 2,396, 15,278
Gillingham, Edith H., 15,009
Gillingham, Elizabeth A. [Mrs. Theodore T.] (1837-1929), 15,278
Gillingham Family, **15,278**
Gillingham, Harrold E. (1864-1954), **15,009**
Gillingham, Theodore T. (1836-1923), 15,278
Gillis, Anna [Mrs. Hudson B.], 500
Gillis, Ethel L. [Mrs. Claude E.], 500
Gillis Family (CA), **500**
Gilman, Etta C., 13,890
Gillum Family (CA), 1,648
Gilma, Robbins, 9,094
Gilman, Anna Canfield (Park) [Mrs. Winthrop S., Jr.], 12,211
Gilman, Caroline (Howard) [Mrs. Samuel] (1794-1888), 317, 850, 3,926, **7,634**, 12,403, **15,475**
Gilman, Catheryne Cooke [Mrs. Robbins] (1880-1954), **9,094**, 9,095, 9,270, 9,297
Gilman, Charlotte Anna (Perkins) [Mrs. George Walter] Stetson [Mrs. George Houghton] (1860-1935), 860, **1,952**, **2,356**, 2,403, 6,392, **6,602**, 7,044, 7,216, 7,227, 11,568, 12,835, **15,382**
Gilman, Daniel Coit (1831-1908), 1,979, 5,728, 5,729, 5,733
Gilman, Dorothy (1923-), 6,060
Gilman, Elisabeth (1867-1950), 2,415, **5,768**
Gilman, Elizabeth Drinker Paxson, 9,095
Gilman, Elizabeth L., 14,421
Gilman, Estella Mae (Trowbridge) [Mrs. Henry Alfred], **17,388**
Gilman Family, 1,504
Gilman Family (NY), **12,211**
Gilman, Frances Paxson, 9,095
Gilman, George Houghton, 2,356, 6,602
Gilman, Helen Ives, 9,095
Gilman, Logan, 9,095
Gilman, Louisa (1797-1868). *See* Loring, Louisa (Gilman) [Mrs. Ellis] (1797-1868)
Gilman, Mildred. *See* Wohlforth, Mildred Gilman [Mrs. Robert]
Gilman, Miss, 2,372
Gilman, Rhoda (Raasch) [Mrs. Logan], 9,095, 9,230
Gilman, Robbins, Family (MN), **9,095**
Gilman, Samuel (1791-1858), **7,634**, 15,468, 15,475
Gilmer, Elizabeth (Meriwether) (1861-1951), 3,110, 5,269, **5,505**, 5,543, 7,209, 17,274, 9,823, **15,871**
Gilmer, Louisa Frederika (Alexander) [Mrs. Jeremy F.], **3,511**

Gilmer, Louisa Porter. *See* Minis, Louisa Porter (Gilmer) [Mrs. J. Florance]
Gilmore, Blanche Basye [Mrs. Eugene], **4,527**
Gilmore, Eugene Allen (1873-1970), **4,527**
Gilmore, George Harrison (1866-1955), **10,463**
Gilmore, Grace [Mrs. Edward] Marron [Mrs. James W.], **10,309**
Gilmore, Helen R., 11,591
Gilmore, Margaret B. [Miss] (1869-1946), **4,528**
Gilmore, Patrick Sarsfield, 2,022
Gilmour, Alice. *See* Abbott, Alice (Gilmour) Young [Mrs. Albert J.]
Gilmour, Jane, 8,295
Gilmour, John A., 8,295
Gilmour, Kate, 8,295
Gilpin County Pioneer Association (CO), **1,776**
Gilpin, Elizabeth, 3,581
Gilpin, Elizabeth (?-1850), **2,049**
Gilpin Family, 11,599
Gilpin, Gertrude, 2,045
Gilpin, Laura (1891-), 11,217, 11,235
Gilroy, Susan M., 1,635
Gilrye, Ann. *See* Muir, Ann (Gilrye)
Gilson, Elnora, 3,967
Gilson Family (CA), **1,299**
Gilson, Mary B., 7,578
Gilson, Mary Barnett [Miss] (1877-1969), **13,015**
Gilstrap, Josie (1858-93). *See* Keeler, Josie (Gilstrap) [Mrs. George B.] (1858-93)
Gilstrap, Julia (Johnson) Whiteturkey [Mrs. Bob]. *See* Dalton, Julia (Johnson) Whiteturkey [Mrs. Bob] Gilstrap [Mrs. Earnest] Lewis [Mrs. Emmett]
Gimbel, Mrs. Bernard, 12,708
Gimble, Elinor, 2,589, 4,970
"Gimme a Pigfoot" (song), 5,533
Gingerich, Mary A. (1908-), **5,050**
Ginsberg, Allen, 11,983, 12,064
Ginsburg, Claire (1897-). *See* Sifton, Claire (Ginsburg) [Mrs. Paul] (1897-)
Giovanni, Nikki (1943-), **6,026**, 9,575, 15,334
Gipsies, 5,655, 12,535
Girdler, Barbara (Kitchell) [Mrs. Reynolds], 1,837
Girdner, Ephraim, 3,354
Girl Graduate, Her Own Book, The, 9,382
Girl Guides, 9,057, 12,093, **12,104**
"Girl in the Lifeboat, The" (story), 6,831
Girl Inside, The (book), 4,987
Girl of the Hills (book), 9,652
Girl Pioneers of America, **12,105**
Girl Reserves, 3,653
Girl Scout Leader (periodical), 12,113
Girl Scout National Council, **12,101**
Girl Scouts, Association of Executive Staff, **1,991**
Girl Scouts Council (IN), **4,564**
Girl Scouts, Huron Valley Council (MI), **7,795**
Girl Scouts, Local Directors' Association, 6,759
Girl Scouts of America, 5,136, 7,148, 8,635, **12,107**, 14,822
Girl Scouts of the USA, 74, 1,525, 1,534, 1,684, 2,109, 2,686, 2,905, **3,531**, **3,600**, 3,653, 3,655, 3,743, 4,165, 5,123, **6,759**, 7,198, 7,290, **8,346**, **8,463**, 8,665, 8,670, 9,104, 9,427, 9,711, 10,889, **12,091**, 12,092, 12,093, 12,094, 12,095, 12,096, 12,098, **12,099**, **12,100**, 12,102, **12,106**, 12,108, **12,109**, **12,110**, **12,111**, **12,113**, 12,738, 12,851, 12,924, 13,446, 13,617, 13,618, 15,251, 17,267
Girl Scouts of the USA, Silver Jubilee Camp, 12,091
Girl Scouts, Raintree Council (IN), **4,499**
Girl Volunteer Aid, 4,769
Girl's Academy (Syenchun, Korea), 14,394
Girls
    education, 169, 11,442
    societies and clubs, **501**, **565**, 2,682, 5,123, **6,178**, 6,806, **7,107**, 11,133, **12,094**, **12,104**, **12,105**, 12,738, **13,847**. *See also* Camp Fire Girls; 4-H clubs; Girl Scouts
Girls City Club (Providence, RI), **15,383**
Girls' Classical School (IN), 4,631, 8,362
Girls' Clubs of America, 5,123
Girls' Friendly Society, **6,178**
Girls' Friendly Society (Baltimore, MD), 5,827
Girls' Friendly Society (NY), **11,598**, 11,686
Girls' Friendly Society, Chicago Chapter (IL), **3,942**

Girls' Friendly Society in the United States of America, **16,025**
Girls High School (San Francisco, CA), 839, 936, **1,300**
Girls' High School (GA), 3,132, 3,153, 3,165, **3,191**, 3,215, 3,224, 3,241, 3,255
Girls' High School (Cawnpore, India), 14,426
Girls' High School (MA), 5,943
Girls High School of Philadelphia (PA), 15,011
Girls' High Times (newspaper), 3,191
Girls homes. *See* Maternity homes
Girls' Latin School (MA), 6,051
Girls League of Milton High School (IA), 4,960
Girls of the Sixties (SC), **15,597**
Girls' Protective Association, 6,467
Girl's State, 13,446
Girls' State (UT), **16,462**
Girls' Tomato Clubs (SC), 15,578
Girls Trade and Technical High School (Milwaukee, WI), 17,841
Girls Trade Education League (MA), 9,964
Girls' Training School (MI), 8,276
Girls Training School (NE), 10,564
Girls' Week Advisory Council (OH), **13,847**
Gish, Lillian (1896-), 575, 2,242, **2,357**, 12,040, 16,157
Gish, Tiny. *See* Carter, Tiny (Gish) [Mrs. Jesse Washington]
Gist, Ariel Idella "Della" Hottel (1870-1928), **261**
Gist, Branford P., 2,358
Gist Family (MD), **2,358**
Gist, George W., 2,358
Gist, Mary S., 2,358
Gist, Mordecai (1743-92), 2,358
Gist, Polly, 2,358
Gist, Richard J. (?-1864), 2,358
Githens, Beverley (1903-71). *See* Dresbach, Beverley (Githens) [Mrs. Glenn Ward] (1903-71)
Gitin, David, 4,636
Gitlin, Nanci Hollander [Mrs. Todd Alan] (1943?-), **17,637**
Gitlin, Todd Allan (1943-), **17,637**
Gittings, Victoria (1879-1965), **5,769**
Given, Annie Rachel [Mrs. John O.], 12,000
Given Family, **12,000**
Given, John O., 12,000
Given, Mrs. B. S., **16,072**
Givens, Spencer H., **9,976**
Gjerset, Knut, **8,737**, **8,764**
Gjertsen, Beatrice (1886-1935). *See* Bessesen, Beatrice (Gjertsen) [Mrs. William A.] (1886-1935)
Gjertsen, Lena. *See* Dahl, Lena (Gjertsen) [Mrs. T. H.]
Gjesdal, Coya (1912-). *See* Knutson, Coya (Gjesdal) [Mrs. Andrew] (1912-)
Gjestvang, T. Andreas, 8,801
Gladden, Rebecca, 1,245
Gladden, Washington, 17,454
"Gladness" (poem), 4,226
Gladstein, Caroline Decker, 1,356, 1,357
Gladstone, William Ewart, 1,647
Gladwin, Mary (1861-1939), **13,729**
Glanton, Willie, 4,869
Glanville-Hicks, Peggy, 12,050
Glaser, Anna Christine (Brown), 10,632
Glaser, Emma (1883-), **9,096**
Glaser, Lulu, 3,100, 4,781
Glasgow, Ellen Anderson Gholson (1873-1945), 267, 2,403, 2,610, 2,617, 2,876, **2,877**, **7,169**, 11,810, 11,944, 11,966, 12,035, 12,648, 17,053, **17,059**, 17,078, 17,114
Glasgow Herald, The, 14,501
Glasier Family (England), 6,565
(Glaspell), Susan Keating [Mrs. George Cram] Cook [Mrs. Norman Häghejm] Matson (1876?-1948), 3,988, **4,323**
Glass factories, **11,186**
Glass, Mabel. *See* Kingsbury, Mabel (Glass) [Mrs. John Adams]
Glass manufacture, 7,491, 11,408, 15,221
Glass, Marion (?-1951). *See* Banister, Marion (Glass) (?-1951)
Glass, Mary Ellen (Miller) (1927-), 10,748, 10,749, **10,755**, 10,787

Glass, Maude Emily (1897-19??), **1,039**
Glass, Meta (1880-1967), 2,067, 13,189
Glass research, 2,738
Glass-workers, **11,408**
Glassberg, Benjamin, 1,722
Glasscock, Anne Bonner (1924-), **962**
Glasscock, Jean, 7,583
Glasscock, William E., 17,482
Glassen, Mary [Mrs. William H.], 11,879
Glasson, Mrs. Josiah, **3,686**
Glassware, 12,182
Glaze, Eleanor [Mrs. William Neal Ellis], **15,893**
Gleason Family, 11,618
Gleason Health Resort (NY), 11,443
Gleason, Henry A., 15,217
Gleason, Ida Riner [Mrs. Frank R.] (1900?-), 1,750, **17,969**
Gleason, Mary Josephine. See Dominga, Sister M.
Gleason, Rachel Brooks, 11,605
Gleason, Sarah (?-1930), **9,097**
Gleiter, Loise Linse (1929-), **17,638**
Glen Cary Lutheran Church (Ham Lake, MN), 8,389
Glen, John, 3,550
Glen, Lenore (1905-). See Offord, Lenore (Glen) (1905-)
Glen, Rose. See Webster, Rose (Glen)
Glenn, Addison N., 9,977
Glenn, Andrew Williams (1852-1937), Family (MN), **9,098**
Glenn, Bella Mitchell [Mrs. Robert C.], 9,977
Glenn Family (MO), **9,977**
Glenn, Isa [Mrs. J. S. Bayard] Schindler (1888-), 3,071
Glenn, John H., 9,977
Glenn, Maria Frances McMillan [Mrs. Andrew William], 9,098
Glenn, Mary E. (1902-), **8,026**
Glenn, Robert C., 9,977
Glennie, Alexander, 15,437
Glennon, Maurade (1926-), **6,027**
Glenny, Esther Ann (Burwell) [Mrs. William H.], **11,347**
Glenny, William H. (?-1882), 11,347
Glenwood Academy (MN), 8,720
Glenwood Seminary (VT), 16,999
Glesne, Elise Torgrimson Fjelde [Mrs. Ole] (1869-1946), **8,738**
Glessner, Frances (Macbeth) [Mrs. John J.] (1848-1932), **3,849**
Glessner, John J., 3,849
Glick, Virginia Kirkus, 2,284
Glicman, Mrs. Henry, 8,769
Glidden, Mabel [Mrs.], 1,663
Glimpses of Heights and Depths (poems), 9,703
Globe (whaleship), mutiny (1824), 7,482
Globe Theatre (NY), 225, 12,444
Gloria Barney (book), 6,091
Glories of Venus, The (book), 1,224
Glorious Company, The (book), 11,931
Glory and the Dream, The (book), 2,318
Glover, Amelia Walton (ca. 1830-post 1903). See Alcorn, Amelia Walton (Glover) [Mrs. James L.] (ca. 1830-post 1903)
Glover, Anna C., **4,386**
Glover, Asenath (?-1896). See Hosford, Asenath (Glover) [Mrs. Chauncey O.] (?-1896)
Glover, Dorothy (pseudonym). See Craigie, Dorothy (1901-)
Glover, Elizabeth Camp [Mrs.], 3,440
Glover, George, 10,808
Glover, Katherine [Miss], 5,122
Glover, Lilly Mae (1906-), **15,894**
Glover, Mary (Baker) [Mrs. George Washington] (1821-1910). See Eddy, Mary (Baker) [Mrs. Asa] Gilbert [Mrs. George Washington] Glover [Mrs. Daniel Patterson] (1821-1910)
Gloyd, Carrie Amelia (Moore) [Mrs. Charles] (1846-1911). See Nation, Carrie Amelia (Moore) [Mrs. Charles] Gloyd [Mrs. David] (1846-1911)
Gluck, Marcia (1903-). See Davenport, Marcia (Gluck) [Mrs. Russell W.] (1903-)
Glud, Anna (Hundley), 385
Glueck, Anitra Joyce (1925-56). See Rosberg, Anitra Joyce (Glueck) (1925-56)

Glueck, Eleanor (Touroff) [Mrs. Sheldon] (1898-1972), 863, **6,260, 6,282**
Glueck, Sheldon, **6,260, 6,282**
Gnagi, Elvira (Marsh) (1830-1910), **502**
Go Down, Death (book), 9,640
"Go to sleep my husky baby" (song), 8,310
Goals for Missouri Commission, 10,194
Goat breeding, 8,456
Goates, Helen (Lee) (1925-), 16,780
"God Bless the Child" (song), 5,530
God in the Dust (book), 6,078
Godat, Mary (1861-1955). See Bellamy, Mary (Godat) (1861-1955)
Godbey, Erma O. (Drumm) [Mrs. Thomas] (1905-), **10,756**
Godbey, Thomas, 10,756
Godchaux, Rebecca, 931
Goddard, Abner S., 9,378, 9,528
Goddard, Catherine McClure Fruit [Mrs. Abner S.]. See Smith, Catherine McClure Fruit [Mrs. Abner S.] Goddard [Mrs. Alexander B.]
Goddard, E., **10,811**
Goddard, Elizabeth (Harrison) [Mrs. George] (1815-1907), **16,682**
Goddard, Elizabeth Hayes [Mrs.], 136
Goddard, Esther C. [Mrs. Robert H.], 11,831
Goddard Family (New England), **6,762**
Goddard, H. H., 13,746
Goddard, Louise. See Whitney, Louise (Goddard) Howe [Mrs. Josiah Dwight]
Goddard, Lucy, 7,274
Goddard, Madeleine. See d'Andigne, Marquise
Goddard, Margaret Hazard [Mrs. Robert H. I., Jr.], 15,385
Goddard, Mehetable, 6,762
Goddard, Robert H. I., 15,385
Goddard, Robert H. I., Jr., 15,385
Goddard, Samuel, 6,762
Goddefroy, Caroline (?-1906). See Lamare, Caroline (Goddefroy) [Mrs. François Nicolas] (?-1906)
Goddesses, 6,542
Godeke, Daisy [Mrs. H. F.], **16,267**
Godey, Louis A., 6,244
Godey's Lady's Book (periodical), 77, 1,275, 1,435, 4,695, 5,827, 6,244, 6,617, 10,027, 11,305, 12,341, 13,528, 13,550, 17,950
Godfrey, Ard (1813-94), Family (MN), **9,099**
Godfrey, Benjamin, 4,374
Godfrey, Dorothy (1893-1975). See Wayman, Dorothy (Godfrey) [Mrs. Charles] (1893-1975)
Godfrey, Harriet (Newell) [Mrs. Ard] (1816-96), 9,099
Godfrey, Harriet R. (1849-1943), 9,099
Godfrey, Helen (1839-1902). See Berry, Helen (Godfrey) [Mrs. Mark] (1839-1902)
Godfrey, Julia, 4,374
Godman, Julia (1907-). See Ruuttila, Julia (Godman) Bertram Eaton (1907-)
Godowsky, Leopold (1870-1938), 2,020
Gods Arrive, The, 4,491
"God's Gentiles" (article), 2,613
"Gods Hand Guides the United States to Free the World from War" (ms), 2,538
God's Waif (book), 799
Godwin, Emma, 4,760
Godwin, Eva, 4,760
Godwin Family, **12,403**
Godwin, Flora, 4,760
Godwin, Parke (1816-1904), 12,403, 12,404, 12,481
Goelet, Mary, 12,440
Goell, Theresa, **11,868**
Goemaere, Mother Mary, **1,513**
Goens, Grace P., 3,290
Goeppert, Maria. See Mayer, Maria (Goeppert) [Mrs. Joseph E.]
Goertzel, Mildred George, 1,525
Goerz, Mrs. R. A. 5,201
Goes, Bertha, 4,727
Goetz, Ruth (Goodman) [Mrs. Augustus] (1912-59), 2,241, **17,798**
Goff Family, 2,532
Goff, Lila J., 9,230
Goff, Myrtle R., 16,648
"Going Steady" (ms), 2,205

"Going to Naples" (story), 9,770, 16,172
Goins, Georgia (Fraser), **2,134**
Goiter, 1,371
Golconda (ship), 15,470
Gold, 5,522
Gold dredging, **959**
Gold, Edith Annie (Benfell) [Mrs. Cyrus Williams] (1893-), **16,683**
Gold, Fay (1907-), **2,765**
Gold Feather, 4,403
Gold, Mary, 8,666
Gold, Mary Sydney (1886-1975), 8,654
Gold miners, 10,297, 10,993, **12,176**, 17,397
Gold mines and mining, 129, 130, 338, 438, 497, 1,393, 1,418, **1,462**, 1,621, 1,633, 1,750, 1,799, 8,373, 9,860, 10,061, 10,244, 10,305, 10,364, 10,763, 16,876
Gold, Rose Bogen (1881-1947), **13,786**
Gold Star Mothers (Chicago, IL). See American Gold Star Mothers
Gold Star Sons (Chicago, IL). See American Gold Star Sons
Goldberg and Torgerson (law firm, MN), 9,525
Goldberg, Dora (1880?-1928). See Bayes, Nora. [Mrs. Otto] Gressing [Mrs. Jack] Norworth [Mrs. Harry] Clarke [Mrs. Arthur A.] Gordon [Mrs. Benjamin L.] Friedland (1880?-1928)
Goldberg, Rebecca. See Holland, Rebecca (Goldberg)
Goldborough, Mary Ellen Lloyd, 5,789
Golden Adventures in California History (book), 315
Golden Books, 8,566
Golden, Diana, 14,497
Golden Gate International Exposition (CA, 1939), 941, 1,377
Golden Gate Kindergarten Association (San Francisco, CA), 11,547
Golden Gate Park Monastery (CA), 1,313
Golden, Mary Katz, **8,649**
Golden Peacock, The (book), 2,183
Golden Press, 14,463
Golden Rule Foundation, American Mothers' Committee, **1,693**
Golden, Verna (1876-1964). See Scott, Verna (Golden) [Mrs. Carlyle McRoberts] (1876-1964)
"Golden Wedding," 5,763
Goldenberg, Joanne (1932-). See Greenberg, Joanne (Goldenberg) (1932-)
Goldfield Women's Club (NV), **10,757**
Goldman, Blanche B., 8,963
Goldman, Emma [Miss] (1869-1940), 702, 825, 1,186, 1,451, 2,396, 2,403, 4,080, 4,145, **4,229, 6,028,** 7,192, **7,223**, 7,923, **7,998**, 8,077, 8,144, 9,900, 11,303, 11,305, 11,812, **12,487**, 12,518, 12,589, 12,699, **12,701**
Goldman, Mary, 1,652
Goldman, Sarah Adler [Mrs. Julius] (1858-1934), **6,603**
Goldmann, Juanita, 639
Goldmark, Alice. See Brandeis Alice (Goldmark) [Mrs. Louise Dembitz]
Goldmark Commission, 11,918
Goldmark Family, **6,604**
Goldmark, Josephine Clara (1877-1950), 2,336, 2,359, 2,504, 6,604, 6,827, 11,771
Goldmark, Pauline (1896-1962), 6,604
Goldmark, Pauline Dorothea (1873?-1962), Family, **2,359**, 2,696
Goldowski, Natasha, 13,333
Goldsboro Female College (NC), 13,458
Goldsborough, Elizabeth (Wirt) [Mrs. Louis M.] (ca. 1807-?), 5,824
Goldsborough, Kitty D. (?-1868). See Mayer, Kitty D. (Goldsborough) [Mrs. Alfred M.] (?-1868)
Goldsmith, Claire, 3,694
Goldsmith, Deborah, 11,726
Goldsmith, Esther, **3,512**
Goldsmith, Hannah (1823-77). See Williams, Hannah Goldsmith (1823-77)
Goldstein, Betty Naomi (1921-). See Friedan, Betty Naomi (Goldstein). [Mrs. Carl] Friedan (1921-)
Goldstein, Fanny [Miss] (1895-1961), **13,787**
Goldstein, Harriet B. L. (1886-1961), **7,531**
Goldstine, Dora, 8,665
Goldstine, Esther (Levitan) [Mrs. Sidney], 17,744

Goldstine, Sidney, 17,744
Goldthwaite, Amanda (Moore) [Mrs. Henry], 54
Goldthwaite, Anne Wilson (1869-1944), **2,766**
Goldthwaite Family (MA), 16,531
Goldthwaite, Lydia (1812-84). *See* Knight, Lydia (Goldthwaite) (1812-84)
Goldthwaite, Nellie E. (1868-1946), **4,387**
Goldwyn, Jennifer (Howard), 556
Golf, **10,510**
Golfers, 997, 4,700, 15,935
Golley, Jenny, 8,206
Goltra, Elizabeth Julia (Ellison) [Mrs. Nelson] (1831-?). *See* Farrington, Elizabeth Julia (Ellison) [Mrs. Nelson] Goltra [Mrs. Keeler] (1831-?)
Gomez Family (NY), **7,532**
Gómez, Francisca, 493
Gomez, Hetty (Hendricks) [Mrs. Aaron Lopez], 7,532
Gomez, Jose Joaquin, 1,289
Gomon, Josephine (Fellows) (1892-1975), **7,796, 8,089**
Gompers, Grace Gleaves Neuscheler [Mrs. Samuel], 16,157
Gompers, Samuel, 2,509, 2,679, 8,122, 11,917, 11,924, 12,485
Gompertz, Helen Marion (1865-1924). *See* Le Conte, Helen Marion (Gompertz) [Mrs. Joseph Nisbet] (1865-1924)
Gone With The Wind (book), 2,488, 3,064, 3,065, 3,070, 3,278, 3,301, 3,555, 3,602
Gone With The Wind (moving-picture), 3,067, **3,192,** 3,210, 3,225, 3,263, 3,301, 3,336, 3,340
Gonne, Maude (1866-1953), 2,660
Gonyaw, Miss, 4,247
Gonzales, Clara, 16,877
Gonzalez, Jane (1918-), **7,797**
Good and evil, **16,584**
"Good Cheer" (column), 14,223
Good Citizenship Bonds, 8,360
Good Counsel Training School (White Plains, NY), 12,932
"Good Grazin'" (story), 15,660
Good Hope Plantation (SC), **15,476**
Good Housekeeping (periodical), 2,205, 6,091, 11,304, 11,491, 11,974, 16,154
Good Housekeeping Institute, 2,596
Good, Jeanne (Stratton), 823
Good, Lydia Belle (Walker), 15,174
Good, Mignon (1899-). *See* Eberhart, Mignon (Good) (1899-)
Good Samaritan Hospital (Lexington, KY), 5,326
Good Samaritan Hospital (Zanesville, OH), 17,820
Good Samaritan Hospital, Inc. (NC), **13,415**
Good Shepherd Community Center (Chicago, IL). *See* Parkway Community House (Chicago, IL)
Good Shepherd Provincial Convent (Cincinnati, OH), **13,866**
Good Shepherd Sisters of Quebec. *See* Servants of the Immaculate Heart of Mary (Saco, ME)
Goodale, Charles, 7,515
Goodale, Dora Reed (1866-?), 7,220, 17,010
Goodale, Elaine (1863-1953). *See* Eastman, Elaine (Goodale) [Mrs. Charles A.] (1863-1953)
Goodale Family (MA), **7,515**
Goodale, Henry S., 7,220
Goodale, Lucy T. (1820-40), 7,515
Goodale, Meliscent (Warren) [Mrs. David] (1797-1861), 7,515
Goodbird, 9,447
Goodbye, Stranger (book), 2,204
Goode, Elle. *See* Hardeman, Elle (Goode)
Goode, Eslanda (1896-1965). *See* Robeson, Eslanda (Goode) (1896-1965)
Goode, Sarah (1822-?). *See* Marshall, Sarah (Goode) (1822-?)
Goodell, Lavinia (1839-80), **5,253**
Goodell, Martha Page (Putnam) (1834-?), **7,376**
Goodenow, Anna Holmes. *See* Willcox Anna Holmes (Goodenow) [Mrs. William Henry]
Goodenow, Mary Reed (Cutler) [Mrs. Robert] (1806-73), 5,676
Goodenow, Robert (1800-74), **5,676**
Goodenow, Valeria. *See* Stone, Valeria (Goodenow)

Goodhue, Anna Willard [Mrs. Benjamin] (1763-1858), 12,695
Goodhue, Benjamin, 12,695
Goodhue, Catharine Rutherfurd (Clarkson) [Mrs. Jonathan] (1794-1861), 12,695
Goodhue, Charles, 12,695
Goodhue, Frances (1779-1808). *See* Ashton, Frances (Goodhue) [Mrs. William] (1779-1808)
Goodhue, Grace Anne (1879-1957). *See* Coolidge, Grace Anne (Goodhue) [Mrs. Calvin] (1879-1957)
Goodhue, Henry, 12,695
Goodhue, Jonathan, 12,695
Goodhue, Martha Hardy (1787-1848). *See* Tucker, Martha Hardy (Goodhue) [Mrs. Gideon] (1787-1848)
Goodhue, Mary (1781-1839). *See* Shreve, Mary (Goodhue) [Mrs. Benjamin, Jr.] (1781-1839)
Goodhue, Sarah (1786-96), 12,695
"Goodies, The," **6,304**
Goodin, Rebecca E., **14,710**
Gooding, Gladys, 9,951, 11,405
Goodloe, Daniel R., 13,587
Goodman, Amelia Levy (?-1916) 938
Goodman, Benny, 5,530, 5,534
Goodman, Clara Browning (1886-), 11,661
Goodman Family (TX), **938**
Goodman, Irvin, 14,656
Goodman, Kenneth Sawyer (?-1918), 3,924
Goodman, Minerva, **1,629**
Goodman, Philip, 17,798
Goodman, Ruth (1912-59). *See* Goetz, Ruth (Goodman) [Mrs. Augustus] (1912-59)
Goodman Theatre (Chicago, IL), **3,924**
Goodnight Family (TX), 16,351
Goodnow, Alice V., 5,878
Goodnow, Hannah Abby (Chase) [Mrs. George Franklin] (1833-?), 10,801
Goodnow, Harriet (Smith) (1787-1869), 7,677
Goodrich, Annie Warburton (1866-1955), 6,122, 6,131, 6,143, 12,351
Goodrich, Bessie Bacon, **8,650**
Goodrich, Caroline (1826-?). *See* Greenman, Caroline (Goodrich) (1826-?)
Goodrich, Chauncey, 8,332
Goodrich, Ellen [Mrs. William Henry], 8,332
Goodrich Family (CT), **1,863**
Goodrich, Frances. [Mrs. Albert] Hackett, **17,799**
Goodrich, Joseph, 17,644
Goodrich, Juliet T. (1881-1963), **6,605**
Goodrich, Margaret "Peggy" Day (Taintor) [Mrs. Robert R.] (1921-), **10,921**
Goodrich, Mary Ann (Welles) [Mrs. Joshua] (1808-73), 1,863
Goodrich, Mary Hopkins (1813-95), 7,508
Goodrich, Mary Reavis, 13,547
Goodrich, Mrs. Levi, 1,314
Goodrich, Sarah [Mrs.], 8,399
Goodrich, Sarah Knox [Mrs.], 1,314
Goodrich School (Chicago, IL), 4,071
Goodrich, William Henry (1825-74), **8,332**
Goodsell, Carolyn [Mrs. Alson] (1890-), **7,332**
Goodsir Family, 9,372
Goodspeed, Joseph H., Jr., 14,447
Goodwater, Leroy, Family (ND, TN, WI), **13,707**
Goodwater, Mamie, 13,707
Goodwill Industries, 10,484
Goodwill Industries of Southeast Iowa, 4,923
Goodwin, Anne (1875-1959). *See* Winslow, Anne (Goodwin) (1875-1959)
Goodwin, Caroline Love (1869?-1943). *See* O'Day, Caroline Love (Goodwin) [Mrs. Daniel] (1869?-1943)
Goodwin, Elizabeth, **5,650**
Goodwin, Emily (Timrod), 15,753
Goodwin, Emma (Philleo). *See* Whipple, Emma (Philleo) Goodwin [Mrs. Charles K.]
Goodwin, Ethel, **5,659**
Goodwin, Hannibal, 11,121
Goodwin, Jane (1831-94). *See* Austin, Jane (Goodwin) (1831-94)
Goodwin, Kathryn, 11,916
Goodwin, Louise Bland [Mrs.], **5,850**
Goodwin, Mary Frances, 17,125
Goodwin, Sarah Augusta [Mrs.], 1,381

Goodwyn Institute (Memphis, TN), 12,479
Goodyear, Andrew, 503
Goodyear, Cynthia (Vaughn) [Mrs. Andrew] (1835-1901), 503
Goodyear Family, **503**
Goold, Abba Louisa (1838-1921). *See* Woolson, Abba Louisa (Goold) (1838-1921)
Goold, Sarah, 12,315
Goold, Sarah C., **12,213**
Goose, Cornelia P., **11,098**
Gooseley, Martha, 17,129
Goostray, Stella (1886-1969), 6,122, **6,141, 6,606**
Gopher (MN), 9,282
Gordan, Juliet Ann (Opie) [Mrs. Alexander George] (1818-1890). *See* Hopkins, Juliet Ann (Opie) [Mrs. Alexander George] Gordan [Mrs. Arthur Frances] (1818-1890)
Gordon, Andrew, 15,172
Gordon, Anna Adams (1853-1931), 4,243, 4,244, 7,866, 14,017
Gordon, Betty, 17,288
Gordon, Beulah (1909-63), **4,332**
Gordon, Caroline Ferguson. [Mrs. Allen] Tate (1895-), 3,986, **11,163,** 15,927, 15,929, 15,934, 15,938
Gordon, Dorothy, 11,909
Gordon, Edith [Mrs. Barry M.], **12,870**
Gordon, Eleanor Elizabeth, 4,958
Gordon, Eleanor Lytle (Kinzie) [Mrs. William Washington, II], 3,594
Gordon, Elizabeth S. [Miss] (1824-1900), **17,640**
Gordon, Emily (Chapman) [Mrs. John Montgomery] (?-ca. 1852), 5,770
Gordon Family, 11,163
Gordon Family (GA), **3,393**
Gordon Family (PA),
Gordon, Fannie (Haralson) [Mrs. John Brown] (1837-1931), **3,394**
Gordon, Gordon, 6,060
Gordon Institute (GA), 3,419
Gordon, John Brown (1832-1904), 3,053, 3,394, 3,521, 3,585
Gordon, John Montgomery (1810-84), 5,770
Gordon, Juliette "Daisy" Magill Kinzie (1860-1927). *See* Low, Juliette "Daisy" Magill Kinzie (Gordon) [Mrs. William Mackay] (1860-1927)
Gordon, Kate M. (1861-1932), 1,308, 5,499
Gordon, Laura (de Force) [Mrs. Charles H.] (1838-1907), **1,611**
Gordon, Linda, **6,607**
Gordon, Major, 11,195
Gordon, Margaret Elizabeth (Schutt) [Mrs. James Frater] (1866-1966), **16,684**
Gordon, Mary Bouhanan [Mrs.] (1848-?), **16,073**
Gordon, Mildred Nixon [Mrs. Gordon] (1912-), 6,060
Gordon, Mrs., 4,761
Gordon, Pearl Avis. *See* Vastal, Pearl Avis (Gordon) [Mrs. C. L.]
Gordon, Rebecca (1841-?). *See* Blackford, Rebecca (Gordon) [Mrs. Eugene] (1841-?)
Gordon, Richard, 11,897
Gordon, Ruth. [Mrs. Garson] Kanin (1896-), 2,336, **2,360,** 12,708, 14,413
Gordon, Sarah Anderson Stiles [Mrs. William Washington], 3,393
Gordon, Susan Fitzhugh [Miss] (1838-58), 5,770
Gordon, Susanna (1824-?). *See* Waddell, Susanna (Gordon) [Mrs. James Alexander] (1824-?)
Gordon, Victoria (1938-), 10,151
Gordon, William Washington, 3,393, 3,521
Gordon, Wyona Eliza Surfus (Stahlnecker) (1878?-?), **14,373, 17,265**
Gore-Booth, Eva (1870-1926), 2,660
Gore, Howard M., 17,473
Gore Land Case (NY), 11,746
Gore, Mary Jeanette (Robison) [Mrs. Charles Levison or Edward H.] (1858-1942). *See* Brown, Mary Jeanette (Robison) [Mrs. Charles Levison or Edward H.] Gore [Mrs. Augustus Homer] (1858-1942)
Gore, Nancie "Granny" (ca. 1821-1917) **9,901**
Gorer, Geoffrey, 6,961

Gorgas, Amelia (Gayle) [Mrs. Josiah] (1826-1913), 105, 106, **107**, 109, **120**
Gorgas Family (AL), **105**
Gorgas, Jessie, 109
Gorgas, Josiah, 107, 120
Gorgas, Marie "Mamie," 105, 109
Gorgas, Mary, 105, 120
Gorham, Annie. *See* Marston, Annie (Gorham)
Gorham, Elizabeth (Jenkins) [Mrs. Jason] (1810-95), 5,897
Gorham Family (MA), **5,897**
Gorham, J. Martin (1830-80), 5,897
Gorham, James W. (1808-81), **17,641**
Gorham, Jason (1787-1881), 5,897
Gorham, May E., 1,302
Gorham, Thelma Thurston, 3,799
Gorky, Arshile, 2,802, 2,816
Gorman, Mary (pseudonym). *See* Palmtag, Mary Gorman (1908-)
Gorman, Peter, 3,000
Gormly, Agnes M. Hays,
Gorum, James W. *See* Gorham, James W.
Goshen College (Goshen, IN), faculty, 4,516
Gosling, Charlotte M., **3,513**
Gosney, Ezra S., 8,634
Goss, Beulah S. [Mrs.] (1898-1974), **17,050**
Goss, Clara, 131
Goss, Margaret Taylor, 3,290
Gosse, Edmund, 2,370
Gosse, Marguerite H. *See* Clark, Marguerite H. Gosse
Goszler, Clara, 2,249
Gotendorf, James Nathan (1811-88), 5,949
Gottheil, Emma L., 12,117
Gottingen University, alumnae, 7,814
Gottschalk, Clara. *See* Peterson, Clara (Gottschalk)
Gottschalk, Louis Moreau, **5,483**
Goucher College (MD), 4,167, 12,737
  alumnae, 13,860
  archives, **5,852**
  faculty, 1,604
Goudge, Elizabeth (1900-), 258
Gougar, Helen Mar (Jackson) [Mrs. John D.] (1843-1907), **4,635**
Gould, Agnes Safley, 1,339
Gould, Alberta Telfair (Welter), 3,518
Gould, Alice Bache (1869-1953), **2,361**, 6,563
Gould, Amos (1808-82), **8,333**
Gould and Curry mine (NV), 1,492
Gould, Annie. *See* Johnson, Annie (Gould) [Mrs. Benoni]
Gould, Beatrice, 11,866
Gould, Benjamin A., 14,895
Gould, Bruce, 11,866
Gould, Catherine Livingston, 11,260
Gould, Eliza William (Chotard) [Mrs. William Proctor] (1798-1878), 67, **12,976**
Gould, Elizabeth Porter (1848-1906), 5,910, **5,929**, 5,934, 5,971, **6,608**, **7,377**
Gould, Elizabeth Wright. *See* Berry, Elizabeth Wright (Gould) [Mrs. William Bogardus]
Gould Family, 11,719, 11,734
Gould Family (NY), 11,260
Gould Farm colony (MA), 2,176
Gould, Hannah Flagg (1789-1865), 17,010
Gould, Hannah (Rodman), 11,600
Gould, Hannah (Wright) [Mrs. John Stanton] (1819-1912), **11,599**, 11,734
Gould, Harriet (Elmendorf), 11,260
Gould, Helen Miller (1868-1938). *See* Shepard, Helen Miller (Gould) [Mrs. Finley S.] (1868-1938)
Gould, Jane Augusta (Holbrook) (1833-1917). *See* Tourtillote, Jane Augusta (Holbrook) Gould (1833-1917)
Gould, Jay, 12,214
Gould, Jennie, 8,333
Gould, John Stanton (1812-74), 11,599, **11,600**, 11,734
Gould, Julia, 12,208
Gould, Lena, 8,333
Gould, Lolita, **4,762**
Gould, Louisa [Mrs. Amos], 8,333
Gould, Margaret (Douglass) [Mrs. Warren H.], **10,759**

Gould, Mary, 8,333
Gould, Mary. *See* Baldwin, Mary (Gould)
Gould, Mary Ashby [Mrs. John Stanton] (1817-43), 11,600
Gould, Mrs. Howard, 1,279
Gould, Prudence Ermina (Hymers) [Mrs. William] (1867-?), 10,759
Gould, Sarah Ashby [Mrs. John Stanton], 11,600
Gould, Stephen, 12,628
Gould, Suzan M., 8,191
Gould, William, 10,759
Gould, William Proctor, 67, 12,976
Goulding, Margaret. *See* Reid, Margaret (Goulding) [Mrs. William Moultrie]
Goulding, Thomas, 15,692
Goulet, Lorrie (1925-), **2,767**
Goulet, Mary Macel (Butler) [Mrs. Alfred W.], 1,666
Gourgas, Adèle. *See* DuBois, Adele Gourgas [Mrs. John]
Gourgas Family, **9,866**
Gourgas, John Mark, 9,866
Govan, Gilbert, 2,488
Gove, Anna Maria [Miss] (1867-1948), **13,243**, 13,610
Gove, George R. (1881-1968), **17,642**
Gove, George W. (1844-1930), **17,642**
Gove, Lucy (Rogers), 9,100
Gove, Marguerite [Mrs. George R.] (ca. 1880-1969), **17,642**
Governesses, 261, 5,786, 5,805, **9,774**, 10,975, 11,602, 13,047, 14,733, 15,711, **17,502**
Government, 14,641
Government advisory bodies. *See* Executive advisory bodies
Government agencies. *See* Administrative agencies
Government attorneys, **1,178**, **3,948**, **10,103**, 13,972. *See also* Attorneys-general; County attorneys
Government buildings. *See* Public buildings
Government commissions. *See* Executive advisory bodies
Government corporations. *See* Corporations, government
Government employees. *See* Civil service; United States, officials and employees; *and as subhead under states, e.g.,* California, officials and employees
Government funding. *See* Grants-in-aid
Government librarians, 342, 1,676, **2,623**, **2,661**, 2,931, 9,694, 10,753, 17,908, 17,918, **17,919**, **18,010**
Government librarians, Afro-American, **17,693**
Government officials. *See* Public officers
"Government Patronage of Indian Missions, 1789-1836" (dissertation), 17,626
Government price regulation. *See* Price regulation
Government publicity, 2,684
Government regulation of railroads. *See* Railroads and state
Government, resistance to, 15,993
Government social functions, 10,083
Governmental investigations, 64, 1,013, 2,379, 3,303, 3,362, 3,771, 5,979, 8,058, 8,971, **11,255**, **11,256**, 11,844, 11,888, 11,895, 11,911, 15,332, 17,281, **17,482**, 17,792. *See also* Legislative hearings; Police
"Governor and the Public, the Press, and the Legislature, The," 504
Governors 102, 105, 106, 110, **145**, **197**, 207, 257, 297, 331, 504, **575**, 645, 1,140, **1,152**, 1,251, 1,430, 1,552, **2,322**, 2,462, **2,526**, 2,527, **2,572**, 2,651, 2,868, 2,886, **2,942**, 2,950, **2,953**, 3,135, **3,158**, 3,266, 3,381, 3,389, **3,394**, 3,429, 3,587, 3,667, 3,687, 3,749, 4,198, 4,322, 4,347, 4,349, 4,351, 4,352, 4,354, 4,357, 4,361, 4,370, 4,417, 4,486, **4,615**, 4,628, 4,700, 4,741, **4,926**, **4,928**, **5,106**, **5,222**, 5,267, 5,343, 5,394, 5,679, 5,750, **5,828**, 6,367, 6,568, 6,937, **7,133**, 7,178, **7,615**, 7,722, 7,729, 7,738, 7,886, 7,914, **8,253**, 8,843, **8,925**, **8,971**, 9,032, 9,035, 9,187, **9,263**, 9,286, **9,287**, **9,297**, **9,303**, **9,371**, 9,467, **9,474**, **9,475**, **9,582**, 9,653, 9,663, 9,688, 9,694, 9,722, **9,867**, 9,869, **9,934**, **9,940**, **9,951**, 9,963, 9,983, **9,985**, **9,995**, 9,996, **10,032**, **10,048**, **10,050**, 10,051, 10,301, 10,303, 10,427, 10,487, **10,649**, 10,753,

10,779, 10,846, 11,070, 11,184, **11,201**, **11,202**, 11,240, 11,514, 11,546, **11,613**, 11,658, 11,795, 11,827, 11,871, 12,210, 12,288, **12,522**, 12,575, **12,697**, 12,963, 13,011, 13,041, 13,070, 13,144, 13,210, **13,371**, 13,414, **13,416**, 13,448, 13,453, 13,454, 13,488, 13,565, **13,565**, **13,566**, 13,567, 13,581, **13,619**, 13,935, **14,046**, 14,062, **14,077**, 14,086, 14,318, 14,594, 14,607, 14,610, **14,619**, **14,810**, **14,815**, 14,820, **14,829**, 14,873, **15,440**, 15,545, **15,563**, 15,755, 15,863, 15,941, 16,014, 16,016, 16,091, 16,313, 16,933, 17,046, 17,083, 17,115, 17,164, **17,217**, 17,226, 17,259, 17,293, **17,335**, **17,376**, 17,409, **17,462**, 17,482, 17,595, **17,629**, **17,670**, 17,908, 17,913, **17,915**, 17,922, 17,941, **18,005**
Governor's Advisory Committee on Children and Youth (CA), 645
Governor's Commission on the Status of Women (IA), 4,861
Governor's Commission on the Status of Women (WI), **17,769**
Governor's Committee on Public School Education (TX), 16,342
Governor's Conference, 18,005
Governor's Council on Aging (WA), 17,245
Governors councils. *See* Executive advisory bodies
Governor's Interracial Commission (MN), 9,276
Governor's Interracial Commission of Minnesota, 8,638
"Governor's Mansion, 1853-1953, A Social History of the Illinois Executive Mansion, The" (ms), 4,355
Governor's Regional Conference on Education (NE), 10,472
Gowen, Abigail (ca. 1794-1845). *See* Brooks, Maria (Gowen) [Mrs. John]. Abigail Gowen. Mary Abigail Brooks (ca. 1794-1845)
Gower, Jean Milne, 1,786
Gower, Lillian (Norton) [Mrs. Frederick Allen] (1857-1914). *See* Nordica, Lillian (Norton) [Mrs. Frederick Allen] Gower [Mrs. Zoltan] Döme [Mrs. George Washington] Young (1857-1914)
Grabau, Mary Antin [Mrs. Amadeus William] (1881-1949), **2,176**
Graber, Albert, Family (MN), **9,101**
Graber, Anna Erb [Mrs. Albert] (1868-?), 9,101
Grabhorn, Jane Bissell (1911-73), **505**, 569, 1,573
Grabhorn Press, 505, 519
Grable, Ella [Mrs.], 1,756
Grace, Abbie T. [Miss], 1,335, 1,358
Grace Baptist Church (Philadelphia, PA), 15,187
Grace, Clara C. [Mrs.], 5,122
Grace E. Frysinger Fellowship, 6,964
Grace Episcopal Church (Canton, MS), 9,706
Grace Episcopal Church (Madison, WI), Ladies Benevolent Society, **17,683**
Grace Evangelical Lutheran Church (Hayes, SD), Sunshine Circle, 15,855
Grace Female Institute (San Francisco, CA), **506**
Grace, Flora. *See* Prince, Flora (Grace)
Grace Hamilton Morrey School of Music, 14,008
Grace Hoper Press, 519
Grace Methodist Church (NY), 12,561
Grace Methodist Episcopal Church (St. Paul, MN), **9,102**
Grace Methodist Episcopal Church (St. Paul, MN), Women's Foreign Missionary Society, 9,102
Grace Notes (newsletter), 15,208
Gracious Lady: The Life of Sara Delano Roosevelt (book), 11,491
Gracy, Alice (Duggan) [Mrs. David C.], **16,268**
Graduate Circle of Alethean Chautauqua (NE), 10,571
Graduate Nurses Association, 17,267
Graduate Nurses' Association of Kalamazoo (MI). *See* Michigan State Nurses' Association
Graduate nursing education, 11,918, 12,077, 12,137
Graduate School of Sacred Theology, 4,640
Graduate students, 5,728, **8,084**
Graduate students, Afro-American, 13,110
Grady, Alice H., 2,336
Grady, Henry W., 2,962
Grady Hospital (GA), 3,216, 3,275
Grady Hospital Aid Association (GA), **3,193**

Graebner, Bertha. *See* Meyer, Bertha (Graebner) [Mrs. R. H. C.]

Graeme, Elizabeth (1737-1801). *See* Ferguson, Elizabeth (Graeme) [Mrs. Henry Hugh] (1737-1801)

Graf, Louise S. (1904-), **17,934**

Graf, Louise Spinner (1933-), **17,905**

Graff, Amalia Kraft, 3,764

Graff, Ella A. (1872-1963), **8,821**

Graff Family (CA), 507

Graff, Louise (Boepple) [Mrs. Ulrich], 507

Graffe, Dorothy (1896-). *See* Van Doren, Dorothy (Graffe) [Mrs. Mark] (1896-)

Graffenried, Clare de [Miss] (1849-1921), 9,618

Grafius, Margaret (1885-1973). *See* Birkhoff, Margaret (Grafius) [Mrs. George David] (1885-1973)

Grafton Female Moral Reform Society (MA), 7,635

Grafton History Club (MA), 7,635

Grafton, Katherine A. (1839-1902). *See* Patterson, Katherine A. (Grafton) [Mrs. Thomas M.] (1839-1902)

Gragg, Bettie M. *See* McLain, Bettie M. (Gragg) [Mrs. William H.]

Gragg, Huldah. *See* Brickett, Huldah (Gragg)

Gragg, Joseph, **14,375**

Gragg, Rosa Lee [Mrs.] (1901-), **8,027**

Graham, Adelaide Elizabeth. *See* Le Conte, Adelaide Elizabeth (Graham) [Mrs. Joseph Nisbet]

Graham, Alberta Powell (1875-1955), **4,988, 5,093**

Graham, Anne (Bancroft), 1,621

Graham, Betsy, 9,025

Graham, Charlotte [Mrs. Frank] (1914-), **15,992**

Graham, Charlotte Meade, 7,534

Graham, Elizabeth (1831-1917). *See* MacDonald, Elizabeth (Graham) [Mrs. Alexander Findlay] (1831-1917)

Graham, Evarts Ambrose, 10,207

Graham Family, **2,162**

Graham Family, 13,031

Graham Family (TX), 16,284

Graham Family (TX), **16,016**

Graham, Frank Porter, 13,264

Graham, Gladys P., 3,799

Graham, Grace. *See* Medinus, Grace (Graham) [Mrs. Carl]

Graham Hall Murder, The (book), 8,962

Graham, Hazel E. (1906-), **8,049**

Graham, Helen (Tredway) [Mrs. Evarts Ambrose] (1890-1971), **10,207**

Graham, Hepzibah, 2,162

Graham, Isabella (Marshall) [Mrs. John] (1742-1814), 12,315

Graham, J. W., 13,031

Graham, James (1773-1829), 2,162

Graham, Jane Maria (1796-?), 2,162

Graham, Jessie Marguarite Pace, 16,890

Graham, John W., 13,449

Graham, Joseph (1759-1836), 2,162

Graham, Katherine (1898-). *See* Howard, Katherine (Graham) (1898-)

Graham, Lucille Ross, **16,074**

Graham, Manta S., **4,989**

Graham, Martha, 2,631, 7,214, 12,050, 17,803

Graham, Mary (Dolliver) (1860-1919), 4,906

Graham, Mary O. 13,436

Graham, Sarah Ann (1807-39?). *See* Alexander, Sarah Ann (Graham) (1807-39?)

Graham, Saundra, 6,336

Graham, Sheilah, 11,907

Graham, Shirley Lola (1906-). *See* Du Bois, Shirley Lola (Graham) (1906-)

Graham, Susan [Mrs. William Alexander], 13,416

Graham, William Alexander, **13,416,** 13,581

Graham, William Grenville (1794-1827), 2,162

Grain, prices, 10,041, 10,059

Grain trade, employees, 14,555

Grains, or, Passages in the Life of Ruth Rover, with Occasional Pictures of Oregon, Natural and Moral, The (book), 14,510

Gramercy Bookshop (NY), 12,001

Gramm, Peg (1954-), **8,699**

Gran, John Peter, 8,693

Grand Army of the Republic. *See* United States (government), Army

Grand Army of the Republic, Connecticut Department, **1,907**

Grand Army of the Republic, John F. Reynolds Post, 13,696

Grand Army of the Republic Memorial Association, 3,922

Grand Forks Federation of Women's Clubs (ND), **13,708**

Grand Isle, history, 17,029

Grand Lodge of Good Templars, 4,164

Grand Lodge of Iowa, 4,696

Grand Music Festival (CA), 1,263

Grand Rapids Alumnae Club (MI), 7,814

Grand Rapids Junior College (MI), faculty, 7,814

Grand Rapids Kindergarten Training School (MI), **7,798,** 7,949, 7,973

Grand Teton National Park, 16,485

Grand Valley State College (Allendale, MI), 7,817

Grandin, Susan. *See* De Camp, Susan (Grandin)

Grandma Called It Carnal (book), 1,082

Grandmaitre, Blanche, **1,301**

"Grandmother, Mother and me" (ms), 10,157

Grandmothers' Club (Ann Arbor, MI), **7,799**

Grandprey, Medora Belle. *See* Petersen, Medora Belle (Grandprey) [Mrs. Hjalmar]

Grandy, Sarah. *See* Briggs, Sarah (Grandy) [Mrs. Thomas Henry, Jr.]

Grandy, Sarah Elizabeth (Ferebee) Lamb, 13,350

Grange. *See* Patrons of Husbandry

Grange Cooperative Wholesale (WA), 17,340

Grange, Mary, 15,716

Granger, Elizabeth, 1,440

Granger, Julia A. (1822-97). *See* Irving, Julia A. (Granger) [Mrs. Sanders] (1822-97)

Granger, Lottie E., 4,696

Granger, Mary (1897-), **3,514**

Granger, Sarah Melissa (1818-98). *See* Kimball, Sarah Melissa (Granger) [Mrs. Hiram S.] (1818-98)

Graniteville Manufacturing Company, 13,135

Granniss, Ruth Shepard [Miss] (1872-1954), **12,002**

Granskou, Ella Odland (1891-), **8,874**

Grant, Adele Gerard (Lewis) (1881-ca. 1967), 10,151, 10,152, 10,153

Grant, Alice, **11,767**

Grant, Alice Eliza (1858-1930), **14,732**

Grant, Anne MacVicar [Mrs.] (1755-1838), 6,609, **12,215**

Grant Avenue United Methodist Church (Denver, CO), 1,700

Grant, Avis (Winchell) [Mrs. Ulysses Sherman] (1872-?), **8,571**

Grant, Blanche Chloe (1874-?), **508**

Grant, Claudius B., 7,722

Grant Collegiate Institute (IL), 3,911

Grant Colored Orphan Asylum (NC), 13,644

Grant County Historical Society (OK), 14,188, 14,192

Grant, Edmonia White, 5,469

Grant, Ella (1854-1939). *See* Wilson, Ella (Grant) (1854-1939)

Grant, Ethel (Watts) Mumford (1878-1940), **12,488**

Grant Family, **7,224**

Grant Family (NY), **14,071**

Grant, Frederick Dent, 12,293

Grant, Heber J., 16,620, 16,676

Grant, Horace J., 16,657

Grant, Ida Honoré [Mrs. Frederick], **6,610**

Grant, Isabel R., **2,904**

Grant, Jane. [Mrs. Harold] Ross (1892-1972), **14,377**

Grant, Jedediah M., 16,479

Grant, John T., Family (GA), 3,045

Grant, Julia (Dent) [Mrs. Ulysses S.] (1826-1902), 3,922, 6,864, 10,165, 15,725

Grant, Julia (Hanscom) Sargent, 5,634

Grant, L. P., 3,218

Grant, Laura, 2,701

Grant, Leila (Moss) [Mrs. Horace J.] (1895-1962). *See* Eldredge, Leila (Moss) [Mrs. Horace J.] Grant [Mrs. John E.] Lee [Mrs. Clarence] (1895-1962)

Grant, Lois. *See* Holman, Lois (Grant)

Grant, Martin Smith, **13,268**

Grant, Mrs. Frederick Dent, 12,293

Grant, Mrs. John T., 3,045

Grant, Mrs. W. D., 3,045, 3,254

Grant, Nell. *See* Gronan, Nell (Grant) [Mrs. William Pigott]

Grant, Nellie. *See* Skidmore, Nellie (Grant)

Grant, Paul (pseudonym). *See* Green, Pyatt [Miss]

Grant, Sarah Jane, 14,071

Grant, Statira (Dickinson), 14,071

Grant, Susan (Boyd), 7,224

Grant, Susan Fairchild (Noble) [Mrs. Jedediah Morgan] (1832-1914), **16,685**

Grant, Ulysses Sherman (1867-1932), 1,251, 1,435, 2,579, 4,953, 6,610, 6,956, 8,571, 10,065, 12,162, 12,326, 12,663, 14,206, 15,725

Grant University (TN), faculty, **9,350**

Grant, Virginia. *See* Barnes, Virginia (Grant)

Grant Wood and Marvin Cone: Artists of an Era (book), 4,976

Grant, Zilpah Polly (1794-1874). *See* Banister, Zilpah Polly (Grant) [Mrs. William] (1794-1874)

Grants-in-aid, 11,911

Granville, Bonita (1923-), 11,907

Granville Female Institute (NC), 13,420

Graphic arts, 2,769

Graphic Arts International Union, **2,122**

Graphic Arts International Union, Project for Equal Progression, 2,122

Graphology, 1,838, 7,648

Grases, James, 727

Grass of the Earth (book), 8,779

Grass research, 10,152, **15,215**

Grass Valley Chamber of Commerce (CA), 687

Grasshopper's Man, The (book), 14,423

Grasso, Ella, 6,710

Gratiot, Susan (Hempstead), **17,643**

Gratz, Benjamin, 7,533

Gratz, Caroline, 15,010

Gratz, Elizabeth, 15,010

Gratz Family (PA), **15,010**

Gratz, Louisa, 15,010

Gratz, Rebecca (1781-1869), **2,362, 7,533,** 12,205, 13,079, 15,153, 15,156

Gratz, Simon (1840-1925), 15,010

Gratz, William, 5,312

Grau, Maurice, 12,321

Graupner, Annabel Elise (Wenzelburger) [Mrs. Adolphus Earhart], 509

Graupner Family (CA), 509

Graupnor, Mrs., 1,237

Gravander, Valborg "Mama" (Mattson) (1888-1978), **510,** 1,068

Graves, Adaline (1835-1906). *See* Earle, Adaline (Graves) [Mrs. Isham Harrison] (1835-1906)

Graves, Ann Jane (Baker) [Mrs. John James], 5,771

Graves, Anna Melissa [Miss] (1875-1964), **8,090,** 15,301, 15,303, **15,305**

Graves, Annie M., 5,771

Graves, Bertha (1881-). *See* Morey, Bertha (Graves) (1881-)

Graves, Calvin, **13,417**

Graves, Caroline, 13,417

Graves, Effie, 16,117

Graves, Eleanor June, 1,431

Graves, Ellen Armistead, **16,075**

Graves Family, 644

Graves Family (MD), **5,771**

Graves Family (TX), **16,357**

Graves, Florence (Carson) [Mrs. Nat], **9,545**

Graves, Frances. *See* Frances (Graves) [Mrs. Thomas Jefferson Jackson]

Graves, Henry M., 5,771

Graves, Janie (Lowrey) Sanford, 9,543

Graves, John James (1800-90), 5,771

Graves, Julia Charlotte Hooper, 13,016

Graves, Juliette Aurelia (1858-?). *See* Adams, Juliette Aurelia (Graves) [Mrs. Crosby] (1858-?)

Graves, Lilly, 5,771

Graves, Louis (1883-1965), **13,016**

Graves, Lucy, 2,196

Graves, Mary (1886-1953). *See* Rees, Mary (Graves) (1886-1953)

Graves, Mildred "Mim" (Moses) [Mrs. Louis] (1892-1976), 13,016

Graves, Mrs., 11,004

Graves, Nat, 9,545
Graves, Theresa M., **7,800**
Graves, William B., 5,771
Gravestones, **3,615**, 7,627
Gravestones of Early New England and the Men Who Made Them (book), 7,627
"Gravestones Wept, The" (story), 16,168
Graville, Winifred [Miss] (1939-70), 11,516
Gray, Abby Jane, 8,962
Gray, Alexina, 9,221
Gray, Alma (Ratliff), **9,633**
Gray, Annette B. [Mrs. W. B. D.], 17,971
Gray, Annie Ruth [Miss] (1900?-), **17,970**
Gray, Arthur F., 14,901
Gray, Asa (1810-88), **6,283**, 6,310, **6,311**, 11,297
Gray, Ben Cottrell, 9,726, 13,119
Gray, Clarence Arthur (1874-1934), **8,334**
Gray, Cora Amelia (1850-1927). *See* Brill, Cora Amelia (Gray) [Mrs. Hascal Russell] (1850-1927)
Gray, Cordelia Lewis (Scales) [Mrs. Ben Cottrell] (1844-1915), **9,726**, **13,119**, 15,895
Gray, Ella Conover (1875/76-1972). *See* Fleck, Ella Conover (Gray) [Mrs. H. Willard] (1875/76-1972)
Gray, Emma P. (Hotchkiss) [Mrs. Horatio Nelson], 1,987
Gray, Ethel Huyler (1877-?), **12,489**
Gray Family, 2,532
Gray, Glen, 5,534
Gray, Grace (Farrington) [Mrs. James] (1871-1935), 9,103
Gray, Horatio Nelson, 1,987
Gray, J. D., 15,636
Gray, James, Family (NY, MN), **9,103**
Gray, Jane Loring [Mrs. Asa] (1821-1909), 6,283, **6,311**, 11,297
Gray, Juanita R. [Mrs. George W., Jr.], **1,777**
Gray, Lucy, 6,653
Gray, Maria (Willey), 511
Gray, Martha Nettie McFarlin (1858-?), 16,076
Gray, Mary Almira. *See* McLench, Mary Almira (Gray) [Mrs. Benjamin Franklin]
Gray, Mary Augusta (Dix) [Mrs. William Henry] (1810-81), 14,566, 17,373
Gray, Nellie Prentice [Mrs. Clarence Arthur], 8,334
Gray, Peter, **6,611**
Gray, Robert, 5,160
Gray, Sadai (Burge), 3,313
Gray, Sophie Stryker [Mrs. James] (1901-52), 9,103
Gray, W. B. D. (1846-1926), **17,971**
Gray, Wil Lou [Miss], 15,609, 15,706
Gray, William Henry (1810-89), **14,566**
Graybiel, Adelaide, 11,361
Graydon, Katherine Merrill, 1,635
Graydon, Nell (Saunders), **13,017**
Grayson, Andrew Jackson (1819-69), **512**
Grayson, Frances Jane (Timmons) [Mrs. Andrew Jackson] (1823-1908). *See* Crane, Frances Jane (Timmons) [Mrs. Andrew Jackson] Grayson [Mrs. George Belden] (1823-1908)
Grayson, Kathryn, 17,943
Grayston, Catherine. *See* Bond, Catherine (Grayston)
Grayston Family (WV), **11,527**
Grayston, James, 11,527
Great Authors in Their Youth (book), 11,993
Great Bands of America (book), 4,988
Great Books Foundation, 10,490
Great Britain, 9,992
  American ambassadors to, 2,388, 2,527, 2,542
  armed forces, women in, 6,850
  civil defense, 2,686
  foreign relations, 12,407
  Friends, Society of, 15,058
  needlework, study and teaching, **12,301**
  suffrage, 4,244
  temperance, 4,244
  women, education, 11,616
Great Diamond Hoax, 1,786
Great Falls Tribune (MT), 10,310
Great Lakes Naval Hospital, 8,260
Great Nemaha Agency, 15,289
Great Northern Railroad Company, 8,690, 9,131
Great Northern Railway, 10,104
Great Reinforcement (OR), 14,596

Great Sahara Mouse Hunt, The (ms), 6,068
Great Sebastians, The (drama), 3,468
Great Southwest Strike, The (book), 15,986
Great Year, The (book), 10,867
Greater Atlanta Council on Human Relations (GA). *See* Community Relations Commission (Atlanta, GA)
Greater Des Moines Chamber of Commerce (IA), **4,990**
Greater Fort Worth Civil Liberties Union (TX), **15,993**
Greater Kalamazoo Federated Women's Club (MI), **8,235**
Greater Lawndale Conservation Commission (IL), **4,093**
Greater Lawrence Young Women's Christian Association (MA), **7,063**
Greater New York Fund, 6,729
Greater St. Louis Prohibition Club (MO), 7,779
Greater St. Paul Community Chest and Council (MN), 8,676
Greater St. Paul United Fund and Council, Incorporated (MN), **9,104**
Greatheart Society, Incorporated (Philadelphia, PA), **15,187**
Greaves, Pauline E., **14,482**
Greble, Edwin, Family (PA), **2,363**
Greble, Sue Volkmar, 2,363
Gree, Eliza (Cary), 2,328
Greece, 12,196
  1944-1949, 17,762
  United Nations, economic assistance, 6,125
Greek-Americans, 5,829
Greek letter societies, 116, 914, **922**, 1,085, 1,404, **1,613**, 1,625, 2,166, 2,446, 2,939, 3,077, **3,779**, 3,799, **3,972**, 4,042, **4,194**, 4,219, **4,220**, 4,383, 4,390, 4,402, 4,403, **4,524**, **4,559**, **4,592**, 4,640, 4,710, **4,718**, **5,046**, 5,064, **6,514**, 7,153, 7,164, 7,576, **7,884**, **8,041**, **8,051**, **8,321**, 8,552, 8,567, **8,579**, 8,607, **8,612**, 8,740, 8,819, **9,038**, 9,829, **9,830**, 9,839, 9,936, 9,951, 9,960, 10,048, 10,060, **10,185**, 10,222, **10,453**, 10,482, **10,663**, 11,218, **11,376**, 11,388, **11,712**, 13,391, 13,945, **14,028**, 14,037, 14,365, 15,186, 16,911, **17,003**, 17,110, **17,288**, 17,541, 17,924
Greek letter societies, Afro-American, 5,064, **10,191**
Greek Royal Order of Beneficence, 4,918
Greek Way, The (book), 11,164
Greeley, Floretta Elmore, **13,018**
Greeley, Gabrielle, **6,612**
Greeley, Horace, 2,406, 6,612, 8,167, 11,741, 12,003, 14,206
Greeley, Robert, 11,983
Greely, Adolphus Washington (1844-1935), **2,364**
Greely, Henrietta (Nesmith) [Mrs. Adolphus Washington), 2,364
Green, A. W., 13,272
Green, Anita (Bryant) [Mrs. Bob] (1941-), 2,932, **14,231**
Green, Ann Maria (Stockwell) [Mrs. George] (1840-1904), **13,928**
Green, Anna Amory Tucker (1803-75), 7,636
Green, Anna Peirce (1702-70), 7,636
Green Bay State Gazette (WI), 17,593
Green, Bob, 14,231
Green, Constance Winsor (McLaughlin) (1897-1975), **2,135**, **2,365**, 7,167
Green County Woman's Democratic Club (MO), 10,012
Green, Edith, 14,504
Green, Edward Henry (1821-1902), 7,636
Green, Elizabeth (1878-1965), 10,163
Green, Emma Edwards, **3,687**
Green Family, 14,059
Green Family (KY), **5,265**
Green Family (MA), **7,636**
Green Family (MS), 9,741
Green Family (NJ), 11,130
Green, Floride, 1,086
Green, George, 13,928
Green Grass of Wyoming (book), 17,999
Green, Halcott Pride, 15,604
Green, Hannah, 7,387

Green, Hattie. *See* Hill, Hattie (Green) [Mrs. William J.]
Green, Hattie (Jones) [Mrs. John], 10,163
Green, Hetty Howland (Robinson) [Mrs. Edward Henry] (1834-1916), 8,064, 16,984
Green, Jennie Scott (1879-1965), 5,265
Green, John (1835-1913), 10,163
Green-Joyce Company, 13,272
Green, Julia (?-1923). *See* Scott, Julia (Green) [Mrs. Matthew] (?-1923)
Green, Julia (Boynton) [Mrs. L. Worthington] (1861-1957), **1,432**
Green Kingdom, The (book), 6,048
Green, Lafayette (1835-1907), 5,265
Green, Letitia (1843-1913). *See* Stevenson, Letitia (Green) [Mrs. Adlai E.] (1843-1913)
Green, Lula S., II, 5,469
Green Mansions (moving-picture), 17,804
Green, Martha [Mrs.], 13,455
Green, Martha M. [Miss], 2,460
Green, Mary Augusta. *See* Tudor, Mary Augusta (Green)
Green, Mary Caroline Tilton, **1,302**
Green, Mary Leonora. *See* Pollard, Mary Leonora Green [Mrs. Horatio Harrison]
Green Mountain College (VT), archives, **17,047**
Green, Mrs. H. Clifford, **13,418**
Green, Mrs. Halcott Pride, 15,604
Green, Mrs. Will S., **513**
Green, Nora B., 14,363
Green, Norma Kidd [Mrs. Roy M.] (1893-1975), **10,465**
Green Pond School (VA), 17,085
Green, Preston Scott (1877-1945), 5,265
Green, Pyatt [Miss], **3,194**
Green, Rebecca Eleanor "Ella" (Scott) [Mrs. Lafayette] (1841-96), 5,265
Green, Robert Scott (1882-1943), **5,265**
Green, Ruth (Tuthill) [Mrs. Thomas H.] (1895-), **7,225**
Green, Sallie B. (Morgan), **514**
Green, Sallie Coles (1849-1929). *See* Heyward, Sallie Coles (Green) [Mrs. Albert Rhett] (1849-1929)
Green, Selina Jewel (East) [Mrs. Theophilus Walton] (1887-1971), **9,634**
Green, Sylvina Maria (Dewey) (1832-?), **12,819**
Green, Theophilus Walton, 9,634
Green, Thomas F., 5,511
Green, Thomas H., 7,225
Green, Thomas Marshall (1837-1904), 5,268
Green Thursday (book), 15,672
Green, Willis (1794?-1862), 5,265
Green, Willis (1870-1944), 5,265
Green, Zoe. *See* Radcliffe, Zoe (Green)
Greenaway, Katherine (1846-1901), 3,927
Greenback-Labor party, 4,854
Greenbaum, Alice (1876-1943). *See* Rosenberg, Alice (Greenbaum) [Mrs. Abraham] (1876-1943)
Greenbaum, Sarah Ackerman [Mrs. Louis], 943
Greenberg, Elizabeth (Pendergast) [Mrs. Henry] (1858-1929), 9,282
Greenberg, Goldie, 4,053
Greenberg, Joanne (Goldenburg) (1932-), **6,029**
Greenbie, Marjorie Barstow [Mrs. Sydney], 14,378
Greenbie, Sydney (1889-1960), **14,378**
Greenblatt, Helen, 2,693
Greene, Abby Lyman [Mrs. William], 13,848
Greene, Catharine (Littlefield) [Mrs. Nathanael]. *See* Miller, Catharine (Littlefield) [Mrs. Nathanael] Greene
Greene, Catherine Ray. *See* Roelker, Catherine Ray (Greene) [Mrs. Frederick]
Greene, Chloe Tyler (Whittle) [Mrs. John Newport], 17,123
Greene, Eleonore (Raoul) (1888-), **3,324**
Greene, Emma [Mrs.], 7,140
Greene Family (MA), **6,613**
Greene Family (VA), **17,123**
Greene, Flora Hartley [Mrs. Charles W.] (1865-1948), **9,978**
Greene, Graham, 11,976
Greene, Henry Copley (1871-1951), 6,613
Greene, Jeanette, **11,423**
Greene, John Morton (1830-1919), 7,163

Greene, John Newport, 17,123
Greene, Katrine R. C. (1912-66), 6,613
Greene, Lida Lisle, 4,842
Greene, Lily Dexter (1868-1942), **4,529**
Greene, Louisa "Lula" (1849-1944). *See* Richards,
  Louisa "Lula" (Greene) [Mrs. Levi Willard]
  (1849-1944)
Greene, Mary. *See* Nye, Mary (Greene)
Greene, Mary Anne (1857-?), **1,103**
Greene, Mary Theresa, **7,801**
Greene, Mary Theresa, 11,754
Greene, Nathanael, 3,534
Greene, Rosalind Huidekoper (1885-1975), 6,613
Greene, Rosaline, 11,909
Greene Street School (RI), 7,631
Greene, William (1797-1883), **13,848**
Greener, Richard Theodore (1844-1922), 5,945
Greenewalt, Mary Elizabeth (Hallock) [Mrs. Frank
  Lindsay] (1871-1950), **2,366**
Greenfield, Albert Monroe (1887-1967), **15,011**
Greenfield, Edna Kraus [Mrs. Albert Monroe], 15,011
Greenfield, Margaret, **515**
Greenfield, Marguerite, **10,311**
Greengard, Bernice (Degginger), 17,282
Greenglass, Ethel (1916-53). *See* Rosenberg, Ethel
  (Greenglass) [Mrs. Julius] (1916-53)
Greenhow, Mary Jane Charlton (1819-?). *See* Lee,
  Mary Jane Charlton (Greenhow) [Mrs. Hugh
  Holmes] (1819-?)
Greenhow, Rose (O'Neale or O'Neal) [Mrs. Robert]
  (ca. 1815-64), 626, 2,444, **13,419**, 13,446
Greenleaf, Daniel, 9,635
Greenleaf, Jean Brooks, 12,834
Greenleaf, Lucy (Cranch) (1767-1846), 7,598
Greenleaf, Matilda (Beaumont) [Mrs. Daniel], **9,635**
Greenleaf, Mary (Longfellow) (1816-1902), 6,330
Greenleaf, Sarah (?-1838). *See* Haven, Sarah
  (Greenleaf) [Mrs. Nathaniel Walker] Appleton
  [Mrs. Joseph] (?-1838)
Greenleaf Woman's Christian Temperance Union
  (ID), **3,688**
Greenman, Caroline (Goodrich) (1826-?), **17,644**
Greenman, Frances Cranmer (1890-), **2,768**, 9,467
Greenough, Annetta, **8,277**
Greenough, Chester Noyes (1874-1938), **6,284**
Greenough, Ruth Hornblower [Mrs. Chester Noyes],
  6,284
Greensboro Female College (NC), 13,345, 13,353,
  13,369, 13,370, 13,463
Greentree, Harriet R., 13,348
Greenville Employment Security Commission (NC),
  13,286
Greenville Female College (SC), 15,643
Greenville Ladies' Association (SC), **15,598**
Greenway, Isabella (Selmes) (1886-1953), 157, 188,
  194, 984, 2,218, 9,155
Greenway, John Campbell (1872-1926), **194**
Greenwich Health Association (CT), 1,837
Greenwich House (NY), 6,885, **12,271**
Greenwich House Music School (NY), 2,664, 15,198
Greenwich Philharmonia, 1,837
Greenwich Village Association (NY), 6,885
Greenwich Village Crumperie Tea Room (NY), 7,209
Greenwich Village Theatre (NY), 7,209
Greenwood, Ada. *See* McLaughlyn, Ada
  (Greenwood)
Greenwood, Annie Pile (1880-1956), **16,686**
Greenwood, Britton, 516
Greenwood Cemetery (NY), 12,494
Greenwood Family (CA), **516**
Greenwood, Grace (pseudonym). *See* Lippincott,
  Sara Jane (Clarke) [Mrs. Leander K.]
  (1823-1904)
Greenwood, Isabel Whittier [Mrs. Chester], **5,626**
Greenwood, James, 10,110
Greenwood, James M., 10,113
Greenwood, Josephine M. [Mrs. James] (?-1920s),
  10,110
Greenwood, Mary Antonia. *See* Reinking, Mary
  Antonia (Greenwood)
Greenwood, Mary Hamer (?-1953), 6,122
Greenwood, May Snowdrop, 1,489
Greenwood, Moses, **5,484**
Greenwood Society (Kansas City, MO), 10,112

Greenwood, William D., 12,310
Greer, Cornelia Jane (Spencer) (1841-1930), 14,567,
  14,668
Greer, Ester Marshall, 10,055
Greer, George, Family (OR), **14,567**
Greer, Germaine, 1,017
Greer, Grace. *See* Nuttall, Grace (Greer)
Greer, John C., 3,089
Greer, Mabel, 11,897
Greer, Margaret Grace (1880-). *See* Nuttall,
  Margaret Grace (Greer) [Mrs. William Albert]
  (1880-)
Greer, Mary Autry, 16,243
Greer Presbyterian Church (SC), **15,599**
Greeting cards, 1,786, 2,220, 8,990
Gregg, David R., 4,362
Gregg, Elinor Delight (1889-1970), **6,142**
Gregg Family, 11,599
Gregg, John Robert (1867-1948), **11,880**
Gregg, Lizzie R. [Miss] (ca. 1861-?), **15,012**
Gregg, Rebecca, 9,842
Gregg, Sarah [Mrs. David R.], **4,362**
Gregorie, Anne K., 15,405
Gregory, Alice (Sterling), 816
Gregory, Alyse, 11,951
Gregory, Annadora Foss (1893-), 10,466
Gregory, Augusta, 1,337
Gregory, Bettie, 13,420
Gregory, Cinderella, 4,300
Gregory, (Doris). *See* Black, Doris (Gregory)
Gregory, Edgar B., 13,929
Gregory, Elizabeth (Hiatt) (1872-1955), **1,040**
Gregory, Emily Lovisa (1841-97), 6,309, 11,297
Gregory Family (NE), **10,466**
Gregory, George Albert (1851-1945), 10,466
Gregory, Hattie Tyng, 17,718
Gregory, Jessica, 13,420
Gregory, John M., 4,381
Gregory, John T., **13,420**
Gregory, Louisa (Allen) [Mrs. John M.] (1856-?),
  4,388
Gregory, Martha Walbridge, 1,337
Gregory, Mary, 13,333
Gregory, Maude, 13,420
Gregory, Molly, 13,616
Gregory, Pernelah, 13,563
Gregory, Sarah E. Franks [Mrs. William D.]
  (1846?-1931), **7,085**
Gregory, Sarah (Mumford) [Mrs. Edgar B.]
  (1855-1950), **13,929**
Gregory, Sarepta, 13,563
Greig, John, 12,824
Greig, Mary, 14,943
Greig, Mrs. John, 12,824
Grenfell expedition (Labrador), 15,776
Grenfell, Joyce, 7,209
Grenfell Mission, 7,209, 7,285
Grenfell, Wilfred 7,285
Grenville Dodge Trust, 4,749
Greshheimer, Laura 6,812
Gress, Ruth A., **14,379**
Gretchen Lamberton Animal Shelter, 9,527
Gretchen's Hill (book), 4,987
Gretter, Lystra E. (1858-1951), 6,122
Greve, Harriet C., 13,189
Grevstad, Mathilde Berg [Mrs.] (1862-1952?), **8,739**
Grew Family (MA), **7,476**
Grew, M., 7,476
Grew, Mary (1813-96), 5,907, 6,244, 6,741
Grey, Jessie [Miss], **10,672**
Grey Lady Corps (CA), 955
Grey, Lucy Jane (1831-64). *See* Latourette,
  Lucy Jane Grey [Mrs. Lyman Daniel Cornwall]
  (1831-64)
Grey Nuns of the Sacred Heart Motherhouse
  (Yardley, PA), **15,356**
Gribble, Mary W. [Mrs. Harry], **2,367**
Gribbons, Jackie Marie, 17,001
Grieco, Rose, **9,496**
Grief, 1,955, 3,295, 7,606, 13,555
Grier, Ada (Bruen) (1848-1924), 10,185
Grierson, Margaret Storrs (1900-), 15,946
Grieve, Lucia Catherine Graeme (1862-1946), **10,974**
Grieve, Martha Lucy (Kinkead) (1838-?), 10,974

Griffen, Gloria Grace (1929-73). *See* Harrison,
  Gloria Grace (Griffen) Cline (1929-73)
Griffin, Abbie T. (1851-?). *See* Dike, Abbie T.
  Griffin [Mrs. S. Clint] (1851-?)
Griffin, Bertha [Miss], 13,294
Griffin, Desire Smith, **14,568**
Griffin, E. H., 583
Griffin, Eleanor, 2,476
Griffin, Elizabeth Gordan [Miss], **13,269**
Griffin, Emily [Mrs. E. H.], 583
Griffin Family, 13,269
Griffin Family, 3,436
Griffin, Isabel K., 11,493
Griffin, Jane (1792-1875). *See* Franklin, Jane
  (Griffin) [Mrs. John] (1792-1875)
Griffin, Lucile Meredith (Mouton), **5,434**
Griffin, Marion Mahony [Mrs. Walter Burley]
  (1871-1962), **3,782**, 12,216
Griffin, Mary (Sands), 11,941
Griffin, Sara Swan, 7,069
Griffin, Vashti Rogers [Mrs. Colin O.], **1,209**
Griffin, Walter Burley (1876-1937), 3,782, **12,216**
Griffing Family (NY), **12,003**
Griffing, Josephine Sophia (White) [Mrs. Charles
  Stockman Spooner] (1814-72), 5,907, 12,003
Griffing, Matilda Coley. *See* Bancroft, Matilda Coley
  (Griffing) [Mrs. Hubert Howe]
Griffis, Guion (1900-). *See* Johnson, Guion (Griffis)
  (1900-)
Griffis, Katharine Lyra (Stanton) [Mrs. William
  Elliot] (1856-98), 10,975
Griffis, Margaret Quandril Clark [Miss] (1838-1913),
  10,975
Griffis, Sarah Francis King [Mrs. William Elliot]
  (1868-1959), 10,975
Griffis, William Elliot (1843-1928), **10,975**
Griffith, Adelaide. *See* Cochrane, Adelaide (Griffith)
Griffith, Alice [Miss], 412, **517**
Griffith Davenport (drama), 11,457
Griffith, David, 5,812
Griffith Family (MS), 17,502
Griffith, Grace (Kellogg) (1885-). *See* Smith, Grace
  (Kellogg) Griffith (1885-)
Griffith, Martha E. (Hutchings) [Mrs. Thomas J.]
  (1842-?), 4,475
Griffith, Millen, 412
Griffith, Mrs. John T., 5,316
Griffith, Nanni (Taylor) [Mrs. David], **5,812**
Griffith School of Music (GA), 3,180
Griffith, Thomas J. (1837-?), **4,475**
Griffiths, Ann Lane (Crittenden), 13,390
Griffiths, Ellen. *See* McClain, Ellen (Griffiths) [Mrs.
  Emlin]
Griffiths, Jane Rio (1810-83). *See* Baker, Jane Rio
  (Griffiths) [Mrs. Henry] (1810-83)
Griffiths, Martha (Wright) [Mrs. Hicks] (1912-),
  2,097, 6,297, 6,710, **7,802**, 7,904
Griffitts, Hannah [Miss] (1727-1817), **15,013**
Griffitts, Mary, 15,013
Grigg, Bessie, 11,753
Grigger, Ann, **2,136**
Griggs, Ann Helen [Miss], 10,976
Griggs, Hazel, 9,234
Griggs, Lillian (Baker) [Mrs. Alfred] (1876-1955),
  13,204
Griggs, Oliver, **10,976**
Grigsby Family (KY), **5,343**
Grigsby, John Warren (?-1877), 5,343
Grigsby, Louisiana, 5,343
Grigsby, Susan Preston (Shelby) [Mrs. John Warren]
  (1830-91), 5,343
Grillo, Clara (Corica) [Mrs. Dominic] (1906-), **9,497**
Grima, Adelaide [Mrs. Felix], 5,485
Grima Family (LA), **5,485**
Grima, Felix, 5,485
Grima, Marie, 5,485
Grimball Family (SC), **13,066**, 15,414
Grimball, John Berkeley (1800-93), 15,414
Grimball, John Berkeley (1800-93). *See* Grimball,
  John Berkeley (1800-93)
Grimball, Margaret Ann "Meta" (Morris) [Mrs. John
  Berkeley] (1810-81), **13,019**, 13,066, 15,414
Grimes Family (IL, NH), **10,812**
Grimes, L. C., 15,303

Grimes, Lucia Isabella (Voorhees) [Mrs. George], **7,803**
Grimké, Angelina Emily (1805-79). *See* Weld, Angelina Emily (Grimké) [Mrs. Theodore Dwight] (1805-79)
Grimké, Angelina Weld (1880-1958), **2,137**, 3,288, 3,290
Grimké, Charlotte L. (Forten) [Mrs. Francis James] (1837-1914), 2,138
Grimké Family, **8,005**
Grimké, Francis James (1850-1937), **2,138**
Grimké, Sarah Moore (1792-1873), 992, **2,368**, 2,501, 2,629, **4,421**, 5,907, 6,741, 7,294, 8,005, 11,590, 11,605, 12,419, 14,836, 14,893, **16,077**
Grimm, Betty Jane, 2,927
Grimsley, Elizabeth (Todd) (1825-95), **4,363**
Grimstvedt, Abr, **9,106**
Grimstvedt, Herborg Kristiansdatter. *See* Klausson, Herborg Kristiansdatter (Grimstvedt) [Mrs.]
Grindley, Sarah A., 8,273
Gringa's Guide to Mexican Cooking, A (book), 18,006
Grinnell College (IA), 2,298, 4,889
    faculty, **4,935**, 4,940
    students, 4,744, 4,886, 4,911
Grinnell, Frank Lansing, 12,490
Grinnell, George Bird (1849-1938), 12,490
Grinnell, George Blake, 12,490
Grinnell, Helen (Lansing) [Mrs. George Blake], **12,490**
Grinnell, Hilda (Wood) [Mrs. Joseph], 518
Grinnell, Joseph (1877-1939), 310, **518**
Grinnell, Mary (Vail) [Mrs. L. J.], 17,039
Gripon, Louise Winslow (Kidder) [Mrs. George Herbert] Sparrow [Mrs. Paul E. H.] (1884-). *See* Sparrow, Louise Winslow (Kidder). [Mrs. George Herbert] Sparrow. [Mrs. Paul E. H.] Gripon (1884-)
Gripon, Paul E. H., 2,585
Gripsholm (ship), 14,396
Griscom, Anna Bassett (1889-1974). *See* Elkinton, Anna Bassett Griscom [Mrs. J. Passmore] (1889-1974)
Grisham, Elizabeth (1826-96). *See* Brown, Elizabeth (Grisham) [Mrs. Joseph Emerson] (1826-96)
Grisso, Walker D., **14,206**
Grist-mills *See* Flour-mills
Griswald, Elijah, Family (NY), 11,440
Griswald, Julia, 11,443
Griswald, Mary Emma, 1,533
Griswold, Augusta Emily. *See* Morris, Augusta Emily (Griswold) [Mrs. John Moses]
Griswold, Emmeline "Emma". *See* Smith, Emmeline "Emma" (Griswold) [Mrs. Joseph, III]
Griswold, Florence (Kressler) (1851-1937), **12,491**
Griswold, Harriet, **9,107**
Griswold, Harriet (Booth) (ca. 1814-1906), **1,303**
Griswold, Mabel E. [Miss], 17,746
Griswold, Marguerite [Mrs. Albert S.], 225
Griswold, Nevada (Hardesty), 10,632
Griswold, Rufus Wilmot (1815-57), 5,914, 5,915, **5,930**, 12,399
Grocers, 3,496, 3,562, 7,084, 8,353, 8,941, 11,053
Grocery trade, 15,441, **17,531**
Groehn, Kathy (1946-). *See* El-Messidi, Kathy (Groehn) Casseboom (1946-)
Groff, Anne M., 2,016
Groff, Florence [Miss], **12,492**
Groff-Smith, Mrs. Everitt (1892-), **14,380**
Groff, William N., 12,492
Grogan, Elmira [Miss], **3,018**
Grolier Club (NY), 12,002
Gronan, Nell (Grant) [Mrs. William Pigott], 6,864
Groomes, Katherine S., 7,757, **7,804**
Gros Ventre Indians, 10,368, **10,369**
Groscurth, Mildred, 14,943
Gross, Esther, 17,282
Gross, Marie Bertrand, **12,493**
Gross, William, 14,269
Grosse Pointe: Race Against Race (book), 8,084
Grossett, Margaret, 14,407
Grossett Studio, 14,407
Grossinger, Jennie, 12,070
Grossman, Gertrude Hubbard, 2,202

Grossman, Jeanette, **13,788**
Grossman, Mary Foley [Mrs.] (ca. 1905-72), **15,200**
Grossman, Mildred, 11,774
Grosvenor, Ebenezer, 11,050
Grosvenor, Elsie May (Bell) [Mrs. Gilbert] (1878-1964), 2,202, 2,420
Grosvenor, Mary H., 12,309
Grotzinger, Laurel [Miss], 4,396
Group Health (MN), 9,180
Group, The (book), 16,160
Grout, Jane M., 9,108
Grout, Julia Rebecca "Jerry" [Miss] (1898-), **13,205**
Grout, Laura Miller [Mrs. Edgar Homer], 8,572
Grout, Ruth Ellen (1901-), **8,572**
Grove, Cora, **8,700**
Grove, Dorothy Haverty [Mrs. Lon], **3,195**
Grove, Roxy Harriette (1889-1952), **16,358**
Grover, E. O., 2,872
Grover, Eldress Ann, 12,309
Grover, Emmeline (1831-1917). *See* Rich, Emmeline (Grover) [Mrs. Charles Coulsen] (1831-1917)
Grover, Katharine (Carruth) (1911-), 519
Grover, Lizzie, 10,211
Grover, Sherwood, **519**
Groves, Adelaide B., 3,826
Groves, Alma Zola (1898-), **4,094**, 4,176
Groves, John Stuart, 16,151
Groves, Mrs. Denison, 4,175
Groves, Phyllis, **8,091**
Grow, Alice (Haynes), 13,432
Grow, Bernadine, 4,625
Grow, Lottie (Lyons) [Mrs. Walter S.] (1884-), **4,625**
Growden, Grace (?-1782). *See* Galloway, Grace (Growden) [Mrs. Joseph] (?-1782)
Growing Pains (book), 17,870
Growth (book), 8,374
"Growth of the Roman Catholic Church in the United States from 1820 to 1840" (dissertation), 17,626
Grubaugh, Orpha Jane, 8,335
Grubb Family (PA), 15,014
Grubb, Henry Bates, 15,014
Grubb, Margaret Day, 1,788
Grubb, Margaret Marian, 1,788
Grubb, Mary (1816-1900). *See* Parker, Mary (Grubb) (1816-1900)
Grubb, Sarah (1818-83). *See* Ogilvia, Sarah (Grubb) (1818-83)
Gruber-Dietmeier, Louise Marie, 9,323
Gruenberg, Benjamin Charles (1875-1965), **2,369**
Gruenberg, Bertha Sanford (1888-), **6,614**
Gruenberg, Sidonie (Matsner) [Mrs. Benjamin] (1881-1974), **2,369**, 2,403, 8,639
Gruening, Dorothy Smith [Mrs. Ernest] (1888-), **6,615**
Gruening, Ernest, 6,615
Grumbling, Sadie, 5,063
Grunbaum, Hannah, 17,282
Grundy, Miss (pseudonym). *See* Snead, Maria Austine [Miss] (?-1888)
Grunsky, Charles, 520
Grunsky, Charlotte Fredericke (1853-1920?), 520
Grunsky, Clotilde (1891-). *See* Taylor, Clotilde (Grunsky) (1891-)
Grunsky Family (CA), 520
Grunsky, Josephine Fredericke Clotilde (Camerer) [Mrs. Charles] (1830-64), 520
Gruppe, Virginia, 12,790
Grzedowska, Mother Veronica, 15,337
Gscheidle, Gertrude, 3,925
Guadalajara As I Know It . . . Live It . . . Love It . . . (book), 18,006
Guadalupe Area Project (St. Paul, MN), 9,210
Guadalupe Center (Kansas City, MO), 10,117
Guajome Rancho (CA), 370
Guaranteed annual wage. *See* Wages, Annual wage
Guard of Honor Society, 11,355
Guardian and ward, 2,206, 5,481, 8,924, 8,946, 9,972, 10,005, 10,976, 11,582, 13,435, 13,570, 16,148. *See also* Adoption
Guardian Angel Society (New Castle, KY), **5,344**
Guardian, The, 17,663
"Guardian, The" (newsletter), 8,490

Guatemala
    coffee plantation workers, American, 11,733
    earthquakes, 11,733
    Indians, 11,733
    insurrections, 16,553
    volunteer workers in social service, **9,389**
Gubisch, Nancy, 15,144
Gudmundsen, Annie Maud Smith (1879-?), 17,924
Gue, Benjamin F. (1828-1904), **4,763**
Gue, Elizabeth Parker [Mrs. Benjamin F.], 4,763
Gue, Mrs. E. H., 3,663
Guenther, Adaline C. (1897-), **521**
Guerard, Adelaide Baynard [Mrs. William P.]. *See* McNish, Adelaide Baynard [Mrs. William P.] Guerard
Guerard, Albert, 1,559
Guerard, Emma B. Moul [Mrs. Peter Godin], 3,515
Guerard Family (GA), **3,515**
Guerard, Mary Emma. *See* Adams, Mary Emma Guerard [Mrs. Richard W.]
Guerard, Mrs. E. B., 3,515
Guerard, Peter Godin, 3,515
Guerard, Sarah C., 3,549
Guerard, William P., 3,549
Guerber, Howard, 1,716
Guerber, Mary Edna Reynolds, **1,716**
Guerber, Mary R., 1,716
Guernsey, Mrs. Egbert, 12,348
Guernsey, S. M. [Mrs. John], 14,515
Guerrillas, 745
Guertin, Florence (1869-1951). *See* Tuttle, Florence (Guertin) (1869-1951)
Guest, Grace, 5,863
Guest in the House (screen play), 17,797
Guest, Ivor, 12,364
Guest, Mary Ann (1797-1855). *See* Reynolds, Mary Ann (Guest) (1797-1855)
Guest, Rebecca (Hall) [Mrs. John], (ca. 1775-?), **5,772**
Guffey, Emma (1874-1970). *See* Miller, Emma (Guffey) [Mrs. Carroll] (1874-1970)
Gugal, Kate Beauregard, 3,583
Guggenheim Fellows, 8,441, 12,362, **14,218**
Guggenheim Foundation, 3,773, 14,744
Guggenheim Jeune, 2,794
Guggenheim Museum, 679
Guggenheim, Peggy, Galleries (London, NY), **2,794**
Guggenheim, Rosalind Mae (1882-1958). *See* Winslow, Rosalind Mae (Guggenheim) (1882-1958)
Guggenheimer, Aimee, 5,809
Guggenheimer, Elinor (Coleman) [Mrs. Randolph] (1912-), 12,078
Guglielmi, O. Louis, 2,463
Guidance Center, 17,716
Guide Book of Art, Architecture, and Historic Interests in Pennsylvania, 14,949
Guided missiles, 11,831
Guides for hunters, fishermen, etc., **5,586**
"Guiding Light, The" (soap opera), 17,705
"Guido, a Tale, and Other Poems," 12,463
Guidon Club, 12,524, 12,525
Guignard, Jane Bruce, 15,429
Guilbert, Yvette, 11,944
Guild, Mary (Eliot) [Mrs. Charles E.], 6,279
Guild of St. Barnabas for Nurses (MO), St. Louis Chapter, 10,145
Guilford College (NC), **13,223**, 13,227
    alumni, **13,224**
    catalogs, 13,225
    dormitories, 13,231
    faculty, 13,225, 13,230, 13,240
    presidents, 13,221
Guilford County Literary and Historical Association (NC), **13,220**
Guilford, Linda Thayer [Miss] (1823-1911), **13,930**
Guilfordian (NC), **13,227**
Guillén, Nicolás, 12,684
Guillet, Elizabeth Maltbie (Eden) [Mrs. Isadore], 12,174
Guillory, Barbara Marie, 5,470, 5,473
Guinan, Sister Mary Gertrude, 10,614
Guiney, Louise Imogen [Miss] (1861-1920), 820, 1,426, **1,433**, **2,370**, 3,927, **4,644**, 5,714, **5,931**, 5,935, 7,585, 7,651, **7,690**

Guinness, Alec, 2,360
Guinzburg, Lenore (1897-). *See* Marshall, Lenore (Guinzburg) [Mrs. James] (1897-)
Guion, Connie Myers (1882-1971), **6,616, 7,226, 11,869, 12,352**
Guion, Cornelia Hall, 9,709
Guion, Ferebe E., **12,140**
Guion, Mary (1782-?). *See* Brown, Mary Guion [Mrs. Samuel] (1782-?)
Guion, Owen Haywood, **13,421**
Guisti, Virginia Boitano (1860-1948), 10,632
Gulager, Catherine Gordon (1829-1910), 15,015
Gulager Family (PA), **15,015**
Gulager, Mary (1836-77), 15,015
Gulager, Mrs. William, Sr. (1760-1835), 15,015
Gulbrandsen, Peter, 705
Gulf, Colorado, and Santa Fe Railroad, **16,237**
Gulf Production Company, 9,728
Gulf Stream, The (book) 43
Gulick, Louisa L., 14,650
Gullah dialect, 15,445, **15,603**
Gulling, Amy (Thompson) (1899-), **10,761**
Gulliver, Sarah Elizabeth (1801-70). *See* Fairbank, Sarah Elizabeth Gulliver [Mrs. Josiah] (1801-70)
Gumb, Katherine "Katie" (Hughes) [Mrs. Daniel J.] (1873-1963), **13,672, 13,724**
Gumby, L. S. Alexander (1885-1961), **12,004**
Gummere, Amelia (Mott) (1859-1937), **14,842**
Gund, Ida May (1868-1951), **10,467**
Gund, Josephine, 10,467
Gundaker, Elizabeth (1823-1902). *See* Black, Elizabeth (Gundaker) [Mrs. William M.] (1823-1902)
Gunderson, Barbara, 5,137
Gundlach, Alexandra, 522
Gundlach, Anita (Hinz) [Mrs. Heini] (1875-1955), **522**
Gundlach, Heini, 522
Gundlach, Jacob, 522
Gunman's Justice (book), 17,942
Gunn, Carol Jeanne Graff (1929-), 16,780
Gunnell, Anne Elia (Wyatt) [Mrs. Franklin L.] *See* Leishman, Anne Eliza (Wyatt) [Mrs. Franklin L.] Gunnell [Mrs. Robert Adamson]
Gunnell, Franklin L., 16,742
Gunnison, Martha E. [Mrs. Arthur G.] (1865-1960), **17,645**
Gunpowder, 2,033
"Guns of Will Sonnett, The" (television program), 5,240
Gunsmiths, **7,143**
"Gunsmoke" (television program), 5,240
Guntekin, Resat, 1,556
Gunterman, Bertha, 14,475
Gunther, Erna (1896-), 920, **17,266**
Gunther, John, 4,476
Gurley, Helen (1922-). *See* Brown, Helen (Gurley)
Gurley, Jane [Mrs.], **13,020**
Gurnee Family (CA), 1,566
Gurnee, Mary Elizabeth, 1,566
Gurney, Eliza Paul (Kirkbride) [Mrs. Joseph John] (1801-1881), 2,448
Gurney, Elizabeth (1780-1845). *See* Fry, Elizabeth (Gurney) [Mrs. Joseph] (1780-1845)
Gurr, Lena (1897-), **2,769**
Gurr, Sarah Elizabeth, 16,417
Gustafson, Phyllis, 11,827
Gustava, Alice (1899-). *See* Smith, Sister Maris Stella (1899-)
Gustavus John Orr, The Man and His Period 1819-1887 (ms), 3,238
Gustin, Ellen, 5,699
Gustine Family (MS), 9,767
Gustine, Margaret, 12,034
Guthrie, Adam, 3,751
Guthrie, Anne (1890-), **6,030**
Guthrie, Charles Claude, Sr. (1880-1963), **9,979**
Guthrie, Fannie Hall, 9,979
Guthrie, Frances "Fannie" Virginia (1885-), 9,979
Guthrie, Jane (Hunter) [Mrs. D. C.], 2,373
Guthrie, Ramon, 10,867
Guthrie, Sylva (D'Arusmont), 2,656
Gutmann Family (CT, IL), **4,422**
Gutmann, Laura Ernestine (1847-1907). *See* Steven,

Laura Ernestine (Gutmann) [Mrs. James, Jr.] (1847-1907)
Gutride, Minnie, 11,774
Guttersen, Alma A. (1865-?), 8,737
Guttersen, Laird, 212
Guttersen, Mrs. Laird, 212
Guttmacher, Alan Frank (1898-), **6,222,** 6,987, 8,634
Guttmacher, Leonore [Mrs. Alan F.], 6,987
Guy Mannering (drama), 3,921
Guyana, missionaries to, Lutheran, 8,869
Guye, Elizabeth W. P., **17,222**
Guyton, Pearl Vivian [Miss], **9,636**
Guzman, Jessie Parkhurst (1898-), **124,** 127
Gvale, Gudrum Hovde [Mrs.], 8,786
Gwinn Family (IL), 4,058
Gwinn, Mary, 14,738
Gwinnett, Ann [Mrs. Button], 3,516
Gwinnett, Button (ca. 1732-77), **3,516**
Gwinnup, Alfred (1808-88), 10,977
Gwinnup, Emma [Miss] (1835?-68), 10,977
Gwinnup Family (NJ), 10,977
Gwinnup, Jabez (1799-1881), 10,977
Gwinnup, Laura [Miss] (1832-1916), 10,977
Gwynn, James, 2,887
Gynecologists, **3,146, 3,309,** 8,634, **11,400,** 14,698
Gynecology, 3,968, 6,219, 6,220, 6,222, **6,232,** 8,996, 12,917
    practice, 3,146, 3,381
    research, 7,274
    study and teaching, 6,225
"Gypsy Earrings" (ms), 6,022
Gypsy, The (periodical), 13,844
H. H. (pseudonym). *See* Jackson, Helen Maria (Fiske) [Mrs. Edward Bissell] Hunt [Mrs. William Sharpless] (1830-85)
Haakon VII, King, 8,777
Haarbauer, Dagmar Frisselle [Mrs.]. Dagmar Desmond (1895-), **970**
Haardt, Sarah Powell. *See* Mencken, Sarah Powell (Haardt) [Mrs. Henry L.]
Haas, Dorothy, 11,375
Haas, Elise (Stern) [Mrs. Walter A.], **523,** 945
Haas, Mary Rosamund, 920
Haas, Rose Greenbaum (1887-). *See* Alschuler, Rose Greenbaum (Haas) [Mrs. Alfred S.] (1887-)
Haas, Sarah Elizabeth. *See* Canfield, Sarah Elizabeth (Haas) [Mrs. Andrew Nahum]
Haas, Walter A., 945
Haase, Ynez, **524**
Habersham, John, 3,509
Habersham, Josephine (Clay) [Mrs. William Neyle], 3,518, **13,021**
Habersham, Leila Elliott, **3,517,** 3,598
Habersham, William Neyle, **3,518**
Habit Training School, The (MA), 6,808
Hacker, Beulah M., 14,856
Hacker, William E., 12,445
Hackett, Albert, **17,799**
Hackett, Alice Payne, 7,583
Hackett, Belle R., 5,345
Hackett Family (KY), **5,345**
Hackett, Joseph, 5,345
Hackett, Mabel, 5,345
Hackley, Emma Azalia (Smith) (1867-1922), 3,294
Hackworthe, Johnnie Mae. [Mrs. Edwin H.] Schaufler (1904-), **16,359, 16,386**
Hadassah (Minneapolis Chapter, MN), **9,109**
Hadassah (PA), **15,245**
Hadassah (Fond du Lac Chapter, WI), **17,646**
Hadassah (Rachel S. Jastrow Chapter, Madison, WI), **17,647**
Hadassah Israel Education Services, 12,117
Hadassah Medical Center (Jerusalem, Palestine), 933
Hadassah Medical Organization, 17,647
Hadassah Medical Relief Association, 12,117
Hadassah, Women's Zionist Organization of America, Inc., **933,** 1,000, 4,149, 5,720, 5,829, **6,920, 9,110,** 11,349, 12,117, 12,118, 13,446, 13,604, 14,908
Haddad, Carol [Mrs.], **5,381**
Haddad, Marie, 9,986
Haddad, Mary Faith (McAdoo) (1920-), 1,530
Hadden, Anne, **1,585**

Hadden, Prudence (Osborn). *See* Vanderbeck, Prudence (Osborn) Hadden
Haddon, Elizabeth. *See* Estaugh, Elizabeth (Haddon) [Mrs. John] (1680-1762)
Haddon Family (NJ), **14,843**
Haddonfield, NJ, founding of, 14,843
Hader, Berta Hoerner [Mrs. Elmer Stanley], 14,381
Hader, Elmer Stanley (1889-), **14,381**
Hadfield, Maria Cecilia Louisa (1759-1838). *See* Cosway, Maria Cecilia Louisa [Mrs. Richard] (1759-1838)
Hadley, Agnes [Mrs. Herbert S.] (1876-1946). *See* Haskell, Agnes [Mrs. Herbert S.] Hadley [Mrs. Henry C.] (1876-1946)
Hadley, E. Amelia (1825-86), **14,483, 14,569**
Hadley, Edith, 17,708
Hadley, Eleanor, 17,074
Hadley, Elizabeth. *See* Wyman, Elizabeth (Hadley) [Mrs. Edward]
Hadley Family (MO), **9,867**
Hadley, Herbert S., 9,983
Hadley, Irene, 13,696
Hadley, Martha, 137
Hadley, Melvina F. *See* Hayes, Melvina F. (Hadley)
Hadley, Moses, 9,867
Hadley, Mrs. E. A., 4,904
Hadley, Rebecca (1820-?). *See* Mills, Rebecca (Hadley) [Mrs. William Clarkson] (1820-?)
Hadley, Rollin van N., 6,185
Hadley Seminary (MA), 7,653
Hadley, Susan [Mrs. Moses], 9,867
Haefele, Ida M., 10,591
Hafen, Ann (Woodbury) [Mrs. Leroy R.] (1893-1970), **16,516**
Hafen, Leroy R., 16,516
Hafen, Orilla W., 16,967
Haffer, Virna. Mrs. Virna M. Randall (1900-74), **17,407**
Haffler, Dew (Flanery) [Mrs. Whayne W.], 5,313
Hagan, Cornelia Juliaette (Benjamin), 2,414
Hagans, Lovella, 4,197
Hagar, Ella (Barrows) [Mrs. Gerald Hanna] (1898-), **525**
Hagar, Gerald Hanna, 525
Hagedorn, Hermann, 2,463
Hagemeyer, Dora (1891-?), 831
Hagen, Betty, 17,288
Hagen, Beulah W., **11,870**
Hagen, Ethel H., 2,849
Hagen, Mrs. Tosten (1877-?), 8,709
Hagen, Petra (1876-1959), **8,740**
Hager, Alice Roberts [Mrs. John Mansfield] (1894-1969), **12,899**
Hager, Lucie Caroline Gilson [Mrs.] (1853-1911), **6,240**
Hagerman, B. F., **9,980**
Hagerman, Linnetta "Linnie" (1852-?), 9,980
Hagerty, James C. (1909-), **5,140**
Haggard, Agnes Barber, 12,005
Haggard, H. Rider, 11,979, **12,005**
Haggin, Eila Butterworth (1894-1939). *See* McKee, Eila Butterworth Haggin [Countess Festeties] de Tolna [Mrs. Robert T.] (1874-1939)
Haggin Family, 1,612
Hagins, Fanny, **4,912**
Hagle, Jane S., 8,231
Hagler, Margaret [Miss], 1,750
Hagner, Elizabeth [Mrs. Henry, Jr.] (1779-1844), 11,786
Hagner Family (NY), **11,786**
Hagner, Henry, Jr., 11,786
Hagner, Phebe, 11,786
Hague, James Duncan (1836-1908), **1,434**
Hague, Mary [Mrs. James Duncan], 1,434
Hague, The, 12,273
Hahn, Elmira H., **10,978**
Hahn, Emilia [Mrs. Ferdinand], **9,111**
Hahn, Emily. [Mrs. Charles R.] Boxer (1905-), **4,476**
Hahn, Ferdinand, 9,111
Hahn, Helena Petrovna (1831-91). *See* Blavatsky, Helena Petrovna (Hahn) [Mrs. Nikifor Vasilievich] (1831-91)
Hahn, Margareta Holl [Mrs. Peter], 9,285
Hahn, Nancy Coonsman, 9,919

Hahnemann Hospital (Chicago, IL), Attending League, 4,015
Hahneman Hospital (Chicago, IL), School of Nursing, 4,009, 4,016
Hahnemann Medical College (Chicago, IL), 17,498
Hahnemann Medical College (PA), alumni, 9,176
Hai-lun, Hseuh (pseudonym). See Snow, Helen Foster (1907-)
Haig, Emily H. [Mrs. Neil] (1890-?), **17,267**
Haigh, Constance, 7,107
Haigh, Florence M. (1907-), 7,109
Haight, Issac C., 16,448
Haight, Iva. See Ruth, Iva (Haight)
Haight, Sarah. See Tompkins, Sarah Haight [Mrs. Edward]
Haight, Sherman, **16,416**
Haile, Mrs. Samuel W., 771
Hails, Frances Mathews, **11**
Haimbach, Ruth, 15,138
Hainan Mission (China), 14,425
Hainan Newsletter, 14,425
Haines, Blanche Moore, 7,920
Haines, E. L. [Miss], 3,969
Haines, Elizabeth Shinn [Mrs. Henry] (1823-83), 15,271, **15,280,** 15,290
Haines, Henry, 15,271
Haines, Joanna Harris, 4,812
Haines School (Chicago, IL), 3,856
Haines Women's Club (AK), **147**
Hains, Frank, 9,768
Hair, care and hygiene, 9,428
Hair preparations, 11,799
Haire, Anna M. (1822-75), **7,805**
Haiti, fauna, 2,714
Hake, Esley D. See Casson, Esley D. (Hake)
Haken, Ines. See Schubert, Ines (Haken)
Halbert, Emma, 8,278
Halbert Family (MI), **8,278**
Halbert, Hattie, 8,278
Halbert, Maria, 8,278
Haldane, Mary (1874 or 1875-1967). See Coleman, Mary (Haldane) [Mrs. George] (1874 or 1875-1967)
Haldeman, Anna (Hostetter) [Mrs. William] (1828-1919). See Addams, Anna (Hostetter) [Mrs. William] Haldeman [Mrs. John Huy] (1828-1919)
Haldeman, Anna Marcet (1887-1941). See (Haldeman)-Julius, Anna Marcet [Mrs. Emanuel] (1887-1941)
Haldeman, Eliza E. [Mrs.] (?-1884), **14,801**
Haldeman Family, 4,095
Haldeman, George Bowman (1861-1909), 4,095, 4,154
Haldeman, Henry Winfield (1838-1905), 4,095, 4,477
Haldeman-Julius, Alice, 5,209
(Haldeman)-Julius, Anna Marcet [Mrs. Emanuel] (1887-1941), 4,095, 4,477, 5,209
Haldeman-Julius, Emanuel (1889-1951), 5,209
Haldeman-Julius Family, **4,095**
Haldeman-Julius Monthly, The (periodical), 4,095, 5,209
Haldeman-Julius Publishing Company (Girard, KS), 4,095
Haldeman, S. S., 14,878
Haldeman, Sarah Alice (Addams) [Mrs. Henry Winfield] (1853-1915), 4,095, 4,154, **4,477**
Haldeman, William (1823-66), 4,095
Hale, Alice. See Hill, Alice (Hale) [Mrs. Nathaniel Peter]
Hale, Alice Little (1811-?). See March, Alice Little (Hale) [Mrs. John C.] (1811-?)
Hale, Allean Lemmon, 9,824, **9,981**
Hale, Ann E., **7,378**
Hale, David, 1,435
Hale, Edward Everett (1822-1909), 2,371, 7,227
Hale, Edward Jones, **13,422,** 13,581
Hale, Ellen, 3,519
Hale, Ellen Day (1854-1940), 1,585, 7,200, 7,227
Hale, Emily, 7,158
Hale, Emma (1804-79). See Bidamon, Emma (Hale) [Mrs. Joseph, Jr.] Smith [Mrs. Lewis C.] (1804-79)
Hale, Eugene B., 217

Hale Family, **2,371,** 7,227
Hale Family (AZ, OH), 217
Hale Family (GA), **3,519**
Hale Family (NH), **10,862**
Hale Family (PA), **15,328**
Hale, Flora Annett Hammond [Mrs. William Dinsmore] (1844-1936), 9,112
Hale, Florence M. [Miss] (1880-?), **5,883**
Hale, George, 10,111
Hale, Geraldine, 5,644
Hale, Horace Morrison, 1,778
Hale, Irving (1861-1930), **1,778**
Hale, John P., 2,406
Hale, John Parker (1806-73), 10,800, 10,862
Hale, Jonathan Harriman, 16,687
Hale, Joshua, 3,519
Hale, Josiah, 3,519
Hale, Laura. See Scott, Laura (Hale)
Hale, Lela [Mrs. Eugene B.], 217
Hale, Lucie, 9,112
Hale, Lucretia Peabody (1820-1900), 3,927, 7,227
Hale, Lucy Lambert (1842-1915). See Chandler, Lucy Lambert (Hale) [Mrs. William E.] (1842-1915)
Hale, Lydia P. [Mrs. Samuel], 10,862
Hale, Martha Elizabeth [Mrs. Horace Morrison], 1,778
Hale, Martha Harriman, 16,687
Hale, Martie, **10,111**
Hale, Mary Taylor [Mrs. Richard], 8,158
Hale, Mary Thayer (1848-1942), 9,354
Hale, Mary Virginia (King) [Mrs. Irving], 1,778
Hale, Mrs. Lyman, 13,294
Hale, Nancy. [Mrs. Fredson] Bowers (1908-), 11,165
Hale, Nathan (1784-1863), 1,572, 2,390, 7,227, **16,517**
Hale, Olive (Boynton) [Mrs. Jonathan Harriman] (1805-46), **16,687**
Hale, Ruth, 11,867, 14,377
Hale, Ruth [Mrs. Nathan], **16,517**
Hale, Ruth (1788-1867). See Williams, Ruth (Hale) [Mrs. Thomas] (1788-1867)
Hale, Ruth Amorette Hatch, 16,492
Hale, Ruth P., **17,860**
Hale, Sadie, **10,111**
Hale, Samuel, 10,862
Hale, Sarah (1817-51), 7,227
Hale, Sarah Josepha (Buell) [Mrs. David] (1788-1879), **1,435, 2,372,** 2,448, 3,764, 3,797, 3,926, 4,695, 5,827, **6,617,** 10,027, 10,853, 12,833, 13,550
Hale, Sarah Preston (Everett) [Mrs. Nathan] (1796-1866), 7,227
Hale, Sarah T. [Mrs.], 1,185
Hale, Susan (1833-1910), 7,227
Hale, Thomas, 3,519
Hale, Virginia, 3,019
Hale, William Dinsmore (1836-1915), Family (MN), **9,112**
Hales, Belle W. [Mrs. Wayne B.], **16,518**
Hales, Mary Isabella (1818-1905). See Horne, Mary Isabella (Hales) [Mrs. Joseph] (1818-1905)
Haley, Adelaide, 5,699
Haley Family (ME), **5,699**
Haley, Lizzie H., 5,699
Haley, Margaret Angela (1861-1939), 3,817, 3,818, 3,890
Haley, Nell, 364
Haley, Nuldah [Miss], 5,699
Half a Century (book), 9,241
Half Century of Freedom of the Negro in Ohio, A (book), 13,945
Halfhill Club (Ontario, CA), 1,092
Halfhill, Mrs. J. M., 1,092
Halfway houses, 6,752, **6,866,** 14,043, 17,821
Hall, Agnes Skidmore [Miss] (1883-1969), 1,786
Hall, Alma, **7,379**
Hall and Mills murder trial (NJ), 5,505, **11,190**
Hall, Ann C., 5,752
Hall, Anna. See Roosevelt, Anna (Hall)
Hall, Anna Marie (Fielding) (1800-81), 6,884
Hall, Anne G. (1864-1943). See Carey, Anne G. (Hall) [Mrs. Francis K.] (1864-1943)
Hall, Anne (Troy) (?-1873), **13,022**
Hall, Bolton (1854-1932), **12,218**

Hall, Carlotta (Case) [Mrs. Harvey Monroe] (1880-?), 526
Hall, Carrie A. (1866-), 1,786
Hall, Carrie May, **6,618**
Hall, Constance H. [Miss] (1886-1973), **6,619**
Hall, Daliah (Brannigan) [Mrs. R.], 2,223
Hall, David Prescott, 6,663
Hall, Dolly Tuttle Davis (1792-1879), 17,044
Hall, Dorothy, 15,990
Hall, Edward Wheeler, 11,034, 11,190
Hall, Eliza, 17,044
Hall, Eliza. See Russell, Eliza (Hall)
Hall, Eliza Calvert (pseudonym). See Obenchain, Lida (Calvert) [Mrs. William Alexander] (1856-1935)
Hall, Elizabeth C. (1898-), 11,297
Hall, Elizabeth VanCleve, 8,954, 9,417
Hall, Ellen May (1848-1935). See Crocker, Ellen May (Hall) [Mrs. Henry Robinson] (1848-1935)
Hall, Emma Amelia (1837-84), **7,806**
Hall Family, 6,663
Hall Family (CT), **1,971**
Hall Family (IN, IA, MI), **8,315**
Hall Family (NY), 11,522
Hall Family (NY), **11,487,** 11,499
Hall Family (Plattsburgh, NY), **12,770**
Hall Family (NC), 13,052
Hall Family (VT), **17,044**
Hall, Florence Gardiner, 11,249
Hall, Florence Marion (Howe) [Mrs. David Prescott] (1845-1922), 6,663
Hall, Frances Delord (Webb) [Mrs. Francis Bloodgood] (1834-1913), 12,770, **12,771**
Hall, Frances (Stevens) [Mrs. Edward Wheeler], 11,190
Hall, Francis Bloodgood (1827-1903), 12,770, 12,771
Hall, Gertrude. [Mrs. William Crary] Brownell, **3,019,** 3,020
Hall, Gordon Langley. See Simmons, Dawn Langley [Mrs. Jean-Paul]
Hall, Grace. [Mrs. Edwin Howland] Blashfield, 3,019, **3,020**
Hall, Grace E. (Adams) (?-1939), **14,382**
Hall, Gwendolyn (Midlo) (1929-), **7,807**
Hall, Harvey Monroe (1874-1932), **526**
Hall, Helen. [Mrs. Paul Underwood] Kellogg (1892-), **8,651,** 8,655, 8,658, 8,659, 8,661, 8,662, 8,668, 8,678, 8,681, 12,008
Hall, Henry Gerary, 5,555
Hall, James, 4,904
Hall, James (1793-1868), 4,444
Hall, James (1811-98), **11,262**
Hall, Josephine (1841-1917). See Bishop, Josephine (Hall) (1841-1917)
Hall, Juanita, 3,290
Hall, Julia A., 10,382
Hall, Ladson, 14,814
Hall, Laura, 1,971
Hall, Leonard W. (1900-), **5,141**
Hall, Louisa Jane (Park) (1802-92), 7,660
Hall, Lucretia Allen, 6,442
Hall, Lucretia Warner [Mrs. Benjamin] (1785-1847), **12,177**
Hall, Lucy M., 2,196
Hall, Lynn (1937-), **4,801, 4,991**
Hall, Maggie, **527**
Hall, Margaret, 12,770
Hall, Margaret (1899-1964), **14,741**
Hall, Margaret Gettys [Mrs.], **6,620**
Hall, Margaret (Hunter) [Mrs. Basil] (1799-1876), **2,373**
Hall, Marion Snelling (1882-), Family (MN), **9,113**
Hall, Martha (1916-?). See Nicolls, Martha (Hall) (1916-?)
Hall, Martha E. Clark [Mrs. Peter], 9,303
Hall, Mary, **10,813**
Hall, Mary [Mrs. Valentine], 11,487
Hall, Mary (1841-?). See Jatta, Mary (Hall) (1841-?)
Hall, Mary A., 6,226
Hall, Mrs., 9,024
Hall, Mrs. Edward Collingwood, 9,304
Hall of Fame for Great Americans, 6,493
Hall of Mirrors (book), 6,050
Hall, Olivia Bigelow, **2,374, 7,808**

Hall, Rebecca (ca. 1775-?). *See* Guest, Rebecca (Hall) [Mrs. John] (ca. 1775-?)
Hall, Rosetta Sherwood, 11,754
Hall, Rubylea, 2,932
Hall, Ruth Julia, 14,907
Hall, Sarah [Miss] (1761-1830), **2,375**
Hall, Sarah Browne [Mrs. Edward] (1758-93), 12,695
Hall, Selina Cole [Mrs.], **3,520**
Hall, Sharlot Mabridth [Miss] (1870-1943), **172, 195**
Hall, Sherwood, 11,754
Hall, Sophie C. [Mrs. George W.], **12,494**
Hall, Susan M. (?-1896). *See* Munroe, Susan M. (Hall) [Mrs. Charles W.] (?-1896)
Hall, Susanna (1715?-95). *See* Morris, Susanna (Hall) [Mrs. Joseph] Harvey [Mrs. John] Rush [Mrs. Richard] (1715?-95)
Hall, Theodosia Burr (1854-1906). *See* Shepherd, Theodosia Burr (Hall) (1854-1906)
Hall, Valentine, 11,487
Hall, Winnie Davis, 3,076
Hallanan, Elizabeth V., 17,442
Halleck, Fitz-Greene, 12,399
Haller, Constance (Reed) [Mrs. Theodore N.], **17,169**
Haller, Theodore N., 17,169
Hallet, Amelia (1830-1906). *See* Hawes, Amelia (Hallet) [Mrs. John] (1830-1906)
Hallet, Anna Eldridge [Mrs. Bangs] (1809-87), 7,693
Hallet, Anner (1830-?). *See* Tripp, Anner (Hallet) [Mrs. Job] (1830-?)
Hallet, Bangs (1807-97), **7,693**
Halley, Elizabeth, 15,345
Halley's comet (1910), 13,398
Halliday, E., 15,436
Halliday, Patricia (1930-), 10,151
Hallie, Harriet Sophia. *See* Hyde, Harriet Sophia (Hallie)
Hallie Q., Brown Community House (St. Paul, MN), **9,114,** 9,467
Hallifax, Lillie S., **8,159**
Hallinan, Vivian, 4,970
Hallman, Bertha B., 14,698
Hallo, Anselm, 12,064
Hallock, Ahlma. *See* Mcdonald, Ahlma (Hallock) [Mrs. Stewart]
Hallock-Greenewalt, Mary Elizabeth (1871-1950). *See* Greenewalt, Mary Elizabeth (Hallock) [Mrs. Frank Lindsay] (1871-1950)
Hallock, Homer H. (1856-1906), **14,570**
Hallock, Joseph H., Family (OR), **14,571**
Hallock, Mary Anna (1847-1938). *See* Foote, Mary Anna (Hallock) [Mrs. Arthur De Wint] (1847-1938)
Hallock, Nannie Nellie Bernardi [Mrs. Homer H.] (1861-?), 14,570
Hallowell, Harriet (?-1943), 15,070
Hallowell, Sarah [Miss], 2,739
Hallowell, Sarah T. (?-1924), 15,070
Halls of fame, **32,** 6,141, 6,493
Halpert, Edith Gregor, 2,662, 2,844
Halprin, Ann, 4,384
Halroyd, Jack, 14,994
Halsell, Grace Eleanor (1923-), **6,031**
Halseth, Martina Marjorie (1847-1912). *See* Bitner, Martina Marjorie (Halseth) [Mrs. Breneman Barr] (1847-1912)
Halsey, Anna, 15,221
Halsey, Ezra, **10,979**
Halsey, Julia Malvina, 12,260
Halsey, Mary (Battey), 3,309
Halstead, Anna (Roosevelt) (1906-75), 411, **11,488, 11,871**
Halstead Family, 14,771
Halsted, Brokaw and Company (NY), 11,099
Halsted, Leonora B., 2,196
Halsted, N. Norris (1816-84), **11,099**
Halsted, Nancy Marsh [Mrs. N. Norris], **11,099**
Halsted, R. H., 8,324
Halverson, Leila (1883-), **9,115,** 9,467
Halverson, Norah. *See* Howe, Norah (Halverson)
Halvorson, Hazel Pearce, 13,682
Halvorson, Wendell, 5,110
Ham, Cornelia Freeman [Mrs. James Madison], 4,913
Ham, James Madison, 4,913
Ham, Maria G., **10,814**

Hamady, Mary (Laird) [Mrs. Walter], 12,879
Hamady, Walter, 12,879
Hamarsbøn Family, 8,779
Hamarsbøn Family (ND), 13,684
Hamberlin, L. R., 13,170
Hamblen, Maria Florilla (Flint), **13,023**
Hamblet, Mary, 14,542
Hamblett, Theora, 9,694
Hamblin, Amarilla (1884-?). *See* Lee, Amarilla (Hamblin) (1884-?)
Hamblin, Harriet Byrle (1820-?). *See* Phillips, Harriet Byrle (Hamblin) [Mrs. Hugh J.] (1820-?)
Hamblin, Herbert, 10,638
Hamblin, Jacob, 16,788, 16,901
Hamburg, Mary, 15,013
Hamer Family (MA), **6,621**
Hamer, Fannie Lou, 9,694
Hamer, Lise (Mitchell) [Mrs. William D.] (1838-1932), **5,518**
Hamer, Thomas, 1,780
Hamer, William D., 5,518
Hamill, Samuel, 1,191
Hamilton, Agnes, 6,622
Hamilton, Alexander (1757-1804), 1,395, **12,495,** 12,554
Hamilton, Alice (1869-1970), 2,336, 2,424, 2,439, 3,828, 3,910, 3,976, 3,977, 4,047, 4,052, 4,089, 4,101, 4,111, 4,143, 4,146, 4,166, 5,870, **6,622,** 7,300, 7,315, 7,923, 8,678, 11,760, 12,534
Hamilton, Allen, 6,622
Hamilton, Amy Vincent [Mrs.], 10,905
Hamilton, Andrew, 15,647
Hamilton, Andrew Holman, 6,622
Hamilton, Betsy (pseudonym). *See* Moore, Idora (McClellan) Plowman (1843-1929)
Hamilton, Cecilia Viets Dakin (1837-1909), 5,350
Hamilton, Clayton Meeker (1881-1946), **12,496**
Hamilton College for Women (Lexington, KY), students, 5,310
Hamilton County Court of Domestic Relations, Ohio Network, **13,874**
Hamilton, Dorothy (1914-). *See* Weisenberger, Dorothy (Hamilton) (1914-)
Hamilton, Edith (1867-1963), 2,242, 6,622, **11,164,** 11,810, 14,738, 17,803
Hamilton, Elisabeth (1903-). *See* Friermood, Elisabeth (Hamilton) (1903-)
Hamilton, Elizabeth "Lizzie" Gwinn (1833-56), **14,162**
Hamilton, Elizabeth (Schuyler) [Mrs. Alexander] (1757-1854), 11,657, 12,192, 12,695
Hamilton, Eloise, **14,383**
Hamilton, Emerine [Mrs. Allen], 6,622
Hamilton Family (IN), 6,622
Hamilton, Florence, **2,376**
Hamilton, Gail (pseudonym). *See* Dodge, Mary Abigail (1833-96)
Hamilton, Gertrude (Pond) [Mrs. Montgomery], 6,622
Hamilton, Gladys Coates [Mrs. Clayton Meeker], 12,496
Hamilton, Gordon [Miss], 8,683
Hamilton, Grace (1877-1962). *See* Morrey, Grace (Hamilton) [Mrs. Charles] (1877-1962)
Hamilton, Grace (Towns) (1907-), **3,293**
Hamilton, Harriet Louise Hubbard, 3,829
Hamilton House (NY). *See* Hamilton-Madison House (NY)
Hamilton, Isabella, **8,279**
Hamilton, Isabelle Caroline [Mrs.], **3,521**
Hamilton, J. G. de Roulhac, 15,585
Hamilton, J. Talmai (1815-?), **17,648**
Hamilton, J. W., 9,782
Hamilton, Jessie, 6,622
Hamilton, John, 2,377
Hamilton, Kay, 13,406
Hamilton Library Association (PA), 14,747
Hamilton-Madison House (NY), **8,652**
Hamilton, Margaret, 6,622
Hamilton, Marian, 3,335
Hamilton, Mary, 12,207
Hamilton, Mary Elizabeth. *See* Carter, Mary Elizabeth (Hamilton) [Mrs. William Alexander]
Hamilton, Montgomery, 6,622
Hamilton, Mrs. Henry, **9,868**

Hamilton, Nancy. *See* Ogden, Nancy (Hamilton)
Hamilton, Norah, 4,047, 6,622
Hamilton, O. C., 13,424
Hamilton, Olivia E., **6,623**
Hamilton, Phoebe (Taber) [Mrs. Andrew Holman], 6,622
Hamilton, Rosanna (Boyd) [Mrs. Hugh] (1789-1872), 2,377
Hamilton, Sarah, 7,140
Hamilton, Weston A., **5,266**
Hamilton, William (1824-96), **2,377**
Hamlin, Anna (?-1925), 2,378
Hamlin, Charles Sumner (1861-1938), **2,378**
Hamlin, Ellen Vesta (Emery) [Mrs. Hannibal] (1832-1920), 5,627
Hamlin Family (ME), **5,627**
Hamlin, Hannibal (1809-91), 5,627
Hamlin, Herbert S., 687
Hamlin, Hilda, 7,151
Hamlin, Huybertie (Pruyn) [Mrs. Charles Sumner] (1874-1964), 2,378, 11,249
Hamlin, Leonora (Austin) [Mrs. Conde], 8,925, 8,971
Hamlin, Margaret Pomeroy, **6,624**
Hamlin, Mrs. L. A., 3,813
Hamlin, Myra Sampson, 5,627
Hamlin, Sarah Purinton Thompson (?-1905), 5,627
Hamlin, Wood Jones, **13,425**
Hamline University (St. Paul, MN), 8,709
 alumnae, 9,385
 faculty, 8,441, 8,638, 9,008, 9,359
Hamm, Carolyn L. (1943-), **7,809**
Hammer, Angela (Hutchinson) (1870-1955?), **218**
Hammer, Bette E. Barber [Mrs. Harry] (?-1968), **9,587**
Hammer, Cecelia. *See* Beckius, Cecelia (Hammer) [Mrs. Michael]
Hammer Galleries (NY), 9,587
Hammer, Harry, 9,587
Hammer, Ina. *See* Hards, Ina (Hammer) [Mrs. Ira A.]
Hammett, Dashiell, 16,156
Hammit, William, 3,764
Hammond, Annie E. *See* Bleckley, Annie E. (Hammond) [Mrs. Sylvester]
Hammond, Aramintha, **8,336**
Hammond, Delia Marcella (1836-1923). *See* Locke, Delia Marcella (Hammond) (1836-1923)
Hammond, Emily (Cumming) [Mrs. Harry], 15,600
Hammond, Eunice (1884-1944). *See* Tietjens, Eunice (Hammond) [Mrs. Paul]. Eunice (Hammond) [Mrs. Paul] Tietjens [Mrs. Cloyd] Head (1884-1944)
Hammond Family (CA), **1,632**
Hammond Family (PA), 9,112
Hammond Family (SC), **15,600**
Hammond, George P., 10,677
Hammond, Harry, 15,600
Hammond, Henry, 15,600
Hammond, Isabelle "Belle" (Boyd) [Mrs. John Swainston] (1844-1900). *See* Harding, Isabelle "Belle" (Boyd) [Mrs. Samuel Wylde, Jr.] Harding [Mrs. John Swainston] Hammond [Mrs. Nathaniel Rue, Jr.] (1844-1900)
Hammond, Julia, 15,600
Hammond, Katharine. *See* Billings, Katharine (Hammond) [Mrs. John Sedgwick]
Hammond, Maria Johns (1862-1949), **5,773**
Hammond, Mary Mildred (1836-?). *See* Sullivan, Mary Mildred (Hammond) (1836-?)
Hammond, Rosetta (1842-1915). *See* Bushnell, Rosetta (Hammond) (1842-1915)
Hammonds, Mamie [Mrs. O. O.], 14,257
Hamp, Julia (1895-1977), **1,684**
Hamp, Sidford, 1,684
Hampden, Walter, 12,559
Hampshire College (CT), 6,914
Hampshire Federalist, The, 9,636
Hampshire Washingtonian Temperance Society (MA), 7,141
Hampson, Clara (1860-1927). *See* Ueland, Clara (Hampson) [Mrs. Andreas] (1860-1927)
Hampton, Caroline, 5,735
Hampton, Charles George (?-1917), **8,337**
Hampton, Christopher, 15,457

Hampton College (Louisville, KY), 5,345
Hampton, Emma (Stark) [Mrs. Charles George] (1843-1925), **8,028**, 8,337
Hampton Family, 8,337
Hampton, Flo. *See* Scott, Flo (Hampton) [Mrs. Charles C.].
Hampton, Frank, 15,601
Hampton High School (IA), 4,828
Hampton Institute (VA), 6,095, 7,590
    faculty, 88
Hampton Institute (VA), School of Nursing, 6,133
"Hampton Institute, Virginia," 3,748
Hampton, Isabel Adams (1860-1910). *See* Robb, Isabel Adams (Hampton) [Mrs. Hunter] (1860-1910)
Hampton, Mary, 9,274
Hampton, Mary Elizabeth [Mrs. Christopher], 15,457
Hampton-Preston home (SC), 15,719
Hampton Roads Port of Embarkation (VA), 14,774
Hampton, Sarah "Sally" Strong (Baxter) [Mrs. Frank] (1833-62), **15,601**
Hampton, Wade, 15,596, 15,601, 15,715, 15,758, 15,769
Hampton, Wade, III, 15,585
Hamwee, Lillian, **17,649**
Hanaford, Phebe Ann (Coffin) [Mrs. Joseph Hibbard] (1829-1921), 1,950, 4,244
Hanalis, Blanche, **17,972**
Hanau, Stella, 6,223, 7,284, 7,320
Hanchett, Mary Hannah (1830-1906). *See* Hunt, Mary Hannah (Hanchett) [Mrs. Leander B.] (1830-1906)
Hancock, Caroline (1785-1847). *See* Preston, Caroline (Hancock) [Mrs. William] (1785-1847)
Hancock, Cornelia (1840-1926), **8,003**, 11,605, 15,281
Hancock Eagle (IL), 4,302
Hancock, Emma Harris, 1,533
Hancock Family, 5,359
Hancock Family, **15,281**
Hancock, John, 3,516
Hancock, Joy Bright, 2,710, **3,022**
Hancock Patriot (newspaper), 4,302
Hancock, Victoria (1880-1967). *See* Jackson, Victoria (Hancock) [Mrs. Jonathan] (1880-1967)
Hancock, Winfield Scott, 17,992
Hand and Flower Press, 4,230
Hand, Cornelia [Mrs. Noah], 15,016
Hand Family (NJ), **15,016**
Hand, Frances (1907-). *See* Ferguson, Frances (Hand) [Mrs. Robert M.] (1907-)
Hand, Mary Muir, 1,635
Hand, Mrs. Thomas Jennings, 12,025
Hand, Noah, 15,016
Handbell ringing, **9,488**
Handbook (University of Wyoming), 17,963
Handbook of Oklahoma Writers, 14,217
Handbook of Texas, The (book), 16,067
Handel, Jensine, **9,116**
Handicapped, 5,401
    clothing, 8,521
    education, 6,808, 7,684, 8,655
    employment, 6,810, 9,381
    rehabilitation, 3,905
    sexual behavior, 8,521
Handicapped children, 9,522, 9,530, **11,830**, 17,463
    education, 1,348, 2,919, 3,787, 4,150, 14,641
    rehabilitation, 5,573
    research, 11,830
Handicrafts of the Modern Indians of Maine, The (book), 7,485
Handy and Harman (silversmiths), 2,831
Handy, Deidre C., 16,164
Handy, Hannah Wall, 8,151
Handy, William Christopher (1873-1958), 6,112
Handy, William J., 16,164
Haner, Sally. *See* Johnson, Sally (Haner) [Mrs. Sidney]
Hanes, T. J., 9,684
Haney, James P., 12,244
Hanford, Mrs. W. H., 2,252
Hanford, Nancy. *See* Cartter, Nancy (Hanford) [Mrs. David Kellogg]
Hanford, Susan (Fowle) [Mrs. Charles] (1802-72), 9,041

Hangchow Christian College (China), administrators, 8,871
Hanger, Francis Marion (Harrow) (1856-1945), **296**
Hanging, 10,721
Hanging Tree, The (book), 5,004
Hankins, Helen, 1,722
Hankinson Family (GA), **3,023**
Hankinson, Margaret, 11,074
Hankinson, Marie Essie, 3,023
Hankinson, Mary C. Speights [Mrs. Stephen], 3,023
Hankinson, Stephen, 3,023
Hanks, Clarrisa Phelps (1822-post 1890), **13,270**
Hanks, Elizabeth Edwards, 16,417
Hanks, Stephen, 8,953
Hanlon, Eleanor (1809-57). *See* Browning, Eleanor (Hanlon) [Mrs. Robert Lewright] (1809-57)
Hanna, Esther Bell [Mrs. Joseph A.], **528**, 1,505, **14,572**, 14,628
Hanna, Esther Belle (McMillan) (1824-78), 15,174
Hanna Family, **2,379**
Hanna, Gertrude, 5,123
Hanna, L. B., 13,652
Hanna, Marcus "Mark" Alonzo (1837-1904), 2,379
Hanna, Mary Carr, 4,482
Hanna, Miss, 1,168
Hanna, Ruth (1880-1944). *See* Simms, Ruth (Hanna) [Mrs. Joseph Medill] McCormick [Mrs. Albert Gallatin] (1880-1944)
Hannaford, Julia (Barnard), **8,338**
Hannaford, William H., 8,338
Hannah, Aloha Margaret. *See* Alvara, Aloha Margaret (Hannah)
Hannah (Bourn) Ingalls, 359
Hannah Family (MT), **10,312**
Hannah Fowler (book), 5,264
Hannah, More, Academy (Resitertown, MD), 5,827
Hannah Neil Home for Children (OH), **13,996**
Hannah Neil Mission and Home of the Friendless (OH), 13,996
Hannah, Robert Bruce (1901-), 10,312
Hannah, William James, 10,312
Hannifin, Dennis, 13,682
Hannon, Michael, 1,241
Hanotte, M., 12,391
Hans Brinker; or the Silver Skates (book), 11,157
Hanschurst, Sarah, **2,380**
Hanscom, Almira (Knight) [Mrs. Sylvester V.] Stoddard [Mrs. George] (1827-1912), 16,598, **16,688**, 16,736
Hanscom, Elizabeth Deering (1865-1960), 7,158
Hanscom, George, 16,688
Hanscom, Julia. *See* Grant, Julia (Hanscom) Sargent
Hansel, Agnes (Johnson) (ca. 1841-?), 8,986
Hansen, Anna Marie. *See* Jamison, Anna Marie (Hansen)
Hansen, Anne M., **8,741**
Hansen, Borghilde "Ole" (Hendricksen) [Mrs. Burnett], 130
Hansen, Doreen V. (1930-). *See* Wilber, Doreen V. (Hansen) (1930-)
Hansen Family (UT), 16,490
Hansen, Florence C., 8,071
Hansen, H. J., **8,741**
Hansen, Julia Butler (1907-), **17,268**
Hansen, Mae, **16,689**
Hansen, Mary Cockshott (1835-1925), 16,490
Hansen School, Town of Montana, School District No. 5, Buffalo County (WI), **17,522**
Hansen, Sylvia Irene, 17,893
Hanshaw, Cella, **2,902**
Hansl, Eva Elise (vom Baur) (1889-), 2,097, **7,228**
Hanson, Agatha Mary Agnes (Tiegel) [Mrs. Olof] (1873-1959), **2,106**
Hanson, Constance Twedt (1919-), **8,875**
Hanson, Edna, 4,085, 4,096
Hanson, Ethel (Ellingson) [Mrs. Oliver] (1896-), **8,701**
Hanson, Florence L., 12,163
Hanson, Harriet Jane (1825-1911). *See* Robinson, Harriet Jane (Hanson) [Mrs. William Stevens] (1825-1911)
Hanson, Isabel (1901-75), **17,269**
Hanson, Laura S. Wolfe [Mrs.] (1888-), 8,518
Hanson, Olof, 2,106

Hanstein, Cornelia (Scandrett) [Mrs. Jack E.] (1912-), 9,437
Hantel, Clara. *See* Brucker, Clara (Hantel) [Mrs. Wilber M.]
Hanus, Mrs. Paul, 6,950
Hanus, Winifred. *See* Whiting, Winifred (Hanus)
Hapgood, Fanny [Mrs.], 2,170
Hapgood, Isabel Florence [Miss] (1850-1928), **12,497**
Hapgood School, Parent-Teacher Association (Athol, MA), **5,889**
"Happiness Insurance" (story), 12,644
Happiness Road (book), 5,273
"Happy Little Family," 5,304
Happy Venture Club (NE). *See* Quill, The (NE)
"Happy Warrior, The" (poem), 7,140
Hara, Ernestine (1896-). *See* Kettler, Ernestine (Hara) (1896-)
Haralson, Fannie (1837-1931). *See* Gordon, Fannie (Haralson) [Mrs. John Brown] (1837-1931)
Haralson, Mrs. J. A., 16,176
Harap, Henry, 11,805
Harben, Kate (1866-?). *See* Jones, Kate (Harben) [Mrs. Archibald A.] (1866-?)
Harbert, Elizabeth (Boynton) (1845-1925), **1,436**, 1,483, **6,526, 6,626**
Harbor Light (newspaper), 1,199
Harcourt, Brace, Jovanovich (publishers), 1,221, 9,769, 14,320, 14,458
Hard, Anne [Mrs. William], 5,120, 5,122
Hard-Boiled Virgin, The (book), 2,969
Hard Ground, Patricia, 10,313
Hard, Kate Jackson, 7,958
Hardaway, Anna Jane (Hunter) [Mrs. John Steger] (?-1941), **13,640**
Hardaway, John Steger (1852-1925), 13,640
Hardee, Elizabeth B., **2,381**
Hardee, Harriett B. [Miss], 3,535
Hardee, Harriett Brailsford, **3,522**, 3,535
Hardeman, Elle (Goode), **13,024**
Harden, Clarissa (1820-1901). *See* Wilhelm, Clarissa (Harden) Lewis Terry (1820-1901)
Harden, Edward (1784-1849), 3,024
Harden Family (GA), **3,024**, 3,025
Harden, Jane LeConte [Mrs.], 14,892
Harden, Mary Elisa Greenhill (1811-87), 3,024
Harden, Nell, **3,025**
Harden, William, **3,025**
Hardenbergh, Ann "Nancy" Maria (1828-60), 10,980
Hardenbergh, Catherine L. (1794-1873), 10,980
Hardenbergh, Catherine Low (1852-1902), 10,980
Hardenbergh, Cornelius L. (1790-1860), 10,980
Hardenbergh Family (NJ), **10,980**
Hardenbergh, Jacob Rutsen (1824-92), 10,980
Hardenburgh, Isabella (ca. 1797-1883). *See* Truth, Sojourner (ca. 1797-1883)
Hardenstein, Hattie, **9,637**
Hardesty, Nevada. *See* Griswold, Nevada (Hardesty)
Hardie Family, **13,025**
Hardie, Jessie Stearns [Mrs. Ledyard Park], 11,392
Hardie, Lucita. *See* Wait, Lucita (Hardie)
Hardin, Charles Henry (1820-92), **9,982**
Hardin College (Mexico, MO), 9,982
Hardin, Ellen (1832-1915). *See* Walworth, Ellen (Hardin) [Mrs. Mansfield Tracy] (1832-1915)
Hardin, John, 4,358
Hardin, John J., 12,847
Hardin, Julia (Stevenson) (1879-1958), 4,375
Hardin, Lemuel, 12,847
Hardin, Martin D., 12,847
Hardin, Martin D., Jr., 11,658
Hardin, Mary B., **13,426**
Hardin, Mary Jenkins [Mrs. Charles Henry], 9,982
Hardin, Sarah E. [Mrs. John J.] (1811-74). *See* Walworth, Sarah E. [Mrs. John J.] Hardin [Mrs. Reuben Hyde] (1811-74)
Harding, Ann, 7,718
Harding, Carrie (Lamoreux) [Mrs. William Lloyd] (1879-1965), **5,106**
Harding, Elizabeth McGavock [Mrs. William Giles], 15,932
Harding Family, 8,374
Harding, Florence (Kling) [Mrs. Warren G.] (1860-1924), 2,596, 2,640, 6,925, 14,004

Harding, George A. (1843-1926), Family (OR), **14,573**
Harding, Harriet, 11,572
Harding, Helene. *See* Rigger, Helene (Harding)
Harding, Helene (Ferrer), 14,573
Harding, Isabelle "Belle" Boyd [Mrs. Samuel Wylde, Jr.] (1844-1900). *See* High, Isabelle "Belle" (Boyd) [Mrs. Samuel Wylde, Jr.] Harding [Mrs. John Swainston] Hammond [Mrs. Nathaniel Rue, Jr.] (1844-1900)
Harding, Jennie (Barlow) [Mrs. George A.], 14,573
Harding, Jennie Imogene (1878-1956). *See* Brodie, Jennie Imogene (Harding) (1878-1956)
Harding, Margaret (Snodgrass) (1885-1976), 8,566
Harding, Nieta Natalie, 14,573
Harding, Rebecca Blaine (1831-1910). *See* Davis, Rebecca Blaine (Harding) [Mrs. Lemuel Clarke] (1831-1910)
Harding, Selene. *See* Jackson, Selene (Harding)
Harding, Warren Gamaliel, 1,424, 6,925, 10,419, 10,660, 13,350, 13,999, 14,004, 14,234, 17,633
Harding, William Giles (1808-86), **15,932**
Harding, William Lloyd (1877-1934), **5,106**
Hardison, Janice [Miss], **13,271**
Hards, Ina (Hammer) [Mrs. Ira A.], 12,006
Hards, Ira A. (1873-1938), **12,006**
Hardware, 1,732
Hardware stores, 9,537
Hardy, Angela Hopkins (1811-97), 3,902
Hardy, Charles Elias, 11,750
Hardy, Elisa B., **6,627**
Hardy, Elizabeth Stanton, 2,166
Hardy, Fannie Pearson (1865-1946). *See* Eckstorm, Fannie Pearson (Hardy) (1865-1946)
Hardy, Genie Steele [Mrs.], **9,638**
Hardy, Harriet (1906-), 6,698
Hardy, Ina [Mrs. I. V.] (ca. 1880-1965), **14,189**
Hardy, Irene, **1,548**, 1,585
Hardy, Jane L., 11,534, 11,750
Hardy, Julia Louisa (1812-82). *See* Lovejoy, Julia Louisa (Hardy) [Mrs. Charles H.] (1812-82)
Hardy, Julia Wrenn, **16,078**
Hardy, Katherine, 5,515
Hardy, Louisa, 11,534, 11,750
Hardy, Mary (1824-1911). *See* Williams, Mary (Hardy) [Mrs. Josiah] (1824-1911)
Hardy, Thomas, 5,711, 16,166
Hardy, Thora M. Plitt, **2,718**
Hare, Alice Iola, **529**
Hare, Constance Parsons, 12,280
Hare, Harriet (Clark), 15,379
Hare, Marie (Surber) (1887-), 10,403
Hare, Maud (Cuney) (1874-1936), **3,294**, 3,298, 5,870
Hare, Stella (Doty) Smith, 801
Hargis, Modeste, **2,903**, **2,904**, 2,946
Hargreaves, Grace Dexter (Bryan), 2,232
Hargreaves, Sheba May (1882-1960), **14,384**, **14,574**
Hargrove, Mrs. R. B., 11,440
Hariford, Jennie E., 3,834
Harju, Walter A. (ca. 1900-73), **9,498**
Harkness, Edward Stephen (1874-1940), **12,498**
Harkness, Georgia (1891-1973), **4,204**
Harkness, Marietta. *See* Pratt, Marietta (Harkness) [Mrs. Walter M.]
Harkness, Mary Emma (Stillman) [Mrs. Edward Stephen] (1874-1950), **12,498**
Harkness, Mrs. E. W., **5,591**
Harkrider, Lois (1923-). *See* Stair, Lois (Harkrider) [Mrs. Ralph Martin] (1923-)
Harlan, Ann Eliza (Peck) [Mrs. James] (1824-84), 4,732, **5,053**, 5,060
Harlan Family (IA), **5,060**
Harlan, James (?-1899), 4,732, 4,747, **5,053**, 5,060
Harlan, Mary Eunice (?-1937). *See* Lincoln, Mary Eunice (Harlan) [Mrs. Robert Todd] (?-1937)
Harland, Hester Ann (Lambert) (1857-1940) 530, **1,304**
Harlem Renaissance, 9,252
Harley, Amanda. *See* Stevens, Amanda (Harley)
Harley, Hannah (Case), 5,710
Harley, Katherine V., 2,452
Harling, Ada May, **3,196**
Harlow, Caroline G., 3,290
Harlow, Dana [Miss], 15,869

Harlow, Mrs. S., 2,448
Harlow's Weekly (periodical), 14,200
Harman, Hattie L., **3,026**
Harman Literary Society (PA), **14,756**
Harmer, Harvey W. (1865-1961), **17,460**
Harmer, Marie [Miss], 10,548
Harmm, Mrs. G. C., 12,830
Harmon, Appleton Milo, 16,495
Harmon Association for the Advancement of Nursing (NY), **11,601**
Harmon, Ellen Gould (1827-1915). *See* White, Ellen Gould (Harmon) [Mrs. James Springer] (1827-1915)
Harmon Family (UT), 16,495
Harmon Foundation (NY), 11,601
Harmon, Juliet, 9,706
Harmon, Mamie, **3,462**
Harmon, Mary Hortense "Tennie" (Keith) [Mrs. Edward N.] (1868-1948), 589
Harmon, Marybell. *See* Anderson, Marybell (Harmon)
Harmon, Millard F., 9,003
Harmon, Nolan B., 9,706
Harmon, Selene Armstrong, **3,027**
Harmonia (NY, PA), **15,259**
Harmony Club (Rochester, IN), 4,661
Harmony College (SC), 15,635
Harmony, Sally, 1,937
Harmony Society (PA), **14,718**
Harned, Clemence Sophia (1813-1888). *See* Lozier, Clemence Sophia (Harned) (1813-1888)
Harned, Harriette C. (1837-1909). *See* Keatinge, Harriette C. (Harned) [Mrs. Henry A.] Veazie [Mrs. Edward C.] (1837-1909)
Harness making and trade, 8,958, 10,434
Harness racing, 6,495
Harney, Eliza Rowan (1815-?). *See* Boone, Eliza Rowan (Harney) [Mrs. William Pendleton] (1815-?)
Harold, Nan (Brooke) (ca. 1888-1958), **17,461**
Harold, Ober, Associates, Inc. (NY), **11,165**
Harolds Club (Reno, NV), 10,738
Harper, Althea, 12,219
Harper and Row (publishers), 5,985, 6,834, 11,036, 11,870, 11,996, **12,499**, 12,661, 12,820, 16,157, 16,163, 16,167, 16,172
Harper, Annie E., **9,639**
Harper Brothers (publishers). *See* Harper and Row (publishers)
Harper, Carrie A., 14,366
Harper, Catharine (Carroll) [Mrs. Robert Goodloe] (1775-1861), 5,774
Harper, Christina A. [Mrs. Samuel B.], 12,219
Harper, Emily Louisa (1812-92), 5,774
Harper, Ernest B., 8,663
Harper Family (NY), **12,219**
Harper, Fletcher, Jr., 12,820
Harper, Frances, 5,774
Harper, Ida A. (Husted) [Mrs. Thomas Winans] (1851-1931), 1,004, 1,427, **1,437**, 1,442, 1,475, 1,488, 2,256, 2,413, 2,447, 2,501, 4,675, **12,500**, 12,811, 12,834, 15,941
Harper, James Philip, 12,219
Harper, Jewell [Mrs.] (ca. 1900-), 8979
Harper, Josephine, 2,540
Harper, Lathrop Colgate (1867-1950), 12,219
Harper, Letitia, 5,774
Harper, Lurline N., 9,639
Harper, Mabel Helen Urner [Mrs. Lathrop Colgate], 12,219
Harper, Margaret, 13,511
Harper, Margaret Cook (Durbin) [Mrs. Fletcher, Jr.] (1830-86), **12,820**
Harper, Margaret (Perego) [Mrs. James Philip], 12,219
Harper, Mary, 5,774
Harper, Mary. *See* Beall, Mary (Harper)
Harper, Mary Diana (1804-18), 5,774
Harper Prize, 2,051
Harper, Robert Goodloe (1765-1825), Family (MD), **5,774**
Harper, Thomas Winans, 1,437
Harper, William Rainey, 4,300
Harper's Bazaar (periodical), 2,037, 9,770, 12,086, 12,500, 12,582, 15,198, 17,387

Harper's Ferry, 7,678
Harper's Magazine (periodical), 3,797, 12,395
Harpham, Josephine Evans, **14,289**
Harpole, Patricia, 9,230
Harpsichord, 468
Harpsichord and Salt Fish (book), 6,061
Harpster, Mary Margaret (Pike) [Mrs. William A.] (1852-?), **10,468**
Harraden, Lydia Anne [Mrs. Benjamin Ives] (1809-81), **7,380**
Harrais, Margaret (Keenan) [Mrs. Martin] (1872-1964), **138**
Harrais, Martin, 138
Harreld, Claudia White, **6,628**
Harrell, Bernard, **15,596**
Harrell, Ellen Maria (1833-1909). *See* Cantrell, Ellen Maria (Harrell) (1833-1909)
Harrell, Laura D. S. [Mrs.], 9,720
Harrell, Nancy. *See* Yancey, Nancy (Harrell) [Mrs. William Lay] Smith
Harrell, Rena [Miss] (1882-1973), **13,178**
Harrie, Florence, 1,662
Harriet Hosmer, Letters and Memoirs (book), 6,659
Harriet Lane, 1830-1903 (book), 14,828
Harriman, Florence "Daisy" Jaffray (Hurst) [Mrs. J. Borden] (1870-1967), **2,382**, 2,679, 8,450, **11,872**
Harrington, Edith (Russell) [Mrs. Herschel R.] (1898-1967), **13,026**
Harrington, Elizabeth Davis Locke [Mrs. Henry Francis] **5,932**
Harrington, Ellen Myra Pendergast [Mrs. Lewis] (1836-1915), **9,282**
Harrington, Fred Harvey, 17,776
Harrington, Henry Francis (1814-87), 5,932
Harrington, Herschel R., 13,026
Harrington, Maria (Ruan) [Mrs. Purnell F.], 14,072
Harrington, Mildred P., 13,890
Harrington, Olive Russell (1861-93). *See* Driggs, Olive Russell (Harrington) [Mrs. Benjamin Woodbury] (1861-93)
Harrington, Purnell F. (1844-1937), **14,072**
Harrington, Ruth [Miss], 17,908, 17,918, 17,919
Harrington-Russell Studios, Complete Pageant Service and Stage Equipment (NC), 13,026
Harriott, Clara Morris (1847-1925). *See* Morris, Clara [Mrs. Frederick C.] Harriott (1847-1925)
Harriott, Frederick C., 6,773
Harris, Agnes Ellen (1883-ca. 1952), **108**
Harris, Anna Rankin, 17,001
Harris, Annie Laurie. *See* Broidrick, Annie Laurie (Harris)
Harris, Annie Pleasants Fisher [Mrs. Wilbur] Dallam [Mrs. John W.] (1823-?), **16,079**
Harris, Barbara Allen (1802-91). *See* Metcalfe, Barbara Allen (Harris) [Mrs. Asa Baldwin] (1802-91)
Harris, Belle (1861-1938). *See* Nelson, Belle (Harris) [Mrs. Clarence] Merrill [Mrs. N. L.] (1861-1938)
Harris, Benjamin G., 5,775
Harris, Bernice (Kelly) (1894-), 13,511
Harris, Beth Kay, **16,519**
Harris, C. W., 3,030
Harris Chapel School (TX), 16,031
Harris, Charles, 15,686
Harris, Corra May (White) [Mrs. Lundy Howard] (1869-1935), 2,975, **3,028**, 3,071, 3,077, 3,117, **3,197**, **3,325**, 13,027, 15,060
Harris, Ellen Matilda (Orbison) [Mrs. John] (1816-1902), 14,824
Harris, Emmeline Blanche (Woodward) [Mrs. James Harvey] (1828-1921). *See* Wells, Emmeline Blanche (Woodward) [Mrs. James Harvey] Harris [Mrs. Newel Kimball] Whitney [Mrs. Daniel Hanmer] (1828-1921)
Harris, Esther, **14,575**
Harris, Eunice Polly (Stewart) [Mrs. Dennison Emer] (1860-1942), **16,690**
Harris, Eusebia (Blodgett) [Mrs. William] (1821-89). *See* Meeks, Eusebia (Blodgett) [Mrs. William] Harris [Mrs. Isaac] (1821-89)
Harris, Faith. *See* Leech, Faith (Harris) [Mrs. Harry]
Harris Family (LA), **5,446**
Harris Family (MS), 9,816

Harris Family (OH, PA, WI), **14,812**
Harris, Fanny, 10,314
Harris, Florence R., **17,270**
Harris, Frances. *See* Runholt, Frances (Harris) [Mrs. Vernon]
Harris, George B., **15,017**
Harris Grove Farmer's Club (IA), 4,839
Harris, Gwen, 10,191
Harris, Hannah, 8,690
Harris, Harry, **13,809**
Harris, Hattie (1873-1959), **5,593**
Harris, Helen, 8,651
Harris, Helen M., 8,681
Harris, Henry, 17,800
Harris Home Association (MO), 10,113
Harris, Isabella Hinton [Mrs. James Henry], 13,428
Harris, Iverson, 1,196
Harris, James, 16,566
Harris, James Harvey, 16,839
Harris, James Henry, **13,428**
Harris, Jane [Miss], 14,812
Harris, Jennie (1871-1922), **16,080**
Harris, Jennie H., 11,754
Harris, Joel Chandler, 3,532
Harris, Judia J., 3,305
Harris, Julia, 11,345
Harris, Julia Florida (Collier) [Mrs. Julian LaRose] (1875-1967), 2,987, 3,326, **7,229**
Harris, Julian LaRose (1874-1963), **3,326**
Harris, Julie (1925-), 7,310, 11,907, 12,039
Harris, Katharine W., 11,566
Harris, Lea, 9,730
Harris, Leah. *See* Sutro, Leah (Harris) [Mrs. Adolph Heinrich Joseph]
Harris, Lola (Wallace, 10,191
Harris, Lucinda (1792 – post 1885). *See* Kennedy, Lucinda (Harris) Eagle (1792-post 1885)
Harris, Lundy Howard, 3,028
Harris, Margaret (1908-). *See* Amsler, Margaret (Harris) [Mrs. Sam] (1908-)
Harris, Martha Elizabeth. *See* Harris, Martha Elizabeth (Harris) [Mrs. Benjamin G.]
Harris, Martha Elizabeth (Harris) [Mrs. Benjamin G.], **5,775**
Harris, Mary. *See* Lester, Mary (Harris) [Mrs. Andrew]
Harris, Mary [Mrs. Stephen], 15,017
Harris, Melissa [Miss], 14,812
Harris, Mrs. Arthur, **3,029**
Harris, Mrs. J. V., 9,722
Harris, Mrs. J. V. S., 9,722
Harris, Mrs. Wilson, 8,454
Harris, Myrtle [Mrs. Helmer], 9,467
Harris, Patricia Roberts (1924-), 2,438, 11,817
Harris, Polly, 5,298
Harris, Priscilla [Mrs.], 14,812
Harris, Rebecca [Mrs.], 14,812
Harris, Reneé [Mrs. Henry] (1876-1969), **17,800**
Harris, Rose [Mrs. Dilue] (1825-1914), **16,081**
Harris, Rosemary, 12,367
Harris, Roxanna Davenport, 14,151
Harris, Safford, **3,030**
Harris, Sallie P., 16,869
Harris, Sarah. *See* Fayerweather, Sarah (Harris)
Harris, Sarah H. [Miss], 3,030
Harris, Sarah Knox. *See* Sager, Sarah (Knox)
Harris, Stephen, 15,017
Harris-Stowe College (St. Louis, MO), **10,149**
Harris, William, 14,151
Harris, William Torrey (1835-1909), **2,383**, 10,149
Harris, Young L. G., 3,060
Harrisburg Area Community College (PA), 14,822
Harrisburg Art Association (PA), 14,822
Harrisburg Charter Commission (PA), 14,822
Harrisburg Female Seminary (PA). *See* Pennsylvania Female College (PA)
Harrisburg Symphony (PA), 14,822
Harrisburg Senators, 11,405
Harrison, Agatha (?-1954), **12,715**
Harrison, Agnes (Schmitt) (1894-1966), **10,469**
Harrison, Anna. *See* Ruder, Anna (Harrison)
Harrison, Anna T., 4,961
Harrison, Belle (Richardson) [Mrs. John Calhoun], 57

Harrison, Benjamin, 4,633, 12,052
Harrison, Bertha (Miller) [Mrs. Clement] (1879-1960), 8,399, **8,403**
Harrison, Burton Norvell (1838-1904), Family, 2,384
Harrison, Caroline "Carrie" Lavinia (Scott) [Mrs. Benjamin] (1832-92), **4,633**
Harrison, Carrie, 2,570
Harrison, Carter Henry, IV (1860-1953), **3,995**
Harrison, Clement (1884-1968), **8,403**
Harrison, Constance (Cary) [Mrs. Burton Norvell] (1843-1920), 2,384
Harrison, Elizabeth (1815-1907). *See* Goddard, Elizabeth (Harrison) [Mrs. George] (1815-1907)
Harrison, Elizabeth Letcher [Miss] (1849-1927), 4,210, **4,211**, 4,212, 7,973
Harrison, Ella (1859-1933), **6,629**, 9,734
Harrison, Emily [Miss], **3,327**
Harrison, Ethelyn, 10,216
Harrison Family (VA), **17,119**
Harrison, Fanny Goodman [Mrs. Learner B.], 13,849
Harrison, Florence L. (1883-1973), **6,630**
Harrison, George L., 5,807
Harrison, George L., Jr., 5,807
Harrison, Henrietta (1865-1950). *See* Rowland, Henrietta (Harrison) [Mrs. Henry A.] (1865-1950)
Harrison, Hetty (Cary) [Mrs. Fairfax], 2,384
Harrison, Irene, 12,715
Harrison, Isabella H. (Ritchie), 17,119
Harrison, Jane H., 12,315
Harrison, Learner B. (1815-1902), **13,849**
Harrison, Louise Colbran, 1,750
Harrison, Lucia [Miss], **8,232**
Harrison, Lucy A. (?-1882). *See* Franklin, Lucy A. (Harrison) (?-1882)
Harrison, Margaret, 13,849
Harrison, Margarita Willets, 15,288
Harrison, Mary S., 11,173
Harrison, Nan Hillary, **16,082**
Harrison, Pat, 9,658
Harrison, William A., 12,370
Harrison, William Henry, 4,961, 7,008
Harrold, Alfred, 14,902
Harroun, Gilbert K., 2,285
Harroun, Margaret, 531
Harrow, Francis Marion (1856-1945). *See* Hanger, Francis Marion (Harrow) (1856-1945)
Harry Garfield's First Forty Years: Man of Action in a Troubled World (book), 2,345
Harry, Ruth [Mrs.], **5,382**
Harsh, Vivian G., **3,915**
Harshaw, Ruth (Hetzel) (1897-1968), **2,385**
Hart, Adelaide Julia (1900-), **7,810**, 7,904, **8,160**
Hart, Alexis Crane, 4,911
Hart, Almira (1793-1844). *See* Phelps, Almira (Hart) [Mrs. Simeon] Lincoln [Mrs. John] (1793-1844)
Hart, Ann Clark [Mrs. Jerome Alfred] (1871-?), **532**
Hart, Anne [Mrs.] (1909-64), 10,238
Hart, Anne [Mrs. Oliver], **11,100**
Hart, Beulah (Craven), 17,232
Hart, Clara Emerson [Mrs. Alexis Crane], 4,911
Hart County News (KY), 5,394
Hart, Doris, 15,371
Hart, Dorothy, 13,890
Hart, Eliza (1807-51). *See* Spalding, Eliza (Hart) [Mrs. Henry Harmon] (1807-51)
Hart, Elizabeth (Biggar) [Mrs. Alexis Crane] (1846-83), 4,911
Hart, Emily (Ellingham) [Mrs. James Henry] (1821-92), **16,691**
Hart, Emma (1787-1870). *See* Willard, Emma (Hart) [Mrs. John]. [Mrs. Christopher] Yates (1787-1870)
Hart Family (IA), **4,911**
Hart Family (KY), 5,343
Hart Family (TX), 16,269
Hart, Irving H., 4,911
Hart, Isabella, 8,279
Hart Jerome Alfred (1854-1937), **532**
Hart, Julia (Duggan) [Mrs. Edward M.] (1873-1970), **16,269**
Hart, Levi, 3,723
Hart, Lucretia (?-1864). *See* Clay, Lucretia (Hart) [Mrs. Henry] (?-1864)

Hart, Lucy Eliza (1814-69). *See* Wilcox, Lucy Eliza (Hart) [Mrs. Abner] (1814-69)
Hart, Malvina A. *See* Bennett, Malvina A. (Hart) [Mrs. William Kirby]
Hart, Margaret (Adams) [Mrs. Leroy], 3,017
Hart, Moss, 4,764, **17,801**
Hart, Pearl M. (1890-1975), **3,852**
Hart, Rebecca Tevis, 5,343
Hart, Sarah M. *See* Jarvis, Sarah M. (Hart) [Mrs. Samuel Farmer]
Hart, Virginia (1809-59). *See* Breckinridge, Virginia (Hart) [Mrs. Alfred] Shelby [Mrs. Robert Jefferson] (1809-59)
Harte, Bret, 1,643, 1,954
Harte, Grace H., **6,527**
Hartford Art Club (CT), **1,949**
Hartford Charitable Society (CT), **1,864**
Hartford Consumers' League (CT), 6,485
Hartford Equal Rights Club (CT), **1,908**
Hartford Female Seminary (CT), **1,865**, 1,951, **6,631**
Hartford Female Seminary (MA), 16,016
Hartford Freedmen's Aid Society (CT), 1,875
Hartford High School (CT), 17,035
Hartford, Nancy (Colburn) (?-1864), 7,677
Hartford North Park Methodist Church, Ladies Aid Society (CT), 1,890
Hartford School of Religious Pedagogy (CT). *See* Hartford Seminary Foundation (CT)
Hartford Seminary Foundation (CT), 1,839, 1,840, 1,841, 1,842, 1,843, 1,844, 1,845, 1,846, 1,847, **1,848**, 1,849, 1,850, 1,851, 1,853, 1,855, 1,856, 1,858, 1,859
    alumnae, 10,926
    students, 13,280
Hartford Seminary Foundation (CT), Kennedy School of Missions. *See* Hartford Seminary Foundation (CT)
Hartford Seminary Foundation (CT), Mackenzie Hall, 1,848
Hartford Seminary Foundation (CT), Woman's Board. *See* Hartford Seminary Foundation (CT)
Hartford Theological Seminary (CT). *See* Hartford Seminary Foundation (CT)
Hartford Wellesley Club (CT), **1,909**
Hartford Women (periodical), 1,910
Hartford Women's Club (CT), **1,910**
Harth, Mary Y. [Mrs. John] (?-1898), **15,602**
Harthan, Annah C. (1853-1938). *See* Fay, Annah C. (Harthan) [Mrs. Arthur] (1853-1938)
Hartigan, Isabel, 1,333
Hartley, Anne Jane (1821-1904). *See* Gilbert, Anne Jane (Hartley) (1821-1904)
Hartley, Emma Frances (1868-?). *See* Angell, Emma Frances (Hartley) [Mrs. Charles August] (1868-?)
Hartley, Helene (Willey) (1893-1963), **12,920**
Hartley, Lucie Klammer [Mrs. Scott] (1911-), **9,117**
Hartley, Marsden, 2,784
Hartley, Sarah Wells (1836-1921). *See* Curtis, Sarah Wells (Hartley) [Mrs. Richard] Soper [Mrs. Lyman] (1836-1921)
Hartman, Edith Kast (1880-1967), 10,639
Hartman, Jo Ann, 3,618
Hartman, Mrs. Peter G., **8,339**
Hartman, Sarah McAllister, 17,271
Hartmann, Sadakichi (1867-1944), **1,124**
Hartness, Helen. *See* Flanders, Helen (Hartness)
Hartrich, Sister Berchmans, 1,007
Hartshorn, Charles W., 4,911
Hartshorn Family (NY), **12,501**
Hartshorn, Florence M. (1869-1943), **17,272**
Hartshorn, George F., 12,501
Hartshorn, Jessie, 12,501
Hartshorn, Margaret Seaton (1776-1823). *See* Densmore, Margaret Seaton (Hartshorn) (1776-1823)
Hartshorn, Martha E., 12,501
Hartshorn, Mary L., 12,501
Hartshorne, Anna Cope (1860-1957), 14,844
Hartshorne, Clementina R., **6,632**
Hartshorne Family (PA), **14,844**
Hartsock, Ernest, 3,167
Hartsough, Mildred Lucille (1898-), 6,203

Hartsuck, Ann S. (Conner) [Mrs. Mark] (1826-1918), **17,273**

Hartsuck, Mrs. Ben, **17,274**

Hartsuff Alice Elliott [Mrs. Albert], 7,811

Hartsuff Family (MI), **7,811**

Hartsuff, Florence, 7,811

Hartt, Augusta Batchelder, 6,759

Hartwell, Anna Burton (1870-1961), 2,018

Hartwell, Eliza H. (Jewett) [Mrs. Jesse] (1837-70), 2,018

Hartwell, Elizabeth (1847-1922). See Delano, Elizabeth (Hartwell) [Mrs. Washington Warren] (1847-1922)

Hartwell, Emily Susan (1858-1951), **2,013**

Hartwell Family, **2,018**

Hartwell Family (CT, MA, RI), 7,520

Hartwell, Mary (1847-1902). See Catherwood, Mary (Hartwell) [Mrs. James Steele] (1847-1902)

Hartwell, Polley [Mrs. Bellows], 1,224

Hartwick Academy (NY), **12,746**

Hartwick College (Oneonta, NY), **12,745**

Hartwick College (Oneonta, NY), Women's Club, 12,745

Hartwick, John Christopher, 12,748

Hartwick Patent (land grant), 12,748

Hartwick Seminary (NY). See Hartwick Academy (NY)

Hartwick Seminary Association (NY), 12,746

Hartwickian, The (periodical), 12,746

Hartwig, Cleo (1911-), **2,770**

Hartzell, Laura Belle (1881-1956), **10,471**

Harvard Botanic Garden (MA), 6,283

Harvard College (MA). See Harvard University (MA)

Harvard College Astronomical Observatory (MA), 6,280, **6,285**, 12,452

Harvard Commission on Western History, 1,496

Harvard Community (MA), 12,309

Harvard Divinity School (MA), 6,251

Harvard Divinity School (MA), Committee on Admission of Women, **6,270**

Harvard Economics Research Project, 6,600

Harvard Field Hospital Unit (England, World War II), 6,153

Harvard Law School (MA), 5,271

   faculty, **6,260, 6,282**

Harvard Law School Crime Survey. See Harvard Survey of Crime and Criminal Justice in Greater Boston (MA)

Harvard Law School Forum, **6,633**

Harvard Museum (MA), 11,897

Harvard Neighbors (MA), 6,265

Harvard-Radcliffe Program in Business Administration (MA), 6,339

Harvard School of Public Health (MA), 6,558, 6,852, 6,987

Harvard Street Baptist Church (Boston, MA), Ladies Aid Society, **7,102**

Harvard Street Church Women's Alliance (Cambridge, MA), **6,252**

Harvard Survey of Crime and Criminal Justice in Greater Boston (MA), 6,263, 6,934

Harvard Teas Association (MA), 6,265

Harvard Unit (France, WWI), 6,152

Harvard University (MA), 2,108, 2,290, 2,429, 6,239, 6,622, 6,651, 6,708, 6,843, 6,870, 6,877, 7,631, 7,639, 7,659, 7,667, 9,042, 14,203, 14,366

   administrators, **6,279**

   admission, **6,270, 6,271, 6,303**

   alumnae, 8,947, 9,445

   alumni, 17,685

   deans, **6,284, 6,899**

   employees, **6,292, 6,304**

   faculty, 1,088, 5,250, **6,268, 6,276, 6,277, 6,280, 6,283, 6,284,** 6,293, **6,302, 6,305,** 6,310, 6,448, 6,782, 8,636, 8,744, 11,473, 12,028, 12,063, 13,134

   presidents, **6,278, 6,291, 6,299,** 7,385

   student housing, **6,288**

   students, 561, 5,271, 7,518, 10,523, 17,637

   students' societies, **6,286**

   tercentenary celebration, 6,986

   women in, **6,306**

Harvard University (MA), Advisor for Harvard Wives, **6,264**

Harvard University (MA), Advisor for Veterans' Wives. See Harvard University (MA), Advisor for Harvard Wives

Harvard University (MA), Business School, Business Historical Society, 6,203

Harvard University (MA), Committee on Admitting Women to the Medical School, **6,271**

Harvard University (MA), Committee on Examinations for Women, **6,272**

Harvard University (MA), Committee on the Harvard-Radcliffe Relationship, **6,275,** 6,482

Harvard University (MA), Committee on the Status of Women at Harvard, **6,482**

Harvard University (MA), Committee on the Status of Women in the Faculty of Arts and Sciences, **6,276**

Harvard University (MA), Faculty of Arts and Sciences. See Harvard University (MA)

Harvard University (MA), Fogg Art Museum, 6,281

Harvard University (MA), Gray Herbarium, 6,277

Harvard University (MA), Houghton Library, 6,396

Harvard University (MA), Housing Office, **6,289**

Harvard University (MA), Library, 12,479

Harvard University (MA), Medical School, 6,225, 6,681

   faculty, 6,933

Harvard University (MA), Museum of American Archaeology and Ethnology, 2,298

Harvard University (MA), Museum of Comparative Zoology, 6,316, **6,321**

Harvard University (MA), Nursery School, **6,287**

Harvard University (MA), Peabody Museum of Archaeology and Ethnology, 6,325

Harvard University (MA), Special Committee on the Petitions Regarding Female Education, **6,303**

Harvard University (MA), Student Record Office, 6,292

Harvard University (MA), Women's Faculty Group, 6,482

Harvard University (MA)-Radcliffe College, relations, **6,274**

Harvardens Village (MA), **6,288,** 6,289

Harvey (book, drama), 14,335

Harvey, Ada, 971

Harvey, Angelina, **533**

Harvey, Ann, 13,338

Harvey, Anne (1928-74). See Sexton, Anne (Harvey) (1928-74)

Harvey, Annie, 971

Harvey, Clarice Collins, 9,575

Harvey, Constance, 971

Harvey, Daniel, 534

Harvey, Dorothy (Dudley) [Mrs. Henry Blodgett] (1884-1962), **12,821**

Harvey, Elizabeth (Mackaness) [Mrs. Thomas], 12,605

Harvey, Eloisa (McLaughlin) [Mrs. William Glenn] Rae [Mrs. Daniel] (1817-84), **534**

Harvey Family (CA), **971**

Harvey Family (GA), 3,612

Harvey Family (NY), **12,605**

Harvey Family (TX), **16,057**

Harvey, Florence [Miss] (ca. 1900-70s), 11,181

Harvey, Frances, 971

Harvey, George B., 11,996

Harvey, Isabella [Miss], 4,137

Harvey, Lewis, 4,354

Harvey, Louise, 971

Harvey, Margaretta A., 15,568

Harvey, Mary. See Rodman, Mary (Harvey) [Mrs. Washington]

Harvey, Mary [Miss], 13,498

Harvey, Nancy, 16,057

Harvey, S. E. [Miss], 13,560

Harvey, Susanna (Hall) [Mrs. Joseph] (1715?-95). See Morris, Susanna (Hall) [Mrs. Joseph] Harvey [Mrs. John] Rush [Mrs. Richard] (1715?-95)

Harvey, Vadae (1884-). See Meekison, Vadae (Harvey) [Mrs. George] (1884-)

Harvey, William, Sr., 971

Harwood, Aurelia, 1,224

Harwood, Burt, 508

Harwood, Clara (1855-1956). See Bradner, Clara (Harwood) (1855-1956)

Harwood, Dorcas Hubbard, 1,900

Harwood, Elizabeth, 508

Harwood, Elizabeth Lloyd, 5,789

Harwood, Margaret Spencer Wilson (1885-), **1,538**

Harwood, Mrs. Harry, 4,597

Harwood-Arrowood, Bertha, **3,198**

Hasbrouk, Mildred, 6,337

Haselmayer, Louis A., 5,068

Haseltine, Florence, 15,134

Hashimoto, Joy, 16,890

Haskell, Agnes [Mrs. Herbert S.] Hadley [Mrs. Henry C.] (1876-1946), **9,983**

Haskell, Anna, 14,122

Haskell, Anna (Fader) [Mrs. Burnette Gregor] (1858-1942), 535

Haskell, Burnette Gregor, 535

Haskell, Edward Wilder, 535

Haskell Family (CA), **535**

Haskell, Harriet C. (1835-1907), 4,361, 4,374

Haskell, Helen (1860-1942). See Thomas, Helen (Haskell) [Mrs. Stephen Seymour] (1860-1942)

Haskell, Henry C., 9,983

Haskell, Jennie Helen (Cryer) [Mrs. Edward Prince], 535

Haskell, Jessie, 5,677

Haskell, Maria Antoinette (Briggs) [Mrs. Edward Wilder] (?-1903), 535

Haskell, Marion Alexander, 3,523

Haskell, Sophia Lovell (1846-1922). See Cheves, Sophia Lovell (Haskell) (1846-1922)

Haskell, Winifred [Miss] (1895-1954), **5,677**

Haskins, Nannie. See Williams, Nannie (Haskins)

Haslam Family, **10,864**

Haslam, Greville, 10,864

Hasler, Alice, **8,742**

Hasler, John, 16,892

Hasler, Louisa (Thalman) [Mrs. John] (1843-97), **16,892**

Hassam, Eleanor (1879-), **7,381**

Hassam Family (MA), **7,382**

Hassam, Nelly Alden (Batchelder), 7,382

Hasselborg, Flora Valeria (1885-), **9,118**

Hasseltine, Ann, 8,304

Hasseltine, Ann (1789-1826). See Judson, Ann (Hasseltine) [Mrs. Adoniram] (1789-1826)

Hasseltine, Nancy (1789-1826). See Judson, Ann (Hasseltine) [Mrs. Adoniram] (1789-1826)

Hassid, Lila B., **934**

Hassler, Charles A., 2,464

Hasslock, Augusta Thekla (1882-1963). See Kemp, Augusta Thekla (Hasslock) [Mrs. John Franklin] (1882-1963)

Hasslock Family, 15,956

Hasslock Family (TX), 16,274

Hasslock, Herman Wilhelm, 15,956

Hasslock, Thekla (Dombois) [Mrs. Herman Wilhelm], 15,956

Haste, Gwendolyn (1889-), **12,502**

Hastings, Ann Eliza (Phipps) (1813-ca. 1915), **6,634**

Hastings College of Law (CA), faculty, 441

Hastings, Harriet B., 3,742

Hastings, Helen King, 2,932

Hastings, Helen. Muzzah Wakon Win, 9,371

Hastings High School (MN), 9,024

Hastings, John Russel (1878-1942), **536**

Hastings, Katharine, 2,004

Hastings Law School (CA), 1,144

Hastings, Mary (1882-1976). See Bradley, Mary (Hastings) (1882-1976)

Hastings, Mary E., 1,572

Hastings, Olivia [Mrs.], 9,564

Hasty, Gladys (1904-). See Carroll, Gladys (Hasty) [Mrs. Herbert Allen] (1904-)

"Hat, The" (story), 5,085

Hat, Cap and Millinery Workers Union, 3,446

Hat trade, 17,459

Hatch, Annie Scarborough, 16,492

Hatch, Cullen B., **13,429**

Hatch, Daisy, **5,182**

Hatch, Dorothy (1902-?). See Langlie, Dorothy (Hatch) [Mrs. Theos A.] (1902-?)

Hatch, Ethel C. [Miss], 1,224

Hatch Family (MI), 7,703
Hatch, Lloyd, 9,169
Hatch, Martha H., 13,429
Hatch, Mrs. Thetis Clay, 9,870
Hatch, Mrs. W. H., 4,961
Hatch, Nelle (Spilsbury), 16,520
Hatch, Olivia Stokes [Mrs. J. D.] (1908-), 7,510
Hatch, Verna, 9,988
Hatchard, Janet (Larke) (1839-?), 11,352
Hatcher, Amelia, 17,884
Hatcher, Lillian, 8,131
Hatcher, Mattie Austin, 16,083
Hatcher, Orie Latham (1868-1946), 12,738, 13,189
Hatchet Gang (MA), 7,336
Hatfield, Alice Chamberlain, 8,262
Hatfield, Henry Drury (1875-1962), 17,462
Hatfield, Mr., 6,610
Hatgren, Thora, 8,743
Hathaway, Agnes, 8,831
Hathaway, Agnes S., 2,701
Hathaway, Anna M., Fund, 1,362
Hathaway, Dame Sybil, 3,226
Hathaway, Eugenie, 10,535
Hathaway Family (NC), 13,044
Hathaway, Katharine (Butler) (1890-1942), 6,635
Hathaway, Louise (1880-?). See Stanley, Louise
   (Hathaway) [Mrs. Charles Alfred] (1880-?)
Hathaway, Margaret. See Jones, Margaret (Hathaway)
Hathway, Marion (1895-1955), 8,653
Hathaway, May [Mrs.], 16,939
Hathaway, Phoebe, 2,315, 11,616
Hathaway, Samuel Gilbert (1780-1867). See
   Hatheway, Samuel Gilbert (1780-1867)
Hathaway School (OH), 14,135
Hathaway, Vera, 8,949
Hathaway, Wealthy, 10,535
Hatheway, Catherine Saxton [Mrs. Samuel Gilbert],
   11,602
Hatheway, Elizabeth Dorothea (1823-1908), 11,602
Hatheway Family (MA), 11,602
Hatheway, Lavinia Matilda (1819-85), 11,602
Hatheway, Samuel Gilbert (1780-1867), 11,602
Hatheway, Sarah (1811-72). See Whitney, Sarah
   (Hatheway) [Mrs. Benajah T.] (1811-72)
Hatheway, Sarah Emerson [Mrs. Samuel Gilbert],
   11,602
Hatheway, Welthea Hannah (1817-55). See Boyd,
   Welthea Hannah (Hatheway) [Mrs. John W.]
   (1817-55)
Hat-makers. See Hatters; Milliners
Hats, 7,587
Hatt, Emma M. [Mrs. John A.], 14,552
Hatt, John A., 14,552
Hatt, Mabel (?-1971), 2,771
Hatten, Margaret, 15,478
Hatters, 6,641, 12,253
Hatton, Bessie, 16,174
Hatton Family (GA), 3,031
Hauck, Hazel Marie (1900-64), 11,603
Haugen, Aase (1851-1910), 8,737
Haugen, Einar, 8,744
Haugen, Gilbert N. (1859-1933), 4,914
Haugen, Kristine [Mrs. John] (1878-1965), 8,744
Haugen, Norma (1888-1959). See Johnson, Norma
   (Haugen) [Mrs. J. O. E.] (1888-1959)
Haugen, Ruth Bergliot (1905-), 8,654
Haun, Catherine Margaret, 1,505
Haun, Mildred Eunice [Miss] (1911-66), 15,927,
   15,929, 15,933
Hauser, Rita E. (1934-), 11,604, 11,817
Hauson, Mary G., 3,533
Hautzinger, Susan O'Brien [Mrs. James] (1939-),
   1,786
Havasupai Indian Reservation (AZ), 153
"Have Ye Room?" (poem), 6,386
Havemeyer, Electra, 2,739
Haven, Caroline T., 11,547
Haven, Elizabeth (1811-91). See Barlow, Elizabeth
   (Haven) [Mrs. Israel] (1811-91)
Haven Hill Garden Club (NH), 10,885
Haven, Jane Stowell [Mrs. Samuel R.], 3,834
Haven, Joseph, 1,392
Haven, Sarah (Greenleaf) [Mrs. Nathaniel Walker]
   Appleton [Mrs. Joseph] (?-1838), 1,392

Havener, Rose (Pendleton), 5,707
Havens, Charles C., 4,395
Havens, Emma, 9,422
Havens, Eva, 9,422
Havens Family, 4,942
Haver, Barbara (1766-1862). See Frietchie, Barbara
   (Haver) [Mrs. John Casper] (1766-1862)
Haver, Jessie (1886-). See Butler, Jessie (Haver)
   (1886-)
Haverhill Academy (MA), 8,526
Haverhill and Bradford Soldiers Relief Society (MA),
   7,637
Haverty, Mary E., 3,199
Haviland, Laura (Smith) [Mrs. Charles, Jr.] (1808-98),
   7,774, 7,939
Havoc, June (1916-), 7,310, 17,816
Havre, Sylvia (1892-). See Raihle, Sylvia (Havre)
   [Mrs. Paul H.] (1892-)
Hawaii, 3,619, 7,225, 9,422
   adult and continuing education, 3,651
   annexation to United States, 10,162
   authors, 3,633
   Catholic schools, 17,820
   child care centers, 3,653
   children of missionaries, 3,639
   church schools, 16,249
   clergy, 3,640
   clergy, Presbyterian, 2,271
   clubs, 3,652
   composers, 3,628, 3,632
   congresswomen, 1,605, 7,262
   corporations, 3,623
   courts martial, 3,620
   diaries and journals, 3,621, 3,643
   education, 3,619
   endowments, 3,626
   folklorists, 3,628, 3,633
   governors, 3,641
   historic sites, conservation and restoration,
      3,644
   historical societies, 3,633
   hotels, taverns, etc., 3,621
   land settlement, 3,621
   leprosy, hospitals, 16,532
   library associations, 3,653
   merchants, 3,647
   missionaries to, 751, 2,002, 2,178, 2,427, 3,636,
      3,637, 3,638, 3,643, 3,645, 3,646, 3,649, 12,185
   missionaries to, Presbyterian, 2,271, 12,185
   missions, 751
   Mormons and Mormonism, 16,651
   newspaper publishers and publishing, 3,640
   nurses, 3,629
   philanthropists, 3,623
   photograph collections, 3,648
   plantations, 8,776
   poets, 3,628
   politics and government, 3,647
   politics, practical, women's activism, 3,625
   public records, 3,619
   queens, 3,620, 3,621, 3,631, 3,632
   registers of births, etc., 3,619
   revolution (1893), 12,350
   shipmasters, 3,647
   social life and customs, 7,479
   teachers, 3,619
   trade and professional associations, 3,629
   universities and colleges, faculty, 3,652
   vital statistics, 3,619
   World War I, civilians' work, 3,635
   World War II, civilians' work, 3,653
Hawaii (moving-picture), 17,804
Hawaii League of Women Voters. See American
   Association of University Women (HI)
Hawaii Library Association, 3,653
Hawaii Public Health Association, 3,653
Hawaiian Evangelical Association, Micronesian
   Mission, 3,642
Hawaiian Historical Commission, 3,633
Hawaiian Legend and Folklore Commission, 3,633
Hawaiians, 3,647
Hawes, Amelia (Hallet) [Mrs. John] (1830-1906),
   7,693
Hawes, Beulah (Nickerson) (1896-), 5,678

Hawes, Evelyn Johnson (1915-), 17,192
Hawes, James Morrison, 13,028
Hawes, Laurence J., 6,923
Hawes, Maria (Southgate) [Mrs. James Morrison]
   (1836-1918), 13,028
Hawes, Mary Jane (1825-1907). See Holmes, Mary
   Jane (Hawes) [Mrs. Daniel] (1825-1907)
Hawes, Mary Jane (1837-1919). See Wilmarth, Mary
   Jane (Hawes) [Mrs. Henry Martin] (1837-1919)
Hawes, Mary Virginia (1830-1922). See Terhune,
   Mary Virginia (Hawes) [Mrs. Edward Payson]
   (1830-1922)
Hawes, Rebecca Williams, 3,716
Hawke, Marlene, 5,083
Hawkes, Ada (Leonard) [Mrs. C. S.], 9,884
Hawkes, Ann (Laurance) [Mrs. George Wright]. See
   Bolton, Ann (Laurance) [Mrs. George Wright]
   Hawkes [Mrs. Daniel]
Hawkes Family (NY), 12,220
Hawkes, George Wright, 12,220
Hawkes, Jean (McCown), 2,016
Hawkes, John, 3,689
Hawkes, Mrs. John, 3,689
Hawkes, Sarah Belknap "Belle" (Sherwood) [Mrs.
   James Woods] (1854-1919), 15,171
Hawkins, Beula [Mrs.], 1,937
Hawkins, Caroline (Norton), 14,576, 14,618
Hawkins, Charlotte (1882-1961). See Brown,
   Charlotte (Hawkins) [Mrs. Edward S.]
   (1882-1961)
Hawkins, Edith, 1,777
Hawkins, Helen Lyon, 537, 538
Hawkins, Jack, 2,284
Hawkins, Janet, 13,430
Hawkins, Lula, 13,430
Hawkins, Madge (Ytrehus) [Mrs. Oscar Ferdinand]
   (1882-), 9,119, 9,129, 9,467
Hawkins, Marion E., 17,859
Hawkins, Marmaduke James, 13,430
Hawkins, Mrs. Marmaduke James, 13,430
Hawkins, Minnie, 1,911
Hawkins, Myrtle [Mrs.], 10,755
Hawkins, Myrtle [Mrs. Ed], 1,534
Hawkins, Oscar Ferdinand (1872-1964), Family (CA,
   MN), 9,119
Hawkins, Ruth (1882-), 9,119
Hawkins, Sally [Mrs. Mark], 17,375
Hawk's Done Gone, The (book), 15,933
Hawks, Esther H., 2,386
Hawk's Flight (book), 12,016
Hawks, J. Milton, 2,386
Hawley, Anne MacDonald (1876-?), 9,120
Hawley, Augustine Boyer, Family (MN), 9,120
Hawley, Edith, 2,673
Hawley, Edward, 9,120
Hawley, Eliza H., 12,834
Hawley, Ella. See Crossett, Ella (Hawley) [Mrs. John
   B.]
Hawley, Emily Elizabeth. See Gillespie, Emily
   Elizabeth (Hawley)
Hawley, Genevieve Lel, 12,834
Hawley, Harriet Ward (Foote) [Mrs. Joseph Rosewell]
   (1831-86), 2,387
Hawley, Mabel B. [Mrs.], 1,122
Hawley, Marianna, 12,192
Hawley, Mary, 12,221
Hawley, May, 4,920
Hawley, S. T and Son, 13,536
Hawn, Jacob, 14,632
Hawn, Laura. See Patterson, Laura A. (Hawn)
Hawn, Mary (1879-). See Bogie, Mary (Hawn)
   (1879-)
Haworth, Evelyn (Martin) [Mrs. Samuel Lee]
   (1877-1967), 13,230
Haworth Family (NC), 13,230
Haworth, Samuel Lee (1868-1957), 13,230
Hawthorn Festival, 9,828
Hawthorne, Alice. See Call, Alice (Hawthorne) [Mrs.
   George R.]
Hawthorne, Elizabeth Manning (1802-83), 1,438,
   7,383
Hawthorne Family (MA), 7,383, 14,165
Hawthorne, Hildegarde (1872-?), 317, 7,383
Hawthorne, Julian, 1,039, 7,383

Hawthorne, Manning, 7,383
Hawthorne, Nathaniel (1804-64), **1,438**, 1,598, **5,933**, 6,329, 6,636, 6,857, 7,025, 7,234, 7,383, 7,477, 12,503
Hawthorne, Rose (1851-1926). *See* Lathrop, Rose (Hawthorne) (Mother Mary Alphonse) (1851-1926)
Hawthorne, Sally, **13,431**
Hawthorne, Sophia Amelia (Peabody) [Mrs. Nathaniel] (1809-71), 1,438, 2,282, 5,925, **5,933**, **6,636**, 7,025, 7,277, 7,383, 7,477, **12,503**, 14,165, 17,010, 17,037
Hawthorne, Una (1844-77), 1,438, 7,025, 7,383, 17,010
Hawxhurst Family (NY), **12,504**
Hawxhurst, James (1775-1854), 12,504
Hawxhurst, Penelope, 12,504
Hawxhurst, Sarah, 12,504
Hawxhurst, Stephen, 12,504
Hawxhurst, Susan C., 12,504
Haxton, Kenneth, 9,769
Hay, 14,558
Hay, Abbie M., 2,160
Hay, Charles Martin (1879-1945), 2,701, **9,984**
Hay, Clara Louise (Stone) [Mrs. John] (1849-1914), 2,388
Hay, Emily Parsons Babcock Hay (?-1937), 589
Hay, Emma (Metcalfe) [Mrs. William Gilbert] (1840-1937), 589
Hay, John (1838-1905), **2,388**, 2,512, 4,365
Hay, Katherine. *See* Humphreys, Katherine (Hay)
Hay, Marion E. (1865-1933), **17,376**
Hay, Mary Garrett (1857-1928), 2,170, 2,501, **12,505**, 12,811
Hay-Silverman Day Care Center (GA), 3,253
Hayakawa, S. I., 18,021
Haycraft, Molly Costain (1911-), **6,032**
Hayden, Agnes, 15,184
Hayden, Alicia (Nearing) [Mrs. W. W.], 11,520
Hayden, Anne Keith (1835-96). *See* Field, Anne Keith (Hayden) [Mrs. Christian] Fader [Mrs. J. C.] (1835-96)
Hayden, Bessie Leach (1886-post 1966), **109**
Hayden, Carl T. (1877-1972), **176**, 181, 188
Hayden, Elmer (1897-1971), 7,148
Hayden expedition (1872), 1,684
Hayden Family, **8,280**
Hayden Family, 535
Hayden Family (MA), **7,148**
Hayden, Ferdinand V., 17,992
Hayden, Gillette (?-1929), **13,997**
Hayden, Hattie Hateful [Mrs. Sumner], 1,224
Hayden, Helen (1906-56), 8,685
Hayden, Jennie (1844-72). *See* Conwell, Jennie (Hayden) [Mrs. Russell H.] (1844-72)
Hayden, Mary Jane, 14,628
Hayden, Mary Logan, **17,275**
Hayden Planetarium, 14,235
Hayden, Sarah Elizabeth Shea [Mrs. Elmer] (1919-), 7,148
Hayden, W. W., 11,520
Haydon, Ione, **7,812**
Hayes, Alice, 12,572
Hayes, Ann Hansen, 16,908
Hayes, Chloe Smith (1762-1847), **14,073**
Hayes, Elizabeth Keen [Mrs. Patrick] (1764-1853), 15,168
Hayes, Esther Rachel, 15,343
Hayes, Eva, 16,876
Hayes, Everis A., 1,359
Hayes Family, 14,080
Hayes Family (PA), 15,168
Hayes, Fanny, 14,079
Hayes, Fanny Arabella (1820-56). *See* Platt, Fanny Arabella (Hayes) (1820-56)
Hayes, Florence [Miss], 13,630
Hayes, Florence Belle Donnelly [Mrs. James Henry], **1,490**
Hayes, Frances (1867-1950), **14,074**
Hayes, Helen (1896-), 1,026, 2,382, 3,921, 7,272, **8,876**, 11,689, 12,129, 16,149, 17,943
Hayes, James Henry, **1,490**
Hayes, Jennie. *See* Field, Jennie (Hayes)

Hayes, Lucy Ware (Webb) [Mrs. Rutherford B.] (1831-89), **14,075**, 14,086, 14,092, 14,206, 16,812
Hayes, Lyman S. (1850-1934), **16,984**
Hayes, Margaret (Jocelyn) [Mrs. Samuel], 1,870
Hayes, Margaret Howell Jefferson (Davis), 3,570, **9,619**, 9,795
Hayes, Mary (Miller) [Mrs. Webb C., I] (1856-1935), **14,076**, 14,091
Hayes, Mary Ann (1838-1925). *See* Bigelow, Mary Ann (Hayes) (1838-1925)
Hayes, Mary H. S., 2,685
Hayes, Melvina F. (Hadley), 14,483
Hayes, Mother Mary Ignatius, 8,483
Hayes, Patrick, 15,168
Hayes, Rose B. (1861-?), **16,521**
Hayes, Russell, 14,060
Hayes, Rutherford, Sr., 14,060
Hayes, Rutherford B. (1822-93), 753, 3,227, 10,165, 14,056, 14,060, 14,073, 14,074, **14,077**, 14,078, 14,079, 14,090, 14,093, 15,959, 16,620, 16,839
Hayes, Sarah Elizabeth (Lumpkin). *See* Bomar, Sarah Elizabeth (Lumpkin) Hayes [Mrs. Benjamin F.]
Hayes, Sophia Birchard (1792-1866), **14,078**
Hayes Textile Company (Oswego, NY), **12,758**
Hayes, Virginia, 13,468
Hayes, Webb C., I, 14,076, 14,091
Haygood, Atticus Greene (1839-96), **3,328**
Haygood, Laura Askew (1845-1900), 3,328
Haygood, Mamie. *See* Ardis, Mamie (Haygood)
Hayler, Guy, Family (CA), **539**
Hayler, Mollie B. [Mrs.], 539
Hayles, Wayne B., 16,518
Hayman, Martha "Mattie" Washington (Knox) [Mrs. Syme], 287
Hayne, Arthur P., 16,893
Hayne Family (SC), 3,280
Hayne, Julia Dean [Mrs. Arthur P.] (1830-68), 7,310, **16,893**
Hayner, Mrs. Earl G., 12,867
Haynes, Alice. *See* Grow, Alice (Haynes)
Haynes, Carrie, 13,432
Haynes, Dora (Fellows) [Mrs. John Randolph], **1,058**
Haynes, Edward (1805-91), 7,491
Haynes Family (NC), **13,432**
Haynes, Harriet J., 5,871
Haynes, Inez (1873-1970). *See* Irwin, Inez (Haynes) [Mrs. Will] (1873-1970)
Haynes, John Randolph, **1,058**
Haynes, Lillian (1873-1971). *See* Tangney, Lillian (Haynes) [Mrs. James H.] (1873-1971)
Haynes, Louisa (Bunker), 13,432
Haynes, Minnie Lee Prince (1881-), 16,780
Haynes, Violet A., 16,030
Haynesworth, Elizabeth, 105
Haynesworth, Malvina Ann (Arthur), 2,180
Haynie, Zillah. *See* Brandon, Zillah (Haynie) [Mrs. Francis Lawson]
Haynsworth, Maria L., **13,029**
Hays, C. M., 3,713
Hays, George P., 5,370
Hays, Mary, 12,206
Hays, Mary (Ludwig). *See* McCauley, Mary (Ludwig) Hays
Hays, Mary Blanche Nichols (1876-1964), **4,802**
Hays, Rosemary, 1,655
Hays, Sarah Ann (1805-94). *See* Mordecai, Sarah Ann (Hays) (1805-94)
Hays, Sue Brown [Mrs.], **9,640**
Hayward, Florence, **10,164**
Hayward Hill and Valley Club (CA), **977**
Hayward, Jeannette. *See* Yeatman, Jeannette (Hayward)
Hayward, Mrs. William, 978
Hayward Union High School (CA), 979
Haywood, "Big Bill," 8,123
Haywood Family (NC), 13,471
Haywood, Martha [Miss], **13,433**
Hayworth, Rita, 592
Hazard, Aline W. [Mrs.] (1895-), **17,650**
Hazard Anna (Rodman) (1761-1845), 15,294
Hazard, Caroline (1856-1945), 2,160, 2,411, **7,569**, 7,574, 15,377
Hazard Family, 9,113
Hazard Family (RI), 7,569

Hazard, Grace Walcott (1878-1958). *See* Conkling, Grace Walcott (Hazard) (1878-1958)
Hazard, Helen. *See* Bacon, Helen (Hazard) [Mrs. Nathaniel Terry]
Hazard, Sarah (1781-1847). *See* Howland, Sarah (Hazard) [Mrs. John Hicks] (1781-1847)
"Hazel" (television program), 17,958
Hazel Green Academy (KY), 5,301
Hazel Green Academy (KY), Former Students Association, 5,301
Hazel, Sister Francesca, 5,399
Hazelrigg Family (GA), 3,032
Hazeltin, Alice Isabel [Miss] (1878-1959), **12,007**
Hazeltine, Mary Emogene [Miss] (1868-1949), **17,770**
Hazeltine, Olivia A. (Brown), 17,651
Hazelton, Alice K., 9,121
Hazelton, Elizabeth Clara (Reynolds) [Mrs. W.E.], **1,439**
Hazelton Family, **1,630**
Hazelwood, Rachel (pseudonym). *See* Kitchelt, Florence Ledyard (Cross) (1874-1961)
Hazelwood School (Lac Qui Parle, MN), 9,316
Hazen, Charlotte de la Saussaye, 2,621
Hazen, Florence. *See* Miller, Florence (Hazen) [Mrs. B. G.]
Hazen, Helen E., 3,767
Hazen, Mildred (McLean). *See* Dewey, Mildred (McLean) Hazen [Mrs. George]
Hazlett, Fanny, 10,680, **10,762**
Hazzard, Alice, 11,746
Hazzard, Florence (Woolsey) (1903-), **6,637**, **7,230**, 7,872, **11,605**
Hazzard, Marion (Lord) (1891-), **5,884**
Hazzard, Mrs. George, 8,953
"He Was Never Seen Again (or Husband's Folly)" (song), 10,540
Head, Alice M., 689
Head, Elizabeth, 15,104
Head Chief, 10,313
Head, Cloyd, 4,005
Head, Edith (1899-), **17,802**
Head Family (GA), **3,033**
Head, Idress Adaline (1874-?). *See* Alvord, Idress Adaline (Head) (1874-?)
Head, Lydia Bush-Brown (1887-), 7,200
Head Start, 8,639, 14,605, 16,259, 17,270
Headhunting in the Solomon Islands Around the Coral Sea (book), 2,500
Headley, Katy (McCaleb), **9,641**
Headman, Mary Hoss, 9,869
Headmistress Association of the Middle West, 11,351
Heald, Sarah Thorp, **9,122**
Healey, Caroline Wells (1822-1912). *See* Dall, Caroline Wells (Healey) (1822-1912)
Healey, Dorothy Ray [Mrs.] (1914-), **993**, 1,654
Health. *See* Hygiene
Health agencies, voluntary. *See* Voluntary health agencies
Health and Hospitals Governing Commission of Cook County (IL), 3,954
Health and Welfare Council, Inc. (Philadelphia, PA), **15,206**
Health associations (non-public). *See* Voluntary health agencies
Health boards, 235, 238, **1,121**, **3,608**, 6,009, 6,123, 8,045, 13,994, **14,912**, **17,515**
  officials and employees, 14,006
Health care. *See* Medical care
Health cooperatives. *See* Health maintenance organizations
Health education, 1,560, 6,642, **11,627**, 17,230
Health facilities, 5,457, 17,826
Health facilities, national, 11,885
Health Food. *See* Food, Natural
Health Forum, 6,123
Health insurance. *See* Insurance, health
Health maintenance organizations, 9,180
Health-officers, 3,482, **6,209**, 8,540, 17,925
Health reports, Municipal. *See* Municipal reports
Health resorts, watering-places, etc., 4,680, 11,443
Health Resources Advisory Commission, 6,919
Health services administration, 11,846
Healy, George Peter Alexander (1813-94), 2,749
Healy, H. Carson, 16,503

Heap, Jane, 17,843
"Hear That Trumpet Talk," 18,000
Heard, Albert 6,196
Heard, Augustine (1827-1905), 7,053
Heard, Elizabeth Ann Farley [Mrs. George
Washington] (1802-63), **7,053**
Heard Family (MA), **6,196**
Heard, George Alexander, 3,404
Heard, John (1824-94), 7,053, 7,054
Heard, Mary, **7,054**
Heard, Mary Livingston [Mrs. Albert], 6,196
Hearn, Jane K., 16,919
Hearnes, Betty Cooper [Mrs. Warren E.], 9,985
Hearnes, Warren E. (1923-), **9,985**
Hearst Castle (San Simeon, CA), 302
Hearst Domestic Industries (CA), 596
Hearst, George (1820-91), 540, 10,137, 17,973
Hearst Historical Schoolhouse (Anaconda, MO),
10,137
Hearst, Millicent Veronica (Willson) [Mrs. William
Randolph, Sr.], 411, 702
Hearst, Mrs. W. R., 17,465
Hearst, Phoebe (Apperson) [Mrs. George]
(1842-1919), 215, 355, 391, **540**, 596, 707, 787,
876, 1,314, 1,474, 1,483, 4,133, 4,695, **10,137**,
10,509, 11,547, **17,973**
Hearst, William Randolph, 540, 678, 1,328, 1,474,
5,505, 10,137, 11,928, 17,973
Hearst, William Randolph, Jr., 10,137, 10,677
Heart
abnormalities and deformities, 11,932
diseases, 11,932
surgery, 8,906
surgery, pediatric, 11,932
Heart Is a Lonely Hunter, The (book), 3,059
"Heart of an Artichoke" (ms), 14,663
Heart of Arethusa, The (book), 5,315
Heart of Rachel, The (book), 692
Heart of Spain (book), 2,423
Heart Throbs of the West (book), 16,525
"Heart to Heart Talk with the Farm Women of
Missouri, A," 9,988
Hearth-Fire (book), 3,159
Hearthstone Club of Hartford (CT), **1,913**
Heartsill, Fannie A., **16,084**
Heat engineering, 11,903
Heat exchangers, design and construction, 15,575
Heat Songs (book), 14,984
Heath, Anna Barnes, **10,165**
Heath, Fannie (Mahood) [Mrs. Frank Arnold]
(1864-1931), **13,653, 13,709**
Heath, Mabel (1885-1949). *See* Palmer, Mabel
(Heath) [Mrs. B. J.] (1885-1949)
Heathen Women's Friend (periodical), 5,173, 8,528
Heathman, Mary (1816-95). *See* Smith, Mary
(Heathman) [Mrs. John A.] (1816-95)
Heaton Family (NY), **11,395**
Heaton, Lucia (ca. 1856-1944), 11,392, 11,395
Heaton, Margaret C., 16,867
Heaton, Mary Marvin (1874-1966). *See* Vorse, Mary
Marvin (Heaton) (1874-1966)
Hebard, Grace Raymond (1861-1936), 14,628,
17,885, **17,906**, 17,908, 17,941, 17,953, **17,974**,
17,985, 17,995
Hebrew, The (CA), 1,002
Hebrew Benevolent Society (Los Angeles, CA), 1,000
Hebrew Female Orphans Dowry Society of the
United States, **7,535**
Hebrew Immigrant Aid Society (Philadelphia, PA),
15,155
Hebrew Ladies Aid Society (CO), 13,790
Hebrew Ladies Aid Society (Rochester, NY), **12,822**
Hebrew Ladies Aid Society (OH), **13,791**
Hebrew Ladies Aid Society (WV), **13,789**
Hebrew Ladies Benevolent Society (GA), **13,792**
Hebrew Ladies' Benevolent Society (St Paul, MN).
See Jewish Relief Society of St. Paul (MN)
Hebrew Ladies Free Loan Society of Seattle (WA),
17,276
Hebrew Sunday School Society (Philadelphia, PA),
2,362, **15,156**
Hebrew Trades Council (IL), 1,656
Hebrew Union College, faculty, **13,810**
Hebrew University (Israel), 7,554

Hebrew University (Israel), Institute for
Contemporary Jewry, 11,915
Hecht House, 6,900
Hecht, Irene W. D., **14,577**
Hecht, Lina Frank (1848-?), 7,525
Hecht, Mrs. Fred, 4,938
Hecht, Winifred. *See* Moffit, Winifred (Hecht) [Mrs.
John T.]
Heck, Barbara (Ruckle) [Mrs. Paul] (1734-1804),
13,434
Heck, Fannie Exile Scudder (1862-1915), 13,434,
13,641
Heck, J. M., **13,434**
Heckle, Mary [Mrs.] (1850-?), 956
Heckler, Margaret, 6,710
Heckman, Pearl (1886-?). *See* Gattini, Pearl
(Heckman) (1886-?)
Hecyra, 9,997
Hedda Gabler (drama), 15,672
Hederman, Ellen [Miss], **9,642**
Hedge, Frederic Henry (1805-90), 6,833
Hedge, Lucy (Pierce) [Mrs. Frederic Henry], 6,833
Hedgerow (book), 6,072
Hedges, Charles H., 12,311
Hedges, Cornelius (1831-1907), 10,315
Hedges, Emma (Shipman) [Mrs. Charles Hedges],
12,311
Hedges Family (MT), **10,315**
Hedges, Virginia Gilkeson, 10,211
Hedgpeth, Ruth, 2,284
Hedlund, Marilou, **3,853**
Hedrick Helen, 12,537
Hedstrom, Olaf G., 10,909
Heeding College (Bloomington, IL). *See* Illinois
Wesleyan University
Heerman, Edward Edson, **9,124**
Heerman, Minnie (1864-?), 2,863, 16,352
Heffelfinger, Elizabeth, **9,307**
Hefferan, Helen Maley [Mrs. William H.]
(1865-1963), 3,785, 3,787
Heflin, James Thomas (1869-1951), **110**
Hegan, Alice Caldwell (1870-1942). *See* Rice, Alice
Caldwell (Hegan) [Mrs. Cale Young] (1870-1942)
Hegeman, Ann Eliza. *See* Rosecrans, Ann Eliza
(Hegeman) [Mrs. William Starke]
Hegeman Family, 1,050
Heger, Mary Lea. *See* Shane, Mary Lea (Heger)
[Mrs. Charles D.]
Hegland, Georgina Dieson [Mrs. Martin] (1882-),
8,806
Hegland, Martin (1880-1967), **8,806**
Hegner, Bertha Hofer [Mrs. Herman Frederick]
(1862-1937), **3,974**
Heiberber, Ida J., 6,697
Heidbreder, Edna, 7,583
Heide, Wilma Scott, 6,794
Heidelburg College (Tiffin, OH), faculty, 17,994
Heidt, Christian I., **3,525**
Heidt Family (GA), **3,524**
Heidt, John, 3,524
Heidt, Leila (Villard) [Mrs. John], 3,524
Heidt, Mary [Mrs. Christian I.], 3,525
Height, Dorothy I. (1912-), 11,817
Heiker, Mother Aloysius, 4,876
Heilbron, Bertha Lion (1895-197?), **9,125**, 9,179,
9,230, 9,251
Hein, Marjorie, 11,913
Hein, Sophie, 9,333
Heineman, Mrs. Walter, 3,787
Heines, Sister Virginia S. C. N. (1896-), **5,372**, 5,373
Heinlen, Anna J., 541
Heinlen Family, **541**
Heinlen, Mary E., 541
Heinrich, Abel, 13,890
Heinsen, Christianne Emilie (1846-1923). *See* Jensen,
Christianne Emilie (Heinsen) [Mrs. Erich
Rickert] (1846-1923)
Heinsen, Dorothea (Pinion) [Mrs. Newton], 982
Heinsen, Emilie (1852-1926). *See* Jensen, Emilie
(Heinsen) [Mrs. Jens Christian] (1852-1926)
Heinsen, Marie (Arfsten), 982
Heinzen, Henriette M., 17,589
Heinzen, Karl Peter (1809-80), **7,999**
Heirs of Old Venice (book), 17,723

Heiskell, Marion Sulzberger [Mrs. Andrew] (1918-),
11,827, 12,078
Heisler, Tibor, **4,029**
Heistad, Anna, 4,127
Heitzer, M., 6,778
Helbig, Agnes, 4,958
Helbig, Esther, 4,958
Helburn, Theresa (1887-1959), 6,008, 12,451, 14,413
Held, Anna (1865?-1918). *See* Ziegfeld, Anna Held
[Mrs. Maximo] Carrera [Mrs. Florenz]
(1865?-1918)
"Held by the Enemy" (story), 9,623
Held in Splendor (book), 15,720
Held in Splendor (drama), 15,700
"Helen and Warren" (stories), 12,219
Helen Keller In Her Story (moving-picture), 11,812
Helena Business Women's Suffrage Club (MT),
10,316
Helena Christian, Princess, 12,301
Helena Herald (MT), 10,305
Helicon Hall (NJ), 3,775
Helicon Home Colony, 8,077
Helicopters, piloting, 31
Heller Committee, 561
Heller, Edmund (1875-1939), **2,719**
Heller, Elizabeth (Wright) [Mrs. John] (1860-1950),
4,958
Heller, Eugenie M. [Miss], **12,506**
Heller, Fredericka, 15,134
Heller, Janet, **17,652**
Heller, John, 4,958
Heller, Judith, 2,205
Hellermen, Helen West, 2,765
Helliwell, Harriet E., 8,617
Hellman, Clarisse Doris [Mrs. Norman Pepper]
(1910-73), **12,009**
Hellman, George S., 12,035
Hellman, Lilian [Miss] (1905-), 60, 556, 2,403,
3,468, 10,992, 11,810, 11,825, **16,156**
Hellriegal, Meta [Miss], 15,869
Helm, Edith (Benham) (1874-1962), 2,340, **2,389**,
2,558
Helm, Elizabeth Sager (1837-1925), **11,606, 14,578**
Helm, Emilie (Todd) [Mrs. Ben Hardin], 2,448, 3,907,
5,291, 5,353
Helm Family (MO), 9,870
Helm, Jane Maria Pope [Mrs. John B.], 9,870
Helm, John B., 9,870
Helm, Martha, 14,578
Helm, Sarah E. "Crumpsie" (Crump), 9,870
Helm, William, 14,578
Helmick, Elizabeth A. [Mrs.], 2,695
Helmin, Nellie, 9,323
Helping Hand Club, 12,865
Helping Hand Club (Dayton, NV), 10,680
Helvie, Clara Cook (1876?-1958), **6,253**
Helwing, Anna [Mrs. Sigmund] (1893-1956), **16,894**
Helwing, Sigmund, 16,894
Hematology, 7,288
Hemenway, Augustus (?-1876), 7,477
Hemenway Family (MA), **7,477**
Hemenway, Francis Dana (1830-84), **4,205**
Hemenway, Mary Porter (Tileston) [Mrs. Augustus]
(1820-94), 7,477
Hemenway, Ruth V. (1894-1974), **7,231**
Hemenway, Sara Bixby [Mrs. Francis Dana], 4,205
Hemingway, Ernest, 3,771, 6,023, 9,126, 11,153,
17,843
Hemingway, Mary Welsh [Mrs. Ernest], **9,126**
Hemming, George, 12,409
Hemmy, Mary L., 8,665
Hempel, Marie. *See* Mezerik, Marie (Hempel) [Mrs.
A. G.]
Hempstead, Susan. *See* Gratiot, Susan (Hempstead)
Hempstead, William, 17,643
Hemsley, Florence. *See* Wood, Florence (Hemsley)
[Mrs. William Halsey]
Hench, Mrs. J. B.,
Hendee, Elizabeth (Russell), **12,716**
Henderson, Alexander S. (1859-1944), **219**
Henderson, Alfred R., **10,981**
Henderson, Archibald (1877-1963), 13,001
Henderson, Arthur, 5,511
Henderson, Artie, 1,186

Henderson, Bena M. [Miss], 3,932
Henderson, Elizabeth, **16,085**
Henderson, Elizabeth (?-1812). See Wertmuller, Elizabeth (Henderson) (?-1812)
Henderson, Elizabeth Brownrigg (1875-1975). See Cotten, Elizabeth Brownrigg (Henderson) [Mrs. Lyman A.] (1875-1975)
Henderson, Elizabeth L., 17,125
Henderson, Ellen, 6,335
Henderson, Eva (Stevens) [Mrs. Alexander S.], 219
Henderson Family, 9,849
Henderson Family (DC), **2,720**
Henderson Family (PA), **15,018**
Henderson Family (TX), 16,085
Henderson Female College (NC), 13,420
Henderson, Fred, 8,141
Henderson, Gertrude [Mrs. Ralph A.] (?-1954), **5,107,** 5,108
Henderson, Harold G., 12,043
Henderson House (MI), 7,955
Henderson, Inez (?-1961). See Pond, Inez (Henderson) [Mrs. Charles McHenry] (?-1961)
Henderson, Isabelle Bowen, 13,446
Henderson, John (?-1792), 15,018
Henderson, John Brooks (1826-1913), 2,720
Henderson, Lucy Ann (1835-1923). See Deady, Lucy Ann (Henderson) [Mrs. Matthew] (1835-1923)
Henderson, Lydia, 15,018
Henderson, Mary (1818-87). See Eastman, Mary (Henderson) [Mrs. Seth] (1818-87)
Henderson, Mary (Foote) [Mrs. John Brooks] (1841-1931), 2,720
Henderson, Miss, 1,334
Henderson, Mrs. W. W., 10,032
Henderson, Ruth, 17,775
Henderson, Samuel, **16,085**
Henderson, Sarah E. [Miss], **4,604**
Henderson, Sister Sabina Mary, 4,709
Henderson, Virginia A. **6,143**
Henderson, William, 14,606
Hendley, Anna E. [Mrs.], 2,597
Hendricks, Camilla (ca. 1898-). See Eames, Camilla (Hendricks) [Mrs. Earl] (ca. 1898-)
Hendricks, Drusilla Dorris [Mrs. James] (1810-81), **16,692**
Hendricks, Hetty. See Gomez, Hetty (Hendricks) [Mrs. Aaron Lopez]
Hendricks, Ida. See Chambers, Ida (Hendricks)
Hendricks, Mrs. Thomas A., 14,618
Hendricks, Pearl, **16,086**
Hendricksen, Borghilde "Ole." See Hansen, Borghilde "Ole" (Hendricksen) [Mrs. Burnett]
Hendrickson, Eleanor, 10,901
Hendrickson, Eva. See Klepper, Eva (Hendrickson)
Hendrickson, Jean [Mrs. Max C.], **16,417**
Hendrickson, Viena Johnson [Mrs. Paul] (1898-), 8,949, **9,127,** 9,467
Hendrix, Lillian Metz, 1,798
Heney, Francis J., **14,579**
Heney, M. Alice, 7,920
Henhan, J. P. K., 2,188
Henkel, Susan, 17,771
Hennen, Ann M. [Mrs. Alfred], 787
Hennepin County Anti-Slavery Society (MN), 9,320
Hennepin County Bar Association (MN), **9,128**
Hennepin County Farmer-Labor Party (MN), 9,381
Hennepin County Farmer-Labor Women's Club (MN), **9,129,** 9,232
Hennepin County Federated Clubs (MN), 8,481
Hennepin County Review, 8,470
Hennepin County Sunday School Association (MN), 9,103
Hennepin County War Finance Committee (MN), Women's Division, **9,130**
Hennepin County War Savings Committee (MN), Women's Division. See Hennepin County War Finance Committee (MN), Women's Division
Hennepin County Women's Conference for Defense (MN), 9,349
Hennessey, Agnes, 1,534
Hennessey, Bishop, 4,873
Hennessy, Mame. See Hennessy, Mary L.
Hennessy, Mary L., **11,607**
Henney, Nella Braddy, 7,560

Hennings, Thomas C., Jr. (1903-60), **9,986**
Hennock, Frieda (1904-60). See Simons, Frieda (Hennock) (1904-60)
Henraus, Felicia, 8,477
Henri, Robert, 2,809
Henrickson, Merle E. (1913-), **8,092**
Henrie, Susan (Coleman) (1839-?), **16,522**
Henrie, Thea Annie (Lund), **16,523**
Henrotin, Charles, 6,638
Henrotin, Ellen (Martin) [Mrs. Charles] (1847-1922), 3,814, 3,816, 3,908, **6,638,** 11,547
Henry, Alice (1857-1943), 2,509
Henry, Ann, **542**
Henry, Aurelia Isabel (1877-1948). See Reinhardt, Aurelia Isabel (Henry) [Mrs. George Frederick] (1877-1948)
Henry Booth House (IL), 4,051, 4,085, **4,096**
Henry, Cammie (Garrett) [Mrs. J. H.], 5,448, 5,450
Henry, Charlotte (Prince) [Mrs. Edwin] (1827-1920s), 11,790
Henry Chauncey (ship), 481
Henry County Woman Suffrage Association (IA), 5,068
Henry, Diana Mara (ca. 1947-), **6,639**
Henry Draper Gold Medal, 2,041
Henry VIII and His Court, or Catherine Parr (book), 38
Henry, Elizabeth (1749-1825), 9,762
Henry, Elvira A. (Cabell) [Mrs. Patrick Jr.] (?-1858). See Bruce, Elvira A. (Cabell) [Mrs. Patrick, Jr.] Henry [Mrs. James] (?-1858)
Henry Family, 9,762
Henry Ford Peace Ship, 7,868, 7,923
Henry George, Citizen of the World (book), 2,301
Henry Grady Hospital (GA), Hughes Spalding Pavilion, 3,293
Henry, Harriet (Alexander) [Mrs. Joseph] (1808-82), 2,721
Henry, Harriet (Buchanan) [Mrs. Robert], 14,968
Henry, Henrietta (Mitchell) [Mrs. Robert H.] (?-1958?), **9,643**
Holt, Henry and Company, 14,416
Henry Hyde (ship), 5,707
Henry James: The Major Phase (book), 12,393
Henry, Jane, 8,934
Henry, Joseph (1797-1878), **2,721**
Henry, Leudivine Carmelite Garrett, 5,552
Henry, Lou (1874-1944). See Hoover, Lou (Henry) [Mrs. Herbert] (1874-1944)
Henry, Louisa Forbes, 9,593
Henry, Marguerite (1902-), 8,531
Henry, Marion (Stephenson) [Mrs. James, Jr.] (1888-). See Olden, Marion (Stephenson) [Mrs. James, Jr.] Henry [Mrs. William K.] DeVictor [Mrs. Paul] Coleman-Norton [Mrs. Roger] (1888-)
Henry, Mary Ann (1834-1903), 2,721
Henry, Mary F., 11,662
Henry, Patrick, 9,762
Henry-Ruffin, M. E. [Mrs.], 54
Henry Street Settlement (NY), 2,309, 6,131, 7,299, 8,651, 8,658, 8,661, 11,897, **12,008,** 12,026
Henry Street Settlement Urban Life Center (NY), **8,655**
Henry Street Visiting Nurse Society (NY), 12,657
Henry, Vera (1909-), **14,385**
Henshaw, Catherine (1784-1806), 7,601
Henshaw, Ellen Wilson (McAdoo) (1915-46), 1,530
Henshaw Family (MA), **7,638**
Henshaw, Grace. See Babcock, Grace (Henshaw) [Mrs. Willoughby M., II], 8,929
Henshaw, Phebe Swan [Mrs. William] (1753-1808), 7,638
Henshaw, Ruth, 5,999
Henshaw, Ruth (1772-1848). See Bascom, Ruth (Henshaw) [Mrs. Ezekiel Lysander] (1772-1848)
Henshaw, William (1735-1820), 7,638
Henslee, Mrs. E. P., 3,034
Hensolt, Edith Ashmore [Mrs. Charles] Elder [Mrs. Fred] (1882-1975), **14,386**
Hensolt, Fred, 14,386
Henson, C. C., 5,543
Henson, Nell [Mrs. C. C.] (?-1965), 5,543

Hentz, Caroline Lee (Whiting) [Mrs. Nicholas Marcellus] (1800-56), **111,** 114, 4,962, 13,049
Hentz, Julia Louisa (ca. 1825-?). See Keyes, Julia Louisa (Hentz) [Mrs. John Washington] (ca. 1825-?)
Hepburn, A. Barton, 11,396
Hepburn, Emily (Eaton) [Mrs. A. Barton] (1886-1955), 11,392, 11,396
Hepburn Family (NY), **11,396**
Hepburn, Katharine (1909-), 4,970, 7,272, 7,289, 12,129
Hepburn, Katharine (Houghton) [Mrs. Thomas Norval] (1878-), 7,320, 12,530
Hepburn, Susan (Preston) Christy, 5,359
Her Garden Was Her Delight (book), 6,646
Herald (Chicago, IL), 17,623
Herald (ME), 5,704
Herald (Boston, MA), 6,948
Herald (MN), 8,443
Herald Tribune (NY). See *New York Herald Tribune*
Herald Tribune Sunday Magazine (NY), 12,045
Heraldry, 15,532
Herb Society of America, 7,465
Herbert C. Moffitt Hospital, 1,379
Herbert, Elizabeth (Willard), 2,558
Herbert, Rietta Hines (1911-73), **12,687**
Herbs, **8,424**
Herbst, Josephine (1897-1969), **4,992**
Here and There in Mexico (book), 5,528
Here and There in Shelby County (book), 4,332
"Here's Help" (newsletter), 1,814
Herfuth Award, 17,776
Hering, Mary [Mrs.], **15,479**
Heriot, Catherine, 15,633
Heriot Family (SC), **15,710**
Heriot, Louisa, 15,633
Heriot, Mary Elizabeth. See Sparkman, Mary Elizabeth Heriot [Mrs. James R.]
Heritage Press, 12,040
Herman Husband, A Story of His Life (book), 15,261
Herman, Maida (1891-). See Solomon, Maida (Herman) [Mrs. Harry Caesar] (1891-)
Hermann-Grima House (New Orleans, LA), 5,510
"Hermit Thrush, The" (song), 17,970
Hermitage Palace (Russia), 6,912
Hermitage, The (residence, TN), 15,948
Herndon, Ann (1811-1901). See Maury, Ann (Herndon) [Mrs. Matthew Fontaine] (1811-1901)
Herndon, Ellen Lewis (1837-80). See Arthur, Ellen Lewis (Herndon) [Mrs. Chester Alan] (1837-80)
Herndon, Sarah "Sallie" (Raymond), **10,246, 10,317**
Herne, Chrystal Katharine (1882-1950), 11,457
Herne, James A. (1839-1901), 11,457
Herne, Julie Adrienne (1880-1955), 11,457
Herney, Marie. See Mueller, Marie (Herney)
Hero, Ann, 5,512
Herod, Elizabeth [Mrs. Joseph], 4,856
Herod, Joseph, 4,856
Heroine of the Prairies; A Story of the Oregon Trail (book), 14,574
Heroines of Jericho, 3,934
Herox, Susan Stafford, **11,348**
Heroy, Anne Pluymert (1855-1939), **10,982**
Herpes Seniplex virus, 10,209
Herpetologists, **2,714,** 2,717, **2,723**
Herpetology, 2,714
Herrera, Felicitas, 9,467
Herreshoff, Constance "Connie" (Mills) [Mrs. James Brown, II] (1880-1966), **1,210**
Herrick, Aurelia (Townsend) [Mrs. Horace] (1811-91), 17,029, 17,036
Herrick, Caroline (Parmerly) [Mrs. Myron T.] (?-1918), **13,931**
Herrick, Elinore (Morehouse) (1895-1964), **6,640,** 12,069
Herrick, Horace, 17,036
Herrick, J. Frank, 5,334
Herrick, Mary Clay [Mrs. J. Frank] (1839-?). See Clay, Mary (1839-?)
Herrick, Mary Josephine (1895-), 3,824, **8,093**
Herrick, Mrs. Gerard, 12,218
Herrick, Mrs. James B., 12,237
Herrick, Myron T., 13,931
Herrick, Una B., 10,214, 10,216, 10,218

Herring, David Wells (1858-1940), 13,288
Herring, Harriet, 13,176
Herring, Susan. *See* Taynton, Susan (Herring) Jeffries
Herrington Family, 4,942
Herrington, Mrs. E. F., 3,319
Herrmann, Sister Carolyn (ca. 1915-), **14,787**, 14,791
Herron, Carrie Rand [Mrs. George Davis], 3,996
Herron School of Art, students, 4,625
Hersch, Virginia, 4,323
"Herschella," 12,560
Hershberger, Helena, 5,049
Hershey, Lewis Blaine, 255
Hershiser, Beulah, 10,673
Hershiser, Nettie P. [Mrs. Anthony Emmett], **10,673**
Hershman, Arlene (1934-), **17,975**
Herstein, Lillian (1886-), **3,854**, 4,032, 8,093, 9,443
Hert, Sally Aley, 5,121
Hertha (book), 5,477
Hertig, Marion, 9,942
Hertzog, Ann Brisky, **14,207**
Hertzog, William, 14,207
"Hervey House," 12,426
Heslop, Daisy, 14,861
Hesperian, The (Salem Academy and College, NC), 13,634
Hesperian Literary Society (IA), **4,993**
Hess, Arlene, **16,524**
Hess, Clara (1859-1945). *See* Foster, Clara (Hess) [Mrs. John Marshall] (1859-1945)
Hess, Cora Ryland [Mrs. George H.], 9,131
Hess, Dame Myra (1890-1965), 931, 2,023
Hess, George H. (1873-?), Family, **9,131**
Hess, Margaret (Steed) (1884-), **16,525**
Hess, Nina D., 3,908
Hess, Stephen H. (1933-), **5,142**
Hess, Whitney L., **4,803**
Hessel, Anne, 6,121
Hesselbein, Frances R., 12,111
Hessian flies, 14,944
Heston, Sarah Tyson (1849-1937). *See* Rorer, Sarah Tyson (Heston) (1849-1937)
Heterodoxy to Marie (book), 6,678
Heustis, James Fountain, 13,030
Heustis, Rachel (Lyons) [Mrs. James Fountain], **13,030**
Hewer, Vivian Humphrey (1908-), **8,573**
Hewes, Clair (Hofer) (1898-), **10,763**
Hewes, Elizabeth (1869-1950). *See* Tilton, Elizabeth (Hewes) [Mrs. William] (1869-1950)
Hewes, Patricia Esther Jackson (1900-76), **6,641**
Hewitt, Charles N., 9,195
Hewitt, Dorothy Caleton (1905-). *See* Hutchinson, Dorothy Caleton (Hewitt) [Mrs. Cranford] (1905-)
Hewitt Family, 2,532
Hewitt, Mary, 11,125
Hewitt, Mary Cornwall (1875-1955). *See* Mitchell, Mary Cornwall (Hewitt) [Mrs. Sydney Knox] (1875-1955)
Hewitt Street Cottage School (CA), 648
Hewson, Mary Stevenson, 14,884, 14,890
Hewton, Marion (Bromley) (1880-ca. 1960), **5,888**
Heydrick, Elizabeth (Coltman) (1769-1831), 992
Heyl, Elizabeth (Mitchell) (1864-1956), **14,079**
Heyl, Fanny, 14,079
Heyman, Gertrude (?-1958), **12,507**
Heymann, Lida Gustava, 1,680, 7,923
Heyneman, Julie Helen [Miss] (1868-?), **543**
Heynemann, Marie, 2,396
Heyward, Albert Rhett, 15,604
Heyward, Dorothy Hartzell (Kuhns) [Mrs. DuBose] (1890-1961), 14,447, 15,480
Heyward, DuBose (1885-1940), 15,480, 15,585, **15,603**
Heyward, Emma Barnwell, 15,498
Heyward, Henrietta, 15,498
Heyward, Jane Screven (1864-1939), 15,480, **15,603**
Heyward, Sallie Coles (Green) [Mrs. Albert Rhett] (1849-1929), **15,604**
Heywood Family, 9,077
Heywood, Joseph L., 16,463, 16,693
Heywood, Martha (Spence) [Mrs. Joseph L.] (1812-?), **16,463**, **16,693**, 16,830, **16,895**
Heywood, Mary S., 9,077

Heywood, Rolland T., 9,360
Heywood, Sarah (1838?-1931). *See* Folwell, Sarah (Heywood) [Mrs. William Watts] (1838?-1931)
Heywood, Sarepta [Mrs. Joseph L.], 16,693
"Hezekiah and Miranda" (paintings), 248
Hiatt, Elizabeth (1872-1955). *See* Gregory, Elizabeth (Hiatt) (1872-1955)
Hibbard, Carlisle V. (?-1954), Family, **17,653**
Hibbard, Esther L., 17,653
Hibbard, Mary Eugenie [Miss], **1,665**
Hibbard, Mrs. William Gold, 4,067
Hibbard, Sue Eugenia Lowell [Mrs. Carlisle V.], 17,653
Hibernian Society, 3,555
Hichborn, Elinor Morton (Hoyt) [Mrs. Philip] (1885-1928). *See* Wylie, Elinor Morton (Hoyt). [Mrs. Philip] Hichborn [Mrs. Horace] Wylie [Mrs. William Rose] Benét (1885-1928)
Hichborn, Philip, 2,658
Hickey, Agnes MacCarthy **2,390**
Hickey, Amanda Sanford, 11,605
Hickey, Bertie (Westbrook) [Mrs. Charles Kennedy], **9,644**
Hickey, Margaret A. (1902-), 2,097, 2,701, 9,823, **10,197**, 10,198
Hickman, Amanda. *See* Hickman, Amanda (Hickman) [Mrs. Thomas H.]
Hickman, Amanda (Hickman) [Mrs. Thomas H.], 9,987
Hickman, Cornelia Ann (Bryan) [Mrs. David M.]. *See* Robinson, Cornelia Ann (Bryan) [Mrs. David M.] Hickman [Mrs. John M.]
Hickman, David H., 9,987
Hickman, David M., 9,987
Hickman, Emily (1880-1947), 8,963
Hickman Family (LA, MO), **9,987**
Hickman, John L., 9,987
Hickman, Louise, 9,987
Hickman, Minerva (Wade) [Mrs. William Adams] (1829-1918). *See* Wade, Minerva (1829-1918)
Hickman, Mrs. Peter T., 9,987
Hickman, Naomi. *See* Hickman, Naomi (Hickman) [Mrs. Thaddeus B.]
Hickman, Naomi (Hickman) [Mrs. Thaddeus B.], 9,987
Hickman, Peter T., 9,987
Hickman, Sarah. *See* Young, Sarah (Hickman) [Mrs. Arch]
Hickman, Sarah Francis (1858-?). *See* Hughes, Sarah Francis (Hickman) (1858-?)
Hickman, Thaddeus B., 9,987
Hickman, Thomas H., 9,987
Hickman, Thomas J. (?-1854), 9,987
Hickman, William Adams, 16,838
Hickman, William P. (?-1842), 9,987
Hickok, Lorena [Miss] (1893-1968), **11,489**
Hicks, Anna Louise, 5,123
Hicks Family, 11,644
Hicks, Frances, 9,694
Hicks, Georgia [Miss], 13,597
Hicks, Henry G., 9,044
Hicks, Mabel Claudia, **11,608**
Hicks, Mary, 3,329
Hicks, Mary Amelia (Dana) [Mrs. Charles Spencer] (1836-1927). *See* Prang, Mary Amelia (Dana) [Mrs. Charles Spencer] Hicks [Mrs. Louis] (1836-1927)
Hicks, Mildred (ca. 1880-?), **3,329**
Hicks, Mrs., 2,372
Hicks, Sarah Frances (1827-). *See* Williams, Sarah Frances (Hicks) [Mrs. Benjamin F.] (1827-)
Hicks, T., 7,045
Hicks, Thomas, 5,750
Hickson, Samuel, 8,164
Hicock, Hanna (1767-1850). *See* Smith, Hannah (Hicock) (1767-1850)
Hidatsa Indians, 9,447
Hidden, Ephraim Nelson, 10,806
Hidden, Mary E. [Mrs.], 12,063
Hidden Tree, The (book), 5,296
Hiddy-doddy (drama), 15,700
Hideaways, The (moving-picture), 17,972
Hides and skins, 2,718

Hielscher, Helen Hughes [Mrs. J. A.] (1863-1935), **9,132**
Hieronymo, Sister, 12,790
Hiester Family (CT), **1,955**
Higbee, Emma Isabella (Carroll) [Mrs. Daniel] Seegmiller [Mrs. Myron D.] (1868-1954), **16,694**
Higbee, Florence (Spilsbury) [Mrs. Myron], **16,418**
Higbee, Harriet A. [Mrs.], 7,655
Higbee, Isabel (?-1915), 9,327
Higbee, Lillian. *See* McFarlane, Lillian (Higbee) [Mrs. Erastus "Rass"]
Higbee, Lorine Isabell Lamb, 16,444
Higbee, Myron D., 16,694
Higbee, Rhea (1886-). *See* Wakeling, Rhea (Higbee) [Mrs. Thomas Alma] (1886-)
Higbee Seminary (Memphis, TN), 15,964
Higgenson, Ella, **17,131**
Higgins, Ella Maria (Rowell) (1852-1904), 2,002
Higgins, Juanda, 11,827
Higgins, Margaret, 1,534
Higgins, Margaret (1879-1966). *See* Sanger, Margaret (Higgins) (1879-1966)
Higgins, Mrs. J. S., 14,618
Higgins, Mrs. John J., 10,889
Higgins, Nancy Meribah (Behunin) [Mrs. Nelson] (1839-1910), **16,695**
Higgins, Verna (Comins) [Mrs. Rosco], 5,644
Higginson, Colonel, 6,443
Higginson, Ella (Rhoades) (1862-1940), 342, **17,277**
Higginson, Mary Potter Thacher (1844-1941), 7,131
Higginson, Thomas Wentworth (1823-1911), 5,922, 5,944, 5,949, 6,587, 6,636, 7,648
High C (drama), 12,651
High, Isabelle "Belle" (Boyd) [Mrs. Samuel Wylde, Jr.] Harding [Mrs. John Swainston] Hammond [Mrs. Nathaniel Rue, Jr.] (1844-1900), 9,919
High Lonesome World (book), 6,006
High, Mary Susan (1875-1958). *See* Brisco, Mary Susan (High) Casey (1875-1958)
High, Pearl (1886-). *See* Stansel, Pearl (High) [Mrs. Horace Sylvan] (1886-)
High Point Garden Club (NC), **13,293**
High school principals, 3,191
High school students, 1,779, 3,831, **5,879**, 5,885, **5,943**, 6,008, 7,773, 7,891, **8,335**, **8,359**, **9,153**, **9,992**, 11,549, 13,430, 17,090
High school teachers, **1,610**, 2,446, 2,868, 3,463, 3,772, **4,124**, **4,181**, **4,268**, **4,625**, 4,814, **4,820**, 6,724, 7,829, **8,042**, 8,476, 8,617, 9,367, **9,636**, **9,724**, 10,087, **10,113**, **10,456**, 11,713, **12,386**, 13,839, 14,152, **15,046**, 15,178, **15,188**, **16,000**, 17,035, **17,140**, 17,393, **17,445**
High school teachers, Afro-American, 4,147
High schools, 78, 789, **1,300**, 1,534, 2,130, 3,132, 3,153, 3,165, **3,191**, 3,215, 3,224, 3,241, 3,255, 3,256, 4,487, 4,660, 5,314, **5,340**, 5,515, 5,519, **5,685**, 6,724, 7,646, 8,044, 8,317, **9,100**, 9,542, 9,636, 9,672, 9,724, 10,975, 13,588, 14,540, 15,011, 15,644, 16,998, 17,841
   alumnae, **5,355**
   curricula, 17,140
High Trails (book), 17,305
Highbaugh, Irma (?-1973), 5,171
Higher education, 2,925
Higher Than the Sky (book), 2,768
Highet, Frank Brewster, 12,222
Highet, Gilbert, 2,331, 11,168, 12,035
Highet, Isabella Boudinot [Mrs. Frank Brewster] (1859-1926), **12,222**
Highland Home College (AL), 114
Highland Park College (IA), alumnae, 4,960
Highland Social Club (IA), 4,960
Highland Turnpike Company, 12,600
Highlander Education and Research Center (Knoxville, TN), 17,691
Highlander Folk School (TN), 6,893, 17,594
   faculty, 15,977
Highlands Folk School, 2,879
Hight, Mary A., **11,609**
Highway beautification. *See* Roadside improvement
Highway construction. *See* Road construction
Highway departments, 5,443, 14,556
Highway law, 12,952
Highway planning, 17,279

Highway relocation, 14,671
Hilbert, Mother Mary Colette, 11,476
Hilbourne, Charlotte, 7,069
Hilburger, Jessie (Cantwell) (1887-1971), **17,170**
Hildebrand, Edith Fly [Mrs. Walter Junius], **16,087**
Hildebrand, Rhea (Boynton), 362
Hildebrand, Walter Junius, 16,087
Hildeburn, Charles R. (1855-1901), **15,019**
Hildegard, Evelyn "Diamond Tooth Lil" [Mrs.], 1,779
Hilger, Sister Inez (1891-), **2,839,** 8,848
Hill, Ada E. S. [Mrs.], **17,160**
Hill, Alberta (Kirchner) [Mrs. Leslie A.] (1898-),
  9,133
Hill, Alice (Hale) [Mrs. Nathaniel Peter], **1,717**
Hill, Alice (Polk) (1854-1921), **1,718**
Hill, Alice (Stewart) [Mrs. Francis B.], **1,786**
Hill, Almoron, 14,628
Hill and Valley Club (Beldenville, WI), **17,856**
Hill, Arthur, 6,756
Hill, Benjamin F., 3,359
Hill, Benjamin Harvey, 3,008
Hill, Bethenia Angelina (Owens) [Mrs. Legrand]
  (1840-1926). *See* (Owens)-Adair, Bethenia
  Angelina [Mrs. Legrand] Hill [Mrs. John]
  (1840-1926)
Hill, Caroline (1854-1914). *See* Behunin, Caroline
  (Hill) [Mrs. Mosiah Steven] (1854-1914)
Hill, Caroline H., 6,619
Hill, Cassie [Mrs.], 956
Hill, Catherine Snedeker [Mrs.] (ca. 1843-90), **4,994**
Hill, Charles, 8,068
Hill, Charles A., 15,439
Hill, Crawford (1862-1922), **1,719**
Hill, Daniel Chapman, Family (TX), 16,272
Hill, Daniel Harvey, Jr., **13,436**
Hill, Edith Naomi (1882-1975), 7,158
Hill, Edward Coke (1866-1961), 14,581
Hill, Elise (Weyerhaeuser) [Mrs. W. B.] (1860-1946),
  9,433
Hill, Elizabeth McDowell, 4,369
Hill, Ella "Billie" (Wilson) [Mrs. Edward Coke]
  (1877-1962), 14,581
Hill, Ethel Osborn [Mrs.] (1880-), **16,197**
Hill, Eunice, **12,223**
Hill, Evelyn (Corthell) [Mrs. John], 17,894
Hill Family, 3,398
Hill Family (OR), **14,387**
Hill Family (SC), **15,439**
Hill Family (TX), 16,271
Hill Family (WA), 17,195
Hill, Frances [Mrs.], 13,429
Hill, Frank Ernest, **12,010**
Hill, Grace (Livingston) [Mrs. Thomas Guthrie
  Franklin]. [Mrs. Flavius J.] Lutz (1865-1947),
  1,224, 14,828
Hill, Hannah, 14,981
Hill, Hattie (Green) [Mrs. William J.], **16,361**
Hill, Heald William Lair, 14,581
Hill, Henry (1847-1905), 14,387
Hill, Ida Linda (Blasienz) [Mrs. Ernest C.] (1895-),
  16,270
Hill Is Level, The (book), 5,011, 12,042
Hill, James Jerome (1838-1916), 8,934
Hill, James Jerome (residence), 9,467
Hill, Jane Louise (Allston) [Mrs. Charles A.]
  (1850-1937), 15,439, 15,440
Hill, Jasper, 14,305
Hill, John, 14,305
Hill, John A. (1858-1912), 11,889
Hill, John W., **13,437**
Hill, Julia (Chandler) [Mrs. William Lair]
  (1844-1932), 14,581
Hill, Kate Alexander (1873-1960), **15,172**
Hill, Kate "Katie" Adele (1900-), **16,271, 16,360**
Hill, Katharine Ledyard, **1,849,** 11,282
Hill Land and Investment Company, 1,719
Hill, Laura Pitcher, 11,440
Hill, Louise Sneed [Mrs. Crawford] (1861-1955),
  1,719
Hill, Mabel Peterson, **8,745**
Hill, Margaret (1736-1816). *See* Morris, Margaret
  (Hill) (1736-1816)

Hill, Margaret (1877-1973). *See* Smith, Margaret
  (Hill) (1877-1973)
Hill, Marie, 13,108
Hill, Mart T. [Mrs. James J.], 13,652
Hill, Mary A., 388
Hill, Mary Theresa Mehegan [Mrs. James Jerome]
  (1846-1921), 9,055
Hill, May Ashmore Thropp [Mrs. William Holcombe]
  (1899-1967), **11,610**
Hill, Mollie (Watson), **14,580**
Hill, Mrs. Crawford, 1,752
Hill, Mrs. Homer, 15,864
Hill, Nathaniel P., 1,719
Hill, Nelle May (1868-1900). *See* Denlinger, Nelle
  May (Hill) (1868-1900)
Hill, Noadiah M., 12,223
Hill, Patty Smith [Miss] (1868-1946), **5,346,** 11,864
Hill, Phoebe (Apperson) (1842-1919), **1,539**
Hill, Rebecca, 13,031
Hill, Reuben Chandler, 14,581
Hill Road, The (book), 4,622
Hill, Ruth (Davis) [Mrs. Roscoe] (1914-67), **10,472**
Hill, Ruth Nickel [Mrs. Frank Ernest], 12,010
Hill, Samuel (?-1859), 13,013
Hill, Samuel H., 4,324
Hill, Sarah, 14,628
Hill, Sarah (1801-54). *See* Fletcher, Sarah (Hill) [Mrs.
  Calvin] (1801-54)
Hill, Sarah Miltia (1895-), **16,272**
Hill Securities, Land and Development Company,
  1,719
Hill, Stella Baker [Mrs. Benjamin], 3,359
Hill, Susan Letitia (Whipple) [Mrs. Zaccheus]
  (1826-94), 9,345
Hill, Therese (Christiansen) [Mrs. Reuben], 7,133
Hill, Thomas B., Jr. (1813-88), 13,031
Hill, Virgie (1915-). *See* Fiveash, Virgie (Hill) [Mrs.
  Wilburn] (1915-)
Hill, William J., **16,361**
Hill, William Lair (1838-1924), **14,581**
Hill, Zina Larsen (1888-), 3,739
Hillard, Harriet [Mrs. John], 12,551
Hillborn, Fanny, 15,271
Hillcrest Children's Center (DC), **2,391**
Hilleboe, Gertrude M. [Miss] (1888-1976), **8,746,**
  8,809, 8,815
Hilleboe, Sjur H., 8,746
Hillel Foundation (MN), 9,218
Hiller, Ada, 14,616
Hilles, Florence (Bayard) [Mrs. William S.]
  (1866-1954), 2,036, 2,063, 6,742, 11,123
Hilles, Gulielma Maria (1822-1907). *See* Howland,
  Gulielma Maria (Hilles) [Mrs. Charles]
  (1822-1907)
Hilles, Margaret H., 2,044
Hilles, Margaret H. (1786-1882), 14,845
Hilles, Martha, 2,044, 2,060
Hillfinger, Deanne, 3,752
Hillhouse High School (Fair Haven, CT), 2,009
Hilliard, Barber, 9,587
Hilliard, Elbert, 9,587
Hilliard, Frances "Fanny" (1841-62), 2,457
Hilliard, Harriet (Low) [Mrs. John H.] (1809-77),
  2,457
Hilliard, Isaac H., Jr., 9,645
Hilliard, Mary (1844-1944). *See* Loines, Mary
  (Hilliard) [Mrs. Stephen] (1844-1944)
Hilliard, Mrs. Isaac H., **9,645**
Hillis, Cora Bussey (1858-1924), 4,805, **4,915,** 4,996
Hillis, Hazel M., 4,915
Hillman, Adelia [Mrs.], 9,553
Hillman, Bessie (Abramowitz) [Mrs. Sidney], 11,809
Hillman Hospital (AL), 21
Hillman Hospital (AL), Board of Lady Managers, 21
Hillman Hospital Training School for Nurses (AL).
  See University of Alabama in Birmingham School
  of Nursing
Hillman, Sidney, 7,300
Hills, Gertrude [Mrs.], 223, 12,282
Hills, Laura Coombe, 3,097, 6,452
Hills of Yesterday, The (book), 10,487
Hillsboro Crusade (OH), **13,998**
Hillsboro Crusade Sketches and Family Records
  (book), 13,963

Hillsborough Military Academy, 15,729
Hillsdale College (MI), 7,929
  faculty, 8,164
Hillsdale Woman's Club (MI), **7,813**
Hillside Home for Boys (MA), 7,477
Hillside Home School (WI), 17,661
Hillyer Family, **3,035**
Hillyer, John, 3,036
Hillyer, Junius (1807-86), 3,035
Hillyer, Mrs. John Freeman, **3,036**
Hilton, Eunice M. (1899-1975). *See* Vreeland, Eunice
  M. [Mrs. John] Freeland (1899-1975)
Hilton Head (SC), 15,744
Hilton, Jane, 17,884
Hilton, Margaret, 1,114
Hilton, Mrs. Afton B. (1873-1958), **8,433**
Himes, Agnes, 14,621
Himes, George H., 14,513, 14,584
Himes, Norman E. (1899-1949), **6,223,** 7,192
Himrod, Anna, **9,134**
Hinchliff, Emerson, 11,670
Hinckley, Caroline. *See* Spear, Caroline (Hinckley)
  [Mrs. John Murray]
Hinckley, Isabella Mack (1842-?), 5,966
Hinckly, Eliza (1819-?). *See* Landon, Eliza (Hinckly)
  (1819-?)
Hindemith, Paul, 468
Hindley, Jane Charters (Robinson) [Mrs. John]
  (1828-1907), **16,696**
Hindman Settlement School (KY), **5,254,** 5,255
Hinds, Alma, 8,340
Hinds County Federation of Woman's Clubs (MS),
  9,673
Hinds, Edna, 8,340
Hinds, Henry Harrison (1840-?), **8,340**
Hinds, Katherine Powell, 9,770
Hinds, Mary Sherwood [Mrs. Henry], 8,340
Hindu Conspiracy Trial, 1,178
Hine, Lewis W., **3,037**
Hines, Earl, 5,534
Hines, Emma Elinor (1869-?). *See* Young, Emma
  Elinor (Hines) (1869-?)
Hines Family, 8,966
Hines, Harvey K., 14,536
Hines, Leone, **13,438**
Hines, Nelle Womack, 3,071
Hines, Wait, **13,438**
Hinkley, Anne (Keemlé) [Mrs. Edward Otis], 5,776
Hinkley, Edward Otis (1824-96), **5,776**
Hinkley, Laura (1875-1949), **4,995**
Hinkson, Katherine (Tynan) (1861-1931), 7,690
Hinman, Eleanor Hamlin [Miss] (1899-), **10,473**
Hinman, Kate (Bailey) [Mrs. George W.]
  (1871-1970), **2,014**
Hinman, Mary Wood, 12,363
Hinman, Porter T., 4,782
Hinsdale Community Service Club (IL), 4,278
Hinsdale, Ellen Clarinda (1864-1958), 7,814
Hinsdale, Ellen Roselle, 1,751
Hinsdale Family (MI), **7,814**
Hinsdale Junior Infant Welfare (IL), 4,278
Hinsdale, Mary Louisa (1866-1946), 7,814
Hinsdale, Mildred (1871-1971), 7,814
Hinsdale Music Club (IL), 4,278
Hinsdale Woman's Club (IL), 4,278
Hinterminster, Miss, 4,233
Hinton, Fanny D. [Miss], **3,200**
Hinton, Isabella. *See* Harris, Isabella Hinton [Mrs.
  James Henry]
Hinton, Leila. *See* Callaway, Leila (Hinton) [Mrs.
  Morgan]
Hinton, Mary Hilliard [Miss] (?-1961), **13,032,** 13,516
Hinton, Richard S., 14,080
Hintz Family (PA), **14,910**
Hintz, Friedrich, 14,910
Hintz, Maria [Mrs. Friedrich], 14,910
Hinz, Anita (1875-1955). *See* Gundlach, Anita
  (Hinz) [Mrs. Heini] (1875-1955)
Hinz, August C., 522
Hinz, Dora Wieger [Mrs. August C.], 522
Hinz, Friedrich. *See* Hintz, Friedrich
Hinz, Helene. *See* Davis, Helene (Hinz) [Mrs. Edwin
  W.]
Hipple, Ruth B. [Mrs.], 15,864, 15,868

Hippodrome Theater (NY), 12,444
Hiram College (OH), students, 13,949
Hiram House (Cleveland, OH), 4,141
Hiram House (Cleveland, OH), Boy's Game Club, 4,141
Hiram, Ida Mae Johnson, 3,038
Hiroshima, 7,212
Hirsch, Elsie. *See* Langsdorf, Elsie (Hirsch) [Mrs. Alexander J.]
Hirsch, Jean E. (1893-1974). *See* Fish, Jean E. (Hirsch) [Mrs. Horace P.] (1893-1974)
Hirsch, Lydia (Becker), **16,362**
Hirsh, Alice [Miss], 2,430
Hirsh, Hazel [Miss], 4,781
Hirsh, Selma, 4,493
Hirshhorn, Olga (Zatorsky) [Mrs. Joseph], 1,837
Hirth, Emma, 8,670
Hirth, Emma P., 12,738
Hirth, William (1875-1940), **9,988**
His Majesty the Queen (book), 12,488
Hisel, Mrs. O. R., **14,208**
Hispanic Society of America, 2,110, 2,112, 11,866
Histamine, 10,207
Historians, **172, 195,** 209, **259,** 395, 974, **1,044,** 1,187, 1,189, **1,333,** 1,420, 1,426, **1,476, 1,496, 1,501,** 1,638, 1,642, **1,676, 1,752,** 1,901, **1,926, 1,939,** 1,958, 1,975, 2,135, **2,173,** 2,174, 2,188, **2,250, 2,275,** 2,333, **2,361, 2,365, 2,411, 2,425, 2,446,** 2,540, 2,550, 2,619, **2,626,** 2,721, **2,744, 2,790, 2,900, 3,418, 3,420,** 3,465, 3,714, **3,998,** 4,408, **4,445,** 4,520, **4,829,** 4,916, 5,414, **5,415, 5,575, 5,578, 5,592, 5,606,** 5,808, 5,824, **5,870, 5,960,** 6,234, **6,301,** 6,336, **6,342, 6,389, 6,448,** 6,518, **6,559, 6,607, 6,684, 6,921,** 7,011, **7,136, 7,144,** 7,167, 7,246, **7,540,** 7,603, 7,615, 7,627, 7,647, **7,804, 7,807, 8,084,** 8,441, 8,591, 8,733, 8,953, 9,077, **9,272, 9,414, 9,672,** 9,697, **9,719, 9,841,** 9,892, 9,944, 10,244, **10,356,** 10,366, 10,449, **10,463,** 10,534, 10,544, 10,608, 10,676, 10,760, 10,779, 10,903, 10,990, **11,040,** 11,299, **11,428, 11,432, 11,514, 11,526, 11,828,** 12,011, **12,240,** 12,460, **12,683,** 12,772, 12,846, **12,863,** 13,176, 13,388, **13,672,** 13,728, **13,942,** 14,046, **14,087, 14,095,** 14,544, **14,655,** 14,680, **14,758, 15,061, 15,107,** 15,129, 15,139, 15,197, 15,361, **15,806, 15,860, 15,882,** 15,902, **15,939, 15,950,** 16,038, **16,041, 16,058, 16,083, 16,086, 16,088, 16,098, 16,129, 16,131, 16,400,** 16,410, 16,434, 16,447, 16,448, 16,485, 16,488, 16,529, **16,564,** 16,712, 16,881, **16,882, 16,924, 16,984,** 17,024, **17,048, 17,181, 17,188,** 17,209, **17,368, 17,373,** 17,495, 17,498, **17,667,** 17,868, **17,885, 17,888,** 17,903, 17,908, **17,918,** 17,977, 17,985, 17,997
Historians, Afro-American, **5,535, 17,693**
Historian's World, An (book), 2,411
Historic buildings, 3,549, 3,561, 9,680, 14,289
conservation and restoration, 1,756, 1,892, 2,197, 3,552, 3,600, 4,501, 5,693, 5,924, 6,907, 9,032, 9,048, 10,113, 10,348, 11,434, **11,436,** 12,988, 14,589, 15,518, 15,719, **17,064**
Historic sites, 4,415, 8,391, 8,399, 9,435, **11,185,** 11,923, 13,897, 14,923, 16,924, 17,136
administration, 14,935, 17,125
conservation and restoration, 990, 991, 1,198, 1,649, 2,931, 3,440, **3,441, 3,644,** 3,879, 4,444, 4,977, 5,082, 5,514, 5,829, 9,813, 10,032, **10,302,** 10,637, 10,662, 10,689, **11,877,** 12,847, **13,514,** 14,666, 15,451, 16,485, 17,475
Historical Commission (Charleston, SC), **15,405**
Historical Data Project (ND), **13,654**
Historical fiction, 1,395, 1,397, 5,733, 6,093, 6,103, 7,486, 17,027
Historical markers, 4,860, 9,833, 17,029
Historical museums, 2,888, 5,693
Historical Pageant of Philadelphia (1912), 15,061
Historical record preservation. *See* Archives
Historical Records Survey, 9,741
Historical research, **335**
Historical researchers, 7,774
Historical Sketches, State Teachers College, Livingston, Ala. (book), 81
Historical societies, 203, 938, **1,076,** 1,078, **1,216,** 1,258, **1,324,** 1,333, 1,526, 1,649, **1,659,** 2,197, 2,411, 2,414, **2,507,** 2,900, 3,131, **3,139,** 3,210,

3,222, 3,225, 3,587, **3,610,** 3,633, **3,916, 3,918,** 3,919, 3,920, **3,929, 4,165,** 4,287, **4,315,** 4,444, 4,684, 5,414, **5,693,** 6,203, 6,501, **7,140,** 7,704, 8,452, 8,458, 8,744, **8,768,** 8,821, 8,833, 8,961, 9,002, **9,032, 9,078,** 9,127, **9,184, 9,229, 9,230, 9,257,** 9,371, 9,385, 9,467, **9,574,** 9,599, 9,672, 9,781, **10,114, 10,115,** 10,135, **10,690, 10,716,** 10,727, 10,826, 10,990, **11,113, 11,227, 11,439, 11,863,** 12,581, 12,751, **12,823,** 13,220, 13,267, 13,440, 13,606, 13,609, 13,661, **13,948,** 14,306, 14,641, 14,676, 15,218, **15,363, 15,579, 15,580,** 15,806, **15,838,** 15,948, 15,975, 16,045, 16,058, 16,133, 16,176, 16,241, 16,430, **16,648,** 17,121, **17,136,** 17,160, 17,162, 17,241, **17,587,** 17,667, **17,918**
Historical societies, Finnish-American, 9,502
Historical Society of York County (PA), Women's Auxiliary, **15,363**
History and Art Club (Buffalo, WY), 17,894
History and Literature Club (Tulsa, OK), **14,262**
"History and Stories of Old Centreville" (ms), 9,667
History Class, The, **12,823**
History Class of 1884 (GA), **3,201**
History of American Life, The (book), 6,921
"History of Arizona Women Lawyers and Judges" (ms), 210
"History of Barry County's Home Economics Clubs" (MO), 9,892
"History of Bishop Jacob Foutz, Sr., and family including a story of the Haun's Mill Massacre, religious and social" (ms), 16,576
History of Bolivar County, A (book), 9,551
History of Costume (book), 17,322
History of Delisle and Its Missions (pamphlet), 9,725
"History of Early Societies in Jacksonville," 4,358
"History of Friendship, New York, The," 16,524
History of Iron County and Parowan, the Mother Town, A (book), 16,410
History of Joseph Smith by his Mother, The (book), 16,505
History of Kobe College (book), 7,212
History of Marcus Aurelius, 1,961
History of Mississippi from Indian Times to the Present Day, The (book), 9,636
History of Newburyport, Mass. (book), 11,315
History of New Haven County, Connecticut (book), 1,998
History of Northampton, From Its Settlement in 1654 (book), 7,144
"History of Reverend William Murphy and His Descendants, 1798-1958," **9,989**
History of Science Society, 4,402, 12,009
History of Shark River Hills (book), 10,921
History of the City of New York (book), 7,246
History of the Czechs (Bohemians) in Nebraska (book), 10,527
History of the Donner Party, A Tragedy of the Sierra (book), 644
"History of the First Twenty Years of the Resident Wives Club, 1941-1961, A," 9,885
History of the Illinois Training School for Nurses, A (book), 4,108
History of the Ohio Branch of the Woman's Missionary Society of the Evangelical Church (book), 10,591
History of the Polaris Expedition (book), 11,315
History of the Rise, Progress and Termination of the American Revolution (book), 2,619
History of the "Soldier's Home," Washington, D. C. (book), 2,174
History of the Wisconsin Federation of Women's Clubs (book), 17,747
History of the Woman's Missionary Association of the United Brethren in Christ, Jubilee Edition (book), 10,586
"History of Woman Suffrage in Arizona" (paper), 210
History of Woman Suffrage, The (book), 2,260, 12,834, 15,941
History of Women in Industry (book), 17,757
History of Women in Medicine (book), 15,129
History of Women in Medicine, The: Vol. 2: Medical Women in the Eastern Hemisphere (book), 6,763

History, periodicals, 5,414, 7,246, 9,599, 9,720, 9,781, 13,388, 17,643, 17,674
Hitch, Annie (Delano) (1849-1926), 11,481, 11,482
Hitchcock, Albert Spear (1865-1936), **15,215**
Hitchcock, Alfred, television program, 5,240
Hitchcock, Ann. *See* Sims, Ann (Hitchcock) [Mrs. William Sowden]
Hitchcock, Charles M. (?-1885), 545
Hitchcock Edward (1793-1864), **5,866**
Hitchcock, Eliza "Lillie" W. (1843-1929). *See* Coit, Eliza "Lillie" W. (Hitchcock) (1843-1929)
Hitchcock, Ethan Allen, 2,282
Hitchcock Family (CA), 545
Hitchcock, Helen Sanborn (Sargent) [Mrs. James Ripley Wellman], 12,011
Hitchcock, James Ripley Wellman (1857-1918), **12,011**
Hitchcock, Jane Elizabeth (1813-96). *See* Jones, Jane Elizabeth (Hitchcock) [Mrs. Benjamin Smith] (1813-96)
Hitchcock, Lucretia (1810-91). *See* Losey, Lucretia (Hitchcock) [Mrs. Nehemiah Homand] (1810-91)
Hitchcock, Margaret (Gale) [Mrs. Henry Ethan] (1831-1914), **4,260,** 11,705
Hitchcock, Martha L. [Miss] (1869-1966), 11,611
Hitchcock, Martha Taliaferro (Hunter) [Mrs. Charles M.], 545, **1,086**
Hitchcock, Mary, 5,866
Hitchcock, Orra White, 5,866
Hitchcock Press (MA), 7,624
Hitchcock, Rebecca (1697-1786). *See* Emery, Rebecca (Hitchcock) (1697-1786)
Hitchcock, Sally (1791-1872). *See* Bliss, Sally (Hitchcock) [Mrs. David] (1791-1872)
Hitchcock, Sophia Stevens [Mrs. Stephen]. *See* Page, Sophia Stevens [Mrs. Stephen] Hitchcock [Mrs. William]
Hitchcock, Stephen, 17,035
Hitchens, Dolores (Birk) Olsen (1907-73), 6,060
Hite House Children's Conference, 8,171
Hite, Kathleen, **5,240**
Hite, Minnie (1900-). *See* Moody, Minnie (Hite) (1900-)
Hitler, Adolf, 8,144, 10,060, 12,701, 17,954
Hittell, Amelia, 546
Hittell, Catherine, 546
Hittell, Charles, 546
Hittell, Elise Christine (Wiehe) [Mrs. Theodore Henry] (?-1900), 546
Hittell Family (CA), **546**
Hittell, Franklin, 546
Hitz, Benjamin, **3,983**
Hively, Sara [Mrs. Andrew Paul], 1,790
Hixon, Adrietta Applegate, 14,628
Hjertaas, Ella (1889-1972). *See* Rose, Ella (Hjertaas) [Mrs. Herman] (1889-1972)
Hjorth, Eric, **4,097**
Hlas Jednoty (periodical), 3,928
Hlavacek, Marus (1908-66). *See* Ptak, Marus (Hlavacek) [Mrs. Victor G.] (1908-66)
Hoadley, Charles Jeremy (1828-1900), 1,866
Hoadley, George Edward (1837-1922), 1,866
Hoag, Amanda Josephine Johnson [Mrs. George W.] (1833-?), **1,305**
Hoag, Betty Lochrie [Mrs.] (1914-), 597
Hoag, Joseph, 15,287
Hoar, Elizabeth, 7,045
Hoar, Samuel, 7,045
Hoard, Margaret A., 3,829
Hoard, Sophronia Conant [Mrs. Samuel], 3,891
Hobart, Alice Tisdale (Nourse) (1882-1967), 4,185, 11,940, **14,388**
Hobart College (NY), 11,467
alumnae, 8,957
Hobart, Elizabeth Wills (Rutter) [Mrs. William Mintzer] (1839-1918), **10,983**
Hobart, Emaline Fletcher, 14,557
Hobart, Emily [Mrs. William Hatfield], **14,389**
Hobart, Enoch, 2,392
Hobart Garden Club (IN), **4,590**
Hobart, Hannah (Pratt) [Mrs Enoch] (?-1804), Family (PA), **2,392**
Hobart, Harriet A., 8,816
Hobart, Inez M. (1885-), **8,575**

Hobart, John Henry (1775-1830), 2,392
Hobart, William Hatfield, 14,389
Hobart, William Mintzer, 10,983
Hobart Woman's Club (IN), **4,591**
Hobart Women's Christian Temperance Union (MN), **8,816**
Hobbes, John Oliver (pseudonym). *See* Craigie, Pearl Mary Teresa (Richards) (1867-1906)
Hobbs, Alice "Judy" Seddon [Mrs. Morris Henry], **5,486**
Hobbs, Ann Mary, 7,677
Hobbs, Bill, 5,486
Hobbs, Emma Augusta (Shaw) (1792?-1875), 7,677
Hobbs Family (NC), **13,231**
Hobbs, Fannie P., **9,871**
Hobbs, Mary (Mendenhall) (1852-1930), 13,223, **13,231**
Hobbs, Morris Henry (1892-1967), **5,486**
"Hobby Horse, The" (radio program), 2,385
Hobby, Oveta (Culp) [Mrs. William Pettus] (1905-), **2,393**, 2,680, 2,699, 5,137, **5,143**, 7,904, 8,685, 9,159, 11,857, 13,406, 16,234
Hobhouse, Emily, 1,559
Hobson, Dorothy Ann (1928-), **14,582**
Hobson, Elizabeth 5,735
Hobson, Katherine Thayer, 11,505
Hochbaum, Elfrieda (1877-1962). *See* Pope, Elfrieda (Hochbaum) [Mrs. Paul Russel] (1877-1962)
Hochman, Julius, 15,332
Hochmuth, Marie, 2,540
Hockderffer, George (1864-1955), **196**
Hockensmith, Mrs. M. S., 547
Hockersmith, Martha J. (Gale) (1826-1903), **14,583**
Hockett Family (NC), **13,229**
Hockett, Rachel Branson [Mrs. William H.], 13,229
Hockett, William H., 13,229
Hocking, Agnes, 11,596
Hocking, Ernest, 6,613
Hoctor, Alice, 11,844
Hodapp, Minnie Josephine (Iverson) [Mrs. Frederick] (1889-?), **16,697**
Hodder, Alan, 6,642
Hodder, Jessie (Donaldson) (1867-1931), 6,544, 6,565, **6,642**
Hodgdon, Abbie L., **8,341**
Hodgdon, Mary A., **14,584**
Hodge, Ann. *See* Rodgers, Ann (Hodge) [Mrs. John]
Hodge, Benjamin, **1,440**
Hodge, C. Esther, 6,947
Hodge, Edna Sanders [Mrs. Melvin] (1909-), 5,394
Hodge, Eliza (Patten) Davis [Mrs. Benjamin], 1,440
Hodge, Frances Eliza, 1,440
Hodge, Frederick W., 11,295
Hodge, Margaret W. [Mrs. Frederick W.]. *See* Magill, Margaret W. [Mrs. Frederick W.] Hodge
Hodge, Maria Louisa, 1,440
Hodge, Mrs. Carroll, 6,337
Hodge, Sarah (Bayard) [Mrs. William L.] 2,556
Hodgen, Margaret T. (1890-1977), 916
Hodges, Barbara (Bailey) [Mrs. J. Stanley] (1909-), **8,656**
Hodges, Clara, 13,439
Hodges Family (NC), 13,439
Hodges, Faustina H. [Miss], 12,331
Hodges, John M., **13,439**
Hodges, Joy, **4,764**
Hodges, Louise (Miller) [Mrs. Clarence] (1901-), 7,151
Hodges, Margaret (1911-), 8,531
Hodges, Margaret Manning. *See* Choate, Margaret Manning (Hodges) [Mrs. George]
Hodges, Millie Pearl (1893-1964). *See* Walker, Millie Pearl (Hodges) [Mrs. Lee O.] (1893-1964)
Hodges, Ruth, **13,439**
Hodgkin's disease, 7,259
Hodgman, Gertrude, 12,850
Hodgman, Martha Elizabeth Densmore [Mrs.] (1838-1908), 9,041
Hodgman, Mildred (1896-). *See* Mahoney, Mildred (Hodgman) [Mrs. John J.] (1896-)
Hodgson, Daisy [Miss], **5,513**
Hodgson, Ellen (1840-1917). *See* Senior, Ellen (Hodgson) [Mrs. Joseph] (1840-1917)
Hodgson, Frances Eliza (1849-1924). *See* Burnett,

Frances Eliza (Hodgson) [Mrs. Swan Moses]. [Mrs. Stephen] Townsend (1849-1924)
Hodgson Hall (GA) 3,587
Hodgson, Jane, 1,984
Hodgson, Margaret Telfair, 3,533
Hodgson, Mary E. [Mrs. Colin], **17,976**
Hodson, Mary F. (Chaplin), 5,617
Hoe, Caroline Phelps, 12,508
Hoe, Elizabeth Woodbridge, 12,508
Hoe Family (NY), **12,508**
Hoe, Laura, 12,508
Hoe, Olivia, 12,508
Hoe, Robert (1784-1833), 12,508
Hoe, Robert (1839-1909), 12,508
Hoerger, Minnie V. [Miss] (1882-1970), **10,474**
Hoeven, Charles B., 5,110
Hoey, Clyde R., 13,282
Hoey, Jane Margueretta (1892-1968), 8,677, 8,685, 11,916
Hofer, Clair (1898-). *See* Hewes, Clair (Hofer) (1898-)
Hofer, Flora Evelyn (Kingsley) [Mrs. Theodore R.], 10,763
Hofer, Theodore R., 10,679
Hoffman, Alice (Green), **13,272**
Hoffman, Alice M., 15,334
Hoffman, Alida, 12,697
Hoffman, Anna Marie (Lederer) [Mrs. Julius] Rosenberg [Mrs. Paul], 9,159, 11,875
Hoffman, Charles Fenns, 12,463
Hoffman, Clara, 4,244
Hoffman, Dora [Mrs. Horace J.], 11,101
Hoffman, Dorothy, 2,927
Hoffman, Eleanor, 7,509
Hoffman, Elwyn Irving (ca. 1870-1949), **1,441**
Hoffman Family (NJ), **11,101**
Hoffman, Gertrude, **11,312**
Hoffman, Gertrude B., 1,666
Hoffman, Horace J., 11,101
Hoffman, Irene (1877-1960), 7,509
Hoffman, John Dell (?-ca. 1869), **2,394**
Hoffman, Malvina (1887-1966), **1,568**, 3,951, 3,953, 15,170
Hoffman, Maria E. Fenno [Mrs. Ogden], 2,362, 7,533
Hoffman, Naomi R., **16,896**
Hoffman, Ogden, 2,362
Hoffman, Sarah, 12,315
Hoffman, Sarah Paine, **4,916**
Hoffman, Sophy. *See* Chester, Sophy (Hoffman) [Mrs. Edward]
Hoffman's Drops, 9,481
Hofheins, Amanda Lucretia (Braffett) [Mrs. Jacob Michael] (1830-1910), **16,698**
Hofheins, Jacob Michael, 16,698
Hofstadter, Richard, **11,912**
Hogan, Elsie. *See* Van Noy, Elsie (Hogan) [Mrs. William Ray]
Hogan, Kathleen, 3,202
Hogan, Maria C. (1851-1926), **14,733**
Hogan, Mary Grace, **3,202**
Hogarth, Paul, 17,478
Hoge, Alicia. *See* Arlen, Alicia [Mrs. James] Hoge [Mrs. Michael]
Hoge, Jane Currie (Blaikie) [Mrs. Abraham Holmes] (1811-90), 3,888, 4,069, 4,135
Hogg Foundation for Mental Health, 16,069
Hogg, Ima, 16,234
Hogstel, Mildred, **8,747**
Hokah Chief (MN), 9,434
Hokya Indians, 12,067
Hol-Tre Producing Company (Ithaca, NY), 11,537
Holberg, Ruth (Langland) (1889-), **14,390**
Holbrook, Frederick (1813-1909), **11,613**
Holbrook, Hal, 10,677
Holbrook, Jane Augusta (1833-1917). *See* Tourtillote, Jane Augusta (Holbrook) Gould (1833-1917)
Holbrook, Lillian (1879-ca. 1965), **5,885**
Holcombe, Beverly, 15,674
Holcombe, Florence, 2,623
Holcombe, Lucy Petway (1832-99). *See* Pickens, Lucy Petway (Holcombe) [Mrs. Francis Wilkinson] (1832-99)
Holcombe, Mrs. A. A., 2,623
Holden, Edward S., 356, 1,340

Holden, Geraldine Weston Dudley, **6,643**
Holden, Miriam Y., 6,947
Holden, Ruth (1890-1917), **6,644**
Holden, Sarah Gilbert [Mrs. George M.], **6,645**
Holder, Christopher, 7,490
Holder, Edward S., 2,464
Holder, Eva, **14,585**
Holder, Imogene, 3,762
Holding companies, **8,972**. *See also* Insurance holding companies
Hole-in-the Day (Native American), 8,940, 9,384
Holeman, Nancy Nash (1806-?), **9,990**
Holiday, Billie, Eleanora Fagan. [Mrs. Joe] Guy [Mrs. Louis] McKay (1915-59), **5,530**
Holiday, Clarence, 5,530
Holidays, 9,117, 9,390
Holinghead, Isabella, 3,114
Holkeboer, Tena (1895-1965), **8,198**
Hollabaugh, Gladys [Miss], 271
Holladay, Ben, 1,621
Holland, Alladean (1928-). *See* Reed, Alladean (Holland) [Mrs. Eldon] (1928-)
Holland, Barbara, 15,198
Holland, Benjamin F., **3,395**
Holland Family (FL), **2,868**
Holland Family (MA), 16,531
Holland, Fanny Virginia [Mrs. B. F.], 2,868
Holland, George, **13,440**
Holland, Hilda, 6,223
Holland, Josiah G., 12,443
Holland, Katrin (pseudonym). *See* Lamon, Heidi Huberta Freybe Loewengard (1911-)
Holland, Mary A. *See* Ryan, Mary A. (Holland)
Holland, Mary Agnes Groover [Mrs. Spessard], 99, 2,868
Holland, Mildred, 11,897
Holland, Miss, 6,911
Holland, Mrs. B. F., 2,870
Holland, Mrs. Josiah G., 12,443
Holland Musicians' Club (MI), **8,194**
Holland, Rebecca (Goldberg), 1,656
Holland Society, 12,201
Holland, Spessard (1892-1971), 2,868, 2,870, 17,465
Holland, Virginia Crenshaw Harper (1838-1932), 16,119
Holland Woman's Literary Club (MI), **8,188**
Hollander, Nanci (1943?-), 17,637
Hollands, Hulda Theodate (St. Bernard) (1837-1910), **8,342**
Hollcroft, Temple Rice (1889-1967), **11,278**, 12,052
Holleman, Wilbur J., 14,377
Holler Family, 15,799
Holler, Mary Louisa Oni Cornwell [Mrs. Adlai Ellwood] (1871-1951), **15,799**
Holley, Alexander Lyman (1831-82), **1,867**
Holley, J. W., 15,377
Holley, Marcia (Coffing), 1,867
Holley, Marietta (1836-1926), 2,196
Holley Mary Austin [Mrs.] (1784-1846), **16,088**
Holley, Sallie (1818-93), 5,907, 7,629, 11,616
Holliday, Norene [Miss], 3,064
Holliday, Virginia, 3,033
Hollingsworth, Ann Maria, 5,777
Hollingsworth, E. Buckner (Kirk), **6,646**
Hollingsworth, Jane [Mrs. William R., Jr.], **9,646**
Hollingsworth, Leta Anna (Stetter) [Mrs. Harry Levi] (1886-1939), **10,475**, **13,742**
Hollingsworth, Loretta Enlow, 4,907
Hollingsworth, Lydia, 5,777
Hollingsworth, Mary Wilson, 15,115
Hollingsworth, Sarah. *See* Gibson, Sarah (Hollingsworth) [Mrs. William]
Hollingsworth, William R. Jr., 9,646
Hollins College, alumnae, 5,470
Hollis, Ernest V., 8,677
Hollis Family (GA), 3,088
Hollis, Harriette V. (French) [Mrs. Abijah], 2,338
Hollister, Elizabeth (?-1958). *See* Frost, Elizabeth (Hollister) [Mrs. Elliott Park] (?-1958)
Hollister, Emily Jane (Areen) (1839-1918), **7,815**
Hollister Family (CA), 548
Hollister, George H., 13,673
Hollister, Jane. *See* Wheelwright, Jane (Hollister) [Mrs. Joseph Balch]

Hollister, Joanna (Randolph) [Mrs. Clark W.] Kelley [Mrs. George H.] (1870-?), **13,673**
Hollister, John James, 548
Hollister, John James, Jr., 548
Hollister, Lottie "Dot" (Steffens) [Mrs. John James] (1872-1956), 548
Hollman, Emilia, 1,534
Holloway, Emma G., **4,605**
Holloway, Jennie Barlow Parr [Mrs. Earl] (1927-), 5,394
Holloway, Mary M. (1831-92). See Wilhite Mary M. Holloway [Mrs. E. A.] (1831-92)
Holloway, Mary "Mother," 1,654
Holloway, Teresa, 2,928, 2,932
Hollowell, Mrs. W. R., 13,247
Holly, Louise R., 3,290
Holly Springs Female Academy (MS), **9,817**
Hollywood, 11,907
Hollywood Community Chorus (CA), 1,038
Hollywood, Edwin L., 11,537
Holm, Celeste (1919-), 11,907
Holm, Jeanne M., 34, **11,876**
Holm, Sax (pseudonym). See Jackson, Helen Maria (Fiske) [Mrs. Edward Bissell] Hunt [Mrs. William Sharpless] (1830-85)
Holman, Albert, 4,804
Holman, Anna E. (ca. 1892-), **6,647**
Holman, Elizabeth (1905-71). See Holman, Libby (1905-71)
Holman Family (TX), 16,261
Holman, Jerome, 4,804
Holman, Libby (1905-71), **6,033**
Holman, Lois (Grant) [Mrs. Palmer], **4,804**, 4,961
Holman, Lottie (1882-1964). See Card, Lottie (Holman) [Mrs. James R.] (1882-1964)
Holman, Lydia (1868-1960), **6,648**
Holmberg, Lottie [Mrs.], **17,907**
Holmes, Adelaide (1853-?), **8,343**
Holmes, Clara [Miss], 5,693
Holmes, Eliza Ford (Gibbes) (1808-75), **15,605**
Holmes, Emilie Rose (Smedes) [Mrs. John Simcox] (?-1950), **13,129**
Holmes Family (NY), **12,759**
Holmes, Fanny Bowditch (Dixwell) [Mrs. Oliver Wendell, Jr.], 6,261
Holmes, Georgianna (Klingle) [Mrs. Benjamin Proctor] (1842?-1940), **2,395**
Holmes, Gladys G., 14,366
Holmes, Grace, 15,134
Holmes, Hazel (Snell) Schreiber, **549**
Holmes, Helen H. (1899-). See Lane, Helen H. (Holmes) (1899-)
Holmes, Huldah Bouton [Mrs. Samuel Leek], **12,510**
Holmes, John (1773-1843), 7,677, **12,509**
Holmes, John Haynes (1897-1964), **2,396**, 7,223, 13,811
Holmes, John Simcox (1868-?), 13,129
Holmes, Julia (1839-?). See Smith, Julia (Holmes) (1839-?)
Holmes, Julia Archibald, 1,790
Holmes, Juliette T., 1,428
Holmes, Kenneth, 14,501
Holmes, Lulu H. [Miss], **550**, 11,902
Holmes, Marjorie [Mrs. Lynn Mighell] (1910-), **5,080**, 5,110, 9,823
Holmes, Mary Bynum. See Ricks, Mary Bynum (Holmes)
Holmes, Mary E., 6,529
Holmes, Mary Jane (Hawes) [Mrs. Daniel] (1825-1907), 1,224, 4,781, 11,036
Holmes, Mary Louise Campbell [Mrs. William L.], **14,586**
Holmes, Minnie (Lenoir), 9,663
Holmes, Mrs. E. K., 15,692
Holmes, Oliver Wendell (1809-94), 1,426, 2,246, 2,569, 2,641, 5,528, 5,815, 6,432, **6,649**, 6,681
Holmes, Oliver Wendell, Jr. (1841-1935), **6,261**
Holmes, Priscilla, **7,816**
Holmes, Rebekah. See Amory, Rebekah (Holmes) [Mrs. Thomas]
Holmes, Roxy [Mrs. Abram], 11,613
Holmes, Sally [Mrs. John], 12,509
Holmes, Samuel Leek, **12,510**
Holmes, Sarah Huntington (Clapp) (1824-69), 7,614

Holmes, William Henry (1846-1933), **2,722**, **2,849**
Holmes, William Henry (1874-1948), 5,693
Holmquist, June D., 9,230
Holocaust, Jewish (1839-1945), 14,497, 17,744
Holocaust, The (book), 15,188
Holsclaw, Mabel, 1,348
Holstein, Anna M., 14,515
Holt, Augustus F., 6,907
Holt, Carol Reid, 6,092
Holt, Catherine, 920
Holt, Constance D'Arcy Mackay [Mrs. Richard], **9,198**
Holt, Emily Burt (1854-1934), 6,650
Holt Family, **6,650**
Holt, Frederick Holford (1867-1929), **8,000**
Holt, Helen [Mrs. Rush D.] (ca. 1918-), **17,463**
Holt, Ivan Lee (1886-1967), **9,991**
Holt, James, 14
Holt, Janice (1909-). See Giles, Janice (Holt) Moore [Mrs. Henry] (1909-)
Holt, Joseph Burt (1828-99), 6,650
Holt, Julia Evelyn Rollins (1829-95), 6,650
Holt, L. B., **13,441**
Holt, Leland Burke [Mrs. Ivan Lee], 9,991
Holt, Lillian (Silk) [Mrs. Frederick Holford] (1869-1949), 8,000
Holt, Luther Emmett (1855-1924), 7,186
Holt, Minnie, 9,819
Holt, Modena M. Rudiswell [Mrs. Ivan Lee], 9,991
Holt, Narcissa Boykin, **3,039**
Holt, Nora Douglas, 3,294
Holt, Starr B. Carrithers [Mrs. Ivan Lee], 9,991
Holten High School (Danvers, MA), 7,009
Holton, Mary 4,743
Holtzman, Elizabeth (1941-). 11,817, **12,148**
Holubnychy, Lydia, 12,012
Holway, Amy Richardson (1894-1949), **6,651**
Holway, Frances Hope (Kerr) (1886-) **6,652**
Holy Child Jesus Convent (Rosemont, PA), **15,265**
Holy Child School for the Retarded (Oklahoma City, OK), 14,226
Holy Family Academy (Chicago, IL), 15,181
Holy Family College (PA), **15,179**
Holy Family College for Women (PA). See Holy Family College (PA)
Holy Family Hospital (Manitowoc, WI), 17,820
Holy Family Institute (Pittsburgh, PA), 15,181
Holy Family Kindergarten (Owensboro, KY), 5,401
Holy Ghost Festival (San Leandro, CA), 1,387
Holy Light Clinic (Shanghai, China), 8,875
Holy Names Sisters, Washington Province, **17,381**
Holyoke, Anna (1735-1812). See Cutts, Anna (Holyoke) (1735-1812)
Holyoke, Edward (1689-1769), 7,385, 7,639
Holyoke, Edward Augustus (1728-1829), 7,385
Holyoke, Elizabeth (1732-1821). See Kneeland, Elizabeth (Holyoke) (1732-1821)
Holyoke, Elizabeth "Betsey" (1771-89), **7,384**
Holyoke Family (MA), 7,385
Holyoke, Margaret (1726-92). See Mascarene, Margaret (Holyoke) (1726-92)
Holyoke, Margaret (1763-1825), 7,385
Holyoke, Margaret Turner, 9,135
Holyoke, Mary (1800-80). See Ward, Mary (Holyoke) (1800-80)
Holyoke, Mary (Epes) [Mrs. Edward] (?-1790), 7,385
Holyoke, Mary (Vial) [Mrs. Edward Augustus] (1738-1802), 7,385
Holyoke, Priscilla (1739-82). See Pearson, Priscilla (Holyoke) [Mrs. Eliphalet] (1739-82)
Holyoke, Susannah (1779-1860). See Ward, Susannah (Holyoke) [Mrs. Joshua] (1779-1860)
Holyoke, William H., **9,135**
Holzhauer, Betty, 3,747, 3,756
Homan, Helen W., 5,123
Home Acres (periodical), 6,964
Home and Garden Club of Russellville (IN), **4,565**
Home and School League of Chester County (PA), **15,344**
Home Circle (Troy, OH), **14,149**
Home Club Milk Commission (CA), 1,251
Home Co-op Club, Inc. (MN), **9,136**
Home Culture Clubs, 11,959

Home demonstration agents **2,682, 10,018, 11,651,** 11,756, 16,558
Home Demonstration Club, 13,446
Home Demonstration Clubs (IN), **4,566**
Home demonstration work, 2,682, 9,530, 9,894, **10,016,** 10,039, **10,217,** 13,285, **13,626,** 15,797, 15,798, **16,271,** 17,927, 17,929
Home economics, 108, 116, 2,704, 3,859, **4,984,** 6,580, 6,672, 6,862, 8,155, 10,707, 11,565, 11,805, 12,737, 13,811, 14,272, 15,183, 16,286, **17,927.** See also Cookery; Dairying; Food; House furnishings; Household appliances; Household workers
accounting, **1,232,** 2,231, 2,673, 3,207, 3,668, **5,683,** 5,953, **6,369,** 6,614, 7,402, 7,411, 7,452, 7,702, 8,327, 9,050, 9,864, 10,801, 11,090, 11,209, 11,533, 11,565, 11,722, 12,025, **12,250,** 12,339, **12,390,** 12,429, **12,975,** 13,312, 14,096, **14,721,** **14,726,** 14,902, 16,303
study and teaching, 1,815, **4,691,** 5,191, 6,188, 8,547, 8,567, 8,578, 8,607, **10,219,** 11,365, 11,661, 11,662, 12,923, 13,479, **14,278,** 14,279, 17,203
teacher training, 7,655
Home Economics Class (Plainfield, IN). See Union Home Economics Club (Plainfield, IN)
Home Economics Club (UT), **16,419**
Home Economics Club of Clinton and Madison Townships (IN), **4,567**
Home economics extension agents, 4,449, **10,261**
Home economics extension work, **3,761,** 4,691, 5,048, 5,871, 6,585, 9,708, 10,016, **10,019,** 11,217, **11,564,** 11,571, 11,651, 11,661, 11,662, 11,756, 13,391, 13,479, 13,618, 13,685, 15,792, 15,797, 15,798, 15,808, **15,820**
Home Economics Movement, The (book), 4,380
Home economics research, 2,673, 8,567, 9,829
Home economics, rural, 2,673, 13,479
Home economics teachers, **4,378, 4,387, 4,397,** 5,662, **8,165, 8,567, 8,596,** 10,605, 10,607, 13,532, **17,194**
Home economists, 1,974, **4,098, 4,378, 4,387, 4,397,** 5,662, **8,165, 8,567, 8,596, 9,788,** 10,605, 10,607, **15,795, 15,798, 15,808,** 15,823, **17,194**
Home for Friendless Children (DE), 2,047
Home for Japanese, 17,285
Home for Respectable Aged Women (NJ), 11,067
Home for the Aged (Chemung County, NY), 11,445
Home for the Friendless (MI), 8,205
Home for the Jewish Aged (PA), 15,161
Home for Working Women (Boston, MA). See Rutland Corner House (MA)
Home Guard, 10,509
Home Institute (New Orleans, LA), 5,426
Home labor, 5,570, 5,900, 6,485, 6,486, **6,869,** 7,664, 15,272, 17,835. See also Sweating system
Home League, The (pamphlet), 3,282
Home Magazine, The. See Arthur's Home Magazine (periodical)
Home Management House (Bozeman, MT), 10,219
"Home Messenger, The" (newsletter), 9,205
Home Missionary (periodical), 5,234
Home Needlework Magazine, 11,304
Home nursing, 232, 236, 247, 2,686, **3,729, 3,904, 4,500, 4,884,** 7,088, 10,015, 11,150, 12,657, 13,994, 16,984, 17,590, **17,733,** 17,826
"Home Our Mutual Effort," 3,978
Home ownership, 7,334
Home Safety Review (periodical), 3,976
Home Scholarship Fund (OR), 14,625
Home School (Athens, GA), **3,094**
Home School for Girls (Sauk Centre, MN), 9,327
Home, Sophie C., 2,202
"Home to the Hills" (story), 11,310
Homemakers, handicapped, 11,565
"Homemaker's Program, The" (radio program), 17,650
Homeopathic Medical College of Pennsylvania, alumni, 4,346
Homeopathic Medical Society of Ohio, 14,000
Homeopathy, hospitals and dispensaries, 2,119
Homer, Eugenie (1854-1940). See Emerson, Eugenie Homer [Mrs. Oliver P.] (1854-1940)

Homer, Louise Dilworth (Beatty) [Mrs. Sidney] (1871-1947), 9,004
Homes for Seniors. *See* Old age homes
Homes, Marian. *See* Dixon, Marian (Homes)
"Homesick" (story), 15,660
Homewood Terrace (CA), 1,327
Homosexuality, 6,760, 15,176
Homosexuals, civil rights, 3,852
Homosexuals in theatre, 12,367
Homsher, Lola M., 17,918, **17,977**
Homsley, Mary E., 17,908
Honduras, 9,354
"Honest Wine Merchant, The" (story), 17,076
Honeyman, Nan (Wood) (1881-1970), 14,362, **14,391, 14,587**
Honeymoon, 1,790, 3,185, 6,553, **7,603**, 9,206, **10,935**, 11,058, 12,200, 12,202, 12,257, 12,286
Honeysett, Caroline E., **8,219**
Hong Kong, 12,195
  missionaries to, Lutheran, 8,869, **8,882, 10,143**
  missionaries to, Methodist, 8,891
Honneyman, Lavinia (1836-1910). *See* Porter, Lavinia (Honneyman) [Mrs. James J.] (1836-1910)
Honnold, Caroline [Mrs. William L.], 5,122
Honor Among Lovers (moving-picture), 1,025
"Honor Among Women," 2,632
Honsinger, Welthy Blakesley (1879-). *See* Fisher, Welthy Blakesley (Honsinger) [Mrs. Frederick] (1879-)
Hoobler, Icie Macy (1892-), **7,817**
Hood Family (MA), **7,003**
Hood, George W., 11,426
Hood, Harriet Parker (1834-?), 7,003
Hood, Helen Dodge (1892-), 7,003
Hood, J. J., 9,619
Hood, Lizzie Frances (1864-?), 7,003
Hood, Rebecca [Mrs. William Henry], **3,330**
Hood River Manufacturing Company (OR), 14,532
Hood, William Henry, 3,330
Hoog, Margaret, 12,336
Hooglandt, Anna, **12,511**
Hook, Elizabeth (1778-?), **7,386**
Hook, Sidney, 8,077
Hooker, Alice (1847-1928). *See* Day, Alice (Hooker) [Mrs. John C.] (1847-1928)
Hooker, Edith Houghton, 6,742
Hooker Family (CA), **551**
Hooker, Isabella (Beecher) [Mrs. John] (1822-1907), 1,896, **1,950**, 1,951, 1,952, 2,542, 5,334, 6,392, 6,526, **6,654**, 6,659, 7,227, 17,043
Hooker, John, 1,896
Hooker, Katharine (Putnam) (1849-1935), 551, **552**
Hooker, Marian Osgood, 551
Hooker, Mary (Treadwell), 1,901
Hooker, Mrs. Edward B., 1,949
Hooker, Mrs. S. I., **17,908**
Hooker, Sarah Brown (1828-?). *See* Capron, Sarah Brown (Hooker) (1828-?)
Hookworm disease, 239
Hoole, Elizabeth Stanley, 15,768
Hooper, Abigail (1788-1885). *See* Trask, Abigail (Hooper) (1788-1885)
Hooper, Alice Forbes (Perkins) [Mrs. William], 1,496
Hooper, Caroline (Mallett) [Mrs. George DeBerniere], **13,033**
Hooper, Elizabeth Amis Cameron (1873-1956). *See* Blanchard, Elizabeth Amis Cameron (Hooper) [Mrs. John Osgood] (1873-1956)
Hooper, Ellen (Sturgis) (1812-48), **6,655**
Hooper, Ethel Pickett, 3,727
Hooper, Florence,
Hooper Foundation, 1,373
Hooper, George DeBerniere, 13,033
Hooper, Jessie Annette (Jack) [Mrs. Ben C.] (1865-1935), **17,654**, 17,749
Hooper, Lucy (1814-41), 11,316, 12,463
Hooper, Lucy Hamilton (1835-93), 12,572
Hooper, Mary (Amis), 12,955
Hooper, William, 1,496
Hoopes, Caroline. *See* Jackson, Caroline (Hoopes)
Hoopes, Eliza [Mrs. Thomas], 15,024
Hoopes Ella Clarinda Hinckley Cardon (1867-?), **3,738**

Hoopes, Thomas, 15,024
"Hoosier Farm Wife Says, The" (column), 6,064
Hooten, Elizabeth. *See* Roberts, Elizabeth (Hooton) [Mrs. Elisha]
Hooton, Elizabeth (1611?-68?), 10,846
Hooven, Edna M., **553**
Hoover Commission on Illiteracy, 5,325
Hoover Dam, 10,781
Hoover, Herbert, 1,321, 1,404, 1,559, 2,542, 2,640, 2,694, 3,302, 3,399, 4,958, **5,119, 5,120, 5,121, 5,122, 5,123**, 5,325, 6,622, 7,031, 10,487, 11,944, 12,052, 12,553, 13,811, 14,387
Hoover, J. Edgar, 10,035
Hoover, Lou (Henry) [Mrs. Herbert] (1874-1944), 1,560, 1,593, 2,640, 5,121, 5,123, 6,759, 9,057, 12,095, 12,108, 12,111, 14,822, 17,978
Hoover luncheons, 54
Hope Adaline [Mrs. Robert], 9,137
Hope, Bob, 14,231
Hope-Clarke, H. E. [Miss], 5,521
Hope College (Holland, MI)
  alumnae, 8,202
  faculty, 8,189, 8,191, 8,192
Hope College (Holland, MI), Women's Glee Club, 8,192
Hope College Vienna Summer School, 8,192
Hope Community Club (ND), 13,672
Hope, Constance. [Mrs. Milton Lionel Berliner] (1908-), **12,013**
Hope diamond, 2,467
Hope Institute, 5,288
Hope, John, 3,302, 5,458
Hope, Lugenia (Burns) [Mrs. John], 3,302
Hope, Robert, 9,137
Hope, Virginia Mae (1921-44), **9,137**
Hope Woman's Club (ND), **13,725**
Hopfenbeck, Elizabeth Ann (White) [Mrs. Alphonzo] (1866-1961), **16,699**
Hopi Indians, 173, **329**, 2,840, 11,222, 11,227, **12,067, 16,864**, 16,865
  agriculture, 16,864
  language, 173
  missions, 5,196
Hopkins Academy (Hadley, MA), 7,135
Hopkins, Arthur, 226
Hopkins, Arthur Francis, 9,803
Hopkins, Augusta. *See* Rice, Augusta (Hopkins) [Mrs. John W.]
Hopkins, Benjamin, 3,527
Hopkins, Charlotte Everett (Wise) [Mrs. Archibald] (1851-1935), **2,397, 6,656**
Hopkins, Cornelia Lee [Mrs. John] (1780-1815), 2,443
Hopkins, Electra Sergeant, 7,591
Hopkins, Ellen Dunlap [Mrs.] (1858-1939), 12,301, 12,577
Hopkins, Elvira [Mrs. Daniel], **9,138**
Hopkins, Emma Santee [Mrs. Alva A.], **11,614**
Hopkins Family (NJ), **14,843**
Hopkins, Flora (Ball), 14,513
Hopkins German Presbyterian Church (Brooklyn, NY), 11,788
Hopkins, H. C., 17,454
Hopkins, Harry, 11,489, 11,853, 11,883
Hopkins, Harry L., 8,662
Hopkins, Helen. *See* Shores, Helen (Hopkins) Keanum
Hopkins Improvement League (MN). *See* Women's Club of Hopkins (MN)
Hopkins, Jane D., **3,526**
Hopkins, Jeanette Hitchcock, **1,549**
Hopkins, Jeannette, 1,600
Hopkins, John L., II, 3,527
Hopkins, John Livingstone, **3,527**
Hopkins, Juliet Ann (Opie) [Mrs. Alexander George] Gordan [Mrs. Arthur Frances] (1818-1890), 99
Hopkins, Lilian Walker Wentworth, 4,279
Hopkins, Maria. *See* Walker, Maria (Hopkins)
Hopkins, Marion, **10,815**
Hopkins, Marjorie Robbins [Mrs. John] (1886-1971), 3,924
Hopkins, Mark (1802-87), **7,591**, 11,520
Hopkins, Martha (Ellis) [Mrs. Arthur Herbert] (1870-1959), **4,606**

Hopkins, Mary Clark [Mrs.], **12,164**
Hopkins, Mary (Cooke) [Mrs. John L., II], 3,527
Hopkins, Mary Curtis [Mrs.], 7,591
Hopkins, Mary Frances. *See* Pond, Mary Frances (Hopkins) [Mrs. Edward Robert]
Hopkins, Mary Hubbell [Mrs. Mark], 7,591
Hopkins, Mary Louisa, 7,591
Hopkins, Miriam, 1,025
Hopkins, Mollie, 3,527
Hopkins, Mrs. Robert (1825-?). *See* Pond, [Mrs. Robert] Hopkins [Mrs. Gideon Hollister] (1825-?)
Hopkins, Robert, 9,293
Hopkins, Ruth Joy [Mrs.], 17,894
Hopkins, Sarah. *See* Kilbourn, Sarah (Hopkins) [Mrs. Dwight C.]
Hopkins, Sarah Ann, 7,140
Hopkins, Susan, 15,042
Hopkinson, Ann (Borden) [Mrs. Francis], 15,020
Hopkinson, Anne (1745-1817). *See* Coale, Anne (Hopkinson) [Mrs. Samuel Stringer] (1745-1817)
Hopkinson, Corinna Prentiss [Mrs. Thomas] **6,657**
Hopkinson, Edwin William, **17,278**
Hopkinson, Elizabeth (1738-?). *See* Duché, Elizabeth (Hopkinson) [Mrs. Jacob] (1738-?)
Hopkinson, Emily (Mifflin) [Mrs. Joseph], 15,020
Hopkinson Family (PA), **5,803, 15,020**
Hopkinson, Francis, 14,753, 15,020
Hopkinson, Jane, 15,079
Hopkinson, Joseph (1770-1842), 15,020
Hopkinson, Mary [Mrs. Edwin William], **17,278**
Hopkinson, Mary (1742-85). *See* Morgan, Mary (Hopkinson) [Mrs. John] (1742-85)
Hopkinson, Mary Elizabeth (Watson), 6,777
Hopkinson, Mary (Johnson) [Mrs. Thomas] (1718-1804), 15,020, 15,079
Hopkinson, Thomas, 15,020
Hopkinson, Thomas, 6,657
Hopkinton, Mary, 11,672
Hopley Family (OH), **13,999**
Hopley, Georgia E. (1858-1944), 13,999
Hopley, Georgiana Rochester [Mrs. John E.], 13,999
Hopley, John Edward, 13,999
Hopley, John Prat (1821-1904) 13,999
Hopper, Arvilla, **11,615**
Hopper Family (Ithaca, NY), 11,615
Hopper, Hedda, 698
Hopper, Isaac T. (1771-1852), 12,576
Hopper, Kathryn [Mrs.] (ca. 1902-74), **10,922**
Hopper, Mrs. John, 12,208
Hopper, Phoebe May (1867-1967), **10,568**
Hopper, Rosa, 14,893
Hops, 11,730, 17,606
Horace (slave, GA), 3,373
Horace Mann Kindergarten (NY), 9,526, 11,864
Horace Mann School (NY), 13,604
Horace S. Stansel Memorial Library (MS), 9,804
Horack, Elizabeth Collins [Mrs. Frank], 4,916
Horack, Frank (1873-1956), **4,917**
Horak, Ella Lilly **9,872**
Horey, Alvin P., 7,539
Horicon Marsh (WI), 17,842
Horn and the Forest, The (ms), 6,001
Horn, Annabel [Miss] (?-1969), **3,463**
Horn, Elizabeth Laura [Mrs. Kirk M.], 14,712
Horn, Elsa, 3,610
Horn, Gertrude Franklin (1857-1948). *See* Atherton, Gertrude Franklin (Horn) [Mrs. Henry Bowen] (1857-1948)
Hornaday, Mary (1906-), 11,493, **17,978**
Hornback, May [Mrs.] (?-1976), **17,772**
Hornbeck, Helen. *See* Tanner, Helen (Hornbeck)
Hornblower, Caroline Bradley, 11,076
Hornbook for Witches, A (book), 5,310
Horne, Alice (Merrill) [Mrs. George Henry] (1868-1948), **16,700**
Horne Committee on the Memorial to the North Carolina Women of the Confederacy, 13,442
Horne, Flora B., **16,701**
Horne, Frank S., 5,458
Horne, Jennie (1846-1932). *See* Turnbull, Jennie (Horne) (1846-1932)
Horne, Joseph, 554, 16,702
Horne, Lena, 4,970, 11,449
Horne, Marilyn (1934-), **994**

Horne, Mary Isabella (Hales) [Mrs. Joseph] (1818-1905), **554**, 16,618, **16,702**
Horne, Mrs. W. J., 1,092
Horner Family (VA), 17,108
Horner, Henry, 17,691
Horner, Julia E., **13,034**
Horner, Mabel (Carlton) [Mrs. John K.] (?-1961), 2,245
Horner, Matina (Souretis) (1940-), **6,658**
Horney, Karen, 6,544
Horrocks, Dilla Basham (?-1954), 286
Horry, Daniel, 15,507
Horry Family (SC), 13,137
Horry, Harriott, 15,507
Horry, Harriott (Pinckney) [Mrs. Daniel] (1748-1830), 2,527, 13,137, 15,681
Horse breeders, 885
Horse breeding, **5,324**, 15,723
Horse stealing, 13,287
Horses, stud-books, 9,711
Horsewomen, **10,428**
Horsfield Family (NY), **12,512**
Horsfield, Sister Elizabeth, 12,512
Horsfield, Timothy, 12,512
Horsley, Frances Jane (1884-?). *See* Shellenberger, Frances Jane (Horsley) (1884-?)
Horstman, Patrice, 157
Horstmann Family (PA), **14,978**
Horstmann, Sigmund H., 14,978
Hort, Mary [Miss] (1796-?), **15,606**
Horticultural research, 8,424
Horticultural societies, 5,559, 6,964, 11,701, 13,709
Horticulture, 5,559, 6,646, **11,297**. *See also* Landscape gardening; Seed industry and trade
Horticulturists, **1,194, 1,218, 1,440, 1,482**, 2,310, 5,268, **5,538**, 7,616, 8,424, 10,152, **10,420, 11,297, 11,701, 11,790, 13,653**
Horton, Elizabeth. *See* Pennell, Elizabeth (Horton) [Mrs. Joseph Stanley]
Horton, Judith Ellen (1840-1910). *See* Foster, Judith Ellen (Horton) [Mrs. Addison] Avery [Mrs. Elijah Caleb O.] (1840-1910)
Horton, Mildred Helen (McAfee), 2,710, 5,719, 7,574, 7,583, 9,986
Horton, Myles, 15,977
Horton, Ruth, 9,908
Horton, Zilphia [Mrs. Myles] (1910-56), 15,977
Horton's Point Lighthouse (Long Island, NY), 12,931
Horvath, Sister Frederica (1897-1970), 1,008
Horwood, Rosemary, **17,279**
Hosach, **10,898**
Hosack, Mary, 12,315
Hosack, Mary Eddy [Mrs. David], 14,884
Hosford, Asenath (Glover) [Mrs. Chauncey O.] (?-1896), **14,588**
Hosford, Frances Juliette [Miss] (1853-1937), **14,123**
Hoskin, Beryl, 830, 1,532
Hosking, Annie (Stelce) [Mrs. Benjamin] (ca. 1900-), 11,181, 11,182
Hoskins, Jane, 14,964
Hoskins, Katherine deMontalant (Lackey) [Mrs. Albert L.] (1909-), **7034**
Hosmer, Ann P. [Mrs.], 3,897
Hosmer, Eliza, 7,055
Hosmer, Elizabeth S. (Viles), **9,992**
Hosmer Family (MA), **7,055**
Hosmer, Frances, 5,709
Hosmer, Harriet, 11,754
Hosmer, Harriet Goodhue (1830-1908), **6,659**, 7,055, 7,182, 7,585
Hosmer, Helen, **12,774**
Hosmer, Jane, 7,055
Hospital administrators, 232, 246, 3,932, 3,967, 4,411, **5,326**, 5,991, 6,140, 6,364, **7,327**, 8,458, 8,518, 8,581, **8,732**, 8,760, **8,761**, 10,732, 12,272, 12,354, 12,759, 15,232, **16,343**, 17,128
Hospital Aid Association (Flint, MI), **8,180**
Hospital and community, 16,343
Hospital and Training School for Nurses (Charleston, SC), 15,430
Hospital auxiliaries. *See* Charitable societies; Volunteer workers in hospitals
Hospital Auxiliary (MN), 8,697

Hospital for the Insane (Independence, IA). *See* Iowa State Hospital (Independence, IA)
Hospital Guild (Elmhurst, IL), 4,197
"Hospital on Peace Street, Foochow, China, The" (pamphlet), 12,776
Hospital records, 1,149, 2,671, **3,932, 3,967, 3,968, 5,213, 5,562, 6,211, 6,212, 6,214**, 7,285, **8,529, 11,149**, 11,443, **12,138**, 12,141, **12,353, 12,354, 12,358**, 14,913, 14,915, 14,916, **15,150, 15,151**
Hospital training schools. *See* Nursing schools
Hospitals, **21**, 153, 447, **472**, 540, 1,374, 1,518, 1,690, 1,753, 1,837, 2,118, 2,542, 2,568, 2,675, 2,945, 3,216, 3,268, 3,275, **3,588**, 3,733, 3,905, 3,958, 4,123, 4,335, 4,506, 5,184, 5,398, 5,410, 5,494, 5,844, 6,222, **6,397**, 6,644, 6,847, 6,968, 7,066, 7,178, **7,274**, 7,694, 8,045, 8,176, **8,184**, 8,535, 8,581, 8,655, 8,732, **8,760, 8,761, 8,770**, 8,860, 8,862, 9,077, 9,132, 9,323, 9,467, 9,477, 9,490, 9,697, 9,956, 10,188, 10,189, 10,220, 10,580, **12,073**, 12,143, 12,802, 13,055, 13,390, **13,415**, 14,625, 14,746, 14,795, **15,842**, 16,092, 16,251, 17,229, 17,415, 17,462, 17,500, **17,569**, 17,578, 17,699, 17,820, 17,831, 17,839. *See also* Almshouses; Children, hospitals; Clinics; Hospitals, ophthalmic and aural; Nursing homes; Psychiatric hospitals; Volunteer workers in hospitals
   administration, 6,797, 8,859, 14,100
   citizen participation, **15,075**
   employees, 5,305
   housing, 9,476
   outpatient service, 12,352
   specifications, 9,476
   staff, 9,476
Hospitals, Afro-American, 3,293, **3,508**, 13,444, 13,559
Hospitals, charities, etc., **15,385**
Hospitals, convalescent, 9,273, 9,460
Hospitals, geriatric, 239
Hospitals, gynecologic and obstetric, **4,010, 4,021, 6,150, 6,213, 6,220**, 6,221, 6,364, 6,407, **6,797, 9,203**, 12,141, **12,353, 12,354**, 12,356, **12,358**, 14,697, **15,148**, 15,150, **15,151**
   laws and legislation, 9,351
Hospitals, Jewish, 14,908
Hospitals, military, 233, 1,408, 2,087, 2,334, 3,172, 4,490, 5,689, 5,991, 6,041, 6,129, 6,153, 6,644, 8,260, 8,310, 8,987, 9,277, 9,286, 11,556, 13,348, 13,889, 14,778, 16,965. *See also* Hospitals, charities, etc.; Medical and sanitary affairs; *under names of wars*
   records and correspondence, 2,671
   women in, 1,348
Hospitals, naval and marine, 5,844
Hospitals, ophthalmic and aural, 5,318
Hosta of Mrs. Frances R. Williams, The (book), 8,424
Hostense, Sophie. *See* Bailly, Sophie (Hostense)
Hostess League (WA), **13,793**
Hostetter, Anna (1828-1919). *See* Addams, Anna (Hostetter) [Mrs. William] Haldeman [Mrs. John Huy] (1828-1919)
Hostetter, Winifred Hager (1926-67), **8,199**
Hostetter's Illustrated US Almanac (1876), 3,540
Hostile Sun, The (book), 11,221
Hotchkiss, Emma P. *See* Gray, Emma P. (Hotchkiss) [Mrs. Horatio Nelson]
Hotchkiss Family (CT), **1,987**
Hotchkiss, Hazel, 997
Hotchkiss, Jennie Jewell [Mrs. Thomas W.], 11,440
Hotchkiss, Levi J., 1,987
Hotchkiss, Lucy, 2,009
Hotchkiss Memorial Church (TX), Women's Missionary Society, 16,059
Hotchkiss School, The (book) 6,111
Hotel and Restaurant International Union, Local 665 (MN), 9,467
Hotel Dieu Hospital (New Orleans, LA), **5,493**
Hotel Dieu School of Nursing (New Orleans, LA), **5,494**
Hotel Minnie (CA), 1,624
Hotel Splendide (CO), 1,750
Hotels, taverns, etc., 400, 413, 438, 1,336, 1,624, 1,750, 2,536, 3,007, 3,148, 3,388, 3,390, 3,425, 3,545, 3,621, 5,644, **5,761**, 6,375, 7,360, 8,455,

8,500, 8,776, 8,957, 8,989, 9,107, 9,214, 9,467, 9,528, 9,686, 9,691, 9,694, 9,841, 9,972, 9,974, 10,789, 10,846, 12,260, 12,601, 13,471, 14,615, 14,642, 14,664, 14,851, 14,945, 15,036, 15,066, 15,532, 16,883, 17,406
   accounting, 13,443
   employees, 982
   law, **11,206**, 11,207
   management, 5,056
"Hotter Than That" (song), 5,529
Houck, Louis, 9,926
Houdini, Harry, 941
Houdlette, Franklin (1815-87), 7,478
Houdlette, Harriet (Lilly) [Mrs. Franklin] (1816-1911), 7,478
Hough, Clara (ca. 1857-?), **17,464**
Hough, Emerson, 4,962
Hough, Henry Beetle, 7,028
Hough, Mrs. B. O., 12,804
Hough, Sue M. Dicke, 9,467
Hough, T. S., 9,847
Houghton Academy (Clinton, NY), students, 14,392
Houghton, Dorothy Deemer [Mrs. Hiram] (1890-1972), **4,918**, 5,110, **6,660**
Houghton, Eliza Poor (Donner) [Mrs. Sherman Otis] (1843-1922), 644
Houghton, Janice G., **14,589**
Houghton, Katharine. *See* Hepburn, Katharine (Houghton) (1878-)
Houghton, Mifflin Company (publishers), 5,699, 5,942, 5,984, 6,093, 14,319, 14,390
Houghton-Mifflin Literary Fellows, 9,583
Houghton, Nancy Manning, **6,661**
Hougstad, Martha Hove [Mrs.] (1867-1945), **8,748**
Houkom, Nellie S. Johnson [Mrs. A.], **8,749**
Hoult, Norah, 267
Houlton Woman's Club (Maine), **6,607**
Hours of labor, 441, 2,504, 5,564, 6,315, 6,486, 8,142, 9,054, 9,473, 9,487, 9,962, 10,953, 11,760, 11,771, 16,237, 17,376
Hourwich, Isaac A., 6,408
House cleaning, 1,299
House Committee on Un-American Activities, 17,792
House Committee to Investigate Un-American Activities, 3,852
House Constitutional Amendments Committee (NC), 13,404
House construction, 5,120, 5,122
House, Elizabeth. *See* Trist, Elizabeth (House) [Mrs. Nicholas]
House furnishings, 7,660, 13,378
   collectors and collecting, 11,899
House Happy, 2,546
"House Is Never Finished, A" (book), 9,126
House, Its Plan, Decoration and Care, The (book), 4,380
House Made of Dawn (book), 11,217
House of Egremont, The (book), 17,098
House of Happiness (Chicago, IL). *See* Benton House (Chicago, IL)
House of Incest (book), 4,232
House of Jacob (synagogue, NC), 13,472
House of John Norton and Sons, 17,129
House of Many Rooms, A (book), 16,462
House of Mercy (MA), 6,175
House of Refuge (Philadelphia, PA), 15,042
House of the Holy Family (White Plains, NY), 12,932
House on Center Street, The (book), 10,251
House, Patricia, 11,857
"House Un-American Activities Committee: Bulwark of Segregation" (booklet), 17,608
House Was Quiet and the World Was Calm, The (book), 13,190
House Without Windows, The (book), 11,991
Houseboat Girl (book), 4,306
Household appliances, 4,064, 6,523, 11,565, 13,446
Household budgets. *See* Home economics, accounting
Household Economics Club (Neenah-Menasha, WI). *See* Neenah-Menasha Federated Woman's Club (WI)
Household Technicians of America, 8,080
Household workers, 1,653, 2,684, 2,975, 6,399, 6,766,

6,892, 6,989, 8,021, 9,701, 9,702, 9,987, 10,203, 11,040, 11,775, 14,593, 15,030, 15,726
Household workers, Afro-American, 1,655, **3,301**, 10,052
Household Workers Association, 4,173
Housekeepers' Alliance, 2,633
Houseman Family, 4,942
Houser, David, **15,834**
Houser, Margaret [Mrs. David], 15,834
Housewives, 62, 66, 67, 156, **296, 502, 594, 1,287, 1,299, 2,040, 2,062,** 3,317, **3,725, 4,333, 4,423, 4,456, 4,474, 4,489, 4,507, 4,532, 5,217, 5,218, 7,016, 7,353, 7,358, 7,391, 7,401, 7,402, 7,405, 7,414,** 7,417, **7,455, 7,589, 7,753, 7,778, 7,782, 7,972,** 8,230, **8,295, 8,339, 8,343, 8,361, 8,373, 8,376, 8,499, 8,501,** 8,518, 8,690, **8,753, 8,763, 8,765, 8,772,** 8,931, **8,979,** 9,005, **9,016,** 9,034, **9,091, 9,314,** 9,421, 9,434, 9,461, 9,521, **9,853, 9,959,** 10,041, **10,052, 10,053, 10,093,** 10,107, **10,167, 10,175, 10,436, 10,468, 10,756, 10,895,** 11,035, **11,048, 11,065, 11,127,** 11,209, **11,211, 11,264, 11,275, 11,276, 11,416, 11,418,** 11,661, **12,458, 12,486, 12,853, 13,228,** 13,231, 13,299, 13,724, **14,179,** 14,180, **14,190, 14,721, 14,734, 14,786, 14,792, 14,793, 15,001, 15,280, 15,605, 15,617, 15,799, 15,809, 15,895, 15,896, 16,068, 16,096, 16,099, 16,109, 16,142, 16,145, 16,300, 16,324, 16,365, 16,379, 16,401, 16,402,** 16,403, **16,410, 16,415, 16,418, 16,420, 16,421, 16,423, 16,427, 16,429, 16,430, 16,435, 16,437,** 16,440, **16,442, 16,447,** 16,965, 16,968, 17,051, 17,195, **17,225, 17,434, 17,441, 17,645, 17,828, 17,830**
Housewives, Afro-American, **8,029**
Housewives Effort for Local Progress (Terre Haute, IN), **4,676**
Housewives League of Detroit (MI), **8,029**
Housing, 470, **517,** 1,317, 1,605, 2,397, 2,504, 3,362, 3,875, 3,879, 3,905, 3,910, 4,003, 4,166, 5,120, 5,839, 7,239, 7,253, 7,678, 7,705, 8,115, 8,646, 8,651, 8,659, 8,661, 8,668, 8,678, 8,681, 8,765, 9,196, 9,407, 10,603, 11,914, 12,870, 13,261, 14,348, 14,671, 15,204
    information services, 11,914
    law and legislation, 4,508, 11,695, 15,205
Housing and health, 15,205
Housing Association of Delaware Valley (PA), **15,201,** 15,205
Housing authorities, 1,837, 3,874, 5,829, 6,656, 6,885, 11,914, 14,605
Housing Authority of Portland (OR), 14,605
Housing, cooperative, 1,654, 6,375, 9,136
Housing management, 140, 2,695, **15,205**
"Housing of Non-Family Women in Chicago, A Survey" (ms), 3,935
Housing policy, citizen participation, **4,129, 15,201**
Housing projects, government. *See* Public housing
Housing subsidies, 1,879
Housman, Ida E., **10,984**
Houston A&M Mothers' Club (TX), **16,198**
Houston Academy (GA), faculty, 14,401
Houston, Charles H., 2,123
Houston, Christopher (1744-1837), 13,006
Houston Community Center (Philadelphia PA), **15,202**
Houston Community College (TX), 16,242
Houston, Elizabeth Lena (Alderson) (1860-1933), **10,247**
Houston, Harriet [Mrs.]. *See* Livingston, Harriet Houston [Mrs. Peter Van Brugh]
Houston, Helen Beall, 16,117
Houston Independent School District (TX), 16,236, 16,242
Houston, Lyda Suydam (1891-), **555,** 11,846
Houston, M. W., **3,528**
Houston-McCallie Family (GA), 3,222
Houston, Margaret Moffette (Lea) [Mrs. Sam] (1819-67), **16,089,** 16,106
Houston Open Forum (TX), 16,236
Houston Post (TX), 2,393
Houston Public Library (TX), 16,239
Houston, Samuel F., 15,202
Houston, Samuel, Jr., 16,089
Houston, Samuel "Sam" (1793-1863), 1,639, 15,463, 15,577, 16,089, 16,097

Houstons of Georgia, The (book), 3,531
Houstoun, Mary Williamson, **3,529**
Houstoun, Mossman, 3,529
Hovda, Jane, **17,280**
Hovey, Anna Maria (Sibley) [Mrs. George Lewis] (1822-65), 7,678
Hovey, Carl, 1,451
Hovey, George Lewis (1810-ca. 1878), 7,678
Hovey, Henriette Russell [Mrs. Richard], 2,610, 10,863
Hovey, Richard (1864-1900), 10,863
Hovey, Susannah. *See* Perkins, Susannah (Hovey) [Mrs. Thomas]
Hoving, Mrs. Walter, 12,708
"How Do Men Look at Women? How Do Women Look at Themselves?," 11,663
"How Do You Like America?" (ms), 6,700
"How I Went to Denver," 1,790
How Many Miles to Babylon (book), 5,992
"How Mother Got Her Forty Acres" (essay), 10,010
How To Be a Successful Advertising Woman (book), 17,623
Howard, Ada, 7,574
Howard, Alice [Mrs. Henry], 5,120
Howard, Augustus, 15,541
Howard, Benoni, 4,812
Howard, Blanche Willis (1847-98). *See* von Teuffel, Blanche Willis (Howard) [Mrs. Julius] (1847-98)
Howard, Caroline (1794-1888). *See* Gilman, Caroline (Howard) [Mrs. Samuel] (1794-1888)
Howard, Cecil Howard Cutts, **7,387**
Howard, Clarina Irene (1810-85). *See* Nichols, Clarina Irene (Howard) [Mrs. Justin] Carpenter [Mrs. George W.] (1810-85)
Howard, Dorothy Cope, 11,471
Howard, Elizabeth "Lizzie" R. *See* Milligan, Elizabeth "Lizzie" R. (Howard) [Mrs. Sam]
Howard, Elizabeth Metzger, 11,940
Howard, Emily Pagelson, 6,662
Howard Family (GA), 3,088
Howard Family (TN), **13,250**
Howard Female College (MO), **9,873,** 10,026, 10,033
Howard, Francis Gilman (1869-1937), **12,513**
Howard, Gertrude (1874-1953). *See* McCormick, Gertrude (Howard) [Mrs. Marlin E.] Olmsted (1874-1953)
Howard, Harriet. *See* Fay, Harriet (Howard)
Howard, Helen Louise (Coe) [Mrs. John Lawrence], 556
Howard, Iva May. *See* Kirk, Iva May Howard [Mrs. William Elwood]
Howard, Jacob, 13,250
Howard, Jean (1880-1955). *See* McDuffie, Jean (Howard) [Mrs. Duncan] (1880-1955)
Howard, Jennifer. *See* Goldwyn, Jennifer (Howard)
Howard, John, 13,250
Howard, Joshua, 8,011
Howard, Katherine Graham [Mrs. Charles P.] (1898-), 5,128, 5,135, **6,662,** 11,857
Howard, Leopoldine "Polly" Blaine (Damrosch) [Mrs. Sidney Coe], 556
Howard, Lilliane Stevens (1872-1958), **4,530, 14,814**
Howard, Lucy [Mrs. Francis Gilman], 12,513
Howard, Martha Taylor, 12,790
Howard, Mary. *See* Schoolcraft, Mary (Howard) [Mrs. Henry Rowe]
Howard Mission Home for Little Wanderers, 11,030
Howard, Mrs. George A., **11,424**
Howard, Mrs. H. C., 12,656
Howard, Robert (1760-1846), 7,663
Howard, Robert Boardman, 761
Howard, Sarah E., 3,379
Howard, Sarah Lue (1868-1948). *See* Bostick, Sarah Lue (Howard) [Mrs. Mancil Mathis] (1868-1948)
Howard, Sidney Coe (1891-1939), **556**
Howard Theatre (GA), 3,267
Howard University (DC), 2,143, 2,149, 10,191
    employees, 8,116
Howard University (DC), Civil Rights Committee, **2,143**
Howard, William G., 6,459
Howarth, Cora Ethel Eaton (1865-1910). *See* McNeil, Cora Ethel Eaton (Howarth) [Mrs. Stephen] Crane [Mrs. Hammon P.] (1865-1910)

Howarth, Ellen Clementine, 11,184
Howe, Abby Waite, 13,881
Howe, Anna B., 4,923
Howe, Clara [Miss], 6,734
Howe, Elizabeth Leavitt [Mrs. Fisher] (1815-99), 12,225
Howe, Evelyn. *See* Porter, Evelyn (Howe)
Howe Family, 6,663
Howe Family, 4,942
Howe Family (MA), 6,621
Howe, Fanny Huntington (Quincy) [Mrs. M. A. DeWolfe] (?-1933), 6,752
Howe, Fisher (1798-1871), **12,225**
Howe, Florence, 15,197
Howe, Florence Hall, 11,114
Howe, Florence Marion (1845-1922). *See* Hall, Florence Marion (Howe) [Mrs. David Prescott] (1845-1922)
Howe, Frances Mae (1892-). *See* Satterlee, Frances Mae (Howe) [Mrs. August N.] (1892-)
Howe, Harold, II, 11,845
Howe, Helen, 6,584
Howe, Henry Clay, 14,392
Howe, Herbert Crombie (1872-1940), **14,392**
Howe, Jonah, 9,414
Howe, Julia (Ward) [Mrs. Samuel Gridley] (1819-1910), 951, 1,426, 1,436, **1,442,** 1,483, 1,896, **2,399,** 2,501, 2,542, 2,605, 3,290, 3,797, 3,862, 3,922, 3,927, 4,304, 4,708, 5,903, **5,934,** 5,965, 5,973, 6,373, 6,587, 6,663, **6,664,** 6,741, 6,762, 6,855, 6,870, 7,044, 7,171, 7,183, 7,232, 7,477, 7,560, 7,648, 7,941, 11,605, 11,658, 11,742, 11,821, 12,467, 12,529, 12,662, 12,807, 14,000, 14,062, 14,895, 17,010, 17,053, 17,197
Howe, Laura Elizabeth (1850-1943). *See* Richards, Laura Elizabeth (Howe) [Mrs. Henry] (1850-1943)
Howe, Letitia Crombie [Mrs. Henry Clay], 14,392
Howe, Lillian, 14,392
Howe, Lois Lilley (1864-1964), 3,781
Howe, Louis, 11,486, 11,853
Howe, Lucy Demaris. *See* Bancroft, Lucy Damaris (Howe)
Howe, Marie Jenney, 16,992
Howe, Mark Antony De Wolfe (1864-1960), 12,035, 17,473
Howe, Mark De Wolfe (1906-1967), 6,261
Howe, Mary (Carlisle) (1882-1964), 2,664
Howe, Maud, 6,870
Howe, Mrs. J. E., 9,333
Howe, Norah (Halverson), 17,862
Howe, Orlando C. (1824-99), **4,765**
Howe, Rose, 3,897
Howe, Samuel Gridley, 1,426, 1,442, 6,663
Howe, Sarah [Mrs. Joel] (1766-1849), **7,333**
Howe, Topssule, 2,314
Howel-Waffle, Willella Earhart (?-1924), **1,521**
Howell, Abigail, 12,779
Howell, Abigail. *See* Luce, Abigail (Howell) [Mrs. Abraham]
Howell, Alfred Elliott (1863-1931), **15,953**
Howell, Anna (Blackwood) [Mrs. Joshua Ladd] (1769-1855), **7,637, 11,209**
Howell, Asher, **10,985**
Howell, Bertha (Wilson) [Mrs. William], 10,985
Howell, Clark, 3,203
Howell, Eliza, 12,779
Howell, Eliza D., **9,792**
Howell, Eliza Dunham [Miss] (1834-1916), 10,985
Howell, Elizabeth, 13,600
Howell, Emma (1862-1937). *See* Jenson, Emma (Howell) [Mrs. Andrew] (1862-1937)
Howell, Evan Park, 3,203
Howell Family (NJ), 10,985
Howell Family (NY), **12,779**
Howell Family (PA), 14,966
Howell Family (PA), 15,021
Howell, Francis Speight Claude, 13,264
Howell House (NC), **13,443**
Howell, Irene Ironheart [Mrs.] (1933-), 8,518
Howell, Isabel [Miss], 15,953
Howell, Jennie (Thompson) [Mrs. Alfred Elliott], 15,953
Howell, Jennie Wright [Mrs.], **3,040,** 3,071

Howell, John Ladd (1739-85), 11,209
Howell, Josephine R., **15,021**
Howell, Joshua Ladd (1762-1818), 7,640
Howell, Julia Adelaide Erwin [Mrs. Evan Park], 3,203
Howell, Julius F., 3,219
Howell, Margaret, 9,737
Howell, Margaret [Mrs. Cornelius D.] (?-1938), 4,099
Howell, Martin A., 10,985
Howell, Mary, 15,134
Howell, Mary Davis Hook [Mrs. Clark], 3,203
Howell Memorial Church (Chicago, IL), 4,099
Howell, Mrs. A., 8,240
Howell, Mrs. H., 4,773
Howell Neighborhood House (Chicago, IL), **4,054, 4,099**
Howell Neighborhood House (Chicago, IL), Women's Auxiliary, 4,054
Howell, Rebecca Elizabeth (1833-1917). *See* Mace, Rebecca Elizabeth (Howell) [Mrs. Wandle] (1833-1917)
Howell, Rosalie, Family (GA), **3,203**
Howell Shad Fisheries, 11,209
Howell, Varina Anne (1826-1906). *See* Davis, Varina Anne (Howell) [Mrs. Jefferson] (1826-1906)
Howell, Virginia Royster, 13,447
Howells, Annie. *See* Frechette, Annie (Howells)
Howells, Aurelia, 14,080
Howells, Elinor Gertrude (Mead) [Mrs. William Dean], 14,080
Howells, Joseph, 10,318
Howells Medal, 11,161
Howells, Mrs. Joseph, 14,080
Howells, Sue [Mrs. Joseph], **10,318**
Howells, Victoria, 14,080
Howells, William Dean (1837-1920), 1,426, 1,954, 5,815, 6,602, 12,021, **14,080**
Hower, Blanche (Bruot) (1862-1953), 13,730
Hower Family (Ohio), **13,730**
Hower, Ralph M., 6,203
Howerton, Merle (Flanery) [Mrs. Davis Monroe], 5,313
Howery Family (MS), 9,816
Howe's Academy (Mount Pleasant, IA), students, 5,058
Howes, Ethel (Puffer) (1872-1950), 6,771
Howes Family, **6,771**
Howey, Laura E., **10,319**, 10,343
Howey, Mrs., 10,317
Howie, Adda F. (1852-1936), **17,655**
Howie, John McFarlane, 11,521
Howland, Abby, 12,397
Howland, Abby. *See* Woolsey, Abby (Howland) [Mrs. G. M.]
Howland, Charles, 14,845
Howland, Deborah Melville (Dowsett) [Mrs. Henry] (1827-53), **3,624**
Howland, Edith, 11,425
Howland, Emily (1827-1929), 5,907, 6,410, **11,279**, 11,605, **11,616**, 15,283, 15,290
Howland Family (NY), **11,425, 15,283**
Howland, Florence King, 2,542
Howland, Gulielma Maria (Hilles) [Mrs. Charles] (1822-1907), 14,845
Howland, Harriet. *See* Roosevelt, Harriet (Howland) [Mrs. James]
Howland, Henry, 3,624
Howland Institute, 14,745
Howland, Isabel (1859-1942), 7,193, **7,232**, 11,508, 11,605, 12,811
Howland, Marie (Stevens) [Mrs. Lyman] Case [Mrs. Edward] (1836?-1921), 2,401
Howland, Sarah (Hazard) [Mrs. John Hicks] (1781-1847), **12,226**
Howland, Susanah, 11,599
Howlett, Angelina, **6,665**
Howorth Family (MS), **6,901**
Howorth, Lucy R. (Somerville) [Mrs. Joseph M.] (1895-), 2,067, 6,901, **9,544, 9,546, 9,647**, 9,734, 13,176
Hoxie Family (IA), **4,919**
Hoxie, Jane (1815-98). *See* Banbury, Jane (Hoxie) [Mrs. James] Robinson [Mrs. Thomas] (1815-98)
Hoxie, Lizzie, 17,010

Hoxie, Vinnie (Ream) [Mrs. Richard Leveridge] (1847-1914), 2,432, 4,919, 9,942, **17,656**
Hoxmeier, Kathryn (Manahan) (1896-), 9,200
Hoyem, Nell M., **8,750**
Hoyt, Catherine (McCann) (1875?-1955), **15,246**
Hoyt, Charles C., 12,021
Hoyt, Elinor Morton (1885-1929). *See* Wylie, Elinor Morton (Hoyt). [Mrs. Philip] Hichborn [Mrs. Horace] Wylie [Mrs. William Rose] Benét (1885-1929)
Hoyt, Esther. *See* Sawyer, Esther (Hoyt) [Mrs. Ansley W.]
Hoyt Family, 4,942
Hoyt Family, 12,431
Hoyt Family (NY), **12,014**
Hoyt, Florence V., 5,119
Hoyt, Helen. *See* Lyman, Helen (Hoyt) [Mrs. William Whittingham]
Hoyt, Herma (1898-). *See* Briffault, Herma (Hoyt) (1898-)
Hoyt, James Otis, 12,014
Hoyt, Janette (Chase) [Mrs. William S.], 2,259
Hoyt, Julia A., **11,617**
Hoyt, Minerva Hamilton (1866-?), 1,594
Hoyt, Mrs. James Otis, 12,014
Hoyt, Nettie Chase, 17,992
Hoyt, Sue E., 8,154
Hsia, Martha So-Shin, 9,986
Hsun, Lu, 174
Hualapai Indians, **16,865**
Huang, Al, 4,384
Hub (NE), 2,340
Hubbard, Alice (Moore) [Mrs. Elbert] (1861-1915), 11,435
Hubbard, Almyra, **9,992**
Hubbard, Annie Ward [Mrs. Theodore], 3,891
Hubbard, Bernice (1897-1975). *See* May, Bernice (Hubbard) [Mrs. Samuel Chester] (1897-1975)
Hubbard, Catherine (1886-1961). *See* Dace, Catherine (Hubbard) Egbert (1886-1961)
Hubbard, Charles, 1,798
Hubbard, Charles J. (1902-1950), 14,447
Hubbard, Charlotte (Moton) (1920-), **2,139**
Hubbard, Cornelia, 12,246
Hubbard, E. Vickery, 17,230
Hubbard, Elbert, 7,012, 11,979, 12,405
Hubbard, Eliza. *See* Smith, Eliza (Hubbard) [Mrs. Ira Gilbert]
Hubbard, Elizabeth Eleanora Thompson [Mrs. John Buford, Jr.] (1908-), 5,394
Hubbard, Ellen Sterling, 12,246
Hubbard, Emeline. *See* Day, Emeline (Hubbard)
Hubbard, Faith (Silliman) [Mrs. Oliver Payson] (1812-87), **10,865**, 12,420
Hubbard Family, **10,864**
Hubbard Family (NY, MA, MI), **12,015**
Hubbard, Frances. *See* Flaherty, Frances (Hubbard) [Mrs. Robert J.]
Hubbard, Frances Cornelia (Smith), 801
Hubbard, Gertrude McCurdy [Mrs. Gardiner Greene], 2,202
Hubbard, Grace, 1,798
Hubbard, Hannah Root, **3,855**
Hubbard, Hazel, 772
Hubbard, Henry Cutler, 426
Hubbard, Hester [Mrs. Thomas], 15,459
Hubbard, John Buford, Jr., 5,394
Hubbard, Leonidas, Jr., 10,864
Hubbard, Lucius Lee (1849-1933), 12,015
Hubbard, Mabel G. (1858-1923). *See* Bell, Mabel G. (Hubbard) [Mrs. Alexander Graham] (1858-1923)
Hubbard, Margaret Carson (ca. 1907-), **10,850**
Hubbard, Martha Dorman. *See* Weaver, Martha Dorman (Hubbard) [Mrs. George Norman]
Hubbard, Mary Hedges [Miss] (1837-1934), **4,364, 12,246**
Hubbard, Mina Benson [Mrs. Leonidas, Jr.]. *See* Ellis, Mina Benson [Mrs. Leonidas, Jr.] Hubbard [Mrs.]
Hubbard, Mrs., 7,109
Hubbard, Mrs. Ward, 12,246
Hubbard, Myrtle S., 4,923
Hubbard, Oliver P., 10,857
Hubbard, Sarah, 13,308

Hubbard, Thomas, 15,459
Hubbard, Ward, Family (NY), 4,364
Hubbel Family. *See* Hubbell Family
Hubbel, Frances Eliza. *See* Berry, Frances Eliza (Hubbel) [Mrs. Charles Henry]
Hubbell Family, 11,618
Hubbell Family (New England), 6,352
Hubbell, Henry Salem (1869-1949), **11,618**
Hubbell, Nellie M., 8,947
Hubbell, Nellie Rose (Strong) [Mrs. Henry Salem], 11,618
Hubbels Family. *See* Hubbell Family
Hubble, Anna G. Johnson [Mrs. Ferdinand], **15,028**
Hubble Family (Mo), **9,993**
Hubble, Janie [Miss], 9,993
Huber, G. Carl (1865-1934), **7,818**
Huber, Lucy. *See* Andrus, Lucy (Huber)
Huber, Lucy (Parker) [Mrs. G. Carl], 7,818
Huber, Marion (Kubic), 7,818
Hubert, Charlotte G., 1,255
Hubley Family (PA), **14,970**
Hubley, Margaret (Burd) (1761-?), 14,970
Hubner, Charles W., 3,204
Hubner, Mary Frances Whitney, 3,204
Hubner, W. Whitney, 3,204
Huckaby, Elizabeth, 11,857
Huddle, Mildred, 14,590
Huddleston, Amelia Edith (1831-1919). *See* Barr, Amelia Edith (Huddleston) (1831-1919)
Hudgins, Mary Dengler [Miss] (1903-), 262
Hudnall, George B., 9,006
Hudnut, William Herbert, III, 4,483
Hudson, Anna (Ridgely) [Mrs. James L.] (1841-1926), 4,365
Hudson, Anna (Rogers) [Mrs. Henry, Sr.], 12,514
Hudson, Dorothy Rose (1887-), **8,577**
Hudson, Erasmus Darwin (1805-80), 7,233
Hudson Family, **7,233**
Hudson Family (NY), **12,514**
Hudson Fortnightly Club (NH), **10,878**
Hudson Guild, 17,716
Hudson, Hannah [Mrs. John Rogers], 12,514
Hudson Historical Society (NH), 10,878
Hudson, John Rogers (1784-?), 12,514
Hudson, Lillian C. [Mrs. Claude] (1892-1976), **1,821**
Hudson, Louise C. [Mrs. Henry, Jr.], 12,514
Hudson, Margaret S., 10,591
Hudson, Mary, 8,936
Hudson, Mary E. (Clemmer) [Mrs. Daniel] Ames [Mrs. Edmund] (1831-84), **6,474**, 12,394, **14,058**
Hudson Memorial School (Cawnpore, India), 14,426
Hudson, Phebe, 12,779
Hudson River School (painting), 2,801, 7,046
Hudson Shore Labor School, 6,893, 17,588
Hudson State Training School (NY), 7,546
Hudson Women's Club (IL),
Hudson's Bay Company, 534, 8,939, 14,549, 14,594, 17,416
Huebsch, Benjamin W. (1876-1964), **2,403**
Huefner, Dixie, 16,971
Hueston, Ethel, 5,070
Huey, Catherine M., **3,396**
Huff, Grace Clementine [Miss], **9,648**
Huff, Sarah [Miss], **3,205**
Huffcut, Lillian, 6,815
Huffman, Edna K., 4,023
Huftalen, Sarah Lorindia (Gillespie) (1865-1952?), **4,920,** 5,029
Hug, Procter R., Sr. (1902-), **10,736**
Huger, Ann (LeJau) [Mrs. Daniel], 15,493
Huger, Benjamin, 15,507
Huger, Daniel, 15,493
Huger, Daniel, 15,499
Huger, Daniel (1779-1858), 15,441
Huger, Esther, **15,781**
Huger Family (SC), **15,441**
Huger Family (SC), **15,493**
Huger, Harriet H., **15,607**
Huger, Julia, 15,441
Huger, Mary Esther (1820-98), **15,608**
Huger, Mary LeJau. *See* Downes, Mary LeJau (Huger) [Mrs. Richard]
Huggins, Anne E. K., 14,549
Huggins, Dorothy H., 395

Huggins, Edward, 14,549
Huggins, Eliza, 9,294
Huggins, Louisa Caroline (1799?-1879). *See* Tuthill, Louisa Caroline (Huggins) [Mrs. Cornelius] (1799?-1879)
Huggins, Mary, 9,294
Huggins, Rosa, **13,035**
Hugh Chatham Memorial Hospital Auxiliary (NC), 13,370
Hughan, Jessie Wallace (1875-1955), 15,313
Hughes, Adella (Prentiss) [Mrs. Felix] (1869-1950), Family (OH), **13,932**
Hughes, Andrew C., 13,672
Hughes, Ann Sarah (Maxcy) [Mrs. George W.] (1812-?), 2,343
Hughes, Antoinette (Carter) [Mrs. Charles Evans] (1864-1945), 2,519
Hughes, C. Amelia, 3,996
Hughes, C. Elizabeth, **8,877**
Hughes, Catherine. *See* Waddell, Catherine (Hughes) [Mrs. Chauncey]
Hughes, Charles Evans, 12,708
Hughes, Constance, 6,336
Hughes Family (PA), **15,052**
Hughes, H. Stuart, 17,637
Hughes High School (OH), 13,839
Hughes, James Langston (1902-67), 3,284, 3,285, **3,287**, 3,288, 6,112, 12,684
Hughes, Josephine Brawley [Mrs. Louis C.] (1838-1926), 197
Hughes, Katherine (1873-1963). *See* Gumb, Katherine (Hughes) [Mrs. Daniel J.] (1873-1963)
Hughes, Katie (1873-1963). *See* Gumb, Katie (Hughes) [Mrs. Dan] (1873-1963)
Hughes, Lillian (?-1962). *See* Prince, Lillian (Hughes) [Mrs. William Meade] (?-1962)
Hughes, Lizzie J. *See* Scott Lizzie J. (Hughes) [Mrs. Robert W.]
Hughes, Louis C. (1842-1915), **197**
Hughes, Louisa Walter Bishop, 6,770
Hughes, Magdalena, 12,316
Hughes, Marija Matich, 2,865
Hughes, Martha (1857-1932). *See* Cannon, Martha (Hughes) [Mrs. Angus Munn] (1857-1932)
Hughes, Mary Gray, 6,035
Hughes, Mrs. Andrew C., 13,672
Human Voice (periodical), 14,368
Hughes, Regina Mary (Olson) [Mrs. Frederick] (1895-), **2,107**
Hughes, Ruby, 15,317
Hughes, Sara (1862-1938). *See* Cornell, Sara (Hughes) (1862-1938)
Hughes, Sarah Francis (Hickman) (1858-?), **9,874**
Hughes, Sarah (Maxcy), 15,052
Hughes, Sarah (Tilghman) [Mrs. George E.] (1896-), 2,067, 2,097, **6,666**, 15,795
Hughes, Ted, 4,485
Hughs, Lucile Smith, 3,206
Hughs, Margaret E., 1,594
Hughs, Susanna M., **3,206**
Huguenin Family, 2,999
Huguenot Society of America, **12,119, 12,120, 12,121,** 12,240, 17,394
Huguenot Society of America, Ladies Committee, 12,121
Huguenot Society of South Carolina, 15,439
Huguenots in America, 12,119, 12,120, 12,121, **15,410**
Hugy, Alice E., **9,139**
Hui of Kahana (HI), 3,623
Huidekoper, Catharine (Cullum) [Mrs. Alfred], 2,286
Huish, Ivie Maude (1891-). *See* Jones, Ivie Maude (Huish) [Mrs. Lorin Franklin] (1891-)
Hulbert Family (CT), **1,972**
Hulbert, Gertrude [Mrs. Edgar Wylie], 3,969
Hulbert, Mary (Huntington), 1,972
Hulet, Catherine (Stoker) [Mrs. Sylvanus Cyrus] (1829-82), **16,703**
Hulet Family (UT), 16,455
Hulett, Alta [Miss] (1854-77), 1,186, **1,188**
Huling, Caroline Alden, 3,862
Hull, Anne A., **2,664**
Hull, Annie E., 2,346
Hull, Charles, 4,062
Hull, Charles H., **11,619**

Hull, Charles Jerold (1820-89), 4,100
Hull, Eliza Ann (1804-32). *See* Staples, Eliza Ann (Hull) (1804-32)
Hull Family (IL), **4,100**
Hull, Hannah Clothier [Mrs. William Isaac] (1872-1958), 5,122, 9,443, 15,301, **15,306,** 15,311, 15,316, 16,121
Hull, Helen Rose (1888-?), **12,016**
Hull-House (Chicago, IL), 3,798, 4,047, 4,052, 4,057, 4,059, 4,071, 4,080, 4,091, 4,100, 4,110, 4,111, 4,116, 4,117, 4,128, 4,134, 4,143, 4,146, 4,156, 4,161, 4,210, 4,330, 4,331, 4,452, 6,622, 6,970, 7,172, 7,300, 9,187, 9,981, 10,603, 11,897, 12,026, 15,303
Hull-House Association (Chicago, IL), 3,803, 4,079, **4,101,** 4,152
Hull-House Music School (Chicago, IL), 4,056, 4,153
Hull-House Players (Chicago, IL), 4,097
Hull-House Women's Club (Chicago, IL), 4,097
Hull, Josephine (Sherwood) (1877?-1957), **6,667,** 11,457
Hull, Julia, 3,052
Hull, Lucy (?-1923). *See* Baldwin, Lucy (Hull) [Mrs. George Johnson] (?-1923)
Hull, Lucy Sizer, 10,449
Hull, Marie, 9,694
Hull, Mary J. [Miss], 11,619
Hull, Phoebe, 4,062
Hull, William "Bill" R., Jr. (1906-77), **9,994**
Hullock, Elizabeth, 16,132
Hulme, Kathryn Cavarly (1900-), 557
Hulsizer, Mary Burr [Miss] (1889-), **10,986**
Hult, Ruby El (1912-), **558, 17,193**
Humaco High School (Puerto Rico), 7,225
Human Betterment Association for Voluntary Sterilization. *See* Association for Voluntary Sterilization
Human Betterment Association of America, 17,716. *See also* Association for Voluntary Sterilization
Human Betterment Foundation, 8,634
Human Freedom League, 2,000
Human reproduction, 2,667, 2,669, 6,222
Human resources, 2,667
Human resources policy, 11,900
Human rights. *See* Civil rights
Human Voice (periodical), 14,368
Humanists, **4,085, 6,408,** 15,900
"Humanities, The: A Means to Educational Unity" (article), 2,936
Humboldt Methodist Church (NE), 10,476
Hume, Emma L., **559**
Hume, Fannie Page (1838-65). *See* Braxton, Fannie Page (Hume) [Mrs. Carter M.] (1838-65)
Hume, Portia (Bell) [Mrs. Samuel James] (1901-), 458, 1,081, 2,086
Hume, Samuel James, 458
Humenna, Dokia (1904-), **9,499**
Humility of Mary Convent (Ottumwa, IA), **5,090**
Humorists, **12,041, 17,806**
Humpal-Zeman, Josefa, 4,057
Humphrey, Doris. [Mrs. Charles F.] Woodford (1895-1958), **12,363**
Humphrey, Edith A. (Lockhart), **10,675**
Humphrey, Ella, 10,714
Humphrey, Emily Barksdale, **9,649**
Humphrey, Helen, 3,911
Humphrey, Helen Florence (1909-63), **6,668**
Humphrey, Horace, 12,363
Humphrey, Hubert Horatio (1911-78), 2,497, 6,765, 8,912, **9,140,** 9,286, 11,827, 15,755, 16,965
Humphrey, Jane. *See* Wilkinson, Jane (Humphrey)
Humphrey, Julia [Mrs. Horace], 12,363
Humphrey, L. B. [Miss], 8,477
Humphrey, Margaret. *See* White, Margaret (Humphrey) [Mrs. Rosman]
Humphrey, Muriel (Buck) [Mrs. Hubert Horatio] 6,765, 9,140, 9,467
Humphrey-Weidman Company, 12,363
Humphrey, Zephine (1874-1956), 17,010
Humphreys, A. E., Sr., 1,720
Humphreys, A. E., Jr., 1,720
Humphreys, Daisy, 2,663
Humphreys, Earle, 9,360
Humphreys Family (CO), **1,720**

Humphreys Harriet L, 17,009
Humphreys, I. B., 1,720
Humphreys, K., 3,499
Humphreys, Katherine (Hay), 12,505
Humphreys, Marie M. (Champney), 6,245
Humphreys, Mildred (Maury), 9,709
Humphreys, Robert, **11,620**
Humphreys, Ruth (Boettcher) [Mrs. A. E., Jr.] (1890-1959), 1,720
Humphreys, Sarah, 11,620
Humphries, Adelaide, 3,000
Huncke, Mary, 4,869
Huncke, Olga H. (1881?-1974), **3,856**
Hundley, Anna. *See* Glud, Anna (Hundley)
Hundley, Ruby M., 3,755
Huneker, James Gibbons (1857-1921), **10,866**
Huneker, Josephine (Lasca), 10,866
Hungarian-Americans, 8,906, 13,933
Hungarian Ladies Charity Club (OH), **13,933**
Hungary
  politics and government, 11,025
  revolution (1848), 5,676
Hunger March (1915), 4,161
Hungry Ghosts, The (book), 11,221
Hungry Hearts (book), 947
Hunkins, Eusebia (Simpson) (1902-), **14,150**
Hunkins-Hallinan, Hazel, 859
Hunley, Mary T. [Mrs.], **13,037**
Hunn, Lydia Jones Sharpless [Mrs. Ezekiel], **15,284**
Hunneman and Company (MA), **6,289**
Hunning, Henrika Bush [Mrs.] (1853-1921), **11,216**
Hunsaker, Marianne (1842-?). *See* D'Arcy, Marianne (Hunsaker) (1842-?)
Hunt, Agnes (1876-1923), 7,158
Hunt, Amelia, 17,037
Hunt, Annie Rubamah (Ludlow) [Mrs. Randell], 17,992
Hunt, Celia (Mounts) [Mrs. Jefferson] (1805-97), **16,704**
Hunt, Edward Bissell, 568, 1,426, 1,443
Hunt, Elizabeth. *See* Palmer, Elizabeth (Hunt)
Hunt, Elizabeth B. Bisbee, 7,234
Hunt, Emma Rebecca. *See* Day, Emma Rebecca (Hunt) [Mrs. John T.] Ewing [Mrs. James Collins]
Hunt, Estelle Louise, **7,819**
Hunt, Euphenia, 11,074
Hunt Family, 9,113
Hunt Family, **7,234**
Hunt, Frances, **14,770**
Hunt, George B., Family, 9,141
Hunt, Helen (1892-1963). *See* West, Helen (Hunt) [Mrs. Byron McG.] (1892-1963)
Hunt, Helen Maria (Fiske) [Mrs. Edward Bissell] (1830-85). *See* Jackson, Helen Maria (Fiske) [Mrs. Edward Bissell] Hunt [Mrs. William Sharpless] (1830-85)
Hunt, Ida (Gibbs) [Mrs. William], 2,140
Hunt, Inez (Whitaker) [Mrs. Nelson V.] (1892-), **1,685,** 1,689
Hunt, Ione, 9,140
Hunt, Irene (1907-), 8,531
Hunt, Jefferson, 16,704
Hunt, Leila Wall (?-1968), **17,194**
Hunt, Lenoir, 17,100
Hunt, Louisa (Lane) [Mrs. Henry Blaine] (1820-97). *See* Drew, Louisa (Lane) [Mrs. Henry Blaine] Hunt [Mrs. George] Mossop [Mrs. John D.] (1820-97)
Hunt, Mabel Leigh, 4,483
Hunt, Marsha, 1,017
Hunt, Mary (1705-77). *See* Pomeroy, Mary Hunt [Mrs. Seth] (1705-77)
Hunt, Mary Ann, 9,741
Hunt, Mary Hannah (Hanchett) [Mrs. Leander B.] (1830-1906), 4,243, **12,515,** 14,017
Hunt, Mary Olive A., 7,234
Hunt, Mrs. Edward L., 15,308
Hunt, Mrs. Ridgely, 2,405
Hunt, Mrs. S. Benton, 11,823
Hunt, Mrs. William Montague, 2,243
Hunt, Nancy A., 14,628
Hunt, Nancy (Zumwalt) Cotton, **560**
Hunt, Priscilla (Coffin) [Mrs. Jabez] (1786-1860).

See Cadwalader, Priscilla (Coffin) [Mrs. Jabez]
   Hunt [Mrs. Joseph] (1786-1860)
Hunt, Randell, 17,992
Hunt, Sarah, **3,041**
Hunt, Sarah Catherine "Kate" S., **17,100**
Hunt, Sarah Ethridge [Mrs.], **9,650**
Hunt, Vedna, 16,868
Hunt, Virginia Livingston [Miss], **2,405**
Hunt, William Henry (1869-1951), **2,140**
Hunter, Aaron Burtis, **13,444**
Hunter, Alice M. (1891-1975), **13,710**
Hunter, Anna Colquitt, **3,530**
Hunter, Anna Jane (?-1941). *See* Hardaway, Anna
   Jane (Hunter) [Mrs. John Steger] (?-1941)
Hunter, Anna (Rogers), 12,514
Hunter, Beatrice Trum (1918-), **6,034**
Hunter, Charles, 8,899
Hunter, Claudia Watkins, 13,189
Hunter, Clora Twedell, 9,875
Hunter College (NY), **12,122,** 12,708, 12,871
   alumnae, 1,283, 1,577
   faculty, 5,460, 6,955
Hunter, Edward, 16,705
Hunter, Eilley (Orrum) [Mrs. Stephen] (1826-1903).
   See Bowers, Eilley (Orrum) [Mrs. Stephen]
   Hunter [Mrs. Alexander] Cowan [Mrs. Lemuel
   Sanford "Sandy"] (1826-1903)
Hunter, Eliza Catherine Finnock, 16,417
Hunter, Elizabeth A. [Mrs.] Cole [Mrs. Thomas
   Meredith], **5,779**
Hunter, Ella Ewing (1870-1935), **14,256**
Hunter, F. W., 2,701
Hunter Family (TX), 16,269
Hunter, Hannah, 8,899
Hunter, Isabella, 3,547
Hunter, Jane, 8,899
Hunter, Jane. *See* Guthrie, Jane (Hunter) [Mrs. D.
   C.]
Hunter, Jane Edna (1882-1971), **13,934,** 13,950,
   15,782
Hunter, Joseph C., 5,555
Hunter, Juanita, 7,889
Hunter, Lydia, 3,518
Hunter, Margaret (1799-1876). *See* Hall, Margaret
   (Hunter) [Mrs. Basil] (1799-1876)
Hunter, Marjorie, 11,916
Hunter, Martha Taliaferro. *See* Hitchcock, Martha
   Taliaferro (Hunter) [Mrs. Charles M.]
Hunter, Mary (1859-1952). *See* Doane, Mary
   (Hunter) [Mrs. Gustavus C.] (1859-1952)
Hunter, Mary (1868-1934). *See* Austin, Mary
   (Hunter) [Mrs. Stafford Wallace] (1868-1934)
Hunter, Mary Ankeney [Mrs. Fred H.], 4,729, 4,859,
   5,002
Hunter, Mattie (1889-). *See* Booth, Mattie (Hunter)
   [Mrs. John A.] (1889-)
Hunter, Nancy (ca. 1820-53). *See* Aiton, Nancy
   (Hunter) [Mrs. John Felix] (ca. 1820-53)
Hunter, Nora (Siens) (1873-1951), 4,464
Hunter, Pearce and Battey (GA), 3,496
Hunter, Robert, 8,899
Hunter, Rodello. *See* Calkins, Rodello Hunter [Mrs.
   Frank]
Hunter, Sallie [Mrs. Nathaniel Wyche], 1,086
Hunter, Sarah Lothrop Taylor [Mrs. Aaron Burtis],
   13,444
Hunter, Susan F., 13,433
Hunter, Susanna (Wann) [Mrs. Edward] (1825-85),
   16,705
Hunter, Thomas Meredith, 5,779
Hunter, Winifred A., 2,724
Hunters Point Project Committee, 517
Hunting, **1,290,** 5,410, **14,296**
Hunting and fishing clubs, 15,595
Hunting, Constance (1925-), **6,035**
Huntingdon Academy (PA), 14,824
Huntingdon Bank (PA), 14,824
Huntingdon College (AL), 12,737
Huntington, Anna Vaughn (Hyatt) [Mrs. Archer
   Milton] (1876-1973), **12,901**
Huntington, Anne (1740-90). *See* Huntington, Anne
   (Huntington) [Mrs. Benjamin] (1740-90)
Huntington, Anne (Huntington) [Mrs. Benjamin]
   (1740-90), 1,868

Huntington, Arabella Duval [Mrs. Collis P.]
   (1851-1924). *See* Huntington, Arabella Duval
   [Mrs. Collis P.] Huntington [Mrs. Henry E.]
   (1851-1924)
Huntington, Arabella Duval [Mrs. Collis P.]
   Huntington [Mrs. Henry E.] (1851-1924), **12,902**
Huntington, Archer Milton, 12,901
Huntington, Benjamin (1736-1800), **1,868**
Huntington, Catharine Sargent (1889-), **6,669**
Huntington, Edna (1895-1965), **11,320**
Huntington College (IN), Auxiliary, 4,594
Huntington, Ellen (1845-1920). *See* Gates, Ellen
   (Huntington) [Mrs. J. E.] (1845-1920)
Huntington, Elvira (Stevens) [Mrs. John S.]
   Woodbury [Mrs. Oliver B.] (1832-1909). *See*
   Barney, Elvira (Stevens) [Mrs. John S.]
   Woodbury [Mrs. Oliver B.] Huntington [Mrs.
   Royal] (1832-1909)
Huntington, Emily Harriet (1895-), **561,** 917
Huntington, Eunice Carew [Mrs. Joseph], 2,009
Huntington Family (CT), **1,972**
Huntington, Frances (Carpenter) [Mrs. William
   Chapin] (1890-1972), 2,247, **7,235**
Huntington, Hannah [Mrs. Samuel] (1770-1818),
   13,935
Huntington, Ida M., 4,766
Huntington Library (CA), 1,425, 11,828, 12,902
Huntington, Margaret, 12,551
Huntington, Margaret Jane (Evans) [Mrs. George]
   (1842-1926), **6,670,** 8,721
Huntington Memorial Hospital (WV), 17,462
Huntington, Oliver B., 16,593
Huntington, Presendia Lathrop (1810-92). *See*
   Kimball, Presendia Lathrop (Huntington) [Mrs.
   Joseph] Smith [Mrs. Heber Chase] (1810-92)
Huntington, Samuel (1765-1817), 13,935
Huntington, William Chapin, 2,247
Huntington, Zina Diantha (1821-1901). *See* Young,
   Zina Diantha (Huntington) [Mrs. Henry Bailey]
   Jacobs [Mrs. Joseph, Jr.] Smith [Mrs. Brigham]
   (1821-1901)
Huntingtonian (IN), 4,595
Huntley, Lenora. *See* Miller, Lenora (Huntley)
Huntley, Lydia Howard (1791-1865). *See* Sigourney,
   Lydia Howard (Huntley) [Mrs. Charles]
   (1791-1865)
Huntley, Marjorie W., 15,766
Hunton, Addie D. (Waites) [Mrs. William Alphaeus]
   (1875-1943), 2,502
Huntsville Female College (AL), 71, 9,698
Huntting, Helen, 1,486
Hupa Indians, 965
Hupp, Emily Bertelsen (1919-). *See* Windsor, Marie
   (1919-)
Huppmann, Ann, 5,842
Hurd, Albert (1823-1906), 4,478
Hurd, Ethel (Edgerton) [Mrs. Tyrus I.] (1845-1929),
   4,261, 9,142, 9,231, 9,327
Hurd, G. H., **17,909**
Hurd, Harriet Sophia (1855-1929). *See* McClure,
   Harriet Sophia (Hurd) [Mrs. Samuel Sidney]
   (1855-1929)
Hurd, J. D., 17,909
Hurd, Kate Campbell (1867-1941). *See* (Hurd)-Mead,
   Kate Campbell [Mrs. William Edward]
   (1867-1941)
Hurd, Mamie (Carpenter) [Mrs. Charles] (ca. 1864-?),
   8,978
Hurd, Mary Charlotte (1859-1949), 4,478
(Hurd)-Mead, Kate Campbell [Mrs. William Edward]
   (1867-1941), **15,129**
Hurd, Sarah D. (Vail) Cutler [Mrs. Whitfield]
   (1811-87), 10,920
Hurd, Whitfield, 10,920
Hurin, Mary Locke (?-1945), 14,144
Hurlburt, Olive E., **6,379**
Hurlbutt, Mary, 8,657, 9,492
Hurley Hospital (Flint, MI), 8,180
Hurley Hospital (Flint, MI), Auxiliary, 8,180
Hurley, James F., 13,001
Hurley, Sister Helen Angela, 9,490
Hurn, Ethel A., 17,743
Hurricane Camille, 9,694
Hurricane, The (plantation), 9,714

Hurricanes, 9,694, 13,266
Hurst, Fannie (1889-1968), 378, 411, 448, 677, 691,
   720, 1,451, 2,403, 2,558, 2,562, **6,671,** 7,209,
   9,443, 11,812, 11,954, 12,013, 12,436, 12,648,
   16,157
Hurst, Florence "Daisy" Jaffray (1870-1967). *See*
   Harriman, Florence "Daisy" Jaffray (Hurst) [Mrs.
   J. Borden] (1870-1967)
Hurston, Zora Neale (1901-60), **2,872,** 2,876, 2,882,
   2,946, 2,948, 5,465, 6,112
Husband, The (drama), 17,793
Huse, Mrs. P. B. P., 6,223
Husk, The (periodical), 5,085
Hussey, Ethel (Fountain) [Mrs. William J.]
   (1865-1915), 7,820
Hussey Family (MI), **7,820**
Hussey, Mary D., 11,114
Hussey, Mrs. Gray, 11,859
Hussey, William J., 7,820
Husted, Ida A. (1851-1931). *See* Harper, Ida A.
   (Husted) [Mrs. Thomas Winans] (1851-1931)
Husted, Marjorie Child [Mrs.], **6,672**
Hustler, Eliza Jane McKean, 14,594
Huston, Charles (1822-97), 2,029
Huston, Charles L. (1856-1951), **2,029**
Hutcheson, Ernest, 2,664
Hutcheson Family, 15,942
Hutchings, Martha E. *See* Griffith, Martha E.
   (Hutchings) [Mrs. Thomas J.]
Hutchings, Mary Emeline "Marie" (1881-). *See*
   Rollins, Mary Emeline "Marie" (Hutchings) [Mrs.
   James Henry] (1881-)
Hutchins, Ephraim, 10,816
Hutchins, Grace (1885-1969), **14,393,** 14,437
Hutchins, Louise Gilman (1911-), 6,987
Hutchins, Magdalene. *See* Claiborne, Magdalene
   (Hutchins) [Mrs. Ferdinand Leigh]
Hutchins, Maude Phelps (McVeigh), **6,036**
Hutchins, Robert, 4,395
Hutchinson, Abigail Jemima (1829-92), 5,907, 6,577
Hutchinson, Angela (1870-1955?). *See* Hammer,
   Angela (Hutchinson) (1870-1955?)
Hutchinson, Ann (Getz) [Mrs. Edward] (ca. 1800-?)
   See Lake, Ann (Getz) [Mrs. Edward] Hutchinson
   [Mrs. Andrew Leech] (ca. 1800-?)
Hutchinson, Anna C. *See* Brown, Anna C.
   (Hutchinson)
Hutchinson, Anne (Marbury) [Mrs. William]
   (1591-ca. 1643), **11,291**
Hutchinson, Clara (Brownlee) (1850-1931), 10,185
Hutchinson, Dorothy (1895-1956), **12,017,** 12,584
Hutchinson, Dorothy Caleton (Hewitt) [Mrs.
   Cranford] (1905-), 15,316
Hutchinson Family (NY), 11,440
Hutchinson, Fred C., 1,235
Hutchinson, Hannah, **7,388**
Hutchinson, Hattie, 8,948
Hutchinson, Isobel Wylie, **14,501**
Hutchinson, Jemima, 6,577
Hutchinson, Josephine, 12,367
Hutchinson, Margaret (1819-47). *See* Sheets,
   Margaret (Hutchinson) [Mrs. Elijah Funk]
   (1819-47)
Hutchinson, Sarah P., **7,388**
Hutchinson, Sophie Lewis (1888-1967). *See* Drinker,
   Sophie Lewis (Hutchinson) [Mrs. Henry
   Sandwith] (1888-1967)
Hutchison, Adam, 13,038
Hutchison, Anne Claire, 15,800
Hutchison Family (SC), **15,800**
Hutchison, Jenny Johnston, 15,800
Hutchison, Phebe Jane (Morrison) [Mrs. John Rogers]
   (1854-1931), **4,423**
Hutchison, Susan Davis (Nye) [Mrs. Adam]
   (1790-1867), **13,038, 13,445**
Hutson, Ethel [Miss], **5,514**
Hutt, Elizabeth L., 14,651
Hutt, Frances E. (1903-70). *See* Dewey, Frances E.
   (Hutt) [Mrs. Thomas E.] (1903-70)
Hutton, Al, 17,377
Hutton, Betty, 1,025
Hutton Family (IL), **3,757**
Hutton, L. L. (?-1927), 3,757

Hutton, Mary Arkwright [Mrs. Al] (ca. 1860-1915), **17,171, 17,377**

Hutton, Mary Blair [Mrs. L. L.] (?-1944), 3,757

Hutton, Pearl. *See* Shrader, Pearl (Hutton) [Mrs. Edwin]

Hutton Settlement (WA), 17,377, 17,380

Huxtable, Ada Louise, **17,979**

Huyck, Sarah, 8,271

Hwa Nan College (China), 14,435
  presidents, 14,419

Hyams, Frances Isabella. *See* Brentano, Frances Isabella (Hyams) [Mrs. Lowell]

Hyatt, Anna Vaughn (1876-1973). *See* Huntington, Anna Vaughn (Hyatt) [Mrs. Archer Milton] (1876-1973)

Hyatt, Virginia (Kingsbury) [Mrs. Belden], 2,424

Hyde, Abigail "Abbie" (1863-1931). *See* Cowley, Abigail "Abbie" (Hyde) [Mrs. Matthias Foss] (1863-1931)

Hyde, Abigail (Bradley), 6,425

Hyde, Agnes Holstad (1899-), **8,878**

Hyde, Anne (Bachman) [Mrs. Charles R.], **13,039**

Hyde, Arthur Mastick (1877-1947), **9,995**, 9,996

Hyde-Bixler Family (CA), 1,233

Hyde, Elizabeth Augusta (1838-1921). *See* Bixler, Elizabeth Augusta (Hyde) (1838-1921)

Hyde, Elizabeth "Beezie." *See* Brownell, Elizabeth "Beezie" (Hyde) [Mrs. Kenneth C.]

Hyde, Elizabeth (Waldo) [Mrs. Alvan Phinney], **1,869**

Hyde Family, 16,961

Hyde Family, **11,621**

Hyde, Florence Elise [Miss], 11,621

Hyde, Harriet "Hallie." *See* Irwin, Harriet "Hallie" (Hyde) [Mrs. Will]

Hyde, Harriet Sophia (Hallie), 1,553

Hyde, Helen (1868-1919), 1,233, **1,306**

Hyde, Ida Henrietta (1857-1945), **2,070**

Hyde, Ira B. (1838-1926), **9,996**

Hyde, Julia E., 12,316

Hyde, Laurance M., 9,996

Hyde, Lavius, 6,425

Hyde, Marietta Butler, 1,233

Hyde, Marinda, 16,852

Hyde, Mary. *See* Field, Mary Hyde [Mrs. William R.]

Hyde, Mary Ann (Price) [Mrs. Orson] (1816-1900), **562**, 16,787

Hyde, Mary Eliza (1854-1934). *See* Willis, Mary Eliza (Hyde) (1854-1934)

Hyde, Orange Percy, 11,621

Hyde, Orson, 562

Hyde Park, 11,853

Hyde Park Current Events Club (MA), **7,050**

Hyde Park High School (Chicago, IL), 3,785, 5,162

Hyde Park Juvenile Protective League, Hyde Park Center (Chicago, IL). *See* Hyde Park Neighborhood Club (Chicago, IL)

Hyde Park Neighborhood Club (Chicago, IL), **4,102**

Hyde Park Neighborhood Club (Chicago, IL), Business and Professional Women's Auxiliary, 4,102

Hyde Park Neighborhood Club (Chicago, IL), Women's Auxiliary, 4,102

Hyde Park Travel Class (IL). *See* Hyde Park Travel Club (IL)

Hyde Park Travel Club (IL), **3,857**

Hyde, Walter Woodburn, 11,621

"Hyenas" (poem), 1,952

Hygeia (periodical). See *Today's Health* (periodical)

Hygiea Female Athenaeum (OH), 13,910

Hygiene, **6,703**, 6,946, 7,317, 8,108, 8,661, 8,743, 12,837, 14,637, 15,802
  study and teaching, 4,116

Hygiene and Physiology of Women, The (book), 1,551

Hygiene, sexual, **6,760**, 6,978, **8,633, 12,736**

Hyland Family (OR), 14,714

Hyland, Hattie. *See* Smith, Hattie (Hyland)

Hylbert, Ethel (Lacey) [Mrs. Lewis C.] (1889-?), **563**, 11,846

Hyman, Libbie Henrietta [Miss], 2,668

Hyman, Shirley Jackson [Mrs. Stanley Edgar] (1919-65). *See* Jackson, Shirley. [Mrs. Stanley Edgar] Hyman (1919-65)

Hyman, Stanley Edgar, 2,410

Hymers, Prudence Ermina (1867-?). *See* Gould, Prudence Ermina (Hymers) [Mrs. William] (1867-?)

Hymn Society of America, 2,626

Hymn writers, **2,350**, 3,969, 5,394, 5,923, 16,486

Hymns, 2,222, **2,544**, 5,364, 6,500, 7,663

Hynes, Anita K., 10,055

Hynes, Sam, 4,237

Hypatia (LA), 5,549

Hypatia Club (Boulder, CO), 1,679

Hypertension, 7,311

Hysing, Else Elisabeth (1832-1918). *See* Koren, Else Elisabeth (Hysing) (1832-1918)

I Am the Fox (book), 5,036, 5,085

IAPW Journal (periodical), 15,124

"I Came A Stranger" (ms), 4,143

"I Didn't Think" (poem), 4,226

I Don't Know—Do You? (book), 10,844

"I Heard an Indian Drum" (ms), 9,041

I, Keturah (book), 6,117

I Knew a Lovely Lady (book), 799

"I Love My Love" (song), 4,689

I Never Sang for My Father (drama), 2,357

I Passed for White (book), 4,061

I Played Their Accompaniments (book), 11,176

"I Pledge Allegiance to My Flag" (song), 1,688

I Remember Me (book), 11,457

"I Tied My Kitty to a Wild Plum Tree" (song), 10,540

"I Tried to Tell You" (song), 10,478

I Was a Savage (book), 6,109

"I Was a WASP" (article), 30

"I Was Teaching in Nebraska" (song), 10,540

Ibáñez, Vicente Blasco, 215

Icarian communities, 4,302

Icarian Community (IL, IA), **4,767**

Ice, 11,429

Iceland, World War II, civilians work, 13,543

Icelandic-Americans, 8,518, 8,690

Ichord, Richard H., 10,062

Ichthyologists, 2,863

Ichthyosaur Paleontological State Monument (NV), 10,726

Ickes, Harold, 8,653

Ickes, Harold L., 2,123, 16,155

I'd Rather Be Right (drama), 4,764

Idaho, 3,664, 3,707, 3,712, 14,680, 16,442
  agricultural laborers, 3,690
  agriculture, 3,739
  authors, **3,657, 3,697, 3,707**
  bibliography, **3,707**
  birds, 3,722
  bookmobiles, 6,858
  businesswomen, 3,682, 17,186
  camping, 3,678
  Catholic Church, societies, etc., **3,655**
  child care centers, 3,690
  church schools, Episcopal, **3,717**
  clubs, **3,660, 3,670, 3,693**
  college trustees, 3,667
  community life, 16,457
  congresswomen, **3,735**
  corporations, **3,682**
  councils and synods, 3,690
  dams, 3,735
  deaf, education, 16,654
  deeds, 3,679
  diaries and journals, 3,678, 16,457, **16,642**
  educational associations, **3,659**
  elections, 3,658
  emblems, 3,687
  executive, **3,698**
  family planning, 3,690
  farm life, 16,530
  foster home care, 3,725
  Friends, 3,688
  governors, 3,667, 3,687, 4,347
  historians, 3,712
  home economics,—accounting, 3,668
  home nursing, **3,729**
  horse breeders, **885**
  housewives, **3,725**
  influenza epidemics, 3,729
  interracial marriage, 3,661

Japanese Americans, evacuation and relocation (1942-1945), 892
  journalism,—societies, **3,694**
  journalists, **3,662, 3,677**
  land settlement, 16,488
  legislators, 3,667, 3,671, **4,468**, 6,858
  librarians, 3,664, **3,696**, 3,713, 6,858
  literary societies, **3,697**
  local church councils, **3,656**
  merchants, 14,449
  midwives, 3,740
  migrant labor, medical care, 3,691
  militia, **3,700**
  mines and mineral resources, 784, 7,935
  mining corporations, 3,698
  minorities, 3,724
  missionaries, **3,706, 3,723**
  monasticism and religious orders for women, Catholic, **17,415**
  monuments, 16,648
  Mormons and Mormonism, 191, **3,738, 3,739**, 3,740, 16,719, 16,803
  musical societies, **3,692**
  Native Americans, 3,731
  newspaper publishers and publishing, **3,669**
  newspapers, sections, columns, etc., 3,662
  Nez Perce Indians
    government relations, **3,665**
    missions, 3,706, 3,723
    reservations, 3,665
  nuns, Catholic, **3,680, 17,415**
  officials and employees, **3,709**
  orphans and orphan asylums, 3,725
  parents' and teachers' associations, **3,695**
  patriotic societies, **3,673, 3,674, 3,699, 3,736**
  pioneers and settlers, **3,671, 3,675, 3,710, 3,726, 3,728, 3,730, 3,731**, 3,736, **3,738**, 16,485, 17,196
  political clubs, **3,658**
  political committees, 6,858
  priories, **3,733**
  public health, 3,690, 3,696
  public nursing, 3,729
  public welfare, 3,677, **3,690, 3,691**
  railroads, 17,183
  ranchers, **3,685**
  ranches, 3,728
  school superintendents and principals, 3,705, **3,709**
  school yearbooks, 3,714
  scrapbooks, 3,689
  senators, United States, 3,667, 3,669, 3,681, 3,684, 3,725, 6,858
  Sheepeater Indians, wars (1878-1879), 3,721
  Shoshone Indians, medical care, 14,763
  silver mines and mining, 17,377
  students' societies, 14,029
  suffrage, 4,481, 6,858
  suffrage societies, **3,681**
  teachers, 3,662, **3,705, 3,714**
  temperance societies, **3,666, 3,688**
  trade-unions, officials and employees, **3,715**
  tuberculosis, prevention, **3,696**
  urban beautification, 3,672

Idaho Chinese Lore (book), 3,680

Idaho Churchman, 3,717

Idaho Council of Churches, Southern Idaho Migrant Ministry, **3,690, 3,691**

Idaho Farm Workers' Service, Inc., 3,677, **3,691**

Idaho Federation of Music Clubs, **3,692**

Idaho Free Press, 3,662

Idaho Press Women, **3,694**

Idaho Spalding Centennial, 3,723

Idaho State College (Pocatello, ID), Chimes, 14,029

Idaho State Federation of Labor, 3,715

Idaho State Federation of Music Clubs, 3,663

Idaho State Historical Society, 3,684, 3,713

Idaho State Parents' and Teachers' Association, **3,695**

Idaho State Tuberculosis Hospital (Gooding, ID), 3,696

Idaho Statesman, 3,669

Idaho Territory, 9,439
  judges, 4,784
  maps, 3,712

Idaho Tuberculosis Association, 3,696

Idaho White Ribboner, 3,666

Idaho Writers' League, **3,697**
Ide, Amanda Sprague, 876
Ide Family, 876
Ide, Mary Eliza (1822-84). *See* Wheeler, Mary Eliza (Ide) [Mrs. Benjamin] (1822-84)
"Idea, An" (ms), 6,087
"Ideal Deaconess, The" (pamphlet), 10,564
Iden, Susan, **13,447**
Identity (drama),
Ideson, Julia (1880-1945), **16,239**
If I Could Fly, 11,618
If My Memory Serves Me Right (book), 12,700
If This Be I, As I Suppose It To Be (book), 2,300
Ignatius Donelly Memorial Association, 9,048
ik ben Nieuwe Neger (i am the New Negro) (book), 2,145
Ike's Travels (book), 10,921
Il Lavoro (newspaper), 12,861
Ilg, Frances Lillian (1902-), 2,168, 2,353
Ill, Charles L., 11,068
I'll Take Texas (book), 16,159
Illegitimacy, 4,141, 6,513, 6,544, 8,456, 8,637, 8,638, 8,647, 11,207, 17,216. *See also* Children of single parents
Illicit (moving-picture play), 17,793
Illington, Margaret. [Mrs. Edward J.] Bowes, 3,745, 4,781
Illini Guides, 4,382
Illini Union, 4,395
Illinois, **3,743**, 3,759, 3,829, **3,851, 3,930,** 3,998, **4,180, 4,245, 4,275, 4,287,** 4,301, **4,302, 4,313, 4,331, 4,450, 4,452**
abortion, legal aspects, 4,046
actors, **4,097**
adoption, 4,103
legal aspects, 3,852
adult education, 3,971, **4,048**
advertising, vocational guidance, **4,171**
aeronautical societies, **3,793**
affirmative action programs, 4,043
Afro-Americans, **3,799, 3,846, 3,934,** 4,073, 4,087, 4,093, 4,142
agricultural experiment stations, 4,386
agriculture, 3,754, **3,756**
alcoholics, hospitals and asylums, **4,164**
altar gilds, **3,936**
animals, treatment of, 4,105
anti-Catholicism, 8,070
arbitration, industrial, 6,531
arboretums, 3,882
architects, 4,336
art
exhibitions, 3,851
exhibitions, traveling, 3,980
galleries and museums, 2,777, 3,980, 12,912
study and teaching, **4,071**
art festivals, 4,275
art patronage, 3,816
art schools, **4,112**
art societies, **3,816, 3,980**
artists, 3,783, 6,597
assessment, 3,947
athletic clubs, 4,213, 4,220
attendance officers, 4,341
attorneys general, **4,094**
authors, 4,143, 4,309, **4,370**
balls (parties), 3,931
bankers, **4,078**
bankruptcy, 12,246
banks and banking, 3,751
bar associations, 4,094
baths, public, 3,875, 4,114
beauty contests, 3,851
beauty operators, 4,336
Bible, societies, **3,808**
Bible colleges, 3,969, **3,970**
bills, legislative, 4,149
bird-song, 3,764
birth control, 4,131
birth control clinics, 4,131
Bohemian-Americans, 4,057
boy scouts, 3,946
businessmen, 3,757, **3,882, 3,893**
Camp Fire Girls, **4,063**

camps, 4,452
Catholic Church
charities, 4,308
societies, **4,447**
Catholic high schools, **4,148**
Catholic hospitals, 15,181
Catholic schools, 4,284, 4,328, 4,335, **4,342,** 4,874, 8,292
Catholic universities and colleges, **3,971,** 4,316
pictorial works, 3,973
caucus, **4,109**
cemeteries, 4,197, 4,302, 4,448
census, 3,945
charitable societies, **3,955, 4,092, 4,118, 4,140, 4,157, 4,372,** 13,785
charitable societies, Jewish, **4,038,** 13,782
charitable uses, trusts, foundations, **4,084**
charities, 3,851, 4,047, **4,072, 4,079,** 4,103, **4,114, 4,150,** 6,748
charities, Jewish, 3,807, **3,865**
charity organization, 3,903
child care, **3,792,** 4,102
child care centers, 3,792, 3,865, 4,054, 4,148, 4,286
child welfare, 3,863, 4,114, 4,166, **12,238**
children
dental care, 4,273
employment, **4,104**
hospitals, **3,932**
law and legislation, 3,887, 3,932, 4,117
children's clubs, **4,136**
Chinese-Americans, 3,856
cholera epidemics, 3,897, 4,347
church colleges, **4,281**
archives, **3,746**
church records and registers, 4,054, 4,099, **4,441**
church societies, 4,147, **4,193,** 16,743
church societies, Episcopal, **3,939, 3,940, 3,941, 3,942,** 4,292
church societies, Lutheran, 3,957, **3,959, 3,960, 3,961, 3,962, 3,963,** 3,965, 4,319
church societies, Methodist, 3,765, 3,766, 3,767, 3,768, **3,769, 3,770,** 4,127
churches, Baptist, 10,812
churches, Lutheran, 4,319, 4,325, 4,326
churches, Methodist, 3,762
cities and towns, 3,753, **3,917, 3,919, 3,920, 3,931**
citizens' associations, 3,792, 3,798, **3,823, 3,824,** 4,073, 4,125, **4,170**
city councilwomen, **3,853, 4,149**
civil rights workers, 3,852
Civil War, 1,408
hospitals, charities, etc., **3,869, 3,888,** 3,897, **4,293,** 4,313, 11,167
clergy, 4,003
clergy, Congregational, 4,436
clergy, German Baptist, 16,365
clergy, Lutheran, 4,319, **4,326**
clergy, Methodist, **4,206**
clergymen's wives, 3,939
clubs, 3,743, **3,750,** 3,783, **3,796,** 3,803, 3,809, **3,820, 3,828,** 3,833, 3,848, 3,851, 3,855, **3,857, 3,868, 3,876, 3,877, 3,891,** 3,899, **3,900, 3,910,** 3,916, 3,917, 3,918, 3,920, 3,930, 3,931, **3,992, 3,997,** 4,044, 4,074, 4,094, 4,163, 4,165, **4,166, 4,171, 4,176, 4,179, 4,187, 4,188, 4,189, 4,190, 4,192, 4,195,** 4,197, 4,273, 4,278, **4,291, 4,298, 4,299, 4,309, 4,310, 4,311, 4,318, 4,334, 4,366, 4,400, 4,401, 4,412, 4,448, 4,451, 4,458, 4,459, 4,462,** 6,748, 11,713, 15,145
clubs, Afro-American, 3,846
coal-miners, **8,091**
coal mines and mining, 10,031
college and school journalism, **4,316, 4,317**
college librarians, **4,398, 4,402**
college presidents, 4,305, 4,326, 4,395
college students, Afro-American, 4,382
college teachers, 2,540, **4,272, 4,304, 4,378,** 4,385, **4,387, 4,389, 4,393, 4,397,** 10,603
college trustees, 4,214, 4,388, 4,411
community and school, 3,787, **3,824**
community centers, **4,054, 4,077, 4,139,** 4,308
community organization, 3,853, **4,093, 4,102, 4,134**
composition (music), **3,790**
concerts, 4,056

congresses and conventions, 4,082, **10,754,** 12,639
congressmen, 2,379, 4,358, 4,375, 12,847
congresswomen, 99, 1,605, 11,225
conservatories of music, **3,788, 3,789,** 4,056, 4,153, 9,467
contemplative orders, **4,329**
convents and nunneries, Catholic, **3,744**
court records, 3,949
courts, 3,760, 4,166
deaconnesses, Episcopal, **3,937**
deans (in schools), **4,042,** 4,181, 4,215, 4,223, **4,382, 4,390**
deeds, 3,871
demonstrations, 4,170
dental hygienists, 4,336
dentists, 4,336, 4,341, 4,373
department stores, management, **13,817**
diaries and journals, 3,834, 3,849, 4,178, **4,294, 8,330**
19th C, **3,776,** 4,348, 4,365, 4,456
travel, **3,763**
disaster relief, 4,072, 4,157
dissertations (academic), 3,790
dormitories, **4,295,** 4,366
draft horses, 3,751
dressmakers, 3,751
dropouts, education, 3,787
dry-goods, 4,184
editors, **4,130,** 4,347, **17,328**
education, 4,166, 14,473
curricula, **3,786,** 4,341
finance, 4,341
education, compulsory, 4,366
education, preschool, **4,116,** 4,128
educational associations, **3,795, 4,048, 4,051, 4,067,** 4,150, **4,407,** 4,452, **12,238**
educators, **4,081,** 6,528
elections, 3,760
emigration and immigration, **3,815**
employment agencies, **3,811, 4,068**
endowments, 3,872, 4,320
equal rights amendment (proposed), 4,124
evening and continuation schools, 6,490
examinations, 4,336
excavations (archaeology), 3,753
executives, **3,927**
executives, Jewish, **13,817**
exhibition buildings, 6,805
exhibitions, 3,912, **4,066,** 4,123, **4,337,** 9,610, 10,343, 13,993, 14,026, 17,468
factories, 4,259
family planning, **3,895**
farm life, 4,294
farmers, 3,757, **4,410, 4,425, 4,430**
federations, financial (social service), **3,905, 4,037,** 4,078, **4,079**
feminists, **3,821**
feminists, Afro-American, **4,132**
fires, 1,036, 3,802, **3,812,** 3,834, 3,897, 6,832, 10,046
foster home care, 4,065, 4,103
fresh-air charity, **4,276**
Friends, 3,762
fund-raising, **3,952,** 4,015, 4,105, 4,128, 4,273
gardening, societies, etc., 4,097, **4,191,** 4,273, **4,454**
gas manufacture and works, 3,898
genealogy, 3,754
government attorneys, **3,946**
governors, 3,749, 4,349, 4,351, 4,352, 4,357, 4,358, 4,361, 4,364, 4,370, 4,417, 10,092, **11,827**
greek letter societies, **3,972, 4,194,** 4,219, **4,220,** 4,403
handicapped children, education, 3,787, 4,150
high school students, 3,831
high school teachers, **4,124, 4,181, 4,268,** 11,713
high school teachers, Afro-American, **4,147**
historians, **3,998**
historic sites, 4,415
conservation and preservation, **4,444**
historical societies, **3,916, 3,918,** 3,919, 3,920, **3,929, 4,165,** 4,287, **4,315, 4,444**
home economics extension agents, 4,449
home economics extension work, **3,761**
home economics, rural, 2,673

home economics teachers, **4,378**
home nursing, **3,904**
hospital administrators, 3,932, 4,411
hospital records, **3,932**, **3,967**, **3,968**
hospitals, 4,123, 4,335, **8,760**, 8,859, 8,862
hospitals, gynecologic and obstetric, **4,010**, **4,021**
housewives, **4,333**, **4,423**, 4,456, **8,330**, 9,434, **10,167**
housing, 4,166
housing authorities, 3,874
housing policy, citizen participation, **4,129**
humanists, **4,085**
hygiene, study and teaching, 4,116
immigrants, **4,110**
immigrants, German, **4,092**
integration (in higher education), 4,017
international education, **4,321**
Japanese-Americans, evacuation and relocation (1942-1945), **4,113**
journalism, societies, etc., **3,862**
journalists, 3,873, 4,060, **4,332**
journalists, Afro-American, **3,835**
judges, **2,255**, 3,785, **4,076**, **4,373**, 4,442
justices of the peace, 4,076
juvenile courts, 3,803, 3,820, 3,823, 3,852
juvenile delinquency, 4,114
juvenile detention homes, 4,114
kindergarten, **3,809**, 3,820, 3,822, 4,099
kindergarten teachers, **3,856**
labor and laboring classes, 4,143
labor law and legislation, 1,188, 4,114
laboratory schools, 4,210
land grants, 13,132
land settlement, 11,704
land titles, registration and transfer, 4,182
lawyers, 1,186, 3,799, **3,852**, **4,060**, **4,076**, **4,269**, **4,290**, **4,351**, 4,361, 4,373, **4,431**, **6,527**, **6,530**, **6,531**, 12,847
legal aid societies, 4,085, **4,144**
legal documents, **3,871**
legislative bodies, 3,858
legislators, 3,745, **3,749**, 3,764, 4,106, 4,149, **4,183**, 4,307, 4,347, **4,349**, 4,361, 4,442
librarians, **3,915**, 3,919, **3,925**
libraries, 4,299
  branches, stations, etc., 3,920
  employees, **3,998**, **4,004**
libraries and state, 4,366
libraries, public, 3,919
library associations, 4,391, 4,396
library schools, **4,023**, 4,391
liquor law, 3,909
literary societies, **3,843**, **3,885**, **4,186**, **4,299**, 4,403
lobbying, 4,170
lobbyists, **3,858**, 4,046, **4,125**
maple syrup, 3,756
maternity homes, **4,088**
mayors, **3,995**
medical colleges, 3,967, **4,027**, **4,217**
medical colleges alumni, **4,225**
medical record librarians, 4,023
midwives, 4,336
militia, 4,416
minorities, 3,851
missions, Lutheran, **3,963**, **3,965**
missions, Mennonite, 4,515, 4,517
monasteries, **4,274**, **4,329**
monasticism and religious orders for women, Catholic, **3,933**, **4,035**, **4,036**, **4,282**, **4,283**, **4,284**, **4,286**, **4,296**, **4,303**, **4,308**, **4,314**, **4,328**, **4,335**, **4,453**, **4,509**
Mormons and Mormonism, 75, 855, 16,540, 16,557, 16,598, 16,636, 16,675, 16,687, 16,692, 16,718, 16,734, 16,749, 16,771, 16,793, 16,798, 16,830, 16,832, **16,835**, 16,853, 16,976
Mormons and Mormonism, Afro-American, **16,708**
municipal government, 3,853
municipal government by city manager, 4,440
municipal officials and employees, **4,182**
  salaries, allowances, etc., 4,078
municipal officials and employees, Afro-American, 10,191
museum directors, **4,123**
music teachers, **4,056**, **4,153**, 8,364

musical revues, comedies, etc., **4,220**
musical societies, **3,838**, 4,056
Native Americans, 3,754
  wars, 3,897
natural history museums, 3,952
  management, 3,953
naturalization records, 3,949
news agencies, Afro-American, 3,799
newspapers, 3,918, 4,165, 4,215, 4,302, 6,080, 6,343
  sections, columns, etc., 3,825, 4,289, 4,379, 6,526
nursery schools, 3,822, **4,049**, 4,081, 4,116, **4,128**
nurses, 3,932, **4,249**, 4,336
nursing, **3,810**
  standards, 3,810
  study and teaching (continuing education), **4,014**
nursing schools, **3,861**, **3,954**, **4,009**, **4,013**, **4,014**, **4,016**, **4,017**, **4,019**, **4,022**, **4,026**, **4,108**, 4,162, **5,843**, 8,862
  alumnae, **4,011**, **4,020**, **4,024**
nutrition, study and teaching, **4,070**
officials and employees, **4,341**, 4,444
old age homes, 4,078, **4,137**, **4,138**, 4,286
old age homes, Jewish, **3,866**
open-air schools, 3,813
opera, 3,838, 3,878
oral history, **4,032**
oriental studies, **4,028**
orphans and orphan asylums, **3,806**, **4,065**, 4,069, **4,107**, 4,286
pageants, 4,332
parents' and teachers' associations, 4,299
parks, 3,753, 3,875
patriotic societies, **3,850**, 4,278, **4,414**, **4,415**
peace societies, **3,814**, 15,316
pediatrics, study and teaching, 3,932
personnel service in education, 8,643
pharmacists, 4,336
philanthropists, **3,882**, **4,214**
photographs, **4,279**, **4,455**
  collections, **4,196**
physical education and training, **4,041**
physicians, 4,111, **4,131**, 4,217, 4,336, **4,346**, **4,377**, 4,698, 7,966
pioneers and settlers, 1,630, **3,754**, 4,255, **4,345**, **4,353**, 4,368, **4,369**, **4,423**, 4,804, 7,678, 7,680, **10,561**, 12,404
poets, **4,000**, **4,200**
Polish-Americans, **3,815**
political activists, women, 3,792, 4,124
politics and government, **3,760**, 4,166, 4,172, 4,994
politics, practical, women's activism, **3,860**, **4,121**, **4,122**, 4,165, **4,426**, **4,427**, 4,440, 6,544
polygamy, 16,794
postgraduate medical education, **3,914**
Presbyterian churches, 3,764
printers, **4,057**
private schools, **3,842**, 4,477
probation officers, 3,852, **4,115**
professional education, 4,336
professions, licenses, **4,336**
prostitution, 3,798
public health, 4,111, 4,440
public health nurses, 4,336
public health nursing, 3,813, 4,085
public housing, 4,077, 4,087, 4,096, 4,147
public institutions, **4,338**
public libraries, **3,925**
public relations consultants, 4,130
public schools, **3,785**
public welfare, law and legislation, 3,858
public works, 4,055
race problems, 4,073, 4,158, 4,170
real estate agents, 4,336
records of births, etc., 3,871
recreation, 3,747, 3,851, 4,166
religious education, 4,468
retirement homes, **3,758**
rhythm bands and orchestras, 3,856
riots, 4,170
sanitation, 4,166
scholarships, **4,150**
school administrators, 4,341
school boards, **3,784**, 3,787, 3,911
school buildings, 4,341

school children, 4,341
school discipline, 4,341
school districts, 3,755
school elections, 4,341
school libraries, 4,391
school nurses, 4,341
school physicians, 4,341
school social work, 8,643
school superintendents and principals, 3,745, 3,785, 3,787, 3,842, **4,272**, 4,305, **4,341**, 4,361, 4,374
schools, **3,755**, 3,911, 4,165, **4,199**, **4,341**, 6,544, 10,564
scrapbooks, 4,280
secretaries, 4,352
self-government (in higher education), 4,213
senators, United States, 2,379, **4,356**, 4,357, 9,170
seniors, societies and clubs, **4,152**
silversmiths, 3,867
singers, **3,878**
single mothers, 4,088
Slovaks, **4,308**
social life and customs, 3,834, 4,178, 4,352, 4,364, **12,246**
social service exchanges, **3,905**
social settlements, **3,791**, **3,801**, **3,809**, 3,820, **3,822**, 3,835, **3,836**, 3,851, **3,874**, **3,875**, **3,894**, 3,901, 4,003, 4,047, 4,052, 4,079, 4,085, **4,087**, **4,096**, **4,099**, 4,100, **4,101**, **4,127**, 4,130, **4,143**, 4,146, 4,158, 6,622, 7,172, 7,300, 11,897, 12,026
social settlements, Presbyterian, **3,837**, **3,845**, **3,892**
social work administration, **4,130**
social work with delinquents and criminals, **4,141**
social workers, 3,826, 3,875, **3,901**, 4,003, 4,056, **4,115**, **4,141**, **4,146**, 8,643
social workers, Afro-American, **3,835**
Socialist parties, **4,080**
Socialists, 4,431
societies, Afro-American, **4,132**
soldiers' homes, **4,338**, **4,339**
strikes and lockouts, 4,080, 6,795
  railroad workers, **4,173**
student counseling, 4,042
student counselors, 4,115, 4,150, 7,545
student financial aid, **4,031**
student housing, 4,394
students' societies, **4,213**, 4,219, **4,220**, 4,382, 14,029
suffrage, 4,290
suffrage societies, 1,436, 3,803, 6,526, 6,536, 6,626
suffrage societies, Afro-American, 4,147
suffragists, 3,851
Sunday-schools, 3,837
surgeons, 4,336
survivors' benefits, **4,338**
Swiss-Americans, charitable societies, **4,157**
symphony orchestras, 4,056
teachers, 3,764, **3,854**, 3,911, 4,279, **4,301**, 4,425, 4,456, 12,233, 14,473
  salaries, pensions, etc., 4,341
teachers colleges, 4,210, 4,211, **4,212**
teachers, training of, 4,341
teachers' unions, 3,787, **3,817**, **3,818**, 3,824, 3,839, 4,124, 8,147
teen age women
  education, 3,785
  institutional care, 4,372
  pregnancy, 3,785
telephone, 3,751, 4,259
temperance, 3,762
temperance societies, **3,819**, **3,909**, 4,054, 4,055, **4,244**, 15,851
theater, 3,847, 3,851, **4,222**, 6,597, 15,901
  little theater movement, 3,994, 4,097
theater programs, **3,921**
theaters, 3,753, **3,924**
theatrical producers and directors, **4,091**
theological seminaries, 4,201, 4,203, 4,206, 4,207, 4,208
trade and professional associations, **3,859**, **3,883**, **4,075**, 4,094, **4,098**, 4,367
trade schools, 4,069
trade-unions, 3,827, 3,839, **4,173**, 6,795

clothing workers, 1,656
officials and employees, 3,854, 3,887, **3,890**
railway workers, **3,805**
trails, 4,289
travelers' aid societies, **4,160**
Ukrainian Americans, 9,501
unemployed, 4,080
United Methodist Church, education, 4,201, 4,206, 4,208
universities and colleges, 3,318, 4,003, 4,123, **4,215**, 4,218, 4,319, 4,379, 4,389, 4,394, 6,527, 6,692, 14,306
archives, **3,741, 4,008, 4,216, 4,285, 4,330**
buildings, 4,395
employees, **4,297, 4,386**
examinations, 4,060
faculty, **4,380, 4,383, 4,388, 4,389, 4,391**, 4,395, **4,396, 4,399, 4,403, 4,404**
graduate work, 4,382
urban beautification, 4,454
urban renewal, citizen participation, 4,101
utopias, 4,302, **4,767**
venereal disease, prevention, 4,111, 4,145
veterans, **4,339**
medical care, 4,339
veterinarians, 4,336
vital statistics, 4,197
voluntary health agencies, **3,813**
volunteer workers in hospitals, 3,932, **4,012, 4,018, 4,025, 15,981**
volunteer workers in social service, **3,807, 3,863, 4,104**
widows, 4,254, **4,338**
women
civil rights, 4,083, 4,166
education, 4,118
women's colleges, 4,050, 4,167, **4,300, 4,374**
women's shelters, **4,069, 4,174**
women's shelters, Afro-American, 4,142
women's studies programs, 4,008
working-women's clubs, **3,956**
working-women's clubs, Afro-American, 3,935
World War I, civilians work, **4,340**
World War II, civilians work, 3,950
Young Women's Christian Association, 3,827, **4,175**
Illinois American Civil Liberties Union (Chicago), 4,083
Illinois Appellate Court, 4,094
Illinois Association of Colored Women, 3,935
Illinois Association of School Librarians, 4,391
Illinois Association Opposed to the Extension of Suffrage to Women, 3,908
Illinois Board of World's Fair Commissioners, **4,337**
Illinois Central Railroad, 4,002
Illinois Child Labor Committee. *See* Illinois Commission on the Employment of Youth
Illinois Children's Home and Aid Society, 4,061, **4,103, 4,163**
Illinois Citizens for the Medical Control of Abortion. *See* Abortion Rights Association of Illinois
Illinois Commission on the Employment of Youth, **4,104, 4,117**
Illinois Commission on the Status of Women, 4,106, 4,124, 4,149
Illinois Committee on Child Welfare Legislation, 4,117
Illinois Conference on Legislation, **3,858**, 4,125
Illinois Congress of Mothers, 3,899
Illinois Congress of Parents and Teachers, Chicago region, 4,149
Illinois Department of Registration and Education, **4,336**
Illinois Emergency Relief Commission, 3,890
Illinois Equal Suffrage Association, 3,803, 6,526, 6,536, 6,626
Illinois Federation of Teachers, 8,147
Illinois Federation of Women's Clubs, 3,857, 3,862, 4,066, **4,366**
Illinois Future Homemakers of America, 3,859
Illinois General Assembly, 3,858
Illinois Home Economics Association, **3,859**
Illinois Hospital Board, 4,125
Illinois House of Representatives, 3,909
Illinois Humane Society, **4,105**

Illinois Industrial Commission, 6,531
Illinois Industrial University, 4,388
Illinois Institution for the Education of Deaf Mutes, 2,308
Illinois International Women's Year Coordinating Committee, **4,106**
Illinois League of Women Voters, **3,860**
Illinois Nurses Association, **4,367**
Illinois Prairie Path, 4,289
Illinois Public Health Committee, 4,440
Illinois Society for the Prevention of Cruelty to Animals. *See* Illinois Humane Society
Illinois Soldiers' and Sailors' Home (Quincy, IL). *See* Illinois Veterans' Home (Quincy, IL)
Illinois Soldiers' Orphans' Home (Normal, IL), **4,107**
Illinois Soldiers' Widows' Home (Wilmington, IL), **4,338**
Illinois State Council of Defense, 4,269, **4,340**
Illinois State Federation of Labor, 3,890
Illinois State Journal, 4,332, 4,347
Illinois State Library Association, 4,396
Illinois State Register, 4,332
Illinois State Sanitary Commission (Springfield, IL), 4,293
Illinois State Testimonial Committee, 14,092
Illinois State University
faculty, 4,304
presidents, **4,305**
Illinois Supreme Court, 2,255, 4,094
Illinois Temperance Council, 4,055
Illinois Training School for Nurses (Chicago, IL), **3,861, 4,108,** 5,843
Illinois Veterans' Home (Quincy, IL), 4,338, **4,339**
Illinois Wesleyan University, archives, 3,746
Illinois Wesleyan University, Woman's Educational Association, 3,746
Illinois Woman Suffrage Association, 1,436
Illinois Women's Athletic Club, 3,897
Illinois Women's Political Caucus, 4,124
Illinois Women's Press Association, **3,862**, 4,061, 4,120
Illiteracy **5,325,** 9,532, 13,309
campaign against, **15,609**
Illiteracy Commission of South Carolina, **15,609**
Illustrated books, children's, 2,805, **8,531**
Illustration of books, 6,059, 12,888, **12,903**
Illustrators, 1,426, **1,434,** 1,581, **1,617,** 1,678, 2,051, 2,198, 2,344, 2,714, 2,726, **2,747, 2,761, 2,780,** 2,792, **2,805, 2,812,** 2,928, 4,161, **4,444,** 5,048, **6,001,** 6,092, **8,179, 8,531,** 10,178, 11,368, 12,879, 12,993, 14,085, **14,215, 14,317, 14,321, 14,326, 14,355, 14,399, 14,407,** 15,445
Image (periodical), 12,789
Imer, Ann (Maurowmet), **15,481**
Immaculate Heart College (Los Angeles, CA), 999, 1,017
students, 895
Immanuel Congregational Church of Hartford Widows Home (CT), 1,889
Immanuel Mission (AZ), 153
Immer, Esther, **4,921**
Immigrant Woman and Her Job, The (bulletin), 2,703
Immigrants, 1,675, 4,055, **4,110,** 5,353, 6,349, 6,695, 6,946, 6,989, 7,063, **8,258,** 8,659, 9,013, 9,138, 9,336, 12,487, **12,517,** 13,765, 15,155, 15,255, 15,869, 17,540. *See also* Emigration and immigration
charities for, **7,537**
Immigrants, American, in Nova Scotia, 7,616, 7,676
Immigrants, Australian, 16,417, 16,486
Immigrants, Austrian, **6,115**
Immigrants, Bohemian, 8,467
Immigrants, British, 2,818, 7,643, **7,728,** 9,427, 10,780, **15,083, 16,433,** 16,468, 16,472, 16,474, 16,477, 16,486, 16,490, 16,906, 16,965, 16,967, **17,099**
Immigrants, Canadian, **13,715**
Immigrants, Chinese, 1,181, 2,683
Immigrants, Czechoslovakian, 10,527, 13,953
Immigrants, Dalmatian, 9,694
Immigrants, Danish, 3,739, **7,708,** 16,486, 16,960, 16,965, 16,967, 16,968
Immigrants, Dutch, **8,265,** 8,518, 9,418, 16,486

Immigrants, Finnish, 8,185, **8,455, 9,175,** 9,467, 9,502, **9,511,** 16,965
Immigrants, French, 1,513, 12,995, 15,258
Immigrants, German, **180, 688, 1,223,** 1,476, **4,092,** 4,346, 5,366, **6,020, 6,106, 6,121, 6,789,** 7,670, **7,890, 7,999,** 8,702, 8,946, 9,063, 9,111, **9,355, 9,433, 9,632,** 10,554, 10,775, 11,216, 14,320, **14,910,** 16,776, 17,379, 17,589, 17,862
Immigrants, Greek, 16,488
Immigrants, Icelandic, **13,711**
Immigrants in the Cities (book), 14,006
Immigrants, Irish, 1,790, 3,270, 6,027, 9,989, 10,355, **15,054,** 15,533, 16,486, 16,967, 16,968
Immigrants, Italian, **3,446,** 6,808, 9,467, 9,495, 10,632, 12,632, 12,862
Immigrants, Japanese, 16,942, 17,285
Immigrants, Jewish, 4,460, 11,915, 15,251, 17,282, 17,744
Immigrants, Latvian, 8,662
Immigrants' Legal Aid Society (IL), 4,100
Immigrants, Lithuanian, 14,908
Immigrants, Luxembourgian, 9,154
Immigrants, Moravian, 16,380
Immigrants, Norwegian, 4,721, **6,611,** 8,690, **8,722, 8,730, 8,731, 8,732, 8,739, 8,743, 8,752, 8,754, 8,757,** 8,803, 9,042, **9,106, 9,263, 9,266,** 9,467, 10,434, **13,684,** 16,486, 17,497
Immigrants, Polish, 13,906, 15,337
Immigrants' Protective League, 2,224, **4,110,** 4,117, 4,146, 10,603
Immigrants, Russian, **650,** 1,749, 5,875, **6,024, 6,081, 6,120,** 8,064, 10,554
Immigrants, Scandinavian, **13,715**
Immigrants, Scottish, **786, 7,181,** 7,628, **9,087,** 9,372, 16,486, 16,967, 16,968
Immigrants' Service League (Chicago, IL), 4,079, 4,146
Immigrants, Sicilian, **6,116**
Immigrants, Slovene, 13,912
Immigrants, Swedish, 8,849, **8,977,** 9,118, 9,155, **9,204, 9,269, 9,322,** 9,467, 10,909, 16,481, 16,486, 16,965, 16,968
Immigrants, Swiss, 8,546, **9,359,** 9,866, 10,010, 16,486, 16,892, 16,968, **17,636**
Immigrants, Ukrainian, **9,501, 14,909**
Immigrants, Welsh, 8,948, **9,952, 15,035,** 16,409, 16,664, 16,946, 16,967, 16,968
Immigrants, Yugoslavian, 10,255
Immigration Commission of Massachusetts, 10,419
Immortal Marriage (book), 1,082
Impeachment, 2,697, 14,257, 16,313, 17,656
Impellitteri, Vincent, 11,895
Imperial Hotel (OR), 14,615
Impey, Catherine, 2,315
Impresarios, **17,333**
Imprints (in books), 2,146
Imus, Charlotte Sophie (1836-1926). *See* Winchell, Charlotte Sophie Imus [Mrs. Newton Horace] (1836-1926)
Imus Family, 9,448
Imus, Genevieve, 8,344
Imus, James, 8,344
Imus, Jennie (Ina) [Mrs. James H.], 8,344
In an Unguarded Moment, 11,038
"In Care of Aggie Horn" (radio program), 6,070
"In Dark New England Days" (story), 5,714
"In Defense of Women" (article), 2,936
In Gay Company (musical comedy), 12,367
"In God We Trust—Christian Foundations of Our Government" (speech), 4,837
"In Her Own Right" (TV program), 6,693
"In Memoriam" (article), 2,936
"In Memorium Voor Hen Die Vielen" (exhibit), 9,587
In the Border Country (book), 7,186
In the Days of McKinley (book), 14,084
In the Days of Victorio (book), 16,497
In the Desert of Waiting (book), 5,349
In This Our Life (book), 17,059
In Thoughtful Mood (book), 4,622
"Ina" (pseudonym). *See* Coolbrith, Ina Donna (1841-1928)
Ina, Amelia, 8,344
Ina Coolbrith Circle (CA), **1,307**

Ina, Emma, 8,344
Ina, Jennie. *See* Imus, Jennie (Ina) [Mrs. James H.]
Ina, Julia, 8,344
Ina, Lyman (?-1883), **8,344**
Ina, Netta, 8,344
Incarnate Word College (TX), 16,277
Incest, 987, 9,877
"Incidentally" (column), 13,468
Incidents in the Life of a Slave Girl (book), 7,561
Income tax, deductions, 9,950
Indentured servants, 7,150, 8,205, 8,276, **12,371,**
    12,423, 13,423, **13,569,** 13,573, 15,626
Indentures, 15,526
Independence Browning Society (MO), **10,085,**
    10,086
Independence Canning Company (IA), 4,899
Independence Female College (MO), 10,026
Independence Hall Association, 11,877
Independence High School (MO), 10,087
Independent (NY), 14,058, 17,210
Independent Funeral Directors Association of Texas,
    Inc., 16,363
Independent Order of B'nai B'rith, Women's Chapter
    267 (MN). *See* B'nai B'rith, Bertha Rutz
    Fiterman Chapter (MN)
Independent Order of Odd Fellows (MD), Rebekah
    Assembly, **5,838**
Independent Order of Odd Fellows (NE), Rebekah
    Assembly, **10,411**
Independent Order of Odd Fellows, International
    Association of Rebekah Assemblies, **10,411**
Independent Productions Corporation, 17,792
Independent Socialist League, 1,283
Independent study, 6,339
Independent, The (periodical), 1,953
Independent, The (MI), 13,929
Independent Voices (book), 8,531
Independent Voters of Minnesota, 2,589, 9,375
Independent Women Olson for Governor League
    (MN), 9,396
Independent Women's Association (NY). *See*
    Association of Women Students (NY)
Index of American Design, 2,732, 2,743
Index of Plays, 8,564
Index, The, 3,927
Index to Short Stories, 8,564
Indexes, 6,122, 8,564
India, 6,978, 12,195
    American consuls in, 9,204
    American teachers in, **7,734, 14,426**
    American travelers in, **6,476**
    Americans in, 6,087
    British occupation (1765-1947), 12,715
    diplomatic and consular service, 4,030
    hospitals, 3,958
    medical colleges, 3,958, 6,875, 11,754
    missionaries to, 1,428, **1,846, 2,261,** 2,394, 3,969,
        4,271, 4,525, 4,529, 4,532, **4,536,** 5,187, **5,993,**
        6,012, 6,868, 7,375, 10,942, 13,949, **14,355,**
        17,189
    missionaries to, Baptist, 11,039
    missionaries to, Lutheran, **14,796, 14,799**
    missionaries to, medical, **3,958**
    missionaries to, medical, Presbyterian, 14,425
    missionaries to, Mennonite, **4,515**
    missionaries to, Methodist, **4,525, 4,529,** 5,171,
        5,993, 6,012, 8,164, **8,879, 14,426**
    missions, 5,713
    missions, Advent Christian, **7,064**
    missions, medical, **6,875**
    partition, 12,891
    passive resistance, 12,715
    physical education and training, 1,035
    retreats, 11,176
    revolutions, 13,801
    universities and colleges, 14,751
India Conciliation Group, 12,715
India Independence Movement, 174
Indian agents, **1,481,** 8,940, 15,278, 16,741, **17,404**
Indian Captive (book), 2,938
Indian Council Fire, 7,220
Indian Defense Association. *See* California League
    for American Indians

Indian Education Research Project, 2,841
Indian Helper, 14,748
"Indian in Minnesota, The," 8,638
Indian Personality and Administration Research
    Project, **2,840**
Indian Rights Association, 2,298
Indian trails, 10,400
Indiana, 4,475, **4,589,** 4,679, 10,031
    Afro-Americans, 4,090
    agricultural administration, 6,343
    agricultural societies, 9,988
    agriculture, 5,366
    archivists, 4,522, 4,530
    art, galleries and museums, 2,778
    artists, **4,620, 4,625**
    assessment, 3,947
    authors, **4,483, 4,537**
    businessmen, 4,469
    camps, 16,257
    Catholic universities and colleges, 4,509, 4,649
        archives, **4,632**
        history, **4,648**
    census, 3,945
    charitable societies, **4,678**
    charitable societies, Jewish, **13,807**
    charities, **4,617, 4,670**
    church societies, 4,469, 4,650
    church societies, Baptist, **4,512,** 4,661
    church societies, Methodist, **4,540, 4,541, 4,542,**
        4,543, 4,544, 4,545, 4,597
    churches, Baptist, 9,906
    cities and towns, civic improvement, **4,676, 4,888**
    citizens' associations, **4,090,** 4,627, **4,671**
    clubs, 4,532, **4,546, 4,548, 4,549, 4,550, 4,553,**
        4,554, 4,555, 4,556, 4,560, 4,561, 4,562, 4,563,
        4,565, 4,566, 4,567, 4,568, 4,570, 4,571, 4,572,
        4,574, 4,575, 4,576, 4,578, 4,579, 4,580, 4,582,
        4,583, 4,584, 4,585, 4,586, 4,587, 4,591, 4,621,
        4,625, 4,630, 4,661, 4,663, 4,664, 4,665, 4,666,
        4,667, 4,668, 4,669, 4,672, 4,673, 4,677, 4,888
    college administrators, **4,495**
    college and school journalism, 4,595
    college librarians, **4,522, 4,523**
    college presidents, **4,521,** 4,598
    college students, **4,612**
    college teachers, 4,489
    college trustees, 4,494, 4,504
    community leadership, **4,502**
    community life, **4,468**
    congresswomen, **4,627**
    contemplative orders, **4,503**
    convents and nunneries, Catholic, 4,466, **4,649**
    court records, **3,949**
    deans (in schools), 4,494, **4,519, 6,941**
    diaries and journals, **4,602, 4,604, 4,607, 4,610,**
        4,613, 4,620, 4,651, **4,656**
    disaster relief, 4,500
    educational associations, **4,498, 4,547, 4,577, 4,588,**
        4,888
    educators, **4,534, 4,535**
    elections, 4,623, 4,628, 4,654
    farm life, 4,607, 4,610
    farmers, **4,651**
    flood control, 4,627
    floods, 4,500
    Friends, 4,651
    gardening, societies, etc., **4,501, 4,590**
    Girl Scouts, **4,499, 4,564**
    governors, 4,486, 4,628
    greek letter societies, **4,524, 4,559, 4,592**
    high school teachers, **4,625**
    high schools, 4,487, 4,660
    historic buildings, conservation and restoration,
        4,501
    home economics, 4,397
    home nursing, **4,500**
    hospitals, 4,506
    housewives, **4,474, 4,507, 4,532**
    housing, law and legislation, 4,508
    Jews, **4,510**
    journalists, **4,622, 4,654, 12,500**
    lawyers, 4,598
    lecturers, 4,630
    legislators, **4,621**

    librarians, **4,528, 4,531, 14,370**
    libraries, 12,479
    literary societies, **4,546, 4,553, 4,556, 4,563, 4,568,**
        4,586, 4,595, 4,663, **4,666, 4,672, 4,673**
    monasteries, **4,503, 4,634**
    monasticism and religious orders for women,
        Catholic, **4,466, 4,497, 4,596, 4,634**
    music teachers, **4,526**
    musical societies, **4,551, 4,573**
    naturalization records, 3,949
    newspapers, 4,538
        sections, columns, etc., 4,622, 6,064
    officials and employees, 6,343
    osteopaths, **4,506**
    patriotic societies, 4,552, **4,557,** 4,661
    physicians, 4,469, **4,496**
    poets, **4,622**
    political activists, women, **4,606,** 4,654
    politicians, **4,662**
    politics, practical, women's activism, **4,569, 4,593,**
        4,623, **4,626,** 4,677
    postal service, postmasters, 4,469
    prisoners, women, examination, 4,628
    prisons for women, officials and employees, **4,624,**
        4,628
    public health nursing, 4,888
    race problems, 4,090
    reformatories (female), 11,003, 15,274
    road construction industry, management, 4,467
    roads, plank, 4,467
    roadside improvement, 4,501
    school boards, 4,623, 4,626
    school physicians, **4,605**
    school superintendents and principals, **4,638,** 8,362,
        13,749
    school yearbooks, 4,595, **4,659**
    schools, 4,471, 8,362
    senators, United States, 4,486
    social life and customs, 4,474, 4,608
    social workers, 4,510
    societies, Jewish, **13,767, 13,796**
    soldiers, Civil War, 3,354
    students' societies, 4,595, 14,029
    suffrage, 14,194
    suffrage societies, **4,618,** 4,626
    teachers, 4,471, 4,527, **4,528, 4,600, 4,604,** 4,613
    teachers' colleges, **4,658**
    teachers of the mentally handicapped, 14,873
    temperance, 4,469
    temperance societies, 4,481, **4,616, 4,619,** 4,650
    theological seminaries, **4,465**
    trade-unions, 8,081, **8,133**
    trails, 4,501
    universities and colleges, 4,481, 4,519, 4,520, **4,522,**
        4,523, 4,527, 4,532, 4,888
        employees, 4,494
        faculty, **4,505**
        finance, 4,594
        history, **4,494**
        utopias, **4,429, 4,433,** 4,435
    volunteer workers in hospitals, **4,581**
    War of 1812, societies, **4,558**
    women, 3,812
        civil rights, 4,469
    World War II, civilians' work, 3,950
    Young Women's Christian Association, **4,674**
Indiana Baptist Women's Missionary Society, 4,512
Indiana Baptist Women's Summer Conferences, 4,512
Indiana Bookplates (book), 4,654
Indiana Farm Board, 9,988
Indiana Federation of Clubs, 4,621, 4,623, 4,625
Indiana Federation of Women's Clubs, 4,623, 4,625
Indiana Girls School, 11,003
Indiana Housing Association, 4,508
Indiana Infantry Volunteers, Company H, Sixty-sixth
    Regiment, 3,354
Indiana League of Women Voters, **4,569, 4,593,**
    4,623, **4,626,** 4,677
Indiana Museum of Modern Art, 2,778
Indiana Reformatory Institute for Women and Girls,
    15,274
Indiana State Board of Agriculture, women's
    department, 6,343
Indiana State Normal School, alumnae, 9,978

Indiana Territory, 14,174
Indiana University
  administration, 4,495
  deans, 4,494, **6,941**
  history, **4,494**
  presidents, 4,494
  students, 4,612, 13,962
  trustees, 4,483, 4,494
Indiana University, Institute for Sex Research, 4,494
Indiana Vassar Club, 4,630
Indiana Women in the World War (book), 4,629
Indianpolis Star (IN), 6,064
Indianapolis Family Welfare Society (IN), 8,637
Indianapolis Woman's Club (IN), 4,630
Indianola Council of Civic Agencies (IN), **4,888**
Indianola Woman's Club (IN), 4,888
Indians. *See* Indians of South America; Native
  Americans
Indians at Work (newsletter), 6,142
Indians of South America, 11,733, 14,897
Indians on Horseback (book), 14,218
Indictments, 178
Indigent Widows and Single Women's Society of
  Philadelphia (PA), **15,022**
Individualist, The, 14,345
Indo-Chinese Women's Conference (Vancouver,
  1971), 17,663
Industrial accidents, 5,564, 11,760, 11,851, 17,214
Industrial arbitration. *See* Arbitration, industrial
Industrial arts, study and teaching, 15,288
Industrial Commission of the State of Oklahoma,
  14,195
Industrial Home for Colored Girls (WV), 17,483
Industrial Home for Girls (Chillicothe, MO), 9,963
Industrial Home for Girls (WV), 17,483
Industrial Home for Negro Girls (Tipton, MO), 9,962,
  9,963
Industrial Home for the Blind, 2,111
Industrial hygiene, 2,703, 3,977, 7,318, 8,075, 11,851
Industrial Institute and College (MS). *See* Mississippi
  State College for Women
Industrial Institute and College for Girls (Chickasaw,
  OK). *See* University of Science and Arts of
  Oklahoma
Industrial medicine, 8,668
Industrial mobilization, 2,700, **2,701**
Industrial nursing, 3,976
Industrial project management, 11,903
Industrial psychiatry, 7,241
Industrial Recovery Act (1935), 6,315
Industrial recreation, **8,134**, 12,721
Industrial relations, 164, 6,668, 6,810, 7,318, 8,658,
  8,678, 12,724, 14,195, 17,214, 17,765
Industrial safety, 2,700, 8,075, 11,771, 17,376
Industrial School (Chicago, IL). *See* Jewish Manual
  Training School of Chicago (IL)
Industrial School and Free Kindergarten Association
  of Elmira (NY), 11,445
Industrial sociology, 7,315, **8,142**
Industrial statistics, 2,672, 2,676, **5,570**
Industrial toxicology, 6,486, 6,622, 11,760
Industrial Union Council (MI), 8,124
Industrial Welfare Commission, 341
Industrial Worker, 8,127
Industrial Workers of the World, 1,652, 1,656, 4,032,
  8,061, 8,072, **8,087, 8,094**, 8,123, 8,127, 8,144,
  9,467, 10,710, 14,503, 14,656, 16,968, 17,274,
  17,278, 17,343, 17,633
Industrialization, **13,175**
  social aspects, 8,123
Industry, 1,034
  social aspects, 12,715, **12,717**
Industry and state, **2,684**, 6,766, 6,982
Industry and women, 16,007
Infant Asylum and Diet Kitchen, 6,598
"Infant Mariner, The: Reminiscences of Voyages in
  the Pacific," 7,479
Infant School Society of Philadelphia (PA), **15,023**
Infant Welfare Society of Chicago (IL), **3,863**, 4,079,
  6,748
Infants
  care and hygiene, 5,846, 13,840, 16,603
  mortality, 2,677, 4,141, 7,660, 8,144, 9,909, 11,916,
  16,060

  nutrition, **14,198**
Infants (premature), 3,968, 11,830, 13,384
  care and hygiene, 238
Infill (Housing Association of Delaware Valley, PA),
  15,201
"Influence of Dorothy Wordsworth on the Poetry of
  Samuel Taylor Coleridge, The" (dissertation), 113
Influenza epidemic (1918), 15,707
Influenza epidemics, 2,421, 3,205, 3,729, 4,016, 4,690,
  12,554, 13,218
*Informal History of St. Clement's Episcopal Church,
  An* (MS), 9,649
Informed History of the DAR, An (book), 18,012
Ingalls, Emma, **10,320**
Ingalls Family (CA), **359**
Ingalls, Marguerite (1888-1971), **7,016**
Ingalls, Mira Kimball, 1,525
Ingalls, William, 3,661
Ingelfinger, Franz J., 6,645
Ingelfinger, Sarah Shurtleff [Mrs. Franz J.], 6,645
Ingelow, Jean (1820-97), 12,467
Ingersoll, Charles Jared (1782-1862), 15,002
Ingersoll, Elizabeth (1815-72). *See* Fisher, Elizabeth
  (Ingersoll) [Mrs. Sidney George] (1815-72)
Ingersoll, Eva. *See* Wakefield, Eva (Ingersoll)
Ingersoll, Eva A. Parker [Mrs. Robert G.] (?-1915),
  17,980
Ingersoll Family (IL, NY), **12,516**
Ingersoll, Henrietta (Crosby) [Mrs. George W.], **2,406**
Ingersoll, Henry, 6,226
Ingersoll, Mary E., 12,740
Ingersoll, Robert Green (1833-99), 11,547, 12,516,
  17,980
Ingersoll, Sarah Brown (1835-96). *See* Cooper, Sarah
  Brown (Ingersoll) [Mrs. Halsey Fenimore]
  (1835-96)
Ingerson, Vera Frances (1890-), 14,394
"Ingham County Must Stay Dry" (pamphlet), 8,175
Ingham, Jenny, 3,996
Inglenook Reading Club (St. Paul, MN), 9,143
Ingles, Thelma (1909-), **13,206**
Inglesby Family (SC), **15,482**
Inglesby, Hilda [Mrs. John], 15,481
Inglesby, John, 15,482
Ingleside Plantation (AL), 77
Ingleside School (New Milford, CT), **2,024**
Inglis, Agnes (1870-1952), 7,997, 7,998, 8,064
Inglis, Elizabeth N. [Mrs. James], **7,821**
Inglis, James, 7,821
Ingols, Margaret Rae, 6,398
Ingraham, Eliza M. [Mrs.] (1883-1957) **8,499**
Ingraham, Isabella, **2,905**
Ingraham, Rosa, 16,132
Ingram, Bess H., 9,426
Ingram, Clara (1879-?). *See* Judson, Clara (Ingram)
  (1879-?)
Ingram, Frances, 8,668
Ingram, Nellie Allen (1866-1945). *See* Walton, Nellie
  Allen (Ingram) [Mrs. Edmund George]
  (1866-1945)
Ingram, Rosa Lee, 12,682
Inheritance and succession, 15,677
  legal aspects, 9,884
Inheritance and succession (Germanic law), 7,469
"Inheritance of Alice Robertson" (ms), 14,197
Inkpaduta (Native American), 4,765
Inland Oil and Refining Company, 1,719
Inland South American Missionary Union (NY),
  14,334
Inman, Elizabeth (Murray) Smith [Mrs. Ralph], 2,191
Inman, Myra (1845-1914), **13,040**
Inman Park Students Club (Atlanta, GA). *See* 1900
  Study Club (Atlanta, GA)
*Inner World of Childhood; The: A Study in
  Analytical Psychology* (book), 2,631
Inner World of Choice, The (book), 2,631
Inner World of Man, The (book), 2,631
"Innocent Bystander" (column), 9,771
Innocent Dreamers (book), 14,388
Inouye, Kay, 1,534
Inquirers (club), 3,305
Inquisitiones post mortem, **11,191**
Insane. *See* Mentally ill

"Insanity: A Sympathetic Accompaniment of Uterine
  Disease" (dissertation), 7,719
Insects, physiology, 8,555
Inspectors of the Jail and Penitentiary House
  (Philadelphia, PA), **14,918**
Institute for Sex Education (IL), **4,111**
Institute for the Study of History, Life, and Culture of
  Black Studies (MS), 9,583
Institute of Design (Chicago, IL), **4,112**
Institute of International Education, 760, 8,621
Institute of Murfreesboro (NC), 13,392
Institute of Pacific Relations (CA), 647, 6,483, 6,874
Institute of Political Engineering, 17,757
Institute of Renaissance Studies, 1,545
Institute of Women's Professional Relations, **6,673,**
  12,739, 13,189
Institute of World Studies, 8,069
Institute on Intercultural Education (1944), 6,751
Institute on World Organization, 6,771
Institute Woman's Council (Chicago, IL), 3,865
Institution libraries, 8,976
Institution management, **11,566**
"Institutional Oppression of Women" (lecture), 15,197
Instructions, 1,513
Instructive District Nursing Association (OH). *See*
  Community Health and Nursing Service (OH)
Insurance, 7,325
  agents, 2,941, **4,257**, 5,394, 5,803, 7,675, 8,690,
  10,980
  societies, etc., 5,394
Insurance companies, 3,229, 8,167, 8,366, 14,674,
  15,123, 15,938, 17,099, 17,465
  employees, 9,488
  management, 1,688
Insurance companies, Afro-American, 5,378
Insurance Company of North America, **15,123**
Insurance Company of North America Corporation,
  15,123
Insurance, deposit, 2,336
Insurance, disability, 11,763
Insurance, group, 6,315
Insurance, health, 659, 1,140, 4,698, 6,315, 8,651,
  8,678, 10,953, 11,591, 11,695, 11,760, 11,885,
  11,916, 14,714
Insurance holding companies, 15,123
Insurance, life, 6,315, 17,914
  societies, etc., **10,412**
Insurance, marine, 14,955, 15,123
Insurance, no-fault automobile, 1,010
Insurance, social. *See* Social security
Insurance, unemployment, 2,672, 6,315, 8,085,
  11,763, 13,972
Insurgency, 13,378
Integration in higher education. *See* Segregation in
  higher education
Intelligence levels, 13,738, 15,585
Intelligence service, World War II, 6,020
Intelligence tests, 11,549, 17,018
Intelligencer (NY), 12,751
"Intemperance" (ms), 7,233
"Intemperance and Tight Lacing Considered in
  Relation to the Laws of Life," 14,152
Intensive care units, 242
Inter-American Commission of Women, 6,908, 6,939,
  6,958, 6,959, **7,236**
Inter-American Conference on Problems of War and
  Peace (1945), 113
Inter-American Congress of Women, 15,316
Inter-Club Council of Western New York, **11,349**
Inter-Community Study Committee, 8,639
Inter-library loans, 11,930
Inter-Municipal Research Committee, 12,517
Inter Nos Study Club (Minneapolis, MN), **9,144**
Inter Ocean (newspaper), 6,343, 6,526
Inter-Tribal Indian Ceremonial Association, **11,231**
Interagency Commission for Agricultural Surplus
  Disposal, 5,145
Intercollegiate Bureau of Occupations (NY), **11,622**
Intercollegiate Socialist Society, 12,705
Intercultural education, 3,283, 6,751, **9,494**
Interdenominational cooperation, 5,841
Interdepartmental Committee on Children and Youth,
  6,860
Interest and usury, 2,397

Interethnic marriage, 199
Interior decorators, 1,068, **2,734, 2,779, 2,859,** 5,394, **6,382, 12,914**
Interlaken Thimble Club (MA), **7,507**
Intermarriage, 16,866, 16,868, 16,876
Intermountain Consumers Service, 11,805
Intermountain Observer, 3,677
Internal revenue, 1,807, 3,947, 9,769, **14,934**
Internal security, 6,720
International agencies, 6,125, **8,657,** 11,852, 11,857, 15,310
International Alliance of Women. *See* International Alliance of Women for Suffrage and Equal Citizenship
International Alliance of Women for Suffrage and Equal Citizenship, 6,746, 6,972, 7,190, 7,205, **7,237,** 7,290, 11,920, 12,415
International Arbitration of Peace Society, 17,916
International Art Union, 12,912
International Assembly of Women, **6,674**
International Association for Personnel Women, **15,124**
International Association of Altrusa Clubs, 250
International Association of Machinists, Ladies Auxiliary 490 (TX), **15,994**
International Association of Medical Illustrators, 3,467
International Association of Medical Museums, 2,088
International Association of Women Preachers,
International Ballet, 17,965
International Ballet Competition (Moscow, USSR), 12,360
International Bar Association, 7,174
International Beacon, 6,778
International Bureau for the Suppression of Traffic in Persons, 8,633
International Bureau of Education, 6,368
International Chiropractors Association, Women's Auxiliary, **4,711**
International Christian University (Japan), 4,918
International Committee for Political Prisoners, **12,518**
International Committee of Young Men's Christian Associations, Women's Auxiliaries, **12,133**
International Conference of Educators of Blind Youth, 7,309
International Conference of Potters and Weavers (1952), 2,828
International Conference of Women, 15,304
International Conference on Alternative Perspectives on Vietnam (1965, MI), **7,822**
International Conference on Education (Geneva, Switzerland, 1935), 2,095
International Conference on Women (The Hague, 1915), 8,009, 17,735
International Congress for the Protection of Childhood, 4,624
International Congress of Americanists, 6,328
International Congress of Women, **1,557,** 8,144, 15,269
International Congress of Women (London, 1899), 17,616
International Congress of Women (1915), 6,812, 7,868, 7,923
International Congresses of Working Women (1919, 1921, 1923), 2,509, 2,878, **7,238**
International cooperation, 1,503, **2,078, 2,407, 2,519,** 4,120, 6,368, 6,380, 6,402, 6,419, **6,674,** 6,730, 6,746, 6,767, 6,865, 6,908, 6,939, 6,958, 6,959, 6,972, 6,973, 6,978, **7,201,** 7,205, **7,207,** 7,236, **7,237,** 7,239, **7,240,** 7,275, 7,290, 7,293, 7,299, **7,322,** 7,885, **8,657,** 9,095, 11,830, 11,920, 11,937, 11,999, **12,115, 12,116,** 12,500, 14,691, 15,570, 17,267
International Council of Nurses, 2,309, 6,123, 6,124, 6,125, 8,553
International Council of Psychologists, **13,735,** 13,739, 13,743, 13,745
International Council of Women, **1,069, 2,407,** 4,631, 4,732, 6,368, 6,978, **7,239,** 7,293, 9,095, 12,500, 17,616
International Council of Women, music committee, 7,299

International Council of Women—National Woman Suffrage Association, 4,156
International Council of Women of the Darker Races of the World, 3,302
International Council on Social Welfare, 10,197
International courts, 6,978, 17,468, 17,654
International Development Advisory Board, 8,613
International Disarmament Conference (1932), 17,468
International education, 58, 2,072, 2,078, **4,067,** 4,577, 6,368, 6,512, 6,702, 6,723, 6,978, 7,885, **8,173,** 13,801, 15,755
International Exhibition of Botanical Art and Illustration (PA), 2,107
International Federation of Business and Professional Women, 6,829, 6,901
International Federation of Business and Professional Women's Clubs, 15,971
International Federation of Library Associations, 11,937
International Federation of University Women, 2,064, **2,071,** 6,419, **7,240,** 9,927, 11,804, 11,999, 15,570
International Federation of University Women Conference (1924), 9,983
International Federation of Women Lawyers, 2,163, 6,789, 7,174
International Federation of Working Women, **6,315, 6,675, 6,795,** 6,812, **7,273**
International Feminist Conference, 6,582
International Glove Workers Union, 3,887
International Harvester, 2,678, 3,849, 3,956, 17,655
International House (CA), 760
International Industrial Relations Association, 6,810
International Industrial Relations Institute, 7,315, 8,142
International Institute, 9,104, 9,333
International Institute for Girls (Spain), 7,567
International Institute of Cleveland (OH), 9,497
International Institute of Detroit (MI), 8,019
International Juridical Association, 6,314
International Kindergarten Union. *See* Association for Childhood Education International
International labor activities, 6,766, 6,982, 9,467, 12,682
International Labor Defense, 640, 1,357, 1,361, 1,654, 9,467, 12,682
International Labor Office, 11,905
International Labor Organization, 6,766, 6,977, 6,982, 7,257
International Labor Organization, Conference of American States (Cuba, 1939), 6,958
International Ladies Auxiliary, 11,897
International Ladies' Garment Workers' Union, 659, 677, 1,779, **3,774,** 4,032, 4,126, 4,492, 8,126, **8,146,** 9,127, 9,467, 9,493, 9,934, 9,962, 11,773, 11,806, 11,897, 12,422, 12,589, 12,704, 12,861, **15,329**
International Ladies' Garment Workers' Union, Local 180 (TX), **15,995**
International Ladies' Garment Workers' Union, Local 214 (TX), **15,996**
International Ladies' Garment Workers' Union, Los Angeles Local (CA), 1,656
International Ladies' Garment Workers' Union, Union Health Center, 6,802
International Ladies' Garment Workers' ⋯ *vs. Dorothy Frocks Company* (TX), **16,090**
International law, 2,163, 6,314, 6,368
International League for Peace and Freedom, 6,966
International League of Press Clubs, 3,862
International Longshoremen's and Warehousemen's Union, 14,656
International Longshoremen's and Warehousemen's Union, Local 6 (CA), **1,280,** 1,357
International Migration Service, 6,973
International Movement for Atlantic Union, 7,885
International Museum of Photography at George Eastman House (NY), **12,789**
International Nursing Index, 6,122
International Order of Good Templars, **14,303,** 17,264
International Order of Job's Daughters, San Francisco Bethel, No. 3 (CA), **565**
International Order of King's Daughters and Sons, Goodwill Circle (Ann Arbor, MI), **7,823**

International Order of Odd Fellows, 8,469
International Order of the King's Daughters and Sons, 5,426, **7,093,** 9,644, **11,410,** 12,520, 13,383, 15,597, **17,113**
International Order of the King's Daughters and Sons (FL), In-As-Much Circle, **2,937**
International Order of the King's Daughters and Sons (New Hampshire Branch), **10,836**
International Order of the King's Daughters and Sons (OH), Mary Pitch Circle, 14,063
International organization, 4,480, 6,379, 7,312
International Organization of Consumers Unions, 11,804, 11,805
International Peace Congress, 15,307
International Planned Parenthood Federation, 6,221, 6,987, 7,289
International Planned Parenthood Federation, "News," 7,197
International Program for Social Workers, 14,016
International Red Cross, 7,188, 8,633
International relations, 1,317, 2,072, 3,799, 4,122, 7,190, 8,658, 8,678, 11,236, **11,848,** 12,020, 13,221
International Relations Club (MA), 7,164
International relief, 6,125, 10,048, 11,593, 13,993
International Review of Missions (periodical), 7,212
International Seamen's Union of America, 3,890
International Social Service, American Branch, **8,657**
International Socialist Congress (Denmark, 1910), 17,722
International Socialist Women's Caucus, 17,975
International Society of Christian Endeavor, **1,631,** 14,468
International Society of the Daughters of the Barons of Runnymede, 4,689
International Statistical Institute, 11,747
International Symposium on Industrial Sterilization (Amsterdam, 1972), 13,259
International Tennis Hall of Fame, 15,371
International Union Against Venereal Diseases, 8,633
International Union for Child Welfare Survey, 6,766
International Visitors Center (TN), 6,767
International Who's Who in Poetry, 5,310
International Woman Suffrage Alliance, 7,306, 17,616
International Woman Suffrage Conference (Berlin, Germany, 1904), 14,814
International Woman Writers Conclave (IL), 6,876
International Women Suffrage Convention (1913), 8,144
International Women's Art Exhibit (NY), 6,876
International Women's Day, 10,020, 17,583
International Women's Year (1974), 12,707
International Women's Year (1975), 6,582, 7,313, 7,699, 8,096, 12,855, 17,619
International Women's Year Conference (Mexico City, Mexico), **12,707**
International Woodworkers of America, District 4, **3,445**
International Workers of the World, 492, 11,927
International Workmen's Association, 535
International Writers Conclave, 7,293
Internment of Japanese Americans (1942-1945). *See* Japanese Americans, Evacuation and relocation (1942-1945)
Interns (education), 14,791
Interns (legislation), 14,622
Interns (medicine), 11,869, 16,226
Interpreter, The (periodical), 4,151
Interprofessional Association for Social Insurance, 8,142
Interracial Commission (MI), 8,148
Interracial family, 9,467
Interracial marriage, 3,421, 3,661, 9,467, 11,897, 12,004, 14,244, 16,588, 16,967, 17,160, 17,420
Interreligious marriage, 16,965
Interstate Association of Commissions on the Status of Women. *See* National Association of Commissions for Women
Interstate Highway 14,220, 17,279
Interstate relations, 6,977
Interurban Woman Suffrage Council (NY), 6,979
Interviewing, 11,829
Interviewing in law enforcement, **5,540**
Interviewing in Social Security, 8,641

Interviews, **1,779**, **6,607**, 17,250, 17,325
Intrepid (ship), 9,120
Invalids, 8,787
Inventories, 2,231, 8,328, **11,455**
Inventors, **2,202**, **2,278**, **2,608**, 2,725, **4,064**, 6,329, **9,760**, 9,979, 10,831, 11,134, 12,053, 12,407, 12,508, 12,770, 13,810, **14,055**, 14,940, 14,942, 17,400
Inventors, Afro-American, **2,142**
Investigator (periodical), 4,809
Investment banking, 14,203
Invinson Memorial Hospital Ladies Auxiliary (WY), **17,981**
Invisible Gods, The (book), 4,007
Invitation to an Inquest (book), 6,079
Iona plantation (MS), 9,794
Ionia Free Fair (MI), **8,345**
Iota Sigma Pi, Mercury Chapter (MN), **8,579**
Iota Study Club (Minneapolis, MN), **9,145**, 9,227
Iowa, 4,707, 4,729, 4,734, 4,765, 4,803, 4,820, 4,857
  abolitionists, 4,940
  abortion, legal aspects, 1,984
  actors and actresses, 4,743
  agricultural education, 4,920
  agricultural societies, **4,687**, 4,839, 4,947
  architecture, domestic, 5,082
  archivists, **5,050**
  armed forces, women's reserves, **5,016**
  art societies, **4,881**
  art teachers, **4,688**
  artists, **4,868**
  associations, institutions, etc., 4,812
  attorneys general, **4,982**
  authors, 4,821, 4,898, **4,950**, 4,957, **4,962**, **4,973**, **5,019**, **5,038**, 5,043, 5,093, **5,094**
  autographs, **4,696**, **4,697**
  bands (music), 5,107
  bankers, **4,707**, 4,899, **4,951**
  basketball for women, 5,062
  billboards, 4,977
  biography, **4,867**, 4,899, **4,958**
  blizzards, 4,958
  boards of trade, **4,990**
  businessmen, 4,799, 4,906, **4,941**, **4,951**
  businesswomen, **4,863**, 4,899, **4,922**
  camps, 4,920
  caterers and catering, **4,939**
  Catholic schools, 4,872, 4,874
  Catholic universities and colleges, **4,709**
  caucus, 4,982, **5,003**
  charitable societies, 4,973, **5,069**
  chautauquas, **5,021**
  child development, **4,996**
  child welfare, 4,915
  church records and registers, **4,774**
  church records and registers, United Brethren, **4,849**
  church societies, **3,961**, **4,724**
  church societies, Baptist, 4,959
  church societies, Episcopal, 4,959
  church societies, Lutheran, 4,959
  church societies, Mennonite, **5,051**, **5,052**
  church societies, Methodist, 4,959, **5,073**, **5,075**, **5,076**, **5,077**, **5,078**
  church societies, Presbyterian, 4,959
  church societies, Unitarian, 4,959
  church societies, United Brethren, 4,849
  churches, Baptist, 4,701
  citizens' associations, **4,899**, 4,921
  city councilwomen, **5,007**
  civil defense, 4,937
  Civil War
    personal narratives, 4,750
    relief of sick and wounded, 4,858
    societies, **4,745**, **4,903**
  clergy, **4,972**
  clergy, Congregational **4,829**, **4,889**
  clergy, German Baptist, 16,365
  clergy, Unitarian, **4,776**, 4,958
  clergymen's wives, **4,721**, 4,779, **8,738**
  clubs, 4,710, **4,711**, **4,719**, **4,723**, **4,725**, 4,729, 4,732, **4,748**, **4,751**, **4,753**, **4,769**, **4,770**, **4,775**, **4,780**, **4,796**, 4,800, 4,815, **4,838**, **4,846**, 4,851,

  4,864, **4,866**, **4,878**, **4,883**, 4,918, **4,923**, 4,957, **4,960**, **4,997**, **4,998**, 5,059, 5,066, 5,087, 5,089, 5,099, 5,109, 5,112, 5,113, 5,117
  clubs, Afro-American, **4,768**
  college administrators, 5,035
  college and school drama, 4,690
  college and school journalism 5,085
  college presidents, 4,709, 5,060
  college teachers, **4,686**, **4,690**, **4,691**, **4,710**, **4,916**, **4,935**, **4,940**, 4,958, **5,035**, **5,063**, **5,068**, **5,070**, **5,079**, **5,082**, **5,083**, **5,084**, **5,085**, **5,101**, **5,102**, **5,103**
  college trustees, **5,063**, **5,065**
  commonplace books, 4,738
  community art centers, 4,977
  composers, 4,689
  congresses and conventions, **4,861**, 4,946
  congressmen, 4,695, 4,747, 4,749, **4,759**, 4,784, 4,906, 4,914
  contemplative orders, **4,871**
  convents and nunneries, Catholic, **4,875**, **5,090**
  country life, 9,975
  county attorneys, 5,109
  county officials and employees, 4,704, 4,899
  deans (in schools), 4,906, 4,969, 5,035, 5,063, **5,101**
  debates and debating, 4,788
  dentists, **4,948**
  diaries and journals, **4,882**, **4,896**, 4,911, **4,925**, 4,964, 5,027
    travel, **4,825**
  divorce, **4,912**
  dolls, collectors and collecting, 5,093
  dramatists, **4,989**
  drug trade, 4,716
  editors, **4,816**, **4,956**
  education, 4,977
  educational associations, **4,712**, **4,726**, 4,815, **4,890**, 5,048, 5,079, **5,097**
  educators, 4,853, **4,946**
  elections, 4,689
  essays, **4,908**
  executive advisory bodies, 4,861, 4,921
  factory inspectors, **4,824**
  family farms, management, 10,445
  farm life, **4,882**, 4,904
  farmers, 4,799, **4,911**, 4,924, 4,952, 4,953, **4,955**, **4,963**
  farmers' institutes, 4,920
  feminists, 4,867
  festivals, 4,981, 8,725
  fiber plants, 4,807
  4-H clubs, 4,947, 4,960, 4,961
  Friends, 4,842, 4,936
  genealogists 4,689, **4,942**
  general stores, 4,892
  governors, 4,741, **4,926**, **4,928**, **5,106**
  greek letter societies, **5,046**, 5,064
  greek letter societies, Afro-American, 5,064
  high school teachers, 4,814, **4,820**
  historians, **4,829**, 4,916
  historic sites, conservation and restoration, 4,977, 5,082
  historical markers, 4,860
  home economics, **4,984**
    study and teaching, **4,691**
  home nursing, **4,884**
  hotels, taverns, etc., management, 5,056
  immigrants, Norwegian, **4,721**, 9,106, **9,266**
  influenza epidemics, 4,690
  itinerancy (church polity), 4,772
  journalism, societies, 4,866, **5,001**
  journalists, **4,957**, **5,019**, 5,107
  judges, 2,545, 4,822, 4,855, **4,856**, 4,934, **4,938**, 9,308
  justices of the peace, 4,924
  labor disputes, 4,855
  land settlement, **5,056**, 5,057, 11,704
  law teachers, 4,765, 4,934
  lawyers, 4,784, 4,831, **4,854**, 4,906, 4,934, **5,104**, **5,106**
  legends, 4,923
  legislators, 4,789, **4,910**, 4,929, 4,951, **4,964**
  librarians, 4,842
  libraries, university and college, **5,034**

  library associations, 4,910, **4,999**
  lieutenant governors, **4,763**
  literary societies, **4,720**, 4,770, **4,886**, 4,960, **4,968**, **4,985**, **4,993**, **5,017**, **5,044**, 5,045, 5,064, **5,096**, 9,098
  local church councils, 4,959
  mayors, 4,729, 4,738, **4,932**, **5,006**, **5,007**
  medical societies, 4,698
  Mennonites, **5,049**, 5,050, **5,051**, **5,052**
  monasticism and religious orders for women, Catholic, 4,696, **4,872**, **4,873**, **4,874**, **4,876**, 15,336
  Mormons and Mormonism, 4,209, 16,636
  mothers, 4,949
  municipal universities and colleges, **5,086**
  murder, 5,108
  museum directors, 5,107
  music teachers, 4,735, **4,901**, **4,944**, 4,949, 5,093, 8,364, 8,748
  musical societies, 4,758, **4,877**
  Native Americans, 5,108
    wars, 4,842
  newspapers, sections, columns, etc., 12,259
  nurses, **5,027**
  nursing schools, **4,880**, 4,969, 4,980
  officials and employees, **4,900**
  old age homes, 4,817
  orphans and orphan asylums, 2,645
  painters, **4,688**
  parents' and teachers' associations, **4,805**, **5,105**
  patriotic societies, **4,745**, **4,787**, 4,815, 4,860, **4,862**, **4,891**, **4,902**, 4,916
  peace societies, **4,754**, 5,068
  periodicals, **4,693**
  philanthropists, 5,072
  photographs, **5,018**
  physicians, **4,945**, 4,952, **4,963**
  pioneers and settlers, 1,770, 4,696, 4,701, 4,706, 4,733, **4,773**, **4,885**, 4,904, **4,972**, **5,108**, 9,106
  poets, 4,732
  political clubs, **4,943**
  politicians, 4,750, **4,869**
  politics and government, 5,038
  politics, practical, women's activism, 4,823, 4,859, **4,931**, **4,932**, **5,005**, 5,024
  postal service
    postmasters, 4,956
    postmistresses, **4,739**
  prayer groups, **4,757**
  psychiatric hospitals, 4,828
  psychiatric nursing, 5,027
  public health, 4,931
  public officers, 4,799, **5,038**, 5,109
  public works, 4,949
  rabbis, 13,810
  radio programs, 4,916
  railroads, 4,820
  real estate agents, **5,104**
  reformatories (female), 4,811
  rewards (prizes, etc.), 4,918
  school buildings, 5,108
  school children, 4,760
  school superintendents and principals, **4,705**, **4,830**, 4,852, 4,899, **4,920**, 4,946, 5,068, 5,086
  schools, **4,813**
    finance, 4,932
  scrapbooks, 4,729, 4,923, **5,095**
  secret societies, 4,697, **4,778**
  senators, United States, 4,732, 4,747, 4,905, 4,906, 5,053, 5,060
  Siouan Indians, wars, 4,765
  social life and customs, 1,770
  social roles, 4,861
  social settlements, **4,823**
  social workers, **4,921**
  societies, etc., **4,699**
  soldiers, Civil War, **4,789**, **4,790**, **4,836**
  students' societies, **4,886**, 4,960, **4,967**, **5,014**, **5,033**, 5,062, **5,064**, 5,068, **5,115**, 14,029
  suffrage, **4,859**, 4,867, 4,887, 4,920, **6,479**, 6,629
  suffrage societies, 1,059, 4,732, 4,786, 4,793, 4,823, 4,831, **4,859**, **4,865**, 4,960, **5,002**, 5,068, 6,479
  suffragists, 4,684, **4,930**
  swimmers, **5,026**

teachers, 4,735, 4,742, **4,744**, 4,815, 4,816, **4,847**, 4,892, 4,906, **4,927**, 4,934, 4,958, 5,048
19th C, **4,739**, **4,783**, **4,819**, 4,842, **4,852**, **4,853**, **4,896**, 11,056
teachers' colleges, 9,318
teachers' unions, **4,777**, **4,806**, 4,830, 4,946, 4,958
temperance, 4,893
temperance societies, **4,786**, 4,793, 4,907, **5,100**, **5,116**
trade and professional associations, **5,000**
traffic safety, 4,947
tuberculosis, hospitals and sanatoriums, 4,950
United Methodist Church, discipline, **4,774**
United Nations associations, 5,024
universities and colleges
alumnae, **5,061**
buildings, 5,018
employees, **5,033**
faculty, **5,033**
records and correspondence, **4,715**
Utopias, 4,701, 4,704, **4,767**, 4,809
volunteer workers in hospitals, **4,713**, **4,879**
water resources, 4,931
water-supply, 4,932
women's colleges, **4,752**
World War I, civilians' work, **5,114**
World War II, civilians' work, 3,950
Young Women's Christian Association, **5,071**, **5,098**
Iowa Arts Council, 5,008
Iowa Association of Colored Women's Clubs, **4,768**
Iowa Band, 4,829, 4,889
Iowa Business Woman, The, 4,922
Iowa Centennial 1846-1946 Poetry Anthology (book), 4,758
Iowa Child Welfare Association, 4,915, 4,996
Iowa City Book Club, 4,960
Iowa City Business and Professional Women's Club (IA), **4,997**
Iowa City First Christian Church, Christian Women's Fellowship (IA), 4,959
Iowa City Unitarian Church, 4,958
Iowa City Woman's Club (IA), 4,923
Iowa Clubwoman, The (periodical), **4,800**
Iowa College (Grinnell, IA). *See* Grinnell College (IA)
Iowa Commission on Children and Youth, 4,921
Iowa Commission on the Status of Women, 4,982
Iowa Confidential Records Council, 5,006
Iowa Congress of Mothers, 4,915
Iowa Congress of Parents and Teachers, **4,805**
Iowa Conservation Education Council, 4,686
Iowa Council of Republican Women, 4,918
Iowa Equal Suffrage Association, 1,059, 4,823, 4,837, 4,859, 4,930
Iowa Equal Suffrage Convention (1902, 1906), 6,479
Iowa Farm Bureau, 4,947
Iowa Federation of Business and Professional Women, **4,922**
Iowa Federation of Business and Professional Women's Clubs, Inc., **4,998**
Iowa Federation of Music Clubs, 4,689, 4,758
Iowa Federation of Republican Women, **4,943**
Iowa Federation of Women's Clubs, 4,748, 4,786, 4,796, 4,846, **4,864**, 4,908, 4,918, **4,923**, 5,112, 5,113
Iowa Historical Building, 4,741
Iowa Indians, 15,289
Iowa League for Nursing, 5,000
Iowa League of American Pen Women, 4,960
Iowa Library Association, 4,910, **4,999**
Iowa Master Farm Homemaker's Guild, **4,687**
Iowa Nurses' Association, **5,000**
Iowa Peace Society, 4,754, 5,068
Iowa Poets Day Association, 4,758
Iowa Press and Authors Club, 4,957
Iowa Press Women, Inc., 4,866, **5,001**
Iowa Salvage Committee, 4,957
Iowa Sanitary Commission, 4,696
Iowa Sanitary Committee 2,645
Iowa State Agricultural College, faculty, 4,691
Iowa State Education Association, English Teachers of the Central District, 5,048
Iowa State Historical Department, 4,747, 4,808, 4,842
Iowa State Hospital, 5,027

Iowa State Hospital (Independence, IA), 4,828
Iowa State Library Commission, 4,727
Iowa State Medical Society, 4,698, 4,732
Iowa State Players, 4,690
Iowa State Senate, 4,789
Iowa (State) Supreme Court, 9,308
Iowa State Teacher's Association, 4,696, **4,806**, 4,830, 4,946, 4,958
Iowa State Teachers College. *See* University of Northern Iowa
Iowa State Teachers College (Cedar Falls, IA), Chimes, 14,029
Iowa State Teacher's College, students, 4,927
Iowa State University
faculty, **4,690**, 15,934
students, 4,685
Iowa Suffrage Memorial Commission, 4,729, 4,859, **5,002**
Iowa Territory, clergy, 4,829
Iowa Wesleyan College (Mount Pleasant, IA), 4,577, 4,815, **5,062**, 5,067, 5,071
alumnae, **5,061**
faculty, 5,061, **5,063**, **5,068**, **5,070**
presidents, 5,060, 5,068
students, 5,053, 5,074
students, Afro-American, 5,064
trustees, **5,065**
Iowa Wesleyan College (Mount Pleasant, IA), Hypatia Literary Society, 5,064
Iowa Wesleyan College (Mount Pleasant IA), Ruthean Literary Society, 5,064, 5,068
Iowa Wesleyan College (Mount Pleasant, IA), Women's Athletic Association, 5,062
Iowa Wesleyan College (Mount Pleasant, IA), Women's Cadet Corps, 5,062
Iowa Woman Suffrage Association, 4,732, 4,793, 4,831
Iowa Woman Suffrage Convention (IA), 4,754
Iowa Woman Suffrage Society, **4,865**
Iowa Women's Political Caucus, 4,982, **5,003**
Iowa Women's Republican Club, Story County unit, 4,815
Iowa X-Ray Club, 4,698
Iowa Yearly Meeting of Friends, Woman's Missionary Union, 4,959
Iowan, The (periodical), 5,082
Ipcar, Dahlov (Zorach) [Mrs. Adolph] (1917-), 2,662
Ipswich Academy (MA). *See* Ipswich Female Seminary (MA)
Ipswich Female Seminary (MA), 7,052, **7,056**, 7,224, 7,494
Iran (Persia), 7,191
foreign relations, 12,407
missionaries to, **11,289**
missionaries to, Presbyterian, **15,171**
Iran's Most Valued Citizen (book), 10,251
Iraq, schools, 10,926, 10,927
Irby, Loulie W., 15,895
Iredell, Annie, 13,454
Iredell, Frances "Fanny" Tredwell [Mrs. James, Jr.], 13,454
Iredell, Hannah (Johnston) [Mrs. James, Sr.], 13,210, 13,454
Iredell, Helen Blair, **13,041**
Iredell, James, 13,041
Iredell, James, Sr. (1751-99), **13,210**
Iredell, James, Sr. (1751-99), Family, 13,454
Iredell, James, Jr. (1788-1853), **13,210**, 13,454
Iredell, Sara (1811-1908). *See* Fleetwood, Sara (Iredell) [Mrs Christian Abraham] (1811-1908)
Irelan, Elma Clementine (1880-1956), **15,907**
Ireland,
American travelers in, 9,601
Friends, Society of, 15,058
political prisoners, **12,567**
riots, 9,279
Ireland forever Club. *See* Erin-Go-Bragh Club
Ireland, Florence, 5,653
Ireland, Irma Thompson [Mrs. Mark] (1880-), **8,172**
Ireland, John, 8,934, 8,956
Ireland, Juliet S., **12,228**
Ireland, Sister Seraphine, 9,490
Ireland, W. H., 12,228
Irene Kaufman Settlement,

Irene Mayer Selznick Company, 6,085
Irion, Eliza Lucy. *See* Neilson, Eliza Lucy (Irion) [Mrs. John Albert]
Irion, Elizabeth Charlotte, 9,651
Irion Family (MS), **9,651**
Irion, James W., 9,651
Irion, McKinney F., Jr., 9,651
Irion, Mrs. McKinney F., Jr., 9,651
Irion, Mrs. Robert, 1,505
Iris Garden Club (GA), 3,187
Irish-Americans, **1,998**, 16,351
Irish, Charles Wood, 4,924
Irish Dew (drama), 7,260
Irish, Elizabeth, 4,924
Irish Family (IA), **4,924**
Irish, Frederick, 4,924
Irish, Gilbert, 4,924
Irish, Jane L., 4,924
Irish, Josie M. (Strawbridge) [Mrs. Gilbert], 4,924
Irish, Ruth, 4,924
Irish, Ruth F., 11,508
Irish, Susanna Abigail (Yarbrough) [Mrs. Charles Wood], 4,92
Iron Eye. *See* La Flesche, Joseph
Iron Eye's Family: The Children of Joseph LaFlesche (book), 10,465
Iron-founding, 15,014
Iron industry and trade, 2,029, **2,031**, 14,816, 16,401, 16,448
Iron Noose, The (book), 962
Iron Will, The, 8,428
Iroquois Indians, antiquities, 11,387
Irrigation, 2,674, 16,486
Irvin, Elizabeth, 14,628
Irvine, Allen (Claywell), 13,016
Irvine, Ann, 11,195
Irvine, Javan Bradley (1831-1904), Family (SD), **15,854**
Irvine, Julia, 7,574
Irvine, Margaret "Maggie" Louisa [Mrs. Javan Bradley], 15,854
Irvine, Sarah "Sallie", 4,729
Irvine, William, 11,195
Irving, Abigail Spicer (Furman) [Mrs. John Treat, Sr.], 12,018, 12,019
Irving College, alumnae, 15,964
Irving, John Beaufain, 15,423
Irving, John Treat (1812-1906), **12,018**
Irving, John Treat, Sr. (1778-1838), 12,018, **12,019**
Irving, Julia A. (Granger) [Mrs. Sanders] (1822-97), **12,824**
Irving, Ruth (Beane), **12,718**
Irving, Sanders (1813-84), 12,824
Irving, Sir Henry, 6,185
Irving, Washington, 10,962, 12,018, 12,019, 12,164, 12,824
Irwin, Agnes (1841-1914), **6,677**
Irwin, Annie, 2,046
Irwin Army Hospital, 5,193
Irwin, Harriet "Hallie" (Hyde) [Mrs. Will], 1,233, 1,306
Irwin, Helen, 4,922
Irwin, Inez (Haynes) [Mrs. Will] (1873-1970), 825, **6,678**, 6,947
Irwin, Janet, 4,123
Irwin, Loretta Hart [Mrs. A. B.], 4,911
Irwin, Margaret, 17,775
Irwin, Mary Ann (ca. 1817-82). *See* Callaway, Mary Ann (Irwin) [Mrs. Merrell Price] (ca. 1817-82)
Irwin, May (1862-1938), 11,453
Irwin, Molly, **1,161**
Irwin Russell Memorial Association (MS), 9,688
Irwin, Will, 1,233
Irwin, William Hyde, 1,233
"Is Biology Women's Destiny?" (speech), 17,710
Isaacks, Maud [Mrs.], **16,214**
Isaacs, Bertha Patience (1865-?), **5,780**
Isaacs, Edith Juliet Rich [Mrs. Lewis] (1878-1956), **17,803**
Isaacs, Hannah, **13,794**
Isaacs, Hermine (1915-68). *See* Popper, Hermine (Isaacs) (1915-68)
Isaacs, Lewis, 17,803
Isaacson, Alice Edith (1874-1955), **5,081**

Isabel Hampton Robb Memorial Fund. *See* Nurses'
   Educational Funds, Inc.
Isabella (pseudonym). *See* Cadwallader, Mary I.
   (Paul) [Mrs. Sylvanus]
Isabella County Girl Scouts, Inc. (MI), **8,346**
Isabella, Queen of Spain, 2,944, 4,647
Isabella Stewart Gardner Museum, 6,452
Isabella Thoburn College, 4,525
Isadora Duncan's Russian Days (book), 12,361
Isbell College and Conservatory of Music (AL), 14
Isbell, Josephine (Walker) [Mrs. John C.], **16,420**
Iselin, Adrian, 11,795
Iselin, Arthur, 11,795
Iselin, Eleanor (Jay) [Mrs. Arthur] (1882-1953),
   11,795
Iselin, Eleanor (O'Donnell) [Mrs. Adrian] (1820-97),
   11,795
Iselin Family (NY), 12,020
Isely, M. Alice, 5,241
Isely, Mildred, **9,877**
Isenberg, Gerda [Mrs. R. A.], 566
Isham, Charles (1853-1919), 3,864
Isham Family (IL), **3,864**
Isham, Leahalma [Mrs. Lincoln], 3,864
Isham, Mary Lincoln, 5,060
Isham, Ruth Eliza (Wales) (1849-1929), **17,657**
Isherwood Family (MO), **9,878**
Ishimoto, Baroness, 8,672
Island County Welfare Board (WA), 17,356
Island Possessed (book), 3,773
Islands, 646, 1,446, 3,132, 5,644, 7,895
Isle La Motte Free Public Library (VT), **17,008**
Isle of Rhodes, Sephardim in, 17,282
Isle Royale Calling (book), 8,314
Isleta Indians, **16,866**
Isn't One Wife Enough? (book), 4,209
Isom, Alice (Parker) [Mrs. George] (1848-1924),
   16,706
Isom, Annie. *See* Matheson, Annie (Isom) [Mrs.
   Christen]
Isom Family (MS), 9,816
Isom, George, 16,706
Isom, Mary Frances (1865-1920), **14,591**
Isoniazid, 11,862
Israel
   American ambassadors to, 12,070
   archives, 11,915
   missionaries to, 14,846
   prime ministers, 12,069, 12,070
   women, 7,301
   women, Arab, 7,301
Israel, Joan L. [Mrs. Kenneth] (1930-), **8,095**
Israel, Rachel Cohen, 17,282
Israel, Rebecca, 17,282
Israel, Victoria, 17,282
Israels, Belle (Lindner) (1877-1933). *See* Moskowitz,
   Belle (Lindner) Israels (1877-1933)
Issaelson, Eva Mae (?-1973), 16,488
Issarescu, Princess Illena, 9,986
Issei, 1,041
Issler, Anne Roller, **567**
Istalilxo, the Lady of Tula (drama), 15,952
Isthmus of Panama, 533, 801
It Changed My Life (book), 6,582
It Pays to Smile (book), 12,488
Italian American Labor Council, 9,493
Italian-American newspapers, 12,861
Italian-Americans, 1,837, 6,727, 9,493, 9,497, 9,507,
   12,860, **12,861**, **15,247**
   evacuation and relocation (1942-1945), 2,702
Italian Art Society (Venice, Italy), 5,118
Italian Cloak, Suit, and Skirt Makers Union, Local 48
   (Staten Island, NY), 12,861
Italian Dress and Waist Makers Union, Local 89
   (Staten Island, NY), 12,861
Italian Mothers' Club (New Haven, CT), 1,997
Italian Sketches (book), 552
Italian Sons and Daughters of America, **15,247**
Italian Welfare League, Inc., **12,862**
"Italians in Milwaukee, The," 9,507
Italo-Ethiopian War (1935-1936), 12,632
Italy, 5,953, 5,954, 6,099, 12,196, 12,285
   American ambassadors to, 2,458, 11,857, 12,022,
      17,116

American artists in, 2,776, 5,906, **6,351**
American sculptors in, **17,338**
American teachers in, 5,171
American travelers in, **5,953**, 6,099, 6,912, 15,063
Americans in, 17,035
cities and towns, 14,744
diplomatic and consular service, 9,277
history (1922-1945), 5,973
international relief, 11,593
politics and government, 12,632
universities and colleges, 9,695
war of 1859, 17,589
World War II, 6,690
   civilians' work, 4,843, 5,131
"Italy Transformed" (ms), 5,973
Itasca County Farm Bureau (MN), 9,377
Itasca State Park (MN),
Ithaca Children's Home (NY), 11,738
Ithaca Church (NE), Woman's Missionary Society,
   10,590
Ithaca City Federation of Women's Organizations
   (NY), **11,623**
Ithaca City Hospital (NY), 11,750
Ithaca College (NY), archives, **11,781**
Ithaca Conservatory (NY), faculty, 11,578
Ithaca Convention (NY, 1894), 7,203
Ithaca High School (NY), 11,658, 11,698, 11,736
Ithaca Methodist Church (NY). *See* St. Paul's United
   Methodist Church (Ithaca, NY)
Ithaca Methodist Church (NY), Foreign Missionary
   Society. *See* St. Paul's United Methodist Church
   (Ithaca, NY), Women's Society of Christian
   Service
Ithaca Methodist Church (NY), India Missionary
   Society. *See* St. Paul's United Methodist Church
   (Ithaca, NY), Women's Society of Christian
   Service
Ithaca Methodist Church (NY), Ladies' Aid Society.
   See St. Paul's United Methodist Church (Ithaca,
   NY), Women's Society of Christian Service
Ithaca Methodist Church (NY), Ladies' and Pastor's
   Christian Union. *See* St. Paul's United
   Methodist Church (Ithaca, NY), Women's
   Society of Christian Service
Ithaca Methodist Church (NY), Ladies' Social Union.
   See St. Paul's United Methodist Church (Ithaca,
   NY), Women's Society of Christian Service
Ithaca Methodist Church (NY), Woman's Home
   Missionary Society. *See* St. Paul's United
   Methodist Church (Ithaca, NY), Women's
   Society of Christian Service
Ithaca Methodist Church (NY), Young Woman's
   Foreign Missionary Society. *See* St. Paul's
   United Methodist Church (Ithaca, NY), Women's
   Society of Christian Service
Ithaca Reconstruction Home (NY), 11,658
Ithaca Woman's Club (NY), 11,623, **11,625**
Itinerancy (church polity), 4,772
   Methodist Church, 1,584, 5,245, **5,801**, 10,879,
      10,908, 11,035
It's a Great War (book), 6,722
It's Different for a Woman (book), 6,108
Ittleson Family Foundation, 5,232
Ivanhoe (book), 2,362
I've Got to Talk With Somebody, God (book), 5,080
Iverson, Andrew, 16,697
Iverson, Caroline Manger, 8,666
Iverson, Julia [Mrs. Andrew], 16,697
Iverson, Lily R., 8,127
Iverson, Minnie Josephine (1889-?). *See* Hodapp,
   Minnie Josephine (Iverson) [Mrs. Frederick]
   (1889-?)
Ives, Eliza, **11,626**
Ives, Elizabeth (Stevenson) [Mrs. Ernest] (1898-),
   4,370, 11,827
Ives, Frances, 2,009
Ives, Margaret (1903-), **13,743**
Ives, Marion, 14,433
Ives, Mrs. Ernest, 13,514
Ives, Robert, 2,009
Ivie, Sallie (Lawing) [Mrs. Thomas G.] (ca. 1845-ca.
   1908), **15,954**
Ivina (slave, SC), 2,126
"Ivory Towers Old and New" (lecture), 1,085

Ivy Club (Bloomsburg, PA), **14,725**
Ivy Garden Club (GA), 3,187
Ivy, H. M., 9,662
Ivy, Irene. *See* Moore, Irena (Ivy)
Ivy, The (Salem Academy and College, NC), 13,634
Iwanska, Alicja, 3,290
Iwo Jima Statue committee, 17,050
Izaak Walton League, 9,467
Izant, Grace Goulder, **14,081**
Izard, Alice De Lancey [Mrs. Ralph, Sr.], 2,408,
   2,621, 15,456, 15,498
Izard, Ann Middleton, 15,456 >6865, **13,078**
Izard, Eliza Lucas (Pinckney) [Mrs. Ralph, Jr.],
   15,456
Izard, Elizabeth (Carter) Banister [Mrs. Thomas Lee]
   Shippen [Mrs. George], 2,574, **15,483**
Izard, Elizabeth (Middleton) [Mrs. Ralph, Jr.], 2,408,
   15,456, 15,483
Izard, George, 2,574
Izard, Margaret (1768-1824). *See* Manigault,
   Margaret (Izard) [Mrs. Gabriel] (1768-1824)
Izard, Ralph, Sr. (1742-1804), Family, 2,408
Izard, Ralph, Jr., 15,456
J. B. Lippincott Company, 14,405
J. B. Lippincott Publishing Company (PA), 14,978
J. G. Sullivan and Company (SC), 15,743
J. H. Bowers (ship), 5,591
J. P. Morgan Company (NY), 11,720
J. Slater and Company Cotton Manufactory (Barre,
   MA). *See* Boston and Barre Manufacturing
   Company (MA)
Ja Ja, Rosella, 6,353
Jack (slave, SC), 15,486
"Jack" (story) 5,970
Jack and Jill (periodical), 14,407
"Jack Benny Show, The" (television program), 17,958
Jack, Jessie Annette (1865-1935). *See* Hooper, Jessie
   Annette (Jack) [Mrs. Ben C.] (1865-1935)
Jack, Mrs. Clyde A., 1,786
Jack, Peter Munro, 14,413
Jack Pine School, Towns of Tilden and Woodmohr,
   Joint School District No. 5, Chippewa County
   (WI), **17,523**
Jackie, Cecilia (1904-69). *See* Martin, Cecilia
   (Jackie) (1904-69)
Jackman, Harold, 3,284, 3,285, 3,288, 3,289, 3,291
Jackman, Ivie A. [Miss], 3,289, 3,290
"Jack's Merry Christmas" (ms), 1,445
Jackson, Abbie Clement [Mrs.], **5,383**
Jackson, Abner (1811-74), **1,956**
Jackson, Ada, **2,409**
Jackson Air Base (MS), 9,587
Jackson, Alice (Day), 1,948
Jackson, Amelia Spencer, 14,857
Jackson, Andrew (1767-1845), 2,312, 2,320, 5,335,
   5,481, 6,539, 9,719, 9,735, 11,746, 12,985,
   15,256, 15,463, 15,577, 15,898, 15,948
Jackson, Angeline. *See* Ashley, Angeline (Jackson)
Jackson, Anne. *See* Williams, Anne (Jackson)
Jackson, Anne E. M., 2,233
Jackson, Anson, 8,957
Jackson, C. D. (1902-64), **5,144**
Jackson, Caroline (Hoopes), 15,024
Jackson Clarion-Ledger (MS), 9,709
Jackson Daily News (MS), 9,599, 9,768
Jackson, Edith Banfield (1895-1977), **6,679**, 8,657
Jackson, Elizabeth (1893-1968), **8,580**
Jackson, Elizabeth Cabot (1836-?). *See* Putnam,
   Elizabeth Cabot (Jackson) (1836-?)
Jackson, Ellen [Mrs.], **6,680**
Jackson, Elvira Evelyna (Worth) (1836-1940). *See*
   Moffitt, Elvira Evelyna (Worth) Jackson Walker
   (1836-1940)
Jackson, Emily Elizabeth (1845-1935). *See* Nicholas,
   Emily Elizabeth (Jackson) [Mrs. Philip N.]
   (1845-1935)
Jackson, Emily Ellsworth [Mrs. Abner] (1816-53),
   1,956
Jackson, Eugenia (Adams) [Mrs. Anson] (ca. 1850-?),
   8,957
Jackson, Eveline Harden (1848-1928), 3,024
Jackson, Evie [Miss], 3,104
Jackson Family (GA), **3,024**
Jackson Family (MA), 6,358

Jackson Family (New England), 6,352
Jackson, Fay, 3,799
Jackson, Frances (Whipple) [Mrs. Frank G.] Craw [Mrs. Freedom W.], 9,437
Jackson, Graham, 3,260
Jackson, Hannah Lowell (1820-79). *See* Cabot, Hannah Lowell (Jackson) [Mrs. Samuel] (1820-79)
Jackson, Harriet N. *See* Ralston, Harriet N. (Jackson) [Mrs. James H.]
Jackson, Harriet R., 8,989
Jackson, Helen Mar (1843-1907). *See* Gougar, Helen Mar (Jackson) [Mrs. John D.] (1843-1907)
Jackson, Helen Maria (Fiske) [Mrs. Edward Bissell] Hunt [Mrs. William Sharpless] (1830-85), **568**, 616, 1,087, 1,340, 1,426, **1,443**, 1,481, 1,635, 1,963, 2,542, 7,131, 7,220, 9,438, 9,965, 11,821, 12,022, 12,403, **12,519**, 14,062
Jackson, Henry, 3,396
Jackson, Henry M., 17,251, 17,409
Jackson, Henry R., 3,540
Jackson Hole Preserve (WY), **11,878**
Jackson Institute (GA), 3,419
Jackson, Irene, 5,466
Jackson, James, **2,954**
Jackson, James, 3,567
Jackson, Jean, **14,395**
Jackson, John, 2,495
Jackson, John Beard (1845-1908), **15,222**
Jackson, Joseph Henry (1895-1955), **569**
Jackson, Josephine Wing [Mrs. Clair] (1877-1972), **8,233**
Jackson, Juanita (1913-). *See* Mitchell, Juanita (Jackson) [Mrs. Clarence] (1913-)
Jackson, Kate [Miss], 2,954, **2,955**
Jackson, Kezia (Stump) [Mrs. Richard I.], 5,811
Jackson, Laura Riding [Mrs. Schuyler B.] (1901-), 454, **4,237**, 15,929, **15,936**, **16,165**, 16,169
Jackson, Leonora (1879-1969). *See* McKim, Leonora Jackson [Mrs. William Duncan] (1879-1969)
Jackson, Lillie May (1889-1975), **5,828**
Jackson, Lucile (Musser), 16,949
Jackson, Lydia (Beals) (1789-1869). *See* Beecher, Lydia (Beals) Jackson (1789-1869)
Jackson, Margaret (1887-). *See* Bovey, Margaret (Jackson) [Mrs. John] (1887-)
Jackson, Margaret A. [Miss], 12,120
Jackson, Maria West (Oden) [Mrs. James] Mullikin [Mrs. Thomas] (ca. 1791-?), 5,797
Jackson, Marilouise (Wheaton) [Mrs. L. J.], 9,434
Jackson, Martha [Miss], 10,712
Jackson, Martha Peeler (1863-?), **9,879**
Jackson, Mary Anna Morrison [Mrs. Thomas J.], 13,327, 13,376, **13,449**
Jackson, Mary Beard, 15,222
Jackson, Mary Louise, 15,222
Jackson, Mercy, **10,248**
Jackson, Mrs. Augie, 3,725
Jackson, Pearl Cashwell [Mrs. J. A.] (1869-1928), **16,091**
Jackson, Rachel (Donelson) Robards [Mrs. Andrew] (1767-1828), 9,722, 11,654, 15,463, 15,948, 16,061
Jackson, Roxana, 8,669
Jackson, Sarah (York) (1806-77), 787
Jackson, Selene (Harding), 15,932
Jackson, Shirley. [Mrs. Stanley Edgar] Hyman (1919-65), 569, **2,410**
Jackson State College (MS). *See* Jackson State University (MS)
Jackson State University (MS), 6,087, 9,575, **9,577**
  catalogs, **9,576**
  faculty, 5,466
  pictorial works, 9,579
Jackson-Thames, Frances, **9,652**
Jackson, Thomas Jonathan, 13,099
Jackson, Thorstina (?-1959). *See* Walters, Thorstina (Jackson) [Mrs. Emile] (?-1959)
Jackson, Vesta Lynn, 16,485
Jackson, Victoria (Hancock) [Mrs. Jonathan] (1880-1967), **16,707**
Jackson, Virginia (1911-). *See* Kiah, Virginia (Jackson) (1911-)

Jackson, W. H., 3,045
Jackson, William Sharpless, 568, 1,426, 1,443
Jacksonville Female Academy (IL), 3,911
Jacksonville State Hospital (IL), 4,411
Jacksonville Woman's Club (FL), **2,885**
Jacob (slave, NC), 2,124
Jacob A. Riis Neighborhood Settlement (NY), **12,520**
Jacob, Frances, **9,146**
Jacob Fugger the Rich (book), 6,203
Jacob, John I., 2,270
Jacob, Max, 12,047
Jacob, Nellie, 17,744
Jacob, Susan M. (1823-1905). *See* Clay, Susan M. (Jacob) [Mrs. James Brown] (1823-1905)
Jacobi, Edith Brandenstein [Mrs. Jacob], 931
Jacobi, Florence. *See* Arnstein, Florence (Jacobi) [Mrs. Lawrence]
Jacobi, Frederick, 931
Jacobi, Mary Corinna (Putnam) [Mrs. Abraham] (1842-1906), 2,542, 6,552, **6,681**, 14,745
Jacobs, Annie E. (Clark), **9,653**
Jacobs, Charles Clark, 9,685
Jacobs, Florence (Burrill) (?-1978), 5,694
Jacobs, Fred Clark, 9,685
Jacobs, Helen Hull (1908-), **12,871**, 15,935
Jacobs, Henry Bailey, 16,860
Jacobs, Jane Emeline, 14,593
Jacobs, Madel. *See* Morgan, Madel (Jacobs) [Mrs. Adlia]
Jacobs, Margaret Flint [Mrs. Lester W.] (1891-1960), 4,445, **5,712**
Jacobs, Maud Leone Openshaw [Mrs. Joseph] (1903-), 16,780
Jacobs, Mrs. Horace T., 15,597
Jacobs, Pattie (Ruffner) [Mrs. Solon Howard] (1875-1935), 48
Jacob's Pillow Dance Festival, 12,365
Jacobs, Sophia (Yarnall) [Mrs. Reginald Robert] (1902-), **6,682**, 16,773
Jacobs, Zina Diantha (Huntington) [Mrs. Henry Bailey] (1821-1901). *See* Young, Zina Diantha (Huntington) [Mrs. Henry Bailey] Jacobs [Mrs. Joseph, Jr.] Smith [Mrs. Brigham] (1821-1901)
Jacobsen, Josephine [Mrs. Eric] (1908-), 5,829
Jacobson, Abraham, 8,751
Jacobson, Clara (1864-1949), **8,751**
Jacobson, Dorothy, 9,140
Jacobson, Dorothy, 9,180
Jacobson, Emilie, 14,414
Jacobson, Marie (1888-). *See* Larson, Marie (Jacobson) (1888-)
Jacobson, Myrtle Saxe (1919-74), **6,683**
Jacocks, Charles W., **13,450**
Jacocks, Mary Caroline. *See* Reed, Mary Caroline (Jacocks)
Jaconetta: Her Loves (book), 5,498
Jacqueline Cochran Cosmetics, 5,132
Jacques, Bertha, 4,288
Jacques, Florence Page, 8,600
Jacquet, Myra Anna, **14,396**, 14,445
Jade, Jerri. *See* Chandler, Mrs. Lloyd
Jaeck, Emma G. (1875-1963), **17,658**
Jaeger, Luth, **9,147**
Jaeger, Mary Ann, 6,337
Jaeger, Nanny (Mattson) [Mrs. Luth] (1859-?), **9,147**, 9,204
Jaeggi, Marie Anna Ruth Annette "Mara" (1951-), 11,956
Jaeggi, Ruth Payne Jewett (Burgess, II) [Mrs. Walter E. A.], 11,956
Jaffa, Adele Solomons (1868-1953), **935**
Jaffe, Sherril, 11,221
Jaffrey, Julia K., 10,679
Jahn, Marie Catherine (Buhlmann) (1897-), 4,899
Jahoda, Gloria, 2,928
"Jailed for Freedom," 6,908
Jailed for Freedom (book), 10,540
Jamaica
  missionaries to, 14,457
  plantations, 15,077
James, Ada Lois (1876-1952), **17,659**, 17,749
James Adger and Company (SC), 15,434
James, Alice, 2,834
James, Alice Howe (Gibbens) [Mrs. William], 551

James, Anna McBride (1826-1907). *See* Edwards, Anna McBride (James) [Mrs. Isaac] (1826-1907)
James, C. H., 9,668
James, Cheryl, **14,592**
James, David G., 17,659
James, Dorothy Biddle, **15,025**
James, Edmund, 4,380
James, Eldon Revare (1875-1949), **6,262**
James, Eleanor, 9,364
James, Elias Olan, 1,085
James, Elizabeth Tillman (1833-81). *See* Seelye, Elizabeth Tillman (James) [Mrs. Julius] (1833-81)
James, Elsie, 12,444
James Family, 12,531
James Family (NY), 12,397
James Family (WA), 17,195
James, Florence B. Mary Florence Bean (1918-72), **17,281**
James, Florida Virginia Hill (1896-), **17,195**
James, Foster, Foundation, 7,967
James, Frank, 9,949, 10,487
James, Genevieve (?-1958), **12,719**
James, George Wharton, 818
James, Grace (1925-), **15,918**
James, Grace Pierson. *See* Beard, Grace Pierson (James)
James Hall of Lincoln's Frontier World (book), 4,445
James, Harlean [Miss], 2,695
James, Henry (1843-1916), 2,643, 4,404, 6,185, 6,419, 6,565, 11,854, 11,979, 12,032, 12,529, 16,166
James, Isabella (Batchelder) (1819-1901), 6,310
James, Jane Elizabeth (Manning) [Mrs. Isaac] (1813-1908), **16,708**
James, Janet Wilson [Mrs.] (1918-), **6,684**
James, Jesse, 10,487
James, Josephine (pseudonym). *See* Lindsay, Barbara
James, Josephine (pseudonym). *See* Sterne, Emma (Gelders) (1894-)
James, Katherine Barber (1834-90). *See* Prince, Katherine Barber (James) [Mrs. William H.] (1834-90)
James, Laura Briggs [Mrs. David G.], 17,659
James Lee Memorial Art Academy (TN). *See* Memphis Academy of Arts (TN)
James, Linda. *See* Benitt, Linda (James) [Mrs. William A.]
James Madison Constitutional Law Institute (Middletown, CT), **1,984**
James, Marcia Lucretia (Ames) [Mrs. William] (1797-1896), 5,713, 5,867
James, Margaret, 12,193
James, Margaret (?-1950). *See* Porter, Margaret (James) [Mrs. Bruce] (?-1950)
James, Mrs. David C., 17,982
James, Mrs. Jesse, Jr., 9,949
James, Phila S. [Mrs. Eldon Revare], 6,262
James, Sue, 157
James Walker Memorial Hospital School of Nursing (Wilmington, NC), **13,630**
James Ward Thorne School of Nursing (Chicago, IL), **4,019**
James Ward Thorne School of Nursing (Chicago, IL), Alumnae Association, **4,020**
James, William (1797-1868), 5,713, **5,867**, 6,565, 6,604, 6,613, 6,681, 6,843, 14,745
James, William (1797-1868), Family (ME), **5,713**
James, Zerald, 10,487
Jameson, Alexander, 1,275
Jameson, Ellen, 1,275
Jameson, John Franklin (1859-1937), **2,411**
Jameson, Laura Maria (1836-93). *See* Dakin, Laura Marie (Jameson) [Mrs. Isaac] (1836-93)
Jameson, Margaret F. [Mrs. Charles Davis], 2,338
Jameson, Marie Butler [Mrs. Patrick] (1831-?), 4,608
Jameson, Mary. *See* Locke, Mary (Jameson) [Mrs. David Morrell]
Jameson, Mary (1851-1930). *See* Judah, Mary (Jameson) [Mrs. John M.] (1851-1930)
Jameson, Sara (Elwell) [Mrs. John Franklin], 2,411
Jameson, Sarah (Locke) [Mrs. Alexander], 1,275
Jamesonian Literary Society, 4,403
Jamestown Academy (NY), 8,934
Jamestown College (ND), presidents, 13,675
Jamestown Exposition (1907), 5,805, 14,535

Jamieson, Donald, 15,332
Jamieson, Irene Templeton Pratt, **981**
Jamison, Anna Marie (Hansen), **5,468**
Jamison, Anne McMeans (1844-?), **9,148**
Janata, Anthony, 4,395
Janauschek, Francesca Romana Magdalena (1829-1904), 12,535
Jane Addams Centennial (1960), 4,047, 4,089, 4,101, 9,127
Jane Addams Memorial Fund, 4,123
Jane Addams Month, 9,187
"Jane Long: The Mother of Texas," 16,082
Jane, Mary Childs (1909-), 5,580, 5,628
"Jane Wyman Show" (television program), 5,240
Janes, Gertrude (?-1954). See Bolton, Gertrude (Janes) [Mrs. Herbert Eugene] (?-1954)
Janeway, Susanna (1853-1930). See Martin, Susanna (Janeway) [Mrs. Zenas] (1853-1930)
Janey, Phyllis, 8,844
Janin, Albert Covington, 1,444
Janin Family, **1,444**
Janin, Violet (Blair) [Mrs. Albert Covington], 1,444
Janis, Joan Gardner (1926-), **17,983**
Janney, Ellen C., 15,610
Janney Family (OH), **14,000**
Janney Family (SC), **15,610**
Janney, Frances. See Derby, Frances (Janney) [Mrs. Samuel C.]
Janney, John Jay (1812-1907), 14,000
Janney, Rebecca Anne Smith [Mrs. John Jay] (1814-86), 14,000
Jansen, Christina, 6,335
Janson, Kristopher, 8,725, 8,994
Janson, Myrtle, 16,404
Janus Lovers, The (ms), 6,068
Janvier, Catherine Anne (Drinker) (1841-1922), 12,403, 12,506
Janzon, Mattiwilda, 5,466
Japan, 5,953, 6,099, 11,545, 12,195
　Allied occupation (1945-1952), **11,902**
　ambassadors to, 15,059
　American consuls in, 1,044, 14,634
　American nurses in, **6,156**
　American travelers in, **5,953**, 6,099
　American tutors in, 10,949
　birth control, 7,189
　civil rights, 11,902
　earthquake (1923), 14,848
　economic conditions, 6,874
　education, higher, 550
　emperors, public opinion, 11,902
　high schools, 10,975
　missionaries to, 4,532, **4,599**, 6,247, **7,280**, 8,203, 9,467, 11,249, 11,440, 13,278, 14,844, 17,653
　missionaries to, Lutheran, 8,858
　missionaries to, Methodist, **13,258**
　missionaries to, Mormon, **12,465**
　missionaries to, Reformed Church, **5,088**
　missionaries to, Universalist, **6,247**, 8,831
　physical education and training, 7,485
　prostitution, 14,848
　social life and customs, 7,212, 7,280, 15,059
　theological seminaries, 14,470
　women, higher education, 11,902
　World War II, 14,848
Japan International Christian University, 15,570
Japanese, 7,197
Japanese-American Association (Salt Lake City, UT), 16,942
Japanese American Citizens League, 166, 566
Japanese-American Evacuation and Resettlement Study (University of California, Berkeley), 570
Japanese-American relations, 1,503
Japanese-American Service Committee (Chicago, IL), **4,113**
Japanese-Americans, 166, **1,041**, **2,702**, 16,890, **16,942**, 17,285, **17,298**, 17,301, 17,902
　evacuation and relocation (1942-1945), 341, 566, **570**, **785**, 892, 1,292, **1,415**, 1,623, **2,702**, **4,113**, 7,212, **9,219**, **9,341**, 9,465, **14,678**, 16,890, 16,942, 17,285
Japanese Baptist Church (Seattle, WA), 17,285
Japanese Cultural Broadcasting Association (KRKD), 17,298

Japanese National Research Council, 14,740
Japanese Presbyterian Church (Watsonville, CA), 5,088
Jaquis, Leta (Dillavou), 5,048
Jarboro, Catarina, 3,290
Jarman, Maria (Bidgood) [Mrs. William] (1832-?). See Ford, Maria (Bidgood) [Mrs. William] Jarman [Mrs. Robert Henry] (1832-?)
Jarman, William, 16,670
Jarnagin, Emily L. (Murrell) [Mrs. Milton Preston], **10,987**
Jarnagin, Milton Preston, 10,987
Jarrett, Mary C. (1877?-1961), **7,241**
Jarvis, Ann M. [Mrs. Grandville E.] (1833-1905), 17,465
Jarvis, Ann M. Reeves, 17,471
Jarvis, Ann Prior [Mrs. George] (1830-85), **16,897**
Jarvis, Anna (1864-1948), 1,224, **12,521**, **17,465**, 17,471
Jarvis, Anna (Moffet) [Mrs. Bruce W.] (1892-), 2,016, **8,879**, 14,397
Jarvis, Bruce W. (1885-1970), **14,397**
Jarvis, Caroline (Dana) [Mrs. Russell] (?-1822), **2,291**
Jarvis, Edward (1803-84), 6,225
Jarvis, Eleanor C. W., **16,898**
Jarvis Family (CO), 1,786
Jarvis Family (CT), **1,914**, **1,957**
Jarvis, George, 16,897
Jarvis, Grandville E., 17,465
Jarvis, Janet, **16,709**
Jarvis, Russell (1790-1853), 2,291
Jarvis, Ruth. See MacKay-Scott, Ruth (Jarvis) [Mrs. Andrew]
Jarvis, Samuel Farmar (1786-1851), 1,914, 1,957
Jarvis, Sarah M. (Hart) [Mrs. Samuel Farmer], 1,914, 1,957
Jarvis, Zora (Smith) [Mrs. Brigham] (1881-1969), **16,710**
Jastrow, Joseph, 17,727
Jastrow, Rachael S. [Mrs.], 17,749
Jastrow, Rachel [Mrs. Joseph], 17,727
Jatta, Mary (Hall) (1841-?), **571**
Jauss, Anne Marie (1907-), 8,531
Jay, Augusta (McVickar) [Mrs. William] (1790-1857), 11,795
Jay Cooke, McCulloch, and Company (London), 4,479
Jay, Eleanor (1882-1953). See Iselin, Eleanor (Jay) [Mrs. Arthur] (1882-1953)
Jay, Eleanor Kingsland (Field) [Mrs. John] (1819-1909), 11,795
Jay Family (NY), **11,795**, **12,020**
Jay, John (1745-1829), 11,795, **12,522**
Jay, Maria (1782-1856). See Banyer, Maria (Jay) [Mrs. Goldsborough] (1782-1856)
Jay, Sarah (Livingston) [Mrs. John], 12,697
Jay, Sarah Louisa, 12,334
Jayhawkers, 9,848
Jazz music, **5,531**, 15,894
Jazz musicians, 5,529, **5,532**
Jeakins, Dorothy (1914-), **17,804**
Jean, Sally Lucas [Miss] (1878-1971), **11,627**
Jeanes, Anna T. [Miss], 11,897
Jeanes, Mary (1804-89), 15,282
Jeanie Winston Opera Company, 9,361
Jeannette Rankin Brigade, 6,846, 14,691, 17,583
Jeannette Rankin Rank and File. See Jeannette Rankin Brigade
Jebe, Sofie, 8,737
Jednota Cesky Vlastenek, 13,965
Jefferis, Ida F. See Fitzgerald, Ida F. (Jefferis)
Jefferis, Plummer Edwards, 1,505
Jeffers, Georgie [Mrs. Ira S.], 8,347
Jeffers, Ira S. (1843-?), **8,347**
Jeffers, Jo, 10,254
Jeffers, Sate [Mrs. Ira S.], 8,347
Jeffers, Sophrona, 8,347
Jeffers, Susie L. (1859-1955), **10,249**
Jeffers, Una (Call) [Mrs. Robinson] (1885-1950), 543, **572**, 794, 816, 831, 1,081, 1,321, 1,507
Jeffers, Winifred [Mrs.], 10,231
Jefferson Avenue Epworth League (MI), 8,366
Jefferson, Catherine, 3,812
Jefferson, Cecile Barefield (1883-1971), **15,919**

Jefferson College (PA), presidents, 5,343
Jefferson Committee (PA), **15,026**
Jefferson County Board of Education (KY), 5,381
Jefferson County Hospital Auxiliary (IA), **4,879**
Jefferson County Hospital School for Nurses (IA), **4,880**
Jefferson Davis, Ex-President of the Confederate States of America, a Memoir by His Wife (book), 4,746, 9,618
Jefferson Davis Memorial Gateway, 9,657
Jefferson Davis Shrine (MS), 9,644
Jefferson-Hillman Hospital School of Nursing (AL). See University of Alabama in Birmingham School of Nursing
Jefferson, Martha (1772-1836). See Randolph, Martha (Jefferson) [Mrs. Thomas Mann, Jr.] (1772-1836)
Jefferson, Martha (Wayles) [Mrs. Bathurst] Skelton [Mrs. Thomas] (1748-82), **13,451**, 17,056, 17,062
Jefferson, Mary "Maria" "Polly." See Eppes, Mary "Maria" "Polly" (Jefferson) [Mrs. John Wayles]
Jefferson Medical College (PA), faculty, 14,809
Jefferson School (PA), **15,027**
Jefferson, Thomas, 2,276, 2,322, 2,359, 2,582, 7,660, 12,600, 13,451, 14,549, 15,039, 15,041, 16,881, 17,056, 17,058, 17,062, 17,083
Jeffery, M. Pauline, 11,754
Jeffires, Rhonda, 15,134
Jeffrey, Alexander, 5,316
Jeffrey Family (KY, LA, NY), **5,316**
Jeffrey, Jennetta A. (Street) [Mrs. Edward C.], **6,685**
Jeffrey, Marianne [Mrs. Frederick R.], 1,837
Jeffrey, Mildred Mesurac (1911-), 8,062, **8,096**, 8,130, 8,139, 8,140
Jeffrey, Newman, 8,096
Jeffrey, Rosa Griffith (Vertner) Johnson [Mrs. Alexander] (1828-94), 5,316, **5,347**, 5,350
Jeffreys, Mary (1821-?). See Bethell, Mary (Jeffreys) (1821-?)
Jeffreys, William Andrew, **13,452**
Jeffries, Benjamin Jay, 4,475
Jeffries, Louise [Mrs. George], 12,431
Jeffries, Mrs. E. S., 9,722
Jeffs, Ralph W., 1,017
Jelenko, Therese, **573**, 942
"Jelly Roll Blues" (song), 5,531
Jemez Pueblo Day School (NM), 11,213, 11,217
Jemima Condict: Her Book, Being a Transcript of the Diary of an Essex County Maid During the Revolutionary War (book), 11,085
Jemison, Caroline Helen (1829-1925). See Plane, Caroline Helen (Jemison) (1829-1925)
Jemne, Elsa, 9,145
Jenckes, Virginia Ellis (1877-1963), 4,627
Jenkins, Alice (Welsh) 15,354
Jenkins, Anna Eliza (1886-), **11,628**
Jenkins, Annie (1877-1967). See Sallee, Annie (Jenkins) [Mrs. William] (1877-1967)
Jenkins, Elizabeth (1810-95). See Gorham, Elizabeth (Jenkins) (1810-95)
Jenkins, Elizabeth (Whipple) [Mrs. James Wright], 5,897
Jenkins Family (MA), **5,897**
Jenkins, James Wright, 5,897
Jenkins, Mamie E. (1875-1957), **13,273**
Jenkins, Mary Eugenia (1820?-65). See Surratt, Mary Eugenia (Jenkins) (1820?-65)
Jenkins, Minnie Kimball [Miss] (1883-), **11,629**
Jenkins, Phebe J., 5,063
Jenkins, Rhoda (Barney), 1,837
Jenkins, Samuel R., **17,440**
Jenks, Agnes M., 9,443
Jenks, Amelia (1818-94). See Bloomer, Amelia (Jenks) [Mrs. Dexter Chamberlain] (1818-94)
Jenks, Delphine Gillette, 1,233
Jenks, Mary R. (Fitch) [Mrs. I. Henry], 7,514
Jenner, Josephine Curtis, 12,350
Jenney, Adeline, 15,869
Jenney, Edmond, 11,318
Jennie Casseday Rest Cottage (KY), **5,348**
"Jennie June" (article), 6,872
Jennifer, Portia Lee (Evans) [Mrs. Harper] Councill] Trenholm, 83, 85
Jennings, Ann A., **17,660**

Jennings, Arthur Bates, 12,229
Jennings, Babette S. [Miss], 3,932
Jennings, Caroline Jerusha (Allen) [Mrs. Arthur Bates], 12,229
Jennings Family (NY), **12,229**
Jennings Family (PA), **15,285**
Jennings, Hannah A. (Clark), 15,285
Jennings, Jane, 6,325
Jennings, May (Mann) [Mrs. William Sherman] (1872-1928), **2,886**
Jennings, Nancy Mores Watts (1913-), 16,133
Jennings, William Sherman, 2,886
Jennison, Ann Elizabeth (1827-69). See Barton, Ann Elizabeth (Jennison) [Mrs. William Sumner] (1827-69)
Jennison Family (MA), **7,641**
Jenny, Adele, 2,726
Jensen, Abby Groesbeck (1875-1963), **16,466**
Jensen, Christianne Emilie (Heinsen) [Mrs. Erich Rickert] (1846-1923), 976
Jensen, Emilie (Heinsen) [Mrs. Jens Christian] (1852-1926), 976
Jensen, Erich Rickert, 976
Jensen Family (CA), **976**
Jensen, Gertrude Glutsch, **14,398**
Jensen, Hanna Bugge [Mrs. Nils E.] (ca. 1841-1921), **8,752**
Jensen, Hannah. See Kempfer, Hannah (Jensen) [Mrs. Charles]
Jensen, Hattie (Critchlow) [Mrs. Ephraim] (1864-1948), **16,711**
Jensen, Jens Christian, 976
Jensen, Kirsten Marie Sorenson (1868-?), 3,739
Jensen, Mrs. O. F., 12,973
Jenson, Andrew, 16,712
Jenson, Emma (Howell) [Mrs. Andrew] (1862-1937), **16,712**
Jenswold, John, 17,548
Jentink, Barbara [Mrs.], 9,488
Jepson, Brenda (Angell) [Mrs. Jesse Nightingale] (1890-1954), **16,713**
Jerabek, Esther, 9,073, 9,230
Jeremy, Lizzie [Miss] (1860-?), **2,412**
Jeritza, Maria (1887-?), 698, 2,968
Jerman, Cornelia (Petty) [Mrs. Palmer] (1874-1946), **13,274**, 13,406, **13,453**
Jerome, Charles Waldron, Family (MN), **9,149**
Jerome, Clare. See Frewen, Clare (Jerome) [Mrs. Moreton]
Jerome, Eva (Sardeson) [Mrs. Charles Waldron] (1875-1966), 9,149
Jerome Family, 12,326
Jerome, Jennie (1854-1921). See Churchill, Jennie (Jerome) [Lady Randolph] (1854-1921)
Jerome, Sister (1852-1922), **9,880**
Jerome, Victor J. See Romaine, Jerome I.
Jerry Rescue (NY), 12,908
Jersey City State College (Trenton, NJ), 10,995
Jerusalem Fellowship (church), 16,386
Jervey, Mrs. Theodore Dehon, **15,484**
Jessamine Withers Home (Bloomington, IL), **3,758**
Jesse Parker Williams Hospital (GA), 3,268
Jesse, Richard H., 10,022
Jesse W. Lilienthal School (CA), 363
Jessee, Adah (Phillips), 16,551
Jessup, Clara Sophia (1824-99). See Moore, Clara Sophia (Jessup) [Mrs. Bloomfield Haynes] (1824-99)
Jessup, Hannah DeLamater, 1,272
Jessup, Helen H., 12,520
Jessup, Julia Clark, 1,444
Jessup, Mary Serena Eliza. See Blair, Mary Serena Eliza (Jessup)
Jessye, Eva, 3,799, 3,800
Jester, Annie Perry [Mrs. J. R.] (?-1970), **15,611**
Jesuits, 5,722, **12,236**
Jet planes, 11,831
Jeter, Annie (1843-?). See Carmouche, Annie (Jeter) [Mrs. Emile A.] (1843-?)
Jeter, John Tinsley (1799-1862), 12,969
Jett, N. E. "Mae" [Mrs. Richard B.], 3,331
Jett, Richard B., **3,331**
Jett, Winona Wilson, 5,171
Jewelers, **2,054**

Jewell, Edward Alden, 357
Jewell, M. H., 13,661
Jewelry, 3,867, 7,012
Jewelry trade, 1,941
Jewett, Annie M. [Mrs. George Washington], 3,734
Jewett, Dora (1853-1939). See Pattee, Dora (Jewett) [Mrs. Edward Sidney] (1853-1939)
Jewett, Elisha Payne, 11,956
Jewett, Eliza H. (1837-70). See Hartwell, Eliza H. (Jewett) [Mrs. Jesse] (1837-70)
Jewett, George Frederick, Sr., **3,734**
Jewett, George Washington (?-1879), 3,734
Jewett, Harriet Kimball (1809-?) **14,593**, 14,618
Jewett, James Richard, 3,734
Jewett, Lucy Kinsman (1757-1837), **7,389**
Jewett, Margaret (Weyerhaeuser) [Mrs. J. R.] (1862-1939), 9,433
Jewett, Mary [Mrs. George Frederick, Sr.], 3,734
Jewett, Mary Gregory [Mrs.], 3,441
Jewett, Mrs. James, 3,734
Jewett, Nathan (1767-1861), 11,956
Jewett, Ruth Payne [Mrs. Nathan] (1769 or 1770-1828), 11,956
Jewett, Ruth Payne (?-1934). See Burgess, Ruth Payne (Jewett) [Mrs. John William] (?-1934)
Jewett, Sarah Orne (1849-1909), **1,445**, 2,643, 3,993, 4,226, 5,650, 5,694, **5,714**, 5,935, 5,966, 6,185, 6,329, 7,185, 7,585, 8,375, 10,853, 11,821, **12,021**, 14,062, 17,010, 17,053
Jewish-Arab relations, 12,117
Jewish Board of Guardians, 7,546
Jewish Center (Los Angeles, CA), 1,003
Jewish charities. See Charities, Jewish
Jewish Child Care Association (NY), **7,536**
Jewish Children's Home (LA), 6,114
Jewish Committee for Personal Service (CA), **574**
Jewish Community Centers of Chicago (IL), **3,865**
Jewish Community Centers of Chicago (IL), Women's Auxiliary, 3,865
Jewish Community Council of Cleveland (OH), 6,082
Jewish Community Federation (Cleveland, OH), Women's Committee, **13,900**
Jewish Community Federation (Cleveland, OH), Women's Organization, **13,899**, 13,901
Jewish Community Relations Council (PA), 13,783
Jewish Community Relations Council of Minnesota, **9,150**
Jewish Congregation (Virginia, MN), Ladies Aid, **9,165**
Jewish Consumptive Relief Society, 17,282
Jewish Exponent, 15,158
Jewish Family Agency (Los Angeles, CA), 1,003
Jewish Family and Children's Service (CO), **13,795**
Jewish Family and Children's Service of Minneapolis (MN), **9,151**
Jewish Family Welfare Society, 17,716
Jewish Federation Council (Los Angeles, CA), 1,000
Jewish Federation of Metropolitan Chicago, Women's Division (IL), **4,037**
Jewish Foster Home (PA), 2,362
Jewish Foster Home and Orphan Asylum (Philadelphia, PA). See Association for Jewish Children (Philadelphia, PA)
Jewish Foundation for the Education of Girls, 12,009
Jewish Home for the Aged (B.M.Z. of Chicago) (IL), **3,866**
Jewish Hospital Association (PA), 15,011
Jewish immigrants, 17,282
Jewish Immigration Committee, **7,537**
Jewish Labor Committee, 4,032
Jewish Ladies Aid Society (GA), **13,797**
Jewish Ladies Aid Society (OH). See Sisterhood of Congregation B'nai Israel (OH)
Jewish Manual Training School of Chicago (IL), 4,039
Jewish Maternity Association (Philadelphia, PA), **13,798**, 15,165
Jewish Maternity Home (Philadelphia, PA), 15,165
Jewish Mothers Alliance (Los Angeles, CA), 1,000
Jewish National Fund, 17,647
Jewish newspapers, **1,002**
Jewish organizations, societies, etc. See Societies, Jewish

Jewish Orphans' Home of Southern California (Los Angeles, CA), 1,327
Jewish People's Institute (Chicago, IL). See Jewish Community Centers of Chicago (IL)
Jewish Publication Society of America, 6,920
Jewish Relief Society of St. Paul (MN), **9,123**
Jewish Service-Organization, 14,497
Jewish Shelter Home (OR), 14,497
Jewish Sheltering Home for Children (MN), 9,151
Jewish Sheltering Home for the Aged (Philadelphia, PA), **15,157**, 15,161
Jewish Sisters Mutual Aid Society (NY), **7,538**
Jewish Social Service Bureau of Jewish Charities, 4,117
Jewish Spectator, The (periodical), 13,834
Jewish Welfare Board, 12,729, 15,101
Jewish Welfare Service, 2,005
Jewish Women's Sewing Society (OR), 14,497
Jews, 601, 619, 1,017, 1,837, **4,510**, 5,828, 5,829, 7,301, 10,763, 12,430, **13,079**, 13,472, 14,686, 15,010, **15,950**, 17,840, 17,890
 civil rights 2,678
 education, 17,282, 17,850
 oral history, **1,001**, **11,817**, **14,497**, **17,744**
 persecutions, 15,159
 social life and customs, 15,158
Jews in Czechoslovakia, 17,744
Jews in Germany (1933-1945), 15,159
Jews in Poland, 15,159
Jews in Russia, 17,744
Jews, The (book), 10,193
Jewson, Ruth H., 8,667
Jicarilla Indians, 11,214
Jimplicuts, The (MO), 10,032
Joan of Arc, 1,024
Joanna Bontecou School (CT), 2,003
Job, Lenore (Peters), 718
Job, Martha, **1,558**
Job placement, 9,662
Jobs for the Over Sixty (book), 6,387
Jocelyn, Dorothea Cornelia. See Foster, Dorothea Cornelia (Jocelyn) [Mrs. William Hammond]
Jocelyn, Elizabeth Hannah. See Cleaveland, Elizabeth Hannah (Jocelyn) [Mrs. James Bradford]
Jocelyn Family (CT), **1,870**
Jocelyn, Frances M. See Peck, Frances M. (Jocelyn) [Mrs. David]
Jocelyn, Margaret. See Hayes, Margaret (Jocelyn) [Mrs. Samuel]
Jocelyn, Sarah. See Wild, Sarah (Jocelyn) [Mrs. Joseph]
Johanneson, Marie, 1,569
Johannson, Alice, 1,569
Johannson, Mamie, 1,569
Johannsson, Anna G., 13,711
Johansen, Dorothy O., **14,594**
John Adams (ship), 15,167
"John and Ann Vanderlee: Promoters and Preservers of Ragtime" (scrapbook), 16,013
John Brown Fort, Removal to Harper's Ferry, 5,924
John C. Campbell Folk School (Brasstown, NC), 5,249
John Crerar Library, 14,386
John Day Company **11,166**, 14,476
John, Emma (1866-1943), 8,388
John Gray Memorial Museum (MI), 8,234
John, Gwen, 12,477
John J. Pratt Memorial Fund, 7
John Jay Homestead, 11,795
John Knox Med-Center (MO), employees, 239
John Knox Press, 97
John Mallett, the Huguenot, and his Descendants, 1694-1894 (book), 1,824
John Marshall High School (Chicago, IL), 3,831
John Marshall Law School (IL), alumnae, 3,852
John, Mary Alice, **14,726**
John Means Institute (GA), 3,013
John Muir Association, 1,634
John Norton and Sons, **17,129**
John O. Meusebach, German Colonizer in Texas (book), 16,366
John Sealy Hospital (Galveston, TX), 16,226
John Watt and Company (LA), 9,713

John Wesley Powell; Canyon's Conqueror (book), 10,262
John Wilson and Son, 6,785
John Wood Case, The, a Novel (book), 5,030
Johnesse, Frank (1869-?), **3,698**
Johnesse, Mary Louise Patton [Mrs. Frank] (1880?-1962?), **3,698**
Johnny (drama), 14,736
Johnny Belinda (drama), 2,112
Johns, Annie E. [Miss] (1831-89), **13,251**
Johns, Ethel, 12,739
Johns, George S., 10,154
Johns Hopkins Hospital (Baltimore, MD), 12,143, 15,566
  obstetrical records, 12,739
Johns Hopkins Hospital (Baltimore, MD), Harriet Lane Home for Invalid Children, 17,118
Johns Hopkins Hospital (Baltimore, MD), School of Nursing, 5,735, 6,136
Johns Hopkins Medical School (Baltimore, MD), 5,729, 7,255, 7,259, 12,143, 14,745
  alumnae, 1,672, 1,724
  faculty, 1,738, 2,090
  students 7,311
Johns Hopkins Unit, 235
Johns Hopkins University (Baltimore, MD), 5,731, 5,815, 6,222, 11,890, 11,932
  admission, **5,725**, 5,728, 5,729
  alumnae, 4,814, 5,836, 10,253, 13,860
  alumni, 14,235
  employees, 10,207
  faculty, 5,727, 5,829
  presidents, 5,728, 5,729, 5,733
  students, 8,574
Johns Hopkins University (Baltimore, MD), Alumni Association, 7,307
Johns Hopkins University (Baltimore, MD), School of Public Health, 6,138, 8,656
Johnson, Ada (Stanley), 14,595
Johnson, Adelaide. Sarah Adeline [Miss] (1859-1955), **2,413**, **2,856**, 7,182
Johnson, Agnes (ca. 1841-?). *See* Hansel, Agnes (Johnson) (ca. 1841-?)
Johnson, Agnes [Mrs. David] (1896-), **9,152**
Johnson, Amanda, 2,009
Johnson, Amelia (1858-?), **8,455**
Johnson, Andrew, 5,750, 12,913, 13,378, 13,610, 17,656
Johnson, Ann [Mrs.], **3,207**
Johnson, Ann (Viley) [Mrs. George W.], 5,332
Johnson, Anna [Miss] (1892-), **16,714**
Johnson, Anna G. *See* Hubble, Anna G. Johnson [Mrs. Ferdinand]
Johnson Anne Louise (?-1944), **1,721**
Johnson, Annie E. (Fisher) Swanson [Mrs. Aron] (1871-), 4,704
Johnson, Annie (Fellows) [Mrs. William "Will" L.] (1863-1931), 4,508, **5,349**
Johnson, Annie (Gould) [Mrs. Benoni], 11,719
Johnson, Arthur B., 8,421
Johnson, Astrid Dodge, 4,169
Johnson, Augusta (Ellis), **7,539**
Johnson, Belle (?-1945), **14,115**
Johnson, Benoni, 11,719
Johnson, Beth, 2,931
Johnson, Beth McCollough [Mrs. George W.] (1909-73), **2,925**
Johnson, Carolina Virginia Marylandia. *See* Frye, Carolina Virginia Marylandia (Johnson) [Mrs. Andrew] Buchanan [Mrs. Nathaniel, Jr.]
Johnson, Carrie Ashton, **6,529**
Johnson, Carrie Fidelia (1860-1947). *See* Aitken, Carrie Fidelia (Johnson) [Mrs. Alvord] (1860-1947)
Johnson, Cecyl (Allen) [Mrs. James W.] (1890-1966), **10,737**
Johnson, Celestia (ca. 1844-?). *See* Sawyer, Celestia (Johnson) (ca. 1844-?)
Johnson, Charles E., **13,454**
Johnson, Charlotte, 8,670
Johnson, Claude M., 5,316
Johnson, Claudia Alta "Lady Bird" (Taylor) [Mrs. Lyndon Baines] (1912-), 64, 1,600, 2,456, 6,899, 13,566, 16,371, 18,012

Johnson County Republican Women's Club (IA), 4,943
Johnson, Dorothea M. (1916-). *See* Funk, Dorothea M. (Johnson) [Mrs. Frank] (1916-)
Johnson, Dorothy M. [Miss] (1905-), **5,004, 10,399**
Johnson, Dorothy Vena, 3,284
Johnson, Eleanor Hope (1871-1969), **1,850**
Johnson, Eliza A. (Clark) [Mrs. Samuel], 8,170
Johnson, Eliza (McCardle) [Mrs. Andrew] (1810-76), 15,876
Johnson, Elizabeth (1833-1913). *See* Blake, Lillie (Devereux) [Mrs. Frank Geoffrey Quay] Umsted [Mrs. Grinfill] (1833-1913)
Johnson, Elizabeth Frieuch [Miss] (1890-), **15,801**
Johnson, Ella H., 3,483
Johnson, Ellen M. (1843-1927). *See* Throop, Ellen M. (Johnson) (1843-1927)
Johnson, Emily Chubbuck [Mrs. Adoniram] (1817-54), **12,785**
Johnson, Emily Cooper [Mrs. Edwin James] (1885-1966), **15,286**
Johnson, Emma [Mrs. Peter G.], 9,152
Johnson, Emma (1879-1944), 15,183
Johnson, Ethel McLean, **5,629**, **6,686**, **6,977**, 6,978
Johnson, Eva. *See* O'Connor, Eva (Johnson) [Mrs. Joseph]
Johnson Family (IA), 4,942
Johnson Family (New England), 1,469
Johnson Family (NY), **12,231**
Johnson Family (OR), 14,500
Johnson, Florence Kendrick, 12,524, 12,525
Johnson, Florence Merriam, 6,131
Johnson, Floria O. [Mrs. Arthur B.] (1924-), **8,421**
Johnson, Floride Cantey [Mrs. John], 13,493
Johnson, Frances (1832-?). *See* Perkins, Frances (Johnson) Beecher [Mrs. James] (1832-?)
Johnson, Frank Edward, 5,060
Johnson, Fritz, 9,467
Johnson, Georgia "Georgia Boy" Douglas (Camp) (1886-1966), 3,284, **3,288**, 3,298, 3,302, 5,870
Johnson, Gladys, 13,300
Johnson, Grace (1887-). *See* Clark, Grace (Johnson) [Mrs. Deane L.] (1887-)
Johnson, Grace A. (1871-1952), **6,978**
Johnson, Grace (Nail), 3,305
Johnson, Guion (Griffis) (1900-), 13,176
Johnson, Guion Griffis [Mrs. Guy B.], 11,844
Johnson, H., 10,977
Johnson, Hannah Gould. *See* Stoddard, Hannah Gould (Johnson)
Johnson, Harriet Mitchell (1867-1934), 11,819
Johnson, Hazel [Miss], **1,912**
Johnson, Helen Louise (Kendrick) [Mrs. Rossiter] (1844-1917), 2,948, **12,524**, 12,525
Johnson, Helene, 3,284, 5,465
Johnson, Henrietta, **15,485**
Johnson High School (St. Paul, MN), **9,153**
Johnson, Hilda, 11,719
Johnson, Hiram Warren (1866-1945), **575**
Johnson Island prison camp, 3,565
Johnson, J. O. E., 4,914
Johnson, James G., 6,827
Johnson, James Weldon, 2,948
Johnson, Jane, **15,287**
Johnson, Janice, 10,477
Johnson, Jerah, 5,541
Johnson, Jessie (Lincoln) [Mrs. Warren] Beckwith [Mrs. Frank Edward] (1875-1948). *See* Randolph, Jessie (Lincoln) [Mrs. Warren] Beckwith [Mrs. Frank Edward] Johnson [Mrs. Robert J.] (1875-1948)
Johnson, Joe, 3,483
Johnson, John, 13,493
Johnson, John A., 9,035
Johnson, John A. B., 8,768
Johnson, John G., 2,475
Johnson, John Reuben (1897-1973), **10,477**
Johnson, Joseph, 3,748
Johnson, Joseph H., 3,483
Johnson, Julia (1814-85). *See* Fisher, Julia (Johnson) [Mrs. William] (1814-85)
Johnson, Kate Ancrum (Burr) [Mrs. Clarence A.] (1881-1968), **13,275**, 13,399

Johnson, Katharine, 12,022
Johnson, Kathryn Ann, 8,958
Johnson, Kathryn M., 2,502
Johnson, Laura Edseth [Mrs. Severin] (1876-1962), **8,753**
Johnson, Laura Virginia, 3,794
Johnson, Lena, 3,157
Johnson, Lila, 9,115
Johnson, Louisa (1833-98). *See* Dyson, Louisa (Johnson) [Mrs. Absalom Roby] (1833-98)
Johnson, Louisa Catherine (1775-1852). *See* Adams, Louisa Catherine (Johnson) [Mrs. John Quincy] (1775-1852)
Johnson, Lucia Beckius (ca. 1893-), **9,154**
Johnson, Lucy (ca. 1850-?). *See* Chambers, Lucy Johnson [Mrs. Clarke] (ca. 1850-?)
Johnson, Lydia (1893-), **576**, 11,846
Johnson, Lynda Bird. *See* Robb, Lynda Bird (Johnson) [Mrs. Charles]
Johnson, Lyndon Baines, 64, 1,600, 2,349, 2,640, 6,031, 6,765, 7,794, 10,197, 11,827, 11,855, 11,916, 15,755, 16,000, 16,317, 16,965
Johnson, Mae Reese [Mrs.], **1,105**
Johnson, Magnus (1871-1936), **9,155**
Johnson, Margot, 14,338
Johnson, Maria (1888-1974), **16,526**
Johnson, Marie Beverly, 5,469
Johnson, Martha Amelia Allen, **3,398**
Johnson, Martin (1884-1937), **5,177**
Johnson, Mary (1718-1804). *See* Hopkinson, Mary (Johnson) [Mrs. Thomas] (1718-1804)
Johnson, Mary Ann, **5,782**
Johnson, Mary B., 3,483
Johnson, Mary (Olmsted) [Mrs. Oakley C.] (1890-1950), 12,884
Johnson, Mary Pay [Mrs.] (1906-), **8,500**
Johnson, Mary Woods Anderson (1813-72), 14,803
Johnson, May Beattie [Mrs.], 11,589
Johnson, Minnie L. (McNeal) [Mrs. Hiram Warren] (1869-1955), 575
Johnson, Morgan, 3,464
Johnson, Mrs. C. M. Watkins (1912-), **16,363**
Johnson, Mrs. Fritz, 9,467
Johnson, Mrs. George W., 5,303
Johnson, Mrs. J. Lee, 2,847
Johnson, Mrs. Jens, 9,190
Johnson, Mrs. Martin, 1,594
Johnson, Mrs. Peter, 3,693
Johnson, Mrs. Sylvanus, 3,484
Johnson, Mrs. Victor R., 13,597
Johnson, Myrtle (1895-). *See* Bell, Myrtle (Johnson) (1895-)
Johnson, Nellie Stone, 9,467
Johnson, Norma (Haugen) [Mrs. J. O. E.] (1888-1959), 4,914
Johnson, Oakley C. (1890-1976), **12,884**
Johnson, Olive, 11,345
Johnson, Olive, 9,106
Johnson, Opha Mae [Mrs.], 2,866
Johnson, Osa Helen (Leighty) [Mrs. Martin] (1894-1953), **5,177**, 8,208
Johnson, Peter G., 9,152
Johnson, Rachel (Steele), 9,371
Johnson, Rhoda M. (1826-1909). *See* Coffin, Rhoda M. (Johnson) [Mrs. Charles Fisher] (1826-1909)
Johnson, Richard Z., 8,986
Johnson, Rita, 37
Johnson, Robert, 15,485
Johnson, Robert Underwood (1853-1937), **577**, 11,996, **12,022**
Johnson, Roland, 2,154
Johnson, Rosa Griffith Vertner [Mrs. Claude M.] (1828-94). *See* Jeffrey, Rosa Griffith Vertner [Mrs. Claude M.] Johnson [Mrs. Alexander] (1828-94)
Johnson, Rosalie Voigt [Mrs. Morgan], **3,464**
Johnson, Rosamond, 3,305
Johnson, Rossiter (1840-1931), **12,525**
Johnson, Ruby, 35
Johnson, Sallie Didd Beck [Mrs. Joseph H.], **3,483**
Johnson, Sally (Haner) [Mrs. Sidney], **8,250**
Johnson, Samuel, 8,170

Johnson, Samuel (1822-82), **7,390**
Johnson, Sarah [Miss], 12,152
Johnson, Sarah Adeline. *See* Johnson, Adelaide.
    Sarah Adeline Johnson
Johnson, Sarah D. [Mrs.] (1805-70), 12,231
Johnson, Sarah Taylor. *See* Boyd, Sarah Taylor
    (Johnson) [Mrs. Alfred Davis, Jr.]
Johnson, Sir William, 11,440
Johnson, Spud, 16,169
Johnson, Stratford, Family, 14,500
Johnson, Susan, 1,425
Johnson, Susan Elvira (Martineau) [Mrs. Benjamin
    Samuel] (1856-1942), **16,715**
Johnson, Viena. *See* Hendrickson, Viena Johnson
    [Mrs. Paul]
Johnson, Vivian W. (1896-), 4,899
Johnson, William Preston, 5,528
Johnson, William S., 1,425
Johnsonian Book Club (NC), 13,410
Johnston, Albert Sidney (1803-62), 5,350
Johnston, Alexander (1739-87), 15,077
Johnston, Alva, 10,992
Johnston, Amy, 3,532
Johnston, Caroline (Gale) [Mrs. George H.] (1874-?),
    9,088, **9,156**
Johnston, Edith Duncan, **3,531**, 12,111
Johnston, Effie, 3,532
Johnston, Effie [Miss], 1,621
Johnston, Elizabeth Maud (1873-1961). *See*
    Nankervis, Elizabeth Maud (Johnston)
    (1873-1961)
Johnston, Elizabeth Pendergrass [Mrs. Marcus], 3,043
Johnston, Eva (1865-1941), 9,934, **9,997, 9,998**
Johnston, Faith (1902-), **8,348**
Johnston Family (IN), **4,508**
Johnston Family (Jamaica), 15,077
Johnston Family (KY, LA), **5,350**
Johnston Family (MD, PA, VA, WV), 2,532
Johnston Family (RI), 15,077
Johnston, Frances Benjamin [Miss] (1864-1952),
    1,475, **2,414**
Johnston, Francis V., 11,941
Johnston, Hannah. *See* Iredell, Hannah (Johnston)
    [Mrs. James, Sr.]
Johnston, Hannah Clark (1839-1923). *See* Bailey,
    Hannah Clark (Johnston) [Mrs. Moses]
    (1839-1923)
Johnston, Harriet (Lane) [Mrs. Henry Elliott]
    (1830-1903), 2,234, 14,863
Johnston, Henrietta, 15,405
Johnston Henrietta (Preston) [Mrs. Albert Sidney],
    5,350, 5,359, 16,014
Johnston, Henry S. (1867-1965), **14,257**
Johnston, Jane (1800-42). *See* Schoolcraft, Jane
    (Johnston) [Mrs. Henry Rowe] (1800-42)
Johnston, Joseph Eggleston (1807-91), **68**
Johnston, Katherin (Aubrey) [Mrs. Mercer Green],
    2,415
Johnston, Lucy (Browne) [Mrs. William Agnew]
    (1846-1937), **5,219**
Johnston, Marcus, 3,043
Johnston, Margaret Afflis (1907-67), **4,628**
Johnston, Margaret Wickliffe (Preston) [Mrs. Philip
    Preston, II] (1885-1964), 5,321
Johnston, Marguerite Kulp (1920-), **578**
Johnston, Mary, 13,608
Johnston, Mary (1870-1936), 12,476, **17,060**
Johnston, Mary A., 13,435
Johnston, Mercer Green (1868-1954), **2,415**
Johnston, Mrs. Lee, 9,962
Johnston, Philip Preston, II, 5,321
Johnston, Rachel A., 13,435
Johnston, Richard Malcolm, 3,043, **3,532**
Johnston, Rosa Duncan [Mrs. William] (1831-85),
    5,350
Johnston, Ruth, 3,532
Johnston, Sarah Anne. *See* Davidson, Sarah Anne
    (Johnston) [Mrs. William F.]
Johnston, Sue Ramsey (1897-). *See* Ferguson, Sue
    Ramsey (Johnston) [Mrs. Raymond S.] (1897-)
Johnston, Susan [Mrs.], 9,411
Johnston, Wade, 1,621
Johnston, William, 5,350
Johnston, William Agnew, 5,219

Johnston, William Bryant, 2,414
Johnston, William Preston (1831-99), 5,350
Johnston, William "Will" L. (?-1892), 4,508
Johnstone, Fanny (Lesesne) [Mrs. Elliott W.], 54
Johnstone, Helen, 11,602
Johnstone, Lillie A. (Armstrong) [Mrs. William]
    (1859-93), 14,173
Johnstone, Samuel, Family (MN), 10,358
Johnstown Flood (1889, PA), 14,860, **14,861**
JOIN, 17,637
Joiner, Jimmy, 6,006
Joiner, W. A., 13,945
Joint Civic Committee on Elections (Chicago, IL),
    4,125
Joint Committee of Organizations Concerned About
    the Status of Women in the Catholic Church,
    6,794
Joint Committee on Higher Education, 13,322
Joint Council for International Cooperation, 6,865
Joint Student Government (NY), 12,916
Jolie, Nancy, 8,936
Joliot-Curie, Frederic, 12,045
Joliot-(Curie) Iréne [Mrs. Frederic], 12,045
Jonah's Gourd Vine (book), 2,872
Jonas, Irene Iris, **2,416**
Jonathan, Brother, 12,367
Jonathan Fisher, Maine Parson 1768-1847 (book),
    5,599
Jones, A. Sheridan, 13,661
Jones, Abbie Maria, 12,527
Jones, Ada Alice (1874-1943), **12,526**
Jones, Ada (Millington) (1849-1930), **579**
Jones, Adalain Kimball [Mrs. Herbert], **4,925**
Jones, Agnes (Blackwell), 2,209
Jones, Agnes Powell [Mrs. Richard] Williams [Mrs.
    Francis] (1827-94). *See* Daniels, Agnes Powell
    [Mrs. Richard] Williams [Mrs. Francis] Jones
    [Mrs. David] (1827-94)
Jones, Albert J., 11,051
Jones Alice (Van Hoosen) (1855-1950). *See*
    Comstock, Alice (Van Hoosen) Jones [Mrs.
    Joseph C.] (1855-1950)
Jones, Ambrose (1809-83), **12,825**
Jones, Amelia. *See* Seabury, Amelia (Jones) [Mrs.
    Samuel]
Jones, Ann. *See* Gardner, Ann (Jones) [Mrs. Robert
    Snow]
Jones, Anna I., 13,111
Jones, Anna M. R. [Mrs.], 1,446
Jones, Anne Catherine "Kate" (Boykin) [Mrs. J. R.],
    13,042
Jones, Avonia, 9,841
Jones, Bessie Judith (Zaban) [Mrs. Howard
    Mumford], 7,169
Jones, Betty Poston, 658
Jones, Britton, 838
Jones, Brownie Lee (1897-), 13,176
Jones, Caroline. *See* Peter, Caroline (Jones) [Mrs.
    Armistead]
Jones, Charles, 14,846
Jones, Charles A., 17,992
Jones, Charles Colcock, Sr. (1804-63), 3,044
Jones, Charles Colcock, Jr. (1831-93), **3,044**
Jones, Charlotte (Ludlow), 17,992
Jones, Christine, 6,335
Jones, Clara Hodges (1883-1972), 5,394
Jones, Clara J. (1900-), **8,880**
Jones, Cleta Mildred [Miss] (1927-), **16,364**
Jones, Corinne, **2,911**
Jones County Junior College (MS), 9,671, 9,672
Jones, Crabtree, **13,455**
Jones, Delia Garlick (1830-1934), 8,934
Jones, Dorothy, **8,097**
Jones, Dunwoody, **3,208**
Jones, E. Elizabeth, 7,583
Jones, Edith Newbold (1862-1937). *See* Wharton,
    Edith Newbold (Jones) [Mrs. Edward Robbins]
    (1862-1937)
Jones, Edward, 13,426
Jones, Elbert P., **1,446**
Jones, Eli, 14,846
Jones, Elissa W., **3,045**
Jones, Eliza [Mrs. George], 12,527
Jones, Eliza (Prescott) [Mrs. Peter S.], 801

Jones, Elizabeth, 13,617
Jones, Elizabeth McLeod [Mrs. Lewis R.] (?-1958),
    9,157
Jones, Elizabeth Orton (1910-), **14,399**
Jones, Elizabeth Sparhawk, 7,210
Jones, Ellen, 14,846
Jones, Ellen C. Lloyd (?-1919), **17,661**
Jones, Emeline Roberts (1836-1916), 1,061
Jones Family (NY), **12,305**
Jones Family (NY?), 12,531
Jones Family (NC), 13,044
Jones Family (PA), **14,846**
Jones Family (PA), 14,966
Jones, Fay, **17,283**
Jones, Flora M., 582
Jones, Francis, 9,952
Jones, George (?-1878), **12,527**
Jones, George Noble, 2,930, 2,943, **3,533**
Jones, Gertrude Flint, 1,348
Jones, Gwladys Webster (1891-), 6,389, **6,687**
Jones, H. G., 13,522
Jones, Hannah D. (1820-78). *See* Orbison, Hannah
    D. (Jones) [Mrs. David W., Sr.] (1820-78)
Jones, Hattie. *See* Green, Hattie (Jones) [Mrs. John]
Jones, Helen [Mrs. Talbot], 2,188
Jones, Helen T., 7,583
Jones, Howard Mumford, 7,169
Jones, Inez, 11,392
Jones, Iva (Rich) [Mrs. Kumen], **16,421**
Jones, Ivie Maude (Huish) [Mrs. Lorin Franklin]
    (1891-), **16,716**
Jones, Jane Elizabeth (Hitchcock) [Mrs. Benjamin
    Smith] (1813-96), 5,866, 5,907, 7,629
Jones, Jane Lloyd (1848-1917), **17,661**
Jones, Jane Margaret (Wood) [Mrs. Paul Tudor]
    (1832-63), **9,778, 15,955**
Jones, Jeannette (1851-1923). *See* Bailey, Jeannette
    (Jones) (1851-1923)
Jones, Jenkin Lloyd, 3,791, 3,835
Jones, Jessie Wilmore (1886-1973). *See* Murton,
    Jessie Wilmore (Jones) (1886-1973)
Jones, John (1815-94), 3,208
Jones, John P., 10,673
Jones, Joseph Piper, 13,131
Jones, Joseph Seawell, 13,593
Jones, Julia (1826-1905). *See* Beecher, Julia (Jones)
    (1826-1905)
Jones, Julia Clinton, 481
Jones, Kate (Harben) [Mrs. Archibald A.] (1866-?),
    13,043
Jones, Katherine H., **9,646**
Jones, Lawrence, 17,544
Jones, LeRoi (1934-). *See* Baraka, Imamu Amira
    (1934-)
Jones, Lois Mailou, 3,298
Jones, Lorin Franklin, 16,716
Jones, Louise, 17,029
Jones, Louise (1901-). *See* DuBose, Louise (Jones)
    (1901-)
Jones, Lucile (Williams) [Mrs. Francis] (1889-), **580,**
    11,846
Jones, Lucy, 16,872
Jones, Lucy, **581**
Jones, Lulie, **9,654**
Jones, M. Agnes, 3,280
Jones, Mahlon Ogden, 2,194
Jones, Margaret, 13,509
Jones, Margaret Bell, 16,176
Jones, Margaret E. M., 12,762
Jones, Margaret (Hathaway), **13,044**
Jones, Margaret (Lee) [Mrs. John Pidding]
    (1821-1900), **16,717**
Jones, Marjory, 3,988
Jones, Marth Ann. *See* Matthews, Marth Ann
    (Jones)
Jones, Martha Burke (1790-1863). *See* Eppes,
    Martha Burke (Jones) [Mrs. John Wayles]
    (1790-1863)
Jones, Mary, 14,884
Jones, Mary [Mrs. William] Nuttall [Mrs. George
    Noble], 2,943
Jones, Mary Alice Lange, **14,400**
Jones, Mary Ann Schuyler [Mrs. Samuel], 12,305

Jones, Mary Ann (Smith) [Mrs. John M.] (1825-1918), 582
Jones, Mary C., 16,092
Jones, Mary Cadwalder [Mrs.], 1,425
Jones, Mary E. [Mrs.], 956
Jones, Mary Eliza (Brown) [Mrs. James A.] Brown [Mrs. Nathaniel Vary] (1836-1916), 16,718
Jones, Mary Katharine (1864-1950). See Bennett, Mary Katharine (Jones) [Mrs. Fred Smith] (1864-1950)
Jones, Mary (Kendall) (1806?-84), 5,259
Jones, Mary "Mother" (Harris) (1830-1930), 2,098, 3,839, 3,890, 4,431, 8,094, 15,330, 17,453, 17,462, 17,482
Jones, Mary Sharpe (1808-69). See Jones, Mary Sharpe (Jones) [Mrs. Charles Colcock, Sr.] (1808-69)
Jones, Mary Sharpe (Jones) [Mrs. Charles Colcock, Sr.] (1808-69), 3,044
Jones, Mary W. [Mrs.], 13,455
Jones, Mary W. (Savage) [Mrs. William B.] Nuttall [Mrs. George Noble], 2,930
Jones, Matilda Jane (1848-1909). See Friend, Matilda Jane (Jones) [Mrs. John S.] (1848-1909)
Jones, May (Chadwick) [Mrs. Charles] (1884-), 16,719
Jones, May F., 13,617
Jones, Mrs. George, 14,399
Jones, Mrs. Ira A., 9,962
Jones, Mrs. Joel, 14,824
Jones, Mrs. John Luther "Casey," 4,700
Jones, Mrs. L. O., 10,600
Jones, Mrs. Lee A., 10,321
Jones, Mrs. Lewis R., 9,073
Jones, Mrs. R. A. Dunwoody, 9,055
Jones, Nathaniel, Family, 582
Jones, Nathaniel Vary, 16,718
Jones, Nell Coate, 2,772
Jones, Nellie Kedzie (1858-1956), 17,662
Jones, Paul Tudor (1828-1904), 15,955
Jones, Paul Tudor, I, 9,778
Jones, Pauline (1896-1965), 14,169
Jones, Perrie (1886-1968), 8,976
Jones, Peter S. (1835-65), 801
Jones, Phyllis, 9,140
Jones, Rebecca, 14,840
Jones, Regine (1894-). See Woody, Regina (Jones) [Mrs. McIver] (1894-)
Jones, Robert E., 2,631
Jones, Ruthe E., 14,646
Jones, Sage (Treaharne) [Mrs. Thomas] (1832-97), 16,747
Jones, Sally (Smith) Shiffer (1791-1871), 801
Jones, Samuel (1770-1853), 12,305
Jones, Samuel Milton (1846-1904), 14,139
Jones, Samuel W., 12,232
Jones, Sarah, 11,630
Jones, Sarah [Mrs.], 9,158
Jones, Sarah (Fletcher) [Mrs. Albert], 16,720
Jones, Sarah Rutgers (Neilson) [Mrs. Willard P.] Voorhees [Mrs. Albert J.] (1853-?), 11,051
Jones, Sarah Van Hoosen (1892-1972), 7,826, 8,161
Jones, Sister Martin Joseph, 11,363, 11,364, 11,365, 11,366, 11,367
Jones, Sister Raphael, 5,494
Jones, Suzanne (Earle) [Mrs. Mahlon Ogden]. See Bartlett, Suzanne (Earle) [Mrs. Mahlon Ogden] Jones [Mrs. Samuel Franklin] Emmons [Mrs. Paul Wayland]
Jones, Sybil (Jones) (1808-73), 14,846, 14,847
Jones, Thomas, 16,747
Jones versus Jones (drama), 6,903
Jones, W. P., 4,215
Jones, William Griffith (?-1906), 583
Jones, William H., 2,279
Jones, Willie, 17,083
Jonesboro High School (NC), 13,588
Joost, Hattie, 490
Joplin Memorial Concert (TX), 16,013
Joralemon, Mary E. (Beaman), 584
Jordan, Barbara, 16,234
Jordan, Constance B. [Mrs. Eldridge] (1896?-1971), 17,984

Jordan, David Starr (1851-1931), 1,547, 1,559, 11,547, 15,307, 17,735
Jordan, Elizabeth Garver [Miss] (1865-1947), 3,993, 12,529
Jordan, Emily, 2,202
Jordan, Frances Reed, 6,484
Jordan, Gail (pseudonym). See Dern, Peggy Gaddis (1895-1966)
Jordan, Helen Dorcas, 8,948
Jordan, Helen M., 6,223
Jordan, Jessie K., 1,585
Jordan, Joan, 17,663
Jordan, John, Jr., 15,006
Jordan, Kathleen B. Smith [Mrs. Lewis], 8,518
Jordan, Lewis, 8,518
Jordan, Mary, 10,098
Jordan, Mary Augusta (1855-1941), 7,158
Jordan, Maude Grimshaw, 8,948
Jordan, Merle. See Moore, Merle (Jordan)
Jordan, Mildred (1901-), 6,037
Jordan, Mildred Salome, 8,948
Jordan, Millicent, 5,466
Jordan, Myra (Beach), 7,896, 7,941
Jordan, Sara Murray (1884-1959), 5,124, 6,688
Jordan, Walter M., 10,347
Jordan, Wilbur Kitchener (1902-), 6,290, 6,339
Jordon, A. B. [Mrs.], 3,608
Jordon, Alice M., 2,370
Jordon, Elizabeth, 17,692
Jordon, Leone P., 9,770
Jorgensen, Florence (Orr) [Mrs. Virgil W.], 585
Jorgensen, Virgil W., Family (CA), 585
Jorgenson, Theodore, 8,788
Joseph, Alice, 2,840
Joseph, Geri, 9,140
Joseph, Mother. Esther Pariseau (1823-1902), 17,229
Joseph, Mother Mary, 11,803
Joseph, Nannine (1889-1976), 11,490
Joscpha (pseudonym). See Maxson, Lydia Harriet (Yates) [Mrs. Thaddeus W.] (1839-1902)
Joset, Joseph, 690
Joslyn, George A. (1848-1916), 10,612
Joslyn, Mary L., 14,618
Joslyn, Matilda (1826-98). See Gage, Matilda (Joslyn) (1826-98)
Joslyn, Sarah Hannah Selleck [Mrs. George A.] (1851-1940), 10,612
Journal (IA), 4,735
Journal (Louisville, KY), 15,952
Journal (St. Charles, MO), 10,134, 10,135
Journal (Knoxville, TN), 15,966
Journal (Milwaukee, WI), 17,725
Journal Herald (Dayton, OH), 14,052
Journal of American History, 13,388
Journal of Forestry, 9,466
Journal of John Woolman (book), 14,842
Journal of Jules Renard (book), 6,073
Journal of Mississippi History, 9,599, 9,720, 9,781
Journal of School Health, The (periodical), 11,627
Journal of Social Hygiene, 8,633
Journal of the American Home Economic Association, 11,656
Journal of the American Institute of Homeopathy, 17,716
Journal of the House of Representatives, 2,697
Journal of the Senate, 2,697
Journal of the Southern Confederacy, The, 9,657
Journalism, 9,913, 11,897. See also Feuilletons awards, 11,862
societies, 720, 1,670, 1,710, 1,761, 1,768, 2,127, 3,117, 3,332, 3,357, 3,694, 3,862, 4,120, 4,169, 4,866, 5,001, 6,767, 8,429, 9,747, 9,823, 9,830, 9,898, 10,060, 10,517, 11,493, 13,406, 13,446, 13,917, 14,040, 16,139, 16,175, 17,716, 17,930, 17,955
Journalism, aeronautical, 1,040
Journalism, labor, 8,126
Journalism, medical, 11,862
Journalism, scientific, 6,056
Journalists, 54, 214, 827, 974, 1,187, 1,193, 1,205, 1,426, 1,437, 1,441, 1,489, 1,564, 1,605, 1,626, 1,638, 1,670, 1,750, 1,790, 2,157, 2,182, 2,192, 2,208, 2,240, 2,247, 2,292, 2,298, 2,331, 2,340, 2,370, 2,420, 2,452, 2,549, 2,560, 2,562, 2,596,

2,604, 2,657, 2,661, 2,715, 2,784, 2,810, 2,879, 2,903, 2,904, 2,928, 3,027, 3,070, 3,117, 3,143, 3,225, 3,251, 3,325, 3,326, 3,327, 3,332, 3,335, 3,338, 3,340, 3,350, 3,357, 3,368, 3,437, 3,488, 3,491, 3,602, 3,622, 3,662, 3,677, 3,825, 3,873, 3,879, 3,969, 3,989, 4,053, 4,060, 4,120, 4,131, 4,161, 4,246, 4,332, 4,409, 4,492, 4,622, 4,654, 4,732, 4,738, 4,957, 5,019, 5,080, 5,107, 5,110, 5,124, 5,269, 5,310, 5,313, 5,451, 5,478, 5,505, 5,514, 5,522, 5,543, 5,662, 5,669, 5,694, 5,869, 5,924, 5,973, 5,987, 5,989, 5,999, 6,025, 6,043, 6,044, 6,056, 6,064, 6,103, 6,104, 6,244, 6,343, 6,344, 6,464, 6,474, 6,492, 6,495, 6,568, 6,601, 6,694, 6,722, 6,767, 6,918, 6,921, 6,933, 6,944, 6,948, 6,952, 6,971, 7,196, 7,199, 7,203, 7,206, 7,229, 7,276, 7,545, 7,691, 7,888, 8,144, 8,658, 8,744, 8,954, 9,035, 9,157, 9,160, 9,175, 9,212, 9,287, 9,436, 9,503, 9,522, 9,527, 9,550, 9,771, 9,826, 9,981, 10,000, 10,060, 10,148, 10,162, 10,235, 10,310, 10,330, 10,354, 10,356, 10,422, 10,444, 10,487, 10,494, 10,544, 10,742, 10,781, 10,784, 10,850, 10,871, 10,874, 11,140, 11,213, 11,269, 11,344, 11,488, 11,493, 11,840, 11,907, 11,926, 11,963, 11,974, 11,989, 11,998, 12,044, 12,061, 12,070, 12,072, 12,130, 12,249, 12,292, 12,395, 12,412, 12,436, 12,485, 12,500, 12,529, 12,535, 12,553, 12,582, 12,619, 12,622, 12,683, 12,702, 12,772, 12,863, 12,911, 13,001, 13,016, 13,108, 13,166, 13,244, 13,264, 13,277, 13,358, 13,616, 13,844, 13,904, 13,961, 13,999, 14,041, 14,046, 14,080, 14,081, 14,082, 14,093, 14,192, 14,195, 14,324, 14,377, 14,384, 14,403, 14,421, 14,422, 14,431, 14,446, 14,451, 14,512, 14,655, 14,872, 14,884, 14,962, 14,964, 15,197, 15,228, 15,273, 15,693, 15,803, 15,871, 15,878, 15,892, 15,966, 16,053, 16,197, 16,248, 16,253, 16,348, 16,354, 16,370, 16,371, 16,387, 16,403, 16,913, 16,965, 17,035, 17,070, 17,078, 17,119, 17,141, 17,379, 17,390, 17,413, 17,436, 17,498, 17,589, 17,614, 17,675, 17,709, 17,716, 17,722, 17,725, 17,731, 17,734, 17,762, 17,803, 17,813, 17,899, 17,947, 17,954, 17,955, 18,009, 18,012
Journalists, Afro-American, 2,315, 3,799, 3,835, 5,535, 10,191, 10,201
Journey into Fame (book), 7,509
Journey into Fame: The Life of Daniel Chester French (book), 2,338
Journey into Fear (moving picture), 17,809
Journey, The (book), 2,879
Journey to America (book), 937
Journey to Boston, A (book), 5,998
Journey to Ohio in 1810, A (book), 13,921
"Journey to Somewhere" (story), 15,660
"Journey to the Future," 12,466
Journeycake, Jane (Sosha), 14,173
Journeycake, Nannie (1843-1924). See Bartles, Nannie (Journeycake) (1843-1924)
Joy, Aryness. (1901-). See Wickens, Aryness (Joy) (1901-)
Joy Bringer, The (book), 415
Joy, Charles, 12,023
Joy, Eleanor (1868-1936), 12,023
Joy, Rachel (?-1868). See Mills, Rachel (Joy) Fisher (?-1868)
Joy, Sallie Elizabeth (1852?-1909). See White, Sallie Elizabeth (Joy) (1852?-1909)
Joy Settlement, 7,307
Joyce, Alice, 11,327
Joyce Chapel (Methodist) (MN), 8,389
Joyce, James, 3,771, 4,234, 11,153, 16,168, 17,843
"Joyce Jordan, M.D." (radio program), 1,026
Joyes Family, 5,359
Joyner, Faith [Mrs. Joseph], 15,836
Joyner, James Yadkin, 13,456
Joyner, Joseph, 15,836
Juarez Latter-day Saints Stake (Mexico), 16,520
Juarez Stake Academy (Mexico), 16,520
Jubalee (drama), 15,700
Jubilee (book), 9,583
Jubilee Inn (LA). See Business Girls' Inn (LA)
Judah, Grace (Seixas), 7,552
Judah L. Magnes Foundation, 2,177
Judah, Mary (Jameson) [Mrs. John M.] (1851-1930), 4,608

"Judaica" (bibliography), 13,787
Judaism (Christian theology), 5,977, 7,545, 13,824
Judd, Dorothy [Mrs. Siegal], **7,827**
Judd, Edith R. [Mrs.], 9
Judd, Elizabeth Kinau (1831-1918). *See* Wilder, Elizabeth Kinau (Judd) [Mrs. Samuel Gardner] (1831-1918)
Judd Family, 3,650
Judd, Harriet (Stewart) [Mrs. Orange] (1822-1907), **586, 11,350, 12,233**
Judd, Helen M., 12,572
Judd, Ida Benfield, 2,376
Judd, Margaret Gay (1831-1912). *See* Clawson, Margaret Gay (Judd) [Mrs. Hiram Bradley] (1831-1912)
Judd, Mary Minerva (Dart) [Mrs. Zadok Knapp] (1838-?), **16,721**
Judd, Orange, 11,350
Judd, Walter Henry (1898-), **9,159**
Judd, Zebulon Vance, Family, 9
Judge, Mr., 6,246
Judge, Thomas A., 15,146
Judges, 64, 297, **400**, 592, 698, 895, 945, **1,031, 1,152**, 1,186, **1,190**, 1,403, 1,783, 2,067, **2,163**, 2,190, 2,252, **2,255, 2,259**, 2,451, 2,545, 2,614, 2,651, 3,214, **3,323**, 3,785, **3,946, 4,076, 4,356, 4,373**, 4,442, 4,765, 4,822, 4,855, **4,856**, 4,934, **4,938**, 5,219, 5,276, 5,281, 5,365, 5,487, 5,736, 5,794, **6,261**, 6,262, 6,346, **6,356, 6,357, 6,385**, 6,544, **6,666**, 6,710, **6,886**, 6,945, 6,956, **6,967, 7,174**, 7,244, 7,266, **7,448**, 7,722, 7,765, **8,363**, 8,941, **8,962**, 8,989, 9,160, **9,206**, 9,212, 9,242, 9,308, 9,520, **9,546**, 9,647, **9,658, 9,929**, 9,996, 10,392, 10,855, 10,920, 10,989, 11,051, **11,076**, 11,242, 11,524, **11,569**, 11,795, 11,855, **11,881**, 11,914, **11,943, 12,019**, 12,069, 12,305, 12,345, 12,418, **12,522, 12,611**, 12,962, 13,080, 13,176, 13,250, 13,272, 13,446, 13,454, **13,846**, 13,904, 13,935, 14,007, 14,212, 14,581, 14,607, 14,648, 14,804, 15,020, 15,252, 15,256, 15,332, 15,565, 16,029, 16,171, **16,264, 16,450**, 16,880, 16,917, 17,108, 17,109, 17,169, 17,453, 17,621. *See also* Courts
Judges, Afro-American, 10,191
Judgments, 986, 1,898, 2,569, 9,206, 11,460, 11,932, 15,548
Judicial statistics, 1,915
Judith (book), 6,115
Judith Montefiore Society (WA). *See* Temple Beth Israel Sisterhood (WA)
Judson, Adelia. *See* Leslie, Adelia (Judson) Olley
Judson, Ann (Hasseltine) [Mrs. Adoniram] (1789-1826), 7,048
Judson, Clara (Ingram) (1879-?), 4,483, 8,531
Judson College (AL), 9,671
  archives, 33
Judson, Emily (Chubbuck) [Mrs. Adoniram] (1817-54), **12,826**
Judson, Katherine B., **13,936**
Judson, Lewis Hubbell (1809-80), **14,596**
Judson, Mary Ann (Prentiss) [Mrs. Oren], 880
Judson, Oren, 880
Judyka, Angeline, 1,534
Judy's Journey (book), 4,306
Juettner, Estelle Bode [Mrs. Otto] (1878-1970), **13,873**
Juettner, Otto (1865-1922), 13,873
Juilliard School of Music (NY), 2,664, **12,124**
  alumnae, 14,150
  students 14,346
Jules, Elise (Jusserand), 9,037
Julia Marlowe: Her Life and Art (book), 2,562
Julian Academy (France), 12,488
Julian, Florence J. (1912-), **8,581**
Julian, Grace Giddings (1865-1938). *See* Clarke, Grace Giddings (Julian) [Mrs. Charles B.] (1865-1938)
Julian Messner, Incorporated (publishers), 14,417
Juliana, Queen (Netherlands), 8,943
Juliette Gordon Low birthplace, 12,109
Juliette Low: Girl Scout Founder (book), 3,073
Juliette Low Museum, 12,109
Juliette Low World Friendship Fund, 12,109
Julius, Emanuel (1889-1951), 4,095, 4,477

Julius Rosenwald Fund, **5,469**
Jumbo Press, 505
Jumel, Eliza (Bowen) [Mrs. Stephen] (1775-1865). *See* Burr, Eliza (Bowen) [Mrs. Stephen] Jumel [Mrs. Aaron] (1775-1865)
Jumel, Stephen, 12,234
Jumping Jupiter (book), 7,202
June, Jennie (pseudonym). *See* Croly, Jane (Cunningham) [Mrs. David Goodman] (1829-1901)
Juneau Woman's Club (AK), 148
Jung, Carl (1875-1961), 2,215, 6,224
Jung Institute (Zurich, Switzerland), 13,261
Junge, Fannie [Mrs. Carl S.], 3,999
Junior Chamber of Commerce (MS), 9,622
Junior colleges, 7,646, 9,672, 11,897, **13,373**, 13,466, 13,474, **17,049**
  administration, **9,671**
  archives, **1,543**
  faculty, 9,664, 13,447. *See also* College teachers, part-time
Junior Epworth League Workers, 10,571
Junior Federated Club (Tama, IA), **5,112**
Junior Federation of Women's Clubs, 4,800
Junior Federation of Women's Clubs (Des Moines, IA), **4,769**
Junior Hadassah, 12,117, 17,647
Junior high schools, 1,713, 2,058
Junior League, 13,446
Junior League (AR), 236
Junior League (GA), **3,209**
Junior League (MN), **8,434**
Junior League (MS), 9,599
Junior League Magazine, 16,899
Junior League of Columbus (OH), **14,001**
Junior League of Salt Lake City (UT), **16,899**
Junior League of the City of New York (NY), **6,689**
Junior League of Waco (TX), 16,374
Junior League of Washington (DC), 2,844
Junior League of Youngstown (OH), **14,171**
Junior Literary Guild, 11,485
Junior Salvage Army, 2,868
Junior Sorosis (Cleveland, OH), 13,916
Junior Woman's City Club (OH), **13,850**
Junior Woman's Club (Aberdeen, MS), **9,536**
Junior Woman's Club (Charlotte, NC), 13,187
Junior Woman's Club of Orange (NJ), 11,141
Junior Women's Clubs (AL), 52
Junkin, Margaret (1820-97). *See* Preston, Margaret (Junkin) [Mrs. John Thomas Lewis] (1820-97)
Juno and the Paycock (drama), 12,367
Jury, 986, **1,185**, 1,817, 5,425, 6,356, 6,742, 8,388, 11,217, 15,819, 16,812, 17,376, 17,884, 17,905, **17,934**
  legal aspects, 15,803
Jusserand, Elise. *See* Jules, Elise (Jusserand)
Just, Emma Thompson, 16,908
"Just Like a Morning Glory" (song), 10,436
Just Wait Till You Have Children of Your Own (book), 17,947
Justice (periodical), 15,329
Justices of the peace, 1,790, 3,414, 4,076, 4,924, 7,618, 8,388, 9,118, 9,976, 12,769, 14,808, **16,411**, 16,425, 17,857, 17,908, **17,910**, 17,933
Justin Boot Company (TX), 16,273
Justin, Enid [Miss], **16,273**
Justin Winsor Prize, 17,667
Justis, Eleanor C., **2,050**
Justitia, Sister Mary, 3,971
Justus, May [Miss] (1898-), **15,879**
Juvenile Aid Society (Philadelphia, PA). *See* Association for Jewish Children (Philadelphia, PA)
Juvenile Court (Memphis, TN), 15,884
Juvenile courts, 1,675, 2,451, 3,803, 3,820, 3,823, 3,852, 4,101, 5,540, 6,789, 11,897, 13,987, 13,988, 17,486
Juvenile delinquency, 2,397, 2,677, 3,362, 3,905, 4,114, 4,921, 6,282, 6,544, 6,666, 6,711, 6,934, 7,031, 7,172, 7,764, 7,967, 8,069, 8,449, 8,676, 8,686, 9,095, 9,299, 10,603, 11,236, 11,974, 12,061, 13,275, 15,246, 17,463, 17,845
  cases, 9,288, 13,874
  prevention, 8,651, 8,655

  public opinion, 6,263
  research, **6,260**, 6,263
Juvenile delinquents, 6,263
Juvenile delinquents (female), 9,222
Juvenile detention homes, 306, 1,525, 1,682, 4,114, 10,741, 13,447
Juvenile-Domestic Relations Court (SC), 15,585
Juvenile Hall (Los Angeles, CA), 306
Juvenile Miscellany (periodical), 11,963, 12,419
Juvenile Protective Association (Chicago, IL), 3,803, 3,833, 4,079, **4,114**, 4,149
Juvenile Protective Association of the District of Columbia, 2,597
Juvonen, Helmi, **17,284**
KALE (radio station, OR), 14,551
KGMD (radio station, CA), 1,626
KSD-TV (St. Louis, MO), 10,191
KTVI-TV (St. Louis, MO), 10,191
Kabotie, Fred, 11,222
Kael, Pauline, 454, 6,584
Kagan, Max, 1,010
Kagan, Mrs. Max, 1,010
Kagawa, Toyohiko, 3,777
Kager, Mary B., **9,655**
Kahler, J. H., **8,824**
Kahn, Claire-Marie Heesacker, 300
Kahn, Dorothy, 8,670
Kahn, Dorothy Caroline, 8,665
Kahn, Ernestine Zadoc, 945
Kahn, Florence (Prag) [Mrs. Julius] (1866-1948), 698, 933, **936**
Kahn, Florence (Ring) [Mrs. Howard] (1883-1964), **5,783**
Kahn, Grace LeBoy, 11,817
Kahn, Hannah, 2,166
Kahn, Julius, 936
Kaibab Indians, **16,867**
Kaiser, John Boynton (1887-1973), **12,024**
Kalakaua, David, King, 3,632
Kalamar, Mary H. (1892-), 11,851
Kalamazoo Business and Professional Women's Club (MI), **8,215**
Kalamazoo Chamber of Commerce (MI), Women's Division. *See* Greater Kalamazoo Federated Women's Club
Kalamazoo College (MI)
  faculty, 11,749
  students, 11,056
Kalamazoo Female Seminary (MI), 7,910
Kalamazoo Labor Council (MI), 8,216
Kalamazoo Michigan Symphony Orchestra, 8,257
Kalamazoo Normal High School (MI), 8,244
Kalamazoo Public Library (MI), 8,236
Kalamazoo Public Museum and Art Institute (MI), 8,211
Kalamazoo Women's Government Caucus (MI), **8,210**
Kaleidograph (periodical), 14,200
Kaleleonalani (1836-85). *See* Emma, Queen. [Mrs. Alexander Liholiho, King Kamehameha IV]. Emma Rooke (1836-85)
Kalich, Lillian, 12,496
Kalich, Molly (1898-). *See* Picon, Molly, [Mrs. Jacob] Kalich (1898-)
Kalisky, Louise, 2,441
Kalkman, Adelaide, **10,166**
Kalkman, Marion E. (1904-), **1,375**
Kallen, Deborah, 7,554, 13,799
Kallen, Horace M. (1882-1974), 5,977, **13,799**
Kallen, Miriam (ca. 1900-), **5,977**
Kallio, Anne (1891-1945), **8,582**
Kalloch, Augusta (1887-). *See* Christie, Augusta (Kalloch) [Mrs. Walter A.] (1887-)
Kalman, Mrs. C. O., 9,467
Kalo Shop (Park Ridge, IL), **3,867**
Kalorama Citizens' Association, 2,633
Kamehameha IV, King. Alexander Liholiho, 3,631
Kaminska, Ida, 7,530
Kammerman, Lillie Fagergren (1882-1944), 16,676
Kampen, Irene Trepel (1922-), **6,038**, 6,045
Kander, John, 12,367
Kander, Lizzie (Black) [Mrs. Simon] (1858-1940), **17,664, 17,744**
Kander, Simon, 17,664, 17,841
Kane, Alice M., 14,813

Kane, Anne (Clark), 15,379
Kane, Elisha Kent (1820-57), **10,861**, **14,891**
Kane Family, 12,314
Kane-Hand Family (NY), **12,025**
Kane-Hand, Oliver, 12,025
Kane, Jane Duval (Leiper), 14,891
Kane, Laura Bartlett, 3,834
Kane, Lucile Marie (1920-), 8,956, 9,002, 9,230
Kane, Rose, 9,361
Kane, Sybil [Miss], **16,527**
Kane, Thomas, 16,527
Kane, Whitford (1882-), **12,530**
Kangas, Jeanne, 6,240
Kanouse, Bessie Bernice (1889-), **7,828**
Kansas, 4,421, 5,182, 5,185, 5,238, 12,404, 12,419
  abortion, legal aspects, 1,981
  accountants, 11,857
  authors, **5,237**
  bankers, 4,095, 4,477
  Baptists, **5,202**
  bishops, 6,784
  boards of trade, **5,181**
  charities, **5,125**
  church colleges, 6,784
    archives, **5,188**, **5,212**
  church records and registers, **5,169**, 5,187, 5,234
  church records and registers, Methodist, **5,171**
  church societies, 10,579
  church societies, Baptist, **5,203**
  church societies, Congregational, **15,948**
  church societies, Episcopal, **5,214**
  church societies, Lutheran, **5,224**
  church societies, Methodist, **5,169**, 5,171, 5,179,
    5,244, **5,247**, **5,248**
  churches, Catholic, **5,239**
  churches, Unitarian, 6,249
  city councilwomen, 5,172
  Civil War, 17,419
    campaigns and battles, 17,584
    societies, 5,176
  clergy, Episcopal, 6,784
  clergymen's wives, **5,220**
  clubs, 4,154, **4,477**, **5,176**, **5,179**, **5,191**, **5,193**,
    5,194, **5,195**, **5,216**
  college and school journalism, 5,188
  college librarians, 5,241
  college teachers, **5,170**, 5,172, **5,211**
  convents and nunneries, Catholic, **5,184**
  county agricultural agents, **5,180**
  court records, 1,808
  creameries, 11,857
  deaf, education, 13,673
  Delaware Indians, 14,175
  diaries and journals, **5,215**, 5,217, **5,218**, 5,219
  disaster relief, 10,620
  editors, **5,243**
  educational associations, 5,176, **5,190**
  experimental farms, 7,224
  4-H clubs, 5,180
  gardening, societies, etc., 5,179
  governors, **5,222**
  hospital records, **5,213**
  housewives, **5,217**, **5,218**
  judges, 5,219
  land settlement, 5,215
  lawyers, 5,162, 5,174, **5,175**, **5,210**
  legislators, 5,239, 8,070
  literary societies, 5,242
  mayors, 5,172
  monasticism and religious orders for women,
    Catholic, **5,164**, **5,178**, **5,184**, **5,186**, **5,204**, **5,236**
  music teachers, **10,120**
  musical societies, 5,179
  Native Americans, 5,182
    missions, 5,247
  newspapers, 10,579
  nuns, Catholic, 5,164, **5,165**, **5,166**, **5,167**
  nursery schools, 5,228
  nursing schools, **5,213**
  patriotic societies, 5,176
  pianists, **10,120**
  pioneers and settlers, **4,972**, 7,678, **9,850**, 15,322
  poets, **5,242**
  politics, practical, women's activism, **5,192**

  prisons, 15,762
  publishers and publishing, 4,095, **5,209**
  riots, 7,737
  school districts, **5,183**
  school superintendents and principals, **5,172**
  schools, records and correspondence, 5,183
  socialist parties, 8,070
  students, Afro-American, 5,209
  students' societies, 5,185, 5,241, 14,029
  suffrage, 6,815
  suffragists, **5,221**
  teachers, 5,183, **5,229**
  teen agers, employment, 10,074
  telephone, directories, 166
  temperance societies, **5,223**
  trade and professional associations, 4,477
  universities and colleges, **5,189**, 9,597
    archives, **5,168**, **5,185**, **5,207**, **5,235**, **5,241**
  volunteer workers in social service, 5,193
  women, civil rights, 5,219
  Wyandotte Indians, mortuary customs, 5,174
Kansas Anti-Saloon League, 5,223
Kansas Authors Club, 5,242
Kansas Baptist Women, **5,203**
Kansas City American Association of University
  Women (MO), 10,112
Kansas City Book Chat Club (MO), 10,112
Kansas City Mothers' Union (MO), **10,108**
Kansas City Quill Club (MO), 10,112
Kansas City School of Law, alumnae, 5,175
Kansas City Star, 9,983, 17,141
"Kansas City Stomp" (song), 5,531
Kansas City Widows and Orphans Home (MO),
  10,115
Kansas Federation of Women's Clubs, 4,477, 5,176
Kansas, Its Interior and Exterior Life (book), 5,222
Kansas Magazine, The (periodical), 4,675
Kansas Sac Indian Reservation, 1,688
Kansas State Bankers Association, 5,209
Kansas State College at Pittsburg
  alumnae, 8,555
  archives, **5,207**
  faculty, **5,211**
Kansas State College at Pittsburg, Faculty
  Association, 5,207
Kansas State College at Pittsburg, Faculty Senate,
  5,207
Kansas State College at Pittsburg, Faculty Wives'
  Club, 5,207
Kansas State College at Pittsburg, Student Assembly,
  5,207
Kansas State Temperance Union, 5,223
Kansas State University (Manhattan, KS), **5,189**
  staff, 5,191
Kansas State University (Manhattan, KS), chimes,
  14,029
Kansas Supreme Court, 5,219
Kansas Territory
  pioneers and settlers, 1,703, 10,879
  politics and government, 5,220
Kansas Wesleyan University (Salina, KS), archives,
  5,212
Kansas Woman's Journal, 9,995
Kansas Wonder Girl. *See* Von Herberg, Eugene
  (Dennis) [Mrs. J. C.] (1901-48)
Kantor, Effie M. [Mrs.] (?-1931), **4,693**
Kantor, Helena, 4,028
Kantor, MacKinlay, 4,693
Kantrowitz, Sadye Ascheim [Mrs. James], 9,254
Kaplan, Ann. *See* Feinberg, Ann (Kaplan) Williams
Kaplan, Ida (1904-). *See* Langman, Ida (Kaplan)
  [Mrs. Oscar] (1904-)
Kapp, Marie F. (1843-1923), 7,158
Kappa Delta, 17,003
Kappa Gamma Pi, 4,640
Kappa Kappa Kappa, Epsilon Zeta Chapter (IN),
  4,592
Karatinos, Gillian, 15,134
Karla, Constance (1892-), 1,068
Karling, Eva Hill LeSeuer, 16,176
Karmandy, Georgiana B., 823
Karmel, Ilona (1925-), **6,039**
Karok Indians, 965, 1,662
  basket making, 1,662

Karow, Anna Belle Welso [Mrs. Edward], **3,534**
Karsten, Helene P. [Mrs. Harold J.] (1898-1972),
  8,189
Käsebier, Gertrude (Stanton) [Mrs. Edward]
  (1852-1934), 12,126
Kashmir Bridge-Woman, The (book), 17,946
Kasper, Ralph, 629
Kassel, Myrna, 4,032
Katayama, May Herd, **17,285**, 17,301
Kate (slave, SC), 15,530
Kate Baldwin Free Kindergarten Association (GA),
  3,574
Kate Baldwin Kindergarten and Alumnae Association
  (GA), **3,535**
Kate Chase (book), 7,892
Kate Richards O'Hare Appeal Fund, 10,177
Kate Sessions, Pioneer Horticulturist (book), 1,189
Katharine Branson School (CA), 760
"Katherine and Myself," 4,228
Katherine Legge Memorial Association, **3,956**
Kato, Shidzue Ishimoto, 7,189, 7,287
Katrina Trask Alliance (Saratoga Springs, NY),
  12,851
Katrina Trask Garden Club (Saratoga Springs, NY),
  12,851
Katy Ferguson Home, 11,030
Katz, Alexander J., **12,532**
Katz, Bernard, 12,692, 16,982
Katz, Ethel (1900-), **2,773**
Katz, Fanny (Bowditch) [Mrs. Johann Rudolf]
  (1874-1967), **6,224**
Katz, Gertrude Price [Mrs. Alexander J.], **12,532**
Katz, Helen. *See* Robeson, Helen (Katz) [Mrs.
  George]
Katz, Hilda, 2,844
Katz, Johann Rudolf (1880-1938), 6,224
Katz, Jonathan, 12,692
Katzenstein, Caroline (ca. 1888-1968), **15,029**
Kauffman, Christmas Carol [Mrs. Nelson E.]
  (1901-69), **4,513**
Kauffman, Nelson E. (1904-), 4,513
Kaufman, Abraham, 15,313
Kaufman, Anna (1894-). *See* Swanke, Anna
  (Kaufman) [Mrs. Ernst Gustav] (1894-)
Kaufman, Bel [Miss], 11,817, **12,533**
Kaufman, George S., 12,367
Kaufman, Lucile B., **177**
Kaufman, Rhode [Miss] (1888-1956), **3,399**
Kaufman, Sarah (?-1941), 14,144
Kaula, Edna Mason, 11,940
Kaup, Elizabeth Dewing (1885-1966), **16,158**
Kautz's Raiders, 17,093
Kavan, Anna, 4,476
Kaweah Cooperative Colony (CA), 623
Kawin, Ethel (1890-1969), **4,115**
Kawin, Irene (1887-), **4,115**
Kaye, Danny, 9,769
Kaylor, Emeline, 9,999
Kaylor, Wesley, **9,999**
Kays, The (book), 2,300
Kazan, Abraham, 11,897
Kazan, Elia (1909-), **1,978**
Kazan, Molly Day (Thacher) [Mrs. Elia] (1907?-63),
  1,978
Ke' a' a' la Family (CA), 740
Keachie Female College (LA), 5,446
Kealhofer, Lutie (1841-76), **13,045**
Kean, Charles, 10,182
Kean, Ellen (Tree) [Mrs. Charles] (1805-80), 10,182
Kean, Julia. *See* Fish, Julia (Kean) [Mrs. Hamilton]
Keanum, Helen (Hopkins). *See* Shores, Helen
  (Hopkins) Keanum
Kearley Family, 15,942
Kearney, Belle (1863-1939), **9,656**, 9,719, 9,821,
  13,046
Kearney Family (MS), 9,656
Kearney, Leonora Marie (1849-1930). *See* Lake,
  Leonora Marie (Kearney) [Mrs. William E.]
  Barry [Mrs. Obadiah Read] (1849-1930)
Kearney Mansion (residence), 970
Kearney, Ruth Elizabeth. *See* Carlson, Ruth
  Elizabeth (Kearney)
Kearns, Mrs. Carroll D., 5,150
Kearny, Philip (1814-62), 4,269

Kearny, Stephen Watts (1794-1848), 4,269
Kearny, Thomas, 4,269
Kearsing Family (CA), **587**
Kearsing, Harriet Amelia. *See* D iaz Pena, Harriet
Amelia (Kearsing)
Kearsing, Mary Ann. *See* Weston, Mary Ann
(Kearsing)
Keasey, Margaret Louise (1885-1931). *See* Keasey,
Mother Boniface (1885-1931)
Keasey, Mother Boniface (1885-1931), **15,146**
Keating, Edward (1875-1965), **1,670**
Keating, Margaret Sloan Medill [Mrs. Edward]
(1875-1939), 1,670
Keating-Owen bill, 9,263
Keating, Sarah "Sally" Sayward (Barrell) [Mrs.
Richard] (1759-1855). *See* Wood, Sarah "Sally"
Sayward (Barrell) [Mrs. Richard] Keating [Mrs.
Abiel] (1759-1855)
Keatinge, Edward, 2,417
Keatinge, Harriette C. (Harned) [Mrs. Henry A.]
Veazie [Mrs. Edward C.] (1837-1909), **2,417**
Keats, John, 5,292, 6,185
Kee, Elizabeth, 17,466
Kee, James, 17,466
Keech, Lillian Sue (Anspach) [Mrs. Edward P.]
(?-1942), 5,784
Keefer, Lubov, 5,829
Keele, Reba, **16,528**
Keeler, Charles Augustus (1871-1937), 544, **588,
1,447**
Keeler, Charles Augustus, Family (CA), **588**
Keeler, Eliza (Shelton) [Mrs. James] (1840-1909),
16,561, **16,722**, 16,836
Keeler, Eloise, 588
Keeler, James (1817-?), 16,561, 16,836
Keeler, Josie (Gilstrap) [Mrs. George B.] (1858-93),
14,173
Keeler, Laura Ann (1859-1909). *See* Thurber, Laura
Ann (Keeler) [Mrs. Joseph Heber] (1859-1909)
Keeler, Louise Mapes (Bunnell) [Mrs. Charles
Augustus] (1877-1907), 588
Keeler, Lucy Elliot (1864-1930), **14,082,** 14,095
Keeler, Merodine. *See* McIntyre, Merodine (Keeler)
Keeler, Ormeida Curtis Harrison [Mrs. Charles
Augustus], 588
Keeler, Sarah I., 588
Keeler, Stephen K., 9,120
Keeley, Carrie Wilhelmina (1859-1942), **17,665**
Keeley, Edmund Burke (?-ca. 1921), 10,000
Keeley, John Paxton, 10,000
Keeley, Mary (Paxton) [Mrs. Edmund Burke]
(1886-), **9,826,** 9,981, **10,000, 10,073,** 10,086
Keelor, Mary, 2,691
Keely, John Worrell, 15,055
Keely motor, 15,055
Keemlé, Anna Maria (Mather) [Mrs. Samuel], 5,776
Keemlé, Anne. *See* Hinkley, Anne (Keemlé) [Mrs.
Edward Otis]
Keemlé, Samuel, 5,776
Keen, Corinne (1868-?). *See* Freeman, Corinne
(Keen) [Mrs. Walter Jackson] (1868-?)
Keen Family (PA), 15,168
Keen, Florence, 14,809
Keen School (Tientsin, China), 14,336, 14,466
Keena, Ruth (Watkins) [Mrs. E. E.] (1892-), **4,506**
Keenan, Margaret (1872-1964). *See* Harrais,
Margaret (Keenan) [Mrs. Martin] (1872-1964)
Keene Academy (NH), 7,653
Keene, Carolyn, 11,185
Keene, Emma. *See* Lourie, Emma (Keene) [Mrs.
Joseph H.]
Keene, Flavins J., 10,278
Keene, Florence R. (1878-?), **1,448**
Keene, Laura (1826-73). [Mrs. John] Taylor [Mrs.
John] Lutz, **2,418,** 2,542
Keene, Myrtle (Pearman), 4,392
Keene Norwegian Evangelical Lutheran Church
(MN), Ladies Aid Society, 9,271
Keener, Anna E. (1895-). *See* Wilton, Anne E.
(Keener) [Mrs. Louis R.] (1895-)
Keeney, Mrs. Harry, 1,901
Keeny, Myrtle, 14,813
Keep, Amelia Holman [Mrs. Josiah], 1,085
Keep, Helen, 14,123

Keep, Rosaline, 1,085
Keetch, Mercy Truth (Barker) [Mrs. Charles
Greenwood] (1835-1922), **16,467, 16,723**
Keets, Louisa Caroline Warburton Fitzherbert, **5,292**
Kefauver, Estes, 8,093
Kefauver, Nancy Paterson Pigott [Mrs. Estes], 2,847
Kefauver, Nannie, 3,527
Keio University (Tokyo, Japan), 11,545
Keisen Girls' School (Tokyo, Japan), 5,088
Keith, Alice (1890-1962), **17,666**
Keith Family, 6,901
Keith Family (CA), **589**
Keith, Frances G. Gibbes (1880-1948), **15,612**
Keith, Marilyn. *See* Bergman, Marilyn (Keith) [Mrs.
Alan]
Keith, Mary Hortense "Tennie" (1868-1948). *See*
Harmon, Mary Hortense "Tennie" (Keith) [Mrs.
Edward N.] (1868-1948)
Keith, Mary (McHenry) [Mrs. William] (1855-1947),
589, 710, **1,308**
Keith, Susan Bacon, 1,997
Keith, William, 14,997
Keith, William, 15,499
Keith, William, 597, 1,308, 1,318, 1,638
Keitt, Anna, 15,835
Keitt, Lawrence M., 15,835
Keitt, Stella Maria, 15,835
Keitt, Suzanne Mandeville Sparks [Mrs. Lawrence
Masillon] (1834-1915), 15,613, 15,835
Keller, Brooke, Jr., 6,691
Keller, Elizabeth (Reed) [Mrs. Phillips Brooks], 6,690
Keller, Ella Platt (1878-), **8,349**
Keller, Helen Adams [Miss] (1880-1968), 863, 1,426,
1,593, 1,963, **2,108,** 2,198, **2,419,** 2,424, 2,432,
2,610, 3,995, 5,122, 5,123, 5,465, 5,603, 6,339,
6,484, **6,691,** 7,171, 7,289, 7,560, 7,684, 11,144,
11,576, 11,810, **11,812,** 12,044, 16,157, 17,010
Keller, John F. (1885-), **10,478**
Keller, P. B., 6,691
Keller, Rosa (Freeman), **5,470,** 5,473
Kellerman, Annette, 11,997
Kellerman, Maude. *See* Swingle, Maude (Kellerman)
[Mrs. Walter T.]
Kellerman, Stella Victoria (Dennis) [Mrs. William
Ashbrook], 15,218
Kellerman, William Ashbrook, 15,218
Kellers, Elsie (Maier) (1890-), 668, 1,068
Kelley, Abigail "Abby" (1810-87). *See* Foster, Abigail
"Abby" (Kelley) [Mrs. Stephen Symonds]
(1810-87)
Kelley, Albert, 12,026
Kelley, Alice, 8,405
Kelley, Belle. *See* Anderson, Belle (Kelley)
Kelley, C. F., 3,775
Kelley, Caroline Bartram (Bonsall) [Mrs. William
Darrah], 12,026, 15,030
Kelley, Clark W., 13,673
Kelley, Cora Scofield [Mrs. Robert J.] (1868-1968),
8,405, 8,406, 8,408
Kelley, Cornelia (1897-1972). *See* Wolfe, Cornelia
Kelley (1897-1972)
Kelley, David Otis, 16,160
Kelley, Edith Packard [Mrs.], 3,760
Kelley, Edith (Summers) [Mrs. Allan] Updegraff
[Mrs. C. F.] (1884-1956), **3,775**
Kelley, Ellen [Mrs. William H.], 10,090
Kelley Family (IL), 4,404
Kelley Family (MA), **7,692**
Kelley Family (MN), **8,405**
Kelley Family (PA), **12,026**
Kelley, Florence. [Mrs. Lazare] Wischnewetzky
(1859-1932), 55, 2,224, 2,336, 2,359, 2,439,
2,499, 2,501, 2,502, 2,504, 4,007, 4,047, 4,143,
6,427, 6,602, 6,604, 6,715, 8,658, 8,668, 8,670,
11,760, 11,771, 12,026, 12,534
Kelley, Henrietta Aiken [Miss], 15,452
Kelley, Joanna (Randolph) [Mrs. Clark W.] (1870-?).
See Hollister, Joanna (Randolph) [Mrs. Clark W.]
Kelley [Mrs. George H.] (1870-?)
Kelley, John Bartram, 12,026
Kelley, Margaret A. [Miss], **590**
Kelley, Margaret Dana, 12,026
Kelley, Mary L. [Mrs. R. S.], **10,322**
Kelley, Mrs. J. S., 8,405

Kelley, Nicholas (1885-1965), 11,897, 12,026, **12,534**
Kelley, Regina, 8,405
Kelley, William Darrah (1814-90), 12,026, **15,030**
Kelley, William H. (1841-1914), **10,090**
Kellie, Luna E. (Sanford) [Mrs. James T.]
(1857-1940), **10,479,** 10,505
Kellner, Esther, **6,040**
Kellner, Louise, 15,057
Kellock, Katharine, 2,166
Kellogg-Briand Pact (1927), 9,160
Kellogg, Charles White (1815-96), 12,235
Kellogg, Charlotte, 5,119, 5,123
Kellogg, Clara Cook [Mrs. Frank Billings]
(1861-1942), 9,160
Kellogg, Clara Louise. [Mrs. Carl] Strakosch
(1842-1916), 12,403, 16,150
Kellogg, Elizabeth R. (1870-1961), **13,851**
Kellogg, Ella Eaton, 7,866
Kellogg, Eva Louise Phelps [Miss] (1862-1942),
17,667
Kellogg Family (NY), **12,235**
Kellogg, Fanny (1848-1947), 12,235
Kellogg, Florence Loeb, 8,678
Kellogg, Frank Billings (1856-1937), **9,160,** 9,277
Kellogg, Frederick (1766-1832), 12,235
Kellogg, Gertrude (1843-1903), 12,235
Kellogg, Grace (1885-). *See* Smith, Grace (Kellogg)
Griffith (1885-)
Kellogg, Harriett S., **4,807**
Kellogg, Jane (Davies) (1830-1922), **14,597**
Kellogg, John Harvey, 8,163
Kellogg, Julia, 4,374
Kellogg, Julia Burwell (Snow) [Mrs. Peter Comstock]
(1842-92), 12,235
Kellogg, Lizzy, **8,162**
Kellogg, Louise (1880-), 310, 526
Kellogg, Louise Phelps. Eva Louise Phelps Kellogg
(1862-1942), 8,953, **17,667**
Kellogg, Lucy Fletcher (1793-1891), **14,124**
Kellogg, Margaret McCauley, 7,920
Kellogg, Maria Parks, 4,812
Kellogg, Mary E. Wills, 7,680
Kellogg, Mary Francis, 1,635
Kellogg, Mrs. Vernon, 2,694
Kellogg, Paul Underwood (1879-1958), 8,649, **8,650,**
8,651, **8,658,** 8,660, 8,662, 8,675, 8,686
Kellogg, Paulina (1813-76). *See* Davis, Paulina
(Kellogg) Wright (1813-76)
Kellogg, Peter Comstock, 12,235
Kellogg, Rhoda, **1,309**
Kellogg, Sarah Ann, 4,842
Kellogg, Tryphena Ely White [Mrs. Frederick]
(1784-1816), 12,235
Kelly, Agnes (1891-). *See* Scott, Agnes (Kelly)
[Mrs. Roderick] (1891-)
Kelly, Albert, Family (OR), **14,598**
Kelly, Ann, **12,149**
Kelly, Bernice (1894-). *See* Harris, Bernice (Kelly)
(1894-)
Kelly, Caroline Bartram, 14,956
Kelly, Daisy. *See* MacCallum, Daisy (Kelly)
Kelly, E. A., 15,551
Kelly, Eliza Lee (Owen), 1,063
Kelly, Endora S., 2,160
Kelly, Eula, 8,237
Kelly Family (PA), 15,053
Kelly, Florence (Finch) [Mrs. Allen P.] (1858-1939),
1,589, 4,101
Kelly-Gadol, Joan (1928-), **11,631**
Kelly, Harry, 12,487
Kelly, Isabel T., 920
Kelly, Jane Bewel [Mrs.], **17,668**
Kelly, John, **10,817**
Kelly, John, Jr., 5,639
Kelly, Katherine Wick. [Mrs. Frederic Charles]
McConnell (1887-1937), 14,413
Kelly, Katie. *See* Bullock, Katie (Kelly) [Mrs.
Dillman S.]
Kelly, Louise, 9,145
Kelly, Lorena [Miss], **13,276**
Kelly, Margaret, 9,467
Kelly, Maria J., 5,063
Kelly, Mary Emily Francis (1867-1945). *See* Pye,

Mary Emily Francis (Kelly) [Mrs. Caleb Enoch] (1867-1945)
Kelly, Mattie E. *See* Plummer, Mattie E. (Kelly) [Mrs. O. P. S.]
Kelly, Maud McLure [Miss] (1887-1973), **20**
Kelly, Mrs. Harold P., 544
Kelly, Nira C. Bingham [Mrs. Albert], 14,598
Kelly, Nora A., 9,467
Kelly, Regina, 4,445
Kelly, Silas G., 14,598
Kelsey, Bessie Catherine Smith (Cook) [Mrs. Leander] (1902-), **16,724**
Kelsey, Blanche, 11,662
Kelsey, Isabel Oliver (Woods) [Mrs. William H.], 13,674
Kelsey, Vera (ca. 1891-1961), **13,674**
Kelsey, William H., 13,674
Kelton, Anna (1877-1964). *See* Wiley, Anna (Kelton) [Mrs. Harvey W.] (1877-1964)
Kelton, John C. (1828-93), 2,633
Kelvinator Company, 8,099
Kemal, Mustapha, 1,556
Kemble, Frances "Fanny" Anne. [Mrs. Pierce] Butler (1809-93), 1,426, **1,449**, 2,643, **3,477**, 3,506, 3,564, 3,889, 6,495, **7,065**, 11,305, **12,027**, 13,008, 15,116, 15,657
Kemp, Alice (?-1881), 5,756
Kemp, Augusta Thekla (Hasslock) [Mrs. John Franklin] (1882-1963), **15,956, 16,274**
Kemp, Harry, 12,006
Kemp, Margaret (1901-63), 7,158
Kemper Hall (IL), 4,383
Kemper Hall (WI), **17,560**
Kempfer, Hannah (Jensen) [Mrs. Charles] (1880-1943), 6,611, **8,456, 8,896**
Kempton-Wace Letters (book), 825
Kenagy, Nina M. (1878-1971), **4,116**, 4,128, 4,146
Kendall, Albert Davis-Messmore, 16,149, 16,150
Kendall, Elizabeth (ca. 1685-1765), **15,031**
Kendall Family, 3,419
Kendall, Louisa Hanson Rogers (Steele) (1804-81), 3,419, 13,376
Kendall, Mary (1806?-84). *See* Jones, Mary (Kendall) (1806?-84)
Kendall, Rita, 8,558
Kendrick, Ann. *See* Benedict, Ann (Kendrick)
Kendrick-Bellamy Company (Denver, CO), 1,698
Kendrick, Caroline. *See* Cooper, Caroline (Kendrick)
Kendrick, Georgia (Avery), 12,524, 12,525
Kendrick, Helen Louise (1844-1917). *See* Johnson, Helen Louise (Kendrick) [Mrs. Rossiter] (1844-1917)
Kendrick, Henrietta (1871-1968). *See* Reeves, Henrietta (Kendrick) [Mrs. John H.] (1871-1968)
Kenmore Association of Virginia, 2,028
Kennan, Emeline Rathbone (Weld) [Mrs. George] (1854?-1940), 2,420
Kennan, George (1845-1924), **2,420, 2,512**
Kennedy, Albert H., 8,651
Kennedy, Albert Joseph (1879-1968), **8,659**
Kennedy, Alice Carey (Traver) Libby (1874-1959), **17,196**
Kennedy, Alice Jacqueline (1907-). *See* Steffan, Alice Jacqueline (Kennedy) (1907-)
Kennedy, Alice Mary (1833-1911). *See* Lynch, Alice Mary (Kennedy) (1833-1911)
Kennedy, Anna (?-1949), **9,161**
Kennedy, Anne, 7,289, 7,312
Kennedy, Anne (1760-1836), **15,783**
Kennedy, Anne M. *See* Cushing, Anne M. (Kennedy)
Kennedy, Annie Ellicott (1839-1918). *See* Bidwell, Annie Ellicott (Kennedy) [Mrs. John] (1839-1918)
Kennedy, Catharine (Morrison) [Mrs. Joseph Camp Griffith] (1834-97), 349
Kennedy, Edward M., 17,230
Kennedy, Elizabeth (ca. 1871-?). *See* Bell, Elizabeth (Kennedy) [Mrs. Robert Mowry] (ca. 1871-?)
Kennedy, Elsie (Parsons) (1903-66), **11,882**
Kennedy Family, 349
Kennedy, Fannie, 15,537
Kennedy, Florynce, 15,197, 15,334
Kennedy, Helen (Weber), **591**

Kennedy, Hetty (1796-1881). *See* McEwen, Hetty (Kennedy) [Mrs. Robert Houston] (1796-1881)
Kennedy, Jacqueline (Bouvier) [Mrs. John Fitzgerald]. *See* Onassis, Jacqueline (Bouvier) [Mrs. John Fitzgerald] Kennedy [Mrs. Aristotle]
Kennedy, John Fitzgerald, 2,108, 2,640, 3,257, 5,829, 6,765, 8,144, 9,286, 10,197, 11,804, 11,827, 11,916, 14,909, 15,755, 16,000
Kennedy, John Pendleton, 12,333
Kennedy, Joseph Camp Griffith, 349
Kennedy, Louise, **16,240**
Kennedy, Lucinda (Harris) Eagle (1792-post 1885), 9,904
Kennedy, Mary Frances (1908-). *See* Fisher, Mary Frances (Kennedy) (1908-)
Kennedy, Mrs. Emilia, 8,215
Kennedy, Robert F., 6,765, 11,827
Kennedy, Sarah Jane (1841-1912). *See* Alexander, Sarah Jane (Kennedy) (1841-1912)
Kennedy, Sarah P. (1842-83). *See* Boone, Sarah P. (Kennedy) [Mrs. William Marshall] (1842-83)
Kennedy School of Missions, 14,443
Kennedy's Gold (book), 962
Kennelly, Sister Antonius, 9,467
Kenney, Edward J., 10,753
Kenney, Edward T., 11,102
Kenney Family (NJ), **11,102**
Kenney, Lona B., **6,041**
Kenny, Lucy Mathilda, 9,919
Kenny, Mary Emerson [Mrs. Jonathon], **7,391**
Kenny, Robert Walker (1901-76), **592**
Kenny, Sister Elizabeth (1886-1952), 8,521, 8,621, 8,943, 9,159, **9,162, 12,142**
Kenosha County Historical Society (WI), 17,566
Kenosha Hospital Training School (WI), 17,561
Kensington (plantation, SC), 15,423
Kensington Stone, 1,604
Kent, Adaline Dutton [Mrs. William] (1900-57), **1,310, 2,774**
Kent, Charlotte Mellen [Mrs. William Austin] (1768-1820), 7,642
Kent, Corita, 999
Kent County Female Anti-Slavery Society (RI), **15,384**
Kent County Sunday School Association (MI), 7,973
Kent, Deborah G., 14,585
Kent, Elizabeth, 6,473
Kent, Elizabeth [Mrs. William], 3278
Kent Family, 12,314
Kent Family (NH), **7,642**
Kent Family (NY), **12,028**
Kent, Hannah (1853-1940). *See* Schoff, Hannah (Kent) [Mrs. Frederic] (1853-1940)
Kent, Horace A., 14,585
Kent, James (1763-1847), 12,028
Kent, Leona (Gelin) [Mrs. William C.], **16,275**
Kent, Louise (Andrews) (1886-1969), **17,027**
Kent, Mary Tucker [Mrs. William Austin] (1776?-1833), 7,642
Kent, Nancy (Young) [Mrs. Daniel] (1786-1860), **16,725**
Kent Place School, 11,698
Kent, Rebecca Prentiss (1808-1905). *See* Packard, Rebecca Prentiss (Kent) (1808-1905)
Kent, Rockwell, 17,478
Kent State University (OH), faculty, 17,858
Kent State University (OH), Faculty Wives Club, **14,108**
Kent State University (OH), Faculty Women's Club, **14,109**
Kent State University (OH), University Women, **14,110**
Kent, William (1858-1910), 12,028
Kent, William Austin (1765-1840), 7,642
Kenton, Edna [Miss] (1876-1954), **12,029**
Kentucky, 5,278, 5,367, 11,748
  abortion, legal aspects, 1,984
  African Methodist Episcopal Church, 5,383
  Afro-Americans, **5,314, 5,383, 5,384, 5,387**
  air pilots, **5,311**
  art, decorative, 13,631

  auctioneers, 5,394
  authors, **5,263, 5,264, 5,342, 5,394**
  bills, legislative, 5,313
  blind, workers for the, **5,318**
  bookmobiles, 5,341
  businesswomen, **5,272**
  Catholic universities and colleges, **5,373**, 5,389
  caucus, 5,330
  caves, 13,250
  child care centers, 5,401
  cholera epidemics, 5,398, 13,173
  Christian Churches (Disciples of Christ), government, **5,300**
  church societies, Methodist, **5,400**
  church societies, Presbyterian, **5,370**
  churches, Baptist, 9,906
  citizens' associations, 3,283
  city councilwomen, **5,386**
  civil rights workers, **5,377**
  Civil War, 5,343
    claims, 5,347
  clergy, 5,285, 5,286, 5,287
  clergy, Christian Churches (Disciples of Christ), 5,262
  clergy, Methodist, 5,271
  clergy, Presbyterian, 5,259
  clubs, 5,301, 5,305, 5,321, **5,352, 5,357, 5,396, 5,405, 5,407**
  college students, 5,306, 5,331
  college teachers, **5,251**, 5,259, **5,372**
  congressmen, 5,267, 5,276, 5,321
  consumers' leagues, **7,208**
  department stores, 5,394
  diaries and journals, **5,259**, 5,279, **5,298, 13,167**
  editors, 5,268
  educational associations, **5,395, 5,403**
  educators, **5,325**, 5,394
  educators, Afro-American, 5,314
  elections, 5,328
  Equal Rights Amendment (proposed), 5,388
  evening and continuation schools, 5,325
  executive advisory bodies, **5,282**
  executives, **5,378**, 5,394
  farmers, 5,262, 5,268, 5,281, **9,917**
  forests and forestry, 2,713
  gas companies, 5,316
  governors, 5,267, 5,343, 5,394
  high schools, 5,314, **5,340**
    alumnae, **5,355**
  horse breeding, **5,324**
  horses, stud-books, 9,711
  hospital administrators, **5,326**
  hospitals, 13,055
    employees, 5,305
  hymn writers, 5,394
  insurance companies, Afro-American, 5,378
  interior decorators, 5,394
  judges, 5,276, 13,250
  kindergarten, 5,346, 5,401
  labor rest homes, **5,348**
  land settlement, 5,265
  lawyers, 5,271, 5,276, 5,277, 5,306, 5,309, 5,320, 5,321, 5,328, 5,394, **6,829**
  legislators, 5,281, **5,313, 5,376**, 5,394, 6,489
  librarians, 5,394
  librarians, Afro-American, **5,379, 5,382**
  libraries, branches, delivery stations, etc., 5,379, 5,382
  library associations, 5,341
  lieutenant-governors, **5,388**, 5,394
  lynching, prevention of, 3,279
  manufacturers, 5,345
  maternal and infant welfare, 6,987
  mayors, **5,356**
  medical societies, 5,318
  memorials, 5,307
  mental hygiene, 5,394
  midwives, 5,252
  military education, 9,645
  military posts, 17,445
  missionaries, lay, **5,300**, 5,394, **17,309**
  missions, Christian Churches (Disciples of Christ), **5,300**
  monasticism and religious orders for women,

Catholic, **5,389**, **5,390**, **5,391**, **5,398**, **5,401**, **5,408**, 10,611
municipal officials and employees, **5,381**
municipal records, 5,356
music teachers, 5,271
musical societies, **5,351**, **5,406**
newspapers, sections, columns, etc., 5,394
nuns, Catholic, **5,380**
nurses, 5,284, **13,301**
nursing schools, 5,284, 5,373
nursing, standards, 5,284
officials and employees, **5,307**
orphans and orphan asylums, 5,393
parks, **5,307**
patriotic societies, 5,326, **5,337**, **5,338**, **5,368**, **5,404**
photographers, **5,257**
physicians, 5,269, 5,394
pianists, 5,394
pioneers and settlers, 9,834, **9,902**, 13,011
poets, 5,394
political activists, women, 5,328, 5,329
political clubs, **5,322**, **5,329**
politicians, **5,334**
politics and government, 5,268, 5,376
prisoners, women, **5,283**
public health laws, 5,318
public officers, 5,394
race problems, 5,377
radio operators, 13,301
reparation, 5,394
right to life movement, **5,385**
rural health services, **5,252**
school boards, 5,381
school integration, 5,381
school superintendents and principals, 5,289, 5,325, 5,394
schools, **5,254**, 5,255, **5,256**, 5,292, **5,293**, 5,301
secret societies, **5,358**, 5,394
secretaries of state, 5,394
segregation, 5,379, 5,382
segregation in education, **5,384**
senators, United States, 5,276, 5,281, 5,333, 5,348, 6,489, 11,131
Shakers, **4,437**, 5,264, **5,298**, **5,364**
sheriffs, **5,272**
social life and customs, 5,271, 5,281
social settlements, 5,255
social workers, 5,394
soldiers, 5,328
storytellers, **5,250**
strikes and lockouts, coal miners, 6,314, 13,273
students' societies, 14,030
suffrage, 5,356, 9,061
suffrage societies, 5,305, 5,329, **5,354**
suffragists, **5,302**
teachers, 844, **5,258**, 5,259, 5,394
teachers, Afro-American, **5,384**
teachers' colleges, 5,313
teachers of the deaf, 13,432
temperance societies, **5,344**
theological seminaries, Baptist, **5,371**
universities and colleges, 5,394, 6,416
curricula, **5,399**
volunteer workers in social service, 5,357, 5,365
women, status, **5,282**
women's colleges, **5,393**
alumnae, **5,392**
women's liberation movement (1960-), **5,330**
World War II, civilians work, 3,950
Kentucky Board of Nursing, **5,284**
Kentucky Board of Nursing Education and Nurse Registration. See Kentucky Board of Nursing
Kentucky Child Labor Commission, 5,302
Kentucky Christian Woman's Board of Missions. See Christian Women's Fellowship
Kentucky Citizens Library Committee. See Friends of Kentucky Libraries
Kentucky Citizens Library League. See Friends of Kentucky Libraries
Kentucky College of Young Ladies, presidents, 5,362
Kentucky Crime Victims Compensation Board, 5,394
Kentucky Democratic Woman's Club, **5,329**
Kentucky Equal Rights Association, 5,302, 5,305, 5,329

Kentucky Federation of Music Clubs, 5,351
Kentucky Federation of Women's Clubs, 5,307
Kentucky Federation of Women's Clubs, Louisville Literature Club, **5,352**
Kentucky House of Representatives, 5,313
Kentucky Library, 5,278
Kentucky Medical Association, 5,318
Kentucky Military Institute, 9,645
Kentucky Mountain Club, 5,301
Kentucky Order of the Eastern Star, 5,394
Kentucky Seminary, **5,293**
Kentucky Society for the Prevention of Blindness, 5,318
Kentucky State, League of Women Voters, 5,329
Kentucky State Park Commission, 5,307
Kentucky Women's Political Caucus, 5,330
Kenwood Improvement Association (Chicago, IL), 3,876
Kenwood Monday Club (Minneapolis, MN), **9,163**
Kenyon, Agnes Robertson, **4,705**
Kenyon, Dorothy (1888-1972), **7,242**, 11,771, 12,069
Kenyon, Eliza Elvira [Miss], 11,025
Kenyon, Helen [Miss] (1884-), **6,170**
Keokuk High School (IA), 4,904
Ker, John, 13,047
Ker, Mary (Baker) [Mrs. John], 13,047
Ker, Mary Susan (1838-1923), **13,047**
Kerby, Elizabeth Poe, **17,805**
Kercher, Alice D. (?-1935), 9,128
Kerfoot Family, 11,717
Kerfoot, Mary Ann, 11,717
Kern, Margaret Ethel Kelley [Mrs. G. T. W.] (1874-1975), **17,086**
Kernahan, Coulson (1858-1943), 7,651
Kerner Report, 12,106
Kernodle, Portia B., 2,309
Kerns, Clarence, 9,763
Kernsky Family, 7,528
Kerr, Alexander (1828-1919), **14,401**
Kerr, Alice Spencer (1858-79), **13,048**
Kerr, Barbara, 11,827
Kerr, Charles, 3,996
Kerr, Dorothy (Fish) [Mrs. William John] (1889-1971), 593
Kerr, Electra (Padden) (1874-1953), **10,250**
Kerr, Elizabeth (Abbott), 5,978
Kerr, Florence (1890-1975), 10,055, **11,883**
Kerr, Frances Hope (1886-). See Holway, Frances Hope (Kerr) (1886-)
Kerr, Helen Culver [Mrs. John Clapperton], **2,421**
Kerr, Jean (Collins) [Mrs. Walter] (1923-), **17,806**
Kerr, Katherine Brown [Mrs. Alexander], 14,401
Kerr, Lizzie, 13,564
Kerr, Marion Adaline (Belnap) [Mrs. Walter Affleck] (1886-1972), **16,726**
Kerr, Mary T. [Mrs.], 3,747
Kerr, May Walden [Mrs. Charles H.] (1865-1960), **3,996**
Kerr, Mrs. Clark, 578
Kerr, Mrs. John Clappertus, 12,347
Kerr, Pamela (Drew), 1,534
Kerr, Rachel Anne (1814-92). See Done, Rachel Anne (Kerr) [Mrs. John Haynie] (1814-92)
Kerr, Sanford S., 4,700
Kerr, Sophie (1880-1965), **12,030**
Kerr, Walter, **17,806**
Kerr, Washington Caruthers, 13,048
Kerr, William John, Family (CA), **593**
Kershaw, Kathryn, 17,251
Kershaw, Newman, **15,486**
Kesler, Donette (Smith) [Mrs. Alonzo Pratt] (1872-1961), **16,727**, 16,789
Kessler, Clara Louise, **3,759**
Kessler Family (IA), 4,942
Kester, Harriet Watkins (?-1926), 12,535
Kester, Paul (1870-1933), **12,535**
Kester, Vaughan (1869-1911), 12,535
Ketcham, Emily B., 5,334
Ketcham Family (NY), 11,440
Ketchan Family, 14,059
Ketchum, Elizabeth. See Swetland, Elizabeth (Ketchum) [Mrs. Henry] Delord [Mrs. William]
Ketchum, Emily. See Bancroft, Emily (Ketchum)
Ketchum, Rebecca, 3,902

Kettering, Eunice Lea (1906-), **10,119**, **11,219**
Kettle, Hazel Olive (Bennet), **1,780**
Kettler, Ernestine (Hara) (1896-), 827, 1,016, 1,652
Kettlewell, Mrs. Frank (1887-), **594**
Keur, Dorothy L., 3,290
Kewannian (school yearbook), 4,659
Kewpie doll cartoons, 10,178
Key, Ellen Karoline Sofia (1849-1926), 1,593
Key, Luella (Gettys) [Mrs. V. A., Jr.], 6,389, **6,692**
Key, Mary Tayloe Lloyd, 5,789
Key, Virginia (Ringgold) (1811-1901), 684
Keyes, Bertha A. [Miss] (1868-1959), **11,351**
Keyes, Dora Ladd, 1,786
Keyes, Elizabeth, 1,786
Keyes Family (AL), 114
Keyes Family (CA), **595**
Keyes, Frances Parkinson (Wheeler) (1885-), 5,511, 7,868, 9,779
Keyes, Jennie Rutledge (ca. 1848-), 69, 70
Keyes, Julia Louisa (Hentz) [Mrs. John Washington] (ca. 1825-?), 70, 114, **13,049**
Keyes, Margaret Naumann (1918-), 5,035, **5,082**
Keyes, Marsden, 5,082
Keyes, Mrs. Arthur, 17,894
Keyes, Rebecca (1736-1812). See Faulkner, Rebecca (Keyes) [Mrs. Francis] (1736-1812)
Keyes, Verna (1893-?), **17,985**
Keyhoe, Mrs., 5,096
Keynes, John Maynard, 13,871
Keyport Literary Club (NJ), **10,899**
Keyport Weekly (NJ), 10,915
Keyser, Amelia. See Stein, Amelia (Keyser)
Keyser, Caroline Dorothea Margrethe (1829-80). See Preus, Caroline Dorothea Margrethe (Keyser) (1829-80)
Keyser, Dora, 1,654
Keyser, Jennie, 10,703
Keyserling, Mary, 8,651
Keyserling, Mary Dublin, 2,504
Khaki Club (KY), 5,357
Khaki Pants and a Tall, Silk Hat (book), 14,610
Khoobyurian, Helen, **1,851**
Kiah, Virginia (Jackson) (1911-), 5,828
Kianu Club (New Concord, OH), 14,118
Kibbee, Betty U., 6,221
Kibbler, William, 1,234
Kidd, Captain, 11,492
Kidd, Catherine (Boulware) [Mrs. John] (?-1867), 3,373
Kidder, Alfred V., 14,897
Kidder, Augusta, 17,651
Kidder, Daniel P. (1815-91), 10,988
Kidder, Electa Emeline (Morse) [Mrs. Thomas B.] (1864-1929), **10,480**
Kidder, Harriette (Smith) [Mrs. Daniel P.] (1816-1915), **10,988**
Kidder, Ida Angeline, 14,277
Kidder, J. P., 13,661
Kidder, Kathryn (1868-1939), 16,150
Kidder, Lilia, 2,997
Kidder, Louise Winslow (1884-). See Sparrow, Louise Winslow (Kidder). [Mrs. Herbert George] Sparrow. [Mrs. Paul E. H.] Gripon (1884-)
Kidder, Mary (1879-1958). See Rak, Mary (Kidder) [Mrs. Charlie] (1879-1958)
Kidoo, Elizabeth M. (1833-71). See Knox, Elizabeth M. (Kidoo) [Mrs. William Franciss] (1833-71)
Kidwell, Jean. See Pestana, Jean (Kidwell)
Kieckhoff, Marion, 14,414
Kiefer, Daniel, 12,705
Kiefer, Lizzie, 5,169
Kiehel, Constance A., 2,701
Kienbusch, Mildred [Mrs.], 11,171
Kierkegaardian Philosophy in the Faith of a Scholar (book), 8,617
Kies, Paul Philemon (1891-1971), **17,197**
Kifer, Martha, 1,533
Kilander, Ellie, **13,712**
Kilbourn, Dwight C. (1837-1914), **1,916**
Kilbourn, Emily (1808-1901). See Cope, Emily (Kilbourn) (1808-1901)
Kilbourn, Sarah (Hopkins) [Mrs. Dwight C.], 1,916
Kilbourne, Emily, 8,174

Kilburn, Ellen, 10,972
Kilgore, Emma (Brownlee) (1848-1925), 10,185
Kilgore, Emma Nettie (1865-?). *See* Montgomery, Emma Nettie (Kilgore) (1865-?)
Kilgour, Dorothy Hewlett, 11,948
Kilham, R. D., 16,165
Killen, Marcella Fitzpatrick [Mrs. Starr] (1909-), 8,984, 9,040, 9,159
Killen, Marcia, 9,375
Killers of the Dream (book), 2,879
Killiam, Lydia A., 16,411
Killian, Amaryllis (Bomar) [Mrs. Charles], 3,154
Killian, Eliza C. [Miss], **13,050**
Killian Family (GA), **3,154**
Killian, Rachel Powell (1851-?), **16,468**
Killough, Lucy, 7,583
Kilmer, Aline (Murray) [Mrs. Joyce] (1888-1941), **2,422**
Kilmer, Joyce (1886-1918), **2,422**
Kilns, 2,796
Kilpatrick, Lucy Webster, 5,061
Kilpatrick, Theresa, 3,922
Kimball, Bertha M., 16,953
Kimball, Doris Fleeson, 11,827
Kimball, Elizabeth McGrew, 7,158
Kimball, Ellen Sanders, 16,701
Kimball, Harriet, 3,829
Kimball, Heber Chase, 16,479, 16,728, 16,729, 16,730, 16,732
Kimball, Helen E., 12,412
Kimball, Helen Mar (1828-96). *See* Whitney, Helen Mar (Kimball) [Mrs. Joseph, Jr.] Smith [Mrs. Horace Kimball] (1828-96)
Kimball, J. N., 3,713
Kimball, Laura Pitkin [Mrs. Heber Chase], **16,728**
Kimball, Lucy (Walker) [Mrs. Joseph] Smith [Mrs. Heber Chase] (1826-1910), **2,581, 16,729**, 16,968
Kimball, Mary (1861-1948). *See* Morgan, Mary (Kimball) [Mrs. William Edgar] (1861-1948)
Kimball, Mary Ellen (Able) [Mrs. Heber Chase] (1818-1902), **16,730**
Kimball, Nancy [Mrs. Jona], 8,164
Kimball, Olive (Woolley) [Mrs. Andrew] (1860-1906), **16,731**
Kimball, Presendia Lathrop (Huntington) [Mrs. Joseph] Smith [Mrs. Heber Chase] (1810-92), 16,667, **16,732**
Kimball, Sarah Melissa (Granger) [Mrs. Hiram S.] (1818-98), **16,733**
Kimball, Victoria E. (Stewart), **596**
Kimball, Vilate, 16,968
Kimber, Abby, 6,842
Kimberly, Jennie [Miss], 1,525
Kimble, Marion (Prescott), 731
Kimbrough, Allan McCaskell (1850-?), 2,296, **9,658**
Kimbrough, Allan McCaskell (1850-?), Family, **9,657, 9,658, 9,793**
Kimbrough, Charlotte Grey [Mrs. O. L.] (1825-?), 9,658
Kimbrough, Emily, 16,773
Kimbrough, Mary Craig (1883-1961). *See* Sinclair, Mary Craig (Kimbrough) [Mrs. Upton Beall] (1883-1961)
Kimbrough, O. L. (1804-81), 9,658
Kimmerle, Marjorie (1906-63), **1,671**
Kimmy, J. E., 11,848
Kimona Club (TX), 16,263
"Kin" (story), 16,172
Kincannon, Alma (Ehrhorn) [Mrs. Claud] (1906-), **16,365**
Kind and Unusual Punishment (book), 16,162
Kindem, Anna Sekse [Mrs. Ingvald] (1896-1976), **8,754**
Kindergarten, 1,385, 3,131, 3,136, 3,137, 3,140, 3,522, 3,535, 3,573, **3,574**, 3,809, 3,820, 3,822, 3,875, **3,974**, 4,099, 4,211, 5,346, 5,394, 5,401, 5,558, 6,288, 6,346, 6,823, 10,149, 10,156, 11,864, 14,732, 15,023, 15,183
  methods and manuals, 1,603, 9,871
Kindergarten teachers, 1,426, 1,721, **2,094**, 2,430, **3,856**, 4,156, **6,951**, 9,202, 9,318, **12,586**, 13,540, **14,731**, 15,225, 15,467

Kindergarten teachers, training of, 540, 2,430, 4,210, 4,211, 4,212, **7,798**, 7,949, 7,973, 11,842
Kindergartens, 509, 1,721, **2,094**, 4,038, 9,103, 9,390, **9,526**, 10,655, **12,076**, 12,431, 12,493, 15,202, 15,205, **15,225**, 17,973
Kinderman, Kathy, **6,693**
Kindienst, Mae, 15,360
Kindsay, Katherine, 7,920
King, Alice, 5,119
King, Ameda Ruth (1893-1972), **4,389**, 4,432
King and I, The (musical), 1,426
King, Ann [Mrs. William], 5,679
King, Anna, 13,294
King, Anna T. Stott (1843-1931), **7,479**
King, Annie Ragan [Miss], 5,415, 13,051
King, Aurelia R., 3,812
King, Benjamin (1765-1840), 2,584
King-Bruwaert House (Hinsdale, IL), 4,078
King, Carl Howie (1898-1967), **13,211**
King, Carol (Weiss) (1895-1952), **6,314**
King, Carolyn St. Clair, 1,750
King, Coretta (Scott) [Mrs. Martin Luther, Jr.] (1927-), 84, 2,438, 4,126, 4,170
King County Council on Aging (WA), 17,341
King, David, 7,392
King, David S., 16,965
King, Edith Follett, **9,794**
King, Edith (Riccius) (1881?-), 7,670
King, Edith Shatto, 8,665
King, Edward L., 9,794
King, Eleanor, 12,363
King, Elizabeth, 14,738
King, Erma (Reinking), 516
King Family, 11,717
King Family (GA), 3,025
King Family (LA), **13,051**
King Family (MS), 9,794
King Family (NY), **12,377**
King, Fay, 941
King, Florence (1859-1939). *See* Lawrence, Florence King [Mrs. John Wilson] (1859-1939)
King Funeral Home (TX). *See* King Tears Mortuary (TX)
King, Georgianna Goddard (1871-1939), **2,423**
King, Grace (1853?-1932), 5,536, 9,600
King, Grace Elizabeth (1853?-1932), 4,695, **4,808**, 5,410, **5,414, 5,415**, 5,498, 13,051
King, Hannah (Tapfield) [Mrs. Thomas Owen] (1807-86), 855, **16,735**, 16,943
King, Harriet H., 6,812
King, Ida M. (Bruner) [Mrs. J. J.], 10,437
King, Irene (Marschall) [Mrs.], **16,366**
King, Jane R., 5,785
King, Jeanette Moore, **15,908**
King, John Glen (1787-1857), 6,738
King, Julia, 2,962
King, Julia [Miss], **3,046**
King, Julia Anne (1838-1919), 7,829
King, Kate [Mrs. David], 7,392
King Lear (drama), 17,804
King, Lucy Buell. *See* Shankland, Lucy Buell (King) [Mrs. Ebenezah Maxwell] Leal [Mrs. William Henry]
King, Margaret A. [Mrs. Philander B.], **4,424**
King, Maria, 14,628
King, Marian, **2,775**
King, Marion (Morrison) [Mrs. Frederick Gore] (1888-1976), 12,695
King, Martin Luther, Jr., 84, 6,834, 11,855, 12,532
King, Mary. *See* Cloon, Mary (King) [Mrs. William G.]
King, Mary (Eskridge) (1901-73), **13,211**
King, Mary Virginia. *See* Hale, Mary Virginia (King) [Mrs. Irving]
King Mongkut (Thailand), 1,426
King, Mrs. Henry C., 12,171
King, Mrs. William, 3,141
King, Mrs. William Neil, 13,990
King, Nina [Miss], 13,051
"King of the Zulus" (song), 5,529
King, Peter B., 12,377
King, Phebe [Miss], 11,279
King, Philander B., 4,424
King, Rose (1884-1967), **17,501**

King, Sarah Van Vleck [Mrs. Peter B.], 12,377
King, Stephen, 14,628
King, Susie (1904-). *See* Smith, Susie (King) [Mrs. O. A.] (1904-)
King Tears Mortuary (TX), 16,363
King, William (1768-1852), **5,679**
King, William Harcourt (1866-1923), 12,471
King, William Woodson, 5,414
Kingdom of Serbs, Croats and Slovenes, American ambassadors to, 14,210
Kingery, Eleanor Eppich [Mrs.], 1,750
Kings and rulers, 1,426, 2,944, 3,631, 6,573, 8,756, 8,777
King's College (England), 6,471
King's Daughters, 12,520. *See also* International Order of the King's Daughters and Sons
King's Daughters (Cortland, NY), **11,410**
King's Daughters (NC), 13,383
King's Daughters (SC), 15,597
King's Daughters (VA), Kate Custis Memorial Circle, **17,113**
King's Daughters and Sons (MS), Frances Ewing Gordon Chapter, 9,644
King's Daughters and Sons of Louisiana, 5,426
"King's Daughters and Sons, The," 8,284
King's Daughters Circle (Middleton, MA), **7,093**
King's Daughters Home for Children (Cortland, NY), 11,410
King's Medal, 12,797
King's Mountain, battle of (1780), 13,583
King's School of Oratory (OH), 14,026
Kingsbury, Alison Mason, 11,505
Kingsbury, Annie (Adams) [Mrs. J. F.], 2,424
Kingsbury, Jean, 2,424
Kingsbury, John Adams (1876-1956), **2,424**
Kingsbury, Letty. *See* Thomas, Letty (Kingsbury)
Kingsbury, Mabel (Glass) [Mrs. John Adams], 2,424
Kingsbury, Mary Melinda (1867-1951). *See* Simkhovitch, Mary Melinda (Kingsbury) (1867-1951)
Kingsbury, Susan Myra (1870-1949), 2,067, 2,068, 2,700, **14,742, 14,758**
Kingsbury, Virginia. *See* Hyatt, Virginia (Kingsbury) [Mrs. Belden]
Kingsford Presbyterian Church (Iron Mountain, MI), Women's Missionary Society, 7,863
Kingsland, Mrs. William M., 12,271
Kingsley, Carter Robie, **11,632**
Kingsley, Flora Evelyn. *See* Hofer, Flora Evelyn (Kingsley) [Mrs. Theodore R.]
Kingsley, Henry, 10,763
Kingsley House (New Orleans, LA), 5,509, **5,515**
Kingsley, Mary (Robie), 11,632
Kingsley, Mrs. Charles, 13,099
Kingsley, Rose, 13,099
Kingsworth, Eliza, **5,786**, 5,805
Kinkead, Beatrice Reynolds (1874-1947), **1,311**
Kinkead, Donald, 1,311
Kinkead, Ludie [Miss], 5,367
Kinkead, Martha Lucy (1838-?). *See* Grieve, Martha Lucy (Kinkead) (1838-?)
Kinkead, Robin, 1,311
Kinloch, Anne Isabella (Cleland), 15,456
Kinloch, Cleland, 15,487
Kinloch, Harriette [Mrs. Cleland], 15,487
Kinloch, Robert A., 15,734
Kinnaird, Emily, 3,969
Kinnan, Marjorie (1896-1953). *See* Baskin, Marjorie (Kinnan) [Mrs. Charles A.] Rawlings [Mrs. Norton] (1896-1953)
Kinney (CT), **1,932**
Kinney, Elizabeth Clementine (Dodge) Stedman [Mrs. William B.] (1810-89), 11,103, 17,010
Kinney Family (NJ), **11,103**
Kinney, Florence, 4,769
Kinney, Grace (Rankin), 6,846
Kinney, Hannah Burnet (1761-1832), 11,103
Kinney, Mary McKain, **7,830**
Kinney, Sara (Thomson) (1842-1922), 1,932, 10,483
Kinney, Thomas T. (1821-1900), 11,103
Kinney, William B. (1799-1880), 11,103
Kinscella, Hazel Gertrude [Miss] (?-1960), **10,481**
Kinsey, Alberta, 5,448
Kinship, 2,832, 2,838

Kinsland, Joshua, 3,047
Kinsland, Mary [Mrs. Joshua], **3,047**
Kinsman, Berthiah Dodge, 7,057
Kinsman Family (MA), **7,393**
Kinsman, Nancy Green [Mrs. William] (1806-86), **7,057**
Kinsman, Nathaniel, 7,277, 7,393
Kinsman, Rebecca (Chase) [Mrs. Nathaniel], **6,197,** 7,277, 7,393
Kinsman, William (1809-88), 7,057
Kinta Years, The (book), 5,264
Kinzie, Eleanor Lytle. *See* Gordon, Eleanor Lytle (Kinzie) [Mrs. William Washington, II]
Kiona-Benton City Canning Club (WA), 17,182
Kiowa-Comanche Reservation (OK), 14,207
Kiowa Indians, 14,207, 14,218, 14,241
Kip, Helen (Culbertson), 423
Kipling, Rudyard, 12,043
Kipnis, Claude, 4,384
Kippen, Manart (1892-1947), **12,536**
Kirby, Durwood, 4,764
Kirby, Georgiana Bruce [Mrs. Richard] (1818-87), **1,312**
Kirby, Richard, 1,312
Kirchner, Albert, 9,133
Kirchner, Alberta (1898-). *See* Hill, Alberta (Kirchner) [Mrs. Leslie A.] (1898-)
Kirchner, Edward, 9,133
Kirchwey, Freda (ca. 1893-1976), 2,336, 2,513, **6,694,** 8,949
Kirk, Alice, 3,911
Kirk, Andy, 5,534
Kirk, Andy, and His Clouds of Joy, 5,534
Kirk, Blair, **17,286**
Kirk, E. Buckner. *See* Hollingsworth, E. Buckner (Kirk)
Kirk, Edward N., 7,025
Kirk, Edwina, 1,186
Kirk, Estelle W., 1,186
Kirk Family, 1,822
Kirk, Hazel M., **1,822**
Kirk, Iva May Howard [Mrs. William Elwood], 14,402
Kirk, Lucy, **17,286**
Kirk, Mary, 6,646
Kirk, Mrs. William, 130
Kirk, Wally, 1,186
Kirk, William Elwood (1868-1937), **14,402**
Kirkbride, Eliza Paul (1801-81). *See* Gurney, Eliza Paul (Kirkbride) [Mrs. Joseph John] (1801-81)
Kirkbride, Elizabeth Butler (1836-1922), **15,203**
Kirkemo, Lillian [Mrs. H. E.], 18,026
Kirkham, Ellis (Musser), 16,949
Kirkham, Francis W., 16,612
Kirkham, Zina Robison, 16,676
Kirkland, Caroline, 7,882
Kirkland, Caroline, 3,994
Kirkland, Helen Marie Upjohn, 7,920
Kirkland, Samuel, 12,338
Kirkland, Winifred, 13,511
Kirkpatrick, Agnes, 15,626
Kirkpatrick, Alice [Mrs.] 3,053
Kirkpatrick, Alma Coffin [Mrs. James], **10,323**
Kirkpatrick, Andrew (1756-1831), **10,989**
Kirkpatrick, Jane (Bayard) [Mrs. Andrew] (1772-1851), 2,582, 10,989
Kirksville Teachers College (MO), faculty, 9,839
Kirkwood, Jane (Clark) [Mrs. Samuel J.], 4,926, 4,958
Kirkwood Rangers (SC), 15,627
Kirkwood, Samuel J. (1813-94), **4,926**
Kirn, Ann, 2,927, 2,928, 2,932
Kirstein, Mina (1896-). *See* Curtiss, Mina (Kirstein) [Mrs. Henry T.] (1896-)
Kirtland, Caroline Amelia (1810-80). *See* Morss, Caroline Amelia (Kirtland) [Mrs. Burton G.] (1810-80)
Kirtland, Frederick W., 11,264
Kirtland, Julia. *See* Sayre, Julia (Kirtland)
Kirtland, Susan Sutton, 7,942
Kiskadden, Margaret, 708
Kiss for Cinderella, A (moving-picture), 18,003
"Kiss, The" (story), 11,145
Kissing Kin (book), 5,031
Kissinger, Henry, 10,197

Kistachie National Forest, 5,443
Kistiakowsky, Vera, 6,335
Kistler, Irene Brady, 14,712
Kitchell, Barbara. *See* Girdler, Barbara (Kitchell) [Mrs. Reynolds]
Kitchell, Myrtle Elizabeth (1917-). *See* Aydelotte, Myrtle Elizabeth (Kitchell) (1917-)
Kitchelt, Florence Ledyard (Cross) [Mrs. Richard] (1874-1961), **6,695,** 6,741, 6,742, 6,864, **7,243,** **11,633**
Kitchelt, Richard, 6,695, 11,633
Kitchener Houses, 543
Kite, Elizabeth Sarah [Miss] (1864-1954), **2,425,** **10,990**
Kite, Mary (1792-1861), 14,853
Kitt, Edith Stratton [Mrs. George F.] (1878-1967), 184, 188, 198, 207, 209
Kitt Family (AZ), **198**
Kitt, George, 184
Kitt, William F. (1842-1904), 198
Kittilsby, Agnes M. [Miss] (1880-1925), **8,755**
Kittlitz, Margaret Emma (1906-), **16,367**
Kittochtinny Magazine, The (periodical), 5,291
Kittredge, Charmian (1883-1955). *See* London, Charmian (Kittredge) [Mrs. Jack] (1883-1955)
Kittredge, Mabel Hyde (1867-1955), **6,696**
Kittredge, Oliva Corinne (1835-1916). *See* Race, Oliva Corinne (Kittredge) [Mrs. George Wesley] (1835-1916)
Kittredge, Susan, 7,455
Kittridge, Elizabeth, **6,697,** 11,511
Kiwanis Club (MS), 9,711
Kizer, Benjamin H. (1878-?), **17,378**
Kizer, Charlotte Elizabeth, 10,482
Kizer Family (NE), **10,482**
Kizer, Jacob R. (1833-1910), 10,482
Kjaer, Helene Anderson Peterson (1805-78). *See* Swanner, Helene Anderson Peterson Kjaer [Mrs. Christian] (1805-78)
Kjelland, Gustava, 8,795
Kjellesvig, Anon, Family, 8,789
Kjer, Minnie [Mrs.] 613
Klasner, Lily (1862-1946), **16,529**
Klauber, Adolph (1879-1933), 12,426
Klausman, Herborg Kristiansdatter (Grimstvedt), 9,106
Kleeman, Rita Halle (1887-1971), **11,491**
Klees, Mrs. John, **2,426**
Klein, Henriette [Miss], 2,086
Kleinberg, Judy, 17,288
Kleine, Carroll, 15,110
Kleinert, Herminie, 2,824
Kleinert, Margaret Noyes (1879-1971), **6,698**
Kleinstuck, Frieda, 7,831
Kleinstueck, Irene [Miss] (1884-1974), **8,238**
Klemm, Mary, 15,308
Klenke, Jeannie (Morgan) (?-1970), **597**
Klepachivska, Maria (Arkas) [Mrs. Konstantyn] (1900-), **9,501**
Klepachivsky, Konstantyn (1887-), **9,501**
Klepper, Eva (Hendrickson), 10,430
Klestadt, Annie, **9,164**
Kletzsch, Elizabeth Schroeder [Mrs.], **1,722**
Kleuser, Louise C. [Miss] (1890-1976), **2,116**
Kleven, Victor, 11,217
Kline, Alma (ca. 1907-), **6,699**
Kline, Christine [Mrs. Emery], **10,620**
Klingle, George (pseudonym). *See* Holmes, Georgianna (Klingle) [Mrs. Benjamin Proctor] (1842?-1940)
Klingle, Georgianna (1842?-1940). *See* Holmes, Georgianna (Klingle) [Mrs. Benjamin Proctor] (1842?-1940)
Klinke, Johanna, 15,704
Klinzing, Ernestine M. (1891-1977), **12,796**
Klio Association (Chicago, IL), **3,868**
Klondike Kate. *See* Rockwell, Kathleen Eloisa (1876-1957)
Klug, Willa. *See* Baum, Willa (Klug)
Klussman, Frieda [Mrs. Hans], **1,313**
Klyce, Carrie Gray, 1,067
Knapp, A. Blair, 15,186
Knapp, Cecile [Miss], 17,589
Knapp, Charlotte C., **2,427**
Knapp, Katherine, 11,532

Knapp, Lizzie Margaret (1863-?), **1,852**
Knapp, Patricia (1915-72), **8,050**
Knappen, Lizzie Brown [Mrs. Eugene], 8,248
Knappen, Theoda [Mrs. Henry], 8,248
Knauer, Virginia, 15,179
Knauf, John, 13,693
Knauff, Ellen [Mrs.], 9,986
Kneeland, Abner (1774-1844), 4,809
Kneeland, Clarissa A., 1,319
Kneeland, Dolly L. Rice [Mrs. Abner], **4,809**
Kneeland, Elizabeth (Holyoke) (1732-1821), 7,385
Kneisel, Franz, 2,020
Kneisel Quartet, 2,020
Knemeyer, Bertha C. (1885-1963), **10,629**
Kner, Elizabeth, 12,879
KneuBuhl, Emily [Miss] (1883-), **6,700**
Knibbs, Henry Herbert, 215
Knickerbocker Publishing Company, 6,932
Knickerbocker, The (periodical), 9,636
Knickerbocker Theater (NY), 12,444
Knight, Adah (1907-). *See* Toombs, Adah (Knight) [Mrs. Henry J.] (1907-)
Knight, Adaline. *See* Belnap, Adaline (Knight)
Knight, Almira (1827-1912). *See* Hanscom, Almira (Knight) [Mrs. Sylvester V.] Stoddard [Mrs. George] (1827-1912)
Knight, Amelia (Stewart) [Mrs. Joel], 17,287, 17,414
Knight, Anna, 4,425
Knight, Dora, 8,296
Knight, Dorothy, 4,098
Knight, Elizabeth Gertrude (1858-1934). *See* Britton, Elizabeth Gertrude (Knight) [Mrs. Nathaniel Lord] (1858-1934)
Knight, Emma, 16,959
Knight Family (ME), **5,673**
Knight Family (OH, IL), **4,425**
Knight Family (WA), **17,414**
Knight, Frances (Beall), **2,776**
Knight, Gladys (Bowman) [Mrs. Leonard R.] (1899-), **3,657**
Knight, Harvey J., 4,425
Knight, Hattie (Madson) (1908-), **16,530**
Knight, Helen, 16,876
Knight, Holly, 11,717
Knight in the Royal Order of the Phoenix (medal), 6,935
Knight, Isabella (Gill) [Mrs. Harvey J.], 4,425
Knight, Joel (1808-67), 17,414
Knight, John H., 17,669
Knight, Lydia (Goldthwaite) (1812-84), **16,531**
Knight, Martha (McBride) [Mrs. Vinson] (1805-1901), 16,598, **16,736,** 16,743
Knight, Martha "Mattie," 4,425
Knight, Mary Lamar (1899-). *See* McConnell, Mary Lamar (Knight) [Mrs. Felton] (1899-)
Knight, Mrs. Allan, 15,315
Knight, Mrs. Edward Dexter, 1,226
Knight, Susan (Clark) [Mrs. John H.], **17,669**
Knight, Susan W., 7,461
Knightoceras kempae, 15,956
Knights and Ladies of Kaleva, Nuoriso Chapter (Ely, MN), **9,500**
Knights of Labor, **598,** 13,661
Knights of Pythias, 14,263
Knights of Pythias (CO), Women's Auxiliary, **1,781**
Knights of Pythias (Ann Arbor, MI), Arbor Temple Number 80, **7,832**
Knights of the Golden Rule (SC), 15,594
Knights of the Modern Maccabees (MI), Tent 419, 8,369
Knights' Ransom (book), 5,042
Knights Templar, 366
Knitters in the Sun (book), 3,993
Knitting Society of Elderly Ladies (CT),
Knobloch, Bertha, 2,160
Knolls Atomic Power Laboratory, 11,903
Knopf, Alfred A. (1892-), 11,897, **12,537,** 12,701, 14,476
Knopf, Alfred A., Publishers, 6,069, 6,518
Knopf, Blanche (Wolf) (1894-1966), 15,208, 16,157
"Knothole, The" (story), 12,473
Knott Family (KY), **5,267**
Knott, Frieda Peterson [Mrs.], 955
Knott, James Proctor (1830-1911), 5,267

Knott, Kate Jeffery, **7,833**
Knott, Maria Irvine (McElroy) (1805-?), 5,267
Knott, Sarah "Sallie" Rosanna (McElroy) [Mrs. James Proctor] (1833-1915), 5,267, 5,291
KNOW, Inc., 7,324
Knower, Mrs. Benjamin, 12,271
Knowland, Josephine (1862-1949). See Laflin, Josephine Knowland [Mrs. Louis Ellsworth] (1862-1949)
Knowles, Constance. See Draper, Constance (Knowles) [Mrs. Jesse]
Knowles Dam (MT), 10,328
Knowles, Etta, 1,590
Knowles, Jennie N., 1,590
Knowlton, Audrey (1904-), **4,531**
Knowlton, Gertrude F., **7,394**
Knowlton, Irene M. ,7,395
Knowlton, Martha Jane (1821-81). See Coray, Martha Jane (Knowlton) [Mrs. Howard] (1821-81)
Knows, William Lee, 4,700
Knox Academy (IL), 4,261
Knox, Aletta V. (Van Doren) [Mrs. John P.] (1816-52), **10,991**
Knox Alumnus, 4,261
Knox, Annie (Reid) [Mrs. William Franklin "Frank"] (1876-1958), 2,429
Knox, Caroline F. (1783-1851). See Swan, Caroline F. (Knox) (1783-1851)
Knox College (IL), 4,252, 4,263, 4,272, 4,416, 4,478, 11,705
    alumnae, 4,271
    faculty, 4,272
    students, 388
Knox, Dorothy Rapiton [Miss] (1896-), **13,277**
Knox, Douglas, 3,712
Knox, Eliza Heritage Washington [Mrs.] 13,437
Knox, Elizabeth C. (Wilson) [Mrs. John], 15,533
Knox, Elizabeth M. (Kidoo) [Mrs. William Franciss] (1833-71), 15,223
Knox, Ella (1868-1964). See Parrish, Ella (Knox) (1868-1964)
Knox, Eudora "Dora" Percival (1849-1921). See Lincoln, Eudora "Dora" Percival (Knox) [Mrs. Charles James] (1849-1921), Family (AR)
Knox, Eudora (Rose), 287
Knox, Eupha Sue (Hixson) [Mrs. John] (1906-), **239**
Knox, Euphemia Helen (?-1909). See Olcott, Euphemia Helen (Knox) [Mrs. John Nathaniel] (?-1909)
Knox Family (CA), **1,314**
Knox, Fannie Rose. See Thomason, Fannie Rose (Knox) [Mrs. Hugh]
Knox Female Institute (IL). See Knox College (IL)
Knox, Georgia Lydia. See Faber, Georgia Lydia (Knox) [Mrs. W. L.]
Knox, Helen M., **11,634**
Knox, Helena (Langslow) [Mrs. Paul] (1888?-1969), **12,797**
Knox, Henry (1750-1806), 5,679, **12,538**
Knox, Jennie, 15,223
Knox, John, 15,533
Knox, John J., 6,701
Knox, John P. (1811-83), 10,991
Knox, Lorraine, 5,137
Knox, Lucy Flucker [Mrs. Henry] (?-1824), 12,538
Knox, Lucy Flucker (1776?-1854), 5,679
Knox, M. A., 15,959
Knox, Martha "Mattie" Washington. See Hayman, Martha "Mattie" Washington (Knox) [Mrs. Syme]
Knox, Maryal (1879-1955), **6,701**
Knox, Mrs. Thomas McAllister, 14,618
Knox, Rose Bell (1879-), **2,428**
Knox, Sarah Curtiss, 6,701
Knox Seminary (IL). See Knox College (IL)
Knox, William Franciss (1831-1915), **15,223, 15,260**
Knox, William Franklin "Frank" (1874-1944), 2,429
Knudsdatter, Birgit, 9,266
Knudson, Carolyn, 11,505
Knudson, Lewis, 11,505
Knuteson, Annetta Verna Marie (Williams) [Mrs. Albert] (1913-), **16,737**
Knutson, Andrew, 8,397

Knutson, Coya (Gjesdal) [Mrs. Andrew] (1912-), **8,397**, 9,040, 9,287, 9,467
Knutson, Mabel (1901-). See Pederson, Mabel (Knutson) [Mrs. Elmer R.] (1901-)
Knutson, Myrtle Bergman [Mrs.] (1906-), **17,561**
Kobe College (Japan), presidents, 7,212
Kobe Theological Seminary for Women (Japan), 14,470
Kobéy, Miriam, 1,786
Koch, Anna-Katherine Barry, 5,063
Koch, Carlota, **599**
Koch, Mrs. Morris, **13,800**
Koch, Theodore, 4,226
Koehler, Irmengarde (Eberle) (1898-), **14,357**
Koehne, Leona E., 3,911
Koenig, Amelia R. See Rannefeld, Amelia R. (Koenig) [Mrs. Hermann]
Koenig, Henry, 12,291
Koerber, Leila Marie (1869?-1934). See Dressler, Marie. [Mrs. George Francis] Hoppert [Mrs. James H.] Dalton (1869?-1934)
Koester, Antoinette, **15,488**
Koesun, Ruth Ann (1928-), 3,856
Kofoed, Leslie S. (1909-), **10,738**
Kofoid, Carrie Prudence (Winter), **600**
Koger, Mary Lou, 3,442
Kohl, Bessie Owens, 16,876
Kohl, Edith Eudora (Ammons) [Mrs. Aaron Wesley] (ca. 1884-1959), 1,750
Kohlberg, Charlotte, 6,223
Kohler, Max James (1871-1934), **7,540**
Kohler, Winifred [Mrs. Max James], 7,540
Kohlman, Edwina, 11,837
Kohlmeyer, Ida, 2,844
Kohn, Esther (Loeb) [Mrs. Alfred D.] (1875-1965), 4,104, 4,110, **4,117**
Kohn, Kathryn (1899-), 8,702
Kohut, George Alexander (1874-1933), **7,541**
Kohut, Rebekah, 7,541
Koinonia Farm, 15,880
Koivisto, Edith (1889-), **9,502**
Kolb, C. William, 967
Kolb, Ethel Daniels, 16,876
Kollen, Martha (Diekema) [Mrs. George E.] (1867-1960), **8,190**
Koller, Alice. See Leopold, Alice (Koller)
Kollock Family (GA), **3,048**
Kollock, Susan M., 3,048
Kollontai, Aleksandra Mikhailovna (1872-1952), 4,080
Kolstad, Annie, 9,025
Kon Kau Indians (CA), 740
Kona Club (New Concord, OH), 14,118
Konick, Julie, 9,508, 9,512
Konikow, Antoinette F., 6,223
Konkin, Frances E., 17,018
Konopka, Gisela (1910-), **8,583**
Konsberg, Annie A. (?-1931), 3,969
Koochiching County Nursing Home (MN), 9,480
Koonce, Lizzie [Miss], **13,458**
Koontz, Elizabeth, 6,584
Kopell, Nancy, 6,335
Kopf, Dorothy (Thompson) [Mrs. Josef] Bard [Mrs. Sinclair] Lewis [Mrs. Maxim] (1894-1961). See Thompson, Dorothy. [Mrs. Josef] Bard [Mrs. Sinclair] Lewis [Mrs. Maxim] Kopf (1894-1961)
Kopp, Barbara (1836-1918), **16,532**
Kopp, Marie E., 6,223
Kops, Jane W. Davidson de Bruyn [Mrs.], 3,526
Korea
    American diplomats in, 11,720
    American educators in, 7,916
    American nurses in, 14,394
    American teachers in, 9,598, 14,394
    medical colleges, 11,754
    missionaries to, 1,822, 5,246, 5,394, 9,597, 13,610, **14,089**
    missionaries to, Methodist, 5,171, 5,394
    missions, Presbyterian, 14,394
Korean War (1950-1953), 5,320
    economic aspects, **1,810**
Koren, Else Elisabeth (Hysing) (1832-1918), **4,717**
Korn, Anna (Brosius), **14,212**
Kornbluh, Joyce, 8,094

Kornitzer, Bela, 5,137
Korpela, Janet W., 8,665
Kortwright, Helen (1739-1819). See Brasher, Helen (Kortwright) [Mrs. Abraham] (1739-1819)
Kory, Rabbi, 13,803
Kosciolowski, Sophie, 4,032
Koshland, Lucile (Wolf) Heming [Mrs. Daniel Edward] (1892-), **601, 6,702**
Kosmer, George, 11,694
Kossuth, Louis, 11,025
Kossuth, Louise. See Ruttkay, Louise (Kossuth)
Kossuth Revolution (Hungary, 1848), 5,676
Kosten, Laurel, **7,834**
Kotschnis, Mrs. Walter, 2,631
Kouts, Gracie, 1,663
Kovarik, Anne, 9,467
Kovarik, Josef J., 9,467
Koverman, Ida R., 5,121, 5,123
Kracaw, Theodora. See Kroeber, Theodora (Kracaw) Brown [Mrs. Alfred Louis]
Kracik, Anne Pauline (1917-73). See Draper, Anne Pauline (Kracik) [Mrs. Hal] (1917-73)
Kraenzel, Carl, 10,251
Kraenzel, Margaret Powell [Mrs. Carl], **10,251**
Kraft, Alice E., 11,889
Kraft, Ruby, **13,713**
Kramer, George W. (1847-1938), **11,105**
Kramer, Harriet Estelle Blackman [Mrs. George W.], **11,105**
Kramer, Herbert G., 9,880
Kramer, Mireille (1932-), 10,151
Krandis, Ruth. See Lewis, Ruth (Krandis)
Kraus Alumni Kindergarten Association (NY), 2,430
Kraus-(Boelté), Maria [Mrs. John] (1836-1918), **2,430**
Kraus, Hertha M., 8,670
Kraus, John, 2,430
Kraushaar, Amalie (1895-). See Nelson, Amalie (Kraushaar) [Mrs. George I.] (1895-)
Krautter, Elisa Bialk (1912-), **14,403**
Kremmeter, Mother Evangelista, **5,165**
Kreps, Juanita, 212
Kress, Idabelle Haughey, **11,106**
Kress, Lauretta, 7,920
Kressler, Florence (1851-1937). See Griswold, Florence (Kressler) (1851-1937)
Krieger, Anna N., 14,577
Kriendler Memorial (NJ), **10,992**
Kristeller, Paul O., 11,990
Kristiansdatter, Susanne [Mrs.], 9,106
Kroeber, Alfred Louis, 602
Kroeber, Theodora (Kracaw) Brown [Mrs. Alfred Louis], 602, 1,751
Kroeze, Barend H. (1868-1960), 13,675
Kroeze, Jeannette "Nettie" Gray [Mrs. Barend H.] (1874-), **13,675**
Kroh, Rosana Margaret (1836-1923). See Alverson, Rosana Margaret (Kroh) Blake (1836-1923)
Kroll, Lucy, **2,431**
Kronberg, Staffan, 1,196
Kropotkin, Peter, 12,701
Kross, Anna (Moskowitz) (1891-), **7,244**, 7,287, 12,069
Krueger, Amy, 4,927
Krueger, Anna Elizabeth Charles, 9,847
Krueger, Cora, 4,927
Krueger Family (IA), **4,927**
Krueger, Mrs. Fred, 4,927
Krueger, Viola, 4,927
Krukoff, Jenny, 8,206
Krull, Frederic, 4,630
Krull, Theresa Vinton (Pierce) [Mrs. Frederic] (1877-1963), **4,630**
Kruse, Kate (1853-1922). See Muller, Kate Kruse [Mrs. Otto] (1853-1922)
Kruskamp, Janet, 1,534
Ku Klux Klan, 7,849, 8,099, 8,517, 9,098, 9,467, 9,806, 11,855, 13,549, 14,133, **14,172**, 15,571, 15,869, 16,965, **17,752**
Ku Klux Klan (Chippewa Falls, WI), Klan Fourteen, **17,550**
Kubic, Marion. See Huber, Marion (Kubic)
Kuemmel, Cornelia A. (1863-?), **9,881**
Kuemmel, Natalia Wagner [Mrs. George F.] (1840-?), **9,882**

Kuenzli, Irvin, 8,093
Kugler, Anna Sarah (1856-1930), **3,958**
Kugler Memorial Hospital (Guntur, India), 3,958
Kugler, Victoria Henrietta (1874-?). *See* Nesbitt, Victoria Henrietta (Kugler) (1874-?)
Kuh, Katherine (1904-), **2,777**
Katherine Kuh Gallery (IL), 2,777
Kuhn, Ed, 14,405
Kuhn Family (WA), 17,390
Kuhn, Louisa A. (?-1877). *See* Wotherspoon, Louisa A. Kuhn [Mrs. Alexander Somerville] (?-1877)
Kuhn, Setty S. [Mrs. Simon], **13,801**
Kuhn, Simon, 13,801
Kuhne, Marie Stafford (Peary) [Mrs. William] (?-1978), 5,694
Kuhns, Dorothy Hartzell (1890-1961). *See* Heyward, Dorothy Hartzell (Kuhns) [Mrs. DuBose] (1890-1961)
Kuitunen, Cecilia, 9,467
Kuliesh, John, 16,011
Kume, Ai, 11,902
Kumi, Masami, 4,384
Kumin, Maxine (Winokur) (1925-), **6,042**, 10,853
Kummer Family (NY), **12,512**
Kummer, Jacob, 12,512
Kummer, Joseph, 12,512
Kunkle, Julia Mitchell [Mrs.], 2,281
Kunze, John C., 12,748
Kupfer, Minna, 2,196
Kurkop, Christina [Mrs. Jacob], 15,489
Kurkop, Jacob, 15,489
Kursheedt, Sarah (Seixas), 7,552
Kurtagh, Emeric, 5,515
Kurtz, Annie Laurie Fuller [Mrs. Wilbur, Sr.], 3,210
Kurtz, Helen, 8,479
Kurtz, Jane Blair Miller, 9,036
Kurtz, Maxine [Miss], 1,779
Kurtz, Wilbur G., Sr., 3,192, 3,210
Kurtz, Wilbur G., Jr., 3,171, **3,210**
Kussy, Sarah (1869-1956), **7,542**
Kutsch, Joyce, 37
Kutter, Elizabeth, 6,336
Kuzma, Genevieve (1910-), 11,851
Kvamme, John Peder, Sr., 8,756
Kvamme, Vera Joyce Fox [Mrs. John Peder], **8,756**
Kyle, Mary, 9,159
Kyser, Kay, 698
"Kysomunique" (periodical), 3,387
L. C. O. (pseudonym). *See* Obenchain, Lida (Calvert) [Mrs. William Alexander] (1856-1935)
Labadie, Joseph Antoine (1850-1933), 7,997
Labels, legal aspects, 2,504
La Boheme Music Club (Seattle, WA), **17,223**
LaBoone, Elizabeth [Miss], 3,106, 3,107
Labor (newspaper), 1,670
Labor and laboring classes, 611, 1,047, 1,605, 2,879, 3,977, 4,003, 4,143, 5,426, **6,812**, 7,323, 8,007, 8,058, 8,076, 8,185, 8,603, 9,462, 12,487, 14,393, 14,437, 14,637, **14,742**, 15,333, 15,585. *See also* Arbitration, industrial; Consumers' Leagues; Discrimination in employment
   dwellings, 396, 7,329, 9,277
   education, 2,878, 4,032, 4,083, 4,126, **6,893**, 6,895, **8,071**, 8,073, 8,074, 8,085, 8,099, 8,126, 8,142, 11,501, **11,762**, 12,422, 13,176, 14,737, 15,332, **17,588**
   political activity, 9,443
   research, 11,924, 11,929
   songs and music, **15,977**
Labor and laboring classes, Afro-American, 835, 15,333
Labor and laboring classes, Chinese-American, 15,762
Labor and laboring classes, Japanese, 835
Labor and laboring classes, Mexican, 835
Labor and laboring classes, Philippine, 835
Labor Argus (WV), 17,482
Labor Assembly for Peace, 1,577
Labor bureaus, 55, **1,917**, 6,365, 6,402, 6,427, 6,468, 6,686, 13,406
Labor contracts, 2,675, 9,717
Labor departments. *See* Labor bureaus
Labor disputes, 348, 1,654, 1,810, 2,502, 2,696, 4,855, 7,303, 9,962, 17,635
Labor economics, 17,757

Labor economists, **12,060**
Labor exchanges. *See* Employment agencies
Labor Extension Service, 7,273
Labor Fact Book, 14,393
Labor injunctions, 6,314
Labor law and legislation, 441, 1,188, 1,283, 1,473, 1,561, 2,120, 2,397, 2,504, 2,509, 2,525, 2,677, 2,684, 2,700, **2,703**, 3,715, 4,047, 4,114, 4,163, 4,173, 4,351, 5,302, 5,330, 5,741, 6,178, 6,365, 6,402, 6,431, 6,485, 6,604, 6,640, 6,686, 6,838, 6,848, 6,966, 6,974, 6,977, 7,208, 7,300, 7,315, 8,137, 8,138, 8,971, 9,477, 9,656, 11,771, 11,905, 13,468, **14,939**, 17,376, 17,486
Labor Problems: A Textbook, 17,757
Labor relations. *See* Industrial relations
Labor Research Association, 14,393, 14,437
Labor rest homes, **5,348**, 12,820
Labor supply, 2,672, 13,262
Labor turnover, 8,140
Labor unions. *See* Trade-unions
Labor World (periodical), 12,702
Laboratories, 14,943
Laboratory schools, 4,210
Laborers Friend, 7,624
Labranche, Brisce Similien, 5,435
Labranche, Jean, **5,435**
Labrie, Rene J., 10,400
LaBudde, Wilhelmine D. [Mrs.] (1880-1955), **17,671**, **17,842**
Lac Qui Parle Mission (MN), 9,293
Lace and lace-making, 2,112
Lace Cuffs and Leather Aprons (book), 6,095
Lacey, Ethel (1889-?). *See* Hylbert, Ethel (Lacey) [Mrs. Lewis C.] (1889-?)
Lacey, John F., 4,759
Lacey, Marey E. [Mrs. Sylvester], 4,773
Lacey, Margaret, 2,610
Lachappelle, Flo, 17,919
Lachlison, Sarah, **3,536**
Lachmeyer, Phoebe J., 2,160
Lachmund, Mrs. Ernest, 9,234
Lackey, Katherine deMontalant (1909-). *See* Hoskins, Katherine deMontalant (Lackey) [Mrs. Albert L.] (1909-)
La Crescenta Women's Club (CA), 901
La Crescenta Women's Club, California history and landmarks department (CA), 901
La Cucarachas (theater), 17,619
Lacy, Adelheid Bertha Marie Zoe Zeller [Mrs. Ilbert O.] (1892-), **11,759**
Lacy-Baker, Marjory, 14,453
Lacy, Benjamin Rice, **13,459**
Lacy, Drury, **13,460**
Lacy, Henry Veere (1886-), **14,404**
Lacy, Ilbert O., 11,759
Lacy, Jessie (Ankeny) [Mrs. Henry Veere], 14,404
La Dame aux Camelias (drama), 3,921
Ladd, Christine (1847-1930). *See* Franklin, Christine (Ladd) [Mrs. Fabian] (1847-1930)
Ladd, Frances C., 11,662
Ladd-Franklin, Christine (1847-1930). *See* Franklin, Christine (Ladd) [Mrs. Fabian] (1847-1930)
Ladenberg, Emily, 12,440
Ladies Aid Club (Morris, MN), 8,696
Ladies Aid Society (MN), 9,467
Ladies Aid Society (Pleasant Valley, NE), **10,569**
Ladies' Aid Society (NC), 13,374
Ladies Aid Society (OR), 14,625
Ladies Aid Society (Philadelphia, PA), 14,972
Ladies Aid Society (Temple Sisterhood of Tree of Life Synagogue, SC), **13,802**
Ladies Aid Society (Oshkosh, WI). *See* Ladies Benevolent Society (Oshkosh, WI)
Ladies' Aid Society of Brocton (OH), **13,937**
Ladies' Aid Society of St. Mary's Episcopal Church (FL), **2,913**
Ladies' American Home Education Society and Temperance Union, **7,245**
"Ladies and King Sorrel, The" (ms), 6,031
Ladies Anti-Polygamy Society of Utah, **16,469**
Ladies' Army Aid Society, 7,295
Ladies' Art Association, 12,446, **15,288**
Ladies Association for Soldiers Relief, 12,169
Ladies Association of Charleston for Commemorating

the Confederate Dead. *See* Ladies Memorial Association (Charleston, SC)
Ladies Association of Garfield Hospital (DC), 2,454
Ladies Auxiliary Missionary Society (NY), 12,237
Ladies Auxiliary Society (MS), **13,803**
Ladies Benevolent Association of South Orange (NJ), 11,133
Ladies Benevolent Society (Somers, CT), 1,900
Ladies Benevolent Society (Danvers, MA), 7,001
Ladies Benevolent Society (Lynn, MA), **7,073**
Ladies Benevolent Society (Newton, MA). *See* Female Benevolent Society (Newton, MA)
Ladies Benevolent Society (MI), **13,804**
Ladies Benevolent Society (Charleston, SC), **15,490**, 15,515, 15,522
Ladies Benevolent Society (Oshkosh, WI), **17,672**
Ladies Benevolent Society of St. Mark's Episcopal Church (NY), **12,237**
Ladies Benevolent Total Abstinence Society (Newton, MA). *See* Female Benevolent Society (Newton, MA)
Ladies Book Club (NJ), **10,994**
Ladies Bureau, The (IA), 4,732
Ladies' Burns Club (GA), **3,211**
Ladies' Church Home Society (Baltimore, MD), 5,827
Ladies Coffee Club (Salem, OR), **14,711**
Ladies Committee of the Smithsonian (DC), 2,850
Ladies Community Club (Harrison, NE), **10,470**
Ladies' Companion (periodical), 11,316
Ladies' Confederate Memorial Association, 5,513
Ladies Coronal, The (periodical), **8,279**
Ladies Domestic Academy (DC), 5,292
Ladies' Education Society (Jacksonville, IL), **4,118**
Ladies Employment Society of Flushing (NY), **11,787**
Ladies First Union Association (PA), 15,069
Ladies Garden Club (GA), **3,050**, 3,082
Ladies Guild of the St. Paul's Mutual Improvement Society (MT), 10,331
Ladies Gunboat Fair (SC), 15,727
Ladies Hearse Society of Wilmont (WI), **17,562**
Ladies Hebrew Association (LA), **13,805**
Ladies Hebrew Benevolent Association (AL), **13,806**
Ladies Hebrew Benevolent Society (IN), **13,807**
Ladies Hebrew Benevolent Society (MI), **13,808**
Ladies Hebrew Social Circle (PA). *See* Ohev Sholom Sisterhood (PA)
Ladies' Heritage Association, 16,061
Ladies' Hermitage Association (SC), 15,405
Ladies Hermitage Association (TN), 15,948
Ladies Home Journal (periodical), 2,205, 3,172, 4,061, 5,048, 6,101, 10,027, 10,197, 11,304, 11,490, 11,866, 12,911
Ladies' Home, The (Atlanta, GA), 15,952
Ladies Hospital Association of Paterson (NJ). *See* Paterson General Hospital Association (NJ)
"Ladies in the Spring" (story), 16,172
Ladies Industrial School Association (IL), **12,238**
Ladies Library Association (Mount Pleasant, IA), **5,066**
Ladies' Library Association (Ann Arbor, MI), **7,836**, 7,919
Ladies' Library Association (Galesburg, MI), 8,213
Ladies' Library Association (Kalamazoo, MI), **8,240**
Ladies Library Association (MI), garden club, 8,211
Ladies' Library Association (Richmond, MI), **8,254**
Ladies Library Association of Phoebe Griffin Noyes Library, Inc. (Old Lyme, CT), **2,025**
Ladies Library of Holly Township (MI), **8,204**
Ladies Literary Circle (MT), 10,402
Ladies Literary Circle (Bloomington, OH), **13,938**
Ladies Literary Club (Rochester, IN), 4,661
Ladies Literary Club (MI), 7,936
Ladies' Literary Club (MI), **8,350**
Ladies' Literary Club (Ypsilanti, MI), **7,837**
Ladies' Literary Club (Cortland, NY), **11,411**, 11,412
Ladies' Literary Club of Wayne (MI). *See* Wayne Literary Club (MI)
"Ladies Meet, The, 1878-1945, The History of the Millard Avenue Woman's Club" (article), 3,929
Ladies Memorial Association (Athens, GA), 2,989, 3,080

Ladies Memorial Association (Atlanta, GA), 3,166, **3,212**
Ladies Memorial Association (Rome, GA), 19
Ladies Memorial Association (NC), **13,053**, 13,344, 13,556
Ladies Memorial Association (Charleston, SC), 15,405, 15,522
Ladies Memorial Association of Mobile (AL), **40**
Ladies' Memorial Association of Wake County (NC), **13,461**
Ladies' Mount Vernon Association, 15,727
Ladies' Musical Club (OH). *See* Women's Music Club (OH)
Ladies Mutual Aid Association (Charleston, SC), **15,491**, 15,727
Ladies of Charity of St. Vincent de Paul (Austin, TX), **16,017**
Ladies of Courage (book), 11,489
Ladies of Kaleva, 9,502
Ladies of Literature (book), 4,995
Ladies of Orange Orphan's Society (NJ), 11,067
Ladies of San Francisco (CA), 390
Ladies of the G.A.R. Home (MN), 9,480
Ladies of the Grand Army of the Republic, 3,699
Ladies of the Grand Army of the Republic, Department of Minnesota, **9,167**
Ladies of the Grand Army of the Republic Monument Association (MN), **9,168**
Ladies of the Senate (DC), 2,868
Ladies of the Maccabees (MI), **8,220, 8,234**
Ladies of the Maccabees (MT), 10,331
Ladies of the Maccabees (WV), Progressive Hive Number Eight, **17,467**
Ladies of the Old Guard of the Gate City Guard (GA), **3,213**
Ladies of the Royal Club (Fort Wayne, IN). *See* Order of Railway Conductors of America, Ladies Auxiliary
Ladies Park Association (TX), 16,263
Ladies' Parlor Reading Circle (Freehold, NJ). *See* Keyport Literary Club (NJ)
Ladies' Patriotic Relief Society (NJ), 7,542
Ladies Physiological Institute of Boston and Vicinity (MA), **6,703**
Ladies Physiological Society (Providence, RI). *See* Providence Physiological Society (RI)
Ladies' Prayer Book and Tract Society (Baltimore, MD), 5,827
Ladies Reading Circle (Columbus, MS), 9,558
Ladies Reading Club (Girard, KS), 4,154
Ladies Reading Club (Niles, MI), **8,384**
Ladies Reading Society (Byfield, MA), **7,397**
Ladies' Relief Society (OH), **14,083**
Ladies Repository (periodical), 5,173
Ladies' Sanitary Society of Eugene (OR), 14,564
Ladies Seminary Society (York, NE), **10,570**
Ladies Sewing Circle (NY), 7,536
Ladies Sewing Society of the German Orphan Asylum (DC), **6,704**
Ladies Silk Culture Society of California, 546
Ladies Social Circle (Iowa City, IA), 4,959
Ladies Society (Danvers, MA), 7,004
Ladies Soldiers' Aid Society (Iowa City, IA), 4,960
Ladies' Springfield Soldiers' Aid Society (IL), **3,869**
Ladies Sustentation Society of the Presbyterian Church of Jackson (MS), **9,660**
Ladies Temperance and Benevolent Union of Elmira (NY), 11,445
Ladies Temperance Society (Newton, MA). *See* Female Benevolent Society (Newton, MA)
Ladies Temperance Union (Adrian, MI), **7,838**
Ladies Union Benevolent Society (Ithaca, NY), 11,619, **11,636**
Ladies Union Relief Society of Albina (OR). *See* Patton Home (OR)
Ladies Universalist Society (Port Huron, MI), **7,839**
Ladies' Ursuline Community (Charleston, SC), **15,492**
Ladies War Committee (IL), 3,897
Ladies' Washington Monument Society (IN), 4,467
Ladwig, Mrs. Otto Worthington (1882-), **17,468**
Lady Aberdeen Fellowship, 6,964
Lady-Doc, The (book), 17,899
"Lady Betty," 17,098
"Lady in Red Slacks" case, 8,115

Lady Possessed (moving-picture), 17,816
Lady Washington (brig), 7,632
Lady Was a Skipper, The (book), 14,470
Lady With a Pen (book), 8,768
Lady's Friend, A Monthly Magazine of Literature and Fashion (periodical), 13,312
Lady's Home Magazine of Literature, Art and Fashion. See *Arthur's Home Magazine* (periodical)
Lady's Life in the Rocky Mountains, A (book), 1,790
Lady's Magazine and Gazette of Fashion (periodical), 13,312
Laengselens Boat (book), 8,788
Laetare Medal, 13,854
La Farge, John, 6,185
La Farge, John (1880-1963), **12,236**
La Farge, Margaret M., 12,236
Lafayette Fund, 12,180
Lafayette Hotel (MN), 8,957
Lafayette, Marie Joseph Paul Yves Roch Gilbert du Motier, Marquis de (1757-1834), 2,550, 11,654, 13,846
Lafcadio Hearn (book), 10,869
La Federation de L'Alliance Francaise aux Etats-Unis et au Canada, 13,331
Lafiat Guild (KY), 5,399
La Flesche Family (NE), 10,459, **10,483**
La Flesche, Francis (?-1932), **2,838**, 6,540, 10,459, 10,483
La Flesche, Joseph, 10,459, 10,483
La Flesche, Marguerite. *See* Diddock, Marguerite (La Flesche) [Mrs. Walter T.]
La Flesche, Mrs. Joseph, 10,029
La Flesche, Rosalie. *See* Farley, Rosalie (La Flesche)
La Flesche, Susan (1865-1915). *See* Picotte, Susan (La Flesche) [Mrs. Henry] (1865-1915)
La Flesche, Susette (1854-1903). *See* Tibbles, Susette (La Flesche) [Mrs. Thomas] (1854-1903)
Laflin Family (IL), **3,870**
Laflin, Josephine Knowland [Mrs. Louis Ellsworth, Sr.] (1862-1949), 3,870, **11,104**
Laflin, Louis Ellsworth, Sr., 11,104
La Follette, Belle (Case) [Mrs. Robert Marion, Sr.] (1859-1931), 2,432, 2,501, 9,386, 17,749
La Follette, Charles Marion, 4,483
La Follette Family, **2,432**
La Follette, Fola (1882-1970). *See* Middleton, Fola (La Follette) [Mrs. George] (1882-1970)
La Follette, Isabel (Bacon) [Mrs. Philip Fox], **6,705**, 17,670
La Follette, Philip Fox (1897-1965), **17,670**
La Follette, Rachel Wilson (Young) [Mrs. Robert Marion, Jr.], 17,761
La Follette, Robert Marion, 1,669, 10,673, 12,597, 17,654, 17,715
La Follette, Robert Marion, Sr. (1855-1925), 2,432
La Follette, Robert Marion, Jr. (1895-1953), 2,432, 12,575, 17,761
La Follette, Suzanne, 12,884
La Follette's Magazine (periodical), 2,432
LaFount, Lenore. *See* Romney, Lenore (LaFount) [Mrs. George]
LaGallienne, Eva, 12,637
Lagerlöf, Selma Ottiliana Lovisa (1858-1940), **4,324**
Lagos, American missionaries to, 14,459
LaGrange College (GA), 3,157, 3,423
    faculty, 3,405
LaGrange Female College (GA). *See* LaGrange College (GA)
LaGrange Plantation (MS), 9,760, 17,502
La Guardia, Fiorello H., 11,841, 11,856, 11,895, 11,914, 11,928
La Guardia, Marie M. [Mrs. Fiorello H.] (1896-), **11,884**, 11,897
Laguna Colony, 16,866
Laguna Indians, **16,868**
    culture, 16,868
    medical care, 153
    missions, 16,868
    relations with whites, 16,868
    religion and mythology, 16,868
    tribal government, 16,868
Lahaina Restoration Foundation (HI), **3,644**

La Harpe, Jacqueline Ellen Violette de (1894-?), **603**
Lahee, Louise Hodge, **6,644**
Lahey Clinic (MA), 6,688
Lahey, Hazel Carter, 10,055
Lahman, Bertha Marion [Mrs. Charles E.] (1872-?), 10,152
Lahman, Marion (Sherwood), **14,213**
Laidlaw, Carrie, 316
Laidlaw Family (CA, WY), **604**
Laidlaw, Harriet Wright (Burton) [Mrs. James Lee] (1873-1949), **6,706**, 12,387
Laidlaw, James Lee, 6,706
Laidler, Harry, 12,705
Laighton, Celia. *See* Thaxter, Celia (Laighton) [Mrs. Levi] (1835-94)
L'Aignoux, Charlotte, 12,220
Laing, Dilys (Bennett) [Mrs. Alexander Kinnan L.] (1906-60), **10,867**
Laing School (SC), 15,281
Laird, Elizabeth Rebecca (1874-1969), 11,813, **11,814**
Laird, Mary. *See* Hamady, Mary (Laird) [Mrs. Walter]
La Jolla Garden Club (CA), **1,211**
La Jolla Woman's Club (GA), **1,193**
Lakaski, Pearl [Mrs.], 4,868
Lake, Ann (Getz) [Mrs. Edward] Hutchinson [Mrs. Andrew Leech] (ca. 1800-?), **1,450**
Lake County Home Bureau (Wauconda, IL), **4,449**
Lake ecology, 4,119
Lake, Edith Janet (1912?-), **8,584**
Lake Erie College (Painesville, OH), 7,224, 11,743, 12,740
    alumnae, 14,123
    faculty, 1,998
Lake Erie Seminary (Painesville, OH). *See* Lake Erie College (Painesville, OH)
Lake Hopatcong Public School (NJ), **11,100**
Lake, Ida, **10,900**
Lake, Leonora Marie (Kearney) [Mrs. William E.] Barry [Mrs. Obadiah Read] (1849-1930),
Lake Michigan, 4,119
Lake Michigan Federation, 4,119
Lake, Mona Keig [Mrs. Myron Charles, Jr.]. *See* Toogood, Mona Keig [Mrs. Myron Charles, Jr.] Lake [Mrs.]
Lake, Mrs., 10,761
Lake, Myron Charles, Jr., 10,721
Lake Park Village Improvement Society (Athol, MA), **5,886**
Lake poets, 12,399
Lake States Forest Experiment Station, 9,466
Lake View Cemetery (Patchogue, NY), 11,792
Lake View Musical Society (Chicago, IL), 4,056
Lakela, Olga (1890-), 8,592
Lakeland Memorial Hospital (Woodruff, WI), 17,699
Lakeside Hospital Unit (France, World War I), 13,889
Lakeside Hospital Unit (World War II), **13,888**
Lakmé (opera), 7,213
LaMama Experimental Theatre, 12,367
Lamar, Caro [Mrs. Charles Augustus Lafayette], 3,400
Lamar, Charles Augustus Lafayette, 3,400
Lamar, Clarinda Huntington (Pendleton) [Mrs. Joseph R.] (1856-1943), 2,679, **3,214**
Lamar, Eliza Anderson, **3,538**
LaMar, Estella, **17,986**
Lamar, Eugenia Dorothy Blount [Mrs. Walter Douglas] (?-1955), **3,465**
Lamar Family (GA), **2,992**
Lamar, Fannie, 9,819
Lamar, Heddy, 11,461
Lamar, Joseph R., 3,214
Lamar, Marta B. [Mrs.] (1902-), **5,538**
Lamar, Mary Ann (1818-99). *See* Cobb, Mary Ann (Lamar) [Mrs. Howell] (1818-99)
Lamar, Mary Ann Robinson [Mrs. Zachariah], 2,992
Lamar, Mrs. Mirabeau B., 16,106
LaMar, Mollie, 9,903
Lamar, Rebecca Ann, **16,093**
Lamar, Rebecca J. *See* McLeod, Rebecca J. (Lamar)
Lamar, Zachariah, 2,992
Lamare, Caroline (Goddefroy) [Mrs. François Nicolas] (?-1906), 589

Lamare, Elizabeth (McHenry) [Mrs. Emmanuel Benjamin] (1850-1907), 589

Lamare Family, 589

Lamarr, Selena, 955

Lamb, Agnes Treat (1811-?). *See* Richards, Agnes Treat (Lamb) [Mrs. Timothy P.] (1811-?)

Lamb, Anthony, 12,239

Lamb, Frank M., 8,306

Lamb, Harriet, **10,167**

Lamb in His Bosom (book), 3,063, 3,174

Lamb, Martha Joanna Reade (Nash) [Mrs. Charles A.] (1826-93), 3,888, **7,136, 7,246**, 12,238, **12,240**, 12,256, 12,403

Lamb, Matilda (ca. 1857-?). *See* Morton, Matilda (Lamb) (ca. 1857-?)

Lamb, Rosamund (1898-), **6,707**

Lamb, Sarah Elizabeth (Ferebee) *See* Grandy, Sarah Elizabeth (Ferebee) Lamb [Mrs.]

Lambard Family (GA), 12,015

Lambda Chi Society, **4,718**

Lambda Rho (WA), **17,288**

Lambda Theta Phi, Zeta Chapter (Stockton, CA), **1,613**

Lamberston, Margaret, 13,462

Lamberston, Mary, 13,462

Lambert, Christine (pseudonym). *See* Lamon, Heidi Huberta Freybe Loewengard (1911-)

Lambert Family (MA), **7,643**

Lambert, George (1913-74), **15,997**

Lambert, Hester. *See* Harland, Hester (Lambert)

Lambert, Isabel St. George, **11,109**

Lambert, Latane (Bartlett) [Mrs. George] (1916-), **15,997, 15,998**

Lambert, Louise Todd (1905-), 1,356, 1,357

Lambert, Mary Alice (Cannon) [Mrs. Charles] (1828-?), **16,738**

Lambert, Sophia A., 9,076

Lamberton, Gretchen (1895-1956), 9,527

Lambeth, Cecelia Panteloon, 16,863

Lambeth, Ida, 9,538

Lambeth, Irma, 9,538

Lambeth, Irma (ca. 1900-70). *See* Milligan, Irma (Lambeth) (ca. 1900-70)

Lambeth, W. B., Family (NC), **13,463**

Lambie, James M., Jr. (1914-), **5,145**

Lamboll, Thomas, **15,526**

Lambson, Julina (1849-1936). *See* Smith, Julina (Lambson) [Mrs. Joseph F.] (1849-1936)

La Mesa Redonda Club (San Francisco, CA), 507

Lamon, A. H., 9,753

Lamont, Corliss (1902-), 6,547, **6,708**, 9,119

Lamont, Florence Haskell (Corliss) (1873-1952), **7,247**

Lamont, Helen Lamb [Mrs. Corliss] (1906-75), 6,547, **6,709**

Lamont, Jane, 8,936

Lamont, Molly, 4,764

La Morada Residence (CA), 1,525

Lamoreux, Carrie (1879-1965). *See* Harding, Carrie (Lamoreux) [Mrs. William Lloyd] (1879-1965)

LaMotte, Ellen Newbold (1873-1961), **2,433**, 5,809

Lamour, Dorothy, 1,025

Lamp in Jerusalem (book), 15,720

Lampe, Ruth Hydon [Mrs. Henry W.], 4,949

Lamphier, Mary (1893-), 16,488

Lampila, Helmi (1890-1974). *See* Mattson, Helmi (Lampila) [Mrs. William] (1890-1974)

Lampkin, Daisy, 2,502

Lampman, Evelyn (Sibley) [Mrs. Herbert S.] (1907-), **14,405**, 14,712

Lampman, Maria Bronck, 11,415

Lamport, Belinda Sophia (1830-?), **8,241**

Lamprey, Louise, 2,166

Lampson, Robin (1900-), **2,204**

Lamson, Albert Henry (1862-1941), 10,851

Lamson Family (NH), **10,851**

Lamson, Peggy [Mrs. Roy], **6,710**

La Mujer En Pie de Lucha (book), 17,619

La Mujer es La Tierre (book), 17,619

Lancaster Current Topics Club (MA), **7,059**

Lancaster, Elsie, 2,858

Lancaster Industrial School for Girls, **6,711**

Lancaster Journal (PA), 14,863

Lancaster Mennonite Conference, Women's Missionary and Service Commission (PA), **14,869**

Lancaster Mennonite Conference, Women's Missionary and Service Commission, Homebuilders (PA), 14,869

Lancaster Town Library (MA), 7,060

Lance, Elizabeth Denison. *See* French, Elizabeth Denison (Lance)

Lance Family (SC), 15,441

Lancraft, Mabel, 2,009

Lanctot, Mother Agnes, 8,425

Land, 8,333
cases, 984

Land, Adelle H. (1901-69), **11,374**

Land, Annie. *See* O'Berry, Annie (Land) [Mrs. Thomas]

Land Beyond the Mountains (book), 5,264

Land development, 8,406

Land, Evangeline Lodge (ca. 1875-1954). *See* Lindbergh, Evangeline Lodge (Land) [Mrs. Charles Augustus] (ca. 1875-1954)

Land Family (GA), **3,379**

Land Family (NC), 13,319

Land grants, 626, **1,145**, 3,246, 3,258, 3,509, 9,539, 12,748, 13,132, **15,969**

Land, Lila. *See* Chunn, Lila (Land) [Mrs. William Augustus]

Land, Mona Ricks Arrington [Mrs. Nathan C.], 3,379

Land, Nathan C. (1812-80), 3,379

Land of Cotton (book), 16,384

"Land of Plenty, The" (radio program), 13,261

Land settlement, 194, 202, 3,621, 4,952, **5,056**, 5,057, 5,215, 5,265, 7,152, 8,280, 8,288, 8,455, 8,517, 8,716, 8,799, 8,920, 9,063, 9,077, 9,158, 9,418, 9,462, 9,467, **9,485, 9,990**, 10,059, 10,227, 10,230, **10,275**, 10,284, **10,292, 10,318**, 10,350, **10,377**, 10,478, 10,533, 10,680, 11,527, 11,574, 11,704, 11,746, 14,185, **14,201**, 14,608, 14,702, 14,910, 15,852, 16,460, 16,488, 16,502, 16,585, 16,715, 17,416, 17,900, **17,948**, 17,982

Land tenure, 11,595
law, 10,459, 11,746

Land, The People, The (book), 6,064

Land titles, 1,273, 3,271, 9,006, 9,618, 9,725, 14,655, 15,492, 15,523. *See also* Deeds
registration and transfer, **2,136**, 4,182, 8,900, 9,398, 9,471, 9,976, 10,010, 10,680, 11,245, 12,643, 14,565, 15,496, 15,511, **15,646**, 16,078, **17,202**
cases, 1,446, 9,076

Land trusts, 88

Land use, planning, 16,231

Land, Velma, 15,308

Land, Yetta, 1,654, 1,656

Landauer, Bella Clara (1874-), **6,712**

Landcraft, Electra S., 2,009

Landen, Elizabeth, 13,600

Lander, Alden M., 2,386

Lander, Frederick, 8,351

Lander, Frederick Charles (?-1863). *See* Lander, Frederick West (?-1863), Family (NV)

Lander, Frederick West (?-1863), Family (NV), **10,764**

Lander, Jean Margaret (Davenport) [Mrs. Frederick West] (1829-1903), **2,434, 8,351**

Lander, Louisa, 10,764

Landers, Ann (pseudonym). *See* Lederer, Esther

Landes, Bertha Knight (1868-1943), 17,257, **17,289**

Landgrebe, Dora, 1,339

Landi, Elissa, 698

Landlord and tenant, 90, **14,959**
cases, 186

Landon, Alfred M., 5,511, 11,621

Landon, Alice E., 17,028

Landon, Eliza (Hinckly) (1819-?), 15,032

Landon Family (PA), **15,032**

Landon Family (VT), **17,028**

Landon, Flora, 17,028

Landon, Margaret Dorothea (Mortenson) [Mrs. Kenneth Perry] (1903-), **2,435**

Landon, Sue (Adams). *See* Vaughan, Sue (Adams) [Mrs. Landon]

Landowska, Wanda, 468

Landreth, Isabella Turnbull (?-1937). *See* Peirce, Isabella Turnbull (Landreth) [Mrs. Benjamin Osgood, Jr.] (?-1937)

Landscape architects, 303, 2,258, **4,393**, 5,442, 7,182, **7,794, 11,711**

Landscape gardening, 1,214, 6,803

Landscape painters, 9,837

Landweer, Lulu Dorothea (Rubke), **605**

Lane, Ann. *See* Petry, Ann (Lane)

Lane, Annie. *See* Blocker, Annie (Lane) [Mrs. J. R.]

Lane, Ashbel, 16,586

Lane Bryant Volunteer Award Committee, 6,555

Lane, Caroline M. Beers, 4,369

Lane, Carrie Clinton (1859-1947). *See* Catt, Carrie Clinton (Lane) [Mrs. Leo] Chapman [Mrs. George William] (1859-1947)

Lane College (TN), 82

Lane County Archives (OR), **14,290**

Lane County Historical Society Oral History Project (OR), **14,291**

Lane County Pioneer Historical Association (OR), 606

Lane Family, 3,054

Lane, Gertrude Battles [Miss] (1874-1941), **2,436**, 2,694, 5,121, 5,122, 5,123

Lane, Harriet (1830-1903). *See* Johnston, Harriet (Lane) [Mrs. Henry Elliott] (1830-1903)

Lane, Harry (1855-1917), 14,362, **14,599**

Lane, Helen H. (Holmes) (1889-), **7,017**

Lane, John, 16,151

Lane, Laura (1913-), **6,713**

Lane, Layle, **8,098**

Lane, Levi Cooper, 1,608

Lane, Louisa (1820-97). *See* Drew, Louisa (Lane) [Mrs. Henry] Blaine [Mrs. George] Mossop [Mrs. John D.] (1820-97)

Lane, Louisa Rebecca. *See* McCrady, Louisa Rebecca (Lane) [Mrs. Edward, Sr.]

Lane, Margaret, 7,868

Lane, Marie, 8,632

Lane, Martha. *See* Boardman, Martha (Lane) [Mrs. William]

Lane, Martha [Mrs.], 15,382

Lane, Mary A., 11,349

Lane, Mrs. A. S., 12,830

Lane, Mrs. M. M., 12,830

Lane, Mrs. W. J. (1843-1910), 13,683

Lane, Nina. *See* McBride, Nina (Lane) [Mrs. Isaac]

Lane, Nina (1884-1945). *See* Faubion, Nina (Lane) (1884-1945)

Lane, Octavia A. (1814-63). *See* Austin, Octavia A. (Lane) [Mrs. Julius Augustus Caesar] (1814-63)

Lane, Pauline C. (Sampson) [Mrs. Levi Cooper] (1837?-1902), **1,608**

Lane, Rose (Wilder) (1887-), 873, 5,123, 10,000, 15,060

L'Année Philologique (periodical), 14,744

Laney, Lucy (Craft) (1854-1933), 3,280

Laney, Margaret L. [Miss], 3,451

Lang, Anne, 14,619

Lang, Anne M., 14,349

Lang, Benjamin J., 12,457

Lang, Elizabeth, 14,619

Lang, Emma Margaret. *See* Morehouse, Emma Margaret Lang [Mrs. Herbert H.]

Lang Family, **11,655**

Lang, Frances Morse (Burrage) [Mrs. Benjamin Johnson] (1839-1934), **5,936**

Lang, Gertrude (1844-?). *See* Garrecht, Gertrude (Lang) (1844-?)

Lang, Ivan, **4,811**

Lang, Julia C., 2,251

Lang, Margaret Ruthven (1867-1972), **5,937**

Lang, Mary [Mrs. Thomas], 14,619

Lang, Matilda, 9,057

Lang, Rosa Christine, 11,655

Lang, Thomas, 14,619

Langdale, Alice, 14,887

Langdon, Caroline (?-1865?). *See* Eustis, Caroline (Langdon) [Mrs. William] (?-1865?)

Langdon, Elvira (?-1898). *See* Cooper, Elvira (Langdon) (?-1898)

Langdon Family (GA), **3,051**

Langdon, Ida [Miss] (1880-1964), **11,637**

Langdon, Olivia Lewis (1810-90), 11,440

Langdon, P. H., 3,051

Lange, Dorothea. [Mrs. Maynard] Taylor [Mrs. Paul Schuster] Dixon (1895-1965), 466, **607**, 6,641, 12,789

Langerman, Flora (1857-1943). *See* Spiegelberg, Flora (Langerman) [Mrs. Willi] (1857-1943)

Langhorne, Ann, **2,141**

Langhorne, Irene. *See* Gibson, Irene (Langhorne) [Mrs. Charles Dana]

Langhorne, Nancy Witcher (1879-1964). *See* Astor, Nancy Witcher (Langhorne) [Mrs. Waldor F.] (1879-1964)

Langland, Ruth (1889-). *See* Holberg, Ruth (Langland) (1889-)

Langley Porter Neuropsychiatric Institute (CA), 458

Langlie, Arthur B., 17,409

Langlie, Dorothy (Hatch) [Mrs. Theos A.] (1902-?), **9,169**

Langmaid, Mrs. George W., **3,700**

Langman, Ida (Kaplan) [Mrs. Oscar] (1904-), **15,216**

Langmuir, Alexander D., 11,571

Langrishe, Jeanette, 8,924

Langsdorf, Alexander S., 10,168

Langsdorf, Elsie (Hirsch) [Mrs. Alexander S.], 10,168

Langton, Harold W., 16,676

Langtry, Lillie (1853-1929), 3,100, **12,539**, 17,197

Language, 4,344

Language and languages, glossaries, vocabularies, etc., 1,497, 2,838, 17,252

Language of Flowers, The (book), 3,023

Languages, artificial, 2,236

Languages, mixed, **1,493**, 5,410, 13,073

Languages, secret, 11,991

Langworthy, Helen, 1,815

Langworthy, Isaac Pendleton, **12,540**

Langworthy, Sarah (Williams) [Mrs. Isaac Pendleton], 12,540

Langzettel, Marian B. [Mrs.] (1861-1929), **12,241**

Lanham, Nell (1892-). *See* Leonian, Nell (Lanham) (1892-)

Lanier, Bette C., **14,140**

Lanier, Eliza Ann, 9,751

Lanier, Elizabeth, 9,812

Lanier, Martha (1815-81). *See* Sykes, Martha (Lanier) [Mrs. James] (1815-81)

Lanier, Mary Day [Mrs. Sidney], 3,436, **3,539**, **5,730**

Lanier, Mary T. [Mrs.], 13,054

Lanier, Sidney, 3,532, 5,730, 5,815, 13,054

Laning, Clair, 11,843

Lanit, Louise, 861

Lanker, Catherine. *See* Walters, Catherine (Lanker)

Lankford, Charlotte J., **2,142**

Lanman, Mary Judith (Gall) Benjamin [Mrs. James] (1777-1848), 11,945

Lann-Carter Hardware Store (MS), **9,537**

Lanneau, Sophie Stephens (1880-1963), **13,642**

La Nouvelle Communauté Icarienne. *See* Icarian Community (IA, IL)

Lanphear, Eliza. *See* Shattuck, Eliza (Lanphear)

Lanphear, Mary. *See* Cummings, Mary (Lanphear) [Mrs. Frank]

Lanphear, Polly, 9,366

Lansburgh, Therese Weil [Mrs. Richard M.] (1919-), **7,248**

Lansing, Eleanor (Foster), 2,519

Lansing, Helen. *See* Grinnell, Helen (Lansing) [Mrs. George Blake]

Lansing, Robert, 11,857

Lansing, Rosadel (Taft) [Mrs. Frank M.], 8,167

Lansing Woman's Club (MI), **8,281**

Lanslow, Helena (1888?-1969). *See* Knox, Helena (Langslow) [Mrs. Paul] (1888?-1969)

Lansoy, Daniel, 9,642

Lantern in Her Hand (book), 10,491

Lantern slides, 11,714

Lantern Slides (book), 1,425

Lantern, The (newsletter), 929

Lantis, Margaret, 920

Lanyon, Ellen, 12,879

Lapham, Increase, 17,689

Lapham, Josephine, 8,916

La pleine lune, or, Mysterious Visitor (NJ), 11,080

La Porte High School (IN), 4,487

Lapp, Mary Agnes, **9,827**

La Purisima Mission (CA), 990, 991

"Laramie" (television program), 5,240

Laramie Woman's Club (WY), 17,940, **17,987**

Laramie-WPA Nursery School (WY), **17,988**

Laramore-Rader Poetry Group, 2,977

Laramore, Vivian Yeiser, **2,437**

La Raza Unida party (TX), 16,368, 16,376

La Razon Mestiza, 17,619

La Razon Mestiza II (periodical), 17,619

Larceny, 987

Larcom, Lucy (1824-93), 1,224, 1,426, 2,196, 3,927, **5,899**, **5,938**, **6,714**, 6,741, 6,859, 7,044, 7,069, 7,131, 7,171, 7,330, **7,398**, 10,796, 12,762, 14,062, 17,010, 17,053

Larisey, Mary Maxine (1909-), 10,151

Larison, Cornelius Wilson, 10,995

Larison, Mary Jane (Sergeant) [Mrs. Cornelius Wilson] (1837-1917), **10,995**

Larke, Alfred, 11,352

Larke Family (NY), **11,352**

Larke, Janet (1839-?). *See* Hatchard, Janet (Larke) (1839-?)

Larke, Margaret [Mrs. Alfred], 11,352

Larkin, Anna Bridget "Brydie" (Nelson) [Mrs. Martin], **8,471**

Larkin, Sister Mary Benedicta (1900-), 17,868

Larned, Elizabeth Rand (1820-80), 7,644

Larned, Ellen Douglas (1825-1912), 1,901, 1,905, **1,918**

Larned Family (MA, RI), **7,644**

Larned, Ruth, 8,657

Larpenteur, A. L., 13,652

Larrabee, Anna Matilda [Mrs. William], 4,928

Larrabee, Augusta. *See* Dolliver, Augusta (Larrabee) [Mrs. Victor]

Larrabee, Helen. *See* Robbins, Helen (Larrabee) [Mrs. Charles B.]

Larrabee, Julia. *See* Love, Julia (Larrabee) [Mrs. Don]

Larrabee, William (1832-1912), **4,928**

Larry and the Freedom Man (book), 1,750

Larsen, A. Margaret, 11,377

Larsen, Anne Marie (Pedersen) [Mrs. Oluf Christian] (1847-1916), 16,739

Larsen, Esther Louise (1901-), 10,152

Larsen, Gunhild Andrine Jacobsdatter [Mrs. Tobias] (1836-1934), **8,757**

Larsen, Hanna Astrup (1873-1945), 4,321, 8,758

Larsen, Hannah [Miss] (1887-1955), **10,484**

Larsen, Karen [Mrs. Laurence] (?-1871), 4,722

Larsen, Karen (1879-1961), **8,758**, 8,768

Larsen, Kirsten, **17,290**

Larsen, Laur, 8,725, 8,758, 8,768

Larsen, May Hunt, 16,903

Larson, Agnes Mathilda [Miss] (1892-1967), **8,759**, 8,768

Larson, Arthur (1910-), **5,146**

Larson, Hazel (Frieda), 13,616

Larson, Marian Louise (Anderson) [Mrs. Robert M.] (1918-), **4,120**

Larson, Marie (Jacobson) (1888-), **8,703**

Larson, Oluf, **16,739**

Larue Holmes Nature Lovers League, 2,395

Las Vegas Age (NV), 10,781

"Las Vegas, Nevada: Its Romance and History" (ms), 10,781

Las Vegas Review-Journal (NV), 10,781

Las Vegas Sun (NV), 10,781

Las Danzas de Haiti (book), 3,773

LaSalle St. Methodist Episcopal Church (NE), Dorcas Methodist Episcopal Ladies Aid, **10,566**

Lasar, Clementine, **11,321**

Lasca, Josephine. *See* Huneker, Josephine (Lasca)

Lasker Foundation, 11,885

Lasker Foundation Awards for Medical Journalism, 11,862

Lasker, Mary [Mrs. Albert D.] (1900-), 7,282, 7,289, 9,140, **11,885**

Laski, Harold, 13,801

Lasky, Jesse L., 14,366

La Soldedad Mission (CA), 779

"Lassie" (television program), 18,000

Lasswell, Mary (1905-), **16,159**

Last Flight (book), 4,681

Last Gentleman, The (book), 10,848

Last, Hettie Mildred (Leavitt) [Mrs. Charles Henry] (1898-), **16,619**

Last letters before death, 7,606

Last Ninety Days of the War, The (book), 13,598

Last of Summer, The (book), 4,235

Last of Summer, The (drama), 4,235

"Last Strike, The" (ms), 2,205

Lataillade, Cesáreo, 599

Latchstring Out (book), 7,718, 17,553

Latest Will (book), 6,050

Latham, Gray, 10,178

Latham, Maude [Mrs. J. E.], 13,440

Latham, Rose Cecil O'Neill [Mrs. Gray] (1874-). *See* Wilson, Rose Cecil O'Neill [Mrs. Gray] Latham [Mrs. Harry Leon] (1874-)

Lathbury, Mary Artemisia (1841-1913), 1,224

Lathe, Nama, 4,868

l'Athénée Louisianais, 5,418

Lathrop, Addie L., 8,286

Lathrop, Bessie (1854-?), 7,149

Lathrop, Clara (?-1907), 7,140, 7,149

Lathrop, Clarissa Stebbins (1823-1908), 7,149

Lathrop, Elizabeth (1825-1910). *See* Gilbert, Elizabeth (Lathrop) [Mrs. John Henry] (1825-1910)

Lathrop Family (MA), **7,149**

Lathrop, George Terrell, 13,244

Lathrop, Helen (Aldis) [Mrs. Bryan], 3,932

Lathrop, Jane Eliza (1828-1905). *See* Stanford, Jane Eliza (Lathrop) [Mrs. Leland] (1828-1905)

Lathrop, Julia, 8,668

Lathrop, Julia Bryan, 4,197

Lathrop, Julia Clifford (1858-1932), 2,224, 2,439, 2,519, 2,681, 3,910, 4,003, 4,047, 4,101, 4,110, 4,117, 4,141, 4,146, 4,166, 4,330, 5,119, 5,120, 5,122, 6,544, **6,715**, 12,534, 13,376

Lathrop, Mary Florence (1865-1951), **1,723**, **1,782**

Lathrop, Mother Mary Alphonsa (1851-1926), 7,025, 7,383, 17,010

Lathrop, Rose (Hawthorne) [Mrs. George Parsons] (1851-1926). *See* Lathrop, Mother Mary Alphonsa (1851-1926)

Lathrop, Suzanne (1860-1938), 7,149

Lathrop, Virginia Terrell [Mrs. Albert H.] (1900-74), **13,244**

Latienne (pseudonym). *See* Mason, Elizabeth Welch (Backus)

Latimer, Alma (Fellows), 4,929

Latimer, Bette D., 3,290

Latimer Family (IA), **4,929**

Latimer, Frances P. [Miss], **13,889**

Latimer, Lucy, 10,055

Latimer, Mary Lee (1898-), 409, 11,846

Latimer, Mrs., 11,171

Latimer, Rebecca Ann (1835-1930). *See* Felton, Rebecca Ann (Latimer) [Mrs. William Harrell] (1835-1930)

Latimer, William, 13,682

Latimore, Magnolia, 9,289

Latin America
    Americans in, 6,031
    international education, 6,702
    rural education in, 1,842

Latino women, **17,619**

La Tour, Onya, **2,778**

Latourette, Ann Eliza Fisher [Mrs. Lyman Daniel Cornwall] (1839-?), 14,600

Latourette, Freda, 14,600

Latourette, Kenneth, 14,600

Latourette, Lucy Jane Grey [Mrs. Lyman Daniel Cornwall] (1831-64), 14,600

Latourette, Lyman Daniel Cornwall (1825-86), Family (OR), **14,600**

Latourette, Lyman Ezra (1872-1963), 14,600

Latourette, Mrs. L. E., 14,600

Latourette, Nellie Edith, 14,600

Latourette, Ruth, 14,600

La Tourrette, Cornelius Wyckoff (1814-1902), **10,993**

La Tourrette, Margaret [Mrs. Cornelius Wyckoff] (1814-1902), 10,993

Latrobe, John Hazelhurst Boneval, 12,963

Latshaw, Sylvia Louise Arrowood [Mrs. Harry F.], **13,055**
Latter-day Saints. *See* Mormons and Mormonism
Latter-day Saints College, students, 16,727
Latter-day Saints High School (UT), 16,591
Lattimer, Emma [Miss], **3,215**
Lattimer Family (GA), 3,215
Lattimore, Eleanore Holgate, 6,630
Latting, Patience (Sewell) [Mrs. Trimble B.] (1918-), **14,236**
Latvian-Americans, **8,604**
Laub, Lillian, 2,396
Lauderdale, Maggie R., **9,661**
Lauerman, Thomas, 210
Laughinghouse, J. J., 13,489
Laughlin, Anne, **10,074**
Laughlin, Clara Elizabeth (1873-1941), **7,249**
Lauhlin, Estelle C., 10,266
Launder, Bessie (1885-1969). *See* Richards, Bessie (Launder) [Mrs. Edwin R.] (1885-1969)
Laundresses, 1,653, 2,514, **6,869**, 9,467
Laundries, 1,776, 8,500
Laundry, 9,872, 17,418
Laundry industry, 2,684
Laundry workers, 2,684
Laura Riding (book), 16,165
Laurance, Ann. *See* Bolton, Ann (Laurence) [Mrs. George Wright] Hawkes [Mrs. Daniel]
Laurance, Elizabeth, 12,220
Laurance, John, 12,220
Laurance, John McDougall, 12,220
Laurel Garden Club (East Hartford, CT), **1,835**
Laurel High School (MS), 9,724
Laurel Hill Association (book), 7,509
Laurel Hill Association (MA), **7,508**
Lauren, Elizabeth M., **3,216**
Lauren, Thomas C., **3,216**
Laurence, Jessie Hughes (1886-1971), **15,802**
Laurens, Caroline Olivia Ball [Mrs. John B.], **13,056**
Laurens, Henry, 15,041
Laurens, John (1754-82), 2,273
Laurens, John B., 13,056
Laurens, Martha (1759-1811). *See* Ramsay, Martha (Laurens) [Mrs. David] (1759-1811)
Laurensville Female College (SC), students, 15,760
Lauri, Mary (1854-1929). *See* Mattoon, Mary (Laurie) (1854-1929)
Lauritsen, Thomas (1915-73), **1,097**
Lausanne (ship), 305, 14,434, 14,528, 14,604, 17,206
Lautz, Catherine Rowley, 11,349
LaVeau, Marie "Voodoo Queen" (1794-1881), 5,410, 5,501
Lavender, Charles, 16,094
Lavender, Eugenie Etiennette [Mrs. Charles] (1817-98), **16,094**
Lavie, Eugenie, 5,485
Lavin Family (NY), **11,287**
Lavin, Mary (Walsh) (1912-). *See* Scott, Mary (Walsh) Lavin [Mrs. Michael MacDonald] (1912-)
"Lavinia—at Pastoral" (poem), 11,078
La Voy, Sister Mary Gerald, 10,732
Lavrova, Nadia. *See* Shapiro, Nadia Lavrova
Law, 202, 6,440. *See also* Actions and defenses; Courts; Lawyers; Legislation; *and specific types of law, e.g.,* Criminal law
  cases, 393, 689, 986, 1,248, 2,009, 2,504, 2,678, **2,990**, 3,149, 3,224, 3,368, 4,798, 4,809, 4,932, 5,505, 6,401, 6,669, 6,849, 6,973, 6,974, 6,993, 8,098, 8,162, 8,953, 9,033, 9,467, 9,728, 9,972, 9,982, 10,096, 10,153, 10,740, 10,800, 11,450, 11,746, 11,897, 12,682, 12,699, 13,468, 13,537, 14,564, 14,579, 14,592, 14,960, 15,548, **16,090**, 16,373, 16,391, **17,218**, 17,792
  United States, colonial period, **1,915**, 1,919
Law, Annie (1840-89), 1,586
Law enforcement, 138, 1,428, 5,121, 6,483, 9,299, 9,372, 12,505, 15,204
Law firms. *See* Law partnership
Law librarians, 2,865
Law, Mabel, 8,634
Law, Margaret L., 7,578
Law, Mildred [Miss] (?-1975), **5,227**
Law, Nellie, 3,911

Law of Citizenship, The (book), 6,692
Law or War (book), 15,307
Law, Philip, 5,399
Law partnership, 4,408, **5,536**, 8,311, 9,525, 12,755, 14,736
Law reporting, 14,687
Law students, 15,773, 15,895
Law students, wives of, **13,198**
Law teachers, 4,765, **6,260**, **6,262**, **6,282**, 11,956, 17,121
Lawes, John, 15,459
Lawing, Sallie (ca. 1845-ca. 1908). *See* Ivie, Sallie (Lawing) [Mrs. Thomas G.] (ca. 1845-ca. 1908)
Lawler, Elsie, 5,735
Lawler, Katherine [Miss] (?-1938), 1,928
Lawler, Kathleen, 2,160
Lawler, Lucille [Mrs. J. T.], 4,315, 4,445
Lawlor, Glenn Joseph "Jake" (1907-), **10,739**
Lawndale-Crawford Historical Society (IL), **3,929**
Lawner, Lynne, 4,485
Lawrence, A. B., 9,728
Lawrence, Archie, 8,222
Lawrence, Caroline Bowne (1827-?). *See* Bedinger, Caroline Bowne (Lawrence) [Mrs. Henry] (1827-?)
Lawrence College (Appleton, WI)
  faculty, 5,061
  students, 1,566
Lawrence, Cora, 17,291
Lawrence, David Herbert, 1,451, 4,476, 11,153, 11,224, 13,871, 16,163, 16,169, 17,803
Lawrence, David L. (1889-1966), **14,815**
Lawrence, Elizabeth, 6,071
Lawrence, Elizabeth [Mrs.], 3,093
Lawrence, Elizabeth "Morning Star" [Mrs. Harry], 9,467
Lawrence, Elsie, 1,525
Lawrence, Emma, 1,525
Lawrence, Emma. *See* Blackwell, Emma (Lawrence)
Lawrence, Esther Copley, 8,237
Lawrence Family (NY), 11,300
Lawrence, Florence King [Mrs. John Wilson] (1859-1939), **13,052**
Lawrence, Frances, 6,233
Lawrence, Frieda (von Richthofen) [Mrs. David Herbert] (1879-1956). *See* Ravagli, Frieda (von Richthofen) [Mrs. David Herbert] Lawrence [Mrs. Angelino] (1879-1956)
Lawrence, Gertrude, 7,214
Lawrence, Jennie Broadhurst [Mrs. George] (1884-), 10,403
Lawrence, John, 12,615
Lawrence, John Wilson, 13,052
Lawrence, Josephine (1897?-), **6,043**
Lawrence, Love Adams, 7,616
Lawrence Manufacturing Company (MA), **6,198**
Lawrence, Margaret Marsden [Mrs. Charles B.] (1829-1918), 3,861
Lawrence, Margery, 12,413
Lawrence, Matilda Van Riper [Mrs. Archie], **8,222**
Lawrence, Mildred, 2,932
Lawrence, Mrs. Alpheus, 4,834
Lawrence, Nancy (1764-1807). *See* DeWolf, Nancy (Lawrence) [Mrs. James] (1764-1807)
Lawrence, Pauline, 12,363
Lawrence, Rebecca (1891-1976). *See* Lowrie, Rebecca (Lawrence) (1891-1976)
Lawrence, Ruth (Williamson) [Mrs. James C.] (1890-1977), 8,622
Lawrence, S. Abbott, 6,208
Lawrence, Sara Tappan Doolittle (1827-1911). *See* Robinson, Sara Tappan Doolittle (Lawrence) [Mrs. Charles] (1827-1911)
Lawrence, Sarah Appleton [Mrs. Amos A.], 6,208
Lawrence, Susan (1871-1952). *See* Skinner, Susan Lawrence [Mrs. James Edwards] (1871-1952)
Lawrence, Vincent, 14,447
Lawrence, Vivian Shirley (1918-74), **12,031**
Lawrew, Ada (Campbell) [Mrs. Charles L.] (1866-1963), **15,957**
Lawson, Alexander, 14,878

Lawson, Alice. *See* McCullough, Alice (Lawson) [Mrs. John W. S.]
Lawson, Andrew Cowper (1861-1952), **608**
Lawson, Helen E., **14,878**
Lawson, Hilda, 5,469
Lawson, Katherine Leslie. *See* Appleby, Katherine Leslie (Lawson)
Lawson, Laura. *See* Blair, Laura (Lawson) [Mrs. Frank] Ellis [Mrs. Gist]
Lawson, Manya, 17,282
Lawson, Marjorie M., 2,678
Lawson, Mary Lockhart. *See* Birckhead, Mary Lockhart (Lawson)
Lawther, Anna (1872-1957), **4,930**
Lawther, William, **4,930**
Lawton, Annie Bryan, 3,376
Lawton, Eba (Anderson) [Mrs. James Marsland] (1830-1919), 2,174, 12,119
Lawton Family, 11,599
Lawton Family (GA, SC), **3,376**
Lawton, Harry, 1,124
Lawton, Helen Fuller [Mrs. Harry C.] (1895-), **9,170**
Lawton, Isaac, 12,628
Lawton, Sarah Gilbert Anderson [Mrs. Alexander Robert] (1826-?), **3,540**
Lawyer in Petticoats (book), 5,175
Lawyers, 20, 53, **64**, 65, 184, **441**, 644, 658, 689, 828, 844, 1,012, 1,016, **1,031**, **1,103**, **1,144**, **1,183**, **1,184**, **1,186**, **1,188**, **1,189**, **1,308**, 1,413, **1,427**, 1,472, 1,507, **1,611**, 1,654, 1,656, 1,669, **1,702**, **1,723**, **1,733**, **1,782**, 1,874, **1,916**, 1,982, 1,983, **1,984**, 1,995, **2,163**, 2,188, **2,206**, 2,211, **2,242**, **2,251**, **2,255**, **2,264**, **2,267**, 2,270, 2,304, 2,312, 2,325, 2,328, 2,343, **2,345**, **2,347**, **2,377**, **2,384**, 2,432, **2,522**, 2,527, **2,528**, **2,587**, 2,614, **2,651**, 2,678, 2,725, **2,857**, **2,873**, **2,887**, 3,158, **3,218**, **3,323**, 3,436, 3,439, 3,799, **3,852**, **4,060**, **4,076**, **4,269**, **4,290**, 4,347, **4,351**, 4,361, 4,373, 4,408, **4,431**, **4,442**, **4,470**, 4,598, 4,603, 4,643, 4,695, 4,708, 4,732, **4,738**, **4,765**, 4,784, 4,831, **4,854**, 4,855, **4,856**, 4,934, 4,949, 5,058, 5,063, 5,068, 5,104, 5,106, 5,162, 5,174, **5,175**, 5,209, 5,210, 5,253, 5,267, 5,271, 5,276, 5,277, 5,281, 5,306, 5,309, 5,320, 5,321, 5,328, **5,394**, **5,473**, **5,476**, 5,499, 5,555, **5,676**, 5,713, 5,736, **5,741**, **5,774**, **5,776**, **5,791**, **5,794**, **5,800**, 5,822, **5,824**, 5,897, **6,261**, **6,262**, **6,314**, 6,330, 6,340, **6,401**, 6,403, 6,432, 6,467, **6,517**, 6,527, **6,530**, **6,531**, 6,533, 6,547, 6,564, 6,603, **6,620**, **6,666**, **6,668**, **6,720**, **6,728**, **6,750**, **6,761**, **6,789**, **6,819**, **6,829**, **6,849**, 6,886, **6,887**, 6,901, 6,915, **6,944**, **6,996**, **7,174**, **7,216**, **7,242**, **7,262**, **7,266**, **7,540**, **7,544**, **7,603**, **7,606**, **7,615**, 7,631, 7,647, **7,672**, **7,802**, 7,853, **8,086**, **8,300**, **8,333**, 8,821, **8,893**, 8,941, **8,949**, **8,971**, **8,989**, 9,074, 9,077, 9,082, **9,083**, **9,181**, **9,200**, **9,206**, 9,263, 9,367, 9,467, **9,501**, 9,520, **9,525**, 9,544, 9,647, 9,658, 9,711, 9,747, **9,864**, **9,929**, **9,957**, **9,972**, **9,980**, **9,982**, **9,984**, 9,986, 9,996, **10,025**, **10,046**, **10,072**, 10,160, **10,197**, 10,270, 10,315, 10,365, 10,384, **10,440**, **10,495**, **10,658**, **10,752**, **10,832**, 10,844, 10,980, **10,989**, 11,041, 11,092, 11,103, **11,121**, 11,122, **11,123**, **11,129**, 11,134, 11,143, 11,242, 11,354, **11,397**, **11,401**, **11,546**, **11,553**, **11,604**, **11,610**, 11,632, **11,657**, **11,710**, 11,817, 11,913, 11,916, 11,932, **11,943**, **11,950**, 12,069, 12,071, **12,163**, **12,174**, **12,218**, 12,234, 12,320, **12,410**, **12,413**, 12,418, 12,419, 12,434, **12,440**, 12,460, 12,461, 12,467, **12,509**, 12,516, **12,534**, **12,616**, **12,658**, **12,755**, 12,847, 12,963, 13,008, 13,033, 13,176, **13,468**, **13,839**, 13,840, **13,846**, **13,848**, **13,904**, 13,999, **14,007**, 14,077, 14,257, 14,353, 14,454, **14,513**, 14,581, 14,600, 14,648, **14,663**, **14,675**, **14,958**, 14,809, 14,820, 14,824, **14,898**, 14,945, **14,958**, 14,976, 14,982, **15,002**, 15,010, 15,197, **15,256**, 15,358, 15,441, **15,502**, 15,634, **15,671**, **15,686**, **15,695**, 16,029, **16,327**, 16,368, **16,450**, 16,917, 16,971, **17,031**, **17,043**, 17,121, 17,169, 17,241, **17,260**, **17,370**, **17,371**, **17,378**, **17,396**, **17,457**, **17,460**, **17,593**, 17,620, **17,732**, 17,867, 17,899, **17,974**
  directories, 4,076
Lawyers, Afro-American, **2,143**, **6,790**, 10,191, 11,494
Lawyer's Club (Essex County, NJ), 11,092

Lawyers, Jewish, **13,784**
Lay apostolate. *See* Catholic action
Lay, Julia Anna Hartness (1819-78), **12,541**
Lay, Mr. J. L., 3,685
Lay, Mrs. J. L., 3,685
Layman, Emma, 5,063
Layne, Mary Katharine (1844-1920). *See* Brandegee, Mary Katharine (Layne) [Mrs. Townshend Stith] Curran (1844-1920)
Layton Art Gallery (Milwaukee, WI), 17,846
Layton Art School (Milwaukee, WI), 17,846
Lazard, Desirie Marks. [Mrs. Harry] Harris, **13,809**
Lazarre (book), 3,985
Lazarus, Celia Rosenthal [Mrs. Fred, Jr.], 11,859
Lazarus, Eleanor, 11,859
Lazarus, Emma (1849-87), 4,732, 7,185, **7,543**, 9,048, **12,032**
Lazarus, Fred, Jr., 11,859
Lazarus, Fred, III, 11,859
Lazarus, Frieda Langer, 15,317
Lazarus, Irma Mendelson [Mrs. Fred, III], 11,859
Lazarus, Margaret, 11,859
Lazarus, Mrs. Ralph, 11,859
Lazell, Julia Ann (Draper) (1808-41). *See* Pratt, Julia Ann (Draper) Lazell (1808-41)
Lazenby, Mary Elinor (1875-?), 2,397, **15,261**
Lazo, Irma Hortensia (1920-). *See* MacKenna, Irma Hortensia (Lazo) de [Mrs. Harold Ruben] (1920-)
Lea, Alice Denny [Mrs.], 13,549
Lea, Anna M. [Miss] (1844-1930), **12,543**
Lea Family, 12,068
Lea, Margaret Moffette (1819-67). *See* Houston, Margaret Moffette (Lea) [Mrs. Sam] (1819-67)
Lea, Nancy Moffette, 16,089
Leach, Agnes Brown [Mrs. Henry Goddard] (1884-1975), **8,660**
Leach, Blake, 3,764
Leach Family (MS), 9,597
Leach, Martha. *See* Curtis, Martha (Leach) [Mrs. William S.]
Leadbeater Family, 14,852
Leadbeater, Mary (Shackleton) (1758-1826), 14,847
Leadership, **7,207**, 12,711, 12,724, **12,729**
Leagazett (newsletter, ID), 3,697
League for Educational Advancement (TX), 16,344
League for Human Rights, 15,121
League for Independent Political Action, 9,443
League for Industrial Democracy, 13,138
League for Mutual Aid, 6,579, 11,806
League for Planned Parenthood (Washtenaw County, MI), **7,840**
League for Political Education, 6,854
League for the Amnesty of Political Prisoners, 12,703
League Items (newsletter), 6,717
League Link (newsletter), 4,426
League of Adult Minors, 11,596
League of American Pen Women, 250, 720, 3,439, 7,868, 13,464, 15,299
League of Coast Guard Women, 12,931
League of Cook County Clubs (IL), 3,899
League of Greencastle Literary Clubs (IN), **4,568**
League of Militant Poets, 12,064
League of Minnesota Poets, 9,043, **9,171**, 9,527
League of Mothers of United Neighborhood Houses (NY), 8,681
League of Nations, 110, 1,680, 6,507, 6,978, 7,078, 7,221, 7,247, 7,312, 9,656, 10,681, 11,249, 11,250, 11,719, 13,686, 13,993, 15,597, 16,252, 17,328, 17,654
  officials and employees, 6,622, 12,070
League of Nations Association, **2,073**
League of Nations Association of Minnesota, 9,197
League of Nations Committee to Defend America by Aiding the Allies, 5,787
League of Nations, Conference for the Reduction and Limitation of Armaments (1932-34), 2,407
League of Nations, Health Organization, 6,622
League of Nations International Institute of Educational Cinematography (1934), 2,407
League of Nations Non-Partisan Association, **5,787**, 11,136, 14,046, 14,745
League of Nations Opium Committee, 2,433

League of Nations societies, 6,966
League of Nations World Disarmament Conference (1932), 6,771
League of Nurses, 233
League of Nursing, 239
League of Ohio Sportsmen, 14,004
League of Red Cross Societies, 2,233, 10,197
League of Republican Women, 2,114
League of Western Writers, 1,282, 3,697
League of Women for Community Service (MA), **6,716**
League of Women in the Ministry, 4,776
League of Women Shoppers, **7,251**, 11,806, 15,333, 17,691
League of Women Voters, 12, 53, 139, 389, 601, 647, 756, 793, 1,356, 1,618, 1,652, 1,669, 1,837, **1,894**, **2,439**, **2,906**, 2,926, **3,217**, 3,308, 3,324, 3,343, 3,356, 3,743, 3,749, 3,899, 4,045, 4,050, 4,089, 4,121, 4,125, 4,197, 4,440, 4,458, **4,569**, 4,815, 4,823, 4,859, **4,931**, 4,932, 5,024, 5,137, 5,329, **5,548**, **5,630**, 5,837, 6,364, 6,405, 6,431, 6,432, 6,530, 6,544, 6,555, 6,596, 6,630, 6,673, 6,687, 6,700, 6,702, 6,706, **6,717**, **6,718**, **6,719**, 6,723, 6,753, 6,837, 6,848, 6,858, 6,860, 6,872, **6,881**, **6,914**, 6,966, 6,968, 6,972, 6,978, 6,980, 6,981, 7,205, **7,252**, 7,284, 7,698, 7,803, 8,092, **8,242**, 8,287, **8,360**, 8,485, 8,493, 8,556, 8,635, 8,696, 8,697, 8,798, 8,896, 8,913, 8,984, 8,991, 9,140, 9,197, 9,211, 9,522, 9,779, **9,851**, 9,930, 9,934, 9,935, 9,946, 9,950, 9,956, 9,958, 9,978, 9,984, 9,995, 10,013, 10,032, 10,050, 10,171, **10,340**, 10,679, **10,765**, 11,018, 11,064, 11,239, 11,240, 11,445, 11,806, 11,865, **11,886**, 11,916, 11,920, **12,056**, **12,057**, **12,058**, 12,505, 12,870, 12,920, 13,176, 13,189, 13,274, **13,510**, 13,604, **13,676**, **13,716**, **13,731**, **13,732**, **13,750**, **14,003**, 14,016, 14,042, 14,052, 14,133, 14,144, 14,671, 15,011, **15,033**, 15,304, 15,381, 15,706, **15,733**, **15,827**, **15,862**, 15,868, 15,997, 16,015, 16,235, 16,239, 16,240, 16,259, 16,260, 16,265, **16,276**, 16,293, **16,422**, 16,789, **17,042**, **17,087**, **17,088**, 17,091, 17,104, 17,246, **17,257**, **17,292**, 17,300, 17,304, 17,314, 17,326, 17,341, 17,348, **17,524**, 17,654, 18,013. *See also* National League of Women Voters
League of Women Voters (CA), 453, 720, **1,316**
League of Women Voters (Berkeley, CA), **610**
League of Women Voters (San Francisco, CA), 485, **1,317**
League of Women Voters (Colorado Springs, CO), **1,682**
League of Women Voters (ID), **3,702**, 3,703
League of Women Voters (Boise, ID), **3,701**
League of Women Voters (Idaho Falls, ID), **3,703**
League of Women Voters (IL), 4,165
League of Women Voters (Champaign County, IL), **4,427**
League of Women Voters (Charleston, IL), **4,426**
League of Women Voters (Chicago, IL), **4,121**
League of Women Voters (McLean County, IL), 3,745
League of Women Voters (Oak Park-River Forest, IL), **4,122**
League of Women Voters (Hobart, IN), **4,593**
League of Women Voters (IA), **5,005**
League of Women Voters (KS), **5,192**
League of Women Voters (Frankfort, KY), 5,307
League of Women Voters (ME), **5,587**
League of Women Voters (Baltimore, MD), 5,828, **5,839**
League of Women Voters (Northampton, MA), **7,253**
League of Women Voters (Ann Arbor, MI), **7,841**
League of Women Voters (Monroe, MI), **7,842**
League of Women Voters (MN), 6,942, **9,231**
League of Women Voters (Duluth, MN), **8,435**
League of Women Voters (MO), 9,918, **10,199**, **10,200**
League of Women Voters (Oxford, MS), **9,818**
League of Women Voters (NH), **10,837**
League of Women Voters (New Brunswick, NJ), **10,996**
League of Women Voters (Brookhaven South, NY), **12,872**
League of Women Voters (Erie County, NY), 11,553

League of Women Voters (North Brookhaven, NY), **12,873**
League of Women Voters (Riverhead, Southold, NY), **12,874**
League of Women Voters (Chapel Hill, NC), **13,058**
League of Women Voters (Cleveland, OH), **13,939**
League of Women Voters (East Cleveland, OH), **13,940**
League of Women Voters (Metropolitan Columbus, OH), **14,002**
League of Women Voters (Dayton, OH), **14,050**
League of Women Voters (Oberlin, OH), **14,125**
League of Women Voters (Youngstown, OH), **14,106**
League of Women Voters (Swarthmore, PA), **15,204**
League of Women Voters (York County, PA), **15,359**
League of Women Voters (College Station, TX), **16,191**
League of Women Voters (Galveston, TX), **16,217**
League of Women Voters (VA), 17,077
League of Women Voters (Charlottesville and Albemarle, VA), **17,061**
League of Women Voters (Oshkosh, WI), **17,702**
League of Women Voters, Overseas Educational Fund, 6,630, 6,702, 6,723, 6,914, 10,199
League of Women Voters of Hawaii, **3,625**
League of Women Voters of Honolulu (HI). *See* American Association of University Women (HI)
League to Enforce Peace, 1,563
League Women's Club, 13,670
Leagueline (newsletter), 15,359
Leahy, Anna C. (1888-1977), **15,999**, **16,000**
Leahy, Kathleen M., **6,144**, 17,291
Leake, Chauncey Depew (1896-), 1,372, 1,376, 1,378
Leake, Phebe, 14,618
Leakes, Adeline, 15,537
Leakey, Mary D., 2,863
Leakin, Annie Middleton (1850?-1942). *See* Sioussat, Annie Middleton (Leakin) [Mrs. Albert W.] (1850?-1942)
Leal, Ebenezah Maxwell, 11,717
Leal Family, 11,717
Leal, Lucy Buell (King) [Mrs. Ebenezah Maxwell]. *See* Shankland, Lucy Buell (King) [Mrs. Ebenezah Maxwell] Leal [Mrs. William Henry]
Leal, Mary Ayres, 11,717
Lealtad, Catherine Deaver, 2,502, 9,295
Leaming, Sarah, 12,034
Leaphart, Benjamin F. Perry, 15,610
Leaphart Family (SC), **15,610**
Leaphart, W. A., 15,596
Lear, Fanny Bassett [Mrs. George Augustine] Washington [Mrs. Tobias], 5,718
Lear, Henrietta S. Sidney, 9,438
Lear, Susanna (1770?-?). *See* Duncan, Susanna (Lear) [Mrs. James] (1770?-?)
Learned Family (MA, RI), 7,644
Learned societies, 6,328, **11,810**, 16,277
Learned, Maria, 2,346
Learned, Marion D., 2,411
Learning disabilities, 11,830
Learning to Know Yourself Series (books), 14,463
Leary, Eliza (Ferry) [Mrs. John] (ca. 1851-1936), **17,293**
Leary, Elizabeth, 11,361
Leary, Ellen, 2,722
Leary, John, 17,293
Leary, Margaret, 3,218
Leary, Mary Ellen, 611
Leas, Nanon Fay. *See* Worcester, Nanon Fay (Leas) [Mrs. Dean Conant]
Lease, Mary Elizabeth (Clyens) [Mrs. Charles L.] (1850-1933), 5,239, 9,048
Lease, Mary Ellen (1850-1933). *See* Lease, Mary Elizabeth (Clyens) [Mrs. Charles L.] (1850-1933)
Leatham, Margaret, **16,944**
Leatham, Mary Evans (Williams) (1851-?), 16,968
Leathers Family (MN), **8,472**
Leathers, Mrs. Harry, 8,472
Leavens, Ella Lamport [Mrs. Robert], **10,324**
Leavens, Robert, 10,324
"Leaves from a war prisoner's devotional diary," 4,518
Leaves of Healing, 4,461

Leavitt, Abbie S. *See* Cairns, Abbie S. Leavitt [Mrs. George W.]

Leavitt Family, 2,733

Leavitt, Henrietta Swan (1868-1921), 6,285

Leavitt, Hettie Mildred (1898-). *See* Last, Hettie Mildred (Leavitt) [Mrs. Charles Henry] (1898-)

Leavitt, Juanita (ca. 1900-). *See* Brooks, Juanita (Leavitt) [Mrs. L. Ernest] Pulsipher [Mrs. William] (ca. 1900-)

Leavitt, Mary, 11,440

Leavitt, Mary Greenleaf (Clement) [Mrs. Thomas Hooker] (1830-1912), 1,224

Leavitt, Mary Luella Abbott [Mrs. Thomas Dudley, Sr.], **10,674**

Leavitt, Mrs. Louis, 4,053

Leavitt, Sarah, 4,112

Leavitt, Sarah Studevant (1798-), **16,900**

Lebanon Plantation (NC), 13,602

LeBaron, Ellice Marie (Bentley) [Mrs. William Farland] (1887-), **16,740**

LeBaron, Marie Helen (Steinacher) [Mrs. Benjamin F.] (1885-), **16,831**

LeBaron, Mary Eva (1867-1958). *See* Bay, Mary Eva (LeBaron) [Mrs. James Willard] (1867-1958)

Le Beau, Emily Beaubien, 3,891

LeBergerie (residence, NY), 12,763

Le Bien Etre du Blesse, **15,385**

LeClerq, Carlotta, 3,100

Le Conte, Adelaide Elizabeth (Graham) [Mrs. Joseph Nisbet], 10,040

Leconte, Anna [Mrs.], 14,802

LeConte, Caroline Eaton (1863-1945), 427, 609

Le Conte, Caroline Elizabeth (Nisbet) [Mrs. Joseph] (ca. 1828-1915), 609

LeConte, Emma. *See* Furman, Emma LeConte [Mrs. Farish Carter]

LeConte, Emma Florence, **13,465**

Le Conte Family (CA), 427, **609**

LeConte Family (GA), **3,541**, 13,144

LeConte Family (PA), **14,892**

Le Conte, Helen Malcolm (1904-), 609

Le Conte, Helen Marion (Gompertz) [Mrs. Joseph Nisbet] (1865-1924), 609, 710

LeConte, John Lawrence (1825-83), 14,892

Le Conte, Joseph (1823-1901), 609, 13,057, 13,144

Le Conte, Joseph Nisbet, 609

Lecturers, 54, 825, 1,040, 1,224, **1,436**, 1,461, **1,499, 1,509**, 1,840, **1,952**, 2,093, **2,119, 2,256, 2,301, 2,339**, 2,420, **2,452**, 2,484, **2,497, 2,547**, 2,655, 3,800, 3,969, 3,996, **4,061**, 4,630, **4,647**, 4,732, 5,736, 5,907, **5,924, 5,939**, 5,956, **5,988, 6,004, 6,011, 6,014, 6,034**, 6,049, 6,065, **6,390, 6,512, 6,522**, 6,573, 6,731, 6,771, **6,823, 6,854, 6,890**, 6,978, 7,146, **7,217, 7,545, 7,629**, 7,648, 7,652, 7,677, **7,941**, 9,077, 9,268, **10,029, 10,155, 10,159, 10,162, 10,863**, 10,873, **10,974**, 11,167, **11,233, 11,578, 11,812, 11,946, 12,446, 12,491**, 12,516, **12,524, 12,525, 12,624, 12,730**, 12,837, **14,223, 14,378**, 14,392, 14,455, **14,630, 14,730**, 15,312, **15,382**, 15,445, 16,438, **16,563, 16,770, 17,583, 17,589**

Lecturers, Afro-American, **2,154**, 5,907

Lecturers, deaf-blind, **2,108**

Lectures and lecturing, 8,070, **11,900, 12,780, 15,197**

Lectures on Cooking (pamphlet), 4,828

Ledbetter, Elizabeth, **13,135**

Ledbetter, Huddie "Leadbelly," 5,552

Ledbetter, Lena Dancy [Mrs.], **16,096**

Lederer, Anna Marie. *See* Hoffman, Anna Marie (Lederer) [Mrs. Julius] Rosenberg [Mrs. Paul]

Lederer, Esther, 4,131

Ledford, Mary Elizabeth Warren, 317

Ledger (IA), 4,816

LeDuc, Alice Sumner (1868-1962), 9,049, 9,173

LeDuc Family (MN), 9,049

LeDuc, Mary (1908-). *See* O'Neill, Mary (LeDuc) (1908-)

LeDuc, William Gates, Family (MN), 9,049, **9,172, 9,173**

Lee, Amarilla (Hamblin) (1884-?), **16,901**

Lee, Amy Freeman, **16,277**

Lee, Ann. Ann Lees. [Mrs. Abraham Standerin].

Mother Ann Lee (1736-84), 7,047, 12,620, 13,955

Lee, Ann Hill Carter [Mrs. Henry], 2,443

Lee, Anna Green [Mrs. Philander], **14,601**

Lee, Anna Maria (Pittman) [Mrs. Jason], 725

Lee, Arthur T., 14,603

Lee, Betty, 10,191

Lee, Bertha Stringer [Mrs.] (1873-1937), **1,318**

Lee, Borghild Lundberg. Margarette Borghild Lundberg (1892-), **14,406**

Lee, Catherine Newton [Mrs. William Little]. *See* Youmans, Catherine Newton [Mrs. William Little] Lee [Mrs. Edward Livingston]

Lee, Charles, 14,603

Lee, Cornelia, **17,673**

Lee, Daniel (1806-95), **14,602**

Lee, Dorothy (McCullough) [Mrs. W. Scott] (1901-), **6,720**, 11,349

Lee, Edmund Trumbull, 14,603

Lee, Eleanor [Miss] (1896-1967), **6,721**

Lee, Elinor, 11,493

Lee, Eliza (Buckminister) [Mrs. R. B.] (ca. 1788-1864), 850, 2,468

Lee, Elizabeth (Blair) [Mrs. Samuel Phillips], 11,154

Lee, Elizabeth Collins [Mrs. Richard Bland], 2,443, 17,673

Lee, Elizabeth Payson Howe [Mrs. William B.], 14,603

Lee, Elsie Fullerton (1878-1937). *See* Zimmerman, Elsie Fullerton (Lee) [Mrs. Paul Irwin] (1878-1937)

Lee, Ester Chan, 9,986

Lee Family, **2,441**

Lee Family, 4,942

Lee Family, **11,154**

Lee Family, 5,359

Lee Family (MS), 3,379

Lee Family (VA), **2,443**, 17,081

Lee, Fitzhugh, 9,678

Lee, Florence, 14,603

Lee, Frances (Patterson), 9,809

Lee, Francis Lightfoot, 15,041

Lee, Francis Wilson, 6,549

Lee, George H., Family (OR), **14,603**

Lee, George Hewit (1859-1951), 14,603

Lee, Harold B., 16,780

Lee, Harold N., 14,603

Lee, Hector H., **1,128**

Lee, Helen (1925-). *See* Goates, Helen (Lee) (1925-)

Lee, Helen K., 6,815

Lee in the Mountains and Other Poems (book), 15,929

Lee, Jason, 14,528, 14,602

Lee, Jennette Perry (1860-1951), 7,158

Lee, John, 7,645

Lee, John Doyle, 16,741

Lee, John E., 16,657

Lee, Leila (Moss) [Mrs. Horace J.] Grant [Mrs. John E.] (1895-1962). *See* Eldredge, Leila (Moss) [Mrs. Horace J.] Grant [Mrs. John E.] Lee [Mrs. Clarence] (1895-1962)

Lee, Lewis Earle, 14,603

Lee, Lila, 11,907

Lee, Louisa, 14,603

Lee, Lucinda (1847-1925). *See* Dalton, Lucinda (Lee) [Mrs. Charles W.] (1847-1925)

Lee, Lucinda "Sukie," **3,401**

Lee, Lucy Chaplin, 15,531

Lee, Manning de Villeneuve (1894-), **14,407**

Lee, Margaret, 4,743

Lee, Margaret, 2,836

Lee, Margaret. *See* Crofts, Margaret (Lee) [Mrs. F. S.]

Lee, Margaret (1821-1900). *See* Jones, Margaret (Lee) [Mrs. John Pidding] (1821-1900)

Lee, Maria T. (Ware), 14,602

Lee, Marston, 14,603

Lee, Martha, **7,399**

Lee, Mary, 2,441

Lee, Mary. *See* Tremain, Mary (Lee)

Lee, Mary (1891-), **6,722**

Lee, Mary Anna Randolph (Custis) [Mrs. Robert

Edward] (1806-73), 2,443, **2,445**, 3,552, 5,350, 17,081

Lee, Mary Custis (1834-?), 9,057

Lee, Mary E. (Brown) (1869-1952), **14,004**

Lee, Mary Elizabeth, 2,441

Lee, Mary Jane Charlton (Greenhow) [Mrs. Hugh Holmes] (1819-?), **2,444**

Lee, Mildred, 13,344

Lee, Minnie Mary. Julia Amanda (Sargent) [Mrs. William Henry] Wood (1825-1903), 8,921

Lee, Mother Ann (1736-84). *See* Lee, Ann. Ann Lees. [Mrs. Abraham Standerin]. Mother Ann Lee (1736-84)

Lee, Mrs. C. C., 13,343

Lee, Nattie Anna (Cooke) [Mrs. George Hewit], 14,603

Lee, Percy Maxim [Mrs. John Glessner] (1906-), **6,723, 11,886**

Lee, Portia, **17,673**

Lee, Rachel Andora (Woolsey) [Mrs. John Doyle] (1825-1912), **16,741**

Lee, Rebecca, 7,645

Lee, Richard Bland, 17,673

Lee, Robert Edward, 2,445, 3,552, 5,513, 13,344, 15,502, 15,608, 17,081

Lee, Ruth, 14,603

Lee, Samuel Phillips (1812-97), 11,154

Lee, Sarah (?-1850), **7,645**

Lee, Sirkka Tuomi (1920-), 5,829

Lee Street Church Ladies Charitable Society (Cambridge, MA), **6,254**

Lee Street Unitarian Church (Cambridge, MA), 6,254

Lee, Susan Palfrey, 2,441

Lee, Susan (Palfrey) [Mrs. William] (?-1834), 2,441

Lee, Vernon (pseudonym). *See* Paget, Violet (1856-1935)

Lee, Wallace Howe, 14,603

Lee, Walter C., 14,603

Lee, William (1770-?), 2,441

Lee, William A. (1778-1848), **15,034**

Lee, William B., 14,603

Lee, William Little, 12,350

Leech, Ann (Getz) [Mrs. Andrew] (ca. 1800-?). *See* Lake, Ann (Getz) [Mrs. Edward] Hutchinson [Mrs. Andrew] Leech (ca. 1800-?)

Leech, Faith (Harris) [Mrs. Harry], 3,028

Leech Lake Indian Reservation (MN), 9,009, 9,042

Leech, Margaret K., **14,084**

Leekley, Richard, **9,174**

Leeper, Mary E. (1887-1965), **2,095**

Lees, Ann (1736-84). *See* Lee, Ann. Ann Lees. [Mrs. Abraham Standerin]. Mother Ann Lee (1736-84)

Lees Family (CA), 612

Lees, Ella (1859-?). *See* Leigh, Ella (Lees) (1859-?)

Lees, Hannah (pseudonym). *See* Fetter, Elizabeth Head (1904-72)

Lees, Isaiah W., 612

Lees, Jane A. (Fisher) [Mrs. Isaiah W.] (1829-97), 612

Lees Junior College (Jackson, KY), 5,402, 17,063

Leese, Jacob, 798

Leese, Rosalia (Vallejo) [Mrs. Jacob], 798

Leeson, Bell, 1,905

LeFetra, Elizabeth Ryles [Miss], **10,997**

LeFevre, Eva J. [Mrs. Owen E.] (1851-1948), **1,783**

Le Fevre Family (CO), 1,698

Le Fevre, Frederica (1884-1963). *See* Bellamy, Frederica (Le Fevre) [Mrs. Harry E.] (1884-1963)

LeFevre, Owen E., 1,783

LeFlore, Basil, 14,214

LeFlore, Carrie, **14,214**

Lefroy, Helena Trench (1878-1962) *See* Caperton, Helena Trench (Lefroy) [Mrs. Clifford Randolph] (1878-1962)

Lefse, 8,754

Left and right (politics). *See* Right and left (politics)

Left Hand Is the Dreamer, The (book), 16,167

Legacies, 7,524, 9,634, 14,020

Legal Action Group (OH), 14,021

Legal aid, 3,903, 9,492, 11,931, 15,176

Legal Aid Bureau (Chicago, IL), 4,085

Legal aid societies, 4,085, **4,144, 12,703**

Legal assistance to prisoners, **17,617**
Legal correspondence, 1,957
Legal documents (general), 3,414, **3,871**, 7,608, 7,611, 7,636, 7,647, **7,653**, 7,660, 7,661, 7,664, 11,318, **11,325**, 11,330, 13,044, 15,438, **15,458**, 15,486, **15,487**, **15,836**, 17,033. *See also* Legal instruments
Legal instruments (used for specific legal acts or agreements), 333, 6,502, **7,076**, 9,345, 10,452, **15,546**
Legal secretaries, **645**, **5,780**, **14,188**, 14,687
Legal Status of Women in the United States, January 1, 1938 (bulletin), 2,703
Le Gallienne, Eva (1899-), 2,625, 3,994, **7,250**, 7,310, 12,367
Le Gallienne, Richard, 16,174
Legare, Anna Goodwyn [Mrs.], 15,597
Legare, Eliza, 12,317
Legend (periodical), 2,936
"Legend of the Yellow Jasmine, A" (poem), 15,741
Legends, 1,750, 3,628, 4,923, 8,921, 10,702
Legends, Celtic, 1,509
Legends of the South (book), 15,952
Legg, Mary, **11,638**
Legge, Alexander, 3,956
Legge, Katherine [Mrs. Alexander] (?-1924), 3,956
Leggroan Family, 16,780
Legion of Merit medal, 2,091
Legislation, **7,287**, 7,323, 8,922, 8,984, 9,155, 9,327, 10,644, 11,486, 12,507, 12,597, 13,473, 17,200. *See also* Bills, legislative; Governmental investigations; Law; Parliamentary practice
Legislative bodies, **2,697**, 3,858, **5,565**, **9,477**, **10,325**, **10,345**, 10,477, 13,322, 13,990, 14,537, **15,543**, 15,617
   committees, 8,456, **9,477**, 9,523, 10,194, 13,322, 17,453
   officials and employees, 14,456
   voting, **11,203**
Legislative Council of Michigan Women, 7,698, 7,803
Legislative councils, 1,406, 7,698, 7,803, 10,280, 17,281
Legislative hearings, 1,141, 17,453
Legislative Ladies League (IA), 4,910
Legislative Voters League of Illinois, 3,798
Legislators, 60, 61, 76, **157**, 178, 184, 196, **453**, 540, 592, 699, 994, 1,010, 1,013, 1,405, 1,413, 1,424, 1,426, 1,430, 1,663, 1,670, 1,673, 1,702, **1,763**, 2,086, 2,235, 2,328, 2,342, **2,925**, 2,931, 3,008, **3,093**, 3,622, 3,671, 3,749, **3,749**, 3,764, 4,106, 4,149, **4,183**, 4,307, 4,347, **4,349**, 4,361, 4,442, 4,468, **4,621**, 4,789, 4,832, **4,910**, 4,929, 4,951, **4,964**, **5,239**, **5,313**, **5,376**, 5,394, **5,641**, 5,736, **5,754**, 5,828, 6,381, 6,573, 6,611, 6,615, 6,720, 6,846, 6,858, 6,901, 7,615, 7,618, 7,625, 8,070, **8,078**, **8,114**, 8,117, **8,119**, 8,171, **8,287**, 8,333, **8,688**, 8,719, 8,846, 8,896, 8,941, 8,971, 9,034, 9,035, 9,036, 9,048, 9,052, 9,076, **9,196**, 9,240, **9,268**, 9,287, 9,367, 9,371, 9,467, 9,511, **9,522**, **9,523**, **9,525**, 9,647, 9,656, 9,697, 9,734, 9,779, 9,804, 9,806, **9,930**, **9,956**, 10,047, 10,168, 10,170, **10,194**, 10,316, 10,345, 10,448, 10,513, 10,548, 10,678, **10,736**, 10,737, 10,738, 11,144, 11,213, 11,217, 11,534, **11,546**, **11,600**, **11,610**, **11,657**, **11,729**, 11,750, 11,928, 11,932, 12,069, 12,153, 12,170, 12,199, 12,209, 12,434, **12,910**, 13,135, 13,168, 13,210, 13,249, 13,282, 13,322, 13,344, 13,468, 13,473, 13,533, **13,564**, 13,728, 13,730, 13,935, 14,015, 14,062, 14,197, **14,318**, 14,392, 14,429, 14,713, 14,763, 15,000, 15,373, 15,440, 15,617, **15,766**, **15,805**, 15,914, **15,976**, 15,988, 16,004, 16,029, **16,214**, 16,225, **16,231**, 16,327, 16,396, 16,473, **16,498**, 16,536, 16,748, 16,880, 16,946, 17,141, **17,201**, 17,254, 17,260, 17,264, 17,268, **17,300**, 17,311, 17,347, 17,356, 17,460, 17,463, 17,616, **17,728**, 17,862, **17,889**, 17,909, **17,940**. *See also* Congressmen; Congresswomen; Senators, United States
Legislators, Afro-American, **2,133**, 2,940, 3,293, 5,473, 10,191
Legitimation of children, 6,259
Le Grand, Ann England, **16,095**
LeGuin, Ursula Kroeber [Mrs. Charles], 14,712
LeHand, Marguerite, 11,853

Lehman, Babette Newgass, 12,069
Lehman, Edith Altschul [Mrs. Herbert H.] (?-1976), 12,069, 12,071
Lehman, Emma Augusta (1841-1922), **13,632**
Lehman, Hartley, 11,868
Lehman, Herbert H. (1878-1963), 6,766, 11,576, **11,875**, **12,069**, 12,521
Lehmann, John, 16,165, 16,172
Lehmann, Lilli (1848-1929), 2,663
Lehmann, Lotte (1888-1976), 831, **1,527**, 6,452, 12,013
Lehmann, Thelma, **17,294**
Lehmer Family (PA), **14,808**
Lehmer, Jacob F. (?-1914), 14,808
Lehmer, Sarah A. (Ditmer) [Mrs. Jacob F.], 14,808
Lehow, Eloise Sargent, 1,803
Leibman, Aline (Meyer), 945
Leicester Academy (MA), 7,601, **7,646**
Leicester Academy (MA), Alumni Association, 7,646
Leider, Mrs., 12,439
Leif Ericson, Explorer (book), 5,041
Leif Erikson Day, 8,777
Leif Erikson League (Oakland, CA), **613**
Leifer, Ann, 15,332
Leifer, Mary E., **15,360**
Leigh, Ada (Bryant) [Mrs. Francis Webster], **16,423**
Leigh, Ella (Berry) [Mrs. William H.] (1879-), **16,424**
Leigh, Ella (Lees) (1859-?), 612
Leigh, Frances (Butler) [Mrs. James Wentworth] (1838-1910), 2,643, 15,117
Leigh, Janet. Jeannette Reames, 1,634, 17,943
Leigh, Nancy, 1,533
Leigh, Vivien (1913-67), 2,360
Leighly, John Barger, **614**
Leighly, Katherine (Edmonds) [Mrs. John Barger] (1904-56), 614
Leighton, Alice Percy [Mrs. Alton Winslow] (1871-1920), **11,674**
Leighton, Alton Winslow, 11,674
Leighton, Clare [Miss] (1901-), 2,736, **2,780**
Leighton, Dorothea Cross (1908-), 2,840, **2,841**
Leighton, Margaret (Carver) (1896-), **14,408**
Leighty, Belle, 5,177
Leighty, Osa Helen (1894-1953). *See* Johnson, Osa Helen (Leighty) [Mrs. Martin] (1894-1953)
Leila Curtis and Company (San Francisco, CA), 1,298
Leinsdorf, Erich, 12,013
Leiper, Jane Duval. *See* Kane, Jane Duval (Leiper)
Leiper, Mary (Taylor) (1885-1973). *See* Moore, Mary (Taylor) Leiper (1885-1973)
Leipzig Conservatorium of Music (German), alumnae, 8,611
Leishman, Anne Eliza (Wyatt) [Mrs. Franklin L.] Gunnell [Mrs. Robert Adamson], **16,742**
Leishman, Robert Adamson, 16,742
Leisler, Jacob, 11,492
Leister, Martha Coplin [Mrs.], 14,931
Leisure, 8,103, 12,738
LeJau, Ann. *See* Huger, Ann (LeJau) [Mrs. Daniel]
LeJau Family (SC), 15,493
LeJau, Francis, I, 15,493
LeJau, Francis, II, 15,493
Le Jazz Hot, 3,773
Lekberg, Barbara, 4,868
Leland, Bernice, **14,409**
Leland, Charles Godfrey, 2,520
Leland, Ellen M. (Gifford) [Mrs. Luther E.], 2,446
Leland Family, 12,867
Leland, Gertrude (Dennis) [Mrs. Waldo Gifford], 2,446
Leland, Mabel Johnson, 8,735, 8,737
Leland, Marine, 7,158
Leland, Minerva Eliza (1859-1926), 2,446, **6,724**
Leland, Mrs., 2,238
Leland, Mrs. Charles F., 2,520
Leland, Waldo Gifford (1879-1966), **2,446**
Leliepre, Madeleine, 2,224
Le Maire, Eleanor (1897-1970), **2,779**
Lemberg, Lauri (1887-1965), **9,175**
Lemberg, Rose, 9,175
Lemberg, Sigrid [Mrs. Lauri], 9,175
Lemcke, Mary Dunbar, 955

Lemen, Elizabeth (1869-1956). *See* Wentz, Elizabeth (Lemen) [Mrs. George H.] (1869-1956)
LeMennier, Josephine Louise (1816-1901). *See* Newcomb, Josephine Louise (LeMennier) [Mrs. Warren] (1816-1901)
Lemmon, Amelia Levy (1930-), 938
Lemmon, Clarence Eugene (1888-1963), **10,001**
Lemmon, Constance Harlan [Mrs. Clarence Eugene] (1887-1972), **10,002**
Lemmon, Hedley F., 10,703
Lemmon, Jack, 12,367
Le Monnier, Josephine Louise (1816-1901). *See* Newcomb, Josephine Louise (LeMennier) [Mrs. Warren] (1816-1901)
Lemoyne, Hannah (DeAngelis) (1802-90). *See* Wells, Hannah (DeAngelis) Lemoyne [Mrs. Chester] (1802-90)
LeMoyne-Owen College (TN), 5,474
Le Moyne, Sarah Cowell, **1,315**
Lemurian (language), 2,236
Lena Dahl Middle School (Sinyang, China), 8,883
Lenawee County Federation of Women's Clubs (MI), **7,696**
L'Enfant, Pierre Charles, 2,425
Lengenegger, Joyce, **16,368**
Lenglen, Suzanne, 15,371, 15,935
Lenin School (Moscow, USSR), students, 17,635
Lennart, Isobel (1915-71), 949, **17,989**
Lennemann, Neta (Oblinger), 10,516
Lenniger, August, 14,410
Lenniger Literary Agency (NY), 14,315, 14,374, 14,385, 14,395, 14,400, **14,410**, 14,417, 14,448, 14,453, 14,464, 14,465
Lennox, Charlotte, 7,310
Lenoir, Dorothy [Miss], **9,662**, 9,744
Lenoir, Evelina [Mrs. Walter R.], 9,883
Lenoir Family (MO), **9,883**
Lenoir Home (MO), 9,981
Lenoir, Minnie. *See* Holmes, Minnie (Lenoir)
Lenoir, Mrs. Robert L., **9,663**
Lenoir, Nannie Jane Walker [Mrs.], 10,056
LeNoire, Rosetta, 3,290
Lenon, Vivion Mercer (1900-). *See* Brewer, Vivion Mercer (Lenon) [Mrs. Joe Robinson] (1900-)
Lenout, Nellie [Mrs. Issac], 8,721
Lenroot, I., 12,575
Lenroot, Katharine Frederica (1891-), 2,693, 5,120, 8,678, 11,916, **12,033**
Lens, Shirley [Mrs. Sidney], 4,168
Lenski, Lois. [Mrs. Arthur] Covey (1893-1974), **615**, **2,938**, **4,306**, 11,368, 12,903, 13,252, 14,215, 17,990
Lente, Mrs. Louis, 16,866
Lentilhon, Eliza Leaycraft (Smith) [Mrs. Antoine] (1802-93), **12,313**
Lenya, Lotte, 12,367
Leo XIII, Pope, 9,695
Leoline, 7,047
Leonard, Abiel (1796-1863), **9,884**, **10,003**
Leonard, Ada. *See* Hawkes, Ada (Leonard) [Mrs. C. S.]
Leonard, Alexander Thomas, **616**
Leonard, Baird. *See* Zogbaum, Leola Baird (Leonard) [Mrs. Harry St. Clair] (1888?-1941)
Leonard, Camilla. *See* Edwards, Camilla (Leonard) [Mrs. Walter]
Leonard, Camilla Davis [Mrs. William H.], 12,242
Leonard Covello Award, 9,497
Leonard, Edgar Cotrell, 11,263
Leonard, Elizabeth F. (Wilson) [Mrs. Edgar Cotrell] (1862-?), **11,263**
Leonard, Ezra, 7,032
Leonard Family (MA), 7,014
Leonard, George, 3,351
Leonard, Helen Louise (1861-1922). *See* Russell, Lillian. Helen Louise (Leonard). [Mrs. Henry] Braham [Mrs. Edward] Solomon [Mrs. John Haley Augustin] Chatterton [Mrs. Alexander Pillock] Moore (1861-1922)
Leonard, Jane Preston [Mrs. William Huntington], 9,176
Leonard, Leola Baird (1888?-1941). *See* Zogbaum, Leola Baird (Leonard) [Mrs. Harry St. Clair] (1888?-1941)

Leonard, Lillian (1861-1922). *See* Russell, Lillian.
Helen Louise (Leonard). [Mrs. Henry] Braham
[Mrs. Edward] Solomon [Mrs. John Haley
Augustin] Chatterton [Mrs. Alexander Pillock]
Moore (1861-1922)

Leonard, Maria (1880-), **4,390**

Leonard, Maria Maud (1883-1938). *See* Walker,
Maria Maud (Leonard) [Mrs. Rex Irving]
McCreery [Mrs. James Walter] (1883-1938)

Leonard, Mary. *See* Everett, Mary (Leonard) [Mrs.
Horace]

Leonard, Mrs. Ira, **8,249**

Leonard, Nancy [Mrs. Ezra], 7,032

Leonard, Priscilla (pseudonym). *See* Bissell, Emily
Perkins [Miss] (1868-1948)

Leonard, Robert Woodward (1843-1929), **12,242**

Leonard, Vernera, 3,794

Leonard, William Edwin (1855-1935), 9,176

Leonard, William Huntington (1825-1907), Family
(MN), **9,176**

Leone, Lucile Petry (1902-), 6,138, **6,145**

Leonhardi, Marie, 12,457

Leonian, Nell (Lanham) (1892-), **17,469**

Leonowens, Anna Harriette (Crawford) [Mrs. T. L.]
(1834-1914), 1,426

Leonowens, T. L., 1,426

Leontovich, Eugene, **2,487**

Leopold, Alice (Koller) (1909-), **6,725**, 11,349

Leopold, Annie, 6,259

Lepko-Kolendro, Melita, 8,604

Le Plongeon, Alice, 4,696

Leprosy, hospitals, 10,144, 16,532

Leray, Father, 9,695

Lerner, Gerda [Mrs. Carl] (1920-), **6,726, 15,917**

LeRoux, Jane. *See* Dick, Jane (LeRoux) [Mrs.
Jackson P., Jr.]

Le Roy Family, 12,342

Le Roy Family (MI, NY, OH, PA), **12,542**

"Les Femmes Peuvent-elles avoir du Genie?"
(pamphlet), 6,746

Lesan, Thankful B. [Mrs. John], 4,803

Lesbian Club (Dover, NH), **10,843**

Lesbianism, 7,324

Lesche Club (LA), **5,447**

Lescott, Frances, 15,485

Lesemann, Louis Frederick William (1869-1941),
4,206

Lesesne, Anne Caroline, **15,494**

Lesesne, Fanny. *See* Johnstone, Fanny (Lesesne)
[Mrs. Elliott W.]

Lesher, Mabel Grier, 8,633

Keslau, Wolf, 853

Lesley College (MA), 6,490

Lesley, J. Peter (1819-1903), **14,893**

Lesley, Susan Lyman [Mrs. J. Peter], 14,893

Leslie, Amy (pseudonym). *See* Buck, Lillie (West)
[Mrs. Harry] Brown [Mrs. Franklyn Howard]
(1855-1939)

Leslie, David, 14,596, **14,604**

Leslie, Frank, 617

Leslie, Lady Constance, 12,053

Leslie, Mabel [Miss], **11,768**

Leslie, Miriam Florence (Folline) [Mrs. David
Charles] Peacock [Mrs. Ephraim George] Squier
[Mrs. Frank] (1836-1914), 617

Leslie, Sarah Adelia (Judson) Olley [Mrs. David],
14,596, **14,604**, 14,715

Leslie Woman Suffrage Commission, **2,447**

Leslie Woman Suffrage Commission (SD), 15,868

Les Natchez (book), 9,603

LeSourd, Leonard Earl, 2,476

LeSourd, Sarah Catherine (Wood) [Mrs. Peter]
Marshall [Mrs. Leonard Earl] (1914-), **2,476**

Lesser Antilles, 2,361

Lesser, Julia Harris, 940

Lesser, Margaret, 14,405, 14,475

Lester, Andrew (1813-89), **12,243**

Lester, Anne (pseudonym). *See* Higgenson, Ella

Lester, Anson Wood (1838?-76), Family, **618**

Lester, Clara Addie (Davis) [Mrs. Anson Wood]
(1850-?), 618

Lester, Emma Service. *See* Chase, Emma Service
(Lester) [Mrs. Lewis Nathaniel]

Luster, Julia. *See* Dillon, Julia (Lester) [Mrs. William
Bennett]

Lester, Lucy (Cooke) [Mrs. Charles] (1827-1921),
12,853

Lester, Mary (Harris) [Mrs. Andrew], 12,243

Lester, Minerva. *See* Powers, Minerva (Lester) [Mrs.
E. Barnham]

L'Estrange (Strang), Family, 12,314

LeSueur, Arthur (1867-1950), **9,177**

LeSueur, Marion Wharton [Mrs. Arthur] (1877-1954),
8,949, 9,177, 9,232

Le Sueur, Meridel, 12,884

Letchworth, John, 11,294

Letitia Rosenberg Women's Home (Galveston, TX),
16,220

LeTourneau College (TX), 16,257

LeTourneau, Evelyn Peterson [Mrs. Robert Gilmore]
(1900-), 16,257

LeTourneau Foundation, 16,257

LeTourneau, Robert Gilmore (1888-1969), **16,257**

Let's Go for Broke (book), 16,159

Letsche, Harry, 11,670

Letter-writing, 14,537

Letters, 3,558, 3,579, 4,961, 17,152

Letters (book), 7,169

Letters (book), 2,969

Letters and Recollections of Alexander H. Stephens
(book), 3,143

Letters from England, 1846-1849 (book), 2,188

Letters from Mississippi (book), 17,726

Letters Home, 4,485

Letters of Abelard and Heloise (book), 1,699

"Letters of the Kollock and Allied Families
(1826-1884)," 3,048

"Letters to her Daughter," 3,872

"Letters to Paw with Love, An Autobiography" (ms),
15,663

Letters to Susan (book), 8,428

Letts, Albina Brockway [Mrs.], **4,771**

"Lettuce Drop and Its Control in the Greenhouse"
(dissertation), 11,628

Levá, Naŭa Yaromila, 2,662

Levang, Ola M., 8,764

Levee Press (publishers, MS), 9,769

Levensohn, Lotte, 12,117

Leverich, Charles P., 12,034

Leverich Family (NY), **12,034**

Leverich, Matilda [Mrs. Charles P.], 12,034

Le Vert, Octavia Celeste Walton (1810-77), 41, 8,189

Levertov, Denise (1923-), 12,877, 12,879

Le Vesconte, Lillie Gibbs, 8,404

Levete, Loleta (1871-1952). *See* Rowan, Loleta
(Levete) [Mrs. Thomas E., Jr.] (1871-1952)

Levey, Jeanette, 12,701

Levi Strauss and Company, 945

Levick (PA), **15,035**

Levien, Sonya. [Mrs. Carl Hovey] (1898-), **1,451**

Levin, Myrtilla Fones (1938-), **5,006**

Levin, Nora (1916-), **15,188**

Levine, Lillian (Epstein) [Mrs. Murray] (1898?-1960),
12,466

Levine, Naomi, **17,295**

Levis, Mary, 15,287

Levis, Rosa Marie (Finnochietti) (1878-1959), **6,727**

Levison, Alice (Gerstle) [Mrs. Jacob Bertha] (1873-?),
619

Levison, Jacob Bertha (1862-1947), 619

Levitan, Esther. *See* Goldstine, Esther (Levitan)
[Mrs. Sidney]

Levitan, Solomon, 17,744

Levitan, Sonia (1934-), **937**

Levitas, Mollie, 4,032

Le Voyage en Icarie (book), 4,767

Levy, Adele (Rosenwald), 5,469

Levy, Amelia. *See* Mayhoff, Amelia (Levy)

Levy, Augusta [Mrs. John M.], **17,674**

Levy, Bilhah Abigail (1696-1756). *See* Franks, Bilhah
Abigail (Levy) [Mrs. Jacob] (1696-1756)

Levy, Estelle Goodman (1892-1963), 938

Levy, Eugenia (1820-1902). *See* Phillips, Eugenia
(Levy) [Mrs. Philip] (1820-1902)

Levy Family (TX), **938**

Levy, Fanny (Yates) [Mrs. Jacob Clavius], 2,522

Levy, Florence Nightingale (1870-1947), **2,781,
12,244, 12,544**

Levy, Harriet Lane (1867-1950), **620**, 931

Levy, Jefferson Monroe (1852-1924), **7,544**

Levy, Leonora. *See* Oberndorfer, Leonora (Levy)

Levy, Louisa F., 17,282

Levy, Martha, 2,522

Levy, Mrs. R. A., **3,542**

Levy, Phebe, 2,522

Levy, Phoebe Yates (1823-1913). *See* Pember,
Phoebe Yates (Levy) [Mrs. Thomas] (1823-1913)

Levy, Suzanne (1926-). *See* Ormond, Suzanne
(Levy) [Mrs. John W.] (1926-)

Lewallan or Llewelyn, Sarah. *See* Boley, Sarah
(Lewallan or Llewelyn) [Mrs. Elijah]

Lewers, Eva Zerline (1895-1956), **14,242**

Lewers, Louise [Mrs. Robert], 9207

Lewers, Robert (1862-1922), **10,766**

Lewes (DE), **15,036**

Lewin-Epstein, Madeline, 12,117

Lewinson, Jean (Flexner) [Mrs. Paul], 2,333

Lewis, Adele Gerard (1881-ca. 1967). *See* Grant,
Adele Gerard (Lewis) (1881-ca. 1967)

Lewis, Alan J., **14,605**

Lewis, Alice. *See* Pearson, Alice (Lewis)

Lewis, Amelia (1799-?). *See* Thomson, Amelia
(Lewis) (1799-?)

Lewis and Clark College (Portland, OR), faculty,
14,460, **14,577**

Lewis and Clark Expedition, 17,736

Lewis and Clark Expedition, sesquicentennial, 2,173

Lewis and Clark Exposition (OR, 1904), 14,549

Lewis and Clark Heritage Foundation, 10,326

Lewis and McGinnis v. Harriet Ames, 13,537

Lewis, Ann Elizabeth. *See* Peter, Ann Elizabeth
(Lewis)

Lewis, Annie, 13,466

Lewis, Austin (1865?-1944), **621**, 1,321

Lewis, Betty, 2,609

Lewis, Dolly Sumner (Lunt) [Mrs. Samuel Harding]
(1817-91). *See* Parks, Dolly Sumner (Lunt) [Mrs.
Samuel Harding] Lewis [Mrs. Thomas] Burge
[Mrs. William Justice] (1817-91)

Lewis, Dorothy Roe, 10,000

Lewis, Dorothy Thompson [Mrs. Sinclair]
(1894-1961). *See* Thompson, Dorothy. [Mrs.
Josef] Bard [Mrs. Sinclair] Lewis [Mrs. Maxim]
Kopf (1894-1961)

Lewis, Edwin J. (1848-1926), **9,178**

Lewis, Eleanor Parke (Custis) [Mrs. Lawrence]
(1779-1852), **15,037**

Lewis, Elizabeth, 9,323

Lewis, Elizabeth Ann Gabriella (1813-62). *See*
Starling, Elizabeth Ann Gabriella (Lewis) [Mrs.
Samuel McDowell] (1813-62)

Lewis, Elise Mae, 5,469

Lewis, Emma, **15,038**

Lewis, Esther Fussell [Mrs. John, Jr.] (1782-1848),
14,873

Lewis, F. Eva, 2,370

Lewis Family, **622**

Lewis Family, 4,942

Lewis Family (KY), **5,268**

Lewis Family (ME), 3,313

Lewis Family (MI), **8,282**

Lewis Family (PA), 14,848

Lewis Family (PA), **14,873**

Lewis, Fielding, 17,064

Lewis, Flora (1921?-), **6,044**

Lewis, Florence Waterman (1899-). *See* May,
Florence Waterman (Lewis) [Mrs. William]
(1899-)

Lewis, Frederica Crane, 11,873

Lewis, Gabriel Jones (1775-1864), 5,268

Lewis, George, 6,102

Lewis, Gertrude Edna. *See* Gates, Gertrude Edna
(Lewis)

Lewis, Grace, **16,098**

Lewis, Grace, 16,157, 16,173

Lewis, Grace Anna (1821-1912), 2,712, 14,873

Lewis, Grace Hegger, 1,458

Lewis, Hannah, 15,567

Lewis, Hannah, **7,516**

Lewis, Hazel J., 2,803

Lewis, Henry (1819-1904), Family, 9,125, **9,179**
Lewis, Hunter, 6,040
Lewis, Hylan Garnet, **5,471**
Lewis, Ida Belle (1887-1969). *See* Main, Ida Belle (Lewis) [Mrs. William A.] (1887-1969)
Lewis, Isabella W., **17,807**
Lewis, James, **1,586**
Lewis, Jane, 1,970
Lewis, Jane Irwin (1913-66), 8,282
Lewis, Janet. [Mrs. Yvor] Winters (1899-), **1,587**
Lewis, John, 12,545
Lewis, John, Jr. (1781-1824), 14,873
Lewis, John L., 8,144
Lewis, John M., 622
Lewis, Julia (Johnson) Whiteturkey [Mrs. Bob] Gilstrap [Mrs. Earnest]. *See* Dalton, Julia (Johnson) Whiteturkey [Mrs. Bob] Gilstrap [Mrs. Earnest] Lewis [Mrs. Emmett]
Lewis, Julie Villiers (1870-1956). *See* Penrose, Julie Villiers (Lewis) [Mrs. James] McMillan [Mrs. Spencer] (1870-1956)
Lewis, K. H., **13,466**
Lewis, Katherine Handy [Mrs. Homer], 11,907
Lewis, Kathryn (1911-), 11,827
Lewis, Lena Morrow [Mrs. Arthur] (1862-1950), 492, **12,702**
Lewis, Lucy Biddle (1861-?), 15,269, 15,316
Lewis, M., 13,548
Lewis, McDaniel, **13,467**
Lewis, Margaret, 16,877
Lewis, Margaret Lynn [Mrs. John], **12,545**, 16,040
Lewis, Maria Newkirk [Mrs. William], 9,372
Lewis, Marie Jones [Mrs. Henry] (?-1891), 9,179
Lewis, Martha Jane "Patty" (Reed) (1838-1923), 644
Lewis, Mary, 17,623
Lewis, Mary, 2,205
Lewis, Mary B., 11,719
Lewis, Mary (Bibb) [Mrs. Gabriel Jones] (1782-1819), 5,268
Lewis, Mary Ellen, **9,108**
Lewis, Mary Thorn (1854-1952). *See* Gannett, Mary Thorn (Lewis) [Mrs. William Channing] (1854-1952)
Lewis, Mildred (Schelde) (1900-73), **8,810**
Lewis, Milla Witter (1809-?), **8,352**
Lewis, Nell Battle, 13,398, 13,446, **13,468**
Lewis, Nelly Parke (Custis), 5,481
Lewis, R. H., 13,468
Lewis, R. W. B., 4,491
Lewis, Rebecca (1820-93). *See* Fussell, Rebecca (Lewis) [Mrs. Edwin] (1820-93)
Lewis, Richard, 13,467
Lewis, Robert A. (1858-?), **199**
Lewis, Roger Gregory, 5,951
Lewis, Russell, **9,180**
Lewis, Ruth E., 8,665
Lewis, Ruth Endicott (1896-1954), 8,685
Lewis, Ruth (Krandis), 623
Lewis, Sarah A. [Miss] (1847-1937), **5,887**
Lewis, Sarah Kimball (1830-72). *See* Baxter, Sarah Kimball (Lewis) [Mrs. James Phinney] (1830-72)
Lewis School (NC), 13,467
Lewis, Sinclair, 2,617, 3,775, 5,209, 5,603, 8,077, 8,144, 9,178, 9,198, 12,476
Lewis, Sophie (Borel) [Mrs. John M.], 622
Lewis, Thelma B. [Mrs. Don], **4,932, 5,007**
Lewis, Thressa. *See* Front, Thressa (Lewis)
Lewis, William, 9,372
Lewis, William, 3,300
Lewiston, Alice, 2,309
Lewiston Normal Training School (ME), 5,609
Lexicographers, **12,667**
Lexington Civic League (KY), 5,302
Lexington Gas Company (KY), 5,316
Lexington Theological Seminary (KY), alumni, 5,319
Lexow, Caroline (1882-). *See* Babcock, Caroline (Lexow) (1882-)
L'Hommedieu, Abigail Reynolds [Mrs. Giles] (1774-1851), 1,901
Libbey, Fannie (Whitenack) (1848-1941), 10,185
Libbey, Laura Jean (1862-1924). *See* Stillwell, Laura Jean (Libbey) [Mrs. Van Mater] (1862-1924)
Libbie Moody Thompson Foundation, 16,221

Libby, A. M. [Miss], **12,245**
Libby, Faith Ward [Mrs. Frederick J.], 15,308
Libby, Frederick J. (1874-1970), 15,308
Libby, Pluma (Plierna), 16,411
Libby Prison (VA), 2,245, 8,028
Libel and slander, cases, 2,873, 2,876
Liberal party (NY), 8,071, 8,126, 12,061
Liberal Union of Minnesota Women, 8,987
Liberator (periodical), 3,297, 13,927
Liberator-Extra, 7,295
Liberia, 2,618
Liberia, Sister M., O.S.F., 10,508
Liberty, 2,483, 6,708, 6,980, 8,058, 10,035, 11,178. *See also* Civil Rights
Liberty (periodical), 12,698
Liberty Bell, 5,907
Liberty Bonds, 8,167
Liberty Chapel Methodist Church (SC), Florence Circuit, **15,614**
Liberty Congregational Church (Trevor, WI), Ladies Aid Society, **17,563**
Liberty Defense Union, 10,177
Liberty Loan Committee, 11,346
Liberty Loans (World War I), 2,886, 4,340, 4,930, 10,509, 11,027, 12,114, 13,617, 13,663, 16,252
Liberty of speech, 915, 7,247
Liberty Prairie Church (Deerfield, WI), 8,724
Liberty School (Greenville County, SC), 15,541
Liberty Seminary (IN), 4,471
Librarians, 11, **123**, 304, **420**, 1,090, **1,190, 1,268, 1,374,** 1,386, **1,429,** 1,525, 1,532, 1,786, **2,260,** 2,370, **2,591,** 2,872, 3,090, 3,308, 3,451, 3,664, **3,684,** 3,713, 3,915, **3,925, 4,528, 4,531,** 4,696, 4,842, 4,850, 5,034, **5,850,** 6,046, 6,053, 6,176, **6,551,** 6,813, 6,858, **7,060,** 7,085, 7,446, **7,605,** 7,636, **7,878, 8,050, 8,551,** 8,564, **8,586,** 8,913, **8,976, 9,020, 9,021,** 9,067, **9,539,** 9,575, 9,781, **9,935,** 10,848, 10,915, **10,923,** 11,123, 11,144, **11,228,** 11,244, **11,268, 11,297, 11,320, 11,327, 11,328, 11,333,** 11,577, **11,594, 11,915, 11,930,** 11,937, **12,002, 12,024, 12,151, 12,479, 12,526,** 12,570, 12,622, **12,654,** 12,803, **13,686,** 13,688, **13,700, 14,099, 14,370, 14,386, 14,591,** 14,698, 14,734, 14,877, 14,931, **15,188, 15,591, 16,239, 16,426,** 16,985, **17,394,** 17,395, **17,603.** *See also* College librarians; Government librarians; Medical librarians; Special librarians
salaries, pensions, etc., 10,012
Librarians, Afro-American, **2,146, 5,379, 5,382,** 5,394
Librarians, interchange of, 11,937
Librarians, Jewish, **13,787**
Libraries, 324, 540, 1,385, 1,786, **1,931,** 2,704, 3,990, 4,299, 4,410, 5,709, 6,241, 6,910, **8,204,** 8,482, 9,077, 9,804, 10,905, 11,893, 12,004, 12,479, 12,902, 13,265, 14,216, 14,222, **14,948,** 16,979, 17,046, 17,110, 17,747
branches, delivery stations, etc., 3,920, 5,379, 5,382, 5,974, 13,787
law and legislation, 4,396
special collections, rare books, 11,921
technical services, 4,402
trustees, 4,477, 14,216
Libraries and community, 1,777, **17,395**
Libraries and state, 4,366
Libraries, children's, 2,069, 15,392
Libraries, county, **2,595**
Libraries, special, 303
Libraries, traveling, 4,366. *See also* Bookmobiles
Libraries, university and college, 107, 4,399, **5,034,** 6,339, 6,396, 6,460, 7,554, **7,571,** 8,588, **11,825,** 11,972, 13,204, **14,277**
Library administration, 1,425, 3,200, 6,460, 12,024, 13,204
Library administrators, 11,140
Library associations, **2,025, 2,924,** 3,653, 4,350, 4,391, 4,396, 4,402, 4,640, **4,727,** 4,910, **4,999, 5,341, 6,241, 6,584,** 7,919, 7,926, 9,020, 9,207, **9,233, 10,012,** 10,331, **10,785, 11,382,** 11,412, **11,936,** 11,937, 12,395, 12,479, 12,526, 12,729, 13,204, 13,686, 14,306, 14,591, **16,288,** 17,394
Library associations, Afro-American, 12,865
Library catalogs, 7,659
Library education, **11,936, 11,938,** 12,024
Library employees, **3,998, 4,004, 11,973**

Library finance, 12,049
Library Journal (periodical), 12,395
Library of Congress, 1,795, 2,798, 14,322
officials and employees, 5,829
Library of Congress, Legislative Reference Service, 2,564
Library resources, 1,425
Library Resources (book), 4,402
Library schools, **4,023,** 4,391, 4,396, **11,333,** 11,930, 12,526, 13,895, 14,217, **14,930**
alumni, **11,955**
Library science, 123, 11,844
Library War Service, 4,350
Library-Zonta Club Oral History Project (Arlington, VA), **17,051**
License system, 15,769
Licenses, 1,119
Lichtenwalter, Geneve [Miss] (1867-1951), **10,120**
Lick Archives (CA), 790
Lick Observatory (Santa Cruz, CA), 790
Lick Old Ladies' Home (San Francisco, CA), 813
Licking, Anna [Mrs.], 10,632
Liddell, Anna Farkes, 2,875
Liddell, Anna Forbes, 2,931
Liddle, Rachel Ann-Ray, 982
Lidgerwood Public Library (ND), 13,688
Lieber, Francis (1798-1872), **1,452**
Lieberman, Annette, 5,842
Liebig, Caroline Louise (Eshman) (1901-), **624**
Liederman, Benjamin, 939
Liederman, Daisy (Cohn) [Mrs. Benjamin] (?-1938), **939**
Lien, Jean Christie (1891-), 8,996
Liepient, Mrs. I. A., 9,216
Lieutenant governors, **1,746,** 2,635, 4,763, 5,394, 8,971, 9,035, 9,048, 9,268, 9,287, 9,478, 9,585, 10,753
Lieutenant's Lady, The (book), 13,651
Life (periodical), 112, 5,242, 7,254, 10,178, 12,891, 15,564, 17,947, 17,991
Life and Labor (periodical), 2,878, 6,835
Life and Letters of Eliza Allen Starr, The (book), 4,647
Life and Letters of George Collier Remey (book), 2,545
Life and Letters of J. Alden Weir, The (book), 16,575
Life and Letters of James Abram Garfield, The (book), 2,348
Life and Letters of Mary Josephine Mason Remey (book), 2,545
Life and Mind of Emily Dickinson, The (book), 12,642
Life and Times of Amelia Bloomer (book), 4,738
Life and Times of Sir Archie: The Story of America's Greatest Thoroughbred, The (book), 12,955
Life and Work of Susan B. Anthony, The (book), 12,834
Life and Works of Mrs. Theresa Robinson (book), 13,754
Life in Colonial America (book), 6,093
"Life in the Fox River Valley," 17,495
Life insurance companies, 9,488, 10,104
Life, Letters and Papers of William Dunbar of Elgin, Morayshire, Scotland and Natchez, Mississippi: Pioneer Scientists of the Southern United States (book), 9,719
Life of a Woman Pioneer (book), 4,345
"Life of Deborah Sampson, the Female Soldier of the Revolution" (ms), 10,876
Life of General Mariano Guadalupe Vallejo, the Portrait of a Man of His Times, The (book), 498
"Life of Joseph Smith" (ms), 4,728
"Life of Mary Southern, The" (radio program), 1,026
Life of the Dead, The (book), 16,165
Life of William Vaughn Moody (book), 11,174
Life on the State: My Personal Experiences (book), 6,773, 7,263
"Life Story of an Oregon Immigrant—1905," 14,643
Life Without Father, 2,546
Lifeboat (drama), 60
"Life's Nexus and Plexus" (ms), 9,767
Lifespan, Inc., **7,843**
Lifting the Curtain (book), 15,029
Liggett, Edith, 8,064

Light and Shadow (book), 3,514
Light at Midnight (book), 6,106
Light, Charlotte Grace. *See* Chilson, Charlotte Grace (Light)
Light, Dorothy B. [Mrs. Jerome], 625
Light, Jerome T., **625**
Light, Maude. *See* Illington, Margaret. [Mrs. Edward J.] Bowes
Light My Candle (book), 14,231
Light Shines, The, a Christmas Play, 5,042
Light Verse and Worse (book), 5,127
Lighter, Esther, 17,282
Lightfoot, Dora Rowell (Maxey) [Mrs. Henry William] (1856-84), 16,029
Lightfoot Family, **15,289**
Lightfoot, Henry William (1846-1901), 16,029
Lightfoot, Mary (Cadwallader) [Mrs. Thomas] (1820-1907), 15,289
Lightfoot, Mildred, 1,655
Lightfoot, Susanna, 15,289
Lightfoot, Thomas (1865-96), 15,289
Lighthouse keepers, 12,931
Lighthouse Settlement (Kensington, PA), 15,208
Lightner, Mary Elizabeth (Rollins) (1818-1913). *See* Smith, Mary Elizabeth (Rollins) Lightner [Mrs. Joseph] (1818-1913)
Lightning in His Hand: Dr. Nikola Tesla (book), 1,685, 1,689
Likens, Sadie M., 1,786
Lilac Day (VT), 17,004
Liles, Meta, **13,469**
Lilford, Lady, 11,826
Liliencrantz, Flora (Sterling), 816
Lilienthal, David, 2,879
Liliuokalani, Queen. [Mrs. John Owen] Dominis. Lydia Kamakaeha Paki (1838-1917), 3,620, 3,626, **3,632**
Liliuokalani Trust, **3,626**
Lill, Jabez, 16,305
Lilliard, Sarah (Davis) Swayne [Mrs. John T.], 4,356
Lillie, Beatrice, 11,449
Lillie, Frances Crane [Mrs. Frank Rattray] (1869-1958), **3,872**
Lillie, Mary Prentice. *See* Barrows, Mary Prentice (Lillie)
Lilly Base Unit, 4,629
Lilly, Dorcas, 15,042
Lilly, Harriet (1816-1911). *See* Houdlette, Harriet (Lilly) [Mrs. Franklin] (1816-1911)
Lilly, Kitty, 2,284
Lilly, Lydia, 7,478
Lilly, Othelia [Miss] (1908-), **1,453**
Lily Dale Woman's Week, 15,283
Lily, The (periodical), **4,655**, 11,305, 12,854
Lima, Martha [Mrs. Ole] (1862-1900), 8,763
Lima, Ole (1860-1931), 8,763
Lima, Ruth. *See* McMahon, Ruth (Lima) [Mrs.]
Limantour, José Yves (?-1885), **626**
Limbach, Sarah, 14,830
Limited Editions Club, 11,891, 12,040
Limon, José, 362, 12,363
Lincklaen, Helen (1845-ca. 1931). *See* Fairchild, Helen (Lincklaen) [Mrs. Charles Stebbins] (1845-ca. 1931)
Lincklaen, Ledyard, **12,247**
Lincklaen, Mrs. Ledyard, **12,247**
Lincoln, Abraham, 1,437, 1,725, 2,129, 2,217, 2,262, 2,388, 2,418, **2,448**, 2,457, 2,512, 2,540, 2,639, 3,171, 3,864, 3,871, 4,348, 4,354, 4,364, 4,365, 4,371, 4,417, 4,423, 4,442, 4,506, 4,994, 5,053, 5,060, 5,094, 5,307, 5,431, 5,750, 7,308, 7,678, 9,308, 9,528, 9,902, 10,748, 11,539, 11,615, 12,246, 12,456, 12,490, 12,594, 14,770, 14,872, 15,006, 15,635, 16,968, 17,479, 17,998
Lincoln Academy (NC), **5,472**
Lincoln Business and Professional Women's Club (NE), 10,471
Lincoln Center (NY), Street Theatre Festival, 12,367
Lincoln, Charles James, 287
Lincoln Council of Churches, Lincoln Council of Church Women (NE), **10,485**
Lincoln Courier (NE), 10,443
Lincoln, Elizabeth (Trumbull) [Mrs. William Sever] (1816-1900), 7,647

Lincoln, Eudora "Dora" Percival (Knox) [Mrs. Charles James] (1849-1921), Family (AR), **287**
Lincoln Family, 8,953
Lincoln Family, 9,388
Lincoln Family (IL), **4,511, 5,060**
Lincoln Family (MA, ME), **7,647**
Lincoln, Fanny (Chandler) (1852-1939), 7,647
Lincoln Foundation (NE), 10,472
Lincoln, Frances (Fiske) [Mrs. Daniel Waldo] (1819-73), 7,650
Lincoln General Hospital School of Nursing (NE), **10,486**
Lincoln, Grace Garrison [Mrs. Pearl] (1871-1970), **17,675**
Lincoln High School (Des Moines, IA), 4,820
Lincoln Institute (MO), 2,130
Lincoln, Jessie (1875-1948). *See* Randolph, Jessie (Lincoln) [Mrs. Warren] Beckwith [Mrs. Frank Edward] Johnson [Mrs. Robert J.] (1875-1948)
Lincoln League (TN), 15,889
Lincoln, Levi (1782-1868), 6,225
Lincoln, Levi, Sr., 7,647
Lincoln, Martha H., **7,844**
Lincoln, Martha (Waldo) [Mrs. Levi, Sr.] (1761-1828), 7,647
Lincoln, Mary Ann (Todd) [Mrs. Abraham] (1818-82), **1,454**, 2,448, **2,449**, 3,743, 3,864, 3,871, 3,907, 3,922, 4,356, 4,357, 4,360, 4,363, **4,371**, 4,417, 4,511, 5,291, **5,353**, 7,553, 11,154, 17,622
Lincoln, Mary Eunice (Harlan) [Mrs. Robert Todd] (?-1937), 5,053, 5,060, 5,061
Lincoln Memorial (DC), 2,338
Lincoln, Olive [Mrs.], 7,844
Lincoln, Pearl, 17,675
Lincoln, Phoebe [Mrs.], 4,716
Lincoln Public Schools (NE), 10,482
Lincoln, Robert Todd (1843-1926), 2,449, 2,512, 3,864, 4,511, 5,053, 5,060
Lincoln-Roosevelt Republican League, 1,599
Lincoln School (Chicago, IL), 3,902
Lincoln School (KY), 5,302
Lincoln Sesquicentennial Commission, 5,126
Lincoln, Tad, 1,454
Lincoln, Thomas, 4,356
Lincoln University (MO), 10,015, 10,020, **10,095**
Lincoln, Victoria, 11,165
"Lincoln Walks Again" (poem), 2,437
Lincoln, William (1839-69), 7,647
Lincoln, William Sever (1811-89), 7,647
Lincoln, Willie, 1,454, 4,360
Lincolnton Female Academy (NC), 13,329
L'Inconnue (pseudonym). *See* French, Lucy Virginia (Smith) [Mrs. John Hopkins] (1825-81)
Lind-Goldschmidt Johanna "Jenny" Maria (1820-87), 1,073, 1,262, **1,588, 1,823**, 1,828, 3,889, **4,325**, 6,329, 7,267, 10,651, 10,909, 12,258, 12,802, **14,906**, 16,150, **17,491**
Lind, Hokan, 9,467
Lind, Jenny (1820-87). *See* Lind-Goldschmidt, Johanna "Jenny" Maria (1820-87)
Lind, Melva, 9,230
Linda (book), 111
Lindbaek, Lise, 8,768, 8,788
Lindbergh, Anne Spencer (Morrow) [Mrs. Charles Augustus, Jr.] (1906-), 1,604, **2,450, 7,170**, 7,264
Lindbergh, Charles Augustus (1858-1924), **9,181**
Lindbergh, Charles Augustus, Jr. (1902-74), 2,365, 9,181, 9,272
Lindbergh, Evangeline Lodge (Land) [Mrs. Charles Augustus] (ca. 1875-1954), 9,181
Lindeke, Mary Proal, 9,486
Lindeman, Anne, 157
Linden Wood Female College (MO). *See* Lindenwood College (MO)
Lindenberger, Edith (Rosenberg), 17,282
Lindenwood College (St. Charles, MO), 9,912, 10,134, **10,169**
  faculty, 8,555
  trustees, 9,956
Linderholm, Natalie Walker, **6,729**
Linderman, Frank B. (1869-1938), **10,327**

Linderman, Winifred B., 11,940
Lindheim, Irma, 12,117
Lindley, Amanda (1836-ca. 1898), **16,099**
Lindley Family (IN), **5,317**
Lindley, Kate, 5,317
Lindley, Martha H., 5,317
Lindley, Mrs. Ernest K., 11,496
Lindley, Thomas Morton, **963**
Lindner, Belle (1877-1933). *See* Moskowitz, Belle (Lindner) Israels (1877-1933)
Lindquist, Maude, 9,230
Lindsay, Barbara, 14,453
Lindsay, Ben B., 14,551
Lindsay, Carrie E. [Mrs.], 8,898
Lindsay, Elizabeth Conner [Mrs. Nicholas Vachel], 16,169, 17,013
Lindsay, Emaline [Mrs. Robert], **16,300**
Lindsay Family (MS), 9,656
Lindsay, Florence, 17,116
Lindsay, John, 12,147, 12,148
Lindsay, Nan, 17,065
Lindsay, Patricia Coffin (?-1974), **17,991**
Lindsay, Perry (pseudonym). *See* Dern, Peggy Gaddis (1895-1966)
Lindsay, Vachel, 11,894, 16,169, 17,473
Lindsey, Bell [Miss], **9,664**
Lindsey, Benjamin Barr (1869-1943), **2,451**
Lindsey Family (NE), 10,454
Lindsey, Georgia. *See* Peek, Georgia (Lindsey) [Mrs. George N.]
Lindsey, Henrietta (Brevoort) [Mrs. Benjamin Barr], 2,451
Lindsey, John, 4,428
Lindsey, Martha M. [Mrs. John], **4,428**
Lindsley, Aaron Ladner, 14,606
Lindsley, Emily. *See* Ross, Emily (Lindsley) [Mrs. James Thorburn]
Lindsley Family (OR), **14,606**
Lindsley, Grant, 12,763
Lindsley, Julia (West) [Mrs. Aaron Ladner], 14,606
Lindsley, Katherine (1918-). *See* Camp, Katherine (Lindsley) [Mrs. William P.] (1918-)
Linehan Family (NC), **13,331**
Linehan, Marie Besson, 13,331
Lines, Daisy, 2,958
Lines Family, **2,958**
Lines, Fanette O'Kell, 5,063
Lines, Sylvanus, 2,958
Linfield College (OR), 14,348
Linford, Velma, 17,901
Linford, Velma [Miss] (1907-), **17,911**
Ling School, Town of Sampson, School District No. 8, Chippewa County (WI), **17,525**
Linge, Lydia (Oden), 14,778
Lingenfelter, Bea (Dally) [Mrs. C. H.], **3,704**
Lingenfelter, C. H., **3,704**
Linguistic research, 1,671, **8,206**, 15,278
Linguists, **2,280**, 11,640, 14,243, **15,789, 17,252**, 17,868
Linington, Elizabeth (1921-), 6,060
Linjenquist, Christiene (1822-1903), 16,490
Linjenquist Family (UT), 16,490
Link, Edwin A. (1904-), **11,288**
Link, Marion (Clayton) [Mrs. Edwin A.], 11,288
Link, Wendell H., 9,415
Linley, Margaret, 3,290
Linn County Medical Society (IA), 4,698
Linn, Elizabeth A. (Relfe) [Mrs. Lewis Fields], 9,929, 10,170
Linn, Lewis Fields (1795-1843), 9,929, **10,170**
Linn, Mary Catherine (Addams), 4,154
Linnea Society (MN), **9,182**
Linton Family (GA), **3,052**
Linton, John S., 3,052
Linton, Laura (1853-1915), **8,822**
Linton, Lucy Ann Hull, 3,052
Linton, Mrs. E. L., 14,860
Lintz, Maria (Sneckner) (1818-89), **12,248**
Linville, Henry Richardson, 8,145
"Lion Gardiner," 12,240
Lion, Oscar, **12,547**
Lion Rubber Company, 12,547
Lions Three, Christians Nothing (book), 5,992

Lipe Family (NY), **11,464**
Lipetz, Lin, **17,296**
Lipids, 1,371
Lipman, Irene Lesser, 940
Lipman, Rowena (1907-), Family, **940**
Lipowsky, Lillian, 11,774
Lippard, Lucy (1937-), **2,782**
Lippincott, Bertha Horstmann (1880-1963). *See*
  Coles, Bertha Horstmann (Lippincott) [Mrs.
  Stricker] (1880-1963)
Lippincott, Christiana, 5,752
Lippincott, Esther Jane (Trimble) (1838-88), 14,873
Lippincott Family (PA), **14,978**
Lippincott, J. B., 5,528, 11,989, 14,476
Lippincott, Kate B., 11,114
Lippincott, Leander K., 1,426
Lippincott, Sara Jane (Clarke) [Mrs. Leander K.]
  (1823-1904), 869, 1,426, **2,452**, 2,542, 11,036,
  17,010
Lippincott, Walter, 14,978
Lippincott's Monthly Magazine (periodical), 2,183,
  9,771, 11,182
Lippman, Ruth (Fessler), 5,121
Lippman, Walter, 2,542
Lippmann, Alice D., 4,005
Lipreading, 10,982
Lipscomb, Ernestine, 2676
Lipscomb, Lamar (Rutherford), 3,350
Lipscomb, Susan B. *See* Wilson, Susan B. (Lipscomb)
  [Mrs. Alpheus Waters]
Lipsky, Louis, 933
Lipton, Estelle L., 2,205
Liquor laws, 2,649, 3,909, 6,484, 10,032, 11,184
Liquor problem, 6,484, 10,032
Lisa (book) 6,981
Lisetor-Lane, Clara A. [Miss], **12,108**
Lisle, Leda R., 1,623
Lisle, Maurice, 14,964
"Listen Professor!," 18,000
Lister, Susanah Ward, 16,417
Liszman, Sarah A., 14,808
Liszt, Franz, 2,665
Litchfield, Elizabeth Pannill (Peirce), 17,089
Litchfield Female Academy (CT), **1,967**, 6,548
Litchfield, Frances Hubbard (1844-1927). *See*
  Turnbull, Frances Hubbard (Litchfield) [Mrs.
  Lawrence] (1844-1927)
Litchfield, Grace Denio (1849-1944), **2,453**, **5,788**,
  5,815
Litchfield, Mrs. C. B., 7,502
Litchfield Seminary (CT), 1,970
Literary agencies, 14,400, **14,410**
Literary agents, 5,273, 5,985, 5,996, **6,045**, 6,085,
  6,100, 6,109, 6,110, 11,036, **11,165**, 11,184,
  11,490, **11,954**, **12,372**, **12,472**, 12,622, 14,313,
  14,315, 14,324, 14,328, 14,338, 14,359, 14,385,
  14,464, 14,465, 15,196, 17,098
Literary Circle (Atlanta, GA). *See* 1900 Study Club
  (Atlanta, GA)
Literary Club (Williamstown, MA), **7,592**
Literary Club (MN), 8,697
Literary Club (Fergus Falls, MN), 8,896
Literary Club (Morris, MN), 8,696
Literary clubs. *See* Literary societies
Literary critics, **1,488**
Literary Life of the Early Friends, The (book), 4,962
"Literary Pathways" (column), 9,771
Literary prizes, 2,051, 2,215, 2,876, 3,771, 5,085,
  5,439, 8,805, 9,583, 9,768, 9,770, 10,262, 11,161,
  11,171, 11,182, 11,309, 11,368, 11,870, 12,473,
  12,484, 12,570, 12,903, 12,915, 15,660, 17,076,
  17,473, 17,614, 17,634. *See also, e.g.,* Pulitzer
  Prize
"Literary Review" (column), 2,596
Literary Review, The (periodical), 11,302
Literary societies, **57**, **75**, 76, **158**, 183, 250, 325,
  1,090, **1,107**, **1,108**, **1,110**, 1,258, 1,282, 1,306,
  1,307, 1,322, **1,625**, **1,641**, 1,749, **1,750**, **1,787**,
  1,789, **1,791**, **1,826**, **1,873**, 2,197, 2,332, **2,914**,
  2,977, 3,159, **3,201**, **3,211**, **3,230**, **3,697**, **3,843**,
  3,885, 3,999, 4,186, **4,299**, 4,403, **4,546**, **4,553**,
  4,556, **4,563**, **4,568**, **4,583**, **4,586**, 4,595, 4,640,
  4,654, **4,663**, **4,666**, **4,672**, **4,673**, **4,720**, 4,770,
  4,886, 4,960, **4,968**, **4,985**, **4,993**, **5,017**, **5,044**,

5,045, 5,064, **5,096**, 5,242, 5,270, 5,418, **5,447**,
5,594, 5,783, **5,795**, **5,912**, 5,913, 5,934, 5,988,
6,014, 6,089, 6,867, 7,166, 7,293, 7,557, **7,592**,
7,593, **7,837**, **8,024**, **8,188**, **8,350**, **8,608**, 9,043,
9,098, **9,171**, **9,217**, **9,243**, **9,255**, 9,527, **9,925**,
9,943, 9,959, **10,497**, **10,498**, **10,512**, **10,525**,
10,563, 10,571, **10,769**, 10,915, **11,110**, 11,271,
12,395, 12,570, 12,893, 12,924, **13,124**, **13,304**,
13,320, **13,464**, **13,511**, **13,554**, **13,656**, 13,674,
13,918, **14,064**, **14,065**, **14,094**, 14,121, **14,148**,
14,149, **14,154**, 14,158, 14,159, **14,423**, **14,747**,
14,756, 15,199, **15,415**, 15,480, **15,786**, **15,872**,
15,965, 16,118, 16,295, 16,395, **16,501**, 17,269,
17,310, **17,426**, 17,696
Literature, 11,905
  history and criticism, 1,433, 1,488, 7,651
  indexes, 8,564
  periodicals, 1,455, 4,732, 15,897
Literature, American, 11,221
Literature, French, 5,632, 12,047
"Literature for an Individual Education," 11,306
Lithographers, **1,254**, **2,755**, **5,952**, **7,667**, 11,213,
  12,637
Lithography, 7,667
Lithuanians in Minnesota, 9,462
Litman, Ray (Frank) (1864 or 1865-1948), **7,545**
Litta, Marie. Marie Eugenia Van Elsner, 3,745
Littell, Anita (Damrosch) [Mrs. Robert], 14,411
Littell, Robert (1896-1963), **14,411**
Little, Anita Gray, 5,582
Little, Ann [Mrs. Ray], 5,642
Little, Ann Hawkins, 13,471
Little, Annis, 9,414
"Little Backstage Gossip, A," 1,750
Little Big Horn, Battle of (1876), 10,213
"Little Bird that Was Caught," 8,404
Little Blue Books, 4,095
Little Brick House Museum (Vandalia, IL),
  4,444
Little, Brown (publishers), 9,769
Little Chevalier, The (book), 5,498
Little Crow, Chief, 9,467
Little Cumbray Island (Scotland), 7,181
Little, Eleanor, 1,936
Little Engine That Could, The (book), 10,444
Little Family (NC), **13,471**
Little Foxes, The (drama), 60, 3,468
Little Garden Club (Wilmette, IL), 4,454
Little, George, 13,471
Little House (CA), 396
Little Jim Crow (book), 6,773
Little, Joan, 13,108
Little, Joann. *See* Little, Joan
"Little Lady," 73
Little Lizzie's Letter, 9,281
Little Lord Fauntleroy (book), 12,409
Little magazines, 17,843
Little, Margaret [Mrs. George], 13,471
Little, Mary Bishop (1836-67), **7,400**
Little May (slave, SC), 15,742
Little Miracle, A (drama), 317
Little Monitor and Parish Guide, The, 434
Little Mose (book), 5,413
Little Musquash Lake (ME), **5,651**
Little Paper, The (periodical), 4,654
Little presses, **1,573**, 4,230
Little, Ray, 5,642
"Little Red Schoolhouse" (article), 11,407
Little Review (periodical), 657, **17,843**
Little River Academy (NC), 13,439
Little Rock Health Department (AR), 235
Little Rock Sanitarium (AR), 230
Little Room, The (Chicago, IL), **3,997**
"Little Sister to the Sioux," 7,220
Little Sisters of the Poor (St. Paul, MN), 9,328
Little, Sophronia (Balch) [Mrs. Josiah] (1793-1872),
  7,401
Little Theater (NY), 12,794
Little Theater Guild of New Haven (CT), **1,996**
Little Theater of the Deaf, 2,104
Little theaters. *See* Theater, Little theater movement
Little Theatre of St. Paul (MN), 9,198
Little Things. *See* *Young Folks Journal*
Little, Thomas, 13,471

"Little Toona-how-i and His Big Gold Watch, A Story
  of Colonial Days in Georgia," 3,009
Little Women (drama), 11,344
Littledale, Clara (Savage) (1891-1956), 6,746
Littlefield, Catharine. *See* Miller, Catharine
  (Littlefield) [Mrs. Nathanael] Greene
Littlefield, Eva [Mrs. Seth], 5,649
Littlefield, Seth, 5,649
Littlejohn, Sarah [Miss], 13,423
Littleton Business and Professional Women's Club
  (CO), **1,817**
Littleton College (NC), 13,285, 13,579
Littleton College (NC), Memorial Association, **13,278**
Littleton Female College (NC). *See* Littleton College
  (NC)
Littleton War Memorial Community Center (CO),
  1,817
Littleton Women's Club (CO), **1,818**
Liturgical language, English, **8,698**, **8,708**
Litwack, Charlotte, **13,472**
Litz, Katherine, 4,384
Liu, Beatrice Exner (1907-), **8,881**
"Live It Up Honey" (song), 9,742
Lively, Mary B. (Sexton) [Mrs. Amos] (1816-91),
  7,935
Lively, Mrs. Charles E., 9,885
Liverance, Sara Vandiver [Mrs.] (1914-), **15,803**
Liveright (publishers), 11,850
Liverman, Elga. *See* Duval, Elga (Liverman)
Livermore, Elizabeth A. (1818-), **10,819**
Livermore, Eunice Hovey [Mrs. Isaac], 2,238
Livermore, Isaac, 2,238
Livermore, Jane Cornelia. *See* Burlingame, Jane
  Cornelia (Livermore) [Mrs. Anson]
Livermore, Mary Ashton (Rice) [Mrs. Daniel Parker]
  (1820-1905), 1,224, 1,409, 1,426, 2,206, 2,501,
  2,542, 3,888, 3,908, 4,135, 4,233, 4,301, 4,695,
  4,732, **5,939**, 5,973, 6,373, **6,731**, 6,741, 7,044,
  7,271, 7,585, **11,167**, 12,819, 14,062
Livermore, Paul S., 11,572
Livermore, Thomas Leonard, 10,819
Livestock, **10,722**
Living My Life (book), 12,487, 12,701
Living Theatre (NY), 964
Living Through Covered Wagon to Space Ship Age
  (book), 6,816
Livingston, Alida (Schuyler) Van Rensselaer [Mrs.
  Robert] (1656-1729), 11,492
Livingston, Ann Home (Shippen) [Mrs. Henry
  Beekman], 2,574
Livingston, Britania J., **9,183**
Livingston, Catharine Livingston [Mrs. Matthew]
  Ridley [Mrs. John] (1751-1813), 12,695
Livingston, Catherine (1752-1849). *See* Garrettson,
  Catherine (Livingston) [Mrs. Freeborn]
  (1752-1849)
Livingston, Catherine "Kitty," 12,697
Livingston, Cornelia, 11,330
Livingston Family, 12,314
Livingston Family (NY), **11,492**
Livingston, Grace. (1865-1947). *See* Hill, Grace
  (Livingston) [Mrs. Thomas Guthrie Franklin].
  [Mrs. Flavius] Lutz (1865-1947)
Livingston, Harriet Houston [Mrs. Peter Van Brugh],
  12,548
Livingston, Henry Beekman, 2,574
Livingston, Janet (1743-1828). *See* Montgomery,
  Janet (Livingston) [Mrs. Richard] (1743-1828)
Livingston Journal (newspaper), 81
Livingston Ladies Aid Military Association, 9,749
Livingston Normal School (AL). *See* Livingston
  University (AL)
Livingston, Peter Van Brugh, **12,548**
Livingston, Philip, **12,548**
Livingston, Priscilla (1881-1957). *See* Evans, Priscilla
  (Livingston) [Mrs. Frank] (1881-1957)
Livingston, Robert, 11,492, 15,745
Livingston, Robert R., 2,281, 12,264
Livingston, Rose, 6,706
Livingston, Sarah. *See* Jay, Sarah (Livingston) [Mrs.
  John]
Livingston, Susan, 12,697
Livingston, Susannah "Sukey" (French) [Mrs.
  William], 12,697

Livingston University (AL), 81
Livingston, William (1723-90), **11,201, 12,697**
Livshis Family, 7,997
Liza (drama), 12,367
Liza Bowe (book), 10,848
Lizzie Borden: A Dance of Death, 12,360
Llano del Rio Cooperative Colony (CA), **1,319**
LL.B (Legal Lore & the Bar) (book), 1,186
Llewelyn, Sarah. *See* Boley, Sarah (Lewallan or
    Llewelyn) [Mrs. Elijah]
Lloyd, Alfred, 7,896
Lloyd, Alice Crocker (1893-1950), **7,845**
Lloyd, Ann Day, 9,034
Lloyd, Edward, IV (1744-96), 5,789
Lloyd, Edward, V (1779-1834), 5,789
Lloyd, Edward, VI (1798-1861), 5,789
Lloyd, Elizabeth C. McBlair, 5,789
Lloyd Family (MD), **5,789**
Lloyd, Hannah, 14,981
Lloyd, Hannah (Breck), 14,961
Lloyd, Lola Maverick (1875-1944), **7,291,** 7,923,
    12,534, **12,617**
Lloyd, Mary, **17,383**
Lloyd, Mrs. Glen Alfred, 11,827
Lloyd, Ola Delight (1880-1958). *See* Cook Ola
    Delight (Lloyd) (1880-1958)
Lloyd, Rebecca. *See* Nicholson, Rebecca (Lloyd)
    [Mrs. Joseph Hopper]
Lloyd, Thomas, 14,873
Lloyd, Abigail, 11,318, 11,322
Lloyd, Bateman, 11,318
Lloyd, Leffert W., 11,318, 11,322
Lloyd, Sara, 11,322
Loan Relief Society (NY), 12,256
Loans, interest free, 7,538
Lobben, Clara, **13,677**
Lobbying, 4,170, 7,139, 9,225, 9,467, 11,904
"Lobbyist, The" (ms), 6,474
Lobbyists, 76, 1,652, **2,074,** 2,075, 2,120, 2,212,
    3,858, 4,046, **4,125,** 6,953, **11,706, 11,760,**
    11,763, 11,769, **11,771,** 11,773, **12,662,** 12,875,
    15,303, 15,819, **17,253**
Lobdell, Adeline (ca. 1887-). *See* Pynchon, Adeline
    (Lobdell) [Mrs. Henry] Atwater [Mrs. Henry C.]
    (ca. 1887-)
Lobdell, Julia, 9,462
Lobner, Corinna del Greco, 17,852
Lobner, Joyce E. [Miss], 1,636
Local church councils, **1,965, 3,137, 3,656,** 4,959,
    5,841, 8,502, 9,305, 10,001, **10,485,** 13,559,
    15,176, 16,038, 17,304
Local Council of Women (Providence, RI), **15,386**
Local Council of Women of New Orleans (LA), **5,500**
Local elections, 1,361, 1,654, 1,829, 5,569, 8,460,
    9,040, 9,327, 9,375, 9,386, 9,984, 10,035, 10,062,
    10,768, 12,680, 13,702, 15,563, 15,596, 15,769,
    16,240, 16,260, 17,324, 17,472. *See also*
    Elections; *and as a subhead under specific names*
    of states, e. g., Louisiana, electing
Local government, 7,253
Local laws, 5,565
Local transit, **7,733**
  law and legislation, 16,231
Lochner, Louis P., 17,735
Lockburne Army Air Base (OH), 36
Locke, Ada Elsie, 5,938
Locke, Alice (1861-?). *See* Park, Alice (Locke)
    (1861-?)
Locke, Delia Marcella (Hammond) (1836-1923),
    1,632
Locke, Edwin (?-1842), 2,002
Locke Family (CA), **1,632**
Locke Family School (CA), 1,632
Locke, Frances Sargent (1811-50). *See* Osgood,
    Frances Sargent (Locke) [Mrs. Samuel Stillman]
    (1811-50)
Locke, Jane E., 7,069
Locke, Jerome G., 10,312
Locke, Lucy Maria (1838-71), 2,002
Locke, Martha Laurens (1840-89), 2,002
Locke, Martha Laurens (Rowell) [Mrs. Edwin]
    (?-1842), 2,002
Locke, Mary (Jameson) [Mrs. David Morrell], 1,275
Locke, Roberta Pratt [Mrs.], **8,391**

Locke, Sarah. *See* Jameson, Sarah (Locke) [Mrs.
    Alexander]
Locke, Theresa (1879-?). *See* Thorpe, Theresa
    (Locke) (1879-?)
Lockeford Band of Hope (CA), 1,632
Lockeford Soldier's Aid Society (CA), 1,632
Lockett, Harwood Alexander, 3,143
Lockett, Julia Kendall, 3,419
Lockett, Myrta. *See* Avary, Myrta (Lockett)
Lockhart, Caroline (1875-1962), 17,899
Lockhart, Dorothy [Miss] **12,549,** 12,612
Lockhart, Edith A. *See* Humphrey, Edith A.
    (Lockhart)
Lockhart, Ella C., 9,665
Lockhart Family (MS), **9,665**
Lockhart, Lucinda [Mrs. Samuel T.], 9,665
Lockhart, Ophelia W., 9,665
Lockhart, Sally (pseudonym). *See* King, Carolyn St.
    Clair
Lockhart, Samuel T., 9,665
Lockley, Frederick E. (1824-1905), **1,455**
Lockley, Frederick E., Jr. (1871-1958), 1,455, **12,249**
Lockley, Laura Simpson [Mrs. Frederick E., Jr.],
    12,249
Locklin, Mary Fokes (1819-1902), **16,100**
Locks and Canals Company (MA), 7,070
Lockwood, Alice Ann (1844-1939). *See* Minick,
    Alice Ann (Lockwood) [Mrs. John S.]
    (1844-1939)
Lockwood, Belva Ann (Bennett) [Mrs. Uriah] McNall
    [Mrs. Ezekiel] (1830-1917), 1,950, 2,170, **2,857,**
    3,908, 4,695, 6,712, **6,732,** 13,661
Lockwood, Debra (Connery), 13,669
Lockwood, Mrs. J. Palmer, **15,804**
Lockwood, Sara Lawrence (1891-1961). *See*
    Williams, Sara Lawrence (Lockwood) [Mrs.
    Walter] (1891-1961)
Lockwood, Sarah S. [Mrs.], **12,250**
Locomotive engineers, 9,517, 9,686
Locomotives, 11,134
Locust Grove Asylum (MA), 7,489
Locusts, 10,458, 14,944, 16,968
Lodge, Carrie Electa (1881-), **627**
Lodge, Henry Cabot, 6,925
Lodge, Martina (Castro) [Mrs. Michael] (1807?-1890),
    627
Loeb, Esther (1875-1965). *See* Kohn, Esther (Loeb)
    [Mrs. Alfred D.] (1875-1965)
Loeb, Therese "Tess" [Mrs. Virgil], **10,171,** 10,200
Loeber, Florence (?-1933), 5,499
Loeffler, Charles Martin, 6,185
Loemker, Dorothy Rowden, 11,844
Loengard, Margery [Mrs. Richard O.], 12,708
Loew, Cora [Mrs. F. A.], 4,594, 4,597
Loewenberg, B. J., 11,306
Loewenthal, Minnie, 2,396
Loew's, Inc. (film company), 17,792
Lofstrand, Esther (1891-1975). *See* Shepherd, Esther
    (Lofstrand) (1891-1975)
Log-books, **1,431,** 1,505, **7,480, 7,481,** 11,481, 14,845
Log Cabin Club (NY), 5,530
Log cabins, 9,214
Log City Days (book), 4,256
Logan, Algernon Sydney, **14,817**
Logan, Ann Armat (1820-95), 15,043
Logan, Benjamin, 5,342
Logan, Deborah (Norris) [Mrs. George] (1761-1839),
    14,817, 14,845, 15,039, **15,040, 15,041,** 15,042
Logan, Eliza, 3,564
Logan, Ernest Alfred, 18,007
Logan Family, **10,004**
Logan Family (PA), 14,817, **15,039**
Logan, Frances [Miss], **15,042**
Logan, Frances D. (1899-), **10,328**
Logan, George, 15,000
Logan, George (1753-1821), 14,817, 15,039, 15,040,
    15,041
Logan, Isabel V. "Belly" Gardner (1864-?), **5,067**
Logan, James (1674-1751), 14,817, 14,845, 15,039,
    15,040
Logan, James O'Neill (1839-1909). *See* Logan, Olive.
    [Mrs. Henry A.] DeLille. [Mrs. William Wirt]
    Sikes. James O'Neill. James O'Neill Logan
    (1839-1909)

Logan, John A., Jr. (1865-99), 2,454
Logan, John Alexander (1826-86), Family, **2,454**
Logan, Joseph Clayton, **3,218**
Logan, Laura, 3,954
Logan, Maria Dickinson (1857-1939), 15,043
Logan, Martha, 10,004
Logan, Mary (ca. 1860-?). *See* Tucker, Mary (Logan)
    [Mrs. William F.] (ca. 1860-?)
Logan, Mary Simmerson (Cunningham) [Mrs. John
    Alexander] (1838-1923), 2,454
Logan, Mary Wynne Wister [Mrs. Algernon Sydney],
    14,817
Logan, Minnie May Swain (1893-1925), 17,924
Logan, Miriam, 5,067
Logan, Mrs. E. W. (Bowling), 4,369
Logan, Olive. [Mrs. Henry A.] DeLille. [Mrs.
    William Wirt] Sikes. James O'Neill. James
    O'Neill Logan (1839-1909), 16,150, 17,616
Logan, Patrick, 14,817
Logan, Robert Restalrig, **14,817**
Logan, Sarah (1751-96). *See* Fisher, Sarah (Logan)
    [Mrs. Thomas] (1751-96)
Logan School (MI), 8,170
Logan, Susie, 15,049
Logan, Yvonne, 10,206
Logic, **11,995**
Logsdon, Richard H., 11,936
Lohr, Josephine Wimsatt [Mrs. Lenox Riley]
    (1888-1975), 4,123
Lohr, Lenox Riley (1891-1968), **4,123**
Lohrer, Alice, **4,391**
Lohrfinck, Rosalind, 10,866, 10,871
Loines, Mary (Hilliard) [Mrs. Stephen] (1844-1944),
    2,457, **6,979**
"Lois Lenski's USA" (map), 2,938
Loitman, Jennie (1891-1969). *See* Barron, Jennie
    (Loitman) (1891-1969)
Lola Montez (drama), 442
Loma, Luisa "Indian Luisa," 1,429
Lombard, Carole. Jane Alice Peters. [Mrs. William]
    Powell [Mrs. Clark] Gable (1908-42), 1,025
Lombard College (IL), 4,255
    alumnae, 4,268
Lombard, Herbert Edwin (1863-1940), 7,681
Lombard, Nellie Montimorenci de Callahan
    (1840-1923), 7,681
London (England), 12,273
London Abolition Society, 14,989
London Anti-Slavery Convention (1840), 7,274
London, Charmian (Kittredge) [Mrs. Jack]
    (1883-1955), 448, 559, 628, 629, 712, 720, 737,
    783, 825, 847, 1,081, 1,082, 1,089, 1,441, 1,455,
    1,499, **4,262, 16,470**
London Daily Telegraph (England), 687
London, Isaac Spencer, **13,473**
London, Jack (1876-1916), 628, **629,** 657, 825, 847,
    1,082, 1,090, 1,441, 1,455, 1,499, 2,330, **16,470**
London, Joan (1901-71), 640
London Naval Conferences (1935-36), 6,771
"London: Past and Present" (ms), 17,616
London School of Economics (England), 11,857
    students, 561, 8,591
London Society of Friends, 7,284
London Yearly Meeting, 14,858
Loneliness, 6,777, 7,425, 8,164, 11,536, 13,409,
    16,385, 17,881
"Lonely Women/Today's Children" (soap opera),
    17,705
Long, Alfred, 11,242
Long, Alice, 15,343
Long, Alice R. Walton [Mrs. Elisha V.], 11,242
Long, Amy Requa, 476
Long, Boaz, 11,242
Long Bridge, The (book), 10,159
Long, Clifford Y., 17,676
Long, Crawford, 3,054, 3,101
Long, Crawford W., Family (GA), **3,054**
Long Day's Journey into Night (drama), 12,367
Long, Elisha V. (1836-1928), 11,242
Long, Elizabeth. *See* Thurmond, Elizabeth (Long)
Long, Ellen (Call) (1826-1904?), 2,931, 2,942
Long Family (GA), 3,054
Long Family (NM), **11,242**
Long, Fannie Blair, Family, **10,005**

Long, Frances "Fannie," 3,054
Long, George S., 11,863
Long Horse, Peter, **10,369**
Long, Huey Pierce, 5,537, 13,163
Long, Isaac, 10,005
Long Island Environmental Council, Inc. (NY), **12,875**
Long Island Federation of Women's Clubs (NY), 11,324
Long Island Forum (periodical), 12,778
Long Island University (NY), archives, **11,332**
Long, J. M. (Underwood) (1842-?), 630
Long, Jane, 16,041, 16,082
Long, Jean Stillman [Mrs. Clifford Y.] (1891-), **17,676**
Long Lane, The (book), 1,208
Long, Lillian Louise, **12,721**
Long, Lily Webb [Miss] (1847-1929), **13,179**, 13,180
Long, Margaret (1873-1957), **1,672, 1,724, 7,255**
Long, Margaret Eleanor (1893-). *See* Whisenand, Margaret Eleanor (Long) (1893-)
Long, Martha White (1829-1909), **9,886**
Long, Mary, 11,242
Long, Mary (1860-1940). *See* Alderson, Mary (Long) [Mrs. Matthew] (1860-1940)
Long, Mary Elitch, 1,751
Long, Mary Jane, 14,628
Long Moment, The (book), 13,945
Long, Mrs. James, 16,106
Long, Mrs. Robert J., 11,857
Long, Priscilla, **6,733**
Long, Richard T., 3,532
Long Roll, The (book), 8,433
Long, Sallie (Applegate), 14,506
Long, Teresa, 11,242
Long-term care of the sick, 3,733, **6,179**
Long Walk at San Francisco State, The (book), 3,771
Long, Walter E., **16,101**
Long, Westray Battle Boyce [Mrs. Willie J.] (1901-72), **10,075**
Long Wharf Theatre, 12,367
Long, William, **13,474**
Long, Willie J., 10,075
Longacre, Eliza [Mrs. James B.], 2,783
Longacre Family (PA), **2,783**
Longacre, James B. (1794-1869), 2,783
Longacre, Lydia (1870-1951), 2,783
Longbrake, George R., 8,541
Longbrake, Gertrude Marie Brandsmark [Mrs. George R.], **8,541**
Longden, Hazel Day [Mrs. Grafton J.], **4,532**
Longfellow, Alice, 6,471
Longfellow, Alice M., 1,224, 6,923
Longfellow, Anne (1810-1901). *See* Pierce, Anne (Longfellow) (1810-1901)
Longfellow, Anne (1855-1934). *See* Thorpe, Anne (Longfellow) (1855-1934)
Longfellow, Annie, **6,734**
Longfellow, Edith (1853-1915). *See* Dana, Edith (Longfellow) (1853-1915)
Longfellow Family, **6,330**
Longfellow, Frances "Fanny" Elizabeth (Appleton) [Mrs. Henry Wadsworth] (1817-61), 6,329, **6,331**, 10,858
Longfellow, Henry Wadsworth (1807-82), 1,426, 5,759, 5,815, 5,970, 6,329, 6,330, 6,331, **6,735**, 10,825, 14,206
Longfellow, Mary (1816-1902). *See* Greenleaf, Mary (Longfellow) (1816-1902)
Longfellow, Mary Alice [Miss] (1850-1928), **6,329**
Longfellow, Stephen, 6,330
Longfellow, Zilpah (Wadsworth) [Mrs. Stephen] (1788-1851), 6,330
Longino, A. H., 9,658
Longino, Marion Buckley, 9,709
Longley, A. S., 4,812
Longley, Alcander, 2,464
Longley, Alfred (?-1851), **9,185**
Longley, Alice L., **4,812**
Longley, Eliza Ann, 4,812
Longley Family (MA), 9,316
Longley, Julia Read [Mrs. Alfred], 9,185
Longley, Martha Anne (Taylor) [Mrs. Thomas], 9,316
Longley, Mary Ann Clark (1813-69). *See* Riggs,

Mary Ann Clark (Longley) [Mrs. Stephen Return] (1813-69)
Longley, Thomas, 9,316
Longman, Evelyn Beatrice, 2,338
Longmans, Green and Company (publishers), 14,388, 14,475
Longscope, Mrs. Charles Septimus, 16,060
Longshore, Hannah E. (Myers) [Mrs. Thomas Ellwood] (1819-1901), **12,139**, 15,144
Longshore, Lucretia (1845-1937). *See* Blankenburg, Lucretia (Longshore) [Mrs. Rudolph] (1845-1937)
Longstreet, Hannah, 15,550
Longstreet, Helen Dortch [Mrs. James] (1863-1962), 3,158, **3,219**
Longstreet, Isabella, 8,366
Longstreet, James, 3,219
Longstreet, Mary (1906-). *See* Wallace, Mary (Longstreet) (1906-)
Longstreet Memorial Association, 3,219
Longstreet, William R., 8,366
Longstreth, Mary Anna (1811-84), 14,950, 15,051
Longview State Hospital (OH), 13,869
Longwood (residence), 2,030
Longwood Gardens, **11,887**
Longwood Meeting of Progressive Quakers (PA), 4,754
Longworth, Alice Lee Roosevelt (1884-), 411, 1,593, 11,922
Longworth, Maria (1849-1932). *See* Storer, Maria (Longworth) [Mrs. George Ward] Nichols [Mrs. Bellamy, Jr.] (1849-1932)
Lonie, Agnes, **1,725**
Lonkeena, 16,877
Lonn, Ella, 2,540
Look (periodical), 17,614, 17,954, 17,991
Look Homeward Angel (drama), 17,797
Look Up and Hope! The Motto of the Volunteer Prison League, the Life of Maud Ballington Booth (book), 5,042
"Looking at Modern Art" (ms), 2,777
Looking Glass Diary (book), 7,316
Lookout, Chief Fred, 14,212
Lookout, Julia, 14,173
Lookout, Nora. *See* Standing Bear, Nora (Lookout)
Loomis, Alice (Green) Whitman [Mrs. Calvin], 880
Loomis, Ann Hendrix. *See* North, Ann Hendrix (Loomis) [Mrs. John W.]
Loomis, Augustus Ward, Family, **11,639**
Loomis, Calvin, 880
Loomis, Charles B., 10,450
Loomis, Elisha (1799-1836), **11,640**
Loomis, Estelle. *See* Burgess, Estelle (Loomis) [Mrs. Gelett]
Loomis, Jerusha Brewster (1806-72). *See* Farnham, Jerusha Brewster (Loomis) [Mrs. Eli] (1806-72)
Loomis, Mabel (1856-1932). *See* Todd, Mabel (Loomis) [Mrs. David Peck] (1856-1932)
Loomis, Maria Sartwell [Mrs. Elisha], 11,640
Loomis, Mary Ann [Mrs. Augustus Ward], 11,639
Loomis, Mildred [Mrs. John], 4,151
Loomis, Mrs., 1,240
Loomis, Pamelia Frances (1865-1945). *See* Benson, Pamelia Frances (Loomis) [Mrs. Simon] (1865-1945)
Loonie, Catherine, 11,440
Loos, Anita. [Mrs. John] Emerson (1893-), 949, 2,331, 2,360, 11,907
Looscan, Adele Lubbock (Briscoe) (1848-1935), **16,102**, 16,241
L'Operaia (newspaper), 12,861
Lord and Taylor, Inc., 6,879, 12,086
Lord, Caroline (1860-1927), 13,836
Lord, Charlotte S., **1,726**
Lord, Edward A., 6,999
Lord, Eleazer, 14,119
Lord, Elizabeth, 14,607
Lord-Heinstein, Lucile, **6,736**
Lord, Helen Cooper, 5,582
Lord, Jeannette (Mather) [Mrs. Frederick P.], **4,933**
Lord, Josephine McCurdy Caroline (1834-1910). *See* Smith, Josephine McCurdy Caroline (Lord) [Mrs. Charles Worcester] (1834-1910)
Lord, Juliette (Montague) [Mrs. William Paine], 14,607

Lord, Louisa, 7,451
Lord, Louisa [Mrs. Samuel], **15,495**
Lord Loveth a Cheerful Liar, The (book), 18,007
Lord, Lucy A., **9,186**
Lord, Lydia (?-1952). *See* Davis, Lydia (Lord) [Mrs. Francis W.] (?-1952)
Lord, Marion (1891-). *See* Hazzard, Marion (Lord) (1891-)
Lord, Mary (?-1874). *See* Floyd-Jones, Mary (Lord) [Mrs. Edward] (?-1874)
Lord, Mary Pillsbury [Mrs. Oswald Bates] (1904-78), **5,147, 6,737**, 9,089, 11,857, 12,078, 12,080
Lord, Montague, 14,607
Lord, Mrs. Eleazer, 14,119
Lord, Mrs. William Wilberforce, **2,455**
Lord, Nancy Ellen Boardman [Mrs. Edward A.] (1825-?), **6,999**
Lord, Pauline. [Mrs. Owen B.] Winters (1890-1950), 12,536, 16,150
Lord, William Paine (1839-1911), Family (OR), **14,607**
Lord, William Paine, Jr., 14,607
Lorenz, Alice B., 6,223
Lorenz, Catherine [Miss], 9,956
Lorenzana, Apolinaria, **631**, 748
Lorenzen, Coral [Mrs. Leslie], 212
Lorenzen, Leslie, 212
"Loretta Young Show, The" (television program), 1,024
Loretto Heights College (CO), 1,779, **1,784**
Lorimer, George Horace (1868-1934), 15,060
Loring, Anna (1830-96). *See* Dresel, Anna (Loring) [Mrs. Otto] (1830-96)
Loring, Cornelia, **6,199**
Loring, Dr., 12,503
Loring, Elizabeth Elaine (Brodt), **17,301**
Loring, Ellis Gray (1803-58), 6,466, **6,738**, 8,002, 12,419
Loring Family (MA), 6,595, 6,738
Loring, Louisa (Gilman) [Mrs. Ellis] (1797-1868), 6,466, 6,738, 7,634
Lorme, Lola (1883-), 10,866
Los Angeles County Juvenile Court (CA), 6,934
Los Angeles County Museum of Art (CA), 624
Los Angeles County Museum of Natural History (CA), 1,004
Los Angeles Feminist Theater (CA), 4,241
Los Angeles Girls' Town (CA), 696
Los Angeles Juvenile Hall (CA), 676
Los Angeles Library School (CA), students, 9,935
Los Angeles Mobilization for Democracy (CA), 1,012
Los Angles Normal School (CA), **1,042**
Los Angeles Philharmonic Orchestra (CA), 1,038
Los Angeles Police Department (CA), officials and employees, 863
Los Angeles Public Library (CA), 1,184
Los Angeles pueblo (CA), 392
Los Angeles Scientific Psychic Research Society (CA), 696
Los Angeles Times (CA), bombing of (1911), 1,507
Los Angeles Woman's Symphony Orchestra (CA), 1,429
Los Angeles Women's Health Center (CA), 6,748
Los Guilucos School for Girls (CA), 1,151
Los Rubios (opera), 1,022
Losey, Lucretia (Hitchcock) [Mrs. Nehemiah Homand] (1810-91), **4,263**
Losey, Nehemiah Homand, 4,263
Lossing, Benson J. (1813-91), 2,445, **14,085**
Lossing, Elizabeth Gurnee Anderson, 1,566
Lossing, Helen (Sweet), 14,085
Lost Angel (drama), 17,989
"Lost Breyfogle" (mine, NV), 10,728
"Lost Cause, The" (poem), 100
Lost Colony, The (drama), 13,100
Lost Father, The (book), 8,735
Lost Island (book), 11,991
Lost Keyes Mine, 10,368
Lost Lyrist, The (book), 12,817
Lost Murphy Mine, 10,724
Lost Sunset, The (moving-picture), 17,966
Lost Wagon Train (1853), 1,505, 14,282, 14,293, 14,294, 14,307, **14,583**

Lothrop, Amy (pseudonym). *See* Warner, Anna Bartlett (1824-1915)
Lothrop, Daniel (1831-92), 5,940
Lothrop, Harriett Mulford (Stone) [Mrs. Daniel] (1844-1924), 1,224, **5,940**, 5,956, 5,959, 7,055
Lothrop, Margaret Mulford (1884-), **5,940**
Lotman, Arline, **15,158**
Lototsky, Helen, 9,508, 9,512
Lott, Abby [Miss], 11,322
Lott, Cathrintie, 11,322
Lott, Edson S., 11,516
Lott, Elsie (Moore), **16,534**
Lott Family (NY), **11,322**
Lott, Jeremiah, 11,322
Lott, John F., 11,322
Lott, Lydia, 11,322
Lott, Maria S. [Miss], 11,322
Lott, Melvina J., **10,329**
Lotta Crabtree, Gold Rush Girl (book), 10,262
Lotta Svard Organization, 8,184
Lotteries, opposition to, **5,502**
Lotwin, Bernice, 2,701
Lotz, Catherine, 17,165
Lotz, George Franklin, 17,165
Lou, Aunt (1843-1926), 3,603
Lou Henry Hoover Girl Scout Fellowship, 6,964
Loucheim, Donald, 2,811
Louchheim, Kathleen "Katie" (Scofield) [Mrs. Walter C. Jr.] (1903-), **2,456**, 6,584, 11,827
Loudon (residence, PA), **15,043**
Loudon Village Anti-Slavery Sewing Circle (NH), 10,818
Loughborough, Louisa Watkins Wright [Mrs.] (1881-1962), **297**
Loughran, Henrietta Adams, **17,297**
Louisa Porter Foundation (GA), **3,543**
Louisburg College (Louisburg, NC), 13,322, 13,328, 13,573, 13,621
Louisburg Female College (Louisburg, NC). *See* Louisburg College (Louisburg, NC)
"Louise" (poem), 5,822
Louisiana, **5,410**, 5,430, 5,434, 5,449, 5,552, 9,699, 9,799, 13,051, 14,124
  abortion, legal aspects, 1,984
  Acadians, 5,410
  Afro-Americans, history, 5,535
  archives, **5,409**, **5,425**
  art, galleries and museums, **5,541**
  art schools, **5,452**
  art societies, **5,488**
  artists, **5,541**, **9,581**
  associations, institutions, etc., **5,421**, **5,500**
  authors, **5,414**, **5,415**, **5,418**, **5,524**, **5,526**, **5,528**, **5,543**, **9,640**
  balls (parties), **5,546**
  bands (music), **5,529**
  bank employees, **5,552**
  birds, 16,304
  bishops, 16,018
  boarding schools, 5,426
  bridges, 5,538, 5,542
  businessmen, 5,431, **9,987**
  carnival, 5,497
  Catholic hospitals, **5,493**
  Catholic schools, **5,556**
  cemeteries, 633
  census, 5,409, 5,497
  ceramists, 5,542
  charitable societies, **5,510**, **5,516**
  charities, 5,484
  charities, Jewish, 6,114
  chatauquas, 5,426
  church and race problems, Catholic Church, 3,844
  church records and registers, Lutheran, **5,433**
  church societies, 5,426, 5,433, 5,544, 5,551
  church societies, Methodist, **5,554**
  citizens' associations, 3,283
  Civil War, 5,412, 5,415, 5,480, 9,594
    campaigns and battles. 5,415
    destruction and pillage, **12,162**
    personal narratives, 5,485
  clergy, Episcopal, **5,492**
  clubs, **5,411**, 5,426, 5,443, **5,445**, **5,508**, **5,545**, **5,546**, 5,549

college librarians, **5,509**
college teachers, **5,432**, **5,512**, **5,550**
college trustees, **5,470**
colonial records, French, **5,436**
commission merchants, 8,781, 9,713
community leadership, **5,538**, **5,540**, **5,542**
community organization, **5,422**, 5,542
composers, 5,531
congresswomen, **5,504**
conservatories of music, 5,543
cookery, 9,799
court records, 5,497, 16,215
courts, colonial, 5,495, **5,496**
Creoles, 5,418
deans (in schools), **5,419**, **5,506**
diaries and journals, 5,553, **13,096**, **13,113**, **13,114**
dramatists, **5,453**
educational associations, **5,429**, **5,438**
educators, **5,426**, 5,543
elections, 5,499, 13,163, 17,992
environmental policy, citizen participation, 5,538, 5,542
epidemics, 5,492
evening and continuation schools, 5,426
exhibitions, 6,664
farmers, 5,549
fishing, 5,410
folk-lore, 5,539
folk-songs, French, 5,539
folklorists, **5,539**
freedmen, 2,154, **9,604**
French-American literature, **5,418**
French in, **5,495**
governors, 12,963
governors, colonial, 5,495
high schools, 5,519
highway departments, 5,443
historians, **5,414**, **5,415**
historians, Afro-American, **5,535**
historical societies, 5,414
history, periodicals, 5,414
horticulturists, **5,538**
hours of labor, 16,237
hunting, 5,410
jazz, 5,531
journalists, **5,451**, **5,514**, **5,522**, 5,543
judges, 5,487
juvenile courts, 5,540
labor and laboring classes, dwellings, **5,544**
languages, mixed, 1,493, 5,410
law partnership, **5,536**
lawyers, **5,476**
legislators, 5,537, 9,605
legislators, Afro-American, 5,473
literary societies, 5,418, **5,447**
lotteries, opposition to, **5,502**
lynching, prevention of, 3,279
martial law, **5,480**
monasticism and religious orders for women, Catholic, **5,427**, **5,428**, **5,503**, **5,556**
municipal government, records and correspondence, 5,538
museums, 5,542
music-halls (variety theaters, etc.), 5,532
musical societies, 5,550
newspaper publishers and publishing, **4,270**
newspapers, 9,771
  sections, columns, etc., 9,600, 9,771
nursing schools, 5,494
officials and employees, **9,572**
old age homes, **5,520**
opera, 5,550
orphans and orphan asylums, 5,426, **5,520**, 6,114
orphans and orphan asylums, Jewish, 13,764
patriotic societies, 5,549
plantation life, 12,969, 13,105
plantations, 5,410, 5,449, 5,490, 5,552, 5,553, 9,594, 9,987
politics and government, 13,163
politics, practical, women's activism, **5,548**
poor, 16,215
private colleges, **5,547**
public health nursing, 3,432
public records, **5,409**, 5,497

public schools, 5,499
public works, **5,422**, **5,424**, **5,425**
real property, cases, 12,162
registers of births, etc., 5,409
reporters and reporting, 6,882
roadside improvement, 5,443
sanitation, 5,499, 5,500
scholarships, 5,545
school integration, 5,470
schools, Afro-American, finance, 3,299
senators, United States, 5,537, 13,163
singers, **5,533**
slave records, 5,440, 5,491
slavery, **5,423**, **5,491**, 5,549
slaves, 5,423
social life and customs, 5,410, 5,490, **5,527**, 12,590, 13,102
social reformers, 5,426
social science research, 16,215
social settlements, 5,515
societies, Jewish, **13,764**, **13,805**
soldiers, 5,481
Spanish in, **5,496**
spiritualism, **5,501**
state boards of education, 5,517
suffrage, 5,514, 6,629
suffrage societies, **5,499**
suffragists, 5,517
synagogues, 13,805
teachers, **2,531**, 5,487
temperance societies, 5,487
theater, 5,410
theaters, 6,882
trade and professional associations, **5,416**, **5,417**
United Methodist Church, **5,551**
universities and colleges, 5,446
  archives, **5,437**, **5,454**
  faculty, **5,539**
  finance, **5,507**, **5,545**
urban beautification, 5,500
urban renewal, 5,540
vital statistics, 5,495, 5,496
voodooism, 5,501
voters, registration of, 5,487
wages, minimum wage, 16,237
widows, 5,520, **5,553**, 13,764
witchcraft, 5,410
women's colleges, 5,517, 5,551
World War II, civilians' work, 16,215
Louisiana Association of Student Nurses, **5,416**
Louisiana Chatauqua, 5,426
Louisiana Federation of Women's Clubs, 5,443, 5,549
Louisiana Folklore Society, **5,539**
Louisiana Highway Commission, 5,443
Louisiana Historical Quarterly (periodical), 5,414
Louisiana Historical Society, 5,414
Louisiana Hour and Health Law for Female Workers (1938), 16,237
Louisiana Lady (book), 5,158
Louisiana Lottery Company, 5,502
Louisiana Minimum Wage Law for Female Workers (1938), 16,237
Louisiana Oil Company, 9,668
Louisiana Purchase Exposition (1904), 2,472
Louisiana Relief Committee, 5,484
Louisiana State Board of Education, 5,517
Louisiana State Museum, 5,542
Louisiana State Normal College. *See* Northwestern State University (LA)
Louisiana State Nurses' Association, 5,416, **5,417**
Louisiana State Tuberculosis Commission, 5,499
Louisiana State University, deans, **5,419**
Louisiana Supreme Court, 5,487
Louisiana Women's War Relief Association, **5,516**
Louisville Courier Journal (KY), 14,093
Louisville Equal Rights Association (KY), **5,354**
Louisville Family Service Organization (KY), 8,637
Louisville Female High School (KY), 17,090
Louisville Free Public Library, West Branch Library (KY), 5,382
Louisville Girls High School, Alumnae Club (KY), **5,355**
Louisville Library Committee (KY), 5,337

Louisville Normal School (KY), alumnae, 5,384
Louisville Textiles (KY), **7,118**
Louk, Ione (1912-), **8,501**
Lounsberry, C. A., 13,661
Lourey, Mary W., 14,515
Lourie, Emma (Keene) [Mrs. Joseph H.], **10,278**
Loussac, Ada, 17,282
Loutrel, Anna, 1,319
Love, Alexander, 2,949
Love and Marriage (book), 16,154
Love as Love, Death as Death (book), 16,165
Love, Cornelia Spencer, 13,176
Love, David S., 14,293
Love Family (CT, NY), **2,020**
Love Family (FL), **2,949**
Love Field (Dallas, TX), 5,311
Love, Georgia, 2,945
Love, Helen Douglas (?-1969). *See* Scranton, Helen Douglas (Love) (?-1969)
Love, Helen Marnie (Stewart) [Mrs. David S.] (1835-73), 606, 1,505, **14,293**, 14,462
"Love Is a Many Splendored Thing" (soap opera), 17,705
Love, James Lee, 13,134
Love, Julia (Larrabee) [Mrs. Don], 4,928
Love, June (Spencer) [Mrs. James Lee], 13,134
Love, Laura, 4,461
Love Letter to Gertrude and Alice, A (book), 819
Love-letters, 1,487, 3,979, 5,940, 7,410, 9,185, 9,651, **9,865, 9,888,** 9,973, 13,030, 13,599, 14,308, **14,518,** 15,768, 16,969
"Love Letters to Rookie-Budd" (ms), 17,400
Love, Lucy Cleveland Prindle [Mrs. Edward Gurley], 2,020
Love, Margaret, 13,448
Love, Maria M. (1839 or 1840-1931), 11,339
"Love or Loyalty? A Story of Lynch Law" (ms), 2,612
Love, Pearl Trogden [Mrs.], 2,949
Love Possessed Juana (book), 12,362
Love Story of Clara and Robert Schumann, The (book), 6,114
Love, Thomas B., 2,635
Love to the Irish (book), 6,017
Love to Vietnam (book), 6,058
Love, W. F., 9,697
Lovejoy, Elizabeth [Mrs.], 14,586
Lovejoy, Esther (Clayson) Pohl (1869-1967), **14,697**
Lovejoy Family (GA), **3,031**
Lovejoy, Julia Louisa (Hardy) [Mrs. Charles H.] (1812-82), **5,220, 10,879**
Lovejoy, Mary Blanche (1905-), 9,467
Lovelace, Maud (Hart) [Mrs. Delos] (1892-), **8,489,** 8,492
Loveland, Bertha Eugenia (1877-1949). *See* Selmon, Bertha Eugenia (Loveland) (1877-1949)
Loveland, Mrs. Frank C., 12,348
Lovell, Emily (Plympton) [Mrs. Mansfield], 1,457
Lovell Family (MA), **12,550**
Lovell, John, Jr., 2,123
Lovell, Laura, 12,550
Lovell, Mansfield (1822-84), **1,457**
Lovell, Martha B., 12,550
Lovell, Mary E. (1840-1925). *See* Carpenter, Mary E. (Lovell) [Mrs. George] (1840-1925)
Lovell, Patience (1725-86). *See* Wright, Patience (Lovell) [Mrs. Joseph] (1725-86)
Lovell, Sylvia [Mrs. Lorenzo Orin] (ca. 1812-?), 8,978
Lovell, Virginia (Lyman), 16,750
Lovell's Polly (book), 111
Loveman, Amy (1881-1955), 2,216, 2,596, 3,290, 4,482, 11,837, **12,035**
Lovering, Elizabeth C., 12,497
"Lover's Serenade, The" (poem), 7,658
"Loves and wives of E. J. Baldwin, The" (ms), 906
Lovett, Beatrice Russel (1898-), **9,187**
Lovett, Elizabeth, 3,333
Lovett, Marietta (Smith) [Mrs. Robert Watkins], 3,333
Lovett, Robert Morss, 4,146
Lovett, Robert Watkins (1818-1912), **3,333**
Lovett, Sarah Isabell (Price) [Mrs. Robert Watkins], 3,333
Lovey, Gertrude (?-1965), **632**

Loving, Sylvia Caroline, 1,533
Low, Annie [Mrs. Seth], 12,036
Low, Ellen (1827-98). *See* Mills, Ellen (Low) [Mrs. Ethelbert Smith] (1827-98)
Low Family (NY), **2,457**
Low, Harriet (1809-77). *See* Hilliard, Harriet (Low) [Mrs. John H.] (1809-77)
Low, Josiah Orne (1821-95), **12,551**
Low, Juliette "Daisy" Magill Kinzie (Gordon) [Mrs. William Mackay] (1860-1927), **2,109,** 3,393, 3,531, 3,594, 3,600, 12,095, 12,108, **12,109,** 12,111
Low, Mary (Fairchild) [Mrs. Fredrick] MacMonnies, 2,739
Low, Minnie F., 7,548
Low, Seth (1850-1916), **12,036,** 12,485
Lowber, Edith Hunn, **2,423**
Lowe, Alice, 7,023
Lowe, Bartley M., 72
Lowe, Berenice (Bryant) (1896-), **7,846, 8,008**
Lowe, Blanche Beal, **9,887**
Lowe, Bridget Ann, 9,887
Lowe, Caroline Ann (1885-1933), **5,210**
Lowe, Edwina, 5,469
Lowe, Joanna Asquisth (1945-), 10,151
Lowe, Kittie, 9,887
Lowe, Maria, 12,251
Lowe, Mary C. (Morrison) [Mrs. George], 1,666
Lowe, Mary Emma [Mrs. Vincent A.], 8,154
Lowe, Mary Louise (Belnap) [Mrs. Joseph], **16,743**
Lowe, Mollie, 13,420
Lowe, Mrs. E. L., **9,188**
Lowe, Peter (1764-1818), **12,251**
Lowe, Sarah (1845-1937), **71**
Lowe, Sophia. *See* Davis, Sophia (Lowe) [Mrs. Nicholas]
Lowe, Vincent A., 8,154
Lowe, William Fletcher, 9,887
Lowell, Abbott Lawrence (1856-1943), **6,291,** 6,484
Lowell, Amy Lawrence (1874-1925), 378, 2,403, 2,643, 4,005, 4,226, 7,319, 10,853, 11,036, 11,254, 11,897, 11,944, 11,969, 15,967, 17,013, 17,053, 17,114, 17,197
Lowell, Charlotte, 2,491
Lowell, Edith (1888-?), 5,580, 5,582
Lowell House Mothers' Club (New Haven, CT), **1,997**
Lowell House Settlement (New Haven, CT), 1,997, 7,243
Lowell, James Russell, 1,426, 6,974, 16,170
Lowell, Joan, 2,205
Lowell, Josephine (Shaw) [Mrs. Charles Russell] (1843-1905), 2,542, 2,549, 6,565, 12,080, **12,252,** 12,375, 12,403, 12,864
Lowell, Leslie M., **14,608**
Lowell, Marcia Johnson (?-1965), **1,853**
Lowell, Mary Chandler (1863-1949), **5,578**
Lowell, Mary Traill Spence (1810-98). *See* Putnam, Mary Traill Spence (Lowell) (1810-98)
Lowell Offering (periodical), 5,899, 11,305
Lowell, Percival, 1,954
Lowenfels, Walter, 12,064
Lowenthal, Esther, 12,815
Lowenthal, Marvin, 933
Lower Deer Creek Mennonite Church (IA), Women's Missionary and Service Auxiliary. *See* Lower Deer Creek Mennonite Church (IA), Women's Missionary Sewing Circle
Lower Deer Creek Mennonite Church (IA), Women's Missionary Sewing Circle, **5,052**
Lower Deer Creek Mennonite Church (IA), Women's Sewing Circle. *See* Lower Deer Creek Mennonite Church (IA), Women's Missionary Sewing Circle
Lower East Side Neighborhood Association (NY), 8,651, **8,661**
Lowery, M. P., 9,684
Lowery, Sarah [Mrs. M. P.], 9,684
Lowman, Mrs. William, 11,440
Lowman, William, 11,440
Lowndes County Board of Health (GA), **3,608**
Lowndes County Historical Society (GA), **3,610**
Lowndes, Marie Adelaide (Belloc) (1868-1947), 16,166, 16,173

Lowndes, Mrs. Belloc, 12,044
Lowndes, Rebecca (?-ca. 1800). *See* Stoddert, Rebecca (Lowndes) [Mrs. Benjamin] (?-ca. 1800)
Lowndes, Sally Scott Lloyd, 5,789
Lowrey, Janie. *See* Graves, Janie (Lowrey) Sanford
Lowrey, M. P., 9,543
Lowrey, Modena (1850-1942). *See* Berry, Modena (Lowrey) (1850-1942)
Lowrie, Helen (Ogden), **12,722**
Lowrie, Mrs. John R., **633**
Lowrie, Rebecca (Lawrence) (1891-1976), 6,416, 6,475, **6,739**
Lowry Air Force Base (CO), 1,769
Lowry, Helen Bullitt, 2,205
Lowry, Kathryn Runge [Mrs.], **9,666**
Lowry, Martha [Mrs.], 11,002
Lowry, Mrs. J. C., **9,667**
Lowther, Margaret. *See* Page, Margaret (Lowther) [Mrs. John]
Loy, Mryna (1905-), 10,393, 11,907
Loyal Orange Ladies' Institution, Purple Star Lodge, No. 131 (Sacramento, CA), **1,155**
Loyal Star of America (GA), Atlanta Lodge Number Fifty-six, **3,220**
Loyal Temperance Legion, 1,668
Loyalists, American, 2,342, 11,980
Loyall, Virginia (1801-70). *See* Farragut, Virginia (Loyall) [Mrs. David] (1801-70)
Loyalty oaths, 561, 811, 916, 2,579, 2,679, 3,521, 7,187
Loyalty Review Board, 64
Loyless, Margaret. *See* Mell, Margaret (Loyless) [Mrs. Patrick]
Lozier, Clemence Sophia (Harned) (1813-88), 12,917
Lubbock Chamber of Commerce (TX), 16,275
Lubbock Council for the United Nations (TX), 16,265
Lubbock Garden Club (TX), 16,278
Lubbock Junior Garden Club (TX), 16,278
Lubbock Needle Club (TX), 16,278
Lubbock, Percy, 4,491
Lubbock Planning and Zoning Commission (TX), 16,259
Lubbock, Richard, 15,483
Lubbock Symphony Orchestra (TX), 16,275
Lubin, Isador, 2,693
Lubin, Simon J., Society, **797**
Luca (ship), 16,611
Lucas, Bertha, **5,723**
Lucas, Elizabeth E., **9,961**
Lucas, Elizabeth "Eliza" (1722?-1793). *See* Pinckney, Elizabeth "Eliza" (Lucas) [Mrs. Charles] (1722?-93)
Lucas, Harriet Annie, 14,814
Lucas, Mary E., 1,086
Lucas, Mrs. F. W., 3,049
Lucas, Robert, 4,958
Lucas, Roy, **1,984**
Lucca, Pauline. *See* Nininger, Pauline
Luccock, Naphtali, 4,208
Luce, Abigail (Howell) [Mrs. Abraham], 12,779
Luce, Abraham (ca. 1789-ca. 1865), 12,779
Luce, Clare (Boothe) [Mrs. George Tuttle] Brokaw [Mrs. Henry Robinson] (1903-), 1,605, 2,097, 2,205, 2,242, **2,458,** 4,233, 4,640, 5,123, 5,135, 5,137, 5,156, 9,823, 11,857, 12,708, 13,406, 14,820, 15,564
"Luce Empire, The," 14,451
Luce Family (NY), **12,779**
Luce, Grace, 1,233
Luce, Henry Robinson, 2,458, 14,451, 15,564
Luce, Nancy (1820-90), **7,026**
Luce, Stephen B., 2,535
Lucia, Carmen (1902-), **3,446, 16,001,** 16,011
Lucier, Ruby Norman, **5,148**
"Luck of Batture Baptiste, The" (ms), 5,526
Luck of the Van Meers, The (ms), 6,046
Lucke, Elmina, 9,492
Luckett, Catherine, Family, **10,006**
Luckett, Maggie C. [Mrs.], **9,668**
Luckett, Tom, 9,668
Luckey, Eunice Waters (Robbins), 14,420, **14,609**
Luckey, Mrs. James C., 14,689
Luckey School for Girls (St. Paul, MN), 9,295

Luckie, Mary O. (Barton) [Mrs. S. Blair] (1862-1964), **6,740**
Lucky Devil (moving-picture), 18,003
Lucy (book), 15,612
Lucy (freedwoman, MO), 9,972
Lucy (slave, NY), 2,141
Lucy (slave, SC), 4,239
Lucy, Autherine (1930-), 112
Lucy Cobb Institute (Athens, GA), 3,024, **3,055,** 3,080, 3,092, 3,266
Lucy Cobb Institute and Home School (Athens, GA), 3,130, 15,729
Lucy Flower Technical High School (Chicago, IL), 4,165
Lucy Gates Opera Company of Salt Lake City (UT), 16,577
Lucy Gayheart (book), 12,414
Lucy Kroll Agency, 2,431
Lucy, Mack, Home for Girls (UT), **16,744**
Lucy, Sister Eleanor, 6,353
"Lucy Somerville Howorth: Legislative Career, 1932-1935" (thesis), 9,544
"Lucy Stone" (drama), 6,981
Lucy Stone, a Chronicle Play, 2,209
Lucy Stone League, 2,205, 6,399, 9,995, 14,377
Ludington, Florabelle (1898-), 7,499, 11,937
Ludington, Katherine, 11,886
Ludlam, Bertha Stewart [Miss], 3,919
Ludlow, Annie Rubamah. *See* Hunt, Annie Rubamah (Ludlow) [Mrs. Randell]
Ludlow, Catherine. *See* Baker, Catherine (Ludlow)
Ludlow, Catherine. *See* Whiteman, Catherine (Ludlow)
Ludlow, Charles, 11,323
Ludlow, Charlotte. *See* Jones, Charlotte (Ludlow)
Ludlow, Clara S., **2,089**
Ludlow, Cornelia, 11,323
Ludlow, Cornelia Ann (ca. 1805-65). *See* Willink, Cornelia Ann (Ludlow) [Mrs. John A.] (ca. 1805-65)
Ludlow, Edward, 11,499
Ludlow, Elizabeth, 15,691
Ludlow, Elizabeth [Miss] (1785?-1867), 11,330, 15,799
Ludlow, Elizabeth Livingston [Mrs. Edward], 11,499
Ludlow Family, 11,499
Ludlow Family, **17,992**
Ludlow Family (NY), **11,323**
Ludlow, Gabriel, 11,323
Ludlow, Israel, 17,992
Ludlow, James C., 17,992
Ludlow, James Chambers, 17,992
Ludlow, James Dunlop, 17,992
Ludlow, John, 11,323
Ludlow, Josephine (Dunlop), 17,992
Ludlow, Mary, 11,323
Ludlow, Sarah Bella (?-1852). *See* Chase, Sarah Bella (Ludlow) [Mrs. Salmon] (?-1852)
Ludlow, Susan (Middlecoff) [Mrs. James Dunlop], 17,992
Ludwig, Mary. *See* McCauley, Mary (Ludwig) Hays
Ludwig, Sister Mileta, 17,572
Lufkin, Emeline Baker (Swain), 634
Lufkin Family (CA), **634**
Luftwaffe (Germany), 11,831
Lugan, Wahleah, 16,873
Lugg, M. Jean, **12,922**
Luhan, Mabel (Ganson) Dodge (1879-1962), 572, 702, 831, 1,451, 2,403, 2,631, 4,476, 8,077, 11,235
Luiseño Indians, 11,293
Luke, Leontine G. [Mrs.] (1909-), **5,540**
Lukens, Carrie E. *See* Smith, Carrie E. (Lukens)
Lukens Family, **5,941**
Lukens, Maggie W. *See* Pratt, Maggie W. (Lukens)
Lukens, Margaret. *See* Adamson, Margaret (Lukens) Smith
Lukens, Rebecca Webb (Pennock) [Mrs. Charles] (1794-1854), 2,029, 2,031
Lukens Steel Company, 2,029
Lulkin, Sheli A., **4,124**
Lullabies, 8,310
Lumbee Indians, 2,883

Lumber camps, **5,651, 5,664,** 9,078, 9,096, 11,863, 14,495
Lumber trade, 8,974, 9,099, 9,424, **9,433,** 10,355, 10,952, 12,420, **14,495,** 17,506
Lumber, transportation, 8,167, 14,305
Lumbering, 497, 5,624, 5,644, 5,689, 8,167, 8,333, 9,078, 9,152, 9,468, 9,694, 10,715, 14,509, 17,274, 17,532, **17,587**
machinery, 11,863
Lumbermen, **8,374, 9,076, 9,078,** 9,096, 9,126, **9,449,** 11,863, **14,565**
songs and music, 5,664, 9,078, 9,387
Lumbert, Charlotte. *See* Wainwright, Charlotte (Lumbert) [Mrs. Peter, Jr.]
Lumm Family, 4,942
Lummis, Charles Fletcher, 215, 1,465, 12,380
Lummis, Dorthea (Rhodes) [Mrs. Charles Fletcher] (ca. 1860-1942). *See* Moore, Dorthea (Rhodes) [Mrs. Charles Fletcher] Lummis [Mrs. Ernest Carroll] (ca. 1860-1942)
Lummis, Elizabeth Fries (1812?-77). *See* Ellet, Elizabeth Fries (Lummis) (1812?-77)
Lummis, Frances Douglas [Mrs. Charles Fletcher] (1870-1969). *See* De Kalb, Frances Douglas [Mrs. Charles Fletcher] Lummis [Mrs. Courtenay] (1870-1969)
Lummus, Lucinda M., 7,075
Lumpkin, Amanda (Boulware) [Mrs. Richardson] (?-1872), 3,373
Lumpkin Family (GA), **3,056**
Lumpkin-Huddleston, Idolene, 3,221
Lumpkin, Joseph Henry, **3,057**
Lumpkin, Katharine Dupre (1897-), 13,176
Lumpkin, Martha, 3,056
Lumpkin, Martha (1827-1917). *See* Compton, Martha (Lumpkin) [Mrs. T. H.] (1827-1917)
Lumpkin, Martha Neville (1844-1915), 15,895
Lumpkin, Mrs. Wilson, 3,381
Lumpkin, Sarah Elizabeth. *See* Bomar, Sarah Elizabeth (Lumpkin) Hayes [Mrs. Benjamin F.]
Lumpkin, William, 3,381
Lumpkin, Wilson, **3,058,** 3,221
Lunarcharskii, Anatolii, 12,361
"Luncheon for Lady Doers," 6,899
Lund, A. C., 16,535
Lund, Cornelia (Sorenson) (1882-1959), **16,535**
Lund, Edla (1867-?), 4,319
Lund, Elizabeth Martha Ellis [Mrs. Francis Marion] (1887-), **16,746**
Lund, Eugene, 9,522
Lund, Joyce Dreton [Mrs. Eugene] (1909-), **9,522**
Lund, Mary Loud, 15,853
Lund, Matilda Barker, **7,402**
Lund, Maxine (1926-). *See* Breinholt, Maxine (Lund) [Mrs. Harvey Cowley] (1926-)
Lund, Rhoda [Mrs. Russell], **9,189**
Lund, Thea Annie. *See* Henrie, Thea Annie (Lund)
Lundberg, Emma Octavia (1880 or 1881-1954), 11,916, **12,037**
Lundberg, Helen Sheldon, 8,174
Lunde, Erling, 9,522
Lunde, Laura Hughes [Mrs. Erling H.] (1886-1966), **4,125**
Lundquist, Mrs. Charles, 9,287
Lundy, Benjamin, 7,751
Lundy, Ida, 16,485
Lung Hwa Camp (China), 1,571
Lungs, diseases, 3,813
Lunney, Grace H., 9,309
Lunsford, Azalea, 13,298
Lunsford, Bascom Lamar (1882-1973), **13,298**
Lunsford, Jennie Louise (1875-1966), 13,298
Lunt, Alice Maude (1876-?). *See* Matheson, Alice Maude (Lunt) [Mrs. Daniel] (1876-?)
Lunt, Belle Waldrip [Mrs. C. L.], **4,772**
Lunt, Cornelia Gray [Miss] (1843-1934), **4,214,** 7,685
Lunt, Dolly Sumner (1817-91). *See* Parks, Dolly Sumner (Lunt) [Mrs. Samuel Harding] Lewis [Mrs. Thomas] Burge [Mrs. William Justice] (1817-91)
Lunt, Henry, 16,402
Lunt, Henry, **16,747**
Lunt, Mary Ann, 16,402
Lunt, Storer B., 11,164

Luquer Family, 12,068
Lurey Caverns, 12,545
Luria, Albert Moses, **13,475**
Lurie, Edith [Mrs. Meyer], 17,282
Lurie, Harry L. (1892-1973), **8,662**
Luscomb, Florence H. (1887-), 6,332, **6,980**
Luscombe, Lucy. *See* Beardsley, Lucy Luscombe [Mrs. Clarence B.]
Lush, L. L., 10,384
Lusk Commission, 11,774
Lusk, Georgia Lee (1893-), **11,243**
Lusk, Juanita (Turner), 848
Luther College (Decorah, IA)
records and correspondence, **4,715**
students, 9,297
Luther College Women's Club (Decorah, IA), **4,719**
Luther, Sally, 9,467
Lutheran Board of Missions, Lutheran Free Church, **8,860**
Lutheran Church, 8,186
biography, 8,856, 8,858, 8,860, 10,142
charities, 8,857, **8,859,** 8,861, **8,863, 8,867**
clergy, 4,319, **4,326,** 8,738, 8,748, 8,749, 8,751, 8,752, 8,774, 8,856, **8,866**
education, 3,962, 4,319, 8,858, 8,860, **8,864,** 8,867
government, 8,793, **8,859**
missionaries, 3,958, 3,962, **8,856, 8,858, 8,860,** 8,868, 8,869, 8,874, 8,875, 8,878, 8,880, 8,882, **8,883, 8,884, 8,887, 8,888, 8,889,** 10,142, 10,143, **14,796, 14,799**
missionaries, medical, 8,875, 9,514
missions, 3,959, 3,962, **3,963, 3,965,** 4,319, 4,870, 5,224, **7,612, 8,858, 8,860,** 8,861, 8,868, 8,869, 8,880, 9,514
publishing, 3,962, 3,966
radio scripts, 3,962
societies, 8,861, 8,865, 8,867
Lutheran Church in America, Lutheran Church Women, **3,959**
Lutheran Church in America, Women of the Illinois Synod, **3,960**
Lutheran Church—Missouri Synod, **10,139**
Lutheran Church—Missouri Synod, Lutheran Women's Missionary League, **10,140, 10,141**
Lutheran Daughters of the Reformation. *See* American Lutheran Church Women
Lutheran Deaconess Home and Hospital (IL), **8,760**
Lutheran Deaconess Home and Hospital (MN), **8,761**
Lutheran Deaconess Home and Hospital (NY), 8,857, 8,859, **8,862,** 8,865
Lutheran Free Church, Diaconate, 8,859
Lutheran Free Churches, 8,867
Lutheran Girls' Home, 8,857, **8,863**
Lutheran Hospital of Manhattan (NY). *See* Lutheran Medical Center (NY)
Lutheran Ladies' Seminary (Red Wing, MN), 4,914, **8,762, 8,817, 8,864**
Lutheran Maternity Home (SD), 8,857
Lutheran Medical Center (NY), **8,770**
Lutheran Memorial Church (Pierre, SD), Ladies Aid Society, 15,855
Lutheran Nurses Guild, **8,865,** 14,797
Lutheran Theological Seminary (PA), faculty, 14,798
Lutheran Women (periodical), 3,959
Lutheran Women's Missionary League, **14,496**
Lutheran Women's Missionary League, Kansas District, **5,224**
Lutheran Women's Work (periodical), 3,966
Lutheran Women's World (periodical), 3,962
Lutt, Hattie, 11,689
Lutz, Alma [Miss] (1890-1973), **6,741, 6,742,** 7,272, 14,377
Lutz, Bertha, 2,714
Lutz, Grace [Mrs. Flavius J.] (1865-1947). *See* Hill, Grace (Livingston) [Mrs. Thomas Guthrie Franklin]. [Mrs. Flavius J.] Lutz (1865-1947)
Lux, Miranda W., 11,547
Luxembourg, American ambassador to, 14,237
Luy, Minnie Ida (Bybee) [Mrs. Fred, Jr.] (1871-1952), **14,484**
Luzadder, Helen Wilson (1867-1963), **3,705**
Lvova, Princess Nadezhda (1826-1904). *See* Turchine, Nadine [Mrs. John Basil] (1826-1904)
Lybeck, Ruth [Mrs.], **1,043**

Lycée Jeane D'Arc (Orleans, France), 13,953
Lydia Baird Home (Carlisle, PA), 14,749
Lydia Estes Pinkham Medicine Company, 6,743
Lydig Family, 12,431
Lydig, Maria (1824-94). See Daly, Maria (Lydig)
    [Mrs. Charles Patrick] (1824-94)
Lyell, Loraine, 12,253
Lykins, Mrs. Johnston, 10,115
Lyman, Alice, 17,918, 17,919
Lyman, Amasa Mason, 16,536, 16,537, 16,749,
    16,751, 16,752, 16,902, 16,945
Lyman, Amy Cassandra (Brown) [Mrs. Richard
    Roswell] (1872-1959), 16,536, 16,748
Lyman, Arthur Theodore, 6,444
Lyman, Butler, 1,505
Lyman, Eliza Maria (Partridge) [Mrs. Joseph] Smith
    [Mrs. Amasa Mason] (1820-86), 16,537, 16,749,
    16,902, 16,945
Lyman, Ella (1866-1934). See Cabot, Ella (Lyman)
    [Mrs. Richard Clarke] (1866-1934)
Lyman, Esther (Brakeman) [Mrs. Joseph]
    (1826-1917). See Butler, Esther (Brakeman)
    [Mrs. Joseph] Lyman [Mrs. Thomas]
    (1826-1917)
Lyman Family (CA), 635
Lyman Family (IL), 4,436
Lyman, Florence Vern (Nielson) [Mrs. Callis]
    (1891-1976), 16,750
Lyman, Francis M., 16,536
Lyman, Helen (Hoyt) [Mrs. William Whittingham],
    635
Lyman, Henry Martyn, 4,436
Lyman House (MA), 6,265
Lyman, Joseph (?-1871), 1,505, 14,294
Lyman, Louisa Maria (Tanner) [Mrs. Amasa Mason]
    (1818-1906), 16,751
Lyman, Lovancia (Pease) [Mrs. Henry Martyn]
    (1821-1912), 4,436
Lyman, Marcia (Dewey) [Mrs. Orange], 4,436
Lyman, Marguerite Rice [Mrs. Bert] (1893 or
    1894-), 10,676
Lyman, Mary, 7,403
Lyman, Orange (?-1851), 4,436
Lyman, Oscar, 16,752
Lyman, Paulina, 16,417
Lyman, Pauline Eliza (Phelps) [Mrs. Amasa Mason]
    (1827-1912), 16,752
Lyman, R. W., 1,230
Lyman, Richard Roswell, 16,536
Lyman, Samuel, 7,403
Lyman, Sarah G., 14,650
Lyman, Stephen, 4,436
Lyman, Theodore, 11,814
Lyman, Thomas, 4,436
Lyman, Virginia. See Lovell, Virginia (Lyman)
Lymphatics, 7,288, 14,900
    tuberculosis, 2,090
Lympus Family, 4,811
Lynam, Mary Louise, 17,937
Lynch, Alice Mary (Kennedy) (1833-1911), 636
Lynch, Anna Charlotte (1815-91). See Botta, Anna
    Charlotte (Lynch) [Mrs. Vincenzo] (1815-91)
Lynch, Deliah, 15,144
Lynch Family, 12,068
Lynch Family (MO), 10,009
Lynch, Harriet Powe, 15,733
Lynch, Helen Gertrude (1902-38), 12,884
Lynch, Julia (1814-79). See Olin, Julia (Lynch) [Mrs.
    Stephen] (1814-79)
Lynch, Mary (Atkins) [Mrs. John] (1819-82), 326
Lynch, Mary H. See Wilkes, Mary H. (Lynch) [Mrs.
    William C.] Bolton [Mrs. Charles]
Lynch, Mother Mary Joseph, 8,705
Lynchburg Methodist Episcopal Church (SC), 15,615
Lynching, 338, 339, 2,315, 2,502, 3,186, 3,283, 9,467,
    12,939, 16,525, 16,540
    prevention of, 3,279, 3,326
Lynd, Helen (Merrell) [Mrs. Robert Staughton]
    (1896-), 2,459, 11,306, 11,888
Lynd, Robert Staughton (1892-), 2,459
Lyndon, Martha Dorothy [Miss], 3,125
Lyndonville Enterprise (NY), 11,269
Lynem, Lillie, 4,085, 4,096
Lynes, Russell, 4,485

Lynett, William, 17,465
Lyngblomsten Retirement Center (St. Paul, MN),
    9,190
Lynn, Ellie, 1,901
Lynn Equal Suffrage Association (MA), 6,825
Lynn Female Fragment Society (MA), 7,074
Lynn Free Church (MA), 7,390
Lynn, Isabelle, 17,251
Lynn, Minnie L., 17,230
Lynn Women's Club (MA), 7,075
Lynne Literary and Social Institute (UT), 16,753
Lyon, Anne Bozeman, 54, 57
Lyon Company, 3,669
Lyon, Eleanor. See Duke, Eleanor (Lyon)
Lyon, Eleanor (Richards) [Mrs. Harvey Blanchard]
    (1889-), 637
Lyon, Helen Ives [Mrs.], 11,407
Lyon, Katherine (1893-). See Mix, Katherine
    (Lyon) [Mrs. Arthur J.] (1893-)
Lyon, Lucy, 7,500
Lyon, Mary (1797-1849), 2,460, 3,764, 7,056, 7,224,
    7,330, 7,493, 12,675, 14,152
Lyon, Mrs. J. S., 3,669
Lyon, Mrs. S. S., 13,683
Lyon, Mrs. Stephen J., 11,641
Lyon, Sophia Blanche (1876-?). See Fahs, Sophia
    Blanche (Lyon) (1876-?)
Lyon, Sophie (1856-?). See Egleston, Sophie (Lyon)
    (1856-?)
Lyon, Stephen J., 11,641
Lyons, Helen M. [Miss], 11,642
Lyons, Lottie (1884-). See Grow, Lottie (Lyons)
    [Mrs. Walter S.] (1884-)
Lyons, Lucia G., 14,650
Lyons, Maritcha (Remond or Raymond) (1848-1929),
    12,688
Lyons, Mary M., 11,123
Lyons, Mrs. R., 9,669
Lyons, Rachel. See Heustis, Rachel (Lyons) [Mrs.
    James Fountain]
Lyons, Ruth, 11,909
Lyons, Veronica, 12,351
Lyric Opera of Chicago, Women's Board (IL), 4,058
Lyric poetry, 1,489, 5,988, 6,007
Lyric, The (periodical), 17,114
Lyric Theatre (MD), 5,828
Lyricists, 14,440, 17,944
Lysne Norwegian Evangelical Lutheran Church
    (Cromwell Township, MN), Ladies Aid, 9,271
Lytle, Alice (1874-1965). See Weber, Alice (Lytle)
    [Mrs. Adam] (1874-1965)
Lytle, Andrew Nelson (1902-), 15,934
Lytle, George, 1,799
Lytle, Mary Jane McAlister, 1,799
M. C. Migel Library, 11,811
M. I. M. (1830-?), 6,521
M Street High School (DC), 2,130
M. T. Stevens and Company, Inc., 7,119
M. W. H. (NC), 13,476
Maahi, Sugi. Miyoshi Sugimachi. [Mrs. Goro
    Yorita], 17,298
Ma'am Jones of the Pecos (book), 16,497
Mabbett Family, 14,059
Mabie, Edith R. [Mrs. Henry C.], 9,070
Mabie, Louise Kennedy, 10,992
McAdoo, Eleanor Randolph (Wilson) [Mrs. William
    Gibbs] (1889-1967), 1,530, 7,868
McAdoo, Ellen Wilson (1915-46). See Henshaw,
    Ellen Wilson (McAdoo) (1915-46)
McAdoo Family, 1,530
McAdoo, Mary Faith (1920-). See Haddad, Mary
    Faith (McAdoo) (1920-)
McAdoo, William Gibbs (1863-1941), 878, 1,530
McAfee, Hannah Douglas, 15,616
McAfee, John T. (1830-79), 15,616
McAfee, Mildred Helen. See Horton, Mildred Helen
    (McAfee)
McAfee, Tom, 10,000
Macalester College (St. Paul, MN), 8,710, 9,388
    alumnae, 9,295
    faculty, 8,441, 9,346
McAlester, J. J., 14,196
Macalester Presbyterian Church (St. Paul, MN),
    Ladies Aid, 9,191

Macalester Presbyterian Church (St. Paul, MN),
    Woman's Home and Foreign Missionary Society,
    9,191
McAliley, Mary [Mrs. Samuel L.] (1848-1901),
    15,617
McAlister, Samantha Cornell (1839-96), 14,536
McAllister, Ada, 8,240
McAllister, Caroline (1806-92). See Winchell,
    Caroline (McAllister) [Mrs. Horace] (1806-92)
McAllister, Daisy [Miss] (1878-1973), 2,910
McAllister, Jane Ellen, 9,575
McAllister, Mrs. Thomas, 11,503
McAllister, Sarabella (Chambers) Dunlop, 17,992
McAlmon, Robert, 12,001
McAlpin, Abby E. (Mason) [Mrs. Orrin Webster]
    (1865-1958), 10,682
McAlpin, Ellen, 3,545
McAlpin Family (GA), 3,544
McAlpin, Mary. See Smith, Mary (McAlpin) [Mrs.
    Erastus M.]
McAlpin, Sallie [Miss], 3,535
Macao, 7,277
MacArthur, Douglas (1880-1964), 194, 1,503, 7,283,
    10,082, 11,874, 15,564, 17,074
MacArthur, Edith H., 11,662
McArthur, Ellen. [Mrs.] Hole-in-the-Day, 8,940
MacArthur, Jean Marie (Faircloth) [Mrs. Douglas],
    17,074
McAtee, Emma Sayles [Mrs.], 11,440
McAuley. Eliza Ann (1835-?). See Egbert, Eliza Ann
    (McAuley) (1835-?)
McAuley, Mother Catherine (1787-?), 298, 9,695,
    15,233
McAvoy, Joseph W., 3,555
McBee, Harriet [Mrs. William Pinckney], 15,618
McBee, Sarah. See Tucker, Sarah (McBee)
McBee, William Pinckney, 15,618
MacBeth, Frances (1848-1932). See Glessner,
    Frances (Macbeth) [Mrs. John J.] (1848-1932)
MacBeth Galley (NY), 2,803
Macbeth, Helen, 3,849
Macbeth, Kate (1833-1915), 3,706, 10,007
Macbeth, Malcolm (1865-?), 15,496, 15,523
Macbeth, Robert, Family (SC), 15,496
McBeth, Susan Law (1830-93), 3,706
"MacBird" (drama), 2,349
McBlair, Charles H., 12,552
McBlair Family (MD), 12,552
McBlair, Fanny (Duncan) [Mrs. Charles H.], 12,552
McBlair, Thomas (?-1857), 12,552
McBlair, Virginia (Myers) [Mrs. William] (1821?-91),
    3,334
McBlair, William, 3,334
McBride, George W., 14,526
McBride, Katharine E., 14,737
McBride, Martha (1805-1901). See Knight, Martha
    (McBride) [Mrs. Vinson] (1805-1901)
McBride, Mary Margaret, 9,823
McBride, Mary Margaret, 7,718
McBride, Nina (Lane) [Mrs. Isaac], 14,599
McBrown, Gertrude P., 3,290
McBryde, Sarah C. [Mrs. Thomas Livingston], 15,619
McBryde, Thomas Livingston (1817-63), 15,619
McCabe, Alice (1911-72), 12,078
McCabe, Charles, 15,331
McCabe, Eliza, 17,299
McCabe Family, 4,942
McCabe, Flora Morgan, 2,461
McCabe, Lida Rose, 12,372
McCaffree, Mary Ellen, 17,300
McCaffree, Mary, Jane, 5,145
McCain, Grace, 1,777
McCain, James Ross, 3,452
McCain-Snow, Margaret, 3,764
McCaine, Helen [Mrs.], 9,233
McCaleb, Katy. See Headley, Katy (McCaleb)
McCall, Ann Margaret, 3,402
McCall, Bertha, 8,670, 8,679
McCall, Charlotte Manigault (Wilcocks), 15,045
McCall, Dorothy Lawson (1888-), 14,610
McCall, Elizabeth Frances (McCall) [Mrs. Benjamin Franklin]
McCall, Elizabeth McMurtrie [Mrs. George A.],
    15,044

McCall Family (PA), **15,044**
McCall, George A. (1802-68), 15,044
McCall, Monica [Miss], **6,045**, 6,085
McCall, Sidney. *See* Fenollosa, Mary McNeill
McCall, Tom, 14,610
McCall, Virginia Nielsen (1909-), **14,412**
McCallie, Elizabeth Hanleiter [Mrs. Samuel Washington], 3,222
McCallie, Samuel Washington (1856-1933), **3,222**
McCalls (periodical), 2,205, 5,048, 6,399, 6,582, 15,228, 16,154
MacCallum, Daisy (Kelly), 1,063
McCallum, Emma (Smith), 10,091
McCallum Family (TX), **16,015**
McCallum, Jane (Yelvington) [Mrs. Arthur Newell] (1878-1957), 16,015, **16,103**
MacCallum, Jean, 1,063
McCamman, Dorothy, 11,916
McCan, Martha Nelson, 9,894
McCandless, Lucy (Cook) (1851-1902), **14,086**
McCann, Catherine (1875?-1955). *See* Hoyt, Catherine (McCann) (1875?-1955)
McCann, Dorothy, 14,772
McCann, Grace Louise (1900-). *See* Morley, Grace Louise (McCann) (1900-)
McCants, Buena Vista, 15,620
McCants Family (SC), **15,620**
McCardle, Eliza (1810-76). *See* Johnson, Eliza (McCardle) [Mrs. Andrew] (1810-76)
McCardy, Joseph J., 9,044
McCarran, Mary, 16,371
McCarthy, Abigail Eleanor (Quigley) [Mrs. Eugene] (1916-), 8,844, **8,850**, 9,192, 9,193
McCarthy, Billy, 16,486
McCarthy, Catherine, 3,284
McCarthy, Clara Field, **17,912**
McCarthy, Consuela Kanaga, 1,081
McCarthy, Eugene, 8,844, 8,850, **9,193**, 13,551
McCarthy for President Committee (St. Cloud, MN), **8,844**
McCarthy hearings, 11,888
McCarthy, Joseph R., 3,667, 7,242, 9,149
McCarthy, Leo T., 1,013
McCarthy, Mary Therese (1912-), **16,160**
McCarthy, Mrs. Joseph R., 14,820
McCarthy, Sister Mary Barbara, 2,540
McCarthyism, 6,547, 11,910
McCartney, Florence. *See* Fitzgerald, Florence (McCartney) [Mrs. Clifford K.]
McCartney, Leah (Brock), 10,191
McCartney, Maida, **10,330**
McCarty, Anne Gambrell (1924-). *See* Braden, Anne Gambrell (McCarty) (1924-)
McCarty, Sister Mary Eva (1882-1970), 17,868
McCary, Sarah Ann, 2,609
McCaslin, Sybil. *See* Bowers, Sybil (McCaslin) [Mrs. Claude Gernade]
McCauley, Eliza, 5,055
McCauley, Mary (Ludwig) Hays, 11,185
McCauley, Rosa Lee (1913-). *See* Parks, Rosa Lee (McCauley) (1913-)
McCauley, Sarah. *See* Davis, Sarah (McCauley) [Mrs. Elkanah]
McCausland, Elizabeth (1899-1965), **2,784**, 11,252
McClain, Donald, 4,949
McClain, Ellen (Griffiths) [Mrs. Emlin], 4,934
McClain, Emlin (1851-1915), **4,934**
McClain, Marjorie Eames (Coast) [Mrs. Donald] (?-ca. 1920), 3,325, 4,949
McClain, Martha Ann (Tuttle) (1827-?), **14,611**
McClain, Rebecca [Mrs. William], 4,934
McClain, William, 4,934
McClary, Anna Eliza Ena Palmer Raymonde Ballantine (1848-84), 10,431
McClatchie, Ann D., 210
McCleery, Mary J., **6,745**
McClellan, Catherine, 2,834
McClellan, Ellen (Marcy) [Mrs. George Brinton, Sr.] (?-1915), 2,462
McClellan, George Brinton, Sr. (1826-85), **2,462**, 16,170, 17,079
McClellan, Idora (1843-1929). *See* Moore, Idora (McClellan) Plowman (1843-1929)

McClellan, Mary (1861-1945). *See* Desprez, Mary (McClellan) [Mrs. Paul] (1861-1945)
McClellan, Sophia (Bird) [Mrs. James L.], 1,062
McClelland, James L., 1,062
McClelland, Lucille, 10,191
McClelland, Pauline Brooks, 11,596
McClench, Elizabeth F. *See* Odell, Elizabeth F. (McClench) [Mrs. Samuel Royal] Thurston [Mrs.]
McClendon, Mary Upshaw (1922-), 8,080
McClendon, Sarah, 9,823
McClintock, Barbara (1902-), 1,095
McClintock, Helen A., **14,087**
McClintock, Margaretta Faber, **14,612**
McCloskey, Betty Charity. *See* Compton, Betty Charity (McCloskey) [Mrs. Arthur Holly]
McCloskey, Eunice Loncoske, 14,828
McCloskey, Eunice M. (1904-), **15,331**
McCloud, Helena, 10,508
McCloud, Susan Evans, **16,754**
McCloy, Helen (1904-), 6,060
McClung, R. E., 1,790
McClure, Annie (Getty) [Mrs. Charles] (?-1926), 11,241
McClure, Charles, 11,241
McClure, Emily (?-1921), 5,065
McClure, Grace (1884-1961), **7,847**
McClure, Harriet Sophia (Hurd) [Mrs. Samuel Sidney] (1855-1929), 4,478
McClure, Marilyn, 9,467
McClure, Martha (1886-1942), 5,065
McClure, Michael, 12,064
McClure, Samuel Sidney (1857-1949), 4,478
McClure, Vida Margaret (1880-?). *See* Boyle, Vida Margaret (McClure) [Mrs. Emmet D.] (1880-?)
McClure's magazine (periodical), 4,484, 7,308, 11,304
McCollum, Elmer V., 11,579, 17,853
McComas, Francis, 414
McComas, Francis John (1874-1938), 1,458
McComas, Gene Frances (Baker) [Mrs. Francis John], **1,458**
McComas, Rosaiie (Cain), 2,241
McComb City Hospital (MS), 9,697
McComb High School (MS), 9,672
McComb, John H., 8,559
McComb, Ruth Elizabeth Eckert [Mrs. John H.] (1905-), **8,559**
McComber, Caroline. *See* Muzzey, Caroline (McComber) [Mrs. Franklin]
McConnell, Delphine Margaret, 5,517
McConnell, Elizabeth Logan (?-1941), 5,517
McConnell Family (LA), **5,517**
McConnell, Frederic Charles (1890-1968), **14,413**
McConnell, Genevieve Knapp, **10,172**
McConnell, Gladys [Miss], **16,425**
McConnell, James, Sr., 5,517
McConnell, Jehiel, 16,425
McConnell, Jennie A., **9,194**
McConnell, Mary Lamar (Knight) [Mrs. Felton] (1899-), **3,332**
McCord Family (SC), 15,457, 15,726
McCord, Julia, 15,457
McCord, Julia. *See* Fielden, Julia (McCord) [Mrs. Henry Wemyss]
McCord, Langdon Cheves, 15,457
McCord, Louisa R., 15,457
McCord, Louisa Susannah (Cheves) [Mrs. David James] (1810-79), 15,457
McCord, Mary, 15,457
McCord, Mary Elizabeth, 15,457
McCord, May Kennedy (1880-), **10,131**
McCormack, John W., 13,282
McCormack, Nancy (Cox) (1885-1967). *See* Cushman, Nancy (Cox) McCormack (1885-1967)
McCormick, Alice (1864-1953). *See* Duniway, Alice (MacCormick) [Mrs. Willis Scott] (1864-1953)
McCormick, Anne (O'Hare) (1882-1954), **12,553**, 17,677
McCormick, Anita (1866-1954). *See* Blaine, Anita (Emmons) McCormick (1866-1954)
McCormick, Cyrus Hall, 4,084, 17,602, 17,678
McCormick, Edith (Rockefeller) [Mrs. Harold Fowler] (1872-1932), 3,880, 3,932
McCormick, Elizabeth (1892-1905), 4,084

McCormick, Ellen (Wirt) [Mrs. Edmund Brooke] Vass [Mrs. Charles] (ca. 1812-?), 5,824
McCormick Family, **2,379**
McCormick, Gertrude (Howard) [Mrs. Marlin E.] Olmsted (1874-1953), 14,822
McCormick, Harriet [Mrs. Cyrus Hall], 4,084, 4,175
McCormick Harvesting Machine Company, 12,574, 17,679
McCormick, Helen P. (1889-1937), **11,397**
McCormick, Joseph Medill (1877-1925), 2,379
McCormick, Katarina. *See* Barnes, Katarina (McCormick)
McCormick, Katharine (Dexter) [Mrs. Stanley] (1875-1967), 6,332, **6,333**, **6,746**, 7,289
McCormick, Ken, 9,769
McCormick, Marie Frances (1878-1964). *See* McGuire, Marie Frances (McCormick) [Mrs. Arthur] (1878-1964)
McCormick, Mary Virginia (1861-1941), **17,678**
McCormick, Mrs. Andrew, 4,369
McCormick, Mrs. Stanley, 6,503
McCormick, Nancy Maria "Nettie" (Fowler) [Mrs. Cyrus Hall] (1835-1923), 17,602, 17,678, **17,679**
McCormick, Patricia, 997
McCormick, R. C., 12,231
McCormick, Ruth (Hanna) [Mrs. Joseph Medill] (1880-1944). *See* Simms, Ruth (Hanna) [Mrs. Joseph Medill] McCormick [Mrs. Albert Gallatin] (1880-1944)
McCormick, Sister Mary Colmcille (1892-), **638**, 11,846
McCormick Theological Seminary (IL), 17,679
McCormick, Virginia Taylor (1873-1957), **17,114**
McCorvey, Mrs. Thomas Chalmers, 13,059
McCorvie, Mary, 3,753
McCourt, Claudia, 1,746
McCourt, Elizabeth Bondvel (1854-1935). *See* Tabor, Elizabeth Bondvel "Baby Doe" (McCourt) [Mrs. Harvey] Doe [Mrs. Horace Austin Warner] (1854-1935)
McCourt, Peter, 1,746
McCowen, Jennie, 4,732
McCown, Jean. *See* Hawkes, Jean (McCown)
McCoy, Bessie, 12,444
McCoy, Emma, **10,998**
McCoy, Irene (ca. 1896-1964). *See* Gaines, Irene (McCoy) (ca. 1896-1964)
McCracken, Elizabeth [Miss], **8,099**
McCrackin, Josephine (Wompner) [Mrs. James A.] Clifford [Mrs. Jackson] (1838-1920), **639**
McCrady, E. M., Jr., 15,621
McCrady, Edward, 15,629
McCrady, Edward, Sr., 15,621
McCrady Family (SC), 15,441
McCrady Family (SC), **15,621**
McCrady, John, 5,488
McCrady, Louisa Rebecca (Lane) [Mrs. Edward, Sr.], 15,621
McCrady, Mary Fraser Davie [Mrs. E. M., Jr.], 15,621
McCrary Family (SC), 15,622
McCrary Jim, **640**
McCrary, John Mathew, **3,223**
McCrary, Mary Boyd [Mrs. John], 3,223
McCrary, Robert, **15,622**
McCray, Bernice Melae, **12,150**
McCray, Dollie Rogers, 3,419
McCrea, Emma, 1,114
McCready, Ann, 12,316
McCreath Family (PA), **14,818**
McCreath, Margaretha Flemming, 14,818
McCreery, Eleanor Alice (Richards) (1877-1967), **17,913**
McCreery, Maria Maud (Leonard) [Mrs. Rex Irving] (1883-1938). *See* Walker, Maria Maud (Leonard) [Mrs. Rex Irving] McCreery [Mrs. James Walter] (1883-1938)
McCrimmon, Elizabeth (Cannon) Porter, **16,946**
McCue, Constance, 11,844
McCue, Honore (1880-1940). *See* Willsie, Honore (McCue) (1880-1940)
McCullers, Carson Smith [Mrs. Reeves] (1917-67), **3,059**, 5,875, 11,810, 12,367, **16,161**
McCullers, Reeves, 16,161

McCulloch, C. R. (1825-1912), 14,088
McCulloch, Catherine Gouger (Waugh) [Mrs. Frank Hathorn] (1862-1945), 4,003, **6,530**, 9,734
McCulloch Family (OH), **14,088**
McCulloch, Frank, 6,530
McCulloch, Hugh (1808-95), **4,479**
McCulloch, Margaret Callender, 5,474
McCulloch, Marie Louise. See Yale, Marie Louise (McCulloch) [Mrs. John Brooks]
McCulloch, Rhoda [Mrs. C. R.] (1826-1905), 14,088
McCulloch, Rhoda E. (1884-?), **7,256**, 7,315
McCulloch, Rollin S., 14,088
McCulloch, Susan Maria (Man) [Mrs. Hugh] (1818-98), 4,479
McCulloh Family (CA), **641**
McCulloh, Frances Jane. See Bartlett, Frances Jane (McCulloh) [Mrs. Carleton T.]
McCulloh, Frank, 641
McCulloh, Hiram William, 641
McCulloh, Jane E. [Mrs. John], 641
McCulloh, John, 641
McCulloh, John G., 641
McCullough, Alice (Lawson) [Mrs. John W. S.], 608
McCullough, Carolyn (1834-1902). See Everhard, Carolyn (McCullough) (1834-1902)
McCullough, Dorothy (1901-). See Lee, Dorothy (McCullough) [Mrs. W. Scott] (1901-)
McCullough, Edith Van Benthuysen (ca. 1880-1965), **17,045**
McCullough, Eliza "Lizzie" Hall (Park) [Mrs. John Giffin] (1848-1938), 17,044, **17,046**
McCullough, Esther Mary, **17,301**
McCullough Family (VT), **17,044**
McCullough, Jessica (1901-63). See Weis, Jessica (McCullough) [Mrs. Charles W., Jr.] (1901-63)
McCullough, Jessie, 14,148
McCullough, John Griffin (1835-1915), 17,046
McCullough, Rosanna, **15,623**
McCullough, Zeline. See Richard, Zeline (McCullough)
McCully, Verna Grisier, 5,048
McCune, Alice Ann (Paxman) [Mrs. George] (1870-1972), 16,648, **16,755**
McCune, Anna. See Schenck, Anna McCune [Mrs. Peter Voorhees]
McCune, Elizabeth Claridge See Rice, Elizabeth Claridge McCune [Mrs. Asaph]
McCune, Florence, **1,727**
McCurdy, Frances, **9,828**
McCurdy, Harold Grier, 11,991
McCutcheon, Evelyn W. [Mrs. Howard C.], **3,224**
McCutcheon, Louise (1880-). See Varése, Louise (McCutcheon) [Mrs. Edgar] (1880-)
McDaniel, Elsie Belle [Mrs. Laurence], 9,956
McDaniel, Hattie, 3,290
McDaniel, John K. (1902-), **8,100**
McDaniel, Laura Winans, 5,123
McDaniel, Orianna (1872-?), **9,195**
McDaniel, Sue Townsend (1919-). See Spencer, Sue Townsend (McDaniel) [Mrs. Robert] (1919-)
McDavid, Mrs. P. A., **15,624**
McDiarmid, Kate R. [Mrs.], 13,606
McDiarmid, Margaret, 15,308
McDill, Harriet (1852-1937). See McLaughlin, Harriet (McDill) (1852-1937)
McDill, Nancy Wilson [Mrs. Robert], 15,896
McDill, Robert, 15,896
McDonald, A. W., 17,456
McDonald, Ahlma (Hallock) [Mrs. Stewart], 14,571
McDonald, Alexander, 12,552
McDonald, Almena Parker, 10,116
McDonald, Blanche (ca. 1870-?), 9,415
McDonald, Charles James (1793-1860), 13,144
Macdonald, Duncan Black (1863-1943), **1,854**
McDonald, E. H., 17,456
McDonald, Elizabeth, 11,662
McDonald, Elizabeth DeHart Bleecker [Mrs. Alexander], **12,554**
MacDonald, Elizabeth (Graham) [Mrs. Alexander Findlay] (1831-1917), **16,756**
McDonald, Eva (1866-1956). See Valesh, Eva (McDonald) [Mrs. Frank]. [Mrs. Benjamin F.] Cross (1866-1956)

McDonald Family, 15,942
McDonald Family (FL, TN), 11,644
MacDonald Farm (Delhi, NY), **11,643**
Macdonald, Flora, 13,446, 13,473
McDonald, Grace [Mrs.], 1,016, 1,656, **11,769**
MacDonald, Harriet M. [Miss], **13,941**
Macdonald, Isabella (1841-1930). See Alden, Isabella (Macdonald) [Mrs. Gustavus Rosinbury] (1841-1930)
McDonald, James G. (1886-1964), **12,070**
MacDonald, Jeanette (1907-65), 3,084, 11,907
McDonald, Julia, 17,456
McDonald, Julie, **5,008**
Macdonald, Lillias, 11,375
MacDonald, Lois (1897-), 13,176
Macdonald, Marcia (pseudonym). See Livingston, Grace. [Mrs. Thomas Guthrie] Franklin [Mrs. Flavius J.] Lutz (1865-1947)
McDonald, Margaret (1925-), **5,009**
McDonald, Marie, **10,252**
McDonald, Marie, **15,625**
McDonald, Martha, 9,860
Macdonald, Mary Leeds Leffingwell (Bartlett) [Mrs. Duncan Black] (1850-1929), 1,854, 1,958
McDonald, Mary M. [Mrs. Ralph] (1881-ca. 1969), **1,728**
McDonald, Mattie W., 9,860
Macdonald, Ranald, 14,549
McDonald, Ruth Seely (Berry) [Mrs. William Naylor, III] (1913-), 11,644
McDonald School, Town of Tilden School District No. 2, Chippewa County (WI), 17,508, **17,526**
McDonald, William Naylor, III, 11,644
MacDonell, Ann Elizabeth Nowlan [Mrs.], 3,546
MacDonell, George G. N., **3,546**
McDonnell Aircraft Corporation v. Sarah J. Bundy et al., 2,678
MacDonnell, Hubert Leon, 13,108
McDonough Family (ND), 13,669
McDonough, John Joseph (1895-1962), **9,196**
McDonough, Marian McIntire [Mrs.], 1,790
McDougal Family (WV), 17,452
McDougal, Jane, 1,505
McDougal, Katherine [Mrs. Edward], 11,827
Macdougall, Allan Ross, 12,361
McDougall, Caroline. See Neilson, Caroline (McDougall)
McDougall, Elizabeth McEvers Rouse [Mrs. Nicholas], 9,716
McDougall, Nancy (1808-?). See Robinson, Nancy (McDougall) [Mrs. Alfred Bassett] (1808-?)
McDougall Nicholas, 9,716
MacDougall, Priscilla Ruth, **17,680**
MacDougall, Ranald, 2,105
McDowall, Mary Nicholson, 16,060
McDowall, Sallie R., **13,060**
McDowell, Agnes Davison. See Richardson, Agnes Davison (McDowell) [Mrs. John Smythe]
McDowell, Allene, 14,174
MacDowell Association, 2,463, 6,867, 12,050
McDowell, Anne Elizabeth (1826-1901), **6,244**
MacDowell, Bessie Fonvielle (1898-1942), 86
MacDowell Colony (NH), 2,463, 4,689, 5,993, 6,011, 7,316, 16,471
McDowell, Davison (1784-1842), **15,626**, 15,695
McDowell, Desha, 5,302
McDowell, Edward, 9,600
MacDowell, Edward Alexander (1861-1908), 2,463, 6,185, 10,852, **12,038**, 16,358, 16,471
McDowell, Eulalie G., 11,493
McDowell Family (KY), 5,279
McDowell Family (NJ), **11,111**
MacDowell, Fanny [Mrs. William Melbourne] (1850-98). See Davenport, Fanny Lily Gypsy (1850-98)
McDowell, Helen, 2,309
McDowell, Katherine Sherwood (Bonner) [Mrs. Edward] (1849-83), 9,600, 9,819
MacDowell, Madeline (1872-1920). See Breckinridge, Madeline (McDowell) [Mrs. Desha] (1872-1920)
MacDowell, Marian Griswold (Nevins) [Mrs. Edward Alexander] (1857-1956), 2,463, 6,867, 7,210, 10,121, 10,852, 12,038, 12,050, **16,471**
McDowell, Mary Ann, 16,176

McDowell, Mary Eliza (1854-1936), 3,814, 3,828, 3,875, 4,003, 4,173
McDowell, Mary Stone [Miss] (1876-1955), **6,747**
McDowell, Mrs. Edward (1897-), 6,503
McDowell, Mrs. R. R. Brevard, 13,347
MacDowell Music Study Club (KY), 5,351
McDowell, Rachel K. (1880-1949), 11,111
McDowell, Sarah Brant (1850-1923). See Preston, Sarah Brant McDowell [Mrs. Wickliffe] (1850-1923)
McDowell, Sue, **15,627**
McDowell, William Anderson (1789-1851), 11,111
McDuffie, Elizabeth [Mrs. Irvin Henry] (1882-1946), **3,301**
McDuffie, George (1790-1851), **15,628**
McDuffie, Irvin Henry (1882-1946), **3,301**
McDuffie, Jean (Howard) [Mrs. Duncan] (1880-1955), 556, 2,694
McDuffie, Mary, 15,722
McDuffie, Mary, 15,628
McDuffie, Mary Singleton, 15,759
Mace, Blanche [Mrs.], **16,426**
Mace, Gladis [Mrs. Russel], 5,643
Mace, Rebecca Elizabeth (Howell) [Mrs. Wandle] (1833-1917), **16,757**
McEachron, Edith (1883-), **17,564**
McElhenney, Jane (1836-74). See Clare, Ada A. Jane (McElhenney) [Mrs. J. Franklin] Noyes (1836-74)
McElmon, Catherine Aikens (1816-92), 14,500
McElroy Family (WA), **17,302**
McElroy, Harry Bates (1861-1928), 17,302
McElroy, Maria Irvine (1805-?). See Knott, Maria Irvine (McElroy) (1805-?)
McElroy, Mary Blythe [Mrs.], 5,361
McElroy, Mary Lennon, 11,242
McElroy, Nellie L. (?-1937), **12,827**
McElroy, Sarah Collins [Mrs. Thornton Fleming] (1827-94), 17,302
McElroy, Sarah "Sallie" Rosanna (1833-1915). See Knott, Sarah "Sallie" Rosanna (McElroy) [Mrs. James Proctor] (1833-1915)
McElroy, Thornton Fleming (1825-85), 17,302
McElwain, Mary Belle (1874-1964), 7,158
McEnerney, Garret W., 642
McEnerney, Genevieve Green Hamilton [Mrs. Garrett W.], **642**
McEnery, Mary A. (1905-74). See Stuhldreher, Mary A. (McEnery) (1905-74)
McEnery, Mary Routh (1856-1917). See Stuart, Ruth (McEnery) [Mrs. Alfred Ogden] (1856-1917)
McEnery, Ruth (1856-1917). See Stuart, Ruth (McEnery) [Mrs. Alfred Ogden] (1856-1917)
McEvoy, Nan, 11,827
McEwan, Inez Puckett (1904-), **17,198**
McEwen, Hetty (Kennedy) [Mrs. Robert Houston] (1796-1881), 15,959
McEwen, Kittie, 15,959
McEwen, Robert Houston (1790-1868), **15,959**
Macey, Eleanor, 3,823
McFadden, Marion Howe (Poole), 6,832
McFadden, Robert Lawrence (1929-), **15,805**
MacFadyen, Alfred, 63
MacFadyen, Irene M. (Ashby) [Mrs. Alfred], 63
McFarland, Emily [Mrs. Ross], 11,830
McFarland, Frances, 8,668
McFarland, J. Horace (1859-1948), 14,819, 14,822
McFarland, Mrs. J. A., 9,669
McFarland, Wilma K. (1890-), 14,408
Macfarlane, Catharine (1877-1969), **14,925**, **15,130**
McFarlane, Ida Krus [Mrs. Frederick] (1873-1940), 1,751
McFarlane, Lillian (Higbee) [Mrs. Erastus "Rass"], **16,427**
McFarlane, Viola (Pratt) Gillette (1871-1956), **16,538**
McFarlin, Elizabeth [Mrs. Peter], 3,414
McFarlin, John G., 16,076
McFarlin, Mary Ann (1838-1929), **10,767**
McFarlin, Peter, 3,414
Macfie, Mary Jane (1832-98). See McMaster, Mary Jane (Macfie) [Mrs. Fitz William] (1832-98)
McGaffey, Christine (1883-1970). See Frederick, Christine (McGaffey) (1883-1970)
McGaffey, Louise A., 2,562

McGary, Ellen Pratt, 16,888

McGee, Amanda, 210

McGee, Anita Newcomb [Mrs. William John] (1864-1940), **2,464**, 2,690

McGee, John (?-1774), 13,219

McGee, Martha McFarlane [Mrs. John] (?-1820). *See* Bell, Martha McFarlane [Mrs. John] McGee [Mrs. William] (?-1820)

McGee, Martha Rector, **17,068**

McGee, Mrs. Tim, 16,865

McGeoy, 9,795

McGettigan, Francisca (Vallejo), 643

McGhee, Rosa [Miss], **8,101**

McGiffert, Gertrude Yates [Mrs. G. R.] (?-1961), **8,436,** 8,446

McGill, Andrew R., 8,925

McGill, Caroline (1879-1959), **10,253**

McGill, Eula (1911-), **3,447,** 13,176

McGill, Lucy Whitehead (1861-1949). *See* Peabody, Lucy Whitehead (McGill) [Mrs. Norman Mather] Waterbury [Mrs. Henry Wayland] (1861-1949)

MacGill, Mary Bell (Peirce) (?-1879), Family (VA), **17,089**

McGill, Ralph, **3,602**

McGill University, 2,088

M'Gillycuddy, Fanny, **15,856**

McGilvra, Caroline Ethel (1858-1932). *See* Burke, Caroline Ethel (McGilvra) [Mrs. Thomas] (1858-1932)

McGilvra, John, 17,241

McGimsey, Laura Cornelia (1840-1920). *See* Warlick, Laura Cornelia (McGimsey) [Mrs. Lewis] (1840-1920)

McGinley, Phyllis [Mrs. Charles] (1905-), 569, 2,166, **12,904**

McGinnis, Esther, **7,848**

McGinnis, Gertrude, **4,813**

McGlashan, Charles Fayette (1847-1931), **644**

McGough, Mary (1885-), **8,102,** 9,467

McGovern, George S., 12,883, 16,965

McGovern, James J., 4,647

MacGowan, Alice, 415

MacGowan Family (CA), 415

MacGowan, Grace (1863-1944). *See* Cooke, Grace (MacGowan) (1863-1944)

McGown, Arthur, 140

McGown, Eva (Montgomery) [Mrs. Arthur] (1884-1972), **140**

McGrath, Edith, 14,437

McGrath, Maria (Davies) (1865-1951), **1,785**

McGrath, Mary A., 17,918, 17,919

McGraw, Eloise Jarvis (1915-), **14,414**

McGraw Family, **11,645**

McGraw, Harrison B., 11,645

McGraw-Hill, Inc., **11,889,** 14,405

McGraw, James H. (1860-1948), 11,889

McGraw, Jennie, 11,558

McGraw, Jennie (1840-81). *See* Fiske, Jennie (McGraw) [Mrs. Willard] (1840-81)

McGraw, John, 11,524

McGraw, John T., 17,465

McGraw, Mrs. Donald C. (1900-), 11,889

McGraw, Natalie, **5,652**

McGraw, Thomas, 11,588

McGreal, Sister Mary Nona (1914-), 17,868

MacGregor, Helen R., **645**

McGregor, Jean (pseudonym). *See* Britten, Evelyn (Barrett) [Mrs. Walter] (1891-1969)

McGrew, Elizabeth, 15,134

McGrew, Martha S., 4,123

McGrew, Mrs. George, 1,790

McGuire, Arthur James, **9,197**

McGuire, John P., 13,062

McGuire, Judith (Brockenbrough) [Mrs. John P.], **13,062**

McGuire, Marie (Collins), 2,086

McGuire, Marie Frances (McCormick) [Mrs. Arthur James] (1878-1964), 9,040, **9,197**

Machado, José Manuel, 748

Machado, Juana de Dios (1814-?). *See* Ridington, Juana de Dios (Machado) Alipás (1814-?)

McHarg, Mrs. T. A., 1,679

McHarg, Rebecca, 9,202

McHenry, Elizabeth (1850-1907). *See* Lamare, Elizabeth (McHenry) [Mrs. Emmanuel Benjamin] (1850-1907)

McHenry, Ellen Josephine (Metcalf), 1,419

McHenry, Ellen (Metcalfe) [Mrs. John] (1827-1922), 589

McHenry, Emma (1857-1934). *See* Pond, Emma (McHenry) [Mrs. Charles Fremont] (1857-1934)

McHenry, Frances, 4,743

McHenry, Margaret (1904-), **15,046,** 15,291

McHenry, Mary (1855-1947). *See* Keith, Mary (McHenry) [Mrs. William] (1855-1947)

Machetanz, Frederick, 14,415

Machetanz, Sara Burleson [Mrs. Frederick] (1918-), **14,415**

Machine and Metal Trades High School (NY), 12,386

Machiz, Herbert (1923-76), **12,039**

McHugh, Anna (1873-1944). *See* McHugh, Sister Antonia (1873-1944)

McHugh, Arona (1924-), **6,046**

McHugh, Sister Antonia (1873-1944), **8,851,** 9,038, 9,490

McIlroy, Lily (1887-1958). *See* Russell, Lily (McIlroy) [Mrs. Junius B.] (1887-1958)

McIlvaine, Caroline (1868-1945), 3,994, **3,998**

McIlvaine Family (MN), **5,010**

McIlvaine, Mrs. Henry B., 5,010

MacInnes, Helen. [Mrs. Gilbert] Highet (1907-), **11,168**

McInnis, Alice, **12,689**

McIntire, Cleopatra (Barzee) [Mrs. E. William] (1892-), **16,758**

McIntire Family (CA), 595

McIntire, Ruth, 5,871

McIntosh Family (GA), 3,410

McIntosh, Mary Ann Dwyer, **3,501**

McIntosh, Millicent Carey (1898-), **11,890**

McIntyre, Emma Jane [Mrs. William J.] (1846?-?), **646**

McIntyre, Florence (1879-1963), 2,520, **15,883**

McIntyre, Jane, 13,569

McIntyre, Julia. *See* Merriman, Julia (McIntyre)

McIntyre, Margaret, 13,569

McIntyre, Merodine (Keeler), 544, 588

McIntyre, Minnie. *See* Wallace, Minnie (McIntyre)

McIntyre, William J., 646

McIver, Annie, 13,245

McIver, Charles Duncan (1860-1906), 13,228, **13,245,** 13,247, 13,248

MacIver, Ivander [Miss], 905

McIver, John J., **15,630**

MacIver, Joyce (pseudonym), **6,047**

McIver, Lula Martin. *See* Dickinson, Lula Martin (McIver) [Mrs. John]

McIver, Lula (Martin) [Mrs. Charles Duncan] (1864-1944), **13,245,** 13,247

McIver, Pearl (1893-1976), **6,146**

McIver, Sarah Witherspoon Ervin [Mrs.] (,26-97), **15,631**

Mac Jennet School (Paris, France), 13,122

McJunkin Advertising Company, 17,623

Mack, Almira (1805-86). *See* Covey, Almira (Mack) [Mrs. Benjamin] (1805-86)

Mack, Catherine Dineen [Mrs. William], 11,407

Mack, Effie Mona (1888-1969), 10,639, **10,677**

Mack, Elizabeth, 10,678

Mack Family (NV), 10,678

Mack, Fannie, 17,647

Mack, Horace, 11,687

Mack, John T., 4,425

Mack, Julia (1879-1962). *See* Riley, Julia (Mack) (1879-1962)

Mack, Lucy. *See* Smith, Lucy (Mack)

Mack, Margaret M. [Miss] (1871-1945), **10,678**

Mack, Martha (Gill) [Mrs. John T.], 4,425

Mack, Mary, **13,477**

Mack, Ruth McCullough, 4,532

Mack, Sarah Emeline [Mrs. O. H.], **10,679**

Mack, Stephen, 16,539

Mack, Temperance (Bond) [Mrs. Stephen] (1771-1850), **16,539, 16,759**

Mack, Thomas Porter, 10,678

McKain, David, 4,237

McKain, Helen [Mrs. William], **8,243**

McKain, William, **8,243**

Mackaness, Elizabeth. *See* Harvey, Elizabeth (Mackaness) [Mrs. Thomas]

Mackaness, Thomas, 12,605

McKay, Alexander, **10,331**

Mackay, Annie A., **12,555**

McKay, Caroline [Mrs. Alexander] (1837-1917), 10,331

Mackay, Catherine J., 4,954

Mackay, Clarence H., **12,843**

McKay, Claude (1890-1948), **3,289,** 6,112

Mackay, Constance D'Arcy. *See* Holt, Constance D'Arcy Mackay [Mrs. Richard]

McKay, David Oman, 16,614, 16,676, 16,760

McKay, Eleanora (1915-1959). *See* Holiday, Billie. [Mrs. Joe] Guy [Mrs. Louis] McKay (1915-1959)

McKay, Eliza, 13,478

Mackay, Eliza Anr. (McQueen) [Mrs. Robert] (1778-1862), **3,547,** 3,567

Mackay, Ellen. *See* Berlin, Ellen (Mackay) [Mrs. Irving]

McKay, Emma Ray (Riggs) [Mrs. David Oman] (1877-1970), 16,676, **16,760**

Mackay Family (GA), **3,548**

McKay Family (NC), **13,478**

McKay, Fawn (1915-). *See* Brodie, Fawn (McKay) [Mrs. Richard] (1915-)

McKay, Flora (1861-1945). *See* McNulty, Flora (McKay) (1861-1945)

McKay, Helen (Willis) [Mrs. William] (1873-1971), **3,627**

Mackay, John, 12,843

Mackay, Katherine Duer [Mrs. Clarence H.] (?-1930). *See* Blake, Katherine Duer [Mrs. Clarence H.] Mackay [Mrs. Joseph] (?-1930)

Mackay, Mary Anne. *See* Stiles, Mary Anne (Mackay)

Mackay, Robert, 3,548

Mackay-Scott, Ruth (Jarvis) [Mrs. Andrew], **6,748**

MacKaye, Arvia (1902-), 10,868

MacKaye, Christy (1909-), 10,868

MacKaye Family, 10,868

MacKaye, Hazel (1880-1944), 10,868

MacKaye, James, 17,757

MacKaye, Marion Morse [Mrs. Percy] (1872-1939), 10,868

MacKaye, Mary Medbery [Mrs. Steele] (1845-1924), 10,868, 12,457

MacKaye, Percy (1875-1956), **6,749**

MacKaye, Percy Wallace, 12,457

McKeaggan, Eulalie, 5,647, **5,653**

McKean, Emma De Garmo, 12,844

McKean, Josephine, 11,902

McKean, May Field, 15,184

McKean, Polly Hicks, 14,594

McKean, Samuel Terry, 14,594

McKee, Alice, 4,741

McKee, Anna M., **1,729**

McKee, Bertha (1890-1974). *See* Dobie, Bertha (McKee) [Mrs. J. Frank] (1890-1974)

McKee, Eila Butterworth Haggin [Countess Festeties] de Tolna [Mrs. Robert T.] (1874-1939), **1,612**

McKee Family, 1,612

McKee, John, 67

McKee, John, 2,465

McKee, Linda Mitchell (1939-). *See* Maloney, Linda Mitchell McKee (1939-)

McKee, Mary T., **2,465**

McKee, Ruth Eleanor (1903-1970?), **1,044,** 2,702

McKee, Sara (Dempster), 4,203

McKeeby Family, 4,942

McKeehan, Mary (1751-1836). *See* Patton, Mary (McKeehan) [Mrs. John] (1751-1836)

McKeesport Feminist (PA), 15,249

McKeever, Jane (Campbell) [Mrs. Matthew] (1800-71), **15,909**

McKeldin, Theodore R., **5,828**

McKellar, Kenneth Douglas, 6,949

McKellar, Mary Belle [Miss] (?-1941), 5,448, **5,451**

McKelvey, Harriet, 8,941

McKelvey, Jean T., **11,770**

McKelvie, Martha (DeArnold) [Mrs. Sam R.] (1887-1976), **10,487**

McKelway, Alexander J., 2,503

McKelway, St. Clair (1845-1915), **12,556**
McKelway, Virginia Brooks Thompson [Mrs. St. Clair], 12,556
McKendree College (Lebanon, IL), archives, **4,285**
McKendree College (Lebanon, IL), Clionian Literary Society, 4,285
McKendree Methodist Episcopal Church (SC), **15,632**
MacKendrick, Lilian (1906-), **2,785**
MacKenna, Irma Hortensia (Lazo) de [Mrs. Harold Ruben] (1920-), **16,761**
McKenny Family (WA), 17,169
McKenzie, Alexander, 13,682
Mackenzie, Arthur Stanley, 11,814
McKenzie College (TX), 16,132
MacKenzie, Elizabeth, 15,633
MacKenzie, Ella (Noland) [Mrs. John Carrerre], **13,063**
McKenzie Family (OR), 14,672
MacKenzie Family (SC), **15,633**
McKenzie, Flora, **7,849**
Mackenzie, Gladys K. Gould, 15,308
Mackenzie Hall (dormitory), 1,848
MacKenzie, Jeanne Daisey [Mrs. Norman Ian] (1922-), **7,257**
MacKenzie, Jemima, 15,633
MacKenzie, John Carrerre (?-1866), 13,063
MacKenzie, John Noland (1853-1925), 13,063
McKenzie, Mrs. T. H., **16,279**
MacKenzie, Tacy Burges (Norbury) [Mrs. Thomas], **5,796**
MacKenzie, Thomas, 5,796
Mackey, Alexander, 15,507
Mackey, Ann Jane, **2,466**
Mackey, Elinor, 15,507
McKibban, Olga (Petrov), 719, 11,997
McKibben, Allison, 9,198
McKibbin, Julia Baldwin (1855-1939), 5,063
McKibbin, May, 8,170
McKie Family (TX), 16,269
Mackie, Helen Holme, 11,508
McKie, Louise (Powers), 9,709
McKim, Leonora Jackson [Mrs. William Duncan] (1879-1969), **5,781**
McKim, William Duncan, 5,781
McKimmon, James, 13,480
McKimmon, Jane (Simpson) (1867-1957), **13,064,** 13,391, 13,408, **13,479, 13,626**
McKimmon, Kate [Miss], **13,480**
McKimmon, W. S., 13,064
Mackinac Island, 8,330
  history, 7,895
McKinley, Ida (Saxton) [Mrs. William] (1847-1907), 11,353
McKinley, Virginia, 11,334
McKinley, William (1843-1901), 2,214, 5,707, 5,854, **11,353,** 15,601, 17,914
McKinney Family, 12,531
McKinney, Louise R. (1900-73), 94
McKinney, Mary Ann (1810-88). See Alexander, Mary Ann (McKinney) [Mrs. William Patterson] (1810-88)
McKinney, Mary E. [Miss], 11,634
McKinnon Family (GA), 3,410
McKinnon, Edna (Rankin), 6,846
McKinnon, Isabella (1833-?), **17,681**
MacKinnon, Lilia, 9,234
McKinstry, Linda, **17,982**
Mackintire, Mary Ann (1824-93). See Salter, Mary Ann Mackintire [Mrs. William] (1824-93)
Mackintosh Family (GA), **3,060**
Mackintosh, Henrietta P., 6,191
McKissick, James Rion (1884-1944), **15,634**
McKittrick, Bernadette A., 1,339
McKittrick, Mary. See Markham, Mary (McKittrick) [Mrs. George D.]
Mackle, Mary, 17,884
McKnight, F. S., 9,535
McKnight, Kate Cassatt, 15,244
McKnight, Reecy [Mrs. M. M.] (1907-), **16,002**
McKown, Sarah Morgan, **17,470**
McLachlan, Mrs. Mab., 5,807
Maclagan, Bridget (pseudonym). See Borden, Mary (1886-1968)
McLain, Bettie M. (Gragg) [Mrs. William H.], 14,375

McLain, William H., 14,375
McLanahan Family (CT), 1,955
McLane, Eliza, 99
McLaren, Anna McVean (1832-86), 9,041
MacLaren Family, 11,130
McLaren, John, 1,634
McLaren, Louise Leonard, 13,189
MacLaren, Mrs. Finley, **12,254**
McLauchlin, Mrs. J. W., **13,481**
McLaughlin, Agnes Winifred (1882-1964), **6,750**
McLaughlin, Alfred, 647
McLaughlin, Andrew C., 7,850
McLaughlin, Constance (1897-1975). See Green, Constance (McLaughlin) [Mrs. Donald Ross] (1897-1975)
McLaughlin, Dorothy [Mrs. Herb], 169
McLaughlin, Eloisa (1817-84). See Harvey, Eloisa (McLaughlin) [Mrs. William Glenn] Rae [Mrs. Daniel] (1817-84)
McLaughlin, Emma (Moffat) [Mrs. Alfred] (1880-1968), **647**
McLaughlin, Frederic (?-1944), 11,537
McLaughlin, Harriet (McDill) (1852-1937), **15,896**
McLaughlin, John, 534
McLaughlin, Lois Thompson (Angell) [Mrs. Andrew C.], **7,850**
McLaughlin, Mary Louise [Miss] (1848-1939), 13,836, **13,852**
McLaughlyn, Ada (Greenwood), **10,113**
McLaurin, A. J., Family, 9,795
McLaurin, Anna Blue, **13,065**
McLaurin, Anselm J., 9,658, 9,740
McLaurin, Benjamin, 11,897
McLaurin, Catherine Louisa, **15,635**
McLaurin, Daisy (1875-1950). See Stevens, Daisy (McLaurin) (1875-1950)
McLaurin, Elvira Raunch, 9,709
McLaurin, Laura Raunch, **9,670**
Maclay, Charles, 426
McLean, Agnes Maria, 648
McLean, Ann, **15,636**
McLean, Charlotte Ellen [Miss] (1835?-?), **1,920**
McLean County Homemakers Extension Association (IL), **3,761**
McLean, Edward, 648
McLean, Eliza J., 8,374
McLean, Eva, **10,332**
McLean, Evalyn (Walsh) [Mrs. Edward "Ned" Beale] (1886-1947), 698, 1,752, **2,467**
McLean Family (CA), **648**
McLean Family (SC), **15,636**
McLean, Fannie Williams, 648, 1,359
McLean, Francis H., 648
McLean, Grace B. (?-1935), **1,855**
McLean, Helen, 3,914
McLean, Hugh, 15,636
McLean, Hulda Hoover, 5,123
McLean, John, 17,992
McLean, John Knox, 703
MacLean, Malcolm Shaw, 6,095
McLean, Margaret A., 15,427
McLean, Mary (1873-1965). See Olney, Mary (McLean) (1873-1965)
McLean, Mary Dyer Williams [Mrs. Charles B.] (1822-1905), 1,881
McLean Mental Hospital (MA), 15,559
McLean, Mildred. See Dewey, Mildred (McLean) Hazen [Mrs. George]
McLean, Mildred Evans, **14,613**
McLean, Sarabella, 17,992
McLean, Sarah E. Chester [Mrs. Edward], 648
MacLeish, Archibald, 2,227, 2,355, 9,779, 11,944, 18,006, 18,021
McLellan, Alice Josephine (1858-1907). See Birney, Alice Josephine (McLellan) [Mrs. Theodore Weld] (1858-1907)
McLelland, Isabel Couper, **14,416**
McLemore, Mrs. H. K., 9,671
McLemore, Nannie Pitts [Mrs. Edward Aubrey] (1900-), 9,671, **9,672**
McLemore, Richard Aubrey (1903-), 9,634, **9,671,** 9,672, **9,673**
McLench, Benjamin Franklin, 14,614
McLench Family (OR), **14,614**

McLench, Mary Almira (Gray) [Mrs. Benjamin Franklin], 14,614
McLendon, Minnie Upson, 12,653
McLenegan, Annie S. [Miss] (1875-1962), **17,495**
McLennan, Dan, 16,356
McLennan, Maggie (1885-). See Gibbons, Maggie (McLennan) (1885-)
McLennan, Neil, Family, 16,356
MacLeod, Annie L. (1883-), **12,923**
Macleod, Charlotte (1852-1950), 6,164
MacLeod, Josephine, 11,596
MacLeod, Leona, **8,165**
McLeod, Mary Jane (1875-1955). See Bethune, Mary Jane (McLeod) (1875-1955)
McLeod, Rebecca J. (Lamar), 2,970
MacLeod, Ruth D., **14,417**
McLeod, W. S., 8,407
McLorn, Olive (Gilbreath), 9,888
Macloskey, Edna Walker, 2,205
McLoughlin, David, 14,549
McLure, Margaret, 3,114
Maclure, William (1763-1840), **4,429**
McMahan, Helen (ca. 1877-1947), **14,190**
MacMahon, Aline (1899-), 11,907, 12,367
McMahon, Mary Alice, 6,215
McMahon, Mrs. Francis E., 4,104
McMahon, Ruth (Lima), **8,763**
McMahon, Susan, 15,198
McMahon, Teresa [Mrs. Edward] (1878-1960?), **17,303**
McMain, Eleanor Laura (1866-1934), 5,509, 5,515
McMann Family (ND), 13,669
McManus, R. Louise (1896-), 12,074
MacManus, Susan R. (Trautwine) (1841-81?), **15,047**
McMaster Family, 8,953
McMaster, Fitz William (1826-99), **15,637**
McMaster, Helen G., 15,638
McMaster, Mary Jane (Macfie) [Mrs. Fitz William] (1832-98), **15,637**
McMaster, Nabbie Howe Young (Clawson) [Mrs. Frank Athol] (1891-), **16,762**
McMeans, Margaret Thompson (1809-84). See Smoot, Margaret Thompson (McMeans) [Mrs. Abraham Owen] (1809-84)
MacMillan, Alice, 9,098
MacMillan Company (publishers), 14,326, 14,352, 16,470
McMillan, Elly (1914-). See Peterson, Elly (McMillan) (1914-)
McMillan, Esther Belle (1824-78). See Hanna, Esther Belle (McMillan) (1824-78)
McMillan Family (WA), 17,390
McMillan, Helen Elvira (Davis) [Mrs. Kenneth] (1909-), **9,523**
McMillan, James, 1,687
McMillan, John G., 17,390
McMillan, Julie Villiers (Lewis) [Mrs. James] (1870-1956). See Penrose, Julie Villiers (Lewis) [Mrs. James] McMillan [Mrs. Spencer] (1870-1956)
McMillan, Kenneth, 9,523
MacMillan, Margaret Burnham (1899-), **8,244**
McMillan, Rubelle, 16,176
McMillin, Martha "Mattie" Jane. See Meharry, Martha "Mattie" Jane (McMillin) [Mrs. Abraham]
McMinnville Ladies Sanitary Aid Society (OR), **14,418**
MacMonnies, Mary (Fairchild) [Mrs. Fredrick]. See Low, Mary (Fairchild) [Mrs. Fredrick] MacMonnies
McMullen, Laura, 17,654
McMullen-McGloin Colony (TX), 16,117
McMullin, Alice (1902-), 11,889
McMullin, Lois, 5,175
MacMurray College (Jacksonville, IL), **4,281**
MacMurray, Mary T. See Fletcher, Mary T. (MacMurray) [Mrs. Donald A.]
McMurtie, Mary, 2,502
McMurtry Family, 256
McNab, John, 1,334
McNabb, Eliza R., **9,674**
McNair, Edith [Mrs. Dayton], 11,181

MacNair, Florence (Wheelock) [Mrs. Francis]
Ayscough [Mrs. Harley Farnsworth] (1878-1942),
1,113
MacNair, Harley Farnsworth, 1,113
McNall, Belva Ann (Bennett) [Mrs. Uriah]
(1830-1917). *See* Lockwood, Belva Ann
(Bennett) [Mrs. Uriah] McNall [Mrs. Ezekiel]
(1830-1917)
McNally, Steve, 2,112
McNamara brothers (CA), 341
McNary, Charles H., 14,683
McNary-Haugen bill, 10,034
McNeal, Hazel L. [Mrs.], 9,594
McNeal, May (Preston) [Mrs. Joshua Vansant]
(1849-1913), **5,800**
McNeal, Minnie L. (1869-1955). *See* Johnson,
Minnie L. (McNeal) [Mrs. Hiram Warren]
(1869-1955)
McNeil, Cora Ethel Eaton (Howarth) [Mrs. Stephen
Crane [Mrs. Hammon P.] (1865-1910), 10,860,
11,978, 11,979
McNeil, Curtis, 3,611
McNeil Family (GA), **3,611**
McNeil, Hammon P., 11,978
McNeil, Laura Virginia Lee. *See* Baker, Laura
Virginia Lee (McNeil) [Mrs. George Varnadoe]
McNeil, Lina, 15,544
McNeill, Anna Matilda (1804-81). *See* Whistler,
Anna Matilda (McNeill) [Mrs. George] (1804-81)
McNeill, Bertha Cannon, 8,091
McNeill Family (NC), 13,439
McNeill, Flora, 13,439
McNeill, John, Sr., 13,439
McNeill, Roxana (Worth), 13,439, 13,619
McNeill, Sarah, 13,439
McNeilly, Tialender Cassandra (Roos) [Mrs. James]
(1874-1964), 9,322
McNish, Adelaide Baynard [Mrs. William P.]
Guerard, **3,549**
McNulty, Flora (McKay) (1861-1945), 10,331, 10,402
McNutt, Ruth J., 4,494
Macomb, Ann Minerva "Nannie" (Rodgers) [Mrs.
John Navarre] (1824-1916), 2,556
Macomb Business and Professional Women's Club
(IL), **4,291**
Macomb, Minerva. *See* Peters, Minerva (Macomb)
[Mrs. Thomas Willing]
Macomb, Rufus K., 16,097
Macon, Jane [Miss], **3,061**
Macon, Nathaniel, **13,482**
Macon Plantation (MS), 9,701
Macon Telegraph (GA), 4,463
MacPhail, Elizabeth (Reinbold) [Mrs. Alfred]
(1912-), **1,189**
McPhee, Clare Mary (?-1960), **10,488**
McPhee, Marguerite Cameron (?-1970), **10,488**
McPherson, Aimee [Mrs. Robert James] Semple [Mrs.
Harold Stewart] (1890-1944), 2,232
McPherson College (KS), archives, **5,188**
McPherson College (KS), Ciceronian Literary Society,
5,188
McPherson College (KS), Moral and Social Reform
Committee, 5,188
McPherson, Elizabeth Weir, **3,612**
McPherson, Jessamyn West, 1,565
McPherson, Primrose, 13,446
McPherson, William F., **1,459**
McPheters, Myrtle. *See* Scribner, Myrtle
(McPheters) [Mrs. John]
McQuade, Clara M., **954**
McQuaid, Kay, 11,827
McQuaid, Mrs. Paul A., 5,349
McQueen, Eliza Ann (1778-1862). *See* Mackay,
Eliza Ann (McQueen) [Mrs. Robert] (1778-1862)
McQueen, Elizabeth, 1,060
McQueen, John J., **3,550**
McQuigg, Esther Hobart (1814-1902). *See* Morris,
Esther Hobart (McQuigg) [Mrs. Artemus] Slack
[Mrs. John] (1814-1902)
McRae, Annie, **288**
McRae Family (MS), 9,597
McRae, Sallie B., **9,796**
Macrae-Smith Company, 14,476

McRaven, Ellen. *See* Charles, Ellen (McRaven)
[Mrs. Thomas C.]
McRaven Family (MS), **9,602**
McRaven, William Henry, 9,705
Macready, William Charley, 11,984
McRoberts, A. J., Family, **10,008**
McRoberts, Mollie Lisk [Mrs. A. J.], 10,008
McTarnahan, Adaline "Addie" Chamberlin [Mrs. J.
C.] (1845-?). *See* Fowler, Adaline "Addie"
Chamberlin [Mrs. J. C.] McTarnahan (1845-?)
McTarnahan, J. C., 1,245
McVan, Alice Jane. [Mrs. Karl Bernard] Stein
(1906-70), **2,110**
McVea, Emilie W., 13,430
MacVeagh, Emily Eames [Mrs. Franklin], 3,816
MacVeagh, Fanny Davenport, 11,560
McVean, Diana Densmore (1808-56), 9,041
McVeigh, Maude Phelps. *See* Hutchins, Maude
Phelps (McVeigh)
McVickar, Augusta (1790-1857). *See* Jay, Augusta
(McVickar) [Mrs. William] (1790-1857)
McVickar Family (NY), 12,020
McVitty, Edward W., 4,480
McVitty, Marion (Etcheverry) [Mrs. Edward W.],
4,480
McWhirter, Luella Frances (Smith) [Mrs. Felix Tony]
(1859-?), **4,481**
McWhirter, Martha (White) [Mrs. George]
(1827-1904), 16,180
McWhorter, Margaret [Mrs.], 3,240
McWhorter, Mrs. Pope, 3,023
McWilliams, Julia (1912-). *See* Child, Julia
(McWilliams) (1912-)
McWilliams, Vera Seeley, **10,869**
McWillie, Catherine (Anderson), 9,709
Macy, Anne Mansfield (Sullivan) [Mrs. John Albert]
(1866-1936), 2,108, **2,111**, 2,390, 7,560, **7,684**,
11,812
Macy, Edith [Mrs. Everit], 5,119
Macy, Edith Carpenter, 12,095
Macy, Ethel Woodruff, 11,077
Macy, George (1900-56), 11,891, **12,040**
Macy, Helen [Mrs. George], **11,891**
Macy, Jesse (1842-1919), **4,935**
Macy, Joanna "Anne" (Sullivan) [Mrs. John Albert]
(1866-1936). *See* Macy, Anne Mansfield
(Sullivan) [Mrs. John Albert] (1866-1936)
Macy, Katharine. *See* Noyes, Katharine (Macy)
Macy, Maude [Mrs. Jesse], 4,935
Madagascar, missionaries to, Lutheran, 8,858
Madame Ambassador (book), 6,030
"Madame Congressman" (ms), 11,016
Madame France (book), 14,365
Madame Talvande's school (SC), 15,737
Madar, Olga (1915-), 8,075, **8,103**, 8,134
Maddalena (drama), 12,413
Maddan, Chester James, 5,654
Maddan, Jessie Flora (Ash) [Mrs. Remington]
(1886-). *See* Maddan, Jessie Flora (Ash) [Mrs.
Remington] Maddan [Mrs. Chester James]
(1886-)
Maddan, Jessie Flora (Ash) [Mrs. Remington]
Maddan [Mrs. Chester James] (1886-), **5,654**
Maddan, Remington, 5,654
Madden, Betty, 4,445
Madden, George (1866-1946). *See* Martin, George
(Madden) [Mrs. Attwood Reading] (1866-1946)
Madden, Georgia May (1866-1946). *See* Martin,
George (Madden) [Mrs. Attwood Reading]
(1866-1946)
Madden, Grace. *See* Braley, Grace (Madden) [Mrs.
Gerald]
Madden, Maude (Whitmore) [Mrs. Milton B.]
(1867-1948), **4,599**
Madden, Milton B. (1869-?), **4,599**
Madden, Mother Camilla, 7,694
Maddonna of Seven Moons, The (book), 12,413
Maddox, Evelyn Bradford (Marshall) [Mrs. Philip],
655
Maddox, Mildred, 1,314
Maddox, Virginia Knox [Mrs. Harry], 1,314
Maddux, Rachel (1912-), **6,048**
Madeira, Jean (1918-72), **15,387**
Madeleva, Sister Mary (1887-1964), 831, 1,224

Madera High School (CA), 952
"Madge Crandall, Girl Heroine of Oakfield" (story),
5,652
Madgett, Naomi Cornelia Long (1923-), **15,920**
Madiera Club (Savannah, GA), 3,585
Madison Abortion Action Coalition (WI), 17,652
Madison, Arnold, 14,475
Madison, Bertha. *See* Smith, Bertha (Madison) [Mrs.
Joseph, III]
Madison Civic Club (WI), **17,682**
Madison, Dorothea "Dolley" (Payne) [Mrs. John, Jr.]
Todd [Mrs. James] (1768-1849), **1,460**, **2,468**,
3,221, **5,294**, 6,653, **11,169**, **12,255**, **13,483**,
14,981
Madison General Hospital (WI), 17,590
Madison, Helene, 997
Madison House (NY). *See* Hamilton-Madison House
(NY)
Madison, James (1751-1836), 1,460, 2,322, 2,464,
2,468, 2,548, 2,582, **11,169**, 12,255, 13,451,
13,483
Madison Ladies' Union League (WI), **17,684**
Madison, Sarah Tate [Mrs. James], 13,451
Madison School (MN), 8,957
Madison Square Presbyterian Church (NY), **12,256**
Madison Valley Woman's Club (MT), **10,254**
Madison Veterans Administration (WI), library,
17,777
Madison Young Republicans (WI), 17,628
Madson, Hattie (1908-). *See* Knight, Hattie
(Madson) (1908-)
Maeser, Eva (1876-1967). *See* Crandall, Eva
(Maeser) [Mrs. Myron E.] (1876-1967)
Maeser, Karl G., 3,738, 16,620, 16,640
Maeser, Mrs. Sherwin, 16,485
Magaw, Adriana, 11,325
Magazine for Women's Clubs (PA), 15,244
Magazine of American History (periodical), 7,246,
12,240
Magdalen, Sister Mary, 17,029
Magdalen Society (PA), **15,048**
Magee, Abbie Eliza [Miss] (1847-1909), **10,999**
Magee, Anna May, 13,942
Magee, Elizabeth S. [Miss] (1899-?), 2,504, 11,771,
13,942
Magee, Emma H. [Mrs.] (1866-1950), **10,401**
Magee, James J. R., 10,999
Magee, Joni, 15,134
Magee, Marie T., 9,007
Magee, Nellie J., 10,543
Magee, Nellie (Throop) [Mrs. Oliver N.] (1874-1962),
10,489, 10,571
Magee, Wiliam A., 13,942
Magelssen Family, 8,764
Magelssen, Thora (?-1968), **8,764**
Maggie, Mary (Scudder), 3,576
Maggio, Graziella (1928-), **2,469**
Magic Circle, The (book), 12,565
Magic in the Alley (book), 4,978
"Magic of America, The" (ms), 12,216
Magic Portholes (book), 11,992
Magicians Wife, The (book), 2,241
Magil, Joseph, 14,908
Magil, Rachel [Mrs. Joseph], 14,908
Magil, Rose I. (1895-1964). *See* Bender, Rose I.
(Magil) (1895-1964)
Magill, Helen (1853-1944). *See* White, Helen
(Magill) [Mrs. Andrew Dickson] (1853-1944)
Magill, Margaret W. [Mrs. Frederick W.] Hodge,
11,295
Maginnis, Patricia, 11,932
Magna Carta, 8,619
Magna Carta Dames (GA), 3,374, 3,439
*Magna Carta: Its Role in the Making of the English
Constitution* (book), 8,619
Magna Charta Dames (Delta, MS), 9,551
Magna Charta Dames (OK), 14,230
Magnes, Beatrice [Mrs. Judah L.] (1879-1968), 11,817
Magnes, Judah Leon, 2,177, 13,801
Magnetism, 11,646
Magnificat (periodical), 10,888
Magnificent Ambersons, The (moving picture), 17,809
Magnolia Community Club (WA), 17,260
Magnuson, Anna. *See* Anderson, Anna (Magnuson)

Magnuson, Mrs. Paul Budd, 11,827
Magnussen, Ann K., 2,087
Magoun, John, 3,754
Magrath Family (SC), 15,497
Magrath, Selina E. Bollin, 15,639
Magrath, Sellina Bollin [Mrs. William Joy] (ca. 1850-?), 15,497
Magrath, William Joy, 15,497
Magraw, Martha [Mrs. Elliot], 9,341
Magriore, Mrs., 6,605
Magruder, Eliza L., 9,675
Magruder, Julia (1854-1907), 17,010
Magruder, Rosalie S., 6,292
Maguire, Grace Adeline (King), 14,216
Maguire, James D., 14,216
Maguire, Sarah Edna (1889-?), 649, 1,068
Mahaffey, Pearl, 17,430
Maharas, Evelyn, 14,174
Mahdesian, Sarah. See Avakian, Sarah (Mahdesian)
Maher, Amy Grace (1883-1965), 14,144
Maher Family (MN), 9,199
Maher, Margaret, 8,021
Mahler, Margaret, 11,908
Mahnkey, Mary Elizabeth (1878-1948), 10,132
Mahoney, Alice Phelan (Doyle) [Mrs. William Patrick] (1923-?), 831
Mahoney, Jay, 558
Mahoney, Margaret, 11,844
Mahoney, Mildred (Hodgman) [Mrs. John J.] (1896-), 6,432, 6,751
Mahoning County Probate Court (OH), Girls Industrial School, 14,105
Mahood, Fannie (1864-1931). See Heath, Fannie (Mahood) [Mrs. Frank Arnold] (1864-1931)
Mahood, Ruth I., 1,004
Maid of Orleans (ship), 7,488
Maiden Creek Friends Meeting (PA), 15,289
Maiden Rachel (book), 17,718
Maier, Elsie (1890-). See Kellers, Elsie (Maier) (1890-)
Maietta, Julia L., 15,321, 15,332
Mail-order business, 4,034
Maimie (1885-?), 6,752
Main Avenue High School (San Antonio, TX), 16,316
Main, Ida Belle (Lewis) [Mrs. William A.] (1887-1969), 14,419
Main, William A., 14,419
Maine, 5,578, 7,647, 7,669
    abolitionists, 5,684
    agriculture, 5,644
        statistics, 5,570
    art societies, 5,558
    associations, institutions, etc., 7,669
    authors, 5,580, 5,590, 5,599, 5,620, 5,694
    autobiographies, 5,678
    biography, indexes, 5,595
    blacksmiths, 5,682
    blind, institutional care, 5,570
    Camp Fire Girls, 5,596
    camp-meetings, 5,614
    camp sites, facilities, etc., 5,614
    camps, 5,654, 6,614
    cemeteries, 5,709
    census, 5,566, 5,570, 5,571
    charitable societies, 5,605, 5,608, 5,686, 5,687, 5,709
    charities, 5,575
    chocolate processing, 6,207
    church societies, 5,604
    churches, Baptist, 5,644
    cities and towns, 5,644
        civic improvement, 5,611
    Civil War, 5,561, 5,689
        personal narratives, 7,669
        registers, lists, etc., 7,669
        relief of sick and wounded, 5,608
    clergy, 5,699
    clergy, Presbyterian, 5,713
    clubs, 5,557, 5,579, 5,607, 5,611, 5,613, 5,614, 5,631, 5,696
    college and school periodicals, 5,685
    college trustees, 5,995
    community centers, 5,709
    community life, 5,688

    composers, 5,582
    congressmen, 2,210, 5,676
    convents and nunneries, Catholic, 5,596
    cooks, 5,651
    country-dance, 5,643
    country music, 5,642, 5,649
    court-houses, 2,507
    court records, 5,568
    criminal statistics, 5,570
    deaf, institutional care, 5,570
    dental clinics, 5,607
    diaries and journals, 5,576, 5,585, 5,623, 5,634, 5,635, 5,671, 5,677, 5,691, 5,715, 5,716
    divining-rod, 5,648
    divorce, 5,568
    dry-goods, accounting, 6,190
    education, 5,570
    educators, 5,615, 5,618
    elections, 11,928
    farm life, 5,644, 5,665
    farmers, 5,672
    festivals, 5,644
    fires, 5,644
    fisheries, fishermen, 5,624
    floods, 5,644
    flower shows, 5,559
    folk tales, 5,652, 5,666
    folklore, 5,655
    genealogy, 6,234, 7,669
    gipsies, 5,655
    governors, 5,679
    guides for hunters, fishermen, etc., 5,586
    handicapped children, rehabilitation, 5,573
    high schools, 5,685
    historians, 5,578, 5,606
    historical museums, 5,693
    historical societies, 5,693
    home economics teachers, 5,662
    home labor, 5,570
    horticultural societies, 5,559
    hotels, taverns, etc., 5,644
    hours of labor, 5,564
    industrial accidents, 5,564
    industrial statistics, 5,570
    islands, 5,644
    journalists, 5,662
    kindergartens, 5,558
    lawyers, 5,676, 12,509
    legislative bodies, 5,565
    legislators, 5,641, 5,676
    libraries, 5,709
    literary societies, 5,594
    local laws, 5,565
    lumber-camps, 5,651, 5,664
    lumbering, 5,624, 5,644, 5,689
    lumbermen, songs and music, 5,664
    manufacturers, 5,704
    maternal and infant welfare, 5,573
    medicines, patent, proprietary, etc., 5,647
    mentally handicapped, institutional care, 5,570
    mentally ill, care and treatment, 5,570
    merchant seamen, missions and charities, 5,605
    midwives, 5,574
    millinery, 6,190
    millinery workers, 5,593
    mills and mill-work, 5,644
    missionaries, Baptist, 5,710
    monasticism and religious orders for women, Catholic, 5,705
    music, 5,657
    musical societies, 5,560, 5,582
    Native Americans, 7,474
        missions, 5,710, 7,597
    newspapers, 5,669
    nurses, 5,583
    nurses' aides, 5,583
    officials and employees, 3,977
    organists, 5,670
    orphans and orphan asylums, 5,570
    patriotic societies, 2,097, 5,597, 5,600, 5,641, 5,717, 7,669
    payrolls, 6,207
    Penobscot Indians, music, 5,658
    photograph collections, 5,596

    pianists, 5,657
    poaching, 5,643
    poets, 5,612
    political activists, women, 5,565
    politicians, 5,627
    politics, practical, women's activism, 5,587, 5,630
    postal service, letter carriers, 5,652
    postmasters, 12,051
    practical nurses, 5,583
    prisoners, 5,570
    private schools, 5,679
    psychiatric hospitals, records, 5,562
    public health nursing, 5,607
    public libraries, 5,558, 5,598
    public welfare, 5,561, 5,573, 5,575
    publishers and publishing, 6,035
    quilting, 5,660
    railroads, 5,689
    refuse removal and disposal, 5,613
    Revolutionary War
        personal narratives, 7,669
        registers, lists, etc., 7,669
    schools, 5,618
    scrapbooks, 5,594
    secretaries, 5,593, 5,647, 5,663
    secretaries of state, 5,569
    senators, United States, 2,210, 5,719, 7,677, 12,509
    shipmasters, 5,675
    shipping, 6,208
    slavery, legal aspects, 5,565
    social life and customs, 5,606, 5,671
    soldiers, 7,669
    speech, research, 5,667
    stores, retail, 5,636
    strikes and lockoutes, 5,704
    suffrage, 4,859, 5,569
        legal aspects, 5,565
        opposition to, 5,680
    suffrage societies, 5,581, 5,626
    suffragists, 5,587
    suicide, 5,702
    summer schools, 3,852
    superstition, 5,664
    teachers, 5,577, 5,584, 12,245
    teachers' colleges, 5,577, 5,609, 5,634
    temperance, legal aspects, 5,565
    temperance societies, 5,641, 5,698
    textile factories, 6,202
    textile workers, 5,596
    universities and colleges, 5,644, 5,708, 5,995
        employees, 5,646, 5,663
    urban beautification, 5,559, 5,613
    vital statistics, 5,563, 5,567, 5,572
    vocational rehabilitation, 5,573
    wages
        household workers, 5,570
        women, 5,564, 5,570
    War of 1812, 7,677
        campaigns and battles, 7,677
        personal narratives, 7,669
        registers, lists, etc., 7,669
    widows, 5,686
    women
        education, 5,679
        employment, 5,564, 5,570
    zoning, 5,607
Maine (ship), 9,032, 15,595
Maine, Adjutant General's Department, 5,561
Maine Association Opposed to Suffrage for Women, 5,680
Maine Department of Vocational Rehabilitation, 5,573
Maine Federation of Music Clubs, 5,582
Maine Federation of Women's Clubs, 5,579, 5,631
Maine Indians
    language and customs, 5,624, 6,375
    missions, 7,597
Maine Woman Suffrage Associations, 5,581, 5,626
Maine Women's Suffrage party, 5,587
Mairs, Clara, 9,145
Mairs, Jane B., 15,640
Major, Agnes. See Park, Agnes (Major) [Mrs. John]
Major Barbara (drama), 17,804
Major, Clare Tree. [Mrs. John D.] Kenardine (1880-1954), 12,557

Major, Grace (Williams), 14,778
Makah Indians, genealogies, 17,266
Maki, Eleanor, **8,104**
Maki, Marjorie, 9,140
Maki, Toini, 9,467
Making of a Lady, The (book), 5,853
"Making the Invisible Woman Visible" (lecture), 15,197
Makocha Study Club (Milbank, SD), **15,847**
Malachowski, Charlotte. *See* Buhler, Charlotte (Malachowski)
Malaco Sound Studios (MS), 9,742
Malanga, Gerald, 12,064
Malarckey, Mary. *See* Cabell, Mary (Malarckey) Cartwright [Mrs. Henry Failing]
Malaysia, American volunteer workers in social service in, 9,286
"Male Attitudes Toward Females: The Politics of Women's Liberation" (lecture), 15,197
Malcolm X College (Chicago, IL), 4,148
Malefactors, The (book), 11,163
Malek, Leona A., **3,873**
Malin Family, 11,746
Malin, Rachel, 11,746
Malina, Judith, 964
Mall, Franklin Paine, 14,900
Mall, Mabel, 1,786
Mallery, Bell. *See* Wright, Bell Mallery [Mrs. W. T.]
Mallett, Anna Smith (1845-1907), **1,824**
Mallett, Caroline. *See* Hooper, Caroline (Mallett) [Mrs. George DeBerniere]
Mallett, Charles Peter, 13,033
Mallet-Prevost, Pauline (ca. 1890-). *See* Ornstein, Pauline (Mallet-Prevost) [Mrs. Leo] (ca. 1890-)
Mallison, Elizabeth, 9,323
Malloch, Helen Miller, 9,823
Mallonian Society (GA), 3,191
Mallory, Angelo Sylvaria Moreno [Mrs. Stephen R.], 2,892
Mallory, Charles (1796-1882), 1,988
Mallory, Clifford Day (1881-1941), 1,988
Mallory, Charles Henry (1818-90), 1,988
Mallory, Cora (1881-1973), **2,907**
Mallory, Cora N. (Pynchon) [Mrs. Henry Rogers] (1854-1938), 1,988
Mallory Family (CT), **1,988**
Mallory Family (FL), **2,892**
Mallory, Helen, 11,440
Mallory, Henry Rogers (1849-1919), 1,988
Mallory, Molla B., 15,935
Mallory, Stephen Russell (1810-73), 2,892, 2,900, 2,907
Malone, Alberta, 3,212
Malone Family (TX), 16,269, 16,341
Malone, Janet H., 4,082
Malone, Katherine D. (1881-), **10,904**
Malone, Mrs. Robert James, 12,184
Malone, Vivian (1943-), **102**
Maloney, Albertine Erickson [Mrs. Michael] (1857-1940), **8,473**
Maloney, Linda Mitchell McKee (1939-), **7,482**
Maloon, Mary Eliza (Warner) (1849-1922), 867, **1,320**
Malott, Deane W., 11,592
Malott, Eleanor S., **11,646**
Malozemoff, Elizabeth (1881-?), **650**
Malsch, Rose [Miss], **17,565**
Malt, 15,070
Maltby, Margaret Eliza (1860-1944), 14,123
Malverne, Gladys, **12,558**
Mama's Bank Account (book), 6,016
Mamas, Helen (1923-). *See* Zotos, Helen (Mamas) [Mrs. Stepheno] (1923-)
Mammals, 2,724
Mammoth Cave (KY), 13,250
Mammoth Life Insurance Company (KY), 5,378
Mamreof, Anna F. [Miss], **7008**
Man Called Peter, A (book), 2,476
Man Called Peter, A (moving-picture), 2,476
Man from the Bitter Roots, The (book), 17,899
Man Named Herne (What They Told Me and What I Remember, A (book), 11,457
Man-Suffrage Association Opposed to Political Suffrage for Women, 12,525

Man, Susan Maria (1818-98). *See* McCulloch, Susan Maria (Man) [Mrs. Hugh] (1818-98)
Man Who Loved His Wife, The, 17,793
Management, 7,315
Manahan, James (1866-1932), Family (MN), **9,200**
Manahan, Kathryn (1896-). *See* Hoxmeier, Kathryn (Manahan) (1896-)
Manahan, Mary [Mrs. James], 9,200
Manchester Academy and Normal School, 4,920
Manchester and District Suffrage Bazaar (England, 1912), 6,889
Manchester Guardian (England), 174
Manchuria, American diplomats in, 11,720
Mandel Brothers Department Store (IL), 13,817
Mandeville, Betty, 1,026
Mandeville, Emma L. (Underhill) [Mrs. Frederick Austin], 11,647
Mandeville Family (NY), **11,647**
Mandeville, Frederick Austin, 11,647
Mangel, Margaret, **9,829**
Mangels, Carrie A., 1,339
Mangold, Frederick R., **13,484**
Mangum, Charity [Mrs. Willie], 13,485
Mangum Family (GA), 3,413
Mangum, Katherine Elizabeth "Lizzie" (1834-?). *See* Osborn, Katherine Elizabeth "Lizzie" (Mangum) [Mrs. James] (1834-?)
Mangum, Willie Person, **13,485**
Manhattan Bank (NY), 12,600
Manhattan Council of the New York State Committee Against Discrimination, 2,587
Manhattan Project, Los Alamos division, 9,146
Manhattan Trade School for Girls (NY), 6,812, 8,671
Manhattanville Nursery (NY), 11,864
Manigault, Ann Ashby, 15,498
Manigault, Charles Izard, 15,498
Manigault, Elizabeth Heyward [Mrs. Charles Izard], 15,498
Manigault Family (SC), **13,066, 15,498,** 15,585
Manigault, Gabriel, 15,498
Manigault, Harriet. *See* Wilcocks, Harriet (Manigault)
Manigault, Margaret (Izard) [Mrs. Gabriel] (1768-1824), 2,408, 13,066, 15,498
Manitou Analecta (book), 8,746, 8,809
Manitou Ripples (school yearbook), 4,659
Manix Family (MT), **10,333**
Mankato College Women's Group (MN). *See* American Association of University Women (Mankato Branch, MN)
Mankato Council of Camp Fire Girls (MN), **8,490**
Mankato Council of Church Women United (MN), **8,502**
Mankato Daily Review (MN), 9,000
Mankato High School (MN), 8,492
Mankato Normal School (MN), 8,498
Mankato Rehabilitation Center Auxiliary (MN), **8,503**
Mankato State College (MN). *See* Mankato State University (MN)
Mankato State Teachers College (MN). *See* Mankato State University (MN)
Mankato State University (MN), 8,492, 8,501, 8,750 faculty, **8,512,** 9,081
Mankato State University (MN), Faculty Wives Association, **8,504**
Mankato Symphony Guild (MN), **8,505**
Mankato Symphony Orchestra (MN), 8,505
Mankell, Natalie, 11,378
Mankin, Helen Douglas, 13,406, 14,046
Mankinen, Vera, 6,761
Manley, Emma Catherine (ca. 1806-63). *See* Embury, Emma Catherine (Manley) (ca. 1806-63)
Manling, Nora, 4,828
Mann Act (1910), 2,193
Mann, Austin Sheuy, 2,886
Mann, Erika, 2,513
Mann Family (CA), 651
Mann Family (OH), **14,165**
Mann, Gladys, 11,774
Mann, Harriet (1831-1918). *See* Miller, Harriet (Mann) [Mrs. Watts Todd] (1831-1918)
Mann, Henry Rice, 651
Mann, Horace, 13,496

Mann, Klaus, 12,042
Mann, Maria R. (1817-?), 2,471
Mann, Mary, 11,125
Mann, Mary Tyler (Peabody) [Mrs. Horace] (1806-87), **2,471,** 7,277, 14,165
Mann, May (1872-1928). *See* Jennings, May (Mann) [Mrs. William Sherman] (1872-1928)
Mann, Mrs. L. N. D., 2,059
Mann, Olive Lucinda (Trobridge) [Mrs. Henry Rice], **651**
Mann, Oreon (?-1907). *See* Smith, Oreon Mann [Mrs. Rufus] (?-1907)
Mann, Thomas, 2,631, 11,969
Mann, Verda [Mrs.], 16,485
Manner, Jane. Jennie Mannheimer, **13,810**
Mannering, Mary, 3,100
Manners, Laurette (Cooney) [Mrs. Charles Alonzo] Taylor [Mrs. Hartley] (1884-1946), 12,476
Manners, Laurette (Cooney) [Mrs. Charles Alonzo] Taylor [Mrs. Hartley] Manners (1884-1946). *See* Taylor, Laurette (Cooney) [Mrs. Charles Alonzo] Taylor. [Mrs. Hartley] Manners (1884-1946)
Mannes, Marya (1904-), **6,049,** 6,065, 11,897
Mannheim, Eunice, **6,753**
Mannheimer, Eugene, 13,810
Mannheimer, Jennie. *See* Manner, Jane. Jennie Mannheimer
Mannheimer, Louise, 13,810
Mannin, Ethel Edith (1900-), 12,487
Manning, Adeline, 7,585
Manning, Anna (1845-1931). *See* Comfort, Anna (Manning) [Mrs. George Fisk] (1845-1931)
Manning, Carrie (1856-75), 11,443, **11,779**
Manning, Daniel (1831-87), **2,472**
Manning, Elizabeth Heard (1808-31), **7,058**
Manning Family (MA), **7,383**
Manning, Harvey, 17,251
Manning, Helen Herron (Taft) [Mrs. Frederick Johnson] (1891-), **2,473,** 2,596, 11,913, 14,889
Manning, Jane (1813-1908). *See* James, Jane Elizabeth (Manning) [Mrs. Isaac] (1813-1908)
Manning, John Heard, 7,058
Manning, Josephine, 17,207
Manning, Malvina Virginia (Van Lear) (1841-1920), **652**
Manning, Margaret [Mrs. Thomas], 7,058
Manning, Maria (1826-1917), 7,383
Manning, Maria Miriam (1786-1814), 7,383
Manning, Mary (1777-1841), 7,383
Manning, Mary Margaretta (Fryer) [Mrs. Daniel] (1845-1928), 2,472
Manning, Mrs. Benjamin, 11,443
Manning, Mrs. John A., 15,576
Manning, Mrs. Michael, 7,151
Manning, Priscilla Miriam (1790-1873). *See* Dike, Priscilla Miriam (Manning) (1790-1873)
Manning, Rebecca B. (1834-1933), 7,383
Manning, Rebecca Dodge (Burnham) (1797-1869), 7,383
Manning, Richard C., Jr., 7,383
Manning, Susan (Dingley), 7,383
Manning, Thomas, 7,058
Manning, W. T. (1866-1949), **12,087**
Manning, Warren H., 14,809
Manning, William Hart, 16,446
Mannington Monthly Meeting, 15,031
"Man's Destiny" (essay), 12,405
Mansfield, Arabella "Belle" Aurelia Babb [Mrs. John Melvin] (1846-1911), **4,533,** 5,063, **5,068**
Mansfield, Beatrice (Cameron) [Mrs. Richard], 9,057, 12,559
Mansfield College (LA), 5,551
Mansfield Family (NY), **11,648**
Mansfield, Katherine (1888-1923), 4,228
Mansfield, Maria Mills (?-1888). *See* White, Maria Mills Mansfield [Mrs. Hugh] (?-1888)
Mansfield, Mary Ann (1859-1949). *See* Bentley, Mary Ann (Mansfield) [Mrs. William Oscar] (1859-1949)
Mansfield, Norma Bicknell [Mrs. Robert S.] (1906-), **14,421**
Mansfield, Rachell K., **10,334**
Mansfield, Richard (1854-1907), **12,559**
Mansfield, Robert S., 14,421

Manship, Paul, 6,185, 9,139
Mansion of Truth (NY), 12,166
Mansion Square Boarding School (Poughkeepsie, NY), 9,277
Manso, Juana, 2,471
Manton-MacDowell Colony (NH), **10,852**
Manton, Robert, 10,852
Manua, Rosa, 15,310
Manual training, 2,313, 12,808, 13,489, 13,916, 13,992
Manufactures, 2,033, 5,345, 7,611, 7,680, 9,962, 12,672, 13,086, 14,532, 14,718, 14,978, **15,953**
Manufactures, **5,704, 14,919**
Manumission of slaves. See Slavery, Emancipation
Manuscript (periodical), 9,769
Manuscripts, 951, **8,531**, 10,992, **11,940**
Manville, Helen A. See Pope, Helen A. (Manville) [Mrs. Charles A.]
Many, Anna Estelle (ca. 1890-), **5,506**
Many Names of Lee Lu, The (book), 8,314
Manz, Helen (1879-?). See Moede, Helen (Manz) (1879-?)
Manzanar Relocation Center (CA), 785
Mao, Tse-Tung, 17,343
Mapes, Mary Elizabeth (1831-1905). See Dodge, Mary Elizabeth (Mapes) [Mrs. William] (1831-1905)
Maple Leaf Fund, 12,797
Maple Street Congregational Church (Danvers, MA), **7,004**
Maple sugar, 5,654, 9,467
Maple syrup, 3,756, 5,644
Mapleson, Henry, 10,793
Maplewood Parents Teacher Association (MN), 8,917
Maps, 499, 1,878, 8,300, 10,037, 11,574, 12,320, 14,206
Marable, Mary Hays, **14,217**
Maracci, Carmelita, 12,360
"Marah" (pseudonym). See Jackson, Helen Maria (Fiske) [Mrs. Edward Bissell] Hunt [Mrs. William Sharpless] (183-85)
Marble, Alice, 997
Marble, Annie Russell [Mrs.] (1864-1936), **7,648**
Marblehead Charitable Society (MA), **7,404**
Marblehead Female Humane Society (MA), **7,086**
Marblehead Garden Club (MA), **7,087**
Marblehead Visiting Nurse Association (MA), **7,088**
Marblehead Women's Club (MA), **7,089**
Marbury, Anne (1591-ca. 1643). See Hutchinson, Anne (Marbury) [Mrs. William] (1591-ca. 1643)
Marbury, Elisabeth (1856-1933), 12,476
Marcet, Jean. See (Haldeman)-Julius, Anna (Marcet) [Mrs. Emanuel]
March, Alice Little (Hale) [Mrs. John C.] (1811-?), **7,405**
March, Charles H., 8,719
March, Florence Eldridge [Mrs. Frederic], 12,040
March of Dimes, 9,522, 10,082, 14,192, 16,911, 17,050
Marchand, Lizzie, **15,049**
Marchand, Marie. See Ross, Marie (Marchand)
Marcley, Jessie [Mrs. W. J.], 8,913
Marconnier, Emily Sims, 2,504
Marcos, Ferdinand, 7,875
Marcus, Grace, 8,665
Marcus, Maria (1928-), **2,786**
Marcus, Minnie, 11,817
Marcus Warland (book), 111
"Marcus Welby, M.D." (television program), 18,020
Marcy, Elizabeth E. (Smith) (1821-1911), 4,127
Marcy, Ellen (?-1915). See McClellan, Ellen (Marcy) [Mrs. George Brinton, Sr.] (?-1915)
Marcy, Mary E., 9,380
Marcy-Newberry Center (IL), **4,127**
Mardis, Mrs. James (1845-?), **10,335**
"Margaret" (ms), 7,197
Margaret (slave, VA), 4,239
Margaret Brown Gallery (MA), **2,787**
Margaret Coffin Prayer Book Society (MA), **6,180**
Margaret Eliza Nast Memorial Hospital (China), 10,580
Margaret Evans Deaconess Home (CO), **1,812**
Margaret Fuller Association, 8,914

Margaret Hickey School for Secretaries (MO), 10,197, **10,198**
Margaret Sage Industrial School (Lawrence, NY). See Five Towns Community House (Lawrence, NY)
Margaret Sanger Clinical Research Bureau. See Planned Parenthood (NY)
Margarita Seminary (NC), 14,577
Margetts, Lucy Marie (Canfield) [Mrs. John W.] Young [Mrs. Ara W.] Sabin [Mrs. Phillip H.] (1846-1915), **16,763**
Margetts, Phillip H., 16,763
Margolis, Edith, 14,315, 14,385, 14,395, **14,400,** 14,410, 14,417, 14,448, 14,453, 14,464
Margot, Antoinette, 2,196
Maria (slave, SC), 15,653
Maria Sanford Junior High (MN), 9,347
Maria, the Potter of San Ildefonso (book), 14,218
Marian Anderson Citizens Committee, 2,123
Marian Anderson Mural Fund Committee, 2,123
Marian College (Indianapolis, IN), 4,649
archives, **4,632**
students, **4,625**
Marian College (Indianapolis, IN), Alumni Association, 4,632
Marian College (Indianapolis, IN), Student Association, 4,632
Marian College Magnet, The, 4,632
Marian Heights Academy (Monroe, CT), 1,985
Marian Sisters Motherhouse (Waverly, NE), **10,618**
Marian, The (yearbook), 4,632
Marianna Club (Springfield, IL), **4,372**
Marianne Moore Festschrift, 16,163
Marianne, Mother (1836-1918). See Kopp, Barbara (1836-1918)
Marie, Mother Marguerite (1897-1970), 14,785
"Marie Rose" (column), 3,070
Marillac House (Chicago, IL), **3,874**
Marlin, Margaret, 13,388
Marine Corps League Auxiliary, Smedley O. Butler Unit (Tulsa, OK), **14,264**
Marine engineering, 14,941
Mariner, John W., Family (WI), **17,685**
Mariner, Mary Fargo Antisdel [Mrs. John W.], 17,685
Mariner's Juvenile Band (AZ), 203
Marines, **11,426**
Marino, Amy (1914-), 7,109
Marinoni, Rosa Zagnoni, 258, 289
Mario, Jessie White, 12,572
Marion, Esther, **15,499**
Marion, Esther (?-1815), **15,641**
Marion Female Institute, 9,801
Marion, Frances (1900-1973), 949, 11,907
Marion, Francis, 15,641
Marital contracts. See Prenuptial contracts
Maritime law, 1,174
Mark, Clara Gould (1882-1966), **14,005**
Mark, Lewis, 14,006
Mark, Mary Louise [Miss] (1878-1975), **14,006**
Mark Twain and the Happy Island (book), 9,425
Mark Twain, Son of Missouri (book), 9,839
Markell, Grace Elizabeth, **2,474**
Markey, Dorothy (1900-), 13,176
Markham, Catherine, 4,000
Markham, Edwin (1852-1940), 2,376, 17,114
Markham Family, 4,942
Markham, James L., 8,470
Markham, Mary (McKittrick) [Mrs. George D.], **10,173**
Markham, O. G., **5,170**
Markham, William, 9,753
Markhus, Ingrid Egge (1848-1918), 8,737
Markle, Florence E., 8,462
Markley, Mary Elizabeth (?-1954), **14,797**
Markoe, Abraham, Jr. (ca. 1740-1808), 15,050
Markoe Family, **2,343, 15,050,** 15,052
Markoe, Margaret H., 14,884
Markoe, Mary (Maxcy) [Mrs. Francis], 2,343, 15,052
Markoff, Sol, 8,686
Markova, Alicia, 3,980
Marks, James Rufus, 10,375
Marks, Jeannette A. (1875-1964), 6,742, **6,754,** 7,499
Marks, Theodora Smith [Mrs. Solon], 17,740
Marlow, Marilyn, 14,414
Marlowe, Alan, 12,894

Marlowe, Julia. Sarah Frances Frost. Fanny Brough. Fancy Brough. [Mrs. Robert] Taber [Mrs. Edward Hugh] Sothern (1866-1950), 2,562, 2,968, 3,100, 10,025, 11,997, **12,173,** 12,535, 12,536, **12,629, 12,630, 12,631,** 12,637, 17,197
Marlton School for the Deaf, Faculty Association, 2,103
Marmon, Mrs. M. A., 3,753
Marmon, Susie, 16,868
Marple, Lorna [Mrs. Warren H.], **17,304**
Marquand, Allan (1853-1924), **11,170**
Marquand, Christina Davenport Sedgwick, 11,560
Marquand, Eleanor (Cross) [Mrs. Allen] (1874-1950), **2,475,** 11,170
Marquis, Don (1878-1937), **12,041**
Marquis, Dorothea Tomlinson [Mrs.], 4,868
Marquis, Marjorie (Vonnegut) [Mrs. Don], 12,041
Marquis, Neeta [Miss], **1,461**
Marr, Josephine, 9,887
Marr, Lizzie, 9,887
Marriage, 685, 1,352, 1,492, 1,657, 1,838, 1,860, 2,451, 2,620, 3,389, 3,988, 4,409, 5,805, 6,653, 7,256, 7,453, **8,200,** 9,376, 9,951, 10,043, 10,101, 11,778, 11,974, 13,427, 13,445, 13,450, 14,753, 15,045, 15,259, 15,323, 17,975. See also Domestic relations; Family; Family life education
annulment, 5,742, 9,934
Marriage Advice (book), 8,929
Marriage and Divorce (book), 10,933
"Marriage and Sex Adjustment," 6,388
Marriage contracts. See Prenuptial contracts
Marriage Council of Philadelphia (PA), 6,987
Marriage counseling, 5,842, 6,223, 6,760, 6,788, 6,987, 7,283, 7,289, 11,932, 14,849
Marriage customs and rites, 13,498
Marriage customs and rites, Native American, 2,832
Marriage law, 2,680, 6,259, 6,530, 6,545, 6,789, 7,199, 8,057, 9,299, 9,934, 10,048, 12,843, 15,745, 17,018
Marriage licenses, **9,784, 11,193,** 11,208
Marriage Manual, 6,232
Marriage of Diamond and Dolls, The, 17,623
Marriage registers. See Registers of births, etc.
Married women
employment, 34, 2,068, 2,684, 6,958, 7,256, 8,664
financial dependency, 15,649
legal status, laws, etc., 4,351, 8,093, 13,376
Marriner, Sarah, 15,036
Marriott, Alice Lee (1910-), 14,218
Marriott, Mrs., 16,629
Marron, Edward, 10,309
Marrón, Felipa Osuña de (1809-?), 653
Marron, Grace [Mrs. Edward]. See Gilmore, Grace [Mrs. Edward] Marron [Mrs. James W.]
Marrs, Evangeline (1860-1930). See Whipple, Evangeline (Marrs) [Mrs. Michael H.] Simpson [Mrs. Henry Benjamin] (1860-1930)
Mars Bluff Methodist Episcopal Church (SC), Women's Missionary Society, Florence District, **15,642**
Mars, Carmelia, **12,560**
Mars Hill Baptist Church (NC), Women's Missionary Union, 13,297
Mars Hill College (NC), archives, **13,300**
Mars, Nancy (1920-). See Freedman, Nancy (Mars) [Mrs. Benedict] (1920-)
Marshall. See also Marshall
Marschall, Cornelia (1895-). See Smith, Cornelia (Marschall) [Mrs. Charles G.] (1895-)
Marschall, Irene. See King, Irene (Marschall)
Marsden, Edward, **1,168**
Marsden, Kate, 12,497
Marsh, Abigail Smith (Tuck) [Mrs. John] (1818-57), 654
Marsh, Alice Frances (1852-1927). See Cameron, Alice Frances (Marsh) [Mrs. William Walker] (1852-1927)
Marsh, Benjamin F., 8,164
Marsh, Dorothy, **1,045**
Marsh, Dorothy (1889-), **15,784**
Marsh, Electa, 1,970
Marsh, Eliza Ann (?-1878). See Robertson, Eliza Ann (Marsh) (?-1878)
Marsh, Elizabeth, 11,519

Marsh, Elizabeth (1873-1964), **10,870**
Marsh, Elvira (1830-1910). *See* Gnagi, Elvira (Marsh) (1830-1910)
Marsh, Emily (Scudder), 3,576
Marsh, Eudocia (Baldwin) (1829-?), **16,540**
Marsh Family, **7,258**
Marsh Family (CA), **654**
Marsh, George, 10,826
Marsh, Helen. *See* Wixson, Helen (Marsh)
Marsh, Jean [Mrs. George], 10,826
Marsh, Jennie E. [Mrs.], 9,262
Marsh, John (1798-1856), 654
Marsh, John Robert, 2,488, 3,065
Marsh, Mae, 11,907
Marsh, Margaret "Peggy" Munnerlyn (Mitchell) [Mrs. Berrien K.] Upshaw [Mrs. John Robert] (1900-49). *See* Mitchell, Margaret "Peggy" Munnerlyn. [Mrs. Berrien K.] Upshaw [Mrs. John Robert] Marsh (1900-49)
Marsh, Marjorie. *See* Enfield, Marjorie (Marsh)
Marsh, Mary B., **6,755**
Marsh, Roberta, 2,202
Marsh, Sarah (1829-57). *See* Cranstone, Sarah (Marsh) (1829-57)
Marsh, Sarah Griswold, 2,202
Marsh, Susan Louise [Mrs.], **9,889**
Marsh Tours, Inc., 7,258
Marshall. *See also* Marschall
Marshall, Andrew, 3,519
Marshall, Ann [Mrs. Robert], 12,561
Marshall, Caroline E. *See* Dodge, Caroline E. (Marshall) [Mrs. George A.]
Marshall, Catherine, 15,269
Marshall, Clara (1847-1931), 15,128, **15,131**
Marshall County Historical Society (IA), 4,772
Marshall County Historical Society (MS), **9,574**
Marshall County Woman Suffrage Association (IA), 4,732
Marshall, Crystal, 1,655
Marshall, Dixie, 1,534
Marshall, Elizabeth. *See* Martin, Elizabeth (Marshall)
Marshall, Elizabeth (1862-83), 15,070
Marshall, Elizabeth Coe (1847-92), 12,759
Marshall, Emma, 5,549
Marshall, Eva. *See* Totah, Eva (Marshall)
Marshall, Evelyn Bradford. *See* Maddox, Evelyn Bradford (Marshall) [Mrs. Philip]
Marshall Family (KY), **5,332**
Marshall Family (LA), **5,549**
Marshall Family (NY), **12,759**
Marshall Female Seminary (MO), 9,854
Marshall, Florence (1869-1964). *See* Stote, Florence (Marshall) [Mrs. William H. R.] (1869-1964)
Marshall, George Catlett (1880-1959), 2,382, 11,874, 17,065, 17,069, 17,071
Marshall, Harriet (Gibbs) (1869-1941), **2,155**
Marshall, Helen Ruffin [Mrs.], **5,550**
Marhshall, Henry (1805-64), 5,549, 5,555
Marshall, Isabella (1742-1814). *See* Graham, Isabella (Marshall) [Mrs. John] (1742-1814)
Marshall Islands, missionaries to, 3,642, 14,470
Marshall, James, 1,582
Marshall, James, 12,042
Marshall, John, **11,892**
Marshall, John Ellis (1785-1838), 12,759
Marshall, John Ellis (1839-1900), 12,759
Marshall, Joseph, Family (MO), **10,009**
Marshall, Katherine Tupper [Mrs. George Catlett] (1882-), **17,069**
Marshall, Lenore (Guinzburg) [Mrs. James] (1897-1971), 2,824, **5,011, 6,050, 12,042**
Marshall, Louise B., **17,305**
Marshall, Margaret, 1,221
Marshall, Margaret, **12,561**
Marshall, Marie (1876-1962). *See* Singer, Marie (Marshall) (1876-1962)
Marshall, Mary Ann (1881-1913), 15,070
Marshall, Millicent Ann (DeAngelis) [Mrs. Orsamus Holmes] (1813-87), 12,759
Marshall, Miriam B., 2,701
Marshall, Mrs., 11,445
Marshall, Mrs. E. C., 11,879
Marshall, Mrs. Hudson Boatner, **16,104**
Marshall, Mrs. John, 11,892

Marshall, Mrs. John, 14,455
Marshall, Myra (Crow) [Mrs. Robert Bradford], 655
Marshall, Nancy, **15,643**
Marshall, Octavia Simpson [Mrs. John Ellis] (?-1894), 12,759
Marshall, Orsamus, 12,763
Marshall, Orsamus Holmes (1812-?), 12,759
Marshall, Peter (1902-49), **2,476**
Marshall, Rachel [Mrs.], 13,470
Marshall, Rebecca Lowry (1830-1925). *See* Cathcart, Rebecca Lowry (Marshall) [Mrs. Alexander Henry] (1830-1925)
Marshall, Robert, 12,561
Marshall, Robert Bradford (1867-1949), **655**
Marshall, Ruth Holmes [Mrs. John Ellis] (1791-1872), 12,759
Marshall, Sadie, 5,549
Marshall, Sarah, 1,533
Marshall, Sarah Catherine (Wood) [Mrs. Peter] (1914-). *See* LeSourd, Sarah Catherine (Wood) [Mrs. Peter] Marshall [Mrs. Leonard Earl] (1914-)
Marshall, Sarah (Goode) (1822-?), **16,541**
Marshall, Thomas, 3,509
Marshall University (Huntington, WV), 11,860
  alumni, 17,438, 17,443
  employees, 17,443
Marshall, Virginia Mann, 655
Marshall, Winifred (1761-1839). *See* Gales, Winifred (Marshall) (1761-1839)
Marshall Woman's Club (OK), 14,223
Marshcall, Nichola (ca. 1833-ca. 1910), 15,954
Marshes of Georgia and Other Poems, The (book), 2,982
Marston, Annie (Gorham), 17,641
Marston, Eleanor Kyme. *See* O'Shaughnessy, Eleanor Kyme (Marston) [Mrs. Arthur William Edgar]
Marston, Elizabeth (1884-). *See* Bade, Elizabeth (Marston) [Mrs. William Frederic] (1884-)
Marston, May Agnes (pseudonym). *See* Johnson, May Beattie [Mrs.]
Marston, Nancy Bates, 2,202
Marston, Philip Bourke, 2,496
Martha Cook Building (MI), **7,852**
"Martha Deane Show" (radio program), 11,402
Martha Washington Benevolent Society (ME), **5,709**
Martha Washington boarding house (OR), 14,642
Martha Washington Club (IN), **4,570**
Martha Washington Home (Chicago, IL), 4,164
Martha Washington Hospital (Chicago, IL), 4,164
Martha's Vineyard Playhouse (MA), 12,623
Marti, Anna M. (Fritz) (1840-?), **10,010**
Martial law, **5,480**, 5,812
Martin (slave, NC), 13,188
Martin, A. E., 9,666
Martin, Adelaide (Barcelon), 1,062
Martin, Amelie, 5,485
Martin and Abraham Lincoln (book), 2,272
Martin, Angelique [Mrs. Giles], 2,818
Martin, Ann Henrietta [Miss] (1875-1951), **656**, 826, 859, 860, **1,321**, 10,668, **10,681**, 10,687, **10,768**
Martin, Anne (Shannon) [Mrs. William A.], 9,613, **9,676**
Martin, Aura E. (?-late 1880s), 1,663
Martin, Azariah, Family (CA), 443
Martin, Betty [Mrs.], 1,017
Martin, Boyce Lokey [Mrs. Harold H.], 3,335
Martin, Cecilia (Jackie) (1904-69), **17,070**
Martin, Clara. *See* Murphree, Clara (Martin)
Martin, Clara B., 12,572
Martin, Cornelia Eliza, **12,344**
Martin, Edward (1879-1967), **14,820**, 14,822
Martin, Elizabeth (Marshall), 3,509
Martin, Elizabeth S., **13,067**
Martin, Ellen (1847-1922). *See* Henrotin, Ellen (Martin) [Mrs. Charles] (1847-1922)
Martin, Ellen Annette (1847-?), **4,290, 7,853**
Martin, Enos Thompson Throop, 12,344
Martin, Esther M., 8,280
Martin, Evaline Throop. *See* Alexander, Evaline Throop (Martin) [Mrs. A. J.]
Martin, Evelyn (1877-1967). *See* Haworth, Evelyn (Martin) [Mrs. Samuel Lee] (1877-1967)

Martin Family (CA), **1,256**
Martin Family (CA), 1,648
Martin Family (NC), **13,230**
Martin Family (TX), 16,085
Martin, Frances Ada (1865-?). *See* Derrickson, Frances Ada (Martin) (1865-?)
Martin, Frederika, **141**
Martin, Giles, 2,818
Martin, George (Madden) [Mrs. Attwood Reading] (1866-1946), 3,020
Martin Handcart Company, 16,433, 16,616, 16,967
Martin, Hannah, 11,093
Martin, Harold H. (1910-), **3,335**
Martin, Helen (Reimensnyder) (1868-1939), 14,828
Martin, Helen W., 8,670
Martin, Ina C. (1874-?), **1,256**
Martin, Inez, 9,131
Martin Institute (GA), 3,101
Martin, Isabella Donaldson (1839-1913), **15,644**
Martin, Jenova [Mrs.], **9,201**
Martin, Jerry, 9,467
Martin, Jimmy Elizabeth (1928-), **240**
Martin, John Ross, 1,256
Martin, Katherine [Mrs. Jerry] (1890-), 9,467
Martin, Lilly (1882-1902). *See* Spencer, Lilly (Martin) [Mrs. Benjamin Rush] (1882-1902)
Martin, Louise Stadtmuller [Mrs. William O'Hara], 656
Martin, Lula (1864-1944). *See* McIver, Lula (Martin) [Mrs. Charles Duncan] (1864-1944)
Martin, Margaret [Mrs. William], 15,723
Martin, Margaret Nickerson (?-1960), 7,846
Martin, Marion [Miss], 9,962
Martin, Marion E., 3,977
Martin, Martha E., 2,679
Martin, Mary (1873-1962). *See* Sloop, Mary (Martin) (1873-1962)
Martin, Mary. [Mrs. Charles] MacArthur, 2,160, 12,367
Martin, Mary Barry (1882-1963). *See* Freeman, Mary Barry (Martin) [Mrs. John Shaw] (1882-1963)
Martin, Mary Emma Cameron [Mrs. John] (1851-1932), 1,256
Martin, Mary Hetty (Bonar) (1860-?), **17,199**
Martin, Mrs. Edward, 14,822
Martin, Mrs. William Clifton, 16,072
Martin, Olive M. *See* Oakes, Olive M. Martin [Mrs. Daniel C.]
Martin, Peter, **15,645**
Martin, Portia, 11,077
Martin, Rosemary, 17,919
Martin, Shirley, 2,931
Martin, Susanna (Janeway) [Mrs. Zenas] (1853-1930), 13,230
Martin, Victoria (Claflin) [Mrs. Canning] Woodhull [Mrs. James Harvey] Blood [Mrs. John Biddulph] (1838-1927). *See* Woodhull, Victoria (Claflin) [Mrs. Canning]. [Mrs. John Harvey] Blood [Mrs. John Biddulph] Martin (1838-1927)
Martin, Vivian, 4,781
Martin, William O'Hara, 656
Martin, Zenas (?-1931), 13,230
Martineau, Harriet (1802-76), 1,426, **2,477**, 3,298, 3,797, 4,904, 5,907, **6,756**, 6,902, 7,185, 7,274, 7,634, 8,375, **9,890**, 11,305, 15,291
Martineau, Susan Elvira (1856-1942). *See* Johnson, Susan Elvira (Martineau) [Mrs. Benjamin Samuel] (1856-1942)
Martinez, Elsie (Whitaker) [Mrs. Xavier] (1890-), **657**
Martinez, Maria, 11,231
Martinez, Xavier, 657
Martini, Teri, 14,475
Martins Ferry Area Historical Society (OH), 14,112
Martinson, Anna Martha, 8,882
Martinson, Cora (1902-), **8,882**
Martinson, Harry, 12,880
Martinson, Martha, **17,527**
"Martinsville Seven" (television script), 5,979
Martson, Mary Olive (1854-1939), **7,851**
Marvel, Elinore, 2,215
Marvin, Lady Blythe, 1,786
Marvin, Lillian Bessie (1876-1961). *See* Swenson,

Lillian Bessie (Marvin) [Mrs. David F.] (1876-1961)
Marvin, Mrs. Walter T., 11,007
Marvin, Rhoda Ann (1813-92). *See* Fullmer, Rhoda Ann (Marvin) [Mrs. David] (1813-92)
Marweb Productions, 2,625
Marx, Erica (1909-69), **4,230**
Marx, Eugenia, 54
Marx, Louisa. *See* Myers, Louisa (Marx) [Mrs. Samuel]
Marx, Stephanie. *See* Curtis, Stephanie (Marx) [Mrs. Charles William]
Marxian economics, 8,082
Marxism and Freedom (book), 8,082
Mary (slave, VA), 4,239
Mary A. Longstreth School and Alumnae Association (PA), **15,051**
Mary Baldwin Seminary (VA), 9,709
Mary Bartelme Home for Girls (Chicago, IL), 4,079
Mary Bennett Ritter Hall (CA), 925
Mary Bridgman Normal School (China), 6,651
Mary Chess cosmetics, 14,351
Mary Crane League (Chicago, IL), 4,079, **4,128**
Mary Crane Nursery (Chicago, IL), 4,047, 4,116, 4,128, 4,210
"Mary Frances Isom: Creative Pioneer in Library Work in the Northwest," 14,591
Mary Green Pomeroy Center (Chicago, IL), 4,152
Mary Hardin-Baylor College (TX). *See* Baylor Female College (TX)
Mary Harlan Lincoln Club (IA), 5,061
Mary Lincoln: Biography of a Marriage, 2,540
Mary McDowell Settlement (Chicago, IL), **3,875,** 4,079
Mary Markley House (MI), **7,854**
"Mary Martin Rebow Letters, The," 17,207
Mary Noble Club (Chicago, IL), **3,876**
Mary of Providence, Mother (1850-1943), 7,049
Mary Paxton Study Class, 10,085, **10,086,** 10,087
Mary Rippon Memorial Fund, 1,674
Mary Rippon Theatre (CO), 1,674
Mary Tenney Gray Travelers Club (KS), 5,176
Mary Thompson Hospital (Chicago, IL), **4,027,** 4,123
Mary Thompson Hospital for Women and Children (Chicago, IL), 4,217
Mary Todd Lincoln, Her Life and Letters (book), 1,454, 4,371
Mary Tyler Moore Enterprises, **17,808**
"Mary Tyler Moore Show, The" (television program), 17,808
Mary, Virgin, shrines, 17,552
Marycrest College (Davenport, IA), archives, **4,709**
Marye, Florence (Nesbit) [Mrs. Phillip Thornton], **3,404**
Maryknoll Sisters (NY), **11,803**
Maryland, 2,228, 3,081, 5,744, 5,825, 5,854
  agriculture, 12,402
  Afro-Americans, education, 12,236
  altar gilds, 5,826
  architects, 5,823
  art, decorative, 13,631
  authors, 5,768, 5,854
  bankers, 17,118
  bible, societies, etc., **5,760**
  birth control clinics, **5,739,** 6,223
  businessmen, 5,743, 5,754, 5,826, 17,118
  canals, 12,402
  cannery workers, 5,829
  Catholic schools, 5,722, 5,778, 5,831
  cemeteries, 5,805
  charitable societies, **5,766**
  child care centers, 5,758, 5,841
  children, hospitals, 17,118
  church records and registers, Episcopal, **5,827**
  church schools, 5,722
  church societies, Episcopal, **5,827**
  churches, Protestant, 5,767
  cities and towns, planning, 5,829, **5,837**
  citizens' associations, 5,829, **5,837**
  city missions, **5,762**
  civil rights workers, Afro-American, **5,828**
  civil service reform, 5,741
  Civil War
    campaigns and battles, 2,223, 5,799

hospitals, charities, etc., 12,165
clergy, 7,674
clergy, Baptist, 5,823
clergy, Methodist, **3,355**
clergymen's wives, 5,823
clubs, **5,738, 5,739, 5,809,** 5,815, **5,825**
college administrators, **5,834**
college presidents, **5,836**
college teachers, 5,829
congressmen, 5,775
conservatories of music, 12,796
consumers leagues, 5,741
convents and nunneries, Catholic, 5,831
country life, 9,594
dairy laws, 5,809
deans (in schools), **5,833**
diaries and journals, 1,425, **5,743, 5,747, 5,749,** 5,754, **5,775, 5,790, 5,799,** 5,819, 5,821
discrimination in public accommodations, 5,828
family planning, **5,842**
farmers, **5,754,** 5,789
Finnish-Americans, 5,829
Friends, 5,746
genealogists, **5,780**
governesses, 5,786
governors, 5,789, **5,828**
Greek-Americans, 5,829
historians, **5,808**
historic sites, conservation and restoration, 5,829
hospitals, 12,143
hotels, taverns, etc., **5,761**
housing authorities, 5,829
interdenominational cooperation, 5,841
Jews, 2,863, 5,829, 7,613
judges, 5,794
law, cases, 16,373
lawyers, **5,741, 5,776,** 5,794, **5,800,** 5,822, 12,963
legal secretaries, **5,780**
legislators, **5,754,** 5,828, 9,036
librarians, **5,850**
literary societies, **5,795**
local church councils, **5,841**
Lumbee Indians, 2,883
mayors, **5,828**
medical colleges, **11,753,** 12,143
medical societies, 11,753
merchants, **12,411,** 12,552
monasteries, **5,722**
monasticism and religious orders for women, Catholic, **5,722, 5,830, 5,832, 5,847, 5,848, 5,851**
Mormons and Mormonism, 5,829
municipal officials and employees, 5,829
museum directors, 5,829
nuns, Catholic, **5,722**
nurses, **5,849**
nurses, Afro-American, 1,779
nursing, 5,723
nursing schools, 5,723, 6,136
oral history, 5,828, **5,829**
patriotic societies, **5,818**
peace societies, 15,316
physicians, 5,771, 13,063
plantations, 5,765, 6,653
poets, 5,771, **5,773, 5,806,** 17,096
Polish-Americans, 5,829
politics, practical, women's activism, 5,828, **5,839, 5,846,** 11,916
postmasters, 5,746
private schools, **5,792**
  records and correspondence, **5,798**
public health, 6,138
public health nurses, 5,829
race problems, 5,828
real property, cases, 5,722
riots, 5,828
school superintendents and principals, 5,785
schools, 1,875, 12,411
  records and correspondence, **14,738**
schools of public health, 6,138
sculptors, **2,826**
secret societies, **5,838**
senators, United States, 5,774
social legislation, 5,840
social life and customs, 5,790

social reformers, 5,768
social service, information services, **5,840**
social settlements, 5,809
socialists, 5,768
student financial aid, 5,825
suffrage societies, **5,833, 6,757,** 16,252
teachers, **5,767, 5,819, 5,850,** 17,096
teachers colleges, 5,835
trade and professional associations, **5,840**
universities and colleges, **5,835**
  admissions, **5,725**
  archives, **5,852, 5,855**
  graduate work, 11,890
urban renewal, 5,837
vocational education, 5,758
Maryland Association for Mental Health, 7,248
Maryland Casualty Company, 14,674
Maryland Committee for Day Care of Children, 7,248
Maryland Conference of Social Concern, **5,840**
Maryland Council of Churches, **5,841**
Maryland Council of Churches, United Church Women, 5,841
Maryland Federation of Women's Clubs, 5,739
Maryland Hospital Training School for Nurses, alumnae, 11,627
Maryland Industrial School for Girls, 5,823
Maryland Institute of Art, students, 5,755
Maryland League of Women Voters, **5,846**
Maryland State Human Relations Commission, 5,828
Maryland Woman's Suffrage Association, 5,833
Marymount College (Tarrytown, NY), archives, **12,926**
Marymount Hospital (Garfield Heights, OH), 14,100
"Mary's Idea" (song), 5,534
Masaryk, Charlotte (Garrigue) [Mrs. Thomas] (1850-1923), 9,023
Mascarene, Margaret (Holyoke) (1726-92), 7,385
Mascoma Overalls Factory (NH), 10,789
Masefield, John (1878-1967), 1,966, 7,247, 16,166
Mask of Solomon (book), 12,441
Masnari, Beatrice Manessari, 9,467
Mason, Abby E. (1865-1958). *See* McAlpin, Abby E. (Mason) [Mrs. Orrin Webster] (1865-1958)
Mason, Alfred, 9,202
Mason, Alice Trumbull (1904-71), **2,788**
Mason, Anne E. (Dann), 12,834
Mason, Anne Murray, 5,789
Mason, Beatrice (Birmingham) [Mrs. Willoughby] (1887-1972). *See* Stanley, Beatrice (Birmingham) [Mrs. Willoughby] Mason [Mrs. Lewis V.] (1887-1972)
Mason, Belle (1865?-1944). *See* Garfield, Belle (Mason) [Mrs. Harry Augustus] (1865?-1944)
Mason, Bertha, 10,191
Mason, Blanch [Mrs.], 17,376
Mason, Caroline (1823-90), 6,758
Mason, Caroline (Atwater) (1853-1939), 1,999, **7,406**
Mason, Charles (1804-82), 2,545, 4,822, 4,958, 9,308
Mason City High School (IA), 4,814
Mason, Edna (1870-1918). *See* Eickbush, Edna (Mason) [Mrs. William Henry] (1870-1918)
Mason, Elias (1811-97), **7,652**
Mason, Elizabeth Welch (Backus), **3,551**
Mason, Elma Briggs [Mrs. Levi S.] (1842-1934), 10,682
Mason, Emelia (Frass) (?-ca. 1969), **10,124**
Mason, Emily V., 5,347
Mason Family, **6,758**
Mason Family (NV), **10,682**
Mason Family (VA), **17,081**
Mason, Harriet "Hattie" Sophia (1878-1975). *See* Mohr, Harriet "Hattie" Sophia (Mason) [Mrs. William] (1878-1975)
Mason, Henrietta, 11,940
Mason, Hodges (ca. 1907-), **8,105**
Mason-Hohl, Elizabeth, 11,511
Mason, John W., 17,465
Mason, Julia [Mrs. Charles], 13,055
Mason, Laura Talmadge (1824-?), **7,855**
Mason, Leila Venable [Mrs. Frank Tucker], 2,218
Mason, Levi S. (1837-1912), 10,682
Mason, Louis Bond, 452
Mason, Louisa, 5,064
Mason, Louisa G., **5,790**

Mason, Lucy Randolph (1882-1959), 2,504, 3,326, 3,347, 11,771, **13,212**

Mason, Margaretta (1772-1838). *See* Brown, Margaretta (Mason) [Mrs. John] (1772-1838)

Mason, Martha Sprague, 13,870

Mason, Mary, 11,493

Mason, Mary Josephine (1845-1938). *See* Remey, Mary Josephine (Mason) [Mrs. George Collier] (1845-1938)

Mason, Mary Mellow [Mrs. Frank] (?-ca. 1967), **11,065**

Mason, Meda (1875-196?), **15,840**

Mason, Mercy B. [Mrs.], 9,737

Mason, Mrs., 13,400

Mason, Mrs. T., 12,316

Mason, Myra (Peters) (1797-1862), **12,257**

Mason, Rachel, 9,202

Mason, Steven, 7,855

Mason, Veda Pauline (Barker) [Mrs. Mirl Reese] (1898-), **16,764**

Mason, William F. (1837-1908), Family (MN), **9,202**

Mason, Willoughby (1871-1935), 17,397

Masonic Order, **1,075**, 8,469, 9,314

Mason's Flowers (St. Louis, MO), 10,191

"Masquerade" (soap opera), 17,705

Mass, Mr., 11,171

Mass media, 2,205

Mass media and women, 8,057

Massachusetts, 1,399, 6,240, **6,871**, 6,872, **7,017, 7,109,** 7,112, 7,144, 7,647, 7,666

  abolitionists, **6,738, 7,072, 7,430**

  abortion, legal aspects, 1,984

  agricultural colleges, 6,624

  agricultural extension work, **5,871**

  agriculture, accounting, 6,206

  albums, **7,135**

  almshouses, 7,142

  American loyalists, 7,659

  art

    collectors and collecting, **5,901**

    galleries and museums, 2,762, **2,787, 6,233**

  art patrons, **6,185**

  art schools, 7,667

  artists, **6,245, 6,308,** 6,364, **7,332, 7,466, 7,601**

  arts and crafts movement, **7,012**

  associations, institutions, etc., **6,760**

  astronomical observatories, **6,285**

  authors, **5,917, 6,242, 6,444, 6,500, 6,696, 7,069, 7,349, 7,377, 7,442, 7,509,** 7,605, 7,648, **7,685**

  autograph albums, **6,998**

  bankers, 7,469, **7,625, 7,680**

  banks and banking, cooperative, 6,808

  bibliographers, **7,647,** 7,681

  biographers, 7,605

  birth control, 6,221, 6,232, 6,364, 6,432, 6,736, 6,987, 7,178, **7,283**

    law and legislation, **6,404**

  bishops, 7,049

  blind

    education, 5,857

    institutional care, 6,346

  blind-deaf, education, 7,684

  book collectors, **7,654**

  boots and shoes, trade and manufacture, 6,192

  botanical illustration, **6,308**

  boys, societies and clubs, 6,665

  broom and brush industry, 7,606

  businessmen, 6,873

  camp-meetings, 7,604

  canals, **7,070**

  census, 7,142

  centennial celebrations, 5,975, **7,010**

  charitable societies, **5,878, 5,898, 6,449, 7,032, 7,073, 7,074,** 7,086, 7,093, 7,095, 7,331, 7,339, 7,348, 7,365, 7,404, 7,431, 7,517, **7,595, 7,637**

  charitable societies, Jewish, **13,812**

  charities, **6,175,** 7,477

  charwomen and cleaners, 6,708

  child care centers, 6,482, 6,808

  child development, 6,420

  child support (law), **6,293**

  child welfare, 6,558

  children

    employment, 6,431, 6,486

  hospitals, **6,150,** 6,407, 6,698

  law, 6,431, 6,486

Christian life, 7,679

church records and registers, **7,092**

church records and registers, Congregational, **7,001, 7,004**

church records and registers, Methodist, 5,894

church records and registers, Unitarian, 5,894

church records and registers, Universalist, **5,859**

church schools, 6,817

church societies, Baptist, 5,894, **7,098, 7,099, 7,100, 7,101,** 7,102, 7,103, 7,104, **7,396**

church societies, Congregational, 4,779, 5,894, **6,169, 6,172, 6,174, 7,001, 7,004, 7,371**

church societies, Episcopal, **6,177, 6,182, 6,183**

church societies, Unitarian, **6,252, 6,254, 6,255, 6,258**

church societies, Universalist, **5,859**

churches, 6,503

churches, Congregational, **7,001, 7,004**

churches, Protestant, **7,092**

cities and towns, **7,635, 7,653**

  civic improvement, 7,508

citizens' associations, **7,508**

civil defense, 7,160

civil service, 6,358

civil service reform, **7,081**

Civil War

  relief of sick and wounded, 7,637

  societies, **5,881**

clergy, 6,500, 6,833, 7,385, **7,390,** 7,472, **7,513,** 7,645, 7,661, **7,676,** 7,681

clergy, Congregational, 5,856, 7,335, 7,616, **7,662, 12,540**

clergy, Unitarian, **6,251**

clergy, Universalist, 5,918

clergymen's wives, 5,918, **6,857,** 7,335, **7,601**

clinics, 6,225, 6,688, 6,847, 7,088

clothing factories, 6,878

clubs, 5,886, 5,893, 5,916, 5,971, 6,265, 6,358, **6,449,** 6,469, 6,494, **6,563,** 6,779, **6,780, 6,781, 6,782, 6,798,** 6,806, 6,822, **6,870,** 6,871, **6,950, 7,000, 7,020, 7,021,** 7,050, **7,051, 7,059,** 7,075, **7,077, 7,078, 7,079, 7,082, 7,089,** 7,132, 7,373, 7,397, **7,434, 7,436, 7,449,** 7,507, **7,512, 7,519, 7,594, 7,596,** 7,635

coeducation, 6,270, 6,271, 6,303, 6,482, **7,646**

college administrators, 6,493

college librarians, 7,499

college presidents, **5,866,** 5,868, **6,290, 6,296, 6,299, 6,346,** 6,436, **6,484,** 6,708, **7,161,** 7,572, **7,574,** 7,639

college registrars, **6,235**

college sports, 7,164

college students, 6,332, 6,338, 7,156, **7,495,** 7,575

college teachers, **5,865, 5,977, 6,296, 6,334, 6,448, 6,590, 6,607,** 6,622, 6,754, 6,870, **7,499**

college teachers, part-time, 6,482

college trustees, **7,165**

commonplace books, 5,929

community leadership, 6,615, 6,727, 6,803, 7,648, 7,659, 7,671

community leadership, Afro-American, **6,716**

congresses and conventions, 7,160

congressmen, 2,238, **2,298,** 5,868, 7,615, 11,602, 14,062

congresswomen, **6,861**

consumers' leagues, 6,486, 6,707, 6,708

correspondence schools and courses, 5,958

cotton manufacture, **5,896**

country music, **5,642**

county officials and employees, 7,610

court-houses, 2,507

court records, **7,106,** 7,659

crime and criminals, 7,142

deans (in schools), **6,189, 6,478, 6,493,** 6,677, 6,769, **7,582**

degrees, academic, **6,273**

diaries and journals, 5,909, 5,943, 5,947, 7,005, 7,047, 7,052, 7,140, 7,376, 7,471, **7,496,** 7,605, 7,644, **8,154**

  18th C, **5,928,** 6,447, **7,346, 7,351,** 7,661, 7,671

  18th-19th C, **7,333, 7,453, 7,460, 7,601,** 7,619, 7,659, 7,660

  19th C, **5,887, 5,909,** 5,918, 5,942, **5,952, 5,955, 6,521,** 6,845, **6,878, 7,008, 7,018, 7,029, 7,057,** 7,061, 7,150, **7,335,** 7,340, **7,341, 7,353,** 7,354, **7,356, 7,357, 7,358, 7,359, 7,368, 7,369, 7,378, 7,380, 7,384, 7,386, 7,388, 7,391, 7,395, 7,399, 7,400, 7,401, 7,402, 7,412, 7,414, 7,415,** 7,417, **7,419, 7,420,** 7,423, **7,425, 7,426,** 7,438, **7,444, 7,454, 7,457, 7,463,** 7,492, 7,606, 7,641, **7,645,** 7,683, **10,788**

  travel, 6,445

discrimination, 6,751

discrimination in employment, 6,751

dissertations, academic, **7,579**

dressmakers, **7,061,** 7,356

drug abuse, treatment, 6,516

education, secondary, **7,668**

educational associations, 6,359, 6,361, **7,071**

educational exchanges, 7,153

educators, **6,444, 12,515**

elections, 17,637

elementary school teachers, **7,491**

emigration and immigration, 10,419

employment agencies, **7,432**

endowments, 7,157

entomologists, **7,467**

Episcopalians, **7,679**

epitaphs, 7,635

fairs, 5,946

family social work, 6,729

farm life, 7,624

farmers, **6,206,** 7,618, 7,632

fires, 7,376

flower shows, 7,519

food processing plants, 7,655

freedwomen, **12,692**

Friends, **7,029, 7,490**

gardening, societies, etc., **7,087**

genealogists, **7,134**

genealogy, **5,876,** 6,234, 7,609, 7,670

general stores, 7,409

geologists, **5,864**

gifted children, education, 6,808

Girl Scouts, **6,759**

girls, societies and clubs, 6,806, **7,107**

glass manufacture, 7,491

governors, **2,322,** 6,937, **7,133,** 7,615, 11,514, 14,062

governors' councils, 6,367

grocers, 7,084

graduate students, 6,482

greek letter societies, 7,153, 7,164

gunsmiths, **7,143**

halfway houses, **6,866**

handicapped, eduducation, 6,808

health boards, 6,009

high school students, **5,879,** 5,885, **5,943,** 9,992

high school teachers, **6,724**

high schools, 6,724, 7,646

historians, **6,448, 7,136**

historical societies, 6,203, **7,140**

home economics

  accounting, **6,369,** 7,402, 7,411, 7,452

  teacher training, **7,655**

home economics extension work, 5,871

home labor, 5,900, 6,486, **6,869**

home nursing, **7,088**

home ownership, 7,334

horticulturists, 7,616

hospital administrators, 6,364

hospital records, **6,211, 6,212, 6,214**

hospitals, 6,128, 6,364, 6,968, **7,274, 8,184**

hospitals, gynecologic and obstetric, **6,150, 6,213, 6,220,** 6,407, **6,797**

hours of labor, 6,486

housewives, **7,016, 7,353, 7,358, 7,391, 7,401, 7,402, 7,405, 7,414,** 7,417, **7,455,** 7,589

hotels, taverns, etc., 7,360

hygiene, **6,703**

hygiene, sexual, **6,760**

illegitimacy, 4,141

immigrants, 7,063

immigrants, Italian, 6,808

indentured servants, 7,150
industrial toxicology, 6,486
infants, mortality, 4,141
insurance, agents, 7,675
intercultural education, 6,751
international education, 6,978
interstate relations, 6,977
Italian Americans, 6,727
journalists, **6,948**
judges, **6,385**
junior colleges, 7,646
justices of the peace, 7,618
kindergarten teachers, training of, 11,842
kindergartens, 6,288, 6,346
labor law and legislation, 6,431, 6,686
land deeds, 7,635
land tenure, law, 11,746
law teachers, **6,260, 6,282**
lawyers, 5,897, **6,728, 6,738, 7,606, 7,615,** 7,631
lecturers, 7,648
legal documents, 7,611, 7,636, 7,653, 7,660, 7,661
legal instruments, **7,076**
legislators, 5,736, 6,615, **6,861, 7,615,** 7,618, 7,625,
    12,153, 14,062
librarians, **7,085, 7,446, 7,605,** 7,636
librarians, Jewish, **13,787**
libraries, 6,241
    branches, delivery stations, etc., 5,974, 13,787
libraries, university and college, 6,396, 6,460, 6,966,
    7,571
library administration, 6,460
library associations, **6,241**
library catalogs, 7,659
literary societies, **5,912,** 5,913, 5,934, 6,014, **7,592,**
    7,593
lithographers, **7,667**
little theater movement, 7,195
lobbying, 7,139
lobbyists, 11,773
local government, 7,253
long-term care of the sick, **6,179**
loyalty oaths, 7,187
manufacturers, 7,611, 7,680, 12,672
maternity homes, 6,175
mayors, 6,185, **6,279**
measles epidemics, 7,346
mechanics (persons), **12,626**
medical colleges, 6,218, 6,225, 6,681, 6,688, 6,698,
    7,677
medical social workers, 8,636
medical societies, **6,226, 6,229**
medicine, cases, clinical reports, statistics, **6,218,**
    7,659
mentally handicapped, 6,225
    education, 5,895
mentally ill, 6,225
merchant seamen, 6,621
merchants, 7,083, 7,483, 7,610, 7,614, 7,616, **7,633,**
    7,636, 7,671, 12,370
milliners, **7,386**
mills and mill-work, 6,859
missionaries, **7,511**
missions, 7,064, **7,080**
monasticism and religious orders for women,
    Catholic, **6,243, 7,033, 7,049, 7,066**
monuments, **6,439**
Mormons and Mormonism, 16,531
municipal government by city manager, 6,717
museum directors, **7,487**
museum registration methods, **6,323**
museums, 6,185, 6,452, 7,571
musical societies, **7,147,** 7,519
Native Americans, missions, 7,511
natural history, study and teaching, 6,346
nautical training-schools, 7,138
newspapers, 6,104, **7,502**
    sections, columns, etc., 6,685, 6,948
novelists, 7,505
nursery schools, **6,287,** 6,288
nurses, employment, **6,230**
nursing, **6,618**
nursing schools, **6,128,** 6,150, 6,152, 6,163, **6,164,**
    6,215, 6,238, 6,618
    alumnae, 6,128

occupational diseases, 6,486
officials and employees, 5,871, 5,884, **6,686, 6,892,**
    10,419
oral history, **7,109, 7,151,** 7,336, **7,510**
orphans and orphan asylums, 7,032, **7,097**
paper making and trade, 7,510
parents' and teachers' associations, **5,889**
patriotic societies, **5,882, 5,946,** 6,368
payrolls, 6,187, 6,195, 6,198
peace societies, 15,304, 15,985
periodicals, 7,610
philanthropists, **5,917,** 7,163
photograph collections, **7,060**
physical education teachers, **7,173**
physicians, 6,164, **6,222, 6,231, 6,698, 6,847,** 7,385,
    7,636, 7,639, **7,654,** 7,660, 12,153
pioneers and settlers, Afro-American, **12,692**
playgrounds, 6,358
poets, **5,612,** 7,605
political parties, 6,980
politics, practical, women's activism, 6,555, **6,717,**
    6,718, 6,753, 6,837, 6,966, 6,968, 6,978, 6,980,
    6,981, **7,253,** 15,304
prayer groups, **6,171**
prayer-meetings, 7,604
prisons, 6,367, 7,142
    officials and employees, **6,642, 7,031**
prisons for women, officials and employees,
    6,934
private schools, 1,885, 2,517, **5,877, 6,397,** 6,487,
    6,818, **7,068,** 12,419
psychiatric hospitals, **6,211, 6,212, 6,214,** 6,900,
    7,489
public health nursing, **6,129, 6,162,** 6,164
public records, **7,142, 11,207**
public relations consultants, **6,407**
public schools, 6,405, 9,992
public welfare, **7,111**
radio programs, 6,034
radio stations, 6,034, 6,658
railroads, employees, 7,680
real estate business, 7,609
real property, valuation, 7,653
reformatories, 6,382, **6,711**
    officials and employees, 6,583
reformatories (female), 6,642, 7,031
reformers, **5,917,** 7,611
religious education, study and teaching,
    6,257
rent, 6,464
reporters and reporting, 7,016
retired teachers, 7,017
revivals, 12,370
Revolutionary War, 14,961
school attendance, 6,486
school boards, 6,376, 6,405, 6,420, 6,497, 6,762
school buildings, 6,805, 7,006
school districts, **5,890**
school management and organization, 7,655
school superintendents and principals, 7,056, **7,494,**
    7,655
schools, **5,728,** 6,051, 6,245, 6,627, **7,056,** 7,135,
    7,433, 7,601, 7,653, 7,658
    accounting, **7,108**
    finance, 6,880
    records and correspondence, **5,895,** 7,646, 7,653
schools of architecture, 7,159
schools of public health, 6,558, 6,852, 6,987
science, exhibitions, **6,986**
scientists, **6,308**
scrapbooks, **5,880, 7,023**
sculptors, 7,055
sculptors, Afro-American, **7,030**
secretaries, **6,873**
selectmen, 6,753
self-government (in higher education), **7,565**
senators, United States, **2,298,** 7,615
seniors, employment, 6,892
Shakers, **7,036, 7,041,** 7,046, **7,047, 12,309**
shipmasters, 5,412, **7,693**
silversmiths, **2,831**
smallpox epidemics, 7,346
social life and customs, 6,421, 6,521, 6,762, 7,514,
    7,516, 8,960, 11,249, 14,961

social security, 6,486
social problems, 7,635
social settlements, 5,079, 6,239, 6,376, **6,516, 6,808**
social workers, **6,729, 6,946,** 14,437
societies, etc., **5,945,** 7,597
sociologists, **6,696**
soldiers, **7,143**
    recreation, 6,477
state boards of education, 7,572
stores, retail, 7,429, **7,437,** 7,633
straw industries, 7,587
strikes and lockouts, 6,315, 6,486, 8,123, 8,144,
    11,927
    textile workers, 7,063, 7,114
student activities, **7,164**
student counselors, **6,264**
student housing, **6,286, 6,289,** 6,482
    married veterans, **6,288**
students
    health and hygiene, 6,482
    part-time, 6,482
    political activity, 7,164
    religious life, 7,164
students' societies, **6,480,** 7,164, **7,576,** 7,646
suffrage, 55, 5,629, 6,364, 6,382, 6,477, 6,565,
    6,825, 6,853, 6,966, 6,970
suffrage societies, 1,948, **4,231, 5,969,** 6,364, 6,477,
    6,685, 6,825, 6,966, 6,969, 6,971, 6,978, 6,980,
    6,981, 6,984, 7,082, **7,096,** 7,139, **7,178,** 11,773,
    15,307, 16,252, 17,226
suffragists, **5,934, 6,469**
summer schools, 6,316, 7,159
Sunday-school teachers, 6,200
surveying, 7,653
swap shops, 6,288
sweating system, 6,486
symphony orchestras, 6,358
tailors, **7,447**
teachers, 369, 2,604, 5,895, 5,972, 6,192, **6,200,**
    6,350, 6,521, 6,923, 6,999, 7,007, 7,014, 7,055,
    7,146, 7,195, **7,332, 7,340,** 7,342, 7,356, **7,389,**
    7,450, 7,599, 7,606, 7,609, 7,610, 7,618, 9,141,
    12,550
teachers' colleges, 6,188, 6,645
teachers' unions, **7,370**
teaching, 8,170
technical education, 6,520
television programs, public service, 6,693
temperance, 7,336
temperance societies, **7,141, 7,374,** 7,601, 12,515
textile factories, **6,187, 6,191, 6,195, 6,198,** 7,070,
    7,113, 7,116, 7,117, 7,118, 7,119, 7,121, 7,122,
    7,123, 7,124, 7,125, 7,126
    fires and fire prevention, 7,120
textile industry, **7,115**
textile workers, **7,067,** 7,070, **7,113, 7,116, 7,117,**
    7,118, 7,119, **7,120, 7,121, 7,122, 7,123, 7,124,**
    7,125, 7,126, 10,813
theater, production and direction, 6,669
theaters, 6,669, 8,351, 12,623
theological seminaries, 6,251
trade and professional associations, **6,147, 6,162,**
    6,164
trade-unions, 6,486
Unitarian churches, education, **6,257, 6,258**
United Methodist Church, 7,604
universities and colleges, **6,237, 6,300,** 6,482, 6,490,
    6,493, **7,048, 7,330, 7,500, 7,564,** 7,573
    administration, **7,570**
    admission, **6,270, 6,271, 6,303,** 7,581
    alumnae, **7,154, 7,498, 7,562**
    alumni, **6,009**
    archives, **6,339, 7,686**
    buildings, **7,155**
    catalogs, 7,110
    centennial celebrations, **7,162**
    curricula, **6,273, 7,580**
    employees, 6,482, 6,708, 6,769, **6,907**
    evaluation, 7,584
    examinations, **6,272**
    faculty, 6,482, 6,782, **7,157, 7,158**
    finance, 7,163, **7,566**
    graduate work, **7,159**
    history, **7,153, 7,160, 7,163, 7,493,** 7,568, **7,583**

job placement, 6,482
university cooperation, **6,274**, **6,275**
urban beautification, 7,087
utopias, 4,434, **7,043**
vacation schools, 6,358
veterans, education, 6,808
vital statistics, 6,216, 7,142, 7,601
vocational education, **6,808**
vocational guidance, **6,808**
voters, registration of, **6,422**
volunteer workers in hospitals, Jewish, **13,812**
wages, 6,192, 6,486
  minimum wage, 11,773
  textile workers, 5,896
weavers, 12,370
whalemen, 7,632
widows, **7,621**, 7,675
wildlife conservation, **7,666**
wills, 7,091
women
  civil rights, 6,482
  education, **6,051**, 6,436, **6,481**, 6,482
  higher education, **5,873**
  institutional care, **6,866**
women's centers and networks, 7,324
women's colleges, 6,346, 6,368, 6,471, 6,482, 6,484
work relief, 6,808
workhouses, 6,206
workmen's compensation, 6,486
World War I
  civilians' work, **7,137**
  hospitals, charities, etc., 6,477
  registers, lists, etc., 7,137
World War II, civilians' work, **7,138**
Young Women's Christian Association, **7,063**
zoological museums, 6,316, **6,321**
Massachusetts Agricultural College, 6,624
Massachusetts Bible Society, 7,597
Massachusetts Birth Control League, 6,364
Massachusetts Board of Health, 6,009
Massachusetts Civil Service Reform Association, 6,561
Massachusetts Civil Service Reform Association, Women's Auxiliary, **7,081**
Massachusetts Colony, governors, 7,127
Massachusetts Commission Against Discrimination, 6,353, 6,751
Massachusetts Commission on Lunacy, **6,225**
Massachusetts Commission to Study the Question of the Support of Dependent Minor Children of Widowed Mothers, **6,293**
Massachusetts Committee for the Ratification of the Child Labor Amendment, 6,431
Massachusetts Committee on Children and Youth, 6,558
Massachusetts Committee on Public Safety, 5,755
Massachusetts Conference on Social Work, 6,358
Massachusetts Cooperative Extension Service, **5,871**
Massachusetts Correctional Institution, 7,031
Massachusetts Council on Women and Children in Industry, 6,686
Massachusetts Department of Education, 6,420
Massachusetts Department of Labor and Industry, 6,686, 6,892
Massachusetts Fair Employment Practices Commission, 6,751
Massachusetts Foreign Policy Association, 6,978
Massachusetts General Hospital, 6,179, 8,636, 13,055, 15,559
Massachusetts General Hospital Unit, 6,722
Massachusetts Governor's Commission for Racial and Religious Understanding, 6,751
Massachusetts Governor's Council, 6,367
Massachusetts Equal Suffrage Association, 6,980
Massachusetts Industrial School for Girls, 6,520
Massachusetts Institute of Technology
  alumnae, 8,424, 8,947
  faculty, 6,334, 6,336, 7,013, 7,286
  students, **6,332**, **6,338**
Massachusetts Institute of Technology, Center for International Studies, 6,709
Massachusetts League of Girls Clubs, 6,806
Massachusetts League of Nations Association, Educational Committee, 6,978

Massachusetts League of Women Workers, 6,806
Massachusetts Library Commission, 7,060
Massachusetts Medical Society, **6,226**
Massachusetts Normal School, students, 17,315
Massachusetts Nurses' Association, **6,147**
Massachusetts Peace Society, 15,304
Massachusetts Progressive Party, 6,980
Massachusetts Public Interests League, 7,187
Massachusetts Reformatory for Women, 6,642
Massachusetts Society for Social Health, **6,760**, 6,900
Massachusetts Society for Social Hygiene. *See* Massachusetts Society for Social Health
Massachusetts Society for the University Education of Women, **6,051**
Massachusetts Spy (periodical), 7,610
Massachusetts State Board of Education, 7,572
Massachusetts State Civil Liberties Union, 6,980
Massachusetts State Federation of Women's Clubs, 6,561, 6,798, 7,050, 7,059
Massachusetts State Federation of Women's Clubs, Education Department, 6,494
Massachusetts Suffrage Association, 6,978, 7,178, 11,773
Massachusetts Superior Court, 6,385
Massachusetts Woman Suffrage Association, **4,231**, 6,364, 6,685, 6,966, 6,971, 6,978, 6,981, **7,139**, 15,307, 17,226
Massachusetts Woman Suffrage Association, First Hampshire Representative District Committee, **7,139**
Massacres, 780, 881, 1,505, 1,751, 1,790, 2,952, 4,696, 4,765, 8,996, 9,467, 16,117, 16,876, 17,173, 17,422
Massage parlors, laws and legislation, 8,633
Massee, May (1889-1966), **11,893**
Massey, Edith [Miss], 9,962
Massey, Elizabeth, 15,646
Massey Family (SC), **15,646**
Massey, James, 15,646
Massey, Mary Elizabeth (1915-74), 99, **15,806**
Massey, Mrs. R. M., 3,141
Massoth, Leona, 8,683
Mastectomy, 5,802
"Master of Doro Plantation—An Epic of the Old South, The" (ms), 9,653
Masters, Alice M., 14,672
Masters, Edgar Lee, 4,675, 11,894, 11,944, 12,642, 12,821
Masters, Elizabeth, 3,751
Masters, Elizabeth, 3,760
Masters, Ellen Coyne [Mrs. Edgar Lee] (1899-), **11,894**
Masterton, Carolina, 11,583
Masterton Family (MS), 9,656
Masterton, Mary, 11,583
Masterson, Mary Margaret (1859-?). *See* Dunn, Mary Margaret (Masterson) (1859-?)
Maston, George A., 10,531
Matawan Journal (NJ), 10,915
Maternal and Child Health Demonstration Project (Taiwan), 6,987
Maternal and infant welfare, 236, 246, **735**, **2,677**, 2,691, 3,904, 5,573, **6,221**, 6,223, 6,431, 6,558, 6,728, **6,987**, 7,283, 7,289, 9,351, 9,962, 11,852, 11,932, 12,736, 12,738, **13,798**, **14,198**, 17,515
Maternal Association (Forest Grove, OR), 14,478
Maternal Association of Marlborough (NH), 7,517
Maternal Association of Sherburn (NH), 7,517
Maternal Health, Committee on. *See* Committee on Maternal Health
Maternal health services, 17,826
Maternity Center Association, Manhattan and Brooklyn (NY), 11,852, 12,738
Maternity Home and Children's Hospital Association (Flint, MI). *See* Hospital Aid Association (Flint, MI)
Maternity homes, 1,672, **4,088**, 6,175, 7,049, 7,546, 8,647, **8,669**, 8,857, **8,863**, 9,424, 10,775, 11,399, **12,316**, 12,355, 13,988, 13,995, **14,367**, 16,029
Maternity homes, Jewish, 15,165
Maternity Hospital (Minneapolis, MN). *See* Ripley Hospital for Women (Minneapolis, MN)
Maternity hospitals, 9,270
Maternity leave, 8,075, 8,137

Mates, Bessie Maher, **9,199**
Mates Family (MN), **9,199**
Mates, Harry James (1879-), **9,199**
Mathematical Association of America, 5,506
Mathematicians, 2,464, **2,570**, **5,728**, **6,815**, 7,328, **13,859**
Mathematics, study and teaching, 1,975, 5,684, 6,354
Matheny, Charles R. (1786-1839), 4,373
Matheny, Fanny (French) [Mrs. James H., Jr.], 4,373
Matheny, James H. (1818-90), **4,373**
Matheny, James H., Jr. (1856-1918), 4,373
Matheon, The (Chicago, IL), **3,877**
Mather, Anna Maria. *See* Keemlé, Anna Maria (Mather) [Mrs. Samuel]
Mather, Flora Stone [Mrs. Samuel] (1852-1909), **13,943**
Mather, Jeannette. *See* Lord, Jeannette (Mather) [Mrs. Frederick P.]
Mather, Melissa, 6,060
Mather, Mrs. F. D., 12,740
Mather, Rachel, 4,936
Mather, Samuel, **4,936**
Mather, Samuel (1851-1931), Family, **13,943**
Mathes, Mary Elizabeth, 1,348
Matheson, Alice Maude (Lunt) [Mrs. Daniel] (1876-?), **16,428**
Matheson, Alva, 16,870
Matheson, Annie (Isom) [Mrs. Christen], **16,429**
Matheson, Belle Fleet [Mrs. Kenneth G.], 3,235
Matheson, Elizabeth Cooper, **8,166**
Matheson, Rhoda. *See* Wood, Rhoda (Matheson) [Mrs. William Henry]
Matheson, Simon Alva (1903-), **16,430**
Matheson, Zella, 16,870
Matheson, Zella (Barnson) [Mrs. Simon Alva], **16,430**
Mathew, Mrs. M. I., 9,323
Mathews, Ann (1753-1830), **15,647**
Mathews, Anthony, **15,526**
Mathews, Jacob, 3,485
Mathews, Mamie. *See* Reese, Mamie (Mathews)
Mathews, Mary [Mrs. John] Musgrove [Mrs. Jacob] (ca. 1700-63). *See* Bosomworth, Mary. Cousaponakeesa. [Mrs. John] Musgrove [Mrs. Jacob] Mathews [Mrs. Thomas] (ca. 1700-63)
Mathews, Nelle J., **15,910**
Mathews, Ophelia. *See* Cary, Ophelia (Mathews) [Mrs. William]
Mathews, Rena A. [Mrs. J. D.] (1874-1962), **200**
Mathews, Shailer, 11,572
Mathias, Edward G., 13,272
Mathias, Mildred Esther. [Mrs. Gerald L.] Hassler (1906-), 10,152, **15,217**
Matilda Berkely, or Family Anecdotes (book), 13,413
Matisse, Henri, 620, 754, 5,721, 6,185, 12,821
Matovick, John, **10,255**
Matrix (periodical), 16,175
Matrons of the Republic, George H. Hoyt Post No. 3 (Athol, MA), **5,882**
Matsner, Sidonie (1881-1974). *See* Gruenberg, Sidonie (Matsner) [Mrs. Benjamin] (1881-1974)
Matson, Susan Keating (Glaspell) (1876?-1948). *See* (Glaspell), Susan Keating. [Mrs. George Cram] Cook [Mrs. Norman Häghejm] Matson (1876?-1948)
Matsuno, Joyce, 16,890
Mattei, Mrs. A. C., 10,679
Matteson, Joel A., 4,352, 4,364
Matteson, Lydia, 4,364
Matthau, Walter, 12,367
Matthay School, 16,358
Matthes, Mary Bewick, 17,616
Matter of Life and Death, A, 6,065
Matthews, Ann, 17,405
Matthews, Annabel (1883-1960), **6,761**
Matthews, Antoinette Johnson [Mrs.], **3,226**
Matthews, Ara E. Branham [Mrs. P. S.] (1887 or 1888-1962), **3,466**
Matthews, Beulah, 17,405
Matthews, Burnita (Shelton) (1894-), **658**
Matthews, Elizabeth (Dennis) [Mrs. Horace], 17,405
Matthews, Elsie Albert, **17,993**
Matthews Family (WA), 17,405
Matthews, Grace Eulalie (1885-1972). *See* Ashmore, Grace Eulalie (Matthews) (1885-1972)

Matthews, Harold Clarke, 17,993
Matthews, Horace, 17,405
Matthews, James Brander (1852-1929), **12,043**
Matthews, John, 14,688
Matthews, Lucille, 761
Matthews, Marth Ann (Jones), 9,709
Matthews, Maryette. *See* Paine, Maryette
  (Matthews)
Matthews, Miriam, 3,290
Matthews, Mrs. William H., 12,654
Matthews, Sarah (Ball) Williams [Mrs. John], 14,688
Matthews, Stella S. (1868-1948), **17,686, 17,831**
Matthews, William H., 12,654
Matthiessen, F. O., 11,832, 12,393
Mattingly, Lenora (1875-1971). *See* Weber, Lenora
  (Mattingly) (1875-1971)
Mattingly, Marie (1883-1943). *See* Meloney, Marie
  (Mattingly) [Mrs. William Brown] (1883-1943)
Mattison, Dorothy, 13,616
Mattison, Lina Wakefield, **15,648**
Mattoon, Mary (Laurie) (1854-1929), 15,174
Mattson, Hans (1832-93), Family (MN), **9,204**
Mattson, Helmi (Lampila) [Mrs. William]
  (1890-1974), **9,503**
Mattson, Kjersti (Perrson) [Mrs. Hans] (1837-1911),
  9,204
Mattson, Nanny (1859-?). *See* Jaeger, Nanny
  (Mattson) [Mrs. Lut
Mattson, Valborg (1888-?). *See* Gravander, Valborg
  (Mattson) (1888-?)
Matyas, Jennie (1895-?), **659**
Mauch, Carrie, 5,063
Mauch, Margaret [Mrs. Rowland C.] (ca. 1905-),
  10,923
Maud (book), 3,776
Maude, Jenny, **12,258**
Maude, Lucy. *See* Alexayeff, Lucy (Maude)
Maude, Mrs. Raymond, 1,588
Maudelle, 3,290
"Maudie's Diary" (radio program), 2,274
Maugham, W. Somerset, 2,617, 17,208
Maughan, Mary Ann (Weston) [Mrs. Peter]
  (1817-1901), **16,472, 16,947**
Maughan, Peter, 16,472, 16,947
Mauk, Charlotte Ellen (1907-73), **660**
Mauldin, Mrs. Thomas J., 15,758
Maule, Jane, 14,847
Mauma Doll, 3,593
Maunsell, Betsey Brown, 12,230
Maurer, Alfred H., 2,734
Maurer, James H., 12,702
Maurer, Katharine, **1,156**
Maurer, Mary Rieman, 4,494
Maurice Porter Memorial Hospital (Chicago, IL). *See*
  Children's Memorial Hospital (Chicago, IL)
Maurowmet, Ann. *See* Imer, Ann (Maurowmet)
Maurowmet, John, 15,481
Maury, Ann (Herndon) [Mrs. Matthew Fontaine]
  (1811-1901), 2,479
Maury, Betty Herndon [Mrs. William A.], **2,478**
Maury Institute (MS), faculty, 10,974
Maury, Jane. *See* Maverick, Jane (Maury) [Mrs.
  Albert]
Maury, Mary H. (1844-1928). *See* Werth, Mary H.
  (Maury) [Mrs. James Rhodes] (1844-1928)
Maury, Matthew Fontaine (1806-73), **2,479**
Maury, Mildred. *See* Humphreys, Mildred (Maury)
Maus, Anna (Russell) [Mrs. L. Mervin], 14,771
Maus Family, 14,771
Maus, L. Mervin, 14,771
Maverick, Ann (Anderson), 12,260
Maverick Family (SC), **15,649**
Maverick Family (TX), 16,117
Maverick, Jane (Maury) [Mrs. Albert], 16,315
Maverick, Lucy [Miss], **16,315**
Maverick, Mary A., 16,049
Maverick, Mary Adams, 16,117
Maw, Margaret (Petersen) (1874-1966), **16,542**
Max, Pearl [Mrs. Louis W.] (1904-), **11,895**
Maxcy, Ann Sarah (1812-?). *See* Hughes, Ann Sarah
  (Maxcy) [Mrs. George W.] (1812-?)
Maxcy Family, **2,343**
Maxcy Family (PA), **15,052**

Maxcy, Mary. *See* Markoe, Mary (Maxcy) [Mrs.
  Francis]
Maxcy, Mary (Galloway) [Mrs. Virgil] (1787-1849),
  2,343, 15,052
Maxcy, Sarah. *See* Hughes, Sarah (Maxcy)
Maxcy, Virgil (1785-1844), 2,343
Maxener, Mrs. J. R., 9,404
Maxey, Dora Rowell (1856-84). *See* Lightfoot, Dora
  Rowell (Maxey) [Mrs. Henry William] (1856-84)
Maxey, Marilda Cassa (Denton) [Mrs. Samuel Bell]
  (1833-1908), 16,029
Maxey, Samuel Bell (1825-95), **16,029**
Maxson, Lydia Harriett (Yates) [Mrs. Thaddeus W.]
  (1839-1902), **12,259**
Maxted, Mattie Cal (1900-), **8,663**
Maxwell, Addie Taylor [Mrs.] (1866-?), 16,486
Maxwell, Anna Caroline (1851-1929), 6,131
Maxwell, Elsa, 1,576
Maxwell Family (GA), 3,025
Maxwell House hotel (Moab, UT), 16,486
Maxwell, James Alexander, 1,730
Maxwell, Lydia, 13,619
Maxwell, Mabel. *See* Brace, Mabel (Maxwell) [Mrs.
  Charles]
Maxwell, Martha A. [Mrs. James Alexander]
  (1831-81), **1,730**, 1,790
Maxwell, S. Annie [Miss], 3,112
Maxwell, Samuel, 10,491
Maxwell Street: Survival in a Bazaar (book), 4,053
Maxwell's Rocky Mountain Museum (CO), 1,730
May, Abigail [Mrs. John] (1754-1824), 7,649
May, Abigail (1775-1800), **5,681**
May, Abigail Williams (1829-88), 6,762
May Arno School of Music and Drama (CO), 1,749
May, Bernice (Hubbard) [Mrs. Samuel Chester]
  (1897-1975), **661**
May, Billy, 6,013
"May Campaign" (VA), 17,091
May, Catherine Dean (Barnes) (1914-). *See* Bedell,
  Catherine Dean (Barnes) May (1914-)
May, Charlotte Augusta (1795-1873), 7,649
May, Clara A., 6,415
May, Edward A., 2,161
May Family (New England), **6,762**
May, Florence Waterman (Lewis) [Mrs. William]
  (1899-), **2,112**
May, Frederick Warren Goddard (1821-1904), 6,762
May, I. Sophie du Pont [Mrs. Ernest N.], 11,887
May, John (1748-1812), 7,649
"May Lou's Mass" (song), 5,534
May, Lovicy Ann (1832-?). *See* Eberhart, Lovicy
  Ann (May) [Mrs. Uriah] (1832-?)
May, Margaret (1869-1958). *See* Dashiell, Margaret
  (May) [Mrs. John Parker] (1869-1958)
May, Mary Davenport (1793-1869), 7,649
May, Mrs. John R., 13,322
May, Phillip Stockton (1891-1969?), **2,873**
May, Samuel (1810-99), 5,907, 5,963, 6,762
May, Samuel Joseph (1797-1871), 6,762, 6,911
May, Sophia (1784-1870), 7,649
"May Women Speak?," 5,370
Maybeck, Annie (White) [Mrs. Bernard Ralph], 662
Maybeck, Bernard Ralph, Family (CA), 662
Mayer, Alfred M., 5,791
Mayer, Bena Frank (1900-), **2,789**
Mayer, Brantz (1809-79), **5,791**
Mayer, Christian, 5,791
Mayer, Eliza C. (Blackwell) [Mrs. Charles F.], 5,791
Mayer, Hannah. *See* Stone, Hannah (Mayer)
Mayer, Katrina (Baum) [Mrs. Christian] (?-1843),
  5,791
Mayer, Kitty D. (Goldsborough) [Mrs. Alfred M.]
  (?-1868), 5,791
Mayer, Maria (Goeppert) [Mrs. Joseph E.], (1906-72),
  1,223, 2,668, 11,813, 11,815, 11,901
Mayer, Mrs. Max, 4,954
Myes, Annie [Miss], 9,677
Mayfield, Sara (1905-), **113**
Mayflower Descendants (MO), 10,112
Mayflower News of North Carolina, 13,580
Mayhall, Jane, 16,163
Mayhew, Elizabeth. *See* Wainwright, Elizabeth
  (Mayhew) [Mrs. Peter, Sr.]
Mayhew, Katherine (Camp), 11,572

Mayhoff, Amelia (Levy), 7,544
Maynard, Frederick A. (1852-1950), 8,353
Maynard, John, 8,353
Maynard, Mary Wilcoxson [Mrs. John], **8,353**
Maynard Walker Gallery (NY), 2,746
Mayne, Virginia, 1,532
Mayne, Winifred Florence (1902-). *See* Van Etten,
  Winifred Florence (1902-)
Maynor, Dorothy (1910-?), 831
Mayo, Charles Edwin (1827-99), **9,205**
Mayo Clinic (Rochester, MN), 247, 3,467
Mayo, Edith Graham [Mrs. Charles H.] (1871-1943),
  8,823, 8,971, 9,038
Mayo, Elizabeth (1793-1865), 12,762
Mayo, Frank (1839-96), 12,471
Mayo, Katherine (1867-1940), 14,828
Mayo, Margot [Miss], **12,260**
Mayo, Minerva, 7,514
Mayo, S., 9,205
Mayo, Virginia, 16,208
Mayors, 895, 2,279, 3,154, 3,203, 3,481, 3,995, 4,729,
  4,738, **4,932, 5,006, 5,007,** 5,172, **5,356, 5,828,**
  6,185, **6,279,** 6,720, 8,089, 8,181, 9,140, 9,196,
  9,686, **9,958,** 10,203, 11,129, 11,134, 11,184,
  11,214, **11,269,** 11,841, 11,856, **11,884,** 11,895,
  11,905, 11,914, 11,928, 11,960, **12,036,** 12,146,
  12,147, 12,148, 12,149, 12,150, 13,728, 13,872,
  13,999, **14,139,** 14,223, **14,236,** 14,552, **14,599,**
  14,619, **14,815,** 14,860, 14,919, 15,077, 15,221,
  15,332, 15,869, 16,914, 17,257, 17,264, **17,289,**
  17,293
Mayor's Advisory Council (Harrisburg, PA), 14,822
Mayor's Committee of Women on National Defense
  (NY), 7,546
Mays Family, 12,531
Mayse, Charles, 201
Mayse, Lola May [Mrs. Charles] (1899-), **201**
Maysville Eagle (KY), 5,306
Mazeppa, 10,717
Mazey, Emil (1913-), **8,137**
Mazyck, Edmund, 15,650
Mazyck, Elizabeth Forcher, 15,650
Mazyck Family (SC), **15,650**
Mazyck, Sarah Livingston, **15,651**
Mazyck, Stephen, 15,650
Mazyck, William, 15,650
Mazzuchelli, Father Samuel O.P. (1806-64), 17,868
Mazzulla, Fred, 1,779
Mboka (book), 6,041
Meacham Family, 4,942
Meachem, Chell (Crozier) [Mrs. Colo W.] (1884-),
  10,490
Mead, Albert S., 3,206
Mead, Belle, 9,058
Mead, Charlotte L. (1871-?). *See* Sanford, Charlotte
  L. (Mead) [Mrs. Edward Rollin] (1871-?)
Mead, Elinor Gertrude. *See* Howells, Elinor
  Gertrude (Mead) [Mrs. William Dean]
Mead, Frances Hughes (1841-ca. 1900), 9,346
Mead, Kate Campbell (Hurd) (1867-1941), **6,763**
Mead, Lucia True (Ames) [Mrs. Edwin Doak]
  (1856-1936), 7,278, 15,298, 15,304, **15,307,**
  15,314, 15,316
Mead, Lucy Irene, **7,407**
Mead, Margaret. [Mrs. Luther Sheeleigh] Cressman.
  [Mrs. Reo] Fortune. [Mrs. Gregory] Bateman
  (1901-78), 212, 2,097, 2,166, 2,513, 2,833, 2,834,
  2,863, 8,208, 11,810, 11,825, 11,897, 12,708,
  13,406, 14,886, **14,894**
Mead, Rhoda E. [Miss], 11,743
Mead, Warren, 9,346
Meade, Ann. *See* Page, Ann (Meade)
Meadville Theological School (PA), faculty, 15,312
Meagher, Ellen Kassim, 5,239
Mealand, Richard L., 14,447
Meals for Millions, 7,287
Means, Alexander (1801-83), **3,405**
Means, Celina Eliza [Mrs.], 15,688
Means, Claudia Hart [Mrs. Edward], 15,652
Means, Edward, 15,652
Means Family (SC), 15,652
Means, Mary D., 13,751
Means, Mary Hart (1835-1916), **15,652**
Means, Matthew Harvey, 3,406

Means, Sarah Virginia [Miss], **3,406**
Meany, Edmund S., 17,164
Meany, Helen, 15,935
Meara, Frank S., 11,869
Mears Family (WI), **17,687**
Mears, Helen Farnsworth [Miss] (1872-1916), 17,687
Mears, Louise. *See* Fargo, Louise (Mears)
Mears, Louise Wilhelmina [Miss] (1874-1925), **10,491**
Mears, Mary, 17,687
Mears, Mary Elizabeth Farnsworth [Mrs. John Hall]
    (1830-1907), 17,687
Mears, Susan V. [Mrs.], 12,527
Measles epidemics, 7,346
Measure, A Journal of Verse, The (periodical), 12,642
Measure of My Days (book), 8,779, 13,684
Meat inspection, 8,223
Meatless and wheatless parties, 54
Mecham, Emma Waitstill (1858-1920). *See* Nielson,
    Emma Waitstill (Mecham) [Mrs. Frihoff
    Godfred] (1858-1920)
Mechanic Arts High School (St. Paul, MN), 9,333
Mechanical drawing, 14,941
Mechanics (persons), **12,626**
Mechanics Educational Society of America, 8,099
Mechanics Fair (CA), 1,263
Mechlin, Leila, 2,844
Mechoopda Indians, marriage rites and customs,
    1,243
Mecklenburg County Board of Education (NC),
    13,184
Mecom, Jane (Franklin) [Mrs. Edward] (1712-ca.
    1794), 14,890
Medal of Honor, 12,913
Medals, 2,091, 4,949, 8,777, 9,057, 17,686
Medals, military and naval, 3,203, 4,843
Medary, Marjorie (1890-), **5,012**
Medford Free Art Fair (OK), 14,192
Medford Progress (OK), 14,188
Medford, Sarah (1786-1849). *See* Clayton, Sarah
    (Medford) (1786-1849)
Media Woman, 17,975
Mediation, international, **17,735**
Mediation and conciliation, industrial, 11,768
Medicaid, 11,932
Medical Art Shop, 8,574
Medical assistants, **16,227**
Medical Association of Montana, 10,402
Medical care, 3,311, 6,124, 6,130, 6,919, 7,324, 8,659,
    13,504
Medical care, cost of, 232, 12,357
Medical care, law and legislation, 9,263
Medical Center (IL), 4,395
Medical centers, 6,748, 11,885
Medical College of Pennsylvania, 15,127, 15,128,
    15,132, 15,135, 15,143
  deans, **15,126, 15,131, 15,140**
  faculty, 15,130
Medical College of South Carolina. *See* Medical
    University of South Carolina
Medical College of the State of South Carolina. *See*
    Medical University of South Carolina
Medical colleges, 1,020, 3,234, 3,958, 3,967, **4,027,**
    4,217, 5,729, 5,844, **6,218,** 6,225, 6,616, 6,679,
    6,681, 6,688, 6,698, 7,255, 7,677, 8,822, 9,195,
    10,616, 11,753, 11,754, 11,869, 12,143, 12,917,
    14,077, **15,132, 15,133, 15,135,** 16,297
  alumni, **4,225**
  faculty, 15,126, 15,130
Medical education, 1,020, 2,333, 7,184, 7,234, 7,274,
    8,636, 10,208, 11,600, 11,754
  finance, 11,885
Medical illustration, **3,467,** 8,574
Medical illustrators, **8,574**
Medical law and legislation, 9,844
Medical librarians, 10,152, **11,591**
Medical libraries, 123, 4,350
Medical literature, 2,609, 4,698, 17,337
Medical museums, 2,088, 2,089
Medical publishing, 10,508
Medical record personnel, 4,023
Medical records, 14, 2,671
Medical research, 2,090, 6,209, **6,216,** 6,221, 6,986,
    9,979, 11,885, 16,236
  legal aspects, 11,885

Medical research personnel, 1,095, **10,207, 10,208,**
    10,209, 10,210
Medical social work, 3,932, 4,117, 6,358, **8,636,**
    8,656, **8,665, 8,666,** 11,593, 15,246
Medical social workers, 8,535, **8,636, 8,666**
Medical societies, 1,045, 1,348, **2,086, 3,273,** 4,698,
    4,732, 5,318, 6,217, **6,226,** 6,229, **6,363,** 6,697,
    6,770, 7,307, 7,920, 9,844, 10,402, 10,405,
    10,508, 11,068, 11,511, 11,753, **11,754,** 11,916,
    12,738, 12,841, **13,679,** 14,697, 14,698, 14,900,
    15,125, 15,141, 15,145, 16,226, 17,831
Medical Society of Westchester County, Women's
    Auxiliary (NY), 12,751
Medical students, 1,380, 1,465, 7,311, 11,511, 11,748,
    13,324, 15,134
Medical teaching personnel, **7,226,** 9,176
Medical technologists, 6,336
Medical technology, 14,033
Medical University of South Carolina
  admissions, 15,429
  students, 15,425
Medical University of South Carolina, College of
    Nursing, **15,426**
Medical Women's Association (OR), 14,698
Medical Women's International Association, 6,770
Medical Women's International Association, Tenth
    General Assembly (Norway, 1960), 6,697
Medical Woman's Journal, 11,753
Medical Women's National Association, 6,697, 7,920
Medicare, 11,916
  legal aspects, 8,085
Medicine, 870, 5,746, 5,849, 14,348, 14,889. *See also*
    Hospitals; Hygiene; Missions, medical; Nurses;
    Nursing
  cases, clinical reports, statistics, **4,475,** 5,555, **6,218,**
    7,659, 8,045, 8,965, 9,008, 9,082, 11,068, 12,825,
    13,605, 16,357, **17,130,** 17,678
  formulae, receipts, prescriptions, 1,299, 2,009,
    2,062, 3,506, **6,369,** 9,176, 9,279, 9,800, 10,053,
    11,513, 13,310, 14,945, 15,343, **15,428, 17,095.**
    See also Medicines, patent, proprietary, etc.
  history, **1,020, 5,724,** 6,407, 6,763, 11,727, **12,073,**
    14,871
  practice, 2,282, 2,541, 5,771, 6,562, 7,660, 7,678,
    9,921, 10,616, 13,132, 13,498, 14,745, 15,022.
    See also Bloodletting; Clinics; Gynecology;
    Nurses; Nursing; Obstetrics
  study and teaching, 409, 11,932, 17,039
  women in, 11,897
Medicine-man, 16,865
Medicine-man, Afro-American, 16,877
Medicine, military, 1,400, 6,511. *See also* Hospitals,
    military; Military nursing
Medicine, preventive, 7,311, 15,136
Medicine, rural, 243, **6,648**
Medicine, state, 232
Medicines, patent, proprietary, etc., **5,647, 6,743,**
    9,868, 13,089
MEDICO (MN), 9,359
Medill, Katharine Patrick [Mrs. Joseph], 3,816
Medinus, Grace (Graham) [Mrs. Carl], 7,133
"Meditations Divine and morall" (ms), 7,127
Mediums, **2,236,** 9,841, 12,513
Medley, Amanda Beckwith [Mrs.], **9,891**
Medley, Mary Louise, 13,629
Medlin, Alisa, 13,591
Medlin, Frances Louise, 9,567
Medora (book), 13,688
Mee, Margaret Ursula (1909-), 10,151
Meecham, Mary, 6,970
Meek, Howard B., 11,521
Meek, Joseph L., 14,594
Meek, Lois Hayden, 2,069
Meekcom, Rachella, 14,497
Meeker, Arvilla Delight Smith [Mrs. Nathan Cook]
    (1815-1905), 1,751
Meeker, Caroline (1813-45). *See* Nichols, Caroline
    (Meeker) [Mrs. John] (1813-45)
Meeker, Ezra, 17,329
Meeker Family (NJ), 10,905
Meeker, Harriet [Miss] (ca. 1900-),11,181
Meeker, Jerusha Cook Harrison [Mrs. Obadiah]
    (1784-1871), 9,036
Meeker, Nathan Cook, 1,751

Meeker, Obadiah (1782-1855), 9,036
Meekison, Vadae (Harvey) [Mrs. George] (1884-),
    14,007
Meeks, Eusebia (Blodgett) [Mrs. William] Harris
    [Mrs. Isaac] (1821-89), 14,150, **14,151**
Meeks, Isaac, 14,151
Meen, Margaret (1775-1824), 10,151
"Meet the Authors" (series), 6,119
Meeter, Lottie [Miss] (1886-), 982
Meeting of Twelve Apostles, **16,765**
Meeting of Women Friends of Grand Isle (1801-22,
    VT), 17,029
Meeuwsen, William, 14,577
Megaw, Elena Elektra (1907-), 10,151
Megel, Carl, 8,093
Meggers, Betty Jane, 2,833
Meginnis Family, 11,730
Megquier, Marie [Mrs.], **5,656**
Megquier, Mary Jane (Cole), **1,462**
Meh Lady (yearbook), **9,561**
Meharry, Abraham Patton (1842-1908), 4,430
Meharry, Charles Leo (1885-), 4,430
Meharry, Clara Esther (Burghardt) [Mrs. Charles
    Leo], 4,430
Meharry Family (IL), **4,430**
Meharry, Isaac, 4,430
Meharry, Martha "Mattie" Jane (McMillin) [Mrs.
    Abraham], 4,430
Meharry Medical College (TN), 3,293
  alumnae, 15,914
  faculty, 15,931
Mehdevi, Anne Marie Sinclair (1921?-), **6,052**
Mehegan, Mary Theresa (1846-1921). *See* Hill, Mary
    Theresa Mehegan [Mrs. James Jerome]
    (1846-1921)
Mehegan, Mother Mary Xavier, 10,892
Mehling, Jessie Reid Garrison, 12,937
Mei Lun Yuen home (San Francisco, CA), 1,236
Meier, Elizabeth B., **13,891**
Meighen, John Felix Dryden (1877-1957), Family
    (MN), **9,206**
Meighen, Joseph P., 9,206
Meighen, Katherine Trusdell [Mrs. William A.] Morin
    [Mrs. John Felix Dryden] (1873-1968), 9,206
Meighen, Thomas V., 9,206
Meigs, Cornelia L. (1884-), **5,013**
Meigs Family (New England), 6,352
Meigs, Louisa (Rodgers) [Mrs. Montgomery
    Cunningham] (1817-79), 2,556
Meigs, Mary. *See* Taylor, Mary (Meigs) [Mrs. Joseph
    Hancock]
Meikleham, David Scott, 17,062
Meikleham Family (VA), 17,062
Meikleham, Septimia Anne Cary (Randolph) [Mrs.
    David Scott] (1814-87), **17,062**
Meiklejohn, John Miller Dow (1836-1902), 7,651
Meili, Anna E. (Passavant) [Mrs. J. Edward]
    (1868-1960), 9,304
Meinal, Aden, 212
Meinal, Marjorie, 212
Meine, Franklin Julius (1896-1968), **3,999**
Meir, Golda, 12,069, 12,070
Meireis, Amy, 11,324
Meitner, Lise (1878-1968), 11,815
Mekeel, Aaron, 11,649
Mekeel, Amy Quinby (1785-1845), 11,649
Mekeel Family (NY), **11,649**
Melancon, Marie Eugenie (1897-1970). *See* Marie,
    Mother Marguerite (1897-1970)
Melba, Nellie, 6,185, 12,440
Meldrim Family (GA), **3,552**
Meldrim, Frances Pamela Bird Casey, 3,552
Melendez, Edith, 16,965
Melendy, Peter, 4,962
Melhinch, Mrs. William, 13,966
Mell Family (GA), **2,986**
Mell, Margaret (Loyless) [Mrs. Patrick], 3,451
Mell, Mrs., 9
Mell, P. H., 3,032
Mellen, George, 663
Mellen, Kathleen (Dickenson) [Mrs. George]
    (1895-1969), 663
Mellen, Queen. *See* Palmer, Queen (Mellen) [Mrs.
    William Jackson]

Mellichamp, Saintlo, Sr., **15,653**
Mellichamp, Thomas, 15,653
Mellish, George H., **1,463**
Mellish, Mary, 1,463
Mellon, Mary Conover, 2,215
Mellon, Paul, 2,215
Meloney, Marie (Mattingly) [Mrs. William Brown] (1883-1943), 5,121, 5,122, 11,822, 12,041, **12,044,** 12,045, 14,819
Meloney, William, **12,045,** 12,046
Melrose (LA), 5,552
Melrose Art School, 4,847
Melvain, Janet F., 10,889
Melville, Elizabeth S., 6,764
Melville, Herman, 6,764
Melvin, Eva (Strode), **10,336**
Member of the Wedding, The (book), 16,161
Memminger, Christopher Gustavus (1803-88), 7,613
Memminger School (Charleston, SC), 15,488
Memo (periodical), 7,321
"Memoir of Ada Comstock With Love, A," 6,484
Memoir of Dr. George Logan of Stenton, A (book), 15,041
Memoirs: Half a Century in Nursing, 6,141
Memoirs of a Baby (book), 7,186
Memoirs of a Sculptor's Wife (book), 2,338, 7,504
Memoirs of Mollie McDowall (book), 16,176
"Memoirs of My Mother and Her Family," 3,031
Memorandum (Housing Association of Delaware Valley, PA), 15,201
Memorial Church (Stratford-on-Avon, England), restoration of, 5,924
Memorial Church Women's Association (MA), **6,294**
Memorial Day, 3,699
"Memorial Day" (poem), 4,636
Memorial of Alice and Phoebe Cary (book), 14,058
Memorial Osteopathic Hospital (IN), 4,506
Memorials, 945, 2,081, **2,646,** 2,972, 3,219, 3,407, 5,307, 5,907, 7,661, 9,596, 9,657, 9,759, **10,992,** 12,561, 12,595, **12,738, 12,834, 13,442,** 13,461, 13,474, 13,584, 15,775, 15,860, 17,980
"Memories and Reminiscences of Early Days at Old Siloam," 9,875
"Memories of a Frontier Childhood" (article), 6,650
Memories of a Southern Woman of Letters (book), 5,536
"Memories of Hopkins" (poem), 8,477
"Memories of Pioneer Days" (ms), 10,430
"Memories of William Halsey Wood," 12,349
Memory of Song, A (book), 3,367
"Memory of the Sage of Yoncalla" (ms), 14,506
Memphis Academy of Arts (TN), 5,474, 15,883
Memphis and Charleston Railroad, 28
Memphis Art Association (TN), 15,883
Memphis Playground Association (TN), 15,884
Memphis State University (TN), 5,394
Memphis State University (TN), Archives, **15,897**
Memphis State University (TN), Columns Gallery, 15,897
Men and Mules (book), 2,872
Men of No Property (book), 11,310
Menashe, Joanna, 14,497
Menasi, Mr., 2,276
Mencken, Henry Louis (1880-1956), **73,** 113, 1,461, 3,326, 5,853, 7,229, 8,433, **10,871,** 11,863, 11,867, 11,894, 12,029, **12,562,** 12,821, 15,564
Mencken, Sara Powell Haardt [Mrs. H. L.] (1898-1935), **73, 5,853**
Mendel, Edith. *See* Stern, Edith (Mendel)
Mendelsohn, Hannah Helen (ca. 1901-). *See* Brown, Hannah Helen (Mendelsohn) [Mrs. Samuel] (ca. 1901-)
Mendelssohn, Felix, 6,185
Mendenhall, Abby Swift [Mrs. Richard Junius] (1832-?), 9,207
Mendenhall, Delphina (1811-post 1880), **13,232**
Mendenhall, Dorothy Mabel (Reed) (1874-1964), 7,255, **7,259,** 7,288
Mendenhall, Eliza T., 16,473
Mendenhall, Emma (1873-1964), 13,836
Mendenhall Family (MT), **10,264**
Mendenhall Family (NC), **13,231,** 13,232
Mendenhall Family (UT), **16,473**
Mendenhall, Gertrude (1861-1926), 13,231

Mendenhall, Jane Johnson, 16,473
Mendenhall, John S., 10,264
Mendenhall, Mary (1852-1930). *See* Hobbs, Mary (Mendenhall) (1852-1930)
Mendenhall, Mary Sue [Mrs. Robert Henry] Smith [Mrs. John S.] (?-1933), 10,264
Mendenhall, Richard Junius (1828-1906), **9,207**
Mendocino Study Club (CA), 1,063
Mengelkoch case, 6,849
Mengers, Marie Christiansen, **5,632**
Mengers, Sue, 950
Menken, Adah Isaacs [Mrs. John Carmel] Keenan [Mrs. Robert Henry] Newell [Mrs. Alexander Isaac] (1835?-68), 1,073
Menken, Alice (Davis) (1870-1936), **7,546**
Menken Family, 7,555
Menlo Academy (CA), 1,066
Menlo Circus Club (CA), 324
Menninger, Catharine "Cay" Wright [Mrs. William C.] (1902-), **5,228**
Menninger, Charles Fredrick, 5,229
Menninger Clinic (KS), 2,134
Menninger, Flora Vesta "Flo V." Knisely [Mrs. Charles Frederick] (1863-1945), 5,229
Menninger Foundation (KS), **5,227,** 5,228, 5,230, 5,231, 5,233, 14,983
Menninger, Jeanetta Lyle [Mrs. Karl] (1901-), **5,230**
Menninger, Karl, 5,229, 11,308
Menninger, William C., 5,228, 5,229
Mennonite Board of Education, 4,513
Mennonite Board of Missions, **4,514**
Mennonite Central Committee, 14,869
Mennonite Church, missionaries, 4,515, **5,197, 5,198, 5,199**
Mennonite Church, Women's Missionary and Service Commission, 4,515, 4,517
Mennonite Historical Society of Iowa, Mennonite Archives, 5,050
Mennonite Publishing House (Scottdale, PA), 4,515
Mennonites, **4,516,** 5,196, **5,197, 5,200, 5,201,** 9,063, **13,759**
clergy, 4,513
missions, **4,514,** 4,515, 4,517, **13,757,** 14,868
publishing, 4,513, 4,515, **14,869**
Mennonites in Iowa, **5,049,** 5,050, **5,051, 5,052**
Menominee Indian Mills, 3,944
Menopause, 7,197
Men's African School Society (DE), 2,044
Men's Garden Club of Atlanta (GA), 3,187
Men's League for Woman Suffrage, 6,706, 11,793, 16,250
Men's League for Woman Suffrage (Des Moines, IA), 4,859
Men's League for Woman Suffrage of the State of California, 1,359
Men's League for Woman Suffrage of the State of Nevada, 10,687
Men's League for Women's Suffrage of the State of New York, 17,217
Men's League for Woman's Suffrage (Birmingham, AL), 49
Men's liberation, 7,324
Men's Liberty Loan Committee, 9,914
Men's Student Government (NY), 12,916
Menstruation, 1,657, 16,876
customs and rites, Native American, 2,832
Mental deficiency, 5,394, 11,830
Mental healers, 10,718
Mental healing, 1,470
Mental health, 74, 2,925, 3,273, 4,040, 4,149, 5,840, 6,260, 6,379, 6,539, 6,544, 6,748, 6,852, 8,108, 9,149, 9,299, 11,063, 11,549, **13,512,** 14,025, 15,251, 16,069, 17,245
research, 11,885
Mental health clinics, 8,655
Mental health laws, 5,394, 6,381, 8,485, 9,351
Mental health services, 243, **458,** 7,546, 9,467, 13,593
Mental illness, 6,260, 9,884, 11,128
treatment, 5,867
Mental retardation. *See* Mental deficiency
Mentally handicapped, 1,348, 2,676, 5,923, 8,638, 9,381, 17,018, **17,678**
care and treatment, 9,403
education, 5,895, 7,764, 8,721, 10,990, 14,226

institutional care, 2,886, 5,570, 9,460
Mentally handicapped children, 11,965, 17,270
care and treatment, 9,490
Mentally ill, 2,539, 2,676, 8,176
care and treatment, 3,529, 5,570, 8,176, 11,600. *See also* Psychiatric hospitals
commitment and detention, 15,544
legal status, laws, etc., 17,463
Mentally ill, Afro-American, 3,381
Mentally ill children, 2,523, 2,631
care and treatment, **2,391,** 5,186
Menter, Sophie (1846-1918), **2,665**
Mentor (periodical), 14,392
Menuhin, Yehudi, 749, 14,670
Menzies, Clark, 3,506
Menzies, Marie W., 3,506
Mera, Phoebe [Mrs. Fergus], 225
Mercer, Anne, 3,290
Mercer, Asa, 17,273
Mercer, Edna, 5,462
Mercer, Eunice Strickland "Birdie" (Abbott) [Mrs. David H.] (1870-1956), 8,893
Mercer Girls, 17,273
Mercer, Jesse, 3,454
Mercer, Patricia, 16,060
Mercer University, 3,218
alumnae, 3,465
Merchant, Abby S. (1883?-), **7,260**
Merchant, Grace (Shepherd) [Mrs. Francis D.] (1869-?), 2,572
Merchant, Jane, 15,879
Merchant, Lina S., 10,427
Merchant, Lizzie Alberta. *See* Ewing, Lizzie Alberta (Merchant)
Merchant marine, 2,535, 15,899
Merchant seamen, 6,621
missions and charities, **5,605,** 8,732
Merchants, **63,** 199, 368, 963, 1,790, **2,268,** 3,033, 3,317, **3,319, 3,344,** 3,352, **3,556,** 3,568, 3,647, **5,688,** 5,793, 5,797, 7,083, 7,483, 7,610, 7,614, 7,616, 7,633, 7,636, 7,671, **7,675, 8,334,** 8,369, 8,719, **8,966, 9,363,** 9,729, 9,836, 9,977, 10,229, 10,515, 10,858, 10,936, 10,968, 11,134, **11,506,** 11,786, 12,034, **12,161, 12,187,** 12,199, 12,219, **12,225, 12,243,** 12,268, 12,288, **12,342,** 12,370, **12,411,** 12,548, **12,551,** 12,552, **12,563,** 12,769, 13,074, 13,771, **13,849,** 13,930, 13,943, 14,449, 14,552, 14,554, 14,600, 14,619, 14,805, 14,884, **14,885,** 14,945, **14,955, 14,973, 14,989,** 15,001, **15,044,** 15,081, **15,089,** 15,104, 15,434, 15,682, **15,959,** 16,071, **16,450, 17,127, 17,129,** 17,435, 17,439, **17,459,** 17,815
Mercier, Germaine, 17,775
"Mercury Theatre of the Air" (radio program), 17,809
Mercy Center of the Arts (PA), 14,794
Mercy Hospital (Philadelphia, PA), 15,011
Mercy Hospital (Pittsburgh, PA), **15,232**
Mercy Montessori School (Erie, PA), 14,794
Mercyhurst College (Erie, PA), 14,786, **14,789, 14,791,** 14,794
alumnae, **14,788,** 14,790
presidents, **14,787**
Meredith College (NC), 13,350, 13,398, 13,404, 13,447, 13,613, 13,618
faculty, 13,255
Meredith, Ellis (1864 or 1865-1955), **1,731**
Meredith, Emily R., **10,337**
Meredith, Georgia Sears [Mrs. Thomas], 13,573
Meredith, Gertrude E., 2,169
Meredith, Gertrude Gouverneur. *See* Biddle, Gertrude Gouverneur (Meredith)
Meredith, John William, 5,245
Meredith, Josephine (Brunyate) [Mrs. Arthur J.] (1879-1965), **14,759**
Meredith, Mamie Jane [Miss] (1888-1966), **10,492**
Meredith, Margaret Maranda (Baker) [Mrs. Thomas Prentiss] Beebe [Mrs. John William] (1853-1942), **5,245**
Meredith, Martha Carpenter [Mrs. Reese], 12,563
Meredith, Mary Moon (1845-1924), **13,233**
Meredith, Reese (1708-99), **12,563**
Meredith, Solomon, 14,776
Meredith, Virginia (Claypool) [Mrs. Henry Clay], **4,609**

Mergen, Anne, 14,046

Merici, St. Angela, 11,808

Merick, Eldridge G., 17,679

Merideth, Mary Louise, **9,547**

Meridian club, 12,524

Merington, Marguerite (1861?-1951), 12,525, **12,564**

Meriweather, Lizzie Avery, 12,552

Meriwether, Charles (1766-1843), **5,269**

Meriwether, Elizabeth (1861-1951). *See* Gilmer,
Elizabeth (Meriwether) (1861-1951)

Meriwether Family (KY), **5,269**, 11,163

Meriwether, Henrietta (Smith), 3,331

Meriwether, Louise, **15,921**

Merkel, Gustav, 12,457

Merli, Madeline, 9,361

Merman, Ethel, 12,367

Mermoud, Willa [Mrs. J. Fred], **9,892**

Merrell, Helen (1896-). *See* Lynd, Helen (Merrell)
[Mrs. Robert Staughton] (1896-)

Merriam, Eve (1916-), 8,531

Merriam, Florence Augusta (1863-1948). *See* Bailey,
Florence Augusta (Merriam) [Mrs. Vernon]
(1863-1948)

Merriam, Lucy Elizabeth. *See* Case, Lucy Elizabeth
(Merriam)

Merriam, Mary B., 17,010

Merriam, Miriam Hooper (Tannatt) (1866-?), 17,209

Merriam, Nancy K., 9,596

Merrick, Caroline Elizabeth (Thomas) [Mrs. Edwin
Thomas] (1825-1908), 5,487

Merrick, David Thomas, 5,487

Merrick, E. R., 11,879

Merrick, Edwin Thomas (1809-?), 5,487

Merrick Family, **5,487**

Merrick Family (MA), **7,650**

Merrick, Maria (1790-?). *See* Allen, Maria (Merrick)
[Mrs. Samuel, Jr.] (1790-?)

Merrick, Mary V. (1886-1955), **2,099**

Merrick, Mrs. E. R., 11,879

Merrick, Nancy (1797-1843). *See* Miller, Nancy
(Merrick) [Mrs. Henry] (1797-1843)

Merrick, Pliny (1755-1814), 7,650

Merrick, Ruth Cutler [Mrs. Pliny] (1770-1841), 7,649

Merrick, Sarah Reed (1832-54), 7,650

Merrifield, Elton E., 462

Merrifield, Harriette (1856-1951). *See* Forbes,
Harriette (Merrifield) (1856-1951)

Merrilies, Meg (pseudonym). *See* Coolbrith, Ina
Donna (1841-1928)

Merrill, Alice (1868-1948). *See* Horne, Alice
(Merrill) [Mrs. George Henry] (1868-1948)

Merrill, Belle (Harris) [Mrs. Clarence] (1861-1938).
See Nelson, Belle (Harris) [Mrs. Clarence]
Merrill [Mrs. N. L.] (1861-1938)

Merrill, Clarence, 16,775

Merrill, Elmer D., 15,217

Merrill, Henry F., 14,380

Merrill, Henry F., 14,552

Merrill, Janie [Miss], 9,624

Merrill, Lila, 8,354

Merrill, Maria M. [Mrs.] (1832-1903), **17,688**

Merrill, Mary Agnes (1869-1963). *See* Chase, Mary
Agnes (Merrill) (1869-1963)

Merrill, Mary (Failing), 14,552

Merrill, Mrs. J. R., 1,092

Merrill, Nathan M. (?-1892), **8,354**

Merrill-Palmer School (Detroit, MI), 7,817, 7,848,
12,738

Merrill, Phyllis (Moulton) (1887-?), **664**

Merrill, Sarah Bradley. *See* Drinkwater, Sarah
Bradley (Merrill) [Mrs. Leoline Howell]

Merrill, Spiro (pseudonym). *See* Gerber, Merrill Joan

Merrill, Winifred H. Edgerton [Mrs. J. H.], 11,825

Merrimac Corporation (Lowell, MA), 10,813

Merriman, Dwight, 8,205

Merriman, Ella "Nellie" Wing (1857-1912). *See*
Sharp, Ella "Nellie" Wing (Merriman) [Mrs. John
C.] (1857-1912)

Merriman, Grace, **14,243**

Merriman, Julia (McIntyre), 646

Merriman, Louise A., 13,441

Merriman, Mary (Wing) [Mrs. Thomas S.]
Farnsworth [Mrs. Dwight] (1822?-92), 8,205

Merriman, Priscilla (1835-1914). *See* Evans, Priscilla
(Merriman) [Mrs. Thomas David] (1835-1914)

Merritt, Alice Jane Tooke [Mrs. Nelson G.], 11,650

Merritt, Anna Mitchell, 11,653

Merritt, Bessie, **11,650**

Merritt, Callie [Miss] (1891-), **9,208**

Merritt, Emma Laura (Sutro) [Mrs. George W.]
(1856-1938), 832

Merritt, Ernest, 11,580

Merritt, Frances (1833-1924). *See* Quick, Frances
(Merritt) [Mrs. A. J.] (1833-1924)

Merritt, Henry, 12,543

Merritt, Lizzie [Mrs. Lucius], 2,893

Merritt, Lucien, 9,208

Merritt, Lucius (1824-93), **2,893**

Merritt, Mollie E. *See* Brown, Mollie E. Merritt
[Mrs. Henry C.]

Merritt, Nehemiah, 11,653

Merritt, Sarah C., 13,622

Merry, Mrs. Blance H., 9,486

Merrymount Press, **1,464**

Mertes, Barbara, 459

Merton, Owen, 16,168

Merton, Thomas, 4,640

Mertz, Barbara Gross (1927-), 6,060

Mertz, Janet, 6,336

Mervine, William McKinley, **15,053**

Merwin, Hester. *See* Ayers, Hester (Merwin) [Mrs.
Edward L.]

Mesa Verde ruins (NM), 11,227

Meseroll, Sarah R., **14,821**

Meservey, Maria Antoinette, 7,677

Mesmerism, 11,602, 11,741

Mespoulet, Marguerite (1880-1965), **12,047**

"Mess-a-Stomp" (song), 5,534

Message, The, 4,481

Messenger, The (periodical), 13,948

Messer, Emma North (1852-1938), 6,650

Messer Family, **6,650**

Messer, Mary Burt (1881-1960), 6,650

Messner, Julian, 14,475

Mesta, George, 14,237

Mesta, Perle Skirvin [Mrs. George] (1892-1975),
2,097, 8,657, 13,406, **14,237**

Meta Mold Aluminum Company (WI), 2,817

Metal Workers Industrial Union, 8,061

Metallurgists, **1,867**

Metaphysics, 764, 11,385

Metcalf, Betsey (1786-1867). *See* Baker, Betsey
(Metcalf) (1786-1867)

Metcalf, E. R., 14,651

Metcalf, Eleanor M. Thomas, **6,764**

Metcalf, Ellen Josephine. *See* McHenry, Ellen
Josephine (Metcalf).

Metcalf, Fannie E., 8,994

Metcalf, Flora (Bates) (1806-?), 1,885

Metcalf, Herbert J., **4,937**

Metcalfe, Augusta [Mrs.] (1881-1971), **14,238**

Metcalfe, Barbara Allen (Harris) [Mrs. Asa Baldwin]
(1802-91), 589

Metcalfe, Ellen (1827-1922). *See* McHenry, Ellen
(Metcalfe) [Mrs. John] (1827-1922)

Metcalfe, Emma (1840-1937). *See* Hay, Emma
(Metcalfe) [Mrs. William Gilbert] (1840-1937)

Metcalfe, Mrs. A. B., **665**

Metco (MA), 6,680

Meteer, Miss M. C., 2,046

Meteor showers, 62

Meteorology, observations, 14,513

Methodism, 3,479, 9,531, 10,988, 11,802, 13,434,
13,473, 16,040

Methodist Board of Missions. *See* United Methodist
Church, Board of Global Ministries, Division of
World Missions

Methodist Church. *See* United Methodist Church

Methodist Church, East Texas Conference, Women's
Missionary Society. *See* United Methodist
Church, United Methodist Women

Methodist Church, Epworth League. *See* United
Methodist Church, Epworth League

Methodist Church, Louisiana Conference. *See* United
Methodist Church, Louisiana Conference

Methodist Church, Nebraska Conference. *See* United
Methodist Church, Nebraska Conference

Methodist Church of Hebron Female Benevolent
Association, 1,889

Methodist Church, South Georgia Conference. *See*
United Methodist Church, South Georgia
Conference

Methodist Church, West Texas Conference. *See*
United Methodist Church, West Texas
Conference

Methodist Church, Winnsboro Circuit Missionary
Society (SC), **15,654**

Methodist Church, Woman's Society of Christian
Service. *See* United Methodist Church, United
Methodist Women

Methodist Church, Women's Board. *See* United
Methodist Church, United Methodist Women

Methodist Church, Women's Foreign Missionary
Society. *See* United Methodist Church, United
Methodist Women

Methodist College (NC), 13,370

Methodist Episcopal Church. *See* United Methodist
Church

Methodist Episcopal Church (CT), Woman's Home
Missionary Society, 1,890

Methodist Episcopal Church (Somers, CT), Ladies
Aid, 1,900

Methodist Episcopal Church (IA), Woman's Foreign
Missionary Society, 4,774

Methodist Episcopal Church (IA), Woman's Home
Missionary Society, 4,774

Methodist Episcopal Church (KS), Woman's Foreign
Missionary Society, **10,565**

Methodist Episcopal Church (MI), Ladies' Aid, 7,862

Methodist Episcopal Church (MI), Woman's Foreign
Missionary Society, 7,862

Methodist Episcopal Church (MI), Woman's Home
Missionary Society, 7,862

Methodist Episcopal Church (MI), Woman's
Missionary Federation, 7,862

Methodist Episcopal Church (MI), Women's Society
of Christian Service, 7,862

Methodist Episcopal Church (Edgar, NE), Woman's
Foreign Missionary Society, **10,457**

Methodist Episcopal Church (Madison, NJ), Women's
Foreign Missionary Society, 10,907

Methodist Episcopal Church (Bucyrus, OH),
Woman's Missionary Society, **13,944**

Methodist Episcopal Church (Grants Pass, OR),
Ladies' Union, **14,485**

Methodist Episcopal Church (Grants Pass, OR),
Sunday School Board, **14,485**

Methodist Episcopal Church (SC), Lynch's Creek
Circuit, **15,655**

Methodist Episcopal Church, Chicago Northern
District (IL). *See* United Methodist Church,
Chicago Northern District (IL)

Methodist Episcopal Church, Ladies Aid. *See* United
Methodist Church, United Methodist Women

Methodist Episcopal Church of New Britain (CT),
Woman's Foreign Missionary Society, 1,889

Methodist Episcopal Church of Newark (NJ), Female
Missionary Society, 10,910

Methodist Episcopal Church, South. *See* United
Methodist Church

Methodist Episcopal Conference, Minnesota. *See*
United Methodist Church, Minnesota Annual
Conference

Methodist Protestant Church. *See* United Methodist
Church

Methodist Woman, The (periodical), 3,479, 9,895

Methodists, **4,204**, **5,072**, 8,900, 14,173, 15,718,
15,914

Methven, Mildred Louise (1899-), **8,586**

Metlakahtla mission (Annette Island, AL), 17,219

Metro Clean Air Committee (MN), **9,209**

Metro-Goldwyn Mayer, 949, 1,451, 14,736, 18,020

Metropolitan Business College (IL), alumnae, 3,852

Metropolitan Fair for the Benefit of the US Sanitary
Commission (NY), **12,261**

Metropolitan Housing and Planning Council (Chicago,
IL), **4,129**, 4,158

Metropolitan League of Women Voters (St. Louis,
MO), **10,200**

Metropolitan Life Insurance Company, 17,642

Metropolitan Museum of Art (NY), 5,118, 11,844

Metropolitan Opera (NY), 2,663, 7,303, 11,782, **12,125,** 15,387
Metropolitan Opera Association, 11,944
Metropolitan Opera Company, 3,275, 6,097, 6,498
Metropolitan Opera Guild, 12,125
Metropolitan Opera House (St. Paul, MN), 9,361
Metropolitan Opera Studio (NY), 3,369
Metropolitan Opera National Company, 7,303
Metropolitan Vocational School (NY), 9,598
Metschan, Anna. *See* Cattanach, Anna (Metschan)
Metschan, Lillian. *See* Flanders, Lillian (Metschan) [Mrs. Jesse Evan]
Metschan, Maria C. [Mrs. Phil], 14,615
Metschan, Phil (1840-1920), Family (OR), **14,615**
Metzel, Katherine. *See* Debs, Katherine (Metzel) [Mrs. Eugene]
Metzger, George (1782-1879), 14,760
Metzger, Henry, 11,666
Metzger Institute (PA), **14,760,** 14,761
Metzger, Mady Ziegler [Mrs. Ludwig], 9,251
Metzger, Sophronia Kennedy, **3,553**
Metzger, Zerline Muhlman [Mrs. Fritz] (1891-), 3,838, **3,878**
Metzroth Clothing Company (St. Cloud, MN), 9,463
Meury, Emily Jane (1865-1912), **11,788**
Meury, John (?-1890), **11,788**
Mew, Charlotte Mary (1869-1928), **2,480**
Mewbourn, Eulalia. *See* Vaughan, Eulalia (Mewbourn) [Mrs. John B.]
Mexia, Ynes Enriquetta Julietta (1870-1938), 364, 10,151, 11,297
Mexican American children, 6,641
Mexican American Farm Workers' Movement, Rio Grande Valley of Texas, **16,003**
Mexican American women, 2,666
Mexican American Women's National Association, **2,666**
Mexican Americans, **968,** 7,797, **9,210,** 9,467, **10,117,** 12,100, 16,009, 16,334, 16,368, 16,965, 17,619
    civil rights, 2,678, **12,682,** 16,376
    education, 5,457, 9,467
    employment, 16,003
    social life and customs, 9,467
Mexican Army Band, 5,418
Mexican Whirlwind (book), 4,983
Mexicans, 206, 480
    missions, 15,173
    oral history, 211
    relations with Navajo Indians, 16,869
Mexicans in California, 1,456
Mexico, 438, 6,023, 6,099, 7,305, 7,457, 16,639, 16,690
    abortion, 6,897
    American ambassadors to, 2,292
    American consuls in, 11,316
    American diplomats in, 7,264
    American sculptors in, 17,338
    American travelers in, 6,099
    Americans in, 6,104, 6,511, **6,641**
    blacks, 835
    bull-fights, 335
    camps, 13,221
    Christmas, 335
    community leadership, 8,635
    congresses and conventions, **12,707**
    foreign relations, 5,748
    frontier troubles, 16,147
    history, 200
        (1910-1946), 215, 745, 1,750, 6,641, 9,467, 16,310, 16,520, 16,808
    Methodist Church, education, 13,260
    missionaries to, **6,862**
    missionaries to, Friends, 13,226
    missionaries to, Methodist, **13,260**
    Mormons and Mormonism, 16,520, 16,769, 16,780, 16,811, 16,844
    officials and employees, 835
    presidents, 335
    silver mines and mining, 745, 2,572
    Sinarquistas, 8,144
    social life and customs, 335
Mexico City (Mexico), 6,582
Meyer, Agnes Elizabeth (Ernst) [Mrs. Eugene, Jr.] (1887-1970), 945, **2,481,** 9,140, 11,896

Meyer, Aline. *See* Leibman, Aline (Meyer)
Meyer, Annie (Nathan) (1867-1951), **13,811**
Meyer, Bertha. *See* Serverin, Bertha (Meyer) [Mrs. William]
Meyer, Bertha (Graebner) [Mrs. R. H. C.], 10,140
Meyer, Carolyn [Miss], 9,893
Meyer, Edith Patterson (1895-), **6,053**
Meyer, Elise. *See* Dantas, Elise (Meyer) Stern de Souze
Meyer, Estelle Reel (1862-1959), **17,914**
Meyer, Eugene (1875-1959), **11,896**
Meyer, Florence. *See* Blumenthal, Florence (Meyer)
Meyer, Georgette L. "Dickey" (1918-65). *See* Chapelle, Georgette L. "Dickey" Meyer [Mrs. Tony] (1918-65)
Meyer, Gladys Eleanor, **12,565**
Meyer, Harriet Newmark, 945
Meyer, Henry C., 3,897
Meyer, Ida, 14,861
Meyer, Lucy Jane (Rider) [Mrs. Josiah Shelly] (1849-1922), 4,026, 4,201
Meyer, Rosalie (1869-1955). *See* Stern, Rosalie (Meyer) [Mrs. Sigmund] (1869-1955)
Meyer, Ruth. *See* Cook, Ruth (Meyer)
Meyercord Decal Company, 2,823
Meyergrins, Andrew, 8,709
Meyers, Nina P. *See* Warren, Nina P. (Meyers) [Mrs. Earl]
Meyers, Sister Anna Marie, 9,467, 9,490
Meyrs, Mrs. Charles, 1,786
Mezerik, A. G., **8,106**
Mezerik, Marie (Hempel) [Mrs. A. G.], **8,106**
Mezey, Gail, 10,897
Mezquida, Anna (Blake) [Mrs. Mateo M.] (?-1965), **666**
Mi Cultura Day Care Center (St. Paul, MN), 9,210, 9,467
Miami University (OH), 14,110
    students, 8,553
Mica miners, 10,789
Miccosukee Indians. *See* Mikasuki Indians
Michael Friendman Gold Medal, 12,577
Michael, Moina [Miss], **3,407**
Michael Reese Hospital (Chicago, IL), 3,968, 4,074, 4,162
Michael Reese Hospital (Chicago, IL), Woman's Aid, 3,968
Michael Reese Hospital (Chicago, IL), Women's Board, 3,968
Michael Reese Hospital (Chicago, IL), Young Ladies' Aid Society. *See* Michael Reese Hospital (Chicago, IL), Woman's Aid
Michaëlis, Karen, 783
Michaels, Barbara (pseudonym). *See* Mertz, Barbara Gross (1927-)
"Michal: the Romance of a King's Daughter," 12,560
Michaux, Joseph, 13,486
Michel, Jane W., 2,208
Michel, Mary. *See* Binckley, Mary (Michel) [Mrs. John Milton]
Michel, Middleton (1822-94), **15,427**
Michelet, Simon Thenistrup (1871-1956), Family (MN), **9,211**
Michelson, Lillian Winter [Mrs.], 1,786
Michelson, Miriam, 10,655
Micheltoreno, Manuel, 493, 626
Michener, Caroll Kinsey (1885-1970), **9,212**
Michener, Daniel K., 9,212
Michener, Ida Blakeslee [Mrs. Daniel K.] (1862-?), 9,212
Michener, James Albert (1907-), **2,482**
Michener, Sarah "Sally" Spensley [Mrs. Carroll Kinsey] (1897-), 9,212
Michigan, 6,514, 8,008, 8,157, 8,342, 12,325, 17,133, 17,445
    abolitionists, 7,751
    abolitionists, Afro-American, 7,846
    abortion, 7,873
        legal aspects, 1,984, **7,856,** 7,864, 7,873
        opposition to, **7822,** 7954
    accountants, 8,366
    Afro-Americans, 8,148, 8,287
        economic conditions, 8,029
    agricultural administration, 8,161, 8,171

agricultural machinery, trade and manufacture, 8,302
    agricultural societies, 7,740, 8,161, 8,171
    agriculture, 7,740, 8,288, 8,302
    anti-Catholicism, 8,070
    antique dealers, **8,358**
    antislavery movement, 7,751
    apportionment (election law), 7,861
    art collectors and collecting, **8,017**
    artists, **8,275**
    associations, institutions, etc., **8,355**
    astronomers, 7,820
    athletic clubs, 7,985, 8,037
    attendance officers, 8,388
    attorneys-general, 8,353
    auditors, 8,062
    audubon societies, 7,874
    authors, 7,718, 7,775, 7,846, **7,888,** 7,892, 8,008, 8,171, **8,274,** 8,314, 8,329, 8,342
    automobile parking, 7,733
    bankers, **8,333**
    banks and banking, 8,224, 8,333
    bar associations, 8,036
    bills, legislative, 8,205
    businessmen, **8,000,** 8,007, **8,374**
    businesswomen, 7,699, 7,875, 8,007, 8,388
    butchers, 8,339
    campaign management, 7,729
    cattle breeders, 7,826, **8,340**
    cattle breeding, 8,161
    caucus, **8,210,** 8,287
    census, 3,945, 4,942, 9,532
    charitable societies, 7,753, 7,913, **7,939,** 8,040
    charitable societies, Jewish, 13,804, 13,808
    charities, 8,031
    child care, 8,095
    child welfare, 8,062, 8,119
    children, development and guidance, 8,040, 8,355
    church records and registers, 7,857
    church records and registers, Baptist, 7,720, 7,759
    church records and registers, Episcopal, **7,905,** 7,907, 7,908, 7,909
    church records and registers, Presbyterian, 7,863, **7,898,** 7,899, 7,900, 7,901, 7,902
    church records and registers, Unitarian, **7,952**
    church societies, 7,720, 8,366, **8,379**
    church societies, Baptist, 7,759, **8,032,** 8,033, 8,034, **8,035**
    church societies, Congregational, 7,857, **8,255**
    church societies, Episcopal, **7,905,** 7,907, 7,908, **7,909**
    church societies, Methodist, 7,862, 7,972
    church societies, Presbyterian, 7,863, 7,898, 7,899, 7,900, 7,901, 7,902, **7,903,** 7,906, **7,989, 7,990**
    church societies, Unitarian, 7,952
    church societies, Universalist, **7,839**
    churches, 7,804
    churches, Baptist, 7,720
    cities and towns, planning, 7,841
    citizens' advisory committees in education, 8,103
    citizens associations, **7,856,** 7,864, 7,967, 8,130, 8,131, 8,148
    city councilwomen, **7,742**
    civil service reform, 7,827
    Civil War, 11,588
        societies, etc., **8,272,** 8,290
    civilian defense, **7,954**
    clergy, **8,223,** 8,332
    clergy, Baptist, **8,304**
    clergy, Methodist, 8,388
    clergymen's wives, **8,285,** 8,367
    clinical psychology, 8,049
    clinics, 8,045
    clubs, 6,546, **7,695,** 7,696, 7,705, 7,726, 7,746, **7,754,** 7,755, 7,771, 7,780, 7,781, 7,787, 7,788, **7,799,** 7,813, 7,836, 7,865, 7,925, 7,934, 7,936, **7,938,** 7,957, 7,960, 7,962, 7,963, 7,971, 7,984, **7,986,** 7,987, 8,014, 8,015, 8,016, 8,018, 8,019, **8,038,** 8,046, 8,047, 8,174, 8,177, 8,187, 8,193, **8,212,** 8,215, 8,218, 8,220, 8,227, 8,234, 8,235, **8,243,** 8,262, 8,263, 8,267, 8,273, 8,281, 8,325, 8,339, 8,349, 8,369, **8,381,** 8,382, 8,384, 8,386
    clubs, Afro-American, **8,029,** 8,284
    clubs, Norwegian-American, **8,769**

college librarians, **7,924**
college students, **7,725**, 7,735, 7,748, 7,814, 7,819, 7,833, 7,893, 8,172
college teachers, **7,747**, **7,818**, 7,873, 7,875, **7,876**, **7,891**, **8,042**, **8,043**, **8,049**, **8,050**, **8,150**, **8,155**, **8,189**, **8,191**, **8,192**, **8,232**, **8,244**, **8,247**, **8,348**
college trustees, 7,714, 8,096, 8,171
community centers, 8,182
community life, 7,716
community organization, 7,926, 8,026, 8,148
community welfare councils, 8,360
congresses and conventions, **7,822**, **10,754**
congressmen, 8,117
congresswomen, 7,802
conservation of natural resources, study and teaching, 7,976
conservationists, 7,794
constitution, 7,749
constitutional conventions, 7,827, 7,841, 7,861, 8,160
continuing education centers, 7,955
convents and nunneries, Catholic, **8,383**
correctional personnel, 7,770, **7,806**
county government, 7,841
county officials and employees, **7,709**, 8,062, **8,226**, 8,293
court records, **3,949**
court reporters, **7,797**
covered bridges, 7,739
deans (in schools), 6,158, **7,845**, **7,872**, **7,959**, 8,053
department heads (universities), **7,727**, 7,829
Depression (1929), 8,148
diaries and journals, **7,706**, **7,762**, **7,782**, **7,812**, 7,815, 7,897, **7,929**, 8,154, **8,217**, **8,229**, **8,246**, **8,248**, **8,249**, **8,252**, 8,294, 8,339, **8,359**, 8,363, 8,365, 8,370
  19th C, **336**, **7,716**, **7,730**, **7,752**, 7,753, **7,778**, **7,805**, 7,928, 7,969, **7,972**, 8,166, **8,214**, **8,219**, **8,221**, **8,225**, **8,230**, **8,231**, **8,237**, **8,239**, **8,241**, **8,250**, **8,251**, **8,256**, 8,279, **8,291**, **8,347**
  travel, **8,222**, **8,326**
discrimination in employment, 8,063
discrimination in housing, 7,794
dormitories, **7,697**, 7,831, **7,852**, **7,854**
dressmakers, **7,732**
education, primary, 8,282
education, secondary, 8,282
educational associations, **7,700**, **7,711**, **8,039**, 8,171, **8,209**
educators, **7,829**, 8,321
elections, 7,914, 8,114, 8,236
emblems, state, 7,749
engravers, 7,789
exceptional children, education, 7,764, 8,030
executive advisory bodies, 8,063
factory inspection, 7,834
fairs, **8,345**
family farms, management, 8,260
family life education, **8,048**
family planning, **7,840**
farm life, 7,812, 8,154, **8,217**, 8,243, 8,344, **8,361**
farmers, **7,826**, 8,157, **8,161**, **8,302**, **8,340**, 8,370, 8,372
Finnish-Americans, **8,185**
fires, 7,877
fishing, 8,167
Friends, 8,166
Friends, Society of, 7,774
fur trade, 8,357
furniture industry and trade, 8,347
gardening, societies, etc., **8,013**, 8,211, 8,360
general stores, 8,151
Girl Scouts, **7,795**, **8,346**
governors, 7,722, 7,729, 7,738, 7,886, 7,914
greek letter societies, **6,514**, **7,884**, **8,041**, **8,051**, **8,321**
grocers, 8,353
health boards, 8,045
high school students, 7,773, 7,891, **8,335**, **8,359**
high school teachers, 8,042
high schools, 8,044, 8,317
historians, **7,804**
historical researchers, 7,774
history, periodicals, 6,514

home economics, accounting, 7,702, 8,327
home economists, **8,165**
hospitals, 8,045
housewives, **7,753**, **7,778**, **7,782**, **7,972**, 8,230, **8,295**, **8,331**, **8,339**, **8,343**, **8,376**
housewives, Afro-American, **8,029**
immigrants, 8,007, **8,258**
immigrants, Danish, **7,708**
immigrants, German, **7,890**
indentured servants, 8,276
insurance agencies, 8,366
insurance companies, 8,167
islands, history, 7,895
journalists, 7,888, **8,314**
judges, 7,722, **8,363**
jury, 8,388
justices of the peace, 8,388
kindergarten teachers, training of, **7,798**, 7,949, 7,973
labor and laboring classes, 8,007
  dwellings, 9,277
labor laws and legislation, 8,137
land, registration and transfer, 10,010
land settlement, 8,280, 8,288
law, cases, 8,162
lawyers, **7,802**, **8,086**, **8,300**, **8,333**, **8,363**
legislative councils, **7,698**, 7,803
legislators, **8,078**, **8,114**, 8,117, **8,119**, 8,171, **8,287**, **8,333**
librarians, **7,878**, **8,050**
libraries, **8,204**
library associations, 7,919, 7,926
literary societies, **7,837**, **8,024**, **8,188**, **8,350**, **8,387**
local church councils, **7,763**
local transit, **7,733**
lumber trade, 8,309
lumber, transportation, 8,167
lumbering, 8,167
lumbermen, **8,374**
mayors, 7,796, 8,089, 8,181
mentally handicapped, education, 7,764
merchants, **8,334**, 8,369
Mexican-Americans, 7,797
militia, 8,313
missionaries, Baptist, **8,304**
missionaries, Presbyterian, 7,932
missionaries, Protestant, 8,164
monasticism and religious orders for women, Catholic, **7,694**, **8,176**, **8,292**, **8,383**
Mormons and Mormonism, 4,209
municipal charters, 7,841
municipal government, 7,796
municipal officials and employees, **7,796**
museum directors, **8,211**
museums, 8,180, 8,211
music teachers, **7,793**, **7,975**, **8,317**, **8,356**, **8,364**
musical societies, 8,189, **8,194**
musicians, **7,975**
Native Americans, 2,566, 8,164
  government relations, 7,945
  missions, 8,304, 10,187
  reservations, 3,944
naturalization records, 3,949
newsletters, 7,723, 8,174
newspapers, 8,369
nurses, **7,873**, **8,366**
nursing schools, 6,158, **8,045**, 8,053
occupational retraining, women, 8,062
officials and employees, 7,797, 7,945, **7,976**, **8,066**, **8,068**
Ojibwe Indians, missions, 7,931
oral history, **8,007**, 8,167, **8,185**
organists, **7,743**
Ottawa Indians, missions, 7,931
pacifists, **7,923**, **8,009**
parks, 8,205, 8,360
parliamentary procedure, **8,179**
party committees, 7,810, 7,883
patriotic societies, **7,768**, **7,858**, **7,860**, **8,011**, **8,178**, **8,271**, 8,301, **8,319**, **8,320**, 8,337, 8,340
peace societies, 7,723, **7,988**, 15,316
physical education and training, **7,772**
physicians, **7,715**, **7,719**, 7,727, **7,801**, **7,872**, 7,920, **7,966**, **8,020**, **8,052**, 8,223

pioneers and settlers, 6,514, 7,632, 7,769, 7,804, **7,855**, **8,153**, **8,156**, 8,164, 8,195, 8,278, 8,291, **8,299**, **8,338**
pioneers and settlers, Afro-American, 8,284
poets, 7,751, 7,789
police and community, 7,794
policewomen, 17,191
political clubs, **7,912**
politics, practical, women's activism, 7,698, **7,841**, **7,842**, **7,861**, **8,242**, **8,360**
pottery, 2,796, 2,821
practical nurses, **7,815**
printing plants, 8,181
prisons for women, records and correspondence, 8,276
property tax, 8,167
psychiatric clinics, 8,049
psychology, forensic, **13,740**
public health nursing, 8,053
public housing, 8,089, 8,104, 8,148
public officers, **8,027**, 8,210
public records, **8,276**
public schools, 7,841
public welfare, 8,148
publishers and publishing, **7,915**
quilts, **8,275**
race relations, 7,742
radio broadcasts, 8,269
radio operators, **8,314**
radio programs, 8,185
railroads, employees, **8,354**
real estate agents, **7,950**, 8,309
reformatories (female), 7,806, 8,276
right to life movement, **7,843**
riots, 8,148
roads, plank, 8,224
sanatoriums, 8,307
scholarships, **7,721**, 8,041, 8,054
school administrators, **7,848**
school boards, 7,913, 7,926, 8,030, 8,170
school census, 8,170
school management and organization, 7,764
school superintendents and principals, 8,044, 8,170, 8,190, 8,293, 9,448
schools, **7,859**, **8,023**, **8,170**, 8,238, **8,245**
  records and correspondence, 8,170
secretaries, 7,796, **7,886**, **8,089**, **8,233**
secretaries of state, 8,062
senators, United States, 7,968
sewing, 7,913
sit-down strikes, 8,081
social life and customs, 8,353
social service, **8,108**
social service administration, 7,709
social workers, 8,148
socialist party, 1,654
societies, etc., 8,057, 8,095
societies, Afro-American, 7,736, 8,068
societies, Jewish, **13,775**
soldiers, **8,313**
  Civil War, 8,380
statues, 8,318
strikes and lockouts, 1,656
  miners, 8,144
student counselors, 8,043
student financial aid, 7,801
student housing, 7,879, 7,959
students, foreign, 8,150
students, part-time, 8,054
students' societies, **7,707**, **7,871**, **7,961**, 8,043
suffrage, 6,546, **7,791**, **7,808**, **8,266**
suffrage societies, 6,414, 7,731, 7,803, **7,894**, 7,921, 7,941, 8,028, 8,266, 16,252
suffragists, **2,374**, **6,414**, **7,791**, **7,803**, **7,808**, **8,009**
Sunday-school teachers, 8,190
surveyors, **8,313**
symphony orchestras, 8,257
tailors, 7,846
taxation, 7,861
teachers, **336**, **802**, **7,710**, **7,756**, **7,757**, **7,758**, **7,767**, **7,796**, **7,930**, **7,934**, **8,019**, **8,025**, **8,027**, **8,030**, **8,104**, **8,159**, **8,160**, **8,162**, **8,169**, **8,170**, **8,195**, **8,217**, **8,229**, **8,231**, **8,306**, **8,308**, **8,342**, **8,377**, **8,380**

legal status, laws, etc., 8,162
  salaries, pensions, etc., 8,293
  teachers, Afro-American, 8,121
teachers' colleges, 8,233, 8,244, 8,310, 8,348, 8,378
temperance, 7,951
temperance societies, 4,244, **7,838**, **7,866**, **7,977,**
  7,978, 7,979, 7,980, 7,982, 7,983, 7,994, 8,166,
  8,175, 8,254, 8,268
trade and professional associations, 7,873, **8,236,**
  8,283, 8,356
trade-unions, **8,107, 8,132,** 8,216
  government employees, 8,063
  household workers, **8,080**
  postal service, 8,026
undertakers and undertaking, **8,334,** 8,369
unemployed, 8,089
universities and colleges, 7,800, **8,152**
  alumnae, **8,054**
  alumni, **7,955, 7,956, 7,957, 7,958**
  archives, **8,174, 8,385**
  centennials, 7,750
  examinations, 7,922
  faculty, **8,047**
  finance, 8,193
  food service, 7,920
  radio broadcasting, 6,625
university extension, 8,150, 8,165
volunteer workers in hospitals, **8,180**
wages, 8,073
War of 1898, societies, etc., **8,289**
women, civil rights, 8,086
women's health centers and clinics, 8,018
working-women's clubs, **7,835**
works councils, 8,124
World War II
  civilians work, 3,950, **7,760**
  civilians work, industrial, Afro-Americans, 8,105
Young Men's Christian Association, **7,993**
Young Women's Christian Association, **7,993,**
  7,995, 7,996, 8,182
Michigan Abortion Referendum Committee, **7,856**
Michigan American Civil Liberties Union, 8,086
Michigan American Revolution Bicentennial
  Commission, 8,312
Michigan Audubon Society, 7,874
Michigan Black Women's Political Caucus, 8,287
Michigan Child Study Association, **8,355**
Michigan Christian Endeavor Union, 7,717
Michigan Civil Service Commission, 7,827
Michigan Commission on Displaced Persons, 9,508,
  9,512
Michigan Congress of Women's Auxiliaries of the
  CIO, 8,124
Michigan Conservation Commission, 7,794
Michigan Constitutional Convention (1961-62), 8,160
Michigan Council on Women in Business and
  Industry, 7,967, 8,131
Michigan Democratic Party, state central committee,
  7,810, 7,883
Michigan Department of Health, 8,045
Michigan Employment Security Commission, 8,068
Michigan Equal Suffrage Association, 6,414, 7,731,
  7,803, 7,941
Michigan Farm Bureau, 8,269
Michigan Federation of Business and Professional
  Women, 7,950
Michigan Federation of Music Clubs, 8,189
Michigan Female College, 7,918
Michigan Female Seminary (Kalamazoo, MI), **7,859,**
  8,238, 8,245
Michigan First Engineers and Mechanics, Company
  M, 8,380
Michigan Grand Army of the Republic Auxiliaries,
  7,860
Michigan Heritage (periodical), 6,514
Michigan History (periodical), 6,514
Michigan League Building Fund, 7,955
Michigan League of Planned Parenthood, 7,967
Michigan League of Women Voters, **7,861**
Michigan League of Women Voters, Children's
  Service, 7,861
Michigan League of Women Voters, Fair Employment
  Practices Commission, 7,861
Michigan Livestock Sanitary Commission, 8,340

Michigan Master Farmers Club, 8,161
Michigan Medical School, students, 9,195
Michigan Music Teachers' Association, **8,356**
Michigan, 1938-1961 (book), 6,514
Michigan Nurses Association, 7,873
Michigan Nursing Association, **8,283**
Michigan Orphan Asylum Association, 7,939
Michigan Parks Association, 7,785, 7,794
Michigan Patron, 8,171
Michigan Reform School for Girls, 8,276
Michigan Reform School for Girls (Adrian, MI),
  7,806
Michigan Right to Life Committee, 7,856, **7,864**
Michigan School for the Blind, 8,181
Michigan School for the Deaf, 8,181
Michigan State Association of Colored Women's
  Clubs, **8,284**
Michigan State Employees Union Council 7, 8,063
Michigan State Federation of Women's Clubs, 5,270,
  7,803, **7,865,** 7,941, 8,177, **8,267**
Michigan State Grange, 7,740
Michigan State Normal College (Ypsilanti, MI), 7,800
  faculty, 7,829
Michigan State Nurses Association, **8,236**
Michigan State University, 8,171
  administration, 8,161
  alumnae, **8,172,** 8,174
  archives, **8,174**
  faculty, **8,150, 8,155,** 8,165
Michigan State University Business Women's Club,
  8,174
Michigan State University, College of Human
  Ecology, **8,152,** 8,155
Michigan State University, Home Economics. *See*
  Michigan State University, College of Human
  Ecology
Michigan State University, Women's Course. *See*
  Michigan State University, College of Human
  Ecology
Michigan Suffrage Association, 8,266
Michigan Territory, deeds, 4,920
Michigan Tool Company, 8,099
Michigan Welfare League, **8,108**
Michigan Woman's Christian Temperance Union,
  7,866
Mickay, Elizabeth Bouchea, **9,213**
Mickcl, C. E., 8,555
Mickey, Margaret Portia [Miss], **14,126**
Mickle, Alice Shaw, **14,616,** 14,618
Micronesia, 7,262
  missionaries to, **3,642**
Microscope and microscopy, 2,718
Mid-Century Conference for Peace, 17,238
Mid-Century White House Conference on Children
  and Youth, 6,860, 12,921
Mid-Day College, 13,932
Mid Pacific Magazine (periodical), 7,275
Middafgh, Cornelia, 11,325
Middafgh, Garrett, 11,325
Middle Ages, history, **15,092**
Middle East
  American nurses in, **6,131**
  American travelers in, 1,841
  political and social conditions, 11,857
Middle Fork Route (western migration), 1,505
Middle States Association of Colleges and Secondary
  Schools, 10,892
Middlebrook, L. Ruth, 2,166
Middlebury College (VT), 12,478, 15,670
Middlecoff, Samuel, 17,992
Middlecoff, Susan. *See* Ludlow, Susan (Middlecoff)
  [Mrs. James Dunlop]
Middlesex County Women Teacher's Association
  (NJ), 10,998
Middleton, Alicia Hopton (Russell) [Mrs. Arthur]
  (?-1840), 15,501, 15,656, 15,657
Middleton, Anna Elizabeth (De Wolf) [Mrs.
  Nathaniel Russell] (1815-?), 15,499, 15,656
Middleton, Anne Manigault (1820-76), 15,656, 15,657
Middleton, Catherine (1812-94), **15,500**
Middleton, Charlotte (1854-?), 15,656
Middleton, Edwardina "Edda" de Normann, 15,656,
  15,658

Middleton, Eleanor Maria. *See* Rutledge, Eleanor
  Maria (Middleton) [Mrs. Benjamin Huger]
Middleton, Elizabeth (?-1784), 15,656
Middleton, Elizabeth (1787-1822). *See* Izard,
  Elizabeth (Middleton) [Mrs. Ralph, Jr.]
  (1787-1822)
Middleton, Emma (1867-1945). *See* Wells, Emma
  (Middleton) [Mrs. Edward Oliver] (1867-1945)
Middleton, Eweretta (1840-99), 15,456
Middleton Family (SC), 13,137, **15,456, 15,656**
Middleton, Fola (La Follette) [Mrs. George]
  (1882-1970), 2,403, 2,432, 6,565, 12,041
Middleton, Harriott, 15,456
Middleton, Henry, 15,500
Middleton, Jane, 11,738
Middleton, Lucy B. [Mrs. Leonidas], **13,487**
Middleton Lyceum (WI), 17,857
Middleton, Maria Louisa (1844-?), 15,656
Middleton, Mary Julia (1829-1904). *See* Read, Mary
  Julia (Middleton) [Mrs. Benjamin Huger]
  (1829-1904)
Middleton, Maude Webster [Mrs.], 17,755
Middleton, Nathaniel, **15,501,** 15,656
Middleton, Nathaniel Russell, Family (SC), **15,501**
Middleton, Ralph Izard, 15,657
Middleton, Susan [Mrs. William] (?-1900),
  15,658
Middleton, Susan Matilda, 15,456
Middleton, Thomas, 15,716
Middleton, William, 15,411
Middleton, William (1809-93), **15,658**
Middletown (book), 11,888
Middletown Center (NY), 11,285
Middletown Female Institute (CT), 1,979
Middletown Female Seminary (CT), 1,979
Midkiff, Mary Weaver [Mrs.] (1885-), 1,786
Midland Chautauqua Company, 4,944
Midland Cooperatives, 9,180
Midland Monthly (periodical), 4,732
Midlo, Gwendolyn (1929-). *See* Hall, Gwendolyn
  (Midlo) (1929-)
Midway Church (GA), 3,415
Midway College (Midway, KY), **5,393**
  alumni, **5,392**
Midway Service Station (Adrian, ND), 13,669
Midwest Academy (Chicago, IL), 3,792
Midwest Association for the Study of Human
  Sexuality, 4,131
Midwest Committee for Protection of Foreign Born,
  The, 3,852
Midwest Population Center (Chicago, IL), 4,131
Midwives, 162, 238, 1,655, 3,482, 3,740, 4,336, 5,252,
  5,574, 6,201, 9,323, 9,542, **9,820, 10,710, 10,978,**
  11,852, 12,423, 12,450, **13,311,** 13,446, 13,522,
  14,048, 14,864, 14,921, 14,945, 15,834, 16,472,
  16,486, 16,765, 16,789, 16,803, **16,815, 16,828,**
  16,838, **16,955,** 16,967, 16,968, 17,528
Mielzinger, Jo (1901-), 6,085
Mier Expedition (1842-1843), 16,147
Miers, Madelin. *See* Phelan, Madelin (Miers)
Mifflin, Anne (Emlen) [Mrs. Warner], 14,991
Mifflin Company. *See* Houghton Mifflin Company
Mifflin, Emily. *See* Hopkinson, Emily (Mifflin) [Mrs.
  Joseph]
Mifflin, George Harrison (1845-1921) 5,942
Mifflin, John F., 15,087
Mifflin, Lemuel, 14,991
Mifflin, Mary Crowninshield [Mrs. Charles] **5,942**
Mifflin, Warner (ca. 1745-98), 14,991
Migel, M. C., 6,691
Mighels, Ella Sterling (Clark) Cummins (1853-1934),
  616, 720, **1,322**
Mignon (opera), 7,213
Migrant agricultural laborers, 11,763, 16,003
  housing, **1,176**
Migrant Health Services, Inc. (MN), 9,467
Migrant labor, 164, 230, 380, 2,504, 4,921, 5,398,
  8,078, 8,144, 9,810, 11,566, 11,730, 11,763,
  11,771, 11,905, 11,965, 14,202, 14,671
  education, 797
  housing, 797
  law and legislation, 10,953, 11,011
  medical care, 3,691
Migrant labor, Mexican American, 16,334

"Migrant Plays," 2,938
Migration, internal, 8,679
Mikasuki Indians, 2,883
"Mike Douglas Show, The" (television program), 17,943
Mikesell, Pearl Adell (Rowell). See Chase, Pearl Adell (Rowell) Mikesell [Mrs. Lewis Nathaniel]
Mikulewicz, Ruth Velzora Benson (1902-), 9,467
Mikulski, Barbara, 6,584
Mikveh Israel Synagogue (Philadelphia, PA), 15,010
Milbank Memorial Fund, 8,572
Mildmay Association for Female Workers (England), 5,079
Mildon, Kay Jon (1933-), **16,766**
Miles, Anna E., 15,457
Miles, Emily Winthrop [Mrs.], **3,062**
Miles Family (SC), 15,457
Miles, Florence Violet (1880-). See Stirling, Florence Violet (Miles) [Mrs. James Y.] (1880-)
Miles, Isadore [Mrs.], **8,109**
Miles, James Warley, 15,457
Miles, Jane Fox Stevenson [Mrs. William Hart] (1842-1924), 16,833
Miles, Josephine [Miss] (1911-), **667,** 710
Miles, Josephine J., 16,648
Miles, L., 15,524
Miles, Luella, **17,172**
Miles Mildred Myrtle (1893-). See Dillman, Mildred Myrtle (Miles) [Mrs. Ray Eugene] (1893-)
Miles, Nancy Teague [Mrs. L.], 15,524
Miles, Nellie, **7,408**
Miles, Virginia, 3,754
Miles Wild Life Sanctuary of the Audubon Society (CT), 3,062
Miles, William Porcher, 15,457
Miley, Mrs. W. J., 16,176
Milford Colony (IA), 4,701, 4,704
Milford Emigration Society (MA). See Milford Western Emigration Society (MA)
Milford Western Emigration Society (MA), 4,701, 4,704
Milhan, Mabel A. [Miss], **11,651**
Milholland, Inez. See Boissevain, Inez (Milholland)
Militant, The, 17,663
Militarism, 12,487
Military camps, 4,359, 4,362
Military Civilian Club of San Antonio (TX), **16,323**
Military courts, 17,453, 17,482
Military departments and divisions, **2,699**
Military drill. See Minor drill and tactics
Military education, 9,645, **11,125,** 14,145, 15,898
Military history, 14,766
Military hygiene, 2,690, 13,966
Military law, **5,480**
Military libraries, **12,654**
Military life, 9,874
Military Life in Dakota (book), 9,002
Military nursing, 238, 242, **382,** 1,779, 1,931, **2,690,** 2,701, 3,203, **4,490, 5,027,** 6,122, **6,127, 6,129, 6,134, 6,145, 6,152, 6,153, 6,159, 6,161, 6,501,** 6,623, 6,826, 8,259, 8,310, 8,446, 8,447, 9,468, **13,206,** 13,336, 13,348, 13,617, 13,618, 17,028, **17,306**
Military occupation, 17,079, 17,092, 17,099, 17,103
Military posts, 311, 1,751, 1,786, 3,302, 3,897, 8,412, 9,113, 9,416, 12,479, 13,024, 14,774, 17,477
Military service, compulsory, 7,723, 8,058, 8,149, 9,312, 14,686, 14,691
  abolition of, 6,379
  opposition to, **15,315**
Military service records. See, e.g., United States (government), Army, records and correspondence
Military social work, 2,280, 8,656, 8,665, 12,728, 13,617, 13,618
Military supplies, 11,978
Military telephone, 6,383
Military transportation, World War I, 8,259
Military Waiting Wives Club of Lincoln (NE), **10,493**
Milk, 3,482, 4,163, 11,629
  prices, 6,896
Milk Commission of the Children's Hospital of

Chicago (IL). See Infant Welfare Society of Chicago (IL)
Milk contamination, 11,579
Milk hygiene, 1,237, 1,251, 2,397, 8,942, 17,517
Milk trade, 7,672
Mill, John Stuart, 12,485
"Mill Valley" (song), 1,068
Mill Valley Library Association (CA), **668**
Mill Valley School District (CA), 649
Millar. See also Miller
Millar, Elizabeth Davison (1830-1913). See Wilson, Elizabeth Davison (Millar) [Mrs. Joseph G.] (1830-1913)
Millar, Margaret, 1,525, 11,165
Millard Fillmore National Landmark House (NY), **11,436**
Millay, Edna St. Vincent (1892-1950), 1,224, **2,483,** 3,988, 5,694, 7,214, 11,810, 11,821, 11,897, 12,451, 12,644, 14,406, 17,010, 17,013, 17,053
Mille-Christine (twins), **13,306**
Mille Lacs Indian Reservation (MN), 8,927
Millean, Jean, 10,721
Millenium Guild, 6,867
Miller. See also Millar
Miller, Adena (1888-1967). See Rich, Adena (Miller) (1888-1967)
Miller, Agnes G. [Mrs.], 169
Miller, Alfred Jacob, 10,357
Miller, Alice (1887-1951). See Pickering, Alice (Miller) [Mrs. John Edson] (1887-1951)
Miller, Alice (Duer) (1874-1942), 15,060
Miller, Annie Louise [Miss] (1860-1945), **10,494**
Miller, Barbara. See Solomon, Barbara (Miller) [Mrs. Peter H.]
Miller, Bernice, 5,123
Miller, Bertha (1879-1960). See Harrison, Bertha (Miller) [Mrs. Clement] (1879-1960)
Miller, Betsy, 9,593
Miller, Caroline [Mrs.], 3,025, 3,028, **3,063,** 3,071, 3,174
Miller, Catharine (Littlefield) [Mrs. Nathanael] Greene, 15,703
Miller, Cattie Lou (1923-), 5,394
Miller, Chris, **16,004**
Miller, Clay V., **17,471**
Miller, Dan, 4,744
Miller, Dayton Clarence, 11,814
Miller, Donna M., 17,230
Miller, Dorothy Canning. See Cahill, Dorothy Canning Miller [Mrs. Holger]
Miller, Dorothy W., 6,760
Miller, Eleanore, 7,109
Miller, Elizabeth Ann (Awbry) [Mrs. John Napper Tandy] (1832-1920), **14,486**
Miller, Elizabeth (Smith) [Mrs. Charles Dudley] (1822-1911), 6,460, 12,625, 12,744, 17,589
Miller, Ellen [Miss], 7,012
Miller, Elmira Pond (1811-?). See William, Elmira Pond Miller [Mrs. Henry] (1811-?)
Miller, Emily (Van Dorn), **9,678**
Miller, Emma [Mrs.], 14,506
Miller, Emma (Guffey) [Mrs. Carroll] (1874-1970), **6,765,** 11,483, 14,377, 14,815, 14,820
Miller, Eunice (1883-). See Bailey, Eunice Miller [Mrs. E. Morgan] (1883-)
Miller, Evylena Nunn (1888-1966), **1,522**
Miller Family (AK, CA), **1,633**
Miller Family (NY), 11,522
Miller Family (NC), 13,319
Miller Family (PA),
Miller, Fannie, 11,789
Miller, Florence (Hazen) [Mrs. B. G.], **10,407**
Miller, Frances Adeline (1805-65). See Seward, Frances Adeline (Miller) [Mrs. William Henry] (1805-65)
Miller, Frances Higbie [Mrs. John Hamlin], **11,789**
Miller, Frieda Segelke (1889-1973), **6,766,** 12,069, 12,071
Miller, Gertrude [Miss], 1,633
Miller, Grace (ca. 1896-), **10,256**
Miller, Grace M., 1,641
Miller, Harriet (Mann) [Mrs. Watts Todd] (1831-1918), **2,484**

Miller, Helen Clarkson (1879-1968). See Davis, Helen Clarkson (Miller) [Mrs. Harvey N.] (1879-1968)
Miller, Helen Guthrie, **9,893,** 10,200
Miller, Helen Hill [Mrs. Francis Pickens] (1899-), **6,767,** 9,449
Miller, Henry Valentine, 4,232, 12,821
Miller, Howard, 5,339
Miller, Hugh, 17,472
Miller, Izetta Jewell [Mrs. William Gay, Jr.] Brown [Mrs. Hugh] (1882-), **17,472**
Miller, Joaquin, 558, 657, 1,089, 1,090, 1,323
Miller, Johanna Strabough, 1,080
Miller, John Hamlin, **11,789**
Miller, Juanita, 616, 712, 1,089, **1,323**
Miller, Kate F. See Peabody, Kate F. (Miller)
Miller, Katherine Browning (Fischer) (1858-1960), **669**
Miller, Katherine E., 9,046
Miller, Lazette Marie. See Worden, Lazette Marie (Miller)
Miller, Lenora (Huntley), 1,633
Miller, Letitia D. (1852-?), **13,069**
Miller, Lidie May, 15,743
Miller, Lois, 14,828
Miller, Lois, 6,336
Miller, Lois Thomas, 16,451
Miller, Louise (1901-). See Hodges, Louise (Miller) (1901-)
Miller, Lucille, 5,124
Miller, Mabel Andreson, 9,527
Miller, Margaret (Akerly) [Mrs. Silvanus], 2,489
Miller, Margaret Spragg, 4,904
Miller, Margaret (Taylor), 17,865
Miller, Marguerite C., 15,502
Miller, Marinda [Mrs. Lois Thomas], 16,451
Miller, Martha, 15,486
Miller, Martha A. 2,575
Miller, Martha "Matt" David, **9,679**
Miller, Mary. See Shufeldt, Mary (Miller)
Miller, Mary (1856-1935). See Hayes, Mary (Miller) [Mrs. Webb C., I] (1856-1935)
Miller, Mary A., **17,306**
Miller, Mary Boykin (1823-86). See Chesnut, Mary Boykin (Miller) [Mrs. James, Jr.] (1823-86)
Miller, Mary Edwards [Mrs. Albert] (1832-1919). See Walker, Mary Edwards [Mrs. Albert] Miller (1832-1919)
Miller, Mary Ellen (1927-). See Glass, Mary Ellen (Miller) (1927-)
Miller, Mary Farnham (1872-1920), 10,151
Miller, Mary Rogers, **11,652**
Miller, Maud, 558
Miller, May Merrill, 12,537
Miller, Minnie Lee (Cardwell), **670**
Miller, Mrs. Guttorm, 8,769
Miller, Mrs. Isadore, 1,080
Miller, Mrs. J. Balfour, **9,680**
Miller, Mrs. Stewart, 15,332
Miller, Nancy L., 7,144
Miller, Nancy (Merrick) [Mrs. Henry] (1797-1843), 7,650
Miller, Olive Kennon (Beaupré) (1883-1968), **2,485, 7,261**
Miller, Olive Thorne (pseudonym). See Miller, Harriet (Mann) [Mrs. Watts Todd] (1831-1918)
Miller, Phoebe, 4,845
Miller, S. Lou [Miss], 12,262
Miller, Sarah (1820-1908). See Schaefer, Sarah (Miller) [Mrs. Jacob] (1820-1908)
Miller, Sarah Ann (1853-1945). See Baker, Sarah Ann (Miller) [Mrs. Edwin Franklin] (1853-1945)
Miller, Sarah Cordelia (1817-97). See Newkirk, Sarah Cordelia (Miller) [Mrs. Thompson] (1817-97)
Miller, Susan, 1,221
Miller, Susan Dixwell [Mrs. Gerrit Smith], 11,596, 11,633
Miller, Thomas Woodnutt (1886-1973), 10,740
Miller, Virginia Larwill (1846-1937). See Ewing, Virginia Larwill (Miller)
Miller, William (1782-1849), 3,742
Miller, William C., **15,502**
Millerites, 11,726

Millers, **10,331**
Millett, Charlotte, **7,409**
Millett, Kate, 11,663
Millette, Minnie Roop, **6,768**
Millican, Arthenia Bates, **15,660**
Millican, Edith, 15,144
Millier, Neva. *See* Moss, Neva (Miller) [Mrs.]
Milligan, Elizabeth "Lizzie" R. (Howard) [Mrs. Sam], 13,250
Milligan, Florence [Miss], 12,276
Milligan, Irma (Lambeth) (ca. 1900-70), **9,538**
Millikan, Greta (Blanchard) [Mrs. Robert Andrews] (1876-?), 1,098
Millikan, Robert Andrews (1868-1953), **1,098**, 11,814
Milliners, **7,386**, 13,217
Millinery, 6,190, 16,726
Millinery workers, **5,593**, 16,006
Millington, Ada (1849-1930). *See* Jones, Ada (Millington) (1849-1930)
Millions of Cats (book), 8,531
Millis Family, 3,408
Millis, John, 3,246, 3,408
Millis, Mary (Raoul) [Mrs. John] (1870-1958), 3,246, **3,408**
Mills, Catherine Jane. *See* Bell, Catherine Jane (Mills)
Mills College (Oakland, CA), 402, 760, 1,404, 4,167, 6,201
   archives, **1,085**
   faculty, 1,088
   presidents, 756, 14,332
   students, 1,610
   trustees, 1,081
Mills College (Oakland, CA), Employees' Association, 1,085
Mills College (Oakland, CA), Mary Atkins Association, 1,085
Mills College (Oakland, CA), Women's Faculty Club, 1,085
Mills, Constance "Connie" (1880-1966). *See* Herreshoff, Constance "Connie" (Mills) [Mrs. James Brown II] (1880-1966)
Mills, Cyrus T., 1,085
Mills, Dorothy. *See* Young, Dorothy (Mills) [Mrs. Gordon Russell]
Mills, Eleanor Reinhardt [Mrs.], 11,034, 11,190
Mills, Elisabeth, 8,665, 8,683
Mills, Elisabeth (1858-1931). *See* Reid, Elisabeth (Mills) [Mrs. Whitelaw] (1858-1931)
Mills, Ellen (Low) [Mrs. Ethelbert Smith] (1827-98), 2,457
Mills, Ethelbert Smith, 2,457
Mills Family (CT), 1,402
Mills Family (HI), 3,640
Mills Family (NY), **2,457**
Mills, Florence (Winfrey). [Mrs. Ulysses S.] Thompson (1895-1927), 12,004
Mills, Harriet May (1857-?), 6,815, 11,605
Mills, Hazel E., 14,591
Mills, Henrietta (Allen), 12,814
Mills Hotel (MN), 9,214
Mills, Julia Sherman (1817-90). *See* Damon, Julia Sherman (Mills) [Mrs. Samuel Chenery] (1817-90)
Mills, Lucius D. (1848-1936), **8,506, 9,214**
Mills, Marjorie. *See* White, Marjorie (Mills)
Mills, Mrs. J. G. M. G., 3,754
"Mills of Long Island, The" (ms), 11,320
Mills, Permelia L. [Mrs.] (1824-1908), 9,214
Mills, Rachel (Joy) Fisher (?-1868), **14,617**
Mills, Rebecca (Hadley) [Mrs. William Clarkson] (1820-?), 4,651
Mills, Sarah, 12,315
Mills Seminary for Girls, 800
Mills Seminary, students, 14,311
Mills, Susan Lincoln (Tolman) [Mrs. Cyrus Taggart] (1825-1912), 823, 876, 1,085
Mills, William Clarkson, **4,651**
Millward, Jesse, 12,832
Millward, Priscilla Jane (pseudonym). *See* Bothwell, Jean (1892?-1977)
Millwheel Turns, The (book), 5,025
Milly (slave, NC), 13,188
Milne, Winifred Murray Deming [Mrs.], 9,032

Milner, Agnes Finding, **1,732**
Milner, Edith (Allen) [Mrs. Charles H
Milner, Vivian Irene, **4,264**
Milnor, Emma, 10,377
Milton Club (Hadley, MA). *See* Colonial Club (Hadley, MA)
Milton, Frances. *See* Trollope, Frances (Milton)
Milton, Jefferson Davis (1861-1947), 220
Milton, Mildred (Taitt) [Mrs. Jefferson Davis] (1879-1963), **220**
"Milton's Poems Adapted for Music," 13,191
Milwaukee Central School of Nursing (WI), 17,701
Milwaukee Children's Betterment League (WI), 17,845
Milwaukee Children's Outing Association (WI), 17,840
Milwaukee County Federation of Women's Clubs (WI), 17,671
Milwaukee County Women's Suffrage Association (WI), 17,828
Milwaukee-Downer College (WI), **17,689, 17,832, 17,844, 17,849**
   presidents, 17,586
Milwaukee Druggists Ladies Club (WI), **17,690**
Milwaukee Endowment Association (WI), 17,747
Milwaukee General Hospital School of Nursing (WI), alumnae, 3,432
Milwaukee Jewish Community Center (WI), 17,841
Milwaukee Jewish Mission (WI), 17,841
Milwaukee News (WI), 2,240
Milwaukee Woman's Suffrage Association (WI), 17,745
Mimi at Camp (book), 5,261
Mims, Bernice (Ashburn), 2,884
Mims, Sue Harper [Mrs. Livingston], **3,227**
Mind and Heart of Frederick Douglass, The (book), 18,004
Mindrum, Beverly, 8,929
Mine Eyes Have Seen the Glory (book), 14,231
Mine management, 1,072, 1,492
Mine, Mill and Smelter Workers' Union, 1,357
Mineau, Hope (Garlick) [Mrs. Wirt], 9,078, 17,587
Miner, Anne Parker, 17,941
Miner, Harold E., 17,656
Miner, Irene. *See* Weisz, Irene (Miner) [Mrs. Charles]
Miner, Myrtilla (1815-64), **2,486**, 12,833
Miner, Virginia Scott [Mrs. Dewey H.] (1901-), **4,482**
Mineral industries, 1,750, 10,638, 10,684, 14,558
   accidents, 8,070
Mineral waters, 5,513
Miners, 190, 1,752, 8,085, 10,315, **10,331, 10,382,** 10,682, 11,853
   medical care, 1,080
Miners, Welsh, 5,457
Miners' Union no. 98 (Kofa, AZ), 15,330
Minerva Society (NJ), 11,110
"Minerva's Daughters" (ms), 11,507
Mines and mineral resources, 202, 412, 413, 745, 1,516, 1,621, 1,627, 1,732, 1,804, 7,935, 9,076, 9,467, 9,468, 10,355, 10,365, 10,684, 10,724, 10,728, 10,731, 11,672, 14,207, 14,564, 16,430, 16,534, 16,968, 17,205, 17,209, 17,249
Minford, Sarah Patterson [Mrs. William Alexander], 15,054
Minford, William Alexander (1881-1946), 15,054
Minga Leper Colony (Zaire), 13,291
Miniature painting, 2,783, **3,097**, 14,949
Minick, Alice Ann (Lockwood) [Mrs. John S.] (1844-1939), **10,495**
Minidoka Desert War Relocation Center Camp (ID), 892
Minimum wage, 4,173
Minimum Wage Board, 2,336
Mining camps, 10,756
Mining claims, 135, 1,334
Mining corporations, 1,675, 1,719, 3,698, **9,273,** 10,354
Mining engineers, **194, 1,434**
Mining law, 1,072
Mining schools and education, **10,024**
Minis, Abigail, 3,509, 3,554
Minis Family (SC), **3,554**

Minis, Louisa Porter (Gilmer) [Mrs. J. Florance], 3,588
Minish, Maude (?-1936). *See* Sutton, Maude (Minish) (?-1936)
Ministers Association of Paterson (NJ), 11,149
Mink, Patsy (Takemoto) (1927-), 1,605, 2,097, 6,710, **7,262**
Minne, Nels, 9,526
Minneapolis Association Opposed to the Further Extension of Suffrage to Women (MN), **9,215**
Minneapolis Audubon Society (MN), **9,216**
Minneapolis Authors' Club (MN), **9,217**
Minneapolis B'nai B'rith Women's Chapter 267 (MN). *See* B'nai B'rith, Bertha Rutz Fiterman Chapter (Minneapolis, MN)
Minneapolis Charter Commission (MN), 8,913
Minneapolis Citizen's Committee on Public Education (MN), 8,984
Minneapolis Committee for World Disarmament (MN), 8,963
Minneapolis Committee on Resettlement of Japanese-Americans (MN), 9,219, 9,392
Minneapolis Community Health Service (MN), 8,713
Minneapolis Council of Americanization, 9,147
Minneapolis Council of Civic Clubs (MN), 9,276
Minneapolis Council of Social Agencies (MN), 9,270, 9,289
Minneapolis Defense Council (MN), labor coordinating committee, 8,984
Minneapolis Federation for Jewish Service (MN), 8,923
Minneapolis Federation of Settlements (MN), 9,289
Minneapolis Female Seminary (MN), 9,354
Minneapolis Friends Meeting (MN), **9,220, 9,221**
Minneapolis Friends Meeting (MN), Margaret Fell Society, 9,220
Minneapolis Friends Meeting (MN), Woman's Missionary Society, 9,220
Minneapolis Guild of Music Teachers Inc. (MN), 8,905
Minneapolis High School (MN), 9,100
Minneapolis Institute of Arts (MN), 8,990
Minneapolis Labor School (MN), 8,984
Minneapolis Library Board (MN), 9,467
Minneapolis Mayor's Council on Human Relations (MN), 9,392
Minneapolis Progressive Education Association (MN), 9,440
Minneapolis Public Library (MN), 8,551, 8,913, 9,020, 9,021
Minneapolis School of Art (MN), 9,157
Minneapolis Society of Friends Women (MN), 9,221
Minneapolis Teachers' Retirement Association (MN), 9,374
Minneapolis Threshing Company (MN), 8,480
Minneapolis Times (MN), 9,103
Minneapolis Town Meeting Association (MN), 9,440
Minneapolis Trades and Labor Assembly (MN), 8,984
Minneapolis Tribune (MN), 6,614
Minneapolis Urban League (MN), 9,276, 9,289
Minneapolis Woman's Club (MN), 8,993
Minneapolis Women's School and Library Organization (MN), 9,291
Minnehaha Grange No. 398 (MN), 8,452
Minnelli, Liza, 12,367
Minnesota, 8,399, **8,452**, 8,462, **8,470**, 8,489, 8,518, 8,692, 8,772, 8,921, 8,964, **8,979**, 9,077, **9,096, 9,117, 9,122,** 9,134, 9,138, **9,169**, 9,229, 9,304, **9,333, 9,377,** 9,384, **9,399, 9,462**, 11,630
   abandoned children, law and legislation, 9,351
   abolitionists, 9,320
   abortion, law and legislation, 8,630, 9,475
   actresses, **9,199**, 9,502
   adoption, 9,166
   adult education, 8,947
   affirmative action programs, 8,550
   Afro-Americans, 9,114, 9,259, 9,467, 9,527
      economic conditions, 9,252, 9,467
   agricultural colleges, **8,578, 8,607**
   agricultural extension, **9,469**
   agricultural extension work, 9,052
   agricultural laborers, **8,467**, 9,467
   agricultural societies, **8,401**, 8,452, 8,517, 8,518, 8,924, 8,937, 8,994, 9,278

agriculture, 8,518, 8,687, 8,693, 9,063, 9,107, 9,154, 9,468
agriculture, cooperative, 8,518
air pollution, 9,209
alcoholism, treatment, 8,984
aliens, **9,481**
Americanization, 9,487
animals, treatment of, 8,474
antisemitism, **9,150**, 9,467
architects, 9,250
architecture, designs and plans, 9,250
architecture, domestic, designs and plans, 9,049
archives, **9,230**
archivists, **9,272**
army wives, 9,041
art, galleries and museums, 8,433, **8,622**
art societies, 8,545, 9,139, 9,525
artists, **8,433**, 8,458, 8,604, **8,990, 9,139**, 9,145, 9,318
assassinations, 9,384
associations, institutions, etc., **9,238**
associations, institutions, etc., Jewish, **8,923**
athletic clubs, **8,570**
attorneys general, 9,416
auditing, **9,480**
audubon societies, **9,216**
authors, 194, **8,428, 8,489, 8,495, 8,600, 9,313**
autopsy, 9,176
bacteriologists, **9,195**
bankers, 8,719, 9,367, 9,401, **9,435**
banks and banking, 8,974
Baptists, **9,070**
bar associations, **8,828, 9,128**, 9,525
beauty culture, **9,483**
beauty operators, **9,483**
beauty queens, 8,476, 8,479
beauty shops, 9,527
beekeeping, 8,456
bills, legislative, 9,232, 9,240, 9,452, 9,467
biographies, 8,493, **8,845, 9,013**
birth control, **8,826**, 9,440
bishops, Episcopal, 9,437, **9,438**
blind, libraries for the, 8,586
blizzards, 9,087
boards of trade, **9,334**, 9,435
boatmen, 9,133
boots and shoes, trade and manufacture, 9,467
botanists, 8,595
Boy Scouts, **8,463**
business, 9,407
businessmen, **8,558**, 8,709, 8,909, **8,943, 9,202, 9,431, 9,435, 9,442**
businesswomen, **9,518**
Camp Fire Girls, **8,490, 8,497**, 8,583
campaigns, political, **8,844**, 9,040
camps, 8,451
capitalists and financiers, **9,055**
carnival, 9,467
cathedrals, 9,022
Catholic schools, 8,425, 9,022, 9,490
Catholic universities and colleges, 9,192, 9,467
   archives, **9,519**
cemeteries, **8,398**
centennial celebrations, 8,767, 8,785, **9,479**
charitable societies, 8,896, **9,166, 9,451, 9,515**
charitable societies, Jewish, **8,906, 9,123, 9,165,** 13,825, 13,826
charitable societies, Scandinavian, **9,182**
charities, 8,481, **8,645, 8,922**, 8,962, 9,140, **9,222, 9,341, 9,351, 9,352, 9,442, 9,460**
charities, Jewish, **9,151**
child care centers, 8,434, 8,836, 9,210, 9,467
child welfare, 8,456, 8,922, 9,015, 9,151, **9,222**
childbirth, 9,467
children
   employment, **8,993**
   hospitals, 8,621
children of immigrants, 9,124
children's clubs, **8,897**
Chinese Americans, 9,390
choirs (music), 8,792, 8,814, **9,338**
Christmas, 9,378
church colleges, **8,817**
church records and registers, **8,938, 9,326**

church records and registers, Baptist, 8,389, **9,070**
church records and registers, Catholic, 8,389
church records and registers, Congregational, 8,389, **9,071, 9,344**
church records and registers, Episcopal, 8,389, **8,901, 8,997, 8,998, 9,093, 9,300, 9,301, 9,329, 9,331, 9,343**
church records and registers, Lutheran, 8,389, **9,271**
church records and registers, Methodist, 8,389, **8,528, 9,072, 9,102, 9,332**
church records and registers, Unitarian, **9,413**
church records and registers, Universalist, **9,406**
church schools, **8,762, 8,864**, 9,413, 9,438
church societies, **8,486**, 8,987, **9,283**, 9,326, **9,406**, 9,448
church societies, Baptist, 9,068, 9,069, **9,070**
church societies, Congregational, **8,951, 9,012**, 9,071, **9,290**, 9,365
church societies, Episcopal, 8,901, **8,997, 8,998**, 9,093, 9,301, 9,331
church societies, Friends, 9,220
church societies, Jewish, **9,218**
church societies, Lutheran, 8,418, 8,731, **8,952, 9,271, 9,405**
church societies, Methodist, 9,072, 9,101, 9,102, 9,332, 9,448
church societies, Presbyterian, **8,487, 9,191, 9,310, 9,432, 9,453, 9,454**
church societies, Unitarian, 9,392, **9,413**
church societies, Universalist, 9,406
church work with women, Catholic Church, 9,491
churches, Congregational, 9,090
churches, Episcopal, 9,120
churches, Lutheran, 8,752
churches, Unitarian, **9,413**
cities and towns, 6,650, **8,470**, 9,354
   civic improvement, 8,481, **8,486, 8,836**, 9,330, 9,347
citizens' associations, 8,630, 8,984, **9,209**, 9,289, **9,342**, 9,435
city attorneys, 8,988
city councilmen, 9,315
civil defense, 9,333, 9,481, **9,486, 9,487**
Civil War, 8,955
clergy, **9,351**
clergy, Baptist, **9,088**
clergy, Congregational, **9,443**
clergy, Episcopal, **9,295, 9,438**
clergy, Methodist, 8,893, **9,246**
clergy, Presbyterian, **8,945, 9,316, 9,317**
clergy, Unitarian, **12,818**
clergymen's wives, **8,432, 8,723, 8,752**
clerks (retail), 8,476, 8,690
clerks of court, 9,369
clinics, 8,645, 8,823, 9,442
clubs, 6,670, 6,700, **8,394, 8,415, 8,416, 8,417, 8,422**, 8,429, **8,431, 8,434, 8,438, 8,445, 8,449, 8,450**, 8,460, 8,476, **8,481**, 8,482, **8,484, 8,488, 8,491, 8,493, 8,504, 8,508, 8,511, 8,562, 8,563**, 8,615, 8,622, 8,696, 8,697, **8,766**, 8,821, **8,825, 8,827, 8,829, 8,832**, 8,833, **8,837**, 8,896, 8,902, 8,919, 8,942, 8,964, 8,972, **9,007, 9,010, 9,027**, 9,080, **9,092**, 9,103, **9,143, 9,144, 9,145, 9,163**, 9,164, **9,188, 9,227, 9,228**, 9,260, **9,267, 9,324**, 9,330, **9,340**, 9,347, 9,349, 9,385, **9,404, 9,455, 9,459**, 9,466, **9,505**, 9,511, **9,516, 9,518**
clubs, Afro-American, **8,898**
coeducation, 8,578
college administrators, **8,395**, 8,544, **8,553**, 8,566, **8,567**
college and school journalism, 8,600, 9,282
college and school periodicals, **8,402**
college librarians, **8,512, 8,564, 8,582, 8,588**, 8,595, **8,604**, 9,467
college presidents, 8,565, **8,851**, 9,077
college registrars, **8,808**
college students, 8,541, 8,601, 8,613, **8,614**, 9,161
   health and hygiene, 8,540
college teachers, **6,835, 8,530, 8,535, 8,538, 8,539**, 8,555, **8,557**, 8,559, 8,575, **8,580**, 8,593, 8,596, **8,597**, 8,603, **8,606**, 8,607, 8,609, **8,611**, 8,617, **8,619**, 8,623, **8,759**, 8,788, **8,805, 8,806, 8,807, 8,809, 8,814, 8,815, 8,913**, 9,052, 9,081, **9,120**, 9,359, 9,467

college trustees, 9,193
communists, 9,467
community centers, 9,104
community churches, **9,275**
community health services, 8,713, 9,467
community health services, Jewish, **8,983**
community leadership, **8,842, 9,275**
community life, 8,518
community organization, **8,486, 8,836, 9,150**
composers, **8,444**, 9,467
concerts, 8,611
congresses and conventions, 8,819, 8,834, 9,061, 9,201, 9,372
congressmen, 9,048, 9,084, 9,155, 9,159, **9,181**, 9,200, 9,225, 9,268, 9,400, **9,421**
congresswomen, **8,397**, 9,040, 9,287, 9,467
conservationists, **9,302**, 9,467
conservatories of music, 8,950
constitution, amendments (proposed), **9,450**
convents and nunneries, Catholic, **8,848**
cooperative societies, **9,136**
county courthouses, 9,258
county officials and employees, 9,304, 9,527
   salaries, allowances, etc., 8,471
cranberries, 9,107
crime and criminals, 9,303
crippled children, institutional care, 8,621
crops, 9,312
cultural relations, 9,467
customs administration, 8,433, 9,205
dairy laws, 8,485
Dakota Indians, 9,371, 9,467
   missions, 9,438
   wars (1862-1865), 9,462
dams, 9,133, 9,464
deaconesses, 8,859
deans (in schools), **6,670, 8,552**, 8,557, **8,594**, 8,721, **8,746**, 9,333
dental hygienists, 9,467
department heads (universities), **8,546, 8,547, 8,611**
department stores, employees, 9,517
diaries and journals, **8,514, 8,516**, 8,937, 9,026, 9,086, 9,099, 9,247, 9,303, **9,461**
   19th C, 7,513, **7,514, 8,895**, 8,945, **9,090**, 9,091, **9,105, 9,207**, 9,294
dieticians, 8,530
dinners and dining, **9,044**
diptheria epidemics, 8,701, 8,709
discrimination in employment, 8,984
disease, 9,312
drug factories, **8,992**
dry-goods, 8,961, 8,982
economic conditions, 9,085
economists, 9,077
editors, 8,566, 8,843, 9,048, **9,434**
education
   curricula, 9,472
   study and teaching, **9,194**
education, bilingual, 9,210
education, rural, 9,442
educational associations, **8,426, 8,485**, 8,492, 8,552, **8,576, 8,819, 8,840, 8,847, 8,902**, 9,392, 9,440, 9,526
educators, **8,102, 8,492**, 8,896
elections, 8,460, 8,706, 9,040, 9,177, 9,197, 9,327, 9,375, 9,386, 9,388
electrification, 8,517
elementary school teachers, **8,841**
emigration and immigration, personal narratives, 9,418
endowments, **8,909**
engineers, 9,074
entertainment, 9,407
Episcopal churches, **9,300, 9,301**
exceptional children, education, 9,467
executive advisory bodies, 8,553, 8,984, **9,237**, 9,276, 9,392, 9,474
executives, 9,401
express highways, public opinion, 9,467
fairs, 8,456, 8,709, 9,154, 9,207, 9,468
family farms, 8,947
family planning, **8,672**
farm life, 8,514, 8,704, 8,978, 9,026
farm management, 1,885

farmers, **8,403, 8,506, 8,961,** 9,155, **9,394**
  political activity, 8,518, 9,278
federations, financial (social service), **9,104**
feminists, **8,495, 9,127**
festivals, **8,479**
Finnish-Americans, **8,455,** 9,462, 9,467, **9,498, 9,500,** 9,502, 9,505
fish inspection, 9,467
fisheries, 9,467
fishing, 8,927, 9,467
folk music, 9,387
food, 9,407
  preservation, 9,467
food adulteration and inspection, 8,486
food prices, 9,138
forest fires, 9,097
forest nurseries, 9,467
forest reserves, **9,397**
foresters, **9,466**
foster home care, 9,351
4-H clubs, 9,469
freedmen, 9,207
Friends, 9,207
Friends, Society of, **9,220, 9,221**
fur trade, 8,709, 9,074
game and game-birds, 9,154
game-laws, 8,456
gardening, societies, etc., **8,390,** 8,481, **8,830**
genealogy, 8,452, **9,527**
genealogy, Native American, 9,296
general stores, 9,467
geologists, 9,448
German-Americans, 8,704
Girl Scouts, **8,463**
girls, societies and clubs, **8,490**
goat breeding, 8,456
governmental investigations, 8,971
governors, 4,322, 8,843, **8,925,** 8,949, 8,971, 9,032, 9,035, 9,187, 9,263, 9,286, 9,287, 9,297, **9,303,** 9,371, 9,467, **9,474, 9,475**
greek letter societies, 8,552, **8,579,** 8,607, **8,612, 9,038**
grocers, 8,941
handbell ringing, **9,488**
handicapped, employment, 9,381
harness making and trade, 8,958
health maintenance organizations, 9,180
health-officers, 8,540
high school students, **9,153**
high school teachers, 8,476, 8,617, 9,367
high schools, records and correspondence, **9,100**
historians, **8,441,** 9,077
historic buildings, conservation and restoration, 9,032, 9,048
historic sites, 8,391, 8,399, 9,435
historical societies, 8,452, 8,458, 8,821, 8,833, **9,032, 9,184, 9,229, 9,230, 9,257,** 9,371, 9,385
holding companies, **8,972**
home economics, study and teaching, 8,547, 8,578, 8,607
hospital administrators, 8,458, 8,518, 8,581
hospital records, **8,529**
hospitals, 8,440, 8,535, 8,581, 8,732, **8,761,** 8,822, 8,862, 9,132, 9,323, 9,467, 9,490
  housing, 9,476
  specifications, 9,476
  staff, 9,476
hospitals, convalescent, 9,273, 9,460
hospitals, gynecologic and obstetric, **9,203**
  laws and legislation, 9,351
hotels, taverns, etc., 8,455, 8,500, 8,957, 9,107, 9,214, 9,467, 9,528
hours of labor, 9,473
housewives, **8,499, 8,501,** 8,518, 8,690, **8,772,** 8,931, **8,979,** 9,005, **9,016,** 9,034, **9,091, 9,314,** 9,421, 9,461, 9,521
housing, 9,196, 9,407
housing, cooperative, 9,136
Hungarian-Americans, 8,906
Icelandic-Americans, 8,518
immigrants, 1,472, 9,013, 9,138, 9,336
immigrants, Bohemian, **8,467**
immigrants, Dutch, 8,518, 9,418
immigrants, English, 9,427

immigrants, Finnish, **9,175,** 9,467, **9,511**
immigrants, German, 8,702, 8,946, 9,063
immigrants, Italian, 9,467
immigrants, Luxembourgian, 9,154
immigrants, Norwegian, 8,690, **8,731, 8,754, 9,263,** 9,467
immigrants, Swedish, **8,977,** 9,118, 9,155, **9,204, 9,322, 9,467**
immigrants, Swiss, **9,359**
Indian agents, 8,940
institution libraries, 8,976
insurance agents, 8,690
insurance companies, employees, 9,488
interracial family, 9,467
interracial marriage, 9,467
Japanese Americans, resettlement and relocation (1941-1945), **9,341**
journalists, **9,157, 9,287, 9,436, 9,522**
judges, 8,941, **8,962,** 8,989, **9,206,** 9,212, 9,242, 9,520
judgments, 9,206
justices of the peace, 9,118
juvenile delinquency, 8,449
juvenile delinquents (female), 9,222
kindergarten, 9,103
kindergarten teachers, 9,202, 9,318
kindergartens, 9,390
labor and laboring classes, 9,462
lampreys, 9,467
land development, 8,406
land settlement, 8,455, 8,517, 8,716, 8,920, 9,063, 9,418, 9,462, 9,467, **9,485,** 14,910
land titles, registration and transfer, 9,076, 9,398, 9,471
laundresses, 9,467
laundries, 8,500
law partnership, 9,525
lawyers, 8,821, **8,893,** 9,074, 9,077, 9,082, **9,083,** 9,181, **9,200, 9,206, 9,263,** 9,367, 9,467, 9,520, **9,525**
legends, 8,921
legislation, 8,922, 9,327
legislative bodies, **9,477**
legislative committees, **9,477,** 9,523
legislators, **6,611, 8,456, 8,688,** 8,719, 8,846, 8,896, 8,971, 9,034, 9,048, 9,052, **9,076,** 9,155, **9,196,** 9,212, 9,237, 9,240, **9,268,** 9,287, **9,327,** 9,367, 9,371, 9,400, 9,452, 9,467, 9,511, **9,522, 9,523, 9,525**
librarians, **8,551, 8,586,** 8,913, **8,976, 9,020, 9,021**
libraries, 8,482
library associations, **9,233**
lieutenant governors, 8,971, 9,035, 9,048, 9,268, 9,287, **9,478**
literary societies, **8,608,** 9,043, **9,171, 9,217, 9,243, 9,255**
Lithuanians, 9,462
liturgical language, English, **8,698, 8,708**
lobbying, 9,467
local church councils, **8,502, 9,305**
log-cabins, 9,214
lumber camps, 9,096, 11,863
lumber industry and trade, 8,974, 9,099, 9,424, **9,433**
lumbering, 9,152, 9,468, **17,587**
lumbermen, **9,076,** 9,096, 9,126
Lutheran Church, education, **8,864**
lynching, 9,467
maple sugar, 9,467
maternity homes, 8,857, 9,424, 9,482
mayors, 9,140, 9,196
medical colleges, 8,822
medical social workers, 8,535, **8,666**
medical teaching personnel, 9,176
medicine, cases, clinical reports, statistics, 8,965, 9,008
Mennonites, 9,063
mental health laws, 9,351
mental health services, 9,467
mentally handicapped
  care and treatment, 9,403
  institutional care, 9,460
mentally handicapped children, care and treatment, 9,490

merchants, 8,719, **9,363**
Mexican Americans, **9,210,** 9,467
military posts, 9,113
mines and mineral resources, 9,467, 9,468
mining corporations, **9,273**
minor drill and tactics, 8,551
minorities, 9,462, 9,467, 9,468
missionaries, **8,926, 9,009,** 9,013, **9,316**
missionaries, Episcopal, 9,042, 9,438
missionaries, Methodist, 8,899, 9,281
missionaries, Presbyterian, **8,945, 9,446**
missionaries, training of, **9,236**
missions, 9,422
monasteries, 8,414
monasticism and religious orders for women, Catholic, **8,425, 8,483, 8,494, 8,839, 8,853,** 9,022, **9,328, 9,490, 9,491**
moving-pictures, censorhsip, 8,486
municipal charters, 8,913, 9,525
municipal officials and employees, 8,476, 8,721, 9,416
  salaries, allowances, etc., 9,196
museum directors, 8,622, 8,929, 9,319
museums, 8,706
music critics, 8,443
music teachers, **8,473,** 8,748, **9,234,** 9,367
musical societies, **8,430,** 8,442, 8,444, **9,234, 9,335, 9,357, 9,488**
Native Americans, 5,457, **8,404,** 8,693, 8,709, 8,929, **9,244,** 9,276, 9,462, 9,468
  education, **8,705**
  history, 8,518
  missions, **9,009,** 9,042, 9,316, **9,446**
  music, 9,467
  reservations, **8,927,** 9,467
  social life and customs, **9,467**
  trading posts, 8,927
  wars, 8,515, 8,718, 9,085, 9,355, 9,419
natural history museums, **8,592**
newsletters, 8,402, 9,130, 9,205
newspaper publishing, 9,157
newspapers, 8,429, 9,287, 9,436
  sections, columns, etc., 2,768, 6,614, 8,443
Norwegian-Americans, 8,994
nuns, Catholic, 8,705, **8,851, 8,853, 8,854,** 9,323, **9,328,** 9,467
nurses, **8,440,** 8,690, 8,823, 9,467
nurses aides, 8,706
nursing audit, 9,484
nursing schools, 8,440, 8,529, 8,547, 8,553, **8,610, 8,818,** 8,822
nursing standards, 8,818
nursing students, 8,584, 8,648
nursing, study and teaching, 9,467
nutrition extension work, 8,575
obstetrics, cases, clinical reports, statistics, 9,064, 9,176, 9,178
officials and employees, 8,586, **8,685, 9,195,** 9,204, 9,319, 9,468
Ojibwe Indians, 8,399, 8,927, 8,940, **9,237**
  land transfers, 9,296
  legal status, laws, etc., 9,296
  missions, 8,926, 9,438
  reservations, 9,296
old age homes, **9,190,** 9,460
oral history, 8,480, **8,517, 8,518,** 8,690, **8,691, 8,692,** 8,701, **8,702, 8,709,** 8,717, 8,956, **9,115, 9,304,** 9,467
ordinance, municipal, 8,129
ornithologists, 9,319
orphans and orphan asylums, **8,930, 9,339,** 9,490, 9,527
pacifists, 9,467
pardon, **9,470**
parents and teachers associations, **8,917, 9,223,** 9,287, 9,385, **9,458**
parks, 8,460
parsonages, 8,752
party committees, **9,239**
patriotic societies, **8,419, 8,453, 8,496, 8,820, 8,907, 9,029, 9,030, 9,031, 9,167, 9,258, 9,337,** 9,385, **9,409**
peace societies, **9,235,** 9,402, **9,456,** 9,467, 15,316
performing arts, 9,468

pharmacists, 8,721, **9,428**
photograph collections, **8,411, 8,476, 9,468**
physical education and training, 8,547
physicians, **8,396,** 8,465, 8,477, 8,518, **8,707,** 8,721, **8,822, 8,965, 8,991,** 9,008, 9,064, 9,082, **9,132, 9,176, 9,178,** 9,203, 9,318, **9,319, 9,323,** 9,359, 9,364
pilots and pilotage, 9,126
pioneers and settlers, **8,406, 8,454, 8,472, 8,482,** 8,515, 8,518, 8,703, 8,709, **8,729, 8,731, 8,783, 8,895,** 8,900, 8,924, **8,939, 8,958, 8,967,** 8,981, **8,982, 9,000,** 9,013, 9,042, **9,065,** 9,066, 9,087, **9,090,** 9,099, 9,122, 9,141, **9,152, 9,154, 9,172, 9,173, 9,183, 9,214, 9,238,** 9,245, 9,249, **9,269,** 9,272, 9,285, **9,294, 9,312,** 9,317, 9,369, 9,378, **9,393, 9,412, 9,418,** 9,419, 9,463, 9,468, **9,524, 9,528, 13,697**
poetry, **8,477**
poets, 9,043, **9,171**
policewomen, 9,252, **9,299**
policewomen, Afro-American, 9,467
poliomyelitis nursing, **8,621**
political activists, women, **2,589, 8,912,** 9,046, **9,084, 9,127, 9,189, 9,276,** 9,392, 9,396, 9,443, 9,467
political clubs, **8,844,** 9,040, **9,129,** 9,232, **9,291, 9,306,** 9,375, 9,396, 9,400
political parties, **9,039, 9,040,** 9,107, 9,467
politics and government, 8,485, 8,493, 8,910, 8,949, 9,149, 9,467, 9,468
politics, practical, women's activism, 6,942, **8,435,** 8,485, 8,493, 8,696, 8,984, 8,991, 9,197, **9,231**
portrait painters, **2,768**
postal service, 9,152
   employees 9,279
postmasters, 9,118
poultry sexing, 8,509
Presbyterian church
   government, 9,453
   missions, **9,454**
priories, **9,489**
prisons, 9,303
private schools, 8,988
public comfort stations, 8,481
public health, 8,572, 8,836, 8,991
public health nursing, 8,648, **8,713,** 9,385
public health officers, 9,008
public health personnel, 8,991
public institutions, auditing and inspection, 9,480
public libraries, 9,205, 9,360
public records, **8,389,** 9,462
public schools, 9,390
   employees, 8,113
public welfare, 8,535, 8,638, 9,462
public works, 8,518, **9,462, 9,463**
publishers and publishing, **8,459**
race discrimination, 9,467
race problems, 8,693, 9,467
radio stations, 9,467
railroads
   construction, 9,419
   employees, 8,518, 9,034, 9,467
real estate agents, 9,427, 9,876
real estate investment, 9,138
real property, 9,424
recreation centers, 9,460
reformatories (female), 9,482
rehabilitation, 9,381
rehabilitation centers, 8,503
religion in the public schools, 9,065
religious education, Jewish, 13,813
relocation (housing), 9,114
reporters and reporting, 8,956, **9,046, 9,415**
research, industrial, 9,349
researchers, **9,125**
resorts, 9,460
retired teachers, **8,687**
rural schools, **8,423**
sauna, 9,467
scholarships, 8,481, 8,625, 9,254
school boards, 9,291, 9,467
school districts, 8,920, 9,208, 9,388
school hygiene, 8,695

school music, 8,505
school superintendents and principals, **8,409,** 8,482, **8,712,** 8,995, 9,422
school supervisors, **9,387**
schools, **8,400,** 8,946, 9,154, 9,273, 9,288, 9,295, 9,317, 9,373, 9,377, 9,442, 9,465
   centralization, 8,517
   finance, 9,196
   records and correspondence, 9,472
scrapbooks, 8,477, **8,478,** 8,568, **8,577,** 9,382
secret societies, 8,469, 8,517, 9,467
secretaries, 8,821
secretaries of state, **8,928,** 9,204
sedition, 9,380
self-government (in education), **8,569, 8,585, 8,616**
self-government (in higher education), **8,625**
senators, United States, **8,895,** 8,949, **9,140,** 9,155, **9,160, 9,193,** 9,211, **9,263,** 9,286, 9,297, 9,303, **9,311, 9,368**
servants, Afro-American, 9,303
sex discrimination in education, **8,549**
sextons, 8,398
single mothers, 9,222
Siouan Indians, wars, 8,720, 8,967, 9,042, **9,056,** 9,245, 9,285
social life and customs, 8,568, **8,700,** 8,957, 8,969, 8,981, 8,982, 8,987, 9,085, 9,101, **9,156,** 9,207, 9,303, **9,366,** 9,436, 9,462, 9,467, 9,521, 17,375
social problems, 9,095
social service exchanges, **8,676**
social settlements, **9,058, 9,094,** 9,095, **9,114,** 9,252, **9,261, 9,270,** 9,467
social settlements, Afro-American, **9,289**
social work administration, 8,638
social workers, 8,654, **9,095,** 9,392, **9,403,** 9,427, 9,467
socialist parties, 9,175, **9,379, 9,380**
socialists, **9,177**
societies, **9,256**
societies, Finnish-American, **9,500**
societies, Jewish, **9,109, 9,110, 9,253,** 9,467, **13,813**
societies, Norwegian-American, **8,767**
soldiers, Civil War, 8,955, 8,958
Spanish-American War, societies, **9,409**
Spanish language, study and teaching, 9,092
state departments of education, **9,472**
state universities and colleges, 9,282
   archives, **9,526**
street-railroads, 9,467
strikes and lockouts, 8,113
   miners, 8,144
   teachers, 8,129, 9,467
   transport workers, 9,467
student counselors, 8,573
student housing, 8,615
student unions, 8,616
students, interchange of, 8,481
students' societies, **8,570, 8,598,** 8,599, **8,624,** 8,809, **8,813,** 14,029
suffrage, 1,652, 8,518, 9,054, 9,061, 9,327, 9,427, 9,468
   legal aspects, 9,320, 9,450, 9,452
   opposition to, **9,215**
suffrage societies, 8,831, 8,896, 9,061, 9,147, **9,225, 9,240, 9,291, 9,292**
suffragists, 2,147, 9,013, **9,142**
Sunday-school conventions, 9,429
Sunday-school teachers, 9,116, **9,298**
Sunday-schools, 9,102, 9,103, 9,220, 9,283, 9,332, **9,429**
surveying, 9,207
Swedish-Americans, 8,690
symphony orchestra societies, **8,505**
symphony orchestras, 9,101
synagogues, **9,251**
taconite, environmental aspects, 9,467
tailors, **9,105**
taxation, 9,006
   law, **9,381**
teachers, **6,611, 8,403,** 8,405, 8,407, **8,497, 8,498, 8,507, 8,510, 8,517,** 8,518, **8,695, 8,710,** 8,712, **8,718, 8,764,** 8,893, 8,941, 8,955, 8,969, 8,980, 8,992, 9,013, 9,034, **9,038, 9,097,** 9,161, **9,265,** 9,282, **9,288,** 9,304, **9,394,** 9,421

legal status, laws, etc., 8,129, 9,467
   salaries, pensions, etc., 9,196
   tenure, 8,059
teachers, Native American, 8,690
teachers' colleges, 8,498
teachers' unions, **8,059,** 8,129, **9,224, 9,298, 9,467,** 16,496
teachers' wives, **8,504**
technical education, 9,055
telegraphers, **8,461**
telephone operators, **9,079**
temperance societies, **8,420, 8,448, 8,816, 8,834,** 8,896, **8,985,** 9,294, 9,295, **9,353,** 9,467
text-books, 8,452
theater management, **9,361**
theatrical producers and directors, 9,175
theological seminaries, 9,438
threshing, 8,690
tobogganing, 9,467
trade and professional associations, **8,437, 8,439,** 8,610, **8,648, 8,666, 9,226**
trade-unions, **8,984, 9,054,** 9,467, 9,468, 9,473
   auxiliaries, **8,842**
   clerks, **9,309**
   clothing workers, **9,408**
   officials and employees, **8,129,** 9,415, 9,467
   restaurants, lunch rooms, etc., 9,467
translators, 9,175
transportation, 8,701
trapping, 8,456
travelers aid societies, **8,680**
trials (murder), 9,303
trust companies, 8,954
tuberculosis, hospitals and sanitoriums, 8,518
Unitarians, 9,282
United Methodist Church, government, **8,528**
universities and colleges, 6,670, 8,492, 8,542, **8,548,** 8,609, 8,740, 8,822, 9,287, 9,371, 9,468
   alumnae, 8,533, 8,534, 8,537, 8,542, 8,543, 8,556, 8,560, 8,600, **9,430**
   buildings, 8,533, 8,558, 8,602, 8,605
   employees, 8,550, 8,602
   faculty, 8,536, 8,554, **8,561, 8,562, 8,563,** 8,572, 8,573, 8,582, 8,592, **8,606, 8,618,** 8,620, 8,622
veterans, 9,059
vocalists, 9,346
voluntary health organizations, 9,385
volunteer workers in social service, **8,503,** 8,583, **8,682**
voters, registration of, 8,913
wages, minimum wage, 9,473
wagons, 8,455
war relief, 8,486
war work, **8,835**
water resources development, 9,464
Welsh, 9,344
wet-nurses, 9,351
widows, **9,107**
wild rice, 8,927
wildlife refuges, **8,973**
wills, 9,206
women
   education, 9,467
   employment, 9,467, 9,487
   status, **8,532**
women's centers and networks, **8,587**
women's colleges, archives, **9,519**
women's studies, 8,501
workmen's compensation, 9,473
World War I, civilians work, **8,447, 9,487**
World War II
   civilians work, 3,950, 9,226
   finance, **9,130**
   prisons and prisoners, 8,690
Young Men's Christian Association, 9,273
Young Women's Christian Association, **8,513,** 8,552, 8,578, **8,627, 8,628, 8,629,** 9,273, **9,465,** 9,467
Minnesota Accredited Schools of Nursing, 8,610
Minnesota Agricultural Agent and Extension Service, **9,469**
Minnesota Anti-Saloon League, 8,896

Minnesota Association of Deans of Women, 8,594, 8,746
Minnesota Association of School Librarians. *See* Minnesota Educational Media Organization
Minnesota Bar Association, 8,828
Minnesota Birth Control League, 9,392, 9,440
Minnesota Birth Control League. *See* Planned Parenthood of Minnesota
"Minnesota Blizzard." *See* Blaisdell, Marie [Mrs. M. J.] (1846-1918)
Minnesota Board of Nursing, 8,818, 9,115
Minnesota Board of Pardons, **9,470**
Minnesota Committee for a Sane Nuclear Policy, 9,127
Minnesota Congress of Parents and Teachers, Eighth District, **9,223**
Minnesota Conservation and Agricultural Development Congress, 9,201
Minnesota Council for the Legal Termination of Pregnancy Inc. *See* Minnesota Organization for the Repeal of Abortion Laws (MORAL)
Minnesota Council of Indian Affairs, 9,392
Minnesota Daily (MN), 9,287
Minnesota Democratic-Farmer-Labor party, 8,603
Minnesota Democratic-Farmer-Labor Women's Study Club (MN), 9,375
Minnesota Department of Conservation, State Land Office, **9,471**
Minnesota Department of Education, **9,472**
Minnesota Department of Labor and Industry, **9,473**
Minnesota Department of Labor and Industry, Bureau of Women and Children, 9,473
Minnesota Department of Public Welfare, officials and employees, 9,403
Minnesota District of the American Association of Hospital Social Workers. *See* National Association of Social Workers, Southern Minnesota Chapter, Medical Social Work Section
Minnesota District of the American Association of Medical Social Workers. *See* National Association of Social Workers, Southern Minnesota Chapter, Medical Social Work Section
Minnesota Education Association, **9,224**, 9,467, 9,526
Minnesota Educational Media Organization, **8,847**
Minnesota Emergency Relief Administration, 9,336
Minnesota Equal Franchise League, **9,225**
Minnesota Fair Employment Practice Commission, 8,984
Minnesota Farmer-Labor Party, 9,386
Minnesota Federation of Business and Professional Women's Clubs, Inc., **9,226**
Minnesota Federation of Women, 8,438
Minnesota Federation of Women's Clubs, 6,670, 8,825, 8,942, 9,080, **9,227**, 9,349, 9,397, 9,455
Minnesota Federation of Women's Clubs, Fifth District, **9,228**
Minnesota Feminists, 8,587
Minnesota Finnish American Historical Society, 9,502
Minnesota Forest Fires Relief Committee, 9,252
Minnesota Geological and Natural History Survey, 8,592
Minnesota, Governor's Commission on the Status of Women, 8,553
Minnesota Governor's Human Rights Commission (1962), 8,929
Minnesota Health Department, Division of Hospital Services, **9,476**
Minnesota Historical Society, 8,441, 8,929, 9,125, **9,229**, 9,251, 9,371, 9,414
Minnesota Historical Society Archives, **9,230**
Minnesota History, 9,125
Minnesota Home for Girls, 9,480
Minnesota Home School for Girls, 9,482
Minnesota House of Representatives, committees, **9,477**
Minnesota House of Representatives, officials and employees, 9,252
Minnesota Leader, 9,386, 9,400
Minnesota League for Nursing, 8,553
Minnesota League for Planned Parenthood, 9,440
Minnesota League of Nursing Service, 8,610
Minnesota Leif Erikson Monument Association, 8,767
Minnesota Library Association, **9,233**
Minnesota May Fete (1911), 8,599, 8,614

"Minnesota Memo to Women" (newsletter), 9,130
Minnesota Mental Hygiene Society, 9,392
Minnesota Mother of the Year, 8,421
Minnesota Mother's Committee, 9,385
Minnesota Music Teachers' Association, Inc., **9,234**
Minnesota Mutual Life Belles, **9,488**
Minnesota Mutual Life Insurance Company, 9,488
Minnesota Negro Council News and Reviews (periodical), 9,252
Minnesota Office of Civilian Defense, 9,333
Minnesota, Office of Civilian Defense, War History Committee, **9,486**
Minnesota Organization for the Repeal of Abortion Laws (MORAL), **8,630**
Minnesota Peace Action Coalition, 9,127
Minnesota Peace Society, **9,235**
Minnesota Plan, 8,587
Minnesota Public Examiner, **9,480**
Minnesota Public Safety Commission, 8,971, **9,481**
Minnesota Registered Nurse, The, 9,132
Minnesota Republican Task Forces, 9,189
Minnesota River, 9,117
Minnesota Save the Children Federation, 9,150
Minnesota School of Missions, **9,236**
Minnesota Seaside Station (Port Renfrew, BC), **9,237**
Minnesota Skyline, 8,600
Minnesota State Advisory Council on Indian Affairs, **9,237**
Minnesota State Board of Control, 8,685, **9,482**
Minnesota State Board of Cosmetology, **9,483**
Minnesota State Board of Examiners of Nurses, **9,484**
Minnesota State Department of Health, division of child hygiene, officials and employees, **8,540**
Minnesota State Department of Public Welfare, officials and employees, 8,535
Minnesota State Emergency Relief Administration, 8,638
Minnesota State Emergency Relief Administration, officials and employees, 8,575, 8,685
Minnesota State Public Library Commission, 9,021
Minnesota State Reform School (St. Paul, MN), 9,317
Minnesota State Teachers College Board, 9,127
Minnesota Statehood Centennial Commission, Women's Committee, **9,479**
Minnesota Supreme Court, 9,242
Minnesota Territorial Pioneer Guild. *See* Minnesota Territorial Pioneers Association
Minnesota Territorial Pioneers Association, 8,953, **9,238**
Minnesota Territory
clergy, Baptist, **9,088**
governors, 9,303
immigrants, German, **9,355**
physicians, **9,423**
pioneers and settlers, **9,366**, **9,370**, 11,520
Minnesota Unitarian Conference, 9,413
Minnesota Unitarian Service Committee, 9,392
Minnesota Valley Community Day Care Center, 8,485
Minnesota Volunteers for Stevenson-Kefauver (Minneapolis, MN), **9,239**
Minnesota White Ribboner, 9,386
Minnesota Woman Suffrage Association, 8,896, **9,240**, 9,291
Minnesota Women for Humphrey, 9,140
Minnesota Women's Reformatory, 9,480
Minnesota Writers (book), 8,600, 9,313
Minns, Susan (1840-1938), 7,666
Minns Wildlife Reservation (MA), 7,666
Minor drill and tactics, 8,551
Minor Hospital, nursing school (Seattle, WA), alumnae, **17,224**
Minor, Julia, **11,000**
Minor, Kate L., 12,034
Minor, Louella (1861-1935), **17,307**
Minor, Mary J., 16,097, **16,105**
Minor, Nellie, 9,467
Minor, Susan St. Clair [Mrs.], **5,384**
Minorities, 168, 203, 365, 496, 592, **968**, 1,428, 1,559, 3,724, 3,851, 6,468, 7,729, 7,889, 8,549, 8,603, 9,462, 9,467, 9,468, 15,209, 16,334, 17,018, **17,507**. *See also* Discrimination
civil rights, 1,012, 7,242, 7,262, 12,473, **12,682**, 17,238

education, 5,457, 11,910
Minott Family (OR), 14,556
Minstrels, 9,841
Minthorn, Matilda [Mrs. J. H.], 5,120, 5,122
Minto, Grace, 3,506
Minto, John, 14,549
Minto, Martha Ann (Morrison) (1832?-?), **671**
Minton Family, 3,896
Mints, 5,434
Minturn, Alice, 12,242
Mintzer, Ethel, 6,544
Minute Men of the Rockies (book), 1,750
Minute Women of America, Inc., 9,150
Miracle at Philadelphia: The Story of the Constitutional Convention, May to September, 1787 (book), 2,219
Miracle in Hellas: The Greeks Fight On (book), 2,622
Miracle, Marilyn, 564
Miracle Worker, The (moving-picture), 2,108
"Mirah's Legacy" (ms), 3,421
Miraj Medical Center (India), 14,425
Miramova, Elena, **2,487**
Mirrielees, Edith Ronald, **1,550**
"Mirror, The," 15,940
Mischko (book), 17,478
Misconduct in office, 197
Mises, Hilda (Geiringer) [Mrs. Richard von] (1893-1973), **6,295**
Mises, Richard von (1883-1953), 6,295
Misprision, 3,620
Miss America, 8,479
Miss America Pageant, 11,897, 17,583
Miss Bates' School (SC), 15,649
Miss Beecher's Domestic Receipt-Book, 3,221
Miss Bucknall's Seminary (NJ), 11,026
Miss Chicago Urban League contest, 4,073
Miss Churchill's School (Richfield Springs, NY), 9,023
Miss Cushing's School (MA), 2,188
Miss de Choiseuls' School (NC), 15,477
Miss Dutton's School (Grove Hall, CT), 2,003
Miss Grant's Private School (Chicago, IL). *See* Grant Collegiate Institute (Chicago, IL)
Miss Hopkins (MN), 8,479
Miss Indian America, 16,873
Miss Ireland's School (MA), 6,563
Miss Isabella's School (SC). *See* Columbia High School for Young Ladies and Little Girls (SC)
Miss Jennie Lee's School (NY), 11,785
Miss Jewell's School (Shanghai, China), 1,571
Miss Kelley's School (Charleston, SC). *See* Charleston Female Seminary (SC)
Miss Kendrick's School for Girls (Cincinnati, OH), students, 5,310
Miss Lulu Bett (book), 17,634
Miss Mercer's Academy (West River, MD), 5,752, 5,757
Miss Minnesota, 8,479
Miss Morgan's school (NH), 5,588
Miss Orton, Private School for Girls (CA), 1,104
Miss Pierce's Academy (Litchfield, CT), 1,970
Miss Pierce's School (Litchfield, CT), 1,901
Miss Pittsburg State Contest (KS), 5,207
Miss Porter's School (Farmington, CT), **1,836**, 12,759
students, 2,345, 5,302
Miss Porter's School (Farmington, CT), Lodge Society, 1,836
Miss Porter's School (Farmington, CT), Sewing Society, 1,836
"Miss Quote" (column), 9,599
Miss Ransom and Miss Bridges School, 11,925
Miss Ransom and Miss Bridges School for Girls (Piedmont, CA), 843
"Miss Sally" (drama), 12,959
Miss Santa Clara beauty contest, 1,534
Miss Sarah Pierce School (CT), 12,389
Miss Sheldon's School (Buffalo, NY), 12,759
Miss Snow's Boarding School for Young Ladies (NY), 12,088
Miss Spafard's School (Philadelphia, PA), 11,602
Miss Spence's School for Girls, 9,346
Miss U.S.A. Pageant, 15,807

Miss Wayland's School (Saratoga Springs, NY), 12,853
Miss Wheelock's Kindergarten Training School (MA), 11,842
Missemma (newspaper), 3,264
Misses Bates' Seminary (SC), **15,503**
Misses Hall School, Alumnae Association (Baltimore, MD), **5,792**
Misses Nichols' School (NY), **12,831**
Misses Skinner School (NC), 13,438
Missing persons, **11,991**
Missing Tidings (periodical), 3,962
Mission Band, Nebraska Branch of the Woman's Missionary Society of the Evangelical Church, **10,572**
Mission Band, Winslow (NE), **10,573**
Mission Dolores (CA), 346
Mission Helpers of the Sacred Heart (Baltimore, MD), **5,830**
Mission Indian Villages (book), 991
Mission Institute (Quincy, IL), 8,899
Mission Kindergarten (GA), 3,137
Mission Neighborhood Centers, Inc. (San Francisco, CA), 501
Mission San Jose (CA), 770
Mission schools, Methodist, 14,396
Mission to Colored Refugees and Children's Home (KS), 5,713
Mission to lepers, 13,291
Missionaries, 44, **45**, **87**, **185**, 292, **313**, **409**, **421**, **555**, 580, **866**, **880**, 1,224, 1,243, 1,428, 1,459, 1,476, **1,498**, **1,504**, **1,571**, 1,652, **1,755**, 1,786, 1,790, 1,822, **1,846**, **1,861**, 2,002, **2,011**, **2,012**, **2,013**, **2,014**, **2,015**, **2,016**, 2,178, **2,261**, 2,304, 2,394, **2,427**, 3,373, **3,464**, 3,619, **3,642**, **3,645**, **3,649**, **3,706**, **3,723**, **3,777**, 3,969, **4,271**, **4,518**, 4,532, **4,536**, **4,538**, **4,597**, **4,599**, 5,187, **5,457**, **6,313**, 6,388, **6,424**, 6,651, 6,652, 6,833, **6,862**, 6,868, **6,875**, **7,129**, 7,191, **7,279**, **7,280**, **7,375**, **7,407**, **7,497**, 7,498, **7,511**, **7,597**, **7,776**, **7,931**, 7,932, **8,198**, **8,199**, **8,203**, 8,366, **8,464**, 8,849, **8,926**, **8,996**, 9,013, 9,185, 9,294, 9,467, 9,543, 9,597, 9,710, 9,782, 10,037, **10,545**, **10,942**, 11,249, 11,260, 11,440, 11,471, **11,640**, **11,846**, 12,540, 12,674, **12,726**, 12,776, **12,826**, 13,121, 13,278, **13,279**, 13,298, 13,610, **13,622**, 13,799, 13,949, 13,951, 13,991, **14,089**, **14,119**, 14,126, **14,129**, **14,243**, **14,334**, **14,355**, 14,397, 14,435, **14,441**, **14,508**, **14,510**, **14,528**, **14,550**, 14,581, **14,604**, **14,650**, **14,667**, **14,715**, 14,844, **14,877**, **14,992**, 15,139, 15,531, 15,550, **15,910**, **16,597**, **16,651**, 16,741, 16,755, 16,915, 17,167, 17,188, 17,189, **17,212**, **17,213**, **17,307**, 17,344, 17,404, 17,419, **17,421**, **17,423**, **17,429**, **17,451**, 17,498, 17,653, 17,908, **17,923**. *See also under names of denominations*
Missionaries, Afro-American, **86**, **15,905**
Missionaries, Coptic, 12,439
Missionaries, domestic, **9,316**, 10,045, 17,315, **17,402**, **17,410**
Missionaries, lay, 4,319, 4,541, **5,300**, **15,669**, **17,309**
Missionaries, medical, **1,840**, **2,010**, **3,958**, **7,231**, 7,293, **8,886**, **9,159**, 10,926, 11,754, **14,425**, **14,442**, **16,367**
Missionaries, Protestant, **3,636**, **3,637**, **3,638**, 3,643, **3,646**, 8,164, **11,289**
Missionaries, training of, **4,201**, **9,236**, 13,641, 16,364
Missionaries wives, **580**, **796**, 2,178, 2,190, 7,678, 8,858, **9,991**, 12,185, **14,389**
Missionary Benedictine Sisters (NE), 10,611
Missionary Benedictine Sisters Motherhouse (Norfolk, NE), **10,610**
Missionary Catechists of Divine Providence, St. Andrew's Convent (San Antonio, TX), **16,319**
Missionary Federation of Muskogee (OK), 14,208
Missionary Herald (periodical), 5,234
Missionary Herald, The (periodical), 2,271
Missionary Medical School for Women (Vellore, India), 3,958
Missionary Monthly (periodical), 4,597
Missionary Servants of the Most Blessed Trinity, 15,146
Missionary Servants of the Most Holy Trinity, 15,146

Missionary Sisters of the Immaculate Conception of the Mother of God (Paterson, NJ), **11,147**
Missionary Sisters of the Most Sacred Heart of Jesus (PA), St. Michael Convent, **15,264**
Missionary Sisters of the Precious Blood Convent (Shillington, PA), **15,267**
Missionary Society of The Dalles (OR), 751
Missionary Society of the Mississippi Conference, Methodist Episcopal Church, 9,750
Missions, 202, 331, **392**, 446, 576, 751, 780, 1,222, 1,384, 1,505, 4,509, 4,596, 4,848, 5,251, 5,300, **5,456**, 6,609, 7,129, 8,837, **8,903**, 9,422, **10,972**, 11,709, 11,750, 11,932, 13,230, 13,980, 14,208, 14,498, 14,846, 15,880, **16,610**, 17,167, **17,219**, 17,301. *See also under names of denominations*
educational work, 1,168, 14,225
finance, **1,904**, 5,604, 7,080, **13,865**
study and teaching, 1,843, 1,849, 1,858
Missions, medical, 409, **6,397**, **6,875**, 8,202, 9,081, 9,425, 10,580
Mississippi, 6,087, 9,551, **9,578**, 9,622, 9,638, 9,688, **9,699**, 9,719, 9,720, 9,799, 9,807, 9,816, 13,046
abortion, legal aspects, 1,984
Afro-Americans, 9,575, 17,600
agricultural administration, 17,714
agricultural colleges, 9,712
agriculture
accounting, 9,787
experimentation, 9,625
air bases, 9,587
archives, 9,739
archivists, **9,599**, 9,634, 9,673
art societies, 9,646
artists, 9,646, 9,694
authors, **9,551**, **9,552**, **9,567**, 9,585, 9,656, 9,694, 9,699, **9,719**, **9,738**, **9,744**, **9,745**, **9,763**, **9,768**, **9,769**, **9,770**
bibliography, 9,746
autograph albums, **9,789**
baccalaureate addresses, **9,563**
Baptists, 5,420, **9,553**
bishops, 9,695
boards of trade, 9,622
businessmen, Afro-American, **2,490**
catalogs, college, **9,555**, **9,576**
charitable societies, Jewish, **13,821**
child care centers, 9,542
Chinese-Americans, 9,550
Choctaw Indians, 2,883, 9,695
church historians, 9,596
church records and registers, 9,728
church records and registers, Baptist, 9,553
church records and registers, Methodist, **9,704**, 9,750
church schools, 5,713, 9,597
church societies, **9,704**, **9,723**, 9,750
church societies, Baptist, **9,659**, 9,811
church societies, Presbyterian, **9,660**
churches, Baptist, 9,697
churches, Episcopal, 9,596, 9,606, **9,649**, 9,706, 9,709
citizens' associations, 3,283
civil engineers, **9,804**
civil rights workers, 9,694, 15,880, **17,599**, **17,600**, **17,714**, 17,726
Civil War, 9,596, 9,751
campaigns and battles, 3,315, 9,586, 9,613, 9,754, 13,123
destruction and pillage, 9,589
personal narratives, **9,584**, 9,586
societies, Confederate, 9,595, **9,615**, 9,644, 9,657, 9,669, 9,719, 9,740, **9,756**, **9,757**, **9,758**, **9,808**
clergy, 9,634
clergy, Baptist, 9,697
clergy, Episcopal, **9,790**
clergy, Methodist, **9,531**, 9,610, 12,941
clergy, Presbyterian, 9,728, 9,801
clubs, **9,536**, **9,540**, **9,541**, 9,551, 9,644, 9,667, **9,673**, **9,681**, **9,682**, **9,689**, **9,691**, 9,708, 9,750, **9,776**, **9,777**, 9,801, **9,805**, 9,811, 9,819, **9,822**
coeducation, 9,699, 9,809
college and school journalism, **9,557**, **9,570**
college librarians, 9,712, 9,803
college presidents, 9,558, 9,610, 9,671, 12,941

college students, 9,569
college teachers, 9,569, 9,610, 9,650
college trustees, 9,785
composers, 5,413
congressmen, 2,638, 9,733
county government, records and correspondence, **9,532**
court records, 9,739
deans (in schools), **9,610**, 9,809
deeds, 9,815
dental hygiene, 1,061
diaries and journals, **9,548**, 9,574, **9,584**, 9,586, 9,588, 9,591, **9,595**, 9,609, **9,743**, 9,796, **9,800**, 9,819, **12,946**
divorce, 9,532
editors, **9,709**, 9,768
education, 9,538, 9,662
educational associations, **9,554**
educators, **9,583**, 9,673
farm management, records and correspondence, 9,538
farmers, **5,420**, 9,582, 9,592, 9,614, **9,760**, 9,803
floods, 3,302, 9,551, 9,694
folk medicine, 9,542
folk music, **9,585**
4-H clubs, 9,708
freedmen, 6,650, 9,717
French in, 9,603
gardening societies, **9,529**, **9,533**, **9,813**
genealogists, **9,697**
genealogy, 9,656, 9,762, 9,816
Girl Scouts, 9,711
governesses, 13,047
government librarians, 9,694
governors, 7,178, **9,582**, 9,629, 9,653, 9,663, 9,688
hardware stores, **9,537**
high school teachers, **9,636**, **9,724**
high schools, 9,542, 9,636, 9,672, 9,724
historians, 9,671, **9,672**, **9,719**
historic buildings, 9,680
historic sites, conservation and restoration, 9,813
historical societies, **9,574**, 9,599, 9,672, 9,781
home demonstration work, 9,530
home economics extension work, 9,708
home economists, **9,788**
hookworm disease, 239
hospital administrators, 246
hospitals, 9,599, 9,697
hotels, taverns, etc., 9,686, 9,691, 9,694
hurricanes, 9,694
illiteracy, 9,532
immigrants, Dalmatian, 9,694
job placement, 9,662
journalists, **9,550**
judges, **9,546**, **9,658**
junior colleges, 9,664, 9,672
administration, **9,671**
faculty, **9,664**
labor contract, 9,717
land grants, 9,539, 9,729
land titles, 9,618, 9,725
law, cases, 9,668
lawyers, **9,544**, **9,647**, 9,658, 9,711, 9,747, 13,176
legislators, 6,901, **9,544**, **9,546**, 9,547, 9,550, 9,552, 9,647, **9,656**, 9,697, **9,734**, **9,779**, 9,804, 9,806
librarians, **9,539**, 9,781
libraries, 9,804
lieutenant governors, 9,585
lumbering, 9,694
lynching, prevention of, 3,279
marriage licenses, **9,784**
mayors, 9,686
memorials, 9,657
midwives, 9,542, **9,820**
monasticism and religious orders for women, Catholic, **9,695**
museums, 9,587, 9,599
Native Americans, missions, 9,782
newspapers, 9,631, 9,641, 9,656, 9,686, 9,709, 9,756, 9,768
sections, columns, etc., 9,550, 9,599
novelists, **5,413**
nuns, Catholic, 9,542
officials and employees, 9,643, 9,647, 9,694

oral history, **9,542, 9,694, 9,820**
pageants, 9,610, 9,648
patriotic societies, 9,596, **9,608, 9,616,** 9,622, 9,638, **9,690,** 9,692, 9,697, 9,731, 9,740, **9,791, 9,816**
pellagra, 239
pensions, 9,816
periodicals, 9,720
photograph collections, **9,540, 9,699**
photography, negatives, **9,535**
physical education teachers, **9,568**
physicians, 9,803, 13,047
peace societies, 15,316
pioneers and settlers, **9,597,** 9,731, **9,797**
plantation life, 9,675, **9,800,** 12,946, 12,955, 13,173
plantations, 3,341, 9,534, 9,588, 9,610, 9,614, 9,625, 9,675, 9,693, 9,701, 9,702, 9,729, 9,760, 9,774, 9,781, 9,794, 17,502
poets, **5,413,** 9,720
political parties, 9,613
politics, practical, women's activism, **9,818**
poultry, 3,161
prisons, 9,613
private schools, 9,641
property tax, 9,795
psychiatric hospitals, 9,643
public libraries, 9,530
public officers, 9,818
public records, **9,739**
public works, 9,688
quilts, **9,732**
rabbis, 13,803
race problems, 16,780
Reconstruction, 9,747, 15,574
reporters and reporting, 9,599
Revolutionary War, registers, lists, etc., 9,816
rural schools, 9,570, 9,628
school boards, 9,711
school superintendents and principals, 9,662
school yearbooks, **9,561, 9,577**
schools, 9,648, 9,687, 9,696, **9,817**
scientists, **9,625**
scrapbooks, **9,569,** 9,611, 9,773
sculptors, **9,735**
seafood processing, 9,694
secret societies, 9,803
segregation in higher education, 9,575
senators, United States, **2,230, 2,638, 9,582**
senators, United States, Afro-American, 1,655, **2,230**
servants, 9,701, 9,702
sharecroppers, Afro-American, 16,780
Sherman's March, 9,621
singers, **9,742**
slave records, 9,656, 9,781
slave trade, 9,803
slavery, 9,641, 11,602
slaves, 9,781
social life and customs, 5,420, 8,154, 12,257, 13,102, 13,463, 17,455
societies, Jewish, **13,803**
soldiers, World War II, **9,758**
state universities and colleges, 9,583, 9,599, 9,607, 9,662, 9,764
archives, **9,809**
statues, 9,735
student etiquette, **9,571**
suffrage, 6,629, 9,734, 9,803
laws and legislation, 9,547
suffrage societies, 6,901, 9,547, 9,656, 9,750
Sunday schools, 13,803
tailors, **9,811**
taxation, legal aspects, 9,544
teachers, 9,363, **9,607, 9,620,** 9,628, 9,634, 9,636, **9,672, 9,687, 9,708,** 9,736, **9,764, 9,807,** 11,589
teachers' colleges, 9,650, 9,764
temperance societies, 6,901, 9,656, 9,707, 9,708, **9,775**
trade and professional societies, 6,901
universities and colleges, 6,087, 9,544, 9,575, 9,597, 9,607, 9,634, 9,671, 9,699
pictorial works, **9,579**
urban beautification, 9,529
veterans, 9,757
volunteer workers in hospitals, 9,530

voters, registration of, 17,599
wills, **9,792**
women, civil rights, 1,627, 6,901, **9,547**
women's colleges, 9,538, 9,556, **9,564, 9,565, 9,566,** 9,614, 9,628
curricula, **9,559**
history **9,543, 9,560, 9,562**
World War II, civilians' work, 9,707
yellow fever epidemics, 5,398, 9,641, 9,675, 9,695
"Mississippi" (poem), 9,773
"Mississippi" (song), 9,719
Mississippi Agricultural and Mechanical College. *See* Mississippi State University
Mississippi Art Association, 9,646
Mississippi Childen's Home (MS), 9,537
Mississippi College, 9,634, 9,671
Mississippi Constitutional Convention (1890), 2,490
Mississippi Dalmatians, 9,694
Mississippi Department of Archives and History, 9,599, 9,719, 9,720, 9,769
Mississippi Federation of Club Women, **9,673**
Mississippi Federation of Women's Clubs, **9,681,** 9,708, 9,750
Mississippi Folk Voices, "Ladies Night" section (series), 9,585
Mississippi Freedom Democratic party, 14,453
Mississippi Genealogical Society, 9,672
Mississippi Historical Society, 9,599, 9,672
Mississippi History (book), 9,558
Mississippi House of Representatives, 9,544, 9,547
Mississippi Industrial Institute and College (Columbus, MS), **9,559, 9,560**
Mississippi Public Lands Committee, officials and employees, 9,544
Mississippi Society of the National Society of Colonial Dames, **9,682**
Mississippi Southern College, 9,671
Mississippi State Board of Development, 6,994, 9,779
Mississippi State College for Women. *See* Mississippi State University for Women
Mississippi State Health Institutions, 9,739
Mississippi State Hospital for the Insane, 9,643
Mississippi State University, 9,712
archives, **9,809**
faculty, 9,803
Mississippi State University for Women, **9,559, 9,560,** 9,597, 9,739, 9,764, 9,802, 9,803, 9,806
Mississippi Story, The (book), 9,672
Mississippi Suffrage Association, 9,547
Mississippi Summer Project (1964), 1,570, 17,691
Mississippi Teachers Association, 9,542
Mississippi Territory, 9,719, 9,729, 9,739
Mississippi Through Four Centuries (book), 483, 9,671
Mississippi University for Women (Columbus, MS), 9,556, **9,564, 9,565, 9,566,** 9,699
alumnae, 9,558
curricula, **9,559**
faculty, **9,568**
history, **9,560, 9,562**
presidents, 9,558
students, **9,569**
Mississippi University for Women (Columbus, MS), Alumnae Association, 9,558
Mississippi Valley Historical Association, 9,002, 17,667
Mississippi Valley Historical Review, 104
Mississippi Valley Suffrage Association Convention (1916), 9,240
Mississippi White Ribbon, The, 9,656
Mississippi Woman Suffrage Association, 6,901, 9,656, 9,750
"Mississippi Woman's Rights Movement, 1889-1923, The" (thesis), **9,547**
Mississippians All (book), 9,733
Missoula Cosmos Club (MT), 10,386
Missouri, 9,845, 9,847, 9,875, 9,883, **10,068,** 10,135, **10,211,** 13,765, 14,212
abortion, legal aspects, 1,984
actresses, **10,176**
Afro-Americans, 10,030, **10,191,** 10,192
agricultural extension work, **10,015**
agricultural societies, 9,988
agriculture, 10,065

apportionment (election law), 9,930, 10,199
apprenticeships, 9,976
archives, **9,861, 10,096**
art centers, Afro-American, 10,163
art festivals, 9,927
art patrons, 10,163
artists, 10,163
attorneys general, 5,267, **9,951,** 9,972
authors, 9,839, **10,126, 10,127, 10,154**
baccalareate addresses, 9,998
bankers, **9,860**
bankruptcy, 9,857
bar associations, 5,175, 6,467
bills, legislative, 10,168
birth control, 9,930
bishops, 9,991
boarding schools, **9,873**
botanical gardens, 10,150, 10,153
business education, **10,198**
businessmen, **9,841, 9,987**
cancer, research, **10,210**
caucus, **9,947**
charities, 9,978
child care centers, 10,013
child welfare, 10,168
legal aspects, 10,161
children, development and guidance, 10,168
church records and registers, 10,055, **10,212**
church records and registers, Methodist, **9,895**
church schools, **10,146,** 10,169
church societies, **10,145, 10,147**
church societies, Methodist, **9,896, 9,923, 10,066**
church work with the sick, Catholic Church, 10,189
churches, 9,989
churches, Baptist, 9,906
cities and towns, 9,907
city councilmen, 9,907
civil defense, **9,894, 10,013**
Civil War, 9,860
economic aspects, 9,836, 9,937
public opinion, 9,061
societies, Confederate, **9,919**
clergy, **9,832**
clergy, Methodist, **9,991**
clergy, Presbyterian, 1,247
clinics, 10,189
clubs, 6,467, **9,843, 9,885,** 9,892, **9,910, 9,915,** 9,918, 9,938, **9,968, 9,969,** 9,978, 9,993, 10,012, 10,032, **10,058, 10,084, 10,085, 10,086, 10,087, 10,108, 10,112,** 10,195
clubs, Afro-American, **10,205**
coeducation, **10,014**
college presidents, **10,022, 10,038**
college students, 9,827, 9,838, 10,022
political activity, 10,020
college teachers, **9,839, 9,857, 9,936, 9,948, 9,960, 9,997, 9,998, 10,027,** 10,049, 10,060, **10,062**
community leadership, **6,467**
community organization, 10,117
congressmen, **9,932, 9,933, 9,938, 9,950, 9,957,** 9,986, **9,994, 9,996,** 10,062
constitutional conventions, 9,855, 10,046, 10,171, 10,199
convents and nunneries, Catholic, **10,129**
corruption (in politics), 10,050
country life, 9,975
county government, records and correspondence, 10,055
court-houses, 2,507
dancers, **10,111**
deans (in schools), **9,829**
diaries and journals, **9,860, 10,051, 10,105, 10,106, 10,107**
discrimination in education, 10,030, 10,159
discrimination in employment, 9,951
distilling, illicit, 9,995
divorce, 9,976
laws and legislation, 9,972
dwellings, **9,907**
editors, 10,027
educational associations, **9,831, 9,927,** 10,112, **10,195**
educators, 10,156
elections, 9,984, 10,062

epidemics, 10,134
equal pay for equal work, **9,831**
executive advisory bodies, 9,930
exhibitions, **10,043**
farmers, **9,884, 9,917, 10,003**, 10,196
feminists, **10,180**
fire fighters, 10,013, 10,111
folk medicine, **9,901**
food adulteration and inspection, 9,893
4-H clubs, 9,892
freedwomen, 9,841, 9,861
gambling, 10,050
gardening societies, 9,918, 10,057
genealogy, 10,068, 10,076
general stores, 9,955
governors, **9,934, 9,940, 9,951, 9,962, 9,963**, 9,982,
    9,983, **9,985, 9,995**, 9,996, **10,032, 10,048,
    10,050**, 10,051
greek letter societies, **9,830**, 9,936, 9,951
greek letter societies, Afro-American, **10,191**
high school teachers, 10,087, **10,113**
historians, **9,841**, 9,892
historic buildings, conservation and restoration,
    10,032, 10,113
historical markers, 9,833
historical societies, **10,114, 10,115**, 10,135
home demonstration agents, **10,018**
home demonstration work, 9,894, **10,016**, 10,039
home economics, accounting, 9,864
home economics extension work, 10,016, **10,019**
hospitals, 9,956, 10,189
hotels, taverns, etc., 9,974
housewives, **9,959, 10,052, 10,053**, 10,107
immigrants, Welsh, **9,952**
itinerancy (church polity), 4,772
journalism, 9,913
    societies, **9,898**, 10,060, 10,126, 10,127
judges, **9,929**, 9,996
judges, Afro-American, 10,191
justices of the peace, 9,976
kindergartens, 10,156
labor and laboring classes, education, 4,083
land settlement, **9,990**
land titles, registration and transfer, 9,976
law, cases, 2,678, 9,972, 9,982, 10,096
lawyers, **9,864, 9,884, 9,929, 9,957, 9,972, 9,980,
    9,982, 9,984**, 9,986, 9,996, **10,003, 10,025,
    10,046**, 10,160
legislative committees, 10,194
legislators, **9,930, 9,956**, 10,047, **10,080**, 10,168,
    10,170, 10,194
librarians, **9,935**
library associations, **10,012**
liquor laws, 10,032
liquor problem, 10,032
literary societies, **9,925**, 9,943, 9,959
local church councils, 10,001
Lutheran Church, biography, **10,142**
lynching, prevention of, 3,279
maps, 10,037
mayors, **9,958**, 10,203
medical law and legislation, 9,844
medical research personnel, **10,207, 10,208, 10,209,
    10,210**
medical societies, 9,844
merchants, 9,836, 9,977
Mexican Americans, **10,117**
militia, 9,884
mining schools and education, **10,024**
monasticism and religious orders for women,
    Catholic, **10,067**, 10,129, 10,134, **10,138, 10,144,
    10,186, 10,187, 10,188, 10,189**
monasticism and religious orders for women,
    Episcopal, **10,146**
Mormons and Mormonism, 4,209, 16,595, 16,636,
    16,675, 16,687, 16,691, 16,692, 16,749, 16,767,
    16,804
museum directors, **9,926**
music teachers, **9,881**
musical societies, 10,179
musicians, **10,179**
Native Americans, relations with whites, 10,045
newspapers, 10,171
    sections, columns, etc., 10,134, 10,135, 10,164

nuns, Catholic, 10,134
nurses, 10,096, **10,145**
nursing service administration, 239
obstetrics, cases, clinical reports, statistics, 9,906
officials and employees, 9,899, **9,912**
    appointments, qualifications, etc., 9,976, 10,032
orphans and orphan asylums, 10,115
parks, 9,974
patriotic societies, **9,953, 10,109**, 10,112, **10,136**
party committees, 9,984
pathologists, **10,208**
peace societies, **10,206**
philanthropists, **10,173**
photography, medical, 9,826
physicians, **9,844, 9,906, 9,909**, 9,916, **10,163,
    10,170**
pioneers and settlers, 7,678, 9,834, 9,842, **9,855,
    9,901**, 9,921, 9,938, **9,952, 9,974**, 10,033
playgrounds, 10,180
poets, 2,637
poets laureate, **9,889, 10,132**
police, **10,160**
political activists, women, 10,050
political clubs, **9,856**, 9,963, 10,048
politicians, **10,046**
politics, practical, women's activism, 6,596, **9,851**,
    9,930, 9,935, **9,946**, 9,978, 9,995, 10,050, 10,171,
    10,199, 10,200
postmistresses, 9,974
premarital examinations, 9,844
prenuptial contracts, 9,861
Presbyterian Church, education, **9,967**
prison reform, **10,174**
prisoners, women, treatment of, 9,940
prisons, 6,811
    hygiene, 10,177
    legal aspects, 10,174
prisons for women, 9,934, 9,951
prohibition, 10,173
public health officers, 9,909
public records, **10,096**
public schools, **10,149**
public welfare, 10,194
public works, **10,055**, 10,163
race discrimination, 10,096
race problems, 10,159, 10,205
railroad companies, 9,956
recreation leadership, 10,180
registers of births, etc., 10,068
retirement homes, 9,981
right of property, 9,861
school attendance, 9,963
school boards, 10,149
school superintendents and principals, 9,972,
    10,110, 10,149, 10,156
schools, 9,841, **9,903, 9,943, 9,945**, 10,134
secession, 7,678
secretaries, 9,858
senators, United States, 9,929, 9,986, 10,170
sex discrimination, 10,096
sex discrimination in government employment,
    9,951
share-cropping, 10,159
singers, **10,166**
slave-trade, 9,976
slavery, 9,883
social life and customs, 10,163, 10,173
societies, etc., **10,204**
societies, Afro-American, **10,203**
soldiers' homes, 10,136
state aid to education, 10,194
state universities and colleges, **9,897, 10,023,
    10,024**, 10,038
    admission, **10,014**, 10,030
student housing, 9,936
students, recreation, 10,024
students' societies, 9,936, 9,943, 14,029
suffrage, 6,442, 6,629, 10,025
    opposition to, **9,924**
suffrage societies, **9,851**, 10,199, 11,865
suicide, 9,909
Sunday schools, 9,855
teachers, 9,858, **9,916, 9,954**, 10,076, **10,105**
teachers colleges, 9,858, **10,149**

teachers' unions, **8,060**
temperance societies, **10,063, 10,116**
text books, 10,037
trade and professional associations, **10,011**
United Methodist Church
    education, 10,066
    membership, 10,066
United States marshal, **10,160**
universities and colleges, **9,939, 10,021**, 10,134
    archives, **9,824, 10,190**
    buildings, 9,938
    employees, 10,022
universities and colleges, Afro-American, **10,095**
university cooperation, 9,942
university extension, **10,015**, 10,019
utopias, **14,268**
vital statistics, 10,055
voters, registration of, 10,096
widows, 9,917, **9,974**
wills, 9,861
witchcraft, 9,909
women
    education, 10,038
    status, 10,017
women's colleges, 9,938, **9,942**, 9,951, 9,964,
    10,026, **10,169**
    administration, 10,035
    archives, **9,825**
working-women's clubs, **10,192**
World War II, civilians work, **10,013**
Young Women's Christian Association, **10,201**
Missouri Association for Social Welfare, 9,934, **10,011**
Missouri Botanical Gardens (St. Louis, MO), 10,150,
    10,153
Missouri and Kansas Dietetic Association, 9,829
Missouri Commission for the Blind, 9,962
Missouri Commission on the Status of Women, 9,930,
    9,951, 9,994, 10,194
Missouri compromise, 12,020
Missouri Constitutional Convention (1943-44), 10,171
Missouri Council of Defense, **9,894**
Missouri Democratic Women's Club, 9,963
Missouri Department of Corrections, Board of
    Probation and Parole, officials and employees,
    9,951
Missouri Equal Suffrage Association, 10,199
Missouri Farm Bureau Federation, 10,047
Missouri Farmers Association, 9,988
Missouri Federation of Music Clubs, 10,179
Missouri Federation of Women's Clubs, 6,467, 9,893,
    9,978, 10,012, 10,032
Missouri Historical Review (periodical), 9,832
Missouri Historical Society, 9,926, 10,046
Missouri Home Economics Association, 9,829
Missouri Library Association, 9,935, **10,012**
Missouri Library Association, Social Responsibilities
    Round Table Task Force on the Status of Women
    in Librarianship, 10,012
Missouri Library Commission, 10,012
Missouri Medical College, faculty, 9,909
Missouri Methodist Church (Columbia, MO), Maria
    Laying Gibson Circle, **9,896**
Missouri Mother of the Year, 9,934
Missouri Pacific Railroad, 9,956
Missouri Press Association, 10,126, 10,127
Missouri Prohibition party, 7,779
Missouri Social Hygiene Association, 9,844
Missouri Society for Crippled Children, 9,978
Missouri State Children's Bureau, 10,032
Missouri State Board of Nursing, 9,934
Missouri State Council of Defense, 9,978, **10,013**
Missouri State Federation of Women's Clubs, 9,910
Missouri State Medical Association, 9,844
Missouri State Penitentiary, 6,811, 9,900, 10,177,
    14,432
Missouri State Penitentiary for Women (Tipton, MO),
    9,951
Missouri State Women's Political Caucus, 9,947
Missouri Supreme Court, 10,003
Missouri University, agricultural experiment station,
    faculty, **9,948**
"Missouri University and I" (essay), 9,959
Missouri University, faculty, **9,960, 9,998**
Missouri Valley Authority, 10,199

Missouri Valley Historical Society (MO), 10,114
Missouri Welfare League, 9,962, **10,174**
Missouri Woman, The, 10,199
Missouri Woman's Legislative Committee, 10,012
Missouri Women's Association of Commerce, 9,993
Missouri Women's Press Club, **9,898,** 10,060
Mistral, Gabriela, 5,815, 15,305
Mitchel, Clara Brown, 16,060
Mitchel, James, 12,046
Mitchel, Jane Verner [Mrs. John], 12,046, 12,567
Mitchel, John (1815-75), **12,046,** 12,567
Mitchel, John Purroy (1879-1918), 12,046
Mitchel, Mary Purroy [Mrs. James], 12,046
Mitchell, Abbie, 3,290
Mitchell, Anna Green. *See* Tilson, Anna Green
   (Mitchell)
Mitchell, Bancroft, 9,242
Mitchell, Benjamin, 11,653
Mitchell, Caroline Pinckney, 15,711
Mitchell, Catherine (Akerly) Cock [Mrs. Samuel
   Latham], **2,489**
Mitchell, Charles Jewett, 5,518
Mitchell Chautauqua Circle (Blue Earth, MN), **8,417**
Mitchell, Christine, 2,946
Mitchell, Clara Edna Lockling Liley [Mrs. Frederick
   A. H. F.] (1892-), **16,767**
Mitchell, Clarence, 15,629
Mitchell, Clarence, 5,828
Mitchell, Cleo, 13,638
Mitchell, Cora Belle Wasson, 1,790
Mitchell, Edith (1906-). *See* Dabbs, Edith
   (Mitchell) (1906-)
Mitchell, Elisha, 12,972
Mitchell, Eliza (1784-1887). *See* Peirce, Eliza
   (Mitchell) (1784-1887)
Mitchell, Elizabeth (1864-1956). *See* Heyl, Elizabeth
   (Mitchell) (1864-1956)
Mitchell, Ella L. (1855-1924), **3,409**
Mitchell, Ellen (1832-). *See* Mitchell, Ellen
   (Mitchell) [Mrs. Francis] (1832-)
Mitchell, Ellen (Mitchell) [Mrs. Francis] (1832-),
   3,787, 11,658
Mitchell, Elsie [Mrs. Thomas M.], **1,733**
Mitchell, Emily Whittlesay [Mrs. William B.]
   (1849-1926), 9,241
Mitchell, Eunice (Barney) [Mrs. Benjamin], 11,653
Mitchell, Ewing Young, Jr. (1873-1954), **10,025**
Mitchell Family, **11,653**
Mitchell, George W., 3,410
Mitchell, Gertrude Bancroft [Mrs. William DeWitt]
   (?-1952), 9,242
Mitchell, Helen H., 4,172
Mitchell, Henrietta (?-1958?). *See* Henry, Henrietta
   (Mitchell) [Mrs. Henry H.] (?-1958?)
Mitchell House (CT), 1,891
Mitchell, Jackie, 11,405
Mitchell, James P. (1900-64), **5,149**
Mitchell, John H., 14,526
Mitchell, John H., 1,998
Mitchell, Juanita (Jackson) [Mrs. Clarence] (1913-),
   2,502, 5,828
Mitchell, Katie (Edwards) [Mrs. John Douglas] Bemo
   [Mrs. L. S.] (1848-1933), **14,244**
Mitchell, L. Pearl (?-1974), **13,945**
Mitchell, L. S., 14,244
Mitchell, Laura (Platt), 14,079
Mitchell, Lise (1838-1932). *See* Hamer, Lise
   (Mitchell) [Mrs. William D.] (1838-1932)
Mitchell, Lucy Bradford [Mrs. Charles Jewett], 5,518
Mitchell, Lucy (Sprague) [Mrs. Wesley Clair]
   (1878-1967), 509, **674,** 11,819, **11,898, 12,048**
Mitchell, Margaret "Maggie" Julia. [Mrs. Henry T.]
   Paddock [Mrs. Charles] Abbott or [Mrs. Charles]
   Mace (1832-1918), 3,100, **12,568**
Mitchell, Margaret "Peggy" Munnerlyn. [Mrs. Berrien
   K.] Upshaw [Mrs. John Robert] Marsh (1900-49),
   556, 2,414, **2,488,** 2,876, 2,879, 2,988, **3,064,**
   3,065, 3,067, 3,070, 3,117, 3,192, **3,225,** 3,263,
   3,278, 3,336, 3,555, 3,602, 14,046
Mitchell, Maria (1818-89), **7,094,** 11,550, 13,339,
   14,895
Mitchell, Martha E. (Webb) [Mrs. Lemuel], 13,450
Mitchell, Mary C., 9,241

Mitchell, Mary Cornwall (Hewitt) [Mrs. Sydney
   Knox] (1875-1955), **1,998**
Mitchell, Mary (Davis) [Mrs. Charles Jewett], 5,518
Mitchell, Mary Louisa (1842-1915). *See* Williamson,
   Mary Louisa (Mitchell) [Mrs. Samuel Thomas]
   (1842-1915)
Mitchell, Minnie A. (1896-), 17,917, **17,920**
Mitchell, Mrs., 8,417
Mitchell, Mrs. C. S., 8,913
Mitchell, Nathaniel R., **3,410**
Mitchell, Peggy (1900-49). *See* Mitchell, Margaret
   "Peggy" Munnerlyn. [Mrs. Berrien K.] Upshaw
   [Mrs. John Robert] Marsh (1900-49)
Mitchell, Ray, 12,095
Mitchell, Rosanna, 3,379
Mitchell, Ruth Comfort (1882-1954), 317, 569, **1,528**
Mitchell, Sydney Knox, 1,998
Mitchell, T. J., 9,643
Mitchell, Thomas, 3,410
Mitchell, Thomas M., **1,733**
Mitchell, Wesley Clair, 12,048
Mitchell, William, 9,242
Mitchell, William (1791-1869), **14,895**
Mitchell, William (1832-1900), 9,242
Mitchell, William Bell, Family (MN), **9,241**
Mitchell, William DeWitt (1874-1955), Family (MN),
   9,242
Mitchell, William L., 11,874
Mitchellville Girl's School (IA), 4,811
Mitchill, Samuel Latham, 2,489
Mitford, Jessica (1918-), **16,162**
Mitnik, Deborah Bertha. *See* Waksman, Deborah
   Bertha (Mitnik) [Mrs. Selman Abraham]
Mittleman, Ann, 2,793
Mix, Arthur J., 11,641
Mix, Isabella, 12,174
Mix, Katherine (Lyon) [Mrs. Arthur J.] (1893-),
   11,641
Mix, Tom, 14,182
Mixed-bloods, 2,674, **10,369**
Mixer, Blanche [Mrs.], 3,608
Mizmoon (?-1974). *See* Soltysik, Patricia Michelle.
   Mizmoon (?-1974)
Mizner, Isabelle. *See* Floyd-Jones, Isabelle (Mizner)
   [Mrs. Charles]
Mizrachi Women's Organization of America, Seattle
   Chapter (WA), 17,282
Mnemosyne, 4,595
Mo Kwong Home for Blind Girls (Canton, China),
   9,543
Moale, Frances North. *See* Gibbons, Frances North
   (Moale) [Mrs. John]
Moale, Mary (Winchester) [Mrs. William Armistead]
   (1812-89), 5,793
Moale, William Armistead (1800-80), 5,793
Moats, Alice Leone (1908-), **6,054**
Mob-Cap, The (book), 111
Mobile (AL), occupation of, Civil War, 78
Mobile Equal Suffrage Association (AL), 42
Mobile Unit Information Center (NY), 12,146
Mobilization for Youth, 8,651
Mobilized Women of Berkeley (CA), **675**
Mobry, Ruby. *See* Pfadenhauer, Ruby (Mobry) [Mrs.
   Herman]
Moccasin, The (periodical), 8,600
Model City Citizen Health Advisory Board (WA),
   17,357
Model League of Nations (1933, 1946), 7,160
"Model Things," 9,317
Modell, Merriam, 6,060
Models, fashion, 11,822, 12,582, 16,569
Modern dance, 402, 1,655, 4,277, 12,363
Modern Language Association, 9,839
Modern Library (publishers), 11,850
Modern Photography, 1,221
Modern Poetry, This (book), 12,441
Modern Priscilla (periodical), 11,304
Modern Priscilla Club (IN), **4,571**
Modern Romances (periodical), 14,374
*Modern Sagas, the Story of the Icelanders in North
   America* (book), 13,692
Modern School (Stelton, NJ), 15,353
Modjeska, Helena. Jadwiga Opid. Helena
   Modrzejewski. [Mrs. Gustave Sinnmayer]

Modrzejewski. [Mrs. Karol Bozenta] Chlapowski
   (1840-1909), 214, 1,409, 1,426, 1,483, **1,523,**
   3,100, 12,798
Modoc Indians, 804
   customs, 1,662
   wars, 804, 1,662
Modrzejewski, Gustav Sinnmayer, 1,426
Modupe, Prince, 6,109
Moe, Karen, 1,534
Moede, Helen (Manz) (1879-?), **676**
Moegart, John H., 3,402
Moellendick, Carrie Lee [Mrs.], 1,722
Moellenhoff, Fritz, 3,914
Moeller, Gladys Elizabeth, 12,532
Moeller, Louisa. *See* Rahm, Louisa (Moeller)
Moeller, Philip, 16,153
Moen, Blanche Elvina (1895-), **8,588**
Moen, Eleanor, 9,140
Moers, Ellen (1928-), **12,049**
Moffat, Adeline [Miss], 11,959
Moffat, Betsy (Barland) [Mrs. George] (1807-88),
   17,502
Moffat, Emma (1880-1968). *See* McLaughlin, Emma
   (Moffat) [Mrs. Alfred] (1880-1968)
Moffat, Emma Louise Presser [Mrs. John Andrew],
   10,683
Moffat Family (NY), **12,306**
Moffat, Tabitha (1780-1858). *See* Brown, Tabitha
   (Moffat) (1780-1858)
Moffet, Anna (1892-). *See* Jarvis, Anna (Moffet)
   [Mrs. Bruce W.] (1892-)
Moffet, Rebecca Virginia (Baker) (1868-?), **8,589**
Moffett, A. L., 17,090
Moffett, Carrie Lena Crawford [Mrs. A. L.] (?-1898),
   17,090
Moffett, Eileen, 1,822
Moffett, Samuel H., 1,822
Moffit, John T. (1862-?), **4,938**
Moffit, Margaret (1897-). *See* Platner, Margaret
   (Moffit) [Mrs. Henry] (1897-)
Moffit, Winifred (Hecht) [Mrs. John T.], 4,938
Moffitt, Elvira Evelyna (Worth) Jackson Walker
   (1836-1940), **13,070,** 13,439, **13,489**
Mofford, Rose (1922-), 168
Mogell, Claire [Mrs.] (1905-), **15,159**
Mohamed, Ethel [Mrs.], **9,683**
Mohave Indians, 1,779, 16,865
Mohawk College (NY), 11,285
Mohawk Indians, 564, 11,440
Mohl, Aurelia Hadley, **16,106**
Mohl, Ruth (ca. 1888-?), **8,590**
Mohn, Anne E. (Ringstad) (1852-1923), 8,811
Mohn, Elsie (Schlueter) (1890-), **8,704**
Moholy-Nagy, Laszlo, 4,112
Moholy-Nagy, Sibyl Dorothy. Dorothea Maria
   Pauline Alice Sibylle (Pietzche) [Mrs. Laszlo]
   (?-1971), **2,790,** 4,112
Mohr, Dennis, 1,182
Mohr, Harriet "Hattie" Sophia (Mason) [Mrs.
   William] (1878-1975), 10,682
Moir, Marian, 9,293
Moisant, Mathilde (?-1964), 11,831
Mokelumne River Ladies Sewing Circle (CA), 1,632
Molan, Hannah Elizabeth "Libbie" [Mrs. Ed M.]
   Emmons [Mrs. Thomas] (1843?-1935), **10,684**
Moldenhauer Archives (Evanston, IL), **4,242**
Molinar, Usule, **6,055**
Molineux, Marie Ada (1857-?), **6,009**
Molitor, Hanna [Mrs. Peter], 9,154
Molitor, Mary, 9,154
Molitor, Peter, 9,154
Moll Well-Baby Clinic, 11,908
Mollenhauer, Margaret H., **16,107**
Moller, Lillian Evelyn (1878-1972). *See* Gilbreth,
   Lillian Evelyn (Moller) [Mrs. Frank B.]
   (1878-1972)
Mollinger, Judy, 15,332
Mollusks, 14,878
Molter, Dorothy, 9,397
Moltzer, Maria (?-1934), 6,224
Momaday, Al, 11,213, 11,217
Momaday, Natachee Scott [Mrs. Al] (1913-), 11,213,
   11,217
Momaday, Scott, 11,217

Mommies Are for Loving (book), 17,956
Moms of America, 10,889
Mona Lisa, The Woman in the Portrait, a Fictional Biography, 113
Monahan, Sherman, 18,002
Monasteries, 831, 998, **1,065,** 1,534, 2,871, **3,601, 4,274, 4,329, 4,503, 4,634,** 4,876, **5,722, 8,414, 11,066, 11,292, 12,845, 12,934, 13,902,** 14,785, **14,870, 17,215**
"Monastery Cookbook," 6,907
Monastery of Poor Clares (Cleveland, OH), **13,902**
Monastery of St. Clare (Evansville, IN), **4,503**
Monastery of Saint Clare (Bloomington, MN), **8,414**
Monastery of St. Clare (Omaha, NE), **10,613**
Monastery of St. Clare (Langhorne, PA), **14,870**
Monastery of St. Dominic (Newark, NJ), **11,066**
Monastery of the Visitation (Snellville, GA), **3,601**
Monastery of the Visitation of Holy Mary (Philadelphia, PA), **15,147**
Monasticism and religious orders for women, Catholic, **24,** 159, 272, 275, 298, 299, 996, 998, 999, **1,007, 1,008, 1,009, 1,066, 1,093,** 1,118, 1,339, **1,369,** 1,513, 1,534, **1,651, 1,690,** 1,750, 1,784, 1,786, **1,819, 1,985,** 2,027, 2,864, **2,919, 2,920,** 3,815, 3,874, **3,933,** 3,971, **4,035, 4,036,** 4,148, **4,274, 4,282, 4,283, 4,284, 4,286, 4,296, 4,303, 4,308, 4,314, 4,328, 4,335, 4,342, 4,453, 4,466, 4,497, 4,509, 4,596, 4,634,** 4,640, 4,643, 4,645, 4,648, **4,696,** 4,709, **4,872, 4,873, 4,874,** 4,876, **5,164, 5,178, 5,184, 5,186, 5,204, 5,236,** 5,373, **5,380, 5,389, 5,390, 5,391, 5,398, 5,401, 5,408, 5,427, 5,428,** 5,493, 5,494, **5,503, 5,556, 5,705, 5,722,** 5,778, **5,830, 5,832, 5,847, 5,848, 5,851, 6,243, 6,888,** 7,033, **7,049, 7,066, 7,694, 8,176, 8,292, 8,383,** 8,414, **8,425, 8,483, 8,494, 8,839, 8,853, 8,855,** 9,022, **9,328, 9,490, 9,491,** 9,542, **9,695,** 10,067, 10,129, 10,134, **10,138, 10,144, 10,186, 10,187, 10,188, 10,189, 10,610, 10,611, 10,614, 10,615, 10,618,** 10,732, **10,880, 10,888, 10,890,** 10,892, **10,893, 11,147, 11,148, 11,232, 11,272, 11,273, 11,298, 11,313, 11,362, 11,404, 11,433, 11,465, 11,476, 11,477, 11,796, 11,803, 11,808, 12,733, 12,749, 12,767, 12,809, 12,810, 12,866, 12,885, 12,932, 12,933, 13,726,** 13,752, **13,763, 13,867, 13,868, 13,902, 13,903, 13,984, 14,044, 14,100, 14,116, 14,130, 14,131, 14,226, 14,259, 14,269, 14,493, 14,494, 14,661, 14,717, 14,719, 14,781, 14,783, 14,794, 14,795, 14,800, 14,859, 14,870,** 14,874, 14,911, 15,146, 15,152, **15,177, 15,178, 15,180,** 15,181, **15,211,** 15,232, **15,233, 15,234, 15,235, 15,264, 15,266, 15,267, 15,336, 15,337, 15,356, 15,369, 15,372, 15,433,** 15,842, **15,844, 15,870, 15,912, 16,020, 16,179, 16,230, 16,251, 16,254, 16,262, 16,319,** 16,343, **16,532, 17,052, 17,145,** 17,215, **17,229, 17,381, 17,415, 17,428, 17,487,** 17,500, **17,552, 17,554, 17,572, 17,578, 17,820, 17,838, 17,839, 17,854, 17,868, 17,871**
rules, 14,795
Monasticism and religious orders for women, Episcopal, **4,732, 5,827, 10,146, 16,026**
Monasticism and religious orders for women, Lutheran, 4,870
Monasticism and religious orders for women, Protestant, 10,212
Monasticism and religious orders for women, United Church of Christ, 10,212
Monday Afternoon Club (CT), **1,921**
Monday Club (AZ), 208
Monday Club (CT), **1,980**
Monday Club (IN), **4,572**
Monday Club (Decorah, IA), **4,720**
Monday Club (Des Moines, IA), **4,775**
Monday Club (Eldora, IA), 4,815
Monday Club (North Adams, MA), 7,112
Monday Club (Williamstown, MA), **7,593**
Monday Club (NH), **10,884**
Monday Literary Club (CO), 1,750, **1,787**
Monday Literary Club (St. Paul, MN), **9,243**
Monday Lunch Club (MA), 6,358
Monday Musicale (Toledo, OH), 14,141
Monday Sewing Class (NY), **12,263**
Monday Sewing Club (NY), 12,297

Monetary policy, 11,857
Money, 14,659
Confederate States of America, 3,262, 9,815, 15,674
United States, 11,857
"Money Blues" (song), 5,533
Money, Hernando, 9,697
Mongan, Agnes, 2,423
Monger, Frieda, 9,230
Monica, Mother Mary, 3,206
Monitor, The (periodical), 17,716
Monk, Penelope, 12,440
Monks, Hanna (Rohrer) [Mrs. Zerah Coston] (1842-1912), 3,337
Monks, Zerah Coston (1841-1909), **3,337**
Monmouth College (IL), 10,185
Monmouth County Historical Association, 12,581
Monmouth County Library (NJ), 10,923
Monnohan, Anna, 17,884
Monogamy, 4,409, 7,174
Monographs of the Society for Research in Child Development, 8,618
Monona Academy (WI), 8,751
Monopolies, 1,017
Monroe. *See also* Munro; Munroe
Monroe, Amelia, 11,440
Monroe, Amelia Phoneta (Bruner) [Mrs. James W.] (1854-?), 10,437
Monroe, Anne Shannon (1877-1942), **14,422**
Monroe County Republican Committee, 6,939
Monroe, Dora E., 677
Monroe, Elizabeth Kortright [Mrs. James] (1768-?), 11,654
Monroe, Fannie [Mrs.], 11,440
Monroe Female Academy (GA), 3,359
Monroe, Harriet, 635
Monroe, Harriet (1842-1927), 3,980
Monroe, Harriet S. [Miss] (1860-1936), 3,797, 3,828, 3,923, 3,986, 3,992, 3,994, 3,997, 4,005, 4,155, 4,226, 5,273, 7,171, 10,029, 11,821, 12,451, 12,821, 15,170, 16,169, 17,011
Monroe, James (1758-1831), 11,654
Monroe, Julia Finney, 14,123
Monroe, Lilla Day, 9,995
Monroe, Lucy. *See* Calhoun, Lucy (Monroe) [Mrs. William James]
Monroe, Will S., **1,589**
Monson, Clara [Mrs. Martin O.] (1888-), **8,765**
Montague, Fanny E. *See* Stockbridge, Fanny E. (Montague)
Montague High School (MI), 8,293
Montague, Juliette. *See* Lord, Juliette (Montague) [Mrs. William Paine]
Montague, Margaret Prescott (1878-1955), **17,473**
Montana, 455, 10,231, 10,244, 10,257, 10,324, 10,332, 10,333, 10,359, 10,388, 10,394, 10,395, 12,502, 14,680
abortion, 10,345
agricultural societies, **10,259,** 10,339
archaeologists, 10,270
athletic clubs, 10,218
attorneys general, **10,342**
authors, **10,232, 10,262,** 10,292, **10,307, 10,332, 10,352,** 10,357, 10,366
bankers, 9,028
bicentennial celebration, **10,338**
businessmen, **10,331,** 10,381
capital and capitol, **10,396**
capital punishment, public opinion, 10,354
cartographers, **10,298**
cattle breeders, 10,336, **10,382**
child welfare, 3,311
church societies, 10,331
church societies, Presbyterian, **10,304**
churches, Episcopal, 10,331
clergy, 10,347
clubs, **10,254, 10,257,** 10,331, **10,339, 10,341, 10,376, 10,396**
congressmen, **2,251**
congresswomen, 9,001, **10,360**
constitution, 10,286
constitutional conventions, 10,285, 10,334, **10,344**
courts, **10,385,** 10,392
dams, 10,328

deans (in schools), **10,216**
diaries and journals, 10,233, **10,234,** 10,265, 10,274, **10,279,** 10,293, 10,362, 10,365, 10,380
dude ranches, 10,238, 10,253, 10,256
education, 10,317
educational associations, **10,273**
Equal Rights Amendment (proposed), 10,345
executive advisory bodies, **10,280**
explorers, 10,236
Flathead Indians, land tenure, 10,272
fur trade, 10,306
gold miners, 10,297
gold mines and mining, 10,244
governors, 10,301, 10,303
greek letter societies, 10,222
Gros Ventre Indians, 10,368, **10,369**
historians, **10,244,** 10,366
historic buildings, conservation and restoration, **10,302,** 10,348
home demonstration work, **10,217**
home economics extension agents, **10,261**
home economics, study and teaching, **10,219**
hospitals, 10,220
immigrants, Yugoslavian, 10,255
journalism, societies, 17,955
journalists, 10,235, 10,310, 10,354, **10,356, 17,955**
judges, 10,392
land settlement, 10,227, 10,230, **10,275,** 10,284, **10,292, 10,318,** 10,350, **10,377,** 16,488
lawyers, 10,270, 10,365
legislative bodies, **10,325, 10,345**
legislative councils, 10,280
legislators, **6,846,** 10,316, **10,320,** 10,345
library associations, 10,331
medical care, 3,311
medical societies, 10,402
merchants, 10,229
millers, **10,331**
miners, **10,331,** 10,382
mines and mineral resources, 10,307
monasticism and religious orders for women, Catholic, **17,415**
motels, 10,362
Native Americans
education, 10,269, 10,398
mixed-bloods, **10,368, 10,369**
trading posts, 10,228
wars, 1,398
newspaper publishers and publishing, 10,305
newspapers, 10,354
nuns, Catholic, **17,415**
nursing schools, **10,220**
officials and employees, **10,346**
oral history, **10,270**
orphans and orphan asylums, **10,299**
patriotic societies, **10,294, 10,295**
physical education and training, **10,218**
physicians, **10,253, 10,274, 10,402**
pioneers and settlers, 1,653, **10,224, 10,234,** 10,237, **10,239, 10,247, 10,248, 10,258, 10,276, 10,277,** 10,283, **10,288, 10,300,** 10,315, **10,321, 10,322, 10,335,** 10,336, **10,338, 10,351, 10,355,** 10,356, **10,364, 10,368, 10,372, 10,374, 10,382, 10,383,** 10,390, **10,400**
politicians, 10,365
politics, practical, women's activism, **10,340**
poets, 10,352
postmistresses, 10,229, 10,231
public records, **10,342**
railroads, 10,240
ranch life, 10,225, 10,233
ranchers, 10,245, 10,272, **10,290,** 10,309, 10,349, **10,371**
ranches, **10,238,** 10,270, **10,278,** 10,379, 10,380
river steamers, 10,265
road construction, management, 10,300
roads, 10,383
school census, 10,367
school districts, **10,367**
school superintendents and principals, 10,263, **10,267,** 10,269, 10,281, **10,306, 10,346,** 10,358, 10,398
schools, 10,237
secretaries, **10,303**

senators, United States, **2,251,** 8,975
social life and customs, 10,323
strikes and lockouts, 10,310
student activities, **10,222**
students' societies, **10,214, 10,221,** 10,222
suffrage, **10,223,** 10,325, 10,345
suffrage societies, **10,316**
surveyors and surveying, **10,298**
teachers, **10,237, 10,242, 10,246,** 10,248, **10,260,**
  10,263, **10,269, 10,282, 10,293,** 10,312, **10,317,**
  10,361, 10,362, 10,373, 10,398, 17,315
trade-unions, 10,310
universities and colleges, 10,216, 10,222
vigilance committees, 10,270, 10,300, 10,364
women, civil rights, 10,271
Young Women's Christian Association, **10,397**
Montana-American Mothers Bicentennial Project,
  10,338
Montana Constitutional Convention, Bill of Rights
  Committee, 10,334
Montana Constitutional Convention Commission,
  10,285
Montana Constitutional Revision Committee, 10,286
Montana Cowbelles, Inc., **10,339**
Montana Department of Institutions, Children's
  Center, **10,299**
Montana Extension Service, 10,261
Montana Institute of the Arts, 10,270
Montana Laundry (Yukon Territory), 135
Montana League of Women Voters, **10,340**
Montana Legislative Assembly, 10,285, 10,286,
  10,325
Montana Legislative Wives Club, **10,341**
Montana Pay Dirt (book), 1,804
Montana Society of Pioneers, 10,402
Montana State Board of World's Fair Managers,
  10,319
Montana State Hospital, 10,220
Montana State Press Women, 17,955
Montana State Tuberculosis Sanitorium, 10,220
Montana State University
  deans, **10,216**
  employees, 10,256
Montana State University, Associated Women
  Students, **10,214,** 10,222
Montana State University, Extension Service, **10,217**
Montana State University, Physical Education
  Department, **10,218**
Montana State University, School of Home
  Economics, **10,219**
Montana State University, School of Nursing, **10,220**
Montana State University, Women's Residence Hall
  Association, 10,222
Montana Stockgrowers Association, 10,339
Montana Supreme Court, **10,385**
Montana Territorial Supreme Court, 10,392
Montana Territory, 10,279
  governors, 10,293, 10,300
Montano, Andres Avelino, 3,628
Montano, Mary Jane Kekulani (Fayerweather) [Mrs.
  Benoni Richmond] Davison [Mrs. Andres
  Avelino] (1842-1930), **3,628**
Montclair High School (NJ), 10,919
Monteagle Assembly (MS), 6,901
Monteith Family (MI), 8,157
Monteith Library Project, 8,050
Monteith, Marion Brown. *See* English, Marion
  Brown (Monteith) [Mrs. Albert D.]
Monterey, Carlotta. *See* O'Neal, Carlotta Monterey
  [Mrs. Eugene]
Monterey History and Art Association (CA), 1,333
Monterey, presidio (CA), 392
Montessori Education Association of New York,
  7,293
Montessori, Maria, 4,211, 5,346, 17,870
Montessori method of education, 299
Montez, Lola. Marie Dolores Eliza Rosanna Gilbert.
  [Mrs. Thomas] James [Mrs. George Trafford]
  [Mrs. Patrick Purdy] Hall. Fanny Gibbons
  (1818-61), 1,077, 1,250, 1,324
Montgomerie, Anne (1864-1954). *See* Traubel, Anne
  (Montgomerie) [Mrs. Horace L.] (1864-1954)
Montgomerie, William, 14,896
Montgomery, Andrew (ca. 1907-), **8,110**

Montgomery, Benjamin, Family (MS), **2,490**
Montgomery, Charlotte (Baker) (1910-), **16,301**
Montgomery County Probate Court (OH), Record of
  Midwives Certificates, **14,048**
Montgomery County Probate Court (OH), Record of
  Registered Nurses, **14,049**
Montgomery, Dorothy Schoell, 15,201
Montgomery, Edmund Duncan, 16,372
Montgomery, Elisabet (Ney) [Mrs. Edmund Duncan]
  (1833-1907). *See* Ney, Elisabet. Franzisca
  Bernadina Wilhelmina Elisabeth. [Mrs. Edmund
  Duncan] Montgomery (1833-1907)
Montgomery, Ella (Sargent), **12,828**
Montgomery, Ellie, 13,573
Montgomery, Emma Nettie (Kilgore) (1865-?), 16,968
Montgomery, Ethel L., **4,657**
Montgomery, Eva (1884-1972). *See* McGown, Eva
  (Montgomery) [Mrs. Arthur] (1884-1972)
Montgomery Family (PA), **14,896**
Montgomery Federation of Women's Clubs (AL), 53
Montgomery, George P., **11,453**
Montgomery, Isaiah T. (1847-1924), **2,490**
Montgomery, Janet, 12,748
Montgomery, Janet (Livingston) [Mrs. Richard]
  (1743-1828), **12,264, 12,569**
Montgomery, Langford, 4,749
Montgomery, Lettie (Dodge), 4,749
Montgomery Lorne Ney, 16,111
Montgomery, Louise [Mrs.], 9,603
Montgomery, Lucille, **17,691**
Montgomery, Mabel, 15,609
Montgomery, Margie [Mrs.], **5,385**
Montgomery, Mary (?-1955). *See* Borglum, Mary
  (Montgomery) [Mrs. John Gutzon de la Mothe]
  (?-1955)
Montgomery, Mary A. C. [Mrs.], 9,741
Montgomery, Mary Cordelia. *See* Booze, Mary
  Cordelia (Montgomery) [Mrs. Eugene P.]
Montgomery, Mary F., **1,376**
Montgomery, Mary Phelps, 14,618
Montgomery, Mary Seymour, 11,534
Montgomery, Mary Virginia (1852-?), 2,490
Montgomery, Maud [Miss], 9,967
Montgomery Mothers' Circle (AL), **74**
Montgomery, Mrs. C. W., 9,684
Montgomery, Mrs. Henry M., 12,830
Montgomery, Richard, 12,569
Montgomery, Rita, 10,191
Montgomery, Ruth (Shick) [Mrs. Robert H.] (1912-),
  11,493, **16,370, 16,371**
Montgomery, Sarah Ann (Purnell), 9,244
Montgomery, Sue Thermutis, 15,768
Monthly (periodical), 12,746
"Monthly News Sheet" (newsletter), 7,239
Monticello College (Godfrey, IL), **4,374,** 4,389
  principals, 4,361
Monticello Female Academy, 9,841
Monticello Hospital (VA), 15,561
Montieth, Charles E., 3,665
Montieth, John B., 3,665
Montieth, Modjeska (1899-). *See* Simkins, Modjeska
  (Montieth) (1899-)
Montis, Lachryma, 858
Montour Family (NY), 11,440
Montour High School (IA), 4,853
Montpelier Institute (Macon, GA), 13,121
Montreal Mission for Friendless Girls, 6,752
Montz, Florence (Stolte) [Mrs. C. R.], 10,140
Monuments, 2,413, 4,467, **6,439,** 9,949, 10,648,
  12,345, 13,340, 13,446, 14,935, 15,683, 16,648,
  17,029
Monuments and Markers (book), 11,320
Mooar, Eva Alberta, **6,769**
Mooar, John Wesley, 16,280
Mooar, John Wright, 16,060
Mooar, Lydia Louise, **16,280**
Mooar, Margaret A., 16,060
"Mood I'm In, The" (song), 5,530
Mood, Julia (1880-1961). *See* Peterkin, Julia (Mood)
  (1880-1961)
Moodie, Belle. *See* Frost, Belle (Moodie) [Mrs.
  William Prescott]
Moody Bible Institute (Chicago, IL), 3,969, **3,970**
Moody, Drusilla. *See* West, Drusilla (Moody)

Moody, Dwight Lyman, 3,969, 6,775
Moody, Helen Wills, 15,935
Moody, Henry, 16,315
Moody, Kathryn Stoner Hicks [Mrs. Lowell H.],
  9,245
Moody, Libbie (1897-). *See* Thompson, Libbie
  (Moody) [Mrs. Clark W.] (1897-)
Moody, Malcolm (1854-1925), 14,619
Moody, Mary Stephenson [Mrs. Zenus Ferry], 14,619
Moody, Maud E., 16,132
Moody, Minnie (Hite) (1900-), 3,071, 3,210, **3,338**
Moody, Mrs. S. J., 4,069
Moody, Ralph E., 14,619
Moody, William H., 14,619
Moody, William Vaughn, 11,174
Moody, Zenus A., 14,619
Moody, Zenus Ferry (1832-1917), Family (OR),
  14,619
Mooney, Isabell (Churchill) [Mrs. Matthew] (1901-),
  7,151
Mooney, Jane, 13,423
Mooney, Rena [Mrs. Thomas Joseph], 677
Mooney, Thomas Joseph (1882-1942), **677**
Mooney, Tom, 492, 1,241, 12,699, 12,702
Moonlight schools, 5,325, 13,309
"Moonstruck" (drama), 6,981
Moore, Abel Buell (1806-79), **12,265**
Moore, Ada, 13,345
Moore, Adella Breckenridge, 9,840
Moore, Al, 5,478
Moore, Alden, 14,039
Moore, Alice (1861-1915). *See* Hubbard, Alice
  (Moore) [Mrs. Elbert] (1861-1915)
Moore, Alice Rigby, 5,079
Moore, Amanda. *See* Goldthwaite, Amanda (Moore)
  [Mrs. Henry]
Moore, Ann Leslie (Nichol) [Mrs. Merrill], 2,491
Moore, Anne Carroll [Miss] (1871-1961), 7,048,
  11,333, **12,570**
Moore, Annie Aubertine Woodward [Mrs.]
  (1841-1929), **17,692**
Moore, Augusta [Mrs.], 3,141
Moore, Augusta C. [Mrs. John Card] (1841 or
  1842-1925), **11,354**
Moore, Bartholomew F., 13,490
Moore, Benjamin (1748-1816), 11,826
Moore, Carrie Amelia (1846-1911). *See* Nation,
  Carrie Amelia (Moore) [Mrs. Charles] Gloyd
  [Mrs. David] (1846-1911)
Moore, Charity (Clarke) [Mrs. Benjamin], 11,826
Moore, Charlotte (Palmer) [Mrs. R. F.], **3,228**
Moore, Clara Sophia (Jessup) [Mrs. Bloomfield
  Haynes] (1824-99), **15,055**
Moore, Clement Clarke (1779-1863), 11,826
Moore College of Art (PA), 14,941
Moore, Cora [Mrs. Louis, Jr.], 9,467
Moore, Cornelia Jackson [Mrs. Wilmer L.], **3,229**
Moore, Cynthia Mosher [Mrs. Alden], 14,039
Moore, Dorothea May, **6,770**
Moore, Dorothy. *See* Anderson, Dorothy (Moore)
  [Mrs. Edgar]
Moore, Dorthea (Rhodes) [Mrs. Charles Fletcher]
  Lummis [Mrs. Ernest Carroll] (ca. 1860-1942),
  1,465
Moore, Dosia (ca. 1850-1940), **5,449**
Moore, Douglas Stuart (1893-1969), **12,050**
Moore, Edith Wyatt, 9,813
Moore, Elisabeth Luce, 7,583
Moore, Elizabeth I. (1832-1930), 17,452, **17,474**
Moore, Ella [Mrs. Addison W.], 4,150
Moore, Elsie. *See* Lott, Elsie (Moore)
Moore, Emily Malone Raymond [Mrs. Isaac Irving],
  1,790
Moore, Erma M., 1,319
Moore, Ernest Carroll, 1,465
Moore, Eron Opha (ca. 1863-1951). *See* Rowland,
  Eron Opha (Moore) [Mrs. Dunbar] (ca.
  1863-1951)
Moore, Eva (Perry) [Mrs. Philip N.] (1852-?), 2,519
Moore Family (IL), 4,404
Moore Family (NY), **11,654**
Moore Family (NY), 12,635
Moore Family (NY?), **12,676**
Moore Family (Savona, NY), **11,595**

Moore, Frances, 2,694
Moore, Genevieve Pearce [Miss] (1889-), **13,071**
Moore, George, 752
Moore, Gertrude (1894-), 7,109
Moore, Gertrude [Mrs. Vernon] (1919-), 5,394
Moore, Grace, 2,207
Moore, Grace [Miss] (1871-1957), 10,626
Moore, Grace. [Mrs. Valentin] Parera (1898-1947), 12,013, **15,874**
Moore, Harriet Ann (1810-?). *See* Ames, Harriet Ann (Moore) [Mrs. Solomon C.] Page [Mrs. Robert] Potter [Mrs. Charles] (1810-?)
Moore, Harriet Ellen. *See* Weakley, Harriet Ellen Moore [Mrs. Thomas P.]
Moore, Helen (1867?-1945). *See* Bristol, Helen (Moore) [Mrs. William Bailey] Thomas [Mrs. Mark Lambert] (1867?-1945)
Moore, Idora (McClellan) Plowman (1843-1929), **13,073**
Moore, Irene (Ivy), **9,797**
Moore, J. E. L., 8,447
Moore, Jacquelyn (1897-1949), 3,229
Moore, James A. G., 11,572
Moore, James Preston, 10,175
Moore, Jessica (Babcock) [Mrs. Gardner S.] (ca. 1860-?), 9,277
Moore, John Card, 11,354
Moore, Julia Merrill [Mrs.], 1,635
Moore, Katherine [Mrs. M. J.], 11,595
Moore, Lillian (1911-67), **12,364**
Moore, Lillie (1870-?). *See* Everett, Lillie (Moore) (1870-?)
Moore, Louis, Jr., 9,467
Moore, Lucy Catherine "Katie," 13,490
Moore, Mahala, 14,618
Moore, Margaret Edgerton, 2,243
Moore, Marianne Craig (1887-1972), 317, 1,221, 2,215, 4,227, 6,344, 11,153, **11,171**, 11,309, 11,810, 11,821, 12,821, **14,761**, **15,170**, 15,198, **16,163**, 18,021
Moore, Marinda Branson, 13,345, 13,496
Moore, Marion [Mrs. O. M.] (1880s-late 1940s), 10,626
Moore, Marion Louise, **13,946**
Moore, Martha "Missouri" (Bishop) [Mrs. James Preston] (1837-81), **10,175**
Moore, Mary Brown (Daniel) [Mrs. John Trotwood] (1875-?), 2,491, 10,026
Moore, Mary Carr (1873-1957), **1,022**
Moore, Mary Evelyn "Mollie" (1852-1909). *See* Davis, Mary Evelyn "Mollie" (Moore) [Mrs. Thomas E.] (1852-1909)
Moore, Mary Taylor, 13,247
Moore, Mary (Taylor) Leiper (1885-1973), 5,278
Moore, Mary Tyler (1937-), **17,808**
Moore, Mary Willie Grace (1898-1947). *See* Moore, Grace. [Mrs. Valentin Parera] (1898-1947)
Moore, Merle (Jordan), **10,347**
Moore, Merrill (1903-57), **2,491**
Moore, Mrs. Cecil, 1,777
Moore, Mrs. Dan K., 13,566
Moore, Mrs. Hugh, 11,582
Moore, Mrs. J. H., 4,699
Moore, Mrs. Jacob, 4,369
Moore, Mrs. James P., 182
Moore, Olietta, 1,777
Moore, Rosa (1849-1924), 10,185
Moore, Rosalie (1910-). *See* Brown, Rosalie (Moore) [Mrs. Bill] (1910-)
Moore, Ruth, **6,056**
Moore, Ruth. *See* Stanley, Ruth (Moore)
Moore, Ruth (ca. 1920-). *See* Garbe, Ruth (Moore) [Mrs. Raymond W.] (ca. 1920-)
Moore, Ruth Huntington, 13,334
Moore, Samuel, **12,051**
Moore, Sarah [Miss], **13,601**
Moore, Stephen Bliss, 16,534
Moore, Susan Maxwell, 17,485
Moore, Susannah (Bolton) [Mrs. William], **3,556**
Moore, Thomas Sturge, 1,751
Moore, Veranus A., 11,579
Moore, Virginia, 4,904
Moore, Willa Mae Dill, 12,532
Moore, William F., 261

Moore, Wilmer L., 3,229
Moore Women's Club (MT), **10,257**
Moorehead, Agnes (1901-74), 7,718, **17,809**
Moorhead Normal School (MN), 8,690
Moorepark, Howard, 6,100
Moores, Althea, **14,424**
Moore's Creek Bridge (NC), Battle of (1776), 13,575
Moores Hill College (IN), students, 4,506, 4,507
Moorfield, Amelia Berndt, **11,112**
Moorland-Spingarn Research Center (DC), 2,146
Moorman, George, 5,528
Moorpark, Howard, 14,460
Moos, Malcolm C. (1916-), **5,146**
Moose, Philip, 13,264
Mooser, Hattie (1878-1970), **941**
Mooser, Minnie, **941**
Mora, F. Luis, 11,835
Mora, Federico, 2,200
Morais, Nina (1855-1918). *See* Cohen, Nina (Morais) (1855-1918)
Moral Rearmament, 17,324
Moran, Catherine E. (1852?-1967?), 6,132
Moran, Dorothy J., **3,411**
Moran, Mary Adelaide (1914-72), **17,308**
Moran, Nina M. K., 17,918, 17,919
Morand, Paul, 8,597
Morand, Ruth Shepard Phelps [Mrs. Paul] (1876-1949), **8,597**
Morani, Alma Dea, 15,134
Moravia, 16,380
Moravian Church (NC), 13,411
Moravian Church, missions, 1,504
Moravian Seminary for Young Ladies (Bethlehem, PA), 10,920, 10,936
Moravian Sisters (PA), 2,544
Moravians, 13,086, 13,149, 13,634, 15,463
Moravians in Pennsylvania, 12,338
Morath, Fred, 1,686
Morath, Gladys "Glad" (Ramsell) [Mrs. Fred] (1896-), **1,686**
Morath, Max, 1,686
Mordecai, Caroline, 13,471, 13,491
Mordecai, Ellen (1790-1884). *See* Mordecai, Ellen (Mordecai) [Mrs. Samuel Fox] (1790-1884)
Mordecai, Ellen (Mordecai) [Mrs. Samuel Fox] (1790-1884), 12,996, 13,074, 13,471, 13,491
Mordecai, Emma, 13,074, 13,491
Mordecai Family, 7,547
Mordecai Family (NC), **13,074, 13,471**
Mordecai Female Seminary (NC), 13,491
Mordecai, Jacob (1762-1838), 13,074, 13,471
Mordecai, Joseph, 13,491
Mordecai, Laura. *See* Summerall, Laura Mordecai
Mordecai, Margaret. *See* Devereux, Margaret (Mordecai) [Mrs. John]
Mordecai, Miriam, 7,547
Mordecai, Pattie, **13,491**
Mordecai, Rachel, 13,491
Mordecai, Rosa, 7,547
Mordecai, Samuel Fox, 12,996, 13,074
Mordecai, Sarah Ann (Hays) (1805-94), **7,534**
"More about 'The Unsinkable Mrs. Brown,'" 1,756
"More Ways Than One: A Book of Songs and Spiritual Dances" (ms), 2,316
More, Thomas, 4,447
Morecock, Misses, 17,125
Morehead Normal School, alumnae, 5,325
Morehouse College (GA), 2,879, 3,451
Morehouse, Elinore (1895-1964). *See* Herrick, Elinore (Morehouse) (1895-1964)
Morehouse Emma Margaret Lang [Mrs. Herbert H.], 11,655
Morehouse Family, **11,655**
Morehouse, Herbert H., 11,655
Morehouse, Lewis Case, **9,246**
Morel-Fatio, Alfred, 9,425
Moreland, Cora. *See* Young, Cora (Moreland) [Mrs. William Wray]
Moreno, Dorinda (ca. 1940-), 17,619
Moreno, Elizabeth [Miss], **2,908**
Moreno, Frances, 4,134
Morey, Bertha (Graves) (1881-), 4,899
Morey, Charles Anson (1851-1904), 9,520
Morey Clay Products Company (IA), 4,899

Morey Family (MN), **9,520**
Morey, Kate (Berry) [Mrs. Charles Anson], 9,520
Morey, Nancy Booker [Mrs. Donald R.] (1903-), **11,656**
Morgan. *See also* Morgin
Morgan, Agnes (Fay) [Mrs. Arthur Ivason] (1884-), **930**
Morgan, Alice (1840-1913). *See* Person, Alice (Morgan) (1840-1913)
Morgan, Angela [Miss] (1873-1957), **7,868**, 7,923, **12,571**
Morgan, Anna (1851-1936), **3,880**
Morgan, Annie E., 11,324
Morgan, Ardita Berry, **16,108**
Morgan, Arthur, 14,174
Morgan, Barbara, 2,751, 2,815, 12,789
Morgan, Benjamin, Jr., 15,000
Morgan, Berry (1919-), **6,057**
Morgan, Caroline, **3,557**
Morgan, Christopher, 12,052
Morgan, Constance Cutter (Morrow) (1913-), 7,264
Morgan, Dale L., 16,881, 16,882
Morgan, Daniel J., 2,461
Morgan, Dorothy Rittenhouse, 15,354
Morgan, Edith Parsons, 12,280
Morgan, Edwin Barber (1806-81), 11,278, **11,280**, 12,052
Morgan, Elisabeth Reeve (Morrow) Morgan (1903-), 7,221, 7,264
Morgan, Elizabeth (Chambers) [Mrs. Thomas J.], 4,431
Morgan, Emma (1906-), **241**
Morgan Family, **6,771**
Morgan Family, 12,607
Morgan Family (MI), **7,869**
Morgan Family (NY), **12,052**
Morgan, Georgia Philipps (1878-). *See* Bullock, Georgia Philipps (Morgan) (1878-)
Morgan, Harriet French Ford (1868-1949), **12,476**, 16,150
Morgan, J. Edward, 12,705
Morgan, J. P., 2,624
Morgan, Jeannie (?-1970). *See* Klenke, Jeannie (Morgan) (?-1970)
Morgan, Jennie Ham [Mrs.], 4,939
Morgan, John, 15,079
Morgan, John H., 2,461
Morgan, John H., 13,054
Morgan, Julia, 3,557
Morgan, Julia (1872-1957), **302, 544, 678, 918**, 932
Morgan, Juliette, 11,855
Morgan, Kate. *See* Brookfield, Kate (Morgan) [Mrs. William]
Morgan, Laura (Puffer) (1874-1962), **6,771**, 15,308
Morgan, Leona (Brooks) [Mrs. Arthur], 14,174
Morgan, Lewis Henry, 11,280
Morgan, Lucille, 1,663
Morgan, Lucy Stow, 7,869, **7,870**
Morgan, Madel (Jacobs) [Mrs. Adlia], **9,685**
Morgan, Mary D., 13,172
Morgan, Mary DeNeale (1868-1948), 597
Morgan, Mary (Hopkinson) [Mrs. John] (1742-85), 15,079
Morgan, Mary (Kimball) [Mrs. William Edgar] (1861-1948), **4,199**
Morgan, Maud, 8,297
Morgan, Minnie (Buerbaum), **13,075**
Morgan, Mrs. J. D., **289**
Morgan, Mrs. Richard Smith, 16,117
Morgan, Mrs. Thomas A., 12,708
Morgan, Nora, 1,124
Morgan Park Woman's Club (IL), 3,930
Morgan, Polly, 7,869
Morgan, Roy, 1,124
Morgan, Sallie B. *See* Green, Sallie B. (Morgan)
Morgan State University (Baltimore, MD), 5,828
Morgan, Thomas J. (1847-1912), **4,431**
Morgan, William C., 2,461
Morgan, William H., 2,296
Morgantown Female Seminary (WV), 17,474
Morgantown High School (WV), 17,445
Morgantown Service League (WV), **17,475**
Morgantown Women's Home Defense Club (WV), **17,476**

Morgen-Posten, 8,736
Morgenblad, 8,801
Morgenstern, Birdie, **12,266**
Morgenstern, Louise, **12,266**
Morgenthau, Henry, Jr., 11,579
Morgenthau, Mrs. Henry, Jr., 2,686
Morgin, Amanda Melvin. *See* Crawford, Amanda Melvin (Morgin)
Morhaime, Rebecca. *See* Mosheatel, Rebecca (Morhaime)
Morian, Lelah May (1881-1963), **1,734**
Morin, Katherine Trusdell [Mrs. William A.] (1873-1968). *See* Meighen, Katherine Trusdell [Mrs. William A.] Morin [Mrs. John Felix Dryden] (1873-1968)
Morin, Richard W., 3,712
Morison, Emily Marshall (Eliot) (1857-?), **6,557**
Morison, Emmy (Eliot) [Mrs. John Holmes], 5,903
Morison, Samuel Eliot, 6,557
Moritz, Mercedes (1896-1977). *See* Randall, Mercedes (Moritz) [Mrs. John Herman, Jr.] (1896-1977)
Morley, Christopher, 4,482, 7,209, 16,153, 16,163, 17,473
Morley, Codelia (1823-1915). *See* Cox, Codelia (Morley) (1823-1915)
Morley, Grace Louise (McCann) (1900-), **679**
Morley, Issac, 16,456
Morley, Sucy Gunn [Mrs. Issac], 16,456
Mormon Battalion, 16,525, 16,590, 16,698, 16,704, 16,838
Mormon Suffrage Association, 16,733
Mormon Tabernacle (Salt Lake City, UT), 15,762
Mormons and Mormonism, 160, 178, 185, 189, 191, 202, 207, 391, 410, 429, 562, 746, **805,** 806, **845,** 855, 856, 904, 1,332, **1,466,** 1,755, 2,581, **3,738,** 3,739, 3,740, 4,209, 4,416, 5,829, 6,092, 6,355, 9,047, 9,308, 10,001, **10,089, 10,090, 10,091,** **10,092, 10,093, 10,094,** 10,162, 10,638, **10,674,** 10,780, 11,536, 12,616, 15,173, 16,060, 16,409, 16,428, **16,431,** 16,438, 16,450, 16,456, **16,458,** 16,475, 16,486, 16,503, 16,504, **16,508, 16,509,** **16,512,** 16,527, 16,531, **16,533,** 16,536, 16,540, **16,541,** 16,543, **16,557,** 16,566, 16,569, 16,572, 16,573, 16,579, 16,580, 16,581, 16,586, **16,592,** 16,595, 16,598, 16,603, 16,607, **16,609, 16,611,** **16,612,** 16,614, 16,616, **16,617, 16,618, 16,620,** **16,625,** 16,629, 16,632, 16,636, 16,638, 16,641, 16,643, 16,649, 16,651, 16,652, 16,653, 16,654, 16,658, 16,660, 16,661, **16,663,** 16,664, 16,665, 16,667, 16,668, 16,673, 16,675, 16,685, 16,686, 16,687, 16,688, 16,689, 16,691, 16,692, 16,693, 16,695, 16,696, 16,698, 16,700, 16,702, 16,705, 16,707, 16,710, 16,711, 16,713, 16,718, 16,719, 16,722, **16,723,** 16,726, 16,727, **16,728, 16,729,** 16,730, 16,731, 16,732, 16,733, 16,734, 16,735, 16,737, 16,740, 16,741, 16,742, 16,743, **16,747,** 16,748, **16,749, 16,750,** 16,751, **16,752,** 16,754, 16,756, 16,757, 16,758, 16,759, 16,760, **16,761,** 16,763, 16,764, **16,765, 16,767,** 16,768, 16,769, **16,770,** 16,771, **16,775, 16,777, 16,778,** 16,779, **16,780, 16,781,** 16,786, **16,789, 16,792,** 16,793, 16,794, 16,798, 16,802, 16,803, **16,804,** 16,805, 16,806, 16,808, **16,809,** 16,811, 16,812, 16,815, 16,818, **16,820, 16,822, 16,823, 16,824, 16,825,** **16,826, 16,830,** 16,832, 16,833, 16,834, **16,835,** **16,836,** 16,837, 16,838, 16,839, **16,840, 16,841,** **16,842,** 16,843, 16,844, 16,846, **16,847, 16,852,** **16,853, 16,854,** 16,855, **16,857,** 16,860, 16,874, 16,876, 16,887, 16,897, 16,898, **16,903,** 16,905, 16,906, **16,909, 16,911,** 16,913, 16,914, 16,916, 16,917, 16,921, 16,932, 16,937, 16,938, 16,939, 16,940, 16,943, 16,945, 16,947, 16,950, 16,952, 16,955, **16,958, 16,959,** 16,961, **16,967,** 16,968, 16,971, **16,973, 16,974,** 16,976. *See also* Church of Jesus Christ of Latter-day Saints; Polygamy
doctrinal and controversial works, 16,465, 16,798
education, 713, 16,620
military history, 845, 16,933
missionaries, 16,711
pictures, illustrations, etc., **16,789**
relations with Native Americans, 16,867
relations with Paiute Indians, 16,870
sacred books, 16,760

Mormons and Mormonism, Afro-American, **16,708,** 16,780
Morning Choral Club (CA), **1,212**
Morning Etude, 10,179
Morning Musicale (IN), **4,573**
Morning News (GA), 3,488
Morning Post, 687
Morning Star VI (ship), 14,470
Morning Study Club (CO), 1,775
Morningside College (Sioux City, IA)
deans, 4,906, 5,101
faculty, 5,102, 5,103
Morongo Indian Reservation (CA), 1,504
Moroz, Josephine, 9,512
Morrah, Mrs. P. Bradley, Sr., 15,747
Morrell, Anna B. [Mrs. Charles Horton] (1785-1855), 12,267
Morrell, Charles Horton (1779-1837), 12,267
Morrell, Charlotte (1816-1901). *See* Boyer, Charlotte (Morrell) [Mrs. Augustine C.] (1816-1901)
Morrell Family (NY), **12,267**
Morrell, Lady Ottoline, 16,173
Morrell, Louisa (1802-?). *See* Cuyler, Louisa (Morrell) [Mrs. Benjamin Ledyard] (1802-?)
Morrell, Louise (Drexel) (1863-1945), 14,781
Morrey, Grace (Hamilton) [Mrs. Charles] (1877-1962), **14,008**
Morrill, Belle Chapman (1882-1972), **1,856**
Morrill, Florence Barry, **2,492**
Morris, Abbie Grace [Mrs. William M.] (1875-1924), 9,247
Morris Academy (Litchfield, CT), 1,970
Morris, Adrienne [Miss], 3,188
Morris, Alice S., 15,198
Morris, Alice Webber (Palmer) [Mrs. Raymond] (1890-?), **17,876**
Morris, Anna, 14,515
Morris, Anna Maria Jackson (De Camp) [Mrs. Gouverneur], 12,191
Morris, Anna Mary (Curtis) (ca. 1830-?), **6,772**
Morris, Anne Cary (Randolph) [Mrs. Gouverneur], 2,493
Morris, Annie, 14,515
Morris, Annie (1860-?), 10,776
Morris, Augusta Emily (Griswold) [Mrs. John Moses], 1,922
Morris, Benjamin (1725-55), 14,977
Morris, Bernice, 1,186
Morris, Beulah, 14,856
Morris Cafritz Memorial Hospital, 8,656
Morris, Charles, 14,515
Morris, Clara. [Mrs. Frederick C.] Harriott (1847-1925), **6,773, 7,263,** 10,025, 10,651
Morris, Deborah (1723 or 1724-93), 14,856, 14,966, 14,977, 15,056
Morris, Edita deToll (1902-), **6,058**
Morris, Elizabeth Carrington [Miss] (1775-1865), 14,944
Morris, Elizabeth (Manigault), 13,066
Morris, Ella Duncan, 16,648
Morris, Esther Hobart (McQuigg) [Mrs. Artemus] Slack [Mrs. John] (1814-1902), 1,790, 17,885, 17,898, 17,908, 17,910, 17,933
Morris Family, 12,314
Morris Family (MS), 9,613
Morris Family (NC), **13,066**
Morris Family (PA), 15,104
Morris Family (SC), 15,622
Morris Family (UT), 16,768
Morris George Q., 16,769
Morris, Gouverneur (1752-1816), **2,493**
Morris, Gulielma (Trueblood) [Mrs. Thomas] (1810-89), **4,610**
Morris Indian School (MN), **8,705**
Morris, Jacob (1755-1844), **11,657**
Morris, Jane T. [Mrs. John], **9,686**
Morris, John, **16,768**
Morris, John (1826-65), 9,686
Morris, John C., 13,448
Morris, John Moses (1837-73), **1,922**
Morris, John T., **15,057**
Morris, Josephine Cushing, 5,794
Morris, Josie, **16,904**
Morris, Ken (1915-), **8,111**

Morris, Levina. *See* Shannon, Levina (Morris) [Mrs. Marmaduke]
Morris, Lewis (1671-1746), 11,070
Morris, Lizzie, 14,515
Morris, Louisa, 14,515
Morris, Lydia Spencer (ca. 1829-1903), 14,857
Morris, Lydia T., **15,057**
Morris, Margaret Ann "Meta" (1810-81). *See* Grimball, Margaret Ann "Meta" (Morris) [Mrs. John Berkeley] (1810-81)
Morris, Margaret Hill (1736-1816), 14,845, 14,847, 14,854
Morris, Margaret Muldoon [Mrs. James] (1828?-93), **10,776**
Morris, Margaretta Hare [Miss] (1797-1867), **14,944**
Morris, Marie Louise. *See* DeMilly, Marie Louise (Morris)
Morris, Martha. *See* Rowley, Martha (Morris) [Mrs. Erastus]
Morris, Martha Elizabeth (Wright) (1832?-1919), **2,494**
Morris, Martha T. (Riggs) [Mrs. Wyllys] (1842-1910), 9,316
Morris, Mary, 11,657
Morris, Mary Lois (Walker) [Mrs. Elias] (1835-1919), 16,769
Morris, Mary (Ormond) [Mrs. William] George [Mrs. John] (1821-92), 16,768
Morris, Mary R., 14,515
Morris, May (1863?-1938), 1,224
Morris, Monia, 10,211
Morris, Pheobe, 14,977
Morris, Rachel W., 14,515
Morris, Ramsay, 12,173
Morris, Robert C., 1,790
Morris, Roland S., 15,059
Morris, Sarah (1842-94), 5,794
Morris, Sarah Andt Sletor [Mrs. Thomas Burnside], 15,059
Morris, Sarah E., 14,515
Morris, Sarah E., 14,831
Morris, Sarah P. (Cushing) [Mrs. Thomas John], 5,794
Morris, Susanna (1682-1755), **15,058**
Morris, Susanna (Hall) [Mrs. Joseph] Harvey [Mrs. John] Rush [Mrs. Richard] (1815?-95), 15,084
Morris, Thomas Burnside (1842-85), **15,059**
Morris, Thomas John (1837-1912), **5,794**
Morris, William, 1,467
Morris, William M., Family (MN), **9,247**
Morrison, Agnes (1893-). *See* Park, Agnes (Morrison) [Mrs. Charles Richardson] (1893-)
Morrison, Alden Leslie, **8,516**
Morrison, Betty, 157
Morrison, Catharine (1834-97). *See* Kennedy, Catharine (Morrison) [Mrs. Joseph Camp Griffith] (1834-97)
Morrison, Clinton (1842-1913), 9,248
Morrison, Dorilus, Family (MN), **9,248**
Morrison, Dottie "Dot" (1845-?), **9,249**
Morrison, Emily (1837-1926). *See* Bondurant, Emily (Morrison) [Mrs. Alexander Joseph] (1837-1926)
Morrison, Ethel (1876-?). *See* Van Derlip, Ethel (Morrison) (1876-?)
Morrison Family, 349
Morrison, Florence, 1,233
Morrison, James, 12,956
Morrison, Julia K. Washburn [Mrs. Clinton], 9,248
Morrison, Mandana [Mrs. Charles] (1816-?), 8,961
Morrison, Marion (1888-1976). *See* King, Marion (Morrison) [Mrs. Frederick Gore] (1888-1976)
Morrison, Martha Ann (1832?-?). *See* Minto, Martha Ann (Morrison) (1832?-?)
Morrison, Mary (Babcock) [Mrs. John Henry] (1857-?), 9,277
Morrison, Mary C. *See* Lowe, Mary C. (Morrison) [Mrs. George]
Morrison, Mary Florence (1850-1921). *See* Walker, Mary Florence (Morrison) [Mrs. Wilbur Fisk] (1850-1921)
Morrison, Mildred, 16,870
Morrison, Mrs., 12,527
Morrison, Mrs. Robert (1839-?), 13,683

Morrison, O. E., 9,249

Morrison, Phebe Jane (1854-1931). *See* Hutchison, Phebe Jane (Morrison) [Mrs. John Rogers] (1854-1931)

Morrison, Sarah Varick (Cozens) [Mrs. William N.] (1814-?), **13,076**

Morrison, William N., 13,076

Morrison, Zedie Jane. *See* Buyse, Zedie Jane (Morrison)

Morriss, Anthony (1654-1721), 14,977, 15,057

Morriss, Margaret, 2,067

Morrissey, Elizabeth, **4,814**

Morrissey, Elizabeth M., **5,943**

Morrissey, Muriel (Earhart), 5,162, 6,550, 11,831

Morrogh, C. T., 11,001

Morrogh, Mary F. [Mrs George] Richmond [Mrs. C. T.], **11,001**

Morrow, Anne Spencer (1906-). *See* Lindbergh, Anne Spencer (Morrow) [Mrs. Charles Augustus] (1906-)

Morrow, Constance Cutter (1913-). *See* Morgan, Constance Cutter (Morrow) (1913-)

Morrow, Dwight, 7,264

Morrow, Dwight, Jr., 7,264

Morrow, Elisabeth Reeve (1903-). *See* Morgan, Elisabeth Reeve (Morrow) (1903-)

Morrow, Elizabeth Reeve (Cutter) (1873-1955), 7,138, 7,161, 7,171, **7,264**

Morrow, Henry A., 14,773

Morrow, Honore Willsie (1880-1940), **5,094**

Morrow, Isabella. *See* Boniface, Isabella (Morrow) [Mrs. John J.]

Morrow, Jean Smith [Mrs. Roger S.], 5,063

Morrow, Maud. *See* Brown, Maud (Morrow) [Mrs. Calvin S.]

Morse, Add, 14,620

Morse, Alice (1851-1911). *See* Earle, Alice (Morse) [Mrs. Henry] (1851-1911)

Morse, Dorothea Clara. *See* Coors, Dorothea Clara (Morse)

Morse, Edward S., 7,467

Morse, Effie Dallas [Mrs. Virgil D.], 11,658

Morse, Electa Emeline (1864-1929). *See* Kidder, Electa Emeline (Morse) [Mrs. Thomas B.] (1864-1929)

Morse, Emily Hall, 17,309

Morse, Ephraim W., 1,197

Morse, Esther (1898-), **14,425**

Morse, Eva S., **16,543**

Morse, F., 12,426

Morse Family (NY), **11,658**

Morse Family (OR), 14,620

Morse, Frances Rollins (1850-1928), **6,774**

Morse, Leonard Blaine, 11,665

Morse, Lucy Smith (1864-1941). *See* Caldwell, Lucy Smith (Morse) [Mrs. Edward] (1864-1941)

Morse, Marion. *See* Davis, Marion (Morse) [Mrs. Elvert M.]

Morse, Mary Ann, 10,480

Morse, Mary Chase Walker [Mrs. Ephraim W.] (1828-99), **1,197**

Morse, Mary Rosie, 7,047

Morse, Nellie, 14,620

Morse, Percy Mulford (1876-1963), 14,620

Morse, Rex L., 14,620

Morse, Robert V., 11,658

Morse, Samuel F. B., 10,920, 15,585

Morse, Wayne, 6,365, 14,504

Morss Burton G., 11,264

Morss, Caroline Amelia (Kirtland) [Mrs. Burton G.] (1810-80), **11,264**

Mortality, 2,317, 2,676

Mortar Board, 13,406, 14,030

Mortar Boards (Black Masque) (NE), **10,606**

Mortara (book), 12,795

Mortenson, Clara E. (1892-). *See* Beyer, Clara E. (Mortenson) (1892-)

Mortenson, Margaret Dorothea (1903-). *See* Landon, Margaret Dorothea (Mortenson) [Mrs. Kenneth Perry] (1903-)

Mortgages, 8,331, **11,204**, 11,523, 15,483

Mortimer Family (NY), 12,020

Mortimer, Mary (1816-77), 17,844

Morton, Abby (1821-1904). *See* Diaz, Abby (Morton) [Mrs. Manuel A.] (1821-1904)

Morton, Annie Malvin (1906-), **4,130**

Morton Arboretum (Lisle, IL), 3,882, 4,289

Morton, Blanche Liffick, **4,629**

Morton, Carl (1865-1900), 3,881

Morton, Carolyn (1915-21), 3,882

Morton, Carrie Lake, 3,881

Morton, Emma Little (1846-192?), **6,775**

Morton Family (IL), **3,881**

Morton, Ferdinand Joseph "Jelly Roll" (1885-1941), **5,531**

Morton, Frances. *See* Froehlicher, Frances Morton

Morton, Frank Thomas, 10,496

Morton, Gertrude Eliza (Tyler), **6,776**

Morton, Hazel Brown [Mrs. Sidney], **8,246**

Morton, Helen, **6,777**

Morton, Helen, 8,651

Morton, J. Sterling (1832-1902), 3,881

Morton, Jean (?-1953). *See* Cudahy, Jean (Morton) [Mrs. Joseph] (?-1953)

Morton, Joy (1855-1934), 3,881

Morton, Katherine A., 17,901

Morton, Levi P., 12,052

Morton, Malvin. *See* Morton, Annie Malvin (1906-)

Morton, Maralyn, **3,707**

Morton, Mark (1858-1951), 3,881

Morton, Mary (18??-1941). *See* Pollock, Mary (Morton) [Mrs. T. E.] (18??-1941)

Morton, Matilda (Lamb) (ca. 1857-?), **13,077**

Morton, Millicent (1925-29), 3,882

Morton, Nancy Jane Fletcher [Mrs. Thomas Frank] (1845-1912). *See* Stevens, Nancy Jane Fletcher [Mrs. Thomas Frank] Morton [Mrs. George W.] (1845-1912)

Morton Salt Company, 3,881

Morton, Sophia Preston Owsley [Mrs. Sterling] (1891-1969), 3,882

Morton, Sterling (1885-1961), **3,882**

Morton, Suzette (1911-), 3,882

Morton, William James (1845-1920), **680**

Mosaic Club (Bridgeport, CT), **1,825**

Mosaics, 2,802, **2,815**

Mosby, Mrs. F. B., 9,737

Moseley, Daisy Haywood (1892-), **13,078**

Moseley, Elizabeth [Mrs. Joseph], **7,483**

Moseley, Hardwick, 2,875

Moseley, Joseph, 7,483

Moseley, Sybil (1792-1848). *See* Bingham, Sybil (Moseley) [Mrs. Hiram] (1792-1848)

Moser, Frances (?-1968), 5,063

Moser, Mother Theresa, **5,166**

Moses (slave, SC), 15,530

Moses, Ann W. [Mrs. Felix], 9,254

Moses, Anna Mary Robertson "Grandma" [Mrs. Thomas Salmon] (1860-1961), **16,997**

Moses, Belle, 5,941

Moses, Bessie, 5,842, 6,223

Moses, Bill, 8,709

Moses Brown school (RI), 7,490

Moses, Clara Cordelia (1839-1926). *See* Cannon, Clara Cordelia (Moses) [Mrs. Angus Munn] (1839-1926)

Moses, George, 10,808

Moses: Man of the Mountain (book), 2,872

Moses, Mary. *See* Claywell, Mary (Moses)

Moses, Mary Edith (Briggs) [Mrs. Bernard], 353

Moses, Mathilde R. (1887-), **14,426**

Moses, Mildred "Mim" (1892-1976). *See* Graves, Mildred "Mim" (Moses) [Mrs. Louis] (1892-1976)

Moses, Miriam Gratz. *See* Cohen, Miriam Gratz Moses [Mrs. Solomon]

Moses, Phoebe Ann (1860-1926). *See* Oakley, Annie. Phoebe Ann Moses. [Mrs. Frank] Butler (1860-1926)

Moses, Robert, 11,914, 11,928

Mosheatel, Rebecca (Morhaime), 17,282

Mosher, Alfreida (1873-1966), **6,778**

Mosher, Clelia Duel (1863-1940), **681, 1,551, 1,560**

Mosher, Cynthia. *See* Moore, Cynthia Mosher [Mrs. Alden]

Mosher, Eliza Maria (1846-1928), **7,872**, 11,605

Mosick, Ruth Ann, 5,063

Moskowitz, Anna (1891-). *See* Kross, Anna (Moskowitz) (1891-)

Moskowitz, Belle (Lindner) [Mrs. Charles Henry] Israels [Mrs. Henry] (1877-1933), 2,336, 7,548, 11,914, 11,928

Mosley, Charles C., Sr., 9,687

Mosley, Jessie B. [Mrs. Charles C., Sr.], **9,687**

Mosquitoes, 2,089

Moss, Leila (1895-1962). *See* Eldredge, Leila (Moss) [Mrs. Horace J.] Grant [Mrs. John E.] Lee [Mrs. Clarence] (1895-1962)

Moss, Luella St. Clair, 10,200

Moss, Mary (1826-73). *See* Keene, Laura [Miss]. [Mrs. John] Taylor. [Mrs. John] Lutz (1826-73)

Moss, Neva (Millier), 4,642

Moss, Samuel, Family, 1,726

Moss Side Plantation (MS), 9,614

Mosshard, Gertrude, 2,694

Mossiker, Frances Sanger (1906-), **6,059, 7,265**

Mossop, Louisa (Lane) [Mrs. Henry Blaine] Hunt [Mrs. George] (1820-97). *See* Drew, Louisa (Lane) [Mrs. Henry Blaine] Hunt [Mrs. George] Mossop [Mrs. John D.] (1820-97)

Motels, 10,362

Moten, Cora Bell, 3,284

Moten, Etta. *See* Barnett, Etta (Moten) [Mrs. Claude A.]

Mother Agnes of Jesus, 828, 829

Mother and child, 17,382

"Mother and Child in American Art" (exhibition), 2,847

"Mother and Daughter Talks" (articles), 13,718

Mother Earth (periodical), 4,145, 4,229, 12,487

Mother Featherlegs monument, 17,961

Mother Jones Rest Home (Hyattsville, MD), 3,839

Mother Joseph (1823-1902), **17,415**

Mother Mary, 5,501

Mother Mary of Jesus, 11,292

Mother Mary of Jesus the Good Shepherd (1842-1902), **15,181**

Mother of Clubs, The (book), 7,294

Mother of Dolores Church (Vandalia, IL), Sir Thomas More Society, **4,447**

Mother of the Year, 4,949

Mother of the Year (IA), 4,918

Mother of the Year (UT), **16,948**

Mother of Washington and Her Times, The (book), 2,187

Mother Seton's Daughters (drama), 1,750

Motherhood Club (Hartford, CT). *See* Hartford Woman's Club (CT)

Motherhood Protective League (MN), 9,440

Mothers, 1,705, 1,860, 4,949

employment, 2,097, 2,677, 2,686, 4,108, 8,664, 11,764

mortality, 8,961, 13,446, 15,633

nutrition, **14,198**

Mother's Book, 13,712

Mothers' Circle (Cambridge, MA), 6,950

Mothers Circle and Child Study Club (AL). *See* Montgomery Mothers' Circle (AL)

Mothers Club (Montgomery, AL). *See* Montgomery Mothers' Circle (AL)

Mothers' Club (Chicago, IL), 3,974

Mother's Club (South Bend, IN), **4,665**

Mothers' Club (MN), 8,917

Mother's Club (Saratoga Springs, NY), 12,851

Mothers' Club of Cambridge (MA), **6,779**

Mothers Club of DeWitt (AR), **273**

Mothers' Congress, 15,270

Mother's Day, 110, 1,224, 9,530, **12,521, 17,465,** 17,471

Mothers' Day International Association, 12,521

Mothers' Discussion Club (MA), 6,358, **6,780**

Mothers' Discussion Club (Cambridge, MA), 6,950

Mothers general, 275, **1,513, 1,515, 1,516, 1,517,** 4,335, 4,649, 7,694, 8,483, 9,695, 12,810, 12,859, 12,934, 13,868, 14,226, 14,874, **15,146, 15,181,** 15,337, 15,866, 15,912, 17,572, 17,854

Mothers general, Afro-American, 17,029

Mother's Health Association, Planned Parenthood of Central Ohio. *See* Planned Parenthood of Central Ohio

Mothers in art, 2,847

Mothers' Meetings (IL), 3,855

Mothers Neighborhood Circle (CT). *See* Northwest Child Welfare Club (CT)

Mothers of America, 9,150

Mothers of Pennsylvania, 15,121

Mothers of the year, 8,421, 10,782, 13,565, **15,799, 17,029**

Mother's Pension Committee (CA), 689

Mothers' Query Club (MA). *See* Mothers' Thursday Club (MA)

Mothers' Study Club (Rochester, IN), 4,661

Mothers' Study Club (MA), **6,781**

Mothers' Study Club (Cambridge, MA), 6,950

Mothers' Thursday Club (MA), **6,782**

Mothers Union (Montgomery, AL). *See* Montgomery Mothers' Circle (AL)

Motion Picture Code, 11,907

Motion Picture Research Council, 1,593, 8,689, 11,944

Motion study, 7,115

Motivation as Related to Personality (book), 13,730

Motley, Constance Baker (1921-), 5,476, 6,710, **7,266**

Motley, Marion, 10,739

Motor bus drivers, 13,217

Motor Products, strike, 8,099

Motor Transport and Allied Workers Industrial Union Local 544 (MN), 9,380

Motor vehicles, safety measures, 9,359

Mott, Amelia (1859-1937). *See* Gummere, Amelia (Mott) (1859-1937)

Mott, Caroline Pitkin [Mrs. Jordan Lawrence, III], 12,053

Mott Family (NY), **12,053**

Mott Family (NY), 11,600

Mott Family (PA), **15,291**

Mott, Frank Luther (1886-1964), **10,027**

Mott, J. L., Jr. *See* Mott, Jordan Lawrence, II (1829-1915)

Mott, James (1788-1868), 15,291

Mott, John R., 11,572

Mott, Jordan Lawrence (1799-?), 12,053

Mott, Jordan Lawrence, II (1829-1915), 12,053

Mott, Jordan Lawrence, III (1881-ca. 1913), 12,053

Mott, Lucretia (Coffin) [Mrs. James] (1793-1880), 1,437, 2,413, **2,495**, 2,501, 2,588, 3,908, 5,907, 5,961, 6,244, 6,589, **6,783**, 7,222, 7,230, 7,430, 7,632, 8,531, 9,023, 11,605, 11,920, 12,003, 12,819, 12,828, 12,857, 15,270, 15,279, 15,283, 15,290, 15,291, 15,292, 15,295, 15,355

Mott, Lydia, 2,588

Mott, Mildred. *See* Wedel, Mildred (Mott)

Mott, Sarah Curtis (pseudonym). *See* Howard, Liliane Stevens [Miss] (1872-1967)

Mott, Sarah "Sallie" [Miss], **11,002**

Mott, Vera Ingram [Mrs. Frank Luther] (1885-1964), 10,027

Mott, Wilbur A., 11,034

Motte, Abraham, 15,512

Motte, Isaac, **15,504**

Motte, Isaac (son), 15,504

Motte, Mary [Mrs. Isaac], 15,504

Motte, Mary (Quince) [Mrs. Abraham], 15,512

Motte, Rebecca (?-1825), 15,441

Motter, Ellen Sitgreaves (Vail), **6,784**

Motzenauer, Margarete, 2,968

Moudy, Alice M., **17,994**

Moudy, Mable Cheney (1878-1972), **17,995**

Moul, Sarah B., 3,515

Mould and Nichol (architects, MN), **9,250**

Moulton, Anna Churchill (1874-1951). *See* Tillinghast, Anna Churchill (Moulton) (1874-1951)

Moulton, Blanche, 4,743

Moulton, Ellen Louise (Chandler) [Mrs. William Upham] (1835-1908), **1,467**, 2,370, **2,496**, 2,520, 2,542, 5,815, **5,944**, 5,959, 6,659, 6,712, **6,785**, 7,131, 7,648, **7,651**, 11,821, 14,062, 17,009

Moulton, L. Josephine (1834-?). *See* Stewart, L. Josephine (Moulton) [Mrs. John] (1834-?)

Moulton, Leonice M. (Sampson) [Mrs. Joseph W.], 5,805

Moulton, Louise (1835-1908). *See* Moulton, Ellen

Louise (Chandler) [Mrs. William Upham] (1835-1908)

Moulton, Phyllis (1887-?). *See* Merrill, Phyllis (Moulton) (1887-?)

Moulton, Susan Whittemore (1856-89), **7,410**

Moulton, William Upham (?-1898), 1,467, 2,496

Mound Road Engine Plant (MI), 8,132

Mount Ararat Plantation (MS), 9,610

Mount Carmel Carnegie Library (IL), 4,299

Mount Carmel Generalate (Lacombe, LA), **5,428**

Mount Carmel Woman's Club (IL), **4,298**

Mount, Charles Wright, **11,199**

Mount Holyoke College (MA), 1,085, 2,460, 4,167, 4,387, 6,754, 7,056, 7,129, 7,496, **7,500**, 7,792, 11,814, 11,905, 12,737, 12,740, 13,962, 17,029, 17,031

alumnae, 2,002, **7,497, 7,498, 7,501**, 8,572, 10,927, 12,675, 14,152

faculty, 949, **7,499**, 7,814, 12,642

history, **7,493**

students, 3,305, 7,350, **7,495**, 8,664, 11,749, 17,653

Mount Holyoke Female Seminary (MA). *See* Mount Holyoke College (MA)

Mount Holyoke Female Seminary (MA), Memorandum Society, **6,786**

Mount Holyoke Seminary and College (MA). *See* Mount Holyoke College (MA)

Mount, Levina (Shannon) [Mrs. Thomas], 9,613

Mount, Mary Jane (ca. 1829-?). *See* Tanner, Mary Jane (Mount) (ca. 1829-?)

Mount Meigs reformatory (AL), 91

Mount Mercy College (Pittsburgh, PA). *See* Carlow College (Pittsburgh, PA)

Mount Pleasant Female Seminary (IA), 5,061

Mount Pleasant German College (IA), students, 5,064

Mount Pleasant High School (IA), 5,068

Mount Pleasant Methodist Episcopal Church (IA), Women's Foreign Mission Society, 4,959

Mount Pleasant Presbyterian Church (Raymilton, PA), 11,626

Mount Pleasant Women's Club (IA), 4,960

Mount Rushmore, 2,218, 6,836

Mount Rushmore Memorial, 2,081

Mount Saint Joseph Ursuline Motherhouse (KY), **5,390**

Mount Saint Mary College (Hooksett, NH), 10,888

Mount St. Mary's College (Los Angeles, CA), **1,006**

Mount St. Paul College (WI), 17,557

Mount St. Scholastica Convent (Atchison, KS), 5,164, 5,165, 5,166, 5,167

Mount Shasta Hotel (CA), 1,661

Mt. Sinai Hospital (NY), 6,222

Mount Sinai Hospital (MA), Ladies Auxiliary, **13,812**

Mt. Tamapais fire (CA, 1929), 405, 471

Mount Vernon, 12,327, 12,847, 15,037

Mount Vernon Association. *See* Mount Vernon Ladies' Association

Mount Vernon Ladies' Association, 297, 6,103, 11,099, 11,602, 15,439, 15,510, 17,293

Mount Vernon Ladies Association of the Union. *See* Mount Vernon Ladies' Association

Mount, William Sidney, 2,744, 10,955

Mount Zion Church (MS), 5,420

Mount Zion Community Club (Rochester, IN), 4,661

Mount Zion Congregational Church (OH), 13,945

Mount Zion Hebrew Congregation (St. Paul, MN), 9,251

Mountain Bell Telephone Company (CO), 10,312

Mountain Dooryards (book), 7,220

Mountain Home School (AL), 29

Mountain House (CA), 438

Mountain Life and Work (book), 5,251

Mountain, Mary (pseudonym). *See* Locke, Mary (Jameson) [Mrs. Charles Morrell]

"Mountain Music" (ms), 1,750

Mountain View Folk Festival, 234

Mountain View Twentieth Century Club (OK), **14,219**

Mountain View Women's Club (Ontario, CA), 1,092

Mountaineers (club), 17,267, 17,305

Mountford, Elizabeth, 5,684

Mountford, Lydia Mary Olive Von Finklestein Mamreov (1848-1917), **16,770**

Mounts, Celia (1805-97). *See* Hunt, Celia (Mounts) [Mrs. Jefferson] (1805-97)

Mourne Family, 12,531

Mouse-Gray Stallion, The (book), 10,262

Mousley, Sarah Maria. *See* Cannon, Sarah Maria (Mousley) [Mrs. Angus M.]

Mouton, Alexander (1853-1938), 5,434

Mouton, Lucile Meredith. *See* Griffin, Lucile Meredith (Mouton)

Movey, Jane, 8,936

Moving-picture industry, 11,537, 11,607

Moving-picture music, 51

Moving-picture plays, 949, 1,451, 3,059, 3,065, 6,000, 6,003, 6,098, 17,972

Moving-picture producers and directors, **1,978, 5,979,** 5,994, 11,989, 12,015, 17,642, **17,791, 17,794, 17,801**

Moving-picture scripts, 11,994

Moving-picture studios, 949, 11,537, 11,907, 14,736

Moving-picture theaters, **12,794**

Moving-pictures, 60, **1,025**, 3,340, 4,473, **8,523,** 9,095, 11,537, 16,774

censorship, 2,242, 8,486, 11,907, 12,061, 13,787

evaluation, 17,326

production and direction, 13,762

Moving-pictures, silent, 11,907

Moving-pictures, talking, 15,897

Moving-pictures and television, 11,907

Moving-pictures in education, 17,642

Mowatt, Anna Cora (Ogden) [Mrs. James]. [Mrs. William Foushee] Ritchie (1819-70), 1,426, **6,787**

Mowatt, James, 1,426

Mowder, Louisa, **4,432**

Mowrer, Edgar Ansel (1892-1977), **2,497**

Mowrer, Lilian (Thomson) [Mrs. Edgar Ansel] (1889-), 2,497

Mowry, Celia, 8,230

Mozier Isabella [Mrs. Joseph], 1,083

Mr. Beardsley's Select School for Girls (MD), 5,796

Mr. Cole's Female School (Salem, MA). *See* Salem Female School (MA)

Mr. Dunham's School (VT), 2,291

Mr. Small (book), 2,938

Mr. U.S.A. Pageant (SC), **15,807**

Mr. W. and I (book), 12,542

Mratchny, Mark. *See* Clevans, Mark

Mrs. Catherine Dineen: Her Life and Contributions (book), 11,407

"Mrs. Eleanor Roosevelt's Contribution to the Status of Women" (memoir), 11,484

Mrs. F. C. Maderia Normal Training School for Kindergarteners (IA), 9,318

"Mrs. Fiske's Definition of Art" (ms), 12,474

Mrs. Flowers' Dog Days (book), 11,992

Mrs. Frost's School (MA), 6,818

Mrs. Hannah's School (Washington, PA), 15,952

Mrs. Howard's School for Young Ladies (Jonesborough, TN), 13,250

"Mrs. Joe Person's Remedy" (medicine), 13,089

Mrs. L. H. Raines Memorial, 3,076

"Mrs. Miniver" (radio program), 2,274

Mrs. Palmer's Honey (book), 10,159

"Mrs. Pep's Diary," 7,254

Mrs. Rivardi's School (PA), 6,504

Mrs. Roosevelt's Press Conference Association, **11,493**

Mrs. Sarazin's Seminary (PA), 15,737

Mrs. Seton's School (Cornish, NH), 2,375

Mrs. Welch's Cookbook, 4,691

Mrs. Wiggs of the Cabbage Patch (book), 5,273, 5,360

Ms. (periodical), 6,079

Mu Sigma Sigma, 1,085

Mudd, Emily Hartshorne (1898-), 6,221, 6,223, **6,788**, 6,987, **14,926**

Mudge, Edwin (1818-90), **7,005**

Mudge Family (NY), **11,412**

Mudge, Florence Augusta (1868-?), 7,001

Mudge, Isadore Gilbert (1875-1957), 11,825, 11,849, 11,930, 11,972, **12,054**

Mudge, John Green, 7,332

Mudge, Mary (1841-89). *See* Collins, Mary (Mudge) (1841-89)

Mudge, Sarah Wilson (1857-1938), **7,005**

Mudgely, Adelaide [Miss], 11,324

Mudget, Helen Parker (1900-62), **8,591**
Mudgett, Mildred Dennett (1888-), **8,664**
Mueller, Kate, 4,494
Mueller, Marie (Herney), 1,186
Mueller, Oscar O., 10,270
Mueller, Ruth, 4,903
Mühlbach, Louise. *See* Mundt, Klara
Muir, Andrew Forest (1916-69), **16,249**
Muir, Anne (Gilrye), 1,468
Muir, Daniel H., 1,468
Muir Family, **1,468**
Muir, Helen. *See* Funk, Helen (Muir)
Muir, John (1838-1914), 490, 589, 710, 1,321, 1,468, **1,635**, 1,640
Muir, Louise Wanda (Strentzel) [Mrs. John], 349
Muirson, Magdalena, 11,941
Mukden shuttle (World War II), 11,861
Mulattos, 2,141, 9,604, 10,134
Mulcahey, Mary, 10,508
Mulder, Gwen, 16,876
Mulford, Elizabeth "Betsey" (1775-1828). *See* Crane, Elizabeth "Betsey" (Mulford) [Mrs. John] (1775-1828)
Mull, Katherine (1904-). *See* Zastrow, Katherine (Mull) [Mrs. Lawrence] Falvey [Mrs. Ralph] (1904-)
Mullan, Maud. *See* Carlgren, Maud (Mullan)
Mullen, Jane H. (1823-1900). *See* Walrad, Jane H. (Mullen) [Mrs. David P.] (1823-1900)
Muller, Edith Squier [Mrs.], 10,905
Müller, Ida, 1,559
Muller, Kate Kruse [Mrs. Otto] (1853-1922), **15,489**
Muller, Maud (1886-1972), 15,299
Muller, Otto, 15,489
Müller, Susanna Rohrer (1756-1815), **14,864**
Muller, Theresa Grace (1895-1962?), **6,148**
Mulligan, Andrew, 13,674
Mulligan, Charlotte (?-1900), **11,355**
Mulligan, Joan E., **7,873**
Mulligan, Mary Margaret (1941-), **10,202**
Mulligen, Caroline E. [Mrs. Charles F.] Park [Mrs. William], 12,211
Mulliken, Ruth [Miss], 10,460
Mullikin, Maria West (Oden) [Mrs. James] (ca. 1791-?). *See* Jackson, Maria West (Oden) [Mrs. James] Mullikin [Mrs. Thomas] (ca. 1791-?)
Mulliner, Maurine, 11,916
Mullins, Helene, 4,000
Multnomah County (OR) Community Action Agency, 14,605
Mulvihill, Mary Margaret, **5,386**
Mumford, Ethel (Watts) (1878-1940). *See* Grant, Ethel (Watts) Mumford (1878-1940)
Mumford, Herbert W., 4,386
Mumford, Sarah (1855-1950). *See* Gregory, Sarah (Mumford) [Mrs. Edgar B.] (1855-1950)
Muncy, Elizabeth. *See* Noggle, Elizabeth (Muncy)
Muncy, Levi, 7,881
Munday, Lucy Sims [Mrs.], 9,841
Mundelein College (Chicago, IL), **3,971**
  pictorial works, **3,973**
Mundelein College (Chicago, IL), Mundelein Weekend College in Residence, 3,971
Mundelein College (Chicago, IL), Nu Theta Epsilon, **3,972**
Mundelein College (MA), 6,493
Mundelein, George Cardinal, 3,971
Mundt, Klara, 38
Munford, Mary Cooke Branch [Mrs.] (1865-1938), **17,091**
Munger, Edith Garnett Cushaway Gotts [Mrs.] (1862-1945), **7,874**
Municipal Art League (Chicago, IL), 3,876
Municipal charters, 7,841, 8,913, 9,525, 11,856
Municipal government, 3,853, 7,796, 11,856, 14,133, 15,683, 16,998
  records and correspondence, **1,119**, **1,120**, **1,933**, 3,384, 5,538, **11,451**, **11,463**
Municipal government by city manager, 4,440, 6,717
Municipal officials and employees, 480, **981**, 1,119, 1,190, **1,650**, 1,721, **1,722**, 2,258, **4,182**, **5,381**, 5,829, 6,720, **6,819**, **7,244**, **7,796**, 8,476, 8,721,

9,416, 10,905, **11,987**, 12,144, 12,146, 12,147, 12,148, 12,149, 13,762, **17,279**
  salaries, allowances, etc., 4,078, 9,196
Municipal officials and employees, Afro-American, 10,191
Municipal records, 5,356
Municipal reports, 6,154
Municipal services, 11,451
"Municipal Theatre in America, The," 7,195
Municipal universities and colleges, **5,086**, 14,822, **16,318**, 17,663
Municipal universities and colleges and city administration, 11,895
Munk, Marie, 6,223, **6,789**
Munro, Annette Gardner, 12,836
Munro, Annette L., 14,778
Munro, Carrie. *See* Baldy, Carrie (Munro)
Munro, Edward V., **3,559**
Munro, Elizabeth [Mrs.], **3,208**
Munro, Evelyn Smith, 13,176
Munroe. *See also* Monroe
Munroe, Henry Smith (1850-1933), **12,055**
Munroe, Kirk (1850-1930), **2,498**
Munroe, Mabel Kittredge (Stearns) Noble [Mrs. Kirk], 2,498
Munroe, Mary (Barr) [Mrs. Kirk] (1853-1922), 2,498
Munroe, Ruth, 11,306
Munroe, Susan. *See* Stowe, Susan (Munroe)
Munroe, Susan Dwight. *See* Smith, Susan Dwight (Munroe) [Mrs. Horatio Southgate]
Munroe, Susan M. (Hall) [Mrs. Charles W.] (?-1896), 2,498
Munsingwear, Inc., 9,349
Munson, Eliza Mariah (Allred) [Mrs. James Willard] (1848-1939), **16,771**
Munson, Gorham (1896-1969), **1,981**
Munson, Margaret Elizabeth (1838-1912). *See* Sangster, Margaret Elizabeth (Munson) [Mrs. George] (1838-1912)
Munson, Mary C. [Mrs.], 12,265
Munson, Samuel, 6,907
Mural painting and decoration, 2,792, 2,802, 7,200
Murat, Katrina Wolf (1824-1910), 1,753
Murat, Princess Achille, 2,931
Murayama, Sada (1901-), 4,495
Murder, 178, 677, 806, 987, 1,254, 2,167, 2,536, 3,171, 3,186, 5,108, 7,160, 8,399, 8,801, 9,624, 10,721, 11,034, 11,190, 12,682, 13,549, 16,806
Murdock Academy (UT), students, 16,810
Murdock Center at Umstead Park (NC), 13,122
Murdock Family, 12,397
Murdock, Louise (Caldwell) [Mrs. Roland Pierpont] (1858-1915), 5,239
Murdock, Margaret, 1,356
Murdock, Marian (1848-1943), **4,776**
Murdock, Mrs. Moore, 16,097
Murdock, Pearl (Allen) [Mrs. Victor] (1875-1940), 2,499
Murdock, Victor (1871-1945), **2,499**
Murdock, Victoria, 5,239
Mure, Frederica Sophia. *See* Broke, Frederica Sophia (Mure) [Mrs. Horatio George]
Mure, James, 12,813
Murff, Mayde R. (ca. 1900-63), **9,539**
Murfree, Mary Noailles [Miss] (1850-1922), 1,426, **3,339**
Murfree, William Law, Sr., 3,339
Muricata Club (Pacific Grove, CA), **1,094**
Murkland, Lois, 11,844
Murphey. *See also* Murphy
Murphey, Archibald D., **13,492**
Murphey, Cornelia Anne, 13,492
Murphree, Clara (Martin), 9,709
Murphy. *See also* Murphey
Murphy, Alyce (Sullivan) (1884-1942), **682**, 828, 829
Murphy, B. "Bert" A. [Miss] (1872-1967), **2,909**
Murphy, Elizabeth, 10,901
Murphy Family, 13,269
Murphy, Frank, 7,765, 7,796, 7,875, 8,089
Murphy, Georgine "Nina" Kelton (1866-?). *See* Darlington, Georgine "Nina" Kelton (Murphy) (1866-?)
Murphy, Irene (Ellis) [Mrs. Harold], 7,875
Murphy, Katherine Prentis (1882-1969), **11,899**

Murphy, Lady Blanche. Elizabeth Mary Anunciata Noel, 12,572
Murphy, Lea, 9,323
Murphy, Lois Barclay [Mrs. Gardner] (1902-), **5,231**, 11,306
Murphy, Mary A., 3,354
Murphy, Mary E., 4,084
Murphy, Patricia Lee, 6,547
Murphy, Ruth (Zagat). Ruth (Zagat) Benton Bernstein Murphy Casselman, 8,631
Murphy, Sarah (Barton) [Mrs. William] (ca. 1748-1817), 9,855, 9,989
Murphy, Sister Evelyn (1881-1955), 17,868
Murphy, Susie (1903-), 5,828
Murphy, Virginia Elizabeth Backenstoe (Reed) [Mrs. John M.] (ca. 1833-1921), 644, **743**
Murray, Aline (1888-1941). *See* Kilmer, Aline (Murray) [Mrs. Joyce] (1888-1941)
Murray, Amelia Matilda, 3,502
Murray, Angela Juanita (Stott) [Mrs. Gerton] Colling [Mrs. James] (1919-). *See* Brennan, Angela Juanita (Stott) [Mrs. Gerton] Colling [Mrs. James] Murray [Mrs. James Arthur] Connery [Mrs. Don] (1919-)
Murray, Anna (?-1882). *See* Douglass, Anna (Murray) [Mrs. Frederick] (?-1882)
Murray, Anna Jane Evans [Mrs. Daniel] (1858-1955), 17,693
Murray, Christina (1896-1948), **17,773**
Murray, Daniel (1852-1925), 17,693
Murray, Dolly. *See* Forbes, Dolly (Murray)
Murray, Dorothy. *See* Forbes, Dorothy (Murray)
Murray, Douglas, 8,348
Murray, Elizabeth. *See* Inman, Elizabeth (Murray) Smith [Mrs. Ralph]
Murray, Elizabeth (Wadsworth) (1815-51), 11,466
Murray, Elsie (1878-1965), **11,659**, **15,319**
Murray, Fanny (Young) [Mrs. Roswell] (1787-1859), **16,772**
Murray, H. J., Family (OR), 14,573
Murray, Hannah, **12,268**
Murray, James, 6,193
Murray, James (?-1949), 13,669
Murray, James Alan, 13,669
Murray, Janette Stevenson (1874-1967), **5,015**
Murray, Jeannette, 9,357
Murray, John, 12,268
Murray, Judith (Sargent) [Mrs. John] Stevens [Mrs. John] (1751-1820), 2,621, 14,884
Murray, Karen Anne. *See* Thompson, Karen Anne (Murray)
Murray, Kate, 14,323
Murray, Katie [Miss], **13,279**
Murray, Kathleen (1891-). *See* Seraphine, Sister M. (1891-)
Murray, Madalyn, 4,151
Murray, Mae (?-1965), 11,907
Murray, Margaret, 8,670
Murray, Margaret James (1865-1925). *See* Washington, Margaret James (Murray) [Mrs. Booker T.] (1865-1925)
Murray, Mary, 12,315
Murray, Mary (1737-1808), **12,268**
Murray, Mary Margaret. *See* Thomas, Mary Margaret (Murray) [Mrs. George]
Murray, Pauli (1910-), **2,143**, **6,790**, **11,494**, 13,176
Murray, Philip, 8,085
Murray, Sarah Elizabeth, 5,789
Murray School (St. Anthony Park, MN), 8,969
Murray, Victoria Colonna (1861-?). *See* Dallin, Victoria Colonna (Murray) [Mrs. Cyrus Edwin] (1861-?)
Murray, Virginia, 13,988
Murray Woman's Club (KY), **5,396**
"Murray's Historical and Biographical Encyclopedia of the Colored Race," 17,693
Murrell, Emily L. *See* Jarnagin, Emily L. (Murrell) [Mrs. Milton Preston]
Murrow, Edward, 5,983
Murtland, Cleo (1873-1965), **7,876**
Murton, Jessie Wilmore (Jones) (1886-1973), **5,270**
Muscatine Community College (IA), **5,086**
Muscatine High School (IA), 4,920
Muse, Jessie [Miss], 3,191

Muse, Viola B., 2,946
Museo Nacional (San Jose, Costa Rica), 14,876
Musetta (opera), 7,213
Museum curators. *See* Museum directors
Museum directors, **182**, 310, 597, 910, 1,004, 1,080,
 1,634, 1,676, 1,827, 2,714, 2,723, 2,808, **4,123**,
 5,107, 5,829, 6,185, **6,281**, **6,319**, 6,321, 6,322,
 7,487, **8,211**, 8,622, 8,929, 9,319, **9,926**, 10,544,
 10,921, **10,955**, 11,238, 11,897, **11,921**, 12,276,
 12,751, 12,863, 13,264, 14,235, 14,343, 15,116,
 15,319, 16,316, 16,388, 17,117, 17,498
Museum of Fine Arts (TX), 16,232
Museum of Fine Arts (Boston, MA), Ladies
 Committee, **6,233**
Museum of Modern Art (NY), 12,901, 17,407
Museum of Modern Art (NY), Department of
 Photography, **12,126**
Museum of Natural History (Minneapolis, MN),
 8,592
Museum of New Mexico, 11,217, 11,238
Museum of New Mexico, Spanish Colonial
 Department, 182
Museum of Science and Industry (IL), 4,123
Museum of Textiles and Clothing (NY), 4,949
Museum registration methods, **6,323**
Museums, 849, 1,465, 1,730, 1,785, 2,131, 2,704,
 2,844, 2,845, 2,846, 2,847, 2,848, 2,849, 2,850,
 2,851, 5,542, 6,185, 6,452, 7,571, 8,180, 8,211,
 8,706, 9,509, 9,587, 9,599, 12,901, 16,388
Museums, Native-American, 7,046
Museums of natural history, management, 3,953
Musgrave, Elizabeth, 17,452
Musgrave, Samuel, 17,452
Musgrove, John, 3,485
Musgrove, Maggie Williams [Mrs.]. *See* Taylor,
 Maggie Williams [Mrs.] Musgrove [Mrs. J. M.]
Musgrove, Mary [Mrs. John] (ca. 1700-63). *See*
 Bosomworth, Mary. Cousaponakeesa. [Mrs.
 John] Musgrove [Mrs. Jacob] Mathews [Mrs.
 Thomas] (ca. 1700-63)
Mushrooms, pictorial works, 4,288, 5,601, 6,307,
 6,308
Music, 74, 1,428, 2,021, 2,804, 3,980, 5,782, 8,659,
 17,384
 competitions, 51
 instruction and study, 51, 1,749, **2,151**, **2,155**,
 4,153, 4,319, 11,844, 14,216, 15,208, 16,381
 manuals, text-books, etc., 5,986
 manuscripts, 4,242, 12,160
 periodicals, 16,358
Music, Afro-American, 3,198, 5,423, 15,445
Music and Women (book), 7,218
Music Arts (UT), **16,432**
Music Arts Association (UT), 16,446
Music clubs. *See* Musical societies
Music critics, **1,210**, **2,295**, 3,878, 8,443, **10,866**,
 11,355
Music festivals, 1,788, **3,708**
Music for Family Fun (book), 5,986
Music-halls (variety-theaters, cabarets, etc.), 396, **941**,
 1,683, 5,532, 10,659
"Music in the Air" (radio program), 17,666
Music in the home, 51
Music, popular (songs, etc.), 11,907
"Music Spillers, The" (musicians), 2,151
Music teachers, 83, 409, 468, 573, 931, **1,686**, 1,788,
 2,023, **2,134**, 2,664, **3,369**, **3,582**, **4,056**, 4,153,
 4,319, **4,526**, 4,735, **4,901**, **4,944**, 4,949, 5,063,
 5,093, 5,271, **5,461**, **7,309**, 7,793, **7,975**, **8,189**,
 8,317, **8,356**, **8,364**, **8,473**, 8,748, **8,905**, 8,981,
 9,234, 9,349, 9,367, **9,881**, **10,120**, **10,121**,
 10,449, **10,481**, 10,919, **11,082**, **11,532**, 12,038,
 12,457, **12,774**, **12,796**, 13,640, **14,189**, 14,311,
 14,346, 14,469, 14,527, **15,364**, **15,367**, 15,368,
 16,062, 16,266, 16,281, 16,341, 16,358, 17,234,
 17,666
Music teachers, Afro-American, 12,690
Music Week, **3,708**
Musical accompaniment, 11,176
Musical American (periodical), 16,358
Musical Arts Association (OH), 13,932
Musical Arts Club (Laramie, WY), **17,996**
Musical instruments, catalogs and collections, 16,562
Musical revues, comedies, etc., **4,220**, 12,360

Musical societies, **17**, **51**, 169, 1,038, 1,123, 1,788,
 1,830, 2,007, 2,020, 3,195, 3,198, 3,229, 3,318,
 3,374, **3,692**, **3,838**, 4,056, 4,278, **4,551**, **4,573**,
 4,758, 4,815, **4,877**, 5,179, **5,351**, **5,406**, 5,550,
 5,560, 5,582, **7,147**, 7,299, 7,519, 8,189, **8,194**,
 8,430, 8,442, 8,444, 9,234, **9,335**, **9,357**, **9,488**,
 10,179, 10,889, 12,125, 12,319, **13,507**, **13,545**,
 13,678, **13,734**, 13,748, 13,932, 13,953, **14,024**,
 14,069, 14,141, 14,150, **14,156**, **14,157**, 14,208,
 14,261, **14,430**, 14,565, **15,073**, 15,364, 15,444,
 15,815, 16,062, **16,136**, 16,266, 16,293, **16,352**,
 16,358, 16,446, **17,132**, **17,134**, **17,223**, 17,380,
 17,484, 17,494, **17,824**, **17,996**
Musical societies, Jewish, 14,908
Musical Union (ME). *See* Philharmonic Club (ME)
Musicians, 156, 171, **468**, 573, 749, **957**, **1,038**, **1,195**,
 1,716, 1,788, **2,134**, **2,276**, 2,665, 2,903, **5,888**,
 5,920, 5,936, **5,937**, **6,185**, **7,267**, 7,299, **7,975**,
 9,234, 10,073, 10,082, **10,179**, 10,418, 10,775,
 11,215, 11,394, 11,435, **11,578**, **12,038**, 12,124,
 12,229, **12,319**, **12,455**, **12,686**, 13,302, 13,331,
 14,670, **14,682**, 14,838, 15,020, **15,953**, **16,269**,
 16,438, **16,446**, **16,562**, 16,780, 16,941, 16,967,
 17,310, **17,494**, 17,692, **17,970**
Musicians, Afro-American, **2,134**, **2,151**, **2,155**,
 12,690
Musicians, British, 6,889
Musicians' Club (Troy, OH), **14,157**
Musicians Club of Phoenix (AZ), 169
Musicians' Society of Denver (CO), 1,788
Musicologists, **7,218**, 9,041
Muskegon Heights Women's Club (MI), **8,381**
Muskegon Office of Educational Opportunity (MI),
 7,797
Muskegon Women's Club (MI), **8,382**
Muskingum College (New Concord, OH), archives,
 14,118
Musser, A. Milton, 16,842
Musser, Ellis. *See* Kirkham, Ellis (Musser)
Musser, Ellis (Shipp) [Mrs. Joseph White], 16,949
Musser Family (UT), **16,949**
Musser, Joseph White (1872-1954), 16,949
Musser, Josephine. *See* Tillotson, Josephine (Musser)
Musser, Lucile. *See* Jackson, Lucile (Musser)
Musser, Samuel Shipp, 16,949
Mussolini, Benito, 3,368, 5,973, 7,210, 10,060, 12,701
Muste, A. J., 8,085, 15,315, 15,332
Mute, 2,676, 10,798
Mutinous Wind, The (book), 6,850
Mutiny, 7,467
Mutton, Mary, 14,618
Mutual Aid Association (VT), 16,998
Muzzah Wakon Win. *See* Hastings, Helen. Muzzah
 Wakon Win
Muzzeniegun; or Literary Voyager, The, 2,566
Muzzey, Caroline (McComber) [Mrs. Franklin], 5,682
Muzzey, Franklin (1806-73), **5,682**
"My Appalachia," 5,304
My Arctic Journal (book), 5,694
My Beloved Zebulon (book), 13,599
My Book House (book), 7,261
My Book of History, 2,485
My Brother Adlai (book), 4,370
My Dear Lady, the Story of Anna Ella Carroll
 (book), 14,378
"My Early Dakota Life" (ms), 10,250
My 80 Years in Atlanta (book), 3,205
My Friend Flicka (book), 17,999
My Grandpa's Farm (book), 11,182
"My Heart" (song), 5,529
"My Home is a Heaven to Me" (song), 10,436
My Life (autobiography), 12,361
"My Life Among the Mormons" (ms), 936
"My Life in Two Continents" (ms), 6,590
"My Little Brother" (song), 10,540
My Memoir (book), 2,640
My Memories of Carson City (book), 10,773
"My Memories of Sharlot Hall," 195
My Mortal Enemy (book), 12,414
My Mother Bids Me Bind My Hair (book), 17,175
"My Mount Pleasant Story, 1864-1881," 5,067
My Old Kentucky Home (residence), 5,277
My Playhouse Was a Concord Coach (book), 354,
 1,544, 1,664

"My Prairie Rose" (song), 13,674
My Religion (book), 2,419
My Roses (book), 15,952
My San Francisco (book), 325
My Story (book), 5,980
"My Three Sons" (television program), 17,966, 18,000
"My time with the General Garibaldi, 1865" (journal),
 16,372
Mycologists, **11,628**
Mycology, 14,273
Myer Myers—Goldsmith (book), 13,820
Myerberg, Michael, 6,047
Myers, Albert Cook, 11,061
Myers, Caroline "Lonny" Rulon. [Mrs. Shu-Yu]
 Wang (1922-), 4,046, **4,131**
Myers, Edna, 3,919
Myers, Elizabeth Kenney, 11,102
Myers, Florence W., **17,201**
Myers, Frances (ca. 1906-64). *See* Bauer, Frances
 (Myers) [Mrs. Edward E.] (ca. 1906-64)
Myers, Hannah E. (1819-1901). *See* Longshore,
 Hannah E. (Myers) [Mrs. Thomas Ellwood]
 (1819-1901)
Myers, Jennie Belle [Mrs.] (?-1950), **3,066**
Myers, John Ephraim, 16,968
Myers, Louisa (Marx) [Mrs. Samuel], 3,334
Myers, M. L. N., 6,562
Myers, Mary Ophelia (Cooper) [Mrs. John Ephraim]
 (1857-?), 16,968
Myers, Michaele "Mike" (1924-74), **4,639**
Myers, Myer, 13,820
Myers, Samuel, 3,334
Myers, Susanna, 12,306
Myers, Thomas J., **13,493**
Myers, Virginia (1821?-91). *See* McBlair, Virginia
 (Myers) [Mrs. William] (1821?-91)
Myerson, Bess, 11,817
Mygatt, Emmie D., **17,997**
Mygatt, Tracy (1885-1973), **11,931**, 15,313,
 15,317
Myles, Harriet (Clark), **9,548**
Myles, Myrtle Tate, 10,724
Myrdal, Gunnar, 8,603
Myrick, Elizabeth T., **683**
Myrick, Hanna G., **6,698**
Myrick, Susan [Miss], 2,995, 3,065, **3,067**,
 3,340
Myron, Nancy, 17,600
"Mystic Star, The" (poetry), **8,771**
Mysticism, 11,385, 14,877, 17,473
Mythology, 14,669
"Mythology for Musicians: Ancient Greece and
 Modern Music, A" (ms), 11,578
Mythology, Greek, 6,500
Mythology, Mexican, 6,768
Mytinger, Caroline, **2,500**
Nack, Sophie, 2,701
Nacona Boot Company (TX), 16,273
Nacoochee Institute (GA). *See* Rabun
 Gap-Nacoochee School (GA)
Nadig, Grace, 15,183
Naegle, John Conrad, 207
Nagel, Elsa, **9,899**
Nagle, Margaret, **10,348**
Nagle, Mother Clare, 4,876
Naglee, Antoinette (1869-1952). *See* Burk,
 Antoinette (Naglee) (1869-1952)
Naglee, Henry Morris (1815-86), Family, **684**
Naglee, Marie Antoinette (Ringgold) [Mrs. Henry
 Morris] (ca. 1846-69), 684
Naglee, Mary (?-1911). *See* Burk, Mary (Naglee)
 [Mrs. James Alexander] (?-1911)
Nagrin, Daniel, 12,366
Nahm, Emanie (1893-). *See* Arling, Emanie (Nahm)
 Sachs (1893-)
Nahm, Helen (1901-), **6,149**
Nail, Grace. *See* Johnson, Grace (Nail)
Nails and spikes, 16,427
Nails and spikes, 16,427
Naisbitt, Catherine Hagell (1850-?), **16,474**
Naisyhdistys Pyrkijä, **9,504**
Naldi, Nita (1902-61), 11,907
Nall, Evelyn E. [Mrs.] (1920-), 94
Names, etymology, 15,789
Names, geographical, 3,381, 10,680

Names, personal, **1,660**
    change of, 6,076
    law, 9,995, **17,598,** 17,680
"Nampa Vignette" (column), 3,662
Nance, Albinus, 10,427
Nance, Ethel Ray [Mrs.], **9,252,** 9,467
Nance, Helen Marie (1877-1966). *See* Anderson,
    Helen Marie (Nance) [Mrs. Walter L.]
    (1877-1966)
Nancy (slave), 4,239
Nankai University (China), 817
Nankervis, Elizabeth Maud (Johnston) (1873-1961),
    685
Nantucket Island, 1,794
Napier, Rebecca, 15,661
Napier, Rebecca [Mrs. Thomas], 15,661
Napier, Thomas (1777-1860), **15,661**
*Napoleon and Josephine: The Biography of a
    Marriage* (book), 6,059
Napton, Baily, **10,028**
Naranjo, Elaine, **16,871,** 16,874
Narcissa (opera), 1,022
Narcotic addicts, rehabilitation, 7,807
Narcotic habit, 2,433, 5,530
Narcotics, 12,515
Narcotics, control of, 5,120
Nardin, Louise [Miss], 9,998
Narr, Erna, 9,986
Narr, Helene, 9,986
Narrow Land, The (book), 6,850
Nasaw, Barbara, 11,847
Nasaw, David, 11,847
Nash, A. H., **8,474**
Nash, Abner, 13,488
Nash, Almeda, 1,590
Nash, Erminia, 1,590
Nash, Even Rupert, **1,590**
Nash Family (CT, NY), 1,590
Nash, Florilla "Rillie," 1,590
Nash, Francis, **13,494**
Nash, Justina Davis [Mrs.] Dobbs [Mrs. Abner],
    13,488
Nash, Lusina (1823-?). *See* Ballard, Lusina (Nash)
    [Mrs. Lyman] (1823-?)
Nash, Marjorie R., 2,701
Nash, Martha Joanna Reade (1826-93). *See* Lamb,
    Martha Joanna Reade (Nash) [Mrs. Charles A.]
    (1826-93)
Nash, Mrs. M. B., 3,712
Nash, Phoebe [Mrs.] (1859-1937), **8,474**
Nash, Sarah B., 1,590
Nash, Susan H., 17,125
Nashville American (TN), 15,966
Nashville and Her Jewry, 1850-1961 (book), 15,950
Nashville College for Young Ladies (TN), 15,960,
    15,964
Nashville Equal Suffrage Association (TN), 15,970
Nashville Female Academy (TN), 15,949
    faculty, 5,287
Nashville Housewives League (TN), **15,961**
Nashville Ladies' College (TN), 15,959
Nashville Protestant School of Industry for the
    Support and Education of Destitute Girls (TN),
    15,959
Nashville Woman Suffrage Association (TN), **15,962**
Nashwauk Finnish Cooperative Women's Guild
    (MN), 9,505
Nashwauk Finnish Socialist Chapter (MN), **9,505**
Nasmyth, Florence, 1,559
Nassau Industrial School (Lawrence, NY). *See* Five
    Towns Community House (Lawrence, NY)
Nasson College (ME), 5,708
Nast, Marie (1880-1971). *See* Wherry, Marie (Nast)
    (1880-1971)
Nat, Anna Marie Ketchum, 16,876
Nat Turner Clubs, 8,065
Natal, South Africa, American missionaries to, **7,129**
Natchez Garden Club (MS), **9,813**
Natchez High School (MS), 9,636
Natchez Institute (MS), 5,419
Natchez Pilgrimage, 9,680, 9,813
Natchez Trace Highway Association, 9,647
Natchitoches Art Colony (LA), **5,452**
Natchitoches Parish (LA), 5,409

Natchitoches Women's Club (LA), 5,445
Nate (slave, NC), 13,188
Nathan, Annie (1867-1951). *See* Meyer, Annie
    (Nathan)(1867-1951)
Nathan, Dorothy Goldeen, **14,427**
Nathan, Elvira (186?-1953). *See* Solis, Elvira
    (Nathan) (186?-1953)
Nathan Family, 7,555
Nathan, Maud (1862-1946). *See* Nathan, Maud
    (Nathan) [Mrs. Frederick] (1862-1946)
Nathan, Maud (Nathan) [Mrs. Frederick]
    (1862-1946), **6,791,** 6,995, 12,835
Nathan, Robert, 13,811
Nathan, Robert, 14,447
Nathoy, Lulu. *See* Bemis, Polly [Mrs. Charles A.]
    (?-1933)
Nation, Carrie Amelia (Moore) [Mrs. Charles] Gloyd
    [Mrs. David] (1846-1911), **1,015,** 13,446
Nation, Elizabeth Ann (1833-?). *See* Champ,
    Elizabeth Ann (Nation) [Mrs. George W.]
    (1833-?)
Nation, The (periodical), 5,861, 6,694, 6,709, 6,841,
    12,572, 12,821
National Abortion Rights Action League, 4,046,
    4,131, 6,582, 6,897, 11,932
National Academy, 11,933
National Academy of Arbitrators, 11,770
National Academy of Broadcasting, 17,666
National Academy of Design (NY), 2,744, **12,131,**
    12,901
*National Academy of Design Exhibition Record,
    1826-1860* (book), 2,744
National Academy of Sciences, 1,738, 2,090, **2,667,
    2,668,** 6,336
National Academy of Television Arts and Sciences,
    1,024
National Advisory Commission on Food and Fiber,
    4,397
National Advisory Committee on Farm Labor,
    8,112
National Advisory Committee on the Education of
    the Deaf, 2,105
National Advisory Council on Adult Education,
    15,889
National Advisory Council on the Education of
    Disadvantaged Children, 16,264
National Aeronautic Committee, 2,421
National Aeronautics and Space Administration,
    5,132
National Alliance for Safer Cities, 6,886
National Alliance of Black Feminists, 4,132
National Alliance of Postal Employees, 8,026
National Alliance of Unitarian and Other Liberal
    Christian Women, 7,941
National American Legion Women's Auxiliary,
    2,193
National American Woman Suffrage Association, 250,
    1,059, 1,069, 1,230, 1,391, 1,950, **2,501,** 2,508,
    2,528, 3,183, 3,681, **3,886,** 4,623, 4,631, 4,859,
    5,305, 6,414, 6,435, 6,455, 6,479, 6,534, 6,536,
    6,560, 6,596, 6,706, 6,746, **6,792,** 6,859, 6,888,
    6,966, 6,971, 6,972, 6,976, 6,978, 6,981, 6,983,
    6,985, 7,205, **7,268,** 7,306, 8,963, 9,142, 9,225,
    9,240, 9,372, 9,750, 10,155, 10,681, 11,904,
    11,916, 12,415, **12,573,** 12,652, 12,811, 12,828,
    12,834, 13,433, 13,604, 13,990, 15,300, 15,312,
    15,857, 15,868, 15,941, 16,015, 16,115, 16,252,
    16,566, 16,789, 17,616, 17,906, 17,953, 18,013
National Angel Flight, Billy Mitchell Squadron,
    University of Iowa, **5,016**
National Anti-Slavery Standard (periodical), 8,002,
    11,963, 12,419
National Anti-Suffrage Association, 13,967
National Arbitration League, 11,616
National Arboretum (DC), 2,107
National Assembly for Social Policy and
    Development. *See* National Assembly of National
    Voluntary Health and Social Welfare
    Organizations
National Assembly of National Voluntary Health and
    Social Welfare Organizations, 8,647, **8,670,**
    17,738
National Association for Mental Health, 5,232,
    13,512

National Association for Nursery Education, 4,049
National Association for Repeal of Abortion Laws.
    See National Abortion Rights Action League
National Association for the Advancement of Colored
    People, 726, 825, 1,654, 2,396, **2,502,** 2,587,
    2,879, 3,915, 5,466, 5,828, 5,870, 6,814, 6,980,
    7,078, 7,266, 7,975, 8,068, 8,116, 8,148, 9,252,
    9,392, 9,467, 11,897, 12,680, 12,865, 13,945,
    15,889, 17,234, 17,245, 17,304
National Association for the Physical Education of
    College Women, 13,254
National Association for the Study and Prevention of
    Tuberculosis, 16,051
National Association for Travelers Aid and Transient
    Service. *See* Travelers Aid Association of
    America
National Association of Broadcasters, 2,953
National Association of Business Women, 12,574
National Association of College Women, 89, 2,149
National Association of Colored Graduate Nurses,
    12,691
National Association of Colored Nurses, Inc., 6,123
National Association of Colored Women, 128, 3,935,
    5,458
National Association of Colored Women's Clubs, Inc.,
    3,302, 3,846, **5,945,** 8,027, 10,205, 16,342, 17,299
National Association of Commissions for Women,
    6,676
National Association of Conservation Districts, Ladies
    Auxiliary, **16,256**
National Association of Consumers, 11,805, 11,806
National Association of Day Nurseries. *See* Child
    Welfare League of America
National Association of Deans of Women, 8,594,
    8,746, 11,906, 12,924, 13,754, 15,186
National Association of Dramatic and Speech Arts,
    5,477
National Association of Hearing and Speech
    Agencies, 2,105
National Association of Homebuilders, 4,918
National Association of Jewish Social Workers, **7,548**
National Association of Junior Republics, 11,596
National Association of Manufacturers, public
    relations, 14,431
National Association of Medical Illustrators, 8,574
National Association of Negro Women, 3,799
National Association of Postal Employees, 8,026
National Association of Principals of Schools for
    Girls, 11,351
National Association of Professional Educators, 2,103
National Association of School Social Workers. *See*
    National Association of Social Workers
National Association of Schools of Music, 16,358
National Association of Schools of Social
    Administration, 8,663
National Association of Social Workers, 2,120, 2,224,
    3,399, **3,883,** 4,158, 4,921, 6,900, 8,637, 8,647,
    8,653, 8,656, **8,665,** 8,683, 9,289, 11,021, **13,313,**
    17,021, 17,244, 17,295
National Association of Social Workers, medical
    social work section, 8,636
National Association of Social Workers, Southern
    Minnesota Chapter, Medical Social Work
    Section, **8,666**
National Association of Student Nurses, 5,416
National Association of Travelers Aid Societies. *See*
    Travelers Aid Association of America
National Association of University Dames, 8,615,
    14,035
National Association of Women Artists, 2,758, 2,761,
    2,772, 3,783, 11,835
National Association of Women Deans and
    Counselors, 5,506, 12,921, 17,354
National Association of Women Journalists, 3,862
National Association of Women Lawyers, 4,076,
    4,094, 5,068, 5,394, 10,440, 14,007
National Association of Women Painters and
    Sculptors, 2,758, 11,956
National Association of Woolen Manufacturers
    (Boston, MA), 14,392
National Association on Service to Unmarried
    Parents, 8,647. *See also* National Council on
    Illegitimacy

National Association Opposed to Woman Suffrage, 5,680, 12,525
National Audubon Society, 9,216
National Birth Control League, 12,705
National Black Feminist Organization, Chicago Chapter (IL), **4,132**
National Board of Charities and Corrections, 15,300
National Board of Popular Education, 14,614
National Board of Prisons and Prison Labor, **11,003**
National Book Award, 11,171
National Broadcasting Company, 2,811, 9,849, 11,493, 13,626
  employees, 2,810
National Business and Professional Women's Club, 9,956
National Business Woman (periodical), 2,705
National Business Woman Conference, 9,956
National Capital Park and Planning Commission, 11,482
National Cathedral School for Girls (DC), 65, 540, 4,914
National Catholic School of Social Service (DC), faculty, 8,656
National Catholic Women's Union, 9,934
National cemeteries, 3,274
National Cemetery (GA), 3,274
National Center for Education in Politics, 6,914
National Chautauqua Movement, 3,282
National Child Labor Committee, **2,503**, 6,486, 8,686
National Child Labor Committee (NY), 14,437
National Child Labor Committee, National Committee on Education of Migrant Children, 8,112
National Citizen and Ballot Box, 14,144
National Citizens Advisory Committee on Recreation and Natural Beauty, 3,293
National Citizens Political Action Committee, 4,970
National Civic Federation, 2,397, 12,517, **12,574**
National Civil Liberties Union, 12,703
National Civil Rights Library, **2,865**
National Civil Service Reform League, 6,561, 7,803
National Clergymen's Advisory Committee, 7,282
National College of Education (Evanston, IL), 4,099, 4,210, 4,211, **4,212**
  deans, 4,128
National College of Education (Evanston, IL), Children's School, 4,210
National Commission on Children and Youth, 4,921, 6,860
National Commission on Law Observance and Enforcement (Wickersham Commission), 5,122, 6,263, 6,484, 6,934
National Committee for a Sane Nuclear Policy. *See* SANE: A Citizens' Organization for a Sane World
National Committee for an Effective Congress, 6,914
National Committee for Fair Play in Bowling, 8,131, 8,134
National Committee for the Extension of Labor Education, 6,893, 15,332, 17,588
National Committee for the Prevention of Blindness, 2,568
National Committee for Young Children, 4,049
National Committee of Jewish Women, 4,050
National Committee on Employment of Youth, 8,686
National Committee on Federal Legislation for Birth Control, 7,192, 7,282, 7,289, 9,440
National Committee on Food Marketing, 17,200
National Committee on Household Employment, 6,766, 8,080
National Committee on Housing, 11,914
National Committee on Maternal Health, 6,221, 6,223, **6,227**, 7,192, 7,198
National Committee on Mental Health, 7,282
National Committee on the Cause and Cure of War, 2,256, 7,190, **7,269**, 7,278, 7,290, 8,963
National Committee to Abolish the House Un-American Activities Committee, 17,608
National Committee to Abolish the Poll Tax, 65, **125**
National Committee to Free Angela Davis, 7,211
National Conference of Christians and Jews, 3,830, 8,963

National Conference on City Planning, 14,819
National Conference on Family Life, 7,848
National Conference on Social Welfare, 2,115, 4,130, 8,647, 10,197, 11,958
National Congress of American Indians, 14,235, 17,266
National Congress of Mothers. *See* National Congress of Parents and Teachers
National Congress of Parents and Teachers, 540, **4,133**, 6,854, 7,174, 10,137
National Conservation Exposition (1913), 3,867
National Consumers' League, 1,652, 1,669, 2,336, 2,359, **2,504**, 2,647, 3,899, 6,427, 6,486, 6,520, 6,791, **6,793**, 8,144, 10,953, **11,771**, 11,897, 13,212, 13,942
National Council Against Conscription, 15,315, 17,939
National Council for Prevention of War, 2,432, 3,074, 15,304, 15,307, **15,308**, 17,254
National Council for War Service, 5,735
National Council of Administrative Women in Education, Wisconsin Branch, **17,694**
National Council of American-Soviet Friendship, 6,730, 8,653
National Council of Catholic Women, 355, 14,671, 17,551
National Council of Catholic Women, Tulsa Deanery Council (OK), 14,259
National Council of Churches of Christ in the U.S.A., 12,907, 15,755
National Council of Churches of Christ in the U.S.A., United Church Women, 164
National Council of Community Chests, 8,428
National Council of Defense, 17,091
National Council of Jewish Women, 938, 2,647, **3,884**, 7,525, 7,537, 7,540, 8,963, **9,253**, 9,467, 13,777, 13,778, 17,342, **17,695**, **17,833**, 17,850
National Council of Jewish Women (MN), Minneapolis Section, **9,254**, **13,813**
National Council of Jewish Women (NY), New York Section, 8,631
National Council of Jewish Women (OH), **13,779**
National Council of Jewish Women (OH), Cleveland Section, **13,915**
National Council of Jewish Women (PA), Pittsburgh Section, **15,248**
National Council of Jewish Women (WA), Seattle Section, **17,247**
National Council of Negro Women, 65, 3,799, 11,817, 12,680, 12,681
National Council of Negro Women, St. Louis Section (MO), **10,203**
National Council of Nurses, 8,610
National Council of Parent Education, 8,639
National Council of Primary Education. *See* Association for Childhood Education International
National Council of Southern Negro Youth Congress, 9,810
National Council of Teachers of English, 12,920, 15,789
National Council of the Metropolitan Opera Association, 12,125
National Council of Women, 8,633
National Council of Women and the Law Center, 6,886
National Council of Women of the United States, **2,076**, 2,193, 2,606, 4,156, 4,631, 5,500, 6,456, 6,682, 6,886, 6,978, 7,201, 7,270, 7,293, 7,299, 11,491, 15,300, 16,681, **16,773**, 16,839, 17,468
National Council of Women of the United States, music committee, 7,299
National Council of Women of the United States, western hemisphere solidarity committee, 11,491
National Council of Women Voters, 17,906
National Council on Agricultural Life and Labor, 2,504, 8,112
National Council on Family Relations, 8,567, **8,667**
National Council on Household Employment, Inc., 11,775
National Council on Illegitimacy, 8,640
National Council on Naturalization and Citizenship. *See* American Immigration and Citizenship Conference

National Council on Social Work Education, 8,677
National Council on the Aging, 8,674
National Council on the Arts, 12,532
National Day Care Program, 7,262
National Defense Committee (NC), 13,557
National Defense Program, 11,504
National Democratic Committee, Colored Division, 8,116
National Dietetic Association, 8,530
National Editorial Association, 3,862
National Education Association, 2,647, 4,211, 4,830, 4,946, 5,325, 5,506, 5,883, 6,237, 7,193, 13,052, 13,677, 17,356
National Education Association, American Alliance for Health, Physical Education and Recreation, Southern District, **12,937**
National Education Association, department of home economics, 17,445
National Education Association, NEA *Journal* (periodical), 4,946
National Educational Policies Committee, 8,058
National Educational Television, 11,845
National Emergency Council, officials and employees, 11,478
National Endowment for the Arts, 17,817
National Endowment for the Arts Award, 15,660
National Farm Workers Association, 842
National Farmers Union, 17,638, 17,676
National Farmers Union, National Department of Junior Education, 13,720
National Federation for Child Study, Chapter 65, 10,168
National Federation for Constitutional Liberties, 12,682
National Federation of Business and Professional Women, 6,901, **8,439**
National Federation of Business and Professional Women's Clubs, 99, **2,705**, 5,130, 6,829, 6,941, 7,699, 15,971
National Federation of Colored Women's Clubs, 128
National Federation of Day Nurseries. *See* Child Welfare League of America
National Federation of Music Clubs, 2,007, 8,442, 12,319, 14,150, 17,134, 17,494
National Federation of Press Women, Inc., 3,694, 4,120, 8,429, **9,823**, 17,930, 17,955
National Federation of Republican Women, 3,658, 5,137, 5,142, 5,143, 5,145, **5,150**, 6,939, 17,141
National Federation of Republican Women, School of Politics, 5,150
National Federation of Settlements. *See* National Federation of Settlements and Neighborhood Centers
National Federation of Settlements and Neighborhood Centers, 4,130, 4,158, 8,646, 8,651, 8,658, 8,659, **8,668**, 9,289
National Federation of Women's Clubs, 6,355
National Federation of Women's Republican Clubs. *See* National Federation of Republican Women
National Florence Crittenton Mission, 2,193, **8,669**
National flowers, 12,910
National Food Company (NY), 7,655
National Foundation for Infantile Paralysis, 8,621, 8,943, 9,522, 16,911
National Freedman's Relief Association, 2,386
National Gentile League, 14,686
National Geographic, 17,614
National Geriatric Hospital, 239
National Get-Out-The-Vote-Club, 9,211
National Guild of Piano Teachers, 16,358
National Health Assembly, 6,919
National Health Council, 6,123, 12,998
National Home Demonstration Council, 13,685
National Homeopathic Hospital (DC), 2,119
National Homeopathic Hospital Association, 2,119
National Honorary Extension Fraternity, 10,039
National Horticultural Society, 13,709
National Independent Student Association, 4,382
National Indian Association, 1,504
National Institute of Arts and Letters. *See* American Academy and Institute of Arts and Letters
National Institutes of Health, officials and employees, 6,336
National Jewish Hospital, 14,908

National Jewish Welfare Board, 7,546, 7,554, 9,083

National Kindergarten and Elementary College (Chicago, IL), alumnae, 3,974

National Kindergarten Association, 3,535, **12,076**

National Labor Relations Board, 6,640, 6,668, 11,905

National Labor Relations Board, officials and employees, 11,484

National League for Civic Education of Women, 12,524

National League for Nursing, 236, 2,686, 3,432, 5,000, 5,494, **5,845**, 6,162, 6,238, 6,594, 8,045, 8,553, 9,976, 12,077, **12,137**, 12,738, 13,880

National League for Nursing, Committee on Historical Source Material in Nursing, 6,721

National League for Opposing Woman Suffrage, 12,524

National League for the Protection of American Institutions, 2,000

National League for Woman's Service, 16,128, 17,392

National League for Woman's Service (WI), 17,685

National League for Woman's Service, Social and Welfare Division, **5,357**

National League of American Pen Women, 54, 325, 1,749, **1,789, 1,826**, 2,844, 2,848, 2,849, 2,977, 3,159, **3,230, 3,885**, 5,270, 5,783, **5,795, 10,497, 10,498, 10,769**, 12,924, **13,656**, 13,674, 17,179, 17,269, **17,310, 17,696**

National League of American Pen Women, Minnesota branch, **9,255**

National League of Families of American Prisoners and Missing in Southeast Asia, 17,731

National League of Girls Clubs, 6,806

National League of Nurses, 5,416

National League of Nursing Education, 6,606, 6,618, 12,074, 12,077. See also National League for Nursing

National League of Women Voters, 2,432, 2,597, 6,596, 6,942, 6,972, 6,978, 6,981. See also League of Women Voters

National League of Women Workers, 6,806, 8,671

National Legion of Mothers of America, 15,121

National Legislative League, 10,844

National Library for the Blind, **2,505**

National Life and Accident Insurance Company, 15,938

National Medical Association, 5,458

National Mother of the Year (1969), 16,257

National Municipal League, 4,125

National Museum (DC), 2,131

National Museum of Natural History, Division of Reptiles and Amphibians, **2,717**

National Music Council, 17,494

National Negro Congress, 1,012, 12,682

National Negro Music Center, 2,155

National Negro Opera Company, 12,686

National Negro Opera Company, New York Guild, 12,685

National Negro Press Association, 2,127

National Newspaper Guild, Great Falls Guild No. 81 (MT), 10,310

National Nonpartisan League, 9,177

National Normal School, alumnae, 5,325

National Notes Magazine, 4,768

National Nursing Accrediting Service, 8,553

National Nursing Planning Committee, 5,735

National Opinion Research Center, **3,975**

National Order of Women Legislators, 12,910

National Organization for Public Health Nursing. See National League for Nursing

National Organization for Women, 3,343, 3,827, 4,241, 6,582, 6,790, **6,794**, 6,849, 7,324, 8,057, 8,095, 8,128, 13,864, **14,009**, 15,197, 15,241, 16,278, **17,774**, 17,975

National Organization for Women (MO), **10,204**

National Organization for Women (Long Island, Nassau Chapter, NY), **12,876**

National Organization for Women (PA), Greater Pittsburgh Area, **15,249**

National Organization for Women (WA), Seattle Chapter, **17,311**

National Organization for Women, Legal Defense and Education Fund, 6,582

National Organization for Women, Legal Defense and Education Fund Public Service Advertising Campaign, 6,794

National Organization of Republican Women, Inc., 14,565

National Organization of University Dames, 13,858

National Organization of Women Legislators, 8,287

National Park Service, 11,877, 11,878

National parks and reserves, **11,877, 11,878**. See also names of parks, e.g., Yellowstone Park

National Peace Conference, **2,077**

National Peace Congress, 3,814

National Peace Convention (1866), 4,754

National Pencil Company (GA), 3,186

National Planning Commission for War Service, 8,610

National Poetry Center, 11,309

National Poetry Day, 5,988, 6,876, 9,629

National Poetry Day Committee (MS), 9,629

National Political Study Club, 2,127

National Popular Education Board, **1,871**

National Popular Government League, 2,432

National Progressive party, 2,589

National Progressive Woman Suffrage Union, 11,261

National Research Council, 2,667

National Research Council, Committee for Research in Problems of Sex, **2,669**

National Research Fellowships in the Natural Sciences, **2,670**

National Research Institute, 17,614

National Resources Planning Board, 11,958

National Retail Druggists Association, Women's Organization, 17,690

National Retail Dry Goods Association, 6,236

National Rural Home Conference, 8,171

National Safety Council, **3,976, 3,977**

National Safety Council, Women's Conference, **3,978**

National Safety Council, Women's Conference, Women of Safety Councils, 3,978

National School of Living, 4,151

National Science Foundation, 5,372, 11,885, 11,901

National Sculpture Society, 12,901

National Secretaries Association, 11,349

National Secretaries Association, Minnesota-Arrow Chapter, **8,437**

National security, 2,679, 2,699, 11,844

National Senior Citizens' Month, 16,000

National Sharecroppers Fund, **8,112**

National Sharecropper's Union, 11,494

National Shorthand Reporters' Association, 13,855

National Silversmithing Workshop Conference, 2,831

National Social Welfare Assembly. See National Assembly of National Voluntary Health and Social Welfare Organizations

National Social Work Council. See National Assembly of National Voluntary Health and Social Welfare Organizations

National socialism, 6,020

National Socialists, book burnings, 13,787

National Society, Colonial Dames of America, 1,444, 1,744, **1,758**, 1,905, 1,948, 1,969, **2,507**, 3,214, 5,805, 7,704, 8,961, **9,608**, 9,692, 9,870, 13,070, **13,379**, 13,446, 13,557, 13,576, 13,629, 14,565, 14,822, 15,439, 16,116

National Society, Colonial Dames of America (GA), **3,509**, 3,597

National Society, Colonial Dames of America (KY), **5,337**

National Society, Colonial Dames of America (MN), **9,257, 9,258**

National Society, Colonial Dames of America (MS), **9,608**

National Society, Colonial Dames of America (OH), Cleveland Circle, **13,948**

National Society, Colonial Dames of America (SC), Columbia Committee, **15,576**

National Society, Colonial Dames of America (TX), 16,176

National Society, Colonial Dames of America (VA), 17,121

National Society, Colonial Dames of America, Committee on Old Houses of Connecticut, **1,892**

National Society, Colonial Dames of America, James Haggard Chapter (TX), **16,296**

National Society, Daughters of the British Empire in Minnesota, **9,256**

National Society for Maintaining American Institutions, 12,524

National Society of Arts and Letters, **2,506**, 5,988

National Society of Children of the American Revolution, 1,444

National Society of Daughters of the Colonial Wars, 14,230

National Society of New England Women (CT), Hartford Colony, **1,923**

National Society of the American Colonists, 14,230

National Society of the Colonial Dames of America. See National Society, Colonial Dames of America

National Society of the Colonial Dames of Mississippi, **9,689**

National Society of the Daughters of Founders and Patriots of America, Georgia Chapter, 3,439

National Society of the Daughters of the American Revolution, 13,365. See also Daughters of the American Revolution

National Society of United States Daughters of 1812, **5,946, 9,690**, 10,032, 15,951

National Society Opposed to Women's Suffrage, 1,444

National Student Council, 3,293

National Symphony Orchestra, 2,743

National Symphony Orchestra Association, 16,358

National Teachers Association, 9,542

National Thanksgiving Association, 9,053

National Theater of Boston (MA), 8,351

National Theatre of the Deaf, 2,104, 2,105, 2,113

National Threshold Theatre Association, 12,557

National Training School for Girls, 2,502

National Travelers Aid Association. See Travelers Aid Association of America

National Tuberculosis Association, 3,813, 7,288

National Tulip Society, 3,233

National Union of Consumers, 11,369

National Union of Marine Cooks and Stewards, **686**

National Urban League, 11,914, 12,066, 15,376

"National Velvet" (television program), 18,000

National W. C. T. U. (periodical), 13,963

National War Garden Commission of Washington, 2,352

National White House Conference on Children and Youth, 4,921

National Woman Suffrage Association. See National American Woman Suffrage Association

National Woman Suffrage Convention (MA, 1850), 4,754

National Woman Suffrage Conventions (1904-1909), 6,479

National Woman's Christian Temperance Union, **7,271, 16,774**. See also Woman's Christian Temperance Union

National Woman's Christian Temperance Union, Plan of Work Institute, 13,677

National Woman's Liberty Loan Committee, 10,680

National Woman's Party, 49, 509, 589, 658, 714, 859, 860, 1,059, 2,043, 2,218, 2,492, 2,502, **2,508,** 2,528, **2,858**, 3,350, 6,379, 6,401, 6,742, 6,754, 6,765, 6,807, **6,894**, 6,941, 6,944, 6,953, 6,959, 6,966, 6,981, **7,272**, 7,273, 7,287, 7,803, 7,868, 8,896, 10,032, 10,681, 10,687, 11,123, 11,143, 11,904, **12,575**, 12,597, **12,856**, 13,997, 14,014, 14,814, 15,029, 17,746

National Women's Advisory Committee on Social Protection, 2,687

National Women's Association of Allied Beverage Industries, Inc., **2,706**

National Women's Committee of 100, 99

National Women's Conference (1977), 4,106

National Women's Emergency Coalition, **12,523**

National Women's Political Caucus, 4,109, 6,582, 8,096, 9,947

National Women's Suffrage Association. See National American Woman Suffrage Association

National Women's Trade Union League, **2,509**, 2,525, 2,878, 3,887, 4,079, 4,173, 8,069, 8,071, 8,126, 12,704, 15,332, 17,588. See also Women's Trade Union League

National Youthworker Education Project, 8,583

Nationalities Services Center, 13,953

Nationalities Service Center of Cleveland, 9,497

"Nationalizing of Business, The" (ms), 6,921
Native Americans, 130, 162, 187, 194, 202, 206, 212,
    337, 349, 370, 434, 451, 491, 496, 497, 538, **564,**
    671, 690, 723, 748, 818, 953, 991, 1,153, 1,271,
    1,305, **1,475,** 1,498, 1,605, 1,664, 1,676, 1,779,
    1,887, **2,841,** 3,485, 3,710, 3,731, 3,754, 3,891,
    4,267, 4,344, 4,368, 4,653, 4,904, 5,108, 5,182,
    5,410, 5,449, 5,821, 6,142, 6,375, 6,609, 6,661,
    6,947, 7,047, 8,164, **8,404,** 8,591, 8,693,˙8,736,
    8,752, 8,929, 8,967, **9,244,** 9,276, 9,462, 9,468,
    9,721, 9,869, 10,054, 10,250, 10,296, **10,313,**
    10,335, 10,355, 10,364, 10,459, 10,608, 10,632,
    10,633, 10,670, 10,680, 10,763, 11,217, 11,223,
    11,226, 11,233, 11,279, **11,296,** 11,443, 11,466,
    11,492, 11,536, 11,974, 13,011, 13,537, 14,006,
    14,165, 14,183, 14,204, 14,212, **14,214,** 14,220,
    14,224, **14,241,** 14,245, 14,288, 14,479, 14,669,
    14,897, 15,025, 15,856, 16,032, 16,060, 16,092,
    16,403, 16,420, 16,455, 16,486, 16,488, 16,604,
    16,789, 16,862, 16,968, 17,249, 17,263, 17,266,
    17,413, 17,418, 17,420, 17,423, 17,643, 17,997.
    See also names of tribes, e.g., Apache Indians
  antiquities, 1,471, 11,295
  art, 1,678, 7,945, 10,657, 11,213
  basket making, 10,657
  captivities (both of and by whites), 1,751, 1,790,
    8,208, 8,515, 9,355, 9,834, 10,098, 10,287,
    10,496, 11,445, 12,545, 14,098, **16,036,** 16,097,
    16,117
  census, 983, 1,175, 1,806, 2,674, 3,944, 14,175,
    15,289, 16,215, 17,216
  civil rights, 1,426, 1,443, 1,526, 2,298, 2,371,
    12,068
  costume and adornment, 2,842
  courts, 1,915
  cultural assimilation, 16,344
  culture, **1,019, 2,842, 11,231**
  dances, 1,779, 9,041
  education, 305, 396, 983, 1,175, 1,806, 2,298,
    2,674, 3,944, 5,457, 7,220, 7,435, 7,945, **8,705,**
    9,347, 10,099, 10,102, 10,134, 10,269, 10,398,
    11,225, 13,540, 14,241, 14,242, 14,246, **14,748,**
    16,215, 16,875, 16,876, 17,216, 17,219
  employment, 1,806, 2,674
  ethnology. *See* Ethnology, Native American
  folk-lore. *See* Folk-lore, Native American
  food, 2,883, 16,876
  government relations, 67, **983, 1,175,** 1,481, 1,780,
    1,806, 2,674, 2,838, **3,944,** 4,953, 6,142, 7,945,
    9,411, **10,098, 10,099, 10,100, 10,101, 10,102,**
    13,448, 14,241, **16,215,** 16,875, **17,216,** 17,219,
    17,997
  health and hygiene, 2,674, 6,142
  history, 191, 8,518, 14,197
  hunting, 16,876
  industries, 7,485, 14,969
  intertribal relations, 12,067
  land tenure, 2,674, 3,944, 10,099, 10,272, 10,459,
    16,215
  land transfers, 6,541, 9,485, 11,574, 13,448
  languages, 1,497, 5,624, 17,252
  legal status, laws, etc., 2,674, 7,945, 10,459, 16,876
  legends, 1,795, 2,566, 17,187, 17,814. *See also*
    Folk-lore, Native American
  marriage rites and customs, 1,243, 2,674, 16,486
  medical care, 983, 1,655, **10,097,** 15,776, 16,215,
    17,216
  medicine, 10,718, 16,876
  missions, 216, 631, 880, 1,171, 1,243, 1,428, 1,476,
    1,504, 1,790, 1,861, 3,382, 5,247, 5,710, **6,177,**
    7,435, 7,511, 8,304, 8,848, 8,899, **9,009,** 9,042,
    9,316, **9,446,** 9,710, 9,782, 10,187, 11,639,
    12,775, 12,784, 14,225, 14,434, 14,457, 14,660,
    15,173, 15,463, 15,845, 15,869, 16,903, 17,229,
    17,315, 17,383, 17,421, 17,422, 17,626, 17,820,
    17,923
  mixed-bloods, 9,316, 9,384, 9,855, 10,281, **10,368**
  mortuary customs, 3,121
  music, 211, 965, 8,444, 9,041, **9,042,** 9,467, 17,814
  names, 723, 16,872
  oral history, 211, **2,883**
  pictorial works, 13,446, **14,201**
  pottery, 2,883
  race identity, 16,875, 16,876

  relations (nongovernmental) with whites, 746,
    2,167, 7,435, 9,078, 10,045, 10,054, 10,374,
    12,338, 16,117, 16,463, 16,525, 16,715, 16,788,
    16,863, 16,867, 16,872, 16,876, 17,402
  religion and mythology, 3,121, 9,041, 16,870,
    16,875, 16,876
  reservations, 153, 155, 740, 1,688, 3,944, 6,650,
    7,220, **8,927,** 9,042, 9,467, **10,101, 10,102,**
    10,433, 11,293, 14,207, 14,225, 14,609, 14,619,
    15,850, 16,872, 16,873, 16,875, 17,183
  social life and customs, 338, 798, 1,475, 2,674,
    3,121, 5,669, 9,032, **9,467,** 11,227, 15,059,
    15,850, 16,873, 17,216
  suffrage, 16,876
  trading posts, 8,927, 10,228, 14,199
  treaties, 14,454
  tribal government, 17,216
  wars, 838, 1,224, 1,229, 1,323, 1,398, 1,475, 1,751,
    1,790, 3,402, 3,829, 4,842, 7,678, 8,515, 8,709,
    8,718, 9,074, 9,085, 9,312, 9,355, 9,366, 9,371,
    9,419, 9,902, 10,029, 10,237, 10,433, 10,496,
    10,557, 10,632, 12,545, 13,612, 14,206, 14,436,
    14,539, 14,657, 14,680, 15,008, 16,064, 16,100,
    16,124, 16,245, 16,310, 16,472, 16,486, 16,876,
    17,271, 17,355, 17,624
Native Americans in literature, 9,047
Native Daughters of Colorado, 1,701
Native Daughters of Oregon, Martha Mulligan Cabin
    Number 3, **14,295**
Native Daughters of Oregon, Tabitha Brown Cabin
    Number 24, **14,621**
Native Daughters of the Golden West, 453, 678, 707,
    1,078
Native Daughters of the Golden West (CA),
    Columbia Parlor Number Seventy, **1,076**
Native Daughters of the Golden West (CA),
    Manzanita Parlor Number Twenty-seven, **1,324**
Native Daughters of the Golden West (CA), Yerba
    Buena Parlor, 1,649
Native Sons of America, **10,115**
Nativistic movements, 7,678
Natural Gas and Water Company (IL), 3,898
Natural history, 1,790, 6,346
  study and teaching, 6,346
Natural history museums, **2,717,** 3,952, **8,592**
Natural history museums, children's, 15,813
Naturalist Club (San Francisco, CA), 535
Naturalists, 668, 1,068, 1,468, **1,730, 2,329,** 2,942,
    4,289, 5,442, **5,633, 6,316, 6,321,** 7,491, 10,534,
    11,297, **11,735, 14,876, 14,877, 14,883,** 14,901,
    14,956, 17,248
Naturalization, 1,645, 3,760, 3,852, 6,808, 6,978,
    8,631, 9,481, 14,230, 14,933. *See also* Aliens
Naturalization records, 162, 986, 1,177, 1,179, 1,180,
    1,809, **2,683,** 3,949, 11,203, 14,938, **17,016**
Nature Conservancy, The, 4,686, 8,715, 8,716
Nature of Nursing, 6,143
Nature study, 2,310
Naughright, Anna De Yoe, **11,004**
Nauman, Gertrude Howard (Olmsted) [Mrs. Spencer
    G.] (1901-73), **14,822**
Nauman, Spencer G., 14,822
Naumberg Award, 5,459
Nauset on Cape Cod (book), 7,023
Nautical training schools, 2,708, 6,850, 7,138
Nauvoo Independent (IL), 4,302
Nauvoo Legion, 16,888
Nauvoo Neighbor (IL), 4,302
Navajo Indian Reservation (AZ), 155
Navajo Indians, 169, 311, 1,779, 2,840, 2,841, 11,227,
    11,231, 12,067, 16,486, 16,865, 16,868, **16,869,**
    16,870, 16,876, 16,877
  missions, 153
  relations with Mexicans, 16,869
Navajo Language Monthly, The (periodical), 7,220
Naval Air Station (Pensacola, FL), 2,910, 9,709
Naval architecture, 14,941
Naval districts, 17,245
Naval Historical Foundation, 2,197
Naval history, **2,535**
Naval Observatory and Hydrographic Office, 2,479
Naval Reserve Midshipmen's School, Smith College
    (Northampton, MA), 2,708, 7,138
Naval Training School (United States), 6,850

Nave, Elizabeth, 10,349
Nave Family (MT), **10,349**
Nave, Jacob, 10,349
Navy League, 8,070
Navy League of the United States, 2,454, 12,263
Navy League of the United States, Department
    Number Six, 2,554
Navy Mothers' Club (MS), **9,691**
Navy-yards and naval stations, safety measures, 2,700
Nay, Charlotte Stimler, 10,714
Nay, Mary Spencer, 2,763
Naylor, Clara Corinne, 11,324
Naylor, Mrs. L. F. Robbins, 11,324
Naylor, Pauline [Mrs. John W.], 16,282
Nazareth Academy (IL), 4,284
Nazareth Academy (OH), 13,903
Nazareth College (Bardstown, KY), Guidance Center
    and Psychological Clinic, 5,373
Nazareth College (Bardstown, KY), students, 5,290
Nazimova, Alla. Golovin, Alla (Leventon) [Mrs.
    Sergei] (1878-1945), 7,310
Neal, Ellen, 13,055
Neal, Eva (Bell), Family (MN), **9,259**
Neal Family (NC), **13,495**
Neal, Margie E., 2,684
Neal, Margie E. (1875-?), 16,132
Neal, Marie C. (1889-1968), 10,151
Neales, Isabel Rose, 1,092
Neall, Adelaide W., **15,060**
Neall, Elizabeth. *See* Gay, Elizabeth (Neall) [Mrs.
    Sydney Howard]
Neall, Hannah Lloyd [Mrs. James], 15,271
Nealy, Mary E., **6,796**
Nealy, Matthew M., 17,465
Near and Far Folk Dance Club (Reno, NV), **10,685**
Near East. *See* Middle East
Near East College Association, 2,233, 11,999
Near North Community Council (Chicago, IL), 4,045
Near, Vida Moss [Miss], 12,290
Near West Side Community Committee (Chicago,
    IL), **4,134**
Near West Side Community Committee (Chicago,
    IL), Women's Auxiliary, 4,134
Near West Side Planning Board (Chicago, IL), 4,101
Nearing, Alicia. *See* Hayden, Alicia (Nearing) [Mrs.
    W. W.]
Nearing Family (NY), 11,520
Nearing, Mary, 11,520
Nearing, Scott, 12,705
Neatherry, Caroline Besson, 13,331
Nebelung, Clara (Bircher), 9,027, **9,260**
Neblett, Lizzie Scott (1833-1917), **16,109**
Nebraska, 10,420, 10,449, 10,452, 10,466, 10,495,
    10,529, 10,544, 10,556
  agricultural societies, 10,479, **10,505**
  agriculture publishing, **10,504**
  allegiance, 10,509
  army wives, 10,493, **10,557**
  art, museums and galleries, 10,612
  art teachers, 10,435
  authors, **10,465, 10,487, 10,491, 10,495, 10,520,**
    10,523, 10,527, 10,529, 10,531, 10,534, 10,608
  Baptists, **10,499**
  beauty operators, **10,469**
  biography, **10,417,** 10,526
  bishops, 10,611
  businessmen, 10,482
  businesswomen, **10,471**
  camps, 10,518
  charities, 10,484, 10,518
  church history, **10,574**
  church records and registers, **10,532, 10,546**
  church records and registers, Congregational,
    10,460, 10,461, 10,464, 10,550
  church records and registers, Methodist, **10,476**
  church records and registers, United Church of
    Christ, **10,501**
  church societies, Baptist, 10,499
  church societies, Congregational, 10,460, 10,461,
    10,464, 10,550
  church societies, Methodist, **10,457,** 10,476, **10,566,**
    10,567, 10,569, 10,572, 10,573, 10,574, 10,575,
    10,576, 10,577, 10,578, 10,579, 10,580, 10,582,
    10,583, 10,584, 10,585, 10,586, 10,587, 10,588,

10,589, 10,590, 10,591, 10,593, 10,594, 10,595, 10,596, 10,597, 10,598, 10,601
citizens' advisory committees in education, 10,472
civil defense, **10,509**
Civil War, societies, etc., **10,619, 10,622**
clubs, 10,101, **10,406, 10,409, 10,413,** 10,415, **10,416,** 10,420, 10,422, **10,423, 10,429, 10,470,** 10,484, **10,506, 10,510, 10,528,** 10,534, **10,536**
college discipline, 10,604
college teachers, **10,477, 10,492, 10,522, 10,554, 10,556, 10,568**
commonplace-books, 12,555
community centers, 10,484
community leadership, 10,469, **10,472, 10,484,** 10,521
composers, **10,478, 10,540,** 10,626
congressmen, **10,513**
contemplative orders, **10,613**
convents and nunneries, Catholic, 10,611
deaconesses, **10,565**
deans (in schools), 11,906, 12,921
department heads (universities), **10,605, 10,607**
ecologists, **10,446**
editors, 10,448
educational associations, 10,424, **10,425**
educational associations, Methodist, **10,600**
educators, 10,466, **10,473, 10,488,** 10,537, **10,562**
family farms, management, 10,471
farm life, 10,420
farmers, 10,466
folklorists, **10,522**
furniture industry and trade, 10,449
genealogists, **10,454, 10,562**
general stores, 10,515
golf, **10,510**
governors, 10,427, 10,487, 11,240
greek letter societies, **10,453,** 10,482
high school teachers, **10,456**
historians, 10,449, **10,463, 10,534, 10,544**
horticulturists, **10,420**
housewives, **10,436, 10,468**
immigrants, Czech, 10,527
immigrants, German-Russian, 10,554
immigrants, Norwegian, 10,434
insurance, life, societies, etc., **10,412**
itinerancy (church polity), 4,772
journalism, societies, etc., **10,517**
journalists, **10,422,** 10,487, **10,494, 10,544**
land settlement, 10,478, 10,533
lawyers, **10,440, 10,495**
League of Women Voters, 11,240
legal instruments, 10,452
legislative bodies, 10,477
legislators, 10,448
literary societies, **10,497, 10,498, 10,512, 10,525, 10,563**
local church councils, **10,485**
locusts, 10,458
medical colleges, **10,616**
medical societies, 10,405, **10,508**
medicine, practice, 10,616
merchants, 9,977, 10,515
Methodists, **10,598**
monasticism and religious orders for women, Catholic, **10,610, 10,614, 10,615, 10,618**
Mormons and Mormonism, 16,820
museum directors, 10,544
music teachers, 10,449, **10,481**
musical societies, **10,418**
Native Americans, wars, 10,496, 10,557
newspaper publishers and publishing, 10,626
newspapers, 10,598
    sections, columns, etc., 10,443
nursing, law and legislation, 10,500
nursing schools, **10,486,** 10,500
officials and employees, **10,422**
old age homes, 17,820
Omaha Indians, 10,459, **10,483**
oral history, **10,403**
ornithology, 10,454
orphans and orphan asylums, **10,621**
parents' and teachers' associations, 10,551
patriotic societies, 10,407, **10,408, 10,410, 10,414, 10,426, 10,451,** 10,463, **10,547, 10,560, 10,625**

peyotism, 12,170
philanthropists, **10,407**
physicians, **10,405, 10,463, 10,538**
pianists, **10,481**
pioneers and settlers, 1,770, **4,744,** 9,325, **10,403, 10,417,** 10,430, **10,437,** 10,439, **10,441, 10,442, 10,458, 10,504, 10,516,** 10,526, **10,535, 10,543, 10,561**
poets, **10,549**
political activists, women, 10,482
politics, practical, women's activism, **10,558**
postmistresses, **10,515**
radiologists, **10,508**
ranchers, **10,431, 10,487**
reformatories, **10,502**
reformatories (female), **10,503**
school and college journalism, **10,623**
school superintendents and principals, **10,488,** 10,626
school supervisors, 10,482
scouts and scouting, 10,514
senators, United States, **10,513, 10,548**
seniors, transportation, **10,404**
Sioux Indians, 10,473
social life and customs, 10,403, 10,489
societies, etc., **10,411**
sod houses, 10,479
students' societies, 10,486, **10,604, 10,606**
suffrage, 1,563, **10,448**
suffrage societies, 10,462, **10,511,** 17,616
suffragists, **17,411**
teachers, 10,403, **10,441,** 10,449, **10,452, 10,453, 10,467, 10,474, 10,490, 10,523, 10,524, 10,541, 10,552,** 10,564
teachers' colleges, 11,906
teachers of the blind, **10,438**
temperance societies, 10,462, 10,474, **10,559**
theological seminaries, Methodist, 10,570
trade and professional associations, 10,471
United Methodist Church
    education, 10,600
    government, **10,565**
    publishing, 10,598
universities and colleges, 10,564, 10,568, 10,600
War of 1898, societies, etc., **10,547, 10,624**
Winnebago Indians, missions, 10,611
working-women's clubs, 10,518
World War II, civilians work, 3,950
Young Women's Christian Association, 10,484, **10,518, 10,609**
"N-E-B-R-A-S-K-A" (song), 10,478
Nebraska Board of Control of State Institutions, 10,422
Nebraska Board of Nursing, **10,500**
Nebraska Capital Mural Commission, 2,802
Nebraska Conference Contingent Fund, Methodist Episcopal Church, 10,584
Nebraska Congress of Parents and Teachers, 10,551
Nebraska Department of Public Institutions, Girls' Training School, **10,502**
Nebraska Department of Public Institutions, Nebraska Industrial Home, **10,503**
Nebraska Farmer (periodical), **10,504**
Nebraska Farmers' Alliance, 10,479, **10,505**
Nebraska Federation of Women's Clubs, 10,101, 10,406, **10,506,** 10,534
Nebraska History (periodical), 10,548
Nebraska Legislative Ladies League, **10,507**
Nebraska Prison Board, 10,440
Nebraska School for the Blind, 10,438
Nebraska Society of Radiological Technologists, **10,508**
Nebraska State Baptist Convention, **10,499**
Nebraska State Board of Cosmetology Examiners, 10,469
Nebraska State Council of Defense, **10,509**
Nebraska State Historical Society, 10,534, 10,544
Nebraska State Hospitals, 10,436
Nebraska State Journal, 10,443, 10,494
Nebraska State Medical Association, 10,405
Nebraska State Student Nurses Association, 10,486
Nebraska Territory, 10,166
Nebraska Wesleyan University, 5,993, 10,568, 10,600

students, 14,402
Nebraska Woman Suffrage Convention, 10,448
Nebraska Women's State Invitational Golf Association, **10,510**
Nebraska Women's Suffrage Association, **10,511,** 17,616
Nebraska Writers Guild, **10,512**
Needham, Christine (Edwards) [Mrs. James Leland] (1897-), **242**
Needham, Grace (Darland) [Mrs. Sherman W.], **4,815,** 4,816
Needham, James Carson, **1,591**
Needham, Sherman W. (1881-1959), 4,815, **4,816**
Needle Pickets (IL), 4,313
Needlecraft Club (IN), **4,574**
Needle's Eye, The (periodical), 15,329
Needlework, 596, 3,804, **5,891,** 7,012, **9,683.** *See also* Embroidery
    study and teaching, **12,301**
Needlework Guild (GA), **3,231**
Needlework Guild of America, 2,193, 10,112, 13,446
Needlework Guild of America (NJ), New Brunswick branch, 11,059
Neeley, Elizabeth Montgomery, **16,110**
Neely, Ann Elizabeth, 8,665, 8,683
Neely, Jane E., **15,662**
Neely, Juanita H. (1889-), **15,808**
Neely, Mary B., **1,719**
Neenah-Menasha Federated Woman's Club (WI), **17,823**
Neenah-Menasha Music Club (WI), **17,824**
Neese, Laura (Aldrich) [Mrs. Albert H., Sr.] (1889-1967), **17,496,** 17,498
Negro Actor's Guild of America, Inc., 3,290, 5,478, 12,685
Negro Community Hospital (MS), 9,599
Negro History Bulletin (periodical), 9,252
Negro in Mississippi, The (book), 9,687
Negro Library Association, 12,865
Negro Women's Club (Baltimore, MD), 5,837
Negro Year Book, 124
Negroes in Columbus (book), 14,006
Nehru, Jawaharlal, 2,108
Nehru: The First Sixty Years (book), 12,905
Neidemeyer, Anna Louise. *See* Wendt, Anna Louise (Neidemeyer)
Neighborhood Affairs Council (Minneapolis, MN), 9,058
Neighborhood Centre (Philadelphia, PA), 15,153, **15,160**
Neighborhood Garden Club (GA), 3,187
Neighborhood House (Elmira, NY), 11,445
Neighborhood House (WA), 17,247
Neighborhood House Association (St. Paul, MN), **9,261**
Neighborhood Teachers Association—National Education Committee for Non-English-Speaking Women, 12,738
Neighborhood Union (GA), **3,302**
Neighbors (book), 5,694
Neighbors' Club (PA), 14,953
Neighbors United, 9,095
Neihardt, Alice, 10,029
Neihardt, John G. (1881-1973), **10,029**
Neihardt, Mona Martinsen [Mrs. John G.], 10,029
Neil, Hannah (1794?-1868), 13,996
Neill (OK), 14,179
Neilson, A. Lou [Miss], **9,692**
Neilson, Caroline (McDougal), **5,757**
Neilson, Catharine (Bleecker) [Mrs. James] (1809-93), 11,005
Neilson, Eliza Lucy (Irion) [Mrs. John Albert], 9,651
Neilson Family (MS), **9,651**
Neilson Family (NJ), **11,005**
Neilson, Gertrude, 7,090
Neilson, Isabelle C., 11,844
Neilson, James (1844-1937), 11,005
Neilson, John, 11,005
Neilson, John Arthur, 9,651
Neilson, Lillian Adelaide, **10,176**
Neilson, Louisa Abert, 9,782
Neilson, Mary Putnam (Woodbury) [Mrs. James] (1846-1914), 11,005
Neilson, Nester, 11,453

Neilson, Sarah Rutgers (1853-?). *See* Jones, Sarah Rutgers (Neilson) [Mrs. Willard P.] Voorhees [Mrs. Albert J.] (1853-?)
Neiman, Carrie [Miss] (1883-1953), 16,210
Neiman-Marcus (TX), 16,210
Neisser, Albert Ludwig Siegmund (1855-1916), 1,383
Nellie Salmon Day Nursery, 9,950
Nellums, Mrs. William, **3,560**
Nelson, Alice, 4,494
Nelson, Amalie (Kraushaar) [Mrs. George I.] (1895-), **14,010**
Nelson, Anna Bridget "Brydie." *See* Larkin, Anna Bridget "Brydie" (Nelson) [Mrs. Martin]
Nelson, Annie Green, **15,663**
Nelson, Belle (Harris) [Mrs. Clarence] Merrill [Mrs. N. L.] (1861-1938), **16,775**
Nelson, Carmen (1891?-). *See* Richards, Carmen (Nelson) (1891?-)
Nelson, Carrie M. [Mrs.], **9,262**
Nelson, Charles Alexander (1839-1933), 11,660
Nelson, Colonel, 9,857
Nelson, Deborah Ann, **13,657**
Nelson, Dwight A. (1911-), **10,741**
Nelson, Earl F. (1884-1945), **10,030**
Nelson, Elba Chase [Mrs.] (1891-1967), **10,872**
Nelson, Ellen, 5,999
Nelson, Elvira Vail (1839-1932), 16,487
Nelson, Emily Serena, 343
Nelson, Emma Ginsberg, 17,282
Nelson, Estella (Bish) (1887-1960), **10,630**
Nelson, Evaline, 1,471
Nelson Family, **343**
Nelson, Florence B., **17,566**
Nelson, Gertrude Jane (1872-1950), **11,660**
Nelson, Harriet, 5,110
Nelson, Helen, 11,805
Nelson, Helene, 12,520
Nelson, Herbert B., 14,510
Nelson, Janet Fowler, 6,223
Nelson, John P., **5,473**
Nelson, Julia (1881-). *See* Bressler, Julia (Nelson) [Mrs. Calvin] (1881-)
Nelson, Julia B., 9,240
Nelson, Kaisa, **7,877**
Nelson, Knute (1843-1923), 9,211, **9,263**, 9,297
Nelson, Margaret (1859-1929). *See* Stephens, Margaret (Nelson) [Mrs. Lawrence "Lon" Vest] (1859-1929)
Nelson, Mary. *See* Williams, Mary (Nelson) [Mrs. Franklin Delano]
Nelson, Mary (1858-?). *See* Felshaw, Mary (Nelson) Johnson (1858-?)
Nelson, Mary E. [Mrs. B. F.], **9,264**
Nelson, Mercedes (1900-), **8,113**
Nelson, Mrs. Hodgson (1886-), 8,709
Nelson, N. L., 16,775
Nelson, Ruth Augusta (1876-?), **11,660**
Nelson, Sarah, 12,161
Nelson, Sylvia, 14,946
Nelson, Vera Joyce (1903-), **14,428**
Nenzel, Ora Adelaid [Mrs. Joseph], **10,686**
Neo-Malthusian League, 7,192
Neprud, Marion C. (1897-1965), **17,697**
Neptune Historical Museum (NJ), 10,921
Neptune Public Library (NJ), 10,921, 10,923
Nerney, May Childs, 2,502
Nerves, peripheral, 10,207
Nervous system, diseases, 11,885
Nesbit, Florence. *See* Marye, Florence (Nesbit) [Mrs. Phillip Thornton]
Nesbitt, Victoria Henrietta (Kugler) (1874-?), **2,510**
Nesmith, Henrietta. *See* Greely, Henrietta (Nesmith) [Mrs. Adolphus Washington]
Ness, Evaline (1911-), **8,531**
Nessenson, Elsa Behaim [Miss] (1877-1969), 17,393
Nest Egg, The (drama), 3,084
Nestell, Ann R., **12,269**
Nestler, Lina Selma (Stock) [Mrs. Friedrich Herman] (1876-1967), **16,776**
Nestor, Agnes (1880-1948), 2,679, **3,887**, 3,890, 4,079, 4,104, 4,173, 11,305
Nestor, Barbara, 1,016, 1,654
Netherlands
    American ambassadors to, 12,273

American diplomats in, 2,322, 12,383
Friends, Society of, 15,058
United Nations economic assistance to, 10,074
Netter, Amy, 13,814
Nettleton, Asahel (1783-1844), **1,857**
Network for Economic Rights, 8,103
Neu, Sallie, 16,041
Neuberg, Karine [Mrs. J. W. Magelssen], 4,722
Neuberger, Maurine (Brown) [Mrs. Richard Lewis] (1907-), 7,904, **14,429, 14,622**
Neuberger, Richard Lewis (1912-60), 14,429, **14,622**
Neuhierl, Sister M. Augustine, 17,145
Neuman, Fannie (1900-), **11,326**
Neuman, St. John, 14,719, 15,069
Neurological nursing, 4,014
Neurologists, **6,843**
Neustaedter, Eleanor, 8,657
Neutral Conference for Continuous Mediation (Stockholm, 1916), 8,000, 17,735
Neutrality, 6,978
Nevada, 10,638, 10,660, 10,661, 10,665, **10,676,** 10,678, 10,693, 10,698, 10,715, 10,727, 10,779, 14,680, 16,639
    abortion, law and legislation, 10,736
    actions and defenses, 1,179
    advertising fliers, **10,659**
    agricultural extension agents, **10,735**
    anthropologists, **10,726**
    anthropology, 10,727
    archaeologists, 10,726
    archaeology, 10,727
    authors, 10,637, 10,759, **10,760, 10,779**
    bankers, 10,748
    bills, legislative, 10,658
    biography, **10,780**
    boundaries, 10,673
    businessmen, 10,752
    businesswomen, 10,680
    capitalists and financiers, **10,776**
    Catholic hospitals, 10,732
    cattle brands, 10,722
    census, 10,723
    charities, 10,747
    children, institutional care, 10,691
    Chinese-Americans, 10,763
    church records and registers, Episcopal, 10,662
    church schools, **1,518**
    cities and towns, 10,686
    city councilmen, 10,743
    civil defense, **10,692**
    civil engineers, 10,678
    clubs, **10,643,** 10,658, 10,679, 10,680, **10,685,** **10,689, 10,705,** 10,720, **10,757, 10,770, 10,771,** 10,782, **10,783**
    coaches (athletics), **10,739**
    coaching, 10,724
    college sports, 10,739
    college students, 10,775
    college teachers, **10,766, 10,775**
    conservation of natural resources, 10,689
    country life, 10,751
    county officials and employees, **10,749,** 12,705
    court records, **1,179**
    curfew, 10,703
    dams, 10,781
    deeds, 10,712
    dental technicians, **10,787**
    department heads (universities), 10,727
    economic conditions, 10,749
    education, 10,707
    educational associations, **10,627, 10,639, 10,640,** **10,641,** 10,707, **10,746,** 10,755
    educators, **10,677,** 10,680, **10,745**
    elections, 10,678, 10,681, 10,768
    engineers, **10,638**
    entertainers, **10,717**
    Episcopal churches, **10,700**
    farmers, 10,748
    floods, 10,686
    foster home care, 10,669
    gambling, 10,711, **10,733,** 10,738
    gardening, societies, etc., **10,704, 10,709**
    geologists, 10,726
    gold mines and mining, 10,763

    government librarians, 10,753
    governors, **10,649,** 10,750, 10,753, 10,779
    greek letter societies, **10,663**
    hanging, 10,721
    historic sites, conservation and restoration, 10,637, 10,662, 10,689
    historical societies, **10,690, 10,716, 10,727**
    home economics, 10,707
    hospital administrators, 10,732
    hospitals, **1,518**
    housewives, **10,756**
    immigrants, 1,472
    Jews, 10,763
    journalists, **10,742,** 10,781
    juvenile detention homes, 10,741
    kindergartens, 10,655
    land settlement, 10,680
    land titles, registration and transfer, 10,680
    lawyers, **10,658, 10,752**
    legends, 10,702
    legislation, 10,644
    legislators, **10,736,** 10,737, 10,738, 10,752, 10,758, **10,787**
    library associations, **10,785**
    literary societies, **10,769**
    little theaters, 10,743
    livestock, **10,722**
    maternity homes, 10,775
    mid-wives, **10,710**
    mine management, 1,492
    mines and mineral resources, 1,621, 10,684, 10,724, 10,728, 10,731
    mining towns, 1,505
    missions, Catholic, **1,514**
    missions, Spanish, 10,680
    monuments, 10,648
    Mormons and Mormonism, 191, **10,674, 10,676**
    murder, 10,721
    music-halls (variety-theaters, cabarets, etc.), 10,659
    Native Americans, 10,670, 10,763
        art, 10,657
    newspapers, **10,694**
    nuns, Catholic, 10,732
    nurses, 10,632, 10,732
    nursing, law and legislation, 10,758
    nursing service administration, 10,732
    officials and employees, **10,638, 10,660,** 10,776
    oral history, **10,714, 10,724,** 10,755
    parades, 10,660
    parks, 10,726
    party committees, 10,752
    patriotic societies, **10,662,** 10,666, 10,679, **10,786**
    peace societies, **10,730**
    photographs, **10,699**
    physicians, 10,632, 10,708, **10,728,** 10,761
    pioneers and settlers, **10,632,** 10,634, **10,636,** 10,680, **10,716,** 10,734, 10,737, 10,749, 10,759, 10,763
    place names, 10,680
    poets laureate, **10,650**
    political activists, women, 10,761
    political clubs, 10,679
    politics and government, 10,748
    politics, practical, women's activism, 10,679
    prisons, **10,652**
        administration, 10,652
    probation officers, **12,705**
    prostitution, 10,656, 10,711, **10,744**
    public relations consultants, **10,738**
    railroads, employees, 10,672
    ranchers, 7,068, **10,713,** 10,719, **10,737,** 10,780, 10,784
    ranches, 10,715
    real estate agents, 10,650
    registers of births, etc., 10,680
    retired teachers, **10,707**
    sanitary engineers, **10,744**
    school superintendents and principals, 10,734
    schools, 10,680, 10,707, 10,778
    secret societies, **10,772**
    senators, United States, **2,528**
    sheep, 10,628
    silver mines and mining, 731
    social life and customs, 10,761

statehood, 10,748
strikes and lockouts, 10,710
student teachers, Afro-American, 10,745
suffrage, 656, **826**, 860, 10,667, 10,668, 10,727, 10,768
  opposition to, 10,687
suffrage societies, 656, 10,679, 10,681, **10,687**, 10,768
suffragists, **10,762**
teachers, 10,628, 10,682, **10,683**, **10,734**, 10,736, 10,749, **10,751**, **10,778**, **10,779**, **10,787**, 17,315
teachers' unions, 10,707
temperance societies, **10,642**, 10,666, 10,673
trade and professional associations, 10,671, **10,688**
traffic safety, study and teaching, 10,689
United States marshals, 10,738
universities and colleges, 10,751
  faculty, **10,755**
veterans, 10,723
water-supply, 10,665
Nevada (poem), 10,650
Nevada Association of Women Opposed to Equal Suffrage, 10,687
Nevada Centennial Committee, 10,759
Nevada Day parades, 10,660
Nevada Education Association, 10,707
Nevada, Emma. Emma Wixom. [Mrs. Raymond Spooner] Palmer (1859-1940), **687**, 800, 1,070, 10,651, 10,680, 10,708, 10,717, **10,729**
Nevada Equal Franchise Society, 2,528. *See also* Nevada Women's Civic League
Nevada Federation of Business and Professional Women's Clubs, **10,688**
Nevada Federation of Women's Clubs, 10,658, **10,689**, 10,720, **10,770**, **10,771**, 10,782
Nevada Historical Society, 10,644, 10,658, 10,727
Nevada Library Association, White Pine District, **10,785**
Nevada Mother of the Year, 10,761, 10,782
Nevada Native Daughters, **10,690**
Nevada Public Service Commission, 10,638
Nevada State Children's Home, **10,691**
Nevada State Council of Defense, **10,692**
Nevada State Park Advisory Commission, 10,726
Nevada State University, faculty, 10,681
Nevada Territory, 8,373
Nevada Volunteers, Company C, 10,703
Nevada Voter's Club, 10,687
Nevada Women's Civic League, 656, 10,681, **10,687**, 10,768
Nevelson, Louise [Miss] (1900-), **2,791**, 3,980
Never Too Late (drama), 4,764
Neville, Emily Cheney (1919-), 8,531
Neville, Linda [Miss] (1873-1961), **5,318**
Neville, Mary, 5,318
Neville, Mary Payne [Mrs.], 5,318
Neville, Thomas, 9,391
Nevin, Blanche, **14,865**
Nevins, Allan, **11,828**
Nevins, Elizabeth West. *See* Perkins, Elizabeth West Nevins [Mrs. Charles Lawrence]
Nevins, Marian Griswold (1857-1956). *See* MacDowell, Marian Griswold (Nevins) [Mrs. Edward A.] (1857-1956)
Nevins, Mary Fleming [Mrs. Allan] (1894-), 11,828
Nevinson, Henry W., 5,726
Nevitte, Emma Dorothy Eliza (1819-99). *See* Southworth, Emma Dorothy Eliza (Nevitte) (1819-99)
Nevius, Catharine Louisa. *See* Demarest, Catharine Louisa (Nevius) [Mrs. David D.]
New Age (CA), 1,655
New Albany Gazette (MS), 9,631
New America Cinema, 17,794
New Beacon Series in Religious Education, 6,250
New Brunswick Board of Recreation (NJ), **11,006**
New Brunswick City Committee on Public Recreation (NJ), **11,007**
New Brunswick City Improvement Society (NJ), 11,007
New Brunswick First Reformed Church (NJ), Ladies Foreign Missionary Society, **11,008**
New Brunswick Theological Seminary (NJ), students, 10,934

New Brunswick Woman's Club (NJ), 11,006, 11,007
New Catholic Encyclopedia, 17,868
New Century Club (Wilmington, DE), 2,058, 6,805
New Century Club (PA), 6,805
New Century Club (SC), **15,664**
New Challenge (periodical), 6,112
New Citizen (newspaper), 4,302
New College (NY), faculty, 2,093
New Concord Female Seminary (OH), 14,118
New Deal, effect on Socialism in America, 11,917
New Deal Homemakers Cooperative, 9,197
New Delhi National Museum (India), 679
New Democracy, 1,981
"New Design for Women's Education, A," 11,306
New England, 7,627
New England Association for Nursery Education, 6,556
New England Clothing Committee, 6,619
New England Conservatory Club (Portland, OR), **14,430**
New England Conservatory of Music (Boston, MA), students, 14,430
New England Diaries 1602-1800: A Descriptive Catalog of Diaries, Orderly Books and Sea Journals (book), 7,627
New England Female Medical College (MA), 6,226, 7,677
New England Female Medical College (MA), Clinical Department, **6,218**
New England Freedmen's Aid Society, 6,943, 7,295
New England Hospital. *See* Dimock Community Health Center (MA)
New England Hospital for Women and Children (MA). *See* Dimock Community Health Center (MA)
New England Institute for International Relations, 7,564
New England School of Social Work, alumnae, 17,018
New England Society of Charleston (SC), 15,522
New England Woman Suffrage Association, 1,950, 6,971
New England Women (Toledo Colony, OH), 14,137
New England Women's Club (MA), 6,762, **6,798**, 7,055
New Englander, The (drama), 7,260
New Garden Boarding School (NC), **13,234**, 13,237
  faculty, 13,238
New Guinea, 2,500
  World War II, civilians' work, 13,543
New Guinea Headhunt (book), 2,500
New Hampshire, **10,789**, 10,797, 10,851
  abolitionists, **10,818**
  anti-slavery movement, 6,577
  artists colonies, **10,852**
  authors, **6,119**, 10,848, **10,853**
  bishops, Episcopal, 10,821
  camping, 10,829
  Catholic universities and colleges, 10,888
  charitable societies, **6,462**
  church societies, **10,836**
  Civil War, personal narratives, 10,819
  clergy, **7,662**
  clergy, Congregational, 10,806
  clergy, Friends, 14,965
  clinics, 10,878
  clothing workers, 10,789
  clubs, 7,517, **10,820**, 10,841, 10,843, 10,845, **10,849**, 10,856, **10,878**, 10,884, **10,886**
  coeducation, 7,662
  communists, **10,872**
  congresses and conventions, 9,368
  congressmen, 10,862, 12,284
  court-houses, 2,507
  curfew, 10,886
  department stores, 7,628
  diaries and journals, 6,487, 7,673, **10,790**, 10,792, 10,795, 10,801, 10,802, 10,803, **10,805**, 10,806, 10,807, 10,810, **10,811**, 10,813, **10,815**, 10,817, **10,819**, 10,821, **10,827**, 10,829, **10,882**
  editors, 10,808
  education, finance, 10,789, 10,886
  educational associations, **10,791**
  elections, 10,844, 10,872
  farm life, **10,790**, 10,807

Friends, 10,846
gardening, societies, etc., **9,145**, **10,842**, **10,883**
genealogy, 6,234
governors, 2,651
home economics, accounting, 10,801
hotels, taverns, etc., 10,789, 10,846
interstate relations, 6,977
judges, 10,855
lawyers, **6,750**, 10,844
legislators, 10,862, 14,763
librarians, 10,848
mica miners, 10,789
monasticism and religious orders for women, Catholic, **10,880**, **10,888**
patriotic societies, **10,840**, 10,887
persecution, 10,846
political clubs, **10,885**
politics, practical, women's activism, **10,837**
public comfort stations, 10,886
refuse and refuse disposal, 10,886
school management and organization, 7,662
school superintendents and principals, 10,865
schools, 7,597, 7,653, 7,662
senators, United States, 2,290, **10,800**, 10,862
Shakers, **4,437**
social life and customs, 9,436
societies, etc., 10,851
soldiers, Civil War, 10,789
suffrage, 6,442, 6,853
suffragists, 10,844
teachers, 7,522, **10,797**, 10,805, 10,810, **10,824**, **10,828**, **10,847**, 10,855
textile factories, **10,881**, 10,882
textile workers, 10,815
trade and professional associations, **10,839**
wages, minimum wage, 6,977
World War I, civilians' work, industrial, 10,789
New Hampshire Commission on Interstate Compacts, 6,977
New Hampshire Conference Seminary, alumnae, 5,079
New Hampshire Federation of Garden Clubs, **10,838**
New Hampshire Federation of Women's Clubs, **10,820**, 10,878, 10,886
New Hampshire League of Nursing Education, **10,839**
New Hampshire Minimum Wage Office, 6,977
New Hampshire Woman Suffrage Association, 10,844
New Harmony (IN), **4,433**, 4,435, 14,880
New Harmony Working Men's Institute (IN), 4,429
New Haven Blind Association (CT), 2,005
New Haven Colony Historical Society (CT), 1,998
New Haven Committee for Retarded Children (CT), 2,005
New Haven Consumers' League (CT), 6,485
New Haven Study Club (CT), **1,999**
New Haven Woman Suffrage Association (CT), **1,872**
New Haven Woman's Club (CT), 2,009
New Hebrides, discovery and exploration, 5,177
New Hope Baptist Church (TX), 16,342
New Idea, The (drama), 537
New Jersey, 10,903, **10,905**, **10,919**, 10,922, **11,181**, 11,184
  abortion, legal aspects, 1,984
  Afro-Americans, 11,013
    education, 11,057
  almshouses, **11,117**
  archives, 11,123, **11,143**
  archivists, 10,943
  artists, **11,136**
  assessment, **11,200**, 14,934
  authors, 10,921, **11,091**, **11,115**, 11,126, **11,182**
  autograph albums, 11,109
  bankers, 10,985, **11,129**
  Baptists, 10,936
  berries, 11,189
  bills, legislative, 11,610
  blind, 10,919
  blizzards, 11,181
  book clubs, **10,994**
  businessmen, **10,920**, 11,005, **11,031**
  capitalists and financiers, **11,074**
  Catholic schools, 10,890
  Catholic universities and colleges, archives, **10,892**
  cemeteries, 10,943

charitable societies, **10,896,** 10,956, **10,965, 10,969,** 10,973, **11,022,** 11,059, **11,067, 11,094,** 11,103, **11,119,** 11,133
charities, 7,542, 11,013
chautauquas, 11,126
child care centers, 10,965
child welfare, 10,945, 11,000
church records and registers, 11,074, **12,378,** 15,006
church records and registers, Methodist, **10,910, 11,095**
church records and registers, Presbyterian, 10,943, **10,956**
church records and registers, Reformed Church, **11,023**
church societies, 7,542, 10,907, **10,910, 11,008, 11,067,** 11,095, **11,107**
church societies, Baptist, 10,900
church societies, Methodist, **10,910**
church societies, Presbyterian, 10,956
church societies, Reformed Church, 11,023
churches, Methodist, **11,095**
cities and towns, civic improvement, **10,917, 10,946**
clergy, **11,102**
clergy, Dutch Reformed Church, 11,086
clergy, Episcopal, 11,034, 11,190
clergy, Presbyterian, 11,099, 11,111
clubs, 2,042, 10,889, **10,891, 10,899, 10,906, 10,918,** 10,919, 10,930, 10,932, **10,994,** 11,006, 11,007, **11,009, 11,010, 11,045,** 11,091, 11,121, **11,126, 11,133, 11,141, 12,598**
college and school periodicals, **11,108**
college librarians, **10,932**
college presidents, **10,928, 10,929**
college teachers, **10,971, 11,170**
commonplace books, **11,078, 11,120, 11,137**
community leadership, **7,542,** 11,170
community organization, **11,006, 11,007**
community welfare councils, **11,013**
congressmen, 11,049
constitution, 11,064
consumer's leagues, **10,953,** 11,011, 11,143
convents and nunneries, Catholic, **10,916**
cookery, **11,089**
county officials and employees, **10,967,** 11,064
court-houses, 2,507
court records, **11,187, 11,205**
crime and criminals, 8,144
deaconesses, 11,140
deans (in schools), 10,928, 10,929, 10,930, **10,931**
debtor and creditor, **11,192**
deeds, **11,188**
diaries and journals, **10,895,** 10,903, **10,914,** 10,950, **10,973,** 10,983, 10,985, 11,041, **11,053, 11,081, 11,085, 11,086,** 11,096, **11,127, 11,211**
    19th C, 10,939, **10,952, 10,957,** 10,959, **10,980, 10,999,** 11,031, **11,048,** 11,050, **11,051,** 11,057, 11,104
educators, **6,387**
elementary school teachers, **10,904**
estates (law), 11,139, **11,189**
executive advisory bodies, **11,011**
executives, **11,073**
farmers, 10,957, **10,959,** 14,981
farms, 10,905
federal aid to the arts, **11,143**
fisheries, 11,209
Friends, 11,048, 15,006
Friends, Society of, **11,033,** 11,120, 11,184, 15,058
genealogy, **11,208**
geologists, 10,954
Girl Scouts, 10,889
girls, societies, clubs, etc., 11,133
glass factories, **11,186**
governors, 2,462, 11,070, 11,184, **11,201, 11,202,** 12,697
grocers, 11,053
hatters, **12,253**
historians, 10,903
historic sites, **11,185**
historical societies, **11,113**
home economics, accounting, 11,090
hospital records, **11,149**
hotels, taverns, etc., 14,851
    law, **11,206**

housewives, **10,895, 11,035, 11,048, 11,065, 11,127, 11,211**
immigrants, Norwegian, **8,743**
inquisitions, post mortem, **11,191**
inventors, 11,134
judges, 10,920, 10,989, 11,051
labor rest homes, 12,820
lawyers, **10,989,** 11,041, 11,092, 11,103, **11,121,** 11,122, **11,129,** 11,134, 11,143
legislative bodies, voting, **11,203**
legislators, 11,144, **11,610**
librarians, 10,915, **10,923,** 11,123, 11,144
libraries, 10,905
library administrators, 11,140
liquor laws, 11,184
literary societies, **11,110**
lumber trade, 10,952
marriage licenses, **11,193**
mayors, 11,129, 11,134, 11,184
medical societies, **11,068**
mentally handicapped, education, 10,990
merchants, 10,936, 11,134, **12,161**
Methodists, 10,922
midwives, **10,978**
migrant labor, law and legislation, 11,011
monasteries, **11,066**
monasticism and religious orders for women, Catholic, **10,890, 10,893, 11,147, 11,148**
mortgages, **11,204**
municipal officials and employees, 10,905
murder, **11,034**
museum directors, **10,921**
music teachers, 10,919, **11,082**
musical societies, 10,889
naturalization records, 11,203
newspapers, **11,080,** 11,122
    sections, columns, etc., 6,043
obstetricians, **11,142**
obstetrics, cases, clinical reports, statistics, 11,019
officials and employees, 2,704, 11,031
oral history, **10,913**
parents' and teachers' associations, 10,905, **11,146**
parks, 11,064
patriotic societies, 10,889, 10,903, **10,960, 10,961,** 10,963, 11,092, **11,112**
peace societies, 10,940, 15,316
pharmacopoeias, 11,068
physicians, 10,903, 10,954, **11,019**
pioneers and settlers, 10,905
poets, 11,077, 11,184
politics, practical, women's activism, **10,996,** 11,018
printers, 11,101, 11,184
private schools, **10,897, 10,947**
public libraries, **10,915,** 10,923
public officers, 11,014
public records, 11,207
recreation, **11,006, 11,007**
registers of births, etc., 11,184
reporters and reporting, 11,111
Revolutionary War (1775-1783), 11,005, 11,045
    finance, commerce, confiscations, **11,196**
    personal narratives, **11,085**
school boards, 6,387, 10,905, **11,118**
school districts, 11,118
school notebooks, **10,901**
school nurses, 10,986
school superintendents and principals, 6,387, **10,904**
school supervisors, 10,986
schools, **4,421,** 6,601, 9,613, 11,074, **11,094, 11,125,** 13,610
schools of social work, 11,021
scrapbooks, **11,135**
shipmasters, 11,134
slave records, 10,939
social life and customs, 10,041, 10,920, 11,044, 14,845
soldiers, 11,134
strikes and lockouts, 6,315, 8,123
    clothing workers, 9,493
    silk industry, 12,705
    textile workers, 8,144
suffrage, 11,200
    opposition to, 11,073, 11,112
suffrage societies, 10,984, **11,114,** 11,124

suffragists, **11,112, 11,123**
Sunday legislation, 10,922
Sunday-school superintendents, **11,072**
Sunday-schools, Afro-American, records, **11,116**
teachers, 10,905, 10,976, **10,984,** 10,997, **11,072, 11,181**
    pensions, 10,984
teachers of mentally handicapped children, 11,181
teachers, training of, 10,995
teachers unions, 10,998
telephone, 11,073
temperance societies, **11,062**
tract societies, 10,970, 11,184
trade and professional associations, **11,012**
trials (murder), **11,190**
universities and colleges
    administration, **10,930**
    history, 10,928, 10,931, 10,932
utopias, 11,028
vital statistics, **11,212**
waxworks, 11,203
wills, **11,189**
women, education, **6,438**
World War II, civilians work, **10,889**
New Jersey Association Opposed to Woman Suffrage, 11,073, 11,112
New Jersey Bell Telephone Company, 11,073
New Jersey Center for Women's Archives, 11,123
New Jersey Child Labor Committee, 14,437
New Jersey College for Women. *See* Douglass College (NJ)
New Jersey Committee on Constitutional Revision, 11,064
New Jersey Committee on the Cause and Cure of War, 10,940
New Jersey Constitutional Foundation, 11,064
New Jersey Consumers' League, 11,064, 11,143, 14,437
New Jersey Federation of Business and Professional Women's Clubs, **11,009**
New Jersey Federation of Business and Professional Women's Clubs, New Brunswick Club, **11,010**
New Jersey Federation of Women's Clubs, 12,598
New Jersey General Assembly, voting, 11,203
New Jersey Governor's Task Force on Migrant Farm Labor, **11,011**
New Jersey Historical Society, **11,113**
New Jersey Home Economics Association, **11,012**
New Jersey State Commission for the Blind, 10,919
New Jersey State Federation of Women's Clubs, 10,930, 10,932
New Jersey State Helping Teachers Rural Supervisor, 6,387
New Jersey State Home for Girls, 13,275
New Jersey State Hospital (Trenton, NJ), 11,610
New Jersey State Normal School (Trenton, NJ). *See* Jersey City State College
New Jersey Supreme Court, **11,205**
New Jersey Teachers Retirement Fund, 10,998
New Jersey Washington Aid Society, 11,099
New Jersey Welfare Council, 11,000
New Jersey Welfare Council, Newark, **11,013**
New Jersey Woman Suffrage Association, **11,114,** 11,124
New Jersey Woman's Press Club, 11,091
New Jerusalem Church, 2,419, 14,733
    education, 14,735
New Jerusalem Church, Theta Alpha, **14,735**
New Latins, The (book), 6,025
New Leader (VA), 17,102
New London High School (IA), 5,071
"New Love"; A True Story of the "New Justice" (drama), 2,451
New Lyme Institute (OH), 13,904
New Market Theater (St. Paul, MN), 9,361
New Mexican (NM), 11,217
New Mexico, 11,223
    Acoma Indians, medical care, 153
    air defense, 14,203
    archives, 11,246
    art schools, 249
    art teachers, 11,217, 11,222, **16,291**
    artists, **2,807,** 11,234, 11,238, **16,291**
    artists' colonies, 11,213

assessment, 1,807
associations, institutions, etc., 11,240
authors, 11,213, **11,214,** 11,222, **11,223,** 11,238
bookmobiles, 11,228
businesswomen, **11,237**
Catholic schools, 1,786
church schools, 1,790
clergymen's wives, 11,246
clubs, 11,222, **11,236**
college teachers, **11,239,** 11,244, **11,246**
colonial period, 11,238
community health services, **11,225**
conductors (music), 11,218
congresswomen, 11,243
court records, 1,808, 1,809
education, 11,213
  finance, 11,213
education, bilingual, 11,217
genealogy, 11,245
historical societies, **11,227**
home economics extension work, 11,217
immigrants, German, 11,216
judges, 11,242
kindergarten teachers, 13,540
Laguna Indians, medical care, 153
land titles, registration and transfer, 11,245
lawyers, 11,242
legislators, **1,424,** 11,213, 11,217
librarians, **11,228**
mayors, 11,214
monasticism and religious orders for women,
  Catholic, **11,232**
Mormons and Mormonism, **16,777,** 16,808
museum directors, 11,238
Native Americans, **11,213,** 11,223, 13,540
  antiquities, 11,295
  medical care, 15,776
newspapers, sections, columns, etc., 11,217
oral history, **11,234**
painters, 11,213, **14,707**
periodicals, 11,213
photographers, 11,217
pioneers and settlers, **221,** 16,529
poets, 11,213
politics, practical, women's activism, 11,239
poor, 16,215
postmasters, 11,242
public health administration, 246
Pueblo Indians, 2,843, 11,217
  art, 11,222
ranchers, 16,529
reformatories (female), 11,236
school superintendents and principals, 11,227,
  11,243
schools, 11,213, 11,229
secretaries of state, 11,239
social science research, 16,215
Spanish-Mexicans, **11,245**
suffrage, 1,424, 11,213
symphony orchestras, 11,217, 11,218
teachers, 11,222
trade and professional associations, 11,237
Ute Indians, 965
vocational education, 11,229
World War II, civilians work, 16,215
New Mexico Association of Indian Affairs, 11,222,
  11,240
New Mexico Civil Air Patrol, 14,203
New Mexico Committee on the Status of Women,
  11,239
New Mexico Cooperative Extension Service, 11,217
New Mexico Federation of Women's Clubs, 11,215,
  11,236
New Mexico Health Foundation, **11,225**
New Mexico House of Representatives, majority
  whip, 11,217
New Mexico Magazine (periodical), 11,213
New Mexico State Records Center and Archives,
  11,246
New Mexico Territory, 1,729
  governors, 4,615
New Mexico War Claims Commission, 11,243
New Moon, The: The Story of Dick Martin's

*Courage, His Silver Sixpence and His Friends in
  the New World* (book), 5,013
New Northwest, The, 13,990
New Northwest, The (Portland, OR), 14,703
New 100 Years War, The (book), 6,025
New Orleans Arts and Crafts Club (LA), **5,488**
New Orleans Bootblacks (LA), 5,529
New Orleans City Council (LA), 5,538
New Orleans Creole Jazz Band (LA), 5,529
New Orleans ERA Club (LA), 5,517
New Orleans Exposition (LA, 1884-85), Women's
  Department, 6,664
New Orleans Girls' High School (LA), Alumnae
  Association, **5,519**
New Orleans, The Place and The People (book),
  5,536
New Orleans Times Democrat (LA), 9,600
New Orleans Wanderers (LA), 5,529
New Republic (periodical), 11,310, 11,720, 14,411,
  14,446
New School for Social Research (NY), 2,738, **11,900**
  faculty, 5,460, 11,490
New South (periodical), 6,547
New Ulm Public Library (MN), 9,360
New University Conference, 17,698
New University Conference, Women's Caucus, 17,698
New World Club (MN), 9,164
New York, 2,228, 11,252, 11,432, 11,492, 11,516,
  11,519, 11,577, 11,630, 11,638, 11,823, 12,186,
  12,209, 12,268, 12,325, 12,330, 12,494, **12,735**
  abolitionists, **11,506**
  abortion, legal aspects, 1,984
  accountants, 12,231
  actresses, **11,607,** 12,235
  advertising, 6,345
  Afro-Americans, 2,141, 11,440, 12,760, **12,865**
  agricultural colleges, 11,703
  agricultural societies, **11,437,** 11,550, 11,650
  agriculture, 9,158, 11,520
    accounting, 11,573
  air raid wardens, **12,668**
  albums, **11,421, 12,332,** 12,603
  alcoholism, study and teaching, 12,806
  almshouses, **12,371, 12,423**
  apprentices, **12,227**
  archaeological societies, 11,387
  archery, 11,445
  arson, 12,175
  art, 11,843
    collectors and collecting, **11,818**
    exhibitions, 6,876
    galleries and museums, 2,734, 2,746, 2,767,
      2,778, **2,794,** 2,803, **2,806,** 2,808, 2,820, 9,587,
      11,844, 12,709, 12,912
    study and teaching (secondary), 12,244
  art education, 12,544
  art patrons, 12,491
  art schools, 1,883, 2,769, 12,301
  art societies, 2,789, 12,446
  art teachers, 11,440
  artists, **11,343,** 11,419, **12,438, 12,506,** 12,870
  assessment, **11,462, 12,849**
  associations, institutions, etc., **2,152, 6,463**
  asylums, 12,156
  attorneys-general, 7,533, 10,948, **11,401**
  auroras, 11,687
  authors, 11,315, **11,343, 12,168, 12,376, 12,430,**
    12,431, 12,460, **12,463, 12,622,** 12,846
  autograph albums, 8,975
  autographs, 12,250
  balls (parties), 12,272
  bankers, 6,833, 11,037, 11,040, 11,396, 11,440,
    11,750, **12,203,** 12,463, 12,490
  bankruptcy, **11,454,** 12,402
  banks and banking, 11,746
  bar associations, 6,819
  bills, legislative, 12,910
  biography, **11,440, 11,798**
  birth control clinics, 12,829
  bishops, 12,933
  bishops, Episcopal, **12,087**
  boarding schools, 12,847
  boards of education, 11,895
  booksellers and bookselling, **12,001**

botanical gardens, **11,297,** 12,431
British in, Revolutionary War, 12,170
business education, **11,379,** 12,271
businessmen, **11,335,** 11,347, 11,700, **11,710,**
  11,875, 12,180, **12,547,** 12,814
camps, 8,684
canals, 1,901
carpenters, 12,432
catalogs, school, 12,088
Catholic hospitals, 11,298
Catholic schools, 12,733
Catholic universities and colleges, **11,807**
  archives, **11,251**
cemeteries, **11,274, 11,441**
census, 1,262, 4,942, **11,797**
charitable societies, 7,319, **11,410,** 11,445, **11,636,**
  11,939, 12,156, **12,263,** 12,315, 12,322, **12,348,**
  12,576, 12,802, 12,830
charitable societies, Jewish, **12,822,** 13,829
charities, 2,568, 12,297, **12,417**
charities, Jewish, 7,525, 7,531, **7,551**
charity organization, 12,252
charity schools, 12,830
chautauqua, 9,103
child care, 12,357
child mental health services, 11,308
child study, 11,756
children
  health and hygiene, 8,671
  hospitals, 7,255, **12,272, 12,356, 12,357**
children's librarians, **12,435, 12,570**
church and race problems, Catholic Church, 3,844
church records and registers, 17,725
church records and registers, Baptist, **11,587,**
  12,378
church records and registers, Methodist, **11,624,**
  11,802
church records and registers, Presbyterian, **12,296,**
  12,781
church societies, 11,443, 12,324
church societies, Baptist, 11,587
church societies, Congregational, **11,697**
church societies, Episcopal, **11,359, 12,084,** 12,088,
  12,237, 12,489
church societies, Methodist, 11,350, 11,624
church societies, Presbyterian, 11,740
churches, Baptist, 12,324
churches, Episcopal, 12,489
churches, Presbyterian, 11,750, **12,256**
cities and towns, 6,755, **12,128**
  civic improvement, 11,270, 12,347
citizens' associations, **5,462, 11,965,** 12,266
city councilmen, 12,297
city councilwomen, **11,987, 12,145**
civil defense, 12,751
Civil War, hospitals, charities, etc., **11,247,** 12,431
clergy, 9,706, 11,314, 12,197, **12,198,** 12,779
clergy, Baptist, 12,966
clergy, Congregational, **3,991**
clergy, Episcopal, 12,083, **12,089**
clergy, Presbyterian, **11,788,** 12,401, 12,770, 12,771
clergy, Reformed Dutch Church, **12,251**
clergy, Unitarian, **12,818**
clergymen's wives, **11,424,** 12,770, **12,771**
clinics, 11,869, 12,079, 12,841
clothing workers, 8,064
clubs, 1,948, 7,302, 8,681, **11,270,** 11,324, **11,334,**
  11,344, **11,349,** 11,351, **11,381, 11,392, 11,406,**
  11,412, **11,413,** 11,417, **11,420,** 11,445, **11,447,**
  11,530, 11,576, **11,581, 11,623, 11,625,** 11,692,
  11,696, 11,794, **11,897, 12,159, 12,208,** 12,297,
  12,323, 12,347, 12,734, **12,804, 12,807, 12,839,**
  12,844, **12,851, 12,882**
coeducation, 12,836
collectors and collecting, 12,376
college administrators, **11,365,** 11,372, 11,375,
  11,386, 11,691
college and school journalism, **11,281,** 11,302,
  11,650
college and school periodicals, 11,281, 12,746
college librarians, **11,371,** 11,824, 11,972, **11,988,**
  12,007, 12,054
college presidents, 6,617, **11,742,** 11,849, 11,910,
  11,930, 12,036, 12,283

college students, **11,302,** 11,641, 11,707, 12,918, **12,919,** 12,922
college teachers, **11,278, 11,282,** 11,285, **11,306, 11,363, 11,364, 11,366, 11,374, 11,383,** 11,526, **11,545, 11,619, 11,631, 11,656,** 11,659, **11,677,** 11,707, **11,739, 11,764, 11,912, 11,957, 11,986, 12,009, 12,016, 12,017, 12,047, 12,049, 12,055, 12,765, 12,923**
college trustees, **11,280,** 11,700
colonial period, 11,492
commonplace books, 7,039, 11,792, **12,228,** 12,580, **12,596**
community centers, 6,701, 7,242, 11,623
community leadership, 12,505, 12,507
community organization, **8,681, 12,078, 12,079,** 12,751
concerts, 11,647
congresses and conventions, **11,663, 12,855, 12,857**
congresswomen, 1,605, 6,939, **11,695, 11,934,** 12,790
conservatories of music, 2,664, **12,124,** 12,796
constitutional amendments, 11,914
consumers, 6,345
consumers' leagues, 1,948, 6,791, 6,982, 11,369, **11,763,** 11,905, 11,916
contemplative orders, 4,881, **11,448, 12,845**
convents and nunneries, Catholic, **12,859**
cookery, 11,573, **12,248, 12,262, 12,306**
coroners, 11,452
corporations, 12,203
court-houses, 2,507
court records, **11,450, 11,460**
courts, 6,886, 7,546
crime and criminals, 8,144, 11,440, **12,175**
dance, 12,260
day nurseries, **6,463**
deaconesses, Shaker, **7,038**
deans (in schools), **6,683,** 11,377, **11,561,** 12,836, 12,921, **12,923**
death, causes, 11,452
deeds, 12,218
department heads (universities), 11,637, 12,050
detectives, 11,440
diaries and journals, 360, **11,429, 11,475,** 11,792, **12,221, 12,295,** 12,326, 12,335, **12,368, 12,374, 12,442, 12,454, 12,586, 12,742**
  18th-19th C, 445, 1,425, **11,284,** 11,316, **11,348, 11,352,** 11,419, 11,443, **11,470, 11,544,** 11,570, **11,609, 11,778, 11,779,** 11,789, 12,170, **12,177, 12,188, 12,217, 12,243,** 12,254, 12,324, 12,430, **12,458,** 12,464, **12,490, 12,541, 12,663, 12,664,** 12,753, **12,793,** 12,824
directories, 12,850, **12,852**
dissertations, academic, **11,303**
domestic relations courts, 11,897
dormitories, **11,680,** 11,687
dramatists, **12,173**
dressmakers, **12,340**
dressmaking, accounting, 12,340
drug abuse, study and teaching, 12,805
druggists, 11,445
editors, **1,325, 12,044,** 12,045, **12,556,** 12,778, **17,328**
education, experimental methods, **4,151**
education, higher, 11,895
education, Jewish, **7,527**
education, secondary, 11,549
educational associations, 2,000, 6,463, 11,509, **12,792,** 15,789
educational tests and measurements, 13,737
educators, **12,544, 12,632**
elections, 11,553, 11,897, 12,680, 12,847
electrocution, 11,445
employment bureaus, **11,787**
endowments, **11,830**
engravers, **12,260, 12,459**
environmentalists, **12,875**
Episcopal Churches, charities, **12,237**
equity pleading and procedure, 11,450, 11,454
estates (law), 11,525
executions, 12,175
exhibitions, 11,326, **12,416,** 13,999
experimental theater, **964**
factories, fires and fire prevention, 11,597

factory inspectors, **11,597**
factory sanitation, 11,597
factory workers, 11,255, 12,760
fairs, 11,650
family planning, **12,829**
farm life, 8,352
farmers, 11,414, 11,415, 12,199
farms, **11,643**
festivals, **11,751**
fresh-air charity, 11,263
friendly societies, **11,598**
Friends, Society of, **11,032, 12,224, 12,627**
fund-raising, **12,261, 12,708,** 12,802
fur trade, 8,357, 11,263
gambling, 12,424
gardening, societies, etc., 12,851, 12,869
genealogy, 11,440
gift-books (annuals, etc.), **12,337**
gifted children, education, 13,742
Girl Scouts, 12,851, 12,924
glass-workers, **11,408**
glassware, 12,182
governmental investigations, **11,255, 11,256,** 11,895
governors, 11,546, 11,795, 11,871, 11,928, 12,210, 12,320, 12,521, **12,522, 12,833**
greek letter societies, **11,376,** 11,388, **11,712**
health-officers, **6,209**
health-resorts, watering-places, etc., 11,443
high school teachers, **12,386**
historians, **11,428,** 12,460, 12,772
historical societies, **11,439,** 12,581, 12,751
home demonstration agents, **11,651**
home economics, 11,565
  accounting, 11,722, **12,250,** 12,339, 12,429
  study and teaching, 11,365
home economics extension, **11,564,** 11,662, 11,756
hops, 11,730
horticulturists, **11,790**
hospital administrators, 12,272, 12,354, 12,759
hospital records, 11,443, **12,138,** 12,141, **12,353, 12,354, 12,358**
hospitals, 2,568, 6,222, **8,770,** 8,857, 8,862, 12,802
hospitals, gynecologic and obstetric, 12,141, **12,353, 12,354,** 12,356, **12,358**
hospitals, military, 6,041
hotels, taverns, etc., 12,601
housewives, **11,264, 11,275, 11,276, 11,416, 11,418, 12,458, 12,486, 12,853**
housing, 12,870
housing authorities, 6,885, 11,914
housing, cooperative, 1,654
ice, 11,429
immigrants, 6,695
  charities for aid to, **7,537**
  economic aspects, 7,557
indentured servants, **12,371**
industry and state, 6,982
industry, social aspects, **12,717**
influenza epidemics, 12,554
interior decorators, **2,779**
inventories, 8,328, **11,455**
inventors, 12,770
Iroquois Indians, antiquities, 11,387
Jews, 12,430
journalists, **11,269, 11,344, 12,061, 12,582, 12,772**
judges, 1,955, 5,476, **6,886,** 7,242, 7,244, 11,524, 11,914, **11,943, 12,019,** 12,069, 12,305, 12,345, **12,611**
judgments, 11,460
justices of the peace, 12,769
juvenile courts, 11,897
kindergarten teachers, **12,586**
kindergartens, 11,864, 12,431
land grants, 12,748
land settlement, 11,746
land titles, registration and transfer, 12,643
law, cases, 11,746
law partnership, 8,311, 12,755
law teachers, 11,956
lawyers, 1,472, **6,314, 6,750, 6,886, 6,887, 6,996,** 7,544, **11,397, 11,546, 11,553, 11,632, 11,657, 11,710, 11,943,** 12,069, **12,163, 12,218, 12,320,** 12,434, **12,440, 12,534, 12,755**
lecturers, **11,946**

lectures and lecturing, **11,900, 12,780**
legal aid, 11,931
legal aid societies, **12,703**
legal documents, 11,318, **11,325,** 11,330
legislative bodies, 11,928
legislators, 6,939, 7,266, 11,534, **11,546, 11,600, 11,657, 11,729,** 11,750, 11,928, 12,170, 12,180, 12,199, **12,209,** 12,434, **12,910,** 14,392
librarians, **11,268, 11,320, 11,328,** 11,577, **11,594, 12,002, 12,151, 12,526**
libraries, special collections, rare books, 11,921
libraries, university and college, **11,825, 11,971**
library associations, **11,382,** 11,412, 12,526
library employees, **11,973**
library finance, 12,049
library schools, **11,333,** 11,930, 12,526
  alumni, **11,955**
lighthouse keepers, 12,931
literary agencies, **14,410**
literary agents, **11,165, 12,372**
literary societies, 7,557, **11,411,** 12,924
lithographers, **2,755**
lobbyists, 2,212, **11,706**
marriage law, 12,843
maternal and infant welfare, 12,738
maternal health services, 12,736
maternity homes, **12,316,** 12,355
mathematicians, **6,815**
mayors, **11,269,** 11,841, 11,856, **11,884,** 11,895, 11,905, 11,914, 11,928, **12,036,** 12,144, 12,147, 12,148, 12,149, 12,150
medical colleges, 6,616, 11,869, 12,917
medical librarians, **11,591**
medical societies, **11,754,** 12,841
medical teaching personnel, **7,226**
memorials, 12,561
mental health services, 7,546
merchants, 10,968, **11,506,** 11,786, 12,034, **12,187,** 12,199, 12,219, **12,225, 12,243,** 12,268, 12,288, **12,342,** 12,548, **12,551,** 12,769, 13,771
midwives, 11,852, 12,450
migrant labor, 11,730
militia, 4,818
missions, Methodist, 10,909
Mohawk Indians, 11,440
monasteries, **11,292, 12,845, 12,934**
monasticism and religious orders for women, Catholic, **11,272, 11,273, 11,298, 11,313, 11,362, 11,404, 11,433, 11,465, 11,469, 11,476, 11,477, 11,796, 11,803, 12,733, 12,749, 12,767, 12,809, 12,810, 12,866, 12,885, 12,932, 12,933,** 14,783
monuments, 12,345
mortgages, 11,523
moving-picture industry, 11,537, 11,607
moving-picture studios, 11,537
moving-picture theaters, **12,794**
municipal charters, 11,856
municipal government, 11,856
  records and correspondence, **11,451, 11,463**
municipal officials and employees, **6,819,** 7,244, **11,841,** 11,895, **11,987,** 12,144, 12,146, 12,147, 12,148, 12,149
municipal services, 11,451
municipal universities and colleges and city administration, 11,895
museum directors, 12,751, 12,863
museums, 9,509, 11,844, 12,901
music critics, **11,355**
music teachers, **11,532, 12,774, 12,796**
musical societies, 2,020
musicians, **12,319**
Native Americans, 11,443
  missions, 1,428, 8,304
newspaper publishers and publishing, 11,512
newspapers, 6,694, **11,311,** 11,443, 11,867
  sections, columns, etc., 10,181, **12,061**
nursery schools, 8,684, **12,878**
nurses, **11,515,** 12,850
nursing, 11,601
  study and teaching, **12,074**
nursing schools, 2,542, 6,131, 6,721, **11,377,** 12,353
  records and correspondence, **12,351**
occupational retraining, **12,271**
occupational retraining for women, 6,799

officials and employees, **6,766**, 6,982, 11,440, 11,504, 11,767, 11,768, 11,770, 12,020, 12,071, 12,790, 14,943, 17,642
old age homes, 11,277, 11,445, **12,287**
old age pensions, 11,939
ombudswomen, 11,545
oral history, **12,760**
organists, **12,291**
orphans and orphan asylums, 11,410, 11,619, **12,355**, 12,759, 12,767
orphans and orphan asylums, Jewish, **7,536**
painters, **2,738**, **2,755**, **2,788**, **2,818**
parks, **12,347**
patriotic societies, **11,317**, **11,319**, **11,409**, **11,438**, **12,189**, **12,776**
peace societies, 7,868, **11,389**, **12,883**, 15,316
pediatricians, Afro-American, **11,390**
pensions, 11,445
periodicals, 11,444
philanthropists, 11,396, **11,777**, 12,069, 12,071, 12,740
photograph collections, **12,081**, **12,127**, **12,129**, **12,130**
photographs, **12,123**, 12,803, **12,887**
physical education teachers, **12,587**
physicians, 11,020, **11,393**, 11,395, **11,423**, 11,440, 11,472, 11,647, 11,666, **11,941**, **12,155**, 12,311, 12,327, 12,345, **12,352**, **12,450**, 12,759, 12,771, **12,825**, **12,841**, **14,146**
pioneers and settlers, **6,505**, 7,143, **7,181**, 11,440, 11,745, 12,235, 12,734, **12,768**
poetry, competitions, 2,469
poets, 5,988, 11,412
police chiefs, **12,434**
police, records and correspondence, 12,827
policewomen, 11,686, **12,827**
political activists, women, 12,069, **12,681**
political parties, 8,071, 8,126, 12,906
politicians, 11,666
politicians, Afro-American, **12,680**
politics and government, 11,553, 12,020
politics, practical, 12,799
politics, practical, women's activism, 11,553, 11,920, **12,056**, **12,057**, **12,058**, **12,872**, **12,873**, **12,874**
poor, 11,738, **12,081**
porcelain, 12,182
postmasters, 12,345
prenatal care, 11,852, 12,357
Presbyterian church, charities, 12,256
printers, 3,991, **12,459**
printing machinery and supplies, 12,508
prisoners, **11,254**
prisons, **12,423**, 12,576
private presses, **12,879**
private schools, **12,750**
probate courts, **11,455**, 11,456
probation officers, **11,788**
prostitution, 12,424
psychiatric hospitals, 12,197
  records and correspondence, 11,254
psychiatrists, **11,308**
public health, **2,152**, 11,571, **12,736**
public health nursing, 6,131, 11,852, 12,078, 12,079
public institutions, **11,254**
public records, **11,452**, 12,775
public schools, 2,758, 12,752
public welfare, 13,692
public welfare administration, 11,695
publishers and publishing, 11,644, **12,384**
rabbis, 6,603, **7,552**
race discrimination, 5,462
race problems, 8,684
radio announcing, **11,402**
radio programs, 11,291
real estate business, 11,882
real property, 12,231, 12,463, 12,611
recreation centers, 12,297
reference services (libraries), **11,972**
reformatories (female), 6,789, 7,546, 11,003, 11,254
reformers, **12,203**, **12,218**
refuse and refuse disposal, 11,229, 12,266
rent, 11,745
rent control, **12,601**

restaurants, lunch rooms, etc., 7,209
revivals, 11,522
riots, 12,487, 12,490
river steamers, 12,330
safe-deposit companies, **11,458**
sanatoriums, 2,542, 12,666
school administrators, 12,244
school attendance, 11,749
school boards, 11,390, 12,847
school buildings, 12,801
school hygiene, 8,572
school physicians, 6,446, **11,357**
school superintendents and principals, **6,507**, 7,527, 11,351, **11,611**, 12,750
school supervisors, 11,532
schools, 7,541, 7,559, 7,653, 11,708, 11,898, **12,152**, 12,241, **12,746**, **12,801**, **12,831**, **12,927**, **12,928**, 13,604, 17,445
  accounting, **12,304**
  administration, **11,673**
  centralization, 12,870
  records and correspondence, **11,257**
scientific societies, **11,248**
scrapbooks, **11,444**, **12,761**, **12,782**
sculptors, **2,814**
secretaries of state, 6,886, 12,790
self-government (in education), 11,561, **11,752**, **11,755**
senators, United States, **2,120**, **11,875**, 12,440, **12,833**
Seneca Indians, **11,294**, 11,440
sewing schools, 12,271
sex discrimination in education, 11,373
Shakers, **4,437**, 7,035, **7,037**, **7,038**, **7,039**, 7,040
singers, 11,427
single mothers, 12,355
slavery, 2,141
  anti-slavery movements, 11,303, 12,908
slaves, 2,141, 11,440
smallpox epidemics, 11,520, 11,718
social action, **12,808**
social legislation, 11,965
social life and customs, 2,033, 8,357, 10,480, 11,249, 11,854, 12,374, 12,412, **12,554**, 15,003
social problems, 11,369
social reformers, **6,791**
social science research, **8,642**
social service, 11,897
social service exchanges, **8,661**
social settlements, 2,309, 6,131, 7,217, 7,243, 7,292, 7,299, **7,557**, **8,646**, **8,652**, **8,681**, 9,095, 11,445, 11,633, 11,897, **12,008**, 12,026, **12,520**, 12,657
social work education, 7,546
social workers, **6,729**, **6,885**, **11,346**, 12,080
social workers, Afro-American, **12,687**
societies, etc., **12,876**
special librarians, 11,407, **12,816**
speech clinics, 11,383
spiritualism, 11,741
street-lighting, **12,266**
streets, maintenance and repair, 12,266
strikes and lockouts, 6,802
  restaurants, lunchrooms, etc., 12,705
student housing, 12,924
student movements, **11,847**
student unions, 11,375
students, 12,152, **12,368**
students' societies, **11,384**, **11,388**, **11,721**, 12,745, 12,746, **12,916**
suffrage, 1,652, 2,212, 4,859, 6,379, 6,706, 6,815, 6,894, 11,261, 11,616, **11,793**
  opposition to, **6,800**, 11,249, 12,524
suffrage societies, 4,156, 6,815, 6,979, **11,258**, 11,443, **11,678**, 11,793, **12,059**, 12,387, **12,743**, 12,834, 12,856, 16,252, 17,217
suffragists, **6,815**, **6,979**, 11,396, 12,129
suicide, 11,440
Sunday school teachers, **11,355**, 11,440
surgeons, 12,279
surveyors, 11,784
tailors, **12,447**
teachers, 369, 2,162, **2,758**, 9,112, **9,158**, 9,448, **11,428**, 11,520, 11,602, **11,724**, **12,209**, **12,510**, **12,533**, 12,688, 12,760, **12,766**, **12,870**

salaries, pensions, etc., 11,706
teachers, Afro-American, **12,687**
teachers' colleges, 1,842, 6,490, **11,378**, **11,819**, 11,842, 11,897, 12,122, 12,470
teachers of the deaf, 11,440
teachers, Shaker, **7,037**
teachers' unions, 8,145, **11,361**, **11,761**, **11,774**
teaching, 8,170
temperance, 11,520
temperance societies, **11,422**, **11,430**, 11,440, **11,801**, **12,608**, **12,741**, 12,790, **12,805**, **12,806**, **12,838**, **12,929**
textile factories, **12,758**
theater, 12,006
  Jews in, 7,530
theater management, **12,444**
theaters, **11,689**, 11,860
theatrical producers and directors, **12,039**
theological seminaries, archives, **12,090**
trade and professional associations, 6,829, **11,601**, 12,738, 12,924
trade schools, Jewish, **7,527**
trade-unions, 6,795, 6,812, **11,772**
  clothing workers, **12,861**
  officials and employees, 8,145, **11,765**
Ukrainian-Americans, **9,509**
universities and colleges, 674, 2,146, 3,257, 6,157, 6,354, 6,416, 6,451, 6,683, 8,085, **11,373**, 11,443, **11,662**, **11,847**, **11,849**, **11,969**, **12,122**, 12,159, 12,740, **12,745**, 12,762, 12,907, 12,917, 12,918, 12,922, 12,923, 13,604, 15,332
  administration, **11,538**, 12,925
  archives, **11,267**, **11,271**, **11,285**, **11,290**, **11,301**, **11,332**, **11,380**, **11,398**, **11,446**, **11,781**, **12,836**
  buildings, 11,694
  employees, 11,642
  faculty, 11,521, **11,581**, 11,835, 11,848
  history, **11,300**, 11,550
university extension, **11,970**
urban economics, 12,149
urban renewal, 11,443
utopias, 1,590, 11,726, **15,259**
vital statistics, **11,441**, 11,443, **11,800**, 12,734
vocational education, 6,812, 8,646, 9,598
vocational rehabilitation, **6,799**
voice culture, **12,322**
volunteer workers in hospitals, 2,384, 11,635, 11,758, 12,506
volunteer workers in social service, **6,689**
voters, registration of, 12,056, 12,057
War of 1812, 12,734
water resources development, 12,057
widows, 11,256, 12,315, 12,511
wills, **11,456**
women
  education, **6,438**
  employment, 6,737
  employment reentry, 6,799
women's colleges, **11,283**, **11,468**, 13,811
  archives, **11,820**, **12,926**
  history, 11,278
women's history, **12,881**
working-women's clubs, 8,684
World War I, civilians work, 11,445, **12,797**
World War II, civilians work, 11,445, **12,797**
yellow fever, 12,260
yellow fever epidemics, 12,514
Young Women's Christian Association, **8,684**
New York Association for Improving the Condition of the Poor. See Community Service Society of New York
New York Association of Neighborhood Workers. See United Neighborhood Houses of New York City
New York Asylum for Lying-In Women, 12,141, **12,354**
New York Botanical Garden, **11,297**, 12,431, 15,217
New York Bureau of Legal Advice, 11,931, **12,703**
New York Charity Organization Society. See Community Service Society (NY)
New York City Babies' Hospital, 7,255
New York City Ballet, 14,239
New York City board of education, 11,765
New York City Bureau of Municipal Research, 11,987

New York City Charter Revision Commission, 11,987
New York City Charter Revision Committee (1935), 11,856
New York City Child Welfare Board, 11,987
New York City Council, 11,987
New York City Department of Welfare, 13,692
New York City Emergency Unemployment Committee, 11,987
New York City Female Union Society for the Promotion of Sabbath Schools, 11,316
New York City Housing Authority, 6,885
New York City Mayor's Committee, 11,987
New York City Opera, 5,479
New York City Woman's Night Court, 7,546
New York City Women's Suffrage party, 12,505
New York Civil Liberties Union, 12,061
New York College Settlement, 7,243
New York Commission of Safety, 11,504
New York Commission on the Education and Employment of Women, 6,737
New York Committee for Young Audiences, 2,205
New York Conference of Social Work, 11,346
New York Conference Seminary (NY), 12,259
New York Consumers' League, 6,791, 6,982
New York Cooperative Extension Service, 11,662
New York Court of Appeals, 12,611
New York Daily Graphic, 14,093
New York Daily Jewish News, 12,705
New York Department of Correctional Services, **11,254**
New York Department of Mental Hygiene, **11,254**
New York Drama Critics Circle, 6,008
New York Dramatic Mirror (periodical), 12,474
New York Evening Post, 2,596, 11,309, 12,403
New York Evening Sun (NY), 11,309
New York Federation of Women's Clubs, 11,576
New York Female Assistance Society for the Relief and Religious Instruction of the Sick Poor, 2,518
New York Herald, The. See New York Herald Tribune
New York Herald Tribune, 2,542, 5,121, 6,640, 7,305, 11,111, 11,223, 11,302, 11,493, 12,466, 12,582, 13,244, 14,237
New York Herald Tribune Sunday Magazine, 12,044
New York Historical Association, 11,706
New York Hospital, 6,616, 7,226, 11,941
New York Hospital, board of governors, 7,226
New York Hospital, School of Nursing, alumnae, 11,515
New York House and School of Industry, **6,799**
New York Infant Asylum, **12,355**
New York Infirmary, 17,618
New York Infirmary for Women and Children, 7,255
New York Journal, 5,505
New York Kindergarten Association, 3,535
New York League of Unitarian Women, 15,270
New York Ledger, **7,276**, 12,394
New York Library Association, 12,526
New York Library School Association, 12,526
New York Medical College for Women, 12,917
New York Mills "Seventy-Five Years of Progress" 1884-1959 (book), 8,455
New York Morning Telegraph, The, 6,694
New York Morning World, The, 12,863
New York National Freedman's Relief Association, 2,313, 7,319, 13,937
New York Nursery and Child's Hospital, **12,272, 12,356**
New York Observer, The, 9,636
New York Post, 12,061, 13,244
New York Prison Association, **12,576**
New York Psychiatric Institute, 11,908
New York Public Library, 12,049, 12,570, 15,600
New York Public Library, Aguilar Branch, 12,654
New York Public Library, Berg Collection, 11,921
New York Public Library School, 11,930
New York Reformatory for Women, 11,003
New York Review of Books, 12,049
New York School for the Deaf, 2,114
New York School of Applied Design for Women, 12,301, **12,577**
New York School of Applied Design for Women, Exhibition of Sculpture by Women (1910), **2,756**

New York School of Fine and Applied Arts, alumnae, 8,779
New York School of Philanthropy, 15,312
New York School of Social Work
   alumnae, 11,501
   faculty, **12,017**
   students, 8,664
New York Security and Trust Company, 12,203
New York Seminary for Kindergartners, 2,430
New York Society for Ethical Culture, 11,946
New York Society for Women Artists, 2,789
New York Sorosis, 13,916
New York State Agricultural and Industrial School (Industry, NY), 11,553
New York State Agricultural Experiment Station, 11,629
New York State Agricultural Society, 11,550
New York State Archaeological Council, 11,387
New York State Association of Applied Psychology, 11,549
New York State Association Opposed to Woman Suffrage, **6,800**, 12,524
New York State Board of Charities, 12,252
New York State Board of Mediation, 11,768, 11,770
New York State Board of Regents, 11,592
New York State Charities Aid Association, 7,319
New York State College of Agriculture, 11,629
   students, 11,703
New York State College of Home Economics, **11,662,** 11,663, 11,739
   faculty, 11,661, 11,691
New York State Commission Against Discrimination, 11,591
New York State Commission Against Discrimination in Employment, 6,886
New York State Committee Against Discrimination, Manhattan Council, 2,587
New York State Council of Rural Women, 11,662
New York State Democratic Coalition, 17,975
New York State Democratic Committee, 6,819
New York State Department of Labor, 6,766
New York State Employment Bureau, 11,440
New York State Factory Investigating Committee, **11,255**
New York State Farm Bureau Women's Committee, **11,664**
New York State Federation of Home Bureaus, 11,662
New York State Federation of Women's Clubs, **11,447,** 11,793
New York State Library School (Albany, NY), 4,396
   alumni, **11,955**
   faculty, **12,526**
   students, 420
New York State Library School Register, 11,955
New York State Preservation Board, 11,387
New York State Psychological Intern Training Program, 11,549
New York State Public Employment Relations Board, 11,767
New York State Reformatory for Women, 7,546
New York State School of Industrial and Labor Relations, faculty, **11,764**
New York State Social Hygiene and Tuberculosis Association, 2,587
New York State Society of Rural Women, 11,393
New York State University, students, 9,358
New York State Woman Suffrage Association, 4,156, 6,979, 7,232, 11,793, 12,834, 12,856, 15,283
New York State Woman Suffrage Party, 7,217, 12,387
New York State Women Suffrage Association. *See* New York State Woman Suffrage Association
New York State Women's Council, 11,729
New York State Women's Political Union, 2,212
New York Sun, 5,048, 5,869
New York Teachers Guild, 8,145
New York Temporary State Commission for Widowed Mothers, **11,256**
New York Theatre Strategy and Women's Theatre Council, 11,221
New York Times, The, 112, 2,340, 4,227, 4,409, 6,120, 6,168, 6,841, 9,706, 11,111, 11,309, 12,466, 12,519, 12,553, 13,108, 13,692, 14,377, 17,677, 17,979
New York Times Book Review, The, 6,110

New York Times Magazine, The, 2,108, 6,075
New York Training School for Community Center Workers, 7,546
New York Training School for Girls, 6,789
New York Tribune, 2,542, 11,998, 12,602, 17,035, 17,141
New York Tribune, Fresh Air Fund, 2,542
New York Tuberculosis and Health Association, Harlem Committee, 2,152
New York University, 12,470
   alumnae, 1,804, 9,558, 11,269
   faculty, 10,894, 12,009
New York University, Hall of Fame, 2,542
New York University Law School, alumnae, 13,904
New York University Medical College, 12,141
New York Urban League, 12,061, 12,680
New York Women's Council, 7,258
New York Women's Trade Union League, 6,812
New York Workmen's Compensation Board, 6,819
New York World, 5,861, 5,869
New York World's Fair, 2,743
New York World's Fair, Advisory Committee on Women's Participation (1939), 9,021
New Yorker, The (periodical), 2,331, 4,476, 5,310, 6,057, 9,736, 9,769, 9,770, 11,316, 12,888, 14,377
New Zealand, 16,782
   American travelers in, 7,488
   archives, **6,801**
New Zealand Women's Archives, 6,801
Newark Academy (NY), Sabbath School for Coloured People, Female Department, **11,116**
Newark Alms House (NJ), **11,117**
Newark Board of Education (NJ), **11,118**
Newark Board of Education (NJ), Committee on Teachers, 11,118
Newark Board of Education (NJ), Teacher's Monthly Institute, 11,118
Newark Daily Advertiser (NJ), 11,103
Newark Deaconess Home (NJ), 11,095
Newark Evening News, The (NJ), 11,111
Newark Female Charitable Society (NJ), 11,067, 11,103, **11,119**
Newark Museum (NJ), 11,140
Newark Public Library (NJ), 11,123, 11,140
Newark Sunday Call (NJ), 6,043
Newark Teacher's Institute (NJ), 11,118
Newark Young Ladies Institute (NJ), students, 11,137
Newberry, Clara (White), 11,742
Newberry, Jane [Mrs.], **14,050**
Newberry Library (IL), 4,004
Newberry, Marie Anna, **7,878**, 11,938
Newbery Medal, 5,694, 11,368, 12,903, 13,252
Newbery Medal books, 4,306, 8,531
Newbold, Caleb, Jr., 9,311
Newbold, Mary Ann, 14,847
Newbold, Rachel. *See* Whitall, Rachel (Newbold) [Mrs. Gilbert]
Newbold, Susan L. *See* Cope, Susan L. (Newbold) [Mrs. William Drinker]
Newburn, Betsy, 1,013
Newbury, Dorothy J., **5,083**
Newbury, Mary (1837-1901). *See* Adams, Mary (Newbury) [Mrs. Austin] (1837-1901)
Newby, J. B., **13,496**
Newby, Sophia A., 13,620
Newcomb, Anita (1864-1940). *See* McGee, Anita (Newcomb) [Mrs. William John] (1864-1940)
Newcomb, Covelle, 4,445
Newcomb, Daniel, 1,469
Newcomb, Eric McGee, 2,464
Newcomb, Harriett Sophie, 5,507
Newcomb, Josephine Louise (LeMennier) [Mrs. Warren] (1816-1901), 5,410, **5,507**, 5,517
Newcomb, Kate Pelham (1886-1956), **17,699**
Newcomb, Lydia, **2,000**, 2,003
Newcomb, Patty, 1,469
Newcomb Relief Unit, 5,506
Newcomb, Samuel P. (1839-ca. 1869), 16,060
Newcomb, Simon, 2,464
Newcomb, Susan E. [Mrs. Samuel P.] (1848-?), 16,060
Newcomers Club (IL), 4,401
Newel, Helen F. [Mrs. Stanford], **12,273**

Newel, Stanford, 12,273
Newell, Barbara Warne, 7,574, 7,583, **7,879**
Newell, Duncan H., 11,014
Newell, Florence (Chase), 2,258
Newell, Frederick Haynes (1862-1932), **2,511**
Newell, Hannah Orme, 3,764
Newell, Harriet (1816-96). *See* Godfrey, Harriet (Newell) [Mrs. Ard] (1816-96)
Newell, Harriet (Atwood) [Mrs. Samuel] (1793-1812), 7,048
Newell, Helen (1866-1930). *See* Garfield, Helen (Newell) [Mrs. James Rudolph] (1866-1930)
Newell, Hope, 2,344
Newell, Julia (Florance) [Mrs. Duncan H.] (1898-), **11,014**
Newell, Robert, 14,594, 14,608
Newfoundland, 6,375
Newhall, Nancy, 12,789
Newhoff, Sarah [Mrs. Lewis], **15,161**
Newkirk, Anna Miller (1841-1918). *See* Place, Anna Miller (Newkirk) [Mrs. James W.] Barker [Mrs. James Keyes] (1841-1918)
Newkirk, Laura, 11,720
Newkirk, Sarah Cordelia (Miller) [Mrs. Thompson] (1817-97), **11,015**, 11,020
Newkirk, Thompson, 11,020
Newlands, Francis G., 10,673
Newman, Edna S., 3,954
Newman, Emma E. [Mrs. Nicholas Newman Emerson], **1,470**
Newman, Frances [Miss] (1883-1928), 2,969, 2,995, 3,167, 3,174, **3,232**
Newman, Irene [Mrs.] 1,832
Newman, Pauline M., 1,779, 6,365, 6,766, **6,802,** 11,917, 12,700, 12,704
Newman, Philip C. (1914-), **12,060**
Newman, Ruth [Mrs. Philip C.], **12,060**
Newman, Sarah, 2,504
Newmark, Mrs. Joseph Solomon, **688**
Newmarket Manufacturing Company (NH), **10,881**
Newport, Anne (1769-1854). *See* Royall, Anne (Newport) [Mrs. William] (1769-1854)
News (periodical), 17,716
News (Chicago, IL), 14,422
News (Tacoma, WA), 14,422
News (Parkersburg, WV), 5,310
News agencies, 169, 250, 3,799, 3,800, 3,851
News agencies, Afro-American, 3,799, 3,800
News and Letters (newspaper), 8,082
News and Mississippian (MS), 9,686
News and Observer (NC), 13,244, 13,390, 13,468
News-Gazette (IL), 4,379
"News in Brief" (newsletter), 7,322
News Print (Buffalo Lake, MN), 8,515
News Republican (New Castle, IN), 4,622
News-Star (OK), 3,382
Newsletter (U.S. Women's Bureau), 2,703
Newsletter, The (OH), 14,024
Newsletters, 4, 929, 1,071, **1,126, 1,129,** 3,230, 4,426, 6,142, 7,197, 7,723, 8,174, 8,402, 9,095, 9,130, 9,205, 13,508, 13,719, 14,024, 14,425, 14,622
Newsom, Emma Ellen (Day) [Mrs. John Edward] (1862-1952), **5,074**
Newsom, John Edward (1856-1930), **5,074**
Newsome, Effie Lee, 3,284
Newspaper Guild, 11,867
Newspaper publishers and publishing, 1,605, 3,640, **3,669, 4,270,** 10,626, 11,512, 14,046, 14,353, **15,229**
Newspaper publishing, 1,455, 2,393, 2,542, 8,070, 9,157, 10,305, 12,394, 15,976
Newspapers, 55, 63, 73, 81, **294, 377, 912, 914,** **1,011, 1,116,** 1,414, 1,757, 1,764, 1,790, 2,128, 3,197, 3,203, 3,227, 3,239, 3,240, 3,271, 3,419, **3,454,** 3,918, **4,086,** 4,165, 4,215, **4,243,** 4,302, 4,538, 5,394, 5,669, 5,999, 6,104, 6,120, **6,167,** 6,344, 6,640, 6,694, **7,502,** 8,369, 8,429, 8,456, 8,816, 9,287, 9,436, 9,636, 9,641, 9,686, 9,703, 9,706, 9,709, 9,717, 9,756, 9,768, 10,171, 10,354, 10,598, **10,694,** 11,122, **11,311,** 11,443, 11,858, 11,867, 11,896, 13,016, 13,692, 13,999, 14,144, 14,216, 14,223, 14,309, 14,582, 14,610, **14,830,** **15,419,** 15,864, 16,403, 16,469, **16,920, 16,977,** 17,379, 17,589

illustrations, **1,617**
indexes, **151, 1,166, 1,535, 1,618**
sections, columns, etc., 100, **1,205,** 1,670, 1,750, 1,800, 2,168, 2,240, 2,596, 2,768, 2,784, 3,070, 3,251, 3,262, 3,276, 3,350, 3,662, 3,825, 4,289, 4,379, 4,622, 5,124, 5,394, 5,505, 6,031, 6,043, 6,044, 6,056, 6,064, 6,526, 6,614, 6,685, 6,841, 6,948, 7,082, 8,070, 8,443, 9,550, 9,599, 9,600, 9,771, 10,134, 10,135, 10,164, 10,181, 10,443, 11,038, 11,213, 11,217, **12,061,** 12,259, 13,390, 13,468, 13,617, 14,058, 14,223, 14,237, 14,512, 14,630, 15,158, 15,966, 16,348, 16,349, 16,371, 16,387, 17,102, 17,267, 17,378, **17,947,** 17,954
Newspapers, Afro-American, 2,879, 3,799, 3,915
Newspapers, Finnish-American, 8,582
Newspapers, Native American, 2,883
Newspapers on microfilm, **1,002**
Newspapers, Socialist, 17,259
Newspapers, Welsh-American, 9,952
Newspapers, women's, **11,080**
Newsreel, 17,637
Newsreel (film company), 17,637
Newton, Agnes (1909-), 4,495
Newton, Catherine [Miss], 2,960
Newton Centre Unitarian Church Women's Auxiliary (MA), **6,255**
Newton, Charlotte [Miss], 3,106, 3,107
Newton, Clara Chipman [Miss] (1848-1937), **13,853**
Newton Equal Franchise Association (MA). *See* Newton Equal Suffrage League (MA)
Newton Equal Suffrage League (MA), **7,096**
Newton Family, 11,599
Newton Family (GA), **2,986**
Newton Female Academy (MA), 7,653
Newton, Gilbert Stuart (1794-1835), **12,274**
Newton High School (MA), 2,446, 6,724
Newton Home for Orphans and Destitute Girls (MA). *See* Rebecca Pomroy Newton Home for Orphan Girls (Newton, MA)
Newton, Kathleen Mitchell (ca. 1900-), **14,296**
Newton, Mildred, 2,828
Newton, Mrs. Scott R., **13,497**
Newton, Willis, 3,434
Newton Woman's Suffrage League (MA). *See* Newton Equal Suffrage League (MA)
Ney, Elisabet. Franzisca Bernadina Wilhelmina Elisabeth. [Mrs. Edmund Duncan] Montgomery (1833-1907), 16,014, **16,021,** 16,032, 16,044, **16,111, 16,372**
Neylan, John Francis (1885-1960), **689**
Neymann, Clara [Mrs.], 7,999
Nez Percé Indians, 1,621, 2,838, 6,541, 10,287, **14,660,** 17,355
government relations, **3,665**
missions, 3,706, 3,723
reservations, 3,665
wars, **17,355**
wars (1877), 3,665, 3,721, 3,730
"Nez Perces Since Lewis and Clark, The" (ms), 3,706
Niagara Falls, 12,734, 12,735, 14,819
Niccolls, Martha (Hall) (1916-?), 526
Nice, Margaret Morse [Mrs. Leonard Blaine] (1883-), **11,665**
Nichol, Ann Leslie. *See* Moore, Ann Leslie (Nichol) [Mrs. Merrill]
Nichol, Elizabeth Pease (1807-97), 5,907
Nichol, Jennie (1845-81), 10,185
Nicholas and the Golden Goose (book), 12,570
Nicholas, Emily Elizabeth (Jackson) [Mrs. Philip N.] (1845-1935), 1,956
Nicholls, Winnie, 13,682
Nichols, Amelia Ann (Ainsworth) [Mrs. Charles Sanders], 7,484
Nichols, Anna Lewis (?-1934), 7,654
Nichols, Arthur H. (1840-1923), 6,803
Nichols, Benjamin, 7,469
Nichols, Caroline (Meeker) [Mrs. John] (1813-45), 9,036
Nichols, Charles Lemuel (1851-1929), **7,654**
Nichols, Charlotte, 7,459
Nichols, Charlotte S., **7,411**
Nichols, Clarina Irene (Howard) [Mrs. Justin] Carpenter [Mrs. George W.] (1810-85), **5,221,** **6,804**

Nichols, Edward L., 11,580
Nichols, Elizabeth F. [Mrs. Arthur H.] (1844-1929), 6,803
Nichols Family (MA), **6,803, 7,484**
Nichols, Fannie (Birch), 9,542
Nichols, Harriet S., **9,265**
Nichols, Harry Pierce, 7,484
Nichols High School (MS), 9,542
Nichols, Jeannette (Paddock) (1890-), 2,160, 2,540
Nichols, John (1812-73), 9,036
Nichols, Lemuel Bliss (1816-83), 7,654
Nichols, Lucy Ann [Mrs.], 10,350
Nichols, Lydia Carter [Mrs. Lemuel Bliss] (?-1888), 7,654
Nichols, Margaret H. (1879-1959). *See* Shurtleff, Margaret H. Nichols (1879-1959)
Nichols, Maria (Longworth) [Mrs. George Ward] (1849-1932). *See* Storer, Maria (Longworth) [Mrs. George Ward] Nichols [Mrs. Bellamy, Jr.] (1849-1932)
Nichols, Marian Clarke (1873-1953), **6,561,** 6,803
Nichols, Mary A., 2,198
Nichols, Mary L. (Costillo), 1,786
Nichols, Minerva (Parker) (1861-1949), **6,805**
Nichols, Minnie P. (1886-1973). *See* Blair, Minnie P. (Nichols) [Mrs. Ernest W.] (1886-1973)
Nichols, Misses, School (NY), **12,801**
Nichols, Rose Standish (1872-1960), 6,803
Nichols, Rowena, 690
Nichols, Ruth Rowland (1901-60), 11,831, 15,008
Nichols, Sarah Pierce (1804-?), **7,412**
Nichols, Susan Farley. *See* Pulsifer, Susan Farley (Nichols) [Mrs. Harold Trowbridge]
Nicholson, Alfred Osborn Pope (1808-76), 13,080
Nicholson, Ann, **11,120**
Nicholson, Ann (1811-88). *See* Scott, Ann (Nicholson) [Mrs. William Anderson] (1811-88)
Nicholson, Caroline (O'Reilly) [Mrs. Alfred Osborn Pope] (1812-?), **13,080**
Nicholson, Ella S., 5,063
Nicholson, Francis (1655-1728), **12,578**
Nicholson, Grace [Miss] (1877-1948), **1,471**
Nicholson, Hannah. *See* Gallatin, Hannah (Nicholson)
Nicholson, John, 15,018
Nicholson, Marie [Mrs. J. J.], **3,233**
Nicholson, Mary [Miss], 4,626
Nicholson, Patricia K. (1900-), **17,312**
Nicholson, Rebecca (Lloyd) [Mrs. Joseph Hopper], 2,574, 5,789
Nicholson, Roberta W., 4,619
Nicholson, William Perrin, **3,234**
Nickel and a Prayer, A (book), 15,782
Nickell, Mary Jane. *See* Rankin, Mary Jane (Nickell) [Mrs. Walter Lowrie]
Nickerson, Beulah (1896-). *See* Hawes, Beulah (Nickerson) (1896-)
Nickerson, Margaret, 2,946
Nickle, Harriet "Hattie" Amelia (Smith) [Mrs. Wesley] (ca. 1841-1923), **4,782**
Nickle, Wesley, 4,782
Nicklin, Sophia Chew (1798-?). *See* Dallas, Sophia Chew (Nicklin) [Mrs. George Mifflin] (1798-?)
Nickman, Jeannette [Mrs. O. A.], 10,101
Nickolls Family, 12,531
Nickolls, Robert H., 15,589
Nicolay, Helen (1866-1954), 2,512, **17,998**
Nicolay, John George (1832-1901), **2,512,** 17,998
Nicolay, Therena (Bates) [Mrs. John George], 2,512
Nicoloro, Mary, 6,336
Nicolson, Marjorie Hope [Miss] (1894-?), 2,166, 7,158, 11,825, 11,969
Nieberding, Velma, **14,220**
Niebuhr, Reinhold (1892-1971), **2,513**
Niedecker, Lorine (1903-70), **6,061**
Nielsen, Helen Bernice (1918-), 6,060
Nielsen, Walter C., 1,788
Nielson, Emma Waitstill (Mecham) [Mrs. Frihoff Godfred] (1858-1920), **16,777**
Nielson, Florence Vern (1891-1976). *See* Lyman, Florence Vern (Nielson) [Mrs. Callis] (1891-1976)
Nielson, Frihoff Godfred, 16,544, 16,777
Nielson, Helga [Mrs.], 9,040, 9,140
Nielson, LaRue. *See* Bates, LaRue (Nielson)

Nielson, Ole, Family (MN), **9,266**
Nielson, Susanna Smart (Parkinson) (1881-), 16,780
Nies, Grace (1895-). *See* Fletcher, Grace (Nies) (1895-)
Nigeria
  American missionaries to, 5,187
  nutrition, 11,603
  universities and colleges, 5,460
Niggler, Elizabeth (?-1876), **8,457**
Niggli, Josephine, 13,511
Night in Acadie, A (book), 10,158
"Night Life" (song), 5,534
Night of the Flaming Guns (book), 17,942
Night of the Hunter, The (drama), 2,357
Night work, 2,700, 11,763, 11,771, 11,851
Nightengale Hall (plantation, SC), 15,440
Nightingale, Florence (1820-1910), **23**, 1,026, 3,954, 4,233, 6,123, 6,141, 6,164, 6,663, 8,553, 9,919, 10,651, 12,073, 12,351, 17,616
Niles, Bertha, 10,821
Niles, Betsy. *See* Breed, Betsy (Niles)
Niles, Blair, 2,863
Niles Family (NH), **10,821**
Niles Family (TX), **16,016**
Niles, Marion [Miss], **6,806**
Niles, Mary, 10,821
Niles, Mary Relief. *See* Scott, Mary Relief (Niles) [Mrs. Emmet Hoyt]
Niles, Thomas, Jr., 7,042
Niles, William W., 10,821
Nillson, Carlotta, **12,579**
Nilsen, Frida R. (1894-), **8,883**
Nilsen, Ole, 8,774
Nilsson, Christine (1843-1921), 17,197
Nilsson, Svein, 8,724
Nin, Anaïs (1903-77), 2,242, **4,232**, 15,198
Nine Days to Christmas (book), 8,531
1900 Study Club (Atlanta, GA), **3,236**
1908 History Club (GA), **3,235**
Nineteenth Amendment, 1,424, 2,492, 2,508, 2,528, 10,511, 13,350, **13,405**, 13,453, 13,516, 15,706, 15,733
Nineteenth Century Class (GA), **3,237**
Nineteenth Century Club (Iowa City, IA), 4,770
Nineteenth Century Club (Minneapolis, MN), **9,267**
"Nineteenth Century Problem—Woman, A" (essay), 4,304
Nineteenth Century Reading Club (MS), 9,570
Nineteenth Century Women's Club of Oak Park (IL), **4,309**
Nineteenth Illinois Infantry, 4,376
Ninety Dozen Glasses, 6,004
"91st Day, The" (television script), 5,979
Ninety Nines, 5,162
Ninety-second Regular Ohio Volunteer Infantry, 2,277
Nininger, Pauline, 9,303
Ninth Ward Civic and Improvement League (LA), 5,540
Nisbet, Caroline Elizabeth (ca. 1828-1915). *See* Le Conte, Caroline Elizabeth (Nisbet) [Mrs. Joseph] (ca. 1828-1915)
Nisbet, Emily Hines. *See* Polhill, Emily Hines (Nisbet)
Nisbet, Maria Alston, 15,681
Nisbet, Sir John, 15,681
Nisei, 9,219
Nismith-Evans, Isabel, 1,695
Nismith Family (CO), 1,695
Nixon, George R., 10,673
Nixon, Richard Milhous (1913-), 7,699, 9,189, 11,592, 14,822, 16,000, 16,965
Nixon School (TX), 16,031
Njaa, Arna, 8,861
Nkrumah, Kwame, 5,460
No Conscription League, 12,699
No Foreign War Committee, 3,219
No Man's Land (OK), 1,790
No More Septembers (book), 6,027
No Name Club (AL), **75, 76**
"No Pigtails for Uncle Sam" (ms), 12,299
No Place for an Angel (book), 9,736

No Strings (musical comedy), 12,367
No Time for Prejudice (book), 2,152
Noall, Claire (1892-1971), **16,905**
Noall, Elizabeth "Libby" Laker, 16,905
Noall Family (UT), 16,905
Noall, Matthew, **16,905**
Nobbs, Lucille, **8,247**
Nobel Peace Prize, 15,301
Nobel Prize, 1,095, 1,098, 4,324, 6,496, 7,558, **11,901**
Noble, Alice W., **7,880**
Noble Collection of Pension Application Files (CT), **1,924**
Noble, Cornelia M., 16,060
Noble, Eugenia Floride, 15,665
Noble Family (SC), **15,665**
Noble, Henrietta, 1,924
Noble, Mabel Kittredge (Stearns). *See* Munroe, Mabel Kittredge (Stearns) Noble [Mrs. Kirk]
Noble, Martha Ann Parker [Mrs. George], 15,495
Noble, Susan Fairchild (1832-1914). *See* Grant, Susan Fairchild (Noble) [Mrs. Jedediah Morgan] (1832-1914)
Noble, William H., 1,924
"Nobody Knows You," 5,533
Nobody's in Town (moving-picture), 17,795
Noe, Louis, 10,913
Noel, Alice (Tye), 9,709
Noel, Elizabeth Mary Anunciata. *See* Murphy, Lady Blanche. Elizabeth Mary Anunciata Noel
Noel, Frances (1873-?), **1,047**
Noel, Jacqueline (1881-1964), **17,394**, 17,395
Noel, Rachel B. [Mrs.], 1,779
Noggle, Elizabeth (Muncy), **7,881**
Nokle, Ermy Corser, 6,215
Nolan, Betty, 1,937
Nolan, Edward J., 14,877
Nolan, Jeannette (Covert) [Mrs. Val Francis] (1897-1974), **4,483**
Nolan, Mary, 15,119
Nolan, Mary, 9,038
Nolan, Rebecca (Weld), 10,093
Nolan, Val Francis (1892-1940), 4,483
Nolan, William Ignatius (1874-1943), **9,268**
Noland, Elizabeth [Mrs. Lloyd], 13,063
Noland, Ella. *See* MacKenzie, Ella (Noland) [Mrs. John Carrerre]
Noland, Lloyd, 13,063
Noland, Mary Ethel, 10,085
Noland, Mary Ethel (1883-1971), **10,076**
Noland, Mrs. Joseph T., 10,076
Noland, Nellie, 10,076
Nolley, Martha Ann. *See* Otey, Martha Ann (Nolley) [Mrs. Armistead George]
None Shall Look Back (book), 11,163
Nones Family, 7,555
Nonpartisan League, 8,070, 9,155, 9,177, 9,200, 9,467, 13,670
Nonpartisan League of Minnesota, 9,400
Non-Partisan League Speaking Bureau, 8,070
Non-Partisan National Woman's Christian Temperance Union, 7,271, 13,976
Nonviolence, 5,828
  moral and religious aspects, 1,859
Noordberg, Henri Gerard, 9,696
Noordhoff, Jeanne (1882-1970), **5,088**
Norbeck, Lydia Anderson [Mrs. Peter] (1873-1961), 15,863
Norbeck, Nell (1902-). *See* Wegner, Nell (Norbeck) (1902-)
Norbeck, Peter (1870-1936), 15,863
Norbury, Tacy Burges. *See* MacKenzie, Tacy Burges (Norbury) [Mrs. Thomas]
Norcott Family, 12,962
Norcott, Mary Biddle (1841-1925). *See* Bryan, Mary Biddle (Norcott) [Mrs. Henry Ravenscroft] (1841-1925)
Norcross, Chancel, 5,673
Norcross Family (ME), **5,673**
Norcum, James, Family (NC), **13,498**
Norcum, Mary Matilda, 13,498
Nordby, Anne Johanne Kristiansdatter [Mrs.], 9,106
Nordhoff, Charles, 7,025
Nordhoff, Lida, 7,025
Nordic Arts Club (MN), **8,766**

Nordica, Lillian. [Mrs. Frederick Allen] Gower [Mrs. Zoltan] Dome [Mrs. George Washington] Young (1857-1914), 3,369, 10,651, 10,793
Nordlyset, 8,757
Norell, Alney (Allbritten) [Mrs. Henry] (1903-), **5,397**
Norfleet Family, 13,031
Norfleet, Virginia, 8,167
Norgaard, Viola, 9,266
Norge Corporation, 4,064
Norgrant, Mrs. Ansel (1910-), 8,518
Normal Advocate, 17,849
Normal and Industrial School (Greensboro, NC), students, 13,111
Normal Park Press (IL), 3,918
Norman, Dorothy Stecher (1905-), **12,061**, **12,905**
Norman, Ellen, 13,499
Norman, Gertrude Branum [Mrs. Rowland] (1908-), 8,706
Norman, Jane (1874-1953). *See* Smith, Jane (Norman) [Mrs. Clarence M.] (1874-1953)
Norman, Julia, 15,436
Norman, Mary, **16,545**
Norman, S. S., 13,499
Norman Transcript (OK), 14,216
Norrel, Mary A., 9,666
Norris, Charles Gilman (1881-1945), 689, 692, **1,592**
Norris, Deborah (1761-1839). *See* Logan, Deborah (Norris) (1761-1839)
Norris, Edwin L., 10,303
Norris, Eliza, 15,013
Norris, Ella Leonard [Mrs. George William], 10,513
Norris Family (CA), **691**, 692
Norris Family (PA), 14,817, 15,039
Norris, Frank (1870?-1902), 692
Norris, George William (1861-1944), **10,513**
Norris, Katharine Augusta (?-1949), **6,807**
Norris, Kathleen (Thompson) [Mrs. Charles Gilman] (1880-1966), 543, 616, 689, 691, **692**, 1,068, **1,592**, 5,123
Norris, Maria Whittlesey, 7,920
Norris, Mark (1796-1862), **7,882**
Norris, Mary, 15,042
Norris, Mary (Parker), 15,042
Norris, Mrs., 1,565
Norris, Roccina B. Vaill [Mrs. Mark], 7,882
Norse-American Centennial Committee, 8,777
Norse American Centennial Daughters of St. Paul (MN), **8,767**
North Adams Normal School (MA). *See* North Adams State College (MA)
North Adams School Department (MA), **7,108**
North Adams State College (MA), 7,110
  students, 7,109
North American Baptist Conference, 16,365
North American Review (periodical), 11,036, 13,413
North, Ann Hendrix (Loomis) [Mrs. John Wesley], 1,472, 8,721
North Atlantic Treaty Organization, 5,130, 11,857
North Beach and Mission Rail Road Company, 1,248
North Beach School (San Francisco, CA), 636
North Bend Community Church (WA), **17,161**
North Bend Study Club (WA). *See* Fall City Study Club (WA)
North Bennet Street Industrial School (MA), **6,808**, 6,880
North Carolina, 20, 9,699, 12,941, 12,967, 12,972, 13,159, **13,287**, 13,322, 13,346, 13,578, 13,609, 13,629
  abortion, legal aspects, 1,984
  actors and actresses, **13,100**
  Afro-Americans, 13,243, 13,636
  education, 5,472, 13,504
  agriculture, 13,322, 13,540
  agriculturists, **13,564**
  architecture, domestic, 12,988
  archivists, **12,988**, **13,411**, 13,522
  art, decorative, 13,631
  art schools, 13,446
  art societies, 13,334
  art teachers, **13,307**
  artists, 13,446
  authors, **12,947**, **12,992**, **13,190**, **13,368**

bankers, **13,339**
Baptist associations, **13,645**
Baptist churches, membership, 13,636
Baptists, **13,635**
Baptists, Afro-American, **13,644**
beauty operators, 13,217
bills, legislative, 13,449
bird watching, 12,973
blacksmiths, 13,402
blind-deaf, institutional care, 12,171
boarding schools, **13,234**, 13,407
bookmobiles, 13,204
businessmen, 13,117
businesswomen, **13,272**, 13,299, 13,610
butchers, 13,217
campaign literature, 13,533
campaign management, 13,266, 13,566
camps, 13,221
catalogs, college, **13,225**, 13,321
charities, 12,738
chemists, 13,531
Cherokee Indians, 13,448
Christian life, 13,270
church colleges, **13,278**, 13,370, 13,552
church historians, **13,411**
church records and registers, 13,635
church records and registers, Baptist, 13,636
church records and registers, Unitarian, **13,182**
church schools, 16,022
church societies, 13,559
church societies, Baptist, 13,297, 13,635, 13,639,
    13,643, 13,645
church societies, Unitarian, 13,182, **13,183**
church work with criminals, 13,639
churches, Unitarian, 13,182
citizens' associations, 3,283
civil defense, 13,617, 13,618
Civil War, 9,661, 12,940, 12,983, 13,287, 13,339,
    13,374, 13,397, 13,526, 13,540, 13,590, 13,593
    Afro-American troops, 6,394
    campaigns and battles, 13,085, 13,374, 13,468,
        13,481, 13,602
    personal narratives, 3,047, **13,268, 13,403**,
        13,431, 13,465, 13,624
    societies, etc., Confederate, 12,940, 13,070,
        13,085, 13,285, 13,571, **13,597**
clergy, Friends, **13,222**
clergy, Presbyterian, 13,292
clubs, 12,941, **12,973, 12,974**, 13,070, **13,083**,
    13,195, 13,198, 13,205, **13,220, 13,253, 13,265**,
    13,274, **13,317**, 13,331, 13,334, 13,352, **13,380**,
    13,383, **13,410**, 13,439, 13,446, 13,447, **13,461**,
    13,468, **13,508, 13,509, 13,511, 13,515, 13,517**,
    13,521, 13,554, 13,557, 13,566, **13,574**, 13,576,
    13,596, 13,604, 13,617, 13,618
coeducation, 13,467
college administrators, **13,187**
college and school journalism, 13,634
college and school periodicals, **13,226, 13,227**,
    13,447
college librarians, **12,935, 13,178, 13,204**, 13,390
college presidents, **13,179, 13,185, 13,186, 13,242**,
    13,245, 13,436
college students, wives of, **13,197**
college teachers, 12,982, 12,998, **13,177, 13,189**,
    13,190, 13,191, 13,192, 13,207, 13,231, 13,243,
    13,261, 13,271, 13,273, 13,289, 13,632
college teachers, wives of, **13,195**
college trustees, 13,244, 13,249, **13,436**
common law marriage, 13,342
community and college, 13,616
community leadership, 13,382, **13,604, 13,615**
community organization, 13,352
congressmen, 13,473
congresswomen, **13,282**
constitution, 13,532
    amendments, 13,404
convict labor, 13,371
corporations, 11,879
councils and synods, 13,230, **13,505**
county government, records and correspondence,
    13,386, 13,448
county school systems, 13,184
court-houses, 2,507

court records, colonial, 13,448
courts, 13,446
criminal law, cases, 13,448
dairy cattle, 13,272
deaf, education, 13,432
deans (in schools), **13,189, 13,191, 13,209**, 13,241,
    13,299, 13,604
deeds, 13,272
desertion, military, 13,567
diaries and journals, **12,954, 12,980, 12,983**, 13,071,
    13,103, 13,230, **13,270**, 13,341, 13,392, **13,403**,
    13,465, 13,624
dollmakers, 13,217
editors, 13,561
education, 13,287
education, curricula, 13,632
educational associations, **12,938, 13,314**, 13,390
educators, **6,430**, 13,217, 13,302, 13,369
elections, 12,952, 13,266, 13,271, 13,286
elementary school teachers, **13,071**
entrepreneurs, **13,637**
Equal Rights Amendment (proposed), 13,322
executive advisory boards, 13,565
extramarital relations, 13,356
family life education, **13,506**
farmers, 13,471
feeds, analysis, 13,531
florists, 13,217
folklorists, **13,143**
food relief, 13,589
foresters, 13,129
4-H clubs, 13,566, 13,618
freedmen, **13,342, 13,428**, 13,573
friendly societies, 13,446
Friends, **13,221**, 13,223, **13,233**, 13,234, **13,236**,
    13,239
Friends, Society of, 13,222, 13,230, 13,232, **13,235**
    education, 13,322
gardening, societies, etc., **13,293, 13,303**
gardens, 12,988
geology, 13,593
governors, 13,041, 13,070, **13,210**, 13,323, 13,371,
    13,416, 13,448, 13,488, **13,565, 13,566**, 13,567,
    13,581, **13,598, 13,619**
high school students, 13,430
high schools, 13,588
highway law, 12,952
historic buildings, conservation and restoration,
    12,988
historic sites, conservation and restoration, **13,514**
historical societies, 13,220, 13,267, 13,440, 13,606,
    13,609
home demonstration work, **13,626**
home economics
    accounting, 13,312
    study and teaching, 13,479
home economics extension work, **13,391**, 13,479,
    13,618
home economics, rural, 13,479
hospitals, 13,390, **13,415**
hospitals, Afro-American, 13,444, 13,559
hotels, taverns, etc., 13,604
    accounting, **13,443**
housewives, 3,317, 13,299
indentured servants, 13,423, **13,569**, 13,573
industries, 11,879, **13,175**
influenza epidemics, 13,218
Jews, 13,472
journalism, societies, 13,446
journalists, **13,001, 13,016, 13,166, 13,244, 13,277**,
    13,358, 13,616
judges, 12,962, 13,446
junior colleges, **13,373**, 13,466, 13,474
    faculty, 13,447
juvenile detention homes, 13,447
labor bureaus, 13,406
land grants, **15,969**
law students, wives of, **13,198**
lawyers, **13,468**
legal documents, 13,044
legislative bodies, 13,322, 13,426
    committees, 13,322
legislators, 13,168, 13,249, 13,322, 13,344, 13,404,
    13,468, 13,533, **13,564**

libraries, 13,265
libraries, university and college, **13,204**
library associations, 13,204
literary societies, **13,304, 13,320, 13,464, 13,511**,
    13,554
local church councils, 13,559
lynching, prevention of, 3,279
manual training, 13,489
medical care, **13,502**
medicine, cases, clinical reports, statistics, 13,605
medicine, rural, **6,648**
memorials, **13,442**
mental health, **13,512**
mental health services, 13,593
merchants, 9,729
Methodism, 13,473
midwives, **13,311**, 13,446, 13,522
military posts, 13,024
militia, ill treatment of women by, 13,567
milliners, 13,217
missions, Baptist, 13,641, 13,643
monuments, 13,446
Moravians, 13,634
mothers , 13,565
motor bus drivers, 13,217
museum directors, 13,264
music teachers, **13,640**
musical societies, **13,507, 13,545**
musicians, 13,302
Native Americans
    government relations, 13,448
    land transfers, 13,448
newspapers, 13,016
    sections, columns, etc., 13,390, 13,468, 13,617
novelists, 13,172, **13,594**
nurses, **12,998**, 13,618, 13,630
nursing schools, 13,630
    alumnae, **13,553**
officials and employees, 8,632, 13,176, 13,255,
    13,274, **13,275, 13,283**, 13,391, 13,399, **13,614**
ophthalmologists, 13,441
ophthalmology, 13,441
oral history, **13,236**
orphans and orphan asylums, 13,569, 13,573
orphans and orphan asylums, Afro-American,
    13,644
pacifists, 13,229
parents' and teachers' associations, **13,247**, 13,618
patriotic societies, **12,994**, 13,085, **13,315, 13,316**,
    13,372, 13,379, 13,393, 13,394, 13,395, 13,439,
    13,446, 13,459, 13,556, 13,557, 13,571, 13,576,
    13,580, 13,597, 13,629
peace societies, **13,503**
physical education and training, **13,200, 13,205**
physicians, 13,262, 13,325, 13,508
plantation life, 13,012, 13,322, 13,347, 13,356,
    13,403, **13,611**
plantations, 7,935, 13,378, 13,602, 13,619
poets, **13,139, 13,190**
policewomen, 13,447
political clubs, 13,271, 13,406, **13,623**
political parties, **13,408**, 13,533
politics, practical, women's activism, **13,063**,
    13,274, **13,510**
potters, 13,446
pottery, 13,361
printers, 13,422
prisoners, 13,585
    recreation, 13,446
prisons, 13,275
    officials and employees, 13,489
property tax, 13,612
public health, **13,513**
public health nursing, 3,432, 6,648
public libraries, 13,204, 13,300
public officers, 13,459, **13,537**
public relations, universities and colleges, 13,244,
    13,616
public welfare, 13,614
    law, 13,504
race problems, 13,222, 13,533, 13,604
railroad companies, management, 13,323
real property, 13,450
Reconstruction, 13,256

religions, 13,217, 13,287
religious education, 13,505
research, **13,501**
Revolutionary War (1775-1783), 13,557, 13,583
  campaigns and battles, 13,575
roads, 12,952
rural schools, 13,456
scholarships, **13,544**, 13,644
school boards, 5,466, **13,181, 13,184**
school buildings, **13,247**
school children, food, 13,249, 13,283
school integration, 13,181, 13,209
school management and organization, 13,249
school physicians, **13,243**, 13,610
school superintendents and principals, **13,329, 13,444**
schools, 5,249, 6,430, **13,128**, 13,322, 13,329, 13,330, 13,345, 13,363, **13,367**, 13,369, 13,377, 13,389, 13,417, 13,423, 13,425, 13,438, 13,452, 13,467, 13,471, 13,477, 13,487, 13,491, 13,496, 13,526, **13,560**, 13,561, 13,563, 13,599, 13,610, 13,625, **13,646**
schools, Afro-American, **5,472**
secession, public opinion, 13,392
secret societies, **13,199**, 13,549
secretaries of state, 13,446
senators, United States, 11,049, 12,965, **13,210**, 13,610
siamese twins, **13,306**
slave records, **2,124**, 13,188
slavery, 13,219
  emancipation, **9,391**, 13,482
  insurrections, 13,262
slaves, 2,124, 9,391, 13,188, 13,342
social life and customs, 13,277, 13,322, 13,446, 13,471, 13,534
social service, 13,604
societies, **13,513**
social work administrators, 17,691
societies, Jewish, 13,446, **13,500**
soldiers
  Civil War, Confederate, **6,394**, 13,629
  World War I, 13,024
  World War II, 13,024
state aid to education, 13,504
state boards of education, 13,249
state universities and colleges, 13,322, 13,390, 13,391, 13,479, 13,581, 13,604
storekeepers, 3,317
strikes and lockouts, 8,144
  textile workers, 17,734
student counselors, 13,071
student financial aid, 13,626
student participation in administration, **13,202**
students, social life, 13,356
students' societies, **13,197, 13,199, 13,202**, 13,226, 13,227, **13,320**
students' societies, Baptist, 13,638, **13,647**
suffrage, 13,533
  opposition to, 13,516
suffrage societies, 13,405, 13,433, 13,446, 13,557, 13,604
suffragists, 13,398
Sunday Schools, 13,182
survivors' benefits, 13,426, 13,449, 13,629
synagogues, 13,472
teachers, **3,314, 13,052**, 13,089, 13,234, **13,245**, 13,299, 13,309, **13,321**, 13,322, 13,345, 13,350, **13,366, 13,400**, 13,418, 13,420, **13,526, 13,535, 13,562**, 13,590, 13,604, 13,610
  salaries, etc., 13,249
teachers' colleges, 13,489, 13,604, 13,610, 13,617, 13,618
technical education, 13,383
temperance societies, 13,226, 13,297, 13,566
textbooks, bias in, 13,459
textile factories, 13,528
trade and professional associations, 13,192, 13,479
trials, **13,108**
trials (arson), 13,468
universities and colleges, 9,583, 13,134, **13,180, 13,186**, 13,189, 13,190, 13,191, 13,192, 13,193, 13,195, 13,196, 13,197, 13,198, 13,199, 13,200, 13,201, 13,202, 13,203, 13,204, 13,205, 13,206,

13,207, 13,208, 13,209, **13,223, 13,227**, 13,242, 13,262, 13,307, 13,322, **13,333**, 13,335, 13,350, 13,390, 13,398, 13,400, **13,401**, 13,430, 13,437, 13,438, 13,439, 13,446, 13,447, 13,453, 13,460, 13,468, 13,470, 13,480, 13,495, 13,499, 13,558, 13,573, 13,584, 13,588, 13,599, 13,616, 13,618, **13,627**
  alumnae, 13,194
  alumni, 13,193, **13,224**
  archives, **13,248, 13,300**
  buildings, 13,613
  centennial celebrations, 13,204
  faculty, 2,727, 13,333
  history, 13,178
  records and correspondence, **13,633**
universities and colleges, Afro-American, 13,444
university extension, **13,253**
Vietnamese Conflict, opposition to, **13,503**
violence, prevention of, 13,615
vital statistics, 13,311, 13,386
vocational guidance, **13,196**
volunteer workers in hospitals, 13,370
weaving, 13,307
widows, 13,445, 13,449, 13,534, 13,582, **13,589**, 13,612
wills, 13,219
witchcraft, 13,287
women
  education, 6,430, 13,496
  status of, 13,565
  women's colleges, **13,201**, 13,228, 13,321, 13,326, 13,328, 13,345, 13,353, 13,364, 13,369, 13,370, 13,381, 13,420, 13,458, 13,462, 13,463, 13,534, **13,542**, 13,579, 13,610, 13,617, 13,621, **13,628**
  women's colleges, Afro-American, **13,215**
  history, **13,216**
World War I, civilians work, **13,617**
World War II, civilians work, **13,618**
yearbooks, college and school, 13,634
Young Men's Christian Association, 13,176
Young Women's Christian Association, 13,176, **13,203**
North Carolina Art Society, 13,334
North Carolina Association of Jewish Women, **13,500**, 13,604
North Carolina Baptist Convention, Woman's Central Committee for Missions, 13,643
North Carolina Baptist Convention, Woman's Missionary Society, 13,645
North Carolina Baptist Convention, Woman's Missionary Union, **13,643**, 13,645
North Carolina Baptist State Sunday School Convention, **13,644**
North Carolina Baptist State Sunday School Convention, Girls' Education Fund, 13,644
North Carolina Bird Club, 12,973
North Carolina Board of Charities and Public Welfare, 13,275
North Carolina Booklet (periodical), 13,032
North Carolina Central University, faculty, 5,466
North Carolina College Conference, Committee on Cooperative Research, **13,501**
North Carolina College for Women, 12,737, 13,617. *See also* University of North Carolina at Greensboro
North Carolina Commission on Patient Care. *See* North Carolina Committee on Patient Care
North Carolina Committee on Interracial Cooperation, 13,222, 13,604
North Carolina Committee on Nursing and Nursing Education. *See* North Carolina Committee on Patient Care
North Carolina Committee on Patient Care, **13,502**
North Carolina Committee to End the War in Indochina, **13,503**
North Carolina Conference for Social Service, **13,504**, 13,604
North Carolina Congress of Parents and Teachers, **13,247**
North Carolina Constitutional Commission, 13,532
North Carolina Council of Churches, 13,230
North Carolina Council of Churches, United Church Women, **13,505**
North Carolina Council of Defense, 13,617

North Carolina Council of Women's Organizations, Inc., **13,253**, 13,510
North Carolina Council on Human Relations, 13,604
North Carolina Credit Union Association, 12,952
North Carolina Democratic Executive Committee, 13,266
North Carolina Democratic Women's Activities, 13,271
North Carolina Employment Office, 13,001
North Carolina Employment Service, officials and employment, 13,406
North Carolina Equal Suffrage Association, 13,446
North Carolina Equal Suffrage League, 13,433
North Carolina Family Life Council, **13,506**
North Carolina Federation of Music Clubs, **13,507**
North Carolina Federation of Women's Clubs, 13,274, 13,275
North Carolina Federation of Women's Clubs, Raleigh Woman's Club, **13,508**
North Carolina General Assembly, 13,322, 13,426
North Carolina Geological and Economic Survey, 12,952
North Carolina Good Roads Association, 12,952
North Carolina Health Officers' Association. *See* North Carolina Public Health Association
North Carolina Home Economics Association, 13,479, **13,509**
North Carolina House, Constitutional Amendments Committee, 13,322
North Carolina League of Women Voters, **13,510**
North Carolina Memorial Hospital, 13,122
North Carolina Mental Health Association, 13,286, **13,512**
North Carolina Museum of Art, 13,264
North Carolina Peace Society, 13,070
North Carolina Press Women, 13,446
North Carolina Prison Advisory Committee, 13,275
North Carolina Public Health Association, **13,513**
North Carolina Public Utilities Commission, officials and employees, **13,111**
North Carolina Railroad Company, 13,323
North Carolina Senate, 13,322
North Carolina Senate, Constitutional Amendments Committee, 13,322
North Carolina Society for the Preservation of Antiquities, **13,514**
North Carolina State Art Gallery. *See* North Carolina Museum of Art
North Carolina State Board of Education, 13,249
North Carolina State Department of Agriculture, officials and employees, 13,531
North Carolina State Home Agents Association, 13,626
North Carolina State Literary and Historical Association, 13,267, **13,511**, 13,606
North Carolina State Mothers Association, **13,515**
North Carolina State Normal and Industrial College, 13,604
North Carolina State Nurses Association, 12,998
North Carolina State Prison, 13,489
North Carolina State University, 13,322, 13,391, 13,479, 13,626
  faculty, 13,255
North Carolina Unemployment Compensation Commission, officials and employees, 13,286
North Carolina Volunteer Infantry, Company C, 39th Regiment, 3,317
North Carolina Woman's Council. *See* North Carolina Council of Women's Organizations, Inc.
North Carolina Woman's Missionary Union, 13,641
North Carolina Woman's Missionary Union, Foreign Mission Board, 13,235
North Carolina Women's Yearly Meeting, 13,232
North Carolina Yearly Meeting, Society of Friends, 13,221, **13,235**, 13,240
North Carolina Young Democrats Club, 13,271
"North Carolina's Claim to Whistler's Mother" (sketch), 13,606
North Cascades Conservation Council (WA), 17,267
North Central Association of Colleges and Secondary Schools, 4,391, 8,573
North China Daily News, 13,674
North Dakota, 13,660, 13,724
  abortion, 13,703

Afro-Americans, 13,682
authors, **13,684**
businesswomen, 13,689
children, adopted, 13,696
church societies, **13,666**
cities and towns, civic improvement, **13,649**
clinics, 13,660
clubs, 13,649, **13,655**, 13,658, 13,659, 13,660,
   13,670, **13,671**, **13,683**, **13,685**, **13,687**, **13,695**,
   13,696, **13,705**, 13,706, **13,708**, 13,713, **13,714**,
   13,725
college teachers, **13,671**, **13,698**
community welfare councils, 13,686
constitutional conventions, 13,690
convents and nunneries, Catholic, **15,845**
corporation law, cases, **10,104**
county government, records and correspondence,
   13,661
court records, 10,103, **10,104**
deaf, education, 13,673, 16,654
diaries and journals, 13,650, 13,652
   travel, **13,651**
dramatists, 13,724
education, 13,718
educational associations, **13,667**, 13,677, **13,698**
elections, 13,702
Equal Rights Amendment (proposed), **13,704**, 13,706,
   13,712
farm life, 8,787
farmers, **13,650**
fires, 13,682
genealogy, 13,684
historians, **13,672**
historical societies, 13,661
home economics extension work, 13,685
horticulturists, **13,653**
housewives, 13,724
Icelandic-Americans, 8,690
immigrants, **13,715**
immigrants, Norwegian, personal narrative, **8,730**
land settlement, 8,799, 9,467
legislators, **13,670**, 13,703
librarians, **6,606**, 13,688, **13,700**
library associations, 13,686
literary societies, 13,656
monasticism and religious orders for women,
   Catholic, **13,726**
musical societies, **13,678**
Native Americans, missions, 15,845
nurses, **13,680**
Oglala Indians, 965
parks, 13,649
physicians, **13,660**, 13,662, **13,693**, **13,710**
pioneers and settlers, 8,779, **8,794**, **13,654**, **13,661**,
   13,662, **13,683**, **13,684**
politics, practical, women's activism, **13,676**, **13,716**
public works, 13,654
rural schools, 13,701
school superintendents and principals, 13,658
schools, 13,682
secret societies, 13,686
soldiers' homes, 13,696
state universities and colleges, 13,698
suffrage, 13,648, 13,668
suffrage societies, 13,664, **13,691**, **13,721**
teachers, **13,700**, **13,701**, **13,718**
teachers of the deaf, **13,673**
temperance societies, 13,648, 13,658, 13,664,
   13,665, 13,668, 13,677, **13,694**
trade and professional associations, **13,679**, **13,680**
universities and colleges, employees, **13,712**
women, civil rights, 13,703
World War I, civilians work, **13,663**, 13,696
World War II, civilians work, 3,950, 13,719
Young Women's Christian Association, **13,681**,
   13,723
North Dakota Association of Registered and
   Graduate Nurses, 13,680
North Dakota Bar Association, 13,693
North Dakota Commission on the Status of Women,
   13,706
North Dakota Coordinating Council for the Equal
   Rights Amendment, **13,704**, 13,706
North Dakota Dames Club, **13,714**

North Dakota Equal Suffrage Association, 13,664
North Dakota Federation of Music Clubs, **13,678**
North Dakota Federation of Nonpartisan League
   Women's Clubs, 13,713
North Dakota Federation of Women's Clubs, 13,658,
   13,660
North Dakota League of Women Voters, **13,716**
North Dakota Nurses Association, **13,679**
North Dakota State Nurses' Association, **13,680**
North Dakota State Senate, 13,693
North Dakota State University
   employees, **13,712**
   students, 13,669
North Dakota State University, Young Women's
   Christian Association, **13,681**
North Dakota Wheat Grower (periodical), 13,698
North Dakota White Ribbon. See *White Ribbon
   Bulletin*
North Dakota Women's Coalition, 13,722
North End Club (New Haven, CT), **2,001**
North End Flower Club (WA), 17,267
North End Industrial Home (MA). *See* North
   Bennet Street Industrial School (MA)
North End Study Club Papers (CT), 1,998
North Family (NY), **11,666**
North, Frank Joshua (1840-85), **10,514**
North, Jane (Petigru), 15,682
North, John Wesley, **1,472**
North Louisiana Historical Association, **5,555**
North Loup Valley Historical Society (NE), 10,439
North, Mary. *See* Bartlett, Mary (North) [Mrs.
   Roswell] Wright [Mrs. Henry E.]
North, Mary M., 2,294
North Mianus Community Center (CT), **1,837**
North, Mrs. Jones A., 10,514
North Reformed Church, Ladies' Benevolent
   Association (NJ), 11,067
North Shore Club (MA), **7,077**
North Shore Mothers' Health Centre (MA), 6,736
North Star News (periodical), 9,073
North Texas Female College, **16,112**
North to the Orient (book), 7,170
North Vietnam, 7,790
North, Wallace [Miss], 3,451
North West Christian University (IN). *See* Butler
   University (IN)
Northampton City Conservation Committee (MA),
   7,137
Northampton Historical Society (MA), **7,140**
Northampton Martha Washington Temperance
   Society (MA), **7,141**
Northampton Total Abstinence Society (MA), 7,141
Northampton War Finance Committee (MA), 7,138
Northcote, Mr., 2,276
Northcott Family (KY), **5,271**
Northcott, Henry Clay (1822-1918), 5,271
Northcott, Martha Catherine "Kate" (1850-89). *See*
   Thomas, Martha Catherine "Kate" (Northcott)
   [Mrs. Bruce F.] (1850-89)
Northeast Missouri Normal School (Kirksville, MO),
   alumnae, 9,839
Northeast Missouri State Teachers College (Kirskville,
   MO), buildings, 9,938
Northeast Neighborhood House (Minneapolis, MN),
   9,094, 9,095, **9,270**
Northeast News (periodical), 15,329
Northeastern Illinois University, archives, **4,008**
Northeastern Iowa Teachers' Association, **4,777**
Northern Arizona Normal School (Flagstaff, AZ).
   See Northern Arizona University (Flagstaff, AZ)
Northern Arizona University (Flagstaff, AZ), faculty,
   224
Northern Association of the City and County of
   Philadelphia for the Relief and Employment of
   Poor Women, **15,292**
Northern California Birth Control Committee of One
   Hundred, 1,596
Northern Cheyenne Reservation, 10,313
Northern Illinois University, 8,087
Northern Iowa Suffrage Society, 4,732, 4,786
Northern Ohio Sanitary Fair (1864), 13,966
Northern Pacific Railroad, 8,520, 15,059
Northern States Cooperative Guilds and Clubs, **9,506**
Northern States Mission, 16,658

Northey, Cynthia (Winslow) (1808-65), 7,413
Northey Family (MA), **7,413**
Northey, Rebekah Maria (1825-?). *See* Buffum,
   Rebekah Maria (Northey) [Mrs. John Henry]
   (1825-?)
Northfield Baptist Church (NJ), 10,905
Northfield School for Girls, 6,875
Northfield Seminary (MA), 3,969
Northman, May L. Scott [Mrs.], **3,709**
Northman, Mother Aloysia, 5,164, **5,167**
Northport Elementary School (AL), 115
Northrup, Cyrus, 8,558, 8,602, 9,120
Northside Improvement Association (Ann Arbor,
   MI), 7,926
Northup, Dorothy Powers, 12,844
"Northwest Archives" (radio program), 17,368
Northwest Child Welfare Club (CT), **1,925**
Northwest Citizens' Defense Committee, 17,278
Northwest Designer Craftsmen, **17,313**
Northwest Indian Congress, 17,383
Northwest Missouri State University, history, 10,126
Northwestern Academy (Evanston, IL), 4,906
Northwestern Bell Telephone Company, 9,011
Northwestern Christian Advocate (periodical), 4,208
Northwestern College (Orange City, IA), Women's
   Auxiliary, **5,089**
Northwestern Female College (IL). *See*
   Northwestern University (IL)
Northwestern Finnish Historical Society, 9,503
Northwestern Freedman's Aid Commission, 8,941
Northwestern Hospital (Minneapolis, MN), 9,195
Northwestern Memorial Hospital (Chicago, IL),
   Prentice Women's Hospital and Maternity
   Center, **4,010**
Northwestern Memorial Hospital (Chicago, IL),
   Service League, **4,025**
Northwestern Memorial Hospital (Chicago, IL),
   Women's Hospital and Maternity Center, **4,021**
Northwestern Miller, 9,057
Northwestern National Life Insurance, 8,574
Northwestern Sanitary Fair (1864), **4,135**
Northwestern School of Chiropractic (OR), 4,816
"Northwestern Sketches" (ms), 4,242
Northwestern Soldiers' Fair (Chicago, 1863), **3,888**,
   3,922
Northwestern State University (LA), faculty, **5,539**
Northwestern State University of Louisiana, archives,
   5,454
Northwestern Union of Telephone Workers, 9,011
Northwestern University (IL), 3,967, 9,137, 13,997,
   14,306
   alumnae, 4,210, 4,927, 5,233
   archives, **4,216**
   deans, 4,223
   examinations, 4,060
   faculty, 4,059
   trustees, 4,214
Northwestern University (IL), Associated Women
   Students, 4,219
Northwestern University (IL), Intercollegiate
   Association of Women Students, 4,219
Northwestern University (IL), Married Women's
   Club, 4,219
Northwestern University (IL), May Week-May Day,
   4,220
Northwestern University (IL), Mortar Board, 4,213
Northwestern University (IL), Office of Student
   Guidance and Counseling, **4,219**
Northwestern University (IL), Panhellenic
   Association, 4,219
Northwestern University (IL), Panhellenic Council,
   4,220
Northwestern University (IL), School of Domestic
   Arts and Sciences, **4,218**
Northwestern University (IL), School of Speech,
   alumnae, 17,815
Northwestern University (IL), Student Governing
   Board, 4,213
Northwestern University (IL), Technological Institute,
   4,221
Northwestern University (IL), WAA-MU Show, **4,220**
Northwestern University (IL), Woman's Medical
   School, **15,133**

Northwestern University (IL), Women's Aid Association, 4,216
Northwestern University (IL), Women's Athletic Association, 4,213, 4,219
Northwestern University (IL), Women's Building, 4,216
Northwestern University (IL), Women's Day, 4,216
Northwestern University (IL), Women's Defense Efforts, 4,219
Northwestern University (IL), Women's Interhouse Council, 4,219
Northwestern University (IL), Women's Invitational Gymnastic Meet, 4,215
Northwestern University (IL), Women's League. See Northwestern University (IL), Student Governing Board
Northwestern University (IL), Women's Medical School, 4,217
 alumnae, 4,225
Northwestern University Settlement (IL), 4,141, 4,163
Northwestern University Settlement (IL), Infant Welfare Station, 4,163
Northwestern Wisconsin Schoolmasters Club, 17,529
Norton, Alice B. (Peloubet) [Mrs. Lewis Mills] (1860-1928), 2,694
Norton, Audree Lauraine (Bennett) [Mrs. Ken] (1927-), 2,113
Norton, Caroline. See Hawkins, Caroline (Norton)
Norton, Charles Eliot, 6,185
Norton, Charles L., 5,414
Norton, Clementine Ursula (1843-1926), 693
Norton, Cordelia, 15,666
Norton, Cortenay, 17,129
Norton, Deacon Lewis Mills (1855-?), 1,926
Norton, Edwin, 11,851
Norton, Elizabeth. See DeHay, Elizabeth (Norton) [Mrs. P. S.]
Norton, Elizabeth. See Philleo, Elizabeth (Norton) [Mrs. Calvin Wheeler]
Norton, Elsie de Witt. See Pettit, Elsie de Witt (Norton)
Norton, Ethel. See Bancroft, Ethel (Norton)
Norton Family (CO), 1,786
Norton, Frank, 7,600
Norton, Grace (1834-1926), 6,427, 6,809
Norton, Helen. See Starr, Helen (Norton) [Mrs. Mark]
Norton, John (1719-77), 17,129
Norton, John Hatley (1745-97), 17,129
Norton, Lillian (1857-1914). See Nordica, Lillian. Lillian (Norton) [Mrs. Frederick Allen] Gower [Mrs. Zoltan] Döme [Mrs. George Washington] Young (1857-1914)
Norton, Maria J. (Elliott), 694
Norton, Mary Adelaide, 5,469
Norton, Mary Catherine (?-1921). See Ayer, Mary Catherine (Norton) (?-1921)
Norton, Mary Florence (Burr) [Mrs. William Harmon] (1852-1950), 5,084
Norton, Mary Teresa (1875-1959), 255, 11,016, 11,123, 13,406
Norton, Nicholas, Jr., 1,235
Norton, Ruth (1903-). See Donnelly, Ruth (Norton) (1903-)
Norton, Tolbert, 14,576
Norton, William Harmon, 5,084
Norway
 American diplomats in, 2,382
 kings, 8,756, 8,777
 women, status of, 6,981
 World War II, civilian relief, 8,769
Norway's New Saga of the Sea (book), 8,788
Norwegian-American Historical Association, 8,733, 8,744, 8,768
Norwegian-American Women's Club of Detroit (MI), 8,769
Norwegian-Americans, 8,733, 8,737, 8,754, 8,768, 8,994, 16,324
Norwegian Evangelical Lutheran Church, 9,405
Norwegian Evangelical Lutheran Church (MN), Ladies Aid of Buffalo River, 9,271
Norwegian Evangelical Lutheran Church in America, 8,793, 8,795

Norwegian Lutheran Church. See also United Norwegian Lutheran Church
Norwegian Lutheran Church (Audubon, MN), 9,419
Norwegian Lutheran Church in America, missions, 8,878, 8,883, 8,888
Norwegian Lutheran Deaconess Institute, 8,859
Norwegian Lutheran Deaconnesses' Home and Hospital (NY). See Lutheran Medical Center (NY)
Norwegian National League, 8,777
Norwich and Worcester Railroad Company, 7,672
Norwich Ladies Literary Society (CT), 1,873
Norwood, Jean Eileen (1919-), 17,314
Not Charity, But Justice (ms), 6,053
Not Slightly (drama), 815
Notable American Women, 1607-1950 (book), 2,365, 6,684, 10,955, 13,895
Notaries, 179, 1,142, 1,334
"Notes on the Anti-Slavery Movement in Maine," 7,669
Notestein, Ada Louise (Comstock) [Mrs. Wallace] (1876-1973). See Comstock, Ada Louise. [Mrs. Wallace] Notestein (1876-1973)
Notestein, Wallace, 6,484
Nothurst, Louise, 7,456
Notre Dame Academy (Chicago, IL), 4,165
Notre Dame College (Baltimore, MD). See College of Notre Dame of Maryland (Baltimore, MD)
Notre Dame Sister, The (periodical), 5,832
Noun, Louise Rosenfield [Mrs.], 4,887
"Nourathar," 2,366
Nourse, Alice Tisdale (1882-1967). See Hobart, Alice Tisdale (Nourse) (1882-1967)
Nourse, Dorothy, 395
Nourse, Edith (1881-1960). See Rogers, Edith (Nourse) [Mrs. John Jacob] (1881-1960)
Nourse, Elizabeth (ca. 1860-1938), 13,836, 13,854
Nova Scotia, 6,975, 6,776
 clergy, 7,676
 immigrants, American, 7,616, 7,676
Novelists, 39, 47, 111, 146, 270, 1,030, 1,390, 1,396, 1,410, 1,416, 1,425, 1,438, 1,447, 1,745, 1,750, 1,978, 2,136, 2,199, 2,482, 2,488, 2,584, 2,601, 2,643, 3,000, 3,075, 3,325, 3,336, 3,338, 4,312, 4,322, 4,323, 4,488, 4,491, 4,732, 4,781, 5,080, 5,085, 5,296, 5,413, 5,441, 5,498, 5,621, 5,694, 5,733, 5,815, 5,924, 5,962, 6,050, 6,060, 6,085, 6,569, 7,169, 7,246, 7,505, 7,626, 7,868, 8,433, 9,503, 9,768, 9,771, 10,000, 10,617, 11,038, 11,163, 11,220, 11,977, 11,994, 12,016, 12,030, 12,042, 12,053, 12,535, 12,991, 13,049, 13,172, 13,267, 13,447, 13,594, 13,608, 14,324, 14,342, 14,388, 14,433, 14,680, 14,712, 14,962, 14,964, 15,196, 15,720, 15,876, 15,893, 15,902, 16,097, 16,151, 16,152, 16,153, 16,157, 16,158, 16,160, 16,161, 16,164, 16,167, 16,172, 16,173, 16,295, 16,384, 16,980, 17,009, 17,059, 17,060, 17,387, 17,473, 17,687, 17,793, 17,795, 17,797, 17,967
Novelists, Afro-American, 5,465
Novelists, British, 267, 5,924
Novelists, Irish, 267
Novelists, Norwegian, 4,321
Novelists, Swedish, 4,324, 14,905
Now I Recollect (book), 2,282
Now Is the Time for All Good Men (drama), 12,367
Nowak, Margaret Collingwood [Mrs. Stanley] (1908-), 8,114
Nowak, Stanley (1903-), 8,114
Nowell, Margaret, 15,533
Nowlin, Annie (1831-91). See Savery, Annie (Nowlin) [Mrs. James] (1831-91)
Noxon, Hannah (Shaw) [Mrs. George] (1834-1920?), 10,515
Noyes, Ada A. [Mrs. J. Franklin] (1836-74). See Clare, Ada A. [Jane (McElhenney)] [Mrs. J. Franklin] Noyes (1836-74)
Noyes, Augusta Maria (1817-71). See Stover, Augusta Maria (Noyes) (1817-71)
Noyes, Blanche, 11,831
Noyes, Clara D., 2,087
Noyes, Constance Pierrepont (1897-). See Robertson, Constance Pierrepont (Noyes) [Mrs. Miles] (1897-)
Noyes, Elizabeth, 7,972

Noyes Family, 12,401
Noyes, Helen Gilman. See Brown, Helen Gilman (Noyes) [Mrs. William Adams]
Noyes, Hilda, 6,223
Noyes, John Humphrey, 12,908
Noyes, Katharine (Macy), 4,935
Noyes, Maria B. (Smith) (1790-1875), 7,677
Noyes, Martha. See Williams, Martha (Noyes)
Noyes School of Rhythm (GA), 3,068
Noyes, William, 6,215
Noyes, William Curtis, 12,755
Nuckolls Family (NE), 10,552
Nuckolls, Lulu (1880-1959). See Wesner, Lulu (Nuckolls) [Mrs. Joy E.] (1880-1959)
Nuclear power. See Atomic power, law and legislation
Nuese, Flora M. [Mrs. Robert Haven] Bishop [Mrs.], 8,954
Nuestra Señora de la Soledad Mission (CA), 695
Nugent, Aimee Webb, 9,762
Nugent, Bruce, 3,288
Nugent, Eleanor Fulkerson (Smith) [Mrs. William Lewis], 6,901
Nugent, Lucy Warfield, 9,549
Nugent, Nellie (1863-1952). See Somerville, Nellie (Nugent) (1863-1952)
Nugent, William Lewis, 6,901
Nuhn, Margie, 4,868
Number One School (PA), 15,012
Nunez, Mrs. Santos, 982
Nunez, Wa-Wa-Chaw, 11,296
Nunn, Emily Bancroft (Trevett), 14,514
Nunn, Robert R., 3,926
Nunn, Romulus A., 13,516
Nunns, Annie A., 395
Nuns, Catholic, 159, 314, 638, 829, 831, 1,006, 1,007, 1,008, 1,510, 1,511, 1,513, 1,514, 1,515, 1,516, 1,517, 1,519, 1,520, 2,895, 3,601, 3,680, 3,971, 4,342, 4,640, 4,643, 4,709, 4,840, 4,873, 4,881, 5,164, 5,165, 5,166, 5,167, 5,372, 5,380, 7,383, 8,705, 8,848, 8,851, 8,853, 8,854, 9,022, 9,323, 9,328, 9,467, 9,490, 9,542, 9,880, 9,938, 10,134, 10,189, 10,614, 10,732, 11,066, 11,232, 11,251, 11,292, 11,476, 11,807, 13,752, 14,671, 14,781, 14,785, 14,786, 14,787, 14,791, 14,800, 15,147, 15,152, 15,181, 15,232, 15,369, 16,018, 16,019, 16,311, 16,343, 17,371, 17,415, 17,572, 17,731, 17,868. See also Mothers general
Nüranen, Margareeta. See Walz, Maggie
"Nurnberg Stove" (story), 2,598
Nurse and doctor, 236
Nurse and patient, 236
Nurse Practice Act, 239, 242
Nurse Practice Act (NV, 1923), 10,758
Nurse-practitioners, 233, 243
Nurse Testing Services, 6,149
Nurseries (horticulture), 1,331, 1,440, 1,481
Nursery and Child's Hospital (NY), 12,357
Nursery Auxiliary (Geneva, IL), 4,273
Nursery schools, 3,822, 4,049, 4,081, 4,116, 4,128, 5,228, 5,346, 5,422, 6,287, 6,288, 8,684, 12,878, 14,226, 17,691
Nursery Training School of Boston (MA), 6,729
Nurses, 23, 99, 107, 141, 174, 230, 231, 232, 233, 235, 236, 238, 239, 242, 243, 247, 340, 447, 631, 1,068, 1,242, 1,243, 1,251, 1,313, 1,379, 1,525, 1,606, 1,655, 1,665, 1,753, 1,906, 2,206, 2,239, 2,309, 2,332, 2,386, 2,387, 2,433, 2,434, 2,454, 2,594, 2,686, 2,895, 2,919, 3,432, 3,444, 3,629, 3,922, 3,932, 4,193, 4,248, 4,249, 4,336, 4,362, 4,490, 4,629, 4,696, 4,732, 4,791, 4,827, 4,843, 4,858, 5,060, 5,081, 5,284, 5,417, 5,493, 5,583, 5,689, 5,764, 5,806, 5,812, 5,817, 5,849, 6,107, 6,122, 6,123, 6,126, 6,129, 6,131, 6,132, 6,137, 6,138, 6,139, 6,140, 6,141, 6,144, 6,148, 6,153, 6,156, 6,157, 6,160, 6,163, 6,336, 6,501, 6,539, 6,618, 6,644, 6,721, 6,826, 6,987, 7,015, 7,019, 7,188, 7,274, 7,285, 7,873, 8,228, 8,277, 8,366, 8,440, 8,454, 8,553, 8,581, 8,648, 8,690, 8,725, 8,823, 8,865, 8,877, 8,890, 8,932, 8,943, 9,059, 9,115, 9,162, 9,212, 9,262, 9,286, 9,467, 9,527, 9,909, 9,919, 10,096, 10,129, 10,145, 10,499, 10,631, 10,632, 10,635, 10,732, 11,277, 11,515, 11,555, 11,852, 12,077, 12,127, 12,814, 12,850, 12,998, 13,301, 13,618, 13,630, 13,657, 13,679,

13,680, 13,729, 13,893, 13,941, **14,049, 14,325,**
14,394, 14,912, **15,224,** 15,281, 15,430, **15,561,**
15,869, **15,931, 16,246, 16,367,** 16,409, 16,417,
16,420, 16,765, 16,789, 16,876, 16,985, 17,028,
17,291, 17,561, 17,596, 17,686, 17,701, 17,784.
See also Deaconesses; Practical nurses
employment, **6,230**
in-service training, 235, 15,559, 15,566
licenses, 1,136
malpractice, 17,022
recruiting, 238, 246, 9,894
registries, 6,123, 6,134
Nurses, Afro-American, 1,779, **2,152, 6,133,** 11,445,
12,683, **12,691,** 15,430, 15,540, **15,782**
Nurses aides, 2,686, **5,583,** 8,706
Nurses aides, Native American, 1,662
Nurses' Associated Alumnae of the United States and
Canada. *See* American Nurses' Association
Nurses' Association, Pennsylvania State, **15,224**
Nurses Association, Territory of Hawaii, **3,629**
Nurses Educational Funds, Inc., **6,151**
Nurses, Jewish, 13,786
Nurses, Latino, 246
Nurses, military, **12,165**
Nurses, Native American, 2,674
Nurses Selective Act, 9,932
Nurses' Settlement (NY). *See* Henry Street
Settlement Urban Life Center (NY)
Nursing, 406, 1,007, 1,121, 1,525, **1,691,** 2,677, 2,686,
2,704, 3,780, **3,810,** 3,977, 4,596, 5,503, 5,723,
5,735, 5,849, **6,122, 6,139, 6,140,** 6,606, **6,618,**
8,584, 9,115, 10,188, **10,839, 12,073,** 12,739,
13,446, 15,233, 17,578. *See also* Obstetrical
nursing; Pediatric nursing; Psychiatric nursing
abstracting and indexing, 6,122, 6,143
cases, clinical reports, statistics, 6,162
economic aspects, 230, 232, 233, 242, 243, 6,122,
6,147, **6,166**
examinations, questions, etc., 230, 238, 6,123,
6,149, 12,137
history, 4,880, 6,136, 6,147, 6,157, 6,160, 6,165,
6,721, 17,291
law and legislation, 239, 1,753, 2,686, 6,134, 6,147,
9,986, 10,500, 10,758, 11,729, 12,074, 14,829
research, 6,122, **6,124,** 6,148
scholarships, fellowships, etc., 6,151, 6,164
social aspects, 236
standards, 238, 242, 3,810, 5,284, 5,417, **8,648,**
8,818, 9,467, 12,137, 12,691, **17,022, 17,748**
study and teaching, 230, 231, 232, 233, 236, 242,
247, 5,494, **5,735,** 5,764, 5,794, 6,126, **6,128,**
6,133, 6,136, 6,137, 6,138, 6,143, 6,145, 6,156,
6,158, 6,165, 6,238, 8,693, 8,980, 9,467, 9,986,
11,065, 11,150, 11,918, **12,074,** 12,137, 14,033,
15,183, 17,701, 17,766
study and teaching (continuing education), 233,
239, **4,014,** 12,137
vocational guidance, **23,** 6,130, 6,140, 6,162, 6,440,
12,077, **14,143**
Nursing audit, 9,484
Nursing education, 2,677, 2,686, 15,972
Nursing ethics, 8,648, 12,077
Nursing Forum, 6,134
Nursing homes, 1,690, **3,239,** 7,066, 9,480, 15,972,
17,590
administration, 242
Nursing Information Bureau, 6,122
Nursing Outlook (periodical), 6,133
Nursing records, 13,994
Nursing recruitment, 2,687
Nursing Research (periodical), 6,122
Nursing schools, **22,** 231, 233, 235, 447, 955, 1,534,
1,739, 1,753, 2,118, **2,306,** 2,542, **3,861, 3,954,**
4,009, 4,013, 4,014, 4,017, 4,019, 4,022,
4,026, 4,108, 4,162, 4,880, **4,969, 4,980,** 5,213,
5,284, 5,373, 5,494, 5,723, **5,843,** 5,844, 6,126,
6,128, 6,131, **6,132,** 6,133, 6,150, 6,152, **6,155,**
6,158, 6,163, **6,164,** 6,165, **6,215, 6,238,** 6,618,
7,274, **8,045,** 8,053, 8,440, 8,529, 8,547, 8,553,
8,610, 8,818, 8,822, 8,862, **10,220,** 10,486,
10,500, **11,377, 12,351,** 12,353, **13,630, 13,877,**
13,887, 13,892, 15,142, **15,149, 15,192, 15,426,**
15,430, **15,734, 15,842,** 15,931, **15,937, 16,333,**
16,946, **17,000,** 17,224, **17,353, 17,385, 17,386,**

17,539, 17,561, **17,568, 17,569,** 17,701, 17,772,
17,773, 17,779, **17,847, 17,848**
accreditation, 5,494, 6,132
administration, 243, **17,297**
alumnae, **4,011, 4,020, 4,024,** 6,128, **13,553, 16,229**
trustees, 15,734
Nursing service administration, 239, 242, 243, 247,
2,332, 3,780, **6,125,** 6,138, 6,141, **6,142, 6,145,**
6,146, 10,732, 16,526
Nursing students, 2,679, 8,584, 8,648, **12,140**
Nursing Studies Index, 6,143
Nursing supervisors, 2,686, 17,737
Nute, Grace Lee (1895-), **8,441,** 9,002, 9,230, **9,272**
Nute, Mary Christie Rogers (1881-1975), 8,996
Nutrition, 1,997, 2,667, 2,692, 4,380, 6,673, 7,817,
8,538, 9,829, 10,015, 11,603, 11,656, 12,923,
13,618, **14,198,** 14,827, 16,288, 16,973
research, 8,575, 17,853
study and teaching, **4,070,** 4,084
Nutrition extension work, 8,575
Nutritionists, **930,** 11,566, 11,656, 12,079
Nutritionists, Jewish, **13,823**
"Nutshell Series," 12,524
Nutt, Carey, 9,693
Nutt, Eliza Hall. *See* Parsley, Eliza Hall (Nutt) [Mrs.
William Murdoch]
Nutt Family (MS), **9,693**
Nutt, Haller, 9,693
Nutt, Julia Augusta Williams [Mrs. Haller], 9,693
Nutt, Mary, 9,693
Nutt, Mary J., 9,580
Nutt, Rush, 9,693
Nuttall, Elisabeth Annie (1881-1968). *See* Baker,
Elisabeth Annie (Nuttall) [Mrs. John Daniel]
(1881-1968)
Nuttall, George Henry Falkiner (1862-1937), 1,378
Nuttall, Grace (Greer) [Mrs. William Albert]
(1880-). *See* Nuttall, Margaret Grace (Greer)
[Mrs. William Albert] (1880-)
Nuttall, Margaret Grace (Greer) [Mrs. William
Albert] (1880-), **16,475, 16,546, 16,778**
Nuttall, Mary W. (Savage) [Mrs. William B.]. *See*
Jones, Mary W. (Savage) [Mrs. William B.]
Nuttall [Mrs. George Noble]
Nuttall, William, 16,475
Nuttall, William B., 2,930, 2,943
Nuttall, Zelia Maria Magdalena. [Mrs. Alphonse
Louis] Pinart (1857-1933), 2,836, 6,323, **6,326,**
7,288, 7,305
Nutten, Mary (Trowbridge) [Mrs. Wilber F.], 13,840
Nutten, Wilber F., 13,840
Nutter, Valentine, **12,275**
Nutting, Elena, **4,234**
Nutting, Helen, **4,234**
Nutting, Lois Anna. *See* Dane, Lois Anna (Nutting)
[Mrs. Ezra]
Nutting, Mary Adelaide (1858-1948), 2,679, 5,735,
6,122, 6,141, 6,606, 12,073, 12,074
Nutting, Mary Olivia (1831-1910), 7,499, 17,029
Nutting, Olive. *See* Berry, Olive (Nutting)
Nutting, Rebecca Hildreth (1835-?). *See* Woodson,
Rebecca Hildreth (Nutting) (1835-?)
Nye, Gertrude, 11,680
Nye, Gorham, 3,630
Nye, Kathryn C., **7,883**
Nye, Lydia Rider (Drew) [Mrs. Gorham], **3,630**
Nye, Mary (Greene), **17,030**
Nye, Susan Davis (1790-1867). *See* Hutchison,
Susan Davis (Nye) [Mrs. Adam] (1790-1867)
Nygaard, Cora (Anderson) (1897-), 8,706
Nystrom, Elvira [Mrs.], **696**
"O, Fair New Mexico" (song), 11,215
O. Henry Award, 17,076
O. Henry Book Club (NC), **13,517**
O.W.L.S. (DC), 2,106
Oahu College (HI), faculty, 14,311
Oak Park Civic League (IL). *See* League of Women
Voters of Oak Park-River Forest (IL)
Oakdale Road (ms), 3,226
Oakdale Tuberculosis Sanitarium (IA), 4,950
Oakes, Daniel C., 1,780
Oakes, Emma [Mrs.] (1867-?), 978
Oakes, Maud, 2,215
Oakes, Olive M. Martin [Mrs. Daniel C.], 1,780

Oakland Art Museum (CA), 14,707
Oakland Episcopal Church (Pittsburgh, PA), 15,226
Oakland Female College of the Pacific (CA), 864
Oakland Female Institute (PA), 13,570
Oakland Free Library (CA), 1,090
Oakland High School (CA), 711
Oakland Homeopathic Hospital and Dispensary
Association (CA), 472
Oakland New Century Club (San Leandro, CA),
1,385
Oakley, Annie. Phoebe Ann Moses. [Mrs. Frank]
Butler (1860-1926), 10,428, **14,101,** 15,935,
16,547, 17,932
Oakley, Cynthia [Mrs. Frank], 17,700
Oakley, Frank W. (1841-1925), **17,700**
Oakley, Violet (1874-1961), **2,792**
Oates, James W., 16,117
Oates, Joyce Carol (1938-), **10,854,** 11,221
Oatman, Mary Ann [Miss], 8,208
Oatman, Olive Ann. [Mrs. John B.] Fairchild
(1838?-1903), 8,208
Obenchain Family (KY), **5,259**
Obenchain, Lida (Calvert) [Mrs. William Alexander]
(1856-1935), 5,259
Obenchain, William Alexander (1814-1916), 5,259
Ober, Carolina Haven (1866?-1929), **17,315**
Ober, Josephine (Robb) (1882-?), **1,325**
Ober, Sarah, 17,315
Oberholtzer, Ellis Paxson (1868-1936), **15,061**
Oberholtzer, Sarah Louise (Vickers) (1841-1930),
15,061
Oberlin Alumni Magazine, 14,123
Oberlin College (OH), 6,975, 8,168, 11,471, 11,616
alumnae, 4,141, 4,146, 4,405, 14,120, 14,126,
17,307
deans, 14,122, 14,123
faculty, 7,300, 14,122, 14,128
presidents, 11,694, 14,124
students, 2,490, 4,436, 13,942
Oberlin College (OH), Order of the Pearls, 14,120
Oberlin Conservatory of Music (OH), **2,155,** 9,042
Oberndorfer, Leonora (Levy), **697**
O'Berry, Annie (Land) [Mrs. Thomas], 13,352
Obertauffer, Delbert, 17,230
Obituaries, 167, 188, 1,956, 6,226, 7,624
Oblate Sisters of Providence, Our Lady of Mount
Providence Convent (Baltimore, MD), **5,831**
Oblate Sisters of the Blessed Sacrament, St.
Sylvester's Convent (Marty, ND), **15,845**
Oblinger, Ella. *See* Roesch, Ella (Oblinger)
Oblinger, Maggie. *See* Sandon, Maggie (Oblinger)
Oblinger, Martha "Mattie" Thomas [Mrs. Uriah
Wesley], 10,516
Oblinger, Neta. *See* Lennemann, Neta (Oblinger)
Oblinger, Uriah Wesley (1842-1901), **10,516**
Obrebsky, Joseph, **5,874**
Obrebsky, Tamara, **5,874**
O'Brien, Driscoll and Raftery (law partnership),
14,736
O'Brien, Frederick, 1,352
O'Brien, Kate (1897-), **4,235**
O'Brien-Moore, Annette Erin Eileen (1908-), **13,081**
O'Brien, Rose, 9,048
O'Brien, Sister Aloysius, 1,516
O'Brien, Sister Antonine, 9,467
O'Bryan, Lawrence, 13,344
O'Bryan, Mrs. Leonel Ross, 1,750
Obscenity (law), 987, 11,178, 17,843
Observatories (astronomy), 790
Observer (NC), 13,358
Obstetrical nursing, 12,140, 16,417
Obstetrical Society of Boston (MA), **6,229**
Obstetricians, **3,309, 7,307,** 8,634, **11,142, 14,198,**
16,417, 16,944, 17,006
Obstetrics, 246, 880, 1,728, 2,609, 2,677, 3,968,
4,475, 6,222, 8,206, **12,141,** 12,739, 14,965,
16,965
cases, clinical reports, statistics, **4,475,** 9,064, 9,176,
9,178, 9,906, **11,019,** 14,864, 15,148
practice, 5,574, 7,677
research, 7,274
study and teaching, 3,482, 5,318, 6,225
O'Casey, Mrs. Sean, 12,367
O'Casey, Sean, 12,367

Occident, The (PA), 1,002
Occidental Mission School and Home (San Francisco, CA), 1,171
Occultists, **2,213**, 4,732
Occupation: Angel, 6,004
Occupational diseases, 11,760
Occupational retraining, **12,271**, **17,448**
Occupational retraining for women, 6,799, 8,062
Occupational therapists, 7,200
Occupational therapy, 2,831, 8,635, 12,808, 17,832
Occupational training, 4,382, 8,079, 8,139, 8,140, 13,816, 15,236
Occupational training for teen age women, **12,720**
Occupations, 2,317, 2,672, 2,676, 6,123, **6,440**, 9,954
Occupations, of teen-age women, 9,964
Ocean Grove Woman's Club (NJ), 10,923
Ocean-Hill, Brownsville integration episode, 8,097
Ocean travel, 326, **358**, 359, 406, 432, 439, 457, 481, 533, 634, **852**, 864, **902**, 1,253, 1,254, 1,262, 1,288, **1,291**, 1,329, 1,336, **1,342**, **1,343**, **1,349**, **1,431**, **1,505**, 1,630, 1987, 1,989, 2,367, 2,630, 2,661, 5,412, **5,591**, 5,681, **5,707**, 6,196, **6,197**, 6,204, 6,205, 6,621, 6,831, 7,277, 7,424, **7,478**, 7,480, 7,481, **7,488**, 7,632, 7,677, 8,373, 10,949, 10,982, 11,002, 11,482, 11,732, 12,000, 12,317, 13,785, 13,931, 14,456, 14,532, **14,560**, 14,604, 14,664, 14,689, **15,083**, 15,167, 16,586, **17,206**, 17,711
  19th C, **3,624**, 3,630
Oceanographers, **2,479**
Oceanography, observation, 7,492
Ockett, Molly, 5,666
O'Connell, Nellie B. (1870-1958). *See* Chisholm, Nellie B. (O'Connell) [Mrs. John A.] (1870-1958)
O'Connor, Agnes, 6,958
O'Connor, Eva (Johnson) [Mrs. Joseph], 12,525
O'Connor, Evelyn (1879-1953), **12,798**
O'Connor, Flannery [Miss] (1925-64), 2,995, 3,177, **3,471**, 15,927, 15,929, 15,934
O'Connor, Hugh (1894-1967), **14,431**
O'Connor, James, 10,611
O'Connor, James Francis Thaddeus (1886-1949), **698**
O'Connor, Joseph, 12,525
O'Connor, Mother Raymond (1882-1943), **1,515**, 1,516
O'Connor, Oleta. *See* Yates, Oleta (O'Connor)
O'Connor School of Nursing (Santa Clara, CA), 1,534
O'Connor, Sister Francis Marie, 4,342
Ocracoke Island, 13,522
Octagon Club (Tama, IA), **5,113**
Octave Thanet Literary Society (IA), **5,017**
Octavia Hill Association, Inc. (Philadelphia, PA), 15,201, **15,205**
O'Day, Caroline Love (Goodwin) [Mrs. Daniel] (1875-1943), 6,687, 11,576
Oddie, Tasker L., 10,673
"Ode to Mississippi" (poem), 9,773
Odegaarden Family (WI), **17,497**
Odegard, Ethel J. [Miss] (1891-), **17,701**
Odell, E. Adeline Allison White [Mrs.], 13,578
Odell, Elizabeth F. (McClench) [Mrs. Samuel Royal] Thurston [Mrs.], **699**
Oden, Benjamin (1762-1836), 5,797
Oden, Lydia. *See* Linge, Lydia (Oden)
Oden, Maria West (ca. 1791-?). *See* Jackson. Maria West (Oden) [Mrs. James] Mullikin [Mrs. Thomas] (ca. 1791-?)
Odencrantz, Louise C. (1884-1969), **6,810**
Odets, Clifford, 11,310
Odilia, Mother Mary (1823-80), 10,134
Odin, Bishop (1800-70), **16,018**
Odland, Lisa, **8,771**
Odlum, Floyd, 5,132
Odlum, Jacqueline Cochran [Mrs. Floyd B.], 6,712, 11,831
O'Donnell, Eleanor (1820-97). *See* Iselin, Eleanor (O'Donnell) [Mrs. Adrian] (1820-97)
O'Donnell, Kitty (1852-1931). *See* O'Donnell, Mother Louis (1852-1931)
O'Donnell, Lillian Udvardy, 6,060
O'Donnell, Mother Louis (1852-1931), 1,515, **1,516**
O'Donnell, Sister Rosalia, 1,516
Odors, 11,605
Odum, Howard, 2,879

Odyssey House (MA), 6,516, 6,517
Oehlberg, Vera R. (1908-), 11,851
Oerting, Ella K. S. (1890-1959), **8,593**
Oess, Mara Ann Pinto, 14,144
Off Duty Magazine, 17,731
Off-the-Street Club (Chicago, IL), **4,136**
Office and Professional Employees International Union, 9,381
Office and Professional Employees International Union, Local 298 (TX), **16,005**
Office Work and Office Workers in 1940 (bulletin), 2,703
Office Workers' Union, 1,357
Offord, Lenore (Glen) (1905-), 569, **700**
O'Flaherty, Kate (1851-1904). *See* Chopin, Kate (O'Flaherty) [Mrs. Oscar] (1851-1904)
Oftedahl, Maria [Mrs. Einar L.] (1861-1948), **8,772**
Ogantz School (PA), 9,970
Ogden, Anna Cora (1819-70). *See* Mowatt, Anna Cora (Ogden) [Mrs. James]. [Mrs. William Foushee] Ritchie (1819-70)
Ogden, Elizabeth Hyatt [Mrs. Albert B.] (?-1922), 1,750
Ogden, Emma K., 9,323
Ogden, Florence (Sillers), **9,550**, 9,551
Ogden, H. Harriet Hudson, 12,779
Ogden, Helen. *See* Lowrie, Helen (Ogden)
Ogden, Marianna Arnot [Mrs. William B.], 11,602
Ogden, Marion G. [Miss] (1875-), **17,845**
Ogden, Nancy (Hamilton), 3,335
Ogden, Nina M. [Mrs.], 3,664
Oge, Marie (1881-1956). *See* Beale, Marie (Oge) [Mrs. Truxtun] (1881-1956)
Ogen, Miriane, 8,154
Ogilvia, Sarah (Grubb) (1818-83), 15,014
Oglala Sioux Indians, 965, 10,433, 10,473
Ogle, Laura. *See* Bacmeister, Laura (Ogle) [Mrs. Theodore]
Oglethorpe College (GA), 3,489
Oglethorpe Park (GA), 3,130
Ogletree, Julia C., **13,518**
Ogontz School (PA), 11,415
Ogran, Tillie, 672
Ogulis, Austra, 8,604
Ogunquit Literary Club (ME). *See* Ogunquit Woman's Club (ME)
Ogunquit Woman's Club (ME), **5,611**
Oh Call Back Yesterday (book), 13,368
"Oh the Man Behind the Man Behind the Gun" (poem), 2,537
O'Hair, Madalyn Murray [Mrs.] (ca. 1919-), **16,373**
O'Hanlon, Margaret Langdon, **13,082**
O'Hanlon, Sister Mary Ellen (1882-1961), 17,868
O'Hara, Edwin V., 14,551
O'Hara Family (PA), **15,221**
O'Hara, Frank, 11,983, 12,894
O'Hara, Mary (1885-), **17,999**
O'Hara, Maureen, 1,576
O'Hare, Anne (1882-1954). *See* McCormick, Anne (O'Hare) (1882-1954)
O'Hare, Francis "Frank" Patrick, 10,177, 15,309
O'Hare, John Myers, **4,000**
O'Hare, Kate (Richards) (1877-1948). *See* Cunningham, Kate (Richards) [Mrs. Francis "Frank" Patrick] O'Hare [Mrs. Charles C.] (1877-1948)
Ohev Sholom Sisterhood (PA), **13,815**
Ohio, **13,897**, 13,954, 14,082, 14,095, 14,111, 14,168
  abolitionists **13,907**, **13,914**, **13,927**, 14,000
  abortion, legal aspects, 1,984
  affirmative action programs, 13,878
  Afro-Americans, 14,140
  agricultural societies, 14,004
  agriculture, 5,366
  air quality, 14,052
  airports, 13,762
  altar guilds, 13,912
  art societies, 13,853
  art teachers, 13,855
  artists, **2,760**, **13,836**, **13,851**, **13,853**, 13,963
  assessment, 3,947

  associations, institutions, etc., 14,004
  asylums, 13,919
  authors, 13,851, 13,963
  ballet dancing, **14,047**
  bankers, 13,930, 14,000, 14,026, **14,114**
  banks and banking, women's, 6,945
  birth control, 14,013
  bishops, 14,117
  blind
    education, 5,857
    employment, 14,155
  Camp Fire Girls, **13,989**
  campaign management, 13,999
  camps, 13,994
  Catholic schools, **13,752**, **13,867**, 13,903, 14,145
  ceramics, **13,852**
  charitable societies, **13,933**, **13,937**, **13,988**, 13,996, **14,083**
  charitable societies, Jewish, **13,772**, **13,791**, **13,822**
  charitable uses, trusts, and foundations, 14,047
  charities, **13,964**, **13,995**, **14,070**
  charities, Jewish, **13,778**
  child care centers, **14,020**
  child psychologists, **14,010**
  child welfare, 13,970, 13,996
  children
    employment, 13,996
    health and hygiene, 8,671
  church societies, **13,980**
  church societies, Baptist, **13,923**
  church societies, Congregational, **13,913**
  church societies, Methodist, **13,944**
  church societies, Presbyterian, **13,951**, **13,952**
  churches, Baptist, 13,991
  cities and towns, civic improvement, 13,991
  citizens' associations, 3,283
  city councilmen, 14,142
  city councilwomen, **13,872**, 13,972
  Civil War, 1,450
  clergy, **7,622**
  clubs, **13,751**, **13,753**, **13,755**, **13,756**, **13,760**, **13,850**, **13,853**, **13,856**, **13,881**, **13,906**, **13,908**, **13,916**, **13,917**, **13,922**, **13,932**, **13,938**, **13,979**, **13,985**, **13,991**, **13,992**, 13,997, **14,001**, **14,022**, **14,023**, **14,029**, **14,030**, **14,031**, **14,032**, **14,035**, **14,036**, **14,043**, **14,067**, **14,108**, **14,109**, **14,110**, **14,147**, **14,160**, **14,171**
  college librarians, **13,954**, **14,128**
  college students, **13,886**, 14,033
  college teachers, **13,746**, **13,749**, **13,755**, **13,870**, **13,879**, **13,882**, **13,883**, **13,891**, **13,895**, **13,896**, **14,006**, 14,122
  communists, 14,002
  community health nursing, **13,994**
  community leadership, 6,881
  community life, 14,061
  community organization, 13,909, **14,021**
  community organization, Jewish, **13,899**, **13,900**, **13,901**
  congressmen, 14,046, 14,077
  congresswomen, **13,911**
  conservationists, **14,052**
  conservatories of music, 2,155, 13,932
  consignment sales shops, **13,841**
  constitution, amendments, 8,118
  consumers' leagues, 13,942
  convents and nunneries, Catholic, **13,727**, **13,866**, **14,145**
  county officials and employees, 13,965
  court records, **3,949**, **13,874**, **14,105**
  courts, 2,163, 6,357, 13,846, 13,930
  deans (in schools), 8,783, **13,754**, **13,892**, 14,122
  demonstrations, **17,858**
  dentists, **13,997**
  department heads (universities), **13,880**, **13,894**
  diaries and journals, **8,322**, 13,919, **13,946**, **13,969**, **14,117**, **14,132**, **14,162**, **16,637**
  disaster relief, 13,729
  divorce, **13,874**
  dormitories, **14,033**
  druggists, **14,089**
  editors, 13,999, **14,052**
  education, experimental methods, **4,151**

educational associations, **13,747, 13,761, 13,986, 13,987, 14,057, 14,107**
educators, 13,999
elections, 1,654, **14,163**
elementary school teachers **14,135**
equal rights amendment (proposed), **14,009, 14,011**
evangelists, **2,613**
exhibitions, **13,863**
expression, schools of, 13,810
family planning, **14,013**
farm life, 8,344
festivals, **14,112**
floods, 13,729
Friends, **13,956**, 14,000
fund-raising, Jewish, **13,900**
game protection, 14,004
gardening, societies, etc., **13,845, 14,068**
geology, **14,005**
girls, societies and clubs, **13,847**
government advisory bodies, 13,909
government attorneys, 13,972
governors, 13,935, 14,046, 14,077, 14,086, 16,068
Greek letter societies, **14,028**
halfway houses, 14,043
health boards, 13,994
    officials and employees, 14,006
high school teachers, 13,839
historians, 13,728, **14,087, 14,095**
historic sites, 13,897
historical societies, **13,948**
home nursing, 13,994
hospital administration, 14,100
hospitals, 17,820
housewives, 14,786
immigrants, Czechoslovakian, **13,953**
immigrants, Slovenian, 13,912
Italian-Americans, 9,497
journalism, societies, 13,917, **14,040**
journalists, **13,844**, 13,961, **13,999, 14,041**
judges, **6,356, 6,357**, 6,967, 13,272, **13,846**, 13,904, 13,935, 14,007
juvenile courts, 13,988
juvenile delinquency, cases, 13,874
land settlements, 7,152
lawyers, 4,643, **6,789**, 11,913, **13,839**, 13,840, **13,846, 13,848**, 13,904, 13,999, **14,007**
legacies, 14,020
legislative bodies, 13,990
legislators, 13,728, 13,730, 13,935, 14,015
librarians, **6,551, 14,099**
libraries, 6,551
library schools, 13,895
literary societies, **13,917, 13,918, 14,034, 14,064, 14,065, 14,094**, 14,118, 14,121, **14,148, 14,149, 14,154**, 14,158, 14,159
maternity homes, 13,988, 13,995
mayors, 13,728, 13,872, 13,999, **14,139**
merchants, **13,849**, 13,930, 17,439
midwives, **14,048**
missionaries, 13,991
missions, finance, **13,865**
monasteries, **13,902**
monasticism and religious orders for women, Catholic, **13,763, 13,867, 13,868, 13,902, 13,903, 13,984, 14,044, 14,100, 14,116, 14,130, 14,131**
municipal reports, 6,154
musical societies, 13,734, 13,748, 13,932, 14,024, 14,069, 14,141, 14,156, 14,157
musicians, 2,155
naturalization records, 3,949
newsletters, 14,024
newspaper publishers and publishing, 14,046
newspapers, 13,999
nurses, **14,049**
nursing records, 13,994
nursing schools, **13,877, 13,887**
officials and employees, **13,970**, 13,999
old age homes, **13,905**
orphans and orphan asylums, 13,945, 14,075
painters, **2,818, 13,854**
patriotic societies, **13,920, 14,045, 14,053, 14,066, 14,167**
pensions, 13,874

petroleum refiners, 5,363
philanthropists, 6,434, **13,857**
philanthropists, Jewish, **13,801**
physical education and training, **13,761**
physicians, **13,860**
physicians, homeopathic, 14,000
pianists, **13,840**
pioneers and settlers, **14,098, 14,153**
poetry, 14,019
poets, **2,172, 13,844**
political clubs, 14,014, 14,015
politicians, 13,840, 14,000, 17,439
politics, practical, women's activism, **13,731, 13,732, 13,750, 13,939, 13,940**, 14,002, 14,003, 14,042, **14,050, 14,106, 14,125**
poor women, aid to, **13,996**
postmasters, 13,999
potters, **13,837, 13,838**
pottery, **13,856**
probation officers, 13,988
public health nursing, **6,154, 14,051**
public libraries, 14,155
public speaking, 14,026
public welfare, 14,025
radio programs, 14,041
real estate agents, **14,014**
reformatories (female), 14,015
religious education, 13,868
school attendance, 14,020
school boards, 13,730, 13,961
school superintendents and principals, Afro-American, **13,909**
schools, 13,930
schools, Afro-American, 13,927
scrapbooks, 13,794
secret societies, **14,172**
secretaries, 14,082
self-government (in higher education), **14,038**
senators, United States, 2,379, 4,643, **11,913**
Shakers, **4,437, 12,620**
shorthand reporters, 13,855
single mothers, 13,995
Slovene-Americans, 13,912
social legislation, 14,025
social life and customs, 8,352, 13,848
social science, study and teaching, 14,006
social settlements, 4,141, 13,934, 13,950, 13,976, **13,996**
social work with delinquents and criminals, 14,010
societies, **13,981**
societies, Afro-American, 17,245
societies, Jewish, 6,082, **13,779, 13,915, 13,993**
soldiers, Civil War, **14,166**
state universities and colleges, 13,997, 14,215
students' societies, 12,713, **14,034, 14,037, 14,038**
suffrage, 7,204, 13,898, **13,990**, 13,999, 14,000, 14,007
    opposition to, 13,967
suffrage societies, 6,815, 6,985, **13,733**, 13,842, 13,967, 13,990, **14,042**, 14,114, 14,168
suffragists, **6,985**, 13,939, **14,133**, 14,142, 14,144
Sunday schools, 13,991
symphony orchestras, 13,932, 13,991
teachers, **2,760, 4,490, 6,768**, 13,843, **13,875, 13,927**, 13,930, 13,960, 14,103
television programs for children, 13,875
temperance, 13,999, 14,164
temperance societies, **13,861, 13,862**, 13,930, **13,973, 13,974, 13,975, 13,976, 13,977, 13,983**, 13,991, **13,998**, 14,000, 14,114, **14,127, 14,164**
trade and professional associations, **14,143**
trade unions
    butchers, 8,118
    cigar makers, 1,656
    officials and employees, 8,118
travelers' aid societies, **13,964**
tuberculosis, prevention, 14,155
United Methodist Church, education, 5,394
universities and colleges, 961
    alumnae, **13,885, 13,890**
    archives, **13,758, 13,876, 13,877, 13,878, 14,118**
    faculty, 14,026

universities and colleges, Afro-American, faculty, **6,997**
utopias, 11,681
War of 1812, societies, **14,097**, 14,137
women
    education, 13,990
    employment, 13,985
    status of, 14,011, **14,012**
women's colleges, **13,884**
World War I, civil defense, 14,006
World War II, civilians work, 3,950
Young Women's Christian Association, 13,843, **13,982, 14,027**
Ohio Anti-Slavery Society, 13,907
Ohio Association Opposed to Woman's Suffrage, 13,967
Ohio Avenue Day Nursery (OH), 14,020
Ohio Bureau of Vital Statistics, 13,999
Ohio Coalition for Equal Rights Amendment, **14,011**
Ohio College Association, Women's Physical Education Section, **13,761**
Ohio Commission on the Status of Women, 14,011, **14,012**
Ohio Conservation Association, 14,052
Ohio Council on Women in Industry, 13,997, 14,144
Ohio Federation of Clubs, 13,932
Ohio Federation of Women's Clubs, 13,917
Ohio Female Seminary, 17,432
Ohio General Assembly, 13,990
Ohio House of Representatives, 13,730
Ohio Landowners' League, 14,004
Ohio League of Women Voters, **13,842**
Ohio Medical College, alumni, 14,151
Ohio Sixth Circuit Court of Appeals, 7,174
Ohio Soldiers' and Sailors' Orphans Home (Xenia, OH), 13,945, 14,075
Ohio State Advisory Committee, 13,999
Ohio State Board of Health, officials and employees, 14,006
Ohio State Board of Medical Registration and Examination, 14,048
Ohio State Democratic League, 3,301
Ohio State Grange, 14,004
Ohio State University, 13,997, 14,215
    alumnae, 4,306, 13,252
    faculty, **13,746, 14,006**, 14,026
Ohio State University (Columbus, OH), Chimes, **14,029**
Ohio State University (Columbus, OH), Mortar Board, **14,030**
Ohio State University (Columbus, OH), Paterson Hall, **14,033**
Ohio State University (Columbus, OH), Philomathean Literary Society, **14,034**
Ohio State University (Columbus, OH), University Dames, **14,035**
Ohio State University (Columbus, OH), University Women's Club, **14,036**
Ohio State University (Columbus, OH), Women's Council, 14,038
Ohio State University (Columbus, OH), Women's Panhellenic Association, **14,037**
Ohio State University (Columbus, OH), Women's Self-Government Association, **14,038**
Ohio State University (Columbus, OH), Young Women's Christian Association, 12,713
Ohio State University Mother's Association, **14,031**
Ohio Suffrage Association, 14,168
Ohio Supreme Court, 2,163, 13,846, 13,930
Ohio University
    alumnae, 13,749
    deans, 13,754
    faculty, **13,755**
Ohio University (Athens, OH), Intercollegiate Association, 13,756
Ohio Wesleyan Female College, presidents, 5,362
Ohio Wesleyan University, 4,399, 11,906
    alumnae, 17,974
Ohio Woman Suffrage Association, 6,815, 6,985, 13,967, 13,990, 14,114
Ohio Woman's Press Association, 13,917
Ohio Women's Club, **14,032**
Ohio Women's Council of Defense, committee of women in industry, 14,006

Ohlinger, Bertha (Schweinfurth) [Mrs. Franklin] (1856-1934), 14,089
Ohlinger, Franklin (1845-1919), **14,089**
Ohm, Howard F., 6,844
Oil for the Lamps of China (book), 4,185
Oil industries
    production, 11,833
    taxation, 11,833
Oil Patch, The (book), 17,959
Ointments, 12,770, 13,259
Ojibwe Indians, 2,566, 8,399, 8,927, 8,940, **9,237, 17,814**
    ethnology, 2,750
    history, 8,591, 9,085
    land transfers, 9,296
    legal status, laws, etc., 9,296
    missions, 7,931, 8,903, 8,926, 9,438
    music, 8,444, 9,042
    property, 9,296
    reservations, 9,296
    social life and customs, 9,085
    treaties, 9,436
O'Keefe, Mary Walsh, 7,151
O'Keeffe, Georgia (1887-), 2,815, 2,844, 5,863, 7,182, 11,235, 11,810
Okemos Women's Prison (MI), 8,276
O'Kill Family (NY), 12,020
Oklahoma, 14,195, **14,196**, 14,217, **14,228**
    abortion, legal aspects, 1,984
    Afro-Americans, 14,241
    agriculture, **14,201**
    authors, **14,195**, 14,205, 14,220, 14,258
    Baptists, 14,173
    bills, legislative, **14,251**
    birth control, **14,221**
    Catholic Church, societies, etc., 14,259
    Cherokee Indians, 243, 247, 10,987, 14,243, 14,246
        history, 14,197, 14,206
    Choctaw Indians, 6,652
    cities and towns, 14,196
    citizens associations, 3,283
    city councilwomen, 14,236
    clergy, German Baptist, 16,365
    clubs, 10,261, 14,177, **14,222**, 14,260, 14,262, **14,265, 14,266, 14,267**
    college teachers, 14,216, **14,217**
    constitutional conventions, **14,247**
    convents and nunneries, Catholic, 14,225
    court records, 1,808, 16,215
    Creek Indians, history, 14,197
    dancers, **14,199**
    diaries and journals, travel, **14,179**
    educational associations, **14,193**, **14,221**
    educators, 10,537
    elections, **14,252**
    executive advisory bodies, **14,249**
    governors, 14,257
    housewives, **14,179**, 14,180, **14,190**
    impeachment, 14,257
    industrial relations, 14,195
    journalists, 6,568, **14,192**, **14,195**
    land settlement, 14,185, 14,201
    lawyers, 14,257
    legislators, 14,197
    libraries, 14,216
    library schools, 14,217
    lynching, prevention of, 3,279
    maps, 14,206
    maternal and infant welfare, **14,198**
    mayors, 14,223, **14,236**
    medicine, rural, 246
    mentally handicapped, education, 14,226
    Methodists, 14,173
    mines and mineral resources, 14,207
    missions, 14,208
    monasticism and religious orders for women, Catholic, **14,226**, **14,259**
    music, instruction and study, 14,216
    music teachers, **14,189**
    musical societies, 14,208, **14,261**
    Native Americans, **14,201**, 14,220, 14,224, **14,241**, 14,245
        education, 14,242, 16,215
        missions, 3,382

    reservations, 14,207, 14,225
    trading posts, 14,199
    newspapers, 14,216
        sections, columns, etc., 14,223
    nursery schools, 14,226
    nursing service administration, 243
    officials and employees, 14,248
    oral history, **14,180**, **14,227**
    painters, **14,238**
    photograph collections, **14,201**, **14,245**
    physicians, **14,198**, 14,200
    pioneers and settlers, **14,174**, **14,176**, **14,181**, **14,194**, 14,204, **14,207**, 14,208, 14,220, 14,241
    poets, **14,200**
    political activists, women, 15,990
    politics and government, **14,250**
    poor, 16,215
    postmistresses, **14,246**
    Presbyterians, 14,208
    prisons, 14,248
    public institutions, **14,248**
    public lands, 14,216
    public records, **14,253**
    ranchers, 14,234
    sanitoriums, 16,215
    school boards, 14,207
    school superintendents and principals, **14,242**
    secretaries, 14,257
    senators, United States, 14,225
    social science research, 16,215
    societies, etc., **14,263**
    statehood, 14,212
    suffrage, 6,455
    suffrage societies, 16,252
    Sunday school teachers, 1,511
    teachers, 14,180, **14,186**, 14,200, **14,207**, 14,224, 14,232, 14,243, **14,244**, **14,246**
    temperance, 14,223
    United Methodist Church, 14,223
    universities and colleges, 14,199, 14,200, 14,201, 14,216
        archives, **14,178**
        faculty, **14,229**, 14,256
    women
        civil rights, **14,253**
        status, **14,249**
    World War II, civilians work, 14,264
Oklahoma Agricultural and Mechanical College, *See* Oklahoma State University (Stillwater, OK)
Oklahoma Art League, 14,230
Oklahoma City University, faculty, **14,229**
Oklahoma Clubwoman (periodical), 14,192
Oklahoma College for Women (Chickasha, OK). *See* University of Science and Arts of Oklahoma (Chickasha, OK)
Oklahoma Department of Charities and Corrections, **14,248**
Oklahoma Farmer, 14,223
Oklahoma Farmer-Stockman, 14,223
Oklahoma Federation of Music Clubs, 14,208
Oklahoma Federation of Women's Clubs, 14,223
Oklahoma Governor's Commission on the Status of Women, **14,249**
Oklahoma Hall of Fame, 14,199
Oklahoma Historical Society, 14,235
Oklahoma Lung Association, 14,192
Oklahoma Pen Women, 14,232
Oklahoma Planned Parenthood Association, **14,221**
Oklahoma Safety Council, 14,232
Oklahoma State University (Stillwater, OK)
    faculty, 14,256
    students, 14,255
Oklahoma Territory, 6,568, 14,216
    Native Americans, 14,183
    pioneers and settlers, 14,183
Oklahoma University, alumnae, 14,184, 14,236
Okuma, Marquis, 10,060
"Ol' Man River Road" (exhibit), 9,587
Olander, Victor A. (1873-1949), **3,890**
Olanoff, Rose [Mrs.], 15,154
Olav II, Saint, 8,756
Olcott, Chauny, 12,476
Olcott, Euphemia Helen (Knox) [Mrs. John Nathaniel] (?-1909), 12,580

Olcott, Euphemia M., **12,580**
Olcott, John Nathaniel (?-1887), 12,580
Olcott Rest Lodge (MN), 9,273
Olcott, W. J., 9,273
Old Academy Girls (WI), **17,861**
Old age, 7,205, 7,270
Old age assistance, 6,728
Old age homes, 813, 877, 1,690, 3,905, 4,078, **4,137, 4,138,** 4,286, 4,817, **5,520,** 7,066, 8,176, 8,862, **9,190,** 9,460, 11,277, 11,445, 12,078, 12,079, **12,287, 13,905, 14,633,** 14,749, 15,404, **16,220,** 17,217, 17,578, 17,672, 17,820
Old age homes, Jewish, **3,866,** 15,157, 15,161
Old age pensions, 1,334, 2,693, 8,644, 11,916, 11,939
Old and New Women's Club (Malden, MA), **7,082**
Old and Old (drama), 815
Old Anti-Slavery Days (book), 7,215
Old Ashburn Place, The (book), 5,712
Old Buffalo Pageant and Bazaar (NY), 11,346
Old Capitol Museum (MS), 9,587
Old Capitol Prison (DC), 12,381
Old Cemetery at Troupville (GA), **3,613**
Old English Tales Retold (book), 5,986
(Old) Farmers' Almanac, The, 5,942
Old Fashioned Women (GA), 3,229
Old Hickory Powder Plant (Nashville, TN), 15,963
Old Homes and Gardens of North Carolina (book), 12,967
Old Ironsides Fair (MA), 5,946
Old Jules (book), 10,529
Old Ladies' Home of Portland (OR), **14,623**
Old North Church (Boston, MA), 6,176
Old Northwest (territory), 6,650
Old Orchard Beach Women's Civic Group (ME), **5,613**
Old Oregon Trail, Inc., 14,285
Old People's Home (Chicago, IL), **1,137, 1,138**
"Old Plantation Days in Mississippi," 16,075
"Old Rose," 13,537
Old Santa Fe Association, 11,240
Old Settlers' Association (IA), 4,812
Old Settler's Association (MN), 9,000, 9,524, 9,527
Old Settlers Association (ND), 13,672
Old Settlers Society of Chicago (IL), 3,891
"Old Settler's Story, An" (essay), 4,908
Old South Bend Cemetery (GA), 3,387
Old South Church Preservation Committee, 5,975
Old Times in Dixie (book), 5,487
Old West and the New, The (book), 17,899
"Old Westport" (article), 9,847
Olden, Marion (Stephenson) [Mrs. James, Jr.] Henry [Mrs. William K.] DeVictor [Mrs. Paul] Coleman-Norton [Mrs. Roger] (1888-), 8,634, **11,017**
Oldenburg, Margaret Elizabeth (1892-1972), **8,595**
Older Americans Act (1975), 7,262
Older, Cora Miranda (Baggerly) [Mrs. Fremont] (1876-1968), 689, **701,** 702, 720
Older, Fremont (1856-1935), 701, **702,** 873
Oldham, Dorothy, 9,819
Oldroyd, Ida Shepherd [Mrs.], **1,575**
Olds, Elizabeth, 9,145
Olds, Fred A., **13,519**
Olds, Leland (1890-1960), **11,495**
Olds, Marion, 11,495
Olds, Maud [Mrs. Leland], 11,495
Oldtown Folks (book), 1,953
Ole Edvart Rølvaag: A Biography, 8,788
O'Leary, Agnes (1907-). *See* Cunningham, Agnes (O'Leary) (1907-)
Olesen, Anna Dickie (1885-1971), 8,910, 8,971
Olier, Eva. *See* Weiniewitz, Eva (Olier)
Olin Family (CT), **1,982**
Olin Family (WI), 11,672
Olin, Helen R., 17,771
Olin, Julia (Lynch) [Mrs. Stephen] (1814-79), 1,982
Olin, Stephen (1797-1851), 1,982
Olin, Stephen Henry (1847-1925), 1,982
Oliphant, Benjamin F., **2,514**
Oliphant, Catherine [Mrs. Benjamin F.], **2,514**
Oliphant, Mary, 2,271
Oliphant, Sarah, 2,271
Olive, Jeannette Ramsey [Mrs. W. E.], **16,281**
Oliver (moving-picture), 17,804

Oliver, Agnes F., 15,588
Oliver, Catherine D. [Miss], **1,326**
Oliver, Curtis, **3,412**
Oliver Family (VA), 17,107
Oliver, Fannie, 10,264
Oliver, Fitch Edward (1819-92), 5,947
Oliver, Frances Motley, **13,520**
Oliver, Harvey, 10,264
Oliver Iron Mining Company (MN), 8,942, **9,273**
Oliver, Matilda, **6,200**
Oliver, Nancy [Mrs. Curtis], 3,412
Oliver, Nola Nance, **15,899**
Oliver, Robert Shaw, 10,673
Oliver, Ruth Law (1891-1970), 11,831
Oliver Street Baptist Church (New York, NY),
    12,324
Oliver, Susan Lawrence Mason [Mrs. Fitch Edward],
    5,947
Oliver, William (1915-), **8,115**
Olivereau, Louise, 17,319
Olivet College (MI), archives, **8,385**
Olivet Community Center (Chicago, IL), **3,892**
Olivet Institute (Chicago, IL). *See* Olivet Community
    Center (Chicago, IL)
Olivetan Benedictine Sisters, Holy Angels Convent
    (Jonesboro, AR), **275**
Olla Podrida Club (NC), **13,521**
Ollerton, Fay, 16,641
Olley, Adelia (Judson). *See* Leslie, Adelia (Judson)
    Olley
Olmstead, Frank, 15,313
Olmstead, Frederick Law, 14,809
Olmsted County Bar Association (MN), 8,828
Olmsted County Federated Women's Club (MN),
    8,825
Olmsted County Historical Society (MN), 8,821,
    8,833
Olmsted, Gertrude Howard (1901-73). *See* Nauman,
    Gertrude Howard (Olmsted) [Mrs. Spencer G.]
    (1901-73)
Olmsted, Gertrude (Howard) [Mrs. Marlin E.]
    (1874-1953). *See* McCormick, Gertrude
    (Howard) [Mrs. Marlin E.] Olmsted (1874-1953)
Olmsted, Marlin E. (1847-1913), 14,822
Olmsted, Mary (1890-1950). *See* Johnson, Mary
    (Olmsted) [Mrs. Oakley C.] (1890-1950)
Olmsted, Mildred (Scott) [Mrs. Allen S.] (1890-),
    8,149, 10,730, 15,315, 15,316
Olney High School (PA), 15,332
Olney, Mary (1821-86). *See* Brown, Mary (Olney)
    [Mrs. Benjamin] (1821-86)
Olney, Mary (McLean) (1873-1965), **703**
Olney, Omen, 3,754
Olney, Zena, 3,754
Olschak, Blanche Christine (1913-), 6,947
Olsen, D. B. (pseudonym). *See* Hitchens, Dolores
    (Birk) Olsen (1907-73)
Olsen, Dolores (Birk) (1907-73). *See* Hitchens,
    Dolores (Birk) Olsen (1907-73)
Olsen, Emily Veblen [Mrs. Sigurd] (ca. 1865-1953),
    8,774
Olsen, Johan, 8,774
Olsen, Lucy Hardee [Mrs.] (1894-), **15,809**
Olsen, Mrs. N. H. F., 8,769
Olsen, Ruth S., 4,229
Olsen, Sigurd, 8,774
Olsen, Tillie (1913-), 7,167
Olson, Betty M., **14,774**
Olson, Edna McElhiney [Mrs.] (?-1969), 10,134,
    10,135
Olson, Eleanora (1870-1946), **8,775**
Olson, Ethel, 8,775
Olson, Florence J. (Peterson) (1913-), **8,706**
Olson, Floyd B., 9,381
Olson, Grace [Mrs. Hubert G.], 8,409
Olson, Hubert G. (1902-64), **8,409**
Olson, Lillian A. (1907-), **8,884**
Olson, Mary, 686
Olson, Regina Jeanette (1885-1971). *See* Tracy,
    Regina Jeanette (Olson) (1885-1971)
Olson, Regina Mary (1895-). *See* Hughes, Regina
    Mary (Olson) [Mrs. Frederick] (1895-)
Olsson, Anna (1866-1946), 4,326
Olsson, Olof (1841-1900), Family (IL), **4,326**

Olympic Games (1972), 5,048
Olympic Peninsula (WA), 17,248
Omaha Community Chest (NE), 10,518
Omaha Indians, 2,838, 10,029, 10,459, **10,483**
Omaha Medical College (NE), 10,616
Omaha Tribe, The (book), 10,459
Omaha Woman's Club (NE), 10,422
Omaha Women's Press Club (NE), **10,517**
Ombudswomen, 11,545
Omega Phi (MI), **7,884**
Omega Psi, 4,220
Omer, Leona (Sutherland) [Mrs. August Gideon]
    (1892-), **16,779**
Omerod, Eleanor (1828-1901), 6,321
Omicron Nu, 8,567
Ommanney, Katharine, 1,815
Omnibus Rail Road Company, 1,248
O'More, Peggy Jeanne (1897-1970). *See* Blocklinger,
    Peggy Jeanne (O'More) (1897-1970)
Omori, Anna B. Shepley [Mrs. Hyozo], **7,485**
Omori, Annie. *See* Omori, Anna B. Shepley [Mrs.
    Hyozo]
Omori, Hyozo (?-1913), 7,485
"On American Women" (article), 2,936
"On Building a Feminist Future in Our Time"
    (speech), 17,712
On Journey (book), 7,292
"On Modern Syphilotherapy with Particular Reference
    to Salversan," 1,383
On the Gorilla Trail (book), 4,061
"On the Prairie" (song), 10,540
"On the Record" (column), 12,911
On the Trail of Negro Folk Songs (book), 16,384
On These I Stand (book), 3,285, 5,465
Onassis, Jacqueline (Bouvier) [Mrs. John Fitzgerald]
    Kennedy [Mrs. Aristotle], 2,640, 5,123, 11,897
Once There Was a Village (book), 2,318
Oncologists, **7,327**
One Cure for Gold Fever (drama), 1,750
One Day at a Time (book), 10,894
One Enchanted Summer (book), 5,206
One God (book), 14,122
100 Hikes (book), 17,305
162nd Regiment, New York, 12,242
One Hundred Tenth Street Neighborhood Club (NY),
    6,701
125th Illinois Regiment, 12,957
100 Years of Wisconsin Authors (book), 17,770
One Night of Love (moving-picture), 14,447
One out of Four (book), 97
One Percent for Art (WA), 17,255, 17,366
One Time, One Place, 9,770
One, Two, Three, Four, Five, Six (book), 17,991
"One Who Cares" (song), 10,478
"One Woman of the 19th Century," 12,409
O'Neal, Evelena O. Marsh (1874-1962), **10,351**
O'Neal, Hettie Tom, **13,522**
Oneal, James, 12,702
Oneal, Marion Sherrard (1884-), **10,352**
O'Neal, Mary, 1,016
O'Neal, Rose (ca. 1815-64). *See* Greenhow, Rose
    (O'Neal) [Mrs. Robert] (ca. 1815-64)
O'Neale, Lila M., 920
O'Neale, Margaret L. (1799?-1879). *See* Eaton,
    Margaret L. (O'Neale) [Mrs. John Henry]. [Mrs.
    John B.] Timberlake [Mrs. Antonio] Buchignani
    (1799?-1879)
Oneida Community, 1,590, 2,464, 6,223, 12,908
Oneida Institute, 11,705
O'Neil, Alta, 7,109
O'Neil, Elizabeth E. (Busick), 10,226, **10,353**
O'Neil, Margaret L. (1799?-1879). *See* Eaton,
    Margaret L. (O'Neale) [Mrs. John Henry]. [Mrs.
    John B.] Timberlake [Mrs. Antonio] Buchignani
    (1799?-1879)
O'Neil, Agnes, 8,144
O'Neill, Carlotta Monterey [Mrs. Eugene], 414,
    1,458, 1,565
O'Neill, Dorothy Kitchen [Mrs.], **2,515**
O'Neill, Egan (pseudonym). *See* Linington, Elizabeth
    (1921-)
O'Neill, Eugene, 1,565, 11,850, 12,367
O'Neill, Fanny (1824-95). *See* O'Neill, Mother
    Aloysia (1824-95)

O'Neill, James A., **1,224**
O'Neill, Lottie Holman [Mrs. William J.]
    (1878-1967), **4,183**
O'Neill, Margaret "Massie" (Orr) [Mrs. Charles]
    (1872-1963), 9,078, 11,863, 17,587
O'Neill, Mary (LeDuc) (1908-), 8,531
O'Neill, Mother Aloysia (1824-95), **1,517**
O'Neill, Nance, 1,073
O'Neill, Rose Cecil. [Mrs. Gray] Latham [Mrs.
    Harry Leon] Wilson (1874-1944), **10,133**, 15,354
O'Neill, Sister Thomas Aquinas (1884-1957), 17,868
*Only One Earth: The Care and Maintenance of a
    Small Planet* (book), 12,072
"Only Texas Girl Ever Pictured on Money" (article),
    15,674
Only the Fear (book), 6,050
*Only the Past Is Ours: The Life Story of Gertrude
    Slaughter* (book), 17,723, 17,771
Onward Neighborhood House (Chicago, IL), **4,139**
Onya La Tour Gallery, 2,778
Open-air schools, 321, 765, 3,226, 3,813, 14,745
Open Eye, The (book), 2,777
Open Sky Players, 14,378
Opera, 51, 819, **994**, 1,022, 1,123, 2,663, 3,198,
    3,838, 3,878, 5,550, **6,097, 6,498, 6,549,** 7,303,
    11,985, **12,125,** 12,374, 12,685, 12,686, 13,932,
    14,150, **14,202,** 14,565
    librettos, 6,116
Opera Association, 12,125
Opera-in-Our-Language, 54
Opera News (periodical), 12,125
Opera singers. *See* Singers
Operation Crossroads Africa, 5,475
Operation Exodus (MA), 6,680
Operation Santa Claus, 17,821, 17,825
Operatives' Magazine and Lowell Album, The
    (periodical), 5,899
Ophthalmologists, 13,441
Ophthalmology, 13,441
Opid, Helena (1840-1909). *See* Modjeska, Helena.
    Jadwiga Opid. [Mrs. Gustav Sinnmayer
    Modrzejewski]. [Mrs. Karol Bozenta
    Chlapowski] (1840-1909)
Opie, Juliet Ann (1818-1890). *See* Hopkins, Juliet
    Ann (Opie) [Mrs. Alexander George] Gordan
    [Mrs. Arthur Frances] (1818-1890)
Opium, 2,433
Opium, smuggling of, 1,174
Oplesch, Hedi (1920-), 9,038
Opp, Julia, 3,100
Oppdalslagets Yearbook, 8,744
Oppenheim, Adelaide, **11,903**
Oppenheim, Mrs. Laurent, 12,299
Oppenheimer, J. Robert, 14,438
Oppermann, Antoinette "Nattie" [Mrs. Gustav F.],
    8,357
Oppermann Fur Company (MI), 8,357
Oppermann, Gustav F. (1863-1932), **8,357**
Opportunities for Professional Transition. *See*
    Bearings for Re-Establishment, Incorporated
Opportunity Bake Shop (OR), 14,497
Opportunity Foundation Corporation, **5,474**
Opsata, Margit, 9,266
Opticians, 4,894
Optimist's Daughter, The (book), 9,770
Opti-Mrs. Club, 2,977
Opti-Mrs. Club (Garden City, KS), 5,179
Oracle, The (opera), 1,022
Oral history, **35, 130, 156,** 157, **168, 169,** 202, 211,
    212, 668, 772, 925, **942, 955, 968,** 982, 1,041,
    1,049, **1,054, 1,068, 1,080,** 1,114, 1,189, **1,345,**
    1,357, 1,532, **1,652, 1,663, 1,837,** 2,710, 2,852,
    2,880, 2,881, 2,882, 2,884, 2,888, 2,910, 2,941,
    3,451, 3,474, 4,032, 4,492, 4,493, 4,494, 4,495,
    5,135, 5,402, **5,719,** 5,828, **5,829,** 6,335, 6,987,
    7,109, 7,151, 7,162, 7,306, 7,336, **7,510, 8,007,**
    8,167, 8,185, 8,480, **8,517, 8,518, 8,690, 8,691,**
    8,692, 8,701, 8,702, 8,709, 8,717, 8,956, 9,115,
    9,304, 9,415, 9,467, 9,542, 9,694, 9,820, 10,270,
    10,311, 10,403, 10,714, 10,724, 10,755, 10,778,
    10,913, 11,234, 11,306, 11,538, 11,661, **11,815,**
    11,817, 11,846, **12,760, 13,175, 13,176, 13,236,**
    14,180, 14,227, 14,270, 14,291, 14,695, 14,811,
    14,861, 15,134, 15,218, **15,332, 15,357,** 15,369,

15,869, **16,012**, **16,181**, **16,204**, **16,205**, **16,206**, **16,207**, **16,208**, **16,238**, **16,374**, **16,408**, **16,485**, **16,488**, 16,548, 16,661, 16,746, **16,780**, **16,863**, **16,864**, **16,865**, **16,866**, 16,867, **16,868**, **16,869**, **16,870**, **16,871**, **16,872**, **16,873**, **16,874**, **16,875**, **16,876**, **16,877**, **16,890**, 16,953, 16,960, 16,965, **17,051**, **17,063**, **17,075**, **17,125**, 17,151, **17,163**, 17,285, 17,379, **17,384**, **17,530**, **17,575**, **17,775**
Oral interpretation, 16,328
Orange (IL), 3,746
Orange Orphan Society (NJ), 10,973
Orange Orphan's Home (NJ), 10,973
Orange Tree, The (book), 848
Orange Winter, a Story of Florida in 1880 (book), 5,012
Oratt, Orson, 16,794
Orbison, David W., Sr., 14,152
Orbison, Eleanor Elliott [Mrs. William], 14,824
Orbison, Ellen Matilda (1816-1902). *See* Harris, Ellen Matilda (Orbison) [Mrs. John] (1816-1902)
Orbison Family (PA), **14,824**
Orbison, Hannah D. (Jones) [Mrs. David W., Sr.] (1820-78), **14,152**
Orbison, Isabella. *See* Siemmons, Isabella (Orbison)
Orbison, William (1777-1857), 14,824
Orchard, Amelia Mandaville, 14,624
Orchard Beach Camp Meeting Association (ME), 5,614
Orchard Family (OR), **14,624**
Orchard, John C., 14,624
Orchard, Sadie, 11,235
Orcutt, Clara [Mrs.], 5,644
Orcutt, Hortense May, 3,535
Ord, George, 14,901
Ord, Maria de las Augustias (de la Guerra) [Mrs. Manuel] Jimeno Cesarin [Mrs. James L.] (1815-?), 626
"Ordained Women and Ministry. An Approach" (ms), 300
Order of Carmel, 10,611
Order of First Families of Virginia, 14,230
Order of Holy Cross, **16,026**
Order of Railway Conductors of America, Ladies Auxiliary, **4,699**
Order of St. Clare, **4,503**, 10,613
Order of St. Helena, 16,026
Order of the Eastern Star, 140, 366, 1,067, **1,075**, 1,078, 1,700, 4,697, **4,778**, 4,960, 6,403, 8,460, 8,469, 9,394, 9,647, 10,720, 13,686
Order of the Eastern Star (Bloomington, IL),
Order of the Eastern Star (IN), Greencastle Chapter Number Two Hundred Fifty-five, **4,561**
Order of the Eastern Star (Garden City, KS), Chapter Three Hundred Fifty-nine, 5,179
Order of the Eastern Star (KY), Naomi Chapter Fourteen, **5,358**
Order of the Eastern Star (NV), Electra Chapter Number Two, **10,772**
Order of the Eastern Star (OR), Adarel Chapter Number Three, 14,486
Order of the Eastern Star, State Secretary-Treasurers' Association of Colorado, **1,796**
Order of the Fleur de Lis, **6,181**
Order of the Sisters of Mercy (Vicksburg, MS), **9,695**
Order of the Unicorn, 7,278
Order of the White Duchy, Duke University (NC), **13,199**
Order of Van Orange-Nassau, 4,918
Ordinances, municipal, 8,129
Ordinaries, 3,379
Ordination, Episcopal, 12,083, 12,085
Ordination of women (Christianity), 300, 17,852
Oread Institute School of Domestic Science (MA), **7,655**
Oregon, 861, 881, 12,249, 14,505, 14,524, 14,541, 14,543, 14,577, 14,680, 16,442, 17,188
abortion, 14,507
actions and defenses, 14,592
adoption, 14,625
agricultural societies, 17,304
agriculture, 14,532
agriculture, cooperative, 14,509
apples, 14,683
authors, **14,285**, **14,289**, **14,333**, **14,460**, 14,462,

14,503, 14,510, 14,574, 14,575, 14,608, 14,610, 14,656, **14,663**, **14,684**, **14,712**, **14,714**, 17,174, 17,400
autobiography, 14,643
baccalaureate addresses, 14,299
bankers, 14,284, 14,552, 14,709
Baptists, 14,302
biographers, 14,680
bishops, 14,269
boarding schools, 14,484
booksellers and bookselling, **12,249**
businessmen, 14,498, **14,507**
Catholic schools, 14,493
census, 14,655
charitable societies, Jewish, 14,497
charities, **14,625**, **14,642**, 14,644, 14,704
child care centers, 14,671, 14,695
child welfare, 14,644
church and race problems, Catholic Church, 3,844
church and social problems, Catholic Church, **14,671**
church societies, **14,439**
church societies, Baptist, 14,595
church societies, Congregational, **14,340**
church societies, Lutheran, **14,496**
church societies, Methodist, **14,485**
citizens' associations, 17,262, 17,304
city attorneys, 14,600
city councilmen, 14,619
city planning, 14,605
civil rights, 14,691
civil rights workers, 14,656, 14,671, **17,262**, **17,304**
Civil War, hospitals, charities, etc., **14,418**
clergy, **14,564**, 14,566, 14,588, 14,603
clergy, Congregational, 14,508
clergy, Methodist, 14,536, 14,668
clergy, Presbyterian, 14,606, 14,664
clubs, **14,281**, **14,287**, **14,295**, 14,336, **14,472**, 14,478, 14,500, 14,564, **14,635**, **14,640**, **14,641**, **14,700**, **14,711**
college librarians, 14,277
college registrars, 14,699
college students, 14,654
college teachers, **14,272**, **14,273**, **14,402**, **14,577**
salaries, pensions, etc., 14,274
college trustees, **14,271**
community leadership, **14,535**, 14,552
community life, 14,695
community organization, 14,605
composers, 17,400
conductors (music), 14,639
congressmen, 699, 14,619
congresswomen, **14,391**, 14,504, **14,587**
conservationists, **14,398**
county officials and employees, 14,554
court records, 14,696
courtship, 14,348
deans (in schools), **14,275**, **14,280**
demography, study and teaching, 14,577
diaries and journals, 14,283, **14,286**, 14,302, 14,305, 14,337, 14,424, 14,461, **14,484**, 14,490, 14,498, 14,514, **14,529**, **14,620**, 14,636, 14,646, **14,649**, **14,702**
docks, 14,555
dramatists, **14,313**, **14,663**
drugstores, 14,573
dwellings, 14,285
editors, 14,581, **14,582**, **14,703**
education, 14,640
educational associations, **14,708**
educators, 14,508, **14,629**
electric utilities, 14,653
employment, 14,671
executives, **14,674**
exhibitions, 14,549
extended care facilities, 14,494
farm life, 14,491
farmers, 14,668, **17,402**
festivals, 1,545
flax, 14,278
floods, 14,656, 14,694
flour-mills, 14,632
flute-players, 14,498
genealogy, 14,506

geology, 14,608
governors, 305, 14,594, 14,607, 14,610, 14,619
grain trade, employees, 14,555
gynecologists, 14,698
handicapped children, education, 14,641
high schools, 14,540
highway departments, 14,556
highway relocation, 14,671
historians, 14,544, **14,655**, 14,680
historic buildings, 14,289
conservation and restoration, 14,589
historic sites, conservation and restoration, 14,666
historical societies, 14,306, 14,641
home economics, study and teaching, **14,278**, 14,279
hospitals, 14,625
hotels, taverns, etc., 14,615, 14,642, 14,664
housing, 14,348, 14,671
housing authorities, 14,605
hunting, **14,296**
inventors, 17,400
Jews, oral history, **14,497**
journalists, 12,249, 14,384, 14,512, **14,655**
judges, 6,956, 14,581, 14,607
land settlement, 14,608, 14,702
land titles, 14,655
registration and transfer, 14,565
law, cases, 14,579
lawyers, **6,720**, 14,353, 14,581, **14,600**, 14,648, **14,663**, **14,675**, **17,371**
legislative bodies, 14,537
officials and employees, 14,456
legislators, 699, 14,429, **14,587**, 14,634, 14,713
librarians, 14,698
libraries, university and college, **14,277**
local church councils, 17,304
lumber, transportation, 14,305
lumbering, 17,214
lumbermen, **14,565**
manufacturers, 14,532
massacres, 780, 881
maternity homes, **14,367**
mayors, 6,720, 14,552, **14,599**, 14,619
medicine, 14,348
merchants, 14,449, 14,552, 14,554, 14,600, 14,619
migrant labor, 14,671
missionaries, 1,498, 1,790, 14,508, **14,528**, **14,550**, 14,581, **14,604**, **14,667**, **14,715**, 17,212, **17,402**, **17,423**
missionaries, Methodist, **14,596**, **14,602**
missionaries, Presbyterian, 14,606
missions, 780, 14,459
missions, Methodist, 14,596, 14,602
missions, Presbyterian, 14,606
monasticism and religious orders for women, Catholic, **14,269**, **14,493**, **14,494**, **14,661**, **17,415**
municipal officials and employees, 6,720
music teachers, **14,346**, **14,527**
musical societies, **14,430**, 14,565
musicians, **14,682**
mythology, 14,669
Native Americans, 671, 690, 14,669
education, 305
missions, 1,498, 14,434, 14,660
relations with whites, 17,402
reservations, 14,609, 14,619
wars, 14,436, **14,539**, 14,657, 14,680
newspaper publishers and publishing, 14,353
newspapers, 1,507, 14,309, 14,582, 14,610
sections, columns, etc., 14,512
Nez Percé Indians, **14,660**
novelists, 14,680, 14,712
nuns, Catholic, 14,671, **17,415**
officials and employees, 14,615
old age homes, **14,633**
opera, 14,565
oral history, **14,270**, **14,497**, **14,695**
orphans and orphan asylums, 14,625
osteopaths, 14,363
parents' and teachers' associations, **14,631**, **14,658**
patriotic societies, **14,349**, **14,376**, **14,481**, **14,492**
peace societies, 14,691, 17,262
philanthropists, **14,704**
photographers, **14,300**, **14,544**

physicians, 1,281, 14,331, 14,473, **14,526, 14,629,** 14,698, 14,699
pioneers and settlers, 305, 410, 583, **606, 671,** 704, **6,956, 12,669, 14,270,** 14,310, **14,341, 14,348, 14,436, 14,477, 14,480, 14,487, 14,488, 14,499,** 14,542, 14,549, **14,588, 14,596,** 14,647, **14,657, 14,669,** 17,212, **17,265, 17,287, 17,330, 17,420**
poets, **14,382, 14,383, 14,428,** 14,656, 14,680
poets, Native American, 14,712
police, records and correspondence, **14,696**
political activists, women, **14,637,** 14,686
political clubs, **14,626**
politicians, **14,541**
politics and government, 14,596
politics, practical, women's activism, 14,533, 14,671, 17,304
population, **14,292**
postmistresses, 6,956
printers, 14,704
private schools, 14,508, **14,638**
prohibition, 14,521
psychiatric hospitals, employees, 14,331
psychiatrists, 14,698
public health, 14,640
public health nursing, 14,356
public records, **14,290**
public schools, 14,508
public welfare, 14,640
  law, 14,551
public works, 14,714
publishers and publishing, 14,545
radio programs, 14,551
railroads, 14,664
ranchers, **14,509, 14,683**
retirement homes, **14,623**
roads, 14,669
rural schools, 14,301
sanatoriums, **14,623**
scholarships, 14,625
school superintendents and principals, 14,668
school supervisors, 14,330
schools, 14,281, 14,348
scientists, 14,508
scrapbooks, 14,502, 14,565, **14,580,** 14,654
secret societies, 14,486
senators, United States, 14,362, **14,429,** 14,504, **14,599, 14,622,** 14,683
sheep ranching, 14,436
social action, 14,605
social life and customs, 671, 14,318, 14,348
social settlements, **14,671**
social workers, **14,356**
societies, **14,621, 14,627, 14,666**
societies, Afro-American, 17,304
soldiers, **14,573**
spiritualists, 14,363
statues, 6,384, 14,549
stock and stock-breeding, 14,554
students' societies, **14,276**
suffrage, 1,308, 14,521, 14,703
suffrage societies, 14,545, 14,547, 17,226
surveyors, 14,619
symphony orchestras, **14,639**
teachers, 704, 6,956, 14,285, **14,306,** 14,363, 14,373, 14,462, **14,479, 14,524, 14,540, 14,557, 14,564,** 14,600, 14,603, **14,609,** 14,614, **14,643,** 14,646, 14,668, **14,682**
teachers' colleges, 14,540
temperance, 14,680
temperance societies, 14,306, **14,361,** 14,471, **14,516, 14,690, 14,692,** 14,713
theater, 14,670
theatrical agencies, **14,670**
trails, 14,669
travel, 14,632
Unitarians, 14,311
United Methodist Church, 14,536
universities and colleges, 14,283, 14,299, 14,375, 14,477, 14,508
  administration, **14,275**
  alumnae, 14,274, **14,699**
urban renewal, 14,671
utopias, **14,268**
violin makers, 14,639

vital statistics, **14,290**
voluntary health agencies, 14,356
War of 1898, societies, **14,701**
winter of 1889-1890, 14,525
women
  civil rights, 14,314
  education, 14,638
  employment, 14,270
  Young Women's Christian Association, **14,694,** 17,262
Oregon Children's Aid Society, **14,625**
Oregon City Chataqua, 14,549
Oregon Civil War Round Table, 14,565
Oregon Congress of Mothers, 14,551
Oregon Daily Journal, 14,551
Oregon Dunes, 14,622
Oregon Federation of Women's Clubs, 14,356
Oregon Girls' Drill Company, 14,535
Oregon Historical Quarterly, 14,462
Oregon Historical Society, 14,641
Oregon Industrial Editors Association, 14,565
Oregon Insane Asylum, 14,331
Oregon Journal, 14,384, 14,615, 17,414
Oregon League of Democratic Women, **14,626**
Oregon Migrant Ministry, 14,459
Oregon Native Daughters, Odell Cabin Number 8, **14,627**
Oregon Normal School (OR), 14,540
Oregon Prison Association, 17,262
Oregon Roadside Council, 14,398
Oregon Sentinel, 14,353
Oregon Shipyards, 14,695
Oregon State College Pan-Hellenic Association, **14,276**
Oregon State Highway Commission, 14,556
Oregon State University (Corvallis, OR)
  alumnae, 14,274
  faculty, **14,272, 14,273**
  library, **14,277**
  students, 14,311
  trustees, **14,271**
Oregon State University (Corvallis, OR), Mother's Club, 14,275
Oregon State University (Corvallis, OR), Office of the Dean of Women, **14,275**
Oregon State University (Corvallis, OR), School of Home Economics, Department of Clothing, Textiles, and Related Arts, **14,278**
Oregon State University (Corvallis, OR), School of Home Economics, Department of Family Life and Home Management, **14,279**
Oregon State University (Corvallis, OR), School of Home Economics, Office of the Dean, **14,280**
Oregon State Woman's Suffrage Association, 14,545
Oregon Supreme Court, 14,607
Oregon Territory, 256, 1,790
Oregon Trail, 1,637, 12,482, 13,384, 14,294, 14,298, 17,293
"Oregon Trail—1849, The" (ms), 14,663
Oregon Tuberculosis Association, 14,356
Oregon Woman Suffrage Association, 17,226
Oregon Women's Industrial Forum, 14,551
Oregon Writers Project, 14,599
Oregonian, 1,699, 14,382, 14,384, 14,460, 14,581
Oregonian (Portland, OR), 14,456
O'Reilly, Alexandro, 5,495
O'Reilly, Caroline (1812-?). *See* Nicholson, Caroline (O'Reilly) [Mrs. Alfred Osborn Pope] (1812-?)
O'Reilly, Leonora (1870-1927), 2,878, 6,354, **6,812**
Orendorff, J. B., 3,754
Orfali, Steffi, **4,460**
Orgain, Sarah Jane, 16,176
Organic gardening, 6,034
Organists, **5,670, 7,743,** 9,951, **12,291,** 15,683
Organization of Arizona Pioneers, 207
Organization of Children's International Summer Villages, 13,869
Organizations. *See* Associations, institutions, etc.
Organized Independent Women (AR), **263**
Oriental-Americans, missions, 15,173
Oriental studies, **4,028**
Orientalists, **1,854, 2,237,** 14,740
Original Club (ND), 13,660

Orkney and Shetland Literary, Social, and Benevolent Society (Chicago, IL), **4,140**
Orleans County Council on the Arts (NY), 11,269
Orleans County Teachers Institute (VT), 17,035
Orleans Gallery (LA), **5,541**
Ormes, Jackie, 13,217
Ormond Family, 16,768
Ormond, Mary (1821-92). *See* Morris, Mary (Ormond) [Mrs. William] George [Mrs. John] (1821-92)
Ormond, Suzanne (Levy) [Mrs. John W.] (1926-), **5,542**
Ormsbeer, Carrie Wyckoff, 15,308
Ormsby, Augusta, **10,695**
Ormsby Family, 10,695
Ormsby, Virginia, 2,932
Ornithologists, **1,447, 2,484, 6,317,** 7,474, 9,319, **11,507, 11,665, 11,701,** 14,873
Ornithology, 518, 5,486, 6,317, 7,666, 10,454
Ornstein, Leo (1892-), **2,021**
Ornstein, Pauline (Mallet-Prevost) [Mrs. Leo] (ca. 1890-), 2,021
Orphan House (Charleston, SC), **15,505**
Orphan Society of Philadelphia (PA), **15,062**
Orphans' Advocate, The (periodical), 7,032
Orphans and orphan asylums, 540, 546, **1,213, 1,236,** 1,605, 1,690, 1,938, 2,013, 2,188, 2,294, 2,362, 2,391, 2,421, 2,645, 2,677, 3,371, 3,488, 3,655, 3,725, **3,806,** 3,905, 4,065, 4,069, 4,079, **4,107,** 4,286, 5,230, 5,393, 5,398, 5,426, 5,475, **5,520,** 5,570, 6,114, 6,359, 6,598, 6,611, 6,704, 7,032, 7,049, 7,066, **7,097,** 8,176, 8,848, **8,930, 9,339,** 9,455, 9,490, 9,527, 10,115, 10,188, **10,299, 10,621,** 10,632, 11,154, 11,410, 11,560, 11,619, **12,355,** 12,759, 12,767, 12,810, 13,284, 13,569, 13,573, 13,696, 13,945, 13,949, 14,075, 14,116, 14,148, 14,625, 14,795, **15,062, 15,122,** 15,181, **15,282,** 15,404, 15,433, **15,505,** 16,251, 16,417, 17,229, 17,377, 17,380, 17,415, 17,422, 17,459, 17,487, 17,839
Orphans and orphan asylums, Afro-American, 13,644
Orphans and orphan asylums, Catholic, **15,705**
Orphans and orphan asylums, Jewish, **1,327, 7,535, 7,536,** 13,764, **15,153**
Orphan's Message (periodical), 3,418
Orr, Charlotte (Pettis) [Mrs. William] (?-1931), 2,516
Orr, Dorothy. *See* Orr, Martha Reynolds "Dorothy"
Orr, Eliza C., 3,342
Orr, Emily (1866-1952). *See* Clifford, Emily (Orr) [Mrs. George S.] (1866-1952)
Orr Family (AZ), 1,373
Orr Family (GA), **3,342**
Orr, Florence. *See* Jorgensen, Florence (Orr) [Mrs. Virgil W.]
Orr, Gustavus John (1819-87), 3,238, 3,342
Orr, Margaret (1872-1963). *See* O'Neill, Margaret (Orr) [Mrs. Charles] (1872-1963)
Orr, Martha Reynolds "Dorothy," 3,238, 3,342
Orr, Mary E., 3,342
Orr, Mrs. James Wallace (1854-?), 585
Orr, Violet (1905-), 1,356, 1,357
Orr, William, 5,289
Orr, William (1860-1939), **2,516**
Orrock, Mary Cumming, 16,910
Orrum, Eilley (1826-1903). *See* Bowers, Eilley (Orrum) [Mrs. Stephen] Hunter [Mrs. Alexander] Cowan [Mrs. Lemuel Sanford "Sandy"] (1826-1903)
Orsment, Nancy, 7,047
Orth, Marion, 949
Orthodox-Congregational Society (Barre, MA), 5,894
Orthodox Jewish Home for the Aged, B.M.A. (Chicago, IL). *See* Jewish Home for the Aged (B.M.Z. of Chicago) (IL)
Ortley, Mary E., 8,936
Orton, Annie B. [Miss], **1,104**
Orton, Fay M., 17,418
Orton, Helen Fuller, 15,319
Orton Society, 15,278
Ortonville Camp (MN), 8,690
Orvis, Ina Leland, 2,205
Orvis, John, 4,434
Orvis, Marianne (Dwight). Mary Ann. [Mrs. John] (1816-1901), **4,434,** 7,043, 12,461, 17,010

Orwig, Mary Sipp [Mrs. Thomas Gilbert] (?-1907), **4,817**
Orwig, Thomas Gilbert, **4,817**
Osage Indians, 2,838, 14,173, 14,212, 14,239
Osborn, Agda Teoline Swenson (1898-), 11,508, **11,667**
Osborn, Augusta, 6,998
Osborn, Chase S., 7,885
Osborn Family (NY), 11,520
Osborn, Genevieve L. [Miss], **5,151**
Osborn, Henry Fairfield (1857-1935), **12,276**
Osborn, Kate Story, 3,413
Osborn, Katherine Elizabeth "Lizzie" (Mangum) [Mrs. James] (1834-?), **3,413**
Osborn, Laura Freele (1867-1955), **8,030**
Osborn, Lucretia "Loulu" Perry [Mrs. Henry Fairfield] (1858-94), 12,276
Osborn, Mary M., **956**
Osborn, Prudence. *See* Vanderbeck, Prudence (Osborn) Hadden
Osborn, Sarah [Mrs. Henry] (1714-96), **7,656**
Osborn, Stella (Brunt) [Mrs. Chase S.] (1894-), 7,718, **7,885**
Osborn, Virginia R. [Mrs. William Henry] (1830-1902), 12,276
Osborn, William Henry (1820-94), 12,276
Osborne, Eric, 11,976
Osborne, Estelle M., 3,290
Osborne, Lucy Eugenia (1879-1955), **6,813**
Osborne, Minnie (1862-?). *See* Fowler, Minnie (Osborne) (1862-?)
Osborne, Nellie [Mrs.], 13,384
Osborne, Sarah Waters (Whittredge) [Mrs. George] (1804-?), **7,414**
Osbourne, Isobel. *See* Field, Isobel (Osbourne) Strong
Osbourne, Katherine D., 12,436
Osgood, Dora (1886-?), **204**
Osgood, Ellen, 12,277
Osgood, Ellen Devereux Sewall, 12,277
Osgood, Ellen Frances, 7,657
Osgood, Ethel B., 6,406
Osgood, Frances Sargent (Locke) [Mrs. Samuel Stillman] (1811-50), **5,948, 7,657**
Osgood, Herbert Levi, 14,758
Osgood, James R., 12,021
Osgood, Joseph, 12,277
Osgood, Joseph Otis (1848-1916), **12,277**
Osgood, Julian. *See* Putnam, Julian (Osgood)
Osgood, Laura, 12,277
Osgood, Martha B. [Mrs. Edmund Charles Genet], 12,210
Osgood, Martha (Usher) (1823-93), 5,689
Osgood Sanders Day Care Center (GA), 3,253
Osgood, Sarah Eva Littlefield [Mrs. Joseph Otis], 12,277
Osgood, Susan Kilteridge. *See* Field, Susan Kilteridge (Osgood) [Mrs. Moses]
Osguthorpe, Sarah Ann (1847-1930). *See* Bitner, Sarah Ann (Osguthorpe) [Mrs. Breneman Barr] (1847-1930)
O'Shaughnessy, Arthur William Edgar (1844-81), **12,062**
O'Shaughnessy, Eleanor Kyme (Marston) [Mrs. Arthur William Edgar], 12,062
Oskaloosa College (IA)
  alumnae, 4,816
  students, 5,074
Osmond, Ann Sammes (ca. 1814-93), 9,274
Osmond, Ella, 9,274
Osmond, Mabel Cross, 18,026
Osmond, Mary, 9,274
Osmond, William R., Family, **9,274**
Ossining Children's Center (NY), 12,751
Ossining Council of Social Agencies (NY), 12,751
Ossining Historical Society (NY), 12,751
Ossining Music Guild (NY), 12,751
Ossining Recreation Commission (NY), 12,751
Ossining School for Girls (NY), **12,750**
Ossining War Council (NY), 12,751
Ostenso, Martha (1900-63), 8,521, 8,805
Osteology. *See* Bones
Osteopaths, 219, **1,045**, 1,111, **4,506**, 14,363
Osterhaven, M. E., **8,201**

Osterman, Marjorie K., **6,062**
Ostrander, Clinton N., 11,669
Ostrander, Dwight H., 11,669
Ostrander, Eveline [Mrs. John], 11,669
Ostrander Family (NY), **11,668**
Ostrander, John B. (1810-79), 11,668
Ostrander, John, Family (NY), **11,669**
Oswald, Caroline "Carrie" (1820-98). *See* Sams, Caroline "Carrie" Oswald [Mrs. Miles Brewton] (1820-98)
Oswald, Marina N. [Mrs. Lee Harvey], 14,504
Oswego Normal and Training School (MI), 11,748
Oswego Normal School (NY), 12,752
Oswego Primary Teachers' Training School (NY). *See* State University College at Oswego (NY)
Otenasek, Mildred, 5,829
Otero, Katherine Stinson, 11,235
Otetela language, 13,276
Otey, George, 9,696
Otey, Martha Ann (Nolley) [Mrs. Armistead George], **9,696**
Other Caroline, The (book), 6,108
Otis, Alfred, 5,162
Otis, Amelia Harris [Mrs. Alfred], 5,162
Otis, Amy. *See* Earhart, Amy (Otis) [Mrs. Edwin S.]
Otis, Edna M., **8,358**
Otis, Elizabeth, 2,205
Otis, Emily Marshall (1832-1906). *See* Eliot, Emily Marshall (Otis) [Mrs. Samuel] (1832-1906)
Otis, Mary Allyne. *See* Gay, Mary Allyne (Otis) [Mrs. Ebenezer]
Otis, Mercy (1728-1814). *See* Warren, Mercy (Otis) [Mrs. James] (1728-1814)
Otken, Charles, 9,697
Otken, Emily Jane Lee [Mrs. Charles], 9,697
Otken, Frances Powell, **9,697**
O'Toole, Ruth [Miss], **13,291**
Ott, Mary, 9,674
Ott, Tess. *See* Weinheim, Tess (Ott)
Ottawa Indians, missions, 7,931
Otte, Frances Phelps, **8,202**
Otten, Sister Mary Carl, 10,732
Otter Tail County Historical Society (MN), 8,458, 8,460
Otto, Carl, 16,011
Otto, Ethel. *See* Sargent, Ethel (Otto)
Otto Family, 12,431
Ottumwa Public Library (IA), 5,093
Ottumwa Shakespeare Club (IA), **5,096**
Ouida (pseudonym). *See* De la Ramée, Louise (1839-1908)
Ouija boards, 10,184
Our Ernie (book), 5,273
Our Faces, Our Words (book), 2,879
Our Gifted Son (book), 332
Our Lady of Bethlehem Academy (IL), 4,284
Our Lady of Guadalupe Catholic Church (St. Paul, MN), 9,210
Our Lady of Holy Cross, Marianite Provincial House (New Orleans, LA), 5,503
Our Lady of Mount Carmel Roman Catholic Church, Ladies Society (Kenosha, WI), 9,507
Our Lady of Perpetual Help Home (GA), **3,239**
Our Lady of the Lake University (TX), 16,230
Our Lady of the Mississippi Abbey (Dubuque, IA), **4,871**
Our Lady of Victory Missionary Sisters (Huntington IN), **4,596**
Our Mountain Heritage (book), 567
Our Nation's Story (book), 9,671, 9,672
Our Own Sevier, A Comprehensive Centennial Volume (book), 16,564
Our Port Folio (newspaper), 11,108
"Our Private World" (soap opera), 17,705
Our Saviour's Lutheran Church (Ham Lake, MN), 8,389
Our Southwest (book), 11,223
"Our Trip to Egypt" (journal), 16,372
"Our Women in the War" (article), 3,262
Our Work for the Church (book), 10,580
Our World of Science (book), 4,975
Ouray, Chief, 16,876
Oursler, Loree [Mrs.] (?-ca. 1975), **5,552**
Ousley Cemetery (GA), 3,615

Ouspenskaya, Maria (1876-1949), **1,048**
Out-of-Doors-School (GA), 3,226
Out of Old Virginia and New England—The Family Story of Jacob Andrus Camp 1823-1900 [and] Elizabeth Francis Osborn Camp 1823-1900, 11,533
Out of the Heart: Poems for Lovers, Young and Old (book), 7,131
Out of the North (book), 5,694
"Out of the Past" (radio program), 11,291
Out of the Shadows (book), 17,718
Out West, 710
Outdoor Art Club (Mill Valley, CA), 1,067
"Outdoor Sketches," 4,821
Outlaw, Albert Timothy, **13,523**
Outlaws. *See* Crime and criminals
Outline of a Course in Good-Will for the Public Schools (book), 6,188
Outline of Careers for Women, An: A Practical Guide to Achievement (book), 2,205
"Outline of Clothing Projects for Girls Clubs," 8,596
Outline of Mississippi History (book), 9,672
"Outline of the Book of Methods of the Baptist Temple" (ms), 15,184
Outlines of Men, Women, and Things (book), 14,058
Outlook Club (NE), 10,484
Outlook, The (periodical), 2,037, 5,274
"Outstanding Women of Quincy," 4,313
Outwater, Eva J. Shedd, 7,920
Outwater, Lucia, 11,742
Outwater, Mary Amanda (1836-87). *See* White, Mary Amanda (Outwater) [Mrs. Andrew D.] (1836-87)
Ovariectomy, 3,146
Ovaries, 7,872
"Over the Line" (hymn), 2,222
Over the Tea Cups (IN), 4,532, **4,575**
Over the Teacups (SC), **15,810**
Overacker, Louise, 7,583
Overbury, Bertha (Van Riper) [Mrs. Frederick], **11,821**
Overheard in Hades (book), 15,720
Overholser Family (NE), **10,519**
Overholser, Forrest E., 10,519
Overholser, Frances, 10,519
Overholser, Winnie [Mrs. Forrest E.], 10,519
Overland journeys to the Pacific, 256, 345, **422**, 478, 489, 512, **527, 528, 547, 560, 571, 579**, 582, **606, 652, 683, 694**, 699, **728, 738, 747, 759**, 780, **782, 867**, 899, **975**, 1,229, **1,267, 1,271, 1,286**, 1,290, **1,297, 1,303, 1,305, 1,320, 1,365**, 1,595, **1,597**, 2,561, 3,902, **5,055**, 7,498, **9,852**, 9,853, 9,949, 10,004, **10,054**, 12,482, 12,669, 14,341, 14,348, **14,372, 14,373**, 14,462, 14,479, 14,483, 14,487, 14,488, 14,489, 14,499, 14,506, 14,513, **14,519**, 14,531, 14,541, 14,545, 14,549, 14,557, **14,561, 14,563, 14,569, 14,572, 14,583, 14,585, 14,597, 14,601, 14,611, 14,612, 14,617, 14,628, 14,662**, 14,668, **14,673, 14,693**, 14,709, **16,543**, 17,167, 17,170, **17,173, 17,176, 17,212, 17,265**, 17,287, 17,329, **17,408**, 17,410, 17,414, 17,418, 17,419, 17,422, 17,423. *See also* Donner Party
Overland Monthly (periodical), 560, 792, 1,340, 6,650
Overlease, Edith, 8,167
Overlease, William, 8,167
Overmann, Mary Lorrain Peters [Mrs. Henry John] (1822-1907), **12,278**
Overseas Press Club, 17,716
Overseers of the Poor (MA), 7,142, 7,150
Overstreet, Bonaro, 1,341
Overtime, 3,449
Overton, Alice, 8,676
Overton, Carrie Burton [Mrs. George W. B.] (1888-1975), **8,116**
Ovington, Mary White (1865-1951), **2,144**, 2,502, 2,587, 5,458, 5,870, **6,814**, 8,116, 15,305
Owen, Eliza Lee. *See* Kelly, Eliza Lee (Owen)
Owen Family (MS), 9,656
Owen Family (PA), 15,104
Owen, Jane Dale. *See* Fauntleroy, Jane Dale (Owen)
Owen, John, **13,524**
Owen, Lou Cretia [Miss], **15,963**
Owen, Margaret, 13,524

Owen, Marie (Bankhead) [Mrs. Thomas M.] (1869-1958), 48, 57, 60, **76**
Owen, Mary Jane Robinson [Mrs. Robert Dale] (1813-71), **4,637**
Owen, Robert Dale (1801-77), 4,433, **4,435**, 4,637, 4,809, 14,718
Owen, Robert L., 14,225
Owen, Ruth Bryan (1885-1954). See Rohde, Ruth (Bryan) Owen [Mrs. Borge] (1885-1954)
Owen, Thomas M., 76
(Owens)-Adair, Bethenia Angelina [Mrs. Legrand] Hill [Mrs. John] (1840-1926), 14,629, 14,698
Owens, Annie Evalina, 7,110
Owens, Bethenia Angelina (1840-1926). See (Owens)-Adair, Bethenia Angelina [Mrs. Legrand] Hill [Mrs. John] (1840-1926)
Owens, Elizabeth McAnulty, 16,117
Owens Family (GA), **3,561**
Owens, George W., 3,561
Owens, Helen (Brewster) [Mrs. Fred] (1881-), **6,815**
Owens, John W., **14,630**
Owens, Lydia, 14,630
Owens, Mary W., 3,561
Owens, Mollie, 14,630
Owens, Rochelle (1936-), **6,063**, 11,221
Owens-Thomas House (GA), 3,561
Owings, Chloe (1883-), **6,816**
Owl in the Cedar Tree (book), 11,213, 11,217
Owl on Every Post, An (book), 5,981
Owls, 15,185
Ownby, Anna [Mrs. Bramble B.], **221**
Ownby, Bramble B., 221
Owne, Walter, 12,489
Oxboro Heath Community League (MN), **9,275**
Oxborough, Mary (Evans) [Mrs. Robert] (1884-), **8,410**
Oxford Area Voter, The (newsletter), 9,818
Oxford, Edward, **3,414**
Oxford Female Academy (NC), 13,450
Oxford Female College, students, 5,306
Oxford Female Seminary (NC), 13,330, 13,417, 13,561, **13,646**
  faculty, 13,640
Oxford University (England), 11,885
Oxford Women's Literary Club (NC), **13,083**
Oyler, Clara (1891-). See Capener, Clara (Oyler) [Mrs. Samuel William] (1891-)
Ozburn, James. See Osborn, James
P. E. O. Record (periodical), 10,128
P. E. O. Sisterhood, 3,743, 4,815, 5,061, 5,064, 5,065, 5,074, **8,173**, **10,128**, 13,718
P. E. O. Sisterhood (IL), Chapter CK, 4,278
P. E. O. Sisterhood (IN), **4,577**
P. E. O. Sisterhood (Chapter G, Ottumwa, IA), **5,097**
P. T. Barnum Circus. See Ringling Brothers and Barnum and Bailey Circus
"Pa 'Delante Mujer" (television program), 17,619
Pace, Ida (1869-1958). See Purdue, Ida (Pace) [Mrs. Albert Homer] (1869-1958)
Pace, Lula (1868-1925), **16,375**
Pace, Patsy Edwina Clark, 9,567
Pace, Pearl (Carter) (1896-1970), 1,605, **5,272**
Pace, Richard, 9,689
Pace, Stanley, 5,272
Pacheco School (CA), 982
Pacific Banner (periodical), 15,300
Pacific Bridge Company, 14,674
Pacific City colony (Mexico), 2,401
Pacific Coast Association of Friends, **705**
Pacific Geographic Society, **1,594**
Pacific, Gertrude, **17,316**
Pacific Hebrew Orphan Asylum and Home Society (CA), **1,327**
Pacific Lutheran University (Tacoma, WA), School of Nursing, **17,385**
Pacific Monthly (periodical), 1,455
Pacific Northwest Library Association, 17,394
Pacific States, **1,595**
Pacific University (OR), 14,477, 14,508
Pacifism, 1,473, 1,561, 2,856, 6,623, 6,867, 7,323, 8,070, 8,658, 8,678, 10,671, 11,018, 11,931, 17,060
Pacifists, **741**, **1,321**, **1,561**, **2,569**, 2,857, 4,897, **6,846**, 7,184, **7,291**, **7,923**, **8,009**, 8,963, 9,467,

10,177, 11,596, 12,652, **12,715**, 13,229, **14,432**, **14,453**, 15,298, 17,262, **17,659**
Pack, Alvin G., **16,781**
Pack, Eliza Walker, 15,667
Pack Family (SC), **15,667**
Pack, John, **16,950**
Pack, Julia [Mrs. John], 16,950
Packard, Charles, 15,506
Packard, Chilion, **15,506**
Packard, Clara Jane (Sanford) (1866-?), 16,967
Packard, M. W., 3,763
Packard, Olive, 15,506
Packard, Rebecca Prentiss (Kent) (1808-1905), 7,642
Packard, Sarah. See Wendell, Sarah (Packard) [Mrs. Philip]
Packard, Sarah Gordon Roulain [Mrs. Chilion], 15,506
Packard, Sophia B. (1824-91), 12,740
Packer Collegiate Institute (NY), 7,217, 11,324
Packer, Dorothy. See Duncan, Dorothy (Packer)
Packer, Martha Suckow (1880-1970), **10,258**
Packer, Thelma [Mrs.], 16,488
Packrow, John, 15,716
Padden, Electra (1874-1953). See Kerr, Electra (Padden) (1874-1953)
Paddlewheels Churning (book), 5,206
Paddock, Ella, 8,924
Paddock, Henry T., 12,568
Paddy, Mary [Mrs.], 3,871
Paden, Irene (Dakin) (1888-1974), 355, **706**, **1,637**
Paderewski, Helena, 15,179
Paderewski, Ignace, 945
Paderewski, Mrs. Ignace, 13,906
Padilla de Sanz, Doña Trina (1864-1957), 15,368
Padilla, Don José Gualberto (1829-96), 15,368
"Padres, Gringoes and Gold" (radio program), 643
Paeff, Bashka, 6,867, 7,182
Paepcke, Elizabeth [Mrs. Walter], 11,827
Page, Ann (Meade), 2,541
Page, Anne F. See Pleasants, Anne F. (Page) [Mrs. Joseph]
Page, Curtis Hidden (1870-1948), 6,754, **12,063**
Page, Edward (1787-1867), 11,035
Page, Esther Cooley, 5,871
Page Family (MA), 7,008, **7,658**
Page Family (VA), **17,115**
Page, Florence Lathrop Field [Mrs. Thomas Nelson] (1858-1911), 17,116
Page, Geraldine (1924-), 11,907
Page, "Grandma," 17,378
Page, Harriet Ann (Moore) [Mrs. Solomon C.] (1810-?). See Ames, Harriet Ann (Moore) [Mrs. Solomon C.] Page [Mrs. Robert] Potter [Mrs. Charles] (1810-?)
Page, Isabel. See Rutter, Isabel (Page) [Mrs. Robert Louis]
Page, John, 17,115
Page, Lucy Burwell (1807-?). See Saunders, Lucy Burwell (Page) [Mrs. Robert] (1807-?)
Page, Margaret (Lowther) [Mrs. John], 17,115
Page, Martha, 7,658
Page, Martha Crosby (1808-32), 7,658
Page, Mary (1806-94). See Putnam, Mary (Page) [Mrs. Alfred] (1806-94)
Page, Mary Ferguson. See Southwick, Mary Ferguson (Page) [Mrs. Philip R. V.]
Page, Myra (pseudonym). See Markey, Dorothy (1900-)
Page, Phyllis, 6,221
Page, Solomon C., 2,167
Page, Sophia Stevens [Mrs. Stephen] Hitchcock [Mrs. William] 17,035
Page, Thomas Nelson (1853-1922), **17,116**
Page, Walter, 5,414
Page, William, 17,035
Pageants, 901, **921**, **2,326**, 4,332, 5,783, 9,349, 9,610, 9,648, 11,897, 12,521, 12,959, 13,026, 14,026, 15,061, 15,164, **15,807**, 16,999, 17,667
Paget, Violet (1856-1935), 5,714
Pahlevi, Reza Shah (1877-1944), 7,191
Paige, Karen E., 17,663
Paige, Mabeth Hurd [Mrs. James] (1870-1961), 8,896, 9,120, 9,231, **9,276**, 9,287, 9,289, 9,302
Pailthorpe, Michele, **17,317**

Pain, Evelyn, 11,907
Paine, Albert Bigelow, 1,493, 1,495, 9,832
Paine, Catherine V. (1829-1908). See Blaine, Catherine V. (Paine) [Mrs. David E.] (1829-1908)
Paine, Cordelia Ayer, 9,075
Paine, Elizabeth (1766-1832). See Trumbull, Elizabeth (Paine) (1766-1832)
Paine, Elizabeth "Mother", 11,440
Paine, Elsie Miriam [Miss] (ca. 1882-), **6,817**
Paine Family (MA), **7,659**
Paine, Fannie Graham, 3,419
Paine Female Institute (TX), **16,113**
Paine, Maryette (Matthews), 17,405
Paine, Samuel (1754-1807), 7,665
Paine, Sarah (Chandler) [Mrs. Timothy] (1726-1811), 7,665
Paine, Thomas, 15,013
Paine, Timothy (1730-93), 7,659, 7,665
Paint Creek coal field (WV), 17,482
Painter, Chloe, 12,653
Painter, Clara (Searle) [Mrs. H. K.] (ca. 1888-), **2,517**, **6,818**, 8,399
Painter, Eleanor. See Strong, Eleanor (Painter)
Painter Family (CT, OH), 12,653
Painter, Polly, 12,653
Painter, Thalia Maria McMahon [Mrs. Alexis], 2,009
Painter, William, 12,653
Painters, 712, **1,522**, **2,207**, **2,218**, **2,662**, **2,729**, **2,730**, **2,731**, **2,736**, **2,738**, **2,739**, **2,740**, **2,741**, **2,744**, **2,747**, **2,755**, **2,761**, **2,763**, **2,765**, **2,766**, **2,769**, **2,772**, **2,773**, **2,774**, **2,778**, **2,785**, **2,786**, **2,788**, **2,789**, **2,792**, **2,793**, **2,795**, **2,798**, **2,799**, **2,803**, **2,809**, **2,816**, **2,818**, **2,819**, **2,822**, **2,829**, 3,415, **4,688**, 5,866, 7,046, 7,200, 8,001, **9,573**, 10,631, 11,233, **11,933**, **12,274**, 12,403, **12,543**, **12,637**, 12,884, **12,914**, **13,854**, 13,860, **14,238**, **14,707**, 15,018, **15,331**, 15,900, 16,486, **16,575**, **17,179**, **17,231**, **17,269**, **17,280**, **17,283**, **17,284**, **17,294**, **17,312**, **17,316**, **17,320**, **17,325**, **17,331**, **17,332**, **17,350**, **17,401**, **17,498**, 17,868, **17,991**
Painters, Afro-American, **3,304**
Painters, Italian, **2,276**
Painters, Jewish, 15,950
Painters, Native American, 11,213, **17,312**
Painting, study and teaching, 11,834
Paintings, 248, 2,736, 2,846, 13,606
  attribution, 12,192
  exhibitions, **17,312**
Paintings, Native American, 11,213
Paisano, Marie, 16,868
Paisley, Marjorie (Flaherty), 10,216
Paiute Indians, 965, 10,713, 11,220, 11,227, 16,486, **16,870**
  legends, 16,870
  medicine, 16,870
  names, 16,870
  relation with whites, 16,870
  social life and customs, 1,243
Pakistan,
  missionaries to, 8,199
  monasteries, 998
Palace Hotel (CA), 1,334
Palaces, 4,393, 6,912
Paladin, Vivian, 10,326
Pa'lante (periodical), **12,064**
Paleobotanists, **6,644**, **14,005**
Paleontologists, **6,320**, **11,262**, 12,276, **14,903**, 15,956
Paleontology, 310, 451, 6,916
Palestine, 2,177, 2,359, 5,720, 8,963, 9,218, 13,801, 14,995, 15,163
  emigration and immigration, 11,915
  history (1917-1948), 3,335
  medical care, 12,117
  missionaries to, 1,652
  occupational training, 13,816
  teachers, 13,799
  vocational education, 12,118
  World War I, civilians work, 6,920, 9,467
  youth movement, 11,915
"Palette of Plants and Its Use" (ms), 4,393
Paley, Dorothy H. [Mrs.], 12,708
Paley, Goldie, 4,053
Palfrey Family, **2,441**

Palfrey, John, 2,441
Palfrey, Susan (?-1834). *See* Lee, Susan (Palfrey) [Mrs. William] (?-1834)
Pallas Club (Athens, OH), **13,751**
Palmer, 3,112
Palmer, A. Mitchell, 7,205
Palmer, Ada, **16,548**
Palmer, Alice Elvira (Freeman) [Mrs. George Herbert] (1855-1902), 6,430, 6,923, **7,572**, 7,574, 7,585, 11,605, 17,010
Palmer, Alice Webber (1890-?). *See* Morris, Alice Webber (Palmer) [Mrs. Raymond] (1890-?)
Palmer, Anna (ca. 1845-1914). *See* Draper, Anna (Palmer) [Mrs. Henry] (ca. 1845-1914)
Palmer, Anna Eliza (Ena) (1848-84). *See* McClary, Anna Eliza (Ena) Palmer Raymonde Ballantine (1848-84)
Palmer, Ardella Hardin [Mrs. W. L. C.], 10,085
Palmer, B. J., 4,710
Palmer, Bertha Honoré [Mrs Potter] (1849-1918), 2,739, **2,922**, 3,816, 3,819, 3,820, 3,880, 3,893, 3,912, 3,923, 4,684
Palmer, Bertha Rachel [Miss], **13,658**
Palmer, Carolyn Hunton, **3,710**
Palmer, Charlotte. *See* Moore, Charlotte (Palmer) [Mrs. R. F.]
Palmer College (IA), 4,710
Palmer, Elizabeth (Hunt), 17,037
Palmer, Elizabeth L. [Mrs.], 2,327
Palmer, Ellen, 3,228
Palmer, Emily (Bancroft). *See* Pierce, Emily (Bancroft) Palmer
Palmer, Etta Sessums [Mrs.], **9,638**
Palmer Family (TN), 13,084
Palmer Family (WI), **17,877**
Palmer Field, 7,831
Palmer, Francis L., 9,009
Palmer, Harriet "Hattie" C. (1854-ca. 1893), **17,878**
Palmer, Harriet Scott, 14,628
Palmer, Hattie Amelia, **15,668**
Palmer, Herbert E., 16,165
Palmer, Jean, 2,710
Palmer, Joanna MacHarg, 1,751
Palmer, John M., 4,351
Palmer, John Williamson, 2,164
Palmer, Laura, 9,025
Palmer, Mabel (Heath) [Mrs. B. J.] (1885-1949), **4,710**
Palmer, Maria Louise (ca. 1830-?). *See* Thomas, Maria Louise (Palmer) [Mrs. Abel Charles] (ca. 1830-?)
Palmer, Mary, 14,515
Palmer, Mary Hunt (1775-1866). *See* Tyler, Mary Hunt (Palmer) [Mrs. Royall] (1775-1866)
Palmer, Maud Alice (1869-1951), **11,670**
Palmer Memorial Institute (NC), 5,459, 6,430
Palmer, Mrs. Edward M., 5,469
Palmer, Mrs. Rodman, 17,877
Palmer, Nannie (1857-1950). *See* Snelling, Nannie (Palmer) [Mrs. William Amos] (1857-1950)
Palmer-Owen bill, 9,263
Palmer, Phoebe (Worrall) [Mrs. Walter Clark] (1807-74), **2,518, 10,911**
Palmer, Potter (1826-1902), 2,922, **3,893**
Palmer, Queen (Mellen) [Mrs. William Jackson], 1,790
Palmer raids, 8,144
Palmer, Raymond S., 10,729
Palmer, Rodman, 17,877
Palmer, Sarah Cornelia (1844-?), **11,671**
Palmer, Sophia French (1853-1920), 6,141
Palmer, Strange N., 2,606
Palmer, Thomas Witherell, 5,334
Palmer, William Jackson, 1,790
Palmer, Zoella. *See* Benson, Zoella (Palmer) [Mrs. Lamont]
Palmes Family (GA), **3,562**
Palmes, Mary [Miss], 3,562
Palmes, Mrs., 3,567
Palmetto Association (SC), 15,634
Palmetto Leaves (book), 1,953
Palmour, Mrs. Oscar, 3,384
PALMS (periodical), 16,169
Palmtag, Mary Gorman (1908-), **14,374**

Palonis, Estelle, 1,623
Paltsits, Victor Hugo (1867-1952), 5,951
Pambrun, Maria, 17,213
Pamphlet Shop (IL), 4,067
Pan-African Conference (London, England), 2,130
Pan American Assembly, 4,120
Pan American Association (PA), 15,216
Pan-American Congress, Women's Auxiliary Conference, **2,519**
Pan American Exposition (Buffalo, NY, 1901), 11,353, 13,999
Pan American Exposition (Buffalo, NY, 1901), Newark Educational Exhibit, 11,118
Pan-American societies, 4,120
Pan-American treaties and conventions, 17,654
Pan-American Treaties of Arbitration, 17,654
Pan-Americanism, 1,604
Pan Pacific and Southeast Asia Women's Association, **2,078, 6,380, 7,275, 7,290**
Pan Pacific Conference (1947), 4,918
Pan-Pacific relations, 2,078, 6,380
Pan Pipes (periodical), 8,612
Pan Republic Congress, 2,000
Panama, 438
Panama Canal, 359, 1,666, 11,466, 12,588
Panama Mail Steamship Company, 902
Panama Pacific International Exposition (CA, 1915), 761, 1,593, 17,616
Panama Railroad Company, 12,588
Panchuck, John (1904-), **9,508**
Pancoast, Lucy A., 2,195
Pandit, Vijaya Lakshmi, 4,030
Panhellenic Association, 17,354
Pankhurst, Adela, 15,307
Pankhurst, Christabel, 9,147, 16,166
Pankhurst, Emmeline Gouden (1858-1928), 2,413, 4,240, 7,222, 14,737, 16,166
Pankhurst, Estelle Sylvia (1882-1960), **4,236**, 5,870, 7,222
Pankhurst, Sylvia (1882-1960). *See* Pankhurst, Estelle Sylvia (1882-1960)
Pankonin, Minnie Schwanke (1875-?), 8,518
Pannell, Anne Gary, 117
Panoplist, The (periodical), 5,234
Pantell, Kate, 11,881
Panton Family, 12,460
Panton, Margaret Wolfe. *See* Duyckinck, Margaret Wolfe (Panton) [Mrs. Evert Augustus]
Paolone, Clementine J., 6,223
Pap test, 4,698
Papa, Nancy, 1,534
Papa Wore No Halo (book), 13,288
Papago Indians, 1,779, 2,840, 3,671
Pape, Nina Anderson, 3,523, **3,563**
Papendreau, Margaret Chant, 4,197
Paper dolls, 8,492
Paper, Lillian Davidson [Mrs. Joseph], 8,983
Paper making and trade, 7,510, **9,433**
Paper, Nina Anderson, 12,095
Papers of the United Church on the Green (CT), 1,998
Paport, Sarah A., 3,481
Parachute Nurses (moving-picture), 13,762
Parachute troops, 1,203, 11,440, 12,010
Parachutists, 13,322
Parades, 1,387, 10,660, 16,320
Paradise (book), 7,138
Paradise Dam (MT), 10,328
"Paradise in the Bering Sea, A" (article), 14,501
Paraguay, American missionaries to, 5,198, **14,334**
Paramount Pictures, 14,366
Parazak, Mary, 9,512
Parcells, Alethea (Crawford) (?-1909). *See* Cox, Alethea (Crawford) Parcells (?-1909)
Pardee, Ariovistus, **14,776**
Pardee, George Cooper (1857-1941), **707**
Pardee, Helen N. (Penniman) [Mrs. George Cooper] (?-1945), 707
Pardon, **9,470**, 13,378, 15,545, 17,086
Pardon My Sarong, 3,773
Parent and child, 2,069, 4,150, 8,639, 8,962, 9,934, 12,738, 17,991
Parent and Child, Native American, 16,876
Parent, George W., 1,196

Parent, Katherine Augusta Westcott [Mrs. Richard Henry] Cook [Mrs. George W.] (1847-1929). *See* Tingley, Katherine Augusta Westcott [Mrs. Richard Henry] Cook [Mrs. George W.] Parent [Mrs. Philo Buchanan] (1847-1929)
Parent, Madeleine, 3,450
Parenthood in a Free Nation (program), 4,115
Parenting, 8,639
Parents (periodical), 6,730, 10,894
Parents' and Teachers' Association, 116, 539, **979**, 1,688, **3,704**, 4,211, 4,299, 7,973, 10,108, 10,137, 13,221, 13,618, 13,870, 14,135, 15,884, 17,973
Parents' and Teachers' Association (IL), 3,785
Parents' and Teachers' Association (Mendota Township, MN), **9,458**
Parents' and Teachers Association (Sparks, NV), 10,689
Parents and Teachers' Association (OR), 14,551
Parents' and Teachers' Association (Russelville, OR), **14,631**
Parents' and Teachers' Association Council, 14,232
Parents' and teachers' associations, 1,304, **1,615**, 1,925, **3,493, 3,695**, 3,704, **4,133**, 4,299, **4,805, 5,105, 5,889**, 6,355, 6,854, 6,926, **8,917, 9,223**, 9,287, 9,385, **9,458**, 10,551, 10,905, **11,146, 13,247, 14,631, 14,658, 15,344**, 17,267, 17,314, 17,318, 17,372, **17,476**, 17,973
"Parents Ask" (column), 2,168
Parents' associations, 11,864
Parera, Valentin, 15,874
Parham, Catherine [Miss] (1901-), **13,280**
Parham, Mollie A., **13,084**
Paris, Dorothy [Miss] (1902-), **2,793**
Paris Exhibition (1906), 4,277
Paris Exposition (1876), 1,790
Paris Exposition (1900-1901), 13,999
Paris, Madame Gaston, 9,425
Paris Opera Ballet, 14,239
Paris Peace Conference (1919), 1,557, 2,186, 2,389
Pariseau, Esther (1823-1902). *See* Mother Joseph (1823-1902)
Parish of St. Stephens (Pineville, SC), 15,465
Parish, Susan Ludlow, 11,499
Parish, Susan (Thompson), 1,505
Parish Visitors of Mary Immaculate, 10,611
Parisi, Angela R. [Mrs. Leo Louison] (1914-61), **6,819**
Park, Agnes (Major) [Mrs. John], 7,660
Park, Agnes (Morrison) [Mrs. Charles Richardson] (1893-), Family (MN), **9,277**
Park, Alice [Mrs.], **1,596**
Park, Alice (Locke) (1861-1961), 1,427, **1,473, 1,561**
Park, Anna Canfield. *See* Gilman, Anna Canfield (Park) [Mrs. Winthrop S., Jr.]
Park, Caroline E. [Mrs. Charles F.]. *See* Mulligan, Caroline E. [Mrs. Charles F.] Park [Mrs. William]
Park, Caroline Hoskins. *See* Strong, Caroline Hoskins (Park) [Mrs. Charles K. W.]
Park College (Kansas City, MO), 5,230
students, 13,241
Park County Poultry Producers Association (MT), **10,259**
Park, Cynthia (Pratt) [Mrs. Luther], 17,044
Park, Eliza "Lizzie" Hall (1848-1938). *See* McCullough, Eliza "Lizzie" Hall (Park) [Mrs. John Griffin] (1848-1938)
Park Family (MA), **7,660**
Park Family (VT), **17,044**
Park, Guy Brasfield (1872-1946), **10,032**
Park, Helen Van Cleave (1889-), 1,068
Park Improvement Committee (San Diego, CA), 9,466
Park, John Cochran (1804-?), 7,660
Park, Laura van der Spiegel Hall [Mrs. Trenor] (1828-75), 17,044
Park, Louisa (Adams) [Mrs. John] (1773-1813), 7,660
Park, Louisa Jane (1802-92). *See* Hall, Louisa Jane (Park) (1802-92)
Park, Luther, 17,044
Park, Marion Edwards, 14,737
Park, Mary, 11,318
Park, Mary Ann (1811-?). *See* Thomas, Mary Ann (Park) (1811-?)
Park, Maud (Wood) [Mrs. Charles Edward]. [Mrs.

Robert] Hunter (1871-1955), 2,209, 2,256, 2,501, 5,120, 5,121, 6,406, 6,966, 6,967, 6,978, **6,981**, 7,205, 10,200, 15,706, 16,252

Park, Maybelle M. (1871-1946), **17,879**

Park, Trenor, 17,044

Parke Family (PA), 15,104

Parker, Achsa Snow, 369

Parker, Alice (1848-1924). *See* Isom, Alice (Parker) [Mrs. George] (1848-1924)

Parker, Amos Andrew, 1,877

Parker, Anna [Miss], 12,234

Parker, Anna Fenn. *See* Pruyn, Anna Fenn (Parker)

Parker, Armeda Jane, 14,628

Parker, Aunt Harriet, 13,322

Parker, Colonel, 1,786

Parker, Cornelia E. (1837-?). *See* Read, Cornelia E. (Parker) (1837-?)

Parker, Cornelia (Stratton) [Mrs. Carleton Hubbell] (1885-1972), **709**, 823

Parker, Cynthia, 16,064

Parker, Dawn (Flanery) [Mrs. H. Leslie], 5,313

Parker, Dorothy Rothschild (1893-1967), 949, 1,025, 3,303, 4,970, 11,810, 11,907, 11,946

Parker, Edith DeBlois Laskey, 7,090

Parker, Emily (1904?-78). *See* Simon, Emily (Parker) [Mrs. Albert] (1904?-78)

Parker Family, 4,942, 8,966, 10,862, 11,599

Parker, Florence, 8,666

Parker, Francis Wayland, 3,842

Parker Genealogical Society (PA), 15,328

Parker, George S., 13,155

Parker, Geraldine, 10,055

Parker, Harriet, 15,540

Parker, Harriet. *See* Campbell, Harriet (Parker) [Mrs. John]

Parker, Henry Middleton, Jr. (1854-1926), **15,669**

Parker, Isaac B., 11,001

Parker, Jamieson, 14,556

Parker, Judge, 14,206

Parker, Julia Evelina (Smith) [Mrs. Amos Andrew] (1792-1886), **1,877**, 1,979, **6,256**

Parker, Katherine H. [Mrs. George W.], **12,065**

Parker, Leonard Fletcher (1825-1911), **4,940**

Parker, Lillian Frances. *See* Wallace, Lillian Frances (Parker)

Parker, Lucy. *See* Huber, Lucy (Parker) [Mrs. G. Carl]

Parker, Lydia Dodge Cabot [Mrs. Theodore], **6,820**

Parker, Maria H., 7,069

Parker, Marianna Rhett, 15,669

Parker, Mary Ann (Coit) [Mrs. Willard], **12,279**

Parker, Mary Brent, 1,786

Parker, Mary Elizabeth (1839-70). *See* Garfield, Mary Elizabeth (Parker) [Mrs. John P.] (1839-70)

Parker, Mary (Grubb) (1816-1900), 15,014

Parker, Minerva (1861-1949). *See* Nichols, Minerva (Parker) (1861-1949)

Parker, Minnie B., **13,281**

Parker, Minnie Lee (Beach) [Mrs. Joseph C.], 9,589

Parker, Nellie B., **3,711**

Parker, Rhoda. *See* Smith, Rhoda (Parker)

Parker, Sarah (Pearse) [Mrs. Leonard Fletcher], 4,940

Parker, Theodore (1810-60), 6,820, 7,233, 12,419

Parker, Warren D., 8,944

Parker, Willard, 12,279

Parkey, Edith, 13,864

Parkhurst, Almira, 11,083

Parkhurst, Emelie Tracy Y., 342

Parkhurst, Helen (1887-1973), 8,064, **17,870**

Parkhurst, Minnie. [Mrs. Ed Rimer] (?-1971), **17,319**

Parkin Family, **12,676**

Parkinson, Samuel, 16,780

Parkinson, Susanna Smart (1881-). *See* Nielson, Susanna Smart (Parkinson) (1881-)

Parkman, Ebenezer (1703-82), 7,661

Parkman Family (MA), **7,661**

Parkman, Francis, 4,172, 5,414, 13,919

Parks, 473, 990, 1,385, 1,526, 1,544, 1,682, 1,817, 1,837, 2,886, 3,130, 3,276, 3,722, 3,753, 3,875, 4,114, **5,307**, 5,443, 8,205, 8,360, 8,460, 9,974, 10,638, 10,726, 11,064, **12,347**, 13,649, 14,819, **14,935**, 16,485, **18,025**, **18,026**

Parks, Dolly Sumner (Lunt) [Mrs. Samuel Harding]

Lewis [Mrs. Thomas] Burge [Mrs. William Justice] (1817-91), 3,313

Parks, Edith Beam [Mrs. John Allen], 978

Parks Family (GA), 3,313

Parks, Lucia (Darling) (1839-1905), **10,260**

Parks, Rosa Lee (McCauley) (1913-), 64, 84, 6,547, **8,117**, 11,855

Parkway Community House (Chicago, IL), **3,894**

Parkway Nursery School (Levittown, NY), **12,878**

Parler, Mary Celestia, 253

Parliamentary law, 7,082

Parliamentary practice, 54, 7,784, 8,025, **8,179**, 14,641

Parmelee, Ruth A., 6,697

Parmenter, Catherine (1905-), 1,750

Parmenter, Christine (Whiting) [Mrs. Kenneth R.] (1877-), 1,750

Parmenter Family (OR), 14,536

Parmenter, Harriet May (1867-1955), **5,716**

Parmerly, Caroline (?-1918). *See* Herrick, Caroline (Parmerly) [Mrs. Myron T.] (?-1918)

Parminter Nellie Mabel (1873-1969). *See* Wetmore, Nellie Mabel (Parminter) [Mrs. Edward M.] (1873-1969)

Parnell, Delia Tudor (Stewart) (?-1898), 3,533

Parochial schools. *See* Church schools

Parole, 1,503, 6,720

Parr, Charles D., **3,069**

Parratt, Edna Martin, 10,681

Parrin, Margaret Perren. *See* Pucell, Margaret Perren (Parrin)

Parrington, Ruth, **6,821**

Parriott, Foster B., 11,833

Parris, Guichard Auguste Bolivar (1903-), **12,066**

Parrish, Anne (1760-1800), 11,144

Parrish, Anne [Miss] (1888-1954?), **2,051**

Parrish, Celestia Susannah (1853-1918), 3,364

Parrish, Ella (Knox) (1868-1964), **3,712**

Parrish, Emily E. (1849-?), **17,202**

Parrish Family (PA), **14,981**

Parrish, Helen (1859-1942), 15,205

Parrish, J. L., 14,566

Parrish, Joseph (1779-1840), 14,981

Parrish, Mary (Pratt) (1908-), 16,780

Parrish, Mrs. Maxfield, 3,071

Parrish, Susannah (Cox) (1788-1851) [Mrs. Joseph], 14,981

Parrish v. the Civil Service Commission (CA), 393

Parrott Family (NH), **10,822**

Parrott, Irma, 15,542

Parrott, John Fabyan, 10,822

Parrott, Katherine Ursula (1902-), 14,431

Parrott, Sarah (?-1886), 10,822

Parry, Armenia, 16,453

Parry, Caroline Keturah (1885-1967). *See* Woolley, Caroline Keturah (Parry) [Mrs. LeGrande] (1885-1967)

Parry Center for Children (OR), 14,551

Parry, John, 16,448

Parry, Mary. *See* Sword, Mary (Parry)

Parsley, Eliza Hall (Nutt) [Mrs. William Murdoch], **13,085**

Parsley, William Murdoch (1840-65), 13,085

Parson, Lillian (1896-), **8,707**

Parsonages, 8,751, 8,752

Parsons, Alice (Beal) [Mrs. Hugh Graham] (1886-1962), **12,906**

Parsons, Alzina (1849-1900). *See* Stevens, Alzina (Parsons) (1849-1900)

Parsons, Anna Quincy (Thaxter), 4,434, 7,043, 7,355, 17,010

Parsons, Anna Reed [Mrs. William B.] (18??-1958), **12,581**

Parsons, Anne A. Spaulding [Mrs. Elijah Chauncey], 7,152

Parsons, Caroline C. *See* Warren, Caroline C. Parsons [Mrs. Waters]

Parsons, Edward Taylor, 710

Parsons, Edwin, J., **3,564**

Parsons, Elijah Chauncey, 7,152

Parsons, Elsie (1903-66). *See* Kennedy, Elsie (Parsons) (1903-66)

Parsons, Elsie (Clews) [Mrs. Herbert] (1875-1941), 6,746, 11,882, **12,067**, **14,897**

Parsons, Emma, 13,949

Parsons Family (CA), **710**

Parsons Family (NY), **12,280**

Parsons Family (OH), **13,949**

Parson's Female Seminary (TX), 16,055

Parsons, Gertrude, 12,280

Parsons, Herbert, 5,010

Parsons, John E. (1849 or 1850-93), 12,280

Parsons, Josiah, Family (MA), **7,152**

Parsons, Louella Rose (Oettinger) (1893-1972), 698, 702, 11,907

Parsons, Lucena Pfuffer, **1,597**

Parsons, Lucretia West [Mrs.], **13,525**

Parsons, Lucy (Gathings) [Mrs. Albert] (1851 or 1853-1942), 4,145, 4,161

Parsons, Margaret, **7,415**

Parsons, Marion Geneth (1871-1968), 6,128, **6,152**

Parsons, Marion (Randall) [Mrs. Edward Taylor] (1878-1953), 710

Parsons, Mary (1864-1940), 12,280

Parsons, Mary Collins, 14,628

Parsons, Mildred F. [Mrs.], **205**

Parsons, Mrs. Ivan, 7,151

Parsons, Myrta, 13,949

Parsons School of Design, alumnae, 1,678

Parsons, Thomas W., 7,690

Part Taken by Women in American History, The (book), 2,454

Parten, Carroll (Borland), **711**

Partheneia, The (CA), **921**

"Parting, The" (story), 12,644

Partington, Blanche [Miss] (?-1951), **712**

Partington, Gertrude, 712

Partington, John Herbert Evelyn, 712

Partington, Phyllis, 712

Partisi, Milli, 1,556

Partners of the Alliance for Progress, 4,120

Partners: The United Nations and Youth (book), 11,485

Parton, James (1912-), **6,201**

Parton, Sara Payson (Willis) [Mrs. Charles H.] Eldredge [Mrs. Samuel P.] Farrington [Mrs. James] (1811-72), 5,694, **7,276**

Partridge, Charles P., **4,818**

Partridge, Charlotte (1881-1975), **17,846**

Partridge, Eliza Maria (1820-86). *See* Lyman, Eliza Maria (Partridge) [Mrs. Joseph] Smith [Mrs. Amasa Mason] (1820-86)

Partridge, Lucy, **4,818**

Partridge, Roi, 425

Partridge, Sophia [Miss], **13,526**

Party affiliation, 9,154

Party committees, **6,342**, 7,810, 7,883, 9,239, 9,984, 10,069, **10,077**, 10,078, 10,752, 17,749

Party Organizer (periodical), 17,635

Parvin, E. P., 11,325

Parvin, Elizabeth, 11,325

Parvin, Theodore Sutton, 4,696

Pasadena Study Club (CA), **1,107**

Paschall, Eliza K., **3,343**

Paschall Family (PA), **15,064**

Paschall, Mary Frances, 15,064

Paschall, Sarah [Miss], **15,065**

Paschen, Henry, 14,239

Pascoe, Mary Elizabeth (1855-1936), **2857**

Passage to India (book), 6,071

Passavant, Anna E. (1868-1960). *See* Meili, Anna E. (Passavant) [Mrs. J. Edward] (1868-1960)

Passavant, Charles, 9,304

Passavant Debutante Cotillion (Chicago, IL), 4,018

Passavant Memorial Hospital Woman's Board (Chicago, IL), **4,018**, 4,021

Passenger Pigeon in New England, The (book), 7,487

Passes (transportation) 2,557, 5,060, 7,055, 9,912

Passion-plays, 3,762

Passions of Uxport, The (book), 6,042

Passive resistance, 2,143, 12,715

Passmore, Elizabeth, 15,343

Passmore, J., 15,279

Past Made Present, A History of Beloit, 1830-1900 (book), 1,349

Past Presidents Club (ND), 13,696

Past Presidents Club (IA), 4,748

Pastel drawing, 7,601

"Pastoral Warriors in Uganda" (speech), 6,992
Patagonia, missionaries to, **12,185**
Patapsco Female Institute (Ellicott City, MD), 5,827, 9,812
Patch, Anna, 7,150
Patch, Edith Marion (1876-1954), **5,633**
Patchen, Kenneth, 12,894
Patchen, Miriam [Mrs. Kenneth], 4,233
Patchin, Elizabeth, [Mrs.], **8,285**
Patchogue Advance (NY), 11,791
Pate, Burwell S., **13,527**
Patee, Doris, 14,352
Patenotre, Jacqueline T., 2,205
Patent Board, 6,919
Patent medicines. *See* Medicines, patent, proprietary, etc. etc.
Patent suits, 11,121
Patents, 194, 9,288, 16,372
Paternity, 8,657
Paterson. *See also* Patterson
Paterson, David, 7,667
Paterson, Dorothy, 15,332
Paterson General Hospital (NJ), **11,149**
Paterson General Hospital Association (NJ), 11,149
Paterson, Isabel (Bowler) (1886-1961), **12,582**
Paterson, Jane E., 12,161
Patha, Darlene Camille, **17,320**
Pathbreaking (book), 14,703
Pathfinder Fund, 6,788
Pathologists, **2,088**, **6,216**, **10,208**, **10,209**, 14,889
Pathology, 7,259, **10,208**
Patience Worth cult (MO), 9,841
Patience Worth Publishing Company, 10,184
Patno, Mary Ellen, 1,751
Patofsky, Jacob, 7,300
Patrick Air Force Base, 2,872
Patrick, Mary A. (Dwight) [Mrs. Matthew], **1,862**
Patrick, Mary Mills (1850-1940), **1,562**
Patrick, Mrs. Edward Thomas, **10,696**
Patrick, Ruth, 4,197
Patriot Review, The (periodical), 6,608
Patriotic literature, 6,608
Patriotic Potato, The (drama), 4,727
Patriotic societies, 40, 145, **279**, **280**, **432**, 1,078, **1,201**, **1,276**, 1,293, 1,423, 1,444, **1,765**, **1,899**, 1,905, 1,907, **1,934**, 1,969, 2,000, **2,123**, 2,193, 2,206, **2,294**, **2,307**, **2,615**, 2,689, **2,896**, 3,169, **3,175**, **3,212**, **3,213**, **3,214**, 3,219, 3,274, 3,358, 3,415, 3,439, 3,465, **3,673**, **3,674**, **3,699**, 3,736, **3,737**, **3,850**, 4,539, 4,689, **4,745**, **4,787**, 4,839, **4,862**, **4,891**, 5,176, 5,308, 5,326, **5,338**, **5,368**, **5,597**, **5,600**, **5,818**, 5,850, **5,882**, **5,946**, **5,975**, **6,354**, 6,355, 6,365, 6,368, 6,901, 6,965, 7,669, 7,704, **7,860**, 8,028, **8,271**, 8,301, **8,319**, **8,320**, 8,337, 8,340, **8,419**, 8,436, **8,453**, **8,820**, 8,835, **8,907**, **9,167**, **9,258**, **9,337**, 9,385, **9,409**, 9,596, **9,608**, **9,616**, 9,617, 9,622, 9,638, 9,647, 9,692, 9,697, 9,706, 9,719, 9,731, 9,779, 9,870, 9,918, 9,962, 10,032, **10,109**, **10,136**, **10,408**, **10,414**, **10,426**, 10,463, **10,547**, **10,560**, 10,625, 10,697, **10,786**, 10,889, 11,092, 11,132, **11,317**, **11,409**, **11,438**, 11,445, 11,555, **12,119**, **12,120**, **12,121**, **12,189**, **12,776**, 12,940, 13,070, 13,085, **13,315**, **13,316**, 13,337, 13,365, **13,372**, **13,375**, **13,379**, 13,388, 13,393, **13,394**, 13,395, 13,439, 13,446, 13,459, 13,556, 13,571, 13,576, **13,580**, 13,595, 13,618, 13,661, 13,696, **14,045**, **14,053**, 14,230, **14,376**, **14,481**, **14,492**, 14,822, **14,986**, **15,342**, 15,439, 15,596, 15,755, 15,865, 15,942, **15,947**, 15,951, 16,014, **16,030**, **16,178**, **16,296**, **16,298**, **16,299**, **17,057**, **17,112**, **17,149**, **17,156**, 17,293, **17,392**, **17,639**, 17,685, **17,751**, **17,755**, 17,830, **17,833**, **17,962**
Patriotism, 1,501, 9,311, 13,451, 13,920
Patriots, **15,084**, 15,783, 17,121
Patrons of Husbandry, 3,756, 7,740, 8,340, **8,401**, 8,452, 8,937, **11,437**, 14,004, 15,596, 17,304
Patrons of Husbandry (MN), Grange Number Four Hundred Eighty-two, **8,401**
Patrons of Husbandry (MN), Pomona Grange Number Twelve, **9,278**
"Patsy the Pioneer," 9,842
Pattee, Dora (Jewett) [Mrs. Edward Sidney] (1853-1939), 9,279

Pattee, Edward Sidney, Family (MN), **9,279**
Patten, Catherine Lane (1845-1914). *See* Dunwoody, Catherine Lane (Patten) [Mrs. William Hood]
Patten, Eliza. *See* Hodge, Eliza (Patten) Davis [Mrs. Benjamin]
Patten, John William (1851-?), 9,055
Pattern (book), 11,994
Patterson. *See also* Paterson
Patterson, Ambrose, 17,321
Patterson, Barbara Ann (1938-), **7,886**
Patterson, Bertha A., 3,794
Patterson, Clara. *See* Todd, Clara (Patterson)
Patterson, Edna B., 16,870, 16,872
Patterson, Eliza, 2,208
Patterson, Elizabeth (1785-1879). *See* Bonaparte, Elizabeth (Patterson) [Mrs. Jerome] (1785-1879)
Patterson Family (NC), **13,528**
Patterson, F. D., 15,377
Patterson Field, 9,137
Patterson, Frances. *See* Lee, Frances (Patterson)
Patterson, Frances Todd, **7,887**
Patterson, Hannah June (1879-1937), 2,679
Patterson, Harriet-Louise H., 13,890
Patterson, Helen H., 14,898
Patterson, Ida (1866-1944), **14,297**
Patterson, Ida S., 10,401
Patterson, J. T., 6,827
Patterson, Joan, 14,278
Patterson, Katherine A. (Grafton) [Mrs. Thomas M.] (1839-1902), 1,673
Patterson, Laura A. (Hawn), **14,632**
Patterson, Louisa, 14,898
Patterson, Louise S., 12,740
Patterson, Margaret. *See* Campbell, Margaret (Patterson)
Patterson, Marguerite [Mrs. W. L.], 8,454, **8,458**
Patterson, Mary (Fries) [Mrs. Rufus Lenoir] (1844-1927), **13,086**, 13,528
Patterson, Nan, 5,505
Patterson, Phoebe, 7,948
Patterson, Rebecca Elizabeth Coy (1911-75), **5,211**
Patterson, Robert A., **13,529**
Patterson, Rufus Lenoir (1830-79), 13,086, 13,528
Patterson, Sam, 13,528
Patterson, Thomas Leiper (1816-1905), **14,898**
Patterson, Thomas M., Family (CO), **1,673**
Patterson, Viola [Mrs. Ambrose], **17,321**
Patterson, W. L., 8,458
Patterson, William, 10,372
Patti, Adelina. [Marquesa de Caux] [Mrs. Ernest] Nicolini [Baroness Rolf] Cederstrom (1843-1919), 3,367, 10,651, 16,150, 17,197
Pattison, Mrs. Frank, 10,932
Pattison, Sallie. *See* Van Sellar, Sallie (Pattison) [Mrs. Henry]
Patton, Annaleone Davis [Mrs.], **713**
Patton, Arrilla, **10,697**
Patton, Delia Annie (Spann) (?-1910), 13,142
Patton, Family (WA), **17,390**
Patton, Francis "Frank" M. (Cook) [Mrs. Thomas McFadden], 14,634
Patton, Grace Espy, 1,814
Patton, Harald Smith, 8,164
Patton Home (OR), **14,633**
Patton, John, 6,500
Patton, Laura [Miss], **9,698**
Patton, Marguerite Irene Taylor [Mrs. Harald Smith], 8,164
Patton, Mary (McKeehan) [Mrs. John] (1751-1836), **15,978**
Patton, Nellie Davis, 1,751
Patton, Sarah (Soule) [Mrs. John G.] McMillan [Mrs. Henry W.], 17,390
Patton, Thomas McFadden (1829-?), **14,634**
Pattridge, Major J. C., 2,623
Patty, Martha. *See* Comfort, Martha (Patty)
Patty Smith Hill Farm, 5,346
Patzig, Cynthia, **14,163**
Paul A. Schmitt Music Company (Minneapolis, MN), 9,348
Paul, Alice (1885-1977), 540, 656, **714**, 827, 859, 860, 2,356, 2,413, 2,499, 2,508, 3,313, 3,681, 6,742, 6,807, 6,858, 7,803, 7,923, 11,123, **11,904**, 12,575, 12,597

Paul Bunyan (book), 17,336
Paul Bunyan legends, 11,863
Paul, Caroline L., 18,026
Paul, Emma V., **3,240**
Paul, George H., 16,130
Paul, Helen M. G., **9,280**
Paul, Mary I. *See* Cadwallader, Mary I. (Paul) [Mrs. Sylvanus]
Paul, Mary Lou (Francis), 5,657
Paul, Susan. *See* Vashon, Susan (Paul)
Paulding, Grace (Bunce) [Mrs. William], 14,777
Paulding, James Kirk, 15,722
Paulding, William, **14,777**
Pauley, Frances (1905-), 13,176
Pauling, Linus, 7,328
Paull, Irene [Mrs. Henry], 8,949
Paulson, Evelina Belden [Mrs. Henry T.] (1885-1966), **4,141**
Paulsson, Bertha (1891-1973), **14,798**
Pavilion Ladies' Aid (MI), 8,243
Pavlova, Anna, 2,968, 3,100
Pavlovna, Marie, Grand Duchess, 12,497
Pawnbroker, The (moving-picture), 12,684
Pawnee Indians, 1,286, 10,514, 14,241
Pawwannee, Cuch, 16,876
Paxman, Alice Ann (1870-1972). *See* McCune, Alice Ann (Paxman) [Mrs. George] (1870-1972)
Paxman, Eva A., 16,889
Paxton, Mary (1886-). *See* Keeley, Mary (Paxton) [Mrs. Edmund Burke] (1886-)
Paxton, Mary Gentry, 10,086
Paxton, Nina Llyr Margaret, **13,301**
Payne, Blanche, 13,604, **17,322**
Payne, Dolley (1768-1849). *See* Madison, Dorothea "Dolley" (Payne) [Mrs. John, Jr.] Todd [Mrs. James] (1768-1849)
Payne, Elizabeth Stanley, 13,447
Payne, Eloise Richards (1787-1819), 12,060
(Payne)-Gaposchkin, Cecilia (1900-), 6,285, 11,815
Payne, Harriet L., 13,604
Payne, Hazel (Dixon), 3,301
Payne, John, 13,121
Payne, John Howard, 3,024, **12,068**
Payne, John Howard (1791-1852), **12,583**
Payne, Kezia, 16,176
Payne, Lucile V., 14,460
Payne, Lucretia [Mrs. Stephen], 1,750
Payne, Martha (Williford) [Mrs. John], 13,121
Payne, Mary (Starling) [Mrs. William Richardson] (1832-96), 5,268
Payne, Moses U. (1807-95), **10,033**
Payne, Nellie Maria de Cottrell (1900-), 8,555
Payne, Ninetta Eames, 559, 16,470
Payne, Robert, 16,153
Payne, Rosana C., 9,396
Payne, Rose, 1,553
Payne, Ruth. *See* Flowers, Ruth (Payne)
Payne, Stephen, 1,750
Payne, Theodora, 1,553
Payne, Virgil, 8,647
Payne, William Richardson, 5,268
Payrolls, 6,187, 6,195, 6,198, 6,202, 6,207
Payson, Elizabeth (1818-78). *See* Prentiss, Elizabeth (Payson) [Mrs. George Lewis] (1818-78)
Payson, Elizabeth Phillips, **6,822**
Payton, Viola, 1,532
Pea, Sarah Dearmon (1814-93). *See* Rich, Sarah Dearmon (Pea) [Mrs. Charles Coulsen] (1814-93)
Peabody, Catherine Endicott (1808-83). *See* Gardner, Catherine Endicott (Peabody) (1808-83)
Peabody, Clarissa (Endicott) [Mrs. George] (1807-91), 7,475
Peabody Conservatory (MD), 12,796
Peabody, Edward T., 333
Peabody, Elizabeth Palmer (1804-94), 1,954, 2,315, 2,542, **5,950**, 6,659, **6,823**, 7,043, 7,277, 7,383, 7,390, **7,416**, 11,616, 11,742, 12,403, 14,165, 17,010, 17,037
Peabody, Elizabeth Preston, 6,738
Peabody, Elizabeth (Smith) [Mrs. John] Shaw [Mrs. Stephen] (1750-1815), 2,571, 7,662
Peabody Family (MA), **7,277**, **14,165**
Peabody, Gertrude (1894-), 15,183, 15,186, 15,189, 15,195

Peabody Hotel (TN), 9,537
Peabody Institute, 5,829
Peabody Institute (TN), 9,672
Peabody Institute Library (MA), 7,010
Peabody, Josephine Preston. [Mrs. Lionel Simon]
    Marks (1874-1922), 1,087, **6,824**, 7,171, 7,567
Peabody, Kate F. (Miller), 11,602
Peabody, Lucy Whitehead (McGill) [Mrs. Norman
    Mather] Waterbury [Mrs. Henry Wayland]
    (1861-1949), 5,121, 12,738
Peabody, Margaret (Tinkham), 7,677
Peabody, Maria Ignacia (Soberanes) [Mrs. Edward
    Turner] de Bale [Mrs. Edward T.], 333
Peabody, Mary S. C. (1817-?), **7,417**
Peabody, Mary Tyler (1806-87). See Mann, Mary
    Tyler (Peabody) [Mrs. Horace] (1806-87)
Peabody, Mrs. Malcom, 2,438
Peabody Museum (MA), 6,327
Peabody, Nancy Leonard (Smith) (1785-1856), 7,677
Peabody Report, 15,770
Peabody School (AR), 232
Peabody, Sophia Amelia (1809-71). See Hawthorne,
    Sophia Amelia (Peabody) (1809-71)
Peabody, Stephen (1741-1819), **7,662**
Peace, 509, 859, 1,563, 1,859, 2,058, 2,170, 2,244,
    2,424, 2,432, 2,538, 2,624, 3,712, 5,305, 5,979,
    6,359, 6,483, 6,534, 6,747, 7,190, 7,221, 7,247,
    7,290, 7,294, 7,298, 7,885, 8,149, 9,020, 9,386,
    11,331, 12,415, 12,507, 12,625, 12,724, 13,468,
    13,898, 14,637, 15,305, 15,31
Peace and Disarmament Committee of the Women's
    International Organizations, **15,310**
Peace and Freedom (periodical), 7,988
Peace College (NC), 13,391, 13,446, 13,460, 13,608,
    13,627
Peace Corps. See United States (government), Peace
    Corps
Peace Council, 14,691
Peace Institute (NC). See Peace Junior College
    (Raleigh, NC)
Peace Junior College (Raleigh, NC), 13,390, 13,436,
    13,447, 13,474
  faculty, 13,245
  students, 13,048
Peace movements, 4,243, 9,467, 16,337
Peace Now Movement, **12,584**
Peace societies, 124, 539, 656, 860, 1,017, 1,018,
    1,530, **1,557**, 1,559, 1,563, 1,577, 1,604, **1,680**,
    2,072, **2,073**, **2,077**, 2,256, 2,432, 3,074, **3,814**,
    4,050, 4,089, 4,143, **4,168**, 4,754, 5,068, **5,787**,
    6,355, 6,368, 6,379, 6,507, 6,538, 6,695, 6,846,
    6,966, 6,978, 7,172, 7,179, 7,190, 7,220, **7,269**,
    7,278, 7,290, 7,321, **7,323**, 7,723, 7,868, 7,923,
    7,988, 8,000, 8,009, **8,149**, 8,658, 8,963, 9,089,
    9,095, 9,119, 9,160, 9,197, 9,287, 9,302, 9,402,
    9,440, **9,456**, 9,467, 10,048, 10,193, **10,206**,
    10,681, 10,730, 10,940, 11,136, 11,299, **11,389**,
    11,616, 11,931, 12,042, 12,518, **12,523**, **12,584**,
    12,652, **12,677**, 12,715, 12,731, **12,883**, 13,439,
    14,393, 14,656, **14,691**, 15,121, **15,298**, 15,300,
    15,301, 15,302, 15,303, 15,304, 15,306, **15,308**,
    15,310, **15,313**, **15,316**, **15,317**, 17,244, 17,254,
    17,262, 17,610, 17,654, 17,691, 17,735, **17,753**,
    17,836, 17,868, 17,916, **17,939**
Peace societies, Chinese-American, 2,746
Peaceways Nonviolent Community (Battle Creek,
    MI), 8,009
Peachtree Papers (periodical), 3,209
Peachtree Park Garden Club (GA), 3,187
Peachy, Mary M., 17,127
Peacock, Cornelia Augusta (1809-79). See Connelly,
    Cornelia Augusta (Peacock) (1809-79)
Peacock, David Charles, 617
Peacock, Miriam Florence (Folline) [Mrs. David
    Charles] (1836-1914). See Leslie, Miriam
    Florence (Folline) [Mrs. David Charles] Peacock
    [Mrs. Ephraim George] Squier [Mrs. Frank]
    (1836-1914)
Peake, Julia Anne, 9,000
Peale, Charles Willson, 12,600
Peale Family (PA), 14,902
Peale, Mary Jane Patterson (1827-1902), **14,899**
Peale, Mrs. E., 12,411
Peale, Norman Vincent, 12,907

Peale, Ruth (Stafford) [Mrs. Norman Vincent]
    (1906-), 5,110, **12,907**
Pearce, Cheryl (1941-), 5,829
Pearce, Christopher Gardner (1811-82), **4,001**
Pearce Family, **7,279**
Pearce Family (IL), 4,197
Pearce, Gladys M. [Miss] (1893-1966), **13,682**
Pearce, Jane Ann (Sackett) [Mrs. Christopher
    Gardner], 4,001
Pearce, Jean Rio (1810-?), **16,906**
Pearce, Jennie Wheeler [Mrs.], 4,215
Pearce, Katharine Standish (1895-), 7,279
Pearce, May Penrose [Miss] (1855-1949), **16,782**
Pearce, Rebecca McClure (Brown) (1860-1911), 7,279
"Pearl Diver, The" (poem), 5,669
Pearl, Gertrude. See Wolfe, Gertrude (Pearl)
Pearl, Helen Z., 1,927
"Pearls" (song), 5,531
Pearmain, Nancy Douglas (Brush) [Mrs. William
    Robert] (1890-). See Bowditch, Nancy Douglas
    (Brush) [Mrs. William Robert] Pearmain (1890-)
Pearmain, William Robert, 2,737
Pearman Family (IL), **4,392**
Pearman, Ida. See Stevens, Ida (Pearman)
Pearman, Minnie, 4,392
Pearman, Myrtle. See Keene, Myrtle (Pearman)
Pearsall, Mary, **15,066**
Pearse, Carroll G. (1858-?), 10,491
Pearse, Sarah. See Parker, Sarah (Pearse) [Mrs.
    Leonard Fletcher]
Pearson, Adelaida Pelley, 14,686
Pearson, Alice (Lewis), 14,848
Pearson, Amanda Caroline Roscoe [Mrs. Philip
    Anderson], 15,964
Pearson, Drew, 15,303
Pearson, Elizabeth (Winsor), 6,354
Pearson, John C., 14,223
Pearson, Josephine Anderson (1868-1944), **15,964**
Pearson, Lola (Clark), **14,223**
Pearson, Philip Anderson, 15,964
Pearson, Priscilla (Holyoke) [Mrs. Eliphalet]
    (1739-82), **7,639**
Pearson, Sarah E., **16,783**
Pearsons, George R., 4,906
Pearsons, Louise (1866-1937). See Dolliver, Louise
    (Pearsons) [Mrs. Jonathan Prentiss] (1866-1937)
Peart, Caroline (1870-1963), **14,862**
Peary, Josephine (Diebitsch) [Mrs. Robert E.]
    (1863-1955), 5,694
Peary, Marie Stafford (?-1978). See Kuhne, Marie
    Stafford (Peary) [Mrs. William] (?-1978)
Peary, Robert E., 5,694
Pease, Arthur Stanley (1881-1964), **6,296**
Pease, Catherine [Mrs. Abraham] Christensen [Mrs.],
    8,994
Pease, Elisha Marshall, 16,016
Pease Family (IL), **4,436**
Pease Family (TX), **16,016**
Pease, Henrietta (Faxon) [Mrs. Arthur Stanley]
    (?-1951), 6,296
Pease, Julia Marie [Miss] (1853-1918), 16,016
Pease, Lovancia (1821-1912). See Lyman, Lovancia
    (Pease) [Mrs. Henry Martyn] (1821-1912)
Pease, Lucadia Niles [Mrs. Elisha Marshall]
    (1813-1905), 16,016
Pease, Marguerite Jenison, 4,445
Pease, Sally Taylor [Mrs. David], 7,145
Pease, Sarah. See Wilson, Sarah (Pease)
Pease, Sarah W., 17,884
Peatfield, Hannah M. (1837-?), **7,418**
Peattie, Donald Culross, 10,677
Peattie, Lisa R., 2,832
Peavey, A. J., Jr., 3,682
Peavey, Mary (Thomas) [Mrs. A. J., Jr.]. See Brooks,
    Mary (Thomas) [Mrs. A. J., Jr.] Peavey [Mrs.]
Pecan Workers' Union of San Antonio (TX), 16,009
Pechak, Lena, **9,509**
Peck, Abel G., 8,164
Peck, Ann Eliza (1824-84). See Harlan, Ann Eliza
    (Peck) [Mrs. James] (1824-84)
Peck, C. Isabel, 12,281
Peck, Clarissa Steadman. See Gayle, Clarissa
    Steadman Peck [Mrs. John]
Peck, Cornelia. See Sweetser, Cornelia (Peck)

Peck Family (CT, NY), **12,281**
Peck Family (NY), **12,585**
Peck Family (Potsdam, NY), **11,672**
Peck Family (NC), **13,237**
Peck, Florence C., **12,586**
Peck, Frances (?-1916). See Burrows, Frances (Peck)
    [Mrs. Julius] (?-1916)
Peck, Frances M. (Jocelyn) [Mrs. David], 1,870
Peck, Harriet (1815-40), 13,237
Peck, Helen Maude (Ames), **12,587**
Peck, Henry W., 12,281
Peck, Henry W., Jr., 12,281
Peck, Janet (1864-1956), **1,328**, 1,474
Peck, Joanna (Platt) [Mrs. Henry W.], 12,281
Peck, John A., 12,281
Peck, Julia S. (1831-?). See Twist, Julia S. (Peck)
    (1831-?)
Peck, Lillie M., 8,651, 8,659, 8,668
Peck, Maria Purdy [Mrs. Washington Freeman]
    (1840-1914), 4,732
Peck, Nancy. See Tuttle, Nancy (Peck) Fairchild
Peck, O. H., 6,559
Peck, Orrin M. (?-1921), **1,474**
Peck, Peren, 13,237
Peck, Ruth (1795-1884). See Fisk, Ruth (Peck) [Mrs.
    Wilbur] (1795-1884)
Peck, Wilda Clair (Strong) (1890-1971), **6,825**
Peck, Williams, 12,585
Peckham, Katherine, 2,397
Peckover, Priscilla Hannah [Miss] (1832 or
    1833-1931), 15,298
Peddy, George, 3,323
Peddy, Zerlina Catherine "Katie" [Mrs. George],
    3,323
Peden, Rachel, **6,064**
Peder Seier (book), 8,788
Peder Victorius (book), 8,788
Pedersen, Anne Marie (1847-1916). See Larsen,
    Anne Marie (Pedersen) [Mrs. Oluf Christian]
    (1847-1916)
Pedersen, Elsa [Mrs.], 142
Pedersen, Marie [Mrs.], 8,398
Pedersen Thyra E. (ca. 1889-), **6,826**
Pederson, Andreas, 8,776
Pederson, Mabel (Knutson) [Mrs. Elmer R.] (1901-),
    8,708
Pederson, Maren Pol [Mrs. Andreas] (1849-1935),
    8,776
Pederson, Mrs. Annie, 9,467
Pederson, Rachel Lyman. (1894-1942). See Field,
    Rachel Lyman. [Mrs. Arthur Siegfried Pederson]
    (1894-1942)
Pediatric nursing, 232
Pediatricians, **11,400**, 11,817, **14,198**, **16,226**
Pediatricians, Afro-American, **11,390**, **15,918**
Pediatrics, 1,348, 1,380, 3,968, 6,209
  research, 7,274
  study and teaching, 3,932, 6,679
Pedrick Family (MA), 7,008
Peeble, Sarah M., 16,060
Peebles, John, 13,438
Peebles, Mary Ann, 16,060
Peebles, Rose Jeffries, 9,563
Peedy Family (GA), 3,323
Peek, George N. (1873-1943), **10,034**
Peek, Georgia (Lindsey) [Mrs. George N.], 10,034
Peeler, Ruth [Mrs.], **17,409**
Peet, Azalia E. (1889-1973), **7,280**
Peet, Elizabeth [Miss] (1874-1961), **2,114**
Peet, Harriet Evens [Mrs. James] (ca. 1828-1914),
    9,281
Peet, Harvey Prindle, 2,114
Peet, Isaac Lewis, 2,114
Peet, James (1828-66), Family (MN), **9,281**
Peet, Lucy Abigail (1837-1900). See Cowley, Lucy
    Abigail (Peet) (1837-1900)
Pegasus Limping (book), 15,956
"Pegleg Smith," 590
Pegler, James Westbrook (1894-1969), **5,124**
Pegler, Julia Harpman [Mrs. James Westbrook], 5,124
Pegler, Maud Towart [Mrs. James Westbrook], 5,124
Pegue, Harriet, 9,574
Pegues, Ella F. [Miss], 9,596
Pegues, Harriet S., 9,819

Peirce, Ann Dabney [Mrs. James N.], 17,089
Peirce, Benjamin Osgood, Jr. (1854-1914), **6,297**
Peirce, David Stuart, 17,089
Peirce, Eliza, 1,598
Peirce, Eliza (Mitchell) (1784-1887), 1,598
Peirce, Elizabeth Pannill. *See* Litchfield, Elizabeth Pannill (Peirce)
Peirce, Emily Mitchell (1839-1923), 1,598
Peirce Family, **1,598**
Peirce, George H., 1,598
Peirce, Hannah Greaves, 15,343
Peirce, Isabella Turnbull (Landreth) [Mrs. Benjamin Osgood, Jr.] (?-1937), 6,297
Peirce, James N., 17,089
Peirce, Lydia Ellen (Eaton) [Mrs. George H.] (1839-1903), 1,598
Peirce, Mary Bell (?-1879). *See* MacGill, Mary Bell (Peirce) (?-1879)
Peirce, Susanna. *See* Zwemer, Susanna (Peirce)
Peirson, Nancy (Richards) (1792-1852), **16,784,** 16,905
Peixotto, Jessica Blanche (1864-1941), 309, 621, 792, 863, 2,679
Peking American School (China), faculty, 1,571
Pelham, Laura Dainty [Mrs. Fred] (1846-1924), 4,097
Pelham, Martha (Coffin) [Mrs. Peter] (1806-75). *See* Wright, Martha (Coffin) [Mrs. Peter] Pelham [Mrs. David] (1806-75)
Pell, Charles J. (1853-1906), **11,121**
Pell, Ethelwyn A., 11,121
Pell, Maria P., **4,779**
Pell, Orlie (?-ca. 1975), **11,018**
Pellagra, 239
Pelletier, 6,746
Pellew Family (NY), 12,020
Pellowe, Esther, 8,237
Peloubet, Alice B. (1860-1928). *See* Norton, Alice B. (Peloubet) [Mrs. Lewis Mills] (1860-1928)
Pelton, Emily O., 6,310
Pember, Phoebe Yates (Levy) [Mrs. Thomas] (1823-1913), 3,511, **13,087**
Pemberton, Anna, 15,067
Pemberton Family (PA), **15,067**
Pemberton, Henry (1826-1910), 15,067
Pemberton, Israel (1813-85), 15,067
Pemberton, John (1783-1847), 8,837
Pemberton, John Clifford (1814-81), 15,067
Pemberton Mill, 7,120
Pemberton Mill Relief Fund, **7,120**
Pemberton, Rebecca Clifford [Mrs. John] (1792-1869), 15,067
Pemberton, Susan Lovering [Mrs. Henry Pemberton, Jr.], 15,067
Pembroke College, 6,769
Pembroke-Country Day School (Kansas City), 4,482
Pen and Pencil (book), 12,376
"Pen-Graphs" (newsletter), 3,230
Pen Points (periodical), 3,862
Pen Woman of the Year, 17,179
Pen Women Club (St. Augustine, FL), 2,875
Peña Family (CA), **587**
Pence, Anna [Mrs.], 1,790
Pence, Anne. *See* Davis, Anne (Pence)
Pencils, 3,186
Pender, Janie (?-1969). *See* Castellaw, Janie (Pender) [Mrs.] (?-1969)
Pendergast, Abigail "Abbie" Lowe Cogswell [Mrs. William Wirt] (1839-1917), 9,282
Pendergast, Edith Myra (1860-78), 9,282
Pendergast, Elizabeth (1858-1929). *See* Greenberg, Elizabeth (Pendergast) [Mrs. Henry] (1858-1929)
Pendergast, Jessie, 9,282
Pendergast, Mary Abbie (1865-?). *See* Vye, Mary Abbie (Pendergast) [Mrs. John A.] (1865-?)
Pendergast, May. *See* White, May (Pendergast) [Mrs. Henry A.]
Pendergast, William Wirt, Family (MA, MN, NH), **9,282**
Pendergrass, S., 3,043
Pendleton, Agnes, 2,596
Pendleton, Amena, 14,734
Pendleton, Augusta, 14,734
Pendleton, Caleb, 8,168
Pendleton, Clarinda Huntington (1856-1943). *See*

Lamar, Clarinda Huntington (Pendleton) [Mrs. Joseph R.] (1856-1943)
Pendleton, Constance, 14,734
Pendleton, Eleora, 14,734
Pendleton, Ellen F., 15,311
Pendleton Ellen Fitz (1864-1936), 7,574
Pendleton, Emily (Perry) [Mrs. Phineas, III], 5,707
Pendleton, Emma W. (ca. 1847-70). *See* Blanchard, Emma W. Pendleton [Mrs. James, Jr.] (ca. 1847-70)
Pendleton Family (MI), **8,168**
Pendleton Female Academy (SC), **15,670**
Pendleton, Freda, 14,734
Pendleton, Korene, 14,734
Pendleton, Lettie, 5,707
Pendleton, Lottie. *See* Bailey, Lottie Pendleton [Mrs. George W.]
Pendleton, Lucy, 5,707
Pendleton, Luelle, 14,734
Pendleton, Rose. *See* Havener, Rose (Pendleton)
Pendleton, Susan, 12,315
Pendleton, Susannah, 11,941
Pendleton, Venita, 14,734
Pendleton, Wertha, 14,734
Pendleton, William F., 14,734
Pendola, Celestine [Mrs.], 1,525
Penelope Club (IN), **4,576**
Penfeather, Penelope (pseudonym). *See* White, Sallie Elizabeth (Joy) (1852?-1909)
Penfield, E. Z., **12,588**
Pengra, Charlotte Emily (Stearns) [Mrs. Byron J.] (1827-?), 606, 1,505, **14,298**
Penguin Books, 1,221
Penikese Summer School (MA), 6,316
Peninsula School (CA), 664
Penn, Ann (Allen) (?-1830), 14,970
Penn, Anne, 15,087
Penn Hall (PA), 13,350
Penn, Letitia, 15,287
Penn, Thomas, 15,041
Penn, William, 11,949, 14,817, 15,039, 15,040
Pennell, Elizabeth (Horton) [Mrs. Joseph Stanley], 14,433
Pennell, Elizabeth (Robins) [Mrs. Joseph] (1855-1936), **2,520,** 4,226, 11,036, 12,282
Pennell Esther (Slocum) [Mrs. Lewis], 12,370
Pennell, Helena Sullivan, 10,283
Pennell, Joseph (1857-1926), **2,520, 12,282**
Pennell, Joseph Stanley (1908-63), **14,433**
Penney Family (FL, England), **5,319**
Penney, J. C., 10,000
Penney, Margaret. *See* Presby, Margaret (Penney) [Mrs. Willard]
Penney, Marian. *See* Winthrop, Marian (Penney) [Mrs. Edward]
Penney, Thomas, 5,319
Pennie, Mary Cheever (ca. 1847-?). *See* Chapin, Mary Cheever (Pennie) (ca. 1847-?)
Penniman, Helen N. (?-1945). *See* Pardee, Helen N. (Penniman) [Mrs. George Cooper] (?-1945)
Pennington Family (NJ), **11,122**
Pennington, Jabez (1827-73), 11,122
Pennington, Mary, 15,290
Pennington, May Williams [Mrs.], **16,114**
Pennington, Ruth, 17,288
Pennington, Samuel (1765-1835), 11,122
Pennock, Isaac, 2,031
Pennock, Rebecca Webb (1794-1854). *See* Lukens, Rebecca Webb (Pennock) [Mrs. Charles] (1794-1854)
Pennoyer, Sylvester, 14,594
Pennsylvania, 2,228, 2,627, 12,268, 14,635, **14,784,** 14,813, 14,816, 14,842, 14,949, 15,004, 16,527
abolitionists, 14,873, 14,953, 14,991, **15,069**
abortion, legal aspects, 1,984, **14,825**
accountants, **15,054**
actresses, 15,193
aeronautical societies, **14,946**
aeronautics, **14,946**
affirmative action programs, 15,236
Afro-Americans, **15,106**
education, 15,023, 15,069
medical care, 15,011
agricultural societies, 14,729

air pilots, 14,946
airports, for women, 14,946
alms houses, 14,913, 14,916
Americanization, 15,023
animals, treatment of, 14,867
art schools, **2,797**
art societies, 14,822
artists, **15,354**
assessment, 14,934
associations, institutions, etc., **14,920,** 15,216
asylums, 15,048
attorneys general, 14,982
authors, **14,828,** 14,949, 14,962, **15,002,** 15,020, **15,111**
autograph albums, 15,065, **15,098**
bankers, **15,011,** 15,221
bible, societies, etc., 15,221
bishops, 15,048, **15,152**
booksellers and bookselling, 12,178
British occupation of Philadelphia, 14,847
business records, **14,945**
businessmen, 14,803, 14,835, 14,977, 14,993, 15,004, **15,222,** 15,257
camps, 2,685
capital and capitol, 2,792
capitalists and financiers, 14,957
carpenters, 3,337, 15,018
Catholic hospitals, 14,794, **15,232**
Catholic schools, 5,759, 14,794, 15,211, 15,235
Catholic universities and colleges, 14,789, 14,794, **15,179**
alumnae, **14,788,** 14,790
archives, **14,911**
pictorial works, **14,791**
census, Afro-American (1840s), 15,069
centennial celebrations, 8,221, 12,346, 12,417, **14,923, 14,924, 14,971,** 15,551
centennial exposition, 16,060
charitable societies, **14,749, 14,841, 14,866, 14,867, 14,947,** 14,953, 14,972, **14,985, 15,022, 15,023, 15,026, 15,048, 15,062, 15,094, 15,187, 15,277, 15,292**
charitable societies, Jewish, **13,776, 13,798, 15,153,** 15,161, **15,165**
charities, 14,924, **15,072, 15,101, 15,206,** 15,251
charities, Jewish, **15,154, 15,155, 15,157,** 15,161
child abuse, 14,867
child care centers, 15,160, **15,206**
child care centers, Jewish, 15,161
child support, 14,916
church records and registers, 15,006, 15,328
church records and registers, Brethren in Christ, 161
church records and registers, Congregational, **14,972**
church societies, **14,735, 15,122, 15,227,** 15,230
church societies, Congregational, 14,972
church societies, Mennonite, **14,869**
church societies, Presbyterian, **14,724, 14,727**
churches, Catholic, 14,909
churches, Congregational, **14,972**
churches, Presbyterian, 11,626
churches, Unitarian, 15,252
cities and towns, **7,664**
city councilmen, 15,000
city councilwomen, **14,983**
civil service, colonial, 15,039
Civil War
  hospitals, charities, etc., 14,824, **14,831**
  personal narratives, **15,047**
  troops, 3,337
  war work, 14,766
clergy, 15,079
clergy, Baptist, **15,184**
clergy, Mennonite, 14,868
clergy, Presbyterian, 14,833
clerks of court, **14,914,** 14,921
clinics, **15,130**
club-houses, 6,805
clubs, 2,643, **14,722, 14,725, 14,746,** 14,822, **14,929,** 14,931, 14,949, 14,953, 14,987, **15,071, 15,076, 15,108, 15,190, 15,194,** 15,207, **15,220, 15,231, 15,243, 15,244, 15,340**
coeducation, **14,752,** 14,941, 15,034

college administrators, **14,889, 15,182**
college and school journalism, 14,748
college presidents, **14,745, 14,787,** 15,212
college students, **14,757,** 15,241, 15,242
college teachers, 11,857, **14,759,** 15,196
college theater, **15,193**
common-place books, 14,951, **14,954,** 15,065
communicable diseases, 14,854
community centers, **15,160**
community health facilities, 15,264
community leadership, **6,682, 15,005**
community organization, 13,783
congressmen, 14,822, 15,020, **15,030**
conservatories of music, **15,208**
constitutional conventions, **15,068**
contemplative orders, **14,782, 14,785, 15,147**
convents and nunneries, Catholic, **14,874, 15,265**
cookery, **15,345**
court records, **14,832, 14,914, 14,921, 14,938,** 15,039
crime and criminals, Afro-American, 15,110
cultural relations, 2,133
customhouse brokers, **15,162**
customs administration, 14,979
cycling, **15,071**
dancing, **15,110**
deaf, Jewish, 15,154
deans (in schools), 14,826 **15,126, 15,131, 15,140, 15,186,** 15,189, **15,237**
delinquency, 15,246
delinquents, Jewish, 15,153
dental clinics, 15,202
dentists, **15,095**
diaries and journals, **14,729, 15,046, 15,049, 15,343**
  18th C, **14,792,** 14,836, **14,961, 14,963, 15,041, 17,082**
  19th C, 1,425, 14,808, **14,899,** 14,950, **14,952,** 15,002, 15,028, **15,047, 15,105, 15,113,** 15,167, **17,660**
disaster relief, 14,860
dissertations, academic, **15,143**
divorce, 15,258
divorce suits, 14,921
domestic relations, cases, 14,914
dressmakers, **15,360**
dry-goods, 15,085
editors, 14,863
education, 14,849
education, bilingual, 15,235
educational associations, **14,750**
educators, 15,051
elections, 14,975
engravers, 2,783
estates (law), 15,018
executive advisory bodies, 14,822, 14,942
executives, **15,000**
exhibitions, 3,234, 7,677, 7,678, 12,346, 12,516, 13,535, **14,940, 14,971,** 15,182, 15,194
fairs, **15,085**
farmers, 14,805, 14,808, 14,835
fire departments, finance, 14,720
floods, 14,860, **14,861**
forestry, 14,809
Friends, **11,061,** 14,977, 14,981, 14,989, 15,001, 15,006, **15,022,** 15,042, **15,089, 15,118, 15,285, 15,294, 15,341**
Friends, Society of, 4,754, 11,120, 14,821, 14,847, **14,849, 14,850, 14,854, 14,858,** 14,965, 15,053, 15,058, 15,352
gardening, societies, etc., **15,074**
genealogists, 15,328
glass manufacture, 15,221
governors, 2,526, **14,810, 14,820, 14,829,** 15,342
health boards, **14,912**
high school teachers, **15,046, 15,188**
high schools, 15,011
historians, **15,061,** 15,107
historic sites, 14,923
historic sites, conservation and restoration, **11,877**
historical societies, **15,363**
home economics, accounting, **14,721, 14,726**
hospital administrators, 6,140, 15,232
hospital records, 14,913, 14,915, 14,916, **15,150, 15,151,** 15,232

hospitals, 14,746
  administration, **15,075**
hospitals, gynecologic and obstetric, **15,142, 15,148,** 15,150, **15,151**
hotels, taverns, etc., 14,945
household workers, 15,030
housewives, **14,721, 14,792, 14,793,** 15,001
housing, 15,204
  law and legislation, 15,205
housing and health, 15,205
housing management, 15,205
housing policy, citizen participation, **15,201**
immigrants, 15,155
immigrants, Irish, **15,054**
insurance companies, 15,000, 17,465
insurance, marine, policies, 14,955
inventions and inventors, 14,940
iron-founding, 15,014
iron industry and trade, 2,031
Jews, 15,010
  social life and customs, 15,158
journalists, **14,964**
judges, 14,648, 14,804, 15,020, 15,252
justices of the peace, 14,808
kindergartens, 15,023, 15,202, 15,205, **15,225**
law, cases, 14,960
law enforcement, 15,204
lawyers, 14,809, 14,824, 14,945, **14,958, 14,976,** 14,982, **15,002, 15,010,** 15,358
legislative bodies, 2,342
legislators, **2,235,** 15,000
legislators, Afro-American, **2,133**
libraries, **14,948**
library schools, **14,930**
literary societies, **14,747, 14,756**
malt, 15,070
manufacturers, 14,718, 14,978
manufactures, **14,919**
marriage counseling, 6,987, **14,849**
maternal and infant welfare, **13,798**
mayors, **14,815,** 14,860, 14,919, 15,077, 15,221, 15,332
medical colleges, 6,698, **15,132, 15,135**
  faculty, 15,126, 15,130
medicine, history, 14,871
merchants, **12,563,** 14,805, 14,884, **14,945, 14,955, 14,973, 14,989,** 15,001, **15,044,** 15,081, **15,089,** 15,104
midwives, **14,864,** 14,921, 14,945
military, 14,994
miniature painters, 14,949
minorities, 15,209
monasteries, 14,785, **14,870**
monasticism and religious orders for women, Catholic, **14,717, 14,719, 14,781, 14,783, 14,794, 14,795, 14,800, 14,859,** 14,874, **15,177, 15,178, 15,211,** 15,232, **15,233, 15,234,** 15,235, 15,264, **15,266, 15,267, 15,336, 15,337, 15,356**
Moravians, 12,338, 12,512, 13,149
municipal universities and colleges, 14,822
museums, 15,116
music, instruction and study, 15,208
musical societies, **15,073**
musicians, 15,020
Native Americans,
  education, **14,748**
  relations with whites, **12,338**
naturalists, **14,956**
nature study, 2,310
newspapers, **14,830**
  sections, columns, etc., 15,158
novelists, 14,962, **14,964**
nuns, Catholic, **14,787**
nurses, 14,912, **15,224**
nursing schools, 15,142, **15,149, 15,192**
obstetrics, cases, clinical reports, statistics, 14,864, 15,148
occupational training of women, 15,236
officials and employees, **14,804,** 14,807, **15,326**
old age homes, 14,749
old age homes, Jewish, **15,157,** 15,161
oral history, **14,811, 14,861, 15,357**
orphans and orphan asylums, **15,062,** 15,181, **15,282**

orphans and orphan asylums, Jewish, **15,153**
race problems, 15,202
real estate agents, 14,945, **14,955**
pageants, 15,061
painters, 15,018
parents' and teachers' associations, **15,344**
patriotic societies, **14,986, 15,342**
peace societies, 15,316
periodicals, **8,921**
philanthropists, 7,533, 12,169, 14,884, **15,011, 15,055, 15,161,** 15,187, 15,251, **15,296**
physicians, **12,139, 14,803,** 14,857, **14,871, 14,889, 14,925, 14,926, 14,927, 14,928,** 14,965, 14,977, 14,981, 15,017, 15,039, 15,040, 15,041, **15,084,** 15,087, **15,117,** 15,260
pioneers and settlers, 14,648, **15,035,** 15,107
playgrounds, 14,746, 15,205
poets, **15,013**
political clubs, 14,987
political parties, 14,987
politicians, 14,957, 14,977
politics, practical, 15,321
politics, practical, women's activism, 15,011, **15,033,** 15,204
poor, 15,022
printers, **14,881**
prisoners, **14,918**
prisons,
  records and correspondence, **14,917,** 14,918
private schools, 6,504, 13,350, **15,051**
probation officers, 15,246
prostitutes, **6,752,** 14,916
public health, **14,983**
public housing, 15,201
public records, **14,922**
public welfare, 14,983
public welfare administration, **14,913, 14,916**
publishers and publishing, **12,178,** 14,945, 14,987
real property, 17,465
recreation, 15,204
reformers, **14,987**
Revolution (1775-1783), 14,839, **15,007**
sanitation, 14,746
school boards, 15,010, 15,027
school superintendents and principals, 8,606, 14,845, 14,949, 15,088
schools, 13,570, 14,851, 14,857, **15,025,** 15,034, 15,204, **15,293,** 17,445
  accounting, 14,762, **15,347**
  records and correspondence, **14,748,** 15,349, 15,350, 15,351, **15,352**
schools, Afro-American, 3,298
schools, Jewish, 15,156
science teachers, **15,216**
scrapbooks,
secretaries, 15,039, **15,163, 15,164**
senators, United States, **2,235,** 14,975, 15,041
sex discrimination in education, 15,237
shipping, 14,960
single mothers, 14,920
sketch books, 14,862
social life and customs, 555, 2,033, 13,066, 14,961, 14,976, 15,041, 15,104, 15,112, 15,118, 15,258, 17,417
social science research, 14,936
social settlements, 7,307, **15,202,** 15,207
social work education, **14,742**
social work with delinquents and criminals, 15,153
social workers, **15,246**
Socialists, 14,830
societies, Italian-American, **15,247**
societies, Jewish, **13,815,** 15,156, **15,248, 15,250**
soldiers, Civil War, **3,337**
spiritualists, **15,082**
state universities and colleges, 13,324
strikes and lockouts, teachers, 15,332
student participation in administration, **14,764**
students' societies, 14,029, 15,237, **15,238,** 15,239
suffrage, **6,632, 15,335**
suffrage societies, 14,814, 15,029, 15,335, **15,361,** 16,252, 17,217
suffragists, **14,728,** 15,252
summer schools, 6,893, 15,011
surveyors, 14,808

symphony orchestras, 14,822
teachers, **3,314**, **3,337**, 9,048, 11,407, 14,873, **15,341**
teachers' unions, 15,200, 15,332
teaching, 8,170
technical education, 14,941
teenagers, employment, 15,202
temperance societies, 14,818, 14,953, **15,254**, **15,346**, **15,362**
tenant and landlord, **14,959**, 15,205
trade and professional associations, **14,826**
trade-unions, 6,795
  clothing workers, **15,321**, 15,329
  electric industry workers, **15,253**
  officials and employees, **15,253**
  political activity, 15,321
United Nations associations, 2,133, 6,682
universities and colleges, 6,987, **14,802**, 14,844, 14,845, 14,857, 14,940, 14,941, **15,183**, 15,195, 15,252
  administration, 14,745, **15,239**
  archives, **14,737**
  faculty, 14,965
  graduate work, 15,241
  history, 15,240
upholstery trade, **15,106**
urban renewal, 11,877, 15,202
utopias, **14,718**, **15,259**
vital statistics, 14,807
vocational guidance, 12,738
voluntary health agencies, 14,746
volunteer workers in hospitals, **14,723**
women's colleges, **14,780**, **15,212**
  alumnae, 15,011
  archives, **14,716**, **15,219**
  records and correspondence, **14,760**
women's studies, 15,236
World War I, civilians work, 15,005
World War II, finance, 14,834
yellow fever epidemics, 15,022
Young Women's Christian Association, 12,710, **14,765**, **15,209**, **15,210**
zoning, 15,204
Pennsylvania Abortion Law Commission, 6,788, **14,825**
Pennsylvania Association of Women Deans and Counselors, **14,826**
Pennsylvania College for Women (Pittsburgh, PA). *See* Chatham College (Pittsburgh, PA)
Pennsylvania Constitutional Convention, **15,068**
Pennsylvania Council of Republican Women, 14,814
Pennsylvania County Woman Suffrage Society, 14,814
Pennsylvania Department of Forestry, 14,809
Pennsylvania Department of Public Welfare, **14,806**
Pennsylvania Department of Records, **14,922**
Pennsylvania Department of State, **14,807**
Pennsylvania Dietetic Association, **14,827**
Pennsylvania Economy League-Bureau of Municipal Research, 14,920
Pennsylvania Electric Company, 14,791
Pennsylvania Female College (Harrisburg, PA), **14,802**
Pennsylvania Female College (Pittsburgh, PA). *See* Chatham College (Pittsburgh, PA)
Pennsylvania Forestry Association, 14,809
Pennsylvania General Hospital, 14,915
Pennsylvania Horticultural Society, 11,701
Pennsylvania Hospital (Philadelphia, PA), 6,140, **15,150**
Pennsylvania Hospital for the Insane, 3,529
Pennsylvania Hospital, Maternity Hospital (Philadelphia, PA), **15,148**
Pennsylvania Hospital of Philadelphia, Women's Medical College, alumnae, 11,043
Pennsylvania Hospital Training School for Nurses (Philadelphia, PA), **15,149**
Pennsylvania Intercollegiate Conference on Government, **14,804**
Pennsylvania Library Club, **14,931**
Pennsylvania Medical College (PA), 4,496
Pennsylvania Men's League for Woman Suffrage, 15,335
Pennsylvania Museum (PA), 15,116
Pennsylvania Mutual Life Insurance Company, 4,257

Pennsylvania Railroad Women's Division of War Relief, **15,103**
Pennsylvania Recorder of Deeds. *See* Pennsylvania Department of Records
Pennsylvania Society for Promoting the Abolition of Slavery, **15,069**
Pennsylvania Society for the Encouragement of Manufactures and the Useful Arts, 14,953
Pennsylvania State Archives, Ethnic Studies Program, Oral History Projects, **14,811**
Pennsylvania State Art Commission, 14,822
Pennsylvania State Council of Republican Women, 15,251
Pennsylvania State Federation of Women's Clubs, 2,643, 14,747
Pennsylvania State Forest Commission, officials and employees, 2,310
Pennsylvania State Reservation Commission, 15,326
Pennsylvania Volunteer Infantry, 2,534, 17,376
Pennsylvania Volunteers, 15,322
Pennsylvania Woman Suffrage Association, 14,814, 15,029, 15,252, 15,335
Pennsylvania Woman Suffrage Party, York County Committee, **15,361**
Pennsylvania Women's Club of Portland (OR), 14,635
Penny Candy (book), 17,806
Penny, John P., 15,229
Penny, Prudence (pseudonym). *See* Malek, Leona A.
"Penny Royal Gazette, The" (newsletter), 9,205
Pennybacker, Anna J. H. [Mrs. Percy V.] (1861-1938), 2,170, **16,115**, 17,654
Pennybacker, Margaret Muse, **17,092**
Pennypacker, Samuel W. (1843-1916), **14,829**
Penobscot Bay Island Project (ME), 5,644
Penobscot Indians, 5,657
  music, **5,658**
Penrod, Doris Bauer [Mrs.], **16,476**
Penrod, Emanuel, 10,669
Penrose, Charles, 15,355
Penrose, Charles W., 16,786
Penrose, Esther Romania (Bunnell) [Mrs. Parley P.] Pratt [Mrs. Charles W.] (1839-1932), **16,786**, 16,839
Penrose, Julie Villiers (Lewis) [Mrs. James] McMillan [Mrs. Spencer] (1870-1956), **1,687**
Penrose, Mary A. [Mrs. James W.], 3,897
Penrose, Mrs., 15,355
Penrose, Romania B. *See* Penrose, Esther Romania (Bunnell) [Mrs. Parley P.] Pratt [Mrs. Charles W.] (1839-1932)
Penrose, Spencer, 1,687
Pensacola Art Club (FL), **2,894**
Pensacola Garden Club (FL), 2,901
Pensacola Girl Scout Council (FL), 2,905
Pensacola Historical Museum (FL), 2,888
Pensions, 2,514, 3,506, 4,360, 8,075, 8,986, 9,000, 9,140, 9,816, 11,445, 13,874, 14,290, 17,278
Pensions, military, 194, 252, 1,907, **1,924**, 2,206, 2,217, 2,229, 2,560, 2,671, 2,698, 2,926, 3,752, 8,324, 8,454, 8,894, **11,194**, 11,197, 13,386, 13,591, 14,454, **15,944**, 17,463
People for Question No. 1 (CT), **1,927**
People to People, International, 5,228
People's Art Center for Negroes (MO), 10,163
People's Church (St. Paul, MN), Women's Foreign Missionary society, **9,283**
People's College (KS), faculty, 9,177
People's Common Sense Medical Adviser, The (book), 3,207
People's Council of America, 7,923
People's Institute (MA), 7,195
People's Institute (OR), 14,644
People's Mandate to Governments to End War, 860, **15,311**
Peoples, Mrs. John, 10,203
People's Paper, The (periodical), 4,654
People's party, 1,255
People's Voice, 5,478
People's Voice (MT), **10,354**
People's Voice, The (Glos Ludowy), 8,114
People's World (periodical), 17,635
People's World thirty-third anniversary (1971), 1,017
Peoria Neighborhood House (IL), 4,130
Pepper, Claude Denson, 255

Pepperell Manufacturing Company (ME), **6,202**
Pepperell Mills (ME), employees, 5,596
Peralta, Frances. *See* Partington, Phyllis
Perch, Mrs. Michael, 1,660
Perchance to Dream (drama), 6,022
Percival, Phebe, 14,851
Percy, Alice (1871-1920). *See* Leighton, Alice Percy [Mrs. Alton Winslow] (1871-1920)
Percy, William Alexander, 9,779
Père Lachaise (book), 825
Perego, Margaret. *See* Harper, Margaret (Perego) [Mrs. James Philip]
Pereira, I. Rice (1907-71), **2,795**
Perennial Bachelor, The (book), 2,051
Pérez, Eulalia (?-1878), **715**
Perez, Rebecca [Mrs.], **16,376**
Performing arts, 1,054, **8,921**, **9,452**, 9,468, 11,444, **11,907**, 12,515, 16,146
Perham, Constance [Mrs.], 1,080
Perini, Hilda, 5,448
Period (IA), 9,098
Periodicals, 77, 163, **278**, 1,410, 1,426, 1,435, 1,451, 1,500, 1,750, **2,043**, **2,055**, 2,127, 2,205, 2,610, 2,611, **2,862**, 2,879, **3,006**, 3,172, 3,209, 3,251, 3,711, 4,145, 4,208, 4,484, **4,655**, **4,693**, 5,629, 5,899, 5,905, 5,907, 5,925, 5,949, 6,057, 6,075, 6,079, 6,081, 6,091, 6,101, 6,112, 6,201, 6,223, 6,343, 6,383, 6,479, 6,514, 6,547, 6,582, 6,601, 6,608, 6,650, 6,694, 6,709, 6,713, 6,730, 6,834, 6,841, 6,867, 6,971, 7,044, 7,610, 8,279, 8,376, 8,428, 9,599, 9,689, 9,736, 9,769, 9,770, 9,771, 11,213, **11,304**, 11,305, 11,331, 11,350, 11,491, 11,720, 11,866, 12,035, **12,064**, 12,236, 12,244, **12,572**, 12,888, **12,891**, 12,911, 13,312, 13,366, 13,400, 13,413, 13,528, 13,550, 13,595, **13,664**, 13,990, 14,200, 14,377, 15,060, 15,554, 15,585, 15,709, 16,169, 17,305, 17,312
Periodicals, Swedish, 12,880
Periodontal disease, prevention, 13,997
Peripatetics of Minneapolis (MN), 9,103
Perishable Press Limited (NY), **12,879**
Peristrome Presbyterian Church (Plattsburgh, NY), 12,770
Perkerson, Angus, 3,070
Perkerson, Medora Field [Mrs. Angus] (1892-1960), 3,065, **3,070**, 3,071
Perkham, Phila M., **11,675**
Perkins, Alice Forbes. *See* Hooper, Alice Forbes (Perkins) [Mrs. William]
Perkins, Ann, 2,190
Perkins, Anna (Weld) [Mrs. George Hamilton], 2,171, 2,521
Perkins, Barbara (1905-76). *See* Gamow, Barbara (Perkins) [Mrs. J. R. de la Torre] Bueno [Mrs. George Antony] (1905-76)
Perkins, Cecile, 11,662
Perkins, Charlotte Anna (1860-1935). *See* Gilman, Charlotte Anna (Perkins) [Mrs. Charles Walter] Stetson [Mrs. George Houghton] (1860-1935)
Perkins, Elizabeth (1765-1844). *See* Wildes, Elizabeth (Perkins) [Mrs. Israel] (1765-1844).
Perkins, Elizabeth S. (?-1971), **2,015**
Perkins, Elizabeth West Nevins [Mrs. Charles Lawrence], **12,270**
Perkins, Emma [Miss], 716
Perkins Family (CA), **716**
Perkins Family (MA), 6,593, 7,659, 7,665
Perkins, Fanny, 1,329
Perkins, Frances. [Mrs. Paul Caldwell] Wilson (1882-1965), 441, 569, 575, 698, 924, 1,451, 2,120, 2,207, 2,336, 2,403, 2,424, 2,439, 2,509, 2,558, 2,681, 2,693, 3,976, 6,365, 6,687, 6,765, 6,766, **6,827**, **6,982**, 8,073, 8,658, 8,678, 9,962, 11,123, 11,483, **11,504**, 11,541, 11,553, **11,676**, 11,760, 11,771, **11,905**, 11,916, 12,044, 12,069, 12,487, 12,700, 12,704, 13,446
Perkins, Frances (Johnson) Beecher [Mrs. James] (1832-?), 6,394
Perkins, Frederick G., 1,743
Perkins, George Clement, **1,329**
Perkins, George Hamilton (1835-99), 2,171, **2,521**
Perkins Institute for the Blind (Watertown, MA). *See* Perkins School for the Blind (Watertown, MA)

Perkins, Isabel Weld (1876-1948). *See* Anderson, Isabel Weld (Perkins) [Mrs. Larz] (1876-1948)
Perkins, Jean Bredin [Mrs. James A.], 11,635
Perkins, Jonathan (1728-1802), 7,663
Perkins, Lu [Mrs. Gale], 9,467
Perkins, Lucy (Fitch) (1865-1937), 8,531
Perkins, Mary [Mrs. Reuben], **12,742**
Perkins, Mary (Beecher) [Mrs. Thomas Clap] (1805-1900), 1,951
Perkins, Mary H., **7,419**
Perkins, Mary Louise Martin [Mrs. Percy Harold, Jr.], (1911-62), **3,415**
Perkins, Maxwell Evarts, 2,875, 2,876, 11,286
Perkins, Mrs. Charles E., 1,954
Perkins, Mrs. R. C., **11,793**
Perkins, Pansy, 1,329
Perkins, Percy Harold, Jr., 3,415
Perkins, Ruth A. Parker [Mrs. George Clement] (?-1921), 1,329
Perkins, Sarah, 6,193
Perkins School for the Blind (Watertown, MA), 5,857, 6,346, 7,309, 7,560, 7,684, 10,798
Perkins, Susan George [Miss] (1838-1911), 2,171
Perkins, Susanna (1757-?), **7,663**
Perkins, Susannah (Hovey) [Mrs. Thomas], 5,691
Perkins, Thomas, 5,691
Perkins, Virginia (Chase) [Mrs. Wallace], 5,694
Perky, Henry D. (1844-1904?), 7,655
Perlin, Paul, 1,017
Perlman, Helen Harris, 8,676
Perlmutter, Rose. *See* Rinder, Rose (Perlmutter) [Mrs. Reuben]
Perls, Eugenia (Riwkin) Söderberg [Mrs. Hugo] (1903-73). *See* Söderberg, Eugenia (Riwkin). [Mrs. Hugo] Perls (1903-73)
Perls, Hugo, 12,880
Permanent Civic Committee of Women's Clubs of Western Pennsylvania, 15,244
Pernicious anemia, 14,900
Peronneau, Alexander, **15,526**
Perot, Joseph, 9,604
Perot Malting Company (PA), **15,070**
Perpich, Rudy, **9,478**
Perricaudet, Julie, 626
Perrigo, E. Stella, 9,323
Perrine, Cordelia Adelaid. *See* Chester, Cordelia Adelaid (Perrine) [Mrs. Lewis] Harvey [Mrs.]
Perrine, Henry, 2,952
Perrine, Hester (1824-post 1885). *See* Walker, Hester (Perrine) (1824-post 1885)
Perrson, Kjersti (1837-1911). *See* Mattson, Kjersti (Perrson) [Mrs. Hans] (1837-1911)
Perry, Ada Jordan (ca. 1880-1958), 957
Perry, Annie (?-1970). *See* Jester, Annie Perry [Mrs. J. R.] (?-1970)
Perry, Augustus, 7,475
Perry, Bell, 6,828
Perry, Benjamin Franklin (1805-86), 13,088, **15,671**
Perry, Bliss (1860-1954), 2,298, 17,009
Perry, Carolina Coronado, 12,403
Perry, Caroline Slidell. *See* Belmont, Caroline Slidell (Perry) [Mrs. August]
Perry, Elizabeth Frances (McCall) [Mrs. Benjamin Franklin], **13,088**, 15,610, 15,671
Perry, Ellen Elizabeth (1828-?). *See* Pierson, Ellen Elizabeth (Perry) (1828-?)
Perry, Eva (1852-?). *See* Moore, Eva (Perry) [Mrs. Philip N.] (1852-?)
Perry Family, 14,059
Perry Family (CT), 1,940
Perry Family (NY), 11,440
Perry, Fredericka D. S., 2,315
Perry, Hally Ballinger (Bryan) [Mrs. Emmett L.] (1868-1955), **16,116**
Perry, Hext M., 15,610
Perry, Jane (Slidell) [Mrs. Matthew Calbraith], **6,828**
Perry, John, 77, 13,256
Perry, Laura L. [Mrs.], **16,377**
Perry, Mary Chase (1867-1961). *See* Stratton, Mary Chase (Perry) [Mrs. William B.] (1867-1961)
Perry, Maude Eleaine (Caldwell) [Mrs. Stuart H.] (1873-1963), **7,888**
Perry, Mrs. Samuel, 9,887
Perry, Nora, 14,058

Perry, Roderick, 5,320
Perry, Sally (Randle) [Mrs. John], **77**
Perry, Sarah (Cornelius), 1,861
Perry, Stuart H., 7,888
Perry, Tulah (Cates), 13,637
Perry, William P., Jr., 5,320
Perry, William Walbridge, 2,821
Persecution, 10,846, 16,525, 16,557, 16,572, 16,718, 16,874, 16,938
Pershing Family, 10,487
Pershing, Helen Frances Warren [Mrs. John Joseph], 17,898
Pershing, John Joseph (1860-1948), 3,699, 4,350, 10,531, 11,944, 14,822, 17,071, 17,379, 17,898
Person, Alice (Morgan) (1840-1913), **13,089**
Person, Jeremiah, 7,669
Personal injuries, 14,195
"Personal Reminiscences of the Old Anti-Slavery Times" (essay), 7,215
Personal Traits of Abraham Lincoln (book), 2,512
Personality, **2,840**
Personius, Catherine Jane (1904-), 11,662, **11,677**
Personnel directors, 6,640, 11,851
Personnel management, 6,810, **15,124**
Personnel service in education, 8,643
Personnel service in higher education, 12,921
Personnel Woman, The (periodical), 15,124
Persons, Irene, **9,284, 9,285**
Persons, Julia E., 8,994
Perston, Jessie, 14,893
Perth Amboy Baptist Church (NJ), 11,057
Pertz, Dorothea F. M. (1859-1939), 10,151
Peru,
  American ambassadors to, 2,590, 7,539
  Americans in, 6,031
  elections, 8,090
  political parties, 8,090
  politicians, **8,090**
Peru State College (NE), 10,491
Pescud, Sue, 13,320
Pesotta, Rose [Miss] (1896-1965), 8,064, 11,305, **12,589**
Pestalozzie Froebel Haus (Berlin, Germany), 3,974
Pestalozzie Froebel Teachers College (Chicago, IL), 3,974
Pestana, Jean (Kidwell), **717**
Pesticides, 10,953
  environmental aspects, 7,976
Petal Pushers (Hopkins, MN), 8,481
Petal Pushers Club (Reno, NV), 10,709
Peter, Ann Elizabeth (Lewis), 385
Peter Brent Brigham Hospital (MA), Nurses Training School, 6,618
Peter Britt House (OR), 14,589
Peter, Caroline (Jones) [Mrs. Armistead], 2,194
Peter Cartwright, Pioneer Circuit Rider (book), 5,037
Peter, Catherine. *See* Evans, Catherine (Peter)
Peter, Frances Dallam, 5,312
Peter, Grace Bakke [Mrs. Louis G.] (1906-), **9,286**
Peter, Robert, 5,312
Peter Skene Ogden (book), 10,760
Peterich, Gerda, 12,789
Peterkin, Julia (Mood) (1880-1961), 2,995, 3,028, 11,821, **15,672**
Peterkin Papers, The, 7,227
Peters, Alice. *See* Wright, Alice (Peters)
Peters, Alice E. H., 7,866
Peters, Anna Marie, 12,590
Peters, Charles H., Sr., 8,357
Peters, Eva, 5,644
Peters Family (CA), **718**
Peters Family (CT, NY, PA), 12,278
Peters Family (LA, NY), **12,590**
Peters, Harriet, 12,590
Peters, Harriet H., 12,316
Peters, James, 4,353
Peters, James A. (1922-72), **2,723**
Peters, Jean, 2,476
Peters, Lenore. *See* Job, Lenore (Peters)
Peters, Lucy Preston (Wilson) (1867-1950), 6,956, **14,636**, 14,689
Peters, Mary, 12,257
Peters, Mary Adelaide (Vallejo), 858

Peters, Minerva (Macomb) [Mrs. Thomas Willing], 2,556
Peters, Mrs. Charles H., Sr., 8,357
Peters, Mrs. James, 4,353
Peters, Mrs. Richard, 3,141
Peters, Myra (1797-1862). *See* Mason, Myra (Peters) (1797-1862)
Peters, Nellie (1851-1919). *See* Black, Nellie (Peters) [Mrs. G. R.] (1851-1919)
Peters, Peter J., 718
Peters, Richard, 3,151, 14,998
Peters, Richard, Family, 3,179
Peters, Roberta. [Mrs. Bertram] Fields (1930-), **11,782**, 11,817
Peters, Sarah [Mrs.], 14,941
Peters, Thomas McClure, 11,030
Peters Wright Creative Dance group, 718
Petersen, Christine L. (1894-), 4,899
Petersen, Hjalmar (1890-1968), 8,843, **9,287**
Petersen, Margaret (1874-1966). *See* Maw, Margaret (Petersen) (1874-1966)
Petersen, Medora Belle (Grandprey) [Mrs. Hjalmar] (ca. 1900-), **8,843**, 9,287
Petersen, Rigmor Christine Laursen (Wosgaard) [Mrs. Hjalmar], 9,287
Petersham Branch Alliance (MA), **7,331**, 7,333
Peterson, Abigail W. (?-1945). *See* Towne, Abigail W. (Peterson) (?-1945)
Peterson, Agnes [Mrs.], 1,358
Peterson, Agnes L., 9,487
Peterson, Anna. *See* Powers, Anna (Peterson) [Mrs. Thomas E.]
Peterson, Antoinette R., 5,861
Peterson, Berthe C. (1872-1941), 8,737, **8,777**
Peterson, Canute (1824-1902), **16,787**
Peterson, Clara (Gottschalk), 5,483
Peterson, Dorothy, 5,465
Peterson, Eda Lien (1892-), **8,507**
Peterson, Elly (McMillan) (1914-), **7,889**
Peterson, Emma (Blome), 14,778
Peterson, Esther, 8,085
Peterson, Esther (1906-), 2,438, 6,365, 6,710, 11,806
Peterson Family (MI), **8,286**
Peterson, Florence J. (1913-). *See* Olson, Florence J. (Peterson) (1913-)
Peterson, Fred, 955
Peterson, H. Martin, **8,475**
Peterson, Hermese (1879-1961), **16,549**
Peterson, Irene, 9,956
Peterson, Johnnie Inez [Miss], 3,040, **3,071**
Peterson, Josephine, **4,819**
Peterson, Julie (1950-), **8,812**
Peterson, Lucille C., 16,458
Peterson, Lydia, 16,965
Peterson, Martha E., **17,776**
Peterson, Mary Helene, 4,819
Peterson, Mary Nellie. *See* Swanson, Mary Nellie (Peterson) [Mrs. Gust E.]
Peterson, Mrs. Edward C., **10,698**
Peterson, Olivia [Miss], 1,245
Peterson, Ruth Middlemiss (1896-1961), 16,676
Peterson, Sadie. *See* Cresswell, Sadie (Peterson)
Peterson, Sarah Ann [Mrs. Canute], 16,787
Peterson, Theresa (Alphin) Taber Wilkinson (1877-1954), 10,631
Peterson, Virgilia. Virgilia Peterson Ross. Princess Paul Sapieha. Virgilia Sapieha (1904-66), **6,065**
Peterson, Zola (1889-1971), **16,550**
Peterson's Magazine. *See* *Arthur's Home Magazine* (periodical)
Pethick-Lawrence, Emmeline, 7,216, 17,616
Pethick-Lawrence, F. W., 7,216
Petigru, Adele. *See* Allston, Adele (Petigru) [Mrs. Robert Francis Withers]
Petigru Family (SC), 15,440
Petigru, James L., 15,554
Petigru, Jane. *See* North, Jane (Petigru)
Petigru, Louise. *See* Porcher, Louise (Petigru)
Petigru, Mrs. M. A., 15,697
Petitdidier, Marie [Mrs.], 4,299
Petitions, 7,664
Petrey, Ann, 3,288, 3,290
Petri, Anna Louise, **10,179**
Petrie, George, 9

"Petrified Man" (story), 9,770
Petrina, Carlotta, 12,040
Petroleum
    refining, 11,550, 11,833
    transportation, 11,833
Petroleum industry and trade, 15,318
Petroleum refineries, 5,363
Petrov, Ivan (1842-96), **719**
Petrov, Olga. *See* McKibban, Olga (Petrov)
Petry, Ann (Lane) (1911-), **6,066**
Petter, Bertha Kinsinger [Mrs.] (1872-1967), 5,199
Petter, Rodolphe, **5,199**
Petterson, Fanny [Mrs.], 2,170
Petterson, Hannah Mary (Bouvier) (1811-70), 1,403
Petticoat Pioneer (book), 9,824, 9,981
Pettigrew, Ann H., 3,298
Pettigrew Family (NC), **13,530**
Pettigrew, Mary Bryan, 13,356
Pettijohn, Eli, Family (MN), 8,981
Pettis, Charlotte. *See* Orr, Charlotte (Pettis) [Mrs.
    William] (?-1931)
Pettit, Elsie de Witt (Norton), **11,265**
Pettit, Katherine [Miss] (1868-1936), 5,254, **5,255,**
    5,256
Petton, Mrs. Ezra, 8,936
Petty, Cornelia (1874-1946). *See* Jerman, Cornelia
    (Petty) [Mrs. Palmer] (1874-1946)
Pew, Ethel [Miss], 8,671
Pewabic Pottery (MI), 2,821
Pews and pew rights, 6,369
Peyote, 10,654
Peyote cult. *See* Peyotism
"Peyote Cult among Wyoming Indians, The" (ms),
    18,011
Peyotism, 12,170
Peyre, Isabella (1803-90). *See* Porcher, Isabella
    (Peyre) [Mrs. William] (1803-90)
Peyton, Annie Coleman [Mrs.] (1852-98), 9,556,
    9,564
Peyton, Lauretta, 3,935
Peyton strike (1959-1961, TX), 16,008
Peyton, Theresa Barbara (1880-1929), **9,288**
Pfabe, Caroline, **7,890**
Pfadenhauer, Ruby (Mobry) [Mrs. Herman], 3,451
Pfankuch, Marjorie (1936-), **17,704**
Pfeiffer, Norma Etta (1889-), 10,152
Pfost, Gracie (Bowers) (1906-63), **3,735**
Phaeton Rogers, 12,525
Phagan, Mary, 3,186
Phar, Katie, 8,094
Pharmaceutical research, 10,207
Pharmacists, 217, 1,311, **2,903,** 4,336, 7,647, 8,721,
    9,428, 11,445, 16,425
    licenses, 1,136
Pharmacopoeias, 11,068
Phases of an Inferior Planet (book), 17,059
Phavant Indians, 16,486
Phebe Anna Thorne Open Air Model School, 14,745
Phegley, Mallie [Miss], 3,725
Phelan, Alice (1860-1912). *See* Sullivan, Alice
    (Phelan) [Mrs. Francis John] (1860-1912)
Phelan, James Duval (1861-1930), 682, **720,** 721, 828
Phelan, Lana Clarke (1920-), 11,932
Phelan, Madelin (Miers), 4,643
Phelan, Mary Louise (?-1933), 720, **721,** 828, 831
Phelps, Almira (Hart) [Mrs. Simeon] Lincoln [Mrs.
    John] (1793-1844), 5,827
Phelps, Anson Greene, 6,910
Phelps, Caroline [Mrs. William], **4,267,** 4,904
Phelps, Cassandra [Mrs. W. G.] (?-1964), **10,261**
Phelps Dodge Corporation Hospital, 1,373
Phelps, Edwin Ledyard, **5,489**
Phelps, Ethel Lowerre (1888-1968), 1,968, **8,596**
Phelps, Guy Fitch, 14,382
Phelps, Jessie (1870-1957), **7,891**
Phelps, John W., **3,299**
Phelps, John Wolcott (1813-85), **12,591**
Phelps, Lucy Fassett (Robinson) Benjamin [Mrs.
    Winthrop H.] (1822-1901), 1,968
Phelps, Elizabeth Stuart (1844-1911). *See* Ward,
    Elizabeth Stuart (Phelps) [Mrs. Herbert
    Dickinson] (1844-1911)
Phelps, Mary Merwin (1865-1944), **7,892**
Phelps Mill (MN), 8,460

Phelphs, Mrs. Timothy Guy, 1,412
Phelps, Orra, 12,848
Phelps, Pauline Eliza (1827-1912). *See* Lyman,
    Pauline Eliza (Phelps) [Mrs. Amasa Mason]
    (1827-1912)
Phelps, Rose [Miss], 4,396
Phelps, Ruth Shepard (1876-1949). *See* Morand,
    Ruth Shepard Phelps [Mrs. Paul] (1876-1949)
Phelps, William, 4,904
Phelps, Winthrop H. (1818-85), **1,968**
Phi Beta Kappa, 2,166, 3,113, 4,402, 4,403, 5,506,
    7,153, 7,576, 8,009
Phi Delta Kappa, 3,799, 8,567
Phi Kappa Phi, 4,402
Phi Kappa Phi Literary Society (MN), **8,813**
Phi Kappa Psi, 7,164
Phi Psi, **11,376**
Phi Upsilon Omicron, 8,567, 8,607, 9,829
Philadelphia (ship), 9,120
Philadelphia Anti-Slavery Society (PA), 14,953
Philadelphia Bicycle Club (PA), **15,071**
Philadelphia Board and Bureau of Health (PA),
    14,912
Philadelphia Board of Education (PA), 15,010
Philadelphia Bulletin, The (PA), 17,899
Philadelphia Bureau of Charities (PA) *See*
    Philadelphia Bureau of Charities and Correction
    (PA)
Philadelphia Bureau of Charities and Correction (PA),
    14,913, 14,916
Philadelphia Bureau of Occupations for Trained
    Women (PA), 12,738
Philadelphia Catalogue of Contributors for Relief of
    the Poor (PA), **15,072**
Philadelphia Centennial Celebration (1876), 8,221
Philadelphia Centennial Celebration (1876), Women's
    Department, 3,234, 14,971
Philadelphia Child Welfare Association (PA), 14,953
Philadelphia Committee on Family Relationships. *See*
    Philadelphia Yearly Meeting, Marriage Counsel
Philadelphia County Medical Society (PA), 7,307
Philadelphia Dancing Assembly (PA), **15,073**
Philadelphia Department of Public Health (PA),
    Bureau of Hospitals, **14,915**
Philadelphia Exposition (1876), 13,837
Philadelphia Federation of Teachers (PA), 15,332
Philadelphia Federation of Teachers (PA), Local
    Three, 15,332
Philadelphia Female Anti-Slavery Society (PA), 2,495,
    15,069
Philadelphia Garden Club (PA), **15,074**
Philadelphia General Hospital, Women's Advisory
    Council (PA), **15,075**
Philadelphia Girls House of Refuge (PA), 8,664
Philadelphia Guardians of the Poor (PA). *See*
    Philadelphia Bureau of Charities and Correction
    (PA)
Philadelphia High School for Girls (PA), 1,279
Philadelphia Hospital for Nurses (PA), 6,215
Philadelphia House of Correction (PA), **14,917**
Phildelphia Housing Association (PA). *See* Housing
    Association of Delaware Valley (PA)
Philadelphia Housing Code (1913), 15,205
Phildelphia Housing Commission (PA). *See* Housing
    Association of Delaware Valley (PA)
Philadelphia Insurance Company, 15,000
Philadelphia International Electrical Exhibition
    (1884), **14,940**
Philadelphia Ladies' Aid Society (PA), 14,824
Philadelphia Lying-In Charity Hospital (PA). *See*
    Pennsylvania Hospital (Philadelphia, PA)
Philadelphia Maternal Health League (PA), 6,223
Philadelphia Orchestra, 15,208
Philadelphia Orphan Society (PA), 2,362
Philadelphia Press (PA), 5,861, 5,869
Philadelphia School of Design for Women. *See*
    Moore Institute of Art, Science, and Industry
Philadelphia Select Council (PA), 15,000
Philadelphia Sewing Circle, **2,147**
Philadelphia Society for Organizing Charity (PA),
    8,664
Philadelphia Society for the Encouragement of
    Domestic Manufacturers (PA), 14,885

Philadelphia Yearly Meeting, Marriage Counsel,
    14,849
Philadelphia Yearly Meeting of the Religious Society
    of Friends (PA), 15,352
Philadelphia Zionist Organization of America, 14,908
Philagorean Debating Society (NC), 13,226
Philalethea Society (Westerville, OH), **14,159**
Philalaethean Society (MO), 10,063
Philanthropist, The, 13,990
Philanthropists, **1,153, 1,193, 1,217, 1,328, 1,474,**
    1,539, 1,544, 1,612, 1,687, 1,747, 1,948, 2,028,
    2,037, 2,196, 2,362, 2,387, 2,395, 2,421, 2,428,
    2,542, 2,549, 2,929, 2,941, 3,321, 3,587, 3,623,
    3,745, 3,872, 3,882, 4,049, 4,214, 4,695, 5,072,
    5,499, 5,500, **5,720, 5,729,** 5,823, **5,917, 6,221,**
    6,329, 6,333, 6,351, 6,434, **6,544, 6,598,** 6,803,
    6,880, 6,910, 6,984, 7,163, **7,167, 7,247, 7,264,**
    7,533, 7,556, 7,611, 9,077, **10,137, 10,407,**
    10,612, 10,858, 11,005, **11,279, 11,280,** 11,283,
    11,396, **11,550, 11,616, 11,720, 11,777,** 11,795,
    11,844, **11,885,** 12,069, 12,071, **12,075, 12,169,**
    12,403, 12,576, 12,577, 12,625, **12,712, 12,744,**
    12,818, **12,820, 12,902,** 13,079, **13,780, 13,857,**
    13,859, 13,943, 14,076, 14,704, 14,741, 14,884,
    15,011, **15,055, 15,161,** 15,187, 15,251, 15,283,
    15,296, 15,377, **16,221, 16,257, 17,171, 17,241,**
    17,377, 17,496, 17,602
Philanthropists, Afro-American, 15,889
Philanthropists, Jewish, **13,801**
Philanthropy. *See* Charities
Philanthropy Club (IA), 4,748
Philbrick, Julia A. [Mrs. John Dudley] (1819-?), **7,006**
Philbrick, Margaret Elder (1914-), **2,798**
Philbrook, Mary [Miss] (1872-1958), 11,114, **11,123,**
    11,143
Philharmonic Club (ME), **5,560**
Philharmonic Society (ME). *See* Philharmonic Club
    (ME)
Philippine Insurrection (1898-1899), war work, Red
    Cross, 13,729
Philippine Islands, 14,771
    American ambassadors to, 7,886
    American army officers in, 1,398
    American diplomats in, 2,192
    American travelers in, 7,488
    child health services, 6,770
    clergy, Episcopal, 2,415
    governors, 2,650, 9,395
    history, 9,003
    Japanese occupation (1942-1945), 1,606, 15,809
    judges, 16,917
    Katipunan Society, 16,132
    missionaries to, 10,499
    missionaries to, Episcopal, **13,269**
    missionaries to, Reformed Church, **8,198**
    monasteries, 998
    officials and employees, 7,992
    politics and government, 7,875
    public health, 5,764
    surgery, psychic, 212
    volunteer workers in social service, 7,297, **17,704**
    World War II, prisoners and prisons, Japanese,
        1,623
Philippine Islands, The (book), 2,553
Philips, Helen, 12,591
Philips, Katherine (1870-1933). *See* Edson, Katherine
    (Philips) (1870-1933)
Philleo, Calvin Wheeler (1822-58), 1,874
Philleo, Elizabeth (Norton) [Mrs. Calvin Wheeler],
    1,874
Philleo, Emma. *See* Whipple, Emma (Philleo)
    Goodwin [Mrs. Charles K.]
Philleo Family, **1,874**
Philleo, Prudence (Crandall) [Mrs. Calvin] (1803-89),
    1,874, **1,898,** 1,918, 3,298, 4,732, 5,907, 6,741,
    11,605
Phillippe de la Noye (ship), 11,481
Phillips Academy (Andover, MA), 5,736
Phillips, Adah. *See* Jessee, Adah (Phillips)
Phillips, Adelaide [Miss] (1833-82), **12,592**
Phillips, Alice, 6,698
Phillips, Amy Carolina Davis (1851-1936), 16,486
Phillips, Ann (Thomas) (1839-1920), **16,551**

Phillips, Anne Terry Greene [Mrs. Wendell] (1813-86), 5,907, 7,476
Phillips, Betty (pseudonym). *See* Way, Elizabeth Penwick
Phillips, Charles, 13,460
Phillips, Cornelia Ann (1825-1908). *See* Spencer, Cornelia Ann (Phillips) [Mrs. James Monroe] (1825-1908)
Phillips, Dorothy, 1,623
Phillips, Elizabeth [Miss], **5,152**
Phillips, Elizabeth [Mrs.], 15,673
Phillips, Elizabeth Cogswell, **6,153**
Phillips, Ella Whitford [Mrs. Ross], 9,439
Phillips, Elsie LaGrange Cole [Mrs. Wilbur Carey] (1879-1961), **8,671**
Phillips, Esther B., 400
Phillips, Eugenia (Levy) [Mrs. Philip] (1820-1902), 2,522, 2,659
Phillips Family, **2,659**
Phillips Family (NY, PA), **7,549**
Phillips Family (SC), 15,673
Phillips, Fannie Fern (1867-1950). *See* Andrews, Fannie Fern (Phillips) [Mrs. Edwin Gasper] (1867-1950)
Phillips Foundation, 11,906
Phillips, Harriet Byrle (Hamblin) [Mrs. Hugh J.] (1920-?), **16,788**
Phillips, Ida Minerva Tarbell [Mrs. John Sanburn] (1857-1944). *See* Tarbell, Ida Minerva. [Mrs. John Sanburn] Phillips (1857-1944)
Phillips, Irna (1901-73), **17,705, 17,810**
Phillips, James, 13,134
Phillips, John Sanburn (1861-1949), **4,484**
Phillips, Julia, 950
Phillips, Julia Macgruder, **7,893**
Phillips, Julia T. (1802-?). *See* Dodge, Julia T. (Phillips) (1802-?)
Phillips, Kathryn Sisson (1879-1968), **11,906**
Phillips, Laurie Kent, **10,520**
Phillips, Lena Madesin (ca. 1881-1955), **6,829**
Phillips, Leslie G., 14,359
Phillips, Mai Rives, 5,553
Phillips, Marcia Louise Sumner [Mrs. B. S.], **17,477**
Phillips, Mary Elizabeth (1857-1945), **5,951,** 5,960, 5,968
Phillips, Mary G., 11,662
Phillips, Mrs. William, 13,585
Phillips, Peggy, **18,000**
Phillips, Philip (1807-84), Family, **2,522**
Phillips, Rosalie (Solomons) [Mrs. Naphtali] (1872-1945), 7,527, 7,549, 12,117
Phillips, Ross, 9,439
Phillips, S. B., 17,477
Phillips, Sampson and Company (publishers), 5,944
Phillips, Sarah Ellen, **13,090**
Phillips, Velma (1891-), **17,203**
Phillips, Wendell (1811-84), 2,303, 5,684, 5,907, **6,830,** 7,233, 7,476, 12,419, 14,206, 17,010
Phillips, Wilbur Carey (1880-1967?), **8,671**
Phillips, William Hallett (1853-97), **2,522**
Phillis Wheatley. *See also* Phyllis Wheatley; Wheatley, Phillis
Phillis Wheatley Association, 13,934
Phillis Wheatley Association (OH), **13,950**
Phillis Wheatley Foundation, 3,799
Phillis Wheatley Institute, 15,782
Philologists, **5,727**
Philomath Club of Roachdale (IN), **4,578**
Philomath College (OR), students, 14,373, 14,375
Philomathean Society, 13,227
Philomaths (MI), **8,212**
Philosophers, 78, 975, 1,413, **2,383, 2,459,** 5,977, 6,210, **6,708,** 7,247, **11,982,** 14,890
Philosophers, Jewish, 13,799
Philosophic Society of Texas, 16,239
Philosophical Society, 14,881
Philosophical Society of Philadelphia (PA),
Philosophical Society of Texas, 16,277
Philotasian Club (PA), **15,076**
Philothea (book), 7,561
Phipps, Laurence, 10,042
Phipps, Margaret (Rogers) [Mrs. Laurence], **10,042**
Phoebe Lincoln Chemical Company (IA), 2,401
Phoenix (periodical), 15,897

Phoenix (ship), 11,134
Phoenix, Alexander (1778-1863), 8,004
Phoenix Coliseum Theater (AZ), 169
Phoenix 1870-1970: In Photographs (book), 169
Phoenix Family (NY), **8,004**
Phoenix Indian School (AZ), 169
Phoenix Soroptimist Club (AZ), 169
Phoenix, The (newspaper), 4,632
Phoenix Women's Club (AZ), 167
Phonograph, 11,907
Phonographic Institute, 13,855
Phonorecords, 5,988, 6,007
Phonotapes, **1,859,** 15,334
Photo Secession, 425
Photograph collections, 978, **1,006, 1,019, 1,064,** 1,079, 1,157, 1,330, 1,531, 1,614, 2,870, 2,923, 2,940, 3,037, 3,648, 4,196, 5,072, 5,596, 7,060, 8,411, 8,476, 9,468, 9,579, 9,699, 11,235, 11,252, 12,081, 12,127, 12,129, 12,130, 13,170, 14,245, 15,867, 16,789, 16,985, 17,532, 17,576
Photographers, 169, 357, 425, 607, 958, **1,266,** 1,330, **1,349,** 1,475, **2,414, 2,423, 2,745,** 3,037, 3,115, 4,028, 5,177, **5,257, 5,638,** 6,075, 6,639, 7,012, 9,082, 9,535, 9,587, 11,217, 11,235, 11,252, 11,466, **11,983,** 12,123, **12,126, 12,127, 12,130, 12,405, 12,789,** 12,842, **12,891, 12,909,** 14,060, **14,115,** 14,201, 14,300, 14,544, 16,398, 17,070, **17,179, 17,250, 17,407**
Photographers, Afro-American, 3,292
Photographic Society of America, 958
Photographs, **206,** 923, 1,475, **2,730,** 3,478, **4,279, 4,455, 6,639, 9,540,** 9,770, **10,699, 12,123, 12,803, 12,887,** 14,876, **15,093, 16,999, 17,489**
collectors and collecting, **12,789**
Native Americans, **2,842**
Photography, 607, 2,784, 7,012, 12,842
exhibitions, 958, 9,587, 14,201
films, 11,121
negatives, **9,535**
societies, etc., 958
Photography, journalistic, **12,891**
Photography, medical, 9,826
Phrenological Journal, The, 11,590
Phrenology, **5,029,** 8,953, 11,600, 11,602, 14,152, 14,630
Phyllis (slave, SC), 15,486
"Phyllis" (television program), 17,808
Phyllis Wheatley. *See also* Phillis Wheatley; Wheatley, Phillis
Phyllis Wheatley Association, **4,142**
Phyllis Wheatley Center. *See* Phyllis Wheatley Community Center (Minneapolis, MN)
Phyllis Wheatley Community Center (Minneapolis, MN), 9,252, **9,289,** 9,467
Phyllis Wheatley Home for Girls (Chicago, IL), 4,142
Phyllis Wheatley Settlement House. *See* Phyllis Wheatley Community Center (Minneapolis, MN)
Phylon (periodical), 3,288
Physical education and training, 1,035, **1,555,** 2,432, 2,686, **4,041,** 7,173, 7,219, 7,317, **7,772,** 8,544, 8,547, 9,877, **10,218,** 12,127, 12,937, **13,200, 13,205, 13,254,** 13,366, **13,761,** 13,894, 13,916, 14,118, 15,183, 17,230
Physical education teachers, **402,** 7,173, **9,568, 12,587, 17,715**
Physical fitness, 6,602
Physical therapists, **2,091,** 3,671
Physical therapy, 8,635
Physically handicapped, 11,765, 17,018
Physician and nurse, 12,074
Physicians, 231, 287, 343, 545, 821, 880, **935,** 1,020, 1,058, 1,062, 1,081, 1,136, 1,219, **1,251,** 1,281, 1,304, **1,348,** 1,374, **1,417,** 1,462, **1,465, 1,521, 1,529, 1,551, 1,560, 1,607,** 1,608, 1,620, **1,629, 1,672,** 1,724, **1,733, 1,738,** 1,779, 1,786, 1,790, **1,840, 2,010, 2,086, 2,088, 2,090,** 2,134, **2,193,** 2,209, **2,277, 2,278, 2,322,** 2,334, 2,386, **2,417, 2,464,** 2,518, 2,574, **2,609,** 2,679, 2,686, 2,690, 2,701, **2,963,** 2,965, 3,007, 3,008, **3,091,** 3,093, 3,146, **3,161, 3,309, 3,310, 3,311, 3,333,** 3,381, **3,464, 3,481, 3,482,** 3,487, 3,608, 3,813, 3,861, **3,926, 3,958,** 3,967, 3,976, 3,977, 4,010, **4,027,** 4,053, 4,101, 4,111, **4,131, 4,145,** 4,196, 4,217, **4,261,** 4,336, **4,346,** 4,352, **4,377,** 4,419, 4,469,

4,475, **4,496, 4,698,** 4,732, **4,945,** 4,948, 4,952, **4,963,** 5,124, 5,269, 5,394, 5,721, 5,724, 5,771, 5,811, 5,842, 5,947, 6,028, 6,150, 6,164, **6,209, 6,216, 6,219, 6,221, 6,222,** 6,223, 6,224, 6,226, **6,231, 6,232, 6,268,** 6,352, 6,363, **6,411,** 6,412, **6,446,** 6,552, 6,564, **6,616, 6,622,** 6,645, **6,649,** 6,662, 6,679, **6,681, 6,688, 6,697, 6,698, 6,736, 6,763, 6,770, 6,777, 6,847,** 6,864, **6,875, 6,983,** 6,987, 7,226, 7,234, **7,255, 7,259, 7,274, 7,288,** 7,311, 7,317, **7,320,** 7,383, 7,385, 7,636, 7,639, **7,654,** 7,660, 7,677, **7,715, 7,719,** 7,727, 7,801, **7,872, 7,920, 7,966, 8,020, 8,052, 8,163,** 8,223, 8,305, **8,396,** 8,465, 8,477, 8,518, 8,667, **8,707,** 8,721, **8,822,** 8,884, **8,965, 8,991,** 9,008, 9,064, 9,082, **9,132, 9,159, 9,176, 9,178,** 9,203, 9,318, **9,319, 9,323,** 9,359, 9,364, **9,423, 9,514,** 9,803, **9,844,** 9,906, 9,909, 9,916, **9,979,** 10,044, 10,163, **10,170,** 10,185, 10,207, 10,210, **10,253, 10,402, 10,405, 10,463, 10,538,** 10,580, 10,632, 10,708, **10,728,** 10,729, 10,761, **10,898,** 10,903, 10,954, **10,970,** 10,976, 10,977, 10,995, 11,001, **11,019,** 11,020, **11,021, 11,043, 11,357, 11,367, 11,393,** 11,395, **11,399, 11,423,** 11,440, **11,467,** 11,472, 11,511, **11,556,** 11,605, 11,647, 11,666, **11,727,** 11,754, 11,857, 11,897, 11,916, **11,941, 11,947,** 12,074, **12,132, 12,139, 12,142,** 12,153, **12,155,** 12,185, 12,311, 12,327, 12,345, **12,352, 12,380,** 12,406, 12,423, **12,450,** 12,753, **12,754,** 12,759, 12,765, 12,771, **12,825, 12,837, 12,840, 12,841,** 12,843, 12,848, **12,913, 12,917, 12,966,** 13,047, 13,063, 13,151, **13,246,** 13,262, 13,325, 13,430, 13,508, 13,662, **13,660, 13,693, 13,710, 13,860,** 14,146, 14,198, 14,200, 14,331, **14,397, 14,425,** 14,463, 14,473, **14,526, 14,629, 14,697,** 14,698, 14,699, **14,763,** 14,803, 14,809, 14,814, 14,817, 14,819, 14,824, 14,857, 14,860, **14,871, 14,889,** 14,892, **14,925, 14,926, 14,927, 14,928,** 14,943, 14,965, 14,977, 14,981, 15,017, 15,039, 15,040, 15,041, 15,077, 15,079, **15,084,** 15,087, **15,117,** 15,125, **15,126, 15,127, 15,129, 15,130, 15,131, 15,133, 15,134, 15,136, 15,137, 15,138, 15,139, 15,140, 15,141,** 15,142, **15,144, 15,260,** 15,423, **15,427,** 15,428, **15,429,** 15,430, 15,467, **15,506,** 15,600, **15,735, 15,749,** 15,776, 15,904, 15,939, 15,951, 16,060, FB16,063, **16,225,** 16,236, 16,342, 16,357, 16,486, **16,786,** 16,839, 16,905, 16,946, 16,949, **16,956,** 16,967, 16,968, 17,121, **17,130,** 17,133, 17,185, 17,278, **17,337, 17,462,** 17,498, 17,528, 17,574, **17,618,** 17,678, **17,699,** 17,875, **17,879, 17,925.** *See also* Obstetricians; Pediatricians
licenses, 1,136
Physicians, Afro-American, 2,134, 3,293, 5,907, 15,430
Physicians, British, 6,889
Physicians, homeopathic, 14,000
Physicians, Native American, 10,029, 10,483
Physicists, **1,096, 1,097, 1,098,** 1,223, **1,540, 1,541,** 6,986, 7,328, **11,813, 11,814,** 11,815, **11,816,** 11,901, 13,333
Physick, Philip, 15,167
Physick, Susan Dillwyn (1803-56). *See* Conner, Susan Dillwyn (Physick) [Mrs. David] (1803-56)
Physick, Susan Syng (1803-56). *See* Conner, Susan Dillwyn (Physick) [Mrs. David] (1803-56)
Physics, 2,344
research, 11,580
Physiologists, **14,900**
Physiology, 11,725, 14,152
research, 10,207
Pi Beta Phi, 5,064, **10,185**
Pi Lambda Theta, 8,567, 9,839, 9,960
Pi Lambda Theta, Alpha Pi Chapter (MI), **8,051**
Pi Mu Epsilon, 4,403
Pianists, 942, **1,021,** 1,686, 2,023, **2,366, 2,641, 2,664, 2,665, 2,908,** 3,294, 3,369, 3,610, 4,056, 4,894, 5,394, **5,529, 5,531, 5,534, 5,657, 5,910,** 9,057, 9,075, 9,517, 10,120, 10,481, 10,835, 11,230, 13,766, 13,840, 14,008, 14,150, 15,367, 16,013, 16,427, 16,577, 17,333, 17,986
Pianists, Afro-American, **2,852**
Piano, instruction and study, **2,908,** 10,481
Piatt, Nadeen, 1,786
Picard, Betty (Brasch) [Mrs. Joseph], 1,569

Picard, Joseph, 1,569
Picard, Lil, **2,799**
Picasso, Pablo, 620, 5,721
Piccard Family, **2,523**
Piccard, Jean Felix (1884-1963), 2,523
Piccard, Jeannette (Ridlon) [Mrs. Jean Felix] (1895-), **2,523**
Pickard, Joseph C., 4,392
Pickel, J. M., **13,531**
Pickens, Andrew, 15,784
Pickens, Kezia Ann Miles, 15,665
Pickens, Lucy Petway (Holcombe) [Mrs. Francis Wilkinson] (1832-99), 15,674, 16,313
Pickens, Rebecca Calhoun [Mrs. Andrew] (1745-1814), **15,784**
Pickens, Ruby. *See* Tartt, Ruby (Pickens) [Mrs. W. P.]
Pickens, William, 5,458
Picker, Jean S. (1921-), **7,281**
Pickering, Alice Miller, 16,648
Pickering, Alice (Miller) [Mrs. John Edson] (1887-1951), **16,790**
Pickering, William, 17,273
Picketing, 6,314
Pickett Family (ID), 3,727
Pickett, Jane E., 9,593
Pickett, Minnie E., 1,319
Pickford, Mary. Gladys Smith. [Mrs. Douglas] Fairbanks, Sr. [Mrs. Charles "Buddy"] Rogers (1893-1979), 720, 3,028, 6,712, 9,878, 11,907, 12,129
Picking, Lelia Grace, **5,153**, 11,857
Pickins, Francis Wilkinson (1805-69), **15,674**
Pickman, Mary Toppan (1816-?), **7,420**
Pickren, Pansy (1904-64?), **2,874**
Picnic Springs Ranch (MT), 10,290
Pico, Maria Inocenta (1811-?). *See* Ávila, Maria Inocenta (Pico) [Mrs. Miguel] (1811-?)
Picon, Clara, 7,550
Picon, Elsie, 8,149
Picon, Molly. [Mrs. Jacob] Kalich (1898-), **7,550, 11,817**
Picot's School for Young Ladies (Philadelphia, PA), 5,343
Picotte, Susan (La Flesche) [Mrs. Henry] (1865-1915), 10,029, 10,483
Pictorial Review (periodical), 11,304, 12,480, 13,027
Picture of Success (book), 6,091
Pictures, **8,527**
Pictures in the Hallway (drama), 12,367
Pidgin, Mrs. William A. (?-1918), **5,683**
"Piece of News, A" (story), 9,770
Piece-work, 5,896, 7,664, 10,795, 10,815, 11,851
Piedmont Park (Atlanta, GA), 3,276
Pieksen, Margot, 2,396
Pier, Caroline (1827-59), 8,934
Pier, Sarah C. (1840-?), **16,378**
Pierce, Adelle P., 7,801
Pierce, Ann, 12,315
Pierce, Ann Elise [Miss] (1892-1967), 5,035
Pierce, Anne (Longfellow) (1810-1901), 6,330
Pierce, Augusta (1833?-95). *See* Tabor, Augusta (Pierce) (1833?-95)
Pierce, Bessie Louise, 3,825
Pierce, Clara Lizette (1859-?). *See* Bell, Clara Lizette (Pierce) [Mrs. James H.] (1859-?)
Pierce, Cornelia Marvin, 14,591, 14,713
Pierce County Library Service Committee (WA), **17,395**
Pierce, De De, 5,532
Pierce, Edith Lovejoy (1904-), 2,396
Pierce, Ella J., 13,300
Pierce, Emily (Bancroft) Palmer, 14,514
Pierce Family, 9,738
Pierce Family (CA), **722**
Pierce Family (MI), 8,167
Pierce, Flora Chase [Mrs. Charles E.], 18,026
Pierce, Florence (1891-1974), **12,726**
Pierce, Franklin (1804-69), **10,823**
Pierce, H. P. [Mrs. Samuel B.], 9,004
Pierce, Henry, 4,630
Pierce, Henry D., 9,738
Pierce, Henry M., 12,283
Pierce, Imogene S., **17,596**

Pierce, Jane Means (Appleton) [Mrs. Franklin] (1806-63), 3,907, 10,170, 10,823
Pierce, John (1773-1849), 6,833
Pierce, Katherine, 15,315
Pierce, Lucy. *See* Hedge, Lucy (Pierce) [Mrs. Frederic Henry]
Pierce, Lucy (Tappan) [Mrs. John], 6,833
Pierce, Margaret (1823-1907). *See* Young, Margaret (Pierce) [Mrs. Morris] Whitesides [Mrs. Brigham] (1823-1907)
Pierce, Margaret (Cameron) [Mrs. James Manning] (1838-1929), 722
Pierce, Mary (1820-1912). *See* Poor, Mary (Pierce) [Mrs. Henry Varnum] (1820-1912)
Pierce, Mary (1883-1971), 10,823
Pierce, Mary Eugenia (1872-1964), 722
Pierce, Mary Jane [Mrs. Henry M.], **12,283**
Pierce, Mrs. Henry, 4,630
Pierce, Sarah (1767-1852), 1,967
Pierce, Susan (?-1974), 10,823
Pierce, Syd, 14,686
Pierce, Theresa Vinton (1877-1963). *See* Krull, Theresa Vinton (Pierce) [Mrs. Frederic] (1877-1963)
Pierce, Vesta Maude (1899-). *See* Crawford, Vesta Maude (Pierce) [Mrs. Arthur Lorenzo] (1899-)
Pierce, Walter M., 14,594
Pierce, Wilhelmina "Billie" [Mrs. De De] (1907-74), **5,532**
Pierce, Winslow S., 4,630
Pierpont, Elias, 1,995
Pierpont, Grace Bradley [Mrs. Elias], 1,995
Pierpont, Hattie (1847-1923). *See* Fuller, Hattie (Pierpont) [Mrs. Austin B.] (1847-1923)
Pierpont, Sarah (1710-58). *See* Edwards, Sarah (Pierpont) [Mrs. Jonathan] (1710-58)
Pierpont, Sarah (Breck) [Mrs. James] (1710-53), 7,661
"Pierre Laval" (television script), 6,111
Pierrepont, Edwards, 15,725
Pierrepont Family (NY), 12,020
Pierrepont, Julia, 11,324
Pierrepont, William Constable, 11,568
Pierson, Bernie Frances, 13,890
Pierson, Ellen Elizabeth (Perry) (1828-?), **7,421**
Pierson Family, 864
Pierson, Harriet, **8,778**
Pierson, Helen. *See* Brower, Helen (Pierson)
Pierson, Mrs. Paul (ca. 1860s-?), 169
Pierson, Nancy A., 14,650
Pierson, Sarah A. (1829-?). *See* Walsworth, Sarah A. (Pierson) [Mrs. Edward Brown] (1829-?)
Pierson, Stephen, 3,225
Pierson, William (1796-1882), **11,019**
Piesinger, Marie, 8,721
Pieters, Jennie A., **8,203**
"Pietism as a Motivating Factor in Women's Participation in the School Board Election of 1895, Xenia, OH" (dissertation), 14,163
Pietists, 14,718
Pietzsche, Dorothea Maria Pauline Alice Sibylle (?-1971). *See* Moholy-Nagy, Dorothea Maria Pauline Alice Sibylle (Pietzsche) [Mrs. Laszlo] (?-1971)
Pigman, Mary (Springman) [Mrs. William Penn], 3,565
Pigman, William Penn, 3,565
Pigou, The (ship), 14,836
Pike, Albert, 266
Pike Beneficial Society of Philadelphia (PA), 14,953
Pike, Elvira, 16,876
Pike, James A., 5,511
Pike, Martha Ellen Goforth Fox [Mrs.] (1861-?), **10,355**
Pike, Mary Margaret (1852-?). *See* Harpster, Mary Margaret (Pike) [Mrs. William A.] (1852-?)
Pike, Miles N., 10,658
Pike's Peak (CO), 1,790
Pilcher, Catherine Berry (1894-). *See* Avery, Catherine Berry (Pilcher) [Mrs. Roy] (1894-)
Pilcher, Nancy (Barrow) (1812-85), 15,939
"Pilgrim Fathers" (poem), 8,477
Pilgrim, Mariette Shaw (1898-), **143**
Pilgrims and pilgrimages, 2,689
Pilkinton, Mrs. C. A., 9,757

Pilling, James Constantine (1864-95), **12,593**
Pillot, Gertrude G., 2,202
Pillsbury, Agnes Hope, 3,828, 4,056
Pillsbury, Dorothy (Pinckney) (1896-1967), **11,226**
Pillsbury, Esther, 4,904
Pillsbury, Frances I. [Mrs. Samuel L.], 4,904
Pillsbury, Parker, 7,233
Pilot Club, 9,779
Pilot Club (AL), 76
Pilot Club (Manhattan, KS), **5,193**
Pilot International, 5,193
Pilots and pilotage, 184, 9,126
Pilsbury, Caroline (1793-?), **5,584**
Pilsbury, Lois C. (1820-1900). *See* Walker, Lois C. (Pilsbury) [Mrs. Galen C.] (1820-1900)
Pilsbury, Moses Cross (1778-?), Family, **2,524**
Pilsbury, Rebecca S. C. [Mrs. Timothy], **13,091**
Pilsbury, Timothy (1780-1858), 13,091
Pinacothea Gallery (NY). *See* Rose Fried Gallery (NY)
Pinart, Alphonse Louis, **723**
Pinchot, Cornelia Elizabeth (Bryce) [Mrs. Gifford] (1881-1960), 2,336, **2,525**, 9,159, 9,466, 14,822
Pinchot, Gifford (1865-1946), 2,464, **2,526**, 6,765, 14,809, 15,176
Pinchot, Mary Eno [Mrs. James W.], 2,526
Pinchot, Mrs. Gifford, 8,083
Pinckney, Ann, 2,556
Pinckney, Anne Randolph McKenna, 15,675
Pinckney, Caroline, 15,675
Pinckney, Charles, 3,567
Pinckney, Charles Cotesworth, 15,456
Pinckney, Charles Cotesworth (1746-1825), 2,527, 15,507, 15,508
Pinckney, Charles Cotesworth, Jr. (1839-1909), **15,675**
Pinckney, Dorothy (1896-1967). *See* Pillsbury, Dorothy (Pinckney) (1896-1967)
Pinckney, Eliza Lucas. *See* Izard, Eliza Lucas (Pinckney) [Mrs. Ralph]
Pinckney, Elizabeth "Eliza" (Lucas) [Mrs. Charles] (1722?-93), 2,527, 3,567, 13,104, 13,137, 15,507, **15,676**, 15,681
Pinckney, Elizabeth Izard (1784-1862), **15,677**
Pinckney Family (SC), **2,527**, 12,028, 13,137, **15,507**, 15,678
Pinckney, Harriott (1776-1866), **15,678**
Pinckney, Harriott Lucas (1748-1830). *See* Horry, Harriott Lucas (Pinckney) [Mrs. Daniel] (1748-1830)
Pinckney, Josephine (1895-1957), **15,679**
Pinckney, Maria Henrietta [Miss] (ca. 1774-?), **15,508**
Pinckney, Mary, 15,675
Pinckney, Mary (Stead) [Mrs. Charles Cotesworth], 2,527
Pinckney, Mrs. Thomas, 15,681
Pinckney, Phoebe Caroline, 15,675
Pinckney, Rebecca R., **15,680**
Pinckney, Sarah Middleton [Mrs. Charles Cotesworth], 15,508
Pinckney, Thomas (1750-1828), 2,527, **15,681**
Pincus, Celia, 15,332
Pine Family (NY), **11,427**
Pine Mountain Settlement School (KY), 2,345, 5,255, **5,256**
Pinède, Alphonse, 12,602
Pinède, Louisa Augusta (Schlossberger) [Mrs. George] Ripley [Mrs. Alphonse], **12,602**
Pinell, Louise R., 2,887
Pinetree Garden Club (GA), 3,187
Pings, Mable Manix (1884-1968), 10,333
Pinion, Dorothea. *See* Heinsen, Dorothea (Pinion) [Mrs. Newton]
Pinker, James B., 10,860
Pinkerton, Ellen Herndon (Arthur) (1875-1915), 2,180
Pinkerton, Fanny, 8,413
Pinkerton High School (Midway, KY), 5,393
Pinkerton's National Police Agency, Female Department, 11,440
Pinkham, Lydia (Estes) (1819-83), 6,743
Pinkham, Wenona Osborne, 6,469
Pinn, Mrs. R. W., 1,777
Pinney, Jean, 8,633

Pioneer (periodical), 7,999
"Pioneer Anniversary" (poem), 862
Pioneer Daughters (ND), **13,683**
Pioneer Daughters of America, **13,659**
Pioneer Days in Idaho County (book), 4,305
Pioneer Historical Society (OR), 14,306
Pioneer Home-makers of the 1840's (book), 14,574
Pioneer Ladies' Aid Society (CO), 1,701, 1,732,
    1,771, 1,785
Pioneer Ladies Aid Society (Denver, CO), **1,735**
Pioneer Memorial State Park (Harrodsburg, KY),
    5,307
"Pioneer Mother" (statue), 6,384
Pioneer Nevada, 10,724
"Pioneer Woman's Story of Illinois, A," 4,313
"Pioneer Women of Afro-American Descent in
    Detroit," 8,284
Pioneer Women of Alaska, 144
Pioneer Women of Arizona (book), 16,504
Pioneer Women of Colorado, 1,785
"Pioneer Women of Colorado—Courage and
    Sacrifice," 1,790
Pioneer Women Teacher Research Project (NE),
    10,453
Pioneer Women, The Women's Labor Zionist
    Organization of America, **13,816**
Pioneer Workers of the Minnesota Federation of
    Women's Clubs, 9,227
Pioneers and Prominent Men of Arizona (book),
    16,504
Pioneers and settlers, **135**, 160, 171, 221, 305, 315,
    410, 457, 538, 562, 583, 591, **606**, 618, **671**, 704,
    724, **798**, 813, **857**, 899, 904, 956, **960**, 971, **975**,
    1,229, 1,235, 1,256, 1,257, 1,278, **1,355**, 1,525,
    1,609, 1,658, **1,661**, **1,703**, 1,736, 2,923, 2,940,
    3,671, **3,675**, **3,710**, **3,726**, **3,728**, **3,730**, **3,731**,
    3,736, 3,737, **3,738**, **3,754**, 4,255, **4,345**, **4,353**,
    4,368, **4,369**, **4,423**, 4,701, 4,706, 4,804, **4,885**,
    4,904, **5,108**, 7,127, 7,676, 7,677, 7,769, 7,804,
    7,855, 8,195, 8,278, 8,291, **8,472**, **8,482**, 8,515,
    8,518, 8,703, 8,709, 8,779, **8,895**, 8,900, 8,924,
    8,958, **8,967**, 8,981, **9,000**, 9,099, 9,245, 9,249,
    9,269, **9,294**, 9,317, 9,378, 9,419, 9,463, **9,524**,
    9,834, 9,842, **9,850**, **9,855**, 9,921, 9,938, **10,224**,
    10,234, 10,237, **10,239**, **10,247**, **10,248**, **10,258**,
    10,276, 10,283, 10,288, 10,296, 10,315, **10,321**,
    10,322, **10,335**, 10,336, **10,338**, **10,351**, **10,355**,
    10,356, **10,364**, **10,368**, **10,372**, **10,374**, **10,382**,
    10,383, 10,390, **10,400**, **10,403**, **10,632**, 10,634,
    10,636, 10,734, 10,737, 10,879, 10,905, 11,520,
    11,745, **11,953**, 12,734, **12,768**, 13,006, 13,011,
    13,697, **14,098**, **14,153**, **14,174**, **14,176**, **14,181**,
    14,183, 14,241, **14,270**, 14,310, **14,341**, **14,348**,
    14,436, **14,477**, **14,480**, **14,487**, **14,488**, **14,499**,
    14,542, 14,549, **14,588**, 14,647, 14,648, 15,059,
    15,322, **15,784**, **15,849**, **15,858**, **16,181**, **16,305**,
    16,460, 16,485, **16,486**, **16,503**, 16,504, **16,508**,
    16,509, **16,512**, **16,513**, **16,522**, 16,525, 16,529,
    16,536, **16,541**, 16,551, 16,560, 16,566, **16,571**,
    16,572, **16,573**, 16,580, 16,602, 16,611, 16,616,
    16,646, 16,647, 16,648, 16,675, 16,682, 16,701,
    16,710, 16,730, 16,739, 16,751, 16,827, 16,862,
    16,887, 16,895, 16,897, **16,912**, 16,913, 16,915,
    16,965, 16,967, **16,968**, **17,151**, 17,170, 17,188,
    17,196, 17,212, 17,397, **17,418**, **17,419**, **17,420**,
    17,558, **17,570**, 17,609, 17,626, **17,632**, 17,664,
    17,887, **17,891**, 17,897, 17,908, **17,912**
Pioneers and settlers, Afro-American, 8,284, **12,692**,
    16,982
Pioneers and settlers, Danish, **17,290**
Pioneers and settlers, German, **16,306**
Pioneers and settlers, Jewish, 13,780
Pioneers and settlers, Polish, **16,307**
Pioneers and settlers, Spanish, 1,396
Pioneers Foundation, Inc. (NM), **11,227**
Pioneer's Home for Women (AK), 17,217
Pioneers in the Arab World (book), 10,927
Pioneers of Alaska Auxiliary, 144
Pioneers of California, 1,634
Piotrowski, Helen [Mrs.], 13,906
Piper, Evelyn (pseudonym). *See* Modell, Merriam
Piper, Helen Jackson (1882-1958), **6,831**
Piper, Lizzie H., **10,824**
Pipes, Susie Fannell, 14,618

Pipkin, Mary, 13,600
Piqua Hebrew Association (OH), 13,791
Pirates, 3,509, 11,492
Piscataqua Pioneers (NH), 10,851
Pischel, Emma, 4,085
Pistol Pete, the Autobiography of Frank Eaton
    (book), 499
Piston, Walter, 6,503
Pitcairn, John, 14,733
Pitcher, Emma Hayes (Bickham) [Mrs. William]
    (1915-), 4,055
Pitcher, Gladys, 5,582
Pitcher, Hazel [Mrs. Charles] (1909-), **14,191**
Pitcher, Molly. *See* McCauley, Mary (Ludwig) Hays
Pitchers (baseball), 11,405
Pitkin, Caroline. *See* Mott, Caroline Pitkin [Mrs.
    Jordan Lawrence, III]
Pitkin, Lorraine J., 4,697
Pitman, Benjamin (1822-1910), **12,594**, 13,855
Pitman Family (OH), **13,855**
Pitman, Melrose (1889-), 13,855
Pitt County Tuberculosis Association (NC), 13,286
Pitt River Indians, 14,677
Pitt, William, 15,219
Pittier, Henry Francois, 14,876
Pittman, Amelia, 725
Pittman, Anna Maria. *See* Lee, Anna Maria
    (Pittman) [Mrs. Jason]
Pittman, Anna (Prince), **9,700**
Pittman Family, **725**
Pittman, George, 725
Pittman, Key (1872-1940), **2,528**, 10,679
Pittman, Lucille, 8,077
Pittman Mimosa (Gates) [Mrs. Key] (1872-1952),
    2,528
Pittman, Tarea Hall, **726**
Pitts Family (TX), 16,269
Pitts, Helen. *See* Douglass, Helen (Pitts) [Mrs.
    Frederick]
Pitts, Lizzie (Craig) [Mrs. Thomas Henry], 3,344
Pitts, Thomas Henry (1834-71), **3,344**
Pittsburgh and Allegheny Kindergarten College (PA(,
    15,225
Pittsburgh Civil Service Commission (PA), 14,804
Pittsburgh Conference of Jewish Women's
    Organizations (PA), **15,250**
Pittsburgh Diocesan Council of Catholic Women,
    4,640
Pittsburgh Female College (PA),
Pittsburgh Hadassah News (PA), 15,245
Pittsburgh Kindergarten Association (PA), **15,225**
Pittsburgh Musical Institute, 3,204
Pittsburgh Select Female Seminary (PA), 15,221
Pittsburgh Training School for Teachers, 15,225
Pittsfield Academy (MA), 6,627
Pius IX, Pope, 13,928
Pius XII, Pope, 15,361
Pizanne, Peggy, 8,936
Pizzini, John, 9,277
Pizzini, Maria Fergus [Mrs. John] (?-1881), 9,277
Pizzuto, Laura, **17,323**
Place, Anna Miller (Newkirk) [Mrs. James W.]
    Barker [Mrs. James Keyes] (1841-1918), **11,020**
"Place Called Morning, A," 5,304
Place, James Keyes, 11,020
Place, Marian Templeton [Mrs. Howard] (1910-),
    10,262, 14,712
Place of Sapphires, The (book), 6,072
"Place of the Family in American Life, The," 10,035
Placenta, 11,830
Placente, Mary, 4,134
Plain Dealer (OH), 13,898, 14,081
Plain News, 4,350
Plane, Caroline Helen (Jemison) (1829-1925), **3,345**
Plank, Betty, 3,844
Planned Parenthood (MN), **8,826**
Planned Parenthood Association (Chicago, IL), **3,895**
Planned Parenthood Association of Oregon, 14,698
Planned Parenthood Federation of America. *See*
    Planned Parenthood-World Population
Planned Parenthood League of Massachusetts, 6,432,
    6,475, 6,987, 7,282, **7,283**
Planned Parenthood of America, 8,633
Planned Parenthood of Central Ohio, 14,013

Planned Parenthood of Maryland, **5,842**
Planned Parenthood of Minnesota, **8,672**
Planned Parenthood of New York City, 6,221, 6,232,
    6,987, **7,192**, 7,289
Planned Parenthood of Rochester and Monroe
    County (NY), **12,829**
Planned Parenthood-World Population, 6,221, 6,222,
    6,223, 6,225, 6,446, 6,987, 7,192, **7,282**, 7,283,
    7,284, 7,289, 7,320, 8,634, 8,647, 8,672, 11,857,
    11,885, 12,736, 14,671
Planning and Counseling Center for Women (MN).
    See Minnesota Women's Center
Plant diseases, **6,472**
Plant, Martha, **13,092**
Plant pathologists, 10,157, 10,180
Plant pathology, 11,628
Plantation life, 260, 2,221, 3,208, 3,313, 3,419, 9,675,
    9,800, 10,975, 11,589, 11,602, 12,944, 12,946,
    12,955, 12,960, 12,969, 13,012, 13,019, 13,105,
    13,173, 13,257, 13,322, 13,347, 13,356, 13,403,
    13,454, 13,530, **13,611**, 14,048, **15,416**, 15,439,
    15,464, 15,474, 15,500, 15,525, 15,562, 15,601,
    15,608, 15,631, 15,635, 15,658, 15,707, 15,712,
    15,746, 15,750, 15,778, 15,781, 15,834, 15,932,
    16,142, 16,244, 17,081, 17,097
Plantation Shadows (book), 9,703
Plantations, 77, 79, 2,527, 2,541, **2,930**, **2,943**, 2,947,
    3,341, 3,348, 3,410, 3,477, 5,410, 5,449, 5,490,
    5,552, 5,553, 5,765, 6,653, 7,935, 8,776, 9,534,
    9,588, 9,594, 9,610, 9,614, 9,625, 9,645, 9,675,
    9,693, 9,701, 9,702, 9,714, 9,729, 9,760, 9,774,
    9,781, 9,794, 9,987, 12,949, 13,091, 13,213,
    13,378, 13,602, 13,619, 15,077, 15,116, 15,401,
    15,414, **15,423**, 15,440, **15,460**, **15,467**, **15,476**,
    15,484, 15,582, 15,678, 15,694, 16,077
Planter's Northern Bride, The (book), 111
Planton, Julia [Mrs.] 14,875, **14,879**
Plants, 2,724, 4,344
Plassman, Martha Edgerton (?-1936), **10,356**
Plastic sculpture, 17,338
Plate of Brass, 762
Plath, Aurelia Schober, 4,485
Plath, Sylvia. [Mrs. Ted] Hughes (1932-63), **4,485**,
    7,185
Platner, Margaret (Moffit) [Mrs. Henry] (1897-),
    4,938
Platt, Erminnie Adele (1836-86). *See* Smith, Erminnie
    Adele (Platt) [Mrs. Simeon H.] (1836-86)
Platt, Fanny Arabella (Hayes) (1820-56), **14,090**
Platt, Joanna. *See* Peck, Joanna (Platt) [Mrs. Henry
    W.]
Platt, Laura. *See* Mitchell, Laura (Platt)
Platt, Mary (Schauffler) (1868-1954), **1,858**
Platt, Mrs. Orville H. (?-1927), 1,928
Platt, Mrs. Rutherford H., 13,988
Platt, Orville H. (1827-1905), **1,928**
Platz, Mrs. Henry, 17,422
Play, 13,738
*Play and Game Theory in Group Work: A
    Collection of Papers by Neva Leona Boyd*
    (book), 4,059
Play, the Child's Response to Life (book), 4,049
Playbill Magazine, 17,958
Player-piano, 11,907
Playfair Family (CA), 1,566
Playford, Pearl [Mrs.], 8,249
Playgrounds, 1,385, 2,000, 2,397, 2,955, 3,875, 3,877,
    4,114, 6,358, 8,486, 10,180, 13,992, 14,746,
    15,205
Playhouse Magazine, The Kendell Playhouse, The,
    4,743
Playwrights. *See* Dramatists
Plaza Church (Los Angeles, CA), 985
"Plea for Industrial Education, A," 9,556
Pleasant Hill School (York, NE), 10,623
Pleasant Hill Seminary (PA), 10,530
Pleasant, Mary Ellen "Mammy" [Mrs. John]
    (1814?-1904), **727**, **1,368**
Pleasant Valley School, Town of Sampson, School
    District No. 12, Chippewa County (WI), **17,533**
Pleasant View Methodist Church (Humboldt, NE),
    10,476
Pleasants, Anne F. (Page) [Mrs. Joseph], **15,063**
Please Don't Eat the Daisies (book), 17,806

Please God, Take Care of the Mule (book), 6,511
Pleiades Club (South Bend, IN), **4,666**
Plierna, Pluma. *See* Libby, Pluma (Plierna)
Plimpton, Harriet [Miss], 5,694
Plitt, Sophie W., 2,234
Plowman, Idora (McClellan) (1843-1929). *See*
    Moore, Idora (McClellan) Plowman (1843-1929)
"Pluck and Perseverance: The History of Women at
    St. Olaf College, 1874-1914" (dissertation), 8,812
Plum Creek Massacre (NE), 10,496
Plum, Hattie (1878-1963). *See* Williams, Hattie
    (Plum) [Mrs. Thomas] (1878-1963)
Plumb, Laura, 7,882
Plumer Family (NY), **12,284**
Plumer, Margaret [Mrs. William, Jr.], 12,284
Plumer, William, Jr. (1789-1854), 12,284
Plummer, Marion. *See* Povey, Marion (Plummer)
    [Mrs. J. Harold]
Plummer, Mary Wright (1856-1916), 11,333
Plummer, Mattie E. (Kelly) [Mrs. O. P. S.], 14,598
Plummer, O. P. S., 14,598
Plunkett, Anne Marie, 9,478
Plunkett, Emma W., 12,937
Plymouth Assembly Plant (MI), 8,132
Plymouth Brethren, missions, 153
Plymouth Congregational Church (Minneapolis, MN),
    9,090
Plymouth Congregational Church (St. Paul, MN),
    Ladies Social Circle, **9,290**
Plymouth Congregational Church (Aberdeen, SD),
    15,839
Plympton, Emily. *See* Lovell, Emily (Plympton)
    [Mrs. Mansfield]
Pneumonia, 1,647
   prevention, 11,571
Poaching, 5,643
Poage, Frances Cotton [Mrs. William Robert "Rob"],
    16,379
Poage, Margaret (1804-72). *See* Williamson, Margaret
    (Poage) [Mrs. Thomas Smith] (1804-72)
Poates, John Lemuel, 11,589
Poates, Sarah Elizabeth (Fitch), 11,589
Poatgieter, A. Hermina, 9,230
Pocahontas Memorial Association, **12,595**
Pocatello Central Labor Union and Building Trades
    Council (ID), 3,715
Pochmann, Virginia Ruth (Fouts) [Mrs. Henry A.]
    (1903-), **16,302**
Pockets, 17,400
Poe, Clarence Hamilton (1881-1964), 13,166, **13,532**
Poe, Edgar Allan (1809-59), 5,948, 5,951, 5,957,
    7,657
Poelman, Eva Beatrice Swain (Squires) [Mrs. Walter
    Jenkins] (1897-), **16,791**
Poelnitz Family (SC), 15,652
Poems (pamphlet), 13,520
Poems and Letters (book), 5,862
Poems: North and South (book), 14,322
Poems of Emma C. Embury, The (book), 12,463
Poems of Gene Derwood, The (book), 4,472
Poems of Passion (book), 16,570
Poetics, 12,815, 14,406
Poetry, 1,426, 3,542, 7,090, 7,651, 7,658, 7,660,
    7,665, **7,674**, **8,477**, **8,771**, 12,462, 13,305,
    14,019, 14,602, 14,981, 15,038, 15,081, **15,109**,
    15,638, 15,668, 16,797
   anthologies, 6,061
   collections. 5,310, 17,013
   competitions, 2,469
   history and criticism, 5,829
   periodicals, 1,448, 1,795, 4,005, 8,600, 10,029,
    12,642, 12,821, 13,844, 14,368, **17,312**, 18,021
   prizes, 15,377
   study and teaching, 1,394
Poetry (periodical), 5,310
Poetry, A Magazine of Verse, 4,005, 10,029, 12,821,
    17,312
Poetry, Russian, 5,875
Poetry Society (Iowa City, IA), 4,960
Poetry Society of America, 2,977, 12,893
Poetry Society of Colorado, 1,749
Poetry Society of Georgia, 2,977
Poetry Society of Kansas, 5,242
PoetrySociety of South Carolina, 15,480, 15,585

Poetry Society of South Carolina, Group A, **15,415**
Poets, 54, 57, 134, 225, **258**, **289**, 436, 635, **667**, 822,
    862, **874**, 889, 931, **1,057**, **1,082**, 1,113, 1,187,
    1,209, **1,221**, **1,268**, **1,282**, 1,323, **1,390**, **1,394**,
    1,397, **1,407**, 1,426, **1,432**, **1,433**, **1,441**, **1,447**,
    1,448, **1,449**, **1,453**, **1,461**, **1,467**, **1,477**, **1,487**,
    1,489, **1,501**, 1,507, **1,508**, 1,525, 1,581, 1,620,
    1,634, 1,646, 1,786, 1,790, **1,795**, **1,966**, **2,056**,
    2,106, **2,107**, **2,171**, **2,172**, **2,184**, **2,204**, **2,220**,
    2,222, **2,227**, **2,253**, **2,260**, **2,282**, **2,316**, 2,319,
    2,324, **2,351**, **2,355**, **2,370**, **2,376**, **2,390**, **2,395**,
    2,398, **2,409**, **2,416**, **2,422**, **2,442**, **2,450**, **2,453**,
    2,466, **2,474**, **2,480**, **2,483**, **2,491**, **2,496**, **2,530**,
    2,537, **2,552**, **2,565**, **2,580**, **2,586**, **2,603**, **2,604**,
    2,610, **2,619**, **2,627**, **2,628**, **2,637**, **2,653**, **2,977**,
    2,982, **3,167**, **3,177**, **3,628**, 3,926, **3,986**, **3,987**,
    4,000, **4,200**, **4,226**, **4,237**, **4,472**, **4,489**, **4,622**,
    4,636, **4,644**, 4,696, 4,732, 4,776, **5,032**, **5,198**,
    5,205, **5,242**, **5,261**, 5,296, **5,347**, **5,374**, 5,394,
    5,413, 5,418, **5,498**, **5,612**, **5,621**, **5,669**, 5,694,
    5,714, 5,730, 5,763, 5,771, **5,773**, **5,783**, **5,784**,
    5,788, **5,806**, 5,815, **5,860**, **5,862**, **5,922**, **5,931**,
    5,949, **5,962**, **5,966**, **5,967**, **5,988**, **6,009**, **6,050**,
    6,061, **6,063**, **6,088**, 6,260, **6,406**, **6,437**, **6,441**,
    6,453, **6,454**, **6,473**, **6,545**, **6,569**, **6,655**, **6,714**,
    6,735, **6,824**, **6,903**, **6,922**, **6,952**, **7,024**, **7,026**,
    7,027, **7,127**, **7,131**, 7,206, **7,458**, 7,508, **7,543**,
    7,545, **7,563**, **7,605**, **7,657**, **7,681**, 7,682, **7,690**,
    7,751, 7,789, **7,868**, 7,997, 8,001, **8,375**, 8,597,
    8,854, 9,043, 9,048, **9,171**, 9,527, **9,583**, 9,720,
    9,771, 9,841, 9,981, **10,000**, **10,029**, **10,148**,
    10,162, **10,183**, 10,352, **10,549**, 10,631, **10,825**,
    10,830, **10,863**, **10,867**, **10,875**, 11,077, 11,103,
    11,145, 11,155, 11,173, 11,174, 11,184, 11,221,
    11,233, **11,307**, **11,309**, **11,338**, **11,385**, 11,394,
    11,401, 11,412, **11,854**, **11,983**, **12,032**, **12,042**,
    12,062, **12,399**, 12,403, **12,441**, **12,443**, **12,451**,
    12,466, **12,502**, **12,648**, 12,684, **12,747**, **12,815**,
    12,893, **12,894**, **12,904**, **12,915**, 12,992, **13,099**,
    13,139, **13,190**, **13,232**, **13,264**, 13,289, **13,844**,
    13,961, 14,019, 14,164, **14,322**, **14,347**, **14,350**,
    14,368, **14,382**, **14,383**, 14,406, **14,423**, **14,428**,
    14,656, **14,679**, 14,680, **14,753**, **14,761**, 14,838,
    14,984, **14,997**, **14,998**, **15,013**, **15,169**, **15,170**,
    15,198, **15,331**, 15,334, **15,368**, 15,377, **15,585**,
    15,612, **15,679**, **15,753**, **15,796**, **15,879**, **15,902**,
    15,920, **15,936**, **15,938**, **15,957**, **15,967**, **16,143**,
    16,152, **16,163**, **16,165**, **16,169**, **16,174**, **16,269**,
    16,560, **16,570**, 16,905, 16,913, 16,941, **17,009**,
    17,011, **17,012**, **17,013**, **17,038**, 17,043,
    17,096, **17,114**, **17,131**, **17,210**, **17,227**, **17,351**,
    17,454, 17,687, 17,964, 17,991, 18,021
   19th C, **15,952**
   20th C, **4,482**, **4,485**, **5,310**
Poets, Afro-American, **2,137**, 2,145, 3,284, **3,285**,
    3,287, **3,288**, **3,289**, 5,260, **5,465**, **5,535**, **6,026**,
    6,112, **12,685**, **14,200**, **16,295**, **16,982**
Poets, British, 7,651, 11,948
Poets, Canadian, **12,290**
Poets, deaf, 2,112
Poets' Guild, 7,166
Poets, Irish, **2,660**
Poets laureate, 289, 1,307, 1,395, 1,416, 1,417, 1,429,
    1,447, 1,489, **1,718**, **2,437**, **3,204**, **3,312**, 3,358,
    3,419, **3,945**, 5,270, **9,889**, **10,132**, **10,650**,
    16,137, **16,349**, 16,566, 17,498
Poets, Native American, 14,712, **17,814**
Poets, Norwegian, **8,735**
Poets' Roundtable, 289
Poets, Swedish-American, **17,327**
Pohl, Emma Ody [Miss] (1880-post 1955), **9,568**
Poindexter, Elizabeth Gale [Mrs. Miles], 17,378
Poindexter, Madeline Romaine Wade, 1,420
Poindexter, Miles, 17,378
Poinsette, Septima (1898-). *See* Clark, Septima
    (Poinsetta) (1898-)
Point Four Program, 10,197
Poirier, Rose Felix, 1,339
Poison Arrows (book), 7,293
Polacheck, Hilda (Satt) [Mrs. William] (1887?-1967),
    4,143
Poland
   American travelers in, 6,912
   history, 7,665

   hospitals, 8,045
   nurses, 8,045
   occupation (1939), 8,144
   teachers' colleges, 8,991
   World War I, civilians work, 9,467
   Young Women's Christian Association, **12,714**
Poletti, Carla Knox, 12,071
Poletti, Charles (1903-), **12,071**
Poletti, Jean Ellis [Mrs. Charles], 12,071
Polhill, Emily Hines (Nisbet), **13,093**
Police, 612, **10,160**, 15,993
   complaints against, 1,122, 6,314
   records and correspondence, **1,122**, 12,827, **14,696**,
    15,537, **17,567**
Police and community, 7,794
Police chiefs, 12,434
Policewomen, 2,687, 7,205, 9,252, **9,299**, 11,440,
    11,686, 12,736, **12,827**, 13,447, 14,814, 15,251,
    17,191, **17,567**
Policewomen, Afro-American, 9,467
Polier, Justine (Wise), 12,069
Poliomyelitis, 1,348, 6,919, 8,621
   personal narratives, 1,152, 9,160
   research, **9,162**
   treatment, 8,943
Poliomyelitis nursing, 8,521, **8,621**
Poliomyelitis vaccine, 5,143
Poliomyelitis vaccine, oral, 8,540
Polish-Americans, 1,837, **3,815**, 3,845, 5,829, **11,367**,
    13,906, 13,960
Polish immigrants, 13,906
Polish Relief Benefit, 13,932
Polite, Carlene Hatcher (1932-), **6,067**
Political activism, 6,067, 8,057
Political activism, Afro-American, 11,494, 15,889
Political activism, children, 10,177
Political activists, women, 972, 1,014, **1,016**, 1,034,
    1,654, 2,189, **2,589**, **2,647**, 3,792, 4,124, **4,126**,
    4,606, 4,654, **5,126**, 5,135, 5,143, 5,156, 5,328,
    5,329, 5,565, 7,187, 8,096, 8,135, **8,912**, 9,046,
    9,084, **9,127**, **9,189**, **9,276**, 9,392, 9,396, 9,443,
    9,467, 9,938, 10,050, 10,127, 10,482, 10,761,
    11,686, 12,069, **12,681**, **14,360**, **14,637**, 14,686,
    15,903, 15,990, 16,006, 16,007, 16,240, **17,319**,
    17,365, 17,472, **17,746**, 17,974
Political activists, women, Afro-American, 2,127,
    7,211
Political Affairs (periodical), 17,635
Political clubs, **133**, 1,464, 1,503, 2,127, 3,301, 3,658,
    3,833, 4,815, **4,943**, 5,123, 5,130, 5,137, 5,142,
    5,143, 5,145, 5,146, **5,150**, 5,155, **5,322**, 5,329,
    6,489, 6,939, **7,912**, **8,844**, 9,040, **9,129**, 9,192,
    9,232, **9,291**, **9,306**, 9,375, **9,856**, 9,963, 10,032,
    10,048, 10,050, 10,679, **10,885**, 11,249, 11,853,
    13,271, 13,406, **13,623**, 14,014, 14,015, 14,565,
    14,626, 14,987, **16,975**, 17,050, 17,141
Political conventions, 1,255, 2,269, 5,006, 6,079,
    6,582, 6,765, 6,939, 7,883, 9,279, 9,400, 11,243,
    11,249, 11,853, 11,857, 11,882, 11,905, 12,680,
    13,266, 13,274, 13,565, 14,587, 17,141, 17,347,
    17,436, 17,472
Political crimes and offenses 17,633
"Political Dimension, The: Is This a Political
    Question?," 11,663
Political Equality Club (CA), 1,629
Political Equality Club (Ann Arbor, MI), **7,894**, 7,921
Political Equality Club (Minneapolis, MN), 9,147,
    9,291
Political Equality Club (Oneida Chapter, NY), **12,743**
Political Equality Club of Independence (IA), 4,859
Political Equality Club of Pierre (SD). *See* Equal
    Suffrage Club of Pierre (SD)
Political Equality Club of Rochester (NY). *See*
    Woman Suffrage Party of Monroe County, Inc.
    (NY)
Political Equality Club of St. Paul (MN), **9,292**
Political Equality League, 1,359
Political Equality League (WI), 17,659, 17,749
Political Equality Society of Bath (NY), **11,678**
Political parties. *See* names of parties, e.g.,
    Democratic Party
Political prisoners, 7,306, 10,177, **12,518**, **12,567**
   East Germany, 6,106
   Russia, 6,106

Political rights of women. *See* Women, civil rights
Political rights of women (essay), 5,689
Political Science Club of Lynn (MA), **7,078**
Political scientists, 2,177, 6,692, 7,328
Political statistics, 15,998
Political Study Club (Ithaca, NY), 11,623
Politicians, 175, **1,010**, 1,397, **1,642**, **1,862**, **1,868,**
    1,874, **1,886**, 2,343, **2,347**, **2,429**, **2,525**, 3,298,
    4,493, **4,662**, 4,750, **4,854**, **4,869**, **5,334**, 5,627,
    5,789, 7,647, **10,046**, 10,324, 10,365, **11,483**,
    11,666, **11,856**, **11,872**, 12,071, **12,174**, 12,478,
    12,481, **12,495**, **13,210**, 13,262, 13,840, **13,859**,
    14,000, **14,541**, 14,683, **14,820**, 14,890, 14,957,
    14,977, 15,039, 15,040, 15,089, **15,674**, **15,681,**
    15,834, **15,835**, 16,007, **16,235**, 16,328, **16,359,**
    16,386, **17,043**, 17,119, 17,238, **17,260**, 17,439,
    17,607
Politicians, Afro-American, **12,680**, 12,690
Politics and education, 13,446, **16,462**
Politics and government, 58, 1,428, 1,728, 6,341,
    6,352, 7,178, 8,333, 8,798, 10,156, 11,550
Politics, practical, **125**, **1,014**, 1,981, 3,293, 3,303,
    5,150, 5,499, 6,067, 6,427, 6,582, 8,485, 9,211,
    9,443, 9,467, 12,799, 15,321, 15,569, 15,706
    public opinion,
Politics, practical, women's activism, **12**, **53**, **139,**
    6,405, 6,431, 6,432, 6,530, **10,558**, 13,676,
    15,706, 17,341
Polk, Alice (1854-1921). *See* Hill, Alice (Polk)
    (1854-1921)
Polk County Republican Women's Association (IA),
    4,780
Polk County Woman Suffrage Society (IA), 4,831,
    4,859
Polk, J. F., 5,750
Polk, James K., Jr., **9,701**, 9,702
Polk, James Knox (1795-1849), **2,529**, 9,722, 13,080,
    14,982
Polk, Juanita "Nita." *See* Denmark, Juanita "Nita"
    (Polk) [Mrs. James W.]
Polk, Leonidas, 5,491, 9,753
Polk, Lucy Eugenia Williams [Mrs. William H.],
    13,534
Polk, Mrs. George W., 9,645
Polk, Mrs. James K., Jr., **9,701**, **9,702**
Polk, Sarah (Childress) [Mrs. James Knox] (1803-91),
    2,529
Poll-tax, 7, 2,868, 3,362, 3,805, 11,855
    abolition of, 65, 125
Pollack, Naomi Newman [Mrs. Reginald] (1930-),
    2,800
Pollack, Reginald, **2,800**
Pollak, Katherine (1905-). *See* Ellickson, Katherine
    (Pollak) [Mrs. John Chester] (1905-)
Pollard, Edward Alfred, 3,346
Pollard, Emily Louise (1896-1972), **13,094**
Pollard, Grace Francis (1893-), 10,403
Pollard, Josephine, **2,530**
Pollard, Marie Antoinette Nathalie [Mrs. Edward
    Alfred] (?-1896?), **3,346**
Pollard, Mary Leonora Green [Mrs. Horatio
    Harrison], 4,422
Pollard, Violet McDougall [Mrs. John Garland]
    (1889-1977), **17,117**
Pollitzer, Anita, 6,807
Pollitzer, Mabel (1885-), 13,176
Pollock, Jessie (Babcock) [Mrs. John] (1865-?), **1,816**
Pollock, John, 1,816
Pollock, Mary (Morton) [Mrs. T. E.] (18??-1941), **222**
Pollock, Sadie. *See* Carlton, Sadie (Pollock) [Mrs.
    Caleb Henry]
Pollock, Sam, **8,118**
Pollution, 611, 8,103, 10,953, 14,002
Polonium, 6,496
Polychromy, 12,898
Polygamy, 185, 207, 410, 416, 562, 730, 746, 805,
    806, 845, 856, 987, **1,466**, 2,581, 3,738, 4,209,
    6,355, 10,102, 10,674, 16,434, 16,450, 16,458,
    16,486, 16,506, 16,512, 16,533, 16,537, 16,544,
    16,561, 16,566, 16,572, 16,598, 16,607, **16,615,**
    16,617, 16,620, 16,641, 16,649, 16,654, 16,665,
    16,668, 16,688, 16,691, 16,693, 16,696, 16,702,
    16,707, 16,722, 16,729, 16,736, 16,740, 16,749,
    16,756, 16,775, 16,777, 16,780, **16,783**, 16,786,

16,792, 16,807, 16,820, 16,835, 16,836, 16,839,
    16,847, 16,876, 16,888, 16,898, 16,907, 16,915,
    16,935, 16,936, 16,938, 16,939, 16,940, 16,945,
    16,949, **16,952**, 16,957, 16,961, 16,965, 16,967,
    16,968, 16,974
    opposition to, **16,469**, 16,537
Pomeroy Family, 14,060
Pomeroy, Hannah Wells (1782-1861), 7,143
Pomeroy, Mary Hunt [Mrs. Seth] (1705-77), 7,143
Pomeroy, Miggs, **6,068**
Pomeroy, Seth (1706-77), **7,143**
Pomo Indians, 965
Pomona College (CA), 6,862
Pomona Fruit and Floral Society (CA), **1,109**
Pompey, Sherman Lee, **9,901**
Pond, Agnes Carson Johnson [Mrs. Robert] Hopkins
    [Mrs. Gideon Hollister] (1825-?), 8,412, 8,413,
    9,293
Pond, Cornelia Eggleston [Mrs. Samuel W.], 9,294
Pond, Edward Robert, 8,407
Pond, Elizabeth Keith (1886-1955), 589
Pond, Ellen [Miss], 12,577
Pond, Emma (McHenry) [Mrs. Charles Fremont]
    (1857-1934), 589
Pond Family (MN), **8,412**, **9,294**
Pond, Gertrude. *See* Hamilton, Gertrude (Pond) [Mrs.
    Montgomery]
Pond, Gideon Hollister (1810-78), 8,412, 9,293, 9,294
Pond, Gideon Hollister, Jr. (1858-?), 9,294
Pond, Inez (Henderson) [Mrs. Charles McHenry]
    (?-1961), 589, **1,638**
Pond, James B., 4,229
Pond, Jennette Cordelia, 9,294
Pond, Mary, 9,921
Pond, Mary Frances (Hopkins) [Mrs. Edward
    Robert], 8,399, 8,412
Pond, Mary M., 9,294
Pond, Mary Virginia. *See* Culbertson, Mary Virginia
    (Pond) [Mrs. Jack Arthur]
Pond, Nina L. [Mrs. J. C.] (1905-), **14,192**
Pond, Rebecca Cordelia (1844-1910). *See* Dean,
    Rebecca Cordelia (Pond) [Mrs. William J.]
    (1844-1910)
Pond, Samuel William (1808-91), 9,294
Pond, Sarah Poage [Mrs. Gideon H.], 9,294
Pond, Scintilla Sexta. *See* Ritchie, Scintilla Sexta
    (Pond) [Mrs. Cyrus]
Ponder, Eleanor (Fox), **9,703**
Ponder Heart, The, 9,768, 9,769, 9,770, 16,172
Ponikarski, Sally, 3,443
Pons, Lily, 12,013
Ponstein, Kathryn Kwak [Mrs. John], 8,518
Pontiac (drama), 7,220
Pontiac High School (MI), 7,891
Pony express, 10,638
Pony Express Courier (CA), 1,621
Ponzo, Doris, 16,872
Pool, Eliza, 13,350, **13,535**
Pool, Rosey Eve (1905-71), **2,145**
Poole, Archibald, 12,865
Poole, Caroline B. [Miss] (1802-44), **2,531**
Poole, Drusilla [Mrs. Archibald] (ca. 1900-67), **12,865**
Poole, Eleanor A. *See* Arnold, Eleanor A. (Poole)
    [Mrs. Henry Harley]
Poole, Elizabeth [Mrs.], 2,179
Poole, Emma Dare,
Poole Family, 1,590
Poole Family (IL), **6,832**
Poole, Jane B., 14,618
Poole, Kitty, 2,875
Poole, Marion Howe. *See* McFadden, Marion Howe
    (Poole)
Poole, Mary 8,665
Poole, Mary Howe, 6,832
Poole, S. Alicia, **7,895**
Pooley, Edith M., 1,067
Poor, 2,676, 11,738, **12,081**, **13,996**, 15,022, **16,215,**
    17,018
Poor, Caroline A., **12,285**
Poor Clare Nuns, Christ the King Monastery (Delray
    Beach, FL), **2,871**
Poor Clares, 8,414, 10,611
Poor Family (New England), **6,833**
Poor, Henry Varnum (1812-1905), 6,833

Poor, Henry William (1844-1915), 6,833
Poor, Jewish, 1,003
Poor laws, 10,603
Poor Little Hearts (book), 7,026
Poor, Mary (Pierce) [Mrs. Henry Varnum]
    (1820-1912), 6,833
Poor People's Campaign (1967), 17,357
Poor People's Corporation, 17,600
Poor Sisters of St. Francis Seraph of Perpetual
    Adoration, 10,611
Poor Thief's Legacy, The (book), 12,441
Poore, B. P., 12,481
Pop art, 2,782
Pope, Annemarie H., 2,848
Pope, Augusta Ann (Sibley) [Mrs. Douglas] (1844-?),
    9,371
Pope, C. Augusta, 5,526
Pope, Earle, 2,875
Pope, Edith (Taylor) [Mrs. Earle] (1905-61), **2,875**
Pope, Elfrieda (Hochbaum) [Mrs. Paul Russel]
    (1877-1962), **11,612**
Pope, Elizabeth, **11,124**
Pope, Elizabeth Law (1773-post 1875), **9,902**
Pope, Emily F., 5,526
Pope, Helen A. (Manville) [Mrs. Charles A.], 1,646
Pope-Hennessy, Una, 2,373
Pope, John, Jr., 5,350, 5,359
Pope, Joseph, 8,164
Pope, Laura Spencer Porter, 6,487
Pope, Lucretia, 1,786
Pope, Lucy Ann [Mrs. John D.], 9,070
Pope, Maria (Preston) [Mrs. John, Jr.] (1805-95),
    5,350, 5,359
Pope, Paul Russel, 11,612
Pope, Sarah A., **7,422**
Pope Wallis, Marie, **11,244**
Pope, William Cox (1841-1917), Family (MN), **9,295**
Popes, 13,928, 15,361
Poppenheim, Christopher Pritchard, 15,509
Poppenheim, Mary Elinor Bouknight [Mrs.
    Christopher Pritchard], **15,509**
Popper, Hermine (Isaacs) (1915-68), **6,834**
Poppy of California (booklet), 1,439
Popular Science (periodical), 8,620, 12,350
Population, **4,082**, 7,289
Population Association of America, 6,223
Population: Boom or Doom (television program),
    17,813
Population control, 9,810
Population Council, 6,987
Population Law Center (Middletown, CT), **1,984**
Population research, 6,223
Populist party, 5,040, 9,046
Porcelain, 12,182
Porcelain League, 13,853
Porcher, Charlotte, **13,095**
Porcher, Ellen Barker, **15,416**
Porcher Family (SC), **15,682**
Porcher, Frances Peyre, 15,428
Porcher, Frederick Adolphus (1809-88), **15,683**
Porcher, James P., 15,527
Porcher, Louise (Petigru), 15,682
Porcher, Virginia Leigh [Miss], **15,510**
Porcher, William (1800-33), 15,428
Pornography, 6,760
Porritt, Annie Gertrude (Webb) (1861-1932), **7,284,**
    7,312
Port Gibson Methodist Episcopal Church, South,
    Methodist Ladies Cooperative Association, **9,704**
Portal, The, 14,408
Porter, Ann Eliza Bacon [Mrs. Joseph] (1821-90),
    17,706
Pomerance, Sally Belfrage (1936-), 1,570, 1,600,
    17,599
Porter, Annie Florence (1862-1907). *See* Gaskill,
    Annie Florence (Porter) [Mrs. Varney]
    (1862-1907)
Porter, Arthur Kingsley (1883-1933), **5,300**
Porter, Charlotte Endymion (1857-1942), 1,589
Porter, Clyde H., **1,476**
Porter, Doris (1892-1971). *See* Caeser, Doris (Porter)
    [Mrs. Harry I.] (1892-1971)
Porter, Dorothy (Burnett) (1905-), **2,146**, 3,290,
    5,469, 9,575

Porter, Elizabeth, **7,423**
Porter, Elizabeth Kerr [Mrs.], **13,892**
Porter, Elizabeth Lee, 14,628
Porter, Ella, 4,185
Porter, Eunice R., **2,532**
Porter, Evelyn (Howe), 4,765
Porter Family (CA), 1,648
Porter Family (MI), 8,167
Porter Family (MO, PA, VA, WV), 2,532
Porter Family (NY), 12,734
Porter, Florence Emeline Foote, **8,169**
Porter, Gertrude. *See* Ashley, Gertrude (Porter) [Mrs. Charles Hart]
Porter, Gustav (1866-69), 1,331
Porter, Hannah (Armstrong) [Mrs. Willard Hall] (1860-1958), **2,052**
Porter, Harriet (?-1835). *See* Beecher, Harriet (Porter) (?-1835)
Porter, Helen Talbot, 2,198
Porter, Henrietta (Curtis) [Mrs. James R.], 3,282
Porter, Ida Estelle (1860-1940). *See* Shaw, Ida Estelle [Mrs. George Moore] (1860-1940)
Porter, Isabel Margaret (1875-1954). *See* Collins, Isabel Margaret (Porter) (1875-1954)
Porter, James J. (ca. 1828-82), 1,331
Porter, Janie (1865-1948). *See* Barrett, Janie (Porter) [Mrs. Harris] (1865-1948)
Porter, Joseph, 17,706
Porter, Julia (Foster) [Mrs. Edward C.] (1846-1936), 3,932
Porter, Katharine (1910-64). *See* Williamson, Katharine (Porter) [Mrs. Harvey] (1910-64)
Porter, Katherine Anne. [Mrs. Albert Russel] Erskine, Jr. (1890-), 2,242, 3,980, 3,986, 4,227, 6,579, 11,153, 11,156, 11,163, 11,810, 11,954, 12,642, 15,927, 15,934, 16,152, **16,164**, 17,053
Porter, Lavinia (Honeyman) [Mrs. James J.] (1836-1910), 728, **1,331**
Porter, Lillian Russell, 17,706
Porter, Lucy Bryant (Wallace) [Mrs. Arthur Kingsley] (1876-1962), 5,300
Porter, Mabel [Mrs.], **5,659**
Porter, Mae (Reed), 1,476, **10,357**
Porter, Margaret (James) [Mrs. Bruce] (?-1950), 543, 551
Porter, Marjorie Lansing (1891-1973), **12,772**
Porter, Mary (1848-1906). *See* Gamewell, Mary (Porter) [Mrs. Francis] (1848-1906)
Porter, Maurice (1868-81), 3,932
Porter, Permelia (Curtis) [Mrs. William Earl] (?-1949), 1,788
Porter, Robert, (ca. 1855-69), 1,331
Porter, Sarah [Miss] (1813-1900), 1,836
Porter, Sarah Jane Clayton, **16,477**
Porter, Winifred [Mrs. Stephen L.], 1,837
Porterfield, Anne (1869-1942). *See* Rankin, Anne (Porterfield) (1869-1942)
Portfolio Club (Mankato, MN), **8,508**
Portland Academy (ME), 5,690
Portland Academy (OR), 14,552, **14,638**, 14,663
Portland Academy and Female Seminary (OR). *See* Portland Academy (OR)
Portland Antislavery Society (ME), **5,684**
Portland Beautification Association, 14,565
Portland Central Labor Council (OR), 14,533
Portland Council of Churches (OR), 17,304
Portland Daily Advertiser (ME), 5,694
Portland Female Provident Association (ME). *See* Portland Provident Association (ME)
Portland Girls' High School (ME), **5,685**
Portland Junior Symphony Orchestra (OR), **14,639**
Portland Labor Temple (OR), 14,533
Portland Metropolitan Steering Committee (OR), 14,605
Portland National Library Association (OR), 14,591
Portland Opera Guild (OR), 14,565
Portland Planning Commission (OR), 14,605
Portland Pro-Musica (OR), 14,565
Portland Provident Association (ME), **5,686**
Portland Public Forum Association (OR), 17,304
Portland Transcript (ME), 5,694
Portland Widows' Wood Society (ME), **5,687**
Portland Women's Club (OR), **14,640**
Portland Women's Research Club (OR), **14,641**

Portland Women's Union (OR), 14,551, **14,642**
Portman, Caroline Bezora (1859-1926). *See* Campbell, Caroline Bezora (Portman) [Mrs. James H.] (1859-1926)
Portmanteau One, The (book), 12,031
Portney, David, 10,192
Portola, Governor, 1,595
Portrait of a Librarian: William Howard Brett (book), 6,551
"Portrait of Israel: A Coming of Age" (photos), 6,075
Portrait-painters, 765, **1,083**, **1,474**, **2,733**, **2,768**, **5,489**, 5,713, 9,467, 9,837, **11,618**, 14,949
Portraits, 2,187
Portraits, American, **2,861**
　indexes, **2,862**
Ports of entry, 2,683, 9,481
Ports of Youth (book), 6,850
Portsmouth Steel Company, 15,333
Portuguese-Americans, 1,532, 1,534
Posednik, Frances (1876-?), **16,380**
Posey, Alice (Puckett), 9,798
Posey, Evie (Stubblefield) [Mrs. H. A.], **9,705**
Posey, Zoe, **9,706**, **9,799**
Posner, Caryl, 3,290
Posner, Henrietta, 2,396
Possession of Joel Delaney, The (moving-picture play), 6,098
Post (CO), 1,699, 1,750, 1,800
Post (KS), 10,000
Post (Boston, MA), 6,948
Post (NY), 3,368
Post (WA), 17,293
Post, Alice T., 6,958
Post, Anna Alice (Thacher) [Mrs. Louis Freeland], 15,301
Post, Anna Coatesworth [Mrs. Henry D.] (?-1907), 8,195
Post, C. W., 2,428
Post Cereal Company, 2,428
Post-Dispatch (MO), 10,193
Post, Emily Price [Mrs. Edwin M.] (1873-1960), **2,533**, 3,117
Post Express (Rochester, NY), 11,512
Post, Jessie M., **1,332**
Post, Marjorie Merriweather (1887-1973), **2,428**
Post, Mary Minturn [Mrs. Henry], 12,286
Post, The (IL), 3,930
Postage stamps, 304
　collectors and collecting, 17,315
　Confederate States of America, 3,262
Postal Auxiliary (NC), 13,446
Postal cards, **14,204**
Postal service, 194, 5,271, 6,348, 9,152
　letter-carriers, 5,652
　officials and employees, 6,348, 9,279
Postal Telegraph Company, 12,843
Posten, Anna Garrison, **1,736**
Postgraduate medical education, **3,914**
Postman Always Rings Twice, The (book), 2,241
Postmasters, 179, 1,746, 2,211, 4,469, 4,956, 5,746, 9,118, 11,242, **12,051**, 12,345, 13,999
Postmistresses, 107, 982, **4,739**, 6,956, **9,755**, 9,972, 9,974, 10,229, 10,231, **10,515**, **14,246**, 16,968
Poston Chronicle (AZ), 1,415
Poston, Eugenia C., 729
"Postscript, The" (column), 12,412
Poteet, Mary, 15,542
Pott, Constance M. [Mrs. Henry], 9,048
Pottawatomie Indians, 3,897, 4,904
Pottawatomie Reservation (OK), 14,225
Potter, Anna Patterson (1861-?), **14,299**
Potter, Beatrix (1866-1943), 12,570
Potter, Cora Urquhart, 16,149
Potter, Ellen Culver (1871-1958), 2,704, 8,670, **11,021**, **15,136**
Potter, Frances (Squire) (1867-1914), **6,835**
Potter, Francis, 8,602
Potter, General Robert, raid (SC), 15,635
Potter, Harriet Ann (Moore) [Mrs. Solomon C.] Page [Mrs. Robert] (1810-?). *See* Ames, Harriet Ann (Moore) [Mrs. Solomon C.] Page [Mrs. Robert] Potter [Mrs. Charles] (1810-?)

Potter, Henry, **13,536**
Potter, Lena [Mrs.], 18,025
Potter, Lorraine, 37
Potter, Louise, **7,896**
Potter, Mary Craig, **12,841**
Potter, Mary. *See* Babcock, Mary (Potter)
Potter, Mary [Mrs. Thomas], 13,450
Potter, Mary Ann, 13,536
Potter, Mary Ann Bailey (1841-1928), **4,706**
Potter, Maud, **12,596**
Potter, Nancy A. J., **6,069**
Potter, Olive Andelin (1868-?), **16,907**
Potter Robert A., 2,167, **13,537**
Potter, Samuel, **2,534**
Potter, Sophie [Mrs. Samuel], 2,534
Potters, **2,828**, 13,446, **13,837**, **13,838**, **17,236**, **17,243**
Pottery, 2,796, 2,821, 13,361, 13,853, **13,856**
Pottery craft, 2,828
Pottery: Its Form and Expression (book), 2,828
Potts, Eugenia Dunlap, **5,295**
Potts, John Morris, 15,056
Pottsmith, Marie M. [Mrs. William F.] (1882-), **14,643**
Poughkeepsie Female Collegiate Seminary (NY), students, 1,581
Poultry, 3,161, 7,026, 16,862
　breeding, 17,278
Poultry Princess Contest (NC), 13,565
Poultry research, 10,215
Poultry sexing, 8,509
Pound, Dorothy, 7,210
Pound, Ezra, 1,124, 7,210, 11,153, 16,169, 17,843, 18,021
Pound, Laura Biddlecombe [Mrs. Stephen] (1841-1928), **10,521**
Pound, Louise (1872-1958), 3,983, 10,425, 10,510, 10,512, 10,518, 10,521, **10,522**, 10,537, **16,552**
Pound, Olivia [Miss] (1874-1961), 10,521, 10,522, **10,523**
Pound, Roscoe, 10,521, 10,522
Pound, Stephen, 10,521
Poverty, 8,057
Povey, J. Harold, 14,598
Povey, Marion (Plummer) [Mrs. J. Harold], 14,598
Powel, Elizabeth Willing [Mrs. Samuel] (1743-1830), 15,077
Powel Family (PA), **15,077**
Powel, John Hare, 15,077
Powel, Mary Edith (1846-1931), **2,535**, 15,077
Powel, Mary (Johnston) [Mrs. Samuel], 15,077
Powel, Samuel (1738-93), 15,077
Powel, Samuel (1818-85), 15,077
Powell, Adam Clayton, Sr., 5,458
Powell, Agnes (1827-94). *See* Daniels, Agnes [Mrs. Richard] Williams [Mrs. Francis] Jones [Mrs. David] (1827-94)
Powell, C. S., 13,540
Powell, Corrie Lee Taylor [Mrs.] (?-1914), **16,381**
Powell, Cuthbert, 1,788
Powell, Eleanor (1912-), **18,001**
Powell, Emma H., 13,440
Powell, Evelyn Knox [Mrs.], **3,241**
Powell, Frances L. A., 3,954
Powell, Fred, 2,536
Powell, Helene (1919-), 1,356, 1,357
Powell, Jane (1929-) **18,002**
Powell, Jane K., **13,539**
Powell, John Wesley, 191
Powell, Kathleen Mackay [Mrs. J. Edward] (?-1974), **3,467**
Powell, Kathryn Summers (1920-), **15,811**
Powell, Lois (Fay) (1883-1960), 7,624, **7,666**
Powell, Louise Mathilde (1871-1943), 8,610
Powell, Mary (Bennion), 730
Powell, Mary (Keane) [Mrs. Fred] (1859-?), **2,536**
Powell, Mary Morrison [Mrs. Cuthbert], 1,788
Powell, Maud. [Mrs. H. Godfrey] Turner (1868-1920), **4,443**
Powell, Mildred (1886-), **17,324**
Powell, Mrs. Aaron Macy, 6,954
Powell, Mrs. C. S., 13,540
Powell, Ransom Judd (1865-1937), **9,296**
Powell, Rosalyn Gale, **17,325**
Powell, Rose (Arnold) (1876-1961), 6,761, **6,836**

Powell, Sarah, 15,056
Powell, Susan Virginia [Miss] (1869-1952), **9,707,**
9,708
Powell, William S., **13,540**
Power, Ellen Louise (1841-1917), **13,096**
Power, Helen, 12,790
Power, Kate M. [Miss] (ca. 1866-1946), **9,709**
Power of attorney, 14,922, 15,661
Power-plants, 3,179
Power, Sarah Helen (1803-78), 17,010
Power, Sister Mary Emily (1844-1909), **17,868**
Power, T. C., 10,242
"Powerful Claw, A" (story), 5,296
Powers, Abigail (1798-1853). *See* Fillmore, Abigail
(Powers) [Mrs. Millard] (1798-1853)
Powers, Anna (Peterson) [Mrs. Thomas E.], **4,819**
Powers, Arvilla Almira (1808-95). *See* Smith, Arvilla
Almira (Powers) [Mrs. George Nelson] (1808-95)
Powers, Beatrice Farnsworth (1880-1967), **7,285**
Powers, Catherine, **2,537**
Powers, E. Barnham, 618
Powers Family, 14,059
Powers Family (GA, VA), **3,436**
Powers, Kate (Ball), 14,513
Powers, Laura Bride (1867-1947), **1,333**
Powers, ·Louise. *See* McKie, Louise (Powers)
Powers, Mary Johnstone, **10,263, 10,358**
Powers Mercantile Company (Minneapolis, MN),
9,463
Powers, Minerva (Lester) [Mrs. E. Barnham], 618
Powers, Sarah M. *See* Whittle, Sarah M. Powers
[Mrs. Lewis Neale]
Powers, Thomas E., **4,819**
Pownall, Dorothy (Ashby) (1895-), **5,019**
Powys, J. Cowper, 12,821
Poydras Home (New Orleans, LA), **5,520**
Poynter, Lida (1832-1919), **15,137**
Practical Nurse School (AR), 242
Practical nurses, **5,583, 7,815,** 16,789, 16,965, 16,968
Practical nursing, 239, **8,598**
Practical X-Ray Treatment (book), 4,698
Practice Club (Saratoga Springs, NY), 12,851
Prag, Florence (1866-1948). *See* Kahn, Florence
(Prag) [Mrs. Julius] (1866-1948)
Prag, Mary Goldsmith (1846-1935), 936
Prager, Ruth E. (1899-), **795**
Prairie Blume Literary Society (TX), **16,118**
Prairie Gold (book), 4,957
Prairie Press, 4,950
Prairie Printer (book), 5,012
Prairie Schooner Detours (book), 706
Prairie Seminary, 7,745
Prairie View Normal and Industrial College (TX),
15,913
Prairie Village Female Moral Reform Society
(Waukesha, WI), **17,707**
Prairies, hardship of life on, 13,537
Prall, David Wight (1886-1940), **1,088**
Prall, Delbert E., 1,088
Prall, Dorothea. *See* Radin, Dorothea (Prall) [Mrs.
Max]
Prall, Elizabeth. *See* Anderson, Elizabeth (Prall)
[Mrs. Sherwood]
Prall, Margaret C. (?-1955), **1,088**
Prang Educational Company (MA), 7,667
Prang, Henriette, 5,952
Prang, Louis (1824-1909), **5,952, 7,667**
Prang, Mary Amelia (Dana) [Mrs. Charles Spencer]
Hicks [Mrs. Louis] (1836-1927), 7,667
Prang Normal Art Classes (MA), 7,667
Prang, Rosa Gerber (?-1898), 5,952
Prather, John Smith, 3,260
Pratt, Amy Wilcken (1890-1927). *See* Romney, Amy
Wilcken (Pratt) [Mrs. Gaskell] (1890-1927)
Pratt, Ann Agatha (Walker) [Mrs. Parley Parker]
(1829-1908), **16,792**
Pratt, Anna Bronson (Alcott) (1831-1893), 7,044
Pratt, Cynthia. *See* Park, Cynthia (Pratt) [Mrs.
Luther]
Pratt, Deborah (1746-96) *See* Ruff, Deborah (Pratt)
[Mrs. Daniel] (1746-96)
Pratt, Eliza Jane, 13,473
Pratt, Elizabeth, **15,684**
Pratt, Esther Romania (Bunnell) [Mrs. Parley Parker]

(1839-1932). *See* Penrose, Esther Romania
(Bunnell) [Mrs. Parley Parker] Pratt [Mrs.
Charles W.] (1839-1932)
Pratt Family, **11,679,** 12,485
Pratt, Grace Elinor Joy (White) [Mrs. Chester], 6,948
Pratt, Hannah (?-1804). *See* Hobart, Hannah (Pratt)
[Mrs. Enoch] (?-1804)
Pratt, Harold W., 16,811
Pratt, Harry Noyes, 1,268
Pratt, Helaman, 16,811
Pratt, Henry, 7,674
Pratt, Hortense Louise Black [Mrs. Schuyler], 11,679
Pratt Institute (NY), 2,795
faculty, 12,009
Pratt Institute (NY), Library, **11,333**
Pratt Institute (NY), School of Library Science,
11,333
alumnae, 12,570
Pratt, Jane [Miss], **13,282**
Pratt, Jonathan, 17,213
Pratt, Joseph Hyde, 13,097
Pratt, Julia Ann (Draper) Lazell (1808-41), 7,618
Pratt, K., 14,010
Pratt, Kate L. (1834-?). *See* Robbins, Kate L. (Pratt)
[Mrs. Abner] (1834-?)
Pratt, Louisa (Barnes) [Mrs. Addison] (1802-80),
16,793
Pratt, Louise (Shedd) [Mrs. Walter I.], 4,941
Pratt, Lucy Agnes, 7,012
Pratt, Maggie W. (Lukens), 5,905, 5,941
Pratt, Margaret, 395
Pratt, Marietta (Harkness) [Mrs Walter M.], **6,837**
Pratt, Martha Elsie (?-1920), **7,897**
Pratt, Mary (1908-). *See* Parrish, Mary (Pratt)
(1908-)
Pratt, Mary (Bayley) [Mrs. Joseph Hyde] (?-1929),
13,097
Pratt, Mary M. S. [Mrs.], 9,323
Pratt, Mary Stark [Mrs. Rey L.], 16,780
Pratt, Matthew (1734-1805), 7,674
Pratt, Mrs. Philo, 8,230
Pratt, Orson, 16,765
Pratt, Parley Parker, 16,786, 16,792
Pratt, Phoebe K. *See* Woodbury, Phoebe K. (Pratt)
Pratt, Rebecca Claypoole [Mrs. Henry], 7,674
Pratt, Rey L., 16,780, 16,811
Pratt, Romania, 16,966
Pratt, S. W., 17,213
Pratt, Sarah (1819-47), **17,708**
Pratt, Sarah Marinda (Bates) [Mrs. Orson] (1817-88),
16,794
Pratt, Sarah Morgan Bryan (1836-1919), 7,131
Pratt, Schuyler, 11,679
Pratt, Thankful Morgan (?-1837), 17,044
Pratt, Viola (1871-1956). *See* McFarlane, Viola
(Pratt) Gillette (1871-1956)
Pratt, Walter I. (1864-1940), **4,941**
Prayer-books, 6,180
Prayer for a Child (book), 14,399
Prayer groups, 4,757, **6,171,** 6,180
Prayer meetings, 7,604, **7,656,** 16,097
Preaching, 7,607
Preble, Mary Kate, 3,891
Preble-Nau, Stella Mae (?-1965), **1,524**
Precious Blood Sisters, 10,611
Prefecture (County) of Los Angeles, Archives (CA),
1,456
Pregnancy, 4,148, **10,898,** 13,446, 15,988, 16,876
complications of, 11,830
Pregnancy counseling, **15,818**
Preisler, Doris B. [Mrs. Paul]. *See* Wheeler, Doris B.
[Mrs. Paul] Preisler [Mrs. Maurice R.]
Preisler, Paul, 8,146
Preistrome Presbyterian Church (Plattsburgh, NY),
12,771
Prejudices and antipathies, 9,149
"Prelude" (ms), 4,242
Premarital examinations, 8,633, 9,844
Prenatal care, 1,607, 10,681, 11,852, 12,357
Prentice, Abbie Cantrill Rockefeller, 4,021
Prentice, Abra Rockefeller, 4,021
Prentice Hall Music Series, 12,050
Prentice, Mrs. A., Jr., 12,830

Prentiss, Adella (1869-1950). *See* Hughes, Adella
(Prentiss) [Mrs. Felix] (1869-1950)
Prentiss, Elizabeth (Payson) [Mrs. George Lewis]
(1818-78), 5,694
Prentiss, Ellen R., 13,932
Prentiss, Mary Ann. *See* Judson, Mary Ann
(Prentiss) [Mrs. Oren]
Prentiss, Mary Eleanor, 7,583
Prentiss, Narcissa (1808-47). *See* Whitman, Narcissa
(Prentiss) [Mrs. Marcus] (1808-47)
Prentiss, Pamela M. *See* French, Pamela M. (Prentiss)
[Mrs. Henry Flagg]
Prenuptial contracts, 333, 2,651, 4,856, 9,861, 13,390
Preparedness Day parade (San Francisco, CA),
12,702
Presby, Margaret (Penney) [Mrs. Willard], 5,319
Presby, Willard, 5,319
Presbyterian Board of Home Missions, 5,251
Presbyterian Church (Athens, GA), Ladies
Benevolent and Missionary Society, 3,049
Presbyterian Church (Waynesboro, GA), Women's
Auxiliary, 3,358
Presbyterian Church (Stony Creek, MI), **7,902**
Presbyterian Church in the U.S.A. *See* United
Presbyterian Church in the United States of
America
Presbyterian Church in the U.S.A., Woman's
Executive Committee of Home Missions. *See*
United Presbyterian Church in the United States
of America, Woman's Board of Home Missions
Presbyterian churches
clergy, 27, 96, 130, 864, **953, 1,243,** 1,247, **2,271,**
2,476, 3,208, **4,089,** 5,259, 5,343, **5,475, 5,713,**
5,867, 7,620, 8,367, **8,945, 9,316, 9,317,** 9,728,
9,801, 10,530, **10,958,** 10,991, 11,099, 11,111,
11,424, **11,788, 12,401,** 12,770, 12,771, 12,956,
13,292, 14,606, 14,833, 15,434, 15,550, **15,692,**
17,373. *See also* United Presbyterian Church in
the United States of America
discipline, 11,669
education, 94, 97, 9,597, **9,967,** 16,125
government, 3,266, 9,453
missionaries, **92, 93, 95,** 1,171, **2,271, 8,412, 8,871,**
8,879, 8,945, 9,446, 11,639, **12,185,** 13,439,
14,606, **15,171, 15,172, 15,173,** 15,174, **15,175,**
15,550, **15,841,** 17,373
missionaries, medical, **14,425**
missions, 95, **1,171,** 4,949, **9,454,** 12,185, 14,394,
14,425, 14,606, **15,841**
publishing, 15,709
Presbyterian Female College (Charlotte, NC), faculty,
13,245
Presbyterian Female Institute (AL), **14**
Presbyterian Foreign Missionary Society and Home
Missionary Society (MN), 9,453
Presbyterian Home for Aged Women (NY), **12,287**
Presbyterian Home for the Chinese, 17,218
Presbyterian Hospital School of Nursing (NY), 6,131,
6,721
Presbyterian Institute, 14
Presbyterian Manual Training Institute (GA), 3,039
Presbyterian Mission Board, 817
Presbyterian Outlook, The (periodical), 15,709
Presbyterian Seminary (SC), 15,619
Presbyterian Synod of Alabama, 9,801
Presbyterians, 8,487, 13,086, 14,208, 14,664, 15,553
Presbytery of Cleveland (OH), Woman's Missionary
Society, **13,952**
Presbytery of Newark (NJ), Woman's Board of
Foreign Missions, 11,067
Pre-school education, 13,875
Prescott, Caroline (1803-?), 6,845
Prescott, Eliza. *See* Jones, Eliza (Prescott) [Mrs. Peter
S.]
Prescott, Elizabeth Ellis. *See* Betton, Elizabeth Ellis
(Prescott)
Prescott, Emma J. Slade [Mrs. Alfred], **3,242**
Prescott, Harriet, 7,345
Prescott, Harriet Elizabeth (1835-1921). *See*
Spofford, Harriet Elizabeth (Prescott) [Mrs.
Richard Smith, Jr.] (1835-1921)
Prescott, Helen B. Crosby, 9,024
Prescott, Helen M., **13,098**
Prescott, Jessie Kennedy, 731

Prescott, Lucy, 8,936
Prescott, Marion. *See* Kimble, Marion (Prescott)
Prescott, Orville, 2,875, 11,637
Presentation Sisters of the Blessed Virgin Mary
    (Aberdeen, SD), **15,844**
Preservation Hall (New Orleans, LA), 5,532
Presidential Cookbook, The, 2,510
Presidents, Confederate States of America, **9,617,**
    9,618, 9,619
Presidents, Mexico, 335
Presidents, United States, 31, 64, 169, 181, 194, 255,
    1,424, 1,435, 1,437, 1,501, **1,502,** 1,507, 1,530,
    1,559, 1,563, 1,666, 2,158, 2,186, 2,214, 2,217,
    2,234, **2,346,** 2,349, 2,389, **2,448,** 2,529, 2,538,
    2,542, **2,559,** 2,582, **2,599,** 2,616, **2,621,** 2,640,
    3,227, 3,257, 3,260, 3,353, 3,469, 3,864, 4,354,
    4,417, 5,060, **5,122,** 5,133, **5,136, 5,137,** 5,151,
    5,750, 5,829, 5,904, 6,403, 6,432, 6,539, 6,622,
    6,720, 6,765, 6,956, **6,957,** 6,976, **7,133,** 7,598,
    7,660, 7,678, 8,096, 8,962, 9,035, 9,308, 9,658,
    9,719, 9,722, 9,779, 9,821, 10,073, 10,082,
    10,197, 10,419, 10,487, 10,748, **10,823,** 11,049,
    11,060, 11,169, 11,177, 11,242, 11,249, 11,340,
    11,345, 11,353, **11,358,** 11,434, 11,436, 11,576,
    11,615, 11,654, 11,746, 11,804, 11,827, 11,883,
    11,916, **11,922,** 11,944, 11,999, **12,184,** 12,203,
    12,299, 12,369, 12,553, 12,663, **12,757,** 12,913,
    13,210, 13,273, 13,350, 13,378, 13,610, 13,811,
    13,904, **13,926,** 13,954, **14,077,** 14,078, 14,838,
    14,872, 15,059, 15,755, 16,000, 16,620, 16,839,
    16,965, 17,029, 17,062, 17,633, 17,735, 17,978
  assassination, 1,725, 2,210, 2,418, 2,449, 3,171,
    4,423, 4,442, 9,286, 9,528, 11,539, 12,456,
    12,490, 12,594, 14,770, 17,479
  biography, 2,129, 2,512, 10,076, 10,079, 10,081,
    14,206
  childhood and youth, 9,902, 11,857
  children, 1,454, 2,345, **2,347,** 2,348, 4,961, 5,053,
    6,610, 10,073, 10,076, 10,082, 10,083, **11,176,**
    11,488, 11,871, 14,074, 17,083
  elections, 110, 349, 680, 793, 1,669, 2,336, 2,432,
    2,449, 2,579, 2,589, 2,663, 2,857, 3,088, 3,293,
    3,301, 3,303, 3,437, 3,778, 4,854, 4,970, 5,121,
    5,128, 5,133, 5,135, 5,265, 5,353, 5,707, **6,403,**
    6,662, 6,732, 6,939, 7,008, 7,889, 8,757, 8,844,
    8,912, 9,189, 9,192, 9,239, 9,464, 9,706, 9,956,
    10,082, 10,862, 11,486, 11,489, 11,502, 11,568,
    11,666, 11,857, 11,928, 12,883, 13,266, 13,274,
    13,286, 13,318, 13,533, 13,551, 13,972, 13,999,
    14,046, 14,683, 14,686, 14,822, 14,909, 15,635,
    17,238, 17,304, 17,455, 17,456
  inauguration, 878, 2,009, 2,457, 2,548, 2,639, 5,307,
    5,459, 10,165, 16,317
  mothers, 11,481, **13,925, 14,968**
  press conferences, 5,137, 11,857
  staff, 753, 1,937, 2,267, 2,312, **2,388, 2,389, 2,510,**
    2,512, 5,137, 5,139, 5,140, 5,142, 5,144, **5,145,**
    5,146, 5,155, 5,159, 5,161, 6,031, 6,662, 11,853,
    11,857, 12,600, 17,998
  staff, Afro-American, **3,301**
  term of office, 6,938, 10,165, 15,889
  wives, 64, 127, 194, **1,454, 1,460,** 1,593, 1,600,
    1,712, 2,123, 2,158, 2,180, 2,340, **2,348, 2,449,**
    2,468, 2,529, **2,640, 2,860, 3,476, 3,569,** 3,743,
    3,907, 3,922, **4,371,** 4,375, **4,633,** 4,695, 4,696,
    5,138, 5,151, 5,161, **5,294, 5,904,** 6,341, 6,432,
    6,653, 6,759, 6,864, 6,899, 6,925, 7,138, **7,337,**
    7,553, 7,598, 7,662, 10,073, 10,076, 10,082,
    10,083, 10,165, 10,823, 11,060, **11,169,** 11,177,
    11,249, 11,339, **11,493,** 11,654, 11,853, 11,914,
    12,153, 12,255, 12,757, **12,867,** 13,391, 13,406,
    13,451, 13,483, 13,566, 14,004, **14,075,** 14,206,
    15,355, 17,029
Presidents, Vietnamese, assassination of, 9,286
President's Commission on Economic Security, 6,973
President's Commission on Equal Opportunity, 8,085,
    11,484
President's Commission on Internal Security and
    Individual Rights, 6,914
President's Commission on the Status of Women,
    2,542, 6,790, **6,838,** 7,325, 8,027, 8,085, 11,484
President's Committee on the White House
    Conference on Education, 10,197
President's Committee on Traffic Safety, 5,155

President's Consumer Advisory Council, 6,723
President's Famine Emergency Campaign, 10,071
President's Task Force on Women's Rights and
    Responsibilities, 7,699
Presidio Hill School (CA), 931
Presidio Open-Air School (San Francisco, CA), 321,
    765
Presley, Ann (Cullen) [Mrs. Walter] (1913-), **243**
Press agents, **6,008, 6,882, 12,659**
Press and Author Club (AL), 76
Press-Enterprise (Riverside, CA),
Press Woman (periodical), 9,823
Pressler, Veannis Maddox (1876-), 16,355
Prestgard, Kristian, 8,764
Preston, Ann (1813-72), 15,144
Preston, C. A., 6,998
Preston, Caroline. *See* Woolley, Caroline (Preston)
    [Mrs. Abram R.]
Preston, Caroline (Hancock) [Mrs. William, Jr.]
    (1785-1847), 5,350, 5,359
Preston, Charles, 4,924
Preston, Elizabeth (1861-1954). *See* Anderson,
    Elizabeth (Preston) [Mrs. James] (1861-1954)
Preston Family (IA), **4,924**
Preston Family (KY, VA), **5,359**
Preston, Frances (Folsom) [Mrs. Grover] Cleveland
    [Mrs. Thomas Jex] (1864-1947). *See* Cleveland,
    Frances (Folsom) [Mrs. Grover]. [Mrs. Thomas
    Jex] Preston (1864-1947)
Preston, Henrietta. *See* Johnston, Henrietta (Preston)
    [Mrs. Albert Sidney]
Preston, John Thomas Lewis, 1,477, 13,099
Preston, Josephine. *See* Rogers, Josephine (Preston)
    [Mrs. James]
Preston, Letitia. *See* Floyd, Letitia (Preston) [Mrs.
    John]
Preston, Lucy, 14,628
Preston, Margaret [Mrs. William], 5,321
Preston, Margaret (Junkin) [Mrs. John Thomas Lewis]
    (1820-97), **1,477,** 5,350, **13,099**
Preston, Margaret (Smith) [Mrs. William P.]
    (1811-80), **5,799,** 5,800
Preston, Margaret Wickliffe (1885-1964). *See*
    Johnston, Margaret Wickliffe (Preston) [Mrs.
    Philip Preston, II] (1885-1964)
Preston, Maria. *See* Pope, Maria (Preston) [Mrs.
    John, Jr.]
Preston, Mary. *See* South, Mary (Preston) [Mrs.
    John M.]
Preston, May (1849-1913). *See* McNeal, May
    (Preston) [Mrs. Joshua Vansant] (1849-1913)
Preston, Mrs. William Campbell (1807-53), **15,685**
Preston, Paul (1724-1806), 14,821
Preston, Ruth (Irish) [Mrs. Charles], 4,924
Preston, Sarah Brant McDowell [Mrs. Wickliffe]
    (1850-1923), 5,321
Preston, Susan. *See* Hepburn, Susan (Preston)
    Christy
Preston, Wickliffe, 5,321
Preston, William, 13,011
Preston, William (1816-87), Family (KY), **5,321**
Preston, William, Jr. (1770-1821), 5,359
Preston, William P. (1811-80), **5,800**
Preston, Zenas, **9,800**
Prestridge, Mary Ann Rebecca Frost, **290**
Pretty Girl Papers, The (book), 7,317
Pretty Idiot, A (drama), 6,602
Preus, Caroline Dorothea Margrethe (Keyser)
    (1829-80), **4,721**
Preus, H. A., 8,817
Preus, Idella Louise Haugen [Mrs. Jacob Aall
    Otteson], 9,297
Preus, Jacob Aall Otteson (1883-1961), Family (MN),
    9,297
Preus, Johan Carl Keyser, **4,722**
Prevas, Pauline (1929-), 5,829
Prevaux, Francis Edward (1822-60), **732**
Prevaux, Lydia Dean (Rowell) [Mrs. Francis Edward],
    732
Previn, Dory, 950
Pribilof Islands, 141, 646
Price, Anna (1835-93). *See* Dillon, Anna (Price)
    [Mrs. John Forest] (1835-93)
Price, Dorothy, 3,604

Price, Elizabeth Fraser (ca. 1860-ca. 1954), 4,451,
    16,553
Price, Eugenia (1916-), **6,070**
Price Family, 9,849
Price Family (New England), 6,352
Price Family (WA), **17,204**
Price, Fanny Lily Gipsy (Davenport) (1850-98). *See*
    Davenport, Fanny Lily Gypsy
Price, Florence Beatrice (Smith) (1888-1953), **264**
Price, George Washington Fergus, 15,960
Price, Hiram, 4,695
Price, Irving, 11,434
Price, John B., 14,552
Price, Leontyne (1927-), 3,788, 9,585, 9,699
Price, Margaret (Bayne) [Mrs. Hickman, Jr.]
    (1912-68), **7,904**
Price, Margaret (Evans) [Mrs. Irving] (1889-1973),
    11,434
Price, Mary (1909-). *See* Adamson, Mary (Price)
    (1909-)
Price, Mary Ann (1816-1900). *See* Hyde, Mary Ann
    (Price) [Mrs. Orson] (1816-1900)
Price, Missoura [Mrs. W. F.], **16,303**
Price, Mrs. A. E., 13,751
Price, Mrs. E. J. (ca. 1828-?), **4,600**
Price, Mrs. Edwin O., 5,063
Price, Mrs. R. E., 9,819
Price, Nellie Harriet Hemenway, 14,684
Price, Nettie, 4,946
Price of Loyalty, The (book), 11,980
Price of Silence, The (book), 5,498
Price regulation, 1,810, 2,509, 2,688, 3,447, 3,805,
    3,931, 8,139
Price, Sarah Frances "Sadie" (1849-1903), 10,152
Price, Sarah Isabell. *See* Lovett, Sarah Isabell (Price)
    [Mrs. Robert Watkins]
Price, Sarah Jane (1841-1922), **10,524**
Price, Vickie, 3,748
Prices, 3,410, 8,743, 8,754, 9,107
Prichard, Hattie Valentine (1862-?), **14,644**
Pride, Hannah T., **9,710**
Pride, Virginia Chapin, 8,961
Pride, William W., **9,710**
Pridgett, Gertrude (1886-1939). *See* Rainey,
    Gertrude (Pridgett) "Ma" (1886-1939)
Priest, Alice L., **6,839**
Priest, Ellen Goodrich (1894-), **10,773**
Priest, Ivy (Baker) (1905-75), **5,154, 6,840,** 10,620
Priestly, Herbert I., 511
Priests, 690, 715, 733, 779, 951, **4,161,** 13,661,
    16,866, 17,868
Priests, Episcopal, 2,523, 13,176
"Prima Donna" (drama), 14,447
Primary Association, 16,667, 16,673
Primary Teacher Steps Out, A (book), 5,977
Primary Teachers' Union (Minneapolis, MN), **9,298**
Prime, Emily (1840-1909). *See* Delafield, Emily
    (Prime) [Mrs. Lewis Levingston] (1840-1909)
Prime Family (NY), 12,020
Prime, Mary Trumbull [Mrs.], 1,962
Prime ministers, 12,069, 12,070
Primers, 5,325
Primitive Baptists, 13,635
Primm, Mrs. Wilson, 9,841
Primrose League, 12,331
Primus Family, **1,875**
Primus Institute (MD), 1,875
Primus, Pearl Eileene, 5,469
Primus, Rebecca (1836-1932). *See* Thomas, Rebecca
    (Primus) [Mrs. Charles H.] (1836-1932)
Prince, Anna. *See* Pittman, Anna (Prince)
Prince, Charlotte (1827-1920s). *See* Henry, Charlotte
    (Prince) [Mrs. Edwin] (1827-1920s)
Prince, Charlotte Collins [Mrs. William Robert],
    12,288
Prince, Della, 12,931
Prince, Elizabeth Oakes (1806-93). *See* Smith,
    Elizabeth Oakes (Prince) [Mrs. Seba] (1806-93)
Prince Family (NY) **11,790, 12,288**
Prince, Flora (Grace), 11,688
Prince, Katherine Barber (James) [Mrs. William H.]
    (1834-90), 5,713, 5,867
Prince, Lillian (Hughes) [Mrs. William Meade]
    (?-1962), **13,100**

Prince, Lucinda Wyman Smith [Mrs. John Tilden]
(1862-1935), 6,236
Prince, Lucy Terry [Mrs. Abisah] (1730-1821),
12,692, 16,982
Prince of Wales Theatre (Australia), 5,911
Prince, William H., 5,713
Prince, William Robert (1795-1869), 11,790, 12,288
Princes, 15,042
"Princess Amber and Her Three Tasks, The" (story),
11,091
Princess Theatre Bulletin, The, 4,743
*Princess Theatre Bulletin, The, Ralph Bellamy
Players*, 4,743
Princesses, 3,260, 12,301
Princeton Theological Seminary (NJ), 10,956
Princeton Theological Seminary, presidents, 10,989
Princeton University (NJ), 8,367, 15,059
employees, 11,151
faculty, 11,170, 11,621
presidents, 11,172
students, **11,151**, 14,835
trustees, 10,989
Princeton University (NJ), Women's Center, 11,151
Princeton University (NJ), Women's Organization,
11,151
Princeton University Press, 2,215
Principals' Club (GA), **3,243**
Principia College (IL), 4,199
Principia Corporation, The (IL), 4,199
Principles of Comparative Psychology (book), 13,744
Prineville (book), 14,610
Pringle, Alva Miller [Mrs.], 1,080
Pringle, Catherine (Sager), 1,505, **17,173**, 17,422
Pringle, Elizabeth Waties (Allston) [Mrs. John Julius]
(1845-1921), 15,439, 15,440, 15,554
Pringle Family (SC), **15,439**
Pringle, John Julius (1753-1845), **15,686**
Pringle, Mr., 6,612
Printed Hearings of the House of Representatives,
2,697
Printed Hearings of the Senate, 2,697
Printers, **505**, 1,358, 3,991, **4,057**, 7,624, 9,175,
11,101, 11,184, **11,640**, **12,459**, 13,422, **14,881,**
14,890, 15,686, 17,302
Printers, Afro-American, **5,535**
Printers' marks, 38
Printing machinery and supplies, 12,508
Printing plants, 8,181
Printmakers, **2,741, 2,750, 2,763, 2,798**, 11,505
Priories, **3,733, 5,851, 9,489**, 13,726, **17,500**
Priory of St. Gertrude (ID), 3,733
Priour, Rosalie Bridget Hart [Mrs.] (1826-?), 16,117
Priscilla Club (IN), **4,579**
Priscilla Embroidery Club (MT). *See* Madison Valley
Woman's Club (MT)
Priscilla Society (NJ), 11,094
Prison reform, 56, 81, 117, 1,473, 1,561, 2,058, 2,562,
3,430, 4,243, 4,652, 4,974, 5,226, 5,522, 5,923,
6,811, 6,830, 7,216, 7,298, 8,223, 9,900, **10,174,**
11,600, 14,000, 14,025, 14,705, **14,755**, 15,274,
15,309, 16,123, 16,252
"Prison Special" (train), 6,959
Prison wardens, 1,312, 2,524
Prisoners, 210, 1,140, 1,147, **1,147**, 5,570, 8,067, **11,254,**
13,585, 13,619, **14,432**, 14,918, 15,309, **15,540,**
17,018, 17,463, 17,635
medical care, 8,028, 17,018
personal narratives, 6,811, 6,959, 7,223, 16,775
recreation, 13,446
Prisoners in the Circle, 17,997
Prisoners, Native American, 2,919
Prisoners of war, 3,721, 5,161, 5,246, 5,272, 5,286,
12,532, 12,913, 14,466
Prisoners, women, **5,283, 9,900**, 14,077
examination, 4,628
treatment, 9,940
Prisons, **165**, 1,939, 2,397, 3,485, 6,367, 9,303, 9,613,
10,652, 11,003, 11,974, 12,375, **12,423**, 12,576,
13,275, 13,468, 14,248, 15,762, 16,789, 17,892
administration, 10,652
hygiene, 10,177
legal aspects, 10,174
officials and employees, 190, 1,147, 1,771, 3,430,
6,263, 6,642, 7,031, 13,489

records and correspondence, **170**, 1,147, 1,149,
1,177, **14,917**, 14,918, **15,540, 17,019**
Prisons for women, 117, 1,140, 1,312, 9,934, 9,951,
17,483
officials and employees, **4,624, 4,628, 6,934, 17,084**
records and correspondence, 1,146, 8,276, **17,020**
Priston, Lizzie, 1,786
Pritchard, Catherine McAlpin (Wray) (1811-88),
13,101
Pritchard, Ellen, **13,563**
Pritchard, Lydia (1887-), **9,299**
Pritchard, Mary, 8,941
Private colleges, **5,547**
archives, 17,430
Private Faces, Public Places (book), 8,850, 9,192
Private Lives (drama), 60, 3,468
Private presses, 519, 2,488, **12,879**
Private Report (book), 5,022
Private schools, 888, 931, 1,104, 1,786, **1,836**, 1,837,
1,885, 1,966, **1,967, 2,003, 2,024**, 2,517, **3,055,**
3,094, 3,130, 3,170, 3,245, **3,264**, 3,266, 3,435,
3,842, 4,477, 5,679, **5,792, 5,798, 6,397**, 6,398,
6,487, 6,504, 6,631, 6,818, **7,068**, 8,988, 9,641,
10,897, 10,947, 12,419, **12,750**, 13,350, 14,508,
14,638, 15,051, 15,503, 17,560
records and correspondence, **5,877**
Prize Stories: The O. Henry Awards, 12,473, 17,076,
17,473
Pro-America, 14,565
Pro-American Republican Women's Club (NV),
10,679
Pro-Arte Musical Association (San Juan, PR), 15,364
Pro Ecclesia and Pontifice, 15,361
Probate courts, **11,455**, 11,456
Probate records, 15,478
Probation officers, 3,852, **4,115, 10,741, 11,788,**
13,988, 15,246
Probert, Ethel, 4,958
Problems of Indian Administration, The (book),
14,006
Probus (ship), 6,197
Procedure (law), 11,855
Proceedings (periodical), 13,501
Proceedings (St. Louis Board of Education, MO),
10,149
Procher, Isabella (Peyre) [Mrs. William] (1803-90),
15,428
Proctor, Edna Dean [Miss] (1829-1923) 9,437, **10,825**
Proctor, Elizabeth (1750-1824), **7,007**
Proctor, Mehetable Cummings (1837-1914). *See*
Baxter, Mehetable Cummings (Proctor) [Mrs.
James Phinney] (1837-1914)
Proctor, Mrs. F. W., 7,140
Professional Art Club, 13,860
Professional education, 7, 4,336, 6,673
Professional Educators of Los Angeles (CA), 2,103
Professional journals. *See* Scholarly periodicals
Professional women, 2,703, 3,183, 6,673, 11,903
Professional Women's Club (Baltimore, MD), 5,837
Professional Workers' Program (MO), 10,163
Professions, licenses, **4,336**
Proffit, Josephine Moore (1914-67), **6,007**
"Profiles of the poor." *See* Social science research
Program Resources, Inc., 8,057
Progress against Cancer (periodical), 7,327
Progress History Club (IN), 4,532, **4,580**
Progressive Education (periodical), 3,772
Progressive Education Association, 3,842
Progressive movement, 1,599
Progressive party, 575, 2,878, 4,970, 8,949, 9,001,
9,177, 9,375, 9,386, 17,238
Progressive party (founded 1948) **5,020**, 8,114, 8,653
Progressive Peace Party, 6,980
Progressive, The (periodical), 2,432
Progressivism (United States politics), 2,432
Prohibition, 349, 870, 1,532, 3,158, 3,205, 3,418,
4,243, 5,120, 5,122, 5,626, 5,829, 6,412, 6,484,
6,830, 6,925, 6,978, 7,172, 7,692, 8,668, 9,035,
9,095, 9,299, 9,327, 9,467, 9,468, 10,173, 10,642,
11,838, 11,928, 13,388, 13,648, 14,521, 15,869,
16,252, 16,337, **16,391**, 17,102, 17,363, 17,460,
17,659
opposition to, 2,030, **6,403, 11,253**, 14,703
repeal, 592, 13,533

"Prohibition and the Child" (ms), 17,750
Prohibition party, 349, 4,244, 7,779, 9,350, 13,533,
13,648, 13,668
"Propensity to Consume, The" (article), 6,601
Proper, Ida S. (1873-1957), 5,580
"Property Baby, The" (ms), 1,745
Property tax, 8,167, 9,795, 13,612
Prophet, Elizabeth, 3,290
Prophet of Peace (book), 15,298
Prophet of Zion-Parnassus, The (book), 13,001
Prophets for a New Day (book), 9,583
Proskauer, Joseph M., **11,881**
Proskowiakoff, Tatiana, 6,325
Prospect House (Cleveland, OH),
Prospecting, 2,528
"Prospects of Mankind" (television serial), 11,497
Prosser, Esther, 6,831
Prosser, William, 6,831
Prostitutes, 2,687, **6,752**, 14,916, 16,393
psychology, 6,752
Prostitution, 167, 186, 400, 870, 987, 1,122, 1,181,
1,751, 1,779, 1,786, 2,451, 2,687, 3,778, 3,798,
3,927, 4,114, 4,145, 4,409, 6,544, 6,638, 6,706,
6,760, 7,172, 7,223, 7,242, 7,257, 8,633, 8,647,
8,669, 9,095, 9,934, 9,962, 10,656, 10,681,
10,692, 10,711, **10,744**, 11,964, **11,978**, 12,424,
12,736, 14,848, 15,451, 16,252, 17,218, 17,377,
17,975
legal aspects, **16,393**
Protection of the Blessed Virgin Mary Ukrainian
Catholic Church (Philadelphia, PA), 14,909
Protective Agency for Women and Children
(Chicago, IL), **4,144**
Protective Land Use Association, 8,517
Proteins, 7,328
Protest songs, **15,977**
Protestant churches, 5,767, **7,092**
Protestant Episcopal Church. *See* Episcopal churches
Protestant Episcopal Church in the USA, **10,700**. *See
also* Episcopal churches
clergy, 9,753
Protestant Episcopal Church, Corporation for the
Relief of Widows and Children/Orphans of
Clergymen, **16,023**
Protestant Episcopal Church, Diocese of Northern
Michigan, Women's Auxiliary, **7,907**
Protestant Episcopal Church, Diocese of Western
Michigan, Conference of Young Women, 7,908
Protestant Episcopal Church, Diocese of Western
Michigan, Women's Auxiliary, 7,908
Protestant Episcopal Church, Society for the Relief of
Widows and Orphans, 15,447
Protestant Episcopal Female Beneficial Society (MD),
5,827
Protestant Episcopal Old Ladies Home (San
Francisco, CA), 877
Protestant Foster Home Society of the City of
Newark (NJ), 11,094
Protestant Home of St. Paul (MN), **9,166**
Protheroe, Lorena Reed, **7,486**
Prothonotaries. *See* Clerks of court
Prothonotary of the Court of Common Pleas (PA),
14,921
Proud, Anna Maria, 5,803
Proud, Eliza (Coale) [Mrs. John Greene] (1786-1838),
5,803
Proud, John Greene (1776-1865), 5,803
"Proud Lady of Stavoren, The" (poem), 5,669
Proud Little Grain of Wheat, The (book), 12,498
"Proud Little Grain of Wheat, The," 12,409
Proud Magazine, 10,191
Proud, Mary Abigail Willing (Coale) [Mrs. William
T.] (?-1831), 5,803
Proud to Be Amish (book), 6,037
Proust Marcel, 7,316
Prouty, Olive Higgins (1882-1974), 4,485, **7,689,**
11,165
Providence College (RI), archives, **15,375**
Providence College (RI), Veridames, 15,375
Providence Day Nursery (Chicago, IL). *See* Benton
House (Chicago, IL)
Providence District Nursing Association (RI), 6,594
Providence Female Charitable Society (RI), **15,388**

Providence Foundation for Training of Normal School Teachers (Poland), 8,991
Providence High School (Chicago, IL), 4,165
Providence Hospital (Waco, TX), 16,343
Providence Physiological Society (RI), **15,389**
Providence Plantations Club (RI), **15,390**
Providence Public Library (RI), 15,392
Providence Society (KS), 5,228
Provident Dispensary (Rochester, NY), 12,841
Provident Loan and Trust Company (Boston, MA), 12,656
Provincetown Players (MA), 6,008, 8,144, 12,029, 17,964
Provincetown Playhouse (MA), 17,494
Provincial Council (PA), 15,039
Provincial Freeman, The, 2,128
Provo School of Beauty Culture (UT), 16,542
Provoker, The (newspaper), 4,431
Provost, Matilda Ann Terril, 1,780
Prowlers of Ashbarrel Street (CA), 377
Prudden, Emily C. [Miss], 5,472
Pruessner, Anna C. [Mrs. J. D.] (1861?-?), **2,538**
Pruett, Elizabeth (1898-). *See* Farrington, Elizabeth (Pruett) (1898-)
Pruette, Lorine Livingston (1896-), 1,652, **6,841**
Pruitt, Helen. *See* Beattie, Helen (Pruitt)
Pruitt, Ida, 1,564
Pruitt, Mary Gardner, 9,462
Prussian Evangelical Church of the Union, 10,212
Pruyn, Anna Fenn (Parker), 11,249
Pruyn, Harriet Langdon (1868-1939). *See* Rice, Harriet Langdon (Pruyn) [Mrs. William Gorham] (1868-1939)
Pruyn, Huybertie (1874-1964). *See* Hamlin, Huybertie (Pruyn) [Mrs. Charles Sumner] (1874-1964)
Pry, Polly (pseudonym). *See* O'Bryan, Mrs. Leonel Ross
Pryor, Anne Augusta (Banister) [Mrs. Archibald Campbell], **17,093**
Pryor, Archibald Campbell, 17,093
Pryor, Helen Brenton, 1,348
Pryor, Margaret. *See* Dailey, Margaret (Pryor)
Pryor, Margaret Evans (1842-1937), 16,409
Pryor Mrs. Roger A., 2,187
Psychiatric clinics, 8,049
Psychiatric hospitals, 4,828, 5,226, 6,900, 7,489, 9,643, **10,097**, 12,197, 14,331, 17,415, 17,892
    employees, 14,331
    records and correspondence, **5,562, 6,211, 6,212, 6,214,** 11,254
Psychiatric nursing, 231, 2,086, 5,027, **6,148**
Psychiatric Nursing (book), 1,375
Psychiatric social work, **6,900**
Psychiatric social workers, **7,241**
Psychiatrists, 755, 2,086, **2,491**, 5,399, 5,713, **6,475, 6,517,** 6,544, 7,030, **11,308**, 14,698, 15,197, 17,604
Psychiatry, **5,225**, 15,429
    study and teaching, **6,224**, 6,679
Psychical phenomena, **5,163**
Psychical research, 2,344, 16,371
Psychoanalysis, 754, **3,914**, 11,885, **11,908**, 13,745
    cases, clinical reports, statistics, 11,908
Psychoanalysts, 15,876
"Psychological Differences Between Men and Women, The," 11,663
Psychologists, 212, **2,353, 2,631, 5,231, 5,232, 5,233, 6,094, 6,263, 6,658,** 6,771, 8,667, **10,475, 11,549, 11,605,** 11,659, 11,661, **12,616,** 13,735, 13,736, **13,737, 13,738, 13,739, 13,740, 13,741, 13,742, 13,743, 13,744, 13,745, 13,746, 13,869**
Psychology, 6,811, 7,648, **11,995**
    cases, clinical reports, statistics, 2,631, 13,737
    experiments, 13,738, 13,741
    societies, etc., 13,735, 13,739, 13,743, 13,745
    study and teaching, 6,379
"Psychology for an Individual Education," 11,306
Psychology forensic, **13,740**
Psychology, industrial, 13,737
Psychology of Women (book), 17,663
Psychometrics, 363, 2,840, 8,573
Psychoses, 11,908
Psychotherapists, feminist, **8,095**

Psychotherapy, 6,841
Ptak Family (OH), **13,953**
Ptak, Marus (Hlavacek) [Mrs. Victor G.] (1908-66), 13,953
Ptak, Victor G., 13,953
Ptapsco Female Institute (Ellicott Mills, MD), **5,798**
Public baths, 4,038
Public buildings, art, 2,801
Public Charities Association of Pennsylvania, 8,637
Public comfort stations, 8,481, 8,486, 10,886, 17,138
Public Education Association of New York, 2,000
Public Education Society (San Francisco, CA), 485
Public Forums of the State of Georgia, 3,117
Public health, 52, 321, 447, **1,148**, 1,779, **2,152**, 2,424, 2,432, 2,680, **2,687**, 2,704, 3,145, 3,273, 3,362, 3,482, 3,690, 3,696, 3,905, 4,111, 4,125, 4,149, 4,440, 4,931, 5,764, 6,446, 6,511, 6,558, 6,622, 6,852, 7,259, 7,286, 7,288, 7,318, 8,436, 8,487, 8,572, **8,633,** 8,668, 8,836, 8,991, 9,477, 11,571, 11,805, 11,932, 12,074, 12,246, 12,574, **12,736,** 12,738, 12,837, 13,261, 13,266, **13,513,** 13,987, 14,429, 14,640, 14,983, 15,431, 17,110
    legal aspects, 11,852, 11,916
Public health administration, 246
Public Health Certification Program, 239
Public health laws, 5,318
Public health nursing, 153, 231, 233, 236, 238, 239, **242, 1,148,** 1,655, 1,706, 1,779, 1,837, 2,347, 2,686, 3,432, 3,729, 3,813, 4,085, 4,888, 5,607, 5,764, 5,829, **6,125,** 6,126, **6,129,** 6,131, 6,135, **6,138, 6,142, 6,146, 6,153,** 6,154, 6,160, 6,162, 6,164, 6,238, **6,511,** 6,594, **6,648,** 8,053, 8,584, 8,648, **8,713,** 9,385, 11,063, 11,852, 12,078, 12,079, **12,657,** 12,738, 12,998, 13,880, **14,051,** 14,356, 16,216, **17,510, 17,511,** 17,515, 17,831
Public Health Nursing Service (OH), **14,051**
Public Health Nursing Service of Dayton and Montgomery County (OH), **6,154**
Public health officers, 9,008, 9,909, **17,517**
Public health personnel, 8,991, 15,429, **17,719**
Public Health Project, 9,195
Public health records, **17,510, 17,511, 17,515, 17,528**
Public housing, **2,695,** 3,293, 4,077, 4,087, 4,096, 4,147, 8,089, 8,104, 8,148, 8,655, 9,289, 11,501, 15,201, **17,697**
Public institutions **3,572, 4,338, 11,254, 14,248**
    auditing and inspection, 9,480
Public institutions, for teenagers, **1,151**
Public lands, 14,216, 14,622
Public libraries, 54, 147, 966, 1,068, **1,114,** 3,919, **3,925,** 5,558, **5,598,** 9,205, 9,360, 9,530, **10,915,** 10,923, 13,204, 13,300, 14,155, 15,795, **16,233, 17,008,** 17,241, 17,486
Public officers, 1,747, 1,779, **2,207, 2,208, 2,240,** 2,345, **2,456, 2,511,** 2,547, 2,608, **4,341,** 4,799, **5,038,** 5,109, 6,573, 6,761, **6,994, 8,027,** 8,210, 9,449, 9,818, **10,072, 10,074,** 10,075, 10,079, 10,342, 11,014, 11,354, 12,619, **12,658,** 13,459, 14,807, 17,376. *See also* Civil service
Public officers, Afro-American, 2,315, 2,880
Public opinion polls, 2,205, **3,975,** 11,866
Public prosecutors, 3,524
Public records, **2,926, 3,119,** 3,619, **5,409,** 5,497, **7,142, 8,276, 8,389,** 9,462, **9,739, 10,096, 11,452,** 12,775, **14,253, 14,922, 15,831, 16,310, 17,509, 17,534.** *See also* Archives
Public relations, 2,684, 2,687, 6,345, **6,399,** 8,057, 8,647, 14,714
    agriculture, 2,682
    charities, 16,222
    police, 863
    universities and colleges, 13,244, 13,616
Public relations consultants, **2,431, 4,120,** 4,130, **6,407, 10,738, 12,013, 12,066, 14,218,** 14,431, **16,222,** 17,125, **17,594,** 17,614
Public relations consultants, Afro-American, **2,139**
Public School Athletic League, Girls Branch, 12,738
Public School Messenger (MO), 10,149
Public schools, 1,010, 1,713, **2,003,** 2,758, 3,088, **3,364, 3,785,** 3,875, 5,499, 7,841, 9,390, 9,992, **10,149,** 12,752, 14,508, 15,543, 16,031, 16,055, 17,048
    employees, 8,113
    history 3,215

Public speaking, 14,026
Public utilities, 17,340
Public Utility District No. 1 (Snohomish County, WA), 17,340
Public welfare, 321, 380, 515, 973, 1,034, 1,049, 1,054, **1,150,** 1,428, **2,684, 2,687,** 3,356, 3,677, **3,690, 3,691,** 3,905, 5,493, 5,515, **5,573, 5,575,** 5,840, 5,846, 6,848, **7,111,** 8,078, 8,148, 8,535, 8,638, 8,670, 9,462, 9,477, 10,194, 11,958, **12,738,** 13,275, 13,614, 13,692, 13,993, 14,025, 14,222, 14,637, 14,640, 14,983, **15,404, 16,297, 17,021,** 17,509, **17,513,** 17,534, 17,738
    accounting,
    law and legislation, 3,858, 9,254, 13,504, 14,551
    research, **8,632**
Public welfare administration, 380, 8,632, **8,641, 8,644,** 8,654, 11,695, **14,913, 14,916,** 17,356, **17,892**
Public Welfare Journal (periodical), 4,130
Public works, 76, **1,798, 2,685, 2,692, 2,704,** 2,904, **3,119, 3,120,** 3,569, 4,055, 4,487, 4,949, 5,107, **5,108, 5,422, 5,424, 5,425,** 6,673, 8,518, 8,697, **9,462, 9,463,** 9,688, 9,699, 9,779, 10,055, 10,163, 10,332, 13,654, 13,715, 14,202, 14,224, 14,713, 15,431, **16,486, 16,968, 17,521,** 17,846
Publishers and publishing, 1,448, **1,464,** 1,719, 1,786, **2,403,** 2,436, 3,109, 3,996, 4,062, 4,095, 4,484, **5,209,** 5,414, 5,699, 5,712, 5,914, 5,940, 5,942, 5,944, **6,035,** 6,093, 6,096, **6,413, 6,694,** 6,785, 7,675, **7,915, 8,459,** 9,001, 9,769, 10,184, 11,153, **11,156,** 11,164, **11,166, 11,221,** 11,644, 11,870, **11,889, 12,172, 12,178, 12,384, 12,395, 12,499, 12,537,** 12,622, 13,929, 14,085, **14,328,** 14,345, **14,377,** 14,451, **14,463,** 14,545, 14,945, 14,987, 15,564, 15,920
Publishers Weekly (periodical), 12,395
Pucell, Margaret Perren (Parrin), **16,433**
Puck (periodical), 10,178
Puckerbrush Press (ME), 6,035
Puckett, Alice. *See* Posey, Alice (Puckett)
Puddington, Grace E., 10,758
Pueblo Chieftain (CO), 1,750, 10,728
Pueblo Indians, 311, 2,840, 2,843, 5,988, 11,213, 11,217, 11,235, 13,540
    art, 11,222
    government relations, 11,236
Pueblos, 1,779, 14,897, 16,874
Puerto Ricans, 6,221
    missions, Presbyterian, 15,173
Puerto Rico, 2,361
    art, galleries and museums, 2,778
    associations, **15,365**
    college teachers, **15,366**
    community centers, 7,225
    composers, 15,367
    health facilities, 5,457
    hospitals, 6,987
    music teachers, **15,364**
    musical societies, 15,364
    physicians, 6,987
    pianists, **15,367**
    poets, **15,368**
    suffrage societies, 15,368
Puffer, Ethel (1872-1950). *See* Howes, Ethel (Puffer) (1872-1950)
Puffer, Laura (1874-1962). *See* Morgan, Laura (Puffer) (1874-1962)
Puget Sound Academy of Science (WA), 17,266
Puget Sound Association of the Deaf (WA), 2,106
Puget Sound Council of Social Studies (WA), 17,341
Pugh, Esther, 4,244
Pugh Family, 12,531
Pugh, Mabel [Miss], 13,447
Pugh, Sarah (1800-84), 3,298, 5,907, **6,842**
Pulitzer, Joseph, 357
Pulitzer Prize, 159, 3,745, 5,694, 9,770, 10,027, 10,760, 11,175, 11,217, 12,553, 15,377, 17,634, 17,799, 17,979
Pulitzer Prize for fiction, 2,876, 9,768
Pulitzer Prize for poetry, 11,171, 14,322, 14,761
Pullen, Catherine (Carson) [Mrs. William H., Jr.], 9,711
Pullen, William H., Jr., **9,711**
Pulley, Mary (1900-), **16,554**

Pulliam, Ann Robertson. *See* Wilson, Ann Robertson (Pulliam) [Mrs. John]
Pulliam, John, 9,689
Pullman Company, 3,955
Pullman, Emily Caroline Minton (1808-92), **3,896**
Pullman, Emma Caroline. *See* Fluhrer, Emma Caroline (Pullman) [Mrs. William F.]
Pullman, George Mortimer, 3,896
Pullman Library (IL), 3,919
Pullman Palace Car Company, 3,156
Pulsifer Family, 4,404
Pulsifer, Susan Farley (Nichols) [Mrs. Harold Trowbridge], 12,695
Pulsipher, Juanita (Leavitt) [Mrs. L. Ernest] (ca. 1900-). *See* Brooks, Juanita (Leavitt) [Mrs. L. Ernest] Pulsipher [Mrs. William] (ca. 1900-)
Pumpelly, Eliza (Shepard) [Mrs. Raphael] (?-1911), 1,478
Pumpelly, Raphael (1837-1923), **1,478**
Pumpkin Flood at Harper's Ferry, The (book), 10,531
Punch (periodical), 112
Puppeteers, 1,534
Puppets and puppet-plays, 11,985
Purcell, Helen Louise, 10,032
Purcell, John B., 14,117
Purdie, Afton, 16,460
Purdie, Mary, 16,460
Purdon, James, **15,078**
Purdon, Maria T., 15,078
Purdue, Albert Homer, 265
Purdue, Ida (Pace) [Mrs. Albert Homer] (1869-1958), **265**
Purdue Research Foundation, 4,681
Purdue University (IN), 4,522, 4,657, 4,681
  faculty, 4,682
  students, 4,430
Purdy, Anne [Mrs. Fred], 130
Purdy, Bertha, [Mrs.], 10,701
Purdy, George S., 12,421
Purdy, Katharine Jerome Purdy [Mrs. Jordan Lawrence, II], 12,053
Pure Food Campaign, 8,486
Purim Association, 7,551
Purisima Concepción Mission (CA), **733**
Puritan Sportswear Company (Altoona, PA), 15,321
Purkett, Mrs. P. B., 4,369
Purnell Funds for Research, 11,656
Purnell, Idella (1901-). *See* Stone, Idella Purnell [Mrs. Remington] (1901-)
Purnell, Sarah Ann. *See* Montgomery, Sarah Ann (Purnell)
Purple Heart, 4,843
Purple William D., 16,612
Purroy, John B., 12,046
Purse, Mrs. Thomas, 3,493
Purvin, Jennie (Franklin) (1873-1958), **13,817**
Purvis, Eliza J. W., 13,541
Purvis, Mrs. Thomas, 1,092
Pusey, Emalea (1853-1948). *See* Warner, Emalea (Pusey) (1853-1948)
Pusey, Nathan Marsh, 6,299, 6,877, 10,197
Putnam, Amelia Mary (Earhart) [Mrs. George Palmer] (1897-1937). *See* Earhart, Amelia Mary. [Mrs. George Palmer] Putnam (1897-1937)
Putnam, Arthur, 543
Putnam, Caroline F. (1826-1917), 2,315, 5,907, 7,629, 11,616, 15,283
Putnam, Catherine, 6,681
Putnam Charles F., 14,645
Putnam, Charles Frederick, III, 17,174
Putnam County Hospital (IN), 4,585
Putnam County Hospital Guild (IN), **4,581**
Putnam, Effie Douglas, 7,267
Putnam, Elias, 7,008
Putnam, Elizabeth, 6,998
Putnam, Elizabeth Cabot (Jackson) (1836-?), 6,565
Putnam, Emily James (Smith) [Mrs. George Haven] (1865-1944), 5,861
Putnam, Emma, 7,001
Putnam, Eva, 8,936
Putnam Family (OR), **14,645**
Putnam, Frederic Ward (1839-1915), 6,326
Putnam, George, 5,162
Putnam, George Haven, 2,457

Putnam, George Palmer, 6,550, 12,289
Putnam, Goldie Van Bibber [Mrs. Charles Frederick, III] (1885-1965), **17,174, 17,205**
Putnam, Herbert, 14,758
Putnam, James Jackson (1846-1918), 6,210, 6,224, **6,843**
Putnam, Joseph, 14,645
Putnam, Julian (Osgood), 12,207
Putnam, Katharine (1849-1935). *See* Hooker, Katharine (Putnam) (1849-1935)
Putnam, Louisa Jane, **7,008**
Putnam, Louisa Lancaster, **7,009**
Putnam, Mabel R. [Mrs. Frank], **6,844**, 12,575, **12,597**
Putnam, Margaret (Sage) (1811-?), 7,424
Putnam, Martha Page (1832-?). *See* Goodell, Martha Page (Putnam) (1832-?)
Putnam, Mary [Mrs. Horace B.], **7,425**
Putnam, Mary Barnard (Clark) (1871-1963), 9,004
Putnam, Mary Corinna (1842-1906). *See* Jacobi, Mary Corinna (Putnam) [Mrs. Abraham] (1842-1906)
Putnam, Mary (Page) [Mrs. Alfred] (1806-94), 7,658
Putnam, Mary Traill Spence (Lowell) (1810-98), 1,426
Putnam, Mrs., 4,211
Putnam, Mrs. Grant C., 8,167
Putnam, Mrs. Haven, 12,208
Putnam, Nathan J., 14,645
Putnam, Persis, 12,739
Putnam, Rozelle (Applegate), 14,645
Putnam, Ruth (1856-1931), **734**, 2,411, 6,681
Putnam, S. B. [Mrs. George], **12,289**
Putnam, Samuel, 17,174
Putnam, Sophie G., 14,515
Putnam, Susan, 14,645
Puzyriskaya, Anna Abramovna. *See* Zon, Anna Abramovna (Puzyriskaya) [Mrs. Raphael]
Pye, Dorothy. *See* Barrett, Dorothy (Pye)
Pye, Mary Emily Francis (Kelly) [Mrs. Calbel Enoch] (1867-1945), **16,797**
Pyle, Gladys, 15,869
Pyle, Howard (1906-), **5,155**
Pyle, Mamie I. Shields [Mrs. John] (1866-1949), **15,868**
Pynchon, Adeline (Lobdell) [Mrs. Henry] Atwater [Mrs. Henry C.] (ca. 1887-), **3,981**
Pynchon, Cora N. (1854-1938). *See* Mallory, Cora N. (Pynchon) [Mrs. Henry Rogers] (1854-1938)
Pynchon Family (CT), 1,988
Pynchon, Henry C., 3,981
Pyne, Robert Stockton, 11,157
Pyper, George D., 16,676
Pythian Sisters (Ann Arbor, MI), Arbor Temple Number Eighty, 7,832
Pythian Sisters (OK), Tulsa Temple, **14,263**
Quachenbush, Sarah [Mrs.], **3,566**
Quaid, Laural, 3,760
Quail, Nellie, 211
Quain, Fannie (Dunn) [Mrs. Eric P.] (1876-1950), **13,660**
Quain-Ramstad Clinic (ND), 13,660
Quaker, a Study in Costume, The (book), 14,842
Qualey, Elizabeth Frances Cummings, 6,353
Quan, Alice (Browne), 14,230
Quandt, Marjorie, 4,023
Quanimptewa, Gloria, 16,864
Quantrill, Sarah King [Mrs. William Clarke], 9,919
Quantrill, William C., 10,879, 17,584
"Quapaw County, The" (booklet), 14,195
Quapaw Indians, 14,241
Quarles, Diana Pittman, 3,071
Quarles, Johanna A., 9,865
Quarries and quarrying, 1,750
Quarterman Family (SC), **15,511**
Quarterman, Leonora, 2,849
Quarterman, Mary, 15,511
Quateh (Cherokee Indian, NC), 13,448
Quayle, Oliver A., III, 12,652
Quealy, Susan J. [Mrs.], 18,014
Quebec (Canada), 1,428
  expedition to (1749), 7,669
Queen, Anne (1911-), 13,176
Queen Catherine of Montour (drama), 11,445

Queen City Chautauqua Circle (TX), **16,119**
Queen City Chautauqua Literary and Scientific Circle (TX), 16,119
"Queen Victoria" (radio program), 1,026
Queens, 2,944, 3,620, 3,621, **3,631, 3,632**, 5,140, 11,509, 12,273, 16,249
Queens College (NY), faculty, 11,029, 11,804, 11,999
Queen's College (Charlotte, NC), **13,542**
  faculty, 13,177, 13,178
Queen's Quire, The (book), 2,319
Query Club (Nashville, TN), 15,965
Quest (periodical), 4,269
"Question of Guilt, A" (ms), 6,115
Quetico-Superior Council (MN), 9,302
Queyrouze, Leona (pseudonym). *See* Barel, Constant Beauvais [Mrs. Pierre M. E.] (1866-1938)
Quick, A. J., 6,845
Quick, Frances (Merritt) [Mrs. A. J.] (1833-1924), **6,845**
Quick, Helen, 8,462
Quick Years, The (book),
Quickert, Margaret [Miss], 5,309
"Quier Kyds, The" (secret society), 7,314
Quiet Hour Club (Metuchen, NJ), **10,918**
Quiet Life of Mrs. General Lane, The (book), 14,333
Quieto, Delilah, 1,532
Quigg, Jane (Townsend) [Mrs. John B.], **5,801**
Quigley, Abigail Eleanor (1916-). *See* McCarthy, Abigail Eleanor (Quigley) [Mrs. Eugene] (1916-)
Quigley, Iola B., **4,820**
Quigley, Robin, 5,719
Quigly, Emma Lucretia. *See* Burr, Emma Lucretia (Quigly) [Mrs. Isaac Post]
Quill, The (NE), 10,525
Quill, The (yearbook), 12,750
Quillen, Jane Lowe, **16,120**
Quillin, Ellen Dorothy (Schulz) [Mrs. Roy W.], **16,316**
Quilting, 1,786, **5,660**, 7,599, **9,732**, 11,211, 14,180, 16,968
Quilts, **8,275**
Quimby, Phineas P. (1802-66), 2,321
Quinby, Hannah [Mrs. William] 11,681
Quinby, Moses, **11,681**
Quinby, William, 11,681
Quince Family (SC), **15,512**
Quince, Mary. *See* Motte, Mary (Quince) [Mrs. Abraham]
Quince, Susannah, 15,512
Quincy, Abby A., **5,953**
Quincy, Fanny Huntington (?-1933). *See* Howe, Fanny Huntington (Quincy) [Mrs. M. A. DeWolfe] (?-1933)
Quincy, Mary Perkins [Miss] (1866-1921), **1,969**
Quiner, Edwin B., 17,709
Quiner, Emilie C. (1840?-?), **17,709**
Quinine, therapeutic use, 10,044
Quinlan, Betsey Lane [Miss], **13,543**
Quinlan, Patrick L, 12,705
Quinn, Frances, 2,502
Quinn, Frank, 496, **965**
Quinn, James R., 1,790
Quinn, Percy E., 9,688
Quintard, May (Shepherd) [Mrs. E. A.], 2,572
Quintessence of Long Speeches, arranged as a Political Catechism, by a Lady, for her God-daughter, The, 15,508
Quinton, Amelia (Stone) (1833-1926), 1,504
Quintuplets, 3,368
Quisinberry, Virginia [Miss], 12,532
Quitman, Eliza (Turner), 9,709
Quitman Select School (MO), **9,903**
Quitzow, Charles, 362
Quitzow Family (CA), 362
Quitzow, OElóel. *See* Braun, OElóel (Quitzow)
Quitzow, Sülgwynn [Mrs. Charles], 362
Quitzow, Vol, 362
Quota Club (GA), 3,265
Quota Club (Davenport, IA), 4,710
R. D. Nesmith and Company, **7,121**
R. H. Macy Company, **6,203**, 13,737
RKO pictures (moving-picture studio), 14,736, 17,792
R. M. Forsman and Company (PA), 17,506
R. R. Bowker Publishing Company (NY), 12,395

Raaen, Aagot [Miss] (1878-1957), **8,779**, **13,684**
Raaen Family, 8,779
Raasch, Rhoda. *See* Gilman, Rhoda (Raasch) [Mrs. Logan]
Rabb, Ellis, 12,367
Rabb, Mary, **16,121**
Rabbis, 933, 6,603, 7,528, **7,552**, 7,559, 11,915, 12,069, 13,803, 13,810, 17,744
Rabinowitz, Tatania Gitel (1887-1963). *See* Robbins, Matilda (1887-1963)
Rabun Gap-Nacoochee Guild (GA), 3,244
Rabun Gap-Nacoochee School (GA), **3,244**
Rabun Gap School (GA). *See* Rabun Gap-Nacoochee School (GA)
Race discrimination, 387, 2,502, 5,462, 6,790, 9,467, 10,096, 16,863, 16,876, 17,663. *See also* Discrimination in education; Discrimination in employment
   law and legislation, 5,470, 5,473
Race discrimination in education, 3,844
Race discrimination in entertainment, 3,773
Race discrimination in higher education, 15,186
Race discrimination in housing, 3,844
Race, George Wesley, 13,102
Race, Olivia Corinne (Kittredge) [Mrs. George Wesley] (1835-1916), **13,102**
Race problems, 62, 124, 164, 203, 232, 1,408, 1,850, 1,859, 2,143, 2,152, 2,879, 2,885, 3,145, 3,155, 3,157, **3,283**, 3,293, 3,302, 3,343, 3,347, 3,357, 3,362, 3,830, 3,875, 4,048, 4,050, 4,073, 4,090, 4,148, 4,158, 4,170, 4,270, 5,377, 5,420, 5,455, 5,460, 5,469, 5,828, 6,490, 6,981, 7,326, 7,329, 7,742, 8,635, 8,638, 8,678, 8,684, 8,693, 9,149, **9,284**, 9,456, 9,464, 9,467, 10,159, 10,203, 10,205, 11,591, 11,855, 11,931, 12,061, 12,236, 12,724, 12,738, 12,939, 13,211, 13,222, 13,262, 13,533, 13,604, 13,982, 14,686, 15,176, 15,202, 15,376, 15,610, 15,683, 15,769, 15,869, 16,356, 16,780, 17,295, 17,341, 17,583. *See also* Discrimination; Intercultural education
   research, 8,659
Rachmaninoff, Sergei, 14,670
Racine Public Library (WI), 17,565
"Racism in Education" Conference, 8,121
Racketty-Packetty House (CA) 941
Radcliffe Chautauqua, 13,366
Radcliffe College (MA), 6,042, 6,188, 6,189, 6,278, **6,300**, 6,368, 6,483, 6,484, 6,493, 6,590, 6,658, 6,667, 6,677, 6,688, 6,691, 6,721, 6,722, 6,776, 6,817, 6,923, 6,986, 7,814, 11,885, 12,737
   alumnae, 2,108, 6,353, 6,556, 6,935, 8,441, 9,392, 12,009
   curricula, **6,273**
   deans, **6,478**
   history, 6,471
   presidents, 4,732, **6,290**, 6,346, 6,436, 7,158, 8,566, 8,689
   students, 561, 1,948, 8,580, 9,839, 11,473, 14,366
   students' societies, **6,286**
   trustees, 2,115, 6,329
Radcliffe College (MA) Alumnae Association, 6,339, 6,556
Radcliffe College (MA) Appointment Bureau, 6,769, 6,907
Radcliffe College (MA), Committee on Instruction and Degrees, **6,273**
Radcliffe College (MA), Education for Action, 6,339
Radcliffe College (MA), Health Center, 6,339
Radcliffe College (MA), Idler Club, 14,366
Radcliffe College (MA), Institute on Historical and Archival Management, 6,339
Radcliffe College (MA), Student Government Association, 6,339
Radcliffe Institute for Independent Study (MA), 6,339
Radcliffe, Mary (Van Wagener) [Mrs. Lewis], **736**
Radcliffe Unit, 6,647
Radcliffe, Zoe (Green), **737**
Rader, Iva [Mrs.], **10,702**
Radford, R. L. (pseudonym). *See* Radford, Ruby Lorraine [Miss]
Radford, Ruby Lorraine [Miss], **3,073**
Radiant Story of Jesus, The (book), 11,179
Radical America, 17,663

Radical United Brethren Church, Woman's Missionary Association, 4,469
Radical Women of New York City (NY), 17,583
Radin, Dorothea (Prall) [Mrs. Max], 1,088
Radio, 4,259, 10,633, 11,907
   censorship, World War II, 11,909
   history, **11,909**
   laws and regulations, 5,120, 11,909
Radio advertising, 6,495
Radio and children, 2,069, 11,909
Radio and music, 51
Radio and television, 11,909
Radio announcing, **11,402**, 17,650
Radio authorship, **6,018**, 6,059, **6,070**, **17,705**
Radio broadcasting, **2,096**, **4,075**, 6,049, 6,082, 10,330, 11,488, 12,900, 13,745, 16,265, 17,298
   moral and religious aspects, 11,909
Radio Free Europe, 17,762
Radio in education, 4,048, 4,383
Radio in propaganda, 6,049
Radio industry and trade, employees, 8,081
Radio operators, **8,314**, 13,301
Radio plays, 1,026, **10,870**, 13,008
Radio programs, 52, 315, **1,026**, 1,786, **2,274**, 2,385, 2,533, 2,714, 4,916, 6,034, 6,070, 6,337, 6,625, 6,658, 7,228, 7,249, 8,185, 8,269, 8,591, 8,867, 9,849, 10,131, 10,330, 10,444, 11,291, 11,496, 11,756, 11,909, 12,426, 13,261, 14,041, 14,551, 15,273, 16,277, 16,845, 17,325, 17,350, 17,368, 17,599, 17,809
   rating, 17,650
Radio scripts, 643, 1,353, 1,795, 2,274, 2,293, 2,681, 3,195, 3,289, 3,432, 4,895, 5,441, 6,049, 6,070, 6,082, 6,100, 6,625, 7,235, 7,550, 11,994, 12,890, 12,900, 15,585
Radio Scripts, Inc., 17,810
Radio serials, 6,070, 6,499
Radio stations, 6,499, 6,658, 9,467, 12,622
Radioactive contamination of milk, 4,492
Radiologic technologists, 1,655
Radiological Society of North America, 4,698
Radiologists, **10,508**
Radium, 6,496, 12,045
   toxicology, 2,504
Radnitz, Gerty Theresa. *See* Cori, Gerty Theresa (Radnitz) [Mrs. Carl F.]
Rae, Eloisa (McLaughlin) [Mrs. William Glenn] (1817-84). *See* Harvey, Eloisa (McLaughlin) [Mrs. William Glenn] Rae [Mrs. Daniel] (1817-84)
Rae, William Glenn, 534
Ragen, Edward, 10,359
Ragen, Mary Ellen [Mrs. Edward] (1867-1961), **10,359**
Ragland, Betty, **9,857**
Rago, Henry, 4,485
Rags, an Orphan of the Storm (book), 5,041
Ragtime music, 16,013
Rahl, Katherine, 8,633
Rahm, Louisa (Moeller), **738**
Rahn, Otto (1881-), **11,682**
Rahoi, Philip (1896-), **8,119**
Rahway Association for the Relief of Sick Poor (NJ), **11,022**
Raicoff, Anna (Duricy) [Mrs. James] (1898-), **16,006**
Raihle, Sylvia (Havre) [Mrs. Paul H.] (1892-), 17,862
Railroad companies, 1,248, 2,984, 3,086, 7,672, 9,956, 10,240, 12,588, 14,745, **16,237**
   management, 13,323
Railroad engineering, 1,770, 15,059
Railroad engineers. *See* Locomotive engineers
Railroad law, 10,104
Railroad societies, 3,220
Railroad travel, 1,235, 1,269, 1,332, 3,486, 7,766, **8,520**, 9,467, 9,858, 10,882, 11,732, 11,795, **14,371**, **14,590**, **15,762**
Railroads 194, 1,790, 3,145, 3,246, 3,268, 4,820, 5,689, 5,821, 7,678, 8,333, 8,712, 8,781, 9,117, 9,686, 10,033, 10,240, 10,638, 11,574, 14,204, 14,664, 14,718, 15,497, 16,968, 17,183
   accidents, **4,694**
   consolidation, 11,769
   construction, 9,419

   employees, 304, 2,696, **3,317**, 3,881, **4,002**, 4,700, 5,319, 5,394, 5,746, 7,177, 7,680, **8,354**, 8,518, 8,690, 8,893, 9,034, **9,131**, 9,401, 9,467, 9,600, 10,672, **14,573**, **15,059**, 17,209
   passes, 2,359
   Pullman cars, 3,156
   sleeping-cars, 3,896
   time-tables, 10,037
   trains, 14,856
Railroads and state, **2,696**
Railway Labor Act, 11,770
Railway Mail Association, Women's Auxiliary (St. Paul, MN), **9,455**
Rain (drama), 60
Rain and rainfall, 16,357
"Rain Pool" (column), 15,966
Rainbow Girls, 13,446
Raine, Colonel, 17,094
Raine, Frances Bouldin (Spragins) (1816-?), **17,094**
Raines, Anna B. [Miss], **8,673**
Raines, Bettie, 3,028
Raines, Trainie, 3,028
Rainey, Gertrude (Pridgett) "Ma" (1886-1939), 5,532, 5,533
Rainey, Glenn Waddington (1907-), **3,347**
Rainey, Homer Price (1896-), **10,035**
Rainey, Ida Lee, 6,223
Rainey, Julian D., 8,116
Rains, Miriam E. (Bliss) [Mrs. J. Frank] (1862-1942), **1,190**, 1,199
Rainy River Country (book), 8,441
Rak, Mary (Kidder) [Mrs. Charlie] (1879-1958), 223
Raleigh Academy (NC), 13,423
Raleigh Academy (NC), Female Department, 13,389
Raleigh Citizens' Defense Corps (NC), 13,618
Raleigh Council of United Church Women (NC), 13,559
Raleigh Equal Suffrage League (NC), 13,274
Raleigh Female Academy (NC), 13,452
Raleigh Female Seminary (NC), 13,487
Raleigh Kiwanis Scholarship Foundation, Inc. (NC), **13,544**
Raleigh Music Club (NC), **13,545**
Raleigh, Sir Walter, 2,485
Raleigh Woman's Club (NC), 13,070, 13,334, 13,446, 13,447
Ralph, Lovina Anderson [Mrs.], **16,478**
Ralston, Esther (1902-), **18,003**
Ralston, Harriet N. (Jackson) [Mrs. James H.], 739
Ralston, Jackson Harvey, **739**
Ralston, Jennie (Craven) [Mrs. Samuel Moffett] (1862-1954), **4,486**
Ralston, Samuel Moffett, 4,486
Ralston, William C., 841
Rama Rau, Lady Dhanvanthi, 7,287
Rama Rau, Santha (1923-), **6,071**
Ramabai, Pundita, 15,283
Ramahdan, 10,927
Ramallah School, 4,176
Raman effect, 11,814
Rambeau, Marjorie, 2,476
Ramblers Club (Ontario, CA), 1,092
Ramon Makes a Trade (book), 18,004
Ramona (book), 12,519
Ramona High School (CA), 789
Ramsay, Andrew, **12,290**
Ramsay, Elizabeth (1857-1924). *See* Fraser, Elizabeth (Ramsay) [Mrs. George] (1857-1924)
Ramsay, J. R. *See* Ramsay, Andrew
Ramsay, Martha (Laurens) [Mrs. David] (1759-1811), **15,687**
Ramsay, Mrs. John B. (1904-), 5,828
Ramsden, Agnes, 8,948
Ramsell, Gladys "Glad" (1896-). *See* Morath, Gladys "Glad" (Ramsell) [Mrs. Fred] (1896-)
Ramsey, Alexander (1815-1903), 4,322, 9,303
Ramsey, Alexander (1815-1903), Family (MN), **9,303**
Ramsey, Anita Earl (1876-1964). *See* Furness, Anita Earl (Ramsey) (1876-1964)
Ramsey, Anna Earl Jenks [Mrs. Alexander] (1826-84), 9,303
Ramsey County Graduate Nurses' Association (MN). *See* Fourth District Minnesota Nurses' Association

Ramsey County Mental Health Services (MN), 9,467
Ramsey County Mental Health Spanish American Project (MN), 9,467
Ramsey County Public Welfare Department (MN), 8,638
Ramsey County Registered Nurses' Association (MN). See Fourth District Minnesota Nurses' Association
Ramsey County Women's Democratic Club (MN), 9,306
Ramsey, J. G. M., 13,546
Ramsey, Justus, 9,303
Ramsey, Katherine, 9,592
Ramsey, Marion (1853-1935). See Furness, Marion (Ramsey) [Mrs. Charles Eliot] (1853-1935)
Ramsey, Mary E. (Wire) (?-1834), 15,174
Ramsland, Margaret Alyce Ruth (Chivers), 740
Ranch life, 1,101, 1,312, 10,225, 10,233, 10,243
Ranch Romances, 14,354
Ranchers, 156, 184, 196, 223, 426, 1,208, 1,634, 1,786, 2,922, 3,685, 9,087, 10,245, 10,272, 10,290, 10,309, 10,349, 10,371, 10,431, 10,487, 10,650, 10,713, 10,719, 10,737, 10,780, 10,784, 11,227, 14,234, 14,509, 14,683, 16,271, 16,434, 16,529, 17,907, 18,015
Ranches, 216, 333, 349, 370, 428, 477, 627, 636, 731, 733, 870, 906, 1,412, 1,441, 1,492, 3,685, 3,728, 5,132, 10,238, 10,270, 10,278, 10,379, 10,380, 10,630, 10,670, 10,680, 10,715, 15,869, 15,985, 16,060, 16,486, 16,904, 17,251
Rancho Los Alamitos (CA), 428
Rancho Santa Fe, 6,375
Rand, Ayn, 1,025, 2,097
Rand, Caroline (?-1918). See Sterling, Caroline (Rand) (?-1918)
Rand, Dorothy, 11,774
Rand Family (WA), 17,175
Rand, Harriet N., 7,514
Rand McNally Company, 14,407
Rand, Rose, 2,539
Randall, Adin, 17,535
Randall, Catherine (ca. 1829-?). See Giddings, Catherine (Randall) [Mrs. Luther?] (ca. 1829-?)
Randall, Catherine (Wirt) [Mrs. Alexander] (ca. 1807-53), 5,802, 5,824
Randall, Elaine Painter [Mrs. James Garfield] (1892-), 2,540
Randall, Elizabeth (ca. 1830-?). See Clunas, Elizabeth (Randall) [Mrs. J. A.?] (ca. 1830-?)
Randall, Elizabeth Wells. See Cumming, Elizabeth Wells (Randall) [Mrs. Alfred]
Randall Family (MD), 5,802
Randall, Florence Engel (1917-), 6,072
Randall, Helen. See Shreve, Helen (Randall)
Randall, Helen McCrary, 3,245
Randall, Henry Stephens (1811-76), 11,683
Randall, James Garfield (1881-1953), 2,540
Randall, James J., 9,904
Randall, Jane Rebecca Polhemus [Mrs. Henry Stephens], 11,683
Randall Junior High School (DC), 2,129
Randall, Laura (Wirt) [Mrs. Thomas] (1803-33), 5,824
Randall, Marion (1878-1953). See Parsons, Marion (Randall) [Mrs. Edward Taylor] (1878-1953)
Randall, Mercedes (Moritz) [Mrs. John Herman, Jr.] (1896-1977), 11,299, 15,301
Randall, Mrs. John G. (1843-1902), 9,070
Randall, Ollie A. (1890-), 8,674, 12,078, 12,079
Randall, Paul, 15,193
Randall, Ruth K., 7,082
Randall, Ruth Painter, 4,445
Randall, Sally (Carlisle) [Mrs. James] (1805-?), 16,798
Randall, Virna M. [Mrs.] (1900-74). See Haffer, Virna. Mrs. Virna M. Randall (1900-74)
Randle, Alola Faye (1880-1952), 14,646
Randle, Bertha Mary (1886-1919), 14,646
Randle, Edith, 14,646
Randle, Ellen Taggert [Mrs. Samuel Arnold], 14,646
Randle Family (OR), 14,646
Randle, George Havelock (1876-1937), 14,646
Randle, Hattie Carol (1887-), 14,646
Randle, Henry Carlyle (1875-1936), 14,646
Randle, Margaret (1882-1956), 14,646
Randle, Nellie Olivia (1878-), 14,646

Randle, Samuel Arnold (1839-1933), 14,646
Randle, Sarah Agnes (1885-), 14,646
Randol, Christiana Terhune [Mrs. James Butterworth] (1845-1919), 1,080
Randolph Academy (MA), 7,668
Randolph, Anne Cary. See Morris, Anne Cary (Randolph) [Mrs. Gouverneur]
Randolph, Elizabeth, 2,541
Randolph, Elizabeth [Mrs. Peter Skipwith] (?-ca. 1810). See Adams, Elizabeth [Mrs. Peter Skipwith] Randolph [Mrs. Richard] (?-ca. 1810)
Randolph, Ellen Wayles (1796-1879). See Coolidge, Ellen Wayles (Randolph) [Mrs. Joseph, IV]
Randolph, Emma (Cady) [Mrs. John M.] (ca. 1860-1940), 8,975
Randolph Family, 4,942
Randolph Family (VA), 1,479, 17,058, 17,062
Randolph, Jane, 17,095
Randolph, Jennings, 17,465
Randolph, Jessie (Lincoln) [Mrs. Warren] Beckwith [Mrs. Frank Edward] Johnson [Mrs. Robert J.] (1875-1948), 5,060
Randolph, Joanna (1870-?). See Hollister, Joanna (Randolph) [Mrs. Clark W.] Kelley [Mrs. George H.] (1870-?)
Randolph, John M., 8,975
Randolph-Macon College (VA), 13,390
Randolph-Macon Woman's College (VA), 11,658
alumnae, 17,608
Randolph, Martha (Jefferson) [Mrs. Thomas Mann, Jr.] (1772-1836), 15,026, 17,056, 17,062
Randolph, Mary Scott, 13,486
Randolph, Pearl, 2,946
Randolph, Peyton, 8,975
Randolph, Richetta, 2,502
Randolph, Robert J., 5,060
Randolph, Septimia Anne Cary (1814-87). See Meikleham, Septimia Anne Cary (Randolph) [Mrs. David Scott] (1814-87)
Randolph, Thomas Mann, 17,062
Randolph, William Beverly (1793-187?), 2,541
Random House (publishers), 11,850, 14,427
"Random Recollections by Harriet Taylor Upton," 13,990
Ranelagh, Lady, 12,264
Ranelagh, Lord, 12,264
Range Symphony Orchestra (MN), 9,101
Rankin, Anne (Porterfield) (1869-1942), 15,966
Rankin, Arthur McKee (1841-1914), 961
Rankin, Belle, 13,189, 15,308, 15,314
Rankin, C. Adela, 17,872
Rankin, Caroline Arabella (1888-1964), 8,181
Rankin, D. C., 13,608
Rankin, Edna. See McKinnon, Edna (Rankin)
Rankin, Ellen B., 684
Rankin, Emily, 11,260
Rankin, Emma Lydia (1838-1908), 13,103, 13,519
Rankin, Everett H., 11,684
Rankin Family, 961
Rankin Family (MO), 10,036
Rankin Family (NY), 11,260
Rankin Family (WI), 17,872, 17,880
Rankin, Francis Hearn (1854-1925), 8,181
Rankin, Grace. See Kinney, Grace (Rankin)
Rankin, J. W., 18,021
Rankin, Jeannette (1880-1973), 741, 2,501, 2,995, 3,074, 4,081, 6,846, 8,975, 9,001, 9,200, 10,316, 10,360, 12,502, 12,523, 15,308, 15,317
Rankin, John William, 10,036
Rankin, Kitty Blanchard [Mrs. Arthur McKee] (1847-1911), 961
Rankin, Louise Spieker [Mrs. Everett H.], 11,684
Rankin, Marjorie (1888-?). See Steurt, Marjorie (Rankin) (1888-?)
Rankin, Mary. See Bragg, Mary (Rankin)
Rankin, Mary Jane (Nickell) [Mrs. Walter Lowrie], 17,880
Rankin, May Nickell (1870-1931), 17,872, 17,880
Rankin, Melinda, 3,764
Rankin, Phyllis (1874-1934), 961
Rankin, Rebecca B., 12,151
Rankin, Walter Lowrie (1841-1910), 17,872, 17,880
Rann, Mary A. [Mrs.], 4,821

Rannefeld, Amelia R. (Koenig) [Mrs. Herrmann], 12,291
Rannefeld, Herrmann, 12,291
Ranoue, Dora Knowlton, 12,525
Ransohoff, Martha (1894-1973), 13,875
Ransom, Eliza Taylor (1867-1955), 6,847
Ransome, Amy (ca. 1872-1942), 1,059
Rantoul Family (MA), 7,426
Rantoul, Hannah Lovett (1821-?), 7,427
Raoul, Eleanore (1888-). See Greene, Eleanore (Raoul) (1888-)
Raoul Family (GA), 3,246, 3,408
Raoul, Mary, 3,246
Raoul, Mary (1870-1958). See Millis, Mary (Raoul) [Mrs. John] (1870-1958)
Raoul, Mary (Wadley), 3,324
Raoul, Norman, 3,246
Raoul, Rosine, 3,246
Raoul, William G., 3,246
Rape, 987, 1,024, 1,122, 4,086, 4,124, 4,132, 9,206, 9,972, 10,342, 11,207, 17,975
law and legislation, 16,231
Rape Crisis Center (Madison, WI), 17,652
Rape crisis centers, 16,259, 17,652
Raphael, Alice Pearl [Mrs.], 16,122
Raphael Art Club (Iowa City, IA), 4,770
Raphael Family, 16,122
Raphaelson, Dorshka, 14,447
Rapidan Community School, 5,122
Rapp-Coudert committee (NY), 11,895
Rapp, Mary Ruth, 10,018
Rappenecker, Sister Mary Helen, 4,709
Raritan Seminary (NJ), 10,980
Raritan Valley "Great Consistory" (NJ), 11,023
Rascob, John J., 48
Rasmussen, Mathilde (1865-1952), 8,780
Rasmussen, P. A., Family, 8,780
Raspberry Day festival (Hopkins, MN), 8,479
Raspberry Press (CA) 914
Ratekin, Mayme, 10,055
Rathbone, Julia, 11,333
Rathbun, Mary Jane (1860-1943), 6,321
Rathburn, Florence [Mrs. William], 10,905
Rationing, consumer, 3,447, 3,931, 7,062, 7,148, 8,369, 10,013, 13,273, 13,617, 16,128, 17,050
Ratliff, Alma. See Gray, Alma (Ratliff)
Rattner, Abraham, 2,738
Raudenbush, David Webb, 9,307
Raudman, Dorothy, 8,359
Rauh, Bertha (Floersheim) [Mrs. Enoch] (1865-1952), 15,251
Rauh Family (PA), 15,251
Rauh, Ida (1877-1970). See Eastman, Ida Rauh (1877-1970)
Rauschenbusch, Pauline E. Rother [Mrs. Walter], 12,786
Rauschenbusch, Walter, 11,572
Rauscher, Pierce Company (TX), 16,038
Raushenbush, Elizabeth (Brandeis) [Mrs. Paul] (1896-), 2,336, 6,848, 11,916
Raushenbush, Esther (1898-), 11,306, 11,910
Raut, Irwin, 10,037
Rautalahti, Thyra [Mrs.], 8,186
Ravagli, Frieda (von Richthofen) [Mrs. David Herbert] Lawrence [Mrs. Angelino] (1879-1956), 572, 1,451, 8,077, 11,224, 12,479, 13,871, 16,169
Raven, William, 15,716
Ravenel, Anna Elizabeth [Mrs. John], 15,689
Ravenel, Beatrice (Witte) (1870-1956), 13,104
Ravenel, Catherine Prioleau, 15,490
Ravenel, Daniel, 15,448
Ravenel, Elizabeth Jane, 15,448
Ravenel, Harriott Horry (Rutledge) (1832-1912), 15,688
Ravenel, John (1793-1862), 15,689
Ravenel, Rose Pringle (1850-1943), 15,690
Ravenswood Women's Club (IL), 3,917
Ravinia Festival (Highland Park, IL), 4,275
Rawalt, Marguerite, 99, 6,849
Rawle, Anna, 15,089
Rawle, Margaret, 15,089
Rawle, Rebecca (Warner) (?-1819). See Shoemaker, Rebecca (Warner) Rawle [Mrs. Samuel] (?-1819)
Rawlings, Charles A., 12,800

Rawlings Family, 15,942
Rawlings, Irena Ingersoll, 11,547
Rawlings, Marjorie (Kinnan) [Mrs. Charles A.]. [Mrs. Norton] Baskin (1896-1953), 556, 2,872, 2,873, 2,875, **2,876**, 2,877, 2,932, **3,075**, 17,114
Rawls, Eugenia. [Mrs. Donald] Seawell (1913-), **13,008**
Rawson, Edward E., 3,247
Rawson, Elizabeth, 5,895
Rawson, Elizabeth Rebecca (1873-1961). *See* Garlick, Elizabeth Rebecca (Rawson) [Mrs. Joseph Elsbury] (1873-1961)
Rawson, Marion Nicholl [Mrs.], **10,826**
Rawson, Mary. *See* Ray, Mary (Rawson) [Mrs. John D.]
Ray, Ethelind (pseudonym). *See* Higgenson, Ella
Ray, Gertrude, 4,099
Ray, Gladys, 8,690
Ray, Hypatia Bowdoin [Mrs.], **3,248**
Ray, John D., 3,247
Ray, June, 3,174
Ray, Mary (Rawson) [Mrs. John D.], **3,247**
Ray, Mary (Stringfield) [Mrs. J. W.], 13,590
Ray, Melinda, 13,374
Ray, Mrs. Jessie, 8,250
Ray Palmer Club (NJ), 11,091, **11,126, 12,598**
Ray, Randolph, 9,706
Ray, Susie, 3,174
Rayburn, J. C., 3,764
Rayburn, Mrs. John Robert, 9,819
Rayburn, Sam, 15,755
Raycraft, Dorothy (1898-), 10,776
Raycraft, Madge Morris, 10,776
Raye, Martha, 1,024
Raymond, Almira Adeline David [Mrs. William W.] (1814-), **14,434, 17,206**
Raymond, Bertha (ca. 1867-?), 17,744
Raymond, Clara (Compton) (1857-?), **13,105**
Raymond, Henry Rodney, **9,801**
Raymond, Maritcha (1848-1929). *See* Lyons, Maritcha (Remond or Raymond) (1848-1929)
Raymond, Mildred, 14,618
Raymond, Paul C., 8,962
Raymond, Ruth (1878-?), 8,547
Raymond, Sarah. *See* Herndon, Sarah (Raymond)
Raymond, Sarah E. *See* Fitzwilliam, Sarah E. (Raymond) [Mrs. Francis J.]
Raymond, William W., 14,434
Raymonde, Anna Eliza (Ena) Palmer (1848-84). *See* McClary, Anna Eliza (Ena) Palmer Raymonde Ballantine (1848-84)
Rayner, Sarah Adella (Crosby) [Mrs. John], 9,025
Rayness, Gerard M. (1898-1946), **4,688**
Rayness, Velma [Mrs. Gerard M.] (1896-1977), **4,688**
Razousky, Cecelia, 8,963
Read, Benjamin Huger, 15,517
Read, Catherine [Mrs. Jacob], 15,691
Read, Cornelia E. (Parker) (1837-?), 3,341
Read, Daniel (1805-78), **10,038**
Read, Deborah (ca. 1707-74). *See* Franklin, Deborah (Read) [Mrs. Benjamin] (ca. 1707-74)
Read, Eliza Jane (1839-1910). *See* Sunderland, Eliza Jane (Read) [Mrs. Jabez T.] (1839-1910)
Read Family (SC), **15,691**
Read, Florence M., 3,290, 12,738, 16,027
Read, George, 15,258
Read, Helen Appleton [Mrs.] (1887-1974), **2,801**, 7,182
Read, Herbert, 12,701
Read, Jacob, 15,691
Read, Julia. *See* Longley, Julia Read [Mrs. Alfred]
Read, Keith, **3,567**
Read, Leslie Stringfellow [Mrs.] (1886-1971), 250
Read, Maria [Mrs. George], 15,258
Read, Mary Julia (Middleton) [Mrs. Benjamin Huger] (1829-1904), 15,517
Read, Mrs. Gordon H., 3,754, 3,762
Read, Naomi (1857-?). *See* Cowan, Naomi (Read) (1857-?)
Reader, Edith, 12,372
Reader's Digest (periodical), 10,894, 11,407, 11,974, 14,411, 17,614
Reading, 5,083, 9,451, 10,010, 15,583
Reading Club (Clarence, IA), 4,960

Reading Club (Dubuque, IA), 4,786
Reading Club (NJ), **11,210**
Reading for Wartime (bulletins), 8,591
Reading interests, **3,107**
Reading Labor Advocate (PA), **14,830**
Reading the Landscape (book), 4,289
Readington Reformed Church (NJ), **11,023**
Readington Reformed Church (NJ), Ladies' Missionary Society, 11,023
Ready, Alice (?-1890), **13,106**
"Real and Ideal in Politics, The" (drama), **6,372**
Real estate agents, 247, 1,655, 1,779, **2,909, 4,177,** 4,336, **5,104, 7,950,** 8,309, 9,427, 9,876, 10,650, 13,176, **14,014,** 14,945, **14,955,** 17,050, 17,664
Real estate business, 3,149, 3,152, 3,270, 5,394, 7,609, 11,882, 13,689
Real estate investment, 1,429, 9,138, **16,046,** 16,130
Real Pioneers of Colorado (ms), 1,785
Real property, 194, 2,635, 2,656, 9,424, 12,174, 12,231, 12,463, 12,611, 13,450, 17,465
cases, 1,811, 5,722, 10,684, 12,162, 15,574
valuation, 7,653
Real, Sister Cathleen, 4,709
Ream, Daniel, 1,663
Ream Family (PA),
Ream, Mary L. [Miss], 10,638
Ream, Vinnie (1847-1914). *See* Hoxie, Vinnie (Ream) [Mrs. Richard Leveridge] (1847-1914)
Reames, Jeannette. *See* Leigh, Janet. Jeannette Reames
Reaper's Club (UT), 16,566
Reapportionment (elections), 5,839
Reardy, Viola, 11,827
Reaugh, Frank, 16,358
Reavis Family (NC), **13,547**
Reavis, Hilliard, 13,547
Reavis, Marie S., 2,502
Reavy, Grace A., 11,553
Rebaleati, Mary Romando, 10,644
Rebaleati-Merialdo Family (NV), 10,644
Rebecca of Sunnybrook Farm (book), 1,426, 5,694
Rebecca Pomroy Newton Home for Orphan Girls (Newton, MA), **7,097**
Rebeccas' Lodge (Santa Clara, CA), 1,532
Rebekahs, 8,469
"Rebel Cruiser *Shenandoah* and the Ships Which She Sank, The", 7,669
Rebel Voices, an IWW Anthology (book), 8,094
Rebellions, 7,333, 11,492, 12,153
Rebow, Mary Martin (1750?-1804), **17,207**
Receipts (acknowledgments), 9,665, 15,436
"Recent Tendencies in the Drama," 3,747
Recession of the Frontier, The (dissertation), 104
Recipe Exchange, The (periodical), 6,964
Recitation From Memory (book), 17,175
Recitations, 7,646
"Reclaiming Our Heritage" (phonotape), 300
Recliffe Plantation (SC), 15,694
Recollections: Conversations about House of Jacob (book), 13,472
Recollections Grave and Gay (book), 2,384
Recollections of My Chinese Days (book), 14,466
Recollections of My Mother (book), 14,893
"Reconcilement of Cross Purposes in the Education of Women" (speech), 6,237
Reconstruction (1865-), 79, 1,440, 2,566, 2,675, 3,007, 3,081, 3,145, 3,227, 3,313, 3,319, 5,617, 6,352, 6,394, 7,206, 7,319, 9,308, 9,639, 9,747, 9,860, 12,979, 13,153, 13,213, 13,239, 13,256, **13,549,** 14,026, 15,401, 15,574, 15,600, 15,602, 15,604, 15,610, 15,667, 15,711, 15,726, 15,769, 16,045, 16,050, 16,097, 16,148, 16,244
Reconstruction (1939-1951)
Europe, 8,144
role of women, **12,294**
Reconstruction Finance Administration, 11,896
Reconstruction in Georgia: Economic, Social and Political, 1920 (book), 3,257
Record, James R., **16,282**
Record, The, 17,207
Recorder (York, NE), **10,623**
Recreation, 1,428, 2,687, 3,747, 3,851, 3,905, 3,910,

4,166, 5,840, 8,646, 8,661, 8,668, 8,681, 9,468, **11,006, 11,007,** 12,725, 13,979, 15,204
Recreation, Afro-Americans, **2,911**
Recreation centers, 945, 1,615, 9,460, 12,297
Recreation leadership, 1,769, 8,174, 10,180, 13,882
Recreation Training School of Chicago (IL), 4,059
Recruiting Officer, The (drama), 15,699
Rector, Emma Cecelia (1870-1964). *See* Flanagan, Emma Cecelia (Rector) [Mrs. Edward E.] (1870-1964)
Rector, General, 9,912
Rector, Mrs., 9,912
Red, Abbie Bell Nicholson [Mrs.], **9,802**
Red Blanket Woman, 9,371
Red Cross. *See also* American Red Cross
Red Cross, Britain, 543, 6,644
Red Cross Committee on Nursing Service, 8,648
Red Cross Medical Corps, Chinese, 174
Red Cross Nurses of America, 5,764
Red Cross Society (NV), **10,703**
Red Is Never a Mouse (book), 17,956
"Red Kate: A Case of Midwestern Socialism" (ms), 13,717
Red Man, The, 14,748
Red Ribbon on a White Horse (book), 6,120, 7,552
Red Ribbon Temperance Union (Battle Creek, MI), 7,978
Red River Runs North! (book), 13,674
"Red Skelton Show, The" (television program), 17,958
Red Wing Lutheran Ladies' Seminary Association (MN). *See* Lutheran Ladies' Seminary (Red Wing, MN)
Red Wing School of Nursing (MN), 8,818
Red Wing Women's Christian Temperance Union (MN). *See* Hobart Women's Christian Temperance Union (MN)
"Redbone" (story), 5,439
Redd, Amasa Jay, **16,434**
Redd, Josephine. *See* Roberts, Josephine (Redd)
Redd, Marietta, 16,876
Redd, Maxine. *See* Front, Maxine (Redd)
Redd, Samuel Hardison, 16,434
Redd, Zillah Lee (Bostick) (1871-1967). *See* Agerton, Zillah Lee (Bostick) Redd (1871-1967)
Reddick, M. A., 13,540
Reddings, Mary Frances Driggs (1864-1950s), **1,334**
Redeen, August (1842-1942), **8,480**
Redeen, Hilda (1879-1973), 8,480
Redemptoristine Nuns, Mother of Perpetual Help Monastery (Esopus, NY), **11,448**
Redfield, Mary (1892-1972). *See* DeHaven, Mary (Redfield) Lindsey (1892-1972)
Redford, Sarah Buell (1848-?), **14,647**
Redhead, Mrs. D. N., 9,667
Redington Family, 864
Redmond, Anna G. (1852-?), **10,914**
Redmond, Eliza Ann. *See* Clarke, Eliza Ann Redmond [Mrs. Thomas], 9,464
Redpath, James (1833-91), **12,292**
Redpath-Kansas City Bureau (KS), 5,021
Redpath Lyceum, 3,880
Redpath Lyceum Bureau (IL), 4,974
Redpath-Vawter Bureau (IA), 5,021
Redway, Virginia Larkin [Mrs. Laurance D.] (1886-1975), **12,751**
Redwood City Public Library (CA), Archives, 1,114
Redwood City Tribune (CA), **1,116**
Redwood, Francis T., 5,803
Redwood, Mary B. (Coale) [Mrs. Francis T.] (1861-1940), 5,803
Redwood, Mrs. Francis T., **15,079**
Reed, Alice Clara (1890-), 742, 11,846
Reed, Alladean (Holland) [Mrs. Eldon] (1928-), **244**
Reed, Bertha (Wilder) [Mrs Robert R.] (1874-?), **11,685**
Reed, Calvin, 16,799
Reed, Constance. *See* Haller, Constance (Reed) [Mrs. Theodore N.]
Reed, Cornelia, 17,043
Reed, Corrine Kelsey-Rider (1877-1947), 14,141
Reed, Dorothy Mabel (1874-1964). *See* Mendenhall, Dorothy Mabel (Reed) (1874-1964)
Reed, Eliza A. L., 10,561

Reed, Elizabeth. *See* Keller, Elizabeth (Reed) [Mrs. Phillips Brooks]
Reed, Elizabeth Freeman (1874-?), **7,669**
Reed, Ella Cartee, **3,713**
Reed, Emily, 17,043
Reed, Eunice Williams [Mrs. Thomas Walter], **3,076**
Reed, Evelyn, **17,710**
Reed Family (GA), 644
Reed Family (VT), 17,043
Reed Family (WA), 17,169
Reed, Hezekiah H., **17,031**
Reed House Young Men's Christian Association (Philadelphia, PA), **15,207**
Reed, Ida McKenny [Mrs. Thomas M.], 17,169
Reed, John (1786-1850), 14,648
Reed, John, Family (OR), **14,648**
Reed, John Henry "Hal" (1824-84), 14,648
Reed, Josephine (1895-), 7,109
Reed, Mabel, 6,375
Reed, Mae. *See* Porter, Mae (Reed)
Reed, Martha (Barnard) [Mrs. Hezekiah H.], 17,043
Reed, Martha Jane "Patty" (1838-1923). *See* Lewis, Martha Jane "Patty" (Reed) (1838-1923)
Reed, Mary, 17,043
Reed, Mary (1806-78). *See* Eastman, Mary (Reed) [Mrs. Ornan] (1806-78)
Reed, Mary Caroline (Jacocks), 13,450
Reed, Mary (Curtis) [Mrs. Clavin] (1821-88), **16,799**
Reed, Mary E., 14,538
Reed, Minnie, **7,910**
Reed, Myron, 1,782
Reed, Myron Winslow, 3,812
Reed, Prudence, **7,911**
Reed, Sarah Ann McDowell [Mrs. John] (1787-1853), 14,648
Reed, Stanley, 5,511
Reed, Thomas B., 14,683
Reed, Thomas M., 17,169
Reed, Virginia Elizabeth Backenstoe (ca. 1833-1921). *See* Murphy, Virginia Elizabeth Backenstoe (Reed) [Mrs. John M.] (ca. 1833-1921)
Reed, William, 11,583
Reeder, Adelaide Staves, **10,361**
Reeder, Hazel Perin [Mrs.], **10,526**
Reeder, Irma Brown (1898-1971), **10,362**
Reeder, Mary, 15,524
Reedick, Mary, 5,160
Reedy, William Marion, 10,154
Reef Point Gardens (Berkeley, CA), **303**
Reehill, Gloria, 15,332
Reel, Estelle, 17,901
Rees, Mary (Graves) (1886-1953), 13,016
Reese Family (IL), 3,077
Reese Family (MS), 9,816
Reese, Jessie F. S., 16,480
Reese, Lizette Woodworth (1856-1935), 17,013, **17,096**, 17,114
Reese, Madge Janet [Miss] (1894-1955), **10,039**
Reese, Mamie (Mathews), **3,417**
Reese, Mrs. John, 1,666
Reese, Nelle [Miss], **3,077**
Reese, Walter O., 3,077
Reese, Woodworth (1856-1935), 17,053
Reeve, Jewell B. [Mrs.], **3,078**
Reeve, Mehetable W., 12,779
Reeve, Sidney Armor (1866-1941), 11,555, **12,599**
Reeves, Agnes Morgan (1839-1901). *See* Appleton, Agnes Morgan (Reeves) [Mrs. James H.] (1839-1901)
Reeves, Andrew J., **13,107**
Reeves, Ann G., 15,287
Reeves, Elizabeth [Mrs. Andrew J.], **13,107**
Reeves, Henrietta (Kendrick) [Mrs. John H.] (1871-1968), **15,967**
Reeves, John M., 13,107
Reeves, Mollie, 13,107
Reeves, Samuel Morgan (1790-1886), 10,936
Reeves, Sarah (Burr) [Mrs. Tapping], 12,174
Reeves, Wealth Millett, 16,433
Reference services (libraries), 2,564, 11,930, **11,972**
Reflected Glory, 60
Reforestation, 8,942
Reform, 8,751
Reform (religion), 8,899

Reform Judaism, 9,251
Reformatories, 91, 3,356, 6,583, **6,711**, 6,789, **10,502**, 11,974, 12,375
officials and employees, 6,583
Reformatories (female), 1,151, 1,979, 3,469, 4,811, 6,642, 7,031, 7,546, 7,806, 8,276, 9,482, **10,503**, 11,003, 11,236, 11,254, 14,015, 15,274, 17,483
Reformatory for Women (MA), 6,934
Reformed Church in America, 8,196, 8,198, 8,199, 8,200, 8,202, 11,023
clergy, 12,470
missionaries, **5,088, 8,198, 8,199, 10,926, 10,927**
missions, 5,088, **10,925, 10,926, 10,927**
Reformed Church in America, Women's Board of Foreign Missions, **10,925**
Reformed Dutch Church, clergy, **12,251**
Reformers, 1,480, 1,483, **1,981, 2,175**, 2,209, **2,262, 2,301, 2,308**, 2,818, **4,161, 4,508, 4,974, 5,226**, 5,907, **5,917, 5,923, 5,950, 6,461, 6,466**, 6,500, **6,508**, 6,561, **6,715**, 6,762, **6,890, 6,918, 6,983, 6,993**, 7,172, **7,180**, 7,611, **7,612**, 8,003, 8,651, **8,686**, 9,347, **10,155, 11,279, 11,616, 11,963**, 12,203, **12,218, 12,445, 12,485**, 12,625, **13,246**, 13,846, 14,000, 14,838, **14,987, 15,286, 15,300, 15,304, 15,305, 15,307**, 17,043. *See also* Social reformers
Refugees, 164, 462, 1,680, 4,918, 6,660, 7,323, 7,326, 8,583, 8,679, 8,963, 9,218, 9,467, 9,492, 9,512, 11,857, 11,908, 12,061, 12,589, 15,316
aid to, 13,795
Refugees, British, 9,888
Refugees, Jewish, 9,164, 9,253, 13,993, 15,164, 16,894, 17,282. *See also* World War II, Jews, rescue
Refugees, Palestinian, 4,176
Refugees, political, 3,835
Refugees, Southern, 69, 2,455, **2,675**, 3,317, 5,484, 5,485, 11,616, 12,303, 13,257, 13,546, 15,590, 15,604
Refugees, Vietnamese, 6,709
Refuse and refuse disposal, 2,397, 3,875, 5,613, 10,886, 11,229, 12,266
Regensteiner, Else Friedsam [Mrs. Berthold] (1906-), 4,112
Regier, Frieda (Voth) (1855-1949). *See* Entz, Frieda (Voth) Regier (1855-1949)
Regier, Marie J. *See* Frantz, Marie J. (Regier)
Regional medical programs, 11,885
Regional planning, 1,173, 1,503, 1,992
Register-Guard (Eugene, OR), 14,309
Register of Debates. See *Congressional Record*
Registers of births, etc., 231, **1,384**, 2,671, 2,675, 2,698, 3,619, 3,871, 5,409, 5,495, 8,486, 9,008, 10,068, 10,099, 10,100, 10,680, 10,700, 11,184, **11,208**, 12,627, 13,386, 14,941, **17,528**, 17,879. *See also* Inquisitions; post mortem; Marriage licenses
Registry of Interpreters for the Deaf, 2,102
Registry of Nurses (MA), **6,230**
Régnier Henri de, 5,632
Rehabilitation, 9,381, 13,866
Rehabilitation Center (Santa Clara, CA), 14,453
Rehabilitation centers, 8,503
Rehabilitation of criminals, 1,270, **7,244**
Rehabilitation of juvenile delinquents, 2,687
Rehm, Leonard, 1,285
Reich, Jacques (1852-1923), **12,293**
Reich, Theodore, 212
Reick, Addie Henry [Mrs.] (?-ca. 1952), **10,040**
Reid, Agnes Just (1886-1976), **16,908**
Reid, Ann, 15,692
Reid, Annie (1876-1958). *See* Knox, Annie (Reid) [Mrs. William Franklin "Frank"] (1876-1958)
Reid, Ava Baltimor, 14,618
Reid, Christine (pseudonym). *See* Tiernan, Frances Christine (Fisher) [Mrs. James Marquis] (1846-1920)
Reid, David S., **13,550**
Reid, Elisabeth (Mills) [Mrs. Whitelaw] (1858-1931), 2,542
Reid Family (GA), 3,612
Reid Family (NY), **2,542**
Reid, Harriet, **6,531**

Reid, Helen (Rogers) [Mrs. Ogden Mills] (1882-1970), 2,542, 5,122, 9,160, 12,087, 12,315
Reid, John Hope, 3,568
Reid, Josephine, 11,976
Reid, Margaret (Goulding) [Mrs. William Moultrie], 15,692
Reid, Marlene Stibal, 16,908
Reid, Mary Martha [Mrs. Robert Raymond], **2,950**
Reid, Mrs. Whitelaw, 12,271
Reid, Ogden Mills (1882-1947), 2,542
Reid, Robert Raymond, 2,950
Reid, Rose Marie Yancey (1910-), 16,780
Reid, Ruth Erwin Welman [Mrs. John Hope] (1799-?), **3,568**
Reid, Ruth Evangeline LaPlant (ca. 1893-), **8,599**
Reid, Sabrie W. [Mrs.], **13,283**
Reid, Samuel Chester, 2,580
Reid, Whitelaw (1837-1912), 2,542
Reid, William Moultrie (1798-1884), **15,692**
Reidesel, Frederika [Mrs. Frederick], 12,848
Reierson, Georg, 8,781
Reierson, Helena [Mrs. Georg], **8,781**
Reiff Family,
Reiff Family (MN), 9,304
Reignolds, Kate (1836-1911). *See* Winslow, Catherine Mary "Kate" (Reignolds) [Mrs. Henry] Farren [Mrs. Alfred Erving] (1836-1911)
Reik, Elsie I., **14,435**
Reiley, Anne Carol, 11,074
Reilly, Caroline I., **6,532**, 7,205
Reilly, Jean Burt, **744**
Reilly, Maryanne, **14,117**
Reimensnyder, Helen (1868-1939). *See* Martin, Helen (Reimensnyder) (1868-1939)
Reimers, Margaret, 14,618
Reinbold, Elizabeth (1912-). *See* MacPhail, Elizabeth (Reinbold) [Mrs. Alfred] (1912-)
Reindeer (ship), **6,204**
Reiner, Bea, 6,353
Reinhardt, Aurelia Isabel (Henry) [Mrs. George Frederick] (1877-1948), 756, 1,085, 5,120, 5,122
Reinking, Erma. *See* King, Erma (Reinking)
Reinking, Mary Antonia (Greenwood), 516
Reissner, Larissa, 9,380
Reisterstown Public Library (MD), Reisterstown Room, 5,850
Reitman, Ben Lewis (1879-1942), **4,145**, 6,028
Reitsch, Hanna, 11,831
Reitz, Beulah M. [Miss], **13,284**
Reizenstein, Jennie, **5,804**
Related Activities Council (Schenectady, NY), 8,637
Relfe, Elizabeth A. *See* Linn, Elizabeth A. (Relfe) [Mrs. Lewis Fields]
Relief Society Magazine, 16,555
Relief Works (Chicago, IL), 4,085
Religio-Philosophical Journal (periodical), 4,062
Religion, 78, 2,038, 6,661, 8,057, 8,798, 9,376, 9,386, 11,236, 12,004, 13,287, 13,322, 13,414. *See also* Spiritual life
controversial literature, 1,500
relations, 9,150
Religion and women, **300**, 1,131
Religion in the public schools, 485, 9,065
Religions, 13,217
Religious and Educational Conference (1957, IA), 4,946
Religious education, 1,839, **1,848**, 1,851, **3,938**, 5,830, **6,258**, 7,645, 8,292, 13,505, 13,868, 16,257, 17,679
study and teaching, **6,257**
text-books for children, Unitarian, 6,250
Religious education, Jewish, 13,813
Religious freedom, 12,119, 12,120, 12,121
Religious life (Christianity), 6,851, 7,679, 11,522, 11,718, 12,633, 13,270, 14,225
Religious literature, 1,513
authorship, 7,300
Religious poetry, 14,997
"Religious Revival and the New Conservatism: Marriage and the Home, 1800-1825" (speech), 6,684
Relocation (housing), 9,114
Reluctant Reformers: The Impact of Racism and

American Social Reform Movements, The (book), 17,583

"Remarkable Exposition of the Position of Woman in the Human Family from Bible Times to the Present Century, A" (ms), 12,795

Remarriage, 46, 5,218, 8,196, **8,200,** 9,902, 9,904, 12,087, 14,522, 15,323, 15,602, 15,616

"Remember the Alamo," 16,317

Remenyi, A., 7,505

Remer, Martha Alice, 10,591

Remey, Charles Mason (1804-82), **9,308**

Remey, Charles Mason (1874-?), 2,545, 9,308

Remey Family, **2,545**

Remey, George Collier (1841-1928), 2,545, 4,822, 4,958, 9,308, **15,080**

Remey, Gertrude Heim [Mrs. Charles Mason] (1888-1932), 4,949, 9,308

Remey, Mary Josephine (Mason) [Mrs. George Collier] (1845-1938), 2,545, 4,822, 4,958, 9,308, **15,080**

Remick, Edith, 5,634

Remick, Fannie, 5,634

Remick, Martha (?-1906), 5,634

Remick, Oliver P. (1853-1913), **5,634**

Remington, Dorothy Child (Cross) (1890-). *See* Zeiger, Dorothy Child (Cross) Remington (1890-)

Remington Family, 4,942

Remington, Helen [Mrs. Loren], **4,942**

"Reminiscences" (ms), 5,472

"Reminiscences—A Schoolmarmian Epic," 9,838

Reminiscences of a Pioneer Woman Judge in Pre-Hitler Germany (ms), 6,789

Reminiscences of a Soldier's Wife (book), 2,454

"Reminiscences of the National Arbitration and Peace Congress" (article), 15,270

Remond, Maritcha (1848-1929). *See* Lyons, Maritcha (Remond or Raymond) (1848-1929)

Remond, Sarah Parker (1826-1887?), 5,907

Remonstrance Against Woman Suffrage, The, 49

Remsen, Henry, Jr., **12,600**

Remy, William H., 5,995

Renard, Julie, 626

Renard, Ysabelle, 626

Reneau, Sallie Eola [Miss] (1837-78), 9,556, 9,564

Renfroe, Mrs. Nathan, 9,589

Renfroe, Nathan, 9,589

Renn, Euticus, 13,551

Renner, Fred, 10,363

Renner, Ginger [Mrs. Fred], **10,363**

Reno Little Theater (NV), 10,743

Reno Women's Civic Club (NV), **10,705**

Renshaw, Julieta Lanteri, 14,819

Renshaw, Maria Jane, **14,649**

Rent, 6,464, 11,745

Rent control, 8,139, **12,601**

Rently, Mrs., 15,529

Renunciation of War Treaty, (Paris, Aug. 27, 1928), 17,654

Renwick, Jane Jeffrey (?-1848). *See* Wilkes, Jane Jeffrey (Renwick) [Mrs. Charles] (?-1848)

Reorganized Church of Jesus Christ of Latter Day Saints, 10,089, 16,959

Reorganized Church of Jesus Christ of Latter Day Saints, Women's Auxiliary, **10,094**

Reorganized Church of Jesus Christ of Latter Day Saints, Women's Council, 10,094

Reparation, 5,394

Repatriation, 8,657

Repeal of legislation, 2,589, 2,649

Report of the Committee on Minimum Wage Board (1912), 6,973

Reporter (periodical), 17,259

Reporters and reporting, 132, 1,507, **5,537,** 6,019, **6,031,** 6,882, 7,016, 8,064, 8,956, 9,046, **9,103, 9,415,** 9,599, 9,736, **9,949,** 10,181, 10,879, 11,111, **11,489,** 11,867, 12,846, 14,377, 15,585, **15,979, 16,222, 17,259,** 17,379, **17,598, 17,805,** 17,829

Reports (St. Louis Board of Education, MO), 10,149

Repplier, Agnes (1855-1950), 1,426, 2,643, 4,226, 15,060, 17,010

Reproduction (human). *See* Human reproduction

Reproductive Freedom League (Lexington, KY), 5,330

Reptiles, 2,717

Republican (Truckee, CA), 644

Republican (MA), 17,594

Republican Action League, 1,829

Republican Congressional Wives Club, 6,489

Republican Convention (1920), 6,939, 11,882

Republican Federation of Women, 9,080

Republican League for Party Efficiency, 1,948

Republican National Committee, 1,605, 2,251, 2,379, 5,121, 5,122, 5,126, **5,141,** 5,150, **5,156,** 5,159, 5,272, 6,662, 7,889, 9,962, 11,857, 17,486

Republican National Committee, women's division, 5,150, 9,276

Republican National Convention (1892), 9,279

Republican National Convention (1936), 17,141

Republican National Convention (1972), 5,006

Republican National Conventions, 9,276

Republican Party, 169, 190, 509, 1,189, 1,404, 1,688, 2,127, 2,262, 2,303, 2,354, 3,734, 4,623, 5,123, 5,135, 5,137, 5,143, 5,995, 6,434, 6,489, 6,662, 6,727, 6,939, 7,699, 7,738, 7,847, 7,889, 9,434, 9,972, 10,427, 10,720, 10,752, 10,761, 11,592, 11,857, 11,879, 11,913, 13,670, 14,683, 15,941, 16,252, 17,141

committees, 2,379, 5,126, 5,141, 5,150, **5,156,** 5,159, 7,889, 8,022, 9,276, 9,962, 11,857, 13,670

Republican Party, California, 1,503

Republican Party, Committee of Policies and Platforms, 17,749

Republican Party, Connecticut, 1,829, 1,837

Republican Party, Idaho, 3,657, 3,658, 6,858

Republican Party, Illinois, 4,347

Republican Party, Indiana, 4,606, 4,654

Republican Party, Iowa, 4,784, 4,838, 4,914, 5,006, 5,009

Republican Party, Massachusetts, 6,925

Republican Party, Michigan, 7,803, 8,022

Republican Party, Minnesota, 8,831, 8,941, 9,015, 9,080, 9,189, 9,385

Republican Party, Mississippi, 9,582

Republican Party, Montana, 10,320

Republican Party, Nevada, 10,706, 10,761

Republican Party, Ohio, 6,434, 13,999, 14,004

Republican Party, Oklahoma, 14,223

Republican Party, Tennessee, 15,889, 15,903

Republican Party Women's Club (Alma, MI), **7,912**

Republican Publishing Company, 1,719

Republican State Central Committee, 9,385, 17,749

Republican State Committee (ID), 6,858

Republican Women's Club (Chicago, IL), 3,833

Republican Women's Club (OH), 14,014

Republican Women's Club of Kentucky, **5,322**

Republican Women's Gazette, 14,004

Republican Women's Meeting (1958), 5,146

Republican Women's National Executive Committee, 12,505

Republicanism, 5,753

Requa, Amy (1895-?), **10,774**

Requa, Mark, 10,774

Reque, Lars Davidson, 8,724

Rescue work, 1,750

Research, 2,215, **2,670,** 7,817, **11,901,** 12,031, **13,501**

Research Commission of the State of Mississippi, 9,647

Research grants, 11,911

Research, industrial, **8,135,** 9,349

Researchers, **1,289,** 7,315, 7,334, **9,125**

Resek, Bella (Fischer), 668, 1,068

Resnik, Muriel (1921?-), **2,546**

Resnikoff, Vladamir, 12,705

Resorts, 169, 9,460

"Responsibility of a Citizen, The" (ms), 9,606

Ressler, Jacob Andrew (1867-1936), **4,515**

Ressler, Lina (Zook) [Mrs. Jacob Andrew] (1869-1948), 4,515

Rest homes, 13,982

Rest rooms. *See* Public comfort stations

Restaurants, lunch rooms, etc., 7,209

Reston, James Barrett, Jr. (1941-), **13,108**

Reston, John R. (?-ca. 1858), 13,068

Reston, Marie Louise (DuBrutz), **13,109**

Reszke, Jean D., 4,307

Retail Clerks International Union, 2,711

Retail Clerks Union (MN), Local Number Two, **9,309**

Retail Clerks Union (MN), Local Number Seven hundred Eighty-nine, **9,309**

Retail Clerks Union (St. Louis, MO), 4,083

Retail, Wholesale and Department Store Union, Local 1199 (NY), **11,772**

Rethlingshafer, Dorothy (1900-69), **13,744**

Retired military personnel, 17,086

Retired teachers, 203, **7,017, 8,687, 9,497, 10,707,** 15,332

Retired Teachers of Nevada, Washoe Unit, Inc., **10,707**

Retirement, 8,664

Retirement homes, **3,758,** 5,186, 9,981, **14,623**

Retreats, 11,176

Retrenchment Society (UT), **16,951**

Return of Lady Brace, The (book), 16,167

Return of Odysseus, The (drama), 8,541

Reuben, Dorothy (1900-). *See* Rosenman, Dorothy (Reuben) [Mrs. Samuel I.] (1900-)

Reul, Santa. *See* Schoof, Santa (Reul)

Reuter, Marie (1861-?). *See* Gallison, Marie (Reuter) [Mrs. Henry] (1861-?)

Reuther, May (Wolf) [Mrs. Walter P.] (1910-70), **8,120**

Reuther, Roy, 8,141

Reuther, Walter P., 8,120, 8,144

Reveille (newspaper, MS), 9,641

Revelation Kiln, 2,796

Reverdy, Pierre, 12,047

"Rev. Robert Blair, Quaker Preacher and Teacher of Falmouth, Maine," 7,669

Revesy, Miriam, 8,906

Review (periodical), 9,689

"Review of the Instructive District Nursing Association, 1886-1951" (ms), 6,962

Reviewer, The (periodical), 113

Reviewers' Club (CO), **1,791**

Reviewer's Matinee (Mount Carmel, IL), **4,299**

Revivals, 11,522, 12,370, 15,666

Revolt of Sarah Perkins, The (book), 6,000

"Revolution in the Education of Women, A", 11,306

Revolution, The (periodical), 4,156, 4,859, 11,305

Revolutionary War (1775-1783). *See* United States, Revolution (1775-1783)

Revolutionary War (1775-1783), loyalists. *See* American loyalists

Revolutionists, 5,949, **17,589**

Revolutions, 5,676, 8,144, 13,801

Rew Family (IL), **3,898**

Rew, Henry C. (1839-1912), 3,898

Rew, Irwin, 3,898

Rew, Katherine Jones [Mrs. Irwin], 3,898

Rew, Prential (Buie) [Mrs. R. G.], 9,597

Rewards (prizes, etc.), 997, 2,041, 2,863, 4,125, 4,918, 5,109, 6,555, 9,496, 9,497, 12,577, 13,535, 16,257, 16,277, 17,667, 17,776, **18,014**

Rewis, Mrs. Millard, **13,552**

Rex Hospital School of Nursing (NC), **13,553**

Rex Hospital School of Nursing (NC), Alumnae Association, 13,553

Reyes-Calderón, Consuelo, 859

Reyher, Rebecca, 859

Reynal, Jeanne (1903-), **2,802**

Reynard, Elizabeth [Miss] (1897-1962), **6,850**

Reynell Family (PA), **14,977**

Reynell, John, 14,977

Reynier, Madeleine Elise. *See* Boyd, Madeleine Elise (Reynier)

Reynolds, Abigail (1774-1851). *See* L'Hommedieu, Abigail Reynolds [Mrs. Giles] (1774-1851)

Reynolds, Alice, 1,716

Reynolds, Alice Louise (1873-1938), 16,528, **16,555, 16,802**

Reynolds, Amelia Harriet Nash, 1,716

Reynolds, Barbara, **17,711**

Reynolds, Bertha C., **6,851**

Reynolds, Catharine, 14,863

Reynolds, Catherine, 13,238

Reynolds, Clara (Geer) [Mrs. Clyde] (1893-1976), **14,014**

Reynolds, Debbie, 12,111

Reynolds, Edith Lindsley, 15,354

Reynolds, Elizabeth Clara. *See* Hazelton, Elizabeth Clara (Reynolds) [Mrs. W. E.]
Reynolds, Elizabeth Johnston (1839-1926). *See* Burt, Elizabeth Johnston (Reynolds) [Mrs. Andrew Sheridan] (1839-1926)
Reynolds, Elizabeth Margaret Carter [Mrs. William B.] (1799-1866), **7,355**
Reynolds, Ellie, 14,863
Reynolds, Emily Simms Bellinger [Mrs. John Schreiner, Jr.], 15,693
Reynolds Family (CA), 1,648
Reynolds Family (Lancaster, PA), **14,863**
Reynolds, Florence, 2,688
Reynolds, Grace (1868-1969), 1,311
Reynolds, Hannah. *See* Watkins, Hannah (Reynolds)
Reynolds, Harriet Dickson, 15,622
Reynolds, Helen (Cowles) [Mrs. Reginald M.], 8,896
Reynolds, Helen Dorothy (Baker) [Mrs. Ralph A.] (1896-), 17,419
Reynolds, Helen M., 6,629
Reynolds, Jane, 14,863
Reynolds, Joan. *See* Faunt, Joan (Reynolds)
Reynolds, John (?-1853), 14,863
Reynolds, John Fulton (1820-63), 14,863
Reynolds, John Schreiner, Jr. (1887-1918), **15,693**
Reynolds, Lily Elizabeth (1866-?), **3,418**
Reynolds, Lydia, 14,863
Reynolds, Mamie, 9,025
Reynolds, Marjorie Richards [Mrs.], **12,294**, 12,295
Reynolds, Mary (1872-1949). *See* Aldis, Mary (Reynolds) (1872-1949)
Reynolds, Mary Ann Guest (1797-1855), **11,024**
Reynolds, Mary L. B., 6,851
Reynolds, Mrs., 12,495
Reynolds, Mrs. O. J., **9,310**
Reynolds, Mrs. R. J., 13,456
Reynolds, Rachel, 2,239
Reynolds, Rebecca Evelina, **7,428**
Reynolds, Rebecca K. [Mrs. William], 14,863
Reynolds, Reginald M., 8,896
Reynolds, Sarah B., 9,025
Reynolds, Sophie M., 15,617, 15,731
Reynolds, Veda, 1,788
Reynolds, William (1815-79), 14,863
Reynolds, William B. (1797-1866), 7,355
Rezanov, Nikolai Petrovich, 1,510
Rhea, C. J., 8,303
Rhea, Martha, 8,303
Rhees, William Jones (1830-1907), **1,480**
Rhet, Sarah [Mrs. William], 15,519
Rhet, William, 15,519
Rhett, Sarah [Mrs. William], 2,169
Rhinah (slave, SC), 15,530
Rhind, Flora Macdonald (1904-), **11,911**
Rhine Revolution (Germany), 17,589
Rhoades, Ella (1862-1940). *See* Higginson, Ella (Rhoades) (1862-1940)
Rhoades, Georgia M., 2,851
Rhoades, Mrs. William J., 3,756
Rhoads, Elizabeth (1770-96). *See* Fisher, Elizabeth (Rhoads) [Mrs. Samuel W.] (1770-96)
Rhoads, Grace [Miss], 15,315
Rhoads, Samuel, 2,486
Rhoads, Sarah Pemberton, 15,000
"Rhoda" (television program), 17,808
Rhode Island, 2,246
  abolitionists, **15,384**
  Afro-Americans, religion, 7,656
  British occupation of (1777), 7,656
  businessmen, 7,608
  charitable societies, **15,388**, **15,397**
  children's librarians, **15,392**
  church societies, **6,173**
  church societies, Baptist, **15,394**, **15,396**
  church societies, Episcopal, **15,380**
  citizens' associations, **15,376**
  clubs, **15,383**, **15,390**
  college teachers, 6,651, **6,733**
  community organization, **15,386**
  court-houses, 2,507
  deans (in schools), **6,165**
  diaries and journals, 15,370
  Friends, Society of, **12,628**
  genealogists, 15,370
  genealogy, 6,234
  general stores, 12,408
  governors, 12,288
  legislators, 15,373
  mayors, 11,960
  merchants, 12,370
  monasticism and religious orders for women, Catholic, **15,369**, **15,372**
  nursing schools, **6,155**, 6,165
  nursing, study and teaching, **6,165**
  politics and government, 6,673, 15,376
  race problems, 15,376
  schools, 7,631
  scientific societies, **15,389**
  senators, United States, **2,160**
  social life and customs, 15,112
  suffrage societies, **15,398**
  suffragists, 15,370
  teachers, 6,587, 7,631, **7,656**
  temperance societies, **15,395**
  trade and professional associations, 6,594
  universities and colleges,
    archives, **15,375**
    curricula, 6,733
  weavers, 12,370
Rhode Island Council of Women, 15,381
Rhode Island Equal Suffrage Association, **15,398**
Rhode Island Hospital School of Nursing, **6,155**
Rhode Island Hospital Training School for Nurses. *See* Rhode Island Hospital School of Nursing
Rhode Island State College, 6,651
Rhodes, Dorthea (ca. 1860-1942). *See* Moore, Dorthea (Rhodes) [Mrs. Charles Fletcher] Lummis [Mrs. Ernest Carroll] (ca. 1860-1942)
Rhodes, Edward A., 1,639
Rhodes, Elisha A., 1,639
Rhodes, Eugene Manlove, 215
Rhodes-Haverty Company (GA), 3,199
Rhodes, John, 175
Rhodes, Mary W. Kimball [Mrs. Elisha A.], 1,639
Rhodes, S. I., 3,376
Rhodes, Sarah Jane [Mrs. George], 3,376
Rhodesia
  missionaries to, Methodist, 13,294
  missions, 13,276
Rhue, Nellie, 3,834
Rhys Family (MS), 9,816
Rhythm bands and orchestras, 3,856
Ribzinski, Charlotte (1881-1978). *See* Xavier, Sister Mary (1881-1978)
Riccius, Adolf Gustav (1841-95?), 7,670
Riccius, Edith (1881?-). *See* King, Edith (Riccius) (1881?-)
Riccius Family (MA), **7,670**
Riccius, Ida Adelia (Barton) [Mrs. Adolf Gustav] (1847-1911), 7,670
Riccius, Saidee F. (?-1959), 2,196, 7,670
Rice, 3,477
  marketing, 15,525
Rice, Alice Caldwell 5
egan) [Mrs. Cale Young] (1870-1942), 138, 5,266, 5,273, **5,274**, 5,275, **5,360**, 11,812
Rice, Anna Virena (1888-1966), **12,727**
Rice, Arthur H., 9,803
Rice, Asaph, 10,676
Rice, Augusta (Hopkins) [Mrs. John W.], 9,803
Rice, Cale Young (1872-1943), 5,266, 5,273, 5,360
Rice, Charles Gorham, Sr., 11,249, 11,250
Rice, David B., 15,543
Rice, Elizabeth Claridge McCune [Mrs. Asaph], 10,676
Rice, Elizabeth Prince [Miss] (1900-), **6,852**
Rice, Emeline (Draper) [Mrs. William E.] (1806-54), 7,618
Rice Family, 8,966
Rice Family (KY), **5,273**
Rice Family (MA), **7,091**, **7,618**
Rice Family (VT), **17,007**
Rice, Fanny, 8,297
Rice, Grantland (1880-1954), **15,935**
Rice, Harriet Langdon (Pruyn) [Mrs. William Gorham, Sr.] (1868-1939), 11,249, **11,250**
Rice, Hazelton, Sr., 17,007
Rice, Henry Mower (1816-94), Family (MN), **9,311**
Rice, James D., 7,618
Rice, Jennie, 4,904, 4,941
Rice, John, 13,333
Rice, John W., 9,803
Rice, Laban Lacy (1870-1973), **5,275**
Rice, Laura, 7,069
Rice, Lilian [Miss] (1888-1938), **1,191**
Rice, Louisa Busenbark [Mrs. Asaph], 10,676
Rice, Lucy W., 7,618
Rice, Lula Bon, 7,977
Rice, Martha, 14,577
Rice, Mary, 17,007
Rice, Mary Ashton (1820-1905). *See* Livermore, Mary Ashton (Rice) (1820-1905)
Rice, Mary Busenbark [Mrs. Asaph], 10,676
Rice, Mary Pamella (Waterman) [Mrs. Hyland Washington] (1850-1925), 870
Rice, Mary Virginia (Rugg) [Mrs. Robert Auerbach] (1881-), 9,311
Rice, Matilda (Whitall) [Mrs. Henry Mower], 9,311
Rice, Melissa Jane Lambson Davis [Mrs. Asaph], 10,676
Rice, Mrs. Frank P., 3,141
Rice, Mrs. Gordon Pryor, **17,097**
Rice, Nannie Herndon [Miss] (1886-1963), **9,712**, **9,803**
Rice, Nell [Mrs. John], 13,333
Rice, Rhoda [Mrs. Hazelton, Sr.], 17,007
Rice, Robert Auerbach, 9,311
Rice, Robertine Howe, 5,995
Rice, Sarah (?-1778), 7,091
Rice, Sarah "Sally" (ca. 1820-?). *See* Alger, Sarah "Sally" (Rice) [Mrs. James] (ca. 1820-?)
Rice, Susan Trowbridge Cleaveland [Mrs. R. L.], 1,870
Rice University, faculty, 16,249
Rice, William E. (1803-82), 7,618
Rice, William E. (1833-1919), 7,618
Rich, Adena (Miller) [Mrs. Kenneth] (1888-1967), 4,047, 4,056, 4,100, 4,101, 4,110, 4,141, **4,146**
Rich, Albina [Mrs. Charles], **4,002**
Rich, Charles, **4,002**
Rich, Charles Coulsen, 16,803, 16,804
Rich, Charlotte, 8,170
Rich, Emmeline (Grover) [Mrs. Charles Coulsen] (1831-1917), **16,803**
Rich, Helen, 1,750
Rich, Lucia, 8,170
Rich, Sarah Dearmon (Pea) [Mrs. Charles Coulsen] (1814-93), **16,804**
Rich Valley Homemaker's Club (ND), **13,685**
Richard, Mrs. George (?-1939), **12,295**
Richard, Zeline (McCullough), **8,121**
Richards, Agnes Treat (Lamb) [Mrs. Timothy P.] (1811-?), **12,239**
Richards, Amasa, Family (MN), **9,312**
Richards, Bertha [Mrs. George S.], **8,442**
Richards, Bertha Julia Stone (1893-), 16,780
Richards, Bessie (Launder) [Mrs. Edwin R.] (1885-1969), **745**
Richards, Carmen Nelson [Mrs. Orrin J.], 8,600, 9,313
Richards, Channing, **10,041**
Richards, Clara Alida [Miss] (1884-1960), **13,686**
Richards, Edith L., 16,876
Richards, Edwin R., 745
Richards, Eleanor (1889-). *See* Lyon, Eleanor (Richards) [Mrs. Harvey Blanchard] (1889-)
Richards, Eleanor Alice (1877-1967). *See* McCreery, Eleanor Alice (Richards) (1877-1967)
Richards, Eliza F. Verplanck [Mrs.], 12,446
Richards, Elizabeth Ney [Mrs.], **6,853**
Richards, Ellen Henrietta (Swallow) [Mrs. Robert Hallowell] (1842-1911), 3,785, 4,380, 6,332, **6,334**, 7,184, 7,274, **7,286**
Richards Family (MA), **7,586**
Richards Family (UT), 16,905
Richards, Franklin O., 746
Richards, George F., 16,620
Richards, Jane (Snyder) [Mrs. Franklin D.] (1823-1912), 746, **16,952**
Richards, Janet Elizabeth Hosmer (1859-1948), **2,119**, **2,547**, 6,854
Richards, John Cushing (1839-1907), 7,586

Richards, Joseph, 6,853
Richards, Julia Hammond (1860-1935), **15,694**
Richards, Kate (1877-1948). *See* Cunningham, Kate
 (Richards) [Mrs. Francis "Frank" Patrick] O'Hare
 [Mrs. Charles C.] (1877-1948)
Richards, Laura Elizabeth (Howe) [Mrs. Henry]
 (1850-1943), 1,426, 1,959, **5,602**, 5,714, **6,855,**
 9,057
Richards, Levi, 16,806
Richards, Linda Anne Judson (1841-1930), 6,122,
 6,141, **6,156**, 7,274, 12,137
Richards, Louisa "Lula" (Greene) [Mrs. Levi Willard]
 (1849-1944), **16,805**, 16,830
Richards, Lydia (Williamson) [Mrs. Channing],
 10,041
Richards, Margaret (1900-), 11,889
Richards, Mary, 9,312
Richards, Mary Ann (1834-69), 7,586
Richards, Mary Haskin Parker [Mrs. Samuel W.]
 (1825-60), **16,909**
Richards, Matilda [Mrs. Robert K.], 12,239
Richards, Minerva (1862-1958). *See* Young, Minerva
 (Richards) [Mrs. Richard Willard] (1862-1958)
Richards, Mrs. George, **6,856**
Richards, Nancy (1792-1852). *See* Peirson, Nancy
 (Richards) (1792-1852)
Richards, Pearl Mary Teresa (1867-1906). *See*
 Craigie, Pearl Mary Teresa (Richards)
 (1867-1906)
Richards, Ruth, 11,746
Richards, Samuel W., 16,909
Richards, Sarah, 11,746
Richards, Sarah Griffith [Mrs. Levi] (1802-92), **16,806**
Richards, Timothy P., 12,239
Richards, Willard, 16,905
Richards, William A., 17,913
Richards, Wolcott, 9,866
Richardson, Agnes Davison (McDowell) [Mrs. John
 Smythe], 15,695
Richardson, Ahira, Family (MN), **9,314**
Richardson, Almer O., 9,315
Richardson, Amy Small [Mrs.], 2,182
Richardson, Ann S., 2,053, 2,060
Richardson, Anna Steese (1865-1949), 5,121
Richardson, Belle. *See* Harrison, Belle (Richardson)
 [Mrs. John Calhoun]
Richardson, Caroline L., **747**
Richardson, Constance (1905-), **2,803**
Richardson, Cora A. Chapman [Mrs.], **11,686**
Richardson, Cora Ella, 13,895
Richardson, Emma Virginia (?-1922). *See* Wharton,
 Emma Virginia (Richardson) [Mrs. Greene
 Lawrence] (?-1922)
Richardson, Eveline Mabel (1900-). *See* Burns,
 Eveline Mabel (Richardson) (1900-)
Richardson Family, 2,315
Richardson Family (DE), **2,053**
Richardson Family (PA), 15,021
Richardson Family (WA), **17,185**
Richardson, Fannie Belle Taylor [Mrs.], **5,157**
Richardson, Georgia Mounts [Mrs. Almer O.]
 (1858-1937), **9,315**
Richardson, Grace, **1,563**
Richardson, Helen L. (Drew) [Mrs. Robert Kimball]
 (ca. 1892-), 8,530, **8,557**, 9,052
Richardson, Henry Hobson, 3,849
Richardson, Jennie S. S., 9,397
Richardson, John P., 17,185
Richardson, John Smythe (1828-94), **15,695**
Richardson, Leon, 1,259
Richardson, Louise, 2,927
Richardson, Margaret (Carpenter) [Mrs. John P.]
 (1910-73), 17,185
Richardson, Margaret E., 6,337
Richardson, Martin, 2,947
Richardson, Mary (1811-97). *See* Walker, Mary
 (Richardson) (1811-97)
Richardson, Mary (Curtis) (1847?-?), **1,335**, 1,358
Richardson, Mary Fletcher [Mrs. Thomas], 10,788
Richardson, Mrs. Ahira, 9,314
Richardson, Nellie (Simpson) (1871-?), **17,032**
Richardson, Nina Maud, 2,463
Richardson, Rebecca, 15,021
Richardson, Robert Kimball, 8,557

Richardson, Sarah, 4,869
Richardson, Sarah Felt (1870-1941), 5,394
Richardson, Sue, **3,348**
Richardson, Thomas, 10,788
Richardson, Thomazine, 2,053
Richardson, Verna, **16,953**
Richardson, William Marchant, 2,338
Richeson, Hazel [Mrs.], 15,308
Richey, Alice, 14,628
Richey, Caleb, 14,628
Richey, F. N., 9,713
Richey Family (OR), 14,500
Richey, Minna (Blair) [Mrs. Stephen Olin], 2,211
Richey, Nancy [Mrs. F. N.], **9,713**
Richey, Stuart (1812-89), 14,500
Richie, Scintilla Sexta (Pond) [Mrs. Cyrus], 8,412
Richland Anti-Tuberculosis Association (SC), 15,754
Richland Center Federation of Clubs (WI), 17,675
Richland Woman's Christian Temperance Union
 (MI), **8,254**
Richman, E. B., 10,976
Richman, Julia (1855-1912), 7,557
Richman Literary Society (NY), 7,557
Richman, Sonya, 15,332
Richmond (ship), 11,002
Richmond Education Association (VA), 17,091
Richmond Enquirer (VA), 17,119
Richmond Fellowship of America, 7,248
Richmond Female Humane Association (VA), 17,111
Richmond Hill House (NY), 12,632
Richmond Ladies Soldiers Aid Society (PA), **14,831**
Richmond, Lizzie [Mrs.], 1,358
Richmond, Mary Ellen (1861-1928), 8,142, 8,641
Richmond, Mary F. [Mrs. George]. *See* Morrogh,
 Mary F. [Mrs. George] Richmond [Mrs. C. T.]
Richmond Palladium (IN), 4,654
Richmond, Rebecca L., **7,913**
Richmond, Sarah Elizabeth [Miss] (1843-1921), **5,833,**
 5,835
Richmond Temperance and Literary Society (NC),
 13,554
Richmond Woman's Christian Association (VA),
 17,111
Richmond Women's Club (VA), 17,091
Richter, Hans, 2,665
Richter, Melissa, 11,306
Rickards, Burt R., 11,571
Rickel, Dora [Mrs. Frank H.], **1,737**
Rickel Family (CO), **1,737**
Rickel, Frank H., **1,737**
Ricker, Marilla Marks (Young) [Mrs. John]
 (1840-1920), **10,844**
Ricketts, Bertha (1890-1970). *See* Sumner, Bertha
 (Ricketts) (1890-1970)
Ricketts, Bertha Burnely, 9,744
Ricketts, Cid (pseudonym). *See* Sumner, Bertha
 (Ricketts) (1890-1970)
Ricketts, Fanny [Mrs. James], **17,073**
Ricketts, James, 17,073
Rickman, Narcissa Nicholson [Mrs.], 13,322
Ricks College (ID), Associated Women Students,
 16,823
Ricks College (ID), faculty, 16,553
Ricks, Mary Bynum (Holmes), **13,110**
Ricks, Mrs. Thomas, **16,807**
Ricks, Mrs. Walter Edward, 5,472
Ricks, P. W. Clark, 15,928
Riddell, Agnes, 5,752
Riddick, Elsie (1879-), **13,111**
Riddick Family, 13,112
Riddick, Frances, 13,112
Riddick, Ivey, **13,112**
Riddick, Margaret [Mrs. Ivey], 13,112
Riddick, Wallace Carl, 13,112
Riddle, Estelle Massey, 12,690
Riddle Family (VA), **17,118**
Riddle, Horace R., 17,115
Riddle, Katherine [Miss], 17,118
Riddle, Nelson, 6,013, 17,796
Riddle, Sarah Elizabeth (1842-1927). *See* Eager,
 Sarah Elizabeth (Riddle) [Mrs. Robert]
 (1842-1927)
Ridenour, Nina. [Mrs. N. Arnold] Boll (1904-),
 5,232

Rider, Lucy (Draper) (1813-?), 7,618
Rider, Lucy Jane (1849-1922). *See* Meyer, Lucy Jane
 (Rider) [Mrs. Josiah Shelly] (1849-1922)
Ridg, Sarah. *See* Schuyler, Sarah Ridg [Mrs. Anthony
 Dry]
Ridgaway, Henry Bascom (1830-95), **4,207**
Ridge Farm Preventorium (Lake Forest, IL), 3,806
Ridge, John Rollin, 14,220
Ridgely, Anna (1841-1926). *See* Hudson, Anna
 (Ridgely) [Mrs. James L.] (1841-1926)
Ridgely, Eliza "Didy". *See* Buckler, Eliza "Didy"
 (Ridgely) [Mrs. John Campbell] White [Mrs.
 Thomas H.]
Ridgely Family (MD), 5,786
Ridgely, Helen West (Stewart) [Mrs. John]
 (1854-1929), **5,805**
Ridgely, John (1851-1938), 5,805
Ridgely, Mildred (Abernathy) [Mrs. Montgomery],
 3,451
Ridgeway, Frances, 11,941
Ridgeways (book), 5,315
Ridgewood Camp (SC), 15,754
Riding clubs, **227**
Riding, Laura (1901-). *See* Jackson, Laura Riding
 [Mrs. Schuyler B.] (1901-)
Ridington, Juana de Dios (Machado) Alipás (1814-?),
 748
Ridley, Anna (1849-1924), **15,696**
Ridley, Bettie (1846-1924), **15,696**
Ridley, Catharine Livingston [Mrs. Matthew]
 (1751-1813). *See* Livingston, Catharine
 Livingston [Mrs. Matthew] Ridley [Mrs. John]
 (1751-1813)
Ridley, Florida R. [Mrs.], 5,945
Ridley, Mrs. Francis T., 15,696
Ridlon, Jeannette (1895-). *See* Piccard, Jeannette
 (Ridlon) [Mrs. Jean Felix] (1895-)
Ridpath, John Clark, 4,530
Ridpath, Martha Jane [Miss] (1855-1926), **4,534**
Riegelhuth, Frank, 10,775
Riegelhuth, Katharina [Mrs. Frank], 10,775
Riegelhuth, Katharine M. (1876-1973), **10,775**
Riegler, Mrs. Ben, 1,017
Ries, Mrs. Thomas Prince Earl, 10,006
Riessman, Frank, 6,834
Rietz, Dorothy, **8,601**
Riewe, Fred, **11,426**
Riewe, Harriet [Mrs. Fred], **11,426**
Rifkin, Lillian (1897-). *See* Blumenfeld, Lillian
 (Rifkin) [Mrs. Gustav] (1897-)
Rigdon, Malissa, 10,055
Rigdon, Sidney, 16,524, 16,822
Rigger, Helene (Harding), 14,573
Riggs, Anna, 9,294
Riggs, Emma Ray (1877-1970). *See* McKay, Emma
 Ray (Riggs) [Mrs. David Oman] (1877-1970)
Riggs, Kate Douglas (Smith) [Mrs. Samuel Bradley]
 Wiggin [Mrs. George Christopher] (1856-1923),
 803, 1,426, **1,603**, 2,663, 3,785, 4,212, **5,603,**
 5,694, 6,712, **6,951**, 7,171, 7,973, 12,493, 12,529,
 17,053
Riggs, Martha, 15,495
Riggs, Martha T. (1842-1910). *See* Morris, Martha T.
 (Riggs) [Mrs. Wyllys] (1842-1910)
Riggs, Mary Ann. *See* Robertson, Mary Ann (Riggs)
Riggs, Mary Ann Clark (Longley) [Mrs. Stephen
 Return] (1813-69), 9,038, **9,185**, 9,316, 9,371
Riggs, Stephen Return (1812-83), **9,185**, **9,316**
Riggs, Stephen Return (1812-83), Family (MN), **9,316**
Riggs, Thomas J., 14,651
Riggs, Williamson, 15,841
Right and left (politics), 1,654, 8,148, 14,686
"Right Flanker, The" (newspaper), 2,465
Right of property, 8,942, 9,861
"Right to Happiness, The" (soap opera), 17,705
Right to life movement, **5,385**, **7,843**, **7,864**, 7,873
Riheldaffer, Catherine (1858-1935), 9,317
Riheldaffer, Helen Gould Wallace [Mrs. David
 Timerman] (1908-), 9,317
Riheldaffer, John Gillan (1818-93), Family (MN),
 9,317
Riheldaffer, Martha Anna (1856-1930), 9,317
Riis, Elizabeth, 4,781
Riis, Jacob August (1849-1914), **2,549**, **12,130**, 12,520

Riis, Mary A. Phillips [Mrs. Jacob] (1877-1967), 12,520
Riis, Roger William (1895-1953), 12,520
Rikk of the Rendahl Clan (book), 4,714
Riley, Edith Dolan (1885-), **17,326**
Riley, Elizabeth M., 14,369
Riley, Franklin L, 9,678
Riley, Gladys, 17,918
Riley, Gladys F., 17,919
Riley, James W., 3,532
Riley, Julia (Mack) (1879-1962), **11,687**
Riley, Mrs. William H., 11,625
Riley, Susan B. (1896-), **266**
Rim Rock (book), 17,997
Rime, Dutch, **12,201**
Rimer, Ed, 17,319
Rinder, Reuben, 933
Rinder, Rose (Perlmutter) [Mrs. Reuben], **749,** 933
Rinehart, Blanche (ca. 1883-1976), **8,122**
Rinehart, Mary (Roberts) (1876-1958), 691, 1,207, 5,123, 10,992, 11,812, 12,044, 12,436, 14,819, 14,828, **15,263**
Ring, Blanche (1872-1961), 11,907
Ring, Elizabeth L. [Mrs. Henry E.], **16,123**
Ring, Florence (1883-1964). *See* Kahn, Florence (Ring) [Mrs. Howard] (1883-1964)
Ring, Frances, 11,897
Ringe Mothers and Daughters Club (MN), **8,827**
Ringgold, Marie Antoinette (ca. 1846-69). *See* Naglee, Marie Antoinette (Ringgold) [Mrs. Henry Morris] (ca. 1846-69)
Ringgold, Virginia (1811-1901). *See* Key, Virginia (Ringgold) (1811-1901)
Ringling, Audrey, 2,931
Ringling Brothers and Barnum and Bailey Circus, 1,827, 9,390, **17,492**
Ringling, Edith, 2,931
Ringling, Mrs. E. Charles, 17,197
Ringold, Rose, 17,282
Rings Around Us (book), 7,202
Ringsrud, Olive A. (1892-1971), **15,859**
Ringstad, Anna E. (1852-1923). *See* Mohn, Anne E. (Ringstad) (1852-1923)
Rinhard, Mattie B., 3,725
Rio Grande Park (CO), 1,817
Rio Pongo (Africa), 15,765
Riordan, Frances, 16,283
Riordan, J. E., Family (TX) **16,283**
Riordan, Josie [Mrs. J. E.], 16,283
Riordan, Mary, 16,283
Riordan, Nellie (1892-1965), 16,283
Riordan, Sallie, 16,283
Riots, 112, 2,502, 3,301, 4,170, 5,828, 6,079, 7,737, 8,148, 9,279, 12,487, 12,490, 16,876
Rip Saw, The (newspaper), 4,675
Ripley, Eleazar Wheelock, 7,128
Ripley, Eliza (?-1868). *See* Buckingham, Eliza (Ripley) [Mrs. William Alfred] (?-1868)
Ripley, Eliza Moore, 5,410
Ripley, Elizabeth B., 7,055
Ripley, George, 6,500, 6,906, 12,602
Ripley Hospital for Women (Minneapolis, MN), **9,203**
Ripley Hospital for Women (Minneapolis, MN), Sarah L. Lara Auxiliary, 9,203
Ripley, Jerome, 7,671
Ripley, John, 11,327
Ripley, Julia Caroline (1825-1913). *See* Dorr, Julia Caroline (Ripley) (1825-1913)
Ripley, Louisa Augusta (Schlossberger) [Mrs. George]. *See* Pinède, Louisa Augusta (Schlossberger) [Mrs. George] Ripley [Mrs. Alphonse]
Ripley, Love (Allen) [Mrs. Eleazar Wheelock] (1786-1820), 7,128
Ripley, Martha George (Rogers) [Mrs. William Warren] (1843-1912), 9,203, 9,323
Ripley, Sally (1785-?). *See* Stearns, Sally (Ripley) [Mrs. Charles] (1785-?)
Ripley, Sarah (1785-?). *See* Stearns, Sally (Ripley) [Mrs. Charles] (1785-?)
Ripley, Sarah Alden (Bradford) [Mrs. Samuel] (1793-1867), **6,857**
Rippin, Jane Deeter, 12,095
Rippon, Mary [Miss] (1850-1935), **1,674**

Ririe, Harriet Olive (1892-). *See* Bradshaw, Harriet Olive (Ririe) [Mrs. Richard] (1892-)
Risberg, Gerda, **17,327**
Risdon, Ruth (1888-). *See* Storer, Ruth (Risdon) [Mrs. Tracy Irwin] (1888-)
Riseman, Meta Rosenberg (1904-), 8,149
Rising Paper Company (MA), 7,510
Risler, E., 12,457
Rister Family (SC), **15,697**
Rister, Martha, 15,697
Ristine, Bella Maria (1855-1953). *See* Wyman, Bella Maria Ristine [Mrs. Oliver Cromwell] (1855-1953)
Ristine, Catherine McMaster [Mrs. Henry] (?-1893), 9,318
Ristine, Henry, Family (MN), **9,318**
Ristori, Adelaide (1822-1906), **5,954**
Ritchie, Adele (1875-1930), 16,150
Ritchie, Anna Cora (Ogden) (1819-70) [Mrs. William Foushee]. *See* Mowatt, Anna Cora (Ogden) [Mrs. James]. [Mrs. William Foushee] Ritchie (1819-70)
Ritchie, Anne, 11,821
Ritchie, Barbara (1943-), **18,004**
Ritchie, Edith [Mrs.], 18,025
Ritchie Family (VA), **17,119**
Ritchie, Isabella Foushee [Mrs. Thomas], 17,119
Ritchie, Isabella H. *See* Harrison, Isabella H. (Ritchie)
Ritchie, Margaret Dewees (Avery) (1930-), 15,939
Ritchie, Mary E. *See* Wallbridge, Mary E. (Ritchie)
Ritchie, Mary Emma, 16,968
Ritchie, Thomas (1778-1854), 17,119
Ritchie, William F., 1,426
Ritchies, Letitia, 9,905
Rittenhouse, Isabella Maud, **3,776**
Rittenhouse, Jessie Bell (1869-1948). *See* Scollard, Jessie Bell Rittenhouse [Mrs. Clinton] (1869-1948)
Rittenhouse, Mrs. Paul, 8,670
Ritter, Mary (1876-1958). *See* Beard, Mary (Ritter) (1876-1958)
Ritter, Mattie W., **8,782**
Ritter, Mrs. William M., 13,988
Ritter, Nellie, 8,251
Rivals, The (drama), 3,921
River Falls Academy (WI), 17,857, 17,861
River Falls Improvement League (WI), **17,863**
River Falls Lyceum (WI), 17,857
River Falls Normal School (WI), students, 17,859, 17,862
River Falls Teachers College (WI), 8,944
River in the Wind (book), 2,875
River Rogue (book), 15,927
River steamers, 259, 5,280, 8,953, 9,124, 10,242, 10,265, 10,306, 10,351, 10,372, 10,374, 10,383, 12,330
River to Pickle Beach, The (book), 5,989
Rivera, Diego, 761
Riverfront Expressway (LA), 5,542
Riverhead Lecture Association (NY), **12,780**
Rivers, Irene [Mrs.], 7,109
Rivers, L. Mendel, 15,755
Rivers, Pauline, 3,013
Riverside Church (NY), 11,835
Riverside Junior College (CA), faculty, 1,123
Riverside Opera Association (CA), 1,123
Riverside Public Library (CA), 8,564
Riverside Reformatory for Women, 17,018
Riverside Sanatorium (Granite Falls, MN), 8,518
Riverside Womancenter (CA),
Riverside Woman's Club (CA), 1,122
Riverside Woman's Club (IL), **4,318**
Riverside Women's Rest Room Association (CA), 1,121
Rives, Amélie (1863-1945). *See* Troubetzkoy, Amélie (Rives) Chandler (1863-1945)
Rives, Blanche Hardee (1887-1973), **13,285**
Rives Family, 9,762
Rives, Henry Macon (1883-1952), **10,776**
Rives, Judith Page (Walker) [Mrs. William Cabell] (1802-82), 2,550
Rives, Lucy Shands. *See* Brown, Lucy Shands (Rives)

Rives, Marguerite Raycraft (1893-), 10,776
Rives, Mary Elizabeth (Carter) (1829-1900), **5,553,** 5,555, **13,113**
Rives, William Cabell (1793-1868), **2,550**
Rivoire, Alice Cecilia (Sanderson), **11,688**
Riwkin, Eugenia (1903-73). *See* Söderberg, Eugenia (Riwkin). [Mrs. Hugo] Perls (1903-73)
Riwkin, Josef, 12,880
Rix, Alfred, **1,336**
Rix, Chastina (Walbridge) [Mrs. Alfred] (1824-57), **1,336,** 1,337
Rix-Walbridge Family (CA), **1,337**
Rizzi, Eva (Byrne). *See* Smith, Eva (Byrne) Rizzi
Rizzio (opera), 1,022
Rizzo, Frank, 15,332
Rizzo School of Music (Chicago, IL), **3,789**
Roach, Emeline, **12,603**
Roach, Mrs., **9,714**
Road construction, 181
Road construction industry, management, 4,467
Road Grows Strange, The (book), 5,694
"Road of Life" (soap opera), 17,705
"Road of Remembrance, The," 4,355
Roads 10,383, 12,952, 14,669, 17,268, 17,564
Roads, plank, 4,467
Roadside improvement, 4,501, 5,443
Roadside Mine (AZ), 215
Roadside Settlement House Association (IA), **4,823**
Roanoke Colony Memorial Association, 13,070
Roanoke Farms Resettlement Administration Project (Halifax, NC), 12,967
Roanoke Island Historical Association, 13,267
Roanoke Island Historical Society, 12,967
Robards, Rachel (Donalson) (1767-1828). *See* Jackson, Rachel (Donalson) Robards [Mrs. Andrew] (1767-1828).
Robb, Agnes R., **750**
Robb, Isabel Adams (Hampton) [Mrs. Hunter] (1860-1910), 4,108, 5,735, 6,151, 12,074, 12,137
Robb, Josephine (1882-?). *See* Ober, Josephine (Robb) (1882-?)
Robb, Lynda Bird (Johnson) [Mrs. Charles], 9,397
"Robber Bridegroom, The" (story), 9,770
Robbins, Abner, 14,436
Robbins, Anne Smith, 6,179
Robbins, Eliza, 12,403
Robbins Eliza (Chapin), 15,358
Robbins, Elizabeth S. [Mrs. Samuel L.], 9,250
Robbins, Eunice Waters. *See* Luckey, Eunice Waters (Robbins)
Robbins, Helen (Larrabee) [Mrs. Charles B.], 4,928
Robbins, Henry A., 2,282
Robbins, Howard C. (1879-1952), **12,089**
Robbins, Jane Elizabeth (1860-1946), 8,668
Robbins, Kate L. (Pratt) [Mrs. Abner] (1834-?), **14,436**
Robbins, Mary Loveridge [Mrs.], 9273
Robbins, Matilda. Tatania Gitel Rabinowitz (1887-1963), 8,064, 8,094, **8,123**
Robbins, Mrs. Raymond, 15,332
Robbins, Phyllis, 2,159
Roberdeau, Buchanan, **15,081**
Roberdeau, Daniel (1727-95), 15,081
Roberdeau, Mary E., 15,081
Roberson, Elizabeth, 13,555
Roberson, Ida Mae. *See* Cullen, Ida Mae (Roberson) [Mrs. Countee]
Roberson, Joseph I., **13,555**
Robert Annys, Poor Priest (book), 13,811
Robert Connor Day Care Center (Owensboro, KY), 5,401
Robert Dale Owen Commission, 4,654
Robert E. Lee Hotel (MS), 9,691
Robert G. Ingersoll Memorial, 17,980
Robert, Jane, 11,318
Robert M. La Follette (book), 2,432
Robert Mills House (SC), 15,518
Robert Taylor Homes Housing Project (Chicago, IL), 4,087
Roberts, A. H., 15,941
Roberts, Belle [Mrs.], **10,708**
Roberts Brothers (Boston, MA), 5,349
Roberts, Carrie (Buchman), 14,618
Roberts, Catherine Border [Mrs. O. M.], 16,144

Roberts, Clara (Fish), **224**
Roberts, Della H., 10,055
Roberts, Dorothy, 15,334
Roberts, Elisha, 14,851
Roberts, Elizabeth (Hooton) [Mrs. Elisha], 14,851
Roberts, Elizabeth Jane (Sadler) [Mrs. John], 9,319
Roberts, Elizabeth Madox (1881-1941), **2,551**, 5,273, **5,361**
Roberts, Ellwyn Clare, **2,552**
Roberts, Ephraim Peters (1825-93), **14,650**
Roberts, Eunice (1903-), 4,495
Roberts Family (CA), 1,648
Roberts Family (PA), **14,851**
Roberts, Flora, **17,811**
Roberts, Frances L., 3,812
Roberts, Jean, **17,712**
Roberts, Josephine (Redd), **16,556**
Roberts, Josie, 5,458
Roberts, Katherine, 15,035
Roberts, Katharine Eggleston (1895-), **5,022**
Roberts, Lou Conway [Mrs. Daniel Webster], **16,124**
Roberts, Margaret (Ashton) [Mrs. Nathan] (1761-1850), 14,951
Roberts, Margaret Stevenson [Miss] (?-1952), **6,858**
Roberts, Mary, 12,137
Roberts, Mary [Miss], 3,608
Roberts, Mary Elizabeth Burroughs (1860-1945). *See* Coolidge, Mary Elizabeth Burroughs (Roberts) Smith [Mrs. Dane] (1860-1945)
Roberts, Mary Fanton (1871-1956), **2,804**
Roberts, Mary May (1877-1959), 6,122, 6,141, **6,157**
Roberts, Mattie, 2,502
Roberts, Mrs. F. C., **13,556**
Roberts, Mrs. Henry M., Jr., 2,123
Roberts, Myra [Miss], 751
Roberts, Myra (Farrington) [Mrs. Ephraim Peters] (1835-1912), 14,650
Roberts, O. M., 16,144
Roberts, Peg, 30
Roberts, Sarah L., 3,812
Roberts, Susanna (1817-?). *See* Townsend, Susanna (Roberts) (1817-?)
Roberts, Thelma Livingston, 2,945
Roberts, Thomas Sadler (1858-1946), 8,592, **9,319**
Roberts, Willa Mae, **10,078**
Robertson, Agnes (1879-1960). *See* Arber, Agnes (Robertson) (1879-1960)
Robertson, Alexander, **15,698**
Robertson, Alice, 14,197
Robertson, Alice Mary [Miss] (1854-1931), 1,928, 14,243, **14,246**
Robertson, Amanda [Mrs.], 10,196
Robertson, Amanda "Mandy", 14,651
Robertson, Amelia. *See* Foss, Amelia (Robertson) [Mrs. Cyrus David]
Robertson, Ann Eliza (Worcester) [Mrs. William Schenck] (1826-1905), **14,243**
Robertson, Caroline B. (Story) [Mrs. George M.], 878
Robertson, Carrie Francis (Weed) [Mrs. Alexander M.] (1852-1941), **4,611**
Robertson, Constance Pierrepont (Noyes) [Mrs. Miles] (1897-), **12,908**
Robertson, Dora (1874-?), 17,886
Robertson, Eliza Ann (Marsh) (?-1878), **13,114**
Robertson, Ethel (1882-?). *See* Whiting, Ethel (Robertson) [Mrs. Henry Hyer] (1882-?)
Robertson Family, 8,966
Robertson Family (OR), **14,651**
Robertson, Frank C., 16,519
Robertson, George M., 878
Robertson, James Alexander (1873-1939), **2,553**, 2,657
Robertson, James P., 14,651
Robertson, LeRoy J., 16,780
Robertson, Margaret Anna (1810-71). *See* Burwell, Margaret Anna (Robertson) [Mrs. Robert] (1810-71)
Robertson, Mary Ann (Riggs), 14,651
Robertson, Myrtle [Miss], 1,339
Robertson, Persis W., 4,868
Robertson, Samuel, 15,495
Robertson, Stuart, 15,196
Robeson, Anna (Rodman) (1787-1848), 15,294

Robeson, Eslanda (Goode) [Mrs. Paul A.] (1896-1965), **3,291**, 3,799, 4,970, 8,949, 9,289
Robeson, Eva Jane [Miss] (1937-), **16,808**
Robeson, Helen (Katz) [Mrs. George], **4,944**
Robeson, Janie (Smith) [Mrs. R. R.], 13,602
Robeson, Mary, 13,437
Robeson, Paul A., 5,478
Robi, Josephine H., **13,818**
Robie, Mary. *See* Kingsley, Mary (Robie)
Robins, C. A., 3,667
Robins, Elizabeth, 6,889
Robins, Elizabeth (1855-1936). *See* Pennell, Elizabeth (Robins) [Mrs. Joseph] (1855-1936)
Robins, Elizabeth (1862-1952), **12,696, 16,166, 17,208**
Robins, Julia Pryor [Miss], **9,715**
Robins, Margaret (Dreier) [Mrs. Raymond] (1868-1945), 2,509, **2,878**, 3,839, 4,003, 4,100, 4,173, 5,121, 6,812, 6,958, 12,704
Robins, Raymond (1873-1955), 2,878
Robinson, Agnes Mary Frances (1857-1944). *See* Duclaux, Agnes Mary Frances (Robinson) (1857-1944)
Robinson, Alexander, 3,891
Robinson, Alfred Bassett, 9,716
Robinson, Alice V., 17,228
Robinson, Amy Josephine Cook (ca. 1882-?), **8,602**
Robinson, Anne [Mrs. George Rowan], 9,057
Robinson, Anne Randolph (ca. 1860-1949). *See* Edgar, Anne Randolph Page (Robinson) [Mrs. William Crowell] (ca. 1860-1949)
Robinson, Augustus, 12,296
Robinson, B. L., 6,277
Robinson, Beverley Randolph (1876-1951), 12,297
Robinson, Carley. *See* Dawson, Carley (Robinson)
Robinson, Caroline [Mrs. L. N.], 6,223
Robinson, Charles (?-1894), **5,222**
Robinson, Clara (Weaver) [Mrs. Nelson], 11,392
Robinson, Corinne (Roosevelt) (1861-1933), 4,000, 7,881, **14,652**
Robinson, Cornelia Ann (Bryan) [Mrs. David M.] Hickman [Mrs. John M.], 9,987
Robinson, Doane (1856-1946), **15,860**
Robinson, Dorothy Clapp (1892-1968), **3,714**
Robinson, Dorothy Medders, 15,316
Robinson, Ednah (1872-1960). *See* Aiken, Ednah (Robinson) (1872-1960)
Robinson, Edward, 12,296
Robinson, Edward Arlington, 2,463, 12,896
Robinson, Edward G., **14,653**
Robinson, Edwin A., 6,503
Robinson, Ellie Bond, **12,604**
Robinson, Emmett E. (1914-), **15,699**
Robinson, Ethel (Blackwell), 2,209
Robinson Family (NY), 12,020, **12,296, 12,297**
Robinson, Florence B., **4,393**
Robinson, Frances [Mrs. Edward G.], 14,653
Robinson, George Rowan, 9,057
Robinson, George W., 16,524
Robinson, Grace Chess, 14,351
Robinson, Hannah [Miss] (1803-78), **2,054**
Robinson Hannah [Mrs. James W.], 12,296
Robinson, Harriet Jane (Hanson) [Mrs. William Stevens] (1825-1911), 6,804, **6,859**, 7,069, 7,082
Robinson, Harriette Lucy (1850-1937). *See* Shattuck, Harriette Lucy (Robinson) [Mrs. Sidney Doane] (1850-1937)
Robinson, Helen Mary, 12,363
Robinson, Helen R. Roosevelt, 11,922
Robinson, Helene, **14,654**
Robinson, Helene Mary (?-1976), 6,321, **6,322**
Robinson, Herman, 12,297
Robinson, Hetty Howland (1834-1916). *See* Green, Hetty Howland (Robinson) [Mrs. Edward H.] (1834-1916)
Robinson, Ida. *See* Cullen, Ida (Robinson) [Mrs. Countee]
Robinson, Ione, 2,207
Robinson, J. LaRue, 10,679
Robinson, James H. (1907-72), **5,475**
Robinson, James W., 12,296
Robinson, Jane A. [Miss] (1827?-?), **17,713**
Robinson, Jane Charters (1828-1907). *See* Hindley, Jane Charters (Robinson) [Mrs. John] (1828-1907)

Robinson, Jane (Hoxie) [Mrs. James] (1815-98). *See* Banbury, Jane (Hoxie) [Mrs. James] Robinson [Mrs. Thomas] (1815-98)
Robinson, Jessie Harvey, 15,175
Robinson, Jo Ann (Ooiman) (1942-), **17,714**
Robinson, John M., 9,987
Robinson, Julia A., 4,727, 4,850
Robinson, Kathleen, 9,170
Robinson, La Petite Sue, 1,073
Robinson Lelia J., **6,533**
Robinson, Lucy Fassett (1822-1901). *See* Phelps, Lucy Fassett (Robinson) Benjamin [Mrs. Winthrop H.] (1822-1901)
Robinson, Lydia S. M., **2,554**
Robinson, Magnus L., 3,295
Robinson, Martha [Mrs.] (ca. 1890-), **5,521**
Robinson, Mary Ann, 16,509
Robinson, Mary (Church), 2,271
Robinson, Mary D. [Mrs.], 5,513
Robinson, Mary Elizabeth (1844-1930). *See* Foster, Mary Elizabeth (Robinson) [Mrs. Thomas R.] (1844-1930)
Robinson, Mary Eve (Byers), 1,757
Robinson, Mortimer, Family (MN), **9,320**
Robinson, Mrs. Douglas, 12,299
Robinson, Mrs. Horace P., 13,514
Robinson, Mrs. John D., 13,523
Robinson, Nancy (McDougall) [Mrs. Alfred Bassett] (1808-?), **9,716**
Robinson, Pat, 17,663
Robinson, Patricia Colbert [Mrs. Emmett E.] (1923-), 15,699, **15,700**, 15,720
Robinson, Pauline, 12,297
Robinson, Rebecca (Dunn), **15,100**
Robinson, Robert, 14,639
Robinson, Rosa Duncan Johnston [Mrs. George Anderson] (1858-1929), 5,350
Robinson, Sara Tappan Doolittle (Lawrence) [Mrs. Charles] (1827-1911), **5,222**
Robinson, Therese Albertine Louise Von Jakob (1797-1870), 12,403
Robinson, William, 17,086
Robinson, William Henry, 12,296
Robison, Bell, 14,776
Robison, Edna (?-1976), 16,485
Robison, Jane, 14,776
Robison, Louise Yates, 16,676
Robkin, Polly Hayden (1912-), 13,176
Robson, Eleanor (1879-). *See* Belmont, Eleanor (Robson) [Mrs. August B.] (1879-)
Robson, Frances [Mrs. Frederick T.] (1885-1949), **958**
Robson, Frederick T., 958
Robson, Harriet Irving, 8,174
Robson, Kate Hester [Mrs.], **3,249**
Robson, Mary. Mary Jeanette Robison. [Mrs. Charles Livingston] Gore [Mrs. Augustus Homer] Brown (1858-1942), **2,555**, 16,150
Robson, May (Waldron) [Mrs. Stuart] (1868-1942), 9,103
Robson, Sadie, 4,760
Roche a Cree Lutheran Church (Arkdale, WI), 8,746
Roche, Emma Langdon, 54
Roche Family, 4,058
Roché, Henri-Pierre, 12,477
Roche, Josephine Aspinwall [Miss] (1886-1976), **1,675**, 9,492, 11,771
Roché, Mrs. Henri-Pierre, 12,477
Rochester, Agatha Jane (1832-96). *See* Strange, Agatha Jane (Rochester) (1832-96)
Rochester, Anna (1880-1966), 14,393, **14,437**
Rochester Barettes (MN), **8,828**
Rochester Business and Professional Women's Club (MN), **8,829**
Rochester City Hospital (NY), 12,822
Rochester Female Academy (NY). *See* Misses Nichols School (NY)
Rochester Female Charitable Society (NY), **12,802, 12,830**
Rochester Female Seminary (NY). *See* Misses Nichols School (NY)
Rochester Flower and Garden Club (MN), **8,830**
Rochester General Hospital (NY), 12,802
Rochester High School (IN), 4,660
Rochester Lyceum Theatre (NY), **11,689**

Rochester Normal University (IN), **4,658**
Rochester Political Equality Club (NY), 12,818, 12,834
Rochester Republican Women's Club (NH), **10,885**
Rochester Republican Women's Organization (NY), 12,790
Rochester State Hospital (MN), 8,822
Rochester Theological Seminary (NY), 14,386
Rochester Woman's Club (IN), 4,661
Rochester Woman's Club (NH), 10,887
Rochester Women's Monday Club (MN), 8,832
Rock Family, 1,504
Rock Hill Jaycee-ettes (SC), **15,812**
Rock Hill Junior Welfare League (SC), **15,813**
Rock Hill Junior Woman's Club (SC), **15,814**
Rock Hill Music Club (SC), **15,815**
Rock, John (1890-), **6,231**
Rock, Lilian D., 17,141
"Rock Me to Sleep" (poem), 5,694
Rockefeller, Abby Greene (Aldrich) [Mrs. John Davison, Jr.] (1874-1948), 2,160, 5,458, 11,843, 12,044, 12,293, 14,819
Rockefeller Commission, 11,918
Rockefeller, Edith (1872-1932). *See* McCormick, Edith (Rockefeller) [Mrs. Harold Fowler] (1872-1932)
Rockefeller Family, 11,878
Rockefeller Foundation, 6,125, 6,126, 6,238, 7,288, 7,326, 11,515, 11,892, 11,911, **12,739, 14,218**
Rockefeller Foundation, China Medical Board, 12,966
Rockefeller Foundation, General Education Board, 12,966
Rockefeller Institute of Medical Research (NY), 1,738, 2,090
Rockefeller, John D. (1839-1937), 2,624, **12,740,** 14,745
Rockefeller, John D., Jr., 6,706, 11,911, 15,564
Rockefeller, John D., III, 11,911
Rockefeller, Laura (Spelman) [Mrs. John D.], 12,738
Rockefeller, Margaretta "Happy" [Mrs. Nelson A.], 14,822
Rockefeller, Nancy (Carnegie) [Mrs. J. Stillman], 1,837
Rockefeller, Nelson A., 10,197, 11,592
Rockets (aeronautics), 11,831
Rockett, Huldah Maybell Hubbard [Mrs.], 13,367
Rockford College (IL), 4,047, 4,477, 6,527, 9,316
  archives, **4,330**
  faculty, 8,557, 9,052
  students, 14,401
Rockford Female Seminary (IL). *See* Rockford College (IL)
Rockport Lodge (MA), 6,806
Rockwell, Betsey (1762-1847), 7,672
Rockwell Family, 11,618
Rockwell Garden Homes (Chicago, IL), 3,874
Rockwell, John Arnold (1803-61), **7,672**
Rockwell, Kathleen Eloisa (1876-1957), 14,398
Rockwell, Loula (Ayres), **13,115**
Rockwell, Lucy [Mrs. Julius], 4,356
Rockwell, Molly Punderson [Mrs. Norman] (1896-), 7,510
Rockwell, Paul Ayres (1889-), 13,115
Rockwell, Vera Cober, 11,596
Rockwell, William S., 3,569
Rockwood, Edith [Miss] (1888-1952), 2,700, **6,860**
Rocky Hill Congregational Church (CT), Elderly Ladies Knitting Society, 2,026
Rocky Hill Congregational Church (CT), Ladies Benevolent Society, **2,026**
Rocky Mount Women's Club (NC), 12,941
"Rocky Mountain Canary Speaks, The" (song), 17,970
Rocky Mountain Fuel Company, 1,675
Rocky Mountain News (CO), 1,670, 1,757, 1,764
Rocky Mountains, rescue work in, 1,750
Rodburn, James A., Family (NY), 11,440
Rodden, Donna (Strickland) (1926-), **11,269**
"Roddy Books," 12,524
Rodemann, Emma (1908-), **8,841**
Roderick, Stella Virginia (ca. 1880-), **17,328**
Rodgers. *See also* Rogers
Rodgers and Hammerstein Award, 6,669
Rodgers, Ann (Hodge) [Mrs. John], 2,556
Rodgers, Ann Minerva "Nannie" (1824-1916). *See*

Macomb, Ann Minerva "Nannie" (Rodgers) [Mrs. John Navarre] (1824-1916)
Rodgers, Dorothy, 11,817
Rodgers, Dorothy (1914-), 4,227
Rodgers, Elizabeth Midland (pseudonym). *See* Bothwell, Jean (1892?-1977)
Rodgers, Emma Washburn, 9,323
Rodgers Family (CT), 1,940
Rodgers Family (MD), **2,556**
Rodgers Family (New England), 6,352
Rodgers Family (TX), 16,085
Rodgers, Isabel King [Mrs.] (1858-?), 16,486
Rodgers, James L., 13,007
Rodgers, John (1773-1838), 2,556
Rodgers, John (1812-82), 2,556
Rodgers, Louisa (1817-79). *See* Meigs, Louisa (Rodgers) [Mrs. Montgomery Cunningham] (1817-79)
Rodgers, Mary (1931-), 8,531
Rodgers, Minerva (Denison) [Mrs. John] (1784-1877), 2,556
Rodgers, Viola, **752**
Rodin, Auguste, 7,030
Rodin, Auguste (1840-1917), 10,029
Rodin, Katherine (1907-), 1,356, 1,357
Rodman, Anna (1761-1845). *See* Hazard, Anna (Rodman) (1761-1845)
Rodman, Anna (1787-1848). *See* Robeson, Anna (Rodman) (1787-1848)
Rodman, Arabella [Mrs. Willoughby], 5,120, 5,122
Rodman, Camille B., 13,557
Rodman, Charity (1766-1824). *See* Rotch, Charity (Rodman) (1766-1824)
Rodman, Elizabeth (1759-1828). *See* Rotch, Elizabeth (Rodman) (1759-1828)
Rodman Family, 11,599, 11,600
Rodman Family (NJ, NY), **12,605**
Rodman Family (NC), **13,557**
Rodman Family (PA), **15,294**
Rodman, Hannah. *See* Gould, Hannah (Rodman)
Rodman, Hannah (1764-1819). *See* Fisher, Hannah (Rodman) (1764-1819)
Rodman, Lida T., 13,376, 13,557
Rodman, Lucy A., 12,605
Rodman, Mary (1781-1813). *See* Fisher, Mary (Rodman) (1781-1813)
Rodman, Mary (Borden) (1729-98), 15,294
Rodman, Mary (Harvey) [Mrs. Washington], 12,605
Rodman, Mary O., 13,557
Rodman, Mrs. W. B., 13,557
Rodman, Sally A., 2,160
Rodman, Sarah (1764-93), 15,294
Rodman, Washington Hendrix (1792-?), 12,605
Rodney, Mary B., 14,515
Rodney, Robert M., 9,839
Rodney, Susan Maria (Fromberger) [Mrs. Thomas McKean] (?-ca. 1863), **2,048**
Rodrigues, Guadalupe, 4,053
Rodrigues, Rosita, 16,097
Rodriguez, Father Antonio José, 779
Roe, Ella (Hjertaas) [Mrs. Herman] (1889-1972), **8,814**
Roe, Gwyneth King [Mrs.] (1868-1968), **17,715**
Roe, M. A., 4,812
Roe, Mrs. E. D., 6,337
Roe v. Wade (TX, 1973), 1,984, 16,396
Roe, Vingie Eve (1879-1958), **14,258**
Roedel, Josephine Forney [Mrs. William D.] (1824-1904), **2,557**
Roeder, Elizabeth A. [Mrs. Henry], **17,329**
Roelker, Catherine Ray (Greene) [Mrs. Frederick], 13,848, 14,890
Roelker, Frederick, 13,848
Roerich Museum, International Art Center (New York, NY), 2,107
Roesch, Ella (Oblinger) 10,516
Roessing, Jennie Bradley [Mrs.] (ca. 1883-1963), **15,252**
Roessler, Ernestine (1861-1936). *See* Schumann-Heink Ernestine (Roessler). [Mrs. Ernst] Heink [Mrs. Paul] Schumann [Mrs. William] Rapp (1861-1936)
Roethke, Theodore, 18,021
Rogé, Charlotte Fiske Bates (1838-1916), 7,131

Rogé v. Borie (PA), 14,960
Roger Ascham School (NY), 6,354
Roger Williams Park Museum (RI), 14,343
Rogers. *See also* Rodgers
Rogers, Anna. *See* Hudson, Anna (Rogers) [Mrs. Henry, Sr.]
Rogers, Anna. *See* Hunter, Anna (Rogers)
Rogers, Aurelia (Spencer) [Mrs. Thomas] (1834-1922), **16,809**
Rogers, Barsina. *See* French, Barsina (Rogers)
Rogers, Betty (Blake) [Mrs. Will], 418
Rogers, Carolyn, 15,082
Rogers, Clara, 12,298
Rogers, Clarissa "Clara" Walbridge, 1,337
Rogers, Colenda Chrilla (1869-?). *See* Adams, Colenda Chrilla (Rogers) [Mrs. Joseph] (1869-?)
Rogers, Daniel (1707-85), 7,673
Rogers, David Camp, 14,758
Rogers, Dorothy Eugenia (1883-1970). *See* Tilly, Dorothy Eugenia (Rogers) [Mrs. Milton Eden] (1883-1970)
Rogers, Edith (Nourse) [Mrs. John Jacob] (1881-1960), 1,605, **6,861,** 13,406
Rogers, Edward S., 11,571
Rogers, Ellen, 12,298
Rogers, Eulalia. *See* Franklin, Eulalia (Rogers)
Rogers Family, **12,676**
Rogers Family (CA), 1,232
Rogers Family (MA), **7,673**
Rogers Family (MO), **9,906**
Rogers Family (NY), **12,298**
Rogers, Frederick, 8,252
Rogers, Ginger, 2,968
Rogers Hall School for Girls (Lowell, MA), **7,068**
Rogers, Harriet M. Francis, 12,298
Rogers, Helen (1882-1970). *See* Reid, Helen (Rogers) [Mrs. Ogden Mills] (1882-1970)
Rogers, Horace, **15,082**
Rogers, Irma Duncan, 12,359, **12,361**
Rogers, John, 12,514
Rogers, John, Jr. (1829-1904), 12,298
Rogers, Josephine (Preston) [Mrs. Jason], 5,359
Rogers, Julia, 14,738
Rogers, Kate [Mrs. Horace], **15,082**
Rogers, Katherine, 8,252
Rogers, Katherine P., 12,298
Rogers, Louisa H., **13,116**
Rogers, Loula Winifred Kendall [Mrs.] (1839-1931), Family (GA), **3,419**
Rogers, Lucy. *See* Gove, Lucy (Rogers)
Rogers, Margaret. *See* Phipps, Margaret (Rogers) [Mrs. Laurence]
Rogers, Martha George (1843-1912). *See* Ripley, Martha George (Rogers) [Mrs. William Warren] (1843-1912)
Rogers, Martha "Patty" (1761-1840), 7,673
Rogers, Mary, 12,514
Rogers, Mary (?-1857). *See* Dunn, Mary (Rogers) (?-1857)
Rogers, Mary [Mrs. Charles "Buddy"]. *See* Pickford, Mary. Gladys Smith. [Mrs. Douglas] Fairbanks, Sr. [Mrs. Charles "Buddy"] Rogers (1893-1979)
Rogers, Mary [Mrs. John, Jr.], 12,514
Rogers, Mary Ann [Mrs. William], 14,688
Rogers, Mary Benjamin [Mrs. H. H.], 11,967
Rogers, Mary Cochrane, 2,198
Rogers, Mary E., **11,127**
Rogers, Mary Jeffreys, **13,558**
Rogers, Mary Josephine. *See* Joseph, Mother Mary
Rogers, Matilda Livingston, **12,606**
Rogers, Peet and Company (NY), 12,179
Rogers, Sarah Ann (1849-1929). *See* Carr, Sarah Ann (Rogers) (1849-1929)
Rogers, Sarah, Ellen Derby, 12,298
Rogers, Will, 1,060
Rogers, William, 14,688
Rogers, William King (1828-93), **753**
Rogers, William P. (1913-), **5,158**
Roget, Elizabeth (1900-), **6,073**
Rogick, Mary Dora, 11,807
Rogoway, Esther (Schreiber), 17,282
Rogstad, Anna, 8,747
Rogstad, Berger, 8,747
Rogue River Indian wars (OR), **14,539,** 14,657

Rogue, The (periodical), 7,316
Rohde, Ruth (Bryan) Owen [Mrs. Borge] (1885-1954), 863, 2,340, 2,590, 3,028, 6,671, 8,450, 11,483
Rohfleisch, Marjorie (Cherry) [Mrs. Kramer] (1910-), **6,862**
Rohfleisch, Peter, 6,862
Rohfleish, Kramer, 6,862
Rohlf, Ida C., 4,945
Rohlf, Lottie (Beed) [Mrs. William A.], 4,945
Rohlf, William A., **4,945**
Rohr, Philip, 9,048
Rohrbough, George E., 4,374
Rohrer, Grace J. [Mrs.], 13,446
Rohrer, Hanna (1842-1912). *See* Monks, Hanna (Rohrer) [Mrs. Zerah Coston] (1842-1912)
Rohrheimer, Rena M., **13,819**
Rokahr, Mary A. (1892-1972), 10,607
Roland, Mrs. Dunbar, 9,819
Role of Women, Their Activities and Organizations, in Lebanon, Egypt, Iraq, Jordan and Syria, The (book), 7,326
Rolfe, Charles W. (1850-1934), 4,394
Rolfe Family (IL), **4,394**
Rolfe, Mary (1881-1974), 4,394
Rolick, Esther (1922-), **2,805**
"Roll Call" (poem), 4,745
"Roll 'Em" (song), 5,534
Rollag, Grace [Mrs. Ole] (1851-1943), **8,783**
Rolland, Madeleine, 15,305
Roller, Elizabeth, 1,786
Rollins College, 5,360
Rollins College (FL), 12,612
Rollins, Helen de St. Prie (Wyman) [Mrs. Daniel] (1857-1949), 5,826
Rollins, Mabel (1909-), 11,661
Rollins, Mary Elizabeth (1818-1913). *See* Smith, Mary Elizabeth (Rollins) [Mrs.] Lightner [Mrs. Joseph] (1818-1913)
Rollins, Mary Emeline "Marie" (Hutchings) [Mrs. James Henry] (1881-), **16,810**
Rollins, Mrs. Roy, **9,717**
Rollinson, Mary Ann (1785-1848). *See* Whittingham, Mary Ann (Rollinson) [Mrs. Richard] (1785-1848)
Roloff, Leland H., 4,228
Rølvaag, Ella Valborg. *See* Tweet, Ella Valborg (Rølvaag)
Rølvaag, Jennie Marie (Berdahl) [Mrs. Ole Edvart], 8,784, 8,795
Rølvaag, Karl F., 9,286, 9,467, **9,474**
Rølvaag, Ole Edvart (1876-1931), 8,744, 8,763, 8,764, **8,784**, 8,786, 8,793, 8,815
Romaine, Jerome I., 12,705
Romance Island (book), 17,634
"Romance of Helen Trent, The" (radio program), 1,026
"Romance of the People, A" (pageant), 15,164
"Romance of Vicksburg (An Epic of the South), The" (poem), 9,590
Romances, 14,354
Romane, Elizabeth, **14,300**
Romans, Viola (Doudna) [Mrs. C. D.] (1863-1946), 14,014, **14,015**
Romantic Forty-Niner Club (CA), 1,355
Romanticism, 1,467
Romberg, Anna, 16,118
Romeo and Juliet (drama), 12,426
Romney, Amy Wilcken (Pratt) [Mrs. Gaskell] (1890-1927), **16,811**
Romney, George W., 7,914, 16,811
Romney, Lenore (LaFount) [Mrs. George], **7,914**
Ronalds, Mary Lorillard (?-1840), **12,607**
Ronalds, Thomas A., 12,607
Ronan, Henrietta, **15,701**
Ronyak, Catherine. *See* Walter, Catherine (Ronyak)
Ronzoni, Ethel, 14,943
Rood, Dorothy Dagmar (Bridgman) [Mrs. Frederick G.] Atkinson [Mrs. John H.] (1890-1965), 8,672, 9,130
Rood, Florence, 8,071
Rood, H. E., 12,437
Rood, Mrs. Ogden N., 12,208
Roody, Mrs. P. E., **16,284**

Rookwood Pottery Company (Cincinnati, OH), **13,837**, 13,838, 13,853, **13,856**
Roorbach, Sophia, 12,460
Roos, Audrey. *See* Roos, Audrey Kelley
Roos, Audrey Kelley, 6,060
Roos, Carl (1805-89), Family (MN), **9,322**
Roos, Carolina Gustafva (1853-1910). *See* Barnes, Carolina Gustafva (Roos) [Mrs. Frank] (1853-1910)
Roos, Celinda Armida (1866-84), 9,322
Roos, Clara Sofia Persdotter [Mrs. Carl] (1827-1910), 9,322
Roos, Cornelia Sophia (1856-ca. 1910), 9,322
Roos, Tialender Cassandra (1874-1964). *See* McNeilly, Tialender Cassandra (Roos) [Mrs. James] (1874-1964)
Roosevelt, Anna. *See* Boettiger, Anna (Roosevelt)
Roosevelt, Anna (1855-1931). *See* Cowles, Anna (Roosevelt) (1855-1931)
Roosevelt, Anna (1906-75). *See* Halsted, Anna (Roosevelt) (1906-75)
Roosevelt, Anna Eleanor (Roosevelt) [Mrs. Franklin Delano] (1884-1962), 64, 127, 194, 378, 575, 592, 1,564, 1,593, 2,097, 2,123, 2,163, 2,189, 2,207, 2,336, 2,340, 2,382, 2,451, 2,502, 2,509, 2,510, 2,640, 2,686, 2,704, 3,117, 3,303, 3,362, **3,569**, 3,772, 3,907, 3,995, 3,996, 4,030, 4,066, 4,067, 4,126, 4,233, 4,639, 4,909, 4,970, 5,124, 5,137, 5,459, 5,469, 5,828, 5,829, 5,863, 5,870, 6,023, 6,432, 6,630, 6,687, 6,907, 7,330, 7,549, 7,904, 8,678, 9,443, 9,779, 9,810, 9,823, 9,963, 10,035, 10,197, 11,144, 11,249, 11,479, 11,483, 11,485, 11,486, 11,487, 11,488, 11,489, 11,490, 11,494, **11,496, 11,497**, 11,499, 11,502, 11,553, 11,576, 11,662, 11,691, 11,812, 11,853, 11,871, 11,875, 11,897, 11,914, 11,916, 11,946, 11,954, 12,044, 12,044, 12,070, 12,071, 12,087, 12,704, 13,241, 13,391, 13,406, 13,532, 13,811, 14,046, 14,391, 14,504, 14,587, 14,819, 14,822, 16,157, 17,197, 17,448, 17,978, 18,006
Roosevelt, Anna (Hall), 11,487
Roosevelt, Belle Wyatt (Willard) [Mrs. Kermit] (1892-1968), 2,558
Roosevelt, Corinne (1861-1933). *See* Robinson, Corinne (Roosevelt) (1861-1933)
Roosevelt, Dorothy K., 8,139
Roosevelt, Edith Kermit (Carow) [Mrs. Theodore] (1861-1948), 194, 2,198, 2,499, 2,558, 2,559, 2,588, 2,596, 3,993, 4,007, 6,925, 12,043, 12,276, 12,299, 17,010
Roosevelt, Eleanor (Roosevelt) [Mrs. Franklin Delano] (1884-1962). *See* Roosevelt, Anna Eleanor (Roosevelt) [Mrs. Franklin Delano] (1884-1962)
Roosevelt, Elliot, 11,871
Roosevelt Family, 11,488, **11,498, 11,499**
Roosevelt, Franklin Delano (1882-1945), 48, 194, 255, 878, 1,340, 1,675, 2,214, 2,378, 2,382, 2,389, 2,405, 2,416, 2,510, 2,542, 2,640, 3,257, 3,260, 3,301, 3,437, 4,909, 5,307, 5,459, 6,432, 8,651, 9,160, 9,779, 11,249, 11,481, 11,482, 11,486, 11,488, 11,490, 11,491, 11,497, 11,498, 11,499, 11,502, 11,504, 11,576, 11,658, 11,853, 11,871, 11,883, 11,914, 11,917, 11,928, 11,999, 12,553, 12,704, 13,241, 13,318, 13,904, 14,587, 14,686
Roosevelt, Gladys L. [Miss], 10,919
Roosevelt, Harriet (Howland) [Mrs. James], **2,400**
Roosevelt, James, 2,400, 11,498, 11,499
Roosevelt, John A., 11,498
Roosevelt, Kermit (1889-1943), Family, **2,558**
Roosevelt, Mary Rebecca (Aspinwall), 11,498
Roosevelt, Mrs. Theodore, Jr., 5,123, 12,695, 13,272
Roosevelt, Rebecca Howland [Mrs. James] (1831-76), 11,498
Roosevelt, Sara (Delano) [Mrs. James] (1857-1941), 1,593, 11,481, 11,498, 11,499, 11,871
Roosevelt, Theodore (1858-1919), 169, 194, 1,437, 1,559, 1,666, 2,549, **2,559**, 2,878, 6,185, 7,847, 8,144, 8,702, 9,658, 11,499, **11,922**, 11,944, 11,969, 12,043, **12,299**
Roosevelt, Theodore, Jr. (1887-), 13,272
Roosevelt University, 4,030

Roosevelt University, Labor Education Division, faculty, 4,126
Roosevelt University Women's Scholarship Association, **4,031**
Roosevelt Women's Democratic Labor Club (NV), 10,680
Root, Anna Metcalf [Mrs. Azariah], 14,128
Root, Anne (Gales) [Mrs. Charles B.], **13,117**
Root, Azariah Smith (1862-1927), **14,128**
Root, Charles B. (1818-?), 13,117
Root, Elihu, 6,800, 13,272
Root, Grace C. [Mrs. Edward Wales], 2,649
Root, Irene Mix, 1,905
Root, Mabel Virginia (1870-1965), 11,555, **11,690**
Root, Margaret, 15,332
Root, Mary Elizabeth (Stafford) (1868-1953), 15,392
Root, Minnie Maes, 7,915
Root, Sarah C., **5,955**
Roots in Adobe (book), 11,226
Roper Hospital (Charleston, SC), 15,425
Roper Public Opinion Research Center (MA),
Ropes, Frances (1883-1969). *See* Williams, Frances (Ropes) [Mrs. Stillman P.] (1883-1969)
Ropes, Marion (1903-), 6,698
Ropes, William Ladd, 2,471, 6,256
Rorem, Marie, 8,760
Rorer, James, 6,863
Rorer, Sarah Tyson (Heston) (1849-1937), **6,863**
Rosa, the Life of an Italian Immigrant (book), 9,495
Rosary College (River Forest, IL), 4,316, 4,317
Rosary College (WI), presidents, 17,868
Rosberg, Anitra Joyce (Glueck) (1925-56), 6,260
Rose (slave, NC), 13,188
Rose, Alice M., **1,599**
Rose, Anna, 12,300
Rose, Anne (1851-?), 13,153
Rose, Annie (Ewer) [Mrs. William J.] (1867-1972), **7,490**
Rose, Arnold M., 8,603
Rose Bank (plantation, SC), 15,440
Rose Bud (periodical), 7,634
Rose, Caroline (Baer) [Mrs. Arnold M.] (1913-75), **8,603**
Rose, Charlotte "Lottie" [Miss], 11,791
Rose, Cornelia (Whipple) [Mrs. William Wilkins] Davis [Mrs. Francis Marion] (1845-84), 9,437
Rose, Elihu, 12,300
Rose, Ernestine Louise Siismondi (Potowski) [Mrs. William Ella] (1810-92), 3,886
Rose, Esther, 12,300
Rose, Eudora. *See* Knox, Eudora (Rose)
Rose Family, **1,291**
Rose Family, (MA), 7,659
Rose Family (NY), **11,791, 12,300**
Rose, Fannie Fargo, 1,291
Rose, Flora [Miss] (1874-1959), 11,521, 11,662, **11,691**, 11,756
Rose, Florence (1902?-69), 1,046, **7,287**, 7,320
Rose, Fried, Gallery, **2,806**
Rose Garden Club (GA), 3,187
Rose Garden Club (Reno, NV), **10,709**
Rose, Hilda, 12,464
Rose Hill (plantation, SC), 15,484
Rose Hill Plantation (VA), 3,348
Rose, James, 15,702
Rose, Julia Rutledge [Mrs. James] (?-1873), **15,702**
Rose Ladies Aid Society (Terre Haute, IN), **4,678**
Rose, Mabel, **11,692**
Rose, Mrs. Nathan, 9,083
Rose, Nancy, 12,300
Rose Resolution No. 106 (bill), 12,910
Rose, Sarah (Strong), 12,300
Rose, Simri (1799-1869), 13,153
Rose Temperance Society (NY), **12,608**
Roseanne (drama), 11,457
Rosebro, Viola, 5,861
Rosebrough Family (MS), 9,762
Rosebud Indian Agency (OK), 14,242
Rosebud Indian Reservation (WY), 10,433
Rosecrans, Adrian L., 1,050
Rosecrans, Ann D., 1,050
Rosecrans, Ann Eliza (Hegeman) [Mrs. William Starke], 1,050

Rosecrans Carl F., 1,050
Rosecrans Family, 1,050
Rosecrans, Lilian, 1,050
Rosecrans, Mary Louise, 1,050
Rosecrans, William Starke (1819-98), **1,050**
Rosecrest Cell, The, 17,793
Roseland PTA, 6,997
Rosemary Hall (CT), 1,837
Rosenbaum, Elsa. *See* Wiel, Elsa (Rosenbaum)
Rosenbaum, Jeanette W., **13,820**
Rosenberg, Abraham, **943**
Rosenberg, Adolph, 943
Rosenberg, Alice (Greenbaum) [Mrs. Abraham] (1876-1943), **943**
Rosenberg, Anna, 11,916
Rosenberg, Anna M., 12,069
Rosenberg, Anna Marie (Lederer) [Mrs. Julius]. *See* Hoffman, Anna Marie (Lederer) [Mrs. Julius] Rosenberg [Mrs. Paul]
Rosenberg, Edith. *See* Lindenberger, Edith (Rosenberg)
Rosenberg, Eth. *See* Clifford, Eth (Rosenberg)
Rosenberg, Ethel (Greenglass) [Mrs. Julius] (1916-53), 5,979, 6,079, 9,150, 17,617
Rosenberg, Julius, 5,979, 6,079, 9,150, 17,617
Rosenberg, Louise. *See* Berman, Louise (Rosenberg) Bransten
Rosenberg, Max, 943
Rosenberger, A. L., 4,828
Rosenberger, Homer Tope, 14,828
Rosenbloom, Clara, 11,693
Rosenbloom Family (NY), **11,693**
Rosenbloom, Isaac, 11,693
Rosenbloom, Marcus, 11,693
Rosenbusch, Louise A., 2,848
Rosencrantz, Esther (1876-1950), **1,377**
Rosenfeld, Sara Emelie (1895-). *See* Ehrmann, Sara Emelie (Rosenfeld) [Mrs. Herbert] (1895-)
Rosenman, Dorothy (Reuben) [Mrs. Samuel I.] (1900-), **11,914**
Rosenman, Samuel I., 11,914
Rosenshine, Annette (1880-1971), **754,** 755, 931
Rosenshine, Edith H. (1895-), **755**
Rosenthal, Eva, 13,604
Rosenthal, Jean (1912-69), **17,812**
Rosenthal, Mattie, 13,604
Rosenthal, Mina. *See* Weil, Mina (Rosenthal) [Mrs. Henry]
Rosenthal, Robert, **9,323**
Rosenthal, Virginia, **12,609**
Rosenwald, Adele. *See* Levy, Adele (Rosenwald)
Rosenwald, Edith. *See* Stern, Edith (Rosenwald)
Rosenwald Fellows, 9,583
Rosenwald Foundation, 3,773
Rosenwald, Julius (1862-1932), 5,469
Rosenwald, Marion. *See* Ascoli, Marion (Rosenwald)
Roses, 12,910
Rosicky, Rose (1875-1954), **10,527**
Rosquist, August, **3,715**
Ross, Ann Woods (1771-1805), 14,803
Ross, Arthur Leonard, 12,701
Ross, Betsy, **4,395**
Ross, Betsy [Mrs. John] (1752-1836). *See* Claypoole, Betsy [Mrs. John] Ross [Mrs. Joseph] Ashburn [Mrs. John] (1752-1836)
Ross, Charles G., 10,073
Ross-Craig, Stella (1906-), 10,151
Ross, Dorothy M. Filbey, 4,385
Ross, E. A., 3,010
Ross, Edgar A. (1850-1929), 13,153
Ross, Edith T., **4,147**
Ross, Elizabeth Magruder, **9,718**
Ross, Ellin A., 2,662
Ross, Emily (Lindsley) [Mrs. James Thorburn], 14,606
Ross Family (IL), **4,280**
Ross Family (OR), **14,606**
Ross Family (SC), **15,417**
Ross, Frank S., 14,774
Ross, Harold, 14,377
Ross, Harold W., 4,476
Ross, Harriet (Chaffee) [Mrs. Frederick R.], 1,786
Ross, Harriet Tubman [Mrs. John] (ca. 1815-1913).

See Tubman, Harriet. [Mrs. John] Ross [Mrs. Nelson] Davis (ca. 1815-1913)
Ross, Helen, 3,914
Ross, Helen (Forbes) [Mrs. E. A.], 3,010
Ross, Hermione. *See* Walker, Hermione (Ross)
Ross, Ishbel, **6,864**
Ross, James Thorburn, 14,606
Ross, Josephine (1906-72), **13,745**
Ross, Katherine (pseudonym). *See* Walter, Dorothy Blake (1908-)
Ross, Louisa A. *See* Shumway, Louisa A. (Ross) [Mrs. John P.]
Ross, Madeline Dane (1902-72), **17,716**
Ross, Margaret (Wheeler) [Mrs. Henry D.] (1867-?), **208,** 210
Ross, Marie (Marchand), 4,767
Ross, Marvin Chauncey, 5,525
Ross, Mary Jane [Miss] (1835-1922), 15,417
Ross, Mary Letitia [Miss] (1885-1971), **3,420**
Ross, Metta J. [Miss] (1890-), **8,191**
Ross, Mrs. J. C., 4,280
Ross, Mrs. Jesse Evans, 11,859
Ross, Nancy Wilson (1905-), 4,227, 8,001, 11,165, **16,167**
Ross, Nellie Tayloe [Mrs. William] (1876-1977), **8,253,** 17,885, 17,908, 17,915, 17,922, 17,941, **18,005**
Ross, Peter, 2,618
Ross, Virgilia Peterson (1904-66). *See* Peterson, Virgilia. Virgilia Peterson Ross. Princess Paul Sapieha. Virgilia Sapieha (1904-66)
Ross, Wilhelmina du Pont (1906-), 11,887
Ross, William, 15,332
Ross, William, 8,253
Rossbach, June (1919-). *See* Bingham, June (Rossbach) [Mrs. Jonathan] (1919-)
Rossetti, Christina, 1,467
Rossi, Alice S., 3,975
Rossi, Arline [Mrs.], 1,186
Rossi, Henrietta. *See* Ashton, Henrietta (Rossi) [Mrs. Thomas B.]
Rossier, Charlotte Beers [Mrs. Henry C.], 2,009
Rossiter, Henry C., 2,009
Rossiter, Thomas P., 2,009
Rossman, Sylvia (pseudonym). *See* Rothchild, Sylvia (1923-)
Rosson, Mary Emma, 16,125
Rost, Ida Sophie (1880-1966), **5,806**
Rotch, Charity (Rodman) (1766-1824), 15,294
Rotch, Elizabeth (Barker) (1764-1858), 15,294
Rotch, Elizabeth (Rodman) (1759-1828), 15,294
Rotch, Helen Gilman Lundington [Mrs. Arthur Grinnell] (?-ca. 1958), **6,865**
Rotch, Lydia (1770-1822). *See* Dean, Lydia (Rotch) (1770-1822)
Rotch, Mary [Miss] (1777-1848), 15,294
Roth, Edith (Douglass) (?-1948), 10,931
Roth, Lillian (1910-), 4,227
Roth, Linda Gage, 7,920
Roth, William M., 505
Rothchild, Sylvia (1923-), **6,074**
Rothermel, Winifred, 2,969
Rothhammer, Keena, 997
Rothrock, J. T., 15,326
Rothrock, Mrs. P. S., 3,219
Rotolante, Elizabeth Ann, 1,750
Rotterdam (ship), 8,518
Rotzien, Kate, 8,462
Roughnecks Home Companion, The (periodical), 3,711
Rouiez, L. [Mrs.], 1,576
Roulain, Tallulah, 15,506
Round Hill Manse (VA), 17,090
Round Lake Association (NY), 12,844
Round Robin Club (Hadley, MA). *See* Colonial Club (Hadley, MA)
"Round Robin Review," 14,041
Round Table Club (CO), **1,792**
Round Table Club (Crete, NE), 10,528
Round Table Club (Hastings, NE), 10,416
Round Table Club (Fargo, ND), 13,687
Round Table Conference on Sterility Testing (London, 1963), 13,259
Round Valley Reservation (CA), 740

Roundabout Club (NY), **12,804**
Roundy, Elizabeth Jeffords (Drake) [Mrs. Daniel] Davis [Mrs. Jared Curtis] (1830-1916), **16,812**
Roundy, Jared Curtis, 16,812
Rounthwaite, Isobelle (Sterling), 414
Rountree, Helen Clark, 16,872
Rourke, Ellen Mary (1885-1943?), **4,824**
Rouse, Benjamin (1795-1871), 13,932
Rouse, Rebecca C. [Mrs. Benjamin] (1799-1887), 13,932, 13,966
Rousseau Family (NV), **10,777**
Rousseau, Margaret Elizabeth "Bessie," 10,777
Rousseau, Margaret Elizabeth Cottle, 10,777
Rousseau, Mrs. J. A., 1,112
Rousseau, Mrs. James, **4,825**
Rousseau, Solomon, 10,777
Routh, Martha (Winter) (1743-1817), 14,847, **15,083**
Rover, Ruth (pseudonym). *See* Bailey, Margaret Jewett (Smith) [Mrs. William J.]
Rover's Club (Excelsior, MN), **9,324**
Row, Arthur William (1878-1961), **12,610**
Row, Peterson and Company, 14,476
Rowan, Andrew S., 1,338
Rowan Family (KY), **5,276**
Rowan, John (1773-1843), 5,276, 5,331
Rowan, John, Jr. (1804-55), 5,276, 5,277
Rowan, Josephine Morris [Mrs.] de Greayer [Mrs. Andrew S.], **1,338**
Rowan, Lorraine (1906-). *See* Cooper, Lorraine (Rowan) [Mrs. John Sherman] (1906-)
Rowan, May (1851?-?), 5,277
Rowan, Rebecca (Carnes) [Mrs. John, Jr.] (1813-97), 5,276, **5,277**
Rowan Vocal Studio (San Diego, CA), 1,192
Rowan, William Atkinson Hill (1838?-1900), 5,277
Rowans, Loleta (Levete) [Mrs. Thomas E., Jr.] (1871-1952), **1,192**
Rowe, Alma Lee, 17,125
Rowe, Mrs. Stanley, 11,913
Rowell, Alice. *See* Rowell, Alice Zbidovsky. [Mrs. Edward] Zbidovsky (?-1931)
Rowell, Alice Zbidovsky. [Mrs. Edward] Zbidovsky (?-1931), 4,099
Rowell, Chester Harvey (1867-1948), **756**
Rowell, Clara Maria (1847-1916), 2,002
Rowell, Eliza Benham [Mrs. Samuel Newell] (?-1864), 2,002
Rowell, Ella Maria (1852-1904). *See* Higgins, Ella Maria (Rowell) (1852-1904)
Rowell, Ellen Louisa (1852-1924), 2,002
Rowell, Frances Eliza (1856-1904). *See* Rowell, Frances Eliza (Rowell) [Mrs. George Addison] (1856-1904)
Rowell, Frances Eliza (Rowell) [Mrs. George Addison] (1856-1904), 2,002
Rowell, George Addison (1850-1904), 2,002
Rowell, George Berkeley (1815-84), Family (NH), **2,002**
Rowell, Hannah Chase [Mrs. Joseph], 2,002
Rowell, Hugh Grant, **12,858**
Rowell, Joseph, 2,002
Rowell, Joseph Cummings (1853-1938), **757**
Rowell, Lydia Dean. *See* Prevaux, Lydia Dean (Rowell) [Mrs. Francis Edward]
Rowell, Malvina Chapin (1843-70), 2,002
Rowell, Malvina Jerusha Chapin [Mrs. George Berkeley] (1816-1901), 2,002
Rowell, Marion Eliza (1848-1912), 2,002
Rowell, Martha Laurens (?-1842). *See* Locke, Martha Laurens (Rowell) [Mrs. Edwin] (?-1842)
Rowell, Mary Adelaide (1853-1932). *See* Stoltz, Mary Adelaide (Rowell) (1853-1932)
Rowell, Pearl Adell. *See* Chase, Pearl Adell (Rowell) Mikesell [Mrs. Lewis Nathaniel]
Rowell, Samuel Newell (1821-93), 2,002
Rowell, Thomas, 16,029
Rowell, William Edwards (1845-1916), 2,002
Rowes, Arlon, 16,889
Rowland, Eron Opha (Moore) [Mrs. Dunbar] (ca. 1863-1951), 9,719, 9,763
Rowland Family, 15,942
Rowland Hall School (UT), **16,954**
Rowland, Henrietta (Harrison) [Mrs. Henry A.] (1865-1950), 5,807

Rowland, Henry A., Jr. (1893-1921), 5,807
Rowland, Kate (Whitehead) (1838-?), **3,349**
Rowland, Margaret [Miss], **17,717**
Rowlands, Gena, 11,449
Rowley, Aaron, 5,362
Rowley, Adelaide A. (1905-), **9,325**
Rowley, Erastus (1814-97), 5,362
Rowley Family, 4,942, **5,362**
Rowley, Grace May (1887-?), **758**, 11,846
Rowley, Martha (Morris) [Mrs. Erastus], 5,362
Rowsell, Harriet, 11,077
Roxana (book), 1,750
Roxborough High School (PA), 15,046
Roxbury Township Historical Society (NJ), 11,181
Roy, Nancy Rebecca, **9,907**
Royal Academy of Music, 2,023
Royal Affinity, A (book), 6,118
Royal Air Force (England), 11,831, 17,450
Royal Astronomical Society of Great Britain, 2,041
Royal College of Music, 1,588
Royal, Denise (1935-), **14,438**
Royal, Emma Cornell, 14,536
Royal Family, The (drama), 12,367
Royal Flush Mine (NV), 10,728
Royal Gazette (SC), 15,419
Royal Geographical Society (England), 2,339
Royal Infirmary (Edinburgh, Scotland), 17,130
Royal Neighbors of America, Fifth District (NE), **10,412**
Royal Neighbors of America, Sixth District (NE), **10,412**
Royal Netherlands Flying School, 9,587
Royal Normal College for the Blind (London, England), 5,857
Royal School (HI), 3,632
Royal School of Art Needlework and School of Applied Design (England), **12,301**
Royal Society of Canada, 7,136
Royal South-Carolina Gazette, 15,419
Royall, Anne (Newport) [Mrs. William] (1769-1854), **2,560**, 9,849, 11,305, 11,821
Royall Family, 9,849
Royall, William, 9,849
Royalton Methodist Episcopal Church (MN), **9,326**
Royalton Methodist Episcopal Church (MN), Ladies Aid, 9,326
Royalty, 8,754, 11,853, 14,684, 14,838, 17,197
Royalty, Margaret (1895-1969). *See* Edwards, Margaret (Royalty) [Mrs. Herbert R.] (1895-1969)
Royce, Hattie, 975
Royce, Josiah, 759, 975, 1,340, 6,444, 6,843, 6,923
Royce, Katherine, 1,340
Royce, Ruth, 975
Royce, Sarah Eleanor (Bayliss) [Mrs. Josiah] (1819-91), **759**, **975**, **2,561**
Roycroft Enterprises, 11,435
Royden, A. Maude, 15,305
Royle, Selena, **18,006**
Royse, George, 10,054
Royse, Mintie Allen (1872-1963), **4,535**
Royster, Virginia. *See* Howell, Virginia Royster
Rozentāls, Magdelēna (1915-), **8,604**
Rozner, Sarah, 1,656
Ruan, Maria. *See* Harrington, Maria (Ruan) [Mrs. Purnell F.]
Rubel, Dorothy, 4,129
Rubenstein, Helena, 3,981
Rubenstein Music Club, 10,179
Rubert, Mrs. John, 8,254
Rubien, Gerel, 11,916
Rubin, Cora, 3,725
Rubio, Luiz, 15,743
Rubio, Mary Sullivan [Mrs. Luiz], 15,743
Rubke, Lulu Dorothea. *See* Landweer, Lulu Dorothea (Rubke)
Rublee, Juliet, 7,289
Ruckelshaus, Jill, 6,584
Ruckle Barbara (1734-1804). *See* Heck, Barbara (Ruckle) [Mrs. Paul] (1734-1804)
Rudd Methodist Episcopal Church (IA), 5,076
Ruddy, Ella (Giles) (1851-1915), **17,718**
Rudene, Elizabeth Cornelius [Mrs. J. O.] (1849-?), **17,330**

Ruder, Anna (Harrison), 4,961
Rudkins, Nettie Penny, 2,536
Rudolph, Adelaide [Miss] (1858-1953), **13,954**
Rudolph, Lucretia (1832-1918). *See* Garfield, Lucretia (Rudolph) [Mrs. James Abram] (1832-1918)
Rudolph, Wilma, 997
Rudulph, Marilou Alston [Mrs. Charles Murray], **3,079**
Rueger, Emily, 11,324
Rueter, Rosalie (1916-). *See* Aars, Rosalie (Rueter) [Mrs. Calvin Pernell] (1916-)
Ruff, Deborah (Pratt) [Mrs. Daniel] (1746-96), **7,674**
Ruffin Family, 3,437
Ruffner, Pattie (1875-1935). *See* Jacobs, Pattie (Ruffner) [Mrs. Solon Howard] (1875-1935)
Rufus, Carl, 7,916
Rufus, Maude [Mrs. Carl], **7,916**
Rugg, Mary Virginia (1881-). *See* Rice, Mary Virginia (Rugg) [Mrs. Robert Auerbach] (1881-)
Ruggieri, Clara Kimball [Mrs.] (1900?-), 16,965
Ruggles, Charles Herman (1789-1865), **12,611**
Ruggles, Samuel B., 12,611
Ruggles, Sarah Colden [Mrs. David], 12,611
Rugs, 7,012
Rugs, braided, **5,645**
Ruidoso (book), 16,497
Ruitter, Nelson, 14,592
Ruitter, Sophia, 14,592
Ruiz-de-Conde, Justina, 7,567
Rukeyser, Muriel (1913-), 6,045
Rule, Sheila. *See* Boyd, Sheila (Rule)
Ruleville Drew Sisterhood (MS), **13,821**
Rumbaugh, Nora, **14,655**
Rumbold, Caroline Thomas (1877-1949), 10,152, 10,157, 10,180
Rumbold, Charlotte, **10,180**
Rumely, Edward Aloysius (1877-?), 4,487
Rumely, Fanny (Scott) [Mrs. Edward Aloysius] (1883-), **4,487**
Rummel, Walter Morse, 12,361
Rumsey, Florence, 17,285, 17,301
Rumsey, Mary Harriman L. [Mrs. Charles Cary] (1881-1934), 6,949
Run into Oklahoma (1889), 14,201
Run Me a River (book), 5,264
Runaway Scrape, 16,035, 16,050
Rungius, Carl, 2,761
Rungius, Elisabeth (1879-1968). *See* Fulda, Elisabeth (Rungius) [Mrs. Carl] (1879-1968)
Runholt, Frances (Harris) [Mrs. Vernon], **8,517**
Runholt, Vernon, **8,517**
Runkle, Maggie, 5,158
Runkle, Ruth, 1,525
Runyon, Florabell (ca. 1906-), **8,605**
Runyon, Sarah C., 3,794
Rupert, Mrs. L. S., 3,764
Rural conditions, 62
Rural electrification, 10,075, 10,354
Rural Electrification Administration, insurance unit, 10,075
Rural Free (book), 6,064
Rural health services, **5,252**, 6,201, 8,598
Rural Home Conference (DC, 1934), 6,585
Rural population, 17,018
Rural schools, **3,244**, **8,423**, 9,570, 9,628, 13,701, 14,301, 17,487
Rural Sun, The (newspaper), 15,952
Rural teenagers, 13,189
Ruscha, Rae (1881-), 17,744
Rush, Alice [Mrs. William], 14,383
Rush, Anne Emily (1779-1850). *See* Cuthbert, Anne Emily (Rush) [Mrs. Ross] (1779-1850)
Rush, Benjamin (1745-1813), **15,084**
Rush, Grace Preyer, 13,890
Rush, Helen, 15,239
Rush, Julia (Stockton) [Mrs. Benjamin] (1759-1848), 15,084
Rush Medical College (Chicago, IL), students, 4,710
Rush, Olive (1873-1966), **2,807**
Rush, Rebecca (1743-93). *See* Stamper, Rebecca (Rush) [Mrs. Thomas] (1743-93)
Rush, Susanna (Hall) [Mrs. Joseph53Mrs. John] (1715?-95). *See* Morris, Susanna (Hall) [Mrs.

Joseph] Harvey [Mrs. John] Rush [Mrs. Richard] (1715?-95)
Rush, Verna, 10,211
Rushlight (periodical), 7,330
Rusk, Henry P., 4,386
Ruskin, Alexander, **5,906**
Ruskin commune (GA), 3,603
Ruskin, John (1819-1900), 5,906
Russel, Fannie Forbes Irvine [Mrs. James R.] (?-1934), **10,364**
Russel, M. Estelle, 14,814
Russell, Abby Osborne (Rust) [Mrs. Charles Edward] (1866-1901), 2,562
Russell, Alicia Hopton (?-1840). *See* Middleton, Alica Hopton (Russell) [Mrs. Arthur] (?-1840)
Russell, Allie (1872-?), **7,917**
Russell, Alys (Smith) [Mrs. Bertrand], 14,745
Russell, Amelia E., 7,043
Russell and Company (MA), 6,196
Russell, Ann, 9,274
Russell, Annie. [Mrs. Eugene Wiley] Presbry. [Mrs. Oswald] Yorke (1864?-1936), 3,100, 12,549, **12,612**
Russell, Bertrand, 11,895, 11,995, 12,400, 12,701, 14,745, 15,305, 15,564
Russell, Charles Edward (1860-1941), **2,562, 12,702**
Russell, Charles M., 10,347, 10,363
Russell, Cornelia, **9,908**
Russell, Edith (1898-1967). *See* Harrington, Edith (Russell) [Mrs. Herschel R.] (1898-1967)
Russell, Eliza (Hall), 1,973
Russell, Elizabeth. *See* Hendee, Elizabeth (Russell)
Russell, Ethelmary (Day), 9,709
Russell Family, 12,314
Russell Family (CT), **1,973**
Russell, Fanny [Miss], 1,973
Russell, Florence (Garfield) [Mrs. George Milo], 9,091
Russell, Harriet Williams (1844-1926). *See* Strong, Harriet Williams (Russell) [Mrs. Charles Lyman] (1844-1926)
Russell, Helen (Crocker) (?-1966), **760**
Russell, Ina Dillard, 3,071
Russell, Irwin, 9,720, 9,769
Russell, James E., 11,864
Russell, Jane [Mrs.], 15,288
Russell, Leila A. [Miss] (1871-1963), **15,816**
Russell, Lillian Helen Louise (Leonard). [Mrs. Henry] Braham [Mrs. Edward] Solomon [Mrs. John Haley Augustin] Chatterton [Mrs. Alexander Pillock] Moore (1861-1922), **4,826**, 16,149
Russell, Lily (McIlroy) [Mrs. Junius B.] (1887-1958), 16,331, **16,382**
Russell, Margaret Rowena. *See* Benning, Margaret Rowena (Russell) [Mrs. Augustus H.]
Russell, Marian, 8,683
Russell, Mary, 3,114
Russell, Mary. *See* Foster, Mary (Russell) [Mrs. Isaac]
Russell, Mary Elizabeth [Miss], **9,720**, 9,769
Russell, Maud, 8,949, 9,119
Russell, Maud (1893-), **8,885**
Russell, Mehitabel (1734-1817). *See* Wadsworth, Mehitabel (Russell) [Mrs. Jeremiah] (1734-1817)
Russell, Nancy, 12,176
Russell, Penelope, 2,188
Russell, Richard B., 15,755
Russell, Rose, 11,774
Russell Sage Foundation, 1,327, 6,130, 7,198, 7,315, 8,142, 8,674
Russell, Seneca Freeman, 8,154
Russell, W. H., 8,588
Russellville Female College (KY), trustees, 5,258
Russia, 6,099, 11,927
 American ambassadors to, 2,590
 American diplomats in, 6,912, 12,640, 15,674
 American travelers in, 6,099, 11,864
 collective settlements, 8,072
 convict labor, 6,106
 English language, study and teaching, 8,090
 foreign relations, 12,012
 palaces, 6,912
 political prisoners, personal narratives, 6,106
 reconstruction (1914-1939), 12,487

Revolution (1917), 9,888
social life and customs, 6,912
women, education, 12,497
World War I, hospitals, 6,644
World War II, civilian relief, 9,218
Young Women's Christian Association, 12,722
"Russian Journals," 12,360
Russian Myth, The (book), 12,487
Russian Orthodox Greek Catholic Church of North America, Diocese of Alaska, **2,563**
Russo-Japanese War (1904-1905), war work, Red Cross, 13,729
Rust, Abby Osborne (1866-1901). *See* Russell, Abby Osborne (Rust) [Mrs. Charles Edward] (1866-1901)
Rust, Clara H. (?-1978), **144**
Rust, Daniel, **7,429**
Rust, Eliza Burgess, 12,790
Rust, Elizabeth, **7,429**
Rust, Horatio Nelson (1828-1906), **1,481**
Rust, Lura Ann (1843-76). *See* Walcott, Lura Ann (Rust) [Mrs. Charles D.] (1843-76)
Rust, Mary, 9,962
Rust, Mary O., 6,310
Rust, Mrs. Lawrence, 11,827
Ruter, Clara, 9,323
Rutgers Female College (NY), 11,539, 12,128, 12,283, 12,740
faculty, **11,084**
presidents, 12,470
students, 11,539
Rutgers Female Institute (NY). *See* Rutgers Female College (NY)
Rutgers State University, faculty, 8,097
Rutgers University (New Brunswick, NJ), 10,931, 10,932, 10,955, 11,021, 17,853
faculty, 10,943, **10,971**
presidents, **10,928, 10,929**
Ruth, Babe, 11,405
Ruth Flower, Institute of Cosmetology, 10,191
Ruth Hall (book), 5,694
Ruth, Iva (Haight), **16,435**
Ruth White Gallery (NY), **2,808**
Rutherford, Elizabeth (1817-99). *See* Savage, Elizabeth (Rutherford) [Mrs. Thomas Stoughton] (1817-99)
Rutherford, Frances A., 7,920
Rutherford, Lamar. *See* Lipscomb, Lamar (Rutherford).
Rutherford, Lamar [Miss], 3,111
Rutherford, Mildred Lewis [Miss] (1851-1928), **3,080$** 3142, 12,120, 15,218, 5011
Rutherford, Ruth I., 8,174
Rutherfurd Family (NJ), **11,128**
Rutherfurd, John (1760-1840), 11,128
Rutherfurd, Robert Walter (1788-1852), 11,128
Rutherfurd, Sabina Morris (1789-1857), 11,128
Rutland Corner House (MA), **6,866**
Rutland Women Reformatory (VT), **17,020**
Rutledge, Benjamin Huger, 15,517
Rutledge, Edward (1749-1800), **15,513, 15,703**
Rutledge, Eleanor Maria (Middleton) [Mrs. Benjamin Huger], 15,517
Rutledge Family (SC), 13,137
Rutledge, Harriott Horry (1832-1912). *See* Ravenel, Harriott Horry (Rutledge) (1832-1912)
Rutledge, Sarah, 15,507, **15,513**, 15,703
Ruttenberg, Harold J. (1914-), **15,333**
Rutter, Charles, 10,983
Rutter, Elizabeth Wills (1839-1918). *See* Hobart, Elizabeth Wills (Rutter) [Mrs. William Mintzer] (1839-1918)
Rutter, Isabel (Page) [Mrs. Robert Louis], 17,378
Rutter, Robert Louis, 17,378
Ruttkay, Louise (Kossuth), **11,025**
Ruuttila, Julia (Godman) Bertram Eaton (1907-), **14,592, 14,656**
Ruxton, George, 10,357
Ryan, Abram J., 54
Ryan, Agnes [Mrs. Henry Bailey Stevens] (1878-1954), **6,867**
Ryan, Anne (1889-1954), **11,145**
Ryan, Beatrice Judd [Mrs.] (ca. 1880-1966), **761,** 1,265

Ryan, Dennis, 8,934
Ryan, Gertrude W., 8,934
Ryan, John, 15,332
Ryan, Martha, **13,118**
Ryan, Mary A. (Holland), 11,602
Ryan, Robert, 12,367
Ryan, Stephen D., 8,934
Rydell, Forbes (pseudonym). *See* Forbes, DeLoris Florine Stanton (1923-)
Rydell, Helen, 6,060
Ryder Community Center (Chicago, IL). *See* Clarence Darrow Community Center (Chicago, IL)
Ryder, Emma B., 11,547
Ryder Memorial Hospital (PR), 6,987
Ryder, Ruth. *See* St. John, Ruth (Ryder)
Ryerson, Margery (1886-), **2,809**
Ryerson, Mrs. Arthur, 4,067
Ryker, Mrs. Darrell W., **9,721**
Ryland Family (GA), 3,373
Ryland, Josephine (Boulware) [Mrs. Robert], 3,373
Ryland, Robert, 3,373
Rylander Family (TX), 16,269
Rypins, Mrs. Isaac L., 9,251
Rypka Zdeňka (Sojka) [Mrs. Walter E.] (1894-1975), **9,510**
S Bar S Ranch (NV), 10,784
S. C. Edward School of Nursing (Fort Smith, AR), 243
"SDS New Left Notes," 10,020
SPARS. *See* United States (government), Women's Reserve of the Coast Guard Reserve
"S. P. C., The. A Bicycle Romance," 2,401
S.S. Belgenland (ship), 4,375
S.S. Hope (ship), 5,398
S.S. Mauretania (ship), 11,614
S.S. Titanic (ship), 11,614
Saar Plebiscite, The (book), 6,935
Saarinen, Aline [Mrs. Eero] (1914-72), **2,810, 2,811**
Saarinen, Eero, **2,811**
Saarinen, Lily Swann, **2,812**
Sabean, Samuel C., 9,139
Sabin, Ara W., 16,763
Sabin, Charlotte, 17,033
Sabin, Dorothy Virginia (Forbes) [Mrs. Joseph Percy], **12,613**
Sabin, Ellen Clara, 17,586, 17,689, 17,844
Sabin Family (VT), **17,033**
Sabin, Florence Rena (1871-1953), **1,738,** 1,779, 1,786, **2,090,** 2,668, 5,724, 7,255, **7,288,** 12,074, **14,900**
Sabin, Henry, 4,853
Sabin, Louisa, 17,033
Sabin, Lucy Marie (Canfield) [Mrs. John W.] Young [Mrs. Ara W.] (1846-1915). *See* Margetts, Lucy Marie (Canfield) [Mrs. John W.] Young [Mrs. Ara W.] Sabin [Mrs. Phillip H.] (1846-1915)
Sabin, Mrs. Charles, 11,253
Sabin, Pauline Morton, 11,621
Sabine, Julia, 11,144
Sabine, Julia A., 17,033
Sabloff, Janet, **8,675**
Sabloniere, Margrit, 2,872
Sac Indians, 7,224, 14,241
Sacajawea (ca. 1786-1812), 2,173, 10,326, 14,714, 17,413, **17,736,** 17,908
Sacajawea Statue Association, 14,549
Sacajawea, The Girl Nobody Knew (book), 17,374
Sacajaweah (ca. 1786-1812). *See* Sacajawea (ca. 1786-1812)
Sacco and Vanzetti case, 2,483, 6,565, 6,669, 6,974, 8,142, 11,867
Sachs, Alice, 14,324
Sachs, Emanie (Nahm) (1893-). *See* Arling, Emanie (Nahm) Sachs (1893-)
Sachs, Mary, 15,097
Sachs, Paul Joseph, 11,897
Sachs, Theodore, 3,813
Sachse, Nancy A., 17,771
Sackett, Emma [Mrs.], **4,827**
Sackett, Fannie (1865-1972). *See* Smith, Fannie (Sackett) [Mrs. William B.] (1865-1972)
Sackett, Jane Ann. *See* Pearce Jane Ann (Sackett) [Mrs. Christopher Gardner)

Sackett, Leonard, 13,682
Sacks, Albert, 6,633
Sackville-West, Victoria, 6,834
Sacramento Orphanage and Children's Home (CA), 1,327
Sacramento Union (CA), 1,166
Sacred Heart Academy and Junior College (Cullman, AL), 24
Sacred Heart Catholic Church (White Deer, TX), 16,307
Sacred Heart Convent, Provincial House (Groton, MA), **7,033**
Sacred Heart School (MO), 10,134
Sacred Scriptures and Religious Philosophy (book), 16,645
Saddle Your Dreams (ms), 9,745
Sadilek, Olga Frances (1878-1952). *See* Stastny, Olga Frances (Sadilek) [Mrs. Charles] (1878-1952)
Sadler, David Hope, Family (SC), **15,817**
Sadler, Elizabeth Jane. *See* Roberts, Elizabeth Jane (Sadler) [Mrs. John]
Sadler, Nellie D., 10,395
Sadtler, Amy (1857-1942). *See* Albrecht, Amy (Sadtler) (1857-1942)
Safe Deposit Company (NY), **11,458**
Safe, Harriet Ives (Gammell) [Mrs. Thomas], **6,591**
Safe, Thomas, 6,591
Safety education, **3,976, 3,977, 3,978,** 12,042
"Safety on the Streets," 3,978
Safford, Clare L. (Wade), 10,392
Safford, Mary Augusta (1851-1927), 4,958
Sag Harbor (drama), 11,457
Sage College for Women, 11,660, 11,674, 11,743
Sage, Elizabeth Manning, **12,614**
Sage, Frances (ca. 1862-1949). *See* Bradley, Frances (Sage) [Mrs. Horace James] (ca. 1862-1949)
Sage, Henry W., 11,531
"Sage in Meditation, The" (article), 2,658
Sage, Margaret (1811-?). *See* Putnam, Margaret (Sage) (1811-?)
Sage, Margaret Olivia (Slocum) [Mrs. Russell B.] (1828-1918), 11,680, 11,742
Sagebrush Symphony Orchestra (OR). *See* Portland Junior Symphony (OR)
Sagen, Ethel (Ames), 762
Sageng, Ole O. (1871-1963), 9,315, **9,327**
Sager, Catherine. *See* Pringle, Catherine (Sager)
Sager Family, 17,422
Sager, Matilda Jane. *See* Delaney, Matilda Jane (Sager)
Sager, Sadie Harris, 9,722
Sager, Sarah Knox (Harris), **9,722**
Saginaw County League of Women Voters (MI), **8,360**
Saginaw Department of Recreation (MI), 8,360
Saginaw Garden Club (MI), 8,360
Saginaw Valley and St. Louis Railroad, 8,354
Saginaw Welfare League (MI), 8,360
Sagwick, Chief, 16,486
Saiki, Sue [Mrs. Taro "Ty"] (1919-), **8,509**
Saiki, Taro "Ty," 8,509
Sailing ships, 1,505
Sailors, 11,199
St. Agnes College (Memphis, TN), faculty, 15,964
St. Agnes Hospital (NC), 13,390, 13,444, 13,559
St. Agnes Service Board (NC), **13,559**
St. Aladie, Sister, **9,328**
Saint Aloysius Academy (OH), **13,752**
St. Aloysius Military Academy (OH), 13,752
St. Andre Convent (ME), 5,596
St. Andrew's Church at Northford (CT), Ladies Association, 1,889
St. Andrews Episcopal Church (Ann Arbor, MI), **7,905**
St. Andrew's Episcopal Church of Meriden (CT), Ladies Sewing Society, 1,889
St. Andrew's Mission (MA), Junior Girls' Club, **7,107**
Saint Andrew's Parish (MS), Woman's Auxiliary, **9,723**
St. Anne's parish (Fort Chartres, IL), 3,871
St. Ansgar church, 8,774
St. Ansgar Seminary, faculty, 8,755
St. Ansgarius Episcopal Church (Minneapolis, MN), **9,329**

St. Anthony Park Association (St. Paul, MN), **9,330**
St. Anthony Park School Union (St. Paul, MN), 9,330
St. Anthony Park Women's Association (St. Paul, MN). *See* St. Anthony Park Association (St. Paul, MN)
St. Augustine's College (Raleigh, NC), 16,022
St. Augustine's Normal and Collegiate Institute (Raleigh, NC), 2,130
St. Augustine's School (Raleigh, NC), 13,444
St. Barnabas Guild for Nurses, **13,893**
St. Barnard, Hulda Theodate (1837-1910). *See* Hollands, Hulda Theodate (St. Barnard) (1837-1910)
Saint Benedict Academy (PA), 15,211
St. Benedict College of Ferdinand (IN), 4,509
St. Benedict's Convent (St. Cloud, MN), **8,848**
St. Catherine's Normal Institute (MD), Holy Cross Alumnae Association, **5,778**
"St. Cecilia" (painting), 12,543
St. Cecilia Society (Charleston, SC), 15,515
St. Charles County Historical Society (MO), 10,135
St. Charles Orpheum Theatre (LA),6,882
St. Charles Parish (LA), 5,409
St. Clair (pseudonym). *See* King, Carolyn St. Clair
St. Clair Bridge Corporation, 15,222
St. Clair, Julia, 11,405
St. Clair, Saide Daniel, 2,125
St. Clara College, faculty, 17,868
St. Clare Convent of the Poor Clares (Omaha, NE), 10,611
St. Cloud Democrat (MN), 9,241
St. Cloud Hospital (MN), 9,323
St. Cloud State Teacher's College (MN), 8,924
St. Cloud State Teachers College (MN), alumnae, 8,517
St. Cloud Visitor (MN), 9,241
St. Croix Bible Society (WI), 8,914
St. Croix-Pierce Counties Federated Women's Club (WI), **17,864**
St. Croix River, 9,096
St. David's Parish (SC), 15,522
St. David's Presbyterian Church (San Francisco, CA), Women's Guild, 763
St. David's Society (Charleston, SC), **15,514**, 15,522
St. Denis, Ruth. [Mrs. Edwin M.] Shawn (1880-1968), **764**, 1,039, **1,051**, 1,081, 1,082, 2,968, 4,384, 7,167, 7,214, 12,365
St. Edward School of Nursing (AR), 243
St. Elizabeth Day Nursery (Chicago, IL), 4,286
St. Frances Academy (Baltimore, MD), 5,831
St. Francis Health Resort (Denville, NJ), 10,893
St. Francis Hospital (WV), 17,487
St. Francis Indians, 5,666
St. Francis of Assisi, 3,201
St. Francis Orphanage (Watsonville, CA), 1,327
St. Francis Xavier College for Women (Chicago, IL), 4,050
St. Geme, Henri de, **5,490**
St. George, Katharine Price Collier [Mrs.] (1896-), 1,605, **11,695**
St. George's Episcopal Church (Macomb, IL), Children's Guild of St. George's Mission. *See* St. George's Episcopal Church (Macomb, IL), St. Agness Guild
St. George's Episcopal Church (Macomb, IL), St. Agness Guild, **4,292**
St. Helena Parish (LA), 5,409
St. Helen's Club (WA), 17,135, **17,138**
St. Helen's Hall (OR), 14,515
St. Hilda's School (Wuchang, China), 14,393
St. Hill, Shirley (1924-). *See* Chisholm, Shirley (St. Hill) (1924-)
St. James African Methodist Episcopal Church (St. Paul, MN), 9,259
St. James Episcopal Church (Marshall, MN), St. Cecelia Guild, **9,331**
St. Johannes Church (Minneapolis, MN), 9,300
St. John, Francis R., 11,936
St. John, Ruth (Ryder), 8,174
St. John's Chapel (Charleston, SC), 15,454
St. John's Church (Baltimore, MD), Altar Society, 5,826

St. John's Episcopal Church (Williamsboro, NC), 12,988
St. John's Evangelical Lutheran Church (SC), Ladies Aid Society, **15,704**
St. John's Lutheran Church (Burns, MN), 8,389
St. John's Lutheran Church (Charleston, SC), 15,495
St. John's Methodist Church (St. Louis, MO), 9,991
St. John's School (Tarrytown-on-Hudson, NY), 7,347
St. John's University (MN), 9,192
    faculty, 11,988
St. Johnsbury Academy (VT), 17,035
St. Joseph Academy (IL), 4,284
St. Joseph Academy (OH), 13,903
St. Joseph Academy (Titusville, PA), 14,794
St. Joseph Home for Aged (West Point, NE), 17,820
St. Joseph Home for the Aged and Crippled (Chicago, IL), 4,286
St. Joseph Hospital (NE), 10,508
St. Joseph Hospital (WV), 17,487
St. Joseph Trail, 12,482
St. Joseph's Academy (Crookston, MN), 8,425
St. Joseph's Academy (St. Paul, MN), 9,022, 9,490
St. Joseph's Academy (MO), 10,138
St. Joseph's Convent (Stillwater, MN), 9,022
St. Joseph's Home for Orphans (NY), 12,767
St. Joseph's Hospital (St. Paul, MN), 9,490
St. Joseph's parish (Prairie de Rocher, IL), 3,871
St. Joseph's School (CA), 1,066
St. Joseph's school (MD), 5,800
St. Jude's Protestant Episcopal Church (NY), 12,660
St. Katherines School (TN), 9,537
St. Lawrence Girls High School (Santa Clara, CA), 1,534
St. Lawrence University (NY)
    alumnae, 17,852
    archives, **11,398**
St. Lawrence University (NY), College of Letters and Sciences, 11,398
St. Lawrence University (NY), Universalist Theological School, alumnae, 11,391, 11,398
St. Levens Lodge (VA), 17,099
St. Louis American (MO), 10,191
St. Louis Association of Colored Women's Clubs (MO), **10,205**
St. Louis Board of Education (MO), 10,149
St. Louis Button Company (MO), 9,918
St. Louis Council for Child Study and Parent Education (MO), 10,168
St. Louis County Child Welfare Board (MN), 8,942
St. Louis County Historical Society (MN), 8,964, 9,208
St. Louis encephalitis, 10,209
St. Louis Female Hospital (MO), 9,909
St. Louis Hotel, 5,514
St. Louis Louisana Purchase Exposition (MO, 1904), 2,859, 9,334, 9,858
St. Louis Louisiana Purchase Exposition (MO, 1904), Educational Exhibit, **10,043**
St. Louis Police Commission (MO), 9,956
St. Louis Woman (drama), 3,285
St. Louis Women's Democratic Club (MO), 10,048
St. Louis World's Fair (1904), 10,201
St. Luke's Hospital (CO), School of Nursing, **1,739**
St. Luke's Hospital (Cedar Rapids, IA), 5,081
St. Luke's Hospital (MN), 8,440
St. Luke's Hospital (St. Louis, MO), 10,146
St. Luke's Hospital (New York, NY), 8,980
St. Luke's Hospital (New York, NY), Training School for Nurses, 12,140
St. Luke's Hospital and School of Nursing (SD), **15,842**
St. Luke's Mission (Neillsville, WI), 17,518
Saint Luke's School of Nursing (Racine, WI), **17,568**
St. Margaret's House, **16,027**
St. Margaret's School (Boise, ID), **3,717**
St. Mark's African Methodist Episcopal Church (Duluth, MN), **9,332**
St. Mark's African Methodist Episcopal Church (Duluth, MN), Sarah Allen Missionary Society, 9,332
St. Mark's Church (St. Paul, MN), St. Mark's Guild, 9,301
St. Mark's Episcopal Church (NY), 12,489
St. Mark's Episcopal Church (Portland, OR), 14,683

St. Mark's Lutheran Church (San Francisco, CA), **1,364**
St. Martha's House (PA), 7,307
Saint Martin's Episcopal Church (Providence, RI), Daughters of Hope, 15,380
St. Martin's Press, 14,438
St. Mary Hospital (WV), 17,487
St. Mary Street College Settlement (PA),
St. Mary's Academy (Denver, CO), **1,740**
St. Mary's Academy (NM), 1,790
St. Mary's Academy (Portland, OR), 14,493, 14,502
St. Mary's Catholic Church (Aberdeen, SD), 15,839
Saint Mary's College (IN), 4,640
St. Mary's College (NC), 13,032, 13,420, 13,430, 13,438, 13,446, 13,468, 13,480, **13,560**, 13,618
St. Mary's College (Raleigh, NC), archives, **13,628**
St. Mary's Convent (San Leandro, CA), 1,387
St. Mary's Convent of the Sacred Heart Mission (OK), 14,225
St. Mary's Hall (Sonoma, CA), 376
St. Mary's Hall (Faribault, MN), 8,924, 9,422, 9,438
St. Mary's Hall (NJ), 9,613, 13,610
St. Mary's High School and Center for Learning (Chicago, IL), **4,148**
St. Mary's High School and Center for Learning (Chicago, IL), Father's Club, 4,148
St. Mary's High School and Center for Learning (Chicago, IL), Mother's Club, 4,148
St. Mary's Hospital (Chicago, IL), 15,181
St. Mary's Hospital (Minneapolis, MN), **8,529**
Saint Mary's Hospital (Reno, NV), **10,732**
Saint Mary's Hospital (Racine, WI), **17,569**
Saint Mary's Hospital Training School (Racine, WI), **17,569**
St. Mary's Junior College (NC), 13,466
Saint Mary's Nurses Alumnae Association (WI), 17,569
St. Mary's School (Knoxville, IL), 3,911
St. Mary's School (Raleigh, NC). *See* St. Mary's College (Raleigh, NC)
Saint Mary's School of Nursing (Milwaukee, WI), **17,847, 17,848**
St. Mary's Seminary (Indianapolis, IN), 4,604
St. Mary's Seminary (MD), 5,744
St. Michael's Parish (SC), 15,645
St. Nicholas Girl program (DC), 3,027
St. Nicholas Magazine (periodical), 1,421, 7,398, 11,157
Saint Nicholas School (NY), 12,733
St. Olaf College (Northfield, MN), 8,754, 8,773, **8,811**, 8,812, 8,861
    alumnae, 8,763, 8,792
    deans, **8,746**
    faculty, 8,755, **8,759**, 8,766, 8,788, 8,793, **8,806, 8,807, 8,809, 8,814, 8,815**
    registrar, **8,808**
    students, 8,740, **8,800**, 8,806, 8,807, **8,810**
St. Olaf Lutheran Choir (MN), 8,792, 8,814
St. Olav Medal, 8,777
St. Paul and Ramsey County War History Committee (MN), **9,333**
St. Paul Chamber of Commerce (MN), **9,334**, 9,435
St. Paul Choral Club (MN), **9,335**
St. Paul City Hospital (MN), 247
St. Paul City Planning Board (MN), **9,336**
St. Paul Clothing Center (MN), 9,104
St. Paul College Club (MN), 8,902
St. Paul College Club (MN), Creative Writing Branch, 8,902
St. Paul College of Law (MN), alumnae, 9,525
St. Paul Commercial Club (MN), 9,334
St. Paul Community Chest (MN), 9,104
St. Paul Council of Churches (MN), **9,305**
St. Paul Council of Human Relations (MN), 8,591
St. Paul Daily News (MN), 8,956
St. Paul Episcopal Church (Virginia City, MT), 10,331
Saint Paul Family Centered Project (MN), **8,676**
St. Paul Federation of Teachers (MN), 8,102, 8,129
St. Paul Female Seminary (MN), 9,317
Saint Paul Forty Years Ago, A Personal Reminiscence, 13,833
St. Paul Free Dispensary (MN), 8,645
St. Paul Free Medical Dispensary (MN), 9,442

St. Paul Guild of Music Teachers, Inc. (MN), 8,905
St. Paul Hermitage (IN), 4,466
St. Paul Ladies Auxiliary (MN), **9,337**
St. Paul Lutheran Church (Fredrick, SD), 15,839
St. Paul Municipal Chorus (MN), **9,338**
St. Paul Protestant Orphan Asylum (MN), **9,339**
St. Paul Public Library (MN), 14,605
Saint Paul Reading Circle (MN), **9,340**
St. Paul Resettlement Committee (MN), **9,341**
St. Paul Resettlement Hostel (MN), 9,341
St. Paul School of Fine Arts (MN), 9,170
St. Paul Teachers Federation (MN), 9,467
St. Paul Trust Company (MN), 8,954
St. Paul Urban League (MN), **9,342**
St. Paul's Chapel (New York, NY), Female
    Missionary Society, 12,088
St. Paul's Episcopal Church (New Orleans, LA),
    5,492
St. Paul's Episcopal Church (Oregon City, OR),
    Women's Guild, **14,439**
St. Paul's Evangelical Church (Clay Center, NE),
    Woman's Missionary Society, **10,593**
St. Paul's Evangelical Lutheran Church (Aberdeen,
    SD), 15,839
St. Paul's Institute (Tarsus, Turkey), 8,996
St. Paul's Priory (St. Paul, MN), **9,489**
St. Paul's United Methodist Church (Ithaca, NY),
    11,624
St. Paul's United Methodist Church (Ithaca, NY),
    Loyal Daughters' Class, 11,624
St. Paul's United Methodist Church (Ithaca, NY),
    Sabbath School Society, 11,624
St. Paul's United Methodist Church (Ithaca, NY),
    Women's Society of Christian Service, 11,624
St. Peter Tribune (MN), 9,000
St. Peter's Mission (MT), 10,333
St. Peter's Presbyterian Church (Rochester, NY),
    11,647
St. Peter's School (SC), 15,412
St. Philip's College (San Antonio, TX), **16,318**
St. Pierre, Sister, 16,019
St. Sigfrid's Episcopal Church (St. Paul, MN), **9,343**
Saint Simon's Island (GA), 3,132, 3,478
St. Stephen's Catholic Church (Anoka, MN), 8,389
St. Teresa's Motherhouse and Novitiate
    (Germantown, NY), **11,469**
St. Therese Academy (OH), 13,903
St. Thomas Episcopal Church (Chicago, IL), 3,934
St. Timothy's School (Baltimore, MD), 2,345
St. Timothy's School (Catonsville, MD), 5,807
St. Ursula Academy (Cincinnati, OH), **13,867**
St. Ursula Convent (Cincinnati, OH), **13,867**
St. Vincent Sisters, Daughters of the Cross Convent
    (Shreveport, LA), **5,556**
St. Vincent's Academy (Helena, MT), 10,237
St. Vincent's Female Orphan Society (SC), **15,705**
St. Vincent's Hospital (NY), 11,298
St. Vincent's Orphanage (Chicago, IL), 4,286
Saints, 4,447, **4,645**, 5,847, 10,144, 13,752
Saladin, 1138-1193, A Biography (book), 17,723
Salaman, Nina Davis (1877-1925), 7,545
Salamanca, Lucy, **2,564**
Salammbô; or, The Sacred Veil (drama), 2,339
Salava, Bozena [Miss], 4,054
Salazar, Fanny Zampini, 4,631
Sale, Elizabeth, **14,889**
Sale, Mary Frances. *See* Edmonson, Mary Frances
    (Sale) [Mrs. Albert G.]
Salem Academy (NC). *See* Salem College (NC)
Salem Academy and College (NC). *See* Salem
    College (NC)
Salem Boarding School (NC). *See* Salem College
    (NC)
Salem Catalog, The (Salem Academy and College,
    NC), 13,634
Salem College (NC), 2,989, 6,662, 13,347, 13,477,
    13,528, 13,558, 13,607, 13,610, 13,618, 13,632,
    13,633, 15,737
  alumnae, 13,245
  faculty, 13,632
Salem College (NC), Alumnae Association, 13,633
Salem Congregational Church (Cambria, MN), **9,344**
Salem Evangelical Church (NE), Platte River
    Conference, Woman's Missionary Society, **10,594**

Salem Female Academy (NC). *See* Salem College
    (NC)
Salem Female Anti-Slavery Society (MA), 7,430
Salem Female Charitable Society (MA), 7,365, **7,431**
Salem Female Employment Society (MA), **7,432**
Salem Female School (MA), **7,433**
Salem Hospital (OR), 14,625
Salem Lutheran Church (MN), Ladies Aid, 9,271
Salem Normal School (MA), 6,188, 7,340
Salem Woman's Club (NY), 11,696
Salem Women's Club (MA), **7,434**
Salem Women's Indian Association (MA), 7,435
Salem Young Women's Association (MA), 7,436
Salemite, The (Salem Academy and College, NC),
    13,634
Sales, Estella, **5,387**
Saleswomen, 11,065
Salinas, Maria Lorenza, 404
Salinas, Pedro, 5,732
Salisbury, D'Estaing (?-1813), 9,345
Salisbury, Helen, **4,828**
Salisbury, Hiram, 9,345
Salisbury, Jane [Miss], 4,781
Salisbury, Leah, 5,465
Salisbury, Lucy (1832-1908). *See* Doolittle, Lucy
    (Salisbury) [Mrs. Myrick H.] (1832-1908)
Salisbury, Marguerite Scott [Miss], **6,868**
Salisbury Post, 13,001
Salisbury, Rebekah Scott (Dean) (1812-43), 7,625
Salisbury, Sarah Brayton (Whipple) [Mrs. Hiram],
    9,345
Salisbury, Susan E. (1854-1930), Family, **9,345**
Salisbury, Susan Letitia (Whipple) (1826-94). *See*
    Hill, Susan Letitia (Whipple) [Mrs. Zaccheus]
    (1826-94)
Salish Indians, 17,252
Sallee, Annie (Jenkins) [Mrs. William] (1877-1967),
    16,383
Salley, A. S., 15,734
Salley, A. S., Jr., **15,515**
Salley, Eulalie Chafee [Mrs. Julian B.] (1883-1975),
    13,176, **15,706**, 15,733
Salley, Mrs. A. S., 15,576
Sally Wister's Journal; a True Narrative (book),
    11,061
Salmagundi Club (Garden City, KS), 5,179
Salmelin, Rose (Lemberg), 9,175
Salmon, George W., **16,126**
Salmon, Hannah, 3,560
Salmon, Lucy Maynard (1853-1927), 2,186, 2,411
Salome of the Tenements (book), 947
Salon des Beaux Arts, 12,912
Salons, 1,426, 1,467, 5,925, 5,944, 7,651
Salt Lake Academy (UT), 13,904
Salt Lake County Detention Center (UT), 16,780
Salt Lake Latter-day Saints Hospital (UT), 16,526
Salt Lake Mission Home (UT), 16,606
Salt Lake Stake Relief Nurses School (UT), alumnae,
    16,789
Salt Lake State Young Women's Mutual Improvement
    Association (UT), 16,916
Salt Lake Theatre (UT), 16,888
Salt Lake Women's Chamber of Commerce (UT),
    16,535
Salter, Mary Ann Mackintire [Mrs. William]
    (1824-93), 4,829
Salter, Mrs., 3,926
Salter, William (1821-1910), **4,829**
Saltonstall, Mary Susan (1807-69), **12,302**
Saltsgiver, Salina, 4,971
Saltzman, Katherine Eleanor (1904-46), **5,023**
Saltzman, Minnie A. (1874-1950). *See*
    (Saltzman)-Stevens, Minnie A. [Mrs. Alexander
    N.] (1874-1950)
(Saltzman)-Stevens, Minnie A. [Mrs. Alexander N.]
    (1874-1950), 3,745, **4,307**
Salubria (IA), 4,809
Salvation Army School for Officers Training, 16,364
Salvation Army, The, 1,078, 3,969, 5,614, 6,515,
    7,203, **12,706**, 12,729, 16,260, 17,868
  missions, 16,364
Salvini, Tomaso, 12,032
Salyards, Zaide (Smith), 10,091
Salz, Ansley K., 765

Salz, Helen, 931, **2,565**
Salz, Helen (Arnstein) [Mrs. Ansley K.], 765, 931,
    2,565
Salzer, Lisel, **17,331**
Salzman, Lorna, 6,336
Sam Davis Memorial Association (TN), 15,943
Samarcand arson case, 13,468
Samarcand Manor (NC), 13,447
*Same Only Different, The: Five Generations of a
    Great Theater Family* (book), 2,625
Sameth, Stella, 17,282
Samizdat, **5,875**
Samples, Sally (pseudonym). *See* Allen, Elizabeth
    (1734-1824)
Sampson College (NY), 11,285
Sampson, Deborah (1760-1827). *See* Gannett,
    Deborah (Sampson) [Mrs. Benjamin] (1760-1827)
Sampson, Edith Spurlock (1901-), 3,799
Sampson, Joanna Stevenson, 1,750
Sampson, Leonice M. *See* Moulton, Leonice M.
    (Sampson) [Mrs. Joseph W.]
Sampson, Myra (1887-), 7,158
Sampson, Pauline C. (1837?-1902). *See* Lane, Pauline
    C. (Sampson) [Mrs. Levi Cooper] (1837?-1902)
Sampter, Jessie, 12,117
Sams, Caroline "Carrie" Oswald [Mrs. Miles Brewton]
    (1820-98), 15,707
Sams, Emmy, 15,707
Sams Family (SC), **15,707**
Sams, Lewis "Luter," 15,707
Sams, Miles Brewton (1811-94), 15,707
Sams, Sarah Jane (1835-1920), **15,708**
Samson, Chloe, **6,869**
Samson, W. H., 11,512
Samter, Thyra (ca. 1885-1961). *See* Winslow, Thyra
    (Samter) (ca. 1885-1961)
Samuel, Irene [Mrs. John], 11,857
Samuel, Merritt, Hospital (CA), **472**
Samuels, Gertrude, **6,075**
Samuelson, Agnes [Miss] (1887-1963), **4,830**, **4,946**
San Angelo Council of United Church Women (TX),
    16,038
San Antonio Art League (TX), 16,315
San Antonio de Padua Mission (CA), **766, 767**
San Antonio Female College (TX), **16,107**
San Antonio Mission, 1,135
San Buenaventura Mission (CA), **768**, 951
San Carlos mission (CA), 1,135
San Diego (CA), presidio, 392
San Diego Children's Home Association (CA), 1,199,
    1,200, 1,213
San Diego County Chamber of Commerce (CA),
    Ladies Annex, **1,214**
San Diego County Federation of Women's Clubs
    (CA), **1,215**
San Diego County War History Committee (CA),
    1,216
San Diego Historical Society (CA), 1,189
San Diego Mission (CA), 631, **769**
San Diego Union (CA), 1,184
San Diego Women's Civic Center (CA), 1,207
San Dieguito Union High School (CA), 1,191
San Francisco (steamer), 2,659
San Francisco Art Association (CA), 939
San Francisco Bay Conservation and Development
    Commission (CA), 661
San Francisco Board of Supervisors (CA), 1,361
San Francisco Boy (book), 4,306
San Francisco Bulletin (CA), 432
San Francisco Center (CA), 485
San Francisco Club (CA), 1,344
San Francisco College for Women (CA), 355
San Francisco Conference (1945), 7,891
San Francisco Daily News (CA), 611
San Francisco de Asis Mission (CA), **770**
San Francisco Examiner (CA), 885
San Francisco Federation of Teachers (CA), 8,128
San Francisco Federation of the Arts (CA), 1,313
San Francisco Foundation (CA), 760
San Francisco Foundling Asylum (CA), 546
San Francisco Museum of Art (CA), 679, 760
San Francisco Planning and Urban Renewal
    Association (CA), 470
San Francisco (CA), presidio, 392

San Francisco Recreation Center (CA), 945
San Francisco Society of Women Artists (CA), 14,707
San Francisco Solano Mission (CA), 319
San Francisco State College (CA), Independent Campus Women, 17,663
San Francisco State College (CA), students, 17,619
San Francisco State University (CA), faculty, 3,771
San Francisco Theological Seminary (CA), faculty, 17,373
San Francisco Women's City Club (CA), 720
San Francisco World's Fair (1917), 16,965
San Gabriel Mission (CA), 715, 985, 1,384, 1,459
San Jacinto, battle of (1836), 16,320
San Joaquin County Federation (CA), 1,341
San Jose pueblo, 392
San Jose State University (CA), alumnae, 1,620
San Juan Bautista Mission (CA), **773**
San Juan Capistrano Mission (CA), **774**
San Juan Island, 17,258
San Juan Women's Club (CO), **1,793**
San Leandro Free Public Library (CA), 1,386
San Leandro Historical-Centennial Committee (CA), **1,387**
San Leandro Memorial Hospital (CA) Auxiliary, **1,388**
San Leandro Symphony League Auxiliary (CA), **1,389**
San Luis Obispo mission (CA), 1,135
San Miguel Mission (CA), **775**
San Quentin prison (CA), 1,146
San Rafael Arcángel Mission (CA), **776**
Sanatoriums, 1,700, 2,542, 3,158, 7,220, 8,176, 8,307, 12,666, **14,623**
Sanborn Family, **10,873**
Sanborn, Katherine "Kate" Abbott (1839-1917), 1,224, 5,736, 5,956, 6,659, 7,044, 10,873
Sanborn, Sarah (1842-1910). *See* Conwell, Sarah (Sanborn) [Mrs. Russell H.] (1842-1910)
Sánchez, Father José, 715
Sanchez, Nellie (Van de Grift) (1856-1935), **777**
Sanchez, Vilma (pseudonym). *See* Jordan, Joan
Sanctificationists, **16,180**
Sand Creek Massacre, 1,790
Sand, Froma, **6,076**
Sand, George, 1,488, 5,939
Sand Sprite (drama), 15,700
Sand, Viki, 9,230
Sandberg, Gladys, 8,462
Sandburg, Carl (1878-1967), 1,461, 4,255, 6,077, 12,405, 12,570, 12,821, 12,915
Sandburg, Helga (1918-), **6,077**
Sandeen, Muriel Ione (1924-63), **13,207**
Sandel, Elias, Jr., **3,614**
Sandel, Mary Eleanor Williams, **3,614**
Sanders, Claudia Thomas [Mrs. James H.], **15,709**
Sanders Family (NY), 12,345
Sanders Family (SC), **15,516**
Sanders, Harriet Peck Fenn [Mrs. W. F.], **10,365**
Sanders, Helen Fitzgerald, **10,366**
Sanders, J. Wilkes, 3,112
Sanders, James H., 15,709
Sanders, Josephine, 3,764
Sanders, Lewis E. (1919-68), **17,719**
Sanders, Luida E. (1917-), **17,719**
Sanders, Marlene, **17,813**
Sanders, Mrs. Bruce G., 1,666
Sanders, Muriel Gurdon (1886-?). *See* Draper, Muriel Gurdon (Sanders) (1886-?)
Sanders, W. F., 10,365
Sanderson, Alice Cecilia. *See* Rivoire, Alice Cecilia (Sanderson)
Sanderson, Cecilia Blandford [Mrs. Dwight], 11,688
Sanderson, Dwight, 11,688
Sanderson, Electa (1822-1901). *See* Dawes, Electa (Sanderson) [Mrs. Henry Laurens] (1822-1901)
Sanderson, Julia, 12,444
Sanderson, Sybil Swift. [Mrs. Antonio] Terry (1865-1903), 1,073
Sandfield, Margery, 5,515
Sando, Halvor Lars, 8,799
Sando, Julia. *See* Vallon, Julia (Sando)
Sandon, Maggie (Oblinger), 10,516

Sandoz, Mari Susette [Miss] (1896?-1966), 1,750, **10,529, 10,608**
"Sandpiper, The," 5,694
Sandro, Barbro, 9,266
Sands, Fanny, 11,941
Sands Home (CO), 1,672
Sands House Sanatorium (CO), 1,700
Sands, Mary. *See* Griffin, Mary (Sands)
Sands, Susan (Bard), 11,941
Sandvig, Elizabeth. *See* Spafford, Elizabeth (Sandvig)
Sandwich Islands, missionaries to, Protestant, 3,637
Sandwich Monthly Meeting (MA), 7,490
Sandwich: The Town That Glass Built (book), 5,986
Sandwith, Elizabeth (1734-1807). *See* Drinker, Elizabeth (Sandwith) [Mrs. Henry] (1734-1807)
"Sandy Bowers' Wife, Queen of the Comstock" (ms), 10,731
Sandy Creek Congregational Church (NY), Ladies' Sewing Society, 11,697
Sandy Creek Congregational Church (NY), Sociable Society, 11,697
SANE: A Citizen's Organization for a Sane World, 12,042, 17,691
Sanford, Albert H., 17,674
Sanford, Amanda, 8,361
Sanford, Amy. *See* Dartt, Amy (Sanford) [Mrs. Josiah]
Sanford, Annie Evaline (1873-1961), **14,799**
Sanford, Bertha B. *See* Gruenberg, Bertha Sanford
Sanford, Charlotte L. (Mead) [Mrs. Edward Rollin] (1871-?), 9,346
Sanford, Clara Jane (1866-?). *See* Packard, Sarah Jane (Sanford) (1866-?)
Sanford, Edith, 11,785
Sanford, Edward Rollin, Family (MN), **9,346**
Sanford Family (IA), **4,702**
Sanford, Frances Hughes (1906-). *See* Anderson, Frances Hughes (Sanford) [Mrs. Robert] (1906-)
Sanford, Hilda Truslow (Berry) (1916-), 11,644, **11,698**
Sanford, Irene (1882-1964). *See* Devan, Irene (Sanford) (1882-1964)
Sanford, John (1906-), **10,742**
Sanford, Julia E. *See* Stoddard, Julia E. Sanford [Mrs. Goodwin]
Sanford, Linda, 8,424
Sanford, Luna E. (1857-1940). *See* Kellie, Luna E. (Sanford) (1857-1940)
Sanford, Maria Louise [Miss] (1836-1920), 8,544, **8,606**, 8,617, 8,896, 9,024, 9,077, 9,103, 9,120, 9,347, 9,455
Sanford, Maude Emily (Tiel) [Mrs. William Ackley] (1866-1941), 4,702
Sanford, Mrs. M. L., **8,361**
Sanford, Olive, 11,144
Sanford, Susan (Howell), 1,901
Sanford, Terry, 16,965
Sanford, Tiel, 4,702
Sanford, William Ackley, 4,702
Sanger, Margaret (Higgins) [Mrs. William]. [Mrs. Noah] Slee (1879-1966), 569, 677, 691, 1,596, 2,403, 2,424, 2,451, 2,558, 3,996, 5,739, 5,870, 6,221, 6,223, 6,404, 6,741, 7,197, 7,282, 7,283, 7,284, 7,287, **7,289**, 7,320, 8,077, 8,144, 8,634, 8,672, 9,440, 9,810, 11,812, 11,897, 11,946, 12,705, 12,837, 17,964
Sanger, Marjory Bartlett, 2,932
Sangster, Margaret Elizabeth (Munson) [Mrs. George] (1838-1912), 1,224
Sangus Seminary (MA), 7,658
Sanitary Commission Great Central Fair (PA), **15,085**
Sanitary engineers, 10,744
Sanitation, 1,997, 3,875, 3,910, 4,166, 4,380, 5,499, 5,500, 8,223, 14,746, 16,224
Sanitoriums, 9,480, 16,215
Sanne, Hertha [Mrs.], 17,589
Sannoner, Ferdinand (1793-1859), 26
Sannoner, Nannie, **26**
Sano, Minna, **17,332**
Sans Souci, Gertrude (1873-1913). *See* Toomey, Gertrude Sans Souci [Mrs. William C.] (1873-1913)
Sansom, Emma, 99

Sanson, Henry, 11,602
"Santa Anita" (ms), 906
Santa Barbara Chamber of Commerce (CA), 1,526
Santa Barbara County Commission on the Status of Women (CA), 1,525
Santa Barbara Indian Defense Association (CA), 1,526
Santa Barbara Mission (CA), **778**
Santa Barbara Trust for Historic Preservation (CA), 1,526
Santa Clara American (CA), 1,535
Santa Clara College (CA), faculty, 1,584
Santa Clara County Genealogical Society (CA), 1,533
Santa Clara Indians, **16,871**
Santa Clara Journal (CA), 1,535
Santa Clara News (CA), 1,535
Santa Clara Sun (CA), 1,535
Santa Clara University (CA), 1,534
Santa Clara Valley Friends of Student Non-Violent Coordinating Committee (CA), 14,453
Santa Fe Art Colony (NM), 11,213
Santa Fe Business and Professional Women's Club (NM), 11,237
Santa Fe Players (NM), 11,222
Santa Fe Women's Club (NM), 11,222
Santa Rosa Junior College (CA), archives, **1,543**
Santa Rosa Junior College (CA), Associated Women Students, 1,543
Santa Rosa Junior College (CA), Women's Center, 1,543
Santangelo, Maria, 2,215
Santayana, George, 6,890
Santiam Academy (OR), 14,646
Santino, Effie (Stranahan) [Mrs. Gustav], 8,721
Santos-Dumont, 14,203
Saperstein, Esther (1903-), **4,149**
Saphhira and the Slave Girl (book), 12,414
Sapieha, Princess Paul (1904-66). *See* Peterson, Virgilia. Virgilia Peterson Ross. Princess Paul Sapieha. Virgilia Sapieha (1904-66)
Saportas, Frances Cabanne [Mrs. Sylvester] Scovel [Mrs. W. F. "Bill"], 10,181
Saportas, W. F. "Bill", 10,181
Saposs, David, 8,085, 15,332
Sapphire Pendant, The (book), 5,694
Sappier, Teresa, 5,658
Sappington, John (1776-1856), **10,044**
Sarah Bradley Tyson Memorial Fellowship, 6,964
Sarah Lawrence College (NY), 12,737
  alumnae, 11,303
  archives, **11,301**
  faculty, **2,784**, 5,231, **11,306**, 11,888, 12,642, 15,917
  history, **11,300**
  presidents, 11,910
  students, 8,812, **11,302**, 17,185
Sarah Lawrence College (NY), Center for Continuing Education, 11,910
Sarah Lawrence College (NY), Early Childhood Center, 11,300
Sarah Porter School, 9,037
"Sarah the Divine," 12,610
Saratoga Board of Education (NY), 12,847
Saratoga Monument Association (NY), 12,847
Saratoga Women's Association (NY). *See* Women's Civic League (Saratoga Springs, NY)
Sarber, Mrs. Joseph, 14,945
Sarcoxie, Frances [Mrs. John], 14,174
Sarcoxie, John, 14,174
Sardeson, Eva (1875-1966). *See* Jerome, Eva (Sardeson) [Mrs. Charles Waldron] (1875-1966)
Sardinia, American ambassadors to, 2,965
Sarfatti, Margherita, 2,207
Sargeant, Hazel [Mrs. John J.], 1,837
Sargent, Aaron Augustus, 12,828
Sargent, Barbara, 1,655
Sargent, Catherine, 6,458, 6,787
Sargent Club (San Francisco, CA), **1,158**
Sargent, David L., **16,436**
Sargent, Ella. *See* Montgomery, Ella (Sargent)
Sargent, Ella S., 9,315
Sargent, Ellen (Cantwell), 9,262
Sargent, Ellen (Clark) [Mrs. Aaron Augustus], 12,828
Sargent, Ethel (Otto), 1,663

Sargent, Helen Durham [Mrs.] (1904-), **5,233**
Sargent, Helen Sanborn. *See* Hitchcock, Helen
   Sanborn (Sargent) [Mrs. James Ripley Wellman]
Sargent, Henrietta, 6,458
Sargent, Jennie (Smith) (1860-1934), **17,176**
Sargent, John Singer, 543, 6,185
Sargent, Judith (1751-1820). *See* Murray, Judith
   (Sargent) [Mrs. John] Stevens [Mrs. John]
   (1751-1820)
Sargent, Julia Amanda (1825-1903). *See* Lee, Minnie
   Mary. Julia Amanda (Sargent) [Mrs. William
   Henry] Wood (1825-1903)
Sargent, Julia (Hanscom). *See* Grant, Julia
   (Hanscom) Sargent
Sargent, Mildred [Mrs. David L.], **16,437**
Sargent, Pamela [Miss] (1948-), **15,199**
Sargent, Shirley, **1,640**
Sargent, William, 17,724
Sarjeant, Ethel (Bascom) (?-1974), 15,106
Sarmiento, Domingo Faustino (1811-88), 2,471
Sarnoff, Dorothy (1914-), **11,699**
Sarrazin Plantation (SC), 15,428
Sarria, Vicente Francisco de (1767-1835), **779**
Sartain, John, 12,376
Sarton, George, 3,097, 12,009
Sarton, Mabel, 3,097
Sarton, May, 3,097, 5,694, 10,853, 11,832
Sartori, Joseph, 5,072
Sartori, Teresa, 5,072
Sartre, Jean Paul, 7,316
Sartwell, Wilbur K., **16,813**
Sasha (pseudonym). *See* Stokes, Rose Pastor. [Mrs.
   James Graham] Phelps [Mrs. Jerome I.] Romaine
   (1879-1933)
Sassoon, Richard, 4,485
Sassoon, Siegfried, 13,871
Sasuly, Elizabeth, 3,442
Sater, Harriett A. [Miss], 5,519
Satersmoen, Alma, 8,462
Sathers, Mrs. Glenn, 5,150
Satir, Virginia, 8,676
Satire, 7,186, 12,341
Satt, Hilda (1887?-1967). *See* Polacheck, Hilda (Satt)
   [Mrs. William] (1887?-1967)
Satterfield, Ellen Steele [Miss], **9,724**
Satterlee, Ann Matthew [Mrs.], 1,476
Satterlee, Emily, 12,303
Satterlee Family (NY), **12,303**
Satterlee, Frances Mae (Howe) [Mrs. August N.]
   (1892-), **9,349**
Satterlee, Marion P., **9,350**
Satterlee, William Wilson (1837-93), **9,350**
Satterthwaite, Adaline Pendleton, 6,987
Satterthwaite, Wella (1901-), 16,488
Saturday Afternoon Club (Downey, CA). *See*
   Woman's Club of Downey (CA)
Saturday Club (Independence, MO), 10,086, **10,087**
"Saturday Cousins," 5,304
Saturday Evening Post (periodical), 4,061, 5,452,
   8,428, 11,491, 11,998, 15,060, 15,228, 17,614
Saturday Home Magazine, 325
Saturday Matinee Musicale (Richmond, KY), **5,406**
Saturday Morning Club (Hartford, CT), **1,954**
Saturday Morning Club (New Haven, CT), 1,992
Saturday Morning Club of Boston (MA), **6,870**
Saturday Review (periodical), 2,658, 5,310, 12,035,
   12,888, 16,153
Saturday Review of Literature (periodical). See
   Saturday Review (periodical)
Saturday's Child (book), 692
Saucier, Corinne Lelia (1890-1960), 5,539
Saucier, John B., 9,725
Saucier, Marie Louise, **9,725**
Saucier, Pierre, 9,725
Sauer, Alice Edmunds (1877-1972), **10,778**
Sauk Centre School for Girls (MN), 8,994
Sauna, 9,467
Saunders, Catharine E. G., **7,518**
Saunders, Charles, 7,518
Saunders, Charles Francis (1859-1941), **1,482**
Saunders Family (VA), **17,115**
Saunders, Laura, 13,561
Saunders, Lizzie C. (Stillwell) (1860-1946), 16,117

Saunders, Lucy Burwell (Page) [Mrs. Robert]
   (1807-?), 17,115
Saunders, Marian, 6,223
Saunders, Mary, 780
Saunders, Mary B. [Mrs. Charles Francis], 1,482
Saunders, Mary Ball (1822-1918), **6,871**
Saunders, Nell. *See* Graydon, Nell (Saunders)
Saunders, Robert (?-1868), 17,115
Saunders, Roberta Page (?-1894), 17,115
Saunders, William Laurance, **13,561**
Saussy, George Nowlan, **3,570**
Sauvegarde de l'Art Francais, 8,545
Savage, Alexander Duncan (?-1935), 12,206
Savage, Augusta, 2,948
Savage, Charles, 8,602
Savage, Clara (1891-1956). *See* Littledale, Clara
   (Savage) (1891-1956)
Savage, Edward P. (1844-1921), **9,351**
Savage, Elizabeth [Mrs. Paul], **5,661**
Savage, Elizabeth (Rutherford) [Mrs. Thomas
   Stoughton] (1817-99), 12,206
Savage, Frank A., **5,363**
Savage, Levi, 16,965
Savage, Mary [Mrs. Frank A.], **5,363**
Savage, Mary W., 2,930
Savage, Pamela, **13,562**
Savage, Thomas Stoughton, 12,206
Savannah Board of Education (GA), 3,481
Savannah Childrens Center (GA), 3,500, **3,572**
Savannah Conservatory of Music (GA), **3,582**
Savannah Evening Press (GA), 3,585
Savannah Federation of Women's Clubs (GA), **3,571**
Savannah Female Asylum (GA). *See* Savannah
   Childrens Center (GA)
Savannah Kindergarten Association (GA), **3,573**
Savannah Kindergarten Club (GA), **3,574**
Savannah Pharmaceutical Association (GA), Women's
   Auxiliary, **3,575**
Savannah River Plantations (book), 3,514
Save Me the Waltz (book), 11,160
Save Our Sons, 4,050
Save the Babies Fresh Air Camps (IA), 4,915
Save the Children Federation, Minnesota Branch,
   9,352
Save the Trees (drama), 4,689
Savenay Base Hospital Centre (France), 2,515
Savery, Annie (Nowlin) [Mrs. James] (1831-91),
   4,708, **4,831**
Savier, Mary Louise (1867-1963). *See* Washburn,
   Mary Louise (Savier) [Mrs. Robert Charles]
   (1867-1963)
Savings-banks, 15,061
Sawdust Days (book), 8,358
Sawtell Family (MI), **7,918**
Sawtelle Girls' School (Bihar, India), 14,426
Sawtelle, Louise Coburn (Burpee) [Mrs. William Otis]
   (?-1941), **5,588**
Sawtooth National Park, 3,722
Sawyer, Alice, **7,437**
Sawyer, Byrd Wall, **10,710, 10,779**
Sawyer, Celestia (Johnson) (ca. 1844-?), 8,986
Sawyer, Esther (Hoyt) [Mrs. Ansley W.], **2,813**
Sawyer Family, 781
Sawyer Family (ME), 7,669
Sawyer, Grant, 10,779
Sawyer, Luella Kenan, **781**
Sawyer, Mrs. Francis H., **782**
Sawyer, Ruth (1880-1970), **8,852**
Sawyer, Susan "Susette" (Fontaine), 9,790
Saxon, Elizabeth Lyle, **5,522**
Saxon, Lyle (1879-1936), 5,511, 5,522
Saxton, Andrew B., **12,747**
Saxton, Catherine. *See* Hatheway, Catherine Saxton
   [Mrs. Samuel Gilbert]
Saxton, Ida (1847-1907). *See* McKinley, Ida (Saxton)
   [Mrs. William] (1847-1907)
Saxton, Martha, 5,863
Saxton, Mr., 12,499
Say, Luce Way (Sistare) [Mrs. Thomas] (1800-86),
   14,880, 14,901
Say the Bells of Old Missions (book), 11,222
Say, Thomas (1787-1834), 14,880, **14,901**
Sayers, Dorothy Leigh (1893-1957), 267, 8,001
Saylor, Adelaide (Baltzelle), 2,966

Saylor, Ann [Mrs. Philip] (1829-68), **4,333**
Saylor, Carol, **6,078**
Saylor, Elizabeth Ann (1789-1868). *See* Yates,
   Elizabeth Ann (Saylor) [Mrs. Joseph]
   (1789-1868)
Saylor, Philip, 4,333
Sayre, E. Berthold, 11,849
Sayre, Elizabeth, 1,564
Sayre, Elizabeth (Dartt) [Mrs. Hal], 1,730
Sayre, Francis B., 5,511
Sayre, Jessie Woodrow (Wilson) (1887-1933), 1,530
Sayre, Julia (Kirtland), 11,264
Sayre, Ruth B. [Mrs. Raymond] (1896-), **4,947**
Sayre, Zelda (1900-48). *See* Fitzgerald, Zelda (Sayre)
   [Mrs. F. Scott] (1900-48)
Scala, Florence, 4,134
Scales, Anne (1883-1958). *See* Benedict, Anne
   (Scales) (1883-1958)
Scales, Cordelia Lewis (1844-1915). *See* Gray,
   Cordelia Lewis (Scales) [Mrs. Ben Cottrell]
   (1844-1915)
Scales, Dabney, 15,895
Scales, John, 10,846
Scales, Laura Lord, 7,158
Scallen, Blanche W., 9,132
Scamman, Edith, 5,701
Scamman Family (ME), **5,701**
Scamman, May Pierce [Mrs. W. C.] (?-1970), 5,065
Scamman, Sarah O., 5,701
Scammon, Richard, 8,574
Scandalabra (drama), 11,160
Scandinavia, Mormons and Mormonism, 6,092,
   16,852
Scandinavian Evangelical Lutheran Church (Red
   Wing, MN), 9,204
Scandinavian Suffrage Association (MN), 9,240
Scandinavian Temperance Union (Fergus Falls, MN),
   8,896
Scadinavian Woman's Suffrage Association, 9,147
Scandinavian Young Women's Christian Temperance
   Union of Minneapolis (MN), **9,353**
Scandrett, Benjamin Wright (1883-1954), 9,437
Scandrett, Bertha Reid [Mrs. Benjamin Wright]
   (1883-), 9,437
Scandrett, Betty, 9,437
Scandrett, Cornelia (1912-). *See* Hanstein, Cornelia
   (Scandrett) [Mrs. Jack E.] (1912-)
Scandrett Family (MN), **9,437**
Scandrett, Henry Alexander (1843-83), 9,437
Scandrett, Henry Alexander, Jr. (1876-1957), 9,437
Scandrett, Jane "Jennie" (Whipple) [Mrs. Henry
   Alexander] (1847-1932), 9,437
Scandrett, Jean, 9,437
Scandrett, Richard, 8,660
Scaravaglione, Concetta (1900-75), **2,814**
Scarborough, Carrie (1832-?). *See* Thompson, Carrie
   (Scarborough) [Mrs. Horace] (1832-?)
Scarborough, Emily Dorothy [Miss] (1878-1935),
   16,384
Scarborough, Katherine (1900-60), **5,808**
Scarlet fever epidemics, 11,653
Scarlet Sister Mary (book), 15,672
Scarlet Thread, The (book), 5,989
Scarletina, 3,373, 12,490
Scarritt College (KS), 9,597
   faculty, 12,731
Scars Make Your Body More Interesting (book),
   11,221
Scarsdale Inquirer, 17,141
Scattergood, Rachel (1832-1903), 14,850
Scattergoods Association (Pasadena, CA), **1,105**
Scenarios. *See* Moving-picture plays
Scent of Violets, The (book), 428
Schackelford, Ida, 10,046
Schackelford, Sarah Harrison [Mrs. Thomas], 10,046
Schackelford, Thomas (1822-1908), **10,046**
Schaddelee, Cornelia Hulst [Mrs.], 8,195
Schaedel, Grace Logan, **18,007**
Schaefer, Beatrice, 8,690
Schaefer, Francesca (1856-?). *See* Winston, Francesca
   (Schaefer) [Mrs. William Overton] (1856-?)
Schaefer, Jacob, Family (MN), **9,354**
Schaefer, Sarah (Miller) [Mrs. Jacob] (1820-1908),
   9,354

Schaeffer, Elaine C. (1903-), **8,710**
Schaeffer, Evelyn (Schuyler), **11,700**
Schaeffer, Frank, Family (MN), 8,710
Schafer, Alice T., 7,583
Schaffer, Helen, **1,023**
Schain, Josephine (1886-1972), 7,269, **7,290**
Schaller Family (SC), **15,729**
Schaller, Frank, 15,729, 15,753
Schaller, Sophie Sosnowski [Mrs. Frank], 2,965,
   3,094, 15,602, 15,729, 15,753
Schanck, Jane Ann, **11,026**
Schappes, Morris, 1,017
Schary, Dore, 4,639
Schaub, Mother Jerome (1856-1942), 5,204
Schaub, Theresa, **7,919**
Schauland, Evelyn, 4,869
Scheele, Leonard Andrew (1907-), 11,857
Scheetz, Francis Harley, Jr. (1894-1968), 11,701
Scheetz, Virginia deMorat Smith [Mrs. Francis
   Harley, Jr.] (1901-), **11,701**
Scheffauer, Ethel (Talbot) [Mrs. Herman George],
   783
Scheffauer, Herman George (1878-1927), **783**
Scheffey, Alice W., 9,397
Scheherezade Cooks! (book), 14,907
Schein, Cecile, 17,647
Schelde, Mildred (1900-73). See Lewis, Mildred
   (Schelde) (1900-73)
Schemm, Ferdinand Ripley, 18,008
Schemm, Mildred Walker [Mrs. Ferdinand Ripley]
   (1905-), **18,008**
Schenck, Anna McCune [Mrs. Peter Voorhees], 9,909
Schenck, Harriet H. [Mrs.], 16,097
Schenck, Henrietta, **11,027**
Schenck, Mary Ethel, 4,948
Schenck, Peter Voorhees (1838-85), **9,909**
Schenck, Walter Leslie (1882-1964), **4,948**
Schenecker, Mary Ellen. See Stott, Mary Ellen
   (Schenecker) [Mrs. Frank E.]
Schenk, Rachel Katherine [Miss], **17,777**
Schenkman, Pamela (Wrinch) (1927-75), 7,328
Schenley, Edward, 15,257
Schenley Family, **15,257**
Schenley, Mary (Croghan) [Mrs. Edward]
   (1826-1903), 15,221, **15,226**, 15,257
Schenley Park (PA), 15,226
Scherer, Minnie (1890-), **8,510**
Scherman, Harry, 11,837
Schermer, Jennie, 17,282
Schermerhorn, Catherine (Yates) [Mrs. John
   Freeman], 10,045
Schermerhorn, Elizabeth L. Spottswood [Mrs. John
   Freeman], 10,045
Schermerhorn, Harriet, 10,045
Schermerhorn, Jane [Mrs. Winfield Scott], 4,832
Schermerhorn, John Freeman (1787-1859), **10,045**
Schermerhorn, Mary, 10,045
Schermerhorn, Mary Y., 10,045
Schermerhorn, Winfield Scott, **4,832**
Schermerhorn, Zella, **4,833**
Scherr, Amy Lay Hall [Mrs.], **11,459**
Scheuer, Lucile, **15,189**
Schevill, Margaret Erwin, 1,082
Schick, Bela (1877-1967), 11,579, 11,817
Schieffelin Family (NY), 12,020
Schieffelin, Hannah (Lawrence), **12,615**
Schiefflin, Corneille [Miss], 3,023
Schildhouse, Ruth (1927-), **14,016**
Schiller, Madeline, 12,457
Schilling, Alice (1890-), 7,510
Schimmelpfennig, Alexander, 14,769
Schimmoler, Lauretta [Miss] (1900-), **13,762**
Schindler, Mrs. J. A. Bayard (1888-). See Glenn,
   Isa. [Mrs. J. S. Bayard] Schindler (1888-)
Schip, Elizabeth, 12,298
Schirmer Family (SC), 15,495
Schism, 1,401, 4,209
Schlager, Sid, 11,537
Schlaifer, Mildred, 1,319
Schlater, Mary Galloway, 9,809
Schleicher, Florence Ernestine (1901-54). See Teed,
   Florence Ernestine (Schleicher) (1901-54)
Schleindlinger, Lena (ca. 1900-), **15,162**
Schlemmer, Hildegarde (1893-), **4,536**

Schlenk, Hugo, 17,587
Schlesinger, Arthur Meier, Sr. (1888-1965), **6,301,**
   6,921
Schlesinger, Elizabeth (Bancroft) [Mrs. Arthur Meier,
   Sr.] (1887-1977), 6,301, **6,872**
Schley, Kate Prentice [Mrs. Reeve, Sr.], 11,129
Schley, Reeve, Sr. (1881-1960), **11,129**
Schlichtmann, Marguerite Elizabeth (Sprado), 1,386
Schliep, Emma, 5,063
Schlingheyde, Clara M., 6,815
Schloss, Ann Lazarus, 11,859
Schlossbach, Isaac, 10,921
Schlossberger, Louisa Augusta. See Pinède, Louisa
   Augusta (Schlossberger) [Mrs. George] Ripley
   [Mrs. Alphonse]
Schlueter, Elsie (1890-). See Mohr, Elsie (Schlueter)
   [Mrs.] (1890-)
Schlundt, Christena, 12,365
Schmid, Elsa (1897-), **2,815**
Schmid, Mother M. Beda, 13,727
Schmid, Pauline Johanna (1903-), 11,508, 11,541,
   11,702
Schmidgall, Floyd (1928-), **8,711**
Schmidgall, Mrs. Floyd (1929-), **8,711**
Schmidt, Albert, 1,569
Schmidt, Esther Ida, 13,816
Schmidt, G. Pearle (Wilson) [Mrs. Louis Bernard]
   (1881-1957), 4,689, 4,834
Schmidt, Katherine, 1,321
Schmidt, Louis Bernard, **4,689**
Schmidt, Louise (Brasch) [Mrs. Albert], 1,569
Schmidt, Mary (Schwandt) [Mrs. William F.]
   (1848-?), **9,355**
Schmitt, Agnes (1894-1966). See Harrison, Agnes
   (Schmitt) (1894-1966)
Schmitt, Clara (Senninger) [Mrs. Otto F.], 10,140,
   10,141
Schmukler, Joan (1949-), **11,703**
Schneeloch, Emelie "Millie" A. (1868-?), **2,022**
Schneeloch, Emma Waleska (1862-?), **2,022**
Schneider, Anna Weinstock (1898-), **11,773**
Schneider, Betty, 3,844
Schneider, Ursula Wolff [Mrs.] (1906-77), 4,028
Schneiderman, Rose, 8,071
Schneiderman, Rose (1882-1972), 2,509, 12,069,
   12,700, **12,704**
Schneir, Miriam [Mrs. Walter], **6,079**
Schneir, Walter, **6,079**
Schock, Anna [Mrs.], **4,174**
Schoedler, Lillian, **6,873**
Schoenberg, Arnold, 468
Schoenborn, Wolfgang, 2,997
Schoene, Katherine M., 13,531
Schoenheit, Mary L., 9,963
Schoff, Hannah (Kent) [Mrs. Fredric] (1853-1940),
   2,451, 3,695
Schofield, Lydia A., 13,120
Schofield, Martha (1839-1916), **13,120**
Scholarly periodicals, 393, 2,093, **2,166**, 2,835, 3,772,
   4,130, 6,122, 6,123, 6,133, 6,134, 6,139, 6,143,
   6,145, 6,150, 6,157, 12,395, 13,501, 14,743
Scholarship and Guidance Association (IL), 4,150
Scholarships, 51, 117, 1,681, 2,064, 2,429, **2,670,**
   3,066, 3,773, 3,865, 4,038, 4,084, **4,150**, 4,176,
   4,217, 4,309, 5,545, 6,136, 6,164, 6,398, 6,456,
   6,493, 6,563, 6,644, 7,032, 7,176, 7,248, **7,721,**
   8,041, 8,054, 8,441, 8,481, 8,485, 8,625, 9,254,
   9,756, 11,526, 11,592, **11,670**, 11,910, 11,911,
   12,362, 12,808, 13,231, 13,261, **13,544**, 13,644,
   14,033, 14,625, 16,413, 17,484, 17,821, 17,822,
   17,825
Scholl, Catherine, 15,134
Schonberg, Bessie. See Varley, Bessie (Schonberg)
   [Mrs. Dimitry V.]
Schoof, Santa (Reul), 5,474
School administrators, 3,474, 4,341, 5,126, **7,848,**
   10,629, 12,244, **14,401**, 17,371
School administrators, Afro-American, **2,155**
School administrators and minority groups, 16,334
School art, 249
School attendance, 4,150, 6,486, 9,473, 9,963, 11,749,
   14,020
School boards, 485, 500, 895, 936, 1,779, 1,829,
   2,123, **3,105**, 3,206, **3,784**, 3,787, 3,911, 4,477,

   4,623, 4,626, 5,381, 5,466, 6,376, 6,387, 6,405,
   6,420, 6,497, 6,762, 6,771, 7,913, 7,926, 7,941,
   8,030, 8,170, 9,291, 9,467, 9,711, 10,149, 10,905,
   11,118, 11,390, 11,895, **13,181**, **13,184**, 13,730,
   13,961, 14,207, 15,010, 15,025, **15,403**, 15,404,
   15,539, 15,544, 15,816, 16,236, **16,242**, **16,453**,
   17,343, 17,357
School buildings, 713, 4,341, 5,108, 6,805, 7,006,
   12,801, **13,247**, 15,816, 16,999
School census, 162, **3,102**, 8,170, 10,367, 17,522,
   17,538
School children, 4,252, 4,341, 4,760, 7,418, 7,419,
   12,389
   food, 1,837, 4,070, 7,198, 8,575, 11,566, 13,249,
   13,283
   health and hygiene, 11,691, 17,517
School Clerks Union of Chicago, 3,818
"School Days" (poem), 8,917
School discipline, 4,341, 4,914, 10,246
School District 14 (MN), 8,400
School District No. 1, Town of Glencoe, Buffalo
   County (WI), 17,538
School District No. 10 (Glasgow, MT), 10,367
School District No. 64 (Clearwater County, MN),
   8,920
School districts, 3,755, **5,183**, **5,890**, 8,920, 9,208,
   9,388, **10,367**, 11,118, 15,993, 16,242, 16,334,
   16,368, 16,376, **17,538**
School drama, 711
School elections, 4,341
School for Christian Service, 16,027
School for Feeble-Minded Youth (Fort Wayne, IN),
   4,605
School for Girls (New York, NY), 11,748
School for Mentally and Physically Handicapped
   Children, Pilot Education Program (OR), 14,641
School for Negro Children (PA), 3,298
School for Non-Violence, 6,867
School for Young Ladies, A (NY), **12,304**
"School Girl Days" (scrapbook), 4,660
School Girls Circle of South Orange (NJ), 11,133
School hygiene, 8,572, 8,695, 17,515
School integration, 295, 5,135, 5,381, 5,455, 5,470,
   7,266, 8,058, 8,097, 9,276, 9,605, 11,390, 13,181,
   13,209, 16,242
School librarians, 1,633, 2,924, **9,572**, 11,702, **15,430**
School libraries, 4,391
School lunches, 2,704, 7,184, 12,808
School lunchrooms, cafeterias, etc., 15,822
School management and organization, 2,155, 7,655,
   7,662, 7,764, 13,249
School music, 3,198, 8,505, 16,062, 16,432
School News, 14,748
School notebooks, 2,034, 2,195, **2,265**, **2,375**, 5,289,
   5,759, 5,786, 5,811, **6,627**, **10,901**, 12,614,
   12,649, 13,363, 13,552, **15,012**, 15,488, **15,517**,
   15,760, 16,600
School nurses, 4,341, 10,986
School nursing, 236
School of Fine Arts (NY), 7,559
School of Living (FL, NY, OH), 4,151
School of Magazine and Newspaper Illustration (San
   Francisco, CA), 712
School of the Good Shepherd (St. Louis, MO), 10,146
School of the Nativity (Flagstaff, AZ), 159
School of the Parents' Education Association (Israel),
   7,554
School of Tropical Medicine (Brussels, Belgium),
   alumnae, 14,443
School physicians, 4,341, **4,605**, 6,446, 6,456, **11,357,**
   13,243, 13,610
School Physiology Journal, The (periodical), 12,515
School Pioneer (CA), 716
School savings-banks, 15,061
School Sisters of Notre Dame, Our Lady of Good
   Counsel Convent (Mankato, MN), **8,494**
School Sisters of Notre Dame Provincial House
   (Baltimore, MD), **5,832**
School Sisters of Notre Dame, South-Central
   Province (TX), **16,254**
School Sisters of St. Francis (Milwaukee, WI), **17,838**
School social work, **8,643**, 8,665
School sports, 8,714
School superintendents and principals, 131, 190, 326,

758, 788, **789**, 1,137, **1,707**, 1,814, 2,015, **2,130,**
2,900, 2,955, 3,080, **3,226**, 3,265, 3,342, **3,409,**
3,705, **3,709**, 3,745, 3,785, 3,787, 3,842, **4,272,**
4,305, **4,341**, 4,361, 4,374, 4,377, **4,638**, 4,649,
4,705, **4,830**, 4,852, 4,899, **4,920**, 4,946, 5,068,
5,086, **5,172**, 5,289, 5,325, 5,394, 5,770, 5,785,
6,387, **6,398**, 6,438, **6,507**, 6,651, **7,011**, 7,056,
7,224, **7,494**, 7,527, 7,655, 8,044, 8,170, 8,190,
8,293, 8,362, **8,409**, 8,482, 8,572, 8,606, **8,712,**
8,995, 9,087, 9,119, 9,422, 9,448, 9,662, 9,801,
9,972, **10,110**, 10,149, 10,156, 10,263, **10,267,**
10,269, 10,281, **10,306**, **10,346**, 10,358, 10,398,
10,488, 10,626, 10,734, 10,751, 10,864, 10,865,
10,904, 11,164, 11,227, **11,243**, 11,351, **11,611,**
11,925, 12,750, 12,859, **13,329**, **13,444**, 13,658,
13,749, **14,242**, 14,393, 14,668, **14,732**, 14,738,
14,802, 14,845, 14,848, 14,949, **15,088**, 15,913,
15,959, 15,964, 16,318, **16,342**, **16,549**, **17,133,**
17,182, **17,512**, 17,516, **17,542**, **17,543**, 17,589,
17,621, 17,889, 17,901, 17,911, 17,914, 18,010
School superintendents and principals,
  Afro-American, 5,472, **13,909**
School supervisors, **9,387**, 10,482, 10,986, 11,532,
  14,330
School yearbooks, **2,939**, 3,435, 3,714, 4,595, 4,632,
  4,659, **9,561**, **9,577**, 11,302, 12,750, 13,194
Schoolcraft, Henry L., 9,356
Schoolcraft, Henry Rowe (1793-1864), 1,480, **2,566,**
  9,356, 9,411
Schoolcraft, Jane A. (1827-?), 2,566
Schoolcraft, Jane (Johnston) [Mrs. Henry Rowe]
  (1800-42), 2,566
Schoolcraft, Mary (Howard) [Mrs. Henry Rowe],
  1,480, 2,566, 9,356
Schoolhouses. *See* School buildings
Schoolmasters' Club (MI), 7,878
Schools, 71, 81, 350, 596, 955, **1,137**, **1,865**, 1,874,
  1,875, 1,876, 1,901, 1,979, **2,006**, 2,013, **2,305,**
  2,486, 2,635, 2,675, 3,039, **3,068**, 3,140, **3,475,**
  3,484, **3,755**, 3,911, **4,199**, **4,341**, **4,421**, 4,471,
  4,489, **4,813**, 4,844, 5,122, 5,249, **5,254**, 5,255,
  5,256, 5,292, **5,293**, 5,301, 5,410, 6,245, 6,354,
  6,405, 6,430, 6,548, 6,601, 6,657, **7,056**, 7,224,
  7,253, **7,433**, 7,537, 7,541, 7,559, 7,597, 7,631,
  7,653, 7,658, 7,662, **7,859**, **8,023**, **8,170**, 8,238,
  8,245, 8,362, **8,400**, 8,926, 9,023, 9,154, 9,273,
  9,295, 9,373, 9,377, 9,442, 9,465, 9,613, 9,648,
  9,687, 9,696, 9,709, **9,817**, 9,841, **9,903**, **9,943,**
  9,945, 10,237, 10,564, 10,680, 10,778, **11,094,**
  11,125, 11,229, 11,708, 11,898, 12,004, **12,152,**
  12,241, 12,411, 12,660, 12,738, 12,740, **12,746,**
  12,801, **12,831**, **13,128**, 13,322, 13,329, 13,330,
  13,345, 13,363, 13,369, 13,377, 13,389, 13,417,
  13,423, 13,425, 13,430, 13,438, 13,450, 13,452,
  13,467, 13,471, 13,473, 13,477, 13,487, 13,491,
  13,496, 13,526, **13,560**, 13,561, 13,563, 13,570,
  13,607, 13,610, 13,625, 13,682, 13,749, 13,930,
  14,281, 14,348, 14,393, 14,850, 14,851, 14,857,
  15,027, 15,034, 15,204, **15,293**, 15,353, **15,541,**
  15,572, 15,589, 15,602, **15,659**, 15,692, **15,731,**
  15,732, 15,799, **15,949**, **16,392**, 16,640, 17,029,
  17,031, 17,035, 17,227, 17,372, 17,415, 17,445,
  17,455, 17,457, **17,485**, 17,564, 17,661, 17,679,
  17,724. *See also* Church schools; Vacation
  schools
  accounting, **7,108**, **12,304**, 14,762, **15,347**
  administration, **11,673**
  centralization, 8,517, 12,870
  finance, 4,932, 6,880, 9,196, 15,834
  records and correspondence, **506**, **3,042**, **3,122,**
    3,397, **3,434**, **3,521**, 4,165, 5,183, 5,474, **5,895,**
    7,646, 7,653, 8,170, **8,705**, 9,288, 9,317, 9,472,
    10,707, 11,074, **11,257**, 12,859, **13,367**, **13,646,**
    14,738, **14,748**, 15,349, 15,350, 15,351, **15,352,**
    15,514, 15,670, **15,767**, **17,508**, 17,522, **17,523,**
    17,525, **17,526**, 17,533, **17,547**
  safety, 3,976
Schools, Afro-American, 3,298, **5,472**, 13,927, 15,281
  finance, 3,299
Schools, Episcopal, **16,954**
Schools, Jewish, 13,827, 15,156
Schools, Native American, 169, 17,415
Schools of architecture, 7,159
Schools of public health, 344, 6,558, 6,852, 6,987

faculty, 6,138
Schools of social work, 6,946, 8,683, 11,021, 14,742
Schoonover, Shirley, **6,080**
Schooten, Sarah (1895-1974), **8,052**
Schopp, N. K. (Carrier) [Mrs. William], 8,164
Schorr, Esther Brann [Mrs. Richard], **14,326**
Schorr, Lisbeth Bamberger, 11,916
Schrader, Pearl Hutton [Mrs.], 17,384
Schrager, Victoria (?-1943), 7,158
Schramm, Dorothy (Daniell) (1908-), 5,024
Schramm Family (IA), **5,024**
Schreiber, Esther. *See* Rogoway, Esther (Schreiber)
Schreiber, Hazel (Snell). *See* Holmes, Hazel (Snell)
  Schreiber
Schreiver, Margery, 5,515
Schricker, Henry F., 4,628
Schroeder, Pat, 4,869
Schroeder, Theodore (1864-1953), **12,616**
Schroll, Mother M. Alfred, 5,164
Schrum, Marion M., 5,110
Schrumpf, Ellen "Brownie" (Brown) [Mrs. William],
  5,662
Schryver, Grace Fay, 4,108
Schubach, Bernice W., **4,178**
Schubert Club (St. Paul, MN), **9,357**
Schubert Club (St. Paul, MN), Education Loan Fund,
  9,357
Schubert Club (St. Paul, MN), Ladies Musicale, 9,357
Schubert, Ines (Haken), 17,862
Schubert's Last Serenade (drama), 12,367
Schulkind, Adelaide. *See* Frank, Adelaide
  (Schulkind)
Schulman, Howard, 12,064
Schulman, Susan H., 12,367
Schultheis, Rose [Mrs. Leo] (1890-1967), **4,679**
Schultz, Catherine, 8,470
Schultz, Cecilia (Augspurger), **17,333**
Schultz, Julia, **10,368**, 10,369
Schultz, Sigrid, 11,817
Schultz, W. C., 1,737
Schultze, Mrs. Theodore, 784
Schulz, Ellen Dorothy. *See* Quillin, Ellen Dorothy
  (Schulz) [Mrs. Roy W.]
Schulz, Martha E., 10,703
Schulze, Edith, **11,028**
Schumaker, Mary (1888-), **8,712**
Schumann, Clara, 12,457
Schumann, Marguerite, 13,244
Schumann-Heink, Ernestine (Roessler). [Mrs. Ernst]
  Heink [Mrs. Paul] Schumann [Mrs. William]
  Rapp (1861-1936), 3,369
Schumpeter, Elizabeth Boody, **6,874**
Schureman, James Wall (?-1852), **2,567**
Schureman, John (1778-1818), **11,029**
Schureman, Julia Ann (Conover) [Mrs. John]
  (1781-1834), 11,029
Schureman, Mary E. [Miss], 2,567
Schurman, Jacob Gould, 11,674
Schurz, Carl, 6,681
Schuster, Edward, 11,556
Schuster, Mary, **3,718**
Schutt, Kate M. [Miss], 11,508
Schutt, Margaret Elizabeth (1866-1966). *See* Gordon,
  Margaret Elizabeth (Schutt) [Mrs. James Frater]
  (1866-1966)
Schutz, Elizabeth Hutchins [Mrs. Augustus], 10,816
Schutz, John G., Family (MN), **9,358**
Schutz, Josephine Amy Hunt [Mrs. John G.]
  (1857-1937), 9,358
Schutz, Louise Elizabeth (1885-), 9,358
Schuyler, Alida (1656-1729). *See* Livingston, Alida
  (Schuyler) Van Rensselaer [Mrs. Robert]
  (1656-1729)
Schuyler, Catherine "Sweet Kitty" (Van Rensselaer)
  [Mrs. Philip John] (1734-1803), 12,848
Schuyler, Elizabeth (1757-1854). *See* Hamilton,
  Elizabeth (Schuyler) [Mrs. Alexander]
  (1757-1854)
Schuyler, Evelyn. *See* Schaeffer, Evelyn (Schuyler)
Schuyler Family (NY), **12,305**
Schuyler, Freda Humphrey, 10,675
Schuyler, George L., 12,203
Schuyler, George Samuel, 11,897
Schuyler, George W., 11,700

Schuyler, Georgina, 6,707
Schuyler, Louisa Lee [Miss] (1837-1926), **2,568,**
  12,252
Schuyler, Philip John, 12,848
Schuyler, Philippa D., 3,290
Schuyler, Sarah, 12,305
Schuyler, Sarah Ridg [Mrs. Anthony Dry], **2,548**
Schwabacher, Babette. *See* Gatzert, Babette
  (Schwabacher) [Mrs. Bailey]
Schwabacher, Ethel (1903-), **2,816**
Schwabacher Family (WA), **495**
Schwandt, Mary (1848-?). *See* Schmidt, Mary
  (Schwandt) [Mrs. William F.] (1848-?)
Schwartz, Charles E., 322
Schwartz, Edith Gertrude (?-1971). *See* Clements,
  Edith Gertrude (Schwartz) [Mrs. Frederick E.]
  (?-1971)
Schwartz, Edna, 9,474
Schwartz, Frances E. (1877-1937), **14,091**
Schwartz, Lily (Garber) [Mrs. Ernest] (1925-),
  15,163
Schwartz, Sarah Roslyn Gensler (1902-42), 9,128
Schwarz, Hermene, 14,047
Schwarz, Josephine, 14,047
Schwarz School of the Dance (OH), 14,047
Schwarzenberg, Anna, 2,309
Schwatt, Herman, 1,749
Schwatt, May Arno [Mrs. Herman], **1,749**
Schweibert, Meta K., 3,845
Schweiger, Clara T., 5,175
Schweinfurth, Bertha (1856-1934). *See* Ohlinger,
  Bertha (Schweinfurth) [Mrs. Franklin]
  (1856-1934)
Schweinhaut, Margaret C. [Mrs.], 2,086
Schweitzer, Albert, 468, 15,900
Schweitzer, John D., 4,374
Schwendener, Hattie A., 7,920
Schwesinger, Gladys C., **785**
Schwigger-Seidel, E., 12,457
Schwimmer, Franciska, 7,291, 7,923
Schwimmer, Rosika. [Mrs.] Bédy (1877-1948), 2,256,
  2,501, 2,569, 4,631, 6,579, **7,291**, 7,923, 8,000,
  8,963, **12,617**
Schwyzer, Arnold (1864-1944), Family (MN), **9,359**
Schwyzer, Johanna Heneggeler [Mrs. Arnold]
  (?-1905), 9,359
Schwyzer, Marguerite (?-1968), 9,359
Schwyzer, Marguerite Mueller [Mrs. Arnold], 9,359
Science, 202, 7,178
  exhibitions, 6,346, **6,986**
Science and Logic (book), 8,082
Science fiction, 15,199
Science Fiction Writers of America, 15,199
Science Hall Home Institute (TX), 16,031
Science Hall Institute (TX), 16,031
Science Hill Academy (Shelbyville, KY), students,
  5,327
Science museums, 310
Science, Science, Everywhere! (book), 5,041
Science teachers, **15,216**
Scientific apparatus and instruments, 13,339
Scientific cryptograms, 15,213
Scientific expeditions, 2,719, 14,903
Scientific illustration, **15,214**
Scientific illustrators, 11,505
Scientific societies, 546, 1,738, 2,041, 2,070, 2,090,
  2,667, **2,668**, **2,669**, 4,119, 7,094, 7,136, 8,831,
  10,459, 10,571, **11,248**, 12,009, 12,923, 13,259,
  14,877, 14,880, 14,944, **15,389**
Scientific Temperance Federation, **14,017**
Scientific Temperance Federation of Boston (MA),
  12,515
Scientific Temperance Journal (periodical), 12,515
Scientists, **1,738**, **2,344**, **2,668**, **2,712**, **2,716**, **2,719,**
  2,721, **2,722**, 3,405, 4,696, 6,103, **6,308**, **6,335,**
  7,013, **9,625**, **9,760**, 10,831, **11,901**, 14,508,
  14,838, 14,873, 14,890, **15,319**, 16,973
Scientists, British, **17,219**
Scipio (slave), 2,156
Scofield, Caroline, 9,278
Scofield, Florence Madilia (1858-1936). *See* Thayer,
  Florence Madilia (Scofield) (1858-1936)
Scofield, James Monroe (1824-71), **7,675**
Scofield, John D., 9,278

Scofield, Kathleen "Katie" (1903-). *See* Louchheim, Kathleen "Katie" (Scofield) [Mrs. Walter C., Jr.] (1903-)
Scofield, Madilia Ney Houche [Mrs. James Monroe] (1830-1913), 7,675
Scollard, Jessie Bell Rittenhouse [Mrs. Clinton] (1869-1948), 4,000, 5,273, 11,036
"Scope of Motherhood, The" (speech), 15,270
Scotland, 4,255, 9,345, 12,285
   intellectual life, 12,215
Scott, Abigail Jane "Jennie" (1834-1915). *See* Duniway, Abigail Jane "Jennie" [Mrs. Benjamin Charles] (1834-1915)
Scott, Agnes (Kelly) [Mrs. Roderick] (1891-), 409, 884, 11,846
Scott, Alice Keyes, 114
Scott, Alma Deivia Schmidt [Mrs.] (1892-), **9,360**
Scott, Amanda (ca. 1835-71). *See* Shober, Amanda (Scott) [Mrs. Herod Jacob] (ca. 1835-71)
Scott, Ann (Nicholson) [Mrs. William Anderson] (1811-88), 787
Scott, Anna Charlotte (Waterman) [Mrs. Irving Murray, Jr.] (1866-?), 530, 870
Scott, Anna Margaret (Tressler) (1850-1922), **14,092**
Scott, Anne Firor, 15,197
Scott, Arcadia Bandini (1885-). *See* Brennan, Arcadia Bandini (Scott) (1885-)
Scott, Blanche Stuart, 12,790
Scott, Carlyle McRoberts, **8,611**
Scott, Caroline "Carrie" Lavinia (1832-92). *See* Harrison, Caroline "Carrie" Lavinia (Scott) [Mrs. Benjamin] (1832-92)
Scott, Carrie Emma (1874-1943), 4,483, 11,938
Scott, Charlotte [Mrs.], 3,753
Scott, Clarice, 2,673
Scott, Clement, 12,539
Scott, Coretta (1927-). *See* King, Coretta (Scott) [Mrs. Martin Luther, Jr.] (1927-)
Scott, Elizabeth Chadwick Roberts [Mrs.] (1784-1847), **10,902**
Scott, Elizabeth N. [Mrs. Louis N.] (ca. 1876-1955), 9,361
Scott, Emily D. (Freeman) [Mrs. George], **10,530**
Scott, Emmet Hoyt, 4,487
Scott, Estelle H., 5,469
Scott, Evelyn (1893-), **16,168**
Scott, Family, 14,092
Scott, Family (NY?), 12,531
Scott, Fanny (1883-). *See* Rumely, Fanny (Scott) [Mrs. Edward Aloysius] (1883-)
Scott, Flo (Hampton) [Mrs. Charles C.], **9,727**
Scott, Flora Murray (1891-), **786**
Scott, Francis Josephine, 13,564
Scott, Francis M., 6,800
Scott, George, 16,385
Scott, George, 10,530
Scott, Gloria D., 12,111
Scott, Grace Leigh, 56
Scott, Hannah L. [Miss], **15,086**
Scott, Harriet, 8,044
Scott, Harriet Virginia (ca. 1824-1917), 16,097
Scott, Hazel, 5,530
Scott, Hugh, 14,822
Scott, James B., 6,908
Scott, Jane, **16,385**
Scott, Jeannette (1864-1937), 6,908
Scott, Jessie E., 8,910
Scott, John, 12,307
Scott, John D., 11,327
Scott, John "Jack" V., 17,230
Scott, Julia Ann (1839-1919), **7,039**
Scott, Julia (Green) [Mrs. Matthew] (?-1923), 11,704
Scott, Julian P., **14,943**
Scott, Laura (Hale), 217
Scott, Lilian, **5,172**
Scott, Lizzie J. (Hughes) [Mrs. Robert W.], 13,564
Scott, Louis N. (1859-1929), Family (MN), **9,361**
Scott, Margaret. *See* Smith, Margaret (Scott) [Mrs. L. M.]
Scott, Margaret, **12,307**
Scott, Marie [Mrs.], 8,399
Scott, Martha, 17,943
Scott, Martha Swan, 4,197
Scott, Mary, 9,369

Scott, Mary Relief (Niles) [Mrs. Emmet Hoyt], 4,487
Scott, Mary (Walsh) Lavin [Mrs. Michael MacDonald] (1912-), **11,287**
Scott, Mary White [Mrs. W. Kerr], 13,566
Scott, Matrena [Mrs. Robert W., Jr.], 13,564
Scott, Matthew T., **11,704**
Scott, Matthew T., Jr. (?-1891), 11,704
Scott, Michael MacDonald, 11,287
Scott, Miss, 11,445
Scott, Mrs. E. B., 12,402
Scott, Mrs. John, **4,835**
Scott, Myrtle Gladys (1905-), 5,035
Scott, Natalie Anderson (1906-), **6,081**
Scott, Polly, 9,369
Scott, Rebecca Eleanor "Ella" (1841-96). *See* Green, Rebecca Eleanor "Ella" (Scott) [Mrs. Lafayette] (1841-96)
Scott, Robert W. (1861-1929), **13,564**
Scott, Robert W., II, **13,565**
Scott, Robert Wilmot (1808-84), 5,265
Scott, Roderick, 884
Scott, Rubamah Chambers, 17,992
Scott, Sir Walter (1771-1832), 2,362, 7,658
Scott Thresher Memorial Hospital (Swatow, China), 2,010
Scott, Verna (Golden) [Mrs. Caryle McRoberts] (1876-1964), 8,611
Scott, W. Kerr, 13,282, **13,566**
Scott, William, 17,992
Scott, William Anderson, **787**
Scott, William, Jr., 12,307
Scotti, Marie, 3,977
Scottsboro (AL) case, 8,144
Scouts and scouting, 10,514, **12,103, 12,112**
Scovel, Frances Cabanne [Mrs. Sylvester]. *See* Saportas, Frances Cabanne [Mrs. Sylvester] Scovel [Mrs. W. F. "Bill"]
Scovel, Sylvester, **10,181**
Scovill, Mary Ann. *See* Curtis, Mary Ann (Scovill) [Mrs. Edmond]
Scranton, Cornelia [Mrs. Joseph], 4,356
Scranton, Helen Douglas (Love) (?-1969), 2,020
Scranton, Mary Worthington [Mrs.], 14,820
Scranton, William, 14,822
Scrapbooks, 56, 430, 514, **926, 980**, 1,698, 1,736, 1,786, **1,838**, 3,248, 3,489, **3,517**, 3,534, 3,689, 4,280, 4,729, 4,923, **4,949**, 5,091, 5,092, 5,094, **5,095, 5,594, 5,880**, 6,311, **7,023**, 8,300, 8,477, **8,478**, 8,534, 8,568, **8,577**, 9,382, **9,569**, 9,611, **9,761**, 9,773, **10,006**, 10,490, **11,135, 11,444, 11,449, 11,453, 11,459**, 12,761, 12,782, 12,890, 13,365, 13,375, 13,457, 13,525, 13,794, 13,800, 14,502, 14,565, **14,580**, 14,654, 15,268, **15,954**, **16,127**, 16,345, 16,831, **17,153, 17,162**, 17,782
Screen Actors Guild, 2,284
Screen Stories, 14,347
Screen writers, 949, 1,025, **1,390, 1,451**, 5,240, 6,008, 6,103, **17,793, 17,797, 17,799**, 17,966, **17,972**, 17,983, **17,989**, 18,000
Screven, Ada, 3,505
Screven, C. B. [Miss], 3,505
Screven, Ellen Buchanan, **3,081**
Screven Family (GA), **3,505**
Screven Family (SC), **15,710**
Screven, H. Georgia (Bryan) [Mrs. James Proctor], 3,505
Scribblers' Club, 2,977
Scribner, Charles, 2,875, 2,876
Scribner, Julia, 2,876
Scribner, Myrtle (McPheters) [Mrs. John], **5,663**
Scribner's (periodical), 2,635
Scribner's Monthly. See *Century Magazine*
Scrimsher, Lila (1900-76), **10,531**
Scripps, Ellen Browning [Miss] (1836-1932), **1,193, 1,217**
Script-writers, 556
Scritchfield, Bessie Belle, **4,612**
Scriver, Helen (1889-), **9,362**
Scroggins, Skip, 1,779
Scrogin, Sara Y., 2,853
Scruggs, Martha (Watkins) [Mrs. W. D.], 10,125
Scruggs, Mary Elfrieda "Mary Lou" (1910-). *See*

Williams, Mary Elfrieda "Mary Lou" (Scruggs) [Mrs. John] (1910-)
Scruggs, Susanne Coulan [Mrs. Thomas M.] (1864-1945), **15,884**
Scruggs, Thomas M., 15,884
Scudder, Amos Picton, 3,576
Scudder, Antoinettea, 11,144
Scudder, Cate, 3,576
Scudder, Cornelia Matilda. *See* Buckner, Cornelia Matilda (Scudder)
Scudder, Dorothy, 6,875
Scudder, Emily. *See* Marsh, Emily (Scudder)
Scudder Family (GA), **3,576**
Scudder, Frances, 11,662
Scudder, Horace E., 1,421, 5,714, 12,021
Scudder, Ida Belle S., 6,875, 15,134
Scudder, Ida Sophia (1870-1960), **6,875**
Scudder, Janet (1869-1940), 12,343
Scudder, Mary. *See* Maggie, Mary (Scudder)
Scudder, Nina (Wilkins), 3,083
Scudder, Nina Wilkins [Miss] (1897-1956), **3,082, 3,083**
Scudder, Sarah, 3,576
Scudder School of Art (GA), 3,082
Scudder, Vida Dutton (1861-1954), 6,516, **7,292**, 7,300, 7,567, 7,585, 11,572, 14,437, 15,305, 15,307
Scully, Alice [Mrs. Frank], 1,600
Scully, Frank, 1,600
Sculptors, 543, 970, 1,426, 1,568, 1,751, **2,170, 2,194, 2,207, 2,218, 2,338, 2,413**, 2,521, **2,585**, 2,646, **2,662, 2,748, 2,750, 2,757, 2,767, 2,770, 2,774**, 2,791, 2,792, **2,799**, 2,814, **2,826, 2,856**, 3,345, 3,775, 3,783, 3,951, 3,953, 4,066, 4,233, **4,238**, 4,919, 5,118, 5,694, **5,755, 5,816**, 6,036, 6,384, **6,499, 6,659, 6,699**, 6,903, 7,055, 7,182, 7,200, **7,210**, 7,503, 7,585, **8,522**, 9,170, 9,735, 9,919, 9,942, 10,029, **10,133**, 10,764, 11,203, 11,235, **11,505**, 11,933, 12,298, **12,709, 12,889, 12,892, 12,895, 12,896, 12,897, 12,898, 12,901, 12,912, 12,914**, 14,865, 15,850, **15,946, 16,021, 16,111, 16,372**, 16,575, 16,934, 17,102, **17,236, 17,338**, 17,350, **17,656**, 17,687, 17,964
   indexes, 8,525
Sculptors, Afro-American, 2,948, **7,030**
Sculptors Guild, 12,892
Sculpture, exhibitions, **2,756**, 2,770, 6,036, 6,699
Scunet, Margaret, 11,324
Scuola d'Industrie Italiane (NY), 12,632
Sea Diver: A Quest for History Under the Sea (book), 11,288
Sea Shore Cottage (NJ), 12,820
Seabrook, Annie, 10,897
Seabrook, C. Pinckney, 15,711
Seabrook Family (SC), **15,711**
Seabrook, Mary, 15,711
Seabury, Amelia (Jones) [Mrs. Samuel], 12,158
Seabury, Caroline, 9,363
Seabury, Channing (1842-1910), Family (MN), **9,363**
Seabury Divinity School, 9,438
Seabury Family (NE), 10,454
Seacoast of Bohemia, The (ms), 6,046
Seafood processing, 9,694
Seagrave, Alice D., 13,890
Seagrave, Sadie Fuller (1882-1972), **4,950, 5,025**
Seal, Lydia, 2,044
Seals Club (IA), **5,026**
Seaman, Elizabeth (Cochrane) [Mrs. Robert L.] (1865?-1922), 7,203
Seamans, Marie, **3,719**
Seaman's Mission Church (NY), 8,732
Seamen, 2,201
Seamstresses, **7,974, 9,105, 9,811**, 10,635, 11,042, **16,401**. *See also* Dressmakers
"Seaplane Cruise in the Canadian Arctic, A" (speech), 6,992
"Search for Beauty" (television program), 1,024
Search for the Hidden Places (book), 17,997
"Search for Tomorrow" (television program), 2,104
Seares, Mabel (Urmy), 1,602
Seares, Susan [Mrs.], 3,599
Searing, Delia, 11,666
Searle, Agnes Chambers (ca. 1825-?), 8,986
Searle, Clara. *See* Painter, Clara (Searle) [Mrs. H. K.]

Searle, Martha (Turner) [Mrs. P. C.], 4,958
Sears, Amelia, 4,060
Sears, Clara Endicott [Miss] (1863-1960), 5,908, **7,046**
Sears, Eleonora, 6,452, 15,371
Sears, Gertrude, 17,010
Sears, Roebuck and Company, catalogs, **4,033**
Sears, Zelda. [Mrs. Louis C.] Wiswell, **3,084**
Sea's Edge (book), 7,888
Seattle Arts Commission (WA), **17,334**
Seattle Audubon Society (WA), 17,267
Seattle Business and Professional Women's Club (WA), **17,177**
Seattle Civic Opera Company (WA), 17,298
Seattle Civic Unity Committee (WA), 17,245
Seattle Co-Arts (WA), 17,269
Seattle Council Against War (WA), 17,254
Seattle Council for Minority Rights (WA), 9,252
Seattle Federation of Women's Clubs (WA), 17,246
Seattle Historical Society (WA), 17,220
Seattle-King County Bar Association (WA), civil rights committee, 17,260
Seattle-King County Economic Opportunity Board (WA), 17,357
Seattle-King County Equal Opportunity Board (WA), 17,357
Seattle-King County Mental Health Association (WA), 17,245
Seattle (WA)-Kobe (Japan) Affiliation Committee, 17,267
Seattle Ladies Auxiliary (WA), 17,282
Seattle Model Cities Program (WA), 17,279
Seattle Observer (WA), 2,106
Seattle Peace Information Center (WA), 17,244
Seattle Radical Women (WA), 4,241
Seattle Repertory Playhouse (WA), 17,281
Seattle Women's Commission (WA), 17,233
Seaver, William A., 4,357
Seawell, Donald (1912-), 3,468, **13,008**
Seawell, Eugenia Rawls [Mrs. Donald] (1913-). *See* Rawls, Eugenia. [Mrs. Donald] Seawell (1913-)
Seawell, Molly Elliot (1860-1916), 4,695, 17,098, **17,120**
Seayrs, Annie (Stakebake) [Mrs. H. J.] (1869-1946). *See* Daniels, Annie (Stakebake) [Mrs. H. J.] Seayrs [Mrs. Benjamin F.] (1869-1946)
Seayrs, H. J., 190
Sebo, Mildred M., **8,785**
Sebo-Myhre Family (MN), 8,785
Seccomb Family (MA), **7,676**
Seccomb, John (1708-92), 7,676
Seccomb, Mercy (1743 or 1744-?), 7,676
Seccomb, Mercy Williams [Mrs. John], 7,676
Secession, 7,678, 15,602, 15,627, 15,634, 15,635, 15,726, 15,749, 15,763, 15,766. *See also* Slavery public opinion, 13,392
Seckar, Alvena V. [Miss] (1916-), **17,478**
Seckinger, Ann Eliza, **3,618**
Secombe, Mrs. David, 9,417
Second Adventists, 10,919
Second Bank of the United States, 5,822
Second Baptist Church (GA), 3,168, 3,170
Second Baptist Church (Detroit, MI), 8,026
Second Charter Convention (Denver, CO), 1,718
Second Church (NH), 7,673
Second Connecticut Volunteer Artillery, 1,968
Second Family (MA), 12,309
Second Iowa Volunteer Infantry, Company D, 4,836
Second Louisiana Regiment, 5,362
Second National Bank, 11,746
Second Ponce de Leon Baptist Church (GA), 3,132
Second Presbyterian Church (Chicago, IL), 3,802
Second Presbyterian Church (New Brunswick, NJ), 10,973
Second Presbyterian Church (Philadelphia, PA), 15,062
Second U. S. Colored Troops, Company H, 3,490
Second (West) Parish church (Marlboro, MA), **7,092**
Secord, Josephine "Jessie" Rigdon, 16,524
Secrest, Mildred, 14,695
Secret of the Old Books (book), 4,966
Secret River, The (book), 2,876
Secret societies, 140, 366, 1,067, **1,075**, 1,078, **1,207**, 1,700, **1,796**, 4,697, **4,778**, 5,179, **5,358**, 5,394,

5,838, 6,403, 7,314, 7,849, 8,469, 8,517, 9,394, 9,647, 10,720, **10,772**, **13,199**, 13,686, **14,172**, 14,486, 16,965, **17,550**. *See also* Greek letter societies
Secretaries, **244**, 578, 753, **1,037**, 1,576, 2,179, 2,260, 2,298, **2,389**, **2,512**, 2,596, 2,685, 3,775, 4,352, **4,386**, 4,700, 5,121, 5,123, 5,129, 5,158, **5,593**, **5,646**, 5,647, **5,663**, **5,668**, 5,829, 6,107, **6,292**, 6,316, 6,321, **6,322**, 6,440, **6,873**, 6,949, **7,559**, 7,796, **7,886**, **8,070**, **8,089**, **8,116**, **8,233**, **8,675**, 8,821, **9,211**, 9,858, **10,303**, 10,871, 11,485, 11,486, 11,490, 11,851, 11,976, **11,981**, **12,150**, **12,588**, 12,600, 12,685, 14,082, 14,091, 14,257, 14,392, 14,740, 15,039, **15,163**, **15,164**, **16,037**, 17,032, **17,117**, 17,214, 17,913
Secretaries of state (state governments), 168, 5,394, **5,569**, 6,886, 8,062, **8,928**, 9,204, 10,740, 11,239, 12,790, 13,446, 15,441, 15,859, 16,015, **16,103**, 17,463
Secretary of Labor for Women, 6,725
Security Disability Program, 4,040
Sedalia Daily Deomocrat, 9,876
Sedgwick, Anne Douglas (1873-1935). *See* Selincourt, Anne Douglas (Sedgwick) [Mrs. Basil] (1873-1935)
Sedgwick, Catherine Maria (1789-1867), 1,224, 7,505, 11,821, 12,403
Sedgwick, Charles, 12,027
Sedgwick Family (MA), **7,505**
Sedgwick Family (MA), **12,618**
Sedgwick Family (NY), 12,020
Sedgwick, Grace, 7,065
Sedgwick, Grace, 12,618
Sedgwick, Lily Cameron, 11,560
Sedgwick, Mollie [Mrs.], **10,370**
Sedgwick, Sarah Cabot [Mrs. William Ellery] (ca. 1906-), 7,510
Sedgwick, Susan Anne [Mrs. Theodore], 12,618
Sedgwick, Theodore, 12,618
Sedition, 5,377, 9,380, 9,894, 11,840, 17,608
See, Anna M. *See* Weeks, Anna M. (See)
See, Frances (Graves) [Mrs. Thomas Jefferson Jackson], 2,570
See, Thomas Jefferson Jackson (1866-1962), **2,570**
Seed and the Glory, The: The Career of Samuel Charles Mazzuchelli, O. P., on the Mid-American Frontier (book), 4,986
Seed industry and trade, 1,052, 1,939
Seed potatoes, **6,472**
Seeds, Corinne Aldine (1889-1969), 708, **788**
Seeds of Hiroshima (book), 6,058
Seegars, Dave, 15,401
Seegars, Tabitha A. E. (Yarbrough) [Mrs. Dave] (1848-1965), 15,401
Seegmiller, Daniel, 16,694
Seegmiller, Emma Isabella (Carroll) [Mrs. Daniel] (1868-1954). *See* Higbee, Emma Isabella (Carroll) [Mrs. Daniel] Seegmiller [Mrs. Myron D.] (1868-1954)
Seegmiller, Mary Jane Orrock, **16,910**
Seeing Eye, The (book), 10,172
Seeley, Elizabeth Sterling (1897-1974), **1,827**
Seeley, Grace Alvana, 11,621
Seeley, Sarah J., 14,628
Seely, Nell (1878-1968), **14,440**
Seelye, Elizabeth Tillman (James) [Mrs. Julius] (1833-81), 5,713, 5,867
Seelye, Julius Hawley (1824-95), **5,868**
Seelye, Laura, 7,510
Seelye, Sarah Emma (1841-98). *See* Edmonds, Sarah Emma (Seelye) (1841-98)
Seery, Hilda, 8,094
Seestrom, Selma, 9,386
Sefhos (school yearbook), 4,659
Segal, Bonnie, 15,332
Segerstrom, Margaret [Mrs. Rangnar] (1903-), **17,720**
Segerstrom, Rangnar (1896-), **17,720**
Segregation, 110, 387, 5,379, 5,382, 7,243, 9,605, 11,178, 13,189, 13,468
Segregation in education, 2,502, **5,384**, 12,694. *See also* Discrimination in education
Segregation in higher education, 89, **102**, **112**, 4,017, 9,576

Segregation in public accommodations. *See* Discrimination in public accommodations
Segregation in transportation, 84, 1,248, 6,547
Seguins (TX), 16,141
Segur, Daniel, Sr. (1812-76), 14,142
Segur Family (OH), **14,142**
Segur, Rosa L. (1833-1906), 14,142, 14,144
Seibert, Elizabeth, 2,932
Seid, Ruth (1913-), **6,082**, 13,945
Seifert, Elizabeth (1897-), **6,083**
Seifert, Shirley Louise (1888-1971), **6,084**
Seiler, Evelyn Norton (1883-), 11,851
Seiler, Laura (Ellsworth) (1891-), 827, 1,652
Seitz, Don Carlos (1862-1935), **12,619**
Seixas, Gershom Mendes (1746-1816), **7,552**
Seixas, Grace. *See* Judah,'Grace (Seixas)
Seixas, Grace (1805-30). *See* Nathan, Grace (Seixas) (1805-30)
Seixas, Sarah. *See* Kursheedt, Sarah (Seixas)
Sekley, Anne Boke, 9,316
Selby Family (MD), **12,308**
Selby, James, 12,308
Selby, John S. (1803-77), 12,308
Selby, Joseph, 12,308
Selby, Margaret [Mrs. John S.], 12,308
Selden, Abigail Jones, 11,705
Selden, Charles, 11,705
Selden, Dixie (1868-1925), 13,836
Selden, Eliza, 11,705
Selden Family (NY), **11,705**
Selden, Harriet (?-1840). *See* Gale, Harriet (Selden) (?-1840)
Selden, Mary, 11,705
Seldes, Gilbert, 12,549
Seldon, Susan W., 12,814
Select Committee on Presidential Campaign Activities, 1,937
Select Committee on the Status of Women (NC), 13,565
Select School for Young Ladies (NC), 13,526
Selected Guide to the Literature on the Flowering Plants of Mexico, A (book), 15,216
Selected Poems, 16,163
Selected Poems, 5,498
Selected Prose Writings of Mrs. Emma C. Embury (book), 12,463
Selective service. *See* Military service, compulsory
Selectmen, 6,753
Selenka, Margaret L., 4,631
Self-government in education, 3,116, 8,569, **8,585**, **8,616**, 11,561, **11,752**, **11,755**
Self-government in higher education, 4,213, 6,339, 7,565, **8,625**, **13,202**, **14,038**, 14,745, 14,764, 15,189
Selig, Clara (1880-1970), **4,184**
Selig, Jeanette, 15,208
Selig, Laura (1890-1951), **4,184**
Seligman, Edwin R. A., 12,485
Seligman, Henry, **7,553**
Seligman, Ruth [Mrs. James L.], 11,234
Seligmann-Lui, Jeanne, 9,037
Seligsberg, Alice, 12,117
Selincourt, Anne Douglas (Sedgwick) [Mrs. Basil] (1873-1935), 1,410
Selincourt, Basil, 1,410
Selix, Leah, 501
Sell, Edward S., **3,085**
Sellers, Ann, 15,064
Sellers, Ann (1785-?), 14,902
Sellers, Anna (1824-1908), 14,902
Sellers, Charles, 14,902
Sellers, Coleman (1781-1834), 14,902
Sellers, Cornelia Well [Mrs.] (1831-1909), 14,902
Sellers, Elizabeth Coleman [Mrs.] (1751-1832), 14,902
Sellers Family (PA), **14,902**
Sellers, George Escol, 14,902
Sellers, Hannah, 14,902
Sellers, J. L., 10,548
Sellers, Jane, 15,064
Sellers, Josie Belle, 5,469
Sellers, Sophonisba Augusciola Peale [Mrs. Coleman] (1786-1859), 14,902
Selma Plantation (MS), 9,774

Selmes, Isabella (1886-1953). *See* Greenway, Isabella (Selmes) (1886-1953)
Selmon, Bertha Eugenia (Loveland) (1877-1949), **7,920, 15,139**
Selznick, Irene Mayer (1910-), **6,085**
Semans, Mary Duke Biddle Trent [Mrs. James H.], 11,879
Semenza, Edwin S. (1910-), **10,743**
Seminars, **950,** 17,583
Seminary for Young Ladies and Children (PA), 14,949
Seminole Indians, 1,475, 2,498, 2,883, 2,947, 14,234, 14,241, 15,494
  costume and dress, 2,951
  food, 2,951
  religion, 2,951
  wars, 2,952, 15,735
Semmingson, Ingrid [Mrs.] (1910-), **8,786**
Semple, Aimee [Mrs. Robert James] (1890-1944). *See* McPherson, Aimee [Mrs. Robert James] Semple [Mrs. Harold Stewart] (1890-1944)
Semple, Ellen Churchill [Miss] (1863-1932), **5,323**
Semple, Eugene (1840-1908), 4,198, 17,226, **17,335**
Semple, Lucy Virginia (1837-1925). *See* Ames, Lucy Virginia (Semple) (1837-1925)
Señan, Father José, 951
Senators, United States, 76, 110, **176,** 181, **255,** 488, 540, 575, 682, 721, 828, 900, 1,430, 1,530, 1,552, 1,669, 1,673, 1,702, 1,746, 2,033, 2,036, 2,120, 2,160, **2,210, 2,230, 2,235, 2,251,** 2,270, 2,290, **2,298,** 2,325, 2,379, 2,408, 2,432, 2,454, 2,489, **2,493,** 2,528, 2,550, **2,638,** 2,651, 2,855, 2,868, 2,875, **3,008,** 3,021, 3,133, 3,389, 3,394, 3,667, 3,669, 3,681, **3,684,** 3,712, 3,722, 3,725, **4,356,** 4,357, 4,486, 4,643, 4,732, 4,747, 4,905, 4,906, 5,053, 5,060, 5,276, 5,281, 5,333, 5,348, 5,537, 5,719, 5,774, 6,489, **6,491,** 6,615, 6,858, 7,242, 7,613, 7,677, 7,745, 7,968, 8,949, 8,975, **9,001,** 9,041, **9,140,** 9,149, 9,155, **9,160,** 9,170, **9,193,** 9,211, **9,263,** 9,286, 9,297, 9,303, **9,311, 9,368, 9,582,** 9,929, 9,942, 9,965, 9,986, 10,137, 10,170, **10,513, 10,548,** 10,800, 10,862, 10,872, 11,049, 11,131, 11,602, 11,827, 11,855, **11,875, 11,913,** 11,956, 12,168, 12,440, 12,481, **12,509,** 12,575, 12,597, 12,828, **12,833,** 12,965, 13,080, 13,163, **13,210,** 13,610, 14,225, 14,362, **14,429,** 14,504, **14,599, 14,622,** 14,683, **14,975,** 15,041, 15,317, 15,583, 15,863, 15,869, 16,029, 17,083, 17,251, 17,378, 17,409, **17,462,** 17,654, **17,732,** 17,973
Senators, United States, Afro-American, 1,655, **2,230**
Seneca Falls Convention, Declaration of Sentiments (1848, NY), 12,857
Seneca Indians, 1,428, **11,294**
Senegal, 9,932
Sengbusch, Anne Walker [Mrs.], 11,377
Sengenberger, Ella [Miss] (1890-1964), **4,268**
Senior Centers of Metropolitan Chicago (IL), **4,152**
Senior Citizens' Hobby Center (Chicago, IL). *See* Senior Centers of Metropolitan Chicago (IL)
Senior, Ellen (Hodgson) [Mrs. Joseph] (1840-1917), **16,814**
Senior History Club (MN), 8,832
Senior women, 8,057
Seniority (employees), 8,075, 8,111, 8,137, 8,140
Senior citizens, 3,905, 8,058, 8,176, 8,655, 11,021, 11,501, 15,176, 15,999, 16,000
  biography, **6,347**
  care and hygiene, 9,987, 16,998
  dwellings, 17,846
  employment, 6,892, 12,271
  hospital care, 8,862
  medical care, 238, 239
  societies and clubs, **4,152**
  transportation, **10,404**
Senkler, Abigail Louise (Dickson) [Mrs. George Easton] (1871-1961), 9,364
Senkler, Ellen Burgess. *See* Brown, Ellen Burgess (Senkler) [Mrs. J. Fuller]
Senkler, George Easton, Family (MN), **9,364**
Senn High School (Chicago, IL), 11,713
Senninger, Clara. *See* Schmitt, Clara (Senninger) [Mrs. Otto F.]
"Sentimental and Melancholy" (song), 5,530
Sentinel (newspaper), 6,343

Sentinels of the Republic, 6,728
Separation (marital relations), 2,574, 10,939, **14,988**
Sephardim, 14,497, 17,282
Sepulchral monuments. *See* Gravestones
Sepulveda, Concepcion Dominguez [Miss], 1,525
"Sequel to Cliquot" (story), 5,413
Seraphine, Sister M. (1891-), 10,732
Serbian Relief Society (CA), 1,328
Sergeant, Abigail (1721-91), 7,511
Sergeant, Caroline, 7,511
Sergeant, Elizabeth Shepley (1881-1965), 17,053
Sergeant, Eunice, 7,511
Sergeant, John (1710-49), **7,511**
Sergeant, Mary, 7,140
Sergeant, Mary Jane (1837-1917). *See* Larison, Mary Jane (Sergeant) [Mrs. Cornelius Wilson] (1837-1917)
Sericulture, 7,467, 16,486, 16,699
Serious Wooing, The (book), 11,977
Serkin, Rudolf, 13,801
Sermons, 2,544, 7,415, 7,484, 7,634, **10,711, 15,295,** 15,654
Seropians, The (booklet), 433
Serrurier, Zenna Leshing (1906-), **789**
Servants, 955, 3,513, 5,281, 12,939. *See also* Household workers
Servants, Afro-American, 9,303
Servants of Mary, 10,611
Servants of Mary Motherhouse (Omaha, NE), **10,614**
Servants of Mary, Our Lady of Sorrows Convent (WI), **17,578**
Servants of the Blessed Sacrament (Pueblo, CO), **1,819**
Servants of the Holy Heart of Mary, Provincial House (IL), **4,283**
Servants of the Immaculate Heart of Mary (Saco, ME), **5,705**
Servants of the Immaculate Heart of Mary (PA), **15,266**
Service Bureau for Intercultural Education, 9,494
Service Bureau for Unemployed Women (IL), 4,055
Service Bureau for Women's Organizations. *See* Auerbach Service Bureau for Connecticut Organizations
Service, Emma Maria [Miss], **13,121**
Service Employees International Union, Local 543 (AL), 3,448
Service Employees International Union, Southern Region, **3,448**
Service, John Hugh James, 13,121
"Service League Follies" (WV), 17,475
Service, Martha (Stackhouse) Williford [Mrs. John Hugh James], 13,121
Service Star, 3,250
Service Star Legion (GA), **3,250**
Serviss, Elizabeth, 8,094
"Sesame Street" (television program), 2,104, 11,845
Sesqui-Centennial International Exhibition (PA), 13,535
Sesquicentennial Exhibition Association (PA), **14,923**
Session, Vivian Siemon, **7,921**
Sessions, Kate Olivia [Miss] (1857-1940), **1,194, 1,218**
Sessions, Patty (Bartlett) [Mrs. Davis] (1795-1892), 16,746, **16,815, 16,955**
"Set a Thief" (story), 14,736
Set designers, 6,085, 17,231
Set Her on a Throne (book), 6,113
Setlow, Jane, 6,336
Seton, Anya (1916-), **6,086**
Seton, Eliza Ann, 12,315
Seton, Ernest Thompson (1860-1946), 6,086
Seton, Grace (Gallatin) [Mrs. Ernest Thompson] (1872-1959), 6,086, **6,876, 7,293**
Seton Hill College, faculty, 14,800
Seton Indians, 1,837
Seton, Robert (1839-1927), Family, **4,645**
Seton, St. Elizabeth Ann (Bayley) (1774-1821), 996, **4,645,** 5,493, 5,774, 5,847, 10,144, 14,800
Settle, Sister Mary, 5,298
Settle, Thomas, **13,567**
Settlement Cook Book, 17,664, 17,840, 17,841
Settlement houses. *See* Social settlements
Settlement Music School (Philadelphia, PA), **15,208**
Settlement Woman's Club (Chicago, IL), 3,875

Settlements (law), 15,533, 15,546, 15,665
Seven Ages of Childhood (book), 6,188
Seven Associated Colleges Alumnae Clubs, **6,877**
Seven Days to Lomaland (book), 6,109
Seven Stories by James Hall (book), 4,445
Seven Sutherland Sisters Hair Restorer, 11,799
Seventeen (periodical), 11,866, 17,614
Seventeenth Connecticut Volunteers, 12,421
Seventh-day Adventist Church, 161, 2,101, 10,602
Seventh-Day Adventists, 53, **8,163**
  education, **2,116**
Seventh-day Adventists, General Conference Ministerial Association, 2,116
Seventh Day Baptists, 11,271
Seventh International Conference of American States on the Political and Civil Rights of Women, 6,908
Severance, Annie (Crittenden), 1,483
Severance, Caroline Maria (Seymour) [Mrs. Theodoric Cordenio] (1820-1914), 1,442, **1,483,** 1,950, 2,818, 4,684, 6,741, 7,222, **7,294,** 11,547
Severance, H. A. (1838-?), **6,878**
Severance, Julia Long, 7,294
Severance, Lena Lillian Hill [Mrs. Frank H.] (1854-1942), **11,706**
Severance, Mary F. (1863-1925), 8,971, 9,268
Severance, Sarah M., 1,255
Severin, Bertha (Meyer) [Mrs. William], 3,897
Severson, Amanda, 9,473
Severson, Bessie [Mrs.], **17,139**
Sevier, Catherine Sherrill [Mrs. John], 9,869
Sevier, Clara Driscoll, 16,072
Sevier, John, 9,722
Sevier, Sarah Hawkins [Mrs. John], 9,869
Sew IT and Wear IT (book), 4,975
Sewall, Elizabeth, 3,051
Sewall, May Eliza (Wright) [Mrs. Edwin W.] Thompson [Mrs. Theodore Lovett] (1844-1920), 2,413, 4,623, **4,631,** 5,334, 7,239, **8,362,** 12,811, 17,616, 17,725
"Sewanee Life" (ms), 15,980
Sewanee Review, 15,934
Seward, Frances Adeline (Miller) [Mrs. William Henry] (1805-65), 12,833
Seward, Frances "Fanny" Adeline (1844-66), 12,833
Seward, Janet McNeil (Watson) [Mrs. William Henry, Jr.], 12,833
Seward, Olive Risley, 12,833
Seward-Saline Inter-County Federation of Women's Clubs (NE), 10,406
Seward, William Henry (1801-72), 2,262, 11,277, 11,280, 11,602, 12,003, 12,052, **12,833**
Sewell, Elizabeth (1919-), **6,087**
Sewell, Margaret Elizabeth (1919-). *See* Sewell, Elizabeth (1919-)
Sewell, Mary Wright, 1,436
Sewell, Patience (1918-). *See* Latting, Patience (Sewell) [Mrs. Trimble B.] (1918-)
Sewing, 2,704, **2,998,** 4,347, 7,913
Sewing Circle (PA), **2,147**
Sewing Club (South Bend, IN), **4,667**
Sewing-machines, 5,758, 14,942
Sewing schools, 12,271
Sewing Society (Newburyport, MA), 9,265
Sex, 459, 12,087
Sex and the Office (book), 7,196
Sex and the Single Girl (book), 7,196
Sex crimes, 9,095
  prevention, 7,738
Sex customs, 8,207
Sex discrimination, 301, 4,124, 6,790, **6,838,** 7,324, 9,984, 10,096, 11,150, 16,226, 17,975
  law and legislation, **1,927,** 6,807, 6,849, 12,707
  cases, 6,790
  legal aspects, 11,695
Sex discrimination in education, 1,125, **8,549,** 11,373, 15,237, 17,698
Sex discrimination in employment, 301, 948, 1,162, 3,451, 11,897
Sex discrimination in government employment, 9,951
Sex discrimination in wages, 5,149, 11,897
Sex education. *See* Sex instruction
Sex in Civilization (book), 6,602

Sex Information and Education Council of the US, 6,446, 6,987
Sex instruction, 2,451, 3,895, **4,111**, 5,842, 6,219, 6,388, 6,446, 6,987, 7,197, 7,283, 7,289, 7,317, 8,637, 8,639, 12,837
Sex research, **2,669**, 6,676
Sex role, 6,898, 7,324
Sex role socialization of women, **5,399**, 15,323
Sex roles, 8,676
Sexism in educational tests and measurements, 11,150
Sexton, Anne (Harvey) (1928-74), **6,088**
Sexton, Caroline (1826-1911), **14,657**
Sexton, Ella May, 317
Sexton Family (AL, CT, MI), 7,935
Sexton, Hannah (?-1848), 7,935
Sexton, Margaret Branch, **3,086**
Sexton, Mary B. (1816-91). *See* Lively, Mary B. (Sexton) [Mrs. Amos] (1816-91)
Sexton, Miranda (1826-1910). *See* Spalding, Miranda (Sexton) [Mrs. William P.] (1826-1910)
Sextons, 8,398
Sexual Barrier: Legal, Medical, Economic and Social Aspects of Sex, The (book), 2,865
Sexual behavior (human). *See* Sexuality
Sexual ethics, 7,174
Sexual freedom, 8,207
"Sexual Politics in the Classroom" (lecture), 15,197
Sexuality, 4,086, 4,131, **8,207**, 8,637
  teen agers, 8,633
Seydell, Mildred (Woolley) (1899-), **3,251**, **3,350**
Seydell Quarterly (periodical), 3,251
Seymore Family, 12,203
Seymour, Caroline Maria (1820-1914). *See* Severance, Caroline Maria (Seymour) [Mrs. Theodoric Cordenio] (1820-1914)
Seymour, Elizabeth, 2,004
Seymour Family (IL), **4,269**
Seymour, Flora Warren [Mrs. George Steele] (1888-1948), 4,269
Seymour, John Lawrence, **16,438**
Seymour, Mary [Mrs.], 11,583
Seymour School of Musical Reeducation (NY), 14,311
Seymour-Smith, Martin, 4,237, 16,165
Sgaw Karen High School (Burma), 6,826
Shabonee (Native American), 3,897
Shackelford, Sara C., **15,712**
Shackford, Martha (Boardman) [Mrs. Seth Ring] (1789-1863), **10,882**
Shackford, Seth Ring, 10,882
Shackleford, Elise (?-1957), **5,324**
Shackleton, Anna W., 2,315
Shackleton, Elizabeth (Carlton) (1726-1804), 14,852
Shackleton Family, **14,852**
Shackleton, Lydia, 2,315
Shackleton, Mary. *See* Leadbeater, Mary (Shackleton)
Shadkhan, Emma. *See* Woytinsky, Emma (Shadkhan) (1893-)
Shadow of a Star, 6,001
Shadow of Eagles, A (book), 5,987
Shadows on the Rock (book), 12,414
Shady Grove (book), 5,264
Shafe, Anne [Miss], **3,252**
Shafer, Helen, 7,574
Shaffer, Rose Jane (Bean), 1,663
Shaffner, John E., 13,568
Shafroth-Palmer Amendment, 6,968, 11,904
Shafter, Toby [Miss], 5,694
Shaftsbury, Anthony Ashley Cooper, First Earl of (1621-83), **15,713**
Shagbark Hill (book), 6,073
Shainess, Natalie, 15,134, 15,197
Shakerag Hounds (GA), 3,374
Shakers, 2,464, 2,626, **4,437**, 5,053, 5,123, 5,264, **5,298**, **5,364**, 7,034, 7,035, 7,036, 7,037, **7,038**, 7,040, **7,041**, 7,046, **7,047**, 10,814, 12,260, **12,309**, 12,363, **12,620**, **13,955**, 14,718
  hymns, **2,626**, 7,047
Shakespeare and Art Club of Mitchell (SD), **15,861**
Shakespeare and Company (book), 11,153
Shakespeare and Company (Paris, France), 11,153
Shakespeare and the Heart of a Child (book), 17,723
Shakespeare Club (Flagstaff, AZ), **158**

Shakespeare Club (Pomona, CA), **1,110**
Shakespeare Club (FL), **2,914**
Shakespeare Club (Williamstown, MA). *See* Literary Club (Williamstown, MA)
Shakespeare Club (Clinton, MO), **9,910**
Shakespeare Club (TX), 16,263
Shakespeare Club (WY), 17,931
Shakespeare Festival (Ashland, OR), 1,545
Shakespeare, William, 16,354
  study, **2,914**
Shakespeare Without Tears (book), 2,625
Shakopee Women's Reformatory (MN), 9,482
Shamberger, Hugh A., 10,665
Shand, Louly (1870-1961), **15,714**
Shand, Mary Wright (1876-1953), **15,715**
Shandorf, Marilyn [Mrs.], 9,488
Shane, Charles D., 790
Shane, Mary Lea (Heger) [Mrs. Charles D.] (1897-), **790**, 11,815
Shanghai American School (China), 8,870, 8,871
"Shanghai Scene" (story), 16,153
Shank, Florence (1901-), 245
Shanker, Albert, 8,097, 8,121
Shankland Family, 11,717
Shankland, Lucy Buell (King) [Mrs. Ebenezah Maxwell] Leal [Mrs. William Henry], 11,717
Shankland, William Henry, 11,717
Shannon, Alice, 9,613
Shannon, Anne. *See* Martin, Anne (Shannon) [Mrs. William A.]
Shannon, Dell (pseudonym). *See* Linington, Elizabeth (1921-)
Shannon, Effie, 12,529
Shannon, Emma. *See* Crutcher, Emma (Shannon) [Mrs. William O.]
Shannon Family (MS), 9,613
Shannon, Grace, 9,613
Shannon, Levina. *See* Mount, Levina (Shannon) [Mrs. Thomas]
Shannon, Levina (Morris) [Mrs. Marmaduke], 9,613
Shannon, Marmaduke, 9,613
Shannon, Marmaduke (son), 9,613
Shannon, Mary, 9,613
Shannon, Mary Ancrum, 15,731
Shannon, Phillip E. (1827-95), **10,712**
Shansi Memorial Association, 14,119
Shape of a Song, The (book), 3,159
Shapiro, Charlotte (1915-). *See* Zolotow, Charlotte (Shapiro) (1915-)
Shapiro, Louis B., 3,914
Shapiro, Nadia Lavrova, 628
Shapsnikoff, Anfesia [Mrs.], 8,206
Share-a-Job Committee (OH), 14,021
Sharecroppers, 10,159
Sharecroppers, Afro-American, 12,682, 16,780
Sharecroppers Union (AL), **90**
Share-cropping, 10,159, 16,377
Sharkey, Minerva (Cage), 9,709
Sharland, Edward, 12,310
Sharland, Emily [Mrs. Edward], **12,310**
Sharon Equal Suffrage League (WI), **17,721**
Sharon, Frederick William (1857-1915), Family, 791
Sharon, Henrietta, 3,284
Sharon, Louise (Tevis) Breckinridge [Mrs. Frederick William] (ca. 1858-1938), 791
Sharp, Abbie Gardner, 4,696
Sharp, Catherine, 11,661
"Sharp Comments," 14,041
Sharp, Doris, 1,339
Sharp, Eleanor P. (Gibbons) [Mrs. Louis H.], **1,298**, 1,358
Sharp, Ella "Nellie" Wing (Merriman) [Mrs. John C.] (1857-1912), **8,205**
Sharp, Estelle Boughton [Mrs. Walter B.], **16,128**
Sharp, Evelyn, 16,166
Sharp, Florence Beatrice (Wines) [Mrs. Lewis, Sr.] (1884-?), **10,633**, 10,636, **10,710**, 10,713
Sharp, Helen Maria [Mrs. John], **4,836**
Sharp, John, **4,836**
Sharp, Katherine Lucinda [Miss] (1865-1914), **4,396**
Sharp, Lewis, **10,713**
Sharp, Lewis, Sr., 10,713
Sharp, Louis H., 1,358
Sharp, Mary McCann, 10,714

Sharp, Mrs. Edgar E., **9,365**
Sharp, Mrs. Walter, 771
Sharp, Susie Marshall [Miss] (1907-), 13,406, 13,446
Sharp, Thelma Fern (1898-1975), **14,041**
Sharpe, Peter, 9,237
Sharpless Family (PA), **14,853**
Sharps, Helen, 1,905
Sharpshooters, **14,101**, **16,547**, **17,932**
Shattuck, E. D., 14,418
Shattuck, Eliza (Lanphear), **9,366**
Shattuck Family (PA), **15,032**
Shattuck, Fredrica (1883-1969), **4,690**
Shattuck, Harriette Lucy (Robinson) [Mrs. Sidney Doane] (1850-1937), **6,859**, 7,082
Shattuck, Helen B., 17,006
Shattuck, Joanna, 12,071
Shattuck School (MN), 9,438
Shattuck School (OR), 14,658
Shaufler, Edwin Henry, **16,386**
Shaufler, Johnnie Mae (Hackworthe) [Mrs. Edwin Henry] (1904-). *See* Hackworthe, Johnnie Mae. [Mrs. Edwin Henry] Shaufler (1904-)
Shaver, Dorothy [Miss] (1899-), **6,879**, 12,086
Shaw (NC), **13,569**
Shaw, Abigail Adams (1790-1859). *See* Felt, Abigail Adams (Shaw) [Mrs. Joseph Barlow] (1790-1859)
Shaw, Adelaide Taber (Young) [Mrs. Farnham Horatio] (1877-1964), **11,707**
Shaw, Ann (1819-91), **8,291**
Shaw, Anna Howard (1847-1919), 49, 55, 349, 826, 1,230, 1,304, 1,308, 1,391, 2,501, 4,631, 5,305, 6,532, **6,534**, 6,536, **6,983**, 7,222, 7,232, 7,268, 7,284, **7,719**, 9,142, 10,687, 11,547, 12,529, 12,588, 12,695, 12,811, 12,834, 12,835, **13,246**, 14,737, 14,745, 15,095, 15,706, 15,733, 15,851, 16,252, 18,013
Shaw, Anna Leonard (Stetson) Smith (1766-1847), 7,677
Shaw, Annette Jane (1853-1920), **11,399**
Shaw, C. A., 13,497
Shaw, D. W., 13,497
Shaw, Edith (1905-), 16,485
Shaw, Elizabeth (Smith) [Mrs. John] (1750-1815). *See* Peabody, Elizabeth (Smith) [Mrs. John] Shaw [Mrs. Stephen] (1750-1815)
Shaw, Emma Augusta (1792?-1875). *See* Hobbs, Emma Augusta (Shaw) (1792?-1875)
Shaw Family, **2,571**
Shaw Family, 12,485
Shaw Family, **12,621**
Shaw Family (MA, ME, NH), 7,677
Shaw Family (NE), **10,533**
Shaw Finger Paint Studio (New York, NY), 13,122
Shaw, Francis G., 12,621
Shaw, George Bernard (1856-1950), 8,619, 11,944, 11,956, 11,979, 12,612, 16,166
Shaw, Hannah (1834-1920?). *See* Noxon, Hannah (Shaw) [Mrs. George] (1834-1920?)
Shaw, Hannah Hicks [Mrs. Stephen P.] (?-1886), 10,533
Shaw, Hannah King (1800-75). *See* Webb, Hannah King (Shaw) (1800-75)
Shaw, Harriet Cornelia Bidwell, 11,246
Shaw, Henry (1800-99), **10,153**
Shaw, Ida Estelle (Porter) [Mrs. George Moore] (1860-1940), 1,331
Shaw, James P., 517
Shaw, Josephine (1843-1905). *See* Lowell, Josephine (Shaw) [Mrs. Charles Russell] (1843-1905)
Shaw, Louise C., 3,506
Shaw, Margretta (1881-). *See* Dietrich, Margretta (Shaw) [Mrs. Charles H.] (1881-)
Shaw, Martha O. (Van Orsdol) [Mrs. John]. *See* Farnsworth, Martha O. (Van Orsdol) [Mrs. John] Shaw [Mrs. Fred C.]
Shaw, Mildred Hart [Mrs.] (1909-), **18,009**
Shaw, Nathaniel Tracy, **11,708**
Shaw, Pauline (Agassiz) [Mrs. Quincy Adams] (1841-1917), 6,808, **6,880**, **6,984**
Shaw, Robert, 2,262
Shaw, Ruth Faison [Miss] (1887-1969), **13,122**, 13,398
Shaw, Sallie Rogers, 3,419

Shaw, Stephen P. (1801-63), 10,533
Shaw University (Releigh, NC), 89
Shaw, William Smith, 2,571
Shawa, Nadonis, **17,814**
Shawhan, Narcissa (Tayloe) [Mrs. Charles S.], 54
Shawl, Helen Livingston, 16,865
Shawn, Edwin M. "Ted" (1891-1972), 764, 12,364, **12,365**
Shawver, C. D., 1,722
Shawver, Ida, **3,720**
Shawver, Lona Thomason [Mrs.], **16,387**
Shay, Jonathan B., 11,117
Shays' Rebellion, 7,333, 12,153
Shea Family, 7,148
Shea, Mabel, 2,596
Shea, Mrs. James M. (1901-), **5,664**
Sheafe, Margarette, 11,708
Shearer, George Martin (1841-90), **3,721**
Shearer, William B., 7,187
Shearson, Mrs. E. L., 13,533
Shedd, Louise. *See* Pratt, Louise (Shedd) [Mrs. Walter I.]
Shedd, Margaret Cochran (1900-), **6,089**
Sheehan, Molly Antoinette, 3,411
Sheeler, Charles, 2,752
Sheen, Fulton J., 14,504
Sheep, 10,628, 16,862
   transportation, 477
Sheep ranches, 1,621
Sheep ranching, 14,436
"Sheepeater Campaign, The: Idaho—1879" (booklet), 3,713
Sheepeater Indians, wars (1878-1879), 3,721
Sheets, Margaret (Hutchinson) [Mrs. Elijah Funk] (1819-47), **16,817**
Sheffield, Anna D. [Miss], **1,929**
Sheftall, Josephine, **3,577**
Sheftall, Mordecai, 3,553
Shehee, Edith Meriwether Washington (1891-1968), **126**
Sheil, Catherine, 9,890
Sheip, Marie Layette, **43**
Sheka, Merle, 16,877
Shelby, Alfred (1804-32), 5,343
Shelby, Isaac, 5,343
Shelby Promoter (MT), 10,336
Shelby, Ruth, 9,950
Shelby, Susan Preston (1830-91). *See* Grigsby, Susan Preston (Shelby) [Mrs. John Warren] (1830-91)
Shelby, Virginia (Hart) [Mrs. Alfred] (1809-59). *See* Breckinridge, Virginia (Hart) [Mrs. Alfred] Shelby [Mrs. Robert Jefferson] (1809-59)
Shelbyville Woman's Club (IL), **4,334**
Sheldon, Addison E., 10,534
Sheldon, Alice Bradley [Mrs. Huntingdon], 4,061
Sheldon, Anna K. [Mrs.], 12,463
Sheldon, Edward Austin (1823-97), **12,762**
Sheldon, Elizabeth, 12,762
Sheldon, Frank M., 11,572
Sheldon, Irene [Mrs. Edwin], **485**
Sheldon, Jennie Maria (Arms) [Mrs. George] (1852-1938), **7,013**
Sheldon, Laura Austin, 12,762
Sheldon, Lucy, 1,970
Sheldon, Margaret (Thompson) [Mrs. Addison E.] (?-1942), **10,534**
Sheldon, Mary, 11,748
Sheldon, Mary Downing (1850-98). *See* Barnes, Mary Downing (Sheldon) [Mrs. Earl] (1850-98)
Sheldon, Mrs. J. O., 220
Sheldon Museum (AK), 147
Sheldon, William E., 11,547
Shellabarger, Abigail W., 1,786
Shellabarger, Blanche Ashley, 1,786
Shellabarger, M. Elizabeth, 1,786
Shellabarger, Mary Elizabeth, **1,741**
Shelland, Annie "Muskeg Annie" (1878-1964). *See* Williams, Annie "Muskeg Annie" (Shelland) [Mrs. Clarence E.] (1878-1964)
Shellenberger, Frances Jane (Horsley) (1884-?), **10,780**
Shellenberger, Hope. *See* Dukes, Hope (Shellenberger)
Shelley, Gertrude Matthews, 2,679

Shelley, Kate (ca. 1866-?), **4,694**, 4,699
Shelley, Mrs. John, 13,966
Shelley, Percy Bysshe, 3,200
Shelley, Rebecca (1887-), 7,868, **7,923, 8,009**
Shelley, Thelma K., 5,469
Shellman, Mary Bostwick (1849-1938), **5,854**
Shells, 14,875, **14,879**, 14,901
   catalogs and collections, 1,575, 1,586
Shelly, Mary, 2,710
Shelnut, Miriah. *See* Cochran, Miriah Shelnut [Mrs. George Washington]
Sheltering Arms Association (GA), 3,135
Sheltering Arms Association of Day Nurseries (GA), **3,253**
Sheltering Arms Children's Service, **11,030**
Sheltering Arms Mission (GA), 3,140
Shelton, Amanda Rhoda. *See* Stewart, Amanda Rhoda (Shelton)
Shelton, Burnita (1894-). *See* Matthews, Burnita (Shelton) (1894-)
Shelton, Eliza (1840-1909). *See* Keeler, Eliza (Shelton) [Mrs. James] (1840-1909)
Shelton, Emma [Mrs.], 9,527
Shelton Family (IA), **5,027**
Shelton Family (NY), **11,709**
Shelton, Maria L. [Miss], **9,728**
Shelton, Mary E., 5,027
Shelton, Wilma Loy (1889-1972), **11,228**
Shenandoah (ship), 15,895
Shenehon, Eleanor, 8,633
Shepard, Anna O., 6,325
Shepard, Eliza, 16,470
Shepard, Eliza (?-1911). *See* Pumpelly, Eliza (Shepard) [Mrs. Raphael] (?-1911)
Shepard, Elizabeth DeAngelis (Wells) [Mrs. Sidney] (1830-1922), 12,763
Shepard Family (NY), **12,763**
Shepard, Finley S., 12,214
Shepard, Flola, 13,333
Shepard, Helen Miller (Gould) [Mrs. Finley S.] (1868-1938), **12,214**
Shepard, Joanna M., 12,034
Shepard, Lulu Loveland, **16,818**
Shepard, May Lucretia. *See* Cheney, May Lucretia (Shepard) [Mrs. Warren]
Shepard, Sidney, 12,763
Shepardson, Mrs. Hill, 8,672
Shephard, Esther (Lofstrand) (1891-1975), **17,336**
Shepherd, Alexander Robey (1835-1902), **2,572**
Shepherd, Edith Carpenter, 7,151
Shepherd, Elizabeth Murray, 4,406
Shepherd Family, 11,522
Shepherd, George F. (1835-65), **17,540**
Shepherd, Grace (1869-?). *See* Merchant, Grace (Shepherd) [Mrs. Francis D.] (1869-?)
Shepherd, Mary Elizabeth (1854-1932). *See* Ashworth, Mary Elizabeth (Shepherd) [Mrs. William Booth] (1854-1932)
Shepherd, May. *See* Quintard, May (Shepherd) [Mrs. E. A.]
Shepherd, May (Young) [Mrs. Alexander Robey] (?-1930), 2,572
Shepherd, Myrtle. *See* Francis, Myrtle (Shepherd)
Shepherd, Theodosia Burr (Hall) (1854-1906), 484, **1,052**
Shepherd, William N. B., 16,916
Shepherd's Fold, 11,030
Sheppard Family, 2,890
Sheppard, George S., **11,710**
Sheppard, Lou Lee, 2,890
Sheppard, Louisa (Campbell) (1848-?), **13,123**
Sheppard, Lucy Gantt [Mrs. William] (1867-1955), 86, **95**
Sheppard, Madeline, **2,148**
Sheppard Memorial Library (Greenville, NC), 13,265
Sheppard, Nettie N. [Mrs.], 13,612
Sheppard-Towner Act (1921), 2,504, 5,587, 6,431, 9,263
Sheppard, William, 95
Shepperd, Juniata L., 8,607
Sheridan, Alice Louise Guerber, 1,716
Sheridan Baptist Church (Lincoln, NE), 10,499
Sheridan, Philip Henry (1831-88), **2,573**, 17,420
Sheridan, Sister Theresa, Frances 5,493

Sheriff, Hilla, 15,429
Sheriffs, 190, **5,272**, 17,452
Sherk, Jessie, 2,260
Sherlock, Mary, **10,371**
Sherlock, W. A., **10,371**
Sherman, Althea Rosina, 2,724
Sherman, Edith Bishop (1889-), **5,028**
Sherman, Ellen Boyle (Ewing) [Mrs. William Tecumseh] (1824-88), **1,484**, 2,325, 2,327, 4,643, 4,646
Sherman, Emma Powell (1856-1938), **11,400**
Sherman, James S., 10,673
Sherman, Joan (pseudonym). *See* Dern, Peggy Gaddis (1895-1966)
Sherman, Margaret (1912-), **8,713**
Sherman, Martha (Williams) [Mrs. H. C.], 12,540, 12,674
Sherman, Mary Jane [Mrs. Salisbury] (1832-1926), **14,487**
Sherman, Mary Nell, 2,850
Sherman, Nettie, 9,467
Sherman, Samary Stedman (1785-?), 7,678
Sherman, Sarah, 11,719
Sherman, William D., 11,330
Sherman, William Tecumseh (1820-91), 62, 2,327, 3,536, 4,646, 15,475, 15,536
Sherman, William Tecumseh (1820-91), Family, **4,646**
Sherman's March to the Sea, 2,277, 3,212, 13,468, 15,590
Sherrard, Mother, 15,860
Sherrill, Evelyn Norcross, 17,114
Sherrill, Harriet (1803-65). *See* Ward, Harriet (Sherrill) (1803-65)
Sherrill, Laura A. (?-1892). *See* Caton, Laura A. (Sherrill) [Mrs. John Dean] (?-1892)
Sherrod, Mrs. Arthur, 8,255
Sherry, Laura Case (1876-1947), **17,815**
Sherwin, Belle (1868-1955), **6,881**, 13,979
Sherwood Eddy Seminary, 13,754
Sherwood, Emily Howland, 11,425
Sherwood, Josephine (1877?-1957). *See* Hull, Josephine (Sherwood) (1877?-1957)
Sherwood, Lillian E. (1913-), **8,124**
Sherwood, Lizzie [Mrs.], 12,168
Sherwood, Lorraine [Miss], 12,120
Sherwood, Mary (1856-1935), 5,809
Sherwood, Mary Elizabeth (Wilson) (1826-1903), 10,834, 11,067, 17,010
Sherwood, Rosamond (1899-), 7,510
Sherwood, Sarah Belknap "Belle" (1854-1919). *See* Hawkes, Sarah Belknap "Belle" (Sherwood) [Mrs. James Woods] (1854-1919)
Sherwood School of Music (Chicago, IL), 14,237
Sherwood Select School, 11,279
Shesler Deaconess Home (Sioux City, IA), 5,073
Shetland, Margaret L. (1906-), **6,158, 8,053**
Shewmake, Oscar Lassiter, 12,987
Shewmake, Susan (Cornwall) [Mrs. Oscar Lassiter] (1825-1905), **12,987**
Shewman, Marguerite, 4,374
Shewsbury, Elizabeth K. *See* Adger, Elizabeth K. Shewsbury [Mrs. John B.]
Shi Family (GA), 3,088
Shick, Ruth (1912-). *See* Montgomery, Ruth (Shick) [Mrs. Robert H.] (1912-)
Shields, Elizabeth (Smallwood) [Mrs. Bernard C.] (1862-1932), **6,882**
Shields, Jane. *See* Freeman, Jane (Shields) [Mrs. Orville]
Shields, Sarah [Miss], **9,729**
Shields, Sarah Coombe, 14,979
Shields, Sarah Elizabeth (?-1919). *See* Fay, Sarah Elizabeth (Shields) [Mrs. Edwin Hedge] (?-1919)
Shields, Mrs. Wilmer H., 9,737
Shillock, Anna Felicia (1866-?), 9,367
Shillock, Daniel G. (1824-?), Family, **9,367**
Shillock, Mathilda [Mrs. Daniel G.], 9,367
Shimer College (Mount Carroll, IL), **4,300**
Shimer, Frances [Mrs. Henry], 4,300
Shimko, Margaret Richards, 11,880
Shinar, Mary, 1,664
Shingleur, Elvira (Flewellen) [Mrs. J. A.], **9,730**
Shingleur, J. A., 9,730
Shinkle, Elizabeth Clark, **1,742**

Shinn, Earl, Sr., 15,271
Shinn Family, 4,933
Shinn, Milicent Washburn (1858-1940), **792, 1,340, 1,540**
Shinn, Rebecca, 15,271
Shinn, Sarah Comfort [Mrs. Earl, Sr.], 15,271
Shinner, Charles, **15,716**
Ship-logs. *See* Log-books
Ship of Fools (book), 16,164
Shipbuilding, 1,988
Shipley, Anna Shinn [Mrs. Samuel R.], 15,271
Shipley, Marie Adelaide (Brown) (1842-1900), **4,327**
Shipley, Maynard (1872-1934), 1,279
Shipley, Miriam Allen De Ford [Mrs. Maynard] (1888-1975), 827, **1,279**, 1,652, 8,077
Shipley, Mrs. E. C., 3,660
Shipley, Samuel R., 15,271
Shipman, Caleb H., 12,311
Shipman, Elizabeth, 12,311
Shipman, Ellen, **11,711**
Shipman, Emma. *See* Hedges, Emma (Shipman) [Mrs. Charles H.]
Shipman Family (NJ, NY), **12,311**
Shipman, Harriett Holden [Mrs. Caleb H.] (1797-1867), 12,312
Shipman, Henry, 12,311
Shipman, Louis, 6,599
Shipman, Mary, 12,311
Shipman, William, 12,311
Shipmasters, **1,431**, 1,987, 1,989, 1,990, 2,575, 2,683, 3,149, 3,624, 3,630, 3,636, 3,647, 3,734, **4,001**, 5,412, 5,591, 5,675, **5,707**, 6,204, 6,205, 6,653, 7,478, 7,480, 7,481, 7,483, 7,488, 7,677, **7,693**, 11,134, 12,000, 14,470, 15,167
Shipp, Bardella (1874-1957). *See* Curtis, Bardella (Shipp) [Mrs. Theodore E.] (1874-1957)
Shipp, Ellis. *See* Musser, Ellis (Shipp) [Mrs. Joseph White]
Shipp, Ellis Reynolds, 16,486, 16,949, **16,956**, 16,966
Shipp, W., 5,749
Shippen, Ann Home. *See* Livingston, Ann Home (Shippen) [Mrs. Henry Beekman]
Shippen, Edward (1758-1809), 2,574, 15,087
Shippen, Elizabeth (Carter) Banister [Mrs. Thomas Lee]. *See* Izard, Elizabeth (Carter) Banister [Mrs. Thomas Lee] Shippen [Mrs. George]
Shippen Family, 12,068
Shippen Family (PA), **2,574, 14,970, 15,087**
Shippen, Louisa S., 2,574
Shippen, Margaret [Mrs. Edward], 15,087
Shippen, Margaret "Peggy" (1760-1804). *See* Arnold, Margaret "Peggy" (Shippen) [Mrs. Benedict] (1760-1804)
Shippen, Nancy, 2,443
Shippen, Rebecca Lloyd [Mrs. Edward], 2,574
Shippen, Sarah (1731-84). *See* Burd, Sarah (Shippen) (1731-84)
Shippen, Susan. *See* Blair, Susan (Shippen)
Shippen, Thomas Lee, 2,574
Shippen, William, 11,172
Shippen, William, 2,574
Shippen, William (son), 11,172
Shipping, 6,208, 11,481, 14,960
Ships, 14,528, 14,604
  cargo, 5,495
Ships' papers, 3,410
Shipstead, Henrik (1881-1960), 8,764, **9,368**
Shipwrecks, 1,756, 2,535, 2,659, 5,237, 5,706, 8,164, **11,614**, 11,653, **12,931**, 13,357, 13,419, 15,058, 17,800
Shipyard Workers Union, 1,577
Shiras, Myrna (1936-), **4,238, 6,883**
Shirley, Anne, 4,764
Shirley Family, 5,780
"Shirley Temple's Storybook" (television program), 17,818
Shirley Uplands and Intervales (book), 7,605
Shirpser, Clara (Garfinkle) [Mrs. Adolph J.] (1901-), **793**
Shirpser, Elsie. *See* Coggins, Elsie (Shirpser)
Shober, Amanda (Scott) [Mrs. Herod Jacob] (ca. 1835-71), 9,369
Shober, Charles E., **13,570**

Shober, Elizabeth (1834-?). *See* Evans, Elizabeth (Shober) [Mrs. William] (1834-?)
Shober, George, Family, **9,369**
Shober, Harriet (ca. 1860-?), 9,369
Shober, Herod Jacob (1821-?), 9,369
Shober, John H. (1832-1925), 9,369
Shocco Academy (NC), 13,625
Shock therapy, **6,220**
Shockley, Ann Allen, 15,920
"Shoe Shiner's Drag" (song), 5,531
Shoemaker, Annie, **15,088**
Shoemaker, Franklin, 15,296
Shoemaker, Henry Wharton (1882-1958), 5,951, 14,809
Shoemaker, Louise (1915-). *See* Stewart, Louise (Shoemaker) [Mrs. Jack] (1915-)
Shoemaker, Mary Howard [Mrs. Franklin] 15,296
Shoemaker, Mary Williams (1861-1957), **15,296**
Shoemaker, Rebecca (Warner) Rawle [Mrs. Samuel] (?-1819), 15,067, **15,089**
Shoemaker, Samuel (1724-1800), **15,089**
Shoemaker, Thomas Howard (1851-?), **15,296**
Shoemakers, 4,701
Shoenfeld, Mrs. Arthur J., 5,543
Shoesmith, Beulah (1880-1959), 3,785
Shoesmith, Earl, 1,341
Shoesmith, Muriel Wilkinson [Mrs. Earl] (?-1975), **1,341**
Shofstall, Dorothy J., 10,048
Shomer, Marion (?-1951). *See* Zemser, Marion (Shomer) (?-1951)
Shonemann, A. C. E., **4,781**
Shoner, Sarah Augusta, 10,874
Shonnard, Eugenie Frederica. [Mrs. E. Gordan] Ludlam (1886-1978), 11,235
Shoppe, Beatrice Bella, 8,479
Shorba, Mary [Mrs.], 8,470
Shore Acres (drama), 11,457
Shore, Marie, 18,001
Shore, Dinah, 18,001
Shore, Pauline, 9,212
Shores, Helen (Hopkins) Keanum, **3,421**
Short, Abigail, **7,438**
Short, Amos, **17,416**
Short, Esther (1806-62), **17,416**
Short History of Julia, A (book),
Short History of Parliament, 1295-1642 (book), 8,619
Short, Marie, 794
Short, Moses, **7,438**
Short, Ruth Isley, 7,438
Short, Sibyl, 12,585
Short stories, 73, 1,426, 1,461, 1,488, 4,319, 6,057, 6,069, 6,091, 6,115, 14,205, 14,354, 14,575, 15,899
Short Wave Research, Inc., 6,049
Shorthand, 6,643, **12,594**
  Gregg, 11,880
Shorthand reporters, 13,855
Shortridge, Clara (1849-1934). *See* Foltz, Clara (Shortridge) [Mrs. Jeremiah Richard] (1849-1934)
Shoshoni Indians, 965, 2,173, 10,631, 10,713, 11,220, 14,763, **16,872, 17,736**, 17,921
  legends, 16,872
  medical care, **10,631**, 14,763
  social life and customs, 16,872
Shotwell, Mary G., 13,617
Shoults, Hattie, 1,525
Shouse, Jouett, 11,621
Shove, Phila (1791-?). *See* Tripp, Phila (Shove) [Mrs. Philip] (1791-?)
Show Boat (drama), 17,795
Showers (parties), 9,376
Showers for Brides and Babies (book), 14,192
Showers, W. E., 14,630
Shrader, Pearl (Hutton) [Mrs. Edwin], **17,380**
Shreve, Helen (Randall), 3,245
Shreve, Mary (Goodhue) [Mrs. Benjamin, Jr.] (1781-1839), 12,695
Shreveport Civic Opera Association (LA), 5,550
Shrewsbury Floral Society (MA), 7,519
Shrewsbury Musical Association (MA), 7,519
Shrewsbury Social Club (MA), 7,519
Shrewsbury Temperance Society (PA), **15,362**
Shrewsbury, Theresa, 12,440
Shrike, The (screen play), 17,797

Shrine of Our Lady (WI), 17,552
Shriver, Eunice, 14,504
Shriver, R. Sargent, 9,286
Shrode, Maria Christina, 1,505
Shropshire, Mollie H., **3,422**
Shubin, Anna Louise (Strong) [Mrs. Joel] (1885-1970), 8,678, 8,949, 9,119, 12,884, 15,305, **17,343**
Shubin, Joel, 17,343
Shubrick, Harriet Cordelia [Mrs. William Branford], 15,717
Shubrick , Mary, 15,487
Shubrick, William Branford (1790-1874), **15,717**
Shufeldt, Mary (Miller), 2,575
Shufeldt, Robert Wilson (1822-95), **2,575**
Shufeldt, Sarah (Abercrombie) [Mrs. Robert Wilson] (?-1871), 2,575
Shuffle Along, 5,478
Shufford, Louisa, 1,659
Shuford, Lowery, **13,571**
Shullo, Joan F., 210
Shuman, Rose, 2,596
Shumway, Augusta M. Johnston [Mrs. Horatio Gates] (?-1884), 9,438
Shumway, John P. (1830-1917), **9,370**
Shumway, Louisa A. (Ross) [Mrs. John P.], 9,370
Shumway, Mary R., **14,659**
Shupe, Ella G., 16,648
Shura, Mary Francis (pseudonym). *See* Craig, Mary Francis (1923-)
Shurtleff Family (MA), 6,561, **6,803**
Shurtleff, Gertrude Hope (1872-?), 6,803
Shurtleff, Margaret H. (Nichols) (1879-1959), 6,803
Shurtleff, Sarah. *See* Ingelfinger, Sarah Shurtleff [Mrs. Franz J.]
Shurtleff, Sarah Ann Keegan, 6,803
Shurtleiff, Robert. *See* Gannett, Deborah (Sampson) [Mrs. Benjamin] (1760-1827)
"Shut Out" (story), 12,678
Shute, H. Josephine, 792
Shwayder Family (CO), 1,786
Shy One, The (book), 14,427
Sialkot Mission, 15,172
Siam. *See* Thailand
Siamese twins, **13,306**, 13,432
  marriage and living arrangements, **13,572**
Sibelius, Jean, 372
Sibell, Muriel (1898-1977). *See* Wolle, Muriel (Sibell) [Mrs. Francis] (1898-1977)
Sibley, Alfred Busch (1866-), 9,371
Sibley, Anna Maria (1822-65). *See* Hovey, Anna Maria (Sibley) [Mrs. George Lewis] (1822-65)
Sibley, Augusta Ann (1844-). *See* Pope, Augusta Ann (Sibley) [Mrs. Douglas] (1844-)
Sibley, Charles Frederic (1860-), 9,371
Sibley, Charlotte Augusta Langdon (Cook) [Mrs. John Langdon] (?-1902?), 6,302
Sibley, Constance Locke [Mrs. Charles F.], 9,371
Sibley, Evelyn (1907-). *See* Lampman, Evelyn (Sibley) [Mrs. Herbert S.] (1907-)
Sibley, George Champlin, 10,134, 10,169
Sibley, George Henry (1821-?), 7,678
Sibley, Henry, 8,515
Sibley, Henry Hastings (1811-91), 9,032, **9,371**
Sibley, John Langdon (1804-85), **6,302**
Sibley, Lucretia Cargill Carter [Mrs. Royal], **7,678**
Sibley, Major, 9,912
Sibley, Marjorie, 9,467
Sibley, Mary Smith (Easton) [Mrs. George Champlin] (1800-78), 10,134, 10,169
Sibley, Mrs., 9,912
Sibley, Persis (1813-91). *See* Black, Persis (Sibley) [Mrs. Charles] Andrews [Mrs. Alvah] (1813-91)
Sibley, Royal (1793-1822), 7,678
Sibley, Samuel Hale (1873-1958), **3,087**
Sibley, Sarah Jane (1851-). *See* Young, Sarah Jane (Sibley) [Mrs. Albert A.] (1851-)
Sibley, Sarah Jane (Steele) [Mrs. Henry Hastings] (?-1969), 9,371
Sibour Family (CT), **1,960**
Sibylline, 5,079
Sick, 7,673, 14,950
  effect upon families, 13,355
Sick-A-Bed (book), 12,488

Sickels, Alice Liliequist [Mrs. Henry James], 9,073
Sickels, Alice Lilliequist [Mrs. Henry Lawrence], 9,333, 9,341
Sides, Johnson, 10,669
Sidney, Margaret (pseudonym). *See* Lothrop, Harriett Mulford (Stone) [Mrs. Daniel] (1844-1924)
Sidon Seminary (Syria), 7,279
Sidway, Charlotte Spaulding, 11,356
Sidway Family (NY), **11,356**
Siedliska, Frances (1842-1902). *See* Mother Mary of Jesus the Good Shepherd (1842-1902)
Siege of Silent Henry, The (book), 4,991
Siegriest, Louis, 761
Siegriest, Lundy, 761
Siemmons, Isabella (Orbison), 14,824
Sienadale Motherhouse (Kenosha, WI), **17,554**
Siens, Nora (1873-1951). *See* Hunter, Nora (Siens) (1873-1951)
Sierra Club, 710, 781, **795**, 17,267
Sierra Club Bulletin, 710
Sierra Leone, Americans in, 115
Sierra Nevada (ship), 457
Siértokanson Kalenteri, 9,175
Sieur de Lhut (drama), 8,444
Sievert, Emily (1893-1958). *See* Weinberg, Emily (Sievert) [Mrs. I. G.] (1893-1958)
Sifton, Claire (Ginsburg) [Mrs. Paul] (1897-), **2,576**
Sifton, Paul (1897-1972), **2,576**
Sights and Insights (Salem Academy and College, NC), 13,634
Sigma Alpha Iota, 11,218
Sigma Alpha Iota, Sigma Sigma Chapter (MN), **8,612**
Sigma Gamma, 17,003
Sigma Gamma Zeta, 17,541
Sigma Kappa, 2,446, 8,552, **11,712**
Sigma Kappa, Alpha Kappa chapter (NE), 10,482
Sigma Phi Chi, 4,710
Sigma Xi, 7,153, 7,576
Sigmund Stern Grove (San Francisco, CA), 945
Sign language, 2,102, 2,103, 2,112, 2,114
Signpost (periodical), 17,305
"Signposts for Freedom" (tract), 3,437
Signton, Peter, 11,318
Sigoigne, Mrs. A., **14,762**
Sigourney, Andrew Maximilian (1831-50), 1,876
Sigourney, Charles (1778-1854), 1,485, 1,876
Sigourney Club (SC), **13,124**
Sigourney, Lydia Howard (Huntley) [Mrs. Charles] (1791-1865), 850, **1,485**, 1,565, 1,866, **1,876**, 1,930, **1,961**, 1,964, 1,998, 3,797, 3,926, **5,957**, 6,741, **6,884**, 7,171, 12,168, 12,178, **12,312**, 12,394, 12,403, 12,461, 15,355, 17,009, 17,010
Sigourney, Sarah B., 12,312
Sikes, George Cushing (1868-1928), **8,613**
Sikes, Madeleine Wallin [Mrs. George Cushing] (1868-1955), **3,899**, 8,613
Sikes, Olive [Mrs. Henry A.] Delille [Mrs. William Wirt] (1839-1909). *See* Logan, Olive [Mrs. Henry A.] Delille [Mrs. William Wirt] Sikes [Mrs. James O'Neill] (1839-1909)
Silberberg, Martin (1895-1966), **10,208**
Silberberg, Ruth [Mrs. Martin] (1906-), **10,208**
Silberman, Rhoda Truax, **6,090**, 15,144
Silcott, Jane [Mrs. John] (1842-95), **14,660**
Silent Singer, The (book), 6,773
Silent Spring (book), 14,452
Silhouettes, 7,601, 7,604
Silk, Lillian (1869-1949). *See* Holt, Lillian (Silk) [Mrs. Frederick Holford] (1869-1949)
Silk Weaving in Spain (book), 2,112
Silkville Co-operative Farm (KS), 7,224
Sill, Elizabeth N. [Mrs. Edward R.], 792
Sill, Mary (Edgar) [Mrs. William Raymond], 9,057
Sill, William Raymond, 9,057
Sillers, Florence. *See* Ogden, Florence (Sillers)
Sillers, Florence (Warfield), **9,551**, 9,567
Sillers, Matilda (Clark), 9,548
Sillers, Mourning Kane [Mrs. Walter], 9,614
Sillers, Mrs. Walter, 9,608, **9,731**
Sillers, Susan. *See* Darden, Susan (Sillers) [Mrs. Jesse H.]
Sillers, Walter, 9,614
Sillers, Walter, Jr., 9,550, 9,552
Silliman, Benjamin (1779-1864), 12,420

Silliman, Faith (1812-87). *See* Hubbard, Faith (Silliman) [Mrs. Oliver Payson] (1812-87)
Silliman, Harriet (Trumbull) [Mrs. Benjamin] (1783-1850), 12,420
Silliman, Henrietta. *See* Dana, Henrietta (Silliman) [Mrs. James Dwight], 12,420
Silliman, Maria Trumbull (1810-80). *See* Church, Maria Trumbull (Silliman) [Mrs. John Barker] (1810-80)
Sills, Beverly (1929-), 11,817
Sills, Marion (1916-), **944**
Silly Girl (book), 12,362
Silsbee, Marianne Cabot (Devereux) [Mrs. Nathaniel] (1812-99), 7,612
Silsby, Mary H., 7,677
Silver, 11,516
Silver Collar Boy (book), 6,118
Silver Cross Hospital (FL), 2,937
Silver Cross of King's Daughters (MN). *See* Junior League (MN)
Silver King Mine, 17,205
Silver mines and mining, 731, 745, 2,572, 16,425, 17,377
Silver question, 1,702
Silver, Reba (1900-), 5,829
Silver Reef mine (UT), 16,425, 16,444
Silver State Historical Society (NV), **10,714**
Silver Thimble Fund, **5,521**
Silver Unicorn (book), 15,720
Silver, William, **7,439**
Silverblatt, Mrs. William, 7,550
Silvercruys, Suzanne, 14,814
Silverheels (legend), 1,750
Silverheels (television script), 1,750
Silverline, Inc. (Fargo, ND), 13,669
Silversmiths, **2,054**, **2,831**, 3,867
Silverthorn Family (OH, PA, WI), **14,812**
Silvola Family (MN), **9,511**
Silvola, Richard, 9,511
Sim Family (NE), **10,535**
Sim, Francis (1821-1907), 10,535
Sim, Sarah (Clarke) [Mrs. Francis] (1824-80), 10,535
Sime, Ruth, **1,162**
Simester, Edith Winifred, **14,441**
Simkhovitch, Mary Melinda (Kingsbury) (1867-1951), 2,120, **6,885**, 8,659, 8,668, 8,681, 12,069
Simkin, Margaret (Timberlake) (1892-?), **796**, 11,846
Simkins, Francis B., 15,585
Simkins, Modjeska (Montieth) (1899-), 13,176
Simmerman, Lulu, 10,211
Simmonds, Sina, 10,134
Simmons, Augusta Emma (1842-1928). *See* Stetson, Augusta Emma (Simmons) [Mrs. Frederick J.] (1842-1928)
Simmons College (MA), 6,223, 6,236, 12,737, 14,386
    alumnae, 6,239
    faculty, 6,900, 6,946, 8,636
    registrar, **6,235**
    students, 6,235
Simmons College (MA) Department of Nursing, **6,238**
Simmons College Corporation, **6,237**
Simmons, Dawn Langley, 15,144
Simmons, Ethel P. [Mrs.], **17,441**
Simmons, Evelyn (Crow), 655
Simmons Family (FL), **2,956**
Simmons Fund, 6,428
Simmons, George F., 6,857
Simmons, John (1796-1870), 6,237
Simmons, Lena. *See* Clark, Lena (Simmons)
Simmons, Martha Virginia Webster Strickland (1836-?), 16,117
Simmons, Mary L., 2,956
Simmons, Maude Inez. *See* Feamster, Maude Inez (Simmons) [Mrs. Claude N.]
Simmons, Mrs., 7,109
Simmons, Mrs. Henry C. (1838-1919), 13,683
Simms, Addie J., 16,097
Simms, Alfred G., 2,379
Simms, Daisy Florence (1873-1923). *See* Simms, Florence (1873-1923)
Simms Family (NM), 11,225
Simms, Florence (1873-1923), 7,329, 12,710
Simms, Margaret (1903-74), **15,922**

Simms, Ruth (Hanna) [Mrs. Joseph Medill] McCormick [Mrs. Albert Gallatin] (1880-1944), 2,379, 2,439, 2,558, 2,602, 4,066, **4,653**, 5,121, 5,123, 11,225
Simon and Schuster, 8,566
Simon, Caroline K., **6,886**, 12,790
Simon, Emily (Parker) [Mrs. Albert] (1904?-78), 15,316
Simon, Paul, 4,059
Simonds, Patience (1794-1862). *See* Cowdery, Patience (Simonds) [Mrs. Warren F.] (1794-1862)
Simons, Algie M. (1870-1950), **17,722**
Simons, Elizabeth Noble, 15,665
Simons Family (SC), **15,718**
Simons, Frieda (Hennock) (1904-60), **6,887**, **10,072**
Simons, Harriet Hyrne, 15,718
Simons, Harriet Stoney [Mrs. Albert] (1896-1971), **15,518**
Simons, James, 15,718
Simons, Jane Kealhofer [Mrs. Arthur St. Julian], **15,719**
Simons, Katherine Drayton Mayrant [Miss] (1892-1968), 15,585, 15,700, **15,720**
Simons, Lena S. [Mrs.], 1,268
Simons, Lizzie H., 16,060
Simons, Maria, 15,718
Simons, Mary (Wood) [Mrs. Algie] (?-1948), 17,722
Simons, Mrs. H. H., **15,721**
Simons, Sara Eliza. *See* Spearman, Sara Eliza (Simons)
Simons, Sarah H., 15,718
Simonson, Joseph, 9,467
Simonson, Mary, 9,462
Simonson, Sylvia [Mrs. Joseph], 9,467
Simonton Family, 3,612
Simopoulos, Artemis, 6,336
Simple Confession (book), 7,254
Simpson, Adele, 12,086
Simpson, Benjamin, 5,700
Simpson, Carrie B., **13,718**
Simpson College (Indianola, IN), 4,888
    faculty, 5,061
    students, 4,847
Simpson, Cora, 2,309
Simpson, David Ferguson, Family (MN), **9,372**
Simpson, Ellen (Burr) [Mrs. Randolph S.], 4,410
Simpson, Eusebia (1902-). *See* Hunkins, Eusebia (Simpson) (1902-)
Simpson, Evangeline (Marrs) [Mrs. Michael H.] (1860-1930). *See* Whipple, Evangeline (Marrs) [Mrs. Michael H.] Simpson [Mrs. Henry Benjamin] (1860-1930)
Simpson Family (NC), **13,573**
Simpson, George Gaylor (1902-), **14,903**
Simpson, Grace Jane (1839-?). *See* Skeeters, Grace Jane (Simpson) (1839-?)
Simpson, J. A., 12,759
Simpson, Jane (1867-1957). *See* McKimmon, Jane (Simpson) (1867-1957)
Simpson, Jessie, 9,372
Simpson, John T., 14,594
Simpson, Josephine Sarles [Mrs. David Ferguson] (1862-1948), 9,372
Simpson, Kate F. [Mrs.], 17,384
Simpson, Leah Reemar (1798-?), **2,915**, **13,125**
Simpson, Mabel B. [Mrs. Albert L.], 1,206, 1,207
Simpson, Margaret [Mrs. Thomas] (1837-88), 9,527
Simpson, Martha Lee. *See* Eastlake, Martha Lee (Simpson)
Simpson, Mary Jean, 17,001, 17,002
Simpson, Mercy, 5,700
Simpson, Mrs. William S., **17,099**
Simpson, Nellie (1871-?). *See* Richardson, Nellie (Simpson) (1871-?)
Simpson, Randolph (?-1918), 4,410
Simpson, Rebecca Calhoun (1800-?), 2,915, **13,125**
Simpson, Theolene, 3,785
Simpson, Thomas, 9,527
Simpson, Wallis (Warfield) (1896-). *See* Windsor, Wallis (Warfield) Simpson (1896-)
Simpson, William S. (1795 or 1796-1868), **17,099**
Sims, Anne (Hitchcock) [Mrs. William Sowden], 2,577
Sims, Bernice Weston, 16,488

Sims, J. Marion, 3,146
Sims, Margaret, 3,799
Sims, Mary Owen [Mrs. John D.], **291**
Sims, William Sowden (1858-1936), **2,577**
Sinclair, Agnes, 16,097
Sinclair, Carrie Bell, **3,578**
Sinclair, Ethel, 3,764
Sinclair, James, 14,608
Sinclair, Jo (pseudonym). *See* Seid, Ruth (1913-)
Sinclair, Mae [Miss], 231
Sinclair, Marguerite, 16,972
Sinclair, Mary Craig (Kimbrough) [Mrs. Upton Beall]
    (1883-1961), **4,488**, 8,077, 9,793
Sinclair, Mary Hunter (Southworth) [Mrs. Allan
    McCaskell], 2,296, 9,657, 9,658, 9,793, 9,795
Sinclair, Meta, 8,077
Sinclair, Upton Beall, 1,559, 3,775, 4,488, 4,493,
    8,077, 11,917, 12,701, 12,705
Sinclairville Fair Grounds Association (NY), 11,650
Sindrey, Daniel, 15,519
Sindrey, Elizabeth [Mrs. Daniel], **15,519**
Sindrey, Sarah. *See* Blake, Sarah (Sindrey) [Mrs.
    Joseph]
Sing at My Wake (book), 6,082
Singapore, Young Women's Christian Association,
    12,726
Singer, Marie (Marshall) (1876-1962), **17,071**
Singer, Maxine, 6,336
Singers, 316, **687**, 712, 722, 800, **967**, **1,070**, **1,123**,
    1,192, **1,238**, **1,244**, 1,262, **1,293**, **1,525**, **1,527**,
    1,588, **1,799**, **1,823**, 2,020, **2,022**, 2,023, **2,663**,
    2,800, **3,267**, 3,367, 3,369, 3,745, **3,800**, 3,838,
    3,878, **4,307**, 4,319, 4,894, 5,466, **5,530**, **5,532**,
    5,533, **5,653**, **5,911**, **5,936**, **6,033**, **6,041**, 6,329,
    6,542, **6,590**, **7,213**, 7,267, **7,303**, **8,775**, **8,950**,
    9,004, 9,303, 9,502, 9,585, 9,699, **9,742**, 10,131,
    10,166, 10,651, 10,680, **10,729**, **10,793**, **10,909**,
    11,106, **11,176**, **11,321**, 11,427, **11,699**, **11,782**,
    11,817, **11,984**, 11,985, 12,125, 12,403, **12,468**,
    12,592, 14,141, **14,231**, 14,284, **14,447**, 14,767,
    14,906, **15,387**, **15,874**, 16,150, 16,402, **16,446**,
    16,538, **16,577**, **16,922**, 17,163, 17,197, **17,298**,
    17,380, **17,491**, 17,801, 17,943, **18,001**, 18,002
Singers, Afro-American, **2,123**, **2,150**, **5,479**, 5,552,
    6,013, **12,685**, 12,690, **13,306**, **15,894**, 17,796
Singers, Jewish, **939**, 13,832
Singers, Lebanese-American, **14,907**
Singers, Swedish, **4,325**
Single mothers, 1,686, **4,088**, 8,583, **8,669**, 9,222,
    11,000, 11,256, 12,017, 12,355, 12,358, 12,706,
    13,995, 14,920, 17,126, 17,511
Single parents, 5,842, **8,647**, 17,991
Single tax, 6,978, 7,222, 8,077
Single Tax Society, 1,279
Single women, 1,655
Singleton, Angelica (1816-77). *See* Van Buren,
    Angelica (Singleton) [Mrs. Abraham] (1816-77)
Singleton, Anne Hinman (Broun) (1848-1932), **13,126**
Singleton Family, **2,578**
Singleton Family (GA), 3,088
Singleton Family (SC), **15,722**, **15,723**
Singleton, Marion (1815-?). *See* Converse, Marion
    (Singleton) [Mrs. Robert Marion] Deveaux [Mrs.
    August L.] (1815-?)
Singleton, Rebecca T. (Coles) [Mrs. Richard]
    (?-1849), 2,578, 2,616
Singleton, Richard (1776-1852), 15,723
Singmaster, Elsie (1879-1958), 14,828, 15,319
Sinks, Julia Lee (1817-1904), **16,129**
Sinnamon, Mrs. Henry Hall, 14,814
Sino-Japanese Conflict (1937-1945), 409, 1,564,
    13,263, 13,279, 13,290
    personal narratives, American, 14,116
Sinsinawa Dominican Congregation of the Most Holy
    Rosary (WI), **17,868**
Siouan Indians, 1,286, 1,761, 1,790, 2,840, 10,473, 15,850
    ethnology, 6,323
    missions, 8,412, **15,841**
    music, 1,497, 8,444
    reservations, 17,191
    social life and customs, women, 10,029
    wars, 4,765, 8,720, 8,967, 9,042, **9,056**, 9,117,
        9,245, 9,249, 9,285
Siouan Indians, Oglala. *See* Oglala Sioux Indians

Sioussat, Annie Middleton (Leakin) [Mrs. Albert W.]
    (1850?-1942), 5,805
Sioussat, Helen, 5,123
Sioux City Diocesan Council of Catholic Women
    (IA), 4,959
Sioux County—Memoirs of Its Pioneers (book),
    10,470
Sipple Family (DE), **12,330**
Sipprell, Clara E. (1886-1975), **12,909**
Sir Walter Cabinet (NC), 13,266, **13,574**
Siris, Evelyn, 1,348
Sirmons, Elizabeth Thame, 3,610
Siroky, Anne (1910-), 11,851
Sirota, Beata, 17,074
Sirridge, Marjorie, 15,134
Sisseton Reservation (Dakota Territory), 8,966
Sistare, Lucy Way (1800-86). *See* Say, Lucy Way
    (Sistare) [Mrs. Thomas] (1800-86)
Sister Kenny Foundation (Minneapolis, MN), 9,162
Sister Kenny Institute (Minneapolis, MN), 8,521,
    8,621, 9,162
*Sister of the Road: The Autobiography of Box-Car
    Bertha* (book), 4,145
Sisterhood of Bethany, 9,417
Sisterhood of Congregation B'nai Israel (OH), **13,822**
Sisterhood of Mount Zion Temple (St. Paul, MN),
    9,251
Sisterhood of St. John, 5,827
Sisterhood of the Good Shepherd (St. Louis, MO),
    10,146
Sisterhoods, 4,732, 9,417
Sisterhoods, Episcopal, 5,827
Sisterhoods, Jewish, **932**, 939, **946**, 17,555
Sisters in the Church at Harvard (MA), **7,041**
Sisters of All Saints, 5,827
Sisters of Charity, 1,750, **2,895**, 5,493, 5,774, 5,827,
    17,383, 17,848
Sisters of Charity (Dubuque, IA), 4,696
Sisters of Charity (Grey Nuns of Montreal)
    (Lexington, MA), **7,066**
Sisters of Charity of Cincinnati, Motherhouse (OH),
    14,116
Sisters of Charity of Leavenworth (KS), **5,186**
Sisters of Charity of Nazareth, 5,373
Sisters of Charity of Nazareth (KY), 5,380, **5,398**
Sisters of Charity of New York (Bronx, NY), **11,298**
Sisters of Charity of Our Lady of Mercy (Charleston,
    SC), **15,433**
Sisters of Charity of St. Augustine (OH), **14,130**
Sisters of Charity of Saint Elizabeth, 10,892
Sisters of Charity of St. Vincent de Paul, 3,874
Sisters of Charity of Seton Hill (Greensburg, PA),
    14,800
Sisters of Charity of the Blessed Virgin Mary, 3,971,
    4,148
Sisters of Charity of the Blessed Virgin Mary (IA),
    4,872
Sisters of Charity of the Incarnate Word,
    Motherhouse (Houston, TX), **16,251**
Sisters of Christian Charity Convent (Mendham, NJ),
    10,916
Sisters of Divine Providence, 10,611
Sisters of Divine Providence (Allison Park, PA),
    14,717
Sisters of Divine Providence, Generalate (Helotes, TX),
    16,230
Sisters of Divine Providence, St. Anne Convent
    (Melbourne, KY), **5,391**
Sisters of Humility, 4,709
Sisters of Jesus Crucified, American Novitiate
    (Devon, PA), **14,782**
Sisters of Loretto, 1,784, 1,786
Sisters of Loretto (Flagstaff, AZ), 159
Sisters of Mercy, **298**, 8,705, 9,542, 10,611, 14,786,
    14,788, 14,789, 15,232, 15,774
Sisters of Mercy (St. Louis, MO), 10,186
Sisters of Mercy (Erie, PA), 14,794
Sisters of Mercy (Merion Station, PA), **14,874**
Sisters of Mercy, Motherhouse (Windham, NH),
    10,888
Sisters of Mercy Motherhouse (Rochester, NY),
    12,809
Sisters of Mercy of Allegheny County (PA), **15,233**
Sisters of Mercy of Amarillo (TX), **16,262**

Sisters of Mercy of Connecticut, **2,027**
Sisters of Mercy of the Union (Dobbs Ferry, NY),
    11,433
Sisters of Mercy, Province of Chicago (IL), **4,035**
Sisters of Mercy, Province of Detroit, **8,176**
Sisters of Mercy, Province of Detroit (Farmington
    Hills, MI), **8,176**
Sisters of Mercy Provincialate (Cumberland, RI),
    15,369
Sisters of Mercy Provincialate, Omaha Province
    (NE), **10,615**
Sisters of Notre Dame, 13,763, **14,661**
Sisters of Notre Dame (CA), **1,651**
Sisters of Notre Dame (Omaha, NE), 10,611
Sisters of Notre Dame de Namur, 2,864
Sisters of Notre Dame de Namur (CA, OR), 299
Sisters of Notre Dame de Namur, Maryland
    Provincial House (Ilchester, MD), **5,848**
Sisters of Notre Dame de Namur, Ohio Province,
    13,868
Sisters of Our Lady of Charity Convent (Hamburg,
    NY), **11,477**
Sisters of Our Lady of Christian Doctrine, Marydell
    Convent (Suffern, NY), **17,386**
Sisters of Our Lady of Mount Carmel, Carmelite
    Monastery (Indianapolis, IN), **4,634**
Sisters of Providence (WA), **17,415**
Sisters of Providence Archives, Sacred Heart Province
    (Seattle, WA), **17,229**
Sisters of Providence of Holyoke, Mother House
    (MA), **7,049**
Sisters of St. Basil the Great, Sacred Heart Province
    (Philadelphia, PA), **15,177**
Sisters of St. Benedict, Convent Immaculate
    Conception (IN), **4,509**
Sisters of St. Benedict, Our Lady of Grace Convent
    (Beech Grove, IN), **4,466**
Sisters of St. Benedict, St. Mary Priory (Nauvoo, IL),
    4,303
Sisters of St. Dominic, Immaculate Conception
    Convent (Great Bend, KS), **5,184**
Sisters of St. Dominic Motherhouse (Caldwell, NJ),
    10,890
Sisters of St. Dominic, Our Lady of the Elms
    Convent (Akron, OH), **13,727**
Sisters of St. Dominic, Siena Center (Racine, WI),
    17,854
Sisters of St. Francis, 4,632, 16,532
Sisters of St. Francis, Assisi Heights, Motherhouse
    (Rochester, MN), **8,839**
Sisters of St. Francis Convent (Oldenburg, IN), **4,649**
Sisters of St. Francis Convent (Tiffin, OH), **14,131**
Sisters of St. Francis Motherhouse (Colorado Springs,
    CO), **1,690**
Sisters of St. Francis of Mary Immaculate (Joliet, IL),
    4,282
Sisters of St. Francis of Millvale, Motherhouse
    (Pittsburgh, PA), **15,234**
Sisters of St. Francis of Penance and Christian
    Charity, Mount Alverno Convent (Redwood
    City, CA), **1,118**
Sisters of St. Francis of Penance and Christian
    Charity, Provincialate (Stella Niagara, NY),
    12,866
Sisters of St. Francis of Philadelphia, Our Lady of
    Angels Convent (PA), **14,719**
Sisters of St. Francis of the Holy Cross, Convent
    (Green Bay, WI), **17,552**
Sisters of St. Francis of the Holy Family (Dubuque,
    IA), **4,873**
Sisters of St. Francis of the Providence of God (PA),
    15,235
Sisters of St. Joseph, 14,911
Sisters of St. Joseph (FL), **2,919**
Sisters of St. Joseph (OH), 13,903
Sisters of St. Joseph (Erie, PA), **14,795**
Sisters of St. Joseph Cluny Provincialate (RI), **15,372**
Sisters of St. Joseph Convent (Kalamazoo, MI), **8,383**
Sisters of St. Joseph Generalate (Buffalo, NY), **11,362**
Sisters of St. Joseph, Marymount Provincial Home
    (Garfield Heights, OH), **14,100**
Sisters of St. Joseph Motherhouse (Rochester, NY),
    12,810

Sisters of St. Joseph Motherhouse (Philadelphia, PA), **15,178**

Sisters of St. Joseph Motherhouse (Superior, WI), **17,871**

Sisters of St Joseph, Nazareth Motherhouse and Novitiate (KS), **5,178**

Sisters of St. Joseph of Boston (MA), **6,243**

Sisters of St. Joseph of Carondelet, 1,006, **8,853**, 9,022

Sisters of St. Joseph of Carondelet (St. Louis, MO), **10,187**

Sisters of St. Joseph of Carondelet, Provincial House (Latham, NY), **11,796**

Sisters of St. Joseph of Carondelet, St. Louis Province (MO), **10,188**

Sisters of St. Joseph of Carondelet, St. Mary's Provincialate (Los Angeles, CA), **1,007**

Sisters of St. Joseph of Carondelet, St. Paul Province (MN), **9,490**

Sisters of St. Joseph of La Grange (IL), **4,284**

Sisters of St. Joseph of Orange (CA), **1,093**

Sisters of St. Joseph of Wheeling (WV), **17,487**

Sisters of St. Joseph Provincial House (Crookston, MN), **8,425**

Sisters of St. Mary of Oregon (Beaverton, OR), **14,269**

Sisters of St. Mary of the Third Order of St. Francis (St. Louis, MO), **10,189**

Sisters of Social Service of Los Angeles Motherhouse (Los Angeles, CA), **1,008**

Sisters of the Blessed Sacrament, 10,611

Sisters of the Blessed Sacrament for Indians and Colored People, 15,152

Sisters of the Blessed Sacrament, St. Elizabeth Convent (Cornwells Heights, PA), **14,781**

Sisters of the Divine Compassion, Good Counsel Convent (White Plains, NY), **12,932**

Sisters of the Good Shepherd, 5,827

Sisters of the Good Shepherd-Magdalenes, 10,611

Sisters of the Good Shepherd, St. Paul Provincialate (MN), **9,491, 11,271**

Sisters of the Holy Cross, 5,778

Sisters of the Holy Family Motherhouse and Novitiate, **6,888**

Sisters of the Holy Family of Nazareth, **15,181**

Sisters of the Holy Family of Nazareth, Immaculate Conception Province, **15,180**

Sisters of the Holy Family of Nazareth, Immaculate Heart of Mary Provincialate (Monroe, CT), **1,985**

Sisters of the Holy Name, Oregon Province, **14,493**

Sisters of the Humility of Mary, Villa Maria Community Center (PA), **15,336**

Sisters of the Immaculate Heart of Mary (Los Angeles, CA), **1,009**

Sisters of the Immaculate Heart of Mary (Santa Barbara, CA), 1,525

Sisters of the Incarnate Word and Blessed Sacrament (Bellaire, TX), **16,179**

Sisters of the Lamb of God, Our Lady of Hope Convent (Owensboro, KY), **5,401**

Sisters of the Most Precious Blood (O'Fallon, MO), 10,134

Sisters of the Most Precious Blood Convent (O'Fallon MO), **10,129**

Sisters of the Order of St. Dominic, Queen of the Rosary Motherhouse (Amityville, NY), **11,273**

Sisters of the Order of Saint Francis, 13,752

Sisters of the Poor of St. Francis, 9,880

Sisters of the Precious Blood (Dayton, OH), **14,044**

Sisters of the Presentation (Dubuque, IA), **4,874**

Sisters of the Presentation Convent (San Francisco, CA), **1,369**

Sisters of the Presentation of Mary, Provincial House (Manchester, NH), **10,880**

Sisters of the Presentation of the Blessed Virgin Mary (SD), 15,842

Sisters of the Resurrection of Our Lord Jesus Christ, Saint Joseph Province (Castleton-on-Hudson, NY), **11,404**

Sisters of the Sorrowful Mother, Milwaukee Province (WI), **17,839**

Sisters of the Sorrowful Mother, Our Lady of Sorrows Convent (Denville, NJ), **10,893**

Sisters of the Visitation (Rock Island, IL), **4,328**

Sisters of Visitation, 4,342

Sisters, Servants of the Immaculate Heart of Mary (Monroe, MI), **8,292**

Sisters, Servants of the Immaculate Heart of Mary (Immaculata, PA), **14,859**

Sisters Under the Sari (book), 4,685

Sit-down strikes, 6,314, 8,081, 8,088, 8,136, 8,144

Sitherwood, 3,747

Sitherwood, Frances G., 3,748, 3,760, 3,763, 3,764

Sitterly, Charlotte Moore (1898-), **1,541**

Sitwell, Dame Edith (1887-1964), 7,226, 16,163, 16,164

Sivley, Jane, **13,127**

Six Horse Hitch (book), 5,264

"Six-Shooter Junction" (ms), 14,205

"Six Years Behind the Magnolia Curtain" (ms), 15,880

Sixkiller, Lena, 16,876

Sixteenth Wisconsin Volunteers, 4,832

Sixth Grace United Presbyterian Church of Chicago (IL), 4,147

Sixth International Congress on Industrial Accidents and Diseases (1931), 7,318

6th Vermont Regiment of Volunteers, Union Army, 1,463

Sixty Years of California Song (book), 316

Sizer, Ellen R., 1,743

Sizer, Ina Cassidy, **1,743**

Sizer, Linda Pyle, **10,372**

Sizer, Nelson (1812-97), **5,029**

Skaggs, Lucinda "Lulu" (1867-84), **14,301**

Skaling, Audrey, 2,808

Skala, Lilia, 7,287

Skarshaug, Pauline Grant Waite (1901-50), **7,924**

Skavlem, Bergit Olsdatter [Mrs. Halvor Gullikson], 17,497

Skavlem, Birgit, 17,497

Skavlem Family (WI), **17,497**

Skavlem, Gunhild, 17,497

Skavlem, Halvor Gullikson, 17,497

Skeen, Augusta. *See* Cooper, Augusta (Skeen) [Mrs. Samuel Inman]

Skeeters, Grace Jane (Simpson) (1839-?), **14,488**

Skells, Lydia Maury, 3,595

Skelton, Bathurst, 13,451

Skelton, M. A., 3,375

Skelton, Martha (Wayles) (1748-82). *See* Jefferson, Martha (Wayles) [Mrs. Bathurst] Skelton [Mrs. Thomas] (1748-82)

Skelton, Mrs. Allen, 9,732

Skerrett, Jane (Armat) [Mrs. William] (?-1856), 15,043

Sketch books, 14,862

Sketch Club (CA), 1,318

Sketch Club (San Francisco, CA), 1,261

Sketches Along Life's Road (book), 4,211

Sketches of Childhood and Girlhood, Chicago, 1847-1864 (book), 7,685

Sketching Club (Ann Arbor, MI), **7,925**

Skewes, Lydia Taylor, 16,876

Skidmore College, 12,737

Skidmore, Nellie (Grant), 17,862

Skiing, 16,965

Skillen, Melita Hamilton [Miss] (1887-), **11,713**

Skilton, Harriet Ingersoll, 11,547

Skin, diseases, 4,475

Skin of Our Teeth, The (drama), 60

Skinner, Annie Lindsay (?-1925), 12,622

Skinner, Avery, 12,764

Skinner, Charlotte (Stebbins) [Mrs. Avery] (1802-88), 12,764

Skinner, Constance Lindsay (1877-1939), **12,622**

Skinner, Cornelia Otis (1901-), 378, 569, 7,310, 8,297, 8,450, 12,496, 12,708, 14,736, 14,889, 16,149

Skinner, Cynthia (1792-?). *See* Walker, Cynthia (Skinner) [Mrs. Hiram] (1792-?)

Skinner, Edith Warman [Mrs. Neil McFee], 12,623

Skinner Family (NY), **12,764**

Skinner, James Edwards (1867-1959), **14,442**

Skinner, Maud Durbin, 4,631

Skinner, Neil McFee, **12,623**

Skinner, Otis, 12,476, 12,529

Skinner, Ruth [Mrs. Timothy], 12,764

Skinner Settlement Project (ME), **5,665**

Skinner, Timothy, 12,764

Skirball, Henry, 11,915

Skirball, Sheba [Mrs. Henry], **11,915**

Skirvin, Perle. *See* Mesta, Perle (Skirvin) [Mrs. George]

Sklodowska, Marie (1867-1934). *See* Curie, Marie (Sklodowska) (1867-1934)

Skolfield, Jane Wilkie Manning, 16,659, 16,967

Skwarra, Elisabeth, 14,943

"Sky, The" (poem), 7,658

Slack, Caroline Lambe [Mrs.] (1850-?), 16,486

Slack, E. Elizabeth (1881-1973), **7,926**

Slack, Esther Hobart (McQuigg) [Mrs. Artemus] (1814-1902). *See* Morris, Esther Hobart (McQuigg) [Mrs. Artemus] Slack [Mrs. John] (1814-1902)

Slade, Amelia Eliza (1854-1936). *See* Bennion, Amelia Eliza (Slade) [Mrs. Alfred] (1854-1936)

Slade, Betsey [Mrs. Peleg] (1781-1882), **11,275**

Slade, Caroline, 5,121

Slade, Ella, 5,183

Slade Family (GA), 13,098

Slade, Governor, 704

Slade, Mrs. F. Louis, 5,123

Slagel, Arthur, 4,516

Slagel, Vesta (Zook) [Mrs. Arthur] (1891-), **4,516**

Slagle, Sarah Elizabeth. *See* York, Sarah Elizabeth (Slagle)

Slanger, Frances Y. (1914-1944), **6,159**

Slappey Family (GA), 3,088

Slappey, George Hiley, **3,088**

Slappey, Pansy Aiken [Mrs. George Hiley], **3,088**

Slate, Frederick, 1,340

Slater, Ilene, 11,857

Slater, Nellie, 1,790

Slater, Renie Collins [Mrs.], 10,905

Slaton, John Marshall, 3,371

Slaton, Sarah Francis Grant [Mrs. John M.], **3,254**

Slaughter, A. B., 16,060

Slaughter, Annie Page Eanes [Mrs. A. B.] (1833-?), 16,060

Slaughter, C. C., 16,285

Slaughter, Carrie Averill [Mrs. C. C.], **16,285**

Slaughter, Elsie Pynchon, 799

Slaughter, Gertrude Elizabeth (Taylor) [Mrs. Moses Stephen] (1870-1963), **17,723**, 17,771

Slaughter, Linda (Warfel) [Mrs. Benjamin Franklin] (1850-1911), **13,661**, 13,682

Slaughter, Mare, 189

Slaughter, Minnie, 17,901, 17,919

Slaughter, Moses Stephen (1860-1923), 17,723

Slaughter, Vestarine W., 3,298

Slave, 2,132

Slave records, **2,124, 2,126, 2,132,** 2,156, 2,527, 2,930, 2,985, 3,099, 3,270, 3,271, 3,300, 3,373, 3,506, 3,529, 3,871, 5,347, 5,440, 5,491, 6,445, 9,656, 9,781, 10,939, 11,207, 11,324, 13,075, 13,188, 15,069, 15,423, **15,442,** 15,458, 15,467, 15,507, 15,524, 15,562, 15,571, 15,834

Slave-trade, 1,350, 2,943, 3,043, **3,089,** 3,152, 3,215, 3,300, **4,239,** 5,491, 7,524, 9,803, 9,976, 9,987, 11,737, 13,250, 15,069, 15,260, 15,445, 15,523, **15,530,** 15,571, 15,602, 15,618, 15,633, 15,636, 15,637, 15,676, 15,736, 15,742, 16,148

Slaveholder's Daughter, A (book), 9,656

Slavery, 1,998, 2,141, **2,221,** 2,388, **2,946, 2,947, 3,118,** 3,298, 3,313, 3,319, 3,396, 3,436, 3,477, **3,478,** 3,502, 5,343, 5,363, **5,423,** 5,440, 5,456, **5,491,** 5,535, 5,549, 5,745, 5,800, 5,821, 6,464, 6,628, 7,270, **7,295,** 7,634, 8,294, 8,781, 9,308, 9,363, 9,641, 9,800, 9,883, 9,884, 10,009, 10,161, 11,412, 11,602, 12,404, **12,693,** 13,091, 13,123, 13,257, 13,269, 13,322, 15,041, 15,414, 15,499, 15,634

anti-slavery movements, 326, 438, **992,** 1,874, 2,495, 2,818, 3,297, 3,897, 5,234, 5,907, 5,926, **5,972,** 6,577, 6,664, 6,943, 6,975, 7,295, 7,629, 7,692, 7,751, 11,125, 11,279, 11,303, 11,600, 11,963, 12,020, 12,419, 12,625, 12,908, 15,470. *See also* Abolitionists

condition of slaves, 2,652, 4,417, 7,678, 9,041, 9,753, 13,445, 13,611, 15,658

controversial literature, 7,678

economic aspects, **15,442,** 15,678

emancipation, 2,038, **2,132**, 2,443, 2,648, 3,300, 4,417, 4,856, 5,495, 5,496, 5,718, 7,232, 7,677, **9,391**, 10,134, 11,207, 11,271, 11,520, 11,602, 12,003, 13,482, 15,653, 16,356
  legal aspects, 5,565
  fugitive slaves, 2,262, 2,947, 5,491, 5,681, 6,738, 6,907, 7,610, 10,794, 11,277, 12,683, 15,445
  insurrections, 7,665, 12,590, 13,262, 15,594, 15,635, 15,658
  law, 3,300, 13,600
  legal status of slaves in free states, 3,300
  social aspects, 3,580
Slavery in Brazil, 69
Slavery in Cuba, 15,601
Slavery in the West Indies, emancipation, 992
Slaves, 2,124, 2,126, 2,132, 2,156, 2,443, 2,947, 3,298, 3,300, 3,373, 4,239, 5,423, 5,440, 5,535, **6,628**, 9,391, 9,781, 10,161, **11,277**, 11,416, 13,188, 13,322, 13,342, 13,482, 15,486, 15,494, 15,495, 15,505, 15,530, 15,546, 15,653, 15,742, 16,356, 17,055
  medical care, 3,594, 15,428, 15,554
Slaves, recolonization of in Africa, 17,055
Slayton, Abbie Cyrena (1884-), 7,927
Slayton Family (MI), **7,927**
Slayton, Helen Elizabeth, 7,927
Slayton, Julia A. [Mrs. William C.] (1829-?), **7,928**
Slayton, Sarah Abbie (Dunn) (1853-1926), 7,927
Slayton, Sarah Augusta (1886-), 7,927, **7,929**
Slayton, William C., 7,928
Sledd, Andrew, 2,884
Sledd, Frances. *See* Blake, Frances (Sledd) [Mrs. John]
Slee, Margaret (Higgins) [Mrs. William] Sanger [Mrs. Noah] (1879-1966). *See* Sanger, Margaret (Higgins) [Mrs. William]. [Mrs. Noah] Slee (1879-1966)
Sletor, Sarah Andt. *See* Morris, Sarah Andt Sletor [Mrs. Thomas Burnside]
Slicer, Mary, 1,174
Slick, Jonathan (pseudonym). *See* Stephens, Ann Sophia (Winterbotham) [Mrs. Edward] (1810-86)
Slidell, Jane. *See* Perry, Jane (Slidell) [Mrs. Matthew Calbraith]
Slidell, John, 5,415
Slides (photography), 7,146, 11,327, 12,842
Sligh, Agnes (1888-). *See* Turnbull, Agnes (Sligh) (1888-)
Slingerland, Effie Brown Earll [Mrs. Mark Vernon] (1868-1950), **11,714**
Slingerland, Mark Vernon, 11,714
Sloan, Edna Wells, 16,676
Sloan, Eleanor B. (1889-), 168, 207
Sloan Family (PA),
Sloan, Marion Louisa [Miss] (1846-1942), **8,831, 9,373**
Sloan Museum (MI), 8,180
Sloan, Richard E., 168, 207
Sloane, Madeleine Edison [Mrs. John Eyre], 11,923
Sloane Maternity Hospital (NY), 12,140
Slobodinsky, Rachelle (1869-1946). *See* Yarros, Rachelle (Slobodinsky) [Mrs. Victor S.] (1869-1946)
Slocum, Charlotte (Adams) [Mrs. Christopher], 12,370
Slocum, Christopher, 12,370
Slocum, Esther. *See* Pennell, Esther (Slocum) [Mrs. Lewis]
Slocum, Margaret Olivia (1828-1918). *See* Sage, Margaret Olivia (Slocum) [Mrs. Russell B.] (1828-1918)
Slocumb, Mary, **13,575**
Slogum House (book), 10,529
Slonimsky, Henry, 3,987
Slonimsky, Marion [Mrs. Stanley] Cummings [Mrs. Henry] (1876-1941), **3,987**, 6,353
Slonimsky, Nicholas, 6,344
Sloop, Mary (Martin) (1873-1962), **13,128**
Sloops, 12,286
Slosberg, Bertha Froma. *See* Sand, Froma
Sloss, Ann Eliza. *See* Coffee, Ann Eliza (Sloss) [Mrs. A. D.]
Sloss Family (AL), 27
Sloss, James L. (?-1844), 27

Sloss, Max C., 1,565, 1,568, 1,592, 1,593
Slosson, Annie Trumbull (1838-1926), 6,321
Slosson, May Preston, 11,605
Slovak-American newspapers, 4,308
Slovak Catholic Charitable Organization of Chicago (IL), 4,308
Slovak Cultural Center (IL), 4,308
Slovaks, **4,308**
Slovene-Americans, 13,912
Slovenian Women's Union, branch 21 (OH), 13,912
Slowe, Lucy Diggs (1885-1937), **2,149**
Slums, 2,549, 6,656
Slusher, H. E. (1893-), **10,047**
Slye, Maud, 4,698
Small business, 1,402
Small, Cecillia Gibson, **10,373**
Small, Fedora. *See* Frank, Fedora (Small)
Small, Herbert P., 15,679
Small, Lena B., 10,055
Smallpox, 4,914, 7,385, 12,514, 15,763
  prevention, 12,223, 15,681
Smallpox epidemics, 5,398, 7,346, 9,363, 11,520, 11,600, 11,718, 16,877
Smallwood, Elizabeth (1862-1932). *See* Shields, Elizabeth (Smallwood) [Mrs. Bernard C.] (1862-1932)
Smallwood, Martha. *See* Field, Martha (Smallwood)
Smart, Helen Hamilton [Mrs. Charles Selden] (1853-1925). *See* Gardener, Helen Hamilton. [Mrs. Charles Selden] Smart [Mrs. Selden Allen] Day (1853-1925)
Smart Set (periodical), 12,562
Smathers, Frank, 2,872
Smaus, Jewel (Spangler), 1,534
Smedberg, Jeanie R., 2,634
Smedes, Emilie Rose (?-1950). *See* Holmes, Emilie Rose (Smedes) [Mrs. John Simcox] (?-1950)
Smedes, Susan (Dabney) (1840-1913), **13,130**
Smedley, Agnes (1894?-1950), 174, 3,986, 4,067, 9,081
Smeltzer Family (PA), 15,227
Smile Please (ms), 9,752
Smiley, John G. (?-1894), 11,780
Smiley, Mrs. Josephine, 4,350
Smiley, Permelia Adelaide "Addie" Weed [Mrs. John G.] (1847-86), **11,780**
Smiley, Sarah F., **13,239, 15,090**
Smilin' Through (drama), 12,426
Smilks, Mildred. *See* Dudley, Mildred (Smilks)
Smilowitz, Anne [Miss] (1909-), **15,164**
Smiraldo, Mrs. Tony, 16,870
Smiraldo, Tony, 16,870
Smiser, Mary Miller (1883-), 10,211
Smith, Aaron, 3,424
Smith, Abigail [Mrs.], 17,382
Smith, Abigail (Adams) (1765-1813), 6,341
Smith, Absalom, 9,887
Smith Act, 9,380
Smith, Ada (Clark) [Mrs. Joseph, III], 10,091
Smith, Adaline, 3,379, 3,424
Smith, Alexander B., 9,378
Smith, Alfred Babington, 14,317
Smith, Alfred E., 110, 6,432, 11,853, 11,928, 11,970, 12,001, 13,274, 14,686
Smith, Alice Maude (1868-1938), **17,337**
Smith, Alice Ravenel Huger (1876-1956), **15,424**
Smith, Alice Waddell, 11,130
Smith, Alys. *See* Russell, Alys (Smith) [Mrs. Bertrand]
Smith, Amanda Barnes [Mrs. Warrne] (1809-86), **16,819**
Smith, Amelia Catherine (1876-?). *See* Calvert, Amelia Catherine (Smith) [Mrs. Philip P.] (1876-?)
Smith, Amos D., 3,580
Smith, Angelia. *See* Whitman, Angelia (Smith)
Smith, Angelina (?-1886). *See* Crews, Angelina (Smith) (?-1866)
Smith, Ann Bryant [Mrs.] (1753-1835), **5,688**
Smith, Ann Fitzhugh [Mrs. Gerrit] (1805-75), 12,744
Smith, Ann White [Mrs.], 2,441
Smith, Anna, 17,516
Smith, Anna K., **7,930**

Smith, Anna Leonard (Stetson) (1766-1847). *See* Shaw, Anna Leonard (Stetson) Smith (1766-1847)
Smith, Anna Maria, 3,091
Smith, Anna Maria Harrison [Miss] (1811-?), 2,582, 11,031
Smith, Annie, 17,064
Smith, Annie Brunson, **15,724**
Smith, Arvilla Almira (Powers) [Mrs. George Nelson] (1808-95), **7,931**
Smith, Asa, 1,790
Smith, Asa Bowen, 1,790, 2,002
Smith, Asa Dodge, 5,858
Smith, Atha C., 3,424
Smith, Audentia. *See* Anderson, Audentia (Smith)
Smith, Audrey Nina (ca. 1887-), **8,614**
Smith, Augustus W. (1802-66), Family, **1,983**
Smith, "Aunt" Catherine [Mrs. Abner] Goddard, 9,528
Smith, Barbara Leigh (1827-91). *See* Bodichon, Barbara Leigh (Smith) (1827-91)
Smith, Bathsheba Wilson (Bigler) [Mrs. George A.] (1822-1910), **16,557**, 16,700, 16,789, **16,820, 16,911, 16,957**
Smith, Belle E., 4,732
Smith, Bertha (Madison) [Mrs. Joseph, III], 10,091
Smith, Bertha Madison [Mrs. Joseph, III], 10,091
Smith, Bess [Miss], 2,596
Smith, Bessie (1894-1937), 5,530, 5,532, **5,533**
Smith, Betty. [Mrs. Joseph Piper] Jones [Mrs. Robert Voris] Finch (1896-1972), **13,131**, 13,511
Smith, Blanche. *See* Ferguson, Blanche (Smith) [Mrs. James H., Jr.]
Smith, Calista Sanders [Mrs. Julius], 4,961
Smith, Caroline Cobb [Mrs. William], 12,626
Smith, Carrie (1861-1944). *See* Weld, Carrie (Smith) (1861-1944)
Smith, Carrie E. (Lukens), 5,941
Smith, Catharine B., **13,956**
Smith, Catherine [Mrs.], 5,668
Smith, Catherine (Childs) [Mrs. Augustus W.] (?-1899), 1,983
Smith, Catherine Delphina "Della" (Fish) [Mrs. Joseph West] (1864-1934), **16,821**
Smith, Catherine McClure Fruit [Mrs. Abner S.] Goddard [Mrs. Alexander B.], 9,378
Smith, Charles Eugene (1890-), **14,443**
Smith, Charles Gardner, 15,221
Smith, Charles Worcester (1828-83), 7,680
Smith, Charlotte (Wilson), 10,191
Smith, Clifton B., **3,423**
Smith College (MA), 2,336, 4,167, 4,487, 6,582, 6,662, 6,724, 6,737, 7,164, 7,166, 7,255, 7,259, 10,677, 11,719, 12,737, 12,740, 13,604, 17,043
  alumnae, 1,998, **7,154**, 7,162, 7,186, 7,264, 8,441, 8,597, 8,689, 14,709, 15,946
  buildings, **7,155**
  centennial celebrations, **7,162**
  endowments, 7,157
  faculty, **7,157, 7,158**, 7,173, 7,328, 10,955, 12,815
  graduate work, **7,159**
  history, **7,153, 7,160, 7,163**
  presidents, **3,362**
  students, 1,995, **7,156**, 8,896, 8,962, 9,004, 9,431, 14,453
  trustees, **7,165**
Smith College (MA), Alumnae Association, 7,154
Smith College (MA), Alumnae College, 7,159
Smith College (MA), Association for Christian Work, 7,164
Smith College (MA), Association of Former Juniors in France, 7,153
Smith College (MA), Faculty Wives Club, 7,157
Smith College (MA), Institute for the Coordination of Women's Interests, 6,771, 12,738
Smith College (MA), Neilson Library, 15,946
Smith College (MA), Relief Unit (World War I), 7,160, 7,307
Smith College (MA), School for Social Work, 7,159, 7,241
Smith College (MA), Women's Liberation, 7,324
Smith College Club (NY), 11,351
Smith, Cornelia (Marschall) [Mrs. Charles G.] (1895-), **16,388**

Smith, Cynthia H., 15,308
Smith, David, 2,750
Smith, David A., 3,911
Smith, Dee (1882-), **9,374**
Smith-Derricotte, Annie, 3,280
Smith, Donette (1872-1961). *See* Kesler, Donette (Smith) [Mrs. Alonzo Pratt] (1872-1961)
Smith, Donna Eloise, **1,378**
Smith, Dorsey B., 14,664
Smith, E. H. [Miss], **6,889**
Smith, E. R., 11,824
Smith, Edith M., 2,157
Smith, Edmund "Ned" Munroe, 12,055
Smith, Edward Hall, 1,342
Smith, Edward Wanton, **14,854**
Smith, Elberta T., 5,065
Smith, Eleanor (1858-1942), 4,047, 4,056, **4,153,** 14,946
Smith, Eleanor Fulkerson. *See* Nugent, Eleanor Fulkerson (Smith) [Mrs. William Lewis]
Smith, Eliza, 7,387
Smith, Eliza A., 3,424
Smith, Eliza (Hubbard) [Mrs. Ira Gilbert], 801
Smith, Eliza Leaycraft (1802-93). *See* Lentilhon, Eliza Leaycraft (Smith) [Mrs. Antoine] (1802-93)
Smith, Eliza Maria (Partridge) [Mrs. Joseph] (1820-86). *See* Lyman, Eliza Maria (Partridge) [Mrs. Joseph] Smith [Mrs. Amasa Mason] (1820-86)
Smith, Eliza Roxey (Snow) [Mrs. Joseph] (1804-87). *See* Young, Eliza Roxey (Snow) [Mrs. Joseph] Smith [Mrs. Brigham] (1804-87)
Smith, Elizabeth (1773-1854), **7,679**
Smith, Elizabeth (1750-1815). *See* Peabody, Elizabeth (Smith) [Mrs. John] Shaw [Mrs. Stephen] (1750-1815)
Smith, Elizabeth (1822-1911). *See* Miller, Elizabeth (Smith) [Mrs. Charles Dudley] (1822-1911)
Smith, Elizabeth B., 3,599
Smith, Elizabeth C. "Bill" Newcom [Mrs.], 9,911
Smith, Elizabeth C. Whitney, 11,560
Smith, Elizabeth (Dixon). *See* Geer, Elizabeth (Dixon) Smith
Smith, Elizabeth E. (1821-1911). *See* Marcy, Elizabeth E. (Smith) (1821-1911)
Smith, Elizabeth H., **800**
Smith, Elizabeth Jennett Smithson [Mrs. James Edward] (1861-?), 16,486
Smith, Elizabeth (Murray). *See* Inman, Elizabeth (Murray) Smith [Mrs. Ralph]
Smith, Elizabeth Oakes (Prince) [Mrs. Seba] (1806-93), 850, 5,694, **6,890, 12,624**
Smith, Ella F. Levengood, **10,374**
Smith, Ella Louise (1859-1949). *See* Badger, Ella Louise (Smith) [Mrs. Robert A.] (1859-1949)
Smith, Ellen [Mrs. Hermon Dunlap], 3,952
Smith, Emily. *See* Warner, Emily (Smith) [Mrs. John]
Smith, Emily. *See* York, Emily (Smith)
Smith, Emily (1902-), 7,510
Smith, Emily James (1865-1944). *See* Putnam, Emily James (Smith) [Mrs. George Haven] (1865-1944)
Smith, Emily Meier Stuart, **12,198**
Smith, Emma, 16,781, 16,822
Smith, Emma (1858-1927). *See* DeVoe, Emma (Smith) (1858-1927)
Smith, Emma. *See* McCallum, Emma (Smith)
Smith, Emma (1838-1912). *See* Woodruff, Emma (Smith) [Mrs. Wilford] (1838-1912)
Smith, Emma Azalia (1867-1922). *See* Hackley, Emma Azalia (Smith) (1867-1922)
Smith, Emma (Hale) [Mrs. Joseph, Jr.] (1804-79). *See* Bidamon, Emma (Hale) [Mrs. Joseph, Jr.] Smith [Mrs. Lewis C.] (1804-79)
Smith, Emmeline "Emma" (Griswold) [Mrs. Joseph, III], 10,091, 10,093
Smith, Erastus M., 13,839
Smith, Erminnie Adele (Platt) [Mrs. Simeon H.] (1836-86), 2,837
Smith, Eva, 9,376
Smith, Eva (Byrne) Rizzi, **10,634**
Smith, Eveline [Mrs.], 17,919
Smith, Evelyn. *See* Bacon, Evelyn (Smith) [Mrs. Walter R.]

Smith, Evelyn Stewart (1871-?), **14,302**
Smith Family, 460
Smith Family (CT), **2,019**
Smith Family (CT), 1,940
Smith Family (GA), **3,424**
Smith Family (GA), **3,599**
Smith Family (IA), 4,842
Smith Family (Ontonagon, MI), **7,932**
Smith Family (Saginaw, MI), 8,374
Smith Family (MN), 9,075
Smith Family (MT), **10,264**
Smith Family (NJ), **11,130**
Smith Family (NY), **12,625**
Smith Family (NY), **12,314**
Smith Family (NY?), 12,531
Smith Family (OR), 14,526
Smith Family (OR), **14,662**
Smith, Fannie Pickelshimer Kerby, **3,425**
Smith, Fannie (Sackett) [Mrs. William B.] (1865-1972), **12,766**
Smith, Fanny C. Whitney, 11,560
Smith, Florence Beatrice (1888-1953). *See* Price, Florence Beatrice (Smith) (1888-1953)
Smith, Forrest (1886-1962), **10,048**
Smith, Frances, 801
Smith, Frances Cornelia. *See* Hubbard, Frances Cornelia (Smith)
Smith, Frances Grace (1871-1948), 7,158
Smith, Francis Monroe, **9,375**
Smith, Frank, 8,225
Smith, Frank E., 16,304
Smith, Frank Ellis, **9,733**
Smith, Gail Preston (1915-), 11,813
Smith, Gamaliel, 12,313
Smith, Garland (1880-1968), **3,090**
Smith, Genevieve Copeland, **4,660**
Smith, Genevieve (Thompson) (1883-1974), **14,663**
Smith, George, 15,623
Smith, George A. (1817-75), Family (UT), 16,557, 16,710, 16,820, 16,826, **16,911,** 16,957
Smith, George Albert, 16,676, 16,825, 16,911
Smith, George Nelson, 7,931
Smith, Gerrit (1797-1874), 6,412, **6,891,** 11,412, 12,625
Smith, Gerrit (1797-1874), Family, **12,744**
Smith, Gilman, 9,041
Smith, Gladys. *See* Pickford, Mary. [Mrs. Douglas] Fairbanks, Sr. [Mrs. Charles "Buddy"] Rogers (1893-1979)
Smith, Gladys Nielsen (1898-1938), 16,676
Smith, Grace (Kellogg) Griffith (1885-), **7,296**
Smith, Grace Ruth, 14,542
Smith, Gusta Evans [Mrs. Frank], **8,225**
Smith, Hannah, 7,387
Smith, Hannah [Mrs. Robert Pearsall], 14,745
Smith, Hannah (1789-?), **7,027**
Smith, Hannah (1861-1941). *See* Allen, Hannah (Smith) [Mrs. Alfred M.] (1861-1941)
Smith, Hannah Cooke, **3,580**
Smith, Hannah Daphne. *See* Dalton, Hannah Daphne (Smith)
Smith, Hannah (Hicock) (1767-1810), 1,901
Smith, Harriet (1787-1869). *See* Goodnow, Harriet (Smith) (1787-1869)
Smith, Harriet "Hattie" Amelia (ca. 1841-1923). *See* Nickle, Harriet "Hattie" Amelia (Smith) [Mrs. Wesley] (ca. 1841-1923)
Smith, Harriette (1816-1915). *See* Kidder, Harriette (Smith) [Mrs. Daniel P.] (1816-1915)
Smith, Hattie (Hyland), **6,892**
Smith, Helen, 4,046
Smith, Helen (1893-?). *See* Giffen, Helen (Smith) (1893-?)
Smith, Helen (1906-). *See* Bevington, Helen (Smith) [Mrs. Merle M.]
Smith, Helen E., 11,940
Smith, Helen Evertson, 12,314
Smith, Helen Fairchild (1837-1926), **11,282**
Smith, Helen Huntington (1902-71), 2,019
Smith, Helen Mar (Kimball) [Mrs. Joseph, Jr.] (1828-96). *See* Whitney, Helen Mar (Kimball) [Mrs. Joseph, Jr.] Smith [Mrs. Horace Kimball] (1828-96)
Smith, Helen Wilkinson, **13,894**

Smith, Henrietta. *See* Meriwether, Henrietta (Smith)
Smith, Henrietta C., **3,426**
Smith, Henry Arthur (1844-?), Family (MN), **9,376**
Smith, Henry Nash (1906-), 328, 11,637
Smith, Herndon, 17,140
Smith, Hilda Worthington [Miss] (1888-), 2,685, **6,893, 11,501,** 13,176, 15,332, 17,588
Smith, Horace, 3,424
Smith, Horatio Southgate, 12,055
Smith, Hyrum, 806, 4,416, 16,505, 16,540, 16,598, 16,635, 16,688, 16,798
Smith, Ida B. Wise, 4,243, **4,837**
Smith, Ida Sauer, **10,715**
Smith, Inez (1846-1941). *See* Soule, Inez (Smith) (1846-1941)
Smith, Inez (1889-1964). *See* Davis, Inez (Smith) (1889-1964)
Smith, Ira Gilbert (1811-89), 801
Smith, Irene, 4,796
Smith, Irene. *See* Calbreath, Irene (Smith) [Mrs. John]
Smith, Irene M., 4,077
Smith, Isabella MacLaren, 11,130
Smith, Isabelle, 17,208
Smith, James I., 7,932
Smith, James Rembert, **3,091**
Smith, Jane (NY), 11,750
Smith, Jane J., **3,427**
Smith, Jane (Norman) [Mrs. Clarence M.] (1874-1953), 6,742, **6,894**
Smith, Jane Rooker. *See* Breeden, Jane Rooker (Smith)
Smith, Janice M. (1906-), **4,397**
Smith, Janie. *See* Robeson, Janie (Smith) [Mrs. R. R.]
Smith, Janie [Miss], 13,374
Smith, Jean Conly [Mrs. G. E.], **3,722**
Smith, Jeanne C. (ca. 1823-1903). *See* Carr, Jeanne C. (Smith) [Mrs. Ezra Slocum] (ca. 1823-1903)
Smith, Jedediah Strong (1799-1831), Family, **801**
Smith, Jennie (1860-1934). *See* Sargent, Jennie (Smith) (1860-1934)
Smith, Jennie L., **802**
Smith, Jessie Ella (Evans) [Mrs. Joseph Fielding] (1902-71), 16,676, 16,754, **16,823**
Smith, Jessie Welborn, 4,758
Smith, Jessica Randolph, 2,579, 2,615, 13,374, **13,576**
Smith, John, **17,724**
Smith, John Israel, 17,012
Smith, John U., 14,526
Smith, Jonathan Bayard Harrison (1810-?), 2,582
Smith, Jose, 7,933
Smith, Joseph F. (1838-1918), 16,533, 16,632, 16,727, 16,786, 16,824, 16,834
Smith, Joseph Fielding (1876-1972), 16,754, 16,823
Smith, Joseph H., 11,715
Smith, Joseph, Jr. (1805-1844), 178, 806, 845, 2,581, 4,416, 10,088, 10,092, 16,505, 16,525, 16,533, 16,536, 16,537, 16,540, 16,545, 16,557, 16,560, 16,581, 16,598, 16,612, 16,635, 16,636, 16,639, 16,688, 16,702, 16,718, 16,729, 16,732, 16,743, 16,752, 16,798, 16,806, 16,815, 16,820, 16,822, 16,830, 16,832, 16,841, 16,852, 16,860, 16,889, 16,902, 16,911, 16,955, 16,959, 16,967, 16,976
Smith, Joseph P., **15,725**
Smith, Joseph, III (1832-1914), 10,091, 10,092, 10,093, 16,813, **16,959**
Smith, Josephine Conly. *See* Vaughn, Josephine Conly (Smith)
Smith, Josephine Groesbeck [Mrs. John Henry] (1857-1948), 16,676
Smith, Josephine McCurdy Caroline (Lord) [Mrs. Charles Worcester] (1834-1910), **7,680**
Smith, Josephine Noble, 19
Smith, Julia [Miss], **16,317**
Smith, Julia A. *See* Clark, Julia A. (Smith) [Mrs. Lincoln]
Smith, Julia Evelina (1792-1886). *See* Parker, Julia Evelina (Smith) [Mrs. Amos Andrew] (1792-1886)
Smith, Julia (Holmes) (1839-?), 3,862
Smith, Julina (Lambson) [Mrs. Joseph F.] (1849-1936), **16,824**

Smith, Juline. *See* Thummel, Juline (Smith)
Smith, Juline E. (Babcock) [Mrs. Peter], 801
Smith, Kate Douglas (1856-1923). *See* Riggs, Kate Douglas (Smith) [Mrs. Samuel Bradley] Wiggin [Mrs. George Christopher] (1856-1923)
Smith, Katherine Moody, 14,096
Smith, Kathryn Muriel, **1,379**
Smith, Kirby, 5,552
Smith, "Lady Martha" (Tunstall) [Mrs. William Tangier], 11,284
Smith, Lady Sybil, 16,166
Smith, Laura (1808-98). *See* Haviland, Laura (Smith) [Mrs. Charles, Jr.] (1808-98)
Smith, Laura Ford, **5,296**
Smith, Letitia Vanderen, 3,093
Smith, Libbie. *See* Killpatrick, Libbie (Smith)
Smith, Lillian Eugenia (1897-1966), 569, **2,879**, 3,290, 3,303, 3,347, **3,351**, 4,126, 5,469
Smith, Lizzie S., 7,135
Smith, Lois Angeline (1844-1921). *See* Bushman, Lois Angeline (Smith) [Mrs. John] (1844-1921)
Smith, Lorna [Mrs.], 1,570
Smith, Lorna Dysart [Mrs. Byron B.] (1897-), **1,600**
Smith, Louisa (Beaman) [Mrs. Joseph] (1815-50). *See* Young, Louisa (Beaman) [Mrs. Joseph] Smith [Mrs. Brigham] (1815-50)
Smith, Louisa Catherine, 12,369
Smith, Louisa Sargent [Mrs. John], **17,724**
Smith, Louise, **17,779**
Smith, Louise Hulbert, **4,154**
Smith, Louise Pettibone, 7,583
Smith, Louise (Von Behren) [Mrs. Dorsey B.] (1890-1964), 14,618, **14,664**
Smith, Lovina [Mrs. Joseph H.], **11,715**
Smith, Lucinda [Mrs. Ferdinand C.], **14,665**
Smith, Lucy, 3,290
Smith, Lucy Ann (1812-67). *See* Tucker, Lucy Ann (Smith) [Mrs. Nathaniel Beverley] (1812-67)
Smith, Lucy Ann (Eastman), 460
Smith, Lucy Emily Woodruff [Mrs. George Albert] (1869-1937), **16,825**, 16,911
Smith, Lucy H. King (Cunningham) [Mrs. Alfred Franklin] (1872-1940), **2,580**
Smith, Lucy Mack, 16,505, 16,539, 16,781
Smith, Lucy Meserve (1817-92). *See* Smith, Lucy Meserve (Smith) [Mrs. George Albert] (1817-92)
Smith, Lucy Meserve (Smith) [Mrs. George Albert] (1817-92), **16,826**, 16,911
Smith, Lucy Virginia (1825-81). *See* French, Lucy Virginia (Smith) [Mrs. John Hopkins] (1825-81)
Smith, Lucy (Walker) [Mrs. Joseph] (1826-1910). *See* Kimball, Lucy (Walker) [Mrs. Joseph] Smith [Mrs. Heber Chase] (1826-1910)
Smith, Luella Frances (1859-?). *See* McWhirter, Luella Frances (Smith) [Mrs. Felix Tony] (1859-?)
Smith, Lura (Case) [Mrs. Jesse], **1,486**
Smith, Lura S., 801
Smith, Luther, 2,583
Smith, Lydia Ann Joslin (1836-1912), 6,643
Smith, Mabel (1877-1933). *See* Douglass, Mabel (Smith) [Mrs. William Shipman] (1877-1933)
Smith, Maggie B., 13,422
Smith, Margaret (slave, NC), 9,391
Smith, Margaret [Mrs. Rowland], 17,176
Smith, Margaret (1811-80). *See* Preston, Margaret (Smith) [Mrs. William P.] (1811-80)
Smith, Margaret Ayer [Mrs. Alfred Babington], **692**
Smith, Margaret (Bayard) [Mrs. Samuel Harrison] (1778-1844), **2,582**, 2,608
Smith, Margaret Chase (1897-), 2,097, 2,163, 5,123, 5,137, 5,569, 5,719, 6,710, 9,932, 11,483, 13,406, 14,820
Smith, Margaret Densmore, 9,041
Smith, Margaret E. [Mrs. Clement], **6,895**
Smith, Margaret G. (1896-1970), **10,209**
Smith, Margaret (Hill) (1877-1973), 14,581
Smith, Margaret Jewett. *See* Bailey, Margaret Jewett (Smith) [Mrs. William J.]
Smith, Margaret (Lukens). *See* Adamson, Margaret (Lukens) Smith
Smith, Margaret (Scott) [Mrs. L. M.], 13,564
Smith, Margaret Seaton Densmore (1835-1919), 9,041
Smith, Margarita, 16,161

Smith, Marguerite Diaz Peña [Mrs. Elliott M.], 587
Smith, Marguerite Waters, 16,161
Smith, Maria. *See* Brown, Maria Smith [Mrs. Morris]
Smith, Maria B. (1790-1875). *See* Noyes, Maria B. (Smith) (1790-1875)
Smith, Maria Elizabeth (Bushman) [Mrs. Silas Derryfield] (1869-?), **16,827**
Smith, Mariah Louisa, 3,424
Smith, Marie T. [Miss], 1,386
Smith, Marietta. *See* Lovett, Marietta (Smith) [Mrs. Robert Watkins]
Smith, Marjorie C. (?-1972), **12,924**
Smith, Martha Ann Grover [Mrs. Edward Hall] (1833-1906), **1,342**
Smith, Martha Baldwin Allen (1831-1922). *See* Battey, Martha Baldwin Allen (Smith) [Mrs. Robert] (1831-1922)
Smith, Martha Bracken [Mrs. James I.], 7,932
Smith, Mary (1741-1811). *See* Cranch, Mary (Smith) (1741-1811)
Smith, Mary Ann [Miss], 2,582
Smith, Mary Ann (1825-1918). *See* Jones, Mary Ann (Smith) [Mrs. John M.] (1825-1918)
Smith, Mary Ann Ripley [Mrs. Thomas], 1,876
Smith, Mary Audentia. *See* Anderson, Mary Audentia (Smith)
Smith, Mary Bainerd, **15,091**
Smith, Mary Bond, 3,091
Smith, Mary Chute, 8,600
Smith, Mary D., 3,500
Smith, Mary E., 16,460
Smith, Mary E., 959
Smith, Mary Elizabeth Burroughs (Roberts) (1860-1945). *See* Coolidge, Mary Elizabeth Burroughs (Roberts) Smith (1860-1945)
Smith, Mary Elizabeth (Rollins) [Mrs.] Lightner [Mrs. Joseph] (1818-1913), **16,533**
Smith, Mary Emma (1891-), **246**
Smith, Mary Fielding [Mrs. Hyrum] (1801-52), 16,781
Smith, Mary (Heathman) [Mrs. John A.] (1816-95), **16,828**
Smith, Mary Jane, 3,424
Smith, Mary (McAlpin) [Mrs. Erastus M.], 13,839
Smith, Mary Morriss [Mrs.] (1802-95), **15,968**
Smith, Mary Rozet (1867?-1934), 3,814, 4,007, 4,047, 4,100
Smith, Mary Ruffin [Miss], **13,132**
Smith, Mary S., 801
Smith, Mary S. D., **1,343**
Smith, Mary Sue [Mrs. Robert Henry] (?-1933). *See* Mendenhall, Mary Sue [Mrs. Robert Henry] Smith [Mrs. John S.] (?-1933)
Smith, Mathilda (1854-1926), 10,151
Smith, May B. (?-1941), **17,180**
Smith, May K. (1881-), **7,934**
Smith Medal, 7,160
Smith, Mercy Rachel (Fielding) [Mrs. Hyrum] (1807-93). *See* Thompson, Mercy Rachel (Fielding) [Mrs. Hyrum] Smith [Mrs. Robert Blashel] (1807-93)
Smith, Mianda, 14,526
Smith, Mildred E. Buller, **6,896**
Smith, Minna Eveline (1860-1929), 12,536
Smith, Minnie L. *See* Bancroft, Minnie L. (Smith) [Mrs. Edward]
Smith, Mrs. Alfred E., 13,533
Smith, Mrs. Aubrey H., 12,417
Smith, Mrs. Charles B., 3,919
Smith, Mrs. Daniel, **2,916**
Smith, Mrs. E. W., 2,059
Smith, Mrs. George Wilson, 12,595
Smith, Mrs. Herman Dunlap, 11,827
Smith, Mrs. J. Hardin, 10,200
Smith, Mrs. S., 1,901
Smith, Mrs. Walter F., **9,377**
Smith, Myra, 8,670
Smith, Myra [Mrs.], 9,741
Smith, Myrtle A., **14,444**
Smith, Nancy [Mrs. Stanton], **8,125**
Smith, Nancy (Harrell) [Mrs. William Lay]. *See* Yancey, Nancy (Harrell) [Mrs. William Lay] Smith
Smith, Nancy J. [Mrs. Aaron], 3,424

Smith, Nancy Leonard (1785-1856). *See* Peabody, Nancy Leonard (Smith) (1785-1856)
Smith, Nancy S. *See* Boston, Nancy S. (Smith) [Mrs. John H.]
Smith, Nellie Angel (1881-1976), 5,394
Smith, Nina (Webster) [Mrs. Leslie D.] (1887-). *See* Dumont, Nina (Webster) [Mrs. Leslie D.] Smith [Mrs. Henry] (1887-)
Smith, Nora Archibald [Miss] (1859-1934), **803**, 12,493
Smith, Olive Cole, 5,065
Smith, Oliver, 12,360
Smith, Oneita Virginia "Jennie" (1862-1946), **3,092**
Smith, Oreon Mann [Mrs. Rufus] (?-1907), 3,405
Smith, Orren Randolph, 13,374
Smith, Orrin F., 9,528
Smith, Orrin F., Family (MN), **9,378**
Smith, Pamela Seward [Mrs. Luther] (1797-?), **2,583**
Smith, Pattie Odom, 2,941
Smith, Pauline Udall, 16,903
Smith, Pearl (Brown) (1879-1957), **804**
Smith, Perry Childs (1827-1903), 1,983
Smith, Peter, 3,093
Smith, Peter (1810-79), 801
Smith, Phebe [Mrs.] (1889-), 16,488
Smith, Presendia Lathrop (Huntington) [Mrs. Joseph] (1810-92). *See* Kimball, Presendia Lathrop (Huntington) [Mrs. Joseph] Smith [Mrs. Heber Chase] (1810-92)
Smith, Rachel, 11,324
Smith, Rachel (1890-). *See* Taylor, Rachel (Smith) [Mrs. Albert LeRoy] (1890-)
Smith, Rachel Jahonnet (1808-80). *See* Spalding, Rachel Jahonnet (Smith) [Mrs. Henry Harmon] (1808-80)
Smith, Reba (Barrett), 8,669
Smith, Rebecca D., **11,131**
Smith, Rescarrick Moore (1804-?), **11,031**
Smith, Rhoda Luann B. (1859-?). *See* Allred, Rhoda Luann B. (Smith) (1859-?)
Smith, Rhoda (Parker), **7,440**
Smith, Rita, 16,161
Smith, Robert Henry, 10,264
Smith, Robert Pearsall, 14,745
Smith, Rowland, 17,176
Smith, Ruby Green, 11,662
Smith, Ruby K., **16,558**
Smith, Rufus, 3,405
Smith, Ruth M., 5,469
Smith, Ruth Newey [Mrs.] (1835-1917), **11,792**
Smith, Ruth Proskauer, 11,881
Smith, S. Myra (Cox) (1822-87), 6,901
Smith, Sallie F., **5,635**
Smith, Sally (1791-1871). *See* Jones, Sally (Smith) Shiffer (1791-1871)
Smith, Samuel, 3,424
Smith, Samuel Francis (1808-95), **1,487**
Smith, Samuel H., 16,545
Smith, Samuel P., 13,573
Smith, Samuel Stanhope (1750-1819), **11,172**
Smith, Sara B., 11,031
Smith, Sarah, 10,036
Smith, Sarah (missionary), 11,440
Smith, Sarah E., 13,370
Smith, Sarah Farr [Mrs. John Henry] (1849-1921), 16,911
Smith, Sarah Gilbert (White) [Mrs. Asa] (1813-55), **1,790**, 2,002, 17,373
Smith, Sarah Grimes, 10,812
Smith, Sarah J., 4,624
Smith, Siba Hand, 12,814
Smith, Sidney, 14,526
Smith, Silas B., 14,549
Smith, Sister Maris Stella (1899-), **8,854**
Smith, Sol, **10,182**
Smith, Sophia (1796-1870), 7,163
Smith, Stanley Barney, 8,256
Smith, Stanton (1905-), **8,125**
Smith, Sue. *See* Beatty, Sue (Smith)
Smith, Susan (1885-), **1,224**
Smith, Susan Bayard [Miss], 2,582
Smith, Susan Crow, 1,274
Smith, Susan Dwight (Munroe) [Mrs. Horatio Southgate], 12,055

Smith, Susan Elizabeth West (1833-1926), 16,911
Smith, Susan Harrison (1804-?), 2,582
Smith, Susie (King) [Mrs. O. A.] (1904-), **4,507**
Smith, Sybil L., 11,656
Smith, Telitha A., 3,424
Smith, Thannie. *See* Wisenbaker, Thannie (Smith)
   [Mrs. E. D.]
Smith, Theodora. *See* Marks, Theodora Smith [Mrs.
   Solon]
Smith, Theodore Clarke, 2,348
Smith, Thomas, 7,355
Smith, Thomas (1745-1809), **3,093**
Smith, Thomas Adams (1781-1844), **9,912**, 17,121
Smith, Tucker, 15,332
Smith, Tullie, 3,226
Smith, V. G., 14,651
Smith, Vera [Mrs. Charles W.] (1878-1969), **10,375**
Smith, Vesta Marie (Eaton) (?-1926). *See* Daniels,
   Vesta Marie (Eaton) Smith (?-1926)
Smith, Viola Leora (Ziegler) [Mrs. Charles Eugene],
   14,443
Smith, Virginia. *See* Berryman, Virginia (Smith)
Smith, W. G., 13,564
Smith, W. H., 16,565
Smith, Walter Bedell, 5,129
Smith, Wilbur F., 3,424
Smith, William, **12,626**
Smith, William, 14,662
Smith, William Benjamin (1850-1934), **10,049**
Smith, William Lay, **13,577**
Smith, William N. H., 13,577
Smith, William Tangier, 11,284
Smith, Williamson Lyncoya, 1,544
Smith, Zaide. *See* Salyards, Zaide (Smith)
Smith, Zilpha Stark [Mrs. George A.], 16,710
Smith, Zina Diantha (Huntington) [Mrs. Henry
   Bailey] Jacobs [Mrs. Joseph, Jr.] (1821 1901).
   See Young, Zina Diantha (Huntington) [Mrs.
   Henry Bailey] Jacobs [Mrs. Joseph, Jr.] Smith
   [Mrs. Brigham] (1821-1901)
Smith, Zora (1881-1969). *See* Jarvis, Zora (Smith)
   [Mrs. Brigham] (1881-1969)
Smithsonian Institution. *See* United States
   (government), Smithsonian Institution (DC)
Smithton School (Bradford, WI), 17,724
Smits, Anna, 8,604
Smock, Harriet, 3,754
"Smoke From My Chimney" (song), 17,970
Smoke, Margaret [Mrs. Ashe], **9,913**
Smoke prevention, 16,535
Smoke Signals (periodical), 2,936
Smoking, 16,845
Smoot, Abraham Owen, 805, 16,842, 16,914
Smoot, Diana Eldredge [Mrs. Abraham O.]
   (1837-1914), 16,914
Smoot, James Edward, **13,578**
Smoot, Maggie Wilson (1870-1954), **2,150**
Smoot, Margaret Thompson (McMeans) [Mrs.
   Abraham Owen] (1809-84), **805**, **16,559**, 16,595,
   16,914
Smoot, Olive (1860-1943). *See* Bean, Olive (Smoot)
   [Mrs. James W.] (1860-1943)
Smorczewska, Maria Robert (Countess). *See* Bullis,
   Maria Robert Smorczewska [Mrs. Harry Ames]
Smorgasbord, 16,324
Smuggling, 1,174, 13,446
Smuts, Jan Christian, 7,247
Smylie, Robert E.. 3,667
Smyth, Annie, 4,951
Smyth Family (SC). *See* Smythe Family (SC)
Smyth, Jane Ann, 15,550
Smyth, Lizzie, 4,951
Smyth, Margaret [Mrs. Robert], 4,951
Smyth, Robert (1814-98), **4,951**
Smyth, Sarah Lanman (1842-?), **13,957**
Smythe Family (SC), **15,418, 15,434, 15,472, 15,550**
Smythe, Hugh (1913-77), **12,694**
Smythe, Jane Adger (1822-99), 15,418
Smythe, Louisa McCord (1845-1928), **15,726**
Smythe, Mabel Murphy [Mrs. Hugh] (1818-), 12,694
Smythe, Margaret Garret (1901-), 409, **8,886**, 11,846
Smythe, Margaret Hall Moffett Adger (1820-1915),
   15,418

Smythe, Margaret Milligan (Adger) [Mrs. Thomas]
   (1807-84), 15,434
Smythe, Mrs. Augustine T., 15,472
Smythe, Mrs. Thomas, 15,550
Smythe, Sarah Ann (1846-1928), 15,434
Smythe, Sarah Annie, 15,418
Smythe, Susan Dunlap Adger (1808-84), 15,418
Smythe, Thomas (1808-64), 15,434
"Snake County Journal, 1827-28," 14,594
Snake Has All the Lines, The (book), 17,806
Snake Pit, The (book), 6,108
Snana. *See* Brass, Maggie
Snark, The (ship), 1,441
Snead, Fayette C., **14,093**
Snead, Maria Austine [Miss] (?-1888), **14,093**
Snedecor, Emily Alston Estes [Mrs. James George]
   (1858-1942), 94, **96**
Snedecor, James George, 96
Sneden, Mrs. Claude M., 2,243
Snediker, Catherine E., 4,374
Sneed, Mrs. Albert, 17,125
Snell, Bertha M. (Denton) [Mrs. Marshall K.]
   (1870-1957), **17,396**
Snell, Florence M., 14,123
Snell, Hazel. *See* Holmes, Hazel (Snell) Schreiber
Snell, Hazel [Miss], 377
Snell, Margaret Comstock, 14,271, 14,274,
   14,277
Snell, Marshall K., 17,396
Snell, Mrs. Holt, **13,579**
Snell, Robert L., **9,914**
Snell, Sarah. *See* Bryant, Sarah (Snell)
Snell, Thomas, 12,404
Snelling Family (GA), **3,352**
Snelling Family (MN), 9,113
Snelling, Josiah, 9,113
Snelling, Lilian (1879-1972), 10,151
Snelling, Nannie (Palmer) [Mrs. William Amos]
   (1857-1950), 3,352
Snelling, Paula (1899-), 3,290, 3,347, 5,469
Snelling, William Amos (1856-1907), **3,352**
Snider, Agnes Meador, 11,227
Snider, Margaret Jo Mitchell [Mrs. Clifton T.]
   (1917-), 5,394
Snipes, Ethel Taylor [Mrs.], **3,255**
Snitzler, Bill, 6,365
Snodgrass, Margaret (1885-1976). *See* Harding,
   Margaret (Snodgrass) (1885-1976)
Snohomish County Legislative Council (WA), 17,238,
   17,340
Snohomish County Public Utility Association (WA),
   17,340
Snook, Mrs., 1,593
Snoqualmie Valley Historical Society (WA), 17,160,
   17,162
Snow, Agnes K. [Mrs. William C.], **17,916**
Snow, Bernella Elizabeth (1866-1952). *See* Gardner,
   Bernella Elizabeth (Snow) [Mrs. Robert Berry]
   (1866-1952)
Snow, Carmel, 12,086
Snow, Clara [Miss], 8,016
Snow Covered Wagons (book), 315
Snow, Dorothy G., 16,890
Snow, Electa (1796-?). *See* Bramer, Electa (Snow)
   (1796-?)
Snow, Eliza Roxey (1804-87). *See* Young, Eliza
   Roxey (Snow) [Mrs. Joseph] Smith [Mrs.
   Brigham] (1804-87)
Snow, Erastus, 16,572, 16,912
Snow, Esther Mac Farlane (1895-1974), **8,192**
Snow Family (UT), 16,686
Snow, Flora (1857-?). *See* Woolley, Flora (Snow)
   [Mrs. Edwin Dilworth] (1857-?)
Snow, Harriet Cecelia (1861-1937). *See* Clapp,
   Harriet Cecelia (Snow) [Mrs. Elisha Drown]
Snow, Helen Foster (1907-), **1,564**
Snow, Jessie (ca. 1886-), 5,787
Snow, Julia Burwell (1842-92). *See* Kellogg, Julia
   Burwell (Snow) (1842-92)
Snow, Julia Josephine Spencer [Mrs. Erastus]
   (1837-1909), **16,912**
Snow, Leta [Mrs.] (1880-), **8,257**
Snow, Myra L., **14,444**

Snow, Peggy (pseudonym). *See* Snow, Helen Foster
   (1907-)
Snow, Phyllis, 16,971
Snow, Sallie A., 807
Snowden Family (CA), 1,648
Snowden, Lois E. (Arnold) [Mrs. Ernest E.], 2,179
Snowden, Louise Hortense, **15,092**
Snowden, Mary Amarinthia (Yates) [Mrs. William]
   (1819-98), 15,535, 15,692, **15,727**
Snowden, William, 15,535
Snowflake Cooperative Tannery (AZ), 16,821
Snyder, Adelaide Craig [Mrs. Harry] (1870-1967),
   9,023
Snyder, Anita, 17,282
Snyder, Anna, **4,783**
Snyder, Charles McCool, **12,765**
Snyder, Dorothy Eastman, **7,487**
Snyder, Harry, 9,023
Snyder, Jane (1823-?). *See* Richards, Jane (Snyder)
   [Mrs. Franklin D.] (1823-?)
Snyder, Jennie W., 1,201
Snyder, Lillian M., 4,302
So Far from Spring (book), 17,959
So You're Going to. . ., 7,249
Soap, 10,052
Soap making, 9,279
Soap operas, **17,705, 17,810**
Soapy Smith, King of the Frontier Con Men (book),
   16,519
Sobell, Helen [Mrs. Morton], 2,513, 12,884, 17,617
Sobell, Morton, 5,979, 17,617
Soberanes, María Ignacia. *See* Peabody, María
   Ignacia (Soberanes) [Mrs. Edward Turner] de
   Bale [Mrs. Edward T.]
Social action, 393, 1,032, **2,782, 12,808**, 13,993,
   14,605, 17,833
Social credit, 1,981
Social Democratic Federation, 12,702
Social-Democratic party, 17,675
Social Ethics (book), 6,602
Social Fraternity (MA), 7,646
Social group work, 4,059, 5,515, **8,646**
Social group workers, **4,059**
Social hygiene. *See* Hygiene, sexual
Social Hygiene Papers, 8,633
Social Hygiene Society (DC), 8,637
Social justice, 2,879
Social legislation, 2,509, 2,647, 5,840, 5,846, 7,315,
   8,666, 9,477, 11,236, 11,965, 12,026, 14,015,
   14,025
"Social life in Tucson in the Early 80's" (ms), 199
Social Literary Circle of East Des Moines (IA), 4,838
Social Literary Club (Athens, OH), 13,753
Social policy, 13,225
Social problems, 1,503, 1,763, 5,456, **6,432**, 6,953,
   7,635, 8,642, 9,095, 9,299, 11,369, **12,424**, 13,468
Social psychiatrists, 2,840, **2,841**
Social reform, 7,698, 8,662
Social Reform Club (NY), 6,354
Social reformers, 56, 104, 109, **117, 1,047**, 1,356,
   1,426, 1,427, 1,473, 1,948, **2,399, 2,401**, 2,403,
   2,415, 2,433, 2,451, 2,481, 2,588, 2,593, 2,594,
   2,643, **2,878**, 2,931, 3,430, **3,841**, 4,732, **4,754**,
   5,426, 5,768, 6,638, 6,663, **6,664, 6,791, 6,812**,
   7,025, 7,229, 7,233, **7,243**, 7,292, **7,300, 7,308**,
   8,658, 9,095, 11,345, **11,547**, 11,720, 11,897,
   12,003, 12,252, 12,419, 12,765, 12,864, 15,281,
   15,283, **15,312**, 17,246, **17,659, 17,756**
Social role, women, 13,847
Social roles, 4,861
Social science research, **2,359**, 6,604, **8,642**, 14,936
Social Science Research Council, 3,302, 11,958
Social sciences, 12,738
   study and teaching, 14,006
Social security, 232, 561, 2,075, 2,504, **2,693**, 6,486,
   6,728, 6,838, 6,973, 6,989, 8,085, 8,641, 8,651,
   11,760, 11,771, **11,916**, 14,429, 14,622, 14,686,
   17,466. *See also* Insurance, health; Survivor's
   benefits
   law and legislation, 8,069, 11,916
Social Security Act (1935), 2,693
Social Security Board. *See* United States, Social
   Security Administration
Social service, 754, 1,054, 6,209, **6,378**, 6,766, 6,984,

8,108, 8,425, 8,658, 8,662, 8,678, 9,468, 11,897, 12,724, 12,738, 13,604
finance, 8,670
information services, **5,840**
legal aspects, 8,638, 8,654
research, 8,665, 8,676
vocational guidance, 2,224, 5,840, 6,440
Social service, rural, 8,112
Social service administration, 7,709
Social service and race problems, 1,842, 3,302
Social Service Club of Maryland, **5,809**
Social service exchanges, **3,905, 8,661, 8,670, 8,676, 8,682**
Social service publicity, **6,928**
Social settlements, 365, 1,426, 1,891, 1,997, 2,309, 2,397, 3,772, **3,791, 3,801, 3,809,** 3,820, **3,822,** 3,835, **3,836,** 3,851, **3,874, 3,875, 3,894,** 3,901, 3,905, 4,003, 4,047, 4,052, 4,056, 4,079, 4,085, **4,087, 4,096, 4,099,** 4,100, **4,101, 4,127,** 4,130, 4,141, 4,143, 4,146, 4,158, 4,163, **4,823,** 5,079, 5,255, **5,515,** 5,809, 6,131, 6,239, 6,376, **6,516,** 6,622, **6,808,** 6,946, 6,970, 7,166, 7,172, 7,217, 7,243, 7,292, 7,299, 7,300, 7,307, **7,557,** 8,635, **8,646, 8,651, 8,652, 8,659,** 8,661, **8,668,** 8,678, **8,681, 9,058,** 9,094, **9,114,** 9,187, 9,252, **9,261, 9,270,** 9,467, 9,981, 10,603, 11,445, 11,633, 11,897, **12,008,** 12,026, **12,520,** 12,657, 12,706, 13,934, 13,950, 13,976, **13,996, 15,202, 15,207,** 15,303, 17,646, 17,716, 17,841
Social settlements, Afro-American, **9,289**
Social settlements, Jewish, 17,247
Social settlements, Presbyterian, **3,837, 3,845, 3,892**
Social structure, American, 6,893
Social Survey Club (SC), **15,728**
Social systems, 8,671
Social work administration, 3,806, **4,130,** 8,583, **8,637,** 8,638, **8,673,** 16,968, 17,691
Social work education, 393, **2,224,** 2,336, 4,051, 4,201, 5,515, 6,852, 7,546, 8,638, 8,641, **8,653,** 8,654, 8,656, **8,663,** 8,664, 8,665, **8,677,** 12,080, **12,723,** 13,882, **14,742**
Social Work Education in the United States: The Report of a Study Made for the National Council on Social Work Education, 8,677
Social Work Research Group. *See* National Association of Social Workers
Social work with children, 8,583
Social work with delinquents and criminals, 4,141, 8,646, 14,010, 15,153
Social work with seniors, 8,646, 8,674
Social work with teen-age women, 8,583
Social work with teenagers, 8,646, **11,596**
Social workers, 648, 689, **957,** 1,426, **1,675,** 1,731, 1,850, **2,424,** 2,498, **3,399,** 3,791, **3,798,** 3,806, 3,826, **3,830, 3,833,** 3,875, **3,901,** 4,003, **4,052,** 4,056, **4,089,** 4,115, **4,141,** 4,146, 4,150, 4,156, **4,158, 4,163,** 4,331, **4,343,** 4,495, 4,510, **4,921,** 5,079, 5,515, **5,925,** 6,239, 6,336, 6,544, 6,565, **6,665,** 6,701, **6,715, 6,729,** 6,814, **6,885, 6,946, 6,958, 6,970,** 7,165, 7,243, **7,248, 7,546,** 7,548, 8,077, **8,148,** 8,583, 8,641, **8,643,** 8,654, 8,658, **8,662, 8,665,** 8,667, 8,674, **8,683, 8,686,** 9,095, 9,270, 9,289, 9,392, **9,403,** 9,427, 9,467, 10,100, **11,021,** 11,063, 11,134, 11,226, **11,346, 11,593,** 11,821, **11,856,** 11,897, 11,904, 11,916, 11,926, 12,008, **12,033, 12,037,** 12,069, **12,075,** 12,078, 12,080, 12,520, 12,534, 12,999, 13,390, **13,945,** 14,144, **14,356, 14,365,** 14,427, **14,437, 14,446, 15,246, 15,880, 15,916, 17,244,** 17,295, **17,581, 17,841,** 17,845
licenses, 1,136
Social workers, Afro-American, **2,153, 3,835,** 5,394, **12,680, 12,687**
Social World, The (AL), 63
Socialism, 1,396, 1,561, 2,610, 3,988, 4,409, 4,433, 5,829, 7,222, 8,963, 11,596, 11,761, 11,950, 14,637, 17,659, 17,675
Socialism and trade-unions, 11,917
Socialist Labor Party of Minnesota, **9,379**
Socialist parties, **4,080, 8,141,** 9,175, 11,897, 11,917, 14,599, 17,365
Socialist Party, 1,654, 3,329, 9,119, 12,702, 14,830
Socialist Party (CA), Alameda County Campaign Committee, **808**

Socialist Workers Party, 1,654, **9,380,** 17,365
Socialist Workers Party, civil rights defense committee, 9,380
Socialists, 492, 825, 1,016, 1,283, **1,499, 2,562,** 3,408, 3,839, **3,996,** 4,032, 4,161, 4,431, 5,768, 6,602, **6,811, 9,177, 9,900,** 10,177, 11,950, **12,700, 12,702, 12,705,** 13,176, **13,717,** 15,309, **17,633, 17,722**
Socialists, Finnish, 8,969
Socialization, 6,781, 6,782
Sociedade Portuguesa Reinha Santa Isabel, Ladies Drill Team and Drum Corps (San Leandro, CA), 1,387
Societies, 144, **1,071, 1,923,** 3,555, 4,467, **4,552, 4,699, 5,684,** 6,223, **6,713,** 7,597, **9,256,** 9,995, 10,032, **10,411,** 12,240, **12,876,** 12,906, 13,855, **13,981, 14,263,** 14,666, 14,676, **15,249,** 15,594, 15,789, 16,400, 16,401, **16,412,** 16,445, 16,447, **17,311, 17,707, 17,774, 17,836, 18,023.** *See also specific types of societies, e.g.,* Musical societies
Societies, Afro-American, 128, 607, 726, 2,127, 2,298, **2,502,** 3,302, 3,799, 3,935, **4,132, 4,142,** 5,458, **5,828,** 5,945, 6,814, 6,980, 7,736, 8,027, 8,116, 8,148, 9,810, **10,203,** 11,491, 11,897, 12,681, 12,865, 13,446, 13,924, 13,945, 15,176, 15,210, 15,889, 16,342, 17,234, 17,266, 17,299, 17,304
Societies, Czechoslovakian-American, 13,953, 13,965
Societies, Finnish-American, **9,500**
Societies, Italian-American, **15,247**
Societies, Jewish, 933, 1,000, 1,018, 2,647, **3,884,** 6,082, **6,920,** 7,540, 7,549, 8,963, 9,083, **9,109,** 9,110, **9,253, 9,254,** 9,467, 11,349, **12,117,** 12,118, 13,446, **13,500,** 13,604, **13,767, 13,775, 13,777, 13,779, 13,790, 13,796, 13,803, 13,805, 13,813, 13,815, 13,816, 13,824, 13,828, 13,830, 13,915, 13,993, 15,156, 15,245, 15,248, 15,250,** 17,276, 17,282, 17,342, **17,646, 17,647, 17,695, 17,833,** 17,850
Societies, Native American, 1,504, **11,231**
Societies, Norwegian-American, **8,767,** 8,777
Societies, Ukrainian-American, 9,513, 14,909
Society Esrath Nashim (Helping Women) (Philadelphia, PA). *See* Jewish Maternity Association (Philadelphia, PA)
Society for Humane Abortion, **6,897,** 11,932
Society for Preservation of Antiquities (NC), 13,440
Society for Preservation of Old Dwellings (Charleston, SC). *See* Charleston Preservation Society (SC)
Society for the Advancement of Christianity in South Carolina, 15,494
Society for the Pro-mulgation of the Education of Aspiring Females (MN), 8,617
Society for the Relief of Orphans and Widows of the Clergy of the Protestant Episcopal Church, **15,520**
Society for the Relief of Poor Widows with Small Children of New York City, **12,315**
Society for the Relief of the Poor (St. Paul, MN), 9,442
Society for the Relief of Widows and Orphans of Deceased Clergymen of the Protestant Episcopal Church, **6,182**
Society for the Study of Child Nature. *See* Family Development Association
Society in America (book), 2,477
Society Islands Mission (San Bernardino, CA), 16,643
Society of American Archivists, 9,599
Society of American Graphic Artists, 2,763, 2,798
Society of Blue and White Needlework (Deerfield, MA). *See* Deerfield Society of Arts and Crafts (MA)
Society of Colorado Pioneers, 1,701
Society of Cornell Dames, **11,716**
Society of Eighty-Eight, 16,625
Society of Fine Arts, Inc. (Mankato, MN), **8,511**
Society of Friends. *See* Friends, Society of
Society of Friends (IN), Plainfield Monthly Meeting, Ladies Aid, 4,650
Society of Hall in the Grove (Blue Earth, MN). *See* Mitchell Chautauqua Circle (Blue Earth, (MN)
Society of Jewish Women of Philadelphia for Lodging the Homeless and Sheltering the Aged

(Hachnasas Orchin Umoshav Z'keinim) (Philadelphia, PA), 15,161
Society of Mayflower Descendants, 4,689, 4,892, 4,942
Society of Mayflower Descendants (NC), **13,580**
Society of Mayflower Descendants (Toledo Colony, OH), 14,137
Society of Midland Authors, 3,999, 4,061, **4,155**
Society of Montana Pioneers, 10,365
Society of Nevada Pioneers, **10,716**
Society of New York State Women, 7,546
Society of the Bull Family of Ashley Hall (SC), 15,521
Society of the Daughters of the US Army, 10,289
Society of the Former Scholars of Mrs. Sigourney (CT), 1,876
Society of the Friends of Music (NY), 2,020
Society of the Hall in the Grove, 10,571
Society of the Lying-In Hospital of the City of New York, **12,358**
Society of the Missionary Sisters of the Catholic Apostolate (Florissant, MO), **10,067**
Society of the New York Asylum for Lying-In Women, **12,316**
Society of the New York Hospital, 12,351, 12,352
Society of the Sacred Heart (San Francisco, CA), **1,066**
Society of the Sacred Heart, Chicago Province (IL), **4,036**
Society of Women Artists, 12,892
Society of Women Engineers, 4,221
Society of Woman Geographers, **2,863,** 14,235
Society of Woman Geographers, Gold Medal, 2,863
Society of Woman Geographers, Outstanding Achievement Award, 2,863
Society of Women Musicians, 7,299
Society to Encourage Studies at Home (MA), **5,958,** 7,286
SOCIO, 16,965
Sociological Society (Hartford, CT), 1,910
Sociologists, 1,779, **2,193, 2,872, 3,356, 4,055,** 4,059, **4,209, 5,471, 5,616, 5,870, 6,223,** 6,544, **6,696, 6,816, 6,841, 6,898,** 8,603, 12,074, **12,491,** 12,574, 13,176, **14,006,** 15,197, **15,323, 15,324,** 17,245
Sociologists for Women in Society, **6,898**
Sociology, 3,988
study and teaching, 15,324
"Socrates of the Ironing Board" (article), 17,947
Sod houses, 10,430, 10,479
Söderberg, Eugenia (Riwkin). [Mrs. Hugo] Perls (1903-73), **12,880**
Soeters, Wilhelmia Tourman [Mrs.] (1888-), **8,258**
Soffel, Sara M. (1887-?), 15,252
Soffin, Estelle Marie (1902-), **15,166**
Soffin, Lena, 15,166
Soffin, Lil, 15,166
Soffin, Rose, 15,166
Soft drink industry, 3,210
"Sogne-Kjerring" (monologue), 8,774
Soil conservation, 7,666
Soiland, Inga, 1,339
Sojka, Zdeňka (1894-1975). *See* Rypka, Zdeňka (Sojka) [Mrs. Walter E.] (1894-1975)
Sojourner, The (book), 2,876, 3,075
Sojourner Truth housing episode, 8,104, 8,148
Sokol Club (Hopkins, MN), 8,476
Sokol Tyrs, 13,953
Sokoloff, Natalie B. *See* Scott, Natalie Anderson
Solano, Isidora Filomena [Mrs.], 798
Solano, Solita [Miss] (1888-1975), 2,331
Solar energy, 212
Solberg, Elizabeth Ronning (1911-), **8,787**
Soldat, Katherine Martha, 15,869
Soldiers, 180, 748, 2,188, 2,190, 2,211, 2,312, 2,558, 2,600, 3,831, 5,481, 5,765, **7,143, 8,296, 8,313, 8,929,** 9,074, 9,079, 9,517, **9,912,** 10,407, **10,876,** 10,903, 11,134, 11,354, 11,445, 11,508, 11,563, 12,307, **12,481,** 13,145, 13,426, 13,926, 14,077, 14,187, **14,573,** 14,766, 14,820, 15,081, 15,258, 16,058, 16,114, 17,435
books and reading, 4,727
Civil War, 80, 119, 1,408, 1,630, **2,185, 2,223,** 2,252, 2,386, **2,514,** 2,534, 3,176, 3,337, 3,354,

3,412, 3,413, 3,565, 4,789, **4,790, 4,817, 4,836,**
4,964, 5,277, 7,148, 7,637, 7,669, 8,164, 8,167,
8,324, 8,372, 8,380, **8,894, 8,955,** 8,958, 8,975,
9,584, 9,679, **9,999,** 10,789, 11,092, 11,101,
11,194, 12,377, 12,953, 12,957, 13,050, 13,343,
14,166, 15,696, 15,749, 15,751, 15,854, 16,060,
16,155, 17,029, 17,540, 17,601, **17,642**
  Confederate, **2,181,** 2,185, 2,254, 2,328, **2,461,**
   3,155, 3,262, **3,315,** 3,317, 3,320, **3,331, 3,344,**
   4,961, 5,277, 5,420, 5,487, 5,812, **6,394,** 9,684,
   10,196, 10,264, 12,308, 12,969, 13,059, 13,061,
   13,065, 13,086, **13,412,** 13,629, 15,695, **15,766,**
   15,768, 15,769, 15,943, **15,944, 15,954, 16,155,**
   17,700
  Civil War, Afro-American, 2,262, **3,299**
  pay, allowances, etc., 4,951
  recreation, 6,477, 15,461, 17,815
  Revolution (1775-1783), 2,273, 2,527, 4,415, 7,669,
   8,271, 9,816, 11,195, 11,441, 13,006, 15,661
  Revolution (1775-1783), Jewish, 7,555
  uniforms, 13,619
  War of 1812, 7,669, 15,959
  War of 1898, 2,904, 11,197
  World War I, 2,554, 3,250, 3,302, 3,407, 5,328,
   6,716, 9,711, 10,784, **13,024, 14,511**
   recreation, **3,635**
  World War I, Jewish, 13,793
  World War II, 3,387, 3,810, 8,348, 8,809, 9,664,
   9,685, 9,724, 9,758, 13,024
Soldiers, Afro-American, 2,262, **2,332, 3,299**
Soldiers' Aid Society, 6,487, 13,392, 13,966
Soldier's Aid Society (Rushville, IL), **4,293**
Soldier's Aid Society (Elsie, MI), 7,753
Soldiers Aid Society (NH), 10,819
Soldiers' Aid Society (Selma, OH), 3,922
Soldier's and Sailor's Club (MA), 6,477
Soldiers' Home (Chicago, IL), 4,135
Soldiers' homes, 543, 1,907, 2,296, 4,338, **4,339,**
  10,136, 13,696, 13,966, **15,538**
Soldiers' monuments, Southern States, 80, 121, 2,218,
  2,961, 3,345, 3,537, 13,053
Soldiers, Native American, 16,872
Soldiers' Relief Association, 15,727
Soldiers' Relief Society (ME), **5,608**
Soldo, Betty Lougaris, **10,717**
Soledad mission (CA), 1,135
Solheim, Ragnhild, 9,266
Solis-Cohen, Emily (1886-), **7,554**
Solis, Elvira (Nathan) (186?-1953), **7,555**
"Solitude," 16,174
Sollie, Allen N., **9,381,** 9,467
Sollie, Violet Johnson [Mrs. Allen N.], **9,381,** 9,467
Solomon, Barbara (Miller) [Mrs. Peter H.], 6,276,
  6,899
Solomon, Edward, 12,832
Solomon, Fred, 12,832
Solomon, Hannah (Greenebaum) [Mrs. Henry]
  (1858-1942), 3,785, 3,884, 3,910, 8,963, 13,993
Solomon, Harriet M., **9,382**
Solomon Islands, discovery and exploration, 5,177
Solomon, Maida (Herman) [Mrs. Harry Caesar]
  (1891-), 6,760, **6,900**
Solomons, Adolphus Simeon (1826-1910), **7,556**
Solomons, Rosalie (1872-1945). *See* Phillips, Rosalie
  (Solomons) (1872-1945)
Solomons, Selina Seixas (1862-1942), 935
Solon Study Club (IA), 4,960
Solon Teacher's Reading Circle (IA), 4,960
Soltysik, Patricia Michelle. Mizmoon (?-1974), **809**
Solum, Nora Olava (1889-1971), 8,784, **8,788, 8,815**
Soman, Florence Jane, **6,091**
"Some Incidents in the Life of Mary Garrett Hay, A
  Wonderful Boss and a Gallant Fighter," 12,505
"Some Memories of Our War" (ms), 15,651
*Some New Light on the Later Life and Last Resting
  Place of Benedict Arnold and his Wife Margaret
  Shippen* (book), 12,373
"Some of the Reasons Against Woman Suffrage,"
  4,172
"Some Opinions of Women" (article), 13,490
*Some Others and Myself: Seven Stories and a
  Memoir* (book), 5,030
"Some Pioneer Women of Mississippi" (ms), 9,596
"Somebody's Darling" (poem), 100

Somerset, Lady Henry (1851-1921), 4,233, 7,271
Somerville College (Oxford, England), alumnae, 8,626
Somerville Family (MS), **6,901**
Somerville, Lucy (1895-). *See* Howorth, Lucy R.
  (Somerville) [Mrs. Joseph M.] (1895-)
Somerville, Mary (1780-1872), 6,659, **6,902**
Somerville, Nellie (Nugent) (1863-1952), 6,901,
  9,544, 9,546, 9,547, **9,734,** 13,176
Something About Yesterday (drama), 12,367
Something Always Happens (moving-picture), 18,003
"Something Beyond" (poem), 14,058
Somewhere the Tempest Fell (book), 4,992
Sommer, Jane, **7,297**
Sommer, Julia K., 11,580
Sommers Family (PA), 15,168
Sommers, Helen, 17,311
Son of Any Wednesday (drama), 2,546
Sondergaard, Gale (1901-), 1,025, **17,792**
Songbook, 5,311
Song-books, Armenian, 330
Song Catcher in Southern Mountains, A (book),
  16,384
Song of Years (book), 4,965
Song Without End (book), 6,114
Song writers, **14,440**
Songs, 211, 1,487, 2,838, 5,988, 6,007, **7,663,** 8,071,
  8,126, 8,146, 9,348, 9,467, 9,719, 9,742, 10,701,
  13,674, 16,931
  collections, 16,384
Songs from the North (phonorecord), 17,692
Songs, Hawaiian, 3,632
"Songs of a Housewife" (poetry), 12,800
Songs of Oklahoma (book), 14,200
"Sonnet in Absence" (poem), 6,112
Sonoma State University (CA)
  faculty, 1,128, 1,130
  students, 1,130
Sonoma State University (CA), Academic Senate
  Committee on the Role of Women, **1,125**
Sonoma State University (CA), Faculty Women and
  Wives Club, **1,127**
Sonoma State University (CA), Women's Studies
  Program, **1,131**
"Sonowoman" (newsletter), **1,129**
Sons and Daughters of Hawaiian Warriors, 3,633
Sons and Daughters of Oregon Pioneers, **14,666**
Sons of Confederate Veterans, 9,657
Sons of Union Veterans Auxiliary (Athold, MA),
  General William T. Sherman Camp, **5,881**
Sons of Union Veterans of the Civil War, Hugh C.
  Irish Camp No. 8, **11,132**
Sons of Union Veterans of the Civil War, Ladies
  Auxiliary No. 3, 11,132
Soochow Baptist Church (China), 13,642
Soper, Richard, 16,646
Soper, Sarah Wells (Hartley) [Mrs. Richard]
  (1836-1921). *See* Curtis, Sarah Wells (Hartley)
  [Mrs. Richard] Soper [Mrs. Lyman] (1836-1921)
Sophie H. Newcomb Memorial College for Women
  (LA), 5,517
  deans, 5,506
Sophograph (IL), 4,392
Sorbier, Cecile Marie, 1,344
Sorbier, Louise Agathe Josephine (Bacon)
  (1847-1929), **1,344**
Sorenson, Amanda Lucinda Pace (1850-1939), 16,430
Sorenson, Cornelia (1882-1959). *See* Lund, Cornelia
  (Sorenson) (1882-1959)
Sorenson, Virginia (Eggertsen) (1912-), **6,092**
Soroptimist Club, 3,439
Sorosis, 2,606, 2,632, 4,732, **7,298**
Sorosis (NY). *See* New York State Federation of
  Women's Clubs
Sorosis Club (NE), **10,536**
Sorosis Club (OH), **14,094**
Sorosis Club (OH), 14,154
Sorosis Club (TX), **16,389**
"Sorrows of Eve, The" (article), 2,936
"Sorry, Wrong Number" (radio play), 1,026
Sosha, Jane. *See* Journeycake, Jane (Sosha)
Sosnowski, Callie [Miss], 2,965, **3,094**
Sosnowski Family (SC), **15,729**
Sosnowski, Sophie. *See* Schaller, Sophie Sosnowski
  [Mrs. Frank]

Sothern, Edward Hugh (1859-1933), 12,065, 12,629,
  12,630, **12,631**
Sothern, Julia Marlowe [Mrs. Edward Hugh]
  (1866-1950). *See* Marlowe, Julia. Sarah Frances
  Frost. Fanny Brough. [Mrs. Edward Hugh]
  Robert] Taber [Mrs. Edward Hugh] Sothern
  (1866-1950)
Sothern, Sarah Frances (Frost) [Mrs. Robert] Taber
  [Mrs. Edward Hugh] (1866-1950). *See* Marlowe,
  Julia. Sarah Frances Frost. Fanny Brough. Fancy
  Brough. [Mrs. Robert] Taber [Mrs. Edward
  Hugh] Sothern (1866-1950)
Sotomayor, Antonio, 761
Souers, Aurelia [Mrs. Webb], 4,740
Soul Sister (book), 6,031
Soule, Elizabeth, 17,291
Soule, Ellen, 4,215
Soule Family (WA), 17,390
Soule, George H., 14,446
Soule, Inez (Smith) (1846-1941), 10,185
Soule, Isobel Walker [Mrs. George H.] (1898-1972),
  14,446
Soule, Sarah. *See* Patton, Sarah (Soule) [Mrs. John
  G.] McMillan [Mrs. Henry W.]
Soulier, Sister Catherine Francis, 11,251
Sound of Music, The (moving-picture), 17,804
Souretis, Matina (1940-). *See* Horner, Matina
  (Souretis) (1940-)
South Africa, missionaries to, 86
South America, 2,790
  American diplomats in, 2,192
  English language, study and teaching, 8,090
  fauna, 2,714
  grass research in, 15,213
  natives, social life and customs, 15,059
  wildlife, 8,164
  Young Women's Christian Association, 12,724,
   12,725
South America Looks at the Future (book), 6,512
South American Wonder Tales (book), 7,235
South Bend Women's Civic Club (IN), **4,668**
South Broad Street USO Club (PA), 15,101
South Carolina, 20, 9,699, 12,247, 15,408, 15,422
  abortion, legal aspects, 15,785
  adult education, 15,798
  Afro-Americans, 13,120, 15,439, 15,451, 15,504,
   15,626, 15,681
   education, 15,541, 15,606, 15,744
  agricultural colleges, 15,780
  agricultural laborers, Afro-American, 15,712
  almshouses, **15,402,** 15,404
  art, 15,498
   galleries and museums, 15,424
  art, decorative, 13,631
  artists, **15,424**
  associations, institutions, etc., 15,570, 15,634,
   15,819
  authors, **13,017, 13,104,** 15,439, **15,445, 15,475,**
   15,573, 15,688, 15,789, 15,796
  autograph albums, 12,483
  ballot, 15,755
  bankers, 15,441, **15,568**
  bankruptcy, 15,768
  Baptists, 15,718
  Bibles, **15,829**
  bills, legislative, 15,686
  bishops, Episcopal, 15,465
  blind, Afro-American, **15,549**
   education, **15,549**
  blind-deaf, personal narratives, **15,587**
  blind, education, **15,549**
  blind, teachers of the, 15,549
  boarding schools, **15,452**
  boards of trade, 15,522
  bombings, 15,709
  businessmen, **15,616, 15,626, 15,637**
  businesswoman, **15,629**
  Catholic Church
   charities, **15,705**
   education, **15,639**
  Catholic schools, 15,497
  census, 15,546
  charitable societies, **15,490, 15,491, 15,520,** 15,727,
   15,775

charitable societies, Jewish, **13,802**
charities, **15,462,** 15,471
church colleges, **15,536, 15,837**
church records and registers, **15,432**
church records and registers, Congregational, **15,453**
church records and registers, Methodist, **15,586, 15,614, 15,615, 15,632, 15,655**
church records and registers, Presbyterian, **15,592, 15,599**
church societies, **15,437**
church societies, Congregational, 15,453
church societies, Episcopal, **15,454,** 15,754
church societies, Lutheran, **15,704**
church societies, Methodist, **15,642, 15,654,** 15,838
church societies, Presbyterian, **15,558, 15,592, 15,593, 15,599**
church work, 15,896
churches, Baptist, 15,093
churches, Presbyterian, 15,553
citizens' associations, 3,283, **15,451**
civil defense, 15,451, 15,755
Civil War, 12,949, 13,019, 13,029, 15,550, 15,600, 15,602, **15,624,** 15,652, 15,667, 15,711, 15,769, 15,817
  campaigns and battles, 15,635
  casualties, 15,749
  defenses, 15,658
  destruction and pillage, 2,417, 15,475, 15,560, 15,597, 15,610, 15,708, 15,714, **15,721,** 15,726, 15,729
  economic aspects, 15,621
  hospitals, charities, etc., **15,598**
  personal narratives, 13,465, 15,651, 15,751
  refugees, 15,604
  societies, Confederate, **15,400,** 15,597, **15,756, 15,757, 15,758**
clergy, **15,435,** 15,634
clergy, Baptist, 13,144
clergy, Episcopal, 15,465
clergy, Methodist, 15,632, 15,837
clergy, Presbyterian, 15,434, **15,692**
clergy, Protestant, 15,447
clergy, Unitarian, 7,634, 15,475
clergymen's wives, 15,475
clubs, 2,904, **15,408, 15,421, 15,422, 15,431, 15,461,** 15,515, **15,522,** 15,578, **15,664, 15,728,** 15,790, **15,791,** 15,797, **15,812, 15,814, 15,912**
coeducation, 15,824
college and school journalism, 15,536
college teachers, **15,683, 15,806, 15,811**
commerce, 15,765
commission merchants, 15,441, 15,532
commonplace books, 15,474
community leadership, **15,790**
community organization, **15,813**
congressmen, **15,695**
convents and nunneries, Catholic, **15,492, 15,639,** 15,696
conveyancing, 15,499
cookery, 15,474
coopers and cooperage, 15,535
coroners, **15,427**
cotton, marketing, 15,723
cotton picking, 15,595
county government, records and correspondence, 15,542, **15,544**
court records, 15,547, **15,548**
crime and criminals, **15,537**
Cusabo Indians, land transfers, 15,713
deaf, Afro-American, education, **15,549**
deaf, education, **15,549**
deans (in schools), **6,423**
death, causes, 15,427
deeds, 15,469, 15,645
diaries and journals, **15,625, 15,640,** 15,724
  19th C, 846, **13,005,** 13,056, **13,057, 15,414, 15,494,** 15,582, **15,595,** 15,608, 15,662, **15,685, 15,746**
disaster relief, **15,471**
disease, 15,474, 15,479
dower, **15,542,** 15,548
earthquakes, 846, 15,471, 15,631, 15,656, 15,707
editors, 15,634, **15,637**

education, 15,422, 15,802
  costs, 15,628
educational associations, **15,555, 15,787,** 15,801
educators, **15,617,** 15,634, **15,789, 15,793,** 15,802
elections, 13,115, 15,563, 15,596, 15,634, 15,769
engineers, **15,618**
epidemics, 15,427
Episcopal church, 15,465, 15,621
Equal Rights Amendment (proposed), **15,794,** 15,805, 15,819
equity pleading and procedure, **15,547**
estates (law), 15,519, 15,641, 15,834
executors, 15,481
fairs, 15,611
family planning, 15,802
farm management, 15,594
farmers, 3,344, 15,439, 15,440, **15,496, 15,529,** 15,616, **15,626, 15,628, 15,677, 15,678,** 15,682, **15,694, 15,695**
feminist credit unions, **15,821**
fires, 15,475
folklore, 15,445
food service
  legal aspects, 15,822
  quality control, **15,822**
food service management, 15,822
food stamp program, aid to applicants, **15,826**
freedmen, **2,136,** 15,630, 15,744
  relations with whites, 15,711
fund raising, 15,730
furniture industry and trade, 15,682
gambling, 15,451
gardening, societies, etc., 5,443, **15,584**
gardens, 12,901
genealogy, 15,521, **15,622,** 15,788
geologists, 12,961
governors, 2,527, 12,410, 15,440, 15,545, 15,563, 16,313
grocery trade, 15,441
Gullah dialect, 15,445
health, 15,802
high schools, 15,644
historians, **15,806**
historic buildings, conservation and restoration, 15,451, 15,518, 15,719
historical societies, **15,579, 15,580,** 15,838
home demonstration work, 15,797, 15,798
home economics extension work, 9,522, 15,792, 15,798, 15,808, **15,820**
home economists, **15,795, 15,798, 15,808,** 15,823
horse breeding, 15,723
hotels, taverns, etc., 15,532
housewives, **15,605, 15,617, 15,799,** 15,809
Huguenots, **15,410**
hunting and fishing clubs, 15,595
illiteracy, campaign against, **15,609**
indentures, 15,526
influenza epidemic (1918), 15,707
islands, 13,120
journalists, **15,803**
judgments, 15,548
jury, 15,819
  legal aspects, 15,803
labor and laboring classes, 15,585
land titles, 15,492, 15,523
  registration and transfer, 15,496, 15,511, **15,646**
law, cases, 15,548
lawyers, 15,441, **15,502,** 15,634, **15,671, 15,686, 15,695**
legal documents, 15,438, **15,458,** 15,486, **15,487, 15,836**
legal instruments, **15,546**
legislative bodies, **15,543,** 15,617
legislators, 13,135, 15,440, **15,671, 15,766, 15,805**
librarians, **15,591**
license systems, 15,769
linguists, **15,789**
literary societies, 13,124, **15,415,** 15,480, **15,786, 15,791,** 15,810
lobbyists, 15,819
lynching, prevention of, 3,279
maps, 12,320
marriage law, 15,745

medicine, receipts, formulae, prescriptions, etc., **15,428**
mentally ill, commitment and detention, 15,544
merchants, **2,268,** 15,434, **15,568,** 15,682
Methodists, 15,718
monasticism and religious orders for women, Catholic, **15,433**
monuments, 15,683
mortgage, 15,483
mothers, **15,799**
municipal government, 15,683
municipal officials and employees, 2,258
musical societies, 15,444, **15,815**
natural history museums, children's, 15,813
newspapers, **15,419**
novelists, **15,720**
nurses, 15,430
nursing schools, **15,426,** 15,430, **15,734**
  trustees, 15,734
officials and employees, 15,686
old age homes, 15,404
organists, 15,683
orphans and orphan asylums, 15,404, **15,505**
orphans and orphan asylums, Catholic, **15,705**
pageants, 12,959, **15,807**
pardon, 15,545
patriotic societies, 15,439, **15,576, 15,581, 15,596,** 15,597, 15,620
periodicals, 15,585
photographs, **15,093**
physicians, **2,417, 15,427,** 15,428, **15,429,** 15,430, 15,467, **15,506, 15,567, 15,735, 15,749,** 15,776
physicians, Afro-American, 15,430
pioneers and settlers, **15,784**
plantation life, 15,439, **15,464,** 15,474, 15,500, 15,525, 15,562, 15,608, 15,631, 15,635, 15,658, 15,712, 15,746, 15,778, 15,781, 15,788, 15,834
plantations, 12,949, 15,401, 15,414, **15,423,** 15,440, **15,460, 15,467, 15,476, 15,484, 15,613,** 15,678, **15,694,** 15,707, 15,750
poets, **15,679, 15,796**
police, records and correspondence, **15,537**
politicians, **15,834, 15,835**
politics and government, 15,610, 15,621
politics, practical, 15,706
politics, practical, women's activism, 15,706, **15,827**
pregnancy counseling, **15,818**
Presbyterian church, **15,599**
Presbyterians, 15,553
printers, 15,686
prisoners, **15,540**
prisons, records and correspondence, **15,540**
private schools, **15,503**
probate records, 15,480
prostitution, 15,451
public health nursing, 3,432
public health personnel, 15,429
public libraries, 15,795
public records, **15,831**
public schools, 15,543, 15,578
public welfare, **15,404**
race problems, 15,610, 15,683, 15,769
real estate agents, 13,176
receipts (acknowledgments), 15,436
Reconstruction, 15,401, 15,600, 15,602, 15,604, 15,610, 15,667, 15,711, 15,769
revivals, 15,666
school boards, **15,403,** 15,404, **15,539,** 15,544
school buildings, 15,816
school librarians, **15,430**
school lunchrooms, cafeterias, etc., **15,822**
school notebooks, 15,488, **15,517,** 15,760
school superintendents and principals, 15,670
schools, **15,541, 15,572, 15,589,** 15,602, 15,659, 15,692, **15,731, 15,732**
  finance, 15,834
  records and correspondence, **15,514, 15,670, 15,767**
schools, Afro-American, 15,281
secession, 15,627, 15,634, 15,635, 15,726, 15,749, 15,763, 15,766
secretaries of state, 15,441
senators, United States, 5,774, 15,583
servants, indentured, 15,626

settlements (law), 15,533, 15,546, 15,665
Sherman's March to the Sea, 15,590
slave records, **2,126**, 15,423, **15,442**, 15,458, 15,467, 15,476, 15,507, 15,524, 15,562, 15,834
slave trade, 2,268, 4,239, 15,445, 15,523, **15,530**, 15,602, 15,618, 15,633, 15,636, 15,637, 15,735, 15,742
slavery, 15,499, 15,634
   conditions, 15,658
   economic aspects, 15,678
   emancipation, 15,653
   insurrections, 15,594, 15,635, 15,658
slaves, 2,126, 4,239, 13,188, 15,486, 15,495, 15,530, 15,546, 15,653, 15,742
   medical care, 15,428
smallpox, 15,763
social life and customs, 2,033, 7,634, 12,270, 12,978, 13,277, 15,414, 15,439, 15,515, 15,525, **15,711**, 15,722
societies, 15,594
soldiers, Civil War, 15,695, 15,749, **15,766**
soldiers, Civil War, Confederate, **15,766**, **15,768**, 15,769
soldiers' homes, **15,538**
state departments of education, **15,541**
state song, 15,804
state universities and colleges, 9,779
   archives, **15,824**
   faculty, **15,801**
strikes and lockouts, Afro-Americans, 15,595
student nurses, **15,425**
students, 15,623, 15,662
suffrage societies, 15,706
suffragists, 13,176, **15,706**
Sunday schools, 13,802
synagogues 13,802
teachers, **13,120**, 15,541, 15,544, **15,606**, 15,637, **15,644**, **15,714**, 15,723, **15,729**, 15,747, 15,767, **15,773**
   certification, 15,539
temperance societies, **15,771**
text books, 15,755
trade and professional associations, **15,823**
trials (murder), 15,610
tricentennial celebration, 15,579
tuberculosis, nursing, 15,754
United Methodist Church, **15,586**, **15,614**, **15,615**, **15,632**, **15,642**, **15,655**, **15,838**
universities and colleges, 6,423, 15,611, **15,777**
   trustees, 15,631
university presses, 15,585
veterans, medical care, 15,538
voluntary health associations, 15,754
voters, 15,747
weddings, 15,479
wildlife preservation, 15,802
wills, **15,504**, 15,534, 15,546
women, education, 15,409
women's colleges, 15,610, **15,648**, **15,730**, **15,736**, **15,770**, 15,824
World War I, effect upon state, 15,800
writ of debt, **15,716**
South-Carolina and American General Gazette, 15,419
South Carolina Business and Professional Women's Clubs, 15,795
South Carolina Clergy Consultation Service on Problem Pregnancies, **15,818**
South Carolina Coeducational Institute, 15,659
South Carolina College, 15,483
   faculty, 15,726
   trustees, 15,631
South Carolina College for Women, **15,730**
South Carolina College, Teachers Institute, 15,557
South Carolina Conference of Social Work, 15,570
South Carolina Council for the Common Good, 15,790, 15,792, 15,795, 15,802, 15,803, **15,819**, **15,820**
South Carolina Court of Common Pleas, **15,548**
South Carolina Department of Corrections, **15,540**
South Carolina Equal Suffrage Association, 15,706
South Carolina Extension Homemakers' Council, 15,797, 15,798

South Carolina Federal Feminist Credit Union, **15,821**
South Carolina Federation of Women's Clubs, 15,790, 15,795, 15,802
South Carolina Female Collegiate Institute, 15,617, 15,637, 15,662, 15,729, **15,731**
South Carolina Food Service Association, **15,822**
South Carolina Garden Clubs, 5,443
South-Carolina Gazette, 15,419
South-Carolina Gazette and Country Journal, 15,419
South Carolina General Assembly, **15,543**
South Carolina Historical Society, 2,527, 15,585
South Carolina Home Economics Association, **15,823**
South Carolina House of Representatives, 15,805
South Carolina Industrial School for White Girls, **15,732**
South Carolina League of Women Voters, **15,733**
South Carolina Magazine, 15,585
South Carolina Medical Association, Women's Auxiliary, **15,431**
South Carolina Penitentiary/Central Correctional Institution, **15,540**
South Carolina Railroad, 15,497
South Carolina School for the Deaf and Blind, **15,549**, 15,587
South Carolina Secretary of State, **15,546**
South Carolina Society for Prevention of Cruelty to Animals, 15,522
South Carolina State Council of Farm Women. *See* South Carolina Extension Homemakers' Council
South Carolina Status of Women Commission, 15,570
South Carolina Status of Women's Clubs, 15,790
South Carolina Status of Women's Conference, 15,795
South Carolina Training School for Nurses, **15,734**
South Carolina Training School for Nurses, Board of Co-operating Lady Members, 15,734
South-Carolina Weekly Gazette, 15,419
South Carolina Women's Council for Common Good, 15,570
South Carolina Women's State Committee, 15,790
"South Carolinians Speak" (column), 15,709
South, Christine Bradley, 5,121
South Congregational Church, 17,971
South Dakota
   abortion, legal aspects, 1,984
   antisemitism, 15,869
   blizzards, 15,869
   businesswomen, **15,840**, 15,869
   Catholic Church, history, 15,870
   Catholic schools, 4,874
   centennial celebrations, **15,853**
   church records and registers, Lutheran, **15,855**
   church societies, Lutheran, **15,855**
   churches, **15,839**
   cities and towns, 15,869
   clubs, **15,846**, **15,847**, 15,851, 15,858, **15,861**
   convents and nunneries, Catholic, **15,866**
   depressions, 15,869
   diaries and journals, 15,856
   droughts, 15,869
   floods, 15,869
   governors, 15,863
   historians, **15,860**
   hospitals, **15,842**
   immigrants, 15,869
   land settlement, 15,852
   maternity homes, 8,857
   mayors, 15,869
   memorials, 15,860
   monasticism and religious orders for women, Catholic, 15,842, **15,844**, 15,870
   Native Americans, 15,856
      medical care, **10,097**
      missions, 15,869
      reservations, 15,850
      social life and customs, 15,850
   nurses, 15,869
   nursing schools, **15,842**
   Oglala Indians, 965
   oral history, **15,869**
   patriotic societies, **15,865**
   photographs, collections, **15,867**

pioneers and settlers, 2,293, 9,325, **15,849**, **15,852**, **15,858**, **15,869**
politics, practical, women's activism, **15,862**
prohibition, 15,869
psychiatric hospitals, **10,097**
race problems, 15,869
ranches, 15,869
secret societies, 15,869
secretaries of state, 15,859
senators, United States, 15,863, 15,869
Siouan Indians, 15,850
   missions, **14,420**
social life and customs, 15,850, 15,856
soldiers, Civil War, **15,854**
suffrage, 4,859, 15,860, **15,864**
suffrage societies, 15,864, 15,868
suffragists, **15,851**, 15,857, **15,868**
teachers, **15,852**, **15,859**, 15,869
temperance societies, **15,843**
tornadoes, 15,869
World War II, civilians work, 3,950
South Dakota Anti-Suffragists, The, 15,864
South Dakota Equal Suffrage Association, 15,851
South Dakota Equal Suffrage Association for Good Government, 15,868
South Dakota Federated Women's Clubs, 15,858
South Dakota Franchise League, 15,868
South Dakota Messenger, 15,864
South Dakota State Historical Society, 15,860
South Dakota Universal Franchise League, 15,864
South Georgia Male and Female College (Dawson, GA), 3,072
South Idaho White Ribboner, 3,666
South Illinois University, faculty, 10,191
South Korea, Americans in, 8,165
South, Mary (Preston) [Mrs. John M.], 14,821
South Moon Under (book), 2,876
South New Market Anti-Slavery Society (NH), 10,818
South of Market Girls' Club (San Francisco, CA), 592
South Philadelphia High School (PA), 15,332
South Philadelphia Women's Liberty Loan Committee (PA), 15,005
South Plains Music Association, 16,062
South Plains Music Teachers Association, 16,266, 16,293
South Rhodesia
   missionaries, Anglican, 13,284
   missionaries, Methodist, **13,284**
   social life and customs, 13,284
South Shore Branch Library (IL), 3,920
South Shore Country Club (Chicago, IL), **3,900**, 4,012
South Shore Historical Society (IL), 3,920
South Shore Scene (Chicago, IL), 3,920
South Today, The (periodical), 2,879
South Vietnam, 7,790
Southack, Blanche Juliette, 810
Southall, Sara E., 2,678, 5,469
Southard Brain study (1925), 6,216
Southeastern Council on Family Relations, 15,811
Southeastern Flower Show (1929), 3,196
Southeastern Folklore Society, 15,585
Southeastern High School (MI), 8,317
Southeastern Montana Cowbelles, **10,376**
Southern Album (book), 5,853
Southern Association for Physical Education of College Women, **13,254**
Southern Association of College Women. *See* American Association of University Women
Southern Association of Colleges for Women, 13,189
Southern Baptist Convention, 3,456, **3,457**
Southern Baptist Convention (1879), 3,147
Southern Baptist Convention Woman's Missionary Union, 13,641
Southern Baptist Convention, Woman's Missionary Union Training School (KY). *See* Carver School of Missions and Social Work (KY)
Southern Baptist Convention, Women's Missionary Union, 3,457
Southern Baptist Foreign Missionary Board, 13,288
Southern Baptist Theological Seminary (Louisville, KY), **5,371**
Southern Benedictine College (Cullman, AL), 24

Southern California Library for Social Studies and Research, 1,015
Southern California Society for Mental Hygiene, 6,748
Southern Christian Institute (MS), 9,687
Southern College of Music (LA), 5,543
Southern Commercial Convention, 76
Southern Committee for People's Rights, 1,654
Southern Conference Educational Fund, **127, 3,303,** 11,840, 11,855, 13,138, 15,877, 17,608
Southern Conference Educational Fund, Committee for North Carolina, 13,176
Southern Conference for Human Welfare. *See* Southern Conference Educational Fund
Southern Conservative, 16,253
Southern Council on Women and Children in Industry, 12,731
Southern Cross of Honor, 9,756, 13,597
Southern Education Board, 15,816
Southern, Eileen (1920-), **15,923**
Southern Fellowships Fund, 11,911
Southern Female College (VA), 13,563
Southern Historical Association, 15,806
Southern Homestead (Nashville, TN), 15,952
Southern Indiana Status of Women Association, 4,502
Southern Ladies' Book, The, 15,952
Southern League for People's Rights, 13,138
Southern League for the Rejection of the Susan B. Anthony Amendment, 13,405, 13,516
Southern Literary Messenger, 15,952
Southern Masonic Female College (GA), **3,428**
presidents, 3,405
Southern Medical College (GA), 3,234
Southern Methodist University, 9,768
Southern Methodist University, Oral History Project, **16,208**
Southern Mountain Project, 17,608
Southern Negro Youth Congress (1946), 89
Southern Patriot, The (newspaper), 17,608
Southern Planter, **13,391**
Southern Presbyterian Board of Missions, 86
Southern Presbyterian Church
missionaries, **44**
missionaries, Afro-American, **45**
Southern Railroad, 9,686
Southern refugees (Civil War). *See* Refugees, Southern
Southern Regional Caucus, 8,101
Southern Regional Council, 65, 3,279, **3,283,** 3,302, 3,347, 3,469, 12,939, 13,222
Southern Regional Education Board, 11,911, 13,255
Southern Review, The (periodical), 9,769
Southern School for Workers, 13,189
Southern Seminary (Buena Vista, VA) faculty, 15,964
Southern States
history (1775-1865), 2,428, **3,341**
industrial recreation, 12,721
race problems, 11,840
secession, public opinion, 12,270
social life and customs, 7,649, **17,105,** 17,106
social service, rural, 12,725
textile workers, 8,085
welfare work in industry, 12,721
women, 11,855
Southern States Art League, **5,523**
Southern states in literature, 11,163
Southern States Insurance Company, 3,229
Southern Summer School for Women Workers in Industry, 3,308, 11,762, 13,176
Southern Tenant Farmers' Union, 13,176
Southern Utah State College, 16,402, 16,414, 16,425, 16,427, 16,448
archives, **16,408**
faculty, **16,413, 16,436**
Southern Woman's League for Rejection of the Susan B. Anthony Amendment. *See* Alabama Woman's Anti-Ratification League.
Southern Woman's Magazine (periodical), 15,966
Southern Women's Educational Alliance, **2,080,** 12,738
Southern Workers Defense League, 4,126
Southey, Robert, 12,399
Southgate, Maria (1836-1918). *See* Hawes, Maria (Southgate) [Mrs. James Morrison] (1836-1918)

Southwest, 183
land settlement, 6,650
Southwest Community Center (NE), 10,484
"Southwest in Print" (column), 16,387
Southwest Indians, 211, 1,396, 1,441
Southwest Museum (CA), 1,404, 1,465
Southwestern Bell Telephone Company, 9,951
Southwestern Library Association, **16,289**
Southwestern Organization Conference of the Office Employees International Union. *See* Office and Professional Employees International Union
"Southwestern Wild Flowers" (ms), 14,213
Southwick, Elaine (Christianson) [Mrs. Edward H.], **16,440**
Southwick, Mary Ferguson (Page) [Mrs. Philip R. V.], **11,035**
Southworth, Edna, 15,308
Southworth, Eli, 9,383
Southworth, Emma Dorothy Eliza (Nevitte) [Mrs. Frederick Hamilton] (1819-99), **2,584**
Southworth, Hunter H. (?-1878), 9,658
Southworth, Mary Hunter. *See* Kimbrough, Mary Hunter (Southworth) [Mrs. Allan McCaskell]
Southworth, Mary Morgan [Mrs. Hunter H.], 9,658
Southworth, Nellie, 9,383
Southworth, Newton, Family (MA, MN), **9,383**
Southworth, Rhoda Sparrow [Mrs. Newton] (1811-?), 9,383
Southworth, Sophie Wing, 9,383
Souvenir (book), 16,154
Sovik, Gertrude (1907-), **8,887**
Sowers, Alice, 13,870
Sowers, Julia Ann (1813-1908). *See* Barclay, Julia Ann (Sowers) [Mrs. James Turner] (1813-1908)
Space Between, The (book), 6,117
Spaeth, Eloise [Mrs. Otto L.] (1904-), **2,817**
Spafford, Elizabeth (Sandvig), 17,288, **17,338**
Spain
American ambassadors to, 2,635
American diplomats in, 5,321, 10,862
American travelers in, 7,651
Civil War, 12,487
Civil War (1936-1939), 6,023, 12,701
personal narratives, 15,793
refugees. *See* Refugees, political women, 12,180
colonies, administration, 1,510
Spalding, A. T., 3,256
Spalding, Adelle, 7,935
Spalding, Bourke, 2,979
Spalding College (KY), **5,373**
Spalding, Eliza (Hart) [Mrs. Henry Harmon] (1807-51), 880, 3,723, 14,667, 17,373, 17,423, 17,908
Spalding, Elizabeth, **1,794**
Spalding, Ella (Barrow) [Mrs. Bourke], 2,979, **13,133**
Spalding Family (AL, CT, MI), **7,935**
Spalding Family (GA), 3,256
Spalding Family (WA), 17,421
Spalding, Henry Harmon (1803-74), **3,723,** 14,566, 14,660, **14,667,** 17,422, **17,423**
Spalding, Mary. *See* Chamberlain, Mary (Spalding) [Mrs. C. P.]
Spalding, Mary (Connally), **3,256**
Spalding, Miranda (Sexton) [Mrs. William P.] (1826-1910), 7,935
Spalding, Rachel Jahonnet (Smith) [Mrs. Henry Harmon] (1808-80), 14,667, 17,423
Spalding, S. I., 7,398
Spalding, Sarah Griswold (1872-1960), **1,744**
Spalding, Virginia Stolte (1916-), 1,068
Spandorf, Lucy, 2,844
Spangler Family, 11,528
Spangler, Jewel. *See* Smaus, Jewel (Spangler)
Spangler, Maude A. [Miss], 8,259
Spanish
in California, 11,822
in Florida, 3,420
in Georgia, 3,420
in Louisiana, **5,496**
oral history, 211
Spanish-American War. *See* United States, War of 1898
Spanish-Americans, **968,** 11,226

education, 11,225
Spanish Cabildo of Louisiana, **5,496**
Spanish Idioms and Their English Equivalents (book), 2,200
Spanish language, study and teaching, 9,092
Spanish-Mexicans, **11,245**
Spanish missions of California, **319,** 346, 657, **673, 695,** 715, **733, 766, 767, 768, 769, 770, 773, 774, 775, 776,** 778, 985, 990, 991, 1,135, 1,459, 1,595, 16,295
Spanish missions of Texas, 16,083
Spann, Delia Annie (?-1910). *See* Patton, Delia Annie (Spann) (?-1910)
Spann, Elizabeth [Mrs. James], 15,735
Spann, James (ca. 1785-1838), 15,735
Spann, Leah Caroline, 13,142
Sparhawk-Jones, Elizabeth, 2,805
Sparkman, Ida Ross, **17,339**
Sparkman, James R. (1815-97), 15,467
Sparkman, Mary A., 15,405
Sparkman, Mary Elizabeth Heriot [Mrs. James R.], 15,467
Sparks, Jared, 13,413
Sparks, Lyra Haisley, **16,130**
Sparks, Marion E. (1872-1929), **4,398**
Sparrow, Louise Winslow (Kidder). [Mrs. Herbert George] Sparrow. [Mrs. Paul E. H.] Gripon (1884-), **2,585, 6,903**
Sparrow, Rhoda (1811-?). *See* Southworth, Rhoda (Sparrow) [Mrs. Newton] (1811-?)
Spartanburg Female College (SC), **15,736**
Spaulding, Anne A. *See* Parsons, Anne A. Spaulding [Mrs. Elijah Chauncey]
Spaulding, Elna B. [Mrs. Asa], 13,615
Spaulding, Eudora Hull, 3,813
Spaulding, Eugenia K., **12,077**
Spaulding, John, 14,523
Spaulding, Mary Cecilia (Swegles) [Mrs. Oliver Lyman], **7,936**
Spaulding, Nancy, 14,523
Speak to Me, Dance with Me (book), 7,214
Spear, Caroline (Hinckley) [Mrs. John Murray], 15,259
Spear, Charles, **6,206**
Spear, Elsa. *See* Byron, Elsa (Spear) Edwards
Spear, John Murray, 15,259
Spear, Katherine, 9,336
Spear, Lillian Sylten (1897-1963), **17,340**
Speare, Dorothy. [Mrs. Franklin B.] Christmas [Mrs. Charles J.] Hubbard (1898-1951), **14,447**
Speare, Edward Ray, 14,447
Speare, Elizabeth George (1908-), 5,999, **6,093**
Speare, Florence Lewis [Mrs. M. Edmund] (1886-1965), **6,904**
Spearman, Sara Eliza (Simons), 801
Spears, Julia A. (Warren) [Mrs. Andrew J.] (1832-?), Family (MN), **9,384**
Special librarians, 11,407, **12,816**
Special libraries, **2,865**
Special Operations Research Organization, 15,323
Special Services Committee of Ann Arbor (MI), 6,895
Spectator (periodical), **9,570**
Speculum (medicine), 4,698
Speech
research, 5,667
study and teaching, 9,828, 13,366
Speech Association of America, 5,477
Speech Can Change Your Life (book), 11,699
Speech clinics, 11,383
Speech Dynamics, Inc. (New York, NY), 11,699
Speech Training for Children (book), 17,604
Speed, Katherine Rhymes, **9,735**
Speedwell Iron Works (NJ), 10,920
Speer, Emma B., 12,738
Speight, Mary Bryan, 13,356
Spektrum (periodical), 12,880
Spell, Lota Mae [Mrs. Jefferson Rea] (1885-), **16,131**
Spellman, Mrs., 11,445
Spelman College, 12,738, 12,740
faculty, 5,466
Spelman, Lucy H., 3,280
Spence, Adam K. (1860-1902), 15,924

Spence, Martha (1812-?). *See* Heywood, Martha (Spence) [Mrs. Joseph L.] (1812-?)
Spence, Mary, **15,924**
Spence, Riley, 11,525
Spence School (NY), 6,507
Spencer, Anna (ca. 1832-1905), 14,857
Spencer, Anna Carpenter (Garlin) [Mrs. William Henry] (1851-1931), 2,519, **15,312,** 15,386
Spencer, Arthur C., III, 14,592
Spencer, Aurelia (1834-1922). *See* Rogers, Aurelia (Spencer) [Mrs. Thomas] (1834-1922)
Spencer, Catherine Curtis, 16,888
Spencer, Cecilia, 14,668
Spencer, Claire. [Mrs. John] Evans, 572
Spencer, Clarissa Hamilton (Young) [Mrs. John D.] (?-1939), 16,486
Spencer, Cornelia Ann (Phillips) [Mrs. James Monroe] (1825-1908), **13,134,** 13,319, 13,359, 13,416, 13,422, 13,528, 13,530, 13,561, **13,581,** 13,593, 13,598, 13,599
Spencer, Cornelia Jane (1841-1930). *See* Greer, Cornelia Jane (Spencer) (1841-1930)
Spencer, Dorothy. *See* Collins, Dorothy (Spencer)
Spencer, Edith, 14,857
Spencer, Elizabeth [Miss] (1921-), 9,567, **9,736**
Spencer Family (OR), **14,668**
Spencer Family (PA), **14,855**
Spencer, Fanny Bixby, 8,127
Spencer, Gwladys (1895-1947), **4,399**
Spencer, Hallie LaFollette [Mrs. W. Russell], 293
Spencer, Herbert, 12,350
Spencer, John (1802-84), 14,668
Spencer, John D., 16,486
Spencer, June. *See* Love, June (Spencer) [Mrs. James Lee]
Spencer, Lillian (White) (ca. 1878-1953), **1,795**
Spencer, Lilly (Martin) [Mrs. Benjamin Rush] (1882-1902), **2,818,** 13,836
Spencer, Mae, 16,486
Spencer, Manlius, 14,668
Spencer, Nannie J. (?-1916), 15,172
Spencer, Orson, 16,888
Spencer, Rachel (1794-1861), 14,857
Spencer, Robert, 115
Spencer, Rose Carolyn Hedlund [Mrs. Milton Leroy] (1891-1967), **9,385**
Spencer, Ruth, 11,746
Spencer, Sarah A., 2,196
Spencer, Sue, 8,663, 8,677
Spencer, Sue Townsend (McDaniel) [Mrs. Robert] (1919-), 115
Spencer, W. Russell, Family (AR), 293
Spencer, Walter B., 5,511
Spencer, William Valentine (1835-1923), 14,567, 14,668
Spensley, Sarah "Sally" (1897-). *See* Michener, Sarah "Sally" Spensley [Mrs. Carroll Kinsey] (1897-)
Speranza, Florence (Colgate) (1873-1951), **12,632**
Sperry, Almeda, 6,028
Sperry, Bryan, 9,517
Sperry, Mary S., 1,308
Sperry, Muriel Frelander [Mrs. Bryan] (1901-54), **9,517**
Sperry, Paul (1879-), 2,419, 2,505
Sperry, Sarah Catherine "Kate" S. *See* Hunt, Sarah Catherine "Kate" S. (Sperry)
Spewack, Bella Loebel (1899-), 11,907
Speyer, Leonora (von Stosch) [Mrs. Edgar] (1872-1956), 1,795, **2,586,** 4,000
Speyer School, P. S. 500 (NY), 13,742
Spice trade, 6,445
Spicer, Rosamond B., 2,840
Spickard, Lisa, 10,211
Spider Monkey, The (book), 10,854
Spiegel Family (IL), **4,039**
Spiegel, Lizzie (1856-?). *See* Barbe, Lizzie (Spiegel) [Mrs. Martin] (1856-?)
Spiegel, Marcus, 4,039
Spiegelberg, Flora (Langerman) [Mrs. Willi] (1857-1943), **11,229**
Spier, William, **17,816**
Spies, **2,444,** 2,522, 2,635, 2,659, 6,811, 9,919,

11,277, 12,381, 12,683, 13,017, **13,419,** 15,610, **17,122,** 17,617
Spiller, Isabele (Taliaferro) [Mrs. William N.] (1888-), **2,151,** 12,690
Spiller School of Music, 2,151
Spiller, William N., 2,151
Spilman, Johnetta Webb [Mrs.], **13,286**
Spilsbury Family (UT), 16,495
Spilsbury, Florence. *See* Higbee, Florence (Spilsbury) [Mrs. Myron]
Spilsbury, Nelle. *See* Hatch, Nelle (Spilsbury)
Spinet Club (ME). *See* Philharmonic Club (ME)
Spingarn, Amy, 5,870
Spingarn, Arthur Barnett (1878-1971), **2,587**
Spingler Institute (NY), students, 11,069
"Spinner in the Sun" (ms), 7,220
Spinners Club (CA), 1,231
Spinney, Anna G., **7,441**
Spinning, 10,052
Spinning, Elizabeth P., **17,225,** 17,226
Spinsters Club (NC), 13,446
"Spinsters' Gazette, The" (newsletter), 17,375
Spinsters of Charleston (SC), 15,515
Spirit and Life (periodical), 10,138
Spirit is Mercy, The: The Story of the Sisters of Mercy in the Archdiocese of Cincinnati, 1858-1958 (book), 4,986
Spirit Lake Business and Professional Women's Club (IA), **5,109**
Spirit Lake Massacre (IA, 1857), 4,696, 4,765
Spirit of Iowa, The (song), 4,689
Spirit writings, 10,184
Spiritual life, 1,857, 5,928, 7,604, 7,611, 7,619, 7,656, 7,661
Spiritualism, 1,351, 2,856, 4,172, **5,501,** 5,939, 11,542, 11,551, 11,741, 12,235, 14,537, 14,565, 17,659, 17,980
Spiritualists 4,062, 11,542, 14,363, **15,082, 17,034,** 17,036
Spirituals (songs), 51
Splawn, Margaret Larsen [Mrs. A. J.], **14,669**
Splint, Sarah F., 2,694
Split Seconds (book), 6,024
Spofford, A. R., 2,512
Spofford, Grace (1888?-1974), **7,299**
Spofford, Harriet Elizabeth (Prescott) [Mrs. Richard Smith, Jr.] (1835-1921), 1,224, **1,488,** 4,226, 4,781, 5,694, 5,714, **5,959,** 5,973, 7,131, 7,442, **7,681,** 11,821, 17,010
Spofford, Richard Smith, Jr. (?-1888), 1,488, 7,681
Spohn, George Weida, 8,815
Spokan Indians, missions, 17,212
Spokane College (WA), 17,380
Spoken Word, The (book), 2,159
Spokesman-Review (WA), 17,379
Spokeswoman Archives, 4,241
Spokeswoman, The (PA), 15,249
Spoon River Anthology (book), 11,894
Spoon River area (CO), 1,779
Spooner, Ella J., 6,691
Spooner, Emily Noyes (1835-99), **7,018**
Spooner, Lucy Jane, 9,316
Spooner, Mary Roche, 9,316
Spooner, Mrs. J. Walter, **10,827**
Spores (botany), 6,308
"Sporting Spirit, The" (leaflet), 15,029
Sports, 7,175
  public opinion, 1,655
Sports Illustrated (periodical), 15,228
Spotlight (periodical), 13,978
Spotts, Florence A., 10,191
Spottswood, Elizabeth L. *See* Schermerhorn, Elizabeth L. Spottswood [Mrs. John Freeman]
Sprado, Marguerite Elizabeth. *See* Schlichtmann, Marguerite Elizabeth (Sprado)
Spragins, Nancy [Mrs. Thomas], 17,094
Spragins, Thomas, 17,094
Sprague, Achsa, **17,034**
Sprauge, Catherine "Kate" Jane (Chase) [Mrs. William] (1840-99), 2,259, 17,992
Sprague, Charles E., 12,160
Sprague, Elizabeth F. (1911-), 10,152
Sprague, Estelle, 2,315
Sprague, Frances [Mrs.], **9,737**

Sprague, Lucy (1878-1967). *See* Mitchell, Lucy Sprague [Mrs. Wesley Clair] (1878-1967)
Sprague, Margaret Graham, 9,618
Sprague, Rosetta (Douglass), 2,315
Sprague, Sarah, 6,353
Spraug, Harriet [Mrs. Frank J.], 1,589
Spreckels, Alma (de Bretteville) (1881-1968), 543
"Spring" (story), 9,770
Spring, Agnes Wright (1894-), 418, **1,676,** 1,750, 1,790, **18,010**
Spring City Oral History Project (UT), **16,960**
Spring Garden Soup Society (PA), **15,094**
Spring Hill School, 1,966
Spring Hotel (Madison, WI), 17,641
Spring, Marcus, 11,125
Spring, Rebecca Buffum (1811-1911), 11,125
Spring Symphony (book), 13,959
Springer Family, 4,811
Springer, Gertrude, 8,678
Springfield Republican (IL), 2,784, 5,869
Springman, Margaret Elizabeth Cooper, 3,565
Springman, Mary. *See* Pigman, Mary (Springman) [Mrs. William Penn]
Springs, Andrew Baxter (1819-86), 13,135, 15,737
Springs Family (NC), **13,135**
Springs Family (SC), **15,737**
Springs, John, 15,737
Springs, John, III (1782-1853), 13,135
Springs, Julia Blandina "Blandie" (Baxter) [Mrs. Andrew Baxter] (1827-1902), 13,135
Springs, Leroy, 15,737
Springs, Mary, 15,737
Springs, Mary Laura, 15,737
Springs, Richard Austin, 15,737
Springs, Sophia C., 15,737
Sproul, Ida (Wittschen) [Mrs. Robert G.] (1891-), **811**
Sproul, Robert Gordon, 750, 811
Spruce Street Settlement House (CT). *See* Mitchell House (CT)
Sprung, Faith Evers [Mrs. William], 8,690
Sprung, William, 8,690
Sprunk, Iva [Mrs. Raymond], **14,095**
Spur, The (MT), 10,221
Spurrier, Mildred. *See* Topp, Mildred (Spurrier)
Spurs (MT), **10,221**
Squier, Ephraim George, 617
Squier, Jonathan, 10,905
Squier, Miriam Florence (Folline) [Mrs. David Charles] Peacock [Mrs. Ephraim George] (1836-1914). *See* Leslie, Miriam Florence (Folline) [Mrs. David Charles] Peacock [Mrs. Ephraim George] Squier [Mrs. Frank] (1836-1914)
Squire, Ally, **12,633**
Squire, Alvin A. (?-1815), 12,633
Squire, Frances (1867-1914). *See* Potter, Frances (Squire) (1867-1914)
Squire, Mrs. Alvin (1788-?), 12,633
Squires, Charles Pemberton (1865-1958), 10,749, **10,781**
Squires, Delphine (Anderson) [Mrs. Charles Pemberton] (1868-1961), 10,781
Squires, Eva Beatrice Swain (1897-). *See* Poelman, Eva Beatrice Swain (Squires) [Mrs. Walter Jenkins] (1897-)
Squires, Florence M. (1890-). *See* Boyer, Florence (Squires) Doherty (1890-)
Sri Aurobindo (Pondicherry, India), 11,176
Srygley, Sara, 2,927
Staats, Sarah (1787-1870). *See* Bayles, Sarah (Staats) (1787-1870)
Stabler, James P. (?-1840), 5,746
Stacey, Elizabeth, 9,323
Stackhouse Family (MS), 13,121
Stackhouse, Martha. *See* Service, Martha (Stackhouse) Williford [Mrs. John Hugh James]
Stackhouse, Verna (Cates), 13,637
Stackpole, Ralph, 765
Stacy, Consider A. (1817-88), **8,363**
Stacy, Loana, 8,363
Stacy, Maria [Mrs. Consider A.], 8,363

Stafford, Jean, 11,954
Stafford, Mary J., **5,810**
Stafford, Ruth (1906-). *See* Peale, Ruth (Stafford) [Mrs. Norman Vincent] (1906-)
Stage lighting, **17,812**
Stage Women's War Relief, **12,634**
Stageberg, Susie (Williamson) [Mrs. Olaf O.] (ca. 1877-1961), 8,949, 9,062, 9,174, 9,375, **9,386,** 9,396, 9,400
"Stages of a Woman's Life from the Cradle to the Grave" (article), 13,308
Stagg, Hunter, 2,877
Stahler, Bonnie (Giberson) (1918-), **8,714**
Stahlnecker, Wyona Eliza Surfus (1878?-?). *See* Gordon, Wyona Eliza Surfus (Stahlnecker) (1878?-?)
Stair, Lois (Harkrider) [Mrs. Ralph Martin] (1923-), 15,176
Stakebake, Annie (1869-1946). *See* Daniels, Annie (Stakebake) [Mrs. H. J.] Seayrs [Mrs. Benjamin F.] (1869-1946)
Staley, Kate Holcomb, 13,881
Stalin, Josef, 6,106, 17,954
Stalleson, Anne Maria (1857-1939). *See* Dorius, Anne Maria (Stalleson) [Mrs. John F. F.] (1857-1939)
Stallings, Edith Langdale [Mrs.], **3,022**
Stallworth, Alma G., **8,287**
Stamp Act (1765), repeal of, 7,639
Stampede to Timberline (book), 1,804
Stamper, Rebecca (Rush) [Mrs. Thomas] (1743-93), 15,084
Stamps, Mary [Mrs.], **13,136**
Stanard, Mary Mann Page Newton (1865-1929), **5,960**
Stanchfield, Bessie Mae (1901-48), **9,387**
Stand by for Danger (book), 17,997
Standard Club (TX), 16,263
Standard Oil Company, 10,104, 15,318
   employees, 11,684
Standard Oil of Atlanta (GA), 3,387
Standerin, Ann Lee [Mrs. Abraham] (1736-84). *See* Lee, Ann. Ann Lees. [Mrs. Abraham] Standerin. Mother Ann Lee (1736-84)
Standing Bear, Nora (Lookout), 14,173
Standing Elk, Fannie, **10,313**
"Standing Orders and Field Guide" (ms), 6,154
Stanford, Jane Eliza (Lathrop) [Mrs. Leland] (1828-1905), **1,552,** 11,547, 11,742
Stanford, John, 11,100
Stanford, Leland G., 1,183, 1,184, 1,185, 1,186, 1,552
Stanford Library (CA), 1,549
Stanford, Margaret, **8,231**
Stanford, Mary M., 13,566
Stanford, May, 13,595
Stanford Mothers' Club (CA), 1,353
Stanford University (CA), 1,551, 1,552, 1,586, 10,658, 10,727, 11,748
   alumnae, 1,620, 5,119, 9,978
   faculty, 337, 1,545, 1,546, 1,548, 1,549, 1,550, 1,560, 1,566, 1,585, 1,595, 14,706
   presidents, 1,547, **1,559**
   students, 420, 656, 1,379, **1,553,** 14,387
Stanford University (CA), Hoover Institution on War, Revolution and Peace, 325
Stanford University (CA), medical school, 1,608
Stanford University (CA), Medical School, alumnae, 3,621
Stanford University (CA), Women's Physical Education Department, **1,555**
Stanford University (CA), Women's Student Health Service, 1,555
Stangland, Arthur G. (1908-), **14,448**
Stanicki, Jane M., **12,925**
Stanislavski, Constantin, 6,834
Stanislawsky, Margaret, 10,687
Stanke, Mrs. Elmer, 8,917
Stanley, Abigail Brothers, **13,287**
Stanley, Ada. *See* Johnson, Ada (Stanley)
Stanley and Livingstone (motion picture), 5,177
Stanley, Beatrice (Birmingham) [Mrs. Willoughby] Mason [Mrs. Lewis V.] (1887-1972), 17,397
Stanley-Brown, Joseph, 2,345

Stanley-Brown, Mary (Garfield) [Mrs. Joseph] (1867-1947), 2,345, 2,346, 2,348
Stanley, Carrie Ellen [Miss] (1886-1962), 5,035
Stanley, Kim. [Mrs. Alfred Ryder] (1925-), 11,907
Stanley, Lee B., 15,332
Stanley, Lewis V. (1876-1956), 17,397
Stanley, Louise (1883-1954), 2,673
Stanley, Louise (Hathaway) [Mrs. Charles Alfred] (1880-?), **812,** 11,846
Stanley, Marie. *See* Sheip, Marie Layette
Stanley, Mr., 2,276
Stanley, Ruth (Moore), **10,537**
Stanly, Mary E., **15,738**
Stanly, Mrs. William, 5,291
Stansbury, Catherine Amanda (1835-94). *See* Washburn, Catherine Amanda (Stansbury) [Mrs. Charles] (1835-94)
Stansel, Horace Sylvan, **9,804**
Stansel, Pearl (High) [Mrs. Horace Sylvan] (1886-), 9,804
Stantial, Edna Lamprey, 2,256, **6,535,** 6,969, 6,980, 18,013
Stanton, Adele Townsend, **5,524**
Stanton, Annie M., 2,370
Stanton, Benjamin, 10,975
Stanton, Edwin, 5,060
Stanton, Elizabeth Brandon [Miss], **9,738**
Stanton, Elizabeth (Cady) [Mrs. Henry Brewster] (1815-1902), 540, 1,004, 1,059, 1,255, 1,436, 1,437, 1,475, 1,837, 1,896, 1,950, 2,175, 2,315, 2,413, 2,501, **2,588,** 3,908, 3,927, 5,939, **5,961,** 6,412, 6,526, 6,830, 6,859, **6,905,** 7,183, 7,203, 7,222, 7,230, 7,295, 9,060, 9,291, 10,155, **10,933,** 11,185, 11,550, 11,605, 11,742, 12,635, 12,811, 12,819, 12,828, 12,833, 12,857, 15,291, 17,411, 17,589, 17,852, 17,898
Stanton Family, 11,600
Stanton Family, 12,635
Stanton Family (OH), 14,059
Stanton, Frank, 3,143
Stanton, Gertrude (1852-1934). *See* Käsebier, Gertrude (Stanton) [Mrs. Edward] (1852-1934)
Stanton, Harriet Eaton (1856-1940). *See* Blatch, Harriot Eaton (Stanton) [Mrs. William Henry] (1856-1940)
Stanton, Jean Austin [Mrs. Seabury], 9,160
Stanton, Jessie (1886-1976), 11,819
Stanton, Katharine Lyra (1856-98) *See* Griffis, Katharine Lyra (Stanton) [Mrs. William Elliott] (1856-98)
Stanton, Lucy May [Miss] (1875-1931), **3,096, 3,097**
Stanton, Mary, 10,718
Stanton, Nora. *See* Barney, Nora (Stanton) [Mrs. Morgan]
Stanton, Phoebe (1914-), 5,829
Stanton, Robert Brewster (1846-1922), **12,635**
Stanton, Theodore (1851-1925), 10,933, **11,036**
Stanwood, Edward (1841-1916), 7,605
Stanwood, Ellen [Mrs.], 6,245
Stanwood, Ethel (1874-1954). *See* Bolton, Ethel (Stanwood) [Mrs. Charles] (1874-1954)
Stanwood Family (MA), **7,605**
Stanwood, Harriet (?-1903). *See* Blaine, Harriet (Stanwood) [Mrs. James Gillespie] (?-1903)
Stanwyck, Barbara, 1,025, 2,241
Staples, Carrie Gertrude Rodgers [Mrs. George Howard] (1864-1955), 9,388
Staples, David Jackson, 813
Staples, Eliza Ann (Hull) (1804-32), 1,901
Staples, George Howard (1858-1944), Family (MN), **9,388**
Staples, Mary Pratt (Winslow) [Mrs. David Jackson], 813
Staples, Milfred Willis (1895-), 9,388
Staples, Myrtle Cole (1890-1927), 9,388
Staples, Robert E., 9,252
Stapleton, Maureen (1925-), 11,907, 12,367
Stapleton, Patience, **1,745**
Stapleton, Susan, **9,389**
Stapp, Emilie Blackmore, 9,819
Star (KS), 4,802
Star (Minneapolis, MN), 9,043
Star Gleams: A Community Christmas Choral, The (drama), 6,904

Star Guild (Hillsdale, MI), **7,938**
Star Lyceum Bureau, 4,897
Star of Hope, Lodge Number Seven (OR), 14,303
Star Telegram (TX), 16,282
Star-Times (MO), 10,171
Starbird, Iantha T. (1860-?). *See* Covel, Iantha T. (Starbird) (1860-?)
Stark, Arcada. *See* Balz, Arcada (Stark) [Mrs. Fred G.]
Stark, Elizabeth, **10,718**
Stark, Emma (1843-1925). *See* Hampton, Emma (Stark) [Mrs. Charles George] (1843-1925)
Stark Family, 8,337
Stark, Lloyd C. (1886-1972), **10,050**
Starke, Juanita G., 3,290
Starkey College (Eddytown, NY), 9,023
Starkey, Marion Lena (1901-), **6,095**
Starkville Woman's Club (MS), 9,801, **9,805**
Starkweather, Elizabeth, **11,717**
Starkweather, John, 10,919
Starkweather, Sarah J. (1835-1915). *See* Churchill, Sarah J. (Starkweather) (1835-1915)
Starling, Anna Irvin (1842-77), 5,268
Starling, Elizabeth Ann Gabriella (Lewis) [Mrs. Samuel McDowell] (1813-62), 5,268
Starling, Lirrel, 1,641
Starling, Mary (1832-96). *See* Payne, Mary (Starling) [Mrs. William Richardson] (1832-96)
Starling, Samuel McDowell (1807-90), 5,268
Starnes, Julia, 9,694
Starr, Augusta, **9,390**
Starr Club (MA), **7,079**
Starr, Dorothy, 14,414
Starr, Eliza Allen (1824-1901), **4,647,** 7,300
Starr, Ellen Gates (1859-1940), 4,047, 4,052, 4,056, 4,071, 4,080, 4,101, 4,161, 4,165, 4,173, 7,172, **7,300**
Starr, Helen (Norton) [Mrs. Mark], 8,071, **8,126,** 15,332
Starr, Jean (1886-). *See* Untermeyer, Jean (Starr) [Mrs. Louis] (1886-)
Starr, Mamie, 3,319
Starr, Mark (1894-), 8,071, **8,126,** 15,332
Starr, Mary Ann (Adams) [Mrs. Cecil Franklin], **16,441**
Starr, Mary Caroline (Dannat) [Mrs. Walter]. *See* Starr, Mother M. Veronica
Starr, Mary M. [Mrs.], 1,931
Starr, Minnie E., **8,364**
Starr, Mother M. Veronica, 12,932
Starr, Sarah E. (1820-80), 7,079
Starr, Shirley, 4,109
Starrett, Agnes, **15,240**
Stars at Noon (book), 5,132
Starvation, 13,537
Stasik, Margaret Darin (ca. 1907-), **15,253**
Stassen, Harold E., 8,433, 9,388
Stastny, Olga Frances (Sadilek) [Mrs. Charles] (1878-1952), 10,453, **10,538**
State aid to education, 13,504
State aid to the arts, 16,111
State Anti-Saloon League of Northern and Central California, 509
State Bank of Girard (KS), 4,477
State Board of Charities (CT). *See* Welfare Department (CT)
State Board of Control (CA), 365
State Board of Education (MN), 9,232
State boards of education, 5,517, 6,420, 7,572, 13,249, 16,062, 17,017, **17,483,** 17,486
State Charities Aid Association of New York, 2,568
State College of Lexington (KY), students, 5,302
State Council of Agriculture and Markets (NY), 11,393
State Defense Council of North Dakota, "Women's Service Bulletins" (newsletters), 13,719
State departments of education, **1,137, 9,472, 15,541, 17,901**
State Education Commission (NC), 13,249
State Education Study Committee (MS), 9,662
State encouragement of science, literature, and art, 2,743, 2,759, 2,784
State Equal Franchise League of Maryland, 6,757
State Farm for Women (CT), 1,906

State Farmer's Alliance (MN), 8,924
State Federation of Home Bureaus (NY), 11,393
State Federation of Pennsylvania Women, 2,310, 14,809, 14,949, 15,244
State Federations of Women's Clubs, 2,117
State Forestry Academy (Mount Alto, PA), 14,809
State Forestry Reservation Commission (PA), 14,809
State governments, 6,692. *See also* Politics and government *under individual states*
  officials and employees, 365, **1,132**, **3,222**, **3,709**, 3,977, **4,341**, **6,766**, 6,848, 6,982, 12,790, 13,391, 14,248, **15,326**, **17,901**, 17,917, **17,918**, **17,920**, 17,977, 18,010
    appointment, qualifications, etc., 1,140
    salaries, allowances, etc., 17,463
State Grange (MI), 8,171
State Historical Museum (MS), 9,599
State Historical Society (IA), 4,908
State Historical Society of Wisconsin, 8,953, 17,603, 17,630
State Hospital for Women and Infants (Philadelphia, PA). *See* Pennsylvania Hospital, Maternity Hospital (Philadelphia, PA)
State Industrial Home for Girls (MI), 8,276
State Industrial Home for Girls (MO), 10,032
State Legislative Council (NC), 13,274
State Library (CT), **1,931**
State libraries, **1,133**, **17,919**
State Lunatic Asylum (NY), 12,197
State Magazine, The, 15,585
State Medical Board, nurses examining committee (OH), 13,994
State Normal and Industrial College for Women (NC). *See* University of North Carolina at Greensboro
State Normal and Industrial School (NC). *See* University of North Carolina at Greensboro
State Normal School (Livingston, AL), deans, 952
State Normal School (Chico, CA), 954
State Normal School (GA), 2,998
State Normal School (ME), 5,634
State Normal School (MA), 6,645, 6,845
State Normal School (Warrensburg, MO), 9,858
State Normal School (NC), 13,610
State Normal University (IL), alumnae, 13,754
State of Georgia, Executive Department (Civil War Section), **3,429**
State of Georgia v. Atlanta Newspapers, Inc., 3,224
State Papers of Vermont, The (book), 17,030
State Records Commission (MO), 10,194
State rights, 6,728, 9,605
State School for the Blind (UT), 16,448
State School for the Deaf (KS), 13,673
State School for the Deaf (ND), 13,673
State songs, New Mexico, 11,215
State songs, South Carolina, 15,804
State Teachers College (AL). *See* Livingston University (AL)
State Teachers College (MS), 9,764
State Teachers College (Dickinson, ND). *See* Dickinson State College (ND)
State universities and colleges, 2,125, **5,189**, 5,394, 5,494, 6,416, 8,244, 8,492, 8,822, 9,282, 9,583, 9,599, 9,607, 9,662, 9,746, 9,764, 9,779, **9,897**, **10,023**, **10,024**, 10,038, 13,322, 13,324, 13,390, 13,391, 13,479, 13,581, 13,604, 13,698, 14,215, 17,315
  administration, 1,779, 8,342
  admission, **10,014**, 10,030
  alumni, **16,414**, **16,424**
  archives, **9,526**, **15,824**, **16,408**
  faculty, **440**, 468, **15,801**, 16,012, **16,413**, **16,436**, 16,448
State University of Iowa, 4,828, 4,958
  alumnae, 4,816, 4,960, 5,048
State University of Iowa, board of education, 4,918
State University of Iowa Equal Suffrage Association, 4,960
State University of New York, 11,903, 12,556
State University of New York at Albany, archives, **11,267**
State University of New York, Binghamton, faculty, 11,285
State University of New York College at Brockport

alumnae, 11,269
archives, **11,290**
State University of New York at Buffalo, Alumnae Association, **11,370**
State University of New York at Buffalo, Cap and Gown, 11,388
State University of New York at Buffalo, Colleges, **11,373**
  archives, **11,380**
  faculty, 11,369, 11,371, 11,374, 11,383
State University College at Buffalo (NY), faculty, 11,363, 11,364, 11,365, **11,366**
State University of New York at Buffalo, Norton Union, 11,375
State University of New York at Buffalo, Panhellenic Council, 11,375
State University of New York at Buffalo, School of Nursing, **11,377**
State University of New York at Buffalo, Secretarial Training Program, **11,379**
State University of New York at Buffalo, Teacher's College, faculty, **11,378**
State University of New York at Buffalo, University Dames, 11,384
State University of New York at Buffalo, Women's Club, **11,381**
State University of New York at Buffalo, Women's Studies College, 11,373
State University College at Oswego (NY), 12,762
  faculty, 12,765
State University of New York College at Potsdam, Crane School of Music, faculty, 12,774
State University of New York at Stony Brook, Women's Club, **12,882**
State University of New York Librarians Association, **11,382**
State v. Tachanatah (NC), 13,448
Statehood (American politics), 4,421, 14,212, 17,477
Statesmen. *See* Diplomats; Politicians
Statesville Female Seminary (NC), 13,377
Statisticians, 349, 2,292, **2,317**, 6,440, 7,198, 7,315, **14,006**, 15,998, 16,038, 17,018
Statler, Helen [Mrs.], 8,236
Statler, Sarah J., 4,773
Statmueller, Father Frederick, 16,866
Stats Tidning (MN), 9,204
Statuary Hall (DC), 15,758
Statue of Liberty, 15,886
Statues, 1,786, 2,338, 2,521, 2,646, 5,118, 6,384, 8,318, 9,455, 9,735, 10,764, 12,988, 14,549, 15,758, 15,886
Staunton Female Seminary (VA), faculty, 10,974
Staupers, Mabel Eloise Doyle Keaton (1890-), **2,152**, 12,691
Stead, Mary. *See* Pinckney, Mary (Stead) [Mrs. Charles]
"Steal of the White Man, The" (song), 9,467
Steamboat travel, **4,251**, 5,262, 5,271
Steamboat up the Missouri (book), 10,262
Steamboats, 3,149, 3,538, 10,400, 11,134
Stearly, Annie [Mrs.], **1,345**
Stearns, Almira [Mrs. Daniel Warren], 14,449
Stearns, Charles (1781-1818), 7,671
Stearns, Charlotte Champe (1843-1929). *See* Eliot, Charlotte Champe (Stearns) [Mrs. Henry Ware] (1843-1929)
Stearns, Charlotte Emily (1827-?). *See* Pengra, Charlotte Emily (Stearns) [Mrs. Byron J.] (1827-?)
Stearns, Daniel Warren (1821-1911), **14,449**
Stearns, Doran H., 14,456
Stearns, Ella A. Stoughton [Mrs. Doran H.] (1857-1944), **14,456**
Stearns Family (OR), 14,487
Stearns, Mabel Kittredge. *See* Munroe, Mabel Kittredge (Stearns) Noble [Mrs. Kirk]
Stearns, Mrs., 7,042
Stearns, Rachel Willard (1813-?), 6,906
Stearns, Sarah "Sally" (Ripley) (1785-?), **6,906, 7,671**
Stearns, Sarah W., **7,443**
Stebbins, Amanda, **11,718**
Stebbins, Caroline, 2,376
Stebbins, Catherine (Fish), 12,834

Stebbins, Charlotte (1802-88). *See* Skinner, Charlotte (Stebbins) [Mrs. Avery] (1802-88)
Stebbins, Clarissa, 7,150
Stebbins, Elizabeth R., **7,939**
Stebbins, Emma (1815-62), 7,585
Stebbins, Laura, 1,900
Stebbins, Lucy Ward (1880-), 372
Stebbins, Sally, 11,718
Stebman, Betty [Miss], 12,708
Stecker, Bertha, 4,948
Stedman, Edith, 6,339
Stedman, Edith G. (ca. 1888-), **6,907**
Stedman, Elizabeth Clementine (Dodge) (1810-89). *See* Kinney, Elizabeth Clementine (Dodge) Stedman (1810-89)
Steece, Ann. *See* Cotton, Ann (Steece) [Mrs. Josiah Dexter]
Steed Family (MA), 16,531
Steed, Margaret (1884-). *See* Hess, Margaret (Steed) (1884-)
Steefel, Genevieve (Fallon) [Mrs. Lawrence D.] (1899-), **2,589**, 9,219, **9,392**
Steel-Brooke, Gertrude (?-1974). *See* Wallis, Gertrude (Steel-Brooke) [Mrs. Ross] (?-1974)
Steel-Brooke, Louise Holmes, 1,219
Steel industry and trade, 6,315
Steel Workers Organizing Committee, 15,333
Steele, Anna Elizabeth (1825-1913). *See* Wright, Anna Elizabeth (Steele) [Mrs. John] (1825-1913)
Steele, Edward S., 14,123
Steele, Elizabeth, 13,411, 13,583
Steele, Eloise, 14,123
Steele, Ephraim, 13,583
Steele, Joan Crawford [Mrs. Alfred], 8,657
Steele, John, **13,583**
Steele, Louisa Hanson Rogers (1804-81). *See* Kendall, Louisa Hanson Rogers (Steele) (1804-81)
Steele, Maria Theresa (Ewing) [Mrs. Clement F.], 2,325
Steele, Mrs. William D., 9,894
Steele, Rachel. *See* Johnson, Rachel (Steele)
Steele, Sarah Jane (?-1969). *See* Sibley, Sarah Jane (Steele) [Mrs. Henry Hastings] (?-1869)
Steelink, Fannia [Mrs. Nicolaas], 8,127
Steelink, Nicolaas (1890-), **8,127**
Steelworkers Union, 1,577
Steep Ascent, The (book), 2,450
Steer, Mattie Enlow [Mrs.], 4,907
Steere, Elizabeth [Mrs. Isaac], 9,393
Steere, Isaac, Family (MN), **9,393**
Steers and Coman (OR), 14,670
Steers, Lois, **14,670**
Stefansson, Vilhjalmur, 12,396
Steffan, Alice Jacqueline (Kennedy) (1907-), **14,450**
Steffens, Alice M., 9,394
Steffens, Charles Hammond (1861-?), Family, **9,394**
Steffens, Charlotte M., **9,394**
Steffens, Ella [Mrs. Lincoln], 1,507
Steffens, Laura (?-1946). *See* Suggett, Laura (Steffens) [Mrs. Allen Holman] (?-1946)
Steffens, Lincoln (1866-1936), 2,595, 8,144, 12,705
Steffens, Lottie "Dot." *See* Hollister, Lottie "Dot" (Steffens) [Mrs. John James] (1872-1956)
Stegner, Wallace, 1,550, **1,601**
Steiber, Anita. *See* Vogel, Anita (Steiber) [Mrs. Rudolf]
Steichen, Clara Smith, 9,894
Steichen, Edward (1879-1973), 6,077
Steichen, Mary (1904-). *See* Calderone, Mary (Steichen) (1904-)
Steichen the Photographer (book), 6,077
Stein, Amelia (Keyser), **814**
Stein, Gertrude [Miss] (1874-1946), 573, 620, 754, 755, 814, **815**, 819, 840, 922, 1,565, 2,331, 4,226, **5,525**, 6,927, 7,171, 11,153, 11,821, 11,897, 11,970, 12,821
Stein, Karl Bernard, 2,110
Stein, Leo, 573, 620, 754
Stein, Marguerite B., 1,186
Stein, Michael, 573, 620, 754, 942
Stein, Mindell W., 1,786
Stein, Sarah, 573, 620, 754, 942
Steinacher, Marie Helen (1885-). *See* LeBaron,

Marie Helen (Steinacher) [Mrs. Benjamin F.] (1885-)
Steinacher, Rudolph, 16,831
Steinbach, Mrs. William E., 10,679
Steinbeck, Mrs. John, 212
Steinberg, Ann, 212
Steinberg, Leon, 212
Steinbrecher, Emelie, 17,282
Steinegger, Marie (1896-), 169
Steiner, Albert, 12,661
Steiner, Clara (Eby) [Mrs. Menno] (1873-1929), 4,514, **4,517**
Steiner, Lisa, 6,335
Steiner, Mrs. G. A. R., 14,618
Steinhardt, Laurence Adolph (1892-1950), **2,590**
Steinhart, Amy (1879-?). See Braden, Amy (Steinhart) [Mrs. Robert] (1879-?)
Stelce, Annie (ca. 1900-). See Hosking, Annie (Stelce) [Mrs. Benjamin] (ca. 1900-)
Stelfax, Mildred A., 5,829
"Stella" (person, NE), **10,539**
Stella Dallas (book), 7,689
Stella Maris House (OR), **14,671**
Stella, Sister Maris, 9,255
Stenberg, Molly Peacock, **18,011**
Stendahl, 7,316
Stenographers, 984, 6,643, 6,752, **11,642**, 11,851, 17,214
Step on the Stair, A (book), 3,993
Stephan, Leslie Bates (1933-), **6,096**
Stephen, Alexander M. (?-1894), 12,067
"Stephen Crane's Lost Helen" (article), 10,860
Stephen F. Austin Colony (TX), 16,088, 16,261
"Stephen, King of England" (dissertation), 9,764
Stephen Markham Company, 16,799
Stephen School of Music (Cleveland, OH), 13,950
Stephen, Virginia (1882-1941). See Woolf, Virginia (Stephen) (1882-1941)
Stephens, Alexander H., 3,008, 3,101, 3,532, 3,584, 13,268
Stephens, Anna Sophia (Winterbotham) [Mrs. Edward] (1810 or 1813-86), 5,694, **12,636**
Stephens College (Columbia, MO), 2,159, 9,938, 9,942, 9,951, 10,035
  administration, 10,035
  archives, **9,825**
  faculty, 4,040, **9,964**
Stephens College (Columbia, MO), Alumnae Club, **9,915**
Stephens College (Columbia, MO), Woman's Foundation, 9,825
Stephens, Eleanor Sharpless, 14,713
Stephens, Hugh, 9,833
Stephens, John Foster, 16,390
Stephens, John H., 14,284
Stephens, John Walter "Chicken," 13,549
Stephens, Lisette "Lizzie" (Bristow) [Mrs. John H.] (1867-1962), 14,284
Stephens, Mary Catherine (1919-), **17,341**
Stephens, Mr., 9,857
Stephens, Mrs. Thomas E., 11,857
Stephens, Pauline (Foster), **16,390**
Stephens, Pauline Francis, 11,948
Stephens, Stephen D., 17,703
Stephens, William A., 7,295
Stephenson, Gladys, 2,309
Stephenson, Marion (1888-). See Olden, Marion (Stephenson) [Mrs. James, Jr.] Henry [Mrs. William K.] DeVictor [Mrs. Paul] Coleman-Norton [Mrs. Roger] (1888-)
Stephenson, Mary. See Moody, Mary Stephenson [Mrs. Zenus Ferry]
Stephenson, Nathaniel W., 2,160
"Stepmother" (radio program), 2,274
Stepping Heavenward (book), 5,694
Stepping Stones (book), 4,710
Sterilization (birth control), 6,221, **8,634**, 9,299, **11,017**, 14,629
  law and legislation, 17,018
  legal aspects, 16,396
  religious aspects, Catholic Church, 8,634
Sterilization League for Human Betterment. See Association for Voluntary Sterilization

Sterilization League of New Jersey. See Association for Voluntary Sterilization
Sterling, Alice. See Gregory, Alice (Sterling)
Sterling, Caroline Dutcher. See Choate, Caroline Dutcher (Sterling) [Mrs. Joseph Hodges]
Sterling, Caroline (Rand) (?-1918), 712
Sterling, Cathy, 13,322
Sterling, Dorothy (1913-), **14,451**
Sterling, Emma (Betts) [Mrs. Frederick A.] (1837-?), **13,958**
Sterling Family (KY), **5,268**
Sterling, Flora. See Liliencrantz, Flora (Sterling)
Sterling, Frederick A., 13,958
Sterling, George (1869-1926), 657, **816**, **1,489**
Sterling, Harriet D. [Mrs. John W.], 17,640
Sterling, Isabella, 8,816
Sterling, Isabelle. See Rounthwaite, Isobelle (Sterling)
Sterling, Philip, **14,452**
Sterling Women's Christian Temperance Union (Burnside, MN), 8,816
Stern, Bernice, **17,342**
Stern, Caroline, **7,301**
Stern, Claire [Mrs.], 12,875
Stern, Edith (Mendel), 2,086
Stern, Edith (Rosenwald), 5,469
Stern, Elise. See Haas, Elise (Stern) [Mrs. Walter A.]
Stern, Frances [Miss] (1873-1947), **13,823**
Stern, Isaac, 749, 17,817
Stern, Jacob B., 4,839
Stern, Laura J., 53
Stern, Lucie, 1,534, 1,585
Stern, Marjorie (1918-), **8,128**
Stern, Millicent B. [Mrs. Jacob B.] (1820-1904), **4,839**
Stern, Philip Van Doren, 17,473
Stern, Rosalie (Meyer) [Mrs. Sigmund] (1869-1955), **945**
Stern, Sigmund, 945
Sternberger, Estelle M., 9,443
Sterne, Emma (Gelders) (1894-), **14,453**
Sterne, Hedda [Miss] (1916-), **2,819**
Sterner, Albert E. (1863-1946), **12,637**
Sterry, Helena Ruth, 11,077
Sterz, Henry E., 103
Stetson, Anna Leonard (1766-1847). See Shaw, Anna Leonard (Stetson) Smith (1766-1847)
Stetson, Augusta Emma (Simmons) [Mrs. Frederick J.] (1842-1928), **1,490**, **1,491**, 1,948
Stetson, Charles Walter, 2,356
Stetson, Charlotte Anna (Perkins) [Mrs. Charles Walter] (1860-1935). See Gilman, Charlotte Anna (Perkins) [Mrs. Charles Walter] Stetson [Mrs. George Houghton] (1860-1935)
Stetson, Ellen, **292**
Stetson, Florence May (Brigham) [Mrs. Harlan True] (?-1956), 6,337
Stetson, Frederick J., 1,491
Stetson, Harlan True (1885-1964), **6,337**
Stetson, John B., 2,657
Stetten, Alice Mayer (1887-1972), 7,239, **7,302**, 9,492
Stetter, Leta Anna (1886-1939). See Hollingsworth, Leta Anna (Stetter) [Mrs. Harry Levi] (1886-1939)
Steuben, Baron, 9,280
Steuben, Phoebe Brownell, 955
Steuenberg, Edith (Farrer) **3,724**
Steurt, Marjorie (Rankin) (1888-), **817**, 11,846
Steven Family (IL), **4,422**
Steven, James, Jr., 4,422
Steven, Laura Ernestine (Gutmann) [Mrs. James, Jr.] (1847-1907), 4,422
Stevens, Alzina (Parsons) (1849-1900), 4,047
Stevens, Amanda (Harley), 5,710
Stevens, Ann LeConte [Mrs.], 14,892
Stevens, Carrie (?-1907). See Walters, Carrie (Stevens) (?-1907)
Stevens, Catharine (Clarkson) [Mrs. Henry H.] (1812-82). See Stevens, Catharine Clarkson (Crosby) [Mrs. Henry H.] (1812-82)
Stevens, Catharine Clarkson (Crosby) [Mrs. Henry H.] (1812-82), **11,037**, **12,183**

Stevens, Catherine [Mrs. William D.] Fairley [Mrs. Melvin James], 11,582
Stevens, Connie, 1,576
Stevens, Daisy (McLaurin) (1875-1950), **9,740**
Stevens, Doris. [Mrs. Jonathan] Mitchell (1892-1963), 5,124, 6,742, **6,908**, 6,947, **10,540**, 14,377
Stevens, Elvira (1832-1909). See Barney, Elvira (Stevens) [Mrs. John S.] Woodbury [Mrs. Oliver B.] Huntington [Mrs. Royal] (1832-1909)
Stevens, Eva. See Henderson, Eva (Stevens) [Mrs. Alexander S.]
Stevens Family, 14,059
Stevens Family, 12,653
Stevens Family (NJ), **11,134**
Stevens Family (NY), **11,582**
Stevens Family (NY, WI), **17,570**
Stevens Family (VT), **17,035**
Stevens, Flora Ellice (Bishop), 1,790
Stevens, George W., 10,496
Stevens, Harry "Ellie" E., 3,831
Stevens, Hazard (1842-1918), **14,454**, 17,164
Stevens, Helen (Bradshaw) [Mrs. Thomas Wood] (1880-1942), **225**
Stevens, Helen N., 14,877
Stevens, Henry, 11,190
Stevens, Henry Bailey, 6,867
Stevens, Henry H., 11,037, 12,183
Stevens, Henry, Sr., 17,035
Stevens, Ida (Pearman), 4,392
Stevens, Isaac Ingalls, 14,318, 14,454, 17,164
Stevens, Jervis Henry, 15,739
Stevens, John (1749-1838), 11,134
Stevens, Judith (Sargent) [Mrs. John] (1751-1820). See Murray, Judith (Sargent) [Mrs. John] Stevens [Mrs. John] (1751-1820)
Stevens, Kate (1852-1941). See Bates, Kate (Stevens) [Mrs. Edward Wingard] Bingham [Mrs. James H. S.] (1852-1941)
Stevens, Lillian Marion Norton (Ames) [Mrs. Michael T.] (1844-1914), 4,243, 14,017
Stevens Linen Works, 7,122
Stevens, Louise Frances (1885-1956). See Bryant, Louise Frances (Stevens) (1885-1956)
Stevens, Lucy Cornelia, 9,316
Stevens, Margaret. See Browne, Margaret (Stevens)
Stevens, Margaret [Mrs.] (1894-), 8,518
Stevens, Margaret Hazard [Mrs. Isaac Ingalls], 14,454
Stevens, Margaret (Nelson) [Mrs. Lawrence "Lon" Vest] (1859-1929), **10,051**
Stevens, Margaret Talbot (1892-1955), **2,591**
Stevens, Marie (1836?-1921). See Howland, Marie (Stevens) [Mrs. Lyman] Case [Mrs. Edward] (1836?-1921)
Stevens, Martha B., 12,242
Stevens, Mary [Miss], **4,882**
Stevens, Mary Ann Elizabeth, **15,739**
Stevens, Matilda Jane Harden [Mrs.], 14,892
Stevens, Melvin James, 11,582
Stevens, Nancy Jane (1846-?), **4,840**
Stevens, Nancy Jane Fletcher [Mrs. Thomas Frank] Morton [Mrs. George W.] (1845-1912), 10,496
Stevens, Risë (1913-), **6,097**, **7,303**
Stevens, Sarah, 12,051
Stevens, Sarah Jane (Christie) (1844-1919), 8,995
Stevens Sophie. See Page, Sophie Stevens [Mrs. Stephen] Hitchcock [Mrs. William]
Stevens, Thaddeus, 2,557, 16,881
Stevens, Thelma (1902-), 13,176
Stevens, Thomas Wood (1880-1942), 225
Stevens, Williamina "Mina" Paton (1857-1911). See Fleming, Williamina "Mina" Paton (Stevens) [Mrs. James Orr] (1857-1911)
Stevens, Willie Carpenter, 11,190
Stevenson, Adlai Ewing, 4,483
Stevenson, Adlai Ewing, I (1835-1914), 4,370, 4,375
Stevenson, Adlai Ewing, II (1900-1965), 3,257, 4,370, 5,511, 6,765, 9,239, 11,827
Stevenson, Alice (Barnett) [Mrs. George Roy], **1,195**
Stevenson, Candace Thurber (1883-1968), **7,304**
Stevenson, Edward, 16,905
Stevenson, Eleanor, 14,360
Stevenson, Elizabeth (1879-). See Ives, Elizabeth (Stevenson) [Mrs. Ernest] (1879-)

Stevenson, Elizabeth Cleghorn (1810-65). *See* Gaskell, Elizabeth Cleghorn (Stevenson) (1810-65)
Stevenson, Elizabeth Jane DuFresne [Mrs. Edward] (1838-1906), 16,905
Stevenson, Ellen Borden, 11,827
Stevenson, Emily Electra (Williams) [Mrs. Edward] (1841-1918), **16,832**
Stevenson Family (IL), **4,375**
Stevenson Family (UT), 16,905
Stevenson, Fanny Matilda (Van De Grift) [Mrs. Robert Louis] (1840-1914), 1,167
Stevenson, Helen Louise (Davis) [Mrs. Lewis Green], 4,370
Stevenson, Janet [Mrs. Philip] (1913-), **14,455**
Stevenson, Julia (1879-1958). *See* Hardin, Julia (Stevenson) (1879-1958)
Stevenson, Letitia (Green) [Mrs. Adlai Ewing] (1843-1913), 4,370, 4,375
Stevenson, Margaret, 2,188
Stevenson, Margaret Isabella Balfour (1829-97), 1,167
Stevenson, Matilda "Tilly" Coxe (Evans) [Mrs. James] (1849-1915), **818**, 2,722, 2,837, **2,843**, 9,437, 15,004
Stevenson, Nancy Anderson [Mrs. Adlai Ewing, III], 11,827
Stevenson, Philip, 14,455
Stevenson, Robert Louis (1850-94), 567, 824, 1,167, 1,579
Stevenson, Robert Louis (1850-94), Family, **1,167**
Stevenson, Sarah Ann Hackett (1841-1909), 3,861, 3,862
Stevenson, Sarah Yorke (1847-1921), 15,116
Stevensons, The: Louis and Fanny (book), 4,995
Steward, Maude Trotter, 3,305
Steward, Sam M., **819**
Stewardesses (air lines). *See* Air lines, flight attendants
Stewards, 12,574
Stewart, A. E., 14,473
Stewart, Addie Osborn [Mrs. Carry E.], 10,377
Stewart, Agnes. *See* Warner, Agnes Stewart [Mrs. Mason]
Stewart, Agnes (1832-1905). *See* Warner, Agnes (Stewart) [Mrs. Thomas] (1832-1905)
Stewart, Alexander, 4,438
Stewart, Alice. *See* Hill, Alice (Stewart) [Mrs. Francis B.]
Stewart, Amanda Rhoda (Shelton), 5,027
Stewart, Amelia. *See* Knight, Amelia (Stewart) [Mrs. Joel]
Stewart, Anita, 11,327
Stewart, Annalee, 8,149
Stewart, Archibald, 10,719
Stewart, Charles A., 10,377
Stewart, Cora (Wilson) (1876-?), **5,325**
Stewart, David, 14,304
Stewart, Delia Tudor (?-1898). *See* Parnell, Delia Tudor (Stewart) (?-1898)
Stewart, Eliza Seelye [Mrs. David] (1841-1911), **14,304**
Stewart, Elizabeth, 17,884
Stewart, Elizabeth Young (1822-1914). *See* Warner, Elizabeth Young (Stewart) (1822-1914)
Stewart, Ella (Seass) (1871-?), **6,536**
Stewart, Emily Smith (1895-1973), 16,911
Stewart, Eunice Polly (1860-1942). *See* Harris, Eunice Polly (Stewart) [Mrs. Dennison Emer] (1860-1942)
Stewart Family (IL, IA, OH), **4,438**
Stewart Family (MT), **10,377**
Stewart, Fannie Aylworth [Mrs. Alexander] (1857-?), 4,438
Stewart, Florence, 12,536
Stewart, Frances Margaret (1842-?). *See* Witte, Frances Margaret (Stewart) [Mrs. Richard] (1842-?)
Stewart, Francis E., **13,584**
Stewart, George R., 730
Stewart, Harriet (1822-1907). *See* Judd, Harriet (Stewart) (1822-1907)
Stewart, Helen. *See* Love, Helen Stewart
Stewart, Helen Augusta (1849-1935), **10,828**
Stewart, Helen Jane Wiser [Mrs. Archibald] (1854-1926), **10,719**

Stewart, Helen Marnie (1835-73). *See* Love, Helen Marnie (Stewart) [Mrs. David S.] (1835-73)
Stewart, Helen West (1854-1929). *See* Ridgely, Helen West (Stewart) [Mrs. John] (1854-1929)
Stewart, I. P., **16,480**
Stewart, Isaac N. (1838-1915), **17,725**
Stewart, Isabel Maitland (1878-1963), 2,309, 5,735, 6,141, **11,918**, 12,074
Stewart, Isabella (1840-1924). *See* Gardner, Isabella (Stewart) [Mrs. John Lowell] (1840-1924)
Stewart, Jack, 169
Stewart, Jessie Hills [Mrs.] (1887-1972), **14,305**
Stewart, John, 14,282
Stewart, Julia Ann Wadsworth [Mrs.] (1854-1933), 16,480
Stewart, L. Josephine (Moulton) [Mrs. John] (1834-?), 5,805
Stewart, Lilian. *See* Burt, Lilian (Stewart) [Mrs. Reynolds J.]
Stewart, Lou Stocking, **10,265**
Stewart, Louise (Shoemaker) [Mrs. Jack] (1915-), 169
Stewart, Lucy Tilden (1873-1940), **4,156**
Stewart, Margaret, 7,109
Stewart, Maria W. [Mrs.] (1803-79), 3,297
Stewart, Mary C. [Miss], 3,932
Stewart, Mary E. (1841-1931), **17,725**
Stewart, Mrs. Archibald, 12,070
Stewart, Mrs. Damon, 4,156
Stewart, Mrs. Francis B., **13,137**
Stewart, Mrs. Paul A., **10,378**
Stewart, Ramona (1922-), **6,098**
Stewart, Rebecca Evans [Mrs.], **16,481**
Stewart, Sarah A., 11,547
Stewart, Teresa. *See* Wilson, Teresa (Stewart)
Stewart, Victoria E. *See* Kimball, Victoria E. (Stewart)
Sthamm, Frances. *See* Fritz, Frances (Sthamm) [Mrs. Philip]
Stickney, Dorothy, 13,662
Stickney Family, 7,445
Stickney Family (ND), **13,662**
Stickney, Frank L., 2,395
Stickney, Lucy Waters (1843-?), **7,444**
Stickney, Matthew Adams, 7,445
Stickney, Molly, **7,445**
Stickney, Prudence, 5,123
Stickney, Victor Hugo, 13,662
Stiefvator, Anne Calwell, **10,379**
Stieglitz, Alfred, 425, 12,405, 12,821
Stier, Rosalie Eugenia. *See* Calvert, Rosalie Eugenia (Stier)
Stiles, Eliza Anne Mackay, 3,567
Stiles, Lydia (1806-87). *See* Foster, Lydia (Stiles) [Mrs. Alfred Dwight] (1806-87)
Stiles, Mary Anne (Mackay), 3,567
Stiles, Maryanne [Mrs. B. E.], **3,581**
Stiles, Mrs. Baxter B., 1,767
Stiles, Nestor L. (1884-1960), **4,707**
"Still Waters" (story), 5,085
Stillman, Bessie G., 1,863
Stillman, Clara F., 1,863
Stillman College (AL), 94
deans, 96
faculty, 97
Stillman, Elizabeth Pamela Goodrich [Mrs. Charles] (1828-1910), 1,863
Stillman Family (CT), **1,863**
Stillman, Isabel G. (?-1894), 1,863
Stillman, Mary Emma (1874-1950). *See* Harkness, Mary Emma (Stillman) [Mrs. Edward Stephen] (1874-1950)
Stillman, Mildred Whitney [Mrs. Ernest G.] (1890-1950), **6,909**
Stillwater High School (MN), 9,076
Stillwell-Kuesel, Mary H., **15,095**
Stillwell, Laura Jean (Libbey) [Mrs. Van Mater] (1862-1924), **11,038**, 12,546
Stillwell, Lizzie C. (1860-1946). *See* Saunders, Lizzie C. (Stillwell) (1860-1946)
Stilman, Janis Carter, 13,890
Stimmenhefte, 7,218
Stimson, Alice W. (Barlett) [Mrs. Henry Albert] 12,318

Stimson, Eleanor. *See* Brooks, Eleanor (Stimson) [Mrs. Van Wyck]
Stimson, Harry, 6,800
Stimson, Henry Albert (1842-1936), **12,318**
Stimson, Henry L., 13,015
Stimson, John Ward, 12,318
Stimson, Julia Catherine (1881-1948), 6,122, 6,141, 12,351
Stimson, Mabel W. [Mrs. Henry L.], 2,650
Stimson, Mrs. Henry C., 12,121
Stimson, Philip Moen (1888-1971), **12,142**
Stingley, Jane C. [Mrs.], 15,574
Stinson, Katherine, 11,831
Stinson, Margaret E. Dayton [Mrs. Jackson L.] (1833-1912), 6,334
Stirling, Elizabeth, 9,274
Stirling, Florence Violet (Miles) [Mrs. James Y.] (1880-), **16,833**
Stirling, Marion I., 2,863
Stites Family (GA), **3,594**
Stitt, Agnes, 15,626
Stitt, Louise, 2,504, 6,766
Stivers, Louise, 1,573
Stock and stock-breeding, 647, 7,680, 14,554, 16,449, 16,450
Stock-exchange, 4,867
Stock, Leo F., 2,411
Stock, Lina Selma (1876-1967). *See* Nestler, Lina Selma (Stock) [Mrs. Friedrich Herman] (1876-1967)
Stockard, Henry Jerome, **13,340**
Stockbridge, Fanny E. (Montague), 14,607
Stockbridge Indians, 7,511
Stockdale, Melissa, 4,369
Stocker, Clara (?-1973), **8,443**, 9,073
Stocker, Stella Prince [Mrs.] (1858-1925), 8,443, **8,444**
Stockgrowers Association, 17,926
Stockheim, Mrs., 6,918
Stockhum, Alice B., 6,626
Stocking, Lucy [Mrs.], 10,265, **10,380**
Stockman, Dora Hall [Mrs.] (1872-?), **8,171**
Stockman, Mrs. Ralph, 12,405
Stockton, Anise Morris (1873-1964). *See* Terhune, Anise Morris (Stockton) [Mrs. Albert Payson] (1873-1964)
Stockton, Annis Boudinot [Mrs. Richard] (1736-?), **11,173**, 14,753
Stockton, Caroline, 11,173
Stockton, Dr., 6,509
Stockton Family (MS), 9,613
Stockton High School (CA), 1,613, 1,632, 1,648
Stockton High School (CA), Parent-Teacher Association, **1,615**
Stockton, Julia (1759-1848). *See* Rush, Julia (Stockton) [Mrs. Benjamin] (1859-1848)
Stockton, Mary (?-1846), 15,084
Stockton Poetry Society (CA), **1,641**
Stockton Presbyterian church (CA), 1,615
Stockton Record (CA), 1,617, **1,618**, 1,626
Stockton, Richard, 11,173
Stockton Tennis Club (CA), **1,616**
Stockton Youth Center (CA), 1,615
Stockwell, Ann Maria (1840-1904). *See* Green, Ann Maria (Stockwell) [Mrs. George] (1840-1904)
Stockwell, Eunice J. [Miss], **9,741**
Stockwell, Madelon Louisa (1845-1924), **7,940**
Stockwell, Maud C., 9,291, 9,467
Stoddard, Almira (Knight) [Mrs. Sylvester V.] (1827-1912). *See* Hanscom, Almira (Knight) [Mrs. Sylvester V.] Stoddard [Mrs. George] (1827-1912)
Stoddard, Anne, 14,421
Stoddard, Bernice "Abie" [Mrs. Lynn], **8,260**
Stoddard, Bertha (1850-?). *See* Whitney, Bertha (Stoddard) [Mrs. Henry] (1850-?)
Stoddard, Caroline, 8,164
Stoddard, Charles H., 10,703
Stoddard, Charles Warren, **820**, 1,333
Stoddard, Charlotte Joy, 11,039
Stoddard, Cora Frances (1872-1936), 4,243, 14,017
Stoddard, Druscilla Chapman (Allen) [Mrs. Ira Joy] (1821-1913), 10,942, 11,039, 11,056
Stoddard, Elizabeth Drew (Barstow) [Mrs. Richard

Henry] (1823-1902), **5,962**, 5,973, 7,682, 17,009, 17,010
Stoddard Family, **11,039**
Stoddard Family, 11,719
Stoddard, Hannah Gould (Johnson), **11,719**
Stoddard, Ira Joy, 10,942, 11,039, 11,056
Stoddard, Joseph Marshall, 2,183
Stoddard, Julia E. Sanford [Mrs. Goodwin], 11,719
Stoddard, Lynn, 8,260
Stoddard, Mary, 10,664
Stoddard, Mary Lavinia [Mrs. John], 3,511
Stoddard, Nancy Cooley, **12,649**
Stoddard, Richard Henry (1825-1903), **7,682**
Stoddard, Sanford, 11,719
Stoddard, Solomon (1643-1729), 7,676
Stoddard, Sylvester V., 16,688
Stoddert, Benjamin, 2,592
Stoddert, Rebecca (Lowndes) [Mrs. Benjamin] (?-ca. 1800), **2,592**
Stodola, Anna [Mrs. Joseph] (1856-1952). *See* Drahosh, Anna [Mrs. Joseph] Stodola [Mrs. Joseph] (1856-1952)
Stodola, Joseph (?-1887), 8,467
Stoermer, Grace S., 1,226
Stogdill, Emily L. (1893-1976), **13,746**
Stokely, France Pope (?-1868). *See* Wilson, Frances Pope (Stokely) [Mrs. Peter] (?-1868)
Stokely, Mountford Samuel, 4,855
Stoker, Catherine (1829-82). *See* Hulet, Catherine (Stoker) [Mrs. Sylvanus Cyrus] (1829-82)
Stoker, Charlotte. *See* Binckley, Charlotte Stoker
Stokes, Anson Phelps (1838-1913), 2,123, 10,974, 11,040
Stokes, Blanche. *See* Eggleston, Blanche (Stokes) [Mrs. William Green]
Stokes, Caroline Phelps (1854-1909), **6,910**
Stokes, Charles E., 9,916
Stokes, Helen Louisa Phelps [Mrs. Anson Phelps] (1846-?), 10,974, **11,040**
Stokes, James, 6,910
Stokes, James Graham Phelps, 12,705
Stokes, Meary, 15,542
Stokes, Montfort, **13,585**
Stokes, Olivia Egleston Phelps (1847-1927), **6,910**
Stokes, Rose Pastor. [Mrs. James Graham] Phelps [Mrs. Jerome I.] Romaine (1879-1933), **12,705**
Stokes, Sallie M., **15,096**
Stokowska, Evangeline. [Mrs. Leopold] Stokowski, 12,066
Stokowska, Olga Samaroff (1882-1948), 17,197
Stokowski, Leopold (1882-), 2,020, 2,123, 12,013
Stolberg, Mildred, 324
Stolen, Lena Kjellesvig [Mrs. Knut] (1869-1937), **8,789**
Stolt, Edna B., 17,901
Stolte, Florence. *See* Montz, Florence (Stolte) [Mrs. C. R.]
Stoltz, Mary Adelaide (Rowell) (1853-1932), 2,002
Stolz, Mary Slattery (1920-), 8,531
Stoltzfus, Amanda (?-1930), 16,132
Stone, Abraham (1890-1959), **6,232**, 7,289
Stone, Alice Homan Osborne (1865-1952), **7,446**
Stone, Amelia (1833-1926). *See* Quinton, Amelia (Stone) (1833-1926)
Stone, Benjamin, 7,014
Stone, Benjamin, 11,419
Stone, Callie M. [Miss], **14,775**
Stone Came Rolling, A (book), 12,992
Stone, Carl L. (1874-1920), Family (MN), **9,395**
Stone, Clara Louise (1849-1914). *See* Hay, Clara Louise (Stone) [Mrs. John] (1849-1914)
Stone, David, **13,586**
Stone, Deborah (Clark) [Mrs. Josiah, Sr.] Fairbank [Mrs. Benjamin], 7,014
Stone, Doris Zemurray [Mrs. Roger T.], 6,323
Stone, E. Elnora [Mrs.], 9,395
Stone, Ellen Maria [Miss] (1846-1927), 2,304
Stone Family, 12,635
Stone Family (MA), 7,014
Stone Family (MS), **9,780**
Stone, Florence (Crosby) [Mrs. Henry], 9,025
Stone, Grace (Zaring) (1896-), **6,099**
Stone, Hannah (Mayer) [Mrs. Abraham] (1894-1941), 6,223, **6,232**, 6,564, 7,289

Stone, Harriett Mulford (1844-1924). *See* Lothrop, Harriett Mulford (Stone) (1844-1924)
Stone, Idella Purnell [Mrs. Remington] (1901-), 1,081, 16,165, **16,169**
Stone, Ikey (pseudonym). *See* Stone, Idella Purnell [Mrs. Remington] (1901-)
Stone, J. M., 9,658
Stone, Jean [Mrs. Irving], 11,828
Stone, John A., 590
Stone, Lucinda (Hinsdale) [Mrs. James Andrus Blinn] (1814-1900), 7,941, 8,240
Stone, Lucy. [Mrs. Henry] Blackwell (1818-93), 530, 1,436, 1,950, 2,196, 2,206, 2,209, 2,315, 2,346, 2,406, 2,542, 2,588, 4,244, 4,304, 4,708, 5,334, **5,963**, 6,009, 6,373, 6,412, 6,413, 6,469, 6,534, 6,589, 6,659, 6,741, 6,758, 6,762, 6,859, 6,870, **6,911**, 6,961, 6,971, 6,975, **7,022**, 7,044, 7,222, 7,268, 7,274, 7,294, 7,390, 7,477, 7,629, 9,060, 9,920, 11,185, 11,605, 12,172, 12,819, 13,204, 14,062, 15,291, 15,312, 15,864, 17,226, 17,411, 17,852, 18,013
Stone, Mabel (1886-). *See* Cartwright, Mabel (Stone) [Mrs. Paul] (1886-)
Stone, Mary, 7,293
Stone, Mary, 4,313
Stone, Mary Allen [Mrs. Benjamin], 11,419
Stone, Mary Gillen, 9,709
Stone, Mary Kent [Mrs. John Seely], 12,028
Stone-masons, 10,670
Stone, May, 5,254
Stone Mountain Confederate Memorial (GA), 17,102
Stone Mountain Confederate Memorial Association (GA), 3,212, 3,345
Stone Mountain Memorial Association (GA), Children's Founders Roll, 3,437
Stone, Myra M. [Mrs. William S.], **11,919**
Stone, Olive Matthews (1897-1977), 1,654, **13,138**, 13,176
Stone, Phoebe Cope [Mrs. John], 8,900
Stone, Rachel, 2,196
Stone, Remington, 16,169
Stone, Sarah [Mrs.], **5,891**
Stone, Sarah (Dashiell) [Mrs. David], 13,586
Stone, Valeria (Goodenow), 5,676
Stone, William B., 6,911
Stoneham, Lois, 16,176
Stoneman's Raid (1865), 13,103, 13,519, 13,528
Stoner, Benjamin, 9,245
Stoner, Cornelia, 8,288
Stoner Family, 9,245
Stoner Family (MI), **8,288**
Stones (book), 5,694
Stones, E. Margaret (1920-), 10,151
Stonewall Jackson Manual Training and Industrial School (NC), 13,383
Stoney, Sarah Barnwell (?-1879), **15,740**
Stoots, Carol Halsey (Cook) [Mrs. William D.], 11,784
Stopes, Marie Carmichael (1841-1929), **1,529**
Stopper, Ruth, 11,349
Storer, Maria (Longworth) [Mrs. George Ward] Nichols [Mrs. Bellamy, Jr.] (1849-1932), 5,421, 13,837, 13,856
Storer, Ruth (Risdon) [Mrs. Tracy Irwin] (1888-), 821
Storer, Tracy Irwin, **821**
Stores, retail, 1,419, 1,837, 7,429, **7,437**, 14,881, 16,101, **16,459**
Storey, Margaret (1833-1915), 16,676
Storm Against the Wall (book), 10,159
Storm, Marian (1892?-1975), **7,305**
Storm, Mrs. Wash, Jr., 3,725
Storm, Willie G. [Mrs. A. F.] (ca. 1870-1965), **5,443**
Storms, Helen [Miss], 10,404
Storms, L. P., 11,554
Storrow, Helen Osborne, 6,759
Storrs, George (1796-1879), **12,638**
Storrs, Lucinda [Mrs. George], 12,638
Story, Ala (1907-72), **2,820**
Story, Caroline B. *See* Robertson, Caroline B. (Story) [Mrs. George M.]
Story, Charles R., 878
Story, Ellen Trent [Mrs. Nelson] (1846-?), **10,381**

Story, Emelyn (Eldridge) [Mrs. William Wetmore] (1821-94), **16,170**
Story, Emma Hayden (Eames) [Mrs. Julian] (1865-1952). *See* Eames, Emma Hayden. [Mrs. Julian] Story. [Mrs. Emilio] de Gogorza (1865-1952)
Story, Enoch, 2,392
"Story in the History of My Community, A" (essay), 4,908
Story, Joseph, 16,171
Story, Julian, 6,549
Story, Mary, 2,392
Story, Nelson, 10,381
Story of a Mission Garden, The (book), 991
Story of an Epoch-Making Movement, The (book), 6,791
Story of Cedar Rapids, The (book), 5,015
Story of Coal and Iron in Alabama, The (book), 15,979
Story of Dante's Divine Comedy, The (book), 7,082
Story of East Africa, The (book), 7,235
Story of Isabel Bevier, The (book), 4,380
Story of Lighthouses, The (book), 5,998
Story of Little Jakey (book), 12,795
"Story of Mary York Cozens, The," 1,790
"Story of My Grandfather, The" (essay), 4,908
"Story of My Grandmother, The" (essay), 4,908
Story of My Life, The (book), 4,233
Story of My Life, The (book), 2,108
Story of Opal, The (book), 14,468
Story of Psychoanalysis, The (book), 6,019
"Story of Shawneetown," 4,315
"Story of Susan O. Hall, The" (story), 9,949
Story, Sarah Waldo (Wetmore) [Mrs. Joseph], **16,171**
Story Teller's Magazine (periodical), 13,366
Story, Thomas Waldo, 16,170
Story, William Cumming (1851-?), **12,639**
Story, William Wetmore, 16,170, 16,171
Storytellers, **5,250**
Storyville (New Orleans, LA), 5,531
Stote, Florence (Marshall) [Mrs. William H. R.] (1869-1964), **1,688**
Stott, Angela Juanita (1919-). *See* Brennan, Angela Juanita (Stott) [Mrs. Gerton] Colling [Mrs. James] Murrary [Mrs. James Arthur] Connery [Mrs. Don] (1919-)
Stott, Frank E., 13,669
Stott, Mary Ellen (Schenecker) [Mrs. Frank E.], 13,669
Stough, A. M. (ca. 1846-?), **14,792**
Stoughton, A. Ella (1857-1944). *See* Stearns, A. Ella Stoughton [Mrs. Doran H.] (1857-1944)
Stoughton, Edward Wallace, 6,912
Stoughton, Edwin Wallace, 12,640
Stoughton, General, 2,635
Stoughton, Louise (1851-86), **6,912**
Stoughton, Mary [Mrs. Edwin Wallace], **12,640**
Stoughton, Samuel (1815-91), 7,683
Stoughton, Sarah Josephine (1848-71), **7,683**
Stout, Anna, 6,310
Stout, George, 6,185
Stout, Ira, 9,955
Stout, Sarah Elizabeth Smith [Mrs. Ira], 9,955
Stoutenburg, Adrien, 822
Stovall, Rosemary McLain, **9,742**
Stovall, Thelma Dewy [Mrs. Lonnie R.] (1919-), **5,388**, 5,394
Stover, Augusta Maria (Noyes) (1817-71), 7,677
Stover, Calista Meader [Mrs. Joseph], **1,989**
Stover, Joseph, 1,989
Stover, Maria Calista, 1,989
Stow, Catharine [Mrs. Uzziel H.], 4,613
Stow, Marietta Lucy [Mrs. J. W.] (ca. 1830-90), **1,091**
Stow, Viola A. *See* Dufour, Viola A. (Stow) [Mrs. Francis R.]
Stowe, Calvin Ellis, 1,426, 6,392
Stowe, Eliza Tyler (1836-?), 6,392
Stowe Family, **6,392**
Stowe, Harriet Elizabeth (Beecher) [Mrs. Calvin Ellis] (1811-96), 1,087, 1,224, 1,426, 1,896, 1,948, 1,950, 1,951, **1,953**, 1,954, 1,963, **2,593**, 2,614, **2,917**, 2,942, 3,298, 3,889, 3,927, 4,226, 4,695, 5,694, 5,939, **5,964**, 6,329, 6,392, 6,712, **6,913**,

7,171, 7,185, 7,274, 7,276, 8,004, 8,526, 11,821, 12,498, **13,587**, 14,062, 15,355, 17,053
Stowe, Harriet Beecher II (1836-?), 6,392
Stowe, Lyman Beecher, 6,392
Stowe, Susan (Munroe), 6,392
Stowell, Emma Augusta (1847-1945). *See* Fox, Emma Augusta (Stowell) (1847-1945)
Stoyomi Ranch (CA), 480
Strachey, Esther Murphy. *See* Arthur, Esther Murphy (Strachey) [Mrs. Chester Alan III]
Strachey, Ray, 14,745
Strahan, Willetta [Miss], 5,086
Straight, Beatrice, 11,459
Straight, Dorothy Payne (Whitney) [Mrs. Willard D.], 11,521, 11,720
Straight, Emma, 11,720
Straight, Willard D. (1880-1918), **11,720**
Strait, Richard Lee, 3,776
Strakosch, Maurice, 12,322
Stranahan, Effie. *See* Santino, Effie (Stranahan) [Mrs. Gustav]
Strand, Jacob Hendrik, 4,319
Strand, Mary. *See* Andreen, Mary (Strand) [Mrs. Gustav Albert]
Strandsness, Elisabeth (1896-), **8,715, 8,716**
Strang Family (IA), 4,842
Strang, Gracie [Miss], 5,644
Strang, James J., 4,209
Strange, Agatha Jane (Rochester) (1832-96), 5,279
Strange Family (KY), **5,279**
Strange Fruit (book), 2,879
Strange Fruit (drama), 3,468
"Strange Fruit" (song), 5,530
"Strange Silence of a Woman" (story), 5,296
Strange, Sister M. Elizabeth, 15,232
Strange Woman, The (drama), 15,612
Stranger, Margaret A., **6,094**
Stranger's Friend Society (HI), 3,640
Stras, Marie, 8,462
Strategy, 5,750
Stratford Hall: The Great House of the Lees (book), 2,443
Stratford, John Ethron, 12,682
Stratosphere, 2,523
Stratton, Ann, 823
Stratton, Cornelia (1885-1972). *See* Parker, Cornelia (Stratton) [Mrs. Carleton Hubbell] (1885-1972)
Stratton, Dorothy, 2,710, 5,719
Stratton Family (CA), 709
Stratton, Frederick Smith (1859-1915), **823**
Stratton, Gene (1863-1924). *See* (Stratton)-Porter, Gene [Mrs. Charles Darwin] (1863-1924)
Stratton, James T., 709
Stratton, Jeanne. *See* Good, Jeanne (Stratton)
Stratton, Mary Chase (Perry) [Mrs. William B.] (1867-1961), 2,796, **2,821**
Stratton, Pauline H. (1814-87), **10,052**
(Stratton)-Porter, Gene [Mrs. Charles Darwin] (1863-1924), 4,226, 4,482
Straus, Nathan, 933
Strauss, Anna Lord (1899-), **6,914**, 11,886, **11,920**
Strauss, Mrs., 12,128
Straw, Amos Gale (1864-1926), 14,763
Straw industries, 7,587
Straw, Zatae Longsdorff [Mrs. Amos Gale] (1866-1955), **14,763**
Strawberries, varieties, 11,757
Strawberry Girl (book), 2,938, 4,306, 11,368, 13,252
Strawbridge Family (IA), **4,952**
Strawbridge Family (PA), **14,856**
Strawbridge, Frank, 4,952
Strawbridge, Jesse K., 4,952
Strawbridge, Josie M. *See* Irish, Josie M. (Strawbridge) [Mrs. Gilbert]
Strawbridge, Susan Adda, 4,952
Strawn, Dorothy R., 17,352
Strayer committee (NY), 11,895
Strayer, Martha [Mrs.], 11,493, **18,012**
Strayhorn, Mary (?-1934). *See* Berry, Mary (Strayhorn) [Mrs. John] (?-1934)
Streator, Isaac, 16,958
Street, Jennetta A. *See* Jeffrey, Jenetta A. (Street) [Mrs. Edward C.]
Street-lighting, 12,266

Street-railroads, 9,467
Street, Rebecca (Wilkinson) (1780-1833), **13,139**
Street, Richard, **13,588**
Street, Sally Kerr, 1,347
Street theater, 12,367
Streeter, Amelia L. Dunwell [Mrs. Benjamin H.], **12,199**
Streeter, Benjamin H. (1826-69), 12,199
Streeter, Bess (1881-1954). *See* Aldrich, Bess (Streeter) [Mrs. Charles S.] (1881-1954)
Streeter, Mary, 11,440
Streeter, Ruth Cheney [Mrs.], 843, 2,867
Streeter, William, 11,440
Streets, maintenance and repair, 12,266
Streidl, Diane, 8,261
Streidl, Jack, **8,261**
Streidl, Mrs. Jack, **8,261**
Stribling, Mary Cary Ambler [Mrs. Robert M.], **17,101**
Stribling, Robert M., 17,101
Stribling, T. S., 11,966
Strickland, Belle (1855-?), 9,574, **9,743**
Strickland, Charity, **13,589**
Strickland, Donna (1926-). *See* Rodden, Donna (Strickland) (1926-)
Strickland, Edward F., 5,336, **6,915**
Strickland, Lillian E., **3,582**
Strickland, Mabel, 8,297
Strickland, Teresa Hammond, **15,741**
Strickle, Elizabeth A., 13,910
Strickler, Florence Dunlop, 1,348
Strickler, Mary Ranson, 9,323
Strike—A Novel of Gastonia (book), 17,734
"Strike the Cymbal" (poem), 4,489
Strikebreakers, Afro-American, 17,232
Strikes and lockouts, 1,357, 1,656, 4,080, 5,302, 5,704, 6,427, 6,486, 6,565, 6,795, 6,802, 8,058, **8,088**, 8,089, 8,113, 8,120, 8,123, 8,144, 10,310, 11,772, 11,905, 11,927, 12,607, 14,446, 14,504, 15,987, 15,992, 15,995, 16,003, 16,008, 16,009, 17,343. *See also* Arbitration, industrial; Sitdown strikes
  actors, 2,284
  agricultural laborers, 842, 1,577
  air pilots, 6,315
  clothing workers, 1,577, 4,173, 6,315, 9,493
  coal miners, 1,731, 6,314, 13,273, **17,453**
  legal aspects, 15,755
  metal-workers, 8,099
  miners, 6,315, 8,070, 8,144
  railroad employees, 4,173, 11,527
  railroads, 3,955
  restaurants, lunchrooms, etc., 12,705
  silk industry, 12,705
  steel industry, 8,144
  teachers, 8,059, 8,129, 8,147, 9,467, 15,332
  telephone, 4,173
  textile workers, 7,063, 7,114, 17,734
  transport workers, 9,467
Strikes and lockouts, Afro-American, 15,595
Stringer, Dorothy O., 14,618
Stringer, Mrs. E. C., 9,454
Stringfield, Mary. *See* Ray, Mary (Stringfield) [Mrs. J. W.]
Stringfield, William Williams, **13,590**
Strip-tease, 9,934
Striving To Make It My Home: The Story of Americans from Africa (book), 6,095
Strobel, Abby Ann, 1,084
Strobel, Emma Cornelia (Clark) [Mrs. William D.] (ca. 1806-?), **1,084**
Strobel Family (SC), **15,420**
Strobel, Mary E., 1,084
Strobel, William D., 1,084
Strode, Eva. *See* Melvin, Eva (Strode)
Strode, Thomas P., 10,336
Strohm, Olivia B., 6,812
"Strolling Along," 5,763
Stron, Susan, 10,651
Strong, Alan Hartwell, **11,041**
Strong, Anna [Mrs. J. F. A.], 145
Strong, Anna Louise (1885-). *See* Shubin, Anna Louise (Strong) [Mrs. Joel] (1885-)
Strong, Anne Harvey (186?-1925), 6,238

Strong, Beulah, 7,158
Strong, Caroline, 3,829
Strong, Caroline, **14,793**
Strong, Caroline Hoskins (Park) [Mrs. Charles K. W.], 12,211
Strong, Charles Lyman, 1,492
Strong, Charles S., 14,324
Strong, Cora, 3,583
Strong, Eleanor (Painter), **13,959**
Strong, Elizabeth, 7,135
Strong, Elizabeth, 824
Strong, Ellen R., 12,261
Strong, Emily Seymour (?-1944), 3,969, 3,970
Strong Family (NY), 12,300
Strong, Harriet Williams (Russell) [Mrs. Charles Lyman] (1844-1926), **1,492**
Strong, Isobel (Osbourne) [Mrs. Joseph Dwight] (1858-1953). *See* Field, Isobel (Osbourne) [Mrs. Joseph Dwight] Strong [Mrs. Edward Salisbury] (1858-1953)
Strong, J. F. A. (1859-1929), **145**
Strong, Jenny (slave, NY), 11,440
Strong, John F. A., 11,897
Strong, Joseph, 12,300
Strong, Joseph Dwight, 824, 1,167
Strong, Julia, 2,190
Strong, Julia Barnard [Mrs. Eben], 2,190
Strong, Kate W. [Miss] (1879-1977), **12,778**
Strong, Louisa Hall [Mrs. Paschal N.], **3,583**
Strong Man (book), 10,531
Strong, Martha Cochrane, 7,920
Strong, Mary Dix (1819-75). *See* Van Dyke, Mary Dix (Strong) [Mrs. John] (1819-75)
Strong Minded Women (book), 4,887
Strong, Nathan, 12,300
Strong, Nellie Rose. *See* Hubbell, Nellie Rose (Strong) [Mrs. Henry Salem]
Strong, Paschal N., 3,583
Strong, Rachel, 7,135
Strong, Ruth Tracy [Mrs. Sidney Dix] (1860-1903), **17,344**
Strong, Sarah. *See* Rose, Sarah (Strong)
Strong, Susan de Lancey Cullen (Van Rensselaer) [Mrs. Alan Hartwell] (1851-1931), 11,041
Strong, Temperance, 12,300
Strong, Wilda Claire (1890-1971). *See* Peck, Wilda Claire (Strong) (1890-1971)
Strother, Dora Dougherty, 30
Strother, William H., **13,591**
Stroud, Melissa Clawson, 14,542
Strout, Irwin Charles (1893-1954), **9,396**
Struck, Susan R., 34
Structural engineering, 9,804
Strudwick, Annie [Miss] (?-ca. 1870), **13,140**
Struggle for World Order (book), 6,512
Strunsky, Anna (1879-1964). *See* Walling, Anna (Strunsky) [Mrs. William English] (1879-1964)
Strunsky, Rose, 12,705
Stryker, Fannie Lou [Mrs.], 17,125
Stryker-Rodda, Harriet (1910-), **11,327**
Stuart, Alfred Ogden, 1,493
Stuart, Charles Macaulay (1853-1932), **4,208**
Stuart, Eleanor Calvert [Mrs. David], 2,443
Stuart, Emma R. Littlefield [Mrs. Charles Macaulay], 4,208
Stuart, Granville (1834-1918), 10,270, 10,382
Stuart, James Ewell Brown "Jeb", 2,635, 17,089
Stuart, John Todd, 4,363
Stuart, Josie A. Wanous [Mrs. Arthur] (1871-1936), **9,428**
Stuart, Leghton, 44
Stuart, Mary. *See* Abbott, Mary (Stuart) [Mrs. E. C. "Teddy Blue"]
Stuart, Mary Horton, **44**
Stuart, Mary M., **15,742**
Stuart, Mrs. John Todd, 4,363
Stuart, Nancy C., 10,382
Stuart, Ruth (McEnery) [Mrs. Alfred Ogden] (1849-1917), **1,493**, 4,631, 5,509, **5,526**
Stuart, Winifred (Bendel), **1,642**
Stuart's Hill (book), 5,023
Stub, Mrs. Valborg Hovind, 17,692

Stubblefield, Evie. *See* Posey, Evie (Stubblefield) [Mrs. H. A.].
Stubblefield, Jean, 3,751
Stubblefield, Mary, **13,141**
Stubborn Fool (book), 183
Student activities, **7,164, 10,222**
Student aid, 51, 1,848, 2,097, **4,031,** 5,469, 5,825, 6,051, **6,151,** 6,339, 7,577, 7,595, 7,801, 11,225, 11,561, 11,897, 13,626, 14,237, 15,296, 17,747
Student aid, to Afro-Americans, 3,280
Student counseling, 4,042
Student counselors, 1,779, **4,040,** 4,115, 4,150, **6,264, 7,545,** 8,043, 8,573, 13,071, 16,989
Student Dancer (book), 10,894
Student etiquette, **9,571**
Student financial aid. *See* Student aid
Student housing, 449, 4,394, **6,289,** 6,482, 7,879, 7,959, 8,615, 8,746, 9,936, 11,531, 12,924, 17,354
married veterans, **6,288**
Student loan funds, 2, 7, 8,485
Student movements, **11,847**
Student Non-Violent Coordinating Committee, 1,570, 14,453, 17,599, 17,600, 17,649, 17,691
Student nurses, **15,425**
Student Nurses' Association of Iowa, 5,000
Student Rights party (WI), 17,628
Student teachers, Afro-American, 10,745
Student unions, 8,616, **11,375,** 16,331, 16,382
Students, 1,263, 3,474, 5,588, **6,306,** 9,860, 11,440, 12,152, **12,368,** 12,925, 13,480, 13,541, 13,563, **13,603,** 14,847, **15,623, 15,643,** 15,662, **15,684, 17,886, 17,904**
health, 6,339, 6,482
political activity, 7,164, 10,214, **17,637**
recreation, 18, 10,024
religious life, 7,164
social life, 13,356
Students, Afro-American, 1,874, 5,209, 7,595
Students, Chinese, 17,315
Students Club (MN), 8,697
Students for a Democratic Society, 993, 10,020, 17,637
Students, foreign, 164, 2,285, 7,582, 8,150, 8,486
Students, interchange of, 8,481
"Students Look at Russia" (article), 2,936
Students, part-time, 6,482, 8,054
Students Review, 17,849
Students' societies, **18, 263, 268,** 578, **908, 925, 927, 1,164,** 1,543, **1,625,** 1,876, 2,106, 2,939, **3,124,** 3,191, 3,281, 3,293, **3,972, 4,213,** 4,219, **4,220,** 4,382, 4,595, 4,632, **4,886,** 4,960, **4,967, 5,014, 5,033,** 5,062, **5,064,** 5,068, **5,115,** 5,185, 5,188, 5,241, **5,416, 6,286,** 6,339, **6,480,** 7,164, **7,576,** 7,646, **7,707, 7,871, 7,961,** 8,043, **8,570, 8,598,** 8,599, 8,608, **8,624,** 8,648, 8,809, **8,813,** 9,936, 9,943, **10,214, 10,221,** 10,222, 10,486, **10,511, 10,604, 10,606,** 11,151, **11,384, 11,388, 11,721,** 11,752, 11,807, **12,099,** 12,745, 12,746, **12,916, 13,197, 13,199, 13,202,** 13,226, 13,227, **13,320,** 13,406, **14,029, 14,030, 14,034, 14,037, 14,038, 14,276,** 15,237, **15,238,** 15,239, **15,872, 17,004,** 17,233, 17,354, **17,449, 17,541, 17,573,** 17,628, **17,790,** 17,963
Students' societies, Baptist, **13,638, 13,647**
Students' wives. *See* College students, Wives
Studies, 8,733
Studies in Citizenship for Georgia Women (book), 3,217
"Studies towards the Life of 'A Business Woman,'" 6,500
Studley, Cordelia Adelaide (1855-87), 6,323, **6,327**
Studley, Ellen, 4,532
Study Club (Warrensburg, MO), 10,211
Study Club (Saratoga Springs, NY), 12,851
Study Club (Charleston, SC), **15,421**
Study Club, The (Niagara Falls, NY), 12,734
Study in English Metrics, A (book), 12,815
"Study in Ethics, A," 1,952
Study in Ethics, A (book), 6,602
Study of Birds, The (book), 4,785
Study of Child Nature, A (book), 4,211
Study of Social Work Education, **8,677**
"Study of the Notions 'Real' and 'Unreal', A" (ms), 2,539

Stuhlcreher, Mary A. (McEnery) (1905-74), **15,228**
Stuhler, Barbara, 9,231
Stull, Daniel, 9,975
Stull, Lydia J. [Mrs.], **2,594**
Stump, Kezia. *See* Jackson, Kezia (Stump) [Mrs. Richard I.]
Stump, Rachel (1806-30). *See* Forwood, Rachel (Stump) [Mrs. S.] (1806-30)
Stunt flying, 11,831
Sturdy Oak, The (book), 12,529
Sturges, Ellen W. Steele, 1,112
Sturges, Ethel (1866-1954). *See* Dummer, Ethel (Sturges) (1866-1954)
Sturges Family (IL), 6,544
Sturges Family (NY), 12,276
Sturges, Gertrude, 6,223
Sturges, Preston, 1,033
Sturges, Quila, 8,011
Sturgis, Dorothy, 11,967
Sturgis, Ellen (1812-48). *See* Hooper, Ellen (Sturgis) (1812-48)
Sturgis Family, 7,659
Sturgis Family (MT), **10,383**
Sturgis, Katharine Rosenbaum Guest Boucot (1903-), **14,927**
Sturgis, Lucy S., **6,916**
Sturgis, Margaret Castex (1885-1962), **14,928**
Sturgis, Mrs. Carroll W., 16,394
Sturgis, Rosanna, 10,383
Sturgis School (Shimonoseki, Japan), 5,088
Sturgis, William, 10,383
Sturtevant, Julia E., **3,584**
Sturvant Family (NH), **10,829**
Sturvant, Lucy Johnson [Mrs. Henry C.] (?-1919 or 1920), 10,829
Stutz, Geraldine, 12,086
Suagee, Dova L. [Mrs. Joel], 14,174
Suagee, Joel, 14,174
"Subjection of Women and The Enfranchisement of Women, The" (speech), 3,362
Suburban Civics and Equal Suffrage Association (IL). *See* League of Women Voters of Oak Park-River Forest (IL)
"Subway Scene" (painting), 2,736
Such a Night, In (book), 12,441
Such Sweet Compulsion (book), 2,663
Suckley, Catherine Rutsen, 12,305
Suckow, Ruth (1892-1960), **5,030**
Sudam, Mary R. C., 12,337
Sudan
    missionaries to, Lutheran, 8,858
    missionaries to, Reformed Church, **8,199**
Sudlow, Phoebe, 4,958
Sudsofloppen, 17,583
Sue (Native American, NC), 13,448
Suez Canal, crisis (1956), 4,480
Suffrage, 49, 110, 176, 200, 346, 349, 437, 441, 530, 540, 575, 589, 648, 658, 826, 860, 868, 870, 900, 1,034, 1,058, 1,153, 1,243, **1,255, 1,359, 1,360, 1,396,** 1,414, 1,424, **1,436,** 1,437, 1,451, 1,452, 1,473, **1,494,** 1,507, 1,544, 1,563, 1,618, 1,673, **1,759,** 2,036, **2,055, 2,063,** 2,075, 2,212, 2,292, 2,315, 2,399, 2,432, 2,451, 2,502, 2,528, 2,542, 2,562, 2,720, **2,860,** 2,942, 2,954, 3,158, 3,169, **3,240,** 3,362, 3,417, 3,820, **3,908,** 3,981, 4,143, 4,156, 4,163, **4,172,** 4,236, 4,244, 4,290, 4,431, 4,481, 4,623, 4,626, 4,677, 4,754, 4,763, **4,859,** 4,867, 4,887, 4,920, 5,302, 5,334, 5,356, 5,444, 5,514, 5,522, 5,569, 5,629, 5,753, 5,829, 5,846, 6,364, 6,366, 6,368, **6,372,** 6,373, 6,374, 6,379, 6,380, 6,382, 6,410, 6,412, 6,432, 6,433, 6,435, 6,442, 6,443, 6,455, 6,469, 6,477, 6,479, **6,524,** 6,530, 6,534, 6,546, 6,565, 6,629, 6,632, 6,638, **6,649,** 6,661, 6,664, 6,678, **6,681,** 6,685, 6,695, 6,706, 6,749, 6,758, 6,791, 6,804, 6,815, 6,825, 6,830, 6,835, **6,839,** 6,846, 6,853, 6,858, 6,894, 6,925, 6,944, 6,948, 6,953, 6,959, 6,960, **6,961,** 6,966, 6,968, 6,974, 6,980, 6,996, 7,078, 7,203, 7,204, 7,216, 7,220, 7,222, 7,237, 7,239, 7,294, **7,306,** 7,308, 7,545, 7,683, 7,692, 7,698, 7,731, 7,791, 7,808, 7,847, 7,946, 8,223, **8,266,** 8,362, 8,484, 8,493, 8,518, 8,925, 8,971, 9,001, 9,020, 9,035, 9,054, 9,061, 9,201, 9,263, 9,268, 9,276, 9,308, 9,327, 9,347, 9,427, 9,468, 9,734, 9,803,

9,821, 9,938, 9,957, 9,996, 10,025, 10,223, 10,325, 10,342, 10,345, 10,402, 10,448, 10,658, 10,667, 10,668, 10,727, 10,768, 11,123, 11,200, 11,213, 11,236, 11,261, 11,271, 11,279, 11,547, 11,616, 11,719, **11,793,** 11,853, 11,905, 11,920, 12,003, 12,406, 12,473, 12,505, 12,574, 12,625, 12,667, 12,704, 12,791, 12,811, 12,818, 12,986, 13,274, 13,318, 13,376, 13,459, 13,468, 13,489, 13,533, 13,648, 13,661, 13,668, 13,898, 13,916, **13,990,** 13,999, 14,000, 14,007, 14,015, 14,077, 14,114, 14,521, 14,579, 14,629, 14,703, 14,740, 14,745, 14,829, 15,166, 15,306, **15,335,** 15,860, **15,864,** 15,869, 15,948, 15,949, 15,970, 16,015, 16,166, **16,250,** 16,337, 16,502, 16,832, 16,883, 17,060, 17,166, 17,181, 17,217, 17,222, 17,225, **17,226,** 17,228, 17,264, **17,411,** 17,417, 17,460, 17,472, 17,675, 17,715, 17,760, 17,882, 17,910, 17,916, 17,922, 17,933, 17,953, **18,013**
    law and legislation, 49, 1,255, 2,356, 2,697, 2,932, 5,587, 6,968, 9,240, 9,547, 10,740, 17,335, 17,895, 17,909, 18,013
    legal aspects, 2,638, 5,565, 9,320, 9,450, 9,452
    literature, 55, **6,537,** 6,632, 15,851, 15,864
    opposition to, 48, 49, 55, 76, 1,435, 1,444, 2,037, 2,063, 2,298, 2,508, 3,234, 3,908, 4,930, **5,680,** 6,746, **6,800, 7,306, 9,215, 9,924,** 10,007, 10,046, 10,687, 11,073, 11,112, 11,249, 12,320, 12,524, 12,525, 13,405, 13,516, 13,811, 13,967, 15,335, **15,964**
Suffrage Archives, 6,433
Suffrage Association of New York State, 12,059
Suffrage Club (Warsaw, NY), 12,834
Suffrage League of Maryland. *See* Maryland League of Women Voters
Suffrage News (periodical), 9,347
Suffrage societies, 5, 42, 49, 55, 176, 250, 530, 648, 656, 1,059, 1,069, **1,158, 1,202,** 1,230, 1,255, 1,344, 1,359, 1,391, 1,436, 1,629, **1,872, 1,896, 1,908,** 1,948, 1,950, **2,042,** 2,218, **2,447, 2,501, 2,508,** 2,528, 2,815, 2,855, 2,858, 3,183, 3,240, 3,350, **3,681,** 3,803, **3,886,** 4,156, 4,173, **4,231, 4,240,** 4,481, **4,618,** 4,626, 4,732, 4,786, 4,793, 4,823, 4,831, **4,859,** 4,865, 4,960, **5,002,** 5,068, 5,305, 5,329, **5,354, 5,499, 5,581,** 5,587, 5,626, 5,833, **5,969,** 6,364, 6,379, 6,401, 6,414, 6,435, 6,455, **6,477,** 6,479, 6,526, 6,534, 6,536, 6,560, 6,596, 6,626, 6,685, 6,706, 6,742, 6,746, 6,754, 6,757, 6,765, 6,792, 6,807, 6,815, 6,825, 6,859, 6,876, 6,888, 6,894, 6,901, 6,941, 6,944, 6,953, 6,959, 6,966, 6,969, 6,971, 6,972, 6,976, 6,978, 6,979, 6,980, 6,981, 6,983, 6,984, 6,985, 7,082, **7,096, 7,139,** 7,178, 7,205, 7,232, **7,268,** 7,272, 7,273, 7,287, 7,306, 7,731, 7,803, **7,894,** 7,921, 7,941, 8,025, 8,028, 8,144, 8,266, 8,484, 8,831, 8,896, 8,963, 9,061, 9,142, 9,147, 9,225, **9,240,** 9,291, 9,292, 9,372, 9,547, 9,656, 9,750, 9,851, 10,032, 10,155, 10,160, 10,199, **10,316,** 10,462, 10,679, 10,681, 10,687, 10,768, 10,984, **11,114,** 11,123, 11,124, 11,143, **11,258,** 11,261, 11,391, 11,443, **11,678,** 11,773, 11,793, 11,865, 11,904, 11,916, **12,059,** 12,387, 12,415, **12,573, 12,575,** 12,597, 12,652, **12,743,** 12,834, 12,843, 12,856, 13,405, 13,433, 13,446, 13,557, 13,604, 13,664, **13,691, 13,721, 13,733,** 13,842, 13,967, 13,990, 13,997, **14,042,** 14,114, 14,168, 14,545, 14,547, 14,637, 14,814, 15,029, 15,283, 15,307, 15,312, 15,335, **15,361,** 15,368, **15,398,** 15,706, 15,733, 15,857, 15,864, 15,868, 15,941, **15,962, 15,970,** 16,015, **16,033,** 16,115, **16,218,** 16,235, 16,250, **16,252,** 16,313, **16,500,** 16,566, 16,733, 16,789, 17,025, 17,042, 17,077, **17,104,** 17,166, 17,217, 17,226, 17,616, 17,659, **17,721,** 17,745, **17,749,** 17,828, 17,895, 17,906, 17,916, 17,953, 18,013
Suffrage societies, Afro-American, 4,147
Suffragette Meeting House (Salem, OH), 14,168
Suffragist, The (periodical), 49, 176, **2,055,** 2,508
Suffragists, 656, 689, 714, **741, 827,** 859, **860, 953,** 1,224, **1,230, 1,255, 1,279, 1,304, 1,308,** 1,309, **1,321, 1,351, 1,391,** 1,404, 1,426, **1,436, 1,442,** 1,452, 1,475, **1,494,** 1,506, **1,652, 1,731, 1,745,** 1,820, **1,950,** 2,128, **2,175,** 2,202, 2,209, **2,212,** 2,240, **2,256,** 2,303, **2,374,** 2,413, 2,432, **2,492, 2,588,** 2,832, 3,324, 3,851, **3,908, 4,261, 4,623, 4,635, 4,654,** 4,684, 4,695, 4,696, **4,708, 4,731,**

4,732, 4,738, **4,742, 4,897, 4,930,** 4,958, **5,221,**
5,302, 5,305, 5,448, 5,517, 5,587, 5,694, 5,907,
5,934, 5,939, 5,963, 6,256, **6,364, 6,373,** 6,414,
6,455, 6,479, 6,508, 6,525, **6,532,** 6,588, 6,654,
6,706, 6,727, **6,731, 6,746, 6,815,** 6,842, **6,853,**
6,859, 6,876, 6,915, **6,932, 6,938, 6,942, 6,949,**
6,959, 6,966, **6,971, 6,976, 6,980, 6,981, 6,985,**
6,994, 7,022, 7,082, **7,180, 7,190,** 7,193, **7,205,**
7,215, **7,217, 7,232,** 7,234, **7,284, 7,290,** 7,306,
7,312, 7,791, 7,803, 7,808, 8,009, 8,362, 8,798,
9,013, **9,142,** 9,147, 9,204, 9,241, **9,288,** 9,406,
10,155, 10,361, 10,540, 10,740, **10,762,** 10,844,
10,912, 10,933, 11,112, 11,123, 11,167, 11,240,
11,391, 11,396, 11,435, 11,865, 12,129, **12,415,**
12,529, **12,624,** 12,652, 12,740, 12,744, **12,791,**
12,811, 12,812, 12,819, 12,828, **12,835, 12,854,**
12,864, 13,176, 13,398, 13,604, **13,904,** 13,939,
14,133, 14,142, 14,144, **14,549, 14,703,** 14,705,
14,728, 14,737, **14,740, 14,741, 14,814, 14,877,**
15,029, 15,252, 15,283, 15,370, **15,706, 15,851,**
15,857, **15,868, 15,980,** 16,235, 16,252, 16,941,
17,025, 17,077, 17,166, 17,171, 17,257, 17,328,
17,376, **17,377,** 17,411, 17,486, **17,589, 17,612,**
17,665, 17,749, **17,828, 17,852, 17,906,** 17,908,
17,953
Suffragists, British 6,889
Sugar-growing, 9,594
Sugar House Relief Society (Salt Lake City, UT), 16,916
Sugars, 8,538
Sugg, Jane A., **13,592**
Sugg, Judith. *See* White, Judith (Sugg)
Suggett, Laura (Steffens) [Mrs. Allen Holman] (?-1946),
     2,595
Suggs, Louise, 4,700
Suicide, 1,352, 4,473, 4,485, **5,702,** 7,160, 9,909,
     10,100, 11,440, 13,055
Sul Ross State College (TX), faculty, **16,272**
Sullivan, Ada. *See* Mother Agnes of Jesus
Sullivan, Alice (Phelan) [Mrs. Francis John]
     (1860-1912), **828,** 829
Sullivan, Alyce (1884-1942). *See* Murphy, Alyce
     (Sullivan) (1884-1942)
Sullivan, Anne Mansfield (1866-1936). *See* Macy,
     Anne Mansfield (Sullivan) [Mrs. John Albert]
     (1866-1936)
Sullivan, Belle Murray [Mrs. William B.], 9,779
Sullivan, Ellen (1887-1971). *See* Woodward, Ellen
     (Sullivan) [Mrs. Albert] (1887-1971)
Sullivan Family (SC), **15,743**
Sullivan, Francis John (1852-1930), 682, **829**
Sullivan, Frank, 15,332
Sullivan, George Hammond, 12,272
Sullivan, Gladys (1889-1933). *See* Doyle, Gladys
     (Sullivan) (1889-1933)
Sullivan, Henry, 8,846
Sullivan, Jeremiah, 12,067
Sullivan, Joanna (1866-1936). *See* Macy, Anne
     Mansfield (Sullivan) [Mrs. John Albert]
     (1866-1936)
Sullivan, John, 10,846
Sullivan, Joseph Augustine (1888-), **830**
Sullivan, Kathryn, **10,384**
Sullivan, Leonor Alice Kretzger, 9,934, 9,938, 10,197
Sullivan, Margery [Mrs. John] (1714-1801), 10,846
Sullivan, Marie (Buchanan) [Mrs. Mark], 2,596
Sullivan, Mark (1874-1952), **2,596**
Sullivan, Mary Mildred (Hammond) (1836-?), 12,272
Sullivan, Noël (1890-1956), **831**
Sullivan, Ruth L. [Mrs. Henry], **8,846**
Sullivan, William, 12,274
Sullivan, William B., 9,779
Sullivan, William Dunklin, 15,743
Sullivan's Indian Campaign (1779), 11,445
Sully, Julia [Miss] (?-1948), **17,102**
Sully, Robert, 17,102
Sully, Thomas, 17,102
Sulzberger, Iphigene Ochs [Mrs. Arthur Hays], 689,
     945, 11,817, 12,708
Summer, Henry, **4,841**
Summer, Matilda, **4,841**
"Summer on a Louisiana Cotton Plantation in 1832,
     A" (ms), 9,766
Summer School for American Women (Oxford,
     England), 13,754

Summer School of Women Workers in Industry,
     11,762
Summer schools, 3,852, 6,316, 6,893, 7,159, 11,501,
     11,762, 13,176, 13,754, 15,011
Summer theaters, 1,751, 17,391
Summer Thunder (book), 3,004
Summerall, Laura Mordecai, 7,547
Summerell, Hope (1870-1960). *See* Chamberlain,
     Hope (Summerell) (1870-1960)
Summerfield, Marie Louise [Mrs.], **10,720**
Summers, Edith (1884-1956). *See* Kelley, Edith
     (Summers) [Mrs. Allan] Updegraff [Mrs. C. F.]
     (1884-1956)
Summers, Eliza A. [Miss] (1844-1900), **15,744**
Summers, Sarah Maria, 15,744
Summerville, Amelia, 8,297
Summey, Polly Mira (Avery) (1779-1857), **13,142**
Summit Avenue Improvement Association (MN),
     9,435
Summit Avenue Methodist Church (NJ), 10,910
Summit County (OH), Woman Suffrage Association,
     13,733
Sumner, Anna Emily [Miss] (1904-), **1,053**
Sumner, Bertha (Ricketts) (1890-1970), **9,744, 9,745**
Sumner, Charles, 1,437, 2,217, 2,262, 2,855, 12,003,
     16,171
Sumner, Cid (Ricketts) (1890-1970). *See* Sumner,
     Bertha (Ricketts) (1890-1970)
Sumner Family (CT, MA, RI), **7,520**
Sumner, Increase, 6,225
Sumner, Mary. *See* Chapman, Mary (Sumner)
Sumner, Mary Brown. *See* Boyd, Mary Brown
     (Sumner)
Sumner, Sarah (1802-53). *See* Broughton, Sarah
     (Sumner) [Mrs. Shebuel] (1802-53)
Sumner, Sarah E. [Mrs.], 2,695
Sumption Prairie Women's Club (IN), **4,669**
Sumter Family (SC), **15,745**
Sumter Guards (SC), 15,749
Sumter, Mary Butler Waties [Mrs. Sebastian], 15,764
Sumter, Natalie de Delage de Volude [Mrs. Thomas,
     Jr.] (1782-1841), 15,585, **15,745,** 15,746
Sun (Baltimore, MD), 5,808
Sun (MI), 8,369
Sun Dials and Roses of Yesterday (book), 4,226
"Sun God Smiled, The," 10,718
Sun, K., 14,010
Sun Yat-sen, Madame (Soong Ching-ling) (1890-),
     174, 1,564, 2,558, 9,081
Sun-spots, 6,337
Sunborg, Vilma (?-1945), **17,345**
Sunday Feature, 17,762
Sunday legislation, 10,922
"Sunday Morning at Aunt Susan's" (radio program),
     2,274
Sunday school conventions, 9,429
Sunday-school literature, 6,107, 10,988
Sunday-school superintendents, **11,072**
Sunday-school teachers, 1,755, 3,991, 4,802, 5,740,
     6,200, 7,332, 7,514, 8,190, 9,116, 9,298, **11,355,**
     11,440, 12,133, 14,192, 17,157
Sunday schools, 107, 1,114, 1,776, 1,890, 1,958,
     3,453, 3,837, 4,849, 8,018, 9,102, 9,103, 9,220,
     9,283, 9,332, **9,429,** 9,855, 10,972, 13,182,
     13,644, 13,802, 13,803, 13,831, 13,926, 13,932,
     13,991, 16,647
Sunday-schools, Afro-American, records, **11,116**
Sunday Sun (NY), 12,500
Sunderland, Eliza Jane (Read) [Mrs. Jabez T.]
     (1839-1910), **7,941**
Sunderland, Jabez T., 7,941
Sundowners, The (drama), 17,989
Sundstrom, Ebba. [Mrs. Victor T.] Nylander
     (1896-), 4,056
Sunny Peak Farm (Elm Grove, WI), 17,655
Sunnycrest Farm for Negro Boys (PA), **15,282**
Sunrise at Campobello (drama), 4,639
Sunrise Farm (NY), 1,654
Sunset (periodical), 710
Sunset Hill Cemetery (GA), 3,615
Sunset Memorial (Fargo, ND), 13,669
Sunshine Cottage, 16,321
Suntzeff, Valentina (1891-1975), **10,210**
Suomi College (MI), 8,185

Suomi Synod, **8,186**
Super Lover, The (drama), 12,367
"Superfluous Women" (lecture), 11,167
Superior Court (CT), 1,915
Superior Court of Cincinnati (OH), 13,846
Superstition, 2,948, 5,664
Supervisory Committee for Recruiting Colored
     Regiments (PA), 3,299
Supreme Commander for Allied Powers, 11,902,
     17,074
Supreme Command of Allied Powers, 550
Supreme Council of Delaware, 15,039
Supreme Court of Appeals of Virginia, 17,109
Supreme Court, Territory of Iowa, 4,856
Supreme Headquarters Allied Expeditionary Forces,
     psychological warfare division, officials and
     employees, 5,144
Supreme Headquarters Allied Expeditionary Forces,
     staff, **5,129**
Surber, Marie (1887-). *See* Hare, Marie (Surber)
     (1887-)
Sure, Ethel Estes, 250
"Sure Road to World Peace" (ms), 3,219
Surgeons, **3,054,** 3,101, **3,310,** 3,967, 3,991, **4,261,**
     4,336, **6,145,** 7,274, 11,172, 11,727, 12,279,
     14,824, **15,914**
Surgery, 3,234, 14,965, 15,535
Surgery, psychic, 212
Surplus government property, **1,811**
Surratt, Mary Eugenia (Jenkins) (1820?-65), 9,528,
     12,594
Survey (periodical), 8,649, 8,650, 8,651, 8,658, 8,660,
     8,675, **8,678**
Survey Associates, Inc. (New York, NY), 2,120,
     8,660, **8,678**
Survey Graphic (periodical), 8,658, 8,678
Survey Midmonthly (periodical), 8,678
*Survey of Women's Employment at Mare Island
     Navy Yard* (book), 1,182
Surveying, 7,653, 9,207
     charts, diagrams, etc., 1,878
Surveyors, 28, 2,498, **3,093,** 5,746, **8,313,** 8,933,
     8,954, 10,298, 11,784, 14,619, 14,803, 14,808,
     14,821, **16,411**
"Survival of the Chivalric Tournament in Southern
     Life and Literature, The" (dissertation), 12,991
Survivors' benefits, 2,693, **2,698,** 2,926, **4,338,** 7,703,
     8,644, 9,932, 9,962, 9,986, 11,916, 13,426,
     13,449, 13,629, **15,944,** 16,698, 16,704
"Survivors '72" (exhibition), 17,236, 17,261, 17,296,
     17,316, 17,323, 17,332, 17,362
Susan B. Anthony Day, 9,227
Susan B. Anthony Forum, 6,836
Susan B. Anthony Forum Foundation, **2,081**
Susan B. Anthony Foundation, **2,597,** 6,836
Susan B. Anthony Memorial Association (NY),
     12,836
Susan B. Anthony Memorial Committee (CA), 1,506
Susan B. Anthony Memorial, Inc., **12,834**
Susan J. Quealy Award, 17,929, **18,014**
Susette La Flesche: Voice of the Omaha Indians
     (book), 4,983
Susman, Amelia Louise (1915-), 14,886
"Suspense Theatre" (radio program), 17,809
Sussman, Mary, 17,282
Sutfin, Ramona (Duck), 982
Sutherland, Alice Mary (1849-?), 14,672
Sutherland, Anne, 11,897
Sutherland, Elizabeth (1925-), 12,064, **17,726**
Sutherland, Evelyn Greenleaf Baker (1855-1908),
     5,965, 12,006, 14,366
Sutherland Family (OR), **14,672**
Sutherland, Fletcher, 11,799
Sutherland, George, 14,672
Sutherland, James, 14,672
Sutherland, Leona (1892-). *See* Omer, Leona
     (Sutherland) [Mrs. August Gideon] (1892-)
Sutherland, Louise C., 9,526
Sutherland, Mary E., 14,672
Sutherland, Roderick (?-1896), 14,672
Sutherland Sisters (NY), **11,799**
Sutherlin, Malinda (1835-1930). *See* Crouch,
     Malinda (Sutherlin) (1835-1930)
Sutliffe, Irene, 16,742

Sutline, John Laffitteau, **3,585**
Sutro, Adolph Heinrich Joseph (1830-98), **832**
Sutro Baths, 832
Sutro, Emma Laura (1856-1938). *See* Merritt, Emma
    Laura (Sutro) [Mrs. George W.] (1856-1938)
Sutro, Florence (Clinton) (1865-1906), 832, **12,319**
Sutro, Leah (Harris) [Mrs. Adolph Heinrich Joseph],
    832
Sutro Library, 832
Sutter, Anna [Mrs. John], 1,346
Sutter, John, **1,346**
Sutter, John A., 1,346
Sutter, Lillian, **9,746**
Sutter, Rosa Schafer (1850-1920), **10,053**
Suttles, Shirley Smith (1922-), **6,100**
Sutton, Emma L., **11,135**
Sutton Family, 5,780
Sutton Family (MI), **7,942**
Sutton, Francena Martin [Mrs.] (ca. 1838-1914),
    16,117
Sutton, Maude (Minish) (?-1936), **13,143**
Sutton, May, 997
Sutton, Sarah, **14,673**
Sutton's Mills, **7,123**
Sutures, 3,146, 16,417
Svendsen, Gro Nielsdatter [Mrs. Ole], 8,768, 9,266
Swadling, Lella (Taylor), **7,943**
Swahili language, 13,280
Swain, Anna Canada [Mrs. Leslie] (1889-), **12,787**
Swain, David Lowry, **13,593**
Swain, Eleanor (White) [Mrs. David L.], 13,581
Swain, Emeline Baker. *See* Lufkin, Emeline Baker
    (Swain)
Swain Family, 3,054
Swain Family (CA), **634**
Swain Family (NY), 11,440
Swain, Joseph, 1,559
Swain, Mary Ann, 7,632
Swain, Reba (1895-ca. 1935), **11,401**
Swain, Rebecca B., 7,632
Swain, Sarah Carpenter [Mrs. William C.], 634
Swain, William C., 634
Swallow, Ellen Henrietta (1842-1911). *See* Richards,
    Ellen Henrietta (Swallow) [Mrs. Robert
    Hallowell] (1842-1911)
Swallow, Shirley, 16,010
Swan, Barbara E. (?1922-), **2,822**
Swan, Caroline F. (Knox) (1783-1851), 7,677
Swan Library (NY), 11,268
Swan, Olive B. [Mrs.], 9,894
Swank, Gladys, 3,694
Swanke, Anna (Kaufman) [Mrs. Ernst Gustav]
    (1894-), **8,717, 8,718**
Swanke, Ernst Gustav, 8,718
Swann, Allie (Cavett), 9,806
Swann, Bess, 9,806
Swann Family (MS), **9,806**
Swann, Penelope, 13,454
Swann, Porter, 9,806
Swann, Thomas, 2,161
Swanner, Helene Anderson Peterson Kjaer [Mrs.
    Jorgen Christian] (1805-78), 16,486
Swanner, Jorgen Christian, 16,486
Swanson, Alexander B., 9,747
Swanson Family (MS), **9,747**
Swanson, Gloria (1899-), 2,242, 11,907
Swanson, Maria (Yates) [Mrs. Alexander B.], 9,747
Swanson, Mary Nellie (Peterson) [Mrs. Gust E.],
    10,541
Swap shops, 6,288
Swap, Sister, 16,603
Swarm, Samuel H., 14,592
Swart, Rose C., **2,598**
Swarthmore College (PA), 11,279, 11,904, 15,269
    deans, 15,270
    employees, 14,740
    faculty, 9,347
    students, 2,424, 15,278, 17,186
    trustees, 2,047
Swarthmore College (PA), Peace Collection, 15,302
Swarthmore Political Action Club, 17,630
Swarthout, Gladys (1904-), 3,788
Swartout, Mrs. Benjamin C., **11,722**
Swayze, Samuel, 9,689

Sweany, Frances Bishop, 10,175
Swear by Apollo (book), 10,848
Swearingen, John Eldred (1875-1957), **15,747**
Swearingen, Mary Haugh [Mrs. John Eldred], 15,747
Swearingen, Richard M., 16,037
Sweating system, 6,486, 10,379. *See also* Consumers'
    leagues
Sweazy, Tessa (1885-). *See* Webb, Tessa (Sweazy)
    [Mrs. Reuben H.] (1885-)
Sweden
    social life and customs, 16,481
    women in, 4,322
Swedenborg, Emanuel, 14,730
Swedish-Americans, 8,690
Swedish Center (San Francisco, CA), 510
Swedish Lutheran Church, 8,518
Sweeney, Esther Emerson, 8,633
Sweeney, Margaret, 8,557
Sweet Briar College (VA), 6,011, 6,616
Sweet, Emma (Biddlecom) [Mrs. Fred G.]
    (1862-1951), **12,835**
Sweet, Gertrude, 14,497
Sweet, Helen. *See* Lossing, Helen (Sweet)
Sweet, Jeanette, 8,948
Sweet, Joshua, 8,948
Sweet, Lottie [Mrs.], **8,519**
Sweet, Mary Eliza. *See* Baber, Mary Eliza (Sweet)
    [Mrs. Ambrose]
"Sweet William" (story), 11,310
Sweet, Winifred (1863-1936). *See* Bonfils, Winifred
    (Sweet) [Mrs. Orlow] Black [Mrs. Frederick G.]
    (1863-1936)
Sweets, Ellen. *See* Dunning, Ellen (Sweets)
Sweets, Melba A., 10,191
Sweetser, Cornelia (Peck), 15,169
Sweetser Family, 15,169
Swegles, John, 7,936
Swegles, Mary Cecilia. *See* Spaulding, Mary Cecilia
    (Swegles) [Mrs. Oliver Lyman]
Swenson, Anna, 9,472
Swenson, David F. (?-1940), 8,617
Swenson, Elfrida, 9,226
Swenson, Gustav, 9,216
Swenson, Hattie, 16,488
Swenson, Lillian Bessie (Marvin) [Mrs. David F.]
    (1876-1961), **8,617**
Swenson, May (1919-), 2,805, 11,810
Swensson House (MN), 8,706
Swensson, Olaf (1843-1923), 8,706
Swetland Elizabeth (Ketchum) [Mrs. Henry] Delord
    [Mrs. William], 12,769, 12,773
Swetland Family (NY), **12,773**
Swetland, William (1782-1864), 12,773
Swett, Helen. *See* Artieda, Helen (Swett)
Swett, Sophie, 1,224
Sweyd, Lester, **11,461**
Swidzinska, Halina [Miss], **13,960**
Swift, Eva [Miss], 10,037
Swift Family (GA), **3,101**
Swift, Frances Dorr (1874-?). *See* Tatnall, Frances
    Dorr (Swift) [Mrs. Henry Lea] (1874-?)
Swift, Gertrude Horton (Dorr) [Mrs. Joseph]
    (1844-1917), **2,056**
Swift, Isaac, 3,101
Swift, Iva Irene, **7,944**
Swift, Louise, **17,346**
Swift, Mildred L., 10,707
Swift, Mrs. Elisha D., **14,833**
Swift, Sister Imelda Therese (1862-1916), 17,868
Swigert, Celia [Mrs. Charles F.], 14,674
Swigert, Charles F. (1862-?), **14,674**
Swiggett, Emma (Bain) [Mrs. Glen Levin], 2,519
Swimmers, 997, 1,534, 4,700, **5,026**, 15,935
Swinburne, A. C., 1,467
Swindler, Mary Hamilton (1884-1967), **14,743**
Swiney, Mary Mae, 2,562
Swinging and swingers (sex customs), 8,207
Swingle, Maude (Kellerman) [Mrs. Walter T.]
    (1888-), **6,917, 15,218**
Swingle, Walter T., 15,218
Swinnerton, Frank Arthur (1884-), 267
Swinton, Marion (?-1938), **11,136**
Swisher, Esther McDowell, 4,949
Swiss-Americans, charitable societies, **4,157**

Swiss Benevolent Society of Chicago (IL), **4,157**
Swiss Benevolent Society of Chicago (IL), Schweizer
    Damen Verein, 4,157
Swisshelm, Dorothy, **15,880**
Swisshelm Family, 9,241
Swisshelm, Jane Grey (Cannon) [Mrs. James]
    (1815-84), **6,918**, 9,048, 9,241, 9,317, **9,398,**
    9,452, 11,305, **15,229**
Switzer, Colleen, 10,441
Switzer, Mary Elizabeth (1900-72), 2,086, 2,115,
    6,919
Switzer, Robert E., 14,463
Switzerland, 5,954, 12,285, 12,289
    American actresses in, 5,954
    Americans in, 6,353, 13,439
    World War I, civilians work, 2,052, 9,037
Switzler Family, 9,849
Switzler, Mary Jane Royall, 9,849
Sword Family (PA), **15,097**
Sword From Galway, A (book), 15,720
Sword in the Mountains, The (drama), 415
Sword, Mary (Parry), 15,097
Sybil Huntington (book), 17,009
Sycamore School (Contra Costa County, CA), 897
Sydenstricker, Grace (1899-). *See* Yaukey, Grace
    (Sydenstricker) (1899-)
Sydenstricker, Pearl (1892-1973). *See* Buck, Pearl
    (Sydenstricker) (1892-1973)
Syford, Amanda O. (Bean) [Mrs. DeWitt N.]
    (1843-1930), 10,542
Syford, Constance Miriam (1887-1965), 10,542
Syford, DeWitt N. (1847-1926), 10,542
Syford, Ethel Corrine (1881-1955), 10,542
Syford Family (NE), **10,542**
Sykes, Ida (1858-91). *See* Billups, Ida (Sykes) [Mrs.
    Thomas Carlton] (1858-91)
Sykes, James (1810-85), **9,812**
Sykes, Jeanette, 9,230
Sykes, Martha (Lanier) [Mrs. James] (1815-81), 9,812
Sykes, Wildie. *See* Billups, Wildie (Sykes) [Mrs.
    Joseph Saunders]
Syllabub (drama), 15,700
Syllogism, 11,995
Sylvarena School (MS), 9,648
Sylvester, Maude (1898-), 8,518
Sylvester, Vida, 5,644
Symbionese Liberation Army, 809
Symbolism, 11,580
Symmes, Anita Day (1872-1962). *See* Blake, Anita
    Day (Symmes) [Mrs. Anson Stiles] (1872-1962)
Symmes Family, 353
Symonds, Eliza Grace (1809-97). *See* Bell, Eliza
    Grace (Symonds) [Mrs. Alexander Melville]
    (1809-97)
Symphony orchestra societies, **1,386, 8,505, 17,425**
Symphony orchestras, 1,038, 1,429, 1,734, 1,788,
    2,743, 3,195, 4,056, 6,358, 8,257, 9,101, 11,217,
    11,218, 13,932, 13,991, **14,639**, 14,822, 16,275,
    16,358, 16,965
Synagogues, **9,251**, 13,472, 13,802, 13,805
Synchronized swimming, 1,534
Syndicalism, 621, 11,927
Syndical Female College (AL), 114
Synodical Female College (Griffin, GA), 3,483
Synodical Female Institute (AL), 14
Synstelian Family, 8,765
Syphilis, 6,900
Syracuse Girl Scout Council (NY), 12,924
Syracuse University (NY), 1,404, 2,134, 12,907,
    12,918, 12,922, 12,923
    alumnae, 11,269
    student housing, 12,924
Syracuse University (NY), College of Fine Arts,
    12,917
Syracuse University (NY), College of Home
    Economics, 12,921, 12,923
Syracuse University (NY), Dean of Women's Office,
    Director of Social Activities, **12,919**
Syracuse University (NY), Youth Development
    Center, 11,592
Syrdal, Borghild Roe (1902-), **8,888**
Syria
    Armenians in, 16,780
    missionaries to, 7,279

Syse, Sophia Stuegaarden [Mrs.] (1866-1947), **8,790**
Szladits, Lola L., **11,921**
Szold, Adele (1876-1940), **17,727**
Szold, Bertha "Betsey," 17,727
Szold, Henrietta (1860-1945), 933, 1,000, **5,720,** **6,920,** 7,525, 7,554, 9,109, 12,117, **12,118,** 13,604, 17,727
Szold, Zip, 12,117
T. T. T. Society, Chapter Iowa A (Mount Pleasant, IA), **5,069**
Tabari, Tokiko [Mrs.] (1898-), 16,942
Taber, Augusta, 15,293
Taber, Ellen Strang [Mrs.] (1846-ca. 1931), **4,842**
Taber, Gladys (Bagg) (1899-), **6,101**
Taber, Phoebe. *See* Hamilton, Phoebe (Taber) [Mrs. Andrew Holman]
Taber, Sarah Frances (Frost) [Mrs. Robert] (1866-1950). *See* Marlowe, Julia. Sarah Frances Frost. Fanny Brough. Fancy Brough. [Mrs. Robert] Taber [Mrs. Edward Hugh] Sothern (1866-1950)
Tabernacle and Purgatory (periodical). *See Spirit and Life* (periodical)
Tabernacle Church (Salem, MA), 7,383
Tabor, Augusta (Pierce) (1833?-95), **833**
Tabor, Elizabeth Bonduel "Baby Doe" (McCourt) [Mrs. Harvey] Doe [Mrs. Horace Austin Warner] (1854-1935), 1,746, 1,752, 1,786
Tabor, Horace Austin Warner (1830-99), **1,746,** 1,752
Tabor, Rosemary Echo Silver Dollar (1889-1925), 1,746
Taccone, Mary, 3,450
Tachau, Jean (Brandeis) [Mrs. Charles G.] (1894-1978), **5,365**
Tack, Minnie (1899-), **8,889**
Tacoma General Hospital (WA), School of Nursing, **17,386**
Tacoma Little Theater (WA), **17,393**
Tacoma Public Library (WA), 17,394, 17,395
Tacoma Times (WA), 12,863
Tacoma Women's Club (WA), 17,412
Tacoma Women's Study Club (WA), 17,412
Taconite, environmental aspects, 9,467
Tadje, Eliza (Walz), 3,740
Tafel, Karl, 5,366
Tafel, Mary Konersman, 5,366
Tafel, Olga A., 15,308
Tafel, Pauline (Autenrieth) [Mrs. Karl] (1833-?), **5,366**
Taft, Ada (Bartlett) [Mrs. Lorado], 9,170
Taft, Anna Sinton [Mrs. Charles P.] (?-1931), **13,857**
Taft, Barbara [Mrs. William H., III], 11,913
Taft, Don C., 4,381
Taft, Emily. *See* Douglas, Emily (Taft) [Mrs. Paul H.]
Taft-Hartley Law, repeal of, 2,589
Taft, Helen "Nellie" (Herron) [Mrs. William Howard] (1861-1943), 1,593, 2,198
Taft, Helen Herron (1891-). *See* Manning, Helen Herron (Taft) [Mrs. Frederick Johnson] (1891-)
Taft, Lorado (1860-1936), 9,170
Taft Museum (OH), 13,845
Taft, Robert Alphonso (1889-1953), 2,473, 11,621, **11,913**
Taft, Rosadel. *See* Lansing, Rosadel (Taft)
Taft, William Howard (1857-1930), 1,559, 2,214, 2,473, 2,596, **2,599,** 2,640, 3,027, 9,821, 11,944
Taggard, Genevieve. [Mrs. Robert L.] Wolf [Mrs. Kenneth] Durant (1894-1948), 317, 635, 831, 1,081, 1,082, 1,507, 4,226, **10,875, 11,307,** **12,641, 12,642**
Taggert, Katherine, 1,553
Taggert, Madge, 11,349
Tagliavia, Father, 9,507
Tagore, Rabindranath, 6,012
Tailors, **7,447,** 12,447
Taintor, Margaret "Peggy" Day (1921-). *See* Goodrich, Margaret "Peggy" Day (Taintor) [Mrs. Robert R.] (1921-)
Tait, Dorothy Fairbairn (?-1972), **6,102**
Tait, Edward, 5,160
Taitt, Mildred (1879-1936). *See* Milton, Mildred (Taitt) [Mrs. Jefferson Davis] (1879-1936)
Taiwan
    maternal and infant welfare, 6,987

missionaries to, 13,279
missionaries to, Lutheran, 8,868, **8,880**
missionaries to, Mennonite, 5,198
missionaries to, Methodist, 8,891
Take Her, She's Mine (drama), 4,764
Takehashi girls high school (Jo-Gakkó) (Japan), 10,975
Takemoto, Patsy (1927-). *See* Mink, Patsy (Takemoto) (1927-)
Talaria (periodical), 2,936
Talbert, Mary B., 2,502
Talbot, Adelaide, 2,600
Talbot, Edith Hull (Armstrong) (1872-?), 7,590, 14,950
Talbot, Ethel. *See* Scheffauer, Ethel (Talbot) [Mrs. Herman George]
Talbot Family, 11,616
Talbot, Marion (1858-1948), 792, 6,009
Talbot, Mary, 12,513
Talbot, Mary L., 2,600
Talbot Mills, **7,124**
Talbot, Mr., 6,936
Talbot, Susan A., **10,386**
Talbot, Theodore (?-1862), **2,600**
Talbot, Violetta T. Bancker, 14,885
Talbott Family, **13,720**
Talboy, Helen H. [Mrs.] (1908-69), **4,843**
Talboys, Millie, **10,266**
Talcott, Mary Kingsbury, 1,948
Tale of a Hero (book), 6,115
Tale of the Alps, A (moving-picture), 18,003
Tale, Terre, 16,208
Talhelm, Anna Stanley [Mrs. Henry P.], 1,790
Taliaferro, Anne, 5,320
Taliaferro, David, 5,280
Taliaferro, Elizabeth "Betsy" (Williamson) [Mrs. James Govan] (1800-50), 5,280
Taliaferro Family (GA), 3,373
Taliaferro Family (KY), **5,280**
Taliaferro, James Govan (1798-1876), 5,280
Taliaferro, John, 9,689
Taliaferro, Mary, 8,936
Taliaferro, Robert, 5,280
Taliaferro, Sally Lyons [Mrs. William], **17,103**
Taliaferro, Susan (Boulware) [Mrs. Alexander], 3,373
Taliaferro, William, 3,373
Taliaferro, William, 17,103
"Talk to Women About Women, A," 9,372
Tall Houses in Winter (book), 5,989
Tall, Lida Lee (1873-1942), **5,834,** 5,835
Talladega College (AL)
    deans, 89
    faculty, 5,477
    students, 5,459
Tallamadge, Julia M., 12,207
Tallant, Alice Weld (1875-1958), 7,307
Tallant, Robert (1909-57), **5,501**
Tallchief, Alexander Joseph, 14,239
Tallchief, Maria. [Mrs. Henry] Paschen (1925-), **14,239,** 16,208
Tallchief, Marjorie, 16,208
Tallchief, Ruth Mary Porter, 14,239
Talley, Elizabeth (Furman), 13,144
Tallmadge, Elizabeth [Mrs. Matthias Burnet], 12,320
Tallmadge, Matthias Burnet (1774-1819), **12,320**
Tallman, Jane Dann, 11,144
Tallulah Falls Industrial School (GA), 3,574
Tally Ho (yearbook), 2,939
Talmage, James E., 3,738
Talmage, Norma, 11,327
Taltavall, Jane Shepard, **1,347**
Tama High School, Young Ladies Debating Society (IA), 5,115
Tamalpais Centre Women's Club (CA), 1,310
Tambimuttu, Thurairajah, 11,171, 16,163
Tamiris, Helen. Helen Becker. [Mrs. Daniel] Nagrin (1905-66), **12,366**
Tamiris-Nagrin Dance Company, 12,366
Tammany Hall, 11,928
    opposition to, 11,853
Tammy in Rome (ms), 9,745
Tammy Tell Me True (screen play), 9,745
Tampa Business and Professional Women's Club (FL), 2,954, 2,955

Tampa Civic Association (FL), 2,955
Tamplet, Serita (Campbell), **9,748**
Tanaka, Tutomu, 11,580
Tanana Valley Fair Association (AK), 140
Tanbara, Ruth [Mrs. Earl], 9,341
Tandy, Jessica. [Mrs. Jack] Hawkins [Mrs. Hume] Cronyn (1909-), **2,284**
Tangney, Lillian (Haynes) [Mrs. James H.] (1873-1971), **7,491**
Tanguay, Eva. [Mrs. John] Ford [Mrs. Chandos] Ksiazkewacz (1850-91), 9,361
Tanguy, Kay Sage, 2,782
Tannatt, Elizabeth Foster Tappan [Mrs. Thomas R.] (1837-?), 17,209
Tannatt Family, **17,209**
Tannatt, Miriam Hooper (1866-?). *See* Merriam, Miriam Hooper (Tannatt) (1866-?)
Tannatt, Thomas R., 17,209
Tanner, Beatrice Stella (1865-1940). *See* Campbell, Beatrice Stella (Tanner) [Mrs. Patrick] (1865-1940)
Tanner, George S., **160**
Tanner, Helen (Hornbeck), **7,945**
Tanner, Henry Ossawa (1859-1937), **3,304**
Tanner, John (1778-?), **16,913**
Tanner, Louisa Maria (1818-1906). *See* Lyman, Louisa Maria (Tanner) [Mrs. Amasa Mason] (1818-1906)
Tanner, Mary Jane (Mount) (1837-90), **834,** 855, **16,482,** 16,913
Tanner, Sara Jane (1832-?), **4,439**
Tanners, 7,614
Tannier, Allen, 4,226
Taoism, 7,407, 14,740
Taos Indians, **16,873**
Taos Pueblo (book), 1,082
Tapestry, 6,382
Tapfield, Hannah (1807-86). *See* King, Hannah (Tapfield) [Mrs. Thomas Owen] (1807-86)
Tapley, Alice, 3,280
Tapley, Lydia P., 6,998
Tappan, Anne, 11,709
Tappan, Benjamin, 6,833
Tappan Family (CO, CT, NJ, NY), 1,822
Tappan Family (NY), 11,709
Tappan, Lucy, 11,709
Tappan, Lucy. *See* Pierce, Lucy (Tappan) [Mrs. John]
Tappan, Mrs. Lewis, 3,296
Tapping, Minnie Ellingson (1867-1949), 9,399
Tapping on the Wall, A (book), 12,016
Tapping, T. Hawley, 7,884
Tarascan language, 7,305
Tarascon, Naneen, 5,331
Tarbell, Ida Minerva. [Mrs. John Sanburn] Phillips (1857-1944), 325, 378, 395, 756, 1,426, 1,565, 2,186, 2,198, 2,499, 2,511, 2,596, 2,694, 3,927, 3,976, 3,993, 4,007, 5,120, 5,273, **6,921,** 7,227, **7,308,** 7,868, 8,953, 11,596, 11,742, 14,828, **14,872, 15,318**
Tarbell, Martha (1862-1948), **4,537**
Tarkington, Booth, 6,452, 12,559
Tarkington, Laurel Louisa (Fletcher) [Mrs. Booth], 12,513
Tarnapowicz, Marie [Mrs. Francis P.], **14,834**
Tarr, Susan, **7,447**
Tart, J. C., 3,452
Tartt, Ruby (Pickens) [Mrs. W. P.], 81
Tarver, Mary. *See* Carroll, Mary (Tarver) [Mrs. M. C.]
Tasmania, 12,567
Tassin, Algernon, 8,116
Tate, Allen, 11,163, 15,927
Tate, Caroline Ferguson (Gordon) [Mrs. Allen] (1895-). *See* Gordon, Caroline Ferguson. [Mrs. Allen] Tate (1895-)
Tate, David, 3,726
Tate, Edna Ferguson [Mrs.], **3,099**
Tate, Emma (1873-1962), **3,726**
Tate Family (GA, NC, VA), 3,099
Tate Family (NC), 13,188
Tate, John P., 3,726
Tatham, Benjamin, 2,486

Tatnall, Frances Forr (Swift) [Mrs. Henry Lea] (1874-?), **2,057**

Tatum, Ella, 4,953

Tatum, Lawrie (1822-1900), **4,953**

Tatum, Mary Ann [Mrs. Lawrie], 4,953

Tatus, Edith, 3,071

Tauch, Waldine, 16,044

Taunton Daily Gazette (MA), 7,016

Tausch, Elizabeth, 1,559

Tausig, Carl, 2,665

Taussig, Helen Brooke (1898-), 11,932

Tauzin, Anna (Durkee) [Mrs. Dominic] (1753-1839). *See* Young, Anna (Durkee) [Mrs. Dominic] Tauzin [Mrs.] (1753-1839)

Tauzin, Dominic, 4,352

Tauzin, Mary. *See* Bartling, Mary (Tauzin) [Mrs. Daniel]

Távarez, Elisa [Mrs.] (1879-1960), **15,367**

Taverner, Margaret B., **1,643**

Tawney, Guy, 4,440

Tawney, Marietta (Busey) [Mrs. Guy] (1879-1949), **4,440**

Tax, Sol, 2,832

Taxation, 162, 194, 2,697, 3,362, **3,947**, 7,251, 7,262, 7,325, 7,861, 9,006, 9,800, 10,199, 14,016, **14,934**, 17,300, 17,463

    law, **6,761**, **9,381**

    legal aspects, 9,544

Taxes. *See* Taxation

Taxidermists, **1,730**, 1,790

Taxonomists, 8,424, **15,217**

Taxonomy, 6,310

Tay Tay's Tales (book), 11,222

Tayloe, John George, 12,373

Tayloe, Narcissa. *See* Shawhan, Narcissa (Tayloe) [Mrs. Charles S.]

Taylor, Ada [Mrs. Joseph J.], 8,164

Taylor and Company, **7,125**

Taylor, Arlene, **2,823**

Taylor, B. Grant, 1,359

Taylor, Barton Stout, 7,946

Taylor, Benjamin F. (1819-87), Family (OH), **13,961**

Taylor, Bernice (Burnet), 10,905

Taylor, Charles E. (1842-1916), 13,640

Taylor, Charles L., **11,723**

Taylor, Claude, 16,876

Taylor, Claudia Alta "Lady Bird" (1912-). *See* Johnson, Claudia Alta "Lady Bird" (Taylor) [Mrs. Lyndon Baines] (1912-)

Taylor, Clotilde (Grunsky) (1891-), 520

Taylor, Cora Best. *See* Williams, Cora Best (Taylor) [Mrs. Jesse Parker]

Taylor, Dorothea Lange. [Mrs. Maynard] Dixon [Mrs. Paul] Schuster (1895-1965), **607**

Taylor, Dorothy, 5,473

Taylor, Edith (1905-61). *See* Pope, Edith (Taylor) [Mrs. Earle] (1905-61)

Taylor, Effie Jane (1874-1970), 5,735, 6,141

Taylor, Eleanor Jane. *See* Calverly, Eleanor Jane (Taylor) [Mrs. Edwin Elliott]

Taylor, Elizabeth Anne (Chase) [Mrs. Marshall S. M.] (1832-1911). *See* Allen, Elizabeth Anne (Chase) [Mrs. Marshall S. M.] Taylor [Mrs. Benjamin Paul] Akers [Mrs. Elijah Marshall] (1832-1911)

Taylor, Ella (Atwater) (1868-?), **17,865**

Taylor, Emma Ahuena (Davison) [Mrs. Albert Pierce] (1866-1937), **3,633**

Taylor, Emma (Dollenmayer) (1859-?), 9,046

Taylor, Estella, 16,876

Taylor, Ethel, 4,168

Taylor, Ethel C., 12,041

Taylor, F., 2,875

Taylor Family (GA), 3,054

Taylor Family (Jamaica), 15,077

Taylor Family (MI), **7,946**

Taylor Family (New England), 6,352

Taylor Family (PA), **14,857**

Taylor Family (UT), 16,961

Taylor, Fan T., **17,817**

Taylor, Florence, 8,665

Taylor, Gertrude Elizabeth (1870-1963). *See* Slaughter, Gertrude Elizabeth (Taylor) [Mrs. Moses Stephen] (1870-1963)

Taylor, Graham (1851-1938), 3,809, 3,901, **4,003**, 4,158

Taylor, Harriet (?-1931), **4,004**

Taylor, Harriet (1853-1945). *See* Upton, Harriet (Taylor) [Mrs. George Whitman] (1853-1945)

Taylor, Harriet (Weaver) [Mrs. Henry] (1859-?), 16,968

Taylor, Hattie (?-1905). *See* Tennent, Hattie Taylor [Mrs. Edward Smith] (?-1905)

Taylor, Helen, 12,485

Taylor, Helen K., 14,455

Taylor, Inez B., 17,918

Taylor, Irita Bradford (1891-1966). *See* Van Doren, Irita Bradford (Taylor) (1891-1966)

Taylor, James, 5,294

Taylor, Jane (Ballantyne) [Mrs. John] (1813-?), 16,961

Taylor, Jane Wilson [Miss], **4,844**

Taylor, John, **12,643**

Taylor, John, 16,533, 16,961, 16,968

Taylor, Joseph W., 14,857

Taylor, Laurette (Cooney) [Mrs. Charles Alonzo]. [Mrs. Hartley] Manners (1884-1946), 12,476

Taylor, Lea Demarest (1883-1975), 3,809, **3,901**, 3,910, 4,003, 4,110, 4,130, 4,141, **4,158**, 4,166, 8,651, 8,658, 8,668

Taylor, Lella. *See* Swadling, Lella (Taylor)

Taylor, Leslie B., 3,711

Taylor, Lillian Horton [Mrs. Charles L.], **11,723**

Taylor, Lily Ross (1886-1970), **14,744**

Taylor, Louisa R., 16,511

Taylor, Lucy E. L., 13,961

Taylor, Maggie Williams [Mrs.] Musgrove [Mrs. J. M.], **9,688**

Taylor, Mamie K., 3,430

Taylor, Margaret. *See* Miller, Margaret (Taylor)

Taylor, Margaret Kirkwood [Mrs. J. Lanning], 11,744

Taylor, Marguerite Irene. *See* Patton, Marguerite Irene Taylor [Mrs. Harald Smith]

Taylor, Maria (1849-?). *See* Beale, Maria (Taylor) (1849-?)

Taylor, Marian Young (1909-75), **11,402**

Taylor, Martha Anne. *See* Longley, Martha Anne (Taylor) [Mrs. Thomas]

Taylor, Mary (1885-1973). *See* Moore, Mary (Taylor) Leiper (1885-1973)

Taylor, Mary Amelia [Mrs. Samuel] (1836-87), **2,287**

Taylor, Mary (Meigs) [Mrs. Joseph Hancock], 2,556

Taylor, Matilda Ormond. *See* Abbey, Matilda Ormond (Taylor) Birchard

Taylor, Maude Sawin (?-1974), **10,782**

Taylor, May,

Taylor, Mildred (Frick) [Mrs. E. Paul] (1905-), **12,910**

Taylor, Minnie Jones (1863-1960), **17,544**

Taylor, Mrs. (NY), 11,442

Taylor, Mrs. B. Grant, 1,359

Taylor, Mrs. Chalmer C., 11,827

Taylor, Mrs. Elmer E., 5,114

Taylor, Nannie. *See* Griffith, Nannie (Taylor) [Mrs. David]

Taylor, Norman, 16,486

Taylor, Paul, 4,384

Taylor, Paul Schuster, **835**

Taylor, Pearl Watts, 16,876

Taylor, Phoebe Atwood (1909-76), 6,060

Taylor, Rachel (ca. 1839-?), **14,489**

Taylor, Rachel (Smith) [Mrs. Albert LeRoy] (1890-), **16,834**

Taylor, Richard, 5,415

Taylor, Rose A., 1,339

Taylor, Sally Elmore (1829-?), **15,748**

Taylor, Samuel, 2,287

Taylor, Sarah K. [Mrs. A. W.], 3,742, 7,064

Taylor, Sydney, 8,531

Taylor, Zachary, 4,855, 11,049

Taylor, Zella [Mrs. C. S.], **972**

Taynton, Susan (Herring) Jeffries, **13,288**

Te Deum, 5,910

Tea Party, The (drama), 7,090

Tea trade, 6,445

Teacher placement agencies, **1,871**, 14,614

Teachers, 111, 130, **143**, 169, 171, 179, **187**, 197, 211, **218**, 326, 336, 369, **381**, 418, **631**, 649, 654, 668, 704, **788, 802, 817,** 844, 942, 955, 956, **957, 969,** 1,068, 1,137, 1,187, 1,193, **1,197,** 1,208, **1,261, 1,275, 1,301, 1,352,** 1,461, **1,522,** 1,532, 1,614, **1,627,** 1,628, 1,634, **1,643, 1,651, 1,655,** 1,713, 1,779, 1,803, 1,863, 1,900, 1,971, 2,119, **2,129,** 2,162, 2,332, 2,457, **2,531,** 2,604, 2,745, **2,751, 2,752, 2,758, 2,760, 2,872, 2,874, 2,891, 2,900, 2,902,** 2,910, **2,912, 3,013, 3,155, 3,215,** 3,265, 3,308, 3,314, 3,329, 3,337, 3,409, 3,413, 3,419, 3,451, 3,474, 3,610, 3,619, 3,662, 3,671, **3,705, 3,714,** 3,764, **3,854,** 3,911, 4,063, 4,279, 4,301, **4,359,** 4,425, 4,456, 4,471, **4,490,** 4,527, **4,528, 4,600, 4,604,** 4,613, 4,732, 4,735, **4,739, 4,742, 4,744,** 4,783, 4,815, 4,816, **4,817, 4,818, 4,819,** 4,842, **4,847, 4,852, 4,853,** 4,892, **4,896, 4,906, 4,927, 4,934, 4,958, 5,048, 5,074,** 5,183, **5,229, 5,245, 5,258,** 5,259, 5,487, 5,493, **5,577, 5,584, 5,711, 5,767, 5,819, 5,850, 5,883,** 5,895, 5,907, **5,938, 5,949, 5,950, 5,956,** 5,972, **5,976, 6,012,** 6,106, 6,107, 6,192, 6,200, **6,261, 6,350, 6,403, 6,506, 6,511, 6,521, 6,587, 6,611, 6,645, 6,650, 6,652, 6,653,** 6,706, **6,768, 6,769, 6,826, 6,842, 6,923,** 6,943, 6,956, **6,999, 7,007, 7,011,** 7,014, 7,045, 7,055, **7,146,** 7,193, 7,195, **7,225, 7,279, 7,332, 7,334, 7,340,** 7,342, 7,356, **7,389,** 7,438, **7,450, 7,522,** 7,599, 7,606, 7,609, 7,610, 7,618, 7,631, 7,652, **7,656, 7,710, 7,734, 7,756, 7,757, 7,758, 7,767, 7,776, 7,777, 7,796, 7,929, 7,930, 7,934,** 7,935, **8,019, 8,025, 8,027, 8,030, 8,104, 8,120, 8,147, 8,159, 8,160, 8,162,** 8,169, **8,170,** 8,195, **8,217, 8,229, 8,231,** 8,286, **8,306, 8,308, 8,342, 8,377, 8,380, 8,403,** 8,405, 8,407, **8,497, 8,498, 8,507, 8,510,** 8,517, 8,518, **8,526, 8,695, 8,710,** 8,712, **8,718, 8,724, 8,725, 8,733, 8,746,** 8,751, **8,764, 8,779,** 8,893, 8,896, 8,941, 8,955, **8,966,** 8,969, 8,980, 9,005, 9,013, **9,017,** 9,034, **9,038,** 9,048, 9,067, **9,097, 9,112,** 9,141, **9,158, 9,161, 9,265, 9,282, 9,288,** 9,304, 9,363, 9,373, **9,394,** 9,421, 9,448, **9,510, 9,598,** 9,607, 9,620, 9,628, 9,634, **9,672, 9,687, 9,708,** 9,764, 9,801, **9,807,** 9,859, 9,867, **9,916, 9,954,** 10,076, 10,081, 10,105, 10,129, 10,228, **10,237, 10,242, 10,246, 10,248, 10,260, 10,263, 10,269, 10,282,** 10,312, **10,317, 10,361, 10,362, 10,373,** 10,398, 10,403, **10,433, 10,441,** 10,449, **10,452, 10,453, 10,467, 10,474, 10,480, 10,490, 10,491, 10,523, 10,524, 10,541, 10,552,** 10,564, 10,628, 10,635, 10,682, **10,683, 10,734,** 10,736, 10,749, **10,751, 10,778, 10,779, 10,787, 10,797, 10,805,** 10,810, **10,824, 10,828,** 10,844, **10,847,** 10,855, 10,905, 10,937, 10,975, 10,976, **10,984,** 10,997, 11,056, **11,072, 11,181,** 11,222, **11,329,** 11,407, **11,428, 11,435,** 11,520, 11,589, 11,602, **11,608,** 11,709, **11,724,** 11,846, **11,963, 11,623,** 12,209, **12,233, 12,245,** 12,370, **12,455, 12,510, 12,533,** 12,550, 12,622, 12,688, **12,694,** 12,760, **12,766, 12,803,** 12,870, 13,038, 13,052, 13,084, 13,089, **13,120,** 13,121, 13,130, **13,158, 13,228,** 13,231, 13,234, **13,237, 13,245,** 13,299, 13,308, 13,309, **13,321,** 13,322, 13,345, 13,350, **13,366, 13,400,** 13,418, 13,420, **13,526, 13,535, 13,562,** 13,590, 13,604, 13,610, **13,700, 13,701, 13,718,** 13,799, **13,843, 13,875, 13,927, 13,930, 13,960,** 14,103, 14,180, **14,186, 14,187, 14,191, 14,200, 14,207, 14,224,** 14,232, 14,243, **14,244, 14,246,** 14,285, **14,301,** 14,306, 14,311, 14,363, 14,373, 14,394, 14,396, 14,416, **14,420, 14,426,** 14,427, **14,435, 14,441,** 14,445, 14,462, 14,473, **14,479, 14,494, 14,524, 14,540, 14,557, 14,564, 14,584,** 14,600, 14,603, **14,609, 14,613,** 14,614, **14,643,** 14,646, 14,668, 14,682, **14,705, 14,730,** 14,734, 14,787, 14,848, 14,873, **15,275,** 15,278, 15,291, **15,341,** 15,541, 15,544, 15,571, **15,606, 15,637, 15,644,** 15,692, **15,714,** 15,723, **15,729, 15,744,** 15,747, 15,767, **15,773, 15,852, 15,859,** 15,869, **15,886, 15,949,** 15,968, 16,053, **16,056,** 16,069, **16,080,** 16,115, 16,117, 16,132, 16,182, **16,214, 16,265,** 16,274, **16,302, 16,334, 16,346, 16,348, 16,353, 16,364, 16,368, 16,392, 16,403, 16,404, 16,415, 16,417, 16,437,** 16,438, 16,440, **16,505, 16,548, 16,549, 16,635, 16,639,** 16,934, 16,953, 16,967, 16,968, 16,981, 17,029, 17,036, 17,051, **17,096,** 17,133, 17,140, 17,163, **17,167, 17,168, 17,189,** 17,195, **17,238, 17,273, 17,280, 17,315,** 17,340,

17,368, **17,369**, **17,374**, 17,379, **17,388**, 17,438, **17,469**, **17,495**, **17,591**, **17,625**, **17,658**, 17,679, **17,708**, 17,862, **17,865**, 17,867, 17,874, **17,887**, **17,949**, 17,995. *See also* Educators
certification, 15,539, 17,017, **17,545**
legal status, laws, etc., 4,934, 8,093, 8,129, 8,162, 9,467
out-of-school activities, 1,197
political activity, 8,058, 11,774
recruitment, 4,118, 8,059, 8,060, 8,526
salaries, pensions, etc., 3,817, 4,341, 8,059, 8,147, 8,293, 9,196, 9,327, 10,984, 11,706, 13,249
selection and appointment, **1,871**
social conditions, 15,649
tenure, 8,058, 8,059, 8,060
Teachers, Afro-American, **2,137**, 2,138, **2,143**, 2,948, 4,768, **5,260**, **5,384**, 5,907, 8,873, **12,687**, **13,909**
Teachers' assistants, **16,376**
Teachers' Association (SC), 15,544
Teachers' associations. *See* Teachers' unions
Teachers College (Morehead, KY), 5,313
Teachers' colleges, 954, **1,042**, 1,842, 2,130, 2,919, 2,986, 3,131, 3,140, **3,363**, **4,210**, 4,211, **4,212**, 4,632, **4,658**, 5,313, 5,469, 5,577, **5,609**, 5,634, **5,835**, 6,188, 6,490, 6,645, 6,651, 6,845, 7,800, 7,829, 8,233, 8,244, 8,310, 8,348, 8,378, 8,492, 8,498, 8,991, 9,318, 9,650, 9,764, 9,858, **10,149**, **11,378**, **11,819**, 11,842, 11,897, 11,906, 12,122, 12,470, 13,489, 13,604, 13,610, 13,617, 13,618, 13,905, 14,540, 16,402, 16,425, 16,427, 16,448, 16,924, 17,381
Teachers, interchange of, 2,072, 8,069
Teachers' Loyalty Oath, 7,187
Teachers, Native American, 8,690
Teachers of handicapped children, 13,055
Teachers of mentally handicapped children, 11,181
Teachers of the blind, **2,111**, **7,309**, **7,684**, **10,438**
Teachers of the deaf, **2,102**, **2,103**, **2,111**, **2,114**, 2,202, 11,440, 13,432, **13,673**
Teachers of the mentally handicapped, 14,873
Teachers Patriotic League (MN), 9,472
Teachers, rating of, 8,058
Teachers' Reading Circle (WI), **17,546**
Teachers, Shaker, **7,037**
Teachers, training of, 4,341, 5,346, 5,390, 9,841, 10,995, 11,724, 12,762, 17,017
Teachers' Union (MN), 9,467
Teacher's Union of Philadelphia (PA), 15,200
Teachers Union of the City of New York (NY), 11,774
Teachers' unions, 203, 1,636, 1,713, 3,308, 3,787, **3,817**, **3,818**, 3,824, 3,839, 4,032, 4,124, **4,777**, **4,806**, 4,830, 4,946, 4,958, **7,370**, **8,058**, **8,059**, **8,060**, 8,069, 8,093, 8,097, 8,098, 8,101, 8,102, 8,104, 8,109, 8,113, 8,120, 8,121, 8,125, 8,126, 8,128, 8,129, 8,145, 8,147, **9,224**, **9,298**, 9,467, 9,542, 10,707, 10,998, **11,361**, **11,761**, **11,774**, 12,738, 15,200, 15,332, 15,789, **17,505**
officials and employees, **8,069**
Teaching, 356, 1,007, 5,427, 8,170, 8,331, 8,944, 9,023, 10,951, 13,445, 15,233, 17,578
aids and devices, 16,440
Teaching, freedom of, 11,178, 11,774
"Teaching the Individual," 11,306
Teagarden, Lyrel G. (1894-), **14,457**
Teague, Abner Griffin, 15,524
Teague, B H., **15,524**
Teague, Isaac Newton, 15,524
Teal, Bessie [Mrs. Joseph Nathan], 14,675
Teal, Clara, 14,675
Teal, Helen, 14,675
Teal, Joseph, 2,359
Teal, Joseph Nathan (1858-1929), **14,675**
Teal, Roleta (Davis) [Mrs. Talmadge Theodore] (1913-), 1,750
Teal, Ruth. *See* Betts, Ruth (Teal)
Teall, Dorothy, 11,951
Teall, Elmira, 11,440
Teapot Dome Scandal, 1,424, 2,467
Tears Are for the Living (book), 5,984
Teasdale, Sara. [Mrs. Ernst B.] Filsinger (1884-1933), 635, 1,390, 1,525, 3,987, 4,000, 4,005, 10,154, **10,183**, 11,821, 11,897, 12,695, 17,010, 17,013
Teatro National de Aztlan, 17,619

Tebbets, Marion, 8,666
Tech Review (Massachusetts Institute of Technology), 6,338
Technical education, 6,520, 9,055, 13,383, 14,941
Technical Services and Library Trends (book), 4,402
Technical writers, **5,820**
Technical writing, 11,889
Tecumseh's Foot (book), 15,952
Ted Shawn and His Men Dancers, 12,365
Tedlock, Anne (1905-). *See* Brooks, Anne (Tedlock) (1905-)
Tedrow, Jane [Mrs.], **4,845**
Tedrow, Sillah, 4,845
Teed, Florence Ernestine (Schleicher) (1901-54), **7,947**
Teen age, **2,083**, 6,432, 6,860, 8,639, 10,035, 11,592
Teen age women
education, 3,785
health, 1,607
institutional care, 4,372
pregnancy, 3,785
Teen agers
employment, **2,685**, 6,765, 8,686, 10,074, 14,202, 15,202
political activity, 11,596
research, 6,934, 10,035, 11,911
welfare, 402
Teigan, Henry George (1881-1941), **9,400**
TEL Sunday school, 2,977
Telegraph, 11,550, 12,396
history, **2,725**
Telegraph Hill Neighborhood Association (CA), 412
Telegraph Hill Neighborhood House (San Francisco, CA), 517
Telegraph operators, 956, 8,286, **8,461**, 8,690, **14,533**, **16,428**, 16,967
Telegram (OR), 14,512
"Telemachus" (poem), 14,998
Telemaque (poem), 14,998
Telephone, 3,751, 4,259, 4,436, **6,383**, 7,670, 8,957, 15,554
directories, **166**
Telephone operators, 1,653, 3,451, 4,034, 4,196, 8,690, **9,079**, 11,445, 16,965, 16,985, 16,999
Telephone systems, 11,073
Television
law and legislation, 10,072
ultrahigh frequency, 10,072
Television advertising, 6,495
Television authorship, **17,810**
Television broadcasters, 4,075
Television broadcasting, **2,096**, 10,077, 10,082, 10,330
Television in education, 4,048, 10,072
Television in higher education, 11,848
Television in preschool education, **11,845**
Television programs, **1,024**, 2,168, 2,811, 6,065, 6,098, 6,465, **11,848**, 12,367, 15,130, 16,660, 17,619, **17,808**, 17,966
Television programs for children, 2,767, 13,875
Television programs, public service, 6,693
Television scripts, 226, 451, 1,750, **5,240**, 5,979, 5,980, 6,008, 6,049, 6,082, 6,100, 6,108, 6,111, 7,550, 11,994, 12,890, 13,008, 13,875, **17,818**, 17,966, 17,972, **18,000**, 18,020
Television serials, 2,839, 11,497
Telfair Academy (GA), 3,597
Telfair Academy of Arts, 3,587
Telfair, Edward, 3,389, 3,587
Telfair Fmily (GA), **3,587**
Telfair Hospital (GA), 3,587
Telfair Hospital (GA) Board of Managers, **3,588**
Telfair, Mary (1798-1875), 3,389, 3,521, 3,533, 3,587, **3,589**
"Tell a Woman" (newsletter), 13,508
"Tell It to Grandma, Mother's Busy" (article), 2,936
Tell My Horse (book), 2,872
"Tell Them I Came" (ms), 6,873
Teller, Harriet, 9,965
Teller, Henry Moore, 1,790, 9,965
Teller, James H., 9,965
Temperance 349, 1,426, 1,436, 1,485, 2,720, 2,818, 2,856, 3,069, 3,453, 3,754, 3,762, **4,159**, **4,243**, 4,469, 4,655, **4,708**, 4,893, 5,305, **5,939**, 6,343, 6,374, 6,418, 6,534, 6,661, 6,731, 6,954, 7,078,

7,232, 7,298, **7,336**, 7,597, 7,643, 7,678, 7,951, **8,183**, 8,995, 9,246, 9,386, 9,477, 9,877, 10,162, 10,988, 11,271, 11,279, 11,520, 11,547, 11,600, 11,616, 11,718, 11,726, 11,746, 11,838, 12,003, 12,415, 12,625, 12,740, 12,744, 12,854, 13,414, 13,916, 13,963, 13,999, 14,132, 14,164, 14,223, 14,680, 15,173, 15,571, 15,773, **16,391**, 17,055, 17,264, 17,486, 17,675
legal aspects, 5,565
Temperance Champion, The (newsletter), 1,071
Temperance Education, Inc., 4,055
Temperance societies, 53, **56**, 138, 197, 203, 400, 453, 509, **1,056**, 1,078, **1,169**, 1,190, **1,199**, 1,632, **1,668**, 1,782, **1,805**, **1,943**, **1,944**, **1,946**, 2,059, 2,607, 2,636, **2,649**, 3,010, 3,069, **3,306**, **3,666**, **3,688**, **3,712**, **3,819**, **3,909**, 3,969, 4,054, 4,055, 4,159, 4,223, **4,244**, 4,469, 4,481, 4,605, **4,616**, **4,619**, 4,650, 4,732, **4,786**, 4,793, 4,907, **5,100**, **5,116**, 5,122, **5,223**, **5,344**, 5,641, **5,698**, 6,343, 6,546, 6,901, 6,926, **7,141**, **7,245**, **7,271**, **7,374**, 7,601, 7,779, **7,838**, **7,866**, 7,948, 7,951, **7,977**, **7,978**, **7,979**, **7,980**, **7,981**, **7,982**, **7,983**, **7,994**, 8,166, **8,175**, **8,254**, **8,268**, **8,420**, **8,448**, **8,816**, **8,834**, **8,985**, 8,992, 9,294, 9,295, **9,353**, 9,421, 9,448, 9,467, 9,656, 9,707, 9,708, 9,719, **9,775**, 9,894, **10,063**, **10,116**, 10,402, 10,462, 10,474, **10,559**, **10,642**, 10,666, 10,673, 10,725, 10,912, 10,972, **11,062**, **11,412**, **11,422**, **11,430**, 11,440, 11,443, **11,801**, 11,838, 12,515, **12,608**, **12,741**, 12,790, **12,805**, **12,806**, **12,838**, 12,844, **12,929**, 13,264, 13,297, 13,398, 13,566, 13,648, 13,658, 13,664, 13,665, 13,668, 13,677, **13,694**, **13,861**, **13,862**, 13,930, 13,963, **13,973**, **13,974**, **13,975**, **13,976**, **13,977**, **13,983**, **13,998**, 14,000, 14,015, **14,017**, 14,075, 14,077, 14,092, 14,104, 14,114, **14,127**, **14,164**, 14,223, **14,303**, 14,306, **14,361**, **14,471**, **14,516**, 14,637, **14,690**, 14,713, 14,818, 14,953, 15,175, **15,254**, 15,346, **15,362**, 15,381, **15,395**, 15,771, **15,843**, 15,851, 15,948, 16,040, 16,391, **16,774**, **16,818**, 16,968, **17,154**, 17,226, 17,376, 17,460, **17,571**, **17,750**, **17,837**, 17,916
Tempest in a Teapot, A (opera), 5,413
Tempest, Ruth [Mrs.], **2,918**
Temple Aaron (CO), 13,790
Temple Beth Israel Sisterhood (WA), **13,824**
Temple B'ne Jeshurun (Milwaukee, WI), 17,664
Temple Buell College (CO). *See* Colorado Women's College
Temple Emanu-El (San Francisco, CA), 749, 933, 939
Temple Emanu-El (Milwaukee, WI), 17,664
Temple Emanuel Ladies Aid Society (MN), **13,825**
Temple Emanuel Sisterhood (MN), **13,826**
Temple Etz Ahayem Sisterhood (AL), **13,827**
Temple, Grace Lincoln, **2,859**
Temple Israel (IN), Women's Auxiliary, **13,830**
Temple Israel Sisterhood (IN), **13,828**
Temple Israel Sisterhood (Marion, OH), **13,778**
Temple Israel Sisterhood (NY), **13,829**
Temple, Jane (ca. 1774-1840). *See* Bettle, Jane (Temple) [Mrs. Samuel] (ca. 1774-1840)
Temple, Mary Boyce [Miss] (1856-1937), **15,881**
Temple, Mary (Fall), **5,297**
Temple of the Wings (CA), 362
Temple Rodef Sholom Sisterhood (TX), **13,831**
Temple, Sarah Gober [Mrs.], **2,994**
Temple, Shirley, **17,818**
Temple Sinai Women's Group (Oakland, CA), **946**
Temple Sinai Women's Group (Oakland, CA), Fruit and Flower Mission, 946
Temple University (PA), 15,184, 15,195, 15,197
administrators, 15,182
deans, **15,186**, 15,189
faculty, **15,190**, 15,196
graduate work, **15,191**
Temple University (PA), Chimes, 14,029
Temple University (PA), College of Education, **15,183**
Temple University (PA), Faculty Women's Club, **15,190**, 15,195
Temple University (PA), Stella Elkins Tyler School of Fine Arts, 15,195
Temple University (PA), Theater, **15,193**
Temple University (PA), Women's Club, 15,186, **15,194**
Temple University Hospital (PA), 15,187, 15,194

Temple University Hospital (PA), School of Nursing, **15,192**
Templeton, Maria, 2,582
Templin, Mildred Clara (1913-), **8,618**
Temporary Homes (CT), 1,938
Ten Broeck Monument (NY), 12,345
Ten Brook, R. K., 3,499
Ten Brook, Sarah, 3,499
Ten Commandments, The (moving-picture), 17,802
Ten Eyck Family, **11,042**
Ten Eyck, Jacob (1733-94), 11,042
Ten Eyck, Margaret [Miss] (1766-1850), 11,042
Ten Grandmothers, The (book), 14,218
"Ten Years in Oregon," 14,602
Ten Years in Washington (book), 14,058
Ten Years of Birth Registration in Ohio (book), 14,006
Tenant and landlord, 15,205
Tenant farming. *See* Farm tenancy
Tenayucca, Emma, 16,009
"Tenement Poor of New York City, The" (dissertation), 11,655
Tenille High School (GA), 3,419
Tennant, Grace Mabel, 9,282
Tennant, Mary Elizabeth, 12,739
Tennent, Ann Martha Smith, 15,749
Tennent, Edward II, 15,749
Tennent, Edward Smith (1819-62), **15,749**
Tennent, Eliza [Mrs. William], 15,749
Tennent Family (SC), **15,750**
Tennent, Hattie Taylor [Mrs. Edward Smith] (?-1905), 15,749, 15,750
Tennent, John Charles, 15,750
Tennent, Madeline Grace "Madge" (Cook) [Mrs. Hugh Cowper] (1889-1972), 3,634
Tennent, Mary Julia, 15,750
Tennent, Susan [Mrs. William Mackey], 15,750
Tennessean (Nashville, TN), 15,966
Tennessee, 122, 9,699, 13,162, 13,450, **15,957**
  art, decorative, 13,631
  art societies, 15,883
  artists, **15,883**
  authors, 3,339, 10,178, **15,878, 15,896, 15,899,**
    15,900, 15,950
    19th C, **15,952**
    19th-20th C, **15,957**
  bankers, Afro-American, 15,889
  bills, legislative, 15,959, 15,971
  boarding schools, **15,940**
  camp meetings, 15,968
  Catholic schools, 15,912
  centennial celebrations, 15,948
  child welfare, 15,884
  cholera epidemics, 5,398, 13,250
  church colleges, **15,960**
  church records and registers, Presbyterian, 161
  church societies, Christian Church (Disciples of Christ), **15,906**
  citizens' associations, 3,283
  Civil War, 12,448, 13,106
    destruction and pillage, 15,952
    personal narratives, 13,072, 13,162, **15,952**
    societies, Confederate, 15,943, 15,951, 15,975
  clubs, 15,897, 15,967, **15,971**
  college and school periodicals, 15,897
  college teachers, 15,924, **15,925**
  community organization, **15,961**
  congresswomen, **15,875**
  court-houses, 2,507
  deans (in schools), **15,922, 15,926, 15,930**
  department heads (universities), **6,924**
  diaries and journals, 3,155, **13,040**
    19th C, **15,952, 15,955**
    20th C, 15,963
  divorce suits, **15,958**
  dormitories, 15,926
  editors, **15,966, 15,976**
  elections, 15,890, 15,941, 15,945
  employment, 15,887
  endowments, **5,474**
  explosives industry, 15,963
  extended care facilities, **15,984**
  family life education, 6,490
  farm life, 8,154

folk medicine, 15,933
folk songs, 15,933
folklore, 15,933
forests and forestry, 2,713
genealogists, **15,951**
genealogy, **15,975**
governors, 9,722, 9,869, 15,887, 15,941
historians, **15,882, 15,902, 15,950**
historical societies, 15,948, 15,975
housewives, 3,317, **15,895, 15,896**
immigrants, 1,472
Jews, **15,950**
journalists, **15,878, 15,892, 15,966**
judges, 13,080
land grants, **15,969**
lawyers, Jewish, **13,784**
legislators, 15,914, **15,976**
literary societies, **15,872, 15,965**
lynching, prevention of, 3,279
manufacturers, **15,953**
merchants, 3,317, **15,959**
monasticism and religious orders for women, Catholic, **15,912**
musicians, **15,953**
newspaper publishing, 15,976
newspapers, sections, columns, etc., 15,966
novelists, **15,902**
nursing education, 15,972
nursing homes, 15,972
nursing schools, 233, **15,937**
officials and employees, 15,887, 15,927, 15,971
patriotic societies, **15,947**, 15,951
pensions, military, **15,944**
philanthropists, Afro-American, 15,889
physical education and training, 12,937
pioneers and settlers, 13,006, **15,888**
plantation life, 15,932
poets, 15,879, **15,952, 15,957, 15,967**
poliomyelitis, 8,621
political activists, Afro-American, 15,889
political activists, women, **15,903**
railroads, employees, 3,317
Reconstruction, 3,155
sanatoriums, 7,220
school superintendents and principals, 15,959, 15,964
schools, 5,474, **15,949**
scrapbooks, **15,954**
social life and customs, 4,608, 15,953, 16,057
soldiers
  Civil War, Confederate, **15,944**
  War of 1812, 15,959
strikes and lockouts, 11,927
  textile workers, 17,734
students' societies, **15,872**
suffrage, 15,941, 15,948
  opposition to, 15,964
suffrage societies, **15,962, 15,970**
suffragists, 6,949, **15,980**
survivors' benefits, **15,944**
teachers, 2,162, **3,155, 15,886, 15,949, 15,968**
temperance societies, 15,948
trade and professional associations, **15,972**
trade-unions, officials and employees, 3,447
universities and colleges, 4,481, 5,474, 9,672
  archives, **15,897**
  employees, **15,919**
urban beautification, 15,961
volunteer workers in hospitals, **15,982, 15,983, 15,984**
Women's colleges, 13,321, **15,960, 15,973**
yellow fever epidemics, 16,246
Tennessee Agricultural and Industrial State College, faculty, **6,924**
Tennessee Board of Pension Examiners, 15,944
Tennessee Centennial Commission, 15,948
Tennessee Centennial Exposition, women's board, 15,948
Tennessee Confederate Pension Board, 15,944
Tennessee Council for Nursing, 15,972
Tennessee Equal Suffrage Association, **15,970**, 15,980
Tennessee Federation of Business and Professional Women's Clubs, Inc., **15,971**

Tennessee Governor's Commission on the Status of Women, 15,971
Tennessee League for Nursing, **15,972**
Tennessee League for Nursing Education. *See* Tennessee League for Nursing
Tennessee Society for Preservation, 15,883
Tennessee State Association Opposed to Woman's Suffrage, 15,964
Tennessee State Industrial Union Council, 3,447
Tennessee Wesleyan College, 4,481
Tenney, Alice, 9,145
Tenney, Anna, 17,593
Tenney Committee (CA), 788
Tenney Family, 4,942
Tenney School (IL), 4,181
Tennis players, 997, 10,784, **12,871, 15,371**, 15,935
Tennyson, Alfred Lord, 6,185, 6,669, 12,381
Tenth Iowa Volunteer Infantry, 4,836
Tenth Street Sisters (San Francisco, CA), 1,339
Tenth United States Cavalry, 211
Tenth Wisconsin Infantry Regiment, 11,101
Teratogenic agents, 11,830
Terekhov, Miguel, 14,240
Terekhov, Yvonne (Chouteau) [Mrs. Miguel] (1929-), **14,199, 14,240**
Teresa, Mother M. Angeline (1894-), 11,469
Terhune, Anise Morris (Stockton) [Mrs. Albert Payson] (1873-1964), 2,601
Terhune, Edward Payson (1872-1942), 1,495, **2,601**
Terhune, Mary Virginia (Hawes) [Mrs. Edward Payson] (1830-1922), **1,495**, 4,244, 12,525
Termehr, Mother Mary Xavier (1831-92), 4,873
Terminal care, 7,359
Terre Haute Post (IN), 4,675
Terrell, Marjory [Miss], 13,145
Terrell, Mary (Church) (1863-1954), **2,153, 2,602**
Terrestrial Air-breathing Mollusks of the United States (book), 14,878
Territorial Centennial Train (MT), 10,370
Territorial Daughters of Colorado, 1,701, 1,775, **1,797**
Territorial Daughters of Washington, Chapter II, **17,156**
Territorial Papers of the United States (book), 2,250
Terry, Elizabeth [Mrs. Reuben], 9,917
Terry, Ellen Alicia (1848-1928), 2,542, 3,100, 3,110, 6,185, 12,359, 12,361, 12,539, 12,610, 13,966, 17,197
Terry, George F., **9,917**
Terry, Luther, 11,579
Terry, Reuben, 9,917
Terry, Roderick, 2,535
Terry, Rose (1827-92). *See* Cooke, Rose (Terry) [Mrs. Rollin H.] (1827-92)
Terry, Ursula [Mrs. George F.], **9,917**
Terwilliger, Elizabeth (Cooper) (1909-), 668, 1,068
Tesdell, Margaret Stanley (1919-), **8,890**
Teshigahara, Kasumi (1932-), 10,151
Tesker, Wanetta (White) [Mrs. Paul] Draper [Mrs. Elmer H.] (1918-), 1,685, **1,689**
Tesmer, Louise M., **17,728**
Tesoro, Giuliana, 6,335
Tested Toy Laboratory (NY), 15,353
Testimonials in advertising, 8,992
Testu, Jeanette (1898-1963), **17,347**
Tetanus, mortality, 106
Teter, Eugene, 247
Teter, Martha Ann Brown [Mrs. Eugene] (1893-), 247
Tetherow, Solomon, 1,505
Tetlow, Elsie, 5,932
Tetlow, Helen Ingersoll (1877-), 5,932, 5,948
Tevis, Henry Lloyd (1856-1931), **836**
Tevis, Lloyd (1824-99), 791
Tevis, Louise (ca. 1858-1938). *See* Sharon, Louise (Tevis) Breckinridge [Mrs. Frederick William] (ca. 1858-1938)
Tewa Indians, 12,067, 14,897, 16,864, **16,874**
Tewksbury, Mary Ellen (1922-), 11,851
Tex-Son Company, 15,995
Texaco, 16,246
Texarkana Pioneer Association (TX), 16,133
Texarkana Pioneer Family Histories (booklet), 16,133
Texas, 2,377, 8,801, 16,035, 16,054, 16,064, 16,080, 16,082, 16,092, 16,096, **16,098**, 16,102, **16,104,**

16,121, 16,122, 16,126, **16,129**, 16,182, **16,206,**
16,207, 16,241, 16,284, **16,345,** 16,353, 16,392
abortion
law and legislation, 16,396
legal aspects, 1,984
Afro-Americans, 16,261, 16,342, 16,351, 16,377
education, **15,913**
history, **16,205**
agricultural statistics, 16,357
agriculture, 16,078, 16,092, 16,095, 16,148
Alamo, 16,314
arbitration, industrial, 16,009
archives, **16,215**
archivists, **16,083**
art, galleries and museums, 16,232
art societies, 16,195, 16,315
artists, **8,179,** 16,145, **16,232, 16,261, 16,277,**
16,304
authors, **8,179,** 16,102, **16,145,** 16,159, 16,274,
16,302
autobiography, **16,120**
balls (parties), 16,321
bankers, **16,040**
Baptists, **16,345**
bells, 16,353
biography, **16,044**
bishops, 9,991, **16,018**
bison, American, 16,060
boarding schools, 16,031
boots and shoes, trade and manufacture, **16,273**
botanists, 16,060
botany, 16,316
boycott, **15,987**
businesswomen, **16,002,** 16,038
camps, 938, 16,257
Catholic Church, societies, **16,017**
Catholic schools, 16,251
Catholic universities and colleges, 16,230
cattle, 16,039, **16,312**
cattle breeders, 875
charitable societies, Jewish, **13,831**
charities, 16,132, 16,260, 16,275, **16,321**
choral societies, **16,223**
church colleges, 16,125
church records and registers, 16,311
church societies, 16,265, 16,278
church societies, Baptist, 16,382
church societies, Methodist, 16,059, **16,084,** 16,209
churches, Baptist, 16,365
cities and towns
civic improvement, 16,302
planning, 16,259
citizens' associations, 3,283, 16,259, 16,342
city councilwomen, **16,002**
civil rights, **15,991, 15,993**
civil supremacy over the military, 16,323
Civil War, 16,016, 16,097, 16,144, 16,261
personal narratives, 16,060
societies, Confederate, 16,114, 16,127, **16,140,**
16,178, 16,261
clergy, 9,597, **16,359, 16,386**
clergy, German Baptist, 16,362, 16,365
clergy, Presbyterian, 9,801
clergymen's wives, 16,014, 16,060
clothing workers, **15,992**
clubs, 938, 11,247, **11,248,** 16,115, **16,119,** 16,126,
16,127, 16,128, **16,138,** 16,145, 16,146, **16,183,**
16,185, 16,186, 16,187, 16,188, 16,189, 16,190,
16,192, 16,193, 16,194, 16,195, 16,196, 16,198,
16,199, 16,200, 16,201, 16,202, 16,203, 16,211,
16,224, 16,228, 16,255, 16,263, 16,267, 16,277,
16,278, 16,279, **16,293,** 16,300, 16,303, **16,309,**
16,313, **16,320, 16,322, 16,323, 16,330,** 16,336,
16,341, **16,350,** 16,354, **16,389, 16,397**
coeducation, 16,031
college and school periodicals, 16,341, 16,369
college librarians, 16,131
college presidents, **2,125**
college students, 16,329, **16,332, 16,338**
college teachers, **15,986, 16,212, 16,249, 16,295,**
16,304, 16,328, 16,347, 16,351, **16,358, 16,360,**
16,385, 16,388
college trustees, 16,225, 16,325
colonial period, 16,083, 16,088, 16,121, 16,310

Comanche Indians, wars, 16,117
community colleges, 16,242
composers, **16,135**
concerts, 16,013
congressmen, 14,284, 16,058, 16,379
conservationists, 16,197
constitution, citizen participation, 16,259, 16,264
corporation law, 16,327
country life, 3,310
court records, 16,215
courts, 6,666
deans (in schools), 16,037, **16,134, 16,288, 16,331,**
16,332, 16,366, 16,382
degrees, academic, **16,340**
department heads (universities), **16,375**
diaries and journals, **16,060,** 16,247, 16,305, 16,378
diseases, 16,117
drug abuse, 16,242
editors, 16,282
education, 16,347
education, bilingual, 16,376
education, rural, 16,132
educational associations, **16,177, 16,184, 16,258,**
16,265, **16,294, 16,326,** 16,344
educators, 2,125, **16,337,** 16,347
elections, 10,035, 16,235, 16,240, 16,260, 16,386
endowments, 16,339
executive advisory bodies, 16,342
executives, **16,273**
farmers, 16,306, 16,357
folklore, 16,261
folklorists, **16,351**
forums and debates, 16,236
freedmen, 16,356
fund-raising, 16,183, 16,185, 16,186, 16,188,
16,189, 16,192, 16,196, 16,198, 16,202
gardening, societies, **16,219,** 16,278
geologists, 15,956, 16,274
governors, 16,000, 16,014, 16,016, 16,313
high school teachers, **16,000**
historians, 16,038, **16,058, 16,083, 16,086, 16,098**
historical societies, 938, 16,058, 16,133, 16,176,
16,241
home demonstration work, **16,271**
home economics, 16,286
hospital administrators, **16,343**
hospital and community, 16,343
hospitals, 16,092, 16,251
housewives, **16,068, 16,096, 16,099, 16,109, 16,142,**
16,145, 16,300, 16,324, 16,365, 16,379
immigrants, German, 1,476
immigrants, Italian, 12,632
immigrants, Moravian, 16,380
impeachment, 16,313
infants, mortality, 16,060
interns (medicine), 16,226
Irish in, 16,351
journalism, societies, etc., **16,139**
journalists, **16,053,** 16,197, **16,248, 16,253, 16,348,**
16,354, 16,387
judges, 6,666, 16,029, **16,264**
land, registration and transfer, 16,078
land use, planning, 16,231
law, cases, **16,090**
lawyers, 6,432, **6,666,** 9,728, **16,029,** 16,327, **16,368**
learned societies, 16,277
legislators, 12,951, **15,988, 16,004,** 16,029, 16,058,
16,214, 16,225, **16,231,** 16,327, **16,396**
librarians, **16,239**
library associations, **16,289**
literary societies, 9,799, 16,295, **16,395**
local church councils, 16,038
local transit, law and legislation, 16,231
lynching, prevention of, 3,279
massacres, 16,117
medical assistants, **16,227**
medicine, cases, clinical reports, statistics, 16,357
mental hygiene, 16,069
merchants, 16,071
Methodism, 16,040
Methodist Church, education, **16,113**
Mexican Americans, 16,334, 16,368
civil rights, 16,376
migrant labor, 230

millinery workers, 16,006
monasticism and religious orders for women,
Catholic, **16,020, 16,179, 16,230, 16,251, 16,254,**
16,262, 16,319
municipal universities and colleges, **16,318**
museum directors, 16,316, 16,388
museums, 16,388
music teachers, **16,062, 16,266, 16,281, 16,341,**
16,358
musical societies, 16,062, **16,136,** 16,266, 16,293,
16,352
musicians, **16,269**
Native Americans, 16,032, 16,060
captivities, 16,117
cultural assimilation, 16,344
relations with whites, 16,117
wars, 838, 16,064, 16,100, 16,124, 16,310
newspapers, sections, columns, etc., 16,348, 16,349,
16,387
Norwegian Americans, 16,324
novelists, 13,172, **16,295**
nuns, Catholic, 16,018, **16,019,** 16,311, **16,343**
nursing schools, **16,333**
alumnae, **16,229**
officials and employees, 16,038, **16,270,** 16,359
old age homes, **16,220**
orphans and orphan asylums, 16,251
oral history, **16,012, 16,181, 16,204, 16,205, 16,206,**
16,238, 16,374
parades, 16,320
patriotic societies, 16,014, **16,030,** 16,040, 16,116,
16,178, 16,265, **16,298, 16,299,** 16,313, 16,382
pediatricians, **16,226**
performing arts, 16,146
philanthropists, **16,221**
physicians, 3,310, 16,060, **16,063, 16,225,** 16,236,
16,342, 16,357
pioneers and settlers, **10,** 1,619, 16,060, **16,071,**
16,074, **16,076, 16,079,** 16,100, 16,117, **16,181,**
16,305, 16,356, 17,626
pioneers and settlers, German, 16,306
pioneers and settlers, Polish, **16,307**
plantation life, 16,142
poets, **16,143, 16,269, 16,295**
poets laureate, **16,137, 16,349**
police, 15,993
political activists, women, 15,990, 16,006, 16,007,
16,240
political parties, 16,368, 16,376
political statistics, 15,998
politicians, 16,007, 16,235, **16,359, 16,386**
politics, practical, women's activism, 16,015,
16,191, 16,217, 16,235, 16,240, 16,259, 16,260,
16,265, **16,276,** 16,293
poor, 16,215
Presbyterian churches, education, 16,125
prison reform, 16,123
prohibition, **16,391**
prostitutes, 16,393
prostitution, legal aspects, **16,393**
public health nursing, 16,216
public libraries, **16,233**
public officers, **13,537**
public records, **16,310**
public relations consultants, **16,222**
public schools, 16,031, 16,055
race problems, 12,939, 16,356
radio broadcasting, 16,265
ragtime music, 16,013
rain and rainfall, 16,357
ranchers, 16,271
ranches, **15,985,** 16,060
rape crisis centers, 16,259
rape, law and legislation, 16,231
real estate investment, **16,046,** 16,130
Reconstruction, 16,097, 16,148
Republic (1836-1846), 1,639, 16,103, 16,117,
16,129, 16,147, 16,261
vice-presidents, 16,058
Revolution (1835-1836), 16,046, 16,050, 16,117,
16,243
Salvation Army, missions, 16,364
school administrators and minority groups, 16,334
school boards, 16,236, **16,242**

school districts, 15,993, 16,242, 16,334, 16,368, 16,376
school integration, 16,242
school music, 16,062
school superintendents and principals, 16,318, **16,342**
schools, **16,392**
scrapbooks, **16,127**
sculptors, **16,021, 16,372**
secession, 9,031
secretaries, **16,037**
secretaries of state, 16,015, **16,103**
senators, United States, 16,029
seniors, 15,999, 16,000
sharecropping, 16,377
slavery, 6,464
    emancipation, 16,356
smorgasbord, 16,324
social life and customs, 16,057, 16,117, 16,145, 16,355
social science research, 16,215
soldiers, 16,114
Spanish missions, 16,083
state aid to the arts, 16,111
state universities and colleges, faculty, 16,012
statisticians, 15,998, 16,038
sterilization (birth control), legal aspects, 16,396
stores, retail, 16,101
strikes and lockouts, 15,987, 15,992, 15,995, 16,008, 16,009
    clothing workers, 1,577
student unions, 16,331, 16,382
suffrage, 16,015
suffrage societies, 16,015, **16,033, 16,218,** 16,235, 16,252, 16,313
suffragists, **16,235**
Sunday-schools, 13,831
symphony orchestras, 16,275, 16,358
teachers, 7,935, **16,053, 16,056,** 16,069, **16,080, 16,115,** 16,117, **16,132,** 16,182, **16,214, 16,265,** 16,274, **16,302, 16,334, 16,346, 16,348, 16,353, 16,364, 16,368, 16,392**
teachers' assistants, 16,376
temperance, **16,391**
tornadoes, 16,259
trade and professional associations, 236, **16,227**
trade-unions, 15,997, **16,007**
    agricultural laborers, **16,003, 16,009**
    clerks, **16,005**
    clothing workers, 15,987, 15,995, 15,996
    hat trade, **16,011**
    machine industry, **15,994**
    officials and employees, 16,007, **16,008**
    packing-house workers, **16,009**
tutors and tutoring, 16,148
undertakers and undertaking, **16,363**
United Nations associations, 16,265
universities and colleges, 2,125, **16,048, 16,107, 16,108, 16,112,** 16,204, **16,287, 16,308**
    buildings, 16,339
universities and colleges, Afro-American, 16,342
urban beautification, citizen participation, **16,394**
urban renewal, 16,259
utopias, **16,180**
vocational education, 16,132
voluntary health agencies, 16,069, 16,284
wages, college employees, 16,325
widows, **16,147**
wild flowers, 16,316
women's colleges, **16,369**
World War II, civilians' work, 16,215
Young Women's Christian Association, 16,275
Texas A&M University (TX), Campus Study Club, **16,190**
Texas A&M University (TX), Newcomers Club, **16,199**
Texas A&M University (TX), Women's Social Club, 16,199, **16,200**
Texas AFL-CIO, **16,007**
Texas Agricultural Extension Service, 16,193
    officials and employees, 16,271
Texas Association for Mental Health, 16,284
Texas Association of College Teachers, 16,212

Texas Association of Deans of Women and Deans of Girls, **16,134**
Texas Baptist Woman's Missionary Union, 16,382
"Texas Centennial" (column), 16,387
Texas Civil Liberties Union, 15,991
Texas Commission on Interracial Cooperation (1940-42), 16,239
Texas Constitutional Revision Commission, 16,264
Texas Constitutional Revision Commission, Lubbock Area Advisory Commission, 16,259
Texas Council of Church Women, 16,265
Texas Department of Education, applied music division, 16,062
Texas Equal Franchise Society, 16,040
Texas Equal Suffrage Association, 16,015, 16,235, 16,252, 16,313
Texas Federation of Music Clubs, 16,062, **16,136**
Texas Federation of Women's Clubs, 16,062, 16,115, 16,127, 16,128, 16,145, **16,267,** 16,293, 16,322
Texas Game and Fish Commision, officials and employees, **16,270**
Texas Genealogical Society, 16,261
Texas Historical and Landmarks Association, 16,058
Texas Home Economics Association, **16,286**
Texas Institute of Letters, 16,295
Texas Interracial Commission, 12,939
Texas Liberal Democrats, 15,997
Texas Literacy Council, 16,271
Texas Memorial Museum, 16,032
Texas Nurses Association, 236
Texas Poet Laureate Contest, **16,137**
Texas Presbyterian College for Girls, 16,125
Texas Prison Centralization Commission, 16,146
Texas Rangers, 16,076, 16,122, 16,124
Texas Society for Crippled Children, 16,132
Texas Society for Mental Health, 16,069
Texas Society for Mental Hygiene. See Texas Society for Mental Health
Texas State Department of Public Health, employees, 16,038
Texas State Historical Association, 16,058, 16,102, 16,241
Texas State Music Festival, 16,062
Texas State Music Teachers Association, 16,062
Texas State Senators' Wives Club, **16,138**
Texas Summer Normal School, 16,132
Texas Teachers' Bureau, 16,115
Texas Tech University (TX), 16,287
    deans, **16,288**
Texas Tech University (TX), Faculty Women's Club, 16,278
Texas Woman Suffrage Association. See Texas Equal Suffrage Association
Texas Woman's University, alumnae, 16,271
Texas Women's Press Association, 16,091, **16,139**
Text Book for Fine Art of Light-Color Play, 2,366
Text-book of the Principles and Practice of Nursing, 6,143
Text-books, 1,898, 1,961, 2,777, 3,434, 3,463, 4,341, 4,710, 5,986, 6,107, 6,141, 6,143, 8,452, 9,558, 10,037, 11,617, 11,889, 11,993, 15,755
    bias in, 13,459
Textbook of Theology (book), 17,307
Textile design, 7,118, 13,307
Textile factories, **6,187, 6,191, 6,195, 6,198,** 7,070, **7,113, 7,114, 7,116, 7,117, 7,118, 7,119, 7,121, 7,122, 7,123, 7,124, 7,125, 7,126, 10,881,** 10,882, **12,758,** 13,528
    fires and fire prevention, 7,120
Textile fibers, synthetic, 8,596
Textile industry, 6,795, **7,115,** 12,574
Textile industry and fabrics, 2,684
    economic aspects, 8,067
Textile industry and fabrics, Spanish, 2,112
Textile workers, 1,426, 5,596, 5,644, **5,899,** 5,938, 6,714, 6,859, **7,067,** 7,070, **7,113, 7,116, 7,117, 7,118, 7,119, 7,120, 7,121, 7,122, 7,123, 7,124, 7,125, 7,126,** 7,680, 8,085, 10,813, 10,815, **12,758,** 15,214, 16,430, 16,965
    diseases and hygiene, 17,007
    wages, 5,896
Textile Workers Industrial Union, 8,061
Textile Workers' Organizing Committee, 13,176

Thacher, Anna Alice. See Post, Anna Alice (Thacher) [Mrs. Louis Freeland]
Thacher, George, **7,448**
Thacher, Molly Day (1907?-63). See Kazan, Molly Day (Thacher) [Mrs. Elia] (1907?-63)
Thacher, Thomas, 9,710
Thackeray, William Makepeace, 6,329, 7,677, 11,993, 12,164, 15,601
Thackray, Ethel M., 2,596
Thailand
    American diplomats in, 2,192, 6,262
    judges, 6,262
    missionaries to, 2,271
    nutrition, 11,603
    tutors and tutoring, 1,426
    women, status of, 6,981
Thailia Club (Charleston, SC), 15,515
Thalidomide, side effects, 11,932
Thalman, Louisa (1843-97). See Hasler, Louisa (Thalman) [Mrs. John] (1843-97)
Thane, Elswyth (1900-). See Beebe, Elswyth Thane [Mrs. William] (1900-)
Thane Miller School (OH), 13,853
Thanksgiving Day, 9,207, 13,550
Tharp, Louise Hall [Mrs.], 10,858
That Remarkable Man, Justice Oliver Wendell Holmes (ms), 6,053
Thatcher, Anne Bell [Mrs. Maurice H.], 1,666
Thatcher, Caine, 4,743
Thatcher, Ebenezer, 5,679
Thatcher, Elizabeth [Miss], **11,724**
Thatcher, George. See Thacher, George
Thatcher, Leora (1894-), 16,485
Thatcher, Mrs. Safford M., 17,665
Thatcher, Paul, **16,914**
Thatcher, Peter Blaney, 12,663
Thatcher, Safford M., 17,665
Thatcher, Sarah Catherine Hopkins, **16,483**
Thatcher, Sarah Maria Davis, 16,914
Thaw, Harry K., 5,505
Thaw, William, 3,706
Thaxter, Anna Quincy. See Parsons, Anna Quincy (Thaxter)
Thaxter, Celia (Laighton) [Mrs. Levi] (1835-94), 1,426, **2,603, 5,032,** 5,694, 5,925, **5,966,** 7,294, 8,375, **10,830,** 10,853, 11,821, 17,010
Thaxter, John, 5,904
Thaxter, Levi, 1,426
Thaxter, Rosamund, 5,694
Thayer, Abby E., **11,725**
Thayer Academy (MA), 6,923
Thayer, Adelaide (De Claire) (1864-1945), 7,997
Thayer, Clarissa, **15,208**
Thayer, Eleanor W. (1908?-), **7,309**
Thayer Family, 4,404
Thayer, Fidelia Hunt [Mrs. Simeon O.], 9,141
Thayer, Florence Madilia (Scofield) (1858-1936), 7,675
Thayer, Harriet, 14,618
Thayer, Hollis, **5,636**
Thayer, Mary Louisa, 12,154
Thayer, Mrs. A. M., 3,751
Thayer, Pauline Revere [Mrs.] (1861-1934), **7,062**
Thayer, Sarah S., 2,604
Thayer, Simeon O., 9,141
Thayer, William Sydney (1830-64), **2,604**
Theater, 60, 1,115, 2,804, 3,145, 3,847, 3,851, **4,222,** 4,473, 4,477, 5,410, **11,453, 11,985,** 12,065, 12,374, 13,026, 14,670, 15,532, 15,901, 16,968, **17,281,** 17,384, 17,964
    awards, 6,669, 11,860
    economic aspects, 6,004
    little theater movement, 1,734, **1,996,** 3,287, 3,847, 3,994, 4,097, 7,195, 8,001, 10,743, 17,393
    reviews, 6,085, 6,104
    study and teaching, 440, 11,907
Theater and society, 11,907
Theater and state, 11,907
Theater audiences, 10,182
Theater, Finnish-American, 9,502
Theater management, 2,418, 3,832, **9,361,** 11,985, **12,444**
Theater managers, 3,084, **12,623**
Theater programs, **2,968, 3,100, 3,921,** 17,807

Theater, Swedish-American, 17,345
Theaters, 169, 203, 225, **1,077**, 1,774, 3,267, 3,753, **3,924**, 6,669, 6,882, 8,144, 8,351, 8,956, **11,689**, 11,860, 11,894, **12,557**, 12,612, 12,623, 16,399
management, 16,888
Theatre Arts Magazine (periodical), 6,834, 13,674, 17,803
Theatre de L'Empire (Paris, France), 17,965
Theatre Guild, 2,284, 6,008, 12,360
Theatre Guild, American Theatre Society, 2,293
"Theatre in Northampton," 7,195
Theatre World Award, 11,860
Theatrical agencies, 6,008, **14,670**
Theatrical agents, **10,182**, **11,461**, **17,811**
Theatrical producers and directors, 871, **1,978, 4,091,** 6,047, 6,085, 6,667, 6,669, 8,001, 9,175, 11,907, **12,006, 12,039,** 12,367, 12,426, 12,474, **12,549,** 12,619, 12,622, **13,008,** 14,413, **15,901,** 16,438, **17,281, 17,800, 17,819**
Theft. *See* Larceny
Their Eyes Were Watching God (book), 2,948
Their Search for God (book), 14,122
Thelander, Hulda Evelyn (1896-), **1,348, 1,380, 9,514**
Thelen, Fanny J. [Mrs. Edmund], 1,213, 1,216
"Then Came the Women" (ms), 109
Theobald, Anna Cole, 9,437
Theocrat, The, 4,461
Theodora Youmans Citizenship award (WI), 17,823
Theodore Frelinghuysen Wolfe (book), 11,182
"Theodore Winthrop, American Writer" (ms), 18,011
Theodore Wirth Park (MN), 8,973
Theologians, **2,513, 4,204, 8,872, 15,358**
Theological seminaries, 1,839, 1,840, 1,842, 1,844, 1,845, 1,846, 1,849, 1,851, 1,853, 1,855, 1,858, 1,859, 3,969, 4,201, 4,203, 4,206, 4,207, 4,208, **4,463,** 4,640, 6,231, 8,724, 10,570, 11,066, 14,470, 17,214, 17,679
archives, **12,090**
Theological seminaries, Baptist, **5,371**
Theological Seminary of Northwestern, alumni, 5,074
Theology, 13,288
Theophilus Trent (book), 13,961
Theosophical Society of America, 1,187, 1,196, 2,213, 4,732, 14,585
Theosophical World-University, 11,580
Theosophists, 1,187, **1,196,** 1,239, **2,213, 6,246,** 14,585, **14,751**
Theosophy, 9,131, 11,580, 17,739
"There Shall Be No Night There" (poem), 2,480
There Was a Garden (book), 14,200
"There's Always Surgery" (ms), 6,841
Thermodynamics, 11,814
"These Are They" (ms), 16,074
"These Were Builders" (booklet), 11,363, 11,364, 11,365, 11,366
Thespians, The (CA), 1,073
Theta Sigma Phi. *See* Women in Communications, Inc.
Thetford Academy (MA?), 7,586
Theus, Simeon, 15,661
"They Gave Us a Job" (ms), 6,082
They Were San Franciscans (book),1,279
Thiele, Merle A., 15,853
Thies, Clarissa Crowninshield [Mrs. Louis] (1810-1907), **7,469**
Thin Man, The (screen play), 17,799
Third Annual Rendezvous of Western Art (MT), 10,363
Third Aviation Instruction Center, American Canteen, 4,350
Third Judicial District Bar Association (MN), 9,525
Third Maryland Cavalry, 2,514
Third Michigan Cavalry, Company G, 8,296
Third National Health Careers Council, 6,123
Third New York Volunteers, 8,929
Third North Carolina Regiment, Confederate States of America, Army, 13,085
Third Presbyterian Church of Newark (NJ), 11,099
Third Ward School (Pittsburgh, PA), 15,226
Thirteenth International Peace Congress (MA, 1904), 15,300

Thirteenth Minnesota regiment, 9,059
Thirty-three Roads to the White House (book), 4,988
Thirty Years of American Dance (book), 12,365
"This Beautiful Stricture, A Play of John S. Calhoun" (drama), 12,959
"This I Believe" (radio program), 15,273
This Is Ohio (book), 14,081
"This Is Your Life" (television program), 15,130
"This Little Light" (radio program), 17,599
"This Throne of Kings" (drama), 12,959
This Tilting Dust (book), 5,310
This Was Tomorrow (book), 5,031
This Week Magazine, 12,044
Thiselton-Dyer, Harriet Anne (1854-1945), 10,151
Thode, Frieda Oelschlaeger [Mrs. E. H.], **10,143**
Thomas, Abel Charles (1807-80), 2,606
Thomas, Ada R., **11,043**
Thomas, Ann (1839-1920). *See* Phillips, Ann (Thomas) (1839-1920)
Thomas, Anna A., **11,137**
Thomas, Anna Hasell (1828-1912), **15,751**
Thomas, Anne (Butler) [Mrs. David Owen], **4,614**
Thomas, Bruce F. (1853?-82), 5,271
Thomas, Caroline (Bedell) [Mrs. Henry M.] (1904-), **7,311**
Thomas, Caroline Elizabeth (1825-1908). *See* Merrick, Caroline Elizabeth (Thomas) [Mrs. Edwin Thomas] (1825-1908)
Thomas, Charles H., 1,875
Thomas, Cora de La Matyr [Miss], **2,605**
Thomas, Danforth W., 8,236
Thomas, Dorothy, **12,644**
Thomas, Dorothy Swaine, 570
Thomas, Dylan, 17,791
Thomas, Edith Matilda (1854-1925), 1,426, **5,967,** 5,973, **6,922,** 17,010, **17,210**
Thomas, Elizabeth (Todhunter) [Mrs. Evan Philip], **5,813**
Thomas, Ella Gertrude (Clanton) (1834-?), **13,213**
Thomas, Eloise (1876-?), **14,676**
Thomas, Eva, 11,548
Thomas, Evan, 15,313
Thomas, Evan Philip, 5,813
Thomas Family, **13,962**
Thomas Family, 4,942
Thomas Family (GA), **3,561**
Thomas Family (NY?), 12,531
Thomas Family (PA), 14,889
Thomas, Fannie Edgar [Miss], **12,321**
Thomas, Harriet, 1,559
Thomas, Helen. *See* Flexner, Helen (Thomas) [Mrs. Simon]
Thomas, Helen. *See* Follett, Helen (Thomas) [Mrs. Wilson]
Thomas, Helen (Haskell) [Mrs. Stephen Seymour] (1860-1942), 535
Thomas, Helen (Moore) [Mrs. William Bailey] (1867?-1945). *See* Bristol, Helen (Moore) [Mrs. William Bailey] Thomas [Mrs. Mark Lambert] (1867?-1945)
Thomas, Henry M. (1891-1966), 7,311
Thomas, James J., 13,999
Thomas, Jeannette Bell (1881-), **5,375**
Thomas Jefferson: An Intimate History (book), 16,881
Thomas, Jennie Manning, 16,967
Thomas, Jessie, **8,365**
Thomas, Joan, **17,348**
Thomas, John, 3,712
Thomas, John (businessman, ID), 3,682
Thomas, John Charles, 2,664
Thomas, John Martin, **10,929**
Thomas, Josephine Elizabeth (1834-?), 6,628
Thomas, Katherine Garford (1883-), **14,096**
Thomas, Letty (Kingsbury), 2,424
Thomas, Lillian, 45
Thomas, Lowell, 14,101
Thomas, Lydia, **15,098**
Thomas, M. Louise, 2,196
Thomas, Margaret [Miss], 3,561
Thomas, Maria Louise (Palmer) [Mrs. Abel Charles] (ca. 1830-?), **2,606**
Thomas, Martha Carey (1857-1935), 2,643, **5,731,**

7,274, 7,315, 11,742, 14,737, 14,738, **14,745,** 14,889, 17,588
Thomas, Martha Catherine "Kate" (Northcott) [Mrs. Bruce F.] (1850-89), 5,271
Thomas, Mary (United States employee). *See* Brooks, Mary (Thomas) [Mrs. A. J., Jr.] Peavey [Mrs.]
Thomas, Mary Ann, 3,529
Thomas, Mary Ann (Park) (1811-?), 7,660
Thomas, Mary B., **15,098**
Thomas, Mary Margaret (Murray) [Mrs. George], 13,669
Thomas, Mildred C., 5,871
Thomas, Mrs. J. G., 3,561
Thomas, Mrs. John, 3,528
Thomas, Naomi, 8,672
Thomas, Norman, 6,544, 8,077, 11,917, 12,701, 12,702
Thomas, Rebecca (Primus) [Mrs. Charles H.] (1836-1932), **1,875**
Thomas, Robert B., 5,942
Thomas, Sarah Putnam, 7,047
Thomas, Stephen Seymour, 535
Thomas, Susan A., 13,962
Thomas, Susan Frances Elder, 3,610
Thomas, W. H., 13,448
Thomas Y. Crowell Company, 2,436, 14,369, 14,390
Thomason, Fannie Rose (Knox) [Mrs. Hugh], 287
Thompson. *See also* Thomson
Thompson, Adelaide, **8,366**
Thompson, Alice, 10,761
Thompson, Almon Harris (1839-1906), 12,645, 16,962
Thompson, Amira Carpenter (ca. 1800-?), 11,440
Thompson, Amos, 9,401
Thompson, Amy (1899-). *See* Gulling, Amy (Thompson) (1899-)
Thompson, Angie, 9,401
Thompson, Anna Boynton (1848-1923), 6,452, **6,923**
Thompson, Anna Young (1851-1932), 15,175
Thompson, Augustus Charles (1812-1901), **1,860**
Thompson, Barbara J. [Mrs.], 17,411
Thompson, Benjamin, 10,831
Thompson, Benjamin F., 6,996
Thompson, C. Mildred (1882-1975), **3,257, 11,502**
Thompson, Caroline Cornelia (Barnum) [Mrs. David W.] (1833-1911), **1,828**
Thompson, Carrie (Scarborough) [Mrs. Horace] (1832-?), 9,401
Thompson, Catherine, 15,258
Thompson, Celia May (Crocker) (1874-?), **837**
Thompson, Claire Warner Churchill, 14,714
Thompson, Cleopatra, 9,575
Thompson, Cornelia Ett (1836-1919). *See* Connett, Cornelia Ett (Thompson) [Mrs. Earl Fairchild] (1836-1919)
Thompson, Delia (?-1918), **14,018**
Thompson, Dr., 11,002
Thompson, Dorothy, 4,151
Thompson, Dorothy. [Mrs. Josef] Bard [Mrs. Sinclair] Lewis [Mrs. Maxim] Kopf (1894-1961), 2,207, 2,336, 2,513, 2,542, 4,482, 9,956, 11,810, 12,044, 12,070, **12,911**
Thompson, Edith, 984
Thompson, Eleanor P., **5,527**
Thompson, Eliza Jane (Trimble) [Mrs. James Henry] (1816-1905), **2,607,** 13,963
Thompson, Elizabeth, 3,114
Thompson, Elizabeth. *See* d'Happart, Elizabeth (Thompson) [Mrs. Joseph St. Leger]
Thompson, Ellen L. "Nellie" (Powell) [Mrs. Almon Harris], **12,645, 16,962**
Thompson, Ellen Powell, 12,573
Thompson, Era Bell, 3,290
Thompson, Ethel, 3,377
Thompson, Faith (1893-1961), **8,619**
Thompson Family (OH), **13,963**
Thompson, Fanny, 15,953
Thompson, Frances Euphemia (ca. 1900-), **6,924**
Thompson, Frances Judith Somes (Trask) (1806-92), **16,392**
Thompson, Frances S., 5,469
Thompson, Frank, 9,749
Thompson, Frank. *See* Edmundson, Sarah Emma (Seelye) (1841-98)

Thompson, Georgia Ann. *See* Broadwick, Tiny. Georgia Ann Thompson
Thompson, Georgia (Cook) [Mrs. Ben], 9,095
Thompson, Glenn, **14,052**
Thompson, Harriet Jane [Mrs. William G.], 4,784
Thompson, Helen, **9,749**
Thompson, Helen, 2,353
Thompson, Henrietta W., **116**
Thompson, Horace (1827-80), Family (MN), **9,401**
Thompson, Hugh Miller, 9,749
Thompson, Ida M., 17,104
Thompson, Irma (1880-). *See* Ireland, Irma Thompson [Mrs. Mark] (1880-)
Thompson, James E., 2,315
Thompson, Jane, 10,452
Thompson, Jean Cebrou, 13,523
Thompson, Jennie. *See* Howell, Jennie (Thompson) [Mrs. Alfred Elliott]
Thompson, Julia, **8,791**
Thompson, Julia F., 12,820
Thompson, "K" [Mrs. Lovell], 7,626
Thompson, Karen Anne (Murray), 13,669
Thompson, Kate, **3,258**
Thompson, Kathleen (1880-1966). *See* Norris, Kathleen (Thompson) [Mrs. Charles G.] (1880-1966)
Thompson, L. C., 3,377
Thompson, Laura, 2,840
Thompson, Leila, 16,999
Thompson, Lewis Thomas (1842-?), **14,677**
Thompson, Libbie (Moody) [Mrs. Clark W.] (1897-), **16,221**
Thompson, Lily Wilkinson [Mrs.], **9,750, 9,821**
Thompson, Louisa A. (?-1912). *See* Evans, Louisa A. (Thompson) [Mrs. Samuel D.] (?-1912)
Thompson, M. Burnette [Miss], **8,792**
Thompson, Malvina, 2,340
Thompson, Margaret (?-1942). *See* Sheldon, Margaret (Thompson) [Mrs. Addison E.] (?-1942)
Thompson, Marguerite (1887-1968). *See* Zorach, Marguerite (Thompson) [Mrs. William] (1887-1968)
Thompson, Maria (Dobie) (1844-1927), 1,860
Thompson, Mary, 14,663
Thompson, Mary (1895-). *See* Fisher, Mary (Thompson) [Mrs. Clyde] (1895-)
Thompson, Mary Angelina [Mrs. James Egbert] (1830-52), 9,401
Thompson, Mary (Dartt) [Mrs. Nathan], 1,730
Thompson, Mary Franklin (Wolfe) [Mrs. Charles] (1886-1970), **11,182**
Thompson, Mary Harris (1829-95), 3,967, 4,027, 4,217
Thompson, Mary J. Stafford, **3,259**
Thompson, Mary McArthur (1849-1916). *See* Tuttle, Mary McArthur (Thompson) (1849-1916)
Thompson, Mary Pickering (1825-94), **10,847, 10,855**
Thompson, Mary Wolfe [Mrs. Charles], **16,983**
Thompson, Mattie, 15,953
Thompson, May (1901-). *See* Evans, May (Thompson) (1901-)
Thompson, May Eliza (Wright) [Mrs. Edwin W.] (1844-1920). *See* Sewall, May Eliza (Wright) [Mrs. Edwin W.] Thompson [Mrs. Theodore Lovett] (1844-1920)
Thompson, May Ringo [Mrs.] (1868-1940), **5,326**
Thompson, Mercy Rachel (Fielding) [Mrs. Hyrum] Smith [Mrs. Robert Blashel] (1807-93), **16,835**
Thompson, Mr., 12,289
Thompson, Mrs., 12,289
Thompson, Mrs. (NV), 10,761
Thompson, Mrs. Joseph, 3,141
Thompson, Mrs. Marshall, 11,829
Thompson, Nancy Christie [Mrs. Amos], 9,401
Thompson, Nellie. *See* Thompson, Ellen L. "Nellie" (Powell) [Mrs. Almon Harris]
Thompson, Peggy, 10,191
Thompson, Rebecca, **15,099**
Thompson, Ruth Gage (ca. 1880-1950), 9,289
Thompson, Ruth P. (1895-?), 1,605
Thompson, Ruth S., **838**
Thompson, Sarah (1764-1821). *See* Dunn, Sarah Thompson [Mrs. Richard] (1764-1821)

Thompson, Sarah (Countess of Rumford) (1774-1852), 10,799, 10,831
Thompson, Sarah Reed, **839**
Thompson, Susan. *See* Parish, Susan (Thompson)
Thompson, Suzy, 5,644
Thompson, Sylvia (Williams), 14,618
Thompson, Sylvie (1868-1975). *See* Thygeson, Sylvie Grace (Thompson) (1868-1975)
Thompson, Te Ata (1895-). *See* Fisher, Mary (Thompson) [Mrs. Clyde] (1895-)
Thompson, W. C., 3,377
Thompson, Walter J., 17,411
Thompson, William G. (1830-1911), **4,784**
Thoms, May De Pree [Mrs. Sharon J.] (1878-1952), **10,926**
Thoms, Sharon J., 10,926
Thomson. *See also* Thompson
Thomson (CT), **1,932**
Thomson, Amelia (Lewis) (1799-?), 6,901
Thomson, Anna Speck, 11,719
Thomson, Elizabeth Anna (Williams) [Mrs. Samuel Steele] (1824-54), **4,489**
Thomson, Fannie (1848-68), 10,185
Thomson, Lilian (1889-). *See* Mowrer, Lilian (Thomson) [Mrs. Edgar Ansel] (1889-)
Thomson, Louise, 3,382
Thomson, Margaret (1809-?). *See* Smoot, Margaret (Thomson) [Mrs. Abraham O.] (1809-?)
Thomson, Margaret M., **9,402**
Thomson, Mary Agnes "Polly" (1885-1960), 11,812
Thomson, Mary Meed, 3,382
Thomson, Mildred [Miss] (1889-), **9,403**
Thomson, Samuel Steele, 4,489
Thomson, Sara (1842-1922). *See* Kinney, Sara (Thomson) (1842-1922)
Thomson, Sarah, **11,044**
Thomson, Susan Belcher [Mrs.] (1809-90), 1,932
Thomson, Virgil, 10,120
Thorburn, Charles E., Family, 5,718
Thorburn Family (OR), 14,606
Thoreau, Henry David, 6,857, 7,055
Thoreau, Mary, 17,010
Thoreau, Sophia E. (1819-76), 7,055, 17,010
Thorn, Katherine (1907-77), **11,383**
Thornbrough, Emma Lou, 2,540
Thornburg, Fannie, 10,228
Thorndike, Lynn, 12,009
Thorne, Alison (Cornish), 16,971
Thorne, Charlotte R., 88
Thorne, Dorothy Lloyd Gilbert [Mrs. Howard Harlan] (1902-76), **13,240**
Thorne, Florence Calvert (1878-1973), 5,119, **11,924**
Thornton, Anna Maria (Brodeau) [Mrs. William] (1774?-?), 2,608
Thornton, Ella Mae [Miss], 3,174, **3,260**
Thornton, Eva [Mrs.], 3,384
Thornton, J. Q., 14,680
Thornton, Jessie Willock [Mrs. Dan] (1912-), 11,857
Thornton, Mrs. Phineas, **15,752**
Thornton, William (1759-1828), **2,608**
Thorp, Polly [Miss], 4,285
Thorp, Vivian Stanley, 9,287
Thorpe, Ann, 8,657
Thorpe, Anne (Longfellow) (1855-1934), 6,330
Thorpe, Mother Catherine Mary Antoninus (1844-79), 12,859
Thorpe, Theresa (Locke) (1879-?), 1,632
Thortvedt, Eva [Mrs.], 8,690
"Those Desert Hills and Other Poems," 10,650
"Those Early Days in Wisconsin" (article), 2,655
Thought and Work Club (Salem, MA), **7,449**
Thought Club (MA), **7,051**
Thousand Ages, A (book), 17,771
Thousand Imitations, A (book), 5,990
Threadcraft, Georgia, **3,590**
Threadcraft, Sallie, **3,590**
Threads of Truth (periodical), 14,869
"Three Observations for Three Woodwinds," 6,503
"Three Old Crows" (poem), **6,373**
"Three Red Hills, The" (ms), 8,796
Three Sisters, The (drama), 17,819
Three Who Loved (book), 6,058
Three Ways of Asian Wisdom (book), 16,167
Three Women (drama), 6,602

Threshing, 8,690
Thrift Garden Project, 8,089
Throop, Ellen M. (Johnson) (1843-1927), **10,543**
Throop, George A., **11,726**
Throop, Nellie (1874-1962). *See* Magee, Nellie (Throop) [Mrs. Oliver N.] (1874-1962)
Thropp, Mary Elizabeth. *See* Cone, Mary Elizabeth (Thropp)
Through Dooms of Love (book), 6,042
Through 150 Years (book), 15,240
Throup, E. T., 12,160
Thumbs Up for Joy and Adventure (book), 2,159
Thummel, Juline (Smith), 801
Thunderhead (book), 17,999
Thurber, James, 4,476
Thurber, Laura Ann (Keeler) [Mrs. Joseph Heber] (1859-1909), **16,561, 16,836**
Thurber, Phebe (Cox), **16,442**
Thurman, Howard (1900-), 6,119
Thurman, Mary E. E., **16,443**
Thurmond, Elizabeth (Long), 3,101
Thurmond Family (GA), **3,101**
Thurmond, Samuel Pinckney, 3,101
Thurmond, Strom, 48, 15,755
Thursby, Alice, 12,322
Thursby, Emma Cecilia (1845-1931), 2,413, **12,322**
Thursby, Ina, 12,322
Thursday Book Club (Newton-Conover, NC), **13,304**
Thursday Club (AL), **15**
Thursday Club (New Haven, CT), **2,004**
Thursday Club (ME), **5,594**
Thursday Club (Winona, MN), 9,520
Thursday Club (Charleston, SC), **15,422**
Thursday Evening Club (NY), **12,323**
Thursday Reading Club (IN), **4,582**
Thurston, Elizabeth F. (McClench) [Mrs. Samuel Royal]. *See* Odell, Elizabeth F. (McClench) [Mrs. Samuel Royal] Thurston [Mrs.]
Thurston, Samuel Royal (1816-51), 699, 14,614
Thurton, Elizabeth, 15,405
Thwing, Mrs. Charles F., 13,979
"Thy Law" (poem), 7,681
"Thy Mercies Will I Sing" (dissertation), 9,695
Thygeson, Sylvie Grace (Thompson) (1868-1975), 827, 1,016, 1,652
Thykesen, Anna (1879-), **8,793**
Tibbets, Mary Ann [Mrs.] (1819-96), **4,601**
Tibbles, Susette (La Flesche) [Mrs. Thomas] (1854-1903), 10,483
Tichenor, Catherine S. *See* Craven, Catherine S. (Tichenor) [Mrs. John Joseph]
Ticknor and Fields (publishers), 7,685
Ticknor, Anna Eliot (1823-1906), 5,958
Ticknor, Caroline (1866-1937), **7,685**
Ticknor, George, 12,239
Ticknor, William Davis (1810-64), 7,685
Tidd, Nannie, 9,918
Tide House (book), 7,888
Tiegel, Agatha Mary Agnes (1873-1959). *See* Hanson, Agatha Mary Agnes (Tiegel) [Mrs. Olof] (1873-1959)
Tiel, Maude Emily (1866-1941). *See* Sanford, Maude Emily (Tiel) [Mrs. William Ackley] (1866-1941)
Tiernan, Frances Christine (Fisher) [Mrs. James Marquis] (1846-1920), **13,594**
Tiernan, James Marquis, 13,594
Tierney, Agnes, 15,283
Tierney, Gene, 1,025
Tietjens, Eunice (Hammond) [Mrs. Paul]. Eunice (Hammond) [Mrs. Paul] Tietjens [Mrs. Cloyd] Head (1884-1944), 3,988, **4,005**
Tiffany, Almira (1888-1966). *See* Bethers, Almira (Tiffany) [Mrs. Albert Francis] (1888-1966)
Tiffany and Company (NY), 9,719
Tiffany Foundation, 11,835
Tiffany, Francis, 12,445
Tiffany, Louis, 11,835
Tiffany, Palmer, **5,056**
Tiffany, Sarah Jane York, 16,604
Tiffin, Edward, 14,086
Tigard Family, 256
"Tiger Rag" (song), 5,531
Tiger's Tail, The: A Story of America's Great Political Cartoonist Thomas Nast (book), 5,037

Tigert, Edith (Bristol) [Mrs. John J.], 2,884
Tigert, John J., 5,458
Tilden, Eleanor Weir, 324
Tilden, Ida [Mrs. William], 4,175
Tilden, Josephine Elizabeth (1869-1957), **8,620,** 14,409
Tilden School, Town of Tilden, School District No. 3, Chippewa County (WI), **17,547**
Tileston, Mary Porter (1820-94). *See* Hemenway, Mary Porter (Tileston) [Mrs. Augustus] (1820-94)
Tileston, Thomas, 7,477
Tilford, Olive (1868-1968). *See* Dargan, Olive (Tilford) [Mrs. Peagram] (1868-1968)
Tilford, Solon, 4,475
Tilghman, Edward, 11,002
Tilghman, Sarah (1896-). *See* Hughes, Sarah (Tilghman) [Mrs. George E.] (1896-)
Tillamook Indians, 17,252
Tilledge, Miriam, 17,125
Tiller, Edith W., **8,459**
Tillett, Gladys (Avery) [Mrs. Charles W.] (1897-), 11,503, 13,176
Tilley, Arthur, 6,471
Tilley, Elizabeth, 9,689
Tilley, Erna Spannagel, 17,398
Tilley, Margaret P. [Miss], **17,398**
Tillich, Paul, 5,511
"Tillie the Toiler" (radio program), 2,274
Tillinghast, Anna Churchill (Moulton) (1874-1951), **6,925**
Tillinghast, Mr., 6,796
Tillman, Benjamin Ryan, 15,563, 15,733
Tillotson College (TX), 2,125
   faculty, 5,468
Tillotson, Josephine (Musser), 16,949
Tillotson, Mrs. Henry B., 9,029
Tillson, Christiana Holmes, 4,313
Tilly, Dorothy Eugenia (Rogers) [Mrs. Milton Eben] (1883-1970), **3,353, 3,469**
Tilson, Anna Green (Mitchell), 3,410
Tilton, Alice (pseudonym). *See* Taylor, Phoebe Atwood (1909-76)
Tilton case, 6,993
Tilton, Elizabeth (Hewes) [Mrs. William] (1869-1950), **6,926**
Tilton, Theodore, 6,395
Timberlake, Alcinda [Miss], **9,751**
Timberlake, John B. (?-1828), 2,320
Timberlake, Margaret (1892-?). *See* Simkin, Margaret (Timberlake) (1892-?)
Timberlake, Margaret L. (O'Neale) [Mrs. John B.] (1799?-1879). *See* Eaton, Margaret L. (O'Neale) [Mrs. John Henry]. [Mrs. John B.] Timberlake [Mrs. Antonio] Buchignani (1799?-1879)
Timberland Times (IL), 4,386
Time (periodical), 15,564
Time in the Sun, A (book), 5,987
Time, Incorporated, 5,144, 14,451, 15,564, 15,565
Time study, 2,673, 4,682, 7,115
Time to Purpose, A (book), 16,306, 16,307
Times (San Jose, CA), 342
Times (Louisville, KY), 17,076, 17,608
Times (MS), 15,899
Times (NC), 13,468
Times and Seasons (newspaper), 4,302
Times-Dispatch (Richmond, VA), 17,076
Times-Gazette (CA), **1,116**
Times-Herald (DC), 17,070
Times Illustrated Hand-Book for 1876, 4,794
Times-Picayune (LA), 9,771
Times-Star (OH), 13,844
Times, The (Charleston, SC), 15,419
Times-Union (NY), 12,800
Timmermann sisters (TX), 16,097
Timmis, William, 8,934
Timmons, Frances Jane (1823-1908). *See* Crane, Frances Jane (Timmons) [Mrs. Andrew Jackson] Grayson [Mrs. George Belden] (1823-1908)
Timothy, Ann [Mrs. Peter] (ca. 1727-92), 15,686
Timpe, Joyce, **17,349**
Timrod, Emily. *See* Goodwin, Emily (Timrod)
Timrod, Henry (1828-67), 13,030, **15,753**
Tin Butterfly, A (book), 16,160
Tingley, Clyde, 11,214

Tingley, Katherine Augusta Westcott [Mrs. Richard Henry] Cook [Mrs. George W.] Parent [Mrs. Philo Buchanan] (1847-1929), 1,187, **1,196**
Tingley, Philo Buchanan, 1,196
Tinker, Katherine, 8,676
Tinkham, Margaret. *See* Peabody, Margaret (Tinkham)
Tinsley, Eleanor, **16,242**
Tinsley, Willa Vaughn, **16,288**
Tintic mining district, 16,534
Tio Pepe (book), 16,159
Tioga Point Museum (Athens, PA), 15,319
Tisdale, Phebe Alden, **12,646**
Tisha (book), 130
Titanic (ship), 2,646, 8,518, 17,800
Titanic disaster, 1,756
Titchener, E. B., 13,741
Title Nine (IX),
Title IX legislation, 6,990
Titles of honor, **3,272,** 9,669, 9,757
Titman, Annie Blair (1867-1952). *See* Cummins, Annie Blair (Titman) [Mrs. George Wyckoff] (1867-1952)
Titman, Margaret Elizabeth Roseberry [Mrs. William Blair] (1844-1940), 10,903
Titus, M. M. [Miss], 4,597
Tjomsland, Anne (1890-1968), **11,727**
Tlingit Indians, **16,875**
"To a Lady by a Female Maniac" (poem), 3,016
"To a Mother Bird" (poem), 3,040
To Catch a Thief (moving-picture), 17,802
To Colorado's Restless Ghosts (book), 1,685, 1,689
To End War (book), 15,308
"To Our Children" (ms), 7,105
"To the Banished Society at Winchester" (poem), 15,042
"To the Discontented and Unquiet" (poem), 7,007
"To the Yukon and Beyond," 12,396
Tobacco manufacture and trade, 12,171
Tobey, Mark, 17,231, 17,280, 17,284
Tobia, Rajee, **8,173**
Tobias, Sheila, 1,975, 11,663, 15,197
Tobin, Margaret. *See* Brown, Margaret (Tobin)
Tobogganing, 9,467
"Today Show" (television program), 6,098
"Today's Children/Women in White" (soap opera), 17,705
Today's Health (periodical), 10,894
Todd (1821-74), **4,405**
Todd, Clara (Patterson), **7,948**
Todd, Della M. (1893-1967), **18,015**
Todd, Dolley (Payne) [Mrs. John, Jr.] (1768-1849). *See* Madison, Dorothea "Dolley" (Payne) [Mrs. John, Jr.] Todd [Mrs. James] (1768-1849)
Todd, Ellen, 11,728
Todd, Eliza, 1,658
Todd, Elizabeth (1825-95). *See* Grimsley, Elizabeth (Todd) (1825-95)
Todd, Elizabeth Parker (1813-88). *See* Edwards, Elizabeth Parker (Todd) [Mrs. Ninian Wirt] (1813-88)
Todd Family (KY), 5,291
Todd Family (KY), **5,327**
Todd Family (NY), **11,728**
Todd Family (NY), 11,440
Todd, Frances R., 11,662
Todd, Jane Hedges (1890-1966), **11,729,** 11,897
Todd, John, 11,583
Todd, John, Jr., 2,468, 13,483
Todd, John Payne (1792-?), 2,468
Todd, Lydia Pendergast, 9,282
Todd, Mabel (Loomis) [Mrs. David Peck] (1856-1932), 5,862, 7,185
Todd, Maria C. Duffie [Mrs. William W.] (1787-1857), **12,324**
Todd, Mary, 9,972
Todd, Mary Ann (1818-82). *See* Lincoln, Mary Ann (Todd) [Mrs. Abraham] (1818-82)
Todd, Matilda (Ferguson) [Mrs. Roger North], 9,972
Todd, Mrs. T. W., 10,029
Todd, Richard, 2,476
Todd, Roger North, 9,972
Todd, Sarah M., 11,728
Todd Shipyards Corporation, 6,640

Todd, Susie L. [Mrs.], 17,622
Todds Valley Gazette, The (CA), 716
Todes, Charlotte, 9,380
Todhunter, Elizabeth. *See* Thomas, Elizabeth (Todhunter) [Mrs. Evan Philip]
Todhunter School, 11,853
Toedteberg, August Frederich, 11,328
Toedteberg, Augusta, 11,328
Toedteberg, Augustus (1825-1909), **11,328**
Toedteberg, Catharine Lagere [Mrs. Augustus] (1821-1905), 11,328
Toedteberg, Emma (1857-1936), **11,328**
Toedteberg, Louisa, 11,328
Together (book), 17,069
Together Magazine Century Club, 10,568
Togno, R. Acelie, 15,731
Toklas, Alice B. [Miss] (1877-1967), 523, 620, 754, 815, 819, **840,** 1,565, 2,331, 4,226, 5,525, 5,863, **6,927,** 11,153
Tokyo Friends Girls School (Japan), 14,848
Tokyo Rose. *See* D'Aquino, Iva Toguri [Mrs.]
Toland, Mary Bertha Morrison [Mrs. Hugh], **1,381**
Tolbert, Marguerite, 13,176
Toldridge, Elizabeth Barnet, **12,647**
Toledano, Ben C., **5,543**
Toledo Consumers League (OH), 14,144
Toledo District Nurses Association (OH), **14,143**
Toledo Normal School (OH), 14,135
Toledo Polytechnical School (OH), alumnae, 14,135
Toledo Woman's Suffrage Association (OH), 14,144
Tolentino, Cecilia T., 9,986
Toll roads, 1,750
Tollefsrude Family, 8,765
Tolles, Mary (ca. 1840-90), **10,790**
Tolley, A. B., 5,161
Tolley, Wilma, 3,751
Tolman, Hannah (Fayerweather) (?-1790). *See* Winthrop, Hannah (Fayerweather) Tolman [Mrs. John] (?-1790)
Tolman, Ruel P., **2,849**
Tolman, Susan Lincoln (1825-1912). *See* Mills, Susan Lincoln (Tolman) [Mrs. Cyrus Taggart] (1825-1912)
Tolmer, Captain A., 8,801
Tolstoy, Countess Alexandra, 5,123
Tolstoy, Olga, 15,305
Tolstoy, Latianer, 1,647
Tolstoy, Leo, 1,647
Toluectin, Edith Newlands, 1,321
Tomasowa, Helena, 9,986
Tombigbee Rifles, First Mississippi Regiment, 9,748
Tomita, Hideto, 14,678
Tomita, Saku [Mrs.] (1900-), **14,678**
Tomkins, Margaret. [Mrs. James Fitzgerald], 17,350
Tomkins, Mary, 10,846
Tomlin, Lily, 4,981
Tomlinson Family, 3,612
Tomlinson Family (NY), 11,709
Tomlinson, Lizzie, **12,325**
Tomlinson, Madeleine Cummings (Baxter) (1879-1938), 5,606
Tomlinson, Sara, 1,339
Tommasi, Gilda, 14,453
Tomorrow Is for You (book), 13,674
Tompkins County Agricultural Society (NY), 11,550
Tompkins County Memorial Hospital (NY), 11,758
Tompkins, Dortha C., 3,755
Tompkins, Edward, 841
Tompkins, Elizabeth Knight [Miss], 841
Tompkins Family (CA), **841**
Tompkins Family (GA), 3,323
Tompkins, Sarah Haight [Mrs. Edward], 841
Tonawanda Indian Mission (NY), 8,304
Tonduz, Adolfo, 14,876
Toner, Joseph Meredith (1825-96), **2,609**
Too Many Girls (musical comedy), 12,367
Too Many Wives (book), 16,686
Too Near the Sun (book), 4,801, 4,991
Toogood, Mona Keig [Mrs. Myron Charles, Jr.] Lake [Mrs.], 10,721
Toohey, Elizabeth [Miss], **209**
Tooke Family (NY), **11,730**
Tooke, Helen. *See* Butler, Helen (Tooke)
Tooke, Manley J., 11,730

Tooke, Mary E., 11,730

Toombs, Adah (Knight) [Mrs. Henry J.] (1907-), **3,430**

Toombs Family, 79

Toombs, Henry J., 3,430

Toombs, Julia A., 3,532

Toombs, Robert, 3,060

Toomer, Jean, 3,288

Toomey, Gertrude Sans Souci [Mrs. William C.] (1873-1913), **9,348**

Toops, H. A., 13,746

Top Hand of Lone Tree Ranch, The (book), 5,261

Topdahl, Manilla P., **8,129**

Topeka Veterans Administration Hospital (KS), 5,233

Topgallant, a Herring Gull (book), 5,012

"Topic of the Day, The," 4,773

Topographers, 191

Topp, Mildred (Spurrier), **9,752**

Topping, Helen F. [Miss] (1889-), **3,777**

Topping, Lucille [Mrs. Tom], **10,387**

Torbenson, Mary Syverson [Mrs. Oscar] (1880-), **8,794**

Torch Press, 1,224, 4,950

Torgerson, Clara (1891-). See Wheeler, Clara (Torgerson) (1891-)

Torgerson, Katherine Virginia Gillespie Geary [Mrs. Loren] (1912-), **9,525**

Torgerson, Loren, 9,525

Törma Family (MN), **9,511**

Törma, Fred, 9,511

Tornadoes, 8,751, 15,869, 16,259

Torre de San Miguel Homes, Inc. (St. Paul, MN), 9,210

Torrence, Francis, 15,226

Torrence, Frederick Ridgely (1874-1950), **11,174**

Torrence, Olivia (Dunbar) [Mrs. Frederick Ridgely] (1873-1953), 11,174

Torrey, Alice, 14,414

Torrey, Dorothea, 1,339

Torrey, Elizabeth [Miss], 10,037

Toscanini, Walter, 12,364

Tosh, Emma Barr, 3,929

Totah, Eva (Marshall), 1,652

Totalitarianism, 2,483

Totherow, Carl D., 13,322

Touchstone Family (GA, LA, MD, MS, NC, SC, VA), 3,614

Tougaloo College (MS), 2,802

faculty, 5,468, 5,477

Tourist Club (Des Moines, IA), **4,846**

Tourist Club (MN), **8,491**

Tourist Club (Minneapolis, MN), **9,404**

Tourist trade, 2,922

Tourists, 9,404

Tourney, The (periodical). See *Colorado Woman, The* (periodical)

Touroff, Eleanor (1898-1972). See Glueck, Eleanor (Touroff) [Mrs. Sheldon] (1898-1972)

Tourtillote, Jane Augusta (Holbrook) Gould (1833-1917), **444**, 4,904

Tousley, Clare M. (1889-), **6,928**, 8,670, 12,078, 12,080

Tousley, May Hewitt, 13,664

Toveritar (newspaper), 9,503

Tovey, Eloyde, **842**

"Toward a New Feminine Psychology" (lecture), 15,197

Toward the Light, Joseph Fels—His Work (book), 14,995

Towell, Emily Fletcher, **3,727**

Towle, Katherine Amelia [Miss] (1898-), **843, 11,925**

Towler, Lewis, **8,367**

Towles, Lois, 3,290

Towley, Charlotte, 8,685

Town, Clarissa E. Leavitt, **9,753**

Town clerks, **16,984**

Town Club (OR), 14,565

Town Down East (book), 5,694

Town Hall Series, 12,549

Town Meeting of the Air, 6,914

Town, Sarah, 17,029

Town Talk (IL), 3,930

Towne, Abigail W. (Peterson) (?-1945), **7,450**

Towne, Alice Christine (1884-). See DeWeese, Alice Christine (Towne) [Mrs. Fred M.] (1884-)

Towne, Charles Hanson (1877-1949), 12,029, **12,648**

Towne, Elizabeth, 2,314

Towne Family (NE), 10,454

Towne, Joseph, 2,314

Towne, Rosa M. (1827-1909), 10,151

Towne, Salem, **7,521**

Towne, Sally [Mrs. Salem, Jr.], 7,521

Townes, Elsie Garrett (1883-), 16,355

Townesend, Frances Eliza (Hodgson) [Mrs. Swan Moses] Burnett [Mrs. Stephen T.] (1849-1924). See Burnett, Frances Eliza (Hodgson) [Mrs. Swan Moses]. [Mrs. Stephen Townesend] (1849-1924)

Townesend, Stephen, 12,409

Towns, George Alexander (1870-1961), **3,305**

Towns, Grace (1907-). See Hamilton, Grace (Towns) (1907-)

Towns, Nellie MacNair [Mrs. George Alexander] (1879-1967), 3,305

Towns of Tintic (book), 16,519

Townsend, Aurelia [Mrs. Alstyne], 17,036

Townsend, Aurelia (1811-91). See Herrick, Aurelia (Townsend) [Mrs. Horace] (1811-91)

Townsend, Caroline Parrish, **12,326**

Townsend, Christina Cornelia Woods (1854-?), 4,255

Townsend, Della, 7,849

Townsend Family (NY), **12,327**

Townsend, Hannah, 12,327

Townsend, Harriet, 12,327

Townsend, Howard (?-1867), 12,327

Townsend, Howard, Jr. (1858-1935), 12,327

Townsend, Isabella (1827-95). See Waterman, Isabella (Townsend) [Mrs. Henry] (1827-95)

Townsend, Jane. See Quigg, Jane (Townsend) [Mrs. John B.]

Townsend, Justine Van Rensselaer [Mrs. Howard], 12,327

Townsend, Lavinia S., 3,911

Townsend, Lora (1878-). See Dickinson, Lora (Townsend) [Mrs. Frederick] (1878-)

Townsend, Mary, 12,327

Townsend, Mary Ashley [Mrs.], **5,528**

Townsend, Peter, 12,326

Townsend, Sarah, 12,327

Townsend, Susan Elizabeth (1817-1906). See Fisher, Susan Elizabeth (Townsend) [Mrs. Hiram] (1817-1906)

Townsend, Susanna (Roberts) (1817-?), **844**

Townsend, Sylvia [Mrs.] (1837-?), 9,262

Townsend, William (1814-64), **17,036**

Towson, Nathan, 5,814

Towson, Sophia (Bingham) [Mrs. Nathan], **5,814**

Towson State University (Baltimore, MD), **5,835**

faculty, 5,833

presidents, 5,834, 5,836

Toy industry, 11,434

Toyiabe Literary Club (NV), 10,689

Toys, 2,069, 15,353

Tozzer, Alfred Marston (1877-1954), **6,328**

Trace of Footprints, A (book), 6,117

Trachoma. See Conjunctivitis, granular

Trachtenberg, Laddie, 14,497

Track and field athletes, 997, 15,935

"Tract Entitled the Duty of Disobedience to the Slave Act, A," 7,561

Tract societies, 10,970, 11,184

Tracts, **8,795**

Tracy, Deborah Woodworth [Mrs.] (1772-1854), **11,276**

Tracy, Eleanor E., 1,628

Tracy Family, 14,056

Tracy, Lois Bartlett, 2,763

Tracy, Martha (1876-1942), 15,128, **15,140**

Tracy, Moses, 845

Tracy, Mrs. Frank, 12,043

Tracy, Nancy N. (Alexander) [Mrs. Moses] (1816-?), **845**

Tracy, Regina Jeanette (Olson) (1885-1971), **14,679**

Trade and Labor Assembly of Chicago (IL). See Chicago Federation of Labor (IL)

Trade and professional associations, 76, 99, 116, 230, 231, 232, 233, 236, 238, 239, 242, 243, 246, **384,** 393, 948, **1,159, 1,160,** 1,344, **1,691, 1,706, 2,097,** 2,205, 2,224, 2,309, **2,506,** 2,673, 2,686, **2,706, 2,833, 2,834, 2,835, 2,836, 2,924,** 3,162, **3,190, 3,361, 3,378,** 3,399, 3,432, 3,439, **3,444,** 3,467, **3,629, 3,780, 3,859, 3,883, 4,075,** 4,094, **4,098, 4,177,** 4,367, 4,380, 4,477, **4,583, 4,692, 5,000,** 5,230, **5,416, 5,417,** 5,477, 5,494, **5,845,** 6,122, 6,123, 6,124, 6,127, 6,134, 6,139, 6,141, 6,147, 6,160, 6,162, 6,164, 6,166, **6,334, 6,345,** 6,387, 6,456, 6,483, 6,523, 6,594, 6,606, 6,618, 6,721, 6,829, 6,900, 6,901, 6,987, 7,873, 7,947, 8,045, 8,142, **8,236, 8,283,** 8,356, **8,437, 8,439,** 8,559, 8,567, 8,574, 8,610, **8,648,** 8,653, **8,665, 8,666,** 8,683, 9,226, 9,599, 9,829, 9,934, 9,978, **10,011,** 10,471, 10,671, **10,688, 10,839, 11,012,** 11,237, 11,349, 11,351, 11,549, **11,601,** 12,074, 12,077, **12,092, 12,137,** 12,574, 12,738, 12,921, 12,923, 12,924, 12,998, 13,189, 13,192, **13,313,** 13,479, 13,661, **13,679, 13,680,** 13,754, 13,855, 13,880, 13,892, **13,893, 14,113, 14,143, 14,826, 14,827, 15,124,** 15,186, 15,199, **15,823, 15,972, 16,175, 16,227,** 17,021, 17,230, 17,244, 17,266, 17,267, 17,291, 17,295, 17,297, 17,354, **17,359,** 17,360, 17,445, **17,529, 17,582,** 17,690, 17,694

Trade and professional associations, Afro-American, 6,123, **12,691**

Trade and professional associations, Jewish, 7,548

Trade schools, 4,069

Trade schools, Jewish, 7,527

Trade-unions, 63, 233, 535, 621, **686,** 1,017, 1,283, 1,356, 1,577, 1,652, **2,122,** 2,502, **2,509,** 2,878, 3,145, 3,158, **3,442,** 3,827, 3,839, 4,047, 4,079, 4,092, 4,101, **4,173,** 4,431, 5,515, **6,315,** 6,365, 6,486, 6,516, **6,795,** 6,812, 6,835, 6,977, 6,982, 7,078, 7,172, 7,257, 7,273, 7,315, 7,729, **8,061,** 8,069, 8,071, **8,072,** 8,074, **8,076, 8,077,** 8,081, **8,085, 8,087, 8,094,** 8,099, **8,107,** 8,114, 8,120, 8,126, **8,131, 8,132, 8,133, 8,135, 8,136, 8,137, 8,138, 8,139, 8,140,** 8,144, 8,216, **8,984, 9,054,** 9,381, 9,467, 9,468, 9,473, 10,032, **10,310, 11,772,** 11,851, 11,870, 11,905, 11,924, 11,926, 11,927, 12,717, 14,503, 14,656, 15,332, 15,333, 15,335, 15,979, 15,997, **16,007,** 17,274, 17,278, 17,343, 17,633, 17,756, 17,843. See also Arbitration, industrial; Yellow dog contract

actors, 2,284, 12,426, 13,832

actors, Afro-American, 3,290, 5,478, 12,685

agricultural laborers, 797, 842, 1,357, 11,494, **16,003, 16,009,** 16,010

air pilots, **8,055**

automobile industry workers, 8,096, 8,103, 8,106, **8,130,** 8,142, 15,998

auxiliaries, **8,842**

boiler-makers, 8,056

butchers, 8,118, 16,008

cigar makers, 1,656

clerks, 1,357, 9,381, **16,005**

clerks (retail trade), 2,711, 8,984, **9,309**

clothing workers, 659, 677, 1,357, 1,656, 1,779, 3,447, **3,774,** 3,839, 4,126, 8,074, 8,126, 8,144, 8,146, 8,984, 9,127, **9,408,** 9,467, 9,934, 9,962, 11,806, **11,809,** 11,897, 12,422, 12,589, 12,704, 12,861, 13,176, **15,321, 15,329, 15,987, 15,995, 15,996,** 15,998

communication and traffic, 3,449, 7,729, **9,011**

electric industry workers, 1,357, **15,253**

fishermen, 466

glove industry, 8,984

government employees, 8,063, **8,092,** 16,373

hat trade, 3,446, 15,998, **16,001, 16,011**

health facilities, 6,802

historiography, 3,446

hosiery workers, 8,984

hotels, taverns, etc., 8,984

household workers, **8,080**

jurisdictional disputes, 3,447

longshoremen, 1,280, 1,357

machine industry, **15,994**

metal-workers, 8,061

mine-workers, 1,357, 2,098, 3,447, 8,142, 15,330

minority membership, **8,056, 8,065,** 8,075, 8,097

municipal employees, 8,984

officials and employees, 63, 640, **1,280,** 1,357, 1,577, 1,656, 1,669, **3,446, 3,447,** 3,448, **3,449,**

3,450, **3,715**, 3,854, **3,887**, **3,890**, 4,032, 4,492,
8,077, **8,083**, **8,085**, **8,092**, **8,093**, **8,096**, 8,100,
8,101, **8,103**, **8,109**, 8,110, **8,111**, 8,118, **8,123**,
8,124, **8,125**, 8,126, **8,128**, **8,129**, 8,131, **8,136**,
8,137, 8,143, **8,145**, **8,146**, **8,147**, 9,011, 9,415,
9,467, **9,493**, **11,484**, 11,494, **11,765**, **11,766**,
11,773, **11,924**, 11,926, **12,422**, **12,589**, 12,704,
13,212, 14,497, **15,327**, **15,330**, **16,001**, 16,007,
16,008, 16,011, 17,635
officials and employees, Afro-American, **8,105**
packing-house workers, **16,009**
political activity, 3,442, **3,443**, 4,970, 8,065, 8,126,
15,321
postal service, 8,026
printing industry, **1,358**
railroad workers, **3,805**, 4,675, **7,177**, 14,533
restaurants, lunch rooms, etc., 9,467
service industries workers, **3,448**
telegraphers, 14,533
telephone workers, 8,984, 9,011
textile workers, **3,450**, 8,061, 8,074, 8,083, 8,123
transport workers, 9,380
woodworkers, **3,445**
Trade-unions and Afro-Americans, 8,121
Trade-unions and communism, 659
Trade-unions and community, 8,068, **8,130**
Trade-unions and social legislation, 11,916
Trade Wind (ship), 864
Traffic safety, 2,925, 3,978, 4,947
study and teaching, 10,689
"Tragedy of Vietnam, The" (pamphlet) 6,709
Trail of the Loup Days (NE), 10,439
Trail of the Three Notched Road, The (book), 17,086
Trails, 1,672, 4,289, 4,501, 8,709, 10,638, 12,482,
14,669
Train, Adeline Dutton (1824-1906). *See* Whitney,
Adeline Dutton (Train) [Mrs. Seth Dunbar]
(1824-1906)
Train for Tecumuh (moving-picture), 17,972
Trained Nurse and Hospital Review, The, 6,139
Training School for Active Workers, 2,878
Training School for Public Service, 6,493
Training School of Visiting Nursing, 6,164
Trains, 10,370
"Traipsin' Woman, The." *See* Thomas, Jeannette Bell
(1881-)
Trammell, Mattie Rivers (1890s-), **91**
Trans-Caspian expedition (1903-04), 1,478
Trans-Mississippi West (photographs), 1,475
Transactions (National Safety Council), 3,976
Transcendentalism, 6,655, 7,044, 11,025, 15,886
Transcendentalists, 5,949, **5,950**, 7,045, 7,046
Transcript (Boston, MA), 5,602
Transeau, Emma L. (1857-1937), 14,017
Translations, 1,877, 6,908, 8,082
Translators, 38, 215, 934, **1,352**, 2,107, 2,112, **2,275**,
2,344, **4,327**, 5,102, **5,732**, 5,815, 5,860, **6,055**,
6,065, 6,116, 6,203, **7,316**, 8,735, 8,788, 9,175,
9,603, 10,937, 11,846, **12,396**, **12,473**, **12,497**,
14,467, **14,753**, **15,218**, **16,122**, 17,692
Transport workers, **304**
Transportation, 202, 1,664, 5,839, 8,701, 8,731, 9,468,
13,414, 15,041, 17,188
research, 6,348
Transvaal
war of 1880-81, 15,472
hospitals, charities, etc., 12,446
Trapier, Hessie (Alston) [Mrs. Richard Shubrick],
2,164
Trapnell, Jean, 708
Trapped in the Old Mine (book), 17,478
Trapping, 8,456
Trask, Abigail (Hooper) (1788-1885) [Mrs. Richard]
(1788-1885), **7,084**, 7,451
Trask Family (MA), **7,451**
Trask, Frances Judith Somes. *See* Thompson,
Frances Judith Somes (Trask) (1806-92)
Trask, Israel, 16,392
Trask, Sarah E. (1828-?), **5,900**
Traubel, Anne (Montgomerie) [Mrs. Horace L.]
(1864-1954), 2,610, 12,547
Traubel, Gertrude, 2,610
Traubel, Horace L. (1858-1919), **2,610**

Traubel, Katherine Grunder [Mrs. Maurice Henry],
2,610
Traubel, Maurice Henry, 2,610
Traut, Sue Elizabeth Cayce [Mrs.], 15,574
Trautwine, Susan (1841-81?). *See* MacManus, Susan
R. (Trautwine) (1841-81?)
Travel, 398, **401**, 423, **452**, 670, 755, **784**, 801, **1,257**,
2,373, 2,997, **3,036**, 3,676, 3,686, 3,716, 3,857,
4,267, 5,343, **5,953**, 6,346, 6,457, **6,992**, 7,249,
7,422, 7,456, 7,475, 7,601, **7,643**, 7,660, 7,816,
8,164, 8,373, **8,491**, 8,747, 8,754, 9,107, **9,148**,
9,373, 10,243, 10,248, 10,249, **10,266**, **10,291**,
10,308, 10,323, **10,337**, 10,353, 10,359, **10,364**,
10,381, **11,535**, 11,550, 11,645, 11,669, 11,690,
11,715, 11,719, 12,286, 12,590, **12,615**, 12,948,
12,951, **13,035**, 13,142, 13,152, 13,414, 13,439,
13,572, 13,819, 14,134, 14,534, 14,608, 14,609,
14,616, 14,632, **15,114**, 15,649, 15,657, 16,091,
17,994
Travel agents, 7,258
Travel Club (Decorah, IA), 4,723
Travel Club (MI), **8,262**
Travel diaries. *See* Diaries and journals, travel
Traveler in the Wilderness (ms), 9,745
Travelers, **1,612**, **2,560**, 4,061, 6,406, 6,444, **14,664**,
15,057, 17,164
Travelers Aid Association of America, 8,670, **8,679**,
15,570
Travelers Aid-International Social Service. *See*
Travelers Aid Association of America
Travelers' aid societies, 4,079, 4,110, **4,160**, 8,670,
8,679, **8,680**, 12,851, **13,964**
Travelers Aid Society, 4,110
Travelers Aid Society (Chicago, IL), 4,079
Travelers Aid Society of Metropolitan Chicago (IL),
4,160
Travelers Aid Society of Minneapolis (MN),
8,680
Traveling Library (ID), 6,858
Travellers Aid (Saratoga Springs, NY), 12,851
Travellers-at-Home-Club (Saratoga Springs, NY),
12,851
Travellers' Club (NJ), **11,045**
Travels in Alaska (book), 710
Travels of a Lady's Maid (book), 6,910
Traver, Alice Carey (1874-1959). *See* Kennedy,
Alice Carey (Traver) Libby (1874-1959)
Traver, Edith Grace [Miss] (1881-), **12,788**, 17,196
Traversity Press, 14,378
Travis, E. L., **13,595**
Trawick, Cora May (1875-?). *See* Court, Cora May
(Trawick) (1875-?)
Traxel, Emma J. [Miss] (1869-1953), **11,731**
Treadcraft, George, 3,590
Treadway, Martha N. (1864-1941?), **4,294**
Treadwell Family (CA), 362
Treadwell, Mary. *See* Hooker, Mary (Treadwell)
Treadwell, Sophie (1890-1970), **226**
Treaharne, Sage (1832-97). *See* Jones, Sage
(Treaharne) [Mrs. Thomas] (1832-97)
Treat, Dr., 2,205
Treat, Essie (1902-). *See* Ward, Essie (Treat)
(1902-)
Treat, Helga [Mrs.], 9,238
Treat, Lucretia Willard (1842-1904), **7,949**, 13,254
Treat, Mary (1830-?), 6,310
Treat, Sarah "Sade" B. *See* Child, Sarah "Sade" B.
(Treat) [Mrs. George]
Treaties, 2,238, 15,311
Treatise on Domestic Economy, A (book), 1,951
Treble Clef Club (IA), 4,815
Tredway, Helen (1890-1971). *See* Graham, Helen
(Tredway) [Mrs. Evarts Ambrose] (1890-1971)
Tree, Ellen (1805-80). *See* Kean, Ellen (Tree) [Mrs.
Charles] (1805-80)
Tree Grows in Brooklyn, A (moving-picture), 17,972
Tree, Marietta [Mrs. Ronald] (1917-), 11,827
"Tree of Freedom," 5,304
Tree-rings, 193
Trees for Tomorrow, 17,823
Trefry, Sarah, **7,452**
Treick, Irene Gerdes, 15,869
Tremain, Mary (Lee), 2,441
Treman, Elizabeth Lovejoy [Mrs. Elias], **11,732**

Treman, Robert Elias, 11,537
Trembisky, Bertha, 11,329
Trenholm, Edwyna, 85
Trenholm, Harper Councill (1900-62), 82, 83, **85**
Trenholm, Portia Lee (Evans) [Mrs. Harper Councill].
See Jennifer, Portia Lee (Evans) [Mrs. Harper
Councill] Trenholm
Trenholm, Virginia Cole, **17,921**
Trenholm, Yvonne, 85
Trent, Lucia, 11,077
Trent, Nellie (1888-1963). *See* Bush, Nellie (Trent)
[Mrs. Joseph E.] (1888-1963)
Trenton College Club (NJ), **11,183**
Trenton Female Tract Society (NY), 11,184
Trenton Library Company (NJ), 11,184
Tresemer, David W.,
Tresham, Jessie, 9,849
Tressler, Anna Margaret (1850-1922). *See* Scott,
Anna Margaret (Tressler) (1850-1922)
Tressler Family, 14,092
Trevelyan, Charles, 17,208
Trevett, Cyrus C., **11,046**
Trevett, Emily Bancroft. *See* Nunn, Emily Bancroft
(Trevett)
Trevett Family (OR), **14,514**
Trevett, Katherine Lucy, 14,514
Trevett, Mary Melissa (Bancroft) (1838-?), 14,514
Trevett, Rebecca Angeline (Clark) [Mrs. Sewell S.]
(1832-?), 11,046
Trevett, Theodore Brooks, 14,514
Trevino, Elizabeth Borton de (1904), **6,104**
Trevor, Emily N., 12,203
Tri-County Co-op Oil Company (Tracy, MN), 8,514
Trial Balances (book), 18,021
Trial of Dr. Spock, The (book), 16,162
Trials, 341, 1,241, 4,431, 4,642, 5,505, 6,736, 7,187,
7,796, 8,127, 8,162, 10,872, 11,207, 11,874,
12,632, **13,108**
Trials (arson), 12,175, 13,468
Trials (conspiracy), 1,178, 12,594, 16,162
Trials (murder), 9,303, 9,624, 11,034, **11,190**, 15,610,
17,343
Trials (robbery), 16,449
Trials (sedition), 10,103, 10,104, 13,717, 15,594,
17,319
Trials (slander), 2,873
Trials (treason), 3,620
Triangle Dairy, 3,726
Triangle Shirtwaist case (NY), 11,255
Tribune (Tampa, FL), 2,955
Tribune (Chicago, IL), 14,422
Tribune (Duluth, MN), 8,443
Tribune (Minneapolis, MN), 2,768, 9,046
Tribune-Herald (Waco, TX), 16,344
Tribute to Rachel Katherine Schenk, A (book), 17,771
Trice, T. S., 16,097
Triem, Eve [Mrs. Paul Ellsworth] (1902-), 2,166,
17,351
Triem, Paul Ellsworth, 17,351
Triennial Conferences of the Associated Country
Women of the World (1936, 1939, 1953), 6,585
Trigg, General, 9,912
Trigg, Sue Pelham [Miss], **9,807**
"Trilby of the Tenements," 3,368
Trilingual Press (Korea), 14,089
Trimble, Eliza Jane (1816-1905). *See* Thompson,
Eliza Jane (Trimble) [Mrs. James Henry]
(1816-1905)
Trimble, Esther Jane (1838-88). *See* Lippincott,
Esther Jane (Trimble) (1838-88)
Trimble, Margaret Spencer, **293**
Trinidad, 12,247
Trinity Cathedral (Newark, NJ), 11,140
Trinity Church (LA), 5,515
Trinity College (CT), 1,921, 1,956
Trinity College (DC), **2,864**
faculty, 5,829
trustees, 4,058
Trinity College (DC), *Alumnae Journal,* 2,864
Trinity College (NC). *See* Duke University
Trinity College, alumnae, 15,228
Trinity College Coordinate College for Women (NC).
See Duke University (NC)

Trinity College of Arts and Sciences (NC). *See* Duke University (NC)
Trinity County Historical Society (CA), **1,659**
Trinity Dredging Company (CA), **959**
Trinity Episcopal Church (San Francisco, CA), **1,370**
Trinity Episcopal Church (San Francisco, CA), St. Mary's Altar Guild, 1,370
Trinity Episcopal Church (Wilmington, DE), 2,038
Trinity Episcopal Church (Hudson, MI), **7,909**
Trinity Episcopal Church (Anoka, MN), 8,389
Trinity Historical Society, 6,501
Trinity Hospital (AR), employees, 247
Trinity Journal (CA), 1,660
Trinity Lutheran Church (St. Paul, MN), Ladies Aid, **9,405**
Trinity Lutheran Church Women (Blue Earth, MN), **8,418**
Trinity Methodist Episcopal Church, South (Atlanta, GA), 3,524
Trinity Protestant Episcopal Church (SC), Daughters of the Holy Cross, **15,754**
Trinka, Anton, 13,688
Trinka, Zdena Irma (1893-1967), **13,688**
Trinkle, Florence A., 1,786
Trio (book), 332, 11,832
"Triple Ridge Farm" (book), 16,302
Tripp, Anner (Hallet) [Mrs. Job] (1830-?), 7,693
Tripp, Helen, 11,596
Tripp, Phila (Shove) [Mrs. Philip] (1791-?), **7,029**
Trippe, Catherine C. [Mrs.], 3,101
"Trips to the North, 1939-1952" (ms), 8,595
Trist, Elizabeth (House) [Mrs. Nicholas], **13,146,** 14,884
Trist, Nicholas Philip, 13,146
Trobridge Family, 651
Trobridge, Olive Lucinda. *See* Mann, Olive Lucinda (Trobridge) [Mrs. Henry Rice]
Trolley buses, 1,313
Trollope, Anthony, 5,924
Trollope, Frances (Milton), 11,305
Trommer, Marie (1895-), **2,611, 11,329**
Tropical medicine, 1,840, 14,459
Tropics, 3,773
Trotskyist movement, 11,917
Trotter, Ada M., **846**
Trotter, Ann Elizabeth, 3,935
Trotter, Ida (Barlow), **9,754**
Trotter, Matthew, **12,328**
Troubetzkoi, Barbara Hutton, 2,205
Troubetzkoy, Amélie (Rives) Chandler (1863-1945), 317
Trouble with Angels, The (moving-picture), 17,972
Trouble with Wives (moving-picture), 18,003
Trout, Edith Sanders (Burt) [Mrs. Harry G.] (1867-?), 2,239
Troutman, Anna (Dicken) [Mrs. Francis] (1839-1909), 5,309
Troutman Family (KY), **5,309**
Troutman, Francis (1820-81), 5,309
Troutman, Frank Simmes, 5,309
Trovatore (ship), 5,706
Trowbridge, Edith, 1,589
Trowbridge, Ella Louise (ca. 1848-1906). *See* Bateman, Ella Louise (Trowbridge) [Mrs. Warner M.] (ca. 1848-1906)
Trowbridge, Estella Mae. *See* Gilman, Estella Mae (Trowbridge) [Mrs. Henry Alfred]
Trowbridge, Mary. *See* Nutten, Mary (Trowbridge) [Mrs. Wilber F.]
Troxell, Belle Alexander, **9,918**
Troxell, Louise (?-1974), **17,783**
Troy Altrurian Club (OH), **14,155**
Troy, Anne (?-1873). *See* Hall, Anne (Troy) (?-1873)
Troy Conference Academy (Poultney, VT). *See* Green Mountain College (VT)
Troy Female Seminary (Oakland, CA), 1,084
Troy Female Seminary (NY), 10,954, 11,039, 11,056
Troy Female Seminary (NY). *See* Emma Willard School (NY, VT)
Troy Female Seminary (VT). *See* Emma Willard School (NY, VT)
Troy High School (NC), 13,320
Troy Music Club (OH), **14,156**
Troy State College (AL), 103

Truancy (schools). *See* School attendance
Truant officers. *See* Attendance officers
Truax, Hawley, 14,377
Truax, Rhoda (pseudonym). *See* Silberman, Rhoda Truax
Trubschenck, Ida [Miss] (1886-), **1,650**
Trudeau Sanatorium, D. O. Mills Training School for Nurses (NY), 2,542
Trudell, Sister Margaret Lillian, 6,119
True, Augusta Isabella, 9,323
True Confessions (periodical), 14,374
True, Martha (ca. 1936-), **3,449**
True, Martha (1834-73). *See* Fargo, Martha (True) [Mrs. Jerome Bonaparte] (1834-73)
True, Ruth, 2,700
True, Sybil, 11,909
"True Tales of Long Island" (story), 12,778
True Union (periodical), 5,823
True, Virginia, 11,662
Trueblood, Benjamin Franklin (1847-1916), 15,298
Trueblood, Gulielma (1810-89). *See* Morris, Gulielma (Trueblood) [Mrs. Thomas] (1810-89)
Trueblood, Lyra. *See* Wolkins, Lyra (Trueblood)
Truett, Velma Stevens [Miss] (1901-67), 10,718, **10,722**
Truffles, 14,273
Truman, Elizabeth "Bess" (Wallace) [Mrs. Harry S.], 2,340, 10,000, 10,073, 10,076, 10,082, 10,083, 13,406, 13,566, 17,978
Truman, Harry S. (1884-1972), 64, 181, 255, 2,389, 2,542, 3,257, 3,353, 3,469, 10,000, 10,073, 10,076, 10,079, **10,080,** 10,081, 10,085, 10,197, 11,914, 14,909, 15,564
Truman, James, 15,095
Truman, Margaret. *See* Daniel, Margaret (Truman) [Mrs. Clifton]
Truman, Mary Martha (1860-1900), 10,081
Truman, Olive Alger (1894-), 16,889
Trumbull, Elizabeth (1816-1900). *See* Lincoln, Elizabeth (Trumbull) [Mrs. William Sever] (1816-1900)
Trumbull, Elizabeth (Paine) (1766-1832), 7,665
Trumbull Family (ME, MA), 7,647
Trumbull Family (NE), 10,454
Trumbull, George Clap (1818-85), 7,665
Trumbull, Harriet (1783-1850). *See* Silliman, Harriet (Trumbull) [Mrs. Benjamin] (1783-1850)
Trumbull, James Russell (1825-99), **7,144**
Trumbull, Laura (Bates) [Mrs. Harry] (1813-?). *See* Van Dorn, Laura (Bates) [Mrs. Harry] Trumbull [Mrs. Isaac] (1813-?)
Trumper, Mary, **10,267**
"Trumpet No End (Blue Skies)" (song), 5,534
Trunkful of Old Letters from Loyalist Ladies in Revolutionary Times, A (book), 15,019
Trusdell, Katherine (1873-1968). *See* Meighen, Katherine Trusdell [Mrs. William A.] Morin [Mrs. John Felix Dryden] (1873-1968)
Trust companies, 8,954
Trusts and trustees, 2,330, 9,933
Trusts, industrial, laws, 4,431
Truth Circle (Grand Island, NE), **10,413**
Truth Is My Country (book), 6,114
Truth o' Women (book), 7,186
Truth, Sojourner (ca. 1797-1883), **2,154,** 5,907, 7,846, **8,010,** 11,412
Tryon, Alice, 11,505
Tryon Palace (NC), 12,988
Tryon Palace Commission (NC), 13,267, 13,440
Tryon, Rolla, 11,505
Tryst (book), 2,110
Tsa-sah-wee-eh. *See* Craddoc, Helen Hardin
Tschida, Katherine, 9,333
Tschudi, Eleanor B. [Miss], 2,996, **3,103**
Tse-Tung, Mao. *See* Mao, Tse-Tung
Tshimakain Mission, 17,212, 17,421
Tsuei, Julia, 6,987
Tuberculosis, 73, 232, 1,377, 1,779, 1,878, 2,152, 5,302, 7,677, 7,678, 7,683, 8,433, 11,862, 13,310, 17,511
  cases, clinical reports, statistics, **3,134**
  hospitals and sanatoriums, 1,672, 3,198, 3,813, 4,950, 7,526, 8,518, 10,220, 15,246, 17,892
  mortality, 481, 10,977

  prevention, **3,696,** 4,084, 14,155, 17,515
  research, 7,255, 7,288, 14,900, 16,051
  treatment, 12,815
Tuberculosis Association of Duval County (FL), 2,885
Tuberculosis Hospital (GA), 3,198
Tuberculosis Institute of Chicago and Cook County (IL). *See* Chicago Lung Association (IL)
Tuberculosis nursing, 233, 15,754
Tubman, Harriet (Ross) [Mrs. John]. [Mrs. Nelson] Davis (ca. 1815-1913), 5,907, **11,277,** 11,605, **12,683**
Tubman, John, 11,277
Tucholka, Lucy Rosalie (1880-1933). *See* Fronczak, Lucy Rosalie (Tucholka) [Mrs. Francis Eustachius] (1880-1933)
Tuck, Abigail Smith (1818-57). *See* Marsh, Abigail Smith (Tuck) [Mrs. John] (1818-57)
Tuck Family, 654
Tuck, Henry Carlton, **3,104**
Tucker, Anita Bracy [Mrs.], 9,467
Tucker, B. Fain (?-1970), 4,176
Tucker, Beatrice, 4,010, 4,053
Tucker, Benjamin R., 12,698
Tucker, C. Delores, 6,584
Tucker, Charlotte Barrell (Cheever) [Mrs. William Jewett] (1858-1944), 7,165
Tucker, Cornelia Dabney Ramseur [Mrs.] (1881-), **15,755**
Tucker, Ebenezer, 11,044
Tucker, Elizabeth, 5,703
Tucker, Ellen Dorothy O'Reilly [Mrs. Irwin St. John] (1883-1953), 4,161
Tucker Family (ME), **5,703**
Tucker Family (VA), **1,479**
Tucker Family (VA), **17,121**
Tucker Family (VA), 17,109
Tucker, Frances Bland (1785-1813). *See* Coalter, Frances Bland (Tucker) [Mrs. John] (1785-1813)
Tucker, Genevieve, 8,721, 9,323
Tucker, Irwin St. John (1886-), **4,161**
Tucker, Jane Roseborough [Mrs.], 15,553
Tucker, Katherine, 2,701
Tucker, Lael (1909-) (pseudonym). *See* Wertenbaker, Lael Tucker (1909-)
Tucker, Lucy Ann (Smith) [Mrs. Nathaniel Beverley] (1812-67), 17,121
Tucker, Lydia E., 5,703
Tucker, Margaret [Mrs.], 13,322
Tucker, Martha Hardy (Goodhue) [Mrs. Gideon] (1787-1848), 12,695
Tucker, Mary, 17,129
Tucker, Mary (Logan) [Mrs. William F.] (ca. 1860-?), 2,454, 16,161
Tucker, Mary Orne [Mrs.] (1775-1806), **7,453**
Tucker, Nathaniel Beverley (1784-1851), 7,592
Tucker, St. George (1752-1827), 17,121
Tucker, Sarah (McBee), 9,709
Tucker School (WI), 17,564
Tucker, Silvia R., **12,649**
Tucker, Sophie. [Mrs. Louis] Tuck [Mrs. Frank] Westphal [Mrs. Al] Lackey (1887-1966), 11,997, **13,832**
Tuckerman, Corinne Marie (1856-1931). *See* Allen, Corinne Marie (Tuckerman) (1856-1931)
Tuckerman, Joseph (1778-1840), 2,200
Tuckerman, Sarah Cary. *See* Becker, Sarah Cary (Tuckerman) [Mrs. Andrew C.]
Tuckerman, Sarah Eliza Sigourney (Cushing) (1831-1915), 6,309
Tuckerman School (Boston, MA), **6,257**
Tuckery, Cynthia Beverley (1832-1908). *See* Coleman, Cynthia Beverley (Tucker) Washington [Mrs. Charles Washington] (1832-1908)
Tuckett, Leila "Lillie" (1855-1937). *See* Freeze, Leila "Lillie" (Tuckett) [Mrs. James Perry] (1855-1937)
Tuckey, Grace, **18,016**
Tucson Committee for Interracial Understanding (AZ), 203
Tucson Festival Society (AZ), 203
Tucson Little Theater (AZ), 203
Tudor, Martha, 17,502
Tudor, Mary Augusta (Green), 12,191
Tudor, Tasha (1915-), 8,531
Tuesday Afternoon Book Club (NC), **13,596**

Tuesday Book Review Club (MI), **8,263**
Tuesday Club (Stockbridge, MA), **7,512**
Tuesday Club (MO), 9,918
Tuesday Club (Dover, NH), **10,845**
Tuesday Club (Bartlesville, OK), **14,177**
Tuesday Evening Club (Dubuque, IA), 4,786
Tuesday Evening Club (MS), 9,811
Tuesday Meetings for the Promotion of Holiness, 10,911
Tuesday Morning Class (CO), 1,786
Tuesday Musical Club (OH), **13,734**
Tuesday Reading Club (IN), **4,583**
Tufts, Anna Louisa, 7,522
Tufts, Anne B., 11,940
Tufts, Cotton, 12,153
Tufts Family (ME, MA, NH), **7,522**
Tufts, Helen (1874-1962). *See* Bailie, Helen (Tufts) (1874-1962)
Tufts, Martha (Adams) (1751-1832), 7,522
Tufts, Mrs. D. A. M. T., **12,650**
Tufts University, 6,556, 6,923
Tufts University (MA), Eliot-Pearson School of Child Study, 6,354, 6,556
Tufts University (MA), medical school, 6,688
Tugboats, 412 ·
Tuke Family (NY). *See* Tooke Family (NY)
Tulalip Indian Agency (WA), 17,387
Tulane University (New Orleans, LA), 3,583, 5,470, 5,473
    department heads, 11,844
    faculty, 5,509, 5,512, 9,794
Tulane University (New Orleans, LA), School of Social Work, 5,515
Tulane University (New Orleans, LA), Sophie H. Newcomb Memorial College for Women, 5,507
Tulane University (New Orleans, LA), Sophie H. Newcomb Memorial College for Women alumnae, 5,504
Tulane University (New Orleans, LA), Women's Association, **5,508**
Tulare County Board of Trade (CA), 623
Tulare County Free Library (CA), 13,688
Tule Lake Relocation Center (CA), 1,623
Tule Lake Segregation Center, 2,702
Tuley, Katherine E., 3,911
Tulip Hill (residence, MD), 2,343
Tulip Study Club (GA), 3,187
Tulips, 3,233
Tull, Maxine (1903-). *See* Boatner, Maxine (Tull) [Mrs. Edmund Burke] (1903-)
Tullahassee Manual Labor Boarding School (OK), 14,244
Tuller, Josephine, 8,633
Tully, Grace, 698, 4,482
Tully, William, 1,425
Tulsa Federation of Women's Clubs (OK), **14,265**
Tulsa Town Club (OK), **14,266**
Tuma, Maria [Mrs.] (1895-), **13,965**
Tumulty, Joseph P., 17,473
Tunnell, Bella [Mrs. Byron], 11,733
Tunnell, Byron, 11,733
Tunnell Family, **11,733**
Tunnell, Mrs. M. F., 11,733
Tunstall, "Lady Martha". *See* Smith, "Lady Martha" (Tunstall) [Mrs. William Tangier]
Tunstall, Nannie Whitemell, **2,612**
Tuomy, Katherine Genevieve (?-1966), **7,950**
Tupelo Hospital (MS), 246
Tuple, Libbie, 14,651
Tupper, Cornelia Moulton (1890-), **3,728**
Turchin, John Basil, 4,376
Turchin, Nadine [Mrs. John Basil] (1826-1904), **4,376**
Turchin's Brigade, 2,277
Tureaud, Alexander P., **5,476**
Turkey (country), 1,562, 12,196, 17,282
    American ambassadors to, 2,590
    American college presidents in, **1,562**
    American college teachers in, **1,556**
    American consuls in, 12,068
    American diplomats in, **2,226**, 2,304, 4,615
    American nurses in, 13,206
    antiquities, 11,868
    history, 1,556
    massacres, 7,498, 8,996, 11,179

Mennonites in, 4,516
missionaries to, 7,279, 7,498, 8,996
missionaries to, Presbyterian, 15,550
missionaries to, Protestant, **11,289**
politics and government, 1,556
Sephardim, 17,282
women, status of, 6,981
World War I, personal narratives, 8,996
Turkeys
    cooperative marketing, 10,215
    grading, 10,215
Turli, Irene (1926-), **8,796**
Turnbull, Agnes (Sligh) (1888-), **6,105**
Turnbull, Belle [Miss], 1,750
Turnbull, Eleanor (1875-1964), **5,732**, 5,815
Turnbull, Frances Hubbard (Litchfield) [Mrs. Lawrence] (1844-1927), **5,733**, 5,815
Turnbull, Grace Hill (1880-1976), **5,816**, **12,912**
Turnbull, Jennie (Horne) (1846-1932), 10,185
Turnbull, Lawrence, 5,815
Turner, Anne Archer [Mrs. Charles], **7,112**
Turner, Annie (1827-1900). *See* Wittenmyer, Annie (Turner) [Mrs. William] (1827-1900)
Turner, Benjamin, 7,951
Turner, Bishop William, 12,933
Turner, Eliza. *See* Quitman, Eliza (Turner)
Turner, Elizabeth, 5,684
Turner, Elizabeth Ann Withrow [Mrs.] (1936-), 94
Turner, Ethel (Duffy) [Mrs. John Kenneth] (1885-1969), **847**, **848**
Turner, Faith, 3,697
Turner, Florence L. [Mrs. George W.] (1878-1965), **973**
Turner, Frederick Jackson (1861-1932), **1,496**, 8,441
Turner, Gertrude E., **8,368**
Turner, Harriet Sutton (1820-1902), 7,942
Turner, Helen Maria (1858-1957), **12,329**
Turner, Janet, **16,304**
Turner, Jennie McMullin [Mrs.], 17,749
Turner, Jessie C. *See* Cordiner, Jessie C. (Turner)
Turner, John, Family (MA), 4,413
Turner, John Kenneth, 847, 848
Turner, Jonathan Baldwin, 4,411
Turner, Juanita. *See* Lusk, Juanita (Turner)
Turner, Justin, 4,371
Turner, Kathleen Walker, 14,682
Turner, Linda, 4,371
Turner, M., 3,377
Turner, Martha, 10,574
Turner, Martha. *See* Searle, Martha (Turner) [Mrs. P. C.]
Turner, Martha Margaret [Miss] (1868-1946), **10,544**
Turner, Mary, 5,644
Turner, Mary [Mrs.], 9,691
Turner, Mary (1845-1928). *See* Carriel, Mary (Turner) [Mrs. H. F.] (1845-1928)
Turner, Mellony [Miss], 13,294
Turner, Nat, 7,665
Turner, Rebecca (Bee) [Mrs. John C.] (1815-98), **11,211**
Turner, Sally, 10,388
Turner, Sarah E. (1834-1939), **7,951**
Turner, Susanna, 17,129
Turnquist, Lucille E., 7,828
Turpin, Frances Lynn, 10,389
Turril, Mary S., 12,350
Tuscaloosa County High School (AL), 115
Tuscaloosa Female Benevolent Society (AL), **118**
Tuscaloosa News (AL), 112
Tusch, Mary, 849
Tusculum College (TN), Alethean Society, 15,872
Tusculum College (TN), Clionian Society, 15,872
Tusculum College (TN), Young Women's Christian Association, **15,873**
Tuskegee Female Academy (AL), 13,148
Tuskegee Institute (AL), 126
    presidents, 15,377
Tuskegee Woman's Club (AL), 126
Tussman, Malka Heifetz, 934
Tuthill, Cornelius, 850
Tuthill Family (CA), **850**
Tuthill Family (NY), 11,440
Tuthill, Jeremiah Goldsmith, 12,212

Tuthill, Louisa Caroline (Huggins) [Mrs. Cornelius] (1799?-1879), 850
Tuthill, Mary E., 850
Tuthill, Ruth (1895-). *See* Green, Ruth (Tuthill) [Mrs. Thomas H.] (1895-)
Tuthill, Sarah J., 850
Tutors and tutoring, 1,426, 1,454, **3,627**, 10,949, 11,050, 11,842, 12,439, 14,706, 16,148, **17,085**
Tutt Family (GA), **3,101**
Tutt, William Duncan, 3,101
Tuttle, Ada Alice [Miss] (1886-1936), **17,729**
Tuttle, Adrianna, 11,144
Tuttle Association of Universalist Women, 9,406
Tuttle, Catherine [Miss], 14,020
Tuttle, Charles Albion (1818-88), **851**
Tuttle, Elizabeth A. (1823?-96), **4,490**
Tuttle Family, 11,717
Tuttle Family (OH), **13,963**
Tuttle, Florence (Guertin) (1869-1951), **7,312**
Tuttle, Hattie, 4,490
Tuttle, Jane Conwell, 15,184
Tuttle, Lucina, 11,717
Tuttle, Maria (Batchelder) [Mrs. Charles Albion] (?-1868), 851
Tuttle, Mary McArthur (Thompson) (1849-1916), 13,963
Tuttle, Nancy (Peck) Fairchild, 7,622
Tuttle, Nima (Conwell) (1868-1950), 15,184
Tuttle Universalist Church (MN), Clara Barton Guild, 9,406
Tuttle Universalist Church (MN), Ladies Aid Society, **9,406**
Tuttle Universalist Church (MN), Women's Association, 9,406
Tutty, Ida, **2,613**
Tutus, Helena, 12,228
Tutwiler, Ida, **13,147**
Tutwiler, Julia Strudwick (1841-1916), 56, 81, 109, **117**, 13,147
Tutwiler's State Normal School (AL), 109
Tuve, Anton, 8,797
Tuve Family, **8,797**
Tuve, George, 8,797
Tuve, Gulbrand, 8,797
Tuve, Merle, 8,797
Tuve, Richard, 8,797
Tuve, Rosemond, 8,797
Tuve, Torbjør, 8,797
Twain, Mark. *See* Clemens, Samuel
Twainian, The (periodical), 10,130
'Twas the Night Before Christmas, 11,826
Twedell, Sam (1903-), **16,008**
Tweet, Ella Valborg (Rølvaag), 8,784
Twelfth Texas Infantry Regiment, 3,310
1200 Broadway, Inc. (CA), 1,327
Twelve Years on a Shoestring (book), 6,907
Twentieth Century Book Club (Garden City, KS), 5,179
Twentieth Century Club, 2,633
Twentieth Century Club (IN), **4,584**
Twentieth Century Club (MI), 8,263
Twentieth Century Club (MN), **8,445**
Twentieth Century Club (Aberdeen, MS), **9,541**
Twentieth Century Club (Cortland, NY), **11,413**
Twentieth Century Club (TX), 16,278
Twentieth Century Club of Reno (NV), 10,689, **10,783**
Twentieth Century-Fox Film Corporation, 325, 1,451
Twentieth Iowa Infantry, 4,784
Twentieth Iowa Volunteer Infantry, 4,359
"Twenty Days with Julian at Lenox," 7,477
Twenty-Eight Club (IL), 4,401
Twenty-fifth Wisconsin Infantry Volunteers, Company F, 17,540
Twenty-first New Hampshire Regiment, 2,289
Twenty-fourth National Anti-Slavery Bazaar, 4,239
29th North Carolina Regiment, 3,176
29th WAC Traffic Regulating Company, 14,774
"Twenty Women Painters and the Landscape Club" (exhibition), 2,849
"Twenty Years After" (poem), 2,409
"Twenty Years at Montana State College" (ms), 10,216
Twerwilliger, Phoebe, 10,638

Tweten, Geneva [Miss] (1901-68), **8,460**
Twiggs County Board of Education (GA), **3,105**
Twilight Sleep Hospitals, 6,847
Twin Cities Business and Professional Women's Club (Neenah-Menasha, WI), **17,825**
Twin City Federation of Settlements, 9,270
Twin City Municipal Exhibit Committee, 9,334
Twine, 9,467
"Twinklin" (song), 5,534
Twins, 11,756, 15,427
Twiss, John Saunders, 16,857
Twiss, Naamah Kendel Jenkins (Carter) [Mrs. John Saunders] (1821-1909). *See* Young, Naamah Kendel Jenkins (Carter) [Mrs. John Saunders] Twiss [Mrs. Brigham] (1821-1909)
Twist, Julia S. (Peck) (1831-?), **852**, 1,349
Two Dot Wilson ranch (MT), 10,245
Two From Galilee (book), 5,080
Two Heroes of Cathay (book), 17,307
Two in the Wilderness (book), 11,182
Two Lives of Edith Wharton, The (book), 7,296
"Two Satans, The" (poem), 1,508
Two Years Before the Mast (book), 6,502
Twyford, Helen (Bailey) [Mrs. Loren C.], 14,173
Twyla: A Novel (book), 5,039
Tye, Alice. *See* Noel, Alice (Tye)
Tye Family (MS), 9,816
Tyler, Adeline (Blanchard) [Mrs. John] (1805-75), **5,817**
Tyler, Alice Sarah [Miss] (1859-1944), **13,895**
Tyler, Annie A. (Dwight) [Mrs. Richard] (?-1936), **13,689**
Tyler, Aphia-Ann Russell. *See* Follansbee, Aphia-Ann Russell (Tyler)
Tyler, Edna Ione Smith (1861-1930), 6,643
Tyler, Elisina Royall [Mrs.], 4,491
Tyler, Elizabeth Ruth, **10,390**
Tyler, Emma [Mrs.], 9,965
Tyler Family, 4,491
Tyler Family (VT), 17,023
Tyler, Frances A. (1899-), 11,851
Tyler, Gertrude Eliza. *See* Morton, Gertrude Eliza (Tyler)
Tyler, Jane [Mrs. C. J.], **10,391**
Tyler, John (1790-1862), 13,210
Tyler, Lyon Gardiner (1853-1935),
Tyler, Mary (1797-?). *See* Chace, Mary (Tyler) [Mrs. Charles, Jr.] (1797-?)
Tyler, Mary Hunt (Palmer) [Mrs. Royall] (1775-1866), 17,037
Tyler, Mrs. Royall, II, 17,037
Tyler, Pauline [Miss] (?-1957), **4,847**
Tyler, Royall (1757-1826), 17,023, **17,037**
Tyler, Sarah (Collins), 5,676
Tyler, Sue Ruffin [Mrs. Lyon Gardiner] (1889-1953),
Tyler, William Royall, 4,491
Tyler's Business College, 6,643
Tyler's Quarterly (periodical),
Tynan, Katherine. *See* Hinkson, Katherine (Tynan) (1861-1931)
Tyner, Doris B., **9,755**
Tyng, Harriet Morgan (?-1952), **17,038**
Type Rider, The (periodical), **163**
Typewriting, 3,713
Typhoid epidemics, 2,991
Typhoid fever, 15,146
Typists, 16,999
Tyree, Tammy, 9,745
Tyron, Louise J. (1863-1942), **4,272**
Tyrone, Mary, 12,367
Tyrrell, Mrs. J. W., **4,848**
Tyson, Edward T., 14,503
Tyson, Harriet Esselstyn (Berry) [Mrs. James Wood] (1883-), 11,644, **11,734**
Tyson, James Wood, 11,644
Tyson, Maryland Allen [Mrs. Edward T.], 14,503
Tyson, Mrs. Russell, 14,819
Tyson, Sarah B. [Mrs. Russell B.], 3,932
UAW. *See* United Automobile, Aerospace, and Agricultural Implement Workers of America
USA v. Na Lay, Alias Annie Kum Chee, 17,218
USS Hunter (ship), 6,850
USS Indianapolis (ship), 3,301

USS New Orleans (ship), 2,630
USS New York (ship), 2,654
USS Relief (ship), 3,051
Uccello, Antonia, 6,710
Uchida, Take [Mrs.] (1890-), 16,942
Uchida, Yoshiko (1921-), 8,531, **14,458**
Udall, Ida Frances Hunt (1858-1915), 16,903
Udin, Sophie, 7,554
Ueland, Brenda, **8,798**
Ueland, Clara (Hampson) [Mrs. Andreas] (1860-1927), 8,798, 9,231
Ueland, Ole Gabriel, 8,798
Uerquhart, John, 10,682
Uhnak, Dorothy, 6,060
Ukrainian-Americans, **9,509**, **9,513**
Ukrainian Catholics in America, Providence Association, 14,909
Ukrainian National Association, 9,513
Ukrainian National Bank, 9,501
Ukrainian National Women's League of America, Inc., 9,508, 9,512
Ukrainian Women's Organization, Daughters of Ukraine, 14,909
Ulbrich, Mrs. Della, 9,467
Ullman, Amelia [Mrs. Joseph], **9,407**, **13,833**
Ulmann, Doris (1884-1935), **5,257**, 5,448
Ullmann, Liv, 950
Ulmer, Laura M. (White) [Mrs. Walter P.] (1896-1974), **10,545**
Ulmer, Margaret Anne, **13,148**
Ulysses (book), 11,153, 17,843
Umatilla Indian Reservation (OR), 14,619
Umbelliferae (botany), 15,217
Umstead, William B., 13,266, 13,282
Umsted, Lillie (Devereux) [Mrs. Frank Geoffrey Quay] (1833-1913). *See* Blake, Lillie (Devereux) [Mrs. Frank Geoffrey Quay] Umsted [Mrs. Grinfill] (1833-1913)
Una (periodical), 11,305
"Una" (pseudonym). *See* Ford, Mary A.
Una Sewing Co-op (Clay County, MS), 17,600
Unbent Twig, The (drama), 7,260
"Uncle Mingo's Speculations" (ms), 1,493
Uncle Remus Day, 3,261
Uncle Remus Memorial Association (GA), **3,261**
"Uncle Scipio's War Story" (ms), 9,633
Uncle Tom's Cabin (book), 1,224, 1,426, 1,953, 2,917, 7,678, 13,587
Uncovered Well, The (ms), 5,816
Under a Glass Bell and Other Stories (book), 4,232
Under Quaker Appointment: The Life of Jane P. Rushmore (book), 15,286
"Under the Prairie Winds" (ms), 13,668
"Under the Tree" (ms), 5,361
Under Three Flags (pageant), 17,667
Undercover operations, 1,122
Underground literature, **12,064**
Underground railroad, 4,601, 14,873
Underground Woman, The (book), 3,771
Underhill, Emma L. *See* Mandeville, Emma L. (Underhill) [Mrs. Frederick Austin]
Underhill, Ruth Murray (1884-), 1,779
Undertakers and undertaking, 8,334, 8,369, **16,363**
Undertow (book), 17,870
Underwater archaeology, 11,288
Underwood, Alice, 2,614
Underwood, Elizabeth Threlkeld (Cox) [Mrs. Joseph Rogers] (1818-84), 5,281
Underwood Family (KY), **5,281**
Underwood, J. M. (1842-?). *See* Long, J. M. (Underwood) (1842-?)
Underwood, John Cox (1840-1913), 5,281
Underwood, John Curtis (1809-73), **2,614**
Underwood, Joseph Rogers (1791-1876), 5,281
Underwood, Maria P. [Mrs. John Curtis], 2,614
Underwood, Sara A., 3,927
Underwood, Warner Lewis (1808-72), 5,281
"Undiplomatic Relations" (ms), 14,362
Undset, Sigrid (1882-1949), 2,876, 4,321
Unemployed, 1,798, 2,424, 2,692, 4,003, 4,055, 4,080, 4,431, 5,120, 5,540, 8,065, 8,089, 8,651, 8,668, 8,678, 8,681, 8,743, 9,468, 10,050, 11,501, 11,504, 11,905, 11,916, 12,008, 12,517, 13,933,

17,278, 17,448. *See also* Economic assistance, domestic; Employment agencies
Unemployed Citizens Council (WA), 17,278
Unemployed Councils, 8,065
Unemployment. *See* Unemployed
Unemployment Committee (Detroit, MI), 7,796
UNESCO. *See* United Nations Educational, Scientific, and Cultural Organization
Unger, Gladys Buchanan (1885-1940), **12,651**
Unicorns, 12,489
Unidentified flying objects. *See* Flying saucers
Uniform state laws, 6,530
Uniforms, military, 14,978
Union (DC), 17,119
Union (Springfield, MA), 11,493
Union Benevolent Association (MI), 7,913
Union Bible School (China), 14,466
Union Center Goodwill Club (WA), **17,211**
Union Circle of King's Daughters (MT), 10,331
Union Classical Institute (NJ), 10,975
Union College (NY), 11,903
    alumnae, 5,362
    faculty, 17,472
Union Colony (CO), 1,751
Union Dorcas Society (Lancaster, PA), **14,866**
Union Girls School (China), 6,826
Union Grove Baptist Church (Columbus, OH), 13,991
Union Home and School for the Children of Volunteers (NY), 12,431
Union Home Economics Club (Plainfield, IN), 4,650
Union Hospital School of Nursing (Terre Haute, IN), alumnae, 4,629
Union label, 4,173
Union Maternal Association of Boston (MA), **6,171**
Union Pacific Railroad, 1,770, 4,749, 15,059
Union Park Forum, 6,900
Union School of Salesmanship (Boston, MA). *See* Prince School of Retailing (Boston, MA)
Union Signal (newspaper), 4,243
Union Signal, The (periodical), 1,668, 13,963, 13,990, 14,164
Union Society (NJ), 11,110
Union Sunday school (CO), 1,776
Union Township Woman's Club of Johnson County (IA), 4,960
Union Village (OH), **12,620**
Union Women's Alliance to Gain Equality, 1,283, 1,577
Unit I (World War I), 4,629
Unitarian Church (Lawrence, KS), 6,249
Unitarian churches, 4,925, **9,413**, 11,279, 11,591, 13,182
    charities, 6,249, **6,254**
    clergy, **2,396**, **4,776**, 4,958, 6,251, 6,253, 6,427, **7,044**, 7,634, 8,345, 12,171, 12,790, **12,818**, 15,312, 15,475
    education, 6,250, **6,257**, **6,258**
    missions, 5,713
    societies, etc., **6,252**, **6,255**, **6,258**
Unitarian Ladies Working Society (Iowa City, IA), 4,959
Unitarian Service Committee, Village Improvement and Leadership Training Program (Awo Amamma, Eastern Nigeria), 11,603
Unitarian Society (Portland, OR), 14,318
Unitarian Sunday School Society, **6,258**
Unitarian Temperance Society, 6,926
Unitarian Universalist Women's Federation, 1,363, 7,331
Unitarianism, 1,392, 6,503, 6,833, 12,818, 13,413, 14,893
Unitarians, 1,363, 7,941, 9,282, 14,311
United Automobile, Aerospace, and Agricultural Implement Workers of America, 1,656, 8,096, 8,100, 8,103, 8,105, 8,106, 8,110, 8,111, 8,120, 8,143, 15,998
United Automobile, Aerospace, and Agricultural Implement Workers of America, auxiliaries, 8,065, 8,088, 8,133, 8,135, 8,136, 8,137
United Automobile, Aerospace, and Agricultural Implement Workers of America, Committee on Political Educaton, 8,130
United Automobile, Aerospace, and Agricultural

Implement Workers of America, Community Relations Department, **8,130**

United Automobile, Aerospace, and Agricultural Implement Workers of America, Congress of Industrial Organizations, Local Two hundred Twelve, 8,137

United Automobile, Aerospace, and Agricultural Implement Workers of America, Congress of Industrial Organizations, National Ford Department, 8,137

United Automobile, Aerospace, and Agricultural Implement Workers of America, Fair Practices and Anti-Discrimination Department, 8,115, **8,131**

United Automobile, Aerospace, and Agricultural Implement Workers of America, Ford Local Six hundred, minority membership, 8,065

United Automobile, Aerospace, and Agricultural Implement Workers of America (IN), Local Six hundred Sixty-two, **8,133**

United Automobile, Aerospace, and Agricultural Implement Workers of America (MI), Local Fifty-one, 8,132

United Automobile, Aerospace, and Agricultural Implement Workers of America, Recreation Department, **8,134**

United Automobile, Aerospace, and Agricultural Implement Workers of America, Research and Engineering Department, 8,135

United Automobile, Aerospace, and Agricultural Implement Workers of America, Unemployment Compensation Department, 8,138

United Automobile, Aerospace, and Agricultural Implement Workers of America, War Policy Division, 8,139, 8,140

United Board for Christian Colleges (China), 11,754

United Brethren Church (Prairie Gem, NE), Woman's Missionary Society. *See* Evangelical United Brethren Church (Prairie Gem, NE), Women's Society of World Service

United Brethren in Christ Church. *See* United Methodist Church

United Brethren in Christ Church, Home Frontier and Foreign Missionary Society. *See* United Methodist Church

United Brethren in Christ Church (IA), Des Moines Conference of Missions. *See* United Methodist Church (IA), Des Moines

United Brethren in Christ Church, Women's Missionary Association. *See* United Methodist Church

United Brethren (Moravian) Church, 12,512, 14,375 clergy, 17,189

United Brothers of Friendship and Sisters of the Mysterious Tens (IL), 3,934

United Cannery, Agricultural, Packing, and Allied Workers of America, District 8, Congress of Industrial Organizations (TX), **16,009**

United Charities of Chicago (IL), **3,903**, 4,055, **4,072**, 4,130, 4,138

United Charities of St. Paul (MN). *See* Family Service of St. Paul (MN)

United Christian Missionary Society, 4,599

United Church (Chester, CT), 1,890

United Church (Chester, CT), Female Praying and Benevolent Society, 1,890

United Church (Chester, CT), Ladies Benevolent Society, 1,890

United Church (Chester, CT), Women's Baptist (Foreign) Missionary Society, 1,890

United Church (Chester, CT), Women's Baptist Home Missionary Society, 1,890

United Church (St. Paul, MN), Elizabeth Eliot Club, 9,413

United Church of Christ, **10,212** clergy, **6,170** publishing, 5,234

United Church of Christ, Congregational American Home Missionary Society, 5,234

United Church of Christ, Kansas-Oklahoma Conference, **5,234**

United Church of Christ, Nebraska Conference, **10,501**

United Church of Christ, Ohio Conference, 2,019

United Church of Christ, Women's Home Missionary Society, 10,501

United Church of Christ, Women's Home Missionary Union of Nebraska, 10,501

United Church Women, 13,872, 16,265

United Church Women (Ann Arbor, MI), **7,953**

United Church Women (Columbia, MO), 10,001

United Church Women of Atlanta (GA), 3,430

United Church Women of Lubbock (TX), 16,278

United Committee to Aid Vermont Marble Workers, 14,446

United Community Services (MI), Women's Committee, **8,031**

United Confederate Veterans, 5,513

United Confederate Veterans, Army of Northern Virginia Department, 15,715

United Council of Church Women, 14,026

United Daughters of North San Juan (CA), 1,078

United Daughters of Rechab, 11,324

United Daughters of the Confederacy, 99, 103, 589, 2,198, 2,292, **2,615**, **2,896**, 2,901, 2,955, 3,076, 3,080, 3,169, 3,219, **3,262**, 3,345, 3,383, 3,419, 3,440, 3,465, 9,596, 9,617, 9,644, 9,657, 9,669, 9,697, 9,740, **9,756**, 9,793, 9,795, 9,918, 9,934, 12,940, 13,070, 13,159, 13,285, 13,337, 13,374, 13,388, 13,459, 13,571, 13,576, **13,597**, 13,617, 13,629, 14,230, 15,975, 16,114, 16,127, 16,178, 16,261, 17,412

United Daughters of the Confederacy (AL), **16, 119**

United Daughters of the Confederacy (AL), Amelia Gayle Gorgas Chapter, 120

United Daughters of the Confederacy (Colusa, CA), Winnie Davis Chapter, 513

United Daughters of the Confederacy (GA), College Park Chapter, 3,262

United Daughters of the Confederacy (GA), Frankie Lyle Chapter, 3,431

United Daughters of the Confederacy (GA), LaGrange Chapter, 3,431

United Daughters of the Confederacy (GA), Lizzie Rutherford Chapter, 3,431

United Daughters of the Confederacy (GA), Margaret Jones Chapter, 3,358

United Daughters of the Confederacy (GA), Peachtree Creek Chapter, 3,431

United Daughters of the Confederacy (GA), Robert E. Lee Chapter, 3,262

United Daughters of the Confederacy (GA), Valdosta Chapter, **3,616**

United Daughters of the Confederacy (Atlanta, GA), 3,262

United Daughters of the Confederacy (MD), **5,818**

United Daughters of the Confederacy (MS), Albert Sidney Johnstone Chapter, 9,596

United Daughters of the Confederacy (MS), Lyda C. Moore Chapter, **9,808**

United Daughters of the Confederacy (MS), Stephen D. Lee Chapter, 9,757

United Daughters of the Confederacy (Beulah, MS), General Charles Clark Chapter, 9,757

United Daughters of the Confederacy (Heidelberg, MS), Jasper County Chapter, **9,669**

United Daughters of the Confederacy (MO), John S. Marmaduke Chapter, **9,919**

United Daughters of the Confederacy (NC), 13,085

United Daughters of the Confederacy (Raleigh, NC), General James Johnston Chapter, 13,597

United Daughters of the Confederacy (SC), **15,758**

United Daughters of the Confederacy (SC), Bethune Chapter, **15,400**

United Daughters of the Confederacy (SC), Marion Chapter, **15,756**

United Daughters of the Confederacy (SC), Secessionville Chapter, James Island, **15,757**

United Daughters of the Confederacy (Columbia, SC), 15,597

United Daughters of the Confederacy (TN), Felix K. Zollicoffer Chapter, 15,943

United Daughters of the Confederacy (TX), Albert Sidney Johnstone Chapter, **16,140**

United Daughters of the Confederacy (Laura Rutherford Chapter), 3,076

United Daughters of the Confederacy, Marking Historical Spots in Georgia, 3,440

United Electrical and Radio Workers of America (PA), Local Six hundred one, 15,253

United Electrical Workers' Union, 1,357

United Evangelical Church (Naponee, NE), Woman's Home and Foreign Missionary Society, **10,581**

United Evangelical Church (York, NE), Woman's Home and Foreign Missionary Society, **10,582**

United Farm Workers' Organizing Committee (TX), 16,003

United Farm Workers Organizing Committee (TX), Fort Worth Boycott, **16,010**

United Farm Workers Union, 842, 1,577

United Federation of Teachers, 8,097

United Fisherman's Union of the Pacific, 466

United Friends of Temperance, 16,391

United Friends of Temperance, Georgia Council, 3,419

United Fund and Council (St. Paul, MN), 9,104

United Fund of Clark County (WA), 17,314

United Garment Workers of America, Local No. 171 (St. Paul, MN), **9,408**

United Garment Workers Union, 15,335

United German Evangelical Lutheran Church (NY), 11,328

United Government Employees Association, 3,301

United Hatters, Cap and Millinery Workers International Union, 13,175, 13,578

United Hatters, Cap and Millinery Workers International Union, Local 125 (TX), **16,011**

United Hebrew Charities, 3,968, **4,162**

United Hebrew Charities, Jochannah Lodge, 4,162

United Hebrew Charities, Sewing Societies, 4,162

United Hospital Fund, 7,198

United Labor League (Philadelphia, PA), 15,335

United Lutheran Church in America, 14,797, 14,799. *See also* Lutheran churches

United Lutheran Church in America, United Lutheran Women of the Iowa Synod, **3,961**

United Lutheran Church in America, Women's Home and Foreign Missionary Society of the Chicago Synod, **3,963**

United Lutheran Church in America, Women's Missionary Society, **3,966**

United Lutheran Church in America, Women's Missionary Society of the Northern Illinois Synod, **3,965**

United Methodist Church, 161, 893, 1,393, **3,479**, 3,746, 4,205, 4,540, 4,541, 4,542, 4,543, 4,545, 4,732, **4,849**, 5,852, 6,901, 7,604, 9,704, **9,895**, 9,984, **10,574**, 10,591, 13,285, 14,223, 14,536, 15,586, **15,614**, 15,615, **15,632**, **15,642**, **15,655**, 16,059, **16,209**, 17,106

charities, 1,889, 1,900, 4,774

clergy, 327, 1,751, **1,976**, **1,977**, **1,982**, 3,091, **3,328**, 3,333, **3,355**, 3,524, **3,546**, 4,201, **4,202**, **4,203**, **4,205**, **4,206**, **4,207**, 4,208, 5,072, 5,074, 5,271, **6,012**, 7,911, 7,947, 8,388, 8,893, **9,246**, **9,531**, 9,610, **9,991**, 10,584, **12,638**, 12,790, 12,941, **13,211**, 14,536, 14,668, 15,632, 15,837, 17,189, **17,227**

deaconesses, **10,564**, 10,598

discipline, **4,774**

education, **4,201**, 4,206, 4,208, 5,394, 8,872, 10,066, 10,564, 10,568, 10,570, **10,600**, 13,260, **16,113**

government, 1,812, 1,813, 4,206, 4,208, **8,528**, 10,565

hymns, 4,205

membership, 10,066, 10,597

missionaries, 2,258, 3,328, **4,203**, **4,525**, **4,529**, 5,171, **5,246**, 5,394, **5,993**, **6,012**, 8,164, **8,745**, **8,876**, **8,879**, **8,891**, **8,892**, **8,899**, 9,281, 10,599, **13,258**, **13,260**, **13,276**, 13,280, **13,284**, **13,290**, **13,291**, 13,294, 13,295, 13,296, **14,325**, 14,336, **14,379**, 14,389, **14,404**, **14,419**, **14,426**, **14,444**, **14,445**, 14,466, **14,596**, 14,602, **17,206**, **17,227**

missions, 421, 1,813, 2,258, 3,307, 3,328, 4,201, 4,203, **4,525**, 4,529, 4,541, **5,171**, 5,394, **5,993**, **6,012**, 8,164, **8,879**, 9,281, **9,750**, 10,564, **10,567**, **10,572**, **10,573**, **10,577**, **10,578**, **10,579**, **10,580**, **10,581**, **10,582**, **10,583**, **10,584**, **10,585**, **10,586**, **10,587**, **10,588**, **10,589**, **10,590**, **10,591**, **10,592**, **10,593**, **10,594**, **10,595**, **10,596**, 10,598, 10,599, **10,601**, 10,909, **13,211**, 13,258, **13,294**, **13,295**,

13,296, 13,944, 14,026, 14,075, 14,325, **14,336,**
14,396, 14,442, 14,596, 14,602
publishing, 3,479, 5,173, 9,895, 10,579, 10,598,
10,988, 11,802
role of women in, 13,211
societies, etc., **10,457, 15,642, 15,654**
United Methodist Church (CO), Woman's Home
Missionary Society, Denver District, 1,813
United Methodist Church (KS), Hutchinson District,
United Methodist Women, **5,248**
United Methodist Church (KY), Louisville Annual
Conference, **5,400**
United Methodist Church (Humboldt, NE), **10,476**
United Methodist Church (Humboldt, NE), Women's
Foreign Missionary Society, 10,476
United Methodist Church, Board of Education, 4,208
United Methodist Church, Board of Global Ministries,
13,295
United Methodist Church, Board of Global Ministries,
Division of World Missions, 8,879, **13,294**
United Methodist Church, Board of Global Ministries,
Woman's Division, 10,621
United Methodist Church, Board of Home Missions
and Church Extension, 1,813
United Methodist Church, Board of Missions and
Church Extension, 3,479
United Methodist Church, Board of Missions,
Woman's Division of Christian Service, 9,895
United Methodist Church, Central Illinois
Conference, Woman's Foreign Missionary
Society, **3,765**
United Methodist Church, Central Illinois
Conference, Woman's Home Missionary Society,
3,767
United Methodist Church, Central Kansas
Conference, Woman's Society of Christian
Service, **5,244**
United Methodist Church, Chicago Northern District
(IL), **4,206**
United Methodist Church, Christian Social Relations,
Women's Division, Board of Missions, 13,176
United Methodist Church, Deaconess Bureau of the
Colorado Conference, **1,812**
United Methodist Church, Epworth League, 5,740
United Methodist Church, Illinois Conference,
Decatur District, Woman's Foreign Missionary
Society, **3,766**
United Methodist Church, Illinois Conference,
Decatur District, Woman's Home Missionary
Society, **3,768**
United Methodist Church, Illinois Conference,
Woman's Society of Christian Service, **3,769**
United Methodist Church, Kansas West Conference,
5,212
United Methodist Church, Kansas West Conference,
Woman's Society of Christian Service, **5,247**
United Methodist Church, Louisiana Conference,
5,551
United Methodist Church, Minnesota Annual
Conference, **8,528**
United Methodist Church, Missouri East Conference,
9,895
United Methodist Church, Nebraska Conference,
10,598
United Methodist Church, Nebraska Conference,
Deaconess Board, **10,565**
United Methodist Church, Nebraska Conference,
Wesleyan Service Guild, **10,576**
United Methodist Church, Nebraska Conference,
Woman's Foreign Missionary Society, **10,580**
United Methodist Church, Nebraska Conference,
Woman's Home Missionary Society, **10,584**
United Methodist Church, North Nebraska
Conference, Woman's Home Missionary Society,
10,585
United Methodist Church, Northeast Iowa
Conference, 5,076
United Methodist Church, Northern New Jersey
Conference, **10,910**
United Methodist Church, Rock River Conference
(IL), United Methodist Women, 4,127
United Methodist Church, School of Missions, 10,066
United Methodist Church, South Carolina
Conference, **15,838**

United Methodist Church, South Georgia Conference,
3,479
United Methodist Church, Sunday School Board,
4,208
United Methodist Church, United Methodist Church
Women, Nebraska Conference, **10,598**
United Methodist Church, United Methodist Women,
421, 1,900, **3,307,** 3,479, **3,770,** 4,127, **4,597,**
4,906, 5,065, 5,072, **5,073, 5,075, 5,076, 5,077,**
5,078, 5,169, **5,173,** 5,544, 5,554, 7,862, 7,947,
9,923, 10,066, 10,910, 11,350, 13,944, 14,426,
14,466, 15,838, 16,084, 16,265
United Methodist Church, Upper Iowa Conference,
5,076
United Methodist Church, West Texas Conference,
16,113
United Methodist Church, Western New York
Conference, **11,802**
United Methodist Church, Woman's Division of
Christian Service, 3,479
United Methodist Church, Woman's Foreign
Missionary Society, **1,813**
United Methodist Church, Woman's Missionary
Association convention, 5,072
United Methodist Church, Women's Organizations of
the Districts of the Nebraska Conference, **10,601**
United Mine Workers hospitals, 13,055
United Mine Workers of America, 1,669, 1,675,
2,098, 3,447, 15,330, 15,979
United Mine Workers Union, 8,142
United Nations, 1,680, 2,072, 2,075, 2,177, 2,407,
5,460, 5,787, 6,674, 6,978, 7,242, 7,247, 7,257,
7,290, **7,313,** 7,323, 8,443, 8,633, 8,651, 8,655,
9,197, 9,385, 11,018, 11,331, 11,389, 11,804,
12,061, 14,453, 14,686, 17,259
armed forces, 4,480
commissions, 5,147
economic assistance, 6,125, 9,779, 10,074
officials and employees, **5,147,** 6,125, 6,766, 8,912,
10,074, 11,827, 11,857, 11,920, 11,999, 14,237
United Nations and learned institutions, societies,
etc., 6,123
United Nations Association, 6,380, 6,914, 7,281
United Nations Association of the USA, Inc., Iowa
Division, 5,024
United Nations associations, 2,133, 2,193, 3,399,
4,480, 5,024, 6,125, 6,380, 6,456, 6,558, 6,682,
6,886, 6,914, 6,978, **6,988,** 7,270, 7,281, 9,449,
11,491, 16,265, 17,246
United Nations, Commission for Social Development,
7,281
United Nations, Commission on Human Rights,
5,147, 6,737, 11,604, 11,827
United Nations, Commission on the Status of
Women, **6,929,** 7,290, 7,313
United Nations, Commissions, 6,737
United Nations Council of Philadelphia (PA), 2,133,
6,682
United Nations, Economic and Social Council, 5,147
United Nations Educational, Scientific, and Cultural
Organization, 679, 760, 2,075, 2,456, 4,957,
7,257, 9,779, 11,331, 11,937, 13,241, 16,911
United Nations Educational, Scientific, and Cultural
Organization Conference (1946), 12,553
United Nations, Emergency Force, 4,480
United Nations, Food and Agriculture Organization,
6,914, 14,272
United Nations, General Assembly, 6,914
officials and employees, 11,497
United Nations International Children's Emergency
Fund, 6,558, 6,766, 10,074, 12,883
officials and employees, 12,033
United Nations, Relief and Rehabilitation
Administration, 2,456, 6,125, 6,994, 8,144, 9,779,
11,857, 17,716
officials and employees, 5,197, 11,244, 11,593
United Nations Scientific Conference on the
Conservation and Utilization of Resources
(1949), 2,525
United Nations Today, The (book), 6,512
United Nations, United States Delegation to the
Economic and Social Council, 7,281
United Nations, United States Mission, 7,281
United Nations Week (RI, 1961), 6,988

United Nations, World Health Organization, 6,558,
6,987, 11,852
officials and employees, 8,572
United Negro College Fund, 3,290, 15,296
United Negro College Fund (NY), **12,708**
United Negro College Fund, Women's Division,
12,708
United Negro Improvement Association, 3,934
United Neighborhood Houses of New York City,
8,681
United Neighborhood Houses of New York, housing
committee, 11,914
United Norwegian Lutheran Church, biography, **8,866**
United Norwegian Lutheran Church, Women's
Missionary Federation, **8,804**
United Order, 10,674, 16,486, 16,489, 16,512, 16,722,
16,867, 16,965, 16,967, 16,968
United Order of True Sisters (CT), New Haven
Lodge Number Four, Jochebed Lodge, **2,005**
United Order of True Sisters (Chicago, IL), Johannah
Lodge Number Nine, **4,038**
United Organized Labor of Ohio, 8,118
United Packinghouse Workers of America, 4,032
United Presbyterian Church in the United States of
America, 98, 3,266, 3,764, 3,892, 4,949, 5,343,
5,370, 9,596, 14,208, 14,664, 15,172, 15,176,
15,599. *See also* Presbyterian churches
charities, 12,256
missions, **1,171,** 15,172, 15,173, **15,174**
United Presbyterian Church in the United States of
America, Board of Foreign Missions, 758
United Presbyterian Church in the United States of
America, Board of National Missions, 15,173
United Presbyterian Church in the United States of
America, Committee on Woman's Work, 92
United Presbyterian Church in the United States of
America, Council on Church and Race, 15,176
United Presbyterian Church in the United States of
America, General Assembly, 3,266
United Presbyterian Church in the United States of
America, Synod of Georgia, **3,416**
United Presbyterian Church in the United States of
America, Woman's Board of Foreign Missions,
1,171
United Presbyterian Church in the United States of
America, Woman's Board of Home Missions,
15,173
United Presbyterian Church of North America. *See*
United Presbyterian Church in the United States
of America
United Presbyterian Women, 15,176
United Press International, 3,332, 11,493
United Public Workers of America, Local 275 (MI),
8,092
United Service Organizations, 1,092, 3,368, 3,388,
3,451, 6,886, 10,192, 10,784, 12,719, 12,725,
13,618, 14,231, **15,101,** 15,121, 15,164, 15,209,
15,210, 16,275
United Service Organizations Labor Plaza, 15,101
United Service Organizations Women's Club, 15,101
United Service Organizations, Young Women's
Christian Association, **12,728**
United Society of Believers in Christ's Second
Appearing, 7,034, 7,047
United Society of Believers in Christ's Second
Appearing, Deaconnesses of the East House,
5,364
United Society of Believers in Christ's Second
Appearing, Sisters of the United Society, 5,364
United Society of Friends Women, 13,235
United Spanish-American War Veterans Ladies
Auxiliary (MI), **8,289**
United Spanish War Veterans (NE), **10,547**
United Spanish War Veterans (NE), Women's
Auxiliary, **10,547**
United Spanish War Veterans (York, NE), Walter
Poor Auxiliary, Number Sixteen, **10,624**
United Spanish War Veterans (OH), Auxiliaries Eight
and Forty, **14,053**
United Spanish War Veterans (Roseburg, OR),
George Starmer Auxiliary Number Eighteen,
14,701
United Spanish War Veterans, A. J. Babcok Ladies
Auxiliary, 8,167

United Spanish War Veterans and Auxiliary, 9,259
United Spanish War Veterans Ladies Auxiliary (MI),
   Guy V. Henry Post, 8,289
United Spanish War Veterans National Auxiliary,
   9,409
United States, 14,905
  air defenses, 2,179
  ambassadors to, Argentinian, 2,471
  ambassadors to, Indian, 4,030
  appropriations and expenditures, 11,695
  armed forces. *See also* United States (government),
    Air Force; United States (government), Army
    demobilization, 8,670
    mobilization, 8,670
    nurses, 238, **382, 6,127, 6,129,** 13,336
    officers, 8,873, 12,615, **15,693**
    pay, allowances, etc., 5,561
    records and correspondence, **2,690,** 4,338,
      11,194, 11,195, 11,196, 11,197, 11,198
    recruiting, enlistment, etc., 162, 2,128, 2,691,
      4,390, 7,198, 13,618
    segregation, 13,189
    surgeons, **6,145**
    women in, 37, 1,203, **6,417,** 6,861, **6,931,** 7,828,
      8,446, 8,447, **9,146,** 9,196, 9,394, **9,457,** 10,013,
      11,876, 12,654, **17,308**
    women's reserves, 4,216, **5,016,** 11,876, 11,925
  bicentennial celebrations, 10,338
  capital and capitol, 3,489
  census, **1,135, 2,676, 5,566, 5,570, 5,571,** 9,410,
    10,723, 14,932, 17,014
  Civil War, 100, 119, 196, 260, 327, 349, 514,
    1,398, 1,450, 1,457, 1,598, 1,770, 1,924, **1,962,**
    2,199, 2,208, 2,327, 2,332, 2,457, **2,462,** 2,479,
    2,514, 2,566, 2,614, 2,659, 2,929, 2,944, 2,950,
    2,967, 2,992, 3,041, 3,081, 3,203, 3,205, 3,269,
    3,313, 3,349, 3,379, 3,412, 3,418, 3,491, **3,495,**
    3,517, **3,599,** 3,829, **3,922,** 3,979, 4,245, 4,301,
    4,333, 4,347, 4,359, 4,365, 4,376, 4,417, 4,423,
    4,735, 4,765, 4,817, 4,832, 4,882, 4,919, 4,925,
    4,958, 4,994, 5,262, 5,334, 5,343, 5,449, 5,456,
    5,467, **5,561,** 5,617, 5,706, 5,742, 5,753, 5,799,
    5,821, 6,352, 6,444, 6,445, 6,457, 6,487, 6,650,
    6,878, 7,206, 7,233, 7,589, **7,613,** 7,677, 7,678,
    7,753, 7,769, 7,935, 8,151, 8,164, 8,166, 8,337,
    8,374, 8,954, 8,975, 9,041, 9,117, 9,294, 9,308,
    9,312, 9,383, 9,401, 9,416, 9,436, 9,444, 9,538,
    9,539, 9,594, 9,596, 9,611, 9,620, 9,636, 9,639,
    9,655, 9,661, 9,677, 9,751, 9,860, 9,874, 10,052,
    10,156, 10,157, 10,164, 10,196, 10,264, 10,445,
    10,803, **11,194,** 11,207, 11,259, 11,443, 11,539,
    11,588, 11,730, 11,777, 11,962, 12,020, 12,333,
    12,404, 12,430, 12,448, 12,458, 12,490, 12,541,
    12,653, 12,663, 12,757, 12,940, 12,944, 12,949,
    12,953, 12,968, 12,969, 12,983, 13,028, 13,029,
    13,039, 13,045, 13,051, 13,077, 13,096, 13,109,
    13,119, 13,169, 13,262, 13,287, 13,322, 13,339,
    13,374, 13,414, 13,518, 13,526, 13,534, 13,540,
    13,546, 13,568, 13,571, 13,576, 13,590, 13,593,
    13,620, 14,111, 14,132, 14,166, 14,246, 14,498,
    14,824, 14,980, 15,008, 15,044, 15,116, 15,414,
    15,420, 15,477, 15,550, 15,552, 15,568, 15,600,
    15,602, 15,606, **15,624,** 15,631, 15,652, 15,667,
    15,673, 15,683, 15,692, 15,711, 15,740, 15,753,
    15,766, 15,769, 15,774, 15,817, 15,895, 15,951,
    15,957, 16,016, 16,032, 16,041, 16,045, 16,047,
    16,050, 16,053, 16,095, 16,097, **16,105,** 16,121,
    16,132, 16,144, 16,261, 16,378, 17,209, 17,388,
    17,419, 17,456, 17,479, 17,622, 17,636, 17,724,
    17,725, **17,743,** 18,007
    addresses, sermons, etc., 6,522
    Afro-American troops, 3,490, 6,394, 13,072
    blockade, 3,583, 13,419, 13,446
    campaigns and battles, 77, 1,408, 1,962, 2,223,
      2,254, 2,358, 2,377, 3,150, 3,170, 3,176, 3,208,
      3,210, 3,219, 3,247, 3,256, 3,271, 3,315, 3,317,
      3,419, 4,490, 5,362, 5,363, 5,413, **5,750,** 7,678,
      9,613, 10,065, 13,090, 13,103, 13,123, 13,268,
      13,348, 13,374, 13,403, 13,468, 13,481, 13,519,
      13,528, 13,602, 14,769, 14,770, 15,322, 15,506,
      15,606, 15,635, 15,696, 15,768, 17,103, 17,477,
      17,584
    casualties (statistics, etc.), 693, 2,289, 2,950,
      3,086, 4,755, 4,961, 8,831, 9,600, 10,196,

    11,554, 11,613, 12,165, 12,381, 13,403, 14,454,
    14,863, 14,969, 15,711, 15,749, 16,243, 17,992
    cavalry operations, 211
    centennial celebrations, etc., **99,** 103, 5,038,
      15,806
    claims, 2,434, 5,347, 13,101
    communications, 79
    desertions, 13,412
    destruction and pillage, 62, 2,417, 2,455, 3,317,
      9,589, 9,848, 9,884, 10,006, **12,162,** 13,037,
      13,493, 15,475, 15,560, 15,597, 15,610, 15,634,
      15,708, 15,714, **15,721,** 15,726, 15,729, 15,952
    economic aspects, 3,176, 9,836, 9,937, 13,213,
      15,588, 15,635
    finance, commerce, confiscations, etc., 2,675,
      3,576
    foreign participants, 17,589
    guerrillas, 10,879
    hospitals, charities, etc., 68, 1,400, 1,408, 1,630,
      2,196, 2,386, 2,494, 2,671, 2,895, 3,752, **3,869,**
      3,888, 3,897, 3,922, 3,991, **4,135, 4,293,** 4,313,
      4,354, 5,689, 5,817, 7,295, 7,319, 9,363, 11,167,
      11,247, 12,165, 12,431, 13,348, **14,418,** 14,775,
      14,824, **14,831,** 15,598, 15,774, 17,672, 17,709
    Jewish participation, 15,950
    juvenile participants, 385, 9,320
    medical and sanitary affairs, 1,413, 2,277, 3,146,
      3,151, 3,170, 3,310, 3,323, **4,490, 5,027,** 8,899,
      10,160, 11,947, 12,233, 12,913, 13,002, **15,561**
    monuments. *See* Soldiers' monuments
    Native American troops, 13,448
    naval operations, 2,201, 2,278
    nurses, 107, **1,242,** 1,243, **1,251,** 2,239, **2,289,**
      2,387, 2,434, 2,454, 2,690, **2,895,** 3,086, 3,922,
      4,248, 4,362, 4,696, 4,732, **4,791, 4,827, 4,858,**
      5,053, 5,060, 5,398, **5,812, 5,817,** 6,539, **7,188,**
      8,003, 9,262, 9,527, **12,165,** 13,002, **13,087,**
      13,251, 14,776, 15,281, 17,709, **17,737**
    personal narratives, 25, **59,** 66, 78, 79, 80, 121,
      283, 1,408, 1,960, 2,185, 2,377, 2,455, 2,478,
      2,890, 2,957, 2,958, 2,978, **2,983,** 2,999, 3,047,
      3,092, 3,129, 3,170, 3,212, **3,242,** 3,315, 3,317,
      3,323, 3,330, 3,331, 3,334, **3,348,** 3,390, 3,436,
      3,536, 3,565, 4,362, 4,442, 4,615, 4,750, 5,312,
      5,485, 5,699, **5,749, 6,370,** 6,394, 6,857, 7,613,
      7,669, 7,678, 8,433, 8,987, 9,204, 9,318, **9,320,**
      9,370, **9,584, 9,586,** 9,630, 9,651, 9,726, 10,045,
      10,065, 10,819, 12,307, 12,381, 12,833, **12,957,**
      12,960, 13,003, **13,037, 13,065,** 13,072, 13,171,
      13,173, 13,250, **13,257, 13,268,** 13,431, 13,465,
      13,624, **14,769, 14,770,** 15,322, 15,449, 15,456,
      15,472, 15,475, 15,509, 15,651, 15,751, **15,952,**
      16,155, 16,244, 16,335, 17,405, 17,540, 17,601
    prisoners and prisons, 2,245, 2,417, 2,465, 2,522,
      2,594, 2,659, 2,893, 3,208, 3,262, 3,565, 5,689,
      7,188, 9,619, 9,684, 9,937, 12,308, **12,381,**
      12,969, 13,061, 13,085, 13,229, 13,257, 15,322,
      15,932, 17,073
    public opinion, 1,639, 2,208, 5,522, 9,061, 9,363,
      12,270, 12,283, 15,768, 17,479
    regimental histories, 3,354
    registers, lists, etc., 20, 3,133, 4,791, 7,669, 8,167,
      13,597
    relief of sick and wounded, 1,423, 2,358, 2,675,
      4,362, **4,858,** 5,608, 5,847, **6,501, 7,637,** 9,363,
      9,891, 11,167, 11,599, 13,624, 13,859, 15,230,
      16,244
    secret service, 2,573
    secret service, Confederate States, **13,419,** 15,610
    societies, **2,294, 4,745, 4,903,** 5,176, **5,881, 6,965,**
      8,272, 8,290, 10,619, 10,622, 14,565, 15,597
    societies, Confederate, 9, 16, 40, 99, 103, **119,**
      120, 513, 589, **1,264,** 2,198, 2,292, **2,580,** 2,901,
      2,955, 3,076, 3,080, 3,104, **3,164,** 3,169, 3,219,
      3,262, 3,345, 3,358, 3,383, 3,419, **3,431,** 3,440,
      3,465, **3,537, 3,616,** 5,513, 9,534, 9,596, **9,615,**
      9,644, 9,657, 9,669, 9,697, 9,719, 9,740, **9,756,**
      9,757, 9,758, 9,793, 9,795, **9,808,** 9,918, **9,919,**
      9,934, 12,940, 13,070, 13,085, 13,159, 13,285,
      13,337, 13,374, 13,388, 13,439, 13,571, 13,576,
      13,597, 13,617, 13,629, 14,230, **15,400,** 15,597,
      15,715, 15,756, 15,757, 15,758, 15,943, 15,951,
      15,954, 15,975, 16,114, 16,127, **16,140, 16,178,**
      16,261, 17,412

  transportation, 15,606
  war work, 10, 68, 1,426, 2,645, 2,690, 3,249,
    4,408, **5,054,** 5,268, 5,939, 6,731, 12,430,
    13,392, 14,766, 15,535, 15,726, 15,806, **15,833**
  colonial period (ca. 1600-1775), 4,383, 11,492,
    12,314
  diplomatic and consular service, **1,044,** 1,475,
    2,441, 2,527, **4,468,** 5,007, 6,391, 6,766, 6,861,
    7,598, 9,179, 14,607, 14,634, 17,629
    appointments, promotions, salaries, etc., 8,912
  economic conditions, 58, 3,449
  economic policy, 2,692
  elections. *See* Elections
  foreign and diplomatic service, officials and
    employees, **1,044**
  foreign relations, 2,075, 5,124, 5,134, 5,745, 9,159,
    11,621, **11,848,** 11,920, 13,801
  history, **11,299**
  imprints, 10,055
  information services, **2,691,** 2,701
  insular possessions, **1,177**
  Italian consuls in, 9,277
  naval militia, 7,138
  officials and employees, 64, 65, **138,** 184, 835,
    1,480, 2,188, 2,189, **2,242,** 2,441, 2,545, **2,623,**
    2,679, 2,715, 2,844, 2,845, **2,848, 2,849,** 2,850,
    2,851, 3,302, 3,682, **4,479,** 4,953, 5,102, **5,130,**
    5,134, 5,394, 5,434, **6,348,** 6,365, 6,662, **6,700,**
    6,709, 6,710, 6,761, **6,827,** 6,838, **6,840,** 6,914,
    6,925, 7,281, **7,468, 7,472,** 7,699, 7,738, **9,546,**
    9,699, 9,781, 10,079, 10,149, 10,763, **10,764,**
    11,250, **11,478, 11,495, 11,504,** 11,839, **11,905,**
    11,909, **11,929,** 12,941, 13,176, **13,614,** 13,999,
    14,203, 14,234, 14,982, 16,357, **17,697,** 17,908
    appointment, qualifications, tenure, 658, **5,160,**
      5,161, 9,932, 11,052
  officials and employees, Afro-American, 8,116
  officials and employees in foreign countries, 9,277
  politics and government, 6,352, 8,754, **17,417**
  postal service, officials and employees, **8,026,**
    16,880. *See also* Postmasters; Postmistresses
  Revolution (1775-1783), 1,924, 2,527, 2,560, 3,234,
    3,389, 3,509, 4,383, 5,765, 5,904, 7,333, 7,385,
    10,903, 11,005, 11,045, 11,184, **11,195,** 11,207,
    11,432, 11,440, 11,492, 12,170, 12,314, 12,848,
    13,210, 13,454, 13,557, 14,753, 14,839, 14,852,
    14,961, 15,001, **15,007,** 15,022, 15,041, 15,079,
    15,221, 15,783, 17,126
    biography, 13,411
    campaigns and battles, 7,638, 13,575, 13,583,
      15,978
    civilian participation, **15,978**
    claims, 3,554
    destruction and pillage, 2,342, 13,454
    economic aspects, 1,411
    finance, commerce, confiscations, **11,196,** 11,203
    French participation, 10,990
    hospitals, charities, etc., 9,834, 14,884
    Jewish participation, 7,555
    personal narratives, **2,257,** 7,669, 10,876, **10,877,**
      11,061, **11,085,** 14,847
    poetry, 11,173
    registers, lists, etc., 7,669, 9,816
  social life and customs, 9,308, 11,829, 12,314
  Southeast, German settlement, **9,632**
  War of 1812, 1,392, 4,352, 9,719, **11,198,** 12,734,
    12,769, 13,426, 15,681, 15,739
    campaigns and battles, 7,677
    destruction and pillage, 15,765
    personal narratives, 2,009, 7,669
    public opinion, 2,408
    registers, lists, etc., 7,669
    societies, 3,439, **9,690,** 10,032, **14,097,** 14,137,
      15,942, 15,951, 17,112
  War of 1898, 1,338, 1,924, 2,302, 2,454, 2,464,
    2,904, 4,735, 7,542, 8,968, 9,091, 9,118, 9,308,
    14,771, 15,707
    hospitals, charities, etc., **5,516, 14,474**
    nurses, 2,690, 2,919, **4,006,** 4,108, 8,648, **9,059,**
      13,729
    personal narratives, **4,006,** 6,162
    relief of sick and wounded, 5,847, **13,968**
    societies, 8,167, **8,289,** 9,259, **9,326,** 10,547,
      10,624, 14,701, 15,848

war work, 7,542
war work, Red Cross, 13,729
War with Mexico (1845-1848), 2,654, 5,335, 5,481,
  5,821, 8,374, 9,074, 9,714, 9,748, 9,911, 11,241,
  16,590
  hospitals, charities, etc., 2,671
  Mormon Battalion, 16,613
  personal narratives, 16,613
United States (government)
  Advisory Commissions on Education Exchange,
    International Education, and Cultural Affairs,
    12,694
  Agency for International Development, 6,209,
    6,402, 8,572
    officials and employees, 7,734, 8,165
  Agricultural Adjustment Administration, 9,197
    officials and employees, 8,947
  Agricultural Research service, officials and
    employees, 2,107
  Agricultural Stabilization and Conservation Service,
    officials and employees, 17,714
  Aid to Dependent Children, 515
  Aid to Dependent Children Program, 8,632, 8,676,
    17,534
  Aid to Families with Dependent Children, 8,062
  Aid to the Blind, 17,534
  Aid to the Disabled, 17,534
  Air Force, 11,831, 11,876
    air pilots, **14,161**
    chaplains, 37
    officials and employees, 15,933
    women in, **30, 34, 35, 36, 37, 9,137,** 11,831,
    14,772
  Air Force Academy, 34, 11,919
  Air Force, Nurse Corps, 34, 37
  Air Force Project, 11,876
  Air Force Reserve, officers, 30
  Air Service, 6,722
  Armed Forces Medical Museum, officials and
    employees, **2,089**
  Army, 180, 1,634, 3,672, 4,259, 8,324, 8,712,
    9,748, 9,884, 11,412, 12,377, 12,421, 17,719
    airborne troops, 37
    appointments and retirements, 2,690
    chaplains, 12,770
    handbooks, manuals, etc., 2,690
    management, 2,690, **2,699**
    military life, 17,445
    nurses, **2,091, 4,006,** 8,690, 9,003, **13,161,**
    13,281, 17,862
    officers, 1,398, **1,423,** 1,463, 1,484, **1,507,** 1,878,
    2,061, **2,174, 2,179, 2,245,** 2,278, **2,286,** 2,327,
    2,364, 2,377, 2,393, 2,454, 2,457, **2,462, 2,567,**
    2,573, 2,650, 2,659, **3,721,** 4,333, 4,408, **4,646,**
    4,784, 4,789, 4,951, 5,268, 5,480, **5,634,** 5,679,
    5,748, 5,779, **8,337,** 9,417, 10,075, 10,082,
    10,236, 10,237, 10,289, 10,519, **10,941,** 11,241,
    11,874, 12,067, 12,071, 12,951, 13,171, 14,454,
    14,766, **14,773,** 14,774, **14,776,** 14,777, 14,863,
    15,008, 15,044, 15,600, 17,065, 17,071, 17,073,
    17,074, 17,079, 17,477, 17,669
    officers, Afro-American, 2,217, **2,223**
    officials and employees, **5,127**
    public relations, 9,598
    records and correspondence, **2,671,** 2,675, 2,689,
    3,172
    recruiting, enlistment, etc., 2,699
    sanitary affairs, **2,690**
    service clubs, integration of, 3,292
    supplies and stores, **2,689**
    surgeons, 419, 2,277, 2,464, 2,654, 4,832, **9,909,**
    12,191, 12,754
    women in, 9,598, **10,075,** 17,719
  Army, Adjutant General's Office, **2,671**
  Army Air Forces, 11,874
    air pilots, **16,292**
  Army Air Forces Training Command, 36
  Army, Artillery, chaplains, **1,968**
  Army Base Hospital Number 5 (France), 6,129
  Army Cadet Nurse Corps, 3,954, 6,145, 13,618
  Army, Cavalry, 211
  Army, Corps of Engineers, 3,408
  Army, Infantry, 14,612
    chaplains, 4,359

  officers, 4,376, 12,157, **14,767, 14,768**
  Army, Medical Corps, officers, 14,771
  Army Military History Institute, 14,766
  Army Nurse Corps, 1,779, 2,690, 2,691, 6,127,
    6,159, 6,861, **6,930,** 8,259, 8,553, 13,618, 14,772,
    14,778
  Army, Office of the Quartermaster General, **2,689**
  Army School of Nursing, 2,690
  Army, Seventh Tennessee Regiment, 15,942
  Atomic Energy Commission, 17,711
    officials and employees, 17,642
  Board of Economic Warfare, 11,857
  Board of Foreign Scholarships, 6,493
  Board of Indian Commissioners, officials and
    employees, 4,269
  Board of Parole, officials and employees, 6,720
  Board of Tax Appeals, officials and employees,
    6,761
  Board of Veterans Appeals, officials and employees,
    9,544
  Books and Authors War Bond Committee,
    7,138
  Bureau of Agricultural Economics, **1,173**
  Bureau of Animal Industry, 2,718
  Bureau of Customs. See United States
    (government), Customs Service
  Bureau of Education, officials and employees,
    2,298
  Bureau of Employment Security, **2,672**
    officials and employees, **6,468**
  Bureau of Family Services, 11,916
  Bureau of Human Nutrition and Home Economics,
    2,673
    officials and employees, 2,673
  Bureau of Immigration and Naturalization Service.
    See United States (government), Immigration and
    Naturalization Service
  Bureau of Indian Affairs, **983, 1,175, 1,806, 2,674,**
    3,944, 6,142, 7,220, 8,705, **9,411, 10,097, 16,215,**
    16,863, 16,877, **17,216**
    officials and employees, 1,779, 2,298, **2,674,**
    8,170, 10,281, 11,220
  Bureau of Indian Affairs, Cheyenne River Agency,
    10,098
  Bureau of Indian Affairs, Lapwai Agency (ID),
    3,665
  Bureau of Indian Affairs, Potawatomi Indian
    Agency, **10,099**
  Bureau of Indian Affairs, Rosebud Agency, **10,100**
  Bureau of Indian Affairs, Winnebago Agency,
    10,101
  Bureau of Indian Affairs, Yankton Agency, **10,102**
  Bureau of Labor, officials and employees, 14,006
  Bureau of Labor Statistics, 6,402, 11,929
    officials and employees, 2,317, 6,600
  Bureau of Land Management, **984,** 14,216
    officials and employees, 20, **984**
  Bureau of Mines, officials and employees, 2,292
  Bureau of Refugees, Freedmen, and Abandoned
    Lands, **2,675,** 6,394, 13,573
  Bureau of Social Service and Rehabilitation,
    officials and employees, **6,919**
  Bureau of the Budget, officials and employees,
    11,478
  Bureau of the Census, **2,676, 3,945, 9,410,** 14,932
    officials and employees, 14,006
  Bureau of the Mint, officials and employees, **8,253,**
    18,005
  Children's Bureau, 231, 341, 2,120, 2,224, 2,504,
    4,330, 8,171, 9,263, 11,916, 13,618
    officials and employees, 863, **1,560,** 1,675, 3,311,
    6,135, 6,402, 6,520, 6,558, 6,715, 6,860, 6,981,
    6,987, 7,259, **9,978, 10,419, 10,603, 12,033,**
    12,037, 14,437, 17,757
  Circuit Court of Appeals, 13,904, 14,007
  Circuit Court of Appeals, Ohio, 6,357
  Civil Rights Commission, 5,828
  Civil Rights Division, officials and employees,
    10,070
  Civil Service Commission, 17,245
    officials and employees, 6,592, 6,976, 6,982,
    11,504
  Civil Works Administration, 10,055
  Civilian Conservation Corps, 3,569, 14,700, 17,513

  Coast Guard, SPARS, 5,719
  Coast Guard, women in, 14,772
  Commission on Civil Rights, **2,865,** 7,827
  Committee on Economic Security, 8,651. See also
    United States (government), Social Security
    Administration
  Committee on Fair Employment, 3,915
  Committee on Fair Employment Practice, **2,678**
  Congress, 3,093, 11,853, 14,994
    chaplains, **2,476, 12,318**
    committees, 993, 2,458, 2,697, 3,303, 3,852,
    5,829, 7,723, 9,368, 9,950, 11,555, 17,792
    officials and employees, 13,173
  Congress, House, **2,697**
  Congress, House Foreign Affairs Committee, 6,861
  Congress, House Joint Economic Committee, 9,950
  Congress, House Judiciary Committee 3,778
  Congress, House Military Affairs Committee, 2,458
  Congress, House Un-American Activities
    Committee, 64, 993, 5,829, 5,979, 7,723, 11,555,
    16,373
  Congress, House Veterans Affairs Committee, 6,861
  Congress, House Ways and Means Committee,
    9,950
  Congress, Senate, **2,697**
  Congress, Senate Committee on Education and
    Labor, 17,453
  Congress, Senate Committee on Foreign Relations,
    7,242, 9,368
  Constitution
    amendments, 1,424, 2,063, 2,492, 2,508, 2,528,
    9,142, 10,511, 10,649, 11,253, 11,621, 11,904,
    13,322, 13,350, **13,404, 13,405,** 13,453, 13,516,
    13,533, 15,317, 15,706, 15,733
    signers, 3,516
  Council of National Defense, officials and
    employees, 2,679
  Council of National Defense, Women's Committee,
    7,954
  Court of Appeals, Fifth Circuit, 16,215
  Customs Service, **1,174**
  Defense Advisory Committee on Women in the
    Services, **6,931**
  Department of Agriculture, 2,688, 10,018, 10,023,
    10,047, 11,629, 15,213, 15,215, 15,218
    officials and employees, 230, 3,123, 4,954, **4,970,**
    10,039, 10,607, 11,628, 13,479, 15,933, **16,342**
  Department of Agriculture, extension service,
    officials and employees, 6,585
  Department of Commerce, 2,789, 12,517
    officials and employees, 212, 16,357, 17,762
  Department of Commerce and Labor. See United
    States (government), Department of Commerce;
    United States (government), Department of
    Labor
  Department of Defense, 2,434, 14,431
    officials and employees, **2,393, 5,984**
  Department of Health, Education and Welfare,
    2,122, 2,680, 6,994, 8,045, 11,857, 11,958, 13,406
    officials and employees, 99, 2,095, 2,115, 2,393,
    2,680, 5,126, 5,137, **5,143,** 9,779, 11,483,
    11,484, 13,255
  Department of Justice, 102, 1,178
  Department of Labor, 2,504, **2,681,** 6,427, 11,929
    officials and employees, 2,681, 6,365, **6,402,**
    6,622, 6,982, 11,676, **11,773,** 12,899, 17,757
  Department of Natural Resources, 2,922
  Department of State, 1,604
    officials and employees, 2,456, 2,625, 2,657,
    3,712, 5,134, 6,720, 9,081, 11,228, 11,478,
    17,398
  Department of the Army, **2,699**
    records and correspondence, **2,699**
  Department of the Interior, officials and employees,
    1,424, 9,573
  Department of the Navy, 17,984
  Department of the Treasury, 2,217
    officials and employees, 1,675, 2,472, 4,855,
    5,130, **5,154,** 6,501, 6,840, 11,486, **12,203,**
    12,255
  Deputy Commissioners, 6,662
  District Court, District of Nevada (Carson City and
    Reno), **1,179**

District Court, Eastern District of California (Sacramento), **1,180**
District Court for Northern Texas, 6,666
District Court for Southern California, 623
District Court, Northern District of California, **1,181**
District Courts, **10,104, 14,938**
Economic Development Administration, 12,148
Employment Service, 1,917, 8,573
  officials and employees, 6,687, 13,406
Farm Security Administration, **1,176**, 14,202
  officials and employees, 607, 9,810, **16,514**
Federal Communications Commission, 11,806
  officials and employees, **6,887**
Federal Extension Service, **2,682**
Federal Maritime Commission, 7,318
Federal Railroad Administration, **2,696**
Federal Reserve Board, 110, 2,378
  officials and employees, **2,378**
Federal Security Agency, 2,115, 9,779
Federal Writers Project, American Guide Series, 2,904
Federal Writers Project, Women in State Development and Folklore, **17,413**
Fish and Wildlife Service, **2,724**
Food Administration, **2,694, 4,850**, 4,930, 4,937, **4,954**, 5,119, 13,617
  officials and employees, 6,236
Food and Drug Administration, 9,349, 11,806
  officials and employees, **13,259**
Food and Drug Administration, Award of Merit, 13,259
Foreign Claims Settlement Commission, officials and employees, 5,272
Foreign Operations Administration, 4,918
Forest Service, officials and employees, **8,715**
General Land Office, **9,485**
Geological Survey, 2,200, 2,292
Head Start, 8,639
High Commission, 7,326
Housing Corporation, **2,695**
Immigration and Naturalization Service, 2,672, **2,683, 14,933**
  officials and employees, 14,006
Information Agency, 7,214
  officials and employees, 9,081, 12,899
Information Agency, European Cooperation Administration, Office of the Special Representative, officials and employees, 17,070
Internal Revenue Service, **1,807, 3,947**, 9,769, **14,934**
  officials and employees, 9,806
Internal Revenue Service, Detroit (MI), officials and employees, 3,947
Job Corps, 4,382, 12,720, 17,191
Land Office. *See* United States (government), Bureau of Land Management
Marine Corps, 11,426, 13,618
  officers, 9,685, 11,925
  women in, 843, 11,925
Marine Corps Reserve, women in, **2,866, 2,867**
Marine Corps, Women's Reserves, 11,925, 14,772
Marshals, 190, **10,103, 10,160**, 10,738
Military Academy, 2,671, 15,008
National Bureau of Standards, 11,806
National Commission for UNESCO, 9,449
National Commission on Law Observance "Wickersham Commission," 7,031
National Herbarium, grass collection, 15,215
National Museum, officials and employees, 6,321
National Museum, Plant division, 15,215
National Park Service, **14,935**
National Recovery Administration, 341, **2,684**, 6,949, 11,905, 12,704
National Recovery Administration, Consumers' Advisory Board, 6,973
National Resources Planning Board, officials and employees, 11,482
National Trail System, 4,289
National War Labor Board, Atlanta Region, officials and employees, 4,126
National War Labor Board, officials and employees, 561

National Youth Administration, **2,685**, 3,946, 6,765, 9,153, 10,074, 14,202, **17,521**
  officials and employees, 2,685, 12,066
National Youth Administration, California State Advisory Committee, 14,202
National Youth Administration, music division, officials and employees, 9,810
Naval Institute, 2,710
Naval Midshipmen's School (MA), 2,867
Navy, **5,718**
  history, **2,707, 2,708, 2,710, 11,500**
  hospitals, 8,260
  officers, **2,226**, 2,229, 2,252, **2,302**, 2,479, **2,521**, 2,545, **2,556, 2,577, 2,630**, 2,654, **2,709, 2,710**, 3,022, **3,181, 3,184**, 4,822, 6,850, 9,986, 10,921, 11,500, 12,191, **12,194**, 12,552, 12,664, 12,871, 13,206, **14,072, 15,080**
  recruiting, enlistment, etc., 13,617
  sea life, 2,201
  surgeons, 2,464
  women in, **3,022, 14,482**
Navy, Cadet Corps of Nurses, 4,026
Navy Nurse Corps, 9,286
Navy, Women's Reserve, **2,707**
Office for Emergency Management, War Manpower Commission, **2,701**
  officials and employees, 2,701
Office for Emergency Management, War Production Board, **2,853**
Office of Child Development, **2,677**, 8,636, 8,647, 8,668
Office of Civil and Defense Mobilization. *See* United States (government), Department of Defense; United States (government), Office of Emergency Planning
Office of Civilian Defense, **2,686**, 5,735, 7,965, 8,446
  officials and employees, 4,493
Office of Community Advisory Services, 2,456
Office of Community War Services, **2,687**
Office of Economic Opportunity, 4,152, 10,404, 11,501, 14,605, 14,671, **14,936**, 16,215
Office of Education, 6,625, 8,572
Office of Education, Federal Board for Vocational Education, Trade and Industrial Education Service, **11,047**
Office of Emergency Planning, 14,431
Office of Government Reports, officials and employees, 11,478
Office of Price Administration. *See* United States (government), Office of Temporary Controls
Office of Price Stabilization, 9,197
Office of Temporary Controls, **2,688**, 6,056, 7,251, 7,965, 11,806, 15,121
  officials and employees, 2,688, 6,056, 6,896, 7,251, 7,965, 11,806, 13,241, 15,121
Office of the Army Surgeon General, 8,656
Office of the Coordinator of Health, Welfare and Related Defense Activities. *See* United States (government), Office of Community War Services
Office of the Surgeon General, **2,690**
Office of War Information, **2,691**, 9,527, 15,121
  officials and employees, 607, 11,478, 14,453
Office of War Mobilization and Reconversion, media programming division, 10,071
Old Age Assistance, 17,534
Patent Office, officials and employees, **2,196**
Peace Corps, 5,475, 8,261, 14,033
  officials and employees, 380, **6,917, 7,297, 7,786, 7,970, 8,261**, 9,286, **9,389, 17,704, 17,759**
President's Committee on Civil Rights (1947-1948), 3,353, 3,469
President's Emergency Committee for Employment. *See* United States (government), President's Organization on Unemployment Relief
President's Organization on Unemployment Relief, **2,692**
Public Health Service, 242, 11,885, 11,916, 13,406, 15,246
  officials and employees, 2,317, **3,466, 6,146, 6,919**, 11,579
Public Service Reserve, 4,937
Reserve Officer Training Corps, 4,216
  women in, 11,876

Secret Service, 11,493
Signal Corps, 6,383
Smithsonian Art Commission, 2,844
Smithsonian Institution (DC), 248, 1,480, 2,107, 2,855, 4,747
  Archives of American Art, 2,065, 2,817
  Archives of American Art, Midwest Area Center (Detroit, MI), **8,017**
  Archives of American Art, New England Area Center (Boston, MA), **5,901**
  Archives of American Art, New York Area Center, **11,818**
  Archives of American Art, West Coast Area Center, **1,225**
  Bureau of Ethnology, 9,042
  Department of Anthropology, **2,837, 2,843**
  Department of Botany, 15,215
  National Collection of Fine Arts, **2,844, 2,846**
  National Collection of Fine Arts, Department of Twentieth-Century Painting and Sculpture, **2,845**
  National Collection of Fine Arts, Office of Exhibition and Design, **2,847**
  National Collection of Fine Arts, Office of the Director, **2,848, 2,849, 2,850**
  National Collection of Fine Arts, Publications, Editor, **2,851**
  National Museum of Natural History, Division of Reptiles and Amphibians, 2,714, 2,723
Social Security Administration, **2,693**, 8,644, 11,958
  officials and employees, 2,693, 5,134, 6,973, 16,373
Social Security Board. *See* United States (government), Social Security Administration
Soil Conservation Service, 4,686
Subversive Activities Control Board, 6,720
Supreme Court, 20, 2,259, 2,651, 2,857, 4,356, 12,522, 17,259
  appointments, qualifications, etc., 15,755
Surveyor's Office, officials and employees, **10,298**
Tennessee Valley Authority, 11,920
  officials and employees, 8,572, **9,733, 15,885**
Veterans' Administration, **2,698**, 6,041, 9,911
  officials and employees, 8,573
Veterans's Administration, nursing service, officials and employees, 6,826
Vocational Rehabilitation Administration, 8,567
Wage and Hour and Public Contracts Division, **14,939**
Wage and Salary Stabilization Boards, Economic Stabilization Agency, **1,810**
War Assets Administration, **1,811**
War Claims Commission, officials and employees, 5,272, 9,647
War Department, 5,755, 9,528, 9,962
  officials and employees, **5,984**, 17,862
War Department, civil affairs division, 10,070
  officials and employees, **10,070**
War Industries Board, officials and employees, 10,034
War Labor Policies Board, 341, **2,700**, 6,402
War Manpower Commission, 659, **1,182, 3,950**, 8,984, 13,406, 13,888, 16,215
  officials and employees, 1,357
War Manpower Commission, Woman's Advisory Committee, 10,197
War Production Board, officials and employees, 15,333
War Relocation Authority, 570, 1,044, **2,702**, 9,219
  officials and employees, 607, 625, **1,044**
Women Accepted for Voluntary Emergency Service, 2,691, **2,707**, 2,708, **2,709**, 2,867, **3,022**, 4,390, **6,850**, 7,138, 7,160, **7,565**, 10,064, 12,871, 13,189, 14,772
  recruiting, 13,618
Women Air Force Service Pilots, **30, 36**, 5,132, **5,311**, 9,137, **14,161, 16,292**
Women, Air Force Service Pilots, Fifth Ferrying Group, 5,311
Women-in-Industry Service, 2,681, 2,703
Women in the Air Forces, **34**
Women's Air Corps, 5,147, 11,932
Women's Air Force, 2,710

Women's Army Auxiliary Corps 2,686, 5,129, 5,737, 9,962
officers, **17,066**, 17,067, **17,068**
Women's Army Corps, 1,618, 2,102, 2,393, 2,663, 2,691, 2,699, 2,701, 3,671, 4,193, 4,390, 6,417, 8,466, 8,665, 9,146, 9,394, 10,064, 10,519, 11,244, 11,644, 11,698, 13,762, 14,714, 14,772, 16,373, 17,719
officers, **14,774**, **17,066**, 17,067, **17,068**, **17,308**
recruiting, 13,618
Women's Army Training Corps, 4,390
Women's Army Volunteer Corps, 3,653
Women's Auxiliary Ferrying Squadron, 36
Women's Bureau, 2,504, 2,681, **2,703**, 5,136, 5,149, 6,365, 6,799, 7,318, 11,305, 11,904, 15,304
officials and employees, 2,703, 6,725, **6,766**, 11,729
Women's Reserve of the Coast Guard Reserve, 2,710, 4,390, 14,772
Work Projects Administration, 76, 231, **1,798**, 2,424, **2,704**, **3,120**, 3,437, 4,055, 4,729, 4,949, 5,410, 5,575, 6,673, 6,893, 6,994, 8,058, 8,067, 8,518, 8,578, 8,622, 8,697, **9,462**, 9,463, 9,688, 9,699, 9,779, 10,163, 10,332, 11,494, 13,654, 14,224, 14,241, 15,054, 16,970
officials and employees, 2,743, **2,754**, 8,066, 8,113, 10,055, 11,489, **11,883**, 14,174, 15,332, 17,846, 17,907
Work Projects Administration, art projects, 2,891, 9,145
Work Projects Administration, Bureau of Home Economics, officials and employees, 2,317
Work Projects Administration, Community Service Division, **5,422**
Work Projects Administration, Education-Recreation Division, 1,798
Work Projects Administration, Ex-Slave Narrative Project (LA), **5,423**
Work Projects Administration, Federal Art Gallery, 2,778
Work Projects Administration, Federal Arts Project, 2,748, 2,795, 11,843
officials and employees, **2,732, 2,742**
Work Projects Administration, Federal Music Project, 2,743, 12,690
Work Projects Administration, Federal Recreation Department, 2,743
Work Projects Administration, Federal Theater Project, 17,281
officials and employees, 2,743, **2,759**, 11,480
Work Projects Administration, Federal Theatre Radio Division, 6,625
Work Projects Administration, Federal Writers Project, 1,798, 2,743, 2,945, 2,946, 2,947, 2,948, 2,951, 9,462, 11,064, **11,143**, **16,436**, 16,519, 16,967, **16,968**, 17,254
officials and employees, 9,498, 10,055, 14,714, 15,585
Work Projects Administration, Historical Data Project, 13,715
Work Projects Administration, Historical Records Survey, 5,107, **5,108**, **5,424**, **5,425**
officials and employees, **10,055**
Work Projects Administration, Indian-Pioneer Project, officials and employees, **14,183**
Work Projects Administration, National Advisory Committee, 14,202
Work Projects Administration, Professional and Service Projects, officials and employees, 3,432
Work Projects Administration, Resident Work Center for Girls (PA), officials and employees, 8,079
Work Projects Administration, Stearns County (MN), Museum Project, **9,412**
Work Projects Administration, Survey of Federal Archives, **5,425**
Work Projects Administration, Women's and Professional Projects, 11,883
Work Projects Administration, Workers Education Service, 11,501
Works Progress Administration. *See* United States (government), Work Projects Administration
Writers' War Board, 16,222
United States (steamboat), 14,993

United States and Russia, The (book), 6,512
United States and Sweden, cultural relations, 4,321
United States Cadet Nurse Corps, **17,784**
United States Catholic Conference, 12,729
United States Centennial Commission, **14,924**
United States-China Friendship Association, 14,691
United States Christian Commission, 2,671, 3,991, 14,418
United States Conference of Mayors, 14,236
United States Courts of Appeals, **14,937**
United States Daughters of 1812, 3,439, 15,942, 17,112
United States Daughters of 1812 (IN), **4,558**
United States Daughters of 1812 (Circleville, OH), Major John Boggs Chapter, **14,097**
United States Daughters of the War of 1812 (MO), James S. Kearney Chapter, 10,109
United States Delegation to the Council of Foreign Ministers, 5,007
United States Education Mission to Japan, 17,356
United States Liaison Committee. *See* Country Women's Council USA
United States Navy League (CT), Admiral Bunce Section, **1,934**
United States Quarantine and Immigration Station (Angel Island, CA), 1,156
United States Sanitary Commission, 1,413, 2,494, 2,568, 3,888, 4,135, 5,060, 5,827, 11,247, 12,431, 12,950, 13,932, 14,418, 14,775
employees, **2,206**, 2,594, 12,233, 12,261
United States Sanitary Commission, Cleveland Branch, Soldier's Aid Society of Northern Ohio, **13,966**
United States Sanitary Commission, Special Relief Department, 13,966
United States Sanitary Commission, Women's Pennsylvania Branch, 14,831
United States Service Club, 14,978
United States Sesquicentennial Exhibition (Philadelphia, 1926), 15,182, 15,194
United States Steel Corporation, 9,273
United States Supreme Court building, 2,354
United States Volunteers, 15,008
United States Western Regional Laboratory (CA), 364
United States Youth Council, 8,670
United Steelworkers of America (Philadelphia, PA), Local Four thousand Eight hundred Eighty nine, 15,332
United Textile Workers of America, **3,450**, 15,977
United Tribes, 1,662
United Ukrainian American Relief Committee, 9,508, **9,512**
United War Work Campaign, 8,447, 10,488, 12,729
United Way of Metropolitan Chicago (IL), 3,901, **3,905**, 4,045, **4,079**, 4,152
United Women Workers (MA), 7,004
United Women's Club (Madison, WI), **17,730**
United Women's Contingent, 17,975
United World Federalists, 9,449
United World Federalists, New York State Branch, **12,652**
Unity Church (Monmouth, IL), **4,441**
Unity Church (Monmouth, IL), Ladies Social Circle, 4,441
Unity Church (Monmouth, IL), Ladies' Society, 4,441
Unity Church (Humboldt, IA), 4,776
Unity Church (St. Paul, MN), **9,413**
Unity Church (St. Paul, MN), Unity Guild, 9,413
Unity Church (St. Paul, MN), Women's Alliance, 8,987, 9,413
Unity School (Honan, China), 8,755
Universal (film company), 949
Universal Peace Union, 11,616, 15,300, 15,302
Universalism, 2,661, 3,381, 7,677, 8,831, 11,669, 11,672, 13,734
Universalist Church (Port Huron, MI), 7,839
Universalist Church of the Good Shepherd (Racine, WI), 17,852
Universalist churches
clergy, 2,606, 4,809, 5,918, **11,391**, **11,403**, 17,852
missionaries, **6,247**, 8,831
missions, 6,247
Universalist Service Committee, 4,077

University and College Women of Illinois
Northeastern Illinois University Chapter, 4,008
Universities and colleges, 1, 81, 97, 674, 760, 786, 917, **923**, 1,163, 1,377, 1,390, 1,404, 1,518, 1,534, 1,552, 1,751, **1,784**, **1,815**, 1,870, 2,125, 2,130, 2,134, 2,143, 2,146, 2,149, 2,680, **2,884**, **3,095**, **3,098**, 3,157, 3,165, 3,218, 3,257, 3,258, 3,305, 3,328, **3,384**, **3,473**, 4,003, 4,123, **4,215**, 4,218, 4,319, 4,379, 4,389, 4,394, 4,470, 4,477, 4,481, 4,519, 4,520, 4,521, 4,522, 4,523, 4,525, 4,527, 4,532, 4,888, 5,446, 5,474, 5,494, 5,644, **5,708**, 5,731, **5,835**, 6,087, 6,157, **6,237**, **6,300**, 6,416, **6,423**, 6,435, 6,451, 6,482, 6,490, 6,493, 6,527, 6,592, 6,670, 6,683, 6,692, 6,708, 6,737, 6,769, 6,848, 6,862, 6,975, **7,048**, 7,094, **7,330**, **7,500**, 7,564, 7,573, 7,800, 7,918, 8,085, **8,152**, 8,226, 8,232, 8,244, 8,247, 8,348, 8,428, 8,542, **8,548**, 8,609, 8,740, 9,023, 9,287, 9,468, 9,544, 9,575, 9,583, 9,597, 9,607, 9,634, 9,671, 9,672, 9,699, 9,768, 9,770, **9,939**, **10,021**, 10,134, 10,564, 10,568, 10,600, 10,751, 11,039, **11,151**, **11,373**, 11,443, **11,662**, **11,847**, **11,849**, **11,969**, 12,048, **12,122**, 12,159, 12,422, 12,737, 12,740, **12,745**, 12,762, 12,907, 12,917, 12,918, 12,922, 12,923, 13,134, **13,180**, **13,186**, 13,189, **13,223**, **13,227**, 13,242, 13,262, 13,307, 13,322, **13,333**, 13,335, 13,350, 13,390, 13,398, 13,400, **13,401**, 13,406, 13,430, 13,437, 13,438, 13,439, 13,446, 13,447, 13,460, 13,468, 13,470, 13,480, 13,484, 13,526, 13,558, 13,573, 13,584, 13,588, 13,599, 13,604, 13,608, 13,616, 13,618, **13,627**, 13,686, 14,199, 14,200, 14,201, 14,216, 14,283, 14,299, 14,306, 14,375, 14,477, 14,508, **14,802**, 14,844, 14,845, 14,857, **15,183**, 15,195, 15,252, 15,332, 15,611, **15,777**, **16,048**, **16,107**, **16,108**, **16,112**, 16,204, **16,287**, **16,308**, **16,408**, 16,423, 16,993, 16,994, 16,996, 17,005, **17,047**, 17,110, 17,167, 17,343, 17,380, 17,532, **17,549**, **17,557**, 17,589, **17,689**, **17,849**. *See also* Agricultural colleges; Bible colleges; Catholic universities and colleges; Church colleges; Coeducation; Greek letter societies; Junior colleges; Municipal universities and colleges; State universities and colleges; Students' societies; Teachers Colleges; Womens' colleges
accounting, 13,196, 16,408
administration, **1,841**, **7,570**, 7,826, **10,930**, 11,538, 12,921, 12,925, **14,275**, 14,745, **15,239**, 16,993, **17,963**
admission, 3,381, **5,725**, **6,270**, **6,271**, **6,303**, **7,581**
alumnae, **2,934**, **5,061**, **6,877**, 7,154, 7,184, 7,286, **7,498**, **7,562**, **8,054**, 8,533, 8,534, 8,537, 8,542, 8,543, 8,556, 8,560, 8,600, **9,430**, **11,370**, 13,194, **13,224**, **13,885**, **13,890**, 14,274, **14,699**
alumni, 4,470, 4,524, **6,009**, 6,339, **6,398**, 6,556, **6,786**, 7,646, **7,955**, **7,956**, **7,957**, **7,958**, **11,508**, 13,193, **16,991**
archives, 33, **1,085**, **1,681**, **1,814**, 2,118, 3,280, **3,470**, **3,741**, **4,008**, **4,216**, **4,285**, **4,330**, **5,168**, **5,185**, **5,207**, **5,235**, **5,241**, **5,437**, **5,454**, **5,852**, **5,855**, **6,339**, 7,686, 8,174, **8,385**, 9,809, **9,824**, 10,190, **11,267**, 11,271, 11,285, 11,290, 11,301, **11,332**, 11,380, 11,398, **11,446**, **11,781**, **12,836**, **13,248**, **13,300**, 13,758, **13,876**, **13,877**, **13,878**, **14,118**, **14,178**, **14,737**, **15,375**, **15,897**, 17,006, **17,142**
buildings, 918, 1,848, 4,395, 5,018, **7,155**, 8,533, 8,558, 8,605, 9,938, 11,694, 13,613, 16,339
centennial celebrations, 7,162, 13,204
curricula, 1,845, **5,399**, **6,273**, 6,733, 7,580, 16,988
directories, 4,048
employees, **2,918**, **4,297**, **4,386**, 4,494, **5,033**, 5,646, 5,663, **6,304**, 6,482, 6,708, **6,907**, 8,602, 10,022, 11,642, **13,712**, **15,919**, 16,986
entrance requirements, 7,184
evaluation, 7,584
examinations, 4,060, 5,318, **6,272**, 7,922
faculty, **228**, **916**, **928**, 2,727, **2,927**, 3,652, **4,380**, **4,381**, **4,383**, **4,384**, **4,388**, 4,391, 4,395, **4,396**, **4,399**, **4,403**, **4,404**, 4,478, **4,505**, **5,033**, **5,539**, 6,482, 6,782, **7,157**, **7,158**, **8,047**, 8,536, 8,550, 8,554, **8,561**, **8,562**, **8,563**, 8,572, 8,573, 8,582, 8,592, **8,606**, **8,618**, 8,620, 8,622, **10,755**, 11,521,

11,581, 11,835, 11,848, 13,333, 14,026, 14,229, 14,256, 14,965, 16,986
faculty, Afro-American, 6,997
finance, 4,594, 5,507, 5,545, 7,163, 7,566, 8,193, 8,746, 12,739
food service, 7,879
graduate work, 4,382, 7,159, 11,846, 11,857, 11,879, 11,890, 13,110, 15,241
history, 126, 3,085, 4,494, 7,153, 7,160, 7,163, 7,493, 7,568, 7,583, 10,928, 10,931, 10,932, 11,300, 11,550, 13,178, 15,240, 17,530, 17,548
law and legislation, 17,442
pictorial records, 9,579
radio broadcasting, 6,625
records and correspondence, 1,095, 4,715, 10,216, 10,222, 13,633, 17,620
religion, 521
Universities and colleges, Afro-American, 2,205, 7,590, 10,095, 13,444, 16,342
finance, 12,708
University Baptist Church (WA), Women's Society, 17,246
University Club (Iowa City, IA), 4,960
University Club (Spokane, WA), 17,375
University cooperation, 6,274, 6,275, 9,942
University Dames (AR), 268
University Dames (Iowa City, IA), 4,960
University Education of Women (conference), 17,785
University Elementary School (Los Angeles, CA), 788, 1,055
University extension, 4,380, 4,383, 6,490, 7,184, 8,150, 8,165, 10,015, 10,019, 11,970, 13,253, 16,484
University Guild (IL), 4,214
University Hall (IL), 4,395
University High School (GA), 2,980
University Hospital (AR), employees, 239
University Hospital School of Nursing (AL). See University of Alabama in Birmingham School of Nursing
University in Transition, A: Florida State College for Women and Florida State University, 1941-1947 (book), 2,928
University Infirmary Association (AR), 269
University Ladies' Club (TX), 16,146
University League (Madison, WI), 17,786
University Lyceum Theater (MN), 8,541
University Methodist Church (TX), Ladies Aid Society, 16,059
University of Alabama (Tuscaloosa, AL), 106, 113, 9,746
admissions, 117
alumni, 103
deans, 108, 116
faculty, 104, 105, 107, 109, 120
students, 89, 115
University of Alabama in Birmingham School of Nursing, 22
University of Arizona, 4,759
University of Arizona (Tucson, AZ), Chimes, 14,029
University of Arizona, Desert Riders, 227
University of Arizona, Faculty Women's Club, 228
University of Arizona, Laboratory of Tree Ring Research, 193
University of Arizona, Steward Observatory, 193
University of Arkansas (Fayetteville, AR), 231, 232, 242, 9,973
alumnae, 265
faculty, 265, 293, 8,663
University of Arkansas (Fayetteville, AR), School of Nursing, deans, 235
University of Berlin (Germany), alumnae, 14,122
University of Bordeaux (France), alumnae, 9,392
University of Bridgeport (CT), Fones School of Dental Hygiene, 1,832
University of Buffalo (NY)
alumnae, 11,357
faculty, 11,366
University of Buffalo (NY) Council, 11,386
University of California, 453, 511, 526, 609, 645, 730, 750, 921, 923, 926, 3,165, 6,188
administration, 449
alumnae, 356, 509, 952, 1,311, 1,341, 3,012, 14,355
buildings, 918

deans, 435, 449, 11,898
faculty, 441, 561, 757, 1,088, 2,660
presidents, 924
students, 605
trustees, 540, 689
University of California, Associated Students, 578
University of California, Associated Women Students, 908
University of California, Berkeley (CA), 17,973
alumnae, 353, 648, 4,682, 8,710, 10,677
deans, 674, 11,925
faculty, 458, 608, 650, 667, 905, 930, 6,928
presidents, 674, 811
students, 420, 525, 561, 647, 703, 711, 726, 790, 809, 810, 843, 1,948, 14,363
University of California, Berkeley (CA), Greek Theatre, 458, 871
University of California, Committee on Music and Drama, 911
University of California, Davis (CA), 811
University of California, Department of Dramatic Art, 913
University of California, extension division, 2,233
University of California, Faculty Women's Club, 1,036
University of California, Free Speech Movement, 915
University of California, Group for Academic Freedom, 916
University of California, Heller Committee for Research in Social Economics, 917
University of California, Los Angeles (CA), 402, 708, 786, 811, 1,053
administrators, 487
alumnae, 667
deans, 1,020
faculty, 440, 788, 1,655, 15,217, 16,881, 16,923
University of California, Los Angeles (CA), Chimes, 14,029
University of California, Los Angeles (CA), Hope for Hearing Foundation, 2,105
University of California, Los Angeles (CA), Near Eastern Center, 853
University of California, Los Angeles (CA), Oral History Program Interviews, 1,054
University of California, Los Angeles (CA), Student Religious Board, 521
University of California, Los Angeles (CA), theater arts department, 440
University of California, Los Angeles (CA), University Religious Conference, 521
University of California, Medical School, 1,348
University of California, Mother's Club, 849
University of California, Museum of Anthropology, 919
University of California, Museum of Paleontology, 310
University of California, Museum of Vertebrate Zoology, 310, 821, 910
University of California, Phi Beta Kappa Society, 922
University of California Press, 11,925
University of California, Prytanean Society, 925
University of California, San Francisco (CA)
faculty, 1,374
students, 1,380
University of California, San Francisco (CA), Doctors' Wives' Association, 1,382
University of California, Santa Barbara (CA), 811
faculty, 2,820
University of California, Santa Barbara (CA), Chimes, 14,029
University of California, school of librarianship, 420
University of California, school of public health, 344
University of California, Women's Dormitory Association, 927
University of California, Women's Faculty Club, 928
University of California, Young Women's Christian Association, 929
University of Cambridge (England), faculty, 5,339
University of Chicago (IL), 2,832, 3,318, 4,003, 4,060, 4,300, 11,894, 11,924, 13,428, 16,375, 17,445
administration, 2,224
alumnae, 2,523, 3,462, 3,463, 3,466, 4,115, 8,597, 8,603, 9,829, 12,422, 13,255

deans, 4,111, 7,572
faculty, 4,115, 4,305, 9,425, 10,603, 11,572, 11,578, 13,015, 14,386
students, 2,446, 3,773, 3,974, 4,049, 4,289, 5,084, 8,553, 8,643
University of Chicago (IL), Extension School, 6,490
University of Chicago (IL), graduate school of social service administration, 2,224, 3,809, 4,047
faculty, 4,146
students, 4,141
University of Chicago (IL), John Dewey Practice School, 11,572
University of Chicago (IL), Oriental Institute, 4,028
University of Chicago (IL), Philanthropic Committee of the Christian Union, 3,875
University of Chicago (IL), Settlement. See Mary McDowell Settlement (Chicago, IL)
University of Cincinnati (OH), 13,857, 13,872, 13,875
faculty, 2,713, 13,869, 13,870
students, 8,553
University of Cincinnati (OH), Affirmative Action Commission, 13,878
University of Cincinnati (OH), Association of Women Administrators, 13,876
University of Cincinnati (OH), College of Nursing and Health, archives, 13,877
University of Cincinnati (OH), Dames, 13,858
University of Cincinnati (OH), Office of University Commitment and Human Resources, 13,878
University of Colorado
administration, 1,779
faculty, 1,671, 1,674, 1,677, 1,678, 1,804
students, 17,653
University of Colorado, Child Research Council, 8,574
University of Colorado, College of Nursing, deans, 17,297
University of Connecticut, faculty, 10,607
University of Dacca (East Pakistan), faculty, 8,586
University of Dallas (TX), faculty, 15,929
University of Denver (CO), 1,751, 12,921
faculty, 8,636
students, 13,155
University of Denver (CO), Women's Faculty Club, 1,786
University of Evansville (IN), Faculty Dames, 4,505
University of Evansville (IN), trustees, 4,504
University of Florida, 2,884
students, Afro-American, 2,880
University of Georgia, 2,962, 3,108, 3,157, 3,258
administrators, 3,058, 3,066, 3,126
admission, 3,381
alumnae, 3,372, 3,415
deans, 3,022, 3,125
employees, 2,988
faculty, 3,123
students, 2,980, 3,107
University of Georgia, Founders Memorial Garden, 3,082
University of Georgia, Homecon Club, 3,124
University of Georgia, Library, 3,063
University of Georgia, Library Book Hour, 3,106
University of Georgia, Library Freshman Reading Survey, 3,107
University of Georgia, Lipscomb Hall, Honor Dormitory, 3,053
University of Georgia, Newcomers Club, 3,127
University of Georgia, Special Collections Department, 2,981
University of Georgia, University Woman's Club, 3,077, 3,127
University of Hawaii at Manoa, 3,651
University of Hawaii at Manoa, Women's Campus Club, 3,652
University of Heidelberg (Germany)
alumnae, 2,070
students, 10,522
University of Helsinki (Finland), faculty, 10,312
University of Houston (TX), 16,236
University of Idaho
faculty, 6,336, 9,839
trustees, 3,667
University of Illinois, 4,123, 4,379, 6,692
alumnae, 4,381, 4,392, 4,394, 13,754

buildings, 4,366, 4,380, 4,395
deans, **4,042, 4,382, 4,390**
employees, **4,386**
faculty, 2,540, 4,040, **4,378, 4,380**, 4,381, **4,383,
4,384**, 4,385, **4,387, 4,388, 4,389, 4,391**, 4,392,
4,393, 4,394, 4,395, **4,396, 4,397**, 4,398, **4,399,
4,402, 4,403, 4,404**, 4,406, 4,432, 4,438, 4,440,
7,545, 8,636
graduate work, 4,382
students, 9,246, 15,936
trustees, 4,411
University of Illinois at Chicago Circle, Activities
Honorary Society, 4,042
University of Illinois at Chicago Circle, Campus
Equal Employment Opportunity Office, 4,043
University of Illinois at Chicago Circle, College of
Health, Physical Education, and Recreation,
4,041
University of Illinois at Chicago Circle, Office of
Student Affairs, Dean of Women, 4,042
University of Illinois at Chicago Circle, Office of the
Chancellor, Committee on the Status of Women,
4,043
University of Illinois at Chicago Circle, University
Dance Committee, 4,042
University of Illinois, Library School, 4,396
University of Illinois, student affairs committee, 4,382
University of Illinois Women's Club at Chicago
Circle, **4,044**
University of Iowa, 4,949
administration, 5,035
alumnae, 5,086, 8,805, 17,974
employees, **5,033**
faculty, 4,040, 4,765, 4,895, **4,916**, 4,934, 4,940,
4,944, 4,962, **5,033, 5,035, 5,082**
students, **4,967**, 5,064
University of Iowa Air Force Reserve Officers
Training Corps, 5,016
University of Iowa, Associated Women Students,
4,967
University of Iowa, College of Nursing, **4,980**
University of Iowa, Committee on International
Women's Year, **4,981**
University of Iowa, Department of Home Economics,
4,984
University of Iowa, Institute of Child Behavior and
Development, **4,996**
University of Iowa, Library, **5,034**
University of Iowa, Mortar Board, Staff and Circle
Chapter, **5,014**
University of Iowa, Women's Forensic Council, **5,045**
University of Iowa, Women's Panhellenic Association,
5,046
University of Kansas
faculty, 2,070
students, 5,209
University of Kentucky, 5,330, 6,416
faculty, 484, 8,654
students, 5,313, 5,326, 5,330
University of Kentucky, alumnae, 5,325
University of Kentucky, Mothers' Club, 5,307
University of Kentucky, Women's Studies Committee,
5,330
University of Latvia, alumnae, 8,604
University of Leipzig (Germany), students, 656, 5,323
University of London (England), students, 656, 8,591
University of Louisville (KY), faculty, 5,380
University of Louisville (KY), medical school, faculty,
15,918
University of Maine, employees, **5,646**, 5,662, 5,663
University of Maryland, 5,834
alumnae, 2,714
University of Massachusetts, 6,607
faculty, 5,466
University of Massachusetts, Advisory Council of
Women, **5,872**
University of Massachusetts, Faculty Senate
Committee on the Status of Women, **5,873**
University of Michigan, 7,773, 7,793, 7,820, 7,822,
7,884, 8,168, 8,342, 11,930
alumnae, 4,304, 7,702, 7,748, 7,777, 7,801, 7,814,
7,853, 7,893, 7,941, 8,009, **11,237**, 14,698
buildings, 7,697, 7,831, **7,852, 7,854**
deans, 7,845, 7,872, **7,959**

examinations, 7,922
faculty, 6,336, 7,727, 7,747, 7,818, 7,873, 7,876,
7,924
food service, 7,879
graduate students, 7,944, 11,387
presidents, 7,704
radio broadcasting, 6,625
students, 3,979, 7,707, 7,717, 7,725, 7,735, 7,739,
7,792, 7,812, 7,819, 7,833, 7,851, 7,879, 7,896,
7,940, 7,966, 17,637
trustees, 7,714, 7,875
University of Michigan, Alumnae Club, 7,955
University of Michigan, Alumnae Council, 7,833
University of Michigan, Alumnae House. *See* Mary
Markley House (MI)
University of Michigan, Alumni Association, 7,955
University of Michigan, Alumni Association, Alumnae
Association, **7,956**
University of Michigan, Alumni Association, Alumnae
Club, Sara Brown Smith group (Ann Arbor, MI),
7,957
University of Michigan, Alumni Association, Saginaw
Valley Alumnae Association, **7,958**
University of Michigan, Barbour Scholarships for
Oriental Women, **7,721**
University of Michigan, Centennial Admission of
Women Committee, **7,750**
University of Michigan, Committee on the Defense
Training Program for Women, **7,760**
University of Michigan, Department of Physical
Education for Women, **7,772**
University of Michigan, Faculty Women's Club, **7,960**
University of Michigan Friends of Student
Non-Violent Coordinating Committee, 17,637
University of Michigan, International Women's Year
Committee, **7,824**
University of Michigan, Labadie Collection, 7,997,
7,998
University of Michigan, League House Directors,
7,959
University of Michigan, Michigan Union, 7,867, 7,937
University of Michigan, Michigras Committee, **7,867**
University of Michigan, Mortar Board, **7,961**
University of Michigan, Mortar Board Alumnae Club,
7,871
University of Michigan, Spring Weekend Committee,
7,937
University of Michigan, University Committee on
National Defense, 7,760
University of Michigan, University Health Service,
7,727
University of Michigan, University War Board, 7,760
University of Michigan, Women's Athletic
Association, 7,772, 7,867, 7,937, **7,985**
University of Michigan, Women's Education Club,
7,987
University of Michigan, Women's League, **7,962**
University of Michigan, Women's Research Club,
7,963
University of Minnesota, 8,542, 8,543, 8,709, 8,942,
8,950, 9,218, 9,371, 9,468, 9,523, 14,409
alumnae, 2,523, 8,391, 8,533, 8,534, 8,537, 8,542,
8,543, 8,555, 8,556, 8,557, 8,560, 8,571, 8,573,
8,584, 8,586, 8,590, 8,591, 8,595, 8,596, 8,600,
8,602, 8,605, 8,607, 8,613, 8,617, 8,713, 8,947,
9,020, 9,296, 9,378, 9,522, 16,288
buildings, 8,533, 8,602, 8,605
deans, **8,552**, 8,557, 8,566, **8,594**
employees, 8,550
faculty, 4,406, 8,441, 8,530, 8,535, 8,536, 8,538,
8,539, 8,540, 8,544, 8,546, 8,550, 8,559, **8,561**,
8,564, 8,565, 8,567, 8,571, 8,572, 8,573, 8,575,
8,580, 8,581, 8,582, 8,588, 8,591, 8,593, 8,595,
8,596, 8,597, 8,603, 8,604, 8,606, 8,608, 8,609,
8,611, 8,617, 8,618, 8,619, 8,620, 8,622, 8,623,
8,636, 8,654, 8,664, 8,893, **8,913**, 8,976, 9,052,
9,120, 9,176, 9,282, 9,347, 9,387, 9,392, 9,467,
11,593
presidents, 9,077, 9,120
students, 8,541, 8,554, 8,574, 8,585, 8,589, 8,599,
8,601, 8,614, 8,689, 8,697, 9,161, 9,169, 9,388
University of Minnesota, Agricultural Faculty
Women's Club, 9,466

University of Minnesota, All-University Student
Council, 8,594
University of Minnesota Arboretum, employees, 8,424
University of Minnesota, Boynton Health Service,
8,540
University of Minnesota, Campus Club, 8,622
University of Minnesota, Center for Continuation
Study, 8,591
University of Minnesota, Center for Youth
Development and Research, 8,583
University of Minnesota, Chimes, 14,029
University of Minnesota, College of Education, **8,547**
University of Minnesota, College of Science,
Literature, and the Arts, **8,548**
University of Minnesota, Commission for Women,
8,549
University of Minnesota (Minneapolis, MN),
Comstock Hall, 8,566
University of Minnesota, Council for University
Women's Progress, **8,550**, 8,603
University of Minnesota, Department of Agriculture.
See University of Minnesota, Institute of
Agriculture
University of Minnesota, Duluth (MN), faculty, 8,592
University of Minnesota, European Club, 8,599
University of Minnesota, Faculty Women's Club,
8,562, 8,622
University of Minnesota, Faculty Women's Dining
Club, **8,563**
University of Minnesota, Girls' Self-Government
Association, Brewster Hall, School of Agriculture,
8,569
University of Minnesota Hospitals, General Hospitals,
8,535, 8,545
University of Minnesota Hospitals, Masonic Hospital,
8,535
University of Minnesota, Institute of Agriculture,
8,578
University of Minnesota, Institute of Technology,
8,609
University of Minnesota, May Fete (1911), 8,543
University of Minnesota, Medical School, alumnae,
8,465, 9,514
University of Minnesota, Meredith Hall Self
Government Association, **8,585**
University of Minnesota, Minnesota Alumni Club,
8,537, 8,600
University of Minnesota, Minnesota Women's Center,
8,587
University of Minnesota, Natural Science Museum,
faculty, 9,319
University of Minnesota Press, 8,566, 9,360
University of Minnesota Regional Writing Fellowship,
9,360
University of Minnesota, St. Paul Campus, Young
Women's Christian Association, 8,628
University of Minnesota, School of Agriculture, **8,607**
University of Minnesota, School of Agriculture,
Estelle Literary Society, **8,608**
University of Minnesota, School of Agriculture, Girls'
Athletic Club, 8,570
University of Minnesota, School of Agriculture, Girls'
Swimming Club, **8,570**
University of Minnesota, School of Agriculture, Home
Economics Association, **8,576**
University of Minnesota, School of Agriculture,
Practical Nurse's and Home Management Club,
8,598
University of Minnesota, School of Agriculture,
Young Women's Christian Association, **8,629**
University of Minnesota, School of Chemistry, **8,609**
University of Minnesota, School of Nursing, **8,610**
faculty, 8,553
University of Minnesota, Society of Minnesota
Dames, **8,615**
University of Minnesota, Student Counseling Bureau,
8,573
University of Minnesota, Student Government
Association. *See* University of Minnesota,
Student Self-Government Association
University of Minnesota, student health center, 9,359
University of Minnesota, Student Self-Government
Association, **8,616**

University of Minnesota, University Artists' Course, 8,611
University of Minnesota, University Gallery, 8,546, **8,622**
University of Minnesota, University Institute of Child Development, 8,618
University of Minnesota, Woman's League. *See* University of Minnesota, Women's Self-Government Association
University of Minnesota, Women's Liberation, **8,624**
University of Minnesota, Women's Self-Government Association, 8,558, **8,625**
University of Mississippi, 9,599, 9,607, 15,895
  employees, **9,822**
University of Mississippi, school of law, alumnae, 9,544
University of Mississippi, University Dames, 9,819, **9,822**
University of Missouri, 9,885, 9,893, **9,897**, 9,913, 9,933, **9,939**, 9,941, 9,972, 9,974, 10,063
  admissions, 9,962, 10,021, 10,030
  alumnae, 9,826, 9,839, 9,935, 9,948, 9,978, 9,981, 10,000
  deans, 9,829, 9,935
  faculty, 9,828, 9,839, **9,936**, 9,969, 9,979, 9,997, **10,049**, 10,062, 14,186, **16,347**
  presidents, **10,022**, **10,038**, 10,060
  students, 9,827, 9,838, **10,020**, 15,964
University of Missouri, Admission of Women Centennial, **10,014**
University of Missouri, agricultural extension service, **10,015**
University of Missouri, agricultural extension service, home demonstration, **10,016**
University of Missouri, Chancellor's Committee on the Status of Women (Columbia, MO), **10,017**
University of Missouri, Cooperative Extension Service, **10,018**, **10,019**
University of Missouri, Graduate School, **10,021**
University of Missouri, Philalathean Society, 9,918
University of Missouri, St. Louis (MO), archives, **10,190**
University of Missouri, St. Louis (MO), Women's Center, 10,190
University of Missouri, School of Home Economics, **10,023**
University of Missouri, School of Mines and Metallurgy, **10,024**
University of Missouri (Columbia, MO), Woman's College, faculty, 15,964
University of Munich (Germany), 6,688
University of Nebraska, 10,452, 10,454, 10,537, 10,564
  administrators, 16,978
  alumnae, 10,419, 10,446, 10,466, 14,425
  buildings, 4,928
  faculty, 10,446, **10,481**, **10,488**, **10,492**, 10,522, **10,554**, **10,607**
  students, 10,425, 10,456, 10,548
University of Nebraska, Associated Women Students, **10,604**
University of Nebraska, college of agriculture, employees, 10,438
University of Nebraska, college of medicine, alumnae, **10,538**
University of Nebraska-Lincoln, 10,482
  faculty, **10,605**
University of Nebraska Medical Center, 10,616
University of Nevada, 10,658, 10,678, 10,707
  faculty, 656, 10,655, 10,677, 10,727
  students, 656
University of Nevada at Reno, 10,751, 10,777
  employees, 10,739
  faculty, 10,743, **10,755**, **10,766**, 10,768, **10,775**
  students, 10,629, 10,775, 10,778
University of New Mexico, 11,217
  faculty, 11,218, 11,228, **11,239**, 11,244, **11,246**
  trustees, 11,236
University of Nigeria, trustees, 5,460
University of North Alabama, buildings, 25
University of North Carolina, 13,132, 13,390, 13,581, 13,626, 15,588
  alumnae, 9,839
  faculty, 12,935, 13,097

students, 12,991, 13,008, 13,055
trustees, 13,249
University of North Carolina at Charlotte, Health Services Training Center, 13,187
University of North Carolina at Charlotte, presidents, 13,185, **13,186**
University of North Carolina at Greensboro, 13,604
  alumnae, 13,244, 13,249
  archives, **13,248**
  deans, 13,241
  faculty, 13,243
  presidents, 13,242, 13,245, 13,247
  students, 13,246
University of North Carolina at Greensboro, Baptist Student Union, **13,647**
University of North Carolina, Chapel Hill, 13,176, 13,228, 13,479
  faculty, 12,982, 13,001, 13,134
University of North Carolina Extension Division, 13,253
University of North Carolina, School of Public Health, faculty, 12,998
University of North Carolina, State Board of Charities, 12,738
University of North Dakota, 13,698
  alumnae, 13,674
University of North Dakota, Faculty Wives and Women's Association, **13,705**
University of Northern Colorado (Greeley, CO), **1,815**
University of Northern Iowa, faculty, 4,920
University of Notre Dame (IN), history, **4,648**
University of Ohio, presidents, 16,978
University of Oklahoma
  faculty, 5,459, 8,663, 14,240, 14,943
  students, 16,164
University of Oklahoma, Oklahoma Family Life Institute, 14,232
University of Oregon, 6,384, 14,299, 14,654
  faculty, 14,332, 14,337, 14,392
  students, 14,468, 17,195
  trustees, 14,461
University of Oregon, Health Sciences Center, 14,698
  alumnae, **14,699**
University of Oregon, Medical School, alumnae, 14,697
University of Oslo (Norway), faculty, **8,786**
University of Paris (France), 9,277
University of Peking (China), 1,558
University of Pennsylvania, 6,987, 13,324
  administrators, 14,889
  alumnae, 15,046, 15,095
  alumni, 14,803
  faculty, 14,965
University of Pittsburgh (PA), 15,236, 15,252
  alumnae, 8,583
  deans, **15,237**
  faculty, 8,653, 9,979
  graduate work, 15,241
  history, 15,240
  students, 15,241
University of Pittsburgh (PA), Advisory Council on Women's Opportunities, **15,236**
University of Pittsburgh (PA), Council for Women's Rights, 15,241
University of Pittsburgh (PA), Institute for Feminist Studies, 15,241
University of Pittsburgh (PA), Office of Student Activities, **15,238**
University of Pittsburgh (PA), Office of Student Affairs, 15,237, **15,239**
University of Pittsburgh (PA), Quo Vadis, 15,239
University of Pittsburgh (PA), Undergraduate Women's Union, 15,238
University of Pittsburgh (PA), University Committee for Women's Rights, 15,241
University of Pittsburgh (PA), Women's Association, 15,242
University of Pittsburgh (PA), Women's Center, 7,013, 15,238
University of Pittsburgh (PA), Women's Council, 15,238
University of Pittsburgh (PA), Women's International Club, **15,243**

University of Pittsburgh (PA), Women's Power Committee, 15,237
University of Pittsburgh (PA), Women's Self-Government Association, 15,237
University of Puerto Rico, faculty, 15,364
University of Rhode Island, Extension, 6,733
University of Rhode Island, School of Nursing, 6,165
University of Richmond (VA), Westhampton College, 13,406
University of Rochester (NY)
  admission, 12,799
  archives, **12,836**
  faculty, 12,817
University of Rochester (NY), Anthony Memorial Hall, 12,836
University of Rochester (NY), Eastman School of Music, 8,792
University of Rochester (NY), Eastman School of Music, Sibley Music Library, 12,816
University of San Francisco (CA), School of Nursing, 6,149
University of Santa Clara (CA), faculty, 1,532
University of Science and Arts of Oklahoma (Chickasha, OK)
  alumnae, 14,235
  archives, **14,178**
  faculty, 11,719
University of Shanghai (China), 13,642
  faculty, 8,870
University of South Carolina, 9,779
  faculty, 15,585
University of South Carolina Press, 15,585
University of South Carolina Society, 15,585
University of Southern California
  faculty, 468, 8,636, 14,455
  students, 17,195
University of Southern California, Chimes 14,029
University of Southern California, School of Dentistry, **1,061**
University of Southern Mississippi, 9,662
  faculty, 9,572
University of Southwestern Louisiana
  archives, **5,437**
  faculty, 5,432
University of Southwestern Louisiana, Intercollegiate Athletics and Oratorical Association, 5,437
University of Tampa (FL), 4,918, 14,378
University of Texas, 10,035, 16,032, 16,101, 16,132, 16,221
  alumnae, 16,038
  deans, 16,037
  employees, **16,037**
  faculty, 16,097, 16,131, 16,146
University of Texas at Arlington (TX), 15,993
  faculty, 16,012
University of Texas at Austin (TX), 15,986
University of Texas at Austin (TX), bureau of research in the social sciences, 15,986
University of Texas at El Paso (TX), faculty, 16,212
University of Texas, Garcia Collection, 16,131
University of Texas, Medical Branch, alumnae, 16,226
University of Texas, Medical Branch, Long Hairs, 16,228
University of Texas, Medical Branch, School of Nursing Alumnae Association, **16,229**
University of Texas, Medical Branch, Short Hairs, 16,228
University of the Pacific (CA)
  alumnae, 541
  faculty, **1,645**
  students, 1,625, 1,634
University of the Pacific (CA), Pacific Center for Western Historical Studies, 1,620
University of the South (TN), 107
  faculty, 15,729, 15,934
University of Toronto (Canada), alumnae, 3,775
University of Utah, 2,828, 16,448
  faculty, 16,890, 16,971
  graduate students, 16,937
University of Vermont, 17,017, 17,035
  archives, **17,006**
  deans, **17,001**
  faculty, **17,002**

University of Vermont, College of Education and Nursing, **17,000**
University of Vermont, Faculty Wives, 17,002
University of Vermont, Ladies of the Faculty, 17,002
University of Vermont, School of Home Economics, **17,005**
University of Vermont, Women's Faculty Club, 17,002
University of Virginia, 9,760, 9,919, 13,079, 15,711, 17,111
　students, 2,578, 13,173
University of Virginia, Institute of Public Affairs, 2,407
University of Washington, 17,231, 17,244, 17,261, 17,288, 17,315
　deans, **17,352**
　faculty, **17,230, 17,240, 17,263, 17,266, 17,303,** 17,315, **17,322,** 17,368
University of Washington, Developmental Psychology Laboratory Preschool, 17,270
University of Washington, Henry Gallery, 17,236, 17,316, 17,323, 17,332, 17,362
University of Washington, School of Art, faculty, 17,288
University of Washington, School of Nursing, **17,353**
　deans, 17,291
　faculty, **17,297**
University of Washington, Women's Commission, Associated Students, 17,233
University of Washington, Women's Studies, **17,354**
University of West Florida, 2,918
University of West Virginia, faculty, 11,366
University of Windsor (Canada), faculty, 11,221
University of Wisconsin, 8,942, 11,885, 17,698, 17,722, 17,725, 17,853
　alumnae, 104, 8,161, 8,593, 8,618, 17,634, 17,667, 17,675
　alumni, 9,372
　deans, 17,723
　faculty, 6,336, 11,748, 14,401, 17,620, 17,626, 17,650, 17,712, 17,723, 17,735, 17,815
　records and correspondence, 17,620
　students, 4,707, 6,239, 14,135, 17,615, **17,628,** 17,636, 17,653, 17,719, 17,727, 17,815
　trustees, 17,507
University of Wisconsin at La Crosse, Associated Women Students, **17,573**
University of Wisconsin at La Crosse, Campus Dames, **17,577**
University of Wisconsin at Stevens Point (WI), faculty, **17,869,** 17,870
University of Wisconsin, Committee to Support the People of South Vietnam, 17,628
University of Wisconsin, Conservative Club, 17,628
University of Wisconsin-Eau Claire (WI), 17,532
　history, **17,548**
　students, **17,541**
University of Wisconsin-Eau Claire: A History, 1916-1976 (book), 17,548
University of Wisconsin-La Crosse (WI), 2,598
University of Wisconsin, Madison (WI), 6,848, 13,686
　deans, **13,494, 17,767, 17,783**
　faculty, **17,764, 17,765, 17,766, 17,768, 17,770, 17,772, 17,773, 17,775, 17,777, 17,788**
　students, 4,914, 17,495, **17,780, 17,781, 17,782, 17,790,** 17,857
University of Wisconsin, Madison (WI), Association of Faculty Women, **17,764**
University of Wisconsin, Madison (WI), Forest Products Laboratory, 17,768
University of Wisconsin, Madison (WI), Library School, 11,893
University of Wisconsin, Madison (WI), school of nursing, 17,773, 17,779
University of Wisconsin, Madison (WI), Women's Self-Government Association, **17,790**
University of Wisconsin, Milwaukee (WI), 17,848
University of Wisconsin-River Falls (WI), faculty, 17,859, 17,860
University of Wisconsin, Senior Swingout **17,778**
University of Wisconsin, Union Theater, 17,817
University of Wisconsin, Wisconsin Farmers Institute, 17,655

University of Wisconsin, Young Republican Club, 17,628
University of Wyoming, 17,922, 17,941, 17,953, 17,988, 18,022
　administration, **17,963**
　alumnae, 17,994
　faculty, 17,906, 17,908, 17,974, 18,019, 18,021
University of Wyoming, Associated Women Students, 17,963
University of Wyoming, Girl's Cadet Organization, **17,968**
University presses, 11,925, 15,585
University Settlement (Philadelphia, PA), 8,651
University Settlement House (NY), 9,095, 12,705
University Settlement Society of New York, **7,557**
University Wives Club (TN), 15,897
University Woman's Club (IL), **4,400**
University Women's League, 7,820
University Women's Tuesday Tea Club (IL), **4,401**
Unruh, Ada [Mrs.], 14,473
Unseen Side of Child Life, The (book), 4,211
Unsinkable Mrs. Brown, The (book), 1,752
Untermeyer, Byrna Ivens, 4,485
Untermeyer, Jean (Starr) [Mrs. Louis] (1886-), 258, 2,463, 2,491
Untermeyer, Louis, 4,482, 8,077
Unthank, Ellen Pusell [Mrs.], 16,967
Unwed mothers. *See* Single mothers
Unwin, Nora Spicer (1907-), 6,119
Up From Poverty (ms), 6,834
Up the Down Staircase (book), 12,533
Up-to-Date Club (Fort Dodge, IA), **4,883**
Updegraff, Allan, 3,775
Updegraff, Edith (Summers) [Mrs. Allan] (1884-1956). *See* Kelley, Edith (Summers) [Mrs. Allan] Updegraff [Mrs. C. F.] (1884-1956)
Updike, Daniel Berkeley (1860-1941), **1,464**
Updike, Mary [Mrs. Donald F.], 1,837
Upham, Henry Pratt (1837-1909), Family (MN), **9,414**
Upham, Mother Mary Geraldine, 4,709
Upholstery trade, **15,106**
Uphsur, Polly, 3,401
Upjohn, Millie Kirby, 7,920
Upland County Court (PA), 15,039
Uplands Sanatorium (TN), 7,220
Upper and Lower Schools (CA), 1,518
Upper Deer Creek Mennonite Church (IA), 5,049
Upshaw, Berrien K., 2,488, 3,065
Upshaw, Margaret "Peggy" Munnerlyn (Mitchell) [Mrs. Berrien K.] (1900-49). *See* Mitchell, Margaret "Peggy" Munnerlyn. [Mrs. Berrien K.] Upshaw [Mrs. John Robert] Marsh (1900-49)
Upson, Arthur, 8,597
Upson Family (CT), **12,653**
Upson, Harvey, 12,653
Upson, Kate (1851-1935). *See* Clark, Kate (Upson) (1851-1935)
Upson, Mary. *See* Avery, Mary (Upson)
Upson, Sam W., 12,653
Upton, Cornelia A. (Babcock) (1854-1941), 7,314
Upton, Eleanor Stuart (1886-1974), 7,314
Upton Family, **7,314**
Upton Family (MA), **7,454**
Upton, George Burr (1882-1942), **11,735**
Upton, Harriet (Taylor) [Mrs. George Whitman] (1853-1945), 5,305, **6,932,** 6,958, **6,985,** 12,811, 12,812, 13,967, 13,990, 14,139, 17,616
Upton, Kate J., 7,454
Upton, Margaret Frances (1890-1967), 7,314
Upton, Mary, 12,051
Upton, Sara K. *See* Edwards, Sara K. (Upton)
Uptown: Poor Whites in Chicago (book), 17,637
Upward Bound, 11,300
Uranium County (book), 1,750
Urbain, George, 5,512
Urban beautification, 2,310, 2,456, **2,921,** 3,672, 4,454, 5,500, 5,559, **5,613,** 7,087, 9,529, 15,961
　citizen participation, **16,394**
Urban Club (NY), 11,324
Urban economics, 12,149
Urban League, 5,828, 8,148
Urban League (GA), 3,302
Urban League (MO), 10,168

Urban League (PA), 6,682
Urban League (VA), 17,091
Urban League (WA), 17,341
Urban League of Portland (OR), 17,262, 17,304
Urban League of Rhode Island, **15,376**
Urban renewal, 470, 3,879, 5,540, 5,837, 7,266, 8,655, 11,443, 11,877, 14,671, 15,202, 16,259
　citizen participation, 4,101
Urban transportation, 1,682, 14,016
Urbanek, Mae (Bobb) (1903-), **18,017**
Urbanization, 2,782
　social aspects, 8,123
Uridge, Margaret D., **854**
Urkevich, Olga Maximoff, 8,064
Urmy, Clarence, **1,602**
Urmy, Mabel. *See* Seares, Mabel (Urmy)
Urquhart, Clara, 3,290
Ursenbach, Maureen (1939-), 16,780
Ursua, Julian, 1,062
Ursuline College (KY), 5,389
Ursuline Convent (SC), 15,639, 15,696
Ursuline Convent (Galveston, TX), 16,019
Ursuline Convent of the Sacred Heart (Toledo, OH), **14,145**
Ursuline Convent School (SC), 15,497
Ursuline nuns, 5,689, 16,018, **16,019**
Ursuline nuns (KY), 10,611
Ursuline nuns (Cincinnati, OH), **13,867**
Ursuline Order, 11,808
Ursulin Sisters Convent (Belleville, IL), **3,744**
Ursuline Sisters Convent (Paola, KS), **5,204**
Ursuline Sisters of the Immaculate Conception (Louisville, KY), **5,389**
Urvina, Carlos, 9,467
Urvina, Marcelina R., 9,467
Use of Books in Libraries, The, 8,588
Usher, Eliza. *See* Berry, Eliza (Usher) [Mrs. William Augustus]
Usher, Ellen. *See* Bacon, Ellen (Usher)
Usher, Ethel Watson, 5,582
Usher Family (CT, MA, RI), 7,520
Usher, Francenia, 12,951
Usher, Jerusha, **7,501**
Usher, Martha. *See* Osgood, Martha (Usher)
Usher, Melissa, **7,501**
Usher, Patrick, 12,951
Usher, Rebecca (1821-1919), **5,689**
Ushers, 12,639
Utah, 554, 562, 16,403, **16,407,** 16,415, 16,418, 16,420, 16,423, 16,425, 16,429, 16,430, 16,437, **16,439,** 16,442, **16,476,** 16,493, 16,515, 16,521, 16,550, 16,556, 16,564, 16,567, 16,611, 16,644, 16,648, 16,677, 16,679, 16,683, 16,694, 16,706, 16,737, 16,854, 16,891
　abortion, legal aspects, 1,984
　actresses, 16,577
　actresses, amateur, 16,410
　agricultural colleges, 16,402
　agricultural societies, **16,963**
　agriculture, 16,486
　alfalfa, 16,486
　art, catalogs, 16,919
　art patronage, 16,965
　artists, **16,916, 16,970**
　authors, **16,440,** 16,442, 16,924, 16,971
　autobiography, **16,967**
　barter, 16,486
　bills, legislative, 16,498
　biography, **16,967**
　birth control, 6,355
　blind, education, 16,448
　boards of trade, 16,419, 16,535
　businessmen, **16,449**
　businesswomen, **16,510**
　charitable societies, **16,657**
　charities, **16,744**
　choral singing, **16,405, 16,406**
　church historians, 16,430
　church societies, 16,430, **16,465, 16,511,** 16,685, 16,731, 16,802, **16,850**
　church societies, Mormon, **16,583,** 16,619, **16,657,** **16,662,** 16,664, 16,679, 16,681, **16,689,** 16,764,

16,769, 16,780, 16,789, **16,801, 16,851,** 16,916, **16,930**
cities and towns, 16,714
   civic improvement, **16,435**
clubs, 6,355, **16,413, 16,419,** 16,444, **16,461,**
   16,542, 16,566, **16,753, 16,879, 16,899,** 16,916,
   16,928, 16,966
college students, 16,810
college teachers, 16,485, **16,971**
community life, 16,488
community music, **16,432,** 16,446
congressmen, 16,965
congresswomen, **16,880**
cooperative societies, 16,489
court records, 1,808
cowboys, **16,450**
crime and criminals, 16,485
cultural relations, 6,355
dairying, 16,436, 16,475
deans (in schools), 16,608, 16,971
department stores, 16,569, 16,888
diaries and journals, 16,495, 16,518, **16,578,** 16,596,
   16,623, 16,650, **16,678,** 16,778
   19th C, 16,463, **16,471,** 16,489, 16,505, **16,513,**
   16,537, 16,559, **16,561,** 16,635, **16,655, 16,656,**
   16,665, 16,671, 16,672, 16,685, **16,691, 16,717,**
   16,728, 16,731, **16,741,** 16,793, **16,848,** 16,909,
   16,915, 16,962
divorce, 16,893
drugstores, 16,425
educational associations, **16,494**
educators, 16,965
employees, **16,928**
Episcopal churches, 16,965
family, 7,174
farmers, **16,411, 16,416, 16,436**
forums (discussion and debate), **16,942**
genealogists, 16,429, **16,434**
genealogy, 16,587
general stores, 16,510
geology, 451
historians, **16,400,** 16,410, 16,434, 16,447, 16,488,
   16,564, 16,924
historic sites 16,924
   restoration and conservation, 16,485
historical societies, 16,430
home demonstration agents, **16,558**
hotels, taverns, etc., 16,883
housewives, **16,401,** 16,402, 16,403, **16,410, 16,415,**
   16,418, 16,420, 16,421, 16,423, 16,427, 16,429,
   16,430, 16,435, 16,437, 16,440, **16,442, 16,447,**
   16,965
immigrants, Australian, 16,417
immigrants, British, 16,490
immigrants, Danish, 16,960, 16,965
immigrants, English, **16,433,** 16,468, 16,474,
   16,477, 16,906, 16,965
immigrants, Finnish, 16,965
immigrants, German, 16,776
immigrants, Swedish, 16,481, 16,965
immigrants, Swiss, 16,892
immigrants, Welsh, 16,409
interracial marriage, 16,588, 16,967
iron industry and trade, 16,401, 16,448
irrigation, 16,486
Japanese-Americans, 16,942
journalists, **16,403,** 16,510
judges, **16,450,** 16,880
justices of the peace, **16,411,** 16,425
land settlement, 16,460, 16,502, 16,585
lawyers, **16,450,** 16,971
legislators, 16,448, 16,473, **16,498,** 16,536, 16,748,
   16,880
librarians, **16,426**
literary societies, **16,501**
locusts, 16,968
mayors, 16,914
merchants, **16,450**
Mexican-Americans, 16,965
midwives, 16,472, 16,789, 16,803, **16,828,** 16,838,
   16,955
mills and mill-work, 16,430
mines and mineral resources, 16,430
missionaries, **16,597,** 16,741

missionaries, Methodist, **8,745**
Mormons and Mormonism, 185, 191, 6,092, 6,355,
   10,004, **10,780,** 11,536, 16,428, **16,431,**
   16,450, 16,458, 16,475, 16,486, 16,569, 16,595,
   16,611, **16,614, 16,620,** 16,653, 16,664, 16,692,
   16,693, 16,696, 16,707, 16,710, 16,713, 16,722,
   16,723, 16,728, 16,730, 16,731, 16,735, 16,737,
   16,741, 16,742, **16,749, 16,750,** 16,756, 16,757,
   16,763, 16,764, 16,768, 16,771, **16,775, 16,777,**
   16,778, 16,779, 16,780, 16,786, 16,789, 16,793,
   16,803, 16,804, 16,815, 16,833, **16,840,** 16,844,
   16,852, 16,854, 16,937, 16,943, 16,945, 16,947,
   16,955, 16,957, **16,958, 16,967**
Mormons and Mormonism, Afro-American, **16,708**
musical societies, 16,446
musicians, **16,446**
Native Americans, 11,536, 16,420, 16,488, 16,862
   marriage rites and customs, 16,486
newspapers, 16,403, **16,920, 16,977**
nurses, 16,409, 16,417, **16,420**
nursing service administration, 16,526
obstetrical nursing, 16,417
obstetricians, 16,417, 16,944
oral history, **16,485, 16,488,** 16,661, 16,746, **16,890,**
   16,953, **16,960, 16,965**
orphans and orphan asylums, 16,417
paleontology, 451
patriotic societies, **3,737,** 6,355
peace societies, 6,355
pharmacists, 16,425
photographers, **16,398**
physicians, **16,786, 16,956,** 16,967
pianists, 16,427
pioneers and settlers, 562, **857,** 904, 3,737, **16,409,**
   16,417, 16,426, 16,430, **16,433,** 16,450, 16,460,
   16,486, 16,503, 16,508, 16,509, **16,512, 16,513,**
   16,522, 16,525, 16,536, **16,541,** 16,551, 16,560,
   16,566, **16,571,** 16,572, **16,573,** 16,602, 16,611,
   16,616, **16,646,** 16,647, 16,648, 16,701, 16,710,
   16,730, 16,739, 16,827, 16,862, **16,887,** 16,895,
   16,897, **16,912,** 16,913, 16,915, 16,965, 16,967,
   16,968
poets laureate, 16,566
political clubs, 16,975
politics and education, **16,462**
politics and government, 16,936
politics, practical, women's activism, **16,422**
polygamy, 730, 16,434, 16,450, 16,506, 16,620,
   16,722, 16,839, 16,935
   opposition to, **16,469**
practical nurses, 16,965
prisoners, personal narrative, 16,775
prisons, 16,789
public works, **16,968**
ranchers, **16,434**
ranching, 16,486
real property, cases, 1,811
refugees, Jewish, 16,894
scholarships, 16,413
school boards, **16,453**
school music, 16,432
school superintendents and principals, **16,549**
schools, 16,640
secret societies, 16,965
senators, United States, 1,702
silver mines and mining, 16,425
singers, 16,402, **16,446, 16,538, 16,577**
smoke prevention, 16,535
social life and customs, 16,720, 16,746, 16,861
societies, 16,400, 16,401, **16,412,** 16,445, 16,447
state universities and colleges
   alumni, **16,414, 16,424**
   archives, **16,408**
   faculty, **16,413, 16,436, 16,448**
stock and stock-breeding, 16,449, 16,450
stores, retail, **16,459**
suffrage, 16,502
suffrage societies, **16,500**
Sunday schools, 16,647
surplus government property, 1,811
surveyors, **16,411**
tailors, **16,401**
teachers, **16,403, 16,404, 16,415,** 16,417, 16,437,

16,440, 16,505, 16,548, 16,549, 16,635, 16,639,
   16,953
teachers' colleges, 16,402, 16,425, 16,427, 16,448,
   16,924
telegraphers, **16,428**
temperance societies, 16,968
Tewa Indians, 16,874
textile workers, 16,965
theaters, 16,399
   management, 16,888
trials (robbery), 16,449
universities and colleges, 16,423
university extension, **16,484**
Ute Indians, 965
volunteers in social service, 16,780
women, education, 16,436
women's centers, 16,971
World War II, civilians work, **16,964**
Utah and Northern Railroad, 10,240
Utah Cattlemen's Association, 16,963
Utah Cowbelles, **16,963**
Utah Expedition (1857-1958), 6,436
Utah Extension Service, **16,484**
Utah Federation of Women's Clubs, 6,355
Utah Heritage Foundation, 16,965
Utah Humanities Research Foundation, **16,915**
Utah Minute Women, **16,964**
Utah Penitentiary, 16,775
Utah Polio Emergency Committee, 16,911
Utah Smokeless Fuel Cooperative Association, 16,535
Utah State College, 16,448
Utah State Historical Society, 16,923
Utah State Industrial Commission, officials and
   employees, 16,890
Utah State University, 16,448
   deans, 16,971
   faculty, 16,485, 16,971
Utah State University League, 16,461
Utah State University Oral History Project, **16,485**
Utah Symphony Orchestra, 16,965
Utah Territory
   census (1850), 10,723
   government attorneys, 16,812
   governors, **16,932,** 16,933
Utah War (1858), 845
Utah Woman's Press Club, 16,566, **16,966**
Utah Woman's Republican League, 16,566
Utah Writers Project, **16,486**
Ute Indians, 311, 965, 1,751, 1,780, 16,868, 16,870,
   16,876
   costume and adornment, 16,876
   dances, 16,876
   health and hygiene, 16,876
   mortuary customs, 16,876
   rites and ceremonies, 16,876
   social life and customs, 16,876
Uterus
   cancer, 4,698
   tumors, 1,281
Utica Female Academy (NY), 7,168, 10,045
Utica Female Seminary, 11,602
Utley, Fentem, 289
Utley, Mrs. Clifton Maxwell, 11,827
Utopia Children's House, 5,346
Utopian Christian Community (Zion, IL), **4,461**
Utopias, 623, **1,319,** 1,426, 1,590, 1,654, 2,464, **2,991,**
   3,603, 4,151, 4,429, 4,433, 4,434, 4,435, **4,437,**
   4,461, 4,701, 4,704, **4,767,** 4,809, **5,364,** 6,223,
   7,043, 8,077, 10,673, 11,028, 11,125, 11,681,
   11,726, 12,309, 12,908, **14,268, 14,718, 15,259,**
   16,180
Utterback, Martha Elizabeth (1904-66), **13,289**
Utvandringen og det utflyttede Norge (book), 8,786
Uxbridge Cotton Mills (MA), **7,126**
Uziel, Perla Bensal, 17,282
V. V. Club (IA), 4,960
"Vacation Camps Give Rest and Instruction to Many
   Farm Women" (government report), 10,023
Vacation schools, 1,385, 2,000, 4,114, 6,358
Vaccination, opposition to, 7,222
Vache Family (NY), **12,331**
Vadnais, Anna, 9,197
Vagabond Voyage Through Brittany (book), 2,258

Vagina, cancer, 4,698
Vail, Alfred (1807-59), 2,725, 10,920
Vail, Alvira (Allen) [Mrs. William], 17,039
Vail, Amanda (Eno) [Mrs. Alfred], **2,725**
Vail, Anna Murray (1863-1955), 11,297
Vail, Ellen Ledlie Bowman [Mrs. Thomas Hubbard], 6,784
Vail, Ellen Sitgreaves. *See* Motter, Ellen Sitgreaves (Vail)
Vail Family (NJ), 11,074
Vail Family (VT), **17,039**
Vail, Laurence, 3,771
Vail, Martha Bartholomew (1803-91), 16,487
Vail, Mary. *See* Grinnell, Mary (Vail) [Mrs. L. J.]
Vail, Rebecca (Warden) [Mrs. Emmor K.] (?-1872), **11,048**
Vail, Sarah D. (1811-87). *See* Hurd, Sarah D. (Vail) Cutler [Mrs. Whitfield] (1811-87)
Vail, Stephen (1780-1864), **10,920**
Vail, Thomas Hubbard, 6,784
Vaill, Asenath B. *See* Barrows, Asenath B. (Vaill) [Mrs. Freeman]
Vaill, Elizabeth. *See* Waldo, Elizabeth (Vaill)
Val Maria (book), 5,815
"Valentine" (song), 10,478
Valentine, Ethel Eyre (1872-1958). *See* Dreier, Ethel Eyre (Valentine) [Mrs. H. Edward] (1872-1958)
Valentine, Jo (pseudonym). *See* Armstrong, Charlotte (1905-69)
Valentines, 8,981, **13,068**
Valentino, Rudolph, 941
Valéry, Paul, 2,215, 11,153
Valesh, Eva (McDonald) [Mrs. Frank]. [Mrs. Benjamin F.] Cross (1866-1956), 8,995, 9,046, 9,048, **9,415, 11,926**
Valiant, Margaret [Mrs.], **9,810**
Valien, Bonita Harrison, 5,469
Valien, Preston, 5,469
Valinat, Margaret, 2,685
Valkill Industries, 11,853
Vallance Family, 12,485
Valle, Marta (1934-), 8,661
Vallejo, Adelayde "Adela" (1837-95). *See* Frisbie, Adelayde "Adela" (Vallejo) [Mrs. Levi C.] (1837-95)
Vallejo, Epifania de Guadalupe "Fannie" (1835-1905). *See* Frisbie, Epifania de Guadalupe "Fannie" (Vallejo) [Mrs. John E.] (1835-1905)
Vallejo Family (CA), 858
Vallejo, Francisca. *See* McGettigan, Francisca (Vallejo)
Vallejo, Francisca Benicia (Carrillo) [Mrs. Mariano Guadalupe] (1815-91), 858
Vallejo, Lily (Wiley) [Mrs. Platón] (1849-85), 858
Vallejo, Luisa Eugenia "Lulu" (1856-1943). *See* Emparán, Luisa Eugenia "Lulu" (Vallejo) [Mrs. Ricardo] de (1856-1943)
Vallejo, Maria Ygnacia (1857-1932). *See* Cutter, Maria Ygnacia (Vallejo) [Mrs. James Harry] (1857-1932)
Vallejo, Mariano Guadalupe (1807-90), 333, 858, 1,222
Vallejo, Mary Adelaide. *See* Peters, Mary Adelaide (Vallejo)
Vallejo, Platón, 858
Vallejo, Rosalia. *See* Leese, Rosalia (Vallejo) [Mrs. Jacob]
Valley Below, The (book), 14,218
Valley Methodist Episcopal Church (Keokuk, IA), Ladies Aid Society, 4,959
Valley Migrant League (OR), 14,671
Valley of the Kings (Egypt), 14,882
Valley of the Mississippi Illustrated, The (book), 9,179
Valley Women's Center (Northampton, MA), 7,324
Vallon, Julia (Sando), **8,799**
Valparaiso University, alumnae, 138
Valsetz Star (OR), 14,582
Van Altena, Edward, 11,327
Van Arsdale, Isabella [Mrs. Martin Van Buren], 4,103
Van Arsdale, Martin Van Buren, 4,103
Vanarsdale, Susan D. (1824-56), **9,920**
van Beethoven, Ludwig, 6,185
Van Benthuysen Family (NY), 17,045

Van Bibber, Lucretia, 5,752
Van Blarcom, Carolyn, 5,735
Van Buren, Abigail, 5,110
Van Buren, Angelica (Singleton) [Mrs. Abraham] (1816-77), **2,616**, 11,534, 15,722, 15,723, **15,759**
Van Buren County Federation of Women's Clubs (MI), **8,187**
Van Buren Family (Kinderhook, NY), 11,534
Van Buren, Lotta (1877-1960). *See* Bizallion, Lotta Van Buren [Mrs. Henry] (1877-1960)
Van Buren, Martin (1782-1862), 2,616, 10,170, 11,534, 12,847, 15,722, 15,759
Van Camp, Dorothy Chalk, 8,141
Van Camp, Lawrence, 8,141
Vance, Angus, 16,487
Vance, Arthur Turner, 13,027
Vance, Elizabeth, 16,890
Vance, Ethel (pseudonym). *See* Stone, Grace (Zaring) (1896-)
Vance, Harriet N. (Espy) [Mrs. Zebulon] (?-1878), 13,446, **13,599**
Vance, Howard Earl, 15,869
Vance, Ruby Harmon [Mrs. Howard Earl], 15,869
Vance, Zebulon Baird, 13,448, 13,567, 13,581, **13,598, 13,599**
Van Cleave, Mina (1879-). *See* Buck, Mina (Van Cleave) [Mrs. Frank] (1879-)
Van Cleef, Eugenia [Miss], 11,736
Van Cleef Family (NY), **11,736**
Van Cleef, Jeannette [Miss], 11,736
Van Cleef, Mynderse, 11,736
Van Cleve, Charlotte Ouisconsin (Clark) [Mrs. Horatio Phillips] (1819-1907), 8,954, 9,229, **9,416**, 9,417
Van Cleve, E. M., 9,417
Van Cleve, Horatio Phillips (1809-91), 8,954, 9,416, **9,417**
Van Cleve, Mary Williams [Mrs. E. M.], 9,417
Van Cleve, Sarah Adams [Mrs. E. M.], 9,417
van Corlaer, Elisabeth, 11,737
Vancouver Operation CIVIC (WA), 17,314
Vandalia Historical Society (IL), 4,444
Vandalia: Wilderness Capital of Lincoln's Land (book), 4,445
Van deBogert, Mattie [Mrs.], 13,665
Van De Grift, Fanny Matilda (1840-1914). *See* Stevenson, Fanny Matilda (Van De Grift) [Mrs. Robert Louis] (1840-1914)
Van de Grift, Nellie (1856-1935). *See* Sanchez, Nellie (Van de Grift) (1856-1935)
Van Deman, Esther Boise (1862-1937), **7,964**
Vandenberg, Hazel Harper (Whittaker) [Mrs. Arthur Hendrick] (1882-1950), **7,968**
Vandenburg, Arthur Hendrick (1884-1951), 7,968, 8,360
Vanderbeck, Prudence (Osborn) Hadden, 12,158
Vanderbilt, Amy, 17,943, 17,991
Vanderbilt, Cornelius (1843-99), 46, 12,335
Vanderbilt, Ellen (Williams), 1,959, 1,964
Vanderbilt Family (NY), **12,335**
Vanderbilt, Frank Armstrong (Crawford) (1839-85), **46**
Vanderbilt, Gertrude (1875-1942). *See* Whitney, Gertrude (Vanderbilt) [Mrs. Harry Payne] (1875-1942)
Vanderbilt, Gertrude L., 11,666
Vanderbilt, Mrs. Cornelius (1839-85), 12,335
Vanderbilt, Mrs. Cornelius II, 17,761
Vanderbilt University (TN)
   alumnae, 3,399
   deans, **15,930**
   dormitories, 15,926
   faculty, 15,929, 15,931
   students, 15,933, 15,953, 15,964
Vanderbilt University (TN), Alumnae Council, 15,926
Vanderbilt University (TN), School of Nursing, **15,937**
Vanderbilt University (TN), Women's Advisory Council, 15,930
Vandergon, Gertrude Braat [Mrs. Nicholas] (1860-1941), **9,418**
Vanderhoof and Company, 17,623
VanderHoof, Emma F., 2,157

VanderHoof, Mable L. (?-1954). *See* Ackerman, Mabel L. (VanderHoof) (?-1954)
Vanderhorst, Adele (Allston) [Mrs. Arnoldus] (1842-1915), 15,440, 15,525
Vanderhorst, Arnoldus, 15,525
Vanderhorst, Frances, **15,525**
Vanderhorst, John, **15,526**
Van derKemp Family, 12,203
Vanderlee, Ann [Mrs. John], **16,013**
Vanderlee, John, **16,013**
Van Derlip, Ethel (Morrison) (1876-?), 9,248
Vanderpoel, James, **12,336**
Vanderveer, Abraham, 11,318
Van der Vrede, Jane (1880-1972), **3,432, 6,160**
Van Deusen, Minnie (1880-), **8,369**
Van Deusen, R. G., 8,369
Van Devender, Bertha (1873-?), 17,924
Van Deventer, Dora E. [Mrs.], **8,370**
Van de Water, Edith, 5,123
Van Diest, Alice, 1,722
Van Dolah, Mrs. L. S.,
Van Doren, Aletta V. (1816-52). *See* Knox, Aletta V. (Van Doren) [Mrs. John P.] (1816-52)
Van Doren, Carl, 14,447
Van Doren Collegiate Institute (NY), 10,991
Van Doren, Dorothy (Graffe) [Mrs. Mark] (1896-), 1,507
Van Doren, Irita Brandford (Taylor) (1891-1966), 2,166, 2,198, 2,542, **2,617**
Van Doren, Mark, 1,507, 16,169
Van Dorn, Earl, 9,678
Van Dorn, Emily. *See* Miller, Emily (Van Dorn)
Van Dorn, Laura (Bates [Mrs. Harry] Trumbull [Mrs. Isaac] (1813-?), 1,885
Van Duren, Margaret Vining, **7,965**
Van Dusen, Albert P., 1,596
Van Duzer, D. C., 10,673
Van Dyke, Fanny [Mrs. James] (?-1928), 9,463
Van Dyke, Henry, 12,529
Van Dyke, John, 11,049
Van Dyke, Mary Dix (Strong) [Mrs. John] (1819-75), **11,049**
Van Dyke, Maude Mary, 9,463
Van Dyke, May. [Mrs. Arthur] Johnson (1888-1963), **11,230**
Van Dyke, Rachel (1793-?), **11,050**
Van Ess, Dorothy Firman [Mrs. John] (1885-1975), **10,927**
Van Etten, Winifred Florence (Mayne) [Mrs. Ben] (1902-), **5,036, 5,085**
Van Gelder Family (NY), **11,427**
Vangen, Christina, **8,800**
Van Gilder, Florence Scott, **1,645**
Van Grunsven, Antone, 14,577
Vanguard: A History (book), 2,365
Vanguard Press, 8,116
Van Hackford, Sarah, 16,876
Van Hoosen, Alice (1855-1950). *See* Comstock, Alice (Van Hoosen) Jones [Mrs. Joseph C.] (1855-1950)
Van Hoosen, Bertha (1863-1952), 7,825, 7,826, **7,966**, 15,125, **15,141**
Van Horn, Ann, 11,318
Van Horn, David, 11,318
Van Horn Family (PA), 15,053
Van Horn, Lucille Wallower, 15,319
Van Horn, Margaret (1790-?). *See* Bell, Margaret (Van Horn) Dwight (1790-?)
Van Horne, Ann, 2,268
Van Horne, Ann Margaret, 11,325
Van Horne, Bernard, 14,591
Van Horne, David, 2,268
Van Horne, Garrit, 11,325
Van Hyning, Lyrl Clark, 14,686
Vanity Fair (moving-picture), 1,996
Vanity Fair (periodical), 425
Vanity of Man, The (drama), 12,562
VanKeuren, Maria D., **12,337**
Van Kleeck, Mary Abby (1883-1972), 2,120, 2,403, 2,424, 2,700, 2,703, 7,273, **7,315**, 8,071, **8,142**, 8,651, 8,653, 8,658, 8,662, 8,665, 8,670, 8,678
Van Lear, Malvina Virginia (1841-1920). *See* Manning, Malvina Virginia (Van Lear) (1841-1920)

Van Lew, Elizabeth L. (1818-1900), **17,122**
van Loon, Elizabeth Ingersoll (Bowditch) [Mrs. Hendrik Willem], **6,933**
van Loon, Hendrik Willem, 6,933, 11,644
Van Matre, Almire Heath, 1,659
Van Matre, Berena Cole, 1,659
Van Metre, Bettie, 17,029
Vann, John, **13,600**
Van Ness Family (NJ), **11,138**
Van Ness, Leslie (1867-1959). *See* Denman, Leslie (Van Ness) [Mrs. William] (1867-1959)
Vannier, Marion Lydia (1878-1966), 8,610
Van Noy, Elsie (Hogan) [Mrs. William Ray], **16,837**
Van Noy, Kathleen (pseudonym). *See* Hogan, Kathleen
Van Noy, Mary Grace (pseudonym). *See* Hogan, Mary Grace
Van Orden, Katherine, 4,970
Van Orsdol, Martha O. *See* Farnsworth, Martha O. (Van Orsdol) [Mrs. John] Shaw [Mrs. Fred C.]
Vanover, Imogene Irwin, 10,714
van Pelt, Ada, 11,547
Van Rensselaer, Catherine G. [Miss], 12,121
Van Rensselaer, Catherine "Sweet Kitty" (1734-1803). *See* Schuyler, Catherine "Sweet Kitty" (Van Rensselaer) [Mrs. Philip John] (1734-1803)
Van Rensselaer, Catherine Visscher. *See* Bonney, Catherine (Van Rensselaer) [Mrs. Samuel W.]
Van Rensselaer, Cornelia Josepha (Codwise) (1810-90), 11,041
Van Rensselaer, Elizabeth, 11,260
Van Rensselaer, Emily Denning, **12,332**
Van Rensselaer, Eugene, 12,333
Van Rensselaer Family (NY), 11,260
Van Rensselaer, Harriet [Mrs. Solomon], 11,260
Van Rensselaer, Jeremiah, 12,215
"Van Rensselaer Manor, The," 12,240
Van Rensselaer, Margaretta, 11,260
Van Rensselaer, Maria, 11,260
Van Rensselaer, Martha (1864-1932), 1,340, 2,694, 5,119, 11,521, 11,579, 11,662, 11,679, 11,691
Van Rensselaer, Sallie B. Pendleton [Mrs. Eugene], **12,333**
Van Rensselaer, Solomon, 11,260
Van Rensselaer, Susan de Lancey Cullen (1851-1931). *See* Strong, Susan de Lancey Cullen (Van Rensselaer) [Mrs. Alan Hartwell] (1851-1931)
Van Riper, Bertha. *See* Overbury, Bertha (Van Riper) [Mrs. Frederick]
Vansandt, Sarah K. [Mrs.], 8,164
Vansant, Irene Allen. [Mrs. Henry Garrison] Carson, **14,254**
Van Santan, Agnes (Burt), 16,614
Van Schaack, Catherine, **12,334**
Van Schaack, Peter, 12,334
van Schaick, Anna, 11,737
van Schaick, Christina, 11,737
van Schaick Family (NY), **11,737**
van Schaick, Maria, 11,737
Vanscoy, James S., 4,845
Van Sellar, Henry (1839-?), **4,442**
Van Sellar, Sallie (Pattison) [Mrs. Henry], 4,442
Van Sickle, Asher, 8,371
Van Sickle, Nellie, **8,371**
Van Striprian, Dorothy, **16,916**
Van Taerlingh, Flooris, 12,377
Vantarlingh, Elizabeth, 12,377
Van Tyne, Helen Belfield (Bates) [Mrs. Josselyn], **7,967**
Van Valkenburgh, Helen. *See* Chesnut, Helen (Van Valkenburgh)
Van Valkenburgh, Mary Wealthy Bradley (?-1866), **3,433**
Van Varick, Margarita [Mrs. Rudolphus], **15,102**
Van Vechten, Carl (1880-1964), 3,285, 3,288, **3,292**, 6,112, 11,897, 12,029
Van Velser, Mary (Fuller), 4,277, 4,279
Van Vleck, Catherine, 12,377
van Vleck, Charlena. *See* Anderson, Charlena (van Vleck) [Mrs. Melville Best]
van Vleck Family (CA), 1,566
van Vleck Family (NY), **12,377**
van Vleck, Mary Marvel. *See* Anderson, Mary Marvel (van Vleck) [Mrs. Balfour H.]

Van Vleck, Mary S. *See* Anderson, Mary S. (Van Vleck) [Mrs. Balfour H.]
Van Volkenburg, Ellen. [Mrs. Maurice] Browne (1882-), 8,001
Van Volkenburg Family, **8,001**
Van Volkenburgh, A., 11,571
Van Voorhis, Louise (1889-1948). *See* Armstrong, Louise (Van Voorhis) (1889-1948)
Van Voris, Jacqueline [Mrs. William] (1922-), 7,162
Van Wagenen, Helen [Miss], 14,146
Van Wagener, Mary. *See* Radcliffe, Mary (Van Wagener) [Mrs. Lewis]
Van Waters, Miriam (1887-1974), **6,263**, 6,544, 6,565, 6,583, 6,760, **6,934**, **7,031**, 8,658, 8,678
Van Wie, Virginia, 15,935
Van Winkle, Mina C., 9,894, 10,679
Van Winkle, Rip (pseudonym). *See* Jackson, Helen Maria (Fiske) [Mrs. Edward Bissell] Hunt [Mrs. William Sharpless] (1830-85)
Van Winter, Lucretia Wilhemine, 2,621
Van Wyck, Charles Henry (1824-95), **10,548**
Van Wyck Family (SC), **15,649**
Van Wyck, Margaret Caroline (Broyles), 15,649
Van Wyke, Lydia [Mrs.], 16,097
Van Wyke, Margaret, 16,097
Varda, Jean, 761
Vardaman, Anna (Buruson), 9,709
Vardaman, James Kimble, 9,620, 9,658
Vardaman, James Money, 9,620
Varden (book), 8,802
Varese, Edgar (1883-1965), 7,316
Varèse, Louise (McCutcheon) [Mrs. Edgar] (1880-), 7,316
Varian, Dorothy (1895-), **2,824**
Variety Club Heart Hospital (Minneapolis, MN), 8,581
"Variety, or; the Vicissitudes of Life" (ms), 2,248
Various Light, The (book), 5,310
Varley, Bessie (Schonberg) [Mrs. Dimitry V.], 11,306
Varney, Maria L. [Mrs. Thomas] (?-1888), 1,350
Varney, Thomas, **1,350**
Varnier, Martha "Mattie", **17,105**
Vasectomy, 4,131
Vashon College and Academy, 17,315
Vashon, Susan (Paul), 10,205
Vass, Ellen (Wirt) [Mrs. Edmund Brooke] (ca. 1812-?). *See* McCormick, Ellen (Wirt) [Mrs. Edmund Brooke] Vass [Mrs. Charles] (ca. 1812-?)
Vassar College, (NY), 3,257, 4,167, 4,614, 6,416, 6,721, 6,739, 7,094, 8,428, 12,737, 12,740, 12,923, 14,386, 16,060
administration, 6,475
alumnae, 4,440, 8,595, 8,671, 9,527, 10,975, 12,009, 13,932, 16,016
deans, **11,502**, 12,525
faculty, 9,563, **11,480**
students, 220, 1,744, 4,049, 13,932, 14,835
Vassar College Associated Alumnae of Indiana, 4,630
Vassar College (NY), Training Camp for Nurses, **6,161**, 9,803
Vassar College (NY), Vassar Alumnae, 13,932
Vassar, Matthew, 6,589
Vassar Summer Institute for Family and Child Care Services in War Time, 10,013
"Vassar, the Pioneer" (article), 15,270
Vassar's Rainbow Division—1918, 6,161
Vastal, Pearl Avis (Gordon) [Mrs. C. L.], 4,958
Vatteng, Hannah. *See* Birkley, Hannah (Vatteng) [Mrs. Iver]
Vatter, Caroline, 14,618
Vaudeville, 4,894, 10,428, 11,907
Vaughan, Benjamin (1751-1835), **14,904**
Vaughan, Ellen Parkman, 11,593
Vaughan, Eulalia (Mewbourn) [Mrs. John B.], 3,109
Vaughan, John, 14,881
Vaughan, John B., **3,109**
Vaughan, Landon, 9,759
Vaughan, Sarah Hallowell (ca. 1727-?), 14,904
Vaughan, Sarah Manning [Mrs. Benjamin] (1754-1834), 14,904
Vaughan, Sue (Adams) Landon [Mrs. Landon], 9,759
Vaughan, Virginia, 12,513

Vaughn, Cynthia (1835-1901). *See* Goodyear, Cynthia (Vaughn) [Mrs. Andrew] (1835-1901)
Vaughn, Etta Bartlett, 17,498
Vaughn Family, 9,318
Vaughn, Jennie [Miss], 9,556
Vaughn, Josephine Conly (Smith), 3,722
Vaughn, Mary, 9,593
Vault, Mrs. William T., 14,645
Vause, Lillie (1854?-1946). *See* Archbell, Lillie (Vause) (1854?-1946)
Vaux Family (PA), 15,104
Vaux, Mary Morris (1860-1940). *See* Walcott, Mary Morris (Vaux) [Mrs. Charles D.] (1860-1940)
Veazie, Harriette C. (Harned) [Mrs. Henry A.] (1837-1909). *See* Keatinge, Harriette C. (Harned) [Mrs. Henry A.] Veazie [Mrs. Edward C.] (1837-1909)
Veblen, Andrew A., 8,774
Veblen, Thorstein, 8,774
Vedder, Jessie Van Vechten (1859-1952), **11,428**
Vedin, Augusta, 17,618
Veeder, Louisa Usher Shaw [Mrs. Uriah], 12,412
Veeder, Mary. *See* Carruth, Mary (Veeder) [Mrs. Oliver Powers]
Veerhusen, Pamela Getz [Mrs. William], 8,672
Veery Very, The (book), 6,061
Vegetarian Settlement Company, 9,850
Vegetarianism, 2,856, 6,867
Veglahn, Nancy (1937-), **5,037**
Veien mot Vest (book), 8,786
Veiller, Lawrence, 11,897, 12,631
Veiller, Marguerite [Mrs. Lawrence], 12,372, 12,631
Vein of Iron (book), 17,059
Velarde, Pablita (1918-), 11,213, 11,217, 11,235
Vellore Christian Medical College (India), 6,875
Velsicol Chemical Corporation, 8,555
Venable Family, 5,359
Venables, Mrs., 9,256
Venables, The (book), 692
Venereal diseases, 1,121, 2,424, 4,145, 6,760, 9,476, 9,962, 10,681, 15,251
clinics, 238
prevention, 592, 2,687, 3,835, 4,111, 4,145, 6,748, 8,633
Venetian Glass Nephew, The (book), 2,658
Venice Biennale (1962), 2,816
Vennemon, Mollie, 16,097
Ventilation, 4,388
Ventress, Charlotte [Mrs. James Alexander] (1815-77), 9,760
Ventress, James Alexander (?-1867), **9,760**
Venture into Darkness (book), 14,388
Venus Through the Ages (book), 2,741
Ver Mehr, Fanny, 376
Veramendi, Juan Martin, 16,310
Veramendi, Maria Josefa Narvaro [Mrs. Juan Martin], 16,310
Verdandi Study Club, 8,768
Verhoeff, Mary [Miss] (1871?-1962), **5,367**
Vermillion, William, 4,815
Vermilyea Family (MN), 9,463
Vermont, **16,998**, 17,024, 17,029, 17,030
abortion, legal aspects, 1,984
administrative agencies, **17,015**, **17,018**, **17,021**, **17,022**
adult education, 17,029
aged, health and hygiene, 16,998
agriculture, 17,014
artists, 16,981
authors, 16,981, **17,025**
beauty shops, law and legislation, **17,015**
census, **17,014**
church societies, **6,169**
clergy, **6,744**
clergymen's wives, 17,029
clubs, 16,984, 16,998, **17,041**
college librarians, 17,002, 17,012
college presidents, **16,992**, **16,993**
college students, **16,990**, **16,995**
college teachers, **17,002**
college trustees, **16,996**
court-houses, 2,507
court records, **17,016**
dancing, study and teaching, **16,987**

deaf, education, 16,998
deans (in schools), **16,988, 17,001,** 17,002
diaries and journals, 17,026, 17,029
dissertations, academic, **16,994**
editors, **17,030, 17,043**
educational associations, **17,040**
eugenics, **17,018**
farm life, 11,259
farmers, **17,007**
Friends, Society of, 17,029
genealogy, 6,234
governors, **11,613,** 17,046
greek letter societies, **17,003**
high schools, 16,998
historians, **16,984, 17,024**
historical markers, 17,029
home economics, rural, 2,673
home nursing, 16,984
lawyers, **17,031, 17,043**
legal documents, 17,033
librarians, 16,985
libraries, 16,979, 17,046
marriage law, 17,018
mentally handicapped, 17,018
minorities, 17,018
monuments, 17,029
mothers general, Afro-American, 17,029
municipal government, 16,998
naturalization records, **17,016**
nurses, 16,985
    malpractice, 17,022
nursing schools, **17,000**
nursing, standards, **17,022**
pageants, 16,999
patriotic societies, 17,048
photographs, **16,999**
    collections, **16,985**
physically handicapped, 17,018
physicians, 17,039
pioneers and settlers, Afro-American, **16,982**
plant diseases, **6,472**
poets, **17,038**
politicians, **17,043**
politics, practical, women's activism, **17,042**
poor, 17,018
prisoners, 17,018
    medical care, 17,018
prisons for women, records and correspondence, **17,020**
prisons, records and correspondence, **17,019**
public libraries, **17,008**
public schools, 17,048
public welfare, **17,021,** 17,029
rural population, 17,018
school buildings, 16,999
schools, **12,927,** 17,035
seed potatoes, **6,472**
social life and customs, 8,352
soldiers, Civil War, 17,029
spiritualists, 17,036
state boards of education, 17,017
sterilization (birth control), law and legislation, 17,018
strikes and lockouts, 14,446
student counselors, 16,989
students' societies, **17,004**
suffrage, 6,373
suffrage societies, 17,025, 17,042
suffragists, **17,025**
teachers, 16,981, 17,029
    certification, 17,017
teachers, training of, 17,017
telephone operators, 16,985, 16,999
titles of honor, 17,029
town clerks, **16,984**
trade and professional associations, 17,021
typists, 16,999
universities and colleges, 16,993, 16,994, 16,996, **17,005, 17,047**
    administration, **16,992,** 16,993
    alumni, **16,991**
    archives, **17,006**
    curricula, 16,988
    employees, **16,986**

faculty, **16,986**
    women, employment, 17,048
Vermont Board of Cosmetology, **17,015**
Vermont Children's Aid Society, 17,018
Vermont Conference on Social Welfare, 17,021
Vermont Department of Classroom Teachers, **17,040**
Vermont Department of Education Teaching Training
    and Certification Program, **17,017**
Vermont Equal Suffrage Association, 17,025, 17,042
Vermont Federation of Women's Clubs, **17,041**
Vermont League of Women Voters, **17,042**
Vermont Social Welfare Department, **17,021**
Vermont State Board of Nursing, **17,022**
Vermont Supreme Court, 17,016
Verner, Elizabeth O'Neill, 15,585
Vernon, Ida, **15,760**
Vernon, Ida Stevenson Weldon [Mrs. W. C.], **16,141**
Vernon, Lillian. *See* de Bosis, Lillian (Vernon) [Mrs.
    Adolfo]
Vernon, Mabel (1883-1975), **859, 860,** 10,740, 15,311
Veronica Club (IN), **4,585**
Verplanck, Mary Eliza Fenno [Mrs. Gulian C.], **12,205**
Verrill, Ruth, **16,563**
Versace, Rocky, 17,731
Versace, Tere Rios (1917-), **17,731**
Versailles, Treaty of (1919), 2,538
Verses (book), 12,815
Verseweavers (Portland, OR), 14,428
Verstille, Charlotte, 15,761
Verstille, Tristram, **15,761**
Vertebrates, brain research, 6,320
Vertees, John J., 15,970
Vertner, Elizabeth [Mrs.], 5,347
Vertner, Mrs. Daniel, 5,316
Vertner, Rosa Griffith (1828-94). *See* Jeffrey, Rosa
    Griffith (Vertner) Johnson [Mrs. Alexander]
    (1828-94)
Very Family (MA), 16,531
Very, Jones, 7,416
Vespucius, Americus, 11,325
Vespucius, Eliza, 11,325
Vespucius, Teresa, 11,325
Vess, Raymond, **8,143**
Vessaria, Miss, 1,261
Vestal, Ophelia D., **14,183**
Vestris, Eliza, 11,985
Vet Students Wives Auxiliary (TX). *See* American
    Veterinary Medical Association, Auxiliary to the
    Texas Student Chapter
Veterans, 1,140, 1,728, 2,206, 2,926, **4,339,** 8,139,
    8,970, 9,059, **9,410,** 9,757, 9,914, **10,547,** 11,236,
    17,086, 17,466. *See also* Bounties, military;
    Pensions, military; Soldiers' homes
    education, 2,698, 6,808
    laws and legislation, 2,698, 6,861, 9,911
    medical care, 233, 2,698, 4,339, 6,826, 8,908, 15,538
Veterans Administration Hospital (Tuskegee, AL), 8,673
Veterans Administration Hospital (AR), 233
Veterans, Confederate, 15,715, 16,148
Veterans, disabled, 6,861
    medical care, 9,132
    rehabilitation, 6,826
    vocational rehabilitation, 543
Veterans Hospital, special service committee (New
    Haven, CT), 2,005
Veterans News (periodical), 10,408
Veterans of Foreign Wars, 9,059
Veterans of Foreign Wars, Auxiliary, 14,188
Veterans of Foreign Wars, ladies auxiliary, 2,205
Veteran's Upward Bound, 13,669
Veterinarians, 4,336
Vial, Mary (1738-1802). *See* Holyoke, Mary (Vial)
    [Mrs. Edward Augustus] (1738-1802)
Vice-presidents, United States, 4,370, 4,375, 5,303,
    9,140, 10,392, 12,410, 14,982, 15,779
    election, 1,091, 9,380
Vickers, Lina, 12,572
Vickers, Sallie [Miss], 3,112
Vickers, Sarah Louise (1841-1930). *See* Oberholtzer,
    Sarah Louise (Vickers) (1841-1930)
"Vicksburg: Home Town Gibralter" (ms), 9,587

Victor Emmanuel II, 13,928
Victor, Frances Auretta (Fuller) [Mrs. Jackson] Barritt
    [Mrs. Henry Clay] (1826-1902), 559, **861, 862,**
    14,314, **14,680**
Victor, Henry Clay, 862
Victoria Mining Company, 10,712
Victoria, Queen of England, 7,213, 11,509
Victoria Regina (drama), 3,921
*Victorian Detective Fiction: A Catalogue of the
    Collection* (book), 11,976
Victorian Newsletter, The, 4,404
Victorian Order of Nurses (Canada), 6,164
Victorian Society of Maine Women (Portland, ME), **5,693**
Victory Aids Association, 8,446
Victory Fleet, 7,318
*Victory: Report of the Women's Liberty Loan
    Committee Tenth Federal Reserve District,* 10,422
Viele, Ann (1884-1967), **11,357**
Vienna News (newspaper), 3,357
Vienna Psychoanalytic Institute, 11,908
Vietnam, 1,017, 7,262
    missionaries to, 5,187
    presidents, assassination, 9,286
Vietnamese Conflict (1961-1975), 459, 1,010, 1,283,
    6,023, 8,624, 9,127, 9,149, 9,467, 9,605, 10,360,
    11,389, 12,523, 15,993, 16,876
    journalists, **17,614**
    opposition to, 741, 1,577, 4,168, 4,170, 10,206,
    12,883, **13,503**
    prisoners and prisons, North Vietnamese, 17,731
    prisoners of war, 212, 10,493
    public opinion, 2,782, 6,709, 6,846, 17,295
*Vietnam's Will to Live: Resistance to Foreign
    Aggression from Early Times Through the
    Nineteenth Century* (book), 6,709
Views, 14,204
Vigen, Helena Carlson [Mrs. Engbret Trond]
    (1861-1935), **9,419**
Vigilance committees, 1,254, 10,270, 10,300, 10,364
Vigilant (whaleship), 7,481
Vigilantes. *See* Vigilance committees
Viking Press, 6,096, 14,455
Vilas, Anna M., 17,732
Vilas, Katherine J. (1919-), 16,488
Vilas, William F. (1840-1908), **17,732**
Viles, Elizabeth S. *See* Hosmer, Elizabeth S. (Viles)
Viles, George, **5,666**
Viley, Ann. *See* Johnson, Ann (Viley) [Mrs. George
    W.]
Villa Branciforte (CA), 392
*Villa Narcisse: The Garden, the Statues, and the
    Pool* (book), 2,398
Villa Serbelloni, 11,892
Villa Teresa Nursery and School (Oklahoma City,
    OK), 14,226
Village Improvement Association (Princeton, NJ),
    11,170
Village Improvement Society (St. Petersburg, FL).
    See Woman's Town Improvement Association
    (St. Petersburg, FL)
Villages, Inc., The, 5,230
Villages, social life and customs, 1,469
Villanova University, deans, 5,110
Villard, Fanny (Garrison) [Mrs. Henry] (1844-1928).
    See Villard, Helen Frances "Fanny" (Garrison)
    [Mrs. Henry] (1844-1928)
Villard, Harriet E., 3,524
Villard, Helen Frances "Fanny" (Garrison) [Mrs.
    Henry] (1844-1928), 5,119, 7,868, 7,923, 11,742,
    12,834, 15,305
Villard, Kate, 3,524
Villard, Leila. *See* Heidt, Leila (Villard) [Mrs. John]
Villette (book), 15,753
Vincent, Ada, 10,905
Vincent, Cecilia. *See* Garrett, Cecilia (Vincent) [Mrs.
    Milton W.]
Vincent, Elizabeth Lee (1897-),
    11,662
Vincent, H. [Mrs. Parker], 5,644
Vincent, Hannah [Mrs. Thomas], 3,567
Vincent, John H. (1832-1920), 6,954
Vincent, Lora Richter [Mrs. T. H.] (?-1948), **10,268**

Vincent, Mrs. George, 8,543
Vincent, Sarah,
Vincent, Thomas, Jr., 10,905
Vinciguerra, Francesca. *See* Winwar, Frances (1900-)
Vineland Training School for Mental Defectives (NJ), 10,990
Vineyard Shore School of Women Workers in Industry, 11,762, 17,588
Vineyard Ward Relief Society (Orem, UT), 16,583
Vining, Italy [Mrs.] (1879-1948), 8,388
Vinson, Clara. *See* Weaver, Clara (Vinson) [Mrs. James Baird]
Vinsonhaler, Mrs. D. M., 10,308
Vinter Hansen, J. M. [Miss], **1,542**
Vinton, John Adams, 10,876
Vinton, Madeleine (1825-98). *See* Dahlgren, Madeleine (Vinton) [Mrs. John Adolphus Bernard] (1825-98)
Viola Thorne Club (Wooster, OH), **14,160**
Violence, prevention of, 13,615
Violet Study Club (Minneapolis, MN), **9,420**
"Violet, The" (poem), 2,466
Violin makers, 14,639
Violin, study and instruction, 10,418
Violinists, 1,788, **4,443**, **5,781**, 9,169, 16,577, 17,817
Viorst, Judith, 8,531
Virden, Helen M., **5,038**
Virginia, 20, 2,228, 2,642, 6,103, 12,247, 17,060
    abortion, legal aspects, 1,984
    actresses, 3,346
    agriculturists, **17,055**
    art, decorative, 13,631
    artists, **17,077**, 17,102
    authors, **6,095**, **17,086**
    bishops, 13,451
    boards of trade, officials and employees, **17,086**
    businesswomen, 12,993
    canteens (war-time, emergency, etc.), **17,072**
    charitable societies, 17,111
    charitable societies, Jewish, **13,781**
    church societies, **17,113**
    citizens' associations, 3,283, 17,110, **17,124**
    Civil War, 8,167, 14,770
        campaigns and battles, 2,223, 17,103, 17,477
        occupation, 17,079, 17,092, 17,099, 17,103
        personal narratives, **3,348**, **13,037**, 16,244, 17,079, 17,100
        prisoners and prisons, 17,073
        social conditions, 17,093
        societies, Confederate, 15,715
    clerks of court, 17,125
    clubs, 13,070, **17,054**, 17,091
    coeducation, 17,091
    college presidents, 6,095, 13,451
    college teachers, **2,125**, **6,095**, 17,115
    congressmen, 2,550
    county officials and employees, 17,050, 17,051
    court-houses, 2,507
    diaries and journals, **2,404**, **13,036**, 17,079, **17,090**, 17,100, **17,101**, 17,103, **17,105**, 17,106, **17,120**, 17,123
    educational associations, 17,091
    executions and executioners, 5,979
    federal aid to the arts, **2,742**
    freedmen, schools for, 7,610
    Friends, 5,746, 14,839
    gardening, societies, etc., 17,110
    governors, 7,561, **12,578**, 13,011, 17,083, 17,115
    greek letter societies, 17,110
    high school students, 17,090
    historic buildings, conservation and restoration, **17,064**
    historic sites, administration, 17,125
    historical societies, 17,121
    hospital administrators, 17,128
    housewives, **10,052**, 17,051
    immigrants, English, **17,099**
    insurance companies, 17,099
    journalists, 17,119

judges, 2,614, 17,108, 17,109
    junior colleges, **17,049**
    law teachers, 17,121
    lawyers, 17,121
    legislators, 2,328, 17,109
    libraries, 17,110
    lieutenant-governors, 2,635
    merchants, **17,129**
    military posts, 17,445
    monasticism and religious orders for women, Catholic, **17,052**
    museum directors, 17,117
    Native Americans, wars, 12,545, 17,624
    newspapers, sections, columns, etc., 17,102
    nursing schools, 6,133
    officials and employees, **17,117**
    oral history, **17,051**, **17,063**, **17,075**, **17,125**
    patriotic societies, **17,057**
    physicians, 17,121, **17,130**
    pioneers and settlers, 10,442, **12,545**, 13,011, 16,060
    plantation life, 16,244, 17,081, 17,097
    plantations, 2,541, 3,348
    poets, **17,114**
    political clubs, 17,050
    politicians, 17,119
    politics, practical, women's activism, 13,176, **17,042**, **17,061**, 17,077, -**17,087**, **17,088**, 17,091, 17,104
    prisons for women, officials and employees, **17,084**
    public health, 17,110
    real estate agents, 17,050
    Reconstruction (1865-), 16,244
    Revolution (1775-1783), 3,234
        economic aspects, 1,411
    schools, 9,709, 15,799
    secretaries of state, 17,463
    senators, United States, 2,550, 17,083
    slave records, **2,132**, 13,075
    slave trade, 1,047
    slavery, condition of slaves, 2,652
    slaves, 2,132, 4,239
    social life and customs, 17,105, 17,106
    state universities and colleges, 2,125
    strikes and lockouts, 6,315, 6,795
    suffrage societies, 16,252, 17,077, **17,104**
    suffragists, **17,077**
    teachers, 17,051
    tobacco manufacture and trade, 12,171
    trade unions
        clothing workers, 8,074
        textile workers, 8,074
    tutors and tutoring, **17,085**
    United Methodist Church, 17,106
    universities and colleges, 6,095, 13,390, 13,406
    women's colleges, 13,563
Virginia Company of London, 14,758
Virginia Cooperative Women's Guilds (MN), 9,511
Virginia Correction Center for Women, 17,084
Virginia Dare Manual Training School (NC), 13,489
Virginia Equal Suffrage League, 17,077
Virginia Federation of Business and Professional Women's Clubs, 17,054
Virginia Girl in the Civil War, A (book), 3,143
Virginia Historical Committee, 16,045
Virginia House of Delegates, 17,109
Virginia Military Institute, 17,111
Virginia Museum of Fine Arts, 17,117
Virginia State Chamber of Commerce, 17,086
Virginia State College, 2,125
Virginia Wright Foundation, 17,366
Virtue, Ethel, 9,230
Virus research, **10,209**
Visconti, Ann, 11,859
Viscoso, Monica Shorten (1923-), **8,626**
"Visit to Florence Nightingale, A" (ms), 6,663
"Visitant, The" (ms), 13,969
Visitation Convent (Dubuque, IA), **4,875**
Visitation Nuns, 15,147
Visiting Nurse Association (Boise, ID), **3,729**
Visiting Nurse Association (Fort Dodge, IA), **4,884**
Visiting Nurse Association (Neenah-Menasha, WI), **17,826**

Visiting Nurse Association of Boston (MA), **6,162**
Visiting Nurse Association of Chicago (IL), 3,813, 3,851, **3,904**, 4,079
Visiting Nurse Association of Dayton (OH). *See* Public Health Nursing Service of Dayton and Montgomery County (OH)
Visiting Nurse Association of Gary (IN), 4,090
Visiting Nurse Association of Southwestern Indiana, **4,500**
Visiting Nurse Service (Madison, WI), 17,733
Visiting Nurses Association, 236, 2,347, 17,831
Visono, Bella (1904-). *See* Dodd, Bella (Visono) (1904-)
Visscher, Gertrude (1899-), 9,467
Visual arts, 8,659
Visual Studies Workshop, Research Center (Rochester, NY), 12,842
Vital statistics, 162, **392**, 432, 1,121, 1,889, 1,933, **1,935**, 3,482, 3,619, 4,197, 5,425, 5,495, 5,496, **5,563**, **5,567**, **5,572**, 7,142, 7,601, 7,609, 7,678, 10,055, 10,100, **11,207**, **11,212**, **11,441**, 11,443, **11,800**, 12,734, 13,311, 13,386, 14,290, 14,807, 17,457, 17,515
Vitamin A, 17,853
Vitamin B, 17,853
Viticulture, 6,403
Vittum, Harriet Elizabeth (1872-1953), 3,910, 4,141, **4,163**, 4,165, 4,166
Vivan, Cassandra, 14,828
Vivisection Investigation League (NY), 12,516
Vivisection, opposition to, 7,222
Vleit, Catherine (Fancher) [Mrs. Frank] (ca. 1880-1970s), 11,181
Vocalists, **5,459**, 9,346, **17,986**
Vocational education, 2,068, 2,069, **2,685**, 2,705, 3,859, **5,758**, 6,236, **6,808**, 6,812, 8,058, 8,069, 8,646, 9,598, 11,047, 11,229, 12,118, 16,132, 16,242
Vocational guidance, 6,134, **6,440**, **6,808**, 9,964, 11,622, 12,724, 12,738, **13,196**, **17,597**, **17,619**
Vocational guidance for girls, 9,964
Vocational guidance for women reentering employment, 17,821
Vocational rehabilitation, **5,573**, **6,799**, 16,911
Vogdes, Ada Adelaide (Adams), **1,497**
Vogel, Anita (Steiber) [Mrs. Rudolf], **1,829**
Vogel, Emma E., **2,091**
Vogel, Louis (Fluetsch) [Mrs. Mort R.] (1914-), **13,690**
Vogler, Lisetta Maria (1820-1903). *See* Fries, Lisetta Maria Vogler [Mrs. Francis] (1820-1903)
Vogue (periodical), 7,182, 11,304, 12,086
Voice culture, 316, 1,068, **1,192**, 11,699, **12,322**
Voice from the South by a Black Woman of the South, A, 2,130
Voice of America, **10,724**
"Voice of American Women" (radio program), 14,551
Voice of the Deaf: A Biography of Edward Miner Gallaudet (book), 2,341
Voice of the Fair (newspaper), 4,135
Voice of the Lute (book), 7,718, 17,553
Voice of Unity, The (periodical), 3,928
Voight, Ellen Bryant, 5,063
Voight, Mrs. A. L., 11,827
Voight, Nell Adams, **8,520**
Voigt, Irma E. (1882-1953), **13,754**
Voigts, Jean Ramsey, 1,339
Voiland, Alice, 8,676
Volcanoes, 955
Vold, Margaret Anna (Bryan), **10,549**
Voline, 8,064
Volk, Mother General M. Augusta, 10,134
Vollmer, August (1876-1955), **863**
Vollmer, Marguerite, 11,627
Volstead, Andrew John (1860-1947), **9,421**
Volstead, Helen Mary Osler Gilruth [Mrs. Andrew John] (1868-1915), 9,421
Voltaire, 14,509
Voluntary Action Center (St. Paul, MN), **8,682**
Voluntary health agencies, 1,700, **3,813**, 4,698, 6,223, 6,760, 6,919, 7,288, **8,633**, **8,634**, 8,670, 8,952, 9,385, 11,445, **11,811**, 11,885, 11,932, 14,192, 14,356, 14,746, 15,754, 16,051, 16,069, 16,284, 16,911, 17,230, 17,238, 17,738

Voluntary Parenthood League, 1,596
Volunteer Bureau, Inc. (St. Paul, MN). *See* Voluntary Action Center (St. Paul, MN)
Volunteer Prison League (TX), 16,128
Volunteer workers in hospitals, 955, **1,388**, 2,384, 3,932, **4,012, 4,018, 4,025, 4,581, 4,713, 4,879, 8,180,** 8,697, 9,385, 9,530, 11,635, 11,758, 12,506, **13,370, 14,723, 15,981, 15,982, 15,983, 15,984, 17,981**
Volunteer workers in social service, 365, **380, 647, 3,807, 3,863, 4,104,** 5,193, 5,357, 5,365, **6,689, 6,774, 8,503,** 8,583, **8,635, 8,682, 15,881,** 16,780, 17,220, **17,840**
Volunteers in Service to America, 16,344
officials and employees, 380, 6,900
Volunteers of America, 4,974, 11,445
"Volunteers Serve in the City" (moving-picture), 8,682
vom Baur, Eva Elise (1889-). *See* Hansl, Eva Elise (vom Baur) (1889-)
Von Behren, Louise (1890-1964). *See* Smith, Louise (Von Behren) [Mrs. Dorsey B.] (1890-1964)
von Bülow, Marie, 2,665
von Bülow, Prince, 2,665
von der Osten, Anna, 14,889
von Elmendorff, Mother Mary Veronica, 13,902
Von Elsner, Marie Eugenia. *See* Litta, Marie. Marie Eugenia Von Elsner
von Grunebaum, Gustave, 853
Von Harten, Emilia, 12,583
Von Herberg, Eugene (Dennis) [Mrs. J. C.] (1901-48), **5,163**
Von Herberg, J. C., 5,163
Von Hesse, Emily MacKaye (1838-?), 10,868
Von Hyning, Lyrl Clark, 9,150
von Kienbusch, Carl O., 11,171
Von Lindeman, Marie, 12,457
von M. Zesch, Leonie, 17,217
Von Meysenburg Family (GA), **3,110**
Vonnegut, Marjorie. *See* Marquis, Marjorie (Vonnegut) [Mrs. Don]
von Pirquet Clinic (Austria), 11,908
Von Richthofen, Baron, 13,277
Von Richthofen, Frieda (1879-1956). *See* Ravagli, Frieda (von Richthofen) [Mrs. David Herbert] Lawrence [Mrs. Angelino] (1879-1956)
Von Saltza, Christine, 1,534
Von Schweinitz Family (NY), 12,020
von Stein, John Peter (1819-1903), **4,955**
von Stein, Sarah, 4,955
von Stosch, Leonora (1872-1956). *See* Speyer, Leonora (von Stosch) [Mrs. Edgar] (1872-1956)
von Suttner, Baroness Berthe, 4,631
von Teuffel, Blanche Willis (Howard) [Mrs. Julius] (1847-98), 5,694
Voodooism, 2,948, 5,501
Voodry, Alva L., **4,851**
Voorhees College (SC), 15,777
Voorhees, Josephine Ludlow Palmer [Mrs. Tracy Stebbins], 11,052
Voorhees, Julia A., **13,150**
Voorhees, Lillian Welch (1894-1972), 3,290, **5,477, 15,925**
Voorhees, Lucia Isabella. *See* Grimes, Lucia Isabella (Voorhees) [Mrs. George]
Voorhees, Sarah Rutgers (Neilson) [Mrs. Willard P.] (1853-?). *See* Jones, Sarah Rutgers (Neilson) [Mrs. Willard P.] Voorhees [Mrs. Albert J.] (1853-?)
Voorhees, Tracy Stebbins (1890-1974), **11,052**
Voorhees, Willard P. (1851-1914), 11,051
Voorheis, Belle [Miss], 8,154
Voorheis Family (CA), **595**
Voorheis, Gertrude. *See* Clark, Gertrude (Voorheis) [Mrs. Baylies Coleman]
Voorhies, Rosseau, 5,525
"Vorbei," 13,811
Vorhies, Marsha Fee [Mrs. J. W.], 5,061
Vorse, Mary Marvin (Heaton). [Mrs. Albert] White (1881-1966), 825, **8,144, 11,927, 17,734**
Vosburg, Edith (1876-1961). *See* Alvord, Edith (Vosburg) (1876-1961)
Vosburgh, Hattie Jensen (1865-1957) **11,429**
Vose Family (MA), 7,014
Voskovec, George, 12,367

Voters, 6,495, 9,933, 11,780, 13,533, 15,747
Voters, Afro-American, 8,116
Voters, registration of, 1,281, 1,933, 3,362, 3,443, 4,073, 5,487, **6,422,** 8,534, 9,211, 10,096, 12,056, 12,057, 17,144, 17,599, 17,960
Votes for Women Club (San Francisco, CA), 935
Votes for Women Club (ND), **13,721**
"Votes for Women" Empire State Campaign Committee (NY), 17,217
Votes for Women League of North Dakota, **13,691**
Voth, H. R., 5,196
Voting, 3,158, 3,219
Vow, The (drama), 7,888
Voyageur, The (book), 8,441
Vreeland, Eunice M. Hilton [Mrs. John] Freeland (1899-1975), **12,921**
Vroom, Garret A., 11,041
Vrooman, Lucy C. (1878-1947). *See* Cooper, Lucy C. (Vrooman) [Mrs. William Jonathan] (1878-1947)
Vrooman, Mrs. Carl S., 11,704
Vuitch, Dr., 1,984
Vye, Mary Abbie (Pendergast) [Mrs. John A.] (1865-?), 9,282
WAACs. *See* United States (government), Women's Army Auxiliary Corps
WAC Mothers' Association, **5,368**
WAC Mother's Club, 17,067
WAFs. *See* Women in the Air Force
WCCO radio (MN), 9,467
WCPO-TV (OH), 13,875
WCTU Messenger, The, 1,668
WEAF (radio station), 6,499
WGBH-FM (MA), 6,658
WGBH-TV (MA), 6,034
WGST (radio station, GA), 3,430
WHA (Madison, WI), 17,650
W. K. Kellogg Foundation, 8,045
WLAG radio (MN). *See* WCCO radio (MN)
WMPL Radio Heritage Line (MI), 8,185
WOR (NY), 11,402
W. S. Housing Corporation, 6,382
WTTW (Chicago, IL), 4,058
W. W. Hodkinson Corporation, 11,537
W. W. Norton Company, 11,164
Wabash College (IN), 4,470, 4,489
Wabash-Maumee River Improvement Association (IN), 4,627
Wabasha County Herald (MN), 9,522
Wabasso Woman's Civic Club (MN), **9,516**
Wachter, Mother Mary Bernardine (1846-1901), 14,494
Wackerbarth, Carrie E., 4,899
Waco Bawdy House License Register (TX), **16,393**
Waco Environmental Task Force, "Beautify Waco" Committee (TX), **16,394**
Waco Human Relations Commission (TX), 16,342
Waco Literary Club (TX), **16,395**
Waco Model City Agency (TX), 16,342
Waco Symphony Orchestra (TX), 16,358
Waco University (TX), 16,338, 16,340
Waddell, Catherine (Hughes) [Mrs. Chauncey], 12,708
Waddell Family, 11,130
Waddell, Francis, 14,510
Waddell, James Alexander, 13,151
Waddell, M. J., 14,510
Waddell, Mrs. Hugh, 13,504
Waddell, Mrs. W. H. Coventry, 12,164
Waddell, Susanna (Gordon) [Mrs. James Alexander] (1824-?), **13,151**
Waddell, William Henry, 3,052
Wade, Andrew, IV, 17,608
Wade, Bernice (Galpin) [Mrs. Decius S.], 10,392
Wade, Catherine E., **2,618**
Wade, Clare L. *See* Safford, Clare L. (Wade)
Wade, Decius S. (1835-1905), 10,392
Wade Family (MT), **10,392**
Wade, Frederica (1901-63). *See* Billings, Frederica (Wade) [Mrs. John Shaw] (1901-63)
Wade, Isaac R., **2,618**
Wade, J. D., **3,434**

Wade, Joanna (pseudonym). *See* Berckman, Evelyn Domenica (1900-)
Wade, Margaretta (1857-1945). *See* Delanci, Margaretta (Wade) (1857-1945)
Wade, Minerva [Miss] (1829-1918), **16,838**
Wade, Mrs. John W. (1844-?), **16,142**
Wade, Peyton, 3,371
Wade, Peyton Lisbey, 15,565
Wade, Sarah Louisa (Atkins) (1806-52), 326
Wadel, Margaret, 3,114
Wadhams, Jane, 1,970
Wadley Family, 3,408
Wadley, Mary. *See* Raoul, Mary (Wadley)
Wadley, Sarah, 3,324
Wadley, Sarah Lois [Miss] (1844-?), **13,152**
Wadley, William M., 3,246
Wadman, Lolita, 9,145
Wadman, Martha [Mrs.], 17,018
Wadsworth, Alice Colden, **12,655**
Wadsworth, Catherine (1774-?), 1,878
Wadsworth, David (1771-1848), 1,878
Wadsworth, Eliza P., **6,163**
Wadsworth, Elizabeth (1815-51). *See* Murray, Elizabeth (Wadsworth) (1815-51)
Wadsworth, Emmeline (Austin) (1808-85), 11,466
Wadsworth Family (CT), **1,878**
Wadsworth Family (NY), **11,466**
Wadsworth, Harriet (1769-93), 1,878
Wadsworth, Jeremiah (1743-1804), 1,878
Wadsworth, Martha (Blow) (1864-1934), 11,466
Wadsworth, Mehitabel (Russell) [Mrs. Jeremiah] (1734-1817), 1,878
Wadsworth, Mrs. Daniel, 12,420
Wadsworth, Permelia Stevens. *See* Buckalew, Permelia Stevens (Wadsworth) [Mrs. Charles Rollin]
Wadsworth, Reverend, 7,001
Wadsworth, Vera (?-1968). *See* Beggs, Vera (Wadsworth) [Mrs. Frederic] (?-1968)
Wadsworth, Zilpah (1788-1851). *See* Longfellow, Zilpah (Wadsworth) [Mrs. Stephen] (1788-1851)
Waerenskjold, Elise Tvede [Mrs. Wilhelm] (1815-95), 8,737, 8,768, 8,781, **8,801**
Waerenskjold, Wilhelm, 8,801
Waffle, Elizabeth, 5,063
Wag on the Wall, The (book), 11,182
Wage Earner's Suffrage League, 4,173
Wagenknecht, Helen. *See* Winter, Helen (Wagenknecht)
Wage-price policy, **1,810,** 2,688
Wager, Charles Henry, 7,300
Wagers, Frances, 3,753
Wages, 398, 1,017, 2,684, 3,805, 5,570, 6,192, 6,486, 7,184, 8,073, 8,142, 8,741, 9,877, 9,997, 11,851, 15,253. *See also* Wage-price policy
annual wage, 8,085
clothing workers, 7,664
college employees, 16,325
household workers, 5,570, 14,593
law and legislation, 6,315
lumbermen, 9,078
minimum wage, 1,034, 2,336, 2,504, 4,117, 5,564, 6,402, 6,485, 6,520, 6,565, 6,686, 6,708, 6,848, 6,892, 6,973, 6,977, 7,208, 8,080, 10,032, 11,760, 11,771, 11,773, 14,939, 16,237
law and legislation, 10,953
servants, 14,784
railroads, 2,696
telephone workers, 9,951
Waggoner, Josephine [Mrs.], 10,433
Waggoner, Maude [Mrs.], **9,761**
Wagnalls, Mabel, 2,376
Wagner, Annie Josephine (1846-1950), 16,132
Wagner, Bea, 10,635
Wagner, Cosima [Mrs. Richard] (1837-1930), 9,438
Wagner, Julia Way, 2,396
Wagner, M. E., 9,975
Wagner, Morris, 1,356
Wagner, Mrs. Carl S., 7,884
Wagner, Robert F. (1877-1953), **2,120,** 11,255
Wagner, Robert F., Jr., 11,895, 12,144, 12,149, 12,150
"Wagon Train" (television program), 5,240

Wagon trains, 1,229, 1,505, 10,004, 10,305, 10,645, 10,695, **14,583**
Wagon Wheels to Denver (book), 1,790
Wagons, 8,455
Wagstaff, Blanche Shoemaker, 4,000
Wagstaff, Julia A. [Mrs. W. G.], **12,528**
Wahab, W. S., 13,522
Wahlquist, P. E., **16,969**
Waif's Home, The (New Orleans, LA), 5,426
Wainwright, Amelia Maria [Mrs. Jonathan Mayhew], 12,656
Wainwright, Charlotte (Lumbert) [Mrs. Peter, Jr.], 12,656
Wainwright, Eliza. *See* Channing, Eliza (Wainwright)
Wainwright, Elizabeth (Mayhew) [Mrs. Peter, Sr.], 12,656
Wainwright Family (MA), **12,656**
Wainwright Family (SC), 15,441
Wainwright, Jonathan Mayhew, 12,656
Wainwright, Peter, Sr., 12,656
Wainwright, Peter, Jr., 12,656
Wait, Lucita (Hardie), 13,025
Wait, Mary, 8,948
Wait, Mary Eliza Hopkins [Mrs. William A.] (1836-1930), 9,422
Wait, Richard, 8,948
Wait, William A., Family (MN), **9,422**
Waite, Caroline E., 3,969, 3,970
Waite, Cordelia M., 10,449
Waite, E. G., 11,547
Waite, Eliza, **7,455**
Waite, Harriet Endicott, 2,825
Waite, John Leman (1840-1924), **4,956**
Waite, Letitia (Williams) [Mrs. John Leman], 4,956
Waite, Lola, 4,956
Waites, Addie D. (1875-1943). *See* Hunton, Addie D. (Waites) [Mrs. William Alphaeus] (1875-1943)
Waites, William, 15,459
"Waitin' with the Dead" (article), 17,734
Waiting Time, The (book), 6,027
Waitt, Daisy Bailey [Miss], 13,381
Wake, Esther [Miss], 13,593
Wake Forest College (Winston-Salem, NC), 7,209, 13,390
  alumni, 13,635
Wake Forest Student (NC), 13,398
Wakefield, Elsie Maud (1886-1972), 10,151
Wakefield, Eva (Ingersoll), 17,980
Wakefield Gallery, 2,735
Wakefield, John L. (1823-74), Family (MN), **9,423**
Wakefield, Mrs. George, 9,462
Wakefield, Sarah F. [Mrs. John L.] (ca. 1833-1901), 9,423
Wakeling, Rhea (Higbee) [Mrs. Thomas Alma] (1886-), **16,444**
Wakeman, Andrew Vergil, 14,459
Wakeman, Antoinette V., 9,048
Wakeman, Katherine. *See* Cooper, Katherine (Wakeman)
Wakeman, Letha Evangeline (Ward) [Mrs. Andrew Vergil] (1898-1974), **14,459**
Wakeman, Mary Eliza (Wilson), 890
Wakoski, Diane (1937-), **4,636**, 11,221
Waksman, Deborah Bertha (Mitnik) [Mrs. Selman Abraham], 7,558
Waksman, Selman Abraham (1888-1973), **7,558**
Walbridge, Chastina (1824-57). *See* Rix, Chastina (Walbridge) [Mrs. Alfred] (1824-57)
Walbridge, Lydia R., 3,716
Walbridge, Sally, 1,337
Walcott, Charles D. (1850-1927), **2,726**
Walcott, Helena B. [Mrs. Charles D.] (1858-1911), 2,726
Walcott, Lura Ann (Rust) [Mrs. Charles D.] (1843-76), 2,726
Walcott, Mary Morris (Vaux) [Mrs. Charles D.] (1860-1940), 2,726, 2,849
Wald, Lillian D. (1867-1940), 2,120, 6,122, 6,131, 6,427, 7,315, 7,868, 8,651, 8,652, 8,655, 8,658, 8,659, 8,668, 8,678, 8,686, 11,897, 11,918, 12,008, 12,069, 12,074, 12,351, 12,534, **12,657**, 15,311
Walden, Katherine (Gesell) [Mrs. Joseph Whitelsen], 2,353

Walden School (NY), 15,353
Walder, Anna, 12,163
Walder, Sarah, 12,163
Waldman, Anne (1945-), **4,636**
Waldo, Elizabeth. *See* Hyde, Elizabeth (Waldo) [Mrs. Alvan Phinney]
Waldo, Elizabeth (Vaill), 9,835
Waldo, Martha (1761-1828). *See* Lincoln, Martha (Waldo) [Mrs. Levi, Sr.] (1761-1828)
Waldo, Mary Jane (1915-67), **14,460**
Waldo, Phoebe M., **7,456**
Waldo, Samuel (1695-1759), **5,690**
Waldo, Sarah Tyng (Winslow) [Mrs. Samuel] (1765-1826). *See* Chase, Sarah Tyng (Winslow) [Mrs. Samuel] Waldo [Mrs. Salmon] (1765-1826)
Waldorf College, faculty, 8,746, 8,755
Waldrip, Isaac, 4,772
Waldron, Mary E., 4,838
Waldron, Sally Ann Maltbie [Mrs. Benjamin], 12,174
Waldson, Mother Mary Patricia, 14,874
Wales, Julia Grace [Miss] (1881-), **17,735**
Wales, Lucy Ann [Miss], 9,972
Wales, Nym (pseudonym). *See* Snow, Helen Foster (1907-)
Wales, Ruth Eliza (1849-1929). *See* Isham, Ruth Eliza (Wales) (1849-1929)
Walgreen, Myrtle, 2,376
Walker, Ada, 15,549
Walker, A'lelia, 3,290
Walker, Alice E., 9,282
Walker, Ann Agatha (1829-1908). *See* Pratt, Ann Agatha (Walker) [Mrs. Parley Parker] (1829-1908)
Walker, Anna, 11,750
Walker, Athalia A., 4,276
Walker, Aurora (1826-1900). *See* Coates, Aurora (Walker) (1826-1900)
Walker, Blanche D., 10,397
Walker, Chief, 16,463, 16,876
Walker, Cynthia (Skinner) [Mrs. Hiram] (1792-?), 12,764
Walker, Edith, 11,837
Walker, Elinor Stevens (1909-), 5,580
Walker, Elkanah, **1,498, 17,212**
Walker, Elvira Evelyna (Worth) Jackson (1836-1940). *See* Moffitt, Elvira Evelyna (Worth) Jackson Walker (1836-1940)
Walker, Emma [Mrs.], 16,488
Walker, Emma Dean (1849-78). *See* Armstrong, Emma Dean (Walker) [Mrs. Samuel Chapman] (1849-78)
Walker, Emma Elizabeth (1864?-1954), **7,317, 12,143**
Walker, F. A., 3,755
Walker Family (MD), **5,753**
Walker Family (MA), **7,523**
Walker Family (MA), 7,590
Walker Family (MO), **10,056**
Walker, Galen C. (?-1856), 2,524
Walker, Grace T., 17,678
Walker, Harriet G. Hulet [Mrs. Thomas Barlow], 9,424
Walker, Helen V. [Miss], 8,177
Walker, Hermione (Ross), 13,153
Walker, Hester (Perrine) (1824-post 1885), **2,952**
Walker, Hiram, 12,764
Walker, James, 11,928
Walker, John James, 9,803
Walker, Josephine. *See* Isbell, Josephine (Walker) [Mrs. John C.]
Walker, Judith Page (1802-82). *See* Rives, Judith Page (Walker) [Mrs. William Cabell] (1802-82)
Walker, Katherine [Mrs.], 1,833
Walker, Kenneth James (1913-65), **4,270**
Walker, Lee O., 14,490
Walker, Lois C. (Pilsbury) [Mrs. Galen C.] (1820-1900), 2,524
Walker, Lucy [Mrs. William Perrin], 4,356
Walker, Lucy (1826-1910). *See* Kimball, Lucy (Walker) [Mrs. Joseph] Smith [Mrs. Heber Chase] (1826-1910)
Walker, Lydia Belle. *See* Good, Lydia Belle (Walker)
Walker, Mabel (1889-1963). *See* Willebrandt, Mabel (Walker) (1889-1963)
Walker, Mae Ross (1876-1970), **14,682**

Walker, Mae S., 17,010
Walker, Margaret, 5,469
Walker, Margaret, 3,290
Walker, Margaret Coulson, **4,785**
Walker, Margaret Isabella (1824-?). *See* Weber, Margaret Isabella (Walker) (1824-?)
Walker, Maria (Hopkins), 9,803
Walker, Maria Maud (Leonard) [Mrs. Rex Irving] McCreery [Mrs. James Walter] (1883-1938), 826
Walker, Mary, 12,363
Walker, Mary, 17,029
Walker, Mary Chase (1828-99). *See* Morse, Mary Chase Walker [Mrs. Ephraim W.] (1828-99)
Walker, Mary E. (1852-1907). *See* Walker, Mary E. (Walker) [Mrs. S. T.] (1852-1907)
Walker, Mary E. (Walker) [Mrs. S. T.] (1852-1907), 2,524
Walker, Mary Edwards. [Mrs. Albert] Miller (1832-1919), 3,908, 12,753, **12,754**, 12,765, **12,913**, 14,814, 15,137
Walker, Mary Florence (Morrison) [Mrs. Wilbur Fisk] (1850-1921), **4,538**
Walker, Mary Hubner, 3,204
Walker, Mary Lois (1835-1919). *See* Morris, Mary Lois (Walker) [Mrs. Elias] (1835-1919)
Walker, Mary (Richardson) [Mrs. Elkanah] (1811-97), 1,498, **14,478**, 14,542, **17,212**, 17,373
Walker, Mattie Jane, **3,591**
Walker, Mercedes, 3,799
Walker, Millie Pearl (Hodges) [Mrs. Lee O.] (1893-1964), **14,490**
Walker, Mrs., 12,527
Walker, Mrs. N. E., 15,549
Walker, Mrs. Thomas, 10,877
Walker, Nellie V., 5,002
Walker, Nellie Verne (1874-?), 3,997
Walker, Noverta, 9,811
Walker, Pamela, **5,039**
Walker, Robert (?-ca. 1820), **17,130**
Walker, Sarah (1814-79). *See* Davis, Sarah (Walker) [Mrs. David] (1814-79)
Walker, Susan, 11,534
Walker, Susan, 11,750
Walker, Susan (1811-87), **13,859**
Walker, Susan Rogers, 9,424
Walker, Sydnor H., 12,738, 12,739
Walker, Tacetta [Mrs.], **18,018**
Walker, Thomas, 10,877
Walker, Thomas Barlow (1840-1928), Family (MN), **9,424**
Walker, Ursula (Genung) [Mrs. Kenneth James] (1913-), **4,270**
Walker, Wilbur Fisk, 4,538
Walker, William Perrin, 4,356
Walker, York, 2,618
Walkill Academy, 4,817
"Walkin' and Swingin'" (song), 5,534
Walking Bull, Montana Hopkins Richards [Mrs. Gilbert C.], 14,712
"Walking Delegate, The" (drama), 4,143
Walkley, Mary A. (1824-97). *See* Beach, Mary A. (Walkley) [Mrs. Joseph Wickliff] (1824-97)
Wall, Annie Cassandra Mackintosh, 3,060
Wall Between, The (book), 15,877, 17,608
Wall, Christina McMillen (1818-94), **4,852**
Wall Family, **11,738**
Wall, Jane, 10,327
Wall, Minnie F., 1,786
Wall Street Mission, Industrial School and Social Center (Sioux City, IA), 5,073
Walla Walla Park and Civic Arts Club (WA), **17,424**
Walla Walla Pioneer Association (WA), 14,676
Walla Walla Symphony Orchestra (WA), 17,425
Walla Walla Symphony Society (WA), **17,425**
Walla Walla Women's Reading Club (WA), **10,957**
Wallace, Aggie, 9,098
Wallace, Anna (Widtsoe) (1899-), 16,973
Wallace, Calla, 4,000
Wallace, Carolyn, 13,055
Wallace, Elizabeth (1865-1960), **9,425**
Wallace, Elizabeth "Bess". *See* Truman, Elizabeth "Bess" (Wallace) [Mrs. Harry S.]
Wallace, Ethel, 14,379
Wallace Family (KY), 5,343

Wallace, Frances (Woolfolk) (1835-?), **13,154**
Wallace, George C., 102
Wallace, George S., 17,453
Wallace, Henry Agard (1888-1965), 2,589, 3,303, 4,970, 17,238, 17,304
Wallace, Lewis (1827-1905), **4,615**, 5,968
Wallace, Lillian Frances (Parker), **13,155**, 13,501
Wallace, Lola. *See* Harris, Lola (Wallace)
Wallace, Lorabel. *See* Wallace, Sister Mary Imelda
Wallace, Lucille [Mrs.] (1897-), 169
Wallace, Lucy Bryant (1876-1962). *See* Porter, Lucy Bryant (Wallace) [Mrs. Arthur Kingsley] (1876-1962)
Wallace, Madge (Gates) [Mrs. George], 10,073, 10,082
Wallace, Martha Louvenia (1862-1947). *See* Donaghey, Martha Louvenia (Wallace) [Mrs. George Washington] (1862-1947)
Wallace, Mary, 14,308
Wallace, Mary (Longstreet) (1906-), **15,196**
Wallace, Mary "May" Southern [Mrs. George Porterfield], 10,087
Wallace, Minnie (McIntyre), 17,498
Wallace, Miriam Amanda (1875-1961). *See* Ferguson, Miriam Amanda "Ma" (Wallace) [Mrs. Jim] (1875-1961)
Wallace, Mrs. Henry E., 325
Wallace, Mrs. John (1898-), 16,965
Wallace, Mrs. Robert M., **15,762**
Wallace, Nancy (Black) (1846-1918), 10,185
Wallace, Sister Mary Imelda, 159
Wallace, Susan (Arnold) Elston [Mrs. Lewis] (1830-1907), 4,615, **5,968**
Wallach, Erica (1922-), **6,106**
Walladoid Academy, 15,959
Wallbridge, Mary E. (Ritchie), 3,518
Walleck, Marguerite C. (1874-1977), 4,310
Waller, Kate Harwood (1857-1925). *See* Barrett, Kate Harwood (Waller) [Mrs. Robert South] (1857-1925)
Waller, Mary Virginia E., **5,819**
Waller, Mrs., 618
Walling, Anna (Strunsky) [Mrs. William English] (1879-1964), **825**, 1,499
Walling, William English (?-1936), 825
Wallingford Community (CT), 1,590
Wallis, Benjamin, 7,488
Wallis, Gertrude (Steel-Brooke) [Mrs. Ross] (?-1974), **1,219**
Wallis, Mary Davis Cook [Mrs. Benjamin], **7,488**
Wallis, Ruth Sawtell, 8,600
Wallis, Wilson D., 433
Walls Came Tumbling Down, The (book), 2,144, 6,006
Walls of Gold (book), 692
Wallworth, Mary Elizabeth (1812-75), 12,847
Waln Family (PA), 15,104
Walnut, 1,229
Walpole, Hugh, 4,482
Walrad, Jane H. (Mullen) [Mrs. David P.] (1823-1900), **14,491**
Walsh, Adelaide [Miss], 3,932
Walsh, Aimee Shands, Family, **9,762**
Walsh, Blanch (1873-1915), 10,651
Walsh, Catherine Louise, 12,658
Walsh, Celia. *See* Bradley, Celia (Walsh)
Walsh, Edward F., **17,355**
Walsh, Evalyn (1886-1947). *See* McLean, Evalyn (Walsh) [Mrs. Edward "Ned" Beale] (1886-1947)
Walsh, Frank P. (1864-1939), **12,658**
Walsh, Grace, 12,658
Walsh, Helen [Mrs. Joseph] Wilshire [Mrs. William J.], 1,837
Walsh, Helen Julia Mason [Mrs. Edward F.], **17,355**
Walsh, Jean H., **9,763**
Walsh, Katherine. *See* Webb, Katherine (Walsh)
Walsh, Katherine O'Flaherty [Mrs. Frank P.], 12,658
Walsh, M., 12,658
Walsh, Mary (1912-). *See* Scott, Mary (Walsh) Lavin [Mrs. Michael MacDonald] (1912-)
Walsh, Mary Blaise (1883-1968). *See* Durkin, Mary Blaise (Walsh) [Mrs. Edmund J., Sr.] (1883-1968)
Walsh, Mary Theresa, 720
Walsh, Mother Augustine, 7,694

Walsh, Mrs. H. (1841-?), 3,730
Walsh, Mrs. James W., 12,658
Walsh, Mrs. T. J., 3,681
Walsh, Pauline Altman, 12,658
Walsh, Phyllis J. (1897-), **10,784**
Walsh, Richard J., 1,564, 1,565
Walsh, Sister Francis Marie, 12,658
Walsh, Sister Mary Joanna, 1,790
Walsh, Townsend (?-1941), **12,659**
Walsh, Virginia, 12,658
Walsworth, Edward Brown (1819-92), 864
Walsworth Family (CA), **864**
Walsworth, Sarah A. (Pierson) [Mrs. Edward Brown] (1829-?), 864
Walt Disney Productions, 5,994
Walt, Mrs., 8,301
Walt Whitman, Builder for America (book), 12,441
Waltemath, Elizabeth (ca. 1870-1900). *See* Welty, Elizabeth (Waltemath) [Mrs. John] (ca. 1870-1900)
Walter, A. F. [Mrs. Paul], 11,234
Walter Baker Chocolate Company, **6,207**
Walter, Bruno, 1,527, 12,013
Walter, Catherine (Ronyak), 17,859
Walter, Dorothy Blake (1908-), **6,107**
Walter, Dorothy C., 17,032
Walter Family (MI), **7,969**
Walter Family (MS), 9,656
Walter, Hulda Sanger (1867-1929), **16,143**
Walter J. Black, Inc. (NY), 11,644
Walter, J. L., 10,471
Walter, Mrs. J. L., 10,471
Walter Reed General Hospital, 2,091, 17,984
Walter, Rosalie (1908-). *See* Wolf, Rosalie (Walter) (1908-)
Walter, Thomas, 15,428
Walter, Valerie Harrise, **2,826**
Walters, Barbara, 17,991
Walters, Carrie (Stevens) (?-1907), 820
Walters, Catherine (Lanker), 1,533
Walters, Ethel, 12,004
Walters, Louise Cook, **3,731**
Walters, Rose, 10,714
Walters, Thorstina (Jackson) [Mrs. Emile] (?-1959), **13,692**
Walthall Family (MS), 9,816
Walthall, Margaret C. "Kate" (1828-1919). *See* Freeman, Margaret C. "Kate" (Walthall) [Mrs. George R.] (1828-1919)
Waltham Training School for Nurses (MA), **6,164**
Waltham Woman Suffrage Society (MA), **5,969**
Walton, Alice R. *See* Long, Alice R. Walton [Mrs. Elisha V.]
Walton, Audrey (1890-), 9,426, 9,427
Walton, Dorothy (1894-). *See* Binder, Dorothy (Walton) [Mrs. Carroll] (1894-)
Walton, Edmund George (1865-1919), **9,426, 9,427**, 9,876
Walton, Edmund George (1865-1919), Family (MN), **9,426, 9,427**
Walton, Elizabeth, 12,738
Walton, Ellen Pauline (1879-1966), **14,306**
Walton, Jesse Pusey, 15,297
Walton, Joseph S., 15,297
Walton, Joshua J., 14,461
Walton, Margaretta (Walton) [Mrs. Jesse Pusey] (1829-1904), **15,297**
Walton, Nellie Allen (Ingram) [Mrs. Edmund George] (1866-1945), 9,426, 9,427, **9,876**
Walton, Pauline (1879-1966), 14,461
Walton, Sophia Peet Glaskin [Mrs. Edmund], 9,427
Walton, William, 11,325
Walulah (drama), 14,575
Walworth, Ann Elizabeth (1817-95), 12,847
Walworth, Clarence Agustus (1820-1900), 12,847
Walworth College (MS), alumnae, 9,556
Walworth, Ellen (Hardin) [Mrs. Mansfield Tracy] (1832-1915), 12,847
Walworth Family (NY), **12,847**
Walworth, Francis DeLord (1834-39), 12,847
Walworth, Maria Averill [Mrs. Reuben Hyde] (1795-1847), 12,847
Walworth, Mansfield Trace (1830-73), 12,847
Walworth, Reuben Hyde (1788-1867), 12,847

Walworth, Sarah E. [Mrs. John J.] Hardin [Mrs. Reuben Hyde] (1811-74), 12,847
Walworth, Sarah Simonds (1815-87), 12,847
Walz, Christina Magdelena (1845-1920), **3,740**
Walz, Eliza. *See* Tadje, Eliza (Walz)
Walz, Maggie, 8,185
Walzer, Michael L., 6,482
Wambaugh, Sarah (1882-1955), **6,935**
"Wanalane or Glimpses of Southern Life" (ms), 9,552
Wanamaker, John, 6,244
Wanamaker, Pearl Anderson (1899-), 17,178, **17,356**
Wanda, Gág, Memorial Fund, 9,360
Wang, Caroline "Lonny" Rulon. *See* Myers, Caroline "Lonny" Rulon. [Mrs. Shu-Yu] Wang (1922-)
Wang, Shu-Yu, 4,131
Wangensteen, Sarah A. Davidson [Mrs. Owen], 8,910
Wann, Susanna (1825-85). *See* Hunter, Susanna (Wann) [Mrs. Edward] (1825-85)
Wanous, Josie A. (1871-1936). *See* Stuart, Josie A. Wanous [Mrs. Arthur] (1871-1936)
Wanton Family, 11,599, 11,600
War, 2,671, 8,144, 8,798, 12,487
  civilian relief, 2,072, 7,191, 17,241
  civilians' work, 4,390, 6,365, 13,193, 15,583
  economics aspects, 1,897, 10,071, 13,350. *See also* Rationing, consumer
  relief of sick and wounded, 54, 3,229, 6,487, 6,644, 7,531, 8,487, **8,835, 15,103**, 17,830, 17,831. *See also* Hospitals, military; Red Cross
War and emergency powers, United States, 15,317
War and literature, 3,980
War brides, **12,718**, 12,729
War Camp Community Service, 6,239, 12,729
War Camp Community Service Club of Savannah (GA), **3,592**
War correspondents, 1,417, 2,207, **2,240, 2,622,** 3,602, 4,061, **6,011**, 6,023, 7,216, **12,553**, 17,379, **17,614**
War Council (CT), **1,936**
War Council (CT), Women's Division, 1,936
War crime trials, 10,070
War Finance Committee, 13,241
War Finance Committee, Fort Pitt Area (PA), 14,834
"War Journal of a Pacifist," 15,290
War Memorial Opera House (San Francisco, CA), 1,293
War memorials, 3,437, 5,608, 6,965, 13,344, 17,102
War Mother's Service Star Legion, 3,250
"War of Survival, The" (poem), 2,552
War poetry, **2,351**
War Production Program, 13,350
War Resisters' League, 11,931, **15,313**, 17,939
War Savings Committee, 17,685
War Savings Stamps, 15,121
War Work Council, 16,128
"War Work of the Women of Duluth, The," 8,447
Warashina, Patti. [Mrs. Bauer], **17,236**
Warber, Esther Maxine, **7,970**
Warburton, Lillian Grace Chadwick (1901-), 16,953
Ward, A. L., 16,360
Ward, Angela Gizzi, 1,357
Ward, Anna, 8,670
Ward, Barbara Mary Lady Jackson [Mrs Robert Gillman Allen J.] (1914-), 4,067, 4,640, 9,449, 12,069, **12,072**
Ward-Belmont School (Nashville, TN), **15,973**
Ward, Carolina, 15,697
Ward, Cynthia Ann Earle, 284
Ward, Dr., 7,458
Ward, Effie [Mrs. Thomas], 14,459
Ward, Elizabeth C. (1839-?), **7,457**
Ward, Elizabeth Phelps, 4,244
Ward, Elizabeth Stuart (Phelps) [Mrs. Herbert Dickinson] (1844-1911), 1,426, **1,500, 5,970,** 6,714, 6,762, **6,936**, 7,398, **7,458**, 12,529, 14,062, 17,010, 17,053
Ward, Ella, **8,214**
Ward, Ellen [Mrs.], 3,398
Ward, Emma, 16,915
Ward, Emma France (1886-1963), 4,684, **7,318**
Ward, Essie (Treat) (1902-), **248**
Ward Family, 6,663
Ward Family, 4,971
Ward, Florence E., 11,662

Ward, Florence J. B., 11,662
Ward, Genevieve (1838-1922), 16,150
Ward, Grace Faulkner, 11,940
Ward, Grace R. (1844-1922), **4,271**
Ward, Harriet (Sherrill) (1803-65), **865**, 1,505
Ward, Henrietta Jaquelina (1814-90). *See* Clarke, Henrietta Jaquelina (Ward) [Mrs. Freeman] (1814-90)
Ward, Henry Dana, **12,660**
Ward, Herbert Dickinson, 1,426, 1,500
Ward, J. E. H., 284
Ward, Julia (1819-1910). *See* Howe, Julia (Ward) [Mrs. Samuel Gridley] (1819-1910)
Ward, Kate, 10,045
Ward, Katherine Bertha B. [Mrs. Ralph] (1900-), **866, 8,891**, 11,846
Ward, Kathleen, 2,284
Ward, Letha Evangeline (1898-1974). *See* Wakeman, Letha Evangeline (Ward) [Mrs. Andrew Vergil] (1898-1974)
Ward, Louisa. *See* Arps, Louisa (Ward)
Ward, Louise (1890-1974). *See* Watkins, Louise (Ward) [Mrs. Edward Francis] (1890-1974)
Ward, Lydia Arms Avery Coonley [Mrs.] (1845-1924), 11,618
Ward, Lyman, 8,116
Ward, Margaret (Beecher), 6,394
Ward, Marjorie (1898-). *See* Falconer, Marjorie (Ward) (1898-)
Ward, Mary Augusta (Arnold) [Mrs. Humphrey] (1851-1920), 12,022, 12,637, **12,661**
Ward, Mary (Holyoke) (1800-80), 7,385
Ward, Mary Jane (1905-), **6,108**
Ward, May (Williams) [Mrs. Merle] (1882-1975), **5,242**
Ward, Morgan, 14,538
Ward, Prudence, 17,010
Ward, Rufus, **9,812**
Ward, Samuel (1814-84), **12,662**
Ward, Sarah Wood, 2,293
Ward Seminary (Nashville, TN). *See* Ward-Belmont School (Nashville, TN)
Ward, Sophia Langdon (1855-?), **7,459**
Ward, Susan (1779-1860). *See* Ward, Susannah (Holyoke) [Mrs Joshua] (1779-1860)
Ward, Susannah (Holyoke) [Mrs. Joshua] (1779-1860), **7,460**
Ward, Thomas, 14,459
Ward, Thornton, 3,246
Ward, Viola, **4,853**
Ward, W. M., 3,102
Ward, William Hayes, 1,433, 17,210, 17,454
Ward, Winifred [Miss] (1884-1975), **4,222, 15,901**
Warde, Beatrice, 1,573
Warde, Mother Frances Xavier (1810?-84), 10,888
Warden, David Bailie (1772-1845), **5,820**
Warden, Mary. *See* Bingham, Mary (Warden) [Mrs. Kingsley Scott]
Warden, Rebecca (?-1872). *See* Vail, Rebecca (Warden) [Mrs. Emmor K.] (?-1872)
Warden, Selina Clark [Mrs.], **8,372**
Warder, Ann [Mrs. John], **15,104**
Warder, E. H. [Miss], **15,105**
Warder, John, 15,104
Wardle, Constance, 11,427
Wardle Family (NY), **11,427**
Wardle, Hazel [Mrs.], 16,876
Wardwell, Florence, 5,122
Wardwell, Frances, 2,694
Wardwell, W. C., 13,652
Ware, Agnes. *See* Bishop, Agnes (Ware) [Mrs. J. L.]
Ware, Caroline Farrar (1899-), 6,895, 11,806
Ware, Carolyn, 1,594
Ware, Clementine (1820-1913). *See* Butler, Clementina (Ware) (1820-1913)
Ware, Elizabeth Roy. *See* Bruchholz, Elizabeth Roy (Ware) [Mrs. Henry]
Ware Family, 3,054
Ware, Florence, **16,970**
Ware, Florentine (1915-), 17,232, **17,357**
Ware, Helen (1877-1939), 536, 16,150
Ware, Henry A., Jr., 6,354
Ware, Maria T. *See* Lee, Maria T. (Ware)
Ware, Mary Coffin (1872-1947). *See* Dennett, Mary

Coffin (Ware) [Mrs. William Hartley] (1872-1947)
Ware, Runa Erwin [Mrs.], **3,111**
Warenski, Marilyn (1931-), **16,971**
Warf Theatre (MA), 12,623
Warfel, Linda (1850-1911). *See* Slaughter, Linda (Warfel) [Mrs. Benjamin Franklin] (1850-1911)
Warfield, Elisha, 9,552
Warfield Family (MS), 9,551
Warfield, Florence. *See* Sillers, Florence (Warfield)
Warfield, Mary Anderson (Carson), 9,545, 9,551, **9,552**
Warfield, Susanna (1797-1890), **5,821**
Warfield, Wallis (1896-). *See* Windsor, Wallis (Warfield) Simpson (1896-)
Warhurst, Mary L. Powelson [Mrs. C. C.] (?-1968), 5,063, **5,070**
Waring, Ethel Bushnell (1887-), **11,739**
Waring, Joseph Frederick, **3,593**
Waring, Lucretia (Cole) [Mrs. Howard S.], 1,032
Waring, Malvina Sarah Black (1842-1930), **15,763**
Waring, Mary D., **78**
Waring, Mrs. Clark, 15,597
Waring, Mrs. L. W., 15,769
Waring, Olive Howard, 1,032
Warley Bascom's Sons (PA), 15,106
Warlick, Laura Cornelia (McGimsey) [Mrs. Lewis] (1840-1920), **13,061**
Warlick, Lewis, 13,061
Warm Spring Indian Reservation (OR), 14,609
Warm Springs, 11,853
Warn, Kate [Mrs.], 11,440
Warne, Colston E. (1900-), 11,805, **11,806**
Warner, Agnes (Stewart) [Mrs. Mason Young] (1832-1905), 606, 1,505, **14,307**, 14,462, 14,628
Warner, Alexander L., 867
Warner, Anna Bartlett (1824-1915), 12,930
Warner, Charles D., 3,665
Warner, Charles Dudley (1829-1900), **1,963**, 5,414, 12,350
Warner, Chester H., 867
Warner, Claire. *See* Churchill, Claire (Warner)
Warner, Edith, 14,448
Warner, Electa. *See* Allen, Electa (Warner)
Warner, Elisabeth "Lilly" (Gillette) [Mrs. George] (1835-1915), 1,948
Warner, Elizabeth Young (Stewart) (1822-1914), 1,505, 14,282, 14,307
Warner, Emalea (Pusey) [Mrs. Alfred D.] (1853-1948), **2,058**
Warner, Emily (Smith) [Mrs. John], **11,928**
Warner, Esther Sietmann (1910-), **6,109**
Warner Family (NY), 12,930
Warner Family (OR), 14,714
Warner, Florence M., 984
Warner, Frank, 16,486
Warner, Mary Eliza (1849-1922). *See* Maloon, Mary Eliza (Warner) (1849-1922)
Warner, Mason Young (1868-1957), **14,462**
Warner, Minnie, **4,680**
Warner, Mrs. Charles Dudley, 1,963, 12,350
Warner, Rebecca (?-1819). *See* Shoemaker, Rebecca (Warner) Rawle [Mrs. Samuel] (?-1819)
Warner, Sarah, 8,164
Warner, Sarah MacKaye (1840-76), 10,868
Warner, Susan Bogert (1819-85), 12,930
Warner, Sylvia Townsend (1893-), 2,403
Warnock, Irvin L. (1892-1974), **16,564**
Warnock, Lexia D. [Mrs. Irvin L.] (1890-), **16,564**
Waroe, Lillie, 9,467
Warr, Vernille DeWitt, **868**
Warren, Alma, 2,882
Warren, Althea [Miss], 1,216
Warren, Audrey [Mrs.], **9,733**
Warren, Caroline C. Parsons [Mrs. Waters], 8,154
Warren, Constance (1880-), 2,067, 11,300, 11,306, 11,910
Warren, Earl, **458**, 504, 645, 1,140, **1,152**, 17,259
Warren, Fred D., 8,070
Warren, Fuller, 2,882
Warren, Gouverneur Kemble (1830-82), 13,039
Warren, Helen Frances. *See* Pershing, Helen Frances Warren [Mrs. John J.]
Warren, Helen M., 14,542

Warren, Irene, **3,263**
Warren, James, 1,501
Warren, James (1757-?), 2,619
Warren, James H., **9,384**
Warren, James Lloyd LaFayette (1805-96), **869**
Warren, Julia A. (1832-?). *See* Spears, Julia A. (Warren) (1832-?)
Warren, Katherine, 2,927
Warren, Lillian P., 11,923
Warren, Lyman, 9,384
Warren, M. Frances, 14,819
Warren, Mary "Molly" (1880-1974). *See* Wilcox, Mary "Molly" (Warren) [Mrs. Edwin F.] (1880-1974)
Warren, Meliscent (1797-1861). *See* Goodale, Meliscent (Warren) [Mrs. David] (1797-1861)
Warren, Mercy (Otis) [Mrs. James] (1728-1814), **1,501, 2,619**, 2,621, 6,741
Warren, Nina Elizabeth "Honeybear," 1,152
Warren, Nina P. (Meyers) [Mrs. Earl], 1,152
Warren, Robert Penn, 2,283, 9,769, 11,832, 11,969, 12,042
Warren Street Mission (MA), 7,064
Warren, Viola Lockhart [Mrs. Stafford L.] (1896-1968), **1,020**
Warren, Waters, 8,154
Warren, William, 9,384
Warrenton Female Academy (NC). *See* Warrenton Female College (NC)
Warrenton Female College (NC), 13,425, 13,471, 13,534, 13,610
Warships, 12,554
Wartels, E., 14,324
Wartenberg, Isabelle von Sazenhofen [Mrs. Robert], **1,383**
Wartime Committee on Personnel in the Social Services, **8,683**
War-time Journal of a Georgia Girl (book), 59
Wartstill, Emma. *See* Nielson, Emma (Wartstill) Mecham [Mrs. Frihoff Godfrey]
Warwick, Anne, 12,413
Waseca County Sunday School Association (MN), **9,429**
Washaki, Chief, 16,488
Washburn, Catherine Amanda (Stansbury) [Mrs. Charles] (1835-94), 606, 1,505
Washburn, Elizabeth Bancroft (Cheever) [Mrs. Ichabod] (1812-98), 7,611
Washburn, Emery (1800-77), 6,937
Washburn, Emily (1870-1958). *See* Dean, Emily (Washburn) (1870-1958)
Washburn, Hannah Blaney Thatcher, **12,663**
Washburn, Ives, 12,542
Washburn, Julia K. *See* Morrison, Julia K. Washburn [Mrs. Clinton]
Washburn, Mae L. [Mrs. George H.], 9,352
Washburn, Margaret Floy [Miss] (1871-1939), 2,668
Washburn, Mary Louise (Savier) [Mrs. Robert Charles] (1867-1963), 14,683
Washburn, Minnie (ca. 1835-?), 6,937
Washburn, Mrs. Abbot McConnell, 11,857
Washburn, Mrs. Samuel B., **12,664**
Washburn, Robert Charles (?-1938), **14,683**
Washburn University (Topeka, KS), 6,784
  archives, 5,235
Washington, 14,546, 17,140, 17,148, 17,153, **17,178**, 17,180, 17,205, 17,272, 17,339, 17,369, 17,401
  abortion
    law and legislation, **17,358**
    legal aspects, 17,367
  actresses, 17,393
  Afro-Americans, 17,163
  agriculture, 17,249, 17,271
  archives, Jewish, **17,282**
  archivists, 17,368
  art
    exhibitions, 17,236, 17,261, 17,296, 17,312, 17,316, 17,323, 17,332, 17,362
    galleries and museums, 17,243, 17,366
  art dealers, **17,243, 17,261**
  art patrons, 17,366
  art societies, 17,179, 17,269, **17,288**
  artists, **17,235, 17,309, 17,312, 17,321, 17,323**, 17,362, 17,413

associations, institutions, etc., 17,245
attorneys general, 17,260
authors, **17,131**, 17,174, **17,248**, **17,259**, 17,343, **17,369**, 17,401
  19th-20th C, 432, 17,221, **17,277**
  20th C, **17,336**, **17,374**, **17,387**
autobiographies, 17,258, **17,339**
automobile agencies, 17,139
automobile mechanics, 17,139
bankers, 17,135, 17,185, **17,370**
bar associations, 17,260
bills, legislative, 17,376
boxing, 17,376
breach of contract, 17,230
building and loan associations, **17,276**
businessmen, 17,293, **17,335**, 17,390
businesswomen, **17,241**
canteens (war-time, emergency, etc.), 17,184
Catholic schools, 17,229
charitable societies, Jewish, **13,793**
charities, 17,220, 17,314
charities, Jewish, **17,247**
child psychology, **17,270**
children, hospitals, 17,241
church records and registers, Methodist, **17,157**
church societies, Baptist, 17,246
churches, 17,227
churches, Baptist, 17,285
cities and towns, civic improvement, **17,138**
citizens associations, 17,314, 17,357
city councilwomen, 17,257, **17,289**, 17,314, 17,324, **17,342**
city planners, **17,279**
civil defense, 17,278
civil rights, 17,245, 17,260, 17,365
civil rights workers, **17,234**, **17,259**, 17,357
clergy, Methodist, **17,227**
clubs, **17,134**, 17,135, **17,136**, **17,138**, **17,158**, **17,177**, **17,211**, **17,228**, 17,246, 17,267, 17,299, 17,375, 17,376, **17,388**, 17,394, **17,399**, **17,412**, **17,424**, **17,611**
coal miners, 17,232
college discipline, 17,354
college librarians, 17,209
college teachers, **17,187**, **17,230**, **17,240**, **17,263**, **17,266**, **17,303**, **17,322**
Colville Indians, **17,383**
Communist party, 17,278
communists, 17,254
community art projects, 17,255, **17,334**, 17,366
community churches, **17,161**
community leadership, **17,237**, 17,260
community organization, 17,357
conductors (music), 17,425
congresswomen, 1,605, **17,200**, **17,268**
conservationists, **17,305**, **17,364**
consumer cooperatives, 17,238, 17,340
county government, records and correspondence, **17,143**
crime and criminals, public opinion, 17,256
deans (in schools), **17,203**, 17,291, **17,352**
department heads (universities), 17,230
diaries and journals, 1,773, 17,135, 17,225
dramatists, **14,313**, **17,391**
educational associations, 17,369
educators, **17,194**, **17,291**, **17,341**
eight-hour movement, 17,376
elections, 17,260, 17,324
employment, 17,233, 17,289
employment agencies, 17,196
equal rights amendment (proposed), **17,253**, 17,317
executive advisory bodies, 17,238, 17,300, 17,340
farm life, 17,199
farmers, 1,773, 17,183
feminists, **17,256**, 17,367
flower shows, 17,146
gardening, societies, etc., **17,137**, **17,146**, **17,147**, **17,155**, 17,314
government librarians, 342
governmental investigations, 17,350
governors, 14,318, 17,226, 17,293, **17,376**, 17,409
greek letter societies, **17,288**
health education, 17,230
high school teachers, **17,140**

high schools, curricula, 17,140
highway planning, 17,279
historians, **17,368**
historical societies, 14,676, **17,136**, 17,160, 17,241
home economics extension work, 5,048
home economists, **17,194**
hospitals, 17,229, 17,415
hotels, taverns, etc., 413, 17,406
hours of labor, 17,376
housewives, 17,195, **17,225**
immigrants, 17,285, 17,379
immigrants, German, 17,379
immigrants, Jewish, 17,282
impresarios, **17,333**
Indian agents, **17,404**
industrial safety, 17,376
interracial marriage, 17,160, 17,162
Japanese Americans, 17,285, 17,301
Jews, social life and customs, 17,282
journalists, 17,343, 17,390, 17,413
jury, 17,376
labor and laboring classes, 17,343
land settlement, 17,416
lawyers, 17,169, 17,241, **17,260**, **17,370**, **17,378**, **17,396**
legislative councils, 17,281
legislators, 17,135, 17,141, **17,201**, **17,254**, 17,260, 17,264, **17,268**, **17,300**, 17,311, **17,347**, 17,356
letters, **17,152**
librarians, **17,394**
libraries and community, **17,395**
library associations, 17,394
literary societies, 17,269, **17,310**, **17,426**
little theaters, 17,393
lobbyists, **17,253**
lumbering, 17,274
massacres, 17,173, 17,422
mayors, 17,257, 17,264, **17,289**, 17,293
mental hygiene, 17,245
mines and mineral resources, 413, 17,249
missionaries, **1,755**, 17,167, **17,213**, 17,404, **17,410**, **17,421**
missionaries, Baptist, **17,285**, 17,301
missionaries, Methodist, **17,227**
missions, 17,167, 17,301
monasteries, **17,215**
monasticism and religious orders for women, Catholic, **17,145**, **17,229**, **17,381**, **17,415**, **17,428**
municipal officials and employees, **17,279**
music, 17,384
music teachers, **17,234**
musical societies, **17,132**, **17,134**, **17,223**, 17,380
Native Americans, 17,249, 17,263, 17,266
  language, 17,252
  missions, 880, 17,421, 17,422
  wars, 17,271, 17,355
naval districts, 17,245
newspapers, sections, columns, etc., 17,267, 17,378
Nez Percé Indians, wars, **17,355**
nuns, Catholic, **17,415**
nurses, **17,291**
nursing, history, 17,291
nursing schools, 17,224, **17,353**, **17,385**, **17,386**
officials and employees, **17,409**
opera, 17,298
oral history, **17,151**, **17,163**, **17,379**, **17,384**
orphans and orphan asylums, 17,377, 17,380, 17,415
pacifists, **17,244**
painters, **17,231**, **17,269**, **17,280**, **17,283**, **17,284**, **17,294**, **17,312**, **17,316**, **17,320**, **17,325**, **17,332**, **17,350**, 17,401
parents' and teachers' associations, 17,314, **17,318**, 17,372
patriotic societies, 14,676, **17,149**, **17,156**, 17,293, 17,390, **17,392**, **17,403**
peace societies, 17,254
philanthropists, **17,241**, **17,377**
photographers, **17,407**
physicians, **17,133**, 17,185, **17,278**, **17,337**
pianists, **17,333**
pioneers and settlers, 538, **17,136**, **17,151**, 17,170, 17,196, **17,242**, **17,258**, **17,271**, **17,273**, **17,275**,

17,329, 17,330, 17,346, 17,349, 17,361, 17,363, 17,401, 17,414, 17,416, 17,418, 17,419
pioneers and settlers, Danish, **17,290**
poets, **17,131**, **17,277**
political activists, women, **17,319**
politicians, 14,683, 17,238, **17,260**
politics and government, 17,368
politics, practical, women's activism, 17,246, 17,257, **17,292**, 17,300, 17,314, 17,326, 17,341, 17,348
potters, **17,243**
poultry breeding, 17,278
printers, 17,302
prohibition, 17,363
prostitution, 17,377
psychiatric hospitals, 17,415
public libraries, 17,241
public officers, 17,245, 17,376
public utilities, **17,340**
public welfare administration, 17,356
radio broadcasting, 17,298
radio programs, 17,368
railroads, officials and employees, 17,209
rationing, consumer, 17,139
reporters and reporting, **17,259**, 17,379
school boards, 17,343, 17,357
school superintendents and principals, **17,133**, **17,182**
schools, 17,227, 17,372, 17,415
schools, Native American, 17,415
scrapbooks, **17,153**, **17,162**
senators, United States, 17,251, 17,378, 17,409
Sephardim, 17,282
singers, 17,163, **17,380**
social life and customs, 14,283, 17,242, 17,302, 17,375
social reformers, **17,246**
social settlements, Jewish, 17,247
social workers, **17,244**, **17,295**
societies, Afro-American, **17,234**, 17,285
societies, etc., **17,311**
societies, Jewish, 17,342
state universities and colleges, 17,315
strikebreakers, Afro-American, 17,232
strikes and lockouts, 17,343
student housing, 17,354
students' societies, 17,233, 17,354
suffrage, 17,166, 17,171, 17,225, 17,228, 17,264, 17,377
suffrage societies, 17,166
suffragists, **17,171**, **17,257**, 17,376
summer theaters, 17,391
Sunday school teachers, 17,157
symphony orchestra societies, **17,425**
taxation, 17,300
teachers, **14,613**, 17,133, **17,140**, 17,163, **17,189**, **17,238**, **17,273**, **17,280**, **17,340**, **17,369**, **17,374**, **17,379**
teachers' colleges, 17,381
temperance, 17,264
temperance societies, **17,154**, 17,376
theater, **17,281**, 17,384
trade and professional associations, 17,230, 17,297, **17,359**, **17,360**
trade-unions, 17,278, 17,376
trials (murder), 17,343
unemployed, 17,278
universities and colleges, 17,167, 17,380
  archives, **17,142**
voluntary health agencies, 17,230
volunteer workers in social service, 17,220
voters, registration of, 17,144
widows, 11,015
wildlife conservation, 17,248, 17,251, 17,267
women
  civil rights, 17,233
  employment, 17,233
women's studies, 17,352, **17,354**
World war II, personal narratives, 17,163
Young Women's Christian Association, 17,141, **17,367**
Washington Advisory Board on Historic Sites, 17,266
Washington, Anita [Miss], 3,264
Washington, Anne, 2,609

Washington, Augustine, 2,187
Washington, Booker T., 2,602, 3,092
Washington Boulevard School of Nursing (Chicago, IL), **4,017**
Washington By-line (book), 2,340
Washington Calling (newsletter), 14,622
Washington, Capital City, 1879-1950 (book), 2,365
Washington Child Research Center (DC), 2,069
Washington Citizens for Abortion Reform (WA), **17,358**
Washington City Orphan Asylum, 11,154
Washington College of Law, alumnae, 4,269
Washington Commonwealth Federation (WA), 17,254, 17,278
Washington Conference on Voting Restrictions (1960), 15,877
Washington Congress of Parents, Teachers, and Students, 17,314, **17,318**
Washington Conservatory of Music (DC), **2,155**
Washington Consumers League (DC), 827
Washington County Historical Society (MS), 9,781
Washington, Cynthia Beverley (Tucker) (1832-1908). *See* Coleman, Cynthia Beverley (Tucker) Washington [Mrs. Charles Washington] (1832-1908)
Washington Disarmament Conference (1921-1922), 6,771
Washington, Elizabeth Foote [Mrs. Lund], 2,620
Washington Environmental Council, 17,305
Washington Equal Rights Amendment campaign, 17,317
Washington Equal Suffrage Association, 17,166, 17,171
Washington Family, **2,620**
Washington Family (TN), 15,974
Washington, Fanny Bassett [Mrs. George Augustine]. *See* Lear, Fanny Bassett [Mrs. George Augustine] Washington [Mrs. Tobias]
Washington Federation of Colored Women's Clubs, 17,299
Washington Female Seminary, 7,932
Washington, Frances [Mrs.], 1,502
Washington, Fredi. [Mrs. H. Anthony] Bell, **5,478**
Washington, George (1732-99), **1,502**, 2,187, 2,257, 2,281, 2,326, 2,620, **2,621**, 2,931, 3,509, 4,506, 7,671, 11,173, 11,184, 12,697, 15,037, 15,041, 15,077, 15,681, 15,703, 16,045, 17,064
Washington, George Augustine, 15,974
Washington, Hannah (Fairfax) (ca. 1738-1810), 2,620
Washington Heights Study Club (Pasadena, CA), **1,106**
Washington, Jane (Smith) [Mrs. George Augustine], 15,974
Washington, Joseph (1770-1848), 15,974
Washington Law School, 10,658
Washington Library Association, 17,394
Washington, Lola [Miss], 3,264
Washington, Lucy H., 12,740
Washington, Margaret James (Murray) [Mrs. Booker T.] (1865-1925), **128**, 2,153, 3,302, 5,917
Washington, Martha (Dandridge) [Mrs. Daniel Parke] Custis [Mrs. George] (1731-1802), 1,024, 1,502, 2,609, 2,620, 2,862, 5,481, 5,718, 15,037
Washington, Mary (Ball) [Mrs. Augustine] (1708-89), **2,187**, 2,609, 2,620
Washington, Mary (Cheatham) (1796-1865), 15,974
Washington National Monument, 4,467
Washington, Olivia A. Davidson [Mrs. Booker T.] (?-1889), 5,917
Washington, Patty W., 8,566
Washington Post (DC), 2,398, 2,467, 6,168, 11,896, 15,979
Washington Public Ownership League, 17,340
Washington, Sarah, 2,609
Washington Seminary (GA). *See* Westminister Schools (GA)
Washington Square Players, 12,705
Washington Star (DC), 2,247, 14,093
Washington State Archives, Oral History Project, **17,163**
Washington State Association of Colored Women, 17,285
Washington State Board Against Discrimination, 17,341

Washington (State) Campaign Committee, Equal Rights Amendment, House Joint Resolution 14,161, **17,253**
Washington State Environmental Council, 17,267
Washington State Federation of Garden Clubs, 17,147, 17,314
Washington State Federation of Music Clubs, 17,134
Washington State Federation of Women's Clubs, 17,246
Washington State Historical Society, 17,396
Washington State League for Nursing, **17,359**
Washington State Nurses Association, **17,360**
Washington State Parks and Recreation Commission, officials and employees, 17,409
Washington State Pension Union, 17,278
Washington State Theater, 17,281
Washington State University
  faculty, 17,187, 17,368
  trustees, 17,209
Washington State University, college of home economics, 17,203
Washington Tapestry (book), 17,954
Washington Territory, 1,431, 14,560, 14,616, 17,275, **17,329**, 17,330, 17,346, 17,363
  governors, 4,198, 14,454, 17,164, 17,273, **17,335**
  militia, 14,668
  mines and mineral resources, 14,564
  officials and employees, 14,454
  suffrage, laws and legislation, 17,335
Washington Territory Infantry, 14,668
Washington Times (DC), 3,027
Washington Trade Union College, 8,069
Washington Training School for Nurses (DC). *See* Capitol City School of Nursing (DC)
Washington University (St. Louis, MO), 10,160
  faculty, 9,979, 14,943
Washington University (St. Louis, MO), Chimes, 14,029
Washington University of St. Louis (MO), George Warren Brown School of Social Work, faculty, 8,685
Washington University School of Medicine (St. Louis, MO), faculty, 10,207, 10,208, 10,209, 10,210
Washington University (Seattle, WA), Intercollegiate Association of Women Students, 17,354
Washington, Val J., 3,290
Washington, Village and Capital, 1800-1878, and Washington, Capital City, 1879-1950 (book), 2,135
Washington Woman, The (WA), 15,864
Washingtonian (periodical), 2,189
Washingtonian Home (Chicago, IL), **4,164**
Washo Indians, 10,680
  language, 10,661
Washtenaw County Juvenile Court (MI), Citizens Advisory Council, 7,967
Washtenaw County Medical Society (MI), Women's Auxiliary, 7,771, **7,971**
Wasik, Anna (Anker) (1949-), **13,722**
Wason, Elizabeth "Betty" (1912-), **2,622**
"WASP Program: An Historical Synopsis, The" (article), 30
Wasp, The (newspaper), 4,302
WASPs. *See* United States (government), Women Air Force Service Pilots
Wasson, Ben, 9,769
Wassor, W. Waltor, 1,786
Wasylowsky, Anna [Mrs. Philip], **9,513**
Wasylowsky, Philip, **9,513**
Watching the World (book), 17,954
Water, fluoridation, 14,686
  fluoridation, opposition to, 14,565
Water resources development, 1,316, 5,475, 5,839, 9,464, 12,057
Water-rights, 16,867, 16,876
Water-supply, 1,492, 4,931, 10,665
Water Witch (ship), 1,343
Waterbury, Charlotte, 12,520
Waterbury Family (NY), **11,740**
Waterbury Family (Livingston County, NY), 11,520
Waterbury, Lucy, 11,740
Waterbury, Lucy Whitehead (McGill) [Mrs. Norman Mather] (1861-1949). *See* Peabody, Lucy

Whitehead (McGill) [Mrs. Norman Mather] Waterbury [Mrs. Henry Wayland] (1861-1949)
Waterbury, Mary, 11,740
Waterbury, Mrs. E. K., 12,189
Waterford (plantation, SC), 15,440
Watergate Affair (1972-), 1,010, **1,937**, 16,965
Waterloo Female Temperance Society (NY), **12,929**
Waterman, Abbie Louisa (1869-?), 870
Waterman, Anna Charlotte (1866-?). *See* Scott, Anna Charlotte (Waterman) [Mrs. Irving Murray, Jr.] (1866-?)
Waterman Family, 7,528
Waterman Family (CA), 870
Waterman Family (CT), **1,990**
Waterman, Florence, 13,890
Waterman, Hazel (Wood) [Mrs. Waldo Sprague] (1866-1948), **1,198**
Waterman, Helen Jane (1856-?), 870
Waterman, Isabella (Townsend) [Mrs. Henry] (1827-95), 17,036
Waterman, Jane (Gardner) [Mrs. Robert Whitney] (1829-1914), 870
Waterman, Joan Cushing [Mrs. Martin] (1795-1845), 1,990
Waterman, L. May [Mrs. R. Burton] (1894-), **5,892**
Waterman, Louise (1874-1947). *See* Wise, Louise (Waterman) [Mrs. Stephen S.] (1874-1947)
Waterman, Martin (1793-1860), 1,990
Waterman, Mary Ann, 7,678
Waterman, Mary Pamelia (1850-1925). *See* Rice, Mary Pamelia (Waterman) [Mrs. Hyland Washington] (1850-1925)
Waterman, Robert Whitney (1826-91), 870, 1,198
Waterman, Silvinia (1772-1835), 1,990
Waterman, Waldo Dean, 1,191, 1,198
Waters, Abigail Devereux, 7,461
Waters, Achsa, 8,164
Waters, Amy L., **12,665**
Waters, Eliza Greenleaf, 7,461
Waters, Ellouise [Miss], 14,069
Waters, Esther, 7,461
Waters, Ethel, 3,292
Waters Family (MA), **7,461**
Waters, Henry Harcourt (1844-1902), **5,492**
Waters, Ida Mae [Mrs.], 2,492
Waters, Lucy, **7,462**
Waters, Marietta, 7,461
Waters, May Carroll [Mrs. Henry Harcourt], **5,492**
Waters, Sibby Ann. *See* Bond, Sibby Ann (Waters) Davis [Mrs. Alvan]
Waters, Susan Louise (Whittredge) (1833-?), **7,463**
Waters, William D., 7,461
Watie, General Stand, 14,206, 14,220
Waties, Anna, 15,718, 15,764
Waties, Charlotte A., **2,156**
Waties Family (SC), **15,764**
Waties, John, 15,764
Waties, Mary Butler. *See* Sumter, Mary Butler Waties [Mrs. Sebastian]
Waties, Thomas, 15,763
Watkins, Abiathar, **12,666**
Watkins, Ann, 14,366, 14,378
Watkins, B. F., 11,962
Watkins, Caroline, 10,125
Watkins, Catherine (1887-). *See* Carrau, Catherine (Watkins) (1887-)
Watkins, Edward Francis, 1,503
Watkins, Emily, **12,666**
Watkins, Ethel, **9,764**
Watkins, Hannah (Reynolds), 13,238
Watkins, Katherine. *See* Atchison, Katherine (Watkins) [Mrs. Jehu B.]
Watkins, Laura Broughton, 11,962
Watkins, Louise (Ward) [Mrs. Edward Francis] (1890-1974), **1,503**
Watkins, Martha. *See* Scruggs, Martha (Watkins) [Mrs. W. D.]
Watkins, Mary Elizabeth "Lizzie." *See* Atchison, Mary Elizabeth "Lizzie" (Watkins) [Mrs. William]
Watkins Mill Association (MO), 10,124
Watkins, Mrs. Herbert B., **9,765**
Watkins, Ruth (1892-). *See* Keena, Ruth (Watkins) [Mrs. E. E.] (1892-)
Watkins, Waltus (1806-84), 10,122, **10,125**

Watson, Alice "Elsie" Theodora (?-1880). *See* Becker, Alice "Elsie" Theodora (Watson) [Mrs. George F.] (?-1880)

Watson, Alice Nevada (1891-1976). *See* Driggs, Alice Nevada (Watson) [Mrs. Burton] (1891-1976)

Watson, Amelia M., 7,065

Watson, Amy [Mrs. Frank D.], 6,223, **11,775**

Watson, Anne Elizabeth [Mrs. Charles Thomas], 2,655

Watson, Annie Clo, 8,657

Watson, Blanche G., 2,396

Watson, Catherine [Mrs. Cyrus], **9,921**

Watson, Cora E. (White) [Mrs. Will] (1843-1911). *See* Carey, Cora E. (White) [Mrs. Will] Watson [Mrs. S. E.] (1843-1911)

Watson, Cyrus, **9,921**

Watson, Elizabeth Lowe [Mrs.] (1843-?), **1,351**

Watson, Ellen, 15,230

Watson, Ellen Murdoch [Miss] (?-1914), **15,230**

Watson, Evelyn M. (1886-1954), 2,419, **11,385**

Watson, Gertrude M., 11,068

Watson, Jane Werner (1915-), **14,463**

Watson, Janet McNeil. *See* Seward, Janet McNeil (Watson) [Mrs. William Henry, Jr.]

Watson, Jennie S. Lathrop, 5,121

Watson, John Fanning (1779-1860), 11,061, **15,107**

Watson Judge, 9,600

Watson, Lucy, 15,107

Watson, Margaret L., **16,144**

Watson, Margaret Wickham (1891-1934), **1,352**

Watson, Martha, 9,149

Watson, Martha Dent (1837-1905), **17,479**

Watson, Mary Elizabeth. *See* Hopkinson, Mary Elizabeth (Watson)

Watson, Mary L., 3,990

Watson, May Greenfield [Mrs.], 13,617

Watson, May Mathis Green [Mrs.] (1883-), **16,145**

Watson, Mollie. *See* Hill, Mollie (Watson)

Watson, Mrs. J. W., 9,600

Watson, Rebecca Haymond [Mrs. Thomas], 17,479

Watson, Sanford, 14,506

Watson, Thomas, 17,479

Watson, Thomas E., 2,984

Watson, Virginia. *See* Applegate, Virginia (Watson)

Watson, Will, 9,600

Watt, Addie, 9,666

Watt, Violet, 2,631

Watters, Hyla (1895-),

Watterston, Eliza, 2,623

Watterston, George (1783-1854), **2,623**

Wattles, August, 4,421

Wattles, Sarah G., 4,421

Watts, Alice, 1,337

Watts, Amelia [Mrs.], **9,766**

Watts, Amelia Thompson [Mrs.] (1799-), 9,762

Watts, Bess, 14,308

Watts, Edith Webb [Mrs.], 9,027

Watts, Edith Weble, 9,260

Watts, Ethel (1878-1940). *See* Grant, Ethel (Watts) Mumford (1878-1940)

Watts, J. O., Family (OR), **14,308**

Watts, Mary, 12,315

Watts, May Theilgaard [Mrs. Raymond] (1893-1975), **4,289**

Watts, Mrs. J. O., 14,308

Watts, Mrs. Robert, 12,237

Watts, Roxanna (Brown) Walbridge, 1,337

Watumull, Ellen [Mrs. G. J.], 6,221, 7,287, 7,289

Waugh, Catharine Gouger (1862-1945). *See* McCulloch, Catharine Gouger (Waugh) [Mrs. Frank Hathorn] (1862-1945)

Waverly Magazine (periodical), 8,376

WAVES. *See* United States (government), Women Accepted for Voluntary Emergency Service

Wawyin Club (New Concord, OH), 14,118

Wax Portraits and Silhouettes (pamphlet), 7,605

Waxworks, 11,203

Way, Elizabeth Fenwick, 6,060, 11,165

Way, Isabel Stewart (1904-), **14,464**

Way, Mrs. W. Lincoln, 2,396

Way, Sarah Sims [Mrs.], **3,112**

Wayles, Martha (1748-82). *See* Jefferson, Martha (Wayles) [Mrs. Bathurst] Skelton [Mrs. Thomas] (1748-82)

Wayman, Dorothy (Godfrey) [Mrs. Charles] (1893-1975), **7,691**

Wayne, Arthur Trezevaut, 15,527

Wayne County Temperance Society (NY), 12,608

Wayne Family (GA), **3,594**

Wayne Literary Club (MI), 8,387

Wayne, Maria L., **15,527**

Wayne State Teachers College (NE), faculty, **10,477**

Wayne State University (MI), 8,041
    alumnae, **8,052, 8,054**
    faculty, **8,043,** 8,046, **8,049, 8,050**
    trustees, 8,096

Wayne State University (MI), College of Nursing, 6,158, **8,045**

Wayne State University (MI), College of Nursing, deans, 8,053

Wayne State University (MI), Faculty Women's Club, **8,047**

Wayne State University (MI), Family Life Project, **8,048**

Wayne State University (MI), Family Life Project, Child Growth and Development Program, 8,048

Wayne State University (MI), Polish Project, 8,045

Waynesboro Garden Club (GA), 3,358

Waynesboro Woman's Club (GA), 3,358

Wayside-Aftermath Club (NY), 11,692

Wayside Home (GA), **13,156**

Wayside Home Association (GA), 3,358

Wayside Hospitals, 15,727

We Americans (book), 17,018

We Called It Culture (book), 14,333

We Have Seen the Best of Our Times (book), 6,069

"We Shall Overcome" (song), 15,977

We Too Are the People (book), 7,709

"We Will Overcome" (song). *See* "We Shall Overcome" (song)

Wead, Eunice (1881-1969), 7,319

Wead Family, **7,319**

Wead, Mary K. [Mrs. Samuel C.] (1812-96), 7,319

Weakley, Eliza (Bedford) [Mrs. Samuel Davies], 28, **13,157**

Weakley Family (AL), **28**

Weakley, Harriet Ellen Moore [Mrs. Thomas P.], **13,072**

Weakley, James Harvey, 28

Weakley, Kate (Thompson), 15,953

Weakley, Samuel Davies (1812-?), 28

Wealth, 3,329

Weapons (drama), 15,612

Wear, Mrs., 1,751

Weather, 7,644
    economic aspects, 7,640

Weatherford, Marion T., 14,504

Weaver, Clara. *See* Robinson, Clara (Weaver) [Mrs. Nelson]

Weaver, Clara (Vinson) [Mrs. James Baird], 4,854, 5,040

Weaver, Elizabeth Caroline (1852-1924). *See* Gerrard, Elizabeth Caroline (Weaver) [Mrs. Leonard] (1852-1924)

Weaver Family (RI), **15,393**

Weaver, George Norman (1851-1907), 15,393

Weaver, Gustine Nancy Courson [Mrs.], 5,448, **9,767**

Weaver, Harriet (1859-?). *See* Taylor, Harriet (Weaver) [Mrs. Henry] (1859-?)

Weaver, James Baird (1833-1912), **4,854, 5,040**

Weaver, Martha Dorman (Hubbard) [Mrs. George Norman], 15,393

Weaver, Mary Watson [Mrs. Powell], **10,121**

Weaver, Powell (1890-1951), 10,121

Weavers, 1,068, 2,662, **2,727,** 12,370

"Weavers, The" (story), 11,145

Weaving, **2,727,** 10,052, 13,141, 13,307

Webb, Alice, 9,289

Webb, Alice [Mrs. Joseph Cheshire, Sr.], 13,031

Webb, Anna Leonard (1821-68). *See* Farris, Anna Leonard (Webb) [Mrs. Thomas C.] (1821-68)

Webb, Annie Gertrude (1861-1932). *See* Porritt, Annie Gertrude (Webb) (1861-1932)

Webb, Cecile Stollenwerck, 9,762

Webb, Cornelia, 13,625

Webb, Edith [Mrs.], 990, **991,** 1,525

Webb, Elizabeth [Miss], 10,037

Webb, Elizabeth (1663-1726), **2,032,** 15,042

Webb, Esther A., 5,063

Webb Family, 2,315

Webb Family (MA, ME, NH), **7,677**

Webb Family (TX), 16,269

Webb, Frances Delord (1834-1913). *See* Hall, Frances Delord (Webb) [Mrs. Francis Bloodgood] (1834-1913)

Webb, Hannah (1809-62), 5,907

Webb, Hannah King (Shaw) (1800-75), 7,677

Webb, James W., 9,796

Webb, Jane W., 11,325

Webb, Jennie [Miss], 3,395

Webb, John, 4,233

Webb, John F., 12,419

Webb, Katherine (Walsh), 12,658

Webb, Laura, 2,045

Webb, Lucy Ware (1831-89). *See* Hayes, Lucy Ware (Webb) [Mrs. Rutherford B.] (1831-89)

Webb, Martha E. *See* Mitchell Martha E. (Webb) [Mrs. Lemuel]

Webb, Mary [Miss], 10,037

Webb, Mary L. [Miss] (1861-?), **2,624**

Webb, Mrs. John, 4,233

Webb, Mrs. Thomas H., **13,602**

Webb, Richard Davis (1805-72), 5,907

Webb, Tessa (Sweazy) [Mrs. Reuben H.] (1885-), **14,019**

Webber, Alice, 8,670

Webber, Mabel L., **15,528**

Webber, Ruby (Clein), 17,282

Weber, Alice (Lytle) [Mrs. Adam] (1874-1965), **1,799**

Weber, Carl J., 5,711

Weber, Charles Maria (1814-81), 591

Weber Family,

Weber Family (MO), **10,057**

Weber, Grace Pauline, 1,750

Weber, Gretchen, **1,800**

Weber, Helen. *See* Kennedy, Helen (Weber)

Weber, Lenora (Mattingly) [Mrs. Albert] (1895-1971), **1,801**

Weber, Margaret Isabella (Walker) (1824-?), **13,158**

Weber, Nan Winston Gardner, 10,057

Weber, Sarah (1817-63). *See* Addams, Sarah (Weber) [Mrs. John Huy] (1817-63)

Weber, Sister M. Anselm, 17,145

Weber State College (UT), 16,448

Weber, Teresa (Frass), 10,123

Weberg, Nancy. *See* Younggren, Nancy (Weberg)

Webster, 12,367

Webster, Ada (Wood) [Mrs. Thomas W.] (1869-1951), **16,445**

Webster and Palmes (GA), 3,562

Webster, Ann V. (1930-), 10,151

Webster, Annette (?-1971). *See* Betenson, Annette (Webster) [Mrs. Leland Stanley] (?-1971)

Webster, Annie Moffett, 10,130

Webster, Benjamin, 2,625

Webster, Caroline Le Roy [Mrs. Daniel], 12,542

Webster, Daniel (1782-1852), 4,408, 5,676, 7,603, **10,832,** 11,602, 15,449

Webster, Daniel (1797-1885), 12,542

Webster, Ellen A. (1863-1965), **6,938**

Webster, Emily H. (1902-), **11,386**

Webster Family, **10,873**

Webster Family (NY?), 12,028

Webster, Fannie, 15,990

Webster, Grace (Fletcher) [Mrs. Daniel] (1781-1828), 10,832

Webster, Harriet. *See* Fowler, Harriet (Webster) [Mrs. William Chauncey]

Webster, Margaret (1831-62). *See* Adams, Margaret (Webster) [Mrs. Hugh] (1831-62)

Webster, Margaret (1905-72), **871, 2,625,** 6,045, **12,367, 17,819**

Webster, Marjorie F., 13,366

Webster, Mary E., 16,890

Webster, Mary L. [Mrs.], **8,373**

Webster, Mel L., 4,971

Webster, Nina (1887-). *See* Dumont, Nina (Webster) [Mrs. Leslie D.] Smith [Mrs. Henry] (1887-)

Webster, Noah (1758-1843), 8,332, 12,478, **12,667**

Webster, Paulette [Mrs.], 9,467
Webster, Rebecca Greenleaf [Mrs. Noah], 12,667
Webster, Rose (Glen), 16,565
Webster, Stella N. [Miss], 10,725
Webster, T. C., 13,603
Webster, Thomas, 3,299
Wecter, Elizabeth, 428
Wedd, A. F. [Miss], 12,206
Wedding anniversaries, 9,878, 12,319
Wedding in Paris (drama), 17,793
Weddings, 872, 5,359, 14,299, 15,479, 15,676
Weddington, Sarah (1945-), 11,932, **16,396**
Wedel, Mildred (Mott), 10,027
Wedlake, Norma M., 11,349
Wednesday Afternoon Musical Club, Inc. (Bridgeport, CT), **1,830**
Wednesday Club (Cape Girardeau, MO), 9,959
Wednesday Evening German Society (Charleston, SC), 15,515
Wednesday Lookout Club (Clarence, IA), 4,960
Wednesday Morning Club (MA), **5,971**
Wednesday Study Club (MO), **10,058**
Weed, Abby, 5,644
Weed, Addie [Miss], 5,644
Weed, Carrie Francis (1852-1941). *See* Robertson, Carrie Francis (Weed) [Mrs. Alexander M.] (1852-1941)
Weed, Ethel, 17,074
Weed Family (GA), **3,595**
Weed, Frances, 12,752
Weed, Henry D., I, 3,595
Weed, Henry D., II, 3,595
Weed, Thurlow, 5,750
Weeds (book), 3,775
Weekly Bulletin (newsletter), 4,850
Weekly Bulletin of Suffrage News, 4,859
Weekly Valley Herald (MN), 9,117
Weeks, Anna M. (See), 2,570
Weeks case, 6,849
Weeks, Clara, 12,351
Weeks, Edward Augustus, 4,485, 12,042
Weeks, Estella T. [Miss], **2,626**
Weeks, Harriet H., 9,237
Weeks, Marcia, 157
Weeks, Marian E. (?-1968), **12,668**
Weeks, Martha, 2,869
Weeks, Mary C., 1,259
Weeks, Mrs. Edwin, 10,108
Weeks, Ruth Mary, 4,727
Wegner, Nell (Norbeck) (1902-), Family, **15,863**
Wehmeyer, Gladys, **17,361**
Wei Ling Girls' Academy (Soochow, China), 13,642
Weicker, Lowell P., Jr. (1931-), 1,937
Weidman, Charles, 12,363, 12,364
Weidman, Jerome, 16,152, 16,156
Weight Lifter of Iron (book), 10,251
Weik, Mary, 4,532
Weil, Gertrude (1879-1971), 13,468, 13,504, **16,184**
Weil, Henry, 13,604
Weil, Janet. *See* Bluethenthal, Janet (Weil) [Mrs. Herbert]
Weil-Kalter Manufacturing Company, 9,962
Weil, Mina (Rosenthal) [Mrs. Henry], 13,500, 13,604
Weil, Sarah (Einstein) [Mrs. Sol], 13,500
Weil, Truda (?-1971), **8,145**
Weill, Kurt, 12,367
Weill, Oscar, 931
Weimar, Rita, 12,372
Weinberg, Emily (Sievert) [Mrs. I. G.] (1893-1958), **14,707**
Weinberg, Helen Joy (1900-), **2,827**
Weinberg, Rose, 12,395
Weiner, Charles, 6,336
Weinheim, Tess (Ott), **2,627**
Weiniewitz, Eva (Olier), 9,542
Weinland, Caroline (Yost) [Mrs. William Henry], 1,504
Weinland, William Henry (1861-?), **1,504**
Weir, Dorothy. *See* Young, Dorothy (Weir)
Weir Family (MS), **9,665**
Weir Family (UT), 16,575
Weir, J. Alden, 16,575
Weir, Mary Wallace, 2,233
Weir, Ruth Cromer (1912-), **5,041**

Weirick, Marjorie [Mrs. Wallace P.], 5,065
Weis, Jessica (McCullough) [Mrs. Charles W., Jr.] (1901-63), 5,150, **6,939**, 12,790
Weisenberger, Dorothy (Hamilton) (1914-), 249
Weisheit, Ingreet Bowen [Mrs. Joseph Elmer], 5,737
Weisiger, Daniel, 17,106
Weisiger, Miss, **17,106**
Weiskopf, Bertha, 9,254
Weislander, Rose Harriet (1879-1933). See Stokes, Rose Pastor. [Mrs. James Graham] Phelps [Mrs. Jerome I.] Romaine (1879-1933)
Weiss, Carol (1895-1952). *See* King, Carol (Weiss) (1895-1952)
Weiss, Edward H., 3,927
Weiss, Myra Tanner, 9,380
Weiss-Rosmarin, Trude (1908-), **13,834**
Weisz, Irene (Miner) [Mrs. Charles], 3,984
Weitz, Alice [Mrs. Frederick], **4,957**
Weitz, Mrs. Fred, 4,729
Welborn, Mrs. John Scott, **13,159**
Welby, Irene, 9,287
Welch Family, 16,830
Welch, Fannie Fredericks [Mrs. Alexander McMillan], **12,202**
Welch, Galbraith, **6,110**
Welch, Harriet, 16,830
Welch, Helen M. (1914-). *See* Tuttle, Helen M. (Welch) (1914-)
Welch, Joseph, 12,360
Welch, Mary B. [Mrs.] (1841-1923), **4,691**
Welch, Marie de Laveaga (1905-74), **2,628**
Welch, Mildred (1898-?). *See* Cranston, Mildred (Welch) (1898-?)
Welch, Mrs. E. Sohier, 1,981
Welch, Robert, 16,830
Welch, Winona Hazel (1896-), **4,539**
Welch Woman's Relief Corps (Ann Arbor, MI), 7,860
Welcher, Amy Ogden [Miss] (1887-), 1,965
Welcome, Verda D., 5,828
Weld, Angelina Emily (Grimké) [Mrs. Theodore Dwight] (1805-79), 992, 2,629, 5,907, 6,940, 8,005, 11,111, 11,605
Weld, Anna. *See* Perkins, Anna (Weld) [Mrs. George Hamilton]
Weld, Carrie (Smith) (1861-1944), 10,091, **10,093**
Weld, Charles S., 8,005
Weld, Emeline Rathbone (1854?-1940). *See* Kennan, Emeline Rathbone (Weld) [Mrs. George] (1854?-1940)
Weld Family, **8,005**
Weld, Harriet. *See* Corning, Harriet (Weld) [Mrs. Erastus]
Weld, Rebecca. *See* Nolan, Rebecca (Weld)
Weld, Theodore Dwight (1803-95), **2,629, 6,858**, 7,294, 8,005
Welders, Afro-American, 8,056
Weldon, Onha, 15,332
Welfare Council of Metropolitan Chicago (IL). *See* United Way of Metropolitan Chicago (IL)
Welfare funds (trade-unions), 659
Welfare Public Relations Forum, 4,130
Welfare rights movement, 393
Welfare work in industry, 1,080, 12,721, 12,725
Well baby clinics. *See* Community health services for children
Wellcome, Sir Henry S. (?-1936), **17,219**
Wellendorf, Mrs. John, 8,989
Weller, Hazel Z. [Mrs.], 367
Welles, Charles F. (1789-1866), 14,835
Welles, Clara Barck [Mrs.] (1868-1965), 3,867
Welles, Ellen J. [Mrs. Charles F.], 14,835
Welles Family (CT), **1,863**
Welles Family (CT) 1,940
Welles Family (PA), **14,835**
Welles, Harriet D. [Mrs. Roger], 2,630
Welles, Mary Ann (1808-73), *See* Goodrich, Mary Ann (Welles) [Mrs. Joshua] (1808-73)
Welles, Mary E., **1,939**
Welles, Mary E., 11,283
Welles, Mercy (Aiken) [Mrs. Roger], 2,630
Welles, Roger (1862-1932), **2,630**
Welles, Sallie Richard Hamilton, **1,940**
Welles, Sumner, 11,853, 15,303
Wellesley Club (Denver, CO), 1,721

Wellesley Club (St. Paul, MN), **9,430**
Wellesley College (MA), 65, 1,224, 6,616, 6,724, 6,877, 7,501, **7,564**, 7,573, 7,577, **7,580**, 7,675, 9,427, 11,748, 11,910, 12,526, 12,737, 12,740
   administration, **7,570**
   admission, **7,581**
   alumnae, **1,909**, 4,906, **7,562**, 8,591, **9,430**, 10,828, 10,927
   deans, **7,582**
   evaluation, **7,584**
   faculty, 1,998, 7,563, **7,567**, 7,851, 11,578, **15,092**, 15,301
   finance, **7,566**
   history, 7,568, **7,583**
   presidents, 7,572, 7,574, 15,377
   students, 1,279, **7,565, 7,575, 7,578**, 8,896, 9,321, 10,974, 11,747, 14,363, 15,341
   trustees, 6,881
Wellesley College (MA), Alumnae Association, 7,562
Wellesley College (MA) (building and endowment), 12,739
Wellesley College (MA), Commission on the Future of the College, 7,584
Wellesley College (MA), Friends of Art, 7,571
Wellesley College (MA), Friends of the Library, 7,571
Wellesley College (MA), Summer Institute for Social Progress, 7,564
Wellesley College (MA) Training Camp and Experiment Station, 6,963
Wellesley College Club, 15,246
"Wellesley College 1875-1975: A Century of Women," 7,583
Wellesley Institute for Foreign Students (MA), 7,564
Wellesley Magazine (periodical), 4,504
"Wellesley: Part of the American Story," 7,583
Wellesley School of Home Making (MA), 6,188
Wellesley Verse Speaking Choir (MA), 7,580
Wellever, Edith, 8,264
Welling, Harriet [Mrs. John], 11,827
Wellington Lake and Reservoir Company (CO), 1,695
Wellington Literary Society (OH), **13,969**
Wellman, Beth Lucy (1895-1952), 5,035
Wellman, Manly Wade, 12,955
Wells, Agnes Ermina (1876-1959), **6,941**
Wells, Amos R., 1,224
Wells-Barnett, Ida Bell. [Mrs. James] Wells [Mrs. Ferdinand Lee] Barnett (1862-1931), 2,315, 4,147, 8,531
Wells, Bettina Borrman, 12,700
Wells, Charles William (1841-93), **8,374**
Wells, Charlotte (Fowler) [Mrs. Samuel Robert] (1814-1901), **11,741**
Wells, Chauncey Wetmore (1872-1933), 7,680
Wells, Chester, 12,763
Wells College (NY), 11,279, 11,281, 12,737
   faculty, 11,278, 11,282, 11,526, 18,008
   history, 11,278, **11,283**
   trustees, 11,280
Wells College (NY) Alumnae, 14,169
Wells College Alumnae News, 14,169
Wells College (NY) Missionary Society, 11,283
Wells College (NY) Philharmonic Club, 11,283
Wells, Daniel H., 16,566, 16,839, 16,840
Wells, Edward Payson (1847-1936), Family (MN), **9,431**
Wells, Elizabeth DeAngelis (1830-1922). *See* Shepard, Elizabeth DeAngelis (Wells) [Mrs. Sidney] (1830-1922)
Wells, Emma (Middleton) [Mrs. Edward Oliver] (1867-1945), **15,975**
Wells, Emmeline Blanche (Woodward) [Mrs. James Harvey] Harris [Mrs. Newel Kimball] Whitney [Mrs. Daniel Hanmer] (1828-1921) 429, 16,500, **16,566**, 16,618, 16,620, 16,787, **16,839**, 16,966
Wells, Evelyn [Miss], **873**
Wells Family (MI), 8,374
Wells Family (NY), **11,590**
Wells, Fargo & Company, 11,278, 11,283
Wells, Florence, 12,763
Wells, Florence [Mrs.], 8,399
Wells, George H., 14,835
Wells, H. G., 7,216, 7,289, 11,979, 16,166

Wells, Hannah Corrilla (Free) [Mrs. Daniel H.] (1829-1913), **16,840**

Wells, Hannah (DeAngelis) Lemoyne [Mrs. Chester] (1802-90), 12,763

Wells, Harry H. (1851-1936), Family (MN), **8,719**

Wells, Heber M., 16,842

Wells, Henry (1805-78), 11,278, 11,280, 11,283

Wells, Herman, 4,494

Wells, Ida Bell [Mrs. James] (1862-1931). *See* Wells-Barnett, Ida Bell. [Mrs. James] Wells [Mrs. Ferdinand Lee] Barnett (1862-1931)

Wells, Junius F., 16,840

Wells, Kate (Gannett) [Mrs. Samuel] (1838-1911), 12,807, 12,818

Wells, Lester G., 2,486

Wells, Lydia, 7,389

Wells, Marguerite Milton (1872-1959), 6,630, **6,942**, 9,231, 9,327, 9,431, 11,886

Wells, Martha C. [Mrs. Cyrus W.], 9,298, 9,404

Wells, Martha P., **13,160**

Wells, Mary [Miss] (1863-1948), **14,702**

Wells, Mary E. *See* Welles, Mary E.

Wells, Mary G., 6,884

Wells, Mary Jane, 14,284

Wells, Mary Prentice [Mrs. Henry] (1829-1908), 11,283

Wells, Melissa [Mrs. Milton], 9,431

Wells, Milton, 9,431

Wells, Mrs. R. H., 9,216

Wells, Nellie, 10,211

Wells, Nellie March Johnson [Mrs. Edward Payson] (1848-1930), 9,431

Wells, Rachel (ca. 1735-96), 11,203

Wells, Roxanna, 6,337

Wells, Sarah E. *See* Champney, Sarah E. (Wells)

Wells Seminary for the Higher Education of Young Women (NY). *See* Wells College (NY)

Wells, Tobias (pseudonym). *See* Forbes, DeLoris Florine Stanton (1923-)

Wells, Wesley Robert, 1,280

Wells, William H., 12,652

Welsch, Emma Bowler, 10,714

Welsh, 9,344

Welsh, Alice. *See* Jenkins, Alice (Welsh)

Welsh, Lilian (1858-1938), 5,809

Welshans, Harriet, **17,480**

Welt, Mildred G. [Mrs. Joseph M.], 9,254

Welter, Alberta Telfair. *See* Gould, Alberta Telfair (Welter)

Welty, Elizabeth (Waltemath) [Mrs. John] (ca. 1870-1900), **10,059**

Welty, Eudora [Miss] (1909-), 3,065, 9,567, 9,585, 9,694, 9,699, **9,768, 9,769, 9,770,** 11,810, 15,927, 15,934, **16,172**

Welty, John, 10,059

Welty, Susan Elizabeth (Fulton) (1905-), **5,042**

Wembo Ngama school (Zaire), 13,291

Wendell, Sarah (Packard) [Mrs. Philip], **12,339**

Wendrell, George, 3,246

Wendover, Jessie May [Miss] (1872-?), **11,053**

Wendover, William (?-1900), 11,053

Wendt, Anna Louise (Neidemeyer), 14,480

Wendt, Emma (1890-). *See* Chase, Emma (Wendt) (1890-)

Wendt, Mathilde F. [Mrs.], 7,999

Wentworth, Lydia G. [Miss] (1858-1947), **15,314**

Wentworth, Marion Craig, 1,525, 9,004

Wentworth, Susan, 7,047

Wentz, Alice K., **13,161**

Wentz, Elizabeth (Lemen) [Mrs. George H.] (1869-1956), **10,551**

Wenz, Julia, 9,512

Wenzel, Caroline, 473

Wenzelburger, Annabel Elise. *See* Graupner, Annabel Elise (Wenzelburger) [Mrs. Adolphus Earhart]

Wergeland, Agnes Matilde (1857-1914), **18,019**

Werlin, Rosella Horewitz [Mrs. Joseph S.] (ca. 1910-), **16,222**

Werner, Adelaide, **11,054**

Werner, Helena, 10,326

Werner, Louis, 11,054

Werner, Ruth M., **13,896**

Werner, Vivian Lescher, **14,465**

Werner, Wilbur P., 10,326

Wertenbaker, Lael Tucker (1909-), **6,111**

Werth, Mary H. (Maury) [Mrs. James Rhodes] (1844-1928), 2,479

Wertmüller, Elizabeth (Henderson) (?-1812), 15,018

Wertmüller Family (PA), **15,018**

Wertz, Adda P., 3,752

Weschler, Anita [Miss] (1903-), **12,914**

Wescott, Angeline, **16,567**

Wesley, Bonnie, 3,265

Wesley College (ND), 13,698

Wesley, Emma, 3,265

Wesley Hospital (Chicago, IL), Wesley Woman's Board. *See* Wesley Memorial Hospital Woman's Board (Chicago, IL)

Wesley, John, 4,202, 10,911

Wesley Memorial Hospital School of Medical Records Librarianship (Chicago, IL), **4,023**

Wesley Memorial Hospital School of Nursing (Chicago, IL), **4,022**

Wesley Memorial Hospital School of Nursing (Chicago ,IL), Alumnae Association, **4,024**

Wesley Memorial Hospital Woman's Board (Chicago, IL), **4,012, 4,025**

Wesley Methodist Church (Paterson, NJ), Women's Society of Christian Service, 10,910

Wesley-Passavant School of Nursing (Chicago, IL), **4,026**, 10,564

Wesley, Rusha, 3,265

Wesley Sisters (GA), **3,265**

Wesleyan Academy (Wilbraham, MA), students, 1,885

Wesleyan College, 3,405

Wesleyan College (Macon, GA), 9,919
alumnae, 3,462, 3,463, 3,464, 3,465, 3,466, 3,467, 3,468, 3,469
deans, 3,463

Wesleyan College (Macon, GA), faculty, **3,459**

Wesleyan College for Women (GA), 12,738

Wesleyan Female College (Macon, GA), 3,125
alumnae, 10,951
students, 3,268, 3,271, 3,406, 3,419

Wesleyan Female College (NC), 13,462, 13,579

Wesleyan Female Collegiate Institute (DE), 13,350

Wesleyan Female Institute (VA), 3,418

Wesleyan Methodist Connection, 5,457

Wesleyan Service Guild (IN), **4,540**

Wesleyan Service Guild (LA), **5,554**

Wesleyan University, 11,350

Wesleyan University, administrators 15,197

Wesleyan University (CT), **1,975**
faculty, wives of, **1,980**
presidents, **1,976,** 1,977, **1,982, 1,983**

Wesleyan University, endowments, 12,233

Wesleyana (IL), 3,746

Wesner, Lulu (Nuckolls) [Mrs. Joy E.] (1880-1959), **10,552**

Wessel, Jennie E. [Miss], **1,941**

Wesselhoft, Selma, **6,943**

Wessyngton (residence, TN), 15,974

West, Anna Sheldon Ogden, 3,897

West Area Business and Professional Women (Chicago, IL), 4,165

West Baden Springs Hotel (IN), 4,680

West Branch Library (KY), 5,379

West China Union University, deans, 893

West, Dorothy (1909-), 3,290, 5,465, **6,112**

West, Drusilla (Moody), 14,619

West, Elizabeth Dickinson. *See* Dowden, Elizabeth Dickinson (West) [Mrs. Edward]

West, Elizabeth Howard [Miss] (1873-1948), **16,289**

West End Institute (New Haven, CT), **2,006**

West End Institute Papers (CT), 1,998

West End Presbyterian Church (NY), 12,561

West Harrisville Relief Society (UT), 16,679

West Hartford Baptist Sewing Society (CT), 1,889

West, Helen (Hunt) [Mrs. Byron McG.] (1892-1963), 6,742, **6,944**

West, Herbert F., 10,869, 10,874

West, I. E., 13,661

West Indies, 12,213

West, Jessamyn (1902-), 569

West, John, 14,606

West, John, 11,728

West, John K., 9,356

West, Julia. *See* Lindsley, Julia (West) [Mrs. Aaron Ladner]

West, Laura McLouth [Mrs. John], 11,728

West, Lillie (1855-1939). *See* Buck, Lillie (West) [Mrs. Harry] Brown [Mrs. Franklyn Howard] (1855-1939)

West, Lucy. *See* Freeman, Lucy (West) [Mrs. Frederick]

West, Mae, 1,025

West, Marie de Laveaga (Welch) [Mrs. George Parsons] (1905-74), 831, **874,** 1,081, 1,082, **2,628**

West, Mary Allen, 4,243

West Michigan Environmental Council, 7,976

West Pakistan, missionaries, medical, Presbyterian, 14,425

West Park Slovenian National Home (OH), 13,912

West Penn Hospital (PA), 15,226

West Philadelphia Reading Society (PA), **15,108**

West Point Military Academy (NY), 15,898, 16,390, 17,081

West, Rebecca (1892-), 267, 325, 2,241, 4,476, 7,214, 11,954, 12,701, 15,564, 16,157

West Seite Frauenverein (Cleveland, OH), 13,905

West Side and Ohio Avenue Day Care Centers (OH), **14,020**

West Side Community Program Center (NY), 7,242

West Side Historical Society (Chicago, IL), **4,165**

West, Stephen, Jr. (1727-90), 5,797

West Suburban Bar Association (IL), 4,076

West Suburban Teachers Union (IL), 8,147

West Union Mennonite Church, West Union Mission Sewing Circle (IA), **5,051**

West Virginia, 17,457
aeronautical societies, 17,450
agricultural laborers, education, 17,448
artists, 17,478
associations, institutions, etc., 17,467
authors, 17,478
blind, law and legislation, 17,463
capital punishment, 17,463
Catholic hospitals, records and correspondence, 17,487
charitable societies, 17,459
charitable societies, Jewish, **13,769, 13,770, 13,774, 13,789**
church historians, 17,471
church work, 13,280
civil engineers, 17,440
Civil War, 12,333
campaigns and battles, 17,477
hospitals, charities, etc., 12,165
public opinion, 17,479
clubs, 6,868, **17,458**
coal mines and mining, **17,482**
college discipline, 17,449
college registrars, 17,443
college students, 17,461
college teachers, 17,463
community organization, **17,475**
congressmen, 17,455, 17,466, 17,472
congresswomen, 17,466
diaries and journals, 13,151, 17,464, 17,470, 17,477, 17,479
education, finance, 17,463
educational associations, 17,433, 17,442, 17,446, **17,447**
educators, **17,474**
elections, 17,472
farmers, 17,472
florists, **17,440**
4-H clubs, **17,481**
fund raising, 17,475
gardening, societies, etc., 17,468
genealogists, 17,444, 17,457
governmental investigations, **17,482**
governors, **17,462,** 17,482
handicapped children, 17,463
high school teachers, **17,445**
historic sites, conservation and restoration, 17,475
hospitals, 17,462
housewives, **17,434, 17,441**
juvenile delinquency, 17,463
lawyers, 17,457, 17,460
legislators, **17,460,** 17,463

mentally ill, law and legislation, 17,463
merchants, **17,459**
Methodism, 17,471
military courts, 17,453, 17,482
miners, 8,085, 11,853
monasticism and religious orders for women,
Catholic, **17,487**
musical societies, **17,484**
novelists, 17,473
occupational retraining, **17,448**
officials and employees, salaries, allowances, etc.,
17,463
orphans and orphan asylums, 17,459
parents' and teachers' associations, **17,476**
physicians, **17,462**
poets, **17,454**
political activists, women, 17,472
political committees, 17,486
prisoners, 17,463
prisons for women, 17,483
private colleges, archives, **17,430**
real property, 17,465
reformatories (female), 17,483
scholarships, 17,484
school superintendents and principals, 17,474
schools, 17,445, 17,455, 17,457, **17,485**
senators, United States, **17,462**
sheriffs, 17,452
social settlements, 3,772
societies, etc., **17,475**
state boards of education, **17,483**, 17,486
state universities and colleges, 9,583
statehood, 17,477
strikes and lockouts, coal mining, **17,453**
students' societies, 14,029, **17,449**
suffrage, 4,859
suffrage societies, 16,252
suffragists, 3,324, 17,486
taxation, 17,463
teachers, 17,438, **17,469**
temperance, 17,486
trade and professional associations, 17,445
unemployed, 17,463
universities and colleges, law and legislation, 17,442
vital statistics, 17,457
workmen's compensation, 17,463
West Virginia Association of Colleges and
Universities, **17,442**
West Virginia Board of Education, 17,486
West Virginia Federation of Women's Clubs, 17,468
West Virginia 4-H Clubs, **17,481**
West Virginia Home Economics Association, 17,445
West Virginia Humane Society, 17,459
West Virginia Mining Investigation Commission,
17,482
West Virginia Prison for Women, 17,483
West Virginia State Board of Control, **17,483**
West Virginia State College, 9,583
West Virginia Training School, 17,463
West Virginia University (Morgantown, WV), 17,445,
17,484
alumnae, 8,603, 17,445
faculty, 17,461
students, **17,449**, 17,469
West Virginia University (Morgantown, WV), Chimes,
14,029
Westbrook, Bertie. *See* Hickey, Bertie (Westbrook)
[Mrs. Charles Kennedy]
Westbrook, C. A., 875
Westbrook Family (TX), **875**
Westchester County Recreation Commission (NY),
2,481
Westchester School (PA), 15,064
Westcoast, Wanda, **17,362**
Westcott, Esther Montgomery, **15,109**
Westcott, Jan Vlachos (1912-), **6,113**
Westcott, Katherine Augusta (1847-1929). *See*
Tingley, Katherine Augusta Westcott [Mrs.
Richard Henry] Cook [Mrs. George W.] Parent
[Mrs. Philo Buchanan] (1847-1929)
Westerfield, Fidelia Burroughs (1846-1915), **4,456**
Westerfield, Peggy, **13,162**
Western (MO), 10,149

Western Association of Collegiate Alumnae. *See*
American Association of University Women
Western Association of Writers, 4,654
Western Athenaeum 1,282
Western Carolina Female College, 13,599
Western College (Toledo, OH), 4,853, 12,737
Western Drama Society, 1,234
Western Federation of Miners, 10,710
Western Female Seminary (Oxford, OH), 9,316
Western House of Refuge (Albion, NY), 11,254
Western Illinois University (Macomb, IL), Grote Hall,
4,295
Western Jewish History Center, 940
Western, Mary Brower. *See* Benjamin, Mary Brower
(Western)
Western Maryland College, archives, **5,855**
Western Michigan University, 8,226, 8,232, 8,244,
8,247
Western Missionary Society of New Jersey, 10,956
Western music. *See* Country music
Western Nevada Teachers' Association, 10,707
Western New York Federation of Women's Clubs,
11,270
Western Newspaper Union, 10,612
Western Normal College (Lincoln, NE), 3,718
Western Products (Fargo, ND), 13,669
Western Reserve University (OH). *See* Case Western
Reserve University (OH)
Western State Normal School (MI), 8,233
Western State Teachers College (MI), 8,244
Western States Mission, 16,651
Western States Missionary Baptist Convention, **1,802**
Western stories, 189, **192**, 1,750, 14,354, **16,290**
Western Telegraph Typewriting Machine Company,
8,928
Western Union, 17,196
Western University of Pennsylvania, students, 15,240
Western Womanhood. See *White Ribbon Bulletin*
Western Women's Club, 720
Western Women's Journal, 10,448
Western World (periodical), 2,497
Western Writers of America award, 10,262
Westervelt, Leonidas, 12,258
Westfall, Elizabeth Bird (1878-1958), **10,635**
Westfeldt, Martha (Gasquet) (1883-1960), **13,163**
Westfield Normal School (MA), 7,342
Westhampton Presbyterian Church (Riverhead, NY),
12,781
Westinghouse Electric Corporation, 15,253
Westlake Family (NY), 11,440
Westminster College, trustees, 9,956
Westminster Presbyterian Church (Big Rapids, MI),
7,899
Westminster Presbyterian Church (Minneapolis, MN),
Ladies Home Mission Society, 9,432
Westminster Presbyterian Church (Minneapolis, MN),
Women's Home Missionary Society, 9,432
Westminster School (Topeka, KS), 5,228
Westminster School of Art, 14,215
Westminster Schools (GA), 3,245, **3,264, 3,435**
Westminster Study Club (Cedar Rapids, IA), 4,959
Weston, Anne Warren (1812-90), 2,629, 5,926, 5,972
Weston, Antonia [Mrs. Paul], 15,529
Weston, Caroline (1808-82), 5,926, 5,972
Weston, Deborah, 5,926, 5,972
Weston, Emma Forbes (1825-?), 5,972
Weston, Faith, 2,793
Weston Family (IL, UT), 16,947
Weston, Harold, 2,793
Weston, Janet, **4,403**
Weston, Lucia (?-1861), 5,972
Weston, Lucy. *See* Gibbs, Lucy (Weston)
Weston, Maria (1806-85). *See* Chapman, Maria
(Weston) [Mrs. Henry Grafton] (1806-85)
Weston, Martha Jane (1838-?). *See* Averill, Martha
Jane (Weston) (1838-?)
Weston, Mary, 15,343
Weston, Mary Ann (1817-1901) *See* Maughan, Mary
Ann (Weston) [Mrs. Peter] (1817-1901)
Weston, Mary Ann (Kearsing), 587
Weston, Paul, **15,529**
Weston School (IL), 4,259
Weston School (PA), 2,195
Westonian, The (periodical), **15,351**

Westover, Carrie Greene [Mrs.], 7,140
Westover School, 6,574
Westport High School (Kansas City, MO), 10,113
Westropp, Clara E. (1886-1965), **6,945**
Westropp, Lillian Mary (1884-1968), **6,945**
Westrum, Gladys [Mrs.], 8,690
"West's Greatest Catastrophe, The" (ms), 187
Westtown School (PA), 14,805, 14,851
accounting, **15,347**
alumnae, 15,351
faculty, 15,341, 15,349
students, **15,348**, 15,349, **15,350**
trustees, **15,352**
Westtown Committee, 15,352
Westward: A Magazine of Verse, 1,448
Westward the Women (book), 16,167
Westwood Garden Club (Evansville, IN), **4,501**
Westwood, Jean M. [Mrs.] (1929-), 16,965
Wet-nurses, 9,351
Wetherbee, Mrs. H. Gardner, 12,348
Wetherell, Elizabeth (pseudonym). *See* Warner,
Susan Bogert (1819-85)
Wetherill, Julia Kern (1857-1931). *See* Baker, Julia
Kern (Wetherill) [Mrs. Marion A.] (1857-1931)
Wetherill, Marietta [Mrs.], 11,227
Wetherill, Thomas M., Family, **9,771**
Wethersfield Academy (CT), 4,489
Wetjen, Albert R., 14,382
Wetman, Josephine, 3,967
Wetmore, Edward M., 4,266
Wetmore, Elizabeth Orne [Mrs. William] (1784-?).
See White, Elizabeth Orne [Mrs. William]
Wetmore [Mrs. Daniel A.] (1784-?)
Wetmore, Maude, 2,397
Wetmore, Nellie Mabel (Parminter) [Mrs. Edward
M.] (1873-1969), **4,266**
Wetmore, Sarah Waldo. *See* Story, Sarah Waldo
(Wetmore) [Mrs. Joseph]
Wetmore, William, 7,464
Wetzel, H. E., 8,663
Wever, Jane Catherine (Dunlop) [Mrs. Caspar W.],
17,992
Wever, Caspar W., 17,992
Wever, Catherine. *See* Collins, Catherine (Wever)
Wexler, Joyce, 4,237
Wexler, Molly, 1,016
Weyerhaeuser, Apollonia (1864-1953). *See* Davis,
Apollonia (Weyerhaeuser) [Mrs. S. S.]
(1864-1953)
Weyerhaeuser, Elise (1860-1946). *See* Hill, Elise
(Weyerhaeuser) [Mrs. W. B.] (1860-1946)
Weyerhaeuser, Elizabeth Sarah Bloedel [Mrs.
Frederick King], 3,734, 9,433
Weyerhaeuser Family (MN), **9,433**
Weyerhaeuser, Frederick King (1834-1914), 9,433
Weyerhaeuser, Margaret (1862-1939). *See* Jewett,
Margaret (Weyerhaeuser) [Mrs. J. R.]
(1862-1939)
Weygand Family, 4,942
Weyler, General, 15,743
Weyman, Catherine, 15,765
Weyman, Edward, 15,765
Weyman Family (SC), **15,765**
Weyman, Lydia C. "Kate," 15,765
Weyman, Mary Rosalie, 15,765
Whaleboats, 634
Whalemen, 3,636, 7,338, 7,492, 7,632
Whalen, Agnes M. [Mrs.], 4,699
Whalen, Philip, 11,983
Whalers, 1,505, 7,481, 7,482, 8,164
Whales, Henry, 15,110
Whales, observation of, 7,492
Whaley, Amy L., 1,061
Whaling, 412, **7,028**, 7,479, 7,632, 11,284, 11,653
Whaling Wives (book), 7,028
Wharton, Anne Hollingsworth (1845-1928), **15,111**
Wharton, Edith Newbold (Jones) [Mrs. Edward
Robbins] (1862-1937), 378, 1,390, 1,425, 2,643,
4,491, 5,734, 5,861, 5,863, 5,956, 7,171, 7,296,
11,156, **11,175**, 11,812, 11,821, 11,854, 11,897,
11,944, 12,637, 14,736, **16,173**, 17,053
Wharton, Emma Virginia (Richardson) [Mrs. Greene
Lawrence] (?-1922), **15,911**
Wharton Family (PA), **14,981**

Wharton, Katherine Johnstone (Brinley) (?-1926), **15,112**

"What a Housewife Can Do" (television program), 1,024

"What America Is Fighting For" (essay), 16,173

"What Are Years?" (poem), 11,171

What Do You Know About the Piano? (moving-picture), 16,562

"What Every Girl Should Know" (lecture), 4,388

What Every Young Bride Should Know (screen play), 6,000

"What Iowa Means to Me" (essay), 4,908

"What Makes a Writer" (lecture), 6,120

"What May Women Do for Development of South" (article), 13,532

"What of the Iowa Poets?", 4,758

What "Our Women in the War" Did and Suffered Within the Lines (pamphlet), 13,556

"What Religion Means to Me" (article), 9,878

"What Should We Teach Our Girls" (lecture), 4,388

"What Sort of North Carolina Rural Civilization Should Farm Women Develop?" (article), 13,532

What the Gulls Knew (drama), 14,313

What to Say When the Spider (book), 16,165

"What Year Is This?" (ms), 9,770

What's Done and Past (book), 13,368

Wheat Grower's Association, 13,698

Wheat, Margaret M., **10,726**

Wheatland, Henry (1812-93), 7,343

Wheatland, Martha (1807-?). *See* Bemis, Martha (Wheatland) [Mrs. R. E.] (1807-?)

Wheatley, Phillis. [Mrs. John] Peters (c. 1753-84), 9,289, 13,214

Wheaton, Anne Williams (1892-), 5,135, **5,159**, 11,857

Wheaton College (Wheaton, IL), faculty, 8,995

Wheaton College (Norton, MA), 7,206, **7,330**, 12,737 faculty, **6,295**

Wheaton, Eliza Baylies (Chapin) [Mrs. Laban Morey] (1809-1905), 7,330

Wheaton Female Seminary (Norton, MA). *See* Wheaton College (Norton, MA)

Wheaton, Gladys (1900-). *See* Ahrens, Gladys (Wheaton) [Mrs. B. F.] (1900-)

Wheaton Herbert E., Family (MN), **9,434**

Wheaton, Laban, 7,330

Wheaton, Laban Morey, 7,330

Wheaton, Marilouise. *See* Jackson, Marilouise (Wheaton) [Mrs. L. J.]

Wheaton, Mary Ann, 533

Wheaton News, 7,330

Wheaton, Sophie [Mrs. Herbert E.], 9,434

Whedon, Helen M. [Mrs. William W.], **7,972**

Whedon, Mary Allen, 13,664

Wheeler, Adade, 4,445

Wheeler, Benjamine Ide (1854-1927), 674, **876**

Wheeler, Burton K., 12,502

Wheeler, Clara (Bradley) [Mrs. N. Milman] (1855-1954). *See* Burdette, Clara (Bradley) [Mrs. N. Milman] Wheeler [Mrs. Presley C.] Baker [Mrs. Robert J.] (1855-1954)

Wheeler, Clara Marian (1861-1946), **7,973**

Wheeler, Clara (Torgerson) (1891-), **8,720**

Wheeler, Cleora Clark (ca. 1883-), 9,003, 9,145, 9,255, 9,435

Wheeler, Cornelia, 6,336

Wheeler, Doris B. [Mrs. Paul] Preisler [Mrs. Maurice R.], **8,146**

Wheeler, Edward Blue, 15,569

Wheeler, Ella (1850-1919). *See* Wilcox, Ella (Wheeler) [Mrs. Robert Marius] (1850-1919)

Wheeler Family, **13,962**

Wheeler Family, 4,811

Wheeler Family, 876

Wheeler, Flora (Atkins) (1815-50), 326

Wheeler, Florence Ida, **16,568**

Wheeler, Frances Parkinson (1885-). *See* Keyes, Frances Parkinson (Wheeler) (1885-)

Wheeler, George Montague, 1,444

Wheeler, H. A., 4,208

Wheeler, Homer, 13,962

Wheeler, John Hill, 13,262

Wheeler, Kate (1833-1912). *See* Cooper, Kate (Wheeler) (1833-1912)

Wheeler, L., 14,645

Wheeler, L. O., **7,974**

Wheeler, Laura Maude (1874-1966) **14,466**

Wheeler, Libbie, 4,811

Wheeler, Lillian (Marsh) [Mrs. Charles Stetson], 876

Wheeler, Lucy James (Blair), 1,444

Wheeler, Marcus P., 17,739

Wheeler, Margaret (1867-?). *See* Ross, Margaret (Wheeler) [Mrs. Henry D.] (1867-?)

Wheeler, Martha A., **10,833**

Wheeler, Mary Ann, **12,340**

Wheeler, Mary Eliza (Ide) [Mrs.] Benjamin (1822-84), 876

Wheeler, Mary Gladding. *See* Benjamin, Mary Gladding (Wheeler) [Mrs. Nathan]

Wheeler, Mary R. (1901-), **8,147**

Wheeler, Maurice R., 8,146

Wheeler, Rush Benjamin (1844-1930), **9,435**

Wheeler, Ruth, 5,505

Wheeler, Samuel Jordan, 13,262, **13,605**

Wheeler-Voegelin, Erminie, 2,835

Wheeler, William F., **17,736**

Wheeler, William F., 10,387

Wheeling Hospital (WV), 17,487

Wheelock, Alice (1885-1960s), **4,457**

Wheelock College (MA), presidents, 2,093

Wheelock, Florence (1878-1942). *See* MacNair, Florence (Wheelock) [Mrs. Francis] Aysscough [Mrs. Harley Farnsworth] (1878-1942)

Wheelock, John Hall, 11,897

Wheelock, Joseph Albert (1831-1906), Family (MN), **9,436**

Wheelock, Kate (French) [Mrs. Joseph Albert], 9,436

Wheelwright, Jane (Hollister) [Mrs. Joseph Balch], 548

Wheelwright, Mary C. [Miss], 5,592

Wheler, Charles L., 3,006

"When Chicago Was Young" (column), 3,825

"When Father Made Root Beer" (song), 10,540

When Michigan Was New (book), 8,342

When the Skies Part (book), 16,165

When the World Ended: The Diary of Emma LeConte (book), 13,057

When We're Green We Grow (book), 13,626

"When You See William", 5,763

"When Your Two Lips Smile at Me" (song), 10,436

"Where You Belong" (story), 15,660

Wherry, Elizabeth (Cripliver) (1893-1956), **5,043**

Wherry, Marie (Nast) (1880-1971), **13,860**

Whetten, Harriet Douglas [Mrs. John], 17,737

Whetten, Harriet Douglas (pre-1822-?). *See* Gamble, Harriet Douglas (Whetten) (pre-1822-?)

Whetten, John, 17,737

Whidbey Island, 17,330

Whig (Quincy, IL), 4,347

Whig Party, Mississippi, 9,582, 9,613

Whimsey, Rachel, 1,573

Whimsical Collection, A (book), 3,078

Whipper, Leigh, 12,685

Whipple, Charles Henry (1849-1932), 9,437

Whipple, Charlotte Lambert (18??-88), **12,669**

Whipple, Cornelia (1845-84). *See* Rose, Cornelia (Whipple) [Mrs. William Wilkins] Davis [Mrs. Francis Marion] (1845-84)

Whipple, Cornelia (Wright) [Mrs. Henry Benjamin] (1816-90), 9,345, 9,437

Whipple, E. P., 12,399

Whipple, Elizabeth. *See* Jenkins, Elizabeth (Whipple) [Mrs. James Wright]

Whipple, Elizabeth (1843-ca. 1918). *See* Farnum, Elizabeth (Whipple) [Mrs. Charles Augustus] (1843-ca. 1918)

Whipple, Emma (Philleo) Goodwin [Mrs. Charles K.], 1,874

Whipple, Evangeline (Marrs) [Mrs. Michael H.] Simpson [Mrs. Henry Benjamin] (1860-1930), 9,437, 9,438

Whipple, Evelyn [Mrs. Charles], 9,437

Whipple Family (MN), 9,345, **9,437**

Whipple, Frances. *See* Jackson, Frances (Whipple) [Mrs. Frank G.] Craw [Mrs. Freedom W.]

Whipple, Henry Benjamin (1822-1901), 9,437, **9,438**

Whipple, Jane "Jennie" (1847-1932). *See* Scandrett, Jane "Jennie" (Whipple) [Mrs. Henry Alexander] (1847-1932)

Whipple, John Hall (?-1878), 9,437

Whipple, Marilyn, **16,569**

Whipple, Mary J. Mills [Mrs. George B.] (?-1911), 9,422

Whipple, Maurine [Miss], **16,972**

Whipple, Sarah Brayton. *See* Salisbury, Sarah Brayton (Whipple) [Mrs. Hiram]

Whirly-Girls, International Women Helicopter Pilots, 31

Whisenand, Margaret Eleanor (Long) (1893-), **10,553**

Whisenton, Zadie Beford [Mrs.] (1935-), 94

Whispering Tongues: A Fanciful Romance of Rio (book), 6,903

Whistler, Anna Matilda (McNeill) [Mrs. George] (1804-81), **12,670**, 13,606

Whistler, Anna Matilda McNeill (1830-76), 2,520

Whistler Family, 12,605

Whistler, Helen, 2,520

Whistler, James Abbot McNeill (1834-1903), 2,520, 6,185, 12,670

"Whistler's Mother" (painting), 13,606

Whitaker, Elizabeth [Mrs. James] (1765-1833), **14,098**

Whitaker, Elsie (1890-). *See* Martinez, Elsie (Whitaker) [Mrs. Xavier] (1890-)

Whitaker, Inez (1892-). *See* Hunt, Inez (Whitaker) [Mrs. Nelson V.] (1892-)

Whitaker, James (17??-1804), **14,098**

Whitaker, Mical, 12,367

Whitaker, Norman, 657

Whitall, Matilda. *See* Rice, Matilda (Whitall) [Mrs. Henry Mower]

Whitall, Rachel (Newbold) [Mrs. Gilbert], 9,311

Whitbeck, Alice, 12,746

Whitby, Beulah [Mrs.], **8,148**

Whitby Literary Society (IA), **5,044**

Whitcher, Benjamin W., 12,341

Whitcher, Frances Miriam (Berry) [Mrs. Benjamin W.] (1811-52), **12,341**

Whitcomb, Anna Gauntlett [Mrs.], 11,645

Whitcomb, Mrs. George F. (?-1935), **8,461**

White, A. Ruth Staples (1895?-), **7,019**

White, Alexina Mease, 12,343

White, Alice, 1,111

White, Alonzo J., **15,530**

White, Amanda. *See* Ferry, Amanda (White) [Mrs. William Montague]

White, Andrew Dickson (1832-1918), 6,617, 11,524, 11,543, 11,575, 11,584, 11,680, **11,742**

White, Ann, 5,822

White, Ann, 12,342

White, Anna M., **3,596**

White, Anne Terry (1896-), **14,467**

White, Bessie Smith [Mrs. Stanford], 12,343

White, Campbell Patrick (1787-1859), **12,342**

White Cap. *See* Continental Group (ConCan)

White, Carrie M., **17,363**

White Citizens' Council (Tuscaloosa, AL), 112

White, Clara. *See* Newberry, Clara (White)

White, Clara Dickson [Mrs. Horace] (1810-82), 11,742

White, Clarence, 607

White Columns in Georgia (book), 3,070

White, Compton I., 3,712

White, Cora E. (1843-1911). *See* Carey, Cora E. (White) [Mrs. Will] Watson [Mrs. S. E.] (1843-1911)

White, Cornelia C., 9,886

White, Cornelia C. (1860-1931), **9,922**

White, Corra May (1869-1935). *See* Harris, Corra May (White) [Mrs. Lundy Howard] (1869-1935)

White, Daisy (Allen), 10,737

White, Dale (pseudonym). *See* Place, Marian T. (ca. 1910-)

White, E. B., 6,416

White Earth Indian Reservation (MN), 8,690, 9,009, 9,042, 9,296

White, Edna N., 12,738

White, Eleanor. *See* Swain, Eleanor (White) [Mrs. David L.]

White, Eliza "Didy" (Ridgely) [Mrs. John Campbell]. *See* Buckler, Eliza "Didy" (Ridgely) [Mrs. John Campbell] White [Mrs. Thomas H.]

White, Eliza Orne (1856-1947), 7,227
White, Elizabeth (Allen), 7,128
White, Elizabeth Ann (1866-1961). *See* Hopfenbeck, Elizabeth Ann (White) [Mrs. Alphonzo] (1866-1961)
White, Elizabeth C. (?-1954), 11,189
White, Elizabeth Orne [Mrs. William] Wetmore [Mrs. Daniel A.] (1784-?), **7,464**
White, Ellen Gould (Harmon) [Mrs. James Springer] (1827-1915), **2,101,** 8,163, **10,602**
White, Elvira T. [Mrs.], 13,322
White, Ernest I., 11,537
White, Esther Griffin [Miss] (1869-1954), **4,654**
White, Eva (Whiting) [Mrs. Wesley Dunn Allen] (1885-1974), **6,239,** 6,760, **6,946**
White Family, **13,962**
White Family (CA), **1,111**
White Family (NY, MD), 12,342
White, Florence Evelyn, **10,652**
White, George Leonard (?-1895), **11,743**
White, Georgia Laura, 11,567, 11,743
White, Gertrude [Mrs. John J.], 1,837
White, Grace Elinor Joy. *See* Pratt, Grace Elinor Joy (White) [Mrs. Chester]
White, Harriet Banyar, 12,342
White, Helen C. (1896-1967), **17,788**
White, Helen McCann, 17,587
White, Helen (Magill) [Mrs. Andrew Dickson] (1853-1944), 2,067, 11,510, 11,742
White, Henrietta S., 7,677
White, Henry, 12,342
White, Henry, 15,335
White, Henry, 5,822
White, Henry Clay, **3,113**
White, Hilda Crystal (1917-), **6,114**
White Horse Leaping (book), 15,720
White House Conference on Aging, 15,570
White House Conference on Child Health and Protection (1930), 5,122, 6,263, 6,420, 9,779
White House Conference on Children and Youth, 1,341, 2,064, **2,083,** 3,399, 7,848, 11,592, 11,744, 11,756, 16,264
White House Conference on Education, 5,143
White House Conference on Food, Nutrition, and Health, 7,817
White House Conference on Home Building and Ownership, 5,122
White House Diary (book), 2,510
White House News Photographers Association, 17,070
White House Office of Social Correspondence, 10,082
White House Office, Office of Special Assistant for Executive Appointments, **5,160**
White House Profile (book), 2,340
White House Social Office, **5,161, 10,083**
White House, The (DC), 2,547, 14,504
White, Hugh (1798-1870), 11,648
White, Hugh L., 9,663
White, Jane, 3,290
White, Jane Strope, 11,445
White, John, 13,446
White, John, 11,318
White, John Campbell, **5,822,** 12,342
White, Josephine Sophia (1814-72). *See* Griffing, Josephine Sophia (White) [Mrs. Charles Stockman Spooner] (1814-72)
White, Judith (Sugg), 9,709
White, Katharine (1906-), 6,416
White, L. Marie, **17,443**
White, Laura M. (1896-1974). *See* Ulmer, Laura M. (White) [Mrs. Walter P.] (1896-1967)
White, Leslie A., 14,897
White, Lida, **14,224**
White, Lillian (ca. 1878-1953). *See* Spencer, Lillian (White) (ca. 1878-1953)
White, Lillian A., 3,850
White, Louisa, **6,165**
White, Lucy Hannah (1842-1900). *See* Flake, Lucy Hannah (White) [Mrs. William Jordan] (1842-1900)
White, Lyman (?-1864), 7,678
White, Mabel E., 1,111
White, Margaret Harding (1823-1903), 6,251
White, Margaret (Humphrey) [Mrs. Rosman], **4,607**

White, Maria Elliot, 3,518
White, Maria Mills Mansfield [Mrs. Hugh] (?-1888), 11,648
White, Marian E. (1921-75), **11,387**
White, Marie Augusta "Minnie Maddern" (Davey) [Mrs. LeGrand] (1865-1932). *See* Fiske, Marie Augusta "Minnie Maddern" (Davey) [Mrs. LeGrand] White [Mrs. Harrison Grey] (1865-1932)
White, Marie S., 3,760
White, Marjorie (1894-1972), 6,542, **6,947,** 11,605
White, Marjorie Mills (ca. 1900-), 668, 1,068
White, Martha (1827-1904). *See* McWhirter, Martha (White) [Mrs. George] (1827-1904)
White, Mary, 1,111
White, Mary. *See* Whitfield, Mary (White)
White, Mary A. [Mrs. Aaron], 7,514
White, Mary Amanda (Outwater) [Mrs. Andrew D.] (1836-87), **11,742**
White, Mary B., 2,701
White, Mary John, 12,342
White, Mary Wilder Foote, 6,251
White, May (Pendergast) [Mrs. Henry A.], 9,282
White Men's Children, 3,288
White, Minnie Maddern (Davey) [Mrs. LeGrand] (1865-1932). *See* Fiske, Marie Augusta "Minnie Maddern" (Davey) [Mrs. LeGrand] White [Mrs. Harrison Grey] (1865-1932)
White, Mrs. Charles Henry, **877**
White, Mrs. J. J., 9,663
White, Mrs. N. D., 9,230
White, Mrs. Robert Leon, **16,146**
White, Myrtle, 7,831
White, Neila Gardner, 14,828
White Oak Presbyterian Church (Coweta County, GA), **3,114**
White, Pearl, 11,607
White, Peter, 8,342
White Pine Copper industry, 10,774
White Pine News (NV), 10,753
"White Plague, The" (story), 8,433
White, Reuben G., 16,060
White Ribbon (newspaper), 8,816
White Ribbon Bulletin (periodical), 9,386, **13,664, 13,665,** 13,668
White River Massacre (CO), 1,751
White, Robert, 12,342
White Rose, The (book), 6,113
White, Ruth (Boericks) [Mrs. Ralston] (1888-?). *See* Bowie, Ruth (Boericks) [Mrs. Ralston] White (1888-?)
White, Ruth M. (1889-). *See* Carr, Ruth M. (White) [Mrs. Clarence] (1889-)
White, Sallie Elizabeth (Joy) (1852?-1909), **6,948**
White, Sallie Lindsay, 2,499
White, Sarah (Caldwell), **13,164**
White, Sarah Gilbert (1813-55). *See* Smith, Sarah Gilbert (White) [Mrs. Asa] (1813-55)
White Slave, The (book), 17,757
"White Slave Traffic, The" (paper), 11,964
White, Sophia A. (Draper) (1811-67), 7,618
White, Sophia May Pendergast [Mrs. Harry A.] (1873-?), 9,282
White, Stanford (1853-1906), 2,810, **12,343**
White, Sue Shelton (1887-1943), **6,949**
White Tiger, The (motion picture), 17,642
White, Tryphena Ely (1784-1816). *See* Kellogg, Tryphena Ely White [Mrs. Frederick] (1784-1816)
White Unicorn, The (book), 15,876, 17,604
White, Viola Chittenden (1890-1977), **17,011, 17,012**
White, W. Wallace (1905-), **10,744**
White, Walter (1893-1955), 2,879, 5,458, 8,116
White, Wanetta (1918-). *See* Tesker, Wanetta (White) [Mrs. Paul] Draper [Mrs. Elmer H.] (1918-)
White, William (1748-1834), 15,048, 15,077
White, William Allen, 17,141
White, William Mansfield, 11,648
White, William O., 7,464
Whitecar, Blanche, 15,187
Whitefield, Fannie B. [Mrs.], **4,200**
Whitefield, George, 4,202
Whitefield, George, 12,170

Whitehead, Helen, 4,085
Whitehead, Kate (1838-?). *See* Rowland, Kate (Whitehead) (1838-?)
Whitehead, Mattie [Mrs.], 3,033
Whitehurst, Mary, **9,772**
Whitehouse, Vivian (Boarman), 12,387
Whiteley, Opal Stanley (1897-), **14,468, 14,684**
Whiteman, Catherine (Ludlow), 17,992
Whitenack, Fannie (1848-1941). *See* Libbey, Fannie (Whitenack) (1848-1941)
Whiteney, Anne (1821-1915), 7,182
Whiteside Family (NY), **11,745**
Whiteside, John, 11,745
Whiteside, Phineas, 11,745
Whiteside, Sarah, 15,117
Whiteside, Walker, 12,476
Whitesides, Margaret (Pierce) [Mrs. Morris] (1823-1907). *See* Young, Margaret (Pierce) [Mrs. Morris] Whitesides [Mrs. Brigham] (1823-1907)
Whitesides, Morris, 16,853
Whiteturkey, Julia (Johnson). *See* Dalton, Julia (Johnson) Whiteturkey [Mrs. Bob] Gilstrap [Mrs. Earnest] Lewis [Mrs. Emmett]
Whiteturkey, Widow (1836 or 1837-1912), 14,173
Whitewater Normal School (WI), students, 17,591
Whitfield, Caroline (Dyer), 9,709
Whitfield, Louise (1857-1946). *See* Carnegie, Louise (Whitfield) [Mrs. Andrew] (1857-1946)
Whitfield, Mary (White), 9,709
Whitford, Ella. *See* Phillips, Ella Whitford [Mrs. Ross]
Whitford, James H., Family, **9,439**
Whiting, Caroline Lee (1800-56). *See* Hentz, Caroline Lee (Whiting) [Mrs. Nicholas Marcellus] (1800-56)
Whiting, Christine (1877-). *See* Parmenter, Christine (Whiting) [Mrs. Kenneth R.] (1877-)
Whiting, Constance F. Gordon, 1,340
Whiting, Elizabeth Braxton, 17,108
Whiting, Elizabeth F. P., **12,671**
Whiting, Emma Mayhew, 7,028
Whiting, Ethel (Robertson) [Mrs. Henry Hyer] (1882-?), 878
Whiting, Eva (1885-1974). *See* White, Eva (Whiting) [Mrs. Wesley Dunn Allen] (1885-1974)
Whiting Family (CA), **878**
Whiting Family (VA), 17,108
Whiting, Henry Hyer, 878
Whiting, Lilian (1847-1942), 5,921, 5,934, 5,939, 5,959, 5,962, 5,967, **5,973,** 7,651, 17,010
Whiting, Margaret [Miss], 7,012
Whiting, Maria [Mrs.] (1827-94), **4,272**
Whiting, Mrs. Giles, 5,123
Whiting, Sarah Frances (1847-1927), 7,567, **11,816**
Whiting, Winifred (Hanus), **6,950**
Whitinger, R. D. (pseudonym). *See* Place, Marian T. (ca. 1910-)
Whitley, Cora [Mrs. Francis], 4,954
Whitley, William, 5,342
Whitlock, Anna (1839-?), **879**
Whitlock, Sarah O., **11,055**
Whitman, Angelia (Smith), **13,165**
Whitman, Ann, 5,137, 5,144, 5,145
Whitman, Augustus, 880
Whitman College (WA), 17,167
Whitman, Elizabeth, 1,397
Whitman, Florence (Lee), 11,392
Whitman grist mill (OR), 14,632
Whitman, Marcus (1802-47), **880,** 1,505, 11,606, **17,213**
Whitman Massacre (1847), 780, 881, 1,505, 14,578, 14,593, 17,422
Whitman Mission (OR), 780
Whitman, Narcissa (Prentiss) [Mrs. Marcus] (1808-47), 880, 1,505, **14,715, 17,213,** 17,373, **17,410,** 17,421, 17,422, 17,908, **17,923**
Whitman, Sarah Helen (Power) (1803-78), 17,010
Whitman, Walt, 1,589, 2,384, 2,610, 12,449, 12,547, 12,698, 17,336, 17,692
Whitmarsh, Martha, 7,140
Whitmore, Emoline, 8,311
Whitmore, Joel, 9,248

Whitmore, Maude (1867-1948). *See* Madden, Maude (Whitmore) [Mrs. Milton B.] (1867-1948)
Whitner, John C., 3,266
Whitner, Sarah Martha (Cobb) [Mrs. John C.], **3,266**
Whitney, Adeline Dutton (Train) [Mrs. Seth Dunbar] (1824-1906), 1,426, 6,659, 6,764, 7,131, 17,010
Whitney, Anita, 9,119
Whitney, Anna B. (1906-), 7,109
Whitney, Anne (1821-1915), 1,426, 4,233, **7,585**
Whitney, Benajah T., 11,602
Whitney, Bennett, 11,056
Whitney, Bertha (Stoddard) [Mrs. Henry] (1850-?), 11,056
Whitney, Charlotte Anita (1867-1955), 640, 689, 756
Whitney, Christina C., 11,560
Whitney, Dorothy Payne. *See* Straight, Dorothy Payne Whitney [Mrs. Willard D.]
Whitney, Eben, 11,056
Whitney, Ellen, 4,445
Whitney, Emmeline Blanch (Woodward) [Mrs. James Harris [Mrs. Newel K.] (1828-1921). *See* Wells, Emmeline Blanch (Woodward) [Mrs. James Harvey] Harris [Mrs. Newel Kimball] Whitney [Mrs. Daniel Hanmer] (1828-1921)
Whitney Family (GA), **3,204**
Whitney Family, 11,039, **11,056**
Whitney, Frank, 17,595
Whitney, Gertrude (Vanderbilt) [Mrs. Harry Payne] (1875-1942), 2,646, 3,783, **12,709**
Whitney, Helen Augusta (Barstow) [Mrs. William Frank] (1831-1924), **17,595, 17,873**
Whitney, Helen Mary (Kimball) [Mrs. Joseph, Jr.] Smith [Mrs. Horace Kimball] (1828-96), **16,841**
Whitney, Henrietta, 3,057
Whitney, Henry, 11,056
Whitney, Horace Kimball, 16,841
Whitney, Josephine (1891-). *See* Duveneck, Josephine (Whitney) (1891-)
Whitney, Louise (Goddard) Howe [Mrs. Josiah Dwight], 371
Whitney, Margaret Mason (?-1953), **882**
Whitney, Mary Traffarn (1852-1940), **11,403**
Whitney Museum of American Art (NY), 2,789, 5,118, 12,709
Whitney, Myra (Clark) [Mrs. William Wallace] (1805-1885). *See* Gaines, Myra (Clark) [Mrs. William Wallace] Whitney [Mrs. Edmund Pendleton] (1805-1885)
Whitney, Myrta V., **17,866**
Whitney, Newel Kimball, 16,566, 16,839
Whitney, Orson Ferguson (1855-1931), 16,841, **16,842**
Whitney, Parkhurst, Family (NY), 12,734
Whitney, Phyllis Ayame (1903-), 6,060, 14,475
Whitney, Sarah (Hatheway) [Mrs. Benajah T.] (1811-72), 11,602
Whitney, Sarah Ware, 1,059
Whitney, Seth Dunbar, 1,426
Whitney Studio Club (NY), 12,709
Whitney, Susan (1839-?), **11,057**
Whitney, William F., 17,873
Whitney, Zina B. Smoot [Mrs. Orson Ferguson], 16,842
Whitsitte, Virginia. *See* Westbrook, Virginia (Whitsitte)
Whittaker, Hazel Harper (1882-1950). *See* Vandenberg, Hazel Harper (Whittaker) [Mrs. Arthur H.] (1882-1950)
Whittaker, Mary Jo, 4,445
Whittemore, Eliza Ann (Cutter) [Mrs. Henry], 12,672
Whittemore Family (MA), **12,672**
Whittemore, Harriet, 16,539
Whittemore, Henry, 12,672
Whitten, Jonathan M., 29
Whitten, Martha L. [Mrs. Jonathan M.] (?-1902), **29**
Whitten, Willie May [Mrs. James H.], **3,267**
Whittier, John Greenleaf (1807-92), 1,426, 2,262, 2,588, 6,663, 7,294, 7,681, **8,375**, 8,526, 10,796, 10,825, 12,003, 13,232, 14,164
Whittier, Ruth [Miss], 10,835
Whittingham, Mary Ann (Rollinson) [Mrs. Richard] (1785-1848), 5,827
Whittingham, William Rollinson, 5,827
Whittington, Dick, 15,876

Whittle, Chloe Tyler. *See* Greene, Chloe Tyler (Whittle) [Mrs. John Newport]
Whittle, Elizabeth Julia, 3,436
Whittle Family (VA), **17,123**
Whittle Family (VA, GA), **3,436**
Whittle, Fortescue, 3,436
Whittle, Grace Latimer, 17,123
Whittle, Lewis Neale, 3,436
Whittle, Mary Ann Davies [Mrs. Fortescue], 3,436
Whittle, Narcissa, 3,436
Whittle, Sarah M. Powers [Mrs. Lewis Neale], 3,436
Whittlesay, Emily (1849-1926). *See* Mitchell, Emily Whittlesay [Mrs. William B.] (1849-1926)
Whittlesey, Miyoka, 1,534
Whittredge, Sarah Waters (1804-?). *See* Osborne, Sarah Waters (Whittredge) [Mrs. George] (1804-?)
Whitty, Dame May, 2,625
Whitworth College (MS), 9,610
"Who Is Becky Thatcher" (article), 9,832
Who Killed Aunt Maggie? (book), 3,070
Who Touches This (book), 14,200
Who Will Buy My Mongoose? (book), 18,004
Whooping-cough epidemics, 11,600
Who's Who awards, 16,277
Who's Who in America, 5,310
Who's Who in American Education, 13,382
Who's Who in Library Service, 11,968
Who's Who of the American Theatre, 3,003
Why Don't They Go Home? (book), 8,802
Why Is an Elephant Called an Elephant? (book), 17,956
"Why Should Women Be Denied Admission to the Bar?" (article), 3,437
"Why Visit Fort Stevens, DC? A Narrative About President Abraham Lincoln That Every One Should Read" (book), 2,129
"Why Women Do Not Want the Ballot" (article), 1,473
Wi-iyohi, 7,220
Wichita Beacon (KS), 12,863
Wichita Falls Daily Times, The (TX), 16,387
Wichita Mountains (mining boom), 14,207
Wichita State University (KS),
    alumnae, 5,243
    archives, **5,241**
Wichita State University (KS), Associated Women Students, 5,241
Wichita State University (KS), Council of University Women, 5,241
Wichita State University (KS), Ladies Advisory Board of the Young Woman's Department, 5,241
Wichita State University, Philmathean Society, 5,241
Wick Family, 12,673
Wick, Grace M. (1888-1958), **14,686**
Wicke, Tempe, 11,185
Wickenden, Elizabeth. [Mrs. Arthur E.] Goldschmid
Wickens, Aryness (Joy), (1901-), 2,681, **11,929**
Wicker, Augusta (French) [Mrs. Cassius] (1849-89), 4,361
Wicker, Cassius, 4,361
Wickersham, Charles, III, 3,111
Wickersham Commission. *See* National Commission on Law Observance and Enforcement (Wickersham Commission)
Wickes, Frances (Gillespy) (1875-1967), **2,631**
Wickes, Gertrude, 2,284
Wickham, Ola Forbes (1889-), **14,184**
Wickliffe Family, **2,659**
Widdemer, Margaret [Miss], 1,087, **12,915**, 14,828
Widditsch, Ann, **17,364**
Widen, Gudrun, **8,802**
Widnall, Sheila, 6,335
"Widow Bedott" (satire), 12,341
Widow of Ephesus (book), 3,514
Widow of the Month Club, 9,986
Widows, 252, 580, 1,860, 1,879, **2,217**, 2,294, 3,370, 3,556, **4,254, 4,338**, 5,520, **5,553**, 5,686, **7,621**, 7,675, **9,107**, 9,512, 9,849, 9,879, 9,904, 9,917, 9,972, **9,974**, 9,986, 10,010, **11,015**, 11,100, 11,180, 11,256, 12,315, 12,511, 13,387, 13,396, 13,401, 13,445, 13,449, 13,450, 13,534, 13,582, 13,589, 13,612, 13,764, 16,144, **16,147**
Widows Homes of Hartford (CT), **1,879**

Widows' pensions. *See* Survivors' benefits
Widtsoe, Anna (1899-). *See* Wallace, Anna (Widtsoe) (1899-)
Widtsoe Family (UT), **16,973**
Widtsoe, John Andreas (1872-1965). *See* Widtsoe, John Andrew (1872-1965)
Widtsoe, John Andrew (1872-1965), 16,843, 16,973
Widtsoe, Leah Eudora (Dunford) [Mrs. John Andrew] (1874-1965), **16,843**, 16,922, 16,973
Wiebeck, Eleanor (Alexander) (1905-), 169
Wieck, Mary C. (1860-96). *See* Folsom, Mary C. Wieck [Mrs. Wyman X.] (1860-96)
Wiecking, Anna M. [Miss] (1887-1973), **8,492**
Wiecking, Emma [Miss] (1894-), **8,512**
Wiecking, H. R., **8,492** .
Wiedefeld, Mary Theresa (1886-), 5,835, **5,836**
Wiehe, Elise Christine (?-1900). *See* Hittell, Elise Christine (Wiehe) [Mrs. Theodore Henry] (?-1900)
Wiel, Elsa (Rosenbaum), **883**
Wien, Ada (Bering) [Mrs. Noel], **14,687**
Wien, Noel, 14,687
Wieners, John, 12,064
Wier, Jeanne Elizabeth [Miss] (1870-1950), 10,655, 10,687, **10,727**, 10,728
Wiersma, Jennie [Mrs.] (1891-), **8,265**
Wieschendorff, Julia (1861-1938). *See* Gerstenberg, Julia (Wieschendorff) [Mrs. E.] (1861-1938)
Wife Is Many Women, A (book), 6,399
Wife of Martin Guerre The (opera), 1,587
Wife of Platt (book), 3,514
Wife swapping. *See* Swinging and swingers (sex customs)
Wiggin, Kate Douglas (Smith) [Mrs. Samuel Bradley] (1856-1923). *See* Riggs, Kate Douglas (Smith) [Mrs. Samuel Bradley] Wiggin [Mrs. George Christopher] (1856-1923)
Wiggin, Samuel Bradley, 1,426
Wiggins, Laura, 6,325
Wiggins, Myra Albert [Mrs.] (1876-1956), **17,179**
Wiggins, Phoebe, 11,318
Wiggins, Roelf, 11,318
Wigglesworth, Anne, 7,476
Wigglesworth, Thomas, 7,476
Wigman, Mary, 2,968
Wilbarger, Margaret Barker [Mrs. Josiah Pugh] (ca. 1802-?). *See* Chambers, Margaret Barker [Mrs. Josiah Pugh] Wilbarger [Mrs. Thomas Washington] (ca. 1802-?)
Wilber, D. T., 11,580
Wilber, Doreen V. (Hansen) (1930-), 5,048
Wilberforce Graduate: A Half Century of Freedom of the Negro in Ohio, 13,945
Wilberforce University, 2,130
Wilbor, Sarah Soule (1804-90), **15,370**
Wilborn, Jane, 13,219
Wilbour, Charlotte Beebe [Mrs. Charles E.] (1833-1914), **2,632**
Wilbur, Julia A., 11,616
Wilbur, Lorraine, **12,001**
Wilbur, Maud Adela, 9,538
Wilbur, R. L., 1,592, 1,593
Wilbur, Robert, **12,001**
Wilchek, Stella (1922-), **6,115**
Wilcocks. *See also* Wilcox
Wilcocks, Charlotte Manigault. *See* McCall, Charlotte Manigault (Wilcocks)
Wilcocks, Harriet (Manigault) [Mrs. Samuel] (1793-?), 13,066, **15,113**
Wilcox. *See also* Wilcocks
Wilcox, Abner (1808-69), **3,649**
Wilcox, Anna B. [Mrs. Albert], **11,058**
Wilcox, Annie Rice [Mrs. Jonathan F.], 16,967
Wilcox, Ella (Wheeler) [Mrs. Robert Marius] (1850-1919), 672, 1,489, 2,413, 3,110, 3,927, 4,226, 4,781, **6,952**, 7,868, 11,821, 12,321, 12,529, **16,174, 16,570**, 17,010, 17,718, **17,739**
Wilcox, Henrietta, 1,880
Wilcox, Howard (1838-83), **1,880**
Wilcox, Hugh B., Family, **9,440**
Wilcox, Jannette Fancher [Mrs. Howard], 1,880
Wilcox, Jean M. [Mrs. Hugh B.], 9,440, 9,456
Wilcox, Jonathan F., 16,967

Wilcox, Lucy Eliza (Hart) [Mrs. Abner] (1814-69), **3,649**
Wilcox, Mary Emily (Donelson) (1829-?), 2,312
Wilcox, Mary "Molly" (Warren) [Mrs. Edwin F.] (1880-1974), **5,243**
Wilcox, Pauline. *See* Burke, Pauline (Wilcox) [Mrs. Moncure]
Wilcox, Phebe Almira, **9,441**
Wilcox, Sarah Catherine, 9,323
Wilcox, Wendell, 840
Wild flowers, 5,601, 13,709, 14,213, 16,316
Wild Geese, 8,805
Wild, Marge [Mrs.], 3,787
Wild, Mary Rosamond (Dana), 6,502
Wild Place, The (book), 557
Wild rice, 8,927
Wild, Sarah (Jocelyn) [Mrs. Joseph], 1,870
Wild west shows, 1,779, 10,428, 14,101
"Wild Woman of Galloria [Galiura] Mountains, The" (story), 189
Wildcat strikes, 11,851
Wilde, Oscar, 1,467
Wildenhain, Marguerite, **2,828**
Wilder, Amherst Holcomb (1828-94), 8,909
Wilder, Amherst Holcomb (1828-94) Family (MN), **9,442**
Wilder, Bertha (1874-?). *See* Reed, Bertha (Wilder) [Mrs. Robert R.] (1874-?)
Wilder, Burt Green, 11,685
Wilder, Cornelia Day (1868-1903). *See* Appleby, Cornelia Day (Wilder) [Mrs. T. E. W. Villiers] (1868-1903)
Wilder, Elizabeth Kinau (Judd) [Mrs. Samuel Gardner] (1831-1918) 3,650
Wilder, Fanny Spencer [Mrs. Amherst Holcomb] (1837-1903), 9,442
Wilder, Gaston Henry, **13,607**
Wilder, Inez Whipple (1871-1929), 7,158
Wilder, Mrs. Frederic (1850-?), 13,683
Wilder, Rose (1887-). *See* Lane, Rose (Wilder) (1887-)
Wilder, Samuel Gardner (1831-88), **3,650**
Wilder, Thornton, 2,463, 2,876, 7,300, 17,803
Wilderness Society, 17,251
Wildes, Elizabeth (Perkins) [Mrs. Israel] (1765-1844), **5,691**
Wildes, Israel, 5,691
Wildlife, 5,487
Wildlife conservation, 50, 1,473, 1,835, **7,666**, 15,802, 17,248, 17,251, 17,267, **17,834**
Wildlife management, 7,666
Wildlife refuges, 2,878, 3,062, 3,327, **8,973**
Wildlife Science Wives Club (TX), **16,201**
Wildlife watching, 7,489
Wildwood, Nellie (pseudonym). *See* Mears, Mary Elizabeth Farnsworth [Mrs. John Hall] (1830-1907)
Wildy, Lois, 4,103
Wile, Ira Solomon (1877-1943), **7,320, 12,837**
Wiles, Alice Bradford, 4,366
Wiley, Alexander, 11,747
Wiley, Anna (Kelton) [Mrs. Harvey W.] (1877-1964), **2,633,** 6,742, **6,953**
Wiley, Calvin H., **13,608**
Wiley, Harvey W. (1844-1930), 2,633
Wiley, I. W., 10,584
Wiley, Lily (1849-85). *See* Vallejo, Lily (Wiley) [Mrs. Platón] (1849-85)
Wiley, Lucia, 9,145
Wiley, Martha [Miss] (1874-1969), 884, 11,846, **17,429**
Wiley, Mary, 13,608
Wiley, Mary C., **13,609**
Wiley, Mary G. (Willcox) [Mrs. Alexander], 11,747
Wilford Ward Primary (UT), 16,662
Wilfred Clarke Company, 9,466
Wilhelm, Clarissa (Harden) Lewis Terry (1820-1901), **16,489,** 16,967
Wilhelm, Crown Prince (Germany), 2,663
Wilhelm II, Kaiser (Germany), 11,956
Wilhelmina, Queen of the Netherlands, 8,950, 12,273
Wilhite, Mary M. Holloway [Mrs. E. A.] (1831-92), **4,496**
Wilkerson, Helen C. (1905-59), **5,419**

Wilkes, Charles (1798-1877), **2,634**
Wilkes, Eliza, 2,634
Wilkes, Jane, 2,634
Wilkes, Jane Jeffrey (Renwick) [Mrs Charles] (?-1848), 2,634
Wilkes, John, 2,634
Wilkes, Louisa Webb [Mrs. Samuel Marion], 15,766
Wilkes, Mary H. (Lynch) [Mrs. William C.] Bolton [Mrs. Charles], 2,634
Wilkes, Samuel Marion (?-1861), **15,766**
Wilkeson, Mary Peters [Mrs. Samuel], 12,278
Wilkie, Mrs. Wendell L., 12,708
Wilkie, Wendell L., 2,617
Wilkin, Matilda Jane (Campbell) [Mrs. George F.] (1846-1943), 8,602, **8,623,** 9,463
Wilkins, Emma Cheves, **3,597**
Wilkins, Hester A. (1809-88). *See* Davis, Hester A. (Wilkins) [Mrs. Allen Bowie] (1809-88)
Wilkins, Kittie (1861-?), **885**
Wilkins, Mary Eleanor (1852-1930) *See* Freeman, Mary Eleanor (Wilkins) [Mrs. Charles M.] (1852-1930)
Wilkins, Nina. *See* Scudder, Nina (Wilkins)
Wilkins, Roy, 2,587, 5,458
Wilkinson, Ann (Biddle) [Mrs. James] (1757-1807), 15,025
Wilkinson, Catharine, 12,315
Wilkinson, F. R. [Miss], 14,809
Wilkinson, Florence, **11,431**
Wilkinson, James, 15,025
Wilkinson, Jane (Humphrey), 15,169
Wilkinson, Jemima (1752-1819), 7,607, 11,440, 11,512, 11,746, **12,768**
Wilkinson, John, 4,358
Wilkinson, Joseph, 16,425
Wilkinson, Leila Fayssoux Davidson [Mrs.] (1881-1958), **15,531**
Wilkinson, Marguerite Ogden Bigelow [Mrs. James G.] (1883-1928), 4,005, 4,226, **17,013**
Wilkinson, Mary Short [Mrs. Micajah], 5,420
Wilkinson, Micajah, **5,420**
Wilkinson, Rebecca (1780-1833). *See* Street, Rebecca (Wilkinson) (1780-1833)
Wilkinson, Virginia Shelton [Mrs.], 3,141
Willamette Iron and Steel Company (OR), 14,674
Willamette Mission (OR), 14,528
Willamette University (OR)
   faculty, 14,402
   students, 14,424
Willamette Valley Southern Railway, 14,573
Willard, Antonia (Ford) [Mrs. Joseph Clapp] (1838-71), 2,635
Willard, Arthur C., 4,395
Willard, Belle Layton (Wyatt) [Mrs. Joseph E.] (?-1954), 2,558, 2,635
Willard, Belle Wyatt (1892-1968). *See* Roosevelt, Belle Wyatt (Willard) [Mrs. Kermit] (1892-1968)
Willard, Catherine. *See* Dickinson, Catherine (Willard) [Mrs. Samuel Philemon]
Willard, Charles Wesley (1827-80), **17,043**
Willard, Elisa, 5,863
Willard, Eliza May, 17,043
Willard, Elizabeth. *See* Herbert, Elizabeth (Willard)
Willard, Emily S., 17,010
Willard, Emma (Hart) [Mrs. John]. [Mrs. Christopher] Yates (1787-1870), 63, 1,084, 2,501, 7,295, 11,605, 11,742, 12,473, 12,790, 12,833, 15,355
Willard Family, **2,635**
Willard, Frances "Frank" Elizabeth Caroline [Miss] (1839-98), 56, 349, 1,224, 1,436, 2,196, 2,315, 2,346, 2,542, 2,605, **2,636,** 3,804, 3,819, 3,862, 3,969, 3,970, 4,062, 4,088, **4,159,** 4,207, 4,215, **4,223,** 4,233, 4,243, 4,244, 5,487, **6,954,** 7,222, 7,239, 7,271, 7,477, 7,585, 7,605, 7,792, 7,866, 7,973, 8,900, 9,241, 9,350, 9,656, 10,725, **10,912,** 11,547, 11,821, 13,963, 14,017, 15,346, 17,226, **17,740,** 18,013
Willard, Frances Langdon, 3,911, 4,377
Willard Hotel (Virginia Hotel Company) 2,635
Willard, Joseph Clapp, 2,635
Willard, Joseph E. (1865-1924), 2,635
Willard, Julius, 4,377
Willard, Mary, 5,863

Willard, Mary, 5,736
Willard, Mary, 17,043
Willard, Mary Bannister, 4,243
Willard, Mary T., 4,244
Willard, Nancy [Mrs. Dustin], 5,420
Willard Parker hospital (NY) 12,506
Willard, Samuel (1821-1913), **4,377**
Willcox. *See also* Wilcocks; Wilcox
Willcox, Alice Eloise Work [Mrs. Walter Francis], 11,747
Willcox, Anne Holmes (Goodenow) [Mrs. William Henry], 11,747
Willcox, Mary Alice (1856-?), 11,747
Willcox, Mary G. *See* Wiley, Mary G. (Willcox) [Mrs. Alexander]
Willcox, Walter Francis (1861-1964), 11,655, **11,747**
Willcox, William Henry, 11,747
Willebrandt, Mabel (Walker) (1889-1963), 1,186, 5,120, 5,121, 5,124, 6,761, 10,740
Willeford, Susannah [Mrs.], 4,958, **5,057**
Willett, Caroline Bronson, 12,398
Willey, Betsy, 14,593
Willey, Maria. *See* Gray, Maria (Willey)
Willey, Samuel Hopkins, 511
William A. Lee Select Seminary (PA), 15,034
William and Alice Hinckley Fund, 17,071
William Appleton and Company (MA), **6,208**
"William Beaumont" (ms), 10,159
"William Burrows House, The" (article), 15,518
William Smith College (Geneva, NY), **11,468**
William, Elizabeth. *See* Chomperey, Elizabeth (William)
William, Elmira Pond Miller [Mrs. Henry] (1811-?), 16,974
William Enston Home for the Aged (Charleston, SC), 15,404
William, Fanny [Mrs. Daniel R.], 4,356
William, Helena Maria. [Mrs. John] Stone (1762-1827), 5,820
William, Henry, **16,974**
William Longstreet and Ludwig General Insurance Agency (MI), 8,366
William Maclure's School of Industry (New Harmony, IN), 4,638
William II, Emperor, 8,950
William Wirt (ship), **6,205**
Williams, Abby, 9,444
Williams, Abigail (Ellsworth) (?-1860), 1,964
Williams, Adelaide. *See* Caldwell, Adelaide Williams [Mrs. Joseph]
Williams, Adele (Cutts) [Mrs. Stephen A.] Douglas [Mrs. Robert] (1835-99), **4,357**
Williams, Agnes Powell [Mrs. Richard] (1827-94) *See* Daniels, Agnes Powell [Mrs. Richard] Williams [Mrs. Francis] Jones [Mrs. David] (1827-94)
Williams, Alice, 7,922
Williams, Alice L. L., **16,490**
Williams, Alice Roeschlaub, 1,788
Williams, Andrew Murray, Jr., 12,299
Williams, Annabelle, **15,114**
Williams, Anne (Jackson), **13,166**
Williams, Annetta Verna Marie (1913-). *See* Knuteson, Annetta Verna Marie (Williams) [Mrs. Albert] (1913-)
Williams, Annie "Meskeg Annie" (Shelland) [Mrs Clarence E.] (1878-1964), 8,482
Williams, Archibald D., **13,611**
Williams, Aubrey, 1,722
Williams, Augusta, 1,964
Williams, Benjamin F., 13,168
Williams, Blanche Colton (1879-1944), **6,955**
Williams, Brenda, 10,191
Williams, Camilla, **5,479**
Williams, Carrie, 11,662
Williams, Charlotte, 11,750
Williams, Clara, 7,590
Williams, Clarinda Boardman. *See* Boltwood, Clarinda Boardman (Williams) [Mrs. Lucius Manlius]
Williams College (MA), 6,813, 7,590
   students, 11,520
Williams College (MA), Chapin Library, 6,813
Williams, Comfort (1783-1825), **1,942**

Williams, Cora Best (Taylor) [Mrs. Jesse Parker], **3,268**

Williams, Cynthia [Miss]. [Mrs. James S.] Dunaway, **16,446**

Williams, Cynthia [Mrs. Lyman], 9,444

Williams, Cyrus (1783-1863), 12,540, **12,674**, 12,675

Williams David, 10,393

Williams, Della Johnson, **10,393**

Williams, Diana Craddock, 11,748

Williams, Edith (1863-1939), 9,445

Williams, Electra, 16,832

Williams, Elizabeth. See Champney, Elizabeth (Williams) [Mrs. James Wells]

Williams, Elizabeth Anna (1824-54). See Thomson, Elizabeth Anna (Williams) [Mrs. Samuel Steele] (1824-54)

Williams, Elizabeth (Bacon) [Mrs. Howard Yolen], 9,443

Williams, Elizabeth Byrne [Mrs. William W.] (1828-1906), 1,881

Williams, Elizabeth Weld (1836-1912). See Dewson, Elizabeth Weld (Williams) (1836-1912)

Williams, Ella, 11,750

Williams, Ellen. See Vanderbilt, Ellen (Williams)

Williams, Emily Electra (1841-1918). See Stevenson, Emily Electra (Williams) [Mrs. Edward] (1841-1918)

Williams, Emma, **886**

Williams, Emma Rigby Jacobs (1872-?), 16,967

Williams, Essie W., **17,867**

Williams, Esther, 4,868

Williams, Esther Baldwin [Mrs. O. E.], 2,829

Williams, Esther (1907-), **2,829**

Williams, Eva Joor (?-post 1940), 9,773

Williams Family (CT), **1,881**

Williams Family (CT), 1,961, **1,964**

Williams Family (GA), 3,489

Williams Family (MA), 7,590

Williams Family (MN), 9,417

Williams Family (MN), 9,443

Williams Family (Corning, NY), **11,749**

Williams Family (Ithaca, NY), 11,534

Williams Family (Weedsport, NY), **11,748**

Williams Family (TX), 16,085

Williams, Fannie (Barrier) [Mrs. S. Laing] (1855-1944), 10,201

Williams, Frances, 2,502

Williams, Frances E. (1844?-1909), **10,728**

Williams, Frances Leigh [Miss] (1909-), **17,078**

Williams, Frances (Ropes) [Mrs. Stillman P.] (1883-1969), **7,465, 8,424**

Williams, Frances Walker (1817-1903), 7,590

Williams, Franklin Delano, 7,589

Williams, G. Mennen, 7,729, 7,886

Williams, George L. (1858-1900), **14,129**

Williams, Gertrude Gideon, **2,637**

Williams, Hannah Goldsmith (1823-77), **12,212**

Williams, Hannah Hopkins (1805-46), 1,881

Williams, Harriet W., 14,659

Williams, Hattie (Plum) [Mrs. Thomas] (1878-1963), **10,554**

Williams, Henry Shaler, 11,534

Williams, Herbert G., 13,015

Williams, Hermann W., 2,744

Williams, Howard Yolen (1889-1973), **9,443**

Williams, Irena Dunn (1856-?), **14,309**

Williams, Irvin, 15,326

Williams, Ivy Currin [Mrs.], **3,732**

Williams, J. Fletcher, 8,926

Williams, Jane, 11,750

Williams, Jean (1876-1965), **14,469**

Williams, Jeanne, **16,290**

Williams, Jesse F., 17,230

Williams, Jesse Parker, **3,268**

Williams, Joanna, 12,674

Williams, John, 5,534

Williams, John, 8,376

Williams, John, Family, **9,444**

Williams, John Sharp (1854-1932), **2,638**, 9,658, 9,697, 9,706

Williams, John T., **14,688**

Williams, Joseph, 14,840

Williams, Joshua Lewis, 4,489

Williams, Josiah (1810-83), 11,750

Williams, Josiah Butler, Family (NY), **11,750**

Williams, Juanita, 5,469

Williams, Juanita (Baldwin) See Foote, Juanita (Baldwin) Williams

Williams, Letitia. See Waite, Letitia (Williams) [Mrs. John Leman]

Williams, Louise, 9,444

Williams, Louise, 11,534

Williams, Louise (1884-), 9,445

Williams, Lucile. See Jones, Lucile (Williams)

Williams, Lucy. See Williams, Lucy (Williams) [Mrs. Comfort]

Williams, Lucy (Williams) [Mrs. Comfort], 1,942

Williams, Margaret Clark, 6,484

Williams, Margaret D. [Miss], **2,639**

Williams, Margery (1881-1944). See Bianco, Margery (Williams) [Mrs. Francesco] (1881-1944)

Williams, Maria D. Stowall [Mrs. Spencer] (?-1868), **8,376**

Williams, Marie E. [Miss] (1866-1961), **7,334**

Williams, Martha. See Sherman, Martha (Williams)

Williams, Martha Ann, 1,798

Williams, Martha (Noyes), 12,755

Williams, Martha Wilder [Mrs. Thomas Hale] (ca. 1814-1910), 9,445

Williams, Mary, 1,964

Williams, Mary (1816-86). See Brayman, Mary (Williams) [Mrs. Mason] (1816-86)

Williams, Mary Alice Moon [Mrs. George L.] (1860-1952), 14,129

Williams, Mary Dyer (1822-1905). See McLean, Mary Dyer Williams [Mrs. Charles B.] (1822-1905)

Williams, Mary Elizabeth "Lizzie" (1825-1902), **7,466**

Williams, Mary Evans (1851-?). See Leatham, Mary Evans (Williams) (1851-?)

Williams, Mary Floyd (1866-1959), **887**

Williams, Mary Gilmare, 11,749

Williams, Mary (Hardy) [Mrs. Josiah] (1824-1911), 11,750

Williams, Mary Lydia Hicks, 13,446

Williams, "Mary Lou" Mary Elfrieda (Scruggs) [Mrs. John] (1910-), **2,852, 5,534**

Williams, Mary (Nelson) [Mrs. Franklin Delano], **7,589**

Williams, Mary Wilhelmine (1878-1944), **1,604**

Williams, May (1882-1975). See Ward, May (Williams) [Mrs. Merle] (1882-1975)

Williams, Maybell. See Benton, Maybell (Williams) [Mrs. John]

Williams, Mildred, 9,575

Williams, Mrs. Beaufort Mathews, **3,269**

Williams, Mrs. Henry L., 7,140

Williams, Mrs. John, 11,879

Williams, Mrs. Theodore L. (1838-1907), 13,683

Williams, Nancy Abigail (Clement) [Mrs. Frederick Granger] (1872-1954), **16,844**

Williams, Nannie (Haskins), 13,167

Williams, Nathan, 9,445

Williams, Nellie, 9,444

Williams, Nellie, 7,140

Williams, Nettie Leona [Miss] (1883-1959), **10,555**

Williams, Olive [Miss] (1890-1971), **11,358**

Williams, Oscar, 4,472

Williams, Otis, 11,750

Williams, Paul A. M., 15,654

Williams, Pearl Allen, 5,346

Williams, Richard, 9,952

Williams, Robert, 7,807

Williams, Roger B., 11,534

Williams, Rosa M. E. (ca. 1799-1853). See Burroughs, Rosa M. E. (Williams) [Mrs. Benjamin] (ca. 1799-1853)

Williams, Ruth (Hale) [Mrs. Thomas] (1788-1867), 9,445

Williams, Ruth Jewett, 8,938

Williams, Samuel McKeehan (1845-1930), 9,445

Williams, Sara Lawrence (Lockwood) [Mrs. Walter] (1891-1961), **8893**

Williams, Sarah. See Langworthy, Sarah (Williams) [Mrs. Isaac Pendleton]

Williams, Sarah [Mrs.], **11,139**

Williams, Sarah (1816-?). See Dobbins, Sarah (Williams) [Mrs. John S.] (1816-?)

Williams, Sarah (1853-1940). See Williams, Sarah (Williams) [Mrs. Samuel McKeehan] (1853-1940)

Williams, Sarah (Ball). See Matthews, Sarah (Ball) Williams [Mrs. John]

Williams, Sarah Broyles, 15,649

Williams, Sarah Elizabeth, 9,445

Williams, Sarah Frances (Hicks) [Mrs. Benjamin F.] (1827-), **13,168**

Williams, Sarah S. L., 14,144

Williams, Sarah (Williams) [Mrs. Samuel McKeehan] (1853-1940), 9,445

Williams, Sophia [Mrs.], 5,869

Williams, Spencer, 8,376

Williams, Stephen, 9,445

Williams, Sylvia. See Thompson Sylvia (Williams)

Williams, Talcott (1849-1928), **5,869**

Williams, Tennessee (1914-), 6,085, 12,367, 16,161, 16,164

Williams, Thomas, 9,445

Williams, Thomas Hale (1813-1901), Family (RI, MN), **9,445**

Williams, Tirzah M., **12,675**

Williams, Vivian Ahlsweh, 2,928

Williams, Walter, 10,060

Williams, William, 13,448

Williams, William Carlos, 4,485, 12,001, 16,152

Williams, William Frederic (1818-71), **11,289**

Williams, Zina Priscenda (Young) [Mrs. Thomas] (1850-1931). See Card, Zina Priscenda (Young) [Mrs. Thomas] Williams [Mrs. Charles Ora] (1850-1931)

Williamsburg Civic League (VA), 17,110, **17,124**

Williamsburg High School (IA), 4,815

Williamsburg Public Library (VA), 17,110

Williamson, Alexander, 1,454

Williamson, Anne A. (1868-), 6,122

Williamson County A&M Mothers' Club (TX), **16,202**

Williamson, Elizabeth "Betsy" (1800-50). See Taliaferro, Elizabeth "Betsy" (Williamson) [Mrs. James Govan] (1800-50)

Williamson, Harry A., 12,688

Williamson, James E., **13,612**

Williamson, Jane Smith (1803-?), 8,903, 9,316, 9,446

Williamson, Jeanette Dildine [Mrs. John], 9,052

Williamson, John Poage, 9,446

Williamson, Julia B. (1894-1945), **11,059**

Williamson, Katharine (Porter) [Mrs. Harvey] (1910-64) **13,970**

Williamson, Lydia. See Richards, Lydia (Williamson) [Mrs. Channing]

Williamson, Margaret (Poage) [Mrs. Thomas Smith] (1804-72), 9,446

Williamson, Martha (1844-?), 9,446

Williamson, Mary, 17,127

Williamson, Mary Louisa (Mitchell) [Mrs. Samuel Thomas] (1842-1915), **79**

Williamson, Myrtle (1898-1958), 94, **97**

Williamson, Nancy Jane, 9,446

Williamson, Nicholas, 10,954

Williamson, Pauline Lyons, 12,688

Williamson, Ruth (1890-1977). See Lawrence, Ruth (Williamson) [Mrs. James C.] (1890-1977)

Williamson, Sarah (Cook) [Mrs. Nicholas] (1849-78), 10,954

Williamson, Susie (1877-1961). See Stageberg, Susie (Williamson) [Mrs. Olaf O.] (ca. 1877-1961)

Williamson, Thomas Smith (1800-79), Family (MN), **9,446**

Williamson, W. H., 13,612

Williamsport Hospital (NY), 11,440

Williamsville Institute (NY), 11,520

Willie Andrews Pioneer Schools Ex-Students (TX), 16,031

Williford, Martha. See Payne, Martha (Williford) [Mrs. John]

Williford, Martha (Stackhouse). See Service, Martha (Stackhouse) Williford [Mrs. John Hugh James]

Williford, William S., 13,121

Willing, Elizabeth Ann, 3,906

Willing, Evelyn P., 3,906

Willing Family (IL), **3,906**

Willing, Frances S., 3,906

Willing, Henry, 3,906

Willing, J. Thomson, 4,226
Willing, Mark, 3,906
Willing, Mary Jane, 3,906
Willingham Family (SC, GA), **3,376**
Willingham, M. A., 3,376
Willink, Cornelia Ann (Ludlow) [Mrs. John A.] (ca. 1805-65), 11,323, 11,330
Willink Family (NY), **11,330**
Willink, John A. (ca. 1805-65), 11,330
Willink, John William, 11,330
Willis, A. F., 10,061
Willis, Bertram Trowbridge (1912-), **16,845**
Willis, Eola [Miss] (1909-56), **15,532**
Willis F. Pierce Memorial Hospital (Foochow, China), 14,316
Willis Family (MO), **10,061**
Willis, Gwendolyn, 17,852
Willis, Helen (1873-1971). See McKay, Helen (Willis) (1873-1971)
Willis, John Henry, 11,391, 17,852
Willis, Mary Eliza (Hyde) (1854-1934) **888**
Willis, Mattie Azalia (1912-70), **7,975**
Willis, Mrs. A. F., 10,061
Willis, Nathaniel Parker, 5,694
Willis, Olympia Brown. See Brown, Olympia. [Mrs. Willis]
Willis, "Queen Ann" Bassett, 1,786
Willis, Sara Payson. Grata Payson (1811-72). See Parton, Sara Payson (Willis) [Mrs. Charles H.] Eldredge [Mrs. Samuel P.] Farrington [Mrs. James] (1811-72)
Willis, Sarah A., 14,618
Willis, William, 5,684
Williston, Constance Bigelow, 6,398
Williston Graded School (SC), **15,767**
Williston, Lyman Richards, 6,398
Willoughby, Barrett (1894-1959). See Willoughby, Florance (Barrett) (1894-1959)
Willoughby, Charles P., 146
Willoughby, Florance (Barrett) (1894-1959), **146**
Willow Hill (book), 14,475
Willowbrook (residence, NY), **12,344**
Wills, 1,177, 3,436, 3,481, 7,091, 9,206, 9,414, **9,792**, 9,861, **11,189, 11,456**, 12,281, 13,219, 13,483, 13,537, **15,102, 15,504**, 15,507, 15,534, 15,546
Wills, Helen, 997, 15,371
Wills, Jesse Ely (1900-), **15,938**
Wills, Rose "Travelin' Lady," 1,534
Willsie, Honore (McCue) (1880-1940), 11,822
Willson, Anne. See Booth, Anne (Willson)
Willson, Edith R. [Mrs. Fred DeSales], 1,666
Willson, Grace Nye, 8,829, **8,833**, 8,838
Willson, Millicent Veronica. See Hearst, Millicent Veronica (Willson) [Mrs. William Randolph, Sr.]
"Willy" (television program), 17,816
Wilman, M. M., 3,500
Wilmarth, Mary Jane (Hawes) [Mrs. Henry Martin] (1837-1919), 3,814
Wilmington College (NC), faculty, 13,230
Wilmington Meeting of Woman Friends (DE), **2,060**
Wilmington-Weldon Railroad (NC), 13,268
Wilshire Family, 1,039
Wilson, A. W., 17,150
Wilson, Ada C., 2,535
Wilson, Adelaide S. [Miss], 5,823
Wilson, Agnes Mae, 9,962
Wilson, Alda H. [Miss], 17,953
Wilson, Alice, 4,729
Wilson, Alpheus Waters (1834-1916), **3,355**
Wilson, Ann, 12,345
Wilson, Ann Robertson (Pulliam) [Mrs. John], 890
Wilson, Augusta Jane (Evans) [Mrs. Lorenzo Madison] (1835-1909), **47, 80**, 99, **121**, 2,199, 13,030
Wilson, Benjamin J. (1825-96), **3,270**
Wilson, Bertha. See Howell, Bertha (Wilson) [Mrs. William]
Wilson Bulletin (periodical), 11,665
Wilson, Carol Green, **1,353**
Wilson, Carrie E., 1,085
Wilson, Catherine M., 15,533
Wilson, Charlotte. See Arthur, Charlotte (Wilson) [Mrs. Chester Alan III]
Wilson, Charlotte. See Smith, Charlotte (Wilson)

Wilson, Clyde (1926-), **10,062**
Wilson College (Chambersburg, PA), **14,780**
alumnae, 1,571
Wilson, Cora (1876-?). See Stewart, Cora (Wilson) (1876-?)
Wilson, Cora P., 8,094
Wilson, David, 11,851
Wilson, Davis D., 4,855
Wilson, Dorothy Clarke (1904-), **5,637**
Wilson, E. Faye, 7,583
Wilson, Edith (Bolling) Galt [Mrs. Woodrow] (1872-1961), 441, 2,186, 2,499, **2,640**, 11,060, 11,176, 11,177, 11,249
Wilson, Edmund, 12,001
Wilson, Eleanor (1891-1972), **14,470**
Wilson, Eleanor Randolph (1889-1967). See McAdoo, Eleanor Randolph (Wilson) [Mrs. William Gibbs] (1889-1967)
Wilson, Elise Munser Beck (1881-), **10,394**
Wilson, Elizabeth C. See Knox, Elizabeth C. (Wilson) [Mrs. John]
Wilson, Elizabeth Davison (Millar) [Mrs. Joseph G.] (1830-1913), **6,956, 14,689**
Wilson, Elizabeth F. (1862-?). See Leonard, Elizabeth F. (Wilson) [Mrs. Edgar Cotrell] (1862-?)
Wilson, Elizabeth (Miller), 704, **14,479**
Wilson, Ella "Billie" (1877-1962). See Hill, Ella "Billie" (Wilson) [Mrs. Edward Coke] (1877-1962)
Wilson, Ella (Grant) (1854-1939), **13,971**
Wilson, Elle (Andrews) [Mrs. James Harrison] (?-1900), **2,061**
Wilson, Ellen "Ellie" Louise (Axson) [Mrs. Woodrow] (1860-1914), **3,476**, 11,177, 12,491, 15,355
Wilson, Emma Webber [Miss] (1897-1970), **5,246**
Wilson, Ethel Brodt, Family (CA), **889**
Wilson, Eveline Gertrude Brown, 15,768
Wilson, Everett Pitt (1868-1956), **10,556**
Wilson Family, **1,530**
Wilson Family, 4,942
Wilson Family (IL), **4,438**
Wilson Family (MD), **5,823**
Wilson Family (NY), **12,345**
Wilson, Fannie, **13,613**
Wilson, Frances, 12,345
Wilson, Frances, 5,171
Wilson, Frances Pope (Stokely) [Mrs. Peter] (?-1868), **4,855**
Wilson, Franklin (1822-96), 5,823
Wilson, G. Pearle (1881-1957). See Schmidt, G. Pearle (Wilson) [Mrs. Louis Bernard] (1881-1957)
Wilson, George, 4,855
Wilson, George (1778-1848), **15,976**
Wilson, Georgia (1886-). See Dingus, Georgia (Wilson) [Mrs. William G.] (1886-)
Wilson, Gilbert Livingston, **9,447**
Wilson, Grace, 7,065
Wilson, Halena [Mrs.], 3,805
Wilson, Harold, 12,345
Wilson, Harry Leon, 10,133, 10,178
Wilson, Hazel Holland. See Beckwith, Hazel Holland Wilson [Mrs. Robert T. Lincoln]
Wilson, Helen Hopekirk [Mrs. William A.] (1856-1945), **2,641**
Wilson, Isabella, 3,506
Wilson, J., **17,349**
Wilson, J. H., 13,090
Wilson, Jack, 10,661
Wilson, James, 15,533
Wilson, James (1742-98), **15,115**
Wilson, James F., **9,827**
Wilson James Grant, 2,512
Wilson, James Harrison, 2,061
Wilson, James, Jr., **10,834**
Wilson, Jane, 4,868
Wilson, Jane, **2,062**
Wilson, Jeanie Woodrow, 11,177
Wilson, Jessie Woodrow (1887-1933). See Sayre, Jessie Woodrow (Wilson) (1887-1933)
Wilson, John (1790-1877), **890**
Wilson, John Appleton (1851-1927), 5,823
Wilson, John G., 16,491

Wilson, Joseph G., 6,956
Wilson, Josephine B. See Bruce, Josephine B. (Wilson) [Mrs. Blanche Kelso]
Wilson, Julia B., 5,713
Wilson, Karle (1878-1960). See Baker, Karle (Wilson) [Mrs. Thomas E.]
Wilson, Katie (Adair) (1846-?), **891**
Wilson, Lila Juliet (Andrews) (1888-), **892**
Wilson, Lorenzo Madison, 2,199
Wilson, Lucy, 7,583
Wilson, Lucy Benson [Mrs. John G.] (1830-1914), **16,491**
Wilson, Lucy Preston (1867-1950). See Peters, Lucy Preston (Wilson) (1867-1950)
Wilson, M. A. C. [Mrs. William F.], 16,147
Wilson, Mabel Zoe, 17,277
Wilson, Margaret (college student), 4,898
Wilson, Margaret (governess), 9,774
Wilson, Margaret Woodrow [Miss] (1882-1944), 1,530, 2,198, **11,176**
Wilson, Martha [Miss], 3,932
Wilson, Mary Ann (Covington) [Mrs. Thomas M.], **13,169**
Wilson, Mary Anne (1834-1909), 16,428
Wilson, Mary E. L., 12,251
Wilson, Mary Eliza. See Wakeman, Mary Eliza (Wilson)
Wilson, Mary Elizabeth (1826-1903). See Sherwood, Mary Elizabeth (Wilson) (1826-1903)
Wilson, Mary Grace (1900-), **13,209**
Wilson, Mary Shelby [Mrs. Samuel M.], 5,328, 5,329
Wilson, Mary Stokely [Mrs. Thomas S.], 4,856
Wilson, Matilda Greer. See Edmundson, Matilda Greer (Wilson) [Mrs. John King]
Wilson, Maude J. [Miss], 1,585
Wilson, Moultrie Reid (1839-1910), **15,768**
Wilson, Mrs. Benjamin J., 3,270
Wilson, Mrs. Degmar, 1,017
Wilson, Mrs. Henry Lumpkin, 3,141
Wilson, Mrs. James McLaughlin, 9,447
Wilson, Mrs. R. J., 2,962
Wilson, Mrs. Wins F., **13,170**
Wilson, Nettie Emery, **10,395**
Wilson Ornithological Society, 11,665
Wilson, Patricia, 11,851
Wilson, Peter, 4,855
Wilson, Rebecca Maltbie (Eden) [Mrs. John Lyde], 12,174
Wilson River Lumber Company, 14,565
Wilson, Robert (1838-1924), **15,533**
Wilson, Rothmell, 16,174
Wilson, Samuel M., 4,855
Wilson, Samuel M. (1871-1940), **5,328**, 5,329
Wilson, Sarah Greer, 15,976
Wilson, Sarah (Pease), 4,436
Wilson, Sophie S., **2,642**
Wilson, Sophire W. [Mrs.], 15,430
Wilson, Susan B. (Lipscomb) [Mrs. Alpheus Waters], 3,355
Wilson, Teddy, 5,530
Wilson, Teresa (Stewart) [Mrs. Wilbur], 4,438
Wilson, Thomas Stokely (1813-94), 4,855, **4,856**
Wilson, Virginia Appleton [Miss] (1881-1957), 5,823
Wilson, Virginia (Appleton) [Mrs. Franklin] (1824-1902), 5,823
Wilson, Virginia Perry, 889
Wilson, Wallace G., 15,976
Wilson, Wilbur (1881-1958), 4,438
Wilson, William, 12,345
Wilson, William B., 2,700
Wilson, William E., **3,115**
Wilson, William F., 16,147
Wilson, William L., 17,456
Wilson, Woodrow (1856-1924), 1,507, 1,530, 1,559, 1,563, 2,186, 2,389, 2,640, 3,027, 3,476, 6,938, **6,957**, 6,976, 9,035, 9,658, 9,719, **11,060**, 11,136, 11,176, **11,177**, 11,236, 11,249, 15,059, 15,355, 17,473, 17,633, 17,735
Wilton, Anne E. (Keener) [Mrs. Louis R.] (1895-), **16,291**
Wilton Library (SC), 15,412
Wily, Penrose, 11,294
Winans, Emma, 12,844
Winans, Pearl (Fosnot) (1891-?), **893**, 11,846

Winchell, Avis (1872-?). *See* Grant, Avis (Winchell) [Mrs. Ulysses Sherman] (1872-?)
Winchell, Caroline (McAllister) [Mrs. Horace] (1806-92), 9,448
Winchell, Charlotte Sophie (Imus) [Mrs. Newton Horace] (1836-1926), 9,448
Winchell, Clarissa (1827-42), 9,448
Winchell, Constance Mabel (1896-), **11,930**, 11,972
Winchell, Ernestine [Mrs.] (1865-1952), **974**
Winchell, Horace (1796-1873), 9,448
Winchell, Ida Belle (1862-?). *See* Winchell, Ida Belle (Winchell) [Mrs. Henry V.] (1862-?)
Winchell, Ida Belle (Winchell) [Mrs. Henry V.] (1862-?), 9,448
Winchell, Newton Horace (1839-1914), Family, 8,571, **9,448**
Winchester, Ann [Mrs. George], 5,793
Winchester, George, 5,793
Winchester, Josiah, 9,737
Winchester, Martha [Miss], 15,495
Winchester, Mary, 5,793
Winchester, Mary (1812-89). *See* Moale, Mary (Winchester) [Mrs. William Armistead] (1812-89)
Winchester, Mrs. Josiah, 9,737
"Wind from the River" (ms), 5,022
Wind, The (book), 16,384
Wind Whispers (book), 15,952
Winder, Anne, 17,435
Winder, Elizabeth Tayloe Lloyd, 5,789
Winder, Mary Ida, 15,308
Windhusen, Anne, 17,254
Windland, Sara J., 35
Windoffer, Melba, **17,365**
Windows in the Sea (book), 11,288
Windows, ventilators for, 13,810
Windsor (plantation, SC), 15,423
Windsor, Marie (1919-), **18,020**
Windsor Park Women's Clubs (IL), 3,920
Windsor, Wallis (Warfield) Simpson (1896-), 6,646
Wine and wine-making, 2,706, 16,968
"Wine from These Grapes," 12,644
Wine of Astonishment, The (book), 4,061
Winegard, Richard Clarence, 270
Winema (Native American), 1,662
Wines, Florence Beatrice (1884-?). *See* Sharp, Florence Beatrice (Wines) [Mrs. Lewis, Sr.] (1884-?)
Wines, Ira Dern, 10,713
Wines, Margaret Taylor [Mrs. Ira D.] (1846-1908), **10,636**, 10,713
Winfrey, Florence (1895-1927). *See* Mills, Florence (Winfrey). [Mrs. Ulysses S.] Thompson (1895-1927)
Wing, Abraham, 8,205
Wing, Amelia Murdock, **4,857**
Wing, Bernice L., 17,029
Wing, Josephine [Miss], **8,377**
Wing, Marie R. [Miss] (ca. 1884-), **13,972**
Wing, Mary (1822?-92). *See* Merriman, Mary (Wing) [Mrs. Thomas S.] Farnsworth [Mrs. Dwight] (1822?-92)
Wing, Willis, 14,329
Wing, Yung (1818-1912), 11,547
Wingate Family (SC), **15,769**
Wingate, Harriet E. [Mrs.], 15,769
Wingate, Willie, 15,769
Wingfield, George, 10,748
Wingreen, Amy Eleanor (1870-1919), **4,006**
Wings Over America (book), 5,311
Wink, Helena Knauf [Mrs. Mathias] (1854-1936), **13,693**
Wink, Mathias (1854-1904), 13,693
Winkler, Mrs. Charles, 3,693
Winn, Beth Wyatt, 16,488
Winn, Cordella, 10,201
Winn, Lulu May [Miss], 9,967
Winn, Mary Elfrieda (1910-). *See* Williams, Mary Lou [Mrs. John] (1910-)
Winne, Caroline (Frey) [Mrs. Charles K.] (1841-1922), **1,354**, **10,557**
Winne, Charles K., 10,557
Winnebago County Mental Health Hospital (WI), 17,824
Winnebago Indians, 9,490, 17,674

commerce, 9,085
missions, 10,611
Winnemucca, Sarah [Mrs. E. C.] Bartlett [Mrs. L. H.] Hopkins (ca. 1844-91), 10,717, 14,165
Winnick, Ann, 15,976
Winningham, William, 15,678
Winnipeg General Hospital (Canada), 11,918
Winokur, Maxine (1925-). *See* Kumin, Maxine (Winokur) (1925-)
Winona Art Club (MN), 9,525
Winona Art Group, 9,527
Winona County Historical Society (MN), 9,385
Winona County Public Health Nursing Advisory Committee (MN), 9,385
Winona High School (MN), Alumni Association, 9,520
Winona Parents' and Teachers' Association (MN), 9,385
Winona State Soldier's Orphan Home (MN), 9,527
Winona State University (MN), 9,520, 9,527
archives, **9,526**
Winona Taxpayers Association (MN), 9,525
Winsborough, Hallie Paxson (1865-1940), 94, **98**
Winser, Beatrice (1869-1947), 11,123, 11,140, 11,144
Winser Family (NJ), **11,140**
Winser, Henry Jacob (1823-96), 11,140
Winser, Natalie, 11,140
Winship, Anna E. *See* Flournoy, Anna E. (Winship) [Mrs. Josiah A.]
Winship Family (GA), **3,271**
Winship, G. B., 13,652
Winslow, Ann (1894-1974), **18,021**
Winslow, Anne (Goodwin) (1875-1959), **15,902**
Winslow, Catherine Mary "Kate" (Reignolds) [Mrs. Henry] Farren [Mrs. Alfred Erving] (1836-1911), **2,543**
Winslow, Cynthia (1808-65). *See* Northey, Cynthia (Winslow) (1808-65)
Winslow Family, 9,373
Winslow Family (NE), 10,452
Winslow, Kate. *See* Davis, Kate (Winslow)
Winslow, Mary N. (1888-1952), **6,958**
Winslow, Mary Pratt. *See* Staples Mary Pratt (Winslow) [Mrs. David Jackson]
Winslow, Ola Elizabeth [Miss] (?-1977), 5,694
Winslow, Rosalind Mae (Guggenheim) (1882-1958), 3,988, **7,199**
Winslow, Sarah Tyng (1765-1826). *See* Chase, Sarah Tyng (Winslow) [Mrs. Samuel] Waldo [Mrs. Salmon] (1765-1826)
Winslow, Thyra (Samter) (ca. 1885-1961), **270**
Winslow, Vienna Y., 3,829
Winsor, Anna. *See* Gauntlett, Anna (Winsor)
Winsor, Annie Ware. *See* Allen Annie Ware (Winsor) [Mrs. Joseph Allen]
Winsor, Elizabeth. *See* Pearson, Elizabeth (Winsor)
Winsor, Fred, 1,790
Winsor, Frederick, 6,354
Winsor, Mary (1869-1956), **6,959**
Winsor, Mary P., 6,354
Winsor, Sarah Alydia Terry (1857-1950), 16,967
Winstanley, Eliza A., 12,670
Winston, Ann Caulfield, 9,567
Winston, Donald O., 9,354
Winston, Elizabeth Martin [Mrs. Donald O.], 9,354
Winston, Ellen Engelman (Black) [Mrs. Sanford] (1903-), 8,632, 10,197, **13,255**, 13,468, 13,614
Winston, Francesca (Schaefer) [Mrs. William Overton] (1856-?), 9,354
Winston, Sanford, 13,255
Winston, William Overton, 9,354
Winter, 10,250
Winter, Alice Vivian (Ames) [Mrs. Thomas Gerald] (1865-1944), 1,594, 5,121, 6,969
Winter, Carrie Prudence. *See* Kofoid, Carrie Prudence (Winter)
Winter, Edward (1908-), **2,830**
Winter, Ella, 873
Winter, Helen (Wagenknecht), 12,884
"Winter in California, A" (ms), 6,602
Winter, Laura (1870-1968). *See* Dean, Laura (Winter) [Mrs. William John] (1870-1968)
Winter, Margery, 1,124
Winter, Marian Boyd [Mrs. James D.], 8,958

Winter, Martha. *See* Routh, Martha (Winter)
Winter, Mary Sarah (Carter) [Mrs. Rogers] (1890-1975), **3,437**
Winter, Nellie Bornstein (1869-?), 17,744
Winter of Artifice (book), 4,232
Winter Study Club of Dearborn (MI), **8,015**
Winter-Telling Stories (book), 14,218
Winter, Thelma [Mrs. Edward], **2,830**
Winter, Una Richardson [Mrs.], **1,506**
Winter, William, 12,559
Winterbotham, Anna Sophia (1810 or 1813-86). *See* Stephens, Anna Sophia (Winterbotham) [Mrs. Edward] (1810 or 1813-86)
Winters, Janet Lewis [Mrs. Yvor] (1899-), 1,573
Winters, John, 13,322
Winters, Sally Kate, 9,819
Winters, Shelley, 11,461
Winters, Theodore, Family, 10,677
Winters, Yvor, 1,587
Winthrop Alumnae Association, Bancroft Johnson Chapter (SC), 15,611
Winthrop, Augusta Temple, 12,676
Winthrop College (SC), 99, 15,585, 15,611, **15,770**
archives, **15,824**
faculty, **15,801**, **15,806**, **15,811**
Winthrop, Edward, 5,319
Winthrop Family, **12,676**
Winthrop, Hannah (Fayerweather) Tolman [Mrs. John] (?-1790), 6,305
Winthrop, John (1588-1649), 7,127
Winthrop, John (1714-79), **6,305**
Winthrop Normal and Industrial School (Rock Hill, SC), faculty, 15,964. *See also* Winthrop College (SC)
Winton Companies, 9,449
Winton, David Judson (1897-), **9,449**
Wintun Indians, 955
Wintzer, A., 12,457
Winwar, Frances (1900-), **6,116**
Wire, Mary E. (?-1834). *See* Ramsey, Mary E. (Wire) (?-1834)
Wire screens, 15,412
Wirt, Agnes C. [Miss] (1815-31), 5,824
Wirt, Catherine (ca. 1807-53). *See* Randall, Catherine (Wirt) [Mrs. Alexander] (ca. 1807-53)
Wirt, Elizabeth (ca. 1807-?). *See* Goldsborough, Elizabeth (Wirt) [Mrs. Louis M.] (ca. 1807-?)
Wirt, Elizabeth (Gamble) [Mrs. William] (1784-1857), 5,824
Wirt, Ellen (ca. 1812-?). *See* McCormick, Ellen (Wirt) [Mrs. Edmund Brooke] Vass [Mrs. Charles] (ca. 1812-?)
Wirt, Laura (1803-33). *See* Randall, Laura (Wirt) [Mrs. Thomas] (1803-33)
Wirt, William (1772-1834), **5,824**
Wirtz, Bill, 6,365
Wirtz, W. Willard, 10,197
Wiscassett Mills (NC), 13,617
Wisconsin, 865, **8,728**, 12,325, 17,527, **17,544**, 17,592, 17,593, 17,629, 17,640, 17,667, 17,725, 17,758
abortion, legal aspects, 1,984
aeronautics, 17,566
affirmative action programs, **17,503**
agricultural societies, 17,720
agriculture, cooperative, 17,676
art
exhibitions, 2,817
galleries and museums, 17,846
art schools, 17,846
artists, **17,496**
assessment, 3,947
attorneys general, 17,680
authors, 17,589, **17,718**, **17,723**, **17,726**
autograph albums, 8,791
Baptists, 8,914
bicentennial celebrations, 8,728
biography, **17,493**
businessmen, **17,535**
businesswomen, **17,496**
Catholic Church, societies, etc., **17,551**, **17,741**
Catholic schools, 17,572
cemeteries, 17,700

charitable societies, **17,562, 17,590, 17,672, 17,684,**
   17,825, **17,833, 17,835**
charities, **17,579, 17,580**
child health services, 17,590
children, health and hygiene, 8,671
children, law and legislation, 17,845
church records and registers, Episcopal, **17,518**
church records and registers, Lutheran, **8,746**
church societies, **9,507, 17,683**
church societies, Congregational, **2,017**
churches, Episcopal, 17,502
   dioceses, **17,518**
circus, **17,489**
cities and towns, civic improvement, 17,863
civil rights, 6,848
Civil War, **17,743**
   personal narratives, 17,601
clergy, **6,435, 11,391**
clergy, Lutheran, 8,751
clergy, Universalist, **17,852**
clergymen's families, 8,751
clergymen's wives, **8,749**
clubs, 1,496, 17,494, **17,546, 17,556, 17,577,**
   17,671, 17,675, **17,682, 17,690, 17,730, 17,742,**
   17,747, 17,786, 17,821, 17,823, 17,825, 17,856,
   17,861, 17,863, 17,864, 17,883
college and school Journalism, **17,849**
college presidents, 17,689, 17,832, 17,868, 17,872,
   17,880
college students, 17,615, **17,628, 17,778, 17,780,**
   17,781, 17,782
college teachers, 1,409, 6,848, **17,520, 17,626,**
   17,712, 17,735, 17,764, 17,765, 17,770, **17,773,**
   17,775, 17,777, 17,788, 17,859, **17,860, 17,869,**
   17,870, 17,872
college theater, 17,817
communicable diseases, 17,515
community centers, **17,827**
community centers, Jewish, 17,664, 17,841
community health nursing, 17,826
congresses and conventions, **17,785**
congressmen, **17,627**
conservation of natural resources, study and
   teaching, 17,842
conservationists, **17,671, 17,842**
convents and nunneries, Catholic, **17,499, 17,552,**
   17,572
country life, 8,373
county officials and employees, **17,511, 17,512,**
   17,542, 17,543, 17,857
court records, 3,949, **17,514**
dairy cattle breeding, **17,655**
deans (in schools), **17,767, 17,776, 17,783**
death
   causes, 17,879
   proof and certification, 17,528
dental clinics, 17,826
department heads (universities), **17,766, 17,772,**
   17,777, 17,788
diaries and journals, 17,591, 17,782, **17,857, 17,859,**
   17,876
   19th C, **2,655,** 17,595, 17,605, 17,668, **17,688,**
      17,703, **17,708,** 17,709, **17,873, 17,875, 17,878**
editors, 17,589
education, directories, **17,537**
educational associations, **17,504, 17,585, 17,586,**
   17,748, 17,763, 17,822
educators 17,494, 17,589
elections, 17,654
employment agencies, 6,705
equal rights amendment (proposed), 17,746
executive advisory bodies, **17,769**
family farms, 2,644
farm income, 17,606
farm life, 17,703
farmers, 17,540, **17,720, 17,724**
farmers' institutes, 17,655
feminists, **17,652**
fish and game licenses, 17,842
forests and forestry, 17,842
fresh air charity, 17,840
fur trade, 17,674
fur traders, **17,519**
governors, 4,354, 17,595, **17,629, 17,670**

grocery trade, **17,531**
health boards, **17,515**
health centers, 17,826
high schools, 17,841
historians, 17,495, 17,498
home labor, 17,835
home nursing, 17,590, **17,733**
hops, 17,606
hospitals, 17,500, **17,569,** 17,578, 17,699, 17,820
housewives, **8,765**
immigrants, 17,540
immigrants, Jewish, 17,744
immigrants, Norwegian, **8,757,** 9,106, 17,497
immigrants, Swiss, **17,636**
Jews, 17,840
   education, 17,850
   oral history, **16,433**
journalists, 17,498, 17,709, **17,725**
judges, 17,621
justices of the peace, 17,857
lawyers, **5,253, 17,593,** 17,620, 17,732, **17,867**
lecturers, 17,589
legislation, 12,575, 12,597
legislators, 4,832, **17,728, 17,862**
librarians, 17,603
libraries, 17,747
lumber camps, 9,078
lumber trade, 17,506
lumbering, 17,532, **17,587**
medical societies, 17,831
midwives, 17,528
military posts, 9,416
minorities, 16,334, **17,507**
monasticism and religious orders for women,
   Catholic, 17,500, **17,552, 17,554, 17,572, 17,578,**
   17,820, 17,838, 17,839, 17,854, **17,868, 17,871**
museum directors, 17,498
musical societies, 17,494, **17,824**
musicians, **17,494**
Native Americans, reservations, 3,944, 6,650
naturalization records, 3,949
newspapers, sections, columns, etc., 2,240
nuns, Catholic, 17,572, 17,868
nurses, **17,561, 17,701, 17,784,** 17,831
nursing
   standards, **17,748**
   study and teaching, 17,766
nursing homes, 17,590
nursing schools, **17,539, 17,568, 17,569,** 17,701,
   17,772, 17,773, 17,779, **17,847, 17,848**
nutrition research, 17,853
occupational therapy, 17,832
officials and employees, 6,705
old age homes, 17,578, 17,672
oral history, **17,530, 17,575, 17,775**
pacifists, **17,659**
painters, 17,498
patriotic societies, **17,639,** 17,685, **17,755, 17,833**
peace societies, 17,654, **17,753, 17,836**
philanthropists, 17,496, **17,602**
photographers, **1,349**
photographs, collections, **17,532, 17,576**
physicians, **11,399,** 17,498, 17,528, 17,574, **17,618,**
   17,699, 17,879
pioneers and settlers, 1,428, **8,742, 8,749,** 9,106,
   17,558, **17,570, 17,609, 17,632,** 17,664, **17,873,**
   17,874, 17,875, **17,877, 17,878**
poets, 17,687
poets laureate, 17,498
police, records and correspondence, 17,567
policewomen, **17,567**
political activists, women, **17,746**
politics, practical, women's activism, 6,719, 6,848,
   17,524, 17,654, **17,702, 17,745**
priories, **17,500**
private schools, **17,560**
public health nursing, **17,510, 17,511**
public health officers, **17,517**
public health personnel, **17,719**
public health records, **17,510, 17,511, 17,515,**
   17,528
public records, **17,509, 17,534**
public welfare **17,509, 17,513, 17,534**
public works, **17,521,** 17,846

rape crisis centers, 17,652
real estate agents, 17,664
registers of births, etc., **17,528,** 17,879
religion, 8,914
reporters and reporting, **17,598, 17,829**
revolutionists, 17,589
roads, 17,564
school census, 17,522, 17,538
school children, health and hygiene, 17,517
school districts, **17,538**
school superintendents and principals, **17,512,**
   17,516, 17,542, 17,543, 17,621
schools, 17,564, 17,589, **17,661,** 17,679, 17,724
   records and correspondence, **17,522, 17,523,**
   17,525, 17,526, 17,533, 17,547
scrapbooks, 17,782
secret societies, **17,550, 17,752**
senators, United States, 2,432, 3,667, **17,732**
seniors, dwellings, 17,846
sex discrimination, law and legislation, 6,844
sisterhoods, Jewish, **17,555**
social life and customs, 8,914, 17,641, 17,651
social problems, **17,756**
social reformers, **17,659**
social settlements, 17,664, 17,841
social workers, **17,841, 17,845**
societies, etc., **17,707**
societies, etc., Jewish, **17,646, 17,647, 17,695**
soldiers, Civil War, 17,540
strikes and lockouts, 6,315
student financial aid, 17,747
students' societies, 14,030, **17,541, 17,573,** 17,628,
   17,790
suffrage, 17,589, 17,882
suffrage societies, 11,391, 16,252, 17,659, **17,721,**
   17,745, **17,749,** 17,828
suffragists, **2,128,** 17,589
taxation, 9,006
teachers, 7,438, 9,005, **17,495, 17,591, 17,625,**
   17,658, 17,708, 17,865, 17,867, 17,874
   certifications, **17,545**
teachers' colleges, 13,905
teachers' unions, **17,505**
temperance societies, **17,571, 17,750, 17,837**
tornadoes, 8,751
trade and professional associations, **17,529,** 17,690,
   17,694
tuberculosis, prevention, 17,515
unemployed, legal aspects, 11,916
universities and colleges, 6,848, 13,686, 17,532,
   17,549, 17,557, 17,689, 17,849
   history, 17,530, **17,548**
   records and correspondence, 17,620
Virgin Mary, shrines, 17,552
vital statistics, 17,515
volunteer workers in social service, **17,840**
Winnebago Indians, 17,674
women, **17,882**
   higher education, **17,789**
women's colleges, **17,844**
World War I, civilians' work, 17,685
World War II, civilians' work, 3,950
Young Women's Christian Association, 17,603,
   17,787, 17,851
Wisconsin Board of Health, 17,719
Wisconsin Composers League, 17,494
Wisconsin Conservation Congress, 17,671
Wisconsin Council of Catholic Women, **17,741**
Wisconsin Department of Vocational and Adult
   Education, officials and employees, 6,705
Wisconsin Dramatic Society, 17,815
Wisconsin Emergency Relief Administration, 17,513
Wisconsin Farmers Union, 17,676, 17,720
Wisconsin Farmers Union, junior program, 17,638
Wisconsin Federation of Business and Professional
   Women's Clubs, **17,742**
Wisconsin Federation of Music Clubs, 17,494
Wisconsin Female College (Fox Lake, WI). *See*
   Milwaukee-Downer College (Milwaukee, WI)
Wisconsin Governor's Commission on Human Rights,
   6,848
Wisconsin Historical Society, 17,624
Wisconsin Historical Society, *Proceedings,* 17,674
Wisconsin History Commission, 17,743

Wisconsin Jewish Oral History Interview Project, **17,744**
Wisconsin League of Women Voters, **17,745**
Wisconsin Magazine of History, 17,643
Wisconsin Players (Milwaukee, WI), 17,815, 17,819
Wisconsin Society for the Equal Rights Amendment, **17,746**
Wisconsin State Colonization Society, 17,620
Wisconsin State Conference of Social Work, 17,654
Wisconsin State Department of Public Welfare, 17,534
Wisconsin State Federation of Women's Clubs, **17,747**
Wisconsin State League of Nursing Education, **17,748**
Wisconsin State Normal School (River Falls, WI), students, 17,866
Wisconsin Student Association, 17,628
Wisconsin Supreme Court, 17,621
Wisconsin Territory, 17,706
Wisconsin Transient Bureau, 17,513
Wisconsin Volunteers (Civil War), 8,167
Wisconsin Woman Suffrage Association, 11,391, **17,659, 17,749**
Wisdom of Life series (lectures), 11,900
Wise, Charlotte Everett (1851-1935). *See* Hopkins, Charlotte Everett (Wise) [Mrs. Archibald] (1851-1935)
Wise, Ethel H., 2,205
Wise, Governor, 7,561
Wise, Jessie [Mrs.], 1,658
Wise, Justine. *See* Polier, Justine (Wise)
Wise, Louise (Waterman) [Mrs. Stephen S.] (1874-1947), 7,528
Wise, Stephen S. (1874-1949), 933, 7,528, 7,559, 12,069
Wisenbaker, Thannie (Smith) [Mrs. E. D.], **3,617**
Wishart, Alfred Wesley (1865-1933), 6,414
Wishes Are Horses (book), 5,261
Wislocki, Florence (Clothier) [Mrs. George] (1903-), 6,416, **6,475,** 6,739
Wisner, Jean (English), 8,157
Wistar, Casper (1761-1818), 14,965
Wistar, Elizabeth Waln, 14,965
Wistar, Ellen, 14,965
Wistein, Rosina, 15,144
Wister Family (PA), **15,116**
Wister, James W., **15,117**
Wister, Mary Channing (1869-1913). *See* Wister, Mary Channing (Wister) [Mrs. Owen] (1869-1913)
Wister, Mary Channing (Wister) [Mrs. Owen] (1869-1913), 2,643
Wister, Owen (1860-1938), **2,643**
Wister, Sarah (Butler) [Mrs. Owen Jones] (1835-1908), 2,643, 15,116
Wister, Sarah "Sally" (1761-1804), **11,061,** 11,305, **15,118**
Wister, Susan, 15,117
Wiswell, Louis C., **3,084**
Witch of Blackbird Pond, The (book), 6,093
Witchcraft, 5,410, 7,626, 9,909, 13,284, 13,287
"Witch's Daughter, The" (story), 12,480
Witfoth, Mabel Rogers, 8,289
With a Quiet Heart (book), 7,250
"With a Rose" (poem), 12,457
With or Without Roses (book), 2,456
Withee, Louisa A. [Mrs. Nisan H.] (1841-?), **1,646, 2,644**
Wither, Jessie, 9,914
Witherow, Gertrude, 955
Withers, Anita (Dwyer) [Mrs. John], **13,171**
Withers, James, 17,129
Withers, Margret Craver, **2,831**
Withers, Mrs. Thomas, 1,790
Witherspoon, Frances (1886-1973), **11,931,** 12,703
Withington, Adelaide [Miss], 11,167
Without My Cloak (drama), 4,235
Withrop, Marian (Penney) [Mrs. Edward], 5,319
Withycombe, James, 14,594
Witing, Captain, 1,899
Witmer, Anna, 11,360
Witmer, Christian, 11,360
Witmer Family (NY), **11,360**
Witmer, Tobias, 11,360
Wit's End (book), 17,947

Witte, Beatrice (1870-1956) *See* Ravenel, Beatrice (Witte) (1870-1956)
Witte, Edwin E., 6,844
Witte, Frances Margaret (Stewart) [Mrs. Richard] (1842-?), **17,881**
Witte Memorial Museum (San Antonio, TX), 16,316
Wittenberg College (Springfield, OH), alumnae, 5,199
Wittenberg, Helen (Gerbich) [Mrs. Ralph K.], 10,741
Wittenmyer, Annie (Turner) [Mrs. William] (1827-1900), **2,645,** 4,244, 4,696, 4,732, **4,858,** 5,027, 14,017
Wittich, Jean [Mrs. Frederick W.], 9,386, 9,396
Wittpen, Caroline Bayard Stevens [Mrs. Otto], 11,134
Wittpen, Otto, 11,134
Wittschen, Ida (1891-). *See* Sproul, Ida (Wittschen) [Mrs. Robert G.] (1891-)
Wixom, Emma (1869-1940). *See* Nevada, Emma. Emma Wixom. [Mrs. Raymond Spooner] Palmer (1859-1940)
Wixom, W. W., 10,708
Wixson, Helen (Marsh), 530
Wodrow, Mary Ann (1762-1841). *See* Archbald, Mary Ann (Wodrow) (1762-1841)
Woerishoffer, Carola, 2,700, 14,745
Wofford, Benjamin (1780-1850), 15,837
Wofford College (Spartanburg, SC), 15,536, **15,837**
Wofford, Emma Lapsley (1861-), 16,132
Woffort, Liola (Craven), 17,232
Wohlforth, Mildred Gilman [Mrs. Robert], **11,867**
Wohlforth, Robert, 11,867
Wolcott, Anna, 1,786
Wolcott, Catherine M., 3,794
Wolcott, Charles, 1,677
Wolcott, Elizabeth. *See* Newberry, Elizabeth (Wolcott)
Wolcott, Jessie L. [Miss], **13,290**
Wolcott, Rosetta Gordon Lipsia (Bell) [Mrs. Charles] (1879-1974), **1,677**
Wolcott School (CO), 1,786
Wold, Blanche. *See* Knopf, Blanche (Wold) (1894-1966)
Wold, Emma, 1,507, 2,432
Woldenberg, Aimee, 1,323
Wolf, Anna, 5,735
Wolf, Blanche (1894-1966). *See* Knopf, Blanche (Wolf) (1894-1966)
Wolf, Chief, 9,447
Wolf, Genevieve Taggard [Mrs. Robert] (1894-1948). *See* Taggard, Genevieve. [Mrs. Robert] Wolf [Mrs. Kenneth] Durant (1894-1948)
Wolf, Lucile. *See* Koshland, Lucile (Wolf) Heming [Mrs. Daniel Edward]
Wolf, May (1910-70). *See* Reuther, May (Wolf) [Mrs. Walter P.] (1910-70)
Wolf, Rosalie (Walter) (1908-), 894
Wolfe, Carolyn S. Williams [Mrs. James H.], 11,503
Wolfe, Cornelia Kelley (1897-1972), **4,404**
Wolfe Family, 12,460
Wolfe, Gertrude (?-1966), **7,559**
Wolfe, Gertrude Franklin, 11,182
Wolfe, Gertrude (Pearl), 17,282
Wolfe Hall (CO), **1,803**
Wolfe, Hannah. *See* Burton, Hannah (Wolfe) [Mrs. Josiah]
Wolfe, Ian, 12,363
Wolfe, Joan, **7,976**
Wolfe, John David, 12,607
Wolfe, Linnie Marsh, 1,634
Wolfe, Marjorie Carlisle, **8,378**
Wolfe, Mary, 6,812
Wolfe, Mary Franklin (1886-1970). *See* Thompson, Mary Franklin (Wolfe) [Mrs. Charles] (1886-1970)
Wolfe, Mrs. John David, 12,607
Wolff, Abe E., 11,689
Wolff, Anna Lee [Mrs. Maurice], 9,467
Wolff, Anna Maria (1803-?). *See* Fahnestock, Anna Maria (Wolff) (1803-?)
Wolff, Ellen, 3,055
Wolff, Mrs. Carl, 8,154
Wolff, Ruth (1909?-72), **6,117**
Wolff, Sister Madeleva (1887-1964), **4,640**
Wolfskill Family, 960
Wolfskill, Frances, 960

Wolfskill, Jennie, 960
Wolfskill, John Reid (1809-97), 960
Wolfskill, Melinda, 960
Wolfskill, Susan Cooper [Mrs. John Reid], 960
Wolfson, Theresa [Miss] (1897-1972), **6,166, 11,776**
Wolkins, Lyra (Trueblood), 15,298
Wolle, Francis, 1,678
Wolle, Muriel (Sibell) [Mrs. Francis] (1898-1977), **1,678, 1,804**
Wollston Congregational Church (Boston, MA), Women's Union, **6,172**
Wolsey, W. W., 1,425
Wolsted, Mabel Ewen, **8,803**
Woltman, Marion O. Hanson [Mrs. Ignatius] Donnelly [Mrs. Henry L.] (1877-1964), 9,048
Wolverine Citizen Printing Company (Flint, MI), 8,181
Wolves, 5,489
"Woman" (poem), 1,268
"Woman a Peer" (ms), 4,761
"Woman as a Metonymy" (essay), 7,284
Woman as Force in History (book), 6,947
"Woman as Nigger" (article), 10,012
Woman at the Crossroads (book), 543
Woman Citizen Corporation, **6,960**
Woman Citizen, The (periodical), 6,971
"Woman Musicians of North Dakota, The" (paper), 13,675
Woman of the Year of Atlanta (GA), **3,272**
Woman of Valor (book), 6,920
Woman Painters of Washington, 17,179
Woman Patriot, The, 10,052
Woman Pays Club, 2,205, 6,399, 17,248
"Woman Pioneers in Democracy" (ms), 11,605
"Woman Power of South Dakota Through Registration, The" (ms), 15,860
Woman Rice Planter, A (book), 15,439
"Woman Secretary, The" (ms), 6,440
Woman Suffrage Association (NY), 6,706
Woman Suffrage Coffee House (MA), 6,477
Woman Suffrage Convention (DC, 1891), 11,605
Woman Suffrage Convention (VT), 6,373
"Woman Suffrage Leaflet," 7,268
Woman Suffrage Party, 6,981, 13,939
Woman Suffrage party (NY), 12,059
Woman Suffrage party (RI), 9,001
Woman Suffrage Party of Monroe County, Inc. (NY), **12,799,** 12,818, 12,835
Woman Suffrage Party of the City of New York, 6,979
Woman Suffrage Procession (1913), 2,063
Woman Suffrage State Central Committee, 8,896
Woman Today, 14,446
Woman Within, The (book), 17,059
Woman Worker, The (U. S. Women's Bureau), 2,703
Womankind (newspaper), 3,821
Woman's Advocate (newspaper), 6,244
Woman's Agricultural Camp (NY), 6,963
Woman's American Baptist Home Mission Society, Watertown Branch (MA), **7,104**
Woman's Anti-Amendment League of Alabama, 49
Woman's Anti-Lottery League (New Orleans, LA), **5,502**
Woman's Art Club (OH), 13,853, 13,860
Woman's Associated Charities of the State of Nebraska, 10,503
Woman's Association for the Betterment of Public School Houses (NC). *See* North Carolina Congress of Parents and Teachers
Woman's Auxiliary (Geneva, IL), 4,273
Woman's Auxiliary, Massachusetts Branch (Episcopal), **6,183**
Woman's Baptist Foreign Mission Society of Michigan, **8,032**
Woman's Baptist Foreign Missionary Society of Rhode Island, **15,394**
Woman's Baptist Foreign Missionary Society of the West (MI), **8,033**
Woman's Baptist Home Mission Society of Michigan, **8,034**
Woman's Baptist Mission Society, 10,499
Woman's Baptist Mission Society of Michigan, **8,035**
Woman's Baptist Mission Society of Southern California, 1,103

Woman's Benefit Association (IL), 4,066
Woman's Benevolent Society (New Brunswick, NJ), 10,973
Woman's Bi-Metallic League (NE), **10,558**
Woman's Board of Missions,
Woman's Board of Missions, Rhode Island Branch, **6,173**
Woman's Building (IL), 4,380
Woman's Centennial Congress (1940), **2,084**, 2,256, 4,100, 4,859, 4,897, 7,217, 9,197, 12,415
Woman's Choral Society of New Haven (CT), **2,007**
Woman's Christian Association. *See* Young Women's Christian Association
Woman's Christian Temperance Society, 1,224
Woman's Christian Temperance Union, 53, 56, 117, 138, 197, 203, 575, 707, 756, 900, 1,078, **1,169,** 1,190, **1,199,** 1,243, 1,782, **1,943, 1,944,** 2,059, 2,607, 2,636, 3,010, **3,306,** 3,358, 3,383, **3,666,** 3,712, **3,909,** 3,969, 4,066, 4,088, **4,243, 4,244,** 4,469, 4,481, 4,605, **4,616,** 4,650, 4,696, 4,732, **4,786,** 4,793, 4,817, 4,837, 4,858, 4,907, 4,930, **5,100,** 5,122, **5,223,** 5,487, 5,641, 6,418, 6,546, 6,901, 7,948, 7,951, **7,977, 7,978, 7,979, 7,980, 7,981, 7,982, 7,983,** 8,175, **8,268, 8,420, 8,448, 8,834,** 9,247, 9,421, 9,448, 9,467, 9,656, 9,719, **9,775,** 9,894, 10,024, **10,063, 10,116,** 10,223, 10,402, 10,462, 10,474, **10,559,** 10,666, 10,673, 10,725, 10,912, 10,972, 11,412, **11,422, 11,430,** 11,440, 11,443, 11,623, **11,801,** 11,838, 12,505, 12,515, 12,790, **12,805, 12,806, 12,838,** 12,844, 13,226, 13,297, 13,398, 13,648, 13,658, 13,668, 13,677, **13,694, 13,861, 13,862,** 13,963, 13,983, 14,015, 14,075, 14,077, 14,104, **14,127,** 14,223, 14,270, 14,306, **14,471,** 14,516, **14,690,** 14,713, 15,175, **15,254,** 15,274, 15,300, 15,315, 15,381, **15,771,** 15,773, **15,843,** 15,851, 15,857, 15,860, 16,040, 16,061, 16,818, 16,968, **17,154,** 17,226, 17,264, 17,376, 17,460, **17,571,** 17,740, **17,750** missions, 13,991, 14,018
Woman's Christian Temperance Union (Duarte, CA), **1,056**
Woman's Christian Temperance Union (Guilford, CT), **1,943**
Woman's Christian Temperance Union (Hartford, CT), **1,944**
Woman's Christian Temperance Union (Middlesex County, NJ), **11,062**
Woman's Christian Temperance Union (Oneida, NY), **12,741**
Woman's Christian Temperance Union (OH), **13,976**
Woman's Christian Temperance Union (Cuyahoga, OH), **13,975**
Woman's Christian Temperance Union (Lake County, OH), **13,974**
Woman's Christian Temperance Union (Lakewood, OH), **13,973**
Woman's Christian Temperance Union (Xenia, OH), **14,164**
Woman's Christian Temperance Union (TX), 16,127
Woman's Christian Temperance Union, Bureau of Scientific Temperance Investigation
Woman's Christian Temperance Union of Chester County (PA), **15,346**
Woman's Christian Temperance Union of Rhode Island, **15,395**
Woman's Christian Temperance Union, Peace Department, 7,278
Woman's Christian Temperance Union, Young Ladies League, 17,571
Woman's *Chronicle* (AR), **294**
Woman's City Club (Chicago, IL), 3,787, 3,803, **3,910,** 4,056, 4,066, 4,125, **4,166,** 16,838
Woman's City Club of Kansas City (MO), 10,032, 10,112
Woman's City Club of Los Angeles (CA), 756
Woman's Civic League of St. Paul (MN), 9,334
Woman's Club (IL), 6,748
Woman's Club (Evanston, IL), 3,783
Woman's Club (Wilmette, IL), 4,458
Woman's Club (IN), **4,586**
Woman's Club (Davenport, IA), 4,732
Woman's Club (Saline, MI), **7,984**
Woman's Club (Columbus, MS), 9,558
Woman's Club (Jackson, MS), 9,673

Woman's Club (VT), 16,998
Woman's Club and Civic League (Rosedale, MS), 9,551
Woman's Club Cemetery Association of Watseka (IL), **4,448**
Woman's Club of Austin (IL), 3,899
Woman's Club of Bellows Falls (VT), 16,984
Woman's Club of Boulder (CO), **1,679**
Woman's Club of Central Kentucky, 5,305, 5,321
Woman's Club of Minneapolis (MN), 9,103, 9,347
Woman's Club of Oak Park (IL), **4,310**
Woman's Club of Orange (NJ), 2,042, **11,141**
Woman's Club of Phoenix (AZ), 210
Woman's Club of the City of Pittsburgh (PA), **15,231**
Woman's Club of Waco (TX), **16,397**
Woman's Club of Waukegan (IL), 4,451
Woman's College (VA), 15,643
Woman's College Board of Chicago (IL), 4,045, 4,058, **4,167**
Woman's College of Alabama, 13,138
Woman's College of Georgia, The. *See* Georgia College
Woman's College of the University of North Carolina. *See* University of North Carolina at Greensboro
Woman's Columbian Exposition Club, 4,411
Woman's Columbian Exposition of Cincinnati (OH), 13,863
Woman's Column, The (MA), 15,864
Woman's Conference on National Safety, 4,947
Woman's Day (periodical), 5,080
Woman's Department Club (Indianapolis, IN), 4,625
Woman's Eastern Shore Society of Maryland, **5,825**
Woman's Education Association, 5,974, 6,428, **6,962**
Woman's Educational Club (Denver, CO), 1,721
Woman's Ethical Club (NY), **12,807**
Woman's Exponent (periodical), 16,566, 16,805
Woman's Farm and Garden Society (Dearborn, MI), **8,016**
Woman's Foreign Missionary Society, **4,541**
Woman's Foundation, 10,035
Woman's Franchise League (IN), 4,481
Woman's Franchise Organization, 10,160
Woman's Free Employment Bureau (Spokane, WA), 17,196
"Woman's History of the World", 4,406
Woman's Home and Foreign Mission Society of the Advent Christian Denomination, 7,064
Woman's Home Companion (periodical), 448, 2,436, 5,048, 5,121, 11,304, 11,974, 12,412
Woman's Home Missionary Society (MI), **8,379**
Woman's Home Missionary Society (NE), 10,601
Woman's Home Missionary Society of the Pittsburgh Presbytery (PA), 15,230
Woman's Hospital (Boston, MA), 1,251
Woman's Hospital of Philadelphia (PA), 15,127, **15,142**
"Woman's Hour, The" (column), 7,082
Woman's Humane League (PA), **14,867**
Woman's Improvement Society at Old Orchard (ME), **5,614**
Woman's Interior Decorators Association, 4,066
Woman's Journal and Suffrage News. See Women's Journal, The
Woman's Journal, The (periodical), 55, 1,451, 2,063, 4,156, 5,629, 6,343, 6,413, 6,479, 6,867, 6,960, 6,971, 9,347, **9,452,** 11,167, 13,990, 15,864
"Woman's Kingdom" (column), 6,526
Woman's Land Army of America, 2,352, **6,963,** 6,964
Woman's Lawyers' Journal, 4,269
Woman's League (IL), 4,382
Woman's League for Political Education, 15,315
Woman's Liberty Loan Committee, 9,914, 13,557, 13,617, 16,127, 17,685
Woman's Literary Club (Baltimore, MD), 5,815
Woman's Literary Club (Holland, MI), 8,190
Woman's Literary Club of Carrington (ND), **13,695**
Woman's Manual of Parliamentary Law (book), 15,664
Woman's March on Washington (1968), 12,523
Woman's Medical College of Pennsylvania, 6,698, 16,221
Woman's Medical Society (Baltimore, MD), 11,753

Woman's Medical Society of Connecticut, 15,145
Woman's Memorial Fund, 12,446
Woman's Missionary Association of the Church of the United Brethren in Christ (NE), **10,586**
Woman's Missionary Society (LA), 5,551
Woman's Missionary Society (MS), **9,776**
Woman's Missionary Society, Beaver Crossing (NE). *See* Woman's Society of World Service
Woman's Missionary Society, Evangelical Association (NE), 4,683, **10,588**
Woman's Missionary Society of the Evangelical Church, 10,572, 10,599
Woman's Missionary Society of the Synod of Minnesota, **9,453**
Woman's Missionary Society Rally, Lincoln District (NE), **10,592**
Woman's Missionary Union of Lynn (MA), **7,080**
Woman's Municipal League, 12,403
Woman's Municipal League (NY), 12,266
Woman's National Committee on Law Enforcement, 5,121
Woman's National Council, 16,566
Woman's National Democratic Club, 1,670
Woman's National Farm and Garden Association, **6,964**
Woman's National Press Club, 1,670
Woman's National Publishing Company, The (MO), 9,001
Woman's National Social Science League, 4,708
Woman's National Weekly, The (periodical), 9,001
Woman's Parliament of Southern California, 1,255
Woman's Parliamentary Club of Hartford (CT), **1,945**
Woman's Party, 4,732
Woman's Peace Party. *See also* Women's International League for Peace and Freedom, 4,047, 8,658, 14,237, 15,301, 15,304
Woman's Philanthropic Union, 13,976
"Woman's Place" (filmstrip), 8,524
Woman's Presbyterial Missionary Society of the St. Paul Presbytery (MN), **9,454**
Woman's Presbyterian Board of Missions of the Northwest, 3,802
Woman's Press Association, 720
Woman's Press Club of Cincinnati (OH), **14,040**
Woman's Press Club of Indiana, 4,630
Woman's Press, The, 12,710
Woman's Progressive League (CA), 1,059
Woman's Pro-League Council, 6,706, 7,868
"Woman's Radio Review," 6,499
Woman's Reading Club (Hobart, IN). *See* Hobart Woman's Club (IN)
Woman's Reading Club (MS), **9,777**
Woman's Reading Club of Sault Ste. Marie (MI), **8,386**
"Woman's Record," 3,926
Woman's Reformatory (Marysville, OH), 14,015
Woman's Relief Corps, **1,201,** 1,423, 1,709, 2,206, 2,454, 3,672, 4,273, 4,732, **4,787,** 4,839, **5,125, 6,965,** 8,028, 8,337, 8,340, 10,463, 10,697, 11,445, 13,661, **14,138,** 17,830
Woman's Relief Corps (CT), 1,907
Woman's Relief Corps (Dakota Territory), 13,696
Woman's Relief Corps (GA), **3,274**
Woman's Relief Corps (IA), 4,960
Woman's Relief Corps (ME), James A. Garfield Post, **5,600**
Woman's Relief Corps (East Tawas, MI), 7,860
Woman's Relief Corps (MN), **8,835**
Woman's Relief Corps (Blue Earth, MN), **8,419**
Woman's Relief Corps (Waterville, MN), **8,453**
Woman's Relief Corps (St. Charles, MO), **10,136**
Woman's Relief Corps (SD), **15,865**
Woman's Relief Corps (WI), **17,579, 17,580**
Woman's Relief Corps, Auten Corps No. 14 (South Bend, IN), **4,670**
Woman's Relief Corps, Burnside Post No. 24 (Medford, OR), **14,481**
Woman's Relief Corps, C. G. Eaton Corps No. 188 (Clyde, OH), **14,070**
Woman's Relief Corps, Chester A. Arthur Chapter No. 34 (Ashland, OR), **14,492**
Woman's Relief Corps, Department of California and Nevada, **10,786**

Woman's Relief Corps, Department of Nebraska, U. S. Grant Chapter, **10,560**
Woman's Relief Corps, Department of North Dakota, John F. Reynolds Corps No. 1, **13,696**
Woman's Relief Corps, Department of Potomac, Washington (DC), **17,751**
Woman's Relief Corps, District No. 3 (NE), **10,414**
Woman's Relief Corps, District of Columbia, **2,307**
Woman's Relief Corps, Kyle Corps No. 195 (Wapakoneta, OH), **14,054**
Woman's Relief Corps, Meade Corps No. 18 (OR), **14,376**
Woman's Relief Corps, No. 5 (York, NE), **10,625**
Woman's Relief Corps, Winchester (IN), No. 46, **4,617**
Woman's Republican Patriotic League (OR), **14,472**
Woman's Rotary Club (IN), **4,630**
Woman's Round Lake Improvement Society (NY), 12,844
Woman's Seamen's Friend Society of Connecticut, **2,008**
Woman's Shakespeare and Literary Club of Barnesville (GA), 3,419
Woman's Society for Christian Service (LA), 5,551
Woman's Society for World Service, **10,596**
Woman's Society of Christian Service (NE), 10,601
Woman's Society of Christian Service and Wesleyan Service Guild, First Methodist Church (NE), **10,597**
Woman's Society of Christian Service of the Methodist Church (IN), **4,543**
Woman's Society of World Service (NE), **10,587**
Woman's Society of World Service, Nebraska Conference, Evangelical United Brethren Church (NE), **10,599**
Woman's South African League, 12,446
Woman's Standard, The (periodical), 1,059, 4,793, 4,859, 15,864
Woman's State Forensic League (IA), **4,788**
Woman's State Temperance Records, 8,175
Woman's Study Club (IN), **4,587**
"Woman's Suffrage" (ms), 10,049
Woman's Suffrage and Temperance Union (OH), 14,000
Woman's Suffrage Association (CA), **1,202**
Woman's Suffrage Association (NY), 6,979
Woman's Suffrage Association (Dayton, OH), **14,042**
Woman's Suffrage Association of Hennepin County (MN), 9,240
Woman's Suffrage Association of Indiana, **4,618**
Woman's Symphony Orchestra (Chicago, IL), 4,056, 4,066
Woman's Tea Company of New York, 6,772
Woman's Temperance Crusade, 15,254
Woman's Temperance Society of Morgan County (OH), **13,977**
Woman's Titanic Memorial Association, **2,646**
Woman's Town Improvement and Health Protection Association (Montclair, NJ), 10,919
Woman's Town Improvement Association (St. Petersburg, FL), **2,921**
Woman's Tribune, The, 1,414, 4,156, 13,990, 15,864, 17,616
Woman's Union Christian College in Foreign Fields (GA), 3,157
Woman's Universal Alliance, 9,995
Woman's Wesleyan Educational Council of Nebraska, **10,600**
Woman's Work in the Civil War (book), 7,295
Woman's World (GA), 3,419
Woman's World's Fair (IL, 1925), 4,018, 6,960
Women, 1,838, 6,684, 8,523, 8,603, **17,882**
    attitudes toward, 13,475
    civil rights, 42, 63, 169, 177, 1,049, 1,350, 1,492, 1,503, 1,507, 1,627, 1,763, 2,193, 2,315, 2,323, 2,602, 2,647, 2,818, 3,282, 3,778, 3,910, 4,047, 4,083, 4,149, 4,163, 4,166, 4,469, 4,495, 4,621, 4,732, 5,122, 5,136, 5,137, 5,219, 5,336, 5,487, 5,689, 5,907, 5,961, 6,089, 6,168, 6,365, 6,368, 6,374, 6,482, 6,535, **6,577, 6,589**, 6,615, 6,654, 6,709, 6,732, 6,741, 6,783, **6,849**, 6,901, 6,905, 6,908, 6,918, **6,966**, 6,968, 6,975, 6,981, 7,172, 7,178, 7,188, **7,189**, 7,190, 7,222, 7,232, 7,294, 7,315, **7,325**, 7,629, 8,010, 8,069, 8,071, 8,083,
    8,085, 8,086, 8,107, 8,126, 8,128, 8,149, 8,962, 8,963, 9,317, **9,547**, 9,841, 9,920, 9,932, 9,996, 10,062, 10,154, 10,155, 10,199, **10,204**, 10,271, 11,025, 11,425, 11,605, 11,897, 12,744, **12,857**, 12,913, 12,917, 13,898, 13,981, 13,993, 14,165, **14,253**, 14,314, 14,553, 14,821, 14,905, 15,260, 15,597, 15,903, 16,077, 16,231, 16,918, 17,217, 17,233, 17,680, 17,843
        legal aspects, **6,990**
    economic status, 1,422, 6,869
    education, 58, **75**, 109, 116, 117, 1,979, 3,245, 3,264, **4,118**, 4,495, 5,679, 5,729, 5,974, 6,009, 6,051, 6,237, 6,278, 6,299, **6,303**, 6,416, 6,418, 6,425, 6,428, 6,430, 6,436, **6,438, 6,481**, 6,482, 6,631, 6,661, **6,856**, 7,094, 7,217, 7,711, 7,882, 8,155, 8,900, 9,077, 9,467, 9,890, 9,945, 9,997, 10,038, 10,564, 10,571, 10,607, 11,300, 11,808, 11,890, 12,174, 12,420, 12,738, 12,854, 12,961, 13,189, 13,228, 13,231, 13,309, 13,398, 13,468, 13,496, 13,573, 13,608, 13,632, 13,990, 14,165, 14,638, 14,745, 14,969, 15,259, 15,409, 15,551, 15,570, 16,436, 17,031
    employment, 210, 246, 1,140, 1,326, **1,653**, 2,045, 2,672, 2,679, 2,684, 2,691, 2,700, 2,701, 2,703, 3,715, 3,821, 4,086, 4,340, 5,564, 5,570, 6,737, 6,742, 6,781, 6,838, 6,989, 6,994, 7,236, 7,325, 8,057, 8,073, 8,100, 8,110, 8,131, 8,142, 8,143, 8,165, 9,467, 9,487, 10,035, 10,050, 11,255, 11,610, 11,851, 11,866, 11,905, 12,807, 13,985, 14,144, 14,270, 15,121, 15,255, 17,048, 17,769. See Home labor; Maternity leave; Mothers, employment; Professional women
        economic aspects, **8,067**
        law and legislation, 9,940
        legal aspects, 8,137
        public opinion,
        role conflict, 1,655
    employment reentry, 3,690, 6,799
    higher education, **5,873, 17,785, 17,789**
    history, 6,301, 6,733, **11,305, 12,881, 15,255**
    information services, **6,991**
    institutional care, **1,146, 6,866**
    legal status, laws, etc., 176, 1,131, 2,068, 2,097, 2,703, 3,183, 3,362, 3,821, 3,887, **6,838**, 9,884, 9,946, 9,972, 12,419, 13,396, 17,217, 17,889
        discriminatory legislation, 17,378
    photographs, 6,639
    role, **3,975**
    status, **5,282**, 6,849, **6,929**, 7,270, 7,298, **8,524, 8,532**, 9,287, 10,017, **14,012**, 14,249
    virtues of, **13,362**
Women Against Rape (OH), 14,021
Women Against War, 4,050
Women Air Force Service Pilots (WASPs). See United States (government), Women Air Force Service Pilots
"Women and Children in the Glass Industry" (paper), 11,964
Women and Leisure (book), 1,652
Women and Missions (book), 14,224
"Women and Professional Elites" (lecture), 15,197
Women and the New East (book), 7,326
Women and World Federalism (book), 7,312
Women Are People, 15,249
Women As Artists in the 20th Century, 3,783
"Women as Lawyers" (lecture), 2,887
"Women at the Polls," 17,911
"Women at Trinity" (NC), 13,208
Women at Work (book), 6,958
Women Citizens' Club (NV), 10,679
Women Etchers of America, 3,783
Women for Humphrey, 7,810
Women for Johnson and Humphrey (1964), 793
Women for Legislative Action, 1,017, 1,018
Women for McCarthy, 9,192
Women for McCarthy, 13,551
Women for Peace, 4,050, **4,168**, 17,691
Women for Wallace, 2,589, 4,970
Women Friends of the New England Yearly Meeting, **14,858**
Women High School Teachers, 8,093
Women Historians of the Midwest, 9,467

"Women in a Changing China: The YWCA" (ms), 2,016
Women-in-Action for the Prevention of Violence and Its Causes, Inc. (NC), **13,615**
Women in agriculture, 6,624
Women in Australia (book), 7,257
Women in Communications, Inc., 914, **4,169**, 4,403, **4,692, 9,830**, 10,060, **16,175**
Women in Community Service, 1,600
Women in historiography, **6,947**
Women in medicine, 6,150, **6,217**, 6,407, 6,763. See also Physicians
Women in Medicine: A Bibliography of the Literature on Women Physicians (book), 15,138
"Women in the Bible" (photographs), 2,730
"Women in the Making of America" (radio program). See "Gallant American Women" (radio program)
Women in the professions. See Professional women
Women in the Twentieth Century: A Study of Their Political, Social and Economic Activities (book), 2,224
Women in trade-unions, **2,122**
"Women in War-Time China," 2,016
Women in World Affairs, 6,901, 6,914
Women, Inc., 17,583
Women Lawyer's Association of Michigan, **8,036**
Women Lawyers' Centennial Celebration, 6,886
Women Lawyer's Journal, 4,076
Women Lawyers of the US, 16,789
Women Leader's Conference with Industry, 15,252
Women Library Workers, 948
Women Marines Association, 2,866
Women Mobilized for Change (Chicago, IL), **4,170**
Women Mobilized for Chicago, 3,827
Women, Muslim, 7,326, 10,927
Women of a State University, The (book), 17,771
Women of Courage (book), 14,427
Women of 1915, The, 17,217
"Women of No Tact," 16,174
Women of the Family, The (book), 8,428
Women of the Ku Klux Klan, Klan Fourteen (Chippewa Falls, WI), **17,752**
"Women of the Sixties" (essay), 16,114
"Women of Virginia" (ms),
Women of Wayne (MI), **8,054**
Women of Wyoming (book), 17,941
Women Peace Officers' Association of California, **1,159**
Women, prehistoric, 6,947
Women Speaking (periodical), 6,947
Women Strike for Peace, 1,017, 1,018, 4,050, 7,278, **7,321**, 7,723, 7,923
Women Studies Students' Association (MN), 8,587
"Women Suffrage: Woman's Rights and White Supremacy," 17,583
"Women Take to Politics," 7,256
Women, The (drama), 16,425
Women, The (moving-picture), 11,461
"Women Today" (conference), 11,663
Women Unemployed Seeking Relief in 1933 (bulletin), 2,703
Women United for the United Nations, **6,988**, 7,270
Women Voters League (TX), 16,040
Women Who Work (book), 799
"Women Will Win If They Work" (article), 9,159
Women's Action Alliance, 4,124
Women's Action Collective (OH), **14,021**
Women's Action Committee, 7,302
Women's Action Movement, 17,652
Women's Advertising Club of Chicago (IL), **4,171**
Women's Advisory Council of the Department of Health (PA). See Philadelphia General Hospital Women's Advisory Council (PA)
Women's Aeronautical Association of the United States of America, 4,066
Women's Air Derby, 1,060
Women's Ambulance and Defense Corps, 1,618
Women's Ambulance and Transport Corps, **1,203**
Women's American Baptist Foreign Mission Society, 12,738
Women's American Baptist Home Missionary Society, 17,301

Women's American Organization for Rehabilitation Training, **13,978**

Women's Anthropological Society of America, 2,464, 2,843

Women's Aquatic Club (MI), **8,037**

Women's Archives, 6,450, 6,899, 11,835

Women's Army Auxiliary Corps. *See* United States (government), Women's Army Auxiliary Corps

Women's Association for the Betterment of Public Schools (NC), 13,070

Women's Association of Commerce (Columbus, OH), **14,022**

Women's Athletic Association, 4,041

Women's Athletic Association (Stanford, CA). *See* Women's Recreation Association (Stanford, CA)

Women's Athletic Association (MT), 10,218

Women's Athletic Association (VT), 17,004

Women's Auxiliary Motor Corps, 4,677

Women's Auxiliary of the Medical Association of Atlanta (GA), **3,273**

Women's Auxiliary to the Board of Missions (Episcopal). *See* Episcopal Churchwomen

Women's Bank, 6,582

Women's Baptist Home Missionary Society, Rhode Island Branch, **15,396**

Women's Bar Association of Illinois, 4,094

Women's Bar Association of Missouri, 5,175

Women's Bar Association of St. Louis (MO), 6,467

Women's Board of Missions, Essex County South Branch (MA), **6,174**

Women's Building of the Cotton States, 3,151

Women's Centennial Committee (PA), **15,119**

Women's Centennial Congress, 7,290, 8,963, 14,814, 18,013

Women's Centennial Executive Committee of Massachusetts, **5,975**

Women's Centennial Society of Danvers (MA), **7,010**

Women's Centennial Union, **12,346**

Women's centers and networks, 1,543, 4,241, 7,324, **8,587**, 16,971

Women's Central Association for Relief for the Army, 12,431

Women's Charter, 6,742

Women's Charter Group, The, 8,142

Women's Choral Club (Galveston, TX), **16,223**

Women's Christian Association (Chicago, IL). *See* Young Women's Christian Association of Metropolitan Chicago (IL)

Women's Christian Association of Minneapolis (MN), **9,451**

Women's Christian Association of Newark (NJ), 11,067

Women's Christian Temperance Union (Davidson County, TN), 15,948

Women's Christian Union of Silverton (CO), **1,805**

Women's City Club (Santa Barbara, CA), 1,525

Women's City Club (NY), 7,217, 7,302, 11,897, 12,061

Women's City Club (Rochester, NY), **12,839**

Women's City Club (Cleveland, OH), 13,932, **13,979**

Women's City Missionary Society (Providence, RI), **15,397**

Women's Civic Club (MS), 9,644

Women's Civic Club (WA), Garden Department, **17,137**

Women's Civic League (Tampa, FL), 2,954

Women's Civic League (Baltimore, MD), 5,837

Women's Civic League (Saratoga Springs, NY), 12,851

Women's Civic League (Galveston, TX), **16,224**

Women's Civic League of Rochester (MN), **8,836**

Women's Club (Chandler, AZ), **149**

Women's Club (Denver, CO), 1,732, 1,741

Women's Club (Adrian, MI), **7,986**

Women's Club (Fergus Falls, MN), 8,896

Women's Club (Hope, ND), 13,672

Women's Club (El Paso, TX), 938

Women's Club (UT). *See* Faculty Ladies Club (UT)

Women's Club Life (PA), 15,244

Women's Club of Camden (NJ), **10,891**

Woman's Club of Downey (CA), **966**

Women's Club of Durham (NH), **10,856**

Women's Club of Forest Hills (NY), **11,794**

Women's Club of Hopkins (MN), 8,481

Women's Club of Livingston (NJ), **10,906**

Women's Club of Richmond (KY), **5,407**

Women's Clubs of Iowa, 4,883

Women's College (Evanston, IL). *See* Northwestern University (IL)

Women's colleges, **14**, 116, 864, 1,906, **2,460, 2,864,** 3,157, 3,268, 3,271, 3,379, **3,392,** 3,422, **3,452,** 4,050, 4,058, **4,167, 4,300, 4,374, 4,752, 5,393,** 5,517, 6,346, 6,368, 6,471, 6,482, 6,483, 6,484, 6,616, 7,279, 9,538, 9,556, **9,564, 9,565, 9,566,** 9,614, 9,628, 9,698, 9,919, 9,938, **9,942,** 9,951, 9,964, 10,026, **10,169,** 10,931, **11,283,** 11,300, **11,468,** 12,737, 12,740, **13,201,** 13,228, 13,278, 13,321, 13,326, 13,328, 13,345, 13,353, **13,364,** 13,369, 13,370, 13,381, 13,420, 13,458, 13,462, 13,463, 13,534, **13,542,** 13,563, 13,579, 13,610, 13,617, 13,621, **13,628,** 13,811, **13,884, 14,780,** **15,212,** 15,610, **15,648,** 15,730, **15,736, 15,770,** 15,824, **15,960, 15,973,** 16,369, 17,832, 17,844

administration, 10,035

alumnae, **5,392**

archives, 1,748, 9,519, 9,825, 11,820, 12,926, **14,716, 15,219**

curricula, 9,559, 12,294

history, **9,543, 9,560, 9,562,** 11,278

records and correspondence, 14,760

Women's colleges, Afro-American

history, **13,216**

records and correspondence, 13,215

Women's Committee for Equal Justice, 17,238

Women's Committee for Permanent Peace, 15,301

Women's Committee for the City Party (PA), 14,987

Women's Committee on the World Court, 7,290

Women's Committee to Oppose Conscription, 7,278, **15,315**

Women's Commonwealth, **16,180**

Women's Community Building (Ithaca, NY), 11,623

Women's Conference Group, 2,205, 6,730

Women's Congress (1873,1887), 7,298

Women's Congress (IL, 1893). *See* World's Columbian Exposition (Chicago, IL, 1893), Women's Congress

Woman's Congress of Missions of the Panama-Pacific International Exposition, 1,170

Women's Congressional Union, 10,681

Women's Conservation League (WI), 17,834

Women's Cooperative Alliance, Inc. (Minneapolis, MN), 9,095, 9,252, 9,466

Women's Cooperative Garage (OH), 14,021

Women's Co-operative Printing Union (San Francisco, CA), **1,358**

Women's Council for Human Relations (South Bend, IN), **4,671**

Women's Council of Duluth (MN). *See* Duluth Women's Club (MN)

Women's Council of National Defense, WWI, 3,214, 8,223

Women's Council of Realtors of the National Association of Realtors, 4,177

Women's Council of the New England Area Young Men's Christian Association, 1,831

Women's Creative Arts Cooperative (OH), 14,021

Women's Democratic Club (MO), 9,938

Women's Democratic Club of King County (WA), **17,228**

Women's Democratic Club of Salt Lake City (UT), **16,975**

Women's Democratic Clubs, 10,050

Women's Democratic State Committee of Missouri, 9,984

Women's Dental Association of the US. *See* Federation of American Women Dentists

Women's Department Club (Terre Haute, IN), 4,677

Women's Dinner Club (Tulsa, OK), 14,267

Women's Educational and Industrial Union, **1,160,** 1,344, 1,464, 6,236, 6,239, 6,946, **6,989,** 7,215, 12,738

Women's Educational and Industrial Union (MA), 6,520

Women's Educational and Industrial Union (NY), **12,808**

Women's Educational and Industrial Union (OH), 14,020

Women's Educational Equality Act (1974), 7,262

Women's Educational Society (CO), 1,681

Women's Emergency Brigade (MI), 1,656, 8,081

Women's Emergency Committee to Open Our Schools (Little Rock, AR), **295,** 7,194

Women's Emergency Corps (OR), **14,474**

Women's Employment Service (PA), 15,251

Women's Equity Action League, 6,849, **6,990,** 9,084, **14,023**

Women's Exchange (OR), 14,642

Women's Faculty Club, University of Denver (CO). *See* University of Denver (CO)

Women's Faculty Group, Harvard University (MA). *See* Harvard University (MA)

Women's Federal Savings and Loan Association (OH), 6,945

Women's Fellowship of the Connecticut Conference of the United Church of Christ, **1,965**

Women's Foreign Missionary Society, 4,817, 11,350

Women's Foreign Missionary Society (Danvers, MA), 7,004

Women's Foreign Missionary Society (MI), 8,330

Women's Foreign Missionary Society (MN), **8,837**

Women's Foreign Missionary Society, Pittsburgh Conference (PA), 15,227

Women's Foundation, 760, 11,897

Women's Franchise League, **4,240**

Women's Freedom League, 17,616

Women's Group System (IL), **4,382**

Women's Hall of Fame (NY), 5,162

Women's Health Action Collective, 14,021

Women's health centers and clinics, 8,018

Women's health centers and services, 2,677

Women's Helena for the Capital Club (MT), **10,396**

Women's Historical Club (MI), **8,038**

Women's History Research Center, Inc. (Berkeley, CA), **18,022**

Women's History Research Center, Inc. (Berkeley, CA), Library, **6,991**

Women's History Research Center Library (MO), 10,012

Women's Home and Foreign Missionary Society of the Augustana Synod (IL), **3,962**

Women's Home Missionary Society, 14,026

Women's Hospital Medical College (Chicago, IL), **4,027**

Women's Improvement Club (Riverside, CA),

Women's Improvement League (Hopkins, MN). *See* Women's Club of Hopkins (MN)

Women's Industrial Exchange (WI), **17,835**

Women's Industrial Home (Salt Lake City, UT), 16,936

Women's Institute of Duluth (MN), **8,450**

Women's Interclub (New Concord, OH), 14,118

Women's International Association of Aeronautics, **1,060**

Women's International Council and Congress (London, 1899), 16,566

Women's International Democratic Federation, **7,322**

Women's International Education Council (MI), **8,039**

Women's International League for Peace and Freedom, 124, 539, 656, 677, 860, 1,018, 1,559, 1,604, **1,680,** 2,432, 4,047, 4,050, 4,089, 4,143, 6,846, 6,978, 7,172, 7,220, **7,323,** 7,868, 7,923, **7,988,** 8,000, **8,149,** 8,963, 9,089, 9,119, 9,160, 9,287, 9,302, 9,402, 9,440, 9,467, 9,494, **10,206,** 10,681, 10,730, 11,299, 11,389, 12,518, 12,705, 12,715, **12,883,** 14,656, **14,691,** 15,299, 15,301, 15,303, 15,306, 15,307, 15,311, **15,316,** 17,238, 17,254, 17,610, 17,715, **17,753,** 17,939

Women's International League for Peace and Freedom, Milwaukee Chapter (WI), **17,836**

Women's International League for Peace and Freedom, Minnesota Branch, **9,456**

Women's International Matteotti Committee, 12,518

Women's International Non-Government Organizations, 7,207

Women's International Organization, 6,538

Women's International Organisations, 2,407

Women's International Suffrage Alliance, 8,144

Women's Joint Congressional Committee, 2,095, 6,981

Women's Joint Congressional Committee (1920), **2,647**

Women's Joint Legislative Committee for Equal
Rights, 6,807
Women's Labor League, San Francisco Assembly
(CA), 598
Women's Land Army, 1,618
Women's Law School of Kansas City (KS), 5,175
Women's League (Kalamazoo, MI), 7,831
Women's League (NY). *See* Association of Women
Students
Women's League (OH), 13,756
Women's League Against Waste, 4,677
Women's League for Good Government (PA), 14,987
Women's League for Hope College (MI), **8,193**
Women's League for Jewish Education (Milwaukee,
WI), **17,850**
Women's League for the Protection of Riverside Park
(NY), **12,347**
Women's liberation. *See* Women's movement
(1960-)
Women's Libraries and Publishing Group (OH),
14,021
Women's Literary Club (South Bend, IN), **4,672**
Women's Little Remembrance Club (MN), **9,515**
Women's Loyal National League, **2,648**
Women's Medical Association, 14,900
Women's Medical College (KS), alumnae, 14,698
Women's Medical College (NY), deans, 14,146
Women's Medical College (PA), alumnae, 10,483
Women's Medical College of Baltimore (MD), **11,753**
Women's Medical College of New York Infirmary,
alumnae, 15,429
Women's Medical College of Pennsylvania, 15,296,
16,486, 16,786
    alumnae, 14,763, 17,618
    students, 14,873
Women's Medical Society of New York State, **11,754,**
12,841
Women's Medical Specialist Corps, officials and
employees, 2,091
Women's Missionary Association (IN), **4,545**
Women's Missionary Federation: the Evangelical
Lutheran, the United Norwegian Lutheran, and
the Lutheran Free Churches, **8,867**
Women's Missionary Friend (periodical), 5,173
Women's Missionary Society of the Methodist
Church, 3,353
Women's Missionary Union of North Carolina,
13,297
Women's Missionary Union of the Cleveland
Churches (OH), **13,980**
Women's movement (1960-), 233, 236, 827, 1,017,
1,681, 3,451, **4,241,** 5,330, 5,388, 5,661, **7,324,**
8,062, 8,524, **8,624, 8,855,** 9,192, 9,467, **13,864,**
14,637, 15,332, 15,988, 17,583, 17,663, 18,022
Women's movement (1960-) and Afro-Americans,
5,387
Women's Municipal League of New York, 2,878
Women's Music Club (OH), **14,024**
Women's Music Club of Morgantown (WV), **17,484**
Women's National Abortion Action Coalition, **17,754**
Women's National Book Association, 12,570
Women's National Committee for Hands Off the
Supreme Court, 7,868
Women's National Committee for Law Enforcement,
15,304
Women's National Democratic Club, 2,844, 11,249
Women's National Indian Association, 2,387, 12,856
Women's National League, 1,230
Women's National Press Club, 2,844, 6,767
Women's National Relief Association, 12,931
Women's National Republican Club, 1,464
Women's News Service, Inc., 250
Women's Nonpartisan Clubs of Minnesota, 9,386,
9,400
Women's Nonpartisan League of Minnesota, 9,396
"Women's Opportunities in the Civil Service," 6,812
Women's Organization for National Prohibition
Reform, 2,649, 7,271, 10,032, **11,253**
Women's Organization for National Prohibition
Reform (IN), **4,619**
Women's Organization for National Prohibition
Reform (VA), 17,102
Women's Organization for War Savings of Hartford
(CT), **1,882**

Women's Overseas Service League, 9,059, 9,374,
9,457, 17,755
Women's Overseas Service League, Tucson unit (AZ),
205
Women's Overseas Service Legion, **10,426**
"Women's Page" (column), 14,223
Women's Part in Defense Plans" (radio program),
2,688
Women's Patriotic Association for Diminishing the
Use of Foreign Luxuries (NY), 12,431
Women's Patriotic Relief Association (NY), **12,348**
Women's Peace Congress, 8,000
Women's Peace Party. *See* Woman's Peace Party;
Women's International League for Peace and
Freedom
Women's Peace Society, 7,868
Women's Peace Union, **12,677, 15,317**
Women's Peace Union of the Western Hemisphere,
6,379
Women's Pharmaceutical Auxiliary, 3,439
"Women's Place in the Labor Movement" (speech),
12,422
Women's Political Union, 1,652
Women's Political Union (NJ), 11,112
Women's Power Conference, 7,729
Women's Presbyterial Society (Flint, MI), 7,989
Women's Presbyterial Society (Lake Huron, MI),
7,989
Women's Presbyterial Society (Lake Superior, MI),
7,989
Women's Presbyterial Society (Lansing, MI), **7,990**
Women's Presbyterial Society (Saginaw, MI), 7,989
Women's Presbyterial Society for Home Missions
(Chicago, IL), 4,099
Women's Press Club, 4,732
Women's Press, The, 17,623
Women's Pressure Group for Safety (NC), 13,446
Women's Prison (IN), 11,003
Women's Prison (NC), 13,446
Women's Prison Council (OR), 14,671
Women's Prison Solidarity Committee (OH), 14,021
Women's Progress Club (Dakota County, MN). *See*
Parents' and Teachers' Association (Mendota
Township, MN)
Women's Progressive Farmers Association of
Missouri, 9,988
Women's Progressive Party Club (MN), 9,129
Women's Protective League, 2,451
"Women's Radio Hour," 8,867
"Women's Radio War Program Guide" (radio
programs), 2,691
*Women's Record: The Only Czech Weekly in
America Devoted to the Interests of Women*
(periodical), **3,928**
Women's Recreation Association (Stanford, CA),
1,554
Women's Relief Corps, **8,290**
Woman's Relief Corps Home Association, 707
Woman's Relief Corps Homes, 1,140
Women's Republican Club of Ohio, 14,015
Women's Republican League, 11,610
"Women's Rights and Community Property in
Arizona" (paper), 210
Women's Rights Conference (PA, 1970), 15,236
Women's Rights Convention (NY, 1848), **12,855,
12,857**
Women's Rights Society of Cleveland (OH), 13,981
Women's Savings and Loan Company of Cleveland
(OH). *See* Women's Federal Savings and Loan
Association (OH)
Women's School Association (New Haven, CT),
2,000, 2,003
Women's School of Horticulture (Ambler, PA),
14,809
Women's Security Council of Eastern Ohio, 8,118
Women's Self-Government Association (Northfield,
MN), 8,809
Women's Sewing Circle (Nashwauk, MN), **9,459**
Women's shelters, **4,069, 4,174**
Women's shelters, Afro-American, 4,142
"Women's Show, The" (radio program), 6,658
Women's Silk Culture Association, The, 7,467
Women's Social Industrial Association (LA), **5,421**
Women's Social Service for Israel, Inc., 6,886

Women's Society (Danvers, MA), 7,004
Women's Society of Christian Service (NE), 10,598
"Women's Sphere of Energy Should be Enlarged"
(essay), 9,942
Women's State Committee of Ohio for Public
Welfare, Health and Education, **14,025**
Women's Student Government Association (GA),
3,116
Women's Student Government Association (VT),
17,004
Women's Student Union (VT), 17,004
Women's studies, 1,125, **1,131, 1,165,** 1,975, 5,873,
8,075, 8,501, 8,624, 11,373, 11,663, **15,197,**
15,236, 17,352, **17,354,** 17,663, **18,022**
Women's studies programs, 4,008
Women's Suffrage Association, 10,462
Women's Suffrage Association (NY), 11,443
Women's Suffrage Committee and Democratic
Caucus, 176
Women's Suffrage Convention (DC, 1891), 17,895
Women's Suffrage League (MO), 11,865
Women's Swope Park Civic Club (MO), 10,112
Women's Synodical Society in the State of Kentucky,
5,370
Women's Teachers' Association of Buffalo (NY),
11,361
Women's Temperance Prayer League (OR), **14,692**
Women's Trade Union Auxiliaries, 1,018
Women's Trade Union League, 1,670, 6,802, 6,835.
See also National Women's Trade Union League
Women's Trade Union League (Chicago, IL), 3,854,
3,901, 4,066, 4,092, **4,173,** 6,795
Women's Trade Union League (MD), 10,032
Women's Trade Union League, Milwaukee Chapter
(WI), **17,756**
Women's Trade Union Leagues (Chicago,
Philadelphia, New York), 6,795
Women's Travel Club, **6,992**
Women's Triennial Council, 16,733
Women's Tuesday Club (Neenah-Menasha, WI). *See*
Young Women's Christian Association
(Neenah-Menasha, WI)
Women's Union (Chicago, IL), 4,085
Women's Union (WA), 8,094
Women's Union Label League, 4,677, 17,376
Women's Union Missionary Society, Cincinnati
Branch (OH), **13,865**
Women's Union of Pullman, **3,955**
Women's Universalist Association of Minnesota,
9,406
"Women's View Point" (column), 14,512
Women's Voice (periodical), 2,127, 14,686
Women's Voter's League, 176
Women's War Work Council (HI), **3,635**
Women's Welfare League, 9,466
Women's Welfare League (Minneapolis, MN), **9,460**
Women's Western Unitarian Conference, 7,941
Women's Work Programs, 17,513
Women's World Fair, 18,005
Women's Worlds Fair, Inc., 4,066
Wompner, Josephine (1838-1920). *See* McCrackin,
Josephine (Wompner) [Mrs. James A.] Clifford
[Mrs. Jackson] (1838-1920)
Wonderful Babies of 1809 and Other Years, The
(book), 6,042
Wonderful Plane Ride, The (book), 5,041
Wood, Ada (1869-1951). *See* Webster, Ada (Wood)
[Mrs. Thomas W.] (1869-1951)
Wood, Alice L., **11,331**
Wood, Annie (1847-1933). *See* Besant, Annie
(Wood) (1847-1933)
Wood, Audrey, 2,284
Wood, Charles, 897
Wood, Charles Erskine Scott (1852-1944), 896, 1,321,
1,507, 14,652
Wood, Charlotte Elmire (1864-?), **897**
Wood, E., 9,630
Wood, Elias M. (1830-?), **10,561**
Wood, Ellen M., 5,735
Wood, Elvira, 6,321
Wood, F. John, **8,626**
Wood Family, 11,163
Wood, Fernando, 5,750

Wood, Florence (Hemsley) [Mrs. William Halsey], 12,349
Wood, G., 12,367
Wood, Grant, 4,847
Wood, H. Curtis, Jr. (1903?-), 8,634
Wood, Hannah, 4,933
Wood, Hazel (1866-1948). *See* Waterman, Hazel (Wood) [Mrs. Waldo Sprague] (1866-1948)
Wood, Hilda. *See* Grinnell, Hilda (Wood) [Mrs. Joseph]
Wood, Horace McGuire, **13,616**
Wood, Ida, 11,897
Wood, James, 10,035
Wood, James J., 13,717
Wood, James Madison, 9,825, 11,897
Wood, Jane Margaret (1832-63). *See* Jones, Jane Margaret (Wood) [Mrs. Paul Tudor] (1832-63)
Wood, Janet Margaret [Miss] (1907-), **11,063**
Wood, Julia Amanda (Sargent) [Mrs. William Henry] (1825-1903). *See* Lee, Minnie Mary. Julia Amanda (Sargent) [Mrs. William Henry] Wood (1825-1903)
Wood, Julia Newton [Mrs. James] (1827-?), **7,991**
Wood, Leonard (1860-1927), **2,650**
Wood, Louise A. (Condit-Smith) [Mrs. Leonard] (1869-1943), 2,650
Wood, Lucy (1841-). *See* Butler, Lucy (Wood) (1841-)
Wood, Marcia, 10,561
Wood, Mary, 5,655
Wood, Mary B., 11,662
Wood, Mary S. [Mrs. William], 12,224
Wood, Maud (1871-1955). *See* Park, Maud (Wood). [Mrs. Charles Edward] Park. [Mrs. Robert] Hunter (1871-1955)
Wood, May (?-1948). *See* Simons, May (Wood) [Mrs. Algie] (?-1948)
Wood, Mrs. Ira Couch, 4,084
Wood, Nan (1881-1970). *See* Honeyman, Nan (Wood) (1881-1970)
Wood, Peggy, 691
Wood, Rhoda (Matheson) [Mrs. William Henry], **16,447**, 16,870
Wood, Samuel, 1,898
Wood, Sara (Field) [Mrs. Ehrgott] Bard [Mrs. Charles Erskine Scott] (1882-1974). *See* Field, Sara. [Mrs. Ehrgott] Bard [Mrs. Charles Erskine Scott] Wood (1882-1974)
Wood, Sarah Catherine (1914-). *See* LeSourd, Sarah Catherine (Wood) [Mrs. Peter] Marshall [Mrs. Leonard Earl] (1914-)
Wood, Sarah "Sally" Sayward (Barrell) [Mrs. Richard] Keating [Mrs. Abiel] (1759-1855), 5,694
Wood, Stella Louise (1865-1949), 9,038, 9,274
Wood, William Halsey (1855-97), **12,349**
Woodard, Marcia (?-1933). *See* Atwater, Marcia (Woodard) [Mrs. Wilbur O.] (?-1933)
Woodberry Forest (VA), 12,971, 17,111
Woodbridge, Caroline Lamar, **3,598**
Woodbridge, Sylvester, **1,172**
Woodburn Female Seminary (WV), 17,452, 17,455, 17,457, 17,474, **17,485**
Woodburn, John, 9,769
Woodbury, Ann (1893-1970). *See* Hafen, Ann (Woodbury) [Mrs. Leroy R.] (1893-1970)
Woodbury, Charles Levi (1820-98), **2,651**
Woodbury, Elizabeth (Clapp) [Mrs. Levi], 2,651
Woodbury, Elvira (Stevens) [Mrs. John S.] (1832-1909). *See* Barney, Elvira (Stevens) [Mrs. John S.] Woodbury [Mrs. Oliver B.] Huntington [Mrs. Royal] (1832-1909)
Woodbury, Helen Laura Sumner [Mrs. Robert Morse] (1876-1933), **17,757**
Woodbury, John S., 16,593
Woodbury, Levi (1789-1851), **2,651**
Woodbury, Lorinda, 8,941
Woodbury, Mary, 5,899
Woodbury, Mary Elizabeth. *See* Blair, Mary Elizabeth (Woodbury) [Mrs. Montgomery]
Woodbury, Mary Putnam (1846-1914). *See* Neilson, Mary Putnam (Woodbury) [Mrs. James] (1846-1914)
Woodbury, Nellie (Forsythe) (1869-post 1922), 4,178

Woodbury, Phoebe K. (Pratt), 16,571
Woodbury, Virginia L. *See* Fox, Virginia L. (Woodbury) [Mrs. Gustavus Vasa]
Woodcock, 8,626
Wood-engravers, 2,780
Woodford, Charles F., 12,363
Woodford College, 9,971
Woodhouse, Mrs. Chase Going, 2,673
Woodhull and Claflin's Weekly, 3,778
Woodhull, Catherine C. (1842-1926), 12,776
Woodhull, Hannah C. (1844-1922), 12,776
Woodhull, Hannah (Conklin) [Mrs. Noah Hallock], 12,776
Woodhull, Noah Hallock, 12,776
Woodhull, Victoria California (Claflin) [Mrs. Canning] Woodhull. [Mrs. John Harvey] Blood [Mrs. John Biddulph] Martin (1838-1927), 1,950, **3,778**, 6,435, **6,993**
Woodland, Blanche Hatch [Mrs.], 16,492
Woodlawn Neighborhood Committee (IL), 3,931
Woodlawn Woman's Club (IL), 3,931
Woodman, Caroline (Bowers) [Mrs. Edward], 5,689
Woodman, Cyrus (1814-89), 5,689
Woodman, Dorothy, 1,564
Woodman Family (ME), 5,689
Woodman, H. Rea (1870-1951), **5,237**
Woodman, Hannah, 5,689
Woodman, Mary, 5,689
Woodman, Mary, **2,652**
Woodman, Norah Durand, 5,689
Woodrow, Harriet, 11,177
Woodrow, Mary, **2,652**
Woodrow Wilson Foundation, 6,914, 11,478
Woodruff, Ada. *See* Anderson, Ada (Woodruff) [Mrs. Oliver Phelps]
Woodruff, Elizabeth S., 2,188
Woodruff, Emma (Smith) [Mrs. Wilford] (1838-1912), **16,846**
Woodruff Family (MA), **7,145**
Woodruff, Louise Lentz, 4,066
Woodruff Manifesto, 16,965
Woodruff, Marietta H. Crane, **11,142**
Woodruff, Martha Charlicana (1863-1961), **7,145**
Woodruff, Maude [Mrs.], 1,169
Woodruff, Mrs. Jerusha A., 7,145
Woodruff, Phebe Whittemore (Carter) [Mrs. Wilford] (1807-85), **898**, 16,847
Woodruff, Sybil (1890-), 5,035
Woodruff, Wilford, 898, 16,533, 16,846, 16,847
Woods, Anna, 1,647
Woods, Campbellina "Cammie," 11,392
Woods, Charles Franklin, 8,564
Woods, Ellcana, 12,450
Woods, George, 14,803
Woods, Helen O'Shea, 7,151
Woods Hole Laboratory (MA), 14,877, 14,943
Woods, Isabel Oliver. *See* Kelsey, Isabel Oliver (Woods) [Mrs. William H.]
Woods, Josie Alma (1892-), **10,787**
Woods, Kate C., 1,339
Woods, Martha J., 9,833
Woods, Rosemary, 1,937
Woods, Virna (?-1903), **1,647**
Woodside, John J., 3,152
Woodside, Nina B., 15,138
Woodsmall, Helen (1879-1959). *See* Eldredge, Helen (Woodsmall)
Woodsmall, Ruth Frances (1883-1963), **7,326**
Woodson Family, 5,359
Woodson, Grandville, 2,618
Woodson, Pascal, 2,618
Woodson, Rebecca Hildreth (Nutting) (1835-?), **899**
Woodson, Sarah Jane, 2,618
Woodward, Adelia, 13,697
Woodward, Albert (?-1925), 9,779
Woodward Award Fund, 5,523
Woodward, Bertha [Mrs.] (1882-), 16,485
Woodward, Camilla, 12,242
Woodward, Catherine Martha, Family (MN), **13,697**
Woodward, Comer McDonald (1874-1960), **3,356**
Woodward, Dorothy (1895-1961), **11,246**
Woodward, Elizabeth, 12,738
Woodward, Ellen (Sullivan) [Mrs. Albert] (1887-1971), 2,693, **6,994**, 9,699, 9,779

Woodward, Emily Barnelia [Miss] (1885-1970), **3,117**, **3,357**
Woodward, Emmeline Blanche (1828-1921). *See* Wells, Emmeline Blanche (Woodward) [Mrs. James Harvey] Harris [Mrs. Newel Kimball] Whitney [Mrs. Daniel Hanmer] (1828-1921)
Woodward, Faith Foster (1883-1963), **5,103**
Woodward, Fred E., 2,470
Woodward, Helen, 3,326
Woodward, Joanne. [Mrs. Paul] Newman (1930-), 11,907, **15,772**
Woodward, Katharine S. (?-1945), 7,158
Woodward, Lucy Louisa, 13,697
Woodward, Lydia [Mrs. George], **9,461**
Woodward, Mary Alethea [Miss], **2,653**
Woodward, Samuel, 8,380
Woodworth, Catherine, 11,260
Woodworth, Ellen L. [Mrs. Samuel] (1833-1914), **8,380**
Woodworth, Olive Newell, **11,432**
Woody, McIver, 10,894
Woody, Regina (Jones) [Mrs. McIver] (1894-), **10,894**
Wooldrik, Mary A. Baasen, 8,928
Wooley, Mary Emma, 5,122
Woolf, Virginia (Stephen) (1882-1941), 11,993, 13,871, 16,166
Woolfolk, Frances (1835-?). *See* Wallace, Frances (Woolfolk) (1835-?)
Woollcott, Alexander, 14,377
Woolley, Alice Snow, 16,449
Woolley, Caroline Keturah (Parry) [Mrs. LeGrande] (1885-1967), **16,448**
Woolley, Caroline (Preston) [Mrs. Abram R.], 5,359
Woolley, Edwin Dilworth, 16,449, 16,450, 16,572
Woolley, Erastus Dilworth, 16,449, **16,450**
Woolley, Florence "Flora" (Snow) [Mrs. Edwin Dilworth] (1857-?), 16,449, **16,572**
Woolley, Maria Lucy (Dewey), **16,976**
Woolley, Mary C. [Mrs.] (1867-?), 4,899
Woolley, Mary Emma (1863-1947), 2,067, 2,411, 7,268, 7,272, 15,311
Woolley, Mary Louisa. *See* Clark, Mary Louisa (Woolley) [Mrs. Joshua Reuben]
Woolley, Mildred (1899-). *See* Seydell, Mildred (Woolley) (1899-)
Woolley, Olive (1860-1906). *See* Kimball, Olive (Woolley) [Mrs. Andrew] (1860-1906)
Woolley, Zina Olivia (Boothe) [Mrs. Dilworth] (1877-1901), **16,848**
Woolman, J., 14,852
Woolman, John Sellman, 11,627
Woolman, Mary S. [Mrs.], 9,909
Woolsey, Abby (Howland) [Mrs. G. M.], 2,400
Woolsey, Florence (1903-). *See* Hazzard, Florence (Woolsey) (1903-)
Woolsey, G. M., 2,400
Woolsey, Mary Hale, 1,534
Woolsey, Rachel Andora (1825-1912). *See* Lee, Rachel Andora (Woolsey) [Mrs. John Doyle] (1825-1912)
Woolsey, Sarah Chauncey (1835-1905), 1,426, 17,010
Woolsey, William Walton, 12,231
Woolson, Abba Louise (Goold) (1838-1921), 5,694, **5,976**, 6,659, 6,870
Woolson, Constance Fenimore (1840-94), 1,963, 9,057, 13,943
Woolworth Building (NY), 2,354
Woonsocket Project (RI), 6,988
Wooster, Earl (1893-1977), **10,745**
Wooster, Lorinda (1821-93). *See* Youngman, Lorinda (Wooster) (1821-93)
Wooster, Raymond, **1,911**
Wooten, Katherine [Miss], **3,275**
Wootten, Bayard, 13,447
Wootten, Mrs. Bayard, **13,172**
Worcester, Alfred (1855-1951), 6,164
Worcester, Ann Eliza (1826-1905). *See* Robertson, Ann Eliza (Worcester) [Mrs. William Schenck] (1826-1905)
Worcester, Dean Conant, 7,992

Worcester, Millie A. [Mrs. Horace L.] (?-1911), **10,887**

Worcester, Nanon Fay (Leas) [Mrs. Dean Conant], **7,992**

Worcester, Noah, 11,975

Word, Lucy [Mrs. M. P.] (1884-), **3,440**

Worden, Lazette Marie (Miller), 12,833

Words by the Way (book), 15,270

Words to Women, 3,666

Work, Alice Eloise. *See* Willcox, Alice Eloise Work [Mrs. Walter Francis]

Work Family, 11,747

Work, Mary A., 4,732

Work, Olivia, 15,343

Work relief, 2,672, **2,692**, **2,704**, 6,420, 6,765, 6,808, 8,079, 10,074, 11,883, 14,202

Workers Chronicle, The (KS), 8,070

Workers' compensation, 8,658

Workers' Defense League, 492, 2,879, 8,077, 8,093

Workers Defense Union, 17,633

Workers Health Bureau, 1,656

Workers Party of America, 640

Workhouses, 6,206

Working class women, housing, **5,544**

Working Girls (moving-picture), 1,025

Working Mother, The (book), 11,764

Working mothers. *See* Mothers, employment

Working-women's clubs, **3,956**, **7,835**, 8,684, **10,192**, 10,518, 12,739

Working-women's clubs, Afro-American, 3,935

Working Women's Protective Union, 12,739

Workingwoman's Industrial Home of Chicago (IL), **4,174**

Workmen's compensation, 2,504, 6,486, 8,075, **8,138**, 11,760, 11,905, 17,463

Works councils, 8,124

Works, John Downey (1847-1928), **900**

Workshop for Cultural Democracy, 9,494

World Affairs Council of Northern California, 647

World Affairs Council of Northern California, library committee, 854

World Anti-Slavery Convention (1840), 6,741, 15,291

World Association of Girl Guides and Girl Scouts, **12,115**, **12,116**

World Center for Women's Archives, Inc., 1,482, **2,085**, 6,389, 6,495, 6,687, **6,995**, 11,143, 11,605, 13,189, 14,900

World Confederation of Organizations of the Teaching Profession, 8,069

World Conference on Education, 5,325

World Congress of Women, 7,322

World Council of Churches, 5,171, 10,001, 13,230

World Council of Peace (India, 1961), 14,455

World Court (The Hague, Netherlands), 110, 6,978, 6,980, 9,160, 13,993, 17,468, 17,654

World Day of Prayer, 3,656, 4,979

World Disarmament Conference (Geneva, 1932), 17,654

World Federalists, U. S. A., United Nations Charter Revision Committee, 4,480

World Federalists, U. S. A., United Nations Liaison Committee, 4,480

World Federation of Education Associations, 13,677

World government. *See* International organizations

World history, juvenile literature, 2,485

World I Breathe, The (moving-picture), 17,791

World News Service, 3,799, 3,800

World of Ellen March, The (book), 4,987

World of Zen, The (book), 16,167

World Organization of the Teaching Profession conference (Glasgow, Scotland, 1947), 3,088

World Organizations on Early Childhood Education, 6,556

World Peaceways, 3,074

World politics (1945-), 8,949

World Population Conference, 6,582

World Rehabilitation Fund, 2,115

World-Telegram, 11,858

World, The (NY), 1,325, 10,181, 11,858, 11,867

World Tomorrow, The, 14,437

World War Auxiliary Club of Johnson County (IA), 4,960

World War I, 1,634, 1,689, 2,429, 2,432, 2,654, 3,181, 3,380, 4,925, 5,803, 6,352, 8,693, 8,712, 8,717,
9,063, 9,067, 9,367, 9,388, 9,608, 9,888, 10,025, 10,202, 10,360, 10,427, 10,506, 11,853, 11,905, 12,449, 12,506, 12,673, 13,657, 14,503, 15,070, 15,304, 15,707, 16,032, 16,092, 16,095, 16,261, 16,554, 17,046, 17,116, 17,413

aerial operations, 11,831

campaigns and battles, 13,889

casualties, 2,554, 2,689, 15,693, 17,450

civil defense, 13,557, 14,006

civilian relief, 1,675, **2,280**, 2,347, 2,352, 2,354, 4,928, 6,613, 6,619, 7,160, 7,191, 7,307, 9,277, 9,430, 11,179, 12,391, 12,729, 13,881

civilians' work, 205, 235, 849, 969, 1,115, **1,206**, 1,688, 1,820, 1,891, 1,931, 2,052, 2,352, 2,421, 2,679, **2,700**, 3,250, **3,383**, **3,635**, 3,931, **4,340**, **4,727**, 4,923, 5,085, **5,114**, 6,716, 6,725, 6,727, 6,963, **7,062**, **7,137**, **8,446**, 9,059, 9,427, **9,487**, **10,509**, 10,538, 10,793, 11,027, 11,236, 11,445, **12,114**, 12,374, **12,797**, 13,398, 13,696, 13,920, 13,993, 15,005, 15,182, **15,378**, 17,071, 17,086, 17,116, 17,685, 17,749

Red Cross, 230, 231, 246, 710, 1,560, 1,772, **2,515**, 3,195, 3,203, 3,343, 3,432, 3,669, 4,258, **4,350**, 4,394, 4,629, 5,451, 5,506, 5,764, 6,594, 6,605, 6,644, 6,646, 6,690, 6,939, 7,332, 8,228, 8,427, 8,436, 8,446, 8,492, 8,651, 9,037, 9,311, **9,362**, 9,374, 9,425, 9,467, 9,709, 10,630, 11,593, 11,719, 13,193, 13,218, 13,243, 13,277, 13,604, 13,617, **13,679**, 13,696, 13,889, 13,941, 14,136, 14,741, 15,009, 15,531, 16,216, 17,984

Salvation Army, 13,663

Young Men's Christian Association, 2,661, 7,003, 7,383, 12,132, 13,663, 14,377, 17,729, 17,815

Young Men's Christian Association, Women's Bureau, **12,134**

Young Women's Christian Association, 8, 2,292, 4,394, 6,920, 10,000, 12,718, **12,719**, 12,725, 13,692, 15,325

civilians' work, industrial, 8,447, 10,789

communications, 6,383

confiscation and contributions, 6,020

conscientious objectors, **9,900**

diplomatic history, 2,665

economic aspects, 1,917, **2,679**, 2,695, **2,700**, 8,070

finance 2,886, 4,340, 4,930, 8,167, 11,027, 11,346, 13,617, 13,663, 13,979, 15,005, 16,252, 17,730

food question, 1,404, 2,352, **2,694**, 3,383, 4,340, **4,850**, **4,954**, 7,062, 9,894, 11,719, 12,114, 13,617

historiography, 1,216, 4,833

hospitals, charities, etc., **2,280**, 5,991, 6,644, 8,310, 9,277, 9,642, 11,727, 12,180, 13,336, 13,617, 13,854, **15,385**, 15,569

human resources, **2,679**, **6,963**, 8,447

libraries (in camps, etc.), 4,350, 8,976

medical and sanitary affairs, 2,679, 6,605, 6,623, 6,722, 11,556

military nursing, 382, **6,129**, 6,152, **6,161**, 6,618, 6,623

nurses, 230, 231, 236, 246, 4,108, **4,629**, **5,081**, **5,764**, 7,015, 7,019, 7,332, **8,932**, **9,059**, 9,311, 11,555, 11,918, 13,336, 13,617, 13,729, 13,887, **14,778**, 15,149, 17,028

opposition to, 741

peace, 14,741

personal narratives, 3,173, **6,470**, 8,996, 15,569

pictorial works, 3,172

posters, 1,062, 1,306, 13,617

prisoners and prisons, 1,557

propaganda, 2,679

public opinion, 6,811, 8,070, 13,398

refugees, 9,437

registers, lists, etc., 7,137

registers of dead, 3,250

relief of sick and wounded, 8,446, 13,277

songs and music, 13,024

transportation, 2,696, 8,259

treaties, 1,557, 2,389, 5,499

World War II, 2,429, 2,891, 2,909, 2,933, 3,219, 3,404, 4,395, 5,269, 5,807, 5,829, 6,352, **6,472**, 7,205, 7,301, 7,891, 8,555, 8,635, 8,704, 8,754, 8,949, 9,003, 9,761, 10,360, 11,644, 11,866, 11,905, 12,584, 13,024, 15,070, 15,172, 16,054, 16,092, 16,379, 16,554, 17,940

aerial operations, 30, 11,831, 11,861
casualties, 17,069

censorship, 3,653, 11,909

charities, **2,263**, 15,446

civilian relief, **2,263**, **3,182**, 8,769, **8,904**, 9,218, 12,180, 13,819, 15,446, 17,445

civilians' work, 54, 205, 1,115, **1,182**, 1,931, 2,558, 2,682, **2,686**, **2,691**, 2,701, 3,451, 3,602, **3,653**, **3,950**, 4,957, **5,152**, 5,207, 5,422, **5,521**, 5,983, **7,138**, **7,760**, 7,965, 8,486, 8,594, **8,999**, 9,226, 9,425, 9,707, **10,013**, **10,889**, 11,236, 11,445, **12,797**, 13,193, **13,618**, 13,719, **14,264**, 16,215, 17,436, 17,582, 17,815, **17,978**

Red Cross, 205, 3,301, 3,343, 3,437, 3,530, 4,843, **5,131**, 7,965, 8,535, 8,651, 9,218, 10,886, 11,063, 13,543, 15,427, 16,216

Young Women's Christian Association, 892, 12,719, 13,618

civilians' work, industrial, **1,182**, **2,701**, **2,853**, 3,437, **5,311**, 8,089, 8,105, 8,135, **8,139**, **8,140**, 9,449, 10,013, **12,114**, 14,497, 14,695, **16,964**, 17,214

civilians' work, industrial, Afro-Americans, 8,089, 8,105

claims, 5,272

economic aspects, **2,688**, **2,853**, 14,203, 15,121

evacuation of civilians, 141, 580, 1,936, 10,692

finance, 2,197, 7,138, 8,999, **9,130**, 9,218, 9,914, 13,979, 14,834, 15,121, 17,730

food question, 1,936, 8,446, 8,999, 10,692, 13,618, 15,121

governments in exile, 12,061

historiography, 9,333

human resources, 2,691, 2,701, **3,950**, 8,132, 8,683, **9,928**, 15,315

information services, 15,121

Jews, rescue, 8,639, 13,819, 15,159

journalists, **2,622**, 6,011

literature and the war, 8,591

medical and sanitary affairs, **1,203**, 3,653, 5,991, 6,153, 6,646, **13,888**

military nursing, 6,122, **6,127**, 6,134, **6,145**, **6,153**, **6,159**, 8,259

naval operations, submarine, 14,505

nurses, 235, 242, **4,843**, 8,045, 9,286, 10,064, 13,618, 13,887, **17,306**, 17,862

occupied territories, 13,819

opposition to, 741

peace, 3,712

personal narratives, 6,523, 9,467, **10,064**, 17,163

photography, 357, 2,622, 12,891

posters, 13,618

prisoners and prisons, 1,606, 4,476, 8,690, 8,884 13,269, 13,642, 14,396, **15,809** *See also* Concentration camps

prisoners and prisons, Japanese, 1,623

propaganda, 1,178, 2,691, 6,049

public opinion, 6,846, 15,121

refugees, 2,263, 13,819, 17,282

registers, lists, etc., 7,138

relief of sick and wounded, 11,854

secret service, 6,020, 13,008

transportation, 1,203, 14,774

"World We Live In—The World We Want, The" (report), 6,674

World Without War Council, 17,244

World Woman's Christian Temperance Union, 4,223, **17,837**

World Woman's Party, 1,059, 6,981

World Woman's Suffrage Conference (1920), 2,292

World's Anti-Slavery Convention (London, 1840), 6,842

World's Columbian Exposition (Chicago, IL, 1893), 2,454, 2,922, 3,923, 4,071, 4,163, **4,224**, 4,337, 4,366, 4,369, 4,704, 4,904, 6,346, 6,805, 7,182, 7,887, 7,941, 8,362, 8,937, 10,343, 12,526, 12,936, 13,993

World's Columbian Exposition (Chicago, IL, 1893), Board of Lady Managers, **3,912**, 4,609, **11,266**

World's Columbian Exposition (Chicago, IL, 1893), Idaho Building, 3,670

World's Columbian Exposition (Chicago, IL, 1893), Illinois Woman's Exposition Board, 4,368

World's Columbian Exposition (Chicago, IL, 1893), Jewish Women's Congress, 3,884

World's Columbian Exposition (Chicago, IL, 1893), Woman's Building, 3,781, 4,786
World's Columbian Exposition (Chicago, IL, 1893), Woman's Dormitory Association, **3,913**
World's Columbian Exposition (Chicago, IL, 1893), World's Congress Auxiliary, 3,923, 4,684
World's Columbian Exposition (Chicago, IL, 1893), World's Congress of Representative Women, 3,923, 7,941, 15,061
World's Education Bureau of America, 12,422
World's Exposition (1884), 5,418
World's Fair (IL, 1893). See World's Columbian Exposition (Chicago, IL, 1893)
World's Fair (Chicago, IL, 1933), 9,705
World's Fair (NY, 1939-40), 11,326
World's Fair (NY, 1939-40), Palestine Pavilion, 14,908
World's Fair (NY, 1964), 10,370
World's Fair, Pacific House (San Francisco, 1939), 441
World's fairs. See Exhibitions
World's Young Women's Christian Association, 6,538
Worley, Dorothy, 2,932
Worley, Katherine Fay (1876-1971). See Allen, Katherine Fay (Worley) [Mrs. Charles] (1876-1971)
Wormer, Grace [Miss] (1886-), 5,034, 5,035
Worrall, Phoebe (1807-74). See Palmer, Phoebe (Worrall) [Mrs. Walter Clark] (1807-74)
Worrell, Emma [Miss] (1834-1931), 2,058, 2,059
Worrell, Ruth Mougey [Mrs. Charles Peters] (1882-?), Family, **14,026**
Worth, Adelaide (1844-?). See Bagley, Adelaide (Worth) (1844-?)
Worth, Elvira Evelyna (1836-1940). See Moffitt, Elvira Evelyna (Worth) Jackson Walker (1836-1940)
Worth Family (NC), 13,439
Worth, James, 13,439
Worth, Jonathan (1802-69), 13,070, 13,439, **13,619**
Worth Literary Club (South Bend, IN), **4,673**
Worth, Patience, **10,184**
Worth, Roxana. See McNeill, Roxana (Worth)
Worthington, Amanda (ca. 1845-?), 9,780, 9,781, 13,173
Worthington, Amanda (Dougherty) [Mrs. Samuel] (1805-?), 9,781, **13,173**
Worthington, Bettie Stone [Mrs. William Mason], 9,780
Worthington Family, 12,314
Worthington Family (MS), **9,780, 9,781**
Worthington Female Seminary (OH), faculty, 10,988
Worthington, Mary, 9,780, 9,781
Worthington, Mary G., 9,780
Worthington, Samuel, 9,781, 13,173
Worthington, Samuel Wheeler, **13,620**
Worthington, Sarah Cahill, 9,048
Worthington, William Mason, 9,780
Worthy Women of Our First Century (book), 2,643, 15,116
Wortman, Doris Nash. [Mrs. Elbert B.] Monroe (1890-1967), 4,078
Wosgaard, Rigmor Christine Laursen. See Petersen, Rigmor Christine Laursen (Wosgaard) [Mrs. Hjalmar]
Wosser, Margaret (1906-?). See Dowd, Margaret (Wosser) (1906-?)
Wotherspoon, Alexander Somerville (?-1854), 2,654
Wotherspoon, Alexander Somerville (1892-), 2,654
Wotherspoon Family, **2,654**
Wotherspoon, Louisa A. Kuhn [Mrs. Alexander Somerville] (?-1877), 2,654
Wotherspoon, Peggy [Mrs. Alexander Somerville], 2,654
Wouk, Herman, 11,981
Wounded Knee Creek, Battle of (1890), 17,891
Wovoka. See Wilson, Jack
Woytinsky, Emma (Shadkan) (1893-), 6,700
Wragg, Ann, 15,534
Wragg, Elizabeth, 15,534
Wragg, Henrietta, 15,534
Wragg, Joseph, 15,534
Wragg, Judith, 15,534
Wragg, Samuel, **15,534**

Wragg, Samuel (son), 15,534
Wrangel Island Expedition (1923), 10,859
Wray, Catherine McAlpin (1811-88). See Pritchard, Catherine McAlpin (Wray) (1811-88)
Wray, Edith, 13,747
Wray Family (GA), **3,599**
Wray Family (GA), 3,030
Wren, Jennie, 1,224
Wright, Agnes R., 17,919
Wright, Alice (Peters), 718
Wright, Alice Spearman (1902-), 13,176
Wright, Allen, 1,751
Wright, Anna Elizabeth (Steele) [Mrs. John] (1825-1913), **2,655**
Wright, Anne (1876-1929), **17,924**
Wright, Bell Mallery [Mrs. W. T.], **14,420**
Wright, Carroll D., 11,372
Wright, Charles, 8,939
Wright, Constance Choate (1897-), **6,118**
Wright, Cornelia (1816-90). See Whipple, Cornelia (Wright) [Mrs. Henry Benjamin] (1816-90)
Wright, David, 9,782
Wright, David McCord, 15,472
Wright, Dorothy Edgerton, **14,099**
Wright, Edgar, **10,731**
Wright, Eliza, 11,442
Wright, Eliza Abert Barry [Mrs. David], 9,782
Wright, Elizabeth, 11,666
Wright, Elizabeth [Miss] (1888-), **10,562**
Wright, Elizabeth (1860-1950). See Heller, Elizabeth (Wright) [Mrs. John] (1860-1950)
Wright, Elizabeth C., 1,822
Wright, Elizabeth Evelyn (1876-1906), **15,777**
Wright, Elizabeth Steele [Mrs.] (1825-1913), **17,758**
Wright, Ella Rupert (1896-1963), **2,897**
Wright Family, 11,522
Wright Family (MS, VT), 9,703
Wright Family (NY), 11,442
Wright Family (NY), 11,599
Wright, Fannie, 7,150
Wright, Fielding L., 9,629
Wright, Frances. [Mrs. Guillaume Sylvan Casimir Phiquepal] D'Arusmont (1795-1852), 2,656, 4,433, 4,435, 4,809, 5,907, 11,776, 13,846
Wright, Frank, 11,831
Wright, Frank Lloyd, 4,958, 17,661
Wright, George Burdick (1835-82), Family (MN), **9,464**
Wright, Grace Duncan (1874-1951). See Capen, Grace Duncan (Wright) [Mrs. Samuel Paul] (1874-1951)
Wright, Grace Radcliffe, 1,666
Wright, Grace Tillston Clarke [Mrs. Vernon Ames] (1874-1950), 9,464
Wright, Hannah (1819-1912). See Gould, Hannah (Wright) [Mrs. John Stanton] (1819-1912)
Wright, Helen, 2,520
Wright, Helen Madeline, **2,023**
Wright, Helen Martha, 10,952, 11,101
Wright, Helen R., 8,677
Wright, Henry, 11,666
Wright, Irene, 2,863
Wright, Irene Aloha [Miss] (1879-1972), 2,553, **2,657**
Wright, J. W. A., 9,782
Wright, Jane C. (1919-), **7,327**
Wright, Jennie. See English, Jennie (Wright)
Wright, John, 2,655
Wright, John, 15,548
Wright, Josepha "Jodie," **16,148**
Wright, Kate H., 901
Wright, Katherine Skelly, 5,473
Wright, Kathleen, 3,323
Wright, Laura E., 9,782
Wright, Louise L., 4,067
Wright, Luella Margaret (1881-1963), **4,962**, 5,035
Wright, Lydia T. (1922-), **11,390**
Wright, Marjorie, 13,108
Wright, Martha (1912-). See Griffiths, Martha (Wright) [Mrs. Hicks] (1912-)
Wright, Martha (Coffin) [Mrs. Peter] Pelham [Mrs. David] (1806-75), 7,222
Wright, Martha Elizabeth (1832?-1919). See Morris, Martha Elizabeth (Wright) (1832?-1919)

Wright, Mary (1777-1855). See Faulkner, Mary (Wright) [Mrs. Winthrop] (1777-1855)
Wright, Mary C., 7,822
Wright, Mary (Featherston), 3,323
Wright, Mary (North) [Mrs. Roswell]. See Bartlett, Mary (North) [Mrs. Roswell] Wright [Mrs. Henry E.]
Wright, May Eliza (1844-1920). See Sewall, May Eliza (Wright) [Mrs. Edwin W.] Thompson [Mrs. Theodore Lovett] (1844-1920)
Wright, Milton, 14,055
Wright, Mrs. Anton P., 15,472
Wright, Mrs. Hugh, 1,080
Wright, Muriel Hazel, 1,751
Wright, Olive Ames, 7,150
Wright, Orville (1871-1948), 11,831, **14,055**
Wright, Patience (Lovell) [Mrs. Joseph] (1725-86), 11,185, 11,203
Wright, Rachel, 17,713
Wright, Rebecca M. (ca. 1839-?). See Bonsal, Rebecca M. Wright (ca. 1839-?)
Wright, Rodema E., 13,226
Wright, Roswell, 11,666
Wright, Sarah (?-1853). See Atkins, Sarah (Wright) (?-1853)
Wright, Sarah Peck [Mrs. Edward] (?-1900), 3,861
Wright, Serena Marie (Ames) [Mrs. George Burdick] (1840-68), 9,464
Wright, Sophie Bell [Miss] (1866-1912), 5,410, **5,426**, 5,500
Wright, Susan, 6,336
Wright, Susan (1816-1904). See Clark, Susan (Wright) [Mrs. Jonas Gilman] (1816-1904)
Wright, Susan Koerner [Mrs. Milton], 14,055
Wright, Susie M., 2,973
Wright, Susie Webb [Mrs. Floyd], **4,860**
Wright, Teresa (1918-), 11,907, 12,367
Wright, Thomas, 11,599
Wright, Vernon Ames (1863-1938), 9,464
Wright, Virginia, **17,366**
Wright, Wilbur (1867-1912), **14,055**
Wrinch, Dorothy (1895-1976), **7,328**
Wrinch, Pamela (1927-75). See Schenkman, Pamela (Wrinch) (1927-75)
Writ of debt, **15,716**
Write, Mrs. Timothy, 12,238
Writer Magazine, The (periodical), 14,414
Writers Book, The, 12,016
Writers' Club (TN), 15,975
Writer's Digest (periodical), 163
Writers Guild, 3,999
Writer's Roundtable, 12,016
Writers Shop Talk Group, 54
Writers War Board (World War II), 11,491
Writing for Love or for Money (book), 16,153, 16,173
Writing of Fiction, The (book), 11,175
Wulfekammer, Verna M., 9,960
Wulkop, Elsie, 6,221
Wurster, Catherine (Bauer) [Mrs. William Wilson] (1905-64), 517
Wurts Family (NY), 12,020
Wurzburg, Jocelyn Maurie Dan (1940-), **15,903**
Wyandotte Indians, 14,098
    mortuary customs, 5,174
    reservations, 5,174
Wyatt, Anne Eliza. See Leishman, Anne Eliza (Wyatt) [Mrs. Franklin L.] Gunnell [Mrs. Robert Adamson]
Wyatt, Belle Layton (?-1954). See Willard, Belle Layton (Wyatt) [Mrs. Joseph E.] (?-1954)
Wyatt, Edith Franklin (1873-1958), 3,990, 3,997, 3,999, **4,007**
Wyatt, Hattie Ophelia (1878-1950). See Caraway, Hattie Ophelia (Wyatt) [Mrs. Thaddeus Horatio] (1878-1950)
Wyatt, Joseph W., 2,635
Wyatt, Marian Cowles, 12,427
Wyatt, Mary. See Gentry, Mary Wyatt [Mrs. Richard Harrison]
Wyatt, Rose M., **14,225**
Wyche Family (AR), **285**
Wyche, Mary Lewis, 13,553
Wycoff, Charlotte Chander, 11,940
Wyckoff, Mary, 12,315

Wyeth, Nathaniel Jarvis, 14,513
Wygal, Winnifred, **12,730**
Wylde, Hazel, 14,630
Wylie, Elinor Morton (Hoyt). [Mrs. Philip] Hichborn [Mrs. Horace] Wylie [Mrs. William Rose] Benét (1885-1929), 2,658, 4,005, 11,821, 17,053
Wylie, Fred, 17,621
Wylie, Horace, 2,658
Wylie, Lollie Belle [Mrs. Hart], 3,141, **3,276**
Wylie, Margaret (1889-1964), **11,756**
Wylly, Alexander Campbell, 3,528
Wyman, Bella Maria Ristine [Mrs. Oliver Cromwell] (1855-1953), 9,318
Wyman, Edward, 9,867
Wyman, Elizabeth (Hadley) [Mrs. Edward], 9,867
Wyman Family, 9,318
Wyman, Helen de St. Prie (1857-1949). *See* Rollins, Helen de St. Prie (Wyman) [Mrs. Daniel] (1857-1949)
Wyman, W. A., **17,925**
Wyman, William (1825-1903), **5,826**
Wymore, Mrs. William, 10,065
Wymore, William, **10,065**
Wyndham, Lee, **14,475**
Wyngard, Rhoda (pseudonym). *See* Silberman, Rhoda Truax
Wynne, Madeline Yale (1847-?), 3,997, 7,012
Wyoming, 8,116, 13,765, 14,680, **17,888, 17,918,** 17,951, 17,976, 17,995, 18,018
  agricultural societies, 17,926
  Americanization, 17,902
  assessment, 1,807
  auditing, **17,917**
  authors, 16,485, 17,908, 17,921, **17,946,** 18,010, **18,011, 18,017**
  charity organization, 17,892
  child care centers, 17,988
  church records and registers, 17,904, 17,962
  church records and registers, Baptist, 17,962
  church records and registers, Methodist, 17,962
  church records and registers, Presbyterian, 17,962
  clergy, Congregational, 17,971
  clubs, 17,894, **17,928,** 17,931, 17,940, **17,987**
  college teachers, **18,019, 18,021**
  convents and nunneries, Catholic, 10,611
  county courts, **17,884**
  county officials and employees, **17,933**
  court records, 1,808, 1,809
  diaries and journals, **16,631,** 17,982, **18,015**
  editors, 17,921
  educational associations, **17,936**
  educators, **17,896, 17,924**
  engineers, 17,889
  flags, 17,985
  government librarians, 1,676, 17,908, 17,918, **17,919, 18,010**
  governors, **8,253,** 17,908, 17,913, **17,915,** 17,922, 17,941, **18,005**
  health-officers, 17,925
  historians, **17,885, 17,888, 17,903,** 17,908, **17,918, 17,977,** 17,985
  historical societies, **17,918**
  home demonstration work, 17,927, 17,929
  home economics, **17,927**
  hotels, taverns, etc., 2,536
  Jews, 17,890
  journalism, societies, 17,930, 18,017
  jury, 17,884, 17,905, **17,934**
  justices of the peace, 17,908, **17,910,** 17,933
  land settlement, 4,952, 17,900, **17,948,** 17,982
  lawyers, 17,899, **17,974**
  legislators, **17,889,** 17,909, **17,940**
  Mormons and Mormonism, 191
  musical societies, **17,996**
  Native Americans, reservations, 10,433
  officials and employees, 10,607, 17,896, **17,901, 17,914, 17,917, 17,918,** 17,920, 17,977, 18,010
  parks, **18,025, 18,026**
  patriotic societies, **17,962**
  physicians, **17,925**
  pioneers and settlers, **2,536, 17,887, 17,891, 17,897,** 17,912
  politics and government, 17,903
  prisons, 17,892
    psychiatric hospitals, 17,892
    public welfare administration, **17,892**
    ranchers, 17,907, **18,015**
    real property, cases, 1,811
    rewards (prizes, etc.), **18,014**
    school superintendents and principals, 17,889, 17,901, 17,911, 18,010
    secretaries, 17,913
    societies, etc., **18,023**
    state departments of education, **17,901**
    state libraries, **17,919**
    students, 17,886, **17,904**
    student's societies, 17,963
    suffrage, 17,910, 17,916, 17,933
      law and legislation, 17,909
    suffragists, **17,898, 17,906**
    surplus government property, 1,811
    teachers, **10,433, 17,887, 17,995**
    tuberculosis, hospitals and sanitoriums, 17,892
    universities and colleges, administration, **17,963**
    volunteer workers in hospitals, **17,981**
    voters, registration of, 17,960
Wyoming Agricultural Extension Service, 17,929
Wyoming Blue Book, 17,903
Wyoming Board of Charities and Reform, **17,892**
Wyoming Children's Home, 17,892
Wyoming Cowbelles Association, **17,926**
Wyoming Day Committee, 17,916
Wyoming Extension Homemakers Council, **17,927, 18,023**
Wyoming Federation of Women's Clubs, **17,928**
Wyoming Homemakers, **17,929**
Wyoming Press Women, **17,930,** 18,017
Wyoming State Archives Department, 17,976
Wyoming State Education Department, **17,901**
Wyoming State Historical Board, 17,918
Wyoming State Mental Hospital, 17,892
Wyoming State Penitentiary, 17,892
Wyoming State Tuberculosis Sanitorium, 17,892
Wyoming Stockman-Journal, 1,676
Wyoming Territory, 1,497, 2,556
Wyoming Territory, justices of the peace, 1,790
Wyoming Wife (book), 16,464
Wyoming Wonderful (book), 18,017
Wyrick, F. H., 4,971
Wyse Family, **2,659**
Wyse, Francis O., 2,659
Wyse, Mrs. Francis O., 2,659
X. Beidler: Vigilante (book), 10,366
X-Ray Technician, The (periodical), 10,508
X-rays, 11,814, 15,120
Xavier, Mother Frances, 15,369
Xavier, Peter, 14,686
Xavier, Sister Mary (1881-1978), 10,732
Yaakers, 10,388
Yadkin Baptist Association Woman's Missionary Union (NC), 13,639
Yadkin College (NC), 13,526
Yakima Indians, wars, 17,188
Yale Award, 9,583
Yale Clinic of Child Development (CT), 2,353
Yale Family (CT), **1,883**
Yale, Horace (1826-95), 1,883
Yale-in-China Hospital, 7,285
Yale, John Brooks, 4,479
Yale, Lilla Charlotte (1855-1929), 1,883
Yale, Madeline. *See* Wynne, Madeline (Yale)
Yale, Marie Louise (McCulloch) [Mrs. John Brooks], 4,479
Yale University (New Haven, CT), 1,167, 1,870, 6,209, 7,680, 8,929
  alumnae, 1,998, 8,572, 13,261
  alumni, 3,898, 9,435, 11,050
  faculty, 1,992, 1,998, 12,420
  students, 11,534, 17,450
Yale University (New Haven, CT), Library, faculty, 1,995
Yale University (New Haven, CT), School of Medicine, 2,353, 6,679, 9,176
Yale University (New Haven, CT), School of Nursing, 6,126, 6,143
Yalta, 11,871
Yalta Conference (1945), 11,488
Yambura, Barbara (Schneider) (1917-), **5,047**
    Yamhill County Woman Suffrage Association (OR), 14,547
Yampolsky, Helene (Boas), 14,886
Yancey, Nancy (Harrell) [Mrs. William Lay] Smith, 13,577
Yankee (periodical), 7,587
"Yankee in an English Village, A" (ms), 6,907
Yankee Stranger (book), 5,031
Yano, Suga [Mrs.], 16,942
Yantis Family (WA), 17,329
Yantis, J. L., 9,945
Yarborough, Mrs. W. F., 9,659
Yarborough, Ralph, 16,328
Yarbrough, Martha Jane, 15,401
Yarbrough, Susannah Abigail. *See* Irish, Susannah Abigail (Yarbrough) [Mrs. Charles Wood]
Yarbrough, Tabitha A. E. (1848-1965). *See* Seegars, Tabitha A. E. (Yarbrough) [Mrs. Dave] (1848-1965)
Yard, William S., 11,184
Yardley, Ralph (1878-1961), **1,617**
Yarmalow, Anna Catherine Drozd (1900-), 5,829
Yarmolinsky, Avrahm, 12,441
Yarnall, Sophia (1902-). *See* Jacobs, Sophia (Yarnall) [Mrs. Reginald Robert] (1902-)
Yarrell, Bell, **13,621**
Yarros, Rachelle (Slobodinsky) [Mrs. Victor S.] (1869-1946), 4,047, 4,111
Yates, Catherine. *See* Schermerhorn, Catherine (Yates) [Mrs. John Freeman]
Yates County Bank (NY), 11,746
Yates County History (book), 11,710
Yates, Eliza Moring [Mrs. Matthew T.], **13,622**
Yates, Elizabeth (1905-), **6,119,** 10,853
Yates, Elizabeth Ann (Saylor) [Mrs. Joseph] (1789-1868), 15,535
Yates, Emma (Hart) [Mrs. John] Willard [Mrs. Christopher] (1787-1870). *See* Willard, Emma (Hart) [Mrs. John]. [Mrs. Christopher] Yates (1787-1870)
Yates Family (MS), **9,747**
Yates Family (SC), **15,535**
Yates, Fanny. *See* Levy, Fanny (Yates) [Mrs. Jacob Clavius]
Yates, Ignatius, 9,747
Yates, Jerome, 9,747
Yates, John Van Ness (1779-1839), **6,996**
Yates, Joseph, 15,535
Yates, Katherine Merritte [Mrs.] (1865-?), **902**
Yates, Lydia Harriett (1839-1902). *See* Maxson, Lydia Harriett (Yates) [Mrs. Thaddeus W.] (1839-1902)
Yates, Martha F. [Miss], **11,757**
Yates, Mary Amarinthia (1819-98). *See* Snowden, Mary Amarinthia (Yates) [Mrs. William] (1819-98)
Yates, Obedience [Mrs. Ignatius], 9,747
Yates, Oleta (O'Connor), **903**
Yates, Richard, 4,357
Yaukey, Grace (Sydenstricker) (1899-), **14,476**
Yavapai Indians, 211, 16,865
Yaw, Ellen Beach. [Mrs. Vere] Goldthwaite [Mrs. Franklin] Cannon (1868-1947), 10,651
Ye Olde Towne Folk (Wilmette, IL), **4,459**
Ye Qualitye Shoppe (TX), 16,101
Yeagley, B. L., 14,860
Yeamans, Annie, 10,717
Year of American Travel, A (book), 12,481
Year of Costa Rican Natural History, A (book), 14,876
Yearbooks, **2,885.** *See also* School yearbooks
Yearbooks, college and school, 13,634
Yeargin, Mary Little (1867-94), **15,773**
Yeargin, Sallie Jane (1857-1949). *See* Atkinson, Sallie Jane (Yeargin) [Mrs.] (1857-1949)
Yearling, The (book), 2,876
"Year's at the Spring, The," 5,910
Years of Grace (drama), 14,736
Yearsley, Mary Ann (1811-1903), **16,573**
Yeatman, Jennette (Hayward) [Mrs. Charles] (1905-), 1,224, 1,407, **1,508**
Yeatman, Reaia (Chatfield) [Mrs. W. E.], **81**

Yeaton, Hopley, 5,585
Yeaton, Mary, **5,585**
Yeats, Elizabeth Corbet (1868-1940), 1,081
Yeats, William Butler, 1,467, 1,954, 2,660, 11,944, 16,165, 17,843
Yello Medicine Agency, 9,423
Yellow dog contract, 6,314
Yellow fever, 3,205, 12,260, 12,402, 15,661, 15,683
Yellow fever epidemics, 1,342, 2,919, 3,564, 5,335, 5,398, 9,641, 9,695, 11,602, 12,514, 12,980, 14,854, 15,022, 15,041, 16,246
Yellow Ribbon Speaker, The, 15,851
Yellow Rose Bush (book), 7,888
Yellowby, H. A., 13,620
Yellowby, Lt. Col., 13,620
Yellowstone National Park, 3,683, 3,686, 10,242, 10,268, 10,287, 10,329, 10,362, 10,389, 13,439, **18,025, 18,026**
Yelvington, Jane (1878-1957). *See* McCallum, Jane (Yelvington) [Mrs. Arthur Newell] (1878-1957)
Yemen, women in, 7,301
Yenching University (China), 6,424, 7,574, 14,336
faculty, 10,060
Yenping Woman's Conference, 5,073
Yeoman, Edna Smith, 801
Yerba Buena Island (CA), 1,446
Yerby, M. O. [Miss], 2,989
Yerby, S. H. [Mrs.], 2,989
Yesharah Society, **16,574**
Yewell, George, 4,919
Yezierska, Anzia (1885-1970), **947, 6,120, 12,678**
Yglesias, Jose, 12,064
Yillard, Edna Holroyd, 1,525
Yoder, Myrtle [Mrs.], **17,931**
Yokoi, Tomoe (1942-), 10,151
Yolles, Tamarath Knigin, 8,555
Yoneda, Elaine Black (1906-), 1,356, 1,357, **1,361**
Yonge, Charlotte (1823-1901), 12,467
Yorck, Ruth Landshoff (1909-66), **6,121**
York County Bar Association (PA), 15,358
York County Children's Nature Museum (SC), 15,813
York County Democratic Women's Club (SC), **15,825**
York County Friends of Food Stamp Applicants (SC), **15,826**
York County League of Women Voters (SC), **15,827**
York County Men's League for Woman Suffrage (PA), **15,361**
York, Emily (Smith), **19**
York Manufacturing Company (Saco, ME), **5,704**
York, Sarah (1806-77). *See* Jackson, Sarah (York) (1806-77)
York, Sarah Elizabeth (Slagle), **14,693**
Yorke, Dane (?-1970), 5,595
Yorke, Elenor, 9,434
Yorke, Oswald, 12,549, 12,612
Yorkville Academy, 15,692
Yosemite, 427
Yosemite Flora, A (book), 526
Yosemite National Park, 401
Yosemite Tomboy (book), 1,640
Yost, Barbara, **17,759**
Yost, Caroline. *See* Weinland, Caroline (Yost) [Mrs. William Henry]
Yost, Lenna Lowe [Mrs. Ellis S.] (1878-1972), 5,121, 5,122, 5,123, **17,486**
Yothers, Merrill A., 14,382
You Have Seen Their Faces (book), 12,891
Youmans, Catherine Newton [Mrs. William Little] Lee [Mrs. Edward Livingston], 12,185, 12,350
Youmans, Edward Livingston (1821-87), **12,350**
Youmans, Eliza A., 12,350
Youmans, Mrs. Henry, 17,747
Youmans, Theodora W. [Mrs.], 17,749
Young, Adelaide Taber (1877-1964). *See* Shaw, Adelaide Taber (Young) [Mrs. Farnham Horatio] (1877-1964)
Young, Alice (Gilmour). *See* Abbott, Alice (Gilmour) Young [Mrs. Albert J.]
Young Americans for Freedom, 13,187
Young, Anna (Durkee) [Mrs. Dominic] Tauzin (1753-1839), 4,352
Young, Brigham (1801-77), 410, 416, 806, 845, 856, 904, 10,004, 10,674, 12,616, 16,479, 16,486,

16,505, 16,511, 16,533, 16,560, 16,620, 16,661, 16,681, 16,725, 16,762, 16,772, 16,812, 16,830, 16,852, 16,853, 16,854, 16,855, 16,857, 16,860, 16,923, 16,941, 16,965, 16,967, 16,968, 17,950
Young, Brigham, Jr., 15,762
Young Business Women (IA), 4,866
Young, Carolyn Sporleder [Mrs.], 1,779
Young, Clara (Decker) [Mrs. Brigham] (1828-89), **904,** 16,701
Young, Clarissa (1895-). *See* Byrne, Clarissa (Young) (1895-)
Young, Clarissa (?-1939). *See* Spencer, Clarissa Hamilton (Young) [Mrs. John D.] (?-1939)
Young Communist League, 993, 17,635
Young, Cora (Moreland) [Mrs. William Wray], 4,963
Young Democratic Club of North Carolina, **13,623**
Young Democratic Clubs (NC), 13,406
Young Democratic-Farmer-Labor Clubs (MN), 9,040
Young Democratic-Farmer-Labor Party, 9,039
Young, Dorothy, 4,963
Young, Dorothy (Mills) [Mrs. Gordon Russell], 2,661
Young, Dorothy (Weir), **16,575**
Young, Eleanor [Miss], **1,648**
Young, Eliza (Adams) [Mrs. Ira] (1810-88), **10,857**
Young, Eliza Roxcy (Snow) [Mrs. Joseph] Smith [Mrs. Brigham] (1804-87), 351, **806, 16,479,** 16,560, 16,667, 16,693, 16,743, 16,763, 16,787, 16,789, 16,815, **16,830,** 16,853, 16,911, 16,955, **16,958**
Young, Ella [Miss] (1867-1956), 635, 831, **905, 1,057,** 1,081, 1,087, 1,448, 1,507, **1,509, 2,660**
Young, Ella (Flagg) [Mrs. William] (1845-1918), 3,787, 3,814, 3,995, 4,305
Young, Emily Dow, 16,789
Young, Emma Elinor (Hines) (1869-?), **906**
Young, Esther, 3,114
Young, Eva M., 13,370
Young, F. G., 14,513
Young Family (NY), **11,573**
Young Family (NC), 13,188
Young Family (SC), **15,774**
Young, Fanny (1787-1859). *See* Murray, Fanny (Young) [Mrs. Roswell] (1787-1859)
Young Female College (Thomasville, GA), 10,974
Young Female Religious Tract Society of Bridgeton (NJ), 10,970
Young Folks Journal (periodical), 5,905, 5,941
Young, Frances Berkeley [Mrs. Karl], 17,760
Young Franklin Roosevelt (book), 11,491
Young, George C., 15,774
Young, Gordon Ray, 16,612
Young, Harriett Decker, 16,701
Young, Hattie [Mrs. Ludwick Craven], 17,761
Young, Helen Anderson, 8,666
Young, Helen S. [Mrs.], 689
Young Housewife's Counsellor, The (book), 13,400
Young Icarians. *See* Icarian Community (IA, IL)
Young, Ida May (Dayton) (1872-?), **12,782**
Young, Ira, 10,857
Young, Jacqueline, 9,632
Young, James A., 15,774
Young, John Graham, **13,624**
Young, John Russell (1840-99), **2,661**
Young, John W., 16,763
Young, Joseph W., 16,467
Young Judea, 17,647
Young, Kimball (1893-), **4,209**
Young Ladies Aid Society (Chicago, IL). *See* Chicago Woman's Aid (IL)
Young Ladies Boarding School (NC), 13,407
Young Ladies' Classical Institute (Newburyport, MA), 7,378
Young Ladies Cooperative Society (GA), **13,835**
Young Ladies Diadem (St. George, UT), **16,977**
Young Ladies' Hospital Association (SC), **15,775**
Young Ladies Institute (PA), 14,891
Young Ladies League for Temperance Education of Cleveland (OH), 13,930
Young Ladies Mutual Improvement Association (UT), 16,444, 16,465
Young Ladies Philalaethian Society (MO), **9,925**
"Young Ladies Remembrancer, The," 1,100
Young Ladies Seminary (Benicia, CA), 326
Young Ladies Seminary (Lexington, MA), 6,245

Young Ladies Temperance League (OH), 13,930
Young Ladies Union Society (Danbury, CT), **8,006**
Young, Lillian (Norton) [Mrs. Frederick Allen] Gower [Mrs. Zoltan] Döme [Mrs. George Washington] (1857-1914). *See* Nordica, Lillian. Lillian (Norton). [Mrs. Frederick Allen] Gower [Mrs. Zoltan] Döme [Mrs. George Washington] Young (1857-1914)
Young, Lillian Rosemary, 4,963
Young, Loretta, 1,025
Young, Louisa (Beaman) [Mrs. Joseph] Smith [Mrs. Brigham] (1815-50), **16,852**
Young, Louise (1892-1974), **12,731,** 13,176
"Young Love" (radio program), 2,274
Young, Lucy Hayes [Mrs.], **9,783**
Young, Lucy Marie (Canfield) [Mrs. John W.] (1846-1915). *See* Margetts, Lucy Marie (Canfield) [Mrs. John W.] Young [Mrs. Ara W.] Sabin [Mrs. Phillip H.] (1846-1915)
Young, Mahonri Mackintosh, 16,575
Young Man With a Horn (book), 332, 11,832
Young, Margaret, 4,085
Young, Margaret A. (1867-1935), 9,128
Young, Margaret (Pierce) [Mrs. Morris] Whitesides [Mrs. Brigham] (1823-1907), **16,853**
Young, Marguerite, 4,483
Young, Marian Willard, 1,790
Young, Marilla Marks (1840-1920). *See* Ricker, Marilla Marks (Young) [Mrs. John] (1840-1920)
Young, Martha (Bowker) [Mrs. Brigham] (1822-90), **16,854**
Young, Martha L. (?-1902). *See* Whitten, Martha L. [Mrs. Jonathan M.] (?-1902)
Young, Mary (1875-1965), **18,024**
Young, Mary A., 4,152
Young, Mary Ann (Angel) [Mrs. Brigham] (1803-82), 16,781, **16,855**
Young, Mary L. [Miss], 15,774
Young, Mary R. [Mrs.], 15,774
Young, Mary Sophie (1872-1919), 16,060
Young, Matilda, 17,761
Young Matrons Circle for Tallulah Falls School (GA), **3,277**
Young Matron's Club (Madison, GA), **3,403**
Young, Maud Jeannie (Fuller) (1826-82), 16,132
Young, May (?-1930). *See* Shepherd, May (Young) [Mrs. Alexander Robey] (?-1930)
Young, May (Dow) [Mrs. George W.] Davids [Mrs. John Russell], 2,661
Young Medics, The (book), 10,894
Young Men So Daring (book), 13,674
Young Men's and Young Ladies' Total Abstinence Society (Harrisburg, PA), 14,818
Young Men's Christian Association, 313, 939, 1,821, 3,905, 6,507, **7,993,** 8,996, 9,205, 9,219, 9,273, 11,324, **12,136,** 12,400, 12,729, 13,176, 17,653
management, **12,135**
officials and employees, **2,516**
Young Men's Christian Association, Expeditionary Force, 4,814
Young Men's Christian Association of Greater Bridgeport (CT), Mother's Club, 1,831
Young Men's Christian Association of Greater Bridgeport (CT), Women's Auxiliary, **1,831**
Young Men's Christian Association, women's auxiliaries, **12,133**
Young Men's Christian Association, Women's Bureau, **12,134**
Young Men's Christian Association, Women's Bureau (Paris, France), 12,132
Young Men's Mutual Improvement Association (UT), 16,465
Young, Mildred Test (1896-), **8,892**
Young, Miller, 4,963
Young, Minerva (Richards) [Mrs. Richard Willard] (1862-1958), **16,856,** 16,917
Young, Mollie, 16,097
Young Mother's Club (Batavia, IL), 3,743
Young Mother's Club (Geneva, IL), 4,273
Young Mule, 10,313
Young, Nancy (1786-1860). *See* Kent, Nancy (Young) [Mrs. Daniel] (1786-1860)
Young, Naomah Kendel Jenkins (Carter) [Mrs. John

Saunders] Twiss [Mrs. Brigham] (1821-1909), **16,857**

Young, Norma Dorothy (1910-63), 5,035

Young, Owen, 2,875

Young People's Association (Chicago, IL), 4,085

Young People's Literary Society (Bangor, ME), 5,589

Young People's Paper (periodical), 5,208

Young People's Temperance Society (Tama, IA), **5,116**

Young, Plummer Barnard, 5,458

Young Poets Series, 14,423

Young Prohibitionists Association, 7,779

Young, Rachel (Barry) Burnap, **13,174**

Young, Rachel Wilson. *See* LaFollette, Rachel Wilson (Young) [Mrs. Robert Marion, Jr.], 17,761

Young, Richard W., Jr., 16,917

Young, Richard Willard (1858-1919), 16,856, **16,917**

Young, Roberta. *See* Brown, Roberta (Young)

Young, Ruth E., 7,158

Young, S. Ella [Miss] (ca. 1895-1948), **14,729**

Young, Sara Louise, 11,707

Young, Sarah [Miss], **13,188**

Young, Sarah Jane (Sibley) [Mrs. Albert A.] (1851-), 9,371

Young, Sarah (Nickman) [Mrs. Arch], 9,987

Young, Susa Amelia (1856-1933). *See* Gates, Susa Amelia (Young) [Mrs. Alma Bailey] Dunford [Mrs. Jacob Forsberry] (1856-1933)

Young, Theodosia, 17,284

Young, W. S., 11,573

Young, William Wray, **4,963**

Young Women's Banner (periodical), 11,407

Young Women's Christian Association, 89, 190, **271,** 380, 387, 389, 525, 540, 576, 592, 720, 756, 793, 892, 929, 1,169, 1,219, 1,534, 1,558, 1,655, 1,684, 1,837, 2,292, 2,298, 2,502, 2,933, 2,939, 3,083, 3,302, 3,305, 3,316, 3,374, 3,383, 3,451, 3,653, 3,734, 3,799, 3,826, 3,827, 3,904, 3,905, 3,969, 4,160, 4,219, 4,394, 4,595, 5,241, 5,635, 6,507, **7,063,** 7,221, 7,256, 7,290, 7,326, **7,329, 7,993, 7,995,** 8,148, **8,451, 8,513,** 8,594, 8,631, 8,633, 8,665, 8,670, 8,679, 8,680, 8,821, 8,833, **8,838,** 8,885, 9,104, 9,219, 9,273, **9,465,** 9,467, 9,570, 9,576, 9,577, 10,484, 10,609, 11,283, 11,349, 11,444, 11,806, **12,136,** 12,526, 12,681, **12,717,** 12,738, 12,739, 12,920, 12,999, 13,176, **13,203,** 13,226, 13,227, 13,391, 13,446, 13,617, 13,618, **13,681,** 13,843, 13,882, 13,991, 14,533, **14,694,** 14,742, 16,275, 16,342, 17,141, 17,262, 17,376, 17,541, 17,588, 17,603, 17,742, 17,896

officials and employees, 2,336, **4,083,** 4,927, 11,906, 15,332

Young Women's Christian Association (South Bend, IN), **4,674**

Young Women's Christian Association (IA), **5,098**

Young Women's Christian Association (Henry County, IA), **5,071**

Young Women's Christian Association (MI), **7,996**

Young Women's Christian Association (Flint, MI), **8,182**

Young Women's Christian Association (MN), 8,552, 8,578

Young Women's Christian Association (Minneapolis, MN), **8,627**

Young Women's Christian Association (Rochester, MN), **8,838**

Young Women's Christian Association (Omaha, NE), **10,518**

Young Women's Christian Association (Trenton, NJ), 11,610

Young Woman's Christian Association (ND), **13,723**

Young Women's Christian Association (OH), **13,982**

Young Women's Christian Association (Columbus, OH), **14,027**

Young Women's Christian Association (Dickinson College, PA), **14,765**

Young Women's Christian Association (TN), **15,873**

Young Women's Christian Association (Milwaukee, WI), **17,851**

Young Women's Christian Association (Neenah-Menasha, WI), 17,827

Young Women's Christian Association, Big Sisters program, 17,827

Young Women's Christian Association, Community Center of Neenah-Menasha (WI), **17,827**

Young Women's Christian Association, Council on Colored Work, 10,201

Young Women's Christian Association, Job Corps, **12,720,** 12,725

Young Women's Christian Association, National Association of Employed Officers, **12,723**

Young Women's Christian Association, National Board, **12,724**

biography, **12,710, 12,711, 12,712, 12,715, 12,716, 12,721, 12,725, 12,726, 12,727, 12,730, 12,731**

Young Women's Christian Association, National Board, War Work Council, **12,729**

Young Women's Christian Association, National Commission on Ethnic Minorities, 3,293

Young Women's Christian Association, Nationalities Service Center, 15,209

Young Women's Christian Association of Metropolitan Chicago (IL), 4,079, 4,170, **4,175**

Young Women's Christian Association of Mount Vernon (NY), **8,684**

Young Women's Christian Association of Philadelphia (PA), 15,209

Young Women's Christian Association of St. Louis (MO), 10,201

Young Women's Christian Association, Old Country Service of the National War Work Council, 12,716, 12,729

Young Women's Christian Association, Phillis Wheatley Branch (St. Louis, MO), 10,192

Young Women's Christian Association, Polish Grey Samaritans, **12,714,** 12,716

Young Women's Christian Association, Professional Writers' Club, 2,197

Young Women's Christian Association, Progressive Club (Dearborn, MI), **8,014**

Young Women's Christian Association, Second War Fund Campaign, 10,397

Young Women's Christian Association, Southwest-Belmont Branch (Philadelphia, PA), **15,210**

Young Women's Christian Association, University Branch (WA), **17,367**

Young Women's Christian Association, University of Wisconsin-Madison, **17,787**

Young Women's Christian Temperance Union (MI), **7,994**

Young Women's Christian Temperance Union (OH), **13,983**

Young Women's Christian Temperance Union (RI), 15,395

Young Women's Christian Temperance Union of Rockville (CT), **1,946**

Young Women's Hebrew Association, 6,920

Young Women's Hospital Aid, The (Ithaca, NY), **11,758**

Young Women's League (Dayton, OH), **14,043**

Young Women's Missionary Society (NE), Miriam Circle, 10,594

Young Women's Union (Philadelphia, PA). *See* Neighborhood Centre (Philadelphia, PA)

Young, Zina Diantha (Huntington) [Mrs. Henry Bailey] Jacobs [Mrs. Joseph, Jr.] Smith [Mrs. Brigham] (1821-1901), 16,667, 16,699, 16,787, 16,789, 16,806, **16,860,** 16,967

Young, Zina Priscenda (1850-1931). *See* Card, Zina Priscenda (Young) [Mrs. Thomas] Williams [Mrs. Charles Ora] (1850-1931)

Youngblood, Richard Singleton, 15,680

Youngdahl, Benjamin Emanuel (1897-1970), **8,685**

Younge, Wyvetter H., 10,191

Younger, J. Arthur, **1,605**

Younger, Maud (1870-1936), 6,678

"Youngest Smiles, The" (book), 16,168

Younggren, Nancy (Weberg), 17,862

Youngjohn, Olive "Girlie" [Miss], 10,905

Younglove Family (KY), **5,259**

Younglove, Jane (1831-61), 5,259

Younglove, Margaret (1829-1920). *See* Calvert, Margaret (Younglove) [Mrs. Thomas] (1829-1920)

Youngman Family (CA), **907**

Youngman, Lorinda (Wooster) (1821-93), 907

Your Secretary, Inc., 2,558

Your Voice and You (book), 11,984

Yourdan, Emma Bile, 9,020

"You're Next" (song), 5,529

You're Well Out of a Hospital (book), 11,994

Youth Authority (CA), 645

Youth centers, 2,687

Youth Consultation Service, 17,594

Youth in Conflict (book), 7,031

Youth Movement for World Recovery, 15,308

Youth movements, 11,915, 15,308

Youth Services Board, 6,432

Youth Services Bureau (OR), 14,605

Youthful Days of Richelieu (drama), 2,543

Youth's Cabinet, 10,193

Youth's Christian Companion (periodical), 4,513

Youth's Companion (periodical), 2,037, 2,108, 7,605, 9,633, 14,082

Youth's Female Missionary Society (Philadelphia PA). *See* Youth's Missionary Society (Philadelphia, PA)

Youth's Missionary Society (Philadelphia, PA), **15,122**

Youtz, May Pardee [Mrs.] (1882-1970), 5,035

Yreka Elementary School Board (CA), 500

Ytrehus, Madge (1882-). *See* Hawkins, Madge (Ytrehus) [Mrs. Oscar Ferdinand] (1882-)

Ytterboe, E. T., 8,746

Yu-Tang, Dr. Lin, 174

Yukon Territory, gold discoveries, 1,633, 10,181

Yuma Territorial Prison (AZ), **165, 170,** 190, 210

Yurka, Blanche, 9,103

Yurok Indians, 965

Yust for Fun, 8,775

Zaban, Bessie Judith. *See* Jones, Bessie Judith (Zaban) [Mrs. Howard Mumford]

Zagat, Ruth. *See* Murphy, Ruth (Zagat). Ruth (Zagat) Casselman Benton Bernstein Murphy

Zaharias, Babe D., 4,700

Zaire
history (1960-), 13,276, 13,280
missionaries to, 45, 15,910
missionaries to, Afro-American, 86
missionaries to, Baptist, 14,443, 14,459
missionaries to, Methodist, 13,276, 13,280, 13,291
missionaries to, Presbyterian, 92, 95
missions, Mennonite, 13,757
missions to lepers, 13,291

Zakrzewska, Marie Elizabeth (1829-1902), 1,483, 6,777, 7,222, 7,274

Zalvidea, Father, 715

Zane, Elizabeth "Betty" [Mrs. John or Henry] McGloughlin [Mrs. Jacob or John] Clark (1766?-1831?), 14,112

Zane, Isaac, 14,977

Zane, Sarah "Sally," 14,977

Zangwill, Israel, 12,701

Zaring, Grace (1896-). *See* Stone, Grace (Zaring) (1896-)

Zastrow, Katherine (Mull) [Mrs. Lawrence] Falvey [Mrs. Ralph] (1904-), **4,910**

Zastrow, Ralph, 4,910

Zatorsky, Olga. *See* Hirshhorn, Olga (Zatorsky) [Mrs. Joseph]

Zaverl, Shirley, 9,040

Zborowski, Hazel, 6,223

Zduleczna, Christine. *See* Fulton, Christine (Zduleczna)

Zebulon Academy (GA), **3,122**

Zebulon Pike Detention Home (Colorado Springs, CO), 1,682

Zeiger, Dorothy Child (Cross) Remington (1890-), 6,997

Zeigler, Babette, 13,331

Zeisler, Fannie (Bloomfield) [Mrs. Sigmund] (1863-1927), 3,997, 9,057

Zeisler, Sigmund, 13,766

Zeller, Adelheid Bertha Marie Zoe (1892-). *See* Lacy, Adelheid Bertha Marie Zoe Zeller [Mrs. Ilbert O.] (1892-)

Zeller, Cornelia (1894-), **11,759**

Zeller, Verena M., 37
Zemach, Margot (1931-), 8,531
Zeman, Josepha Humpal [Mrs.] (1870-?), 3,928
Zemser, Marion (Shomer) (?-1951), **12,679**
Ženské Listy, Jediný Český Týdenník v Americe Věnovaný Zájmum Žen (periodical) (Chicago, IL), **3,928**, 4,057
"Zero Hour" (radio program), 1,178
Zeta Phi Beta, 3,799
Zeta Phi Eta, 4,220, 14,235
Zeta Tau Alpha, 5,064
Zetalethan Literary Society (IN), 4,595
Zetasophian "Zeta" Society (NY), 12,746
Zetetic Club (MN), **8,493**
Zetetic Club (NE), **10,563**
Zicafoose, Myrtle [Miss], **13,291**
Ziegfeld, Anna Held [Mrs. Maximo] Carrera [Mrs. Florenz] (1865?-1918), 4,781, 11,453
Ziegfield, Florenz, 2,330
Ziegler, Amelia, 14,698
Ziegler, Viola Leora. *See* Smith, Viola Leora (Ziegler) [Mrs. Charles Eugene]
Zimand, Gertrude (Folks) [Mrs. Savel] (1894?-1966), **8,686**
Zimand, Savel (1891-1967), 8,686
Zimbalist, Efrem, 14,670, 14,995
Zimmer, Orpha Spicer, 11,508
Zimmerman, Elsie Fullerton (Lee) [Mrs. Paul Irwin] (1878-1937), **2,442**
Zimmerman, Mary (1870-1953), 4,165
Zimmerman, Mrs. Simpson, 15,576

Zimmerman, Paul Irwin, 2,442
Zinsser, Hans, 11,579
Zion Banner, 4,461
Zion Baptist Church (CO), 1,777, 1,802
Zion Evangelical Church (Laurel, IA), 5,075
Zion Woman's Club (IL), **4,462**
Zionism, 13,801, **14,908**
Zionists, 1,000, 4,510, **5,720**, 7,528, **12,117**, **12,118**, **14,908**, 17,646, 17,744
Zion's Cooperative Mercantile Institute (UT), 16,569, 16,888
Zipperer, Nathaniel A., **3,618**
Zitron, Celia, 11,774
Zlac Rowing Club (CA), 1,191
Zoar Community (OH), 11,681
Zogbaum, Leola Baird (Leonard) [Mrs. Harry St. Clair] (1888?-1941), **7,254**
Zollicoffer, 13,625
Zolotow, Charlotte (Shapiro) (1915-) 8,531
Zon, Anna Abramovna (Puzyriskaya) [Mrs. Raphael], 9,466
Zon, Henry, 9,466
Zon, Leo, 9,466
Zon, Raphael (1874-1956), **9,466**
Zoning, 5,607, 15,204
Zonta Club, 4,094
Zonta Club (Buffalo, NY), 11,344
Zonta Club of Chicago Loop (IL), **4,176**
Zonta Club of Detroit (MI), **8,040**
Zonta International, 4,176
Zook, Laura (Brown) (1868-1944), **10,269**, **10,398**

Zook, Lina (1869-1948). *See* Ressler, Lina (Zook) [Mrs. Jacob Andrew] (1869-1948)
Zook, Vesta (1891-). *See* Slagel, Vesta (Zook) [Mrs. Arthur] (1891-)
Zoological museums, **910**, 6,316, **6,321**
Zoological research, **8,626**
Zoological Station, American Woman's Table (Naples), 2,070
Zoologists, **2,070**, 6,321, **8,555**, **8,626**, 11,747, **14,876**, 14,943
Zoology, 310
"Zóphiël" (poem), 12,002
Zora, Lucia. *See* Alispaw, Lucia Zora [Mrs. Fred]
Zorach, Dahlov (1917-). *See* Ipcar, Dahlov (Zorach) [Mrs. Adolph] (1917-)
Zorach, Marguerite (Thompson) [Mrs. William] (1887-1968), 2,662, 2,845, 11,933
Zorach, William (1887-1966), **2,662**, **11,933**
Zorbaugh, Grace Stone McClure, 13,890
Zotos, Helen (Mamas). [Mrs. Stephano] Zotos (1923-), **17,762**
Zotos, Stephano, 17,762
Zuleika Dobson (drama), 14,413
Zumwalt, Nancy. *See* Hunt, Nancy (Zumwalt) Cotton
Zuni Indians, 2,841, 16,868, **16,877**
antiquities, 11,295
Zuska of the Burning Hills (book), 17,478
Zuvekas, Ann, 9,467
Zwemer, Susanna (Peirce), **11,064**